McDougal Littell

# THE LANGUAGE OF
# LITERATURE

## AMERICAN LITERATURE

## TEACHER'S EDITION

**McDougal Littell**
A HOUGHTON MIFFLIN COMPANY
Evanston, Illinois • Boston • Dallas

ISBN 0-618-60147-3

1 2 3 4 5 6 7 8 9 – DWO – 09 08 07 06

# Senior Consultants

The senior consultants guided the conceptual development for *The Language of Literature* series. They participated actively in shaping prototype materials for major components, and they reviewed completed prototypes and/or completed units to ensure consistency with current research and the philosophy of the series.

*Arthur N. Applebee* Professor of Education, State University of New York at Albany; Director, National Research Center on English Learning and Achievement; Senior Fellow, Center for Writing and Literacy

*Andrea B. Bermúdez* Professor of Studies in Language and Culture; Director, Research Center for Language and Culture; Chair, Foundations and Professional Studies, University of Houston–Clear Lake

*Sheridan Blau* Senior Lecturer in English and Education and former Director of Composition, University of California at Santa Barbara; Director, South Coast Writing Project; Director, Literature Institute for Teachers; Past President, National Council of Teachers of English

*Rebekah Caplan* Coordinator, English Language Arts K-12, Oakland Unified School District, Oakland, California; Teacher-Consultant, Bay Area Writing Project, University of California at Berkeley; served on the California State English Assessment Development Team for Language Arts

*Peter Elbow* Professor of English; University of Massachusetts at Amherst; Fellow, Bard Center for Writing and Thinking

*Susan Hynds* Professor and Director of English Education, Syracuse University, Syracuse, New York

*Judith A. Langer* Professor of Education, State University of New York at Albany; Director, National Research Center on English Learning and Achievement; Albany Institute for Research on Education; Senior Fellow, Center for Writing and Literacy

*James Marshall* Professor of English and English Education, University of Iowa, Iowa City

# Contributing Consultants

*Linda Diamond* Executive Vice President, Consortium on Reading Excellence (CORE); co-author of *Building a Powerful Reading Program*

*Lucila A. Garza* ESL Consultant, Austin, Texas

*Jeffrey N. Golub* Assistant Professor of English Education, University of South Florida, Tampa

*William L. McBride, Ph.D.* Reading and Curriculum Specialist; former middle and high school English instructor

*Sharon Sicinski-Skeans, Ph.D.* Assistant Professor of Reading, University of Houston–Clear Lake; primary consultant on *The InterActive Reader*

# THE LANGUAGE OF LITERATURE

## Experience the Language of Literature

I want to change
people's minds...

I want to love what I do...

I want to make
a statement...

# Experience

# THE LANGUAGE OF LITERATURE

## Experience the Language of Literature

*The Language of Literature* provides students with high-interest selections and a variety of opportunities to interact with the literature, analyze what they read, and enjoy the experiences that great literature has to offer.

### Skillfully Crafted Instruction

A variety of skills and strategies "bookend" each selection to support students before and after they read and help them connect to the literature.

### Interactive Strategies

Critical reading, writing, and thinking strategies are interwoven throughout the text to help students build comprehension and develop their writing skills.

### Solid Literary Analysis

Students learn how to analyze literature from a number of genres, interpret a variety of literary themes, and apply the analyses to their own experiences.

### Flexible Ongoing Assessment

Assessment options in both print and electronic formats are integrated with the selections to help students be better prepared and more successful.

Experience the possibilities. Experience success.
Experience *The Language of Literature*.

I want to see the world...

I want to
create a memory...

# Skillfully Crafted Instruction

Specific reading and literary strategies appear before each selection and are mirrored at the end to give students a complete literature experience.

**Connect to Your Life** helps students identify with the characters, plots, and themes and relate what they read to their own lives.

I want to try new things...

**Literary Analysis** provides the definitions of specific literary terms and supports those definitions with literary examples.

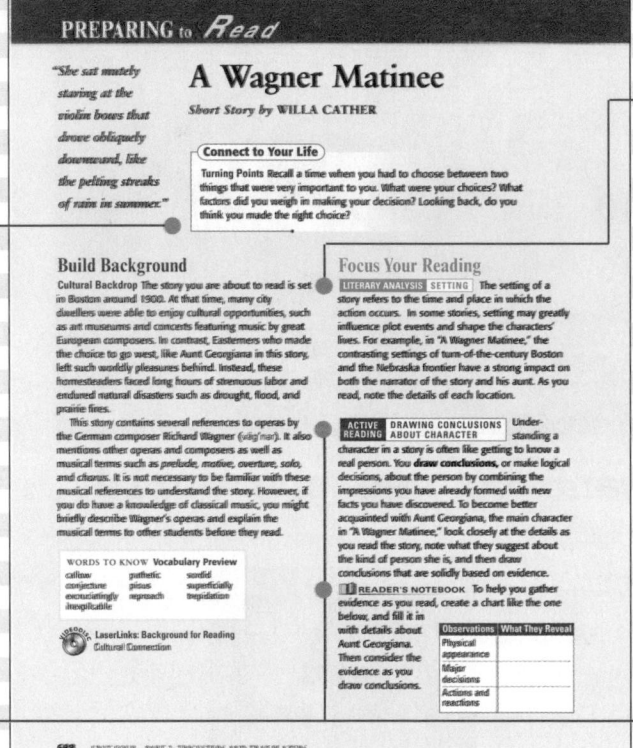

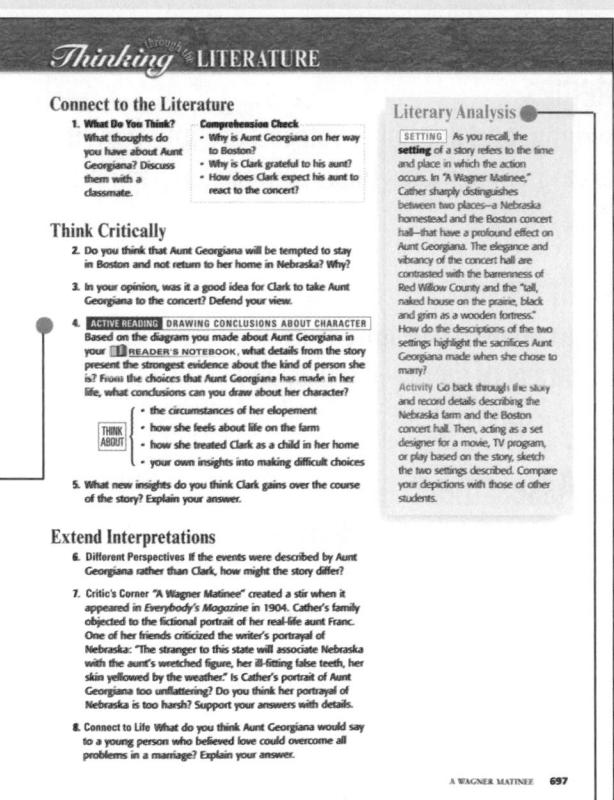

The **Active Reading** strand prepares students to focus on a concept they will encounter in the selection and incorporates graphic organizers through the **Reader's Notebook**. Students are then asked to review their notes and journal entries from their **Reader's Notebook**.

**Key literary concepts** such as Setting "bookend" the selection. The concepts are introduced before reading and reinforced and practiced after reading.

# Interactive Strategies

Interwoven support increases comprehension, improves writing skills, and makes the literature experience more meaningful.

The InterActive Reader™ Plus consumable worktext takes core selections from the main anthology and breaks them into manageable reading chunks to increase comprehension. Also available with differentiated support in **The InterActive Reader Plus with Additional Support** and **The InterActive Reader Plus for English Learners**.

Students receive **focused instruction** on specific reading skills and have the opportunity to **mark up** the text with their own notes.

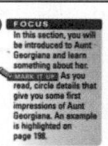

**Writing Workshops**, prompted by the literature, build skills and establish rubrics for different types of writing.

Literary, professional, and student models show skills in context and provide a wide range of practice opportunities in literary analysis.

**Graphic organizers** visually represent specific writing lessons.

Interactive

# Solid Literary Analysis

Students compare and contrast ideas as they learn to interpret and analyze literature within a variety of themes and genres.

**Comparing Literature** shows students how to compare and contrast two literature selections from different genres or cultures.

**Assessment practice** prepares students for standardized tests with a compare-and-contrast focus.

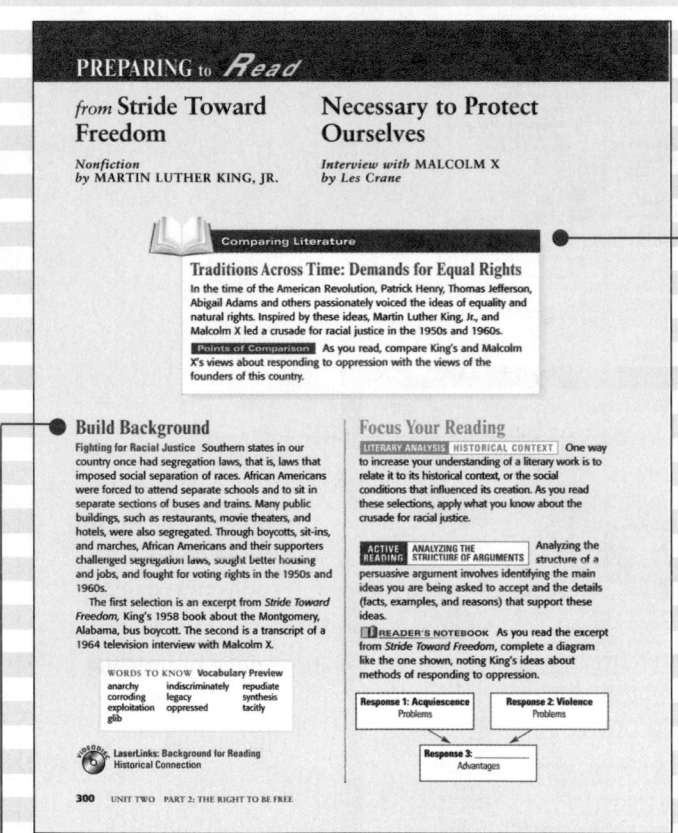

## PREPARING to *Read*

*from* **Stride Toward Freedom**

Nonfiction
by MARTIN LUTHER KING, JR.

**Necessary to Protect Ourselves**

Interview with MALCOLM X
by Les Crane

### Comparing Literature

**Traditions Across Time: Demands for Equal Rights**

In the time of the American Revolution, Patrick Henry, Thomas Jefferson, Abigail Adams and others passionately voiced the ideas of equality and natural rights. Inspired by these ideas, Martin Luther King, Jr., and Malcolm X led a crusade for racial justice in the 1950s and 1960s.

**Points of Comparison** As you read, compare King's and Malcolm X's views about responding to oppression with the views of the founders of this country.

### Build Background

**Fighting for Racial Justice** Southern states in our country once had segregation laws, that is, laws that imposed social separation of races. African Americans were forced to attend separate schools and to sit in separate sections of buses and trains. Many public buildings, such as restaurants, movie theaters, and hotels, were also segregated. Through boycotts, sit-ins, and marches, African Americans and their supporters challenged segregation laws, sought better housing and jobs, and fought for voting rights in the 1950s and 1960s.

The first selection is an excerpt from *Stride Toward Freedom*, King's 1958 book about the Montgomery, Alabama, bus boycott. The second is a transcript of a 1964 television interview with Malcolm X.

WORDS TO KNOW Vocabulary Preview

| | |
|---|---|
| anarchy | indiscriminately | repudiate |
| corroding | legacy | synthesis |
| exploitation | oppressed | tacitly |
| glib | | |

LaserLinks: Background for Reading
Historical Connection

### Focus Your Reading

**LITERARY ANALYSIS** **HISTORICAL CONTEXT** One way to increase your understanding of a literary work is to relate it to its historical context, or the social conditions that influenced its creation. As you read these selections, apply what you know about the crusade for racial justice.

**ACTIVE READING** **ANALYZING THE STRUCTURE OF ARGUMENTS** Analyzing the structure of a persuasive argument involves identifying the main ideas you are being asked to accept and the details (facts, examples, and reasons) that support these ideas.

**READER'S NOTEBOOK** As you read the excerpt from *Stride Toward Freedom*, complete a diagram like the one shown, noting King's ideas about methods of responding to oppression.

| Response 1: Acquiescence | Response 2: Violence |
|---|---|
| Problems | Problems |

| Response 3: _____ |
|---|
| Advantages |

**300** UNIT TWO PART 2: THE RIGHT TO BE FREE

**Build Background** provides students with a context for the selections that helps them analyze and compare two approaches to an issue or story.

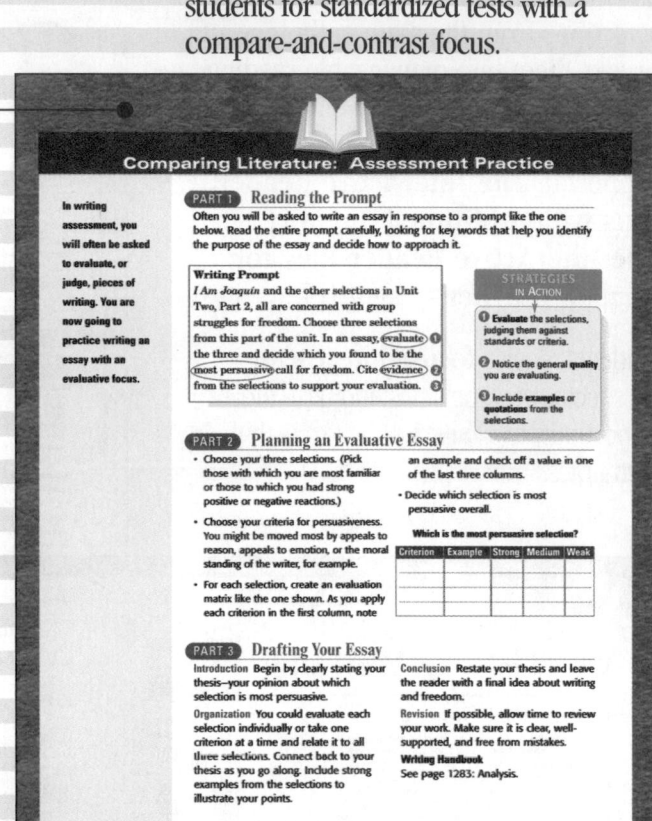

### Comparing Literature: Assessment Practice

In writing assessment, you will often be asked to evaluate, or judge, pieces of writing. You are now going to practice writing an essay with an evaluative focus.

**PART 1** **Reading the Prompt**

Often you will be asked to write an essay in response to a prompt like the one below. Read the entire prompt carefully, looking for key words that help you identify the purpose of the essay and decide how to approach it.

**Writing Prompt**
*I Am Joaquín* and the other selections in Unit Two, Part 2, all are concerned with group struggles for freedom. Choose three selections from this part of the unit. In an essay, evaluate the three and decide which you found to be the most persuasive call for freedom. Cite evidence from the selections to support your evaluation.

**STRATEGIES IN ACTION**
1. **Evaluate** the selections, judging them against standards or criteria.
2. Notice the general **quality** you are evaluating.
3. Include **examples** or **quotations** from the selections.

**PART 2** **Planning an Evaluative Essay**

- Choose your three selections. (Pick those with which you are most familiar or those to which you had strong positive or negative reactions.)

- Choose your criteria for persuasiveness. You might be moved most by appeals to reason, appeals to emotion, or the moral standing of the writer, for example.

- For each selection, create an evaluation matrix like the one shown. As you apply each criterion in the first column, note

an example and check off a value in one of the last three columns.

- Decide which selection is most persuasive overall.

**Which is the most persuasive selection?**

| Criterion | Example | Strong | Medium | Weak |
|---|---|---|---|---|
| | | | | |
| | | | | |
| | | | | |

**PART 3** **Drafting Your Essay**

**Introduction** Begin by clearly stating your thesis—your opinion about which selection is most persuasive.

**Organization** You could evaluate each selection individually or take one criterion at a time and relate it to all three selections. Connect back to your thesis as you go along. Include strong examples from the selections to illustrate your points.

**Conclusion** Restate your thesis and leave the reader with a final idea about writing and freedom.

**Revision** If possible, allow time to review your work. Make sure it is clear, well-supported, and free from mistakes.

**Writing Handbook**
See page 1283: Analysis.

**318** UNIT TWO PART 2: THE RIGHT TO BE FREE

I want a challenge...

# Literary

# Flexible, Ongoing Assessment

A variety of assessment options meets the needs of a broad range of students as they acquire essential skills and prepare for standardized tests.

**Assessment practice and strategies are supported in each unit of the *Pupil's Edition*.**

---

## Reading & Writing for Assessment

When you studied strategies for reading a test selection on pages 330–335, you practiced techniques for success on reading and writing assessments. These kinds of tests are often important end-of-course examinations. The following pages will give you more practice with test-taking strategies. Work through the models to practice applying each of the following strategies.

### PART 1   How to Read a Test Selection

Here are the basic strategies you studied earlier along with several new ones based on a different type of reading selection. By applying basic test-taking strategies, by taking notes, and by highlighting or underscoring passages as you read, you can focus on the key information you need to know.

#### STRATEGIES FOR READING A TEST SELECTION

- **Before you begin reading, skim the questions that follow the passage.** These can help focus your reading.
- **Think about the title.** What does it suggest about the overall message and tone of the passage?
- **Use your active reading strategies, such as analyzing, predicting, and questioning.** Make notes in the margin to help you focus your reading. You may do this only if the test directions allow you to mark on the test itself.
- **Look for main ideas.** These are often stated at the beginnings or ends of paragraphs. Sometimes main ideas are implied, not stated. After reading each paragraph, ask "What was this passage about?"
- **Note the literary elements and techniques used by the writer.** You might consider the tone (writer's attitude toward the subject), the structure (how the writer organizes details into a single message), or the use of techniques like foreshadowing or depiction of people. Then ask yourself what effect the writer achieves with each choice.
- **Examine the sequence of ideas.** Are the ideas developed in chronological order, presented in order of importance, or organized in some other way? What does the sequence of ideas suggest about the writer's message?
- **Think about the message and writer's purpose.** What questions does the selection answer? What new questions does it imply? Can you make any generalizations?

---

### Reading Selection

#### An English Foothold in North America

1   England's first significant attempt to carve out a colony of its own in North America (after an earlier failed attempt at Roanoke) nearly collapsed, as disease and starvation threatened the new settlement. However, through the determination of its colonists and the development of a marketable crop, ① England's first permanent settlement in North America took shape.

2   **The Business of Colonization** The rulers of England— unlike the Spanish—decided not to fund the risky venture of colonizing the Americas. Instead, King James I in 1606 granted a charter, or official permit, to two joint-stock companies, the Virginia companies of London and Plymouth. Numerous investors had pooled their wealth in order to finance the trip to North America. The Virginia Company of Plymouth soon disbanded, leaving only the Virginia Company of London, later simply called the Virginia Company.

3   ② The Virginia Company had lured financial supporters with the chance of reaping wealth in the form of gold or silver for a relatively small investment. England was to get something from the expedition, too. The King's charter guaranteed that the English monarch would receive one-fifth of all gold and silver found by the colonists.

4   In April of 1607, nearly four months after the Virginia Company's three ships—and nearly 150 passengers and crew members—had pushed out of an English harbor, the North American shore rose on the horizon. Reaching the coast of Virginia, the vessels slipped into a broad coastal river and sailed inland until they reached a small peninsula. There, the colonists climbed off their ships and claimed the land as theirs. They named the settlement Jamestown and the river the James, in honor of their king.

5   **A Disastrous Start** ③ John Smith sensed trouble from the beginning. Nearly all of the settlers seemed to be consumed by one thought—the discovery of gold. Because the investors in the colony demanded a quick return on their investment, the colonists directed much of their energy toward searching the land for riches. As Smith later put it, "There was no talk, no hope, no work, but dig gold, wash gold, refine gold, load gold." Smith warned of disaster, but few listened to the arrogant captain, who had made few friends on the voyage over.

---

#### STRATEGIES IN ACTION

**① Read actively— predict.**

**ONE STUDENT'S THOUGHTS**
"This selection will explain how England's first permanent colony in North America got started."

**YOUR TURN**
Based on paragraph 1, what topics can you predict will become main ideas in the rest of the passage?

**② Read actively— analyze.**
"For a small investment, the Virginia Company promised wealth. People must have expected to get rich easily. I wonder how that will work out."

**③ Note literary elements such as tone and foreshadowing.**
"Now the writer gives us John Smith's point of view."

**YOUR TURN**
Based on John Smith's concerns, what kind of future do you think lies ahead for the colony?

ASSESSMENT   **733**

---

**The Teacher's Guide to Assessment and Portfolio Use** includes portfolio assessment, writing rubrics, and other forms of open-ended assessment.

The **Test Generator CD-ROM** contains a variety of pre-made tests and a test bank of items that allows teachers to create customized tests.

**eTest Plus Online** allows teachers to take tests created with the *Test Generator* and publish them to an online service. Students can take their tests online where they are automatically scored. Reports can be generated for individual students or the whole class. All reports can be correlated to national and state standards.

The **Formal Assessment** and **Integrated Assessment** booklets provide selection tests, part tests, a mid-year test, and end-of-year tests, writing rubrics, and practice questions for standardized tests.

# Assessment

# THE LANGUAGE OF LITERATURE
## Time-Saving Teaching Support

### *The Language of Literature* Comprehensive Teacher's Edition

The annotated *Teacher's Edition* serves as a complete reference tool for the classroom. Each page contains a wealth of information that includes a lesson overview, teaching strategies, background information, and references to ancillary materials.

### The InterActive Reader™ Plus
### The InterActive Reader™ Plus with Additional Support
### The InterActive Reader™ Plus for English Learners

*The Interactive Reader™ Plus* is a consumable worktext that reinforces active reading strategies, encourages writing during reading, and increases comprehension by breaking core selections from *The Language of Literature* anthology into manageable reading chunks. The *Teacher's Guide* contains complete lesson plans for each selection, activities, mini-lessons, and graphic organizers.

### The Reading Toolkit

*The Reading Toolkit* is a valuable collection of teacher tools, mini-lessons, copymasters, and transparencies that helps teachers diagnose students' abilities and provides them with guidelines for direct instruction in reading comprehension skills and strategies.

### *Literature Connections*

Each *Literature Connections* volume contains a complete novel or play with five to eight theme-related readings that represent a variety of genres. Each title is supported by a *Teacher's SourceBook* that includes background material, author biographies, discussion starters, and suggested essay questions.

## Unit Resource Books

The *Unit Resource Books,* one per unit, provide additional skills work and extensions of activities and exercises. Contents include a family and community involvement section; a selection summary; SkillBuilders in active reading, literary analysis, vocabulary, grammar, and spelling; a selection quiz; a Writing Workshop; a reflect and assess segment; and answer keys.

## Resource Management Guide

This organizational guide helps teachers match ancillary materials to each selection.

## Lesson Planning Guide

This booklet helps teachers organize resources, keep track of daily objectives and activities, and track standards met.

## Professional Development and Planning Guide

This guide for teachers includes lesson plans for regular and block scheduling.

## Formal Assessment

This booklet offers selection tests, part tests, a mid-year test, an end-of-year test, writing rubrics, and standardized test practice questions.

## Integrated Assessment

Features of this booklet include Unit Integrated Assessments, an End-of-Year Integrated Assessment, and a record of student thinking and planning.

## Teacher's Guide to Assessment and Portfolio Use

This guide includes portfolio assessment, writing rubrics, and other forms of open-ended assessment.

## English Learners/Students Acquiring English Resources

*The Language of Literature* offers solid support for the English Learner.

**EL/SAE Spanish Study Guide**

**EL/SAE Teacher's SourceBook for Language Development**

**EL/SAE: Test Preparation Copymasters**

**EL/SAE: English Grammar Survival Kit with Audio CD**

**Selection Summaries in English, Spanish, and Haitian Creole**

## Skills Transparencies and Copymasters

A variety of transparencies and copymasters help teachers enhance their lessons in the following areas:

**Writing**

**Grammar**

**Vocabulary**

**Communications**
  (includes Fine Art transparencies)

**Literary Analysis**

**Reading and Critical Thinking**

# THE LANGUAGE OF LITERATURE
## Integrated Technology

### Literature in Performance

This video series helps students compare written selections to film adaptations of literature. The *Video Resource Book* provides activities that motivate students to think critically about what they have viewed.

### Audio Library

Professional recordings of selections from the anthology help students develop strategies for critical listening. These audio CDs enrich the literary experience for all students and provide extra support to less-proficient readers, students acquiring English, and auditory learners.

### eEdition Plus Online

*eEdition Plus Online* offers students an online version of *The Language of Literature* that can be used both at school and at home. Features include an interactive reader's notebook, interactive vocabulary practice, video clips, and audio summaries.

### EasyPlanner CD-ROM

This CD-ROM allows teachers to view, edit, and customize pre-made lesson plans and access all of the printed teacher resources. The resources can be searched by skill or topic.

### Test Generator CD-ROM

This CD-ROM contains a variety of pre-made tests and a test bank of items that allows teachers to create customized tests. The program provides tools that walk the user through the searching and editing steps and help correlate the tests to national and state standards.

### NetActivities CD-ROM

This CD-ROM contains extension activities for each Author Study in the text and offers additional information about featured authors through links to related Web sites.

I want to share ideas...

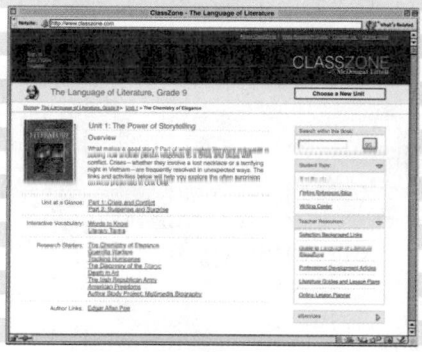

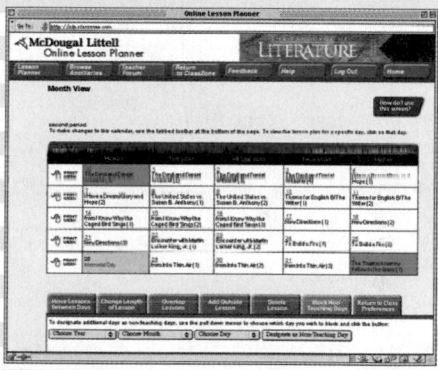

## Power Presentations CD-ROM
This CD-ROM contains PowerPoint® presentations that are tied to the Writing Workshops found in the *Pupil's Edition*.

## Electronic Library CD-ROM
This CD-ROM collection lets teachers customize instruction by choosing the works of a favorite author from over 200 additional pieces of classic literature.

## classzone.com
*ClassZone* is an online guide to *The Language of Literature* that provides access to a variety of Internet resources. This companion Web site offers links correlated to the textbook, an Internet research tutorial, vocabulary flipcards and other activities, author background, spelling practice, a *Teacher Center* and access to the *Online Lesson Planner*.

## Online Lesson Planner
The *Online Lesson Planner* allows teachers to conveniently create, edit, and customize lesson plans on the Internet. Lessons can be modified to incorporate activities from the *Teacher's Edition* or customized to meet specific classroom needs. A correlation feature allows the plans to be correlated to specific state standards or guidelines.

McDougal Littell

# THE LANGUAGE OF
# LITERATURE

## AMERICAN LITERATURE

Arthur N. Applebee

Andrea B. Bermúdez

Sheridan Blau

Rebekah Caplan

Peter Elbow

Susan Hynds

Judith A. Langer

James Marshall

McDougal Littell
A HOUGHTON MIFFLIN COMPANY
Evanston, Illinois • Boston • Dallas

# Acknowledgments

**Unit One**

**Harcourt Brace & Company:** "A Worn Path," from *A Curtain of Green and Other Stories* by Eudora Welty. Copyright 1941 and renewed © 1969 by Eudora Welty. Reprinted by permission of Harcourt Brace & Company.

**McGraw-Hill Companies:** Excerpt from "The World on the Turtle's Back," from *The Great Tree and the Longhouse* by Hazel W. Hertzberg. Copyright © 1966 by the American Anthropological Association. Reprinted with the permission of The McGraw-Hill Companies.

Excerpt from *The Log of Christopher Columbus* by Christopher Columbus, edited by Robert Fuson, originally published by International Marine Publishing Company. Copyright © 1987 by Robert H. Fuson. All rights reserved. Reprinted with the permission of The McGraw-Hill Companies.

**Sunstone Press:** "Song of the Sky Loom" from *Songs of the Tewa*, translated by Herbert Joseph Spinden. Courtesy of Sunstone Press, Box 2321, Santa Fe, NM 87504-2321.

**University of Nebraska Press:** "Coyote and the Buffalo" and "Fox and Coyote and Whale," from *Coyote Stories* by Mourning Dove. Reprinted by permission of the University of Nebraska Press.

*Continued on page 1435*

ISBN 0-618-60139-2

# Senior Consultants

The senior consultants guided the conceptual development for *The Language of Literature* series. They participated actively in shaping prototype materials for major components, and they reviewed completed prototypes and/or completed units to ensure consistency with current research and the philosophy of the series.

*Arthur N. Applebee* Professor of Education, State University of New York at Albany; Director, Center for the Learning and Teaching of Literature; Senior Fellow, Center for Writing and Literacy

*Andrea B. Bermúdez* Professor of Studies in Language and Culture; Director, Research Center for Language and Culture; Chair, Foundations and Professional Studies, University of Houston-Clear Lake

*Sheridan Blau* Senior Lecturer in English and Education and former Director of Composition, University of California at Santa Barbara; Director, South Coast Writing Project; Director, Literature Institute for Teachers; Former President, National Council of Teachers of English

*Rebekah Caplan* Senior Associate for Language Arts for middle school and high school literacy, National Center on Education and the Economy, Washington, D.C.; served on the California State English Assessment Development Team for Language Arts; former co-director of the Bay Area Writing Project, University of California at Berkeley

*Peter Elbow* Emeritus Professor of English, University of Massachusetts at Amherst; Fellow, Bard Center for Writing and Thinking

*Susan Hynds* Professor and Director of English Education, Syracuse University, Syracuse, New York

*Judith A. Langer* Professor of Education, State University of New York at Albany; Co-director, Center for the Learning and Teaching of Literature; Senior Fellow, Center for Writing and Literacy

*James Marshall* Professor of English and English Education; Chair, Division of Curriculum and Instruction, University of Iowa, Iowa City

# Contributing Consultants

*Linda Diamond* Executive Vice President, Consortium on Reading Excellence (CORE); co-author of *Building a Powerful Reading Program*

*Lucila A. Garza* ESL Consultant, Austin, Texas

*Jeffrey N. Golub* Assistant Professor of English Education, University of South Florida, Tampa

*William L. McBride, Ph.D.* Reading and Curriculum Specialist; former middle and high school English instructor

*Sharon Sicinski-Skeans, Ph.D.* Assistant Professor of Reading, University of Houston-Clear Lake; primary consultant on *The InterActive Reader*

## Student Board

The student board members read and evaluated selections to assess their appeal for 11th-grade students.

*Joanne Cheng,*  Spanish River High School, Boca Raton, Florida

*Sharon Garnett Counts,*  Lake Worth High School, Lake Worth, Florida

*Shericko Davis,*  Ramsey High School, Birmingham, Alabama

*Leigh Ann Gordon,*  Plantation High School, Plantation, Florida

*Jennifer Halbert,*  Peoria High School, Peoria, Illinois

*Denise Harris,*  Phineas Banning High School, Wilmington, California

*Robbie Hay,*  Butler High School, Louisville, Kentucky

*Michael Scott,*  Westerville North High School, Westerville, Ohio

*Calvin Yu,*  Ramsey Alternative High School, Birmingham, Alabama

## Student Resource Bank

## Literature Connections

Each of the books in the *Literature Connections* series combines a novel or play with related readings—poems, stories, plays, personal essays, articles—that add new perspectives on the theme or subject matter of the longer work.

Listed below are some of the most popular choices to accompany the Grade 11 anthology:

## THE LANGUAGE OF LITERATURE

# *Reading Strategies*

# UNIT ONE

# Origins and Encounters
## 2000 B.C.–A.D. 1620

Accounts of Exploration and Exploitation

# Part 2 First Encounters

INTERNET
CONNECTION

# UNIT TWO

# From Colony To Country
## 1620 — 1800

American Gothic
# Part 2  The Dark Side of Individualism

# UNIT FOUR

# *Conflict* and *Expansion*
## 1850–1900

*Cliffs Beyond Abiquiu, Dry Waterfall* (1943), Georgia O'Keeffe. Oil on canvas, 76.2 cm × 40.6 cm. The Cleveland (Ohio) Museum of Art, bequest of Georgia O'Keeffe (87.141). Copyright © 1996 The Georgia O'Keeffe Foundation/Artists Rights Society (ARS), New York. Photo Copyright © The Cleveland Museum of Art.

Modernism

## Part 2   Alienation of the Individual

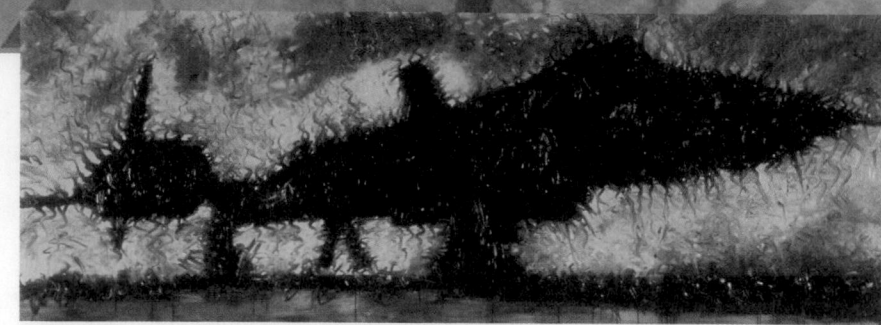

# UNIT SEVEN *War Abroad and Conflict at Home*

## 1940–PRESENT

# Student *Resource Bank*

# *Selections* by Genre

# Poetry

xxvii

## Drama

## Electronic Library

The *Electronic Library* is a CD-ROM that contains additional fiction, nonfiction, poetry, and drama for each unit in *The Language of Literature*. Here is a sampling from the titles included in Grade 11.

**What Happened Till the First Supply,** *from* The General History of Virginia
   John Smith

**Huswifery**
   Edward Taylor

*from* **Common Sense**
   Thomas Paine

**Rip Van Winkle**
   Washington Irving

**Thanatopsis**
   William Cullen Bryant

**Hymn at Concord Monument**
   Ralph Waldo Emerson

**Conclusion,** *from* Walden
   Henry David Thoreau

**Walden**
   E. B. White

**The Minster's Black Veil**
   Nathaniel Hawthorne

**Bartleby, the Scrivener**
   Herman Melville

**Swing Low, Sweet Chariot**
   Negro Spiritual

**Farewell to His Army**
   Robert E. Lee

**O Captain! My Captain!**
   Walt Whitman

**The Outcasts of Poker Flat**
   Bret Harte

**The Open Boat**
   Stephen Crane

**Disappointment Is the Lot of Women**
   Lucy Stone

**Roman Fever**
   Edith Wharton

**Beehive**
   Jean Toomer

**Sophistication**
   Sherwood Anderson

**He**
   Katherine Anne Porter

# *Special Features* in This Book

# THE *Language* OF LITERATURE

## Traditions Across Time

*The legacy of America is a legacy of traditions—trends, themes, and issues that have occurred throughout our history. The literature of America reflects these traditions, serving as a record of the conflicts, failures, and triumphs of a country and its people. Look at the images and quotations below. What kinds of issues and themes are represented?*

Clockwise from top: Civil War soldiers; Vietnam War soldiers; World War II soldiers

**"A Bayonet's contrition is nothing to the Dead."**

*Emily Dickinson*
*19th-century poet*

**"Never think that war, no matter how necessary, nor how justified, is not a crime."**

*Ernest Hemingway*
*20th-century novelist*

"Though the flame of liberty may sometimes cease to shine, the coal can never expire."

*Thomas Paine*
*18th-century patriot*

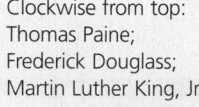

Clockwise from top:
Thomas Paine;
Frederick Douglass;
Martin Luther King, Jr.

"Oppressed people cannot remain oppressed forever. The yearning for freedom eventually manifests itself."

*Martin Luther King, Jr.*
*20th-century political activist*

- **How can literature teach you about the traditions and issues of American culture?**
- **How can a piece of literature from generations ago still capture our imaginations, our minds, and our emotions?**
- **How can YOU find relevance in literature from earlier times?**

*The answers lie on the next few pages.*

# THE Language OF LITERATURE

# Get Involved with the Literature

*Think of any activity you enjoy—sports, music, traveling, painting.
How did you really learn to understand and appreciate it? By watching
others, or by participating yourself? Just about any activity is richer, more
interesting, and more exciting when you are actively involved. The same is
true with literature. You can't simply sit back and absorb the words on a page.
You have to jump into the stories and participate.*

## Your Reader's Notebook

Almost any kind of notebook can be used to help you
interact with literature. Use your Reader's Notebook
to keep track of what's going on inside your mind as
you read. Here are three ways to interact.

**READING MODEL**

Alongside "A Worn Path" are transcripts of the spoken comments made b
11th-grade students, Robert Lewis and Gesenia Veizaga, while they were rea
the story. Their comments provide a glimpse into the minds of readers active
engaged in the process of reading. You'll notice that in the course of their re
Robert and Gesenia quite naturally used the Strategies for Reading that were
introduced on page 7.

To benefit most from this model of active reading, read the story first, jott
down your own responses in your reading log. (Cover up the side comments
a sheet of paper if you're tempted to peek.) Then read Robert's and Gesenia'
comments and compare their processes of reading with your own.

### ① Record Your Thoughts

In your 📖 **READER'S NOTEBOOK** , jot
down ideas, responses, connections,
and questions before, while, and after
you read a selection. (See "Strategies
for Reading," page 7.) Summarize
important passages, and include
sketches and charts, too, if they will
help. If you wish, compare your ideas
with those of a classmate.

# A Worn Path
## EUDORA WELTY

Detail of *Sharecropper* (1970),
Elizabeth Catlett. Linoleum cut on paper,
National Museum of American Art,
Smithsonian Institution, Washington
D.C./Art Resource, New York.

**Robert:** *That's a neat image comparing
her to a pendulum. I wonder if that
means she measures time somehow.*
**EVALUATING/QUESTIONING**

t was December a bright frozen day in the early morning. Fa
in the country there was an old Negro woman with her head
in a red rag, coming along a path through the pinewoods. He
name was Phoenix Jackson. She was very old and small and s
walked slowly in the dark pine shadows, moving a little from
to side in her steps, with the balanced heaviness and lightness of
pendulum in a grandfather clock. She carried a thin, small cane
from an umbrella, and with this she kept tapping the frozen eart
front of her. This made a grave and persistent noise in the still ai
that seemed meditative like the chirping of a solitary little bird.

She wore a dark striped dress reaching down to her shoe tops
an equally long apron of bleached sugar sacks, with a full pocke
neat and tidy, but every time she took a step she might have falle
over her shoelaces, which dragged from her unlaced shoes. She lo
straight ahead. Her eyes were blue with age. Her skin had a patt
all its own of numberless branching wrinkles and as though a w

**Gesenia:** *But she's so tidy. Why
would she be sloppy with her shoes?*
**QUESTIONING**

READING MODEL

"A Worn Path"
by Eudora Welty

(page 7) The old woman closed her eyes, yet she made it
across the log. How was she able to do that?

(page 13) On one level, this story makes me feel sorry for
the old woman. But I'm also so amazed at how strong-
willed and determined she is. I feel like she's a real survivor.

## ❷ Improve Your Reading Skills

Complete the specific 📖 READER'S NOTEBOOK activity on the first page of each literature lesson. This activity will help you apply an important skill as you read the selection.

## ❸ Collect Ideas for Writing

Be aware of intriguing themes, passages, and thoughts of your own as you read or complete follow-up activities. In a special section of your 📖 READER'S NOTEBOOK, jot down anything that may later be a springboard to your own writing.

le tree stood in the middle of her forehead, but a golden color ran …derneath, and the two knobs of her cheeks were illumined by a yel-…w burning under the dark. Under the red rag her hair came down on …r neck in the frailest of ringlets, still black, and with an odor like copper. …Now and then there was a quivering in the thicket. Old Phoenix …d, "Out of my way, all you foxes, owls, beetles, jack rabbits, coons …d wild animals! . . . Keep out from under these feet, little bob-…aites. . . . Keep the big wild hogs out of my path. Don't let none of …ose come running my direction. I got a long way." Under her small …ack freckled hand her cane, limber as a buggy whip, would switch …the brush as if to rouse up any hiding things.

…On she went. The woods were deep and still. The sun made the …e needles almost too bright to look at, up where the wind rocked. …e cones dropped as light as feathers. Down in the hollow was the …urning dove—it was not too late for him.

…The path ran up a hill. "Seem like there is chains about my feet, …e I get this far," she said, in the voice of argument old people keep …use with themselves. "Something always take a hold of me on this …—pleads I should stay."

…After she got to the top she turned and gave a full, severe look …hind her where she had come. "Up through pines," she said at …gth. "Now down through oaks."

…Her eyes opened their widest, and she started down gently. But …fore she got to the bottom of the hill a bush caught her dress.

…Her fingers were busy and intent, but her skirts were full and long, …that before she could pull them free in one place they were caught …another. It was not possible to allow the dress to tear. "I in the …orny bush," she said. "Thorns, you doing your appointed work. …ver want to let folks pass, no sir. Old eyes thought you was a …tty little *green* bush."

…Finally, trembling all over, she stood free, and after a moment dared …stoop for her cane.

…"Sun so high!" she cried, leaning back and looking, while the thick …rs went over her eyes. "The time getting all gone here."

…At the foot of this hill was a place where a log was laid across the creek.

…"Now comes the trial," said Phoenix.

…Putting her right foot out, she mounted the log and shut her eyes. …ting her skirt, leveling her cane fiercely before her, like a festival …ure in some parade, she began to march across. Then she opened … eyes and she was safe on the other side.

…"I wasn't as old as I thought," she said.

…But she sat down to rest. She spread her skirts on the bank around … and folded her hands over her knees. Up above her was a tree in …early cloud of mistletoe. She did not dare to close her eyes, and …en a little boy brought her a plate with a slice of marble-cake on it

**Gesenia:** *You can really picture her skin color from this description.*
VISUALIZING

**Robert:** *Phoenix seems like a down to-earth person. She just goes abou… her business.*
EVALUATING

**Robert:** *Phoenix has made this trip before.*
CLARIFYING

**Gesenia:** *This author uses a lot of description. I'd better pay attention to details so I get a clear picture of what's happening in this story.*
MONITORING

**Gesenia:** *She's not grumpy like some old people. She sees that the thorns are just doing what they do. It doesn't make her mad.*
EVALUATING/CONNECTING

**Gesenia:** *Why would she close her eyes? Usually that's for when you do something for the first time, and she's been here before.*
QUESTIONING/CONNECTING

A WORN PATH    **9**

*"A Worn Path"*
*by Eudora Welty*

Writing Ideas
The author is so good at describing this woman and what she
goes through minute by minute. I'd like to try writing a character sketch of a person and using this much detail. It makes the
woman seem so real.

## Your Working Portfolio

Artists and writers keep portfolios in which they store works in progress or the works they are most proud of. Your portfolio can be a folder, a box, or a notebook—the form doesn't matter. Just make sure to keep adding to it—with drafts of your writing experiments, summaries of your projects, and your own goals and accomplishments as a reader and writer. Later in this book, on the Reflect and Assess pages, you will choose your best or favorite work to place in a **Presentation Portfolio**.

# Become an Active Reader

*The strategies you need to become an active reader are already within your grasp. In fact, you use them every day to make sense of the images and the events in your world. And you really exercise them when you are watching a television program or a movie!*

Take a look at this photograph. The four strategies shown here—Clarify, Question, Predict, and Evaluate—are among those you can use to understand and interpret the situation portrayed. These and other reading strategies listed on the next page can help you interact with literature as well.

**Clarify** *From the way the people are dressed, I'd say it was the 1930s.*

**Question** *I wonder what the little girl is looking at. And why does she seem sad?*

**Predict** *I wonder if the woman will comfort the girl.*

**Evaluate** *I like this photo because it leaves you asking a lot of questions.*

# Strategies for Reading

Following are specific reading strategies that are introduced and applied throughout this book. Use them when you read and interact with the various literature selections. Occasionally **monitor** how well the strategies are working for you and, if desired, modify them to suit your needs.

**PREDICT** Try to figure out what will happen next and how the selection might end. Then read on to see how accurate your guesses were.

**VISUALIZE** Visualize characters, events, and setting to help you understand what's happening. When you read nonfiction, pay attention to the images that form in your mind as you read.

**CONNECT** Connect personally with what you're reading. Think of similarities between the descriptions in the selection and what you have personally experienced, heard about, and read about.

**QUESTION** Question what happens while you read. Searching for reasons behind events and characters' feelings can help you feel closer to what you are reading.

**CLARIFY** Stop occasionally to review what you understand, and expect to have your understanding change and develop as you read on. Reread and use resources to help you clarify your understanding. Also watch for answers to questions you had earlier.

**EVALUATE** Form opinions about what you read, both while you're reading and after you've finished. Develop your own ideas about characters and events.

**On the next page, you will see how two readers applied these strategies to the story "A Worn Path."**

**Go Beyond the Text** If you really become an active reader, your involvement doesn't stop with the last line of the text. Decide what else you'd like to know. Discuss your ideas with others, do some research, or jump on the Internet.

**More Online**
www.mcdougallittell.com

Alongside "A Worn Path" are transcripts of the spoken comments made by two 11th-grade students, Robert Lewis and Gesenia Veizaga, while they were reading the story. Their comments provide a glimpse into the minds of readers actively engaged in the process of reading. You'll notice that in the course of their reading, Robert and Gesenia quite naturally used the Strategies for Reading that were introduced on page 7.

To benefit most from this model of active reading, read the story first, jotting down your own responses in your reading log. (Cover up the side comments with a sheet of paper if you're tempted to peek.) Then read Robert's and Gesenia's comments and compare their processes of reading with your own.

# A Worn Path
## — EUDORA WELTY —

Detail of *Sharecropper* (1970), Elizabeth Catlett. Linoleum cut on paper, National Museum of American Art, Smithsonian Institution, Washington D.C./Art Resource, New York.

**Robert:** *That's a neat image comparing her to a pendulum. I wonder if that means she measures time somehow.*
**EVALUATING/QUESTIONING**

**Gesenia:** *But she's so tidy. Why would she be sloppy with her shoes?*
**QUESTIONING**

It was December—a bright frozen day in the early morning. Far out in the country there was an old Negro woman with her head tied in a red rag, coming along a path through the pinewoods. Her name was Phoenix Jackson. She was very old and small and she walked slowly in the dark pine shadows, moving a little from side to side in her steps, with the balanced heaviness and lightness of a pendulum in a grandfather clock. She carried a thin, small cane made from an umbrella, and with this she kept tapping the frozen earth in front of her. This made a grave and persistent noise in the still air, that seemed meditative like the chirping of a solitary little bird.

She wore a dark striped dress reaching down to her shoe tops, and an equally long apron of bleached sugar sacks, with a full pocket: all neat and tidy, but every time she took a step she might have fallen over her shoelaces, which dragged from her unlaced shoes. She looked straight ahead. Her eyes were blue with age. Her skin had a pattern all its own of numberless branching wrinkles and as though a whole little tree stood in the middle of her forehead, but a golden color ran underneath, and the two knobs of her cheeks were illumined by a yellow burning under the dark. Under the red rag her hair came down on her neck in the frailest of ringlets, still black, and with an odor like copper.

Now and then there was a quivering in the thicket. Old Phoenix said, "Out of my way, all you foxes, owls, beetles, jack rabbits, coons and wild animals! . . . Keep out from under these feet, little bobwhites. . . . Keep the big wild hogs out of my path. Don't let none of those come running my direction. I got a long way." Under her small black-freckled hand her cane, limber as a buggy whip, would switch at the brush as if to rouse up any hiding things.

On she went. The woods were deep and still. The sun made the pine needles almost too bright to look at, up where the wind rocked. The cones dropped as light as feathers. Down in the hollow was the mourning dove—it was not too late for him.

The path ran up a hill. "Seem like there is chains about my feet, time I get this far," she said, in the voice of argument old people keep to use with themselves. "Something always take a hold of me on this hill—pleads I should stay."

After she got to the top she turned and gave a full, severe look behind her where she had come. "Up through pines," she said at length. "Now down through oaks."

Her eyes opened their widest, and she started down gently. But before she got to the bottom of the hill a bush caught her dress.

Her fingers were busy and intent, but her skirts were full and long, so that before she could pull them free in one place they were caught in another. It was not possible to allow the dress to tear. "I in the thorny bush," she said. "Thorns, you doing your appointed work. Never want to let folks pass, no sir. Old eyes thought you was a pretty little *green* bush."

Finally, trembling all over, she stood free, and after a moment dared to stoop for her cane.

"Sun so high!" she cried, leaning back and looking, while the thick tears went over her eyes. "The time getting all gone here."

At the foot of this hill was a place where a log was laid across the creek.

"Now comes the trial," said Phoenix.

Putting her right foot out, she mounted the log and shut her eyes. Lifting her skirt, leveling her cane fiercely before her, like a festival figure in some parade, she began to march across. Then she opened her eyes and she was safe on the other side.

"I wasn't as old as I thought," she said.

But she sat down to rest. She spread her skirts on the bank around her and folded her hands over her knees. Up above her was a tree in a pearly cloud of mistletoe. She did not dare to close her eyes, and when a little boy brought her a plate with a slice of marble-cake on it

**Gesenia:** *You can really picture her skin color from this description.*
VISUALIZING

**Robert:** *Phoenix seems like a down-to-earth person. She just goes about her business.*
EVALUATING

**Robert:** *Phoenix has made this trip before.*
CLARIFYING

**Gesenia:** *This author uses a lot of description. I'd better pay attention to details so I get a clear picture of what's happening in this story.*
MONITORING

**Gesenia:** *She's not grumpy like some old people. She sees that the thorns are just doing what they do. It doesn't make her mad.*
EVALUATING/CONNECTING

**Gesenia:** *Why would she close her eyes? Usually that's for when you do something for the first time, and she's been here before.*
QUESTIONING/CONNECTING

she spoke to him. "That would be acceptable," she said. But when she went to take it there was just her own hand in the air.

So she left that tree, and had to go through a barbed-wire fence. There she had to creep and crawl, spreading her knees and stretching her fingers like a baby trying to climb the steps. But she talked loudly to herself: she could not let her dress be torn now, so late in the day, and she could not pay for having her arm or her leg sawed off if she got caught fast where she was.

At last she was safe through the fence and risen up out in the clearing. Big dead trees, like black men with one arm, were standing in the purple stalks of the withered cotton field. There sat a buzzard.

"Who you watching?"

In the furrow she made her way along.

"Glad this not the season for bulls," she said, looking sideways, "and the good Lord made his snakes to curl up and sleep in the winter. A pleasure I don't see no two-headed snake coming around that tree, where it come once. It took a while to get by him, back in the summer."

She passed through the old cotton and went into a field of dead corn. It whispered and shook and was taller than her head. "Through the maze now," she said, for there was no path.

Then there was something tall, black, and skinny there, moving before her.

At first she took it for a man. It could have been a man dancing in the field. But she stood still and listened, and it did not make a sound. It was as silent as a ghost.

"Ghost," she said sharply, "who be you the ghost of? For I have heard of nary death close by."

But there was no answer—only the ragged dancing in the wind.

She shut her eyes, reached out her hand, and touched a sleeve. She found a coat and inside that an emptiness, cold as ice.

"You scarecrow," she said. Her face lighted. "I ought to be shut up for good," she said with laughter. "My senses is gone. I too old. I the oldest people I ever know. Dance, old scarecrow," she said, "while I dancing with you."

She kicked her foot over the furrow, and with mouth drawn down, shook her head once or twice in a little strutting way. Some husks blew down and whirled in streamers about her skirts.

Then she went on, parting her way from side to side with the cane, through the whispering field. At last she came to the end, to a wagon track where the silver grass blew between the red ruts. The quail were walking around like pullets, seeming all dainty and unseen.

"Walk pretty," she said. "This the easy place. This the easy going."

She followed the track, swaying through the quiet bare fields, through the little strings of trees silver in their dead leaves, past cabins silver from weather, with the doors and windows boarded shut, all like old women under a spell sitting there. "I walking in their sleep," she said, nodding her head vigorously.

In a ravine she went where a spring was silently flowing through a hollow log. Old Phoenix bent and drank. "Sweet-gum makes the water sweet," she said, and drank more. "Nobody know who made this well, for it was here when I was born."

The track crossed a swampy part where the moss hung as white as lace from every limb. "Sleep on, alligators, and blow your bubbles." Then the track went into the road.

Deep, deep the road went down between the high green-colored banks. Overhead the live-oaks met, and it was as dark as a cave.

A black dog with a lolling tongue came up out of the weeds by the ditch. She was meditating, and not ready, and when he came at her she only hit him a little with her cane. Over she went in the ditch, like a little puff of milkweed.

Down there, her senses drifted away. A dream visited her, and she reached her hand up, but nothing reached down and gave her a pull. So she lay there and presently went to talking. "Old woman," she said to herself, "that black dog come up out of the weeds to stall you off, and now there he sitting on his fine tail, smiling at you."

A white man finally came along and found her—a hunter, a young man, with his dog on a chain.

"Well, Granny!" he laughed. "What are you doing there?"

"Lying on my back like a June-bug waiting to be turned over, mister," she said, reaching up her hand.

He lifted her up, gave her a swing in the air, and set her down. "Anything broken, Granny?"

"No sir, them old dead weeds is springy enough," said Phoenix, when she had got her breath. "I thank you for your trouble."

"Where do you live, Granny?" he asked, while the two dogs were growling at each other.

"Away back yonder, sir, behind the ridge. You can't even see it from here."

"On your way home?"

"No sir, I going to town."

"Why, that's too far! That's as far as I walk when I come out myself, and I get something for my trouble." He patted the stuffed bag he carried, and there hung down a little closed claw. It was one of the bob-whites, with its beak hooked bitterly to show it was dead. "Now you go on home, Granny!"

"I bound to go to town, mister," said Phoenix. "The time come around."

*Robert:* Phoenix is a good name for her character—she's old and enduring. But I wonder what ashes she will rise from.
**EVALUATING/QUESTIONING**

*Robert:* She's hallucinating again, but she's wishful for help. She's not afraid, not imagining terrible things.
**EVALUATING**

*Gesenia:* She seems to be getting older and more feeble. At first she was just striding along, but now she needs help even to get up.
**CLARIFYING**

*Robert:* He's so condescending. He's younger but he shows her no respect. His attitude doesn't bother her, though.
**EVALUATING**

*Gesenia:* Now I don't like this guy. He's being bossy to Phoenix.
**EVALUATING**

*Georgia Landscape* (about 1934–1935), Hale Woodruff. National Museum of American Art, Smithsonian Institution, Washington D.C./Art Resource, New York.

**Robert:** *He's a racist, too. What a jerk.*
EVALUATING

**Gesenia:** *The hunter is pretty nosy, asking her so many questions.*
EVALUATING

**Gesenia:** *It's hard for her to stoop down, even. But she's able to cross all those obstacles.*
CLARIFYING

**Robert:** *A nickel is a big deal to her. She must be real poor, or maybe the story happens a long time ago.*
CLARIFYING

He gave another laugh, filling the whole landscape. "I know you old colored people! Wouldn't miss going to town to see Santa Claus!"

But something held old Phoenix very still. The deep lines in her face went into a fierce and different radiation. Without warning, she had seen with her own eyes a flashing nickel fall out of the man's pocket onto the ground.

"How old are you, Granny?" he was saying.

"There is no telling, mister," she said, "no telling."

Then she gave a little cry and clapped her hands and said, "Git on away from here, dog! Look! Look at that dog!" She laughed as if in admiration. "He ain't scared of nobody. He a big black dog." She whispered, "Sic him!"

"Watch me get rid of that cur," said the man. "Sic him, Pete! Sic him!"

Phoenix heard the dogs fighting, and heard the man running and throwing sticks. She even heard a gunshot. But she was slowly bending forward by that time, further and further forward, the lids stretched down over her eyes, as if she were doing this in her sleep. Her chin was lowered almost to her knees. The yellow palm of her hand came out from the fold of her apron. Her fingers slid down and along the ground under the piece of money with the grace and care they would have in lifting an egg from under a setting hen. Then she slowly straightened up, she stood erect, and the nickel was in her apron pocket. A bird flew by. Her lips moved. "God watching me the whole time. I come to stealing."

The man came back, and his own dog panted about them. "Well, I scared him off that time," he said, and then he laughed and lifted his gun and pointed it at Phoenix.

She stood straight and faced him.

"Doesn't the gun scare you?" he said, still pointing it.

"No, sir, I seen plenty go off closer by, in my day, and for less than what I done," she said, holding utterly still.

He smiled, and shouldered the gun. "Well, Granny," he said, "you must be a hundred years old, and scared of nothing. I'd give you a dime if I had any money with me. But you take my advice and stay home, and nothing will happen to you."

"I bound to go on my way, mister," said Phoenix. She inclined her head in the red rag. Then they went in different directions, but she could hear the gun shooting again and again over the hill.

She walked on. The shadows hung from the oak trees to the road like curtains. Then she smelled wood-smoke, and smelled the river, and she saw a steeple and the cabins on their steep steps. Dozens of little black children whirled around her. There ahead was Natchez shining. Bells were ringing. She walked on.

In the paved city it was Christmas time. There were red and green electric lights strung and crisscrossed everywhere, and all turned on in the daytime. Old Phoenix would have been lost if she had not distrusted her eyesight and depended on her feet to know where to take her.

She paused quietly on the sidewalk where people were passing by. A lady came along in the crowd, carrying an armful of red-, green-and silver-wrapped presents; she gave off perfume like the red roses in hot summer, and Phoenix stopped her.

"Please, missy, will you lace up my shoe?" She held up her foot.

"What do you want, Grandma?"

"See my shoe," said Phoenix. "Do all right for out in the country, but wouldn't look right to go in a big building."

"Stand still then, Grandma," said the lady. She put her packages down on the sidewalk beside her and laced and tied both shoes tightly.

"Can't lace 'em with a cane," said Phoenix. "Thank you, missy. I doesn't mind asking a nice lady to tie up my shoe, when I gets out on the street."

Moving slowly and from side to side, she went into the big building, and into a tower of steps, where she walked up and around and around until her feet knew to stop.

She entered a door, and there she saw nailed up on the wall the

**Robert:** That's a neat way to say that Phoenix has an image of this place in her mind.
EVALUATING

document that had been stamped with the gold seal and framed in the gold frame, which matched the dream that was hung up in her head.

"Here I be," she said. There was a fixed and ceremonial stiffness over her body.

"A charity case, I suppose," said an attendant who sat at the desk before her.

But Phoenix only looked above her head. There was sweat on her face, the wrinkles in her skin shone like a bright net.

**Gesenia:** The attendant is so rude.
EVALUATING

**Robert:** The attendant looks down on Phoenix—treats her like she's not really a person.
EVALUATING

"Speak up, Grandma," the woman said. "What's your name? We must have your history, you know. Have you been here before? What seems to be the trouble with you?"

Old Phoenix only gave a twitch to her face as if a fly were bothering her.

"Are you deaf?" cried the attendant.

But then the nurse came in.

"Oh, that's just old Aunt Phoenix," she said. "She doesn't come for herself—she has a little grandson. She makes these trips just as regular as clockwork. She lives away back off the Old Natchez Trace." She bent down. "Well, Aunt Phoenix, why don't you just take a seat? We won't keep you standing after your long trip." She pointed.

**Gesenia:** People don't talk about "clockwork" if something happens every week. I'll bet she comes about once a year.
CONNECTING/CLARIFYING

The old woman sat down, bolt upright in the chair.

"Now, how is the boy?" asked the nurse.

Old Phoenix did not speak.

"I said, how is the boy?"

**Gesenia:** She's changed now. On the way, she talked to everything, but now she's motionless. What's wrong?
QUESTIONING

But Phoenix only waited and stared straight ahead, her face very solemn and withdrawn into rigidity.

"Is his throat any better?" asked the nurse. "Aunt Phoenix, don't you hear me? Is your grandson's throat any better since the last time you came for the medicine?"

With her hands on her knees, the old woman waited, silent, erect and motionless, just as if she were in armor.

"You mustn't take up our time this way, Aunt Phoenix," the nurse said. "Tell us quickly about your grandson, and get it over. He isn't dead, is he?"

**Robert:** Phoenix definitely has a senility problem or a loss of alertness.
EVALUATING

At last there came a flicker and then a flame of comprehension across her face, and she spoke.

"My grandson. It was my memory had left me. There I sat and forgot why I made my long trip."

"Forgot?" The nurse frowned. "After you came so far?"

**Robert:** I like how she's so dignified. My grandparents went through Alzheimer's, and they were both like that—being dignified as they could, knowing they can't help what's happening.
EVALUATING/CONNECTING

Then Phoenix was like an old woman begging a dignified forgiveness for waking up frightened in the night. "I never did go to school, I was too old at the Surrender," she said in a soft voice. "I'm an old woman without an education. It was my memory fail me. My little grandson, he is just the same, and I forgot it in the coming."

"Throat never heals, does it?" said the nurse, speaking in a loud, sure voice to old Phoenix. By now she had a card with something written on it, a little list. "Yes. Swallowed lye. When was it?—January—two-three years ago—"

Phoenix spoke unasked now. "No, missy, he not dead, he just the same. Every little while his throat begin to close up again, and he not able to swallow. He not get his breath. He not able to help himself. So the time come around, and I go on another trip for the soothing medicine."

"All right. The doctor said as long as you came to get it, you could have it," said the nurse. "But it's an obstinate case."

"My little grandson, he sit up there in the house all wrapped up, waiting by himself," Phoenix went on. "We is the only two left in the world. He suffer and it don't seem to put him back at all. He got a sweet look. He going to last. He wear a little patch quilt and peep out holding his mouth open like a little bird. I remembers so plain now. I not going to forget him again, no, the whole enduring time. I could tell him from all the others in creation."

"All right." The nurse was trying to hush her now. She brought her a bottle of medicine. "Charity," she said, making a check mark in a book.

Old Phoenix held the bottle close to her eyes, and then carefully put it into her pocket.

"I thank you," she said.

"It's Christmas time, Grandma," said the attendant. "Could I give you a few pennies out of my purse?"

"Five pennies is a nickel," said Phoenix stiffly.

"Here's a nickel," said the attendant.

Phoenix rose carefully and held out her hand. She received the nickel and then fished the other nickel out of her pocket and laid it beside the new one. She stared at her palm closely, with her head on one side.

Then she gave a tap with her cane on the floor.

"This is what come to me to do," she said. "I going to the store and buy my child a little windmill they sells, made out of paper. He going to find it hard to believe there such a thing in the world. I'll march myself back where he waiting, holding it straight up in this hand."

She lifted her free hand, gave a little nod, turned around, and walked out of the doctor's office. Then her slow step began on the stairs, going down.

*Gesenia:* She blames her lack of education, but I'm not sure that's why. My great grandmother just sits sometimes when you ask her questions, but then she gets interested and joins in the talk.
**EVALUATING/CONNECTING**

*Robert:* So that's the important errand.
**CLARIFYING**

*Gesenia:* The story is getting a serious tone now. The grandson is sick and alone at home, and Phoenix has to go back through all those obstacles.
**CLARIFYING**

*Robert:* She knows what she wants. She doesn't shy away except with that memory lapse earlier. She's very gutsy.
**EVALUATING**

*Robert:* She has a hard road ahead. The struggle keeps going, and that fits with the title of the story.
**CLARIFYING**

*Gesenia:* Is she going to make it back at all? She's so forgetful.
**QUESTIONING/EVALUATING**

## Origins and Encounters

The selections in Unit One explore some beliefs of Native Americans before European contact and the experiences of early Europeans and Africans in North America. The unit is divided into two parts in an effort to do justice to the disparate cultures that came into contact in North America after 1492.

### ———— Part 1 ————

**In Harmony with Nature** This part contains a sample of literature from the Native American oral tradition. The selections in the **Traditions Across Time** section show how contemporary Native American writers have used the ancient traditions of their people to inform and enrich their work.

### ———— Part 2 ————

**First Encounters** This part includes important historical documents by some of the first Europeans in North America as well as one of the first slave narratives. All of these selections focus on the encounter between different cultures. The selections in **Traditions Across Time** show how the tradition of writing about personal explorations has continued into the present.

# ORIGINS AND ENCOUNTERS

Pleasant it looked,
this newly created world.
Along the entire length and breadth
of the earth, our grandmother,
extended the green reflection
of her covering
and the escaping odors
were pleasant to inhale.

**WINNEBAGO**
*an Algonkian people*

Let us... go
to the place that
God will show
us to possess in
peace and plenty,
a land more like
the Garden of
Eden, which the
Lord planted,
than any part else
of all the earth.

**REVEREND WILLIAM SYMONDS**
*Puritan minister*

Giovanni da Verrazano becoming the first European
to enter New York Bay, 1524. Lithograph done
in 1868 by an unknown American artist.
The Granger Collection, New York.

16

---

 **Mini Lesson** ## Viewing and Representing

*Giovanni da Verrazano becoming the first European to enter New York Bay, 1524,* **anonymous**

**ART APPRECIATION**
**Instruction** Created in 1868, this drawing is a lithograph. In the lithographic process, an image is drawn in crayon or grease pencil directly onto a flat surface, often a stone. The surface is dampened with water, which will not stick to the greased image. An oil-based ink is then applied to the surface with a roller, and only the greased image absorbs the ink. A special press then prints the inked image onto a paper sheet. Color lithographs must repeat the procedure for each color.

Verrazano (c. 1485–c. 1528), an Italian navigator in the service of France, explored the long eastern coast of North America in 1524. He was the first European to enter what became New York Bay, and he wrote of the "very pleasant place . . . through which there ran to the sea an exceedingly great stream of water. . . ."

To help students explore connections among the art, the quotations, and the unit theme, have them consider the following questions:

**Ask: How does this painting suggest the theme of origins and encounters?**
Possible Response: The painting shows how a now-urbanized area of North America looked at the time of arrival of Europeans. The interest of the Native Americans in the approaching ship implies that the natives will have contact with the newcomers.

Although the two quotations on this page each address the land in its primordial beauty, they reflect significant cultural differences between the Winnebago and the early English settlers.

**Ask: How do the groups differ in the way they view the land and their place on it?**
Possible Response: The Winnebago mention a personal connection with the land, calling it "our grandmother," and they praise it. Though the English recognize its beauty, they think of land in terms of ownership, as the word *possess* indicates.

**Ask: What kinds of stories and experiences might you expect to read about in this unit?**
Possible Response: This unit may contain stories of how traditions began and what effect a meeting of people from different traditions will have on each of them.

**Ask: What have been your experiences when you've encountered something or someone new?**
Possible Response: Accept all reasonable responses. Students may mention feelings of excitement, apprehension, curiosity, disappointment, discovery, or some combination of these. Their encounters may have had positive or negative results.

Use the following question to help develop students' visual literacy.
**Ask: How would you describe the boat's and human figures' relations to the landscape?**
Possible Response: The boat seems high and distant—an outsider; in contrast, in the foreground, lying and sitting among foliage, the Native Americans appear as a natural part of the landscape.

| Features and Selections | Literary Analysis | Reading and Critical Thinking | Writing Opportunities | |
|---|---|---|---|---|
| **Origins and Encounters**<br>**Time Line**<br>**Historical Background/**<br>In Harmony with Nature | | | | |
| IROQUOIS MYTH<br>The World on the Turtle's Back | Creation Myths, 24, 31 | Causes and Effects, 24, 31 | Essay on Harmony, 32<br>Opinion Essay, 32<br>Alternate Ending, 32 | |
| TEWA SONG & NAVAJO SONG<br>Song of the Sky Loom<br>Hunting Song/Dinni-e Sin | Repetition, 33, 37 | Native American Songs, 33, 37 | Definition Essay, 38<br>Siren Song, 38<br>Reflective Essay, 38 | |
| OKANOGAN FOLK TALES<br>Coyote Stories | Trickster Tales, 39, 46 | Trickster Tales, 39, 46<br><br>Informal Assess., 47 | Magazine Article, 47<br>Trickster Tale, 47 | |
| SHORT STORY<br>**Comparing Literature**<br>The Man to Send Rain Clouds | Conflict, 48, 53 | Making Inferences, 48, 53<br>Informal Assess., 54 | Performance Review, 54<br>Description of Rites, 54 | |
| NONFICTION<br>**Comparing Literature**<br>The Way to Rainy Mountain | Setting, 55, 62 | Structure, 55, 62<br>Sequential Order, 63 | Eulogy, 63<br>Points of Comparison, 63 | |
| Comparing Literature<br>**Assessment Practice** | | | Comparison Essay, 64 | |

LEGEND  DLS – Daily Language SkillBuilder
CCL – Cross Curricular Link    Green type – Teacher's Edition

| Features and Selections | Literary Analysis | Reading and Critical Thinking | Writing Opportunities | |
|---|---|---|---|---|
| **Historical Background/ First Encounters** | | | | |
| **Learning the Language of Literature** Historical Narratives | Historical Narratives, 70 | Strategies for Reading, 71 | | |
| REPORT *from* La Relación | Audience, 72, 78 Review: Setting, 78 | Text Organizers, 72, 78 | Firsthand Account, 79 Leadership Essay, 79  Report, 79 Informal Assess., 79 | |
| CHRONICLE *from* Of Plymouth Plantation  **Related Reading** Women and Children First: The Mayflower Pilgrims | Primary and Secondary Sources, 81, 88 Review: Conflict, 88 | Summarizing, 81, 88  Informal Assess., 87   Women and Children First: The Mayflower Pilgrims, 91 | Diary, 89 Eyewitness Account, 89  Interview, 89 | |
| SLAVE NARRATIVE *from* The Interesting Narrative of the Life of Olaudah Equiano | Slave Narratives, 93, 98  Review: Audience, 98 Review: Primary and Secondary Sources, 98 | Analyzing Details, 93, 98  Informal Assess., 99 | Song of Freedom, 99 Narrative Summary, 99 | |
| TRAVELOGUE **Comparing Literature** *from* Blue Highways | Author's Purpose, 100, 107 | Organizing Details, 100, 107  Fact and Nonfact, 106 | Hopi Dialogue, 108 Personal Essay, 108  Points of Comparison, 108 | |
| AUTOBIOGRAPHY **Comparing Literature** My Sojourn in the Lands of My Ancestors | Autobiography, 109, 116 Review: Author's Purpose, 116 | Autobiography, 109, 116  Test Practice, 115 | Description of Place, 117  Poetry of Experience, 117 Points of Comparison, 117 | |
| **Comparing Literature** **Assessment Practice** | | | Synthesis Essay, 118 | |
| **Writing Workshop: Eyewitness Report** **Assessment Practice** **Building Vocabulary** **Sentence Crafting** | | | Standards for Writing, 120 Eyewitness Report, 123 | |
| **Reflect and Assess** Origins and Encounters | Reviewing Literary Concepts, 129 | | Old Beliefs, New Literature, 128 Building Your Portfolio, 129 | |

To introduce the theme/literary period of this unit, use Fine Art Transparencies T17–19 in the Communications Transparencies and Copymasters.

| | Unit Resource Book | Assessment | Integrated Technology and Media | Additional Support — Literary Analysis Transparencies |
|---|---|---|---|---|
| **The World on the Turtle's Back** *pp. 24–32* | • Summary p. 8<br>• Active Reading p. 9<br>• Literary Analysis p. 10<br>• Words to Know p. 11<br>• Selection Quiz p. 12 | • Selection Test, Formal Assessment pp. 7–8<br>⊙ Test Generator | ◯ Audio Library | • Legends, Myths, and Folk Tales T24 |
| **Song of the Sky Loom Hunting Song/Dinni-e Sin** *pp. 33–38* | • Active Reading p. 13<br>• Literary Analysis p. 14 | • Selection Test, Formal Assessment p. 9<br>⊙ Test Generator | ◯ Audio Library | • Legends, Myths, and Folk Tales T24 |
| **Coyote Stories Coyote and the Buffalo Fox and Coyote and Whale** *pp. 39–47* | • Summary (Coyote and the Buffalo) p. 15<br>• Summary (Fox and Coyote and Whale) p. 16<br>• Active Reading p. 17<br>• Literary Analysis p. 18<br>• Selection Quiz p. 19 | • Selection Test, Formal Assessment pp. 11–12<br>⊙ Test Generator | ◯ Audio Library<br><br>▭ Video: Literature in Performance, Video Resource Book pp. 3–8 | • Legends, Myths, and Folk Tales T24 |
| **The Man to Send Rain Clouds (1969)** *pp. 48–54* | • Summary p. 20<br>• Active Reading p. 21<br>• Literary Analysis p. 22<br>• Words to Know p. 23<br>• Selection Quiz p. 24 | • Selection Test, Formal Assessment pp. 13–14<br>⊙ Test Generator | ◯ Audio Library | • Social Conflict/Issues T14 |
| *from* **The Way to Rainy Mountain (1969)** *pp. 55–63* | • Summary p. 25<br>• Active Reading p. 26<br>• Literary Analysis p. 27<br>• Words to Know p. 28<br>• Selection Quiz p. 29<br>• Comparing Literature p. 30 | • Selection Test, Formal Assessment pp. 15–16<br>⊙ Test Generator | ◯ Audio Library | • Setting T13 |
| | | **Unit Assessment**<br>• Unit One, Part 1 Test, Formal Assessment pp. 17–18<br>⊙ Test Generator<br>• Unit One Integrated Test, Integrated Assessment pp. 1–9 | **Unit Technology**<br>ⓘ ClassZone www.mcdougallittell.com<br>⊙ EasyPlanner CD-ROM<br>⊙ Electronic Library | |

| Reading and Critical Thinking Transparencies | Grammar Transparencies and Copymasters | Vocabulary Transparencies and Copymasters | Writing Transparencies and Copymasters | Communications Transparencies and Copymasters |
|---|---|---|---|---|
| • Cause and Effect T1<br>• Sequence Chain T49<br>• Organizational Chart: Horizontal T51 | • Daily Language SkillBuilder T1<br>• Diagnostic: Parts of Speech C61 | • Personal Word List C17<br>• Expanding Vocabulary C19 | • Literary Interpretation C30<br>• Compare and Contrast C31<br>• Opinion Statement C34 | • Impromptu Speaking: Dialogue, Role-Play, Debate T13 |
| • Compare and Contrast T15<br>• Locating Information Using Print References T32 | • Daily Language SkillBuilder T1<br>• Possessive Nouns T38<br>• Forming Plurals and Distinguishing Plurals from Possessives C64 | • Context Clues C18 | | • Evaluating Roles in Groups T8<br>• Dramatic Reading T12 |
| • Compare and Contrast T15<br>• Cluster Diagram T48 | • Daily Language SkillBuilder T1<br>• Kinds of Sentences C74<br>• Capitalizing Proper Nouns and Proper Adjectives C142 | • Expanding Vocabulary C19 | • Short Story C29 | • Evaluation Matrix: Film/Video T7<br>• Nonverbal Strategies T15 |
| • Making Inferences T7 | • Daily Language SkillBuilder T2<br>• Capitalizing the First Word of a Sentence C146 | • Word Origins C22 | • Opinion Statement C34 | |
| • Evaluating Story Elements T6<br>• Analyzing Text Structure T17 | • Daily Language SkillBuilder T2<br>• Types of Pronouns C65<br>• Simple and Compound Predicates C77 | • The Connotative Power of Words C26 | • Compare and Contrast C32 | |

## STUDENTS ACQUIRING ENGLISH

The **Spanish Study Guide,** pp. 1–19, includes language support for the following pages:
• Family and Community Involvement (per unit)

• Selection Summaries and Vocabulary
• Active Reading
• Literary Analysis

To introduce the theme/literary period of this unit, use Fine Art Transparencies T17–19 in the Communications Transparencies and Copymasters.

| | Unit Resource Book | Assessment | Integrated Technology and Media | Additional Support — Literary Analysis Transparencies |
|---|---|---|---|---|
| *from* **La Relación** pp. 72–80 | • Summary p. 31 • Active Reading p. 32 • Literary Analysis p. 33 • Words to Know p. 34 • Selection Quiz p. 35 | • Selection Test, Formal Assessment pp. 19–20 • Test Generator | Audio Library  Research Starter www.mcdougallittell.com | • Historical Narrative T1 |
| *from* **Of Plymouth Plantation** pp. 81–90 | • Summary p. 36 • Active Reading p. 37 • Literary Analysis p. 38 • Words to Know p. 39 • Selection Quiz p. 40 | • Selection Test, Formal Assessment pp. 21–22 • Test Generator | Audio Library | • Historical Narrative T1 • Historical Narrative: Sequencing T2 |
| *from* **The Interesting Narrative of the Life of Olaudah Equiano** pp. 93–99 | • Summary p. 41 • Active Reading p. 42 • Literary Analysis p. 43 • Words to Know p. 44 • Selection Quiz p. 45 | • Selection Test, Formal Assessment pp. 23–24 • Test Generator | Audio Library | • Historical Narrative T1 • Historical Narrative: Sequencing T2 |
| *from* **Blue Highways (1982)** pp. 100–108 | • Summary p. 46 • Active Reading p. 47 • Literary Analysis p. 48 • Words to Know p. 49 • Selection Quiz p. 50 | • Selection Test, Formal Assessment pp. 25–26 • Test Generator | Audio Library | • Compare/Contrast Themes and Conflicts T16 |
| **My Sojourn in the Lands of My Ancestors** pp. 109–117 | • Summary p. 51 • Active Reading p. 52 • Literary Analysis p. 53 • Words to Know p. 54 • Selection Quiz p. 55 • Comparing Literature p. 56 | • Selection Test, Formal Assessment pp. 27–28 • Test Generator | | |

## Writing Workshop: Eyewitness Report

**Unit One Resource Book**
• Prewriting p. 57
• Drafting and Elaboration p. 58
• Peer Response Guide pp. 59–60
• Revising, Editing, and Proofreading p. 61
• Student Models pp. 62–67
• Rubric for Evaluation p. 68

 **Power Presentations CD-ROM**
**Writing Transparencies and Copymasters** T11, T20, C25
**Teacher's Guide to Assessment and Portfolio Use**

### Unit Assessment
• Unit One, Part 2 Test, Formal Assessment pp. 29–30
 Test Generator
• Unit One Integrated Test, Integrated Assessment p. 1–9

### Unit Technology
 ClassZone www.mcdougallittell.com
 EasyPlanner CD-ROM
 Electronic Library

| Reading and Critical Thinking Transparencies | Grammar Transparencies and Copymasters | Vocabulary Transparencies and Copymasters | Writing Transparencies and Copymasters | Communications Transparencies and Copymasters |
|---|---|---|---|---|
| • Reading for Details T16<br>• Organizing and Interpreting Information on Bar Graphs T37 | • Daily Language SkillBuilder T3<br>• Sentence Fragments T42<br>• Parts of Speech C62<br>• Simple Sentences C75 | • Meanings of Prefixes and Roots C27 | • Opinion Statement C34<br>• Autobiographical Incident C35 | • Evaluating Roles in Groups T8<br>• Impromptu Speaking: Dialogue, Role-Play, Debate T13 |
| • Summarizing T10<br>• Determining Author's Purpose and Audience T19<br>• Determining Author's Bias T22 | • Daily Language SkillBuilder T3<br>• Sentence Fragments I C107<br>• Run-on Sentences C109 | • Word Origins C22 | • Eyewitness Report C25 | • Appreciative Listening T2 |
| • Summarizing T10<br>• Observation Chart T46 | • Daily Language SkillBuilder T3<br>• Compound Sentences C110 | | | |
| • Determining Author's Purpose and Audience T19<br>• Cluster Diagram T48<br>• Evaluation Matrix T55 | • Daily Language SkillBuilder T4<br>• Complex Sentences C111<br>• Pronouns C125 | • Meanings of Prefixes and Roots C27 | • The Uses of Dialogue T24 | |
| • Observation Chart T46 | • Daily Language SkillBuilder T4 | | • The Uses of Dialogue T24 | • Reading Aloud T11 |

## STUDENTS ACQUIRING ENGLISH

The **Spanish Study Guide,** pp. 20–34, includes language support for the following pages:
• Family and Community Involvement (per unit)
• Selection Summaries and Vocabulary
• Active Reading
• Literary Analysis

| Selection | SkillBuilder Sentences | Suggested Answers |
|---|---|---|
| The World on the Turtle's Back | 1. "Hey Carlos, James said, whats the assignment for english class tomorrow." | 1. "Hey, Carlos," James said, "what's the assignment for **E**nglish class tomorrow?" |
| | 2. Carlos replyed, we're supposed to read an iroquois myth write a poem and studying for a spelling test. | 2. Carlos **replied**, "**We**'re supposed to read an **I**roquois myth, write a poem, and **study** for a spelling test." |
| Song of the Sky Loom Hunting Song/Dinni-e Sin | 1. "Song of the Sky Loom" is an apparantly simple yet truely complex poem that espresses peoples longing to be as pure as the natural world. | 1. "Song of the Sky Loom" is an **apparently** simple yet **truly** complex poem that **expresses** people**'s** longing to be as pure as the natural world. |
| | 2. If we could really understand in what sence our mother is the earth and our father is the sky, than we would be more respectfull of nature. | 2. If we could really understand in what **sense** our mother is the earth and our father is the sky, **then** we would be more **respectful** of nature. |
| Coyote Stories Coyote and the Buffalo Fox and Coyote and Whale | 1. many native american cultures have there own versions of Coyote Storys. | 1. **M**any **N**ative **A**merican cultures have **their** own versions of Coyote **stories**. |
| | 2. Coyote and the buffalo is a story that is funny entertaining and it is scary. | 2. "Coyote and the **B**uffalo" is a story that is funny, entertaining, and scary. |
| The Man to Send Rain Clouds | 1. did you go to the bank she asked? | 1. "**D**id you go to the bank?" she asked. |
| | 2. When a author writes a short story, they may have to do some research. | 2. When **an** author writes a short story, **he or she** may have to do some research. |

| Selection | SkillBuilder Sentences | Suggested Answers |
|---|---|---|
| *from* The Way to Rainy Mountain | 1. Having died in the Spring, Momaday returned to Rainy mountain in july to mourn his grandmother. | 1. Momaday returned to Rainy **M**ountain in **J**uly to mourn his grandmother, **who had died in the spring.** |
| | 2. If I remember correct, that were a beutiful story of a man who cared deeply for his ancesturs, and so returned to the land where he was born at. | 2. If I remember **correctly**, that **was** a **beautiful** story of a man who cared deeply for his **ancestors**, and so returned to the land where he was **born**. |
| *from* La Relación | 1. Alvar Núñez Cabeza de Vaca was a Spanish explorer made an extraordinary journy then years later he wrote about it. | 1. Alvar Núñez Cabeza de Vaca was a Spanish explorer **who** made an extraordinary **journey. Then**, years later, he wrote about it. |
| | 2. Members of Cabeza de Vacas group sailed in ships, rode horseback, foot travel, and drifting in barges before finally reaching Mexico city. | 2. Members of Cabeza de Vaca**'s** group sailed in ships, rode horseback, **traveled on foot**, and **drifted** in barges before finally reaching Mexico **C**ity. |
| *from* Of Plymouth Plantation | 1. Of Plymouth plantation a book by William Bradford describes the experiences of the pilgrim settlers in north America. | 1. <u>**Of Plymouth Plantation**</u>, a book by William Bradford, describes the experiences of the **P**ilgrim settlers in **N**orth America. |
| | 2. The settlers of the new land was further from home than theyd ever been before and they faced many challenges. | 2. The settlers of the new land **were farther** from home than they**'d** ever been before, and they faced many challenges. |

| Selection | SkillBuilder Sentences | Suggested Answers |
|---|---|---|
| *from* The Interesting Narrative of the Life of Olaudah Equiano | **1.** "Ava did you know that Olaudah Equiano grew up in west Africa, in a village called essaka"? Roger asked.<br><br>**2.** "He wouldve growed up to rule that village" said Ava "but he was kidnapped and made a slave." | **1.** "Ava, did you know that Olaudah Equiano grew up in **W**est Africa, in a village called **E**ssaka?" Roger asked.<br><br>**2.** "He would**'ve grown** up to rule that village," said Ava**,** "but he was kidnapped and made a slave." |
| *from* Blue Highways | **1.** The word blue in the title of blue highways does not refer to the color of the asfault in Utah.<br><br>**2.** William Least Heat-Moon suggests to Fritz that he is more tolerant than many other. | **1.** The word **blue** in the title of **Blue Highways** does not refer to the color of the **asphalt** in Utah.<br><br>**2.** William Least Heat-Moon suggests to Fritz that he is more tolerant than many **others**. |
| My Sojourn in the Lands of My Ancestors | **1.** My sojourn in the Lands of my Ancestors is from Maya Angelous book "All Gods Children need Traveling Shoes."<br><br>**2.** Angelou has been a dancer, writer an actress and singer she read her poem <u>on the Pulse of Morning</u> at president Clinton's inauguration. | **1.** "My **S**ojourn in the Lands of **M**y Ancestors" is from Maya Angelou**'s** book **All God's Children Need Traveling Shoes**.<br><br>**2.** Angelou has been a dancer, **a** writer, an actress, and **a** singer. **S**he read her poem "**O**n the Pulse of Morning" at **P**resident Clinton's inauguration. |

| | Unit One | Unit Two | Unit Three | Unit Four | Unit Five | Unit Six | Unit Seven |
|---|---|---|---|---|---|---|---|
| **Grammar Focus by Unit** | Parts of a Sentence | Verbs | Phrases | Clauses, Part I | Clauses, Part II | Special Sentence Structures, Part I | Special Sentence Structures, Part II |

*The Language of Literature* offers several options for integrating grammar instruction and literature.

- Each literature unit has a grammar focus. The Teacher's Edition includes Mini Lessons for each selection that help develop the grammar focus for the unit and spring from the content of the specific literature.
- The Pupil Edition includes several full-page lessons on Sentence Crafting. These lessons are related to both the literature and the grammar focus for the unit and help students use grammar in their own writing.
- Daily Language SkillBuilders in the Teacher's Edition provide students with ongoing proofreading practice and reinforce punctuation, spelling, grammar and usage, and capitalization.
- Grammar Copymasters and Transparencies, which may be used to complement or extend lessons in the Teacher's Edition, present grammar in a traditional, systematic sequence. References to appropriate copymasters or transparencies are included at point of use in the Teacher's Edition Mini Lessons.

TE Mini Lessons shown in green
**PE instruction shown in black**

## Part 1

**Parts of Speech**

**Diagnostic**
"The World on the Turtle's Back," p. 30

**Forming Plurals**

**Distinguishing Plurals from Possessives**
"Song of the Sky Loom," "Hunting Song," p. 34

**Pronouns**
from *The Way to Rainy Mountain,* p. 57

**Parts of the Sentence**

**Kinds of Sentences**
Coyote Stories, p. 44

**Predicates, Compound and Simple**
from *The Way to Rainy Mountain,* p. 60

**Capitalization**

**Capitalizing Proper Nouns and Proper Adjectives**
Coyote Stories, p. 43

**Capitalizing First Word in Sentence**
"The Man to Send Rain Clouds," p. 54

## Part 2

**Parts of Speech**

**Review**
from *La Relación,* p. 80

**Pronouns**
from *Blue Highways,* p. 108

**Parts of the Sentence**

**Sentence Variety**
Sentence Crafting, p. 127

**Simple Sentences: Subject and Predicate**
from *La Relación,* p. 75

**Using Phrases**

**Placement of Prepositional Phrases**

**Participles and Participial Phrases**
Writing Workshop, p. 125

**Using Clauses**

**Sentence Fragments**
from *Of Plymouth Plantation,* p. 83

**Run-on Sentences**
from *Of Plymouth Plantation,* p. 89

**Structure: Compound Sentences**
from *The Interesting Narrative of the Life of Olaudah Equiano,* p. 95
Writing Workshop, p. 125

**Structure: Complex Sentences**
from *Blue Highways,* p. 103

**Structure: Compound-Complex Sentences**
"My Sojourn in the Lands of My Ancestors," p. 113

**Using Modifiers**

**Problems with Modifiers: Double Negatives**
Writing Workshop, p. 125

**Style**

**The Need for Sentence Variety**
Sentence Crafting, p. 127

This time line shows major dates and events in the early development of North America, from the end of the Ice Age to the signing of the Mayflower Compact. Guide students to an understanding that this period is characterized worldwide by explorations and discoveries, advances in learning, and the increased interaction of differing cultures. Additional information about selected people and events is provided below.

### 2000–1000 B.C.

**A** Maize was essential to life in the Southwest. Dried kernels were stripped from the ear, placed on a stone, and ground into a flour. Cornmeal was so fundamental to the Hopi diet that a prospective bride had to spend four days grinding in the household of her betrothed to prove she was qualified to be a wife.

### North America: c. A.D. 500

**B** In conducting trade, Native Americans often bartered goods, but some also used *wampumpeag*—small cylindrical beads made from polished shells and fashioned into belts or strings—as currency. Wampum was also used in ceremonies or as jewelry.

### World: c. 250

**C** Mayan culture in southern Mexico and Guatemala reached its height in its Classic Period, during which great cities of spectacular pyramids and temples were built. Then around 880, the culture mysteriously declined, and most cities were abandoned. Among its achievements were a system of writing, an accurate calendar, and impressive architecture and stone carvings.

### World: 630

**D** According to Muslim belief, around 610, the Meccan trader Muhammad was told that he was a messenger of God by the voice of the angel Gabriel. Convinced that this God was Allah, Muhammad began to preach. Forced to leave Mecca in 622, Muhammad and his followers settled in Medina, 200 miles to the north, but returned to conquer Mecca in 630, unifying the Arabian Peninsula under Islam.

# ORIGINS AND ENCOUNTERS

## EVENTS IN AMERICAN LITERATURE

| 2000–1000 B.C. | 0 | A.D. 1000 |
|---|---|---|

## EVENTS IN NORTH AMERICA

| 2000–1000 B.C. | 0 | A.D. 1000 |
|---|---|---|

**A c.2000–1000 B.C.** Native Americans in Southwest cultivate maize, a forerunner of corn

**c.400 B.C.** Olmec civilization begins decline in central Mexico

**B c.A.D. 500** Native American tribes in Eastern woodlands establish agricultural economy and widespread trade

**c.800** Mound Builder culture develops along Mississippi River (to c. 1500s)

**E c.1000** Anasazi build elaborate, multistory cliff dwellings in Southwest canyons (to c. 1300)

**1492** Christopher Columbus sets foot in Bahamas

## EVENTS IN THE WORLD

| 2000–1000 B.C. | 0 | A.D. 1000 |
|---|---|---|

**c.1790 B.C.** Hammurabi, king of Babylon, codifies set of laws

**c.753 B.C.** City of Rome founded

**483 B.C.** The Buddha dies

**334 B.C.** Alexander the Great begins conquest of Persia (to 323 B.C.)

**c.A.D. 30** Jesus crucified

**105** Chinese invent paper

**C c.250** Mayan civilization begins Classic Period (to c. 880)

**c.476** Western Roman Empire falls

**D 630** Prophet Muhammad conquers Mecca, which becomes holiest city of Islam

**800** Charlemagne unites much of Europe and is crowned Holy Roman Emperor

**1095** First of nine "holy wars," known as Crusades, begins

**1206** Genghis Khan begins Mongol conquest of Asia (to 1227)

**F 1215** In England, King John agrees to Magna Carta

**c.1300** Renaissance begins in Italy

**1453** Ottomans conquer Constantinople

**G 1455** Gutenberg Bible produced on printing press

### North America: c. 1000

**E** From around 1000 to nearly 1300, the Anasazi built villages in sheltered areas of cliffs. These community dwellings had up to four stories and from 20 to 1,000 rooms. These dwellings were abandoned in the late 13th century, possibly due to a long drought and the influx of Navajo and Apache tribes from the North.

### World: 1215

**F** Rebelling nobles forced King John to sign the Magna Carta ("Great Charter"). It was originally drafted to protect only nobles' rights but eventually came to guarantee basic rights to all English citizens. Because King John was so unpopular, he is the only king whose name is not given to potential heirs to the English throne.

## PERIOD PIECES

Compass used for navigation in the 15th century

Pilgrim foot warmer

**H** The Anko Calendar from the Kiowa people

---

**1500**      **1600**

**1521** Hernándo Cortés writes to king of Spain describing Aztec gifts

**I** **1537** Upon returning to Spain, Álvar Núñez Cabeza de Vaca reports to Spanish king about harrowing North American journey

**1620** William Bradford describes journey across Atlantic and Pilgrims' settlement in *Of Plymouth Plantation*

---

**1500**      **1600**

**1502** Amerigo Vespucci returns from second exploration of South America and declares it a New World; the Americas are named after him.

**1521** Hernándo Cortés conquers Aztecs and claims territory for Spain

**1535** Jacques Cartier explores St. Lawrence River and claims Quebec and Montreal for France

**1540** Horses introduced on large scale by Spanish explorers

**J** **1607** First permanent English colony set up in Jamestown, Virginia

**1618** Virginia governor Samuel Argall declares all colonists who fail to attend church will be locked in guardhouse

**K** **1619** Africans first arrive in Virginia as indentured servants

**L** **1620** Before landing at Plymouth, Pilgrims sign Mayflower Compact, establishing government by will of majority

---

**1500**      **1600**

**1502** First enslaved Africans taken to the Americas

**1517** Martin Luther begins Protestant Reformation

**1522** Magellan sails around world

**1526** Babur founds Mughal Empire in India

**1543** Copernicus publishes theory that sun is center of universe

**1588** Spanish Armada sails for England

**1603** Tokugawa Ieyasu unites Japan

**1613** Michael Romanov elected Russian czar, founding the Romanov dynasty

**1615** Italian scientist Galileo Galilei condemned by Inquisition for supporting Copernicus's theory

TIME LINE    **19**

---

### World: 1455

**G** The Bible printed by German printer Johann Gutenberg (c. 1397–1468) is arguably the first book printed with movable types cast in molds. He divided the Bible into two volumes with a total of 1,282 pages. A single copy of the Bible had previously taken months to write out by hand. Gutenberg could now make numerous copies in a short period of time. He produced several hundred copies, of which about 40 are still surviving.

### PERIOD PIECES

**H** Kiowans, nomadic people of the Plains, were known for their "calendar histories"—pictographic portrayals of important tribal events. The "moons," or lunar months, are shown by crescents. The black strips mark winters. Today about 10,000 Kiowans survive, living mostly in Oklahoma.

### Literature: 1537

**I** Cabeza de Vaca's report, known as *La Relación* (*The Relation*—that is, *The Narrative*), was not published until 1542. Today the narrative is viewed as Cabeza de Vaca's attempt to reconcile his own uncertain feelings about his Native American captors and what the nature of his countrymen's future contacts with them should be.

### North America: 1607

**J** John Smith (c. 1580–1631) assumed leadership of the colony of Jamestown, Virginia, in 1608. He made peace with the Powhatan Indians, who then taught the colonists to plant corn. The story of his being saved from certain death at the hands of the Powhatans by the intervention of the chief's daughter, Pocahontas, is probably exaggerated, as Smith's first written account of this adventure does not mention her.

### North America: 1619

**K** A Dutch ship brought to Jamestown 20 Africans from the West African region later known as the Slave Coast. Within 40 years Africans were enslaved for life in the English colonies. This system of slavery lasted for more than two centuries.

### North America 1620

**L** This compact, though not an actual constitution, had great impact. It created the first settlement in North America to be governed by a social contract, creating a "civil Body Politick" to frame equitable laws that would then bind all signers. It remained the basis of Plymouth's operations for 10 years and served as the model for all of the colony's successive governments.

# In Harmony with Nature

## Native American Traditions

**Introduction**
This article places the selections in Part 1 of this unit in a historical and literary context. It explains the evolution of the Native American literary tradition and briefly traces its history through the present day. An example from this tradition, the Pawnee tale "The Lesson of the Birds," appears in **Voices from the Times.**

## Teaching Nonfiction

**Reading Skills and Strategies**
**ESTABLISHING A PURPOSE FOR READING**

Explain that this article introduces students to Native American oral literature as the first American literature. Have students review the article and establish a purpose for reading (to find out specifics of exploration and exploitation).

**IDENTIFYING MAIN IDEAS**
The two subheadings of "In Harmony with Nature" form sections that become the main ideas of the article. Have students approach the article by reading one section at a time, summarizing each section by identifying its main idea and noting the supporting ideas.

**NOTETAKING**
Encourage students to take notes to better understand the article as they read. They may want to note important concepts, unfamiliar vocabulary, and proper names that occur in the article.

**DISCUSSING**
Students should be prepared to discuss the article in class. Discussion could focus on the possible changes made in the Native American stories and myths as they are passed down orally through the generations (i.e., whether oral literature is affected in any way by current events) and how this method differs from written literature.

The first American literature was created by the first people to live here—the Native Americans, who inhabited North America thousands of years before the first Europeans arrived. To be sure, the Native Americans did not think of themselves as living in a single nation, as most Americans do today. Rather, the original native peoples belonged to more than 200 distinct groups who spoke more than 500 different languages. They called themselves names such as Anishinabe, Diné, and Lakota—each of which means "the people." Their ways of life, dictated by their natural surroundings, varied greatly. They had complex religious beliefs, sophisticated political systems, and strong social values, all reflected in their literatures.

Literature is not limited to what is written down in books. Native American literatures were primarily oral, passed down from generation to generation by storytelling and performances.

Some widespread types of Native American oral literature are creation myths, which explain the beginning of the world; tales of heroes and tricksters who transformed the world to its present state; and the ritual songs and chants that are part 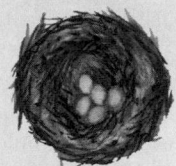 of ceremonies.

This part of Unit One presents a small sampling of works from Native American oral traditions: a creation myth from the Iroquois of the Northeast, two ancient songs from the Tewa and the Navajo of the Southwest, and two trickster tales from the Okanogan of the Pacific Northwest. Preceding these, in Voices from the Times, is a fable from the Pawnee of the central plains.

As readers of a textbook, you will not be experiencing these works as you would if you belonged to the cultures they came from. You will not be hearing them or seeing them performed; you will be reading them on a page, in a language different from the languages in which they were created. These pieces were collected in the early 1900s and translated into English by anthropologists—or in the case of the Okanogan stories, by a bilingual member of the tribe with the help of white editors. Despite the limitations of translations, they remain the best way to expose a wide audience to the beauty, wisdom, and humor of Native American oral literature.

Although traditional Native American literature has many forms and functions, much of it emphasizes the importance of living in harmony with the natural world. In Native American belief, human beings have a kinship with animals, plants, the land, heavenly bodies, and the elements. All of these things are seen as alive and aware, as when singers address Mother Earth and Father Sky in the Tewa "Song of the Sky Loom." Furthermore, the human and the nonhuman are seen as parts of a sacred whole. To Native Americans, human beings do not have dominion over nature; they are part of nature and must act to maintain a right relationship with the world around them. Notice

## Voices from the Times

### THE LESSON OF THE BIRDS
Pawnee

One day a man whose mind was open to the teaching of the powers wandered on the prairie. As he walked, his eyes upon the ground, he spied a bird's nest hidden in the grass, and arrested his feet just in time to prevent stepping on it. He paused to look at the little nest tucked away so snug and warm, and noted that it held six eggs and that a peeping sound came from some of them. While he watched, one moved and soon a tiny bill pushed through the shell, uttering a shrill cry. At once the parent birds answered and he looked up to see where they were. They were not far off; they were flying about in search of food, chirping the while to each other and now and then calling to the little one in the nest.

The homely scene stirred the heart and the thoughts of the man as he stood there under the clear sky, glancing upward toward the old birds and then down to the helpless young in the nest at his feet. As he looked he thought of his people, who were so often careless and thoughtless of their children's needs, and his mind brooded over the matter. After many days he desired to see the nest again. So he went to the place where he had found it, and there it was as safe as when he left it. But a change had taken place. It was now full to overflowing with little birds, who were stretching

## Making Connections

### Anthropology
**A** While it is true that there are more than 200 Native American language families, recent studies support the idea that America was settled by only three migrations over the Bering land bridge: the Na-Dene (nä-dĕn´ē), the Eskimos, and the Aleuts. Linguist Joseph Greenberg has claimed that all Native American languages can be grouped into these three phyla.

### Literature
**B** Remind students that everyone's first exposure to literature is oral—lullabies, bedtime stories, and nursery rhymes. However, in Native American culture, the oral tradition was the means by which the young learned tribal history and beliefs. The oral literature required long periods of memorization, so Native Americans often used drum music as well as pictographs, knotted strings, and coded wampum belts as memory aids.

### Literature
**C** Many Native American songs used rhythmic repetition rather than rhyme. This repetition was thought to enable the singer to communicate with animals, nature, and the world of the spirit. Translators try to suggest these Native American cadences through the repetition of words and the placement of lines on the page.

### History
**D** Many Native American peoples developed animal clans or societies. The Mohawks, for example, had three animal clans: Wolf, Bear, and Turtle. People frequently attributed the characteristics of these animals to clan members. Thus members of the Bear clan were said to be strong and dangerous, while people in the Turtle clan were reserved and methodical.

### SUMMARIZING

Have students summarize in their own words the article's contents. Remind students that a summary recounts the most important information in a text, leaving out less important details and personal opinions of the reader.

### MAIN IDEAS AND SUPPORTING DETAILS

The article as a whole gives a history of the Native American oral literary tradition. Ask students to find details in the article supporting the idea that traditional oral literature has been adapted in order to fit modern times and reach a wider audience.

**Possible Response:** Anthropologists and tribal members with the help of white editors translated oral native American works into English and printed them in the early 1900s. Modern Native Americans are writing today in English.

### CONNECTING

**Have students describe what the man learns from watching the birds' nest.**

**Possible Responses:** Humans should care for children's needs; caring for children keeps a people strong.

---

### Voices *from the* TIMES

their wings, balancing on their little legs and making ready to fly, while the parents with encouraging calls were coaxing the fledglings to venture forth.

"Ah!" said the man, "if my people would only learn of the birds, and, like them, care for their young and provide for their future, homes would be full and happy, and our tribe be strong and prosperous."

When this man became a priest, he told the story of the bird's nest and sang its song; and so it has come down to us from the days of our fathers.

*Translated by Alice C. Fletcher*

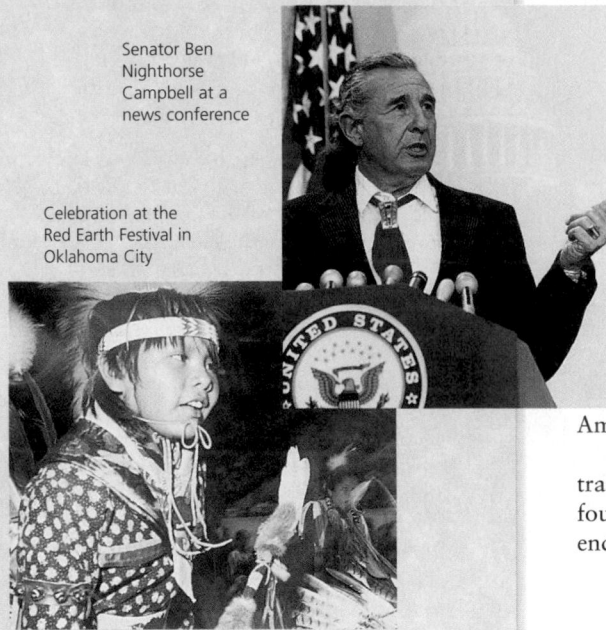

Senator Ben Nighthorse Campbell at a news conference

Celebration at the Red Earth Festival in Oklahoma City

---

this perspective as you read the examples of traditional oral literature in this book.

### Traditions Across Time: Harmonizing Old and New

Native Americans and their traditions have not disappeared from this country. Although some cultures were lost to the diseases and violence of the Europeans, others have survived—changed but not destroyed by forced religious conversion, forced relocation, and forced education. Today, Native Americans live in cities and suburbs as well as on reservations. They are keeping oral traditions alive by singing songs and telling stories, but they are also writing in English.

A new generation of such writers is enjoying unprecedented respect and popularity. They include N. Scott Momaday (whose 1969 novel *House Made of Dawn* won a Pulitzer Prize), Leslie Marmon Silko, Paula Gunn Allen, Simon Ortiz, Louise Erdrich, and Michael Dorris.

Most of these writers display a powerful interest in the problems of harmonizing the old and the new. In many of their works, such as Silko's story "The Man to Send Rain Clouds," characters or speakers are shown reconciling old traditions with new practices. Moreover, the structures of the works themselves are often based on a blend of oral techniques and new literary forms. For example, in *The Way to Rainy Mountain*, Momaday braids together mythology, oral history, and personal reflections. His novel *House Made of Dawn* and Silko's novel *Ceremony* both are constructed around traditional Native American ceremonies.

That these writers continue to draw on traditional sources for inspiration and have found such wide acclaim demonstrates the enduring value of our country's first literature.

## Native American Traditions

23

# OVERVIEW

## Objectives
1. understand and appreciate a **creation myth (Literary Analysis)**
2. identify **causes and effects (Active Reading)**

## Summary
Before the earth's creation, a vast ocean lies below a Sky-World inhabited by humanlike gods. One day a woman accidentally falls through the floor of the Sky-World. Birds catch her and set her down on the back of a great sea turtle. A muskrat dives to the bottom of the ocean and brings her a handful of soil, which the woman uses to make the land. She gives birth to a daughter, who grows up and bears twin boys. The boys are always at odds because the right-handed one is honest and upright and the left-handed one is devious and rebellious. In a final duel, the honest brother defeats the devious one, who goes on to control the underworld.

## Thematic Link
This Iroquois myth explains how the world was created. It also expresses a **Native American** ideal of people living **in harmony with nature.**

## 5-Minute Warm-Up

### *Daily Language SkillBuilder*

Have students **proofread** the display sentences on page 17i and write them correctly. The sentences also appear on Transparency 1 of **Grammar Transparencies and Copymasters.**

# The World on the Turtle's Back

IROQUOIS (ĭr′ə-kwoi′) MYTH

## Connect to Your Life

**Mysterious Origins** In all times and places, people have wondered how the world was created. What different accounts of creation—biblical narratives, scientific theories, or stories from other cultures, for example—have you heard or read? With a group of classmates, summarize as many of these accounts as you know.

## Build Background

**The Iroquois League** "The World on the Turtle's Back" is an Iroquois explanation of how the world was created. The term *Iroquois* refers to a league of five separate Native American peoples—the Seneca, Cayuga, Oneida, Onondaga, and Mohawk—who united in a confederation in the 14th century. (In the 18th century, a sixth group, the Tuscarora, joined the Iroquois League.) The ancestors of today's Iroquois lived in the woodlands of what is now New York State, the region roughly extending from the Hudson River in the east to the Great Lakes in the west.

The Iroquois groups spoke similar languages, held similar beliefs, and followed similar ways of life. They lived in longhouses made of pole frames covered with elm bark, and they built fences around their villages for protection. The women cultivated squash, beans, and corn and gathered berries and nuts. The men hunted, fished, and fought with the neighboring Mahican people. Warfare, an important part of Iroquois culture, gave men power and prestige. The Iroquois League was created primarily to end fighting among the nations that formed the alliance.

WORDS TO KNOW
**Vocabulary Preview**

| | |
|---|---|
| contend | succumb |
| devious | void |
| ritual | |

## Focus Your Reading

**LITERARY ANALYSIS** **CREATION MYTHS**
A **myth** is a traditional story, passed down through generations, that explains why the world is the way it is. In myths, events usually result from the actions of supernatural beings. A **creation myth** explains how the universe, earth, and life began. As you read this Iroquois creation myth, note the supernatural explanations of the world's origin.

**ACTIVE READING** **CAUSES AND EFFECTS**
Creation myths, to some extent, are imaginative stories of cause and effect. When events have a **cause-and-effect** relationship, one (the cause) directly brings about the other (the effect). In this Iroquois myth, the actions of supernatural beings cause the present features of the world to exist.

**READER'S NOTEBOOK** As you read, fill in a chart like the one started below to record what caused the existence of various things in the world, according to the myth.

| What Exists | What Caused It to Be |
|---|---|
| The earth | It grew when a woman walked in a circle around dirt brought up from the ocean floor and placed on a turtle's back. |

# LESSON RESOURCES

**UNIT ONE RESOURCE BOOK,** pp. 8–12

### ASSESSMENT RESOURCES
**Formal Assessment,** pp. 7–8
**Teacher's Guide to Assessment and Portfolio Use**
**Test Generator**

### SKILLS TRANSPARENCIES AND COPYMASTERS
**Literary Analysis**
• Legends, Myths, and Folk Tales, T24 (for Cooperative Learning Activity, p. 31)

**Reading and Critical Thinking**
• Cause and Effect, T1 (for Active Reading, p. 24)

**Grammar**
• Diagnostic: Parts of Speech, C61 (for Mini Lesson, p. 26)

**Vocabulary**
• Expanding Vocabulary, C19 (for Vocabulary in Action, p. 32)

**Writing**
• Literary Interpretation, C30 (for Writing Option 1, p. 32)
• Compare and Contrast, C31 (for Extend Interpretations 5, p. 31)
• Opinion Statement, C34 (for Writing Option 2, p. 32)

**Communications**
• Impromptu Speaking: Dialogue, Role-Play, Debate, T13 (Activities & Explorations 1, p. 32)

### INTEGRATED TECHNOLOGY
**Audio Library**
**LaserLinks**
• Geographical Connection: Iroquois Lands
• Visual Vocabulary. See **Teacher's SourceBook,** p. 8.
**Visit our website:**
www.mcdougallittell.com

# The WORLD on the TURTLE'S BACK

*IROQUOIS*

◆

In the beginning there was no world, no land, no creatures of the kind that are around us now, and there were no men. But there was a great ocean which occupied space as far as anyone could see. Above the ocean was a great void of air. And in the air there lived the birds of the sea; in the ocean lived the fish and the creatures of the deep. Far above this unpeopled world, there was a Sky-World. Here lived gods who were like people—like Iroquois.

In the Sky-World there was a man who had a wife, and the wife was expecting a child. The woman became hungry for all kinds of strange delicacies, as women do when they are with child. She kept her husband busy almost to distraction finding delicious things for her to eat.

In the middle of the Sky-World there grew a Great Tree which was not like any of the trees that we know. It was tremendous; it had grown there forever. It had enormous roots that spread out from the floor of the Sky-World. And on its branches there were many different kinds of leaves and different kinds of fruits and flowers. The tree was not supposed to be marked or mutilated by any of the beings who dwelt in the Sky-World. It was a sacred tree that stood at the center of the universe.

The woman decided that she wanted some bark from one of the roots of the Great Tree—perhaps as a food or as a medicine, we don't know. She told her husband this. He didn't like the idea. He knew it was wrong. But she insisted, and he gave in. So he dug a hole among the roots of this great sky tree, and he bared some of its roots. But the floor of the Sky-World wasn't very thick, and he broke a hole through it. He was terrified, for he had never expected to find empty space underneath the world.

WORDS TO KNOW   **void** (void) *n.* an empty space

25

### Reading Skills and Strategies: PREVIEW

Remind students that a creation myth is an attempt to describe how the universe, the earth, and life on earth began and that most of the world's cultures have their own stories explaining these mysteries. Tell students to keep the purpose of the selection in mind as they read it.

### Literary Analysis  CREATION MYTHS

**A** Some students may be puzzled by the lack of precision in this part of the story. Explain that because myths were originally passed on through oral storytelling, there are many different versions of each myth. The narrator is calling attention to this common characteristic of myths.

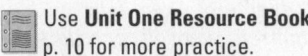 Use **Unit One Resource Book**, p. 10 for more practice.

### Active Reading  CAUSES AND EFFECTS

**B** Point out that the cause and effect listed in the sample chart on PE page 24 is contained in this part of the myth. Remind students to record further causes and their effects in their charts as they continue reading.

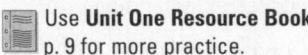 Use **Unit One Resource Book**, p. 9 for more practice.

### Literary Analysis: SYMBOLISM

**C** Ask students what the woman's actions might symbolize.

**Possible Responses:** the development of agriculture; the geological formation of the earth

---

But his wife was filled with curiosity. He wouldn't get any of the roots for her, so she set out to do it herself. She bent over and she looked down, and she saw the ocean far below. She leaned down and stuck her head through the hole and looked all around. No one knows just what happened next. Some say she slipped. Some say that her husband, fed up with all the demands she had made on him, pushed her.

So she fell through the hole. As she fell, she frantically grabbed at its edges, but her hands slipped. However, between her fingers there clung bits of things that were growing on the floor of the Sky-World and bits of the root tips of the Great Tree. And so she began to fall toward the great ocean far below.

---

$T$o keep the earth growing,
the woman walked as the sun goes,
moving in the direction
that the people still move
in the dance rituals.

---

The birds of the sea saw the woman falling, and they immediately consulted with each other as to what they could do to help her. Flying wingtip to wingtip they made a great feathery raft in the sky to support her, and thus they broke her fall. But of course it was not possible for them to carry the woman very long. Some of the other birds of the sky flew down to the surface of the ocean and called up the ocean creatures to see what they could do to help. The great sea turtle came and agreed to receive her on his back. The birds placed her gently on the shell of the turtle, and now the turtle floated about on the huge ocean with the woman safely on his back.

The beings up in the Sky-World paid no attention to this. They knew what was happening, but they chose to ignore it.

When the woman recovered from her shock and terror, she looked around her. All that she could see were the birds and the sea creatures and the sky and the ocean.

And the woman said to herself that she would die. But the creatures of the sea came to her and said that they would try to help her and asked her what they could do. She told them that if they could find some soil, she could plant the roots stuck between her fingers, and from them plants would grow. The sea animals said perhaps there was dirt at the bottom of the ocean, but no one had ever been down there so they could not be sure.

If there was dirt at the bottom of the ocean, it was far, far below the surface in the cold deeps. But the animals said they would try to get some. One by one the diving birds and animals tried and failed. They went to the limits of their endurance, but they could not get to the bottom of the ocean. Finally, the muskrat said he would try. He dived and disappeared. All the creatures waited, holding their breath, but he did not return. After a long time, his little body floated up to the surface of the ocean, a tiny crumb of earth clutched in his paw. He seemed to be dead. They pulled him up on the turtle's back and they sang and prayed over him and breathed air into his mouth, and finally, he stirred. Thus it was the muskrat, the Earth-Diver, who brought from the bottom of the ocean the soil from which the earth was to grow.

The woman took the tiny clod of dirt and placed it on the middle of the great sea turtle's back. Then the woman began to walk in a circle around it, moving in the direction that the sun goes. The earth began to grow. When the earth was big enough, she planted the roots she had clutched between her fingers when she fell from the Sky-World. Thus the plants grew on the earth.

To keep the earth growing, the woman walked as the sun goes, moving in the direction that the people still move in the dance <u>rituals</u>. She

WORDS TO KNOW  **ritual** (rĭch′ōō-əl) *n.* a ceremonial act or a series of such acts

---

## Teaching Options

 **Grammar**

**DIAGNOSTIC: PARTS OF SPEECH Instruction**
Words in the English language may be divided into eight categories, called parts of speech. These are nouns, pronouns, verbs, adjectives, adverbs, prepositions, conjunctions, and interjections. Articles such as *the, a,* and *an* are not generally considered parts of speech.

On the chalkboard or a transparency, write the eight parts of speech and the three sentences shown below. Underline the word *land* in each sentence.

A turtle swims; a tortoise is a <u>land</u> mammal.
Because the birds broke her fall, the woman was able to <u>land</u> softly.

In the past, people's lives were more closely connected to the <u>land</u>.

Explain that the way a word is used in a sentence determines its part of speech. Have students explain how *land* is used in each sentence and identify the part of speech for each use.

**Diagnostic Exercise** Display the following passage and have students identify the part of speech of each word.

Farmers in Onondaga worried about their corn, which was possibly ruined by heavy rains in June. "Well, we'll harvest the crop in August," said one Iroquois, "and then we'll know the results."

*Creation Legend*, Tom (Two Arrows) Dorsey. Philbrook Museum of Art, Tulsa, Oklahoma (46.24).

THE WORLD ON THE TURTLE'S BACK **27**

**Students Acquiring English**

**1** Make sure students understand the expression *broke her fall.* If necessary, explain that to break a fall means to stop a falling object from hitting the ground, or to make it fall more slowly and gently.

**2** Explain that a muskrat is a rodent that lives in the water, native to the United States and Canada.

**Answers:** Nouns—*Farmers, Onondaga, corn, rains, June, crop, August, Iroquois, results;* pronouns—*which, we;* verbs—*worried, was ruined, 'll harvest, said, 'll know;* adjectives—*their, heavy, one;* adverbs—*possibly, then;* prepositions—*in, about, by;* conjunction—*and;* interjection—*Well.*

 Use **Grammar Transparencies and Copymasters**, p. 61.

 Use McDougal Littell's ***Language Network,*** "Parts of Speech," for more instruction and practice in parts of speech.

**A** Point out that events usually have multiple causes and effects. Ask students to list two causes and two effects of the death of the twins' mother.

**Possible Responses:** Causes: The left-handed twin wanted to head for the light he saw; he was born through his mother's armpit. Effects: Useful plants grew from the mother's grave; the right-handed twin was angry at his brother for killing their mother.

**Literary Analysis: SYMBOLISM**

**B** Ask students what the buried mother, from whose body plants grow, might represent. *(Possible responses: Mother Earth; agriculture; fertility)*

**Literary Analysis** CREATION MYTHS

**C** Remind students that creation myths provide answers about how things came to be. Ask them what answer this myth gives to the question *How was the earth created?*

**Answer:** The muskrat brought soil from the bottom of the ocean, and the woman grew the earth from it.

Have students formulate a question that is answered by the story of the left-handed and right-handed twins.

**Possible Responses:** Why is the world made up of forces that seem to be in opposition to one another?

---

gathered roots and plants to eat and built herself a little hut. After a while, the woman's time came, and she was delivered of a daughter. The woman and her daughter kept walking in a circle around the earth, so that the earth and plants would continue to grow. They lived on the plants and roots they gathered. The girl grew up with her mother, cut off forever from the Sky-World above, knowing only the birds and the creatures of the sea, seeing no other beings like herself.

One day, when the girl had grown to womanhood, a man appeared. No one knows for sure who this man was. He had something to do with the gods above. Perhaps he was the West Wind. As the girl looked at him, she was filled with terror, and amazement, and warmth, and she fainted dead away. As she lay on the ground, the man reached into his quiver, and he took out two arrows, one sharp and one blunt, and he laid them across the body of the girl, and quietly went away.

When the girl awoke from her faint, she and her mother continued to walk around the earth. After a while, they knew that the girl was to bear a child. They did not know it, but the girl was to bear twins.

Within the girl's body, the twins began to argue and quarrel with one another. There could be no peace between them. As the time approached for them to be born, the twins fought about their birth. The right-handed twin wanted to be born in the normal way, as all

children are born. But the left-handed twin said no. He said he saw light in another direction, and said he would be born that way. The right-handed twin beseeched him not to, saying that he would kill their mother. But the left-handed twin was stubborn. He went in the direction where he saw light. But he could not be born through his mother's mouth or her nose. He was born through her left armpit, and killed her. And meanwhile, the right-handed twin was born in the normal way, as all children are born.

The twins met in the world outside, and the right-handed twin accused his brother of murdering their mother. But the grandmother told them to stop their quarreling. They buried their mother. And from her grave grew the plants which the people still use. From her head grew the corn, the beans, and the squash—"our supporters, the three sisters." And from her heart grew the sacred tobacco, which the people still use in the ceremonies and by whose upward-floating smoke they send thanks. The women call her "our mother," and they dance and sing in the rituals so that the corn, the beans, and the squash may grow to feed the people.

But the conflict of the twins did not end at the grave of their mother. And, strangely enough, the grandmother favored the left-handed twin.

The right-handed twin was angry, and he grew more angry as he thought how his brother had killed their mother. The right-handed twin was the one who did everything just as he should. He said what he meant, and he meant what he said. He always told the truth, and he always tried to accomplish what seemed to be right and reasonable. The left-handed twin never said what he meant or meant what he said. He always lied, and he always did things backward. You could never tell what he was trying to do because he always made it look as if he were doing the opposite. He was the <u>devious</u> one.

These two brothers, as they grew up, represented two ways of the world which are in

WORDS
TO
KNOW     **devious** (dē'vē-əs) *adj.* shifty; not straightforward

28

---

## BLOCK SCHEDULING: MANAGING TIME

**If your schedule requires that you cover the lesson objectives in a shorter time, use . . .**
- Preparing to Read, p. 24
- Thinking Through the Literature, p. 31
- Vocabulary in Action, p. 32

**If you want to take advantage of longer class times, use . . .**
- TE Teaching Options: Preteaching Vocabulary, p. 25 (can be done as a group activity); Viewing and Representing, p. 29
- Choices & Challenges, p. 32

all people. The Indians did not call these the right and the wrong. They called them the straight mind and the crooked mind, the upright man and the devious man, the right and the left.

The twins had creative powers. They took clay and modeled it into animals, and they gave these animals life. And in this they <u>contended</u> with one another. The right-handed twin made the deer, and the left-handed twin made the mountain lion which kills the deer. But the right-handed twin knew there would always be more deer than mountain lions. And he made another animal.

> The world the twins made
> was a balanced
> and orderly world,
> and this was good.

He made the ground squirrel. The left-handed twin saw that the mountain lion could not get to the ground squirrel, who digs a hole, so he made the weasel. And although the weasel can go into the ground squirrel's hole and kill him, there are lots of ground squirrels and not so many weasels. Next the right-handed twin decided he would make an animal that the weasel could not kill, so he made the porcupine. But the left-handed twin made the bear, who flips the porcupine over on his back and tears out his belly.

And the right-handed twin made berries and fruits of other kinds for his creatures to live on. The left-handed twin made briars and poison ivy, and the poisonous plants like the baneberry and the dogberry, and the suicide root with which people kill themselves when they go out of their minds. And the left-handed twin made medicines, for good and for evil, for doctoring and for witchcraft.

And finally, the right-handed twin made man.

The people do not know just how much the left-handed twin had to do with making man. Man was made of clay, like pottery, and baked in the fire. . . .

The world the twins made was a balanced and orderly world, and this was good. The plant-eating animals created by the right-handed twin would eat up all the vegetation if their number was not kept down by the meat-eating animals, which the left-handed twin created. But if these carnivorous animals ate too many other animals, then they would starve, for they would run out of meat. So the right- and the left-handed twins built balance into the world.

As the twins became men full grown, they still contested with one another. No one had won, and no one had lost. And they knew that the conflict was becoming sharper and sharper, and one of them would have to vanquish the other.

And so they came to the duel. They started with gambling. They took a wooden bowl, and in it they put wild plum pits. One side of the pits was burned black, and by tossing the pits in the bowl and betting on how these would fall, they gambled against one another, as the people still do in the New Year's rites. All through the morning they gambled at this game, and all through the afternoon, and the sun went down. And when the sun went down, the game was done, and neither one had won.

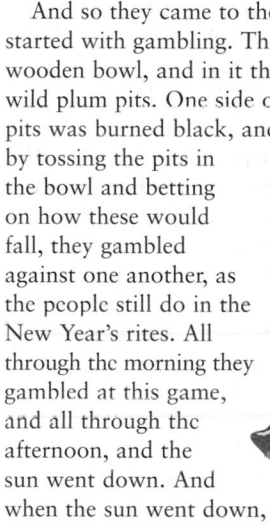

29

## Customizing Instruction

### Students Acquiring English

**1** Clarify that *quiver* is used here to mean "a case for carrying arrows" rather than "to shake."

### Less Proficient Readers

**2** Guide students' comprehension of the myth by asking the following questions.

• Which god accidentally falls out of the sky?

**Answer:** a pregnant woman

• How does the woman create land on the turtle's back?

**Answer:** She places dirt from the bottom of the ocean on the turtle's back and causes the land to grow by walking around it.

• What happens when the twins are born?

**Answer:** The left-handed twin is born through his mother's left armpit, and she dies as a result.

 **Mini Lesson** ## Viewing and Representing

*Creation Legend* **by Tom Two-Arrows**

**ART APPRECIATION** Tom Two-Arrows is an Onondaga artist. His *Creation Legend,* on page 27, is a visual retelling of "The World on the Turtle's Back." **Instruction** *Creation Legend* tells the story of "The World on the Turtle's Back" in picture form. After students have finished reading the myth, ask them the following questions to discuss *Creation Legend.*

• What characters or events do you recognize in the painting?

**Possible Response:** turtle, twins, birds, woman, arrows

• Does the painting address the issue of balance? If so, how?

**Possible Response:** Balance is represented in the symmetry of the painting, with the right-handed twin on one side and the left-handed twin on the other.

**Literary Analysis** | CREATION MYTHS

 Tell students that the transformation of a character is a common element in mythology, often used to explain natural phenomena. Ask what natural feature is explained by the grandmother's transformation.

**Answer:** the moon

So they went on to battle one another at the lacrosse[1] game. And they contested all day, and the sun went down, and the game was done. And neither had won.

And now they battled with clubs, and they fought all day, and the sun went down, and the fight was done. But neither had won.

And they went from one duel to another to see which one would <u>succumb</u>. Each one knew in his deepest mind that there was something, somewhere, that would vanquish the other. But what was it? Where to find it?

Each knew somewhere in his mind what it was that was his own weak point. They talked about this as they contested in these duels, day after day, and somehow the deep mind of each entered into the other. And the deep mind of the right-handed twin lied to his brother, and the deep mind of the left-handed twin told the truth.

On the last day of the duel, as they stood, they at last knew how the right-handed twin was to kill his brother. Each selected his weapon. The left-handed twin chose a mere stick that would do him no good. But the right-handed twin picked out the deer antler, and with one touch he destroyed his brother. And the left-handed twin died, but he died and he didn't die. The right-handed twin picked up the body and cast it off the edge of the earth. And some place below the world, the left-handed twin still lives and reigns.

When the sun rises from the east and travels in a huge arc along the sky dome, which rests like a great upside-down cup on the saucer of the earth, the people are in the daylight realm of the right-handed twin. But when the sun slips down in the west at nightfall and the dome lifts to let it escape at the western rim, the people are again in the domain of the left-handed twin—the fearful realm of night.

Having killed his brother, the right-handed twin returned home to his grandmother. And she met him in anger. She threw the food out of the cabin onto the ground and said that he was a murderer, for he had killed his brother. He grew angry and told her she had always helped his brother, who had killed their mother. In his anger, he grabbed her by the throat and cut her head off. Her body he threw into the ocean, and her head, into the sky. There, "Our Grandmother, the Moon" still keeps watch at night over the realm of her favorite grandson.

The right-handed twin has many names. One of them is Sapling. It means smooth, young, green and fresh and innocent, straightforward, straight-growing, soft and pliable, teachable and trainable. These are the old ways of describing him. But since he has gone away, he has other names. He is called "He Holds Up the Skies," "Master of Life," and "Great Creator."

The left-handed twin also has many names. One of them is Flint. He is called the devious one, the one covered with boils. Old Warty. He is stubborn. He is thought of as being dark in color.

These two beings rule the world and keep an eye on the affairs of men. The right-handed twin, the Master of Life, lives in the Sky-World. He is content with the world he helped to create and with his favorite creatures, the humans. The scent of sacred tobacco rising from the earth comes gloriously to his nostrils.

In the world below lives the left-handed twin. He knows the world of men, and he finds contentment in it. He hears the sounds of warfare and torture, and he finds them good.

In the daytime, the people have rituals which honor the right-handed twin. Through the daytime rituals, they thank the Master of Life. In the nighttime, the people dance and sing for the left-handed twin. ❖

---

1. **lacrosse** (lə-krôs′): a game of Native American origin, played on a field by two teams, in which participants use long-handled sticks with webbed pouches to maneuver a ball into the opposing team's goal.

WORDS
TO
KNOW     **succumb** (sə-kŭm′) v. to give up or give in; yield

30

 **Mini Lesson** ### Grammar

**PARTS OF SPEECH**

**Instruction** Review with students the roles that nouns, pronouns, verbs, adjectives, and adverbs play in sentences. A noun names a person, place, or thing; a pronoun refers to or takes the place of a noun; a verb describes action or states of being; adjectives modify nouns; and adverbs modify verbs, adjectives, or other adverbs.

Use **Grammar Transparencies and Copymasters**, p. 62.

Use McDougal Littell's *Language Network*, "Parts of Speech," for more instruction and practice in parts of speech.

# *Thinking* through the LITERATURE

## Connect to the Literature

**1. What Do You Think?**
What are your thoughts about this creation myth?

**Comprehension Check**
- How did the animals help the woman who fell from the sky?
- What are the differences between the twins?
- What was the outcome of the duels between the twins?

## Think Critically

**2.** **ACTIVE READING** **CAUSES AND EFFECTS** Look over the chart you made in your  **READER'S NOTEBOOK** as you read this **myth.** What caused various things in the world to come into being? Discuss the cause and effect you found most interesting.

**3.** What are the most important things you learned about the values and way of life of the Iroquois from reading this myth?

**THINK ABOUT**
- their attitude toward nature
- their view of their gods
- important foods, rituals, and games
- the roles of men and women

**4.** Why do you think the Iroquois honor both the left-handed twin and the right-handed twin?

## Extend Interpretations

**5. Comparing Texts** How does this Iroquois creation myth compare with the other accounts of creation that you discussed earlier?

**6. Connect to Life** How would you relate the left-handed and right-handed twins to your own concept of good and evil?

## Literary Analysis

**CREATION MYTHS** As you recall, a **creation myth** explains how the universe, earth, and life began. Creation myths, like all myths, can be viewed as essentially religious, presenting the cosmic views of the cultural groups that create them. According to the scholar Joseph Campbell, myths have four functions:
- to instill a sense of awe toward the mystery of the universe
- to explain the workings of the natural world
- to support and validate social customs
- to guide people through the trials of living

**Cooperative Learning Activity** Do you think "The World on the Turtle's Back" serves the functions of myths noted by Joseph Campbell? Meet in small groups to discuss this question. Support your responses with examples from the selection.

| Function | Examples |
|---|---|
| to instill awe | |
| to explain world | |
| to support customs | |
| to guide people | |

## Extend Interpretations

**Comparing Texts** Students' responses should clearly describe ways in which the selection is similar to and different from other creation myths.
**Connect to Life** Possible Responses: The left-handed and right-handed twins are more complex than a concept of good versus evil. The twins show that even bad things usually have something good or useful in them. Good needs to be balanced by evil.

## Connect to the Literature

**1. What Do You Think?**
Students may comment on whether they found the myth interesting or how well they think it explained natural phenomena.

**Comprehension Check**
- The birds broke her fall, the sea turtle gave her a place to rest, and the muskrat brought her soil to make the earth and grow plants.
- One is devious and crooked and the other is honest and upright.
- The right-handed twin won the final duel and cast his brother's body off the earth. He now rules the day, and the left-handed twin rules the night.

 Use Selection Quiz in
**Unit One Resource Book,** p. 12.

## Think Critically

**2.** Students' responses should describe a valid cause-and-effect relationship and explain what is interesting about it.
**3.** Students may discuss respect for the balance of nature, belief in the world's creation by a higher power, ritual dancing, and prayer for plentiful harvests.
**4.** Possible Responses: The Iroquois acknowledge "crooked" and "straight" minds as being necessary to a balanced world. They see neither twin as wholly good or wholly evil and give thanks to each for his creations.

## Literary Analysis

**Creation Myths** Students might point out the transformation of the twins' grandmother into the Moon as an example of how this myth explains the origin of a natural phenomenon. The twins, one left-handed and the other right-handed, are the source of opposed forces in the world.

## Writing Options

**1. Essay on Harmony** Students' essays may mention the woman's cooperating with the animals to make the earth, the people's gratitude for the fruits of the earth, and their respect for the delicate balance of the natural world.

**2. Opinion Essay** Students' essays should state their opinions clearly and provide thoughtful reasons for them.

**3. Alternate Ending** Students' writing should reflect an understanding of how the left-handed twin differs from his brother. **To get students started on the assignment,** have them skim the selection and make a list of things the left-handed twin did and created. Suggest that they think about the kind of world he'd like to rule.

## Activities & Explorations

**1. Oral Storytelling** Students' presentations should clearly and dramatically convey the events taking place in the story.

**2. Narrative Pictographs** Students should be able to explain how elements in their pictographs represent events in the myth. The pictographs should be very simple line drawings.

**3. Food Chain Diagram** Students' diagrams should include deer, mountain lions, ground squirrels, weasels, porcupines, bears, and humans.

## Inquiry & Research

**Creation Stories Compared** Students can research some creation myths on the Internet. For example, a Tohono O'odham creation story is available at http://www.hanksville.phast.umass.edu /poems/Papagocreation.html. More creation stories are indexed at http://www.indians.org/welker/ legend.htm.

## Art Connection

**Every Picture Tells a Story** Characters from the myth include the woman from the Sky-World, the great sea turtle, the birds, and the twins. Events include the birds' forming a feathery raft and the left-handed twin's coming to rule over the night.

## Writing Options

**1. Essay on Harmony** The Iroquois, like most native peoples of North America, emphasized the importance of living in harmony with the natural world. Write a short expository essay in which you explain how the Iroquois myth expresses this relationship toward all living things.

**Writing Handbook**
See page 1283: Analysis

**2. Opinion Essay** The twins in this myth represent "two ways of the world which are in all people"— the "straight mind" and the "crooked mind." Draft a short reflective essay in which you agree or disagree with this view of human character. Support your opinion with examples.

**3. Alternate Ending** If the left-handed twin had killed the right-handed twin, what kind of world might have resulted? Write an alternate ending to this Iroquois myth.

## Activities & Explorations

**1. Oral Storytelling** Iroquois traditions, rituals, and history have been passed down orally from generation to generation. Present an oral interpretation of part of this Iroquois myth for the class. ~ **SPEAKING AND LISTENING**

**2. Narrative Pictographs** Native American groups without written languages often used pictographs —pictures that represent objects and ideas—to help them remember important events and stories. The pictograph shown here, from the Lenni Lenape group, represents the creation of the sun, the moon, and the stars. Create your own pictographs to represent significant events in "The World on the Turtle's Back." Display your work in the classroom. ~ **ART**

**3. Food Chain Diagram** A food chain shows the sequence of food relationships among plants and animals. In rural areas, for example, some snakes eat mice, which feed on grain. Draw a diagram of a food chain based on the animal and plant life the twins created in the Iroquois myth. Think of each plant and animal as a link in the chain. Refer to diagrams of food chains in a biology textbook or encyclopedia as models. ~ **SCIENCE, ART**

## Inquiry & Research

**Creation Stories Compared** Read or listen to a creation myth from a culture other than the Iroquois—for example, the Navajo from the southwestern United States or the Norse from Scandinavia. In a chart or essay, explore similarities and differences between this myth and the Iroquois myth.

## Art Connection

**Every Picture Tells a Story** Look at the picture *Creation Legend* by Tom (Two-Arrows) Dorsey on page 27. What characters and events from "The World on the Turtle's Back" are portrayed?

## Vocabulary in Action

**EXERCISE A: ASSESSMENT PRACTICE** Review the list of Words to Know. On your paper, write the vocabulary word that is a synonym of each word below. Then write a sentence containing the vocabulary word.

1. dishonest
2. strive
3. vacuum
4. quit
5. ceremony

**EXERCISE B** With a partner, make up a story that contains at least three of the Words to Know. Then practice telling the story, partly in words and partly in pantomime. Perform the story for your classmates, and have them try to figure out which vocabulary words it contains.

**Building Vocabulary**
For an in-depth lesson on how to expand your vocabulary, see page 126.

| WORDS TO KNOW | | | |
|---|---|---|---|
| | contend | ritual | void |
| | devious | succumb | |

## Vocabulary in Action

1. devious
2. contend
3. void
4. succumb
5. ritual

# Song of the Sky Loom

TEWA (tä'wə) SONG

# Hunting Song / Dinni-e Sin

NAVAJO (năv'ə-hō') SONG

### Connect to Your Life

**Sacred Words** Many cultures have spiritual songs and poetry that are used in worship or thanksgiving. Write down the words of a prayer, psalm, vow, hymn, or some other form of sacred expression in your culture. Study the words carefully. What, in your opinion, distinguishes sacred language from ordinary language?

## Build Background

**Tewa and Navajo Songs** These selections are sacred songs of two Native American groups of the Southwest. The Tewa are a group of Pueblo Indians, so called because they live in pueblos—villages of stone or adobe dwellings. The Tewa live in six pueblos north of Santa Fe, New Mexico: Tesque, Nambe, Pojoaque, San Ildefonso, Santa Clara, and San Juan. "Song of the Sky Loom" is one of many Tewa songs that are sung in religious rituals. The translator, Herbert Spinden, states that *sky loom* refers to "small desert rains which resemble a loom hung from the sky."

"Dinni-e Sin" ("Hunting Song" in English translation) is a song of the Navajo. The Navajo were originally hunters and gatherers, but after migrating to the Southwest in the 11th century, they gradually adopted a more settled life of herding and farming. According to the Navajo, "Hunting Song" was given to them by Hastyeyalti, the god of the sunrise and of game animals. Navajo men prepared for the hunt by praying and singing hunting songs, in the belief that if they sang well, they would have success.

## Focus Your Reading

**LITERARY ANALYSIS** | **REPETITION** **Repetition** is the recurrence of words, phrases, or lines in a piece of literature. Notice the repetition in the following lines from "Hunting Song":

> *Comes the deer to my singing,*
> *Comes the deer to my song,*
> *Comes the deer to my singing.*

Consider how this repetition affects you. Look for other examples of repetition in the songs.

**ACTIVE READING** | **STRATEGIES FOR READING NATIVE AMERICAN SONGS** It is important to remember that the texts you are about to read are not fully representative of these songs. They are lyrics, translated from the original languages, unaccompanied by music and movement, and taken out of the context of the ceremonies they are a part of. Still, there is enough left to appreciate. The following strategies will help you accomplish this:

- Read the songs aloud.
- Try to **visualize** the singers and the occasions for which the songs were sung.
- **Speculate** about the deeper, nonliteral meaning of words such as "garment of brightness."
- Be aware of the feelings the songs express about nature and the universe. Record your impressions in your ▯▯ **READER'S NOTEBOOK.**

### Objectives
1. understand and appreciate sacred **songs (Literary Analysis)**
2. appreciate author's use of **repetition (Literary Analysis)**
3. apply **strategies for reading Native American songs (Active Reading)**

### Summary
"Song of the Sky Loom": The Tewa bring offerings to Mother the Earth and Father the Sky. They ask in return that Mother the Earth and Father the Sky weave a symbolic garment out of the white light of morning and the red light of evening, and out of the rain and the rainbow. "Hunting Song": The Navajo hunter imitates the singing of the blackbird, favorite companion of the deer. His song calls the deer to come down from the mountain.

### Thematic Link
Both songs eloquently express the Native American desire to live **in harmony with nature.** For the Tewa this means wearing a mystical "garment" woven by nature itself. For the Navajo it means coaxing the deer to participate in a cycle in which death in one part of the natural world brings life and sustenance in another.

### 5-Minute Warm-Up

*Daily Language SkillBuilder*

Have students **proofread** the display sentences on page 17i and write them correctly. The sentences also appear on Transparency 1 of **Grammar Transparencies and Copymasters.**

## LESSON RESOURCES

**UNIT ONE RESOURCE BOOK,** pp. 13–14

**ASSESSMENT RESOURCES**
**Formal Assessment,** p. 9
**Teacher's Guide to Assessment and Portfolio Use**
**Test Generator**

**SKILLS TRANSPARENCIES AND COPYMASTERS**
**Literary Analysis**
- Legends, Myths, and Folk Tales, T24 (for Extend Interpretations, items 5 and 6, p. 37)

**Reading and Critical Thinking**
- Compare and Contrast, T15 (for Extend Interpretations, items 5 and 6, p. 37)

**Grammar**
- Possessive Nouns, T38 (for Mini Lesson, p. 34)
- Forming Plurals and Distinguishing Plurals from Possessives, C64 (for Mini Lesson, p. 34)

**Vocabulary**
- Context Clues, C18 (for Mini Lesson, p. 35)

**Communications**
- Evaluating Roles in Groups, T8 (for Activities & Explorations 1, p. 38)
- Dramatic Reading, T12 (for Activities & Explorations 1, p. 38)

**INTEGRATED TECHNOLOGY**
**Audio Library**
**LaserLinks**
- Cultural Connection: The Tewa People
- Cultural Connection: The Navajo. See **Teacher's SourceBook,** p. 9.

**Visit our website:**
www.mcdougallittell.com

## Reading and Analyzing

**Literary Analysis** `REPETITION`

Have students find repeated phrases in each song.

**Possible Responses:** "Song of the Sky Loom": The first and last lines are identical; "may the [noun] be . . ."; "that we may walk fittingly where . . ."
"Hunting Song": All lines show repetition of some kind except 4–5, 20–21, and 23–24.

Ask students to consider why the songs use repetition.

 Use **Unit One Resource Book**, p. 14 for more practice.

### Active Reading

STRATEGIES FOR READING
NATIVE AMERICAN SONGS

Have volunteers read "Song of the Sky Loom" and "Hunting Song" aloud. Ask:

• What do you think the singers look like as they sing?

**Possible Responses:** "Song of the Sky Loom": They look like people who are relaxing after working hard, gathered together in a ceremony; they look pleased, happy, fulfilled. "Hunting Song": The singer looks hungry but hopeful.

• What are the deeper, nonliteral meanings of interesting phrases in the songs?

**Possible Response:** The blackbird, beloved of the deer, may represent a desire that draws one to death.

• What general feelings do the songs express about nature and the universe?

**Possible Response:** oneness with the universe, or at least a working relationship with nature

 Use **Unit One Resource Book**, p. 13 for more practice.

## Teaching Options

# Song of the Sky Loom

## TEWA

Oh our Mother the Earth, oh our Father the Sky,
Your children are we, and with tired backs
We bring you the gifts that you love.
Then weave for us a garment of brightness;
5  May the warp[1] be the white light of morning,
May the weft[2] be the red light of evening,
May the fringes be the falling rain,
May the border be the standing rainbow.
Thus weave for us a garment of brightness
10  That we may walk fittingly where birds sing,
That we may walk fittingly where grass is green,
Oh our Mother the Earth, oh our Father the Sky!

---

1. **warp:** the threads that run lengthwise in a woven fabric.
2. **weft:** the threads interlaced at right angles through the warp threads in a woven fabric.

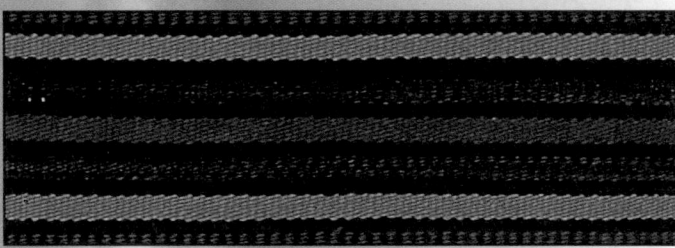

Copyright © School of American Research Press. Photo by Deborah Flynn.

### Thinking Through the Literature

1. What feeling are you left with after reading "Song of the Sky Loom"?

2. The Tewa ask the earth and the sky for a "garment of brightness." What do you think this phrase means?

THINK ABOUT { • the four parts of the garment (lines 5–8)
• why they ask for the garment (lines 10 and 11)

3. How is this sacred song like the examples of sacred expression you wrote down before you read?

  **Grammar**

**FORMING PLURALS AND DISTINGUISHING PLURALS FROM POSSESSIVES**

**Instruction** Review with students the rules for forming plurals. Also review with students the rules for forming possessives. Point out that plurals are not formed with apostrophes, while possessives are. Possessives of plurals, however, will have apostrophes.

Use **Grammar Transparencies and Copymasters**, p. 64.

Use McDougal Littell's **Language Network**, Chapter 10, for more instruction in forming possessives.

# HUNTING SONG

NAVAJO

Comes the deer to my singing,
Comes the deer to my song,
Comes the deer to my singing.

He, the blackbird, he am I,
5   Bird beloved of the wild deer,
Comes the deer to my singing.

From the Mountain Black,
From the summit,
Down the trail, coming, coming now,
10   Comes the deer to my singing.

Through the blossoms,
Through the flowers, coming, coming now,
Comes the deer to my singing.

Through the flower dew-drops,
15   Coming, coming now,
Comes the deer to my singing.

Through the pollen, flower pollen,
Coming, coming now,
Comes the deer to my singing.

*(continued)*

# DINNI-E SIN

Ye shakaikatal, i-ne-yanga,
Ye shakaikatal, ai-ye-lo,
Ye shakaikatal, i-ne-yanga.

Ka' aiyash-te tilyilch-ye
5   Shini shlini ko-lo,
Ye shakaikatal, i-ne yanga

Dsichl-tilyilch-iye
Bakashte
Ka' ta-adetin 'shte lo,
10   Ye shakaikatal, i-ne yanga

Tshilatra hozhoni-ye
Bitra 'shte lo,
Ye shakaikatal, i-ne yanga

Bi datro-iye
15   Bitra 'shte lo,
Ye shakaikatal, i-ne yanga

Ka' bi tradetin-iye
Bitra 'shte lo,
Ye shakaikatal, i-ne yanga

*(continued)*

**Less Proficient Readers**
**Set a Purpose** Ask students to look, as they read, for clues that show how the singers feel about nature.
**Possible Responses:** "Song of the Sky Loom": The singers view earth and sky reverently as their parents, deserving of gifts, and able to bestow gifts in return. "Hunting Song": The singer views nature as very much a part of his world; he believes that he can communicate with it and influence it by singing.

**Students Acquiring English**
Write the words *garment, fringe,* and *border* on the chalkboard. Have students indicate what these words mean by pointing out examples in the classroom or by drawing pictures on the chalkboard. Demonstrate the meaning of *warp* and *weft* by drawing a series of long lines to represent the warp and a series of shorter lines running across the warp to represent the weft. Then show students how these lines correspond to the woven lines of thread in fabric.

 Use **Spanish Study Guide** for additional support, pp. 7–9.

---

 **Mini Lesson  Vocabulary Strategy**

**USING CONTEXT CLUES** Readers can rely on context to determine the meanings of phrases that include figurative language.
**Instruction** Discuss the term *figurative language:* an expression that describes one thing as if it were something else. Then point out the figurative phrases *Mother the Earth* and *Father the Sky.* Demonstrate three steps that students can use to determine the meaning of figurative language.
1. Identify exactly what makes the language figurative.
   *(The earth and sky are called parents)*
2. Determine how the context restates what is suggested by the figurative language.

*(The singers look upon themselves as children who need the care of the earth and sky.)*
3. List specific elements of the context that support your interpretation.
   *(The "tired backs" suggest that singers have worked to bring the offering described as "the gifts that you love." That they give gifts, and ask for gifts in return, indicates reverence and intimacy.)*

 Use **Vocabulary Transparencies and Copymasters**, p. 92.

A lesson on context clues appears on page 326 in the Pupil's Edition.

## Active Reading

### STRATEGIES FOR READING NATIVE AMERICAN SONGS

**A** Explain to students that speculating involves drawing tentative conclusions based on evidence that is not strong enough to support firm conclusions. Often in reading poetry and songs, the reader must speculate about the meanings of certain details. Ask students to speculate about why the deer stamps on the blossoms and flowers mentioned in "Hunting Song."

**Possible Response:** The deer, instinctively sensing danger, may have picked up the scent of the hunter—the whiff of death.

Students should be prepared to modify this and other strategies if their understanding breaks down.

### Reading Skills and Strategies: CONNECTING

In a class discussion, explore any experiences with nature that the songs call to mind.

**Possible Responses:** Seeing spectacular sunsets, rainbows, or night skies, or experiencing a close relationship with nature while hiking or hunting.

*Born Free*, Edwin Salomon. Courtesy, Jacques Soussana Graphics, Jerusalem, Israel.

20 Starting with his left fore-foot,
 Stamping, turns the frightened deer,
    Comes the deer to my singing.

    Quarry mine, blessed am I
    In the luck of the chase,
25     Comes the deer to my singing.

    Comes the deer to my singing,
    Comes the deer to my song,
    Comes the deer to my singing.

20 Dinnitshe-bekan-iye
    Bitzil-le deshklashdji-lo
    Ye shakaikatal, i-ne yanga

    Bisedje
    Ka' shinosin-ku lo,
25     Ye shakaikatal, i-ne-yanga

    Ye shakaikatal, i-ne-yanga,
    Ye shakaikatal, ai-ye-lo,
    Ye shakaikatal, i-ne-yanga.

## Teaching Options

### Mini Lesson: Viewing and Representing

#### *Born Free* by Edwin Salomon

**ART APPRECIATION** Painter and printmaker Edwin Salomon, born in 1935, grew up in Romania. After graduating from art school in Romania, he studied at the Sorbonne in Paris. *Born Free* is a serigraph (a color silkscreen print) printed by hand in 40 colors.

**Instruction** Point out that shape, line, color, and texture all communicate the meaning of a visual image. Ask students to describe how each of these elements communicate meaning in the serigraph *Born Free.*

**Possible Responses:** The shapes of the deer proceed from left to right in the direction the deer are facing, indicating forward movement. They also progress from a standing, alert position through all the phases of running. This conveys alarm and flight. The lines are exaggerated, like those in cave paintings, conveying the primal nature of the deer's fear. The deer is an unnatural blood-red color, suggesting both vitality and death. The textures are flat and muted, suggesting symbolism and universality rather than realism and specific, individual deer.

# Thinking through the LITERATURE

## Connect to the Literature

1. **What Do You Think?** What distinctive features of "Hunting Song" did you notice? Discuss your impressions with a classmate.

> **Comprehension Check**
> • What is the purpose of "Hunting Song"?

## Think Critically

2. Describe your interpretation of the deer hunt as it is portrayed in the song.

**THINK ABOUT**
- what attracts the deer
- the hunter's comparison of himself to the bird loved by the deer
- the use of the words "blessed" and "luck"
- the hunter's feelings about the deer

3. What kinds of movement or what larger rituals do you think accompanied "Hunting Song" and "Song of the Sky Loom"? Describe what you visualized and why.

4. **ACTIVE READING  STRATEGIES FOR READING NATIVE AMERICAN SONGS**  Refer to the notes you made in your 📖 **READER'S NOTEBOOK**. What attitude toward nature and the universe do you see expressed in the songs? Discuss why the Navajo might consider these songs sacred.

## Extend Interpretations

5. **Comparing Texts** How would you compare "Hunting Song" and "Song of the Sky Loom"?

**THINK ABOUT**
- the singers
- the purposes of the songs
- the attitudes expressed toward nature

6. **Comparing Texts** How does the relationship between humans and animals suggested in "Hunting Song" compare with the relationship between humans and animals suggested in "The World on the Turtle's Back"?

7. **Connect to Life** How do the attitudes toward nature expressed in these songs compare with the attitudes toward nature common in American society today?

## Literary Analysis

**REPETITION**  One obvious feature of these songs is **repetition**—the recurrence of words, phrases, or lines. For example, the first line of "Song of the Sky Loom" is the same as the last line.

Some songs and poems feature **incremental repetition:** the structure of a line or stanza is repeated a certain number of times, with a slight variation in wording each time. The sequence "May the warp be. . . / May the weft be. . . / May the border be. . ." is an example of incremental repetition. Find examples of incremental repetition in "Hunting Song." Identify any repetition used in the examples of sacred speech and song you noted for the Connect to Your Life activity on page 33.

**Cooperative Learning Activity** Scholars of Native American song have proposed that repetition creates a regular rhythm for dancing, reinforces important ideas, makes a song easier to remember, gives power to a song, and has a hypnotic effect on consciousness. Gather in small groups and discuss which of these purposes for repetition is apparent in "Song of the Sky Loom" and "Hunting Song." Write down specific examples to support your answers.

| Function of Repetition | Examples |
|---|---|
| Creates regular rhythm | |
| Reinforces ideas | |
| Makes memorable | |
| Gives power | |
| Has hypnotic effect | |

## Connect to the Literature

1. **What Do You Think?** Students may mention such techniques as repetition, the inversion of subject and verb, the images from nature, or the overall flow of the sound and rhythms.

**Comprehension Check**
• To induce the deer to appear

## Think Critically

2. Possible Responses: The process of hunting deer involves identifying with the blackbird, a bird that deer love; it involves waiting patiently for the approach of the deer; and it is successful because the hunter sings well and is blessed with luck, signifying the connection with some higher force.

3. Possible Responses: "Song of the Sky Loom": a ritual in which the Tewa make offerings to the earth and sky at harvest time, including movements that represent giving or offering. "Hunting Song": movements that show the deer descending from the mountain, the blackbird fluttering and calling, and the hunter stealthily stalking his prey.

4. Possible Responses: The songs show an openness to and awareness of nature and how it interacts with human life. The Navajo might consider their songs sacred because the songs celebrate the Navajo relationship with nature.

## Literary Analysis

**Repetition** The repetition of the line "Oh our Mother the Earth , oh our Father the Sky" helps to frame the petitions of the Tewa. The line "Comes the deer to my singing" in "Hunting Song" creates a hypnotic, chantlike effect.

## Extend Interpretations

**Comparing Texts** Possible Response: "Song of the Sky Loom" is a generalized prayer for a good life, while "Hunting Song" is a specific prayer for a successful hunt. Both songs reflect a feeling of oneness with and respect for nature.

**Comparing Texts** Possible Response: "The World on the Turtle's Back" focuses on the relationship between gods and plants, humans, and animals; "Hunting Song" focuses on the predator-prey relationship. Both works, however, see the predator-prey relationship as part of the harmony of nature.

**Connect to Life** Possible Response: People today are much more likely to see themselves as being outside of or opposed to nature than the Tewa or the Navajo apparently did. Modern people would expect technology to provide them with a good life rather than farming, hunting, or other activities close to nature.

## Writing Options

1. **Definition Essay** Students' responses should tackle the problem of converting the metaphor of "walking fittingly" into modern, practical terms. They may include analysis of whether what is "fitting" today is measured by an internal standard or by an external one. **To get students started on this assignment,** suggest that they make two lists—one that lists internal qualities—such as honesty, kindness, mercy, and justice—and another that lists qualities bestowed by or won from others, such as fame, wealth, and power. They should then use these lists to describe what they believe it would mean to "walk fittingly" in today's society.

2. **Siren Song** Students' responses can reflect either a practical plan to get what they want or a magical process such as that described in the Navajo song.

3. **Reflective Essay** Student essays should explore the relationship between the Tewa and Navajo songs and some other form of sacred expression familiar to them. They should make conclusive statements about the nature of sacred language.

## Activities & Explorations

1. **Oral Reading** Reasons offered may include performance criteria such as clarity of recitation or the use of appropriate gestures.

2. **Visual Storytelling** Student work should reflect at least some of the following stages: The deer on the summit of the mountain, the blackbird calling to the deer, the deer descending the trail through the blossoms, the deer stamping as it becomes frightened, the hunter about to kill the deer. Encourage students to use a drawing program to create images and assemble them into a video adaptation of this text.

---

## Writing Options

1. **Definition Essay** In "Song of the Sky Loom," the Tewa express a wish to "walk fittingly." Draft a definition essay describing how a person might walk fittingly in today's society. Place the essay into your **Working Portfolio.** 🗂

2. **Siren Song** The singer in "Hunting Song" attempts to draw a deer to himself. Compose your own hunting song in which you lure what you most desire to yourself.

3. **Reflective Essay** Review the ideas about sacred language you recorded in your Reader's Notebook. Has studying these Native American songs given you new ideas about sacred language and how it differs from ordinary language? What comparisons can you make between these songs and forms of sacred expression in your own culture? Share your thoughts in a reflective essay.

## Activities & Explorations

1. **Oral Reading** With a small group of classmates, prepare oral readings of these two songs and perform them for the class. Include movement if you wish. After the performances, ask the class to vote on which reading they liked the best, giving reasons for their choice. **~ SPEAKING AND LISTENING**

2. **Visual Storytelling** Make a sequence of drawings, in panels, that show stages of the deer hunt in "Hunting Song." **~ VIEWING AND REPRESENTING**

*My hunting song*

## Inquiry & Research

1. **Mapping the Music** Recall that the term *sky loom* refers to desert rains. Point out images in "Song of the Sky Loom" that relate to rain. Why would rain be important to a farming culture in the Southwest? Research the terrain and climate of New Mexico. Draw a map on which you represent the different terrains and climates with various materials. Predict what other things might be subjects of Tewa songs.

2. **Thrill of the Hunt** Find out how the techniques and attitudes of modern hunters compare with those found in "Hunting Song." Give an oral report to the class based on research you conduct, on an interview with a hunter or local game warden, or on your own personal experiences.

3. **Hear My Song** If possible, bring in and play a recording of a traditional Tewa or Navajo song. (If you live in Arizona or New Mexico, perhaps you might invite a Tewa or Navajo singer to class.) What is the song about, and when is it usually sung? What aspects of the song could not be captured in a written translation of the lyrics? How does the song compare, in style and theme, to either of the songs you studied?

---

## Inquiry & Research

**Mapping the Music** Maps could be either three dimensional or two dimensional, with varying terrain and climate zones indicated in various colors or patterns. **Sources of information** include atlases with climate, vegetation, and relief maps of the Southwest, as well as books about the Southwest as a region.

**Thrill of the Hunt** Students might point out that despite a modern reliance on advanced weaponry in hunting, including telescopic sights and high-powered rifles, the hunter often has an experience of nature during the hunt. Some students may find hunting a disturbing topic and may wish to describe birding, "photo safaris," or other nonlethal stalking activities rather than sporting trips in which animals are killed. **Sources of information** include book-length accounts by hunters and columns or articles in hunting magazines. Nonlethal hunting is covered in birding magazines and journals such as *National Geographic.*

**Hear My Song** Aspects of such a song that might not be captured in the written version include its rhythmic or incantational nature.

# Coyote Stories

OKANOGAN (ō′kə-nŏg′ən) FOLK TALES

*Retold by* MOURNING DOVE

### Connect to Your Life

**Coyotes—Fact and Fiction** A coyote is a small, wolflike animal that is native to western North America and found in many other regions of the continent. You might have observed coyotes in the wild or in a zoo, or you might have seen them depicted in Westerns or cartoons. What traits do you associate with coyotes? Record your impressions in a word web, with the word coyote in the center of the web.

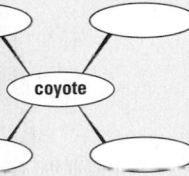

## Build Background

**Okanogan Storytelling** The homeland of the Okanogan people is north central Washington State and southern British Columbia. Many of the Okanogan now live on the Colville Reservation in Washington. "Coyote and the Buffalo" and "Fox and Coyote and Whale" are two folk tales originally told by Okanogan storytellers who traveled from village to village. They told these stories in Salish, their native language, and referred to places along the Columbia River, where they lived. Mourning Dove's retellings include Salish words and place names, spelled in a way that reflects their pronunciation.

Both tales belong to an oral tradition of the history of the Animal People, a race of supernatural beings believed to have been the first inhabitants of the world. The Animal People had magical powers and could alter their shapes. They usually appeared in animal form but could also take human form. When human beings appeared on earth, the Animal People were changed into different animal species. Coyote, one of the most important Animal People, is a central figure in these stories. He is thought to have made the world habitable for humans by killing monsters and bringing fire and salmon, among other deeds. Coyote stories are told in many Native American cultures across the western states.

## Focus Your Reading

**LITERARY ANALYSIS** **TRICKSTER TALES** Like myths, **folk tales** are stories handed down, usually by word of mouth, from generation to generation. In fact, some scholars regard myths—religious stories offering supernatural explanations of the world—as a special category of folk tale. **Trickster tales** are folk tales that feature an animal or human character who engages in deceit, violence, and magic. Often trickster tales are mythic, explaining features of the world. As you read these two stories, notice how Coyote demonstrates the trickster's contradictory qualities: he is foolish yet clever, greedy yet helpful, immoral yet moral. Also notice what Coyote creates.

**ACTIVE READING** **STRATEGIES FOR READING TRICKSTER TALES**

Using the following strategies as you read will help you get the most from these trickster tales:

- Read them aloud, or imagine a storyteller's voice.
- See the footnotes for explanations of Salish words.
- Accept magical transformations and animals who behave as humans.
- Note mysteries of nature that are explained.
- Infer the social values taught through the characters and situations.
- Note details that reveal other aspects of Okanogan culture.

**READER'S NOTEBOOK** As you use the last three strategies, jot down your notes in a three-column chart with these headings: **Explanations, Social Values, Cultural Details.**

## OVERVIEW

### Objectives
1. understand and appreciate **trickster tales** (Literary Analysis)
2. use **strategies for reading trickster tales** (Active Reading)

### Summary
"Coyote and the Buffalo": Coyote finds the skull of his enemy Buffalo Bull and plays with it in an insulting manner. Buffalo Bull comes back to life and chases Coyote over the plains until Coyote offers to make him new horns. In return for the horns, Buffalo Bull then gives Coyote a buffalo cow. He tells Coyote not to kill her when he is hungry but to eat her fat. When Coyote kills the cow, Buffalo Bull refuses to give him another one. Coyote thus returns alone to his home along the Columbia River, where to this day no buffalo have ever lived.

"Fox and Coyote and Whale": Fox's wife falls in love with Whale. After she vanishes one day, Fox and Coyote learn that Whale has stolen her. They retrieve her from Whale's lodge and cut off the monster's head, causing a permanent rift between Land People and Water People.

### Thematic Link
In these **traditional Native American** tales, no sharp distinction is drawn between humans and the rest of the natural world, suggesting a philosophy that views humans as **in harmony with nature.**

### 5-Minute Warm-Up

*Daily Language SkillBuilder*

Have students **proofread** the display sentences on page 17i and write them correctly. The sentences also appear on Transparency 1 of **Grammar Transparencies and Copymasters.**

---

### LESSON RESOURCES

**Reading Skills and Strategies: PREVIEW**

Tell students that trickster tales often have a cause-and-effect structure on two levels. First, the entire story explains the cause of some aspect of the natural world. Second, the plot of the tale unfolds as a series of causally related events. Ask students to identify the larger cause-and-effect structure in this tale.

**Possible Response:** The tale explains the absence of buffalo around the Columbia River.

### Active Reading

**STRATEGIES FOR READING TRICKSTER TALES**

 **A** Remind students of these characteristics of trickster tales: magical transformations, animals that act like humans, and explanations of natural phenomena. Have them identify these characteristics in "Coyote and the Buffalo."

**Possible Response:** Buffalo Bull is transformed from a skull into a living animal; Coyote talks and takes revenge on his old enemy; the tale promises to explain why no buffalo live near the Columbia River.

Encourage students to refer to the strategies on p. 39 if their understanding breaks down.

Use **Unit One Resource Book**, p. 17 for more practice.

### Literary Analysis  TRICKSTER TALES

**B** Ask students what Coyote creates in this tale.

**Answer:** He creates a pair of heavy horns with sharp points for Buffalo, which are the ones worn by all buffalo after that.

Use **Unit One Resource Book**, p. 18 for more practice.

---

### COYOTE STORIES
## OKANOGAN

# COYOTE and the BUFFALO

**Retold by Mourning Dove**

Buffalo skull. Private collection. Photo by John Oldenkamp.

No buffalo ever lived in the *Swah-netk'-qhu*[1] country. That was Coyote's fault. If he had not been so foolish and greedy, the people beside the *Swah-netk'-qhu* would not have had to cross the Rockies to hunt the *quas-peet-za*[2] (curled-hairs).

This is the way it happened:

 **A**

**COYOTE** was traveling over the plains beyond the big mountains. He came to a flat. There he found an old buffalo skull. It was the skull of Buffalo Bull. Coyote always had been afraid of Buffalo Bull. He remembered the many times Bull Buffalo had scared him, and he laughed upon seeing the old skull there on the flat.

"Now I will have some fun," Coyote remarked. "I will have revenge for the times Buffalo made me run."

He picked up the skull and threw it into the air; he kicked it and spat on it; he threw dust in the eye sockets. He did these things many times, until he grew tired. Then he went his way. Soon he heard a rumbling behind him. He thought it was thunder, and he looked at the sky. The sky was clear. Thinking he must have imagined the sound, he walked on, singing. He heard the rumbling again, only much closer and louder. Turning around, he saw Buffalo Bull pounding along after him, chasing him. His old enemy had come to life!

Coyote ran, faster than he thought he could run, but Buffalo gained steadily. Soon Buffalo was right at his heels. Coyote felt his hot breath.

"Oh, *Squas-tenk'*,[3] help me!" Coyote

---

1. *Swah-netk'-qhu:* the Salish name for Kettle Falls on the Columbia River or for the river itself.

2. *quas-peet-za:* a Salish word for buffalo.

3. *Squas-tenk':* a Salish word that refers to Coyote's power or spirit helper.

---

## Teaching Options

### Mini Lesson  Vocabulary

**USING CONTEXT CLUES AND FOOTNOTES** Display the following sentence from "Coyote and the Buffalo."

No buffalo ever lived in the *Swah-netk'-qhu* country.

Point out that context clues such as the phrase *lived in,* the word *country,* and capitalization rules pertaining to proper nouns suggest that the word *Swah-netk'-qhu* is the name of a place.

Now have students locate the sentence on page 40 of their textbooks. Tell them that the superscript number *1* after the word *Swah-netk'-qhu* indicates that there is a footnote associated with it. Footnotes provide extra information about a word, phrase, or idea in a text. They are located at the bottom of a page. Ask a volunteer to read the footnote aloud, and ask the class whether it confirms what they had concluded from context clues about the word's meaning. Have students continue to use context and footnotes as they read.

 Use **Vocabulary Transparencies and Copymasters**, p. 20.

A lesson on context clues appears on p. 326 in the Pupil's Edition.

begged, and his power answered by putting three trees in front of him. They were there in the wink of an eye. Coyote jumped and caught a branch of the first tree and swung out of Buffalo's way. Buffalo rammed the tree hard, and it shook as if in a strong wind. Then Buffalo chopped at the trunk with his horns, first with one horn and then the other. He chopped fast, and in a little while over went the tree, and with it went Coyote. But he was up and into the second tree before Buffalo Bull could reach him. Buffalo soon laid that tree low, but he was not quick enough to catch Coyote, who scrambled into the third and last tree.

"Buffalo, my friend, let me talk with you," said Coyote, as his enemy hacked away at the tree's trunk. "Let me smoke my pipe. I like the *kinnikinnick*.[4] Let me smoke. Then I can die more content."

"You may have time for one smoke," grunted Bull Buffalo, resting from his chopping.

Coyote spoke to his medicine-power, and a pipe, loaded and lighted, was given to him. He puffed on it once and held out the pipe to Buffalo Bull.

"No, I will not smoke with you," said that one. "You made fun of my bones. I have enough enemies without you. Young Buffalo is one of them. He killed me and stole all my fine herd."

"My uncle,"[5] said Coyote, "you need new horns. Let me make new horns for you. Then you can kill Young Buffalo. Those old horns are dull and worn."

Bull Buffalo was pleased with that talk. He decided he did not want to kill Coyote. He told Coyote to get down out of the tree and make the new horns. Coyote jumped down and called to his power. It scolded him for getting into trouble, but it gave him a flint knife and a stump of pitchwood.[6] From this stump Coyote carved a pair of fine heavy horns with sharp points. He gave them to Buffalo Bull. All buffalo bulls have worn the same kind of horns since.

**BUFFALO BULL** was very proud of his new horns. He liked their sharpness and weight and their pitch-black color. He tried them out on what was left of the pitchwood stump. He made one toss and the stump flew high in the air, and he forgave Coyote for his mischief. They became good friends right there. Coyote said he would go along with Buffalo Bull to find Young Buffalo.

They soon came upon Young Buffalo and the big herd he had won from Buffalo Bull. Young Buffalo laughed when he saw his old enemy, and he walked out to meet him. He did not know, of course, about the new horns. It was not much of a fight, that fight between Young Buffalo and Buffalo Bull. With the fine new horns, Buffalo Bull killed the other easily, and then he took back his herd, all his former wives and their children. He gave Coyote a young cow, the youngest cow, and he said:

**He** heard the rumbling again, only much closer and louder. Turning around, he saw Buffalo Bull pounding along after him, chasing him. His old enemy had come to life!

"Never kill her, *Sin-ka-lip'*![7] Take good care of her and she will supply you with meat forever. When you get hungry, just slice off some choice fat with a flint knife. Then rub ashes on the wound and the cut will heal at once."

Coyote promised to remember that, and they parted. Coyote started back to his own country, and the cow followed. For a few suns he ate only the fat when he was hungry. But after awhile he became

---

4. *kinnikinnick:* the Salish word for the bearberry, a shrub that is native to North America and Eurasia. The Okanogan toasted bearberry leaves and then crumbled and mixed them with tobacco for pipe smoking.

5. **my uncle:** Native Americans commonly use terms such as *uncle, cousin, brother,* and *sister* to express affection or respect or to flatter someone. Coyote uses this term of endearment to flatter Buffalo Bull.

6. **pitchwood:** the sap-filled wood of a pine or fir tree.

7. *Sin-ka-lip':* the Salish name for Coyote; it means "Imitator."

**Literary Analysis: CHARACTERIZATION**

Ask students to create cluster diagrams listing Coyote's human characteristics. Have them create similar diagrams for Buffalo Bull.

**Literary Analysis** [ TRICKSTER TALES ]

**A** Ask who else, besides Coyote, is a trickster in this tale.

**Answer:** the old woman

**Literary Analysis: IRONY**

**B** Ask students to explain what is ironic about Coyote's returning to Buffalo Bull's herd and seeing his cow.

**Answer:** Coyote killed the cow, but now he finds it alive and well.

# Thinking Through the Literature

1. **Comprehension Check** Coyote loses everything that his greed made him pursue.

2. **Possible Responses:** The tale teaches that it pays to befriend one's enemies, that greed will eventually be punished, and that a person can usually be tricked only once before wising up.

3. For people who are hungry on a cold winter night, the story teaches patience and wisdom.

 Use Selection Quiz in
**Unit One Resource Book**, p.19.

---

tired of eating fat, and he began to long for the sweet marrow-bones and the other good parts of the buffalo. He smacked his lips at the thought of having some warm liver.

"Buffalo Bull will never know," Coyote told himself, and he took his young cow down beside a creek and killed her.

As he peeled off the hide, crows and magpies came from all directions. They settled on the carcass and picked at the meat. Coyote tried to chase them away, but there were too many of them. While he was chasing some, others returned and ate the meat. It was not long until they had devoured every bit of the meat.

"Well, I can get some good from the bones and marrow-fat," Coyote remarked, and he built a fire to cook the bones. Then he saw an old woman walking toward him. She came up to the fire.

"*Sin-ka-lip'*," she said, "you are a brave warrior, a great chief. Why should you do woman's work? Let me cook the bones while you rest."

Vain Coyote! He was flattered. He believed she spoke her true mind. He stretched out to rest and he fell asleep. In his sleep he had a bad dream. It awoke him, and he saw the old woman running away with the marrow-fat and the

---

## VAIN COYOTE!

He was flattered. He believed she spoke her true mind. He stretched out to rest and he fell asleep. In his sleep he had a bad dream.

---

boiled grease. He looked into the cooking-basket. There was not a drop of soup left in it. He chased the old woman. He would punish her! But she could run, too, and she easily kept ahead of him. Every once in awhile she stopped and held up the marrow-fat and shouted: "*Sin-ka-lip'*, do you want this?"

Finally Coyote gave up trying to catch her. He went back to get the bones. He thought he would boil them again. He found the bones scattered all around, so he gathered them up and put them into the cooking-basket. Needing some more water to boil them in, he went to the creek for it, and when he got back, there were no bones in the basket! In place of the bones was a little pile of tree limbs!

Coyote thought he might be able to get another cow from Buffalo Bull, so he set out to find him. When he came to the herd, he was astonished to see the cow he had killed. She was there with the others! She refused to go with Coyote again, and Buffalo Bull would not give him another cow. Coyote had to return to his own country without a buffalo.

That is why there never have been any buffalo along the *Swah-netk'-qhu*. ❖

**A**

**B**

**1**

---

## Thinking Through the Literature

1. **Comprehension Check** What happens when Coyote disobeys Buffalo Bull's order?

2. Folk tales often serve to teach or explain. In your view, what does "Coyote and the Buffalo" teach or explain? Refer to the chart you made in your
   📖 **READER'S NOTEBOOK** as you read.

   [THINK ABOUT]
   - what actions are rewarded or punished
   - what changes occur in the characters
   - the first and last paragraphs of the tale

3. Okanogan storytellers might tell "Coyote and the Buffalo" during a winter night. Why do you think people would want to hear this story over and over again?

---

## Teaching Options

 **Mini Lesson** **Vocabulary Strategy**

**EXPANDING VOCABULARY THROUGH WIDE READING**

**Instruction** Tell students that as they read new materials, they are constantly expanding and strengthening their vocabularies. They should use context clues to figure out the meanings of new words. Have them locate the word *magpies* on page 42. Ask them to find a synonym for this word in the surrounding text.

**Answer:** crows

How does this help them understand *magpies*?

**Answer:** Magpies, like crows, are scavenger birds.

**Practice** Suggest that students jot down new Vocabulary words and their definitions in a Vocabulary notebook. Have students locate the word *contented* on PE page 45. What words in the surrounding text are synonyms for *contented*?

**Answers:** *happy, glad*

Have students look up *contented* in a dictionary to confirm its exact definition.

📄 Use **Vocabulary Transparencies and Copymasters**, p. 20.

# F O X
## and
## C O Y O T E
## and
## W H A L E

**Retold by Mourning Dove**

**FOX** had a beautiful wife. He was very much in love with her, but she had stopped caring for him. Fox was a great hunter, and every day he brought home food and fine skins for his wife to make into robes and clothing. He did not know that, while he was away hunting, his wife would sit beside the *Swah-netk'-qhu* and sing love songs to the water. Painting her face with bright colors, she would pour out her love thoughts in song.

Coyote came to visit his twin brother, and he soon noticed the strange actions of his sister-in-law. He spoke to Fox. "*Why-ay'-looh,*"[1] he said, "I think your wife is in love with somebody else." But Fox could not believe she loved anyone but him. He was blinded by his love for her. Then, one sun, he and Coyote returned from a hunt and she was not in the lodge. So Fox started to look for her. He walked down toward

Nootka wood whale effigy rattle (about 1870). Courtesy, Morning Star Gallery, Santa Fe, New Mexico. Photo by Addison Doty.

the river and there he saw his wife. She was sitting on the river bank, singing a love song. She did not see Fox. He watched her.

As Fox watched, the water began to rise. Slowly it rose, higher and higher, and soon, out of the middle of the river, appeared a big monster of the fish-kind. The monster was *En-hah-et'-qhu,* the Spirit of the Water—Whale. It swam to the shore. As it

---

1. *Why-ay'-looh:* the Salish name for Fox.

---

**Less Proficient Readers**

**1** Have students outline the sequence of events that answers the question *Why are there no buffalo in Coyote's country?*

**Possible Response:** Coyote insults Buffalo's bones; Buffalo comes back to life and chases him; to save his own life, Coyote offers to make Buffalo new horns; Buffalo gives Coyote a cow; Coyote kills the cow; Buffalo refuses to give him another cow; Coyote returns to his country alone.

**Students Acquiring English**

**2** Help students understand the poetic use of language in this tale. For example, Fox's wife is said to "pour out her love thoughts in song," meaning that her singing expresses her feelings of love. Fox is "blinded by his love," meaning that he is so in love with his wife that he cannot see that she is in love with someone else. The phrase *one sun* is used to mean "one day."

**Less Proficient Readers**

**3** Ask a student to summarize what Fox's wife has been doing.

**Possible Response:** While Fox is away hunting each day, she goes to the river and sings to her lover, Whale, who arises from the water and comes to her.

**Set a Purpose** Have students read to find out how the tale explains the great force of Kettle Falls and why whales don't live in fresh water.

---

 **Grammar**

## CAPITALIZATION OF PROPER NOUNS AND ADJECTIVES

**Instruction** Explain that a proper noun is the name of a particular person, place, thing, or idea. Examples include *Maya Angelou, Coyote, Columbia River, Empire State Building,* and *Christianity.* A proper adjective is an adjective formed from a proper noun, such as *Dickensian* (from *Dickens*) and *North American.* Display the following passage and ask students to explain why each underlined word is or is not capitalized.

Each <u>day</u> this week our class has read a folk tale. On <u>Tuesday</u> we read two <u>Okanogan</u> tales

featuring a clever <u>trickster</u>. The <u>storyteller</u> explains why <u>buffalo</u> have <u>sharp</u> horns by describing the actions of <u>Coyote</u> long ago. The language that <u>Mourning Dove</u> uses in her stories is <u>vivid</u> and poetic.

**Application** Have students form groups of four. Have each student write four sentences with capitalization errors in them. Have them exchange papers and correct the errors.

📃 Use **Grammar Transparencies and Copymasters,** p. 142.

Use McDougal Littell's *Language Network,* Chapter 8, for more instruction in capitalization.

**A** Ask students what human qualities Fox demonstrates in this passage.

**Possible Responses:** love, sadness, worry, jealousy

### Active Reading:

**STRATEGIES FOR READING TRICKSTER TALES**

**B** Read aloud or ask a student volunteer to read the passage on page 44 from *A few suns later* to *"He is bad."* Have students discuss how listening to this part of the story affected their experience of it. What does hearing the story read aloud add to the telling?

**Possible Responses:** The story is dramatic and suspenseful. An oral storyteller can add to the drama using his or her voice. Hearing this passage read aloud also conveys the musical quality of the Water Maidens' song.

### Literary Analysis TRICKSTER TALES

**C** After Fox gets the information he wants from the Water Maidens, he breaks their necks and steals their clothes. Ask students what these actions show about Fox and about tricksters in general.

**Possible Responses:** Fox is violent and cruel. Tricksters can be dangerous as well as playful.

Have students compare and contrast Coyote's role in each story.

**Possible Response:** In both stories Coyote is very clever and he can think on his feet. However, in "Coyote and the Buffalo," Coyote is more devious and cruel than he is in "Fox and Coyote and Whale"; in the latter he is more noble and a good brother.

---

touched dry land, it changed into a tall handsome man with long braided hair. This monster-man made love to the wife of Fox.

**A** Sad at heart, Fox turned away. He went to his lodge. He said nothing, but he wondered how he could win back his wife's love. He worried about her as the suns passed. She grew pale and thin. Nothing that Fox could do pleased her. Her thoughts always were with the man who was not a man but a monster. One day when Fox and Coyote came home from hunting, she was gone, and the fire in the lodge was cold. Fox called and called. He got no answer. His heart was heavy.

**B** A few suns later Fox looked up the river and saw an odd-shaped canoe coming. It was only half of a canoe. Two Water Maidens were standing in it, rocking it from side to side. They were singing:

> We come for food,
> Food for the Chief's stolen wife.
> The water-food does not suit her.
> That is why we come! We come!

 As the Water Maidens approached, Fox and Coyote hid in the tepee. The maidens beached the half-canoe and entered the lodge. They began to pick up dried meat to take to the stolen wife. Coyote and Fox sprang from their hiding places and caught the maidens, and Fox asked about his wife—where she was and how to get to her. The maidens were silent. Then the brothers threatened to kill them unless they answered, and the maidens said:

"To find the person who stole her, you must go over the Big Falls[2] and under the water. His lodge is under the falls, under the water—a dangerous trip for Land People. Every trail is watched. Even if you get there, the mighty Whale chief will kill you. He is bad."

**C** The Water Maidens had told all they knew, so Fox broke their necks. He and Coyote dressed in the maidens' robes and started down the river in the half-canoe. Standing on the sides of the strange craft, they rocked it as they had seen the maidens do, and rode it down the river and over the roaring falls. "Let me do all the talking," Fox warned Coyote. "I know better what to say." Down through the pouring, flashing waters they shot with the half-canoe. The thunder of the falls hurt their ears. And then, suddenly, they were landing at a great encampment of Water People, a strange kind of 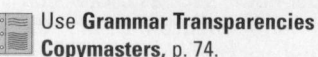 people to them. All of the people were strange except *Gou-kouh-whay'-na*—Mouse. She was there. She knew them and they knew her. Fox jumped ashore. Coyote, following, tripped and touched the water, and Mouse, the Sly One, laughed. "Ha-ha!" said Mouse, "Coyote nearly fell into the water."

"Do not speak," Fox whispered to Mouse. "Say nothing. I will pay you well."

But some of the Water People had heard. "What, *Gou-kouh-whay'-na*, did you say?" they inquired.

"Nothing," Mouse answered. "Nothing of importance. I was just joking."

"Yes, you did say something," said a Water Person. "You said that Coyote nearly fell into the water. You cannot fool me."

**MOUSE** insisted that she had not said that, and the other Water People believed her. They  knew she was a fickle person and giddy, and they did not think much of her because she went everywhere to steal. She went everywhere, and that is why she understood all the different languages.

Carrying packs of dried meat and berries they had brought with them, Coyote and Fox made their way to the lodge of Whale, the chief. He and the stolen wife sat side by side in the lodge. The wife was glad to get the meat and berries, her kind of food.

---

2. **Big Falls:** Kettle Falls on the Columbia River in northeastern Washington.

---

## Teaching Options

### Mini Lesson Grammar

**IDENTIFYING DIFFERENT TYPES OF SENTENCES**

**Instruction** Review the different kinds of sentences using the following examples.

| Kind of Sentence | Example |
|---|---|
| Declarative (statement) | Buffalo Bull chased Coyote. |
| Exclamatory (strong feeling) | Leave me alone! |
| Imperative (request or command) | Give me some soup. |
| Interrogative (question) | Why did you kill the cow? |

Discuss the kinds of end punctuation that may be used for each sentence type: A declarative sentence ends with a period; an exclamatory sentence ends with an exclamation point; an imperative sentence ends with a period or an exclamation point; an interrogative sentence ends with a question mark.

**Practice** Have students work in cooperative groups to search through "Coyote and the Buffalo" and "Fox and Coyote and Whale" for two examples of each sentence type.

Use **Grammar Transparencies and Copymasters**, p. 74.

Use McDougal Littell's *Language Network*, Chapter 9, for more instruction on end punctuation.

**FOX AND COYOTE** kept their robes over their faces until everyone else was asleep. Then, when everything was quiet, Fox slipped up to Whale and cut off the monster's head with a flint knife. At the same time Coyote picked up the stolen wife and ran for the broken canoe. The noise they made awoke the camp, and the people rushed out of their lodges to see Coyote carrying off Fox's wife and Fox close behind, carrying the head of their chief. The people chased them, but the three got into the broken canoe, and Fox quickly put Coyote and the woman into his *shoo'-mesh*[3] pipe. Then Fox pushed the half-canoe into the water and it shot up to the river's surface below the falls. There Fox landed. He took Coyote and his twice-stolen wife out of the medicine pipe, and the head of the Whale Monster he threw toward the setting sun.

"In the Big Salt Water (ocean) shall Whale Monster stay," said Fox. "No longer shall he live in the smaller waters, in the rivers, where he can make love to the wives of men, where he can lure wives from their husbands."

As Fox and his wife and brother walked up the bank to their tepee, the headless body of Whale Monster turned over and over in the depths of the river, making the Big Falls of the *Swah-netk'-qhu* more fearful and thunderous, the way they are today, spilling with such force over the great rocks.

The wife of Fox became contented and happy again, glad to be back in her husband's lodge. But since that day Whale Monster was vanquished the Land People and the Water People have not loved each other. Fox made it so. ❖

Mask for Coyote Dance. Courtesy, University of Texas at Austin. Photo by Donald Codry.

---

3. *shoo'-mesh:* the Salish word for medicine, or magic power.

---

## Mini Lesson  Viewing and Representing

*Nootka Wood Whale Effigy Rattle,* **anonymous, c. 1870** *Mask for a Coyote Dance,* **anonymous**

**ART APPRECIATION** The Nootka of the Northwest Coast are renowned artists. They carve and paint wood, bone, antler, and other materials. This mask was made in southern Mexico for use in Aztec Coyote Dances. Three small coyote heads grow out of the main head, from which the Coyote's tongue also protrudes.

**Instruction** Ask students: What does this mask suggest about coyotes? Compare it with your impressions of Coyote from reading the two Okanogan tales.
**Possible Response:** The coyote mask is both scary, with its big teeth and staring eyes, and humorous, with the animal's laughing expression and protruding tongue. The image supports the characterization of Coyote as a trickster because it has contradictory traits and suggests a tricky, untrustworthy, but powerful spirit.

**GUIDING STUDENT RESPONSE**

## Connect to the Literature

**1. What Do You Think?**
Possible Response: The climactic scene of the story, in which Fox and Coyote rescue Fox's wife and cut off Whale's head, is memorable for several reasons. First, it is the most physically dramatic scene in the story; second, it may bring issues of family loyalty to mind; third, it solidifies Fox and Coyote's camaraderie and heroism.

**Comprehension Check**
- They go to rescue Fox's wife and return her to her real home.
- The powerful force of Kettle Falls is caused by the headless body of the Whale Monster turning over and over again.
- Fox threw Whale's head toward the setting sun and proclaimed that the Whale must live in "the Big Salt Water" and not in the "smaller waters," or rivers.

 Use Selection Quiz in **Unit One Resource Book**, p. 19.

## Think Critically

**2.** Possible Response: This story is really about family values and family loyalty. Fox's wife betrayed him, but his twin brother saved the day. The purpose of this story may be to remind the Okanogan of the importance of family.

**3.** Possible Responses: The Okanogan believe in marriage, value friendship, disapprove of greed, use canoes, and eat meat.

**4.** Possible Responses: Yes and no. In "Coyote and the Buffalo" he is selfish, cruel, greedy, and witty; he is more entertaining than admirable. However, in "Fox and Coyote and Whale," he is loyal, hard-working, and wise; here he is very admirable.

## Literary Analysis

**Trickster Tale** Possible Response: Students may state that Coyote emerges as a numskull in "Coyote and the Buffalo" because he foolishly kills the cow that would have provided food forever. In "Fox and Coyote and Whale," on the other hand, Coyote emerges as a cultural hero who helps Fox regain his kidnapped wife.

## Connect to the Literature

**1. What Do You Think?**
What did you feel was most memorable about "Fox and Coyote and Whale"?

**Comprehension Check**
- Why do Fox and Coyote go to the world of the Water People?
- What caused the powerful force of Kettle Falls, according to the story?
- Why don't whales live in fresh waters, according to the story?

## Think Critically

**2.** What might be Okanogan storytellers' purpose for telling this story?

**3.**  **ACTIVE READING** | **STRATEGIES FOR READING TRICKSTER TALES** Share details about Okanogan culture that you recorded in your 📖 **READER'S NOTEBOOK** as you read the story. What did you learn about the Okanogan people and their way of life?

**THINK ABOUT** {
- their values, attitudes, and beliefs
- geographical features of their area
- the ways they adapt to their environment
}

**4.** Do you view Coyote as admirable? Explain why or why not.

## Extend Interpretations

**5. Comparing Texts** What do these Coyote stories have in common with other folk tales you know?

**6. Different Perspectives** Some Native Americans have argued that stories about the Animal People constitute "the first history of America." Do you agree? Support your opinion.

**7. Connect to Life** Compare Coyote in these stories with your previous mental image of a coyote. Refer to the word web you were asked to make on page 39.

## Literary Analysis

**TRICKSTER TALE** A **trickster tale** is a folk tale about an animal or person who engages in deceit, violence, and magic. Besides Coyote, tricksters in Native American oral traditions also include Raven, Mink, Hare, and Blue Jay. In tales from other world cultures, the trickster is a spider, a rabbit, or a fox. According to the folklorist Stith Thompson, a trickster "may appear in any one of three roles: the beneficent culture hero, the clever deceiver, or the numskull."

**Paired Activity** Create a three-column chart that classifies tricksters according to Stith Thompson's categories. Then meet with a partner to analyze the roles that Coyote plays in "Coyote and the Buffalo" and "Fox and Coyote and Whale." Fill in the chart with examples to support your findings. In each tale, which role of trickster seems the most dominant?

| Culture Hero | Clever Deceiver | Numskull |
|---|---|---|
| | | |
| | | |
| | | |

## Extend Interpretations

**Comparing Texts** Students might focus on the morals of the stories or their purpose in the society in which each was told. Others may focus on supernatural aspects of the stories or on their entertainment value.

**Different Perspectives** Some students may disagree, saying that the tales focus too much on the supernatural to provide valid history; others may say that these stories impart much information about early Native American life.

**Connect to Life** Students may be struck by how much personification influences their answer to this question. Their previous mental images of coyotes will probably be vastly different from the character they met in these tales, who can talk and play tricks on his friends.

# Choices & CHALLENGES

## Writing Options

**1. Magazine Article** Meet with two other students to brainstorm a list of four tricksters who are popular today. Then compare and contrast them with Coyote. Use your discussion to outline a magazine article about one of these tricksters.

**Writing Handbook**
See page 1281: Compare and Contrast

**2. Updated Trickster Tale** Some modern American writers have used the figure of Coyote in their own stories and poetry, updating  the traditional tales for their own times. Drawing on the characters and plot structures of the Coyote tales you have just read, write your own contemporary trickster tale.

*A Trickster Tale*

## Activities & Explorations

**1. Creative Pantomime** It was customary for storytellers to visit different villages and tell stories about the Animal People to children. To help dramatize the stories, the storytellers used facial expressions and gestures. Choose one of the two Coyote tales, and use creative movement and gestures to act it out for your classmates as a partner reads aloud. ~ **PERFORMING**

**2. Coyote on Video** When the Nez Perce anthropologist Archie Phinney recorded his people's animal stories in writing, he felt that their spirit had been lost. He said, "When I read my story mechanically I find only the cold corpse." View the video of storyteller Terry Tafoya's performance of "Coyote's Eyes." What would be lost if the performance were transferred to the printed page? ~ **VIEWING AND REPRESENTING**

 **Literature in Performance**

---

## Mourning Dove
### 1888?–1936

**Other Works**
*Mourning Dove: A Salishan Autobiography*
*Mourning Dove's Stories*

**Echoes of the Past** "Mourning Dove" was the pen name of Christine Quintasket, who grew up on the Colville Reservation in north central Washington State. As a child, she listened eagerly to the stories told by her mother, Lucy; her father, Joseph; Broken Nose Abraham; Long Woman; and other storytellers. In the preface to *Coyote Stories*, she reflects on what these storytellers taught her about the Animal People:

> *Vividly I recall old S'whist-kane (Lost-Head), also known as Old Narciss, and how, in the course of a narrative, he would jump up and mimic his characters, speaking or singing in a strong or weak voice, just as the Animal Persons were supposed to have done. And he would dance around the fire in the tule-mat covered lodge until the pines rang with the gleeful shouts of the smallest listeners.*

**Determined to Write** Mourning Dove not only was educated in her people's oral traditions but also had some formal education at government and Catholic mission schools. Determined to be a writer, she learned to write English and later attended secretarial school in Canada to learn how to type. She drafted a novel in 1912 but put it away for several years, until she met Lucullus Virgil McWhorter, an author and Native American–rights activist, who offered to edit it. *Cogewea, the Half-Blood* was published in 1927.

**A Storyteller's Legacy** McWhorter encouraged Mourning Dove to record the traditional stories of the Okanogan and the other Colville tribes. Although Mourning Dove was a migrant worker, picking apples ten hours a day, she managed to write at night. *Coyote Stories*, which McWhorter and the journalist Heister Dean Guie helped edit, was published in 1933. By collecting and preserving some of the stories that tell the history of her people, Mourning Dove in her own way carried on the work of the storytellers she had heard as a child.

---

## Writing Options

**1. Magazine Article** Students' articles should discuss personality traits that they believe are essential to tricksters. **To get students started on this assignment,** suggest that they list all the traits that they attribute to tricksters in general *before* they choose their four current-day tricksters. Then, when students choose their contemporary tricksters, have them justify their choices by discussing both personality traits and relationships with others.

**2. Updated Trickster Tale** Students' stories should demonstrate a knowledge of the conventions of trickster tales, such as a central trickster character, magical events, explanations of natural phenomena, and moral lessons. **To get students started on this assignment,** have them focus on these conventions. Suggest that they think about questions such as *What aspect of the natural world do I want to explain? How will the trickster's actions bring about a permanent change in the world?*

## Activities & Explorations

**1. Creative Pantomime** This activity is well suited to **kinesthetic learners.** Have students compare and contrast the various performances given by their classmates. Ask them to discuss what the pantomimes added to their experience of the story as compared to reading it silently. Interested students may want to present a video of their pantomime.

**2. Coyote on Video** Have students list the different methods that Terry Tafoya uses in the video to dramatize the story of "Coyote's Eyes." Possible Responses: Facial expressions, gestures, body movement, different voices and intonations for different characters in the story.

See Literature in Performance: Teachers' Resource Book.

---

☑ **Assessment** **Informal Assessment**

**ARRANGE EVENTS IN SEQUENTIAL ORDER** Many standardized exams test students' understanding of the sequence of events in a narrative passage. Display the items below and ask students to number them in the proper sequence.

Coyote offers to make Buffalo Bull new horns. *(3)*

An old woman tricks Coyote out of his soup. *(5)*

Coyote insults Buffalo Bull by playing with his skull. *(1)*

Buffalo Bull chases Coyote. *(2)*

Buffalo refuses to give Coyote a cow. *(6)*

Coyote kills a cow. *(4)*

**Exercises** Have students answer the following: Which event happens first in "Fox and Coyote and Whale"?

**A.** Whale emerges from the river to meet Fox's wife.

**B.** Coyote suspects that Fox's wife loves someone else.

**C.** Fox declares that Whale shall never live in the river again.

**D.** Water Maidens arrive in a canoe.

## Objectives

1. understand and appreciate a **short story (Literary Analysis)**
2. recognize author's use of **conflict (Literary Analysis)**
3. make **inferences** based on information presented in a story **(Active Reading)**

## Summary

In an arroyo in New Mexico, Leon and his brother-in-law, Ken, find the body of Leon's grandfather, Teofilo, who died while herding sheep. In accordance with tradition, they put a feather in the dead man's hair, paint his face, and ask him to send rain. Driving back with the body, they meet Father Paul, the local Catholic priest, who asks about Teofilo. Leon does not reveal that the old man has died. The family has a traditional funeral presided over by medicine men. Afterward, Leon asks Father Paul to sprinkle holy water on the grave so that Teofilo won't be thirsty. Father Paul at first resists, but he finally consents to Leon's request. Leon is happy, believing that Teofilo will send rain.

## Thematic Link

Leon and his family insist on burying his grandfather according to their ancient **traditions.** Their lives have been influenced by European ways, however, and they decide to incorporate a Christian element into the rite. The burial thus expresses **harmony with nature,** with Laguna tradition, and with the family's white neighbors.

### 5-Minute Warm-Up

**Daily Language SkillBuilder**

Have students **proofread** the display sentences on page 17i and write them correctly. The sentences also appear on Transparency 2 of **Grammar Transparencies and Copymasters.**

# The Man to Send Rain Clouds

*Short Story by* LESLIE MARMON SILKO

**Comparing Literature**

## Traditions Across Time: Harmonizing Old and New

"The Man to Send Rain Clouds" is not traditional oral literature but a short story, in a modern setting, by a contemporary Native American writer. Still, like the earlier pieces you have read, the story reflects ancient beliefs and ceremonies.

**Points of Comparison** As you read, compare the Laguna characters' spiritual views with those expressed in other Native American cultures. Also notice the impact of Christianity on traditional Laguna ways.

## Build Background

The story depicts funeral ceremonies held among the Laguna people of western New Mexico. Like the Tewa, the Laguna are a Pueblo group, but they speak a Keresan language. Pueblo groups had settled in the Southwest thousands of years before the first Spanish conquistadors arrived in 1540. The Spanish came to establish a colony and to convert the Pueblos to Catholicism but were driven away in 1680 during the Pueblo Rebellion. The Spanish soon returned, however, completing their re-conquest of New Mexico in 1692. The Laguna pueblo was founded in 1699 by emigrants from other pueblos to the north. In the 1700s and 1800s, the Laguna and other Pueblo groups were harassed by Mexican slavers; raiders from the Navajo, Apache, and Ute tribes; and Protestant settlers from the United States.

Despite being influenced by outside cultures, the Laguna have kept many of their values and beliefs. For example, they perform traditional ceremonies when a person dies because they believe that dead persons' spirits will become Shiwanna —Cloud People—who bring the precious gift of rain.

## Focus Your Reading

**LITERARY ANALYSIS    CONFLICT** A **conflict** is a struggle between opposing forces that is the basis of a story's plot. A character can be in conflict with an outside force, such as nature, society or another character. One of the conflicts in this story is between the characters Leon and Father Paul. Conflict can also occur within a character. Notice the different kinds of conflict in this story.

**ACTIVE READING    MAKING INFERENCES** An **inference** is a logical guess based on evidence. By using information from your reading and from your own experience, you can make inferences about things left unstated in a work of literature.

**READER'S NOTEBOOK** Use a chart like the one started below to record the ceremonies, or prescribed acts, that people either perform or want performed after Teofilo's death. Use the second or third column to indicate which tradition you infer that the ceremony belongs to, Laguna or European.

| Ceremony | Laguna | European |
|---|---|---|
| painting on face | X | |

## LESSON RESOURCES

**UNIT ONE RESOURCE BOOK,** pp. 20–24

**ASSESSMENT RESOURCES**
**Formal Assessment,** pp. 13–14
**Teacher's Guide to Assessment and Portfolio Use**
**Test Generator**

**SKILLS TRANSPARENCIES AND COPYMASTERS**
**Literary Analysis**
• Social Conflict/Issues, T14 (for Literary Analysis, p. 48)

**Reading and Critical Thinking**
• Making Inferences, T7 (for Active Reading, p. 48)

**Grammar**
• Capitalizing the First Word of a Sentence, C146 (for Mini Lesson, p. 52)

**Vocabulary**
• Word Origins, C22 (for Vocabulary in Action, p. 54)

**Writing**
• Opinion Statement, C34 (for Think Critically, item 5, p. 53)

**INTEGRATED TECHNOLOGY**

**Audio Library**
**LaserLinks**
• Cultural Connection: Pueblo Culture
• Art Gallery: Art of the Southwest. See **Teacher's SourceBook,** pp. 11–12.

**Visit our website:**
www.mcdougallittell.com

# THE MAN TO SEND RAIN CLOUDS

### Leslie Marmon Silko

**THEY FOUND HIM UNDER A BIG COTTONWOOD TREE.** His Levi jacket and pants were faded light-blue so that he had been easy to find. The big cottonwood tree stood apart from a small grove of winterbare cottonwoods which grew in the wide, sandy arroyo. He had been dead for a day or more, and the sheep had wandered and scattered up and down the arroyo. Leon and his brother-in-law, Ken, gathered the sheep and left them in the pen at the sheep camp before they returned to the cottonwood tree. Leon waited under the tree while Ken drove the truck through the deep sand to the edge of the arroyo. He squinted up at the sun and unzipped his jacket—it sure was hot for this time of year. But high and northwest the blue mountains were still deep in snow. Ken came sliding down the low, crumbling bank about fifty yards down, and he was bringing the red blanket.

Before they wrapped the old man, Leon took a piece of string out of his pocket and tied a small gray feather in the old man's long white hair. Ken gave him the paint. Across the brown wrinkled forehead he drew a streak of white and along the high cheekbones he drew a strip of blue paint. He paused and watched Ken throw pinches of corn meal and pollen into the wind that fluttered the small gray feather. Then Leon painted with yellow under the old man's broad nose, and finally, when he had painted green across the chin, he smiled.

"Send us rain clouds, Grandfather." They laid the bundle in the back of the pickup and covered it with a heavy tarp before they started back to the pueblo.

They turned off the highway onto the sandy pueblo road. Not long after they passed the store and post office they saw Father Paul's car coming toward them. When he recognized their faces he slowed his car and waved for them to stop. The young priest rolled down the car window.

"Did you find old Teofilo?" he asked loudly.

Leon stopped the truck. "Good morning, Father. We were just out to the sheep camp. Everything is O.K. now."

WORDS TO KNOW — **arroyo** (ə-roi′ō) *n.* a deep gully cut by an intermittent stream; a dry gulch

49

---

---

Tell students that this story describes a conflict between people who belong to different cultures. As they read, students should consider the cultural values that are important to these characters.

### Active Reading:

**MAKING INFERENCES**

**A** Ask students what inference Father Paul makes about Teofilo from Leon's comments. Have them support their inferences with evidence from the text and/or personal experience.

**Possible Response:** He infers that Teofilo has been found alive.

**B** Ask students what they can infer about Louise from the fact that she wants Father Paul to sprinkle holy water for Teofilo.

**Possible Response:** Although she honors the traditions of her people, she also respects those of the Christian faith.

Use **Unit One Resource Book,** p. 21 for more practice.

### Literary Analysis | CONFLICT |

Remind students that conflict can take place between two or more characters or within the mind of a single character. Ask them what external conflict exists in this story, and between whom.

**Answer:** Father Paul is in conflict with Leon and the Laguna community over the proper way to bury Teofilo.

Use **Unit One Resource Book,** p. 22 for more practice.

---

"Thank God for that. Teofilo is a very old man. You really shouldn't allow him to stay at the sheep camp alone."

"No, he won't do that any more now."

**A** "Well, I'm glad you understand. I hope I'll be seeing you at Mass this week—we missed you last Sunday. See if you can get old Teofilo to come with you." The priest smiled and waved at them as they drove away.

Louise and Teresa were waiting. The table was set for lunch, and the coffee was boiling on the black iron stove. Leon looked at Louise and then at Teresa.

"We found him under a cottonwood tree in the big arroyo near sheep camp. I guess he sat down to rest in the shade and never got up again." Leon walked toward the old man's bed. The red plaid shawl had been shaken and spread carefully over the bed, and a new brown flannel shirt and pair of stiff new Levis were arranged neatly beside the pillow. Louise held the screen door open while Leon and Ken carried in the red blanket. He looked small and shriveled, and after they dressed him in the new shirt and pants he seemed more shrunken.

It was noontime now because the church bells rang the Angelus.[1] They ate the beans with hot bread, and nobody said anything until after Teresa poured the coffee.

Ken stood up and put on his jacket. "I'll see about the gravediggers. Only the top layer of soil is frozen. I think it can be ready before dark."

Leon nodded his head and finished his coffee. After Ken had been gone for a while, the neighbors and clanspeople came quietly to embrace Teofilo's family and to leave food on the table because the gravediggers would come to eat when they were finished.

The sky in the west was full of pale-yellow light. Louise stood outside with her hands in the pockets of Leon's green army jacket that was too big for her. The funeral was over, and the old men had taken their candles and medicine bags[2]

and were gone. She waited until the body was laid into the pickup before she said anything to Leon. She touched his arm, and he noticed that her hands were still dusty from the corn meal that she had sprinkled around the old man. When she spoke, Leon could not hear her.

"What did you say? I didn't hear you."

"I said that I had been thinking about something."

"About what?"

"About the priest sprinkling holy water[3] for Grandpa. So he won't be thirsty." **B**

Leon stared at the new moccasins that Teofilo had made for the ceremonial dances in the summer. They were nearly hidden by the red blanket. It was getting colder, and the wind pushed gray dust down the narrow pueblo road. The sun was approaching the long <u>mesa</u> where it disappeared during the winter. Louise stood there shivering and watching his face. Then he zipped up his jacket and opened the truck door. "I'll see if he's there."

**K**en stopped the pickup at the church, and Leon got out; and then Ken drove down the hill to the graveyard where people were waiting. Leon knocked at the old carved door with its symbols of the Lamb. While he waited he looked up at the twin bells from the king of Spain with the last sunlight pouring around them in their tower.

The priest opened the door and smiled when he saw who it was. "Come in! What brings you here this evening?"

The priest walked toward the kitchen, and

---

1. **rang the Angelus** (ăn′jə-ləs): was rung to remind Roman Catholics to recite a prayer in commemoration of the Annunciation, the archangel Gabriel's announcing to the Virgin Mary that she had conceived Jesus, the Son of God.

2. **medicine bags:** pouches containing collections of sacred items believed to possess magical influence.

3. **holy water:** water blessed by a priest and used for religious purposes.

| WORDS TO KNOW | **mesa** (mā′ sə) *n.* a broad, flat-topped hill with clifflike sides |
| --- | --- |

50

---

## Cross Curricular Link **History**

**LAGUNA PUEBLO** The Laguna Pueblo is located about 45 miles west of Albuquerque, New Mexico. The name *Laguna* is Spanish for "lake" and refers to a large pond near the site of the pueblo. In the early 1700s, the main pueblo of Laguna and several surrounding villages had a total population of about 480. Today the Laguna population numbers about 8,000, and the main pueblo is still used for ceremonial purposes and as a political center. Laguna tradition holds that the founders of the pueblo migrated there from the north, looking to escape drought conditions. The history, farming lifestyle, and desert home of the Laguna thus contribute to a cultural focus on the importance of rain. For example, the traditional initiation ceremony for young men included dances in which they impersonated rain gods. Members of medicine societies also performed ceremonies and dances to bring good crops and control the weather.

*Between Heaven and Earth; Earth and Sky* (1976), Frank LaPena. Acrylic on canvas, 24″ × 18″, WINTU-NOMTIPOM.

Leon stood with his cap in his hand, playing with the earflaps and examining the living room—the brown sofa, the green armchair, and the brass lamp that hung down from the ceiling by links of chain. The priest dragged a chair out of the kitchen and offered it to Leon.

"No thank you, Father. I only came to ask you if you would bring your holy water to the graveyard."

The priest turned away from Leon and looked out the window at the patio full of shadows and the dining-room windows of the nuns' <u>cloister</u> across the patio. The curtains were heavy, and the light from within faintly penetrated; it was impossible to see the nuns inside eating supper. "Why didn't you tell me he was dead? I could have brought the Last Rites[4] anyway."

Leon smiled. "It wasn't necessary, Father."

The priest stared down at his scuffed brown loafers and the worn hem of his <u>cassock</u>. "For a Christian burial it was necessary."

His voice was distant, and Leon thought that his blue eyes looked tired.

"It's O.K. Father, we just want him to have plenty of water."

---

4. **Last Rites:** a sacrament in which a priest anoints a dying person with holy oil and prays for his or her salvation.

WORDS
TO
KNOW

**cloister** (kloi'stər) *n.* a place devoted to religious seclusion; a monastery or convent

**cassock** (kăs'ək) *n.* an ankle-length garment, with close-fitting waist and sleeves, worn by clergymen

51

## Viewing and Representing
*Mini Lesson*

*Between Heaven and Earth; Earth and Sky,* by **Frank LaPeña (1937– )**

**ART APPRECIATION** Frank LaPeña, a Wintu-Nomtipom artist, was born in San Francisco. Although he received a master's degree, his training with tribal elders and his participation in ceremonies and dances were also an essential part of his education.
**Instruction** Ask students what clues the title *Between Heaven and Earth; Earth and Sky* offers about the meaning of this painting. Ask students to consider how they might interpret the painting without knowing its title. Taking the title into consideration, what do they think the artist is saying about his relationship to the universe?

**Possible Responses:** Without knowing the title, students might comment on the more abstract qualities of the painting: the geometric shapes, the colors, and so on. The title makes the meaning behind the painting more concrete. The artist may be expressing his feeling of being suspended between an earthly or bodily existence and a heavenly or spiritual one. The circle with the cross may represent the artist himself, and the white lines show his connections to the earth, to the sky, and to other people and animals whose spirits are likewise suspended in bodily existence.

**Literary Analysis** `CONFLICT`

**A** What internal conflict is Father Paul facing?

**Possible Response:** He is not sure whether to grant Leon's request. He knows that to sprinkle holy water at Teofilo's grave violates the rules of his church, but he wants to take part in the burial because he knew and cared about the old man.

**Literary Analysis: SYMBOLISM**

A symbol is a person, place, or thing that stands for something beyond itself, such as an idea or a feeling. Ask students to speculate about the symbolic meaning of the corn meal and pollen that are scattered to mark Teofilo's death.

**Possible Response:** They represent fertility; they link Teofilo's death to new life.

**Reading Skills and Strategies:**
**COMPARING AND CONTRASTING CULTURES**

Have students list similarities and differences between the Laguna and European cultures as portrayed in the story.

**Possible Responses:** Father Paul knows he is going against his own tradition when he sprinkles the holy water, but he also realizes that he is fulfilling the needs of his parish by doing so. Leon knows that holy water is not part of his own tradition, but he still asks for it.

---

**He felt good because it was finished, and he was happy about the sprinkling of the holy water; now the old man could send them big thunderclouds for sure.**

The priest sank down into the green chair and picked up a glossy missionary magazine. He turned the colored pages full of lepers and pagans without looking at them.

**A** "You know I can't do that, Leon. There should have been the Last Rites and a funeral Mass at the very least."

Leon put on his green cap and pulled the flaps down over his ears. "It's getting late, Father. I've got to go."

When Leon opened the door Father Paul stood up and said, "Wait." He left the room and came back wearing a long brown overcoat. He followed Leon out the door and across the dim churchyard to the adobe steps in front of the church. They both stooped to fit through the low adobe entrance. And when they started down the hill to the graveyard only half of the sun was visible above the mesa.

The priest approached the grave slowly, wondering how they had managed to dig into the frozen ground; and then he remembered that this was New Mexico, and saw the pile of cold loose sand beside the hole. The people stood close to each other with little clouds of steam puffing from their faces. The priest looked at them and saw a pile of jackets, gloves, and scarves in the yellow, dry tumbleweeds that grew in the graveyard. He looked at the red blanket, not sure that Teofilo was so small, wondering if it wasn't some <u>perverse</u> Indian trick—something they did in March to ensure a good harvest—wondering if maybe old Teofilo was actually at sheep camp corralling the sheep for the night. But there he was, facing into a cold dry wind and squinting at the last sunlight, ready to bury a red wool blanket while the faces of his

parishioners were in shadow with the last warmth of the sun on their backs.

His fingers were stiff, and it took him a long time to twist the lid off the holy water. Drops of water fell on the red blanket and soaked into dark icy spots. He sprinkled the grave and the water disappeared almost before it touched the dim, cold sand; it reminded him of something—he tried to remember what it was, because he thought if he could remember he might understand this. He sprinkled more water; he shook the container until it was empty, and the water fell through the light from sundown like August rain that fell while the sun was still shining, almost evaporating before it touched the wilted squash flowers.

The wind pulled at the priest's brown Franciscan robe[5] and swirled away the corn meal and pollen that had been sprinkled on the blanket. They lowered the bundle into the ground, and they didn't bother to untie the stiff pieces of new rope that were tied around the ends of the blanket. The sun was gone, and over on the highway the eastbound lane was full of headlights. The priest walked away slowly. Leon watched him climb the hill, and when he had disappeared within the tall, thick walls, Leon turned to look up at the high blue mountains in the deep snow that reflected a faint red light from the west. He felt good because it was finished, and he was happy about the sprinkling of the holy water; now the old man could send them big thunderclouds for sure. ❖

---

5. **Franciscan robe:** the distinctive garment of a Roman Catholic religious order founded by Saint Francis of Assisi in 1209. After Spain established a colony in New Mexico in 1598, Franciscan missionaries began to settle there and build churches in the pueblos.

---

WORDS
TO
KNOW

**perverse** (pər-vûrs´) *adj.* stubbornly opposed to what is right or reasonable; wrong-headed

52

---

## Teaching Options

 **Mini Lesson** **Grammar**

**CAPITALIZING FIRST WORD OF SENTENCE**

**Instruction** Remind students that a sentence expresses a complete thought, and that it always begins with a capital letter and ends with a period, question mark, or exclamation point. A direct quotation embedded in a longer sentence also begins with a capital letter.

**Practice** Display the following sentence and work through it with students as a model.

The priest shook his head and said, "You know I can't do that, Leon."

Use **Grammar Transparencies and Copymasters,** p. 144.

Use McDougal Littell's *Language Network,* Chapter 8, for more instruction and practice in capitalization.

## Connect to the Literature

**1. What Do You Think?**
Did Teofilo have a "good" funeral? Share your impressions.

**Comprehension Check**
- Who is Teofilo and what has happened to him?
- What do Teofilo's relatives want Father Paul to do?
- Why is it necessary for Teofilo to have plenty of water?

## Think Critically

**2.** Why do you think Leon and Ken do not tell Father Paul about Teofilo's death right away?

**3.** Louise and Leon want Father Paul to sprinkle holy water on Teofilo's grave. Why do you think this act is so important to them?

**4.** ACTIVE READING | MAKING INFERENCES | Of the two kinds of ceremonies surrounding Teofilo's death—Laguna and European—which do you think is more important to his people? Refer to the chart you were asked to make in your  READER'S NOTEBOOK.

**5.** In your opinion, does Father Paul do the right thing at the end of the story? Consider the evidence.

THINK ABOUT {
- his attitude toward Laguna ceremonies
- his attitude toward Christian burial
- possible reasons for his decision
}

## Extend Interpretations

**6. What If?** Suppose Father Paul had been a Laguna man who had lived in the pueblo as a youth, left to study for the priesthood, and then returned. How might the **conflicts** in this story be different?

**7. Connect to Life** Name important ceremonies in your own culture; for example, the passing out of diplomas at a graduation. What do you believe is the function of ceremonies? When do you think a ceremony should be changed, if ever?

**8.** Points of Comparison Judging from this story, how would you describe the Laguna people's spiritual views and relationship to nature? Compare their beliefs with those of the Iroquois, Tewa, or Navajo.

## Literary Analysis

CONFLICT As you recall, the basis of a story's plot is **conflict**, or a struggle between opposing forces. An **external conflict** pits a character against nature, society, or another character. An **internal conflict** is between opposing forces within a character. In "Coyote and the Buffalo," for example, Coyote's struggle to keep Buffalo Bull from killing him is an external conflict, whereas Coyote's struggle to decide whether to kill and eat the buffalo cow is an internal conflict.

**Cooperative Learning Activity** In a small group, discuss the conflicts you see in "The Man to Send Rain Clouds." Summarize them on a chart like the one below, and classify each as external or internal. Are the conflicts resolved? If so, tell how.

| Conflict | Internal or External? | How Resolved |
|---|---|---|
|  |  |  |
|  |  |  |
|  |  |  |

---

### Connect to the Literature

**1. What Do You Think?**
Some students may focus on the "best of both worlds" aspect of this funeral. Others may think that Teofilo's family should have followed one tradition and not have tried to blend the two.

**Comprehension Check**
- Teofilo is Leon's grandfather. He died while herding sheep.
- They want him to sprinkle holy water over Teofilo's grave.
- His family doesn't want him to be thirsty, and they hope that he will send rain for their crops.

 Use Selection Quiz in **Unit One Resource Book,** p. 24

### Think Critically

**2.** Possible Responses: They wanted to avoid a conflict over what kind of funeral Teofilo would have; they feared that Father Paul would take over the funeral and do it his way rather than theirs.

**3.** Possible Responses: Water is essential to life in the desert, and Laguna tradition holds that the dead will send rain to help the living. Louise and Leon also respect Christian traditions and want to incorporate them into the funeral.

**4.** Possible Response: The Laguna ceremonies are more important to Teofilo's family. Only one Christian element, the sprinkling of holy water, is included in the burial rite.

**5.** Students' responses should weigh Father Paul's disregard for the rituals of his own faith against the fact that he did what his heart told him was right in a unique situation.

### Literary Analysis

**Conflict** Have students discuss the plot development. Possible Responses: Major internal conflicts are those of Leon and Louise, each debating whether to ask for the holy water, and of Father Paul, deciding whether to use it. The main external conflict is between Leon and Father Paul about Teofilo's funeral ceremony. Leon prevails when Father Paul agrees to sprinkle holy water over Teofilo and his grave.

---

### Extend Interpretations

**What If?** Possible Responses: In this scenario, Father Paul would not even question the use of the holy water in the ceremony. Through empathy and familiarity, he would better understand the needs of the parish.

**Connect to Life** Possible Responses: They mark rites of passage, family occasions, and times when a person is especially honored or appreciated.

Ceremonies should be changed if they become insensitive or offensive to people.

**Points of Comparison** The Laguna people believe that humans are closely connected with the life-fostering events of the natural world. For example, their rituals emphasize that the dead directly help the living by providing rain to an arid land.

## Writing Options

**1. Performance Review** Tell students that performance reviews are a common type of business writing. Students' responses should reflect the events of the story as well as the perspective of the writer.

**2. Description of Rites** Students' responses should contain adequate detail for the specified audience, someone who has never seen the ceremony. **To adapt this activity for Visual Learners,** have students draw or paint a picture of the ceremony, including details that show symbolic elements.

## Activities & Explorations

**1. Illustrative Scene** Students' drawings should accurately reflect what happened in the story but may also include details that express their personal reactions.

**2. Points of Comparison** Students may mention the modern prose style and the realistic setting and characters in "The Man to Send Rain Clouds." Unlike the Coyote stories they have read, this story does not set out to explain the origin of any natural phenomena.

## Vocabulary in Action

1. perverse    4. arroyo
2. cassock    5. mesa
3. cloister

## Author Activity

**To make this assignment more challenging,** have students compare and contrast the Laguna with another Native American culture, based on stories and myths from both traditions.

## Writing Options

**1. Performance Review** Assuming the role either of Father Paul's religious superior or of a leader of the Laguna community, write an evaluation of Father Paul, assessing his relationship with the community he serves.

**2. Description of Rites** Think about a ceremony that is familiar to you, such as graduation, wedding, or coming-of-age ceremony, and write a detailed description of it for someone who has never seen it before. If you can, explain any symbolic actions, garments, or colors associated with the ceremony. Put your writing in your **Working Portfolio.**

**Writing Handbook**
See page 1277: Description

## Activities & Explorations

**1. Illustrative Scene** Draw or paint a scene from the story, including specific objects and colors mentioned in relation to Teofilo's death. Then display your picture, explaining significant details to the class. ~ **ART**

**2. Points of Comparison** Listen as a class member reads the first three paragraphs of this story aloud. Discuss how the story differs in style from the traditional oral literature you read earlier in the unit.

## Vocabulary in Action

**EXERCISE: RELATED WORDS** On your paper, fill in each blank with the word or words that belong in each group below. Then with a partner, practice using the words in a conversation.

Group A: irrational, obstinate, ___(1)___
Group B: mission, ___(2)___, ___(3)___
Group C: desert, ___(4)___, ___(5)___

**Building Vocabulary**
Two of the Words to Know come from Spanish. For an in-depth study of word origins, see page 550.

| WORDS TO KNOW | | |
|---|---|---|
| arroyo | cloister | perverse |
| cassock | mesa | |

## Leslie Marmon Silko
1948–

**Other Works**
*Laguna Woman, Ceremony, Almanac of the Dead*

**Girl from Laguna** Leslie Marmon Silko grew up in the pueblo of Old Laguna, about 45 miles west of Albuquerque, New Mexico. Although she is of mixed European, Laguna, and Mexican ancestry, Silko derives inspiration for her stories, poems, and novels from the traditional Native American myths and tales she learned as a child. "I grew up at Laguna listening," she has said, "and I hear the ancient stories, I hear them very clearly in the stories we are telling right now. Most important, I feel the power which the stories still have, to bring us together, especially when there is loss and grief."

**Stories as a Natural Resource** In *Storyteller*, which was published in 1981 and includes the story "The Man to Send Rain Clouds," Silko pays tribute to Native American storytelling traditions, weaving together poems, photographs, ancient tales, stories about her family, and stories about memorable characters like Father Paul and Leon. As she told an interviewer, "Storytelling for Indians is like a natural resource. Some places have oil, some have a lot of water or timber or gold, but around here, it's the ear that has developed."

**Award Winner** Silko, who was educated at the University of New Mexico, considered a law career before becoming a writer and a teacher. She has won numerous grants and awards for her poetry and fiction.

## Author Activity

**Silko the Storyteller** Find a copy of Silko's book *Storyteller*, and choose two other stories from it to read aloud in class. As a group, discuss what more you learn about the Laguna people from the stories.

---

## Teaching Options

✓ **Assessment Informal Assessment**

**IDENTIFYING IMPLIED MAIN IDEA** Students have had several opportunities to make inferences while reading this story. They can also apply this skill to determine the main idea of a selection. Students should think about the selection as a whole, identifying the most important idea rather than specific details.
**Practice** Have students select the best answer to this question and explain their choice.
What is the main idea of "The Man to Send Rain Clouds"?

A. Certain cultures have nothing in common with each other, which leads to conflict.
B. The Laguna scatter corn meal in the wind when someone dies.
C. A major event, such as a death, can make cultural differences seem less important.
D. When people die, they go to heaven.

**Answer:** The best answer is C. Items A and D are not implied anywhere in the story, and item B is too specific to apply to the story as a whole. Item C summarizes a major theme of the story.

# PREPARING to *Read*

## *from* The Way to Rainy Mountain

*Nonfiction by* N. SCOTT MOMADAY

### Comparing Literature

### Traditions Across Time: Harmonizing Old and New

The selection you are about to read is a personal and historical narrative by N. Scott Momaday, one of the most important modern voices of Kiowa culture. Momaday's writing, like Leslie Marmon Silko's, draws on Native American history and traditions and reflects a love of the land.

**Points of Comparison** Compare Momaday to Silko as you read. Also notice how the stories embedded in Momaday's narrative are similar to the earlier Native American literature you have read.

### Build Background

**The Kiowa** In the 1600s, after a bitter dispute between two chiefs, a band of Kiowa moved from what is now western Montana to South Dakota's Black Hills. About 1785, the Kiowa migrated farther south to escape frequent attacks by neighboring tribes, settling in what is now western Kansas and Oklahoma. Like other Plains Indian groups, the Kiowa hunted buffalo, lived in tepees, had warrior societies, and observed the annual Sun Dance as an important religious ceremony.

With their Comanche allies, the Kiowa ruled the southern Great Plains for about 100 years, until their survival was threatened by deadly smallpox and cholera epidemics, the decline of buffalo herds, and bloody conflicts with other tribes and with U.S. soldiers. One of the last tribes of Plains Indians to be defeated by the U.S. government, the Kiowa surrendered at Fort Sill in 1875 and were forced onto a reservation in the southwestern part of the Indian Territory (now Oklahoma), where today members of the tribe farm and lease mining rights.

**WORDS TO KNOW  Vocabulary Preview**

| | | |
|---|---|---|
| engender | nomadic | servitude |
| inherently | opaque | unrelenting |
| linear | preeminently | |
| luxuriant | profusion | |

### Focus Your Reading

**LITERARY ANALYSIS  SETTING**  The **setting** of a literary work consists of the time and place in which the events unfold. Notice how, in the opening sentence of this selection, Momaday uses details to establish the setting:

> *A single knoll rises out of the plain in Oklahoma, north and west of the Wichita Range.*

As you read the selection, be aware that Momaday weaves together events from several different times and places. Use details to help you visualize each time period and landscape that he describes.

**ACTIVE READING  UNDERSTANDING STRUCTURE**
The **structure** of a literary work is the arrangement of its parts—its pattern of organization. Momaday interweaves three distinct strands throughout his narrative:

- geographical details about the landscape
- historical details about the rise and fall of the Kiowa
- personal details about his grandmother Aho

**READER'S NOTEBOOK**  Create a three column chart with the following headings: **The Landscape, The Kiowa, Momaday's Grandmother.** As you read each paragraph in this selection, write down one or two things you learn about any of these topics.

### OVERVIEW

**Objectives**
1. understand and appreciate a **personal narrative (Literary Analysis)**
2. appreciate author's use of **setting (Literary Analysis)**
3. **understand** the **structure** of a personal narrative **(Active Reading)**

**Summary**
N. Scott Momaday, a writer of Kiowa descent, describes his pilgrimage to Rainy Mountain after the death of his grandmother. Weaving together the history of his people, a description of his ancestral lands, and details about his beloved grandmother, Aho, he creates a moving tribute to the Kiowa, to the Great Plains, and to Aho herself.

**Thematic Link**
Momaday describes **Native American traditions** such as the worship of the Sun Dance Doll and the legend of Devil's Tower. Relating his people to the land they once ruled, he shows how they lived **in harmony with nature** on the open plains as riders of horses and hunters of bison.

### 5-Minute Warm-Up

***Daily Language SkillBuilder***

Have students **proofread** the display sentences on page 17j and write them correctly. The sentences also appear on Transparency 2 of **Grammar Transparencies and Copymasters.**

**Mini Lesson  Preteaching Vocabulary**
If you would like to preteach the WORDS TO KNOW for this selection, use the Mini Lesson, p. 56.

### LESSON RESOURCES

**UNIT ONE RESOURCE BOOK,** pp. 25–30

**ASSESSMENT RESOURCES**
**Formal Assessment,** pp. 15–16
**Teacher's Guide to Assessment and Portfolio Use**
**Test Generator**

**SKILLS TRANSPARENCIES AND COPYMASTERS**
**Literary Analysis**
• Setting, T13 (for Literary Analysis, p. 55)

**Reading and Critical Thinking**
• Evaluating Story Elements, T6 (for Active Reading, p. 55)

**Grammar**
• Types of Pronouns, C65 (for Mini Lesson, p. 57)
• Simple and Compound Predicates, C77 (for Mini Lesson, p. 60)

**Vocabulary**
• The Connotative Power of Words, C26 (for Mini Lesson, p. 58)

**Writing**
• Compare and Contrast, C32 (for Writing Option 2, p. 63)

**INTEGRATED TECHNOLOGY**

**Audio Library**
**Visit our website:**
www.mcdougallittell.com

**Active Reading**

UNDERSTANDING STRUCTURE Have students use the graphic organizer as a "road map" of the structure of the selection. As they read, have them consider how this structure influences their understanding.

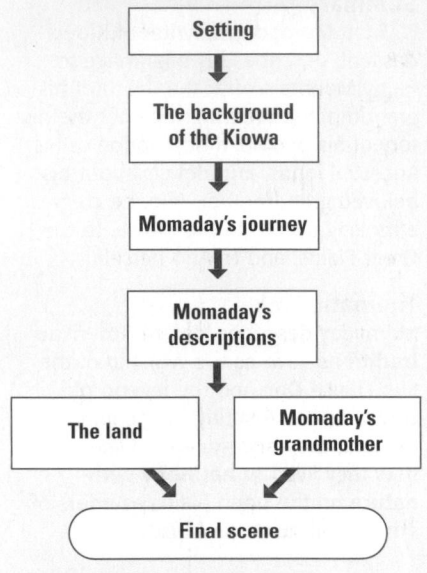

```
┌─────────────────┐
│     Setting     │
└─────────────────┘
         │
         ▼
┌─────────────────┐
│  The background │
│   of the Kiowa  │
└─────────────────┘
         │
         ▼
┌─────────────────┐
│ Momaday's journey│
└─────────────────┘
         │
         ▼
┌─────────────────┐
│    Momaday's    │
│   descriptions  │
└─────────────────┘
         │
    ┌────┴────┐
    ▼         ▼
┌────────┐ ┌──────────┐
│The land│ │ Momaday's│
│        │ │grandmother│
└────────┘ └──────────┘
    │         │
    └────┬────┘
         ▼
┌─────────────────┐
│   Final scene   │
└─────────────────┘
```

 Use **Unit One Resource Book,** p. 26 for additional support.

**Literary Analysis** SETTING

Briefly summarize the essay and its setting. Suggest that as they read students note details about the setting and consider how Momaday's account would be different if it were set on the Gulf Coast of Texas or in Alaska.

 Use **Unit One Resource Book,** p. 27 for additional support.

---

*from* The Way to
# RAINY MOUNTAIN

## N. Scott Momaday

*Wun-Pan-To-Mee, The White Weasel* (1836), George Catlin. Watercolor on paper, 5¼″ × 5⅛″. Gilcrease Museum, Tulsa, Oklahoma (0226.1493).

A single knoll[1] rises out of the plain in Oklahoma, north and west of the Wichita Range. For my people, the Kiowas, it is an old landmark, and they gave it the name Rainy Mountain. The hardest weather in the world is there. Winter brings blizzards, hot tornadic winds arise in the spring, and in summer the prairie is an anvil's edge. The grass turns brittle and brown, and it cracks beneath your feet. There are green belts along the rivers and creeks, <u>linear</u> groves of hickory and pecan, willow and witch hazel. At a distance in July or August the steaming foliage seems almost to writhe in fire. Great green and yellow grasshoppers are everywhere in the tall grass, popping up like corn to sting the flesh, and tortoises crawl about on the red earth, going nowhere in the plenty of time. Loneliness is an aspect of the land. All things in the plain are isolate; there is no confusion of objects in the eye, but one hill or one tree or one man. To look upon that landscape in the early morning, with the sun at your back, is to

---

1. **knoll** (nōl): a small round hill.

WORDS TO KNOW    **linear** (lĭn′ē-ər) *adj.* resembling or arranged in a line

---

## Teaching Options

 **Mini Lesson** ## Preteaching Vocabulary

**USING REFERENCE MATERIALS** Call students' attention to the list of WORDS TO KNOW. Remind them that reference materials such as glossaries, dictionaries, and thesauruses can help them find precise meanings for words. When they look up a word in a dictionary, they will sometimes find several listed meanings. The context in which a word is used determines which meaning is appropriate. Demonstrate the strategy for them using the following model.

**Model Sentence**

Instead of instilling courage in his players' hearts, the coach's tirade <u>engendered</u> fear.

**Instruction**

- Write the model sentence on the chalkboard.
- Ask a volunteer to look up the word *engender* in a dictionary and read the definitions aloud. Write these definitions on the chalkboard.
- Have students determine which is the best definition of the word in the context of the model sentence.
- Have students work in cooperative groups to use the same process with each of the Words to Know.

 Use **Unit One Resource Book,** p. 28 for additional support.

lose the sense of proportion. Your imagination comes to life, and this, you think, is where Creation was begun.

I returned to Rainy Mountain in July. My grandmother had died in the spring, and I wanted to be at her grave. She had lived to be very old and at last infirm. Her only living daughter was with her when she died, and I was told that in death her face was that of a child.

## Her forebears *came down from the high country in western Montana nearly three centuries ago.*

I like to think of her as a child. When she was born, the Kiowas were living the last great moment of their history. For more than a hundred years they had controlled the open range from the Smoky Hill River to the Red, from the headwaters of the Canadian to the fork of the Arkansas and Cimarron. In alliance with the Comanches, they had ruled the whole of the southern Plains. War was their sacred business, and they were among the finest horsemen the world has ever known. But warfare for the Kiowas was <u>preeminently</u> a matter of disposition rather than of survival, and they never understood the grim, <u>unrelenting</u> advance of the U.S. Cavalry. When at last, divided and ill-provisioned, they were driven onto the Staked Plains in the cold rains of autumn, they fell into panic. In Palo Duro Canyon they abandoned their crucial stores to pillage and had nothing then but their lives. In order to save themselves, they surrendered to the soldiers at Fort Sill[2] and were imprisoned in the old stone corral that now stands as a military museum. My grandmother was spared the humiliation of those high gray

walls by eight or ten years, but she must have known from birth the affliction of defeat, the dark brooding of old warriors.

Her name was Aho, and she belonged to the last culture to evolve in North America. Her forebears came down from the high country in western Montana nearly three centuries ago. They were a mountain people, a mysterious tribe of hunters whose language has never been positively classified in any major group. In the late seventeenth century they began a long migration to the south and east. It was a journey toward the dawn, and it led to a golden age. Along the way the Kiowas were befriended by the Crows,[3] who gave them the culture and religion of the Plains. They acquired horses, and their ancient <u>nomadic</u> spirit was suddenly free of the ground. They acquired Tai-me, the sacred Sun Dance doll, from that moment the object and symbol of their worship, and so shared in the divinity of the sun. Not least, they acquired the sense of destiny, therefore courage and pride. When they entered upon the southern Plains they had been transformed. No longer were they slaves to the simple necessity of survival; they were a lordly and dangerous society of fighters and thieves, hunters and priests of the sun. According to their origin myth, they entered the world through a hollow log. From one point of view, their migration was the fruit of an old prophecy, for indeed they emerged from a sunless world.

Although my grandmother lived out her long life in the shadow of Rainy Mountain, the immense landscape of the continental interior lay

---

2. **Fort Sill:** a U.S. Army post established in 1869 in the Indian Territory (now Oklahoma).

3. **Crows:** a group of Native Americans who once inhabited the region between the Platte and Yellowstone rivers in the northern Great Plains and who are now settled in Montana.

---

WORDS
TO
KNOW
**preeminently** (prē-ĕm′ə-nənt-lē) *adv.* above all; most importantly
**unrelenting** (ŭn′rĭ-lĕn′tĭng) *adj.* not stopping or weakening
**nomadic** (nō-măd′ĭk) *adj.* without a fixed home; wandering

**57**

**Less Proficient Readers**
Prepare students by explaining that the selection is not a story in which events follow one after another and build a narrative. Copy the following themes on the chalkboard, and then ask students to identify which themes are covered in each paragraph. Description of the land; Grandmother Aho; the history of the Kiowa; Kiowa legend and religion; houses and Aho's house; mourning for Aho.

**Students Acquiring English**
Explain that the selection is about a Kiowa woman and her people. Prepare students to expect words that describe both history and the natural landscape. Words that they may find unfamiliar or difficult include *Wichita Range, Kiowa, Crows, Tai-me, Sun Dance, Blackfeet.*

Use **Spanish Study Guide** for additional support, pp. 17–19.

**Multiple Learning Styles**
**Interpersonal Learners**

Ask students to think about Momaday's relationship with his grandmother as they read.

## Grammar

**PRONOUNS** Review with students the definitions of personal, indefinite, and reflexive pronouns. Then write the following sentences on the chalkboard:
He did not think anyone cared about anything other than the latest news. He himself paid no attention to it, keeping his head in legends of the Kiowa and Crow.
Have students indicate the personal, indefinite, and reflexive pronouns in these sentences. *(personal—He, it; indefinite—anyone, anything; reflexive—himself )*

**Exercise** Have students indicate whether the pronouns in the following sentence are personal, indefinite, or reflexive.
We know more than anyone thinks we know, yet he knows more than we, and he himself knows it. *(personal—We, he, it; indefinite—anyone; reflexive—himself)*

 Use **Grammar Transparencies and Copymasters**, p. 66.

 Use McDougal Littell's **Language Network**, Chapter 6, for more instruction and practice in pronouns.

## Reading Skills and Strategies: VISUALIZING

**A** As students read, have them visualize—that is, create a mental picture of—the terrain and the events that Momaday is describing. Explain that many people make a habit of just "reading the words" for sense without taking the time to imagine what the writer is describing. To help improve students' visualizing ability, read aloud the paragraph describing the slopes of the Rockies and the plains. Pause after each sentence, asking students to close their eyes and imagine the scene. Then ask them to redescribe in their own words the scene they have visualized.

## Active Reading

### UNDERSTANDING STRUCTURE

**B** Point out to students that Momaday re-creates the journey of the Kiowa from their oldest homelands in the Rockies to the Black Hills. Have students follow the progress of the Kiowa on the map.

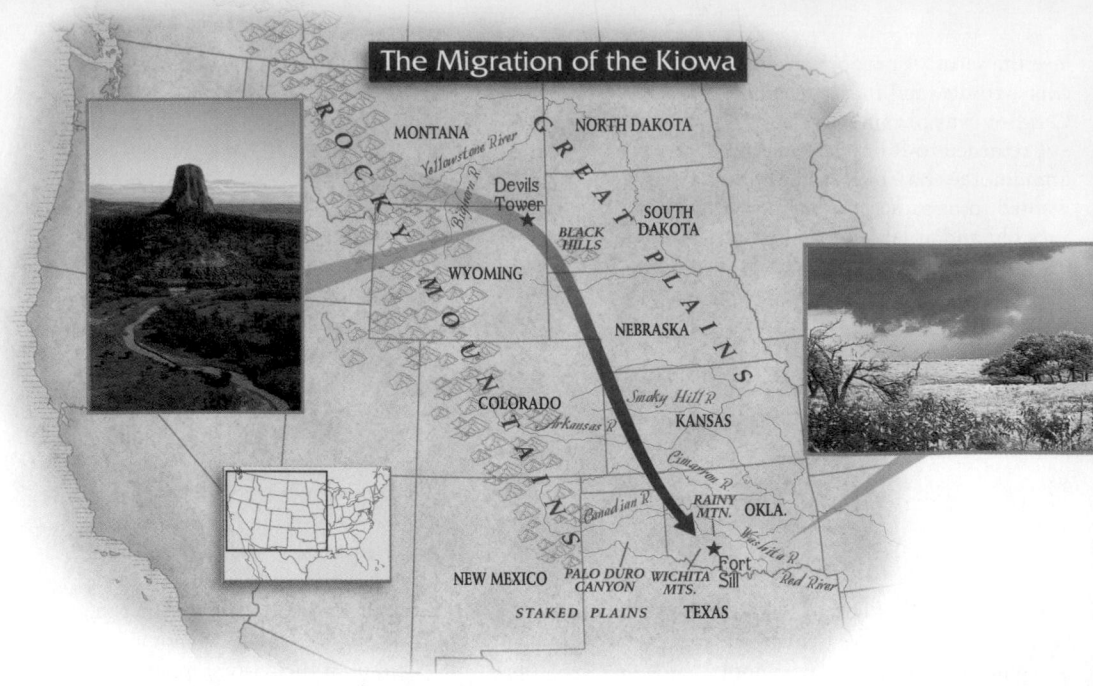

### The Migration of the Kiowa

like memory in her blood. She could tell of the Crows, whom she had never seen, and of the Black Hills, where she had never been. I wanted to see in reality what she had seen more perfectly in the mind's eye, and traveled fifteen hundred miles to begin my pilgrimage.

Yellowstone, it seemed to me, was the top of the world, a region of deep lakes and dark timber, canyons and waterfalls. But, beautiful as it is, one might have the sense of confinement there. The skyline in all directions is close at hand, the high wall of the woods and deep cleavages of shade. There is a perfect freedom in the mountains, but it belongs to the eagle and the elk, the badger and the bear. The Kiowas reckoned their stature by the distance they could see, and they were bent and blind in the wilderness.

**A** Descending eastward, the highland meadows are a stairway to the plain. In July the inland slope of the Rockies is <u>luxuriant</u> with flax and buckwheat, stonecrop and larkspur. The earth unfolds and the limit of the land recedes. Clusters of trees, and animals grazing far in the distance, cause the vision to reach away and wonder to build upon the mind. The sun follows a longer course in the day, and the sky is immense beyond all comparison. The great billowing clouds that sail upon it are shadows that move upon the grain like water, dividing light. Farther down, in the land of the Crows and Blackfeet,[4] the plain is yellow. Sweet clover takes hold of the hills and bends upon itself to cover and seal the soil. There the Kiowas paused on their way; they had come to the place where they must change their lives. The sun is at home

**B**

---

4. **Blackfeet:** a group of Native Americans who once inhabited a region now occupied by parts of Montana, Alberta, and Saskatchewan.

WORDS TO KNOW **luxuriant** (lŭg-zhŏŏr'ē-ənt) *adj.* characterized by abundant growth

58

## Teaching Options

### Mini Lesson **Vocabulary Strategy**

**INTERPRETING CONNOTATIONS Instruction** The denotative meaning of a word or term is the literal, dictionary, or explicit meaning. The connotative meaning of a word or term also expresses any attitudes or emotions associated with the word. Have students discuss the differences between the connotative and denotative meanings of the following terms and the different impressions they get from the connotations: car/automobile; pickup/light utility truck; sneaker/running shoe; drink/beverage; burger/ground beef.
**Exercise** Have students copy this table into their notebooks and fill in the second and third columns.

| Word | Denotative Meaning | Connotative Meaning |
|------|-------------------|---------------------|
| stature | (quality or status) | (loftiness, uprightness, pride, righteousness, worthiness) |
| clusters | (groups) | (richness, fertility, great quantity) |
| billowing | (rolling like a great wave) | (hugeness, power, suddenness) |

Use **Vocabulary Transparencies and Copymasters**, p. 20.

A lesson on connotations appears on page 908 in the Pupil's Edition.

on the plains. Precisely there does it have the certain character of a god. When the Kiowas came to the land of the Crows, they could see the dark lees[5] of the hills at dawn across the Bighorn River, the profusion of light on the grain shelves, the oldest deity ranging after the solstices.[6] Not yet would they veer southward to the caldron[7] of the land that lay below; they must wean their blood from the northern winter and hold the mountains a while longer in their view. They bore Tai-me in procession to the east.

A dark mist lay over the Black Hills, and the land was like iron. At the top of a ridge I caught sight of Devil's Tower upthrust against the gray sky as if in the birth of time the core of the earth had broken through its crust and the motion of the world was begun. There are things in nature that engender an awful quiet in the heart of man; Devil's Tower is one of them. Two centuries ago, because they could not do otherwise, the Kiowas made a legend at the base of the rock. My grandmother said:

*Eight children were there at play, seven sisters and their brother. Suddenly the boy was struck dumb; he trembled and began to run upon his hands and feet. His fingers became claws, and his body was covered with fur. Directly there was a bear where the boy had been. The sisters were terrified; they ran, and the bear after them. They came to the stump of a great tree, and the tree spoke to them. It bade them climb upon it, and as they did so it began to rise into the air. The bear came to kill them, but they were just beyond its reach. It reared against the tree and scored the bark all around with its claws. The seven sisters were borne into the sky, and they became the stars of the Big Dipper.*

From that moment, and so long as the legend lives, the Kiowas have kinsmen in the night sky. Whatever they were in the mountains, they could be no more. However tenuous their well-being, however much they had suffered and would suffer again, they had found a way out of the wilderness.

My grandmother had a reverence for the sun,  a holy regard that now is all but gone out of mankind. There was a wariness in her, and an ancient awe. She was a Christian in her later years, but she had come a long way about, and she never forgot her birthright. As a child she had been to the Sun Dances; she had taken part in those annual rites, and by them she had learned the restoration of her people in the presence of Tai-me. She was about seven when the last Kiowa Sun Dance was held in 1887 on the Washita River above Rainy Mountain Creek. The buffalo were gone. In order to consummate the ancient sacrifice—to impale the head of a buffalo bull upon the medicine tree—a delegation of old men journeyed into Texas, there to beg and barter for an animal from the Goodnight herd. She was ten when the Kiowas came together for the last time as a living Sun Dance culture. They could find no buffalo; they had to hang an old hide from the sacred tree. Before the dance could begin, a company of soldiers rode out from Fort Sill under orders to disperse the tribe. Forbidden without cause the essential act of their faith, having seen the wild herds slaughtered and left to rot upon the ground, the Kiowas backed away forever from the medicine tree. That was July 20, 1890, at the

---

5. **lees:** sides sheltered from the wind.

6. **solstices** (sŏl'stĭs-ĭz): the times of year—about June 21 and December 21—when days are longest and shortest in the Northern Hemisphere, marking the beginnings of summer and winter.

7. **caldron** (kôl'drən): a large kettle for boiling things—here, the term is used figuratively.

---

WORDS
TO
KNOW

**profusion** (prə-fyōō'zhən) *n.* abundance; lavishness
**engender** (ĕn-jĕn'dər) *v.* to produce; bring about

59

**Mini Lesson** ## Speaking and Listening

**PRESENTING INTERPRETATIONS**
**Prepare** Point out that the legend of the Devil's Tower is well suited to oral reading and dramatic performance. Give students the following guidelines to help them prepare for a speaking/acting performance of the Devil's Tower legend.
• Read the material silently to be sure you understand it.
• With other members of your group, improvise a dialogue to accompany the events of the story.
• Choose a reader and assign the parts of the seven sisters, the brother, and the great tree.

• Use effective nonverbal strategies such as pitch and tone of voice, posture, and eye contact.
• Rehearse together several times. Ask someone to watch and critique.
**Perform** Divide the class into groups and have students use the guidelines to perform the Devil's Tower legend. After the performances, discuss the various techniques used by different groups to convey the information of the story. Ask students to justify their choice of actions in the performance.

## Reading and Analyzing

**Reading Skills and Strategies: CONNECT TO LITERATURE**

**A** Actively comparing the setting of a selection with a familiar area is a good way to engage with the work of the writer. Ask the following questions.

- How is the Oklahoma setting described by Momaday similar to or different from your own home area? *(Responses should compare and contrast the violent heat and cold, the groves of trees along the creeks, the wildlife, and the gray, weather-beaten houses with students' environs.)*
- How would you feel about living in the area Momaday describes? *(Responses should indicate an awareness of the features of the landscape.)*

**Literary Analysis: SYMBOLISM**

**B** Point out to students that Momaday uses a description of the houses near Rainy Mountain as a powerful symbol. To explore this symbolism, ask the following questions.

- Name two things the houses described in the essay might symbolize.

**Possible Responses:** They might symbolize the old, weathered condition of Kiowa strength and culture, or Aho herself, who is described as becoming very aged toward the end of her life.

- Explain what the symbolism means if the houses stand for Kiowa culture.

**Possible Responses:** Like the houses, Kiowa culture has undergone intense stress in its environment and shows the effect of that stress; you might imagine Kiowa culture to be like the houses, full of ghosts. However, just as Aho's house was once full of life, the culture was a vital force on the Great Plains and continues to inspire people like Momaday.

*Kiowa Sun Dance,* Sharron Ahtone. Photo by Sandy Settle. Private collection.

great bend of the Washita. My grandmother was there. Without bitterness, and for as long as she lived, she bore a vision of deicide.[8]

Now that I can have her only in memory, I see my grandmother in the several postures that were peculiar to her: standing at the wood stove on a winter morning and turning meat in a great iron skillet; sitting at the south window, bent above her beadwork, and afterwards, when her vision failed, looking down for a long time into the fold of her hands; going out upon a cane, very slowly as she did when the weight of age came upon her; praying. I remember her most often at prayer. She made long, rambling prayers out of suffering and hope, having seen many things. I was never sure that I had the right to hear, so exclusive were they of all mere custom and company. The last time I saw her she prayed standing by the side of her bed at night, naked to the waist, the light of a kerosene lamp moving upon her dark skin. Her long, black hair, always

drawn and braided in the day, lay upon her shoulders and against her breasts like a shawl. I do not speak Kiowa, and I never understood her prayers, but there was something <u>inherently</u> sad in the sound, some merest hesitation upon the syllables of sorrow. She began in a high and descending pitch, exhausting her breath to silence; then again and again—and always the same intensity of effort, of something that is, and is not, like urgency in the human voice. Transported so in the dancing light among the shadows of her room, she seemed beyond the reach of time. But that was illusion; I think I knew then that I should not see her again.

Houses are like sentinels[9] in the plain, old keepers of the weather watch. There, in a very little while, wood takes on the appearance of great age. All colors wear soon away in the wind

**A**

**B**

---

8. **deicide** (dē′ə-sīd′): the destruction of a god.
9. **sentinels:** sentries; watchmen.

WORDS
TO
KNOW

**inherently** (ĭn-hîr′ənt-lē) *adv.* essentially

60

## Teaching Options

 **Mini Lesson** ## Grammar

**COMPOUND AND SIMPLE PREDICATES**

**Instruction** A predicate is the part of a sentence that tells what a subject is or does. A simple predicate has no connector such as *and* or *or.* A compound predicate contains a connector. Write the following sentence on the chalkboard. Have students indicate which part is the predicate and whether the predicate is simple or compound.

The medicine tree broke into a thousand pieces and was never whole again. *(Compound predicate: "broke into a thousand pieces and was never whole again")*

**Exercises** In each sentence below, have students identify the predicate and tell whether it is simple

or compound.

1. Sing the greatest song that ever was. *(Simple predicate: "Sing the greatest song that ever was")*
2. The sisters flew into the sky and became the Big Dipper. *(Compound predicate: "flew into the sky and became the Big Dipper")*

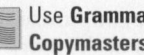 Use **Grammar Transparencies and Copymasters,** p. 77.

Use McDougal Littell's *Language Network,* Chapter 1, for more instruction and practice in predicates.

and rain, and then the wood is burned gray and the grain appears and the nails turn red with rust. The windowpanes are black and <u>opaque</u>; you imagine there is nothing within, and indeed there are many ghosts, bones given up to the land. They stand here and there against the sky, and you approach them for a longer time than you expect. They belong in the distance; it is their domain.

Once there was a lot of sound in my grandmother's house, a lot of coming and going, feasting and talk. The summers there were full of excitement and reunion. The Kiowas are a summer people; they abide the cold and keep to themselves, but when the season turns and the land becomes warm and vital they cannot hold still; an old love of going returns upon them. The aged visitors who came to my grandmother's house when I was a child were made of lean and leather, and they bore themselves upright. They wore great black hats and bright ample shirts that shook in the wind. They rubbed fat upon their hair and wound their braids with strips of colored cloth. Some of them painted their faces and carried the scars of old and cherished enmities.[10] They were an old council of warlords, come to remind and be reminded of who they were. Their wives and daughters served them well. The women might indulge themselves; gossip was at once the mark and compensation of their <u>servitude</u>. They made loud and elaborate talk among themselves, full of jest and gesture, fright and false alarm. They went abroad in fringed and flowered shawls, bright beadwork and German silver. They were at home in the kitchen, and they prepared meals that were banquets.

There were frequent prayer meetings, and great nocturnal[11] feasts. When I was a child I played with my cousins outside, where the lamplight fell upon the ground and the singing of the old people rose up around us and carried away into the darkness. There were a lot of good things to eat, a lot of laughter and surprise. And afterwards, when the quiet returned, I lay down with my grandmother and could hear the frogs away by the river and feel the motion of the air.

Now there is a funeral silence in the rooms, **2** the endless wake of some final word. The walls have closed in upon my grandmother's house. When I returned to it in mourning, I saw for the first time in my life how small it was. It was late at night, and there was a white moon, nearly full. I sat for a long time on the stone steps by the kitchen door. From there I could see out across the land; I could see the long row of trees by the creek, the low light upon the rolling plains, and the stars of the Big Dipper. Once I looked at the moon and caught sight of a strange thing. A cricket had perched upon the handrail, only a few inches away from me. My line of vision was such that the creature filled the moon like a fossil. It had gone there, I thought, to live and die, for there, of all places, was its small definition made whole and eternal. A warm wind rose up and purled[12] like the longing within me.

The next morning I awoke at dawn and went out on the dirt road to Rainy Mountain. It was already hot, and the grasshoppers began to fill the air. Still, it was early in the morning, and the birds sang out of the shadows. The long yellow grass on the mountain shone in the bright light, and a scissortail[13] hied[14] above the land. There, where it ought to be, at the end of a long and legendary way, was my grandmother's grave. Here and there on the dark stones were ancestral names. Looking back once, I saw the mountain and came away. ❖

---

10. **enmities** (ĕn'mĭ-tēz): hatreds.
11. **nocturnal:** occurring at night.
12. **purled:** flowed with a murmuring sound.
13. **scissortail:** a bird with a long, forked tail, native to the southwestern United States.
14. **hied** (hīd): hurried.

| WORDS TO KNOW | **opaque** (ō-pāk') *adj.* not allowing light to pass through<br>**servitude** (sûr'vĭ-tōōd') *n.* the condition of one who is subject to a master; lack of freedom |
|---|---|

61

## Customizing Instruction

**Less Proficient Readers**
Ask students to make a list of the people mentioned in the last two pages of the essay. This list will help them keep their reading focused and enable them to sort out the characters. *(Characters mentioned include Momaday as an adult; Aho; the aged Kiowa visitors, both old warlords and their wives and daughters; Momaday as a child; and Momaday's cousins.)*

**Students Acquiring English**
**1** Point out the difference between the terms *jest* ("a joke") and *gesture* ("a motion of the hand or body expressive of an emotion or idea"); between *fright* ("fear") and *false alarm* ("mistaken fear"); and between *meal* ("any regular eating") and *banquet* ("a special feast"). Explain that Momaday enjoys playing on subtle shades of meaning in the words he chooses, and suggest that students ask about the connotations of a word if they feel they are missing something.

**Gifted and Talented Students**
**2** Have students examine the description of the silence in Aho's house as "the endless wake of some final word." Ask: What does Momaday mean by this?

**⟲ Cross Curricular Link** **Science**

**THE ROOTS OF THE PLAINS** The prairie is a place of almost unimaginable natural wealth. It includes more than 100 grasses, including big bluestem, Indian grass, and switchgrass. Nongrass plants include purple poppy mallow, butterfly milkweed, catclaw brier, moth mullein, dogwood, and oak; they total well over 300 varieties. Lichens and other types of mossy plants add up to 100 more species. The root system of these prairie plants is enormous. The first 8 inches of its depth is so tightly interwoven that early nonnative settlers cut it into blocks and made houses from it. Other roots stretch down between 12 and 20 *feet* underground. A single grass plant may have 14 billion root hairs, forming a total of miles of root length. In fact, 75 to 85 percent of the prairie's biomass, or mass of living matter, is underground.

This underground root system forms an enormous factory for producing fertility. For thousands of years, from the last ice age to the beginning of nonnative settlement, this root system produced a vast area of rich soil that became the backbone of American wealth. Furthermore, the prairie draws carbon dioxide from the air, turning it into carbon in the soil with great efficiency.

## GUIDING STUDENT RESPONSE

## Connect to the Literature

**1. What Do You Think?**
Possible Response: Full of the recollections of the suffering of her people, yet not bitter; deeply religious

**Comprehension Check**
- to visit his grandmother's grave
- the origin of Devil's Tower and the Big Dipper
- The buffalo herds were slaughtered, and U. S. soldiers dispersed the tribe.

 Use **Unit One Resource Book,** p. 29 for additional support.

## Think Critically

**2.** Possible Responses: Momaday's relationship with his grandmother is warm and meaningful. He loved her both as a person and as the embodiment of his Kiowa heritage.

**3.** Possible Responses: In their discussion, have students consider how the structure influenced their understanding of Momaday's work. Important events in Kiowa history include their migration from western Montana in the late 17th century, their entering the southern Plains, and the last Kiowa Sun Dance in 1887. Tai-me, the sacred Sun Dance doll, is the symbol of their worship. A deeply religious people, the Kiowa hold the sun in reverence.

**4.** Some students may state that Momaday learns to appreciate his grandmother's abiding influence upon him. Others may say that Momaday's pilgrimage enables him to relive his people's glorious triumphs and tragic losses.

**5.** Possible Responses: To Momaday, the cricket might symbolize his grandmother's spirit. Just as the cricket perched on the handrail seems "whole and eternal," so his grandmother's spirit seems timeless because of its connection with Rainy Mountain.

## Connect to the Literature

**1. What Do You Think?**
What are your impressions of Momaday's grandmother Aho? Describe her in a few words or phrases.

**Comprehension Check**
- Why does Momaday return to Rainy Mountain?
- What two natural phenomena does the Kiowa story about the seven sisters and their brother explain?
- Why did the Kiowa stop holding the annual Sun Dance ritual?

## Think Critically

**2.** How would you characterize Momaday's relationship with his grandmother?

**3.**   Review the chart you created in your  **READER'S NOTEBOOK.** What are some things you learned about the Kiowa from this selection?

**THINK ABOUT**
- important events in their history
- their beliefs, traditions, and customs
- their origin myth
- the story about the seven sisters and their brother
- the personal habits of Momaday's grandmother

**4.** What do you think is the most important insight that Momaday gains during his pilgrimage from Yellowstone to his grandmother's grave at Rainy Mountain? Explain your response.

**5.** A **symbol** is a person, place, or object that has a concrete meaning in itself and also stands for something beyond itself, such as an idea or a feeling. What might the cricket mentioned at the end of this selection symbolize to Momaday?

## Extend Interpretations

**6. Connect to Life** Momaday values his close relationship with his grandmother. Discuss what young people today can learn or gain from older relatives, giving examples from your own or others' experience.

**7.** **Points of Comparison** What similarities of **style, subject,** or **theme** do you see in the excerpt from *The Way to Rainy Mountain* and Leslie Marmon Silko's story "The Man to Send Rain Clouds"?

**62**   UNIT ONE   PART 1: IN HARMONY WITH NATURE

## Literary Analysis

**SETTING** In some fiction and nonfiction works, **setting**—the particular time and place in which the action occurs—is no more than a backdrop for events. In others, setting is very important. A writer may use setting to create a mood or may make it a driving force in a story—one that influences events or affects how the characters act and feel. In Momaday's narrative, the Great Plains landscape plays a central role.

**Paired Activity** With a partner, review the details about the plains landscape and about Kiowa history and culture that you recorded in your 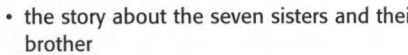 **READER'S NOTEBOOK.** In what ways did the landscape influence the lives of the Kiowa? In what ways does it affect Momaday as he travels? Jot down your ideas and share them with other pairs of students.

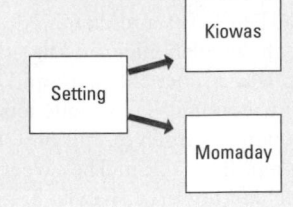

## Extend Interpretations

**Connect to Life** Responses will vary. Students may mention that they learn certain values from older relatives. Others may point out that their older relatives, like Momaday's grandmother, help them appreciate their heritage and are a cherished fund of family stories.

**Points of Comparison** Responses will vary. Both selections deal with conflicts between a Native American people—the Kiowa and the Laguna—and a European culture; both present important tribal ceremonies—the Sun Dance ritual and a Laguna funeral service; both provide many descriptive details about the landscape.

## Literary Analysis

**Conflict** Possible Response: The landscape—"The sun is at home on the plains"—helped to foster in the Kiowa a reverence for the sun. As he relives his people's odyssey, Momaday is filled with awe, especially when he sees the Devil's Tower.

# Choices & CHALLENGES

## Writing Options

**1. A Fitting Eulogy** Write a eulogy for Momaday's grandmother Aho or for the culture of the Kiowa as she knew it in her childhood. Deliver the eulogy to classmates, then place it in your **Working Portfolio.**

**2.** [ **Points of Comparison** ] In an essay, compare the Kiowa values conveyed in the excerpt from *The Way to Rainy Mountain* with the Iroquois values conveyed in "The World on the Turtle's Back."

## Activities & Explorations

[ **Points of Comparison** ] Momaday's father, Al, illustrated *The Way to Rainy Mountain.* Create two illustrations of your own—one to accompany this excerpt from Momaday's book and one to accompany another selection in this part of Unit One. Display your artwork in the classroom, along with a brief explanation of how your illustrations reflect the selections' content and the values of different Native American cultures. ~ ART

## Vocabulary in Action

**EXERCISE: ASSESSMENT PRACTICE** On your paper, write the vocabulary word that best completes each analogy.

1. GLASS: TRANSPARENT:: paper : _____
2. FARMERS: SETTLED:: herders : _____
3. HAPPILY: JOYFULLY:: especially : _____
4. POVERTY: WEALTH:: freedom : _____
5. DESERT: BARREN:: jungle : _____
6. WHEEL: CIRCULAR:: street : _____
7. INSUFFICIENT: INADEQUATE:: endless : _____
8. OBSERVE: EXAMINE:: produce : _____
9. WEARINESS: VITALITY:: scarcity : _____
10. LARGELY: MOSTLY:: essentially : _____

| WORDS TO KNOW | engender | inherently | linear |
|---|---|---|---|
| | luxuriant | nomadic | opaque |
| | preeminently | profusion | servitude |
| | unrelenting | | |

## N. Scott Momaday
### 1934–

**Other Works**
*Angle of Geese and Other Poems*
*The Names: A Memoir*
*The Ancient Child*
*The Man Made of Words*

**Native American Roots** Born in Lawton, Oklahoma, on February 27, 1934, N. Scott Momaday grew up on Native American reservations in the Southwest. His father, a Kiowa, was a well-known artist and art teacher. His mother, of English, French, and Cherokee ancestry, was a teacher and writer. Although his parents moved away from the Kiowa community when he was two years old, Momaday developed a strong ethnic identity. In his childhood, his parents taught him about the culture, history, and traditions of the Kiowa people, and they took him on a journey to Devils Tower. During the summer months, he frequently returned to Oklahoma to visit his grandfather Mammedaty, his grandmother Aho, and other Kiowa relations.

**Voice of the Kiowa** Momaday wrote his first poem, a tribute to a pet dog, when he was nine years old. Later he became the first Native American to receive a Pulitzer Prize, which he was awarded for his novel *House Made of Dawn* (1968). In one of his favorite works, *The Way to Rainy Mountain* (1969), he mixes Kiowa myths, legends, and history with autobiographical details. When asked by an interviewer how his heritage has affected his work, Momaday answered, "When I was growing up on the reservations of the Southwest, I saw people who were deeply involved in their traditional life, in the memories of their blood. They had, as far as I could see, a certain strength and beauty that I find missing in the modern world at large. I like to celebrate that involvement in my writing."

**Building Vocabulary**
For an in-depth lesson on analogies, see page 254.

## Writing Options

**1. A Fitting Eulogy** Students' responses should include details that describe the character of Aho and the culture of the Kiowa. **To get students started on this assignment,** suggest that they make a paragraph-by-paragraph outline of the selection, listing facts about Aho or the Kiowa that they can use in their eulogy. They should then reorganize the information under appropriate headings and retell it.

**2. Points of Comparison** Students' essays should give a balanced sketch of the values expressed in each piece and exhibit awareness of similarities and differences between them. To make the assignment more challenging, have students create a myth or legend that fuses elements of Iroquois and Kiowa belief.

## Activities & Explorations

**Points of Comparison** Values of Native American cultures illustrated might include spirituality, connection with the land, and reliance upon close-knit family structure. Artwork may illustrate this either indirectly (for example, a landscape painting of the plains region) or symbolically (for example, a drawing of the Kiowa Sun Dance god Tai-me). Encourage students to use a computer drawing program to generate their illustrations.

## Vocabulary in Action

1. opaque
2. nomadic
3. preeminently
4. servitude
5. luxuriant
6. linear
7. unrelenting
8. engender
9. profusion
10. inherently

---

## ✓ Assessment  Informal Assessment

**ARRANGING EVENTS IN SEQUENTIAL ORDER**
Many standardized tests include items that require students to indicate the order in which events in a passage took place. You can give students practice in this skill by writing the following exercise on the chalkboard and asking them to choose the option that shows the correct sequence of events at the end of *The Way to Rainy Mountain.*

  **I.** Momaday sits on the steps of the house.
  **II.** Momaday walks to the graveyard.
  **III.** Momaday returns to his grandmother's house.
  **IV.** Momaday sees the cricket against the moon.

The proper order of the above events is:
**A.** I, II, III, IV
**B.** IV, III, II, I
**C.** III, I, IV, II
**D.** None of the above

Discuss the options with students, guiding them to realize that the correct choice is C. Suggest that they can solve such a problem by eliminating all the incorrect options and double-checking the remaining option. In this case, students should note that Momaday's walk to the graveyard is the very last of the events listed.

## PART 1 Reading the Prompt

Model the process of reading a prompt:

- Read through the entire prompt.
- List key words and phrases of the assignment on the board ("compare," "qualities, transformations, and explanations," "generalize").
- Define each key word using the Strategies in Action to show how students can restate the prompt in their own words.

## PART 2 Planning a Comparison Essay

- In their charts, students might note character traits, actions, quotations, and examples.
- Suggest that students begin by first identifying obvious features in the Kiowa story. Then have them look for corresponding features in the other story.
- Encourage students to question each feature, asking themselves, for instance, "In what ways are these characters alike?"

## PART 3 Drafting Your Essay

**Introduction** Suggest that students begin by making a general statement about traditional Native American stories. Then they can state their opinions about the common elements that the stories have.

**Organization** Students can read down each column in the chart—first the "Kiowa Story" column, and then the other story column—for a subject-by-subject organization. Moving left to right across the rows creates a feature-by-feature organization.

**Conclusion** Students may conclude that people are a part of nature and are on the same level as its other parts.

**Revision** Remind students that the names of stories are written inside quotation marks. Also, encourage them to use words that signal similarities, such as *both*, *like*, *also*, and *neither*.

---

# Comparing Literature: Assessment Practice

Many assessment prompts ask you to compare literary elements in two or more selections. You will now practice writing an essay with a comparison focus.

### PART 1 Reading the Prompt

Often you will be asked to write in response to a prompt like the one below. Pay close attention to the wording of the prompt. Look for clues that help you identify the purpose and the scope of your essay and the kind of information to include.

**Writing Prompt**

In *The Way to Rainy Mountain*, Momaday retells a traditional Kiowa story about seven sisters and their brother. In an essay compare this story and another traditional Native American story you have read—for example, the Iroquois creation myth or one of the Okanogan Coyote stories. Consider the qualities of the characters, the transformations that occur, and the explanations offered in the stories. Then generalize about the relationship between humans and nature that the stories suggest.

**STRATEGIES IN ACTION**

1. **Compare**, or find similarities in, two stories.

2. Notice the **features** you will be comparing.

3. **Generalize**, making a statement that applies to more than one example.

### PART 2 Planning an Comparison Essay

- In a graphic, note details about features you will compare—characters, transformations, and explanations.

- Identify similarities to make a general statement about humans and nature.

**Stories Being Compared**

| Features | Kiowa Story | Iroquois or Okanogan Story | |
|---|---|---|---|
| characters | | | Generalization about humans and nature |
| transformations | | | |
| explanations | | | |

### PART 3 Drafting Your Essay

**Introduction** State the two stories you will compare and the features you will examine in each.

**Organization** You might write a **subject-by-subject** comparison in which you write about one story first and then the other. Or, you might write a **feature-by-feature** comparison in which you discuss the characters in both stories, the transformations in both stories, and so on.

**Conclusion** Summarize what you learned from the comparison. Write a general statement about the relationship between humans and nature in the two stories.

**Revision** Allow time to review your work. Make sure it is clear, well-supported, and free from mistakes.

**Writing Handbook**
See page 1281: Compare and Contrast

**64** UNIT ONE PART 1: IN HARMONY WITH NATURE

---

 **Mini Lesson** Grammar

**QUOTATIONS WITHIN QUOTATIONS**

**Instruction** When material that contains dialogue is quoted, double quotation marks are placed around the entire quotation. Single quotation marks are placed around the internal dialogue.

Fox and Coyote are almost unmasked by the Sly One's observation: "'Ha-Ha!' said Mouse, 'Coyote nearly fell into the water.'"

**Activity** Write the preceding sentence on the chalkboard without the single and double quotations. Then ask students to rewrite it with proper puncuation.

## Fools Crow

### JAMES WELCH

Set in Montana during the late 19th century, this coming-of-age story features a young warrior, Fools Crow, whose haunting vision foretells the dying culture of Native Americans. As a member of the Blackfeet, Fools Crow will face a key decision—either to defend his people's land and way of life or to suffer an immense loss of cultural identity. Loosely based on true events, the novel portrays the world of James Welch's ancestors—their landscape and their history.

## American Indian Myths and Legends

### EDITED BY RICHARD ERDOES AND ALFONSO ORTIZ

This collection of 160 Native American tales keeps the past alive. Drawing from a rich oral tradition, the editors have captured the voices of storytellers from a wide range of tribal groups across the United States. These stories provide a glimpse into Native Americans' diverse cultural heritage—their views of human behavior and relationships, the mysterious origins of life, heroes and war, animals, and the natural environment.

**Reading Skills and Strategies**
**SUSTAINED SILENT READING**
Encourage students to select one of the books as an opportunity to read silently over a period of time.

## And Even *More* . . .

**Books**

**Growing Up Native American**
EDITED BY PATRICIA RILEY
An anthology of stories and personal histories about the passage of youth to maturity, told from the perspective of Native Americans.

**The Way to Rainy Mountain**
N. SCOTT MOMADAY
This autobiographical work inventively mixes poetry, legend, history, and artwork.

**Native American Almanac**
ARLENE HIRSCHFELDER AND MARTHA KREIPE DE MONTANO
Comprehensive information and fascinating facts on Native American history, culture, and perspectives.

**Other Media**

**Smoke Signals**
This 1998 feature film—the first written, directed, and produced by Native Americans—explores the lives of two men from an Idaho reservation. Miramax Films. (VIDEOCASSETTE)

**More Than Bows and Arrows**
Author N. Scott Momaday narrates this critically acclaimed documentary focusing on Native American culture. Camera One. (VIDEOCASSETTE)

**The American Indian**
This product presents a panoramic view of Native American history through audio clips, images, and text. Facts on File. (CD-ROM)

## Spider Woman's Granddaughters

### EDITED BY PAULA GUNN ALLEN

Remnants of the past and the realities of the present are brought to life in this anthology of tales, essays, and short stories. Louise Erdrich and Leslie Marmon Silko are among the contributors who give voice to the experiences of Native American women.

## OVERVIEW

**Introduction**
This article provides the historical context for the literature selections in Part 2 of this unit. It examines the interactions among and experiences of the various cultural groups that existed in America beginning in the late fifteenth century. The primary-source sidebar **Voices from the Times** enables students to analyze a European perspective on an initial encounter between two different cultures.

## Teaching Nonfiction

**Reading Skills and Strategies**
**ESTABLISHING A PURPOSE FOR READING**
Explain to students that this article introduces students to three of the cultural groups who inhabited North America following the fifteenth century. Have students review the article and establish a purpose for reading (to find out).

**IDENTIFYING MAIN IDEAS**
The first section of "First Encounters" contains the main ideas of the article. Have students produce summaries by identifying the main ideas and supporting details. Students should note examples of exploration and exploitation.
**Possible Response:** Accounts of exploration include the arrivals in the Americas of Columbus and other Spanish and Portuguese explorers. Accounts of exploitation include explorers' desires to acquire the Americas' riches, the forceful conversion of Indian peoples to Christianity, and the enslaving of Africans.

**NOTETAKING**
Encourage students to take notes to better understand the article as they read. They may want to note important concepts, unfamiliar vocabulary, and proper names that occur in the article.

**DISCUSSING**
Encourage students to discuss the article in class. A possible focus for the discussion could be comparing and contrasting the lives of Native Americans, Europeans, and Africans in America using the information provided in this article and the article in Part 1 of this unit.

# First Encounters

## Accounts of Exploration and Exploitation

**(A)** When Christopher Columbus landed on a tiny Caribbean island in 1492, he called the inhabitants Indians because he thought he was near the East Indies. One of the first men to try to communicate with Columbus inadvertently cut his hand on Columbus's sword because he didn't know what a sword was. Such events—mistaken identity and injury—marked the first recorded encounter between the native people of the Americas and the Europeans who were to come in increasing numbers over the next 500 years.

Although the first explorers' motivations for coming to the Americas were complex, many came for the reason people often seek out dangers and challenges: a desire for fame and adventure. In addition, the early explorers expected to find great riches. European rulers had already sent explorers to India and China to bring back spices, silks, gold, jewelry, and other luxuries. Columbus, of course, was looking for a shortcut to these countries when he unexpectedly bumped into a new world. Once the **(B)** European monarchs realized that Columbus had led the way to two previously unknown continents, they put their best explorers to work finding out what wealth they could gain from these new lands.

Not all motivations for coming to the Americas were selfish ones, however. Reports of the existence of people in the Americas stirred many to come to spread Christianity. Others, such as the English Puritans, came seeking the religious freedom that they were denied in their homeland. Nevertheless, for both Catholics and Protestants, Christianity was the only true religion. People who

The Landing of Columbus at San Salvador (Guanahani), October 12, 1492. The Granger Collection.

**Mini Lesson** ## Viewing and Representing

*The Landing of Columbus at San Salvador (Guanahani), October 12, 1492*

**ART APPRECIATION**
**Instruction** This anonymous steel engraving from 1856 is based on the famous painting by John Vanderlyn that hangs in the Capitol Rotunda in Washington, D.C. In 1837 Congress commissioned the huge painting (12′ × 18′) for $10,000. Vanderlyn based his scene on the romanticized description of Columbus's arrival in Washington Irving's biography of the explorer. To

it, Vanderlyn added embellishments of his own, including a friar with a crucifix (there was no friar on the voyage) and the background of sailors on their knees looking for treasures in the sand and others dancing in celebration. The image, though, has been viewed by millions of visitors who undoubtedly assume this is what Columbus's landfall looked like.

Use the following question to help develop students' visual literacy.
**Ask: How would you describe the engraver's use of light and dark?**

were not Christian had to be converted by persuasion or by force. Those who rejected Christianity were considered enemies of God, suitable only for enslavement or death.

The story of cultural contact, like the story of America itself, would not be complete without the experiences of the Africans who were brought here as slaves. The European trade in enslaved Africans had been started by the Portuguese during the 1400s, and enslaved Africans accompanied most of the Spanish and Portuguese explorers in the Americas. In fact, one of the three men who survived with Cabeza de Vaca on his disastrous journey was an enslaved African named Estéban.

Africans were first brought in large numbers to the West Indies to provide labor for the vast sugar plantations. At first, the Spanish plantation owners had tried to use Indian labor, but the native peoples proved too susceptible to European diseases and unable to withstand the harsh treatment of their masters. Africans took their place. Before long, English colonists were also participating in the slave trade. In 1619, twelve years after the founding of Jamestown, Virginia—the first permanent English

## Voices from the TIMES

from *The Log of Christopher Columbus*

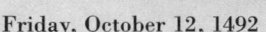

**Friday, October 12, 1492**

No sooner had we concluded the formalities of taking possession of the island than people began to come to the beach, all as naked as their mothers bore them, and the women also, although I did not see more than one very young girl. All those that I saw were young people, none of whom was over 30 years old. They are very well-built people, with handsome bodies and very fine faces, though their appearance is marred somewhat by very broad heads and foreheads, more so than I have ever seen in any other race. Their eyes are large and very pretty, and their skin is the color of Canary Islanders or of sunburned peasants, not at all black, as would be expected because we are on an east-west line with Hierro in the Canaries. These are tall people and their legs, with no exceptions, are quite straight, and none of them has a paunch. They are, in fact, well proportioned. Their hair is not kinky, but straight, and coarse like horsehair. They wear it short over the eyebrows, but they have a long hank in the back that they never cut. Many of the natives paint their faces; others paint their whole bodies; some, only the eyes or nose. Some are painted black, some white, some red; others are of different colors.

The people here called this island *Guanahaní* in their language, and their speech is very fluent, although I do not understand any of it. They are friendly and well-dispositioned people who bear no arms except for small spears, and they have no iron. I showed one my sword, and through ignorance he grabbed it by the blade and cut himself. Their spears are made of wood, to which they attach a fish tooth at one end, or some other sharp thing.

HISTORICAL BACKGROUND    **67**

## Making Connections

### Culture

**A** When two such different groups as Native Americans and Spaniards meet, it is perhaps inevitable that there should be "mistaken identity and injury." A classic example is the 1519 encounter, in central Mexico, between the conquistador Cortés and Aztec ruler Montezuma. When the Aztecs first saw Cortés in his glittery armor, they hailed him as the god Quetzalcoatl, whose arrival had been predicted by Aztec legend. Similarly, when Cortés saw the gold and jewels of Montezuma's capital city, Tenochtitlán (the site of modern-day Mexico City), he determined to seize the treasure. By 1521, the Aztec civilization was destroyed.

### History

**B** Upon Columbus's return to Spain, he was congratulated by the king and queen, knighted, and declared "Admiral of the Ocean Sea." However, the Atlantic was soon alive with explorers from other countries, robbing Columbus of future discoveries in the Americas, even though he managed three more voyages there himself between 1493 and 1504. Columbus is quoted as saying that people "made fun of my plan then; now even tailors wish to discover."

### Religion

**C** Slavery was commonplace around the world. All organized religions at the time accepted slavery as a normal part of life. Then American Quakers became abolitionists. In 1696, at their annual meeting in Philadelphia, they discouraged members from engaging in any aspect of the slave trade. Changing people's attitudes was slow, but between 1758 and 1800, nearly all Quakers voluntarily released their slaves. With this action, the Quakers became the first religious body to effectively oppose slavery.

### History

**D** The Americas had been isolated from nearly all diseases that had long affected Europe. But just as smallpox was waning in Europe in the early 1500s, it arrived with the Spaniards in the Americas with a vengeance. In 1518, it began spreading westward from Spanish ports in Puerto Rico and Cuba. It is estimated that the native population of central Mexico in 1519 was 25.3 million; by 1605, it had been reduced to 1 million. By 1534, smallpox covered the Americas as far north as the Great Lakes.

## SUMMARIZING

Have the students use their notes to summarize the contents of the article in their own words. Remind them that a summary includes main ideas and suporting details. It does not include personal opinions or unimportant details.

## VOICES FROM THE TIMES

**Ask: What does Columbus find interesting about the indigenous people he encounters?**

**Possible Response:** He notes their physical appearance, their friendliness, and their apparent lack of religious belief.

**Ask: What can you tell about their civilization?**

**Possible Responses:** They know how to use and make dugout canoes; they are unfamiliar with iron; they may be agricultural because they grow cotton and tobacco.

**Ask: Do you think Columbus is an explorer or an exploiter?**

**Possible Responses:** an explorer—he describes the people and their land vividly and is fascinated by what he encounters; an exploiter—he never considers the point of view of these people he encounters

## First Encounters

The first interactions between Europeans and Native Americans were marred by misunderstanding and at times outright cruelty. Show students this video presentation featuring explorers and inhabitants to give students an idea of what those first meetings were like.

See Teacher's SourceBook p. 13 for bar codes.

---

### Voices from the TIMES

I want the natives to develop a friendly attitude toward us because I know that they are a people who can be made free and converted to our Holy Faith more by love than by force. I therefore gave red caps to some and glass beads to others. They hung the beads around their necks, along with some other things of slight value that I gave them. And they took great pleasure in this and became so friendly that it was a marvel. They traded and gave everything they had with good will, but it seems to me that they have very little and are poor in everything. I warned my men to take nothing from the people without giving something in exchange.

This afternoon the people of San Salvador[1] came swimming to our ships and in boats made from one log. They brought us parrots, balls of cotton thread, spears, and many other things, including a kind of dry leaf[2] that they hold in great esteem. For these items we swapped them little glass beads and hawks' bells.

Many of the men I have seen have scars on their bodies, and when I made signs to them to find out how this happened, they indicated that people from other nearby islands come to San Salvador to capture them; they defend themselves the best they can. I believe that people from the mainland come here to take them as slaves. They ought to make good and skilled servants, for they repeat very quickly whatever we say to them. I think they can easily be made Christians, for they seem to have no religion. If it pleases Our Lord, I will take six of them to Your Highnesses when I depart, in order that they may learn our language.

***Translated by Robert H. Fuson***

---

1. **San Salvador** (săn săl'və-dôr'): the name that Columbus gave the island he first landed on; it means "Holy Savior" in Spanish.

2. **dry leaf:** tobacco

---

Slave ship diagram, 1798

settlement in the Americas—20 Africans were brought there as indentured servants. Eighteen years later, the first American-built slave ship, the *Desire,* set sail from Marblehead, Massachusetts.

One of the few firsthand accounts of the perilous two months that enslaved Africans spent packed in ships bound for the Americas is that of Olaudah Equiano. You will read about his experiences in this part of the unit.

## Traditions Across Time: The New Explorers

The tradition of writing about the exploration of a new place and what is encountered there has continued up to the present day. But what, you might ask, is left to explore in a world of jet propulsion, TV, computers, and fiber optics? In the remaining selections in this part of Unit One, you will read about some contemporary explorations: William Least Heat-Moon's exploration of forgotten areas of his own country, and Maya Angelou's journey across the ocean to discover the Africa of her ancestors.

## Accounts of Exploration and Exploitation

#### Objectives
- understand the following literary terms:
  historical narrative
  primary source
  secondary source
  slave narrative
- experience events in history by reading varied sources such as journals, letters, speeches, and other primary and secondary sources
- interpret the influences of historical context on literary works
- recognize distinctive characteristics of cultures that are reflected in different types of historical narratives
- understand how some historical narratives reflect the personal qualities and motives of their writers

### Teaching the Lesson

Students will be reading a variety of historical narratives that share the experiences of people in early American history. Together these narratives present different perspectives on the early years of European exploration and settlement in the Americas. This lesson will give students some background on the historical narrative as a literary form.

#### Introducing the Concepts
Historical narratives can be valuable tools in helping students understand people and events of the past. Through these narratives, they can "experience" episodes in history and learn from mistakes, challenges, and accomplishments. In this unit, students will read about difficult journeys at sea, exciting explorations of a new world, challenges faced by colonists in an unfamiliar world, and the ordeals of Africans who were captured and brought to the Americas as slaves. As students read these narratives, ask them to interpret the possible influences of the historical context on the literary works. Have them consider the following questions:

How do the challenges faced by people in early America compare to challenges people face in today's world?
**Possible Response:** People in early America had some issues of basic survival to contend with that most people in the United states do not face today.

# LEARNING the Language of Literature

## Historical Narratives

### Recording the American Experience
Imagine living in a world with no electronic media. For many of us, it would be quite a stretch to imagine living like that. However, for all people, this was the basic condition of life more than 400 years ago, when people from very different parts of the world first interacted with each other in America.

Many records of these interactions still exist and provide insights into the past. **Historical narratives** are accounts of real-life historical experiences, given either by a person who experienced those events or by someone who has studied or observed them. In many cases, the narratives are key historical documents, existing as our principal record of events. Historical narratives take two basic forms:

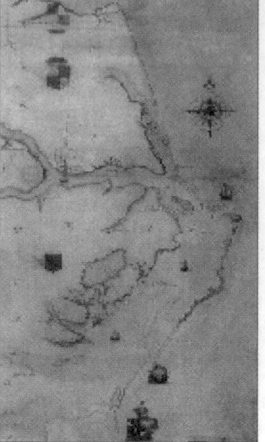

John White and Thomas Harriot, Roanoke colonists, rendered this map of Virginia in about 1588. Copyright © British Museum.

**PRIMARY SOURCES** Historical narratives can take the form of documents, such as letters, diaries, journals, and autobiographies, that present direct, firsthand knowledge of a subject; these are known as a primary sources.

**SECONDARY SOURCES** These types of narratives provide indirect, secondhand knowledge. Histories and biographies are examples of secondary sources.

### Records of Real Life
The first Americans, the Native Americans, had been recording information for thousands of years through picture symbols (in the form of pictographs, animal skin drawings, Mayan *glyphs,* and wampum belts), and through oral language. The myth "The World on the Turtle's Back"

(page 24), the sacred song "Song of the Sky Loom" (page 33), and the selection of coyote stories (page 39) represent a tiny part of the wealth of this oral tradition.

In the late 15th century, Europeans began voyages by ship to the Americas and reported news of their explorations and settlement. Many historical narratives of these times were survivors' tales, gripping adventure stories written down in journals and letters. Álvar Núñez Cabeza de Vaca was one of many explorers who sailed to the New World after Christopher Columbus. The historical narrative *La Relación* was Cabeza de Vaca's report to the King of Spain. Note the details conveyed in this passage:

> When night fell, only the navigator and I remained able to tend the barge. Two hours after dark he told me I must take over; he believed he was going to die that night.
>
> —Álvar Núñez Cabeza de Vaca

The use of vivid, sensory details makes historical narratives come to life. In 1620, the Puritans survived a journey across the Atlantic in *The Mayflower* and landed at Cape Cod. In 1630, William Bradford, the Plymouth Colony's second governor, began writing *Of Plymouth Plantation,* a chronicle of his colony's experiences. This is Bradford's description of the colony's first winter:

> The weather was very cold and it froze so hard as the spray of the sea lighting on their coats, they were as if they had been glazed.
>
> —William Bradford

What personal qualities did Europeans need to survive in the New World? Which narrators are most admirable?
**Possible Response:** the ability to improvise, strong belief in one's goals, and fearlessness in the face of the unknown; because of surviving life-threatening circumstances, Álvar Núñez Cabeza de Vaca and Olaudah Equiano are particularly admirable.

What important lessons can be learned from the positive and negative experiences described by these narratives?
**Possible Response:** Acquiring an understanding of and a respect for all cultures is an important goal for people who are interacting.

As they finish reading these historical narratives, students can write reactions to these questions and keep their responses in their Working Portfolios.

As American colonies expanded from the 16th through the 18th centuries, the slave trade expanded as well. Olaudah Equiano, one of the millions of Africans captured and transported to the Americas, survived his ordeal and published his autobiography in 1789. (It is also a slave narrative, a literary form that is discussed in detail in the box on the right). These lines from *The Interesting Narrative of the Life of Olaudah Equiano* describe his first reactions to going below the decks of a slave ship:

> There I received such a salutation in my nostrils as I had never experienced in my life; so that, with the loathsomeness of the stench, and crying together, I became so sick and low that I was not able to eat, nor had I the least desire to taste anything.
>
> —Olaudah Equiano

**YOUR TURN** On the basis of these three excerpts, what personal qualities do you think the writers share?

## "Remarkable Productions"

The **slave narrative** is an American literary genre that portrays the daily life of slaves as written by the slaves themselves after having gained their freedom. Some 6,000 slave narratives are known to exist. The Reverend Ephraim Peabody, writing in 1849 about five recently published slave narratives, wrote:

> We place these volumes without hesitation among the most remarkable productions of the age—remarkable as being pictures of slavery by the slave, remarkable as disclosing under a new light the mixed elements of American civilization, and not less remarkable as a vivid exhibition of the force and working of the native love of freedom in the individual mind.
>
> —The Reverend Ephraim Peabody

Probably the most influential example of the genre is the autobiography of Frederick Douglass, *Narrative of the Life of Frederick Douglass, an American Slave* (1845). Harriet Tubman's *Scenes in the Life of Harriet Tubman* (1869) is another important example of the genre.

## Strategies for Reading: Historical Narratives

1. Look for clues to a narrative's organization, such as the use of headings and bold type.
2. Determine a document's origin. Check for the use of ellipses [. . .], a clue that words or lines have been cut from the original narrative. Be aware of the original audience and purpose.
3. Keep track of the events described. If necessary, make a time line.
4. Reread and paraphrase (restate in your own words) to help you understand unfamiliar words or sentence structures.
5. Let yourself "experience" the narrative.
6. Briefly state the main idea of the narrative in your own words.
7. Take into account the time a work was written, and try to understand the background, perspective, and even the motives of the writer.
8. Remember to use your Strategies for Active Reading: **monitor, predict, visualize, connect, question, clarify,** and **evaluate.**

### Presenting the Concepts
Read through the strategies aloud or project them on a transparency. Ask students to identify modern narratives that provide valuable information about some aspect of their own society. They should consider primary sources such as letters, editorials, journals, or autobiographies; or secondary sources such as documentary films, biographies, or essays describing current events or events in the recent past. Model how to use the strategies provided to analyze each narrative.

### The Oral Narrative and Literature
The oral tradition has inspired stories, poems, and songs that provide a wealth of information about American history.

### Tall Tales
These stories feature exaggerated characters, called folk heroes, in wild, often humorous adventures. Many of America's most famous tall tales grew from oral tales passed around on the American frontier beginning in the 1820s. One of the most well-known folk heroes is the giant Paul Bunyan. His experiences reflect many of the challenges faced by real lumberjacks on the frontier. Other American tall tales describe heroes such as Pecos Bill. Beyond being larger-than-life stories, these adventures give readers an idea about 19th-century American concerns.

### Ballads
Ballads, both folk and literary, are narrative poems or songs that tell stories. The former are usually anonymous and feature legends. For example, "John Henry" describes a folk hero who worked to lay railroad tracks across the country. The ballad "Casey Jones" reflects the growing nation's fascination with railroads in the 19th century. Among American literary ballads, none is more famous than Longfellow's poem about Paul Revere, which made the latter a legend. Though not historically accurate, it captures the excitement of the American revolution and inspires patriotism.

### Spirituals
These religious songs grew primarily from the African-American oral tradition. African Americans held as slaves found identification in Bible stories that told of the Israelites seeking freedom from slavery in Egypt. Spirituals describing an escape to "the promised land" have double meaning. While slave owners assumed these songs referred only to Heaven, slaves meant them to refer to a free earthly land. One such spiritual, "Follow the Drinking Gourd," even provided clues about how a slave might escape from the South to the North. The drinking gourd represents the Big Dipper, a constellation pointing north.

As students read the selections in Part 2, have them imagine how each might inspire a tall tale, ballad, or song.

### Objectives

1. read a **nonfiction report** (Literary Analysis)
2. examine how **audience** influences the author **(Literary Analysis)**
3. use text organizers **(Active Reading)**

### Summary

The selection opens with Cabeza de Vaca and his company adrift on a barge in November of 1528. Starving, freezing, and deathly ill, the men finally drift ashore on Galveston Island. There they meet the Karankawas, who keep them alive with generous gifts of food. The Spaniards decide to try their luck on the ocean again, but with disastrous results. They barely leave shore before their barge is smashed by large waves, drowning three men and leaving the rest naked and without possessions. Once again the Karankawas save them, even taking them to their village. The Spaniards are relieved not to be killed as human sacrifices—a fear planted in their minds by tales of the Aztecs—but they are puzzled by the Karankawas' insistence that they serve as medicine men for the community. The Spaniards incorporate Christian elements into the Karankawas' rituals, breathing on the sick and praying to God for their recovery.

### Thematic Link

A mission of **exploration** becomes a test of survival in *La Relación.* Cabeza de Vaca's **first encounter** with the Karankawas leads to a mutually beneficial relationship between representatives of vastly different cultures.

---

### 5-Minute Warm-Up

***Daily Language SkillBuilder***

Have students **proofread** the display sentences on page 17j and write them correctly. The sentences also appear on Transparency 3 of **Grammar Transparencies and Copymasters.**

# *from* La Relación

*Report by* ÁLVAR NÚÑEZ CABEZA DE VACA
(äl′vär noo′nyĕs kä-bĕ′sä dĕ vä′kä)

**Connect to Your Life**

**Conquistadors—Popular Images** Lured by the prospect of vast lands filled with gold and silver, Spanish explorers known as conquistadors (conquerors) took to the seas to claim new colonies for Spain. What image do you have of conquistadors? What did they look like? How did they act? Share your ideas with classmates.

## Build Background

**A Doomed Expedition** In 1527, Pánfilo de Narváez, a Spanish conquistador, led a five-ship, 600-man expedition to Florida. His second in command was Álvar Núñez Cabeza de Vaca. The expedition was a disaster from the moment the Spaniards entered the Caribbean. After the loss of two ships in a hurricane and over 200 men by drowning and desertion, the Narváez expedition finally made its way to the west coast of Florida. Against the advice of Cabeza de Vaca, Narváez separated 300 of his men from the ships and marched these forces overland. Narváez intended for the ships to meet the land forces at a Spanish settlement on the coast of central Mexico, but he had grossly underestimated the vastness of the territory and the difficulty of crossing it. Eventually, overwhelmed by hunger, disease, and Indian attacks, the land forces decided to build five crude barges to get them to Mexico more quickly. These barges, each carrying about 50 men, soon drifted apart, and the one commanded by Cabeza de Vaca was shipwrecked on Galveston Island, off the coast of what is now Texas.

Ultimately, Cabeza de Vaca and three companions were the only survivors of the Narváez expedition. They wandered for more than eight years before reaching Mexico City and thus became the first Europeans to cross North America. After returning to Spain in 1537, Cabeza de Vaca wrote *La Relación,* a report addressed to the king of Spain.

**WORDS TO KNOW**
**Vocabulary Preview**

| | |
|---|---|
| beseech | ingratiate |
| cauterize | inundate |
| comply | placate |
| embody | lament |
| infirmity | scoff |

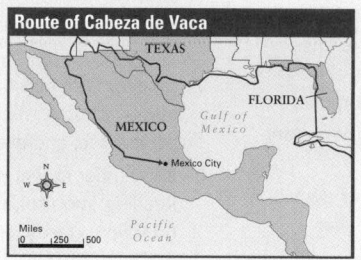

**Route of Cabeza de Vaca**

## Focus Your Reading

**LITERARY ANALYSIS   AUDIENCE**

The **audience** for a piece of writing is the person or persons intended to read it. Cabeza de Vaca wrote *La Relación* for a specific audience—the king of Spain. As you read, notice how Cabeza de Vaca's sense of audience determined the content, format, and organization of his report.

**ACTIVE READING   USING TEXT ORGANIZERS**

Aids—such as italics, boldfaced headings, and colored type—that help emphasize, clarify, or structure ideas in a piece of writing are called **text organizers.** For example, in *La Relación* the italicized paragraphs on pages 73 and 76 provide important background information and introduce the excerpts. The boldfaced headings organize the report by breaking it down into topics. Each heading announces what the section is about.

**READER'S NOTEBOOK** As you read this report, turn each boldfaced heading into a question. Then take notes, searching for the key details that answer the question and jotting them down.

---

### LESSON RESOURCES

*from*

# La Relación

*At this point in the account, Narvaez's barge has abandoned the rest, and Cabeza de Vaca's barge has joined one commanded by two other officers. The next three chapters describe the crew's shipwreck on Galveston Island and their encounter with the Karankawa Indians who lived there.*

## A Sinking and a Landing

Our two barges continued in company for four days, each man eating a ration of half a handful of raw corn a day. Then the other barge was lost in a storm. Nothing but God's great mercy kept us from going down, too.

It was winter and bitterly cold, and we had suffered hunger and the heavy beating of the waves for many days. Next day, the men began to collapse. By sunset, all in my barge had fallen over on one another, close to death. Few were any longer conscious. Not five could stand. When night fell, only the navigator and I remained able to tend the barge. Two hours after dark he told me I must take over; he believed he was going to die that night.

So I took the tiller.[1] After midnight I moved over to see if he were dead. He said no, in fact was better, and would steer till daylight. In that hour I would have welcomed death rather than see so many around me in such a condition. When I had returned the helm[2] to the navigator, I lay down to rest—but without much rest, for nothing was farther from my mind than sleep.

Near dawn I seemed to hear breakers[3] resounding; the coast lying low, they roared louder. Surprised at this, I called to the navigator, who said he thought we were coming close to land. We sounded[4] and found ourselves in seven fathoms.[5] The navigator felt we should stay clear of the shore till daylight; so I took an oar and pulled it on the shore side, wheeling the stern to seaward about a league[6] out.

As we drifted into shore, a wave caught us and heaved the barge a horseshoe-throw [about 42 feet] out of the water. The jolt when it hit brought the dead-looking men to. Seeing land at hand, they crawled through the surf to some rocks. Here we made a fire and parched some of our corn. We also found rain water. The men began to regain their senses, their locomotion, and their hope.

This day of our landing was November 6.

## What Befell Oviedo with the Indians [2]

After we ate, I ordered Lope de Oviedo, our strongest man, to climb one of the trees not far off and ascertain the lay of the land. He complied and found out from the treetop that we were on

---

1. **tiller:** a lever used to turn a rudder and steer a boat.
2. **helm:** the steering gear of a boat.
3. **breakers:** waves breaking against a shoreline.
4. **sounded:** measured the depth of the water.
5. **fathoms** (făth'əmz): units used in measuring the depth of water; a fathom is equal to 6 feet (1.83 meters).
6. **league:** a unit of distance; Cabeza de Vaca probably used the Spanish league, equal to 3.1 miles (5 kilometers).

WORDS
TO
KNOW     **comply** (kəm-plī') *v.* to obey another's command, request, rule, or wish

**73**

---

---

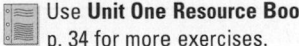

## Preteaching Vocabulary

**USING CONTEXT CLUES** Call students' attention to the list of WORDS TO KNOW on page 80. Remind them that sometimes they can determine the meaning of an unfamiliar word by analyzing a **cause-and-effect** relationship in the text. A causal relationship may be stated directly or implied. Demonstrate the strategy using the following model.

**Model Sentence**
After the travelers had <u>complied</u> with their hosts' requests, they were given food and shelter.

**Instruction**
- Write the model sentence on the chalkboard.
- Ask a volunteer to tell what cause-and-effect relationship is implied in the sentence.

**Possible Response:** The travelers complied with their hosts' requests, and as a result they received food and shelter.
- Have students use their understanding of the cause-and-effect relationship to guess the meaning of *comply.*
- Ask a volunteer to create a new sentence using *comply.*

Use **Unit One Resource Book,** p. 34 for more exercises.

A lesson on context clues appears on page 326 in the Pupil's Edition.

Indians forced to carry baggage and supplies of the Spanish invaders (1590), Theodor de Bry. Rare Books and Manuscripts Division, The New York Public Library, Astor, Lenox, and Tilden Foundations.

not half a dozen of us could even stand up.

The Inspector [Solís] and I walked out and greeted them. They advanced, and we did our best to placate and ingratiate. We gave them beads and bells, and each one of them gave us an arrow in pledge of friendship. They told us by signs that they would return at sunrise and bring food, having none then.

an island. [This was Galveston Island.] He also said that the ground looked as if cattle had trampled it and therefore that this must be a country of Christians.

I sent him back for a closer look, to see if he could find any worn trails, but warned him not to risk going too far. He went and came upon a path which he followed for half a league to some empty huts. The Indians were gone to shoal-flats[7] [to dig roots]. He took an earthen pot, a little dog, and a few mullets[8] and started back.

We had begun to worry what might have happened to him, so I detailed another two men to check. They met him shortly and saw three Indians with bows and arrows following him. The Indians were calling to him and he was gesturing them to keep coming. When he reached us, the Indians held back and sat down on the shore.

Half an hour later a hundred bowmen reinforced the first three individuals. Whatever their stature, they looked like giants to us in our fright. We could not hope to defend ourselves;

### The Indians' Hospitality Before and After a New Calamity

As the sun rose next morning, the Indians appeared as they promised, bringing an abundance of fish and of certain roots which taste like nuts, some bigger than walnuts, some smaller, mostly grubbed from the water with great labor.

That evening they came again with more fish and roots and brought their women and children to look at us. They thought themselves rich with the little bells and beads we gave them, and they repeated their visits on other days.

Being provided with what we needed, we thought to embark again. It was a struggle to dig our barge out of the sand it had sunk in, and another struggle to launch her. For the work in the water while launching, we stripped and stowed our clothes in the craft.

---

7. **shoal-flats:** stretches of level ground under shallow water.
8. **mullets** (mŭl'ĭts): a kind of edible fish.

WORDS
TO
KNOW

**placate** (plā'kāt') *v.* to soothe another's feelings; appease
**ingratiate** (ĭn-grā'shē-āt') *v.* to gain another's favor by deliberate effort

74

Quickly clambering in and grabbing our oars, we had rowed two crossbow shots from shore when a wave <u>inundated</u> us. Being naked and the cold intense, we let our oars go. The next big wave capsized the barge. The Inspector and two others held fast, but that only carried them more certainly underneath, where they drowned.

A single roll of the sea tossed the rest of the men into the rushing surf and back onto shore half-drowned.

We lost only those the barge took down; but the survivors escaped as naked as they were born, with the loss of everything we had. That was not much, but valuable to us in that bitter November cold, our bodies so emaciated we could easily count every bone and looked the very picture of death. I can say for myself that from the month of May I had eaten nothing but corn, and that sometimes raw. I never could bring myself to eat any of the horse-meat at the time our beasts were slaughtered; and fish I did not taste ten times. On top of everything else, a cruel north wind commenced to complete our killing.

The Lord willed that we should find embers while searching the remnants of our former fire. We found more wood and soon had big fires raging. Before them, with flowing tears, we prayed for mercy and pardon, each filled with pity not only for himself but for all his wretched fellows.

At sunset the Indians, not knowing we had gone, came again with food. When they saw us looking so strangely different, they turned back in alarm. I went after them calling, and they returned, though frightened. I explained to them by signs that our barge had sunk and three of our number drowned. They could see at their feet two of the dead men who had washed ashore. They could also see that the rest of us were not far from joining these two.

The Indians, understanding our full plight, sat down and <u>lamented</u> for half an hour so loudly they could have been heard a long way off. It was amazing to see these wild, untaught savages

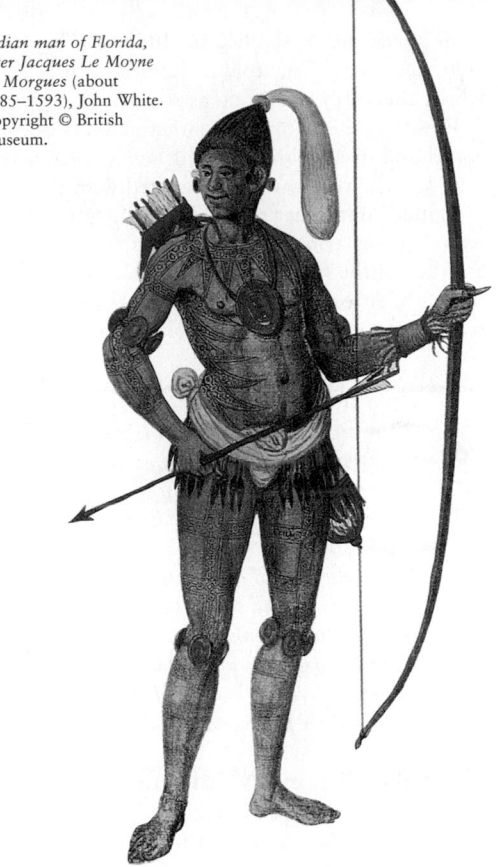

*Indian man of Florida, after Jacques Le Moyne de Morgues* (about 1585–1593), John White. Copyright © British Museum.

howling like brutes in compassion for us. It intensified my own grief at our calamity and had the same effect on the other victims.

When the cries died down, I conferred with the Christians about asking the Indians to take us to their homes. Some of our number who had been to New Spain warned that the Indians would sacrifice us to their idols.[9] But death being surer and nearer if we stayed where we were, I

---

9. **New Spain . . . their idols:** New Spain included what is now the southwest United States, Mexico, Central America north of Panama, and some West Indian islands. In Mexico, conquistadors had encountered Aztecs who practiced human sacrifice.

| WORDS TO KNOW | **inundate** (ĭn′ŭn-dāt′) *v.* to cover with water; overwhelm |
|---|---|
| | **lament** (lə-mĕnt′) *v.* to grieve; wail |

75

## Customizing Instruction

### Students Acquiring English
**1** Help students understand this passage by explaining the following words and idioms.
- *detailed*: selected to perform a particular job
- *shortly*: in a short time
- *gesturing*: making hand signals or using body language
- *held back*: stayed a distance away

### Less Proficient Readers
**2** Be sure that students understand the Spaniards' fear of the Karankawas by asking the following questions.
- Why does the author compare the Karankawas to giants?

**Possible Response:** Even normal-sized men seemed huge to the tired, frightened Spaniards.
- Why do the Spaniards give the Karankawas beads and bells?

**Possible Response:** They want to show that their intentions are friendly.

**Set a Purpose** Have students read on to see whether the Karankawas keep their promise to help the Spaniards.

### Multiple Learning Styles
**Kinesthetic Learners**
**3** Have students work in pairs to use visual signs, gestures, or body language to mimic Cabeza de Vaca's report to the Karankawas about what happened to the Spaniards when they tried to get their barge out to sea.

---

 **Mini Lesson** **Grammar**

### SIMPLE SENTENCES: SUBJECT, PREDICATE
**Instruction** A simple sentence has one independent clause and no subordinate clauses. The independent clause contains both a subject and a predicate. The subject tells whom or what the sentence is about; the predicate tells what the subject is or does. The following chart shows the basic parts of four simple sentences.

| SUBJECT | PREDICATE |
|---|---|
| We | ran. |
| Everyone | was hungry. |
| The Indians | brought us food. |
| Our strongest man | climbed one of the trees. |

**Exercises** Ask students whether each of the following phrases is a sentence, and have them identify the underlined words as the subject or the predicate.
1. Only <u>the navigator</u> was able to control the barge. *(sentence; subject)*
2. The tired men <u>crawled through the surf to shore</u>. *(sentence; predicate)*
3. <u>Álvar Núñez Cabeza de Vaca, Lope de Oviedo, and the other men</u> frozen by the November wind. *(not a sentence; subject)*

 Use **Grammar Transparencies and Copymasters**, p. 75.

 Use McDougal Littell's *Language Network*, Chapter 1, for more instruction and practice in simple sentences.

LA RELACIÓ'

**A** Point out the heading for the last section of text, "How We Became Medicine-Men." Have students develop a list of questions that this heading raises in their minds.

**Possible Responses:** What is a medicine man? How will Cabeza de Vaca and his crew become medicine men? Will they heal anyone? Will they decide to stay with the Karankawas after they become medicine men?

**Set a Purpose** Have students read on to find the answers to their questions. After they have finished the selection, ask them whether anything in the last section surprised them and, if so, why.

**Literary Analysis: CONFLICT**

**B** Ask students to identify the internal and external conflicts introduced here.

**Possible Responses:** external—their hosts insist that the Spaniards perform medical rites before they receive food; internal—the Spaniards don't believe that Karankawa healing rites can work, but they want to be useful to their hosts

**Link Across Cultures**
**from *The Travels of Marco Polo***

This selection offers an opportunity for students to compare similar themes, genres, and literary concepts across cultures. Ask students to point out the similarities and differences between *La Relación* and *The Travels of Marco Polo*. What are the narrators' attitudes toward the inhabitants of the foreign lands? What are the purposes of their expeditions?

---

went ahead and beseeched the Indians. They were delighted. They told us to tarry a little while, then they would do as we wished.

Presently thirty of them gathered loads of wood and disappeared to their huts, which were a long walk away; while we waited with the remainder until near nightfall. Then, supporting us under our arms, they hurried us from one to another of the four big fires they had built along the path. At each fire, when we regained a little warmth and strength, they took us on so swiftly our feet hardly touched ground.

Thus we made their village, where we saw they had erected a hut for us with many fires inside. An hour later they began a dance celebration that lasted all night. For us there was no joy, feasting, or sleep, as we waited the hour they should make us victims.

In the morning, when they brought us fish and roots and acted in every way hospitably, we felt reassured and somewhat lost our anxiety of the sacrificial knife.

---

**C**ABEZA DE VACA *learned that men from one of the other barges had also landed on the island, bringing the number of Europeans there to about 90. In a matter of weeks, all but 16 of them died of disease, which spread to the Karankawas and killed half of them as well. Some of the Karankawas wanted to put the remaining Europeans to death but were dissuaded by Cabeza de Vaca's host. Cabeza de Vaca and his men were later forced to act as healers.*

### **A** How We Became Medicine-Men

The islanders wanted to make physicians of us without examination or a review of diplomas. Their method of cure is to blow on the sick, the breath and the laying-on of hands supposedly **B** casting out the infirmity. They insisted we should do this too and be of some use to them. We scoffed at their cures and at the idea we knew how to heal. But they withheld food from us until we complied. An Indian told me I knew not **2** whereof I spoke in saying their methods had no effect. Stones and other things growing about in the fields, he said, had a virtue whereby passing a pebble along the stomach could take away pain and heal; surely extraordinary men like us **3** embodied such powers over nature. Hunger forced us to obey, but disclaiming any responsibility for our failure or success.

An Indian, falling sick, would send for a medicine-man, who would apply his cure. The patient would then give the medicine-man all he had and seek more from his relatives to give. The medicine-man makes incisions over the point of the pain, sucks the wound, and cauterizes it. This remedy enjoys high repute among the Indians. I have, as a matter of fact, tried it on myself with good results. The medicine-men blow on the spot they have treated, as a finishing touch, and the patient regards himself relieved.

Our method, however, was to bless the sick, breathe upon them, recite a *Pater noster* and *Ave Maria*,[10] and pray earnestly to God our Lord for their recovery. When we concluded with the sign of the cross, He willed that our patients should directly spread the news that they had been restored to health.

In consequence, the Indians treated us kindly. They deprived themselves of food to give to us, and presented us skins and other tokens of gratitude. ❖

*Translated by Cyclone Covey*

---

10. *Pater noster* (pä′tər-nŏs′tər) **and** *Ave Maria* (ä′vä mə-rē′ə): the Lord's Prayer and the Hail Mary, so called from the prayers' opening words in Latin.

---

WORDS
TO
KNOW

**beseech** (bĭ-sēch′) *v.* to implore; beg
**infirmity** (ĭn-fûr′mĭ-tē) *n.* a sickness or weakness
**scoff** (skŏf) *v.* to mock
**embody** (ĕm-bŏd′ē) *v.* to represent in bodily form
**cauterize** (kô′tə-rīz′) *v.* to burn or sear to destroy abnormal tissue

76

---

 **Mini Lesson** **Vocabulary Strategy**

**APPLYING PREFIX AND ROOT WORD MEANINGS**

**Instruction** The word *infirmity* comprises smaller meaningful elements—root, prefix, and suffix. Students can use knowledge of the root *firm*, "strong," and the prefix *in-*, "not," to determine the meaning of *infirmity*, "lack of strength."

**Application** Have students work in pairs to analyze the prefixes and roots for *embody* and *inundate*. Note that, in these cases, the prefixes *em-* (or *en-*) and *in-* share the meaning "in" or "into" (rather than "not"). Ask students to use a dictionary to find three words using each prefix

meaning "into" (*em-*, *en-*, and *in-*) and to use each word in a sentence. Ask students to describe how they can use their knowledge of the two meanings of the prefix *in-* to help determine the meanings of unfamiliar words.

Use **Vocabulary Transparencies and Copymasters**, p. 21.

# *from* The Travels of Marco Polo

*In 1271, when he was about 17 years old, the Italian trader Marco Polo began his famous journey to Asia. He spent 17 years in China as a guest of the emperor, Kublai Khan; visited islands in the Pacific and Indian oceans; and traveled to India and Persia before returning to Venice in 1295. The first printed version of* The Travels of Marco Polo *appeared in 1477. This book of colorful stories inspired Columbus and other European explorers and served as a model for later travel accounts, such as* La Relación.

---

*Of the third kingdom, named Samara.*

Leaving Basman, you enter the kingdom of Samara,[1] being another of those into which the island is divided. In this Marco Polo resided five months, during which, exceedingly against his inclination, he was detained by contrary winds. The north star is not visible here, nor even the stars that are in the wain.[2] The people are idolaters[3]; they are governed by a powerful prince, who professes himself the vassal of the grand khan.[4]

As it was necessary to continue for so long a time at this island Marco Polo established himself on shore, with a party of about 2,000 men; and in order to guard against mischief from the savage natives, who seek for opportunities of seizing stragglers, putting them to death, and eating them, he caused a large and deep ditch to be dug around him on the land side, in such manner that each of its extremities terminated in the port, where the shipping lay. This ditch he strengthened by erecting several blockhouses or redoubts[5] of wood, the country affording an abundant supply of that material; and being defended by this kind of fortification, he kept the party in complete security during the five months of their residence. Such was the confidence inspired amongst the natives, that they furnished supplies of victuals[6] and other necessary articles according to an agreement made with them.

No finer fish for the table can be met with in any part of the world than are found here. There is no wheat produced, but the people live upon rice. Wine is not made; but from a species of tree resembling the date-bearing palm they procure an excellent beverage in the following manner. They cut off a branch, and put over the place a vessel to receive the juice as it distils from the wound, which is filled in the course of a day and a night. So wholesome are the qualities of this liquor, that it affords relief in dropsical complaints,[7] as well as in those of the lungs and of the spleen. When these shoots that have been cut are perceived not to yield any more juice, they contrive to water the trees, by bringing from the river, in pipes or channels, so much water as is sufficient for the purpose; and upon this being done, the juice runs again as it did at first. Some trees naturally yield it of a reddish, and others of a pale colour. The Indian nuts[8] also grow here, of the size of a man's head, containing an edible substance that is sweet and pleasant to the taste, and white as milk.

1. **Basman . . . Samara:** kingdoms on the island of Sumatra (now part of Indonesia).

2. **the wain:** the group of stars more commonly known as the Big Dipper—so called because its shape resembles that of a wain, or farm wagon.

3. **idolaters** (ī´dŏl´ə-tərz): people who worship idols. Polo uses the term to refer to various sorts of non-Christians.

4. **the vassal of the grand khan:** a lord subject to the authority of Kublai Khan, the Mongol emperor of China.

5. **blockhouses or redoubts:** forts.

6. **victuals** (vĭt´lz): food.

7. **dropsical complaints:** symptoms of dropsy, an illness characterized by a buildup of fluids in body tissues.

8. **Indian nuts:** coconuts.

THE TRAVELS OF MARCO POLO **77**

**Less Proficient Readers**

**1** Ask students to summarize the Karankawas' method for transporting the Spaniards safely to their village.

**Possible Response:** They built fires in several places along the route from the shore to the village. Then they carried the Spaniards to the first fire, allowed them to warm themselves, carried them to the next fire, and so on.

**Students Acquiring English**

**2** Point out that the phrase *I knew not whereof I spoke* is a formal way of saying "I didn't know what I was talking about."

**Gifted and Talented**

**3** Ask students what this comment suggests about the Karankawas' view of the Spaniards.

**Less Proficient Readers**

**4** Make sure that students appreciate the humor in the story of how the Spaniards became medicine men. Ask them the following questions.

• Why did the Karankawas think the Spaniards would make good medicine men?

**Possible Response:** They seemed so strange that the Karankawas thought they must have special powers.

• Why did the Spaniards object to breathing and laying hands upon the sick?

**Possible Response:** They didn't believe this was an effective medical procedure.

• Why did the Spaniards have to comply with the Karankawas' request?

**Possible Response:** The Karankawas withheld food until they did.

---

 **Speaking and Listening**

**DRAMATIC READING AND RETELLING**

**Prepare** Ask students to select a favorite passage from the narrative to present to the class. Explain that they'll present the passage in two ways: first, they will read it as written; then they'll retell the story in their own words as though they were telling the story to a friend. Explain that the written passage is intended for the king; their retelling assumes a more informal audience. Discuss what nonverbal strategies—such as pitch and tone of voice, posture, gestures, and eye contact—would enhance each kind of presentation.

**Present** Have students present their dramatic reading and improvised retellings. Students should be able to justify their choice of verbal and nonverbal performance techniques by referring to the narrative and to their interpretation of Cabeza de Vaca's character. Audience members should evaluate how the performance increases their understanding of the narrative and its author.

**BLOCK SCHEDULING** This activity is particularly well-suited for longer class periods.

## Connect to the Literature

**1. What Do You Think?**
Students should be able to explain what was surprising about the event they choose.

**Comprehension Check**
• The barge sank, some drowned, and others washed ashore naked and freezing.
• They were afraid of being sacrificed.
• They forced the Spaniards to act as medicine men.

 Use Selection Quiz in
**Unit One Resource Book**, p. 35.

## Think Critically

2. Students' responses should show an awareness of the thought processes they use while reading and how the questions served as study guides.
3. Students should explain the images they had of conquistadors before reading the selection and tell how these images were reinforced or contradicted by the selection.
4. Possible Responses: They felt anxiety when lost at sea; gratitude upon reaching land; fear at seeing armed natives; hope when they were fed; sorrow when their friends drowned; fear and hope as they were taken to the village.
5. Possible Response: They viewed themselves as civilized Christians and the Karankawas as savages.
6. Possible Response: They were in awe of the Spaniards, sometimes feeling afraid of them and at other times wanting to harness the Spaniards' imagined powers.

## Literary Analysis

**Audience** Students might comment on the following differences: in the diary, absence of unnecessary explanation, such as the comment that Lope de Oviedo was "our strongest man."
**Review Setting** The physical setting plays a large role in the survival of Cabeza de Vaca and his crew. Many Spaniards die from cold and starvation on barges at sea, and others later drown when a large wave capsizes the barge; the land offers the survivors food, and shelter.

---

## Connect to the Literature

**1. What Do You Think?**
What event or idea in Cabeza de Vaca's account did you find the most surprising?

**Comprehension Check**
• What happened when the Spaniards tried to leave Galveston Island on their barge?
• Why were the Spaniards afraid to go to the Karankawa village?
• How did the Native Americans force the Spaniards to be useful to them?

## Think Critically

2. **ACTIVE READING** **USING TEXT ORGANIZERS** Share with a classmate the headings that you rewrote as questions in your **READER'S NOTEBOOK**, and compare your responses. How did these questions act as guides for reading the text?

3. How closely do Cabeza de Vaca and his men fit your image of conquistadors?

4. What can you **infer** about the feelings of Cabeza de Vaca and his men as they went through their ordeals?

5. How would you say Cabeza de Vaca and his men viewed themselves in relation to the Karankawa Indians they met?

 THINK ABOUT
{
• the reason Lope de Oviedo assumed that the island was a country of Christians
• the terms Cabeza de Vaca uses to describe his men, and those he uses to describe the Karankawas
• Cabeza de Vaca's opinion of the Karankawas' method of healing
}

6. How do you think the Karankawas viewed Cabeza de Vaca and his men? What parts of the report support your interpretation?

## Extend Interpretations

7. **Comparing Texts** Read the excerpt from *The Travels of Marco Polo* on page 77, and compare Cabeza de Vaca's and Marco Polo's encounters with native peoples. What similarities and differences do you see in their attitudes?

8. **Connect to Life** Sixteenth-century conquistadors described, mapped, and claimed territory that was previously unknown to them. They also replaced traditional belief systems with their own. Who are the present-day equivalents of conquistadors, and what do they explore or conquer?

## Extend Interpretations

**Comparing Texts** Students may point out that both Cabeza de Vaca and Marco Polo fear that the native peoples intend to kill them as human sacrifices. Both regard the native peoples as savages. Out of necessity, however, Cabeza de Vaca, shipwrecked and half starved, develops a closer relationship with the natives than does Marco Polo, who ensconces himself and his 2,000 men behind a trench and a blockhouse.

**Connect to Life** Responses will vary. Some students may compare the conquistadors, who explore a distant continent, to research scientists who explore the mysteries of the cosmos.

---

## Literary Analysis

**AUDIENCE** In writing *La Relación*, Cabeza de Vaca was keenly aware of his **audience**—the king of Spain. To gain insight into the relationship between the writer and his audience, imagine that Cabeza de Vaca considered the following questions while he was drafting his report:
• What does the king already know about my situation?
• What more do I want him to know and why?
• What **details** would he find most interesting?
• How can I make the information easy for him to follow?
• What kind of language will be most appropriate?

The form Cabeza de Vaca chose, the details he included, the level of **diction** he used, and the attitude he expressed toward his subject all were determined by his knowledge of who his reader would be.

**Paired Activity** How might Cabeza de Vaca's account have been changed if he had chosen a different audience? Imagine he had decided to tell about one of his ordeals in a letter to his wife. Choose a brief passage from the selection to rewrite as a personal letter. Exchange your letter with a partner, and discuss the differences between the rewritten passage and the original account.

**REVIEW** **SETTING** As you recall, **setting** is the time and place of the action in a literary work. How does the physical setting determine the events that Cabeza de Vaca recounts in this selection?

## Writing Options

**1. Firsthand Account** Imagine you are a member of Cabeza de Vaca's expedition. Write a firsthand account of the most difficult ordeal you endure. Include details from one of the passages of *La Relación*. Put your account in your **Working Portfolio.**

**2. Essay on Leadership** From your reading of this selection, do you think Cabeza de Vaca was a good leader? Draft a short persuasive essay in which you state your opinion and support it with reasons.

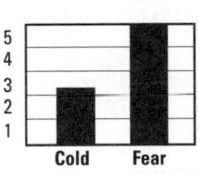

*A Good Leader*

**3. Report to the President** Imagine you are an astronaut who has just returned from a daring space mission. Using *La Relación* as a model, write a brief report describing your exploration to the president of the United States.

## Activities & Explorations

**1. Miniseries Storyboard** Imagine that you are planning a television miniseries based on the adventures of Cabeza de Vaca. Prepare a storyboard—a series of rough sketches—depicting any scene from this selection.

Combine your work with classmates' to make a bulletin-board display. ~ **ART**

**2. Karankawa Speech** Speaking as one of the Karankawas who met the shipwrecked Spaniards, make an informal speech to members of a neighboring clan, giving your impressions of the strangers. ~ **SPEAKING AND LISTENING**

**3. Informal Debate** With a small group of classmates, stage an informal debate in which you discuss the pros and cons of whether the Karankawas should take the shipwrecked strangers to their homes. ~ **SPEAKING AND LISTENING**

**4. Bar Graph** Working with a partner, create a bar graph like the one started below. List five physical or mental challenges that Cabeza de Vaca and his men faced and numbers to indicate degrees of success. Then draw bars to show the degrees to which the men were able to overcome the challenges. ~ **VIEWING AND REPRESENTING**

| | Cold | Fear |
|---|---|---|
| 5 | | |
| 4 | | |
| 3 | | |
| 2 | | |
| 1 | | |

## Inquiry & Research

**Early Explorers** Research the following 16th-century Spanish explorers: Juan Ponce de Leon, Vasco Nuñez de Balboa, Hernando Cortés, Ferdinand Magellan, Francisco Pizarro, and Hernando de Soto. Organize your findings in a chart with the following headings: *Explorer, Date of Exploration, Goal,* and *Achievement.*

> **More Online: Research Starter**
> www.mcdougallittell.com

## Art Connection

**History Through Art** Like the reports of 16th-century European explorers, the renderings by European artists who came to America served a documentary purpose. For instance, English artist John White made drawings of native people, plants, and wildlife (see his painting of a Florida man on page 75). Theodor de Bry, a Flemish artist, made engravings based on the works of White and others (see page 74). Discuss what these works document—what can you tell about the man in White's painting? What do you learn from de Bry's scene?

Indians forced to carry baggage and supplies of the Spanish invaders (1590).

---

**1. Firsthand Account To get students started on this assignment,** have them consider times when they experienced hardship in their own lives, such as during storms when their homes lost power or during other emergencies.

**2. Essay on Leadership To get students started on this assignment,** have them brainstorm a list of qualities that a good leader has, such as strong interpersonal skills, intelligence, the ability to delegate responsibility, and so on.

**3. Report to the President** Students who are visual learners may choose to illustrate their report.

## Activities & Explorations

**1. Miniseries Storyboard** Explain that a storyboard is a visual outline of a movie containing one drawing per camera shot. A storyboard should include instructions for camera angles, character positions, costumes, props, gestures, and backgrounds. Suggest students use the glossary from the Literature in Performance Resource Book.

**2. Karankawa Speech** Students should decide at what point in the sequence of events the speech will take place—before or after the barge sinks, before or after the epidemic is spread by the Spaniards, or after all the events have taken place.

**3. Informal Debate** Students should divide their groups in half. Each side should brainstorm the defense of its position and anticipate its opponents' arguments.

**4. Bar Graph** Other challenges that students might graph include the sea, exhaustion, hunger, grief, and despair.

## Inquiry & Research

Students may also want to research who funded these explorers and why.

## Art Connection

Have students compare and contrast the images of Native Americans in the two paintings.

---

## ✓ Assessment   **Informal Assessment**

**CHARACTER EMPATHY** You can informally assess students' understanding of the narrative by asking them to place themselves in the narrator's position. Ask them to list four physical or mental challenges that Cabeza de Vaca faced during his ordeal. Then ask students to write sentences, using the first-person voice, that explain how successfully "they" met each challenge.

### RUBRIC

**3  Full Accomplishment** Students accurately list four challenges from the selection, and their

sentences reflect a clear understanding of the narrator.

**2  Substantial Accomplishment** Students list fewer challenges and/or their sentences may not fully reflect an understanding of the narrator.

**1  Little or Partial Accomplishment** Students have difficulty identifying challenges and/or their sentences show little understanding of the narrator.

## Vocabulary in Action

1. cauterize
2. infirmity
3. inundate
4. beseech
5. lament
6. scoff
7. embody
8. comply
9. placate
10. ingratiate

## Vocabulary in Action

**EXERCISE: CONTEXT CLUES** Write the vocabulary word that is closest in meaning to the italicized word or phrase in each sentence.

1. The Indians learned to *burn* a wound to make it stop bleeding.
2. Starvation caused *illness* among many of the conquistadors.
3. Huge waves threatened to *flood* the barges and capsize them.
4. Why did the navigator *beg* Cabeza de Vaca to take control of the barge?
5. Cabeza de Vaca did not expect the Indians to *express sorrow* for the conquistadors' predicament.
6. The conquistadors learned not to *sneer* at the Indians' healing methods.
7. Cabeza de Vaca seems to *personify* many positive qualities.
8. When Cabeza de Vaca gave an order, his men had no choice but to *obey*.
9. How did the conquistadors *calm* the Indians who were carrying bows?
10. The conquistadors gave away bells and beads to *gain favor for* themselves with the Indians.

| WORDS TO KNOW | comply | lament | embody |
|---|---|---|---|
| | placate | beseech | cauterize |
| | ingratiate | infirmity | |
| | inundate | scoff | |

**Building Vocabulary**
For an in-depth lesson on context clues, see page 326.

## Álvar Núñez Cabeza de Vaca
1490?–1557?

**A Rising Star** As a young man, Cabeza de Vaca joined the Spanish army and fought in many battles. His military successes eventually led to his appointment as an officer of the Narváez expedition to Florida. His report of this ill-fated expedition, *La Relación,* describes his adventures as he crossed the North American continent, living with various Native American tribes and trading shells, beads, skins, and other items to survive. He was the first European to describe a Caribbean hurricane, the Mississippi River, and herds of buffalo.

**A Fallen Hero** In 1540, Cabeza de Vaca returned to the Americas as governor of the province of Río de la Plata in South America. While there, he led a yearlong expedition 1,000 miles across the continent, becoming the first European to cross both North and South America on foot. As governor, he prohibited the mistreatment of Native Americans by Spaniards. For that reason and others, he was thrown out of office by a group of rebels in 1543 and sent back to Spain two years later. In 1551 he was tried and found guilty of the charges that the rebels had brought against him. He was sentenced to an eight-year exile in Africa, stripped of his titles, and ordered to pay damages to his accusers. In 1556 the king of Spain pardoned him and awarded him a small pension, but his last years were marked by illness and poverty.

## Author Activity

**Just Like Fiction** The scholar William T. Pilkington writes, "*La Relación* possesses many of the attributes of a good novel, especially its subtle presentation of character and its dramatic tension." Read other passages from *La Relación,* and find examples of characterization and plot development that resemble the techniques a novelist uses in writing a well-crafted story.

**80** UNIT ONE PART 2: FIRST ENCOUNTERS

 **Mini Lesson** **Grammar**

**REVIEW: PARTS OF SPEECH**
**Instruction** Help students compile a list of the eight parts of speech: nouns, pronouns, verbs, adjectives, adverbs, prepositions, conjunctions, and interjections. If necessary, review the way in which each part of speech is used.
**Exercises** Ask students to identify the part of speech of each underlined word.

1. <u>After</u> midnight we crept <u>from</u> the camp and moved <u>toward</u> the sea. *(prepositions)*
2. The Karankawas <u>expected</u> us to cure them, although we <u>knew</u> nothing of medicine and <u>had</u> no training. *(verbs)*

3. <u>He</u> and <u>I</u> both tried to tell <u>them</u> about <u>it</u>, but <u>they</u> couldn't understand Spanish. *(pronouns)*
4. We gathered <u>dry</u> wood and built a <u>big</u>, <u>raging</u> fire, which made us feel quite <u>warm</u>. *(adjectives)*
5. We had gone <u>far</u>, stumbling <u>blindly</u> through the trees until we became <u>very</u> tired. *(adverbs)*

 Use **Grammar Transparencies and Copymasters**, p. 62.

 Use McDougal Littell's *Language Network,* "Parts of Speech," for more instruction and practice in parts of speech.

# *from* Of Plymouth Plantation

### *Chronicle by* WILLIAM BRADFORD

> **Connect to Your Life**
>
> **The Pilgrims** What do you know about the Pilgrims? How, when, and why did they come to North America? With a small group of classmates, discuss facts and images that come to mind when you think of the Pilgrims. Collect the group's impressions in a cluster diagram.

## Build Background

In England during the 1500s and 1600s, a group of Protestants called Puritans led a movement to "purify" the Church of England. One group of Puritans, the Separatists, wanted to withdraw from the established church. Separatist groups were declared illegal, and members faced arrest for practicing their beliefs. One congregation of Separatists, known today as the Pilgrims, fled from England to Holland and eventually migrated to America. In September 1620, this group sailed across the Atlantic on the *Mayflower.* Blown off course, the *Mayflower* reached the tip of Cape Cod, in what is now Massachusetts, in early November. While the ship was moored in Provincetown Harbor, some of the group set out in a smaller boat to search for a good place to build a settlement. About a month later, the colonists built their first shelter at Plymouth.

Nearly half of the colonists died during the first brutal winter, but the entire colony might have perished without the aid of the Wampanoag and other Native American groups. Under Governor William Bradford's leadership, the colony not only survived but also grew to about 300 people by 1630. Bradford wrote about the Pilgrims' long journey and their settlement at Plymouth.

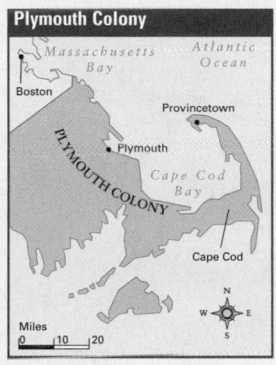

**Plymouth Colony**

Massachusetts Bay — Atlantic Ocean — Boston — Provincetown — Plymouth — PLYMOUTH COLONY — Cape Cod Bay — Cape Cod

Miles 0 10 20

WORDS TO KNOW
**Vocabulary Preview**

| | |
|---|---|
| aloof | providence |
| commodity | procure |
| desolate | sentinel |
| feigned | solace |
| hue | vanquish |

## Focus Your Reading

**LITERARY ANALYSIS  PRIMARY SOURCES**

**Primary sources** are written or created by people who observed or participated in an historical event. Primary sources include letters, diaries, speeches, newspaper articles, and eyewitness accounts. *Of Plymouth Plantation,* William Bradford's chronicle of Pilgrim settlers in North America, is an example of a primary source. The passages you are about to read provide direct, firsthand knowledge about a small band of Pilgrims who founded Plymouth colony. As you read this primary source for factual information, also note Bradford's opinions, biases, assumptions, and point of view.

**ACTIVE READING  SUMMARIZING**

**Summarizing** means condensing what you read into fewer words. As you summarize, you restate the main ideas and most important details. Summarizing helps clarify your understanding of the key information in a piece of writing. The process will be especially useful for reading *Of Plymouth Plantation,* in which the long, complex sentences may divert you from grasping the most essential points.

**READER'S NOTEBOOK** This selection has five sections, each labeled with a boldfaced heading. Copy the boldfaced headings onto a page of your notebook, leaving writing space below each one. Then, as you read, write a one- or two-sentence summary of each section. Restate the key ideas in your own words.

---

---

## Reading and Analyzing

**Reading Skills and Strategies:**
**PREVIEW**

Explain that this selection is taken from the writings of one of the pilgrims who sailed to America on the *Mayflower*.

**Literary Analysis** | PRIMARY SOURCES |

 When reading a primary source, students should try to distinguish factual information from the author's opinions, biases, assumptions, and personal point of view. In the first section of the selection, in which Bradford describes the safe arrival of the Pilgrims at Cape Cod, what factual information does he present about the voyage?

**Answer:** The Pilgrims crossed the ocean from England and landed in a safe port on Cape Cod.

What descriptions show Bradford's personal opinion or point of view?

**Possible Responses:** Bradford describes Native Americans as "savage barbarians," the weather as "sharp and violent," and the wilderness as "hideous and desolate." He also describes the ocean as separating the Pilgrims from all "civil" parts of the world.

Use **Unit One Resource Book**, p. 38 for additional support.

**Active Reading:** | SUMMARIZING |

 Summarize the events leading up to the arrival in America of the *Mayflower*. Suggest students keep notes as they read, putting main events and ideas into shorter, simpler sentences.

Use **Unit One Resource Book**, p. 37 for additional support.

---

FROM

# OF PLYMOUTH PLANTATION

## WILLIAM BRADFORD

### THEIR SAFE ARRIVAL AT CAPE COD

But to omit other things (that I may be brief) after long beating at sea they[1] fell with that land which is called Cape Cod; the which being made and certainly known to be it, they were not a little joyful. . . .

Being thus arrived in a good harbor, and brought safe to land, they fell upon their knees and blessed the God of Heaven who had brought them over the vast and furious ocean, and delivered them from all the perils and miseries thereof, again to set their feet on the firm and stable earth, their proper element. . . .

But here I cannot but stay and make a pause, and stand half amazed at this

---

1. **they:** Bradford refers to the Pilgrims in the third person even though he is one of them.

---

## Teaching Options

 **Preteaching Vocabulary**

**USING CONTEXT CLUES** Call students' attention to the list of WORDS TO KNOW. Remind them that sometimes they can understand the meaning of an unfamiliar word by examining the context in which the word is used. Write the following sentence on the chalkboard:

After months of research, the historian was able to *procure* the information he needed.

**Instruction**

• Ask a volunteer to state the situation described in the sentence.

• Have students infer from this situation the meaning of the word *procure*.

• Ask a volunteer to use *procure* in a sentence.

**Exercises** Ask students to use context clues to determine the meanings of the underlined term in each sentence.

1. Jackson was usually talkative and friendly, but lately he seemed quiet and <u>aloof</u>.

2. Sara's basketball team lost the championship game, but she took <u>solace</u> in the fact that they played well.

Use **Unit One Resource Book**, p. 39 for more exercises.

A lesson on context clues appears on p. 326 in the **Pupil's Edition**.

poor people's present condition; and so I think will the reader, too, when he well considers the same. Being thus passed the vast ocean, and a sea of troubles before in their preparation (as may be remembered by that which went before), they had now no friends to welcome them nor inns to entertain or refresh their weatherbeaten bodies; no houses or much less towns to repair to, to seek for succor.[2] It is recorded in Scripture as a mercy to the Apostle and his shipwrecked company, that the barbarians showed them no small kindness in refreshing them,[3] but these savage barbarians, when they met with them (as after will appear) were readier to fill their sides full of arrows than otherwise. And for the season it was winter, and they that know the winters of that country know them to be sharp and violent, and subject to cruel and fierce storms, dangerous to travel to known places, much more to search an unknown coast. Besides, what could they see but a hideous and <u>desolate</u> wilderness, full of wild beasts and wild men—and what multitudes there might be of them they knew not. Neither could they, as it were, go up to the top of Pisgah[4] to view from this wilderness a more goodly country to feed their hopes; for which way soever they turned their eyes (save upward to the heavens) they could have little <u>solace</u> or content in respect of any outward objects. For summer being done, all things stand upon them with a weatherbeaten face, and the whole country, full of woods and thickets, represented a wild and savage <u>hue</u>. If they looked behind them, there was the mighty ocean which they had passed and was now as a main bar and gulf to separate them from all the civil parts of the world. . . .

## THE FIRST ENCOUNTER

Being thus arrived at Cape Cod the 11th of November, and necessity calling them to look out a place for habitation (as well as the master's and mariners' importunity); they having brought a large shallop[5] with them out of England, stowed in quarters in the ship, they now got her out and set their carpenters to work to trim her up; but being much bruised and shattered in the ship with foul weather, they saw she would be long in mending. Whereupon a few of them tendered themselves to go by land and discover those nearest places, whilst the shallop was in mending; . . .

After this, the shallop being got ready, they set out again for the better discovery of this place, and the master of the ship desired to go himself. So there went some thirty men but found it to be no harbor for ships but only for boats. There was also found two of their [the Indians'] houses covered with mats, and sundry of their implements in them, but the people were run away and could not be seen. Also there was found more of their corn and of their beans of various colors; the corn and beans they [the English] brought away, purposing to give them [the Indians] full satisfaction when they should meet with any of them, as, about some six months afterward they did, to their good content.[6]

And here is to be noted a special <u>providence</u> of God, and a great mercy to this poor people, that here they got seed to plant them corn the next year, or else they might have starved, for they had none nor any likelihood to get any till

---

2. **succor** (sŭk′ər): help; relief.

3. **It is . . . refreshing them:** a reference to the biblical account of the courteous reception of Paul and his companions by the inhabitants of Malta (Acts 27:41–28:2).

4. **Pisgah** (pĭz′gə): the mountain from whose peak Moses saw the Promised Land (Deuteronomy 34:1–4).

5. **shallop** (shăl′əp): an open boat usually used in shallow waters.

6. **purposing . . . content:** intending to repay the Nauset Indians whose corn and beans they took, as they in fact did, to the Indians' satisfaction, six months later.

WORDS TO KNOW

**desolate** (dĕs′ə-lĭt) *adj.* without inhabitants; barren
**solace** (sŏl′ĭs) *n.* comfort in sorrow or distress
**hue** (hyōō) *n.* appearance; color
**providence** (prŏv′ĭ-dəns) *n.* an instance of divine care or guidance

83

## Grammar

### SENTENCE FRAGMENTS

**Instruction** A sentence fragment is a group of words that does not express a complete thought. A sentence fragment might lack a subject, a predicate, or both. You can correct a sentence fragment by adding the missing element to complete the thought. When a fragment is a phrase or a subordinate clause, you can often connect it to a complete sentence by simply changing the punctuation. Write the following items on the chalkboard. Then ask students to explain how any sentence fragments might be corrected.

**Practice** In 1620. Pilgrims arrived in what is now Massachusetts. (*In 1620, Pilgrims arrived in what is now Massachusetts.*)
The Pilgrims stepped off their ship. Did not expect to be in such a wilderness. Even the leaders. (*The Pilgrims stepped off their ship. They did not expect to be in such a wilderness. Even the leaders were surprised and frightened.*)

 Use **Grammar Transparencies and Copymasters**, p. 107.

 Use McDougal Littell's **Language Network**, Chapter 3, for more instruction and practice in sentence fragments.

### Literary Analysis | PRIMARY SOURCES

**A** How does William Bradford interpret the Pilgrims' discovery of Native Americans' corn and beans? What does this tell you about his beliefs and feelings?

**Possible Response:** He believes that God led them to find the food in order to save them from starving. Bradford believes that God plays an active role in the Pilgrims' daily lives. This belief creates a feeling of intimacy, trust, and love between the Pilgrims and their God.

### Reading Skills and Strategies: TAKING NOTES

**B** Explain to students the importance of taking notes as they read important sections of challenging texts. Note-taking can help them organize and remember important details. Have students make notes about the exploring party's encounter with Native Americans. What are some important details in this scene?

**Possible Response:** Students might jot down the chain of events, how the exploring party reacted, and Bradford's descriptive details.

*View of Plymouth* (1627), Cal Sachs. American Heritage Picture Collection, New York.

the season had been past, as the sequel did manifest. Neither is it likely they had had this, if the first voyage had not been made, for the ground was now all covered with snow and hard **A** frozen; but the Lord is never wanting unto His in their greatest needs; let His holy name have all the praise.

The month of November being spent in these affairs, and much foul weather falling in, the 6th of December they sent out their shallop again with ten of their principal men and some **1** seamen, upon further discovery, intending to circulate that deep bay of Cape Cod. The weather was very cold and it froze so hard as the spray of the sea lighting on their coats, they were as if they had been glazed. . . . [The next night

they landed and] made them a barricado[7] as usually they did every night, with logs, stakes, and thick pine boughs, the height of a man, leaving it open to leeward,[8] partly to shelter **2** them from the cold and wind (making their fire in the middle and lying round about it) and partly to defend them from any sudden assaults **3** of the savages, if they should surround them; so being very weary, they betook them to rest. But about midnight they heard a hideous and great cry, and their <u>sentinel</u> called "Arm! arm!" So they bestirred them and stood to their arms and

---

7. **barricado** (băr´ĭ-kä´dō): a barrier for defense.
8. **to leeward** (lē´wərd): on the side sheltered from the wind.

| WORDS TO KNOW | **sentinel** (sĕn´tə-nəl) *n.* a guard |
|---|---|

84

---

**Viewing and Representing**

### *View of Plymouth, 1627* by Cal Sachs

#### ART APPRECIATION

**Instruction** This panoramic view of the colony some seven years after its founding shows houses crowded close together and surrounded by a palisade of wooden pilings.

**Interpretation** Describe this artist's depiction of Plymouth colony and ask students the following questions. What does this image help you understand about the colony?

**Possible Response:** The settlement was small and abutted the sea. People lived close together within the confines of sturdy protective walls. What evidence do you see that the colony was thriving and well protected?

**Possible Response:** The colony seems organized and tidy. It is protected on all sides by walls and at one end by guns and cannons.

shot off a couple of muskets, and then the noise ceased. They concluded it was a company of wolves or such like wild beasts, for one of the seamen told them he had often heard such a noise in Newfoundland.

So they rested till about five of the clock in the morning; for the tide, and their purpose to go from thence, made them be stirring betimes. So after prayer they prepared for breakfast, and it being day dawning it was thought best to be carrying things down to the boat. But some said it was not best to carry the arms down, others said they would be the readier, for they had lapped them up in their coats from the dew; but some three or four would not carry theirs till they went themselves. Yet as it fell out, the water being not high enough, they laid them down on the bank side and came up to breakfast.

But presently, all on the sudden, they heard a great and strange cry, which they knew to be the same voices they heard in the night, though they varied their notes; and one of their company being abroad came running in and cried, "Men, Indians! Indians!" And withal, their arrows came flying amongst them. Their men ran with all speed to recover their arms, as by the good providence of God they did. In the meantime, of those that were there ready, two muskets were discharged at them, and two more stood ready in the entrance of their rendezvous[9] but were commanded not to shoot till they could take full aim at them. And the other two charged again with all speed, for there were only four had arms there, and defended the barricado, which was first assaulted. The cry of the Indians was dreadful, especially when they [the Indians] saw their men [the English] run out of the rendezvous toward the shallop to recover their arms, the Indians wheeling about upon them. But some running out with coats of mail on, and cutlasses[10] in their hands, they [the English] soon got their arms and let fly amongst them [the Indians] and quickly stopped their violence. . . .

Thus it pleased God to vanquish their enemies and give them deliverance; and by His special providence so to dispose that not any one of them were either hurt or hit, though their arrows came close by them and on every side [of] them; and sundry of their coats, which hung up in the barricado, were shot through and through. Afterwards they gave God solemn thanks and praise for their deliverance, and gathered up a bundle of their arrows and sent them into England afterward by the master of the ship, and called that place the First Encounter. . . .

## THE STARVING TIME

But that which was most sad and lamentable was, that in two or three months' time half of their company died, especially in January and February, being the depth of winter, and wanting houses and other comforts; being infected with the scurvy[11] and other diseases which this long voyage and their inaccommodate condition had brought upon them. So as there died some times two or three of a day in the foresaid time, that of 100 and odd persons, scarce fifty remained. And of these, in the time of most distress, there was but six or seven sound persons who to their great commendations, be it spoken, spared no pains night nor day, but with abundance of toil and hazard of their own health fetched them wood, made them fires, dressed them meat, made their beds, washed their loathsome clothes, clothed and unclothed them. . . . In a word, did all the homely and necessary offices for them which dainty and queasy stomachs cannot endure to hear named; and all this willingly and cheerfully, without any grudging in the least, showing herein their true love unto their friends

---

9. **rendezvous** (rän'dā-vōō'): a gathering place; here used to denote the Pilgrims' encampment.

10. **coats of mail . . . and cutlasses:** armor made of joined metal links, and short curved swords.

11. **scurvy** (skûr'vē): a disease caused by lack of vitamin C.

WORDS
TO
KNOW    **vanquish** (văng'kwĭsh) v. to defeat in battle

85

B

## Speaking and Listening

**ORAL HISTORY**

**Instruction** Family or community memories, collected via tape-recorded interviews, are important sources of historical information. For example, in the *Foxfire Journals*, the students of Rabun County High School in Georgia published oral histories collected from the people of the Appalachians. Have students research their own family history—including that of adoptive parents or guardians—interviewing parents and older relatives to establish when, where, and why they came to this country. Before conducting their interviews, stu-

dents can get together in small groups to brainstorm a list of questions to ask.
**Present** After students have completed their research, have volunteers deliver five-minute oral reports to the class. Have the listeners evaluate the speakers' presentations. After each report, invite students to comment about the most interesting aspects of what they have heard. Then ask students to discuss why keeping a family's history and traditions alive is a worthwhile activity.

**BLOCK SCHEDULING** This activity is particularly well-suited for longer class periods.

**Literary Analysis: CHARACTERIZATION**

**A** Characterization is a technique a writer uses to create and develop a character. Ask students what methods Bradford uses to characterize the heroic colonists who helped the sick.

**Possible Response:** the characters' actions; the narrator's direct comments; the feelings of other characters

**Literary Analysis** | PRIMARY SOURCES |

**B** Because Bradford observed the events he narrates here, his report is considered a primary source. His use of third person allows the reader to forget that Bradford himself was one of the Pilgrims. To illustrate this point, you might have students read this paragraph aloud sentence by sentence, substituting *we, us,* and *our* for the appropriate third-person pronouns.

**Active Reading:** | SUMMARIZING |

**C** Ask students to summarize how the Pilgrims' relationship with Native Americans changed. Remind them to include the main ideas and important details.

**Possible Response:** An English-speaking Native American named Samoset visited the colonists. He shared important information with them and brought them into contact with other Native Americans. As a result of his visit, the Pilgrims began to enjoy more peaceful relations with the Native Americans. They even developed a peace agreement with Massasoit. Squanto, a Native American who stayed with the Pilgrims for years, taught them how to plant and fish and served as an interpreter.

and brethren; a rare example and worthy to be remembered. Two of these seven were Mr. William Brewster, their reverend Elder, and Myles Standish, their Captain and military commander, unto whom myself and many others were much beholden in our low and sick condition. And yet the Lord so upheld these persons as in this general calamity they were not at all infected either with sickness or lameness. . . .

## INDIAN RELATIONS

All this while the Indians came skulking about them, and would sometimes show themselves aloof off, but when any approached near them, they would run away; and once they [the Indians] stole away their [the colonists'] tools where they had been at work and were gone to dinner. But about the 16th of March, a certain Indian came boldly amongst them and spoke to them in broken English, which they could well understand but marveled at it. At length they understood by discourse with him, that he was not of these parts, but belonged to the eastern parts where some English ships came to fish, with whom he was acquainted and could name sundry of them by their names, amongst whom he had got his language. He became profitable to them in acquainting them with many things concerning the state of the country in the east parts where he lived, which was afterwards profitable unto them; as also of the people here, of their names, number and strength, of their situation and distance from this place, and who was chief amongst them. His name was Samoset. He told them also of another Indian whose name was Squanto, a native of this place, who had been in England and could speak better English than himself.

Being, after some time of entertainment and gifts dismissed, a while after he came again, and five more with him, and they brought again all the tools that were stolen away before, and made way for the coming of their great Sachem,[12] called Massasoit. Who, about four or five days after, came with the chief of his friends and other attendance, with the aforesaid Squanto. With whom, after friendly entertainment and some gifts given him, they made a peace with him (which hath now continued this 24 years) in these terms:

**1.** That neither he nor any of his should injure or do hurt to any of their people.

**2.** That if any of his did hurt to any of theirs, he should send the offender, that they might punish him.

**3.** That if anything were taken away from any of theirs, he should cause it to be restored; and they should do the like to his.

**4.** If any did unjustly war against him, they would aid him; if any did war against them, he should aid them.

**5.** He should send to his neighbors confederates to certify them of this, that they might not wrong them, but might be likewise comprised in the conditions of peace.[13]

**6.** That when their men came to them, they should leave their bows and arrows behind them.

After these things he returned to his place called Sowams,[14] some 40 miles from this place, but Squanto continued with them and was their interpreter and was a special instrument sent of God for their good beyond their expectation. He directed them how to set their corn, where to take fish, and to procure other commodities, and was also their pilot to bring them to unknown places for their profit, and never left them till he died.

---

12. **Sachem** (sā′chəm): chief.

13. **He should . . . peace:** Massasoit was to send representatives to inform other tribes of the compact with the Pilgrims so other tribes might also keep peace with them.

14. **Sowams** (sō′ämz): near the site of present-day Barrington, Rhode Island.

| WORDS | **aloof** (ə-lōōf′) *adj.* distant |
| TO | **procure** (prō-kyŏŏr′) *v.* to get by special effort; obtain |
| KNOW | **commodity** (kə-mŏd′ĭ-tē) *n.* something useful; an article of commerce |

86

**Cross Curricular Link** **Social Studies**

**SQUANTO** Squanto, also known as Tisquantum, was born a member of the Pawtuxet tribe, which occupied lands in what is today Massachusetts and Rhode Island. In 1615 he and other Native Americans were captured by explorer Captain Thomas Hunt, brought to the Mediterranean port of Malaga, Spain, and sold into slavery. Squanto was able to escape to England, where he spent two years. In 1619 he returned to North America and found that disease had killed every member of his tribe. Squanto died on Cape Cod in 1622.

The Bettmann Archive, New York.

## Customizing Instruction

**Students Acquiring English**

**1** Have students work with partners to paraphrase one of the numbered items in the peace treaty. Help them to clarify to whom the pronouns *he, his, they,* and *them* refer in these sentences.

**Less Proficient Readers**

**2** Ask students how the Native Americans helped the Pilgrims to survive.

**Answer:** Squanto taught them how to find and grow food; a local tribe made a peace treaty with them.

**3** Have students summarize how the Pilgrims' lives in America have changed by the end of the selection.

**Possible Responses:** They are able to get enough food by growing corn, hunting, and fishing; they have established good relations with local Native Americans; they are no longer sick; they can write back to friends in England and say that they are doing well.

## FIRST THANKSGIVING

They began now to gather in the small harvest they had, and to fit up their houses and dwellings against winter, being all well recovered in health and strength and had all things in good plenty. For as some were thus employed in affairs abroad, others were exercised in fishing, about cod and bass and other fish, of which they took good store, of which every family had their portion. All the summer there was no want; and now began to come in store of fowl, as winter approached, of which this place did abound when they came first (but afterward decreased by degrees). And besides waterfowl there was great store of wild turkeys, of which they took many, besides venison, etc. Besides they had about a peck[15] a meal a week to a person, or now since harvest, Indian corn to that proportion. Which made many afterwards write so largely of their plenty here to their friends in England, which **3** were not <u>feigned</u> but true reports. ❖

---

15. **peck:** a unit of measurement equal to eight dry quarts.

WORDS
TO
KNOW    **feigned** (fānd) *adj.* not real; pretended

**87**

---

☑ Assessment **Informal Assessment**

**PARALLEL ACCOUNT** You can informally assess your students' understanding of the selection by asking them to write a parallel account from the Native American perspective. Students can assume that the writer observed all the events in the selection and knew Samoset, Squanto, and Massasoit. Have students do this individually or in small groups, sharing the planning and writing.

**RUBRIC**

**3** **Full Accomplishment** Students create convincing stories that present all of the same events from the Native American perspective.

**2** **Substantial Accomplishment** Students represent most of the events.

**1** **Little or Partial Accomplishment** Students have difficulty creating stories and fail to include essential events.

## GUIDING STUDENT RESPONSE

## Connect to the Literature

**1. What Do You Think?**
Possible Response: The Pilgrims were brave people so committed to their religious beliefs that even harsh weather, danger, and starvation could not make them unfaithful.

**Comprehension Check**
- They saw a desolate wilderness full of dense, dark woods and thickets.
- They faced severe winter weather. The constant wind was wet and bitterly cold.
- They showed the Pilgrims how to plant corn, where to fish, and generally how to use the natural resources.

 Use Selection Quiz in **Unit One Resource Book,** p. 40.

## Think Critically

2. Encourage students to note whether their summaries were clear and interesting, containing only the main ideas and important details.

3. Possible Responses: The Pilgrims felt nature was something to be feared; they felt God observed everything they did and either punished or rewarded them for their deeds; they were afraid of the Native Americans but eventually appreciated their knowledge and willingness to help.

4. Possible Responses: Some students will say that the treaty was fair because it fostered a peaceful relationship and both sides promised to protect each other against attack. Others might say the treaty was not fair because it provided more protection for the Pilgrims than for the Wampanoag.

## Literary Analysis

**Primary Sources** Possible Response: Students may state that Bradford's purpose is to recount the key events in the history of the colony. He provides a third-person narrative with interpretive commentary. He assumes that the colonists are God's special people, divinely protected. Among his biases is the view that Native Americans are "savage barbarians."

**Review Conflict** Students may state that the conflicts in this excerpt are mostly external, as the Pilgrims struggle to establish a settlement in the wilderness.

## Connect to the Literature

**1. What Do You Think?**
What is your impression of the Pilgrims after reading these excerpts from *Of Plymouth Plantation?*

**Comprehension Check**
- How did the Pilgrims view the landscape of Cape Cod when they first arrived?
- What kind of weather did the Pilgrims face after they landed?
- How did the Native Americans help the Pilgrims survive?

## Think Critically

2. **ACTIVE READING** **SUMMARIZING** Share your section **summaries** from your **READER'S NOTEBOOK** with a partner. Do they include the most important information? Were all unnecessary details dropped?

3. On the basis of these excerpts, what conclusions can you draw about the Pilgrims' way of looking at the world?

 **THINK ABOUT**
- their attitude toward nature
- their attitude toward God
- their attitude toward Native Americans

4. Do you think the treaty between the Wampanoag and the Pilgrims was fair? Why or why not? Support your answers with references from the selection.

## Extend Interpretations

5. **What If?** What do you think might have happened if Squanto had not helped the Pilgrims? Explain your opinion, using evidence from the selection.

6. **Comparing Texts** Both *Of Plymouth Plantation* and *La Relación* describe Europeans' encounters with Native Americans. Compare the ways in which the Pilgrims and Cabeza de Vaca's men interacted with the Native Americans they met. What do you think accounts for any similarities or differences?

7. **Connect to Life** Religious persecution forced the Pilgrims to flee from England to Holland and later to settle in North America. Think of another group of people who faced persecution for their religious or political beliefs. Briefly explain what happened to them, and compare and contrast their experiences with the Pilgrims' ordeals.

## Literary Analysis

**PRIMARY SOURCES** **Primary sources,** such as diaries and personal histories, often reveal the beliefs and motives of the people involved in an historical event, their ability to overcome obstacles, and the distinctive features of time and place in which they lived. *Of Plymouth Plantation* provides a glimpse of the past through the eyes of William Bradford. As governor of the Plymouth colony and eyewitness to the events he describes, William Bradford is considered a reliable source of information.

**Paired Activity** Work with a partner to analyze *Of Plymouth Plantation* as a primary source. Consider Bradford's purpose (reason for writing), point of view (narrative perspective from which events are told), assumptions (preconceived ideas) and biases (personal prejudices). Make and fill in a chart like the one shown to record your analyses.

| Source | Purpose | Point of View | Assumptions | Biases |
|---|---|---|---|---|
| *Of Plymouth Plantation* | | | | |

**REVIEW** **CONFLICT** **Conflict,** as you remember, is a struggle between opposing forces. **Internal conflicts** are within a character; **external conflicts** pit a character against nature, society, or another character. What conflicts are described in this excerpt from *Of Plymouth Plantation.* Are they mostly internal or external?

## Extend Interpretations

**What If?** Most students will say that without the help of Squanto, the Pilgrims would not have adapted to the area as quickly and might not have survived. Evidence supporting this opinion includes the following details from the selection: The Pilgrims were unfamiliar with the land and not yet accustomed to the weather in the region. They feared the Native Americans, and this fear created an antagonistic relationship between the two groups. Squanto helped foster a peaceful relationship between the Pilgrims and the Native Americans. With the help and cooperation of Native Americans, the Pilgrims were able to fish, grow corn, and gain knowledge of their surroundings.

**Comparing Texts** Students should point out that unlike the armed Pilgrims, de Vaca's men were helpless and defenseless and could not risk antagonizing the Native Americans. Both groups, however, relied on the Native Americans' knowledge of and adaptation to the region. In their responses, students should consider what they know about the different historical contexts.

**Connect to Life** To help students effectively answer this question, you might hold a class brainstorming session focused on historical and current events. You might also give students a chance to use computer and library resources to research the topic.

## Writing Options

**1. Squanto's Diary** Imagine that you are Squanto. Write a diary entry that reveals why you helped the Pilgrims and chose to live with them.

**2. Eyewitness Account** How do you think the majority of the Wampanoags viewed the arrival and settlement of the Pilgrims? From the Native Americans' point of view, write an eyewitness account of any incident in this selection. Then place the account in your **Working Portfolio.**

**3. Interview Questions** If you could speak to one of the Pilgrims or Native Americans you have read about, what would you ask him or her? Write five interview questions that you might ask William Bradford, Samoset, or another person. Then write the answers that the person might give.

## Activities & Explorations

**1. Pilgrim Memorial** Design a memorial—such as a statue, monument, or historical marker—for the Pilgrims who died either aboard the *Mayflower* or during the first winter at Plymouth. Then work with classmates to display your memorial designs. **~ ART**

**2. Musical Soundtrack** Think about the mood conveyed by each of the excerpts from *Of Plymouth Plantation.* Then work with a partner to create and record a musical soundtrack that evokes these different moods. **~ MUSIC**

**3. Time Line** Create a time line, beginning in November 1620 and ending in March 1621, to show important events that happened after the Pilgrims reached Cape Cod. **~ HISTORY**

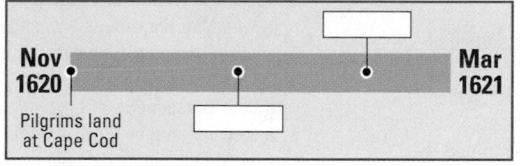

Nov 1620    Pilgrims land at Cape Cod    Mar 1621

## Inquiry & Research

**The Voyage of the Pilgrims** Find out more about the Pilgrims' voyage on the *Mayflower*. For example, to get a sense of how crowded the 102 passengers were, you might find estimates of the ship's dimensions, make an outline of the deck, and invite other classes to stand with you inside the outline. Learn how women and children fared on the journey by turning to the Related Reading on page 91.

## Art Connection

Look at the illustration of the Plymouth colony in 1627 on page 84. Notice where the Puritans set up their military fortification. Why do you think they had it so far inland instead of near the sea?

---

## Writing Options

**1. Squanto's Diary** Students' responses should reflect an understanding of Squanto's possible motivations. **To get students started on this assignment,** suggest that they freewrite for several minutes about possible reasons for Squanto's actions. Ask them to think about how a relationship with the Pilgrims might have been beneficial to him, and how he must have felt in his role.

**2. Eyewitness Account** Students' accounts should show an understanding of the events of the selection, as well as the ability to think about the events from the point of view of Native Americans. **To get students started on this assignment,** suggest that they make a chart of key events in the selection.

**3. Interview Questions** Students' questions should reflect an understanding of these characters' roles in the selection. **To get students started on this assignment,** have them create a character chart in which they record names and important details about key characters. Then have each student brainstorm a list of questions for the character that interests him or her the most.

## Activities & Explorations

**1. Pilgrim Memorial** Students should make a list of images and ideas that seem to reflect the Pilgrims' experience. These key details should be incorporated into their memorial designs. Students should recall memorials they have seen and appreciated, asking themselves why these memorials are impressive.

**2. Musical Soundtrack** Before searching for music, students might want to reread the excerpts aloud, thinking about the mood conveyed by each one.

**3. Time Line** Students might want to illustrate their time lines to make them more interesting. Invite students to share and compare their finished time lines.

## Art Connection

Possible Response: The Pilgrims felt they had to protect themselves from what lurked in the wilderness of their new land.

---

**Mini Lesson** ## Grammar

### RUN-ON SENTENCES

**Instruction** Remind students that a run-on sentence consists of two or more sentences incorrectly joined. A run-on sentence is confusing and unclear because a reader cannot tell where one idea ends and the next begins.

One way to correct a run-on sentence is to form two separate sentences by adding a period or other end punctuation after the first complete thought. If the ideas expressed in a run-on sentence are closely related, they can be combined to form one compound sentence.

Write the following run-on sentences on the chalkboard. Ask students to correct them.

The Pilgrims were joyful when they reached Cape Cod, they had been at sea for a long time. *(The Pilgrims were joyful when they reached Cape Cod. They had been at sea for a long time.)*

They wanted to feel immediately at home in the new area all they saw was wilderness. *(They wanted to feel immediately at home in the new area, but all they saw was wilderness.)*

Use **Grammar Transparencies and Copymasters,** p. 109.

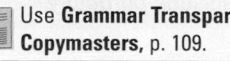
Use McDougal Littell's *Language Network,* Chapter 3, for more instruction in run-on sentences.

## Vocabulary in Action

1. vanquish
2. commodity
3. providence
4. aloof
5. sentinel
6. desolate
7. hue
8. solace
9. feigned
10. procure

## Vocabulary in Action

**EXERCISE A: MATCHING MEANINGS** Write the vocabulary word that most clearly relates to the situation expressed by each sentence below.

1. The Pilgrims were able to drive the hostile Indians away.

2. The Pilgrims brought with them some necessities, such as flour for baking bread.

3. The Pilgrims felt that God had helped the colony survive through the first harsh winter.

4. At first, the Indians were reluctant to have contact with the Pilgrims and so didn't come near them.

5. When the Pilgrims explored Cape Cod, some of the men kept watch while the others slept.

6. Vast stretches of seemingly uninhabitable wilderness greeted the Pilgrims.

7. In the fall, the leaves on the trees turned scarlet, orange, and golden yellow.

8. Squanto comforted the Pilgrims by befriending them and helping them learn about the new land.

9. Historians generally believe William Bradford's account and do not think he misrepresented anything.

10. Fortunately, after the first winter the Pilgrims were able to get what they needed to survive by hunting and farming.

**EXERCISE B:** With a small group of classmates, play a game of charades, acting out the words *desolate, sentinel, vanquish, aloof,* and *feigned.*

### Building Vocabulary

For an in-depth lesson on word connotation and denotation, see page 908.

| WORDS TO KNOW | | | | |
|---|---|---|---|---|
| | aloof | feigned | providence | vanquish |
| | commodity | hue | sentinel | |
| | desolate | procure | solace | |

## William Bradford

### 1590–1657

**Other Works**
*Dialogues*

**Religious Rebel** When the Pilgrims settled at Plymouth, William Bradford was 30 years old and had already endured grave hardship. Orphaned as a young child, he ran off to join an outlawed religious group when he was 12. He joined the Separatists at the age of 16 and two years later followed them to Holland. In 1620, Bradford was among the Separatists and non-Separatists who set sail on the *Mayflower* to start a colony in North America. Bradford likely helped write the Mayflower Compact, the agreement that set up the government of the colony.

**Political Leader** Bradford joined the initial expeditions to explore Cape Cod but returned from his exploration to find that his young wife, Dorothy May, had drowned while the *Mayflower* was moored in Provincetown Harbor. Despite his difficulties, Bradford kept his faith in God and in the struggling colony. In the spring of 1621, he was elected governor, a post he held for 30 years. Under his leadership, the colony grew into a thriving community.

**Scholar and Historian** Largely self-taught, Bradford read widely in English, as well as in Dutch, French, Greek, and Hebrew. He wrote the first ten chapters of his history of the Separatists in 1630, beginning with their persecution in England and concluding with their landing in North America in 1620. He continued to work on *Of Plymouth Plantation* over the next 17 years, but his 500-page manuscript remained unpublished until 1856.

## Author Activity

**Profiles in Courage** Historian Samuel Eliot Morison described *Of Plymouth Plantation* as "a story of simple people inspired by an ardent faith to a dauntless courage in danger, a resourcefulness in dealing with new problems . . . ." Read additional selections from *Of Plymouth Plantation,* and find examples that support Morison's claim.

## Teaching Options

 **Vocabulary Strategy**

**RESEARCHING WORD ORIGINS** *PURITAN*
**Instruction** Tell students that the word *Puritan* is based on the Latin root *puritas,* which means "purity." In the 17th century, the Puritans, a sect in the Church of England, sought to purify their church by removing all traces of the Roman Catholic rite and the practice of elaborately decorating places of worship. They wanted to practice a form of Christianity that they felt was pure. Words with similar origins include *purgatory, purge, purify,* and *purist.*

**Practice** Have students work in pairs to define *purgatory, purge, purify,* and *purist.* Ask them to use each word in a sentence. Tell students a knowledge of the root word *puritas* can help them remember the meanings of these words.

 Use **Vocabulary Transparencies and Copymasters,** p. 22.

*from*

# Women and Children First: The Mayflower Pilgrims

### by Alicia Crane Williams

When the ship *Mayflower* sailed from Plymouth, England, in September 1620 on her voyage into history, she carried 102 passengers, of which nearly half were women and children. Eighteen of the passengers were wives accompanying their husbands to the New World; with them they brought thirty-one children ranging in age from a nursing infant to teenagers. In addition, at least three of the women were pregnant during the voyage. . . .

 Elizabeth Hopkins gave birth to her son Occanus at sea while also mothering her two-year-old daughter Damaris and her stepchildren, thirteen-year-old Constance and ten-year-old Giles. Miraculously, all survived the voyage and the first winter, though Oceanus and Damaris did not live to adulthood. Five more children eventually were born to the Hopkinses in this inhospitable new land. . . .

In early December 1620, Susanna White gave birth to her son Peregrine on board the *Mayflower* while it was anchored in the shelter of Cape Cod. Two months later her husband William died, leaving her with the baby and their five-year-old son Resolved. In May, Susanna married Edward Winslow, whose first wife had died during the winter. Susanna and Edward's marriage, the first performed in the new colony, produced five children, though only two survived their childhoods. Resolved and Peregrine lived to adulthood, married women of the colony, and fathered fifteen children between them.

Dorothy Bradford, William's wife, left behind her only child, two-year-old John, when she accompanied her husband to the New World. She fell overboard from the *Mayflower*, anchored near Cape Cod, while William was away searching for a settlement site. Although Bradford and his contemporaries recorded the event as accidental, rumors persist to the present day that Dorothy actually committed suicide. . . .

## Reading for Information

Curious about the past? Much of our knowledge about past events comes from primary and secondary sources.

- **Primary Source** William Bradford's *Of Plymouth Plantation* is a primary source. It offers firsthand information on the Pilgrims.

- **Secondary Source** In 1993, genealogist Alicia Crane Williams wrote on the same topic. Unlike Bradford, however, Williams did not experience the events she describes. Her article is a secondary source.

**PRIMARY AND SECONDARY SOURCES** Secondary sources are more likely than primary sources to present a longer view of the history of events. To help you get the most from Williams's article, use these suggestions and activities:

❶ **Comparing Sources** Bradford himself would have known most of the details that Williams provides about Elizabeth and her children. What information does Williams give that Bradford may not have known?

❷ Williams has chosen to focus on the women and children among the Pilgrims. What can you infer about her choice, based on the details she provides?

## Objectives
- read and analyze secondary sources
- read to be informed about the women and children who traveled on the Mayflower
- evaluate the credibility of information sources including how the writer's motivation may affect that credibility
- compare and contrast the elements of primary and secondary source articles

## Further Background
The author of this article, Alicia Crane Williams, is a descendant of John and Priscilla Alden, two passengers featured at the end of her article.

The name of Elizabeth Hopkins's son born at sea, "Oceanus" (in Greek mythology, the river that followed around the earth), sounds highly unusual today but is an example of the common practice of association in the naming of Puritan children in the 17th century.

## Connecting to the Literature
This article expands on the history of the pilgrims told by William Bradford in "Of Plymouth Plantation." Together, these readings give a more complete picture of the hardships the pilgrims encountered in the New World.

## Reading for Information
As you read through this article with students, have them use the material in the right-hand column as a guide to reading secondary and primary sources. The following are possible responses to the four questions.

**PRIMARY AND SECONDARY SOURCES**
**1. Comparing Sources**
**Possible Response:** Bradford may not have known that Oceanus and Damaris died before reaching adulthood. Since Bradford died in 1657, he definitely never knew about the grandchildren and great-grandchildren of other Mayflower pilgrims as Williams does.
**2.** Students should support their inferences with text evidence.

**Possible Response:** From her concentration on births and deaths, we can infer that Williams is interested in the genealogy of the *Mayflower* pilgrims. From her focus on only women and children, we can infer that she wants to get the neglected history of these equally courageous pilgrims on record.

**3.** Student response should evaluate the credibility of the information sources, including how the writer's motivation may affect that credibility. **Possible Response:** Williams uses Bradford's words to give credibility to her own information about the Billingtons. By quoting from Bradford, an eyewitness to the behavior of the Billingtons, Williams has support for her assertion that John Billington was a troublemaker.

**4. Possible Response:** Bradford's account of his experiences in *Of Plymouth Plantation* is colored by his emotions, which were an integral part of the events about which he writes. The tone of his account is emotional as he tries to share the feelings of the pilgrims through his descriptions of their experiences. Williams's account is based mainly on research gathered from sources such as Bradford's or from other secondary sources. She is far removed from the emotions involved in the births, deaths, and other hardships that made up the lives of the pilgrims.

## COMPARING TEXTS
Possible Response: Both accounts emphasize how difficult and hazardous life was for the pilgrims. Life on Plymouth Plantation obviously required great courage, fortitude, and ingenuity. Bradford's description and commentary highlight the dangers of the life, and Williams's factual accounting of early deaths provides concrete proof of the precariousness of life. Bradford's account is highly involving because it is in the form of a story. Bradford's account could be considered more moving because of the emotions involved in his retelling of his experiences, but Williams's account is also moving because of her anecdotal information and her detailing of the fate of various individuals such as Dorothy Bradford, John Billington, and Priscilla Mullins.

**Editor's Note:** With the permission of the copyright holder, this selection was excerpted from a longer work. Material was deleted to shorten and focus the selection.

Forty-one-year-old Elinor Billington and her family numbered among the "Strangers" aboard the *Mayflower*. Bradford called the Billingtons "one of the profanest families among us" and could not imagine how they "shuffled into [our] company." John Billington constantly quarreled with Bradford and other leaders and kept company with troublemakers. In 1630 he was convicted of murder, gaining the distinction of being the first person executed by hanging in the New World.

The Billingtons' two sons—John, sixteen years old, and Francis, some years younger—apparently terrorized the other passengers throughout the voyage. Francis endangered the ship by firing his father's fowling piece, igniting a fire that almost spread to nearby barrels of gunpowder. And young John got lost in the woods in May 1621, only to be rescued by Indians and returned to a ten-man search party sent from the colony. The troublesome youth died a few years later, but Francis survived to marry and father nine children.

Priscilla Mullins—today probably the best-known of all the *Mayflower* colonists—would have been about sixteen years old when she supposedly attracted the simultaneous attention of friends John Alden, a cooper hired by the company in Southampton, and Miles Standish, a man of military experience who looked after the colony's defense. Priscilla had arrived in New England with her parents, William and Alice, and her brother Joseph, all of whom perished during that first winter. Captain Standish, who was one of only two people not afflicted with the illness that took so many lives, had lost his wife Rose to the epidemic.

Henry Wadsworth Longfellow's poem *The Courtship of Miles Standish* immortalized the legend of how Standish asked Alden to carry his marriage proposal to Priscilla, who replied, "Why don't you speak for yourself, John?" Married soon after, John and Priscilla had ten children, who in turn produced sixty-nine grandchildren and nearly four hundred great-grandchildren. Miles Standish found a bride elsewhere and fathered seven children.

**3** The Billingtons, Williams quotes from Bradford, are "one of the profanest families among us." What does the quotation from Bradford's account add to Williams's own account of the Billington family?

**4** Bradford's narrative comes alive with interpretive commentary based on his observations of events, while Williams's is an objective, factual narrative. How would you account for the differences in tone between the two narratives?

**Comparing Texts** After reading Bradford's account and Williams's narrative, what is your reaction to the experiences of the Plymouth colonists? Did you find one of the accounts more informative than the other? more interesting? more moving? Record your responses.

## *from* The Interesting Narrative of the Life of Olaudah Equiano

*Slave Narrative by* OLAUDAH EQUIANO (ō-lou′də ĕk′wē-än′ō)

Detail of *The Slave Ship* (1956), Robert Riggs.

## Build Background

**The Middle Passage** The expansion of European colonies in North and South America led to the growth of the transatlantic slave trade. Large plantations needed great numbers of workers to produce sugar, tobacco, and cotton for sale in Europe. Following a triangular route, traders carried manufactured goods (such as cloth and guns) from Europe to Africa, slaves from Africa to the Americas, and raw materials from the Americas to Europe.

Historians estimate that between 10 million and 20 million Africans were enslaved to work in the Americas. During the Middle Passage, the horrific two-month voyage from Africa to the West Indies, millions of enslaved Africans died from the effects of overcrowding, bad food, harsh treatment, disease, and despair. Chained in the dark, airless holds of slave ships, the Africans lay packed side by side. They were allowed on deck only briefly. Olaudah Equiano was one of those who survived the Middle Passage. In the following excerpts, he tells what happened when, as a child, he was shipped to the island of Barbados in the West Indies.

**WORDS TO KNOW** Vocabulary Preview

| | | |
|---|---|---|
| anguish | copious | pestilential |
| apprehension | countenance | stench |
| avarice | nominal | wretched |
| consternation | | |

## Focus Your Reading

**LITERARY ANALYSIS** SLAVE NARRATIVES

**Slave narratives** are autobiographical accounts by persons who suffered the horrors of slavery. Equiano's book was one of the earliest American slave narratives. As you read, use your imagination to recreate the horrors he described.

**ACTIVE READING** ANALYZING DETAILS

**Descriptive details** in pieces of writing help readers to imagine and understand characters' experiences. In this selection, Olaudah Equiano uses **sensory details**— ones that appeal to the five senses—to bring to life his first encounter with white men and his ordeal aboard a slave ship.

📖 **READER'S NOTEBOOK** As you read, use a chart similar to the one shown to jot down the sensory details that make his experience come alive for you.

| Sensory Details |
|---|
| **Hearing:** shrieks of the women |
| **Sight:** |
| **Taste:** |
| **Smell:** |
| **Touch:** |

**Reading Skills and Strategies: PREVIEW**

Explain that Olaudah Equiano is an adult looking back on his experience of being kidnapped and sold into slavery as a young boy.

**Active Reading:** ANALYZING DETAILS

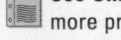 Remind students that sensory details help make writing vibrant and real to readers. Ask students to cite some of the details in this passage.

**Possible Response:** Students may cite details relating to the smell below deck, the sound of crying, Equiano's loss of appetite, and his being flogged.

What do these details tell about the ship's environment and Equiano's experience?

**Possible Response:** His experience is extremely frightening and miserable. The ship is a violent, filthy, and horrid place.

Use **Unit One Resource Book,** p. 42 for more practice.

**Literary Analysis** SLAVE NARRATIVES

 Remind students that slave narratives are autobiographical accounts. People who wrote them experienced the horrors of slavery and sought to share their experiences with readers. Point out that Equiano's slave narrative contains direct, firsthand information about the slave trade. Ask students how Equiano's involvement may make his description different from that of an outsider.

**Possible Responses:** more vivid, more emotional, more personal

Use **Unit One Resource Book,** p. 43 for more practice.

---

*from*

# The INTERESTING NARRATIVE *of the* Life of OLAUDAH EQUIANO

### OLAUDAH EQUIANO

*When Olaudah Equiano was eleven years old, he and his sister were kidnapped while the adults in his village were working in the fields. After being forced to travel for several days, Equiano and his sister were separated. For the next six or seven months, Equiano was sold to several African masters in different countries. He was eventually taken to the west coast of Africa and carried aboard a slave ship bound for the West Indies.*

THE FIRST OBJECT WHICH SALUTED MY EYES WHEN I ARRIVED ON THE COAST, WAS THE SEA, AND A SLAVE SHIP, WHICH WAS THEN RIDING AT ANCHOR, AND WAITING FOR ITS CARGO. THESE filled me with astonishment, which was soon converted into terror, when I was carried on board. I was immediately handled, and tossed up to see if I were sound, by some of the crew; and I was now persuaded that I had gotten into a world of bad spirits, and that they were going to kill me. Their complexions, too, differing so much from ours, their long hair, and the language they spoke (which was very different from any I had ever heard), united to confirm me in this belief. Indeed, such were the horrors of my views and fears at the moment, that, if ten thousand worlds had been my own, I would have freely parted with them all to have exchanged my condition with that of the meanest slave in my own country. When I looked round the ship too, and saw a large furnace of copper boiling, and a multitude of black people of every description chained together, every one of their countenances expressing dejection and sorrow, I no longer doubted of my fate; and, quite overpowered with horror and anguish, I fell motionless on the deck and fainted. When I recovered a little, I found some black people about me, who I believed were some of those who had brought me on board, and had been receiving their pay; they talked to me in order to cheer me, but all in vain. I asked them if we were not to be eaten by those white men with horrible looks, red faces, and long hair. They told me I was not, and one of the crew brought me a small portion of spirituous liquor in a wine glass; but, being afraid of him, I would not take it out of his hand. One of the blacks, therefore, took it from him and gave it to me, and I took a little down my palate, which, instead of reviving me, as they thought it would, threw me into the greatest consternation at the strange feeling it produced, having never tasted any such liquor before. Soon after this, the blacks who brought me on board went off, and left me abandoned to despair.

WORDS TO KNOW
**anguish** (ăng′gwĭsh) *n.* agonizing physical or mental pain
**consternation** (kŏn′stər-nā′shən) *n.* a state of paralyzing dismay; fear

94

---

## Teaching Options

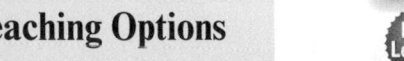 **Preteaching Vocabulary**

**USING CONTEXT CLUES AND REFERENCE MATERIALS**
Call students' attention to the list of WORDS TO KNOW. Remind them that reference materials such as glossaries, dictionaries, and thesauruses can help them find precise meanings for words. When they look up a word in a dictionary, they will sometimes find several listed meanings. The context in which a word is used determines which meaning is appropriate. Demonstrate the strategy for them using the following model.

**Model Sentence**
He was the nominal mayor, but others did more than he did to lead and improve the town.

**Instruction**
- Write the model sentence on the chalkboard.
- Ask a volunteer to look up the word *nominal* in a dictionary and read the definitions aloud. Write these definitions on the chalkboard.
- Have students determine which is the best definition of the word in the context of the model sentence.
- Have students work in cooperative groups to use the same process with each of the Words to Know.

 Use **Unit One Resource Book,** p. 44 for additional support.

I now saw myself deprived of all chance of returning to my native country, or even the least glimpse of hope of gaining the shore, which I now considered as friendly; and I even wished for my former slavery in preference to my present situation, which was filled with horrors of every kind, still heightened by my ignorance of what I was to undergo. I was not long suffered to indulge my grief; I was soon put down under the decks, and there I received such a salutation in my nostrils as I had never experienced in my life; so that, with the loathsomeness of the <u>stench</u>, and crying together, I became so sick and low that I was not able to eat, nor had I the least desire to taste anything. I now wished for the last friend, death, to relieve me; but soon, to my grief, two of the white men offered me eatables; and, on my refusing to eat, one of them held me fast by the hands, and laid me across, I think, the windlass,[1] and tied my feet, while the other flogged[2] me severely. I had never experienced anything of this kind before, and, although not being used to the water, I naturally feared that element the first time I saw it, yet, nevertheless, could I have got over the nettings,[3] I would have jumped over the side, but I could not; and besides, the crew used to watch us very closely who were not chained down to the decks, lest we should leap into the water; and I have seen some of these poor African prisoners most severely cut, for attempting to do so, and hourly whipped for not eating. This indeed was often the case with myself. In a little time after, amongst the poor chained men, I found some of my own nation, which in a small degree gave ease to my mind. I inquired of these what was to be done with us? They gave me to understand, we were to be carried to these white people's country to work for them. I then was a little revived, and thought, if it were no worse than working, my situation was not so desperate; but still I feared I should be put to death, the white people looked and acted, as I thought, in so

savage a manner; for I had never seen among any people such instances of brutal cruelty; and this not only shown towards us blacks, but also to some of the whites themselves. One white man in particular I saw, when we were permitted to be on deck, flogged so unmercifully with a large rope near the foremast,[4] that he died in consequence of it; and they tossed him over the side as they would have done a brute. This made me fear these people the more; and I expected nothing less than to be treated in the same manner. I could not help expressing my fears and <u>apprehensions</u> to some of my countrymen; I asked them if these people had no country, but lived in this hollow place (the ship)? They told me they did not, but came from a distant one. "Then," said I, "how comes it in all our country  we never heard of them?" They told me because they lived so very far off. I then asked where were their women? had they any like themselves? I was told they had. "And why," said I, "do we not see them?" They answered, because they were left behind. I asked how the vessel could go? They told me they could not tell; but that there was cloth put upon the masts by the help of the ropes I saw, and then the vessel went on; and the white men had some spell or magic they put in the water when they liked, in order to stop the vessel. I was exceedingly amazed at this account, and really thought they were spirits. I therefore wished much to be from amongst them, for I expected they would sacrifice me; but my wishes were vain—for we were so quartered that it was impossible for any of us to make our escape. . . .

---

1. **windlass** (wĭnd'ləs): a device for raising and lowering a ship's anchor.

2. **flogged:** beat severely with a whip or rod.

3. **nettings:** networks of small ropes on the sides of a ship used for various purposes, such as to prevent boarding or to stow sails. On slave ships, the nettings helped keep slaves from jumping overboard.

4. **foremast** (fôr'məst): the mast (tall pole that supports sails and rigging) nearest the forward end of a sailing ship.

WORDS
TO
KNOW
**stench** (stĕnch) *n.* a strong, foul odor
**apprehension** (ăp'rĭ-hĕn'shən) *n.* a suspicion of future evil; dread

95

## Mini Lesson **Grammar**

**STRUCTURE: COMPOUND SENTENCES**
**Instruction** Compound sentences consist of two or more independent clauses. In a compound sentence, the independent clauses may be joined by a comma and a coordinating conjunction, by a semicolon, or by a conjunctive adverb or transition followed by a comma. Write the following sentence pairs on the chalkboard. Ask students to combine each pair to make a compound sentence.
Equiano had never seen water before. He was fearful of the water. *(Equiano had never seen water before, so he was fearful of the water.)*

Some slaves were able to come up from below deck. Breathing fresh air was a welcome relief. *(Some slaves were able to come up from below deck; breathing fresh air was a welcome relief.)*

**Exercises** Have students combine each of the following sentence pairs to form compound sentences.
1. Equiano was a young boy. He had already lived through many unfortunate experiences. *(Equiano was a young boy, but he had already lived through many unfortunate experiences.)*

2. Many slaves had trouble eating while on the ship. The ship's unsanitary conditions made food unappealing. *(Many slaves had trouble eating while on the ship; the ship's unsanitary conditions made food unappealing.)*

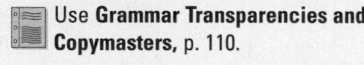

Use **Grammar Transparencies and Copymasters**, p. 110.

Use McDougal Littell's *Language Network*, Chapter 3, for more instruction and practice in compound sentences.

## Reading and Analyzing

### Literary Analysis: IMAGERY

**A** Remind students that imagery consists of descriptive words and phrases that appeal to the five senses. Point out how the imagery in this passage shows rather than tells the reader Equiano's experiences by presenting sights, sounds, smells, and other physical sensations. Have students reread the passage while trying to visualize Equiano's ordeal at the moment the ship sets sail.

### Reading Skills and Strategies: CONSTRUCTING A GRAPHIC ORGANIZER

**B** The images in this passage help readers envision what life was like for Equiano and others aboard the slave ship. Have students construct graphic organizers to display the details Equiano uses to describe the ship.

**Possible Responses:** A sample word web is provided below.

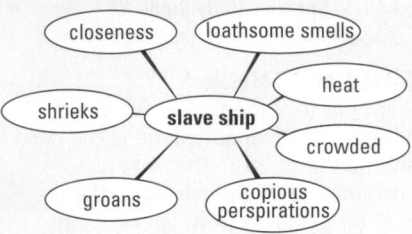

### Literary Analysis: IMAGERY

**C** Ask students to locate imagery in this passage.

**Possible Responses:** the beat of the drum, the noise and clamor, the eagerness in the buyers' faces

Ask how, on the basis of these images, students visualize the slave action. Have students decide how it would feel to be there.

### Literary Analysis  SLAVE NARRATIVES

Ask students to identify the writer's purpose in this passage and explain why his words are so emotionally charged.

**Possible Response:** After showing his readers the horrors of slavery through images, the writer wants to confront directly those who are responsible for it. He is perhaps hoping his words will elicit shame. The words are emotionally charged because the writer has a personal stake in the issue.

Detail of *The Slave Ship* (1956), Robert Riggs, N.A. Courtesy of Les Mansfield, Cincinnati, Ohio.

**A** At last, when the ship we were in, had got in all her cargo, they made ready with many fearful noises, and we were all put under deck, so that we could not see how they managed the vessel. But this disappointment was the least of my sorrow. The stench of the hold while we were on the coast was so intolerably loathsome, that it was dangerous to remain there for any time, and some of us had been permitted to stay on the deck for the fresh air; but now that the whole ship's cargo were confined together, it became absolutely <u>pestilential</u>. The closeness of the place, and the heat of the climate, added to the number in the ship, which was so crowded that each had scarcely room to turn himself, almost suffocated us. This produced <u>copious</u> perspirations, so that the air soon became unfit for respiration, from a variety of loathsome smells, and brought on a sickness among the slaves, of which many died. . . . This <u>wretched</u> situation was again aggravated by the galling[5] of the chains. . . . The shrieks of the women, and the groans of the dying, rendered the whole a scene of horror almost inconceivable. Happily perhaps, for myself, I was soon reduced so low here that it was thought necessary to keep me almost always on deck; and from my extreme youth I was not put in fetters.[6] In this situation I expected every **B** hour to share the fate of my companions, some

---

5. **galling** (gô'lĭng): causing skin sores by rubbing.
6. **fetters:** chains or shackles for the ankles.

> WORDS   **pestilential** (pĕs'tə-lĕn'shəl) *adj.* deadly; poisonous
> TO      **copious** (kō'pē-əs) *adj.* in large amounts; abundant
> KNOW    **wretched** (rĕch'ĭd) *adj.* miserable

96

---

## Teaching Options

 **Mini Lesson**  ## Viewing and Representing

### *The Slave Ship* (detail) by Robert Riggs

**ART APPRECIATION** A painter and lithographer, Robert Riggs (1876–1970) painted this scene, which appeared in an issue of *Life* magazine on slavery in early America. It portrays action on the open deck as well as the scene in the dark hold below deck.

**Instruction** An artist can use shape, colors, and composition to evoke a certain mood in the viewer. What mood does this painting evoke? How does the artist achieve this mood?

**Possible Response:** The mood is one of anguish and brutal confinement. Arms are flailing. The slaves appear to be calling out in pain, while the white men appear cold and harsh.

What thoughts or feeling does the painting evoke in you?

**Possible Response:** The painting's disturbing scene evokes feelings of pity and anger.

What is this painter trying to emphasize about the slave trade?

**Possible Response:** the suffering of the slaves

of whom were almost daily brought upon deck at the point of death, which I began to hope would soon put an end to my miseries. . . .

One day they had taken a number of fishes; and when they had killed and satisfied themselves with as many as they thought fit, to our astonishment who were on deck, rather than give any of them to us to eat, as we expected, they tossed the remaining fish into the sea again, although we begged and prayed for some as well as we could, but in vain; and some of my countrymen, being pressed by hunger, took an opportunity, when they thought no one saw them, of trying to get a little privately; but they were discovered, and the attempt procured them some very severe floggings. One day, when we had a smooth sea and moderate wind, two of my wearied countrymen who were chained together (I was near them at the time), preferring death to such a life of misery, somehow made through the nettings and jumped into the sea; immediately, another quite dejected fellow, who, on account of his illness, was suffered to be out of irons, also followed their example; and I believe many more would very soon have done the same, if they had not been prevented by the ship's crew, who were instantly alarmed. . . .

**1**

*During the rest of his voyage to the West Indies, Equiano continued to endure hardships. After the ship anchored on the coast of Barbados, Equiano and the other slaves were brought ashore and herded together in a slave merchant's yard to be sold.*

W E WERE NOT MANY DAYS IN THE MERCHANT'S CUSTODY, BEFORE WE WERE SOLD AFTER THEIR USUAL MANNER, WHICH IS THIS: ON A SIGNAL GIVEN (as the beat of a drum), the buyers rush at once into the yard where the slaves are confined, and make choice of that parcel[7] they like best. The noise and clamor with which this is attended, and the eagerness visible in the countenances of the buyers, serve not a little to increase the apprehension of terrified Africans, who may well be supposed to consider them as the ministers of that destruction to which they think themselves devoted. In this manner, without scruple, are relations and friends separated, most of them never to see each other again. I remember, in the vessel in which I was brought over, in the men's apartment, there were several brothers, who, in the sale, were sold in different lots; and it was very moving on this occasion, to see and hear their cries at parting. O, ye <u>nominal</u> Christians! might not an African ask you—Learned you this from your God, who says unto you, Do unto all men as you would men should do unto you? Is it not enough that we are torn from our country and friends, to toil for your luxury and lust of gain? Must every tender feeling be likewise sacrificed to your <u>avarice</u>? Are the dearest friends and relations now rendered more dear by their separation from their kindred, still to be parted from each other, and thus prevented from cheering the gloom of slavery, with the small comfort of being together, and mingling their sufferings and sorrows? Why are parents to lose their children, brothers their sisters, or husbands their wives? Surely, this is a new refinement in cruelty, which . . . thus aggravates distress, and adds fresh horrors even to the wretchedness of slavery. ❖

**C**

**D**

**2**

---

7. **parcel:** group of slaves offered for sale.

WORDS TO KNOW
**countenance** (koun′tə-nəns) *n.* the face, especially as an indicator of emotion
**nominal** (nŏm′ə-nəl) *adj.* in name but not in reality
**avarice** (ăv′ə-rĭs) *n.* greed

97

## Customizing Instruction

### Multiple Learning Styles
**Visual/Kinesthetic Learners**

Have students compare the art on page 96 with Equiano's description of the slave ship thus far. Ask what events and scenes from Equiano's narrative are depicted in the painting. Ask students to create a drawing, painting, or sculpture that both depicts some aspect of life on the slave ship and conveys a particular emotion.

### Less Proficient Readers

**1** Ask students to describe Equiano's emotions as reflected thus far in the selection.
**Possible Responses:** fear, confusion, disgust

Ask why Equiano feels this way.
**Possible Response:** He is surrounded by squalor and treated cruelly by people of a race he has never encountered.

### Gifted and Talented

**2** Have students discuss whether Equiano's closing argument was persuasive. Ask which of his persuasive tactics were especially convincing. Which were least convincing?

**Cross Curricular Link** **History**

**SLAVERY** Writings from Mesopotamian cultures show that the practice of slavery existed at the dawn of recorded history. Egyptian, Greek, and Roman civilizations all exploited the labor of enslaved people. The conquest and colonization of the New World, however, created a new demand for human labor, a demand so huge that the enslavement of Native American people failed to meet it. As disease and inhumane treatment diminished the native populations, other people were brought from Africa to replace them. Between 1500 and 1800, the slave trade carried approximately 12 million Africans to the Americas. About sixty-five percent of these people went to Brazil, Cuba, Jamaica, and Haiti; 6 percent were brought to what is now the United States. The proportion of slaves who died on the ships transporting them to the Americas ran as high as 20 percent.

# GUIDING STUDENT RESPONSE

## Connect to the Literature

**1. What Do You Think?**
Possible Response: The selection helped me understand some of the horrors of slavery. It is frightening to know that humans are capable of such evil.

**Comprehension Check**
• Equiano believes he will be eaten by the Europeans.
• His captors allow him fresh air and an escape from the stench of the hold because he is ill.
• Equiano accuses his captors of separating families—parents from children, brothers from sisters, and husbands from wives.

 Use Selection Quiz
**Unit One Resource Book,** p. 45.

## Think Critically

**2.** Possible Response: This was a system based on exploitation and cruelty.

**3.** Possible Response: Being forced to eat when I felt sick from the stench of the ship's hold would be hardest to endure.

**4.** Possible Responses: The crew probably viewed the captive Africans as property and less than human; there were many more Africans than crew members; some Africans responded with fear and reserve, while others tried to take food or escape the ship.

**5.** Possible Response: Equiano is talking about people who practice slavery yet claim to be guided by Christian values—Christians in name only. Most students will agree that holding human beings as slaves is not morally acceptable behavior.

**6.** Possible Response: To survive, a person needed the inner strength to withstand terrible physical and psychological pain and the ability to look beyond the present horrors and envision a better future.

## Literary Analysis

**Review Primary and Secondary Sources**
Encourage students to compile their points of comparison using a spreadsheet or a chart in a word processing program.

## Connect to the Literature

**1. What Do You Think?**
What impact did this selection have on you? Share your response with others.

**Comprehension Check**
• What does Equiano think will happen to him when he is brought on board ship?
• Why is Equiano allowed to be kept on deck rather than in the hold?
• What new "refinement in cruelty" does Equiano accuse his captors of practicing?

## Think Critically

**2.** Recall some of the ideas about slave ships you discussed before reading this selection. How did reading Equiano's account affect your view of the slave trade?

**3.**  **ACTIVE READING** **ANALYZING DETAILS** Look back in your **READER'S NOTEBOOK** at the chart that lists the **sensory details** you found most gripping. Which of the experiences that Equiano described would be hardest for you to endure? Explain why.

**4.** Why do you think the captive Africans were treated so brutally?

> **THINK ABOUT**
> • how the crew probably viewed them
> • how the number of crew members compared with the number of Africans
> • how the Africans reacted to their situation

**5.** Who do you think are the "nominal Christians" that Equiano refers to in the last paragraph? Do you agree with his **epithet?** Support your answer with evidence from the selection.

**6.** What qualities do you think the captured Africans needed in order to survive the Middle Passage?

## Extend Interpretations

**7. Comparing Texts** How would you compare the experiences of captured Africans brought to North America on slave ships with the experiences of the Pilgrims or Cabeza de Vaca's men?

**8. Connect to Life** At what age do you think American students should learn about slavery in the United States, and what do you think they should be told?

## Literary Analysis

**SLAVE NARRATIVES** Equiano's book is an example of a **slave narrative,** or an autobiographical account by someone who suffered the misery of slavery and lived to write about it. Writers of slave narratives often use sensory details to recreate their experiences. For example, to depict the horror of confinement in the hold of a slave ship, Equiano gives the reader such details as "the galling of the chains" and "the groans of the dying."

**Cooperative Learning Activity**
Working in a small group, go back through this selection and choose a passage that you think gives an especially vivid picture of slavery. As a guide, use the chart that you completed in your **READER'S NOTEBOOK.** Select the details that you find most vivid and discuss why they are so effective. Then prepare a **choral reading** of the passage to convey the power of Equiano's details to the class.

**REVIEW** **AUDIENCE** Who do you suppose was Equiano's intended audience? Support your opinion with evidence.

**REVIEW** **PRIMARY AND SECONDARY SOURCES**
**Primary sources,** such as Equiano's narrative, are written or created by people who observed or participated in a historical event. **Secondary sources,** such as scholarly articles or textbooks, are written after the event, by nonparticipants. Compare what you learn about Equiano from his own words with what you learn about him from the biography on page 99.

## Extend Interpretations

**Comparing Texts** Encourage students to consider what they know about the historical contexts as they respond to this question. Students should understand that the major difference between the experiences of African slaves and those of Pilgrims is that the Pilgrims chose to make their journey. Although they were escaping persecution, they were making a conscious decision for themselves and for their families. Cabeza de Vaca's men likewise had a voice in deciding their futures, although their decisions brought them severe suffering.
**Connect to Life** Possible Response: American students should learn about slavery in the United

States when they are old enough to begin studying their country's history. At a young age, they should receive factual information about the slave trade. When they are older, they should read firsthand narratives that depict the personal horrors endured by slaves.

## Literary Analysis

**Review Audience** Possible Response: Equiano's intended audience was European or American readers who might be stirred to take action against the slave trade.

# *Choices* & CHALLENGES

## Writing Options

**1. Song of Freedom** Imagine that you are Equiano or another captured African chained below deck on a slave ship. Write a song to express your feelings about freedom.

**2. Narrative Summary** Write a summary of this selection for someone who has not read it and wants to know what Equiano's experience was like.

**Writing Handbook**
See page 1279: Narrative Writing

## Activities & Explorations

**Museum Exhibit** In a small group, plan and sketch a museum exhibit designed to show some of the horrors of the Middle Passage that you learned about in this selection. In your sketch, include the pictures, models, and artifacts you would use, and write descriptions of any nonvisual features, such as sound recordings. ~ **VIEWING AND REPRESENTING**

## Vocabulary in Action

**EXERCISE: ASSESSMENT PRACTICE** On your paper, write the vocabulary word that belongs in each group of synonyms below.

1. dread, anxiety, _____
2. odor, _____, stink
3. _____, torment, agony
4. deplorable, terrible, _____
5. _____, plentiful, ample
6. selfishness, _____, greed
7. _____, diseased, polluted
8. alarm, _____, dismay
9. _____, so-called, ostensible
10. expression, visage, _____

**Building Vocabulary**
For an in-depth lesson on how to expand your vocabulary, see page 126.

| WORDS TO KNOW | anguish apprehension avarice consternation | copious countenance nominal | pestilential stench wretched |
| --- | --- | --- | --- |

## Olaudah Equiano
### 1745?–1797

**A Leader's Son** Olaudah Equiano grew up in the West African kingdom of Benin in the area that is now eastern Nigeria. His father ruled the village of Essaka, which Equiano himself would have ruled one day had he not been kidnapped by African slave traders and sent first to Barbados, then to colonial Virginia.

**Traveling the World** After a short time in Virginia, Equiano was sold to a British naval officer, with whom he traveled as far as Nova Scotia, London, and the Mediterranean. In 1763, he was sold again, to a merchant from Philadelphia who allowed him to work as a clerk and captain's assistant on slave and merchant ships. With the extra money that he was able to earn, Equiano bought his freedom in 1766. Working as a barber, sailor, and free servant, he traveled extensively, from England to the Arctic, but never returned to Africa.

**A Voice of Protest** During his years of captivity, Equiano had learned to speak and read English. As a free man, he became involved in the antislavery movement, lecturing against British slave holders. From 1787 to 1788 he worked on his autobiography, *The Interesting Narrative of the Life of Olaudah Equiano, or Gustavus Vassa, the African,* which was first published in London in 1789 and quickly became popular.

## Author Activity

**Personal and Political** Discuss the reasons that Equiano's account and other slave narratives were so important to the antislavery movement.

## Writing Options

**1. Song of Freedom** Students' songs should demonstrate an appreciation of the importance of freedom to those who are denied it. **To get students started on this assignment,** have them write the word *freedom* at the top of a sheet of paper and then freewrite about words and thoughts that come to mind.

**2. Narrative Summary** Students' summaries should show an understanding of the important details of the selection. **To get students started on this assignment,** have them reread the selection, taking notes about the most important details. From these notes, students can devise an outline for a summary.

## Activities & Explorations

**Museum Exhibit** As they plan their exhibits, students should ask themselves how they can make the experience real and moving to others, particularly to those learning about this historical period for the first time. Students might want to consult other sources to see what information and artifacts they might include. Suggest that interested students prepare a seven-to-ten minute video documentary explaining the middle passage to engage an audience of middle school students.

## Author Activity

Slave narratives gave a voice to slaves and enabled them to be seen as people, with the same feelings, hopes, and beliefs as their readers. They gave a firsthand account of the evils of slavery.

---

☑ **Assessment** **Informal Assessment**

**OPEN-ENDED TEST QUESTIONS** Many standardized tests include questions that call for students to formulate a complete response to a reading rather than select a correct response from a list. For this type of question, students often must support their responses with details or facts from the reading. Read the following description from the selection. Then have students respond to the open-ended question that follows.

This wretched situation was again aggravated by the galling of the chains. . . . The shrieks of the women, and the groans of the dying, rendered the whole a scene of horror almost inconceivable.

Have students explain how the underlined words help establish the mood in this part of the essay.
**Possible Response:** The words all reflect the suffering of the slaves. These images suggest misery, noise, and pain. They make the reader feel horrified, sad, and angry.

### Objectives

1. appreciate a **travelogue** (Literary Analysis)
2. examine **author's purpose** (Literary Analysis)
3. **organize details** (Active Reading)

### Summary

During the author's travels around the country, he spends the night on a mountain in Utah. The next morning, at a university cafeteria, he meets a Hopi named Kendrick Fritz, who is studying chemistry and wants to be a doctor. They discuss issues concerning Native Americans. Among other topics, Fritz talks about Hopi culture, explaining that it emphasizes harmony. He invites the author to his dorm room and offers him piki, a traditional Hopi corn bread. He explains that the Hopi believe that life is a series of journeys and that humanity has evolved through four worlds. When the author asks if it is difficult for a Hopi to enter the technologically complex field of medicine, Fritz replies that the Hopi believe the spirit can go anywhere—that in fact the spirit is compelled to travel, change, and emerge anew.

### Thematic Link

William Least Heat-Moon undertook his journey on the "blue highways" in order to **encounter** rural America. In his discussion with Kendrick Fritz, he **explores** the Hopi Way, discovering how a Native American combines modern and traditional ways of life.

### 5-Minute Warm-Up

***Daily Language SkillBuilder***

Have students **proofread** the display sentences on page 17k and write them correctly. The sentences also appear on Transparency 4 of **Grammar Transparencies and Copymasters.**

---

## PREPARING to *Read*

### *from* Blue Highways

*Travelogue by* WILLIAM LEAST HEAT-MOON

**Comparing Literature**

#### Traditions Across Time: The New Explorers

Like early voyagers to America, the contemporary writer William Least Heat-Moon undertook his own journey of discovery—to explore the heart of rural America. He traveled the backroads of this country in a pickup truck, stopping in small towns and talking to ordinary people. In this excerpt from *Blue Highways,* he describes an interview with Kendrick Fritz, a Hopi medical student who reveals his people's values and standards of conduct.

**Points of Comparison** As you read about this encounter between two strangers, compare it with the other first encounters you read about earlier.

### Build Background

This selection describes some cultural traditions of the Hopi (hō′pē) of northeastern Arizona. For more than four centuries, the Hopi have been pressured to adopt European ways, first by Spanish colonizers and Catholic missionaries, then by settlers from the United States. In response to the Hopi's appeal, the U.S. government made Hopi lands a protected reservation in 1882. However, the government also forced Hopi children to attend government schools, a policy that threatened the Hopi way of life and created a division between traditional and progressive Hopi that still exists today. Despite these pressures, the Hopi have kept alive many of their cultural traditions.

| WORDS TO KNOW | **Vocabulary Preview** | |
| --- | --- | --- |
| begrudge | evolve | precipitately |
| contempt | genetic | theology |
| emergence | materialism | variant |
| ethical | | |

### Focus Your Reading

**LITERARY ANALYSIS** **AUTHOR'S PURPOSE** The **author's purpose** is the author's reason for writing: to entertain, to inform, to express himself or herself, or to persuade, for example. Frequently an author writes to accomplish two or more of these purposes. To help you determine Heat-Moon's primary purpose for writing, notice the incidents he recounts, the people he describes, and language that indicates his stance toward his subject.

**ACTIVE READING** **ORGANIZING DETAILS** In this selection, Kendrick Fritz gives the reader an insider's view of Hopi culture, providing details about important foods, objects, practices, beliefs, and concepts—what Fritz calls the Hopi Way.

**READER'S NOTEBOOK**
As you read, create a cluster diagram like the one started here to organize these details. You will use them later as you discuss the Hopi Way.

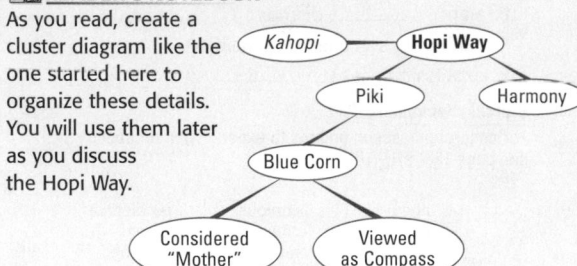

---

## LESSON RESOURCES

**UNIT ONE RESOURCE BOOK,** pp. 46–50

**ASSESSMENT RESOURCES**
**Formal Assessment,** pp. 25–26
**Teacher's Guide to Assessment and Portfolio Use**
**Test Generator**

**SKILLS TRANSPARENCIES AND COPYMASTERS**
**Literary Analysis**
• Compare/Contrast Themes and Conflicts, T16 (for Writing Option 3, p. 108)

**Reading and Critical Thinking**
• Determining Author's Purpose and Audience, T19 (for Cooperative Learning Activity, p. 107)

**Grammar**
• Complex Sentences, C111 (for Mini Lesson, p. 103)
• Pronouns, C125 (for Mini Lesson, p. 108)

**Vocabulary**
• Meanings of Prefixes and Roots, C27 (for Mini Lesson, p. 105)

**Writing**
• The Uses of Dialogue, T24 (for Writing Option 1, p. 108)

**INTEGRATED TECHNOLOGY**

**Audio Library**
**LaserLinks**
• Cultural Connection: The Hopi. See **Teacher's SourceBook,** p. 18.

**Visit our website:**
www.mcdougallittell.com

*Road Past the View I* (1964), Georgia O'Keeffe. Oil on canvas, 24″ × 30″. Copyright © 1996 The Georgia O'Keeffe Foundation/Artists Rights Society (ARS), New York. Photo Copyright © Malcolm Varon.

from

# BLUE HIGHWAYS

### William Least Heat-Moon

W*hen William Least Heat-Moon set out on a long circular trip around the United States, he drove the back roads—the two-lane highways that were colored blue on old road maps. His goal was to learn about America by seeing the small towns and talking to the people he met there. He was not always successful, however. In Tuba City, Arizona, for instance, he failed to strike up a conversation with several Navajos. This chapter begins a few days later, with Heat-Moon at the top of a snowy mountain pass in Utah. He has slept in his van overnight rather than risk driving down the mountain in the dark.*

## Customizing Instruction

### Less Proficient Readers
Create interest by asking students to read the introductory text on page 101.
**Set a Purpose** Have students read on to find out how the author gets down from the mountain pass and whom he meets.

### Students Acquiring English
• Ask volunteers how they integrate their native culture with the one in which they now live. Tell them that the selection is about just such a challenge, as faced by a Hopi student.
• If possible, use a road map to show students the type of roads that the author refers to as "blue highways." The highways shown in blue are local roads, not superhighways. Explain that this is a term invented by the author and is not in common use.

 Use **Spanish Study Guide** for additional support, pp. 29–31.

### Gifted and Talented
Have students consider the difficulties faced by Kendrick Fritz in his quest to help his people. Ask students to observe qualities of love, caring, responsibility, and discipline in Fritz's actions and statements.

---

 **Mini Lesson** **Preteaching Vocabulary**

**CONTEXT CLUES** Have students review the list of WORDS TO KNOW for this selection. Remind them that when they see an unfamiliar word in their reading, they can often find clues in the surrounding text to figure out what the word means. Demonstrate the strategy by using the following model.
**Model Sentence**
The sides of the cliff plunged <u>precipitately</u>, so that even following a well-worn path to the bottom was dangerous.

**Instruction**
• Write the model sentence on the chalkboard.
• Ask a volunteer to state the situation described in the sentence.
• Have students infer from this situation the meaning of *precipitately.*
• Ask a volunteer to use *precipitately* in a new sentence.

Use **Unit One Resource Book,** p. 50 for more exercises.

A lesson in context clues appears on page 326 in the Pupil's Edition.

Tell students that this selection informs readers about the way one Native American reconciles the clash of his culture with Anglo culture.

**Active Reading** | ORGANIZING DETAILS

**A** Suggest to students that one way to organize details in a text is to list events that are related as cause and effect. With students, list in a table some cause-and-effect relationships mentioned on this page.

| Effect | Cause |
|---|---|
| Author feels stiff. | Sleeping coiled |
| Author buys large breakfast. | He needs to celebrate being alive. |
| Author could not start conversation in Tuba City. | He was seen as a tourist. |

Use **Unit One Resource Book,** p. 47 for more practice.

**Literary Analysis** | AUTHOR'S PURPOSE

**B** Authors may write for several purposes: to entertain, to inform, to express themselves, or to persuade. Analyzing an author's purpose is often easier in a nonfiction work than in a piece of fiction. In a nonfiction work, one clue to an author's purpose is the topic he or she chooses to treat. Ask students to identify Heat-Moon's topic in this selection.

**Answer:** He describes the clash between traditional Hopi values and modern "Anglo" values.

Use **Unit One Resource Book,** p. 48 for more practice.

---

**A** **D**irty and hard, the morning light could have been old concrete. Twenty-nine degrees inside. I tried to figure a way to drive down the mountain without leaving the sleeping bag. I was stiff—not from the cold so much as from having slept coiled like a grub. Creaking open and pinching toes and fingers to check for frostbite, I counted to ten (twice) before shouting and leaping for my clothes. Shouting distracts the agony. Underwear, trousers, and shirt so cold they felt wet.

I went outside to relieve myself. . . . Then to work chipping clear the windows. Somewhere off this mountain, people still lay warm in their blankets and not yet ready to get up to a hot breakfast. So what if they spent the day selling imprinted ballpoint pens? Weren't they down off mountains?

Down. I had to try it. And down it was, Utah 14 a complication of twists and drops descending the west side more <u>precipitately</u> than the east. A good thing I hadn't attempted it in the dark. After a mile, snow on the pavement became slush, then water, and finally at six thousand feet, dry and sunny blacktop.

Cedar City, a tidy Mormon town, lay at the base of the mountains on the edge of the Escalante Desert. Ah, desert! I pulled in for gas, snow still melting off my rig. "See you spent the night in the Breaks," the attendant said. "You people never believe the sign at the bottom."

"I believed, but it said something about winter months. May isn't winter."

"It is up there. You Easterners just don't know what a mountain is."

I didn't say anything, but I knew what a mountain was: a high pile of windy rocks with its own weather.

In the cafeteria of Southern Utah State College, I bought a breakfast of scrambled eggs, pancakes, bacon, oatmeal, grapefruit, orange juice, milk, and a cinnamon roll. A celebration of being alive. I was full of victory.

Across the table sat an Indian student named Kendrick Fritz, who was studying chemistry and wanted to become a physician. He had grown up in Moenkopi, Arizona, just across the highway from Tuba City. I said, "Are you Navajo or Hopi?"

"Hopi. You can tell by my size. Hopis are smaller than Navajos."

His voice was gentle, his words considered, and smile timid. He seemed open to questions. "Fritz doesn't sound like a Hopi name."

"My father took it when he was in the Army in the Second World War. Hopis usually have Anglo[1] first names and long Hopi last names that are hard for other people to pronounce."

I told him of my difficulty in rousing a conversation in Tuba City. He said, "I can't speak for Navajos about prejudice, but I know Hopis who believe we survived Spaniards, missionaries, a thousand years of other Indians, even the BIA.[2] But tourists?" He smiled. "Smallpox would be better."

**B** "Do you—yourself—think most whites are prejudiced against Indians?"

"About fifty-fifty. Half show <u>contempt</u> because they saw a drunk squaw at the Circle K. Another half think we're noble savages—they may be worse because if an Indian makes a mistake they hate him for being human. Who wants to be somebody's ideal myth?"

"My grandfather used to say the Big Vision made the Indian, but the white man invented him."

"Relations are okay here, but I wouldn't call them good, and I'm not one to go around looking for prejudice. I try not to."

"Maybe you're more tolerant of Anglo ways than some others."

---

1. **Anglo:** European-American.
2. **BIA:** the Bureau of Indian Affairs, established in 1824 by the United States government to supervise Native American reservations; many Native Americans feel that the bureau has interfered too much in their lives.

| WORDS TO KNOW | **precipitately** (prĭ-sĭp′ĭ-tĭt-lē) *adv.* steeply |
|---|---|
| | **contempt** (kən-tĕmpt′) *n.* scorn; disdain |

---

## Teaching Options

### BLOCK SCHEDULING: MANAGING TIME

| If your schedule requires that you cover the lesson objectives in a shorter time, use . . . | If you would like to take advantage of longer class times, use . . . |
|---|---|
| • Preparing to Read, p. 100<br>• Thinking Through the Literature, p. 107<br>• Vocabulary in Action, p. 108 | • TE Teaching Options: Preteaching Vocabulary, p. 101 (can be done as a group activity); Cross-Curricular Link, p. 104; Informal Assessment, p. 106<br>• Choices & Challenges, p. 108 |

"Could be. I mean, I *am* studying to be a doctor and not a medicine man. But I'm no apple Indian—red outside and white underneath. I lived up in Brigham City, Utah, when I went to the Intermountain School run by the BIA. It was too easy though. Too much time to goof around. So I switched to Box Elder—that's a public school. I learned there. And I lived in Dallas a few months. What I'm saying is that I've lived on Hopi land and I've lived away. I hear  Indians talk about being red all the way through criticizing others for acting like Anglos, and all the time they're sitting in a pickup at a drive-in. But don't tell them to trade the truck for a horse."

 "The Spanish brought the horse."

He nodded. "To me, being Indian means being responsible to my people. Helping with the best tools. Who invented penicillin doesn't matter."

"What happens after you finish school?"

 "I used to want out of Tuba, but since I've been away, I've come to see how our land really is our Sacred Circle—it's our strength. Now, I want to go back and practice general medicine. At the Indian hospital in Tuba where my mother and sister are nurse's aides, there aren't any Indian M.D.'s, and that's no good. I don't respect people who don't help themselves. Hopi land is no place to make big

> "To me, being Indian means being responsible to my people. Helping with the best tools. Who invented penicillin doesn't matter."

Kendrick Fritz in Cedar City, Utah. From *Blue Highways* by William Least Heat-Moon.

money, but I'm not interested anyway."

"You don't use the word *reservation*."

"We don't think of it as a reservation since we  were never ordered there. We found it through Hopi prophecies. We're unusual because we've always held onto our original land—most of it anyway. One time my grandfather pointed out the old boundaries to me. We were way up on a mesa. I've forgotten what they are except for the San Francisco Peaks. But in the last eighty years, the government's given a lot of our land to Navajos, and now we're in a hard spot—eight thousand Hopis are surrounded and outnumbered twenty-five to one. I don't begrudge the Navajo anything, but I think Hopis should be in on making the decisions. Maybe you know that Congress didn't even admit Indians to citizenship until about nineteen twenty. Incredible—live someplace a thousand years and then find out you're a foreigner."

"I know an Osage who says, 'Don't Americanize me and I won't Americanize you.' He means everybody in the country came from someplace else."

"Hopi legends are full of migrations."

"Will other Hopis be suspicious of you when you go home as a doctor?"

"Some might be, but not my family. But for a

| WORDS TO KNOW | **begrudge** (bĭ-grŭj′) *v.* to resent another person's possession of something |

**Multiple Learning Styles**
**Kinesthetic Learners**
**1** Invite volunteers to read this passage aloud, using body language, tone of voice, and facial expression to convey Fritz's irony as he points out the hypocrisy of the behavior he is criticizing.

**Less Proficient Readers**
**2** Ask students why the author points out that the Spanish brought the horse to the Americas.
**Answer:** He is making the point that the horse, like the pickup truck, is something Indian culture adopted.

**Gifted and Talented Students**
**3** Remind students of the irony that Fritz speaks for a traditional way of life while at college preparing to enter medical school. Have students ask themselves if it will be possible for Fritz to combine two such different ways of living, thinking, and feeling. Ask whether Fritz will eventually be won over to the modern way or succeed in bringing the traditional Hopi Way into the technological world.

**Students Acquiring English**
**4** Explain to students that Kendrick Fritz defines the word *reservation* in his own way. Discuss with students what his definition is.
**Answer:** A reservation is an area to which Natives Americans were forced to move from some other place. Suggest that if students define a word according to their personal interpretation in this manner, they should be able to justify their definitions.

## Grammar
*Mini Lesson*

### COMPLEX SENTENCES

**Instruction:** A complex sentence contains one independent clause and at least one subordinate clause. A subordinate clause states an idea that is less important than the main idea of a sentence. It often begins with a subordinating conjunction such as *after, although, because, if, since, when, wherever, where,* or *while,* or a relative pronoun such as *who, whom, whose, which,* or *that.* Write the following models on the board (without underlining) and ask students to underline the subordinate clauses.

Across the table sat Kendrick Fritz, who was studying chemistry.

He looked like a Hopi rather than a Navajo because he was small.

Although Heat-Moon could not get an interview in Tuba City, he could get an interview in Cedar City.

Use **Grammar Transparencies and Copymasters,** p. 111.

Use McDougal Littell's **Language Network,** Chapter 3, for more instruction and practice in complex sentences.

**Literary Analysis: METAPHOR**

(A) Fritz describes the traditional Hopi prayer or meditation as "sitting in pictures." Ask students to explain this metaphor.

**Possible Response:** In prayer, the Hopi sit and make images or mental pictures of whatever they are praying for, as if they were placing themselves in the desired condition.

**Reading Skills and Strategies: DRAWING ON BACKGROUND**

(B) Ask students if there is a traditional food or meal in their families.

**Possible Responses:** Thanksgiving turkey, Fourth of July cherry pie, or foods not related to specific celebrations such as potato salad or gingerbread

Ask how such foods compare to the traditional Hopi bread, piki.

**Possible Response:** Such traditional foods, like piki, form a link with previous generations.

lot of Hopis, the worst thing to call a man is *kahopi*, 'not Hopi.' Nowadays, though, we all have to choose either the new ways or the Hopi way, and it's split up whole villages. A lot of us try to find the best in both places. We've always learned from other people. If we hadn't, we'd be extinct like some other tribes."

"Medicine's a pretty good survival technique."

"Sure, but I also like Jethro Tull and the Moody Blues.[3] That's not survival."

"Is the old religion a survival technique?"

"If you live it."

"Do you?"

"Most Hopis follow our religion, at least in some ways, because it reminds us who we are and it's part of the land. I'll tell you, in the rainy season when the desert turns green, it's beautiful there. The land is medicine too."

"If you don't mind telling me, what's the religion like?"

"Like any religion in one way—different clans believe different things."

"There must be something they all share, something common."

"That's hard to say."

"Could you try?"

He thought a moment.

"Maybe the idea of harmony. And the way a Hopi prays. A good life, a harmonious life, is a prayer. We don't just pray for ourselves, we pray for all things. We're famous for the Snake Dances, but a lot of people don't realize those ceremonies are prayers for rain and crops, prayers for life. We also pray for rain by (A) sitting and thinking about rain. We sit and picture wet things like streams and clouds. It's sitting in pictures."

He picked up his tray to go. "I could give you a taste of the old Hopi Way. But maybe you're

> **H**uman existence is essentially a series of journeys, and the emergence symbol is a kind of map of the wandering soul, an image of a process.

too full after that breakfast. You always eat so much?"

"The mountain caused that." I got up. "What do you mean by 'taste'?"

"I'll show you."

We went to his dormitory room. Other than several Kachina dolls[4] he had carved from cottonwood and a picture of a Sioux warrior, it was just another collegiate dorm room—maybe cleaner than most. He pulled a shoebox from under his bed and opened it carefully. I must have been watching a little wide-eyed because he said, "It isn't live rattlesnakes." From the box he took a long cylinder wrapped in waxed paper and held it as if trying not to touch it. "Will you eat this? It's very special." He was smiling. "If you won't, I can't share the old Hopi Way with you."

"Okay, but if it's dried scorpions, I'm going to speak with a forked tongue."

"Open your hands." He unwrapped the cylinder and ever so gently laid across my palms an airy tube the color of a thunderhead. It was about ten inches long and an inch in diameter. "There you go," he said.

"You first."

"I'm not having any right now."

So I bit the end off the blue-gray tube. It was many intricately rolled layers of something with less substance than butterfly wings. The bite crumbled to flakes that stuck to my lips. "Now tell me what I'm eating."

"Do you like it?"

"I think so. Except it disappears like cotton candy just as I get ready to chew. But I think I taste corn and maybe ashes."

"Hopis were eating that before horses came to (B) America. It's piki. Hopi bread you might say. Made from blue-corn flour and ashes from

---

3. **Jethro Tull . . . Moody Blues:** British rock bands popular from the 1960s to the 1980s.

4. **Kachina** (kə-chē′nə) **dolls:** dolls representing kachinas— spirits of Hopi ancestors that the Hopi believe live in mountains near their lands.

### Cross Curricular Link **History**

**THE INDIAN CITIZENSHIP ACT OF 1924** By as early as 1917, two-thirds of all Native Americans in the United States had acquired citizenship by fulfilling certain legal requirements. The Indian Citizenship Act, passed in 1924, guaranteed United States citizenship to all Native Americans born within the boundaries of the United States. The *New York Times* observed the irony of this act in much the same way as Kendrick Fritz: "If there are cynics among the Indians, they may receive the news of their new citizenship with wry smiles. The white race, having robbed them of a continent, and having sought to deprive them of freedom of action, freedom of social custom, and freedom of worship, now at last gives them the same legal basis as their conquerors."

greasewood or sagebrush. Baked on an oiled stone by my mother. She sends piki every so often. It takes time and great skill to make. We call it Hopi cornflakes."

"Unbelievably thin." I laid a piece on a page of his chemistry book. The words showed through.

"We consider corn our mother. The blue variety is what you might call our compass— wherever it grows, we can go. Blue corn directed our migrations. Navajos cultivate a yellow species that's soft and easy to grind, but ours is hard. You plant it much deeper than other corns, and it survives where they would die. It's a genetic variant the Hopi developed."

"Why is it blue? That must be symbolic."

"We like the color blue. Corn's our most important ritual ingredient."

"The piki's good, but it's making me thirsty. Where's a water fountain?"

When I came back from the fountain, Fritz said, "I'll tell you what I think the heart of our religion is—it's the Four Worlds."

Over the next hour, he talked about the Hopi Way, and showed pictures and passages from *Book of the Hopi*. The key seemed to be emergence. Carved in a rock near the village of Shipolovi is the ancient symbol for it:

With variations, the symbol appears among other Indians of the Americas. Its lines represent the course a person follows on his "road of life" as he passes through birth, death, rebirth. Human existence is essentially a series of journeys, and the emergence symbol is a kind of map of the wandering soul, an image of a

process; but it is also, like most Hopi symbols and ceremonies, a reminder of cosmic patterns that all human beings move in.

The Hopi believes mankind has evolved through four worlds: the first a shadowy realm of contentment; the second a place so comfortable the people forgot where they had come from and began worshipping material goods. The third world was a pleasant land too, but the people, bewildered by their past and fearful for their future, thought only of their own earthly plans. At last, the Spider Grandmother, who oversees the emergences, told them: "You have forgotten what you should have remembered, and now you have to leave this place. Things will be harder." In the fourth and present world, life is difficult for mankind, and he struggles to remember his source because materialism and selfishness block a greater vision. The newly born infant comes into the fourth world with the door of his mind open (evident in the cranial soft spot[5]), but as he ages, the door closes and he must work at remaining receptive to the great forces. A human being's grandest task is to keep from breaking with things outside himself.

"A Hopi learns that he belongs to two families," Fritz said, "his natural clan and that of all things. As he gets older, he's supposed to move closer to the greater family. In the Hopi Way, each person tries to recognize his part in the whole."

"At breakfast you said you hunted rabbits and pigeons and robins, but I don't see how you can

---

5. **cranial** (krā′nē-əl) **soft spot:** the soft area on top of an infant's head, a result of the as yet incomplete formation of the bones of the skull (cranium).

---

| | |
|---|---|
| WORDS TO KNOW | **genetic** (jə-nĕt′ĭk) *adj.* relating to genes, the units that determine and transmit hereditary characteristics |
| | **variant** (vâr′ē-ənt) *n.* something that differs slightly from others of its kind |
| | **emergence** (ĭ-mûr′jəns) *n.* the process of coming forth or coming into existence |
| | **evolve** (ĭ-vŏlv′) *v.* to develop gradually |
| | **materialism** (mə-tîr′ē-ə-lĭz′əm) *n.* a preoccupation with worldly rather than spiritual concerns |

105

### Less Proficient Readers
**1** Have students give one descriptive word for each of the four worlds.
**Possible Response:** contented; comfortable or forgetful; fearful; materialistic or selfish

### Multiple Learning Styles
**Visual/Kinesthetic Learners**
**2** Have students construct a graphic or artistic representation of the four worlds of Hopi legend.

### Students Acquiring English
**3** Point out the idiom *break with*. Tell students that this means "to end a relationship with." In this context it does not mean to physically break something into pieces.

### Less Proficient Readers
Ask students which of the items in Kendrick's room reveal his Hopi heritage.
**Answer:** Kachina dolls, picture of a Sioux warrior, piki

Ask students to summarize what Fritz says about the Hopi Way.
**Possible Response:** The Hopi Way reminds people to respect everything and not to give in to materialism.

## Mini Lesson: Vocabulary Strategy

### PREFIXES, SUFFIXES, AND ROOTS WORDS
**Instruction** Explain to students that they can use prefixes, suffixes, and root words to better understand the meaning of several WORDS TO KNOW for this selection, including *contempt, emergence, evolve, materialism, precipitately,* and *theology.* Point out the prefixes *con-, e-,* and *pre-*; and the suffixes *-ism* and *-ology.* Copy the following table on the board to show students how prefixes and suffixes affect the meaning of roots.

| Word | Prefix or Suffix | Meaning of Prefix or Suffix | Root | Meaning of Root | Meaning of Root with Prefix or Suffix |
|---|---|---|---|---|---|
| contempt | con- | very much | -temp-, -temn- | to despise | to despise intently |
| emergence | e- | out of | -merse | to plunge | plunge out of, rise out of |
| theology | -ology | study of | theo- | of God | the study of religion |

**Literary Analysis: MYTH**

**A** Ask students what two rules Spider Grandmother gave people.

**Answer:** "Don't go around hurting each other," and "Try to understand things."

How would the world be different if people followed these rules?

**Possible Response:** There would be no war or racial prejudice.

What is the purpose of the Hopi myth?

**Possible Response:** to help people live together in harmony

shoot a bird if you believe in the union of life."

"A Hopi hunter asks the animal to forgive him for killing it. Only life can feed life. The robin knows that."

"How does robin taste, by the way?"

"Tastes good."

"The religion doesn't seem to have much of an <u>ethical</u> code."

**A** "It's there. We watch what the Kachinas say and do. But the Spider Grandmother did give two rules. To all men, not just Hopis. If you look at them, they cover everything. She said, 'Don't go around hurting each other,' and she said, 'Try to understand things.'"

"I like them. I like them very much."

"Our religion keeps reminding us that we aren't just will and thoughts. We're also sand and wind and thunder. Rain. The seasons. All those things. You learn to respect everything because you *are* everything. If you respect yourself, you respect all things. That's why we have so many songs of creation to remind us where we came from. If the fourth world forgets that, we'll disappear in the wilderness like the third world, where people decided they had created themselves."

"Pride's the deadliest of the Seven Deadly Sins in old Christian <u>theology</u>."

"It's *kahopi* to set yourself above things. It causes divisions."

Fritz had to go to class. As we walked across campus, I said, "I guess it's hard to be a Hopi in Cedar City—especially if you're studying biochemistry."

"It's hard to be a Hopi anywhere."

"I mean, difficult to carry your Hopi heritage into a world as technological as medicine is."

"Heritage? My heritage is the Hopi Way, and that's a way of the spirit. Spirit can go anywhere. In fact, it has to go places so it can change and emerge like in the migrations. That's the whole idea." ❖

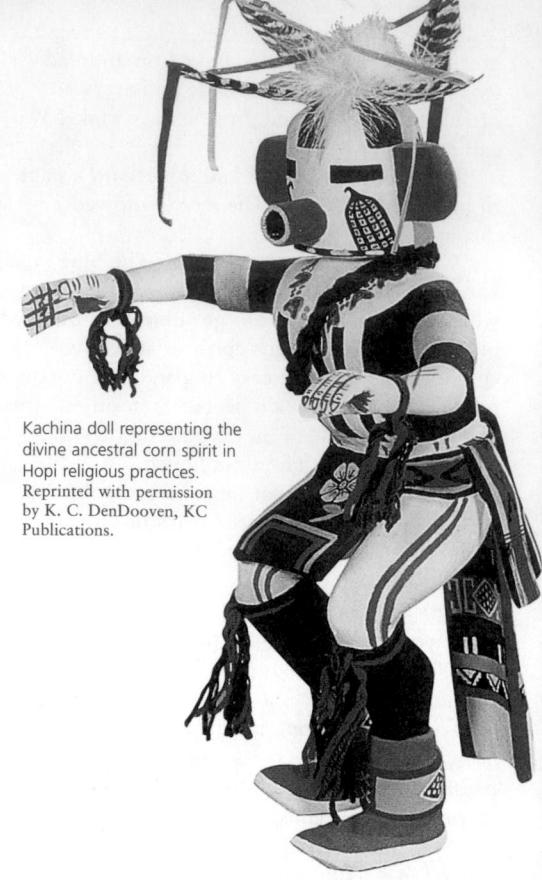

Kachina doll representing the divine ancestral corn spirit in Hopi religious practices. Reprinted with permission by K. C. DenDooven, KC Publications.

> **"The Spider Grandmother did give two rules.**
> **To all men, not just Hopis.**
> **If you look at them, they cover everything.**
> **She said,**
> **'Don't go around hurting each other,'**
> **and she said,**
> **'Try to understand things.'"**

| WORDS TO KNOW | **ethical** (ĕth′ĭ-kəl) *adj.* dealing with principles of right and wrong; moral<br>**theology** (thē-ŏl′ə-jē) *n.* a system of religious beliefs |
| --- | --- |

106

---

✓ **Assessment** **Informal Assessment**

**DISTINGUISHING BETWEEN FACT AND NONFACT**
Many standardized tests include items that require students to decide whether a statement is a fact. Write the following sentences on the board and have students choose which is NOT a fact, based on their reading of the excerpt from *Blue Highways*.

**A.** The author is afraid to drive down the mountain at night.

**B.** Kendrick says that it is wrong to set yourself above things.

**C.** Kendrick will make a superb doctor.

During the discussion, point out that the last option is an opinion. Although this prediction may prove to be correct, it is still only one person's estimation of Kendrick's potential as a doctor. The other options are statements of fact. Students may think B is an opinion; if so, point out that it is a statement of fact because you can determine whether it is true or false by consulting the selection.

# *Thinking* through the LITERATURE

## Connect to the Literature

1. **What Do You Think?**
   What interests you most about Kendrick Fritz? Discuss your impressions with your classmates.

   **Comprehension Check**
   - Why does Fritz invite the author to his room?
   - What does Fritz say is the heart of the Hopi religion?
   - What two rules did the Spider Grandmother give?

## Think Critically

2. **ACTIVE READING** **ORGANIZING DETAILS**  Review the cluster diagram you created in your 📖 **READER'S NOTEBOOK.** In your own words, tell what you learned about the Hopi Way.

3. What is your opinion of the Hopi Way? For example, what ways would be easy for you to follow and what ways would be difficult?

4. Fritz says, "It's hard to be a Hopi anywhere." What do you think makes it difficult to be a Hopi?

**THINK ABOUT**
{
- how most whites view Native Americans
- how some Native Americans view others for "acting like Anglos"
- how the Hopi and other Native Americans have historically been treated

5. The author mentions his grandfather's statement that "the Big Vision made the Indian, but the white man invented him." How would you explain this distinction?

6. At the end of the selection, the author tells Fritz that it is difficult to carry his Hopi heritage "into a world as technological as medicine is." How successful do you think Fritz will be in remaining true to the Hopi Way as a doctor? Explain your views.

## Extend Interpretations

7. **Connect to Life** How would you compare the Hopi experience with that of other minority groups in the United States?

8. **Points of Comparison**  How would you compare the experiences and attitudes of William Least Heat-Moon, William Bradford, and Álvar Núñez Cabeza de Vaca as they explored America?

## Literary Analysis

**AUTHOR'S PURPOSE**  A writer usually writes for one or more of the following **purposes:** to inform, to entertain, to express himself or herself, or to persuade readers to believe or do something. For example, in *The Interesting Narrative of the Life of Olaudah Equiano*, the author's purpose is primarily to inform readers about the horrors of the Middle Passage.

**Cooperative Learning Activity**
Review the selection and identify two or more reasons why you think Heat-Moon wrote it. For each reason you identify, record the evidence on a chart like the one shown. Then get together with a group of classmates to compare charts and to discuss your choices. What would you say is Heat-Moon's primary purpose for writing this selection?

Purpose 1:
Evidence:
Purpose 2:
Evidence:

## Extend Interpretations

**Connect to Life** Possible Response: The Hopi experience parallels that of other Native Americans in the United States because they were subjected to Anglo pressures to give up their traditional way of life. Unlike many Native Americans, the Hopi have held on to most of their original land.

**Points of Comparison** Possible Responses: William Least Heat-Moon has a greater respect for and interest in Native American culture; Bradford and de Vaca are wary of Native Americans, regarding them as barbarians whose way of life is inferior to Western European culture; Least Heat-Moon is less judgmental and more interested in learning about the Native American way of life; all have experienced some degree of suffering from the rugged American landscape.

## Literary Analysis

**Author's Purpose** Possible Responses: Most will agree that Heat-Moon wants to inform the readers about the Hopi Way and about Hopi attitudes toward whites; others may suggest that he also wants to express his admiration for Kendrick Fritz, who is striving to combine modern technology with a traditional way of life.

# Writing Options

1. **Hopi Dialogue** Students' responses should include an expression of the plausible points of view of the parties mentioned. **To get students started on this assignment,** you might have them break into groups of three and improvise a dialogue among the speakers. This may provide them with thoughts and expressions to use in their written dialogues.

2. **Personal Essay on Beliefs** Students' essays should relate a Hopi belief to their own experiences. **To get students started on this assignment,** have them choose the Hopi belief that interests them most. Then have them do brief research in other sources for myths that seem to present parallel teachings. For instance, the myth of the Four Worlds is parallel to ancient Greek and Roman myths of the Four Ages of the world—Golden, Silver, Bronze, and Iron—and to Judeo-Christian myths about the world before and after the Flood.

3. **Points of Comparison** Students' report cards should evaluate Squanto's conduct explicitly in terms of Spider Grandmother's standards. Squanto's willingness to help the Pilgrims adjust to life in a foreign environment certainly fulfills Spider Grandmother's first rule. **To make this assignment more challenging,** have students also grade the Pilgrim settlers' conduct.

# Vocabulary in Action

**EXERCISE: RELATED WORDS**

1. d
2. b
3. c
4. b
5. b
6. c
7. c
8. c
9. d
10. c

# Writing Options

1. **Hopi Dialogue** Write an imagined dialogue among three speakers: Kendrick Fritz, an older Hopi with traditional values, and a young Hopi who plans to move away from Hopi lands.

2. **Personal Essay on Beliefs** Draft a personal essay about an aspect of Hopi belief described in this selection. You might compare the belief with one of your own beliefs or explain how the belief applies to your own experience.
**Writing Handbook**
See page 1281: Explanatory Writing

3. **Points of Comparison** Consider the standards of conduct that the Spider Grandmother gave to humans. By these standards, how would you evaluate Squanto's conduct toward the Pilgrims, as recounted in *Of Plymouth Plantation*? Present your evaluations as a report card with comments.

# Vocabulary in Action

**EXERCISE: RELATED WORDS** On your paper, write the letter of the word that does not belong in the group.

1. (a) theology (b) doctrine (c) religion (d) unbelief
2. (a) respect (b) contempt (c) admiration (d) regard
3. (a) immoral (b) improper (c) ethical (d) dishonest
4. (a) materialism (b) spirituality (c) greed (d) consumerism
5. (a) duplicate (b) variant (c) twin (d) replica
6. (a) resent (b) begrudge (c) esteem (d) envy
7. (a) extinction (b) termination (c) emergence (d) disappearance
8. (a) genetic (b) hereditary (c) artificial (d) inheritable
9. (a) precipitately (b) steeply (c) abruptly (d) gradually
10. (a) evolve (b) develop (c) perish (d) unfold

| WORDS TO KNOW | begrudge contempt emergence ethical | evolve genetic materialism precipitately | theology variant |
|---|---|---|---|

## William Least Heat-Moon
1939–

**Other Works**
*PrairyErth*

**His Pen Name** "William Least Heat-Moon" is the pen name of William Trogdon, who is of mixed European-American and Native American ancestry. As he explains in *Blue Highways,* "My father calls himself Heat Moon, my elder brother Little Heat Moon. I, coming last, am therefore Least." Heat-Moon says that his father advised him to use his Anglo name for official business, such as paying taxes, and his Native American name for spiritual matters. His choice of pen name therefore indicates the spiritual quality of the journey that he recorded in *Blue Highways.*

**His Odyssey** Feeling isolated and tired of the commercialism he saw in mainstream American culture, Heat-Moon traveled in search of "places where change did not mean ruin and where time and men and deeds connected." He made his three-month, 13,000-mile journey in a Ford van that he named Ghost Dancing, a reference to a ceremony of the Plains Indians in which they danced for the return of their old, harmonious way of life. Equipped with a tape recorder, a camera, notebooks, Walt Whitman's *Leaves of Grass,* and John Neihardt's *Black Elk Speaks,* Heat-Moon followed the back roads, interviewing people he met along the way.

**Literary Success** After compiling his interviews, Heat-Moon spent the next four years editing his tapes and notebooks to capture "the details of ordinary lives that shape, control, and reveal the nature of an existence." His compelling portrait of rural America, *Blue Highways,* won several awards, became a bestseller, and earned critical acclaim.

---

## Grammar

**PRONOUNS** Remind students that personal pronouns have three cases: nominative, objective, and possessive. Copy the following chart on the chalkboard to demonstrate the cases.

| Person | Nominative | Objective | Possessive |
|---|---|---|---|
| First | I, we | me, us | my, our(s) |
| Second | You | you | your(s) |
| Third | he, she, it, they | him, her, it, them | his, her(s), its, theirs |

Nominative case pronouns are used as subjects, objective case pronouns are used as direct objects or objects of prepositions, and possessive case pronouns are used to indicate ownership. Have students correct the model sentence for practice.

**Model Sentence**
Him doesn't think the piki is she's. *(He doesn't think the piki is hers.)*

 Use **Grammar Transparencies and Copymasters,** p. 125.

 Use McDougal Littell's *Language Network,* Chapter 6, for more instruction and practice in pronouns.

# My Sojourn in the Lands of My Ancestors

*Autobiography by* MAYA ANGELOU

## Comparing Literature

### Traditions Across Time: The New Explorers

Earlier you read Olaudah Equiano's account of his terrible journey from Africa to America in a slave ship. More than 200 years later, the African-American writer Maya Angelou made a reverse journey—to West Africa, the land of her enslaved ancestors.

**Points of Comparison** As you read Angelou's account, notice how she remains affected by the events of history.

## Build Background

**African Slave Trade** In the 1400s, Europeans began to come to West Africa to trade for pepper, gold, and ivory. Over the years, they built more than 40 massive forts along the African coast to protect their trade and to store goods. As the slave trade grew, these European forts were also used to house enslaved Africans, who were branded, chained, and crowded into hot, dark, bat-infested dungeons for months at a time until they were shipped to colonies in the Americas. Two such forts are Elmina Castle and Cape Coast Castle in Ghana. Today, both forts are popular tourist attractions.

| WORDS TO KNOW | **Vocabulary Preview** | | |
|---|---|---|---|
| career | mincing | reverberate | wane |
| environs | purging | suffuse | |
| impervious | rebuff | surreptitious | |

## Focus Your Reading

**LITERARY ANALYSIS** **AUTOBIOGRAPHY** An **autobiography** is the story of a person's life, written by that person. Generally told from the first-person point of view, autobiographies vary in style from straightforward chronological accounts to impressionistic narratives. The following autobiographical selection focuses on Maya Angelou's experiences as she searches for her roots to the past. You will notice how her account jumps unexpectedly from narration of events to description of her own inner thoughts and reactions.

**ACTIVE READING** **STRATEGIES FOR READING AUTOBIOGRAPHY**
When you read an autobiography, you learn something about the author as an individual. To discover what "My Sojourn in the Lands of My Ancestors" reveals about Maya Angelou, ask these questions as you read:

- What events has Angelou chosen to describe?
- What feelings and associations do these events trigger in her mind?
- How do these events change her?

**READER'S NOTEBOOK** Fill in a chart like the one started below to show how the events Angelou writes about reveal the kind of person she is.

| Event | Reaction | Impact |
|---|---|---|
| Viewing Cape Coast Castle | Imagining her ancestors imprisoned there | Realizing the legacy of slavery |
| | | |

## LESSON RESOURCES

**UNIT ONE RESOURCE BOOK,**
pp. 51–56

**ASSESSMENT RESOURCES**
**Formal Assessment,** pp. 27–28
**Teacher's Guide to Assessment and Portfolio Use**
**Test Generator**

**SKILLS TRANSPARENCIES AND COPYMASTERS**
**Reading and Critical Thinking**
- Observation Chart, T46 (for Writing Option 1, p. 117)
**Writing**
- The Uses of Dialogue, T24 (for Writing Option 3, p. 117)
**Communications**
- Reading Aloud, T11 (for Mini Lesson, p. 117)

**INTEGRATED TECHNOLOGY**
**LaserLinks**
- Cultural Connection: Modern Ghana
- Art Gallery: West African Art. See **Teacher's SourceBook,** p. 19.
**Visit our website:**
www.mcdougallittell.com

### Objectives
1. understand and appreciate an **autobiography** (Literary Analysis)
2. apply **strategies for reading autobiography** (Active Reading)

### Summary
Maya Angelou, an African-American writer living in Ghana in 1962, explains that she did not feel at home there because she was an American. At the start of the narrative, Angelou travels through Cape Coast, the site of two castles once used as holding forts for enslaved Africans. She contemplates what her ancestors must have felt and thought as they were torn from their families and homeland. Angelou then reaches the village of Dunkwa and asks a woman on the street about a place to stay and is quickly welcomed into the woman's community. Angelou finds parallels between the way she is treated in the village and the way African Americans were welcomed in her grandmother's home in Arkansas in the time of segregation. Angelou is pleased that her hosts assume she is a native African instead of someone from the United States. As a descendant of African slaves, she is pleased to be recognized as part of Africa.

### Thematic Link
Angelou is haunted by images of her ancestors' **first encounter** with Europeans, which resulted in **exploitation** and slavery.

### 5-Minute Warm-Up

***Daily Language SkillBuilder***

Have students **proofread** the display sentences on page 17k and write them correctly. The sentences also appear on Transparency 4 of **Grammar Transparencies and Copymasters.**

### Preteaching Vocabulary
If you would like to preteach the WORDS TO KNOW for this selection, use the Mini Lesson, p. 110.

**Active Reading**

STRATEGIES FOR READING
AUTOBIOGRAPHY

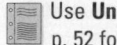 Remind students that when reading an autobiography, they should note what events the author describes and how he or she reacts to them. Ask students where Maya Angelou stops for gas and what the historical significance of this place is.

**Answer:** She stops in Cape Coast, where African captives were held before they were shipped to America as slaves.

Have students describe how Angelou reacts to passing through Cape Coast.

**Answer:** After passing through the town, she finds herself weeping. She stops the car and allows images of her ancestors' suffering to surface in her mind.

Use **Unit One Resource Book,** p. 52 for more practice.

**Literary Analysis** | AUTOBIOGRAPHY |

The historical context of the writer's life often has an important influence on autobiographies. Remind students of the historical context of the early 1960s, when Angelou was in Ghana: many African countries had recently gained independence; John F. Kennedy was president of the United States; African Americans were demanding equal rights and expressing racial pride. Ask students to interpret the possible influences of this historical context on Angelou's writing.

Use **Unit One Resource Book,** p. 53 for more practice.

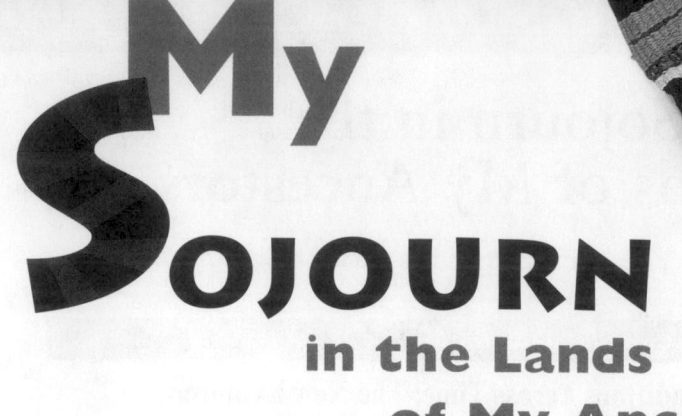

# My SOJOURN
## in the Lands
## of My Ancestors

## MAYA ANGELOU

*During the early sixties in New York City, I met, fell in love with, and married a South African Freedom Fighter who was petitioning the United Nations over the issue of apartheid.[1] A year later, my 15-year-old son, Guy, and I followed my new husband to North Africa.*

*I worked as a journalist in Cairo and managed a home that was a haven to Freedom Fighters still trying to rid their countries of colonialism. I was a moderately good mother to a growingly distant teenager and a faithful, if not loving, wife. I watched my romance <u>wane</u> and my marriage end in the shadows of the Great Pyramid.*

*In 1962, my son and I left Egypt for Ghana, where he was to enter the university and I was*

*to continue to a promised job in Liberia.[2] An automobile accident left Guy with a broken neck and me with the responsibility of securing work and a place for him to recover. Within months I did have a job, a house, and a circle of black American friends who had come to Africa before me. With them I, too, became a hunter for that elusive and much longed-for place the heart could call home.*

*Despite our sincerity and eagerness, we were often <u>rebuffed</u>. The pain of rejection in Africa caused the spiritual that black slaves sang about their oppressors to come to my mind:*

*I'm going to tell God
How you treat me
When I get home.*

*On the delicious and rare occasions when we were accepted, our ecstasy was boundless, and we could have said with our foreparents in the words of another spiritual:*

---

1. **apartheid** (ə-pärt′hīt′): an official policy of racial segregation practiced from 1948 to 1991 in South Africa, involving discrimination against nonwhites.
2. **Liberia** (lī-bîr′ē-ə): a West African country; it is on the Atlantic coast to the west of Ghana.

WORDS TO KNOW

**wane** (wān) *v.* to decrease in size, intensity, or degree
**rebuff** (rĭ-bŭf′) *v.* to reject bluntly; snub

110

---

## Teaching Options

### Mini Lesson Preteaching Vocabulary

**USING CONTEXT CLUES AND REFERENCE MATERIALS**
Call students' attention to the list of WORDS TO KNOW. Remind students that reference materials such as glossaries, dictionaries, and thesauruses can help them find the exact meaning of words. When looking up a word in a dictionary, students sometimes will find several definitions. The context in which a word is used determines which meaning is appropriate. Demonstrate this strategy by using the following model.

**Model Sentence**
As the school year *waned,* students' thoughts turned to their plans for summer vacation.

**Instruction**
• Write the model sentence on the chalkboard.
• Ask a volunteer to look up the word *wane* in a dictionary and read the listed definitions aloud. Write these definitions on the chalkboard.
• Have students determine which definition best suits the context of the model sentence.

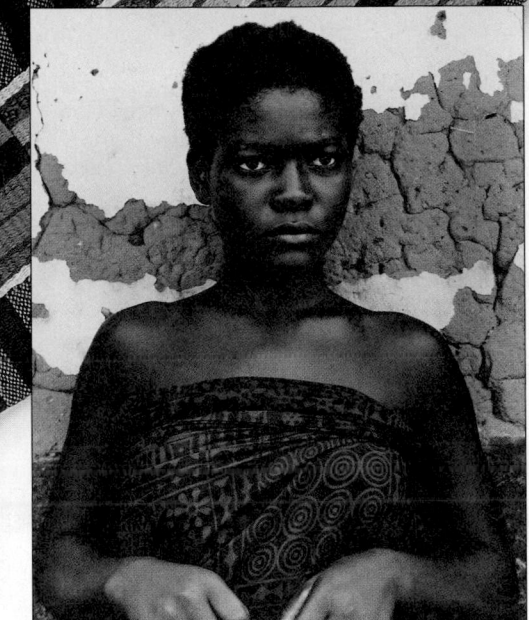

Afi Negble, Asenema, Ghana, 1964, Paul Strand. Copyright © 1971, Aperture Foundation Inc., Paul Strand Archive.

*My soul got happy*
*When I came out of the wilderness*
*Came out of the wilderness*
*Came out of the wilderness.*
*My soul got happy*
*When I came out of the wilderness*
*And up to the welcome table.*

**1** I had a long weekend, money in my purse, and working command of Fanti.[3] After a year in Accra,[4] I needed country quiet, so I decided to travel into the bush. I bought roasted plantain stuffed with boiled peanuts, a quart of Club beer, and headed my little car west. The stretch was a highway from Accra to Cape Coast, filled with trucks and private cars passing from lane to lane with abandon. People hung out of windows of the crowded mammie lorries,[5] and I could hear singing and shouting when the drivers careened

those antique vehicles up and down hills as if each was a little train out to prove it could. **2**

I stopped in Cape Coast only for gas. Although many black Americans had headed for the town as soon as they touched ground in Ghana, I successfully avoided it for a year. Cape Coast Castle and the nearby Elmina Castle had been holding forts for captured slaves. The captives had been imprisoned in dungeons beneath the massive buildings, and friends of mine who had felt called upon to make the trek reported that they felt the thick stone walls still echoed with old cries. **A**

The palm-tree-lined streets and fine white-stone buildings did not tempt me to remain any longer than necessary. Once out of the town and again onto the tarred roads, I knew I had not made a clean escape. Despite my hurry, history had invaded my little car. Pangs of self-pity and a sorrow for my unknown relatives <u>suffused</u> me. Tears made the highway waver and were salty on my tongue.

What did they think and feel, my grandfathers, caught on those green savannas, under the baobab trees? How long did their families search for them? Did the dungeon wall feel chilly and its slickness strange to my grand-mothers, who were used to the rush of air against bamboo huts and the sound of birds rattling their green roofs?

I had to pull off the road. Just passing near Cape Coast Castle had plunged me back into the eternal melodrama.

There would be no <u>purging</u>, I knew, unless I asked all the questions. Only then

---

3. **Fanti** (făn′tē): the dialect of the Fanti, one of the many ethnic groups who inhabit Ghana.
4. **Accra** (ăk′rə): the capital and largest city of Ghana.
5. **mammie lorries:** small trucks or open-sided buses used for public transportation in West Africa.

---

| WORDS | **careen** (kə-rēn′) *v.* to swerve, or cause to swerve, from side to side while in motion |
| TO | **suffuse** (sə-fyōōz′) *v.* to spread through |
| KNOW | **purging** (pûr′jĭng) *n.* getting rid of something unwanted; cleansing **purge** *v.* |

**111**

---

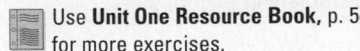

**Literary Analysis FLASHBACK**

**A** Point out that this paragraph interrupts the narrative to describe events that took place at an earlier time. Ask students how this scene helps the reader understand the narrator's present situation.

**Possible Response:** The disturbing images and scenes that the narrator imagines explain why she is weeping.

**Literary Analysis IMAGERY**

**B** Ask students to find words that give the scene a sense of motion (*"moving quietly," "rippling"*) and color (*"black water," "bright sun," "a rippling cloth of lamé"*). Then have them find other passages on this page in which the author paints vivid word pictures.

**Possible Responses:** The paragraphs beginning "I allowed the shapes to come" and "As usual, in the towns of Ghana"

**Literary Analysis METAPHOR**

**C** Remind students that a metaphor is a figure of speech that compares two things and, by doing so, suggests that they have a common characteristic. Then ask students what the Fanti name *Nkran* compares the city to.

**Answer:** a large anthill with millions of ants

Ask students what the name implies about people's attitudes toward life in the city.

**Possible Response:** The name suggests that people live there crowded together without being recognized as individuals.

would the spirits understand that I was feeding them. It was a crumb, but it was all I had.

I allowed the shapes to come to my imagination; children passed, tied together by ropes and chains, tears abashed, stumbling in a dull exhaustion, then women, hair uncombed, bodies gritted with sand, and sagging in defeat. Men, muscles without memory, minds dimmed, plodding, leaving bloodied footprints in the dirt. The quiet was awful. None of them cried, or yelled, or bellowed. No moans came from them. They lived in a mute territory, dead to feeling and protest. These were the legions, sold by sisters, stolen by brothers, bought by strangers, enslaved by the greedy, and betrayed by history.

For a long time I sat as in an open-air auditorium watching a troupe of tragic players enter and exit the stage.

The visions faded as my tears ceased. Light returned and I started the car, turned off the main road, and headed for the interior. Using rutted track roads, and lanes a little larger than footpaths, I found the River Pra. The black water moving quietly, ringed with the tall trees, seemed enchanted. A fear of snakes kept me in the car, but I parked and watched the bright sun turn the water surface into a rippling cloth of lamé.[6] I passed through villages that were little more than collections of thatch huts, with goats and small children wandering in the lanes. The noise of my car brought smiling adults out to wave at me.

In the late afternoon I reached the thriving town that was my destination. A student whom I had met at Legon (where the University of Ghana is located) had spoken to me often of the gold-mining area, of Dunkwa, his birthplace. His reports had so glowed with the town's virtues, I had chosen that spot for my first journey.

My skin color, features, and the Ghana cloth I wore would make me look like any young Ghanaian woman. I could pass if I didn't talk too much.

As usual, in the towns of Ghana, the streets were filled with vendors selling their wares of tinned pat milk, hot spicy Killi Willis (fried, ripe plantain chips), Pond's cold cream, and antimosquito incense rings. Farmers were returning home, children returning from school. Young boys grinned at <u>mincing</u> girls, and always there were the market women, huge and <u>impervious</u>. I searched for a hotel sign in vain and as the day lengthened, I started to worry. I didn't have enough gas to get to Koforidua, a large town east of Dunkwa, where there would certainly be hotels, and I didn't have the address of my student's family. I parked the car a little out of the town center and stopped a woman carrying a bucket of water on her head and a baby on her back.

"Good day." I spoke in Fanti and she responded. I continued, "I beg you, I am a stranger looking for a place to stay."

She repeated, "Stranger?" and laughed. "You are a stranger? No. No."

To many Africans, only whites could be strangers. All Africans belonged somewhere, to some clan. All Akan[7]-speaking people belong to one of eight blood lines (Abosua) and one of eight spirit lines (Ntoro).

I said, "I am not from here."

For a second, fear darted in her eyes. There was the possibility that I was a witch or some unhappy ghost from the country of the dead. I quickly said, "I am from Accra." She gave me a good smile. "Oh, one Accra. Without a home." She laughed. The Fanti word *Nkran*, for which

---

6. **lamé** (lă-mā´): a glittering fabric containing metallic threads.

7. **Akan** (ä´kän´): a language spoken in southern Ghana, of which Fanti is a dialect.

WORDS TO KNOW
**mincing** (mĭn´sĭng) *adj.* acting refined or dainty
**impervious** (ĭm-pûr´vē-əs) *adj.* incapable of being affected

## Teaching Options

### BLOCK SCHEDULING: MANAGING TIME

**If your schedule requires that you cover the lesson objectives in a shorter time, use . . .**
- Preparing to Read, p. 109
- Thinking Through the Literature, p. 116
- Vocabulary in Action, p. 117

**If you would like to take advantage of longer class times, use . . .**
- TE Teaching Options: Preteaching Vocabulary, p. 110 (can be done as a group activity); Cross-Curricular Link, p. 114; Standardized Test Practice, p. 115; Speaking and Listening, p. 117
- Choices & Challenges, p. 117

the capital was named, means the large ant that builds 10-foot-high domes of red clay and lives with millions of other ants.

"Come with me." She turned quickly, steadying the bucket on her head, and led me between two corrugated tin shacks. The baby bounced and slept on her back, secured by the large piece of cloth wrapped around her body. We passed a compound where women were pounding the dinner *foo foo*[8] in wooden bowls.

The woman shouted, "Look what I have found. One Nkran which has no place to sleep tonight." The women laughed and asked, "One Nkran? I don't believe it."

"Are you taking it to the old man?"

"Of course."

"Sleep well, alone, Nkran, if you can." My guide stopped before a small house. She put the water on the ground and told me to wait while she entered the house. She returned immediately, followed by a man who rubbed his eyes as if he had just been awakened.

He walked close and peered hard at my face. "This is the Nkran?" The woman was adjusting the bucket on her head.

"Yes, Uncle. I have brought her." She looked at me, "Good-bye, Nkran. Sleep in peace. Uncle, I am going." The man said, "Go and come, child," and resumed studying my face. "You are not Ga."[9] He was reading my features.

A few small children had collected around his knees. They could barely hold back their giggles as he interrogated me.

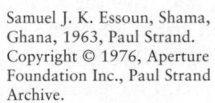

Samuel J. K. Essoun, Shama, Ghana, 1963, Paul Strand. Copyright © 1976, Aperture Foundation Inc., Paul Strand Archive.

"Aflao?"

I said, "No."

"Brong-ahafo?"

I said, "No. I am . . ." I meant to tell him the truth, but he said, "Don't tell me. I will soon know." He continued staring at me. "Speak more. I will know from your Fanti."

"Well, I have come from Accra and I need to rent a room for the night. I told that woman that I was a stranger . . ."

He laughed. "And you are. Now, I know. You are Bambara from Liberia. It is clear you are Bambara." He laughed again. "I always can tell. I am not easily fooled." He shook my hand. "Yes, we will find you a place for the night. Come." He touched a boy at his right. "Find Patience Aduah and bring her to me."

The children laughed, and all ran away as the man led me into the house. He pointed me to a seat in the neat little parlor and shouted, "Foriwa, we have a guest. Bring beer." A small black woman with an imperial air entered the room. Her knowing face told me that she had witnessed the scene in her front yard.

She spoke to her husband. "And, Kobina, did

---

8. *foo foo*: a starchy dough made from mashed yams, cassavas, or plantains.
9. **Ga** (gä): like *Aflao, Brong-ahafo,* and *Bambara* in the following sentences, the name of a West African ethnic group.

MY SOJOURN IN THE LANDS OF MY ANCESTORS **113**

---

---

 **Mini Lesson** ## Grammar

**COMPOUND-COMPLEX SENTENCES** Review the difference between main clauses and subordinate clauses. Write the following sentence on the board:

Africans who were captured and sold into slavery were imprisoned in Cape Coast Castle.

Point out that the main clause (*Africans were imprisoned in Cape Coast Castle*) expresses a complete idea and can stand alone as a sentence. The subordinate clause (*who were captured and sold into slavery*) doesn't express a complete idea and can't stand alone as a sentence.

A compound sentence contains at least two main clauses, while a complex sentence contains one main clause and at least one subordinate clause.

A compound-complex sentence contains at least two main clauses *and* at least one subordinate clause.

Write the following compound-complex sentence on the board. Then underline the main clauses and place the subordinate clause within parentheses.

(When I journeyed through Africa), I came to understand my ancestor's suffering, and I also learned something about myself.

 Use **Grammar Transparencies and Copymasters,** p. 112.

 Use McDougal Littell's *Language Network,* Chapter 3, for more instruction in compound-complex sentences.

## Reading Skills and Strategies: MAKING JUDGMENTS

**A** By not correcting her hosts' mistake, Angelou in effect tells a lie. Ask students to discuss why she does this and if they think she is wrong to do so.

**Possible Responses:** She doesn't want to embarrass her hosts or spoil their delight in identifying her; also, she is pleased to be taken for an African.

Some students may say that to lie is wrong under any circumstances; others may excuse this lie because it harms no one and allows Angelou to experience a much-needed sense of belonging.

## Active Reading:

> STRATEGIES FOR READING AUTOBIOGRAPHY

**B** Remind students that in an autobiography, the writer often describes memories that he or she associates with events in the main narrative. Ask students to explain how Angelou's **flashback** to her childhood in Arkansas helps the reader understand her present thoughts and feelings in Ghana.

**Possible Response:** Angelou remembers people in her Arkansas community bringing food to her grandmother for the African-American travelers staying at her home. In this flashback Angelou compares the welcome that African-American travelers received in Arkansas during segregation and the welcome she receives as a traveler in Ghana, where she is treated as a guest and shown generous hospitality.

## Literary Analysis IMAGERY

**C** Point out how the author conveys a sense of the children's physical presence by using vivid verbs such as *bobbed* and *jumped* to describe their energetic activity.

---

you find who the stranger was?" She walked to me. I stood and shook her hand. "Welcome, stranger." We both laughed. "Now don't tell me, Kobina, I have ears, also. Sit down, sister, beer is coming. Let me hear you speak."

We sat facing each other while her husband stood over us smiling. "You, Foriwa, you will never get it."

I told her my story, adding a few more words I had recently learned. She laughed grandly. "She is Bambara. I could have told you when Abaa first brought her. See how tall she is? See her head? See her color? Men, huh. They only look at a woman's shape."

Two children brought beer and glasses to the man, who poured and handed the glasses around. "Sister, I am Kobina Artey; this is my wife, Foriwa, and some of my children."

**A** I introduced myself, but because they had taken such relish in detecting my tribal origin I couldn't tell them that they were wrong. Or, less admirably, at the moment I didn't want to remember that I was an American. For the first time since my arrival, I was very nearly home. Not a Ghanaian, but at least accepted for an African. The sensation was worth a lie.

Voices came to the house from the yard.

"Brother Kobina," "Uncle," "Auntie."

Foriwa opened the door to a group of people, who entered, speaking fast and looking at me.

"So this is the Bambara woman? The stranger?" They looked me over and talked with my hosts. I understood some of their conversation. They said that I was nice-looking and old enough to have a little wisdom. They announced that my car was parked a few blocks away. Kobina told them that I would spend the night with the newlyweds,

**1** Patience and Kwame Duodu. Yes, they could see clearly that I was a Bambara.

"Give us the keys to your car, sister; someone will bring your bag."

I gave up the keys and all resistance. I was either at home with friends or I would die wishing that to be so.

Later, Patience, her husband, Kwame, and I

---

sat out in the yard around a cooking fire near to their thatched house, which was much smaller than the Artey bungalow. They explained that Kobina Artey was not a chief, but a member of the village council, and all small matters in that area of Dunkwa were taken to him. As Patience stirred the stew in the pot that was balanced over the fire, children and women appeared sporadically out of the darkness carrying covered plates. Each time Patience thanked the bearers and directed them to the house, I felt the distance narrow between my past and present.

**B** In the United States, during segregation, black American travelers, unable to stay in hotels restricted to white patrons, stopped at churches and told the black ministers or

Nana Oparabea, High Priestess, Larteh, Ghana, 1963, Paul Strand. Copyright © 1976, Aperture Foundation Inc., Paul Strand Archive.

---

# Teaching Options

## Cross Curricular Link  History

**MANHATTAN'S AFRICAN BURIAL GROUND** In 1991, construction workers, excavating the site of a new federal office building in New York City, discovered the remains of an 18th-century burial ground containing the graves of hundreds of enslaved Africans. This site, now a historical landmark called the African Burial Ground, provides a rare and valuable glimpse into the lives of people whose labor helped to create a great city out of a wilderness.

A controversy arose over who would control the study and interpretation of the human remains and artifacts. The General Services Administration agreed to fund a thorough study based at Howard University in Washington, D.C.

Results of the study have been both disturbing and uplifting. Analysis of the skeletons reveals that many children as well as adults in this African community endured the excessive physical demands of slave labor, such as carrying heavy loads on their shoulders and heads. On the other hand, the existence of such a large burial ground and the fact that many people were buried according to African customs show that there was a strong, supportive community of Africans in New York in the 1700s. Despite the inhuman conditions of slavery, Africans created a vibrant cultural and social life for themselves in the New World.

deacons of their predicaments. Church officials would select a home and then inform the unexpecting hosts of the decision. There was never a protest, but the new hosts relied on the generosity of their neighbors to help feed and even entertain their guests. After the travelers were settled, surreptitious knocks would sound on the back door.

In Stamps, Arkansas, I heard so often, "Sister Henderson, I know you've got guests. Here's a pan of biscuits."

"Sister Henderson, Mama sent a half a cake for your visitors."

"Sister Henderson, I made a lot of macaroni and cheese. Maybe this will help with your visitors."

My grandmother would whisper her thanks and finally when the family and guests sat down at the table, the offerings were so different and plentiful, it appeared that days had been spent preparing the meal.

Patience invited me inside, and when I saw the table I was confirmed in my earlier impression. Groundnut stew, garden egg stew, hot pepper soup, *kenke, kotomre,* fried plantain, *dukuno,* shrimp, fish cakes, and more, all crowded together on variously patterned plates.

In Arkansas, the guests would never suggest, although they knew better, that the host had not prepared every scrap of food, especially for them.

I said to Patience, "Oh, sister, you went to such trouble."

She laughed. "It is nothing, sister. We don't want our Bambara relative to think herself a stranger anymore. Come let us wash and eat."

After dinner, I followed Patience to the outdoor toilet; then they gave me a cot in a very small room.

In the morning, I wrapped my cloth under my arms, sarong fashion, and walked with Patience to the bathhouse. We joined about 20 women in a walled enclosure which had no ceiling. The greetings were loud and cheerful as we soaped ourselves and poured buckets of water over our shoulders.

Patience introduced me. "This is our Bambara sister."

"She's a tall one, all right. Welcome, sister."

"I like her color."

"How many children, sister?" The woman was looking at my breasts.

I apologized, "I only have one."

"One?"

"One?"

"One!" Shouts reverberated over the splashing water. I said, "One, but I'm trying."

They laughed. "Try hard, sister. Keep trying."

We ate leftovers from the last night feast, and I said a sad good-bye to my hosts. The children walked me back to my car, with the oldest boy carrying my bag. I couldn't offer money to my hosts, Arkansas had taught me that, but I gave change to the children. They bobbed and jumped and grinned.

"Good-bye, Bambara Auntie."

"Go and come, Auntie."

"Go and come."

I drove into Cape Coast before I thought of the gruesome castle and out of its environs before the ghosts of slavery caught me. Perhaps their attempts had been halfhearted. After all, in Dunkwa, although I had let a lie speak for me, I had proved that one of their descendants, at least one, could just briefly return to Africa, and that despite cruel betrayals, bitter ocean voyages, and hurtful centuries, we were still recognizable. ❖

| WORDS | **surreptitious** (sûr´əp-tĭsh´əs) *adj.* secret; stealthy |
| TO | **reverberate** (rĭ-vûr´bə-rāt´) *v.* to echo |
| KNOW | **environs** (ĕn-vī´rənz) *n.* a surrounding region |

**115**

## Customizing Instruction

**Less Proficient Readers**

**1** Ask students to identify the feelings that Angelou's visit to Dunkwa has evoked thus far.

**Possible Responses:** She is comforted by the community's welcome; she enjoys being identified as an African, invited into the house, and addressed as "sister."

**Set a Purpose** Have students read on to see how Angelou is welcomed by the newlyweds and how she feels about their welcome.

**2** Ask students to summarize what Angelou's community in Arkansas did when black American travelers could not stay in hotels.

**Possible Response:** The community invited travelers into their homes, giving them food and a place to stay.

Then ask them how this behavior is similar to how Angelou is treated in Dunkwa.

**Possible Response:** The people of Dunkwa also take in a traveler, contribute to a feast in her honor, and give her a place to stay.

---

## ✓ Assessment  Standardized Test Practice

**CHOOSING THE BEST SUMMARY** Many standardized tests include items that require students to select the best summary statement for a passage they have read. Write the following statements on the chalkboard and ask students to discuss which is the best summary of "My Sojourn in the Lands of My Ancestors."

**A.** Maya Angelou is welcomed into the community at Dunkwa and feels grateful to be recognized as an African.

**B.** Maya Angelou is haunted by images of her ancestors' suffering during the African slave trade.

**C.** Maya Angelou travels through Ghana and connects with her African heritage in both painful and heartwarming ways.

During the discussion, point out that all three statements contain true information about the selection. Statement C is the best summary because it applies to the selection as a whole, whereas statements A and B apply only to specific parts of the selection.

# *Thinking* through the **LITERATURE**

## GUIDING STUDENT RESPONSE

### Connect to the Literature

**1. What Do You Think?**
Possible Response: The account made me think about how isolated people are today. I can't imagine going into a town and having strangers take care of me. It would be wonderful if everyone were as hospitable as the people of Dunkwa.

**Comprehension Check**
- Her marriage had ended, and she traveled to Ghana with her son, who planned to attend the university there.
- They were used as holding forts for captured African slaves.
- The people welcomed her warmly, inviting her to their homes and giving her food and shelter.

Use Selection Quiz
**Unit One Resource Book**, p. 55.

### Think Critically

**2.** Angelou has a feeling of hope that she and other African Americans can reconnect with their heritage.

**3.** Possible Responses: She is fed and sheltered, identified as an African, and addressed as "sister"; she is reminded of the Arkansas home in which she grew up.

**4.** Possible Responses: No, because the people of Dunkwa wanted to believe she was a "sister" and take care of her. Yes, because meaningful relationships must be built on the truth.

**5.** Possible Response: She knew about the terrible history of that place but tried to avoid confronting it. When she passed by the castle, she could no longer repress the images of suffering. She realized that she had to make peace with her ancestors who had suffered the horror of slavery.

**6.** Possible Responses: When she sees that there are no hotels in Dunkwa, she feels worried and realizes that she must ask people in the community for help. When the people of Dunkwa assume she is African, she does not correct them, realizing her deep need to be accepted by the community. When the community of Dunkwa welcomes her, she feels relieved, happy, and connected to her ancestors.

**116** UNIT ONE PART 2

---

## Connect to the Literature

**1. What Do You Think?**
What thoughts or feelings do you have about Angelou's experiences in Dunkwa? Describe your impressions to a classmate.

**Comprehension Check**
- Why did Angelou leave Egypt and move to Ghana?
- What was the historical significance of the two castles located on the Cape Coast?
- How did the people of Dunkwa welcome Angelou?

## Think Critically

**2.** Why do you think it matters to Angelou that she "had proved that one of their descendants, at least one, could just briefly return to Africa, and that despite cruel betrayals, bitter ocean voyages, and hurtful centuries, we were still recognizable"?

**3.** What makes Dunkwa seem like home to Angelou?

**4.** Do you think Angelou should have revealed that she was an American? Explain your opinion.

**5.** How do you interpret Angelou's strong reaction the first time she passed by Cape Coast Castle?

> THINK ABOUT
> - why she avoided the town for a year
> - the scenes from the past she imagined
> - her references to "purging" and "feeding the spirits"

**6.** **ACTIVE READING** **STRATEGIES FOR READING AUTOBIOGRAPHY** Review the chart you made in your **READER'S NOTEBOOK**. Which events had the greatest impact on Angelou? How do you think they changed her?

## Extend Interpretations

**7. Connect to Life** While living in Africa, Angelou explored the lands of her ancestors. If you could visit the home of your ancestors, what would you most like to find out? Why?

**8.** **Points of Comparison** Imagine a conversation between Maya Angelou and Olaudah Equiano, the African who was kidnapped and sent to the Americas on a slave ship (see page 93). What do you think they might say to each other?

**116** UNIT ONE PART 2: FIRST ENCOUNTERS

---

## Literary Analysis

**AUTOBIOGRAPHY** As you recall, an **autobiography** is the story of a person's life, written by that person. Writers of autobiographies draw from moments in their lives that are especially compelling, dramatic, or exciting. In "My Sojourn in the Lands of My Ancestors," Angelou recounts some of her powerful memories and explores their personal meaning. Like all writers of autobiographies, she is both a storyteller and an interpreter of events.

**Paired Activity** Imagine that Maya Angelou considered the following question as she was writing this autobiographical selection: Will the telling of these memories reveal something significant about who I am? Working with a partner, create a personality profile of Angelou, based on what you have learned about her.

**REVIEW** **AUTHOR'S PURPOSE**
What do you think is Angelou's purpose for writing this selection? How does her purpose compare with William Least Heat-Moon's purpose in *Blue Highways*?

---

## Extend Interpretations

**Connect to Life** Students may say that they would like to find out the names of their ancestors and visit the places where they lived and worked to experience what their lives were like. Others might like to discover distant relatives still living in the place and sharing the family name.

**Points of Comparison** Possible Responses: Angelou might ask Equiano the questions that were in her mind after seeing Cape Coast, such as what he thought and felt when he was captured, how long he thought his family searched for him, and how the dungeon wall felt to him. She might also ask him whether living in America and speaking and writing in English made him feel disconnected from his African roots.

## Literary Analysis

**Autobiography** Students' personality profiles of Angelou should mention her need to experience vicariously her ancestors' suffering and to feel at home in Ghana.

**Review Author's Purpose** Angelou's purpose is to express her thoughts and feelings as a traveler in western Ghana, the home of her ancestors; Heat-Moon's purpose is to inform the reader about Hopi beliefs.

## Writing Options

**1. Description of Place** What makes a place feel like home? Write a description of a place (other than your own home) that feels like home to you. Use sensory details—details that appeal to the five senses—to make the place come to life for your readers.

**2. Poetry of Experience** Angelou was moved by her journey to her ancestors' lands. Draft a poem that captures her feelings about Cape Coast Castle, her visit to Dunkwa, or some other aspect of her experiences. As an alternative, you might draft a poem about your own response to Angelou's journey.

**3. ▌Points of Comparison** Based on your answer to discussion question 8, write an imagined dialogue between Angelou and Equiano.

## Vocabulary in Action

**EXERCISE: MATCHING MEANINGS** On a piece of paper, write the word that most clearly relates to each phrase below. Then write a sentence containing both the phrase and the vocabulary word.

1. an out-of-control car
2. a map of Accra and its suburbs
3. the light at sunset
4. a stone that is undamaged by harsh weather
5. a slave's secret plan of escape
6. the villagers' loud singing
7. an unwanted offer of money
8. the scent of hot pepper soup
9. sorrow that needs release
10. villagers who try to act sophisticated in front of strangers

**Building Vocabulary**

For an in-depth lesson on word connotation and denotation, see page 908.

| WORDS TO KNOW | careen | mincing | reverberate | wane |
| --- | --- | --- | --- | --- |
| | environs | purging | suffuse | |
| | impervious | rebuff | surreptitious | |

## Maya Angelou
### 1928–

**Other Works**
*I Know Why the Caged Bird Sings, The Heart of a Woman, The Complete Collected Poems of Maya Angelou*

**Unlimited Potential** Maya Angelou's formal education ended with high school, but she has continued to search for knowledge of herself and the world around her. Her search has taken her from rural Stamps, Arkansas, where as a child she lived with her grandmother, to as far away as Ghana and Egypt. She has said in *Black Women Writers at Work*, "I believe all things are possible for a human being, and I don't think there's anything in the world I can't do." Angelou's life bears witness that she lives by this philosophy.

**Performing Artist** After high school, Angelou studied dance in New York City, where she eventually worked under the celebrated performer and teacher Martha Graham. She soon made her mark as a dancer, actress, singer, director, and producer, both in the United States and abroad.

**Versatile Writer** Angelou, who began writing in the 1960s, has written poems, plays, songs, short stories, screenplays, articles, and television specials. She has also written five autobiographical works, including *All God's Children Need Traveling Shoes,* the source of this selection. "I had not consciously come to Ghana to find the roots of my beginnings," Angelou states in this book, "but I had continually and accidentally tripped over them or fallen upon them in my everyday life." One of the highlights of Angelou's career was composing and reciting the poem "On the Pulse of Morning" for President Bill Clinton's inauguration in 1993.

## Writing Options

1. **Description of Place** Students' responses should include sensory details that convey what home means to them. **To get students started on this assignment,** suggest that they make a five-column chart with the five senses as column headings—sight, hearing, smell, taste, and touch. Students can fill in the chart by listing the sensory details that they might include in their written descriptions. Advise students to list several details as they fill in the chart, and then select the most vivid ones to use in their writing.

2. **Poetry of Experience** Students' poems should demonstrate an appreciation of the feelings Angelou shares in the selection. **To get students started on this assignment,** have them skim the selection looking for specific words or phrases that Angelou uses to convey her feelings. Students should consider how these words affect their response to the selection.

3. **Points of Comparison** Students' dialogues should reflect an understanding of the historical contexts and concerns of both Angelou and Equiano. **To make this assignment more challenging,** have students work with partners to perform their completed dialogues before the class.

## Vocabulary in Action

1. careen
2. environs
3. wane
4. impervious
5. surreptitious
6. reverberate
7. rebuff
8. suffuse
9. purging
10. mincing

##  Speaking and Listening

**POETRY READING**

**Prepare** The Million Man March took place on October 16, 1995, in Washington, D.C. Its purpose was to assemble a large group of African-American men who would commit themselves to improving the lives of their families and communities. Maya Angelou wrote a poem for the event and read it before the crowd. Have students find copies of her "Million Man March Poem" and prepare an oral reading for the class. Suggest that they keep in mind the legacy of slavery that Angelou describes in "My Sojourn in the Lands of My Ancestors." Have students consider the emotions that Angelou's reading might have stirred in her audience and the speaking techniques she might have used to create this effect. Students may work with partners to practice their readings.

**Present** Have students take turns reading lines of the poem for the class. Students in the audience should listen carefully, appreciating the emotional effect that each reading creates. When all students have read, lead a discussion of the techniques various students used and how well they worked.

**BLOCK SCHEDULING** This activity is particularly well suited to longer class periods.

## PART 1 Reading the Prompt

Model the process of reading a prompt:
- Read the entire prompt aloud.
- List key words of the assignment on the board ("encounters between people of different cultures," "examples from the three selections," "develop recommendations").
- Define key words using the Strategies in Action to show how students can restate the prompt for themselves.

## PART 2 Planning a Synthesis Essay

- Have students begin by choosing two other selections.
- Suggest that they create charts that are large enough to accommodate detailed notes.
- After completing their charts, students should select the evidence that they will use. Urge them to consider their recommendations as they select details.

## PART 3 Drafting Your Essay

**Introduction** Suggest that students try beginning with a question or interesting detail that will catch readers' interest. Then they can tell the purpose of their essays: to give recommendations for positive cross-cultural encounters.

**Organization** Have students consider different organizational patterns before they begin writing. Besides using order of importance or chronological order, they might think about creating a section for each recommendation.

**Conclusion** Students may conclude that fear or anxiety is common in encounters with unknown people, but that acts of kindness often win people over and create positive relationships.

**Revision** Students should check their essays to make sure they have used possessive forms correctly. They should use an apostrophe and *s* after an individual author's name, or a simple apostrophe if they are referring to "authors."

---

# Comparing Literature: Assessment Practice

In writing assessment, you will sometimes be asked to synthesize, or pull together, information from a number of selections and make a generalization about what you've learned. You are now going to practice writing an essay with this kind of focus.

## PART 1 Reading the Prompt

Often you will be asked to write in response to a prompt like the one below. First, read the entire prompt carefully. Then read through it again, looking for key words that help you identify the purpose of the essay and decide how to approach it.

> **Writing Prompt**
>
> Think about the encounters between people of **❶** different cultures in "My Sojourn in the Lands of My Ancestors" and two other selections you have read in Unit One, Part Two. Using examples from **❷** the three selections, develop recommendations **❸** for anyone wanting to have a positive cross-cultural encounter.

> **STRATEGIES IN ACTION**
>
> **❶** Consider your **topic**—cross-cultural encounters.
>
> **❷** Cite **examples** of behavior from three selections.
>
> **❸** **Synthesize**, or pull together, information to set guidelines for cross-cultural encounters.

## PART 2 Planning a Synthesis Essay

- Create a diagram to organize your sources of information.
- In each selection, identify the passages related to your topic—cross-cultural encounters.
- Look for examples of positive behavior to imitate or negative behavior to avoid.
- Draw parallels among the various examples.
- Make generalizations and recommendations about positive cross-cultural encounters.

| My Sojourn | Other Selection | Other Selection |
|---|---|---|
| Positive Examples | Positive Examples | Positive Examples |
| Negative Examples | Negative Examples | Negative Examples |

Generalizations / Recommendations

## PART 3 Drafting Your Essay

**Introduction** Begin by stating your topic—guidelines for cross-cultural encounters. Identify the three selections you will use for illustration.

**Organization** Present your recommendations in a logical order, perhaps from most important to least important, or from those followed at first contact to those followed later. Use examples from all three selections to support your recommendations.

**Conclusion** End your essay by restating the topic of your paper and summarizing your recommendations.

**Revision** Allow time to review your work. Make sure it is clear, well-supported, and free from mistakes.

**Writing Handbook**
See page 1281: Explanatory Writing

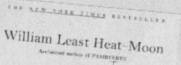

## The Great Explorers

SAMUEL ELIOT MORISON

The voyages of Christopher Columbus, Ferdinand Magellan, Sir Francis Drake, and other famous European navigators come alive in Morison's critically acclaimed book. A notable historian and scholar, Morison details the enormous challenges of their hazardous sea journeys, their courage to explore the unknown, and their extraordinary navigational achievements. The book also includes several maps showing the routes of historic voyages.

## Blue Highways

WILLIAM LEAST HEAT-MOON

Go beyond the excerpt on page 100 and read more from *Blue Highways,* Heat-Moon's chronicle of his 13,000-mile road trip through the United States. Riding in a van he named "Ghost Dancing," Heat-Moon takes the scenic route, traveling down rural roads and meeting a colorful cast of small-town characters. Heat-Moon's eloquent descriptions provide a panoramic view of the American landscape.

The *Electronic Library* is a CD-ROM that contains additional fiction, nonfiction, poetry, and drama for each unit in *The Language of Literature.*

This is the additional selection found in Unit 1 of the *Electronic Library.*

John Smith
**What Happened Till the First Supply,** *from* **The General History of Virginia**

**Reading Skills and Strategies**
**SUSTAINED SILENT READING**
Encourage students to select one of the books as an opportunity to read silently over a period of time.

## And Even *More* . . .

### Books
**The Buried Mirror**
CARLOS FUENTES
Illustrated essay on Spain's influence in the New World.

**The Whole World Guide to Culture Learning**
J. DANIEL HESS
Informative book for contemporary travelers who encounter people from new cultures.

**Endangered Peoples**
ART DAVIDSON
The voices and faces of diverse native peoples who caution against destroying their cultures.

### Other Media
**1492: Conquest of Paradise**
A feature film portraying the history-making explorations of Christopher Columbus. Panavision. (VIDEOCASSETTE)

**A Son of Africa: The Slave Narrative of Olaudah Equiano**
A film adaptation of Equiano's autobiography chronicling his experiences from his abduction in Africa to his role in the anti-slavery movement. California Newsreel. (VIDEOCASSETTE)

**Lewis and Clark**
A documentary by Ken Burns dramatizing moments from the historic expedition. Florentine Films and WETA, Washington, D.C. (VIDEOCASSETTE)

### The Journals of Lewis and Clark

EDITED BY BERNARD DE VOTO

Imagine a cross-country trip from Missouri to Oregon—without a car or a map. In their journals, explorers Meriwether Lewis and William Clark vividly record their 1804–1806 expedition to find a western route to the Pacific coast.

## Objectives
- write an Eyewitness Report
- use a written text as a model for writing
- revise a draft to add sensory details
- place modifiers as close as possible to the words they modify

## Introducing the Workshop

**A Eyewitness Report** Explain that eyewitness reports are firsthand accounts of events that have personal or historical significance. Newspaper and magazine articles as well as television and film documentaries include eyewitness reports. These reports acquaint us with interesting local, national, and international events. Have students briefly summarize a few eyewitness reports they have heard or read, and write the topics on the board. Do these reports fit in any particular categories, such as national or international politics, sports, the environment, local community, family, etc.? Point out that through writing an eyewitness report, students, too, will be able to inform their readers of newsworthy events to which they might otherwise never be exposed.

Establish some criteria for what makes an eyewitness report worth telling. Students may be interested in sharing information about a school event. Some may want to raise the social consciousness of their readers by describing a situation in a certain locality. Still others may be interested in letting others know about local and community events.

## Basics in a Box

**B Using the Graphic** The components of an eyewitness report work together to create an overall impression of an event. The graphic offers suggestions that students can use to draft an effective eyewitness report.

**C Presenting the Rubric** To better understand the assignment, students can refer to the Standards for Writing a Successful Eyewitness Report. You may also want to share with them the complete rubric, which describes several levels of proficiency.

---

# *Writing* Workshop — Eyewitness Report

## A Describing what you have seen . . .

**From Reading to Writing** Upon arriving in North America for the first time, William Bradford described the land as "a hideous and desolate wilderness, full of wild beasts." Bradford's **eyewitness report** is a firsthand account of the events he observed and experienced as an English colonist in North America. Writers of eyewitness reports use compelling details and sensory language to describe events. Today, eyewitness accounts written by professional journalists are published daily in newspapers and magazines.

### For Your Portfolio

**WRITING PROMPT** Write an eyewitness report describing an event that has personal or historical significance.

**Purpose:** To inform
**Audience:** Classmates, family, or general readers

---

### Basics in a Box

**B Eyewitness Report at a Glance**

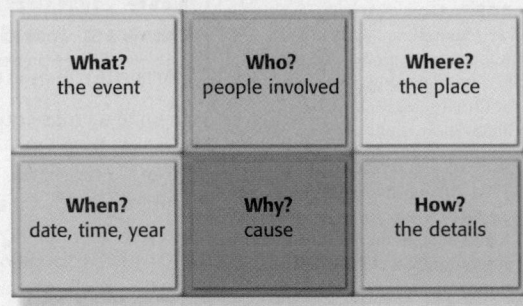

| What? the event | Who? people involved | Where? the place |
| --- | --- | --- |
| When? date, time, year | Why? cause | How? the details |

= **Re-creation of Event**

**C RUBRIC Standards for Writing**

**A successful eyewitness report should**
- focus on an event that has personal or historical significance
- answer the five W's: *who, what, when, where,* and *why*
- create a sense of immediacy using precise language and sensory images
- present events in a clear, logical order
- capture the mood of the event

---

## LESSON RESOURCES

**USING PRINT RESOURCES**
**Unit One Resource Book**
- Prewriting, p. 57
- Drafting, p. 58
- Peer Response, pp. 59–60
- Revising, Editing, and Proofreading, p. 61
- Student Models, pp. 62–67
- Rubric, p. 68

**Writing Transparencies and Copymasters**
- Writing Process Transparencies, pp. 1, 2
- Writing Style Transparencies, p. 14
- Writing Template Copymasters, p. 25

**USING MEDIA RESOURCES**
**Visit our website:** www.mcdougallittell.com

For a complete view of Lesson Resources, see page 17g.

# Analyzing a Student Model

Joseph Saroufim
West End High School

### Far from the Land of Opportunity

On July 27, 1993, my family and I journeyed to the Middle East to the small country of Lebanon, my father's birthplace. On the day of our departure, Lebanon had just been hit with a massive air, land, and sea attack, and our plane landed on a runway made invisible by thick black smoke. As we waited for the jammed cargo doors of the plane to be forcibly opened to claim our luggage, I went in search of a bathroom. Things were not looking good. The bathroom looked even worse. Because of the ongoing war in Lebanon, much was in disrepair and this bathroom was no exception. The doors to the stalls were torn off and the room was completely pitch black. Toilet paper seemed to be considered a luxury. My most memorable summer vacation had begun.

My father had always told us that he grew up in the countryside of Lebanon. Throughout the one-hour ride at high speed on winding mountain roads that overlooked sheer drops of 10,000 feet, I imagined a peaceful village with hens and chickens, and maybe a lamb or two. When we arrived, I was amazed to see that the house was on the main road connecting Beirut, the capital of Lebanon, to Damascus, the capital of Syria. It was like living on the median strip of a major highway. That night, it was impossible to sleep. We were all crowded in the same room with our good friends, the transparent lizards and the bloodsucking mosquitoes. After finally dozing before dawn, I was wakened by the sounds of the Moslem call to prayer at a nearby mosque, a distant bomb, a caravan of large trucks, and a rooster. Well, this was the country, right? Day two, and I was ready to return home.

The incident that occurred the next morning was highly unexpected. As my family was getting ready to go out, we heard a startling bang and shatter. We all rushed to the front balcony. On the busy street in front of our house we saw a tightly compressed blue BMW with red blotches on the windshield belonging to the driver. Lying on its side in front of the car was a giant potato truck. The road was covered with smashed potatoes and little old ladies screaming at something and scurrying to pick up potatoes for a free dinner. As we found out, this would be one of the small surprises in our exciting vacation.

**D**

## RUBRIC
### IN ACTION

**❶** This writer sets the scene by telling *who, what, when,* and *where.*

**❷** Uses precise language and sensory details to create a vivid picture

**❸** Includes sound images to recreate the scene for the reader

**❹** Orders events chronologically

**❺** Uses precise words and images to present a vivid picture

## Teaching the Lesson

### Analyzing the Model
#### "Far from the Land of Opportunity"

**D** The student writer, a high-school boy, recounts a visit to Lebanon, his father's birthplace. The writer includes a visit to the ancient city of Baalbek, where the ruins of Roman temples still stand. Baalbek is in the Bekka, a fertile valley in eastern Lebanon.

Have students read the model aloud then discuss the Rubric in Action. Point out key words and phrases in the student model that correspond to the elements mentioned in the Rubric in Action.

1. Explain that Lebanon is a narrow strip of land along the eastern shore of the Mediterranean Sea, and is bordered by Syria and Israel. The population is mostly Arab. Over half of the three million people are Muslims, and the rest are Christians.
2. Point out that from the mid 1970s until 1991 there was a civil war, and Lebanon is still involved in fighting.
5. Ask students to point out words in the text that create a vivid scene of the crash.
   **Possible Response:** bang; shatter; tightly compressed BMW; red blotches; smashed potatoes; old ladies screaming and scurrying

Use McDougal Littell's *Language Network,* Chapter 18, for more instruction on writing an eyewitness report.

To engage students visually, use **Power Presentation** 1, Eyewitness Report.

6. Explain that the writer knows his readers will be able to contrast his experience in Lebanon with their own experiences.
7. Point out that in an eyewitness report, a description of the mood helps the reader "experience" the event.
8. Point out that when the writer contrasts his summer in Lebanon with life in the United States, he comes to appreciate his own freedom.

Lebanon is the most beautiful country that I have ever seen, but the war has taken its toll. During our four-week stay, we had no hot water, no drinking water that we didn't have to boil, and electricity for six-hour intervals. Much of our socializing was done with flashlights and candles. Besides these inconveniences, what disturbed me was the lack of personal freedom. In Lebanon, you cannot drive on the road for more than five miles without arriving at an army checkpoint where your papers are examined and, in some cases, your entire car is searched. Male Lebanese citizens over the age of 18 are pulled out of their vehicles and immediately put in the service of the army.

**❻** Gives examples to develop a point—the lack of personal freedom

Besides the lack of freedom and the lack of amenities, what bothered me even more was the lack of safety. It seemed as if there were no laws. There were 12-year-old kids driving cars, and there were no stop signs or traffic signals. This might seem like a fantasy for many teenagers in the United States, but as a cautious ten-year-old I was as nervous as can be.

**❼** Captures the fearful mood with specific details

We decided to visit the old Lebanese city of Baalbek. There were beautiful pieces of architecture and carved stones, not to mention breathtaking cliffs and bottomless pits just lying in the middle of the dehydrating walk-through tour. My two-year-old cousin nearly ran into a deep hole but, luckily, my aunt caught her in the nick of time.

However, what struck me the most was the resilience of the Lebanese people. Throughout all of these hardships, they faced each day with a smile and a song. Listening to them play music on their rhythmical drums brought a joyful smile to my face. No matter how little they may have, they will always have that little extra for a relative or a friend. They laugh, they sing, they dance, and they make the most of what God has given them. We, in the land of opportunity, should take a long hard look at our Middle Eastern neighbors and learn that we have much to be thankful for and little to complain about. No matter how down or deprived I sometimes feel, whether I'm grounded, can't watch TV, or can't play sports, I look back at my Lebanon summer and realize that I really have a lot to live for.

**❽** Summarizes the personal significance of the experience in the conclusion
**Other Options:**
· Begin the report by explaining the significance.
· Comment throughout the report on what the experiences mean.

## Viewing and Representing

**PICTURING TEXT STRUCTURE**
**Instruction** Word choice and ideas are important parts of effective writing. However, the structure of the text—the way in which the words and ideas are organized—also adds to the effectiveness of a written piece.
**Activity** Have students analyze the text structure of the student model by constructing a graphic organizer that reflects how the student writer has organized his piece. Students might first write a note about each paragraph to see how the paragraphs relate to one another and to the whole report.

They should conclude by discussing how the text structure influences their understanding.

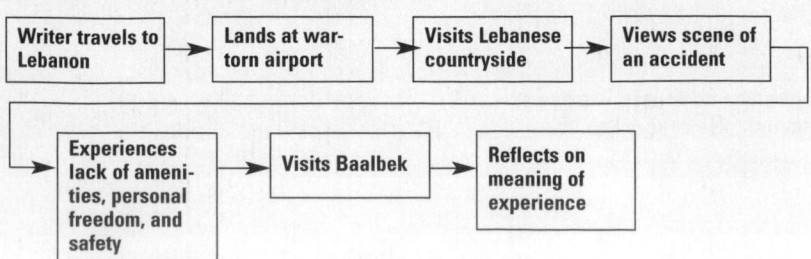

# Writing Your Eyewitness Report

## ❶ Prewriting

> *I can only report on what I know.*
> **Max Frisch, Swiss writer**

Eyewitness reporting is about being there and being aware. Jot down school, community, and family events that are coming up in the near future. Ask yourself whether any of these events are newsworthy. Might you have a unique opportunity to witness something that few others experience? Plan to attend those events that seem interesting.

When you go to an event, attend as a keen observer. In your notebook, record details, sensory images, snippets of conversations, and anything else that will help you re-create this experience for your readers. See the **Idea Bank** for more suggestions. Then choose one event and follow the steps below.

### Planning Your Eyewitness Report

▶ **1. Get the facts.** Use a chart like the one at the right to record the basic facts about the event.

| Who? | |
| --- | --- |
| What? | |
| When? | |
| Where? | |
| Why? | |

▶ **2. Capture the mood.** Sensory details and vivid images will help you capture the mood of the event. Think about the sights, sounds, smells, tastes, and textures that you experience.

▶ **3. Record what is said.** Direct quotations can often give readers a sense of being at the event.

▶ **4. Make it clear why this is significant.** Reflect on what happens and why it is important to you or to others. Make sure you let your reader know the significance of the event.

## ❷ Drafting

Use your notes to get going. You might pick a real attention grabber—such as a startling image or a humorous quote—to capture your readers' attention early in your report.

Many eyewitness reports use **chronological order**—telling events in the order they occurred. This structure makes the experience easy for readers to follow. You might want to create a sense of intrigue by starting at the end and then filling in what happened to get there. Think about your choices and try different approaches until one works for you. To get started, look for examples of eyewitness reports in newspapers and magazines. Study one or two reports to see how they are organized and what kinds of details are included.

### Ask Your Peer Reader

- What event am I describing? When and where does it take place?
- Why do you think I chose to report on the event?
- How would you describe the mood of the event?
- Which details made the greatest impression on you? Why?
- Which details, if any, seem unnecessary?
- Is the order of events clear?

WRITING WORKSHOP **123**

---

**1. Your Working Portfolio** 🗁
Build on one of the Writing Options you completed earlier in this unit:

- **Firsthand Account,** p. 79
- **Eyewitness Account,** p. 89

**2. Calendar Check**
Check a community, school, or sports calendar for interesting upcoming events. Plan to attend one of them and write an eyewitness account.

**3. Ace Reporter**
For the next week, carry a notebook. Report on both planned and spontaneous events. Take notes!

**Have a question?**
See the **Writing Handbook,** p. 1278

---

## Guiding Student Writing

### Prewriting

#### Choosing a Subject
If after reading the Idea Bank students are having difficulty choosing their subjects, suggest they try the following:

- Ask friends and family members if they know of any upcoming events that may be of interest.
- Check the weekend guide of your local newspaper for a list of events.
- Read the community service bulletin board at the library for information about upcoming events.

#### Planning the Eyewitness Report

1. Suggest that students carry a notebook to the event and write down everything they observe, even details that seem insignificant. After the event, they can use their notes to fill in a chart like the one pictured.
2. Have students record descriptive words for each of the five senses.
3. Encourage students to write down the reactions of others to the event as well as their words. This will enhance the reader's sense of "being there" at the event.

### Drafting

#### Organizing the Draft
Point out that as students draft, they should focus on including the important details of the event. Have them consider the dominant feeling or mood they want to convey, then choose details that fit that mood.

Encourage students to prepare first drafts using a word processing program. That will make revision and editing—even rearranging sentences and paragraphs—much easier.

#### Teaching Tip
Some students might find it helpful to bring a tape recorder or camera to the event, but caution them not to use these devices as a replacement for their notes.

## Revising
### ELABORATING WITH SENSORY DETAIL

Point out that in the example, the writer includes two similes—"like being on a film set when the director calls, 'Action!'" and "like a huge herd of cattle on the verge of a stampede." Both similes add details that appeal to the sense of sight and sound.

Other sound images include taxis "bleating their horns." Images that appeal to the sense of smell include "the smells of asphalt and exhaust" and "hot dogs roasting."

## Editing and Proofreading
### MODIFIER PLACEMENT

Remind students that misplaced modifiers appear to be modifying the wrong word. Dangling modifiers do not seem to modify any particular word. Errors in the example include the following:

- *Looking at people in the city* is a dangling modifier. It is not clear *who* is looking at people in the city. Adding the phrase *I noticed that* corrects the error.
- *Walking into office buildings* is misplaced; it modifies the phrase *business men and women.*
- *In trendy restaurants* is misplaced because it modifies the noun *people.*
- *Wearing comfortable jeans or shorts* is misplaced. It modifies the word *myself. Midtown* should be capitalized because it is the first word in the sentence.

## Reflecting

 Have students write a brief note addressing their writing experience. They can clip their assessment to the essay itself and place both in their working porfolios.

---

**Need revising help?**

Review the **Rubric,** p. 120.

Consider **peer reader** comments.

Check **Revising, Editing, and Proofreading,** p. 1269.

**Maddened by modifiers?**

See the **Grammar Handbook,** pp. 1312–1314.

## Publishing
### IDEAS

- Publish your eyewitness report in your school or community newspaper.
- E-mail your report to friends or pen pals.

**More Online: Publishing Options** www.mcdougallittell.com

---

## ❸ Revising

**TARGET SKILL ▶ ELABORATING WITH SENSORY DETAILS** In descriptive writing, such as an eyewitness report, try to use details that appeal to the senses—sights, sounds, smells, textures, and flavors. Concrete nouns, and strong verbs and adjectives, help make images vivid.

> *like being on a film set when the director calls, "Action!"*
> Standing on a busy street during rush hour in New York City is ~~an~~
> ~~amazing experience.~~ *speed* Taxis ~~drive~~ by constantly. *bleating their horns* Bicycle messengers
> weave in and out of pedestrian traffic on the sidewalks. Pedestrians
> *like a huge herd of cattle on the verge of a stampede.*
> walk down the block ~~in huge groups.~~
>
> *The smells of asphalt and exhaust mingle with that of hot dogs roasting at outdoor stands.*

## ❹ Editing and Proofreading

**TARGET SKILL ▶ MODIFIER PLACEMENT** After adding well-chosen details, be sure to check the placement of modifiers. In general, you should place modifiers as close as possible to the words they modify. Two common errors are **misplaced modifiers,** which are placed too far from the words they modify, and **dangling modifiers,** which do not clearly modify any noun or pronoun in the sentence.

> *I noticed that*
> Looking at people in the city, a few styles of dress stand out.
> Businessmen and women look serious in their dark suits and white
> shirts walking into office buildings. Young people wear everything
> from long flowered skirts and tank tops to baggy pants and neon-
> colored shirts in trendy restaurants. Wearing comfortable jeans or
> shorts, midtown Manhattan is full of tourists like myself.

## ❺ Reflecting

**FOR YOUR WORKING PORTFOLIO** What did you learn about being a good observer while writing your eyewitness report? How did writing the report help you become a better observer? Attach your answer to your finished work. Save your eyewitness report in your **Working Portfolio.**

## Assessment Practice Revising & Editing

Read this passage from the first draft of an eyewitness report. The underlined sections may include the following kinds of errors:

- **lack of detail**
- **correctly written sentences that should be combined**
- **misplaced modifiers**
- **double negatives**

For each underlined phrase or sentence, choose the revision that most improves the writing.

> From my vantage point I saw the entire incident on the bridge. The first
> (1)
> thing I noticed was white smoke rising from the boat's engine. Then came the
> (2)
> smell. I called to the passengers. The passengers did not hear me. Then the motor
> (3)
> burst into flames. At first the passengers stood motionless in panic, but that
> didn't last long. The captain soon took control and checked that everyone was on
> the boat wearing a life jacket . One crew member used the fire extinguisher, but
> (4)
> it wasn't ineffective against the growing fire. I heard the captain shout. One by
> (5)                                                    (6)
> one, the passengers jumped into the icy lake.

1. **A.** From my vantage point on the bridge, I saw the entire incident.
   **B.** From my vantage point I saw the entire incident from the bridge.
   **C.** On the bridge, I saw the entire incident from my vantage point.
   **D.** Correct as is

2. **A.** Then came the smell from the mist.
   **B.** Then came the sharp smell of smoke and gas.
   **C.** Then the smell came quickly.
   **D.** Correct as is

3. **A.** I called to the passengers, they did not hear me.
   **B.** I called to the passengers but the passengers did not hear me.
   **C.** I called to the passengers, but they did not hear me.
   **D.** Correct as is

4. **A.** everyone was wearing a life jacket on the boat.
   **B.** on the boat everyone was wearing a life jacket.
   **C.** everyone on the boat was wearing a life jacket.
   **D.** Correct as is

5. **A.** was ineffective
   **B.** was effective
   **C.** wasn't hardly effective
   **D.** Correct as is

6. **A.** I heard the captain's shout.
   **B.** I heard the captain shout the order to abandon ship.
   **C.** I barely heard the captain shout the order.
   **D.** Correct as is

**Need extra help?**

See the **Grammar Handbook:**

Modifiers, p. 1312;

The Sentence and Its Parts, p. 1316.

---

## Assessment Practice

Demonstrate how students can eliminate incorrect choices for the first question.

**B.** This choice is incorrect because the modifier *from the bridge* belongs near *vantage point.*

**C.** This choice is incorrect because the phrase *on the bridge* is a dangling modifier. It does not seem to modify any noun or pronoun in the sentence.

**D.** This choice is incorrect because it sounds as though the incident took place on the bridge.

**A.** This is the best choice because the modifiers are in the correct place.

**Answers:**

1. A; **2.** B; **3.** C; **4.** C; **5.** A; **6.** B

## Objectives

- expand vocabulary by using strategies to ascertain word meaning
- rely on context to determine the meanings of words
- apply meanings of prefixes, roots, and suffixes in order to comprehend
- figure out the meaning of related words
- use reference materials to determine precise meaning and usage

# Strategies for Building Vocabulary

### EXERCISE

You may need to point out to students the way the etymology for *navigator* was compiled in the sample. A dictionary has no etymology for *navigator* per se, and therefore its root or basic form, *navigate*, must be consulted for the first two syllables. The affix third syllable, the word's suffix *-or*, is defined where it falls alphabetically in a dictionary.

## *Expanding Word Power*

Building an extensive vocabulary is like building stronger muscles—it helps to have a workout strategy. When you encounter an unfamiliar word, there are certain strategies you can use to determine its meaning and make the word your own. For instance, what words and phrases serve as clues to help you determine the meaning of *ascertain* in the passage on the right?

Details like "ordered . . . to climb one of the trees," "the lay of the land," and "found out . . . we were on an island" can help you infer that *ascertain* probably

> After we ate, I ordered Lope de Oviedo, our strongest man, to climb one of the trees not far off and ascertain the lay of the land. He complied and found out from the treetop that we were on an island.
> —Álvar Núñez Cabeza de Vaca, *La Relación*

means "to find out" or "to discover." Remember that strategies like noting context clues can help you ascertain the meanings of many unfamiliar words as you read.

### Strategies for Building Vocabulary

There are a number of useful strategies you can use to strengthen your vocabulary.

**❶ Consider the Context** Inference clues, like those that were used to infer the meaning of *ascertain,* are one type of context clue that can help you learn new words. Others include definition or restatement clues, comparison or contrast clues, description clues, and example clues. For more information on using context clues, see page 326.

**❷ Recognize Word Parts** Sometimes the familiar roots or affixes in words will suggest their meanings. For example, in *The Interesting Narrative of the Life of Olaudah Equiano,* Equiano speaks of a man who was "flogged unmercifully." *Unmercifully* contains the base word *mercy.* The prefix *un-* means "not," and the suffix *-ly* indicates that the word is an adverb and therefore describes an action. You can use what you know about roots and affixes to conclude that the man was flogged without mercy. To learn more about roots and affixes, see pages 444 and 1130.

**❸ Build Word Families** Words that are built from the same base word or root can be grouped together as a "family." For example, the words *incision, precision,* and *concise* all contain the root *cise,* which comes from the Latin verb *caedere,* "to cut." It is useful to know that the sense of the root *cise* has survived in these words: the meaning of each is based on an idea of physical or mental sharpness. Try to make connections like these as

you encounter new words. For more about roots and word families, see page 444.

**❹ Check a Dictionary** Even if you have guessed the meaning of an unfamiliar word, a dictionary can still help you to refine your understanding of the word's meaning, usage, and parts. Of course, it will also tell you if your guess was wrong. See page 990 for more about using reference aids to unlock word meanings.

**❺ Record and Use New Words** A good way to remember new words is to make diagrams like the one below in your 📖 **READER'S NOTEBOOK.** Make it a point to review your word diagrams frequently and to use the words in your conversation and writing until they are a natural part of your vocabulary.

| NAVIGATOR |
| --- |
| **Definition:** one who plans and monitors a ship's course |
| **Etymology:** *navis* "ship" + *agere* "to drive" + *-or* "one who" |
| **Example:** I called to the navigator, who said we were coming close to land. |

**Related Words:** naval, navigable, navigate, navy

**EXERCISE** Create diagrams like the one above to record five words, from the selections you have read in this book, that you would like to add to your vocabulary.

## Grammar from Literature

Experienced writers add interest and rhythm to their writing by using a variety of sentence types and sentences of different lengths. Look at the following passage. The sentence types are identified by color. They are paired with the definitions below.

> It was winter and bitterly cold, and we had suffered hunger and the heavy beating of the waves for many days. Next day the men began to collapse. By sunset, all had fallen over on one another, close to death. Few were any longer conscious. Not five could stand. When night fell, only the navigator and I remained able to tend the barge. Two hours after dark he told me I must take over; he believed he was going to die that night.
> — *La Relación*, translated by Cyclone Covey

Notice that the translator of this work used all of the four kinds of sentences in English.

A **simple** sentence has one independent clause or main clause. An independent clause can stand alone as a complete thought.

A **compound** sentence contains two or more independent clauses joined by a conjunction or semicolon.

A **complex** sentence has one independent clause and one or more subordinate clauses, or clauses that cannot stand alone as a sentence.

A **compound complex** sentence has two or more independent clauses and one or more subordinate clauses.

---

**WRITING EXERCISE** Combine each pair of simple sentences following the directions in parentheses.

1. Is Oviedo lost? Has he been captured? (Form a compound sentence by joining with a comma and a conjunction such as *and, but,* or *or.* )
2. The Pilgrims sailed across the Atlantic. They arrived at Cape Cod in November. (Form a compound sentence.)
3. Conditions were very hard the first year. Many of the colonists died. (Form a complex sentence. Begin with *because,* and put a comma after the first clause.)
4. Maya Angelou followed her husband to North Africa and supported his efforts. Her marriage failed in spite of her efforts. (Form a compound sentence.)

**Using Sentence Variety in Your Writing** As you revise your own writing, look at the kind and the length of sentences you have used. If many of your sentences are short, experiment with combining ideas.

> LACKING SENTENCE VARIETY
> The Pilgrims arrived on November 11. Soon they set about repairing the boat. They saw the extensive damage. They knew the repair would take a long time.
>
> REVISED
> Soon after the Pilgrims arrived on November 11, they set about mending the boat. They saw the extensive damage, and they knew the repair would take a long time.

**Usage Tip** As you try using various types of sentences, avoid sentence fragments. Be sure each sentence has a subject, has a verb, and expresses a complete thought. Remember that although a subordinate clause has a subject and verb, it does not express a complete thought and cannot stand alone as a sentence.

> INCORRECT
> verb                         verb
> Gave the Spaniards shelter and fed them. (no subject)
>
> CORRECT
>       subject   verb                    verb
> The Indians gave the Spaniards shelter and fed them.

> INCORRECT
> As we drifted into shore. (A subordinate clause cannot stand alone.)
>
> CORRECT
> As we drifted into shore, a wave pushed us forward.

5. Olaudah Equiano saw whites for the first time. He thought they were evil spirits. (Form a complex sentence. Begin with *when,* and put a comma after the first clause.)

**GRAMMAR EXERCISE** Rewrite these sentences, changing fragments into sentences. You may need to add words.

1. The Spanish explorer Cabeza de Vaca.
2. Because the Pilgrims were weakened during their first winter.
3. Sailed from England to gain more religious freedom.
4. Although Olaudah Equiano survived a voyage on a slave ship.
5. To the Cape Coast Castle and nearby Elmina Castle.

---

### Objectives
- use varied sentence structure to express meanings and achieve desired effect
- demonstrate mastery of simple, compound, complex, and compound complex sentences.
- change sentence fragments into complete sentences

### WRITING EXERCISE
1. Is Oviedo lost, or has he been captured?
2. The Pilgrims sailed across the Atlantic, and they arrived at Cape Cod in November.
3. Because conditions were very hard the first year, many of the colonists died.
4. Maya Angelou followed her husband to North Africa and supported his efforts, but her marriage failed in spite of her efforts.
5. When Olaudah Equiano saw whites for the first time, he thought they were evil spirits.

### GRAMMAR ACTIVITY
The following are possible responses.
1. The Spanish explorer Cabeza de Vaca was one of the first Europeans to cross North America.
2. The Pilgrims weakened and starved during their first winter.
3. The Pilgrims sailed from England to gain more religious freedom.
4. Olaudah Equiano survived a voyage on a slave ship only to be sold at an auction in Barbados.
5. For a year Maya Angelou avoided visiting Cape Coast Castle and nearby Elmina Castle.

## Objectives

- reflect on and assess understanding of the unit
- recognize distinctive characteristics of cultures through reading
- reflect on and assess understanding of such literary concepts as conflict and resolution
- reflect on and assess understanding of literary forms such as historical narratives
- assess and build portfolios

## Reflecting on the Unit

### OPTION 1

A successful response will
- identify which selections in the unit are ancient and which are contemporary.
- select ancient values that are seen continuing in the present.
- analyze how these values have been altered to fit contemporary needs.

### OPTION 2

A successful response will
- identify what was encountered for the first time in each selection in Part 2.
- note the similarities and differences in the first-time encounters.
- decide whether any selection in Part 2 does not relate to the Part 2 title and, if not, offer reasons why.

### OPTION 3

In a group of six, each member might initially consider only one of the three topics with regard to one of the unit parts. Then the group as a whole could analyze the similarities and differences between the parts.

### Self Assessment

Be sure that students develop working definitions of *explorer* so that they can judge, for example, whether William Least Heat-Moon is an explorer according to their definitions.

# Origins and Encounters

What did you learn about Native American culture from reading this unit? Did you find out anything new about the first Europeans and Africans to come to this continent? Choose one or more of the options in each of these sections to help you explore how your thinking has developed.

## Reflecting on the Unit

### OPTION 1

**Old Beliefs, New Literature**  Consider how the ancient Native American selections relate to the more contemporary ones in the first part of this unit. What traditions—such as values, beliefs, and forms of storytelling— do you see continuing into the present? How have these traditions been adapted, or changed, to fit contemporary needs? Write a few paragraphs to explain your ideas.

### OPTION 2

**Explorers and Exploiters**  Think back over the selections in Part 2 of this unit. What things was each author encountering for the first time? What similarities and differences between the different encounters do you notice? Do any of the selections seem unrelated to the title "First Encounters"? Get together with a partner to discuss these questions, and jot down your conclusions.

### OPTION 3

**Different World Views**  How do the attitudes expressed in Part 1, "In Harmony with Nature," differ from those expressed in Part 2, "First Encounters"? With a small group of classmates, discuss the differences.

THINK ABOUT
- ideas about nature
- ideas about good and evil
- ideas about how human beings should behave

## Self ASSESSMENT

📖 **READER'S NOTEBOOK**
To explore how your understanding has developed as you read this unit, create a two-column chart. In the first column, list what you knew about Native Americans and explorers before you read the selections. In the second column, list important facts and concepts you discovered.

## Reviewing Literary Concepts

OPTION 1 **Considering Conflict** You know that conflict forms the basis of a plot and that the resolution of the conflict often concludes a story. To help you analyze the conflicts in the stories that you read in this unit, make a chart like the one shown. Then write a few sentences telling why you particularly liked the way one or two of the conflicts were resolved. Write a few more sentences, telling which resolutions, if any, you found unsatisfying and giving reasons for your opinion.

| Selection | Conflict | How Conflict Is Resolved |
|---|---|---|
| "The World on the Turtle's Back" | Twins struggle to overcome each other. | Straight-minded twin kills his brother, but both continue to have power over different parts of the world. |

OPTION 2 **Oral Literature and Historical Narratives** In this unit you have read not only Native American oral literature—myths, tales, and songs—but also historical narratives written by some of the first nonnative people in North America. How do these two kinds of literature differ? With a small group of classmates, discuss what each kind of literature contributes to your understanding of early America.

## Building Your Portfolio

- **QuickWrites** Several of the Writing Options in this unit asked you to relate the ideas presented in selections to your own ideas and experiences. Choose two pieces that you feel present particularly insightful or interesting connections. Write a cover note explaining your choices. Then attach your note to the pieces and add them to your Presentation Portfolio.

- **Writing Workshop** In this unit you wrote an Eyewitness Report about an event of personal or historical significance. Reread the report and assess the quality of your writing. Where is your writing most vivid? Attach a note with your thoughts about your work, and place the report in your **Presentation Portfolio.**

- **Additional Activities** Review the assignments you completed under **Activities & Explorations** and **Inquiry & Research.** Keep a record in your portfolio of any assignments that you think are representative of your best work.

### Self ASSESSMENT

**READER'S NOTEBOOK**
Did you understand *conflict, oral literature,* and *historical narratives* well enough to complete one of the options at left? Copy the following list of literary terms introduced in this unit. Next to each, rate your understanding of the concept from 1 (none at all) to 5 (absolute mastery). Review the terms you are not sure about in the **Glossary of Literary Terms** (page 1342).

myth
creation myth
repetition
folk tale
trickster tale
setting

primary and
  secondary
  sources
slave narrative
author's purpose
audience
autobiography

### Self ASSESSMENT

At this point, you may just be beginning your **Presentation Portfolio.** Are the pieces you have included so far ones you think you'll keep, or do you think you will replace them as the year goes on?

### Setting GOALS

As you thought about the selections in this unit, did you want to know more about the original inhabitants of North America and about the Europeans and Africans who came later? Jot down a few questions you would like to investigate on your own.

## Reviewing Literary Concepts

OPTION 1

Use the Unit One Resource Book p. 71 to provide students a ready-made, full-depth chart for recording conflicts and resolutions that will form the basis of their opinion sentences on satisfying and unsatisfying conflict resolutions.

OPTION 2

A successful response will
- categorize the unit's literature into Native American oral literature and historical narratives written by some nonnative people.
- examine the differences between the two kinds of literature.
- involve a discussion of how each kind of literature contributes to the understanding of early America.

## Building Your Portfolio

Students will use their Presentation Portfolios to file what they consider their highest quality work—the very best projects and activities from their Working Portfolios.

For more information on using writing and assessing portfolios, see the *Teacher's Guide to Assessment and Portfolio Use* beginning on page 53.

## From Colony to Country

The selections in Unit Two present some of the great minds that shaped the early years of this country, exploring the authors' wit, wisdom, and experience on a variety of topics. The unit is divided into two sections to better represent the social, political, and economic upheavals of the era.

### Part 1

**Between Heaven and Hell** This part contains a survey of literature from Puritan writers. The wide variety of genres—poetry, nonfiction, and a sermon—affords students a useful introduction to the age. The full-length play in **Traditions Across Time** shows the viewpoint of a 20th-century American writer on the Puritan experience.

### Part 2

**The Right to Be Free** This part features important historical documents from the period, including an excerpt from Patrick Henry's famous speech in the Virginia Convention, as well as selections that offer insight into the revolutionary spirit. In addition, the articles, letters, and essays in this part of the unit underscore the attempt of many 18th-century writers to define America and the American spirit. The selections in the **Traditions Across Time** section reveal how the struggle for freedom and equality continues today.

From Colony to Country

130

 **Mini Lesson** **Viewing and Representing**

*A Morning View of Blue Hill Village*
**by Jonathan Fisher**

**ART APPRECIATION**

**Instruction** Jonathan Fisher (1768–1847) was born in Massachusetts and, after his education, served in Maine as a minister in the newly established village of Blue Hill. He remained in Blue Hill for the rest of his life, pursuing his interests in art, science, farming, and writing. *A Morning View of Blue Hill Village,* painted in 1824, was his most celebrated work.

In this painting, Fisher combines his artist's view with moral interpretation. He re-creates the details of his surroundings to reflect his view that progress and civilization were fast approaching the Maine coast. Biblical allusions give the landscape a deeper significance. Have students analyze the painting to get to its main idea.

Use the following questions to help develop students' visual literacy.

A *Morning View of Blue Hill Village* (1824), Jonathan Fisher. William A Farnsworth Library and Art Museum, Rockland, Maine, museum purchase, 1965 (1465.134).

*The Lord will make our name a praise and glory, so that men shall say of succeeding plantations: "The Lord make it like that of New England." For we must consider that we shall be like a City upon a Hill; the eyes of all people are on us.*

JOHN WINTHROP
*First Governor of the Massachusetts Bay Colony*

131

## Making Connections

To help students explore connections among the art, the quotation, and the unit title found in this unit-opening spread, have them consider the following questions.

**Ask: What can you infer about the Puritans' attitude toward their mission in the New World from Governor Winthrop's words?**
**Possible Response:** The Puritans believed that their mission was sanctioned and protected by God. Winthrop's words show that he believed the Puritans would succeed as colonists and serve as a model for all succeeding generations.

**Ask: Based on the quotation and the painting, what types of literature do you think were most prevalent in the New World at this time?**
**Possible Responses:** sermons, religious writings, poems, letters, essays

**Ask: What do you think might be the most difficult aspects of colonizing a foreign land? Why?**
**Possible Responses:** physical danger, homesickness, disease, resistance from the indigenous population, culture and language barriers

**Ask: What adjectives do you think best describe the type of person who could leave home in order to start a colony in an unknown land?**
**Possible Responses:** intrepid, desperate, religious, restless, adventurous

**Ask: What symbols of progress and industry do you see in the painting?**
**Possible Responses:** the ship sailing into the harbor on the far left; indications of boat making industry on the harbor shore; tree stumps indicate the remnants of a forest that was cut to make way for the cultivation of the fields

**Ask: What examples of religious symbolism are contained in the painting.**
**Possible Responses:** the snake being driven out of the area like the Biblical serpent in the Garden of Eden; the church on a rise in the background overlooking the village; the stone walls that surround the village keeping evil out and goodness in

| Features and Selections | Literary Analysis | Reading and Critical Thinking | Writing Opportunities | |
|---|---|---|---|---|
| **From Colony to Country**<br>**Time Line**<br>**Historical Background/Essay** | | | | |
| POETRY<br>To My Dear and Loving Husband<br>Upon the Burning of Our House,<br>July 10th, 1666 | Meter, 138, 142 | Clarifying Meaning, 138, 142<br>Informal Assess., 141 | Lyric Poem, 143<br>Personal Analogy, 143 | |
| SALEM COURT DOCUMENTS, 1692<br>The Examination of Sarah Good<br><br>**Related Reading**<br>History Clashes with Commercialism | Transcript, 144, 148 | Detecting Bias, 144, 148<br><br>Distinguishing Fact from Opinion, 150 | Courtroom Drama, 149<br>Plea for Mercy, 149<br>Explanation of Motives, 149 | |
| SERMON<br>*from* Sinners in the Hands of an<br>Angry God | Persuasive Writing, 152, 158 | Analyzing Emotional Language, 152, 158<br>Test Preparation, 159 | Letter of Opinion, 159<br>Vivid Comparison, 159<br>Public Service Announcement, 159 | |
| **Learning the Language of Literature**<br>The Conventions of Drama | Conventions of Drama, 161 | Reading Strategies, 162 | | |
| DRAMA<br>**Comparing Literature**<br>The Crucible | Stage Directions, 163, 190<br><br>Dialogue, 206<br><br>Foil, 228<br><br>Plot and Conflict, 243<br><br>Test Practice, 227 | Graphic Organizer, 163, 190, 206<br>Test Practice, 168, 184, 224<br>Sequential Order, 196<br>Cause and Effect, 204<br>CCL: Logic, 218<br>Making Inferences, 238 | Points of Comparison, 244<br>Missing Scene, 244<br>Editorial, 244<br>Capsule Review, 244<br>Alternative Ending, 188, 240<br>Court Reporter, 214 | |
| **Comparing Literature**<br>**Assessment Practice** | | Reading the Prompt, 246 | Comparison-Contrast Essay, 246 | |
| **Writing Workshop:** **Critical Review**<br>**Assessment Practice**<br>**Building Vocabulary**<br>**Sentence Crafting** | Critical Review, 248 | Analyzing a Professional Model, 249 | Critical Review, 251<br><br><br>Avoiding Circular Reasoning, 252 | |

| | | | | |
|---|---|---|---|---|
| **The Right to Be Free**<br>**Historical Background/Essay** | | | | |
| **Learning the Language of Literature**<br>Persuasive Rhetoric | Argument, 260 | Reading Strategies, 261 | | |

LEGEND    **DLS – Daily Language SkillBuilder**
**CCL – Cross Curricular Link**        **Green type – Teacher's Edition**

| Features and Selections | Literary Analysis | Reading and Critical Thinking | Writing Opportunities | |
|---|---|---|---|---|
| **SPEECH** Speech in the Virginia Convention | Allusion, 262, 267 Review: Repetition, 267 | Rhetorical Questions and Persuasion, 262, 267 | Newspaper Report, 268 Character Sketch, 268 Rebuttal Speech, 268 | |
| **DOCUMENT** Declaration of Independence | Parallelism, 270, 279 | Paraphrasing, 270, 279 Making Inferences / Drawing Conclusions, 274 | Modern Paraphrase, 280 Teenager's Declaration, 280 Personal Response, 280 | |
| **LETTER** Letter to the Rev. Samson Occom Letter to John Adams | Figurative Language, 282, 287 | Literary Letters, 282, 287 | Literary Letter, 288 | |
| **ESSAY** What Is an American? | Theme, 289, 293 Review: Figurative Language, 293 | Analyzing Contrast, 289, 293 Test Practice, 292 | Draft of Article, 294 Local Definition, 294 | |
| **SPEECH** Lecture to a Missionary | Tone, 295, 298 Theme, 298 | Drawing Conclusions about Tone, 295, 298 | Mediator's Recommendations, 299 Cram's Response, 299 Tolerance Pamphlet, 299 | |
| **NONFICTION** Comparing Literature *from* Stride Toward Freedom Necessary to Protect Ourselves | Historical Context, 300, 307 Allusion, 307 | Analyzing the Structure of Arguments, 300, 304, 307 Main Idea, 303 | Points of Comparison, 308 | |
| **POETRY** Comparing Literature *from* I Am Joaquín/Yo Soy Joaquín | Epic Poem, 309, 316 Informal Assess., 315 | Reading Epic Poetry, 309, 316 | Book Review, 317 Points of Comparison, 317 | |
| Comparing Literature **Assessment Practice** | | Reading a Prompt, 318 | Evaluative Essay, 318 | |
| Writing Workshop: **Persuasion** **Assessment Practice** **Building Vocabulary** **Sentence Crafting** | | Analyzing a Student Model, 321 | Persuasion, 323 Supporting Personal Opinions with Facts, 324 | |
| Reflect and Assess | Reviewing Literary Concepts, 329 | | Strong Beliefs, 328 Building Your Portfolio, 329 To Form a More Perfect Union, 328 | |
| Reading and Writing for Assessment | | Test-Taking Strategies, 330 | Test-Taking Strategies, 334 | |

**LEGEND**   DLS – Daily Language SkillBuilder
CCL – Cross Curricular Link        Green type – Teacher's Edition

To introduce the theme/literary period of this unit, use Fine Art Transparencies T20–22 in the Communications Transparencies and Copymasters.

| | Unit Resource Book | Assessment | Integrated Technology and Media | Literary Analysis Transparencies |
|---|---|---|---|---|
| **To My Dear and Loving Husband Upon the Burning of Our House, July 10, 1666** *pp. 138–143* | • Active Reading p. 4<br>• Literary Analysis p. 5 | • Selection Test, Formal Assessment pp. 31–32<br>  Test Generator | Audio Library | • Form in Poetry: Structure T11 |
| **The Examination of Sarah Good** *pp. 144–149* | • Summary p. 6<br>• Active Reading p. 7<br>• Literary Analysis p. 8<br>• Selection Quiz p. 9 | • Selection Test, Formal Assessment pp. 33–34<br>  Test Generator | Audio Library<br><br>Research Starter<br>www.mcdougallittell.com | |
| *from* **Sinners in the Hands of an Angry God** *pp. 152–160* | • Summary p. 10<br>• Active Reading p. 11<br>• Literary Analysis p. 12<br>• Words to Know p. 13<br>• Selection Quiz p. 14 | • Selection Test, Formal Assessment pp. 35–36<br>  Test Generator | Audio Library | • Persuasion: Types of Appeals T9 |
| **The Crucible (1953)**<br>• Act 1<br>• Act 2<br>• Act 3<br>• Act 4<br>*pp. 163–245* | • Summary pp. 15, 20, 25, 30<br>• Active Reading pp. 16, 21, 26, 31<br>• Literary Analysis pp. 17, 22, 27, 32<br>• Words to Know pp. 18, 23, 28, 33<br>• Selection Quiz pp. 19, 24, 29, 34<br>• Comparing Literature p. 35 | • Selection Test, Formal Assessment pp. 37–44<br>  Test Generator | Research Starter<br>www.mcdougallittell.com | • Drama: Basics T3<br>• Drama: Dialogue T4<br>• Drama: Plot Development T5 |

## Writing Workshop: Critical Review

| | | | | |
|---|---|---|---|---|
| **Unit Two Resource Book**<br>• Prewriting p. 36<br>• Drafting and Elaboration p. 37<br>• Peer Response Guide pp. 38–39<br>• Revising, Editing, and Proofreading p. 40<br>• Student Models pp. 41–46<br>• Rubric for Evaluation p. 47 | **Power Presentations CD-ROM**<br>**Writing Transparencies and Copymasters** T11, T20, C26<br>**Teacher's Guide to Assessment and Portfolio Use** | **Unit Assessment**<br>• Unit Two, Part 1 Test, Formal Assessment pp. 45–46<br>  Test Generator<br>• Unit Two Integrated Test, Integrated Assessment pp. 11–18 | **Unit Technology**<br>ClassZone<br>www.mcdougallittell.com<br>EasyPlanner CD-ROM<br>Electronic Library | |

| Reading and Critical Thinking Transparencies | Grammar Transparencies and Copymasters | Vocabulary Transparencies and Copymasters | Writing Transparencies and Copymasters | Communications Transparencies and Copymasters |
|---|---|---|---|---|
| • Compare and Contrast T15<br>• Generating Research Questions T26 | • Daily Language SkillBuilder T5<br>• Verbs–Using Correct Verb Forms T45<br>• Auxiliary Verbs C67 | • Analogies C24 | | • Appreciative Listening T2 |
| • Determining Author's Bias T22 | • Daily Language SkillBuilder T5<br>• Overuse of the Verb *To Be* C163 | • Idioms C25 | • The Uses of Dialogue T24<br>• Persuasive Essay C27 | • Interviewing T9<br>• Impromptu Speaking: Dialogue, Role-Play, Debate T13 |
| • Compare and Contrast T15<br>• Analyzing Emotional Appeals T18 | • Daily Language SkillBuilder T5<br>• Agreement of Subject and Verb T47<br>• Subject-Verb Agreement I C123 | • The Connotative Power of Words C26 | • Persuasive Essay C27 | • Dramatic Reading T12<br>• Verbal Strategies T14 |
| • Evaluating Story Elements T6<br>• Compare and Contrast T15<br>• Organizational Chart: Vertical T52 | • Daily Language SkillBuilder T6<br>• Interjections C72<br>• Regular and Irregular Verbs C113<br>• Principal Parts of Verbs C114<br>• Perfect Tenses of Verbs I C115<br>• Correcting Comma Splices C147 | • Meanings of Prefixes and Roots C27 | • Critical Review C26<br>• Opinion Statement C34 | • Dramatic Reading T12<br>• Verbal Strategies T14 |

## STUDENTS ACQUIRING ENGLISH

The **Spanish Study Guide,** pp. 35–58, includes language support for the following pages:
• Family and Community Involvement (per unit)

• Selection Summaries and Vocabulary
• Active Reading
• Literary Analysis

UNIT TWO
# RESOURCE MANAGEMENT GUIDE
## PART 2

To introduce the theme/literary period of this unit, use Fine Art Transparencies T20–22 in the Communications Transparencies and Copymasters.

| | Unit Resource Book | Assessment | Integrated Technology and Media | Additional Support — Literary Analysis Transparencies |
|---|---|---|---|---|
| **Speech in the Virginia Convention** *pp. 262–269* | • Summary p. 50<br>• Active Reading p. 51<br>• Literary Analysis p. 52<br>• Words to Know p. 53<br>• Selection Quiz p. 54 | • Selection Test, Formal Assessment pp. 47–48<br>Test Generator | Audio Library<br><br>Research Starter www.mcdougallittell.com | • Persuasion: Types of Appeals T9 |
| **The Declaration of Independence** *pp. 270–281* | • Summary p. 55<br>• Active Reading p. 56<br>• Literary Analysis p. 57<br>• Words to Know p. 58<br>• Selection Quiz p. 59 | • Selection Test, Formal Assessment pp. 49–50<br>Test Generator | Audio Library | • Persuasive Techniques T10 |
| **Letter to the Rev. Samson Occom / Letter to John Adams** *pp. 282–288* | • Summary (Letter to the Rev. Occom) p. 60<br>• Summary (Letter to John Adams) p. 61<br>• Active Reading p. 62<br>• Literary Analysis p. 63<br>• Words to Know p. 64<br>• Selection Quiz p. 65 | • Selection Test, Formal Assessment pp. 51–52<br>Test Generator | Audio Library | |
| **What Is an American?** *pp. 289–294* | • Summary p. 66<br>• Active Reading p. 67<br>• Literary Analysis p. 68<br>• Words to Know p. 69<br>• Selection Quiz p. 70 | • Selection Test, Formal Assessment p. 53<br>Test Generator | Audio Library | • Theme in Nonfiction T22 |
| **Lecture to a Missionary** *pp. 295–299* | • Summary p. 71<br>• Active Reading p. 72<br>• Literary Analysis p. 73<br>• Selection Quiz p. 74 | • Selection Test, Formal Assessment p. 55<br>Test Generator | Audio Library | • Tone T19 |
| *from* **Stride Toward Freedom (1958) / Necessary to Protect Ourselves (1964)** *pp. 300–308* | • Summary (from Stride Toward Freedom) p. 75<br>• Summary (Necessary to Protect Ourselves) p. 76<br>• Active Reading p. 77<br>• Literary Analysis p. 78<br>• Words to Know p. 79<br>• Selection Quiz p. 80 | • Selection Test, Formal Assessment pp. 57–58<br>Test Generator | Audio Library | • Compare/Contrast Themes and Conflicts T16 |
| *from* **I Am Joaquín/Soy Joaquín (1967)** *pp. 309–317* | • Active Reading p. 81<br>• Literary Analysis p. 82<br>• Comparing Literature p. 83 | • Selection Test, Formal Assessment pp. 59–60<br>Test Generator | Audio Library | • Compare/Contrast Themes and Conflicts T16 |

## Writing Workshop: Persuasion

| | Unit Assessment | Unit Technology |
|---|---|---|
| **Unit Two Resource Book**<br>• Prewriting p. 84<br>• Drafting and Elaboration p. 85<br>• Peer Response Guide pp. 86–87<br>• Revising, Editing, and Proofreading p. 88<br>• Student Models pp. 00–04<br>• Rubric for Evaluation p. 95<br><br>**Power Presentations CD-ROM**<br>**Writing Transparencies and Copymasters** T11, T20, C27<br>**Teacher's Guide to Assessment and Portfolio Use** | • Unit Two, Part 2 Test, Formal Assessment pp. 61–62<br>Test Generator<br><br>• Unit Two Integrated Test, Integrated Assessment pp. 11–16 | ClassZone www.mcdougallittell.com<br>EasyPlanner CD-ROM<br>Electronic Library |

| Reading and Critical Thinking Transparencies | Grammar Transparencies and Copymasters | Vocabulary Transparencies and Copymasters | Writing Transparencies and Copymasters | Communications Transparencies and Copymasters |
|---|---|---|---|---|
| • Evaluating Argumentation I and II T20, T21<br>• Sequence Chain T49<br>• Dialoguing Frame T54 | • Daily Language SkillBuilder T6<br>• Perfect Tenses of Verbs II C116 | • Context Clues C92 | • Opinion Statement C34 | • Evaluating Roles in Groups T8<br>• Dramatic Reading T12<br>• Nonverbal Strategies T15 |
| • Paraphrasing and Summarizing T41 | • Daily Language SkillBuilder T7<br>• Avoiding Shifts in Tense, Mood, and Voice C120<br>• Capitalization I C144 | • Using a Thesaurus C31 | | • Dramatic Reading T12<br>• Impromptu Speaking: Dialogue, Role-Play, Debate T13 |
| • Making Inferences T7 | • Daily Language SkillBuilder T7<br>• Verbs–Using Correct Verb Forms T45<br>• Correct Verb Forms C117 | | • Identifying Writing Variables T2 | • Interviewing T9<br>• Impromptu Speaking: Dialogue, Role-Play, Debate T13 |
| • Compare and Contrast T15<br>• Venn Diagram T50 | • Daily Language SkillBuilder T7<br>• Verbs: Voice and Mood C119 | | • Elaboration T10 | |
| • Drawing Conclusions T4 | • Daily Language SkillBuilder T8<br>• Commonly Confused Verbs C122 | • Figurative Language C32 | • Persuasive Essay C27 | • Reading Aloud T11<br>• Dramatic Reading T12<br>• Verbal Strategies T14 |
| • Analyzing Text Structure T17<br>• Evaluating Argumentation II T21<br>• Comparing Authors' Views T23 | • Daily Language SkillBuilder T8<br>• Verbs–Using Correct Verb Forms T45<br>• Perfect Tenses of Verbs II C116 | • Idioms C36 | • Persuasive Essay C27 | • Impromptu Speaking: Dialogue, Role-Play, Debate T13 |
| • Reading for Details T16<br>• Evaluation Matrix T55 | • Daily Language SkillBuilder T9<br>• Avoiding Shifts in Tense T46<br>• Verbs: Tense Shifts C121 | • Word Origins C43 | • Critical Review C26 | • Dramatic Reading T12<br>• Impromptu Speaking: Dialogue, Role-Play, Debate T13 |

## STUDENTS ACQUIRING ENGLISH

The **Spanish Study Guide,** pp. 60–81, includes language support for the following pages:
• Family and Community Involvement (per unit)

• Selection Summaries and Vocabulary
• Active Reading
• Literary Analysis

| Selection | SkillBuilder Sentences | Suggested Answers |
|---|---|---|
| To My Dear and Loving Husband / Upon the Burning of Our House, July 10th, 1666 | 1. You must of read other lyric poems. <br><br> 2. To My dear and loving Husband was published after she died, because before, when anne was alive she thought they were too private for public view. | 1. You must **have** read other lyric poems. <br><br> 2. "To My **D**ear and **L**oving Husband" was published after she died, because when **A**nne was alive, she thought **it was** too private for public view. |
| The Examination of Sarah Good Documents, 1692 | 1. Having been hanged, the town eventually expressed regret for Sarah's death, <br><br> 2. Muttering isn't no crime we now recognize that. | 1. **After Sarah was hanged**, the town eventually expressed regret for **her** death. <br><br> 2. Muttering **is** no crime; we now recognize that. |
| *from* Sinners in the Hands of an Angry God | 1. Sinners In The Hands Of An Angry God is Jonathan Edwards famousest sermon. <br><br> 2. Edwards write sermons and philosophical works and religious works. | 1. "Sinners in the Hands of an Angry God" is Jonathan Edwards**'s most famous** sermon. <br><br> 2. Edwards **wrote** sermons and **philosophical and religious works**. |
| The Crucible | 1. Of all Arthur Miller plays I like The Crucible better. <br><br> 2. In puritan times they thought hanging witchs was right today few people woud agree. | 1. Of all Arthur Miller**'s** plays, I like **The Crucible best**. <br><br> 2. **The Puritans thought** hanging witch**es** was right. **T**oday few people **would** agree. |

| Selection | SkillBuilder Sentences | Suggested Answers |
|---|---|---|
| Speech in the Virginia Convention | **1.** What were the sequence of events leading to the declaration of independance! | **1.** What **was** the sequence of events leading to the **Declaration** of **Independence?** |
| | **2.** Some of the colonists in Virginia that Spring was ready to fight. | **2.** Some of the colonists in Virginia that **spring were** ready to fight. |
| The Declaration of Independence | **1.** American Colonist's engaged in heated debates about weather they should rebell against Englend. | **1.** American **colonists** engaged in heated debates about **whether** they should **rebel** against **England**. |
| | **2.** Many learned people was influenced by philosopher, John Locke's, notion of "natural rights." | **2.** Many learned people **were** influenced by philosopher John Locke's notion of "natural rights." |
| Letter to the Rev. Samson Occom Letter to John Adams | **1.** Around the time of the American revolution women was not aloud to make public speeches. | **1.** Around the time of the American **Revolution,** women **were** not **allowed** to make public speeches. |
| | **2.** Phillis Wheatleys book of poetry has been published in london, in 1773. | **2.** Phillis Wheatley**'s** book of poetry **was** published in **London** in 1773. |
| What Is an American? | **1.** What is an American? is a essay about America in the 1700s. When many people left Europe to settle their and make new lives for themselves. | **1.** "What **Is** an American?" is **an** essay about America in the 1700s, **w**hen many people left Europe to settle **there** and make new lives for themselves. |
| | **2.** Many in this early group of settlers was in search of freedom opportunities and equal rights not gave to them in Europe. | **2.** Many in this early group of settlers **were** in search of freedom, opportunities, and equal rights not **given** to them in Europe. |

| Selection | SkillBuilder Sentences | Suggested Answers |
|---|---|---|
| Lecture to a Missionary | 1. Red Jacket a seneca chief was knowed for his ability to speak eloquent he used this skill to protect the rights of Native Americans.<br><br>2. Christian missionarys wanted Native Americans to abandon there traditional religious beliefs. And adopt Christian beliefs. | 1. Red Jacket, a **Seneca** chief, was **known** for his ability to speak **eloquently. He** used this skill to protect the rights of Native Americans.<br><br>2. Christian **missionaries** wanted Native Americans to abandon **their** traditional religious beliefs **and** adopt Christian beliefs. |
| *from* Stride Toward Freedom<br>Necessary to Protect Ourselves | 1. Both Martin Luther King, jr and Malcolm X worked tireless for equal rights.<br><br>2. You must of heard some of Dr Kings speeches. | 1. Both Martin Luther King, **Jr.,** and Malcolm X worked **tirelessly** for equal rights.<br><br>2. You must **have** heard some of Dr. King**'s** speeches. |
| *from* I Am Joaquín/Yo Soy Joaquín | 1. On tuesday would you like to go to the main street cultural center with Renata and I, there is a exhibit honoring Mexican American history.<br><br>2. These exhibit will learn the community about Chicano poets artists and political activists such as Rodolfo Gonzales. | 1. On **Tuesday** would you like to go to the **Main Street Cultural Center** with Renata and **me? There** is an exhibit honoring Mexican-American history.<br><br>2. **This** exhibit will **teach** the community about Chicano poets, artists, and political activists, such as Rodolfo Gonzales. |

| Grammar Focus by Unit | Unit One | Unit Two | Unit Three | Unit Four | Unit Five | Unit Six | Unit Seven |
|---|---|---|---|---|---|---|---|
| | Parts of a Sentence | Verbs | Phrases | Clauses, Part I | Clauses, Part II | Special Sentence Structures, Part I | Special Sentence Structures, Part II |

*The Language of Literature* offers several options for integrating grammar instruction and literature.

- Each literature unit has a grammar focus. The Teacher's Edition includes Mini Lessons for each selection that help develop the grammar focus for the unit and spring from the content of the specific literature.

- The Pupil Edition includes several full-page lessons on Sentence Crafting. These lessons are related to both the literature and the grammar focus for the unit and help students use grammar in their own writing.

- Daily Language SkillBuilders in the Teacher's Edition provide students with ongoing proofreading practice and reinforce punctuation, spelling, grammar and usage, and capitalization.

- Grammar Copymasters and Transparencies, which may be used to complement or extend lessons in the Teacher's Edition, present grammar in a traditional, systematic sequence. References to appropriate copymasters or transparencies are included at point of use in the Teacher's Edition Mini Lessons.

TE Mini Lessons shown in green
PE instruction shown in black

## Part 1

### Parts of Speech

**Auxiliary Verbs**
"To My Dear and Loving Husband"
"Upon the Burning of Our House, July 10th, 1666," p. 143

**Adverbials: The Qualifiers**
Writing Workshop, p. 253

**Interjections**
*The Crucible*, p. 170

### Using Clauses

**Sentence Fragments**
Writing Workshop, p. 253

### Verb Usage

**Principal Parts of Verbs: Regular and Irregular Verbs**
*The Crucible*, p. 178

**Principal Parts of Verbs: Present, Present Participle, Past, Past Participle**
*The Crucible*, p. 200

**Perfect Verb Tenses**
*The Crucible*, p. 222

**Subject-Verb Agreement**
from *Sinners in the Hands of an Angry God*, p. 160

### End Marks and Commas

**Avoiding Comma Splices**
*The Crucible*, pp. 244–245
Sentence Crafting, p. 255

**Commas, Interrupters: Parenthetical Expressions**
Writing Workshop, p. 253

### Style

**Verbs: Overuse of *Be***
"The Examination of Sarah Good," p. 149

## Part 2

### Parts of Speech

**Distinguishing Plurals from Possessives**

**Pronouns**
Writing Workshop, p. 325

### Verb Usage

**Verb Tenses**
Sentence Crafting, p. 327

**Perfect Verb Tenses**
"Speech in the Virginia Convention," p. 269

**Verbs: Using Correct Forms**
"Letter to the Rev. Samson Occom,"
"Letter to John Adams," p. 288

**Verb Tenses: Special Uses of Past Perfect**
from *Stride Toward Freedom*,
"Necessary to Protect Ourselves," p. 308
Sentence Crafting, p. 327

**Using Verbs: Voice and Mood**
The Declaration of Independence, pp. 280–281
"What Is an American?" p. 294

**Verbs: Avoiding Shifts in Tense**
The Declaration of Independence, pp. 280–281

**Problems in Using Verb Tenses**
from *I am Joaquín/Yo Soy Joaquín*, p. 317

**Using Verbs: Commonly Confused Verbs**
"Lecture to a Missionary," p. 299

**Subject-Verb Agreement**
Writing Workshop, p. 325

**Capitalization**
The Declaration of Independence, p. 277

This time line shows some major dates and events in the struggle that led to the founding of the United States, from the establishment of the Massachusetts Bay Colony to the creation of a federal government under the Constitution. Help students recognize that this period was characterized worldwide by political upheaval and the evolution of political philosophy.

## From Colony to Country

### EVENTS IN AMERICAN LITERATURE

**1620**      **1700**

**1624** Captain John Smith writes *General History in Virginia*

**1640** *Bay Psalm Book* is first book printed in America

**1666** Anne Bradstreet, first notable colonial poet, writes "Upon the Burning of Our House"

**1678** Bradstreet publishes "To My Dear and Loving Husband," not originally intended for "public view"

**1704** *Boston Newsletter*, first American newspaper is established

**1732** Benjamin Franklin initiates a circulating library in Philadelphia; Franklin's *Poor Richard's Almanack* is published

**1741** Jonathan Edwards delivers sermon called "Sinners in the Hands of an Angry God"

### EVENTS IN NORTH AMERICA

**1620**      **1700**

**Ⓐ** **1630** About 1,000 Puritans establish Massachusetts Bay Colony

**1676** Puritans' victory in King Philip's War ends Native American resistance in New England colonies

**Ⓓ** **1682** Quakers led by William Penn begin living in peace with Native Americans in Pennsylvania (to c. 1752)

**1688** Quakers voice opposition to slavery

**1691** New charter provides for religious tolerance in Massachusetts, weakening Puritans' control

**1692** Witchcraft trials take place in Salem, Massachusetts

**Ⓕ** **1763** British defeat French in French and Indian War, and claim land east of Mississippi River, including Canada

**1765** British Parliament passes Stamp Act, which levies tax on colonies to help pay off British debts

### EVENTS IN THE WORLD

**1620**      **1700**

**Ⓑ** **1632** Indian emperor Shah Jahan builds Taj Mahal, over the next 22 years

**1643** Louis XIV begins 72-year reign in France

**Ⓔ** **1649** Oliver Cromwell and Puritans execute King Charles I of England

**1687** Sir Isaac Newton presents law of gravity

**1721** Edo (Tokyo) in Japan becomes world's largest city

**1748** French philosopher Baron de Montesquieu publishes *Spirit of the Laws*

### North America: 1630

**Ⓐ** The Massachusetts Bay Colony was named for the Massachuset tribe—a Native American group of the Algonquin language family. Once a great tribe in New England, the Massachuset lost their cultural identity when colonists converted them to Christianity.

### World: 1632

**Ⓑ** Mughal emperor Shah Jahan (1592–1666) began construction of the Taj Mahal to honor his wife, who died in childbirth after 19 years of marriage. Architects from India, Persia, Central Asia, and other parts of the world formed a council to design the mausoleum situated on the banks of the Yamuna River in northern India. More than 20,000 laborers worked on the structure daily for 22 years. The Taj Mahal is still regarded as one of the most beautiful buildings in the world.

### Literature: 1666

**Ⓒ** Celebrated for being one of the first poets to compose English verse in the American colonies, Anne Bradstreet (c. 1612–1672) wrote while raising eight children and acting as hostess for her husband, who became governor of Massachusetts. Her later poems, written for her family, trace her spiritual progress toward greater acceptance of the Puritan faith.

### North America: 1682

**Ⓓ** Within five years 12,000 people had moved to Pennsylvania. Its fertile soil attracted farmers, and the planned city of Philadelphia attracted merchants and artisans. By the early 1700s, the City of Brotherly Love rivaled Boston as a major colonial urban center.

### World: 1649

**Ⓔ** After years of civil war, the English army assumed control of the country's government in late 1648. The army held King Charles I responsible for the country's troubles and demanded that he be tried for high treason. He was condemned to death and was beheaded on January 30, 1649. According to spectators, the crowd that gathered to watch the execution groaned aloud when the axe struck—"such a groan," wrote one, "as I never heard before, and desire I may never hear again."

### North America: 1763

**Ⓕ** George Washington (1732–1799) learned to identify flaws in British military strategy when he led a colonial regiment fighting alongside the British army during the French and Indian War. His knowledge later helped the ragged, outnumbered Continental troops on the battlefields of the American Revolution.

# PERIOD PIECES

Paul Revere silver tea pot

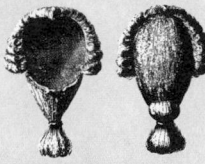

Popular style of wig in the 18th century

Puritan pocket watch

**1773** In London, Phillis Wheatley's *Poems on Various Subjects, Religious and Moral* appears, the first book of poetry published by an African American

**1775** In speech to the Second Virginia Convention, Patrick Henry makes plea for armed resistance against British

**1776** Thomas Paine publishes *Common Sense*, claiming that independence from England is "destiny"; Declaration of Independence is written by Thomas Jefferson; Abigail Adams proclaims power of "ladies" in letter to husband John

**1782** Michel-Guillaume Jean de Crèvecoeur publishes *Letters from an American Farmer*, a collection of 12 essays on life in America

**1789** *The Interesting Narrative of the Life of Olaudah Equiano* is published

**1773** To protest new British tax on tea, enraged colonists stage Boston Tea Party, dumping huge amounts of tea into Boston Harbor

**1775** "Shot heard round the world" is fired on Lexington Green in Massachusetts, starting Revolutionary War

**1781** British surrender to General George Washington at Yorktown, ending Revolutionary War

**1789** George Washington is elected first president of United States (to 1797)

**1791** Bill of Rights becomes part of U.S. Constitution

**1793** Eli Whitney invents cotton gin

**1796** Washington declines to run for third term and establishes presidential succession

**1762** Catherine the Great begins rule of Russia (to 1796)

**1776** Adam Smith publishes *The Wealth of Nations*

**1789** French Revolution begins (to 1794)

**1793** French King Louis XVI is executed by guillotine

**1795** Poland disappears from map of Europe after last partition

## PURITAN POCKET WATCH FROM 1635

**L** The art of watchmaking in the 17th century required a stunning degree of skill. All watch parts, including the intricate inner ones, had to be painstakingly crafted by hand.

## PAUL REVERE SILVER TEA POT

**G** In 1768, John Singleton Copley (1738–1815), a renowned artist of the colonial period, painted silversmith Paul Revere holding a silver tea pot similar to the one pictured. Copley's distinctive painting now hangs in the Museum of Fine Arts in Boston.

### Literature: 1773

**H** Born in Africa, Phillis Wheatley (c. 1753–1784) was brought to Boston and sold as a slave when she was eight years old. The tailor who purchased her recognized her intelligence and educated her with his family. Her poetry began attracting attention while she was still a teen. Her works were later used by abolitionists as evidence of the intellectual potential of African Americans.

### North America: 1775

**I** Patience Wright (1725–1786), American sculptor and outspoken patriot, found an unusual way to help the American war effort. While living in the whirl of high society in London, she spied on her clients and contacts, then shipped her messages to Philadelphia concealed in the heads of her wax sculptures.

### World: 1762

**J** Catherine II (1729–1796) became empress of Russia when she forced her husband, Czar Peter III, to abdicate. A native of Germany, he had inherited the throne of Russia through his grandfather Peter the Great. During Peter III's short reign, he made no secret of his disdain for Russia and its people. Catherine raised troops against her husband, forced him to abdicate, and had herself proclaimed empress. Eight days later Peter was assassinated by Catherine's supporters.

### Literature: 1782

**M** A citizen of the American colonies, Michel-Guillaume Jean de Crèvecoeur (1735–1813), also known as J. Hector St. John, found himself in a dangerous position when the American Revolution broke out. His wife was from a loyalist family while his friends and neighbors were supporters of the Revolution. To escape persecution by both sides, he sailed to Europe with one son, where he published *Letters from an American Farmer*. When he returned to North America in 1783, he found his home burned, his wife dead, and his two remaining children dispersed.

### Literature: 1776

**K** The first successful newspaper in the colonies, the *Boston NewsLetter*, was forced to shut down when its loyalist publisher fled the city during the British evacuation of Boston.

#### Introduction
This essay places the selections in Part 1 of this unit in historical context by providing students with an overview of the Puritans and their traditions in this country during the 17th century. The primary source selection in **Voices from the Times** enables students to interpret the possible influences of historical contexts on literary works.

### Teaching Nonfiction

#### Reading Skills and Strategies:
#### ESTABLISHING A PURPOSE FOR READING
Explain that this article introduces students to the Puritans' way of life and their belief system. Have students review the article and establish a purpose for reading.

#### IDENTIFYING MAIN IDEAS
The subheadings in **Between Heaven and Hell** relate to the main idea in each section. Have students approach the article by reading one section at a time, summarizing each section by identifying its main idea and noting the supporting ideas.

#### NOTETAKING
To better understand the article, encourage students to take notes as they read. They should note the Puritans' accomplishments, elements of their religious beliefs, and the values by which they lived. Graphic organizers that create visual connections can also help students remember important concepts and ideas.

#### DISCUSSING
Allow students time to discuss the article in class. A possible starting point could be a discussion of their perceptions of Puritans before reading this article. Discussion could also focus on the system of beliefs held by Puritans and the role it played in their lives and in politics. Ask students to draw upon their own backgrounds to compare this role of religion with the role of religion in daily life and politics today.

# Between Heaven and Hell

## The Puritan Tradition

**P**uritans too often have the reputation of being black-clad moralists self-righteously proclaiming the values of thrift and hard work. According to the American writer and humorist H. L. Mencken, a Puritan is one who suspects that "somewhere someone is having a good time." To call someone a puritan is usually not a compliment.

This negative image, however, is based on a stereotype of the 16th-century Puritans that, like most stereotypes, is full of half-truths and misconceptions. True, the Puritans did value hard work and self-sacrifice, but they also honored material success. Wealth was considered to be the reward of a virtuous life. Some Puritans, especially the early Pilgrims, wore severe black clothing because that was all they had. Those who settled the Massachusetts Bay Colony after 1630, however, were better off financially. They could afford decorative and colorful clothing—when they could find it in the colony, that is. These Puritans were even known to drink beer and other alcoholic beverages on occasion.

Puritans also valued family life, community service, art, and literature. They were the first in the colonies to establish a printing press, free public grammar schools, and a college (Harvard).

On the other hand, the Puritans *were* arrogant in their religious faith and completely intolerant of viewpoints different from their own. Puritans who remained in England

Tombstone design
from Puritan
New England

134

*Mrs. Freake and Baby Mary* (1674), unknown artist. The Granger Collection, New York.

participated in a revolution that not only toppled the king but had him beheaded as well. Those who had come to North America had even freer rein for their beliefs. With supreme confidence and self-consciousness, they went about setting up their institutions as though not only God but the whole world were watching. "The eyes of all people are on us," proclaimed John Winthrop, the first governor of the Massachusetts Bay

 D

# Puritan Beliefs

The key to the Puritan heart and soul is religious belief. What follows is a brief explanation of the Puritans' basic convictions:

• *Human beings are inherently evil and so must struggle to overcome their sinful nature.* This belief in original sin was one of the first things a Puritan child learned. "In Adam's fall / We sinned all" is the rhyme that teaches the letter *A* in *The New England Primer.*

• *Personal salvation depends solely on the grace of God, not on individual effort.* Puritans believed in predestination, the doctrine that only those people who are "elected" by God are saved and go to heaven. The only way an individual could know that he or she was saved was by directly experiencing God's grace in a religious conversion.

E

• *The Bible is the supreme authority on earth.* Puritans argued that the Bible was the sole guide not only in governing the moral and spiritual life but also in governing the church and society as a whole. One effect of this belief was to make Puritan churches more democratic, organized around their congregations rather than around ruling bishops. On the other hand, it led the Puritans to be more repressive in their political systems and more intolerant of others. For example, they used the Bible to justify their occupation of the land and their use of force against Native Americans: "Whosoever therefore resisteth the power, resisteth the ordinance of God: and they that resist shall receive to themselves damnation" (Romans 13:2). In short, the Puritans saw themselves as God's chosen people, like the "children of Israel" in the Old Testament.

F

### Literature
A Puritan literature is often stereotyped as overly pious, gloomy, and unimaginative. This judgment may apply to some works of the period, but Puritans have made fine literary contributions. English Puritan John Milton's (1608–1658) *Paradise Lost* is perhaps the most acclaimed imaginative work of the period. Anne Bradstreet's sensitive lyrics and Puritan cultivation of a straight-forward prose style are other notable achievements.

### Sociology
B The Puritans envisioned their society as a Christian "commonwealth" in which each person put the good of the group ahead of personal concerns. They established a strict moral code that provided a sense of common mission and cultural cohesion. Education was highly valued as a way to fight atheism and to instill in children the value of hard work.

### Religion
C Puritans often focused on other Christians in their efforts to root out the devil. Quakers and other dissenters received harsh punishments, including execution, for their beliefs. Puritan reformers like Anne Hutchinson (1591–1643) were excommunicated from the church and driven out of the community.

### Government
D Many variations of John Winthrop's (1588–1649) "city of God" experiment were tried in the colonies. A number of groups besides Puritans had come to America fleeing religious persecution and had set up religious establishments of their own. In fact, most colonies had some form of religion supported by the government in the revolutionary period. Massachusetts retained a limited version of Protestant government until well into the 1800s, despite the Constitution's restriction on the establishment of religion.

### Religion
E The Puritans believed that repentance, like personal salvation, depended on the grace of God. They also believed that, since humans were inherently evil, sin could never be eradicated. They saw guilt and remorse as signs of God's grace. Thus they examined themselves and their lives constantly, always looking for evidence of their election.

### History
F Puritan leader Roger Williams (c. 1603–1683) was banished from the Massachusetts Bay Colony in 1635 for challenging the strict religious code and the government's right to confiscate Native American land without compensation. He befriended the Narragansett tribe, learned its language, and purchased land from two of its chiefs. In 1636, he founded the colony of Providence and established the first government policy in the colonies guaranteeing political and religious freedom.

## SUMMARIZING

Have students summarize in their own words the article's contents. Remind students that a summary recounts the most important information in a text, leaving out less important details. Remind them that a summary does not include their opinions.

## MAIN IDEAS AND SUPPORTING DETAILS

This article gives the history of the Puritan tradition in colonial America. Ask students to read several paragraphs at a time and then identify the main ideas and supporting details in these paragraphs. Ask students to produce summaries of the text based on their identification of these elements.

## COMPARING AND CONTRASTING

Explain to students that they are expected to analyze text structures for how they influence understanding of the material. Point out to students that the phrases *however* and *on the other hand* usually signal a contrast to what has just been stated. Ask students to note what contrasts are signaled by these phrases in the article, how these contrasts relate to the article as a whole, and how the use of this technique influences their understanding of the material.

## USING TEXT ORGANIZERS

If students need more support, have them scan the article, noting the basic text organizers: title, overview, subheads, images and captions, and sidebar commentaries. Ask students to describe what information they would expect to locate in each section. As they read, have students use the subheads to make an outline or graphic organizer. Have them categorize information from the article under the appropriate heading. Remind students to use text organizers to locate and categorize information as they do independent research.

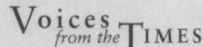

## Voices from the TIMES

### from *The New England Primer*

*The New England Primer* is a famous American schoolbook that dates from before 1690. The sale of more than 2 million copies of the book during the 18th century is an indication of how widely the primer was used.

136

Colony. And so it was that in New England during the 1600s Puritanism gained its fullest and perhaps purest development.

The selections in this part of Unit Two represent the Puritan tradition over a span of approximately 100 years. The poet Anne Bradstreet gives a sense of what ordinary Puritan lives were like. Her voice expresses the view of a heaven ruled by a just God—a goal to which all Puritans aspired. The grace of Bradstreet's voice is followed by the harshness of the judges' voices at the Salem witch trials, an example of the darker aspects of Puritanism. The last Puritan represented is the passionate minister Jonathan Edwards, threatening his congregation with the torments of hell in an excerpt from his famous sermon "Sinners in the Hands of an Angry God."

## Traditions Across Time: Another Look at the Puritans

Many American writers have been fascinated by the Puritans. Nathaniel Hawthorne, one of whose ancestors had been a presiding judge at the Salem witch trials, set his novel *The Scarlet Letter* and many of his short stories in Puritan times to explore the psychological effects of sin and guilt.

In the 1950s, the playwright Arthur Miller dramatized the Salem witchcraft trials in *The Crucible*. The play was written partly in response to the anti-Communist "witch hunts" of the period. Miller's drama not only personalizes the events of Salem but also warns against similar injustices in our own time.

**VOICES FROM THE TIMES**

**Ask: What things besides the alphabet does the New England Primer teach children?**

**Possible Responses:** reading, morality, religious values, Bible stories, patience, the value of hard work

**Ask: How does education today compare with education in colonial times?**

**Possible Responses:** religion not taught in public schools; separate public, private, and parochial schools

## The Puritan Tradition

Detail of chair-seat cover (about 1725), embroidered by a member of Anne Bradstreet's family.

137

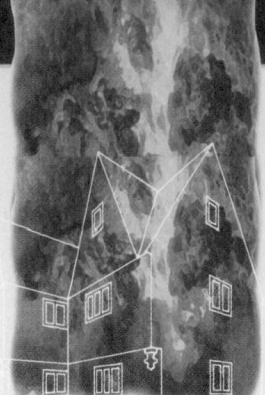

# To My Dear and Loving Husband
*and*

# Upon the Burning of Our House, July 10th, 1666

*Poetry by* ANNE BRADSTREET

**Connect to Your Life**

## OVERVIEW

### Objectives
1. understand and appreciate **lyric poetry** (Literary Analysis)
2. appreciate author's use of **meter** (Literary Analysis)
3. **clarify meaning** of archaic language (Active Reading)

### Summary
"To My Dear and Loving Husband" is both a love poem and a tribute to Anne Bradstreet's husband. Written many years into their marriage, it is one of the poems that Bradstreet did not want published because she did not consider it appropriate for public view. Both her husband and her father served as governor of Massachusetts and as such were very public figures. This poem is a private testimony to the profound love she knew with her husband. "Upon the Burning of Our House, July 10th, 1666" is the poet's chronicle of a domestic tragedy.

### Thematic Link
"To My Dear and Loving Husband" is an example of the **Puritan** belief that domestic bliss was a blessing that came from God. "Upon the Burning of Our House" reveals Bradstreet's struggle to reconcile herself with a devastating material loss.

## Reading and Analyzing

### GUIDE FOR READING
**A** **Possible Response:** Couples who are loving and constant on earth will attain eternal life in heaven.

### 5-Minute Warm-Up

*Daily Language SkillBuilder*

Have students **proofread** the display sentences on page 131i and write them correctly. The sentences also appear on Transparency 5 of **Grammar Transparencies and Copymasters.**

**Connect to Your Life**

**Prized Persons and Possessions** Think about a person or a possession that means a lot to you. What comparison would express the emotions you feel toward this person or thing? On a sheet of paper, complete the following sentence:
_____ means more to me than _____.

## Build Background

**Puritan Poetry** You may be surprised to learn that Anne Bradstreet was not only the first notable American woman poet—she was essentially the first notable American poet. In the two poems presented here, Bradstreet expresses her intense feelings about her husband and about the loss of her home in a destructive fire. Although Bradstreet's poetic language may seem a bit stiff to you, you'll be able to understand the recognizable emotions of love and sadness she expresses.

Poetry in 17th-century New England was almost exclusively devotional in nature and, as such, was highly recommended reading for the Puritan community. What sets Bradstreet's poems apart from other Puritan verse is their personal subject matter. She focused primarily on the realities of her life—her husband, her children, and her house, for example. However, like any conscientious Puritan, Bradstreet always viewed her life within a spiritual context: every event, no matter how trivial, bore a divine message; every misfortune served to remind her of God's will and the path to salvation. In her poetry, Bradstreet gave us a lasting impression of what it felt like to be a Puritan.

## Focus Your Reading

**LITERARY ANALYSIS  METER**  If you read Bradstreet's two poems aloud, you will hear a distinct rhythm. **Meter** is the repetition of a regular rhythmic unit in a line of poetry. Each unit, known as a foot, has one stressed syllable (indicated by a ´) and either one or two unstressed syllables (indicated by a ˘). Read the beginning lines of both poems aloud, tapping out the rhythm. Note which words or syllables are stressed and how many stresses there are.

**ACTIVE READING  CLARIFYING MEANING**
**Archaic language** consists of words that were once commonly used in the past but are now considered old-fashioned or out-of-date. For example, note that Bradstreet uses the pronouns *thee, ye,* and *thou,* rather than *you.* Also, like other early American poets, Bradstreet often uses **inverted syntax**—meaning that she reverses the expected order of words. In the first line of "Upon the Burning of Our House," for example, she writes "when rest I took" rather than "when I took rest."

**READER'S NOTEBOOK**  As you read "Upon the Burning of Our House," note other lines with archaic language and inverted syntax, and paraphrase (restate) them using contemporary vocabulary and conventional word order.

138  UNIT TWO  PART 1: BETWEEN HEAVEN AND HELL

## LESSON RESOURCES

**UNIT TWO RESOURCE BOOK,** pp. 4–5

**ASSESSMENT RESOURCES**
**Formal Assessment,** pp. 31–32
**Teacher's Guide to Assessment and Portfolio Use**
**Test Generator**

**SKILLS TRANSPARENCIES AND COPYMASTERS**
Literary Analysis
• Form in Poetry: Structure, T11 (for Paired Activity, p. 142)

**Reading and Critical Thinking**
• Compare and Contrast, T15 (for Extend Interpretations, item 7, p. 142)

**Grammar**
• Verbs—Using Correct Verb Forms, T45 (for Mini Lesson, p. 143)
• Auxiliary Verbs, C67 (for Mini Lesson, p. 143)

**Vocabulary**
• Analogies, C24 (for Mini Lesson, p. 140)

**Communications**
• Appreciative Listening, T2 (for Activities & Explorations 2, p. 143)

**INTEGRATED TECHNOLOGY**
**Audio Library**
**LaserLinks**
• Cultural Connection: The Puritans in North America. See **Teacher's SourceBook,** p. 23.
**Visit our website:**
www.mcdougallittell.com

ANNE BRADSTREET

# To My  Dear and Loving Husband

Chair-seat cover (about 1725), embroidered by a member of the Bradstreet family. Cotton threads, linen warp, wool embroidery, 43 cm × 47 cm. Gift of Samuel Bradstreet, courtesy of Museum of Fine Arts, Boston.

If ever two were one, then surely we.
If ever man were loved by wife, then thee;
If ever wife was happy in a man,
Compare with me, ye women, if you can.
5   I prize thy love more than whole mines of gold
Or all the riches that the East doth hold.
My love is such that rivers cannot quench,
Nor ought but love from thee, give recompense.
Thy love is such I can no way repay,
10  The heavens reward thee manifold, I pray.
Then while we live, in love let's so persevere
That when we live no more, we may live ever.

**GUIDE FOR READING**

**8 recompense** (rĕk'əm-pĕns'): payment in return for something, such as a service.

**9–12** What relationship is seen between earthly love and eternal life?

**11 persevere:** In Bradstreet's time, *persevere* would have been pronounced pûr-sĕv'ər, which rhymes with *ever*.

## Thinking Through the Literature

1. **Comprehension Check** What is valued more than gold in this poem?
2. What do you think Bradstreet is saying in the last two lines of the poem?
3. What emotions does Bradstreet express toward her husband? Point out the words that make you think so.
4. Do you know any couples who regard each other as Bradstreet and her husband do? Describe them.

TO MY DEAR AND LOVING HUSBAND   **139**

---

**Reading Skills and Strategies:
PREVIEW**

Have students read poems aloud to get
a sense of the meter and to familiarize
themselves with the archaic language.

**Active Reading:** CLARIFYING MEANING

 **A** Have students locate examples of
**inverted syntax** in the first stanza of
the poem and rewrite these lines the
way they would normally expect to see
them.

**Possible Responses:** "when rest I
took" (line 1) becomes "when I took
rest"; "For sorrow near I did not look"
(line 2) becomes "I did not look for
sorrow near"; "I wakened was" (line 3)
becomes "I was wakened"

Use **Unit Two Resource Book,**
p. 4 for more exercises.

**Literary Analysis** METER

 **B** Have students read the first stanza
aloud, tapping out the rhythm. Ask
them to analyze the meter and compare and contrast it with the meter
used in "To My Dear and Loving
Husband."

**Possible Responses:** As in the previous
poem, every other syllable is stressed.
Instead of five stressed syllables per
line, this poem has four.

Use **Unit Two Resource Book,**
p. 5 for more practice.

**GUIDE FOR READING**

**C** **Possible Response:** God gave her
what she had; because her possessions
really belonged to Him, it was not
unfair of Him to take them away.

**D** **Possible Response:** things that she
stored in her trunk and chest; the people who can no longer gather in the
house to talk and eat

**E** **Possible Responses:** heaven; that
God makes heaven a permanent home
for believers

---

ANNE BRADSTREET

# $U$PON the $B$URNING of Our $H$OUSE,

## July 10th, 1666

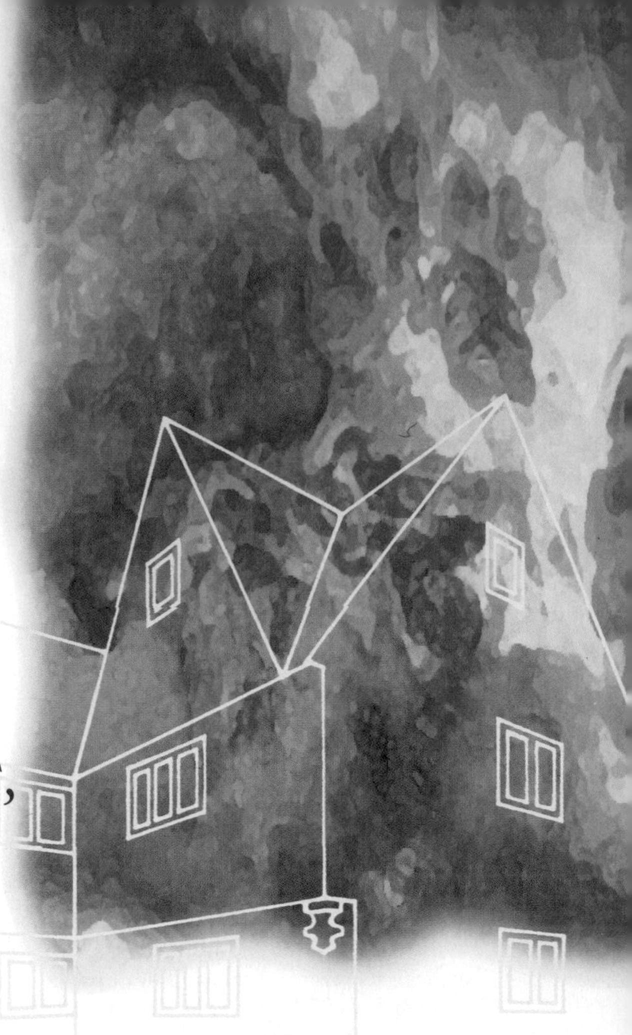

$I$n silent night when rest I took
For sorrow near I did not look
I wakened was with thund'ring noise
And piteous shrieks of dreadful voice.
5   That fearful sound of "Fire!" and "Fire!"
Let no man know is my desire.

I, starting up, the light did spy,
And to my God my heart did cry
To strengthen me in my distress
10   And not to leave me succorless.
Then, coming out, beheld a space
The flame consume my dwelling place.

**GUIDE FOR READING**

**10 succorless** (sŭk'ər-lĭs): without
help or relief.

**140**   UNIT TWO   PART 1: BETWEEN HEAVEN AND HELL

---

**Teaching Options**

 **Vocabulary Strategy**

**READING AND UNDERSTANDING ANALOGIES**
**Instruction** Analogies enable students to enrich
their vocabularies. An analogy consists of two
pairs of words that are related to each other in
the same way.
Write this analogy on the chalkboard:
    SHRIEK : PITEOUS :: sob : mournful
Ask students to determine how *shriek* and *piteous*
are related to each other. Have a volunteer state
the relationship in a sentence, such as "A shriek

often sounds piteous." Finally, insert the second
pair of words into the sentence ("A sob often
sounds mournful") and have students confirm that
the same relationship exists between them.

Use **Vocabulary Transparencies and
Copymasters,** p. 24.

**A lesson on analogies appears on p. 254 in
the Pupil's Edition.**

And when I could no longer look,
I blest His name that gave and took,
That laid my goods now in the dust:
Yea, so it was, and so 'twas just.
It was His own, it was not mine,
Far be it that I should repine;

He might of all justly bereft,
But yet sufficient for us left.
When by the ruins oft I past,
My sorrowing eyes aside did cast,
And here and there the places spy
Where oft I sat and long did lie:

Here stood that trunk and there that chest,
There lay that store I counted best.
My pleasant things in ashes lie,
And them behold no more shall I.
Under thy roof no guest shall sit,
Nor at thy table eat a bit.

No pleasant tale shall e'er be told,
Nor things recounted done of old.
No candle e'er shall shine in thee,
Nor bridegroom's voice e'er heard shall be.
In silence ever shalt thou lie;
Adieu, Adieu, all's vanity.

Then straight I 'gin my heart to chide,
And did thy wealth on earth abide?
Didst fix thy hope on mold'ring dust?
The arm of flesh didst make thy trust?
Raise up thy thoughts above the sky
That dunghill mists away may fly.

Thou hast an house on high erect,
Framed by that mighty Architect,
With glory richly furnishèd,
Stands permanent though this be fled.
It's purchasèd and paid for too
By Him who hath enough to do.

A price so vast as is unknown
Yet by His gift is made thine own;
There's wealth enough, I need no more,
Farewell, my pelf, farewell my store.
The world no longer let me love,
My hope and treasure lies above.

15
20
25
30
35
40
45
50

**14 I . . . took:** an allusion to Job 1:21—"The Lord gave, and the Lord hath taken away; blessed be the name of the Lord."

**13–18** How does Bradstreet view her loss? **C**

**18 repine:** to complain or fret; to long for something.

**21–36** What does Bradstreet miss about her house? **D**

**36 all's vanity:** an allusion to Ecclesiastes 1:2, "All is vanity," meaning that all is temporary and meaningless.

**37 chide:** to scold mildly so as to correct or improve.

**43–54** What is Bradstreet comparing to a house? What ideas are suggested by this comparison? **F**

**52 pelf:** wealth or riches, especially when dishonestly acquired.

UPON THE BURNING OF OUR HOUSE **141**

## Customizing Instruction

### Students Acquiring English
Defining the following words and phrases will help students understand the poem.
Line 7: *starting up* suggests that Bradstreet has been startled from sleep and is getting out of bed. *Spy* means "to catch sight of, glimpse, or quickly see"; line 12: *dwelling place* means "home"; line 19: *bereft* means the same as *bereaved*, "deprived of"; line 38: *abide*, as it is used here, might best be translated as "remain."

### Less Proficient Readers
**1** Ask students to paraphrase lines 13–18 as simply as possible.
**Possible Response:** God's will be done.
Encourage them to work together to find other places in the poem where Bradstreet expresses spiritual values.

### Multiple Learning Styles
**Visual Learners**
**2** Ask students to imagine what Bradstreet saw when she woke up to a house on fire. Ask students what feelings those images evoke. Reread lines 21–28 and ask: What would it have been like for Bradstreet when she went back to the charred remains? What did she see there?

## Informal Assessment

✓ Assessment

**JOURNAL ENTRY** You can informally assess your students' understanding of the poems by asking them to respond to the following scenario. This activity also allows students to draw inferences and support them with textual evidence and experience. *Imagine that you are a close friend of Anne Bradstreet. Write a journal entry about the night her house burned and how she responded to the tragedy. Be sure to include your feelings about her reaction and make some mention of her husband in your entry.*

**RUBRIC**

**3 Full Accomplishment** Response conveys Bradstreet's emotional change from sorrow to acceptance, accurately evokes her love for her husband, and comments on the appropriateness of her response to the tragedy.

**2 Substantial Accomplishment** Response shows some understanding of Bradstreet's reactions and her feelings for her husband, but it does not convey the full range of her emotions.

**1 Little or Partial Accomplishment** Response does not accurately convey Bradstreet's feelings.

## GUIDING STUDENT RESPONSE

## Connect to the Literature

**1. What Do You Think?** Students who have experienced the destruction of their own homes from fire or natural disaster may be more compassionate. Others might wonder aloud how they would respond in a similar situation. A highly perceptive response will point out that the extent of Bradstreet's inner conflict attests to her spiritual strength.

**Comprehension Check**
- She cries out to God for help and courage.
- The reason is that God willed it to happen.
- in heaven, or in God's love

## Think Critically

**2. Possible Response:** She comes to believe that material wealth is not as valuable as spiritual wealth, and all that happens is God's will.

**3. Possible Responses:** fear (lines 3–6); distress (lines 7–10); horror (line 13); sorrow, grief (lines 21–36); humility (lines 37–38); hope (lines 43–54)

**4. Possible Responses:** She would have written a poem to eulogize her dead husband, and in it find peace knowing he was now with God and that she would join him when her time came.

**5. Possible Response:** For this Puritan woman, belief in the will of God takes precedence over every detail of her life. In her daily life, the things she values most are simple: a trunk, a chest, friends eating at table, telling stories, and so on.

**6. Possible Responses:** Rewriting the poem disrupts the meter and rhyme scheme, making it less pleasing to the ear.

## Literary Analysis

**Meter** Have one student read aloud while the other quietly taps out the beat. Ask:
- How many feet are in each line? *(4)*
- What is the pattern of stressed and unstressed syllables? *(unstressed, stressed)*
- What is the meter of the lines? *(iambic tetrameter)*

---

## Connect to the Literature

**1. What Do You Think**
What do you make of Bradstreet's reaction to her loss? Share your thoughts with a classmate.

**Comprehension Check**
- What is Bradstreet's initial reaction when she learns her house is on fire?
- What does she conclude about the reason for the fire?
- Where does she expect to find a permanent home?

## Think Critically

**2.** Explain in your own words why Bradstreet feels the way she does at the end of the poem.

- her attitude toward wealth and material goods
- her religious beliefs and values

**3.** What different emotions does Bradstreet express at various points in the poem? Point out lines in the poem that support your ideas.

**4.** If Bradstreet had lost her husband in the fire, how might the poem be different?

**5.** What did you learn about Bradstreet's daily life from reading this poem?

**6.** **ACTIVE READING** **CLARIFYING MEANING** Share lines from the poem that you paraphrased using contemporary language and conventional word order. How do your versions compare with the original lines? By changing Bradstreet's syntax, how did you alter the **rhyme scheme**—the pattern of rhyme at the end of each line?

## Extend Interpretations

**7. Comparing Texts** On the basis of "To My Dear and Loving Husband" and "Upon the Burning of Our House," how would you describe Bradstreet's views of God and heaven?

**8. Connect to Life** Think of someone you know whose spiritual values are a source of strength during trying times. Briefly describe that person, and compare him or her to the speaker in "Upon the Burning of Our House."

---

## Literary Analysis

**METER** Bradstreet's two poems follow a regular pattern, or **meter,** of accented and unaccented syllables. In a poetic line, each unit, known as a foot, has one stressed syllable (indicated by a ´) and either one or two unstressed syllables (indicated by a ˘), as shown in the chart below:

| Foot | Syllables | Example |
|------|-----------|---------|
| iamb | unstressed, stressed | to͝dáy |
| trochee | stressed, unstressed | láte͝r |
| anapest | unstressed, unstressed, stressed | ͝inter͝fére |
| dactyl | stressed, unstressed, unstressed | pérma͝ne͝nt |

Two words are used to identify the meter of a line. The first word describes the type of metrical foot—iambic, trochaic, anapestic, or dactylic— and the second word describes the number of feet in a line, as follows:

one foot: **monometer**      four feet: **tetrameter**
two feet: **dimeter**         five feet: **pentameter**
three feet: **trimeter**      six feet: **hexameter**

If you were to analyze, or scan, line 2 of "To My Dear and Loving Husband," it would look like this:

*If* ˘évĕr mán ˘wĕre lovéd bў ˘wífe ˘thĕn thée
  1     2      3      4     5

"To My Dear and Loving Husband" is an example of **iambic pentameter**, the most common meter in English poetry.

**Paired Activity** What is the meter of "Upon the Burning of Our House"? Working with a partner, scan the first two lines, count the stressed syllables, and refer to the charts. Then write two lines of poetry that duplicate the meter of either Bradstreet poem.

---

## Extend Interpretations

**Comparing Texts** Students may notice that objects, no matter how dear, will never make it to heaven, but the people we love do. In "To My Dear and Loving Husband," Bradstreet views heaven as the reward for a loving marriage. In "Upon the Burning of Our House," she views God as the only source of love that is essential; Bradstreet lets go of all earthly attachments. It is interesting to note here that she makes no mention at all of her husband, nor of her children or grandchildren who might have been visiting at the time of the fire.

**Connect to Life** Responses will vary. Encourage students to focus their descriptions on the qualities of the person that enable him or her to resolve inner conflict.

## Writing Options

**1. Lyric Poem** Both of Bradstreet's poems are called lyric poems because they are short and express the thoughts and feelings of one speaker. Write a lyric poem that expresses your emotions toward the person or possession you described for the Connect to Your Life activity on page 138. Imitate Bradstreet's style if you wish.

**2. Personal Analogy** In the last two stanzas of "Upon the Burning of Our House," Bradstreet compares heaven to a house. Develop an analogy, an extended comparison of two things that have certain similarities, to explain your personal view of one of the following concepts: heaven, love, home, loss, marriage, wealth.

## Activities & Explorations

**1. Storyboard Illustrations** Working with a small group of classmates, create a series of drawings to illustrate the sentiments in "To My Dear and Loving Husband" or the events in "Upon the Burning of Our House." Show your storyboard to the class, identifying specific lines that you illustrated. ~ **ART**

**2. Musical Adaptation** Bradstreet's poetry was influenced by a book of biblical psalms set to the melodies of familiar hymns. Create a song by setting one of Bradstreet's poems to music with an appropriate rhythm and mood. Make a tape recording of the song, and share it with the class. ~ **MUSIC**

## Inquiry & Research

**1. Puritan Women** The Puritan emphasis on reading the Bible encouraged a higher rate of literacy among Puritan women in New England than in England or other British colonies. Locate information on the education of Puritan women and the roles they played in the Puritan community.

**2. Puritan Homes** Puritans were artistic interior decorators. For instance, the women wove beautifully designed bedspreads and embroidered colorful chair-seat covers, such as the one shown on page 139. Find out more about the beautiful objects that adorned Puritan homes.

---

## Anne Bradstreet
(1612?–1672)

**Other Works**
"Before the Birth of One of Her Children"
"As Weary Pilgrim"
"To My Dear Children"

**A Privileged Upbringing** The first noteworthy poet in the American colonies, Anne Dudley Bradstreet was born in England. She grew up among educated aristocrats because her father, Thomas Dudley, was steward, or manager of affairs, for the Earl of Lincoln. Bradstreet's father provided her with tutors and access to the Earl's extensive library, and he taught her Greek, Latin, Hebrew, and French.

**Life in the Colonies** In 1628, 16-year-old Anne married Simon Bradstreet. Two years later, the young couple sailed for the Massachusetts Bay Colony. The Bradstreets eventually settled in North Andover, where they raised eight children. Despite Anne Bradstreet's domestic and religious responsibilities and persistent illnesses, she managed to find time to write.

**America's First English-Speaking Poet** In 1647, Bradstreet's brother-in-law, John Woodbridge, went to England with verses that she had copied for members of her family. Without her knowledge, he had the verses published in London in 1650, in a volume titled *The Tenth Muse Lately Sprung Up in America*. A second edition, published in 1678, contained Bradstreet's corrections and personal poems, including "To My Dear and Loving Husband," which she had not intended for "public view." A third edition, printed in 1867, contained additional poems, including "Upon the Burning of Our House."

---

 **Mini Lesson**

## Grammar

**AUXILIARY VERBS** An auxiliary verb is used with another verb to indicate voice, mood, or tense. Auxiliary verbs include *be, have, can, may, must, might, shall, will, could, should, would,* and *do.* A main verb and one or more auxiliary verbs constitute a verb phrase. Illustrate this point with a chart such as the following:

| Auxiliary | Main Verb | Verb Phrase |
|---|---|---|
| was | burning | was burning |
| is | destroyed | is destroyed |
| would have | grieved | would have grieved |
| will | endure | will endure |

 Use **Grammar Transparencies and Copymasters**, p. 67.

 Use McDougal Littell's ***Language Network***, Chapter 4, for more instruction and practice in auxiliary verbs.

---

## Writing Options

**1. Lyric Poem** To qualify as lyric, students' poems should sound musical, have one speaker, and be longer than a haiku. The language should be emotionally charged, expressing thoughts and feelings through the images. **To get students started on this activity,** suggest that they brainstorm a list of words and phrases associated with the person or possession.

**2. Personal Analogy** Responses will vary. Have students explain the common characteristics or functions between two otherwise dissimilar things. **To make this assignment more challenging,** have them put their analogies into poems.

## Activities & Explorations

**1. Storyboard Illustrations** Encourage students to explain why they rendered certain lines of the poems as they did.

**2. Musical Adaptation** For an extension activity, students might compare the meter of Langston Hughes's poetry to rhythm and blues music, which influenced his writing.

## Inquiry & Research

**1. Puritan Women** Remind students that they can locate appropriate print information using a technical resource such as a library database. For example, they might locate the 11-volume set *The Young Oxford History of Women in the United States* (New York: Oxford University Press, 1995), especially volume 2, *The Colonial Mosaic: American Women 1600–1760*, by Jane Kamensky, and volume 3, *The Limits of Independence: American Women 1760–1800*, by Marylynn Salmon.

**2. Puritan Homes** Students can find relevant information in the book *American Colonial: Puritan Simplicity to Georgian Grace*, by Wendell Garrett (New York: Monacelli Press, 1995).

# The Examination of Sarah Good

SALEM COURT DOCUMENTS, 1692

## Objectives

1. understand and appreciate a court **transcript (Literary Analysis)**
2. **detect bias** in a speaker's language **(Active Reading)**

## Summary

As recorded in Salem court documents of 1692, Sarah Good is charged with using witchcraft on several children. She denies the charges, even though the children confront her and go into convulsions in her presence. In the transcript of her testimony, she denies the court's accusations that she has communicated with the devil. She also accuses Sarah Osborne of being a witch. Her testimony, however, is described as wicked and spiteful, and it is stated that her husband believes she is or soon will be a witch.

## Thematic Link

Although Americans often give too much weight to the witchcraft episode in assessing colonial history, it does form a part of the **Puritan tradition.** Alert readers will appreciate how Sarah Good struggles ineffectively to clear her name. She desperately resorts to lies that only arouse deeper suspicions in her accusers, who view the proceedings as a conflict **between heaven and hell.**

### 5-Minute Warm-Up

*Daily Language SkillBuilder*

Have students **proofread** the display sentences on page 131i and write them correctly. The sentences also appear on Transparency 5 of **Grammar Transparencies and Copymasters.**

## Connect to Your Life

**Justice Denied** Have you ever been accused of doing something that you didn't do, or do you know of someone else who was falsely accused? If so, how did you feel about the accusation? Why do you think it was made? Was it ever disproved? With your classmates, discuss the causes and effects of false accusations.

## Build Background

**Mass Hysteria in Salem** In 1692, the Massachusetts Bay Colony settlement of Salem was gripped by panic after a group of adolescent girls suffered mysterious symptoms such as convulsive fits, hallucinations, loss of appetite, and the temporary loss of hearing, sight, and speech. Diagnosed as being victims of witchcraft, the girls denounced certain townspeople for this crime, including a woman named Sarah Good. The selection you will read consists of excerpts from the court records of Sarah Good's preliminary examination on March 1, 1692, at the Salem meeting house. Good was later jailed, tried in court, and found guilty; she was hanged on July 19, 1692.

Between 1692 and 1693, more than 400 people in Salem and nearby towns were accused of being witches. Ultimately, 19 men and women were found guilty and hanged. When Puritan leaders began to doubt the accusers and their evidence, the Salem witch trials finally ended. Over the next 20 years, most of those falsely accused were pardoned and awarded financial compensation.

## Focus Your Reading

**LITERARY ANALYSIS** **TRANSCRIPT** A **transcript** is a written record of information communicated orally, such as a **speech**, an **interview**, or **legal testimony**. The transcript of Sarah Good's examination provides the actual questions she was asked and the answers she gave. Think of this document as the script of a real-life drama. Imagine the voices of Sarah Good and her questioners and the motives for their remarks. Also notice how the introductory summary, a brief description of events written by those who questioned Good, differs from the transcript as a source of information.

**ACTIVE READING** **DETECTING BIAS** A **bias** is a prejudice or mental leaning toward or against some topic, issue, or person. Writers can reveal their biases by using **loaded language,** words with strong emotional associations. The description "poor tormented children" reveals the writer's sympathetic attitude, or positive bias, toward the accusing girls. Similarly, interrogators can reveal their biases by asking **loaded questions**—questions that make unwarranted presumptions or that force a certain answer. For example, the question, "Why do you hurt these children?" assumes Good's guilt.

**READER'S NOTEBOOK** As you read, note examples of loaded language or loaded questions that reveal the biases of court officials.

## LESSON RESOURCES

**UNIT TWO RESOURCE BOOK,** pp. 6–9

**ASSESSMENT RESOURCES**
**Formal Assessment,** pp. 33–34
**Teacher's Guide to Assessment and Portfolio Use**
**Test Generator**

**SKILLS TRANSPARENCIES AND COPYMASTERS**
**Reading and Critical Thinking**
• Determining Author's Bias, T22 (for Active Reading, p. 144)

**Grammar**
• Overuse of the Verb *To Be,* C163 (for Mini Lesson, p. 149)
**Vocabulary**
• Idioms, C25 (for Mini Lesson, p. 146)
**Writing**
• The Uses of Dialogue, T24 (for Writing Option 1, p. 149)
• Persuasive Essay, C27 (for Writing Option 2, p. 149)
**Communications**
• Interviewing, T9 (for Activities & Explorations 2, p. 149)

• Impromptu Speaking: Dialogue, Role-Play, Debate, T13 (for Activities & Explorations 3, p. 149)

**INTEGRATED TECHNOLOGY**
**Audio Library**
**LaserLinks**
• Historical Connection: The Salem Witch Trials. See **Teacher's SourceBook,** p. 24.
**Internet: Research Starter**
**Visit our website:**
www.mcdougallittell.com

# The EXAMINATION of SARAH GOOD

## SALEM COURT DOCUMENTS, 1692

## SUMMARY

SALEM VILLAGE, MARCH THE 1ST, 1691–92.

Sarah Good, the wife of William Good of Salem Village, Laborer. Brought before us by George Locker, Constable in Salem, to Answer, Joseph Hutchinson, Thomas Putnam, etc., of Salem Village, yeomen[1] (Complainants[2] on behalf of their Majesties) against said Sarah Good for Suspicion of witchcraft by her Committed and thereby much Injury done to the Bodies of Elizabeth Parris, Abigail Williams, Ann Putnam, and Elizabeth Hubbard, all of Salem Village aforesaid according to their Complaints as per warrants.

---

1. **yeomen** (yō′mən): farmers who cultivate their own land.
2. **complainants** (kəm-plā′nənts): people who make a complaint or file a formal charge in court.

## Reading and Analyzing

### Reading Skills and Strategies: PREVIEW

Have students go over Preparing to Read to help them understand the context of the Salem Witch trials.

### Literary Analysis [TRANSCRIPT]

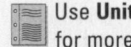 Have students compare this section of the Summary to what is recorded in the transcript.

**Possible Response:** The Summary implies that Good accused Sarah Osborne immediately after Good was asked who tortured the children. The transcript reveals Good's reluctance to make the accusation, which is dragged out of her after several questions.

Use **Unit Two Resource Book**, p. 8 for more exercises.

### Active Reading [DETECTING BIAS]

 Point out to students the phrasing of these questions. Rather than asking *whether* Sarah Good hurt the children, the questioner assumes that she did and simply asks *why* and *how* she hurt them. Thus his questions indicate his bias. Ask students to remain alert to other examples of bias as they read. In particular, they should recognize deceptive modes of persuasion such as loaded language—words or phrases chosen to appeal to emotions, to create a prejudice in the mind of the hearer, or to control an answer to a question. Loaded language often works through the connotative power of words.

Use **Unit Two Resource Book**, p. 7 for more practice.

Sarah Good upon Examination denieth the matter of fact (viz.) that she ever used any witchcraft or hurt the abovesaid children or any of them.

The above-named Children being all present positively accused her of hurting of them Sundry[3] times with this two months and also that morning.

Sarah Good denied that she had been at their houses in said time or near them, or had done them any hurt. All the abovesaid children then present accused her face to face, upon which they were all dreadfully tortured and tormented for a short space of time, and the affliction and tortures being over, they charged said Sarah Good again that she had then so tortured them, and came to them and did it, although she was personally then kept at a Considerable distance from them.

Sarah Good being Asked if, that she did not then hurt them who did it. And the children being again tortured, she looked

upon them And said that it was one of them we brought into the house with us. We Asked her who it was: She then Answered and said it was Sarah Osborne, and Sarah Osborne was then under Custody and not in the house; And the children being quickly after recovered out of their fit said that it was Sarah Good and also Sarah Osborne that then did hurt & torment or afflict them—although both of them at the same time at a distance or Remote from them personally—there were also sundry other Questions put to her and Answers given thereunto by her according as is also given in.

JOHN HATHORNE
JONATHAN CORWIN } ASSISTANTS

---

3. **sundry** (sŭn′drē): various.

---

# TRANSCRIPT

THE EXAMINATION OF SARAH GOOD BEFORE THE WORSHIPFUL ASSISTANTS JOHN HATHORNE, JONATHAN CORWIN.

Q. Sarah Good, what evil Spirit have you familiarity with?

A. None.

Q. Have you made no contract with the Devil?

Good answered no.

Q. Why do you hurt these children?

A. I do not hurt them. I scorn it.

Q. Who do you employ then to do it?

A. I employ nobody.

Q. What creature do you employ then?

A. No creature, but I am falsely accused.

Q. Why did you go away muttering from Mr. Parris, his house?

## Teaching Options

### Mini Lesson **Vocabulary Strategy**

**USING CONTEXT TO DETERMINE THE MEANING OF IDIOMS** An idiom is a widely used expression that cannot be understood by defining its individual words. Examples in the selection are *take someone in a lie* and *not in this nature*. Students can rely on context to determine the meanings of idiomatic phrases. Demonstrate the strategy by using the following model:

**Model Sentence**

When asked whether he had seen his wife commit witchcraft, Good said that he had not seen anything <u>in this nature</u>, but that she had behaved badly.

**Instruction**

- Write the model sentence on the chalkboard.
- Ask students what the context suggests about the phrase *in this nature*.
- Guide students to see that *in this nature* means "of this kind." Good did not see his wife commit witchcraft, so he says that he saw nothing of that kind of behavior.

 Use **Vocabulary Transparencies and Copymasters**, p. 25.

A. I did not mutter, but I thanked him for what he gave my child.

Q. Have you made no contract with the devil?

A. No.

H[athorne] desired the children, all of them, to look upon her and see if this were the person that had hurt them, and so they all did look upon her and said this was one of the persons that did torment them—presently they were all tormented.

Q. Sarah Good, do you not see now what you have done? Why do you not tell us the truth? Why do you thus torment these poor children?

A. I do not torment them.

Q. Who do you employ then?

A. I employ nobody. I scorn it.

Q. How came they thus tormented?

A. What do I know? You bring others here and now you charge me with it.

Q. Why, who was it?

A. I do not know, but it was some you brought into the meeting house with you.

Q. We brought you into the meeting house.

A. But you brought in two more.

Q. Who was it then that tormented the children?

A. It was Osborne.

Q. What is it you say when you go muttering away from persons' houses?

A. If I must tell, I will tell.

Q. Do tell us then.

A. If I must tell, I will tell. It is the commandments. I may say my commandments I hope.

Q. What commandment is it?

A. If I must tell, I will tell. It is a psalm.

Q. What psalm?

After a long time she muttered over some part of a psalm.

Q. Who do you serve?

Q. **Why do you hurt these children?**
A. **I do not hurt them. I scorn it.**

A. I serve God.

Q. What God do you serve?

A. The God that made heaven and earth, though she was not willing to mention the word *God*. Her answers were in a very wicked spiteful manner, reflecting and retorting against the authority with base and abusive words, and many lies she was taken in. It was here said that her husband had said that he was afraid that she either was a witch or would be one very quickly. The worshipful Mr. Hathorne asked him his reason why he said so of her, whether he had ever seen anything by her. He answered no, not in this nature, but it was her bad carriage[4] to him and indeed, said he, I may say with tears that she is an enemy to all good.

SALEM VILLAGE, MARCH THE 1ST, 1691–92

WRITTEN BY EZEKIEL CHEEVER

---

4. **carriage:** conduct.

### Students Acquiring English

**1** The Summary contains many sentences made up of multiple clauses. To keep track of the information, students should read each long, complex sentence as a series of short sentences. Also tell students that *abovesaid* is an adjective meaning "mentioned before."

### Less Proficient Readers

**2** The archaic language of this document includes the capitalization of words in the middle of sentences and unusual sentence construction. Remind students that a capitalized word (such as *Asked* in this sentence) does not necessarily signal the start of a new sentence; they should look for end punctuation such as periods and question marks to determine where sentences end. Read the sentence aloud and ask a volunteer to paraphrase it in modern English.

**Possible Response:** Sarah Good was asked who hurt the children, if it was not she who did it.

**3** Sarah Good says several times, "I scorn it." Explain to students that *I scorn it* means "I reject your accusation and view it with contempt." Ask students what effect this statement might have had on the judges.

**Possible Response:** Good may have sounded proud and defiant when she said this, making the judges feel more inclined to convict her.

---

 **Assessment** **Test Preparation**

**UNDERSTANDING MULTIPLE-MEANING WORDS**
Some standardized tests ask students to use context clues to choose the appropriate meaning of a multiple-meaning word. Have students answer this question:
The children <u>recovered</u> out of their fit and said that both Sarah Good and Sarah Osborne had tormented them.
In this sentence, the word *recovered* means

**A.** covered again

**B.** returned to normal

**C.** saved something from being lost

**D.** accused

Discuss why B is correct: When the children returned to normal, they were able to explain that they thought Sarah Good and Sarah Osborne had caused their fit.

**Application** Have students apply their skill to this additional question.
Cheever thought that Sarah Good's behavior <u>reflected against</u> the authority of the court.
The word *reflected against* means

**A.** thought calmly and carefully

**B.** brought a curse upon

**C.** caused something to appear a certain way

**D.** turned away from or rejected

**Answer:** D is the best choice.

## GUIDING STUDENT RESPONSE

## Connect to the Literature

**1. What Do You Think?**
Possible Response: Sarah Good seems to have been misunderstood, mistreated, and condemned because she did not have a pleasant personality or know how to deal with the accusations brought against her.

**Comprehension Check**
- Sarah Good's alleged victims are four girls of Salem.
- Good denies that she ever used any witchcraft or hurt the children.

 Use Selection Quiz **Unit Two Resource Book** p. 9.

## Think Critically

**2.** Possible Response: The court officials are prejudiced against Good. She is asked leading questions in loaded language, and the statement at the end of the transcript indicates that the officials have made up their minds that she is an "enemy of good," though there is no evidence but hearsay.

**3.** Possible Response: The officials are frightened and full of superstition. They want to protect Salem from witchcraft, and they may possibly have a grudge against Good.

**4.** Possible Response: Good is desperately trying to shift blame from herself.

**5.** Possible Response: Good's husband seems to have had trouble dealing with Good, who was probably a difficult and stubborn person.

**6.** Possible Response: The convulsions were the result of mass hysteria or were willingly faked by the children, who had started the panic and did not know how to stop and admit their fault.

## Connect to the Literature

**1. What Do You Think?**
What is your reaction to Sarah Good's examination?

**Comprehension Check**
- Who are Sarah Good's alleged victims?
- What charges made against her does Good deny?

## Think Critically

**2.** **ACTIVE READING** **DETECTING BIAS** How would you describe the court officials' attitude toward Sarah Good? Support your answer with evidence from your 📖 **READER'S NOTEBOOK**.

 THINK ABOUT {
- the questions Good is asked
- the comments made about her at the end of the transcript

**3.** What do you think accounts for the court officials' attitude?

**4.** Why do you think Sarah Good accuses Sarah Osborne of being a witch?

**5.** Why do you think Sarah Good's husband testifies against her?

**6.** What explanation can you offer for the apparent torments suffered by the girls who accuse Sarah Good?

## Extend Interpretations

**7.** **Different Perspectives** In the preface to her book on the Salem witch trials, the 20th-century historian Marion L. Starkey writes, "Who in my day has a right to be indignant with people in Salem of 1692?" Why might she have made this comment? Do you agree that people of our time cannot or should not make judgments about people of earlier times?

**8.** **Connect to Life** Do you think that something similar to the Salem witch trials could happen in your community today? Why or why not? Consider the Connect to Your Life activity in which you discussed false accusations.

## Literary Analysis

**TRANSCRIPT** A **transcript** is a written record of information that was originally spoken aloud. The **summary** of Sarah Good's examination you read first provides a brief narrative account of what occurred in the courtroom. The transcript that followed shows what was actually said in the courtroom. The phrasing of the questions and answers are in the interrogators' and Good's own words. Did reading the transcript change your view of the trial?

**Activity** Compare and contrast the summary and the transcript. What did you learn or infer from the transcript that you didn't learn from the summary? What did the summary tell you that the questions and answers on the transcript did not? What parts of the summary accurately reflect the transcript, in your view? Record differences and similarities in a large Venn diagram, as shown. Then decide which document seems to be the more **credible,** or trustworthy, source of information about the trial. Consider the possible **motivations** of the persons who wrote each document and the kind of information included. Discuss your opinion with classmates.

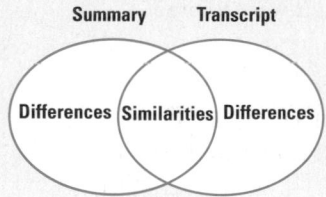

## Extend Interpretations

**Different Perspectives** Possible Response: Starkey may mean that we have our own forms of mass hysteria and witch-hunting in the twentieth century. It is necessary to make judgments about people of earlier times for the very reason that we are constantly repeating many of their mistakes today. By judging them, we become less likely to make the errors they made.

**Connect to Life** Possible Response: Yes; people are still very capable of making false accusations and creating a form of panic against individuals within a community. This is clear from news reports about accusations leveled against private individuals and public officials.

## Literary Analysis

**Transcript** Possible Responses: The beginning Summary is objective; the questions are slanted, presupposing that Good is guilty of witchcraft; the language following the final answer is inflammatory, containing phrases such as "wicked spiteful manner" and "base and abusive words."

# Choices & CHALLENGES

## Writing Options

**1. Courtroom Drama** Rewrite part of the transcript as a dramatic scene from a play. Using a script form, include the name of each character who is speaking and stage directions that show the character's tone of voice, feelings, gestures, or actions.

**2. Plea for Mercy** Write a letter of appeal asking panel members to reconsider their decision to hang Sarah Good. Tell why the court documents you have read do not convince you of her guilt. Save your writing in your **Working Portfolio.**

**3. Explanation of Motives** Write a brief essay in which you explain the possible motivations of either the girls who accused Good of witchcraft, the men who pressed charges against Good, or the men who conducted Good's preliminary examination.

**Writing Handbook**
See page 1283: Analysis

## Activities & Explorations

**1. Courtroom Sketches** Assume the duties of a courtroom artist and draw sketches of the people and events involved in Good's examination. ~ **ART**

**2. Media Coverage** With a group of classmates, create a newscast in which you report on Sarah Good's examination. At the beginning of the newscast, have a news anchor recap what has happened so far. Then have reporters interview Sarah Good, the examiners, the afflicted girls, and Salem residents. If possible, make a videotape of the interviews. ~ **SPEAKING AND LISTENING**

*Dear Panel Members:*
*Sarah Good does not deserve hanging.*

**3. Legal Discussion** A basic premise of the U.S. legal system is that a person charged with a crime is presumed innocent until proven guilty. Also, the Bill of Rights in the Constitution provides that a defendant is not required to testify against himself or herself. Meet in a small group to discuss why you think such ideas became so important in our legal system. Base your discussion on Sarah Good's experiences with the justice system in Puritan New England. ~ **GOVERNMENT**

## Inquiry & Research

**1. Salem Witch Trials** Find out more about the Salem witch trials, researching questions such as these:

- Which girls in the community were afflicted?
- Whom else did they accuse?
- How many people confessed?
- How was a person's guilt proven in court?

Report your findings to the class.

**2. Salem Memorials** Find out how the town of Salem has memorialized those people who were executed as witches. You might research the memorial park that was built in 1992, exactly 300 years after the trials. Also look at the Related Reading on page 150, which describes a clash over ways to commemorate Salem's history.

**More Online: Research Starter**
www.mcdougallittell.com

## Art Connection

**Mental Picture** The engraving on page 145 depicts the examination of an accused witch in Salem. How closely does it match the image of the courtroom you formed as you read about Sarah Good's examination?

---

 **Mini Lesson** **Grammar**

### OVERUSE OF THE VERB *TO BE*

**Instruction** Poor writing often depends upon some form of the verb *to be* with one or more adjectives. Write the following sentence on the chalkboard:

Good was evasive towards her questioners, and they were doubtful about her testimony.

Have students rewrite the passage without using forms of the verb *to be*.

**Possible Response:** Good evaded her questioners, and they doubted her testimony.

**Exercises** Have students rewrite the following sentences without using the verb *to be*.

**1.** When Good came into the room she was bold,

scowling, and glaring at everyone. (Good entered the room boldly and scowled and glared at everyone.)

**2.** The dog was barking and biting the old woman, who was loud and shouting and smacking the dog with a broom. (The dog barked and bit the old woman, who shouted loudly and smacked the dog with a broom.)

 Use **Grammar Transparencies and Copymasters,** p. 163 to project these sentences.

Use McDougal Littell's *Language Network*, Chapter 15, for more instruction in the overuse of the verb *to be*.

---

## Writing Options

**1. Courtroom Drama** Students' plays should reflect the give-and-take of the original transcript, with the addition of plausible stage directions. **To make this assignment more challenging,** have students write a complete one-act play culminating in Good's condemnation.

**2. Plea for Mercy** Student letters should contain persuasive language aimed at overcoming the prejudice and fear of the judge's era.

**3. Explanation of Motives** Students should be able to develop a psychologically plausible analysis of the motives of one of the groups mentioned. **To get students started on this assignment,** divide the class into small groups to discuss the motivations of the participants in the event.

## Activities & Explorations

**1. Courtroom Sketches** Students' work should reflect the personalities of people involved and depict events in a plausible fashion.

**2. Media Coverage** Student work should be a serious effort to capture the pain and suffering of the participants in the Salem witchcraft trial.

**3. Legal Discussion** In their discussions, students should note that Good was presumed to be guilty before she was tried. Students should see that the presumption of innocence and the right not to testify are valuable principles that help protect citizens.

## Inquiry & Research

**1. Salem Witch Trials** Student reports should include accurate information on the topics listed as well as other relevant and interesting questions.

**2. Salem Memorials** Have Visual Learners design a memorial to Sarah Good and other victims of prejudice and superstition.

## Art Connection

**Mental Picture** Students should be able to compare and contrast their own mental image with the image presented by the engraver.

Primary Source

## Objectives
- read and analyze newspaper articles
- evaluate the credibility of information sources including how the writer's motivation may affect that credibility
- connect secondary sources to historical contexts

## Further Background
"History Clashes with Commercialism" by Craig Wilson discusses how the witch trials of 17th-century Salem, like the one related in "The Examination of Sarah Good," have been turned into big business by 20th-century inhabitants of Salem, Massachusetts. Wilson describes the controversy caused by the commercialization of this dark period of Salem's history and quotes from supporters of both sides of the controversy. Articles such as Wilson's help students realize the close connection between history and life in today's world.

## Reading for Information
As you read through this article with students, have them use the material in the right-hand column as a guide to reading newspaper articles.

## Distinguishing Fact from Opinion
1. **Possible Response:** Wilson's word choice indicates his bias regarding the controversy. In his initial description of Salem, he uses positive words such as *historic* and *home.* His second description uses negative-sounding words and phrases such as *tacky, rife, second rate,* and *fly-by-night.* His choice of words might cause the students' initial reactions to be against the festival. The introduction could be made more evenhanded by taking out the initial contrasts and beginning the article with a factual description of the controversy.
2. **Possible Responses:** Additional facts and opinions from the article can be included in the chart.

# History Clashes with Commercialism
by Craig Wilson
USA TODAY

*Salem, Massachusetts, has been the scene of a conflict between two citizens' groups. One group, capitalizing on the fame of Salem's 17th-century witchcraft trials, has staged an annual money-making Halloween festival in the town. According to the other group, such commercialism serves only to tarnish Salem's historical heritage. Craig Wilson wrote this article about the controversy in* USA Today.

SALEM, MA *(USA Today)*—One a historic New England seaport, home to Nathaniel Hawthorne, Federal-style homes, and the infamous 1692 witch trials.

**❶** The other a tacky tourist town, rife with hot dog vendors, second rate wax museums, and fly-by-night haunted houses. And shops. Shops selling everything from $300 witches' capes and herbal potions to T-shirts that proclaim "Born-Again Pagan."

Both are Salem, Massachusetts.

**❷** This is also a tale of history vs. commercialism, and some here think Salem's rich heritage is coming up the loser.

Salem's 24-day Haunted Happenings peaks next weekend when thousands will flock here for Halloween. As many as 200,000 overrun this town of 38,000 during the annual event, which in 15 years has grown from a one-night Halloween party to a three-week carnival. It now brings in $5 million . . . .

Salem's struggle between revenue for today and reverence for yesterday has become so touchy several people refused to go on the record about the flourishing witch business.

And *Witch City*, a documentary that takes an unflattering look at Salem's "witch industry," has only added fuel to the fire. The film has become an unwelcome guest at the party.

Filmmaker Joe Cultrera, a native son who now lives in New York, calls Salem "a company town," the company being the witch-related tourism that he says does much to line the pockets of local merchants but little to tell the true story of the 20 people executed here in 1692 during the witch trials.

To tourism director Mariellen Norris that's a bunch of bunk.

"This isn't about the witch hysteria, it's about Halloween," she says. "It's about fun. . . . What we're trying to do here is make it a wholesome family event."

## Reading for Information
Journalists often resemble tightrope walkers at a circus: both strive for balance to accomplish their tasks. Reporters need balance in their writing so that readers can form clear judgments about the news.

**DISTINGUISHING FACT FROM OPINION**
News reports are filled with facts and opinions that readers must be able to recognize and evaluate. Use the questions and activities below to help you distinguish between fact and opinion in this article.

**❶** One guide to a writer's opinion or bias is the writer's **word choice,** or **diction**—especially the **connotations** of (feelings associated with) the words he or she uses. Examine the adjectives Wilson used in describing the two views of Salem. Did his word choice influence your initial reaction to the conflict? Why or why not? How might the introduction be changed to make it seem more evenhanded?

**❷** A **fact** is something that can be proved to be true or untrue. One fact in the article is that the Halloween festival takes place in Salem. An **opinion** is something a person believes, such as "Salem's rich heritage is coming up the loser." Make a two-column chart, with one column headed "Facts" and the other "Opinions." Then reread the article, and list the facts and opinions it contains in the appropriate columns. Next to each entry identify the person responsible for the statement.

| Facts | Opinions |
|---|---|
| • Haunted Happenings event "brings in $5 million" (author Craig Wilson) | • "I don't think they care about Salem's historical legacy." (Professor Donna Vinson) |
| • "a Salem native had made a movie" (Mayor Neil Harrington) | • "It's about fun. . . . What we're trying to do here is make it a wholesome family event." (tourism director Mariellen Norris) |
| • "the Salem Witch Museum . . . gets 350,000 visitors a year" (author Craig Wilson) | • "you don't get that story, you get spectacle and gross generalizations and haunted house music" (Professor Tad Baker) |

Helen Gifford, city editor of *The Salem Evening News*, agrees. Earlier this month she told her readers to lighten up.

"Shall we all observe Halloween in Salem by holding candlelight vigils at the Witch Trials Memorial, while we recall our ancestral sins of bigotry and intolerance?" she asked.

Salem Mayor Neil Harrington, meanwhile, is running for re-election and trying desperately to steer clear of the whole topic. When asked about the documentary, he says he only knew "a Salem native had made a movie."

"But I don't know anything about it," he quickly adds, despite the fact *Witch City* is the talk of Salem, and stories about it have run everywhere from *The Boston Globe* to the front page of Salem's *Evening News*. . . .

Norris says it [the movie] "doesn't really tell us what Salem is about."

Others say it shows present-day Salem all too clearly.

Donna Vinson, a Salem resident and history professor at Salem State College, is one.

"I don't think they care about Salem's historical legacy," she says of Salem's elected officials and witch-industry promoters. "They don't know anything about it, and they don't care to know. . . ."

"There are a lot of people in town who care and want to do the right thing," says Patty MacLeod, director of the Salem Witch Museum, which gets 350,000 visitors a year. "It's in our best interest to do the best job we can or they won't come."

The Salem Witch Museum

Many in town have complained that the four-year-old Salem Wax Museum of Witches & Seafarers, adjacent to the city's 1637 Old Burying Point Cemetery, blares haunted house sounds from its rooftop and has rubber-masked employees dressed as ghouls and goblins at the entrance to the historic cemetery and the adjoining memorial.

Wax museum director Barbara Fanning admits "it's like a carnival this time of year," but adds, "it's good for Salem.". . .

Tad Baker, another history professor at Salem State whose specialty is witchcraft, says he's concerned. . . .

"When you go to the {witch trial} memorial you should get that—that people were willing to die for their beliefs. . . . That's an important story, but you don't get that story, you get spectacle and gross generalizations and haunted house music. . . . That's what a lot of people here object to."

**③ Analyzing Opinions** To be able to judge an opinion, a reader needs sufficient knowledge of the person expressing the opinion. Donna Vinson, for example, is identified as a history professor at Salem State College before she is quoted as saying, "I don't think they care about Salem's historical legacy." Use the chart you made to help you answer the following questions about each person quoted in the article: What is the person's occupation? What are the person's credentials? What motivation might the person have to hold the opinions he or she expresses?

**Forming Opinions** You have now identified the facts and the opinions in the article. Which side of the argument would you be on if you lived in Salem? Why? What facts and opinions in the article helped you form your opinion?

**Analyzing Opinions**

3. Student responses should evaluate the credibility of information sources, including how the writer's motivation may affect credibility.

**Possible Responses** Filmmaker Joe Cultrera is a native of Salem and is against the commercialization of the town. He might be resentful of changes made in his hometown.

Mariellen Norris is the tourism director for the town. It is her job to promote Salem as a popular tourist attraction, so she would probably support any event or idea that would accomplish this.

Helen Gifford is the city editor of the *Salem Evening News.* She would probably be in favor of any plan that would increase the amount of money being spent in the town, since this would translate into more money for the local businesses and her newspaper.

Mayor Neil Harrington steered clear of stating an opinion on the matter since he did not want to offend any potential voters.

Donna Vinson and Tad Baker are both history professors and probably care mainly about Salem's historical integrity, which they feel is not a high priority for the promoters of the Salem events.

**Forming Opinions**

**Possible Responses:** Students could decide to support those who are in favor of commercializing Salem's past since it provides money and a livelihood for today's residents of the city. The article implies that Salem depends on the money spent by tourists every year, and that fact is emphasized by the supporters of the celebration. Students could support those who favor a lessening of the commercialization by stating that the festival denigrates the serious historical legacy of Salem and makes what happened in the 17th century seem less serious. The implied and stated opinions of the author and the history professors are persuasive.

*Editor's Note: With the permission of the copyright holder, this selection was excerpted from a longer work. Material was deleted to shorten and focus the selection.*

## OVERVIEW

 This selection is included in the **Grade 11 InterActive Reader.**

### Objectives
1. analyze an 18th-century **sermon** (Literary Analysis)
2. appreciate author's use of **persuasive writing (Literary Analysis)**
3. **analyze emotional language (Active Reading)**

### Summary
In this fiery sermon, Jonathan Edwards describes the wretchedness of humans, who are all sinners in danger of eternal condemnation. Edwards uses powerful images to describe the plight of sinners: sinners are standing over the pit of hell on a rotted cover that may give way without warning; God's arrow of death is pointed at human hearts, and He can release it at any moment; God holds sinners suspended over hell as humans might hold a spider above a fiery pit. Furthermore, Edwards emphasizes that the torments of hell are everlasting, with no hope of deliverance. Edwards does offer hope at the end of his sermon, however, by declaring that Christ has made it possible for sinners to receive mercy. By accepting Christ, humans can avoid hell and rejoice in God.

### Thematic Link
Edwards preaches that all humans are sinners poised **between heaven and hell.** Those who believe in and accept Christ, Edwards declares, will go to heaven; those who refuse Christ will be condemned to hell.

---

#### 5-Minute Warm-Up

***Daily Language SkillBuilder***

Have students **proofread** the display sentences on page 131i and write them correctly. The sentences also appear on Transparency 5 of **Grammar Transparencies and Copymasters.**

---

*"God has so many different unsearchable ways of taking wicked men out of the world . . . "*

# *from* Sinners in the Hands of an Angry God

*Sermon by* JONATHAN EDWARDS

### Connect to Your Life

**Power of Persuasion** Think about someone who recently persuaded you to do something—perhaps a parent, friend, teacher, coach, or salesperson. What method of persuasion did this person use? For example, what was emphasized—the benefits of taking the action or the drawbacks of not taking the action? Did this person appeal to your emotions, such as love, fear, or pride? Or did this person appeal to principles, such as justice, efficiency, or frugality? Write down what you were persuaded to do, and analyze the method of persuasion that worked on you. With your classmates, talk about effective methods of persuasion.

### Build Background

**Great Awakening** One hundred years after a group of Puritans came to colonial America for religious freedom, some Puritans felt that their congregations had grown too complacent, or self-satisfied. To rekindle the fervor that the early settlers had, Jonathan Edwards and other Puritan ministers led the Great Awakening, a religious revival that swept through New England from 1734 to 1750. Edwards's most famous sermon, "Sinners in the Hands of an Angry God," was delivered in Enfield, Connecticut, in 1741. In it he warned his congregation that being church members would not automatically save them from hell. He tried to persuade them that they had to personally experience conversion, a transforming moment in which they felt God's grace.

> **WORDS TO KNOW**
> **Vocabulary Preview**
> abhor            incense
> abominable       inconceivable
> appease          loathsome
> ascribe          mitigation
> deliverance      wrath

### Focus Your Reading

**LITERARY ANALYSIS  PERSUASIVE WRITING** Edwards's sermon is an example of **persuasive writing,** which is intended to convince a reader to adopt a particular opinion or to perform a certain action. Persuasive writing can take many forms, including sermons, political speeches, newspaper editorials, and advertisements. As you read Edwards's sermon, analyze his methods of persuasion: What does he want his audience to do and why does he want them to do it?

**ACTIVE READING  ANALYZING EMOTIONAL LANGUAGE** Persuasive writing often contains **loaded language**—words with strong connotations, or emotional associations. For example, contrast the word *child* with the more loaded words *brat* and *cherub*. A writer would use *brat* to create a negative feeling in the reader and *cherub* to create a positive feeling. Part of what makes Edwards's sermon so effective is his choice of loaded words.

**READER'S NOTEBOOK** Monitor how you feel as you read the sermon. Create a chart like the one below to list examples of specific words, phrases, and images that Edwards uses to achieve the greatest emotional effect on his audience.

| Example | Emotional Impact |
|---------|------------------|
|         |                  |
|         |                  |

**152**  UNIT TWO  PART 1: BETWEEN HEAVEN AND HELL

---

### LESSON RESOURCES

**UNIT TWO RESOURCE BOOK,** pp. 10–14

**ASSESSMENT RESOURCES**
**Formal Assessment,** pp. 35–36
**Teacher's Guide to Assessment and Portfolio Use**
**Test Generator**

**SKILLS TRANSPARENCIES AND COPYMASTERS**
**Literary Analysis**
• Persuasion: Types of Appeals, T9 (for Cooperative Learning Activity, p. 158)

**Reading and Critical Thinking**
• Compare and Contrast, T15 (for Extend Interpretations, item 7, p. 158)

**Grammar**
• Agreement of Subject and Verb, T47 (for Mini Lesson, p. 160)
• Subject-Verb Agreement I, C123 (for Mini Lesson, p. 160)

**Vocabulary**
• The Connotative Power of Words, C26 (for Mini Lesson, p. 156)

**Writing**
• Persuasive Essay, C27 (for Writing Option 3, p. 159)

**Communications**
• Dramatic Reading, T12 (for Activities & Explorations 1, p. 159)
• Verbal Strategies, T14 (for Activities & Explorations 1, p. 159)

**INTEGRATED TECHNOLOGY**
**Audio Library**
**Visit our website:**
www.mcdougallittell.com

# from Sinners
## in the Hands of an Angry God

JONATHAN EDWARDS

We find it easy to tread on and crush a worm that we see crawling on the earth; so it is easy for us to cut or singe a slender thread that any thing hangs by; thus easy is it for God when he pleases to cast his enemies down to hell. . . .

They[1] are now the objects of that very same *anger* and <u>wrath</u> of God, that is expressed in the torments of hell. And the reason why they do not go down to hell at each moment, is not because God, in whose power they are, is not then very angry with them; as angry as he is with many miserable creatures now tormented in hell, who there feel and bear the fierceness of his wrath. Yea, God is a great deal more angry with great numbers that are now on earth; yea, doubtless, with many that are now in this congregation,[2] who it may be are at ease, than he is with many of those who are now in the flames of hell.

So that it is not because God is unmindful of

their wickedness, and does not resent it, that he does not let loose his hand and cut them off. God is not altogether such an one as themselves, though they may imagine him to be so. The wrath of God burns against them, their damnation does not slumber; the pit is prepared, the fire is made ready, the furnace is now hot, ready to receive them; the flames do now rage and glow. The glittering sword is whet,[3] and held over them, and the pit hath opened its mouth under them. . . .

---

1. **they:** Earlier in the sermon, Edwards refers to all "unconverted men," whom he considers God's enemies. Unconverted men are people who have not been "born again," meaning that they have not accepted Jesus Christ and consequently have not experienced a sense of God's grace and an assurance of salvation.

2. **this congregation:** the Puritans attending the church service at which Edwards spoke.

3. **whet:** sharpened.

WORDS
TO
KNOW    **wrath** (răth) *n.* fierce anger, or punishment resulting from such anger

153

---

### TEACHING THE LITERATURE
#### Customizing Instruction

**Less Proficient Readers**
Prepare students to read this sermon by explaining that Edwards uses long sentences filled with fiery images and difficult vocabulary. Read aloud the first paragraph and the first sentence of the second paragraph.

**Set a Purpose** Tell students to read to find out how Edwards describes God's wrath.

**Students Acquiring English**
Discuss the title of the sermon and make sure students understand the Puritan beliefs of sinful nature and personal salvation that would make this sermon so powerful to its listeners. Explain that this sermon was delivered in the 1700s and that some of the words are no longer used today. Explain the meaning of words such as *yea, whet,* and *fain,* and point out the use of *an* instead of *a* in expressions such as "such an one."

Use **Spanish Study Guide** for additional support, pp. 44–46.

**Gifted and Talented**
Explain to students that one of the tenets of Calvinism (Edwards's religion) was predestination, the belief that one's salvation is unalterably determined before birth. Encourage students to consider the relationship between predestination and Edwards's message as they read the selection.

---

**Mini Lesson**   ## Preteaching Vocabulary

**USING CONTEXT CLUES** When students encounter an unfamiliar word while reading, they can often use the context, or surrounding words and sentences, to determine its meaning.

**Instruction** Display the following sentence and ask a volunteer to state the situation described in the sentence.

    The student demonstrated <u>abominable</u> behavior by interrupting the teacher and shouting in class.

Have students infer the meaning of the word *abominable.* Then ask a volunteer to use the word *abominable* in a new sentence.

**Exercises** Have students work in pairs and use context clues to determine the meanings of underlined

terms. They can then use a dictionary to check their definitions.

1. He was <u>incensed</u> when his brand-new car was hit by a careless driver.

2. It can be very difficult to <u>appease</u> crying infants; sometimes they cry despite any comfort.

3. Some people <u>abhor</u> vegetables even though they are very nutritious.

Use **Unit Two Resource Book** p. 13 for additional support.

A lesson on context clues appears on p. 326 in the Pupil's Edition.

### Reading Skills and Strategies: PREVIEW

Have students go over Preparing to Read to understand the context for Edwards's sermon.

### Literary Analysis  PERSUASIVE WRITING

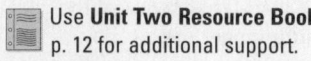 **A** Ask students what frightening powers Edwards attributes to God. Have them explain what emotions this view of God creates, and what Edwards was trying to persuade his audience to do.

**Possible Responses:** Edwards claims that God is able to take wicked people out of the world and send them to hell at any time. By saying that God's wrath is directed at "unconverted men," Edwards is trying to persuade his listeners to become born again and thus escape this wrath.

📄 Use **Unit Two Resource Book**, p. 12 for additional support.

### Active Reading
ANALYZING EMOTIONAL LANGUAGE

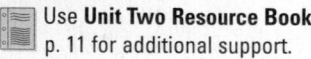 **B** Edwards chooses his language very carefully to achieve the greatest emotional effect on his listeners. Ask students to identify loaded words and phrases that Edwards uses to convey God's view of human beings.

**Possible Response:** Language such as *loathsome insect, worthy of nothing else, abhors,* and *abominable* shows God's distaste for human beings. *Dreadfully provoked* and *wrath* show His anger. All of these words depict the wickedness of people who have not been "born again" through Christ. Edwards's listeners would have felt guilty and afraid, making them more likely to do what he recommended to avoid going to hell.

📄 Use **Unit Two Resource Book**, p. 11 for additional support.

---

**A** **1** Unconverted men walk over the pit of hell on a rotten covering, and there are innumerable places in this covering so weak that they will not bear their weight, and these places are not seen. The arrows of death fly unseen at noonday; the sharpest sight cannot discern them. God has so many different unsearchable ways of taking wicked men out of the world and sending them to hell, that there is nothing to make it appear, that God had need to be at the expense of a miracle, or go out of the ordinary course of his providence, to destroy any wicked man, at any moment. . . .

**2** So that, thus it is that natural men[4] are held in the hand of God, over the pit of hell; they have deserved the fiery pit, and are already sentenced to it; and God is dreadfully provoked, his anger is as great towards them as to those that are actually suffering the executions of the fierceness of his wrath in hell; and they have done nothing in the least to appease or abate that anger, neither is God in the least bound by any promise to hold them up one moment; the devil is waiting for them, hell is gaping for them, the flames gather and flash about them, and would fain[5] lay hold on them, and swallow them up; the fire pent up in their own hearts is struggling to break out: and they have no interest in any Mediator,[6] there are no means within reach that can be any security to them. In short, they have no refuge, nothing to take hold of. . . .

The bow of God's wrath is bent, and the arrow made ready on the string, and justice bends the arrow at your heart, and strains the bow, and it is nothing but the mere pleasure of God, and that of an angry God, without any promise or obligation at all, that keeps the arrow one moment from being made drunk with your blood. Thus all you that never passed under a great change of heart, by the mighty power of the Spirit of God upon your souls; all you that were never born again, and made new creatures, and raised from being dead in sin, to a state of new, and before altogether unexperienced light and life, are in the hands of an angry God. However you may have reformed your life in many things, and may have had religious affections,[7] and may keep up a form of religion in your families and closets,[8] and in the house of God, it is nothing but his mere pleasure that keeps you from being this moment swallowed up in everlasting destruction. . . .

The God that holds you over the pit of hell, much as one holds a spider, or some loathsome insect over the fire, abhors you, and is dreadfully provoked: his wrath towards you burns like fire; he looks upon you as worthy of nothing else, but to be cast into the fire; he is of purer eyes than to bear to have you in his sight; you are ten thousand times more abominable in his eyes, than the most hateful venomous serpent is in ours. You have offended him infinitely more than ever a stubborn rebel did his prince; and yet it is nothing but his hand that holds you from falling into the fire every moment. It is to be ascribed to nothing else, that you did not go to hell the last night; that you was suffered[9] to awake again in this world, after you closed your eyes to sleep. And there is no other reason to be given, why you have not dropped into hell since you arose in the morning, but that God's hand has held you up. There is no other reason to be given why you

---

4. **natural men:** people who have not been "born again."
5. **fain:** rather.
6. **Mediator:** Jesus Christ, who mediates, or is the means of bringing about, salvation.
7. **affections:** feelings or emotions.
8. **closets:** private rooms for meditation.
9. **suffered:** permitted.

---

WORDS TO KNOW

**appease** (ə-pēz′) *v.* to bring peace, quiet, or calm to; soothe
**loathsome** (lōth′səm) *adj.* arousing great dislike
**abhor** (ăb-hôr′) *v.* to regard with disgust
**abominable** (ə-bŏm′ə-nə-bəl) *adj.* thoroughly detestable
**ascribe** (ə-skrīb′) *v.* to attribute to a specified cause or source

154

---

## Teaching Options

### BLOCK SCHEDULING: MANAGING TIME

**If your schedule requires that you cover the lesson objectives in a shorter time, use . . .**
- Preparing to Read, p. 152
- Thinking Through the Literature, p. 158
- Vocabulary in Action, p. 159

**If you want to take advantage of longer class times, use . . .**
- TE Teaching Options: Preteaching Vocabulary, p. 153; Viewing and Representing, p. 155; Vocabulary Strategy, p. 156; Cross-Curricular Link, p. 157; Test Preparation, p. 159
- Choices & Challenges and Author Activity, pp. 159–160

*Un quadro di fuochi preziosi* [A painting of precious fires] (1983), Enzo Cucchi. Oil on canvas with neon, 117½" × 153½", private collection, courtesy of Sperone Westwater, New York.

The **pit** is prepared,

the **fire** is made ready,

the **furnace** is now hot,

ready to receive them;

the **flames** do now

**rage** and **glow**.

155

## Viewing and Representing

*Un quadro di fuochi preziosi* [A painting of precious fires] **by Enzo Cucchi**

**ART APPRECIATION** Born in 1950, Enzo Cucchi lives and works in Italy. This 1983 oil painting shows a dark pit illuminated by rings of distinct flames.

**Instruction** Point out the colors Cucchi uses in his oil painting: mainly red and black. Ask students to describe what meanings are communicated through the artist's use of these colors.

**Possible Response:** Red is frequently associated with fire, passion, and anger; black is often associated with death, despair, and nothingness.

**Application** Have students describe the images and movement they see in this painting. Ask them to discuss whether they think Edwards would have liked to use the painting as part of his sermon.

**Possible Response:** The burning flames move in a circular fashion, like people descending into a dark pit. This painting perfectly suits Edwards's "fire and brimstone" sermon. It could easily be a depiction of the pit of hell where sinners go after death to suffer the fiery wrath of God.

### Literary Analysis: REPETITION

**A** Point out the repetition of the word *nothing*. Ask students why Edwards repeats this word.

**Possible Response:** The repetition of the word alerts listeners, emphasizing that human beings are nothing and can do nothing.

### Literary Analysis

> **PERSUASIVE WRITING**

**B** To be most effective, persuasive writing must anticipate the counter-arguments that readers or listeners might have. Ask students what idea Edwards is refuting in this passage.

**Possible Response:** Listeners might think that they do not need to be "born again" because they already live according to God's principles. Edwards says that this is not enough to save them from hell.

### Active Reading

> **ANALYZING EMOTIONAL LANGUAGE**

**C** Ask students to identify emotionally powerful words and phrases that Edwards uses to describe the state of those who heed Christ's call. What effect would this language have had on his listeners?

**Possible Response:** He uses language such as *door of mercy wide open, happy state, hearts filled with love, rejoicing in hope of the glory of God,* and *singing for joy of heart.* These words would have made the congregation long to share in the happiness of the converted.

---

have not gone to hell, since you have sat here in the house of God, provoking his pure eyes by your sinful wicked manner of attending his solemn worship. Yea, there is nothing else that is to be given as a reason why you do not this very moment drop down into hell.

O sinner! Consider the fearful danger you are in: it is a great furnace of wrath, a wide and bottomless pit, full of the fire of wrath, that you are held over in the hand of that God, whose wrath is provoked and <u>incensed</u> as much against you, as against many of the damned in hell. You hang by a slender thread, with the flames of divine wrath flashing about it, and ready every moment to singe it, and burn it asunder;[10] and you have no interest in any Mediator, and nothing to lay hold of to save yourself, nothing to keep off the flames of wrath, nothing of your own, nothing that you ever have done, nothing that you can do, to induce God to spare you one moment. . . .

It is *everlasting* wrath. It would be dreadful to suffer this fierceness and wrath of Almighty God one moment; but you must suffer it to all eternity. There will be no end to this exquisite[11] horrible misery. When you look forward, you shall see a long forever, a boundless duration before you, which will swallow up your thoughts, and amaze your soul; and you will absolutely despair of ever having any <u>deliverance</u>, any end, any <u>mitigation</u>, any rest at all. You will know certainly that you must wear out long ages, millions of millions of ages, in wrestling and conflicting with this almighty merciless vengeance; and then when you have so done, when so many ages have actually been spent by you in this manner, you will know that all is but a point to what remains. So that your punishment will indeed be infinite. Oh, who can express what the state of a soul in such circumstances is! All that we can possibly say about it, gives but a very feeble, faint representation of it; it is inexpressible and <u>inconceivable</u>: For "who knows the power of God's anger?"[12]

How dreadful is the state of those that are daily and hourly in the danger of this great wrath and infinite misery! But this is the dismal case of every soul in this congregation that has not been born again, however moral and strict, sober and religious, they may otherwise be. . . .

And now you have an extraordinary opportunity, a day wherein Christ has thrown the door of mercy wide open, and stands in the door calling and crying with a loud voice to poor sinners; a day wherein many are flocking to him, and pressing into the kingdom of God. Many are daily coming[13] from the east, west, north, and south; many that were very lately in the same miserable condition that you are in, are now in a happy state, with their hearts filled with love to him who has loved them, and washed them from their sins in his own blood, and rejoicing in hope of the glory of God. How awful is it to be left behind at such a day! To see so many others feasting, while you are pining and perishing! To see so many rejoicing and singing for joy of heart, while you have cause to mourn for sorrow of heart, and howl for vexation of spirit! How can you rest one moment in such a condition? . . .

Therefore, let every one that is out of Christ, now awake and fly from the wrath to come. . . . ❖

---

10. **asunder** (ə-sŭn′dər): into separate parts or pieces.

11. **exquisite** (ĕk′skwĭ-zĭt): sharply intense.

12. **"who knows . . . anger?":** an allusion to Psalm 90:11, "Who knoweth the power of thine anger?"

13. **Many . . . coming:** Edwards is referring to the hundreds of people who were being converted during the Great Awakening.

---

WORDS TO KNOW

**incense** (ĭn-sĕns′) *v.* to cause to be extremely angry
**deliverance** (dĭ-lĭv′ər-əns) *n.* rescue from danger
**mitigation** (mĭt′ĭ-gā′shən) *n.* lessening of something that causes suffering
**inconceivable** (ĭn′kən-sē′və-bəl) *adj.* not able to be understood or imagined

156

---

## Teaching Options

###  Mini Lesson **Vocabulary Strategy**

#### INTERPRETING THE CONNOTATIVE POWER OF WORDS

**Instruction** Connotation refers to the associated meanings or emotions that a word evokes. Ask students to share the associations they have with each of the following words.

| irritation | rage | indignance | wrath |
|---|---|---|---|
|  |  |  |  |
|  |  |  |  |
|  |  |  |  |

**Possible Responses:** *irritation*—mild, related to issues of minor importance; *rage*—out of control, passionate; *indignance*—happens when someone is offended, related to moral issues; *wrath*—strong, frightening, righteous

Edwards understood the connotations of the words he chose. Have students consider how the phrase *great furnace of wrath* would lose much of its effect if *irritation* were substituted for *wrath*. Students can rely on context to determine the connotations of words they encounter while reading.

 Use **Vocabulary Transparencies and Copymasters,** p. 26.

The God that holds you over the pit of **hell,**

much as one holds a **spider,**

or some loathsome insect over the **fire,**

# abhors you...

his wrath toward you burns like **fire;**

he looks upon you as worthy of nothing else,

but to be cast into the **fire.**

## Cross Curricular Link **History**

**PURITAN INTOLERANCE** The harsh religious views preached by Jonathan Edwards were in conflict with the impulse toward religious freedom that had led to the establishment of many of the original 13 colonies. Several colonies even began as refuges from the religious intolerance of the Puritans, who had sought religious freedom for themselves but did not tolerate other religions within their jurisdiction.

• **1632—Lord Baltimore** establishes the colony of Maryland as a haven for persecuted Roman Catholics.

• **1636**—Colonists leave Puritan Massachusetts to seek religious freedom in Connecticut (led by **Thomas Hooker**) and Rhode Island (led by **Roger Williams**).

• **1660s**—The New Jersey colony, established by **John Berkeley** and **George Carteret,** begins a 50-year legal battle to win religious and political freedom from the local Puritan jurisdiction.

• **1682**—Quaker **William Penn**'s Pennsylvania becomes a model of religious and political tolerance.

## GUIDING STUDENT RESPONSE

### Connect to the Literature

**1. What Do You Think?**
Possible Response: The most vivid image is that God holds people over the pit of hell as humans would hold a spider over a fire.

**Comprehension Check**
• All human beings are in danger of being sent to hell by God at any moment.
• People who have undergone a change of heart and been born again are spared God's wrath.
• Sinners who love and accept Christ can save themselves.

 Use Selection Quiz
**Unit Two Resource Book,** p. 14.

### Think Critically

**2.** Possible Responses: Yes, because Edwards is a strong, emotional speaker who truly believes in what he preaches. No, because his speeches are too harsh and they evoke feelings of fear.

**3.** Possible Response: The two phrases that are the most emotionally charged are *loathsome insect* and *worthy of nothing else.* Edwards chooses his words carefully to make his message more powerful. His words emphasize the lowliness of humans and the torments of hell.

**4.** Possible Response: Edwards's sermon persuaded people to change their lives for several reasons. First, Edwards convinced many of God's power over human beings by comparing it to our ease in crushing a worm. Second, despite the threat of being sent to hell by God at any moment, Edwards offers hope and an escape from hell through Jesus.

**5.** Students should support their answers with textual evidence. Possible Response: The people who belonged to Edwards's congregation believed that human beings are inherently evil and can only escape hell through God's grace, not by anything they do themselves.

**6.** Possible Response: In this sermon, human beings are presented as powerless to control their own lives or help themselves; God is presented as powerful and threatening.

### Connect to the Literature

**1. What Do You Think?**
Describe the most vivid image from this sermon and how it made you feel.

**Comprehension Check**
• According to this sermon, what is a constant threat to all human beings?
• According to this sermon, which people are spared God's wrath?
• What does Edwards say sinners can do to save themselves?

### Think Critically

**2.** Would you want to hear another of Edwards's sermons? Explain why or why not.

**3.**  **ACTIVE READING** | **ANALYZING EMOTIONAL LANGUAGE** Review your list of loaded words and phrases, and identify two that you think are the most emotionally charged. Discuss with a classmate their intended effect on the audience. How do you think Edwards's choice of words affects the overall impact of his message?

**4.** Why do you think people were persuaded to change their lives as a result of Edwards's sermon?

**THINK ABOUT**
{ • what he wants his congregation to do and why
• the emotions he appeals to in the first paragraphs and in the last paragraphs of the excerpt

**5.** What conclusions can you draw about the spiritual beliefs and values of the people who belonged to Edwards's congregation?

**6.** How would you describe the view of human beings and the view of God presented in this sermon?

### Extend Interpretations

**7. Comparing Texts** In your view, is Jonathan Edwards's conception of God consistent with Anne Bradstreet's conception of God? Explain your opinion.

**8. Connect to Life** Are Edwards's methods of persuasion ones that are likely to work on you? Consider what you wrote for the Connect to Your Life activity on page 152.

### Literary Analysis

**PERSUASIVE WRITING** The goal of **persuasive writing** is to convince a reader to adopt a particular opinion or perform a certain action. The overriding purpose of Edwards's sermon is to change the behavior of his audience and to show them the path toward salvation. Generally, persuasive writing uses both logical and emotional appeals. **Logical appeals** imply that if the readers are reasonable people, they will do or think what the writer desires. **Emotional appeals** sometimes contain very little factual information and instead often rely on highly charged language that triggers intense feelings, such as fear, insecurity, and so on.

**Cooperative Learning Activity**
Reread Edwards's sermon and find examples of emotional appeals. Responding to criticism of his appeal to emotions rather than reason, Edwards said: "I think it is a reasonable thing to fright persons away from hell. They stand upon its brink, and are just ready to fall into it, and are senseless of their danger. Is it not a reasonable thing to fright a person out of a house on fire?" Meet in small groups to debate whether or not you believe his use of scare tactics is justified, considering his goal.

### Extend Interpretations

**Comparing Texts** Possible Response: No, because Edwards views God as wrathful, whereas Bradstreet views God as just and loving; yes, because both view God as being in control and all-powerful.

**Connect to Life** Some students may say that Edwards's persuasive methods would not work on them because they respond to facts, not emotions. Other students may say his methods would work because the only way they will change is if they're scared.

### Literary Analysis

**Persuasive Writing** Students should consider whether Edwards's goal of saving his congregation from eternal damnation justifies his use of language that instills terror.

## Writing Options

**1. Letter of Opinion** Draft a letter to Edwards, giving your personal response to the religious views presented in his sermon.

*Humans are like ___*

**2. Vivid Comparison** Edwards compares a sinful human being to "a spider, or some loathsome insect" held over a fire. Develop a comparison to describe your own view of human beings.

**3. Public Service Announcement** Take a strong moral stand on an issue that concerns you, such as high school dropouts or a social injustice. Using Edwards's sermon as a model, write a public service announcement in which you motivate the audience to adopt your views.

## Activities & Explorations

**1. Live Performance** Jonathan Edwards reportedly read his sermon in a calm, level voice, with his sermon book in his left hand. Imagine what he would do if he had his own television ministry and were giving the sermon today. Present part of this sermon as an oral performance, making it as powerful as you can for a contemporary audience.
**~ SPEAKING AND LISTENING**

**2. Jacket Cover** If you were going to publish "Sinners in the Hands of an Angry God" as a religious tract, how would you illustrate it? Design a cover that suggests important ideas in the sermon. **~ ART**

## Inquiry & Research

**1. Inspirational Speakers** Find out more about a modern-day religious or political leader whose powerful speeches have swayed audiences. Compare this leader with Edwards.

**2. Artistic Visions** Examine paintings, such as Peter Brueghel's *Dulle Griet* (Mad Meg) or Michelangelo's mural on the Sistine Chapel, that depict the fate of evildoers. Compare the mood and images in the paintings with Edwards's sermon.

## Vocabulary in Action

**EXERCISE: ASSESSMENT PRACTICE** Decide if the following pairs of words are synonyms or antonyms. Number your paper from 1 to 10, and write *S* for synonyms or *A* for antonyms.

1. alleviation—mitigation
2. upset—appease
3. inconceivable—knowable
4. damnation—deliverance
5. pleasant—loathsome
6. blessing—wrath
7. attribute—ascribe
8. adore—abhor
9. agreeable—abominable
10. enrage—incense

**Building Vocabulary**
For an in-depth lesson on word denotation and connotation, see page 908.

| WORDS TO KNOW | abhor | appease | deliverance | inconceivable | mitigation |
|---|---|---|---|---|---|
| | abominable | ascribe | incense | loathsome | wrath |

## Writing Options

**1. Letter of Opinion** Students' letters should reflect their opinions about human beings as sinners who need to be saved. **To get students started on this assignment,** have them jot down some of their own beliefs to compare them with Edwards's.

**2. Vivid Comparison** Students' comparisons should employ effective images, metaphors, or analogies. **To get students started on this assignment,** have them write down five adjectives that they think describe human beings.

**3. Public Service Announcement** Students' public service announcements should demonstrate an understanding of persuasive writing techniques. **To make this assignment more challenging,** have students deliver their messages to the class, keeping in mind the tone they use to persuade their audience (emotional, logical, etc.).

## Activities & Explorations

**1. Oral Performance** Students should justify their choice of verbal and nonverbal performance techniques by referring to their interpretations of the sermon.

**2. Jacket Cover** Covers might show images of hell, insects or people being held over a fire, and other images depicted in the sermon.

## Vocabulary in Action

1. synonym
2. antonym
3. antonym
4. antonym
5. antonym
6. antonym
7. synonym
8. antonym
9. antonym
10. synonym

## ✓ Assessment **Test Preparation**

**CHOOSING THE BEST SUMMARY** Many standardized tests require students to select the best summary statement for a passage. You can give students practice in this skill by asking them to discuss which of the following is the best summary of "Sinners in the Hands of an Angry God."

**A.** Jonathan Edwards says that God has the power to send any man to hell whenever He wants.

**B.** Jonathan Edwards preaches that all human beings are sinners who will be sent to hell by God if they do not accept Jesus Christ.

**C.** Jonathan Edwards talks about hell as an everlasting place of damnation.

During the discussion, point out that all three statements contain true information about the selection. What makes statement B the best summary is the fact that it applies to the selection as a whole; statements A and C summarize only part of what Edwards says.

## Author Activity

**A Vision of Terror and Beauty** Students may express surprise that Edwards emphasizes the positive and beautiful aspects of divinity rather than the negative outcomes of God's wrath.

## Jonathan Edwards

1703–1758

**Other Works**
*Images or Shadows of Divine Things*
*Personal Narrative*

**Brilliant Beginnings** Jonathan Edwards, the only son in a family of 11 children, was born in East Windsor, Connecticut. Intellectually curious as a child, Edwards wrote "Of Insects," a study of the behavior of spiders, when he was 11 years old. Just before turning 13, Edwards entered what is now Yale University. While a graduate student there, he had a conversion experience that greatly influenced his religious views.

**Religious Calling** In 1722, after finishing his education, Edwards launched a career in ministry, following the path of his father and his maternal grandfather, both of whom were Puritan ministers. In 1726, Edwards assisted his grandfather as a minister at the church in Northampton, Massachusetts, and three years later became the church's pastor after his grandfather's death. There, he developed a reputation as a powerful preacher. After his accounts of some "surprising conversions" in Northampton from 1734 to 1735, Edwards found himself at the center of a religious revival, the Great Awakening.

**Righteous Works** Throughout his life, Edwards wrote sermons, as well as philosophical and religious works. In his most famous sermon, "Sinners in the Hands of an Angry God," Edwards captured the intensity of the Great Awakening. Although Edwards inspired thousands, he was dismissed from the Northampton church in 1750 because he wanted to limit church membership to those who had undergone conversion, or had been "born again." A year later, Edwards and his family moved to Stockbridge, where he became a missionary to a Native American settlement. In 1757, Edwards accepted an appointment as president of what is now Princeton University.

## Author Activity

**A Vision of Terror and Beauty** Read Edwards's essay "The Beauty of the World" in *Images or Shadows of Divine Things.* Do the ideas that Edwards expresses in this piece change your impression of him? Explain.

## Teaching Options

 **Grammar**

**SUBJECT-VERB AGREEMENT** In every sentence, the verb must agree with its subject in number. Singular subjects take singular verbs, and plural subjects take plural verbs. Write this sentence on the chalkboard:

> <u>Worms</u> crawling on the sidewalk <u>are</u> easily <u>crushed</u> by pedestrians.

Underline the subject and verb as shown. Point out that *worms* is the subject of the sentence and *are crushed* is the verb. In this sentence, both the subject and the verb are plural.

**Exercises** In each of the following sentences, ask students to underline the subject and verb and determine whether they agree in number. If not, have students change the verb so that it agrees with the subject.

1. <u>Jonathan Edwards are</u> the author of "Sinners in the Hands of an Angry God." *(change* are *to* is*)*
2. <u>Edwards persuades</u> people that hell is everlasting and tormenting. *(correct)*
3. <u>The Puritans</u> in Edwards's congregation <u>believes</u> that humans are sinners. *(change* believes *to* believe*)*
4. <u>Jonathan Edwards's sermon appeals</u> to the emotions. *(correct)*

 Use **Grammar Transparencies and Copymasters,** p. 123, for more exercises.

 Use McDougal Littell's *Language Network,* Chapter 5, for more instruction and practice in subject-verb agreement.

# The Conventions of Drama

## The Rise of American Drama

Have you ever acted in a school play or been spellbound by an award-winning film? If so, then you've already experienced the thrill of dramatic performances. **Drama** is a form of literature that is written to be performed for an audience, whether on stage or in front of cameras. The two main types of drama are tragedy and comedy: a **tragedy** unveils the downfall of a main character, and a **comedy** is light and often humorous in tone. Many dramas combine elements of both tragedy and comedy.

Drama was one of the last of the literary genres to develop in the United States. The Puritans in New England regarded theatrical performances as frivolous, so few plays were staged in the 1600s. During the 18th and 19th centuries, drama gradually became an accepted form of entertainment. However, most of the plays performed in the United States were imported from Europe or were adapted from novels.

In 1920 the Broadway production of Eugene O'Neill's *Beyond the Horizon* marked a turning point. This important play used a realistic setting to present true-to-life characters who were struggling to understand their lives. Building on O'Neill's achievement, American playwrights Thornton Wilder, Lillian Hellman, Tennessee Williams, and Arthur Miller created dramas in the 1930s and 1940s that met with critical and popular success. Following World War II, American dramatists Edward Albee and Lorraine Hansberry made significant contributions to the theater. Today, hit plays by contemporary

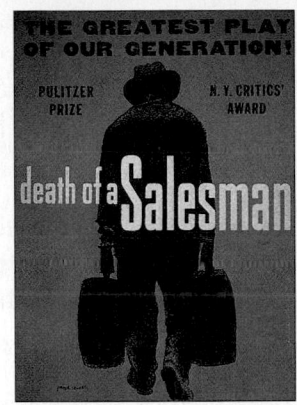

Arthur Miller's *Death of a Salesman* (1949) explores the tragic aspects of the American Dream.

playwrights, including Sam Shepard, David Mamet, August Wilson, Wendy Wasserstein, and Tony Kushner, are performed in theaters across the country. Drama has become a thriving art form in the United States.

## Conventions of Drama

Most dramas follow similar conventions, or rules, in how they are presented. An understanding of basic dramatic conventions can help you imagine the staging of the performance as you read. You may recognize that drama and fiction share a common set of elements: **plot, setting, character,** and **theme.**

**ACTS AND SCENES** Dramatic plots are divided into **acts** and **scenes,** with each scene establishing a different time or place. As in fiction, the **plot** in a drama introduces interactions that produce a **conflict,** or struggle, between opposing forces. The action intensifies, reaches a peak, and is eventually resolved. The elements of plot in drama—**exposition, rising action, climax, falling action,** and **resolution**—parallel those in fiction.

**THE CAST OF CHARACTERS** A play lists the **cast of characters** in the beginning, before the action starts. Many of the same types of characters that populate fiction are also found in drama. The **protagonist** is the central character of the play. This character is at the center of the conflict and often undergoes radical changes during the course of the play. The **antagonist** is the character who opposes the main character. Some plays also include a **foil,** a minor character whose traits contrast sharply with those of the main character. The interplay among these characters heightens the dramatic tension as the play develops.

THE CONVENTIONS OF DRAMA **161**

## OVERVIEW

**Objectives**
- understand the following literary terms:

| | |
|---|---|
| Drama | Tragedy |
| Comedy | Plot |
| Setting | Character |
| Theme | Act |
| Scene | Conflict |
| Cast of Characters | Protagonist |
| Antagonist | Foil |
| Playwright | Stage Directions |
| Dialogue | Monologue |
| Soliloquy | Aside |

- appreciate a playwright's craft
- increase knowledge of American culture by studying the development of drama as a popular literary form in the United States
- connect an American drama to historical contexts and to current events

## Teaching the Lesson

This lesson will give students some background on the conventions of drama.

**Introducing the Concepts**
As students read *The Crucible,* have them consider the following questions.

What themes, characters, or situations in the play might concern people today?
**Possible Response:** Students might be able to draw parallels with recent political events.

How is drama different from other literary forms?
**Possible Response:** Plays are meant to be performed whereas novels and most poetry is meant primarily for reading.

As they finish reading the play, students can write reactions to these questions and keep their responses in their Working Portfolios.

**Presenting the Concepts**
Read through the strategies aloud or project them on a transparency. Then work with students to read the opening scene from *The Crucible,* using the strategies as a guide.

# Making Connections

## DRAMA ACROSS CULTURES

### The Origins of Western Drama

Although drama was not a popular literary genre in the United States until the 19th century, drama has existed in the world for centuries. Share with students the following background information on the origins of drama in the Western world.

### Drama in Ancient Greece

Ancient Greece is considered the birthplace of drama in Western culture. Greek drama evolved from religious festivals honoring Dionysus, the god of wine and celebration. These festivals included performances by choruses—troupes of performers who sang, danced, and chanted. According to legend, the actor was created in the 6th century B.C. by a Greek chorus member named Thespis. In performances, he began separating himself from the chorus to give speeches and to exchange dialogue with the chorus leader. Today, actors are sometimes called thespians in honor of his contribution. Considered the two greatest playwrights of ancient Greece, Aeschylus (c. 525–456 B.C.) introduced a second actor, and Sophocles (c. 496–406 B.C.) introduced a third actor.

### Conventions of Drama in Greece

Greek dramatic performances often included costumes, scenery, and music. Actors in ancient Greek dramas wore masks to portray different characters, which meant that they depended on body movements and changes in voice to communicate emotions.

Early Greek comedies often centered around satires of people, particularly public figures. It then evolved to include characters that represented ordinary people and plots centered on love stories. Greek tragedies, which depicted the fall of a flawed character, were considered cathartic, or emotionally cleansing, for audiences. The Greek philosopher Aristotle (c. 384–322 B.C.) thought that the audience would feel sorrow and pity for the tragic hero and thus release themselves from these emotions.

Another important feature of Greek drama was its use of choruses. Many early plays included interludes in which a chorus danced and gave singing commentaries on the characters and action of a play.

**STAGE DIRECTIONS** The italicized instructions in a play are written by the **playwright,** or author, and are called **stage directions.** Stage directions describe the **setting** of the play and suggest the use of props, lighting, scenery, sound effects, and costumes. Stage directions also describe the entrances and the exits of characters, and how the characters look, speak, and react to events or to others. Excerpted below are stage directions from *The Crucible* that describe the stage set at the beginning of Act Four.

> (*A cell in Salem jail, that fall.*)
>
> (*At the back is a high barred window; near it, a great, heavy door. Along the walls are two benches.*)
>
> (*The place is in darkness but for the moonlight seeping through the bars. It appears empty. Presently footsteps are heard coming down a corridor beyond the wall, keys rattle, and the door swings open. Marshal Herrick enters with a lantern.*)

**YOUR TURN** What is the effect of the marshal's entrance on the scene?

**SPEECH DEVICES** In drama, the playwright develops the story line through the characters' actions and dialogue. **Dialogue,** or conversation between characters, is the lifeblood of drama. Virtually everything of consequence—from the plot details to the character revelations—flows from dialogue.

Other **speech devices** used by playwrights, in addition to dialogue, include

- the **monologue:** a long speech spoken by a single character to himself or herself, or to the audience;
- the **soliloquy:** a monologue in which a character speaks his or her private thoughts aloud and appears to be unaware of the audience;
- the **aside:** a short speech or comment that is delivered by a character to the audience, but that is beyond the hearing of other characters who are present.

## Strategies for Reading: Drama

1. Review the cast of characters and read the opening stage directions carefully. Remember that the opening scene usually introduces the main conflict.
2. Try to picture the characters and the action as if you were watching the play being performed. Use stage directions to help you "see" the setting and characters, and use dialogue to help you "hear" how characters speak.
3. Follow the dialogue to keep track of the plot and to learn more about the characters.
4. Analyze how the characters interact. What motivates their actions and speech?
5. First read the play silently; then read parts of it aloud to yourself or with others.
6. **Monitor** your reading strategies and modify them when your understanding breaks down. Remember to use your Strategies for Active Reading: **predict, visualize, connect, question, clarify,** and **evaluate.**

# PREPARING to *Read*

# The Crucible

*Drama by* ARTHUR MILLER

**Comparing Literature**

## Traditions Across Time: Another Look at the Puritans

*The Crucible*, a modern play by Arthur Miller, is based on the witch trials that took place in Salem, Massachusetts, in 1692. The play is faithful to the historical period and to Puritan beliefs. Miller actually visited Salem in the course of his research for *The Crucible*, and most of the characters in the play were drawn from those named in the Salem court documents.

**Points of Comparison** As you read *The Crucible*, use your knowledge of history and of Puritan beliefs to help you interpret the characters' motives and actions.

## Build Background

**The Puritan Mindset** In the Salem witch trials, spectral evidence—the testimony of a church member who claimed to have seen a person's spirit performing witchcraft—was enough to sentence the accused to death. Innocent people were tried and convicted on "evidence" that certain things they did caused children to become sick. Belief in witchcraft fueled a climate of hysteria and suspicion, turning neighbor against neighbor, casting doubts even on those of spotless reputation. Miller vividly depicts this climate in this play.

WORDS TO KNOW
**Vocabulary Preview**

| | |
|---|---|
| afflicted | fanatic |
| arbitrate | immaculate |
| ascertain | inaudibly |
| calamity | indictment |
| contentious | indignant |
| deposition | iniquity |
| disproportionate | plaintiff |
| effrontery | predilection |
| empower | subservient |
| excommunication | unintelligible |

## Focus Your Reading

**LITERARY ANALYSIS** **STAGE DIRECTIONS** Located at the beginning of a script and throughout, **stage directions** may identify the setting; tell actors how to speak and move; or describe the characters, the scenery, or the arrangement of props. In *The Crucible*, Miller also uses the stage directions to convey historical background, occasionally drawing parallels to the American political scene of the 1950s.

**ACTIVE READING** **USING A GRAPHIC ORGANIZER** **Graphic organizers**—visual representations of information in a text—include charts, diagrams, and time lines. By using a graphic organizer as you read, you can keep track of details and relationships.

**READER'S NOTEBOOK** Create a chart like this one for each of the following characters: John Proctor, Abigail Williams, and Reverend Hale. Fill in the charts by jotting down important character traits and evidence that reveals these traits. This evidence may be from the characters' actions or dialogue or from the stage directions. As you continue to read the play, add information to your charts and create new charts for the important characters you meet in later acts: Elizabeth Proctor and Deputy Governor Danforth.

| John Proctor | |
|---|---|
| **Trait:** _____ | **Trait:** _____ |
| Evidence: | Evidence: |

THE CRUCIBLE **163**

## OVERVIEW

 An excerpt of this selection is included in the **Grade 11 InterActive Reader.**

### Objectives
1. understand and appreciate a **drama** (Literary Analysis)
2. understand author's use of **stage directions** (Literary Analysis)
3. use a **graphic organizer** to keep track of details in a play (**Active Reading**)

### Summary
This play dramatizes the tragic Salem witch trials of 1692. When Reverend Parris's daughter, Betty, falls ill, the fear is that witchcraft is the cause, and an expert, Reverend Hale, is summoned. Hysteria soon flares up, as Betty, Abigail Williams, and other girls accuse innocent people of witchery. Among the accused is John Proctor's wife, Elizabeth, who dismissed Abigail from her service after discovering her husband's infidelity with the girl. When Proctor defends his wife, he is also accused and convicted. Reverend Hale finally denounces the court and encourages the accused to confess to a lie in order to save their lives. Refusing to give the judges his signed confession, Proctor goes to the gallows with other innocent people.

### Thematic Link
The way to **heaven** is unclear for the people of Salem who are accused of witchcraft. They can save their lives by confessing to crimes they did not commit, knowing that God will judge them for this perjury; or they can refuse to confess and go to the gallows with clear consciences, leaving their loved ones to endure the **hell** of losing them.

### 5-Minute Warm-Up

*Daily Language SkillBuilder*

Have students **proofread** the display sentences on page 131i and write them correctly. The sentences also appear on Transparency 6 of **Grammar Transparencies and Copymasters.**

 **Mini Lesson** **Preteaching Vocabulary**

If you would like to preteach the WORDS TO KNOW for this selection, use the Mini Lesson, pp. 164–165.

THE CRUCIBLE **163**

## LESSON RESOURCES

**UNIT TWO RESOURCE BOOK,** pp. 15–35

**ASSESSMENT RESOURCES**
**Formal Assessment,** pp. 37–44
**Teacher's Guide to Assessment and Portfolio Use**
**Test Generator**

**SKILLS TRANSPARENCIES AND COPYMASTERS**
**Literary Analysis**
• Drama: Basics, T3 (for Literary Analysis, pp. 190, 206, 228, 243)
**Reading and Critical Thinking**
• Evaluating Story Elements, T6 (for Writing Option 4, p. 244)

**Grammar**
• Interjections, C72 (for Mini Lesson, p. 170)
• Regular and Irregular Verbs, C113 (for Mini Lesson, p. 178)
• Principal Parts of Verbs, C114 (for Mini Lesson, p. 200)
• Perfect Tenses of Verbs I, C115 (for Mini Lesson, p. 222)
• Correcting Comma Splices, C147 (for Mini Lesson, p. 244)
**Vocabulary**
• Meanings of Prefixes and Roots, C27 (for Mini Lesson, p. 172)
**Writing**
• Critical Review, C26 (for Writing Option 4, p. 244)

• Opinion Statement, C34 (for Writing Option 3, p. 244)
**Communications**
• Dramatic Reading, T12 (for Mini Lessons, pp. 220 and 236)
• Verbal Strategies, T14 (for Mini Lesson, p. 235)

**INTEGRATED TECHNOLOGY**
**Internet: Research Starter**
**Visit our website:**
www.mcdougallittell.com

### Reading and Analyzing

**Literary Analysis** STAGE DIRECTIONS

Usually, the cast of characters is listed at the beginning of the script. Have students review the characters' names and think about how various characters might be related to each other (for example, Reverend Samuel Parris and Betty Parris, and John Proctor and Elizabeth Proctor). Point out that some characters have titles—Reverend, Marshal, Judge, Deputy Governor—and have students predict what roles these characters will have in the witch trials.

 Use **Unit Two Resource Book,** p. 17 for additional support.

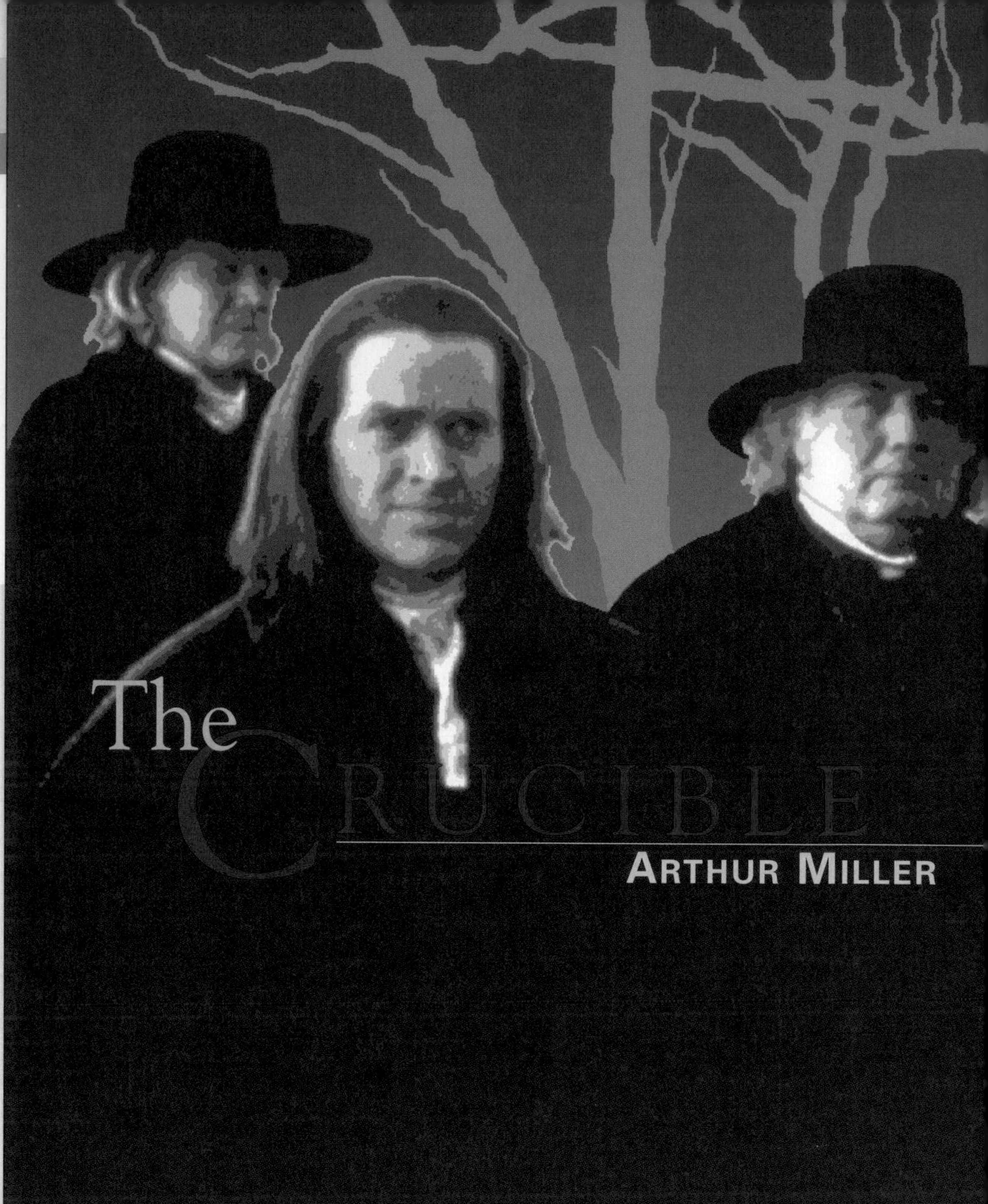

# The CRUCIBLE

## ARTHUR MILLER

## Teaching Options

 **Mini Lesson** **Preteaching Vocabulary**

**USING REFERENCE MATERIALS** Students can use reference materials such as glossaries, dictionaries, thesauruses, and available technology to determine the exact meanings of words. When students look up a word in a dictionary, they may find several definitions listed. The context in which a word is used determines which definition is appropriate. Use the model sentence to demonstrate the strategy.

**Model Sentence**

The <u>indictment</u> was sitting on the lawyer's desk, waiting to be read.

**Instruction**

• Write the model sentence on the chalkboard.

• Ask a volunteer to look up the word *indictment* in a dictionary and read the definitions aloud. Write these definitions on the chalkboard.

• Have students determine which is the best definition for *indictment* considering the context of the model sentence.

• Ask volunteers to create sentences for each definition of *indictment*.

**Exercises** Ask students to use context clues to create a working definition for each underlined word.

## Cast of Characters (order of appearance)

Reverend Samuel Parris
Betty Parris
Tituba
Abigail Williams
John Proctor
Elizabeth Proctor
Susanna Walcott
Mrs. Ann Putnam

Thomas Putnam
Mercy Lewis
Mary Warren
Rebecca Nurse
Giles Corey
Reverend John Hale
Francis Nurse

Ezekiel Cheever
Marshal Herrick
Judge Hathorne
Martha Corey
Deputy Governor Danforth
Girls of Salem
Sarah Good

THE CRUCIBLE **165**

### Less Proficient Readers

Prepare students by explaining that they are about to read a drama, and they will learn about each character's traits and feelings through dialogue (conversation between the characters) and stage directions. Have students keep these questions in mind as they read:

• Who is speaking?
• Where is the character?
• What do the stage directions tell me about how the character feels?

### Students Acquiring English

Have students consider the title of the play and the somber image on the opening page. Explain that a crucible is a container in which metals or ores are melted. The word *crucible* also means "a severe test or trial." In 1692, Salem, Massachusetts, was a crucible for those who were accused of witchcraft. Inform students that although characters in the play speak English, they use archaic phrases and words such as *aye* ("yes") that we no longer use.

 Use **Spanish Study Guide** for additional support, pp. 47–58.

### Gifted and Talented

Theocracy is a form of government that combines political and religious power. Explain to students that in Puritan Salem, if a person did not belong to the church, he could not vote. Why did the founders of the United States insist upon a separation between church and state? How does *The Crucible* illuminate the dangers of combining the powers of church and state?

Then have them use a dictionary to look up precise meanings.

1. Sophie had spent hours cleaning her room, so it was <u>immaculate</u>.
2. The officer at the crime scene tried to <u>ascertain</u> what had happened.
3. The company president became <u>indignant</u> when he was unfairly accused of embezzling money.
4. The two brothers could not settle their disagreement, so they asked their mother to <u>arbitrate</u>.
5. The president is <u>empowered</u> to rule the armed forces.

 Use **Unit Two Resource Book,** p. 18 for additional support.

Read over the first stage directions for a sense of setting. Explain that the opening narration is important for understanding the context of the play.

**Literary Analysis** STAGE DIRECTIONS

**A** Ask students what the setting of Act One is. What do the stage directions regarding Parris's bedroom suggest about his house?

**Possible Responses:** The setting is Salem, Massachusetts, in the spring of 1692, in one of Reverend Parris's small upstairs bedrooms. The stage directions suggest that his house is minimally furnished, containing only the necessities.

**Active Reading**
USING A GRAPHIC ORGANIZER

Students can create web diagrams such as the one below to characterize the town of Salem.

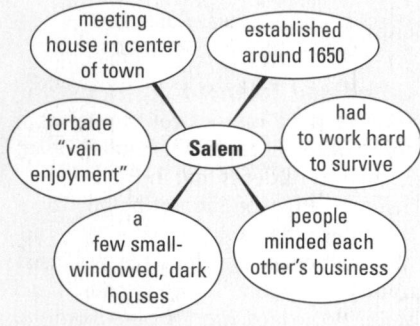

Use **Unit Two Resource Book,** p. 16 for additional support.

# ACT ONE
## An Overture

(*A small upper bedroom in the home of Reverend Samuel Parris, Salem, Massachusetts, in the spring of the year 1692.*)

 (*There is a narrow window at the left. Through its leaded panes the morning sunlight streams. A candle still burns near the bed, which is at the right. A chest, a chair, and a small table are the other furnishings. At the back a door opens on the landing of the stairway to the ground floor. The room gives off an air of clean spareness. The roof rafters are exposed, and the wood colors are raw and unmellowed.*)

(*As the curtain rises, Reverend Parris is discovered kneeling beside the bed, evidently in prayer. His daughter, Betty Parris, aged ten, is lying on the bed, inert.*)

At the time of these events Parris was in his middle forties. In history he cut a villainous path, and there is very little good to be said for him. He believed he was being persecuted wherever he went, despite his best efforts to win people and God to his side. In meeting, he felt insulted if someone rose to shut the door without first asking his permission. He was a widower with no interest in children, or talent with them. He regarded them as young adults, and until this strange crisis he, like the rest of Salem, never conceived that the children were anything but thankful for being permitted to walk straight, eyes slightly lowered, arms at the sides, and mouths shut until bidden to speak.

## Teaching Options

### Mini Lesson Viewing and Representing

**Instruction** Have students study the picture of the bedroom and compare it to the description in the stage directions. Would they visualize the bedroom in the same way?

**Possible Response:** The text description does not convey the neatness, barrenness, or loneliness in the same way that a picture does. The picture allows a viewer to imagine the lives of the people who live in the house.

**Application** This picture represents Betty's bedroom, the set for Act One. Ask students to create

set designs, based on the stage directions and their own imagination. Ask students what colors they would use to depict the mood of the scene. What feelings do students think this set would evoke in the audience? Have students keep their set designs to use for presenting a scene later on.

**Possible Responses:** Students are likely to use somber colors like brown, black, and gray. The set would probably create feelings of seriousness and melancholy in the audience.

His house stood in the "town"—but we today would hardly call it a village. The meeting house[1] was nearby, and from this point outward— toward the bay or inland—there were a few small-windowed, dark houses snuggling against the raw Massachusetts winter. Salem had been established hardly forty years before. To the European world the whole province was a barbaric frontier inhabited by a sect of fanatics who, nevertheless, were shipping out products of slowly increasing quantity and value.

No one can really know what their lives were like. They had no novelists—and would not have permitted anyone to read a novel if one were handy. Their creed forbade anything resembling a theater or "vain enjoyment." They did not celebrate Christmas, and a holiday from work meant only that they must concentrate even more upon prayer.

Which is not to say that nothing broke into this strict and somber way of life. When a new farmhouse was built, friends assembled to "raise the roof," and there would be special foods cooked and probably some potent cider passed around. There was a good supply of ne'er-do-wells in Salem, who dallied at the shovelboard[2] in Bridget Bishop's tavern. Probably more than the creed, hard work kept the morals of the place from spoiling, for the people were forced to fight the land like heroes for every grain of corn, and no man had very much time for fooling around.

That there were some jokers, however, is indicated by the practice of appointing a two-man patrol whose duty was to "walk forth in the time of God's worship to take notice of such as either lye about the meeting house, without attending to the word and ordinances, or that lye at home or in the fields without giving good account thereof, and to take the names of such persons, and to present them to the magistrates, whereby they may be accordingly proceeded against." This predilection for minding other people's business was time-honored among the people of Salem, and it undoubtedly created many of the suspicions which were to feed the coming madness. It was also, in my opinion, one of the things that a John Proctor would rebel against, for the time of the armed camp had almost passed, and since the country was reasonably—although not wholly—safe, the old disciplines were beginning to rankle. But, as in all such matters, the issue was not clear-cut, for danger was still a possibility, and in unity still lay the best promise of safety.

The edge of the wilderness was close by. The American continent stretched endlessly west, and it was full of mystery for them. It stood, dark and threatening, over their shoulders night and day, for out of it Indian tribes marauded[3] from time to time, and Reverend Parris had parishioners who had lost relatives to these heathen.

The parochial snobbery of these people was partly responsible for their failure to convert the Indians. Probably they also preferred to take land from heathens rather than from fellow Christians. At any rate, very few Indians were converted, and the Salem folk believed that the virgin forest was the Devil's last preserve, his home base and the citadel of his final stand. To the best of their knowledge the American forest was the last place on earth that was not paying homage to God.

For these reasons, among others, they carried about an air of innate resistance, even of persecution. Their fathers had, of course, been persecuted in England. So now they and their church found it necessary to deny any other sect its freedom, lest their New Jerusalem[4] be defiled and corrupted by wrong ways and deceitful ideas.

---

1. **meeting house:** the most important building in a Puritan community, used both for worship and for meetings.

2. **shovelboard:** a game in which a coin or disc is shoved across a board by hand.

3. **marauded** (mə-rôd´ĭd): attacked and raided.

4. **New Jerusalem:** in Christianity, a heavenly city and the last resting place of the souls saved by Jesus. It was considered the ideal city, and Puritans modeled their communities after it.

| WORDS TO KNOW | **fanatic** (fē-năt´ĭk) _n._ a person possessed by an excessive and irrational zeal, especially for a religious or political cause |
| | **predilection** (prĕd´l-ĕk´shən) _n._ a personal preference |

**167**

**Reading Skills and Strategies:**
**SUMMARIZING**

**A** Ask students to summarize the main reasons Miller cites for the witch-hunts.

**Possible Response:** The witch-hunts occurred mainly because of people's fear of individual freedom, people's desire to publicly confess their sins while hiding behind accusations of others, and people's need for personal vengeance.

**Literary Analysis** STAGE DIRECTIONS

**B** Ask students what is the mood or atmosphere of this opening scene, and what details in the stage directions create this mood.

**Possible Response:** It is a somber mood. Reverend Parris is crying and praying for his daughter to get better.

**Reading Skills and Strategies:**
**MAKING INFERENCES**

**C** Ask students to infer what they think the doctor means by "unnatural things."

**Possible Response:** The doctor means evil spirits or witchery. He cannot find a cure for Betty's symptoms in his medical texts, so he believes that the cause of her illness lies beyond the natural world.

They believed, in short, that they held in their steady hands the candle that would light the world. We have inherited this belief, and it has helped and hurt us. It helped them with the discipline it gave them. They were a dedicated folk, by and large, and they had to be to survive the life they had chosen or been born into in this country.

The proof of their belief's value to them may be taken from the opposite character of the first Jamestown settlement, farther south, in Virginia. The Englishmen who landed there were motivated mainly by a hunt for profit. They had thought to pick off the wealth of the new country and then return rich to England. They were a band of individualists, and a much more ingratiating group than the Massachusetts men. But Virginia destroyed them. Massachusetts tried to kill off the Puritans, but they combined; they set up a communal society which, in the beginning, was little more than an armed camp with an autocratic and very devoted leadership. It was, however, an autocracy by consent, for they were united from top to bottom by a commonly held ideology whose perpetuation was the reason and justification for all their sufferings. So their self-denial, their purposefulness, their suspicion of all vain pursuits, their hardhanded justice, were altogether perfect instruments for the conquest of this space so antagonistic to man.

But the people of Salem in 1692 were not quite the dedicated folk that arrived on the Mayflower. A vast differentiation had taken place, and in their own time a revolution had unseated the royal government and substituted a junta[5] which was at this moment in power. The times, to their eyes, must have been out of joint, and to the common folk must have seemed as insoluble and complicated as do ours today. It is not hard to see how easily many could have been led to believe that the time of confusion had been brought upon them by deep and darkling forces. No hint of such speculation appears on the court record, but social disorder in any age breeds such mystical suspicions, and when, as in Salem, wonders are brought forth from below the social surface, it is too much to expect people to hold back very long from laying on the victims with all the force of their frustrations.

The Salem tragedy, which is about to begin in these pages, developed from a paradox.[6] It is a paradox in whose grip we still live, and there is no prospect yet that we will discover its resolution. Simply, it was this: for good purposes, even high purposes, the people of Salem developed a theocracy, a combine of state and religious power whose function was to keep the community together, and to prevent any kind of disunity that might open it to destruction by material or ideological enemies. It was forged for a necessary purpose and accomplished that purpose. But all organization is and must be grounded on the idea of exclusion and prohibition, just as two objects cannot occupy the same space. Evidently the time came in New England when the repressions of order were heavier than seemed warranted by the dangers against which the order was organized. The witch-hunt was a perverse manifestation of the panic which set in among all classes when the balance began to turn toward greater individual freedom.

When one rises above the individual villainy displayed, one can only pity them all, just as we shall be pitied someday. It is still impossible for man to organize his social life without repressions, and the balance has yet to be struck between order and freedom.

The witch-hunt was not, however, a mere repression. It was also, and as importantly, a long overdue opportunity for everyone so inclined to express publicly his guilt and sins, under the cover of accusations against the victims. It suddenly became possible—and patriotic and holy—for a man to say that Martha Corey had come into his bedroom at night, and that, while his wife was sleeping at his side, Martha laid herself down on

---

5. **junta** (hŏŏn'tə): a Spanish term meaning a small, elite ruling council; in this case the group that led England's Glorious Revolution of 1688–1689.

6. **paradox:** a seemingly contradictory statement that is in fact true.

✓ **Assessment** **Standardized Test Practice**

**RECOGNIZING FACTS AND DETAILS** For some standardized tests, students will be asked to recognize facts and details in a passage. Read aloud or write on the chalkboard the following question:
Which form of government did the people of Salem establish?
**A.** autocracy
**B.** democracy
**C.** theocracy

Lead students through the process of choosing the correct answer. Autocracy is mentioned in Miller's background information, but this form of government was established by people who arrived on the Mayflower. Democracy is the form of government that we have in the United States today. C is the correct answer; the passage states that the people of Salem established a theocracy, a combination of church and state.

his chest and "nearly suffocated him." Of course it was her spirit only, but his satisfaction at confessing himself was no lighter than if it had been Martha herself. One could not ordinarily speak such things in public.

Long-held hatreds of neighbors could now be openly expressed, and vengeance taken, despite the Bible's charitable injunctions.[7] Land-lust which had been expressed before by constant bickering over boundaries and deeds, could now be elevated to the arena of morality; one could cry witch against one's neighbor and feel perfectly justified in the bargain. Old scores could be settled on a plane of heavenly combat between Lucifer and the Lord; suspicions and the envy of the miserable toward the happy could and did burst out in the general revenge.

(*Reverend Parris is praying now, and, though we cannot hear his words, a sense of his confusion hangs about him. He mumbles, then seems about to weep; then he weeps, then prays again; but his daughter does not stir on the bed.*)

(*The door opens, and his Negro slave enters. Tituba is in her forties. Parris brought her with him from Barbados,[8] where he spent some years as a merchant before entering the ministry. She enters as one does who can no longer bear to be barred from the sight of her beloved, but she is also very frightened because her slave sense has warned her that, as always, trouble in this house eventually lands on her back.*)

**Tituba** (*already taking a step backward*). My Betty be hearty soon?

**Parris.** Out of here!

**Tituba** (*backing to the door*). My Betty not goin' die . . .

**Parris** (*scrambling to his feet in a fury*). Out of my sight! (*She is gone.*) Out of my—(*He is overcome with sobs. He clamps his teeth against them and closes the door and leans against it, exhausted.*) Oh, my God! God help me! (*Quaking with fear, mumbling to himself through his sobs, he goes to the bed and gently takes Betty's hand.*) Betty. Child. Dear child. Will you wake, will you open up your eyes! Betty, little one . . .

(*He is bending to kneel again when his niece,* Abigail Williams, *seventeen, enters—a strikingly beautiful girl, an orphan, with an endless capacity for dissembling.[9] Now she is all worry and apprehension and propriety.*)

**Abigail.** Uncle? (*He looks to her.*) Susanna Walcott's here from Doctor Griggs.

**Parris.** Oh? Let her come, let her come.

**Abigail** (*leaning out the door to call to Susanna, who is down the hall a few steps*). Come in, Susanna.

(Susanna Walcott, *a little younger than* Abigail, *a nervous, hurried girl, enters.*)

**Parris** (*eagerly*). What does the doctor say, child?

**Susanna** (*craning around Parris to get a look at Betty*). He bid me come and tell you, reverend sir, that he cannot discover no medicine for it in his books.

**Parris.** Then he must search on.

**Susanna.** Aye, sir, he have been searchin' his books since he left you, sir. But he bid me tell you, that you might look to unnatural things for the cause of it.

---

7. **injunctions** (ĭn-jŭngk′shənz): commands; orders.

8. **Barbados** (bär-bā′dōs): an island in the West Indies under British rule until 1966.

9. **dissembling:** disguising the truth about something.

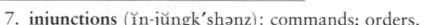
Abigail

## Customizing Instruction

### Students Acquiring English
**1** Help students understand difficult words and phrases in this passage.
- *ingratiating:* pleasing, likable
- *communal:* sharing everything with the whole community
- *autocratic:* ruled by one person who has absolute power
- *Ideology:* a system of ideas or way of thinking
- *perpetuation:* continuation, keeping something going
- *vain pursuits:* activities not related to work or religion
- *antagonistic:* hostile, fighting against
- *out of joint:* wrong, messed up, out of order
- *insoluble:* not able to be solved or fixed

### Gifted and Talented
**2** Have students explain why the Salem witch trials are paradoxical.
**Possible Response:** The people of Salem created a theocracy to make sure that their community stayed together and lived according to Christian principles, but this very theocracy made possible the witch trials, which tore the community apart and led to the slaughter of innocent victims.

### Less Proficient Readers
**3** Make sure students understand the gist of Miller's explanation: Salem was a community organized on Christian principles, but its strictness eventually led people to revolt. The people of Salem had the same problems and desires that all people do, but they had no way to express or deal with them. The witch trials gave them a way to vent their frustrations and talk publicly (although in the guise of accusing others of witchcraft) about their own failures.

**A** Ask students why they think both Abigail and Parris do not want Susanna to speak of the doctor's suspicions in the village.

**Possible Response:** They both want to protect themselves and their reputations. If the townspeople think Betty is ill due to witchery, Abigail may be accused of witchcraft and Parris may be held responsible for allowing the Devil to enter his community.

### Reading Skills and Strategies: DRAWING INFERENCES

**B** Ask students to infer what Abigail and Tituba were doing in the forest and to support their inferences with textual evidence.

**Possible Response:** They were performing a ceremony or rite of some kind; they were performing witchcraft; they were dancing just to have fun—something they could not do openly in Salem.

### Literary Analysis | STAGE DIRECTIONS

**C** What do these stage directions suggest about Abigail?

**Possible Response:** She is a liar and a skillful actress, and she is trying to hide what really happened in the forest. She acts innocent when Parris asks about the dress, and her terror when Parris says he saw someone naked suggests that she doesn't want him to know this.

---

**Parris** (*his eyes going wide*). No—no. There be no unnatural cause here. Tell him I have sent for Reverend Hale of Beverly, and Mr. Hale will surely confirm that. Let him look to medicine and put out all thought of unnatural causes here. There be none.

**Susanna.** Aye, sir. He bid me tell you. (*She turns to go.*)

**Abigail.** Speak nothin' of it in the village, Susanna.

**Parris.** Go directly home and speak nothing of unnatural causes.

**Susanna.** Aye, sir. I pray for her. (*She goes out.*)

**Abigail.** Uncle, the rumor of witchcraft is all about; I think you'd best go down and deny it yourself. The parlor's packed with people, sir. I'll sit with her.

**Parris** (*pressed, turns on her*). And what shall I say to them? That my daughter and my niece I discovered dancing like heathen in the forest?

**Abigail.** Uncle, we did dance; let you tell them I confessed it—and I'll be whipped if I must be. But they're speakin' of witchcraft. Betty's not witched.

**Parris.** Abigail, I cannot go before the congregation when I know you have not opened with me. What did you do with her in the forest?

**Abigail.** We did dance, uncle, and when you leaped out of the bush so suddenly, Betty was frightened and then she fainted. And there's the whole of it.

**Parris.** Child, sit you down.

**Abigail** (*quavering, as she sits*). I would never hurt Betty. I love her dearly.

**Parris.** Now look you, child, your punishment will come in its time. But if you trafficked with[10] spirits in the forest I must know it now, for surely my enemies will, and they will ruin me with it.

**Abigail.** But we never conjured spirits.

**Parris.** Then why can she not move herself since midnight? This child is desperate! (Abigail low-

ers her eyes.) It must come out—my enemies will bring it out. Let me know what you done there. Abigail, do you understand that I have many enemies?

**Abigail.** I have heard of it, uncle.

**Parris.** There is a faction that is sworn to drive me from my pulpit. Do you understand that?

**Abigail.** I think so, sir.

**Parris.** Now then, in the midst of such disruption, my own household is discovered to be the very center of some obscene practice. Abominations[11] are done in the forest—

**Abigail.** It were sport, uncle!

**Parris** (*pointing at* Betty). You call this sport? (*She lowers her eyes. He pleads*). Abigail, if you know something that may help the doctor, for God's sake tell it to me. (*She is silent.*) I saw Tituba waving her arms over the fire when I came on you. Why was she doing that? And I heard a screeching and gibberish coming from her mouth. She were swaying like a dumb beast over that fire!

**Abigail.** She always sings her Barbados songs, and we dance.

**Parris.** I cannot blink what I saw, Abigail, for my enemies will not blink it. I saw a dress lying on the grass.

**Abigail** (*innocently*). A dress?

**Parris** (*it is very hard to say*). Aye, a dress. And I thought I saw—someone naked running through the trees!

**Abigail** (*in terror*). No one was naked! You mistake yourself, uncle!

**Parris** (*with anger*). I saw it! (*He moves from her. Then, resolved*). Now tell me true, Abigail. And I pray you feel the weight of truth upon you, for now my ministry's at stake, my ministry and perhaps your cousin's life. Whatever abomina-

---

10. **trafficked with:** met.
11. **abominations:** dreadful and immoral things.

## Teaching Options

 **Mini Lesson** **Grammar**

**INTERJECTIONS** An interjection is a word that expresses sudden emotion. A strong interjection is followed by an exclamation point; a mild one is set off by a comma or commas. An interjection has no grammatical relation to the surrounding text. Write this example on the chalkboard:

Wow! Betty is really sick, and she might not get better.

Have students identify the interjection and explain why it is followed by an exclamation point.

**Answer:** *Wow* is the interjection; it is followed by an exclamation point because it shows strong emotion.

**Exercises** Have students underline any interjections they find in these sentences.

1. Ugh! Abigail does not want to tell Parris the truth about the forest. (*Ugh*)

2. Secretly, Tituba sang her songs while the girls danced. (*No interjection*)

3. Well, do you think Parris believes Abigail's story? (*Well*)

## Customizing Instruction

**Students Acquiring English**

**1** Help students understand the expression *I know you have not opened with me* ("I know you have not been honest with me") and the words *sport* ("fun") and *blink* ("ignore").

**Less Proficient Readers**

**2** To help students understand this passage, ask the following questions. Before they answer the second question, discuss what feelings or characteristics are associated with the color white, such as pureness and innocence.

• Why is Parris upset with Abigail?

**Possible Response:** It has taken him a long time to gain the respect of his parish, and he's afraid that what the girls have done will take away his respect.

• What do you think Parris means by his question?

**Possible Response:** He's asking Abigail if she has a reputation of innocence in the town.

tion you have done, give me all of it now, for I dare not be taken unaware when I go before them down there.

**Abigail.** There is nothin' more. I swear it, uncle.

**Parris** (*studies her, then nods, half convinced*). Abigail, I have fought here three long years to bend these stiff-necked people to me, and now, just now when some good respect is rising for me in the parish, you compromise my very character. I have given you a home, child, I have put clothes upon your back—now give me upright answer. Your name in the town—it is entirely white, is it not?

**Abigail** (*with an edge of resentment*). Why, I am sure it is, sir. There be no blush about my name.[12]

**Parris** (*to the point*). Abigail, is there any other cause than you have told me, for your being discharged from Goody[13] Proctor's service? I have heard it said, and I tell you as I heard it,

that she comes so rarely to the church this year for she will not sit so close to something soiled. What signified that remark?

**Abigail.** She hates me, uncle, she must, for I would not be her slave. It's a bitter woman, a lying, cold, sniveling woman, and I will not work for such a woman!

**Parris.** She may be. And yet it has troubled me that you are now seven month out of their house, and in all this time no other family has ever called for your service.

**Abigail.** They want slaves, not such as I. Let them send to Barbados for that. I will not black my face for any of them! (*With ill-concealed resentment at him.*) Do you begrudge my bed, uncle?

---

12. **There be . . . my name:** There is nothing wrong with my reputation.

13. **Goody:** short for Goodwife, the Puritan equivalent of Mrs.

4. Oh! Susanna must not tell that the doctor suspects unnatural causes. *(Oh)*

5. Ah, Reverend Hale will be coming to town. *(Ah)*

 Use **Grammar Transparencies and Copymasters**, p. 72.

Use McDougal Littell's *Language Network*, Chapter 9, for more instruction and practice in the use of end marks.

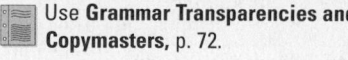

**Literary Analysis: FORESHADOWING**

**A** Ask students to discuss what Reverend Hale's arrival may foreshadow, based on his reputation.

**Possible Response:** Reverend Hale "found a witch" in Beverly. Considering the events that are transpiring in Salem, it is probable that some Salem residents will be found guilty of witchcraft, too.

**Reading Skills and Strategies: DRAWING INFERENCES**

**B** Have students draw inferences about what Abigail is doing here and support their inferences with textual evidence.

**Possible Response:** Abigail is lying about what the girls did in forest; she is implicating Tituba and Ruth to protect herself. The stage directions have described her as having "an endless capacity for dissembling," and she has already shown great reluctance to tell the truth about what happened in the forest. She reveals information only when she knows it is safe to do so, and she lies whenever it will profit her.

---

**Parris.** No—no.

**Abigail** (*in a temper*). My name is good in the village! I will not have it said my name is soiled! Goody Proctor is a gossiping liar!

(*Enter Mrs. Ann Putnam. She is a twisted soul of forty-five, a death-ridden woman, haunted by dreams.*)

**1**

**Parris** (*as soon as the door begins to open*). No—no, I cannot have anyone. (*He sees her, and a certain deference springs into him, although his worry remains.*) Why, Goody Putnam, come in.

**Mrs. Putnam** (*full of breath, shiny-eyed*). It is a marvel. It is surely a stroke of hell upon you.

**Parris.** No, Goody Putnam, it is—

**Mrs. Putnam** (*glancing at* Betty). How high did she fly, how high?

**Parris.** No, no, she never flew—

**Mrs. Putnam** (*very pleased with it*). Why, it's sure she did. Mr. Collins saw her goin' over Ingersoll's barn, and come down light as bird, he says!

**Parris.** Now, look you, Goody Putnam, she never—(*Enter* Thomas Putnam, *a well-to-do, hardhanded landowner, near fifty.*) Oh, good morning, Mr. Putnam.

**Putnam.** It is a providence[14] the thing is out now! It is a providence. (*He goes directly to the bed.*)

**Parris.** What's out, sir, what's—?

(*Mrs. Putnam goes to the bed.*)

**Putnam** (*looking down at* Betty). Why, her eyes is closed! Look you, Ann.

**Mrs. Putnam.** Why, that's strange. (*To Parris*). Ours is open.

**Parris** (*shocked*). Your Ruth is sick?

**Mrs. Putnam** (*with vicious certainty*). I'd not call it sick; the Devil's touch is heavier than sick. It's death, y'know, it's death drivin' into them, forked and hoofed.

**Parris.** Oh, pray not! Why, how does Ruth ail?

**Mrs. Putnam.** She ails as she must—she never waked this morning, but her eyes open and she

walks, and hears naught, sees naught, and cannot eat. Her soul is taken, surely.

(*Parris is struck.*)

**Putnam** (*as though for further details*). They say you've sent for Reverend Hale of Beverly?

**Parris** (*with dwindling conviction now*). A precaution only. He has much experience in all demonic arts, and I—

**Mrs. Putnam.** He has indeed; and found a witch in Beverly last year, and let you remember that.

**Parris.** Now, Goody Ann, they only thought that were a witch, and I am certain there be no element of witchcraft here.

**Putnam.** No witchcraft! Now look you, Mr. Parris—

**Parris.** Thomas, Thomas, I pray you, leap not to witchcraft. I know that you—you least of all, Thomas, would ever wish so disastrous a charge laid upon me. We cannot leap to witchcraft. They will howl me out of Salem for such corruption in my house.

**A** word about Thomas Putnam. He was a man with many grievances, at least one of which appears justified. Some time before, his wife's brother-in-law, James Bayley, had been turned down as minister of Salem. Bayley had all the qualifications, and a two-thirds vote into the bargain, but a faction stopped his acceptance, for reasons that are not clear.

Thomas Putnam was the eldest son of the richest man in the village. He had fought the Indians at Narragansett, and was deeply interested in parish affairs. He undoubtedly felt it poor payment that the village should so blatantly disregard his candidate for one of its more important offices, especially since he regarded himself as the intellectual superior of most of the people around him.

---

14. **providence** (prŏv′ĭ-dəns): sign of good fortune.

---

## Teaching Options

 **Mini Lesson** ## Vocabulary Strategy

**APPLYING MEANINGS OF PREFIXES AND ROOT WORDS**

**Instruction** Students can apply meanings of root words and prefixes in order to figure out the meaning of an unfamiliar word. For example, the word *disproportionate* is based on the Latin root *proportio,* which means "a portion of," and the prefix *dis-,* which means "away, off, or opposing." Putnam was upset because he felt that the portion of his father's estate received by his stepbrother was unfair. Other words based on the same root wood are *proportion* and *disproportion.*

Other words with the prefix *dis-* are *disabled, disarray,* and *discredit.*

**Application** Have students determine the meanings of the following words: *proportionate, disproportion, disabled, disarray,* and *discredit.* Ask them to use each word in a sentence.

Use **Vocabulary Transparencies and Copymasters,** p. 27.

A lesson on word parts appears on p. 1130 in the **Pupil's Edition.**

His vindictive[15] nature was demonstrated long before the witchcraft began. Another former Salem minister, George Burroughs, had had to borrow money to pay for his wife's funeral, and, since the parish was remiss in his salary, he was soon bankrupt. Thomas and his brother John had Burroughs jailed for debts the man did not owe. The incident is important only in that Burroughs succeeded in becoming minister where Bayley, Thomas Putnam's brother-in-law, had been rejected; the motif of resentment is clear here. Thomas Putnam felt that his own name and the honor of his family had been smirched[16] by the village, and he meant to right matters however he could.

Another reason to believe him a deeply embittered man was his attempt to break his father's will, which left a disproportionate amount to a stepbrother. As with every other public cause in which he tried to force his way, he failed in this.

So it is not surprising to find that so many accusations against people are in the handwriting of Thomas Putnam, or that his name is so often found as a witness corroborating the supernatural testimony, or that his daughter led the crying-out at the most opportune junctures of the trials, especially when—But we'll speak of that when we come to it.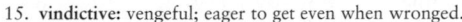

**Putnam** (*at the moment he is intent upon getting* Parris, *for whom he has only contempt, to move toward the abyss*). Mr. Parris, I have taken your part in all contention here, and I would continue; but I cannot if you hold back in this. There are hurtful, vengeful spirits layin' hands on these children.

**Parris.** But, Thomas, you cannot—

**Putnam.** Ann! Tell Mr. Parris what you have done.

**Mrs. Putnam.** Reverend Parris, I have laid seven babies unbaptized in the earth. Believe me, sir, you never saw more hearty babies born. And yet, each would wither in my arms the very night of their birth. I have spoke nothin', but my heart has clamored intimations.[17] And now, this year, my Ruth, my only—I see her turning strange. A secret child she has become this year, and shrivels like a sucking mouth were pullin' on her life too. And so I thought to send her to your Tituba—

**Parris.** To Tituba! What may Tituba—?

**Mrs. Putnam.** Tituba knows how to speak to the dead, Mr. Parris.

**Parris.** Goody Ann, it is a formidable sin to conjure up the dead!

**Mrs. Putnam.** I take it on my soul, but who else may surely tell us what person murdered my babies?

**Parris** (*horrified*). Woman!

**Mrs. Putnam.** They were murdered, Mr. Parris! And mark this proof! Mark it! Last night my Ruth were ever so close to their little spirits; I know it, sir. For how else is she struck dumb now except some power of darkness would stop her mouth? It is a marvelous sign, Mr. Parris!

**Putnam.** Don't you understand it, sir? There is a murdering witch among us, bound to keep herself in the dark. (Parris *turns to* Betty, *a frantic terror rising in him.*) Let your enemies make of it what they will, you cannot blink it more.

**Parris** (*to* Abigail). Then you were conjuring spirits last night.

**Abigail** (*whispering*). Not I, sir—Tituba and Ruth.

**Parris** (*turns now, with new fear, and goes to* Betty, *looks down at her, and then, gazing off*) Oh, Abigail, what proper payment for my charity! Now I am undone.[18]

---

15. **vindictive:** vengeful; eager to get even when wronged.

16. **smirched:** soiled; reduced in value.

17. **clamored intimations** (klăm′ərd ĭn′tə-mā′shənz): nagging suspicions.

18. **undone:** ruined.

| WORDS TO KNOW | **disproportionate** (dĭs′prə-pôr′shə-nĭt) *adj.* out of proportion; of an unequal size or amount |
| --- | --- |

**Multiple Learning Styles**
**Visual Learners**

**1** Based on the description of Mrs. Putnam in the stage directions, have students visualize in detail what they think she looks like. Discuss these visualizations with them, or invite students to draw Mrs. Putnam.

**Less Proficient Readers**

**2** Tell students that Miller is saying that Thomas Putnam accused many people of evil doings because of bitterness and revenge. Have them give evidence of Putnam's vindictiveness.

**Possible Response:** Putnam jailed a minister for debts he did not owe, and he tried to break his father's will.

### Reading Skills and Strategies: VISUALIZING

 **A** Ask students to construct an image of Mary Warren based on her dialogue and details in the stage direction. Then ask students to talk about how Mary is different from Abigail and Mercy.

**Possible Response:** Mary is shy, naive, and submissive. Students may picture her as having a slumped posture and lowered eyes, or as flitting around nervously and speaking in a high-pitched voice. Abigail and Mercy, by contrast, are sly, experienced, and dominant. They keep their cool, speak with authority, and have few nervous gestures.

### Active Reading

**USING A GRAPHIC ORGANIZER**

**B** Remind students to add information about Abigail to the graphic organizer in their Reader's Notebook. Tell them that evidence can be drawn from her dialogue or from stage directions.

#### Abigail Williams

| Trait: intimidating; mean | Trait: |
|---|---|
| Evidence: threatens to harm the girls if they will not support her story and lie | Evidence: |

---

**Putnam.** You are not undone! Let you take hold here. Wait for no one to charge you—declare it yourself. You have discovered witchcraft—

**Parris.** In my house? In my house, Thomas? They will topple me with this! They will make of it a—

(*Enter* Mercy Lewis, *the Putnams' servant, a fat, sly, merciless girl of eighteen.*)

**Mercy.** Your pardons. I only thought to see how Betty is.

**Putnam.** Why aren't you home? Who's with Ruth?

**Mercy.** Her grandma come. She's improved a little, I think—she give a powerful sneeze before.

**Mrs. Putnam.** Ah, there's a sign of life!

**1 Mercy.** I'd fear no more, Goody Putnam. It were a grand sneeze; another like it will shake her wits together, I'm sure. (*She goes to the bed to look.*)

**Parris.** Will you leave me now, Thomas? I would pray a while alone.

**Abigail.** Uncle, you've prayed since midnight. Why do you not go down and—

**Parris.** No—no. (*To* Putnam). I have no answer for that crowd. I'll wait till Mr. Hale arrives. (*To get* Mrs. Putnam *to leave.*) If you will, Goody Ann . . .

**Putnam.** Now look you, sir. Let you strike out against the Devil, and the village will bless you for it! Come down, speak to them—pray with them. They're thirsting for your word, Mister! Surely you'll pray with them.

**Parris** (*swayed*). I'll lead them in a psalm, but let you say nothing of witchcraft yet. I will not discuss it. The cause is yet unknown. I have had enough contention since I came; I want no more.

**Mrs. Putnam.** Mercy, you go home to Ruth, d'y'-hear?

**Mercy.** Aye, mum.

(Mrs. Putnam *goes out.*)

---

**Parris** (*to* Abigail). If she starts for the window, cry for me at once.

**Abigail.** I will, uncle.

**Parris** (*to* Putnam). There is a terrible power in her arms today. (*He goes out with* Putnam.)

**Abigail** (*with hushed trepidation*).[19] How is Ruth sick?

**Mercy.** It's weirdish, I know not—she seems to walk like a dead one since last night.

**Abigail** (*turns at once and goes to* Betty, *and now, with fear in her voice*). Betty? (Betty *doesn't move. She shakes her.*) Now stop this! Betty! Sit up now!

(Betty *doesn't stir.* Mercy *comes over.*)

**Mercy.** Have you tried beatin' her? I gave Ruth a good one and it waked her for a minute. Here, let me have her.

**Abigail** (*holding* Mercy *back*). No, he'll be comin' up. Listen, now; if they be questioning us, tell them we danced—I told him as much already.

**Mercy.** Aye. And what more?

**Abigail.** He knows Tituba conjured Ruth's sisters to come out of the grave.

**Mercy.** And what more?

**Abigail.** He saw you naked.

**Mercy** (*clapping her hands together with a frightened laugh*). Oh, Jesus!

(*Enter* Mary Warren, *breathless. She is seventeen, a <u>subservient</u>, naive, lonely girl.*)

**Mary Warren.** What'll we do? The village is out! I just come from the farm; the whole country's talkin' witchcraft! They'll be callin' us witches, Abby!

**Mercy** (*pointing and looking at* Mary Warren). She means to tell, I know it.

**Mary Warren.** Abby, we've got to tell. Witchery's a hangin' error, a hangin' like they done in

---

19. **trepidation** (trĕp′ĭ-dā′shən): alarm or dread.

WORDS TO KNOW

**subservient** (səb-sûr′vē-ənt) *adj.* acting like a servant

---

## Teaching Options

### Mini Lesson — Vocabulary Strategy

#### APPLYING MEANINGS OF PREFIXES AND ROOT WORDS

**Instruction** The word *subservient* is based on the Latin root *servire,* which means "to serve," and the prefix *sub-,* which means "under." When Mary Warren is described as subservient, it means she has a personality that serves others; she is "under" people. Other words based on the same root are *servant, servile, serviceable,* and *servitude.* Other words with the prefix *sub-* are *submarine, submit, subconscious,* and *subway.*

**Application** Have students work in pairs to find the meanings of *servant, servile, serviceable,* and *subconscious.* Ask them to use each word in a sentence.

Boston two year ago! We must tell the truth, Abby! You'll only be whipped for dancin', and the other things!

**Abigail.** Oh, we'll be whipped!

**Mary Warren.** I never done none of it, Abby. I only looked!

**Mercy** (*moving menacingly toward Mary*). Oh, you're a great one for lookin', aren't you, Mary Warren? What a grand peeping courage you have!

(Betty, *on the bed, whimpers.* Abigail *turns to her at once.*)

**Abigail.** Betty? (*She goes to Betty.*) Now, Betty, dear, wake up now. It's Abigail. (*She sits Betty up and furiously shakes her.*) I'll beat you, Betty! (*Betty whimpers.*) My, you seem improving. I talked to your papa and I told him everything. So there's nothing to—

**Betty** (*darts off the bed, frightened of* Abigail, *and flattens herself against the wall*). I want my mama!

**Abigail** (*with alarm, as she cautiously approaches* Betty). What ails you, Betty? Your mama's dead and buried.

**Betty.** I'll fly to Mama. Let me fly! (*She raises her arms as though to fly, and streaks for the window, gets one leg out.*)

**Abigail** (*pulling her away from the window*). I told him everything; he knows now, he knows everything we—

**Betty.** You drank blood, Abby! You didn't tell him that!

**Abigail.** Betty, you never say that again! You will never—

**Betty.** You did, you did! You drank a charm to kill John Proctor's wife! You drank a charm to kill Goody Proctor!

**Abigail** (*smashes her across the face*). Shut it! Now shut it!

**Betty** (*collapsing on the bed*). Mama, Mama! (*She dissolves into sobs.*)

**Abigail.** Now look you. All of you. We danced. And Tituba conjured Ruth Putnam's dead sisters. And that is all. And mark this. Let either of you breathe a word, or the edge of a word, about the other things, and I will come to you in the black of some terrible night and I will bring a pointy reckoning that will shudder you.[20] And you know I can do it; I saw Indians smash my dear parents' heads on the pillow next to mine, and I have seen some reddish work done at night, and I can make you wish you had never seen the sun go down! (*She goes to Betty and roughly sits her up.*) Now, you— sit up and stop this!

(*But* Betty *collapses in her hands and lies inert on the bed.*)

**Mary Warren** (*with hysterical fright*). What's got her? (Abigail *stares in fright at* Betty.) Abby, she's going to die! It's a sin to conjure, and we—

**Abigail** (*starting for* Mary). I say shut it, Mary Warren!

(*Enter* John Proctor. *On seeing him,* Mary Warren *leaps in fright.*)

Proctor was a farmer in his middle thirties. He need not have been a partisan of any faction in the town, but there is evidence to suggest that he had a sharp and biting way with hypocrites. He was the kind of man—powerful of body, even-tempered, and not easily led—who cannot refuse support to partisans without drawing their deepest resentment. In Proctor's presence a fool felt his foolishness instantly—and a Proctor is always marked for calumny[21] therefore.

But as we shall see, the steady manner he displays does not spring from an untroubled soul. He is a sinner, a sinner not only against the moral fashion of the time, but against his own vision of decent conduct. These people had no ritual for the

---

20. **bring . . . shudder you:** inflict a terrifying punishment on you.

21. **calumny** (kăl′əm-nē): slander; lies about someone.

**Less Proficient Readers**

**1** Ask students why they think Putnam wants Parris to declare that he's discovered witchcraft. Is he genuinely concerned for Parris, or could it be something else?

**Possible Response:** Putnam resents anyone who becomes minister of Salem because his brother-in-law, James Bayley, was denied the position. Putnam wants Parris to declare witchcraft because he knows it will probably ruin Parris's reputation, thus making everyone see that things would have been better under Bayley.

**Students Acquiring English**

The following words and phrases may be difficult for students acquiring English.

- *contention:* fighting, disagreements, trouble
- *d'y'hear:* do you hear, do you understand
- *hangin' error:* a crime punishable by hanging
- *grand peeping courage:* courage only to watch, not to act; no courage at all
- *breathe a word:* say anything
- *reddish work:* bloody, violent acts
- *partisan:* member of a group with certain goals or beliefs
- *faction:* group that stands separate or divided from others

## Literary Analysis STAGE DIRECTIONS

**A** What do the stage directions reveal about how Abigail and John each feel about their relationship?

**Possible Response:** Abigail still has passionate feelings for John and thinks they have a future together. John has some fond memories of their time together but considers the relationship over.

## Active Reading
### USING A GRAPHIC ORGANIZER

**B** Help students further develop their character chart for Abigail. What does this passage tell them about Abigail?

### Abigail Williams

| Trait: intimidating; mean | Trait: flirtatious; tempting |
|---|---|
| Evidence: threatens to harm the girls if they will not support her story and lie | Evidence: looks feverishly at John and moves close to him when she speaks |

## Literary Analysis: CHARACTERIZATION

**C** Abigail's characterization of Elizabeth Proctor differs from how other people would describe Elizabeth. Ask students to discuss how Abigail characterizes Elizabeth. Why do you think Abigail would speak of Elizabeth in this manner?

**Possible Response:** Abigail says that Elizabeth is a poor wife and a cold, sniveling woman. She is angry that Elizabeth made her leave the Proctors' house and that Elizabeth knows the truth about Abigail's character. Furthermore, she wants John Proctor for herself and is jealous of his wife.

---

washing away of sins. It is another trait we inherited from them, and it has helped to discipline us as well as to breed hypocrisy among us. Proctor, respected and even feared in Salem, has come to regard himself as a kind of fraud. But no hint of this has yet appeared on the surface, and as he enters from the crowded parlor below it is a man in his prime we see, with a quiet confidence and an unexpressed, hidden force. Mary Warren, his servant, can barely speak for embarrassment and fear.

**Mary Warren.** Oh! I'm just going home, Mr. Proctor.

**Proctor.** Be you foolish, Mary Warren? Be you deaf? I forbid you leave the house, did I not? Why shall I pay you? I am looking for you more often than my cows!

**Mary Warren.** I only come to see the great doings in the world.

**Proctor.** I'll show you a great doin' on your arse one of these days. Now get you home; my wife is waitin' with your work! (*Trying to retain a shred of dignity, she goes slowly out.*)

**Mercy Lewis** (*both afraid of him and strangely titillated*). I'd best be off. I have my Ruth to watch. Good morning, Mr. Proctor.

(*Mercy sidles out. Since* Proctor's *entrance, Abigail has stood as though on tiptoe, absorbing his presence, wide-eyed. He glances at her, then goes to* Betty *on the bed.*)

**A** **Abigail.** Gah! I'd almost forgot how strong you are, John Proctor!

**Proctor** (*looking at* Abigail *now, the faintest suggestion of a knowing smile on his face*). What's this mischief here?

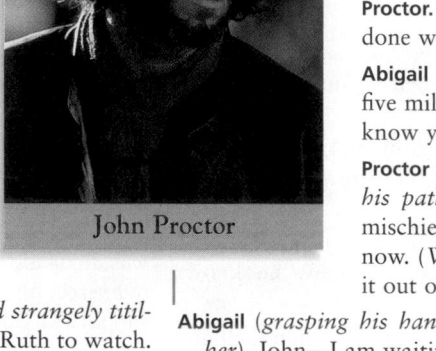
John Proctor

**Abigail** (*with a nervous laugh*). Oh, she's only gone silly somehow.

**Proctor.** The road past my house is a pilgrimage[22] to Salem all morning. The town's mumbling witchcraft.

**Abigail.** Oh, posh! (*Winningly she comes a little closer, with a confidential, wicked air.*) We were dancin' in the woods last night, and my uncle leaped in on us. She took fright, is all.

**Proctor** (*his smile widening*). Ah, you're wicked yet, aren't y'! (*A trill of expectant laughter escapes her, and she dares come closer, feverishly looking into his eyes.*) You'll be clapped in the stocks before you're twenty.

(*He takes a step to go, and she springs into his path.*)

**Abigail.** Give me a word, John. A soft word. (*Her concentrated desire destroys his smile.*)

**Proctor.** No, no, Abby. That's done with.

**Abigail** (*tauntingly*). You come five mile to see a silly girl fly? I know you better.

**Proctor** (*setting her firmly out of his path*). I come to see what mischief your uncle's brewin' now. (*With final emphasis.*) Put it out of mind, Abby.

**Abigail** (*grasping his hand before he can release her*). John—I am waitin' for you every night.

**Proctor.** Abby, I never give you hope to wait for me.

**Abigail** (*now beginning to anger—she can't believe it*). I have something better than hope, I think!

**Proctor.** Abby, you'll put it out of mind. I'll not be comin' for you more.

---

22. **pilgrimage:** a journey to a religious shrine, often made in groups.

**Abigail.** You're surely sportin' with me.

**Proctor.** You know me better.

**Abigail.** I know how you clutched my back behind your house and sweated like a stallion whenever I come near! Or did I dream that? It's she put me out, you cannot pretend it were you. I saw your face when she put me out, and you loved me then and you do now!

**Proctor.** Abby, that's a wild thing to say—

**Abigail.** A wild thing may say wild things. But not so wild, I think. I have seen you since she put me out; I have seen you nights.

**Proctor.** I have hardly stepped off my farm this sevenmonth.

**Abigail.** I have a sense for heat, John, and yours has drawn me to my window, and I have seen you looking up, burning in your loneliness. Do you tell me you've never looked up at my window?

**Proctor.** I may have looked up.

**Abigail** (*now softening*). And you must. You are no wintry man. I know you, John. I know you. (*She is weeping.*) I cannot sleep for dreamin'; I cannot dream but I wake and walk about the house as though I'd find you comin' through some door. (*She clutches him desperately.*)

**Proctor** (*gently pressing her from him, with great sympathy but firmly*). Child—

**Abigail** (*with a flash of anger*). How do you call me child!

**Proctor.** Abby, I may think of you softly from time to time. But I will cut off my hand before I'll ever reach for you again. Wipe it out of mind. We never touched, Abby.

**Abigail.** Aye, but we did.

**Proctor.** Aye, but we did not.

**Abigail** (*with a bitter anger*). Oh, I marvel how such a strong man may let such a sickly wife be—

**Proctor** (*angered—at himself as well*). You'll speak nothin' of Elizabeth!

**Abigail.** She is blackening my name in the village! She is telling lies about me! She is a cold, sniveling woman, and you bend to her! Let her turn you like a—

**Proctor** (*shaking her*). Do you look for whippin'?

(*A psalm is heard being sung below.*)

**Abigail** (*in tears*). I look for John Proctor that took me from my sleep and put knowledge in my heart! I never knew what pretense Salem was, I never knew the lying lessons I was taught by all these Christian women and their covenanted[23] men! And now you bid me tear the light out of my eyes? I will not, I cannot! You loved me, John Proctor, and whatever sin it is, you love me yet! (*He turns abruptly to go out. She rushes to him.*) John, pity me, pity me!

(*The words "going up to Jesus" are heard in the psalm, and* Betty *claps her ears suddenly and whines loudly.*)

**Abigail.** Betty? (*She hurries to* Betty, *who is now sitting up and screaming.* Proctor *goes to* Betty *as* Abigail *is trying to pull her hands down, calling "Betty!"*)

**Proctor** (*growing unnerved*). What's she doing? Girl, what ails you? Stop that wailing!

(*The singing has stopped in the midst of this, and now* Parris *rushes in.*)

**Parris.** What happened? What are you doing to her? Betty! (*He rushes to the bed, crying, "Betty, Betty!"* Mrs. Putnam *enters, feverish with curiosity, and with her* Thomas Putnam *and* Mercy Lewis. Parris, *at the bed, keeps lightly slapping* Betty's *face, while she moans and tries to get up.*)

**Abigail.** She heard you singin' and suddenly she's up and screamin'.

**Mrs. Putnam.** The psalm! The psalm! She cannot bear to hear the Lord's name!

---

23. **covenanted** (kŭv′ə-nən′tĭd): in Puritan religious practice, the men of a congregation would make an agreement, or a covenant, to govern the community.

**C**

**1**

**C**

## Customizing Instruction

### Students Acquiring English

**1** Students might not understand what Abigail means when she says, "You are no wintry man." She refers to winter, the coldest season of the year, to describe a human personality that is cold and without passion. She is saying that John Proctor is not like this—he is warm and passionate.

### Gifted and Talented

Ask students to recognize and analyze the persuasive techniques Abigail uses to win Proctor's affection. What arguments does she present, and what emotional tactics does she employ?

## Literary Analysis | STAGE DIRECTIONS

**A** What do the stage directions tell about Rebecca Nurse? What kind of person is she? How do you picture her?

**Possible Response:** Rebecca is an elderly and well-respected member of the community. She is 72 years old, white-haired, and walks with a cane. Everyone is quiet while she approaches Betty, and her presence seems to calm the child. She probably has a kind, wise face and alert, intelligent eyes.

## Reading Skills and Strategies: TAKING NOTES

**B** Have students use study strategies, such as notetaking, to better understand what the history between the Putnams and the Nurses adds to the plot of the play. Have them take notes on these stage directions.

**Possible Response:** The Putnams and the Nurses disputed over land ownership. The Nurses had been part of the group that prevented Bayley, Putnam's brother-in-law, from becoming minister. Friends and kin of the Nurses had broken away from Salem and established Topsfield, a separation that the Putnams likely resented.

## Active Reading
### USING A GRAPHIC ORGANIZER

**C** Students can use a graphic organizer to keep track of which characters believe there is witchcraft afoot in Salem and which do not.

| Believe there is witchcraft in Salem | Do not see evidence of witchcraft |
|---|---|
| Reverend Parris | Rebecca Nurse |
| Thomas Putnam | John Proctor |
| Mrs. Ann Putnam | |

---

**Parris.** No. God forbid. Mercy, run to the doctor! Tell him what's happened here! (*Mercy Lewis rushes out.*)

**Mrs. Putnam.** Mark it for a sign, mark it!

**A** (*Rebecca Nurse, seventy-two, enters. She is white-haired, leaning upon her walking-stick.*)

**Putnam** (*pointing at the whimpering* Betty). That is a notorious sign of witchcraft afoot, Goody Nurse, a prodigious[24] sign!

**Mrs. Putnam.** My mother told me that! When they cannot bear to hear the name of—

**Parris** (*trembling*). Rebecca, Rebecca, go to her, we're lost. She suddenly cannot bear to hear the Lord's—

**1** (*Giles Corey, eighty-three, enters. He is knotted with muscle, canny, inquisitive, and still powerful.*)

**Rebecca.** There is hard sickness here, Giles Corey, so please to keep the quiet.

**Giles.** I've not said a word. No one here can testify I've said a word. Is she going to fly again? I hear she flies.

**Putnam.** Man, be quiet now!

**A** (*Everything is quiet. Rebecca walks across the room to the bed. Gentleness exudes from her. Betty is quietly whimpering, eyes shut. Rebecca simply stands over the child, who gradually quiets.*)

And while they are so absorbed, we may put a word in for Rebecca. Rebecca was the wife of Francis Nurse, who, from all accounts, was one of those men for whom both sides of the argument had to have respect. He was called upon to <u>arbitrate</u> disputes as though he were an unofficial judge, and Rebecca also enjoyed the high opinion most people had for him. By the time of the delusion,[25] they had three hundred acres, and their children were settled in separate homesteads within the same estate. However, Francis had originally rented the land, and one theory has it that, as he gradually paid for it and raised his social status, there were those who resented his rise.

Another suggestion to explain the systematic campaign against Rebecca, and inferentially against Francis, is the land war he fought with his neighbors, one of whom was a Putnam. This squabble grew to the proportions of a battle in the woods between partisans of both sides, and it is said to have lasted for two days. As for Rebecca herself, the general opinion of her character was so high that to explain how anyone dared cry her out for a witch—and more, how adults could bring themselves to lay hands on her—we must look to the fields and boundaries of that time.

As we have seen, Thomas Putnam's man for the Salem ministry was Bayley. The Nurse clan had been in the faction that prevented Bayley's taking office. In addition, certain families allied to the Nurses by blood or friendship, and whose farms were contiguous with the Nurse farm or close to it, combined to break away from the Salem town authority and set up Topsfield, a new and independent entity whose existence was resented by old Salemites.

That the guiding hand behind the outcry was Putnam's is indicated by the fact that, as soon as it began, this Topsfield-Nurse faction absented themselves from church in protest and disbelief. It was Edward and Jonathan Putnam who signed the first complaint against Rebecca; and Thomas Putnam's little daughter was the one who fell into a fit at the hearing and pointed to Rebecca as her attacker. To top it all, Mrs. Putnam—who is now staring at the bewitched child on the bed—soon accused Rebecca's spirit of "tempting her to <u>iniquity</u>," a charge that had more truth in it than Mrs. Putnam could know. 🐦

---

24. **prodigious** (prə-dĭj′əs): extraordinary.
25. **delusion** (dĭ-lōō′zhən): witchcraft.

WORDS TO KNOW
**arbitrate** (är′bĭ-trāt) *v.* to judge or act as referee
**iniquity** (ĭ-nĭk′wĭ-tē) *n.* wickedness; immorality

178

---

## Teaching Options

### Mini Lesson — Grammar

**REGULAR AND IRREGULAR VERBS** Verbs can be either regular or irregular. A verb is regular if it forms the past and past participle by adding *-d* or *-ed* to the infinitive. A verb is irregular if it forms the past and past participle in some other way. Write these two sentences on the chalkboard:

Rebecca <u>asked</u> Giles Corey to keep quiet.
Giles had not <u>said</u> a word.

Underline the verbs as shown. Have students identify *asked* as the regular verb because it forms the past by adding *-ed,* and *said* as the irregular verb because it does not follow that rule.

**Exercises** In each sentence, have students underline the verb and identify it as regular or irregular.

1. Reverend Hale <u>studied</u> witchcraft. (*regular*)
2. Abigail <u>gazed</u> into John Proctor's eyes. (*regular*)

**Mrs. Putnam** (*astonished*). What have you done?

(Rebecca, *in thought, now leaves the bedside and sits.*)

**Parris** (*wondrous and relieved*). What do you make of it, Rebecca?

**Putnam** (*eagerly*). Goody Nurse, will you go to my Ruth and see if you can wake her?

**Rebecca** (*sitting*). I think she'll wake in time. Pray calm yourselves. I have eleven children, and I am twenty-six times a grandma, and I have seen them all through their silly seasons, and when it come on them they will run the Devil bow-legged keeping up with their mischief. I think she'll wake when she tires of it. A child's spirit is like a child, you can never catch it by running after it; you must stand still, and, for love, it will soon itself come back.

**Proctor.** Aye, that's the truth of it, Rebecca.

**Mrs. Putnam.** This is no silly season, Rebecca. My Ruth is bewildered, Rebecca; she cannot eat.

**Rebecca.** Perhaps she is not hungered yet. (*To Parris*) I hope you are not decided to go in search of loose spirits, Mr. Parris. I've heard promise of that outside.

**Parris.** A wide opinion's running in the parish that the Devil may be among us, and I would satisfy them that they are wrong.

**Proctor.** Then let you come out and call them wrong. Did you consult the wardens[26] before you called this minister to look for devils?

**Parris.** He is not coming to look for devils!

**Proctor.** Then what's he coming for?

**Putnam.** There be children dyin' in the village, Mister!

---

26. **wardens:** officers appointed to keep order.

The Nurse House

---

**Customizing Instruction**

**Students Acquiring English**

**1** Enable students to better understand Giles Corey by explaining the terms *canny* and *inquisitive*. *Canny* means "clever or knowing" and *inquisitive* means "intellectually curious."

**Less Proficient Readers**

**2** Use these questions to help students understand the characters' differing points of view on the children's illness.

• How does Rebecca explain Betty's and Ruth's sickness?

**Possible Response:** Rebecca feels that Betty is just acting like a child and that she will awaken when she is ready. She suggests that perhaps Ruth is not eating because she is not hungry.

• What is Putnam's interpretation of the children's condition?

**Possible Response:** He suspects that witchcraft or "loose spirits" are behind the illnesses.

• What is Proctor's opinion on the matter?

**Possible Response:** He agrees with Rebecca and sees no reason to suspect witchcraft.

---

**3.** Tituba <u>sang</u> her Barbados songs. (*irregular*)

**4.** The girls <u>danced</u> in the woods. (*regular*)

**5.** Thomas Putnam <u>spoke</u> negatively of many townspeople. (*irregular*)

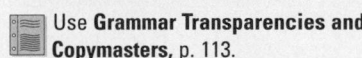 Use **Grammar Transparencies and Copymasters**, p. 113.

 Use McDougal Littell's *Language Network* for more instruction and practice on verbs.

**Literary Analysis: CHARACTERIZATION**

**A** Ask students what this dialogue reveals about Reverend Parris and about John Proctor.

**Possible Response:** Parris has a fragile ego and feels threatened by anyone who questions or challenges him. As a Harvard-educated minister, he feels that he deserves better pay and greater respect from his parish. Proctor is insightful, self-confident, and has a strong sense of justice. He distrusts Parris and criticizes him openly.

**Proctor.** I seen none dyin'. This society will not be a bag to swing around your head, Mr. Putnam. (*To Parris*) Did you call a meeting before you—?

**Putnam.** I am sick of meetings; cannot the man turn his head without he have a meeting?

**Proctor.** He may turn his head, but not to Hell!

**Rebecca.** Pray, John, be calm. (*Pause. He defers to her.*) Mr. Parris, I think you'd best send Reverend Hale back as soon as he come. This will set us all to arguin' again in the society, and we thought to have peace this year. I think we ought rely on the doctor now, and good prayer.

**Mrs. Putnam.** Rebecca, the doctor's baffled!

**Rebecca.** If so he is, then let us go to God for the cause of it. There is prodigious danger in the seeking of loose spirits. I fear it, I fear it. Let us rather blame ourselves and—

**1**

**Putnam.** How may we blame ourselves? I am one of nine sons; the Putnam seed have peopled this province. And yet I have but one child left of eight—and now she shrivels!

**Rebecca.** I cannot fathom that.

**Mrs. Putnam** (*with a growing edge of sarcasm*). But I must! You think it God's work you should never lose a child, nor grandchild either, and I bury all but one? There are wheels within wheels in this village, and fires within fires!

**Putnam** (*to Parris*). When Reverend Hale comes, you will proceed to look for signs of witchcraft here.

**2**

**Proctor** (*to Putnam*). You cannot command Mr. Parris. We vote by name in this society, not by acreage.

**Putnam.** I never heard you worried so on this society, Mr. Proctor. I do not think I saw you at Sabbath meeting since snow flew.

**3**

**Proctor.** I have trouble enough without I come five mile to hear him preach only hellfire and bloody damnation. Take it to heart, Mr. Parris. There are many others who stay away from church these days because you hardly ever mention God any more.

**Parris** (*now aroused*). Why, that's a drastic charge!

**Rebecca.** It's somewhat true; there are many that quail[27] to bring their children—

**Parris.** I do not preach for children, Rebecca. It is not the children who are unmindful of their obligations toward this ministry.

**Rebecca.** Are there really those unmindful?

**Parris.** I should say the better half of Salem village—

**Putnam.** And more than that!

**Parris.** Where is my wood? My contract provides I be supplied with all my firewood. I am waiting since November for a stick, and even in November I had to show my frostbitten hands like some London beggar!

**Giles.** You are allowed six pound a year to buy your wood, Mr. Parris.

**Parris.** I regard that six pound as part of my salary. I am paid little enough without I spend six pound on firewood.

**Proctor.** Sixty, plus six for firewood—

**Parris.** The salary is sixty-six pound, Mr. Proctor! I am not some preaching farmer with a book under my arm; I am a graduate of Harvard College.

**Giles.** Aye, and well instructed in arithmetic!

**Parris.** Mr. Corey, you will look far for a man of my kind at sixty pound a year! I am not used to this poverty; I left a thrifty business in the Barbados to serve the Lord. I do not fathom it, why am I persecuted here? I cannot offer one proposition but there be a howling riot of argument. I have often wondered if the Devil be in it somewhere; I cannot understand you people otherwise.

**Proctor.** Mr. Parris, you are the first minister ever did demand the deed to this house—

---

27. **quail:** fear.

**Parris.** Man! Don't a minister deserve a house to live in?

**Proctor.** To live in, yes. But to ask ownership is like you shall own the meeting house itself; the last meeting I were at you spoke so long on deeds and mortgages I thought it were an auction.

**Parris.** I want a mark of confidence, is all! I am your third preacher in seven years. I do not wish to be put out like the cat whenever some majority feels the whim. You people seem not to comprehend that a minister is the Lord's man in the parish; a minister is not to be so lightly crossed and contradicted—

**Putnam.** Aye!

**Parris.** There is either obedience or the church will burn like Hell is burning!

**Proctor.** Can you speak one minute without we land in Hell again? I am sick of Hell!

**Parris.** It is not for you to say what is good for you to hear!

**Proctor.** I may speak my heart, I think!

**Parris** (*in a fury*). What, are we Quakers?[28] We are not Quakers here yet, Mr. Proctor. And you may tell that to your followers!

**Proctor.** My followers!

**Parris** (*now he's out with it*). There is a party in this church. I am not blind; there is a faction and a party.

**Proctor.** Against you?

**Putnam.** Against him and all authority!

**Proctor.** Why, then I must find it and join it.

(*There is shock among the others.*)

**Rebecca.** He does not mean that.

**Putnam.** He confessed it now!

**Proctor.** I mean it solemnly, Rebecca; I like not the smell of this "authority."

**Rebecca.** No, you cannot break charity[29] with your minister. You are another kind, John. Clasp his hand, make your peace.

**Proctor.** I have a crop to sow and lumber to drag home. (*He goes angrily to the door and turns to*

Corey *with a smile*.) What say you, Giles, let's find the party. He says there's a party.

**Giles.** I've changed my opinion of this man, John. Mr. Parris, I beg your pardon. I never thought you had so much iron in you.

**Parris** (*surprised*). Why, thank you, Giles!

**Giles.** It suggests to the mind what the trouble be among us all these years. (*To all*) Think on it. Wherefore is everybody suing everybody else? Think on it now, it's a deep thing, and dark as a pit. I have been six time in court this year—

**Proctor** (*familiarly, with warmth, although he knows he is approaching the edge of Giles' tolerance with this*). Is it the Devil's fault that a man cannot say you good morning without you clap him for defamation?[30] You're old, Giles, and you're not hearin' so well as you did.

**Giles** (*he cannot be crossed*). John Proctor, I have only last month collected four pound damages for you publicly sayin' I burned the roof off your house, and I—

**Proctor** (*laughing*). I never said no such thing, but I've paid you for it, so I hope I can call you deaf without charge. Now come along, Giles, and help me drag my lumber home.

**Putnam.** A moment, Mr. Proctor. What lumber is that you're draggin', if I may ask you?

**Proctor.** My lumber. From out my forest by the riverside.

**Putnam.** Why, we are surely gone wild this year. What anarchy[31] is this? That tract is in my bounds, it's in my bounds, Mr. Proctor.

**Proctor.** In your bounds! (*Indicating* Rebecca) I bought that tract from Goody Nurse's husband five months ago.

---

28. **Quakers:** a radical English religious sect, much hated by the Puritans, who often "spoke their heart" during their religious meetings.

29. **break charity:** break off; end the relationship.

30. **clap . . . defamation** (klăp . . . dĕf'ə-mā'shən): imprison him for slander.

31. **anarchy** (ăn'ər-kē): disorder and confusion.

## Customizing Instruction

### Students Acquiring English

**1** Help students better understand the dialogue between Mrs. Putnam and Rebecca by explaining the words *baffled, prodigious,* and *fathom. Baffled* means "confused," *fathom* means "comprehend fully," and *prodigious* means "appalling."

The following words and phrases may also be difficult for Students Acquiring English:

- *acreage:* the amount of land a person owns
- *pound:* a British unit of money used in the American colonies
- *contradicted:* challenged, fought with
- *wherefore:* why
- *in my bounds:* part of my property

### Less Proficient Readers

**2** Ask students to rephrase Proctor's statement in their own words.

**Possible Response:** Putnam cannot tell Parris whether or not to proceed with the witch-hunt. In Salem, each person has a vote on such matters; the wealthiest person does not decide by himself.

**3** Ask students to discuss Putnam's accusation of Proctor.

**Possible Response:** Putnam says that Proctor has not attended church since last winter.

What reason does Proctor give for avoiding church?

**Possible Response:** Proctor does not go to church because Parris preaches only about hell and damnation.

**Literary Analysis: FORESHADOWING**

**(A)** Hale is thought to be an expert in detecting witchery. Have students read this passage and tell what Reverend Hale's experience with the "witch in his parish" may foreshadow.

**Possible Response:** Hale jumped incorrectly to the conclusion of witchcraft before, and he may do so again. On the other hand, he applied "searching scrutiny" to the woman in his parish and decided that she was not a witch after all, so perhaps he will show moderation and good judgment in Salem.

**Reading Skills and Strategies: TAKING NOTES**

Students can use study strategies such as notetaking to better understand this text. Have them take notes on the information Miller has offered thus far. Give them the following prompts for each paragraph.

• Why is the Devil a necessity for most people?

**Possible Response:** because it is difficult to conceive of good unless we can contrast it with evil; because the Devil can be used as a weapon to control people

• In what situations, besides Salem in 1692, has the Devil been used against people?

**Possible Response:** The Catholic Church used the Devil to justify the Inquisition; Luther was accused of alliance with the Devil and accused his enemies of the same; Communist countries in the 1950s viewed capitalism as diabolical; Americans in the 1950s demonized communism.°

**Putnam.** He had no right to sell it. It stands clear in my grandfather's will that all the land between the river and—

**Proctor.** Your grandfather had a habit of willing land that never belonged to him, if I may say it plain.

**Giles.** That's God's truth; he nearly willed away my north pasture but he knew I'd break his fingers before he'd set his name to it. Let's get your lumber home, John. I feel a sudden will to work coming on.

**Putnam.** You load one oak of mine and you'll fight to drag it home!

**Giles.** Aye, and we'll win too, Putnam—this fool and I. Come on! (*He turns to* Proctor *and starts out.*)

**Putnam.** I'll have my men on you, Corey! I'll clap a writ on you!

(*Enter* Reverend John Hale *of Beverly.*)

Reverend Hale

Mr. Hale is nearing forty, a tight-skinned, eager-eyed intellectual. This is a beloved errand for him; on being called here to <u>ascertain</u> witchcraft he felt the pride of the specialist whose unique knowledge has at last been publicly called for. Like almost all men of learning, he spent a good deal of his time pondering the invisible world, especially since he had himself encountered a witch in his parish not long before. That **(A)** woman, however, turned into a mere pest under his searching scrutiny, and the child she had allegedly been afflicting recovered her normal behavior after Hale had given her his kindness and a few days of rest in his own house. However, that experience never raised a doubt in his mind as to the reality of the underworld or the existence of Lucifer's many-faced lieutenants. And his belief is not to his discredit. Better minds than Hale's were—and still are—convinced that there is a society of spirits beyond our ken. One cannot help noting that one of his lines has never yet raised a laugh in any audience that has seen this play; it is his assurance that "We cannot look to superstition in this. The Devil is precise." Evidently we are not quite certain even now whether diabolism is holy and not to be scoffed at. And it is no accident that we should be so bemused.

Like Reverend Hale and the others on this stage, we conceive the Devil as a necessary part of a respectable view of cosmology.[32] Ours is a divided empire in which certain ideas and emotions and actions are of God, and their opposites are of Lucifer. It is as impossible for most men to conceive of a morality without sin as of an earth without "sky." Since 1692 a great but superficial change has wiped out God's beard and the Devil's horns, but the world is still gripped between two diametrically opposed absolutes. The concept of unity, in which positive and negative are attributes of the same force, in which good and evil are relative, ever-changing, and always joined to the same phenomenon—such a concept is still reserved to the physical sciences and to the few who have grasped the history of ideas. When it is recalled that until the Christian era the underworld was never regarded as a hostile area, that all gods were useful and essentially friendly to man despite occasional lapses; when we see the steady and methodical inculcation into humanity of the idea

---

32. **cosmology** (kŏz-mŏl'ə-jē): a branch of philosophy dealing with the structure of the universe.

WORDS TO KNOW    **ascertain** (ăs'ər-tān') *v.* to find out

of man's worthlessness—until redeemed—the necessity of the Devil may become evident as a weapon, a weapon designed and used time and time again in every age to whip men into a surrender to a particular church or church-state.

Our difficulty in believing the—for want of a better word—political inspiration of the Devil is due in great part to the fact that he is called up and damned not only by our social antagonists but by our own side, whatever it may be. The Catholic Church, through its Inquisition,[33] is famous for cultivating Lucifer as the arch-fiend, but the Church's enemies relied no less upon the Old Boy to keep the human mind enthralled. Luther[34] was himself accused of alliance with Hell, and he in turn accused his enemies. To complicate matters further, he believed that he had had contact with the Devil and had argued theology with him. I am not surprised at this, for at my own university a professor of history—a Lutheran, by the way—used to assemble his graduate students, draw the shades, and commune in the classroom with Erasmus.[35] He was never, to my knowledge, officially scoffed at for this, the reason being that the university officials, like most of us, are the children of a history which still sucks at the Devil's teats. At this writing, only England has held back before the temptations of contemporary diabolism. In the countries of the Communist ideology, all resistance of any import is linked to the totally malign capitalist succubi, and in America any man who is not reactionary in his views is open to the charge of alliance with the Red hell. Political opposition, thereby, is given an inhumane overlay which then justifies the abrogation of all normally applied customs of civilized intercourse. A political policy is equated with moral right, and opposition to it with diabolical malevolence. Once such an equation is effectively made, society becomes a congerie of plots and counterplots, and the main role of government changes from that of the arbiter to that of the scourge of God.

The results of this process are no different now from what they ever were, except sometimes in the degree of cruelty inflicted, and not always even in that department. Normally the actions and deeds of a man were all that society felt comfortable in judging. The secret intent of an action was left to the ministers, priests, and rabbis to deal with. When diabolism rises, however, actions are the least important manifests of the true nature of a man. The Devil, as Reverend Hale said, is a wily one, and, until an hour before he fell, even God thought him beautiful in Heaven.

The analogy, however, seems to falter when one considers that, while there were no witches then, there are Communists and capitalists now, and in each camp there is certain proof that spies of each side are at work undermining the other. But this is a snobbish objection and not at all warranted by the facts. I have no doubt that people *were* communing with, and even worshiping, the Devil in Salem, and if the whole truth could be known in this case, as it is in others, we should discover a regular and conventionalized propitiation of the dark spirit. One certain evidence of this is the confession of Tituba, the slave of Reverend Parris, and another is the behavior of the children who were known to have indulged in sorceries with her.

There are accounts of similar *klatches* in Europe, where the daughters of the towns would assemble at night and, sometimes with fetishes, sometimes with a selected young man, give themselves to love, with some bastardly results. The Church, sharp-eyed as it must be when gods long dead are brought to life, condemned these orgies as witchcraft and interpreted them, rightly, as a resurgence of the Dionysiac[36] forces it had crushed long before. Sex, sin, and the Devil were early

---

33. **Inquisition** (ĭn′kwĭ-zĭsh′ən): a tribunal in the Roman Catholic Church dedicated to the discovery and punishment of heresy.

34. **Luther:** Martin Luther (1483–1546), the German theologian who led the Protestant Reformation.

35. **Erasmus** (ĭ-răz′məs): Desiderius Erasmus (1466?–1536), a Dutch scholar and humanist who sought to restore simple Christian faith by a study of the Scriptures and classical texts.

36. **Dionysiac** (dī′-ə-nĭs′ē-ăk′) **wild and chaotic;** refers to Dionysus, the Greek god of wine and madness.

THE CRUCIBLE  **183**

**A** What important details do these stage directions reveal about Hale's view of himself and his mission in Salem?

**Possible Response:** Hale believes that his intellectual achievements put him in league with the best minds of Europe. He has a lofty view of his mission; he is eager to do whatever is necessary, including fight with the Devil, to ensure that goodness prevails in Salem.

### Reading Skills and Strategies: SUMMARIZING

**B** Ask students to summarize how Hale has described the Devil.

**Possible Response:** Hale says that the Devil leaves precise marks. By consulting scholarly books, it is possible to recognize these marks and find the Devil beneath his many disguises. The Devil can be defeated only if he can be detected and challenged.

---

linked, and so they continued to be in Salem, and are today. From all accounts there are no more puritanical mores in the world than those enforced by the Communists in Russia, where women's fashions, for instance, are as prudent and all-covering as any American Baptist would desire. The divorce laws lay a tremendous responsibility on the father for the care of his children. Even the laxity of divorce regulations in the early years of the revolution was undoubtedly a revulsion from the nineteenth-century Victorian immobility of marriage and the consequent hypocrisy that developed from it. If for no other reasons, a state so powerful, so jealous of the uniformity of its citizens, cannot long tolerate the atomization of the family. And yet, in American eyes at least, there remains the conviction that the Russian attitude toward women is lascivious. It is the Devil working again, just as he is working within the Slav[37] who is shocked at the very idea of a woman's disrobing herself in a burlesque show. Our opposites are always robed in sexual sin, and it is from this unconscious conviction that demonology gains both its attractive sensuality and its capacity to infuriate and frighten.

Coming into Salem now, Reverend Hale conceives of himself much as a young doctor on his first call. His painfully acquired armory of symptoms, catchwords, and diagnostic procedures are now to be put to use at last. The road from Beverly is unusually busy this morning, and he has passed a hundred rumors that make him smile at the ignorance of the yeomanry[38] in this most precise science. He feels himself allied with the best minds of Europe—kings, philosophers, scientists, and ecclesiasts[39] of all churches. His goal is light, goodness and its preservation, and he knows the exaltation of the blessed whose intelligence, sharpened by minute examinations of enormous tracts, is finally called upon to face what may be a bloody fight with the Fiend himself. 🔥

*(He appears loaded down with half a dozen heavy books.)*

**Hale.** Pray you, someone take these!

**Parris** (*delighted*). Mr. Hale! Oh! it's good to see you again! (*Taking some books*) My, they're heavy!

**Hale** (*setting down his books*). They must be; they are weighted with authority.

**Parris** (*a little scared*). Well, you do come prepared!

**Hale.** We shall need hard study if it comes to tracking down the Old Boy. (*Noticing* Rebecca) You cannot be Rebecca Nurse?

**Rebecca.** I am, sir. Do you know me?

**Hale.** It's strange how I knew you, but I suppose you look as such a good soul should. We have all heard of your great charities in Beverly.

**Parris.** Do you know this gentleman? Mr. Thomas Putnam. And his good wife Ann.

**Hale.** Putnam! I had not expected such distinguished company, sir.

**Putnam** (*pleased*). It does not seem to help us today, Mr. Hale. We look to you to come to our house and save our child.

**Hale.** Your child ails too?

**Mrs. Putnam.** Her soul, her soul seems flown away. She sleeps and yet she walks . . .

**Putnam.** She cannot eat.

**Hale.** Cannot eat! (*Thinks on it. Then, to* Proctor *and* Giles Corey) Do you men have afflicted children?

**Parris.** No, no, these are farmers. John Proctor—

**Giles Corey.** He don't believe in witches.

**Proctor** (*to* Hale). I never spoke on witches one way or the other. Will you come, Giles?

**Giles.** No—no, John, I think not. I have some few queer questions of my own to ask this fellow.

---

37. **Slav** (släv): a generic reference to Russians and other Slavic-speaking peoples of Eastern Europe who were under the control of the former Soviet Union.

38. **yeomanry** (yō′mən-rē): the farmers; common people.

39. **ecclesiasts** (ĭ-klē′zē-ăsts): religious officials; clergy.

---

## Teaching Options

### ✓ Assessment **Standardized Test Practice**

**MAKING INFERENCES AND DRAWING CONCLUSIONS** Many standardized tests ask students to make inferences and draw conclusions. Both of these skills require that the student go beyond what is directly stated in the text. Read aloud or write on the chalkboard the following question: Which word best describes how Rebecca feels about Hale's intention to determine whether Betty is afflicted by the Devil?

**A.** angry
**B.** appalled
**C.** supportive

Encourage students to return to the text to find clues. Discuss each possible answer and the textual evidence for or against it. A does not seem accurate, because there are no stage directions implying that Rebecca is angry, and she says, "I go to God for

**Proctor.** I've heard you to be a sensible man, Mr. Hale. I hope you'll leave some of it in Salem.

(Proctor *goes*. Hale *stands embarrassed for an instant*.)

**Parris** (*quickly*). Will you look at my daughter, sir? (*Leads* Hale *to the bed*.) She has tried to leap out the window; we discovered her this morning on the highroad, waving her arms as though she'd fly.

**Hale** (*narrowing his eyes*). Tries to fly.

**Putnam.** She cannot bear to hear the Lord's name, Mr. Hale; that's a sure sign of witchcraft afloat.

**Hale** (*holding up his hands*). No, no. Now let me instruct you. We cannot look to superstition in this. The Devil is precise; the marks of his presence are definite as stone, and I must tell you all that I shall not proceed unless you are prepared to believe me if I should find no bruise of hell upon her.

**Parris.** It is agreed, sir—it is agreed—we will abide by your judgment.

**Hale.** Good then. (*He goes to the bed, looks down at* Betty. *To* Parris) Now, sir, what were your first warning of this strangeness?

**Parris.** Why, sir—I discovered her—(*indicating* Abigail) and my niece and ten or twelve of the other girls, dancing in the forest last night.

**Hale** (*surprised*). You permit dancing?

**Parris.** No, no, it were secret—

**Mrs. Putnam** (*unable to wait*). Mr. Parris's slave has knowledge of conjurin', sir.

**Parris** (*to* Mrs. Putnam). We cannot be sure of that, Goody Ann—

**Mrs. Putnam** (*frightened, very softly*). I know it, sir. I sent my child—she should learn from Tituba who murdered her sisters.

**Rebecca** (*horrified*). Goody Ann! You sent a child to conjure up the dead?

**Mrs. Putnam.** Let God blame me, not you, not you, Rebecca! I'll not have you judging me any more! (*To* Hale) Is it a natural work to lose seven children before they live a day?

**Parris.** Sssh!

(Rebecca, *with great pain, turns her face away. There is a pause*.)

**Hale.** Seven dead in childbirth.

**Mrs. Putnam** (*softly*). Aye. (*Her voice breaks; she looks up at him. Silence.* Hale *is impressed.* Parris *looks to him. He goes to his books, opens one, turns pages, then reads. All wait, avidly.*)

**Parris** (*hushed*). What book is that?

**Mrs. Putnam.** What's there, sir?

**Hale** (*with a tasty love of intellectual pursuit*). Here is all the invisible world, caught, defined, and calculated. In these books the Devil stands stripped of all his brute disguises. Here are all your familiar spirits—your incubi and succubi;[40] your witches that go by land, by air, and by sea; your wizards of the night and of the day. Have no fear now—we shall find him out if he has come among us, and I mean to crush him utterly if he has shown his face! (*He starts for the bed*.)

**Rebecca.** Will it hurt the child, sir?

**Hale.** I cannot tell. If she is truly in the Devil's grip we may have to rip and tear to get her free.

**Rebecca.** I think I'll go, then. I am too old for this. (*She rises*.)

**Parris** (*striving for conviction*). Why, Rebecca, we may open up the boil of all our troubles today!

**Rebecca.** Let us hope for that. I go to God for you, sir.

**Parris** (*with trepidation—and resentment*). I hope you do not mean we go to Satan here! (*Slight pause*.)

**Rebecca.** I wish I knew. (*She goes out; they feel resentful of her note of moral superiority*.)

**Putnam** (*abruptly*). Come, Mr. Hale, let's get on. Sit you here.

B

---

40. **incubi** (ĭn′kyə-bī′) **and succubi** (sŭk′yə-bī′): male and female demons.

### Students Acquiring English

**1** Explain that *pray you* is an archaic expression that means "please." Then discuss the phrase *weighted with authority*. Hale is playing with the word *weight*. Parris says the books are heavy, and Hale responds that they are "weighted" (heavy) because they have so much authority.

### Multiple Learning Styles
**Kinesthetic Learners**

**2** Have students consider the stage directions and dialogue involving Reverend Hale to this point and consider what kind of presence he might have on stage. Ask volunteers to act out a few lines of dialogue, using gestures, postures, and facial expressions that aptly characterize Hale. Suggest that they infuse their characterizations with subtle humor if appropriate.

you, sir." C is incorrect because Rebecca indicates that she is not sure whether Hale and the others are doing the Devil's work. B is the best choice, because Rebecca leaves the room rather than witness Hale's work, and she makes a remark indicating her moral superiority as she goes.

## Reading and Analyzing

### Literary Analysis: FORESHADOWING

**A** Ask students to discuss what Giles Corey's statement may foreshadow.

**Possible Response:** Giles says that when his wife reads, he cannot pray, and when she stops reading, he is able to pray again. Perhaps people will regard this as evidence that his wife is a witch.

### Literary Analysis: CHARACTERIZATION

**B** Discuss with students how Giles Corey is portrayed in this passage.

**Possible Response:** Giles Corey was an elderly man the townspeople always suspected of wrongdoing. He cared little about what others thought of him, nor did he care much about church. He irritated people, but he was brave and innocent at the same time.

**Giles.** Mr. Hale, I have always wanted to ask a learned man—what signifies the readin' of strange books?

**Hale.** What books?

**Giles.** I cannot tell; she hides them.

**Hale.** Who does this?

**Giles.** Martha, my wife. I have waked at night many a time and found her in a corner, readin' of a book. Now what do you make of that?

**Hale.** Why, that's not necessarily—

**Giles.** It discomfits me! Last night—mark this—I tried and tried and could not say my prayers. And then she close her book and walks out of the house, and suddenly—mark this—I could pray again!

Old Giles must be spoken for, if only because his fate was to be so remarkable and so different from that of all the others. He was in his early eighties at this time, and was the most comical hero in the history. No man has ever been blamed for so much. If a cow was missed, the first thought was to look for her around Corey's house; a fire blazing up at night brought suspicion of arson to his door. He didn't give a hoot for public opinion, and only in his last years—after he had married Martha—did he bother much with the church. That she stopped his prayer is very probable, but he forgot to say that he'd only recently learned any prayers and it didn't take much to make him stumble over them. He was a crank and a nuisance, but withal a deeply innocent and brave man. In court once, he was asked if it were true that he had been frightened by the strange behavior of a hog and had then said he knew it to be the Devil in an animal's shape. "What frighted you?" he was asked. He forgot everything but the word "frighted," and instantly replied, "I do not know that I ever spoke that word in my life."

**Hale.** Ah! The stoppage of prayer—that is strange. I'll speak further on that with you.

**Giles.** I'm not sayin' she's touched the Devil, now, but I'd admire to know what books she reads and why she hides them. She'll not answer me, y' see.

**Hale.** Aye, we'll discuss it. (*To all*) Now mark me, if the Devil is in her you will witness some frightful wonders in this room, so please to keep your wits about you. Mr. Putnam, stand close in case she flies. Now, Betty, dear, will you sit up? (Putnam *comes in closer, ready-handed.* Hale *sits* Betty *up, but she hangs limp in his hands.*) Hmmm. (*He observes her carefully. The others watch breathlessly.*) Can you hear me? I am John Hale, minister of Beverly. I have come to help you, dear. Do you remember my two little girls in Beverly? (*She does not stir in his hands.*)

**Parris** (*in fright*). How can it be the Devil? Why would he choose my house to strike? We have all manner of licentious[41] people in the village!

**Hale.** What victory would the Devil have to win a soul already bad? It is the best the Devil wants, and who is better than the minister?

**Giles.** That's deep, Mr. Parris, deep, deep!

**Parris** (*with resolution now*). Betty! Answer Mr. Hale! Betty!

**Hale.** Does someone afflict you, child? It need not be a woman, mind you, or a man. Perhaps some bird invisible to others comes to you—perhaps a pig, a mouse, or any beast at all. Is there some figure bids you fly? (*The child remains limp in his hands. In silence he lays her back on the pillow. Now, holding out his hands toward her, he intones*) In nomine Domini Sabaoth sui filiique ite ad infernos.[42] (*She does not stir. He turns to* Abigail, *his eyes narrowing.*) Abigail, what sort of dancing were you doing with her in the forest?

---

41. **licentious** (lĭ-sĕn′shəs): lacking moral restraint.
42. **In . . . infernos** *Latin:* "In the name of the Father and Son, get thee back to Hell."

## Teaching Options

### Cross Curricular Link **History**

**BARBADOS** Tituba was from Barbados, an island in the West Indies. Barbados was originally inhabited by the Arawak and the Carib, although it was uninhabited when the first white settlers arrived from England in 1627. West African slaves were brought there during the 1600s and the 1700s. Africans brought to the West Indies cultural practices that contributed to the development of voodoo, which is characterized by sorcery and spirit possession. The Puritans did not know or understand Tituba's culture, and anything they did not know, they assumed to be evil. Therefore, Tituba was the perfect target for accusations of witchery.

**Abigail.** Why—common dancing is all.

**Parris.** I think I ought to say that I—I saw a kettle in the grass where they were dancing.

**Abigail.** That were only soup.

**Hale.** What sort of soup were in this kettle, Abigail?

**Abigail.** Why, it were beans—and lentils, I think, and—

**Hale.** Mr. Parris, you did not notice, did you, any living thing in the kettle? A mouse, perhaps, a spider, a frog—?

**Parris** (*fearfully*). I—do believe there were some movement—in the soup.

**Abigail.** That jumped in, we never put it in!

**Hale** (*quickly*). What jumped in?

**Abigail.** Why, a very little frog jumped—

**Parris.** A frog, Abby!

**Hale** (*grasping* Abigail). Abigail, it may be your cousin is dying. Did you call the Devil last night?

**Abigail.** I never called him! Tituba, Tituba . . .

**Parris** (*blanched*).[43] She called the Devil?

**Hale.** I should like to speak with Tituba.

**Parris.** Goody Ann, will you bring her up? (*Mrs. Putnam* exits.)

**Hale.** How did she call him?

**Abigail.** I know not—she spoke Barbados.

**Hale.** Did you feel any strangeness when she called him? A sudden cold wind, perhaps? A trembling below the ground?

**Abigail.** I didn't see no Devil! (*Shaking* Betty) Betty, wake up. Betty! Betty!

**Hale.** You cannot evade me, Abigail. Did your cousin drink any of the brew in that kettle?

**Abigail.** She never drank it!

**Hale.** Did you drink it?

**Abigail.** No, sir!

**Hale.** Did Tituba ask you to drink it?

**Abigail.** She tried, but I refused.

**Hale.** Why are you concealing? Have you sold yourself to Lucifer?

**Abigail.** I never sold myself! I'm a good girl! I'm a proper girl!

(*Mrs. Putnam* enters with Tituba, *and instantly* Abigail *points at* Tituba.)

**Abigail.** She made me do it! She made Betty do it!

**Tituba** (*shocked and angry*). Abby!

**Abigail.** She makes me drink blood!

**Parris.** Blood!!

**Mrs. Putnam.** My baby's blood?

**Tituba.** No, no, chicken blood. I give she chicken blood!

**Hale.** Woman, have you enlisted these children for the Devil?

**Tituba.** No, no, sir, I don't truck with no Devil!

**Hale.** Why can she not wake? Are you silencing this child?

**Tituba.** I love me Betty!

**Hale.** You have sent your spirit out upon this child, have you not? Are you gathering souls for the Devil?

**Abigail.** She sends her spirit on me in church; she makes me laugh at prayer!

**Parris.** She have often laughed at prayer!

**Abigail.** She comes to me every night to go and drink blood!

**Tituba.** You beg me to conjure! She beg me make charm—

**Abigail.** Don't lie! (*To* Hale) She comes to me while I sleep; she's always making me dream corruptions![44]

**Tituba.** Why you say that, Abby?

**Abigail.** Sometimes I wake and find myself standing in the open doorway and not a stitch on my body! I always hear her laughing in my sleep. I hear her singing her Barbados songs and tempting me with—

---

43. **blanched:** turned pale with shock or fear.

44. **corruptions:** evil, immoral thoughts.

## Reading Skills and Strategies: DRAWING CONCLUSIONS

**A** Have students draw a conclusion about why Tituba makes these particular claims. If necessary, suggest that they refer back to the last two paragraphs of Miller's stage directions on pages 168–169.

**Possible Response:** Tituba is drawing on her own fantasies of revenge against her master, who took her away from her home in Barbados and holds the power of life and death over her. She herself, not the Devil, sees him as a cruel man who deserves death, and she has dreamed of killing him and returning home.

## Active Reading

**USING A GRAPHIC ORGANIZER**

This drama has an overall plot, but each act also has a self-contained plot with a problem and a resolution. Help students organize information from Act One by filling in a story map like the one below. Students can work in pairs, and they can use their story maps to retell the events in this act to one another.

### Story Map

| Setting |
|---|
| Main Characters |
| Problem |
| Events |
| Resolution |

---

**Tituba.** Mister Reverend, I never—

**Hale** (*resolved now*). Tituba, I want you to wake this child.

**Tituba.** I have no power on this child, sir.

**Hale.** You most certainly do, and you will free her from it now! When did you compact with the Devil?

**Tituba.** I don't compact with no Devil!

**Parris.** You will confess yourself or I will take you out and whip you to your death, Tituba!

**Putnam.** This woman must be hanged! She must be taken and hanged!

**Tituba** (*terrified, falls to her knees*). No, no, don't hang Tituba! I tell him I don't desire to work for him, sir.

**Parris.** The Devil?

**Hale.** Then you saw him! (Tituba *weeps*.) Now Tituba, I know that when we bind ourselves to Hell it is very hard to break with it. We are going to help you tear yourself free—

**1** **Tituba** (*frightened by the coming process*). Mister Reverend, I do believe somebody else be witchin' these children.

**Hale.** Who?

**Tituba.** I don't know, sir, but the Devil got him numerous witches.

**Hale.** Does he! It is a clue. Tituba, look into my eyes. Come, look into me. (*She raises her eyes to his fearfully.*) You would be a good Christian woman, would you not, Tituba?

**Tituba.** Aye, sir, a good Christian woman.

**Hale.** And you love these little children?

**Tituba.** Oh, yes, sir, I don't desire to hurt little children.

**Hale.** And you love God, Tituba?

**Tituba.** I love God with all my bein'.

**Hale.** Now, in God's holy name—

**Tituba.** Bless Him. Bless Him. (*She is rocking on her knees, sobbing in terror.*)

**Hale.** And to His glory—

**Tituba.** Eternal glory. Bless Him—bless God . . .

**Hale.** Open yourself, Tituba—open yourself and let God's holy light shine on you.

**Tituba.** Oh, bless the Lord.

**Hale.** When the Devil comes to you does he ever come—with another person? (*She stares up into his face.*) Perhaps another person in the village? Someone you know.

**Parris.** Who came with him?

**Putnam.** Sarah Good? Did you ever see Sarah Good with him? Or Osburn?

**Parris.** Was it man or woman came with him?

**Tituba.** Man or woman. Was—was woman.

**Parris.** What woman? A woman, you said. What woman?

**Tituba.** It was black dark, and I—

**Parris.** You could see him, why could you not see her?

**Tituba.** Well, they was always talking; they was always runnin' round and carryin' on—

**Parris.** You mean out of Salem? Salem witches?

**Tituba.** I believe so, yes, sir.

(*Now Hale takes her hand. She is surprised.*)

**Hale.** Tituba. You must have no fear to tell us who they are, do you understand? We will protect you. The Devil can never overcome a minister. You know that, do you not?

**Tituba** (*kisses Hale's hand*). Aye, sir, oh, I do.

**Hale.** You have confessed yourself to witchcraft, and that speaks a wish to come to Heaven's side. And we will bless you, Tituba.

**Tituba** (*deeply relieved*). Oh, God bless you, Mr. Hale!

**Hale** (*with rising exaltation*). You are God's instrument put in our hands to discover the Devil's agents among us. You are selected, Tituba, you are chosen to help us cleanse our village. So speak utterly, Tituba, turn your back on him and face God—face God, Tituba, and God will protect you.

---

## Teaching Options

### ✓ Assessment Informal Assessment

**ALTERNATIVE ENDING** You can informally assess students' understanding of the selection by having them imagine an alternative ending in which Tituba does not confess to witchcraft. Students' writing might describe, for example, an honest testimony by Tituba that focuses Hale's attention back on Abigail.

**RUBRIC**

**3 Full Accomplishment** Student writing reflects a full understanding of Abigail's character and the events leading up to Abigail's accusation of Tituba.

**2 Substantial Accomplishment** Student writing shows a general understanding of the events but does not fully reflect the character of Abigail.

**1 Little or Partial Accomplishment** Student writing displays little or no understanding of the events surrounding the accusation against Tituba or the character of Abigail.

**Tituba** (*joining with him*). Oh, God, protect Tituba!

**Hale** (*kindly*). Who came to you with the Devil? Two? Three? Four? How many?

(*Tituba pants, and begins rocking back and forth again, staring ahead.*)

**Tituba.** There was four. There was four.

**Parris** (*pressing in on her*). Who? Who? Their names, their names!

**Tituba** (*suddenly bursting out*). Oh, how many times he bid me kill you, Mr. Parris!

**Parris.** Kill me!

**Tituba** (*in a fury*). He say Mr. Parris must be kill! Mr. Parris no goodly man, Mr. Parris mean man and no gentle man, and he bid me rise out of my bed and cut your throat! (*They gasp.*) But I tell him "No! I don't hate that man. I don't want kill that man." But he say, "You work for me, Tituba, and I make you free! I give you pretty dress to wear, and put you way high up in the air, and you gone fly back to Barbados!" And I say, "You lie, Devil, you lie!" And then he come one stormy night to me, and he say, "Look! I have white people belong to me." And I look—and there was Goody Good.

**Parris.** Sarah Good!

**Tituba** (*rocking and weeping*). Aye, sir, and Goody Osburn.

**Mrs. Putnam.** I knew it! Goody Osburn were midwife to me three times. I begged you, Thomas, did I not? I begged him not to call Osburn because I feared her. My babies always shriveled in her hands!

**Hale.** Take courage, you must give us all their names. How can you bear to see this child suffering? Look at her, Tituba. (*He is indicating Betty on the bed.*) Look at her God-given innocence; her soul is so tender; we must protect her, Tituba; the Devil is out and preying on her like a beast upon the flesh of the pure lamb. God will bless you for your help.

(*Abigail rises, staring as though inspired, and cries out.*)

**Abigail.** I want to open myself! (*They turn to her, startled. She is enraptured, as though in a pearly light.*) I want the light of God, I want the sweet love of Jesus! I danced for the Devil; I saw him; I wrote in his book; I go back to Jesus; I kiss His hand. I saw Sarah Good with the Devil! I saw Goody Osburn with the Devil! I saw Bridget Bishop with the Devil!

(*As she is speaking, Betty is rising from the bed, a fever in her eyes, and picks up the chant.*)

**Betty** (*staring too*). I saw George Jacobs with the Devil! I saw Goody Howe with the Devil!

**Parris.** She speaks! (*He rushes to embrace* Betty.) She speaks!

**Hale.** Glory to God! It is broken, they are free!

**Betty** (*calling out hysterically and with great relief*). I saw Martha Bellows with the Devil!

**Abigail.** I saw Goody Sibber with the Devil! (*It is rising to a great glee.*)

**Putnam.** The marshal, I'll call the marshal!

(*Parris is shouting a prayer of thanksgiving.*)

**Betty.** I saw Alice Barrow with the Devil!

(*The curtain begins to fall.*)

**Hale** (*as Putnam goes out*). Let the marshal bring irons![45]

**Abigail.** I saw Goody Hawkins with the Devil!

**Betty.** I saw Goody Bibber with the Devil!

**Abigail.** I saw Goody Booth with the Devil!

(*On their ecstatic cries*)

**the curtain falls**

---

45. **irons:** iron chains and manacles for criminals.

## GUIDING STUDENT RESPONSE

### Connect to the Literature

**1. What Do You Think?**
Students should support their opinions with textual evidence.

**Comprehension Check**
- Reverend Parris
- The afflicted girls see nothing although their eyes are open.
- Parris sent for Reverend Hale to determine whether Betty is a victim of witchcraft.

 Use Selection Quiz
**Unit Two Resource Book,** p. 19.

### Think Critically

**2. Possible Response:** Tituba realizes that she can save her life by confessing and implicating others; she is so intimidated that she decides to tell Reverend Hale and the others what they expect to hear.

**3. Possible Response:** Abigail is assertive, vengeful, and devious. She leads Betty Parris and the other girls in Salem to violate Puritan standards of conduct by dancing in the woods and drinking blood; she is determined to continue her affair with John Proctor, even though he tells her it is over, and is bitter toward his wife for dismissing her from the Proctor home; she lies about Tituba's evil influence upon her and accuses others of being in league with the Devil.

**4. Possible Responses:** Yes, Proctor is admirable because he thinks for himself, has the courage to speak out against Mr. Parris, is honest to Abigail about his feelings for her, and sees through the girls' charade. No, Proctor is guilty of infidelity with Abigail, who still believes that he desires her.

**5. Possible Response:** The fear of witchcraft probably will exacerbate the underlying tensions and festering resentments within this community, turning neighbor against neighbor.

---

### Connect to the Literature

**1. What Do You Think?**
Do you believe the accusations made at the end of this act? Why or why not?

> **Comprehension Check**
> - Who discovers Betty and the other girls dancing in the forest?
> - Name one symptom shown by the afflicted girls—Betty Parris and Ruth Putnam.
> - Why does Reverend Hale come to Salem?

### Think Critically

**2.** Why do you think Tituba admits so quickly to having practiced witchcraft?

**3.** **ACTIVE READING** **USING A GRAPHIC ORGANIZER** Refer to the chart you made in your **READER'S NOTEBOOK.** How would you describe Abigail Williams's most important **character traits?**

 **THINK ABOUT**
- her conduct in the woods
- her attitude toward Reverend Parris
- her comments about Elizabeth Proctor
- her conversation with John Proctor
- her accusations at the end of this act

**4.** Is John Proctor basically an admirable **character,** or not? Support your opinion with evidence from this act.

**5.** Throughout this act, Miller includes information about land disputes, lawsuits, and job appointments. What effect do you predict this new crisis of suspected witchcraft will have on the community?

### Extend Interpretations

**6. What If?** What do you think would have happened if Tituba had not confessed to practicing witchcraft?

**7. Connect to Life** At the end of this act, Tituba, Abigail, and others accuse some of their neighbors of afflicting them. Give examples of individuals or groups today who accuse others of causing their problems. How would you evaluate their accusations?

**8. Points of Comparison** Consider the Puritan beliefs that you explored while reading and discussing the excerpt from Jonathan Edwards's sermon "Sinners in the Hands of an Angry God." Which of those beliefs do you see reflected in Reverend Hale's motives and actions?

**190** UNIT TWO PART 1: BETWEEN HEAVEN AND HELL

---

### Literary Analysis

**STAGE DIRECTIONS** The **stage directions** of a play—the instructions for the director, the performers, and the stage crew—provide information about any or all of the following:
- the time and place of the action
- how characters look, move, speak, and feel
- the scenery, props, lighting, costumes, music, and other sound effects used in a performance

In *The Crucible,* Miller's stage directions sometimes become "mini-essays," providing historical background about the Puritans and their beliefs, biographical information about the historical figures upon whom the characters are based, or social commentary drawing parallels between circumstances in Salem and those in America after World War II. For example, in the stage directions just after Reverend Hale's entrance, Miller provides social commentary, observing that in the America of his day "any man who is not reactionary in his views is open to the charge of alliance with the Red hell."

**Cooperative Learning Activity**
Get together with a small group of classmates and review the stage directions for this act. Then create a chart with two columns. In the first column, list at least three details that helped you imagine one of the important characters in the play, such as Abigail Williams or John Proctor. In the second column, list three or more insights about America after the second world war that Miller conveys to his readers. Share your charts with other groups.

---

### Extend Interpretations

**What If?** Possible Response: Tituba would have been jailed, perhaps tortured, and even killed in an attempt to extort a confession from her.
**Connect to Life** Accept all reasonable responses.
**Points of Comparison** Puritan beliefs reflected in the play include the innate depravity of humans, the continual war between the forces of good and evil, the loss of one's soul to the powers of darkness, and the need for confession and repentance of sin.

### Literary Analysis

**Stage Directions** For Abigail Williams, students' charts might include an array of details, such as "strikingly beautiful" "feverishly looking into his [Proctor's] eyes," and "enraptured, as though in a pearly light." Students should reread the stage directions on pages 182–184 for insights about postwar America.

# A CT TWO

**1** (*The common room of* Proctor's *house, eight days later.*)

(*At the right is a door opening on the fields outside. A fireplace is at the left, and behind it a stairway leading upstairs. It is the low, dark, and rather long living room of the time. As the curtain rises, the room is empty. From above,* Elizabeth *is heard softly singing to the children. Presently the door opens and* John Proctor *enters, carrying his gun. He glances about the room as he comes toward the fireplace, then halts for an instant as he hears her singing. He continues on to the fireplace, leans the gun against the wall as he swings a pot out of the fire and smells it. Then he lifts out the ladle and tastes. He is not quite pleased. He reaches to a cupboard, takes a pinch of salt, and drops it into the pot. As he is tasting again, her footsteps are heard on the stair. He swings the pot into the fireplace and goes to a basin and washes his hands and face.* Elizabeth *enters.*)

**2**

**3**

### Less Proficient Readers
**1** Tell students that when a new act begins, the scenery usually changes. Have them keep the following questions in mind as they begin Act Two.

• Where is the setting of this scene?

**Answer:** the common room at the Proctors' house

• How does John feel about his wife? What actions of his reveal this?

**Possible Response:** He loves her, because when he seasons the soup, he is sure not to let her see so that her feelings won't be hurt.

### Multiple Learning Styles
**Visual Learners**

**2** Have students listen to the description of the Proctors' common room without looking at the picture. Ask them to draw the room as they see it.

### Gifted and Talented
**3** Ask students what these actions of John Proctor might symbolize about his relationship with his wife.

**Elizabeth.** What keeps you so late? It's almost dark.

**Proctor.** I were planting far out to the forest edge.

**Elizabeth.** Oh, you're done then.

**Proctor.** Aye, the farm is seeded. The boys asleep?

**Elizabeth.** They will be soon. (*And she goes to the fireplace, proceeds to ladle up stew in a dish.*)

**Proctor.** Pray now for a fair summer.

**Elizabeth.** Aye.

**Proctor.** Are you well today?

THE CRUCIBLE **191**

 **Viewing and Representing**

**Instruction** Have students read the stage directions carefully and compare the description of the common room in the Proctors' house to the set in the photograph on page 191. Suggest that students take notes about what they might do differently if they were designing a set for Act Two.

**Application** Have students create detailed drawings of their sets, showing walls, doors, fireplace, stairway, and the placement of furniture. You might consider having volunteers build a miniature model of the set based on the design they created for Act One or Act Two.

## Reading and Analyzing

### Literary Analysis DIALOGUE

 Ask students to discuss how this dialogue reflects Elizabeth's and John's feelings for each other.

**Possible Response:** John wants very much to please Elizabeth, perhaps in an attempt to atone for his past transgression. He compliments her on the meal, promises to buy her a heifer (a female calf), and tries to involve her in his work. Elizabeth tries to be solicitous toward John, but she seems distracted. She forgets the cider and the flowers.

Use **Unit Two Resource Book**, p. 22 for additional support.

### Literary Analysis STAGE DIRECTIONS

**B** Discuss with students what this stage direction suggests about Elizabeth and John's relationship.

**Possible Response:** It indicates a distancing—as if something has come between them. They don't feel comfortable speaking about their true feelings.

---

**Elizabeth.** I am. (*She brings the plate to the table, and, indicating the food*) It is a rabbit.

**Proctor** (*going to the table*). Oh, is it! In Jonathan's trap?

**Elizabeth.** No, she walked into the house this afternoon; I found her sittin' in the corner like she come to visit.

**Proctor.** Oh, that's a good sign walkin' in.

**Elizabeth.** Pray God. It hurt my heart to strip her, poor rabbit. (*She sits and watches him taste it.*)

**Proctor.** It's well seasoned.

**Elizabeth** (*blushing with pleasure*). I took great care. She's tender?

**Proctor.** Aye. (*He eats. She watches him.*) I think we'll see green fields soon. It's warm as blood beneath the clods.

**Elizabeth.** That's well.

(*Proctor eats, then looks up.*)

**Proctor.** If the crop is good I'll buy George Jacob's heifer. How would that please you?

**Elizabeth.** Aye, it would.

**Proctor** (*with a grin*). I mean to please you, Elizabeth.

**Elizabeth** (*it is hard to say*). I know it, John.

**A** (*He gets up, goes to her, kisses her. She receives it. With a certain disappointment, he returns to the table.*)

**Proctor** (*as gently as he can*). Cider?

**Elizabeth** (*with a sense of reprimanding herself for having forgot*). Aye! (*She gets up and goes and pours a glass for him. He now arches his back.*)

**Proctor.** This farm's a continent when you go foot by foot droppin' seeds in it.

**Elizabeth** (*coming with the cider*). It must be.

**Proctor** (*drinks a long draught, then, putting the glass down*). You ought to bring some flowers in the house.

**Elizabeth.** Oh! I forgot! I will tomorrow.

**Proctor.** It's winter in here yet. On Sunday let you come with me, and we'll walk the farm together;

I never see such a load of flowers on the earth. (*With good feeling he goes and looks up at the sky through the open doorway.*) Lilacs have a purple smell. Lilac is the smell of nightfall, I think. Massachusetts is a beauty in the spring!

**Elizabeth.** Aye, it is.(*There is a pause. She is watching him from the table as he stands there absorbing the night. It is as though she would speak but cannot. Instead, now, she takes up his plate and glass and fork and goes with them to the basin. Her back is turned to him. He turns to her and watches her. A sense of their separation rises.*)

**Proctor.** I think you're sad again. Are you?

**Elizabeth** (*she doesn't want friction, and yet she must*). You come so late I thought you'd gone to Salem this afternoon.

**Proctor.** Why? I have no business in Salem.

**Elizabeth.** You did speak of going, earlier this week.

**Proctor** (*he knows what she means*). I thought better of it since.

**Elizabeth.** Mary Warren's there today.

**Proctor.** Why'd you let her? You heard me forbid her go to Salem any more!

**Elizabeth.** I couldn't stop her.

**Proctor** (*holding back a full condemnation of her*). It is a fault, it is a fault, Elizabeth—you're the mistress here, not Mary Warren.

**Elizabeth.** She frightened all my strength away.

**Proctor.** How may that mouse frighten you, Elizabeth? You—

**Elizabeth.** It is a mouse no more. I forbid her go, and she raises up her chin like the daughter of a prince and says to me, "I must go to Salem, Goody Proctor; I am an official of thc court!"

**Proctor.** Court! What court?

**Elizabeth.** Aye, it is a proper court they have now. They've sent four judges out of Boston, she says, weighty magistrates of the General Court, and at the head sits the Deputy Governor of the Province.

---

## Teaching Options

 **Vocabulary Strategy**

**USING CONTEXT CLUES** Students can rely on context to determine the meanings of unfamiliar words. Use the following sentences to demonstrate the strategy of using context clues that provide synonyms.

After making a million dollars in the stock market, he became <u>ostentatious</u>. His diamond-studded watch and new sportscar seemed especially <u>showy</u>.

**Instruction**

- Ask a volunteer to summarize the meaning of the sentences.
- Help students recognize that *showy* is a synonym for *ostentatious*.

**Exercises** Ask students to use context clues such as synonyms to determine the meanings of the underlined words.

**1.** He was <u>indignant</u> about being unjustly fired. In fact, he was so incensed that he threatened to sue.

**Proctor** (*astonished*). Why, she's mad.

**Elizabeth.** I would to God she were. There be fourteen people in the jail now, she says. (*Proctor simply looks at her, unable to grasp it.*) And they'll be tried, and the court have power to hang them too, she says.

**Proctor** (*scoffing, but without conviction*). Ah, they'd never hang—

**Elizabeth.** The Deputy Governor promise hangin' if they'll not confess, John. The town's gone wild, I think. She speak of Abigail, and I thought she were a saint, to hear her. Abigail brings the other girls into the court, and where she walks the crowd will part like the sea for Israel. And folks are brought before them, and if they scream and howl and fall to the floor— the person's clapped in the jail for bewitchin' them.

**Proctor** (*wide-eyed*). Oh, it is a black mischief.

**Elizabeth.** I think you must go to Salem, John. (*He turns to her.*) I think so. You must tell them it is a fraud.

**Proctor** (*thinking beyond this*). Aye, it is, it is surely.

**Elizabeth.** Let you go to Ezekiel Cheever—he knows you well. And tell him what she said to you last week in her uncle's house. She said it had naught to do with witchcraft, did she not?

**Proctor** (*in thought*). Aye, she did, she did. (*Now, a pause.*)

**Elizabeth** (*quietly, fearing to anger him by prodding*). God forbid you keep that from the court, John. I think they must be told.

**Proctor** (*quietly, struggling with his thought*). Aye, they must, they must. It is a wonder they do believe her.

**Elizabeth.** I would go to Salem now, John—let you go tonight.

**Proctor.** I'll think on it.

**Elizabeth** (*with her courage now*). You cannot keep it, John.

**Proctor** (*angering*). I know I cannot keep it. I say I will think on it!

**Elizabeth** (*hurt, and very coldly*). Good, then, let you think on it. (*She stands and starts to walk out of the room.*)

Elizabeth Proctor

**Proctor.** I am only wondering how I may prove what she told me, Elizabeth. If the girl's a saint now, I think it is not easy to prove she's fraud, and the town gone so silly. She told it to me in a room alone—I have no proof for it.

**Elizabeth.** You were alone with her?

**Proctor** (*stubbornly*). For a moment alone, aye.

**Elizabeth.** Why, then, it is not as you told me.

**Proctor** (*his anger rising*). For a moment, I say. The others come in soon after.

**Elizabeth** (*quietly—she has suddenly lost all faith in him*). Do as you wish, then. (*She starts to turn.*)

**Proctor.** Woman. (*She turns to him.*) I'll not have your suspicion any more.

**Elizabeth** (*a little loftily*). I have no—

**Proctor.** I'll not have it!

**Elizabeth.** Then let you not earn it.

**Proctor** (*with a violent undertone*). You doubt me yet?

**Elizabeth** (*with a smile, to keep her dignity*). John, if it were not Abigail that you must go to hurt, would you falter now? I think not.

**Proctor.** Now look you—

THE CRUCIBLE **193**

**2.** The earthquake in Japan was a <u>calamity</u>. People in every economic class suffered because of this catastrophe.

Use **Unit One Resource Book,** p. 23 for additional support.

**A lesson on context clues appears on p. 326 in the Pupil's Edition.**

## Reading and Analyzing

### Active Reading

> **USING A GRAPHIC ORGANIZER**

**A** Have students analyze the conversation between John and Elizabeth. Ask them to identify a character trait for Proctor and to list that trait and evidence of it in their graphic organizers.

#### John Proctor

| Trait: defensive | Trait: |
|---|---|
| **Evidence:** He feels guilty about his sin, yet he becomes defensive with Elizabeth and tells her she should improve herself by learning charity before she judges him. He also points out his excellent behavior since Abigail's departure. | **Evidence:** |

### Reading Skills and Strategies: VISUALIZING

**B** Have students visualize Proctor's behavior during his argument with Elizabeth and when Mary appears. Have them use stage directions and dialogue to imagine how he would act and move about the stage.

### Reading Skills and Strategies: SUMMARIZING

**C** Ask students to summarize the events that took place in court.

**Possible Response:** Thirty-nine women have been arrested. Goody Osburn will hang. Sarah Good escaped the gallows because she confessed that she made a compact with Lucifer. She was convicted on evidence that Mary provided and on her inability to recite one commandment.

---

**Elizabeth.** I see what I see, John.

**Proctor** (*with solemn warning*). You will not judge me more, Elizabeth. I have good reason to think before I charge fraud on Abigail, and I will think on it. Let you look to your own improvement before you go to judge your husband any more. I have forgot Abigail, and—

**Elizabeth.** And I.

**Proctor.** Spare me! You forget nothin' and forgive nothin'. Learn charity, woman. I have gone tiptoe in this house all seven month since she is gone. I have not moved from there to there without I think to please you, and still an everlasting funeral marches round your heart. I cannot speak but I am doubted, every moment judged for lies, as though I come into a court when I come into this house!

**Elizabeth.** John, you are not open with me. You saw her with a crowd, you said. Now you—

**Proctor.** I'll plead my honesty no more, Elizabeth.

**Elizabeth** (*now she would justify herself*). John, I am only—

**Proctor.** No more! I should have roared you down when first you told me your suspicion. But I wilted, and, like a Christian, I confessed. Confessed! Some dream I had must have mistaken you for God that day. But you're not, you're not, and let you remember it! Let you look sometimes for the goodness in me, and judge me not.

**Elizabeth.** I do not judge you. The magistrate sits in your heart that judges you. I never thought you but a good man, John—(*with a smile*)—only somewhat bewildered.

**Proctor** (*laughing bitterly*). Oh, Elizabeth, your justice would freeze beer![46] (*He turns suddenly toward a sound outside. He starts for the door as Mary Warren enters. As soon as he sees her, he goes directly to her and grabs her by her cloak, furious.*) How do you go to Salem when I forbid it? Do you mock me? (*Shaking her.*) I'll whip you if you dare leave this house again!

(*Strangely, she doesn't resist him, but hangs limply by his grip.*)

**Mary Warren.** I am sick, I am sick, Mr. Proctor. Pray, pray, hurt me not. (*Her strangeness throws him off, and her evident pallor and weakness. He frees her.*) My insides are all shuddery; I am in the proceedings all day, sir.

**Proctor** (*with draining anger—his curiosity is draining it*). And what of these proceedings here? When will you proceed to keep this house, as you are paid nine pound a year to do—and my wife not wholly well?

(*As though to compensate, Mary Warren goes to Elizabeth with a small rag doll.*)

**Mary Warren.** I made a gift for you today, Goody Proctor. I had to sit long hours in a chair, and passed the time with sewing.

**Elizabeth** (*perplexed, looking at the doll*). Why, thank you, it's a fair poppet.[47]

**Mary Warren** (*with a trembling, decayed voice*). We must all love each other now, Goody Proctor.

**Elizabeth** (*amazed at her strangeness*). Aye, indeed we must.

**Mary Warren** (*glancing at the room*). I'll get up early in the morning and clean the house. I must sleep now. (*She turns and starts off.*)

**Proctor.** Mary. (*She halts.*) Is it true? There be fourteen women arrested?

**Mary Warren.** No, sir. There be thirty-nine now—(*She suddenly breaks off and sobs and sits down, exhausted.*)

**Elizabeth.** Why, she's weepin'! What ails you, child?

**Mary Warren.** Goody Osburn—will hang!

(*There is a shocked pause, while she sobs.*)

---

46. **your justice . . . beer:** alcoholic beverages freeze at very low temperatures, so Proctor is sarcastically calling his wife cold-hearted.

47. **fair poppet:** pretty doll.

---

## Teaching Options

**Proctor.** Hang! (*He calls into her face.*) Hang, y'say?

**Mary Warren** (*through her weeping*). Aye.

**Proctor.** The Deputy Governor will permit it?

**Mary Warren.** He sentenced her. He must. (*To ameliorate[48] it.*) But not Sarah Good. For Sarah Good confessed, y'see.

**Proctor.** Confessed! To what?

**Mary Warren.** That she—(*in horror at the memory*)—she sometimes made a compact with Lucifer, and wrote her name in his black book—with her blood—and bound herself to torment Christians till God's thrown down—and we all must worship Hell forevermore.

(*Pause.*)

**Proctor.** But—surely you know what a jabberer she is. Did you tell them that?

**Mary Warren.** Mr. Proctor, in open court she near to choked us all to death.

**Proctor.** How, choked you?

**Mary Warren.** She sent her spirit out.

**Elizabeth.** Oh, Mary, Mary, surely you—

**Mary Warren** (*with an indignant edge*). She tried to kill me many times, Goody Proctor!

**Elizabeth.** Why, I never heard you mention that before.

**Mary Warren.** I never knew it before. I never knew anything before. When she come into the court I say to myself, I must not accuse this woman, for she sleep in ditches, and so very old and poor. But then—then she sit there, denying and denying, and I feel a misty coldness climbin' up my back, and the skin on my skull begin to creep, and I feel a clamp around my neck and I cannot breathe air; and then—(*entranced*)—I hear a voice, a screamin' voice, and it were my voice—and all at once I remembered everything she done to me!

**Proctor.** Why? What did she do to you?

**Mary Warren** (*like one awakened to a marvelous secret insight*). So many time, Mr. Proctor, she come to this very door, beggin' bread and a cup of cider—and mark this: whenever I turned her away empty, she mumbled.

**Elizabeth.** Mumbled! She may mumble if she's hungry.

**Mary Warren.** But what does she mumble? You must remember, Goody Proctor. Last month—a Monday, I think—she walked away, and I thought my guts would burst for two days after. Do you remember it?

**Elizabeth.** Why—I do, I think, but—

**Mary Warren.** And so I told that to Judge Hathorne, and he asks her so. "Sarah Good," says he, "what curse do you mumble that this girl must fall sick after turning you away?" (*And then she replies—mimicking an old crone*)—"Why, your excellence, no curse at all. I only say my commandments;[49] I hope I may say my commandments," says she!

**Elizabeth.** And that's an upright answer.

**Mary Warren.** Aye, but then Judge Hathorne say, "Recite for us your commandments!"—(*leaning avidly toward them*)—and of all the ten she could not say a single one. She never knew no commandments, and they had her in a flat lie!

**Proctor.** And so condemned her?

**Mary Warren** (*now a little strained, seeing his stubborn doubt*). Why, they must when she condemned herself.

**Proctor.** But the proof, the proof!

**Mary Warren** (*with greater impatience with him*). I told you the proof. It's hard proof, hard as rock, the judges said.

**Proctor** (*pauses an instant, then*). You will not go to court again, Mary Warren.

---

48. **ameliorate** (ə-mēl′yə-rāt′): improve.

49. **commandments:** the biblical Ten Commandments.

---

| WORDS TO KNOW | **indignant** (ĭn-dĭg′nənt) *adj.* filled with anger caused by something unjust or mean |
| --- | --- |

**195**

---

---

## Mini Lesson  Vocabulary Strategy

### APPLYING PREFIXES AND ROOT WORDS

**Instruction** Have students apply meanings of prefixes and root words in order to comprehend the meanings of words. The word *indignant* is based on the Latin root *dignus,* meaning "worthy," and the prefix *in-*, which means "not." Mary becomes indignant with the Proctors when she thinks that their opinions of her are unjustified. She believes that she is "not worthy" of their criticism. Other words based on the same root are *indignity, dignity,* and *dignitary.*

**Exercises** Have students work in pairs to find the meanings of *indignity, dignity,* and *dignitary.* Ask them to use each word in a sentence. Ask students to describe how they can use knowledge of the prefix *in-* and the root word *dignitas* to remember the meanings of these words.

Use **Vocabulary Transparencies and Copymasters,** p. 27.

**A lesson on prefixes and root words appears on p. 444 in the Pupil's Edition.**

**A** Ask students to explain what Elizabeth means by "the noose." Then ask them to identify the person to whom the pronoun *she* refers when Elizabeth says, "She wants me dead."

**Possible Response:** The noose refers to her hanging. Elizabeth believes she'll be hanged because of Abigail's accusation.

**Active Reading**

USING A GRAPHIC ORGANIZER

**B** Have students add information about Elizabeth Proctor to the character charts they are keeping in their notebooks.

### Elizabeth Proctor

| Trait: insightful | Trait: |
|---|---|
| **Evidence:** She understands that Abigail dreams of taking her place as John's wife, and she knows that John still has feelings for Abigail even though he hotly denies it. | **Evidence:** |

**Reading Skills and Strategies:
PREDICTING**

**C** Ask students to recall what Mary has told Elizabeth about the court proceedings. Then ask students what might happen after Hale arrives at the Proctors' home.

**Possible Response:** Mary told Elizabeth that someone had mentioned her name. Hale might question Elizabeth to try to form his own opinion about whether she is guilty of witchcraft.

---

**Mary Warren.** I must tell you, sir, I will be gone every day now. I am amazed you do not see what weighty work we do.

**Proctor.** What work you do! It's strange work for a Christian girl to hang old women!

**Mary Warren.** But, Mr. Proctor, they will not hang them if they confess. Sarah Good will only sit in jail some time—(*recalling*)—and here's a wonder for you; think on this. Goody Good is pregnant!

**Elizabeth.** Pregnant! Are they mad? The woman's near to sixty!

**Mary Warren.** They had Doctor Griggs examine her, and she's full to the brim. And smokin' a pipe all these years, and no husband either! But she's safe, thank God, for they'll not hurt the innocent child. But be that not a marvel? You must see it, sir, it's God's work we do. So I'll be gone every day for some time. I'm—I am an official of the court, they say, and I—(*She has been edging toward offstage.*)

**Proctor.** I'll official you! (*He strides to the mantel, takes down the whip hanging there.*)

**Mary Warren** (*terrified, but coming erect, striving for her authority*). I'll not stand whipping any more!

**Elizabeth** (*hurriedly, as* Proctor *approaches*). Mary, promise now you'll stay at home—

**Mary Warren** (*backing from him, but keeping her erect posture, striving, striving for her way*). The Devil's loose in Salem, Mr. Proctor; we must discover where he's hiding!

**Proctor.** I'll whip the Devil out of you! (*With whip raised he reaches out for her, and she streaks away and yells.*)

**Mary Warren** (*pointing at* Elizabeth). I saved her life today!

(*Silence. His whip comes down.*)

**Elizabeth** (*softly*). I am accused?

**Mary Warren** (*quaking*). Somewhat mentioned. But I said I never see no sign you ever sent your spirit out to hurt no one, and seeing I do live so closely with you, they dismissed it.

**Elizabeth.** Who accused me?

**Mary Warren.** I am bound by law, I cannot tell it. (*To* Proctor) I only hope you'll not be so sarcastical no more. Four judges and the King's deputy sat to dinner with us but an hour ago. I—I would have you speak civilly to me, from this out.

**Proctor** (*in horror, muttering in disgust at her*). Go to bed.

**Mary Warren** (*with a stamp of her foot*). I'll not be ordered to bed no more, Mr. Proctor! I am eighteen and a woman, however single!

**Proctor.** Do you wish to sit up? Then sit up.

**Mary Warren.** I wish to go to bed!

**Proctor** (*in anger*). Good night, then!

**Mary Warren.** Good night. (*Dissatisfied, uncertain of herself, she goes out. Wide-eyed, both,* Proctor *and* Elizabeth *stand staring.*)

**Elizabeth** (*quietly*). Oh, the noose, the noose is up!

**Proctor.** There'll be no noose.

**Elizabeth.** She wants me dead. I knew all week it would come to this!

**Proctor** (*without conviction*). They dismissed it. You heard her say—

**Elizabeth.** And what of tomorrow? She will cry me out until they take me!

**Proctor.** Sit you down.

**Elizabeth.** She wants me dead, John, you know it!

**Proctor.** I say sit down! (*She sits, trembling. He speaks quietly, trying to keep his wits.*) Now we must be wise, Elizabeth.

**Elizabeth** (*with sarcasm, and a sense of being lost*). Oh, indeed, indeed!

**Proctor.** Fear nothing. I'll find Ezekiel Cheever. I'll tell him she said it were all sport.

**Elizabeth.** John, with so many in the jail, more than Cheever's help is needed now, I think. Would you favor me with this? Go to Abigail.

---

# Teaching Options

✓ **Assessment** ## Standardized Test Practice

**ARRANGING EVENTS IN SEQUENTIAL ORDER** In certain test situations, students will be asked to arrange events in sequential order. To practice, read aloud or write on the chalkboard the following question and possible answers:

Which of these does Mary Warren do *first*?

**A.** She tells Elizabeth her name was mentioned in court.

**B.** She cries because Goody Osburn is going to hang.

**C.** She gives Elizabeth a poppet she made in court.

Help students determine the proper sequence by first relying on their memory of events and then checking their answer against the text.

**Answer:** C

**Proctor** (*his soul hardening as he senses . . .*). What have I to say to Abigail?

**Elizabeth** (*delicately*). John—grant me this. You have a faulty understanding of young girls. There is a promise made in any bed—

**Proctor** (*striving against his anger*). What promise!

**Elizabeth.** Spoke or silent, a promise is surely made. And she may dote on it now—I am sure she does—and thinks to kill me, then to take my place.

(*Proctor's anger is rising; he cannot speak.*)

**Elizabeth.** It is her dearest hope, John, I know it. There be a thousand names; why does she call mine? There be a certain danger in calling such a name—I am no Goody Good that sleeps in ditches, nor Osburn, drunk and half-witted. She'd dare not call out such a farmer's wife but there be monstrous[50] profit in it. She thinks to take my place, John.

**Proctor.** She cannot think it! (*He knows it is true.*)

**Elizabeth** (*"reasonably"*). John, have you ever shown her somewhat of contempt? She cannot pass you in the church but you will blush—

**Proctor.** I may blush for my sin.

**Elizabeth.** I think she sees another meaning in that blush.

**Proctor.** And what see you? What see you, Elizabeth?

**Elizabeth** (*"conceding"*). I think you be somewhat ashamed, for I am there, and she so close.

**Proctor.** When will you know me, woman? Were I stone I would have cracked for shame this seven month!

**Elizabeth.** Then go and tell her she's a whore. Whatever promise she may sense—break it, John, break it.

**Proctor** (*between his teeth*). Good, then. I'll go. (*He starts for his rifle.*)

**Elizabeth** (*trembling, fearfully*). Oh, how unwillingly!

**Proctor** (*turning on her, rifle in hand*). I will curse her hotter than the oldest cinder in hell. But pray, begrudge me not my anger!

**Elizabeth.** Your anger! I only ask you—

**Proctor.** Woman, am I so base?[51] Do you truly think me base?

**Elizabeth.** I never called you base.

**Proctor.** Then how do you charge me with such a promise? The promise that a stallion gives a mare I gave that girl!

**Elizabeth.** Then why do you anger with me when I bid you break it?

**Proctor.** Because it speaks deceit, and I am honest! But I'll plead no more! I see now your spirit twists around the single error of my life, and I will never tear it free!

**Elizabeth** (*crying out*). You'll tear it free—when you come to know that I will be your only wife, or no wife at all! She has an arrow in you yet, John Proctor, and you know it well!

(*Quite suddenly, as though from the air, a figure appears in the doorway. They start slightly. It is Mr. Hale. He is different now—drawn a little, and there is a quality of deference, even of guilt, about his manner now.*)

**Hale.** Good evening.

**Proctor** (*still in his shock*). Why, Mr. Hale! Good evening to you, sir. Come in, come in.

**Hale** (*to Elizabeth*). I hope I do not startle you.

**Elizabeth.** No, no, it's only that I heard no horse—

**Hale.** You are Goodwife Proctor.

**Proctor.** Aye; Elizabeth.

**Hale** (*nods, then*). I hope you're not off to bed yet.

**Proctor** (*setting down his gun*). No, no. (*Hale comes further into the room. And Proctor, to explain his nervousness*) We are not used to visitors after dark, but you're welcome here. Will you sit you down, sir?

---

50. **monstrous:** tremendous.
51. **base:** having low moral standards.

## Literary Analysis: DIALECT

**A** Point out to the students that dialect is the distinct form of a language as it is spoken in one geographical area or by a particular social or ethnic group. Miller creates a dialect to reflect the way he imagines the people of Salem spoke in 1692. For example, they dropped the *g* sound from words ending in *-ing* and used contractions such as *y'know;* they used plural verb forms with singular subjects (*it hurt*) and present-tense verb forms to refer to past events (*he preach*); and they used archaic phrases such as *I tell you true.* Have students work in pairs to rewrite John's dialect in their own language and then share their translations with the class.

## Literary Analysis | STAGE DIRECTIONS

**B** Have students think about these stage directions. Proctor certainly did not hide his anger in Act One; why would he try to hide his feelings of resentment now?

**Possible Response:** John knows that Hale has influence with the town authorities. He realizes the potentially dangerous situation Elizabeth is in, and he does not want to offend Hale.

---

**Hale.** I will. (*He sits.*) Let you sit, Goodwife Proctor. (*She does, never letting him out of her sight. There is a pause as* Hale *looks about the room.*)

**Proctor** (*to break the silence*). Will you drink cider, Mr. Hale?

**Hale.** No, it rebels[52] my stomach; I have some further traveling yet tonight. Sit you down, sir. (Proctor *sits.*) I will not keep you long, but I have some business with you.

**Proctor.** Business of the court?

**Hale.** No—no, I come of my own, without the court's authority. Hear me. (*He wets his lips.*) I know not if you are aware, but your wife's name is—mentioned in the court.

**Proctor.** We know it, sir. Our Mary Warren told us. We are entirely amazed.

**Hale.** I am a stranger here, as you know. And in my ignorance I find it hard to draw a clear opinion of them that come accused before the court. And so this afternoon, and now tonight, I go from house to house—I come now from Rebecca Nurse's house and—

**Elizabeth** (*shocked*). Rebecca's charged!

**Hale.** God forbid such a one be charged. She is, however—mentioned somewhat.

**Elizabeth** (*with an attempt at a laugh*). You will never believe, I hope, that Rebecca trafficked with the Devil.

**Hale.** Woman, it is possible.

**Proctor** (*taken aback*). Surely you cannot think so.

**Hale.** This is a strange time, Mister. No man may longer doubt the powers of the dark are gathered in monstrous attack upon this village. There is too much evidence now to deny it. You will agree, sir?

**Proctor** (*evading*). I—have no knowledge in that line. But it's hard to think so pious[53] a woman be secretly a Devil's bitch after seventy year of such good prayer.

**Hale.** Aye. But the Devil is a wily one, you cannot deny it. However, she is far from accused, and I know she will not be. (*Pause.*) I thought, sir, to put some questions as to the Christian character of this house, if you'll permit me.

**Proctor** (*coldly, resentful*). Why, we—have no fear of questions, sir.

**Hale.** Good, then. (*He makes himself more comfortable.*) In the book of record that Mr. Parris keeps, I note that you are rarely in the church on Sabbath Day.

**Proctor.** No, sir, you are mistaken.

**Hale.** Twenty-six time in seventeen month, sir. I must call that rare. Will you tell me why you are so absent?

**Proctor.** Mr. Hale, I never knew I must account to that man for I come to church or stay at home. My wife were sick this winter.

**Hale.** So I am told. But you, Mister, why could you not come alone?

**Proctor.** I surely did come when I could, and when I could not I prayed in this house.

**Hale.** Mr. Proctor, your house is not a church; your theology must tell you that.

**Proctor.** It does, sir, it does; and it tells me that a minister may pray to God without he have golden candlesticks upon the altar.

**Hale.** What golden candlesticks?

**Proctor.** Since we built the church there were pewter candlesticks upon the altar; Francis Nurse made them, y'know, and a sweeter hand never touched the metal. But Parris came, and for twenty week he preach nothin' but golden candlesticks until he had them. I labor the earth from dawn of day to blink of night, and I tell you true, when I look to heaven and see my money glaring at his elbows—it hurt my prayer, sir, it hurt my prayer. I think, sometimes, the man dreams cathedrals, not clapboard meetin' houses.

---

52. **rebels:** upsets.
53. **pious** (pī′əs): religious.

**Hale** (*thinks, then*). And yet, Mister, a Christian on Sabbath Day must be in church. (*Pause.*) Tell me—you have three children?

**Proctor.** Aye. Boys.

**Hale.** How comes it that only two are baptized?

**Proctor** (*starts to speak, then stops, then, as though unable to restrain this*). I like it not that Mr. Parris should lay his hand upon my baby. I see no light of God in that man. I'll not conceal it.

**Hale.** I must say it, Mr. Proctor; that is not for you to decide. The man's ordained, therefore the light of God is in him.

**Proctor** (*flushed with resentment but trying to smile*). What's your suspicion, Mr. Hale?

**Hale.** No, no, I have no—

**Proctor.** I nailed the roof upon the church, I hung the door—

**Hale.** Oh, did you! That's a good sign, then.

**Proctor.** It may be I have been too quick to bring the man to book,[54] but you cannot think we ever desired the destruction of religion. I think that's in your mind, is it not?

**Hale** (*not altogether giving way*). I—have—there is a softness in your record, sir, a softness.

**Elizabeth.** I think, maybe, we have been too hard with Mr. Parris. I think so. But sure we never loved the Devil here.

**Hale** (*nods, deliberating this. Then, with the voice of one administering a secret test*). Do you know your Commandments, Elizabeth?

**Elizabeth** (*without hesitation, even eagerly*). I surely do. There be no mark of blame upon my life, Mr. Hale. I am a convenanted Christian woman.

**Hale.** And you, Mister?

**Proctor** (*a trifle unsteadily*). I—am sure I do, sir.

**Hale** (*glances at her open face, then at John, then*). Let you repeat them, if you will.

**Proctor.** The Commandments.

**Hale.** Aye.

**Proctor** (*looking off, beginning to sweat*). Thou shalt not kill.

**Hale.** Aye.

**Proctor** (*counting on his fingers*). Thou shalt not steal. Thou shalt not covet thy neighbor's goods, nor make unto thee any graven image. Thou shalt not take the name of the Lord in vain; thou shalt have no other gods before me. (*With some hesitation.*) Thou shalt remember the Sabbath Day and keep it holy. (*Pause. Then.*) Thou shalt honor thy father and mother. Thou shalt not bear false witness. (*He is stuck. He counts back on his fingers, knowing one is missing.*) Thou shalt not make unto thee any graven image.

**Hale.** You have said that twice, sir.

**Proctor** (*lost*). Aye. (*He is flailing[55] for it.*)

**Elizabeth** (*delicately*). Adultery, John.

**Proctor** (*as though a secret arrow had pained his heart*). Aye. (*Trying to grin it away—to* Hale) You see, sir, between the two of us we do know them all. (Hale *only looks at* Proctor, *deep in his attempt to define this man.* Proctor *grows more uneasy.*) I think it be a small fault.

**Hale.** Theology, sir, is a fortress; no crack in a fortress may be accounted small. (*He rises; he seems worried now. He paces a little, in deep thought.*)

**Proctor.** There be no love for Satan in this house, Mister.

**Hale.** I pray it, I pray it dearly. (*He looks to both of them, an attempt at a smile on his face, but his misgivings are clear.*) Well, then—I'll bid you good night.

**Elizabeth** (*unable to restrain herself*). Mr. Hale. (*He turns.*) I do think you are suspecting me somewhat? Are you not?

**Hale** (*obviously disturbed—and evasive*). Goody Proctor, I do not judge you. My duty is to add

---

54. **bring the man to book:** judge the man.
55. **flailing:** struggling.

## Literary Analysis: CHARACTERIZATION

**A** Ask students to discuss how Elizabeth characterizes herself. Have them consider how her characterization of herself could be dangerous.

**Possible Response:** Elizabeth claims to be a good woman. She says she does not believe a woman who does good like herself could have secret relations with Satan, and therefore if she is called a witch, then she does not believe in witches. This is a dangerous statement because she seems to be contradicting the Bible, and during a witch-hunt this might be enough to condemn her.

## Reading Skills and Strategies: PREDICTING

**B** Ask students to predict what might happen after Ezekiel Cheever's arrival at the Proctors' home.

**Possible Response:** Cheever will arrest Elizabeth because she has been formally accused.

---

what I may to the godly wisdom of the court. I pray you both good health and good fortune. (*To* John) Good night, sir. (*He starts out.*)

**Elizabeth** (*with a note of desperation*). I think you must tell him, John.

**Hale.** What's that?

**Elizabeth** (*restraining a call*). Will you tell him?

(*Slight pause.* Hale *looks questioningly at* John.)

**Proctor** (*with difficulty*). I—I have no witness and cannot prove it, except my word be taken. But I know the children's sickness had naught to do with witchcraft.

**Hale** (*stopped, struck*). Naught to do—?

**Proctor.** Mr. Parris discovered them sportin' in the woods. They were startled and took sick.

(*Pause.*)

**Hale.** Who told you this?

**Proctor** (*hesitates, then*). Abigail Williams.

**Hale.** Abigail!

**Proctor.** Aye.

**Hale** (*his eyes wide*). Abigail Williams told you it had naught to do with witchcraft!

**Proctor.** She told me the day you came, sir.

**Hale** (*suspiciously*). Why—why did you keep this?

**Proctor.** I never knew until tonight that the world is gone daft[56] with this nonsense.

**Hale.** Nonsense! Mister, I have myself examined Tituba, Sarah Good, and numerous others that have confessed to dealing with the Devil. They have confessed it.

**Proctor.** And why not, if they must hang for denyin' it? There are them that will swear to anything before they'll hang; have you never thought of that?

**Hale.** I have. I—I have indeed. (*It is his own suspicion, but he resists it. He glances at* Elizabeth, *then at* John.) And you—would you testify to this in court?

**Proctor.** I—had not reckoned with goin' into court. But if I must I will.

**Hale.** Do you falter[57] here?

**Proctor.** I falter nothing, but I may wonder if my story will be credited in such a court. I do wonder on it, when such a steady-minded minister as you will suspicion such a woman that never lied, and cannot, and the world knows she cannot! I may falter somewhat, Mister; I am no fool.

**Hale** (*quietly—it has impressed him*). Proctor, let you open with me now, for I have a rumor that troubles me. It's said you hold no belief that there may even be witches in the world. Is that true, sir?

**Proctor** (*he knows this is critical, and is striving against his disgust with* Hale *and with himself for even answering*). I know not what I have said, I may have said it. I have wondered if there be witches in the world—although I cannot believe they come among us now.

**Hale.** Then you do not believe—

**Proctor.** I have no knowledge of it; the Bible speaks of witches, and I will not deny them.

**Hale.** And you, woman?

**Elizabeth.** I—I cannot believe it.

**Hale** (*shocked*). You cannot!

**Proctor.** Elizabeth, you bewilder him!

**Elizabeth** (*to* Hale). I cannot think the Devil may own a woman's soul, Mr. Hale, when she keeps an upright way, as I have. I am a good woman, I know it; and if you believe I may do only good work in the world, and yet be secretly bound to Satan, then I must tell you, sir, I do not believe it.

**Hale.** But, woman, you do believe there are witches in—

**Elizabeth.** If you think that I am one, then I say there are none.

---

56. **daft:** crazy; mad.
57. **falter:** hesitate.

## Teaching Options

 **Mini Lesson** Grammar

**PRINCIPAL PARTS OF VERBS** Every verb has four principal parts: the present, the present participle, the past, and the past participle. All other verb forms are made from these four principal parts. On the chalkboard, write the principal parts of the regular verb *walk* and the irregular verb *see*.

| Present | Present Participle | Past | Past Participle |
|---------|-------------------|------|-----------------|
| walk | (is) walking | walked | (has) walked |
| see | (is) seeing | saw | (has) seen |

**Exercises** Have students underline the verb and identify which principal part it represents.

1. Reverend Hale <u>questioned</u> Elizabeth Proctor. *(past)*
2. The witch trials <u>have begun</u> in Salem. *(past participle)*
3. John <u>is reprimanding</u> Elizabeth for her leniency. *(present participle)*

**Hale.** You surely do not fly against the Gospel,[58] the Gospel—

**Proctor.** She believe in the Gospel, every word!

**Elizabeth.** Question Abigail Williams about the Gospel, not myself!

(Hale *stares at her.*)

**Proctor.** She do not mean to doubt the Gospel, sir, you cannot think it. This be a Christian house, sir, a Christian house.

**Hale.** God keep you both; let the third child be quickly baptized, and go you without fail each Sunday in to Sabbath prayer; and keep a solemn, quiet way among you. I think—

(Giles Corey *appears in doorway.*)

**Giles.** John!

**Proctor.** Giles! What's the matter?

**Giles.** They take my wife.

(Francis Nurse *enters.*)

**Giles.** And his Rebecca!

**Proctor** (*to* Francis). Rebecca's in the jail!

**Francis.** Aye, Cheever come and take her in his wagon. We've only now come from the jail, and they'll not even let us in to see them.

**Elizabeth.** They've surely gone wild now, Mr. Hale!

**Francis** (*going to* Hale). Reverend Hale! Can you not speak to the Deputy Governor? I'm sure he mistakes these people—

**Hale.** Pray calm yourself, Mr. Nurse.

**Francis.** My wife is the very brick and mortar of the church, Mr. Hale—(*indicating* Giles)—and Martha Corey, there cannot be a woman closer yet to God than Martha.

**Hale.** How is Rebecca charged, Mr. Nurse?

**Francis** (*with a mocking, half-hearted laugh*). For murder, she's charged! (*Mockingly quoting the warrant*) "For the marvelous and supernatural murder of Goody Putnam's babies." What am I to do, Mr. Hale?

**Hale** (*turns from* Francis, *deeply troubled, then*). Believe me, Mr. Nurse, if Rebecca Nurse be tainted, then nothing's left to stop the whole green world from burning. Let you rest upon the justice of the court; the court will send her home, I know it.

**Francis.** You cannot mean she will be tried in court!

**Hale** (*pleading*). Nurse, though our hearts break, we cannot flinch; these are new times, sir. There is a misty plot afoot so subtle we should be criminal to cling to old respects and ancient friendships. I have seen too many frightful proofs in court—the Devil is alive in Salem, and we dare not quail to follow wherever the accusing finger points!

**Proctor** (*angered*). How may such a woman murder children?

**Hale** (*in great pain*). Man, remember, until an hour before the Devil fell, God thought him beautiful in Heaven.[59]

**Giles.** I never said my wife were a witch, Mr. Hale; I only said she were reading books!

**Hale.** Mr. Corey, exactly what complaint were made on your wife?

**Giles.** That bloody mongrel Walcott charge her. Y'see, he buy a pig of my wife four or five year ago, and the pig died soon after. So he come dancin' in for his money back. So my Martha, she says to him, "Walcott, if you haven't the wit to feed a pig properly, you'll not live to own many," she says. Now he goes to court and claims that from that day to this he cannot keep a pig alive for more than four weeks because my Martha bewitch them with her books!

(*Enter* Ezekiel Cheever. *A shocked silence.*)

**Cheever.** Good evening to you, Proctor.

**Proctor.** Why, Mr. Cheever. Good evening.

---

58. **the Gospel:** in the Bible, the first four books of the New Testament.

59. **an hour . . . Heaven:** alludes to the Christian belief that Satan was God's favorite angel until Satan rebelled and was cast out of heaven.

THE CRUCIBLE **201**

Use **Grammar Transparencies and Copymasters**, p. 114.

Use McDougal Littell's *Language Network*, Chapter 4, for more instruction and practice in verbs.

---

## Customizing Instruction

### Students Acquiring English

**1** Explain that when Francis refers to his wife as the "the very brick and mortar of the church," he means that she embodies its principles and that she is the foundation on which the church in Salem stands. Her being accused of witchery is ridiculous, he argues, because she is so godly and so essential to Salem's religious community.

### Less Proficient Readers

**2** Make sure students understand Hale's defense of the court by asking them to restate his remarks in their own words.

**Possible Response:** As painful as it is, we must allow the court to go forward. The Devil's work is difficult to see, and we cannot let our feelings for friends and family get in the way of finding him out. There has been so much proof of witchery presented in court that we cannot ignore it. The Devil is so tricky that he was even able to deceive God for a time.

**3** Ask students the following questions to guide their understanding of why Giles's wife was really accused of witchery:

• Who charged Martha Corey?
**Answer:** Walcott

• What reasons did he give for his accusation?

**Possible Response:** He claims that he cannot keep any pig alive for more than four weeks because Martha bewitches them with her books.

• According to Giles, what is the real reason Walcott accused her?

**Possible Response:** Walcott bought a pig from Martha, and the pig died. Giles believes Walcott's accusation is motivated by revenge.

**Reading Skills and Strategies:**
**PREDICTING**

**A** Have students predict what will be the significance of the poppet.

**Possible Response:** Since Cheever asks about it specifically, it must be related to Abigail's accusation of Elizabeth. The poppet will probably be used as evidence against Elizabeth. Perhaps Mary planted the doll in the Proctors' house with evil intent.

**Reading Skills and Strategies:**
**MAKING INFERENCES**

**B** Ask students to suggest possible causes behind Abigail's attack.

**Possible Response:** Abigail knew that Mary had given the poppet to Elizabeth. She placed the needle in her own belly to implicate Elizabeth, knowing that the court officers would find the poppet and consider it proof of witchcraft.

**Reading Skills and Strategies:**
**SUMMARIZING**

**C** Have students summarize what Mary says about the doll. Ask them to discuss whether they think that Mary knows about Abigail's actions.

**Possible Response:** Mary made the doll for Elizabeth in court, and she says she meant nothing by the needle. When Hale suggests she may be conjured to say this, she innocently says she is not and offers Abigail as her witness. This suggests she knows nothing of Abigail's intentions.

**Cheever.** Good evening, all. Good evening, Mr. Hale.

**Proctor.** I hope you come not on business of the court.

**Cheever.** I do, Proctor, aye. I am clerk of the court now, y'know.

(*Enter Marshal Herrick, a man in his early thirties, who is somewhat shamefaced at the moment.*)

**Giles.** It's a pity, Ezekiel, that an honest tailor might have gone to Heaven must burn in Hell. You'll burn for this, do you know it?

**Cheever.** You know yourself I must do as I'm told. You surely know that, Giles. And I'd as lief[60] you'd not be sending me to Hell. I like not the sound of it, I tell you; I like not the sound of it. (*He fears Proctor, but starts to reach inside his coat.*) Now believe me, Proctor, how heavy be the law, all its tonnage I do carry on my back tonight. (*He takes out a warrant.*) I have a warrant for your wife.

**Proctor** (*to* Hale). You said she were not charged!

**Hale.** I know nothin' of it. (*To* Cheever) When were she charged?

**Cheever.** I am given sixteen warrant tonight, sir, and she is one.

**Proctor.** Who charged her?

**Cheever.** Why, Abigail Williams charge her.

**Proctor.** On what proof, what proof?

**Cheever** (*looking about the room*). Mr. Proctor, I have little time. The court bid me search your house, but I like not to search a house. So will you hand me any poppets that your wife may keep here?

**A** **Proctor.** Poppets?

**Elizabeth.** I never kept no poppets, not since I were a girl.

**Cheever** (*embarrassed, glancing toward the mantel where sits* Mary Warren's *poppet*). I spy a poppet, Goody Proctor.

**Elizabeth.** Oh! (*Going for it:*) Why, this is Mary's.

**Cheever** (*shyly*). Would you please to give it to me?

**Elizabeth** (*handing it to him, asks* Hale). Has the court discovered a text in poppets now?

**Cheever** (*carefully holding the poppet*). Do you keep any others in this house?

**Proctor.** No, nor this one either till tonight. What signifies a poppet?

**Cheever.** Why, a poppet—(*he gingerly turns the poppet over*)—a poppet may signify—Now, woman, will you please to come with me?

**Proctor.** She will not! (*To* Elizabeth) Fetch Mary here.

**Cheever** (*ineptly reaching toward* Elizabeth). No, no, I am forbid to leave her from my sight.

**Proctor** (*pushing his arm away*). You'll leave her out of sight and out of mind, Mister. Fetch Mary, Elizabeth. (Elizabeth *goes upstairs.*)

**Hale.** What signifies a poppet, Mr. Cheever?

**Cheever** (*turning the poppet over in his hands*). Why, they say it may signify that she—(*He has lifted the poppet's skirt, and his eyes widen in astonished fear.*) Why, this, this—

**Proctor** (*reaching for the poppet*). What's there?

**Cheever.** Why—(*He draws out a long needle from the poppet*)—it is a needle! Herrick, Herrick, it is a needle!

(Herrick *comes toward him.*)

**Proctor** (*angrily, bewildered*). And what signifies a needle!

**Cheever** (*his hands shaking*). Why, this go hard with her, Proctor, this—I had my doubts, Proctor, I had my doubts, but here's calamity. (*To* Hale, *showing the needle*) You see it, sir, it is a needle!

**Hale.** Why? What meanin' has it?

---

60. **as lief** (ăz lēf): rather.

**Cheever** (*wide-eyed, trembling*). The girl, the Williams girl, Abigail Williams, sir. She sat to dinner in Reverend Parris's house tonight, and without word nor warnin' she falls to the floor. Like a struck beast, he says, and screamed a scream that a bull would weep to hear. And he goes to save her, and, stuck two inches in the flesh of her belly, he draw a needle out. And demandin' of her how she come to be so stabbed, she—(*to* Proctor *now*)—testify it were your wife's familiar spirit[61] pushed it in.

**Proctor.** Why, she done it herself! (*To* Hale) I hope you're not takin' this for proof, Mister!

(Hale, *struck by the proof, is silent.*)

**Cheever.** 'Tis hard proof! (*To* Hale) I find here a poppet Goody Proctor keeps. I have found it, sir. And in the belly of the poppet a needle's stuck. I tell you true, Proctor, I never warranted to see such proof of Hell, and I bid you obstruct me not, for I—

(*Enter* Elizabeth *with* Mary Warren. Proctor, *seeing* Mary Warren, *draws her by the arm to* Hale.)

**Proctor.** Here now! Mary, how did this poppet come into my house?

**Mary Warren** (*frightened for herself, her voice very small*). What poppet's that, sir?

**Proctor** (*impatiently, pointing at the doll in* Cheever's *hand*). This poppet, this poppet.

**Mary Warren** (*evasively, looking at it*). Why, I—I think it is mine.

**Proctor.** It is your poppet, is it not?

**Mary Warren** (*not understanding the direction of this*). It—is, sir.

**Proctor.** And how did it come into this house?

**Mary Warren** (*glancing about at the avid faces*). Why—I made it in the court, sir, and—give it to Goody Proctor tonight.

**Proctor** (*to* Hale). Now, sir—do you have it?

**Hale.** Mary Warren, a needle have been found inside this poppet.

**Mary Warren** (*bewildered*). Why, I meant no harm by it, sir.

**Proctor** (*quickly*). You stuck that needle in yourself?

**Mary Warren.** I—I believe I did, sir, I—

**Proctor** (*to* Hale). What say you now?

**Hale** (*watching* Mary Warren *closely*). Child, you are certain this be your natural memory? May it be, perhaps, that someone conjures you even now to say this?

**Mary Warren.** Conjures me? Why, no, sir, I am entirely myself, I think. Let you ask Susanna Walcott—she saw me sewin' it in court. Or better still: Ask Abby, Abby sat beside me when I made it.

**Proctor** (*to* Hale, *of* Cheever). Bid him begone. Your mind is surely settled now. Bid him out, Mr. Hale.

**Elizabeth.** What signifies a needle?

**Hale.** Mary—you charge a cold and cruel murder on Abigail.

**Mary Warren.** Murder! I charge no—

**Hale.** Abigail were stabbed tonight; a needle were found stuck into her belly—

**Elizabeth.** And she charges me?

**Hale.** Aye.

**Elizabeth** (*her breath knocked out*). Why—! The girl is murder! She must be ripped out of the world!

**Cheever** (*pointing at* Elizabeth). You've heard that, sir! Ripped out of the world! Herrick, you heard it!

**Proctor** (*suddenly snatching the warrant out of* Cheever's *hands*). Out with you.

**Cheever.** Proctor, you dare not touch the warrant.

**Proctor** (*ripping the warrant*). Out with you!

**Cheever.** You've ripped the Deputy Governor's warrant, man!

**Proctor.** Damn the Deputy Governor! Out of my house!

---

61. **familiar spirit:** the spirit or demon, most usually in the form of an animal such as a black cat, that was a companion and helper to a witch.

## Customizing Instruction

**Students Acquiring English**

**1** Proctor asks, "What signifies a poppet?" This question may be rephrased, "What does it mean when a doll is discovered in someone's house?"

## Literary Analysis | STAGE DIRECTIONS

**A** Ask students to consider how these stage directions inform their understanding of the scene. Have them use the stage directions to describe the atmosphere in the room and the characters' feelings.

**Possible Response:** The atmosphere is chaotic, with everyone full of fear or doubt. Hale feels unsure of what he's doing, Mary is frightened and weeping, Elizabeth is terrified, Giles is yelling at Hale, and Proctor is enraged.

## Active Reading

### USING A GRAPHIC ORGANIZER

**B** Refer students back to their character chart for John Proctor. Ask them to identify another trait and provide evidence for it, and then add this information to their charts.

### John Proctor

| **Trait:** defensive | **Trait:** protective; brave |
|---|---|
| **Evidence:** He feels guilty about his sin, yet he becomes defensive with Elizabeth and tells her she should improve herself by learning charity before she judges him. He also points out his excellent behavior since Abigail's departure. | **Evidence:** He is willing to go to court and expose both himself and Abigail as adulterers in order to save Elizabeth. He will not allow Elizabeth to suffer for him, and he will force Mary to tell the truth. |

## Reading Skills and Strategies: TAKING NOTES

Have students take notes to understand the play better, in particular what has happened since Cheever came to the house. Ask them to use their notes to give a plot summary.

---

**Hale.** Now, Proctor, Proctor!

**Proctor.** Get y'gone with them! You are a broken minister.

**Hale.** Proctor, if she is innocent, the court—

**Proctor.** If she is innocent! Why do you never wonder if Parris be innocent, or Abigail? Is the accuser always holy now? Were they born this morning as clean as God's fingers? I'll tell you what's walking Salem—vengeance is walking Salem. We are what we always were in Salem, but now the little crazy children are jangling the keys of the kingdom, and common vengeance writes the law! This warrant's vengeance! I'll not give my wife to vengeance!

**Elizabeth.** I'll go, John—

**Proctor.** You will not go!

**Herrick.** I have nine men outside. You cannot keep her. The law binds me, John, I cannot budge.

**Proctor** (*to Hale, ready to break him*). Will you see her taken?

**1** **Hale.** Proctor, the court is just—

**Proctor.** Pontius Pilate![62] God will not let you wash your hands of this!

**Elizabeth.** John—I think I must go with them. (*He cannot bear to look at her.*) Mary, there is bread enough for the morning; you will bake, in the afternoon. Help Mr. Proctor as you were his daughter—you owe me that, and much more. (*She is fighting her weeping. To* Proctor) When the children wake, speak nothing of witchcraft—it will frighten them. (*She cannot go on.*)

**Proctor.** I will bring you home. I will bring you soon.

**Elizabeth.** Oh, John, bring me soon!

**Proctor.** I will fall like an ocean on that court! Fear nothing, Elizabeth.

**A** **Elizabeth** (*with great fear*). I will fear nothing. (*She looks about the room, as though to fix it in her mind.*) Tell the children I have gone to visit someone sick.

(*She walks out the door,* Herrick *and* Cheever *behind her. For a moment,* Proctor *watches from the doorway. The clank of chain is heard.*)

**Proctor.** Herrick! Herrick, don't chain her! (*He rushes out the door. From outside*) Damn you, man, you will not chain her! Off with them! I'll not have it! I will not have her chained!

(*There are other men's voices against his.* Hale, *in a fever of guilt and uncertainty, turns from the door to avoid the sight;* Mary Warren *bursts into tears and sits weeping.* Giles Corey *calls to* Hale.)

**A**

**Giles.** And yet silent, minister? It is fraud, you know it is fraud! What keeps you, man?

(Proctor *is half braced, half pushed into the room by two deputies and* Herrick.)

**Proctor.** I'll pay you, Herrick, I will surely pay you!

**Herrick** (*panting*). In God's name, John, I cannot help myself. I must chain them all. Now let you keep inside this house till I am gone! (*He goes out with his deputies.*)

(Proctor *stands there, gulping air. Horses and a wagon creaking are heard.*)

**Hale** (*in great uncertainty*). Mr. Proctor—

**Proctor.** Out of my sight!

**Hale.** Charity, Proctor, charity. What I have heard in her favor, I will not fear to testify in court. God help me, I cannot judge her guilty or innocent—I know not. Only this consider: the world goes mad, and it profit nothing you should lay the cause to the vengeance of a little girl.

**Proctor.** You are a coward! Though you be ordained in God's own tears, you are a coward now!

**Hale.** Proctor, I cannot think God be provoked so grandly by such a petty cause. The jails are packed—our greatest judges sit in Salem now—

---

62. **Pontius Pilate** (pŏn'chəs pī'lət): the Roman governor who presided over the trial and sentencing of Christ. Pilate publicly washed his hands to absolve himself of responsibility for Christ's death.

---

## Teaching Options

### ✓ Assessment Standardized Test Practice

**PERCEIVING CAUSE AND EFFECT RELATIONSHIPS**
In many test situations, students will be asked to perceive cause-and-effect relationships. To provide students with practice, read aloud or write on the chalkboard the following question:
On what evidence is Elizabeth arrested?
**A.** Elizabeth tells Hale that she does not believe in witches.
**B.** Abigail claims that a needle in her stomach came from Elizabeth's spirit, and the men find a poppet and needle in Elizabeth's house.

**C.** Martha Giles and Rebecca Nurse have been forced to testify against her.
Lead students through the process of selecting the best answer. Point out that C is not true at all. Although statements A and B are both true, B is the better choice because it contains the concrete evidence that convinces Cheever to arrest Elizabeth.

and hangin's promised. Man, we must look to cause proportionate. Were there murder done, perhaps, and never brought to light? Abomination? Some secret blasphemy that stinks to Heaven? Think on cause, man, and let you help me to discover it. For there's your way, believe it, there is your only way, when such confusion strikes upon the world. *(He goes to* Giles *and* Francis.*)* Let you counsel among yourselves; think on your village and what may have drawn from heaven such thundering wrath upon you all. I shall pray God open up our eyes.

*(Hale goes out.)*

**Francis** *(struck by* Hale's *mood).* I never heard no murder done in Salem.

**Proctor** *(he has been reached by* Hale's *words).* Leave me, Francis, leave me.

**Giles** *(shaken).* John—tell me, are we lost?

**Proctor.** Go home now, Giles. We'll speak on it tomorrow.

**Giles.** Let you think on it. We'll come early, eh?

**Proctor.** Aye. Go now, Giles.

**Giles.** Good night, then.

*(Giles Corey goes out. After a moment)*

**Mary Warren** *(in a fearful squeak of a voice).* Mr. Proctor, very likely they'll let her come home once they're given proper evidence.

**Proctor.** You're coming to the court with me, Mary. You will tell it in the court.

**Mary Warren.** I cannot charge murder on Abigail.

**Proctor** *(moving menacingly toward her).* You will tell the court how that poppet come here and who stuck the needle in.

**Mary Warren.** She'll kill me for sayin' that! *(Proctor continues toward her.)* Abby'll charge lechery[63] on you, Mr. Proctor!

**Proctor** *(halting).* She's told you!

**Mary Warren.** I have known it, sir. She'll ruin you with it, I know she will.

**Proctor** *(hesitating, and with deep hatred of himself).* Good. Then her saintliness is done with. *(Mary backs from him.)* We will slide together into our pit; you will tell the court what you know.

**Mary Warren** *(in terror).* I cannot, they'll turn on me—

*(Proctor strides and catches her, and she is repeating, "I cannot, I cannot!")*

**Proctor.** My wife will never die for me! I will bring your guts into your mouth but that goodness will not die for me!

**Mary Warren** *(struggling to escape him).* I cannot do it, I cannot!

**Proctor** *(grasping her by the throat as though he would strangle her).* Make your peace with it! Now Hell and Heaven grapple[64] on our backs, and all our old pretense is ripped away—make your peace! *(He throws her to the floor, where she sobs, "I cannot, I cannot . . ." And now, half to himself, staring, and turning to the open door)* Peace. It is a providence, and no great change; we are only what we always were, but naked now. *(He walks as though toward a great horror, facing the open sky.)* Aye, naked! And the wind, God's icy wind, will blow!

*(And she is over and over again sobbing, "I cannot, I cannot, I cannot," as)*

**the curtain falls**

---

63. **lechery** (lĕch′ə-rē): excessive or illicit sexual activity.
64. **grapple:** struggle.

THE CRUCIBLE **205**

---

## Customizing Instruction

### Students Acquiring English

**1** Help students interpret the figurative language in this passage.

• *Were they born this morning as clean as God's fingers?*: Proctor is being sarcastic here and pointing out that those doing the accusing are sinners themselves.

• *the little crazy children are jangling the keys of the kingdom*: The girls making accusations are directing what the adults do.

• *common vengeance writes the law*: The Salem court is not following the law but acting on the vengeful feelings of certain citizens.

• *God will not let you wash your hands of this*: Hale may get away with supporting the witch-hunt while he is alive, but God knows he is guilty of allowing innocent people to be hanged and will punish him for it.

• *I will fall like an ocean on that court*: Proctor will overwhelm the court with his righteous anger and his testimony about Abigail.

### Less Proficient Readers

**2** Ask students to restate the reason Hale gives for the outbreak of witchery in Salem. Then have them consider how Hale's beliefs might affect Proctor.

**Possible Response:** Hale believes the witch trials are God's way of punishing Salem for some murder that went untried, or for some disgusting act or word against God. Proctor might believe that his affair with Abigail is the root cause of the witch-hunt, and he may decide to reveal his sin in order to save Elizabeth.

---

## Cross Curricular Link **History**

**McCARTHY HEARINGS** Wisconsin senator Joseph Raymond McCarthy led an aggressive anti-Communist campaign between 1950 and 1954. This period coincided with the escalation of the cold war, when the United States struggled for international influence against the Soviet Union. Americans feared a world dominated by Soviet Communism, and they also dreaded a conflict that could spark another world war. McCarthy began to denounce individual citizens as communists just when people in America feared that Communism was threatening all aspects of human life. In a speech given on February 9, 1950, Senator McCarthy announced that he had a list of 205 U.S. State Department employees known to be "card-carrying communists." He did not, however, have his own proof. He based his accusations on 205 FBI security investigations, most of which were discounted or were focused on individuals no longer in the department. Out of fear, America fell victim to many ridiculous charges made by McCarthy, and the country entered an era, much like 17th-century Salem, when fear overwhelmed reason. In fact, McCarthy's critics frequently referred to his activities as "witch-hunts."

THE CRUCIBLE **205**

## GUIDING STUDENT RESPONSE

## Connect to the Literature

**1. What Do You Think?**
Students should support their reactions with textual evidence.

**Comprehension Check**
• a small rag doll
• the Ten Commandments
• Rebecca Nurse and Martha Corey

 Use Selection Quiz in
**Unit Two Resource Book**, p. 24.

## Think Critically

**2.** Possible Response: John Proctor learns that his actions have consequences. His affair with and rejection of Abigail has set in motion her vengeance, which has now claimed his innocent wife as a victim.

**3.** Possible Response: Elizabeth is a concerned wife and caring mother who feels ill at ease in her relationship with her husband because of his past affair with Abigail. According to her husband, Elizabeth's outstanding trait is honesty.

**4.** Possible Response: Elizabeth and John Proctor maintain a strained relationship, haunted by the specter of John's infidelity. Elizabeth feels that she cannot trust him. John feels that no matter what he does, his wife still suspects him of desiring Abigail. John's guilty passion for Abigail has damaged his relationship with his wife.

**5.** Possible Responses: Yes, Reverend Hale believes that any human, even the most saintly, can succumb to the powers of evil; no, he believes Proctor's statements about Elizabeth's honesty but cannot accept that the hysteria might be a hoax.

**6.** Possible Response: Proctor's statement "vengeance is walking Salem" suggests that personal spite is the underlying cause of all the arrests. Abigail and the other girls, once subject to punishment for their wayward conduct in the woods, are now esteemed as community benefactors and relish their new status. Their newfound power silences all doubters, allowing the girls the opportunity to take revenge on their enemies. Abigail has the public backing to go after anyone opposed to her, even Elizabeth Proctor.

## Connect to the Literature

**1. What Do You Think?**
How did you react to Elizabeth Proctor's arrest at the end of this act?

**Comprehension Check**
• What object does Mary Warren give Elizabeth Proctor?
• What does Reverend Hale ask John Proctor to recite?
• Whom does Ezekiel Cheever arrest besides Elizabeth Proctor?

## Think Critically

**2.** What do you think is the most important thing that John Proctor learns about himself by the end of this act? Explain your answer, using details from the play.

**3.** **ACTIVE READING  USING A GRAPHIC ORGANIZER**  How would you describe Elizabeth Proctor's **character traits**? Refer to the chart you made for her character in your  **READER'S NOTEBOOK.**

**4.** Evaluate the relationship between Elizabeth and John Proctor. Who is more to blame for their marital problems?

**5.** Do you think Reverend Hale believes that Elizabeth Proctor is practicing witchcraft? Support your opinion.

**6.** Why do you suppose so many people have been arrested? What do you think is motivating the officials of Salem?

> **THINK ABOUT**
> • who is making the accusations and why
> • why no one speaks out against the accusers
> • the types of women who have been accused and how the pattern of accusation has changed
> • which **characters** seem sincere in their beliefs about witches

## Extend Interpretations

**7. Critic's Corner**  Critic Sheila Huftel points out that Miller is not content with simply writing a dramatic story about the Salem witch trials but seems to find it "necessary to explain why these things take place and how, in fact, people come to believe in witches." Based on the evidence in the first two acts, how do people come to suspect others of being witches?

**8. What If?**  What, if anything, do you think John Proctor might have done to prevent his wife's arrest? Explain.

**9. Connect to Life**  Puritan society pressured individuals to adhere to strict standards of conduct and belief. To what extent do you think society expects you to conform today? Explain.

## Literary Analysis

> **DIALOGUE**  **Dialogue** is written conversation between two or more **characters.** Found in all forms of literature but most important in drama, dialogue moves the **plot** forward and provides clues about characters' motives and relationships. For example, consider the following dialogue between Elizabeth and John Proctor.

> **Elizabeth.** You were alone with her [Abigail Williams]?
> **Proctor.** (*stubbornly*): For a moment alone, aye.
> **Elizabeth.** Why, then, it is not as you told me.

Why does Elizabeth react so strongly to the news that John was alone with Abigail? What does Proctor's stubborn reply reveal about him? You might infer that John and Elizabeth are both uneasy about John's relationship with Abigail—John feels guilty about what happened between them, and Elizabeth does not trust her husband.

**Cooperative Learning Activity**  With two classmates, examine other passages of dialogue in Act Two: the exchanges between Mary Warren, Proctor, and Elizabeth in which Mary reveals Sarah Good's confession of witchcraft (page 195); the exchanges between Mr. Hale, Proctor, and Elizabeth in which Proctor tries to recite the Commandments (page 199); the exchange between Proctor and Mary Warren at the end of the act (page 205). Read these exchanges aloud. Then discuss with the rest of the class how the dialogue moves the plot forward or what it reveals about the characters.

## Extend Interpretations

**Critic's Corner** Possible Response: People look for scapegoats to account for their own misfortunes. Ann Putnam, for example, who has lost seven children in childbirth, targets Rebecca Nurse, who has several children and grandchildren, as a witch. Mary Warren connects her mysterious stomach cramps with Sarah Good's mumbling, which probably made Mary feel uncomfortable and guilty for turning Good away without food.
**What If?** Possible Response: It was only a matter of time before the witchcraft hysteria claimed Elizabeth, Abigail's enemy. Still, if Proctor had gone to Salem earlier and accused Abigail of fraud, he might have damaged her credibility before she gained the power to accuse his wife.
**Connect to Life** Accept all reasonable responses.

## Literary Analysis:

**Dialogue** Students should cite particular lines as supporting evidence for their insights about the characters.

# ACT THREE

*(The vestry room[65] of the Salem meeting house, now serving as the ante-room of the General Court.)*

*(As the curtain rises, the room is empty, but for sunlight pouring through two high windows in the back wall. The room is solemn, even forbidding. Heavy beams jut out, boards of random widths make up the walls. At the right are two doors leading into the meeting house proper, where the court is being held. At the left another door leads outside.)*

*(There is a plain bench at the left, and another at the right. In the center a rather long meeting table, with stools and a considerable armchair snugged up to it.)*

*(Through the partitioning wall at the right we hear a prosecutor's voice, Judge Hathorne's, asking a question; then a woman's voice, Martha Corey's, replying.)*

**Hathorne's Voice.** Now, Martha Corey, there is abundant evidence in our hands to show that you have given yourself to the reading of fortunes. Do you deny it?

**Martha Corey's Voice.** I am innocent to a witch. I know not what a witch is.

**Hathorne's Voice.** How do you know, then, that you are not a witch?

**Martha Corey's Voice.** If I were, I would know it.

**Hathorne's Voice.** Why do you hurt these children?

**Martha Corey's Voice.** I do not hurt them. I scorn it!

**Giles' Voice** *(roaring)*. I have evidence for the court!

---

65. **vestry room:** a room in a church used for nonreligious meetings or church business.

THE CRUCIBLE   **207**

## BLOCK SCHEDULING: MANAGING TIME

**If your schedule requires that you cover the lesson objectives in a shorter time, use . . .**
• Thinking Through the Literature, p. 228

**If you want to take advantage of longer class time, use . . .**
• TE Teaching Options: Vocabulary Strategy, pp. 208–209, 210; Speaking and Listening, p. 220; Cross-Curricular Link, pp. 212, 218, 226; Informal Assessment, p. 214; Standardized Test Practice, pp. 224, 227

## TEACHING THE LITERATURE
### Customizing Instruction

**Students Acquiring English**
Prepare students for Act Three by explaining that it takes place in a court-room and that much of the dialogue consists of questions and answers. The characters Hathorne, Danforth, and Hale are trying to decide who is guilty of witchcraft, so their questions are aimed at getting relevant information from various witnesses.

**Multiple Learning Styles**
**Visual Learners**
**1** Draw students' attention to the picture of the outside of the Salem meeting house. Have students construct an image based on text descriptions of the vestry room's interior. They may share their sketches with other students to compare how each imagined the interior room.

**Less Proficient Readers**
**2** Remind students that the setting changes with the beginning of each new act. Review the settings of the last two scenes. Then ask the following questions to help acquaint them with Act Three:

• What is the setting?
**Answer:** the vestry room in a Salem meeting house, which serves as an anteroom

• What do you think is happening?
**Possible Response:** Martha Corey is standing trial for witchery.

## Literary Analysis [FOIL]

The word *foil* refers to a jeweler's practice of placing a thin sheet of bright metal under a gem to increase the jewel's brilliance. In literature, the word refers to a character that enhances another character through contrast, making that character's attributes stand out more sharply. Ask students to consider the play's cast of characters and suggest a character who functions as a foil for another.

**Possible Response:** Elizabeth can be seen as a foil for Abigail. Mrs. Proctor's honesty and essential goodness stand in sharp contrast to Abigail's vindictive, manipulative nature.

Use **Unit Two Resource Book,** p. 27 for more practice.

## Reading Skills and Strategies: VISUALIZING

**A** Read the description of Deputy Governor Danforth aloud to students. Ask them to visualize what he looks like in more detail than is given. Encourage students to share their visualizations and to compare and contrast their perceptions of Danforth.

## Literary Analysis: CHARACTERIZATION

**B** Have students discuss how the author reveals Deputy Governor Danforth's character as the deputy questions both Giles and Francis.

**Possible Response:** Danforth's questions indicate that he's filled with a sense of officious self-importance. He speaks condescendingly to both Giles and Francis, as if they do not realize how important he and his decisions are.

---

(*Voices of townspeople rise in excitement.*)

**Danforth's Voice.** You will keep your seat!

**Giles' Voice.** Thomas Putnam is reaching out for land!

**Danforth's Voice.** Remove that man, Marshal!

**Giles' Voice.** You're hearing lies, lies!

(*A roaring goes up from the people.*)

**Hathorne's Voice.** Arrest him, excellency!

**Giles' Voice.** I have evidence. Why will you not hear my evidence?

(*The door opens and* Giles *is half carried into the vestry room by* Herrick.)

**Giles.** Hands off, damn you, let me go!

**Herrick.** Giles, Giles!

**Giles.** Out of my way, Herrick! I bring evidence—

**Herrick.** You cannot go in there, Giles; it's a court!

(*Enter* Hale *from the court.*)

**Hale.** Pray be calm a moment.

**Giles.** You, Mr. Hale, go in there and demand I speak.

**Hale.** A moment, sir, a moment.

**Giles.** They'll be hangin' my wife!

 (Judge Hathorne *enters. He is in his sixties, a bitter, remorseless Salem judge.*)

**Hathorne.** How do you dare come roarin' into this court! Are you gone daft, Corey?

**Giles.** You're not a Boston judge yet, Hathorne. You'll not call me daft!

**A** (*Enter* Deputy Governor Danforth *and, behind him,* Ezekiel Cheever *and* Parris. *On his appearance, silence falls.* Danforth *is a grave man in his sixties, of some humor and sophistication that does not, however, interfere with an exact loyalty to his position and his cause. He comes down to* Giles, *who awaits his wrath.*)

**Danforth** (*looking directly at* Giles). Who is this man?

**Parris.** Giles Corey, sir, and a more <u>contentious</u>—

---

**Giles** (*to* Parris). I am asked the question, and I am old enough to answer it! (*To* Danforth, *who impresses him and to whom he smiles through his strain*) My name is Corey, sir, Giles Corey. I have six hundred acres, and timber in addition. It is my wife you be condemning now. (*He indicates the courtroom.*)

**Danforth.** And how do you imagine to help her cause with such contemptuous riot?[66] Now be gone. Your old age alone keeps you out of jail for this.

**Giles** (*beginning to plead*). They be tellin' lies about my wife, sir, I— **B**

**Danforth.** Do you take it upon yourself to determine what this court shall believe and what it shall set aside?

**Giles.** Your Excellency, we mean no disrespect for—

**Danforth.** Disrespect indeed! It is disruption, Mister. This is the highest court of the supreme government of this province, do you know it?

**Giles** (*beginning to weep*). Your Excellency, I only said she were readin' books, sir, and they come and take her out of my house for—

**Danforth** (*mystified*). Books! What books?

**Giles** (*through helpless sobs*). It is my third wife, sir; I never had no wife that be so taken with books, and I thought to find the cause of it, d'y'see, but it were no witch I blamed her for. (*He is openly weeping.*) I have broke charity with the woman, I have broke charity with her. (*He covers his face, ashamed.* Danforth *is respectfully silent.*)

**Hale.** Excellency, he claims hard evidence for his wife's defense. I think that in all justice you must—

**Danforth.** Then let him submit his evidence in proper affidavit. You are certainly aware of our

---

66. **contemptuous** (kən-tĕmp′chŏō-əs) **riot:** disrespectful, outrageous behavior.

---

WORDS
TO     **contentious** (kən-tĕn′shəs) *adj.* quarrelsome
KNOW

**208**

---

## Teaching Options

### (Mini Lesson) **Vocabulary Strategy**

**USING CONTEXT CLUES** There are many types of context clues that can help students determine the meanings of unfamiliar words. Use the model sentence to demonstrate how to use context clues that provide comparisons or contrasts.

#### Model Sentence

Unlike her friend Mary, who is usually cooperative, Abigail is a <u>contentious</u> girl.

#### Instruction

- Write the model sentence on the chalkboard.
- Ask a volunteer to summarize the meaning of the sentence.
- Have students use the contrasting word, *cooperative*, to determine the meaning of *contentious*.
- Ask a volunteer to use the word *contentious* in a sentence.

procedure here, Mr. Hale. (*To* Herrick) Clear this room.

**Herrick.** Come now, Giles. (*He gently pushes Corey out.*)

**Francis.** We are desperate, sir; we come here three days now and cannot be heard.

**Danforth.** Who is this man?

**Francis.** Francis Nurse, Your Excellency.

**Hale.** His wife's Rebecca that were condemned this morning.

**Danforth.** Indeed! I am amazed to find you in such uproar. I have only good report of your character, Mr. Nurse.

**Hathorne.** I think they must both be arrested in contempt, sir.

**Danforth** (*to* Francis). Let you write your plea, and in due time I will—

**Francis.** Excellency, we have proof for your eyes; God forbid you shut them to it. The girls, sir, the girls are frauds.

**Danforth.** What's that?

**Francis.** We have proof of it, sir. They are all deceiving you.

(Danforth *is shocked, but studying* Francis.)

**Hathorne.** This is contempt, sir, contempt!

**Danforth.** Peace, Judge Hathorne. Do you know who I am, Mr. Nurse?

**Francis.** I surely do, sir, and I think you must be a wise judge to be what you are.

4

B

THE CRUCIBLE **209**

## Customizing Instruction

### Students Acquiring English

**1** Explain that *remorseless* means "without mercy." Hathorne has no pity or concern for the people he condemns.

**2** Explain that when Giles says he "broke charity" with his wife, he means that he acted unlovingly by giving testimony about her book reading—evidence that allowed them to charge her with witchery.

**3** An *affidavit* is a legal document containing a sworn statement made in the presence of a court official. Danforth is telling Hale that Giles must follow the proper procedure for submitting evidence, rather than simply bursting into court on his own.

**4** Point out that the idiom *in due time* means "eventually" or "when it is appropriate."

**Exercises** Ask students to use context clues to determine the meanings of underlined terms in the following sentences.

1. Elizabeth has an <u>immaculate</u> reputation in Salem; like Rebecca, Elizabeth is known for always doing the right thing.

2. Mary spoke <u>inaudibly</u> during her testimony, but Danforth spoke so clearly that everyone could hear him.

3. The girls acted as though <u>afflicted</u>, screaming in pain and torment.

4. Mercy's speech was <u>unintelligible</u> during her outburst and sounded like gibberish.

5. The students acted with disrespectful boldness toward the substitute teacher. Their regular teacher, however, would not tolerate such <u>effrontery</u>.

**A lesson on context clues appears on p. 326 in the Pupil's Edition.**

### Active Reading
**USING A GRAPHIC ORGANIZER**

 **A** Ask students to consider these words spoken by Deputy Governor Danforth. In their Reader's Notebooks, have them use their graphic organizers to describe a trait of Danforth and list evidence to support it.

#### Deputy Governor Danforth

| Trait: rigid; close-minded | Trait: |
|---|---|
| **Evidence:** He has already approved the hangings of seventy-two people, and he has no reason to think he's wrong. Instead of welcoming new evidence, he'd prefer to disregard it. | **Evidence:** |

Use **Unit Two Resource Book,** p. 26 for additional support.

### Literary Analysis:
#### FIGURATIVE LANGUAGE

**B** Ask students to interpret this figurative language and discuss how it is related to the play's title. If necessary, have them use a dictionary to check multiple meanings of the word *crucible*.

**Possible Response:** Danforth is comparing his court to a hot fire. In other words, the court pursues facts so relentlessly that it will destroy any witness's attempt to hide the truth. A crucible is literally a container used to melt metals at extremely high temperatures in order to purify or alter them in some way. In a figurative sense, a crucible is a situation in which people's souls are tested and changed through hardship.

---

**Danforth.** And do you know that near to four hundred are in the jails from Marblehead to Lynn,[62] and upon my signature?

**Francis.** I—

**Danforth.** And seventy-two condemned to hang by that signature?

**Francis.** Excellency, I never thought to say it to such a weighty judge, but you are deceived.

(*Enter* Giles Corey *from left. All turn to see as he beckons in* Mary Warren *with* Proctor. Mary *is keeping her eyes to the ground;* Proctor *has her elbow as though she were near collapse.*)

**Parris** (*on seeing her, in shock*). Mary Warren! (*He goes directly to bend close to her face.*) What are you about here?

**Proctor** (*pressing* Parris *away from her with a gentle but firm motion of protectiveness*). She would speak with the Deputy Governor.

**Danforth** (*shocked by this, turns to* Herrick). Did you not tell me Mary Warren were sick in bed?

**Herrick.** She were, Your Honor. When I go to fetch her to the court last week, she said she were sick.

**Giles.** She has been strivin' with her soul all week, Your Honor; she comes now to tell the truth of this to you.

**Danforth.** Who is this?

**Proctor.** John Proctor, sir. Elizabeth Proctor is my wife.

**Parris.** Beware this man, Your Excellency, this man is mischief.

**Hale** (*excitedly*). I think you must hear the girl, sir, she—

**Danforth** (*who has become very interested in* Mary Warren *and only raises a hand toward* Hale). Peace. What would you tell us, Mary Warren?

(Proctor *looks at her, but she cannot speak.*)

**Proctor.** She never saw no spirits, sir.

**Danforth** (*with great alarm and surprise, to* Mary). Never saw no spirits!

**Giles** (*eagerly*). Never.

**Proctor** (*reaching into his jacket*). She has signed a deposition, sir—

**Danforth** (*instantly*). No, no, I accept no depositions. (*He is rapidly calculating this; he turns from her to* Proctor.) Tell me, Mr. Proctor, have you given out this story in the village?

**Proctor.** We have not.

**Parris.** They've come to overthrow the court, sir! This man is—

**Danforth.** I pray you, Mr. Parris. Do you know, Mr. Proctor, that the entire contention of the state in these trials is that the voice of Heaven is speaking through the children?

**Proctor.** I know that, sir.

**Danforth** (*thinks, staring at* Proctor, *then turns to* Mary Warren). And you, Mary Warren, how came you to cry out people for sending their spirits against you?

**Mary Warren.** It were pretense, sir.

**Danforth.** I cannot hear you.

**Proctor.** It were pretense, she says.

**Danforth.** Ah? And the other girls? Susanna Walcott, and—the others? They are also pretending?

**Mary Warren.** Aye, sir.

**Danforth** (*wide-eyed*). Indeed. (*Pause. He is baffled by this. He turns to study* Proctor's *face.*)

**Parris** (*in a sweat*). Excellency, you surely cannot think to let so vile a lie be spread in open court!

**Danforth.** Indeed not, but it strike hard upon me that she will dare come here with such a tale. Now, Mr. Proctor, before I decide whether I shall hear you or not, it is my duty to tell you this. We burn a hot fire here; it melts down all concealment.

**Proctor.** I know that, sir.

---

67. **Marblehead to Lynn:** two coastal towns in Massachusetts, near Salem.

**WORDS TO KNOW**    **deposition** (dĕp′ə-zĭsh′ən) *n.* a written statement by a witness

210

---

## Teaching Options

### Mini Lesson **Vocabulary Strategy**

**UNDERSTANDING MULTIPLE-MEANING WORDS**
**Instruction** Many words have more than one meaning. The correct meaning in any case is determined by context. For example, the most frequently used definition for *deposition* is "a sworn written statement that can be used in court." Another meaning is "the act of removing from a position of power or authority." When Proctor says that Mary has signed a deposition and Danforth replies, "I accept no depositions," they are referring to a written statement signed by Mary. Thus the first definition is correct for this context.

**Application** Have students use a dictionary to find multiple meanings of *disinterested, swift, furnish, mind,* and *fare.* Challenge them to write sentences using the various meanings of each word.

**Danforth.** Let me continue. I understand well, a husband's tenderness may drive him to extravagance in defense of a wife. Are you certain in your conscience, Mister, that your evidence is the truth?

**Proctor.** It is. And you will surely know it.

**Danforth.** And you thought to declare this revelation in the open court before the public?

**Proctor.** I thought I would, aye—with your permission.

**Danforth** (*his eyes narrowing*). Now, sir, what is your purpose in so doing?

**Proctor.** Why, I—I would free my wife, sir.

**Danforth.** There lurks nowhere in your heart, nor hidden in your spirit, any desire to undermine this court?

**Proctor** (*with the faintest faltering*). Why, no, sir.

**Cheever** (*clears his throat, awakening*). I—Your Excellency.

**Danforth.** Mr. Cheever.

**Cheever.** I think it be my duty, sir—(*Kindly, to* Proctor) You'll not deny it, John. (*To* Danforth) When we come to take his wife, he damned the court and ripped your warrant.

**Parris.** Now you have it!

**Danforth.** He did that, Mr. Hale?

**Hale** (*takes a breath*). Aye, he did.

**Proctor.** It were a temper, sir. I knew not what I did.

**Danforth** (*studying him*). Mr. Proctor.

**Proctor.** Aye, sir.

**Danforth** (*straight into his eyes*). Have you ever seen the Devil?

**Proctor.** No, sir.

**Danforth.** You are in all respects a Gospel Christian?[68]

**Proctor.** I am, sir.

**Parris.** Such a Christian that will not come to church but once in a month!

**Danforth** (*restrained—he is curious*). Not come to church?

**Proctor.** I—I have no love for Mr. Parris. It is no secret. But God I surely love.

**Cheever.** He plow on Sunday, sir.

**Danforth.** Plow on Sunday!

**Cheever** (*apologetically*). I think it be evidence, John. I am an official of the court, I cannot keep it.

**Proctor.** I—I have once or twice plowed on Sunday. I have three children, sir, and until last year my land give little.

**Giles.** You'll find other Christians that do plow on Sunday if the truth be known.

**Hale.** Your Honor, I cannot think you may judge the man on such evidence.

**Danforth.** I judge nothing. (*Pause. He keeps watching* Proctor, *who tries to meet his gaze.*) I tell you straight, Mister—I have seen marvels in this court. I have seen people choked before my eyes by spirits; I have seen them stuck by pins and slashed by daggers. I have until this moment not the slightest reason to suspect that the children may be deceiving me. Do you understand my meaning?

**Proctor.** Excellency, does it not strike upon you that so many of these women have lived so long with such upright reputation, and—

**Parris.** Do you read the Gospel, Mr. Proctor?

**Proctor.** I read the Gospel.

**Parris.** I think not, or you should surely know that Cain were an upright man, and yet he did kill Abel.

**Proctor.** Aye, God tells us that. (*To* Danforth.) But who tells us Rebecca Nurse murdered seven babies by sending out her spirit on them? It is the children only, and this one will swear she lied to you.

---

68. **a Gospel Christian:** a true Christian.

**Literary Analysis: FORESHADOWING**

**A** Have students take note of this brief exchange between Proctor and Danforth, in which Proctor reinforces his conviction that Elizabeth could never lie. Have students keep these statements in mind when Elizabeth is later called to testify.

**Literary Analysis: CHARACTERIZATION**

**B** Ask students to analyze Proctor's behavior in the court. How does his behavior show that he has changed?

**Possible Response:** Proctor is acting principled, even noble. He wants to help his friends defend their wives. Before, he remained aloof from town affairs.

**Literary Analysis: MOOD**

**C** Have students analyze the mood created by this exchange.

**Possible Response:** The mood is one of horror and foreboding. The reader shares Francis's fear for the honest people who have signed the testament in defense of Rebecca, Elizabeth, and Martha. The scene shows that the witch hysteria has grown to such proportions that no one is safe.

**Literary Analysis** FOIL

**D** Have students review Hale's interjections during the proceedings. Ask them to explain how he might be functioning as a foil.

**Possible Response:** Hale's comments function as the voice of reason, which contrasts with both the fanaticism of Parris and the dogmatism of Danforth.

(Danforth *considers, then beckons* Hathorne *to him.* Hathorne *leans in, and he speaks in his ear.* Hathorne *nods.*)

**Hathorne.** Aye, she's the one.

**Danforth.** Mr. Proctor, this morning, your wife send me a claim in which she states that she is pregnant now.

**Proctor.** My wife pregnant!

**Danforth.** There be no sign of it—we have examined her body.

**Proctor.** But if she say she is pregnant, then she must be! That woman will never lie, Mr. Danforth.

**Danforth.** She will not?

**Proctor.** Never, sir, never.

**Danforth.** We have thought it too convenient to be credited. However, if I should tell you now that I will let her be kept another month; and if she begin to show her natural signs, you shall have her living yet another year until she is delivered—what say you to that? (John Proctor *is struck silent.*) Come now. You say your only purpose is to save your wife. Good, then, she is saved at least this year, and a year is long. What say you, sir? It is done now. (*In conflict,* Proctor *glances at* Francis *and* Giles.) Will you drop this charge?

**Proctor.** I—I think I cannot.

**Danforth** (*now an almost imperceptible hardness in his voice*). Then your purpose is somewhat larger.

**Parris.** He's come to overthrow this court, Your Honor!

**Proctor.** These are my friends. Their wives are also accused—

**Danforth** (*with a sudden briskness of manner*). I judge you not, sir. I am ready to hear your evidence.

**Proctor.** I come not to hurt the court; I only—

**Danforth** (*cutting him off*). Marshal, go into the court and bid Judge Stoughton and Judge Sewall declare recess for one hour. And let them go to the tavern, if they will. All witnesses and prisoners are to be kept in the building.

**Herrick.** Aye, sir. (*Very deferentially*) If I may say it, sir, I know this man all my life. It is a good man, sir.

**Danforth** (*it is the reflection on himself he resents*). I am sure of it, Marshal. (Herrick *nods, then goes out.*) Now, what deposition do you have for us, Mr. Proctor? And I beg you be clear, open as the sky, and honest.

**Proctor** (*as he takes out several papers*). I am no lawyer, so I'll—

**Danforth.** The pure in heart need no lawyers. Proceed as you will.

**Proctor** (*handing* Danforth *a paper*). Will you read this first, sir? It's a sort of testament. The people signing it declare their good opinion of Rebecca, and my wife, and Martha Corey. (Danforth *looks down at the paper.*)

**Parris** (*to enlist* Danforth's *sarcasm*). Their good opinion! (*But* Danforth *goes on reading, and* Proctor *is heartened.*)

**Proctor.** These are all landholding farmers, members of the church. (*Delicately, trying to point out a paragraph*). If you'll notice, sir—they've known the women many years and never saw no sign they had dealings with the Devil.

(Parris *nervously moves over and reads over* Danforth's *shoulder.*)

**Danforth** (*glancing down a long list*). How many names are here?

**Francis.** Ninety-one, Your Excellency.

**Parris** (*sweating*). These people should be summoned. (Danforth *looks up at him questioningly.*) For questioning.

**Francis** (*trembling with anger*). Mr. Danforth, I gave them all my word no harm would come to them for signing this.

**Parris.** This is a clear attack upon the court!

**Hale** (*to* Parris, *trying to contain himself*). Is every defense an attack upon the court? Can no one—?

**Cross Curricular Link History**

**WITCHCRAFT TRIALS** The witchcraft trials in Salem in 1692 created mass hysteria because of a culturally ingrained fear of witchcraft. The people of Salem believed in the presence of witches and demons, as did the people of Europe. In fact, a Great Witch Hunt began in central Europe in the mid-16th century. In the witch trials of Europe and New England, the defendants were usually women. For every man executed for witchcraft, three or more women were sent to their death. This disproportionate persecution of women stemmed from another cultural belief: that women were the weaker sex—physically, mentally, and morally—and therefore were more susceptible to the Devil.

Eventually, the Salem courts were forbidden to base their condemnations on "spectral evidence." Lacking any other evidence on which to base prosecutions, the courts soon dissolved. Over time, most Salem court officials confessed their errors. Twenty years after the trials, the Massachusetts legislature annulled the convictions and awarded compensation to the victims' heirs.

**Parris.** All innocent and Christian people are happy for the courts in Salem! These people are gloomy for it. (*To* Danforth *directly*) And I think you will want to know, from each and every one of them, what discontents them with you!

**Hathorne.** I think they ought to be examined, sir.

**Danforth.** It is not necessarily an attack, I think. Yet—

**Francis.** These are all covenanted Christians, sir.

**Danforth.** Then I am sure they may have nothing to fear. (*Hands* Cheever *the paper*.) Mr. Cheever, have warrants drawn for all of these—arrest for examination. (*To* Proctor) Now, Mister, what other information do you have for us? (Francis *is still standing, horrified*.) You may sit, Mr. Nurse.

**Francis.** I have brought trouble on these people; I have—

**Danforth.** No, old man, you have not hurt these people if they are of good conscience. But you must understand, sir, that a person is either with this court or he must be counted against it, there be no road between. This is a sharp time, now, a precise time—we live no longer in the dusky afternoon when evil mixed itself with good and befuddled the world. Now, by God's grace, the shining sun is up, and them that fear not light will surely praise it. I hope you will be one of those. (Mary Warren *suddenly sobs*.) She's not hearty,[69] I see.

**Proctor.** No, she's not, sir. (*To* Mary, *bending to her, holding her hand, quietly*) Now remember what the angel Raphael said to the boy Tobias.[70] Remember it.

**Mary Warren** (*hardly audible*). Aye.

**Proctor.** "Do that which is good, and no harm shall come to thee."

**Mary Warren.** Aye.

**Danforth.** Come, man, we wait you.

(Marshal Herrick *returns, and takes his post at the door*.)

**Giles.** John, my deposition, give him mine.

**Proctor.** Aye. (*He hands* Danforth *another paper*.) This is Mr. Corey's deposition.

**Danforth.** Oh? (*He looks down at it. Now* Hathorne *comes behind him and reads with him*.)

**Hathorne** (*suspiciously*). What lawyer drew this, Corey?

**Giles.** You know I never hired a lawyer in my life, Hathorne.

**Danforth** (*finishing the reading*). It is very well phrased. My compliments. Mr. Parris, if Mr. Putnam is in the court, will you bring him in? (Hathorne *takes the deposition, and walks to the window with it*. Parris *goes into the court*.) You have no legal training, Mr. Corey?

**Giles** (*very pleased*). I have the best, sir—I am thirty-three time in court in my life. And always plaintiff, too.

**Danforth.** Oh, then you're much put-upon.

**Giles.** I am never put-upon; I know my rights, sir, and I will have them. You know, your father tried a case of mine—might be thirty-five year ago, I think.

**Danforth.** Indeed.

**Giles.** He never spoke to you of it?

**Danforth.** No, I cannot recall it.

**Giles.** That's strange, he give me nine pound damages. He were a fair judge, your father. Y'see, I had a white mare that time, and this fellow

---

69. **She's not hearty:** She's not well.

70. **what the angel said . . . to Tobias:** from the Book of Tobit in the Apocrypha; Tobit's son Tobias was attacked on the Tigris River by a fish, which he caught at the bidding of the angel Raphael. Raphael cured Tobit's blindness by applying the gall of the fish to Tobit's eyes. When Tobit and Tobias were about to reward Raphael, the angel revealed his identity and returned to Heaven.

---

WORDS TO KNOW **plaintiff** (plăn′tĭf) *n.* the party that institutes a suit in court

213

**Literary Analysis: IRONY**

**A** Ask students to point out the irony in the situation Giles now finds himself in.

**Possible Response:** Giles considers himself an expert in legal matters, and in the past he's frequently used the courts for his own advantage. Now, in trying to expose the truth and honor his promise to protect his neighbor, he finds himself facing arrest.

**Literary Analysis: CHARACTERIZATION**

**B** Have students discuss how Hale has changed since he first arrived in Salem. Ask them to explain why Hale now seems to be trying to help Proctor.

**Possible Response:** When Hale came to Salem, he was eager to discover witches and was convinced that Salem was in danger. Now he begins to doubt the process, and he sees that Proctor may have valid evidence.

come to borrow the mare—(*Enter* Parris *with* Thomas Putnam. *When he sees* Putnam, Giles' *ease goes; he is hard.*) Aye, there he is.

**Danforth.** Mr. Putnam, I have here an accusation by Mr. Corey against you. He states that you coldly prompted your daughter to cry witchery upon George Jacobs that is now in jail.

**Putnam.** It is a lie.

**Danforth** (*turning to* Giles). Mr. Putnam states your charge is a lie. What say you to that?

**Giles** (*furious, his fists clenched*). A fart on Thomas Putnam, that is what I say to that!

**Danforth.** What proof do you submit for your charge, sir?

**Giles.** My proof is there! (*Pointing to the paper.*) If Jacobs hangs for a witch he forfeit up his property—that's law! And there is none but Putnam with the coin to buy so great a piece. This man is killing his neighbors for their land!

**Danforth.** But proof, sir, proof.

**Giles** (*pointing at his deposition*). The proof is there! I have it from an honest man who heard Putnam say it! The day his daughter cried out on Jacobs, he said she'd given him a fair gift of land.

**Hathorne.** And the name of this man?

**Giles** (*taken aback*). What name?

**Hathorne.** The man that give you this information.

**Giles** (*hesitates, then*). Why, I—I cannot give you his name.

**Hathorne.** And why not?

**Giles** (*hesitates, then bursts out*). You know well why not! He'll lay in jail if I give his name!

**Hathorne.** This is contempt of the court, Mr. Danforth!

**Danforth** (*to avoid that*). You will surely tell us the name.

**Giles.** I will not give you no name. I mentioned my wife's name once and I'll burn in hell long enough for that. I stand mute.

**Danforth.** In that case, I have no choice but to arrest you for contempt of this court, do you know that?

**Giles.** This is a hearing; you cannot clap me for contempt of a hearing.

**Danforth.** Oh, it is a proper lawyer![71] Do you wish me to declare the court in full session here? Or will you give me good reply?

**Giles** (*faltering*). I cannot give you no name, sir, I cannot.

**Danforth.** You are a foolish old man. Mr. Cheever, begin the record. The court is now in session. I ask you, Mr. Corey—

**Proctor** (*breaking in*). Your Honor—he has the story in confidence, sir, and he—

**Parris.** The Devil lives on such confidences! (*To* Danforth) Without confidences there could be no conspiracy, Your Honor!

**Hathorne.** I think it must be broken, sir.

**Danforth** (*to* Giles). Old man, if your informant tells the truth let him come here openly like a decent man. But if he hide in anonymity I must know why. Now sir, the government and central church demand of you the name of him who reported Mr. Thomas Putnam a common murderer.

**Hale.** Excellency—

**Danforth.** Mr. Hale.

**Hale.** We cannot blink it more. There is a prodigious fear of this court in the country—

**Danforth.** Then there is a prodigious guilt in the country. Are you afraid to be questioned here?

**Hale.** I may only fear the Lord, sir, but there is fear in the country nevertheless.

**Danforth** (*angered now*). Reproach me not with the fear in the country; there is fear in the country because there is a moving plot[72] to topple Christ in the country!

71. **Oh . . . lawyer:** Oh, he thinks he is a real lawyer.
72. **moving:** active.

## ✓ Assessment **Informal Assessment**

**COURT REPORTER** You can informally assess students' understanding of the selection by having them summarize the events of Act Three so far. You might have them assume the role of court reporters and prepare news reports that cover the most important events.

**RUBRIC**

**3 Full Accomplishment** Response reflects a full understanding of the court proceedings, including these details: who has been condemned of witchcraft and what Giles, Francis, and John are doing to try to save their wives.

**2 Substantial Accomplishment** Response shows a reasonable understanding of events but may not fully explain the reasons behind characters' actions.

**1 Little or Partial Accomplishment** Response shows little understanding of events or of character motivation.

**Hale.** But it does not follow that everyone accused is part of it.

**Danforth.** No uncorrupted man may fear this court, Mr. Hale! None! (*To* Giles.) You are under arrest in contempt of this court. Now sit you down and take counsel with yourself, or you will be set in the jail until you decide to answer all questions.

(Giles Corey *makes a rush for* Putnam. Proctor *lunges and holds him.*)

**Proctor.** No, Giles!

**Giles** (*over* Proctor's *shoulder at* Putnam). I'll cut your throat, Putnam, I'll kill you yet!

**Proctor** (*forcing him into a chair*). Peace, Giles, peace. (*Releasing him.*) We'll prove ourselves. Now we will. (*He starts to turn to* Danforth.)

**Giles.** Say nothin' more, John. (*Pointing at* Danforth.) He's only playin' you! He means to hang us all!

(Mary Warren *bursts into sobs.*)

**Danforth.** This is a court of law, Mister. I'll have no effrontery here!

**Proctor.** Forgive him, sir, for his old age. Peace, Giles, we'll prove it all now. (*He lifts up* Mary's *chin.*) You cannot weep, Mary. Remember the angel, what he say to the boy. Hold to it, now; there is your rock. (Mary *quiets. He takes out a paper, and turns to* Danforth.) This is Mary Warren's deposition. I—I would ask you remember, sir, while you read it, that until two week ago she were no different than the other children are today. (*He is speaking reasonably, restraining all his fears, his anger, his anxiety.*) You saw her scream, she howled, she swore familiar spirits choked her; she even testified that Satan, in the form of women now in jail, tried to win her soul away, and then when she refused—

**Danforth.** We know all this.

**Proctor.** Aye, sir. She swears now that she never saw Satan; nor any spirit, vague or clear, that Satan may have sent to hurt her. And she declares her friends are lying now.

(Proctor *starts to hand* Danforth *the deposition, and* Hale *comes up to* Danforth *in a trembling state.*)

**Hale.** Excellency, a moment. I think this goes to the heart of the matter.

**Danforth** (*with deep misgivings*). It surely does.

**Hale.** I cannot say he is an honest man; I know him little. But in all justice, sir, a claim so weighty cannot be argued by a farmer. In God's name, sir, stop here; send him home and let him come again with a lawyer—

**Danforth** (*patiently*). Now look you, Mr. Hale—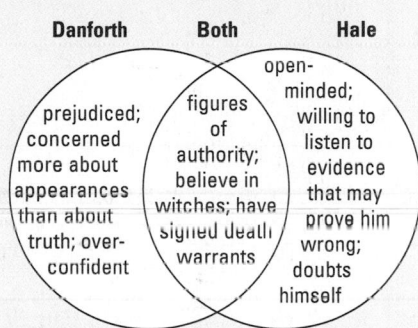

**Hale.** Excellency, I have signed seventy-two death warrants; I am a minister of the Lord, and I dare not take a life without there be a proof so immaculate no slightest qualm of conscience may doubt it.

**Danforth.** Mr. Hale, you surely do not doubt my justice.

**Hale.** I have this morning signed away the soul of Rebecca Nurse, Your Honor. I'll not conceal it, my hand shakes yet as with a wound! I pray you, sir, this argument let lawyers present to you.

**Danforth.** Mr. Hale, believe me; for a man of such terrible learning you are most bewildered—I hope you will forgive me. I have been thirty-two year at the bar, sir, and I should be confounded were I called upon to defend these people. Let you consider, now—(*To* Proctor *and the others.*) And I bid you all do likewise. In an ordinary crime, how does one defend the accused? One calls up witnesses to prove his innocence. But witchcraft is ipso facto,[73] on its face and by its nature, an invisible crime, is it not? Therefore, who may possibly be witness to

---

73. **ipso facto** *Latin:* by that very fact.

---

**215**

---

**A** Have students monitor their own comprehension by questioning Parris's behavior. Ask them to suggest possible motives for his response to the evidence. If they are unable to do so, suggest that they modify their reading strategies to correct this breakdown in understanding—for example, by rereading.

**Possible Response:** Parris acts openly doubtful of the evidence that could save Elizabeth Proctor. He even defends Abigail's behavior in the church by saying she was under Tituba's control. He may be doing this because he dislikes Proctor and because if the girls are discovered to be lying, then his reputation could be permanently marred since one of the accusers is his niece and another is his daughter.

---

it? The witch and the victim. None other. Now we cannot hope the witch will accuse herself; granted? Therefore, we must rely upon her victims—and they do testify, the children certainly do testify. As for the witches, none will deny that we are most eager for all their confessions. Therefore, what is left for a lawyer to bring out? I think I have made my point. Have I not?

**Hale.** But this child claims the girls are not truthful, and if they are not—

**Danforth.** That is precisely what I am about to consider, sir. What more may you ask of me? Unless you doubt my probity?[74]

**Hale** (*defeated*). I surely do not, sir. Let you consider it, then.

**Danforth.** And let you put your heart to rest. Her deposition, Mr. Proctor.

(Proctor *hands it to him.* Hathorne *rises, goes beside* Danforth, *and starts reading.* Parris *comes to his other side.* Danforth *looks at* John Proctor, *then proceeds to read.* Hale *gets up, finds position near the judge, reads too.* Proctor *glances at* Giles. Francis *prays silently, hands pressed together.* Cheever *waits placidly, the sublime official, dutiful.* Mary Warren *sobs once.* John Proctor *touches her head reassuringly. Presently* Danforth *lifts his eyes, stands up, takes out a kerchief and blows his nose. The others stand aside as he moves in thought toward the window.*)

**Parris** (*hardly able to contain his anger and fear*). I should like to question—

**Danforth** (*his first real outburst, in which his contempt for* Parris *is clear*). Mr. Parris, I bid you be silent! (*He stands in silence, looking out the window. Now, having established that he will set the gait.*) Mr. Cheever, will you go into the court and bring the children here? (Cheever *gets up and goes out upstage.* Danforth *now turns to* Mary.) Mary Warren, how came you to this turnabout? Has Mr. Proctor threatened you for this deposition?

**Mary Warren.** No, sir.

**Danforth.** Has he ever threatened you?

**Mary Warren** (*weaker*). No, sir.

**Danforth** (*sensing a weakening*). Has he threatened you?

**Mary Warren.** No, sir.

**Danforth.** Then you tell me that you sat in my court, callously lying, when you knew that people would hang by your evidence? (*She does not answer.*) Answer me!

**Mary Warren** (*almost inaudibly*). I did, sir.

**Danforth.** How were you instructed in your life? Do you not know that God damns all liars? (*She cannot speak.*) Or is it now that you lie?

**Mary Warren.** No, sir—I am with God now.

**Danforth.** You are with God now.

**Mary Warren.** Aye, sir.

**Danforth** (*containing himself*). I will tell you this— you are either lying now, or you were lying in the court, and in either case you have committed perjury and you will go to jail for it. You cannot lightly say you lied, Mary. Do you know that?

**Mary Warren.** I cannot lie no more. I am with God, I am with God.

(*But she breaks into sobs at the thought of it, and the right door opens, and enter* Susanna Walcott, Mercy Lewis, Betty Parris, *and finally* Abigail. Cheever *comes to* Danforth.)

**Cheever.** Ruth Putnam's not in the court, sir, nor the other children.

**Danforth.** These will be sufficient. Sit you down, children. (*Silently they sit.*) Your friend, Mary Warren, has given us a deposition. In which she swears that she never saw familiar spirits, apparitions, nor any manifest of the Devil. She claims as well that none of you have seen these

---

74. **probity** (prō′bĭ-tē): complete honesty; integrity.

WORDS
TO     **inaudibly** (ĭn-ô′də-blē) *adv.* unable to be heard clearly
KNOW

things either. (*Slight pause.*) Now, children, this is a court of law. The law, based upon the Bible, and the Bible, writ by Almighty God, forbid the practice of witchcraft, and describe death as the penalty thereof. But likewise, children, the law and Bible damn all bearers of false witness. (*Slight pause.*) Now then. It does not escape me that this deposition may be devised to blind us; it may well be that Mary Warren has been conquered by Satan, who sends her here to distract our sacred purpose. If so, her neck will break for it. But if she speak true, I bid you now drop your guile and confess your pretense, for a quick confession will go easier with you. (*Pause.*) Abigail Williams, rise. (Abigail *slowly rises.*) Is there any truth in this?

**Abigail.** No, sir.

**Danforth** (*thinks, glances at* Mary, *then back to* Abigail). Children, a very auger[75] bit will now be turned into your souls until your honesty is proved. Will either of you change your positions now, or do you force me to hard questioning?

**Abigail.** I have naught to change, sir. She lies.

**Danforth** (*to* Mary). You would still go on with this?

**Mary Warren** (*faintly*). Aye, sir.

**Danforth** (*turning to* Abigail). A poppet were discovered in Mr. Proctor's house, stabbed by a needle. Mary Warren claims that you sat beside her in the court when she made it, and that you saw her make it and witnessed how she herself stuck her needle into it for safe-keeping. What say you to that?

**Abigail** (*with a slight note of indignation*). It is a lie, sir.

**Danforth** (*after a slight pause*). While you worked for Mr. Proctor, did you see poppets in that house?

**Abigail.** Goody Proctor always kept poppets.

**Proctor.** Your Honor, my wife never kept no poppets. Mary Warren confesses it was her poppet.

**Cheever.** Your Excellency.

**Danforth.** Mr. Cheever.

**Cheever.** When I spoke with Goody Proctor in that house, she said she never kept no poppets. But she said she did keep poppets when she were a girl.

**Proctor.** She has not been a girl these fifteen years, Your Honor.

**Hathorne.** But a poppet will keep fifteen years, will it not?

**Proctor.** It will keep if it is kept, but Mary Warren swears she never saw no poppets in my house, nor anyone else.

**Parris.** Why could there not have been poppets hid where no one ever saw them?

**Proctor** (*furious*). There might also be a dragon with five legs in my house, but no one has ever seen it.

**Parris.** We are here, Your Honor, precisely to discover what no one has ever seen.

**Proctor.** Mr. Danforth, what profit this girl to turn herself about? What may Mary Warren gain but hard questioning and worse?

**Danforth.** You are charging Abigail Williams with a marvelous cool plot to murder, do you understand that?

**Proctor.** I do, sir. I believe she means to murder.

**Danforth** (*pointing at* Abigail, *incredulously*). This child would murder your wife?

**Proctor.** It is not a child. Now hear me, sir. In the sight of the congregation she were twice this year put out of this meetin' house for laughter during prayer.

**Danforth** (*shocked, turning to* Abigail). What's this? Laughter during—!

**Parris.** Excellency, she were under Tituba's power at that time, but she is solemn now.

**Giles.** Aye, now she is solemn and goes to hang people!

**Danforth.** Quiet, man.

---

75. **auger** (ô'gər) **bit:** sharp drill.

## Customizing Instruction

### Students Acquiring English
**1** Explain that *perjury* means "to give false testimony under oath." Danforth is telling Mary that she has testified falsely in court and, as punishment, will go to jail.

### Less Proficient Readers
**2** Have students summarize in their own words what Danforth tells the girls before he allows any of them to speak.
**Possible Response:** First, he tells them that Mary has testified against them. He tells the girls that the law is based upon the Bible and that both the law and the Bible forbid witchery and lying. He knows that the Devil may have conquered Mary Warren and may be using her to prevent justice from occurring. However, he demands that the girls tell the truth and says that if they confess, he will be easier on them.

### Literary Analysis [FOIL]

**A** Have students consider how Parris reacts when he is questioned about the girls' dancing and how much he knew about it. Suggest that they keep this scene in mind as they continue reading so that they can contrast his behavior with John Proctor's.

**Possible Response:** Parris is evasive and confesses to witnessing the dancing only under duress. He is still lying, in fact, by saying that he saw no one naked. Getting to the truth of the matter is not important to him—he merely wants to protect himself.

### Reading Skills and Strategies: MAKING INFERENCES

**B** Point out that Abigail acts insulted that Danforth would dare suggest she is lying. Ask students to explain why Abigail begins to act as she does.

**Possible Response:** To convince the court of her righteousness, Abigail first adopts the attitude that, because of her suffering, she should be beyond reproach and should not be doubted. Then she pretends to be afflicted by spirits to "prove" that she is not lying and to implicate Mary.

---

**Hathorne.** Surely it have no bearing on the question, sir. He charges contemplation of murder.

**Danforth.** Aye. (*He studies* Abigail *for a moment, then*) Continue, Mr. Proctor.

**Proctor.** Mary. Now tell the Governor how you danced in the woods.

**Parris** (*instantly*). Excellency, since I come to Salem this man is blackening my name. He—

**Danforth.** In a moment, sir. (*To* Mary Warren, *sternly, and surprised.*) What is this dancing?

**Mary Warren.** I—(*She glances at* Abigail, *who is staring down at her remorselessly. Then, appealing to* Proctor) Mr. Proctor—

**Proctor** (*taking it right up*). Abigail leads the girls to the woods, Your Honor, and they have danced there naked—

**Parris.** Your Honor, this—

**Proctor** (*at once*). Mr. Parris discovered them himself in the dead of night! There's the "child" she is!

**Danforth** (*it is growing into a nightmare, and he turns, astonished, to* Parris). Mr. Parris—

**Parris.** I can only say, sir, that I never found any of them naked, and this man is—

**Danforth.** But you discovered them dancing in the woods? (*Eyes on* Parris, *he points at* Abigail.) Abigail?

**A** **Hale.** Excellency, when I first arrived from Beverly, Mr. Parris told me that.

**Danforth.** Do you deny it, Mr. Parris?

**Parris.** I do not, sir, but I never saw any of them naked.

**Danforth.** But she have *danced?*

**Parris** (*unwillingly*). Aye, sir.

(Danforth, *as though with new eyes, looks at* Abigail.)

**Hathorne.** Excellency, will you permit me? (*He points at* Mary Warren.)

**Danforth** (*with great worry*). Pray, proceed.

**Hathorne.** You say you never saw no spirits, Mary, were never threatened or <u>afflicted</u> by any manifest of the Devil or the Devil's agents.

**Mary Warren** (*very faintly*). No, sir.

**Hathorne** (*with a gleam of victory*). And yet, when people accused of witchery confronted you in court, you would faint, saying their spirits came out of their bodies and choked you—

**Mary Warren.** That were pretense, sir.

**Danforth.** I cannot hear you.

**Mary Warren.** Pretense, sir.

**Parris.** But you did turn cold, did you not? I myself picked you up many times, and your skin were icy. Mr. Danforth, you—

**Danforth.** I saw that many times.

**Proctor.** She only pretended to faint, Your Excellency. They're all marvelous pretenders.

**Hathorne.** Then can she pretend to faint now?

**Proctor.** Now?

**Parris.** Why not? Now there are no spirits attacking her, for none in this room is accused of witchcraft. So let her turn herself cold now, let her pretend she is attacked now, let her faint. (*He turns to* Mary Warren.) Faint!

**Mary Warren.** Faint?

**Parris.** Aye, faint. Prove to us how you pretended in the court so many times.

**Mary Warren** (*looking to* Proctor). I—cannot faint now, sir.

**Proctor** (*alarmed, quietly*). Can you not pretend it?

**Mary Warren.** I—(*She looks about as though searching for the passion to faint.*) I—have no sense of it now, I—

**Danforth.** Why? What is lacking now?

**Mary Warren.** I—cannot tell, sir, I—

**Danforth.** Might it be that here we have no afflicting spirit loose, but in the court there were some?

**Mary Warren.** I never saw no spirits.

---

WORDS
TO
KNOW      **afflict** (ə-flĭkt′) *v.* to trouble or attack, causing physical or mental suffering

---

## Teaching Options

**Cross Curricular Link  Logic**

**INDUCTIVE AND DEDUCTIVE REASONING** Two common forms of reasoning are the inductive and deductive methods. Induction moves from the particular to the general. For example, from the fact that many people in Salem were hanged as suspected witches, you can conclude that witchcraft was regarded as a terrible crime, punishable by death. Deductive reasoning is just the opposite. It involves the process of drawing a particular conclusion from a general statement. For example, if all humans are capable of evil and Abigail is human, it follows that Abigail is capable of evil. Have interested students study more about inductive and deductive reasoning and apply what they've learned to the Salem witch trials.

**Parris.** Then see no spirits now, and prove to us that you can faint by your own will, as you claim.

**Mary Warren** (*stares, searching for the emotion of it, and then shakes her head*). I—cannot do it.

**Parris.** Then you will confess, will you not? It were attacking spirits made you faint!

**Mary Warren.** No, sir, I—

**Parris.** Your Excellency, this is a trick to blind the court!

**Mary Warren.** It's not a trick! (*She stands.*) I—I used to faint because I—I thought I saw spirits.

**Danforth.** Thought you saw them!

**Mary Warren.** But I did not, Your Honor.

**Hathorne.** How could you think you saw them unless you saw them?

**Mary Warren.** I—I cannot tell how, but I did. I—I heard the other girls screaming, and you, Your Honor, you seemed to believe them, and I—It were only sport in the beginning, sir, but then the whole world cried spirits, spirits, and I—I promise you, Mr. Danforth, I only thought I saw them but I did not.

(*Danforth peers at her.*)

**Parris** (*smiling, but nervous because Danforth seems to be struck by Mary Warren's story*). Surely Your Excellency is not taken by this simple lie.

**Danforth** (*turning worriedly to Abigail*). Abigail. I bid you now search your heart and tell me this—and beware of it, child, to God every soul is precious and His vengeance is terrible on them that take life without cause. Is it possible, child, that the spirits you have seen are illusion only, some deception that may cross your mind when—

**Abigail.** Why, this—this—is a base question, sir.

**Danforth.** Child, I would have you consider it—

**Abigail.** I have been hurt, Mr. Danforth; I have seen my blood runnin' out! I have been near to murdered every day because I done my duty pointing out the Devil's people—and this is my reward? To be mistrusted, denied, questioned like a—

**Danforth** (*weakening*). Child, I do not mistrust you—

**Abigail** (*in an open threat*). Let you beware, Mr. Danforth. Think you to be so mighty that the power of Hell may not turn your wits? Beware of it! There is—(*Suddenly, from an accusatory attitude, her face turns, looking into the air above—it is truly frightened.*)

**Danforth** (*apprehensively*). What is it, child?

**Abigail** (*looking about in the air, clasping her arms about her as though cold*). I—I know not. A wind, a cold wind, has come. (*Her eyes fall on Mary Warren.*)

**Mary Warren** (*terrified, pleading*). Abby!

**Mercy Lewis** (*shivering*). Your Honor, I freeze!

**Proctor.** They're pretending!

**Hathorne** (*touching Abigail's hand*). She is cold, Your Honor, touch her!

**Mercy Lewis** (*through chattering teeth*). Mary, do you send this shadow on me?

**Mary Warren.** Lord, save me!

**Susanna Walcott.** I freeze, I freeze!

**Abigail** (*shivering visibly*). It is a wind, a wind!

**Mary Warren.** Abby, don't do that!

**Danforth** (*himself engaged and entered by Abigail*). Mary Warren, do you witch her? I say to you, do you send your spirit out?

(*With a hysterical cry Mary Warren starts to run. Proctor catches her.*)

**Mary Warren** (*almost collapsing*). Let me go, Mr. Proctor, I cannot, I cannot—

**Abigail** (*crying to Heaven*). Oh, Heavenly Father, take away this shadow!

(*Without warning or hesitation, Proctor leaps at Abigail and, grabbing her by the hair, pulls her to her feet. She screams in pain. Danforth, astonished, cries, "What are you about?" and Hathorne and Parris call, "Take your hands off her!" and out of it all comes Proctor's roaring voice.*)

## Customizing Instruction

### Students Acquiring English

**1** Explain that a *pretense* is a make-believe act, or the act of pretending. Mary is admitting to Danforth that she and the girls were pretending to be afflicted by spirits.

### Less Proficient Readers

**2** Ask students the following questions to be certain they understand what is happening to Mary:

• What does Parris ask Mary to do? Why?

**Possible Response:** Parris asks Mary to faint. He thinks that if she is telling the truth, she should be able to pretend to faint.

• Why is Mary not able to faint?

**Possible Response:** She is afraid. With all eyes on her, she cannot pretend as she does when she is with the other girls, imitating their actions.

• What do you think Mary means when she says that she only thought she saw spirits, but she really didn't?

**Possible Response:** Mary made herself believe in them only because that's what the other girls did, and she was overtaken by the emotional situation.

### Gifted and Talented

**3** Have students note Abigail's warning to Danforth. Ask them to compare Abigail's attitude toward Danforth with the attitudes of others who have testified before him. What allows her to assume this attitude?

**Literary Analysis: PROTAGONIST**

**A** Remind students that the protagonist is the main character in a literary work. Have students analyze how Proctor approaches this revelation of his shameful truth. What motivates him to reveal his affair with Abigail?

**Possible Response:** He is motivated by his desire to save Elizabeth and by his need to unburden his soul. When he reveals the truth, he reveals all of it, even emphasizing his own shame and culpability. He no longer cares what happens to him—he must do what is right. He confesses his sin and pleads with Danforth to see the truth about Abigail. At great sacrifice to himself, he struggles to expose the truth and save people's lives.

**Literary Analysis: CHARACTERIZATION**

**B** Ask students to explain how the author characterizes Elizabeth's feelings during this inquisition by Danforth.

**Possible Response:** The hesitancy in her speech and her nervous actions indicate that she is uncomfortable and unsure of what to say. She feels protective of her husband's honor, not wanting to reveal the real reason she dismissed Abigail.

**Proctor.** How do you call Heaven! Whore! Whore! (Herrick *breaks* Proctor *from her.*)

**Herrick.** John!

**Danforth.** Man! Man, what do you—

**Proctor** (*breathless and in agony*). It is a whore!

**Danforth** (*dumfounded*).[76] You charge—?

**Abigail.** Mr. Danforth, he is lying!

**Proctor.** Mark her! Now she'll suck a scream to stab me with, but—

**Danforth.** You will prove this! This will not pass!

**Proctor** (*trembling, his life collapsing about him*). I have known her, sir. I have known her.

**Danforth.** You—you are a lecher?

**Francis** (*horrified*). John, you cannot say such a—

**Proctor.** Oh, Francis, I wish you had some evil in you that you might know me! (*To* Danforth) A man will not cast away his good name. You surely know that.

**Danforth** (*dumfounded*). In—in what time? In what place?

**Proctor** (*his voice about to break, and his shame great*). In the proper place—where my beasts are bedded. On the last night of my joy, some eight months past. She used to serve me in my house, sir. (*He has to clamp his jaw to keep from weeping.*) A man may think God sleeps, but God sees everything, I know it now. I beg you, sir, I beg you—see her what she is. My wife, my dear good wife, took this girl soon after, sir, and put her out on the highroad. And being what she is, a lump of vanity, sir—(*He is being overcome.*) Excellency, forgive me, forgive me. (*Angrily against himself, he turns away from the* Governor *for a moment. Then, as though to cry out is his only means of speech left.*) She thinks to dance with me on my wife's

**1**

---

76. **dumfounded:** shocked.

## Teaching Options

 **Speaking and Listening**

**ROLE-PLAYING** Have students prepare an interpretation of the scene in which Proctor confesses his adulterous affair with Abigail and Danforth calls Elizabeth to see if she supports Proctor's confession. Assign parts for Proctor, Danforth, Abigail, Parris, Cheever, and Elizabeth. Make sure the actors consider all stage directions to help each actor communicate his or her character's feelings—they should be able to justify their choices of verbal and nonverbal performance techniques by referring to analysis of the text.

**Present** Students can decide when they are ready to perform this scene for an audience. They can present their interpretations for a variety of audiences, including their classmates, students from other classes, parents, and teachers. Ask students in the audience to evaluate the performance and explain how it increased their understanding of this scene and the characters.

**BLOCK SCHEDULING** This activity is particularly well-suited for longer class periods.

**A** grave! And well she might, for I thought of her softly. God help me, I lusted, and there is a promise in such sweat. But it is a whore's vengeance, and you must see it; I set myself entirely in your hands. I know you must see it now.

**Danforth** (*blanched, in horror, turning to* Abigail). You deny every scrap and tittle[77] of this?

**Abigail.** If I must answer that, I will leave and I will not come back again!

(Danforth *seems unsteady*.)

**Proctor.** I have made a bell of my honor! I have rung the doom of my good name—you will believe me, Mr. Danforth! My wife is innocent, except she knew a whore when she saw one!

**Abigail** (*stepping up to* Danforth). What look do you give me? (Danforth *cannot speak*.) I'll not have such looks! (*She turns and starts for the door.*)

**Danforth.** You will remain where you are! (Herrick *steps into her path. She comes up short, fire in her eyes*.) Mr. Parris, go into the court and bring Goodwife Proctor out.

**Parris** (*objecting*). Your Honor, this is all a—

**Danforth** (*sharply to* Parris). Bring her out! And tell her not one word of what's been spoken here. And let you knock before you enter. (Parris *goes out*.) Now we shall touch the bottom of this swamp. (*To* Proctor) Your wife, you say, is an honest woman.

**Proctor.** In her life, sir, she have never lied. There are them that cannot sing, and them that cannot weep—my wife cannot lie. I have paid much to learn it, sir.

**Danforth.** And when she put this girl out of your house, she put her out for a harlot?[78]

**Proctor.** Aye, sir.

**Danforth.** And knew her for a harlot?

**Proctor.** Aye, sir, she knew her for a harlot.

**Danforth.** Good then. (*To* Abigail) And if she tell me, child, it were for harlotry, may God spread His mercy on you! (*There is a knock. He calls to the door*.) Hold! (*To* Abigail) Turn your back. Turn your back. (*To* Proctor) Do likewise. (*Both turn their backs—*Abigail *with indignant slowness*.) Now let neither of you turn to face Goody Proctor. No one in this room is to speak one word, or raise a gesture aye or nay. (*He turns toward the door, calls*.) Enter! (*The door opens.* Elizabeth *enters with* Parris. Parris *leaves her. She stands alone, her eyes looking for* Proctor.) Mr. Cheever, report this testimony in all exactness. Are you ready?

**Cheever.** Ready, sir.

**Danforth.** Come here, woman. (Elizabeth *comes to him, glancing at* Proctor's *back*.) Look at me only, not at your husband. In my eyes only.

**Elizabeth** (*faintly*). Good, sir.

**Danforth.** We are given to understand that at one time you dismissed your servant, Abigail Williams.

**Elizabeth.** That is true, sir.

**Danforth.** For what cause did you dismiss her? (*Slight pause. Then* Elizabeth *tries to glance at* Proctor.) You will look in my eyes only and not at your husband. The answer is in your memory and you need no help to give it to me. Why did you dismiss Abigail Williams?

**Elizabeth** (*not knowing what to say, sensing a situation, wetting her lips to stall for time*). She—dissatisfied me. (*Pause.*) And my husband. **B**

**Danforth.** In what way dissatisfied you?

**Elizabeth.** She were—(*She glances at* Proctor *for a cue*.)

**Danforth.** Woman, look at me! (Elizabeth *does*.) Were she slovenly?[79] Lazy? What disturbance did she cause?

**Elizabeth.** Your Honor, I—in that time I were sick. And I—My husband is a good and righteous man. He is never drunk as some are, nor

---

77. **tittle:** tiniest bit.

78. **harlot** (här′lət): a woman of low morals.

79. **slovenly:** untidy.

### Students Acquiring English

**1** Explain what John means when he says that "a man will not cast away his good name." He is saying that a man would not voluntarily ruin his reputation. In other words, John would not lie about his relationship with Abigail.

**2** Explain that Proctor likens his honor to a bell. By exposing his past relationship with Abigail, he has rung this bell, causing his reputation to be ruined.

### Multiple Learning Styles
**Interpersonal Learners**

Ask students to explain why Danforth insists that Elizabeth meet his eyes while testifying. Ask them to consider how eye contact influences people in conversations.

**Possible Response:** Danforth not only wants to evaluate her truthfulness; he also wants to make sure that Elizabeth receives no indication from John or Abigail that might influence her response. In conversation, eye contact often signals attentiveness and sincerity.

**Literary Analysis: IRONY**

Ⓐ Ask students to discuss the irony in Elizabeth's situation. Have them consider her upright character and why she is being questioned.

**Possible Response:** The irony is that if Elizabeth tells the truth, which she always does, the truth will set her free. Instead, she uncharacteristically lies, which she never does, to protect her husband's reputation. Her actions further implicate both her and John, which is the complete opposite of what she hoped to accomplish.

**Active Reading**

USING A GRAPHIC ORGANIZER

Ⓑ Have students review the way Danforth conducts his questioning. Then ask them to add another trait and supporting evidence to his character chart.

### Deputy Governor Danforth

| Trait: rigid; close-minded | Trait: manipulative |
|---|---|
| Evidence: He has already approved the hangings of seventy-two people, and he has no reason to think he's wrong. Instead of welcoming new evidence, he'd prefer to disregard it. | Evidence: He will not acknowledge the difficult position he has put Elizabeth in. When he hears John tell Elizabeth he confessed, he disregards their interchange and only accepts her actual testimony, which was given under duress. |

# View and Compare
## The Crucible

What can the film version of *The Crucible* show you about the setting and characters that a stage version cannot?

222

## Teaching Options

**Mini Lesson** ## Grammar

**PERFECT TENSES** The tense of a verb tells when an action happens. Verbs have six tenses, and three of those tenses are the perfect tenses. Perfect tenses combine the past participle of the verb with one of the following auxiliary verbs: *has, have, had, shall have,* or *will have.* Write the perfect tenses for *jump* on the chalkboard.

| Present Perfect | Past Perfect | Future Perfect |
|---|---|---|
| I have jumped | I had jumped | I will have jumped |

Explain that the future perfect tense contains both *will* and *have* because it indicates an action that

will be completed in the future before another action occurs. Remind students that when they write, they should keep verb tenses consistent.

**Exercises** Have students underline the verbs and identify their tenses.

1. Martha Corey <u>has maintained</u> her innocence. *(present perfect)*
2. Danforth <u>will have listened</u> to many witnesses by the end of the trial. *(future perfect)*

 Use McDougal Littell's *Language Network,* Chapter 4, for more instruction and practice in perfect tenses.

wastin' his time at the shovelboard, but always at his work. But in my sickness—you see, sir, I were a long time sick after my last baby, and I thought I saw my husband somewhat turning from me. And this girl— (*She turns to* Abigail.)

**Danforth.** Look at me.

**Elizabeth.** Aye, sir. Abigail Williams—(*She breaks off.*)

**Danforth.** What of Abigail Williams?

**Elizabeth.** I came to think he fancied her. And so one night I lost my wits, I think, and put her out on the high-road.

**Danforth.** Your husband—did he indeed turn from you?

**Elizabeth** (*in agony*). My husband—is a goodly man, sir.

**Danforth.** Then he did not turn from you.

**Elizabeth** (*starting to glance at* Proctor). He—

**Danforth** (*reaches out and holds her face, then*). Look at me! To your own knowledge, has John Proctor ever committed the crime of lechery? (*In a crisis of indecision she cannot speak.*) Answer my question! Is your husband a lecher!

**Elizabeth** (*faintly*). No, sir.

**Danforth.** Remove her, Marshal.

**Proctor.** Elizabeth, tell the truth!

**Danforth.** She has spoken. Remove her!

**Proctor** (*crying out*). Elizabeth, I have confessed it!

**Elizabeth.** Oh, God! (*The door closes behind her.*)

**Proctor.** She only thought to save my name!

**Hale.** Excellency, it is a natural lie to tell; I beg you, stop now before another is condemned! I may shut my conscience to it no more—private vengeance is working through this testimony! From the beginning this man has struck me true. By my oath to Heaven, I believe him now, and I pray you call back his wife before we—

**Danforth.** She spoke nothing of lechery, and this man has lied!

**Hale.** I believe him! (*Pointing at* Abigail). This girl has always struck me false! She has—

(Abigail, *with a weird, wild, chilling cry, screams up to the ceiling.*)

**Abigail.** You will not! Begone! Begone, I say!

The 1996 American film version of *The Crucible*, with Winona Ryder.

A 1990 British production of *The Crucible* by the National Theatre, London.

## Customizing Instruction

**Less Proficient Readers**

**1** Ask students to discuss how Hale's opinion of the Proctors has changed.

**Possible Response:** When Hale first visited with the Proctors to question Elizabeth, he doubted them both. Now, he believes that John and Elizabeth are honest people and that Abigail is lying for her own benefit.

**Students Acquiring English**

**2** Point out that when Hale uses the idiom *struck me,* he means "impressed me as" or "created a feeling."

**Reading Skills and Strategies:**
**VISUALIZING**

**A** Have students visualize and attempt to replicate the facial expressions that Abigail and the other girls assumed during their "possession." What feelings would these expressions instill in others?

**Possible Response:** People would feel discomfort, fear, and uncertainty.

**Reading Skills and Strategies:**
**CONNECTING**

**B** Abigail and the other girls are using a familiar childhood method of taunting: they are repeating everything Mary says and does. Suggest that students consider how Mary might be feeling in the midst of this. If they were ever the victim of such taunting when they were younger, have them connect their own experience with Mary's.

**Literary Analysis: CHARACTERIZATION**

**C** What clues does the author give us that Mary may not be able to withstand the pressure from the other girls?

**Possible Response:** The stage directions and Mary's dialogue indicate that she is becoming increasingly distressed.

**Reading Skills and Strategies:**
**QUESTIONING**

**D** Have students ask themselves why Proctor is saying these things to Mary.

**Possible Response:** Proctor sees her wavering, and he refers to religious beliefs in an attempt to make Mary adhere to the truth.

---

**1**

**Danforth.** What is it, child? (*But* Abigail, *pointing with fear, is now raising up her frightened eyes, her awed face, toward the ceiling—the girls are doing the same—and now* Hathorne, Hale, Putnam, Cheever, Herrick, *and* Danforth *do the same.*) What's there? (*He lowers his eyes from the ceiling, and now he is frightened; there is real tension in his voice.*) Child! (*She is transfixed*[80]—*with all the girls, she is whimpering open-mouthed, agape at the ceiling.*) Girls! Why do you—?

**Mercy Lewis** (*pointing*). It's on the beam! Behind the rafter!

**Danforth** (*looking up*). Where!

**Abigail.** Why—? (*She gulps.*) Why do you come, yellow bird?

**Proctor.** Where's a bird? I see no bird!

**Abigail** (*to the ceiling*). My face? My face?

**Proctor.** Mr. Hale—

**Danforth.** Be quiet!

**Proctor** (*to Hale*). Do you see a bird?

**Danforth.** Be quiet!!

**Abigail** (*to the ceiling, in a genuine conversation with the "bird," as though trying to talk it out of attacking her*). But God made my face; you cannot want to tear my face. Envy is a deadly sin, Mary.

**Mary Warren** (*on her feet with a spring, and horrified, pleading*). Abby!

**Abigail** (*unperturbed, continuing to the "bird"*). Oh, Mary, this is a black art[81] to change your shape. No, I cannot, I cannot stop my mouth; it's God's work I do.

**Mary Warren.** Abby, I'm here!

**Proctor** (*frantically*). They're pretending, Mr. Danforth!

**Abigail** (*now she takes a backward step, as though in fear the bird will swoop down momentarily*). Oh, please, Mary! Don't come down.

**Susanna Walcott.** Her claws, she's stretching her claws!

**Proctor.** Lies, lies.

**Abigail** (*backing further, eyes still fixed above*). Mary, please don't hurt me!

**Mary Warren** (*to Danforth*). I'm not hurting her!

**Danforth** (*to Mary Warren*). Why does she see this **A** vision?

**Mary Warren.** She sees nothin'!

**Abigail** (*now staring full front as though hypnotized, and mimicking the exact tone of Mary Warren's cry*). She sees nothin'!

**Mary Warren** (*pleading*). Abby, you mustn't!

**Abigail and All the Girls** (*all transfixed*). Abby, you mustn't!

**Mary Warren** (*to all the girls*). I'm here, I'm here!

**Girls.** I'm here, I'm here!

**Danforth** (*horrified*). Mary Warren! Draw back your spirit out of them!

**Mary Warren.** Mr. Danforth!

**Girls** (*cutting her off*). Mr. Danforth!

**Danforth.** Have you compacted[82] with the Devil? Have you?

**Mary Warren.** Never, never!

**Girls.** Never, never!

**Danforth** (*growing hysterical*). Why can they only repeat you?

**Proctor.** Give me a whip—I'll stop it!

**Mary Warren.** They're sporting.[83] They—!

**Girls.** They're sporting!

**Mary Warren** (*turning on them all hysterically and stamping her feet*). Abby, stop it!

**Girls** (*stamping their feet*). Abby, stop it!

**Mary Warren.** Stop it!

**Girls.** Stop it!

**Mary Warren** (*screaming it out at the top of her*

---

80. **transfixed:** paralyzed with horror or shock.
81. **a black art:** sorcery.
82. **compacted:** made an agreement.
83. **sporting:** playing a game.

---

## Teaching Options

✓**Assessment Standardized Test Practice**

**PREDICTING PROBABLE FUTURE ACTIONS** For some standardized tests, students will be asked to predict probable future actions of a character. Read aloud or write on the chalkboard the following question:

You can tell from the way Mary responds to the girls that she is most likely to _____.

**A.** keep accusing the girls and declaring the truth

**B.** feel badly for the girls and try to help them

**C.** become frightened of what the girls will do to her and rejoin them

Help students consider each choice, and encourage them to read stage directions for help in predicting Mary's future behavior. Point out that although Mary could choose any of the options, the choice that is most in keeping with her character and behavior is C.

**Students Acquiring English**

**1** Explain that when Danforth asks Mary why she did "turn about," he wants to know why she changed her story.

**2** Point out that the phrase *made compact* means "reached an agreement."

*lungs, and raising her fists*). Stop it!!

**Girls** (*raising their fists*). Stop it!!

(Mary Warren, *utterly confounded, and becoming overwhelmed by Abigail's—and the girls'—utter conviction, starts to whimper, hands half raised, powerless, and all the girls begin whimpering exactly as she does.*)

**Danforth.** A little while ago you were afflicted. Now it seems you afflict others; where did you find this power?

**Mary Warren** (*staring at Abigail*). I—have no power.

**Girls.** I have no power.

**Proctor.** They're gulling you,[84] Mister!

**Danforth.** Why did you turn about this past two weeks? You have seen the Devil, have you not?

**Hale** (*indicating Abigail and the girls*). You cannot believe them!

**Mary Warren.** I—

**Proctor** (*sensing her weakening*). Mary, God damns all liars!

**Danforth** (*pounding it into her*). You have seen the Devil, you have made compact with Lucifer, have you not?

**Proctor.** God damns liars, Mary!

(Mary *utters something* unintelligible, *staring at* Abigail, *who keeps watching the "bird" above.*)

**Danforth.** I cannot hear you. What do you say? (Mary *utters again unintelligibly.*) You will confess yourself or you will hang! (*He turns her roughly to face him.*) Do you know who I am? I say you will hang if you do not open with me!

**Proctor.** Mary, remember the angel Raphael—do that which is good and—

---

84. **gulling:** deceiving.

WORDS
TO
KNOW
    **unintelligible** (ŭn'ĭn-tĕl'ĭ-jə-bəl) *adj.* incomprehensible; unable to be understood

225

## Reading Skills and Strategies: CONNECTING

**A** Have students draw upon their own backgrounds to provide a connection to the text. Discuss peer pressure, and discuss how Mary finally succumbs because she can no longer resist the pressure. Explain that people often find it difficult to maintain their individuality.

## Reading Skills and Strategies: SUMMARIZING

**B** Have students summarize what happens after Abigail pretends to see the "bird."

**Possible Response:** Mary turns on John Proctor and accuses him of threatening to kill her unless she went with him to overthrow the court; she aligns John with the Devil. John is so distraught at what is happening that he declares God is dead.

## Reading Skills and Strategies

USING A GRAPHIC ORGANIZER

Have students use a graphic organizer such as the one below to show how Parris serves as Proctor's foil in this act.

|  | Proctor | Parris |
|---|---|---|
| **Personality** | forthright; sincere | deceitful; pompous |
| **Values** | values his wife more than his reputation | values his reputation and status above all else |
| **Opinion of himself** | feels unworthy and sinful; has low self-esteem | self-righteous; conceited |

---

**Abigail** (*pointing upward*). The wings! Her wings are spreading! Mary, please, don't, don't—!

**Hale.** I see nothing, Your Honor!

**Danforth.** Do you confess this power! (*He is an inch from her face.*) Speak!

**Abigail.** She's going to come down! She's walking the beam!

**Danforth.** Will you speak!

**Mary Warren** (*staring in horror*). I cannot!

**Girls.** I cannot!

**Parris.** Cast the Devil out! Look him in the face! Trample him! We'll save you, Mary, only stand fast against him and—

**Abigail** (*looking up*). Look out! She's coming down!

(*She and all the girls run to one wall, shielding their eyes. And now, as though cornered, they let out a gigantic scream, and Mary, as though infected, opens her mouth and screams with them. Gradually Abigail and the girls leave off, until only Mary is left there, staring up at the "bird," screaming madly. All watch her, horrified by this evident fit. Proctor strides to her.*)

**Proctor.** Mary, tell the Governor what they—(*He has hardly got a word out, when, seeing him coming for her, she rushes out of his reach, screaming in horror.*)

**Mary Warren.** Don't touch me—don't touch me! (*At which the girls halt at the door.*)

**Proctor** (*astonished*). Mary!

**Mary Warren** (*pointing at Proctor*). You're the Devil's man! (*He is stopped in his tracks.*)

**Parris.** Praise God!

**Girls.** Praise God!

**Proctor** (*numbed*). Mary, how—?

**Mary Warren.** I'll not hang with you! I love God, I love God.

**Danforth** (*to Mary*). He bid you do the Devil's work?

**Mary Warren** (*hysterically, indicating Proctor*). He come at me by night and every day to sign, to sign, to—

**Danforth.** Sign what?

**Parris.** The Devil's book? He come with a book?

**Mary Warren** (*hysterically, pointing at Proctor, fearful of him*). My name, he want my name. "I'll murder you," he says, "if my wife hangs! We must go and overthrow the court," he says!

(*Danforth's head jerks toward Proctor, shock and horror in his face.*)

**Proctor** (*turning, appealing to Hale*). Mr. Hale!

**Mary Warren** (*her sobs beginning*). He wake me every night, his eyes were like coals and his fingers claw my neck, and I sign, I sign . . .

**Hale.** Excellency, this child's gone wild!

**Proctor** (*as Danforth's wide eyes pour on him*). Mary, Mary!

**Mary Warren** (*screaming at him*). No, I love God; I go your way no more. I love God, I bless God. (*Sobbing, she rushes to Abigail.*) Abby, Abby, I'll never hurt you more! (*They all watch, as Abigail, out of her infinite charity, reaches out and draws the sobbing Mary to her, and then looks up to Danforth.*)

**Danforth** (*to Proctor*). What are you? (*Proctor is beyond speech in his anger.*) You are combined with anti-Christ,[85] are you not? I have seen your power; you will not deny it! What say you, Mister?

**Hale.** Excellency—

**Danforth.** I will have nothing from you, Mr. Hale! (*To Proctor*) Will you confess yourself befouled with Hell, or do you keep that black allegiance yet? What say you?

**Proctor** (*his mind wild, breathless*). I say—I say—God is dead!

**Parris.** Hear it, hear it!

---

85. **combined with anti-Christ:** working with the Devil.

---

# Teaching Options

## Cross Curricular Link **Psychology**

**HYSTERIA** Hysteria is a form of neurosis that often includes symptoms of physical illness without actual physiological disease to account for the symptoms. People who suffer from hysteria are emotionally upset, and they demonstrate an unusual variety of symptoms. In ancient times, physicians felt that hysteria affected only women. By the 17th century, people realized that hysteria occurred in males as well. One type of hysteria is characterized by pseudo-psychotic symptoms, like hysterical amnesia, hysterical stupors, trances, and similar states.

During the time of the witchcraft trials, hysteria was not recognized as a psychological condition. It gained notoriety in the late 1800s, when the French neurologist Jean Martin Charcot and Sigmund Freud began more accurately diagnosing the condition. Hysterical neurotic reactions to combat were seen in World War I and World War II and defined as "shell shock." Some soldiers exhibited various psychological conditions that served to erase the horrors of battle.

**Proctor** (*laughs insanely, then*). A fire, a fire is burning! I hear the boot of Lucifer, I see his filthy face! And it is my face, and yours, Danforth! For them that quail to bring men out of ignorance, as I have quailed, and as you quail now when you know in all your black hearts that this be fraud—God damns our kind especially, and we will burn, we will burn together!

**Danforth.** Marshal! Take him and Corey with him to the jail!

**Hale** (*starting across to the door*). I denounce these proceedings!

**Proctor.** You are pulling Heaven down and raising up a whore!

**Hale.** I denounce these proceedings, I quit this court! (*He slams the door to the outside behind him.*)

**Danforth** (*calling to him in a fury*). Mr. Hale! Mr.  Hale!

*the curtain falls*

THE CRUCIBLE **227**

## Customizing Instruction

**Less Proficient Readers**
**1** Ask students the following questions to help them grasp what Mary has done:
• Of what does Mary accuse Proctor?
**Possible Response:** Mary accuses Proctor of forcing her to come to court and threatening her with murder if she didn't.
• With whom does Mary realign herself?
**Answer:** She realigns herself with Abigail and the other girls.
• What dreadful consequences could this have for Elizabeth and John?
**Possible Response:** Mary was their only witness that Abigail and the other girls were lying, and now both John and Elizabeth may be convicted of perjury and witchery.

**Students Acquiring English**
**2** Help students understand what Danforth says to Proctor by explaining that *befouled* means "covered with filth" and *black allegiance* refers to Proctor's alleged loyalty to the Devil. In other words, Danforth is asking Proctor whether he will admit his relationship with the Devil or continue to protect it.

✔ **Assessment Standardized Test Practice**

**DESCRIBING CHARACTER** Some standardized tests ask students to describe a character in a particular text. To provide students with practice, read aloud or write on the chalkboard the following question: At the end of Act Three, how would you describe John Proctor?

**A.** He is enraged because he cannot believe what the courts are doing to innocent people in Salem.

**B.** He is angry at what is happening to innocent people, and he intends to bring forth more evidence to free them.

**C.** He is confident that the truth will eventually come out.

Lead students through the process of choosing the most accurate description. Consider each choice. Point out that although all of the descriptions fit him at some point during the play, A best describes his attitude at the end of Act Three.

## GUIDING STUDENT RESPONSE

## Connect to the Literature

**1. What Do You Think?**
Accept all reasonable responses.

**Comprehension Check**
- Mary Warren testifies that Abigail and the other girls are only pretending to see spirits.
- lechery
- Mary Warren accuses Proctor of having sent his spirit to torment her.

 Use Selection Quiz in **Unit Two Resource Book**, p. 29.

## Think Critically

**2. Possible Response:** Mary Warren is intimidated by Abigail Williams and the other girls, who pretend that Mary's spirit has taken the form of a yellow bird about to swoop down on them. Mary sides with Abigail and her peers, who are now in power, and not with Proctor, a desperate opponent of the court.

**3. Possible Response:** Elizabeth lies to save her husband's good name. Out of love for him, she does something she has never done before—tell a lie. She knows that her reputation as an honest women will cause the community to believe her. By lying, she can save her husband from public scorn as a lecher, denounced by his own wife.

**4. Possible Response:** At the beginning of the play, Reverend Hale is intolerant and rigid, like the other representatives of the Puritan establishment. Yet by the end of Act Two, some major changes are taking place within him. He seems ambivalent about the arrest of Elizabeth Proctor as his doubts about the witch-hunt begin to surface. In Act Three, he is haunted by guilt for having sentenced so many to die. He is appalled at the extent of the witch-hunt, the saintly people it now claims, Danforth's use of Proctor's depositions against him, and Abigail's manipulation of the court.

**5. Possible Response:** Corey is a man of principle who speaks his mind, taking pride in his forensic skills. He shows great courage but little tact in his dealings with the Salem judges.

## Connect to the Literature

**1. What Do You Think?**
What event or speech in this act made the strongest impression on you? Why?

**Comprehension Check**
- What testimony about the girls' behavior does Mary Warren give the court?
- What sin does John Proctor admit that he committed?
- Why is Proctor arrested at the end of the act?

## Think Critically

**2.** Why do you suppose Mary Warren changes her testimony at the end of this act?

**3.** Why does Elizabeth Proctor lie to Danforth about her husband's relationship with Abigail?

 THINK ABOUT
- her feelings toward her husband
- her reputation in Salem
- the social and religious consequences of adultery

**4.** How would you account for the way Reverend Hale has changed since the beginning of the play?

**5.** Evaluate Giles Corey's behavior in court. Do you think he handles himself well or recklessly? Cite lines from the play to support your opinion.

## Extend Interpretations

**6. What If?** What do you think might have happened if Elizabeth Proctor had told the court the truth about her husband's relationship with Abigail?

**7. Connect to Life** Mary Warren is subjected to intense peer pressure from Abigail Williams and the other girls. How would you compare the intensity of the peer pressure she faces with that exerted on many young people today?

**8. Points of Comparison** Judging from your reading of the Salem court documents earlier in the unit, how accurately do you think Arthur Miller portrays the court proceedings? Discuss any additional insights you have gained about the participants' behavior.

## Literary Analysis

**FOIL** A **foil** is a character who provides a striking contrast to another character. A writer might use a foil to emphasize certain traits of another character or simply to set off or enhance this character through contrast. For example, consider contrasts between Reverend Parris and Reverend Hale, two Puritan ministers. Reverend Parris, paranoid and self-centered, is obsessed with maintaining his position in Salem and is supportive of the witch trials. On the other hand, Reverend Hale is an outsider who, at first deeply disturbed by the mounting evidence of witchcraft, eventually comes to doubt the afflicted girls' credibility.

**Paired Activity** Working with a partner, consider ways that Elizabeth Proctor and Abigail Williams contrast. Refer to the charts of each **character's traits** that you made in your READER'S NOTEBOOK. Then create a new chart like the one below, jotting down details about how these characters differ in personality, values, and their feelings for John Proctor. After you have completed the chart, discuss what Miller emphasizes about Elizabeth by presenting Abigail as her foil.

| | Elizabeth | Abigail |
|---|---|---|
| Personality | | |
| Values | | |
| Feelings for Proctor | | |

## Extend Interpretations

**What If?** Possible Response: By telling the truth, Elizabeth might have discredited Abigail and thereby have saved the people whom she and the others have accused; on the other hand, the wily Abigail might have found a way to retain her credibility and power, perhaps by alleging that Elizabeth's testimony is prompted by the Devil.
**Connect to Life** Accept all reasonable responses.
**Points of Comparison** Possible Response: Miller shows the apparent torture of the victims in the presence of a supposed witch in the courtroom, as mentioned in the court documents. He also shows the tendency of the accused to try to save themselves by incriminating others.

## Literary Analysis

**Foil** Students' charts might describe Elizabeth as honest and loving and Abigail as devious and self-centered.

# ACT FOUR

(A cell in Salem jail, that fall.)

(At the back is a high barred window; near it, a great, heavy door. Along the walls are two benches.)

(The place is in darkness but for the moonlight seeping through the bars. It appears empty. Presently footsteps are heard coming down a corridor beyond the wall, keys rattle, and the door swings open. Marshal Herrick enters with a lantern.)

**1**

(He is nearly drunk, and heavy-footed. He goes to a bench and nudges a bundle of rags lying on it.)

---

**Herrick.** Sarah, wake up! Sarah Good! (He then crosses to the other bench.)

**Sarah Good** (rising in her rags). Oh, Majesty! Comin', comin'! Tituba, he's here, His Majesty's come!

**Herrick.** Go to the north cell; this place is wanted now. (He hangs his lantern on the wall. Tituba sits up.)

**Tituba.** That don't look to me like His Majesty; look to me like the marshal.

**Herrick** (taking out a flask). Get along with you now, clear this place. (He drinks, and Sarah Good comes and peers up into his face.)

**Sarah Good.** Oh, is it you, Marshal! I thought sure you be the devil comin' for us. Could I have a sip of cider for me goin'-away?

**Herrick** (handing her the flask). And where are you off to, Sarah?

**Tituba** (as Sarah drinks). We goin' to Barbados, soon the Devil gits here with the feathers and the wings.

---

## TEACHING THE LITERATURE
### Customizing Instruction

**Less Proficient Readers**

**1** Ask these questions to help students focus on the setting of this act.

• Where is the setting of this act?

**Answer:** The setting is in a Salem jail in the fall.

• What season did the play begin in?

**Answer:** It was spring when the play began.

• What might the change from spring to fall symbolize?

**Possible Response:** Spring is generally a time of rebirth, and fall is a time when things start to die. Fall might symbolize that people will start dying.

**Students Acquiring English**

**2** Tell students that the *bundle of rags* Herrick nudges is actually Sarah Good. Help them recognize that *His Majesty* is a title of address used for kings, and that here Sarah and Tituba use it to refer to the Devil.

---

## BLOCK SCHEDULING: MANAGING TIME

**If your schedule requires that you cover the lesson objectives in a shorter time, use . . .**

• Thinking Through the Literature, p. 243
• Vocabulary in Action, p. 245

**If you want to take advantage of longer class time, use . . .**

• TE Teaching Options: Vocabulary Strategy, pp. 230–231, 232; Viewing and Representing, p. 241; Speaking and Listening, pp. 235, 236; Workplace Link, p. 234; Standardized Test Practice, p. 238; Informal Assessment, p. 240
• Choices & Challenges, p. 244

**Literary Analysis: IRONY**

 **A** Have students explain the irony in this dialogue.

**Possible Response:** Although Sarah Good and Tituba are innocent of making contracts with the Devil, they are now speaking as though they expect him to arrive at any moment to rescue them from jail. Either they have lost their sense of reality, or they are being deliberately ironic in their conversation with Herrick.

**Literary Analysis: MOOD**

**B** Discuss Cheever's description of the town. Ask students how they would characterize the mood created by this description.

**Possible Response:** The image of cows wandering the road implies a mood of chaos in the town—everything is out of order, and people are fighting with each other.

**Literary Analysis** PLOT AND CONFLICT

**C** Have students describe the development of the plot in Act Four so far. What information does Parris give to Danforth that adds an interesting twist to the plot?

**Possible Response:** Parris tells Danforth that Abigail and Mercy are missing, and he thinks they have left town on a ship. Up to this point, these girls have been the "proof" that witchery is at play, and now they are gone. Their sneaky disappearance and Abigail's theft of Parris's money make them seem suspicious.

Use **Unit Two Resource Book,** p. 32 for additional support.

---

**Herrick.** Oh? A happy voyage to you.

**Sarah Good.** A pair of bluebirds wingin' southerly, the two of us! Oh, it be a grand transformation, Marshal! (*She raises the flask to drink again.*)

**Herrick** (*taking the flask from her lips*). You'd best give me that or you'll never rise off the ground. Come along now.

**Tituba.** I'll speak to him for you, if you desires to come along, Marshal.

**Herrick.** I'd not refuse it, Tituba; it's the proper morning to fly into Hell.

**Tituba.** Oh, it be no Hell in Barbados. Devil, him be pleasureman in Barbados, him be singin' and dancin' in Barbados. It's you folks—you riles him up 'round here; it be too cold 'round here for that Old Boy. He freeze his soul in Massachusetts, but in Barbados he just as sweet and—(*A bellowing cow is heard, and* Tituba *leaps up and calls to the window.*) Aye, sir! That's him, Sarah!

**Sarah Good.** I'm here, Majesty! (*They hurriedly pick up their rags as* Hopkins, *a guard, enters.*)

**Hopkins.** The Deputy Governor's arrived.

**Herrick** (*grabbing* Tituba). Come along, come along.

**Tituba** (*resisting him*). No, he comin' for me. I goin' home!

**Herrick** (*pulling her to the door*). That's not Satan, just a poor old cow with a hatful of milk. Come along now, out with you!

**Tituba** (*calling to the window*). Take me home, Devil! Take me home!

**Sarah Good** (*following the shouting* Tituba *out*). Tell him I'm goin', Tituba! Now you tell him Sarah Good is goin' too!

(*In the corridor outside* Tituba *calls on*—"*Take me home, Devil; Devil take me home!*" *and* Hopkins' *voice orders her to move on.* Herrick *returns and begins to push old rags and straw into a corner. Hearing footsteps, he turns, and enter* Danforth *and Judge Hathorne. They are in greatcoats and wear hats against the bitter cold. They are followed in by Cheever, who carries a dispatch case[86] and a flat wooden box containing his writing materials.*)

**Herrick.** Good morning, Excellency.

**Danforth.** Where is Mr. Parris?

**Herrick.** I'll fetch him. (*He starts for the door.*)

**Danforth.** Marshal. (Herrick *stops.*) When did Reverend Hale arrive?

**Herrick.** It were toward midnight, I think.

**Danforth** (*suspiciously*). What is he about here?

**Herrick.** He goes among them that will hang, sir. And he prays with them. He sits with Goody Nurse now. And Mr. Parris with him.

**Danforth.** Indeed. That man have no authority to enter here, Marshal. Why have you let him in?

**Herrick.** Why, Mr. Parris command me, sir. I cannot deny him.

**Danforth.** Are you drunk, Marshal?

**Herrick.** No, sir; it is a bitter night, and I have no fire here.

**Danforth** (*containing his anger*). Fetch Mr. Parris.

**Herrick.** Aye, sir.

**Danforth.** There is a prodigious stench in this place. ▎1

**Herrick.** I have only now cleared the people out for you.

**Danforth.** Beware hard drink, Marshal.

**Herrick.** Aye, sir. (*He waits an instant for further orders. But* Danforth, *in dissatisfaction, turns his back on him, and* Herrick *goes out. There is a pause.* Danforth *stands in thought.*)

**Hathorne.** Let you question Hale, Excellency; I should not be surprised he have been preaching in Andover lately. ▎2

**Danforth.** We'll come to that; speak nothing of Andover. Parris prays with him. That's strange. (*He blows on his hands, moves toward the window, and looks out.*)

---

86. **dispatch case:** a case for carrying documents.

---

 **Vocabulary Strategy**

**USING CONTEXT CLUES** One type of context clue that students can use to determine the meaning of an unfamiliar word is restatement. In some contexts, a difficult word will be restated in simpler language. Use the model sentence to demonstrate how to use this type of context clue.

**Model Sentence**

The minister's <u>excommunication</u> baffled his congregation; they couldn't imagine what had caused his banishment from the church.

**Instruction**

• Write the model sentence on the chalkboard.
• Ask a volunteer to summarize the situation described in the sentence.
• Have students identify the restatement of the word *excommunication,* which provides its meaning.
• Ask a volunteer to use *excommunication* in a sentence.

**Hathorne.** Excellency, I wonder if it be wise to let Mr. Parris so continuously with the prisoners. (Danforth *turns to him, interested.*) I think, sometimes, the man has a mad look these days.

**Danforth.** Mad?

**Hathorne.** I met him yesterday coming out of his house, and I bid him good morning—and he wept and went his way. I think it is not well the village sees him so unsteady.

**Danforth.** Perhaps he have some sorrow.

**Cheever** (*stamping his feet against the cold*). I think it be the cows, sir.

**Danforth.** Cows?

**Cheever.** There be so many cows wanderin' the highroads, now their masters are in the jails, and much disagreement who they will belong to now. I know Mr. Parris be arguin' with farmers all yesterday—there is great contention,[87] sir, about the cows. Contention make him weep, sir; it were always a man that weep for contention. (*He turns, as do Hathorne and Danforth, hearing someone coming up the corridor. Danforth raises his head as Parris enters. He is gaunt, frightened, and sweating in his greatcoat.*)

**Parris** (*to Danforth, instantly*). Oh, good morning, sir, thank you for coming, I beg your pardon wakin' you so early. Good morning, Judge Hathorne.

**Danforth.** Reverend Hale have no right to enter this—

**Parris.** Excellency, a moment. (*He hurries back and shuts the door.*)

**Hathorne.** Do you leave him alone with the prisoners?

**Danforth.** What's his business here?

**Parris** (*prayerfully holding up his hands*). Excellency, hear me. It is a providence. Reverend Hale has returned to bring Rebecca Nurse to God.

**Danforth** (*surprised*). He bids her confess?

**Parris** (*sitting*). Hear me. Rebecca have not given me a word this three month since she came. Now she sits with him, and her sister and Martha Corey and two or three others, and he pleads with them, confess their crimes and save their lives.

**Danforth.** Why—this is indeed a providence. And they soften, they soften?

**Parris.** Not yet, not yet. But I thought to summon you, sir, that we might think on whether it be not wise, to—(*He dares not say it.*) I had thought to put a question, sir, and I hope you will not—

**Danforth.** Mr. Parris, be plain, what troubles you?

**Parris.** There is news, sir, that the court—the court must reckon with. My niece, sir, my niece—I believe she has vanished.

**Danforth.** Vanished!

**Parris.** I had thought to advise you of it earlier in the week, but—

**Danforth.** Why? How long is she gone?

**Parris.** This be the third night. You see, sir, she told me she would stay a night with Mercy Lewis. And next day, when she does not return, I send to Mr. Lewis to inquire. Mercy told him she would sleep in my house for a night.

**Danforth.** They are both gone?!

**Parris** (*in fear of him*). They are, sir.

**Danforth** (*alarmed*). I will send a party for them. Where may they be?

**Parris.** Excellency, I think they be aboard a ship. (*Danforth stands agape.*) My daughter tells me how she heard them speaking of ships last week, and tonight I discover my—my strong-box[88] is broke into. (*He presses his fingers against his eyes to keep back tears.*)

**Hathorne** (*astonished*). She have robbed you?

**Parris.** Thirty-one pound is gone. I am penniless. (*He covers his face and sobs.*)

---

87. **contention:** controversy.

88. **strongbox:** a reinforced box for storing valuables.

## Customizing Instruction

### Students Acquiring English

**1** Explain *prodigious stench* to students to help them understand the condition of the jail. In this phrase, *prodigious* means "enormous" and *stench* means "odor or smell." Danforth is reacting to the odor left by the prisoners' unwashed bodies.

### Less Proficient Readers

**2** Ask students what attitude Hathorne has toward Hale now.
**Possible Response:** He seems very suspicious of him and suggests that Danforth bring him in for questioning.
**Set a Purpose** Tell students that Andover is a town in Massachusetts about 20 miles from Salem. Have them read to find out why "preaching in Andover" is a suspicious activity in Hathorne's eyes.

**3** Ask students the following questions to prompt them to discuss Hale's newfound role and Parris's opinion of Hale:
• What is Reverend Hale doing in the jail?
**Possible Response:** He is trying to get the condemned prisoners to confess so that they will not be hanged.
• What is odd or ironic about Parris's delivering the message about Hale to Danforth?
**Possible Response:** Parris approves of what Hale is doing and is defending his actions. It is ironic because these two men disagreed bitterly about the girls' accusations, but now they seem to be on the same side.

**Application** Have students work in pairs to use context clues to determine the meanings of underlined terms.

1. The prosecutor read over the <u>indictment</u> of Jim. This formal charge stated that Jim had extorted money from clients.

2. I am <u>empowered</u> to make this decision by myself. I am also authorized to see that it is carried out.

**A lesson on context clues appears on p. 326 in the Pupil's Edition.**

## Reading and Analyzing

**Reading Skills and Strategies: EVALUATING**

**(A)** Have students evaluate the change in Parris's character and viewpoint in this scene as opposed to previous scenes. Have them also consider ways in which he has not changed.

**Possible Response:** Parris is no longer confident about the witch trials. He opposes Danforth and Hathorne and pleads with them to postpone the hangings. Abigail's and Mercy's flight and the rising discontent among the people of Salem have caused this change in viewpoint, but as always his first concern is his own well-being. He fears for his reputation and safety.

**Literary Analysis** `PLOT AND CONFLICT`

**(B)** Ask students what is the main external conflict in Act Four.

**Possible Response:** It is the day when Rebecca Nurse and John Proctor are scheduled to hang. Parris argues for a postponement, and Danforth refuses. Many people of Salem apparently oppose the hangings as well.

**Literary Analysis: IRONY**

**(C)** Ask students what is ironic about Danforth's reasoning behind refusing to pardon the remaining seven people or postpone their hangings.

**Possible Response:** Danforth says it would be unjust to pardon these people when twelve have already been hanged. It is ironic that his idea of justice extends more to those who have already been hanged than to those who are still alive.

---

**Danforth.** Mr. Parris, you are a brainless man! (*He walks in thought, deeply worried.*)

**Parris.** Excellency, it profit nothing you should blame me. I cannot think they would run off except they fear to keep in Salem any more. (*He is pleading.*) Mark it, sir, Abigail had close knowledge of the town, and since the news of Andover has broken here—

**Danforth.** Andover is remedied.[89] The court returns there on Friday, and will resume examinations.

**1** **Parris.** I am sure of it, sir. But the rumor here speaks rebellion in Andover, and it—

**Danforth.** There is no rebellion in Andover!

**Parris.** I tell you what is said here, sir. Andover have thrown out the court, they say, and will have no part of witchcraft. There be a faction here, feeding on that news, and I tell you true, sir, I fear there will be riot here.

**Hathorne.** Riot! Why at every execution I have seen naught but high satisfaction in the town.

**Parris.** Judge Hathorne—it were another sort that hanged till now. Rebecca Nurse is no Bridget that lived three year with Bishop before she married him. John Proctor is not Isaac Ward that drank his family to ruin. (*To Danforth*) I would to God it were not so, Excellency, but these people have great weight yet in the town. Let Rebecca stand upon the gibbet[90] and send up some righteous prayer, and I fear she'll wake a vengeance on you.

**(A)** **Hathorne.** Excellency, she is condemned a witch. The court have—

**Danforth** (*in deep concern, raising a hand to Hathorne*). Pray you. (*To Parris.*) How do you propose, then?

**Parris.** Excellency, I would postpone these hangin's for a time.

**Danforth.** There will be no postponement.

**Parris.** Now Mr. Hale's returned, there is hope, I think—for if he bring even one of these to God, that confession surely damns the others in the public eye, and none may doubt more that they are all linked to Hell. This way, unconfessed and claiming innocence, doubts are multiplied, many honest people will weep for them, and our good purpose is lost in their tears.

**Danforth** (*after thinking a moment, then going to Cheever*). Give me the list.

(*Cheever opens the dispatch case, searches.*)

**Parris.** It cannot be forgot, sir, that when I summoned the congregation for John Proctor's <u>excommunication</u> there were hardly thirty people come to hear it. That speak a discontent, I think, and—

**Danforth** (*studying the list*). There will be no postponement.

**Parris.** Excellency—

**Danforth.** Now, sir—which of these in your opinion may be brought to God? I will myself strive[91] with him till dawn. (*He hands the list to Parris, who merely glances at it.*)

**Parris.** There is not sufficient time till dawn.

**Danforth.** I shall do my utmost. Which of them do you have hope for?

**Parris** (*not even glancing at the list now, and in a quavering voice, quietly*). Excellency—a dagger—(*He chokes up.*)

**Danforth.** What do you say?

**Parris.** Tonight, when I open my door to leave my house—a dagger clattered to the ground. **(B)** (*Silence. Danforth absorbs this. Now Parris cries out.*) You cannot hang this sort. There is danger for me. I dare not step outside at night!

(*Reverend Hale enters. They look at him for an instant in silence. He is steeped in sorrow, exhausted, and more direct than he ever was.*)

---

89. **remedied:** no longer a problem.

90. **gibbet** (jĭb′ĭt): a structure for hanging criminals; the gallows.

91. **strive:** struggle (in prayer).

> WORDS TO KNOW
>
> **excommunication** (ĕks′kə-myōō′nĭ-kā′shən) *n.* banishment from a church

232

---

## Teaching Options

**Mini Lesson** **Vocabulary Strategy**

**RESEARCHING WORD ORIGINS** Have students research word origins to aid their understanding of word meanings. The word *excommunicate* comes from the Latin root *communicare,* which means "to communicate," and *ex,* meaning "out from." The precise meaning of *excommunicate* is "to banish from the Christian sacraments or from communication with the faithful."

**Application** Have students work in pairs to find the origins of the following words: *volcano, autobiography, avarice, Goody* (as in "Goody Proctor") and *sophisticated.* Ask students to use each word in a sentence. Ask students to describe how researching word origins can help them to remember the meanings of words.

**A lesson on word origins appears on p. 550 in the Pupil's Edition.**

**Danforth.** Accept my congratulations, Reverend Hale; we are gladdened to see you returned to your good work.

**Hale** (*coming to* Danforth *now*). You must pardon them. They will not budge.

(Herrick *enters, waits.*)

**Danforth** (*conciliatory*).[92] You misunderstand, sir; I cannot pardon these when twelve are already hanged for the same crime. It is not just.

**Parris** (*with failing heart*). Rebecca will not confess?

**Hale.** The sun will rise in a few minutes. Excellency, I must have more time.

**Danforth.** Now hear me, and beguile[93] yourselves no more. I will not receive a single plea for pardon or postponement. Them that will not confess will hang. Twelve are already executed; the names of these seven are given out, and the village expects to see them die this morning. Postponement now speaks a floundering on my part; reprieve or pardon must cast doubt upon the guilt of them that died till now. While I speak God's law, I will not crack its voice with whimpering. If retaliation is your fear, know this—I should hang ten thousand that dared to rise against the law, and an ocean of salt tears could not melt the resolution of the statutes. Now draw yourselves up like men and help me, as you are bound by Heaven to do. Have you spoken with them all, Mr. Hale?

**Hale.** All but Proctor. He is in the dungeon.

**Danforth** (*to* Herrick). What's Proctor's way now?

**Herrick.** He sits like some great bird; you'd not know he lived except he will take food from time to time.

**Danforth** (*after thinking a moment*). His wife—his wife must be well on with child now.

**Herrick.** She is, sir.

**Danforth.** What think you, Mr. Parris? You have closer knowledge of this man; might her presence soften him?

**Parris.** It is possible, sir. He have not laid eyes on her these three months. I should summon her.

**Danforth** (*to* Herrick). Is he yet adamant? Has he struck at you again?

**Herrick.** He cannot, sir, he is chained to the wall now.

**Danforth** (*after thinking on it*). Fetch Goody Proctor to me. Then let you bring him up.

**Herrick.** Aye, sir. (Herrick *goes. There is silence.*)

**Hale.** Excellency, if you postpone a week and publish to the town that you are striving for their confessions, that speak mercy on your part, not faltering.

**Danforth.** Mr. Hale, as God have not empowered me like Joshua to stop this sun from rising,[94] so I cannot withhold from them the perfection of their punishment.

**Hale** (*harder now*). If you think God wills you to raise rebellion, Mr. Danforth, you are mistaken!

**Danforth** (*instantly*). You have heard rebellion spoken in the town?

**Hale.** Excellency, there are orphans wandering from house to house; abandoned cattle bellow on the highroads, the stink of rotting crops hangs everywhere, and no man knows when the harlots' cry will end his life—and you wonder yet if rebellion's spoke? Better you should marvel how they do not burn your province!

**Danforth.** Mr. Hale, have you preached in Andover this month?

**Hale.** Thank God they have no need of me in Andover.

**Danforth.** You baffle me, sir. Why have you returned here?

---

92. **conciliatory** (kən-sĭl′ə-tôr′ē): showing goodwill to end an argument.

93. **beguile** (bĭ-gīl′): deceive.

94. **like Joshua . . . rising:** According to the Bible, after the death of Moses, Joshua became the leader of the Israelites, defeating the Amorites and leading his people to the Promised Land while the sun stood still.

**A** What is ironic about what Hale is doing?

**Possible Response:** Hale is a Christian minister who is asking people to lie, or commit a sin, in order to save their lives. It is also ironic that he helped set the witch-hunt in motion, and now he is doing everything in his power to reverse the court's actions.

### Literary Analysis  PLOT AND CONFLICT

**B** Remind students that conflicts are struggles between opposing forces and that characters can have internal and external struggles. Have students describe Elizabeth's internal conflict.

**Possible Response:** Elizabeth has been asked to convince her husband to confess to witchery so that he will not hang. Elizabeth must decide whether she will urge him to lie or let him make his own decision. She is caught between her love for her husband and her Christian principles.

### Literary Analysis: MOOD

**C** Have students describe the mood suggested by this stage direction.

**Possible Response:** It is a mood of both horror and love. The sight of John Proctor so changed by his time in prison is horrifying and painful, but the feelings of love and concern that flow between Elizabeth and John are even more powerful. It is a tragic, bittersweet scene.

---

**Hale.** Why, it is all simple. I come to do the Devil's work. I come to counsel Christians they should belie[95] themselves. (*His sarcasm collapses.*) There is blood on my head! Can you not see the blood on my head!!

**Parris.** Hush! (*For he has heard footsteps. They all face the door.* Herrick *enters with* Elizabeth. *Her wrists are linked by heavy chain, which* Herrick *now removes. Her clothes are dirty; her face is pale and gaunt.* Herrick *goes out.*)

**Danforth** (*very politely*). Goody Proctor. (*She is silent.*) I hope you are hearty?

**Elizabeth** (*as a warning reminder*). I am yet six month before my time.

**Danforth.** Pray be at your ease, we come not for your life. We—(*uncertain how to plead, for he is not accustomed to it.*) Mr. Hale, will you speak with the woman?

**Hale.** Goody Proctor, your husband is marked to hang this morning.

(*Pause.*)

**Elizabeth** (*quietly*). I have heard it.

**Hale.** You know, do you not, that I have no connection with the court? (*She seems to doubt it.*) I come of my own, Goody Proctor. I would save your husband's life, for if he is taken I count myself his murderer. Do you understand me?

**Elizabeth.** What do you want of me?

**Hale.** Goody Proctor, I have gone this three month like our Lord into the wilderness.[96] I have sought a Christian way, for damnation's doubled on a minister who counsels men to lie.

**Hathorne.** It is no lie, you cannot speak of lies.

**Hale.** It is a lie! They are innocent!

**Danforth.** I'll hear no more of that!

**Hale** (*continuing to* Elizabeth). Let you not mistake your duty as I mistook my own. I came into this village like a bridegroom to his beloved, bearing gifts of high religion; the very crowns of holy law I brought, and what I touched with my bright confidence, it died; and where I turned the eye of my great faith, blood flowed up. Beware, Goody Proctor—cleave to no faith when faith brings blood. It is mistaken law that leads you to sacrifice. Life, woman, life is God's most precious gift; no principle, however glorious, may justify the taking of it. I beg you, woman, prevail upon your husband to confess. Let him give his lie. Quail not before God's judgment in this, for it may well be God damns a liar less than he that throws his life away for pride. Will you plead with him? I cannot think he will listen to another.

**Elizabeth** (*quietly*). I think that be the Devil's argument.

**Hale** (*with a climactic desperation*). Woman, before the laws of God we are as swine! We cannot read His will!

**Elizabeth.** I cannot dispute with you, sir; I lack learning for it.

**Danforth** (*going to her*). Goody Proctor, you are not summoned here for disputation. Be there no wifely tenderness within you? He will die with the sunrise. Your husband. Do you understand it? (*She only looks at him.*) What say you? Will you contend with him? (*She is silent.*) Are you stone? I tell you true, woman, had I no other proof of your unnatural life, your dry eyes now would be sufficient evidence that you delivered up your soul to Hell! A very ape would weep at such calamity! Have the devil dried up any tear of pity in you? (*She is silent.*) Take her out. It profit nothing she should speak to him!

**Elizabeth** (*quietly*). Let me speak with him, Excellency.

**Parris** (*with hope*). You'll strive with him? (*She hesitates.*)

**Danforth.** Will you plead for his confession or will you not?

**Elizabeth.** I promise nothing. Let me speak with him.

---

95. **belie:** slander; defame.
96. **like our Lord . . . wilderness:** According to the New Testament, Jesus spent 40 days wandering in the wilderness.

---

### Workplace Link  Communicating

Communicating persuasively is an important skill in the workplace, whether that communication takes place in a conversation—such as the one between Reverend Hale and Elizabeth Proctor—or in a written document such as a memo. Have students list some of the arguments and techniques Hale uses to persuade Elizabeth to talk her husband into confessing.

**Possible Responses:** He humbly confesses his own mistakes and urges her not to repeat them; he appeals to common sense and reason when he talks about the value of life; he appeals to her love for her husband when he asks her to persuade Proctor to confess.

Other persuasive methods include making a concession, using statistics and other facts, and appealing to a sense of fairness.

**Application** Divide students into groups and have each group imagine that they are a company committee whose task is to determine a company policy regarding, for example, child-care leave, carpooling, smoking, or flexible work scheduling. Have group members work together to decide on a policy and then draft a recommendation to the boss explaining why that policy is necessary and how it will benefit the company and its workers.

**C** (A sound—the sibilance[97] of dragging feet on stone. They turn. A pause. Herrick enters with John Proctor. *His wrists are chained. He is another man, bearded, filthy, his eyes misty as though webs had overgrown them. He halts inside the doorway, his eye caught by the sight of* Elizabeth. *The emotion flowing between them prevents anyone from speaking for an instant. Now* Hale, *visibly affected, goes to* Danforth *and speaks quietly.*)

**Hale.** Pray, leave them, Excellency.

**Danforth** (*pressing* Hale *impatiently aside*). Mr. Proctor, you have been notified, have you not? (Proctor *is silent, staring at* Elizabeth.) I see light in the sky, Mister; let you counsel with your wife, and may God help you turn your back on Hell. (Proctor *is silent, staring at* Elizabeth.)

**Hale** (*quietly*). Excellency, let—

(Danforth *brushes past* Hale *and walks out.* Hale *follows.* Cheever *stands and follows,* Hathorne *behind.* Herrick *goes.* Parris, *from a safe distance, offers*)

**Parris.** If you desire a cup of cider, Mr. Proctor, I am sure I—(Proctor *turns an icy stare at him, and he breaks off.* Parris *raises his palms toward* Proctor.) God lead you now. (Parris *goes out.*)

(*Alone.* Proctor *walks to her, halts. It is as though they stood in a spinning world. It is beyond sorrow, above it. He reaches out his hand as though toward an embodiment not quite real, and as he touches her, a strange soft sound, half laughter, half amazement, comes from his throat. He pats her hand. She covers his hand with hers. And then, weak, he sits. Then she sits, facing him.*)

**Proctor.** The child?

**Elizabeth.** It grows.

**Proctor.** There is no word of the boys?

**Elizabeth.** They're well. Rebecca's Samuel keeps them.

**Proctor.** You have not seen them?

**Elizabeth.** I have not. (*She catches a weakening in herself and downs it.*)

**Proctor.** You are a—marvel, Elizabeth.

**Elizabeth.** You—have been tortured?

**Proctor.** Aye. (*Pause. She will not let herself be drowned in the sea that threatens her.*) They come for my life now.

**Elizabeth.** I know it.

(*Pause.*)

**Proctor.** None—have yet confessed?

**Elizabeth.** There be many confessed.

**Proctor.** Who are they?

**Elizabeth.** There be a hundred or more, they say. Goody Ballard is one; Isaiah Goodkind is one. There be many.

**Proctor.** Rebecca?

**Elizabeth.** Not Rebecca. She is one foot in Heaven now; naught may hurt her more.

**Proctor.** And Giles?

**Elizabeth.** You have not heard of it?

**Proctor.** I hear nothin', where I am kept.

**Elizabeth.** Giles is dead.

(*He looks at her incredulously.*)

**Proctor.** When were he hanged?

**Elizabeth** (*quietly, factually*). He were not hanged. He would not answer aye or nay to his indictment; for if he denied the charge they'd hang him surely, and auction out his property. So he stand mute, and died Christian under the law. And so his sons will have his farm. It is the law, for he could not be condemned a wizard without he answer the indictment, aye or nay. **3**

**Proctor.** Then how does he die?

**Elizabeth** (*gently*). They press him, John.

**Proctor.** Press?

---

97. **sibilance:** a hissing sound.

WORDS
TO **indictment** (ĭn-dīt′mənt) *n.* accusation
KNOW

**235**

**Students Acquiring English**

**1** Point out that *hearty* means "in good health " and *before my time* means "before my baby is due to be born." Make sure students understand the warning tone in Elizabeth's voice: it would be a sin to hang a pregnant woman and kill her innocent baby as well.

**2** Explain that *disputation* means "the act of debating or arguing." Danforth is telling Elizabeth that he does not want her to debate God's will with him; he wants her to save her husband.

**Less Proficient Readers**

**3** Ask students to summarize what has been happening to the accused since Proctor has been in jail. Point out that *wizard* is a term sometimes used for a male witch.

**Possible Response:** One hundred people have confessed. Rebecca Nurse has not confessed, nor does she ever intend to. Giles Corey was pressed to death for refusing to answer yes or no to his indictment.

## **Speaking and Listening**

**STAGING A MOCK TRIAL** Tell students that they are going to stage a mock trial of one of the characters in Act Four. Have them form groups and discuss which character they will put on trial and on what charges. For example, they might try Reverend Parris for his involvement in the conviction of innocent people and have the prosecutor present as evidence the fact that Abigail has run away, casting doubt on her own integrity as well as Parris's. Groups should work together to assign roles and write scripts for their mock trials.

**Present** Students can either memorize their scripts, read from their scripts, or use their scripts as guidelines for improvisation. Have each group present their trial in turn, and when all groups have presented, encourage them to discuss and critique each other's work.

**BLOCK SCHEDULING** This activity is particularly well suited for longer class periods.

### Active Reading

**USING A GRAPHIC ORGANIZER**

**A** Have students copy this graphic into their Reader's Notebooks. Ask them to write down what they think John Proctor's internal conflict is.

#### John Proctor

| Internal Conflict | External Conflict |
|---|---|
| Individual vs. self: Proctor struggles with his own definition of himself and tries to decide whether or not he should confess. | |

### Reading Skills and Strategies: CONNECTING

**B** Have students put themselves in the place of John Proctor and discuss whether they would confess to a lie to save their lives or not.

**Possible Responses:** Yes, I would confess because then at least I would be alive to parent and protect my three sons, especially since their mother is in jail. No, I would not confess, because it would be a sin and because it would lend legitimacy to the witch trials.

---

**Elizabeth.** Great stones they lay upon his chest until he plead aye or nay. (*With a tender smile for the old man.*) They say he give them but two words. "More weight," he says. And died.

**Proctor** (*numbed—a thread to weave into his agony*). "More weight."

**Elizabeth.** Aye. It were a fearsome[98] man, Giles Corey.

(*Pause.*)

**Proctor** (*with great force of will, but not quite looking at her*). I have been thinking I would confess to them, Elizabeth. (*She shows nothing.*) What say you? If I give them that?

**Elizabeth.** I cannot judge you, John.

(*Pause.*)

**Proctor** (*simply—a pure question*). What would you have me do?

**Elizabeth.** As you will, I would have it. (*Slight pause.*) I want you living, John. That's sure.

**Proctor** (*pauses, then with a flailing of hope*). Giles' wife? Have she confessed?

**Elizabeth.** She will not.

(*Pause.*)

**Proctor.** It is a pretense, Elizabeth.

**Elizabeth.** What is?

 **Proctor.** I cannot mount the gibbet like a saint. It is a fraud. I am not that man. (*She is silent.*) My honesty is broke, Elizabeth; I am no good man. Nothing's spoiled by giving them this lie that were not rotten long before.

**Elizabeth.** And yet you've not confessed till now. That speak goodness in you.

**Proctor.** Spite only keeps me silent. It is hard to give a lie to dogs. (*Pause, for the first time he turns directly to her.*) I would have your forgiveness, Elizabeth.

**Elizabeth.** It is not for me to give, John, I am—

**Proctor.** I'd have you see some honesty in it. Let them that never lied die now to keep their souls. It is pretense for me, a vanity that will

not blind God nor keep my children out of the wind. (*Pause.*) What say you?

**Elizabeth** (*upon a heaving sob that always threatens*). John, it come to naught that I should forgive you, if you'll not forgive yourself. (*Now he turns away a little, in great agony.*) It is not my soul, John, it is yours. (*He stands, as though in physical pain, slowly rising to his feet with a great immortal longing to find his answer. It is difficult to say, and she is on the verge of tears.*) Only be sure of this, for I know it now: Whatever you will do, it is a good man does it. (*He turns his doubting, searching gaze upon her.*) I have read my heart this three month, John. (*Pause.*) I have sins of my own to count. It needs a cold wife to prompt lechery.

**Proctor** (*in great pain*). Enough, enough—

**Elizabeth** (*now pouring out her heart*). Better you should know me!

**Proctor.** I will not hear it! I know you!

**Elizabeth.** You take my sins upon you, John—

**Proctor** (*in agony*). No, I take my own, my own!

**Elizabeth.** John, I counted myself so plain, so poorly made, no honest love could come to me! Suspicion kissed you when I did; I never knew how I should say my love. It were a cold house I kept! (*In fright, she swerves, as Hathorne enters.*)

**Hathorne.** What say you, Proctor? The sun is soon up.

(*Proctor, his chest heaving, stares, turns to Elizabeth. She comes to him as though to plead, her voice quaking.*)

**Elizabeth.** Do what you will. But let none be your judge. There be no higher judge under Heaven than Proctor is! Forgive me, forgive me, John— I never knew such goodness in the world! (*She covers her face, weeping.*)

(*Proctor turns from her to Hathorne; he is off the earth, his voice hollow.*)

---

98. **fearsome:** courageous.

---

## Teaching Options

### Mini Lesson  Speaking and Listening

**PERFORMING THE CLIMACTIC SCENE** Help students prepare to present the last scene of Act Four, beginning with Proctor's telling Hathorne that he wants his life. Students should be able to justify both their verbal and nonverbal performance techniques by referring to their interpretations of the text. Assign all character parts. Have students work together to read through the scene and interpret the characters before they perform it. Have them consider all the stage directions so that they can better portray their characters both verbally and nonverbally. Have students discuss how the drumrolls affect the mood of the scene and the feelings of the characters.

**Present** Students can decide how they will present their dramatic performance. Students who are audience members should evaluate how the performance enhances their appreciation and understanding of the final scene in *The Crucible*.

**BLOCK SCHEDULING** This activity is particularly well-suited for longer class periods.

**Proctor.** I want my life.

**Hathorne** (*electrified, surprised*). You'll confess yourself?

**Proctor.** I will have my life.

**Hathorne** (*with a mystical tone*). God be praised! It is a providence! (*He rushes out the door, and his voice is heard calling down the corridor.*) He will confess! Proctor will confess!

**Proctor** (*with a cry, as he strides to the door*). Why do you cry it? (*In great pain he turns back to her.*) It is evil, is it not? It is evil.

**Elizabeth** (*in terror, weeping*). I cannot judge you, John, I cannot!

**Proctor.** Then who will judge me? (*Suddenly clasping his hands.*) God in Heaven, what is John Proctor, what is John Proctor? (*He moves as an animal, and a fury is riding in him, a tantalized search.*) I think it is honest, I think so; I am no saint. (*As though she had denied this he calls angrily at her.*) Let Rebecca go like a saint; for me it is fraud!

(*Voices are heard in the hall, speaking together in suppressed excitement.*)

**Elizabeth.** I am not your judge, I cannot be. (*As though giving him release.*) Do as you will, do as you will!

**Proctor.** Would you give them such a lie? Say it. Would you ever give them this? (*She cannot answer.*) You would not; if tongs of fire were singeing you you would not! It is evil. Good, then—it is evil, and I do it!

(*Hathorne enters with* Danforth, *and, with them,* Cheever, Parris, *and* Hale. *It is a businesslike, rapid entrance, as though the ice had been broken.*)

**Danforth** (*with great relief and gratitude*). Praise to God, man, praise to God; you shall be blessed in Heaven for this. (*Cheever has hurried to the bench with pen, ink, and paper. Proctor watches him.*) Now then, let us have it. Are you ready, Mr. Cheever?

**Proctor** (*with a cold, cold horror at their efficiency*). Why must it be written?

**Danforth.** Why, for the good instruction of the village, Mister; this we shall post upon the church door! (*To Parris, urgently.*) Where is the marshal?

**Parris** (*runs to the door and calls down the corridor*). Marshal! Hurry!

**Danforth.** Now, then, Mister, will you speak slowly, and directly to the point, for Mr. Cheever's sake. (*He is on record now, and is really dictating to Cheever, who writes.*) Mr. Proctor, have you seen the Devil in your life? (*Proctor's jaws lock.*) Come, man, there is light in the sky; the town waits at the scaffold; I would give out this news. Did you see the Devil?

**Proctor.** I did.

**Parris.** Praise God!

**Danforth.** And when he come to you, what were his demand? (*Proctor is silent. Danforth helps.*) Did he bid you to do his work upon the earth?

**Proctor.** He did.

**Danforth.** And you bound yourself to his service? (*Danforth turns, as Rebecca Nurse enters, with Herrick helping to support her. She is barely able to walk.*) Come in, come in, woman!

**Rebecca** (*brightening as she sees Proctor*). Ah, John! You are well, then, eh?

(*Proctor turns his face to the wall.*)

**Danforth.** Courage, man, courage—let her witness your good example that she may come to God herself. Now hear it, Goody Nurse! Say on, Mr. Proctor. Did you bind yourself to the Devil's service?

**Rebecca** (*astonished*). Why, John!

**Proctor** (*through his teeth, his face turned from Rebecca*). I did.

**Danforth.** Now, woman, you surely see it profit nothin' to keep this conspiracy any further. Will you confess yourself with him?

**Rebecca.** Oh, John—God send his mercy on you!

**Danforth.** I say, will you confess yourself, Goody Nurse?

**Rebecca.** Why, it is a lie, it is a lie; how may I damn myself? I cannot, I cannot.

**Active Reading**

USING A GRAPHIC ORGANIZER

**A** Have students add John Proctor's external conflict to their graphic organizers.

### John Proctor

| Internal Conflict | External Conflict |
|---|---|
| Individual vs. self: Proctor struggles with his own definition of himself and tries to decide whether or not he should confess. | Individual vs. individual or society: Proctor fights against the authorities and refuses to besmirch others with his confession. |

**Danforth.** Mr. Proctor. When the Devil came to you did you see Rebecca Nurse in his company? (*Proctor is silent.*) Come, man, take courage—did you ever see her with the Devil?

**Proctor** (*almost inaudibly*). No.

(Danforth, *now sensing trouble, glances at John and goes to the table, and picks up a sheet—the list of condemned.*)

**A** **Danforth.** Did you ever see her sister, Mary Easty, with the Devil?

**Proctor.** No, I did not.

**Danforth** (*his eyes narrow on* Proctor). Did you ever see Martha Corey with the Devil?

**Proctor.** I did not.

**Danforth** (*realizing, slowly putting the sheet down*). Did you ever see anyone with the Devil?

**Proctor.** I did not.

**Danforth.** Proctor, you mistake me. I am not empowered to trade your life for a lie. You have most certainly seen some person with the Devil. (Proctor *is silent.*) Mr. Proctor, a score of people have already testified they saw this woman with the Devil.

**Proctor.** Then it is proved. Why must I say it?

**Danforth.** Why "must" you say it! Why, you should rejoice to say it if your soul is truly purged of any love for Hell!

**Proctor.** They think to go like saints. I like not to spoil their names.

**Danforth** (*inquiring, incredulous*).[99] Mr. Proctor, do you think they go like saints?

---

99. **incredulous:** disbelieving.

WORDS
TO
KNOW

**empower** (ĕm-pou′ər) *v.* to invest with authority

238

---

## Teaching Options

✓ Assessment **Standardized Test Practice**

**MAKING INFERENCES** For some standardized tests, students will be asked to make inferences. To provide students with practice in this skill, read aloud or write on the chalkboard the following question:

Which word best describes Danforth's feelings toward Proctor as he is questioning him?

**A.** indignant

**B.** bemused

**C.** authoritative

Lead students through the process of choosing the correct inference. Consider each choice. Point out that while all the answers have validity, the best choice is that which most accurately describes Danforth's exact feelings at that moment. For that reason, A is the best choice.

**Proctor** (*evading*). This woman never thought she done the Devil's work.

**Danforth.** Look you, sir. I think you mistake your duty here. It matters nothing what she thought—she is convicted of the unnatural murder of children, and you for sending your spirit out upon Mary Warren. Your soul alone is the issue here, Mister, and you will prove its whiteness or you cannot live in a Christian country. Will you tell me now what persons conspired with you in the Devil's company? (Proctor *is silent.*) To your knowledge was Rebecca Nurse ever—

**Proctor.** I speak my own sins; I cannot judge another. (*Crying out, with hatred*) I have no tongue for it.

**Hale** (*quickly to* Danforth). Excellency, it is enough he confess himself. Let him sign it, let him sign it.

**Parris** (*feverishly*). It is a great service, sir. It is a weighty name; it will strike the village that Proctor confess. I beg you, let him sign it. The sun is up, Excellency!

**Danforth** (*considers; then with dissatisfaction*). Come, then, sign your testimony. (*To* Cheever) Give it to him. (Cheever *goes to* Proctor, *the confession and a pen in hand.* Proctor *does not look at it.*) Come, man, sign it.

**Proctor** (*after glancing at the confession*). You have all witnessed it—it is enough.

**Danforth.** You will not sign it?

**Proctor.** You have all witnessed it; what more is needed?

**Danforth.** Do you sport with me? You will sign your name or it is no confession, Mister! (*His breast heaving with agonized breathing,* Proctor *now lays the paper down and signs his name.*)

**Parris.** Praise be to the Lord!

(Proctor *has just finished signing when* Danforth *reaches for the paper. But* Proctor *snatches it up, and now a wild terror is rising in him, and a boundless anger.*)

**Danforth** (*perplexed, but politely extending his hand*). If you please, sir.

**Proctor.** No.

**Danforth** (*as though* Proctor *did not understand*). Mr. Proctor, I must have—

**Proctor.** No, no. I have signed it. You have seen me. It is done! You have no need for this.

**Parris.** Proctor, the village must have proof that—

**Proctor.** Damn the village! I confess to God, and God has seen my name on this! It is enough!

**Danforth.** No, sir, it is—

**Proctor.** You came to save my soul, did you not? Here! I have confessed myself; it is enough!

**Danforth.** You have not con—

**Proctor.** I have confessed myself! Is there no good penitence[100] but it be public? God does not need my name nailed upon the church! God sees my name; God knows how black my sins are! It is enough!

**Danforth.** Mr. Proctor—

**Proctor.** You will not use me! I am no Sarah Good or Tituba, I am John Proctor! You will not use me! It is no part of salvation that you should use me!

**Danforth.** I do not wish to—

**Proctor.** I have three children—how may I teach them to walk like men in the world, and I sold my friends?

**Danforth.** You have not sold your friends—

**Proctor.** Beguile me not! I blacken all of them when this is nailed to the church the very day they hang for silence!

**Danforth.** Mr. Proctor, I must have good and legal proof that you—

**Proctor.** You are the high court, your word is good enough! Tell them I confessed myself; say Proctor broke his knees and wept like a woman; say what you will, but my name cannot—

---

100. **penitence:** regret for one's sins.

### Reading Skills and Strategies: CONNECTING

**A** Remind students that when John Proctor originally decided to confess, he did not know that Danforth would require him to give the names of others. Ask students to put themselves in Proctor's place. Would they give the confession Danforth required or would they refuse?

**Possible Response:** I would refuse to give that confession because I would not be able to live with myself for turning others in.

### Literary Analysis: RESOLUTION

**B** How does Proctor resolve both his inner and outer conflicts?

**Possible Response:** Proctor sees some goodness in himself and determines that he can die for the truth. The authorities still exercise their power to execute him, but they do not win what they really want—Proctor's confession, which would help them avoid a revolt by the people of Salem.

---

**Danforth** (*with suspicion*). It is the same, is it not? If I report it or you sign to it?

**Proctor** (*he knows it is insane*). No, it is not the same! What others say and what I sign to is not the same!

**Danforth.** Why? Do you mean to deny this confession when you are free?

**Proctor.** I mean to deny nothing!

**Danforth.** Then explain to me, Mr. Proctor, why you will not let—

**Proctor** (*with a cry of his whole soul*). Because it is my name! Because I cannot have another in my life! Because I lie and sign myself to lies! Because I am not worth the dust on the feet of them that hang! How may I live without my name? I have given you my soul; leave me my name!

**A** **Danforth** (*pointing at the confession in* Proctor's *hand*). Is that document a lie? If it is a lie I will not accept it! What say you? I will not deal in lies, Mister! (Proctor *is motionless.*) You will give me your honest confession in my hand, or I cannot keep you from the rope. (Proctor *does not reply.*) Which way do you go, Mister?

(*His breast heaving, his eyes staring,* Proctor *tears the paper and crumples it, and he is weeping in fury, but erect.*)

**Danforth.** Marshal!

**Parris** (*hysterically, as though the tearing paper were his life*). Proctor, Proctor!

**Hale.** Man, you will hang! You cannot!

**B** **Proctor** (*his eyes full of tears*). I can. And there's your first marvel, that I can. You have made your magic now, for now I do think I see some shred of goodness in John Proctor. Not enough to weave a banner with, but white enough to keep it from such dogs. (Elizabeth, *in a burst of terror, rushes to him and weeps against his hand.*) Give them no tear! Tears pleasure them! Show honor now, show a stony heart and sink them with it! (*He has lifted her, and kisses her now with great passion.*)

**Rebecca.** Let you fear nothing! Another judgment waits us all!

**Danforth.** Hang them high over the town! Who weeps for these, weeps for corruption! (*He sweeps out past them.* Herrick *starts to lead* Rebecca, *who almost collapses, but* Proctor *catches her, and she glances up at him apologetically.*)

**Rebecca.** I've had no breakfast.

**Herrick.** Come, man.

(Herrick *escorts them out,* Hathorne *and* Cheever *behind them.* Elizabeth *stands staring at the empty doorway.*)

**Parris** (*in deadly fear, to* Elizabeth). Go to him, Goody Proctor! There is yet time!

(*From outside a drumroll strikes the air.* Parris *is startled.* Elizabeth *jerks about toward the window.*)

**Parris.** Go to him! (*He rushes out the door, as though to hold back his fate.*) Proctor! Proctor!

(*Again, a short burst of drums.*)

**Hale.** Woman, plead with him! (*He starts to rush out the door, and then goes back to her.*) Woman! It is pride, it is vanity. (*She avoids his eyes, and moves to the window. He drops to his knees.*) Be his helper!—What profit him to bleed? Shall the dust praise him? Shall the worms declare his truth? Go to him, take his shame away!

**Elizabeth** (*supporting herself against collapse, grips the bars of the window, and with a cry*). He have his goodness now. God forbid I take it from him!

(*The final drumroll crashes, then heightens violently.* Hale *weeps in frantic prayer, and the new sun is pouring in upon her face, and the drums rattle like bones in the morning air.*)

**1**
**2**

**the curtain falls**

---

## Teaching Options

✓ Assessment **Informal Assessment**

**ALTERNATIVE ENDING** You can informally assess students' understanding of the selection by having them imagine an alternative ending in which John Proctor does not rip up his confession. Students' writing could take the form of a narrative telling how John Proctor and his family were treated in town after he confessed.

### RUBRIC

**3 Full Accomplishment** Response reflects a full understanding of the effects a confession

would have on the character of John Proctor as well as on the reputation of his family.

**2 Substantial Accomplishment** Response shows a general understanding of the effects a confession could have on John Proctor, but misses some of the implications of this in the community.

**1 Little or Partial Accomplishment** Response shows little understanding of the effects a confession would have on the character of John Proctor or on the reputation of his family.

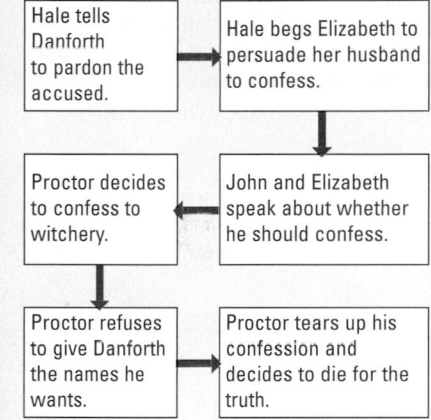

### Less Proficient Readers

**1** Point out the simile to students. Explain that the sound of the drums is being compared to the sound of rattling bones. In other words, the drums are the sound of death.

### Multiple Learning Styles
#### Visual or Spatial Learners

**2** Have students construct a graphic organizer based on text descriptions of the events that occur between the time that Hale tells Danforth to pardon the accused and John Proctor refuses to confess. Graphic organizers should contain events in the order shown.

| | | | |
|---|---|---|---|
| Hale tells Danforth to pardon the accused. | → | Hale begs Elizabeth to persuade her husband to confess. | |
| | | ↓ | |
| Proctor decides to confess to witchery. | ← | John and Elizabeth speak about whether he should confess. | |
| ↓ | | | |
| Proctor refuses to give Danforth the names he wants. | → | Proctor tears up his confession and decides to die for the truth. | |

 **Mini Lesson** # Viewing and Representing

**DARKNESS AND LIGHT** Remind students that an artist's use of darkness and light can communicate meaning. In *The Crucible,* Arthur Miller's stage directions tell set designers how he envisioned each setting, including whether a place is shrouded in darkness or flooded with light.

**Application** Have students review the stage directions and the photographs on pages 229 and 241. Do the photographs accurately reflect the stage directions?

**Possible Responses:** The darkness of the jail cell creates a somber mood and suggests the igno-

rance and evil intentions that have landed so many innocent people in jail. The photograph on page 229 captures this. At the end of the play, the light streaming in upon Elizabeth's face symbolizes the victory of truth over evil, because Elizabeth is watching John do the right thing. The photograph on page 241 does not create a feeling of triumph, however; the light seems harsh on Proctor's ravaged face. The way the play version ended is preferable, because the audience never actually sees Proctor go to the gallows, only Elizabeth's triumphant reaction.

**Literary Analysis: IRONY**

Ask students to discuss what is ironic about the entire premise of the witch trials.

**Possible Response:** All of the accusers called themselves Puritans, and yet they lied and gave false testimonies—sins in the Bible. The people who were wrongly accused were also Puritans, and they tried to tell the truth—something required by the Bible—and they were hanged for it. Finally, the authorities, who were supposed to follow the Bible and rational principles of justice, did the exact opposite and condoned the killing of innocent people. The Salem witch trials occurred in the name of Christianity, and yet these trials embodied the very sins that Christianity condemns.

# View and Compare
## The Crucible

In your opinion, which movie poster better reflects the content and atmosphere of *The Crucible*?

Poster for the 1996 film version of *The Crucible*.

Poster for a 1957 French film based on *The Crucible*.

242

## Connect to the Literature

**1. What Do You Think?**
What was your reaction to John Proctor's final choice?

**Comprehension Check**
• What becomes of Abigail Williams and Mercy Lewis?
• How is Giles Corey killed?
• What does John Proctor do when asked to sign a confession?

## Think Critically

**2.** At the end of the play, Elizabeth Proctor says that her husband has "his goodness now." What do you think she means?

THINK ABOUT

• why he at first agrees to confess after having resisted so long
• why he believes his signed confession would blacken his friends' reputations
• what gives him the strength to die

**3.** Explain, in your own words, why Reverend Hale urges the prisoners to confess to a lie. What does this suggest to you about the way he has changed?

**4.** Who do you think is the most courageous **character** in the play, and why?

**5.** The word *crucible* means "a severe test or trial." Why do you think Miller chose to give his play this **title**?

## Extend Interpretations

**6. Critic's Corner** According to critic Penelope Curtis, "The most interesting feature of *The Crucible* is that it is so impressively a play about evil forces, despite the fact that it *seems* to be a play discrediting belief in such forces." How would you describe the evil forces that Miller presents in this play?

**7. Different Perspectives** *The Crucible* was first produced in 1953, during Senator Joseph McCarthy's congressional investigations to root out suspected Communists in the State Department, the entertainment industry, and the U.S. Army. In his pursuit of Communists, McCarthy sometimes accused individuals on the basis of flimsy evidence and innuendo. In what ways do you think *The Crucible* is a criticism of McCarthy and his ways? Support your opinion with details from the play.

**8. Connect to Life** Think of a 20th-century person who suffered or died for his or her beliefs, and compare this person to John Proctor.

## Literary Analysis

**PLOT AND CONFLICT** The **plot** is the sequence of events in a literary work. Generally, plots are built around a **conflict**—a struggle between opposing forces. An **external conflict** pits a character against nature, society, or another character. For example, the courtroom confrontation between Mary Warren and Abigail Williams over who is telling the truth is an external conflict. An **internal conflict** is a struggle between opposing forces within a character. For example, Reverend Hale at first supports the proceedings in Salem. Soon, however, he doubts whether the afflicted girls are truthful. As more and more people are accused, his doubts grow, and he eventually quits the court.

In a plot structure, the **climax** is the moment when interest and emotional force reach a peak. Usually occurring toward the end of a story or a drama, the climax often results in a change in the characters or a solution to a conflict.

**Paired Activity** Working with a partner, create a diagram to show the internal and the external conflicts of John Proctor. Then create a second diagram for Elizabeth Proctor. After you complete both diagrams, identify the conflict that is resolved at the climax. Discuss whether the other conflicts are resolved by the end of the play.

---

## Extend Interpretations

**Critic's Corner** Possible Responses: Miller explores such evil forces as arrogance, intolerance, vengeance, and coldness of heart. Characters such as Danforth, Parris, and Hathorne, who uphold the Puritan establishment, assume they have a lock on the truth, refusing to tolerate dissent and non-conformity. Characters such as Putnam and Abigail Williams use the hysteria to further their own personal vendettas.

**Different Perspectives** Possible Responses: Elizabeth Proctor is arrested because Abigail Williams has accused her of attempted murder through witchcraft. The only "evidence" is the small rag doll with a needle stuck in it that Mary Warren planted in the Proctor home. Danforth sees anyone who questions his methods as enemies and potential suspects. Like McCarthy, he seems motivated more by personal ambition than by a sincere desire to learn the truth.

**Connect to Life** Accept all reasonable responses. For example, students might draw parallels between Proctor and Martin Luther King, Jr.

---

## Connect to the Literature

**1. What Do You Think?**
Some students will be surprised at Proctor's sacrifice; others will find his decision in keeping with his character.

**Comprehension Check**
• They abscond from Salem with Mr. Parris's money.
• Giles Corey is pressed to death with heavy stones laid on his chest.
• He signs it, then refuses to hand it over, and finally tears it up.

 Use Selection Quiz in **Unit Two Resource Book,** p. 34.

## Think Critically

**2.** Possible Response: She means that John Proctor has regained his integrity, which he thought he had forfeited forever because of his affair. At first he agrees to confess because he longs to live with Elizabeth, who has forgiven him. But he tears up his signed confession so that the court cannot use it to cast doubt upon the innocence of Rebecca Nurse and the others who chose death rather than confess to a lie.

**3.** Possible Response: Reverend Hale urges the prisoners to confess to a lie because he realizes that his conduct has led to the shedding of innocent blood. Finally convinced that life is God's most precious gift, he disavows his allegiance to Puritanism.

**4.** Possible Response: Anyone who goes against the crowd, refusing to support the witch-hunt, is a courageous character.

**5.** Possible Responses: Those accused of witchcraft face a terrible dilemma: they can refuse to confess and hang, or save their lives by lying and incriminating others. By making such a confession, however, they sacrifice their integrity and imperil their souls.

## Literary Analysis:

**Plot and Conflict** Students should note that Elizabeth's final line in the play— "He [Proctor] have his goodness now"— suggests that the conflict between her husband and herself has been resolved. She is convinced that Proctor has regained his honor.

# Writing Options

**1. Points of Comparison** Students' responses should demonstrate a clear understanding of Puritan beliefs as reflected in both works. **To get students started on this assignment,** ask them to review Edwards's sermon. Then have students think about how the people of Salem viewed the human soul, evil spirits, and the confession of sins. Have students consider how fear affected Edwards's audience and the townspeople in Salem.

**2. Missing Scene** Students' dialogue should reflect an understanding of both characters. **To get students started on this assignment,** have them review the scene in which the Proctors learn that Abigail is responsible for accusing Elizabeth. Then, ask students whether they think John might have demanded that Abigail rescind her accusation. Or do they think he would have tried to deceive her by making false promises to get her to change her testimony?

**3. Editorial on Hysteria** Students' editorials should express opinions backed by an understanding of the meaning of hysteria and how it is demonstrated in Miller's play.

**4. Capsule Review** In reviewing the play, students should use their personal responses as a starting point. Students may focus on a literary element—such as character, conflict, and theme—or Miller's criticism of postwar America.

# Activities & Explorations

**1. Historical Fashions** Students' costume designs should look like genuine clothing from the 17th century, specifically with regard to color and modesty.

**2. Set Design** Students' dioramas should mirror a set from the play, with special attention to color and lighting.

**3. Dramatic Reading** Students' readings should show an understanding of the characters' motives and interactions.

**4. Salem Game Show** Students' game show should include thoughtful questions and answers about the events and characters in the play.

---

# *Choices* & CHALLENGES

## Writing Options

**1. [Points of Comparison]**
Think about the views of Puritan life you formed after reading Jonathan Edwards's sermon "Sinners in the Hands of an Angry God," on pages 152–156. In what ways did reading *The Crucible* confirm or challenge these views? Write a personal response to answer this question, using the diagram below to structure your writing.

| Edwards's sermon | Miller's play |
|---|---|
| My views of Puritan life | What confirms or changes my views |
| 1. | 1. |
| 2. | 2. |
| 3. | 3. |

**2. Missing Scene** Act Two of *The Crucible* originally consisted of two scenes. The second scene dramatized a meeting between John Proctor and Abigail Williams. Miller later omitted this scene from the published version, and it is not usually performed. Write your own scene between Proctor and Abigail to serve as a bridge between Acts Two and Three.

**3. Editorial on Hysteria** Write a newspaper editorial expressing your opinion about the causes of the witchcraft hysteria in Salem more than 300 years ago. For evidence, draw upon events in Miller's play and your own knowledge of the witchcraft hysteria.

**4. Capsule Review** Write a brief evaluation of *The Crucible,* telling what you think the play achieved or did not achieve. Support your opinion with evidence. Save your review in your **Working Portfolio.**

## Activities & Explorations

**1. Historical Fashions** Create a costume design for one of the characters in a production of *The Crucible.* To make your design as historically accurate as possible, research 17th-century American fashions typically worn by Puritans, ministers, judges, household servants, farmers, and so forth. ~ **HISTORY, ART**

**2. Set Design** With a small group of classmates, create a three-dimensional diorama of one of the sets for the play. First, review details given in the stage directions to visualize the setting. Then consult reference books on colonial homes in New England for ideas on decor. Display your finished diorama in the classroom. ~ **HISTORY, ART**

**3. Dramatic Reading** Readers Theater requires no props, no costumes, and no memorization. Instead, performers read aloud from a script, using only their voices to convey their interpretations of characters and events. With a group of classmates, stage a Readers Theater performance of a favorite passage from this play. Use the stage directions to help you determine how the characters act and speak. Then rehearse your reading and present it to the class. ~ **PERFORMING**

**4. Salem Game Show** With a small group, create a television game show in which contestants answer questions relating to events or characters in Miller's play. One student should act as emcee and the other members of the group as contestants. ~ **SPEAKING AND LISTENING**

## Inquiry & Research

**1. Drama v. History** Do some historical research to find out how faithfully Miller depicts the actual people and events from the Salem witch trials. For example, did you know that the real Abigail Williams was only 11 years old at the time? Present an oral report to share your findings.

 **More Online: Research Starter**
www.mcdougallittell.com

**2. McCarthyism** The McCarthy hearings of the 1950s, often described as "witch hunts," inspired Miller's writing of *The Crucible.* With a small group of classmates, find out more about what led to the hearings, how they were conducted, and what happened to the accused.

---

## Teaching Options

 **Mini Lesson** **Grammar**

**COMMA SPLICES** Explain to students that a comma splice occurs when two sentences are linked together with a comma when a stronger form of punctuation is needed, such as an end mark or a semicolon. Write the following example on the chalkboard:

**Comma splice:** Last winter I went to Bermuda for vacation, this winter I plan to go to Mexico.

**Correct sentences:** Last winter I went to Bermuda for vacation. This winter I plan to go to Mexico.

**Exercise** Ask students to identify and properly punctuate the sentences that contain comma splices.

**1.** Tituba, Reverend Parris's slave, is in the Salem jail. *(no comma splice; appositive)*

**2.** Reverend Hale asked Danforth to pardon the prisoners, he did not think they should be hanged. *(comma splice; replace comma with a period or a semicolon)*

# Vocabulary in Action

**EXERCISE A: CONTEXT CLUES** Review the Words to Know on page 163. On your paper, write the vocabulary word that best answers each riddle.

1. I am a terrible event that harms many people.
2. I describe the behavior of an ideal butler.
3. I will do anything in support of my beliefs.
4. I am issued against a suspected criminal.
5. I am a punishment for religious wrongdoing.
6. I describe something clean and without blemish.
7. I might be a person who accuses you of crime.
8. I am the statement of a witness.
9. I describe something that cannot be understood.
10. I fill the soul of a wicked person.

**EXERCISE B: ASSESSMENT PRACTICE** Write the vocabulary word that fits best in each group.

1. authorize, grant, entitle, _____
2. troublesome, contrary, argumentative, _____
3. boldness, rudeness, impudence, _____
4. distress, torment, harass, _____
5. partiality, taste, liking, _____
6. irregular, unbalanced, unfair, _____
7. decide, negotiate, judge, _____
8. angry, outraged, insulted, _____
9. learn, discern, discover, _____
10. silently, soundlessly, quietly, _____

## Arthur Miller
### 1915–

**Other Works**
*All My Sons*
*Death of a Salesman*
*A View from the Bridge*

**Growing Up in the Depression** Arthur Miller was born in New York City on October 17, 1915. As a boy, he showed little interest in writing or reading literature. Instead, he played football, baseball, and other sports. When he was 13, his father suffered business losses during the Great Depression, and the family was forced to move from a large apartment in Harlem to a tiny house in Brooklyn. Miller graduated from high school in 1932, but his parents could not afford to send him to college. For the next two years, he worked at a variety of odd jobs, including shipping clerk in an automobile parts warehouse. While riding the subway to and from work, he read voraciously.

**Aspiring Playwright** After saving money for college, Miller enrolled as a journalism student at the University of Michigan. After graduating in 1938, He returned to New York. Following his debut on Broadway with *The Man Who Had All the Luck* in

1944, Miller's career began to soar. His play *All My Sons* (1947) captured numerous awards. The drama introduced one of his main motifs—the haunting influence of a guilty past. This motif also informed his next work, *Death of a Salesman* (1949), a Pulitzer Prize-winning play that met with enormous critical and popular acclaim.

**On Trial** The inspiration for Miller's next play, *The Crucible* (1953), came from the McCarthy era in American politics. Miller wrote the play to warn against mass hysteria and to plead for freedom and tolerance. Ironically, Miller himself was subpoenaed to appear before McCarthy's committee in 1956 and was questioned about his activities with the American Communist Party. Miller refused to provide testimony that might implicate others. He said, "My conscience will not permit me to use the name of another person and bring trouble to him." For his refusal, he was cited for contempt of Congress—a conviction that was later overturned.

**Years of Triumph** Since the mid-1960s, Miller has published more than a dozen plays. *Broken Glass*, his play about an American Jewish couple's reaction to Nazi atrocities during World War II, appeared on Broadway in 1994—50 years after his first Broadway play premiered.

# Vocabulary in Action

**Exercise A**
1. calamity
2. subservient
3. fanatic
4. indictment
5. excommunication
6. immaculate
7. plaintiff
8. deposition
9. unintelligible
10. iniquity

**Exercise B**
1. empower
2. contentious
3. effrontery
4. afflict
5. predilection
6. disproportionate
7. arbitrate
8. indignant
9. ascertain
10. inaudibly

3. Where are John and Elizabeth, they are in a room speaking privately. *(comma splice; replace comma with question mark)*
4. Rebecca Nurse, Elizabeth Proctor, and Sarah Good have all been accused of witchery. *(no comma splice; items in a series)*
5. John Proctor is determined to protect his friends, he does not want to sign a confession. *(comma splice; replace comma with a period or a semicolon)*

 Use McDougal Littell's *Language Network,* Chapter 3, for more instruction and practice in avoiding comma splices.

## PART 1 Reading the Prompt

Model the process of reading a prompt:

- Read through the prompt in its entirety.
- List the assignment's key words and phrases on the board (*"compare and contrast," "qualities,"* and *"which relationship better reflects the Puritan ideal"*).
- Define each key word using the Strategies in Action to show how students can restate the prompt in their own words.

## PART 2 Planning a Comparison-Contrast Essay

- Students can define the Puritan ideal of marriage. Suggest that they list qualities that such a marriage might have.
- Have students first jot down their main impressions of the three qualities identified in the prompt. Then encourage them to look at the selections again for supporting evidence. Evidence might include both words and actions.

## PART 3 Drafting Your Essay

**Introduction** Suggest that students begin by describing an ideal Puritan marriage. Then they can state their view as to which relationship best reflects that ideal.

**Organization** Students may find it helpful to make two or more informal outlines, each reflecting a different type of organization mentioned in Part 3. Once they have chosen a framework they can better select which examples and transitions to include.

**Conclusion** Students may conclude that Bradstreet's marriage more closely reflects the Puritan ideal: it is genuinely loving without negative undercurrents.

**Revision** Remind students to punctuate quotations correctly and to include logical transitions that will make their organization clear. These might include such words as *similarly, both, however,* and *while.*

---

# Comparing Literature: Assessment Practice

In writing assessments, you will often be asked to compare and contrast two works of literature. The purpose of the comparison may be to evaluate the works against a standard. You will now practice writing a comparison-contrast essay with an evaluative focus.

## PART 1 Reading the Prompt

Often you will be asked to write in response to a prompt like the one below. Examine the wording carefully to see what is required in your response.

> **Writing Prompt**
>
> Both Arthur Miller's play *The Crucible* and Anne Bradstreet's poem "To My Dear and Loving Husband" depict a husband-and-wife relationship in Puritan times. In an essay, compare and contrast ① these relationships. Consider such qualities as the ② following: the depth of love, the degree of commitment, and the amount of personal fulfillment. Conclude by telling which relationship better reflects the Puritan ideal—a love that brings the ③ individual closer to God.

### STRATEGIES IN ACTION

① **Compare** and **contrast**, stating similarities and differences.

② Notice the **qualities**, or characteristics, of relationships you will examine.

③ **Evaluate** the relationships against a given standard.

## PART 2 Planning a Comparison-Contrast Essay

- Create a Venn diagram to organize similarities and differences.
- Write characteristics shared by both relationships in the overlapping area, and write characteristics not shared outside this area.
- Evaluate each relationship against the criteria in the prompt. Decide which relationship brings the partners closer to God.

The Bradstreets in "To My Dear and Loving Husband" — The Proctors in *The Crucible*

Differences — Differences

Similarities

## PART 3 Drafting Your Essay

**Introduction** Introduce the subject—husband-and-wife relationships in the two selections—and describe the ideal against which you will evaluate the relationships.

**Organization** You might first describe one relationship, then describe the other, and then explain their similarities and differences. Or, you might present first all the similarities and then all the differences. Include examples from the play and the poem to illustrate your ideas. Use transitional words and phrases such as *similarly* or *however* to connect ideas within and between paragraphs.

**Conclusion** State an opinion about which relationship is closer to the Puritan ideal.

**Revision** Allow some time to review your work. Make sure it is clear, well-supported, and free from mistakes.

**Writing Handbook**
See page 1281: Compare and Contrast.

---

## Mini Lesson Punctuation

### QUOTING LINES OF POETRY

**Instruction** When two or more lines of poetry are quoted, they are usually set line-for-line in a block that is separated from the main text and indented. For block quotations, no quotation marks are used. However, a poetry quotation of just a few lines may also be run into the main text. In this case, double quotation marks are used before and after the lines; a slash mark, with a space before and after it, identifies line breaks.

**Application** Students will probably use quotations from the poem to support the conclusions that they draw. Remind them to use double quotation marks when they quote one line of poetry and slashes when they quote two lines.

### LITERATURE CONNECTIONS

## The Scarlet Letter

NATHANIEL HAWTHORNE

These thematically related readings are provided along with *The Scarlet Letter*:

**For each ecstatic instant / Mine Enemy is growing old**
EMILY DICKINSON

**The Lottery**
SHIRLEY JACKSON

**Concerns Raised on "Scarlet Letter" for Drunk Drivers**
TONY LOCY

**Muddy Brains**
JOHN DUNTON

*from* **The Classics Reclassified**
RICHARD ARMOUR

**A Respectable Woman**
KATE CHOPIN

## The Crucible

ARTHUR MILLER

These thematically related readings are provided along with *The Crucible*:

**Conversation with an American Writer**
YEVGENY YEVTUSHENKO

**Guilt**
CLIFFORD LINDSEY ALDERMAN

**How to Spot a Witch**
ADAM GOODHEART

**Young Goodman Brown**
NATHANIEL HAWTHORNE

**The Great Fear**
J. RONALD OAKLEY

**Justice Denied in Massachusetts**
EDNA ST. VINCENT MILLAY

**The Very Proper Gander**
JAMES THURBER

**A Piece of String**
GUY DE MAUPASSANT

## And Even *More* . . .

**Books**

**Hester: A Novel About the Early Hester Prynne**
CHRISTOPHER BIGSBY
This imaginative prequel to *The Scarlet Letter* recounts the beginnings of Hester and Dimmesdale's relationship and their years of separation.

**Everyday Life in Early America**
DAVID FREEMAN HAWKES
A fascinating assortment of details about the daily routines of 17th-century American colonists covers such topics as housing, foods, fashions, and superstitions.

**Salem-Village Witchcraft**
PAUL BOYER AND STEPHEN NISSENBAUM
This highly informative book provides a documentary record of the witchcraft hysteria that gripped colonial New England.

**Other Media**

**The Scarlet Letter**
A PBS production of the novel, starring Meg Foster and John Heard. WGBH Boston. (VIDEOCASSETTE)

**The Puritan Experience: Making of a New World**
A brief videodisc providing insights into the Puritans and the communities they founded. LCA Releases. (VIDEODISC)

**McCarthy: Death of a Witch Hunter**
The downfall of the famous 1950s anti-communist activist. Film Archives. (VIDEOCASSETTE)

### The Witchcraft of Salem Village

SHIRLEY JACKSON

This versatile author, who often explored supernatural happenings and the sinister side of human nature in her fiction, investigates Salem's outbreak of witchcraft hysteria in this intriguing nonfiction work.

The *Electronic Library* is a CD-ROM that contains additional fiction, nonfiction, poetry, and drama for each unit in *The Language of Literature*.

These are the additional selections found in Unit 2 of the *Electronic Library* that apply to Part 1.

Edward Taylor
**Upon a Spider Catching a Fly**
**Huswifery**

**Reading Skills and Strategies**
**SUSTAINED SILENT READING**
Encourage students to select one of the books as an opportunity to read silently over a period of time.

## Writing Workshop
### Critical Review

**Objectives**
- write a Critical Review
- use a written text as a model
- revise a draft to avoid circular reasoning
- eliminate unnecessary qualifiers that weaken the message

## Introducing the Workshop

**A** **Critical Review** Students encounter critical reviews in newspapers and magazines, as well as on television and radio. Critical reviews can cover television programs, movies, books, theatrical presentations, and concerts. Critical reviews give us insight into the reviewer's opinion of the work. Reviews done by professionals can also influence the success of the work being reviewed. Have students name a few well-known professional reviewers as well as works for which they have read reviews. Establish some criteria for what makes a good review.

Point out that through writing a critical review, students, too, will be able to give their opinion on a book or film. Some students may be interested in reviewing current movies or books. Others, like the professional reviewer in the model, may prefer to review a classical piece of literature or old movie.

**Basics in a Box**
**B** **Using the Graphic** The graphic illustrates the three parts of a critical review: the introduction, which identifies the work being reviewed; the body, which states the criteria for judgment and evidence to support it; and the conclusion, which offers an opinion of whether the work is worthwhile.

**C** **Presenting the Rubric** To better understand the assignment, students can refer to the Standards for Writing a Successful Critical Review. You may also want to share with them the complete rubric, which describes several levels of proficiency.

 To engage students visually, use **Power Presentation** 2, Critical Review.

---

## Writing Workshop — Critical Review

### You be the judge . . .

**From Reading to Writing** Both *The Crucible* and "The Examination of Sarah Good" are writings that excite strong reader responses—either positive or negative. You can present your response to books, movies, or performances in a **critical review** of the work. In writing a review, you use evidence from the work to support your opinion. You already form opinions of what you read and see every day. In this workshop, you will learn to put them on paper.

**For Your Portfolio**

**WRITING PROMPT** Write a review of a piece of literature or a film you feel strongly about. You will establish evaluation criteria and express your opinion of the piece.

**Purpose:** To share your opinion
**Audience:** Your classmates or a reading group

### Basics in a Box

**Critical Review at a Glance**

**Introduction**
- Identify author and subject
- State overall evaluation

↓

**Body**
- Briefly summarize selection
- Establish criteria for judging work
- Give evidence to support evaluation

↓

**Conclusion**
Make a recommendation

**RUBRIC** **Standards for Writing**

**A successful critical review should**
- identify and give a brief summary of the work
- state your opinion of the work and make clear the criteria you used to judge it
- support your opinion with well-chosen details and examples from the text
- organize arguments and supporting details in a way that is easy to follow
- conclude with a recommendation to the reader regarding the work

**248** UNIT TWO PART 1: BETWEEN HEAVEN AND HELL

---

## LESSON RESOURCES

**USING PRINT RESOURCES**
**Unit Two Resource Book**
- Prewriting, p. 36
- Drafting, p. 37
- Peer Response, pp. 38–39
- Revising, Editing, and Proofreading, p. 40
- Student Models, pp. 41–46
- Rubric, p. 47

**Writing Transparencies and Copymasters**
- Writing Process, pp. 1–4
- Writing Structure, p. 6
- Writing Style, p. 21
- Writing Template, p. 26

**USING MEDIA RESOURCES**
**Visit our website:**
www.mcdougallittell.com

For a complete view of Lesson Resources, see page 131e.

# Analyzing a Professional Model

**RUBRIC**
IN ACTION

To demonstrate my empathy with the themes of _The Crucible,_ I'm going to engage in a bit of heresy of my own: I don't think Arthur Miller's play is particularly good. I'm not suggesting that it is dated, as other critics have done. Irrational fear and extremism are alive and well in America today. The ideas in _The Crucible_ were never the issue, but those weighty issues overwhelmed underdeveloped characters. Productions of _The Crucible_ have lived or died on the ability of the actors to invest the material with feeling missing from the page, and this first English-language film of the play is no different. Fortunately, the cast is very strong, and the conventions of cinema give the energy level a much needed boost. Flawed as it may be, _The Crucible_ still has moments of undeniable power.

Set in 1692 in Salem, Massachusetts, _The Crucible_ begins with a gathering in the woods where several young girls, led by Abigail Williams (Winona Ryder) play at conjuring spirits. The fun ends when they are discovered by Reverend Parris (Bruce Davison) and the Reverend's own daughter is frightened into a catatonic state. To save themselves from punishment, the girls begin accusing Salem's women of witchcraft, naming names indiscriminately. Abigail, however, has one specific name in mind: Elizabeth Proctor (Joan Allen), wife of her former employer and lover, John Proctor (Daniel Day-Lewis). As Salem becomes a town ruled by paranoia, Judge Danforth (Paul Scofield) arrives to try the accused witches. Only a few men like Proctor are brave enough to challenge the court.

Miller's 1953 play is well-known as an allegory for the "Red Scare" and the blacklisting of the 1950s, but Miller's own screen adaptation attempts to make the story less specific to that era, while also making it more visual. The girls' ritual gathering, only described by other characters in the play, is shown in graphic detail, as is an incident in which Abigail stabs herself with a needle and accuses Elizabeth of hexing her. The scenes are not included simply for shock value, but to emphasize the active hypocrisy of the accusers. They also make Abigail less a creature of youthful spite and more a deeply disturbed young woman caught up in the attention and admiration she receives for pointing out the witches of Salem. Winona

**❶** Identifies the work to be evaluated

**❷** This writer hooks the reader with a bold statement.

**Other Options:**
· Quote a professional critic about the work
· Describe a striking scene from the work

**❸** States his overall evaluation

**❹** Summarizes the story without giving away the ending

**❺** Clearly states first supporting point and illustrates it with details from the film

## Analyzing the Model
### Movie Review of _The Crucible_

The professional model is a review of the 1996 film version of _The Crucible,_ a play written by Arthur Miller in 1953. It deals with the Salem witch trials of 1692. At that time, in Salem, Massachusetts, jurors in a special court erroneously convicted 27 townspeople for witchcraft and executed 20 of them. After many years as a play, _The Crucible_ was adapted for the large screen.

At the time _The Crucible_ was written, the United States experienced a heightened fear of communism. The "Red Scare" mentioned in the review included Senator Joseph R. McCarthy's irrational accusations labeling government officials as communists despite a lack of credible evidence. Unable to substantiate his claims, McCarthy was eventually discredited in 1954.

Have students read the professional model, then discuss the Rubric in Action. Point out the key words and phrases in the model that correspond to elements mentioned in the Rubric in Action.

2. Have students suggest an alternate opening based on the other options listed.

   **Possible Response:** One of the most riveting scenes in the film version of Arthur Miller's _The Crucible_ occurs when Elizabeth Proctor is questioned about witchcraft.

3. Ask students if the review is positive or negative.

   **Possible Response:** It is mostly positive. The reviewer acknowledges that there are some flaws, but sees the overall strength of the film.

5. Explain that an _allegory_ is a work of literature in which people and events stand for abstract qualities. The reviewer acknowledges that the play _The Crucible_ is an allegory for the communist scare that occurred in the United States during the 1950s; however, the reviewer doesn't think that the film is meant to refer specifically to that communist scare. Rather, the film takes advantage of the camera's ability to visually expand the scenes, exploring the characters and their motives in greater depth than the play.

---

**Mini Lesson** ## Viewing and Representing

**PICTURING TEXT STRUCTURE**
Have students analyze the structure of the professional model by constructing an image such as a graphic organizer. The graphic students construct should reflect how the professional reviewer has organized his piece. Students might first write a note about each paragraph to see how the paragraphs relate to one another and to the entire review. They should conclude by discussing how this text structure influences their understanding.

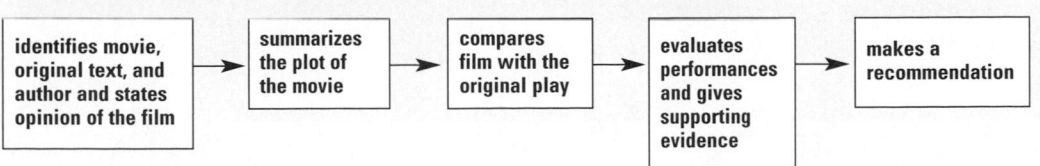

identifies movie, original text, and author and states opinion of the film → summarizes the plot of the movie → compares film with the original play → evaluates performances and gives supporting evidence → makes a recommendation

**6.** Ask students to summarize the reviewer's second point.

**Possible Response** The reviewer says that cast members Winona Ryder, Paul Scofield, and Joan Allen all give strong performances. However, the reviewer is disappointed in the performance of Daniel Day-Lewis.

**8.** Have students define *iconoclastic*, and explain how it relates to the review. Then have volunteers restate the reviewer's recommendation.

**Possible Response:** An iconoclast is one who destroys traditional or popular ideas. The reviewer is saying that Hytner's direction does not destroy the original message of the play; instead, it enhances it. He gives the film a favorable review.

---

Ryder does some of her best work ever in the role, shedding the restrained quality of her previous period-film performances. Here she lets loose like an animal—desperate, haunted, and dangerous.

Ryder is one part of a <u>cast that gives its all</u> to *The Crucible*, beginning with Paul Scofield as Danforth. Scofield brings a commanding, weathered presence to the role of Salem's Grand Inquisitor and a conviction that the judge's work is good and proper. He also gives lines a punch few other actors could muster; when he announces that he intends to "touch the bottom of this swamp" of accusations and counter-accusations, he utters the word "swamp" with a fearsome authority. Joan Allen's steady, cool Elizabeth is just what the part calls for, and she shows that passive-aggressive behavior is not a uniquely 20th-century phenomenon. Surprisingly, the weak link in the cast is Daniel Day-Lewis. In both the play and the movie, Proctor is an underwritten role. However, in the movie there is too much self-righteous heroism in Day-Lewis's reading. When he delivers his final plea to avoid a public confession, literally foaming at the mouth, he almost seems to believe he deserves special consideration.

**❻** Makes second supporting point and illustrates it with details and examples

<u>Underwritten characters and underdeveloped relationships are the main faults of *The Crucible* as a text;</u> at times, it feels nearly as plot-driven as a Michael Crichton novel. The story is meant to provoke outrage at the lives destroyed by false accusers and complicit authority figures, but it only takes a couple of scenes to make this point. After this, the children's accusations begin to seem repetitive. Still, there are a couple of scenes in *The Crucible* which can get any audience to hold its breath, notably a tense questioning of Elizabeth for which there can be no correct answer. Director Nicholas Hytner (*The Madness of King George*) offers an interpretation which isn't in the least iconoclastic, but he knows where to use George Fenton's score or a lingering close-up to give a scene added weight. <u>*The Crucible* is a good (though not great) adaptation of a good (though not great) play which still has the ability to cast its own spell.</u>

**❼** Summarizes the criteria for his review.

**❽** Concludes by making a recommendation

# Writing Your Critical Review

## ❶ Prewriting

*It is as hard to find a neutral critic as it is a neutral country in time of war. I suppose if a critic were neutral, he wouldn't trouble to write anything.*

**Katherine Anne Porter, short story writer**

Begin by choosing a piece of literature or a film that strongly affected you—either positively or negatively. Perhaps you want to examine a film based on a literary work. You might select a work you've read for class, another selection by an author you liked, or a memorable piece of literature you've read in the past. See the **Idea Bank** in the margin for more suggestions. After you've chosen a subject, follow the steps below.

### Planning Your Evaluation

▶ 1. **Explore your overall reaction to the work.** Did you generally feel positively or negatively? Why? If you had both positive and negative reactions, which were stronger? Discuss your impressions with a friend. How did his or her reactions differ from yours?

▶ 2. **List the criteria you will use to judge the work.** How did you judge elements of the work such as plot, characters, language, setting and visual elements, or theme? For example, do the characters seem realistic? Does the setting make sense with the plot?

▶ 3. **Gather evidence from the work to support your review.** What facts, examples, quotations, and other details from the work support your opinion of each element? If you find evidence that contradicts your view, will you include and respond to it in your review? You might create a chart like the one below to list your evaluation and your evidence.

| Element | Criteria | Critical Evaluation | Supporting Evidence |
|---|---|---|---|
| plot | | | |
| characters | | | |
| language | | | |
| setting | | | |
| theme | | | |

▶ 4. **Evaluate and organize your evidence.** For which criteria do you have the strongest evidence? Which less strongly supported criteria might you not want to include in your review?

## IDEABank

**1. Your Working Portfolio** 📁
Look for ideas in this **Writing Option** which you completed earlier in this unit:
• Capsule Review, p. 244

**2. Screen the Screen**
Look at the movie section of your local newspaper or visit a video store to remind yourself of movies you've seen.

**3. Jog Your Memory**
Look in your Readers Notebook to find a story you felt strongly about.

## Guiding Student Writing

### Prewriting
#### Choosing a Subject
If after reading the Idea Bank students are having difficulty choosing their subjects, suggest they try the following:

• Look through the book review section of the Sunday newspaper for new books or authors that interest you.
• Work with a small group of students. Brainstorm a list of movies that members of the group have seen.
• Collect book or film reviews from newspapers and magazines.
• Watch the movie reviewers on television, or read reviews that are available online.

#### Planning the Critical Review
2. Other questions students might consider are these: How important is the theme and how well is it conveyed in the work? Are the characters presented as complex people or are they one-dimensional?

3. Suggest that students take notes as they read or watch the movie. Remind them that they may have to return to key parts in the book or movie to make sure quotations and details are accurate.

## Drafting

### Organizing the Draft

There is no one "correct" way to write a draft. Some students may be comfortable with freewriting. Others may prefer to make a writing plan or outline to guide them in the drafting stage. Remind them, however, to stay open to new ideas as they draft. Students should feel free to revise or even discard their writing plan if they find their writing taking a new direction.

## Revising

### AVOIDING CIRCULAR REASONING

Some words in the example merely restate the main idea of the sentence without any evidence to support that idea. Have students point out those words in each sentence. Discuss how the revision improves the writing.

If students need more help in understanding circular reasoning, write the following sentence on the chalkboard:

• *This remake of the movie is the best. It is superior to the others.*

Have students rewrite the above sentences, providing supporting evidence for each claim. Then ask volunteers for other examples of circular reasoning.

## Editing and Proofreading

### ELIMINATING QUALIFIERS

Have students read aloud the example both before and after changes were made to eliminate qualifiers. Discuss the differences that they hear in each version. Have students check their own writing to eliminate unnecessary qualifiers.

## Reflecting

Have students write a brief note addressing their writing experience. They may also wish to consider how they selected their topic and how they decided upon their criteria for evaluation. Have them clip their assessment to their essay and put both in their working portfolio.

Also ask students to analyze a written review of the film or work of literature they have selected and compare it with their own response. Direct them to use the criteria established on page 248.

---

## ❷ Drafting

You might want to begin your draft by **freewriting** about each of your criteria, one by one. At some point, you will also need to state your **overall opinion** of the work and think of an interest-grabbing way to begin your review. In the body of the review, you will present your **criteria for judgment** and the **evidence** that supports them. Start with your freewriting and organize and refine it. You can either begin with your strongest point or build to it at the end of your review. Try to give a balanced view of the work by including a discussion of both its strengths and its weaknesses. Be sure to include a **clear recommendation** in your conclusion.

### Ask Your Peer Reader

• What criteria for evaluation was I using?

• Which parts of my review are most convincing?

• Which of my statements need additional support?

• How can I improve my organization?

**Need revising help?**

Review the **Rubric,** p. 248

Consider **peer reader** comments

Check **Revision Guidelines,** p. 1269

## ❸ Revising

**TARGET SKILL ▶ AVOIDING CIRCULAR REASONING** To be convincing, your review must show clear thinking. Avoid circular reasoning or trying to prove a statement merely by restating it in different words. Be sure to include detailed evidence to support your statements.

> Winona Ryder does some of her best work ever in the role ~~because~~ *shedding* *the restrained quality of* ~~she never acted as well in~~ her previous period-film performances. *desperate, haunted, and dangerous.* Here she lets loose like an animal—~~totally beastlike~~.

## ❹ Editing and Proofreading

**TARGET SKILL ▶ ELIMINATING QUALIFIERS** When writing a review, you should state your opinions firmly and clearly. Eliminate unnecessary qualifiers—such as the conditional verbs *could* and *might;* the adverbs *nearly, somewhat, possibly,* and *probably;* and phrases like *It seems to me*—that express indecision and weaken your message.

> ~~It seems to me that~~ the scenes are ~~probably~~ not included simply for shock value, but ~~possibly~~ to emphasize the ~~somewhat~~ active hypocrisy of the accusers.

## ❺ Reflecting

**FOR YOUR WORKING PORTFOLIO** How did your opinions change as you wrote your review? What will you do differently the next time you write a review? Write answers to these questions and save them with your review in your **Working Portfolio.**

**Publishing IDEAS**

• Submit your review to an online journal with literary or film reviews.

• Meet with classmates who wrote reviews of the same work or a work by the same author. Analyze your classmates' reviews and compare them to your own reactions.

**More Online: Publishing Options** www.mcdougallittell.com

## Option

### Managing the Paper Load

Have students use a highlighter to indicate the name of the work being reviewed, their overall evaluation, and their recommendation. This will help as you scan the paper for organizational structure.

Read this paragraph from the first draft of a review. The underlined sections may include the following kinds of errors:

- **capitalization errors**
- **comma errors**
- **unnecessary qualifiers**
- **sentence fragments**

For each underlined section, choose the revision that most improves the writing.

> Nathaniel Hawthorne's <u>daughter, Una provided</u> inspiration for the
> (1)
> character of <u>Pearl in *the Scarlet letter.*</u> Pearl's wild and willful nature <u>seems to</u>
> (2)                                                                                     (3)
> <u>be</u> an exaggerated version of Una's lively personality. <u>In his journal. Hawthorne</u>
> <u>describes Una and her brother play-acting.</u> "There is something that almost
> (4)
> frightens me about the child," he writes. "I know not whether elfish or angelic,
> but, at all events, supernatural." In my opinion, the parallels between Una and
> Pearl are <u>pretty clear.</u> <u>Pearl's behavior like Una's can be described as</u>
> (5)                  (6)
> <u>supernatural.</u>

1. **A.** daughter Una provided
   **B.** daughter. Una, provided
   **C.** daughter Una, provided
   **D.** Correct as is

2. **A.** pearl in *the Scarlet Letter*
   **B.** Pearl in *The Scarlet letter*
   **C.** Pearl in *The Scarlet Letter*
   **D.** Correct as is

3. **A.** must surely be
   **B.** is almost
   **C.** is
   **D.** Correct as is

4. **A.** In his journal, Hawthorne describes Una and her brother play-acting.
   **B.** In his journal Hawthorne describes Una and her brother, play-acting.
   **C.** In his journal Hawthorne describes Una, and her brother, play-acting.
   **D.** Correct as is

5. **A.** fairly clear
   **B.** clear
   **C.** pretty
   **D.** Correct as is

6. **A.** Pearl's behavior like Una's, can be described as supernatural.
   **B.** Pearl's behavior, like Una's, can be described as supernatural.
   **C.** Pearl's behavior, like Una's can be described, as supernatural.
   **D.** Correct as is

**Need extra help?**

See the **Grammar Handbook**

Capitalization Chart, p. 1329

Punctuation Chart, pp. 1327–1328

Correcting Fragments, p. 1323

### Objectives

- read and understand analogies
- understand analogy as the basis of literary metaphor
- realize that words can be related by function
- recognize and distinguish different types of analogies
- practice completing and classifying analogies

## Strategies for Building Vocabulary

### EXERCISE

Students should correctly identify the relationships involved. Answers will vary.

**1.** soothe (synonyms)
**2.** suffering (action to object)
**3.** worshiper (whole to part)
**4.** tolerance (cause to effect)
**5.** apathy (synonyms)

## Recognizing Relationships

When we encounter a new thing, we mentally connect and compare it with things we already know and understand. One type of comparison between objects or situations is called an **analogy**.

The Puritans of colonial Massachusetts constantly compared their own lives, communities, and behavior to those recorded in the Bible, and they often used analogies to make those comparisons clear. For example, in the excerpt at the right, the poet Anne Bradstreet likens heaven to "a house on high erect."

> Thou hast an house on high erect,
> Framed by that mighty Architect,
> With glory richly furnishéd,
> Stands permanent though this be fled.
> —Anne Bradstreet,
> "Upon the Burning of Our House"

She is saying, in effect, that just as a house shelters those who live in it, so heaven shelters saved souls. Metaphors like this one compare things or ideas that have certain similarities.

## Strategies for Building Vocabulary

Not only are analogies the basis of literary metaphors; expressed as word formulas, they can be used to test your ability to make logical connections. For example, an analogy comparing the lava that flows from a volcano to ketchup that flows from a bottle would be expressed as follows:

LAVA : VOLCANO :: ketchup : bottle

To read this, you would say, "Lava is to a volcano as ketchup is to a bottle."

**❶ Determine Word Relationships** The first step in analyzing an analogy is to determine the relationship between the first pair of words in the analogy. What, for example, do you think is the relationship between these two words?

PURITANISM : PROTESTANTISM

Once you see that the relationship is one of classification (Puritanism is a type of Protestantism), you can determine which of the following word pairs best completes this analogy. Which pair would you choose?

(A) joy : rapture     (C) anarchy : order
(B) leaf : plant     (D) dirge : song

Although each pair expresses a relationship, pair D best completes the analogy, since a dirge is classified as a type of song.

**❷ Distinguish Types of Analogies** Many standardized tests include items that require you to complete analogies. This chart will help you become familiar with some of the more common types of analogies.

### Common Relationships in Analogies

| Type | Example | Relationship |
|---|---|---|
| Classification | COTTAGE : HOUSE | is a type of |
| Description | INTOLERANT : FANATIC | describes |
| Worker to Creation | MINISTER : SERMON | is one who creates or makes |
| Sequence or Time | CHILDHOOD : ADOLESCENCE | occurs before (or after) |
| Synonyms | AFFLUENCE : PROSPERITY | means the same as |
| Part to Whole | MAST : SAILBOAT | is a part of |
| Cause to Effect | CRIME : PUNISHMENT | results in or leads to |
| Action to Object | CULTIVATE : PLANTS | is what you do to |
| Grammar | WHO : WHOM | is a grammatical form related to |

**EXERCISE** Complete and classify these five analogies.

**1.** PROVOKE : INFLAME :: appease : _____
**2.** REDUCE : PRESSURE :: mitigate : _____
**3.** ARMY : SOLDIER :: congregation: _____
**4.** BIGOTRY : PERSECUTION :: empathy : _____
**5.** BELIEF : CONVICTION :: indifference : _____

## Grammar from Literature

Notice the words in blue in the passages below from *The Crucible* by Arthur Miller. At first glance they may appear to be verbs. A closer look reveals that they are verb forms used as nouns; in other words, they are gerunds.

> gerund as subject
> The **singing** has stopped in the midst of this, and now Parris rushes in.
>
> gerund as direct object
> And I heard a **screeching** and gibberish coming from her mouth.
>
> gerund as object of a preposition
> Oh, you're a great one for **lookin'** aren't you, Mary Warren?
>
> gerund phrase as object of a preposition
> This predilection for **minding other people's business** was time-honored among the people of Salem.

**Gerunds** can take the form of single words or phrases. A gerund phrase may consist of a gerund with modifiers, objects, or complements. In the example above, the gerund *minding* is followed by a direct object, *business.*

You can see from the examples above that writers use gerunds and gerund phrases in all the ways that they use nouns and noun phrases.

**Using Gerunds in Your Writing** Sometimes, you can eliminate awkwardness and be more concise by using a gerund. Longer phrases and clauses can be reduced to a gerund. The examples at the top of the next column show ways this can be done.

> ORIGINAL
> Jonathan Edwards paints a vivid picture of the consequences when someone commits a sin.
>
> REVISED USING A GERUND
> Jonathan Edwards paints a vivid picture of the consequences of **sinning**.
>
> ORIGINAL
> Proctor finds the fact that he must sign his name to the confession very difficult and very distasteful.
>
> REVISED USING A GERUND
> Proctor finds **signing** his name to the confession very difficult and very distasteful.

**Usage Tip** A pronoun that modifies a gerund must be in the possessive case. Similarly, a proper noun in the possessive case is used to modify a gerund.

> INCORRECT
> proper noun gerund
> The Nurse family prevents **Bayley** taking office.
>
> pronoun gerund
> The Nurse family prevents **him** taking office.
>
> CORRECT
> possessive gerund
> The Nurse family prevents **Bayley's** taking office.
>
> possessive gerund
> The Nurse family prevents **his** taking office.

**Punctuation** When you combine two short sentences that have gerund subjects be careful to avoid comma splices. Remember that you cannot join two complete ideas with just a comma. Use a semicolon or use a comma and a coordinating conjunction.

> INCORRECT
> Suspecting is bad, knowing is worse.
>
> CORRECT
> Suspecting is bad; knowing is worse.

---

**WRITING EXERCISE** Rewrite each sentence, changing the underlined words to a gerund or gerund phrase.

1. Prior to <u>the time when he became a minister,</u> Samuel Parris was a merchant in Barbados.
2. Abigail seems to enjoy <u>it when she taunts John Proctor.</u>
3. <u>Acts of prayer</u> and <u>acts of worship</u> are regular parts of Parris's daily life.
4. <u>The fact that the girls danced in the woods</u> outrages Parris.
5. In <u>the talk that she has</u> with the other girls, Abigail reveals her true nature.

**GRAMMAR EXERCISE** Rewrite these sentences, correcting any errors in punctuation and usage.

1. Believing is fine, taking action is even better.
2. Samuel Parris praying has little effect on the unconscious child.
3. Mrs. Putnam offers a reason for the child screaming.
4. Lying to friends and family is one thing, lying on the witness stand is quite another.
5. The other men are rattled by him arriving at that moment.

---

**Objectives**
- recognize gerunds as verb forms used as nouns
- revise drafts by using gerunds and gerund phrases for more concise writing
- practice using proper nouns and pronouns in the possessive case to modify a gerund
- revise using proper punctuation, such as semicolons instead of commas

**WRITING EXERCISE**

1. Prior to becoming a minister, Samuel Parris was a merchant in Barbados.
2. Abigail seems to enjoy <u>taunting John Proctor</u>.
3. <u>Praying and worshiping</u> are regular parts of Parris's daily life.
4. <u>The girls' dancing in the woods</u> outrages Parris.
5. In <u>talking with the other girls</u>, Abigail reveals her true nature.

**GRAMMAR EXERCISE**

1. Believing is <u>fine; taking</u> action is even better.
2. Samuel <u>Parris's</u> praying has little effect on the unconscious child.
3. Mrs. Putnam offers a reason for the <u>child's</u> screaming.
4. Lying to friends and family is one thing, <u>but</u> lying on the witness stand is quite another.
5. The other men are rattled by <u>his</u> arriving at that moment.

### Introduction

This article provides a historical and literary context for the Revolutionary War–era selections and for the selections written by 20th-century advocates of equality and cultural pride. The primary source selections in **Voices from the Times** help students interpret the possible influences of historical contexts on a literary work.

## Teaching Nonfiction

### Reading Skills and Strategies
### ESTABLISHING A PURPOSE FOR READING

Explain to students that this article introduces them to the conflict between England and her American colonies in the 18th century. Have students review the article and establish a purpose for reading (to find out).

### MONITORING AND MODIFYING READING STRATEGIES

Have the students read through the article silently. Ask them to monitor their comprehension of the information and, if necessary, modify their strategies when understanding breaks down. Suggest rereading the article as a way to increase comprehension.

### ANALYZING TEXT STRUCTURE

Encourage students to analyze the text structure of the article for how it influences their understanding of the issues facing Americans before, during, and after the Revolution. Ask students to note how the author has organized the material in the article and to consider whether this structure influenced their understanding of the material.

# The Right to Be Free

## Writers in the Time of Revolution

"*No* taxation without representation!" "Give me liberty, or give me death!" "We hold these truths to be self-evident. . . ." "We the people . . ." Many famous phrases have come from the rhetoric of the American Revolution, along with many of our favorite national anecdotes—the Boston Tea Party, "the shot heard round the world," and George Washington at Valley Forge. Behind the rhetoric and the mythologizing of the Revolution, however, lie major philosophical ideas that not only transformed 13 British colonies into a nation but laid the groundwork for democratic institutions throughout the world.

On the surface, the conflict between England and her **(A)** American colonies was about money—specifically, what the colonists considered unlawful taxation. On a deeper level, what gave the rebellious colonists the mental preparedness and moral strength needed for such a dangerous undertaking as revolution came essentially from two sources: the writings of English philosopher John Locke and the Bible. **(B)**

Central to John Locke's theory was the notion of "natural rights." In addition to life and liberty, the right to own property was considered a natural right. If any government abridged that right to property—by levying taxes without the consent of the property owners, for example—then the people could organize a new government. **(C)**

You can see the spirit of Locke reflected in Jefferson's eloquent opening to the Declaration of Independence. Locke's ideas of property rights were echoed in the wording of the U.S. Constitution. The Revolutionary writers in this part of Unit Two—particularly Patrick Henry, Phillis Wheatley, Abigail Adams, and Michel-Guillaume Jean de Crèvecoeur—all appealed to natural rights in their arguments for freedom.

The American Revolution was not solely the enterprise of learned

Statue of John Locke in the classical style

Portrait of Thomas Jefferson

**Silhouette of Abigail Adams**

men and women of the day, however. Ordinary people were caught up in the struggle and used the Bible to help them make hard decisions about their country and their lives.

From the time of the early Pilgrims, successive generations of Protestant ministers had proclaimed from their pulpits that no man need obey a government that violated the will of God as defined in the Bible. During the Revolution, many preachers recounted Bible stories of unjust rulers who burdened the people with high taxes and unjust laws. While much of the political writing during this time contained lofty philosophical ideas, it also vibrated with the fiery passion of a Puritan minister. In Patrick Henry's famous "Give me liberty, or give me death" speech, you'll hear more references to God and the Bible than to Locke's ideas of natural rights.

The philosophical and religious ideas that spurred the American Revolution also raised other important issues—the most important being slavery. The philosophy of democracy is as much an attack on the institution of slavery as it is on political tyranny. However, the entire plantation economy of the South was dependent on slaves, who were considered the property of plantation owners. As powerful Southern landowners exerted their influence in the new government, reform that might have prohibited slavery was halted.

Another issue for the Founding Fathers was what to do about Native Americans. In the early years of the nation, the policy of the U.S. government was to assimilate Native Americans

## Voices from the TIMES

We hold these truths to be self-evident:— That all men are created equal; that they are endowed by their Creator with certain unalienable rights; that among these are life, liberty, and the pursuit of happiness.

**Thomas Jefferson**
*from* the Declaration of Independence

These are the times that try men's souls. The summer soldier and the sunshine patriot will in this crisis, shrink from the service of his country; but he that stands it Now, deserves the love and thanks of man and woman.

**Thomas Paine**
*from* Common Sense

Yankee doodle went to town,
A-riding on a pony,
Stuck a feather in his cap
And called it Macaroni.
Yankee Doodle, keep it up,
Yankee Doodle Dandy,
Mind the music and the step
And with the girls be handy.

**Anonymous patriotic song**

## Making Connections

### Law
**A** Although much of the rhetoric that fueled the American Revolution was derived from the theories of Enlightenment philosophers and thinkers, the idea that taxes should not be levied without consent of the taxpayer is a principle in English law that dates back to the Magna Carta (1215).

### History
**B** With the Battle of Lexington and Concord behind them and the siege of Boston still raging, a majority in the Second Continental Congress—including George Washington—opposed independence. However, pressure from John Adams, Benjamin Franklin, and most of the New England delegates ultimately convinced the other delegates to adopt the Declaration of Independence in July 1776.

### Philosophy
**C** John Locke's (1632–1704) theories on just government provided a blueprint for colonial leaders. In addition to his theory of "natural rights," Locke proposed a system of government in three parts—legislative, executive, and judicial, with the legislative holding the most power because it reflected the will of the people. He also advocated separation of church and state.

### Religion
**D** The local church was a hub of social and political as well as religious activity. Ordinary people who worked hard all week looked forward to the Sabbath as a day of rest. They gathered to worship and discuss events of the day with neighbors. The church provided a forum for political discussion and debate unavailable to many of them in their daily lives.

### Philosophy
**E** In *The Wealth of Nations,* published in 1776, Scottish economist and philosopher Adam Smith (1723–1790) argued that slavery and the plantation system were inefficient uses of land and labor. Slaves did not have an incentive to produce, Smith held, because they did not profit from their labor. He also believed that the human desire to dominate and the money to be made in cotton and tobacco were reasons that slavery continued. While Smith was not an abolitionist, he was an early critic of the theory that slavery was economically efficient.

### OUTLINING

Have students create an outline of the article as a study strategy to better understand the text. Ask students to note the main ideas of the text as well as supporting details.

### SUMMARIZING

Ask students to write a summary of the article in their own words. Remind them to avoid inserting personal opinions and extraneous details. Encourage them to use their outlines as a guide for their summaries.

**LaserLinks**

**Historical Literary Connection: Writers in the Time of Revolution**

Introduce your students to some of the great writers of this period by presenting these images of American orators, poets, and thinkers.

See Teacher's SourceBook p. 25 for bar codes.

---

## Voices from the TIMES

The United States of America have exhibited, perhaps, the first example of governments erected on the simple principles of nature; and if men are now sufficiently enlightened to disabuse themselves of artifice, imposture, hypocrisy, and superstition, they will consider this event as an era in their history.

**John Adams**
*from* Defense of the Constitutions of Government of the United States of America

When Israel was in Egypt's land,
    Let my people go;
Oppressed so hard they could
    not stand,
Let my people go.
            CHORUS
*Go down, Moses, way down
    in Egypt's land;
Tell old Pharaoh, to let my people go.*

**Anonymous Negro spiritual**

JOIN, or DIE.

**Benjamin Franklin** created this woodcut in 1754 to warn the colonies to unite in their common defense.

---

into Anglo culture. To this end, government officials worked with existing missions set up by the principal churches of the time to teach Native Americans Christian theology, reading, and writing as well as to train them in agriculture.

Although some Native Americans resisted such efforts—most notably Seneca chief Red Jacket—the U.S. policy worked for a while. However in 1830, U.S. policy toward Native Americans changed. The Indian Removal Act authorized the relocation of tribes from the Southeastern states to land west of the Mississippi River, in order to free up the well-cultivated Indian farmland for white settlers.

## Traditions Across Time: Demands for Equal Rights

Even though the ideals of equality and natural rights promised by the American Revolution did not fully materialize after the war, the noble words had been written—and they remained to haunt the country. The conflicts also remained for subsequent generations of Americans to resolve—first during the Civil War and later in the civil rights movement of the 20th century. When you read the words of Martin Luther King, Jr., and Malcolm X as they contemplate the meaning of equal rights in their own time, you'll be able to recognize the American tradition of political thought that dates back to the beginnings of our country.

Rodolfo Gonzales in his 1967 poem *I Am Joaquín* speaks as eloquently for his people—Chicanos— as Patrick Henry did for his.

---

### VOICES FROM THE TIMES

**Ask: What ideals do the Declaration of Independence and the anonymous Negro spiritual share?**

**Possible Responses:** liberty, freedom from oppression

**Ask: What did Thomas Paine mean by "summer soldier" and "sunshine patriot"?**

**Possible Responses:** These terms referred to people who would fight only when it suited them, people who would join the fight when the conditions (i.e. weather, geography) were comfortable, or people who would support the fight only when a successful outcome seemed assured.

**Ask: To what sentiments or emotions was Thomas Paine appealing?**

**Possible Responses:** patriotism, pride, courage, love of liberty

## Writers in the Time of Revolution

> **COMPARING LITERATURE**
> *Traditions Across Time: Demands for Equal Rights*
>

## OVERVIEW

### Objectives

- understand the following literary terms:

  | | |
  |---|---|
  | Rhetoric | Persuasive rhetoric |
  | Logical appeal | Deductive |
  | Generalization | Premise |
  | Inductive | Emotional appeal |
  | Ethical appeal | Elevated language |
  | Repetition | Parallelism |
  | Rhetorical question | |

- recognize logical modes of persuasion in text
- evaluate the credibility of information sources, including how a writer's motivation may affect that credibility
- analyze how reasoned arguments are structured in persuasive rhetoric
- analyze the characteristics of clearly written texts

## Teaching the Lesson

In this section, students will be introduced to persuasive rhetoric in a variety of speeches and writings. This lesson will outline modes and styles of persuasive rhetoric.

### Introducing the Concepts

Throughout history, people have understood the power of language and used it to influence how people think and act. Writers and speakers today who aim to move people with persuasive rhetoric use many of the same techniques that helped people like Thomas Jefferson, Patrick Henry, and Martin Luther King, Jr., influence dramatic changes in society. As students read the persuasive rhetoric in this unit, they should recognize logical, deceptive, and faulty modes of persuasion. Ask them to consider the following questions:

Based on speeches and talks you've heard, what persuasive technique affects you most as a reader or listener?
**Possible Responses:** Generalization, repetition, ethical appeals, and emotional appeals will be the most common.

---

# Persuasive Rhetoric

### Beyond "Please!"

If old news footage of speeches by John F. Kennedy or Martin Luther King, Jr., never fails to capture your attention, you have experienced the power of persuasive language. The aim of persuasive writing or speaking is to convince people to adopt an opinion, perform an action, or both. **Rhetoric** is the art of communicating ideas. **Persuasive rhetoric** consists of reasoned arguments in favor of or against particular beliefs or courses of action.

The pamphlets of Thomas Paine (1737-1809) urged American colonists to seek independence.

### The Workings of an Argument

To be effectively persuasive, a work generally has to engage both the mind and the emotions of its audience, making them think that the problem the work deals with is important enough for them to care how it is resolved. (See "Persuasion in

Action" below.) Furthermore, the writer needs to show that his or her position has a firm moral basis. The Declaration of Independence (page 270) provides examples of the three basic types of appeals used in persuasive arguments:

**LOGICAL APPEALS** Generally based on sets of assumptions, **logical appeals** provide rational arguments to support writers' claims—for instance, the assumption that "all men are created equal"—and are supported with objective evidence, such as the list of "injuries and usurpations" committed by King George III. A writer can develop an argument **deductively,** by beginning with a **generalization,** or **premise,** and proceeding to marshal examples and facts that support it (as in the Declaration of Independence), or **inductively,** by beginning with examples or facts and proceeding to draw a

---

## *P*ersuasion in Action

To be effective, a persuasive writer:

- clearly states the issue and a position
- gives an opinion and supports it with facts and reasons
- takes opposing views into account
- uses sound logic and effective language
- concludes by summing up reasons or calling for action

"When, in the course of human events, it becomes necessary for one people to dissolve . . . political bands . . . they should declare the causes which impel them to the separation."
—Thomas Jefferson

"I cannot say that I think you are very generous to the ladies; for, whilst you are proclaiming peace and good-will to men, emancipating all nations, you insist upon retaining an absolute power over wives."
—Abigail Adams

"With nonviolent resistance, no individual or group need submit to any wrong, nor need anyone resort to violence in order to right a wrong."
—Martin Luther King, Jr.

**YOUR TURN** Pick one of the quotes above. Identify which of the bulleted standards to the left apply.

---

Which speaker or writer in this section is most persuasive, and why? What specific modes of persuasion did the speaker use?
**Possible Response:** Students can choose any writer in the section as long as they support their answer with evidence.

Which people in the world today make regular use of persuasive rhetoric?
**Possible Responses:** politicians, religious leaders, teachers

### Presenting the Concepts

Read through the strategies aloud or project them on a transparency. Then show students a modern newspaper editorial, letter, or column that attempts to convince people to adopt an opinion or take an action. Have students use the strategies to analyze the writing in the piece. Ask them to identify what techniques the writer uses to make an argument and express ideas.

conclusion from them. Analyzing the reasoning of an argument can help you evaluate its soundness.

**EMOTIONAL APPEALS** Appeals to emotion are often based on specific examples of suffering or potential threats, as in Jefferson's statement that King George is attempting "to complete the works of death, desolation, and tyranny." Emotional appeals can also include "loaded language"—language that is rich in connotations and vivid images.

**ETHICAL APPEALS** Based on shared moral values, ethical appeals call forth the audience's sense of right, justice, and virtue. Jefferson, for example, reminded people that independence was a last resort, after the failure of other measures: "In every stage of these oppressions we have petitioned for redress, in the most humble terms; our repeated petitions have been answered only by repeated injury."

## Styles of Persuasion
Persuasive writers and speakers use a number of techniques.

**ELEVATED LANGUAGE** Formal words and phrases can lend a serious tone to a discussion. In her "Declaration of the Rights of Woman" (page 277), written during the French Revolution, Olympe de Gouges used the political terminology of the time to stir women to action: "The powerful empire of nature is no longer surrounded by prejudice, fanaticism, superstition, and lies. The flame of truth has dispersed all the clouds of folly and usurpation."

**RHETORICAL QUESTIONS** Think of these as questions that don't require answers. Writers pose rhetorical questions to show that their arguments make the answers obvious. Patrick Henry's speech in the Virginia Convention (page 262), for example, includes a variety of questions whose answers Henry considers self-evident, such as "Is life so dear, or peace so sweet, as to be purchased at the price of chains and slavery?"

**REPETITION** Repeating a point tells the audience that it is especially important; repeating a form of expression tells the audience that the ideas expressed in the same way are related. **Parallelism,** a form of repetition, is used very effectively in the Declaration of Independence. Notice the parallel clauses beginning with *that* in the following famous passage.

> We hold these truths to be self-evident:—That all men are created equal; that they are endowed by their Creator with certain unalienable rights; that among these are life, liberty, and the pursuit of happiness.
>
> —Thomas Jefferson

## Strategies for Reading: Persuasive Rhetoric

1. Identify the problem that is addressed and the solution that is proposed. Restate them in your own words.

2. Analyze the writer's presentation of his or her argument. What rhetorical tools does the writer use?

3. Analyze the evidence used to support the argument. What facts support the writer's opinions?

4. Consider how the writer appeals to the logic, emotions, and ethics of the audience.

5. Evaluate the credibility of the writer. What motivations might lie behind the work?

6. **Monitor** your reading strategies and modify them when your understanding breaks down. Remember to use the Strategies for Active Reading: **predict, visualize, connect, question, clarify,** and **evaluate.**

PERSUASIVE RHETORIC **261**

### History and Social Studies: Truth in Rhetoric
Rhetoric as a formal study began in the Greek cities of Sicily in the 5th century B.C. A group of teachers known as Sophists taught the art of speaking and received fees for their lectures. Although some Sophists were respected, others were criticized by well-known Greek philosophers such as Plato and Aristotle. These philosophers viewed the Sophists' rhetorical techniques with suspicion, believing that Sophists were more interested in the political uses of rhetoric than in using language to pursue and spread truth. Because of these early criticisms, the term *rhetoric* is sometimes used to suggest verbal trickery, or language that is showy and complicated but without sincerity or truthfulness. The term *sophist* is often used to refer to people who use this type of language.

Rhetorical techniques can be used to create oral or written pieces that are artificial or insincere but can also be used to make valid arguments and achieve positive ends. Ask students when they've experienced positive and negative rhetoric. Then ask them how they recognize the various modes of persuasion and how they know the difference. Remind students that some examples of oral or written language might combine elements of both truth and exaggeration.

# OVERVIEW

 This selection is included in the **Grade 11 InterActive Reader.**

## Objectives
1. understand a persuasive **speech** (Literary Analysis)
2. appreciate the use of **allusion** (Literary Analysis)
3. analyze the use of **rhetorical questions and persuasion** (Active Reading)

## Summary
Patrick Henry delivered this famous speech in March 1775, at a time when the colonists in America were faced with the choice of openly revolting against Britain or attempting some sort of compromise with the mother country. Henry says that he is obligated to speak out or consider himself guilty of treason toward his country and disloyalty to God. He points out that although the colonies' most recent petition to Britain has been received politely, Britain is making preparations for war by sending fleets and armies to the colonies. Noting that the colonists have tried arguments and petitions for ten years, he concludes that if the colonies wish to be free, they must fight.

## Thematic Link
The question that Henry addresses in his speech is essentially "Do we choose freedom, or do we choose oppression?" British rule has become an intolerable and untenable tyranny. To protect their **right to be free,** the colonists must take a stand and openly resist the British.

---

### 5-Minute Warm-Up

***Daily Language SkillBuilder***

Have students **proofread** the display sentences on page 131j and write them correctly. The sentences also appear on Transparency 6 of **Grammar Transparencies and Copymasters.**

# Speech in the Virginia Convention

*Speech by* PATRICK HENRY

### Connect to Your Life

**Patriotism and Battle** Think about what *patriotism* means to you. Then list at least three reasons a patriot might give for fighting in a war. Circle the reason that seems most compelling to you. With a partner, discuss the reasons that you listed and circled.

## Build Background

**Heading Toward War** Until the mid-1700s, American colonists largely had been content to be under British rule. However, tension grew between Great Britain and her American colonies after the end of the French and Indian War in 1763. Although Britain had defeated the French and their Indian allies, thousands of British troops remained quartered in the colonies, which caused resentment among the colonists. Their resentment increased and angry protests ensued when, beginning in 1764, the British Parliament passed a series of harsh laws and taxes.

To discuss the growing crisis, the First Continental Congress, composed of delegates from all 13 colonies except Georgia, met in Philadelphia in 1774. The delegates held out hope that they could restore the colonies' relationship with Great Britain, and they sent formal petitions to King George III and the British people, asking for their rights as British subjects. Six months after this meeting, in March 1775, the Second Virginia Provincial Convention was called to vote on whether Virginia should take up arms to defend against a feared British attack. Patrick Henry, the most famous orator of the American Revolution, delivered a fiery speech to convince delegates of the need for armed resistance.

> WORDS TO KNOW **Vocabulary Preview**
> | | | |
> |---|---|---|
> | adversary | irresolution | tyrannical |
> | formidable | martial | vigilant |
> | insidious | subjugation | |
> | invincible | spurn | |

## Focus Your Reading

**LITERARY ANALYSIS** **ALLUSION**

An **allusion** is an indirect reference to a person, place, event, or literary work with which the author believes the reader will be familiar. Refer to the Guide for Reading for an explanation of the allusions in Patrick Henry's speech. Consider what this technique contributes to Henry's argument.

**ACTIVE READING** **RHETORICAL QUESTIONS AND PERSUASION**

A **rhetorical question** is a question to which no answer is expected because the answer is obvious. Rhetorical questions are often used in persuasive writing to emphasize a point or create an emotional effect. For example, Patrick Henry asks this rhetorical question in his speech: "Is life so dear, or peace so sweet, as to be purchased at the price of chains and slavery?" The obvious answer is no, and the effect of the question is to stir his listeners to act decisively against the British.

**READER'S NOTEBOOK** As you read Henry's famous speech, list some examples of rhetorical questions.

---

## LESSON RESOURCES

**UNIT TWO RESOURCE BOOK,** pp. 50–54

**ASSESSMENT RESOURCES**
**Formal Assessment,** pp. 47–48
**Teacher's Guide to Assessment and Portfolio Use**
**Test Generator**

**SKILLS TRANSPARENCIES AND COPYMASTERS**
**Literary Analysis**
• Persuasion: Types of Appeals, T9 (for Active Reading, p. 262)
**Reading and Critical Thinking**
• Evaluating Argumentation I and II, T20, T21 (for Think Critically, item 2, p. 267)

**Grammar**
• Perfect Tenses of Verbs II, C116 (for Mini Lesson, p. 269)
**Vocabulary**
• Context Clues, C92 (for Mini Lesson, p. 263)
**Writing**
• Opinion Statement, C34 (for Extend Interpretations 7, p. 267)
**Communications**
• Evaluating Roles in Groups, T8 (for Activities & Explorations 4, p. 268)
• Dramatic Reading, T12 (for Activities & Explorations 3, p. 268)

• Nonverbal Strategies, T15 (for Activities & Explorations 3, p. 268)

**INTEGRATED TECHNOLOGY**
**Audio Library**
**LaserLinks**
• Historical Connection: Colonial Rebellion
• Art Gallery: The American Revolution. See **Teacher's SourceBook,** pp. 27–28.
**Internet: Research Starter**
Visit our website:
www.mcdougallittell.com

# SPEECH *in the* VIRGINIA CONVENTION

## PATRICK HENRY

### TEACHING THE LITERATURE

### Customizing Instruction

**Students Acquiring English**
The long sentences in this speech may challenge students' understanding. Advise them to break difficult sentences into manageable clauses, and to stop and paraphrase often.

Use **Spanish Study Guide** for additional support, pp. 59–61.

**Less Proficient Readers**
Review with students the historical context (page 262). Have them imagine that they are delegates to the Second Virginia Provincial Convention, at which Patrick Henry is about to give his speech.
**Set a Purpose** Have students read to find out what Henry says about the colonists' efforts so far and about the actions they should now take.

**Gifted and Talented**
Henry used allusions to the Bible and to classical Greek literature because his audience was very familiar with these works. Such allusions were like shorthand that Henry could use to evoke the deep, complex emotions associated with ancient stories. Have students analyze a contemporary political speech for similar "cultural shorthand." What are some of the stories and issues that Americans today recognize from a mere word or phrase?

### GUIDE FOR READING
**A Possible Response:** to make them see Henry as a fair, reasonable person

March 23, 1775

Mr. President: No man thinks more highly than I do of the patriotism, as well as abilities, of the very worthy gentlemen who have just addressed the House. But different men often see the same subject in different lights; and, therefore, I hope that it will not be
5 thought disrespectful to those gentlemen, if, entertaining as I do opinions of a character very opposite to theirs, I shall speak forth my sentiments freely and without reserve. This is no time for ceremony. The question before the House is one of awful moment to this country. For my own part I consider it as nothing less than a
10 question of freedom or slavery; and in proportion to the magnitude of the subject ought to be the freedom of the debate. It is only in this way that we can hope to arrive at truth, and fulfill the great responsibility which we hold to God and our country. Should I keep back my opinions at such a time, through fear of giving
15 offense, I should consider myself as guilty of treason towards my country, and of an act of disloyalty towards the majesty of heaven, which I revere above all earthly kings.

Mr. President, it is natural to man to indulge in the illusions of hope. We are apt to shut our eyes against a painful truth, and lis-
20 ten to the song of that siren, till she transforms us into beasts. Is this the part of wise men, engaged in a great and arduous struggle for liberty? Are we disposed to be of the number of those who,

### GUIDE FOR READING

**1 Mr. President:** the president of the Virginia Convention, Peyton Randolph.

**5 entertaining:** holding in mind.

**1–7** Henry states his respect for the previous speakers, a technique called "concession to the opposition." What effect might this have on the audience?

**8 The question before the House:** Henry proposed resolutions to prepare the Virginia colony for war and gave this speech to support those resolutions.

**20 song . . . beasts:** an allusion to Homer's *Odyssey*. The sirens' seductive song lured sailors to their deaths. The goddess Circe lured men to her island and then magically transformed them into pigs. Henry compares "the illusions of hope" to these dangerous mythical creatures.

---

 **Preteaching Vocabulary**

**CONTEXT CLUES** Remind students that they can figure out the meaning of an unfamiliar word by considering the context in which the word is used. Write the following sentence on the chalkboard and guide students through the process of using context clues to determine the meaning of *insidious* ("treacherous").

> The stranger had an <u>insidious</u> smile that seemed charming at first, but Marissa had a feeling that he was up to no good.

**Application** Have students work in pairs to determine the meanings of the underlined words. Students should use context clues first and then

check their answers in a dictionary.

1. The goal of the invading army was the <u>subjugation</u> of a weaker nation.
2. How could you <u>spurn</u> Seth's invitation so coldly?
3. West Central's hockey team was a <u>formidable adversary</u>, but Cindy was convinced that her team was better.

 Use **Unit Two Resource Book,** p. 53 for more exercises.

A lesson on context clues appears on p. 326 in the **Pupil's Edition.**

### Reading Skills and Strategies: PREVIEW

Have students review Preparing to Read to understand the context of Patrick Henry's speech.

### Literary Analysis 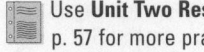 ALLUSION

**A** Why might Henry have chosen to use this biblical allusion?

**Possible Response:** Henry wants the colonists to feel that they are on the side of God, menaced by the forces of evil.

Use **Unit Two Resource Book,** p. 57 for more practice.

### Active Reading

**RHETORICAL QUESTIONS AND PERSUASION**

**B** What emotions is Henry trying to evoke through these rhetorical questions? What rational argument is he making?

**Possible Response:** The questions are intended to evoke feelings of outrage. Henry is arguing that the British government is treating the colonists unfairly and dishonestly. The British say that they want reconciliation, but their military activities suggest otherwise.

Use **Unit Two Resource Book,** p. 57 for additional support.

### GUIDE FOR READING

**C** Henry says that the British intend to control the colonists by force.

**D Possible Response:** This technique grabs attention, makes a deeper impression than simple statements, and persuades listeners that negotiating will not work.

---

having eyes, see not, and having ears, hear not, the things which so nearly concern their temporal salvation? For my part, whatever
25 anguish of spirit it may cost, I am willing to know the whole truth—to know the worst and to provide for it.

I have but one lamp by which my feet are guided; and that is the lamp of experience. I know of no way of judging of the future but by the past. And judging by the past, I wish to know what there has
30 been in the conduct of the British ministry for the last ten years, to justify those hopes with which gentlemen have been pleased to solace themselves and the House? Is it that insidious smile with which our petition has been lately received? Trust it not, sir; it will prove a snare to your feet. Suffer not yourselves to be betrayed with
35 a kiss.

Ask yourselves how this gracious reception of our petition comports with these warlike preparations which cover our waters and darken our land. Are fleets and armies necessary to a work of love and reconciliation? Have we shown ourselves so unwilling to be
40 reconciled that force must be called in to win back our love? Let us not deceive ourselves, sir. These are the implements of war and subjugation—the last arguments to which kings resort. I ask gentlemen, sir, what means this martial array, if its purpose be not to force us to submission? Can gentlemen assign any other possible
45 motives for it? Has Great Britain any enemy, in this quarter of the world, to call for all this accumulation of navies and armies? No, sir, she has none. They are meant for us; they can be meant for no other. They are sent over to bind and rivet upon us those chains which the British ministry have been so long forging.
50 And what have we to oppose to them? Shall we try argument? Sir, we have been trying that for the last ten years. Have we anything new to offer on the subject? Nothing. We have held the subject up in every light of which it is capable; but it has been all in vain. Shall we resort to entreaty and humble supplication? What
55 terms shall we find which have not been already exhausted? Let us not, I beseech you, sir, deceive ourselves longer.

Sir, we have done everything that could be done to avert the storm which is now coming on. We have petitioned; we have remonstrated; we have supplicated; we have prostrated ourselves
60 before the throne, and have implored its interposition to arrest the tyrannical hands of the ministry and Parliament. Our petitions have been slighted; our remonstrances have produced additional violence and insult; our supplications have been disregarded; and we have been spurned, with contempt, from the foot of the throne.

---

**23 having eyes . . . hear not:** an allusion to Ezekiel 12:2.

**24 temporal:** worldly.

**32 solace** (sŏl′ĭs): comfort.

**34 snare:** trap.

**35 betrayed with a kiss:** a biblical allusion to the Apostle Judas, who betrayed Jesus. When soldiers came to arrest Jesus, Judas identified him by kissing him.

**38–49** What does Henry say is the reason for the British military buildup in America?

**50–55** Notice how Henry uses rhetorical questions to anticipate the arguments of his opponents. How effective is this technique?

**54 entreaty** (ĕn-trē′tē): earnest request; plea; **supplication** (sŭp′lĭ-kā′shən): the act of asking for something humbly or earnestly.

**59 remonstrated** (rĭ-mŏn′strā-tĭd): objected.

**60 interposition:** intervention.

---

WORDS
TO
KNOW

**insidious** (ĭn-sĭd′ē-əs) *adj.* treacherous
**subjugation** (sŭb′jə-gā′shən) *n.* control by conquering
**martial** (mär′shəl) *adj.* warlike
**tyrannical** (tĭ-răn′ĭ-kəl) *adj.* harsh; oppressive
**spurn** (spûrn) *v.* to reject scornfully

264

---

### BLOCK SCHEDULING: MANAGING TIME

**If your schedule requires that you cover the lesson objectives in a shorter time, use . . .**
- Preparing to Read, p. 262
- Thinking Through the Literature, p. 267
- Vocabulary in Action, p. 268

**If you want to take advantage of longer class time, use . . .**
- TE Teaching Options: Preteaching Vocabulary, p. 263; Viewing and Representing, p. 265; Cross-Curricular Link, p. 266; Standardized Test Practice, p. 268
- Choices & Challenges, pp. 268–269

*Patrick Henry Before the Virginia House of Burgesses* (1851), Peter F. Rothermel. Red Hill, The Patrick Henry National Memorial, Brookneal, Virginia.

## Mini Lesson · Viewing and Representing

**Patrick Henry Before the Virginia House of Burgesses** by Peter F. Rothermel

**ART APPRECIATION** Peter Rothermel was renowned as a painter of historical subjects. A master of compositions involving masses of figures, he used color as a major means of expression.

**Instruction** Have students describe how the composition, color, and light communicate meaning in this work. Encourage students to consider what is the focal point of the painting and which colors catch their attention.

**Possible Response:** The composition draws attention to Patrick Henry, dressed in a vibrant red robe, which contrasts with the drab colors of his listeners. The composition creates a flow along the line of his outstretched arm, suggesting that his voice projects over his audience. Henry is lit from the right; his face is the focal point of light in the painting, and his shadow is cast over those who seem to doubt him.

**Application** This painting is very dramatic, like a freeze frame from an exciting film. Ask students to study the people in the painting, their facial expressions and gestures. What sort of emotions do they convey?

**Possible Responses:** The artist has painted a range of emotional responses to Henry's speech: outrage, frowning disagreement, suspicion, revelation, curiosity.

### GUIDE FOR READING

**A** He wants his listeners to vote in favor of assembling an army to defend itself against Britain.

### Active Reading

| RHETORICAL QUESTIONS |
| AND PERSUASION |

**B** Have students review Henry's use of rhetorical questions in this passage. What attitude does he convey toward people who argue that the colonies are too weak to challenge the British?

**Possible Response:** His attitude is sarcastic and scornful. He portrays those people as weaklings who would "lie supinely on [their] backs" while the British dominate them.

### GUIDE FOR READING

**C** Waiting will weaken the colonists' position; the colonists are strong, and God will bring allies to help; war is inevitable.

### Literary Analysis | ALLUSION |

**D** Direct students to line 93: "Their clanking may be heard on the plains of Boston!" Henry alludes to recent events in Boston where, in response to protests, the British amassed troops to police the area. Encourage students to contrast allusions within this text. How is this allusion different from the allusion in lines 34–35?

**Possible Response:** The earlier allusion to Jesus' betrayal is religious and literary; this one alludes to current events.

### GUIDE FOR READING

**E** Possible Responses: patriotism, courage, religious faith

65 In vain, after these things, may we indulge the fond hope of peace and reconciliation. There is no longer any room for hope.

If we wish to be free—if we mean to preserve inviolate those inestimable privileges for which we have been so long contend- ing—if we mean not basely to abandon the noble struggle in which 70 we have been so long engaged, and which we have pledged our- selves never to abandon until the glorious object of our contest shall be obtained, we must fight! I repeat it, sir, we must fight! An appeal to arms and to the God of Hosts is all that is left us!

They tell us, sir, that we are weak—unable to cope with so 75 formidable an adversary. But when shall we be stronger? Will it be the next week, or the next year? Will it be when we are totally disarmed, and when a British guard shall be stationed in every house? Shall we gather strength by irresolution and inaction? Shall we acquire the means of effectual resistance, by lying supinely on 80 our backs, and hugging the delusive phantom of hope, until our enemies shall have bound us hand and foot?

Sir, we are not weak, if we make a proper use of those means which the God of nature hath placed in our power. Three millions of people, armed in the holy cause of liberty, and in such a coun- 85 try as that which we possess, are invincible by any force which our enemy can send against us. Besides, sir, we shall not fight our bat- tles alone. There is a just God who presides over the destinies of nations, and who will raise up friends to fight our battles for us. The battle, sir, is not to the strong alone; it is to the vigilant, the 90 active, the brave. Besides, sir, we have no election. If we were base enough to desire it, it is now too late to retire from the contest. There is no retreat but in submission and slavery! Our chains are forged! Their clanking may be heard on the plains of Boston! The war is inevitable—and let it come! I repeat it, sir, let it come!

95 It is in vain, sir, to extenuate the matter. Gentlemen may cry, "Peace! peace!"—but there is no peace. The war is actually begun! The next gale that sweeps from the north will bring to our ears the clash of resounding arms! Our brethren are already in the field! Why stand we here idle? What is it that gentlemen wish? What 100 would they have? Is life so dear, or peace so sweet, as to be pur- chased at the price of chains and slavery? Forbid it, Almighty God! I know not what course others may take; but as for me, give me liberty, or give me death! ❖

**67 inviolate** (ĭn-vī′ə-lĭt): not violated; intact.

**68 inestimable** (ĭn-ĕs′tə-mə-bəl): extremely valuable.

**69 basely** (bās′lē): dishonorably.

**72–73** Henry has reached the main point of his speech. What is Henry trying to convince his listeners to do?

**74–94** In these two paragraphs, what reasons does Henry give for taking military action now?

**89 battle . . . strong alone:** an allusion to Ecclesiastes 9:11— "the race is not to the swift, nor the battle to the strong."

**90 election:** choice.

**95 extenuate** (ĭk-stĕn′yōō-āt′): to lessen the seriousness of, especially by providing partial excuses.

**97 the next gale . . . north:** Some colonists in Massachusetts had already shown open resistance to the British and were on the brink of war.

**102–103** What emotions does Henry appeal to with the last lines of his speech?

| | **formidable** (fôr′mĭ-də-bəl) *adj.* difficult to defeat |
| WORDS | **adversary** (ăd′vər-sĕr′ē) *n.* an opponent |
| TO | **irresolution** (ĭ-rĕz′ə-lōō′shən) *n.* uncertainty; indecision |
| KNOW | **invincible** (ĭn-vĭn′sə-bəl) *adj.* unbeatable |
| | **vigilant** (vĭj′ə-lənt) *adj.* alert; watchful |

266

### Cross Curricular Link  **American History**

**PATRICK HENRY** The paradox here is that Patrick Henry, like many Revolutionaries, claimed to be fighting for freedom from tyranny and oppression, and yet he was a man who could not have man- aged to be a member of the House of Burgesses— as a member of Virginia's landed elite, he was entitled to speak—if he had not enslaved men and women to work his fields. Indeed, many celebrat- ed leaders of the American Revolution—George Washington, Thomas Jefferson—amassed vast wealth by exploiting slave labor. How did they live with this paradox: to demand freedom while denying the very same to so many? While Patrick Henry admitted in a letter to Quaker and anti- slavery leader Robert Pleasants that slavery was an "abominable practice," he had to concede: "Would anyone believe I am the master of slaves of my own purchase? I am drawn along by the general inconvenience of living without them."

## Connect to the Literature

**1. What Do You Think?**
After hearing Henry's speech, would you have voted to prepare for war?

**Comprehension Check**
• What does Henry warn the colonists about?
• What does Henry urge the colonists to do?

## Think Critically

**2.** In your view, what is the most convincing point Henry makes in his argument?

 THINK ABOUT
• the main points he makes in the speech
• whether his reason for wanting to fight is the one you circled as the most compelling

**3.** **ACTIVE READING** **RHETORICAL QUESTIONS AND PERSUASION**
Review the examples of rhetorical questions you copied in your **READER'S NOTEBOOK**. Choose one of these rhetorical questions and reread the passage of the speech in which it is found. How does the use of a rhetorical question strengthen the persuasive force of this passage?

**4.** Think about Henry's famous statement, "Give me liberty, or give me death!" Do you agree that liberty is more important than life itself? Explain your answer.

## Extend Interpretations

**5. Different Perspectives** Imagine how each of these people might have responded to Henry's speech:

• an American-born colonist whose grandparents were British
• a Loyalist, meaning an American colonist who sides with the British
• an African enslaved in the Virginia colony
• a Native American

**6. Comparing Texts** How would you compare Patrick Henry's speech and Jonathan Edwards's sermon as examples of persuasion? Consider the purpose of each speech and the emotions to which it appeals.

**7. Connect to Life** Patrick Henry argued that the actions of King George III and the British Parliament posed major threats to the liberty of the American colonists. In your opinion, what are the major threats to the liberty of Americans today?

## Literary Analysis

**ALLUSION** An **allusion** is an indirect reference to a person, place, event, or literary work with which the author believes the reader will be familiar. Many works contain allusions to the Bible, classical mythology, or other works of literature. By using allusions, writers tap the knowledge and memory of the reader, drawing upon associations already in the reader's mind. For example, Patrick Henry warns colonists not to be "betrayed with a kiss." This biblical allusion refers to the Apostle Judas, who betrayed Jesus by kissing him. Henry used this brief, powerful allusion to suggest that there might be something sinister behind Great Britain's friendly gestures.

**Paired Activity** Work with a partner to investigate Henry's allusions in this speech. Review the Guide for Reading notes that explain the allusions to Homer's *Odyssey* and to Ecclesiastes. Each of you should choose one of these allusions to research, locating the particular passage in the original source, reading it carefully, and then expanding the note given in the Guide for Reading. Share your new note with your partner and with the rest of the class.

**REVIEW** **REPETITION** Reread the paragraph that begins "Sir, we have done everything . . ." (pages 264–266). What words, phrases, and sentence patterns are repeated in this paragraph? What effect does this repetition have?

---

## Connect to the Literature

**1. What Do You Think?**
Possible Responses: Yes, the colonists should rebel against an unjust government and defend themselves against the British troops. No, war should be avoided at all costs.

**Comprehension Check**
• He warns the colonists that the British are preparing to use military force against them.
• He urges the colonists to take up arms against British rule.

 Use Selection Quiz
**Unit Resource Book Two,** p. 54.

## Think Critically

**2.** Possible Responses: The oppressor is preparing to use force; freedom is more important than even life itself; the colonists can wait no longer for a peaceful resolution—they have waited long enough, and the situation is getting worse.

**3.** To help students answer this question, suggest that they first read the passage without including the rhetorical question and then reread it with the rhetorical question included.

**4.** Make sure students define their understanding of liberty in explaining their answers.

## Literary Analysis

**Allusion** In sharing their notes with the class, students might read aloud the entire passage in the original source to which Henry alludes.

**Repetition** Students should notice that Henry creates a pattern by using different past participles in the following construction: "We have petitioned; we have remonstrated; we have supplicated;"

---

## Extend Interpretations

**Different Perspectives** Possible Responses:
• An American-born colonist with British grandparents may have felt conflicted at first. Only two out of five actively supported the Revolution.
• A Loyalist would have been outraged to hear Henry's treasonous speech.
• An enslaved African might have found Henry's references to bondage ironic, since some of the white colonists who Henry says might become "enslaved" to the British were themselves guilty of enslaving many Africans.

• Some Native Americans supported the French, others the British. Any call to arms meant troops, more war, and a threat to their way of life.

**Comparing Texts** Students may compare different sources of persuasive power: the use of allusion or figurative language, rhetorical questions, choice of language, or repetition. Some students might point out that both Edwards and Henry exploit the fear of their respective audiences.

**Connect to Life** Students might state that greed, poverty, and racism are major threats to liberty today.

## Writing Options

1. **Newspaper Report** Remind students to state the most important facts in the lead paragraph. **To get students started on this assignment,** suggest that they jot down answers to *who, what, when, where, why,* and *how.*

2. **Character Sketch** Possible Response: Henry would be described at worst as a traitor, at best as a victim of youthful folly.

3. **Rebuttal Speech** Students might include such arguments as the terrible cost in lives that war would entail and the lack of consensus among the colonists as to necessity of waging war.

## Activities & Explorations

1. **Political Advertisement** Students may create colonial-style ads or may update the style.

2. **Liberty Poster** The famous concluding paragraph of the speech may be a popular choice. Encourage a variety of visual approaches, such as collage and cartoon.

3. **Dramatic Reading** Encourage students to recall electrifying speakers they have heard and to "pull out all the stops" in delivering their speeches.

4. **Independence Discussion** Responses will vary widely and may include a number of groups—for example, the peoples of several former Soviet republics. Generally, these groups have used ethnic, religious, or historical differences to support their movements of self-determination; they stand to gain independence, but often at the cost of many lives.

## Art Connection

Possible Response: Henry is standing on the right, in front of three groups of listeners. The lighting and the listeners' rapt attention focus the viewer's eye on him. Each group displays a different reaction: shock, suspicion, and admiration.

## Inquiry & Research

**Countdown to Revolution** Suggest that students work in pairs to review their American history materials and design their time lines. Major events include the French and Indian War, the Stamp Act, the First Continental Congress, the Townshend Acts, and the Declaration of Independence.

## Writing Options

1. **Newspaper Report** Write the first paragraphs of a newspaper report about Henry's speech that might have been published in the colonial *Virginia Gazette.* Describe the speech and its probable effect on the audience.

2. **Character Sketch** It has been said that history is written by the winners. Patrick Henry is regarded as a patriot today, but if the British had won the Revolutionary War, how would he be described? Write a brief sketch of Henry as it might appear in a current British history textbook.

3. **Rebuttal Speech** Draft a rebuttal opposing Henry's point of view. Offer a counterargument in favor of peaceful compromise with the British. Place this piece in your **Working Portfolio.**

**Writing Handbook**
See page 1285: Persuasive Writing

## Activities & Explorations

1. **Political Advertisement** Plan a political advertisement for television that promotes one or more ideas from Henry's speech.

Select fitting visual images, music, or slogans to use in the ad. Then share your TV spot with classmates. **~ VIEWING AND REPRESENTING**

2. **Liberty Poster** Which images in Henry's speech do you think are the most powerful? Create a poster that conveys Henry's message, using illustrations and quotations that best capture the spirit of his speech. Use a computer to experiment with different type fonts and type sizes for your poster. **~ ART**

3. **Dramatic Reading** Prepare and give a dramatic reading of Henry's speech, using gestures and varying your tone of voice to make the speech effective. **~ PERFORMING**

4. **Independence Discussion** Take part in a roundtable discussion in which you identify groups of people who have recently fought or are now fighting for independence from another nation. What arguments have they used to support their cause? What do they stand to lose or gain? **~ SPEAKING AND LISTENING**

## Art Connection

Patrick Henry earned fame as an orator long before he made the speech reprinted here. In the painting on page 265, Peter F. Rothermel portrays Henry giving a speech in Virginia's House of Burgesses, which was Virginia's colonial legislature before the Revolution. Look for techniques that make this scene dramatic. What features of the painting focus attention on Henry?

## Inquiry & Research

**Countdown to Revolution** What events led up to the conflict between Great Britain and the American colonists? What events happened after Patrick Henry called for war on March 23, 1775? Use an encyclopedia or an American history textbook to find out about important events that occurred before and after Henry gave his speech. Then make a time line of these events to share with the class.

 **More Online: Research Starter** www.mcdougallittell.com

## Vocabulary in Action

**EXERCISE: CLASSIFYING WORDS** On your paper, copy the chart shown. Then review the Words to Know. Which vocabulary words best fit the American colonists' view of the British? Write these words in the first column of the chart. Which words best fit the colonists' view of themselves? Write them in the second column. Be ready to explain your choices in class.

| British | Colonists |
|---|---|
|  |  |
|  |  |

| WORDS TO KNOW | | | |
|---|---|---|---|
| adversary | irresolution | tyrannical |
| formidable | martial | vigilant |
| insidious | spurn | |
| invincible | subjugation | |

## Teaching Options    Standardized Test Practice

**UNDERSTANDING MULTIPLE-MEANING WORDS**
Using context clues to figure out the meanings of multiple-meaning words is a required skill on some standardized tests. Give students practice in this skill by directing their attention to line 30 of Henry's speech and presenting the following test item.
In this passage, the word <u>ministry</u> means
**A.** giving aid or service
**B.** a government department

**C.** a body of religious officials
**D.** the duties and functions of a minister
Help them use context clues in the passage to determine the correct answer. Prompt them by asking who has received the colonists' petition (lines 32–33). The correct answer is B: the "British ministry" Henry mentions is the government department in charge of the American colonies.

## Patrick Henry
### 1736–1799

**Fiery Orator** American patriot Patrick Henry was a self-taught lawyer whose gift of oration helped spark the American Revolution. In acknowledging Henry's gift, fellow Virginian Thomas Jefferson said: "Call it oratory or what you will, but I never heard anything like it. He had more command over the passions than any man I ever knew." An eloquent defender of colonial rights, Henry spent more than 30 years in public life and took part in the creation of a new nation.

**A Voice of Protest** In 1765, at the age of 28, Henry joined the House of Burgesses, the lower house of Virginia's colonial legislature. Just nine days after becoming a burgess, Henry introduced the Stamp Act Resolves. He opposed the Stamp Act, which required colonists to buy stamps to put on taxable paper items, on the grounds that only the colonial legislature—not the British Parliament—had the right to tax colonists. Virginia became the first colony to officially protest the Stamp Act.

**Revolutionary Activities** Ten years later, Henry again proposed resolutions that led toward American independence. At the Second Virginia Provincial Convention, he gave the impassioned speech you have just read. His resolutions to prepare for war passed by five votes, and he was named chairman of a committee to implement the plan to arm Virginia. In 1776, while the American Revolution raged, Henry helped draw up Virginia's first state constitution and was elected Virginia's first governor.

**Later Years** After the Revolution had ended and the U.S. Constitution had been ratified, Henry resumed his law practice. Then, in 1794, he retired to his Virginia estate, Red Hill. Although he was offered a U.S. Senate seat, posts as minister to Spain and to France, and the positions of Secretary of State and Chief Justice, he did not return to politics until George Washington urged him to run for representative in the Virginia state legislature in 1799. Henry won the election, but he died before taking office.

## Vocabulary in Action
**EXERCISE: CLASSIFYING WORDS**

**Possible Responses**

**British**
adversary
insidious
tyrannical

**Colonists**
formidable
invincible
vigilant

---

 ## Grammar
### Mini Lesson

**PERFECT TENSES** The perfect tense refers to completed actions, whether in the past, the present, or the future. The following chart shows the first-person perfect tenses of the verb *to watch*, in both the active and passive voices.

| Tense | Active Voice | Passive Voice |
|---|---|---|
| Present Perfect | I have watched. | I have been watched. |
| Past Perfect | I had watched. | I had been watched. |
| Future Perfect | I shall have watched. | I shall have been watched. |

**Application** Have students read the last paragraph on page 264, lines 57–64. Ask students what verb tense predominates. *(present perfect)* Ask why Henry chose the present perfect verb tense ("we have petitioned") instead of the simple present ("we petition") or the present progressive ("we are petitioning").

**Possible Response:** The present perfect tense suggests that these actions have been completed at an indefinite time in the past. Henry does not see petitioning as an ongoing process; he is convinced that it is time to abandon that strategy and take up arms.

 Use **Grammar Transparencies and Copymasters,** p. 115.

 Use McDougal Littell's *Language Network,* Chapter 4, for more instruction and practice in perfect tenses.

## OVERVIEW

### Objectives

1. understand a **document** of critical importance in U.S. history (**Literary Analysis**)
2. recognize examples of **parallelism** (**Literary Analysis**)
3. construct meaning by **paraphrasing** difficult passages (**Active Reading**)

### Summary

The Declaration of Independence asserts that when a government violates the unalienable rights of the people, it is the people's duty to abolish that government and form a new one. A long list of grievances against the King of England follows, such as his demand that people relinquish their representation in the legislature, his decree prohibiting immigrants from becoming citizens, his quartering of armed troops in the colonies, his cutting off of trade with other countries, and his imposing of taxes without the consent of the people. These policies are characterized as the acts of a tyrant. The document concludes with the declaration that the United Colonies are free and independent states. All allegiance to the British Crown is said to be dissolved.

### Thematic Link

The ideals of freedom and equality espoused by writers in the **time of revolution** found bold expression in the Declaration of Independence. Through the years, this document has been a beacon for those who claim the **right to be free.**

## Reading and Analyzing

### GUIDE FOR READING

**A** Respect for world opinion required it.

### 5-Minute Warm-Up

*Daily Language SkillBuilder*

Have students **proofread** the display sentences on page 131j and write them correctly. The sentences also appear on Transparency 7 of **Grammar Transparencies and Copymasters.**

---

*"We hold these truths to be self-evident. . . ."*

# Declaration of Independence

*Document by* THOMAS JEFFERSON

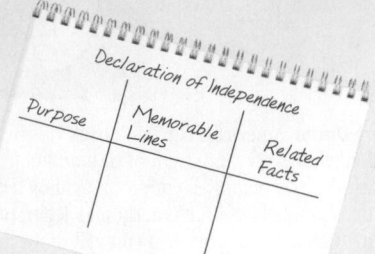

**Connect to Your Life**

**A Treasured Document** With a small group of your classmates, explore what you already know about the Declaration of Independence by filling in a chart like this one. Then read this selection to find out more about the Declaration of Independence.

*Declaration of Independence*

| Purpose | Memorable Lines | Related Facts |
|---|---|---|
| | | |

## Build Background

**Let Freedom Ring** In 1775, simmering tensions between Great Britain and her American colonies exploded in violent clashes. By the spring of 1776, many colonial Americans believed that the only solution to the conflict was to break away from British rule. At the Second Continental Congress held in Philadelphia, a five-member committee was appointed to draft an official statement of the reasons for independence. Thomas Jefferson, a 33-year-old Virginia lawyer with a keen talent for writing, prepared the first draft. After voting for independence on July 2, the full Congress debated the Declaration for two days, making a few more changes before adopting it on July 4.

The final version of the Declaration has four main parts:

- a preamble, or foreword, that announces the reason for the document
- a declaration of people's natural rights and relationship to government
- a long list of complaints against George III, the British king
- a conclusion that formally states America's independence

> **WORDS TO KNOW** **Vocabulary Preview**
> abdicate   impel         mercenary
> arbitrary   insurrection

## Focus Your Reading

**LITERARY ANALYSIS** **PARALLELISM** When a writer uses similar grammatical forms or sentence patterns to express ideas of equal importance, this technique is called **parallelism.** Patrick Henry's famous line, "Give me liberty, or give me death!" is an example of parallelism. Notice other examples in the Declaration of Independence.

**ACTIVE READING** **PARAPHRASING** A **paraphrase** restates someone else's ideas in simpler words. To paraphrase a passage, determine its main idea and replace difficult words with easier ones. Consider the following passage from the Declaration of Independence:

> *Prudence, indeed, will dictate that governments long established should not be changed for light and transient causes.*

Here is a paraphrase of the same passage that restates the main idea in simpler language:

> Common sense tells us that governments that have existed for a long time should not be changed for minor reasons.

**READER'S NOTEBOOK** As you read the Declaration of Independence, pause from time to time to paraphrase difficult passages, replacing difficult words with easier ones.

---

## LESSON RESOURCES

**UNIT TWO RESOURCE BOOK,** pp. 55–59

**ASSESSMENT RESOURCES**
**Formal Assessment,** pp. 49–50
**Teacher's Guide to Assessment and Portfolio Use**
**Test Generator**

**SKILLS TRANSPARENCIES AND COPYMASTERS**
**Literary Analysis**
- Persuasive Techniques, T10 (for Writing Option 2, p. 280)

**Reading and Critical Thinking**
- Paraphrasing and Summarizing, T41 (for Active Reading, p. 270)

**Grammar**
- Avoiding Shifts in Tense, Mood, and Voice, C120 (for Mini Lesson, p. 280)
- Capitalization I, C144 (for Mini Lesson, p. 277)

**Vocabulary**
- Using a Thesaurus, C31 (for Mini Lesson, p. 275)

**Communications**
- Dramatic Reading, T12 (for Writing Option 2, p. 280)
- Impromptu Speaking: Dialogue, Role-Play, Debate, T13 (for Activities & Explorations 1, p. 280)

**INTEGRATED TECHNOLOGY**

**Audio Library**
**Visit our website:**
www.mcdougallittell.com

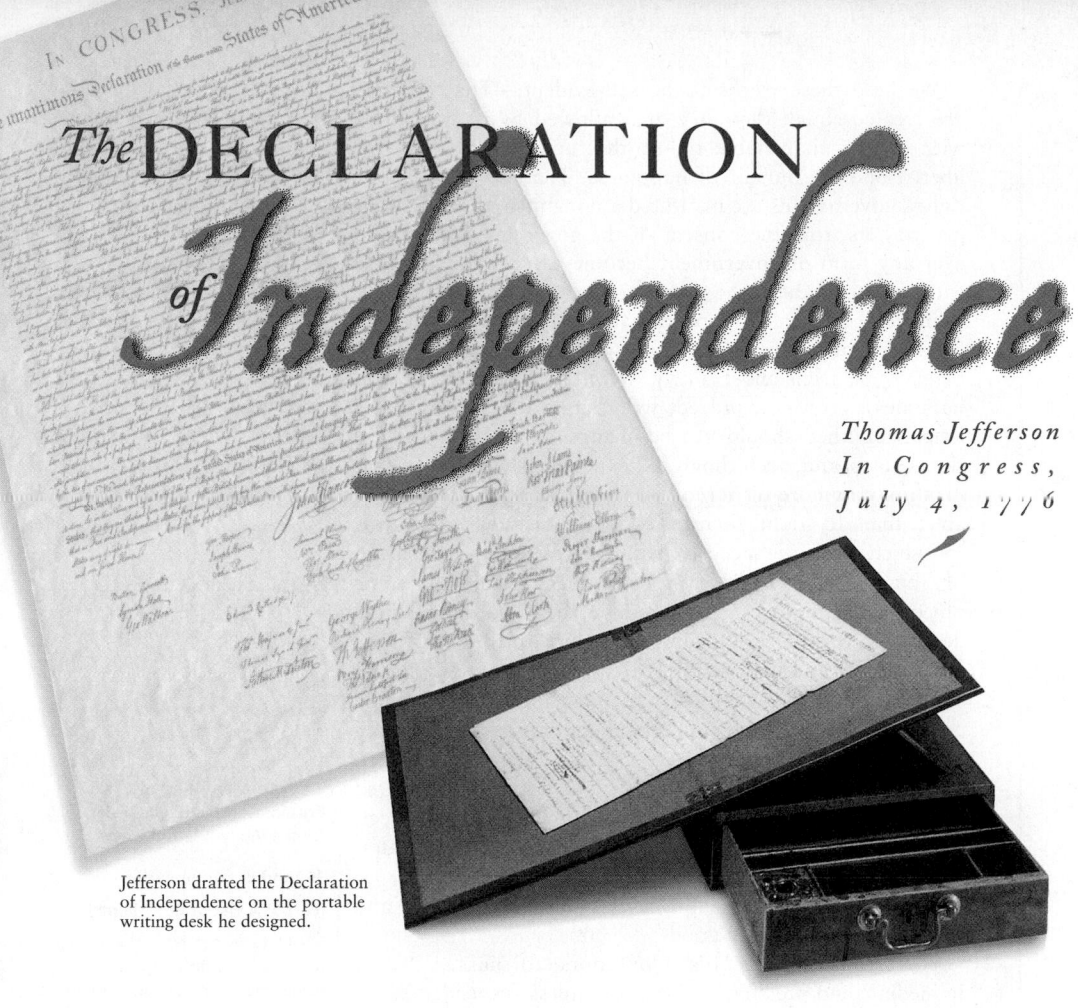

# The DECLARATION of *Independence*

Thomas Jefferson
In Congress,
July 4, 1776

Jefferson drafted the Declaration
of Independence on the portable
writing desk he designed.

When, in the course of human events, it becomes necessary
for one people to dissolve the political bands which have
connected them with another, and to assume, among the
powers of the earth, the separate and equal station to
5   which the laws of nature and of nature's God entitle
them, a decent respect to the opinions of mankind requires
that they should declare the causes which impel them to the
separation.

**GUIDE FOR READING**

[Part 1: The Preamble]

**1–8** The colonists felt they must
explain their reasons to the world.
Why?   **A**

WORDS
TO    **impel** (ĭm-pĕl') v. to drive forward; force
KNOW

**271**

---

**Mini Lesson** Preteaching Vocabulary

**USING CONTEXT CLUES** Remind students that
sometimes they can rely on context to determine
the meaning of words. Write the following sentence on the chalkboard:

The king's advisers warned him that if he
ignored the rebels, he would abdicate his
authority over them, and they would take the
government into their own hands.

**Instruction** Have students look for clues that help
them determine the meaning of the word *abdicate.*

**Application** Have students use context clues to
determine the meanings of the underlined words.

1. The colonists, who had no voice in creating the
laws imposed on them, considered such laws
totally arbitrary.
2. The colonists asserted that the tyrant's unjust
treatment seemed designed to impel them to
rebel.
3. The people were ready to engage in an armed
insurrection to overthrow the tyrant.

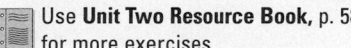 Use **Unit Two Resource Book,** p. 58
for more exercises.

**A lesson on context clues appears on
page 326 in the Pupil's Edition.**

THE DECLARATION OF INDEPENDENCE   **271**

---

## TEACHING THE LITERATURE

### Customizing Instruction

**Less Proficient Readers**
Help students establish and adjust their
purpose for reading. Tell students to
refer to the Guide for Reading to help
them understand the selection better.
**Set a Purpose** Tell students to read to
find out the answers to these questions:
• To whom is the Declaration of
Independence addressed?
• Why was the Declaration of
Independence written?
• What are the most important points
made in the Declaration?

**Students Acquiring English**
Help students connect the literature to
the historical context by discussing the
historical background of the document.
Make sure students understand the
meaning of the document's title.
Because the formal style and archaic
vocabulary may pose special difficulties,
you may wish to allow students to
read in pairs or small groups, with
frequent pauses to paraphrase or clarify
information.

Use **Spanish Study Guide** for
additional support, pp. 62–64.

**Gifted and Talented**
Encourage students to interpret the
connotative power of words by pointing out the contrast between such
phrases as the "patient sufferance" of
the colonies and the "absolute tyranny"
of the king. Have students summarize
the overall effect of Jefferson's use of
words with negative connotations in
listing the grievances against the King
of England.

Have students review Preparing to
Read for background.

### Active Reading

**A** When students encounter difficult
wording, they can figure out the meaning by putting each sentence into their
own words. Ask students to paraphrase
the main ideas of Part 2: "A Declaration
of Rights."

Use **Unit Two Resource Book** p. 56
for more practice.

### GUIDE FOR READING

**B** to ensure basic rights, such as life,
liberty, and the pursuit of happiness
**C** when it destroys basic rights
**D** for trivial reasons

### Literary Analysis

**E** Have students point out examples
of parallelism in this list of grievances.
**Possible Response:** "He has refused . . .
He has forbidden . . ."

Ask students what effect this technique
creates for the reader.
**Possible Response:** It emphasizes that
the king's crimes are of equal worth as
evidence of his tyranny.

Use **Unit Two Resource Book** p. 57
for more practice.

### GUIDE FOR READING

**F** Governors refused to pass needed
laws, called meetings at inconvenient
places, dissolved assemblies, and did
not provide for new elections.
**G** The king refused to approve laws to
establish courts and made judges' terms
in office and their salaries uncertain.

---

**A**

We hold these truths to be self-evident:—That all men
10  are created equal; that they are endowed by their Creator
with certain unalienable rights; that among these are life,
liberty, and the pursuit of happiness. That, to secure these
rights, governments are instituted among men, deriving their
just powers from the consent of the governed; that, when-
15  ever any form of government becomes destructive of these
ends, it is the right of the people to alter or to abolish it, and
to institute a new government, laying its foundation on such
principles, and organizing its powers in such form, as to
them shall seem most likely to effect their safety and
20  happiness. Prudence, indeed, will dictate that governments
long established should not be changed for light and transient causes; and, accordingly, all experience hath shown that
mankind are more disposed to suffer, while evils are sufferable, than to right themselves by abolishing the forms
25  to which they are accustomed. But, when a long train
of abuses and usurpations, pursuing invariably the same
object, evinces a design to reduce them under absolute
despotism, it is their right, it is their duty, to throw off such
government, and to provide new guards for their future
30  security. Such has been the patient sufferance of these
colonies; and such is now the necessity that constrains them
to alter their former systems of government. The history of
the present King of Great Britain is a history of repeated
injuries and usurpations, all having, in direct object,
35  the establishment of an absolute tyranny over these States.
To prove this, let facts be submitted to a candid world.

He has refused his assent to laws the most wholesome and
necessary for the public good.

He has forbidden his Governors to pass laws of
40  immediate and pressing importance, unless suspended in
their operation till his assent should be obtained; and, when
so suspended, he has utterly neglected to attend to them.

He has refused to pass other laws for the accommodation
of large districts of people, unless these people would

**E**  45  relinquish the right of representation in the legislature—a
right inestimable to them, and formidable to tyrants only.

He has called together legislative bodies at places unusual,
uncomfortable, and distant from the depository of their
public records, for the sole purpose of fatiguing them into
50  compliance with his measure.

He has dissolved representative houses repeatedly, for
opposing, with manly firmness, his invasions on the rights of
the people.

---

**[Part 2: A Declaration of Rights]**

**11 unalienable** (un āl' yən ə bəl):
that may not be taken away.

**12–14** What is the purpose of
government? **B**

**15–17** When is it right to
overthrow a government? **C**

**20–22** When is it not right to
change a government? **D**

**22 transient** (trăn'shənt): passing
away with time; temporary.

**26 usurpations** (yōō'sər-pā'shənz):
acts of wrongfully taking over a
right or power that belongs to
someone else.

**33 the present King of Great
Britain:** George III, who reigned
from 1760 to 1820.

**36 candid:** fair; impartial.

**[Part 3: A List of Complaints]**

**37–42** Laws passed in the colonies
needed the king's approval;
sometimes it took years for laws to
be approved or rejected.

**39–59** Royal colonial governors
created hardships for the colonial
assemblies. What were some of
these hardships? **F**

**39 Governors:** officials appointed
by the king to govern individual
colonies.

---

## Teaching Options

*Signing the Declaration of Independence*, John Trumbull. Corbis-Bettmann.

He has refused, for a long time after such dissolutions,
55  to cause others to be elected; whereby the legislative powers, incapable of annihilation, have returned to the people at large for their exercise; the State remaining, in the meantime, exposed to all dangers of invasion from without, and convulsions within.

60  He has endeavored to prevent the population of these States; for that purpose obstructing the laws for the natural ization of foreigners; refusing to pass others to encourage their migration hither, and raising the conditions of new appropriations of lands.

65  He has obstructed the administration of justice, by refusing his assent to laws for establishing judiciary powers.

He has made judges dependent on his will alone for the tenure of their offices, and the amount and payment of their salaries.

70  He has erected a multitude of new offices, and sent hither swarms of officers to harass our people and eat out their substance.

**60–64** The king had decreed that no more immigrants to America could become citizens, and he had raised the purchase price of frontierland.

**65–69** The British had created hardships for the colonial courts. What were these hardships?

**66 judiciary** (jōō-dĭsh'ē-ĕr'ē): relating to courts of law.

**67–68 the tenure** (tĕn'yər) **of their offices:** their job security.

**71 officers:** tax gatherers and law enforcers.

**71–72 eat out their substance:** use up their resources.

THE DECLARATION OF INDEPENDENCE   **273**

## Customizing Instruction

### Students Acquiring English
**1** Help students understand the meanings of difficult terms. Point out that *evinces* means "shows" and *despotism* means "tyranny."

### Multiple Learning Styles
**Auditory Learners**
**2** Have volunteers read aloud the list of grievances against the king. Encourage readers to emphasize the first three words of each item. Discuss how the parallel sentence structure creates a cadence, or a steady beat. Point out that it isn't necessary to grasp the fine points of every grievance in order to understand the overall message.

### Gifted and Talented
**3** Encourage students to analyze Jefferson's word choice. Discuss Jefferson's use of strong verbs with negative connotations throughout this section. Have students list these verbs and then use a thesaurus to find a weaker, or neutral, verb for each one. Discuss how substituting weaker verbs affects the tone and the message conveyed in this passage.

## Mini Lesson **Viewing and Representing**

*Signing the Declaration of Independence*
**by John Trumbull**

**ART APPRECIATION** Tell students that this painting by John Trumbull (1746–1843) measures only 30 inches wide, yet Trumbull includes 48 figures in this small space.

**Instruction** Explain that John Hancock is seated at the table and standing in front of him (left to right) are John Adams, Roger Sherman, Robert R. Livingston, Thomas Jefferson, and Benjamin Franklin.

**Application** Explain to students that artists communicate meaning through certain elements of design. Ask students how, with so many figures in such a small space, the artist focuses attention on the document itself.

**Possible Response:** The play of light and dark focuses attention on the document, which, flanked by the most prominent figures in the painting, almost seems to glow. The light, which spreads upward and outward from the document, is accentuated by the sweep of the banner on the wall.

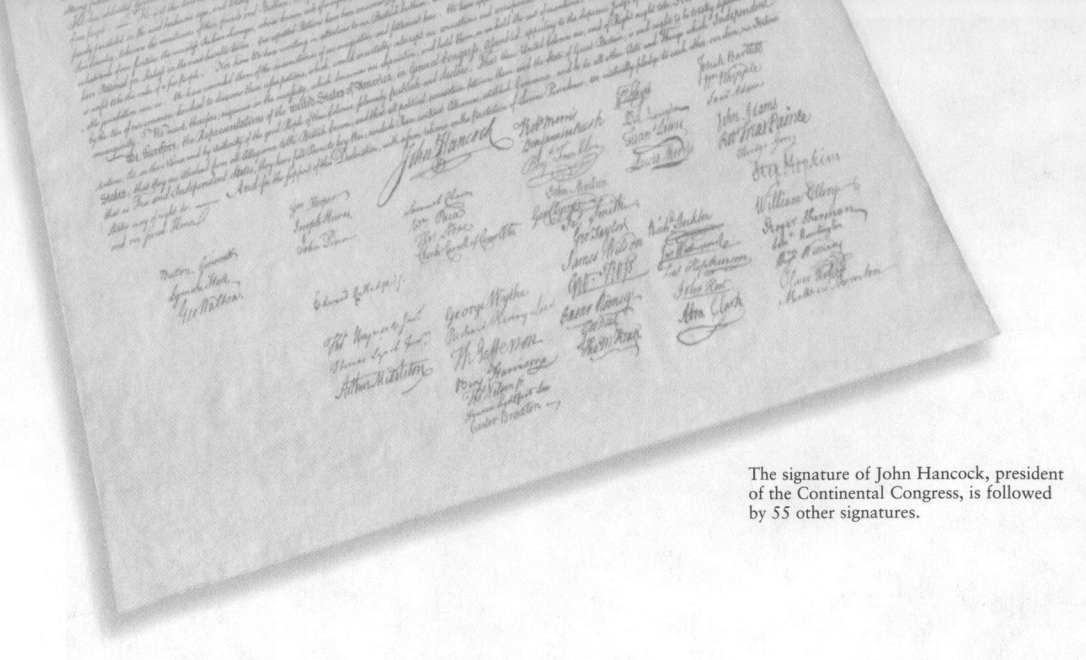

The signature of John Hancock, president of the Continental Congress, is followed by 55 other signatures.

### GUIDE FOR READING

**A** The colonial legislatures had not consented to their presence; they were dangerous because they were protected from prosecution for wrongdoing.

**B** Laws were abolished; legislatures were suspended.

### Active Reading | PARAPHRASING

**C** Have students work in pairs or small groups to paraphrase this portion of the list of grievances. Encourage the use of reference materials such as a dictionary or thesaurus to find precise meanings and synonyms for difficult words.

**Possible Response:** Now he is sending large armies of hired troops from another country to finish his evil work. Having acted more cruelly than most barbarians, he is not worthy to lead a civilized nation.

---

He has kept among us, in times of peace, standing armies, without the consent of our legislatures.

75 He has affected to render the military independent of, and superior to, the civil power.

He has combined with others to subject us to a jurisdiction foreign to our constitutions, and unacknowledged by our laws; giving his assent to their acts of pretended

80 legislation:

For quartering large bodies of armed troops among us;

For protecting them, by a mock trial, from punishment for any murders which they should commit on the inhabitants of these States;

85 For cutting off our trade with all parts of the world;

For imposing taxes on us without our consent;

For depriving us, in many cases, of the benefits of trial by jury;

For transporting us beyond the seas, to be tried for

90 pretended offenses;

For abolishing the free system of English laws in a neighboring province, establishing there an <u>arbitrary</u> government, and enlarging its boundaries, so as to render it at once an

**77–79** Parliament had passed the Declaratory Act in 1766, stating that the King and Parliament could make all the laws for the colonies.

**81–84** What objections did the colonists have about British soldiers in America? **A**

**85–101** What additional hardships were put on colonial lawmakers? **B**

**91 92 a neighboring province:** the province of Quebec, which at the time extended south to the Ohio River and west to the Mississippi.

| WORDS TO KNOW | **arbitrary** (är′bĭ-trĕr′ē) adj. based on unpredictable decisions rather than on reason or law |
|---|---|

274

---

## Teaching Options

### ✓ Assessment **Standardized Test Practice**

**MAKING INFERENCES AND DRAWING CONCLUSIONS**
Tell students that some standardized tests require them to make inferences or draw conclusions based on their reading. They must support their inferences or conclusions with evidence from the text and their own experience. To give students practice with this skill, read aloud or write on the chalkboard the following question:

Which of the following statements best describes the mood of the framers of the Declaration of Independence?

**A.** Overall, they were content with the English government.

**B.** They were indignant because the English government refused to recognize their rights.

**C.** They were pessimistic and downtrodden after years of British oppression.

Lead students through the process of choosing the best response. Consider each choice and ask students if they can support it with details from the selection. Point out that only B can be supported by textual evidence.

example and fit instrument for introducing the same
95 absolute rule into these colonies;

For taking away our charters, abolishing our most valuable laws, and altering, fundamentally, the forms of our
governments;

For suspending our own legislatures, and declaring
100 themselves invested with power to legislate for us in all cases
whatsoever.

He has abdicated government here, by declaring us out of
his protection, and waging war against us.

He has plundered our seas, ravaged our coasts, burnt our
105 towns, and destroyed the lives of our people.

He is at this time transporting large armies of foreign
mercenaries to complete the works of death, desolation, and
tyranny, already begun with circumstances of cruelty and
perfidy scarcely paralleled in the most barbarous ages, and
110 totally unworthy the head of a civilized nation.

He has constrained our fellow citizens, taken captive on
the high seas, to bear arms against their country, to become
the executioners of their friends and brethren, or to fall
themselves by their hands.

**104–105** American seaports, such as Norfolk, Virginia, had already been shelled.

**106–107** The British hired thirty thousand German soldiers to fight in America.

**109 perfidy** (pûr′fĭ-dē): betrayal; treachery.

*We mutually pledge to each other our lives, our fortunes, and our sacred honor.*

The signers used this silver inkwell, made by Philip Syng in 1752.

WORDS
TO
KNOW

**abdicate** (ăb′dĭ-kāt′) v. to give up responsibility for
**mercenary** (mûr′sə-něr′ē) n. a professional soldier hired to fight in a foreign army

275

**Customizing Instruction**

**Less Proficient Readers**
 Make sure that students understand archaic or formal terms, such
as *render* for "make" (line 76) and
*quartering* for "housing" (line 82).
Encourage students to use a dictionary
for difficult terms, and help them
choose the best synonyms.

 **Vocabulary Strategy**

**USING A THESAURUS TO DETERMINE SYNONYMS**
Write the sentence that begins on line 105 on the
chalkboard, and underline the verbs *plundered,
ravaged,* and *destroyed.* Point out that these verbs
have strong connotations.
**Instruction** Circle the word *plundered* and ask a
volunteer to look up the correct form of the word
(e.g., verb, rather than noun) in a thesaurus.
• Ask students to find a synonym with a more
neutral connotation (for example, *despoiled* or
*preyed upon*).
• Have students substitute various choices in the
sentence to test them for sense. Tell students

that if they are unsure of the connotation of a
word, they can look it up in a dictionary to
determine the precise usage.
**Application** Have students work in pairs to find
"neutral" synonyms for the verbs *ravaged* and
*destroyed.* (Possibilities are *ruined* and *marred.*)
Tell students to rewrite the sentence, using their
synonyms. Have them compare the "toned down"
sentence with the original and discuss how connotations reflect the author's attitude.

Use **Vocabulary Transparencies and
Copymasters,** p. 31.

**Literary Analysis: REPETITION**

**A** Point out Jefferson's repeated references to *tyranny* or *tyrants* (lines 35, 47, 109, 125). Why does he repeat the words so often?

**Possible Response:** A tyrant is cruel and oppressive. Jefferson is making the case that the colonists are justified in rebelling. He wants to make it clear that the king's cruel and oppressive acts have caused the rebellion.

**Literary Analysis: CAUSE AND EFFECT**

**B** As students read lines 126 to 138, have them construct a cause-and-effect graphic organizer to help them analyze the events/causes that led to the colonists' separation from the British people.

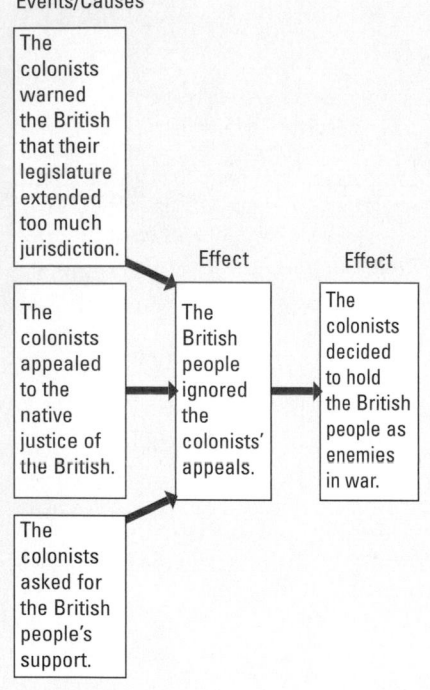

Events/Causes

The colonists warned the British that their legislature extended too much jurisdiction.

The colonists appealed to the native justice of the British.

The colonists asked for the British people's support.

Effect — The British people ignored the colonists' appeals.

Effect — The colonists decided to hold the British people as enemies in war.

---

115 He has excited domestic <u>insurrection</u> amongst us, and has endeavored to bring on the inhabitants of our frontiers the merciless Indian savages, whose known rule of warfare is an undistinguished destruction of all ages, sexes, and conditions.

120 In every stage of these oppressions we have petitioned for redress, in the most humble terms; our repeated petitions have been answered only by repeated injury. A prince whose character is thus marked by every act which may define a tyrant is unfit to be the ruler of a free people.

**A**

125 Nor have we been wanting in our attentions to our British brethren. We have warned them, from time to time, of attempts by their legislature to extend an unwarrantable jurisdiction over us. We have reminded them of the circumstances of our emigration and settlement here. We

**B**
130 have appealed to their native justice and magnanimity; and we have conjured them, by the ties of our common kindred, to disavow these usurpations, which would inevitably interrupt our connections and correspondence.

They, too, have been deaf to the voice of justice and of
135 consanguinity. We must, therefore, acquiesce in the necessity
**1** which denounces our separation; and hold them, as we hold the rest of mankind, enemies in war, in peace friends.

WE, THEREFORE, THE REPRESENTATIVES OF THE UNITED STATES OF AMERICA, in General Congress assembled,
140 appealing to the Supreme Judge of the world for the rectitude of our intentions, do, in the name and by the authority of the good people of these colonies, solemnly publish and declare, that these United Colonies are, and of right ought to be, FREE AND INDEPENDENT STATES; that they are absolved
145 from all allegiance to the British crown, and that all political connection between them and the state of Great Britain is, and ought to be, totally dissolved; and that, as free and independent states, they have full power to alliances, establish commerce, and to do all other acts and
150 things which independent states may of right do. And, for the support of this declaration, with a firm reliance on the protection of Divine Providence, we mutually pledge to each other our lives, our fortunes, and our sacred honor. ❖

**115 domestic insurrection:** George III had encouraged slaves to rebel against their masters.

**121 redress:** the correction of a wrong.

**130 native:** natural; inborn.

**[Part 4: A Statement of Independence]**

**131 conjured:** appealed to.

**135 consanguinity** (kŏn'săn-gwĭn'ĭ-tē): blood relationship.

**135–136 acquiesce** (ăk'wē-ĕs') **in the necessity which denounces:** recognize that we must demand.

**138–139** Some historians believe that this is the first appearance of the name "United States of America" in a document.

**140 Supreme Judge of the world:** God.

**144** Notice the word *states.* America would not become one united country until 1789.

**152 Divine Providence:** God in his role of controller and guardian of the world.

WORDS
TO
KNOW    **insurrection** (ĭn'sə-rĕk'shən) *n.* rebellion

276

---

## Teaching Options

### Cross Curricular Link   **History**

**THE AGE OF ENLIGHTENMENT** The 18th century, also known as the Age of Reason, was a time of optimism, discovery, and questioning. Scientists such as Isaac Newton were discovering the laws of the universe, and people began to rely on reason to analyze both the natural world and human society. Writers and philosophers such as John Locke promoted the value of education through observation and logic. In their quest for improvement, leaders of the Enlightenment began to question social values and structures. This social and cultural ferment climaxed with the Declaration of Independence. The ideals that sparked the American Revolution were the ideals of the Enlightenment. Even though many people were later appalled at the violence of the French Revolution (1789–1794), the Enlightenment's central belief in progress continued to inspire writers, thinkers, and explorers.

# *from* THE DECLARATION OF THE RIGHTS OF WOMAN

### Olympe de Gouges (ô-lamp' də goozh')

*The Declaration of Independence asserted that the people could overthrow a government if it did not protect their natural rights. In 1789, the common people in France did just that, rebelling against their king and setting up a government of their own. In August of that year, the Declaration of the Rights of Man and of the Citizen proclaimed the ideals that inspired the French Revolution. Responding to this document in 1791, the French writer and revolutionary Olympe de Gouges urged that political rights be extended to women.*

## Preamble

Mothers, daughters, sisters [and] representatives of the nation demand to be constituted into a national assembly. Believing that ignorance, omission, or scorn for the rights of woman are the only causes of public misfortunes and of the corruption of governments, [the women] have resolved to set forth in a solemn declaration the natural, inalienable,[1] and sacred rights of woman in order that this declaration, constantly exposed before all the members of the society, will ceaselessly remind them of their rights and duties; in order that the authoritative acts of women and the authoritative acts of men may be at any moment compared with and respectful of the purpose of all political institutions; and in order that citizens' demands, henceforth based on simple and incontestable principles, will always support the constitution, good morals, and the happiness of all.

Consequently, the sex that is as superior in beauty as it is in courage during the sufferings of maternity recognizes and declares in the presence and under the auspices of the Supreme Being, the following Rights of Woman and of Female Citizens.

**Article I.** Woman is born free and lives equal to man in her rights. Social distinctions can be based only on the common utility.

**Article II.** The purpose of any political association is the conservation of the natural and imprescriptible[2] rights of woman and man; these rights are liberty, property, security, and especially resistance to oppression.

**Article III.** The principle of all sovereignty rests essentially with the nation, which is nothing but the union of woman and man; no body and no individual can exercise any authority which does not come expressly from it [the nation].

**Article IV.** Liberty and justice consist of restoring all that belongs to others; thus, the only limits on the exercise of the natural rights of woman are perpetual male tyranny; these limits are to be reformed by the laws of nature and reason.

**Article V.** Laws of nature and reason proscribe all acts harmful to society; everything which is not prohibited by these wise and divine laws cannot be prevented, and no one can be constrained to do what they do not command.

**Article VI.** The law must be the expression of the general will; all female and male citizens must contribute either personally or through their representatives to its formation; it must be the same for all: male and female citizens, being equal in the eyes of the law, must be equally admitted to all honors, positions, and public employment according to their capacity and without other distinctions besides those of their virtues and talents.

---

1. **inalienable** (ĭn-āl′yə-nə-bəl): not to be taken away.
2. **imprescriptible** (ĭm′prē-skrĭp′tə-bəl): inalienable.

## Customizing Instruction

### Less Proficient Readers

**1** The use of the word *denounces* may leave students confused about Jefferson's attitude toward the British. Explain that an obsolete definition of *denounce* is "to announce, especially in a menacing way."

**2** Help students compare this document with the Declaration of Independence by asking the following questions:

- What is the purpose of this document as stated in the Preamble?
  **Answer:** The women intend to declare their rights.

- In the Articles, who is accused of tyranny?
  **Answer:** males

- What laws are cited to back up the women's claims?
  **Answer:** the laws of nature and reason

### Students Acquiring English

**3** Help students understand the meaning of difficult terms such as *incontestable*. Explain that the women feel that their demands are based on principles so basic that they cannot be disputed.

---

 ## Grammar

**CAPITALIZATION** Remind students to capitalize the names of historical documents, periods, and events in their writing.

**Exercises** Have students correct the capitalization in the following sentences.

1. The american revolution took place during a period of history that is often called the age of reason, or the age of enlightenment. *(American Revolution, Age of Reason, Age of Enlightenment)*

2. The stamp act, passed by the British government in 1765, was considered an unfair tax by the colonists. *(Stamp Act)*

3. Colonial objections to the townshend acts of 1767 led to the 1770 boston massacre. *(Townshend Acts, Boston Massacre)*

4. Several battles, including the battle of bunker hill, took place before the second continental congress declared independence. *(Battle of Bunker Hill, Second Continental Congress)*

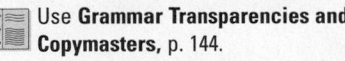 Use **Grammar Transparencies and Copymasters,** p. 144.

Use McDougal Littell's *Language Network*, Chapter 8, for more instruction and practice in capitalization.

## Literary Analysis: COMPARISON AND CONTRAST

**A** Have students consider the point the author is making with this comparison. Ask these questions: In what way is a rostrum like a scaffold? With what do you associate a scaffold? a rostrum?

**Possible Response:** They are both raised platforms around which crowds gather. The scaffold is associated with punishment and death; a rostrum might be associated with making a speech and disseminating ideas. If women are held accountable for offenses against the law and can be punished by death on the scaffold, then that same law should allow them the right to speak out in public.

## Active Reading | PARAPHRASING

**B** Ask students to paraphrase Article XVI. Then ask students to describe why this document is challenging the validity of the new government.

**Possible Response:** A majority of people in the country were not allowed to help draft the country's constitution.

**C** Ask students to paraphrase the main ideas of the Postscript. Then ask them to explain its main purpose.

**Possible Response:** Its purpose is to call women to action.

---

**Article VII.** No woman is an exception; she is accused, arrested, and detained in cases determined by law. Women, like men, obey this rigorous law.

**Article VIII.** The law must establish only those penalties that are strictly and obviously necessary, and no one can be punished except by virtue of a law established and promulgated[3] prior to the crime and legally applicable to women.

**Article IX.** Once any woman is declared guilty, complete rigor is [to be] exercised by the law.

**Article X.** No one is to be disquieted for his very basic opinions; woman has the right to mount the scaffold; she must equally have the right to mount the rostrum,[4] provided that her demonstrations do not disturb the legally established public order.

**Article XI.** The free communication of thoughts and opinions is one of the most precious rights of woman, since that liberty assures the recognition of children by their fathers. Any female citizen thus may say freely, I am the mother of a child which belongs to you, without being forced by a barbarous prejudice to hide the truth; [an exception may be made] to respond to the abuse of this liberty in cases determined by the law.

**Article XII.** The guarantee of the rights of woman and the female citizen implies a major benefit; this guarantee must be instituted for the advantage of all, and not for the particular benefit of those to whom it is entrusted.

**Article XIII.** For the support of the public force and the expenses of administration, the contributions of woman and man are equal; she shares all the duties [*corvées*] and all the painful tasks; therefore, she must have the same share in the distribution of positions, employment, offices, honors, and jobs [*industrie*].

**Article XIV.** Female and male citizens have the right to verify, either by themselves or through their representatives, the necessity of the public contribution. . . .

**Article XV.** The collectivity of women, joined for tax purposes to the aggregate of men, has the right to demand an accounting of his administration from any public agent.

**Article XVI.** No society has a constitution without the guarantee of rights and the separation of powers; the constitution is null if the majority of individuals comprising the nation have not cooperated in drafting it.

**Article XVII.** Property belongs to both sexes whether united or separate; for each it is an inviolable and sacred right; no one can be deprived of it, since it is the true patrimony[5] of nature, unless the legally determined public need obviously dictates it, and then only with a just and prior indemnity.[6]

### Postscript

Woman, wake up; the tocsin[7] of reason is being heard throughout the whole universe; discover your rights. The powerful empire of nature is no longer surrounded by prejudice, fanaticism, superstition, and lies. The flame of truth has dispersed all the clouds of folly and usurpation. Enslaved man has multiplied his strength and needs recourse to yours to break his chains. Having become free, he has become unjust to his companion. Oh, women, women! When will you cease to be blind? What advantage have you received from the Revolution? . . . Regardless of what barriers confront you, it is in your power to free yourselves; you have only to want to.

---

3. **promulgated** (prŏm′əl-gā′tĭd): announced publicly.
4. **rostrum** (rŏs′trəm): a raised platform for public speaking.
5. **patrimony** (păt′rə-mō′nē): inheritance; legacy.
6. **indemnity** (ĭn-dĕm′nĭ-tē): compensation for loss.
7. **tocsin** (tŏk′sĭn): alarm bell.

---

# Teaching Options

## Cross Curricular Link **History**

**LEGAL RIGHTS OF WOMEN IN 1776** At the time of the American Revolution, colonial women had very few rights. The unalienable rights proclaimed in the Declaration of Independence did not extend to women. They were discouraged from obtaining an education and were expected to pursue pastimes such as sewing, drawing, and music. In a few colonies, women had voting rights, based on the ownership of land. By 1787, however, women in all states except New Jersey had lost the right to vote. In 1807, women in New Jersey also lost that right. Voting rights would not be extended to women in all the states until 1920, when the Nineteenth Amendment was ratified.

## Connect to the Literature

**1. What Do You Think?** What did you learn about the Declaration of Independence that you didn't know before?

**Comprehension Check**
- What main reason for writing the Declaration is stated in the Preamble?
- According to the Declaration, what three rights do all people have?
- What are three complaints the colonists had against the king?

## Think Critically

**2.** Which reason for breaking away from British rule strikes you as most important, and why?

**THINK ABOUT**
- the colonists' philosophical ideals
- the economic and political hardships colonists suffered as a result of British policies
- the king's response to colonists' complaints

**3.** Jefferson makes it clear that America has complaints against George III, not against the British people. In what ways does the Declaration emphasize this difference, and why do you think this distinction was made?

**4.** The Enlightenment, or the Age of Reason, was a period in which logic, reason, and rational thought prevailed. What phrases and sentences in the Declaration suggest that this document was a product of the Age of Reason?

**5.** **ACTIVE READING** **PARAPHRASING** Read aloud a passage that you paraphrased in your **READER'S NOTEBOOK** and compare the paraphrase with the original passage. How does the effect on the reader change?

**6.** How do you think the statement "all men are created equal" was interpreted at the time it was written? How do Americans interpret the words today?

## Extend Interpretations

**7. Comparing Texts** What influences from the Declaration of Independence do you see on Olympe de Gouges's Declaration of the Rights of Woman (page 277)? How do the two documents differ?

**8. Connect to Life** The Declaration of Independence states the purpose of government and the conditions under which a government should be changed. How would you evaluate your local government or the present federal government, based on Jefferson's standards?

## Literary Analysis

**PARALLELISM** The use of similar grammatical forms or sentence patterns to express ideas of equal importance is called **parallelism.** Parallelism generally makes both written and spoken expression more concise and powerful. In the Declaration of Independence, for example, Jefferson uses the parallel constructions *He has refused . . . , He has forbidden . . . , He has dissolved . . .* in his list of complaints against George III. By using parallelism, Jefferson emphasizes that each of the colonists' grievances is equally important, and he cumulatively builds a case against the king.

**Paired Activity** Work with a partner to find three or more sets of parallel phrases in the Declaration of Independence. Then create a diagram like the one shown for each set of parallelisms that you find. Later, find examples of parallelism in modern political speeches or advertisements.

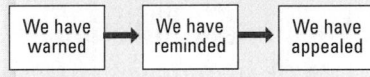

We have warned → We have reminded → We have appealed

---

## Connect to the Literature

**1. What Do You Think?**
All responses are valid.

**Comprehension Check**
- The colonists want to explain to the world their reasons for separating from England.
- life, liberty, and the pursuit of happiness
- He dissolved representative houses, refused to pass necessary laws, and kept standing armies in the colonies.

Use Selection Quiz in **Unit Two Resource Book**, p. 59.

## Think Critically

**2.** Some students will feel that having soldiers controlling the colonists was the most important reason to want independence from Britain. Other students will cite the king's unwillingness to pass important laws or even listen to the colonists' concerns. Still others will remember "taxation without representation" and the cutting off colonists' trade.

**3. Possible Responses:** The complaints all refer to the king's offenses. Jefferson may have directed his criticisms against the king in the hope of winning the support of the British people to the colonists' cause.

**4.** Students may cite the thorough and carefully thought-out language of the Preamble. Others will mention the way Jefferson logically describes the situation before talking about separating from the British government. Still others may mention the emphasis upon natural rights.

**5.** Students may mention that their paraphrases, though easier to understand, lack the elegance and eloquence of the original.

**6. Possible Responses:** When written, the statement merely stated the common assumption that free citizens were politically equal. It was not intended to mean that all had the same ability or ought to have equal wealth. It obviously did not apply to women, who could not vote, or to African Americans, many of whom were slaves. Today, the sentence suggests the right to equality of opportunity.

---

## Extend Interpretations

**Comparing Texts** Possible Responses: Influences from the Declaration of Independence include the following ideas: the authority of a government derives from the governed; the laws of nature and reason are supreme; to be just, a law must express the will of all the people. One difference is that Jefferson cites specific grievances against George III to justify the decisive step taken by the colonists; Olympe de Gouges, on the other hand, reasons from general principles—for instance, that people subject to the law must also be allowed to express their views freely.

**Connect to Life** Students may mention that one reason to change a government is its failure to protect people's rights.

## Literary Analysis

**Parallelism** Students might mention as examples of parallelism the sequence of gerund phrases found in lines 82–92: "For quartering . . . ," "For protecting . . . ," "For cutting off . . . ," and so on.

# Writing Options

1. **Modern Paraphrase** Student responses should use formal language, avoiding slang or street language. **Multiple Learning Styles**: For auditory learners, have students work in pairs; they can take turns reading aloud both the original passage and their paraphrases.

2. **Teenager's Declaration** Students' declarations should use forceful language and be logically organized. **To get students started on this assignment,** have each group brainstorm ideas. Encourage students to list all suggestions and then to evaluate them. Students should also consider listing the rights in the order of importance.

3. **Personal Response** Students' essays should be organized, with a clear beginning, middle, and end. Ideas should be clearly stated, and the voice and tone should be consistent and appropriate to the audience. Suggest that students try organizing their ideas in an outline before beginning to write.

# Activities & Explorations

1. **Taking Sides** Before they begin the debate, have the entire class brainstorm to develop a list of arguments for each side. Make sure that students listen carefully to one another and follow the established rules for the debate.

2. **First Draft Blues** Students may be tempted to make this a comedy skit. While the skit may include some humor, it should also demonstrate an understanding of the issues and challenges that Jefferson faced.

3. **Colonial Cartoon** Cartoons should be neatly drawn, with clearly legible printing. **Multiple Learning Styles: Auditory/Interpersonal**: Invite cartoonists to explain to the class how they came up with their ideas.

# Vocabulary in Action

1. incorrect
2. correct
3. incorrect
4. correct
5. correct

---

# Choices & Challenges

## Writing Options

1. **Modern Paraphrase** Looking back at the passages you paraphrased in your 📖 **READER'S NOTEBOOK**, write a more polished paraphrase of one section of the Declaration of Independence. Choose either the preamble, the declaration of rights, or the conclusion. Then share your paraphrase with the class.

2. **Teenager's Declaration** With a small group of classmates, write a declaration of independence for teenagers, following Jefferson's or de Gouges's style. Include a brief declaration of teen rights, a list of at least ten complaints, and a concluding statement of independence. Have a member of your group read the declaration to the class.

3. **Personal Response** Choose a famous phrase from the Declaration of Independence— "all men are created equal" or "life, liberty, and the pursuit of happiness"—and explore what the phrase means to you in a personal essay. You might tell how you interpret the words or whether you believe them.

## Activities & Explorations

1. **Taking Sides** With your classmates, role play an informal debate between colonists who

support independence and those who feel loyal to Great Britain, using points brought out in the Declaration to frame your argument. ~ **SPEAKING AND LISTENING**

2. **First Draft Blues** Thomas Jefferson spent two weeks writing a draft of the Declaration of Independence. Imagine that he used the same writing process as you do. Present a one-person skit for your class that shows Jefferson talking to himself as he writes. Use your own writing experiences as a guide. ~ **PERFORMING**

3. **Colonial Cartoon** Imagine that you are an 18th-century cartoonist who either supports or rejects the ideas in the Declaration of Independence. Draw an editorial cartoon that expresses your point of view. Then display your cartoon on a classroom bulletin board. ~ **ART**

## Vocabulary in Action

**EXERCISE: CONTEXT CLUES** For each sentence, determine whether the boldfaced word is used correctly or incorrectly. Write *correct* or *incorrect* on your paper.

1. Jefferson believed that King George needed to **abdicate** Benjamin Franklin in France.

2. Jefferson wrote the Declaration of Independence during a colonial **insurrection** against the king.

3. The British troops tried to **impel** their cannons at the Battle of Lexington.

4. Colonists felt that many British actions were **arbitrary,** or taken without justification.

5. Many a colonial family was forced to provide lodging to a **mercenary** in the British army.

**Building Vocabulary**

For an in-depth lesson on context clues, see page 326.

| WORDS TO KNOW | | | | |
|---|---|---|---|---|
| abdicate | arbitrary | impel | insurrection | mercenary |

---

## Teaching Options    Mini Lesson   Grammar

**VERBS: AVOIDING SHIFTS IN TENSE, MOOD, AND VOICE** Tell students that abrupt, unnecessary shifts of tense, mood, and voice make a piece of writing confusing and difficult to read.

**Instruction** Remind students to check their verbs carefully to avoid such shifts. Tell them that reading sentences aloud will often make such errors obvious. Write the following sentence on the chalkboard:

> Thomas Jefferson <u>wrote</u> the first draft of the Declaration of Independence and then changes <u>are made</u> by other members of Congress.

Underline the verbs as shown. Have students identify that the problem in this sentence is a shift from past to present tense.

**Exercises** Have students underline the verbs and then correct each sentence. Ask for volunteers to read aloud the incorrect and the correct versions of the sentences and to explain the reason for each correction.

1. The king violated the rights of the people, and it was not liked by them. (*Violated is active voice; it was not liked by them is passive. Change passive to active—they did not like it.*)

## Thomas Jefferson
### 1743–1826

**Renaissance Man** Few in American history have better fit the ideal of the Renaissance man, or a man who develops talents in many areas, than Thomas Jefferson. He was a lawmaker and writer, the author of the Virginia laws on religious freedom and of the Declaration of Independence. He was a talented scientist, with notable accomplishments in botany and agriculture. He was an architect whose Virginia home—Monticello—is considered an architectural masterpiece. An inventor, he designed such practical devices as the dumbwaiter, a revolving music stand, a better type of plow, a machine that made copies of letters, and a portable writing desk on which he probably drafted the Declaration.

**A Man of Contradictions** Jefferson was not only versatile, but he was also a complex man who often showed contradictions in his actions. He was one of the young radicals who pushed for a break with Great Britain, but he had no interest in the military, and he did not fight in the Revolutionary War. He spoke out frequently against slavery, yet he owned slaves all his life. Although he was a wealthy landowner from a prominent Southern family, he neglected to pay his debts and was plagued by financial troubles, and he passionately championed the rights of the small farmer and the average citizen.

**Early Years** Jefferson was born in Albermarle County, Virginia, on April 13, 1743. His father was a successful planter, surveyor, and mapmaker, and his mother was a member of a respected Virginia family. As a young man, he was educated at small, private schools and attended the College of William and Mary in Williamsburg. After finishing college,

Jefferson studied law. He launched a successful career as a lawyer in 1767, practicing until the American Revolution closed the courts in 1774. A few years after establishing his law practice, he married a wealthy young widow, Martha Skelton. Tragically, after only ten years of marriage, Mrs. Jefferson died, and four of the couple's six children died in childhood. Jefferson did not marry again but devoted his energies to his two surviving daughters and to public life.

**The Statesman** Jefferson distinguished himself in politics. At the age of 26, he was elected to Virginia's colonial legislature, where he befriended Patrick Henry and became an outspoken advocate of American rights. As a delegate to the Second Continental Congress, he was chosen to draft the Declaration of Independence. During the Revolutionary War, Jefferson was elected Virginia's governor in 1779. He later served as United States minister to France during the unfolding French Revolution, as the nation's first secretary of state, and as vice-president under John Adams before being elected the third president of the United States in 1800. Among his accomplishments as president were the Louisiana Purchase, which nearly doubled the size of the United States, and the Lewis and Clark expedition, which brought back invaluable scientific and cultural information about the West.

**Later Years** After two terms in office, Jefferson retired to Monticello in 1809, where he read voraciously, studied mathematics, conducted scientific experiments in farming, played the violin, and collected paintings. He founded the University of Virginia, designing the course of study as well as many of the buildings. To prevent plunging into bankruptcy, he sold his 10,000-volume library to the United States, his library formed the basis of the Library of Congress. With dramatic appropriateness, Thomas Jefferson died just hours before fellow patriot John Adams on July 4, 1826, the 50th anniversary of the adoption of the Declaration of Independence.

2. If I was one of the colonists under King George III, I would have supported independence. (*The hypothetical situation calls for subjunctive mood. Change* was *to* were.)

3. The colonists feel compelled to declare their independence because the king was a tyrant. (*Feel is present tense;* was *is past tense. Change* feel *to* felt.)

4. Jefferson wanted to include a statement about slavery in the Declaration, but the decision was made by Congress to delete it. (*Wanted is active voice;* the decision was made by Congress *is passive. Change passive to active—*Congress decided.)

 Use **Grammar Transparencies and Copymasters,** p. 120.

 Use McDougal Littell's **Language Network,** Chapter 4, for more instruction and practice in using verbs.

## OVERVIEW

### Objectives

1. understand and appreciate **literary letters** (Literary Analysis)
2. appreciate author's use of **figurative language** (Literary Analysis)
3. use strategies for reading **literary letters** (Active Reading)

### Summary

In the first letter, Phillis Wheatley replies to a letter from a clergyman in which he has defended the natural rights of Africans. Agreeing with the clergyman's arguments against slavery, she writes that civil and religious liberty are linked and that God has instilled a desire for freedom in every human. She would like to convince those who call for liberty while oppressing others that there is an inherent contradiction in their conduct.

In the second letter, Abigail Adams writes to her husband, John Adams, who is away from their Massachusetts home attending the Second Continental Congress in Philadelphia. She urges that the rebel government declare its sovereignty to the world. Finally, she takes issue with the view that men should retain absolute power over their wives, pointing out that it contradicts the rebels' calls for emancipation.

### Thematic Link

Inspired by the widespread discussion of natural rights during the **time of the Revolution,** both Phillis Wheatley and Abigail Adams argue that the **right to be free** must be extended to all, regardless of race or gender.

### 5-Minute Warm-Up

*Daily Language SkillBuilder*

Have students **proofread** the display sentences on page 131j and write them correctly. The sentences also appear on Transparency 7 of **Grammar Transparencies and Copymasters.**

# Letter to the Rev. Samson Occom

*by* PHILLIS WHEATLEY

# Letter to John Adams

*by* ABIGAIL ADAMS

**Connect to Your Life**

**What Freedom Means** What ideas and phrases come to mind when you think of the words *liberty* and *freedom?* What kinds of liberty and freedom do you believe people should have? Should all people have the same liberties and freedoms? Discuss your thoughts with a small group of classmates.

## Build Background

**Letters by Colonial Women** The two letters you are about to read are concerned with the issues of liberty and freedom. Both were written at the time of the American Revolution and provide insights into colonial life during the struggle for independence. The first letter is by Phillis Wheatley, a former slave in Boston who was the first African American to have a book of poetry published. It is believed that she was writing to her friend the Reverend Samson Occom, a converted Mohegan Indian minister, in response to his written protest against slave-owning ministers. This letter was dated February 11, 1774, and was published later in the *Connecticut Gazette* and other colonial newspapers.

The second letter is by Abigail Adams, the wife of John Adams, who became the second president of the United States. It was written to her husband shortly before the Declaration of Independence was signed. He had left their Massachusetts home in 1774 to become a delegate to the First Continental Congress in Philadelphia, and they saw each other only rarely in the ten years afterward. During this time, however, they exchanged more than 300 letters, including the one you will read. A grandson saved the letters and first published them in 1840.

> **WORDS TO KNOW**
> **Vocabulary Preview**
>
> | | |
> |---|---|
> | acquiescing | precept |
> | countenance | probity |
> | dispensation | ruminating |
> | emancipate | solicitous |
> | lethargy | vindication |

## Focus Your Reading

**LITERARY ANALYSIS   FIGURATIVE LANGUAGE**

Language that communicates ideas beyond the literal meaning of words is known as **figurative language.** Both Wheatley's and Adams's letters contain figurative language. For example, a line from Adams's letter states that one's country is a "secondary god" and the "first and greatest parent." Notice other examples of figurative language in the letters.

**ACTIVE READING   LITERARY LETTERS**

A **literary letter** is a personal letter that has been published because a well-known figure wrote it and/or because it provides information about the period in which it was written. Not only do literary letters reveal a writer's personal concerns, but they may also cast light on public issues of the writer's time.

**READER'S NOTEBOOK** As you read each letter, fill in a diagram like the one shown to separate the private and public issues that are addressed.

> **Public**
> **Private**

---

**UNIT TWO RESOURCE BOOK,** pp. 60–65

**ASSESSMENT RESOURCES**
**Formal Assessment,** pp. 51–52
**Teacher's Guide to Assessment and Portfolio Use**
**Test Generator**

**SKILLS TRANSPARENCIES AND COPYMASTERS**
**Reading and Critical Thinking**
• Making Inferences, T7 (for Active Reading, p. 282)

**Grammar**
• Verbs—Using Correct Verb Forms, T45 (for Mini Lesson, p. 288)
• Correct Verb Forms, C117 (for Mini Lesson, p. 288)

**Writing**
• Identifying Writing Variables, T2 (for Writing Options, p. 288)

**Communications**
• Interviewing, T9 (for Activities & Explorations, p. 288)

• Impromptu Speaking: Dialogue, Role-Play, Debate, T13 (for Activities & Explorations, p. 288)

**INTEGRATED TECHNOLOGY**

**Audio Library**
**LaserLinks**
• Historical Connection: Lives of Two Colonial Women Writers. See **Teacher's SourceBook,** p. 29.

**Visit our website:**
www.mcdougallittell.com

# Letter

## to the Rev. Samson Occom

Phillis Wheatley

An engraving of Phillis Wheatley. Reproduced from the collections of the Library of Congress.

Reverend and honored Sir,

"I have this day received your obliging kind epistle,[1] and am greatly satisfied with your reasons respecting the negroes, and think highly reasonable what you offer in <u>vindication</u> of their natural rights: Those that invade them cannot be insensible[2] that the divine light is chasing away the thick darkness which broods over the land of Africa;[3] and the chaos which has reigned so long, is converting into beautiful order, and reveals more and more clearly the glorious

---

1. **epistle:** letter.
2. **insensible:** unaware.
3. **divine light . . . Africa:** Wheatley is referring to the spread of Christianity to areas of Africa where it had not been practiced.

WORDS
TO
KNOW

**vindication** (vĭn′dĭ-kā′shən) *n.* the defense or justification of something, such as one's rights

283

---

### Mini Lesson  Preteaching Vocabulary

**USING CONTEXT CLUES** Call students' attention to the list of WORDS TO KNOW. Remind students that sometimes they can find clues to the meaning of a word by examining the context in which it is used. Use the model sentence to demonstrate the strategy of using context clues to make **inferences** about word meaning.

**Model Sentence**
Phillis Wheatley thought it was hypocritical for people to talk about liberty and still <u>countenance</u> the holding of slaves.

**Instruction**
• Write the model sentence on the chalkboard.
• Ask a volunteer to summarize the meaning of the sentence.
• Have students use the meaning of the sentence to infer the meaning of *countenance.*
• Ask volunteers to use *countenance* in a sentence.

Use **Unit Two Resource Book,** p. 64 for more exercises.

## TEACHING THE LITERATURE

### Customizing Instruction

**Less Proficient Readers**
Help students connect these letters to their historical context by explaining that the letters were written at a time when natural rights, equality, and personal freedom were revolutionary ideas.
**Set a Purpose** Have students read to understand Wheatley's views on freedom and equality.

**Students Acquiring English**
Students may have trouble with the formal and sometimes dated language of these letters and with the long, complex sentences. Read each letter aloud, stopping to ask volunteers to rephrase difficult passages in simpler, more contemporary language and form.

Use **Spanish Study Guide** for additional support, pp. 65–68.

**Gifted and Talented**
Invite students to note, as they read, the sentence structure and vocabulary in these 18th-century letters. Ask students to make some generalizations based on their observations. Have them hypothesize about why American usage has changed over the last two centuries.

### Reading Skills and Strategies: PREVIEW

Have students review Preparing to Read and author biographies to help understand the context of these letters.

### Active Reading  LITERARY LETTERS

 **A** Point out to students that this biblical allusion is particularly appropriate to Wheatley's audience—a clergyman. Explain that when reading a literary letter, it is helpful to keep in mind what is known about the intended recipient of the letter.

Use **Unit Two Resource Book**, p. 62 for more practice.

### Literary Analysis

FIGURATIVE LANGUAGE

 **B** Ask students to explain the visual image Wheatley creates when she personifies the principle she calls "love of freedom." What words does she use to make it seem to be alive?

**Possible Response:** The principle seems to be a great, noble beast, perhaps a lion. It "is impatient," it "pants for deliverance," and it "lives in us."

Use **Unit Two Resource Book**, p. 63 for more exercises.

## Thinking Through The Literature

1. **Comprehension Check** It isn't hard to see that demanding liberty for yourself and denying liberty to your slaves don't fit together.

2. **Possible Responses:** Her attitude toward Occom is respectful. Her attitude toward slaveholders is one of tempered anger.

3. **Possible Response:** God gave every human a love of freedom; she hopes God will make slaveholders see how absurd it is to demand freedom for themselves but to deny freedom to slaves.

---

*For in every human breast God has implanted a principle, which we call love of freedom.*

dispensation of civil and religious liberty, which are so inseparably united, that there is little or no enjoyment of one without the other: **A** Otherwise, perhaps, the Israelites had been less <u>solicitous</u> for their freedom from Egyptian slavery;[4] I do not say they would have been contented without it, by no means; for in every human breast God **B** has implanted a principle, which we call love of freedom; it is impatient of oppression, and pants for deliverance; and by the leave of our modern Egyptians[5] I will assert, that the same principle lives in us. God grant deliverance in his own way and time, and get him honor upon all those whose avarice impels them to <u>countenance</u> and help forward the calamities of their fellow creatures. This I desire not for their hurt, but to convince them of the strange absurdity of their conduct, whose words and actions are so diametrically opposite. How well the cry for liberty, and the reverse disposition for the exercise of oppressive power over others agree—I humbly think it does not require the penetration[6] of a philosopher to determine."—

*Phillis Wheatley*

---

4. **Israelites . . . Egyptian slavery:** a biblical allusion to the enslaved Jews who were led out of Egypt by Moses sometime between 1300 and 1200 B.C.

5. **modern Egyptians:** this comparison refers to the owners of African slaves.

6. **penetration:** understanding; insight.

---

## Thinking Through the Literature

1. **Comprehension Check** Paraphrase the last sentence of this letter. You could begin the paraphrase with "It doesn't take a rocket scientist. . . ."

2. How would you describe Wheatley's attitude toward Occom? toward slaveholders? Support your answer with evidence from the text.

3. How would you evaluate the case that Wheatley makes against slavery?

   THINK ABOUT
   - what she says is happening in Africa
   - what relationship she sees between civil and religious liberty
   - what she hopes God will do

---

WORDS
TO
KNOW

**dispensation** (dĭs′pən-sā′shən) *n.* distribution; giving out
**solicitous** (sə-lĭs′ĭ-təs) *adj.* full of desire; eager
**countenance** (koun′tə-nəns) *v.* to give or express approval; support

284

# Letter
## to John Adams

### Abigail Adams

This 1775 British cartoon ridicules a group of North Carolina women who, in support of the patriot cause, signed a pledge not to drink tea. Courtesy of the State Department of Cultural Resources, Divison of Archives and History, Raleigh, North Carolina.

raintree, 7 May, 1776.

How many are the solitary hours I spend, ruminating upon the past, and anticipating the future, whilst you, overwhelmed with the cares of state, have but a few moments you can devote to any individual. All domestic pleasures and enjoyments are absorbed in the great and important duty you owe your country, "for our country is, as it were, a secondary god, and the first and greatest parent. It is to be preferred to parents, wives, children, friends, and all things, the gods only excepted; for, if our country perishes, it is as impossible to save an individual, as to preserve one of the fingers of a mortified[1] hand." Thus do I suppress every wish, and silence every murmur, acquiescing in a painful

separation from the companion of my youth, and the friend of my heart.

I believe 't is near ten days since I wrote you a line. I have not felt in a humor to entertain you if I had taken up my pen. Perhaps some unbecoming invective[2] might have fallen from it. The eyes of our rulers have been closed, and a lethargy has seized almost every member. I fear a fatal security has taken possession of them. Whilst the building is in flames, they tremble at the expense of water to quench it. In short, two months have elapsed since the evacuation of

---

1. **mortified:** decayed; having gangrene.
2. **invective:** abusive language.

| WORDS TO KNOW | **ruminating** (rōō′mə-nā-tĭng) *adj.* turning a matter over and over in the mind **ruminate** *v.* |
|---|---|
| | **acquiescing** (ăk′wē-ĕs′ĭng) *adj.* consenting passively or without protest **acquiesce** *v.* |
| | **lethargy** (lĕth′ər-jē) *n.* a state of sluggishness and inactivity |

285

---

## Literary Analysis
### FIGURATIVE LANGUAGE

**A** Ask students to paraphrase this simile.

**Possible Response:** Power and liberty, like heat and moisture, need to balance each other out; too much of a good thing isn't good.

## Reading Skills and Strategies: MAKING INFERENCES

**B** Ask students to infer what Adams means in this sentence. What is the word that Congress is "hesitating so long at"?

**Possible Response:** *independence*

## Literary Analysis: AUDIENCE

**C** Invite students to discuss why Adams's letter is still read today. What contemporary audiences might be most interested in the letter?

**Possible Responses:** historians, feminists

## Active Reading | LITERARY LETTERS

**D** Point out that in literary letters to intimates, writers may jump from serious discussion of national issues to personal concerns that may or may not be related to larger issues. When reading literary letters, it is necessary to keep in mind the circumstances surrounding the letter. Tell students to ask questions such as the following:

- Do the writer and the recipient have a formal or an informal/intimate relationship?
- What problems or serious topics does the writer mention?
- What is the tone of the letter? What seems to be the mood of the writer?

---

**A** Boston,[3] and very little has been done in that time to secure it, or the harbor, from future invasion. The people are all in a flame, and no one among us, that I have heard of, even mentions expense. They think, universally, that there has been an amazing neglect somewhere. Many have turned out as volunteers to work upon Noddle's Island, and many more would go upon Nantasket, if the business was once set on foot. "'T is a maxim of state,[4] that power and liberty are like heat and moisture. Where they are well mixed, every thing prospers; where they are single, they are destructive."

A government of more stability is much wanted in this colony, and they are ready to receive it from the hands of the Congress. And since I have begun with maxims of state, I will add another, namely, that a people may let a king[5] fall, yet still remain a people; but, if a king let his people slip from him, he is no longer a king. And as this is most certainly our case, why not proclaim to the world, in decisive terms, your own importance?

**B** Shall we not be despised by foreign powers, for hesitating so long at a word?

**C** I cannot say that I think you are very generous to the ladies; for, whilst you are proclaiming peace and good-will to men, emancipating all nations, you insist upon retaining an absolute power over wives. But you must remember, that arbitrary power is like most other things which are very hard, very liable to be broken; and, notwithstanding all your wise laws and maxims, we have it in our power, not only to free ourselves, but to subdue our masters, and, without violence, throw both your natural and legal authority at our feet;—

"Charm by accepting, by submitting sway, Yet have our humor most when we obey."[6]
I thank you for several letters which I have received since I wrote last; they alleviate a tedious absence, and I long earnestly for a Saturday evening, and experience a similar pleasure to that which I used to find in the return of my friend upon that day after a week's absence. The idea of a year dissolves all my philosophy.

**D** Our little ones, whom you so often recommend to my care and instruction, shall not be deficient in virtue or probity, if the precepts of a mother have their desired effect; but they would be doubly enforced, could they be indulged with the example of a father alternately before them. I often point them to their sire,

"engaged in a corrupted state, Wrestling with vice and faction."[7]

*A. Adams*

---

3. **two months . . . Boston:** British troops under General William Howe and more than a thousand Loyalists evacuated Boston on March 17, 1776.

4. **maxim of state:** rule or short saying related to government.

5. **king:** Adams is referring to the British king George III, who ignored colonists' protests and put Massachusetts under military rule.

6. **"Charm . . . obey":** a couplet taken from Alexander Pope's poem *Moral Essays*.

7. **vice and faction:** corruption and conflict within a nation.

---

| WORDS TO KNOW | |
|---|---|
| **emancipate** (ĭ-măn′sə-pāt′) *v.* to free; liberate |
| **probity** (prō′bĭ-tē) *n.* honesty; integrity |
| **precept** (prē′sĕpt′) *n.* a rule or principle prescribing a particular course of action |

---

## Teaching Options

### ✓ Assessment **Informal Assessment**

Invite students to create a collage expressing Adams's and Wheatley's views on liberty. Students may use sketches, magazine cutouts, or any other medium to represent the authors' views. Have them share their collages in class, explaining which elements represent Adams's views and which represent Wheatley's. Ask how they decided to represent each element as they did.

**RUBRIC**

**3 Full Accomplishment** Student presents a collage that reflects full understanding of the issues raised in each letter.

**2 Substantial Accomplishment** Student presents a collage with an adequate, but less than thorough, representation of the issues.

**1 Little or Partial Accomplishment** Student presents a collage that demonstrates little or no understanding of the issues.

## Connect to the Literature

**1. What Do You Think?**
What impression of Abigail Adams do you get from her letter? Share your ideas with classmates.

> **Comprehension Check**
> • What does Adams warn will result from the congressmen's treatment of the ladies?
> • According to Adams, what should take precedence, public responsibilities or personal concerns?

## Think Critically

2. **ACTIVE READING** **LITERARY LETTERS** What private issues and what public issues do you see addressed in Adams's letter? Refer to the diagram you made in your  **READER'S NOTEBOOK.**

3. How would you describe Adams's attitude toward her husband and his work? Support your answer with evidence from the letter.

4. What can you **infer** about Adams's views on public issues?

**THINK ABOUT**
- her description of the local colonial government
- her maxim about power and liberty
- her maxim about people and a king
- her comments about women

## Extend Interpretations

5. **Comparing Texts** How similar are the purposes of Wheatley's letter and Adams's letter? Consider the private and public issues they address.

6. **What If?** If Phillis Wheatley or Abigail Adams were living today, what public issues do you think they would have addressed? What stand do you think they would have taken on these issues?

7. **Connect to Life** Adams and Wheatley did not intend their letters to be published, but many people have read and enjoyed them. Name a contemporary woman whose letters or diaries you think might be read 200 years from now, and explain why.

## Literary Analysis

 **FIGURATIVE LANGUAGE**

**Figurative language** is language that communicates ideas beyond the literal meaning of words. Two common forms of figurative language—metaphors and similes—make comparisons between two unlike things that have something in common. A **metaphor** makes the comparison directly: "Our country is a parent," for example. A **simile** states the comparison using *like* or *as*: "Our country is like a parent." Metaphors and similes in prose can make descriptions more interesting and also make unfamiliar ideas easier to understand.

**Cooperative Learning Activity**
Working with a small group of classmates, find three or four examples of figurative language in these two letters. Copy each one into a chart like the one shown. Classify each example as a simile or a metaphor, and explain what ideas the comparison suggests. Share your chart with other groups.

| Example | Simile or Metaphor? | Ideas Suggested |
|---|---|---|
|  |  |  |
|  |  |  |
|  |  |  |

---

### Connect to the Literature

**1. What Do You Think?**
Possible Responses: Adams is concerned with both personal and political matters. She seems very well-informed and educated.

**Comprehension Check**
• Possible Response: She warns that arbitrary power is usually broken, and that women will not only free themselves but subdue their "masters."
• Answer: public responsibilities

Use Selection Quiz in **Unit Two Resource Book**, p. 65.

### Think Critically

2. Possible Response: Private issues include her loneliness at being separated from her husband and their children's upbringing; public issues include the vulnerability of Boston to invasion, lack of government stability and the need to create a stable and assertive government to support liberty, and the rights of women.

3. Possible Response: She loves Adams and supports his work; later, she's ironic about his absence and his attitude toward women.

4. Possible Responses: is impatient and dissatisfied with the actions of the Congress; favors declaring sovereignty; has little respect for the king; disagrees with her husband on the rights of women

---

## Extend Interpretations

**Comparing Texts** Wheatley is more concerned with freedom for slaves, Adams with the rights of women; both support freedom for all people. Adams's letter to her husband contains personal matters.

**What If?** Possible Response: Wheatley would address continuing issues of discrimination and civil rights; Adams would address feminist issues. Both women would probably overlap in their concerns, arguing for equal rights for all oppressed groups.

**Connect to Life** Possible Responses: Mother Theresa, Oprah Winfrey, Sandra Day O'Connor, Maya Angelou. Students should be prepared to defend their choices.

## Literary Analysis

**Figurative language** helps emphasize ideas and evoke emotions. Tell students that by speaking of things as though they are other than they are, figurative language can shock us into new insights.

## Writing Options

**Literary Letter** Before they begin to write, have students identify their audience. The letter should have an appropriate tone for the chosen audience. Also, suggest that students include both public and private issues in their letters. **To make this assignment more challenging,** suggest that students write two letters, one formal and one informal. Have them compare the two letters.

## Activities & Explorations

**Talk Show** To prepare for the talk show, allow students to brainstorm questions they would like to ask the guests. Students may vote on the questions that the host will ask. Remaining questions might be put on cards, and each audience member may draw a card to use during the open-question period. Encourage students to ask follow-up questions or to depart from the prepared list of questions as needed.

## Vocabulary in Action

eager—solicitous
favor—countenance
justification—vindication
law—precept
drowsiness—lethargy
consenting—acquiescing
honesty—probity
freeing—emancipating
gift—dispensation
thinking—ruminating

---

## Writing Options

**Literary Letter** Write your own literary letter addressing the topic of liberty. As a starting point, use the comments you made in the Connect to Your Life activity (page 282). Then consider the ideas that the letters by Wheatley and Adams suggest to you. Publish your letter by displaying it in the classroom or by submitting it to the school newspaper or literary magazine. Place this piece in your **Working Portfolio.**

## Activities & Explorations

**Talk Show** With other members of your class, stage a colonial talk show with guests Phillis Wheatley and Abigail Adams. The host can introduce the guests and ask a few questions, then open up the questioning to the rest of the audience. ~ **SPEAKING AND LISTENING**

## Vocabulary in Action

**EXERCISE: ASSESSMENT PRACTICE** Read this fictitious letter by an 18th-century patriot. Rewrite the letter, replacing the underlined word or phrase with the vocabulary word that is a synonym.

> I am <u>eager</u> to learn your views on the burning issue of freedom. While I do not <u>favor</u> violence, I do think there is <u>justification</u> for recent events. It is a fundamental <u>law</u> that those who are attacked must defend themselves if they wish to escape destruction. We must shake off our <u>drowsiness</u> and prepare for war. We should neither be politely <u>consenting</u> to the king's taxes nor blindly trusting his <u>honesty</u> as he says one thing to us and does another. What choice do we have left but to prepare for <u>freeing</u> ourselves from his choking grasp? He will offer no kind <u>gift</u> of freedom, to be sure. While <u>thinking</u> about possible conflict, I pray for God's guidance.

### Building Vocabulary

Most of the Words to Know in this lesson come from Latin. For an in-depth study of word origins, see page 550.

| WORDS TO KNOW | | | |
|---|---|---|---|
| | acquiescing | lethargy | |
| | countenance | precept | solicitous |
| | dispensation | probity | vindication |
| | emancipate | ruminating | |

---

## Phillis Wheatley
### 1753?–1784

**African-born Poet** After being kidnapped by slave traders in 1761, Phillis Wheatley was brought from Africa to Boston on the slave ship *Phillis* and was bought by Susanna Wheatley, the wife of a wealthy merchant. While living at the Wheatleys, she learned English and Latin and studied literature, and she began to write poetry at about age 12. Her only book, *Poems on Various Subjects, Religious and Moral,* was published in London in 1773. That same year, she received her freedom, and a short time later she wrote the antislavery letter you have just read.

## Abigail Adams
### 1744–1818

**Colonial Commentator** Abigail Adams was the wife of President John Adams and the mother of President John Quincy Adams. Educated at home, Adams studied the works of John Milton, Alexander Pope, and William Shakespeare. When she was 15, she met John Adams, a 26-year-old Massachusetts lawyer. Five years later, in 1764, they were married. From 1774 to 1784, John was often away from home, serving first as a delegate to the Continental Congress in Philadelphia and later as a diplomat in Europe. During this period, Abigail raised four children, managed family business matters, and carried on a lively correspondence with her husband. Her letters today provide us with a vivid portrait of 18th-century life as a new nation was being born.

---

## Teaching Options

**Mini Lesson** ## Grammar

**USING CORRECT VERB FORMS** The past-tense form of a regular verb is formed by adding -ed to the infinitive. A form of the auxiliary verb *be* is used with the present participle, and a form of the auxiliary verb *have* is used with the past participle. Write this sentence on the chalkboard:

"The ink <u>has spilled</u> all over my letter!" she <u>exclaimed</u>.

Underline the verbs as shown and ask students to identify the past participle *(has spilled)* and the past tense *(exclaimed)*.

**Exercises** Have students put the verbs in parentheses into the correct past-tense form.

1. Phillis Wheatley (agree) with Reverend Occom about the rights of Africans. *(agreed)*
2. Some people who talked of natural rights and (demand) liberty for themselves (are) guilty of enslaving others. *(demanded; were)*
3. The letters that Abigail Adams (write) to her husband (has) been (publish). *(wrote; have; published)*

 Use **Grammar Transparencies and Copymasters,** p. 117.

 Use McDougal Littell's *Language Network,* Chapter 4, for more instruction and practice in verb forms.

# What Is an American?

*Essay by* MICHEL-GUILLAUME JEAN DE CRÈVECOEUR
(mē-shĕl′ gē-yōm′ zhän də-krĕv-kœr′)

### Connect to Your Life

**Defining an American** What words and phrases come to mind when you hear the word *American*? What different traits or qualities do you associate with Americans? Create a word web to explore your associations. Then as a class, discuss the question, What is an American?

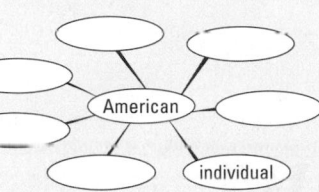

## Build Background

**An Immigrant's Impressions** During the mid-1700s, many people left Europe for the opportunity and challenge of North America. Some came to escape crowded cities, to own their own land, and to earn a better living. Others came in search of religious freedom, a life with less government interference, and the chance to have a greater voice in government.

Michel-Guillaume Jean de Crèvecoeur was a French immigrant who arrived in New York in 1759. For ten years, he traveled widely throughout the British colonies as a surveyor and a trader, finally settling on a farm he bought in New York. There, he began to write down his impressions of life in America. In 1782, under the name of J. Hector St. John, he published a collection of 12 essays called *Letters from an American Farmer*. These letters were very well received in Europe and were read by many people—some considering the voyage to America and some just curious. The selection you will read is an excerpt from one of the best known of these letters, in which de Crèvecoeur offers his definition of an American.

**WORDS TO KNOW**
**Vocabulary Preview**
allurement
despotic
kindred
servile
subsistence

## Focus Your Reading

**LITERARY ANALYSIS** | **THEME** The **theme** of a literary work is the central idea the writer wishes to share with the reader. For example, the theme of Phillis Wheatley's "Letter to the Rev. Samson Occom" is that the love of freedom is inborn in all humans. As you read this essay, consider de Crèvecoeur's ideas and think about which one is most important.

**ACTIVE READING** | **ANALYZING CONTRAST** "What Is an American?" is structured as a series of contrasts: de Crèvecoeur contrasts America and Americans with Europe and Europeans. To **contrast** two things is to state or show how they are dissimilar.

**READER'S NOTEBOOK** Copy in your notebook the chart shown. Then as you read de Crèvecoeur's essay, complete the chart by noting the contrasts he makes.

| Category | Europe/European | America/American |
|---|---|---|
| Government | "despotic prince" | a new government |
| Work | | |
| Quality of Life | | |
| Ethnic Background | | |
| Religion | | |

# OVERVIEW

 This selection is included in the **Grade 11 InterActive Reader.**

### Objectives
1. understand and appreciate an **essay** (Literary Analysis)
2. understand and appreciate use of **theme** (Literary Analysis)
3. **analyze contrast** in an essay (Active Reading)

### Summary
In this brief essay published in the 1700s, de Crèvecoeur explains that most Americans or their forebears were once the poor and oppressed of Europe. Most owned no land and had few or no political rights. Moving to America, they became citizens and were given a chance at prosperity. De Crèvecoeur believes that Americans ought to love their new country, since it offers them rewards for their labor. He concludes that an American is a new person who acts on new principles and is open to new ideas and beliefs.

### Thematic Link
Writing around the **time of the Revolution,** de Crèvecoeur describes America as a refuge for people who were poor and oppressed in Europe. In America, people of all backgrounds can prosper and enjoy their natural **right to be free.**

### 5-Minute Warm-Up

***Daily Language SkillBuilder***

Have students **proofread** the display sentences on page 131j and write them correctly. The sentences also appear on Transparency 7 of **Grammar Transparencies and Copymasters.**

---

## LESSON RESOURCES

**UNIT TWO RESOURCE BOOK,** pp. 66–70

**ASSESSMENT RESOURCES**
**Formal Assessment,** p. 53
**Teacher's Guide to Assessment and Portfolio Use**
**Test Generator**

**SKILLS TRANSPARENCIES AND COPYMASTERS**
**Literary Analysis**
• Theme in Nonfiction, T22 (for Paired Activity, p. 293)

**Reading and Critical Thinking**
• Compare and Contrast, T15 (for Active Reading, p. 289)

**Grammar**
• Verbs: Voice and Mood, C119 (for Mini Lesson, p. 294)

**Writing**
• Elaboration, T10 (for Writing Option 2, p. 294)

**INTEGRATED TECHNOLOGY**

**Audio Library**
**LaserLinks**
• Art Gallery: The "Ideal" American. See **Teacher's SourceBook,** p. 30.

**Visit our website:**
www.mcdougallittell.com

 **Preteaching Vocabulary**

If you would like to preteach the WORDS TO KNOW for this selection, use the Mini Lesson, p. 290.

**Reading Skills and Strategies:
PREVIEW**

Have students familiarize themselves
with the definitions of the WORDS TO
KNOW and footnoted words in the text
to help them understand the essay.

**Literary Analysis** THEME

Ask students the following questions:

• How, according to de Crèvecoeur, are
the poor in Europe affected by the
hardships in their lives?

**Possible Response:** They are filled with
"want, hunger, and war." They are
unable to prosper or feel fully alive and
feel no attachment to their country.

• How do the conditions in America
affect the lives of formerly poor
Europeans?

**Possible Response:** They flourish as
citizens of the new country.

 Use **Unit Two Resource Book** p. 68 for
more practice.

**Active Reading** ANALYZING CONTRAST

Ⓐ Discuss how de Crèvecoeur uses a
compare-and-contrast structure to convey his picture of America. Have students identify the contrasts between
Europe and America that he describes
in the first paragraph.

**Possible Responses:** De Crèvecoeur
says that in Europe the poor have no
country because the countries where
they live provide nothing for them. By
contrast, America provides "new laws, a
new mode of living, a new social system." They are able to flourish as citizens in America, whereas in Europe
they wilt and die.

 Use **Unit Two Resource Book** p. 67 for
more practice.

## Teaching Options

# What Is an  American?

Michel-Guillaume Jean de Crèvecoeur

Ⓐ

**In** this great American asylum,[1] the poor of
Europe have by some means met together, and in
consequence of various causes; to what purpose
should they ask one another, what countrymen
they are? Alas, two-thirds of them had no country.
Can a wretch who wanders about, who works and
starves, whose life is a continual scene of sore
affliction or pinching penury[2]—can that man call
England or any other kingdom his country? A
country that had no bread for him, whose fields
procured him no harvest, who met with nothing
but the frowns of the rich, the severity of the laws,
with jails and punishments, who owned not a
single foot of the extensive surface of this planet?
No! urged by a variety of motives, here they came.
Everything has tended to regenerate them: new
laws, a new mode of living, a new social system.
Here they are become men; in Europe they were as
so many useless plants, wanting vegetative mold[3]
and refreshing showers; they withered and were
mowed down by want, hunger, and war. But now,
by the power of transplantation, like all other
plants, they have taken root and flourished!
Formerly they were not numbered in any civil list
of their country, except in those of the poor; here
they rank as citizens. . . .

What attachment can a poor European emigrant
have for a country where he had nothing? The
knowledge of the language, the love of a few

1

---

1. **asylum** (ə-sī′ləm): a shelter.
2. **penury** (pĕn′yə-rē): extreme poverty.
3. **vegetative mold:** loose, crumbly soil that is rich in
   nutrients and helps plants grow.

 **Mini Lesson** **Preteaching Vocabulary**

**USING CONTEXT CLUES** Signal words for comparisons (*like, as, similar to*) and contrasts (*but, not,
although, however, on the other hand*) can be
used to determine meanings. Write the following
sentence on the chalkboard and help students
use context clues to determine the meaning of
*despotic.*

The leader's <u>despotic</u> actions were similar to the
actions of a bully on a playground.

**Exercises** Use context clues to determine the
meaning of the underlined words.

1. Most of the country's citizens were proud and
   independent, not meek and <u>servile</u>.
2. The patient's <u>kindred</u> were allowed into the
   hospital room, but friends were told to sit in
   the waiting room.
3. To the young actor, the <u>allurement</u> of a theater
   was like a room full of new toys to a small child.

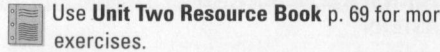 Use **Unit Two Resource Book** p. 69 for more
exercises.

**A lesson on context clues appears on page 326 in the
Pupil's Edition.**

Van Bergen Overmantel (1732–1733), attributed to John Heaten. Oil on wood (fireboard), 15¼" × 73½", New York State Historical Association, Cooperstown, New York. Photo Copyright © New York State Historical Association, Cooperstown, New York.

<u>kindred</u> as poor as himself were the only cords that tied him. His country is now that which gives him land, bread, protection, and consequence.[4] *Ubi panis ibi patria* [where my bread is earned, there is my country] is the motto of all emigrants. What then is the American, this new man? He is either a European or the descendant of a European; hence that strange mixture of blood which you will find in no other country. I could point out to you a man whose grandfather was an Englishman, whose wife was Dutch, whose son married a French woman, and whose present four sons have now four wives of different nations. *He* is an American who, leaving behind him all his ancient prejudices and manners, receives new ones from the new mode of life he has embraced, the new government he obeys, and the new rank he holds. He becomes an American by being received in the broad lap of our great alma mater.[5]

Here individuals of all nations are melted into a new race of men, whose labors and posterity will one day cause great change in the world. Americans are the western pilgrims who are carrying along with them that great mass of arts, sciences, vigor, and industry[6] which began long since in the east; they will finish the great circle. The Americans were once scattered all over Europe; here they are incorporated into one of the finest systems of population which has ever appeared, and which

will hereafter become distinct by the power of the different climates they inhabit. The American ought, therefore, to love this country much better than that wherein either he or his forefathers were born. Here the rewards of his industry follow with equal steps the progress of his labor; his labor is founded on the basis of nature, self-interest. Can it want a stronger <u>allurement</u>? Wives and children, who before in vain demanded of him a morsel of bread, now, fat and frolicsome, gladly help their father to clear those fields whence exuberant crops are to arise to feed and to clothe them all, without any part being claimed, either by a <u>despotic</u> prince, a rich abbot,[7] or a mighty lord. Here, religion demands but little of him; a small voluntary salary to the minister, and gratitude to God. Can he refuse these?

The American is a new man, who acts upon new principles; he must, therefore, entertain new ideas and form new opinions. From involuntary idleness, <u>servile</u> dependence, penury, and useless labor he has passed to toils of a very different nature, rewarded by ample <u>subsistence</u>. This is an American. ❖

---

4. **consequence:** importance.
5. **alma mater** (ăl′mə mä′tər): A Latin phrase that literally means "nourishing mother."
6. **industry:** energetic devotion to a task or endeavor; diligence.
7. **abbot** (ăb′ət): the head of a monastery.

| | WORDS TO KNOW |
|---|---|
| | **kindred** (kĭn′drĭd) *n.* relatives or family |
| | **allurement** (ə-lŏŏr′mənt) *n.* attraction; enticement |
| | **despotic** (dĭ-spŏt′ĭk) *adj.* like a dictator |
| | **servile** (sur′vəl) *adj.* humbly submissive; slavish |
| | **subsistence** (səb-sĭs′təns) *n.* livelihood |

**291**

**Active Reading** `ANALYZING CONTRAST`
Ask students what different aspects of life the proverbs address. Have them give examples of how some of the proverbs address these areas.
**Possible Response:** They address work, money, time, friendship, making use of time, and dealing with friends. The proverb "Lost time is never found again" emphasizes the value of time and the danger in wasting it.

**Reading Skills and Strategies:**
**MAKING JUDGMENTS**
**(A)** Tell students they can draw upon their own backgrounds to provide connections to the text. Do they agree with Franklin's attitude toward friends, neighbors, and visitors? Why? Have their own experiences given them different ideas about how to deal with people?
**Possible Response:** Some students might say that Franklin's attitude is cynical but accurate; others might say that Franklin is too negative. Students should refer to specific proverbs and support their opinions with examples from their own lives.

**Literary Analysis** `THEME`
**(B)** Tell students that they can compare elements across texts to help their understanding of both texts. For example, de Crèvecoeur maintains that an American enjoys freedom to work and prosper. Which of Franklin's proverbs in this section address this theme?
**Possible Responses:** "Never leave that till tomorrow . . ."; "A penny saved . . ."; "A rolling stone . . ."; "Make hay . . ."; "Little strokes . . ."

---

*from*

# Poor Richard's Almanack

Benjamin Franklin

He that cannot obey cannot command.

Don't count your chickens before they are hatched.

A mob's a monster; heads enough but no brains.

Well done is better than well said.

Lost time is never found again.

Early to bed, early to rise, makes a man healthy, wealthy and wise.

If you would know the worth of money, go and try to borrow some.

A friend in need is a friend indeed.

Fish and visitors smell in three days.

Love your neighbor; yet don't pull down your hedge.

God helps them that help themselves.

If you would keep your secret from an enemy, tell it not to a friend.

Be slow in choosing a friend, slower in changing.

Don't throw stones at your neighbors', if your own windows are glass.

Eat to live and not live to eat.

Love your enemies, for they tell you your faults.

Better slip with foot than tongue.

Three may keep a secret, if two of them are dead.

Never leave that till tomorrow, which you can do today.

A penny saved is a penny earned.

A rolling stone gathers no moss.

Make hay while the sun shines.

Beware of little expenses; a small leak will sink a great ship.

He that goes a borrowing goes a sorrowing.

Honesty is the best policy.

Little strokes fell big oaks.

He that lies down with dogs shall rise up with fleas.

**292**    UNIT TWO    PART 2: THE RIGHT TO BE FREE

---

## Teaching Options

✓ **Assessment** **Standardized Test Practice**

**PERCEIVING CAUSE AND EFFECT** For some standardized tests, students will be asked to identify cause-and-effect relationships within a work. Read aloud or write on the chalkboard the following questions:

According to de Crèvecoeur, what was the main reason why many Europeans were eager to leave the countries of their birth?

**A.** They resented the taxes they had to pay.

**B.** They lived in poverty and were not respected as equal citizens.

**C.** They resented being forced to farm land.

**D.** They felt living in America would be an exciting adventure.

**Answer:** B

What did de Crèvecoeur believe was an effect of early America's unique ethnic mix?

**A** Americans did not have a single identity or loyalty to the new society.

**B.** People enjoyed economic prosperity.

**C.** People felt ethnic tension.

**D.** People abandoned old prejudices and embraced new ideas.

**Answer:** D

## Connect to the Literature

1. **What Do You Think?**
What impressions of America and Americans do you get from de Crèvecoeur's essay?

**Comprehension Check**
• What does de Crèvecoeur say life was like for the poor of Europe?
• According to de Crèvecoeur, why should Americans love their country?

## Think Critically

2.  **ACTIVE READING** **ANALYZING CONTRAST** Refer to the chart you made in your **READER'S NOTEBOOK** to discuss the contrasts de Crèvecoeur sees between America and Europe. What do you think is the main reason that de Crèvecoeur prefers America to Europe?

3. Why do you think de Crèvecoeur feels that the American must be a "new man"?

4. To what extent do you think de Crèvecoeur's definition of an American still applies today?

**THINK ABOUT**
• groups that Crèvecoeur does not mention
• goals and lifestyles popular in America today
• how you and your classmates defined an American in the Connect to Your Life activity

## Extend Interpretations

5. **Comparing Texts** Consider what the proverbs from *Poor Richard's Almanack* (page 292) suggest about the concerns of 18th-century Americans. Is Franklin's picture of Americans consistent with de Crèvecoeur's? Explain your opinion.

6. **Critic's Corner** Critics have noted that when de Crèvecoeur writes, "Here individuals of all nations are melted into a new race," he anticipates the "melting pot" **metaphor** commonly used to describe America. Do you think "melting pot" is a good metaphor for this country? Explain why or why not. What other metaphors can you think of to describe America?

7. **Connect to Life** How similar are the motives of 18th-century immigrants and today's immigrants to the United States? Support your answer.

---

## Literary Analysis

**THEME** As you recall, the **theme** of a literary work is the central idea the writer wishes to share with the reader. This idea may be a lesson about life or about people and their actions. Sometimes, writers state the theme directly. Often, however, the reader must infer the central message. Different readers may even discover different themes in the same work. Sometimes, the title of a literary work may provide a clue about its theme.

**Paired Activity** Working with a partner, review the chart of contrasts you made in your **READER'S NOTEBOOK.** Based on these contrasts, discuss what you think is the central idea of "What Is an American?" Then write a statement that expresses de Crèvecoeur's theme. Share this statement with other pairs of classmates.

**REVIEW** **FIGURATIVE LANGUAGE**
Point out the figurative language that de Crèvecoeur uses to convey his ideas about life in Europe and America. Do you think he makes good comparisons?

---

## Connect to the Literature

1. **What Do You Think?**
Possible Response: Students might say that the essay characterizes America as a land of freedom and opportunity for poor and oppressed immigrants. Americans are portrayed as ambitious, hardworking people open to new ideas.

**Comprehension Check**
• The poor of Europe did not own land, had no political rights, and were often treated unfairly by those who were rich and powerful.
• They can own land and support their families; they need not fear tyranny.

Use Selection Quiz
**Unit Two Resource Book,** p. 70.

## Think Critically

2. **Possible Responses:** economic, social, and religious freedom; chances for prosperity; exciting new experiences; diversity of population
3. **Possible Response:** An American leaves behind "ancient prejudices and manners" to join a new society, governed by new principles and new ideas. Americans are also "new" because their mixture of ethnic backgrounds is truly unique.
4. **Possible Responses:** Students might say that Americans are still known for their ideals of freedom and individual prosperity and for ethnic diversity. Others might feel that America has become more factionalized.

## Literary Analysis

**Theme** Possible Response: The essay's central theme is that America is a land where people of different ethnic backgrounds can work hard and enjoy freedom, opportunities, prosperity, and new ideas.

**Figurative Language** Possible Response: Students should point out specific examples of figurative language, including the descriptions of America as a both a shelter and as a place in which people of different backgrounds melt together, and the description of new Americans as plants that withered in Europe but took root and flourished in America.

---

## Extend Interpretations

**Comparing Texts** Possible Response: The writings of both Franklin and de Crèvecoeur emphasize the value of hard work and self-reliance in achieving material success.

**Critic's Corner** Some students will say that America is a melting pot because people of all ethnic backgrounds come together to form one "American culture," characterized by its own unique ideals and customs. Other students might say that "melting pot" is not an accurate metaphor because people of different ethnic backgrounds do not simply blend together and abandon their individual beliefs and customs. Students should think of interesting metaphors that describe Americans as a group. For example, some students might call America a mosaic, a salad bowl, or a patchwork quilt.

**Connect to Life** Students might say that, like 18th-century immigrants, many of today's immigrants come to America for new work opportunities, for excitement, or for the purpose of making better lives for themselves and for their families.

## Writing Options

**1. Draft of Article** Students' responses should reflect an understanding of de Crèvecoeur's definition of America and an ability to define their own ideas about America. **To get students started on this assignment,** suggest that they create a rough outline that lists similarities and differences between their ideas about America and de Crèvecoeur's ideas. **To make this assignment more challenging,** ask students to read their completed magazine articles aloud to the rest of the class. Then conduct a discussion based on the articles, in which students discuss the different ideas people have about America.

**2. Local Definition** Students' letters should include concrete details about the areas in which they live. **To get students started on this assignment,** suggest that they write the name of their city or state at the top of a sheet of paper and then freewrite words and phrases that come to mind when they think of where they live. **If you wish to make this assignment easier,** have students work in pairs to create their letters.

## Vocabulary in Action

1. allurement
2. subsistence
3. servile
4. despotic
5. kindred

---

## Writing Options

**1. Draft of Article** Review the word web you created for the Connect to Your Life activity. Write a draft of a magazine article comparing and contrasting de Crèvecoeur's definition of an American with your own definition.

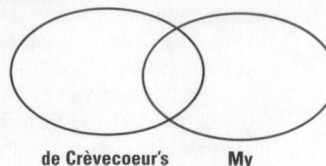

de Crèvecoeur's
Definition            My
                    Definition

**2. Local Definition** Using "What Is an American?" as a model, write a short letter to a friend who lives outside your state, defining what it means to be a resident of your area. You might answer the question "What Is a Texan?" or "What Is a Detroiter?" for example.

**Writing Handbook**
See page 1281: Explanatory Writing

## Vocabulary in Action

**EXERCISE: CONTEXT CLUES** Read the sentences below. On your paper, write the vocabulary word that best completes each sentence.

1. Immigrants found being rewarded fairly for their labor a great _____.
2. Fertile land and good weather offered farmers a good _____.
3. Colonists gladly left behind their _____ existence in Europe.
4. Immigrants often left countries that were ruled by a _____ government.
5. American colonists were frequently separated from their _____ forever.

**Building Vocabulary**
For an in-depth study of context clues see page 326.

| WORDS TO KNOW | allurement despotic | kindred servile | subsistence |
|---|---|---|---|

---

## Michel-Guillaume Jean de Crèvecoeur
### 1735–1813

**Other Works**
Sketches of Eighteenth Century America

**Coming to America** Born in Caen, France, Michel-Guillaume Jean de Crèvecoeur was educated in a Jesuit school and traveled to England as a young man. In 1755, he left England for Canada, where he enlisted in the French militia. During the French and Indian War, he served as a surveyor and a mapmaker. In 1759, de Crèvecoeur came to New York; ten years later, he married an American woman and settled down to farm.

**A Perceptive Essayist** During the period in which de Crèvecoeur lived on his farm in New York, he wrote the essays that were published in 1782 in *Letters from an American Farmer.* An immediate success in Europe, de Crèvecoeur's book provided an eyewitness account of American life in places ranging from Massachusetts to South Carolina.

**Tragic Upheavals** During the American Revolution, both the patriots and the British suspected de Crèvecoeur's loyalty because he seemed sympathetic to the British side but would not openly state his feelings. He was arrested as a spy and imprisoned by the British army in New York before sailing for Europe with his elder son in 1780. It was not until 1783, after being appointed French consul to New York, New Jersey, and Connecticut, that de Crèvecoeur was able to return to America. He found his farm burned, his wife dead, and his two other children housed with strangers in Boston. Reunited with his children in 1784, de Crèvecoeur remained in America until 1790. In that year, the "American farmer" returned to France, where he spent the last 23 years of his life.

---

## Teaching Options

## Grammar

**USING VERBS: VOICE AND MOOD** **Voice** is the form a verb takes to show whether its subject carries out the action or receives the action. Write the following sentences on the chalkboard. Underline the verbs and identify the voice of each.

European immigrants established their own rules in America. *(active)*

Individuals of all nations were melted into a new race. *(passive)*

**Mood** is the form a verb takes to show the manner in which the verb is used. Write these sentences on the chalkboard. Underline the verbs and identify their mood as shown.

The settlers planted crops. Did their farms prosper? *(indicative)*

Accept new ideas and form new opinions in America. *(imperative)*

In Europe, some wished they were living in a more democratic society. In America, leaders recommended that old ideas be changed. *(subjunctive)*

 Use **Grammar Transparencies and Copymasters,** p. 119.

 Use McDougal Littell's *Language Network,* Chapter 4, for more instruction and practice in using verbs.

# Lecture to a Missionary

*Speech by* RED JACKET

### Connect to Your Life

**Europeans and Native Americans** What do you know about the history of relations between Native Americans and white settlers? How would you describe the relationship between Native Americans and other Americans today? Discuss your ideas with a group of classmates.

## Build Background

**A Clash of Cultures** Early relations between Native Americans and white settlers were marked by the missionary impulse. In the mid-1600s, Catholic missionaries from Spain and France and Puritans from England sought to convert Native Americans to Christianity. As the United States became a nation in the late 1700s and early 1800s, a number of Protestant missionary societies sent workers to establish churches and schools on Iroquois reservations. At the time, the Iroquois consisted of six separate nations: the Seneca, Cayuga, Oneida, Onondaga, Mohawk, and Tuscarora. In the summer of 1805, Reverend Cram of the Boston Missionary Society met with Iroquois chiefs assembled at Buffalo Creek in New York and offered to instruct the Iroquois on "how to worship the Great Spirit agreeably." In the speech you are about to read, Red Jacket, a Seneca chief, responds to this offer.

## Focus Your Reading

**LITERARY ANALYSIS** **TONE** **Tone** is a writer's attitude toward his or her subject. A writer's tone might be respectful, angry, or amused, for example. Tone can be communicated through word connotations, choice of details, and direct statements of a writer's position. Consider the tone established in the first words of this speech:

> *Friend and Brother, it was the will of the Great Spirit that we should meet together this day.*

What seems to be Red Jacket's attitude toward Missionary Cram and his offer?

**ACTIVE READING** **DRAWING CONCLUSIONS ABOUT TONE** To **draw a conclusion** is to pull together pieces of information from your reading and your own experiences to make some final decision or judgment. To draw conclusions about tone, look for word connotations, revealing details, and direct statements that express the writer's or speaker's attitude. These clues may become more obvious to you if you read the speech aloud, noting the emotions you convey.

**READER'S NOTEBOOK** As you read, jot down specific words, revealing details, and direct statements that suggest Red Jacket's tone.

---

## Reading and Analyzing

**Reading Skills and Strategies:
PREVIEW**
Have students review Preparing to
Read for context.

**Literary Analysis** [TONE]

 Ask students how they would characterize Red Jacket's attitude toward
Reverend Cram and the council meeting. What specific words and phrases
convey the speaker's attitude?
**Possible Responses:** respectful, serious, friendly, patronizing. His manner of
directly addressing the missionary as
"friend" and "brother," and brief, definite sentences convey his attitude.

Use **Unit Two Resource Book**,
p. 73 for more practice.

**Active Reading**

DRAWING CONCLUSIONS
ABOUT TONE

 Draw conclusions about the tone of
this paragraph, based on Red Jacket's
choice of words and direct statements.
What is his attitude toward the missionary's goal?
**Possible Response:** Red Jacket's tone
is bitter, hurt, accusing, and sad. He
uses figurative language about Native
Americans' having no room to spread
their blanket to emphasize their desperate situation.

**C** Discuss Red Jacket's tone in this
paragraph. Does he really feel that religion will change his white neighbors?
**Possible Response:** Red Jacket is being
sarcastic. He does not seem to feel that
a change will actually occur.

Use **Unit Two Resource Book**,
p. 72 for more exercises.

## Teaching Options

# RED JACKET

# LECTURE TO A MISSIONARY

**A** Friend and Brother, it was the will of the Great Spirit that we should meet together this day. He orders all things, and has given us a fine day for our Council. He has taken his garment from before the sun, and caused it to shine with brightness upon us. Our eyes are opened, that we see clearly; our ears are unstopped, that we have been able to hear dis-tinctly the words you have spoken. For all these favors we thank the Great Spirit and Him only.

Brother, this council fire was kindled by you. It was at your request that we came together at this time. We have listened with attention to what you have said. You requested us to speak our minds freely. This gives us great joy; for we now consider that we stand upright before you, and can speak what we think. All have heard your voice, and all speak to you now as one man. Our minds are agreed.

Brother, you say you want an answer to your talk before you leave this place. It is right you should have one; as you are a great distance from home, and we do not wish to detain you. But we will first look back a little, and tell you what our fathers have told us, and what we have heard from the white people.

Brother, listen to what we say. There was a time when our forefathers owned this great island. Their seats extended from the rising to the setting sun. The Great Spirit had made it for the use of Indians. He had created the buffalo, the deer, and other animals for food. He had made the bear and the beaver. Their skins served

us for clothing. He had scattered them over the country, and taught us how to take them. He had caused the earth to produce corn for bread. All this He had done for his red children, because he loved them. If we had some disputes about our hunting ground, they were generally settled without the shedding of much blood. But an evil day came upon us. Your forefathers crossed the great water and landed on this island. Their numbers were small. They found friends and not enemies. They told us they had fled from their own country for fear of wicked men, and had come here to enjoy their religion. They asked for a small seat. We took pity on them; granted their request; and they sat down amongst us. We gave them corn and meat; they gave us poison [rum] in return.

The white people, Brother, had now found our country. Tidings were carried back, and more came amongst us. Yet we did not fear them. We took them to be friends. They called us brothers. We believed them and gave them a larger seat. At length their numbers had greatly increased. They wanted more land; they wanted our country. Our eyes were opened, and our minds became uneasy. Wars took place. Indians were hired to fight against Indians, and many of our people were destroyed. They also brought strong liquor amongst us. It was strong and powerful, and has slain thousands.

Brother, our seats were once large and yours were small. You have now become a great people, and we have scarcely a place left to spread our blankets. You have got our country, but are not

 **B**

### Mini Lesson **Vocabulary Strategy**

**UNDERSTANDING FIGURATIVE LANGUAGE**
**Instruction** Figurative language communicates
meaning beyond the literal meanings of the
words. Tell students that they can rely on context
to determine the meaning of figurative language
in a work. For example, Red Jacket states, "There
was a time when our forefathers owned this great
island. Their seats extended from the rising to the
setting sun." Students can use context clues to figure out that Red Jacket's forefathers once owned
land all over North America, from the east coast to
the west coast.

**Application** Ask students to identify the figurative
language in the passages below and rely on context clues to determine meanings.
• He (the Great Spirit) orders all things, and has
given us a fine day for our Council. He has taken
his garment from before the sun, and caused it
to shine with brightness upon us.
• Our eyes are opened, that we see clearly; our
ears are unstopped, that we have been able to
hear distinctly the words you have spoken.

Use **Vocabulary Transparencies and
Copymasters**, p. 32.

satisfied; you want to force your religion upon us.

Brother, continue to listen. You say that you are sent to instruct us how to worship the Great Spirit agreeably to his mind, and, if we do not take hold of the religion which you white people teach, we shall be unhappy hereafter. You say that you are right and we are lost. How do we know this to be true? We understand that your religion is written in a book. If it was intended for us as well as you, why has not the Great Spirit given to us, and not only to us, but why did he not give to our forefathers, the knowledge of that book, with the means of understanding it rightly? We only know what you tell us about it. How shall we know when to believe, being so often deceived by the white people?

Brother, you say there is but one way to worship and serve the Great Spirit. If there is but one religion, why do you white people differ so much about it? Why not all agreed, as you can all read the book?

Brother, we do not understand these things. We are told that your religion was given to your forefathers, and has been handed down from father to son. We also have a religion, which was given to our forefathers, and has been handed down to us their children. We worship in that way. It teaches us to be thankful for all the favors we receive; to love each other, and to be united. We never quarrel about religion.

Brother, the Great Spirit has made us all, but He has made a great difference between his white and red children. He has given us different complexions and different customs. To you

He has given the arts. To these He has not opened our eyes. We know these things to be true. Since He has made so great a difference between us in other things, why may we not conclude that he has given us a different religion according to our understanding? The Great Spirit does right. He knows what is best for his children; we are satisfied.

Brother, we do not wish to destroy your religion, or take it from you. We only want to enjoy our own.

Brother, you say you have not come to get our land or our money, but to enlighten our minds. I will now tell you that I have been at your meetings, and saw you collect money from the meeting. I cannot tell what this money was intended for, but suppose that it was for your minister, and if we should conform to your way of thinking, perhaps you may want some from us.

Brother, we are told that you have been preaching to the white people in this place. These people are our neighbors. We are acquainted with them. We will wait a little while, and see what effect your preaching has upon them. If we find it does them good, makes them honest and less disposed to cheat Indians, we will then consider again of what you have said.

Brother, you have now heard our answer to your talk, and this is all we have to say at present. As we are going to part, we will come and take you by the hand, and hope the Great Spirit will protect you on your journey, and return you safe to your friends. ❖

YOU SAY THAT **YOU** ARE **RIGHT** AND **WE** ARE **LOST.** HOW DO WE KNOW THIS TO BE **TRUE?**

LECTURE TO A MISSIONARY **297**

---

## Mini Lesson **Speaking and Listening**

**SPEECH** Tell students that "Lecture to a Missionary" is an effective speech because its speaker, Red Jacket, believes in its message and takes the time to make his argument logical and clear. Ask students to think about a world, national, or local issue that concerns them. Have each student work individually to prepare a short speech that first informs readers and listeners about the topic and then persuades people to understand his or her point of view. In preparing their speeches, students might use some of the techniques used by Red Jacket, such as asking rhetorical questions, using figurative language, presenting facts that appeal to

readers' emotions, using irony, and directly addressing a particular listener.

**Present** Have students read their speeches for the class. Remind them to use effective verbal and non-verbal strategies such as making eye contact, using gestures, and speaking clearly and at a reasonable pace. Students in the audience should provide appropriate feedback after each performance. Encourage students to apply the criteria in the rubrics in the Communication Handbook, page 1301, as they evaluate speakers' messages.

 This activity is particularly well-suited for longer class periods.

## Customizing Instruction

**Less Proficient Readers**
Tell students that the purpose of Red Jacket's "Lecture to a Missionary" is to send a strong message to white missionaries who wish to convert Native Americans to Christianity. In the speech, Red Jacket gives specific reasons why he and his people will not abandon their own religious traditions.

**Set a Purpose** Have students read to find out what Red Jacket's specific reasons against conversion are and how Red Jacket feels about the relationship between white settlers and his people.

**Students Acquiring English**
Discuss Red Jacket's use of the word *brother* throughout the selection. Red Jacket's use of this word to directly address the missionary is meant to sound friendly, but it could also have another meaning. The word, which implies a close, familiar relationship, is ironic or sarcastic because the Native Americans have not been treated as brothers by white settlers.

Use **Spanish Study Guide** for additional support, pp. 72–74.

**Gifted and Talented**
Tell students that they can recognize the distinctive characteristics of cultures through reading. As they read Red Jacket's speech, what observations can they make about the values and beliefs of Red Jacket and the Seneca people? Encourage students to consider specific references to nature, heritage, and religion. They should also note how Red Jacket and his people reacted to the needs of white settlers when they first arrived.

## GUIDING STUDENT RESPONSE

### Connect to the Literature

**1. What Do You Think?**
Students should be able to explain their opinions of Red Jacket's lecture and support their opinions with details from the text.

**Comprehension Check**
- Reverend Cram wants the Iroquois to convert to Christianity.
- The Europeans brought liquor and war.

Use Selection Quiz
**Unit Two Resource Book,** p. 74.

### Think Critically

**2.** Possible Responses: respectful, politely rejecting, ironic, distrustful

**3.** Possible Responses: He already has his own religion; Christianity is written in a book not intended for the Iroquois; historically, whites have lied to them; the missionaries have asked for money in church, despite their claim that they didn't want anything from their converts.

**4.** Possible Responses: Relations were strained, because Red Jacket mentions so many grievances against whites. Or, the peaceful, polite conduct of the council shows that relations were not that bad.

**5.** Students should support their opinions with details from the text.

---

### Connect to the Literature

**1. What Do You Think?**
What did you think of Red Jacket's lecture? Share some comments with your classmates.

**Comprehension Check**
- What does Reverend Cram want the Iroquois to do?
- State one "evil" that the Europeans brought to the Iroquois, according to Red Jacket.

### Think Critically

**2.**  **ACTIVE READING** **DRAWING CONCLUSIONS ABOUT TONE**
Review the words and passages you copied into your ▯▯**READER'S NOTEBOOK** as clues to **tone.** How would you describe Red Jacket's overall attitude toward Reverend Cram and his proposal?

**3.** In your own words, explain Red Jacket's reasons for not converting to Reverend Cram's religion. Which of these reasons seems most persuasive to you?

 **THINK ABOUT**
- the questions Red Jacket asked
- his view of his own religion and of the Great Spirit
- his observations about the missionary's meetings and about the Senecas' white neighbors

**4.** What can you **infer** from Red Jacket's speech about relations between Senecas and white settlers at the time?

**5.** What is your impression of Red Jacket as a leader? Cite passages from his speech that support your impression.

### Extend Interpretations

**6. Comparing Texts** Compare Red Jacket's speech to Reverend Cram with Patrick Henry's speech to delegates at the Virginia Convention (page 263). How are the topics of the two speeches alike, and how are they different? Is Red Jacket's attitude toward white settlers similar to or different from Henry's attitude toward the British? Explain.

**7. Connect to Life** Differences in religious views caused friction between the Senecas and the Christian missionaries who sought to convert them. What are some issues that cause conflict between Native Americans and other Americans today?

---

### Literary Analysis

**TONE** As you recall, **tone** is a writer's attitude toward a subject. De Crèvecoeur's tone in "What Is an American?" was enthusiastic; Abigail Adams's tone in her letter to her husband was alternately loving and critical, depending on the subject she was discussing. Tone is conveyed by what a writer says about a subject as well as how he or she says it. For example, de Crèvecoeur's enthusiasm for America was conveyed by his inclusion of details about free, productive farmers instead of slaves or indentured servants. His use of positive terms such as "new man" also helped convey his tone.

**Activity** Again review the clues to tone—word connotations, revealing details, and direct statements—that you put in your ▯▯**READER'S NOTEBOOK.** Then imagine you are Red Jacket's speech-writing consultant. If Red Jacket wanted to express a friendlier tone, what changes would you suggest? If he wanted to express a more defiant tone, what would you suggest? Share your recommendations with classmates.

**REVIEW** **THEME** How would you state the theme, or central idea, of Red Jacket's speech in a single sentence?

---

### Extend Interpretations

**Comparing Texts** Possible Response: Both speeches involve the liberty of an oppressed people. Henry is addressing his peers in an attempt to unite them against an adversary. Red Jacket is addressing someone from another culture who is seeking to change Red Jacket's beliefs. Henry's tone is more openly hostile than Red Jacket's.
**Connect to Life** Possible Responses: Points of conflict include land rights, fishing rights, economic development, cultural traditions, education, reparations.

### Literary Analysis

**Tone** To create a friendlier tone, Red Jacket might have softened or glossed over references to the harm done by Europeans, such as the statement "But an evil day came upon us." To create a more defiant tone, he might have openly accused the missionary of hypocrisy.
**Theme** Possible Response: Red Jacket is asking European settlers to give the Iroquois people the same rights and freedoms that settlers left Europe to find for themselves, including the freedom to choose their own religion.

# Choices & CHALLENGES

## Writing Options

**1. Mediator's Recommendations**
Consider the points of conflict between the Senecas and their white neighbors as revealed in Red Jacket's speech. Then think about ways that relations between the two groups could be improved. Write a list of recommendations that you would propose.

*Recommendations*
*1*
*2*
*3*

**2. Cram's Response** After Red Jacket spoke, he and other Senecas walked over to shake hands with Reverend Cram. The missionary refused to shake hands with them, saying there was "no fellowship between the religion of God and the devil." If, the next day, Cram had written a response to Red Jacket, what do you think he might have said? Draft a response that tries to answer Red Jacket's objections.

**3. Tolerance Pamphlet** Create a pamphlet that argues for religious tolerance. Refer to or quote Red Jacket's speech within the pamphlet.

**Writing Handbook**
See page 1285: Persuasive Writing

## Activities & Explorations

**1. Re-created Speech** Do a dramatic reading of this lecture for your class. As you prepare, keep in mind the occasion for Red Jacket's speech, and the words and phrases that most strongly communicate his tone.
~ SPEAKING AND LISTENING

**2. Mural of Seneca History** Draw a sketch that depicts an aspect of the history of the Senecas as recounted by Red Jacket in his speech. Then work with your classmates to design a mural.
~ ART

---

## Red Jacket
### 1756?–1830

**Seneca Orator** Red Jacket, whose Iroquois name, Sagoyewatha, means "He Keeps Them Awake," was a Seneca chief known for eloquent oratory. Although he did not distinguish himself in battle, he did use his oratorical skills to wage war against the European influence on Iroquois culture. Vehemently opposed to efforts to convert the Iroquois to Christianity, he led the effort to evict a local missionary after the New York legislature passed a law in 1821 forbidding white settlers from living on reservation lands.

**His English Name** During the American Revolution, the Senecas and most other Iroquois nations sided with the British. Sagoyewatha came to be known as Red Jacket after he began wearing the red military coats that British soldiers gave him. After the war, he advocated peace with the Americans. In 1792, he went to Philadelphia with other Iroquois chiefs to meet President George Washington, who gave him a silver medal.

**Ironic End** Toward the end of his life, Red Jacket experienced much turmoil. He left his wife for a few months after she became a Christian. As his power waned and his dependence on alcohol grew, he lost his chieftainship in 1827. When he died, Red Jacket, despite his wishes to the contrary, was given a Christian funeral and was buried in a missionary cemetery.

LECTURE TO A MISSIONARY **299**

---

## Writing Options

**1. Mediator's Recommendations To get students started on this assignment**, suggest that they make a list of the points of conflict between the Senecas and their white neighbors. Then ask them to think of the reason behind each conflict and brainstorm possible solutions. **If you wish to make this assignment easier,** allow students to work together in pairs or small groups to create their list of recommendations.

**2. Cram's Response To get students started on this assignment,** suggest that they consider Reverend Cram's beliefs, why he feels the Senecas must convert, and what explanation he might give for the actions of white people. **To make this assignment more challenging,** tell students to think about what tone Cram's response would have. Ask them to write their response to reflect this tone.

**3. Tolerance Pamphlet** To get students started on this assignment, ask them to review Red Jacket's speech and think about what ideas and specific lines are most moving. Then have them freewrite for several minutes about the idea of religious tolerance.

## Activities & Explorations

**1. Re-created Speech** Students should spend time preparing their interpretations and rehearsing the speech, perhaps in pairs or in small groups. They also might want to photocopy the speech and then make marks on the copy to indicate what words and phrases should be emphasized and where they might take dramatic pauses as they read. Remind students that making eye contact with the audience and using gestures can make the delivery of a speech more effective.

**2. Mural of Seneca History** Have students hold a discussion about the history of the Senecas, as described by Red Jacket. Then have them discuss what aspect of this history would make the most visually appealing mural.

---

**COMMONLY CONFUSED VERBS** The verb pairs listed below are often confused.
*affect*: "to influence"; *effect*: "to cause"
*lie*: "to rest in a flat position" or "to be in a certain place"; *lay*: "to put or place"
*sit*: "to be in a seated position"; *set*: "to put or place"
*rise*: "to move upward"; *raise*: "to move something upward"
*learn*: "to gain knowledge or skill"; *teach*: "to help someone learn"

**Exercises** For each sentence, have students choose the correct verb from the pair in parentheses.

1. Their land once extended from the (raising, <u>rising</u>) sun to the setting sun.
2. White settlers (<u>affected</u>, effected) the Senecas in a negative way.
3. Missionaries hoped that the Seneca would (<u>set</u>, sit) aside their traditional beliefs.
4. Red Jacket wanted to (<u>teach</u>, learn) the missionaries about his Great Spirit.

 Use **Grammar Transparencies and Copymasters**, p. 122.

 Use McDougal Littell's *Language Network*, Chapter 4, for more instruction and practice in verbs.

LECTURE TO A MISSIONARY **299**

## Objectives

1. understand and appreciate an **excerpt** and a **transcript of an interview** (Literary Analysis)
2. understand the **historical context** of a literary work (**Literary Analysis**)
3. analyze the structure of arguments (**Active Reading**)

## Summary

In the excerpt from *Stride Toward Freedom,* Dr. Martin Luther King, Jr., defends nonviolent resistance as a means for African Americans to achieve equality and civil rights. He states that both passive acceptance and physical violence are ineffective and immoral responses to oppression. For integration to succeed, King argues, African Americans must organize a mass movement that is both militant and nonviolent. In "Necessary to Protect Ourselves," Malcolm X argues that African Americans have the right to defend themselves in the parts of the country where the government cannot or will not protect their lives and property. He denies advocating anarchy, explaining that he respects law and order but feels that African Americans should do what is necessary to protect themselves. In closing, Malcolm X argues that the United States came into existence because oppressed people revolted and that it is only fair to expect African Americans to act in the same self-respecting way.

## Thematic Link

Martin Luther King, Jr., and Malcolm X express different views about how African Americans can protect their **right to be free.** King advocates nonviolent resistance as a response to oppression, while Malcolm X argues that African Americans should use any means possible to fight injustice.

### 5-Minute Warm-Up

***Daily Language SkillBuilder***

Have students **proofread** the display sentences on page 131k and write them correctly. The sentences also appear on Transparency 8 of **Grammar Transparencies and Copymasters.**

---

# PREPARING to *Read*

## *from* Stride Toward Freedom

*Nonfiction*
*by* MARTIN LUTHER KING, JR.

## Necessary to Protect Ourselves

*Interview with* MALCOLM X
*by Les Crane*

**Comparing Literature**

### Traditions Across Time: Demands for Equal Rights

In the time of the American Revolution, Patrick Henry, Thomas Jefferson, Abigail Adams, and others passionately voiced the ideas of equality and natural rights. Inspired by these ideas, Martin Luther King, Jr., and Malcolm X led a crusade for racial justice in the 1950s and 1960s.

**Points of Comparison** As you read, compare King's and Malcolm X's views about responding to oppression with the views of the founders of this country.

## Build Background

**Fighting for Racial Justice** Southern states in our country once had segregation laws—that is, laws that imposed social separation of races. African Americans were forced to attend separate schools and to sit in separate sections of buses and trains. Many public buildings, such as restaurants, movie theaters, and hotels, were also segregated. Through boycotts, sit-ins, and marches, African Americans and their supporters challenged segregation laws, sought better housing and jobs, and fought for voting rights in the 1950s and 1960s.

The first selection is an excerpt from *Stride Toward Freedom,* King's 1958 book about the Montgomery, Alabama, bus boycott. The second is a transcript of a 1964 television interview with Malcolm X.

| WORDS TO KNOW | **Vocabulary Preview** | |
|---|---|---|
| anarchy | indiscriminately | repudiate |
| corroding | legacy | synthesis |
| exploitation | oppressed | tacitly |
| glib | | |

## Focus Your Reading

**LITERARY ANALYSIS** **HISTORICAL CONTEXT** One way to increase your understanding of a literary work is to relate it to its **historical context,** or the social conditions that influenced its creation. As you read these selections, apply what you know about the crusade for racial justice.

**ACTIVE READING** **ANALYZING THE STRUCTURE OF ARGUMENTS** Analyzing the **structure** of a persuasive argument involves identifying the main ideas you are being asked to accept and the details (facts, examples, and reasons) that support these ideas.

**READER'S NOTEBOOK** As you read the excerpt from *Stride Toward Freedom,* complete a diagram like the one shown, noting King's ideas about methods of responding to oppression.

| Response 1: Acquiescence | Response 2: Violence |
|---|---|
| Problems | Problems |

| Response 3: _____ |
|---|
| Advantages |

---

## LESSON RESOURCES

**UNIT TWO RESOURCE BOOK,** pp. 75–80

**ASSESSMENT RESOURCES**
**Formal Assessment,** pp. 57–58
**Teacher's Guide to Assessment and Portfolio Use**
**Test Generator**

**SKILLS TRANSPARENCIES AND COPYMASTERS**
**Literary Analysis**
• Compare/Contrast Themes and Conflicts, T16 (for Extend Interpretations, item 8, p. 307)

**Reading and Critical Thinking**
• Analyzing Text Structure, T17 (for Active Reading, p. 300)

**Grammar**
• Verbs—Using Correct Verb Forms, T45 (for Mini Lesson, p. 308)
• Perfect Tenses of Verbs II, C116 (for Mini Lesson, p. 308)

**Vocabulary**
• Idioms, C36 (for Mini Lesson, p. 306)

**Writing**
• Persuasive Essay, C27 (for Writing Options, p. 308)

**Communications**
• Impromptu Speaking: Dialogue, Role-Play, Debate, T13 (for Mini Lesson, p. 305)

**INTEGRATED TECHNOLOGY**

**Audio Library**
**LaserLinks**
• Historical Connection: The Civil Rights Movement
• Author Background: Malcolm X. See **Teacher's SourceBook,** p. 32.

**Visit our website:**
www.mcdougallittell.com

from

# stride toward freedom

**Martin Luther King, Jr.**

**O**ppressed people deal with their oppression in three characteristic ways. One way is acquiescence: the oppressed resign themselves to their doom. They tacitly adjust themselves to oppression, and thereby become conditioned to it. In every movement toward freedom some of the oppressed prefer to remain oppressed. Almost 2800 years ago Moses set out to lead the children of Israel from the slavery of Egypt to the freedom of the promised land.[1] He soon discovered that slaves do not always welcome their deliverers. They become accustomed to being slaves. They would rather bear those ills they have, as Shakespeare pointed out, than flee to others that they know not of.[2] They prefer the "fleshpots of Egypt" to the ordeals of emancipation.

There is such a thing as the freedom of exhaustion. Some people are so worn down by the yoke of oppression that they give up. A few years ago in the slum areas of Atlanta, a Negro guitarist used to sing almost daily: "Been down so long that down don't bother me." This is the type of negative freedom and resignation that often engulfs the life of the oppressed.

But this is not the way out. To accept passively an unjust system is to cooperate with that system; thereby the oppressed become as evil as the oppressor. Noncooperation with evil is as much a moral obligation as is cooperation with good. The oppressed must never allow the conscience of the oppressor to slumber. Religion reminds every man that he is his brother's keeper.[3] To accept injustice or segregation passively is to say to the oppressor that his actions are morally right. It is a way of allowing his

---

1. **promised land:** in general, a longed-for place where complete satisfaction and happiness will be achieved. In the Old Testament of the Bible, the Promised Land is the land of Canaan, promised by the Lord to Abraham's descendants.

2. **bear those ills they have . . . know not of:** an allusion to a line in Act III, Scene I, of *Hamlet* by William Shakespeare.

3. **his brother's keeper:** an allusion to the biblical story of the brothers Cain and Abel. After Cain murdered Abel, God asked him where his brother was. Cain replied, "I know not; am I my brother's keeper?" In general, the saying refers to people's reluctance to accept responsibility for the welfare of others.

WORDS TO KNOW   **oppressed** (ə-prĕst') *adj.* kept down by severe and unjust use of force or authority **oppress** *v.*
**tacitly** (tăs'ĭt-lē) *adv.* silently

**301**

## TEACHING THE LITERATURE

### Customizing Instruction

**Less Proficient Readers**
Have a volunteer read the first sentence aloud. Ask what important idea the sentence states.
**Answer:** There are three ways in which people deal with oppression.
**Set a Purpose** Invite students to speculate about what the three ways are and to find out about them by reading further.

**Students Acquiring English**
Students might find the formal language of the selection challenging in places. Prepare them by discussing the main purpose of the selection. Tell students that the excerpt from *Stride Toward Freedom* describes Martin Luther King, Jr.'s beliefs about the best way for African Americans to fight oppression and injustice. You might also tell them that King makes several important allusions, or references, which are explained in the footnotes.

 Use **Spanish Study Guide** for additional support, pp. 75–78.

**Gifted and Talented**
King states that "noncooperation with evil is as much a moral obligation as is cooperation with good." Although King does not condone violence under any circumstances, he feels that people should actively resist injustice. Have students think about why cooperating with unjust policies can be just as evil as committing a violent act.

 **Preteaching Vocabulary**
Mini Lesson

**USING CONTEXT CLUES** Students can rely on context to determine the meanings of unfamiliar words. In some cases, they might find nearby words that are **synonyms**. Write the following sentences on the chalkboard and have students find a synonym for *repudiate.*

   Dr. King wanted African Americans to <u>repudiate</u> violence. He believed that they would win respect and support from other citizens only if they rejected violent tactics.
   **Answer:** *rejected*

**Exercises** Have students figure out the meanings of the underlined words.

1. People believed the speaker's words would cause <u>anarchy</u>, but no such chaos or lawlessness occurred.
2. The final plan was a combination of many different ideas, and this <u>synthesis</u> proved to be successful.
3. He <u>tacitly</u> approved of the proposal, nodding and smiling but remaining silent.
4. Some people thought her response was too <u>glib</u>, but we thought her answer was anything but thoughtless.

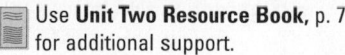 Use **Unit Two Resource Book**, p. 79 for additional support.

### Active Reading

**ANALYZING THE STRUCTURE OF ARGUMENTS**

**A** In this passage, what is King's main argument against acquiescence? What emotionally charged language does he use to appeal to the conscience of readers and make his argument stronger?

**Possible Response:** King states that African Americans will never win the respect of oppressors if they continue to acquiesce. They will only help their oppressors to become more arrogant. King appeals to the conscience of readers by accusing people who acquiesce of selling the future of their children for their own comfort.

Use **Unit Two Resource Book,** p. 77 for more practice.

### Literary Analysis

**HISTORICAL CONTEXT**

**B** Have students interpret the influences of the historical context on King's essay. Use the phrase *the present crisis* as an opportunity to ask volunteers to review their knowledge of the civil rights struggle of the 1950s and 1960s. The struggle at that time focused on overturning segregation laws, called Jim Crow laws. A turning point in the legal battle against segregation was the 1954 decision of the U.S. Supreme Court in *Brown v. Board of Education.* In this decision, the Court declared that "separate but equal" education, which had been a keystone of segregationist policy, was inherently discriminatory.

Use **Unit Two Resource Book,** p. 78 for more practice.

---

**A** conscience to fall asleep. At this moment the oppressed fails to be his brother's keeper. So acquiescence—while often the easier way—is not the moral way. It is the way of the coward. The Negro cannot win the respect of his oppressor by acquiescing; he merely increases the oppressor's arrogance and contempt. Acquiescence is interpreted as proof of the Negro's inferiority. The Negro cannot win the respect of the white people of the South or the peoples of the world if he is willing to sell the future of his children for his personal and immediate comfort and safety.

**A** second way that oppressed people sometimes deal with oppression is to resort to physical violence and corroding hatred. Violence often brings about momentary results. Nations have frequently won their independence in battle. But in spite of temporary victories, violence never brings permanent peace. It solves no social problem; it merely creates new and more complicated ones.

Violence as a way of achieving racial justice is both impractical and immoral. It is impractical because it is a descending spiral ending in destruction for all. The old law of an eye for an eye[4] leaves everybody blind. It is immoral because it seeks to humiliate the opponent rather than win his understanding; it seeks to annihilate rather than to convert. Violence is immoral  because it thrives on hatred rather than love. It destroys community and makes brotherhood impossible. It leaves society in monologue rather than dialogue. Violence ends by defeating itself. It creates bitterness in the survivors and brutality in the destroyers. A voice echoes through time saying to every potential Peter, "Put up your sword."[5] History is cluttered with the wreckage of nations that failed to follow this command.

If the American Negro and other victims of oppression succumb to the temptation of using violence in the struggle for freedom, future generations will be the recipients of a desolate night of bitterness, and our chief legacy to them will be an endless reign of meaningless chaos. Violence is not the way.

The third way open to oppressed people in their quest for freedom is the way of nonviolent resistance. Like the synthesis in Hegelian philosophy,[6] the principle of nonviolent resistance seeks to reconcile the truths of two opposites—acquiescence and violence—while avoiding the extremes and immoralities of both. The nonviolent resister agrees with the person who acquiesces that one should not be physically aggressive toward his opponent but he balances the equation by agreeing with the person of violence that evil must be resisted. He avoids the nonresistance of the former and the violent resistance of the latter. With nonviolent resistance, no individual or group need submit to any wrong, nor need anyone resort to violence in order to right a wrong.

It seems to me that this is the method that must guide the actions of the Negro in the present crisis in race relations. Through nonviolent resistance the Negro will be able to rise to the noble height of opposing the unjust system while loving the perpetrators of the system. The Negro must work passionately and unrelentingly for full stature as a citizen, but he must not use inferior methods to gain it. He **B**

---

4. **an eye for an eye:** an allusion to Exodus 21:23–25—"You shall give life for life, eye for eye, tooth for tooth, hand for hand, foot for foot."

5. **Peter . . . sword:** Peter, one of the 12 disciples of Jesus, drew his sword to protect Jesus from the soldiers who came to arrest him in the Garden of Gethsemane, but Jesus condemned Peter's use of violence.

6. **Hegelian** (hā-gā′lē-ĭn) **philosophy:** Georg Hegel (1770–1831) was a German philosopher who proposed the theory that for each idea or situation there is an opposite and that these two will eventually merge to form a unified whole.

**WORDS TO KNOW**
**corroding** (kə-rō′dĭng) *adj.* gradually destructive **corrode** *v.*
**legacy** (lĕg′ə-sē) *n.* something handed down from an ancestor or a predecessor or from the past
**synthesis** (sĭn′thĭ-sĭs) *n.* the combining of separate elements or substances to form a coherent whole

302

---

## Teaching Options

### BLOCK SCHEDULING: MANAGING TIME

**If your schedule requires that you cover the lesson objectives in a shorter time, use . . .**
- Preparing to Read, p. 300
- Thinking Through the Literature, pp. 304, 307
- Vocabulary in Action, p. 308

**If you want to take advantage of longer class time, use . . .**
- TE Teaching Options: Preteaching Vocabulary, p. 301; Test Preparation, p. 303; Speaking and Listening, p. 305; Vocabulary Strategy, p. 306
- Choices & Challenges, p. 308

" To accept passively an **unjust** system is to cooperate with that system; thereby the oppressed become as **evil** as the oppressor. "

Martin Luther King, Jr., on the march from Selma to Montgomery, Alabama, in 1965 to protest voting restrictions on African Americans.
Copyright © Bruce Davidson/Magnum Photos.

✓ **Assessment** **Test Preparation**

**IDENTIFYING THE MAIN IDEA** For some standardized tests, students will be asked to choose the main idea of a passage. To provide students with practice, read aloud or write on the chalkboard the following question:

> What is the main idea of the passage in which Dr. King shares his beliefs about the passive acceptance of injustice?

**A.** People who are worn down by oppression are often not capable of fighting injustice.

**B.** Passive acceptance of injustice is cowardly and shows support for the evil actions of the oppressor.

**C.** Passive acceptance is preferable to violence in most situations.

**D.** There are times when people will accept injustice passively in order to protect themselves.

Help students through the process of choosing B as the correct answer. Point out that, although several statements express important ideas found in the passage, the best answer is the statement that completely expresses the main idea.

**A** Ask students to use their knowledge of history to interpret this paragraph and answer the following questions: Why would African Americans be encouraged to leave the South at this time? Why would simply avoiding the South go against Dr. King's beliefs?

**Possible Response:** Jim Crow laws existed in the South. Leaving the South at a time when it was filled with hatred and segregation would have shown passivity. Dr. King believed that not challenging unjust and abusive laws was cowardly and immoral.

**Active Reading**

ANALYZING THE STRUCTURE OF ARGUMENTS

**B** Students should analyze Dr. King's argument for using his methods to achieve racial equality. What three elements does King say are indispensable to racial progress?

**Answer:** mass movement, militancy, and nonviolence

Invite students to analyze and discuss King's use of the word *militant* in combination with *nonviolent*. What message is he trying to send?

**Possible Response:** *Militant* means "aggressive, vigorous, ready to fight," but King refers to moral, not physical, fighting. He wants people to understand that they can be militant without being violent.

---

must never come to terms with falsehood, malice, hate, or destruction.

**A** Nonviolent resistance makes it possible for the Negro to remain in the South and struggle for his rights. The Negro's problem will not be solved by running away. He cannot listen to the glib suggestion of those who would urge him to migrate en masse[7] to other sections of the country. By grasping his great opportunity in the South he can make a lasting contribution to the moral strength of the nation and set a sublime example of courage for generations yet unborn.

**B** By nonviolent resistance, the Negro can also enlist all men of good will in his struggle for equality. The problem is not a purely racial one, with Negroes set against whites. In the end, it is not a struggle between people at all, but a tension between justice and injustice. Nonviolent resistance is not aimed against oppressors but against oppression. Under its banner consciences, not racial groups, are enlisted.

**B** If the Negro is to achieve the goal of integration, he must organize himself into a militant and nonviolent mass movement. All three elements are indispensable. The movement for equality and justice can only be a success if it has both a mass and militant character; the barriers to be overcome require both. Nonviolence is an imperative in order to bring about ultimate community.

A mass movement of a militant quality that is not at the same time committed to nonviolence tends to generate conflict, which in turn breeds anarchy. The support of the participants and the sympathy of the uncommitted are both inhibited by the threat that bloodshed will engulf the community. This reaction in turn encourages the opposition to threaten and resort to force. When, however, the mass movement repudiates violence while moving resolutely toward its goal, its opponents are revealed as the instigators and practitioners of violence if it occurs. Then public support is magnetically attracted to the advocates of nonviolence, while those who employ violence are literally disarmed by overwhelming sentiment against their stand. ❖

---

7. **en masse** (ŏn măs′): in one group or body; all together.

### Thinking Through the Literature

1. **Comprehension Check** Which two methods of responding to oppression does King oppose, and which does he support?

2. ACTIVE READING   ANALYZING STRUCTURE   Refer to the diagram you made in your 📖 READER'S NOTEBOOK. What are King's reasons for opposing the first two methods he discusses?

3. Of the reasons King favors the third response to oppression, which reason do you find the most persuasive, and why?

WORDS TO KNOW
**glib** (glĭb) *adj.* showing little thought, preparation, or concern
**anarchy** (ăn′ər-kē) *n.* absence of any form of political authority
**repudiate** (rĭ-pyōō′dē-āt′) *v.* to reject the validity or authority of

---

## Teaching Options

### Thinking Through the Literature

1. **Comprehension Check** King opposes violence and acquiescence. He supports nonviolent resistance.

2. Possible Responses: Problems with acquiescence—it makes people part of an evil system; it suggests oppression is moral; it can't win respect. Problems with violence—it doesn't solve problems in the long run; it's immoral; it leads to destruction, not understanding.

3. Possible Response: Students should support their responses with solid reasons. Some students might feel that the fact that nonviolent resistance is noble and attracts people to a cause is persuasive. An important part of waging a successful campaign is winning support.

# necessary to protect ourselves

## Malcolm X

**Interviewed by Les Crane**

**Crane:** You've been a critic of some of the Negro leadership in this country—Martin Luther King, Roy Wilkins, Abernathy,[1] and others—have you changed in your feelings toward them of late?

**Malcolm X:** I think all of us should be critics of each other. Whenever you can't stand criticism you can never grow. I don't think that it serves any purpose for the leaders of our people to waste their time fighting each other needlessly. I think that we accomplish more when we sit down in private and iron out whatever differences that may exist and try and then do something constructive for the benefit of our people. But on the other hand, I don't think that we should be above criticism. I don't think that anyone should be above criticism.

**Crane:** Violence or the threat of violence has always surrounded you. Speeches that you've made have been interpreted as being threats. You have made statements reported in the press about how the Negroes should go out and arm themselves, form militias of their own. I read a thing once, a statement I believe you made that every Negro should belong to the National Rifle Association—

**Malcolm X:** No, I said this: That in areas of this country where the government has proven its—either its inability or its unwillingness to protect the lives and property of our people, then it's only fair to expect us to do whatever is necessary

to protect ourselves. And in situations like Mississippi, places like Mississippi where the government actually has proven its inability to protect us—and it has been proven that ofttimes the police officers and sheriffs themselves are involved in the murder that takes place against our people—then I feel, and I say that anywhere, that our people should start doing what is necessary to protect ourselves. This doesn't mean that we should buy rifles and go out and initiate attacks indiscriminately against whites. But it does mean that we should get whatever is necessary to protect ourselves in a country or in an area where the governmental ability to protect us has broken down—

---

1. **Roy Wilkins, Abernathy:** Roy Wilkins (1901–1981) was executive secretary of the National Association for the Advancement of Colored People (NAACP) from 1955 to 1977. Ralph Abernathy (1926–1990) was a close friend of Martin Luther King, Jr., and helped him found the Southern Christian Leadership Conference to combat racism.

WORDS TO KNOW

**indiscriminately** (ĭn′dĭ-skrĭm′ə-nĭt-lē) *adv.* randomly

305

---

**Mini Lesson** **Speaking and Listening**

**DEBATE** Have students prepare to debate this question: In resisting oppression, should people use only nonviolent measures, or should they resort to more aggressive measures in certain situations? Students should draw upon the ideas and arguments presented by King and Malcolm X. Divide the class into two groups according to their views about this issue. Each side should formulate an argument and support it with reasons and examples.

**Debate** After students have prepared their arguments, ask both sides to meet for a debate. In conducting the debate, follow a pattern of allowing one side to make a point and the other side to offer its rebuttal. Students on both sides should show that they clearly understand both arguments and that they have used critical thinking to build strong cases.

**BLOCK SCHEDULING** This activity is particularly well-suited for longer class periods.

## Active Reading

### ANALYZING THE STRUCTURE OF ARGUMENTS

**(A)** Tell students that an effective argument is always supported by concrete reasons and examples. Why does Malcolm X mention the FBI? How does this reference help to support his argument?

**Possible Response:** The FBI, which is supposed to be the strongest law enforcement agency in the country, has failed to protect African Americans. His point is that if this agency won't protect him, he must do what he can to protect himself.

**(B)** What examples does Malcolm X provide to support his argument for justified violence? Do students feel that these examples support his argument?

**Possible Response:** He describes vigilante committees organized in New York to protect neighborhoods, and he describes the revolt of the American colonists against British rule. Students might say that the examples help to validate Malcolm X's argument—that African Americans should have the same rights as others to defend themselves.

### Reading Skills and Strategies: COMPARING AND CONTRASTING

Invite students to compare and contrast the language and form of King's essay with the language and form of this interview. What did students like or dislike about each form? Did they feel one was more informative than the other? What was the main difference in language and word choice?

**Possible Responses:** Students might say that the essay used formal and vivid language, while the interview transcript was more conversational. While one form is a finished piece, the other form allows for more spontaneity.

## Teaching Options

---

**"My belief in brotherhood would never restrain me in any way from protecting myself in a society from a people whose disrespect for brotherhood makes them feel inclined to put my neck on a tree at the end of a rope."**

Malcolm X with his daughters Qubilah and Attallah in 1962. Photo by Robert L. Haggins.

**Crane:** Therefore you do not agree with Dr. King's Gandhian philosophy[2]—

**Malcolm X:** My belief in brotherhood would never restrain me in any way from protecting myself in a society from a people whose disrespect for brotherhood makes them feel inclined to put my neck on a tree at the end of a rope.[3] *[Applause]*

**Crane:** Well, it sounds as though you could be preaching a sort of an anarchy—

**(A)** **Malcolm X:** No, no. I respect government and respect law. But does the government and the law respect us? If the FBI, which is what people depend upon on a national scale to protect the morale and the property and the lives of the people, can't do so when the property and lives of Negroes and whites who try and help Negroes are concerned, then I think that it's only fair to expect elements to do whatever is necessary to protect themselves.

And this is no departure from normal procedure. Because right here in New York City you have vigilante committees[4] that have been set up by groups who see where their neighborhood community is endangered and the law can't do anything about it. So—and even their lives aren't at stake. So—but the fear, Les, seems to come into existence only when someone says Negroes should form vigilante committees to protect their lives and their property.

I'm not advocating the breaking of any laws. But I say that our people will never be respected as human beings until we react as other normal, intelligent human beings do. And this country came into existence by people who were tired of tyranny and oppression and exploitation and the brutality that was being inflicted upon them by powers higher than they, and I think that it is only fair to expect us, sooner or later, to do likewise. ❖

---

2. **Gandhian** (gän′dē-ĭn) **philosophy:** Mohandas Gandhi (1869–1948) was an Indian nationalist and spiritual leader who developed the practice of nonviolent civil disobedience that forced Great Britain to grant independence to India in 1947.

3. **put my neck . . . rope:** an allusion to the practice of lynching. Many African Americans were executed by whites without due process of law, especially by hanging.

4. **vigilante** (vĭj′ə-lăn′tē) **committees:** volunteer groups of citizens that without lawful authority assume powers such as pursuing and punishing suspected criminals or offenders.

WORDS TO KNOW

**exploitation** (ĕk′sploi-tā′shən) *n.* use of another person or group for selfish purposes

306

---

## Mini Lesson **Vocabulary Strategy**

### UNDERSTANDING CONNOTATIONS AND IDIOMS

**Instruction** Denotation is the literal meaning of a word. Connotation refers to the emotional response evoked by a word. Writers use words that not only express ideas, but also evoke emotional associations. For example, Martin Luther King, Jr., writes that African Americans must work "passionately" for full stature as citizens. A word similar in denotation to *passionately* is *enthusiastically*. While *enthusiastically* connotes an action that is cheerfully spirited, *passionately* connotes a more serious action, driven by emotion and need.

An idiom is an expression whose meaning differs from the meanings of the individual words. For example, Martin Luther King, Jr., refers to the Israelites leaving Egypt for the "promised land." The phrase "going to the promised land" has become an idiom meaning "going to a desired place where happiness will be found."

**Practice** Have students work in pairs to find the denotative and connotative meanings of the following words from the selections: *evil, corroding, freedom,* and *brutality.*

Use **Vocabulary Transparencies and Copymasters,** p. 33.

# *Thinking* through the LITERATURE

## Connect to the Literature

**1. What Do You Think?**
What is your response to the ideas Malcolm X expresses in this interview? Share your first thoughts in a small group.

**Comprehension Check**
• According to Malcolm X, when is violence justifiable?
• In explaining what to expect from African Americans, to what historical event does Malcolm X refer?

## Think Critically

**2.**  **ACTIVE READING | ANALYZING STRUCTURE** What are the main positions Malcolm X takes in this interview, and what are his supporting reasons? Create a diagram to represent his argument.

**3.** Malcolm X compares the oppression of African Americans with that of American colonists under King George III. He believes that "it is only fair to expect" African Americans to react to tyranny as the revolutionaries did. Do you agree?

**4.** Based on these two selections, which leader do you regard as more persuasive—King or Malcolm X?

 **THINK ABOUT** { • each leader's intellectual arguments
• each leader's emotional appeals
• each leader's **tone,** or attitude

**5.** Which leader do you think is more revolutionary—King or Malcolm X?

**THINK ABOUT** { • what "revolutionary" means to you
• each leader's arguments and results

**6.** In your view, are the similarities between King and Malcolm X more important, or are the differences? Explain.

## Extend Interpretations

**7. Connect to Life** Both King and Malcolm X fought for justice for African Americans in the 1950s and 1960s. Name political, religious, or social causes that people are fighting for in the United States today. What are the most effective methods used to promote these causes?

**8.** **Points of Comparison** Based on "Speech in the Virginia Convention," what do you imagine Patrick Henry might have said about King's advocacy of nonviolent resistance?

## Literary Analysis

**HISTORICAL CONTEXT**
The **historical context** of a literary work refers to the social conditions that inspired or influenced its creation. Patrick Henry, for example, protested against the British military buildup in the colonies in his "Speech in the Virginia Convention" on page 263. In *Stride Toward Freedom,* King uses the phrase "the present crisis in race relations." To understand this phrase, readers must apply what they know about the civil rights struggle of the 1950s and 1960s. This struggle sought to overturn segregation laws in the South—laws which, as you learned in Build Background on page 300, sanctioned racial separation.

**Cooperative Learning Activity**
Working in a small group, reread "Necessary to Protect Ourselves." Identify sentences in the selection that refer to events or conditions at the time of the interview or to public figures that Malcolm X is reacting to. To interpret comments in their historical context, research each of these events, conditions, or individuals. Then write a note that provides useful background information. Compile the notes in a Guide for Reading, modeled on the one that accompanies "Speech in the Virginia Convention," on page 263.

**REVIEW | ALLUSION** Identify the Biblical **allusions** in the excerpt from *Stride Toward Freedom.* How do they make King's writing more persuasive? Which one do you think is most important to the selection, and why?

---

## Extend Interpretations

**Connect to Life** Responses will vary. Students' responses should focus on what methods of promoting causes seem to be effective and why. Students should relate these methods to the ideas expressed by King or Malcolm X.
**Points of Comparison** Possible Response: Patrick Henry would have rejected nonviolent resistance as ineffective when the oppressor is armed and ready to use force.

## Literary Analysis

**Historical Context** Tell students that they can locate relevant print and nonprint information using technical resources such as the Internet or a library database.
**Allusion** Students should list King's references to Moses and the "promised land," to Cain and Abel, to the "eye for an eye" philosophy, and to Peter, who drew his sword to protect Jesus. Students should explain how these allusions support King's ideas.

---

## Connect to the Literature

**1. What Do You Think?**
Some students may agree that people who are oppressed in a society should stop at nothing to fight for their civil rights, while others may feel that violence is an inappropriate response to any situation.

**Comprehension Check**
• Violence is justifiable when citizens must protect themselves from injustice because the government has failed to do so.
• Malcolm X refers to the American Revolution.

## Think Critically

**2.** Possible Response: Malcolm X takes the position that people must protect themselves when their government fails to do so. He argues that it is only fair and understandable that African Americans try to protect themselves and stand up for their rights as other groups of people have done. He states that in the long run, this is the only way that African Americans will earn respect as equal human beings.

**3.** Possible Response: Students may say the two situations are comparable and that violence is a justifiable means to an end. Others may disagree, saying that many African Americans followed Dr. King's leadership, refusing to resort to violence.

**4.** Possible Response: Some students will find King more persuasive because of his highly moral stance and his carefully reasoned arguments. Others may find Malcolm X more persuasive because of his practicality and his call for self-respect.

**5.** Accept all reasonable, well-supported responses.

**6.** Possible Response: Some students may say that although King and Malcolm X have different views about how to achieve civil rights, their beliefs that society must change and that African Americans must be relentless in their pursuit of equality are similar. Other students might feel that King's and Malcolm X's views about the use of violence set them far apart.

# Writing Options

**Points of Comparison To get students started on this assignment,** suggest that they make a chart in which they list each speaker's main points about the use of violence to achieve a goal. Under each main point, students should list each speaker's supporting arguments. Students can review this chart and then reach their own conclusions about this issue. **To make this assignment more challenging,** invite volunteers to read their essays aloud. Students listening can ask questions and try to challenge the reader's assertions.

# Author Background

**The Montgomery Bus Boycott**
The 1955 bus boycott in Montgomery, Alabama, was sparked by an incident involving Rosa Parks, an African American who was riding home on a city bus after a hard day's work. On all buses in Montgomery at the time, whites sat in the front seats and African Americans sat in the back. Parks was sitting in the front row of the African American section of the bus, when the driver ordered her to move so that a white passenger could sit. Parks, who was tired, refused to move for the man. She was promptly arrested for breaking a Jim Crow Law. Her arrest sparked anger among African Americans. They protested by boycotting Montgomery's bus system. The boycott, led by twenty-six-year-old Martin Luther King, Jr., was an effective form of nonviolent resistance, as most of the bus system's passengers were African Americans. Despite the loss of money, the bus system refused to revoke its Jim Crow laws. African Americans firmly held their stance, opting to walk, organize car pools, or take taxis to work. Finally, one year later, the U.S. Supreme Court stepped in and declared segregation on city buses unconstitutional. This boycott was an impressive and important victory for the African American community.

# Writing Options

**Points of Comparison** Write notes and organize them for a persuasive essay about the use of violence to achieve a goal. As you develop your views, consider the ideas of King and Malcolm X as well as those of Patrick Henry. Place this piece in your **Working Portfolio.**

**Writing Handbook**
See page 1285: Persuasive Writing

## Martin Luther King, Jr.
**1929–1968**

**Other Works**
"Letter from Birmingham Jail"
(See excerpt on pages 1137–1145.)
*Why We Can't Wait*
*Where Do We Go from Here*

**Called to Leadership** The Reverend Dr. Martin Luther King, Jr., was the pastor of a Baptist church in Montgomery, Alabama, in 1955 when a woman named Rosa Parks was arrested for refusing to give up her bus seat to a white passenger as the local segregation law then required. Civil rights activists in Montgomery organized a boycott of buses by African Americans and selected King as their leader. A little over a year after the boycott began, the U.S. Supreme Court determined that segregated seating on public buses in Montgomery violated the Constitution.

**Crusader for Justice** The successful Montgomery bus boycott launched King's career in the civil rights movement. He went on to develop a reputation as a powerful leader and a brilliant orator. In his most famous speech, "I Have a Dream," he electrified more than 200,000 demonstrators gathered for the March on Washington in August 1963. The following year, Congress passed the landmark Civil Rights Act of 1964, and King received the Nobel Peace Prize. For the rest of his life, King continued to work for justice and equality. He was killed by an assassin's bullet on April 4, 1968, in Memphis, Tennessee.

# Vocabulary in Action

**EXERCISE: WORD KNOWLEDGE** For each vocabulary word, write a sentence describing a situation in which the word could be applied.

1. oppressed
2. tacitly
3. corroding
4. legacy
5. synthesis
6. glib
7. anarchy
8. repudiate
9. indiscriminately
10. exploitation

**Building Vocabulary**
For an in-depth lesson on how to expand your vocabulary, see page 126.

## Malcolm X
**1925–1965**

**Other Works**
*The Autobiography of Malcolm X*
*Malcolm X Talks to Young People*

**Symbolic Name** While in prison for burglary from 1946 to 1952, Malcolm Little converted to the faith of the Nation of Islam (popularly known as the Black Muslims), a militant religious and cultural community that believed in black separatism. Like many members of that group, he took the name "X" as a symbol of his lost African name.

**Dynamic Speaker** Malcolm X was one of the most powerful speakers of his time, and he won many converts to the Nation of Islam. However, in 1964, after a disagreement with Nation of Islam leader Elijah Muhammad, Malcolm X left the sect and founded his own organization. On a pilgrimage to Mecca, he saw Muslims of all races joined in common faith and soon embraced the possibility of cooperation among races.

**Final Years** The rivalry between Malcolm X and the Nation of Islam grew, resulting in violence and threats against his life. On February 21, 1965, some members of the organization shot Malcolm X to death as he spoke at a rally in Harlem.

## Mini Lesson Grammar

**PAST PERFECT TENSE** The past perfect tense is used to describe a past action that happened before another past action. This tense consists of the auxiliary verb *had* and the past participle of a verb. Display the following sentence:

> Yesterday we watched that documentary on Malcolm X because our teacher <u>had told</u> us it was interesting.

**Exercise** Ask students to identify the past perfect tenses in the following paragraph and explain why this tense was used in each situation.

> We read books about Martin Luther King, Jr., and Malcolm X yesterday because we <u>had</u> <u>heard</u> about their lives in school last week. If Martin Luther King, Jr., <u>had chosen</u> another profession in his youth, the civil rights movement would not have benefited from his energy and brilliance. People were drawn to his powerful speeches and his commitment to nonviolent protest. Many people chose to join the movement only after they <u>had heard</u> his ideas.

 Use **Grammar Transparencies and Copymasters,** p. 115.

 Use McDougal Littell's *Language Network*, Chapter 4, for more instruction and practice in verb tenses.

## *from* I Am Joaquín / Yo Soy Joaquín

### Poetry *by* RODOLFO GONZALES

**Comparing Literature**

## Traditions Across Time: Demands for Equal Rights

"The Declaration of Independence" proclaimed the basic rights of all citizens to life, liberty, and the pursuit of happiness. To extend these rights to African Americans, Martin Luther King, Jr., Malcolm X, and others spearheaded the civil rights movement in the 1950s and 1960s. Inspired by this movement, other minority groups asserted their right to equality. *I Am Joaquín / Yo Soy Joaquín,* by Rodolfo Gonzales, is a famous poem associated with the Chicano movement.

**Points of Comparison**  Consider what this poem has to do with revolution and what it has in common with the other selections in this part of Unit Two.

## Build Background

During the 1960s, Chicanos—residents of the United States who trace their ancestry to Mexico—demanded economic justice and equal rights. In California, Cesar Chavez organized the United Farm Workers Union and led a successful strike against grape growers. New political groups such as the Alianza in New Mexico, La Raza Unida in Texas, and the Crusade for Justice in Colorado spoke out for the rights of Chicanos. Groups of Chicano students throughout the southwestern states that were once part of Mexico protested unfair treatment and promoted pride in their Chicano heritage.

The Chicano movement inspired much new poetry, prose, and drama. *I Am Joaquín/Yo Soy Joaquín* is one of the earliest and most widely read works associated with the movement. Reprinted here are excerpts from the beginning and the end of this book length poem by social activist Rodolfo Gonzales. In its entirety the poem describes the modern dilemma of Chicanos in the 1960s, then outlines 2,000 years of Mexican and Mexican-American history, highlighting the different, often opposing strains that make up the Chicano heritage.

## Focus Your Reading

**LITERARY ANALYSIS  EPIC POEM**  An **epic** is a long narrative poem on a serious subject presented in an elevated or formal style. Ancient epic poems, such as *The Odyssey,* trace the adventures of a hero who performs courageous, even superhuman deeds. As you read *I Am Joaquín,* a modern epic poem, consider what makes the speaker heroic.

**ACTIVE READING  STRATEGIES FOR READING EPIC POETRY**  The length of an epic poem poses challenges to the reader, who must keep track of many events and details. One way to increase your understanding of Gonzales's poem is to identify its epic characteristics.

**READER'S NOTEBOOK**  While reading, fill in a chart like the one shown. Jot down evidence from the poem for each of the characteristics listed.

| Epic Characteristics | Evidence |
| --- | --- |
| **1.** Hero with high ideals | |
| **2.** Courageous deeds | |
| **3.** Large-scale setting | |
| **4.** Universal ideas | |

## Reading and Analyzing

**Reading Skills and Strategies:
PREVIEW**
Have students read the poem quickly the first time through to get a sense of the speaker and issues being raised.

**Active Reading**

**STRATEGIES FOR READING EPIC POETRY**

 As students begin reading, have them explore why *I Am Joaquín* is appropriately classified as a modern epic poem. Remind students that an epic is a long, serious narrative poem that often traces the adventures of a brave hero. Encourage students to create a chart on a separate sheet of paper in which they can list heroic qualities of the speaker and details that characterize the poem as an epic.

Use **Unit Two Resource Book**,
p. 81 for more practice.

**Literary Analysis** EPIC POEM

**B** In some epic poems, the actions of the epic hero often determine the fate of a nation or a group of people. Judging from this passage, whose fate is hanging in the balance? What struggle does Joaquín, speaking for this group of people, face?

**Possible Response:** The fate of Chicano people is in question. The speaker and other Chicano people must struggle to maintain a cultural identity in a world that does not seem to value Chicano culture or goals that don't involve gaining material wealth.

Use **Unit Two Resource Book**,
p. 82 for more practice.

# I AM JOAQUÍN

*Rodolfo Gonzales*

### from **I Am Joaquín**

I am Joaquín,
lost in a world of confusion,
caught up in the whirl of a
            gringo society,
5   confused by the rules,
scorned by attitudes,
suppressed by manipulation,
and destroyed by modern society.
My fathers
10     have lost the economic battle
and won
        the struggle of cultural survival.
And now!
    I must choose
15                between
    the paradox of
victory of the spirit,
despite physical hunger,
            or
20     to exist in the grasp
of American social neurosis,
sterilization of the soul
        and a full stomach. . . .

**1**

### de **Yo Soy Joaquín**

Yo soy Joaquín,
perdido en un mundo de confusión,
enganchado en el remolino de una
            sociedad gringa,
5   confundido por las reglas,
despreciado por las actitudes,
sofocado por manipulaciones,
y destrozado por la sociedad moderna.
Mis padres
10     perdieron la batalla económica
y conquistaron
        la lucha de supervivencia cultural.
Y ¡ahora!
    yo tengo que escojer
15                en medio
    de la paradoja de
triunfo del espíritu,
a despecho de hambre física,
            o
20     existir en la empuñada
de la neurosis social americana,
esterilización del alma
        y un estómago repleto. . . .

## Teaching Options

### BLOCK SCHEDULING: MANAGING TIME

**If your schedule requires that you cover the lesson objectives in a shorter time, use . . .**
• Preparing to Read, p. 309
• Thinking Through the Literature, p. 316

**If you want to take advantage of longer class time, use . . .**
• TE Teaching Options: Viewing and Representing, p. 311; Speaking and Listening, p. 312; Cross-Curricular Link, p. 313; Vocabulary Strategy, p. 314; Informal Assessment, p. 315
• Choices & Challenges and Author Activity, p. 317

Detail of *The Farmworkers of Guadalupe* (1990), Judith F. Baca. From *The Guadalupe Mural*, acrylic on plywood, 8′ × 7′. Copyright © J. Baca, photo by R. Rolle.

## Customizing Instruction

**Less Proficient Readers**

**1** Have students read the first eight lines and then stop to discuss Joaquín's feelings.

**Set a Purpose** Have students continue to read to find out how Joaquín feels about his place in American culture.

**Students Acquiring English**
Invite Spanish-speaking students to choose stanzas to read aloud in the original Spanish and then to summarize in English what the stanzas mean to them.

Use **Spanish Study Guide** for additional support, pp. 79–81.

**Gifted and Talented**
Students should practice comparing and contrasting literary elements such as theme, conflict, and style across texts that are similar in form. For example, suggest that students compare and contrast these excerpts from *I Am Joaquín* with other epic poems they may be familiar with, such as *The Odyssey* or *The Iliad*. What does the epic hero in this poem seem to have in common with other epic heroes? In what ways is his experience different from that of other heroes?

**Less Proficient Readers**

**2** Ask students to summarize Joaquín's feelings toward himself and society so far.

**Possible Response:** He feels that he has to struggle for cultural survival in an unfriendly society.

|  |  |
|---|---|
| I shed the tears of anguish<br>25   as I see my children disappear<br>behind the shroud of mediocrity,<br>never to look back to remember me.<br>I am Joaquín.<br>     I must fight<br>30         and win this struggle<br>        for my sons, and they<br>        must know from me<br>        who I am. **B** **2** | Lloro lágrimas de angustia<br>25   cuando veo a mis hijos desaparecer<br>detrás de la mortaja de mediocridad,<br>para jamás reflexionar o acordarse de mí.<br>Yo soy Joaquín.<br>     Debo pelear<br>30         y ganar la lucha<br>        para mis hijos, y ellos<br>        deben saber de mí,<br>        quien soy yo. |

I AM JOAQUÍN   **311**

---

**Mini Lesson**  ## Viewing and Representing

*The Farmworkers of Guadalupe* **by Judith F. Baca**

**ART APPRECIATION** This detail is from a mural in Leroy Park, Guadalupe, Mexico.

**Instruction** Tell students it is important to notice the ways in which figures are arranged. Why do students think the artist shows workers both in the distance and up close?

**Possible Responses:** The artist wants people to view the people in the painting both as a group and as individuals. Allowing viewers to look into the faces of individual workers helps them con-

nect to the people in the painting.

**Application** Ask students what the choice of colors implies about the artist's attitude toward her subject.

**Possible Response:** The predominant colors are blue and green. The workers themselves, the conveyor belt, and the crates are painted in contrasting tones of yellow and orange. The artist may be suggesting that the workers have been severed from their connection to nature by the mechanized work they are forced to do.

## Reading and Analyzing

### Reading Skills and Strategies: AUTHOR'S PURPOSE

 **A** Tell students they can learn to recognize distinctive characteristics of cultures through reading. What do they learn about Chicano heritage in this passage? What was the author's purpose for including this information?

**Possible Response:** As a people Chicanos have had to fight other cultures for survival for many years. The author might have included this information so that readers would appreciate the trying experiences of this culture as well as the speaker's anger and determination.

### Literary Analysis: POINT OF VIEW

Ask students to characterize the point of view of the speaker. Make sure they understand that Joaquín speaks not just for himself, but for all Chicanos.

**Possible Response:** The speaker is a strong survivor who has endured many hardships.

### Literary Analysis  EPIC POEM

Point out to students that *I Am Joaquín*, like other epic poems, recounts courageous and heroic deeds that represent the ideals and values of a particular culture. Ask students what values these deeds in *I Am Joaquín* seem to represent.

**Possible Responses:** endurance, hard work, persistence, determination, hope

### Active Reading

STRATEGIES FOR READING EPIC POETRY

Ask students to find evidence of adventure, courageousness, and high ideals in this passage.

Copyright © 1978 George Ballis/Take Stock, San Rafael, California.

Part of the blood that runs deep in me
35  could not be vanquished by the Moors.[1]
I defeated them after five hundred years,
and I endured.
    Part of the blood that is mine
    has labored endlessly four hundred
40  years under the heel of lustful
        Europeans.[2]
        I am still here!
I have endured in the rugged mountains
    of our country.
45  I have survived the toils and slavery
    of the fields.
        I have existed
in the barrios of the city
in the suburbs of bigotry
50  in the mines of social snobbery
in the prisons of dejection
in the muck of exploitation
and
in the fierce heat of racial hatred.
55  And now the trumpet sounds,
the music of the people stirs the
        revolution.
Like a sleeping giant it slowly  **1**
rears its head
60  to the sound of
                tramping feet
                clamoring voices
                mariachi strains
        **2**     fiery tequila explosions
65          the smell of chile verde and
        soft brown eyes of expectation for a
                        better life.

**A**

_____

1. **Moors** (mōōrz): followers of the religion of Islam who conquered Spain during the 700s and who lost most of their territory there by the late 1200s.
2. **labored . . . Europeans:** In 1521, Hernándo Cortés, a Spanish conquistador, conquered the Aztec empire, located in the area around present-day Mexico City. The speaker suggests that the native population has been dominated by Europeans ever since.

**312**  UNIT TWO  PART 2: THE RIGHT TO BE FREE

## Teaching Options

(Mini Lesson) **Speaking and Listening**

**POETRY READING WORKSHOP** Explain to students that the language of poetry is meant to be read and heard aloud. Organize students into pairs and have each pair practice reading excerpts from *I Am Joaquín* aloud. As students practice reading their poems aloud, they should concentrate on hearing rhythms and on changing pace and pitch to match content.

**Present** Have students present interpretations of the poem. Students in each pair can take turns reading lines. Discuss as a class the different interpretations of the same poem. Students should show that they've used effective listening strategies.

BLOCK SCHEDULING  This activity is particularly well-suited for longer class periods.

Parte de la sangre que corre hondo en mí
35  no pudo ser vencida por los moros.
Los derroté después de quinientos años,
y yo perduré.
            La parte de sangre que es mía
            ha obrado infinitamente cuatrocientos
40          años debajo el talón de europeos
                lujuriosos.
                      ¡Yo todavía estoy aquí!
He perdurado en las montañas escarpadas
    de nuestro país.
45  He sobrevivido los trabajos y esclavitud
    de los campos.
                Yo he existido
en los barrios de la ciudad
en los suburbios de intolerancia
50  en las minas de snobismo social
en las prisiones de desaliento
en la porquería de explotación
y
en el calor feroz de odio racial.
55  Y ahora suena la trompeta,
la música de la gente incita la
                revolución.
Como un gigantón soñoliento lentamente
alza su cabeza
60  al sonido de
                patulladas
                voces clamorosas
                tañido de mariachis
            explosiones ardientes de tequila
65      el aroma de chile verde y
    ojos morenos, esperanzosos de una
                    vida mejor.

313

### Cross Curricular Link    History

**CESAR CHAVEZ** Cesar Chavez (1927–1993) was a Chicano labor leader known for his work with migrant farm workers. Born in Yuma, Arizona, Chavez grew up working in migrant labor camps and knew firsthand the hardships migrant workers faced. Chavez's work for migrant farm workers began in 1962, when he organized a union that eventually became known as the United Farm Workers (UFW). The union fought unfair working conditions using nonviolent types of protest such as fasts, picketing, marches, and boycotts. Chavez and the UFW were able to get some growers to create workers' contracts, raise pay, and improve living conditions for workers. One of Chavez's most successful protest campaigns was launched in 1965, against California grape growers. Chavez convinced people all over the country to boycott grapes until growers agreed, in 1970, to improve working conditions for laborers.

## Customizing Instruction

### Gifted and Talented
Ask students to discuss other ethnic groups, in the present and in the past, that have experienced oppression and the effects of prejudice. Ask them to compare and contrast the experiences of these groups with the experiences described in this poem. Why do they think this type of oppression occurs?

### Less Proficient Readers
**1** Be sure students understand the writer's image of the sleeping giant raising its head. Explain to them that the writer is comparing the impending revolution to a sleeping giant who is slowly awakening. Ask them the following questions: In what ways, according to the speaker in previous lines, has the revolutionary spirit been "asleep"? By comparing the revolution to a "giant" rather than to an average person, what is the speaker saying about the size and force of the impending revolution?

### Multiple Learning Styles
**Visual Learners**
**2** In lines 58–67, the writer is trying to paint a picture with words of the impending revolution of Chicano culture. Ask students to close their eyes and try to picture the image of revolution and of Chicano culture that the writer creates. Then ask them to think of their own images of revolution.

# Reading and Analyzing

## Literary Analysis  EPIC POEM

Ask students who the hero of this poem is. Make sure they understand that the hero is the Chicano race as a group rather than any single man. Have students discuss what makes the Chicano people heroic in the poem.

**Possible Responses:** their survival, persistence, hard work, courage

## Reading Skills and Strategies: AUTHOR'S PURPOSE

**(A)** Have students read the last two lines of the poem aloud. Ask them to explain the author's purpose in ending the poem with capital letters and exclamation points. What attitude is the author trying to express at the conclusion of the poem and why?

**Possible Responses:** The poet is trying to express a defiant, determined, celebratory, and hopeful attitude. He wants readers to feel that the Chicano culture is triumphant and will survive.

## Active Reading

STRATEGIES FOR READING EPIC POETRY

Ask students to name one universal idea expressed by this modern epic poem.

**Possible Responses:** triumph of the oppressed over the oppressor; the fight against mediocrity; the fight to maintain one's identity against odds

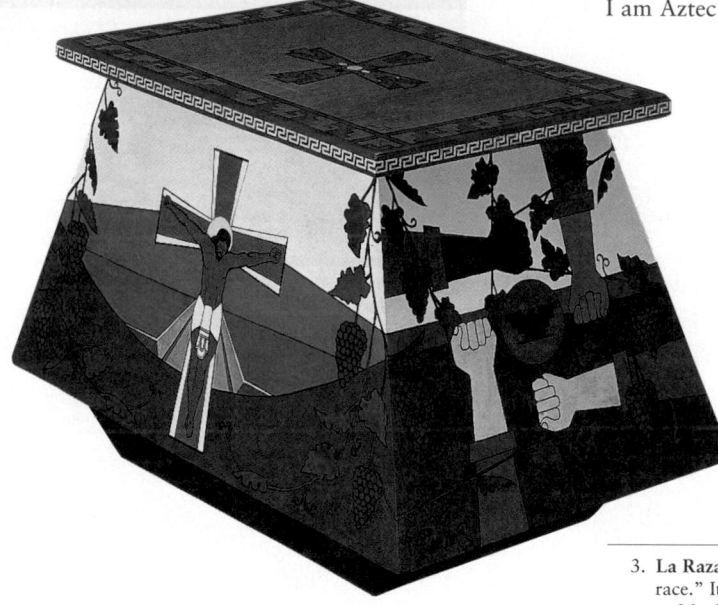

*Farm Workers' Altar* (1967), Emanuel Martinez. Acrylic on wood, 37½″ × 53″ × 35½″, UCLA at The Armand Hammer Museum of Art and Cultural Center, Los Angeles.

And in all the fertile farmlands,
        the barren plains,
70  the mountain villages,
smoke-smeared cities,
      we start to MOVE.
    La Raza![3]
Méjicano!
75    Español!
      Latino!
        Hispano!
          Chicano!
or whatever I call myself,
80           I look the same
           I feel the same
           I cry
             and
           sing the same.
85 I am the masses of my people and
I refuse to be absorbed.
        I am Joaquín.
The odds are great
but my spirit is strong,
90           my faith unbreakable,
           my blood is pure.
I am Aztec prince and Christian Christ.
      I SHALL ENDURE!   **A**
      I WILL ENDURE!

---

3. **La Raza** (lä rä′sä): literally, the term means "the race." It refers to people who trace their heritage to Mexico.

---

# Teaching Options

 **Mini Lesson** ## Vocabulary Strategy

**RESEARCHING WORD ORIGINS: *Epic*** Tell students that researching word origins can help them understand word meanings and the derivations of certain words. Explain that the word *epic* is based on the Latin root *epicus,* from the Greek *epikos,* from *epos,* which means "song" or "word." In addition to detailing heroic feats, epics are characterized by their oral tradition. *Epic* is also a derivative of the Indo-European root *wek* ("to speak"), along with *vocal, advocate, vocation,* and *provoke.*

**Application** Have students work in pairs to define *vocal, advocate, vocation,* and *provoke* and then write a short paragraph that uses each word in a sentence. Ask students to describe how they can use knowledge of the roots *epos* and *wek* to remember the meanings of these words.

📄 Use **Vocabulary Transparencies and Copymasters,** p. 34.

**A lesson on word origins appears on p. 550 in the Pupil's Edition.**

Y en todos los terrenos fértiles,
                        los llanos áridos,
70  los pueblos montañeros,
ciudades ahumadas,
                empezamos a AVANZAR.
    ¡La Raza!
¡Méjicano!
75  ¡Español!
        ¡Latino!
            ¡Hispano!
                ¡Chicano!
o lo que me llame yo,
80              yo parezco lo mismo
                yo siento lo mismo
                yo lloro
                        y
                canto lo mismo.
85  Yo soy el bulto de mi gente y
yo renuncio ser absorbido.
            Yo soy Joaquín.
Las desigualdades son grandes
pero mi espíritu es firme,
90                  mi fé impenetrable,
                    mi sangre pura.
Soy príncipe azteca y Cristo cristiano.
            ¡YO PERDURARÉ!
            ¡YO PERDURARÉ!

Copyright © 1978 George Ballis/Take Stock, San Rafael, California.

## Customizing Instruction

### Students Acquiring English
Write the terms *la raza, méjicano, español, latino, hispano,* and *chicano* on the chalkboard. Ask Spanish-speaking students to explain the differences between these terms and to tell which they prefer to use.

### Less Proficient Readers
Ask students to summarize what Joaquín asserts about the past and the future of the Chicano people.
**Possible Response:** that they have survived oppression and that they will endure as a proud people

### Multiple Learning Styles
**Auditory Learners**
Have students listen to the audiotape of *Yo Soy Joaquín,* paying attention to how the poem's rhythm and sound convey its emotions. Students might also want to prepare their own audiotapes of the poem.

✓Assessment **Informal Assessment**

**DEFINING CHARACTER** Ask students to work in pairs to elaborate on the sentence "I Am Joaquín," creating an extended definition of the narrator. Have the partners take turns making a statement beginning "I Am Joaquín" and then giving an item of information and interpretation— for example, "I Am Joaquín. My heritage is part Native American, part Spanish." If partners disagree about each other's interpretations, they should work to understand each other's reasoning.

**RUBRIC**

**3 Full Accomplishment** The pair generates numerous statements demonstrating understanding of the poem and its narrator.

**2 Substantial Accomplishment** The pair generates statements demonstrating accurate, but superficial, understanding of the poem and its narrator.

**1 Little or Partial Accomplishment** The pair generates few statements and shows little understanding of the poem and its narrator.

## Connect to the Literature

**1. What Do You Think?**
Guidelines for student response: Students should articulate specific thoughts based on the text.

**Comprehension Check**
- According to the speaker, his fathers have lost the economic battle and won the battle of cultural survival.
- The speaker wishes that his children will have cultural identity and pride in their Chicano heritage.

## Think Critically

**2.** Possible Responses: Some students may envision a political rebellion. Others may see a spiritual revolution leading to increased cultural awareness.

**3.** Possible Response: Students should give concrete examples of Joaquín's heroic qualities and ideas. For the second part of the question, some students may say that Joaquín represents all Chicano people. Others may say that he represents a certain hero from Mexican history or that he represents a fictional individual.

**4.** Students' responses should show careful thought about the difference between achieving economic success and achieving spiritual/cultural growth. Students should explain why economic success might interfere with cultural survival, using elements of the text to defend or clarify their positions. Students might also draw from their own experiences or from the experiences of people they know.

**5.** Possible Response: Some students will say that the intended audience is the Chicano people and that the intended effect is to foster pride in heritage, along with positive social action. Others may say the poem was also written to express the feelings of Chicano people to a general audience.

## Connect to the Literature

**1. What Do You Think?**
What immediate thoughts or questions do you have after reading these excerpts? Share them in class.

**Comprehension Check**
- According to the speaker, what struggle have his fathers won and what struggle have they lost?
- What does the speaker wish for his children?

## Think Critically

**2.** What kind of revolution do you think the speaker is calling for? Explain.

**3.** **ACTIVE READING** | **STRATEGIES FOR READING EPIC POETRY**
What evidence do you see that Joaquín is a hero with high ideals? Refer to the chart you made in your **READER'S NOTEBOOK.** Then tell whom or what you think Joaquín represents.

**THINK ABOUT** {
- who the speaker says he is
- the references to the past and future

**4.** In lines 9–23, the speaker suggests that economic success is incompatible with cultural and spiritual survival. Do you agree with this view? Give reasons to support your opinion.

**5.** Analyze this poem as an effort to persuade. Who do you believe is the intended audience, and what do you think the poet wants the audience to do, think, or feel?

## Extend Interpretations

**6. Critic's Corner** In his introduction to *I Am Joaquín/Yo Soy Joaquín,* Rodolfo Gonzales has written, "Ultimately, there are no revolutions without poets." What do you think he means by this? In what way would his poem contribute to a revolution?

**7.** **Points of Comparison** Both "What Is an American?" and *I Am Joaquín/Yo Soy Joaquín* attempt to define a new race of people. Compare and contrast the "new men" idealized in each work, paying special attention to the forces that created them.

## Literary Analysis

**EPIC POEM** *I Am Joaquín/Yo Soy Joaquín* is subtitled *An Epic Poem.* As you remember, an **epic poem** is a long narrative poem on a serious subject presented in an elevated or formal style. An epic poem traces the adventures of a hero who performs courageous, even superhuman, deeds. Such deeds often represent the ideals and values of a group of people, such as a nation or a race.

For example, Odysseus, the hero of Homer's ancient epic *The Odyssey,* is supremely clever, defeating monsters and other enemies by tricking them. He also is a great warrior, killing all the men who have pursued his wife while he was away. Odysseus' deeds show that the ancient Greeks valued wit, fighting skill, and fidelity.

**Cooperative Learning Activity**
Get together with a small group of classmates to review the charts you made in your **READER'S NOTEBOOK.** Then discuss Joaquín's deeds—his triumphs and sufferings. What can you conclude about the ideals and values of Mexican Americans, based on Joaquín's deeds? Write a group statement and share it with other groups. If you are ambitious, you might obtain the full text of *I Am Joaquín* to better see its epic elements.

## Extend Interpretations

**Critic's Corner** Possible Response: Poets can move people to social activism by appealing to their emotions and giving voice to their sense of cultural pride.

**Points of Comparison** In "What Is an American?" Americans are a new kind of people, open to new ideas and beliefs, people who have come to the United States to escape the oppression of their homes in Europe; de Crèvecoeur sees America as a place where people are rewarded for their hard work. In "Yo Soy Joaquín," Chicanos do not enjoy the freedom and prosperity of those earlier European immigrants. They must struggle to maintain their cultural identity and overcome oppression in America.

## Literary Analysis

**Epic Poem** Have students discuss the values and ideals of Joaquín and the Chicano people. How do they compare or contrast to other familiar epic heroes like Odysseus?

# *Choices &* CHALLENGES

## Writing Options

**1. Book Review** *I Am Joaquín/Yo Soy Joaquín* was first published in 1967. Based on the excerpts you have read, how relevant do you believe the poem is today? Explain your opinion in a book review.

**2.** **Points of Comparison**
Of the other works in this part of the unit, "The Right to Be Free," which do think is closest in spirit to Gonzales's poem? Defend your choice in a brief essay,

pointing out the connections you see. Place this piece in your **Working Portfolio.**

## Activities & Explorations

**1. Choral Reading** Many theater groups have performed dramatizations of *I Am Joaquín/ Yo Soy Joaquín.* With a group of classmates, plan and present a dramatic reading of these excerpts from the poem. Consider assigning

different voices or groups of voices to different phrases or verses.
~ **SPEAKING AND LISTENING**

**2. Language Study** Compare the English and Spanish versions of the poem. Do you notice words that are similar in two languages? Are there similarities in word order? If you know Spanish, evaluate how well this poem has been translated. Are there lines you would render differently in English? ~ **WORLD LANGUAGES**

---

## Rodolfo Gonzales
1928–

**Chicano Voice** A poet and a leader of the Chicano movement, Rodolfo "Corky' Gonzales has devoted his life to promoting the pride and power of the Chicano people. He founded the Crusade for Justice, an organization based in Denver, Colorado, to promote political action among Chicano youth. During the 1968 Poor People's March, Gonzales presented the "Plan of the Barrio," a declaration demanding rights for Chicanos. Later, the Crusade for Justice proposed "The Spiritual Plan of Aztlán," which identified the Southwestern United States as Aztlán, the mythical place of origin of the Aztecs. By linking Chicano identity to pre-Columbian history, Gonzales connected modern Chicano concerns to the long history of the Chicano people.

**Former Boxer** Born in Denver to a family of migrant workers, Gonzales began working in the fields in the spring and summer by the time he was ten. During the fall and winter, he went to

public school in Denver, graduating from high school at age 16. Gonzales, a skilled boxer, won a Golden Gloves championship and a National Amateur Athletic Union championship, then turned professional. Before he retired from the ring in 1955, he was a contender for the world featherweight championship.

**Social Activist** After he left professional boxing, Gonzales became active in politics. He organized the Viva Kennedy presidential campaign in Colorado during the 1960 elections and subsequently served in a variety of government posts. In 1966, however, he left government service to devote himself full time to promoting Chicano issues.

### Author Activity

Think again about Gonzales's statement, "Ultimately, there are no revolutions without poets." Discuss other individuals who merge art with social activism as Gonzales does.

---

## **Mini Lesson** Grammar

**PROBLEMS IN USING VERB TENSES** A shift in verb tense is needed when two events occur at different times or out of sequence. The tenses of the verbs should clearly show that one action occurred before the other. Show students the following sentence:

> I **felt** that the poem **was** interesting to read, and I know that next year's students **will enjoy** it. (*The speaker has already read the poem, so this part of the sentence uses past tense. Other students will read the poem in the future, so this part of the sentence is in future tense.*)

**Exercises** Have students rewrite the following

sentences, choosing the correct verb from each pair in parentheses.

**1.** *I Am Joaquín* explores the experiences of Chicano people; the poet (felt, <u>feels</u>) that young people today do not know their heritage.

**2.** The poet says his culture is in danger and (struggled, <u>struggles</u>) for survival.

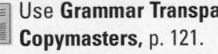 Use **Grammar Transparencies and Copymasters,** p. 121.

 Use McDougal Littell's *Language Network,* Chapter 4, for more instruction and practice in using verb tenses.

---

## Writing Options

**1. Book Review** Student responses should touch on current issues of equality, such as affirmative action. **To get students started on this assignment,** have them discuss different issues that affect immigrants and ethnic groups today. Then have students connect these issues to those faced by the speaker of the poem. You might ask them to consider whether maintaining one's cultural identity in the United States today seems to be easier or harder than it was in 1967, when this poem was published.

**2. Points of Comparison** Essays should reflect shared issues, such as cultural identity, American identity, and oppression. **To get students started on this assignment,** suggest that they review each of the works in this part of the unit, taking brief notes as they read. Their notes should reflect the main ideas in each work.

## Activities & Explorations

**1. Choral Reading** Give students time to rehearse their dramatic readings in their groups. Students in each group who are **musical learners** might want to choose appropriate background music or sound effects to accompany the dramatic reading.

**2. Language Study** Invite students to try reading the Spanish version of the poem aloud to appreciate the sound of the language. If there are Spanish-speaking students in the classroom, you might have them read the poem first so that other students can hear how words should be pronounced. If there are no Spanish-speaking students in the classroom, you might briefly go over with them the pronunciation of certain words.

## Author Activity

Possible Responses: Picasso, Pablo Casals, Isabel Allende, Andre Brink, and Rigoberta Menchu. Have students look up artists in an encyclopedia to get more information on their activism.

## PART 1 Reading the Prompt

Model the process of reading a prompt:

- Read the entire prompt aloud.
- List key words and phrases of the assignment on the board (*"evaluate," "most persuasive," "evidence"*).
- Define key words using the Strategies in Action to show how students can restate the prompt for themselves.

## PART 2 Planning an Evaluative Essay

- Encourage students to choose at least one selection that has personal relevance for them.
- Students might want to brainstorm more criteria, such as appeals to largest group, appeals to people today, or appeals to fairness.
- Remind students that each chart should contain the same criteria.

## PART 3 Drafting Your Essay

**Introduction** Suggest that students begin with a general statement about the types of selections that they considered. Then they can state their opinions as to which is the most persuasive selection.

**Organization** If students organize by selecting one criterion at a time, they might arrange these by order of importance. For example, they could begin with the least important and then build to the most important. Encourage them to consider several examples from each piece and then to select the best.

**Conclusion** In their conclusions, students may want not only to identify the selections that they found most persuasive but also to explain how such a piece affects a free society.

**Revision** Remind students to use double quotation marks around selection titles and around quotations used as evidence.

---

## Comparing Literature: Assessment Practice

### PART 1 Reading the Prompt

In writing assessment, you will often be asked to evaluate, or judge, pieces of writing. You are now going to practice writing an essay with an evaluative focus.

Often you will be asked to write an essay in response to a prompt like the one below. Read the entire prompt carefully, looking for key words that help you identify the purpose of the essay and decide how to approach it.

> **Writing Prompt**
> *I Am Joaquín* and the other selections in Unit Two, Part 2, all are concerned with group struggles for freedom. Choose three selections from this part of the unit. In an essay, evaluate ❶ the three and decide which you found to be the most persuasive call for freedom. Cite evidence ❷ from the selections to support your evaluation. ❸

> **STRATEGIES IN ACTION**
> ❶ **Evaluate** the selections, judging them against standards or criteria.
> ❷ Notice the general **quality** you are evaluating.
> ❸ Include **examples** or **quotations** from the selections.

### PART 2 Planning an Evaluative Essay

- Choose your three selections. (Pick those with which you are most familiar or those to which you had strong positive or negative reactions.)
- Choose your criteria for persuasiveness. You might be moved most by appeals to reason, appeals to emotion, or the moral standing of the writer, for example.
- For each selection, create an evaluation matrix like the one shown. As you apply each criterion in the first column, note an example and check off a value in one of the last three columns.
- Decide which selection is most persuasive overall.

**Which is the most persuasive selection?**

| Criterion | Example | Strong | Medium | Weak |
|-----------|---------|--------|--------|------|
|           |         |        |        |      |
|           |         |        |        |      |
|           |         |        |        |      |

### PART 3 Drafting Your Essay

**Introduction** Begin by clearly stating your thesis—your opinion about which selection is most persuasive.

**Organization** You could evaluate each selection individually or take one criterion at a time and relate it to all three selections. Connect back to your thesis as you go along. Include strong examples from the selections to illustrate your points.

**Conclusion** Restate your thesis and leave the reader with a final idea about writing and freedom.

**Revision** If possible, allow time to review your work. Make sure it is clear, well-supported, and free from mistakes.

**Writing Handbook**
See page 1283: Analysis.

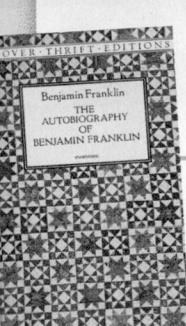

## The Autobiography of Benjamin Franklin

Benjamin Franklin—inventor, writer, statesman, and diplomat—tells his life history with wit, charm, and intellect. An American success story, Franklin describes his climb from anonymity and poverty to fame and fortune. Full of concrete suggestions and ideas on how to achieve moral perfection, *The Autobiography* stands as a monument to the ideals of reason, order, and human perfectibility that typified Enlightenment thought of the 18th century. Franklin wrote this book as a model that might guide readers to follow his example.

## The American Revolutionaries: A History in Their Own Words

EDITED BY MILTON MELTZER

A sweeping collection of primary sources, this book captures the spirit of '76 through the voices of people who joined the struggle for independence. A cross-section of American society—for example, teenagers in combat, women revolutionaries, commanding officers, religious leaders, immigrants, and slaves—provide firsthand accounts of this critical time in the nation's history. They show how the Revolutionary War touched the lives of all Americans, not just the troops fighting on the battlefield and the leaders forging a democratic government.

The *Electronic Library* is a CD-ROM that contains additional fiction, nonfiction, poetry, and drama for each unit in *The Language of Literature*.

These are the additional selections found in Unit 2 of the *Electronic Library* that apply to Part 2.

Benjamin Franklin
**Moral Perfection, *from* The Autobiography**

Thomas Paine
***from* Common Sense**
**The Crisis, Number 1**

**Reading Skills and Strategies**
**SUSTAINED SILENT READING**
Encourage students to select one of the books as an opportunity to read silently over a period of time.

## And Even *More* . . .

**Books**
**The Poems of Phillis Wheatley**
PHILLIS WHEATLEY
A collection of Wheatley's poems on a broad range of topics, including patriotic themes.

**Angel in the Whirlwind: The Triumph of the American Revolution**
BENSON BOBRICK
Engaging historical account, filled with interesting quotations from key political and military leaders.

**The American Revolution in Drawings and Prints**
COMPILED BY
DONALD H. CRESSWELL
A pictorial history of the struggle for independence.

**Other Media**
**1776**
Film version of a smash-hit Broadway musical, tracing events that spurred the American colonies to declare their independence from Britain. Columbia. (VIDEOCASSETTE)

**Liberty! The American Revolution**
A documentary of the dramatic events that culminated in the founding of a new nation. PBS Home Video. (VIDEOCASSETTE)

**Thomas Jefferson**
A film by Ken Burns profiling Jefferson's life and political career. PBS Home Video. (VIDEOCASSETTE)

### April Morning

HOWARD FAST
This historical novel focuses on Adam Cooper, a 15-year-old boy who comes to grips with his fears during the Revolutionary War. Fast skillfully weaves fact with fiction. Through Adam's eyes, readers experience the real-life Battle of Lexington, fought in April 1775.

### Objectives
- write a Persuasive Essay
- use a written text as a model for writing
- revise a draft to add factual information
- use pronouns that agree with their antecedents

## Introducing the Workshop

**A Persuasion** Explain that students are already familiar with persuasive writing and speech. Television and radio commercials bombard consumers with reasons to purchase certain products. Politicians urge voters to support their issues. Newspaper editorials and letters to the editor promote certain opinions. Students may try to persuade each other to go to a dance, buy a particular video game CD, or root for a favorite team. Discuss why some people or campaigns are successful at persuading others. Do these people use reason or emotion to convince others? Point out that through writing a persuasive essay, students, too, will have a chance to take a stand on an issue and influence the attitudes and actions of others.

Discuss the kinds of issues that concern students. What really makes them angry? What would they like to change? Some students may be primarily concerned with school-related issues. Others may be interested in environmental issues or politics.

### Basics in a Box

**B Using the Graphic** Like the pillars that hold up a building, the supporting evidence in a persuasive essay substantiates the writer's opinion and gives the opinion credibility. Without supporting evidence, the opinion would not be valid.

**C Presenting the Rubric** To better understand the assignment, students can refer to the Standards for Writing a Successful Persuasive Essay. You may also want to share with them the complete rubric, which describes several layers of proficiency.

---

# Writing Workshop  Persuasion

## Writing to Persuade Others . . .

**A** **From Reading to Writing** Thomas Jefferson, Martin Luther King, Jr., and Malcolm X had powerful ideas about political and social problems, and they believed that one way to solve them was by persuading others to think and act as they did. All **persuasive writing** serves this basic purpose, although it is not always about such world-shaking issues. Advertising, fund-raising campaigns, editorials, and political speeches are examples of persuasive writing.

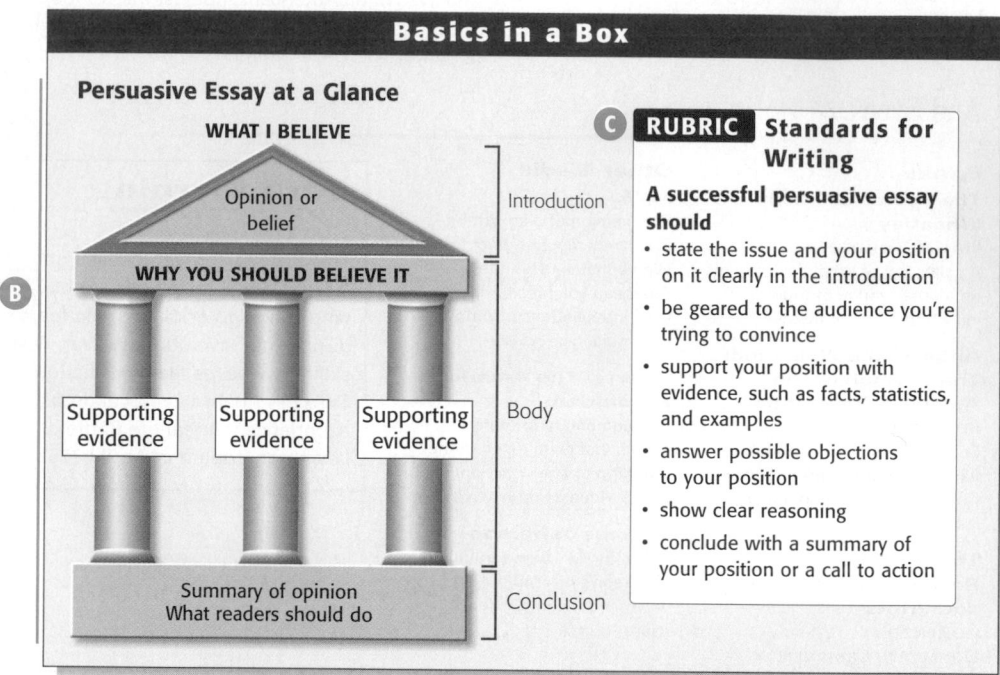

### Basics in a Box

**Persuasive Essay at a Glance**

WHAT I BELIEVE

Opinion or belief — Introduction

WHY YOU SHOULD BELIEVE IT

Supporting evidence | Supporting evidence | Supporting evidence — Body

Summary of opinion
What readers should do — Conclusion

**C RUBRIC Standards for Writing**

**A successful persuasive essay should**

- state the issue and your position on it clearly in the introduction
- be geared to the audience you're trying to convince
- support your position with evidence, such as facts, statistics, and examples
- answer possible objections to your position
- show clear reasoning
- conclude with a summary of your position or a call to action

320  UNIT TWO   PART 2: THE RIGHT TO BE FREE

---

## LESSON RESOURCES

**USING PRINT RESOURCES**
**Unit Two Resource Book**
- Prewriting, p. 84
- Drafting, p. 85
- Peer Response, pp. 86–87
- Revising, Editing, and Proofreading, p. 88
- Student Models, pp. 89–94
- Rubrics, p. 95

**Writing Transparencies and Copymasters**
- Writing Process Transparencies, pp. 1–4
- Writing Style Transparencies, pp. 13, 20
- Writing Template Copymasters, p. 27

**USING MEDIA RESOURCES**
**Visit our website:**
www.mcdougallittell.com
For a complete view of Lesson Resources, see page 131e.

# Analyzing a Student Model

**Jim Meyer
Fenwick High School**

## Security Cameras in Schools

Today, reports of improved test scores and of successful community service projects are only one part of the news from our public schools. Frequently, it seems, we also hear reports of dangers faced by students and teachers, from violence to drugs to vandalism. There's no question that students and faculty should feel safe at school and that whenever safety is in doubt, the quality of education is jeopardized. So how do you provide the needed security? Some schools have installed security cameras to ensure safety among faculty and students. However, the idea of security cameras is not universally accepted. While some students feel the cameras are a violation of their rights, I maintain their right to learn and work in a safe environment is more important.

According to a study published by the Office of the Attorney General in the state of South Carolina, the top offenses in schools since 1995 included controlled substance violations, possession of pagers, weapons offenses, aggravated assaults, thefts, vandalism, and threatening students and school officials. Security cameras can reduce these crimes significantly. Alan Page, systems engineer for North Miami Beach High School, reports that the rate of theft and vandalism dropped 85 percent in those Miami-area schools where security cameras had been installed. The students also reported feeling safer with the cameras watching over the school.

Opponents of security cameras claim they are too expensive. I do not agree. A proper installation costs from $10,000 to $20,000—less than the annual salary of one security guard according to *American School and University,* Oct. 1996. Security cameras don't need fringe benefits, vacations, or retirement, either. The money schools would save on property insurance premiums alone would more than cover the cost of installation. For example, an article in *Security Management,* March 1996, notes that the Huntsville, Alabama, school district installed an elaborate microwave-based surveillance system throughout the district for $1.7 million. That's a huge investment, but in just two years, the district saved $700,000 on insurance premiums alone. The installation cost of a security system is, at best, a weak argument for not having cameras watching over the school.

### RUBRIC
### IN ACTION

**❶** This writer introduces the issue with a straightforward statement of the problem.

**Other Options:**
- Quote an expert
- Present an anecdote
- Cite an example or give statistics

**❷** Clearly states position on the issue

**❸** Gives statistics and an example to support the position

**❹** States opposing view

**❺** Answers opposing view with facts and statistics

WRITING WORKSHOP **321**

---

Use McDougal Littell's **Language Network,** Chapter 21, for more instruction on writing a persuasive essay.

To engage students visually, use **Power Presentation** 3, Persuasion.

---

## Teaching the Lesson

### Analyzing the Model
### "Security Cameras in Schools"

**D** The student model introduces the reader to an issue of concern in many of today's schools—the use of video surveillance cameras for security purposes. Explain that some people feel the use of these cameras is a violation of the rights granted by the First Amendment of the U. S. Constitution, which guarantees freedom of speech and peaceable assembly.

Ask students if they are familiar with this issue, or know of any schools using such cameras. Invite them to share their opinions on this topic.

Have students read the student model, then discuss the Rubric in Action. Point out key words and phrases in the model that correspond to the elements mentioned in the Rubric in Action.

1. Have students suggest an alternate opening based on the other options listed.

   **Possible Response:** According to Alan Page, systems engineer for North Miami Beach High School, the rate of theft and vandalism has dropped 85 percent in those Miami area schools where security cameras have been installed.

2. Point out that the writer uses first person and states his opinion clearly and firmly.

3. The student writer uses statistics to support his conclusion. Ask students what additional statistics or examples he could have used.

   **Possible Responses:** The writer could include statistics about the schools that did not use security cameras. Evidence that those schools had higher rates of theft and vandalism would have strengthened his case. In addition, he could include an example of a student who had been a victim of an unsolved school incident, and show how the incident affected him or her.

4. Ask students why they should include the opposing view.

   **Possible Response:** The writer needs to be ready to counter any arguments against his or her position. Including the opposing view shows the reader that the writer has thought about the entire issue and is making an informed stand.

6. Ask students how facts and statistics like these strengthen the writer's position.

**Possible Response:** Readers will want to know the benefits of having security cameras. These facts and statistics show positive changes at a school.

7. Have students compare and contrast how the writer refuted the two opposing viewpoints.

**Possible Response:** The writer uses statistics and logic to refute the first opposing viewpoint while he uses personal opinion combined with facts to refute the second opposing viewpoint.

8. Explain that the ACLU is a national, non-profit, non-partisan association founded in the United States in 1920. The organization provides legal assistance to individuals or groups in cases involving violations of civil rights or liberties. The ACLU played a leading role in cases concerning freedom of speech, the right to privacy, desegregation, and separation of Church and State.

9. Ask students what action the writer could have urged his readers to take.

**Possible Response:** He could have asked his readers to find out more about the use of surveillance cameras in their own school. He could have urged his readers to state their opinion on this issue by writing to their principal and school board.

The fact is, cameras can actually save money for a school district. The same *Security Management* article reported that one high school in Chicago was spending $35,000 each year just to paint over graffiti. After cameras were installed, the annual cost dropped to $2,000. The savings are being used for school beautification projects. This same school also had a long history of students transferring to other schools because students and parents considered it dangerous. Because of the cameras, that perception has changed. The school is now seen as a safe learning environment and the student population is again growing.

❻ Provides additional facts and statistics to answer opposing view

Students in some California schools have objected to security cameras on the grounds that they are an invasion of privacy. They claim the cameras create a prison-like atmosphere in the school. The students feel security cameras in every hallway convey the feeling that Big Brother is watching every move they make. They say having the cameras is like having a prison guard observing them constantly, waiting for them to make a mistake. I might concede this point if the cameras were installed in a private area, but I fail to see what could possibly be private about a public area like a hallway. Do the security cameras in local department stores create a prison-like atmosphere that drives customers away? I fully support the Constitution of the United States, but I question the students' interpretation of the rights the Constitution guarantees. There is no privacy in an area intended for public use.

❼ Presents and answers another opposing view

The American Civil Liberties Union, a staunch and untiring guardian of American rights, has, in fact, raised some questions about the legal use of cameras in schools and how much or how little they infringe on the rights of students. But even the ACLU has stated that surveillance cameras, when properly installed and used in correct situations, are neither illegal nor bad policy.

❽ Gives additional facts to refute opposing view

Although some students and faculty in the United States feel security cameras are a bad idea, other schools are installing these systems in order to improve their schools. Whether the argument is about a prison-like atmosphere or too much spending, without security measures teachers will have to take on more responsibility for the safety of students. They will have less time for teaching. The right to learn is one of the most powerful rights Americans have. This right should not be taken away from us because some feel their need for privacy is more important. I believe in my right to learn in a safe environment, and cameras will help to ensure safety for every student who is under their watchful eye.

❾ This writer concludes by summing up arguments and restating his position.

**Another Option:**
· Urge readers to take action.

---

**Mini Lesson** ## Viewing and Representing

**PICTURING TEXT STRUCTURE**

**Instruction** The structure of a text—the way in which the words and ideas are organized—adds to the effectiveness of a written piece.

**Activity** Have students analyze the text structure of the student model by constructing an image such as a graphic organizer. The graphic students construct should reflect how the student writer has organized his piece. Students should conclude this activity by discussing how this text structure influences their understanding of the structure of an argument. A sample graphic is shown.

**Opinion: Security cameras should be installed in schools to ensure safety**

↓

**Supporting evidence: security cameras reduced theft and vandalism by 85% in Miami-area schools**

↓

**States first and second counterarguments and refutes each of them with facts and statistics**

↓

**Conclusion: summarizes arguments and restates position**

# Writing Your Persuasive Essay

## ❶ Prewriting

> *Writing comes more easily if you have something to say.*
> **Sholem Asch, novelist**

Look for an issue that's important to you and about which people disagree. Try brainstorming for ideas with a friend or looking for controversial issues in the news. See the **Idea Bank** in the margin for more suggestions. After you've chosen an issue, follow the steps below.

### Planning Your Persuasive Essay

▶ **1. Clarify your position.** What do you believe about your topic? Why do you hold that belief?

▶ **2. Identify your audience.** What do they know about the topic? What is their position on it? How can you answer opposing views?

▶ **3. Use evidence to support your arguments.** What facts, statistics, and examples support your position? What reference books or experts will offer more information?

## ❷ Drafting

Continue exploring your ideas as you begin drafting. Don't be afraid to rethink or revise your opinion as you work. At some point, you must state your position clearly and support it with evidence, such as **facts, statistics, examples, observations, anecdotes,** or **quotations.** Make your case strongly, but beware of using unfair language and faulty reasoning. Watch out for these illogical arguments and faulty and deceptive uses of language.

- **circular reasoning**—just restating something in other words without offering proof (We need a new traffic light at the corner because it's necessary.)

- **over-generalization**—making a statement that's too broad to prove (Everybody likes chocolate.)

- **either-or fallacy**—stating that there are only two possible alternatives (Either I get into Ivy League U. or my future is ruined.)

- **cause-and-effect fallacy**—assuming that because event B followed event A, A caused B (I flunked the test because I wore my unlucky shirt.)

- **bandwagon appeal**—trying to persuade people to follow the crowd (Everyone wears Spike brand of athletic shoes.)

- **name-calling**—attacking the person, not the idea (Joe won't be a good representative because he is a nerd.)

### IDEABank

**1. Your Working Portfolio**
Look for ideas in the **Writing Options** you completed earlier in this unit:

- **Rebuttal Speech,** p. 268
- **Literary Letter,** p. 288
- **Points of Comparison,** p. 308
- **Points of Comparison,** p. 317

**2. What's Your Opinion?**
Interview several classmates and adults to find out what current issue they think is most important and controversial.

**3. Fill in the Blanks.**
Complete this statement: If we don't do something about _____ soon, _____.

Have you used language fairly?

See the **Writing Handbook** Persuasive Writing, pp. 1285–1286

### Ask Your Peer Reader

- What is my position on this issue?
- What more do you need to know to understand the issue?
- What arguments do you find most convincing?
- What arguments are not convincing?

---

## Guiding Student Writing

## Prewriting

### Choosing an Issue
If after reading the Idea Bank students are having difficulty choosing an issue, suggest they try the following:

- Watch one or more of the political talk shows on television. Take notes on the issues and the positions of the speakers.
- Read the editorial pages of a newspaper or one of the weekly or monthly news magazines.
- Look for online chat groups that discuss current issues. If more than one topic is equally appealing to you, freewrite on both to see which issue you could better support.

### Planning the Persuasive Essay

1. Have students work with a small group of classmates to discuss their positions on their issues. Suggest that students listen carefully to what others have to say about the stand they take on their issues. Students might find during this discussion that they want to change their position on an issue or pursue another issue instead.

2. Explain that students need to understand the opposing side in order to present effective counterarguments. Students might make a list of opposing viewpoints and conduct some preliminary research for facts that support and oppose their position.

3. Tell students to gather information about their issue from books, newspapers and magazines. Suggest that they consult the school or public librarian for assistance in finding additional materials. Depending on their issues, police reports and minutes of school board meetings may also be helpful. They may also want to interview people who are familiar with the issue.

## Drafting

### Organizing the Draft
Review the types of illogical arguments and faulty and deceptive uses of language. Ask students to give additional examples of each type.

Suggest that students make a checklist for the components of the persuasive essay—facts, statistics, examples, observations, anecdotes, quotations—and check each off as they include it in their drafts. Remind them to also state opposing arguments and refute them with facts and examples.

## Revising

### SUPPORTING PERSONAL OPINIONS WITH FACTS

In the unrevised example, the writer does not mention the cost of the security cameras. It would be hard to refute that the cost of security cameras is too expensive unless the writer states what the actual cost is. By comparing the cost of security cameras with the annual salary of one security guard, the writer successfully refutes this opposing point.

## Editing and Proofreading

### PRONOUN-ANTECEDENT AGREEMENT

Remind students that a pronoun is a word that takes the place of a noun or another pronoun. The first sentence of the example contains an error in person. The antecedent *some* is an indefinite pronoun that refers to the people who oppose the use of surveillance cameras. The sentence needs the third-person pronoun *their. Our* is incorrect because *our* is a first person pronoun. In the second sentence, the word *cameras* is the antecedent. Since *cameras* is plural, the plural pronoun *their* should be used instead of the singular pronoun *its.*

## Reflecting

Encourage students to recognize and evaluate the way in which they approached writing their persuasive essays. Which comments from their peer readers helped them clarify their opinions? Have them add these self-evaluations to their working portfolios.

---

**Need revising help?**

Review the **Rubric,** p. 320

Consider **peer reader** comments

Check **Revision Guidelines,** p. 1269

**Stumped by pronoun-antecedent agreement?**

See the **Grammar Handbook,** p. 1307

### Publishing IDEAS

- Submit your essay to your local or school newspaper.
- Post your essay on your school's Web page.

**More Online: Publishing Options** www.mcdougallittell.com

---

### ❸ Revising

TARGET SKILL ▶ **SUPPORTING PERSONAL OPINIONS WITH FACTS**
While experts' opinions can provide strong support for your arguments, you must back up your own opinions with facts.

> Opponents of security cameras claim they are too expensive. I do not
>
> *A proper installation costs from $10,000 to $20,000—less than*
> agree. The installation cost of a security system is, at best, a weak
>
> *the annual salary of one security guard.*
> argument for not having cameras watching over the school.

### ❹ Editing and Proofreading

TARGET SKILL ▶ **PRONOUN-ANTECEDENT AGREEMENT** In doing persuasive writing, you're focusing on solid reasoning and objective arguments, and it's easy to over-look pronoun-antecedent agreement. When you edit and proofread, make sure pronouns agree with their antecedents in number, gender, and person so your writing is clear and unambiguous.

> This right should not be taken away from us because some feel ~~our~~ *their*
>
> need for privacy is more important. I believe in my right to learn in a
>
> safe environment, and cameras will help ensure safety for every
>
> student who is under ~~its~~ *their* watchful eye.

### ❺ Reflecting

**FOR YOUR WORKING PORTFOLIO** What do I like most about my finished essay? How has my opinion on this issue been changed by writing about it? Which aspect of this writing assignment was most difficult for me? Write responses to these questions and keep them with your persuasive essay in your **Working Portfolio.**

# Assessment Practice Revising & Editing

Read this paragraph from the first draft of a persuasive essay. The underlined sections may include the following kinds of errors:

- **unsupported opinions**
- **lack of pronoun-antecedent agreement**
- **lack of subject-verb agreement**
- **incorrect possessive forms**

For each underlined section, choose the revision that most improves the writing.

> School uniforms unfairly restrict students's freedom of choice and
> _____(1)
> expression. Restricting free choice isn't good. Everyone has a right to choose
> _____(2)
> their own clothes, and uniforms take away this right. Teens who are allowed to
> ___(3)___                _____(4)
> wear whatever they choose can pick clothes that reflects their personality and
> _____(5)
> judgment. On the other hand, a teen who must wear a uniform is denied the
> _____(6)
> chance to make their own decisions.

1. **A.** student's
   **B.** students'
   **C.** students
   **D.** Correct as is

2. **A.** Restricting free choice isn't good because it prevents students from practicing real-world decision-making skills.
   **B.** Restricting free choice isn't good because it's harmful to students.
   **C.** In my opinion, restricting free choice isn't good.
   **D.** Correct as is

3. **A.** theirs
   **B.** his or her
   **C.** your
   **D.** Correct as is

4. **A.** a uniform takes away
   **B.** a uniform take away
   **C.** uniform's take aways
   **D.** Correct as is

5. **A.** reflects his or her personality and judgment
   **B.** are reflecting their personality and judgment
   **C.** reflect their personality and judgment
   **D.** Correct as is

6. **A.** the chance to make his or her own decisions
   **B.** the chance to make its own decision
   **C.** the chance to make your own decisions
   **D.** Correct as is

**Need extra help?**

See the **Grammar Handbook**

Pronouns, p. 1307

Subject-Verb Agreement, p. 1324

Possessives, p. 1306

---

## Assessment Practice

Remind students to read all the choices before they answer each question.

**Answers:**
1. B; 2. A; 3. B; 4. A ; 5. C; 6. A.

**Note:** Letter D in question 4 is technically correct; however, stylistically letter A is a better choice. Since the word *everyone* is singular, each student would probably have only one *uniform*.

### Objectives

- develop a variety of strategies to ascertain word meanings
- rely on context clues to determine the meanings of words
- recognize types of context clues: definition or restatement, example, comparison and contrast, inference

### EXERCISE

1. "agreement;" clues include the phrase "proposals for changes" and the signal word *but* (inference clue)
2. "an oppressor" or "an absolute ruler who governs without restrictions;" clues are the comma and the phrase "an oppressor" (restatement clue)
3. "speaking readily but without thought;" clues include the phrases "joked about the issues" and "showed no knowledge of the facts" (example clue)
4. "silently" or "without protest;" clues include the signal words "while some" and "others" and the contrast clue "speak out" (contrast clue)
5. "to reject or disavow;" clue is the phrase "is to reject" (restatement clue)

## Meaning from Details

By now you have developed a variety of strategies to help you figure out the meanings of unfamiliar words. Often, you can find hints to the meaning of a word in the words and sentences that surround it. These hints are called **context clues.** For example, you can determine that *acquiescence* in the quotation on the right means "resignation" or "giving in" because Martin Luther King, Jr., restates his meaning immediately after the word appears.

> Oppressed people deal with their oppression in three characteristic ways. One way is acquiescence: the oppressed resign themselves to their doom.
> —Martin Luther King, Jr., *Stride Toward Freedom*

## Strategies for Building Vocabulary

Familiarity with context clues like the ones explained in the following paragraphs can help you expand your vocabulary.

**❶ Definition or Restatement Clues** The passage quoted above demonstrates that a writer sometimes provides a clue to a word's meaning by restating the meaning in a simpler and defining way. Words like *or, that is, in other words,* and *also called* often signal definition or restatement clues.

**❷ Example Clues** Sometimes a writer follows an unfamiliar word with examples that illustrate its meaning. At other times, an unfamiliar word may occur within a series of examples and be explained by the other examples that surround it. In the passage below, the phrases "to be underpaid for the work they do," "tied to menial jobs," and "to be used" help you determine that *exploitation* means "a selfish and unfair use of a person or group".

> Some groups in society fail to appreciate the effects of exploitation. They do not know what it is like to be underpaid for the work they do or to be tied to the most menial jobs. They do not know what it feels like to be used.

**❸ Comparison and Contrast Clues** A word's meaning may also be clarified by comparing or contrasting it with a more familiar word. Comparisons are often signaled by words like *like, as,* and *than;* contrasts, by words like *although, but, yet, however,* and *on the other hand.* For example,

in the sentence "He called for order rather than anarchy," the words *rather than* signal that *anarchy* contrasts with *order.*

**❹ Inference Clues** The meaning of a word is sometimes clarified by the general sense of the words and sentences that surround it. For example, in lines 20–22 of the Declaration of Independence, Jefferson writes that "Prudence, indeed, will dictate that governments long established should not be changed for light and transient causes." The reference to the "long established" governments and Jefferson's warning that they should not be changed for "light and transient causes" helps you to infer that *transient* means "temporary."

**EXERCISE** Explain the meaning of the italicized word in each sentence. Then identify the type of context clue and the details that helped you to define it.

1. The colonists presented their proposals for changes in the laws, but the angry king refused his *assent.*
2. Jefferson considered the king to be a *tyrant,* an oppressor.
3. The speaker's response was *glib.* She joked about the issues and showed no knowledge of the facts.
4. While some people *tacitly* accept oppression, others speak out against it.
5. To *repudiate* authority is to reject its values.

## Grammar from Literature

Writers use different verb tenses in the same sentence for a variety of reasons.

- To establish a time frame for events—past, present, or future.
- To show a chronological or conditional relationship.

Notice in the following sentences how different forms of the verbs, or tenses, have been used to show variations in the time of action or state of being.

> simple present
> **It becomes necessary for one people to dissolve the**
> present perfect
> **political bands which have connected them with another.**
> —The Declaration of Independence
>
> present progressive                    simple future
> **As we are going to part, we will come and take you by**
> **the hand.**          —Red Jacket, "Lecture to a Missionary"

When writing about events that happened at different times, it is important to use the right combination of verb tenses. The order of the verb tenses within a sentence is called the **sequence of tenses.**

In the first example, Thomas Jefferson begins by relating a present situation and then switches to the present perfect tense to talk about a continuing action that began in the past. In the second passage, Red Jacket switches to the future tense to talk about something that will happen after the first action mentioned in the sentence (*are going*).

Writers also use shifts in tense to express conditional relationships—that is, relationships in which one event will occur only if another does. In the following sentence, the shift in tense shows that the action indicated by *will fight* will occur after the action indicated by *continues*.

> **If the tyranny continues, we will fight.**

Remember that all verbs have three simple tenses and three perfect tenses. The list below illustrates forms of the verb *walk* in the simple and perfect verb tenses.

| Simple Tenses | Regular Verb | Irregular Verb |
|---|---|---|
| Present | walk | begin |
| Past | walked | began |
| Future | (shall) will walk | (shall) will begin |
| **Perfect Tenses** | | |
| Present Perfect | has walked | has or have begun |
| Past Perfect | had walked | had begun |
| Future Perfect | will have walked | will have begun |

**Using Verb Sequences in Your Writing**  Many writing situations involve recording actions that happened at various times. By carefully structuring the sequence of the tenses you choose, you can avoid confusion and give your reader a clear picture of events and relationships.

> **Letters and journal entries give us a picture of events that happened in day to day life over two centuries ago, but events in the future will tell if we have learned anything from history.**

**Usage Tip**  If one event in the past clearly happened before another, use the past perfect tense for the event that happened first. Form the past perfect tense by combining the word *had* with the past participle of the verb.

> INCORRECT
> simple past          simple past
> **They told us they fled from their own country for fear of wicked men.**
>
> CORRECT
> simple past          past perfect
> **They told us they had fled from their own country for fear of wicked men.**
> —Red Jacket, "Lecture to a Missionary"

---

**WRITING EXERCISE**  Rewrite the following sentences, correcting errors in sequence of verb tenses.

1. Patrick Henry had felt that under some circumstances it is better to die than to live.
2. The words of the Declaration of Independence will remain a model for nations who sought democracy.
3. Phillis Wheatley will say that some people have oppressed others in the name of liberty.
4. If we read carefully the words of Martin Luther King, Jr., we come to understand his greatness.
5. Dr. King discussed the three ways in which people dealt with oppression in the past.

---

**Objectives**

- use different verb tenses in the same sentence to show variations in time of action or state of being
- use the correct verb tense and practice shifting verb tenses to express conditional relationships
- revise drafts by carefully structuring the sequence of verb tenses in order to make events and relationships clear
- practice using the past perfect tense in writing

**WRITING ACTIVITY**

Answers will vary. Accept responses that meet the criteria and are grammatically correct.

1. Patrick Henry <u>felt</u> that under some circumstances it <u>was</u> better to die than to live.
2. The words of the Declaration of Independence <u>remain</u> a model for nations who seek democracy.
3. Phillis Wheatley <u>said</u> that some people <u>oppressed</u> others in the name of liberty.
4. If we read carefully the words of Martin Luther King, Jr., we <u>can</u> understand his greatness.
5. Dr. King discussed the three ways in which people <u>had dealt</u> with oppression in the past.

UNIT TWO  *Reflect* and Assess

## Objectives

- reflect on and assess understanding of the unit
- compare text events with student's own and other readers' experiences
- understand such literary concepts as persuasion and tone
- assess and build portfolios

## Reflecting on the Unit

### OPTION 1

A successful response will

- choose two selections from the unit in which writers give a differing perspective on a topic or event.
- include a chart which lists the topic or event, the important points each writer makes, and a summary of his or her opinion.
- identify which perspective most closely matches the student's.

### OPTION 2

A successful response will

- include a discussion of the principles and values upon which the United States was founded.
- assess whether those ideas and values are still important today.
- include examples from the selections as well as the students' previous knowledge to support their answers.

### OPTION 3

You may want to use the following rubric to evaluate students' letters:

**3 Full Accomplishment** Identifies the key values of at least four writers and relates them to the current government policies.

**2 Substantial Accomplishment** Identifies the key values of a few writers and relates them to current government policies.

**1 Little or Partial Accomplishment** Identifies a few key values but does not attribute them to specific writers and fails to relate them to current government policies.

## Self Assessment

Ask students to list their insights in order of importance.

# From Colony to Country

*A Morning View of Blue Hill Village* (1824), Jonathan Fisher. William A. Farnsworth Library and Art Museum, Rockford, Maine.

As a result of reading the selections in this unit, have you gained any new insights into the principles and beliefs of the Puritans and the American revolutionaries? What did you learn about the power of persuasion as you read the examples of persuasive writing? Choose one or more of the options in each of the following sections to explore what you've learned.

## Reflecting on the Unit

### OPTION 1

**Strong Beliefs** Many of the selections in this unit express the strong religious and political beliefs held by early Americans. List some of these beliefs, noting the people or groups who supported them. Which of the beliefs do you agree with most? Which do you disagree with? In a few paragraphs, identify your choices and explain why you chose them.

### OPTION 2

**The American Way** With a small group of classmates, discuss the principles and values that you believe were the most important in the creation of the United States as a nation. Are those principles and values still important today? Use examples from the selections to support your opinions, but also draw on your previous knowledge.

### OPTION 3

**To Form a More Perfect Union** Choose four or more writers from this unit, both historical and contemporary, that have had the greatest influence on your opinions about the values central to American democracy. Using the ideas of these writers as support, write a letter to the President of the United States, commenting on the current government's political and moral policies.

### Self ASSESSMENT

📖 **READER'S NOTEBOOK**

To document what you have learned by reading the selections in this unit, make a list of the insights into the development of the nation that you have gained.

## Reviewing Literary Concepts

### OPTION 1

**Analyzing Drama** In this unit, you read *The Crucible,* a modern play, and learned literary concepts associated with drama. To test your understanding, write one or two sentences applying each of the following literary terms to *The Crucible:* **setting, internal conflict, external conflict, plot, climax, resolution, characters, protagonist, antagonist, foil, dialogue, stage directions.** For example, you might write, "The **setting** of *The Crucible* is Salem, Massachusetts, in 1692." To extend your knowledge further, apply the same terms to a film or television show you saw recently.

### OPTION 2

**Understanding Persuasion** Most of the selections in this unit contain persuasive arguments. Make a chart like the one shown here, noting the main points of the writer's argument in each selection you have read. Also note how each writer attempts to persuade the reader—for example, by appeals to reason or emotion, by biblical allusions, by loaded language, or by rhetorical questions. Then write a short paragraph explaining which two or three arguments you found most persuasive and why.

| Selection | Points Argued For | Author's Persuasive Tactics |
|---|---|---|
| "Speech in the Virginia Convention" | The need to arm and fight the British | Biblical allusions, rhetorical questions, appeals to patriotism, appeals to reason |

## Building Your Portfolio

- **Writing Options** Several of the Writing Options in this unit asked for your personal responses to the beliefs and principles presented in the selections. Choose the response that best expresses your opinion about a belief or principle important to you, and explain your choice in a cover note. Attach the note to the response and put them in your **Presentation Portfolio.**

- **Writing Workshop** In this unit, you wrote a Review of a literary work or a film. You also wrote a Persuasive Essay about an issue important to you. Reread these pieces and decide which is more successful at presenting and defending your opinions. Explain your choice in a note attached to the preferred one. Place this piece in your **Presentation Portfolio.**

- **Additional Activities** Think back to any of the assignments you completed under **Activities & Explorations** and **Inquiry & Research.** Keep a record in your portfolio of any assignments you would like to do further work on in the future.

### Self ASSESSMENT

📖 **READER'S NOTEBOOK**

In addition to dramatic terms, other literary terms were discussed in Unit Two. Copy this list and place an X next to those terms you understand well. Review the terms you are not sure about in the **Glossary of Literary Terms** (page 1244).

| | |
|---|---|
| meter | metaphor |
| iambic pentameter | simile |
| | theme |
| transcript | tone |
| allusion | historical context |
| rhetorical question | epic poem |
| parallelism | |
| figurative language | |

### Self ASSESSMENT

Now that you have some pieces of writing in your **Presentation Portfolio,** look them over and decide which kinds of writing contain your strongest work. What kinds of writing would you like more practice in as the year goes on?

**Setting GOALS**

Look back through this unit's selections, your portfolio, and your notebook, identifying the literary genres that you would like to read more examples of or would like to experiment with in your writing.

---

## Reviewing Literary Concepts

### OPTION 1

In addition to applying the dramatic terms to a film or television show, have students apply each of the literary terms under Self Assessment to selections from the unit.

### OPTION 2

Use the Unit Two Resource Book, p. 98, to provide students a ready-made, full-depth chart for examining persuasion.

## 📁 Building Your Portfolio

Students will use their Presentation Portfolios to file what they consider their highest quality work—the very best projects and activities from their Working Portfolios.

📑 For more information on using writing and assessing portfolios, see the *Teacher's Guide to Assessment and Portfolio Use,* p. 53.

The Reading and Writing for Assessment feature provides practice in taking standardized tests. As students work through this lesson, they will learn strategies for reading comprehension questions, multiple-choice questions, and essay and short-answer questions. Boxed strategies located alongside the text will help guide students through the activities. These strategies model processes students can use as they take standardized tests.

This feature is based on and will help to prepare students for state assessments, including end-of-course assessments. It will also prepare students for the reading comprehension questions used on such college board examinations as the Scholastic Aptitude Test (SAT) and the American College Test (ACT).

## Objectives

- understand and apply strategies for reading a test selection
- recognize literary techniques in a test selection
- understand and apply strategies for answering multiple-choice questions about a test selection
- respond to a writing prompt and present ideas in a logical order
- understand and apply strategies for revising and proofreading a test response

# Reading&Writing   for Assessment

Throughout high school, you will be tested on your ability to read and understand many different kinds of reading selections. These tests will assess your basic understanding of ideas and knowledge of vocabulary. They will also check your ability to analyze and evaluate both the message of the text and the techniques the writer uses in getting that message across.

The following pages will give you test-taking strategies. Practice applying these strategies by working through each of the models provided.

### PART 1   How to Read a Test Selection

In many tests, you will read a passage and then answer multiple-choice questions about it. Applying the basic test-taking strategies that follow, taking notes, and highlighting or underscoring passages as you read can help you focus on the information you will need to know.

---

**STRATEGIES FOR READING A TEST SELECTION**

▶ **Before you begin reading, skim the questions that follow the passage.** These can help focus your reading.

▶ **Use your active reading strategies such as analyzing, predicting, and questioning.** Make notes in the margin to help you focus your reading. You may do this only if the test directions allow you to mark on the test itself.

▶ **Think about the title.** What does it suggest about the overall message or theme of the selection?

▶ **Look for main ideas.** These are often stated at the beginnings or ends of paragraphs. Sometimes they are implied, not stated. After reading each paragraph, ask "What was this passage about?"

▶ **Note the literary elements and techniques used by the writer.** You might consider structure, the writer's portrayal of people, or techniques the writer used to create humor or suspense. Then ask yourself what effect the writer achieves with each choice.

▶ **Unlock word meanings.** Use context clues and word parts to help you unlock the meaning of unfamiliar words.

▶ **Think about the message or theme.** What larger lesson can you draw from the passage? Can you infer anything or make generalizations about other similar situations, human beings, or life in general?

---

330

## A Boy's School Project Aims to Revise History: New Focus on Case of a 1945 War Disaster

By Lizette Alvarez

1   It took the cruiser *Indianapolis* just 12 minutes to go down, pierced by three Japanese torpedoes in the Pacific on July 30, 1945. Hundreds of the ship's 1,169 crewmen managed to scurry overboard and spent four days and five nights fending off sharks and hallucinations.

2   For 53 years, the 316 survivors of the single worst disaster at sea in American naval history have pursued one goal: to wipe clean the 1946 court-martial conviction of Capt. Charles Butler McVay 3d, their skipper. Now a 12-year-old Florida boy could be the impetus for the ❶ exoneration of a captain whose crew considered him a scapegoat for the Navy's own culpability.

3   The boy, Hunter Scott of Cantonment, on the outskirts of Pensacola, a Navy town in the Florida panhandle, was watching the movie *Jaws* when he got the inspiration for a history project. Now through a combination of luck, gumption and the appeal only a 12-year-old could carry off, ❷ Hunter has become a sensation, attracting the interest of politicians, reporters and documentarians around the world.

4   "We have tried and tried and it didn't get anywhere," said Maurice G. Bell, 73, one of the 150 remaining survivors of the *Indianapolis,* the ship that ferried the atom bomb Little Boy to Guam. "And here you've got this young 12-year-old boy and they listen to him a little bit better. This is the best chance we've ever had. If we don't get it now, I don't think we ever will."

5   Last week, with Hunter in Washington, Representative Joe Scarborough, whose district includes the town where Hunter lives, introduced a bill to exonerate Captain McVay.

6   Hunter toted his hundreds of letters, interviews, documents and newspaper clippings around the Capitol, meeting with numerous lawmakers, including Speaker Newt Gingrich, who was instantly smitten and told the boy he expected to push for the bill after a review by the House National Security Committee. Senator Daniel K. Inouye, Democrat of Hawaii, said he would sponsor the bill in the Senate, and Senator Robert C. Smith, Republican of New Hampshire, said he would help.

7   "Is your evidence solid?" Senator Smith asked Hunter, during their one-on-one chat.

8   "Like a rock, sir," Hunter replied, without missing a beat.

9   Wise to the ways of Washington, Hunter even made his pitch at a full-fledged news conference there, ❸ shrugging off microphones that all but obscured his head.

---

❶ **Use context clues to understand vocabulary.**

**ONE STUDENT'S THOUGHTS**

"*Exoneration* must mean that Captain McVay's name would be cleared if his court-martial conviction is set aside."

❷ **Note literary elements that build interest.**

"I've read three paragraphs and all I have are questions. Why has Hunter become a sensation? Why was Captain McVay court-martialed?"

**YOUR TURN**

What questions do the first three paragraphs leave you with? Why would the writer want you to ask these questions?

❸ **Note how the writer shows character traits.**

"Hunter must be very confident—all those microphones would make me nervous!"

**YOUR TURN**

What else does the writer show about Hunter by telling us how Hunter reacted to the microphones?

---

## Strategies in Action

Begin by previewing the text. Note the title and identify the subject of the reading selection. Read through the questions and prompts at the end of the text. Ask students what they will need to look for as they read.

1   Students do not need to know the meaning of every word in a selection. However, when an unfamiliar word is used to explain or describe a key event, idea, or concept, students will need to decipher the word's meaning. Use the following questions to help students unlock the meaning of unfamiliar words:

- Does the sentence or paragraph offer any clues to the word's meaning?
- Does the sentence restate or extend information provided earlier in the selection?
- Are any parts of the word familiar? Is the word similar to other words that might have similar meanings?

2   Remind students that a way to monitor and modify reading strategies is by asking questions as they read. Students can predict what questions might be asked if they note the structure of a selection and the amount of space the writer uses to discuss each idea. The three paragraphs of the introduction use about one-fourth of the selection. Students can infer from this that the introduction is important and is likely to be covered on a test.

**YOUR TURN** What happened aboard the *Indianapolis*? Why was McVay court-martialed? How is Hunter's history project connected with McVay and the *Indianapolis*? The writer wants to build suspense and wants the reader to seek answers to those questions.

3   Instead of explaining Hunter's character traits, the writer reveals Hunter's character with his actions. Understanding his personality can also help the reader grasp the story.

**YOUR TURN** Hunter might shrug off the microphones because he prefers to speak directly to people. The writer may be trying to show that Hunter is confident in his ideas.

4 When a test selection contains anecdotes and dialogue, it can be harder to identify main ideas. Some main ideas may be stated in quotations, rather than stated directly by the writer.

5 To save time on a test, students should read the questions that follow the test selection first. Then they can look for answers to the questions as they read. In this case, the lesson Hunter learns from his project may also be one of the messages the writer hopes to convey.

## Customizing for Less Proficient Readers

6 Reading comprehension tests often assess students' ability to recognize bias in a test selection. Use the following questions to guide less proficient readers to recognize bias.

• How many sides are there to this story?

**Possible Response:** Two—the Navy's side and that of the *Indianapolis* survivors and Hunter Scott

• Whose point of view is presented in this selection?

**Possible Response:** Hunter Scott's point of view

• What information does the writer leave out of the story?

**Possible Response:** Any evidence suggesting Captain McVay was at fault

**YOUR TURN** He supports McVay and claims he's amassed a large amount of evidence. He seems to have examined both sides of the issue.

---

10   To the chagrin of the Navy, Hunter, who cannot help winding up his sentences with "ma'am" and "sir," has stayed resolutely "on-message."

11   Back home, he said: "A lot of people in the Navy don't want to reopen this. That's politics. ❹ They had to have a scapegoat to appease the public and they chose Captain McVay. I'm not going to let that stop me."

12   In a statement yesterday, a Navy spokesman said that in 1996 the Navy had reviewed the court-martial proceeding and concluded that it was "accurate," and that "no further actions are appropriate."

13   ❺ And what exactly has Hunter learned from his blockbuster history project? "I found out how hard it is to right an injustice," he said. . . .

14   The Navy has long maintained that Captain McVay was at fault for failing to follow a zigzag course in a submarine-infested patch of the Pacific. He was convicted of that charge, although the Secretary of the Navy, taking note of Captain McVay's illustrious record, remitted the sentence and gave him a desk job. The Navy refused, however, to expunge his conviction.

15   Subsequent evidence, though, cast doubt on the Government's position. One 1993 report, for example, indicated that the Navy knew there were Japanese submarines in the area but never told Mr. McVay and sent the ship to sea unescorted. ❻ The Navy disputes that conclusion. . . .

16   Hunter, a seventh-grader at Ransom Middle School, spent what seemed like a lifetime to him—"since sixth grade"—compiling all the information he could get his hands on.

17   Mr. Scarborough exhibited Hunter's research in his office, and in no time, word spread about the project.

18   None of this has fazed Hunter, who says he never gets nervous, even when he makes the rounds on morning television news programs and tells his story to the BBC.

19   The idea for the project zapped Hunter while he watched *Jaws,* and heard Quint, the scurrilous shark hunter, recount his hair-raising battle with sharks after the *Indianapolis* went down. Hunter's father suggested he start a research project, and Hunter put an advertisement in the local Navy newspaper seeking survivors. . . .

20   His schoolmates predict that Hunter will be President one day. But Hunter has other plans. He wants to join the Navy as a doctor or lawyer, then "get a bunch of land in New Mexico and hunt and fish every day."

**❹ Look for main ideas.**

"In this paragraph, the writer lets Hunter speak for himself about why he thinks Captain McVay was court-martialed."

**❺ Skim the questions that follow the passage.**

"There is a question about the larger lessons the writer hopes to convey. This statement talks about what Hunter learns. Perhaps there is a clue here."

**❻ Read actively by analyzing.**

"Expunging his conviction won't do Captain McVay any good. Hunter must be doing this just because he thinks people should know the truth."

**YOUR TURN**

*Do you think Hunter examined the evidence neutrally? Or was he biased? What is the basis for your opinion?*

---

## Check Your Understanding

Have students use the following questions to test their understanding of the selection before they answer the questions in their texts.

• What were the main ideas in the selection?

• How does the writer encourage readers to care about the information she presents?

• What structure does the writer use for the selection?

• Did the selection answer all your questions about the subject? If not, what questions remain unanswered?

Use the strategies in the box and notes in the side column to help you answer the questions below and on the following pages.

Based on the selection you have just read, choose the best answer for each of the following questions.

1. The main idea expressed by this selection is that
   A. the Indianapolis disaster was a great tragedy.
   B. Captain McVay was scapegoated by the Navy.
   C. The survivors of the Indianapolis have been ignored.
   D. Hunter Scott is a good student.

2. Why do you think that the writer chooses to tell us that Hunter "cannot help winding up his sentences with 'ma'am' and 'sir'"?
   A. to show that Hunter is respectful
   B. to make fun of Hunter
   C. to show Hunter's youth
   D. all of the above

3. Hunter tells Senator Smith that his evidence is as solid as a rock. Why does the writer include this detail in the selection?
   A. to show that Hunter will say anything to make his case
   B. to show that Hunter has a sense of humor
   C. to show that Hunter feels intimidated by the Senator
   D. to show that Hunter feels confident about stating his case

4. What literary element does the writer add to the selection by telling us that the time period "since sixth grade" seems like a lifetime to Hunter?
   A. plot
   B. foreshadowing
   C. humor
   D. suspense

5. Which of the following might be one of the larger lessons the writer hopes to convey through this story?
   A. It's never too late to reverse an injustice.
   B. With a fresh approach, a child may succeed where adults have failed.
   C. It's hard to fight a large institution.
   D. All of the above.

---

**STRATEGIES** FOR ANSWERING MULTIPLE-CHOICE QUESTIONS

▶ **Ask questions** that help you eliminate some of the choices.
▶ **Pay attention to choices** such as "all of the above" or "none of the above." To eliminate them, all you need to find is one answer that doesn't fit.
▶ **Skim your notes.** Details you noticed as you read may provide answers.

**STRATEGIES** IN ACTION

**Pay attention to choices such as "all of the above."**

**ONE STUDENT'S THOUGHTS**
"The writer seems to admire Hunter—I don't think she would make fun of him. *So I can eliminate choice B. That means I can also eliminate choice D.*"

**YOUR TURN**
*What other choice doesn't make sense?*

**Skim your notes.**

**ONE STUDENT'S THOUGHTS**
"The writer doesn't go on to say anything that would suggest Hunter is likely to spend a lifetime on this project. I don't think this detail is foreshadowing anything. *So I can eliminate choice B.*"

**YOUR TURN**
*Which of the three remaining choices makes the most sense?*

---

## Guiding Student Response

**Multiple-Choice Questions**
1. D
2. A

**YOUR TURN** Choice C doesn't make sense because you don't necessarily have to be young to say "ma'am" or "sir."
3. D
4. C

**YOUR TURN** Choice C makes the most sense. Calling one year a lifetime is an example of humorous exaggeration.
5. D

## Short-Answer Question

By not telling Hunter's story in chrono-logical order, the writer creates a sense of mystery. The writer hopes that the reader will want to read further to find out what happened to the *Indianapolis,* and how Hunter got involved. If the writer had started with the history of the *Indianapolis,* the reader might have lost interest before reaching the end of the article.

**YOUR TURN** The end of the article explains Hunter got the idea for his project by watching the movie *Jaws.* The writer mentions *Jaws* at the begin-ning but doesn't explain the connec-tion. The reader may continue reading, wondering what *Jaws* has to do with the history of World War II.

## Essay Question

Hunter seems confident, intelligent, and caring. With help from his father, he came up with the idea for a research project about the *Indianapolis,* and his actions during the project reveal his character traits.

   He worked on this project for a year, prepared research and evidence, and spoke to U. S. Senators and Representatives about it. This demon-strated that he cares about the project, that he's confident in his goals, and that he seems to care about truth and justice.

   Hunter has also shown that he's able to talk to people, even reporters, about what he believes. He's respectful and seems to want to make his case through hard evidence and polite words—not inflamed rhetoric.

**YOUR TURN** The writer tells us that Hunter always ends his sentences with "ma'am" and "sir," suggesting that Hunter is respectful. The writer also tells us that Hunter wants to join the Navy, which suggests that Hunter respects the institution even though he disagrees with the decision about Captain McVay.

---

**PART 3** **How To Respond in Writing**

You may also be asked to write answers to questions about a reading passage. Short-answer questions usually ask you to answer in a sentence or two. Essay questions require a fully developed piece of writing.

### Short-Answer Question

**STRATEGIES** FOR RESPONDING TO SHORT-ANSWER QUESTIONS

▸ **Identify the key words** in the writing prompt that tell you the ideas to discuss. Make sure you know what is meant by each.
▸ **State your response directly** and to the point.
▸ **Support your ideas** by using evidence from the selection.
▸ **Use correct grammar.**

> **Sample Question**
> Answer the following question in one or two sentences.
>
> Why does the writer not tell Hunter's story in chronological order? How does the writer's decision to save important information for the end of the article affect the reader?

### Essay Question

**STRATEGIES** FOR ANSWERING ESSAY QUESTIONS

▸ **Look for direction words** in the writing prompt, such as *essay, analyze, describe,* or *compare and contrast,* that tell you how to respond directly to the prompt.
▸ **List the points** you want to make before beginning to write.
▸ **Write an interesting introduction** that presents your main point.
▸ **Develop your ideas** by using evidence from the selection that supports the statements you make.
▸ **Present the ideas** in a logical order.
▸ **Write a conclusion** that summarizes your points.
▸ **Check your work** for correct grammar.

> **Sample Prompt**
>
> The writer describes Hunter as having a combination of "luck, gumption, and appeal." Write an essay in which you analyze Hunter's character using evidence provided by the writer.

**334**

---

**STRATEGIES**
IN ACTION

**Identify the key words.**

**ONE STUDENT'S THOUGHTS**
"This question is asking about the structure of the selection. The key words seem to be *chronological* and *important information.*"

**YOUR TURN**
*What is the important information at the end of the article? Why isn't it put at the beginning?*

**Develop your ideas by using evidence from the selection.**

**ONE STUDENT'S THOUGHTS**
"The writer says that Hunter compiled a file containing letters, interviews, documents, and newspaper clippings. Hunter must have worked on this project a long time. He must have been very determined—and organized."

**YOUR TURN**
*What other details does the writer provide that suggest insights into Hunter's character?*

Here is a student's first draft in response to the writing prompt at the bottom of page 334. Read it and answer the multiple-choice questions that follow.

| 1 | Hunter is a determined kid. He has worked on his project for a |
| 2 | year and has taken his case to Washington. To be that determined, |
| 3 | he must really think that Captain McVay is innocent and should |
| 4 | have his name cleared. He seems to care about truth and justice— |
| 5 | and he doesn't think much of politics. |
| 6 | Hunter not only cares about this project, but he also has what |
| 7 | it takes. The character traits that might help him to succeed. He |
| 8 | is organized, confident, and ready to talk to people. Hunter seems |
| 9 | to want to make his case through hard evidence and polite words. |
| 10 | He doesn't want to stir people up with inflamed rhetoric. |

1. What is the BEST way to revise the sentence in lines 2–4 to make it clear who is referred to by the pronoun "his"? ("To be... must...name cleared.")

   A. He must really think that Captain McVay is innocent and should have McVay's name cleared.

   B. Hunter must really think Captain McVay is innocent and should have his name cleared.

   C. Hunter must want Captain McVay's name to be cleared because he (McVay) is innocent.

   D. Make no change.

2. What is the BEST change, if any, to the sentences in lines 6 and 7? ("Hunter not only...to succeed.")

   A. Hunter not only cares about this project, but he also has what it takes; the character traits that might help him to succeed.

   B. Hunter not only cares about this project, but he also has: the character traits that might help him to succeed.

   C. Hunter not only cares about this project, but he also has the character traits that might help him to succeed.

   D. Make no change.

3. What is the BEST way to combine the sentences in lines 8–10? ("Hunter seems...inflamed rhetoric.")

   A. Hunter uses hard evidence and polite words to make his case. Never inflamed rhetoric.

   B. Hunter wants to make his case using hard evidence, but not using inflamed rhetoric, and using polite words.

   C. Hunter seems to want to make his case through hard evidence and polite words, not with inflamed rhetoric.

   D. Make no change.

**STRATEGIES** FOR REVISING, EDITING, AND PROOFREADING

▶ **Read the passage carefully.**
▶ **Note the parts that are confusing** or don't make sense. What kinds of errors would that signal?
▶ **Look for errors** in grammar, usage, spelling, and capitalization. Common errors include:
  • run-on sentences
  • sentence fragments
  • subject-verb agreement
  • unclear pronoun antecedents
  • lack of transition words

**Answers**
1. C
2. C
3. C

**Check Your Understanding**
Have students reread their own responses to the short-answer and essay questions. Then have students use the following questions to guide themselves as they revise and edit their own work.

• Have I responded directly to the direction words in the writing prompt?
• Have I supported my ideas with evidence from the selection?
• Have I presented my ideas in a logical order?
• Have I included an introduction and a conclusion?
• Have I used correct grammar?

## The Spirit of Individualism

The selections in Unit Three explore some of the ideals and issues that evolved in America and elsewhere in the first half of the 19th century. The two sections of the unit examine different aspects of the spirit of the age.

### ——— Part 1 ———

**Celebrations of the Self** The literature in this part of the unit explores the development of a distinctive literary tradition in America in the early years of the 19th century. These poems, short stories, and essays reveal how many of the American writers of this time emphasized the examination of inner feelings and emotions over reason, logic, and scientific observation. The selections in the **Traditions Across Time** section show how 20th-century writers have continued this exploration of self.

### ——— Part 2 ———

**The Dark Side of Individualism** The selections in this part examine the underside of Romanticism: the terror of the soul. An **Author Study** on Edgar Allan Poe leads off this part. The rest of the works—offering the conventions of crumbling mansions, mad scientists, and horrifying apparitions—mark the growth of the horror story and its fascination with evil and the supernatural. The selections in **Traditions Across Time** show how the Gothic tradition has influenced 20th-century writers in the American South.

# The Spirit of Individualism

If a man does not keep pace

with his companions,

perhaps it is because

he hears a different drummer.

Let him step to the music

which he hears, however measured

or far away.

HENRY DAVID THOREAU

*Naturalist and writer*

*The Wanderer* (1818), Caspar David Friedrich, Kunsthalle, Hamburg, Germany, Bridgeman/Art Resource, New York.

336

## Viewing and Representing

*The Wanderer*
**by Caspar David Friedrich**

### ART APPRECIATION

**Instruction** German artist Caspar David Friedrich (1774–1840) was one of the earliest and most influential Romantic painters. He created a series of vast, barren landscapes that show how powerless people are against the forces of nature. He produced his first important work, *The Cross in the Mountains,* in 1807, and it established his mature style. His work fell into obscurity soon after his passing, but interest in it was revived in the 20th century.

*The Wanderer* (1818) is typical of Friedrich's realistic but symbolic landscapes, where eerie light seems to emanate from the spiritual natures of silent, desolate images. Friedrich once said, "The artist should paint not only what he sees before him but also what he sees within him."

Use the following question to develop students' visual literacy.

To help students explore connections among the art, the quotation, and the unit theme, have them consider the following questions.

**Ask: What was Henry David Thoreau advocating in this quotation? How does this quotation relate to the unit as a whole?**

**Possible Responses:** Thoreau was urging his readers to follow their own conscience rather than mindlessly conforming to the rules of society. He was implying that being an individual means making up one's own mind. The quotation urges people to follow their inner voice; it makes individuality acceptable.

**Ask: How do you think the central figure in the painting relates to the theme of individualism in this unit?**

**Possible Responses:** His isolation on the mountain suggests his separateness from the crowd. The clarity with which he is painted stands out against the fogginess that characterizes the rest of the painting, suggesting that he has defined himself while the rest of the world is lost in the mists of conformity and group thinking.

**Ask: How do you define individualism?**

**Possible Responses:** following your own conscience; having the strength to resist peer pressure; being creative

**Ask: Based on the unit title, the quotation, and the painting on this page, what kinds of stories and poems do you expect to read in this unit?**

**Possible Responses:** stories and poems that describe individuals and support individualism

**Ask: Based on this painting, how do you think Friedrich viewed individualism?**

**Possible Responses:** He supported the Romantic view that individualism often required one to be isolated, away from the crowd; individualism is born of inner contemplation and distant reflections.

| Features and Selections | Literary Analysis | Reading and Critical Thinking | Writing Opportunities |
|---|---|---|---|
| POETRY<br>A Psalm of Life | Stanza and Rhyme Scheme, 344, 347 | Strategies for Reading Traditional Poetry, 344, 347 | Personal Response, 348<br>Longfellow Parody, 348 |
| SHORT STORY<br>The Devil and Tom Walker | Imagery, 349, 360<br><br>Narrator, 360<br>Author Activity, 362 | Visualizing, 349, 360<br>Informal Assess., 358<br>Test Practice, 361 | Reflective Essay, 361<br>Fitting Proverbs, 361<br>Updated Faust Legend, 361 |
| ESSAY<br>from Self-Reliance | Aphorism, 363, 367 | Summarizing, 363, 367<br>Author Activity, 368<br>Test Practice, 366 | Personal Essay, 368<br>Update of Emerson, 368 |
| ESSAY<br>from Civil Disobedience | Essay, 369, 378 | Strategies for Reading Essays, 369, 378<br>Photographs, 375<br>Informal Assess., 377 | Comparison, 379<br>Personal Response, 379<br>Essay, 379 |
| ESSAY<br>from Walden | Nature Writing, 381, 392<br><br>Figurative Language, 392 | Evaluating Author's Observations, 381, 392<br>Test Practice, 386<br>Informal Assess., 391 | Walden Pond Letter, 393<br>Interpretive Essay, 393<br>Nature Writing, 393<br>Workplace Link, 387 |
| **Learning the Language of Literature**<br>Form in Poetry | Form in Poetry, 394 | Form in Poetry, 394 | |
| POETRY<br>I Hear America Singing<br>I Sit and Look Out<br>from Song of Myself | Free Verse, 396, 404 | Strategies for Reading Free Verse, 396, 404<br>Author Activity, 405 | Literary Review, 405<br>Free-Verse Poem, 405 |
| POETRY<br>**Comparing Literature**<br>Danse Russe<br>anyone lived in a pretty how town | Experimental Poetry, 410, 414 | Making Inferences, 410, 414 | Diary Confession, 415<br>Headstone, 415<br>Points of Comparison, 415<br>Informal Assess., 415 |
| POETRY<br>**Comparing Literature**<br>Ending Poem<br>Tía Chucha | Speaker, 416, 421<br><br>Tone, 421 | Structure and Form in Poetry, 416, 421 | Points of Comparison, 422<br>Autobio. Sketch, 422<br><br>Contrast Essay, 422<br>Test Practice, 423 |
| AUTOBIOGRAPHICAL STORY<br>**Comparing Literature**<br>Gary Keillor | Humor, 424, 434 | Purpose for Reading, 424, 434<br>Informal Assess., 433 | Points of Comparison, 435<br>Story Sequel, 435<br>Literary Review, 435 |
| Comparing Literature<br>**Assessment Practice** | | Reading the Prompt, 436<br>Planning Essay, 436 | Drafting Essay, 436 |
| Writing Workshop: **Reflective Essay**<br>**Sentence Crafting** | | Reflective Essay, 438 | Reflective Essay, 438 |

LEGEND    DLS – Daily Language SkillBuilder
CCL – Cross Curricular Link          Green type – Teacher's Edition

| Features and Selections | Literary Analysis | Reading and Critical Thinking | Writing Opportunities | |
|---|---|---|---|---|
| **AUTHOR STUDY**<br>**Edgar Allan Poe** | | | | |
| SHORT STORY<br>The Masque of the Red Death | Allegory, 454, 462 | Meaning, 454, 462 | Editorial, 463<br><br>Retelling, 463<br>Report, 463 | |
| ESSAY<br>*from* Danse Macabre | Paradox, 464 | | | |
| POETRY<br>The Raven | Sound Devices, 466, 471 | Conclusions, 466, 471<br>Informal Assess., 470 | Description, 472<br>Diary Entry, 472<br>Parody, 472 | |
| SHORT STORY<br>The Fall of the House of Usher | Mood, 473, 496 | Complex Sentences, 473, 496<br>Test Practice, 484<br>Informal Assess., 494 | Letter, 498<br>Comparing, 498<br>Retelling, 498 | |
| The Author's Style<br>Author Study Project | | Points of View, 497 | Style in Action, 497 | |
| SHORT STORY<br>Dr. Heidegger's Experiment | Foreshadowing, 500, 514<br><br>Review: Mood, 514 | Allegory, 500, 514<br><br>Informal Assess., 513<br>Test Practice, 512 | Warning Label, 515<br>Science News, 515<br>Story Ending, 515 | |
| SHORT STORY<br>Comparing Literature<br>A Rose for Emily | Characterization, 516, 525<br><br>Review: Foreshadowing, 525 | Sequencing, 516, 525 | Obituary, 526<br>Diary, 526<br>Points of Comparison, 526<br>Workplace Link, 519<br>Informal Assess., 522 | |
| SHORT STORY<br>Comparing Literature<br>The Life You Save<br>May Be Your Own | Irony, 528, 539<br>Review: Characterization, 539 | Conclusions, 528, 539<br>Test Practice, 534<br>Storyboard, 541 | Letter, 540<br>Sequel, 540<br>Points of Comparison, 540 | |
| Comparing Literature<br>Assessment Practice | Literary Analysis, 542 | Reading a Prompt, 542 | Analytical Essay, 542 | |
| Writing Workshop: Short Story<br>Assessment Practice<br>Building Vocabulary<br>Sentence Crafting | | | Short Story, 547 | |
| Reflect and Assess<br>The Spirit of Individualism | Reviewing Literary Concepts, 553 | Reflect and Assess, 552 | Visions, 552<br>Building Your Portfolio, 553 | |

LEGEND    DLS = Daily Language SkillBuilder
CCL - Cross Curricular Link          Green type - Teacher's Edition

| | Unit Resource Book | Assessment | Integrated Technology and Media | Additional Support — Literary Analysis Transparencies |
|---|---|---|---|---|
| **A Psalm of Life** *pp. 344–348* | • Active Reading p. 4<br>• Literary Analysis p. 5 | • Selection Test, Formal Assessment pp. 63–64<br>Test Generator | Audio Library | • Form in Poetry: Structure T11 |
| **The Devil and Tom Walker** *pp. 349–362* | • Summary p. 6<br>• Active Reading p. 7<br>• Literary Analysis p. 8<br>• Words to Know p. 9<br>• Selection Quiz p. 10 | • Selection Test, Formal Assessment pp. 65–66<br>Test Generator | Audio Library | • Point of View T20 |
| *from* **Self Reliance** *pp. 363–368* | • Summary p. 11<br>• Active Reading p. 12<br>• Literary Analysis p. 13<br>• Words to Know p. 14<br>• Selection Quiz p. 15 | • Selection Test, Formal Assessment pp. 67–68<br>Test Generator | Audio Library | |
| *from* **Civil Disobedience** *pp. 369–380* | • Summary p. 16<br>• Active Reading p. 17<br>• Literary Analysis p. 18<br>• Words to Know p. 19<br>• Selection Quiz p. 20 | • Selection Test, Formal Assessment pp. 69–70<br>Test Generator | Audio Library<br><br>Research Starter www.mcdougallittell.com | • Persuasion T8<br>• Persuasion: Types of Appeals T9 |
| *from* **Walden** *pp. 381–393* | • Summary p. 21<br>• Active Reading p. 22<br>• Literary Analysis p. 23<br>• Words to Know p. 24<br>• Selection Quiz p. 25 | • Selection Test, Formal Assessment pp. 71–72<br>Test Generator | Audio Library<br><br>Research Starter www.mcdougallittell.com | • Persuasion T8<br>• Theme in Nonfiction T22 |
| **Selected Poems by Walt Whitman** *pp. 396–405* | • Active Reading p. 26<br>• Literary Analysis p. 27 | • Selection Test, Formal Assessment pp. 73–74<br>Test Generator | Audio Library | • Poetic Devices T12 |
| **Danse Russe (1916) anyone lived in a pretty how town (1940)** *pp. 410–415* | • Active Reading p. 28<br>• Literary Analysis p. 29 | • Selection Test, Formal Assessment pp. 75–76<br>Test Generator | Audio Library | • Style and Voice T23 |
| **Ending Poem (1986) Tía Chucha (1991)** *pp. 416–423* | • Active Reading p. 30<br>• Literary Analysis p. 31 | • Selection Test, Formal Assessment pp. 77–78<br>Test Generator | Audio Library<br><br>Research Starter www.mcdougallittell.com | • Form in Poetry: Structure T11<br>• Point of View T20 |
| **Gary Keillor** *pp. 424–435* | • Summary p. 32<br>• Active Reading p. 33<br>• Literary Analysis p. 34<br>• Selection Quiz p. 35<br>• Comparing Literature p. 36 | • Selection Test, Formal Assessment pp. 79–80<br>Test Generator | | |

## Writing Workshop: Reflective Essay

| | | Unit Assessment | Unit Technology | |
|---|---|---|---|---|
| **Unit Three Resource Book**<br>• Prewriting p. 37<br>• Drafting and Elaboration p. 38<br>• Peer Response Guide pp. 39–40<br>• Revising, Editing, and Proofreading p. 41<br>• Student Models pp. 42–47<br>• Rubric for Evaluation p. 48 | **Power Presentations CD-ROM**<br>**Writing Transparencies and Copymasters** T11, T20, C28<br>**Teacher's Guide to Assessment and Portfolio Use** | • Unit Three, Part 1 Test, Formal Assessment pp. 81–82<br>Test Generator<br>• Unit Three Integrated Test, Integrated Assessment pp. 19–29 | ClassZone www.mcdougallittell.com<br><br>EasyPlanner CD-ROM<br><br>Electronic Library | |

| Reading and Critical Thinking Transparencies | Grammar Transparencies and Copymasters | Vocabulary Transparencies and Copymasters | Writing Transparencies and Copymasters | Communications Transparencies and Copymasters |
|---|---|---|---|---|
| • Organizational Chart: Horizontal T51 | • Daily Language SkillBuilder T9<br>• Noun Phrases C80 | • Homonyms C35 | | |
| • Visualizing T8 | • Daily Language SkillBuilder T9<br>• Modifiers C127 | • Idioms C36 | • Reflective Essay T28<br>• Short Story T29 | |
| • Summarizing T10 | • Daily Language SkillBuilder T10<br>• Adjective and Adverb Phrases I C82 | • Prefixes and Meanings of Roots C21 | • Levels of Language T12 | • Formal Presentations T10 |
| • Compare and Contrast T15<br>• Evaluating Argumentation I T20 | • Daily Language SkillBuilder T10<br>• Punctuating a Series of Clauses C156 | • Denotation and Connotation C38 | • Compare-Contrast C32 | • Evaluating Roles in Groups T8<br>• Impromptu Speaking: Dialogue, Role-Play, Debate T13 |
| • Observation Chart T46 | • Daily Language SkillBuilder T11<br>• Nouns Used as Adjectives C69<br>• Double Negatives C137<br>• Modifiers: *Good* and *Well* C136 | • Homonyms C35 | • Interpretive Essay C36 | • Impromptu Speaking: Dialogue, Role-Play, Debate T13 |
| • Compare and Contrast T15 | • Daily Language SkillBuilder T11<br>• Prepositional Phrases C84 | • Analogies C48 | • Critical Review C28 | • Nonverbal Strategies T15 |
| • Making Inferences T7 | • Daily Language SkillBuilder T11 | | • Point of View T23 | |
| • Compare and Contrast T15 | • Daily Language SkillBuilder T12 | • Using Reference Materials C40 | • The Uses of Dialogue T24<br>• Compare-Contrast C31<br><br>• Short Story C29 | • Dramatic Reading T12<br>• Impromptu Speaking: Dialogue, Role-Play, Debate T13<br>• Verbal Strategies T14<br>• Nonverbal Strategies T15 |
| • Comparing Authors' Views T23 | • Daily Language SkillBuilder T12<br>• Commas with Nonessential Elements T55<br>• Appositives and Appositive Phrases C85<br>• Commas with Parenthetical Expressions C148 | • Idioms C41 | | • Impromptu Speaking: Dialogue, Role-Play, Debate T13 |

## STUDENTS ACQUIRING ENGLISH

The **Spanish Study Guide**, pp. 82–111, includes language support for the following pages:
• Family and Community Involvement (per unit)

• Selection Summaries and Vocabulary
• Active Reading
• Literary Analysis

UNIT THREE
# RESOURCE MANAGEMENT GUIDE
## PART 2

To introduce the theme/literary period of this unit, use Fine Art Transparencies T23–25 in the Communications Transparencies and Copymasters.

| | Unit Resource Book | Assessment | Integrated Technology and Media | Additional Support — Literary Analysis Transparencies |
|---|---|---|---|---|
| **The Masque of the Red Death** *pp. 454–463* | • Summary p. 51<br>• Active Reading p. 52<br>• Literary Analysis p. 53<br>• Words to Know p. 54<br>• Selection Quiz p. 55 | • Selection Test, Formal Assessment pp. 83–84<br>Test Generator | Audio Library<br><br>Research Starter www.mcdougallittell.com<br>NetActivities | |
| **The Raven** *pp. 466–472* | • Summary p. 56<br>• Active Reading p. 57<br>• Literary Analysis p. 58<br>• Words to Know p. 59<br>• Selection Quiz p. 60 | • Selection Test, Formal Assessment pp. 85–86<br>Test Generator | Audio Library<br>NetActivities | • Poetic Devices T12 |
| **The Fall of the House of Usher** *pp. 473–499* | • Summary p. 61<br>• Active Reading p. 62<br>• Literary Analysis p. 63<br>• Words to Know p. 64<br>• Selection Quiz p. 65 | • Selection Test, Formal Assessment pp. 87–88<br>Test Generator | Audio Library<br>NetActivities | • Mood T18 |
| **Dr. Heidegger's Experiment** *pp. 500–515* | • Summary p. 66<br>• Active Reading p. 67<br>• Literary Analysis p. 68<br>• Words to Know p. 69<br>• Selection Quiz p. 70 | • Selection Test, Formal Assessment pp. 89–90<br>Test Generator | Audio Library | |
| **A Rose for Emily (1930)** *pp. 516–527* | • Summary p. 71<br>• Active Reading p. 72<br>• Literary Analysis p. 73<br>• Words to Know p. 74<br>• Selection Quiz p. 75 | • Selection Test, Formal Assessment pp. 91–92<br>Test Generator | Audio Library<br>Video: Literature in Performance, Video Resource Book pp. 9–14 | • Characterization T6 |
| **The Life You Save May Be Your Own (1953)** *pp. 528–541* | • Summary p. 76<br>• Active Reading p. 77<br>• Literary Analysis p. 78<br>• Words to Know p. 79<br>• Selection Quiz p. 80<br>• Comparing Literature p. 81 | • Selection Test, Formal Assessment pp. 93–94<br>Test Generator | Audio Library | • Irony T21 |

## Writing Workshop: Short Story

| | Unit Assessment | Unit Technology | |
|---|---|---|---|
| **Unit Three Resource Book**<br>• Prewriting p. 82<br>• Drafting and Elaboration p. 83<br>• Peer Response Guide pp. 84–85<br>• Revising, Editing, and Proofreading p. 86<br>• Student Models pp. 87–92<br>• Rubric for Evaluation p. 93<br><br>**Power Presentations CD-ROM**<br>**Writing Transparencies and Copymasters** T11, T20, C29<br>**Teacher's Guide to Assessment and Portfolio Use** | • Unit Three, Part 2 Test, Formal Assessment pp. 95–96<br>• Mid-Year Test, Formal Assessment pp. 97–103<br>Test Generator<br>• Unit Three Integrated Test, Integrated Assessment pp. 19–29 | ClassZone www.mcdougallittell.com<br>EasyPlanner CD-ROM<br>Electronic Library | |

| Reading and Critical Thinking Transparencies | Grammar Transparencies and Copymasters | Vocabulary Transparencies and Copymasters | Writing Transparencies and Copymasters | Communications Transparencies and Copymasters |
|---|---|---|---|---|
| • Summarizing T10 | • Daily Language SkillBuilder T13<br>• Participles and Participial Phrases C86<br>• Past and Present Participles C87 | • Meanings of Latin Roots C42 | • Opinion Statement C34 | • Impromptu Speaking: Dialogue, Role-Play, Debate T13 |
| • Drawing Conclusions I4 | • Daily Language SkillBuilder T13<br>• Comparison of Regular and Irregular Adjectives and Adverbs T52<br>• Comparative Forms of Adjectives and Adverbs C128 | | • Sensory Word List T14 | • Impromptu Speaking: Dialogue, Role-Play, Debate T13 |
| • Main Idea and Supporting Details T12<br>• Compare and Contrast T15<br>• Sequence Chain T49 | • Daily Language SkillBuilder T13<br>• Comparison of Regular and Irregular Adjectives and Adverbs T52<br>• Comparisons of Irregular Adjectives and Adverbs C129<br>• Apostrophes: Possessive Compounds C160<br>• Dashes C161 | • Figurative Language C50 | • Compare-Contrast C31 | • Dramatic Reading T12 |
| • Predicting Outcomes T2<br>• Compare and Contrast T15 | • Daily Language SkillBuilder T14<br>• Comparison of Regular and Irregular Adjectives and Adverbs T52 | • Suffixes C46 | • Short Story C29 | • Nonverbal Strategies T15 |
| • Sequencing T13<br>• Compare and Contrast T15 | • Daily Language SkillBuilder T14<br>• Illogical Comparisons C134 | • Connotation C47 | • Achieving Conciseness T21 | |
| • Drawing Conclusions T4 | • Daily Language SkillBuilder T15<br>• Double Negatives T53<br>• Double Negatives C137 | • Analogies C48 | • Compare-Contrast C31<br>• Opinion Statement C34 | • Evaluating Roles in Groups T8 |

## STUDENTS ACQUIRING ENGLISH

The **Spanish Study Guide,** pp. 112–129, includes language support for the following pages:
• Family and Community Involvement (per unit)

• Selection Summaries and Vocabulary
• Active Reading
• Literary Analysis

| Selection | SkillBuilder Sentences | Suggested Answers |
|---|---|---|
| A Psalm of Life | 1. What are some of you're favorite poems wrote by Longfellow. | 1. What are some of **your** favorite poems **written** by Longfellow**?** |
| | 2. Him and other romantic writers of the early 1800s tried to often encourage an appreciation for life. | 2. **He** and other romantic writers of the early 1800s **often tried to encourage** an appreciation for life. |
| The Devil and Tom Walker | 1. Jolene which enjoys Washington Irvings writing suggested that Gina and me read his work. | 1. Jolene, **who** enjoys Washington Irving**'s** writing, suggested that Gina and **I** read his work. |
| | 2. "One of his storys she said are called 'The Devil and Tom Walker'" | 2. "One of his **stories,**" she said, "**is** called 'The Devil and Tom Walker.'" |
| *from* Self-Reliance | 1. People say who study Emerson that his ideas our real interesting and inspiring. | 1. People **who study Emerson say** that his ideas **are really** interesting and inspiring. |
| | 2. I hope to this afternoon read all of Self-Reliance. One of my favorite essays. | 2. **This afternoon, I hope to read** all of "Self-Reliance,**"** one of my favorite essays. |
| *from* Civil Disobedience | 1. Among great American essays about the responsibilitys of citizens are Henry David Thoreaus "Civil Disobedience." Wrote in the 1800s. | 1. Among great American essays about the **responsibilities** of citizens **is** Henry David Thoreau's "Civil Disobedience,**"** **written** in the 1800s. |
| | 2. The essay states that all Americans needed to monitor the actions of his or her government. | 2. The essay states that all Americans **need** to monitor the actions of **their** government. |
| *from* Walden | 1. Any nature lover whom is required to read "Walden" will ultimately want their own copy. | 1. Any nature lover **who** is required to read <u>Walden</u> will ultimately want **his or her** own copy. |
| | 2. In terms of financial gain Thoreau was not richly compinsated for his experiences at walden pond, he was richly compinsated in terms of personal growth. | 2. In terms of financial gain, Thoreau was not richly **compensated** for his experiences at **W**alden **P**ond, **but** he was richly **compensated** in terms of personal growth. |

| Selection | SkillBuilder Sentences | Suggested Answers |
|---|---|---|
| Selected Poems by Walt Whitman | **1.** Walt Whitman does not attempt to conceal the harshness of america in his poetry he shows the pain and meaness of existance.<br><br>**2.** The speaker answer's the child's question about the grass. By saying I guess it must be the flag of my disposition. | **1.** Walt Whitman does not attempt to conceal the harshness of **America. In** his poetry he shows the pain and **meanness** of **existence**.<br><br>**2.** The speaker **answers** the child's question about the grass **by saying,** "I guess it must be the flag of my disposition." |
| Danse Russe<br>anyone lived in a pretty how town | **1.** While the wife, the baby and kathleen slept William Carlos Williams' character in danse russe dancing in front of a mirror.<br><br>**2.** Experimental Poets like E. E. cummings write clever in order to create figures of speech and other literary affects in their poems. | **1.** While the wife, the baby, and **Kathleen** slept, William Carlos Williams**'s** character in "**D**anse **Russe**" **danced** in front of a mirror.<br><br>**2.** Experimental poets like E. E. **Cummings** write **cleverly** in order to create figures of speech and other literary **effects** in their poems. |
| Ending Poem<br>Tia Chucha | **1.** In Ending Poem the Poets comtemplate the many strands of their ancestry Puerto Rican, new yorker, californian, Jewish, and Caribean.<br><br>**2.** If my mother and me wrote a poem together about our childhood, we can talk about how we were raised different. | **1.** In "Ending Poem," the **p**oets contemplate the many strands of their ancestry: Puerto Rican, **New Yorker, C**alifornian, Jewish, and **Caribbean**.<br><br>**2.** If my mother and **I** wrote a poem together about our childhood**s**, we **could** talk about how we were raised different**ly**. |
| Gary Keillor | **1.** In this story Gary Keillor recite the poem O Captain! My Captain at the talent show.<br><br>**2.** Keillor reads an article about Colorado in National Geographic, then he wants to go their. | **1.** In this story, Gary Keillor **recites** the poem "O Captain! My Captain!" at the talent show.<br><br>**2.** Keillor reads an article about Colorado in **National Geographic, and** then he wants to go **there**. |
| The Masque of the Red Death | **1.** Prince prospero was a fearless man. Who defied death and disease by throwing a bizarre party.<br><br>**2.** He invited a thousand friend's, sealed the iron gates of the abbey, and dancing was provided, and music. | **1.** Prince **P**rospero was a fearless **man who** defied death and disease by throwing a bizarre party.<br><br>**2.** He invited a thousand **friends,** sealed the iron gates of the abbey, **and provided dancing and music**. |

| Selection | SkillBuilder Sentences | Suggested Answers |
|---|---|---|
| The Raven | 1. Most think of Edgar Allan Poe as a writer of mystery or horror tales but he also wrote poetry literary criticism even science fiction.<br><br>2. Poe wrote harsh, negative reviews of many of the more famous, american writers of his time. | 1. Most **people** think of Edgar Allan Poe as a writer of mystery or horror tales, but he also wrote poetry, literary criticism, **and** even science fiction.<br><br>2. Poe wrote harsh, negative reviews of many of the **most famous American** writers of his time. |
| The Fall of the House of Usher | 1. The Fall of the house of usher were published in 1839.<br><br>2. Written by Edgar allan poe the story takes place in a spooky gothic mansion. | 1. "The Fall of the **H**ouse of **U**sher" **was** published in 1839.<br><br>2. Written by Edgar **A**llan **P**oe, the story takes place in a spooky **G**othic mansion. |
| Dr. Heidegger's Experment | 1. Dr. heideggers guests' all have pasts that are less then admirable.<br><br>2. Although dr Heidegger warns his visitors before the experement takes place. They ignore his advice. | 1. Dr. **H**eidegger**'s guests** all have pasts that are less **than** admirable.<br><br>2. Although **Dr.** Heidegger warns his visitors before the **experiment** takes place, **t**hey ignore his advice. |
| A Rose for Emily | 1. Miss Emily couldn't hardly wait to go for a ride.<br><br>2. Some say love is efemeral while others insists its eternal. | 1. Miss Emily **could not wait** to go for a ride.<br><br>2. Some say love is **ephemeral**, while others insist **it's** eternal. |
| The Life You Save May Be Your Own | 1. The old car in the shed, it was a ford maid in 1929.<br><br>2. Mr. Shiftlet said that "it were the law that doesnt satisfy him." | 1. The old car in the shed was a **Ford made** in 1929.<br><br>2. Mr. Shiftlet said that it **was** the law that **didn't** satisfy him. |

| Grammar Focus by Unit | Unit One | Unit Two | Unit Three | Unit Four | Unit Five | Unit Six | Unit Seven |
|---|---|---|---|---|---|---|---|
| | Parts of a Sentence | Verbs | Phrases | Clauses, Part I | Clauses, Part II | Special Sentence Structures, Part I | Special Sentence Structures, Part II |

*The Language of Literature* offers several options for integrating grammar instruction and literature.

- Each literature unit has a grammar focus. The Teacher's Edition includes Mini Lessons for each selection that help develop the grammar focus for the unit and spring from the content of the specific literature.

- The Pupil Edition includes several full-page lessons on Sentence Crafting. These lessons are related to both the literature and the grammar focus for the unit and help students use grammar in their own writing.

- Daily Language SkillBuilders in the Teacher's Edition provide students with ongoing proofreading practice and reinforce punctuation, spelling, grammar and usage, and capitalization.

- Grammar Copymasters and Transparencies, which may be used to complement or extend lessons in the Teacher's Edition, present grammar in a traditional, systematic sequence. References to appropriate copymasters or transparencies are included at point of use in the Teacher's Edition Mini Lessons.

TE Mini Lessons shown in green
PE instruction shown in black

## Part 1

### Parts of Speech
**Review: Parts of Speech**
Sentence Crafting, p. 445
**Forming Plurals**
**Distinguishing Plurals from Possessives**
Writing Workshop, p. 443
**Nouns as Adjectives**
from *Walden*, p. 390

### Using Phrases
**Modifiers: Adjective and Adverb Phrases**
from *Self-Reliance*, p. 368
from *Civil Disobedience*, p. 376
Sentence Crafting, p. 445
**Prepositional Phrases**
Whitman poems, p. 401
**Appositives and Appositive Phrases**
"Gary Keillor," p. 430
**Participles and Participial Phrases**
"The Devil and Tom Walker," pp. 352–353

### Verb Usage
**Verb Tenses**
**Problems in Using Verb Tenses**
Writing Workshop, p. 443

### Using Modifiers
**Using Modifiers**
"The Devil and Tom Walker," p. 362
**Problems with Modifiers:** *good* and *well*
from *Walden*, p. 388
**Problems with Modifiers: Double Negatives**
from *Walden*, p. 393

### End Marks and Commas
**Commas, Interrupters: Parenthetical Expressions**
"Gary Keillor," p. 432

### Other Punctuation
**Hyphens: Compound Adjectives**
from *Walden*, p. 380

### Style
**Noun Phrases**
"A Psalm of Life," p. 348

## Part 2

### Parts of Speech
**Review: Parts of Speech**
Sentence Crafting, p. 551
**Pronouns**
Writing Workshop, p. 549

### Using Phrases
**Modifiers: Adjective and Adverb Phrases**
Sentence Crafting, p. 551
**Placement of Prepositional Phrases**
Writing Workshop, p. 549
**Participles and Participial Phrases**
"The Masque of the Red Death," p. 457
**Participles and Participial Phrases: Past and Present Participles**
"The Masque of the Red Death," p. 463

### Using Modifiers
**Comparisons of Irregular Adjectives and Adverbs**
"The Fall of the House of Usher," p. 486
**Modifiers: Positive, Comparative, and Superlative Degrees**
"The Raven," p. 472
"Dr. Heidegger's Experiment," p. 502
"A Rose for Emily," p. 521
**Modifiers: Illogical Comparisons**
"Dr. Heidegger's Experiment," p. 515
**Problems with Modifiers: Double Negatives**
"The Life You Save May Be Your Own," p. 540

### Other Punctuation
**Apostrophes: Possessive Compounds**
"The Fall of the House of Usher," p. 490
**Quotation Marks in Dialogue**
Writing Workshop, p. 549

### Style
**Creating Compound Sentences**
Writing Workshop, p. 549

## TIME LINE 1800-1855

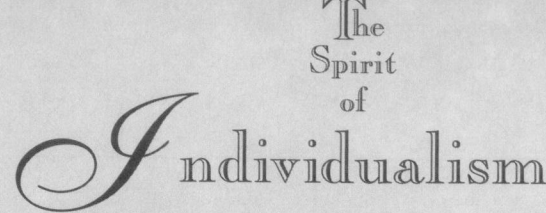

The
Spirit
of
*Individualism*

### EVENTS IN AMERICAN LITERATURE

| 1800 | 1810 | 1820 |
|---|---|---|

**1809** Washington Irving publishes *A History of New York*

**1824** Irving's "The Devil and Tom Walker" is published

**1826** James Fenimore Cooper publishes *The Last of the Mohicans*

**1827** *Freedom's Journal*, first African-American newspaper, is founded

**D** **1828** *American Dictionary of the English Language* is published by Noah Webster

### EVENTS IN THE UNITED STATES

| 1800 | 1810 | 1820 |
|---|---|---|

**1801** Thomas Jefferson becomes president

**A** **1803** Jefferson doubles size of United States by buying Louisiana territory from France

**1804** Meriwether Lewis and William Clark begin explorations of Louisiana territory and beyond to Pacific coast (to 1806)

**1807** Robert Fulton launches *Clermont*, the first steamboat

**1808** United States bans slave trade

**1812** United States declares war on Great Britain

**C** **1814** After witnessing naval battle during War of 1812, Francis Scott Key composes "The Star Spangled Banner"

**1820** Missouri Compromise prohibits slavery in western territory north of Missouri's southern border and allows slavery in Arkansas territory and Louisiana

**E** **1821** Sequoyah develops a system for writing the Cherokee language

**1823** President James Monroe issues Monroe Doctrine, banning European colonization in Americas

**1825** Erie Canal, a 363-mile waterway linking Lake Erie with the Hudson River, is opened

### EVENTS IN THE WORLD

| 1800 | 1810 | 1820 |
|---|---|---|

**B** **1804** Napoleon crowned emperor of France

**1807** British slave trade is abolished

**1812** Napoleon invades Russia

**1815** Napoleon is defeated at Battle of Waterloo

**1819** Zulu kingdom controls southeastern Africa

**1821** Mexico declares independence from Spain

**F** **1823** Beethoven completes Ninth Symphony

**338**    UNIT THREE    THE SPIRIT OF INDIVIDUALISM (1800–1855)

---

This time line shows some major dates and events of the first half of the 19th century in the United States and in the world. Help students recognize that this period was remarkable for its innovations and spirit of adventure.

### United States: 1803

**A** The American envoys to France, who had been instructed by Jefferson to try purchasing New Orleans and western Florida, were caught off guard when Napoleon suddenly offered the entire Louisiana Territory—for $15 million, or about $18 a square mile.

### World: 1804

**B** Although the Republicans won the Revolution in France, their original ideals of liberty and political freedom failed to become permanent. Political clubs were banned and elections became meaningless through fraud. In 1804, the pretense of republicanism was discarded when Bonaparte crowned himself emperor.

### United States: 1814

**C** While witnessing a successful defense of Fort McHenry against British bombardment in Baltimore Harbor on September 13–14 (the War of 1812 lasted until 1815), lawyer and poet Francis Scott Key wrote the words of "The Star-Spangled Banner" to the tune of a popular British song of the day. The song, though, did not become the official U.S. national anthem until 1931.

### Literature: 1828

**D** Noah Webster's first publication of his two-volume dictionary sold out in just over a year despite criticisms of its "Americanisms," its use of unconventional spellings, and the inclusion of technical terms that were considered nonliterary. About half of the dictionary's 70,000 entries had never been in any previous dictionary. An enlarged version, the "Unabridged," appeared in 1840. Webster is credited with giving American English a unique character and vitality.

### United States: 1821

**E** The writing system of Cherokee leader Sequoyah (c. 1766–1843) consisted of 85 symbols, one for each consonant/vowel combination. His system was used to publish parts of the Bible and a newspaper, *The Cherokee Phoenix*.

### World: 1823

**F** Beethoven's music is seen as encompassing the spirit of individualism and innovation that characterized his era. His *Ninth Symphony* (1817–1823), also known as the *Choral Symphony*, is distinguished by its unprecedented combination of vocal and instrumental music. Remarkably, Beethoven composed most of the work while completely deaf, his gradual loss of hearing becoming total in 1819.

## PERIOD PIECES

The cotton gin invented by Eli Whitney in 1793

Levi Strauss designed the first blue jeans, which were worn by prospectors in the 1850s

G

Mahogany tall-case clock

**1830**     **1840**     **1850**

H **1835** Ralph Waldo Emerson, Henry David Thoreau, Margaret Fuller, and others form the Transcendental Club

**1838** Henry Wadsworth Longfellow's "A Psalm of Life" is published

**1839** Edgar Allan Poe's "The Fall of the House of Usher" is published

**1845** Henry David Thoreau begins living on shore of Walden Pond (to 1847)

**1846** Herman Melville's first novel, *Typee*, is published

**1847** Thoreau publishes essay later known as "Civil Disobedience"

K **1850** Nathaniel Hawthorne's *The Scarlet Letter* is published

**1855** Walt Whitman publishes poetry collection *Leaves of Grass*

---

**1830**     **1840**

**1830** Indian Removal Act authorizes relocation of southeastern Native American tribes—including the Cherokee, Chickasaw, Choctaw, Creek, and Seminole—to territories west of Mississippi River

**1837** John Deere produces first steel-bladed plow, which makes large-scale farming possible in heavy soil in Midwest and West

I **1844** Samuel F. B. Morse sends first telegraph message from Baltimore to Washington, D.C.

**1848** United States defeats Mexico in Mexican War and claims land that is now Nevada, California, and part of New Mexico and Arizona

J **1848** Gold discoveries in California lead to first gold rush

**1850** Congress passes Fugitive Slave Act, forcing officials in Northern states to return escaped slaves to owners; Compromise of 1850 is passed, which supposedly settles controversy over slavery between slave and free states

---

**1830**     **1840**     **1850**

**1839** Britain and China fight first Opium War

**1848** Mass of revolutions sweep Europe; Karl Marx and Friedrich Engels publish *Communist Manifesto*

**1850** Taiping rebellion in China begins (to 1864)

TIME LINE    **339**

---

## PERIOD PIECES

G Pendulum clocks enclosed in tall, narrow cabinets came to be called "grandfather clocks." The name derives from the song "My Grandfather's Clock" by Henry Clay Work (1832–1884), a songwriter known for his pro-Union songs written during the Civil War.

### Literature: 1835

H An early feminist, Margaret Fuller (1810–1850) was the first editor of *The Dial*, the journal of the transcendentalists. In 1845 she published *Woman in the Nineteenth Century*, which demanded political equality and attempted to give women a defined, fulfilling place in society. She later became America's first woman foreign correspondent when she reported on her European travels for the *New York Tribune*. She died tragically in a shipwreck while returning from Italy.

### United States: 1844

I An excellent painter as well as an inventor, Samuel Morse (1791–1872) probably had the first working model of his telegraph by 1835. He invented the "code" that bears his name in 1838. The first telegraph message was "What hath God wrought!"

### United States: 1848

J At least 250,000 "Forty Niners" sought gold in California from 1848 to 1853, extracting about $300 million worth of the metal. The original discoverer of gold was James Marshall, a carpenter who was building a sawmill on John Sutter's land. Marshall's and Sutter's claims were ignored and overrun, the sawmill failed, and neither man ended his days wealthy.

---

### Literature: 1850

K The tragic heroine of Hawthorne's novel embodies the spirit of individualism that so concerned writers and artists of the early 19th century. It directly inspired fellow author Herman Melville, who published his own tragedy, *Moby Dick*.

**Introduction**

This article provides a historical background for the romantic and transcendentalist writers of the 19th century—notably Longfellow, Irving, Emerson, Fuller, Thoreau, and Whitman. Within the theme of celebrating the self, it also introduces some 20th-century "New Expressions of the Self." This first part of the unit deals with romanticism, which emphasized individual self-expression, and transcendentalism, which stressed "the all in each" (Emerson).

## Teaching Nonfiction

**Reading Skills and Strategies**
**ESTABLISHING A PURPOSE FOR READING**

Explain to the students that this article introduces them to the literary movements of romanticism and transcendentalism. Have students review the article and establish a purpose for reading *(to find out about the specific features of these movements and to understand their underlying philosophies).*

**USING REFERENCE MATERIALS**

Encourage students to note unfamiliar words as they read through the text of this article. Students are expected to use reference materials such as glossaries, dictionaries, and available technology to determine precise usages and definitions.

**MONITORING AND MODIFYING READING STRATEGIES**

Explain to students that this article contains some difficult words and complicated explanations. Encourage them to monitor their reading strategies and, if necessary, modify them when their understanding breaks down. Suggest they reread the article several times and ask questions in order to clarify their understanding of the material.

# Celebrations of the Self

## Romanticism and Transcendentalism

*Ralph Waldo Emerson*

**A** "Good men must not obey the laws too well," Ralph Waldo Emerson said. His aphorism illustrates a vital key to the American character—after all, if the original colonists *had* obeyed the laws, the American Revolution would never have occurred, and the country might never have existed. This rebelliousness—so much a part of our heritage—reflects an essential aspect of Emerson's philosophy of transcendentalism, a distinctively American offshoot of the romantic movement.

Around the beginning of the 19th century, the movement known as romanticism sprang up in both Europe and America as a reaction to everything that had come before it: the rationalism of the 18th-century

**American authors of the 19th century.** *Seated from left:* Henry Wadsworth Longfellow, William Cullen Bryant, Washington Irving (at the end of the table), and Margaret Fuller (slightly behind Irving). *Seated in right foreground:* Harriet Beecher Stowe.

*Standing from left:* Edgar Allan Poe (in profile facing left) and Nathaniel Hawthorne (in profile facing right). *Standing from right:* James Russell Lowell (with beard facing front) and Ralph Waldo Emerson. The Bettmann Archive.

Age of Reason and, especially in America, the strict doctrines of Puritanism. Romantic artists, philosophers, and writers saw the limitations of reason and celebrated instead the glories of the individual spirit, the emotions, and the imagination as basic elements of human nature. The splendors of nature inspired the romantics more than the fear of God, and some of them felt a fascination with the supernatural.

In the first half of the century, as the U.S. **B** population exploded and the country's borders spread westward, the romantic spirit guided American writers in their efforts to capture the energy and character of the new country. Henry Wadsworth Longfellow and Washington Irving were by far the most popular American writers of the time. Their works exhibit a typical romantic preoccupation with atmosphere, sentiment, and optimism.

*Henry Wadsworth Longfellow* **C**

Although Washington Irving was the first American writer to achieve international fame, the first really distinctive American literature came from the transcendentalists. The philosophy of transcendentalism, derived in part from German romanticism, was based on a belief that "transcendent forms" of truth exist beyond reason and experience. However, Ralph Waldo Emerson gave this philosophy a peculiarly American spin: he said that every individual is capable of discovering this higher truth on his or her own, through intuition.

*Washington Irving*

# Voices from the TIMES

The groves were God's first temples. Ere man learned
To hew the shaft, and lay the architrave,
And spread the roof above them—ere he framed
The lofty vault, to gather and roll back
The sound of anthems; in the darkling wood,
Amid the cool and silence, he knelt down,
And offered to the Mightiest solemn thanks
And supplication.

     **William Cullen Bryant**
     from "A Forest Hymn"

By the shores of Gitche Gumee,
By the shining Big-Sea-Water,
Stood the wigwam of Nokomis,
Daughter of the Moon, Nokomis.
Dark behind it rose the forest,
Rose the black and gloomy pine-trees,
Rose the firs with cones upon them;
Bright before it beat the water,
Beat the clear and sunny water,
Beat the shining Big-Sea-Water.

     **Henry Wadsworth Longfellow**
     from *The Song of Hiawatha*

I know I am august,
I do not trouble my spirit to vindicate itself or be understood,
I see that the elementary laws never apologize,
(I reckon I behave no prouder than the level I plant my house by, after all.)

     **Walt Whitman**
     from "Song of Myself"

HISTORICAL BACKGROUND   **341**

## Making Connections

### Politics
**A** Emerson's aphorism and the rebelliousness in the American character are well illustrated in Thoreau's famous essay "Civil Disobedience," which arose from the night he spent in jail for refusing to pay a tax. According to Thoreau, "Under a government which imprisons any unjustly, the true place for a just man is also a prison."

### Statistics
**B** There was explosive growth in the United States in the first half of the 19th century. Between 1800 and 1850, the area of the country increased from roughly 867,000 square miles to 2,944,000. The population grew from a little over five million in 1800 to a little over 23 million in 1850. The expansion no doubt created energy and optimism, but this was not the whole story. One reason that so many joined the gold rush in 1848 was social instability in the east.

### Literature
**C** Longfellow, especially, was popular beyond imagining. When this "household poet" died, schools were closed and the nation went into mourning.

### Philosophy
**D** Traced back to around 1830, the American transcendental movement was comprised of a loosely knit group of mostly New England poets and philosophers. Its beliefs were never formally articulated, but the followers wanted to "go beyond" the limitations of the senses and everyday experience. Their means of doing this was intuition, by which they hoped to discover higher truths and insights. A Transcendental Club was formed in 1835, and its magazine, *The Dial,* flourished from 1840 to 1844 as an important showcase for the more obscure poets. The club dissolved around 1844, and by 1855 the movement had lost steam, the energy of its ideas of freedom and individualism having been transferred from literary thought to abolitionist zeal.

## SUMMARIZING

Ask students to identify the main ideas and supporting details of this article. Then ask them to produce summaries of the article in their own words, paying particular attention to the elements of romanticism and transcendentalism.

## DISCUSSING

Because the material in this article is fairly complicated, give students the opportunity to discuss it in class. A starting point might be a discussion of the distinctions between romanticism and transcendentalism. It may also help to emphasize the historical context of these movements by discussing them as reactions against what came before them.

## ANALYZING

Ask students how Emerson's advice fits into the theme of the unit.

**Possible Responses:** He is advocating self-reflection; he is advising young people to do what is difficult rather than fall into what comes easily.

Have students compare Emerson's advice with the opening passage from Melville's *Moby Dick.* What is the connection between them?

**Possible Response:** Both quotations reflect a spirit of adventure. Emerson advocates daring by confronting fears, while Ishmael is drawn to the adventures of life on the sea.

---

# Voices from the TIMES

It was a high counsel that I once heard given to a young person, "Always do what you are afraid to do."

**Ralph Waldo Emerson**

Call me Ishmael. Some years ago—never mind how long precisely—having little or no money in my purse, and nothing particular to interest me on shore, I thought I would sail about a little and see the watery part of the world. It is a way I have of driving off the spleen, and regulating the circulation. Whenever I find myself growing grim about the mouth; whenever it is a damp, drizzly November in my soul; whenever I find myself involuntarily pausing before coffin warehouses, and bringing up the rear of every funeral I meet; and especially whenever my hypos [hypochondria] get such an upper hand of me, that it requires a strong moral principle to prevent me from deliberately stepping into the street, and methodically knocking people's hats off—then, I account it high time to get to sea as soon as I can.

**Herman Melville**
from *Moby-Dick*

---

Henry David Thoreau, Emerson's young friend and colleague, proved a prickly but brilliant embodiment of transcendentalist ideals as, militantly turning his back on material rewards, he devoted his life to the study of nature and his own individual spirit. His *Walden,* an account of the two years he lived alone in a one-room shack in the country (although dining regularly at Emerson's Boston house), remains a genuine American masterwork.

Walt Whitman was championed at the beginning of his career by Emerson for the ideas and style that Emerson believed the new American poetry required. Still, influential as Whitman has been in the 20th century, he waited a long time for his contribution to be recognized by the larger public in his own time. In 1855 he had to print the first collection of his poems, *Leaves of Grass,* himself. Able to sell only a few copies of the book, he gave virtually all of the 795 copies away. Meanwhile, in that same year, Longfellow published *The Song of Hiawatha,* which like his earlier books of poetry, sold thousands and became a bestseller.

## Traditions Across Time: Whitman's Heirs Express the Self

The celebration of individualism that began with romanticism and flourished with transcendentalism has remained at the core of American literature to the present day. During the first half of the 20th century, the poetry of William Carlos Williams and E. E. Cummings, among others, emphasized the spirit and power of solitary individuals. Contemporary writers, however, tend to temper their celebrations of the individual with more ambiguity. Rosario and Aurora Morales, for instance, try to find a new unity in their separate voices as mother and daughter, and the poet Luis J. Rodriguez makes readers view his eccentric aunt with a mixture of admiration and shock. The down-home voice of Garrison Keillor is shaped by the humorous ironies that are a trademark of our time.

## Romanticism and Transcendentalism

## Objectives

1. understand and appreciate a classic **lyric poem (Literary Analysis)**
2. examine **stanza and rhyme scheme (Literary Analysis)**
3. use **strategies for reading traditional poetry (Active Reading)**

## Summary

"A Psalm of Life" is an inspirational poem that celebrates the gift of life. Longfellow rejects the notion that life is an "empty dream" to be endured or wasted until death. He believes that people should appreciate their life on earth as precious and real—a time in which they should act to make a spiritual, moral, or intellectual mark on the world. He urges people not to waste the short time that they have behaving as "dumb, driven cattle" but rather to act as "heroes" amid earth's strife.

## Thematic Link

"A Psalm of Life" reflects the **romanticism** and optimism that existed in early nineteenth-century America. Longfellow's sentimental poem encourages readers to **celebrate** life and to work toward personal achievement.

## Reading Skills and Strategies: PREVIEW

Discuss the quotations by Plato, Stevenson, Wilde, and the character Forrest Gump. Explain that this short poem by Longfellow describes his view of life. As students read Longfellow's views, have them consider whether any of these people describe the truth or part of the truth about life. What, if anything, would they add to these views of life?

### 5-Minute Warm-Up

**Daily Language SkillBuilder**

Have students **proofread** the display sentences on page 337i and write them correctly. The sentences also appear on Transparency 9 of **Grammar Transparencies and Copymasters.**

---

# PREPARING to *Read*

# A Psalm of Life

*Poetry by* HENRY WADSWORTH LONGFELLOW

**Connect to Your Life**

**What Life Is All About** Each of the quotations on this page presents a way of looking at life. Which one comes closest to expressing your own philosophy of life?

> The life which is unexamined is not worth living.
> *Plato*

> To be what we are, and to become what we are capable of becoming, is the only end of life.
> *Robert Louis Stevenson*

> Life is far too important a thing ever to talk seriously about.
> *Oscar Wilde*

> Life is like a box of chocolates. You never know what you're going to get.
> *Forrest Gump*

## Build Background

**Uplifting Poetry** Henry Wadsworth Longfellow was the most popular and famous member of a group of New England romantic writers known as the Fireside Poets—a group that also included Oliver Wendell Holmes, James Russell Lowell, and John Greenleaf Whittier. The name of the group refers to a popular family pastime of the period: reading poetry aloud in front of the fireplace after dinner. Longfellow and his fellow Fireside Poets wrote poems that were morally uplifting and often sentimental.

One summer morning, Longfellow wrote "A Psalm of Life" in the blank spaces of an invitation. After it was published in *Knickerbocker* magazine in October 1838, the poem swept the country and became known around the world. Although widely parodied, even by Longfellow himself, it celebrates an optimistic view of life and reflects the aims of Americans at the time.

## Focus Your Reading

**LITERARY ANALYSIS** | **STANZA AND RHYME SCHEME** A **stanza** is a group of lines that form a unit in a poem. "A Psalm of Life" is written in four-line stanzas. A **rhyme scheme** is the pattern of end rhyme (rhyming of words at the end of lines) in a stanza or an entire poem. Traditional poems, such as "A Psalm of Life," contain stanzas with a regular rhyme scheme. In addition to having a regular rhyme scheme, much of the poetry written by the Fireside Poets has a regular **meter** (a repeated sequence of stressed and unstressed syllables).

**ACTIVE READING** | **STRATEGIES FOR READING TRADITIONAL POETRY** To appreciate the musical qualities of "A Psalm of Life," try these strategies:

- Read the poem silently to understand the basic meaning.
- Then read the poem aloud, paying attention to its patterns of sound. Notice the pattern of end rhymes in each stanza.
- Tap out the meter, or the rhythm of the poem.

### LESSON RESOURCES

**UNIT THREE RESOURCE BOOK,** pp. 4–5

**ASSESSMENT RESOURCES**
**Formal Assessment,** pp. 63–64
**Teacher's Guide to Assessment and Portfolio Use**
**Test Generator**

**SKILLS TRANSPARENCIES AND COPYMASTERS**
**Literary Analysis**
- Form in Poetry: Structure, T11 (for Paired Activity, p. 347)

**Reading and Critical Thinking**
- Organizational Chart: Horizontal, T51 (for Writing Option 1, p. 348)

**Grammar**
- Noun Phrases, C80 (for Mini Lesson, p. 348)

**Vocabulary**
- Homonyms, C35 (for Mini Lesson, p. 346)

**INTEGRATED TECHNOLOGY**

**Audio Library**
**LaserLinks**
- Biographical Connection: The Fireside Poets. See **Teacher's SourceBook,** p. 36.

**Visit our website:**
www.mcdougallittell.com

*En Mer* [At sea] (1898), Max Bohm. Courtesy of Alfred J. Walker Fine Art, Boston.

# A Psalm of Life

HENRY
WADSWORTH
LONGFELLOW

*What the Heart of the Young Man
Said to the Psalmist*[1]

Tell me not, in mournful numbers,[2]
   Life is but an empty dream!—
For the soul is dead that slumbers,
   And things are not what they seem.

5  Life is real! Life is earnest!
   And the grave is not its goal;
Dust thou art, to dust returnest,
   Was not spoken of the soul.

Not enjoyment, and not sorrow,
10  Is our destined end or way;
But to act, that each tomorrow
   Find us farther than today.

---

1. **Psalmist** (sä′mĭst): the author of the poems in the
biblical Book of Psalms, many of which comment on
the fleeting nature of life. Traditionally, most of the
psalms have been ascribed to King David of Israel.
2. **numbers:** metrical feet or lines; verses.

## Mini Lesson — Viewing and Representing

*En Mer [At Sea]* **by Max Bohm**

**ART APPRECIATION** Max Bohm (1868–1923) won a gold medal for this painting at a Paris exhibition in 1898.

**Instruction** Artists often use various elements of design to convey meaning. Have students describe the image of the men at sea. How does the artist use light and shadow? What details in the picture suggest the power of the sea? What details suggest the courage of the men?

**Possible Responses:** the white and gray churning water; the way in which the water gathers around the boat; the men's posture as they struggle to stay in control of the boat

**Application** In what way does this picture relate to Longfellow's view of life?

**Possible Response:** Longfellow feels that people should have the courage to live life to the fullest. The men in the picture are not giving up—they are fighting to stay afloat with all of their strength.

## Reading and Analyzing

### Active Reading

**STRATEGIES FOR READING TRADITIONAL POETRY**

After students have read the poem silently, have them take turns reading stanzas aloud so that they can analyze the evocative rhythms of literary language. Ask students who are listening to quietly tap out the rhythm of the poem at their desks. Then have them explain how reading aloud increases their appreciation of the poem.

 Use **Unit Three Resource Book**, p. 4 for more practice.

### Literary Analysis

**STANZA AND RHYME SCHEME**

Have students identify the poem's structure.

**Answer:** nine four-line stanzas, *abab* rhyme scheme

Have them analyze how this structure influences their understanding of the poem.

**Possible Response:** The short stanzas, strong rhymes, and pulsing rhythm give a sense of urgency and excitement that supports the speaker's message of living heroically and fully.

 Use **Unit Three Resource Book**, p. 5 for more practice.

### Literary Analysis: FIGURATIVE LANGUAGE

**A** Students can rely on context clues to determine the meaning of figurative language, such as Longfellow's image of "footprints on the sands of time." How does the image relate to Longfellow's message? Who is the "forlorn and shipwrecked brother"?

**Possible Responses:** Longfellow is comparing personal achievements to footprints in the sand. He is saying that great achievements can have a lasting effect on the world and can help guide and influence others. The "forlorn and shipwrecked brother" is a person in trouble who can benefit from the example of another person's life.

---

Art is long, and Time is fleeting,
  And our hearts, though stout and brave,
15 Still, like muffled drums, are beating
  Funeral marches to the grave.

In the world's broad field of battle,
  In the bivouac[3] of Life,
Be not like dumb, driven cattle!
20  Be a hero in the strife!

Trust no Future, howe'er pleasant!
  Let the dead Past bury its dead!
Act—act in the living Present!
  Heart within, and God o'erhead!

25 Lives of great men all remind us
  We can make our lives sublime,[4]
And, departing, leave behind us
  Footprints on the sands of time;

Footprints, that perhaps another,
30  Sailing o'er life's solemn main,[5]
A forlorn and shipwrecked brother,
  Seeing, shall take heart again.

Let us, then, be up and doing,
  With a heart for any fate;
35 Still achieving, still pursuing,
  Learn to labor and to wait.

---

3. **bivouac** (bĭv′ŏŏ-ăk′): a temporary encampment of troops.
4. **sublime:** of high spiritual, moral, or intellectual worth.
5. **main:** open ocean.

---

## Teaching Options

**Mini Lesson** **Vocabulary**

### HOMONYMS

**Instruction** Homonyms are two or more words with the same pronunciation and often the same spelling, but with different meanings. Tell students that they can rely on context clues to determine the separate meanings of homonyms.

**Application** Ask students to explain the meanings of the words *numbers* and *main* that are most familiar to them. Then ask them to use context clues to define the homonyms of these words that appear in the poem. Have students work in pairs to come up with a list of familiar homonyms in the English language. They should try to use at least three sets of homonyms in complete sentences.

 Use **Vocabulary Transparencies and Copymasters**, p. 35.

**A lesson on homonyms appears on p. 728 in the Pupil's Edition.**

# *Thinking* through the LITERATURE

## Connect to the Literature

**1. What Do You Think?**
What are your thoughts about the form or the message of this poem?

> **Comprehension Check**
> What, according to the speaker, is "our destined end," or purpose?

## Think Critically

**2.** How does the **speaker's** view of life compare with your own view?

**THINK ABOUT**

- what the speaker says life is not
- the command "Act—act in the living Present!" (line 23)
- the last four lines of the poem
- the quotation you chose as closest to your philosophy

**3.** In your own words, summarize what the speaker says about the value of the lives of great people (lines 25–32). Do you agree with the speaker? Explain.

**4.** **ACTIVE READING** | **STRATEGIES FOR READING TRADITIONAL POETRY** Read the poem aloud in class, with a different person taking each stanza. If the poem were to be sung, what style of music do you think would fit best with its **meter** and **theme**? Explain your choice.

## Extend Interpretations

**5. Comparing Texts** How do you think a Puritan writer such as Anne Bradstreet (page 139) or Jonathan Edwards (page 152) might have responded to the ideas presented in "A Psalm of Life"?

**6. What If?** Imagine that Longfellow were a counselor at your school. Based on the message of "A Psalm of Life," do you think he would be a successful counselor or not? Explain your opinion.

**7. Connect to Life** Do you think that Americans today still share the values expressed in "A Psalm of Life"? Point out lines in the poem that you think contemporary Americans might or might not agree with.

## Literary Analysis

**STANZA AND RHYME SCHEME**
You can mark the **rhyme scheme** of a stanza or a poem by using letters (beginning with *a*) to designate the lines, assigning the same letter to lines that end with the same sound. Here is the first stanza of an Anne Bradstreet poem:

| | |
|---|---|
| In silent night when rest I <u>took</u> | a |
| For sorrow near I did not <u>look</u> | a |
| I wakened was with thund'ring <u>noise</u> | b |
| And piteous shrieks of dreadful <u>voice</u>. | b |
| That fearful sound of "Fire!" and "<u>Fire!</u>" | c |
| Let no man know is my <u>desire</u>. | c |

Notice that the letters change each time the end rhyme changes. The rhyme scheme of this stanza is *aabbcc*.

**Paired Activity** Working with a partner, identify the rhyme scheme used in "A Psalm of Life" by marking it for the first two stanzas. Then look at the poem as a whole. What words or ideas does the rhyme scheme emphasize?

**REVIEW** A **metaphor** is a figure of speech that compares two things that have something in common. Consider the metaphor in lines 17–18. How is the world like a field of battle? How is life like a bivouac in this battlefield?

A PSALM OF LIFE   **347**

---

## GUIDING STUDENT RESPONSE

## Connect to the Literature

**1. What Do You Think?**
Possible Responses: Some students may feel that the form of the poem makes it seem silly, or sing songy, but that the message is serious and meaningful.

**Comprehension Check**
- taking bold action; striving for accomplishment

## Think Critically

**2.** Ask students to use evidence from the poem to support their opinions about the speaker's attitudes. Their writing should address the bulleted items.

**3.** Possible Responses: The speaker says that the achievements ("footprints") of the great can serve as an inspiration to others. Some students will agree; others may insist that everyone has to find his or her own way.

**4.** Possible Responses: Students may conclude that aesthetic elements such as regular rhyme and military images would make marching music an appropriate accompaniment.

## Literary Analysis

**Stanza and Rhyme Scheme** The rhyme scheme is abab cdcd efef, and so on through qrqr. The rhyming emphasizes key words in the poet's argument. These key words state and restate the main idea that, because of the soul's immortality and the fleetness of time, life is something to be taken seriously.

**Review Metaphor** Possible Responses: The world is filled with many challenges; life provides us with temporary shelter as we join in the struggle.

---

## Extend Interpretations

**Comparing Texts** Possible Response: Both Bradstreet's poems and Edwards's sermon stressed the importance of worshiping God, the meaninglessness of material wealth, and the need to be humble in this life so that one can look forward to the next. Since Longfellow's poem stresses personal achievement on earth and suggests that people can look to one another, as well as to God, for inspiration, it is possible that Bradstreet and Edwards would find Longfellow misguided or too worldly.

**What If?** Possible Responses: Yes, he would make a good counselor because he has such a strong view of life and many students would find him inspiring. No, because he doesn't leave room for students to develop their own views.

**Connect to Life** Most students are likely to agree that Americans today believe in the importance of achievement during one's life.

A PSALM OF LIFE   **347**

## Writing Options

1. **Personal Response** If writing a poem does not appeal to students, suggest that they explain their views in a journal entry or a letter to a friend.

2. **Longfellow Parody** Remind students that a parody is an imitation designed to mock the original. Harriet Fleischman's parody, for example, suggests that what we leave behind may be more embarrassing than inspiring. **To get students started on this assignment,** suggest that they experiment with substituting different words in several stanzas of the original.

## Activities & Explorations

1. **Photo Collage** Ask students to collect images suggesting themes of heroism, courage, hope, endurance, and aspiration. Some students may prefer to take their own photos or search for images on the Internet.

2. **Bumper Sticker** Students should be able to recall clever bumper stickers they have seen. After students work together to create text for the bumper sticker, one student can choose colors and do the lettering; another student might speak for the group to the class. Encourage students to use a word processing program and clip art to create their own bumper sticker designs.

## Author Activity

Possible Responses: Longfellow's poetry is inspiring and optimistic and expresses the shared values of most Americans at that time. His themes are universal and accessible. The rhythmic nature of his poems makes them easy to memorize and recite.

## Writing Options

1. **Personal Response** How do you think life should be lived? Think about the quotation you chose and the ideas you discussed in responding to question 2. Then in a personal response to Longfellow, perhaps in the form of a poem, explain your philosophy of life. Place this piece in your **Working Portfolio.**

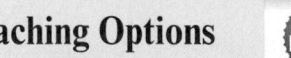

Philosophy of Life
Longfellow's Views | My Views

2. **Longfellow Parody** "A Psalm of Life" is among the most parodied poems in the English language. Here is an example by Harriet Fleischman:

*Lives of great men all remind us*
*As we history's pages turn*
*That we often leave behind us*
*Letters which we ought to burn.*

Write a stanza or two of parody in the style of "A Psalm of Life."

## Activities & Explorations

1. **Photo Collage** Find a photograph or an illustration that suggests an idea or theme in "A Psalm of Life." Combine the images found by the class to create a bulletin-board collage.
~ VIEWING AND REPRESENTING

2. **Bumper Sticker** Work with a partner to design a bumper sticker that expresses the philosophy of life suggested by the poem. Present your design to the class and explain why it is appropriate. ~ ART

## Henry Wadsworth Longfellow
### 1807–1882

**Other Works**
*The Courtship of Miles Standish*
*Evangeline*
*The Song of Hiawatha*
"Paul Revere's Ride"
"The Wreck of the Hesperus"
"The Village Blacksmith"

**Aspiring Poet** Henry Wadsworth Longfellow, the most famous American poet of the 1800s, had a career that spanned more than 50 years. His first poem was published in a Maine newspaper when he was 13. Two years later, he entered Bowdoin College, where, like his classmate Nathaniel Hawthorne, he decided to become a writer. From college, Longfellow wrote his father, "I most eagerly aspire after further eminence in literature." Eventually he was to fulfill his aspirations.

**College Professor** A brilliant scholar, the 18-year-old Longfellow was offered Bowdoin's first established professorship in modern languages when he graduated in 1825. Since the field was so new, he had to create his own textbooks. Several years later he accepted a similar position at Harvard, where he remained until 1854, when he resigned to write full time.

**Literary Eminence** Longfellow's first book of poetry, *Voices of the Night,* was published when he was 32. As his popularity grew, many of his poems became household favorites. A beloved poet and a scholar able to speak and read ten languages, Longfellow was respected all over the world. He was the first American writer to be honored with a bust in the Poets' Corner of London's Westminster Abbey.

## Author Activity

Do you recognize any of the other Longfellow works listed? Can you quote lines from them? Discuss what has made Longfellow's poetry so popular.

## Teaching Options

**Mini Lesson** ## Grammar

**NOUN PHRASES** A noun phrase is a group of related words that functions as a noun and that does not contain both a subject and a verb. Remind students that a noun indicates a person, place, thing, or idea. Write the following sentence on the chalkboard. Ask students to identify the noun phrase. Then ask them to explain how they know the word group is a noun phrase.

Striving to accomplish great things is crucial, according to Longfellow.

**Answer:** This group of words does not have a subject and a verb (and thus is not a clause), and it functions as the subject of the sentence.

**Application** Ask students to work in pairs to write five sentences about "A Psalm of Life" that contain noun phrases. Ask them to underline the noun phrases in each of their sentences.

 Use **Grammar Transparencies and Copymasters,** p. 80.

 Use McDougal Littell's *Language Network,* Chapter 2, for more instruction in noun phrases.

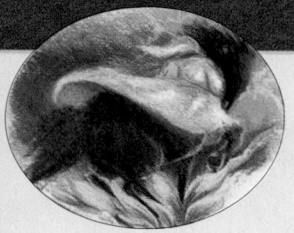

# PREPARING to Read

# The Devil and Tom Walker

*Short Story by* WASHINGTON IRVING

### Connect to Your Life

**Money Matters** Should people pursue wealth? Why or why not? How important is wealth to you? What limits, if any, would you put on your own pursuit of wealth? Discuss your answers to these questions with a small group of classmates.

## Build Background

**The Faust Legend** The first American writer esteemed abroad, Washington Irving is known for his humorous essays and stories. In "The Devil and Tom Walker," Irving adapted the Germanic legend of Johann Faust, a 16th-century magician and alchemist who was said to have sold his soul to the devil in exchange for worldly power and wealth. For his comic retelling, Irving created an American character who strikes the same bargain and faces the same consequences in an American setting. The story takes place in the environs of Boston in the early 1700s, when the Puritans still dominated Massachusetts society.

### WORDS TO KNOW
**Vocabulary Preview**

| | | |
|---|---|---|
| abode | ostentation | prowess |
| censurer | parsimony | repose |
| daunted | peculiar | resolute |
| dolefully | piety | singular |
| melancholy | propitious | surmise |

## Focus Your Reading

**LITERARY ANALYSIS** **IMAGERY** Imagery is words and phrases that appeal to the five senses, helping you to imagine precisely what people, places, and events in a literary work are like. The majority of images are visual, serving to stimulate pictures in your mind. Consider this descriptive paragraph from Irving's story:

> . . . *there lived near this place a meager, miserly fellow, of the name of Tom Walker. He had a wife as miserly as himself.* . . . *They lived in a forlorn-looking house that stood alone and had an air of starvation. A few straggling savin trees, emblems of sterility, grew near it; no smoke ever curled from its chimney; no traveler stopped at its door. A miserable horse, whose ribs were as articulate as the bars of a gridiron, stalked about a field.*

The images of the forlorn house, the straggling trees, and the starved horse show you just how miserly Tom and his wife are.

**ACTIVE READING** **VISUALIZING** Irving provides much description in "The Devil and Tom Walker," so an understanding of the imagery is crucial to an understanding of the story—and to an enjoyment of its humor.

**READER'S NOTEBOOK** As you read, try to visualize, or form mental pictures of, the characters, settings, and events. Jot down some of the images that describe Tom and the character trait that each image helps you to picture.

## OVERVIEW

### Objectives
1. understand and appreciate a **short story (Literary Analysis)**
2. identify **imagery** in a short story (Literary Analysis)
3. **visualize** the characters, settings, and events in a short story (**Active Reading**)

### Summary
One day at dusk, while taking a short-cut home through a swamp, miserly Tom Walker encounters the devil. Old Scratch offers Tom the buried gold of the pirate Kidd on certain conditions. Tom shares this secret with his greedy wife, who sets off to bargain for the gold herself, but she disappears and is never seen again. Eventually, Tom agrees to the bargain, which includes acting as the devil's usurer; he lends money to people in need and takes everything they own when they cannot repay the loan. Toward the end of his life, Tom regrets his deal with the devil. He becomes aggressively religious in an attempt to escape his fate. One day, as Tom is completing a cruel transaction, the devil takes Tom's soul and reduces his fortune to ashes.

### Thematic Link
Like other **romantic** writers of his time, Washington Irving uses supernatural elements and striking details to create atmosphere.

### 5-Minute Warm-Up

*Daily*
*Language*
*SkillBuilder*

Have students **proofread** the display sentences on page 337i and write them correctly. The sentences also appear on Transparency 9 of **Grammar Transparencies and Copymasters.**

**Mini Lesson** **Preteaching Vocabulary**
If you would like to preteach the WORDS TO KNOW for this selection, use the Mini Lesson, p. 350.

**Reading Skills and Strategies: PREVIEW**

Have students read the Preparing to Read page. Tell students that as they visualize the images, they might draw quick sketches of them in their notebooks. They should also notice particular sounds, physical sensations, and smells, and write down their emotional reactions to them. Students should ask themselves these questions about the images in each passage:

• What pictures do they form in my imagination?
• Are the pictures related in any way?
• What ideas do I associate with them?

**Literary Analysis** IMAGERY

Throughout the story, Irving creates images of darkness, decay, hidden danger, and ugliness. Ask students to find examples of such sensory language in the opening paragraphs. Then ask them to look for more of this language as they read.

**Set a Purpose** Have students read to find out how images of darkness, decay, hidden danger, and ugliness relate to the writer's theme, or main idea.

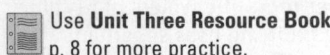 Use **Unit Three Resource Book**, p. 8 for more practice.

**Active Reading** VISUALIZING

Irving describes key locations in vivid detail. As students read, they should pause from time to time, close their eyes, and try to picture in their minds the settings that Irving's descriptive language creates.

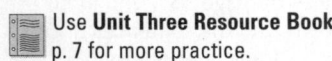 Use **Unit Three Resource Book**, p. 7 for more practice.

## Teaching Options

# The Devil and Tom Walker

## Washington Irving

A few miles from Boston in Massachusetts, there is a deep inlet, winding several miles into the interior of the country from Charles Bay, and terminating in a thickly wooded swamp or morass. On one side of this inlet is a beautiful dark grove; on the opposite side the land rises abruptly from the water's edge into a high ridge, on which grow a few scattered oaks of great age and immense size. Under one of these gigantic

350

 **Mini Lesson** **Preteaching Vocabulary**

**USING CONTEXT CLUES** When students encounter an unfamiliar word in their reading, they can try to figure out the word's meaning by making inferences based on the context, or the surrounding words. Write the model sentence on the chalkboard. Ask a volunteer to point out specific words that provide clues about the meaning of *censurer*.

**Model Sentence**
Acting as a <u>censurer</u> of his friends and neighbors made him quite unpopular. He was always criticizing, finding faults, and expressing disapproval.

**Exercises** Ask students to use context clues to define the underlined terms.
1. The soldier was constantly bragging about his <u>prowess</u>. He told people that he was stronger, braver, and more daring than most people.
2. The leader seemed firm and unwavering in his values and beliefs. People respected the fact that he was so <u>resolute</u>.

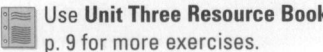 Use **Unit Three Resource Book**, p. 9 for more exercises.

A lesson on context clues appears on p. 326 in the Pupil's Edition.

trees, according to old stories, there was a great amount of treasure buried by Kidd the pirate. The inlet allowed a facility to bring the money in a boat secretly and at night to the very foot of the hill; the elevation of the place permitted a good lookout to be kept that no one was at hand; while the remarkable trees formed good landmarks by which the place might easily be found again. The old stories add, moreover, that the devil presided at the hiding of the money and took it under his guardianship; but this, it is well-known, he always does with buried treasure, particularly when it has been ill-gotten. Be that as it may, Kidd never returned to recover his wealth; being shortly after seized at Boston, sent out to England, and there hanged for a pirate.

About the year 1727, just at the time that earthquakes were prevalent in New England, and shook many tall sinners down upon their knees, there lived near this place a meager, miserly fellow, of the name of Tom Walker. He had a wife as miserly as himself: they were so miserly that they even conspired to cheat each other. Whatever the woman could lay hands on, she hid away; a hen could not cackle but she was on the alert to secure the new-laid egg. Her husband was continually prying about to detect her secret hoards, and many and fierce were the conflicts that took place about what ought

to have been common property. They lived in a forlorn-looking house that stood alone and had an air of starvation. A few straggling savin trees, emblems of sterility, grew near it; no smoke ever curled from its chimney; no traveler stopped at its door. A miserable horse, whose ribs were as articulate as the bars of a gridiron,[1] stalked about a field, where a thin carpet of moss, scarcely covering the ragged beds of pudding-stone,[2] tantalized and balked his hunger; and sometimes he would lean his head over the fence, look piteously at the passerby and seem to petition deliverance from this land of famine.

The house and its inmates had altogether a bad name. Tom's wife was a tall termagant,[3] fierce of temper, loud of tongue, and strong of arm. Her voice was often heard in wordy warfare with her husband; and his face sometimes showed signs that their conflicts were not confined to words. No one ventured, however, to interfere between them. The lonely wayfarer shrunk within himself at the horrid clamor and clapper-clawing;[4] eyed the den of discord askance;[5] and hurried on his way, rejoicing, if a bachelor, in his celibacy.

One day that Tom Walker had been to a distant part of the neighborhood, he took what he considered a shortcut homeward, through the swamp. Like most shortcuts, it was an ill-chosen route. The swamp was thickly grown with great

---

1. **as articulate . . . gridiron:** as clearly separated as the bars of a grill.
2. **puddingstone:** a rock consisting of pebbles and gravel cemented together.
3. **termagant** (tûr′mə-gənt): a quarrelsome, scolding woman.
4. **clapper-clawing:** scratching or clawing with the fingernails.
5. **eyed . . . askance** (ə-skăns′): looked disapprovingly at the house filled with arguing.

THE DEVIL AND TOM WALKER **351**

## Customizing Instruction

### Less Proficient Readers
Ask students to think about a time when they felt hopelessly trapped in a deal that they shouldn't have made or a situation they didn't like. What did they do? What happened? Have students compare their experience with Tom's as they read this story.

**Set a Purpose** Have students read to find out where Tom stops on his way home.

### Students Acquiring English
- Point out that the devil is a symbol of evil.
- Irving's humorous tone may be overlooked and his euphemisms and sarcasm misunderstood by students who are struggling to understand his unfamiliar sentence structure and dated language. You may wish to discuss Irving's tone and style before students begin reading.

 Use **Spanish Study Guide** for additional support, pp. 88–90.

### Gifted and Talented
As they read the selection, students should note similarities between the Faust legend and the story of Tom Walker.

## BLOCK SCHEDULING: MANAGING TIME

**If your schedule requires that you cover the lesson objectives in a shorter time, use . . .**
- Preparing to Read, p. 349
- Thinking Through the Literature, p. 360
- Vocabulary in Action, p. 361

**If you want to take advantage of longer class time, use . . .**
- TE Teaching Options: Preteaching Vocabulary, p. 350; Vocabulary Strategies, pp. 354, 357; Multicultural Link, p. 355; Economics Link, p. 356; Informal Assessment, p. 358; Test Preparation, p. 361
- Choices & Challenges, pp. 361–362

## Active Reading  VISUALIZING

Remind students that authors often use sensory details to appeal to a reader's five senses. Suggest that students fill in a word web like the one shown below to help them visualize Tom's experience in the swamp. Have them complete the web with words and phrases used on page 352 to describe the swamp.

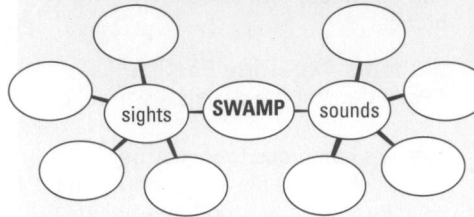

## Literary Analysis  IMAGERY

**A** Ask students what impression of the swamp is suggested by these descriptive details.

**Possible Responses:** dreary, unpleasant, dangerous, frightening, haunted

## Literary Analysis: SYMBOLISM

**B** A symbol is something that represents or suggests something else. Ask students what the great tree scored with the name of Deacon Peabody and "fair and flourishing without, but rotten at the core" represents.

**Possible Response:** It represents Deacon Peabody's hypocrisy. Although externally he appears respectable and successful and thus blessed by God, he is actually wicked underneath.

---

**A** gloomy pines and hemlocks, some of them ninety feet high, which made it dark at noonday, and a retreat for all the owls of the neighborhood. It was full of pits and quagmires, partly covered with weeds and mosses, where the green surface often betrayed the traveler into a gulf of black, smothering mud; there were also dark and stagnant pools, the <u>abodes</u> of the tadpole, the bullfrog, and the water snake; where the trunks of pines and hemlocks lay half-drowned, half-rotting, looking like alligators sleeping in the mire.

Tom had long been picking his way cautiously through this treacherous forest; stepping from tuft to tuft of rushes and roots, which afforded precarious footholds among deep sloughs; or pacing carefully, like a cat, along the prostrate trunks of trees; startled now and then by the sudden screaming of the bittern,[6] or the quacking of wild duck rising on the wind from some solitary pool. At length he arrived at a firm piece of ground, which ran out like a peninsula into the deep bosom of the swamp. It had been one of the strongholds of the Indians during their wars with the first colonists. Here they had thrown up a kind of fort, which they had looked upon as almost impregnable, and had used as a place of refuge for their squaws and children.

Nothing remained of the old Indian fort but a few embankments,

gradually sinking to the level of the surrounding earth, and already overgrown in part by oaks and other forest trees, the foliage of which formed a contrast to the dark pines and hemlocks of the swamp.

It was late in the dusk of evening when Tom Walker reached the old fort, and he paused there awhile to rest himself. Anyone but he would have felt unwilling to linger in this lonely, <u>melancholy</u> place, for the common people had a bad opinion of it, from the stories handed down from the time of the Indian wars, when it was asserted that the savages held incantations[7] here, and made sacrifices to the evil spirit.

Tom Walker, however, was not a man to be troubled with any fears of the kind. He <u>reposed</u> himself for some time on the trunk of a fallen hemlock, listening to the boding cry of the tree toad, and delving with his walking staff into a mound of black mold at his feet. As he turned up the soil unconsciously, his staff struck against something hard. He raked it out of the vegetable mold, and lo! a cloven skull, with an Indian tomahawk buried deep in it, lay before him. The rust on the weapon showed the time that had elapsed since this death-blow had been given. It was a dreary memento of the fierce struggle that had taken place in this last foothold of the Indian warriors.

"Humph!" said Tom Walker, as he gave it a kick to shake the dirt from it.

"Let that skull alone!" said a gruff voice. Tom lifted up his eyes, and beheld a great black man seated directly opposite him, on the stump of a tree. He was exceedingly surprised, having neither heard nor seen anyone approach; and he was still more perplexed on observing, as well as the gathering gloom would permit, that the stranger was neither Negro nor Indian. It is true he was dressed in a rude half-Indian garb, and

---

6. **bittern:** a wading bird with mottled, brownish plumage and a deep, booming cry.

7. **incantations:** verbal charms or spells recited to produce a magic effect.

---

WORDS
TO
KNOW

**abode** (ə-bōd') *n.* a dwelling place; home
**melancholy** (mĕl'ən-kŏl'ē) *adj.* gloomy; sad
**repose** (rĭ-pōz') *v.* to rest or relax

352

---

**Mini Lesson** ## Grammar

**VERBAL PHRASES: INFINITIVES, GERUNDS, AND PARTICIPLES** A verbal is a verb form that functions in a sentence as a noun, an adjective, or an adverb. Verbals include infinitives, gerunds, and participles. Share the following definitions and examples with students. Verb phrases are in bold. An infinitive is a verb form made up of the word *to* and the base form of a verb. An infinitive functions as a noun, an adjective, or an adverb.

Tom loves **to bargain.**
The quarrels between Tom and his wife were frightful **to hear.**

A gerund is a verb form that ends in *-ing* and always acts as a noun.

**Arguing** fills the Walker household.
To save his soul, Tom tried **praying.**

A participle ends in *-ing* or *-ed* and functions as an adjective.

**Walking,** Tom made his way through the dense forest.
Tom, **defeated and frightened,** made his final journey.

A verbal phrase consists of a verbal, its modifiers, and its complements.

had a red belt or sash swathed round his body; but his face was neither black nor copper-color, but swarthy and dingy, and begrimed with soot, as if he had been accustomed to toil among fires and forges. He had a shock of coarse black hair, that stood out from his head in all directions, and bore an ax on his shoulder.

He scowled for a moment at Tom with a pair of great red eyes.

"What are you doing on my grounds?" said the black man, with a hoarse, growling voice.

"Your grounds!" said Tom, with a sneer, "no more your grounds than mine; they belong to Deacon Peabody."

"Deacon Peabody be d—d," said the stranger, "as I flatter myself he will be, if he does not look more to his own sins and less to those of his neighbors. Look yonder, and see how Deacon Peabody is faring."

Tom looked in the direction that the stranger pointed, and beheld one of the great trees, fair and flourishing without, but rotten at the core, and saw that it had been nearly hewn through, so that the first high wind was likely to blow it down. On the bark of the tree was scored the name of Deacon Peabody, an eminent man, who had waxed wealthy by driving shrewd bargains with the Indians. He now looked around, and found most of the tall trees marked with the name of some great man of the colony, and all more or less scored by the ax. The one on which he had been seated, and which had evidently just been hewn down, bore the name of Crowninshield; and he recollected a mighty rich man of that name, who made a vulgar display of wealth, which it was whispered he had acquired by buccaneering.[8]

"He's just ready for burning!" said the black man, with a growl of triumph. "You see, I am likely to have a good stock of firewood for winter."

"But what right have you," said Tom, "to cut down Deacon Peabody's timber?"

---

8. **buccaneering:** robbing ships at sea; piracy.

Ⓐ Be sure students notice the humorous attitude the author takes toward Tom's reaction to meeting the devil face-to-face. According to the narrator, why does Tom not fear the devil?

**Possible Response:** He is hardened after living so many years with his wife. Even the devil is not frightening compared to Tom's wife.

**Literary Analysis: CHARACTERIZATION**

Ⓑ Ask students what Tom's refusal to agree to the devil's bargain at this point in the story suggests about his character.

**Possible Response:** He is even more contrary and spiteful than he is greedy; he would rather deny himself riches than please his wife by acquiring them.

**Literary Analysis: TONE**

Ⓒ Ask students what attitude the author takes toward Tom in this brief passage.

**Possible Response:** The author's attitude is humorously critical; he suggests that Tom cares more about the silver than about his wife's safety.

**Literary Analysis** IMAGERY

Ⓓ Ask students to identify the sounds and their sources in this passage. What effect are these sounds intended to create?

**Possible Response:** The screaming of the bittern, the croaking of the bullfrog, the hooting of the owls, and the clamor of the carrion crows create a mood of uneasy loneliness and anticipation.

---

"The right of a prior claim," said the other. "This woodland belonged to me long before one of your white-faced race put foot upon the soil."

"And pray, who are you, if I may be so bold?" said Tom.

"Oh, I go by various names. I am the wild huntsman in some countries; the black miner in others. In this neighborhood I am he to whom the red men consecrated this spot, and in honor of whom they now and then roasted a white man, by way of sweet-smelling sacrifice. Since the red men have been exterminated by you white savages, I amuse myself by presiding at the persecutions of Quakers and Anabaptists;[9] I am the great patron and prompter of slave dealers, and the grand master of the Salem witches."

*"The upshot of all which is that, if I mistake not," said Tom, sturdily, "you are he commonly called Old Scratch."*

"The upshot of all which is that, if I mistake not," said Tom, sturdily, "you are he commonly called Old Scratch."[10]

"The same, at your service!" replied the black man, with a half-civil nod.

Such was the opening of this interview, according to the old story; though it has almost too familiar an air to be credited. One would think that to meet with such a singular personage, in this wild, lonely place, would have shaken any man's nerves; but Tom was a hard-minded fellow, not easily <u>daunted</u>, and he had lived so long with a termagant wife that he did not even fear the devil.

It is said that after this commencement they had a long and earnest conversation together, as Tom returned homeward. The black man told him of great sums of money buried by Kidd the pirate, under the oak trees on the high ridge, not far from the morass. All these were under his command, and protected by his power, so that none could find them but such as propitiated his favor. These he offered to place within Tom Walker's reach, having conceived an especial kindness for him; but they were to be had only on certain conditions. What these conditions were may be easily <u>surmised</u>, though Tom never disclosed them publicly. They must have been very hard, for he required time to think of them, and he was not a man to stick at trifles when money was in view. When they had reached the edge of the swamp, the stranger paused. "What proof have I that all you have been telling me is true?" said Tom. "There's my signature," said the black man, pressing his finger on Tom's forehead. So saying, he turned off among the thickets of the swamp, and seemed, as Tom said, to go down, down, down, into the earth, until nothing but his head and shoulders could be seen, and so on, until he totally disappeared.

When Tom reached home, he found the black print of a finger burnt, as it were, into his forehead, which nothing could obliterate.

The first news his wife had to tell him was the sudden death of Absalom Crowninshield, the rich buccaneer. It was announced in the papers

---

9. **presiding . . . Anabaptists:** exercising authority over the oppression of Christian groups that the Puritans considered radical.

10. **Old Scratch:** a nickname for the devil.

---

| WORDS TO KNOW | **singular** (sǐng'gyə-lər) *adj.* unusual or remarkable; unique |
| | **daunted** (dôn'tĭd) *adj.* intimidated or frightened **daunt** *v.* |
| | **surmise** (sər-mīz') *v.* to guess |

354

---

 **Mini Lesson** ## Vocabulary Strategy

**IDIOMS** An idiom is an expression whose meaning differs from the meanings of the individual words in the expression. Idioms are often the products of regional or cultural influences on language. Idioms can pose difficulty for non-native speakers of a language or for anyone reading a selection from other historical periods. Tell students that they can use context clues to figure out the meanings of unfamiliar idioms. For example, after the devil describes his many roles, Tom says, "The upshot of all which is that, if I mistake not . . . you are he commonly called Old Scratch." The expression *the upshot of all that* is an idiom that means the "the result, or conclusion of that. . . ." Students can use context clues to figure out that Tom is reaching a conclusion based on the devil's information.

**Application** Have students explain the idiomatic expressions in these passages: "The house and its inmates had altogether a bad name"; "Give the devil his due"; "loud of tongue." Then ask them to work in pairs to come up with a list of idiomatic expressions they use in their daily lives.

📋 Use **Vocabulary Transparencies and Copymasters,** p. 36.

with the usual flourish that "a great man had fallen in Israel."[11]

Tom recollected the tree which his black friend had just hewn down and which was ready for burning. "Let the freebooter[12] roast," said Tom; "who cares!" He now felt convinced that all he had heard and seen was no illusion.

He was not prone to let his wife into his confidence; but as this was an uneasy secret, he willingly shared it with her. All her avarice was awakened at the mention of hidden gold, and she urged her husband to comply with the black man's terms, and secure what would make them wealthy for life. However Tom might have felt disposed to sell himself to the devil, he was determined not to do so to oblige his wife; so he flatly refused, out of the mere spirit of contradiction. Many and bitter were the quarrels they had on the subject; but the more she talked, the more <u>resolute</u> was Tom not to be damned to please her.

At length she determined to drive the bargain on her own account, and if she succeeded, to keep all the gain to herself. Being of the same fearless temper as her husband, she set off for the old Indian fort toward the close of a summer's day. She was many hours absent. When she came back, she was reserved and sullen in her replies. She spoke something of a black man, whom she met about twilight hewing at the root of a tall tree. He was sulky, however, and would not come to terms; she was to go again with a propitiatory offering, but what it was she forbore to say.

The next evening she set off again for the swamp, with her apron heavily laden. Tom waited and waited for her, but in vain; midnight came, but she did not make her appearance; morning, noon, night returned, but still she did not come. Tom now grew uneasy for her safety, especially as he found she had carried off in her apron the silver teapot and spoons, and every portable article of value. Another night elapsed,

another morning came; but no wife. In a word, she was never heard of more.

What was her real fate nobody knows, in consequence of so many pretending to know. It is one of those facts which have become confounded by a variety of historians. Some asserted that she lost her way among the tangled mazes of the swamp, and sank into some pit or slough; others, more uncharitable, hinted that she had eloped with the household booty and made off to some other province; while others surmised that the tempter had decoyed her into a dismal quagmire, on the top of which her hat was found lying. In confirmation of this, it was said a great black man, with an ax on his shoulder, was seen late that very evening coming out of the swamp, carrying a bundle tied in a check apron, with an air of surly triumph.

The most current and probable story, however, observes that Tom Walker grew so anxious about the fate of his wife and his property that he set out at length to seek them both at the Indian fort. During a long summer's afternoon he searched about the gloomy place, but no wife was to be seen. He called her name repeatedly, but she was nowhere to be heard. The bittern alone responded to his voice, as they flew screaming by; or the bullfrog croaked <u>dolefully</u> from a neighboring pool. At length, it is said, just in the brown hour of twilight, when the owls began to hoot, and the bats to flit about, his attention was attracted by the clamor of carrion crows[13] hovering about a cypress tree. He looked up, and beheld a bundle tied in a check apron, and hanging in the branches of the tree, with a great vulture perched hard by, as if

_____

11. **a great man . . . Israel:** a biblical reference—"Know ye not that there is a prince and a great man fallen this day in Israel?" (2 Samuel 3:38)—used, with unconscious irony, by the papers to mean that an important member of God's people on earth has passed away.

12. **freebooter:** pirate.

13. **carrion crows:** crows that feed on dead or decaying flesh.

WORDS TO KNOW
**resolute** (rĕz′ə-lōōt′) *adj.* firm or determined; unwavering
**dolefully** (dōl′fə-lē) *adv.* mournfully

355

## Customizing Instruction

**Students Acquiring English**
**1** This passage describing Tom's important conversation with the devil moves quickly and contains difficult language. You might want to read the passage aloud with students, defining the following words and phrases: *propitiated his favor* ("satisfied his wishes"); *conceived* ("established"); *especial* ("special"); *trifles* ("small details"). You might have students answer the following questions:

• What money does the devil describe? Where is the money?
  **Answer:** Captain Kidd's treasure, which is buried not far from the swamp

• What does the devil offer to do with the money?
  **Answer:** allow Tom to have it

• What decision must Tom make? How do readers know it is a difficult decision?
  **Answer:** He must decide whether or not to sell his soul to the devil. It must be a difficult decision because Tom is a greedy person who normally would not hesitate when offered money.

**Less Proficient Readers**
**2** Ask students who Old Scratch is, what he offers to Tom Walker, and what he wants in return.
  **Answer:** Old Scratch is the devil; he offers Walker treasure in return for his soul.

**Set a Purpose** Have students read to find out how Tom Walker's wife reacts to the devil's offer.

## Multicultural Link

**FOLKLORE** Folklore consists of a culture's customs, legends, beliefs, and orally transmitted stories, ballads, poems, and songs. People who study folklore often regard it as a reflection of a civilization's values and attitudes. The formal study of folklore began in the early nineteenth century, with the rise of Romanticism in Europe. The ideals of Romantic writers in Europe spread to America, where writers such as Washington Irving were

living and working. Irving himself is well-known for his use of folklore in his short stories. Readers familiar with his stories can understand his fascination with the quirky legends and tales that were transmitted from generation to generation in both Europe and America. In American folklore appear such heroes as Paul Bunyan the woodcutter, John Henry the railroad worker, and Pecos Bill the cowboy.

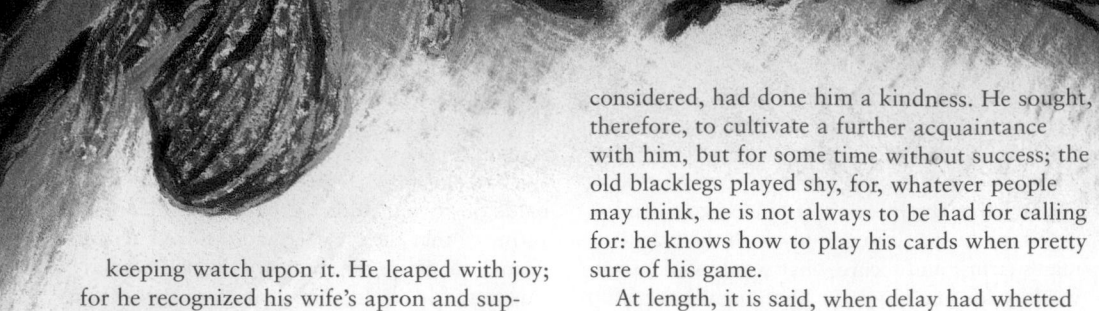

## Reading and Analyzing

## Reading and Analyzing

### Literary Analysis: OMNISCIENT NARRATOR

**A** Point out the narrator's access to Tom's thoughts and feelings. Ask students what the narrator's omniscience adds to the story.

**Possible Responses:** It strengthens the story's moral message because the narrator can reveal Tom's wicked character and the reasons for his ultimate punishment; it offers more opportunities for humor because the narrator can reveal the ironic truths about Tom, his wife, and his fellow townspeople.

### Reading Skills and Strategies: SUMMARIZING

**B** Students should be able to summarize by identifying main ideas and supporting details. Ask students to describe the situation in the colony that makes it advantageous for Tom Walker to lend money.

**Possible Response:** Times are hard; a period of wild speculation, in which people lost money in get-rich-quick land schemes, has just ended; many people lost borrowed money and desperately need to borrow more money to pay off their debts.

### Literary Analysis: TONE

**C** Point out Irving's humorous attitude toward Tom's business practices in this passage. Explain that Irving uses humor to teach readers what is morally right. By mocking Tom and thus getting readers to laugh at him, Irving helps readers recognize the error of behaving like Tom.

keeping watch upon it. He leaped with joy; for he recognized his wife's apron and supposed it to contain the household valuables.

"Let us get hold of the property," said he consolingly to himself, "and we will endeavor to do without the woman."

As he scrambled up the tree, the vulture spread its wide wings, and sailed off screaming into the deep shadows of the forest. Tom seized the checked apron, but, woeful sight! found nothing but a heart and liver tied up in it!

**1** Such, according to this most authentic old story, was all that was to be found of Tom's wife. She had probably attempted to deal with the black man as she had been accustomed to deal with her husband; but though a female scold is generally considered a match for the devil, yet in this instance she appears to have had the worst of it. She must have died game, however; for it is said Tom noticed many prints of cloven feet stamped upon the tree, and found handfuls of hair that looked as if they had been plucked from the coarse black shock of the woodman. Tom knew his wife's prowess by experience. He shrugged his shoulders, as he looked at the signs of a fierce clapper-clawing. "Egad," said he to himself, "Old Scratch must have had a tough time of it!"

**A** Tom consoled himself for the loss of his property with the loss of his wife, for he was a man of fortitude. He even felt something like gratitude towards the black woodman, who, he considered, had done him a kindness. He sought, therefore, to cultivate a further acquaintance with him, but for some time without success; the old blacklegs played shy, for, whatever people may think, he is not always to be had for calling for: he knows how to play his cards when pretty sure of his game.

At length, it is said, when delay had whetted Tom's eagerness to the quick, and prepared him to agree to anything rather than not gain the promised treasure, he met the black man one evening in his usual woodsman's dress, with his ax on his shoulder, sauntering along the swamp, and humming a tune. He affected to receive Tom's advances with great indifference, made brief replies, and went on humming his tune.

By degrees, however, Tom brought him to business, and they began to haggle about the terms on which the former was to have the pirate's treasure. There was one condition which need not be mentioned, being generally understood in all cases where the devil grants favors; but there were others about which, though of less importance, he was inflexibly obstinate. He insisted that the money found through his means should be employed in his service. He proposed, therefore, that Tom should employ it in the black traffic; that is to say, that he should fit out a slave ship. This, however, Tom resolutely refused: he was bad enough in all conscience; but the devil himself could not tempt him to turn slave trader.

Finding Tom so squeamish on this point, he did not insist upon it, but proposed, instead, that he should turn usurer;[14] the devil being extremely

---

14. **usurer** (yōō′zhər-ər): one who lends money, especially at an unusually or unlawfully high rate of interest.

WORDS
TO
KNOW

**prowess** (prou′ĭs) *n.* superior strength, courage, or daring, especially in battle

356

---

## Teaching Options

 **Cross Curricular Link** **Economics**

**USURY** Interest is a fee, usually a percentage of the amount loaned, that a borrower must pay to a lender in return for the use of the money. Lending at excessively high rates of interest has traditionally been condemned as *usury,* because high interest can make a debt virtually impossible to repay. High interest can also hurt a country's economy by making it more difficult for consumers and businesses to obtain loans. Usury has been in practice since ancient times. In some cultures and institutions, charging interest was actually forbidden as an unethical business practice. In the United States today, people obtaining loans are routinely charged interest, but a distinction is made between high-interest-rate loans and low-interest-rate loans. Bonds and mortgages are assets that an individual might pledge today as security, or collateral, to obtain a loan. If the borrower fails to repay the loan and interest within the agreed-upon time, he or she gives up these assets to the lender. For example, a mortgage on a house, if not repaid, would allow the lender to foreclose on, or take possession of, the house.

anxious for the increase of usurers, looking upon them as his <u>peculiar</u> people.

To this no objections were made, for it was just to Tom's taste.

"You shall open a broker's shop in Boston next month," said the black man.

"I'll do it tomorrow, if you wish," said Tom Walker.

"You shall lend money at two percent a month."

"Egad, I'll charge four!" replied Tom Walker.

"You shall extort bonds, foreclose mortgages, drive the merchants to bankruptcy—"

"I'll drive them to the d——l," cried Tom Walker.

"You are the usurer for my money!" said blacklegs with delight. "When will you want the rhino[15]?"

"This very night."

"Done!" said the devil.

"Done!" said Tom Walker. So they shook hands and struck a bargain.

A few days' time saw Tom Walker seated behind his desk in a countinghouse[16] in Boston.

His reputation for a ready-moneyed man, who would lend money out for a good consideration, soon spread abroad. Everybody remembers the time of Governor Belcher, when money was particularly scarce. It was a time of paper credit. The country had been deluged with government bills; the famous Land Bank[17] had been established; there had been a rage for speculating; the people had run mad with schemes for new settlements; for building cities in the wilderness; land-jobbers[18] went about with maps of grants, and townships, and Eldorados[19] lying nobody knew where, but which everybody was ready to purchase. In a word, the great speculating fever, which breaks out every now and then in the country, had raged to an alarming degree, and everybody was dreaming of making sudden fortunes from nothing. As usual the fever had

subsided; the dream had gone off, and the imaginary fortunes with it; the patients were left in doleful plight, and the whole country resounded with the consequent cry of "hard times."

At this <u>propitious</u> time of public distress did Tom Walker set up as usurer in Boston. His door was soon thronged by customers. The needy and adventurous, the gambling speculator, the dreaming land-jobber, the thriftless tradesman, the merchant with cracked credit; in short, everyone driven to raise money by desperate means and desperate sacrifices hurried to Tom Walker.

Thus Tom was the universal friend of the needy and acted like a "friend in need"; that is to say, he always exacted good pay and good security. In proportion to the distress of the applicant was the hardness of his terms. He accumulated bonds and mortgages; gradually squeezed his customers closer and closer; and sent them at length, dry as a sponge, from his door.

In this way he made money hand over hand, became a rich and mighty man, and exalted his cocked hat upon 'Change.[20] He built himself, as usual, a vast house, out of <u>ostentation</u>; but left the greater part of it unfinished and unfurnished,

---

15. **rhino:** a slang term for money.

16. **countinghouse:** an office in which a business firm conducts its bookkeeping, correspondence, and similar activities.

17. **Land Bank:** Boston merchants organized the Land Bank in 1739. Landowners could take out mortgages on their property and then repay the loans with cash or manufactured goods. When the Land Bank was outlawed in 1741, many colonists lost money.

18. **land-jobbers:** people who buy and sell land for profit.

19. **Eldorados:** places of fabulous wealth or great opportunity. Early Spanish explorers sought a legendary country named El Dorado, which was rumored to be rich with gold.

20. **exalted . . . 'Change:** proudly raised himself to a position of importance as a trader on the stock exchange.

---

WORDS
TO
KNOW

**peculiar** (pĭ-kyōōl'yər) *adj.* belonging particularly or primarily to one person, group, or kind
**propitious** (prə-pĭsh'əs) *adj.* helpful or advantageous; favorable
**ostentation** (ŏs'tĕn-tā'shən) *n.* display meant to impress others; boastful showiness

357

## Customizing Instruction

**Less Proficient Readers**

**1** Use the following questions to help students make inferences about this section of the story.

• Why did Tom's wife go into the forest with the household valuables?
**Answer:** to make an offering to the devil and gain his good will

• Whose heart and liver were tied up in the checked apron?
**Answer:** the wife's

• What has happened to the wife?
**Answer:** She has been killed by the devil.

**Set a Purpose** Have students read to see what bargain Tom makes with the devil and what comes of it.

**Students Acquiring English**

**2** Explain that the "one condition" refers to the fact that Tom had to sell his soul to the devil. In other words, at death he would go to hell instead of heaven.

**Gifted and Talented**

**3** Ask students to describe Tom's attitude toward becoming a slave trader. Does his attitude surprise students, given Tom's character? What does his response to the idea of slavery suggest about attitudes toward slavery in the North at the time? If possible, have students read briefly about slavery in the United States in the early 1800s.

## Mini Lesson   Vocabulary Strategy

**WORD ORIGINS** Tell students they can research word origins as a way to understand word meanings and derivations. Explain that the word *melancholy* derives from the Greek words *melas,* meaning "black," and *khole,* meaning "bile" or "gall." In medieval medicine, bile was one of the four fluids, called humors, believed to influence a person's health and disposition. *Melancholy* referred to black bile, an excess of which was thought to cause gloominess and depression. Although people no longer believe in the humors, the word *melancholy* is still used to describe a person who is gloomy and

sad. Another humor, *choler,* referred to yellow bile, which was believed to cause anger and irritability.

**Application** Ask students to work in pairs to research the meaning of *melanin, melanite, melanoma, cholera,* and *cholesterol.* Ask them to use each word in a sentence that shows they understand its meaning. Then ask students to explain how these words are related to the word *melancholy,* and how the root words *melas* and *khole* provide clues to the meaning of these words.

**A lesson on word origins appears on p. 550 in the Pupil's Edition.**

**Literary Analysis** [IMAGERY]

**A** Have students describe the image of Tom driving his carriage. In what condition are the horses? What sounds do the carriage wheels make? What effect does this image create?

**Possible Responses:** The horses are starving, and the carriage wheels groan and screech. The image gives an impression of Tom's cruelty and miserliness.

**Reading Skills and Strategies: PREDICTING**

**B** Ask students whether they think Tom's practice of religion is likely to save him from his bargain with the devil.

**Possible Response:** His motives are insincere and therefore cannot save him. His practice of religion is as selfish as his pursuit of wealth.

**Active Reading** [VISUALIZING]

**C** Ask students to jot down the words and phrases that help them visualize Tom's final capture. How does Irving make this capture seem dramatic?

**Possible Response:** Tom is whisked away like a child, during a thunderstorm, on the back of a black galloping horse. Fire flies from the horse's hoofs. The devil's disappearance while no one is looking creates a sense of shock and wonder.

**A** **1** out of <u>parsimony</u>. He even set up a carriage in the fullness of his vainglory,[21] though he nearly starved the horses which drew it; and as the ungreased wheels groaned and screeched on the axletrees, you would have thought you heard the souls of the poor debtors he was squeezing.

As Tom waxed old, however, he grew thoughtful. Having secured the good things of this world, he began to feel anxious about those of the next. He thought with regret on the bargain he had made with his black friend, and set his wits to work to cheat him out of the conditions. He became, therefore, all of a sudden, a violent churchgoer. He prayed loudly and strenuously, as if heaven were to be taken by force of lungs. Indeed, one might always tell when he had sinned most during the week, by the clamor of his Sunday devotion. The quiet Christians who had been modestly and steadfastly traveling Zionward[22] were struck with self-reproach at seeing themselves so suddenly outstripped in their career by this new-made convert. Tom was as rigid in religious as in money matters; he was a stern supervisor and <u>censurer</u> of his neighbors, and seemed to think every sin entered up to their account became a credit on his own side of the page. He even talked of the expediency of reviving the persecution of Quakers and Anabaptists. In a word, Tom's zeal became as notorious as his riches.

**B** Still, in spite of all this strenuous attention to forms, Tom had a lurking dread that the devil, after all, would have his due.[23] That he might not be taken unawares, therefore, it is said he always carried a small Bible in his coat pocket. He had also a great folio Bible on his countinghouse desk, and would frequently be found reading it when people called on business; on such occasions he would lay his green spectacles in the book, to mark the place, while he turned round to drive some usurious bargain.

Some say that Tom grew a little crackbrained

## Tom's zeal became as notorious as his riches.

in his old days, and that fancying his end approaching, he had his horse new shod, saddled and bridled, and buried with his feet uppermost; because he supposed that at the last day the world would be turned upside down; in which case he should find his horse standing ready for mounting, and he was determined at the worst to give his old friend a run for it. This, however, is probably a mere old wives' fable. If he really did take such a precaution, it was totally superfluous; at least so says the authentic old legend, which closes his story in the following manner:

**2** One hot summer afternoon in the dog days, just as a terrible black thundergust was coming up, Tom sat in his countinghouse, in his white linen cap and India silk morning gown. He was on the point of foreclosing a mortgage, by which he would complete the ruin of an unlucky land speculator for whom he had professed the greatest friendship. The poor land-jobber begged him to grant a few months' indulgence. Tom had grown testy and irritated, and refused another day.

"My family will be ruined and brought upon the parish," said the land-jobber. "Charity begins at home," replied Tom; "I must take care of myself in these hard times."

"You have made so much money out of me," said the speculator.

---

21. **vainglory:** boastful, undeserved pride in one's accomplishments or qualities.

22. **Zionward:** toward heaven.

23. **the devil . . . due:** a reference to the proverb "Give the devil his due," used to mean "Give even a disagreeable person the credit he or she deserves." Here, of course, the expression is used literally rather than figuratively.

WORDS TO KNOW

**parsimony** (pär'sə-mō'nē) *n.* extreme economy; stinginess
**censurer** (sĕn'shər-ər) *n.* one who expresses strong disapproval or harsh criticism

**358**

✓ **Assessment** **Informal Assessment**

**STORY MAP** You can informally assess your students' understanding by having them create story maps. To visualize the sequence of events, students should draw a box for each setting listed here. In each box, students should write a summary of the corresponding events.

1. The swamp
2. Tom's house
3. The swamp
4. Tom's house
5. The swamp
6. Tom's counting house in Boston
7. The street outside his counting house
8. The swamp

**RUBRIC**

**3** **Full Accomplishment** Students create story maps that accurately summarize events of the story.

**2** **Substantial Accomplishment** Students create story maps that present most of the essential events of the story.

**1** **Little or Partial Accomplishment** Students create partial story maps or cannot accurately summarize the plot.

Tom lost his patience and his piety. "The devil take me," said he, "if I have made a farthing!"[24]

Just then there were three loud knocks at the street door. He stepped out to see who was there. A black man was holding a black horse, which neighed and stamped with impatience.

"Tom, you're come for," said the black fellow, gruffly. Tom shrank back, but too late. He had left his little Bible at the bottom of his coat pocket, and his big Bible on the desk buried under the mortgage he was about to foreclose; never was a sinner taken more unawares. The black man whisked him like a child into the saddle, gave the horse the lash, and away he galloped, with Tom on his back, in the midst of the thunderstorm. The clerks stuck their pens behind their ears, and stared after him from the windows. Away went Tom Walker, dashing down the streets; his white cap bobbing up and down, his morning gown fluttering in the wind, and his steed striking fire out of the pavement at every bound. When the clerks turned to look for the black man, he had disappeared.

Tom Walker never returned to foreclose the mortgage. A countryman, who lived on the border of the swamp, reported that in the height of the thundergust he had heard a great clattering of hoofs and a howling along the road, and running to the window caught sight of a figure, such as I have described, on a horse that galloped like mad across the fields, over the hills, and down into the black hemlock swamp toward the old Indian fort; and that shortly after a thunderbolt falling in that direction seemed to set the whole forest in a blaze.

The good people of Boston shook their heads and shrugged their shoulders, but had been so much accustomed to witches and goblins, and tricks of the devil, in all kinds of shapes, from the first settlement of the colony, that they were not so much horror-struck as might have been expected. Trustees were appointed to take charge of Tom's effects. There was nothing, however, to administer upon. On searching his coffers[25] all his bonds and mortgages were found reduced to cinders. In place of gold and silver, his iron chest was filled with chips and shavings; two skeletons lay in his stable instead of his half-starved horses, and the very next day his great house took fire and burnt to the ground.

Such was the end of Tom Walker and his ill-gotten wealth. Let all griping money brokers lay this story to heart. The truth of it is not to be doubted. The very hole under the oak trees whence he dug Kidd's money is to be seen to this day; and the neighboring swamp and old Indian fort are often haunted in stormy nights by a figure on horseback, in morning gown and white cap, which is doubtless the troubled spirit of the usurer. In fact the story has resolved itself into a proverb so prevalent throughout New England, of "The Devil and Tom Walker." ❖

---

24. **farthing:** a coin worth one-fourth of a penny, formerly used throughout the British Empire.

25. **coffers:** safes or strongboxes designed to hold money or other valuable items.

| WORDS TO KNOW | **piety** (pī′ĭ-tē) *n.* religious devotion; reverence for God |
|---|---|

**359**

## GUIDING STUDENT RESPONSE

# Connect to the Literature

## 1. What Do You Think?
Possible Response: Many students may have reactions of satisfaction that such a cruel man is punished.

## Comprehension Check
- The devil offers Captain Kidd's buried treasure in exchange for Tom's soul.
- He goes to church, begins reading the Bible, and condemns the sins of others.
- Tom is taken away by the devil, and his money is reduced to chips and shavings.

Use Selection Quiz
**Unit Three Resource Book,** p. 10.

# Think Critically

2. Some students may say that Tom could have escaped by repenting and restoring his ill-gotten wealth to those whom he had ruined; others may say that no one can escape a voluntary pact with the devil.

3. Possible Response: The images describing Tom's house and horse suggest the selfishness and miserliness of the owner.

4. Some students may say that many of the Puritans were intolerant hypocrites, so Tom Walker was no worse than the rest.

5. Possible Response: Irving's purpose was to show the corruption of apparently righteous Puritans.

# Literary Analysis

**Imagery** Possible Responses:

- supports theme by highlighting the hypocrisy of the pillars of the community
- supports characterization and mood by showing how Tom felt about his wife and presenting the swamp as a treacherous place
- supports characterization and theme by highlighting Tom's avarice and stinginess
- supports plot and theme by bringing Tom to a deserved end

**Narrator** The narrator's attitude is one of amused sarcasm. The narrator's omniscience makes the story more humorous by revealing ironic truths about characters, and it strengthens the moral message by revealing the inner vice that leads to Tom's dire fate.

---

# Connect to the Literature

**1. What Do You Think?** What comments do you have about the ending of this story? Share them with classmates.

**Comprehension Check**
- What does Old Scratch offer Tom and what does he want in return?
- How does Tom try to get out of his bargain?
- What happens to Tom at the end?

# Think Critically

2. In your opinion, could Tom Walker have escaped the consequences of his bargain with Old Scratch? Explain?

3. **ACTIVE READING  VISUALIZING**  How did you visualize Tom Walker from the **images** used to describe him? What **character traits** are suggested by these images? Refer to the notes from your 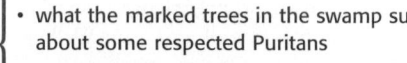 **READER'S NOTEBOOK.**

4. Do you consider Tom Walker better or worse than the other prominent Puritans in Boston? Consider the evidence.

**THINK ABOUT**
- the Puritans' treatment of Native Americans, Quakers, and Anabaptists
- what the marked trees in the swamp suggest about some respected Puritans
- why land speculators have "run mad with schemes for new settlements"
- how other Christians react to Tom's religious zeal

5. What do you think was Irving's **purpose** in writing this story?

# Extend Interpretations

6. **Critic's Corner** It has been noted that Washington Irving received critical acclaim as a writer because in his stories he managed to impart insights about human nature that were amusing without being too moralistic. Agree or disagree, basing your answer on "The Devil and Tom Walker."

7. **The Writer's Style** Writers use a variety of elements to create humor, including ridiculous characters, absurd situations and images, exaggeration, understatement, and **situational irony.** What makes this story humorous?

8. **Connect to Life** Driven by greed, Tom Walker literally sells his soul to gain wealth. What real person or fictional character reminds you of Tom Walker? Explain your choice.

# Extend Interpretations

**Critic's Corner** Possible Response: The whole story is meant to entertain, particularly the passages showing Tom's attitude toward his wife; passages relating to the devil and Tom's fate are also meant to instruct.

**The Writer's Style** Have students work in pairs to identify passages in the story that they found particularly funny. Partners should reread the passages individually and then work together to identify the sources of humor.

**Connect to Life** Point out that the character of Tom is exaggerated. Few people are all good or all bad.

# Literary Analysis

**IMAGERY** For the Active Reading activity on page 349, you were asked to pay close attention to Irving's **imagery**—the descriptive words and phrases a writer uses to re-create sensory experiences. Think of imagery as a multimedia presentation in your mind. The pictures, sounds, physical sensations, and sometimes tastes and smells that you imagine as you read help you interpret what is going on in a story.

**Cooperative Activity** Identify the imagery in the following passages, and discuss how it supports **characterization, plot,** or **theme.**
- the description of the trees marked with the names of men in the colony (page 353)
- the description of Tom's search for his wife in the forest (pages 355–356)
- the description of Tom's house, horses, and carriage (pages 357–358)
- the description of Tom's being carried off by the devil (page 359)

**NARRATOR** Another interesting element of this story is its **omniscient** (all-knowing) **narrator,** who stands outside the action of the story and reports what different characters are thinking. What seems to be the narrator's attitude toward the events of the story? What does Irving gain by using this type of narrator rather than having Tom relate the events?

# Choices & CHALLENGES

## Writing Options

**1. Reflective Essay on Wealth** Drawing on your reading of this story and on your notes for Connect to Your Life activity on page 349, draft a reflective essay on the pursuit of wealth. Place this piece in your **Working Portfolio.**

**2. Fitting Proverbs** Write a set of three proverbs—such as "Money is the root of all evil"—that help explain the lesson or moral of "The Devil and Tom Walker."

**3. Updated Faust Legend** Write your own version of the Faust legend, as Irving did. Create a modern character in a present-day setting who makes a bargain he or she shouldn't.

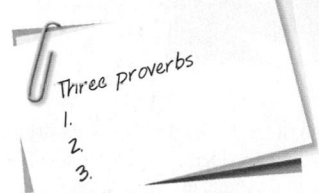

Three proverbs
1.
2.
3.

## Activities & Explorations

**Board Game** With a small group of classmates, design a board game, a video game, or a computer game based on the major events and characters in "The Devil and Tom Walker." Use the imagery in the story to help you depict specific settings, such as Deacon Peabody's woods. In class, show the game and explain the rules.
~ VIEWING AND REPRESENTING

## Vocabulary in Action

**EXERCISE A: ASSESSMENT PRACTICE** Review the Words to Know. Then, for each item below, write the letter of the word pair that expresses a relationship similar to that of the capitalized pair.

**1.** ABODE : COTTAGE ::
   (a) nest : bird    (c) vehicle : car
   (b) nail : hammer    (d) trumpet : music

**2.** SINGULAR : ORDINARY ::
   (a) whole : complete    (c) warm : hot
   (b) chapter : book    (d) flexible : rigid

**3.** PIETY : NUN ::
   (a) poverty : banker    (c) warmth : humidity
   (b) dishonesty : crook (d) simplicity : puzzle

**4.** DOLEFULLY : GRIEVE ::
   (a) loudly : whisper    (c) joyfully : celebrate
   (b) humbly : brag    (d) rapidly : stroll

**5.** OSTENTATION : FLAUNT ::
   (a) cowardice : sneak    (c) give : generosity
   (b) love : emotion    (d) humility : boast

### Building Vocabulary
For an in-depth lesson on analogies, see page 254.

**EXERCISE B: MEANING CLUES** Write the vocabulary word, not used in Exercise A, that is suggested by each description below.

**1.** If you don't give way, give in, or give an inch, and you never say die, this describes you.

**2.** Facing a vicious dog or having to perform a solo could make a person feel this way.

**3.** Walking five miles to buy beans at a discount is an example of this.

**4.** This is someone who finds fault, comes down hard, and rakes people over the coals.

**5.** This is what sunny skies are for picnic planners, storm clouds are for farmers in need of rain.

**6.** Clues help a detective do this about a suspect's guilt.

**7.** Listening to mournful music on a gray, cloudy day could make you feel this way.

**8.** Odysseus, Crazy Horse, Davy Crockett, and Hercules all had plenty of this.

**9.** One could tell workers to do this by saying "Take a break."

**10.** This could describe an accent, a style of dressing, or a way of celebrating a holiday.

| WORDS TO KNOW | abode | dolefully | parsimony | propitious | resolute |
|---|---|---|---|---|---|
| | censurer | melancholy | peculiar | prowess | singular |
| | daunted | ostentation | piety | repose | surmise |

---

## ✓ Assessment Test Preparation

**RECOGNIZE FACTS AND DETAILS** For some standardized tests, students will be asked to show that they recognize important facts and details in a text. To help students practice this skill, have them answer the following multiple-choice questions.

**1.** What was the main reason why Tom Walker at first decided not to accept the devil's offer?
   **A.** He was afraid of what would happen to him in the afterlife.
   **B.** He wanted to spite his wife.
   **C.** He did not want to go against his values.
   **D.** He was afraid the devil was not who he said he was.
   **Answer:** B

**2.** What was Tom Walker about to do just before he was carried off by the devil?
   **A.** foreclose a mortgage
   **B.** go to church
   **C.** go for a ride in his carriage
   **D.** break his pact with the devil
   **Answer:** A

---

## Writing Options

**1. Reflective Essay on Wealth** Remind students that reflective essays can be informal and that this one should express their own ideas and feelings about the pursuit of wealth. Students can use elements of the story to clarify their responses. They can also draw from their own experiences.

**2. Fitting Proverbs** Remind students that a proverb is a concise sentence summarizing a general idea, understood as a bit of traditional wisdom. **To make this assignment easier,** suggest that students work in pairs or small groups to discuss the lesson or moral of the story and then create interesting proverbs to reflect the moral.

**3. Updated Faust Legend** Have students review Build Background on page 348 for a summary of the legend. Point out that the main character eventually comes to regret his deal with the devil and tries to escape the consequences of the pact.

## Activities & Explorations

**Board Game** Students' games should accurately reflect the events, characters, and imagery in the text. **To help students get started,** tell each group to first come up with a concept and rules for their game, and then divide the project work among group members. One student should record the instructions and rules for the game as the group generates them; another student should make a list of the major settings in the story and their important imagery; a third should illustrate those scenes deemed appropriate by the group.

## Vocabulary in Action

**EXERCISE A**
1. c    4. c
2. d    5. a
3. b

**EXERCISE B**
1. resolute
2. daunted
3. parsimony
4. censurer
5. propitious
6. surmise
7. melancholy
8. prowess
9. repose
10. peculiar

## Author Activity

All three stories are humorous with a fairy-tale atmosphere and an American setting. Like Tom Walker, both Rip Van Winkle and Ichabod Crane are distinctly American types—caricatures, rather than three-dimensional characters—who find themselves in extreme, but comic, predicaments.

## Washington Irving
### 1783–1859

**Other Works**
*Diedrich Knickerbocker's History of New York*
*Tales of a Traveller*

**Literary Pioneer** Born at the end of the American Revolution and named after our first president, Washington Irving made many contributions to American literature. He set an example for humorous writing, pioneered the short story as a literary form, influenced important writers—particularly Nathaniel Hawthorne—and put America on the literary map.

**An Eye for Detail** While growing up in a large, prosperous New York family, Irving came to know American society intimately. Besides learning to appreciate literature, art, theater, and opera, he loved to explore the countryside along the Hudson River. Gifted with an eye for the pictorial, he considered painting as a career but instead used his talent to write about the American landscapes he knew so well.

**World Traveler** Ironically, this first notable American writer spent much of his life abroad. After studying law for 6 years, Irving joined the family exporting business and was sent to work in its British office in 1815. Although the business failed, he stayed in Europe for the next 17 years, traveling extensively and serving as a U.S. diplomat.

**Creator of Classic Tales** Irving captured his European experiences in much of his writing, but American life provided him with some of his richest stories and most memorable characters. In *The Sketch Book of Geoffrey Crayon, Gent.* (1819–1820), he created the first distinctively American tales, such as "Rip Van Winkle" and "The Legend of Sleepy Hollow." Irving spent the last years of his life at his New York estate, Sunnyside, near his beloved Hudson River.

## Author Activity

**Tales Compared** Recall or reread "Rip Van Winkle" and "The Legend of Sleepy Hollow." What do these stories have in common with "The Devil and Tom Walker"?

## Teaching Options

 **Mini Lesson** ## Grammar

**USING MODIFIERS CORRECTLY** An adjective modifies—that is, describes or limits—a noun or a pronoun. An adverb modifies a verb, an adjective, or another adverb.

**Instruction** An adjective modifies the subject of a linking verb such as *am, is, are, was, were, be, been,* and *being.*

> Tom Walker was **greedy.**
> The Devil said, "You will be **wealthy** and **powerful.**"

An adverb modifies an action verb.

> Tom Walker worked **greedily** at his job.
> The devil called **loudly.**

**Exercises** Ask students to choose the correct modifier in each sentence.

1. Tom Walker walked (slow, <u>slowly</u>) through the woods.
2. The black figure was (<u>angry</u>, angrily) when Tom touched the skull.
3. (Careful, <u>Carefully</u>), Tom counted his money.
4. The wind blew (fierce, <u>fiercely</u>) through the countinghouse.

 Use **Grammar Transparencies and Copymasters**, p. 127.

 Use McDougal Littell's ***Language Network***, Chapter 7, for more instruction and practice in modifiers.

# PREPARING to *Read*

## *from* Self-Reliance

Essay by RALPH WALDO EMERSON

**Connect to Your Life**

**Self-Reliance Defined** What do you think *self-reliance* means? Which people in the world today seem to have this quality? What are some advantages and disadvantages of being self-reliant? Discuss these questions with a small group of classmates.

## Build Background

**Voice of Transcendentalism** Ralph Waldo Emerson was one of 19th-century America's greatest writers and thinkers. In 1836, Emerson formed the Transcendental Club with a group of friends, including Henry David Thoreau and the feminist writer and critic Margaret Fuller. As the intellectual leader of the transcendentalists, he defined many of his original ideas in lectures, poems, and essays. Part of the appeal of Emerson's lectures and essays was his poetic style and elegant way with words. This excerpt from the essay "Self-Reliance" is a series of loosely related thoughts and extracts from lectures and journals that Emerson had written in the years between 1832 and 1840. Published in 1841, the essay elaborates Emerson's belief in the importance of the individual.

| WORDS TO KNOW | Vocabulary Preview | |
|---|---|---|
| absolve | aversion | bestowed |
| nonconformist | predominate | |

## Focus Your Reading

**LITERARY ANALYSIS** **APHORISM** An **aphorism** is a brief statement, usually one sentence long, that expresses a general principle or truth about life. For example, in *Poor Richard's Almanack,* Franklin uses several aphorisms, such as "Honesty is the best policy." Notice Emerson's aphorisms in this essay.

**ACTIVE READING** **SUMMARIZING** To summarize a piece of writing is to state its main ideas briefly in your own words, omitting less important details. These guidelines will help you summarize Emerson's essay.

- In each paragraph, identify the one or two most important phrases or statements.
- Write a sentence of your own to express the main idea of each statement you identified.
- Pull your sentences together into a single summary.

**READER'S NOTEBOOK** After reading this excerpt from "Self-Reliance," summarize Emerson's main ideas in a few sentences.

---

---

**Literary Analysis** APHORISM

An aphorism is a brief statement that expresses a truth about life. "Self-Reliance" is full of statements that could be classified as aphorisms. As students read, they should write down aphorisms.

 Use **Unit Three Resource Book** p. 13 for more practice.

**Active Reading** SUMMARIZING

**A** Producing summaries of texts involves identifying main ideas and supporting details. Ask students to summarize the first two paragraphs of "Self-Reliance" using this technique.

**Possible Response:** Each person must ultimately rely on himself or herself, because nothing good comes of envying or imitating someone else, and a person can only profit from his or her own work. One must accept one's unique place in the world and have faith that God is working through oneself in a unique way.

 Use **Unit Three Resource Book** p. 12 for more practice.

**GUIDE FOR READING**

**B** **Possible Response:** One's own impulses must be honored as if they came from God; following your nature is crucial in order to be a self-reliant individual.

**C** **Possible Response:** It is easy to live by your own ideas when alone and to conform when you are with others. A great person refuses to conform even in a crowd.

---

FROM

# Self-Reliance

RALPH
WALDO
EMERSON

There is a time in every man's education when he arrives at the conviction that envy is ignorance; that imitation is suicide; that he must take himself for better for worse as his portion; that though the wide universe is full of good, no kernel of nourishing corn can come to him but through his toil bestowed on that plot of ground which is given to him to till. . . .

Trust thyself: every heart vibrates to that iron string. Accept the place the divine providence has found for you, the society of
10 your contemporaries, the connection of events. Great men have always done so, and confided themselves childlike to the genius of their age, betraying their perception that the absolutely trustworthy was seated at their heart, working through their hands, predominating in all their being. . . .

15 Whoso would be a man, must be a nonconformist. He who would gather immortal palms must not be hindered by the name of goodness, but must explore if it be goodness. Nothing is at last sacred but the integrity of your own mind. Absolve you to yourself, and you shall have the suffrage of the world. I remember an
20 answer which when quite young I was prompted to make to a valued adviser who was wont to importune me with the dear old doctrines of the church. On my saying, "What have I to do with the sacredness of traditions, if I live wholly from within?" my friend suggested—"But these impulses may be from below, not
25 from above." I replied, "They do not seem to me to be such; but if I am the Devil's child, I will live then from the Devil." No law can be sacred to me but that of my nature. Good and bad are but names very readily transferable to that or this; the only right is what is after my constitution; the only wrong what is against it. . . .

**GUIDE FOR READING**

**A**

**9 the divine providence:** God.

**12–13 betraying . . . trustworthy:** revealing their awareness that God.

**16 immortal palms:** everlasting triumph and honor. In ancient times, people carried palm leaves as a symbol of victory, success, or joy.

**19 suffrage:** approval; support.

**21 wont to importune me:** accustomed to trouble me.

**26–29** What is implied by Emerson's use of the word *sacred*? Why does he believe that one should follow his or her own nature? **B**

**29 after my constitution:** consistent with my physical and mental nature.

WORDS
TO
KNOW

**bestowed** (bǐ-stōd´) *adj.* applied; used **bestow** *v.*
**predominate** (prǐ-dǒm´ə-nāt´) *v.* to have controlling power or influence
**nonconformist** (nǒn´kən-fôr´mǐst) *n.* one who does not follow generally accepted beliefs, customs, or practices
**absolve** (əb-zǒlv´) *v.* to clear of guilt or blame

364

---

 **Preteaching Vocabulary**

**USING CONTEXT CLUES** Students can determine the meanings of unfamiliar words by using context clues that suggest cause-and-effect relationships. Write the following sentence on the chalkboard and ask a volunteer to identify a cause-and-effect relationship in it. Have students use the meaning of the sentence to suggest meanings for the word *bestow*.

The wealthy family plans to bestow money on the museum so that it can expand and add new art.

**Cause:** Money will be bestowed.

**Effect:** The museum will expand as a result of money being bestowed.

**Exercises** Ask students to use their understanding of cause-and-effect relationships to figure out the meanings of underlined terms.

1. Her ideas seem to predominate, so she will probably win the election next week.
2. After the judge decided to absolve the prisoner, he was released from prison.
3. Because she has an aversion to loud noise and crowds, she never attends concerts.

 Use **Unit Three Resource Book** p. 14 for additional support.

A lesson on using context clues appears on p. 326 in the Pupil's Edition.

*Kindred Spirits* (1849), Asher B. Durand. Oil on canvas, collection of The New York Public Library, Astor, Lenox and Tilden Foundations.

30    What I must do is all that concerns me, not what the people think. This rule, equally arduous in actual and in intellectual life, may serve for the whole distinction between greatness and meanness. It is the harder because you will always find those who think they know what is your duty

35    better than you know it. It is easy in the world to live after the world's opinion; it is easy in solitude to live after our own; but the great man is he who in the midst of the crowd keeps with perfect sweetness the independence of solitude. . . .

**33 meanness:** the state of being inferior in quality, character, or value.

**35–38** What does Emerson say is easy to do? What does he say a great person is able to do?

---

 **Mini Lesson**   **Viewing and Representing**

*Kindred Spirits* by **Asher B. Durand**

**ART APPRECIATION** Asher Durand (1796–1886) was a leader of the Hudson River School of painting. These artists portrayed the grandeur of nature and the concept of a wilderness in which people were an insignificant intrusion in the landscape.

**Instruction** Encourage students to analyze the ideas represented in this painting. How are natural elements portrayed? What does the composition of the painting suggest about the importance of people in this landscape?

**Possible Responses:** The people are small and not the focus of the painting. Their faces are not clear, while the details of their natural surroundings—running water, contour of the rocks, leaves on the trees—are quite clear and occupy most of the canvas.

**Application** What do you suppose the people are talking about? What sounds do you imagine the people are hearing? If you were in that setting, what would you feel?

**Possible Response:** Accept all reasonable responses. Students might say the people hear the sounds of moving water and birds.

## Customizing Instruction

### Less Proficient Readers
**Set a Purpose** Have students read to learn Emerson's beliefs about nonconformity, or refusing to do what everyone else does.

### Students Acquiring English
Students may find Emerson's long, complex sentences challenging. You may wish to help them paraphrase certain passages aloud to ensure comprehension.

Use **Spanish Study Guide** for additional support, pp. 91–93

### Gifted and Talented
Students may be interested in reading more of "Self-Reliance" and evaluating the relevance of Emerson's ideas to high school students today.

### Students Acquiring English
**1** Explain that *arduous* means "very difficult." Ask students to explain the difference between *actual life* and *intellectual life.* Help them paraphrase this sentence.

## Literary Analysis [APORISM]

**A** Ask students to explain what makes this statement particularly memorable.
**Possible Response:** the strong image of the world "whipping" someone who doesn't fit in

### GUIDE FOR READING

**B** **Possible Responses:** displeasure of others; sour faces; aversion

**C** **Possible Response:** because inconsistency would expose us to criticism from others

## LITERARY LINK

### Reading Skills and Strategies: COMPARE

Have students compare the theme of the excerpt from "Memoirs" to that of "Self-Reliance."
**Possible Response:** The theme of "Memoirs" is that truth is the most important thing, even when it is difficult to bear. In "Self-Reliance," Emerson expresses a similar idea in his emphasis on finding what is true for oneself as a unique individual.

### Margaret Fuller

Primarily a journalist and critic, Fuller edited *The Dial,* the journal of Emerson's Transcendental Club. Fuller's feminist views are expressed in her book *Woman in the Nineteenth Century,* published in 1845.

---

**A** **40** For nonconformity the world whips you with its displeasure. And therefore a man must know how to estimate a sour face. The by-standers look askance on him in the public street or in the friend's parlor. If this <u>aversion</u> had its origin in contempt and resistance like his own he might well go home with a sad countenance; but the sour faces of the multitude, like **45** their sweet faces, have no deep cause, but are put on and off as the wind blows and a newspaper directs. . . .

The other terror that scares us from self-trust is our consistency; a reverence for our past act or word because the eyes of others have no other data for computing our orbit than our past **50** acts, and we are loth to disappoint them. . . .

A foolish consistency is the hobgoblin of little minds, adored by little statesmen and philosophers and divines. With consistency a great soul has simply nothing to do. He may as well concern himself with his shadow on the wall. Speak what you **55** think now in hard words and to-morrow speak what to-morrow thinks in hard words again, though it contradict every thing you said today.—"Ah, so you shall be sure to be misunderstood."— Is it so bad then to be misunderstood? Pythagoras was misunderstood, and Socrates, and Jesus, and Luther, and Copernicus, **60** and Galileo, and Newton, and every pure and wise spirit that ever took flesh. To be great is to be misunderstood. ❖

**B** **39–42** What does Emerson say is one consequence of being a nonconformist?

**41 askance** (ə-skăns'): with disapproval, suspicion, or distrust.

**C** **47–52** Why does consistency scare us from trusting ourselves?

**50 loth** (lōth): unwilling; reluctant.

**51 hobgoblin:** a source of fear or dread. Notice that Emerson does not criticize all consistency, only "foolish" consistency that does not allow for change or progress.

**52 divines:** religious leaders.

**58–60 Pythagoras . . . Newton:** great thinkers whose radical theories and viewpoints caused controversy.

---

## LITERARY LINK

### *from* Memoirs
#### MARGARET FULLER

In the chamber
of death, I prayed
in very early years,
"Give me truth;
**5** cheat me by no illusion."
O, the granting of
this prayer is
sometimes terrible to me!

I walk over the
**10** burning ploughshares,[1]
and they sear[2]
my feet. Yet nothing but
the truth will do.

1. **ploughshares** (plou'shârz'): the cutting blades of plows.
2. **sear:** scorch; burn.

WORDS TO KNOW
**aversion** (ə-vûr'zhən) *n.* a strong dislike

**366**

---

## Teaching Options

**RECOGNIZE THE AUTHOR'S POINT OF VIEW AND PURPOSE** Some standardized tests ask students to show that they can recognize the author's point of view and purpose. To provide students with practice, read aloud or write on the chalkboard the following questions:

1. You can tell from "Self-Reliance" that the author believes some traditions and old doctrines

   A. are worth preserving and using as a guide for behavior.

✓ Assessment **Standardized Test Practice**

   B. help shape the lives of great thinkers.
   C. keep people from following their own impulses and seeking out their own truths.
   D. help him look within himself to find his own place and function in the world.
   **Answer:** C

2. The author's main purpose in warning people against "foolish consistency" is to
   A. encourage people to be open-minded and willing to contradict their past atti-

   tudes.
   B. help people earn more respect among their peers.
   C. encourage a return to traditional beliefs and attitudes.
   D. warn people against listening too closely to the inaccurate advice of others.
   **Answer:** A

## Connect to the Literature

**1. What Do You Think?**
What kind of impact did this essay have on you? Share your reaction with your classmates.

**Comprehension Check**
- Which does Emerson value more—original thought or traditional wisdom?
- According to Emerson, which virtue does society demand most—truth, conformity, creativity, or self-reliance?
- What is the only law that Emerson says can be sacred to him?

## Think Critically

**2.** `ACTIVE READING` `SUMMARIZING` How did you summarize Emerson's main ideas in this excerpt? Share what you wrote in your 📖 **READER'S NOTEBOOK.**

**3.** Describe situations or aspects of your own life in which Emerson's ideas about the importance of the individual might apply.

**THINK ABOUT**
- his idea that all people should be nonconformists
- his disregard for consistency in thought and deed
- peer pressures to conform to certain standards of appearance or behavior

**4.** If you had heard this essay as a public lecture, what questions would you have liked to ask Emerson directly about his philosophy?

## Extend Interpretations

**5. Critic's Corner** The noted writer Henry James said that Emerson "had no great sense of wrong... no sense of the dark, the foul, the base." How do you think Emerson might have defended his views against this charge?

**6. What If?** If Emerson had specifically addressed the institution of slavery in this essay, what do you think he would have said about it?

**7. Comparing Texts** How do Margaret Fuller's ideas in the Literary Link poem on page 366 compare with Emerson's ideas in "Self-Reliance"?

**8. Connect to Life** Refer to the ideas you wrote about self-reliance for the Connect to Your Life activity on page 363. How do the ideas in Emerson's essay compare with your own?

## Literary Analysis

`APHORISM` "Self-Reliance" is sprinkled with memorable sayings or **aphorisms**—brief statements, usually one sentence long, that express a general principle or truth about life. "A foolish consistency is the hobgoblin of little minds" is one of the most frequently quoted aphorisms from American literature. Emerson's aphorisms are interesting for their shock value. They proclaim his radical ideas in clear, concise sentences. His idea about consistency, for example, is distilled into one easy-to-remember aphorism and thereby immortalized.

**Cooperative Learning Activity** With a small group of classmates, identify at least three other aphorisms from "Self-Reliance," then list them on a sheet of paper. Compare your list with those of other groups. How similar are the ideas expressed in different aphorisms?

Emerson's Aphorisms
1.
2.
3.

## Writing Options

1. **Personal Essay** Essay should reflect a complete understanding of the chosen aphorism. **To get students started on this assignment,** have students organize the essay in three paragraphs, first quoting the aphorism, then explaining it in a paraphrase, and then connecting it with their own experience.

2. **Update of Emerson** Students will be successful if they present an accurate, interesting paraphrase with appeal to a contemporary young audience. **To get students started on this assignment,** remind them that they need not "translate" the entire piece; only the main ideas are required. **Students who are interpersonal learners** might want to present their piece orally to the rest of the class.

## Inquiry & Research

**History** Students should locate appropriate print and nonprint information using both text resources and technical resources.

## Vocabulary in Action

1. one that puzzled you
2. independence
3. bossy
4. avoid the person
5. guilty but sorry, or completely innocent

## Author Activity

The poet John Greenleaf Whittier called Emerson "the one American who is sure of being remembered in a thousand years." In "The American Scholar," a speech at Harvard in 1837, Emerson told Americans that they should develop their own distinctive philosophy rather than continue to imitate European models. Oliver Wendell Holmes called the address America's "Intellectual Declaration of Independence." Writers in the Realist movement, such as Henry James, Stephen Crane, and Theodore Dreiser, rejected Transcendentalist beliefs.

## Writing Options

1. **Personal Essay** Choose your favorite aphorism from "Self-Reliance," and draft a personal essay to explain why it is significant to you. Support your explanation with examples drawn from your life. Place this piece in your **Working Portfolio.**

2. **Update of Emerson** Imagine that Emerson has come to you and asked for your help in bringing his message about the importance of the individual to an audience of contemporary teenagers. Paraphrase his ideas for a teenage audience and provide up-to-date examples.

## Inquiry & Research

**History** In the last paragraph of the selection, Emerson names several historical figures who were misunderstood. Choose one to learn more about and present your findings in an oral report.

## Vocabulary in Action

**EXERCISE: MEANING CLUES** Review the Words to Know and then answer the following questions.

1. Would you be most likely to **bestow** a great deal of thought on a matter that revolted you, one that puzzled you, or one that bored you?

2. What is likely to be most important to a **nonconformist**—tradition, independence, or approval?

3. Is a person who **predominates** in too many situations wimpy, sneaky, or bossy?

4. If you have an **aversion** to a person, are you most likely to avoid the person, ignore the person, or seek the person out?

5. Is a judge most likely to **absolve** an accused criminal if the judge knows that the accused is guilty but sorry, guilty and not sorry, or completely innocent?

**Building Vocabulary**
For an in-depth study of word parts and root words, see page 444.

# Ralph Waldo Emerson
1803–1882

**Other Works**
*The Poet*
*The American Scholar*
*Concord Hymn*

**Early Struggles** The distinguished poet, essayist, and lecturer Ralph Waldo Emerson was born in Boston, Massachusetts. As a child, he experienced illness, poverty, and the death of a parent. His father, a Unitarian minister, died when Emerson was 8 years old, and his mother struggled to raise five boys—including a mentally retarded son—alone. With the aid of several grants, however, Emerson was able to enter Harvard College when he was 14. To pay for other expenses, he worked as a tutor, a messenger, and a waiter at the college.

**Spiritual Challenges** After graduating, Emerson taught for several years at his brother's school for girls. He returned to Harvard to study for the ministry and became a Unitarian minister in 1829. Unfortunately, his brief career as a minister was marred by religious doubt and by his wife's death in 1831. Because he felt that he could no longer perform certain church rituals in good faith, he resigned his ministry in 1832.

**Popular Lecturer** After traveling in Europe for a year, Emerson returned to the United States to devote himself to lecturing and writing. In 1835, he remarried and settled in Concord, and a year later he celebrated the birth of his first child as well as the publication of his first book, *Nature*.

## Author Activity

Emerson was the most important spiritual voice of his generation. Find out which other writers Emerson influenced, in addition to Thoreau and Fuller. Which writers rejected his beliefs?

---

**Mini Lesson** ## Grammar

**MODIFIERS: ADJECTIVE AND ADVERB PHRASES**
An adjective phrase is a prepositional phrase that modifies a noun or pronoun. The adjective phrase tells what type, which one, or how many:
  **Examples:**
  A foolish consistency is the hobgoblin **of little minds.**
  Everyone **in the world** must live to find truth.
An adverb phrase is a prepositional phrase that modifies a verb, an adjective, or an adverb. The adverb phrase tells when, where, why, how, or to what extent:

**Examples:**
The ideas of transcendentalism were discussed **at the lecture.**
Emerson was tired **of conformity.**

 Use **Grammar Transparencies and Copymasters,** p. 82.

Use McDougal Littell's *Language Network,* Chapter 7, for more instruction and practice in modifiers.

# *from* Civil Disobedience

### *Essay by* HENRY DAVID THOREAU

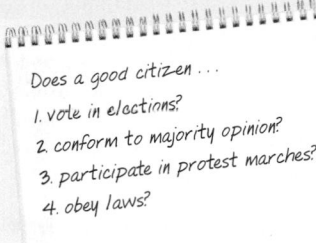

**Connect to Your Life**

**Civic Duty** With a small group of classmates, discuss what it means to be a good citizen. Consider the actions listed, and add others to the list. Indicate whether a good citizen would **always, usually, sometimes,** or **never** perform each action.

*Does a good citizen . . .*
*1. vote in elections?*
*2. conform to majority opinion?*
*3. participate in protest marches?*
*4. obey laws?*

## Build Background

**Nonviolent Resistance** Henry David Thoreau put into practice the ideas expressed in Emerson's "Self-Reliance." Thoreau spent a night in jail for refusing to pay a poll tax used to finance a government that condoned the institution of slavery and waged war against Mexico. Like many Americans at the time, Thoreau viewed the Mexican War (1846–1848) as a conflict in which a stronger country sought to overpower a weaker one simply to expand its own borders. Inspired by his experience in jail, Thoreau in 1847 published an essay originally titled "Resistance to Civil Government." In this essay, which became popularly known as "Civil Disobedience," Thoreau affirmed individual conscience and advocated nonviolent acts of political resistance to protest government policy.

**WORDS TO KNOW**
**Vocabulary Preview**

| | |
|---|---|
| blunder | flourish |
| conclude | inexpedient |
| confront | meditation |
| conscientious | multitude |
| endeavor | unscrupulous |

## Focus Your Reading

**LITERARY ANALYSIS** **ESSAY** An **essay** is a short work of nonfiction that deals with a single subject, usually presenting the personal views of the writer. "Civil Disobedience" is a persuasive essay. It presents political ideas that Thoreau hopes his readers will adopt, and at the same time, it reveals much about Thoreau's personality.

**ACTIVE READING** **STRATEGIES FOR READING ESSAYS** Using these strategies will help you get the most from this essay:

• Keep the **historical context** in mind.
• Use the Guide for Reading alongside the text.
• Keep reading a paragraph even if a sentence stumps you, but read the entire essay more than once.
• Throughout, notice what Thoreau favors and opposes.
• Keep track of the **main ideas** and the **supporting details** that develop them.

**READER'S NOTEBOOK** One of Thoreau's main ideas in this excerpt is that there are three ways in which citizens serve the state. As you read, identify the three ways on a chart like the one shown. Fill in examples of each, and mark what Thoreau believes is the best way.

**Ways to Serve the State**

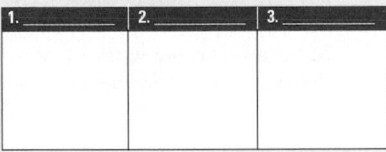

| 1. | 2. | 3. |
|---|---|---|
| | | |

## LESSON RESOURCES

**UNIT THREE RESOURCE BOOK,** pp. 16–20

**ASSESSMENT RESOURCES**
**Formal Assessment,** pp. 69–70
**Teacher's Guide to Assessment and Portfolio Use**
**Test Generator**

**SKILLS TRANSPARENCIES AND COPYMASTERS**
**Literary Analysis**
• Persuasion, T8 (for Cooperative Learning Activity, p. 378)

**Reading and Critical Thinking**
• Compare and Contrast, T15 (for Writing Option 1, p. 379)
**Grammar**
• Punctuating a Series of Clauses, C156 (for Mini Lesson, p. 380)
**Vocabulary**
• Denotation and Connotation, C38 (for Mini Lesson, p. 373)
**Writing**
• Compare-Contrast, C32 (for Writing Option 1, p. 379)
**Communications**
• Evaluating Roles in Groups, T8 (for Activities & Explorations 1, p. 379)

• Impromptu Speaking: Dialogue, Role-Play, Debate, T13 (for Activities & Explorations 2, p. 379)

**INTEGRATED TECHNOLOGY**

**Audio Library**
**Internet: Research Starter**
**Visit our website:**
www.mcdougallittell.com

**Objectives**
1. understand and appreciate a persuasive **essay (Literary Analysis)**
2. use **strategies for reading essays (Active Reading)**

**Summary**
Thoreau's essay challenges people to fight government injustice with civil disobedience. Thoreau complains that Americans' tax dollars go to support unjust causes such as slavery and the war against Mexico. Citizens have the power to create a better government, but they are afraid to take a stand and make changes without the support of a majority. Thoreau advocates withholding tax money as a sign of protest, believing that if enough people gather the courage to do so, government will be forced to improve itself. Thoreau tells of his own experience in jail after he refused to pay taxes. Despite the fact that he was behind bars, he felt free because his conscience was clear and he was obeying his own personal laws.

**Thematic Link**
"Civil Disobedience" expresses the **transcendental** belief that all people must live as individuals, not as mindless parts of a society that may or may not be just.

**5-Minute Warm-Up**

*Daily*
*Language*
*SkillBuilder*

Have students **proofread** the display sentences on page 337i and write them correctly. The sentences also appear on Transparency 10 of **Grammar Transparencies and Copymasters.**

**Mini Lesson** **Preteaching Vocabulary**

If you would like to preteach the WORDS TO KNOW for this selection, use the Mini Lesson, p. 370.

**Reading Skills and Strategies: PREVIEW**

 **A** Have students read the first sentences in each paragraph to get an overall sense of Thoreau's argument.

**Literary Analysis** ESSAY

Have students note the opening lines of the essay. Thoreau captures readers' attention by making a strong and potentially radical statement about government. These lines are effective because they spark emotion and interest, both in those who agree and in those who disagree. Thoreau establishes through these lines that his essay will explore the proper role of government.

Use **Unit Three Resource Book,** p. 18 for more practice.

**GUIDE FOR READING**

**B** **Possible Response:** The main idea is that government should be merely a tool for carrying out the will of the people, but it can become a tool of abusive power.

**Active Reading**

STRATEGIES FOR READING ESSAYS

 **C** Thoreau clarifies his position in this passage. Ask students to explain what Thoreau favors and what he opposes.

**Possible Response:** He opposes abolishing government immediately; he favors improving government immediately.

Use **Unit Three Resource Book** p. 17 for more practice.

**GUIDE FOR READING**

**D** individual conscience

---

*from*

# Civil Disobedience
# Henry David Thoreau

**A**

heartily accept the motto, "That government is best which governs least;" and I should like to see it acted up to more rapidly and systematically. Carried out, it finally amounts
5    to this, which also I believe,—"That government is best which governs not at all;" and when men are prepared for it, that will be the kind of government which they will have. Government is at best but an expedient; but most governments are usually, and all governments are sometimes, <u>inexpedient</u>. The objections
10   which have been brought against a standing army, and they are many and weighty, and deserve to prevail, may also at last be brought against a standing government. The standing army is only an arm of the standing government. The government itself, which is only the mode which the people have chosen to
15   execute their will, is equally liable to be abused and perverted before the people can act through it. Witness the present Mexican war, the work of comparatively a few individuals using the standing government as their tool; for, in the outset, the people would not have consented to this measure. . . .

Nelson Mandela, imprisoned for 27 years by the South African government for his antiapartheid activities, recalls his confinement in this 1994 photo.

**GUIDE FOR READING**

**8 expedient** (ĭk-spē′dē-ənt): a means to an end.

**1–9** How would you restate Thoreau's attitude toward government?  **B**

**16–17 the present Mexican war:** the 1846–1848 war between the United States and Mexico.

WORDS TO KNOW        **inexpedient** (ĭn′ĭk-spē′dē-ənt) adj. not useful for achieving a goal

370

---

## Teaching Options

**USING CONTEXT CLUES** Difficult words are sometimes restated in simpler language in the surrounding text. Sometimes restatements are signaled by words and phrases such as *that is, or,* or *in other words.* Dashes and parentheses can serve as signals, or a restatement might appear as an appositive phrase set off by commas. Write the following sentence on the chalkboard and ask students to identify the restatement of *inexpedient.*

**Mini Lesson** ## Preteaching Vocabulary

He feels government is <u>inexpedient</u>; in other words, it is not useful for achieving goals.
  **Answer:** "not useful for achieving goals"

**Exercises** Ask students to use their understanding of restatement to figure out the meanings of underlined terms in these sentences.

1. I've never known anyone so <u>conscientious</u>; that is, he's the most honest and dependable person I've ever met.

2. The label said that those plants will <u>flourish</u>, or thrive, in direct sunlight.

3. Their <u>blunder</u>, the biggest mistake of the year, cost the business thousands of dollars.

4. When we finally <u>confront</u> them next week— when we meet them face to face—we will definitely make our wishes known.

Use **Unit Three Resource Book** p. 19 for more exercises.

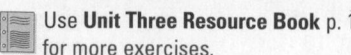 **A lesson using context clues appears on p. 326 in the Pupil's Edition.**

20 But, to speak practically and as a citizen, unlike those who call themselves no-government men, I ask for, not at once no government, but *at once* a better government. Let every man make known what kind of government would command his respect, and that will be one step toward obtaining it.

25 After all, the practical reason why, when the power is once in the hands of the people, a majority are permitted, and for a long period continue, to rule is not because they are most likely to be in the right, nor because this seems fairest to the minority, but because they are physically the strongest. But a government 30 in which the majority rule in all cases cannot be based on justice, even as far as men understand it. Can there not be a government in which majorities do not virtually decide right and wrong, but conscience?—in which majorities decide only those questions to which the rule of expediency is applicable? 35 Must the citizen ever for a moment, or in the least degree, resign his conscience to the legislator? Why has every man a

**29–37** What position does Thoreau take on the conflict between majority rule and individual conscience?

In Tianenmen Square in 1989, Chinese demonstrators support prodemocracy students on a hunger strike.

A young man strapped to logs protests the cutting of California redwoods in 1990.

CIVIL DISOBEDIENCE **371**

**Cross Curricular Link  History**

**U.S.-MEXICAN WAR** As the new United States prospered and grew in the 19th century, people began to believe in Manifest Destiny—the idea that the country should continue expanding and one day occupy territory from coast to coast. Part of achieving this goal meant acquiring southwestern territories that belonged to Mexico.
In 1845 President James Polk attempted to purchase the territories that are now California and New Mexico. When Mexico would not agree to the purchase, Polk prepared to fight for the territories. In 1846 American General Zachary Taylor occupied an area called Point Isabel on the Rio Grande. Mexico claimed this area and crossed the Rio Grande to shell an American fort, causing President Polk to declare war on May 13, 1846. About two years later, American troops finally defeated Mexican troops. On February 2, 1848, the treaty of Guadalupe Hidalgo was signed to officially end the war. As part of the treaty, Mexico was forced to cede about half of its territory to the United States in return for $15 million. The war against Mexico was criticized by some Americans, particularly Democrats and Whigs, because President Polk proceeded without having Congress officially declare war.

### Active Reading

STRATEGIES FOR READING ESSAYS

**A** Have students interpret the influence of historical context on this essay. Ask them to explain Thoreau's purpose in making direct references to people in the military. Why might this passage have struck a chord with many Americans at the time? What different ways might these remarks have affected people?

**Possible Responses:** Americans were in the midst of fighting a controversial war with Mexico, so people would be especially sensitive to these remarks. Some people probably felt angry and resentful after reading these comments, while others might have agreed with Thoreau's statements and been more receptive to his call to action.

### GUIDE FOR READING

**B** People can become "agents of injustice" by upholding morally wrong laws.

**C** Thoreau approves of those who serve with their conscience (heroes, patriots, martyrs, and reformers); he condemns those who serve with their bodies and heads, without conscience (e.g., militia and politicians).

conscience, then? I think that we should be men first, and subjects afterward. It is not desirable to cultivate a respect for the law, so much as for the right. The only obligation which I have a right to assume is to do at any time what I think right. It is truly enough said, that a corporation has no conscience; but a corporation of <u>conscientious</u> men is a corporation *with* a conscience. Law never made men a whit more just; and, by means of their respect for it, even the well-disposed are daily made the agents of injustice. A common and natural result of an undue respect for law is, that you may see a file of soldiers, colonel, captain, corporal, privates, powder-monkeys, and all, marching in admirable order over hill and dale to the wars, against their wills, ay, against their common sense and consciences, which makes it very steep marching indeed, and produces a palpitation of the heart. They have no doubt that it is a damnable business in which they are concerned; they are all peaceably inclined. Now, what are they? Men at all? or small movable forts and magazines, at the service of some <u>unscrupulous</u> man in power? Visit the Navy-Yard, and behold a marine, such a man as an American government can make, or such as it can make a man with its black arts—a mere shadow and reminiscence of humanity, a man laid out alive and standing, and already, as one may say, buried under arms with funeral accompaniments, though it may be,—

> "Not a drum was heard, not a funeral note,
>    As his corse to the rampart we hurried;
> Not a soldier discharged his farewell shot
>    O'er the grave where our hero we buried."

The mass of men serve the state thus, not as men mainly, but as machines, with their bodies. They are the standing army, and the militia, jailers, constables, *posse comitatus*, etc. In most cases there is no free exercise whatever of the judgment or of the moral sense; but they put themselves on a level with wood and earth and stones; and wooden men can perhaps be manufactured that will serve the purpose as well. Such command no more respect than men of straw or a lump of dirt. They have the same sort of worth only as horses and dogs. Yet such as these even are commonly esteemed good citizens. Others—as most legislators, politicians, lawyers, ministers, and office-holders—serve the state chiefly with their heads; and, as they rarely make any moral distinctions, they are as likely to serve the Devil, without *intending* it, as God. A very few—as heroes, patriots, martyrs, reformers in the great

**42 corporation:** group.

**43 a whit:** the least bit.

**43–45** What can be the consequences of having too much respect for the law? **B**

**47 powder-monkeys:** boys with the job of carrying gunpowder to artillery crews.

**51 palpitation** (pǎl′pǐ-tā′shən): irregular, rapid beating.

**54 magazines:** places where ammunition is stored.

**57 black arts:** witchcraft.

**61–64 "Not a drum . . . we buried":** the opening lines of "The Burial of Sir John Moore After Corunna" by the Irish poet Charles Wolfe.

**65–82** Which way of serving the state does Thoreau approve of? Which ways does he condemn? **C**

**67 *posse comitatus*** (pŏs′ē kŏm′ĭ-tŏt′əs) *Latin:* power of the county—a term used to refer to the group of people that can be called on by a sheriff to help enforce the law.

| WORDS TO KNOW | **conscientious** (kŏn′shē-ĕn′shəs) *adj.* guided by conscience; honest<br>**unscrupulous** (ŭn-skrōō′pyə-ləs) *adj.* without principles; dishonorable |
|---|---|

372

---

## Teaching Options

**BLOCK SCHEDULING: MANAGING TIME**

**If your schedule requires that you cover the lesson objectives in a shorter time, use . . .**
- Preparing to Read, p. 369
- Thinking Through the Literature, p. 378
- Vocabulary in Action, p. 380

**If you want to take advantage of longer class time, use . . .**
- TE Teaching Options: Preteaching Vocabulary, p. 370; Cross-Curricular Link, pp. 371, 374; Vocabulary Strategy, p. 372; Viewing and Representing, p. 375; Informal Assessment, p. 377; Inquiry & Research, p. 379
- Choices & Challenges, p. 379

sense, and *men*—serve the state with their consciences also, and so necessarily resist it for the most part; and they are commonly treated as enemies by it. . . .

Unjust laws exist: shall we be content to obey them, or shall we <u>endeavor</u> to amend them, and obey them until we have succeeded or shall we transgress them at once? Men generally, under such a government as this, think that they ought to wait until they have persuaded the majority to alter them. They think that, if they should resist, the remedy would be worse than the evil. But it is the fault of the government itself that the remedy *is* worse than the evil. *It* makes it worse. Why is it not more apt to anticipate and provide for reform? Why does it not cherish its wise minority? Why does it cry and resist before it is hurt? Why does it not encourage its citizens to be on the alert to point out its faults, and *do* better than it would have them? Why does it always crucify Christ, and excommunicate Copernicus and Luther, and pronounce Washington and Franklin rebels? . . .

```
Let your life be

a counter-friction

to stop the machine.
```

If the injustice is part of the necessary friction of the machine of government, let it go, let it go: perchance it will wear smooth, —certainly the machine will wear out. If the injustice has a spring, or a pulley, or a rope, or a crank, exclusively for itself, then perhaps you may consider whether the remedy will not be worse than the evil; but if it is of such a nature that it requires you to be the agent of injustice to another, then, I say, break the law. Let your life be a counter-friction to stop the machine. What I have to do is to see, at any rate, that I do not lend myself to the wrong which I condemn. . . .

I meet this American government, or its representative, the state government, directly, and face to face, once a year—no more—in the person of its tax-gatherer; this is the only mode in which a man situated as I am necessarily meets it; and it then says distinctly, Recognize me; and the simplest, most effectual, and, in the present posture of affairs, the indispensablest mode of treating with it on this head, of expressing your little satisfaction with and love for it, is to deny it then. My civil neighbor, the tax-gatherer, is the very man I have to deal with,—

---

**96-97 Copernicus** (kō-pûr′nə-kəs) **and Luther:** Nicolaus Copernicus (1473–1543), a Polish astronomer who theorized that the sun rather than the earth is the center of our planetary system, and Martin Luther (1483–1546), a German theologian who was a leader in the Protestant Reformation. Both men were excommunicated (barred from participation in religious rites) by the Roman Catholic Church.

**100-106** In this metaphor Thoreau compares injustice within government to friction in the workings of a machine—both are often unavoidable byproducts of the workings of a complex system.

**114-122** What does Thoreau consider the most effective way of expressing his displeasure with the government? **D**

**119 posture of affairs:** situation.

---

WORDS
TO
KNOW
**endeavor** (ĕn-dĕv′ər) v. to make an earnest effort; strive

**373**

## Customizing Instruction

### Less Proficient Readers

**1** Ask students to explain what Thoreau feels is more important than obeying the law.
**Possible Response:** doing what one knows is right

**2** Help students answer the following questions.
- For which people in his society does Thoreau have little respect?
  **Answer:** soldiers, jailers, constables, legislators, politicians, lawyers, ministers, office holders
- What types of people does Thoreau respect?
  **Answer:** heroes, reformers, martyrs
- What reasons does he give for his feelings?
  **Answer:** He respects people who follow their consciences, even if it leads them to take unpopular positions in society. He believes that people who blindly follow the law, or who lead without making moral distinctions, are not true men.

**Set a Purpose** Have students read to find out what Thoreau believes is the correct way to deal with injustice.

### Students Acquiring English

**3** Explain to students Thoreau's comparison of government to a machine. Thoreau is questioning whether injustice is a necessary part of the machine of government. If it is, he says, it is a moral person's job to stop the machine.

---

## Vocabulary Strategy

**UNDERSTANDING THE CONNOTATIVE AND DENOTATIVE MEANINGS OF WORDS** Denotation refers to the dictionary definition of a word; connotation refers to the feelings and attitudes a word evokes. Two words can have similar denotative meanings but convey very different feelings and attitudes. Students can rely on context to determine both the denotative and connotative meanings of words. For example, the words *blunder* and *mistake* both mean "an error or oversight," but *blunder* connotes a clumsy, foolish, or rather stupid misdeed, while *mistake* connotes a simple error of judgment. Point out to students that Thoreau carefully chooses the word *blunder* to describe the actions of townspeople he calls "underbred," who do not understand his beliefs.

**Application** Have students work in pairs to list a denotative meaning and a connotative meaning for each of the following words: *flourish, meditation, endeavor, evil,* and *conscience.* Then ask them to use each word in a sentence that shows its connotative meaning.

Use **Vocabulary Transparencies and Copymasters,** p. 38.

A lesson on connotation and denotation appears on p. 908 in the Pupil's Edition.

### Active Reading

#### STRATEGIES FOR READING ESSAYS

**A** Noting the feelings and attitudes Thoreau expresses will help students understand his point of view. Ask students to describe Thoreau's attitude toward the tax collector and then explain the reasons behind his attitude.

**Possible Response:** He dislikes the tax collector because the man chooses to be the agent of an unfair government.

### Literary Analysis [ESSAY]

**B** Students should be able to recognize logical modes of persuasion in Thoreau's essay. Thoreau uses this portion of the essay to explain the reasons for civil disobedience. Ask students to summarize the arguments Thoreau uses to convince people that civil disobedience is the only sensible and moral course of action to take.

**Possible Response:** Truth holds power; people should not be afraid to stop supporting a government that is unjust; people should use their whole influence to fight for change, not just talk about or vote for change; if they experience some injustice themselves, it will only make them more effective and eloquent as protesters; if a thousand men decided to go to prison rather than support the government, the government would change.

#### GUIDE FOR READING

**C** Thoreau's anecdote illustrates that a jailed person with a clear conscience is freer than someone blindly serving an unjust system. It also emphasizes the personal rewards of standing up for one's beliefs.

---

for it is, after all, with men and not with parchment that I quarrel,—and he has voluntarily chosen to be an agent of the government. How shall he ever know well what he is and does as an officer of the government, or as a man, until he is obliged to consider whether he shall treat me, his neighbor, for whom he has respect, as a neighbor and well-disposed man, or as a maniac and disturber of the peace, and see if he can get over this obstruction to his neighborliness without a ruder and more impetuous thought or speech corresponding with his action. I know this well, that if one thousand, if one hundred, if ten men whom I could name,—if ten *honest* men only,—ay, if *one* HONEST man, in this State of Massachusetts, *ceasing to hold slaves,* were actually to withdraw from this copartnership, and be locked up in the county jail therefor, it would be the abolition of slavery in America. For it matters not how small the beginning may seem to be: what is once well done is done forever. But we love better to talk about it: that we say is our mission. Reform keeps many scores of newspapers in its service, but not one man. . . .

Under a government which imprisons any unjustly, the true place for a just man is also a prison. The proper place today, the only place which Massachusetts has provided for her freer and less desponding spirits, is in her prisons, to be put out and locked out of the State by her own act, as they have already put themselves out by their principles. It is there that the fugitive slave, and the Mexican prisoner on parole, and the Indian come to plead the wrongs of his race should find them; on that separate, but more free and honorable ground, where the State places those who are not *with* her, but *against* her,— the only house in a slave State in which a free man can abide with honor. If any think that their influence would be lost there, and their voices no longer afflict the ear of the State, that they would not be as an enemy within its walls, they do not know by how much truth is stronger than error, nor how much more eloquently and effectively he can combat injustice who has experienced a little in his own person. Cast your whole vote, not a strip of paper merely, but your whole influence. A minority is powerless while it conforms to the majority; it is not even a minority then; but it is irresistible when it clogs by its whole weight. If the alternative is to keep all just men in prison, or give up war and slavery, the State will not hesitate which to choose. If a thousand men were not to pay their tax bills this year, that would not be a violent and bloody measure, as it would be to pay them, and enable the State to commit violence and shed innocent blood. This is, in fact, the definition

**132-139** Note that Thoreau advocates refusing to go along with the "copartnership of the individual and government if the government acts against an individual's conscience." Although abolitionists in Thoreau's time did not act on his suggestion, civil rights leaders more than one hundred years later, in the 1960s, staged protests and went to jail to oppose unjust segregation laws and practices.

**374** UNIT THREE PART 1: CELEBRATIONS OF THE SELF

---

## Teaching Options

### Cross Curricular Link **Social Studies**

**FEMALE LEADERS OF SOCIAL PROTEST** Along with Thoreau and other men, many American women in the 19th century were effective leaders in the fight for social justice. At this time, women were not allowed to vote or take part in government. When antislavery sentiment began to grow in the North, many women became part of the abolition movement. In working for the rights of African Americans, women realized that they too deserved the rights and privileges that the U.S. Constitution promised.

Sarah Moore Grimké and her sister Angelina Emily Grimké were born to a wealthy slaveholding family in the South and became the first women to speak out against slavery and promote women's rights. Lucretia Coffin Mott fought for labor rights and abolition, protested against war, and helped runaway slaves. She also helped to form the Philadelphia Female Anti-Slavery Society. Elizabeth Cady Stanton and Susan B. Anthony led the women's suffrage movement in America. In 1848 Stanton, Anthony, and Mott were among the women who organized the first women's rights convention in Seneca Falls, New York.

**Students Acquiring English**

**1** Be sure students understand Thoreau's description of his unhappy relationship with the tax collector. Explain that Thoreau feels people should stop paying taxes to protest unjust government policies. Tell them that this is a form of civil disobedience.

**Set a Purpose** Have students read to find out why he feels withholding taxes is an effective form of protest.

**2** Explain that when Thoreau refers to reform in this instance, he is talking about reform movements in which people talk about making change but do not take drastic measures to force change.

**Less Proficient Readers**

**3** Ask students to tell why Thoreau refused to pay his taxes.

**Possible Response:** He felt that government was unfair, and he should not support it.

**Set a Purpose** Have students read to find out how Thoreau feels about his beliefs as he sits in prison.

of a peaceable revolution, if any such is possible. If the tax-gatherer, or any other public officer, asks me, as one has done, "But what shall I do?" my answer is, "If you really wish to do anything, resign your office." When the subject has refused allegiance, and the officer has resigned his office, then the revolution is accomplished. But even suppose blood should flow. Is there not a sort of blood shed when the conscience is wounded? Through this wound a man's real manhood and immortality flow out, and he bleeds to an everlasting death. I see this blood flowing now. . . .

I have paid no poll-tax for six years. I was put into a jail once on this account, for one night; and, as I stood considering the walls of solid stone, two or three feet thick, the door of wood and iron, a foot thick, and the iron grating which strained the light, I could not help being struck with the foolishness of that institution which treated me as if I were mere flesh and blood and bones, to be locked up. I wondered that it should have <u>concluded</u> at length that this was the best use it could put me to, and had never thought to avail itself of my services in some way. I saw that, if there was a wall of stone between me and my townsmen, there was a still more difficult one to climb or break through before they could get to be as free as I was. I did not for a moment feel confined, and

A 1981 march for nuclear disarmament in London's West End.

Rosa Parks, whose arrest for refusing to move to the back of a segregated bus touched off the Montgomery, Alabama, bus boycott in 1955.

In the early 1900s, suffragists demonstrate for women's voting rights outside Buckingham Palace in London.

**178–205** Why do you think Thoreau includes this personal anecdote about his one night in jail? **C**

**178 poll-tax:** a tax that one had to pay in order to vote.

---

WORDS
TO
KNOW

**conclude** (kən-klōōd′) *v.* to arrive at a judgment or decision

**375**

---

**(Mini Lesson) Viewing and Representing**

The photographs show an anti-nuclear weapons protest, Rosa Parks, and a women's suffrage demonstration.

**Instruction** Ask students to analyze the different ways in which important ideas are represented in photographs. Ask them to compare and contrast the subjects and the action shown in each of the photographs. What emotions are expressed by the crowd in the nuclear protest picture? What message is sent by the photo of Rosa Parks sitting by herself on the bus? Explain the image of the tall fence in the women's suffrage photo.

**Possible Responses:** The anti-nuclear photo shows an energetic rally. People send their message with signs and banners. Rosa Parks sits by herself, but sends the message that one person can make a difference. The fence represents the barriers faced by women working for voting rights.

**Application** What common theme do these photos express?

**Possible Responses:** courage, determination, the strength of people acting according to their own consciences

### Literary Analysis ESSAY

**A** What does Thoreau's description of the townspeople and of his time in jail reveal about his personality?
**Possible Responses:** He is sure of himself and angry with people who do not agree with him.

### GUIDE FOR READING

**B** **Possible Response:** He will not give in to the government's demand for money. He must obey his own laws or he will die.

### Reading Skills and Strategies: CHALLENGE

Ask students to challenge Thoreau's idea that it is acceptable to break the law to correct an injustice. Have them suggest other possible ways in which Thoreau could make his point and be true to his nature.
**Possible Responses:** Thoreau isolates himself and does not listen to other opinions. Students might feel that Thoreau could work within the law.

## Link Across Cultures

### Reading Skills and Strategies: COMPARE AND CONTRAST

Have students note the similarities and differences between the situations in 19th-century America and 20th-century India. How is Gandhi's call for civil disobedience similar to that of Thoreau?

---

the walls seemed a great waste of stone and mortar. I felt as if I alone of all my townsmen had paid my tax. They plainly did not know how to treat me, but behaved like persons who are underbred. In every threat and in every compliment there was a
195 <u>blunder</u>; for they thought that my chief desire was to stand the other side of that stone wall. I could not but smile to see how industriously they locked the door on my <u>meditations</u>, which followed them out again without let or hindrance, and *they* were really all that was dangerous. As they could not reach me,
 200 they had resolved to punish my body; just as boys, if they cannot come at some person against whom they have a spite, will abuse his dog. I saw that the State was half-witted, that it was timid as a lone woman with her silver spoons, and that it did not know its friends from its foes, and I lost all my
205 remaining respect for it, and pitied it.

    Thus the State never intentionally <u>confronts</u> a man's sense, intellectual or moral, but only his body, his senses. It is not armed with superior wit or honesty, but with superior physical strength. I was not born to be forced. I will breathe after my
210 own fashion. Let us see who is the strongest. What force has a <u>multitude</u>? They only can force me who obey a higher law than I. They force me to become like themselves. I do not hear of *men* being *forced* to live this way or that by masses of men. What sort of life were that to live? When I meet a government
215 which says to me, "Your money or your life," why should I be in haste to give it my money? It may be in a great strait, and not know what to do: I cannot help that. It must help itself; do as I do. It is not worth the while to snivel about it. I am not responsible for the successful working of the machinery of
220 society. I am not the son of the engineer. I perceive that, when an acorn and a chestnut fall side by side, the one does not remain inert to make way for the other, but both obey their own laws, and spring and grow and <u>flourish</u> as best they can, till one, perchance, overshadows and destroys the other. If a
225 plant cannot live according to its nature, it dies; and so a man.

194 **underbred:** ill-mannered.

198 **without let or hindrance** (hĭn′drəns): without encountering obstacles.

201 **spite:** grudge.

**220-225** What message does Thoreau convey through this example of the acorn and the chestnut?

```
If a plant cannot live according to its nature; it dies;
                                    and so a man.
```

| | |
|---|---|
| WORDS TO KNOW | **blunder** (blŭn′dər) n. a mistake<br>**meditation** (mĕd′ĭ-tā′shən) n. a thought or reflection<br>**confront** (kən-frŭnt′) v. to come up against; meet face to face<br>**multitude** (mŭl′tĭ-tōōd′) n. a great number of people<br>**flourish** (flûr′ĭsh) v. to thrive |

376

---

## Teaching Options

 **Grammar**

### MODIFIERS: ADJECTIVE AND ADVERB PHRASES

**Instruction** An adjective phrase is a prepositional phrase that modifies a noun or pronoun. An adverb phrase is a prepositional phrase that modifies a verb, an adjective, or an adverb. Write the following examples on the chalkboard and help students analyze the way each phrase functions in its sentence.

Adjective phrase: Thoreau spoke to everyone <u>in the town</u>. (modifies the pronoun *everyone*)

Adverb phrase: The students were impressed <u>with his beliefs</u>. (modifies the adjective *impressed*)

**Application** Have each student write a brief letter to Thoreau expressing his or her ideas about Thoreau's essay. In their letters, students should use at least four adjective phrases and four adverb phrases. Have them underline the adjective phrases and circle the adverb phrases. Students may share their letters with the rest of the class.

 Use **Grammar Transparencies and Copymasters,** pp. 82–83.

Use McDougal Littell's *Language Network,* Chapter 7, for more instruction and practice in modifiers.

# ON CIVIL DISOBEDIENCE

*Mohandas K. Gandhi*

*Mohandas K. Gandhi (1869-1948), called Mahatma ("Great Soul"), helped free India of British rule. As a student, he greatly admired Thoreau's essay "Civil Disobedience." Thoreau's ideas helped shape Gandhi's key principle—satyagraha (sə-tyä′ grə-hə), or "truth-force." In the following excerpt from a 1916 speech, Gandhi describes this powerful weapon for fighting oppression.*

July 27, 1916

There are two ways of countering injustice. One way is to smash the head of the man who perpetrates injustice and to get your own head smashed in the process. All strong people in the world adopt this course. Everywhere wars are fought and millions of people are killed. The consequence is not the progress of a nation but its decline. . . . No country has ever become, or will ever become, happy through victory in war. A nation does not rise that way, it only falls further. In fact, what comes to it is defeat, not victory. And if, perchance, either our act or our purpose was ill-conceived, it brings disaster to both belligerents.[1]

But through the other method of combating injustice, we alone suffer the consequences of our mistakes, and the other side is wholly spared. This other method is *satyagraha.*[2] One who resorts to it does not have to break another's head; he may merely have his own head broken. He has to be prepared to die himself suffering all the pain. In opposing the atrocious laws of the Government of South Africa, it was this method that we adopted. We made it clear to the said Government that we would never bow to its outrageous laws. No clapping is possible without two hands to do it, and no quarrel without two persons to make it. Similarly, no State is possible without two entities, the rulers and the ruled. You are our sovereign, our Government, only so long as we consider ourselves your subjects. When we are not subjects, you are not the sovereign either. So long as it is your endeavour to control us with justice and love, we will let you to do so. But if you wish to strike at us from behind, we cannot permit it. Whatever you do in other matters, you will have to ask our opinion about the laws that concern us. If you make laws to keep us suppressed in a wrongful manner and without taking us into confidence, these laws will merely adorn the statute-books.[3] We will never obey them. Award us for it what punishment you like, we will put up with it. Send us to prison and we will live there as in a paradise. Ask us to mount the scaffold[4] and we will do so laughing. Shower what sufferings you like upon us, we will calmly endure all and not hurt a hair of your body. We will gladly die and will not so much as touch you. But so long as there is yet life in these our bones, we will never comply with your arbitrary laws.

---

1. **belligerents** (bə-lĭj′ər-ənts): participants in a war.
2. **satyagraha** (sə-tyä′grə-hə) *Sanskrit:* insistence on truth—a term used by Gandhi to describe his policy of seeking reform by means of nonviolent resistance.
3. **statute-books:** books of laws.
4. **scaffold:** a platform on which people are executed by hanging.

---

**Less Proficient Readers**
Have students identify the theme of Gandhi's speech.
**Possible Response:** Nonviolent resistance is the best way to fight injustice.

Ask students to point out similarities and differences between Gandhi's speech and Thoreau's essay.
**Possible Responses:** Both Gandhi and Thoreau advocate civil disobedience and believe that violence is no way to solve disagreements. Both argue that it is morally wrong to participate in a system of unjust laws. Gandhi's argument against violence is stated more strongly; he says that it is better to suffer violence against oneself than to take responsibility for violence against someone else. He says that he and his supporters will "gladly die" before they obey unjust laws.

---

## ✓ Assessment Informal Assessment

**IDEA CHART** You can informally assess students' understanding of the essay by asking them to complete an idea chart with information about Thoreau's views. Their charts should contain the following heads.
1. Government
2. Taxes
3. Slavery
4. War with Mexico
5. Civil Disobedience
Have students describe Thoreau's specific views on each of these issues.

**RUBRIC**
**3** **Full Accomplishment** Students show a full understanding of Thoreau's views on each of the major issues.
**2** **Substantial Accomplishment** Students show a full understanding of Thoreau's views on only some of the major issues.
**1** **Little or Partial Accomplishment** Students show little understanding of Thoreau's views on the major issues.

## GUIDING STUDENT RESPONSE

## Connect to the Literature

**1. What Do You Think?**
Students will offer an initial opinion of Thoreau's views on disobeying unjust laws. Good responses might address the following: Are Thoreau's beliefs practical or impractical, patriotic or unpatriotic, democratic or anarchistic?

**Comprehension Check**

• A person's conscience; knowledge of right and wrong.
• Disobey an unjust law.
• Thoreau does not feel confined and believes the only true place for a just man is prison.

 Use Selection Quiz
**Unit Three Resource Book,** p. 20.

## Think Critically

**2.** Students who find Thoreau's argument convincing might offer the following support: every individual must follow his or her own conscience; an individual can become an important minority by refusing to comply with laws that cause injustice to others. Students who find Thoreau's argument unconvincing might cite these reasons: Thoreau's idea of civil disobedience is unrealistic and gives individuals too much authority.

**3.** Thoreau describes three ways of serving the state: with one's body; with one's mind; or with one's conscience.

**4.** Thoreau's threatening ideas might include diminishing the role of government and encouraging people to work outside the legal system.

## Literary Analysis

**Essay** Possible Response: Thoreau's anecdotes about his personal experience lend credence to his position. His night in jail shows that he lives by his philosophy.

---

## Connect to the Literature

**1. What Do You Think?** What is your first reaction to Thoreau's views on civil disobedience, or nonviolent resistance?

**Comprehension Check**
• According to Thoreau, what should be respected more than the law?
• What should a citizen do about an unjust law?
• How does Thoreau respond to being jailed?

## Think Critically

**2.** How convincing do you find Thoreau's argument?

 **THINK ABOUT**
• Thoreau's comment that a man must live according to his nature
• circumstances under which he advocates breaking the law
• his views on majority rule

**3.** **ACTIVE READING** **STRATEGIES FOR READING ESSAYS** Refer to the chart you made in your **READER'S NOTEBOOK.** How important to Thoreau's argument is his idea about the different ways of serving the state? Explain your answer.

**4.** What might some find threatening about Thoreau's ideas?

## Extend Interpretations

**5.** **The Writer's Style** A **paradox** is a statement that seems to contradict itself but may nevertheless suggest an important truth. "Civil Disobedience" is based on the paradox that a good citizen must be a lawbreaker under certain circumstances. Find other paradoxes in the essay that reinforce and extend this basic paradox.

**6.** **Critic's Corner** Critic Leon Edel states that Thoreau's theory of nonviolent resistance does not work in all conditions and that it "presupposes . . . a society which has moved beyond barbarism." Explain what you think Edel means. Does his view affect your opinion of Thoreau's argument?

**7.** **Comparing Texts** Thoreau's ideas influenced many 20th-century reformers, notably Mohandas Gandhi, the Indian nationalist and spiritual leader. What connections do you see between Thoreau's views and Gandhi's in the excerpt "On Civil Disobedience," on page 377?

**8.** **Connect to Life** How would you compare Thoreau's views on good citizenship with your own?

**378** UNIT THREE PART 1: CELEBRATIONS OF THE SELF

---

## Literary Analysis

**ESSAY** An **essay** is a short work of nonfiction that deals with a single subject. The term comes from the French word *essai,* meaning "attempt." The purpose of an essay may be to express ideas and feelings, to analyze, to inform, to entertain, or to persuade. For example, de Crèvecoeur's essay "What Is an American?" was written to inform Europeans about a new breed of people, the Americans. Thoreau's purpose in "Civil Disobedience," on the other hand, is to persuade his audience to use nonviolent resistance to oppose unjust laws.

Even when they discuss serious ideas, essays are often informal, loosely structured, and highly personal. Consider the picture you get of Thoreau the man as you digest the political views in his essay.

**Cooperative Learning Activity**
Working in small groups, locate passages in which Thoreau refers to himself—identifying his personal opinions or recounting personal experiences, such as the night he spent in jail. How do these passages influence your acceptance of his arguments? Discuss what effect omitting these passages would have on the essay.

---

## Extend Interpretations

**The Writer's Style** Students may cite the following paradoxes: "That government is best that governs least." "I saw that, if there was a wall of stone between me and my townsmen, there was still a more difficult one to climb or break through before they could get to be as free as I was."
**Critic's Corner** Students might say that Edel means Thoreau's concept is applicable to only civilized societies in which the government tolerates dissenters rather than killing them. Students who change their opinion based on Edel's interpretation may say that Thoreau's argument has a narrow scope because nonviolent resistance works only in a place that values humane efforts.
**Comparing Texts** Possible Response: Both Thoreau and Gandhi advocate the use of civil disobedience rather than violence to effect change.
**Connect to Life** Some students may say that Thoreau's essay has broadened their definition of good citizenship. Others may respond that good citizenship demands loyalty to the government.

## Writing Options

**1. Comparison of Emerson and Thoreau** Ralph Waldo Emerson was Thoreau's mentor and friend. Compare Thoreau's and Emerson's messages about the importance of the individual, as expressed in "Civil Disobedience" and "Self-Reliance." From their writings, make a generalization about the romantic view of the individual.

**Writing Handbook**
See page 1201: Comparison and Contrast

**2. Personal Response** Select a paradox you identified for question 5 on the Writer's Style (page 378). Then write a personal response, explaining what this paradox means to you.

**3. Essay on Citizenship** Imagine that a local civic group is sponsoring an essay contest about good citizenship. Drawing upon your views and Thoreau's, write an essay exploring ways to serve the community or the nation with your conscience.

*Good CHIZenship*

*A good citizen tries to create a good environment for all.*

## Activities & Explorations

**1. Group Discussion** Thoreau acted on his beliefs by going to jail rather than paying taxes to help finance the war against Mexico or slavery in the South. What present-day causes do you think Thoreau might have supported? With five or six classmates, explore this question in a discussion. Choose one of the causes, and in a chart list two strategies that you believe Thoreau would have used to support this cause and two that he would not have used.
**~ SPEAKING AND LISTENING**

| Cause: | |
|---|---|
| Strategies to Use | Strategies to Avoid |
| | |
| | |

**2. Drama in a Jailhouse** With a small group of classmates, stage a reenactment of Thoreau's arrest, his night in jail, and his subsequent release. Feel free to add imaginative touches such as an interview by a journalist questioning Thoreau about his motives or a visit by one of Thoreau's friends, such as Emerson. Make sure that your characterization of Thoreau is consistent with the message of this essay. **~ PERFORMING**

**3. Political Poster** Design a political poster based on your reading of this essay. Include a slogan and visual images that convey Thoreau's political views. Display your poster in the classroom. **~ ART**

## Inquiry & Research

**Resisting Injustice** Working with a small group, research situations in which protesters have used nonviolent resistance as a means of opposing injustice. Consider situations in the following countries:

- India in the 1920s and 1930s
- Germany in the late 1930s
- the United States in the 1960s
- the Philippines in 1987
- China in 1989

Gather information from resources such as history books and print or on-line encyclopedias. Then, based on your group's research, form an opinion about the effectiveness of nonviolent resistance. Present an oral report to share your findings.

 **More Online: Research Starter**
www.mcdougallittell.com

## Writing Options

**1. Comparison of Emerson and Thoreau To get students started on this assignment,** suggest that they reread Emerson's essay and then make a list of similarities between it and Thoreau's essay. Ask them to think about what generalizations they can make based on their lists.

**2. Personal Response** Invite students to express their personal opinions.

**3. Essay on Citizenship To make this assignment easier,** invite students to work in pairs to brainstorm ideas. **To make this assignment more challenging,** ask students to read their essays aloud to the rest of the class.

## Activities & Explorations

**1. Group Discussion** Encourage students to think about current events and issues in the world today. They might want to review newspapers or magazines.

**2. Drama in a Jailhouse** Give students time to brainstorm ideas for their reenactments. Invite classmates or people from outside the classroom to view and critique the reenactments.

**3. Political Poster** Students should think about effective political posters they have seen. They should ask themselves what techniques people use to sell their political ideas.

## Inquiry & Research

**Resisting Injustice** Students are expected to locate appropriate print and nonprint information. They should draw conclusions from information gathered.

 **Mini Lesson** **Inquiry and Research**

**GENERATING RELEVANT QUESTIONS** When conducting an inquiry on a specific topic, it is valuable to develop questions to guide both research and analysis of data. The Inquiry & Research project on page 379 of the Pupil's Edition provides a bulleted list of items that can be translated into researchable questions—for example, What nonviolent resistance occurred in India in the 1920s and 1930s? After students have researched these topics, they should generate a list of relevant questions that will help them analyze the information they find.

**Application** Suggest that students work with their groups to develop lists of questions that will help them decide, based on their research, whether nonviolent resistance is an effective means of protest. Encourage them to think about what constitutes success in the realm of political protest.

**Possible Responses:** What did the protesters want to change? What happened when they used nonviolent resistance? Did they accomplish all or some of their goals? Was the result of protesting worth the cost?

## Vocabulary in Action

## Vocabulary in Action

**Exercise A**

1. meditation
2. inexpedient
3. flourish
4. endeavor
5. conclude

**Exercise B**

1. S
2. S
3. A
4. S
5. A

**EXERCISE A: CONTEXT CLUES** Write the Word to Know that best completes the meaning of each sentence.

1. Thoreau's "Civil Disobedience" is a _____ on the relationship between citizen and government.
2. Thoreau believes that government leaders sometimes find it _____ to do what is morally right.
3. Thoreau wants a society in which individual liberty would _____ .
4. Thoreau says that Americans should _____ to change unjust laws.
5. Some might _____ that Thoreau wants a revolution.

**EXERCISE B: SYNONYMS AND ANTONYMS** For each pair of words, write *S* if the words are synonyms or *A* if they are antonyms.

1. blunder—error
2. conscientious—principled
3. multitude—individual
4. confront—encounter
5. unscrupulous—honorable

| WORDS TO KNOW | blunder | endeavor | meditation |
|---|---|---|---|
| | conclude | flourish | multitude |
| | confront | inexpedient | unscrupulous |
| | conscientious | | |

**Building Vocabulary**

For an in-depth lesson on context clues, see page 326.

## Henry David Thoreau
### 1817–1862

**Other Works**
*Walden*
*A Week on the Concord and Merrimack Rivers*
*The Collected Poems of Henry Thoreau*

**Philosopher and Scholar** Henry David Thoreau was born and raised in Concord, Massachusetts, where he lived almost all of his life. He studied classics and natural history at Harvard University. After graduating at the age of 20, he returned to Concord to teach school. Although some of Thoreau's neighbors viewed him as a cranky eccentric, he was a careful observer and a deep thinker, who recorded his thoughts and observations in his journal. Taking to heart the ideas of Ralph Waldo Emerson, Thoreau tried to live by his own values rather than society's values, which he considered materialistic.

**Dedicated Nonconformist** Thoreau's life was full of examples of his independent spirit. As a Harvard student, he was required to wear a black coat but sported a green one instead. In his first year of teaching, he refused to punish his students

physically and resigned his post. In 1845, he conducted his famous experiment, living simply and frugally in a small cabin that he had built himself on the shores of Walden Pond. In 1846, he was arrested and spent a night in jail for refusing to pay a poll tax.

**Social Reformer** Despite his love of solitude and country life, Thoreau took an active part in social causes. During the 1840s and 1850s, he became passionately involved in the abolitionist movement. He lectured at antislavery rallies and served as a conductor on the Underground Railroad, hiding fugitive slaves in his family's house. Although he did not advocate violence, he publicly defended John Brown, the fiery abolitionist who had led a bloody raid on Harpers Ferry.

**Posthumous Praise** During his lifetime, Thoreau published only two books, both of which sold poorly. In the years since his death, however, his reputation has grown tremendously. His observations about nature, the importance of the individual, and the value of a simple life are more and more relevant today, as environmental abuses multiply, the pressure to conform increases, and the pace of life continues to speed up.

 **Mini Lesson** ## Grammar

**COMPOUND ADJECTIVES** Compound adjectives are word combinations that work together to modify a noun. Most two-word and three-word compound adjectives are separated by a hyphen. The hyphen keeps the reader from confusing compound adjectives with coordinate adjectives, which are strings of adjectives that work separately to modify a noun.
Coordinate adjectives: <u>long, slow, difficult</u> journey
Compound adjectives: <u>well-written</u> essay; <u>sooner-than-expected</u> victory

When a proper name modifies a noun, it is not hyphenated: a <u>Henry David Thoreau</u> fan

**Exercises** Ask students to punctuate the following sentences correctly with hyphens or commas.

1. He was a quiet thoughtful man. *(quiet, thoughtful)*
2. The writer had a well thought out philosophy. *(well-thought-out)*
3. People accused him of being an arrogant selfish rebellious man. *(arrogant, selfish, rebellious)*

 Use **Grammar Transparencies and Copymasters,** p. 70 for more exercises.

 Use McDougal Littell's *Language Network,* Chapter 7, for more instruction in compound adjectives.

# PREPARING to *Read*

## from Walden

*Essay by* HENRY DAVID THOREAU

### Connect to Your Life

**Future Experiences** What do you want to experience in your life? Think of some experiences you look forward to, such as working for the Peace Corps, learning to play the guitar, inventing a computer game, seeing the Rocky Mountains, or appearing on TV. Pick three of the experiences and explain to a small group of your classmates why you want to have each one.

## Build Background

**Thoreau's Experiment** Like Ralph Waldo Emerson and other transcendentalists, Thoreau felt a need to confirm his unity with nature. On July 4, 1845, he began his famous experiment in what he thought of as "essential" living—living simply, studying the natural world, and seeking truth within himself. On land owned by Emerson near Concord, Massachusetts, Thoreau built a small cabin by Walden Pond and lived there for more than two years, writing and studying nature. *Walden*—a mixture of philosophy, autobiography, and meditation upon nature—is the record of Thoreau's experiences at the pond.

WORDS TO KNOW
**Vocabulary Preview**

| | | |
|---|---|---|
| abject | magnanimity | resignation |
| congenial | mean | rudiment |
| deliberately | misgiving | serenity |
| disreputable | perennial | sublime |
| dissipation | perturbation | vulgar |

## Focus Your Reading

**LITERARY ANALYSIS** **NATURE WRITING** The term **nature writing** describes a type of essay in which the writer uses firsthand observations to explore his or her relationship with the natural world. *Walden* is one of the best known examples of nature writing. Find out what Thoreau learns from his experiences with nature.

**ACTIVE READING** **EVALUATING AUTHOR'S OBSERVATIONS** Good readers look for connections between what they read and their own experiences. They also challenge the text, forming their own opinions about the writer's observations. As Emerson did in "Self-Reliance," Thoreau often uses aphorisms—brief statements that express general principles or truths about life—to convey his observations.

| Aphorism | Do I Agree? |
|---|---|
| "An honest man has hardly need to count more than his ten fingers." | |

**READER'S NOTEBOOK** As you read, jot down some of Thoreau's aphorisms. Then, after you finish reading, write a brief evaluation of each aphorism, explaining whether or not you agree with it.

### Objectives
1. understand and appreciate a classic example of **nature writing (Literary Analysis)**
2. **evaluate the author's observations** in an essay **(Active Reading)**

### Summary
These passages from *Walden* contain many of Thoreau's key ideas. He explains that he went to live at Walden Pond to experience the essentials of life and not let life pass him by while he got lost in details. In a passage on solitude, he describes feeling in tune with nature, alert to all that happens around him. Thoreau states that he left Walden because he had "several more lives to live." He had learned from his own experience that by following their dreams, people can transform their lives and values. By recounting the story of a bug that hatched from a wooden table after lying dormant for sixty years, Thoreau offers hope for human resurrection and revival.

### Thematic Link
Thoreau's devotion to finding truth through the deliberate study of nature is characteristic of American **transcendentalism**.

### 5-Minute Warm-Up

*Daily Language SkillBuilder*

Have students **proofread** the display sentences on page 337i and write them correctly. The sentences also appear on Transparency 11 of **Grammar Transparencies and Copymasters**.

**Mini Lesson** **Preteaching Vocabulary**

If you would like to preteach the WORDS TO KNOW for this selection, use the Mini Lesson, p. 382.

---

## LESSON RESOURCES

**UNIT THREE RESOURCE BOOK,** pp. 21–25

**ASSESSMENT RESOURCES**
**Formal Assessment,** pp. 71–72
**Teacher's Guide to Assessment and Portfolio Use**
**Test Generator**

**SKILLS TRANSPARENCIES AND COPYMASTERS**
**Literary Analysis**
• Persuasion, T8 (for Writing Option 1, p. 393)

**Reading and Critical Thinking**
• Observation Chart, T46 (for Writing Option 3, p. 393)

**Grammar**
• Nouns Used as Adjectives, C69 (for Mini Lesson, p. 390)
• Double Negatives, C137 (for Mini Lesson, p. 393)
• Modifiers: *Good* and *Well*, C136 (for Mini Lesson, p. 388)

**Vocabulary**
• Homonyms, C35 (for Mini Lesson, p. 384)

**Writing**
• Interpretive Essay, C36 (for Writing Option 2, p. 393)

**Communications**
• Impromptu Speaking: Dialogue, Role-Play, Debate, T13 (for Inquiry & Research, p. 393)

**INTEGRATED TECHNOLOGY**
**Audio Library**
**LaserLinks**
• Contemporary Connection: Walden Today. See **Teacher's SourceBook**, p. 40.
**Internet: Research Starter**
**Visit our website:**
www.mcdougallittell.com

**Literary Analysis** NATURE WRITING

Have students read to appreciate Thoreau's craft as a nature writer. As they read, they should make brief notes in a chart similar to the one below about each image of nature and its meaning for Thoreau.

| Image | Meaning |
|-------|---------|
|       |         |
|       |         |
|       |         |
|       |         |

 Use **Unit Three Resource Book,** p. 23 for more practice.

**Active Reading**

EVALUATING AUTHOR'S OBSERVATIONS

**A** Thoreau refers to the place where the first shots of the American Revolution were fired. In what ways does the setting of *Walden,* so close to the symbolic beginning of the American Revolution, seem appropriate?
**Possible Responses:** Thoreau's rebellious and independent spirit is in keeping with the spirit of the American revolutionaries.

 Use **Unit Three Resource Book,** p. 22 for more practice.

**GUIDE FOR READING**

**B** **Possible Response:** to live simply and deliberately; to experience the essence of life

**C** **Possible Responses:** simplifying our lives; eliminating unnecessary activities

**Teaching Options**

F R O M

# *Walden*

H E N R Y   D A V I D   T H O R E A U

F R O M

## *Where I Lived, and What I Lived For*

When first I took up my abode in the woods, that is, began to spend my nights as well as days there, which, by accident, was on Independence day, or the fourth of July, 1845, my house was not finished for winter, but was merely a defense against the rain, without plastering or chimney, the walls being of rough weather-stained boards, with wide chinks, which made it cool at night. The upright white hewn studs and freshly planed door and window casings gave it a clean and airy look, especially in the morning, when its timbers were saturated with dew, so that I fancied that by noon some sweet gum would exude from them. . . .

5

10

 **Preteaching Vocabulary**

USING CONTEXT CLUES When students encounter an unknown word, one strategy is to continue reading to see if the word's meaning is summarized in another part of the sentence or paragraph. Write the word *deliberately* on the chalkboard and read the following passage aloud. Then ask students to summarize the meaning of *deliberately.* People noticed that Rolf worked <u>deliberately</u> at his job. He never hurried to get something done; instead, he approached every task in a thoughtful way. His high-quality work reflected the care that he put into it.
**Exercises** Have students use their understanding of summary statements to figure out the mean-

ings of underlined terms.
1. Townspeople in the flooded area had a feeling of <u>resignation</u> as more rain fell. They walked with their heads down in silent acceptance of the power of nature.
2. The band played songs that were <u>perennial</u> favorites. People clapped and danced to songs they had listened to and enjoyed for years.

 Use **Unit Three Resource Book,** p. 24 for more exercises.

A lesson on context clues appears on page 326 in the Pupil's Edition.

I was seated by the shore of a small pond, about a mile and a
15 half south of the village of Concord and somewhat higher than
it, in the midst of an extensive wood between that town and
Lincoln, and about two miles south of that our only field
known to fame, Concord Battle Ground; but I was so low in the
woods that the opposite shore, half a mile off, like the rest, cov-
20 ered with wood, was my most distant horizon. For the first
week, whenever I looked out on the pond it impressed me like a
tarn high up on the side of a mountain, its bottom far above the
surface of other lakes, and, as the sun arose, I saw it throwing
off its nightly clothing of mist, and here and there, by degrees,
25 its soft ripples or its smooth reflecting surface was revealed,
while the mists, like ghosts, were stealthily withdrawing in every
direction into the woods, as at the breaking up of some nocturnal conventicle. The very dew seemed to hang upon the trees
later into the day than usual, as on the sides of mountains. . . .
30 I went to the woods because I wished to live deliberately, to
front only the essential facts of life, and see if I could not learn
what it had to teach, and not, when I came to die, discover that
I had not lived. I did not wish to live what was not life, living is
so dear; nor did I wish to practice resignation, unless it was
35 quite necessary. I wanted to live deep and suck out all the marrow of life, to live so sturdily and Spartan-like as to put to rout
all that was not life, to cut a broad swath and shave close, to
drive life into a corner, and reduce it to its lowest terms, and, if
it proved to be mean, why then to get the whole and genuine
40 meanness of it, and publish its meanness to the world; or if it
were sublime, to know it by experience, and be able to give a
true account of it in my next excursion. For most men, it
appears to me, are in a strange uncertainty about it, whether it
is of the devil or of God, and have *somewhat hastily* concluded
45 that it is the chief end of man here to "glorify God and enjoy
him forever."

Still we live meanly, like ants; though the fable tells us that
we were long ago changed into men; like pygmies we fight with
cranes; it is error upon error, and clout upon clout, and our best
50 virtue has for its occasion a superfluous and evitable wretchedness. Our life is frittered away by detail. An honest man has
hardly need to count more than his ten fingers, or in extreme
cases he may add his ten toes, and lump the rest. Simplicity,
simplicity, simplicity! I say, let your affairs be as two or three,
55 and not a hundred or a thousand; instead of a million count

**22 tarn:** a small mountain lake or
pool.

**27–28 nocturnal conventicle**
(kən-věn'tĭ-kəl): a secret religious
meeting held at night.

**30–42** What are Thoreau's reasons
for moving to the woods?

**35–36 marrow:** the central, most
essential part; literally, the soft
tissue inside a bone.

**36 Spartan-like:** in a simple,
economical, and disciplined way,
like the inhabitants of the ancient
Greek city-state of Sparta.

**37 cut a broad swath and shave
close:** gather as much of the
essence of life as possible.

**45 chief end of man here:** most
important purpose of human life
on earth.

**47 the fable:** a Greek myth in
which Zeus changes ants into men.

**48–49 like pygmies . . . cranes:** a
reference to a legend, mentioned
in Homer's *Iliad,* about the
continual battles fought by a race
of dwarfs against cranes.

**50 evitable** (ĕv'ĭ-tə-bəl):
avoidable.

**53–54** What is Thoreau's remedy
for our hectic, detail-crowded
lives?

| WORDS TO KNOW | **deliberately** (dĭ-lĭb'ər-ĭt-lē) *adv.* in an unhurried and thoughtful manner |
|---|---|
| | **resignation** (rĕz'ĭg-nā'shən) *n.* an acceptance of something as unavoidable |
| | **mean** (mēn) *adj.* inferior in quality, value, or importance |
| | **sublime** (sə-blīm') *adj.* of high spiritual, moral, or intellectual worth; noble |

**383**

### Literary Analysis: FIGURATIVE LANGUAGE

**A** Point out this extended metaphor, in which Thoreau likens civilized life to a rough sea. Ask students what the clouds and storms of life might be, and how one might "founder and go to the bottom" in civilized life.

**Possible Responses:** The storms of life could be problems with family, jobs, and so on; everyday demands might cause one to "founder"—to lose a job, to fail in school, or to overlook the meaning of life.

### GUIDE FOR READING

**B** **Possible Response:** He exaggerates the importance that the average person gives to the daily news.

**C** **Possible Response:** The offer of "a penny for your thoughts" is never taken literally. However, the penny-post seems to take the expression literally and charges a penny to deliver the worthless thoughts expressed in many letters.

### Literary Analysis: STYLE

**D** Have students evaluate the effectiveness of Thoreau's use of many examples.

**Possible Responses:** The style imitates modern life, overwhelming the reader with many news items.

### GUIDE FOR READING

**E** **Possible Response:** Thoreau wants to spend his time figuring out the "secret of things." He feels he can use his intellect to delve deep into whatever situation he is in to uncover the answers he seeks.

---

**A** half a dozen, and keep your accounts on your thumbnail. In the midst of this chopping sea of civilized life, such are the clouds and storms and quicksands and thousand-and-one items to be allowed for, that a man has to live, if he would not founder and
60 go to the bottom and not make his port at all, by dead reckoning, and he must be a great calculator indeed who succeeds. Simplify, simplify. Instead of three meals a day, if it be necessary eat but one; instead of a hundred dishes, five; and reduce other things in proportion. . . .

**1** 65 Why should we live with such hurry and waste of life? We are determined to be starved before we are hungry. Men say that a stitch in time saves nine, and so they take a thousand stitches today to save nine to-morrow. As for *work*, we haven't any of any consequence. We have the Saint Vitus' dance, and
70 cannot possibly keep our heads still. If I should only give a few pulls at the parish bell-rope, as for a fire, that is, without setting the bell, there is hardly a man on his farm in the outskirts of Concord, notwithstanding that press of engagements which was his excuse so many times this morning, nor a boy, nor a
75 woman, I might almost say, but would forsake all and follow that sound, not mainly to save property from the flames, but, if **2** we will confess the truth, much more to see it burn, since burn it must, and we, be it known, did not set it on fire,—or to see it put out, and have a hand in it, if that is done as handsomely;
80 yes, even if it were the parish church itself. Hardly a man takes a half hour's nap after dinner, but when he wakes he holds up his head and asks, "What's the news?" as if the rest of mankind had stood his sentinels. Some give directions to be waked every half hour, doubtless for no other purpose; and then, to pay for
85 it, they tell what they have dreamed. After a night's sleep the news is as indispensable as the breakfast. "Pray tell me any thing new that has happened to a man any where on this globe,"—and he reads it over his coffee and rolls, that a man has had his eyes gouged out this morning on the Wachito River;
90 never dreaming the while that he lives in the dark unfathomed mammoth cave of this world, and has but the <u>rudiment</u> of an eye himself.

For my part, I could easily do without the post-office. I think that there are very few important communications made
95 through it. To speak critically, I never received more than one or two letters in my life—I wrote this some years ago—that were worth the postage. The penny-post is, commonly, an institution through which you seriously offer a man that penny for his

**59 founder:** to sink like a ship.

**60–61 dead reckoning:** guesswork. The term, used by sailors, describes a method of estimating a ship's position when the stars cannot be seen.

**69 Saint Vitus'** (vī'təs) **dance:** a disorder of the nervous system, characterized by rapid, jerky, involuntary movements.

**80–92** What situation is Thoreau exaggerating here? **B**

**89 Wachito River:** a river (now called the Ouachita) in northern Louisiana and southern Arkansas. In Thoreau's time, it was believed that violent men went to that region to escape from the law.

**97–99** Thoreau jokingly connects the postage rate (a penny per letter at the time) with the phrase "a penny for your thoughts." What is the point of his joke? **C**

| WORDS |
| TO | **rudiment** (rōō'də-mənt) *n.* an imperfect or undeveloped form
| KNOW |

384

---

## Teaching Options

 **Mini Lesson** **Vocabulary Strategy**

### HOMONYMS

**Instruction** Many word pairs in the English language have the same spelling and pronunciation but different meanings. These word pairs are called homonyms. For example, the word *calf* can refer either to a young cow or to the back part of a person's leg. In *Walden,* Thoreau uses the adjective *mean* to describe something that is inferior or poor in value. Have students think of other meanings for this word that are more familiar to them ("cruel," "average"). Tell students that they can avoid confusion with homonyms if they learn to rely on context clues to determine meaning.

**Application** Have students work in pairs to find other homonyms in the selection from *Walden.* If necessary, they can consult a dictionary to check on the spellings and meanings of words. Have them use these words in sentences that show their different meanings.

**Possible Responses:** *upright, seated, wood, reflecting, front, drive, account, end, lump, consequence, sound, rolls*

Use **Vocabulary Transparencies and Copymasters,** p. 35.

A lesson on homonyms appears on p. 728 in the Pupil's Edition.

Photo by Ernst Haas. Copyright © Tony Stone Images

thoughts which is so often safely offered in jest. And I am sure
100 that I never read any memorable news in a newspaper. If we
read of one man robbed, or murdered, or killed by accident, or
one house burned, or one vessel wrecked, or one steamboat
blown up, or one cow run over on the Western Railroad, or one
mad dog killed, or one lot of grasshoppers in the winter,—we
105 never need read of another. One is enough. . . .

    Let us spend one day as deliberately as Nature, and not be
thrown off the track by every nutshell and mosquito's wing that
falls on the rails. Let us rise early and fast, or break fast, gently
and without perturbation; let company come and let company
110 go, let the bells ring and the children cry,—determined to make
a day of it. . . .

    Time is but the stream I go a-fishing in. I drink at it; but
while I drink I see the sandy bottom and detect how shallow it

**112–126** Thoreau says that we do
not have much time on earth.
What does he say he wants to
spend his time trying to understand? How does he feel that he
can find some of the answers
he seeks?

**E**

> WORDS
> TO      **perturbation** (pûr′tər-bā′shən) *n.* a disturbance of the emotions; agitation; uneasiness
> KNOW

**385**

---

**A** Ask students to discuss Thoreau's belief that a baby is wiser than an adult. What do they think he means?

**Possible Response:** Thoreau felt that the impact of civilization—learning such tasks as counting and reading—distances the young child from spiritual awareness.

Point out that Romantics generally considered unspoiled human nature, represented by childhood, to be pure and good; they considered society and its institutions to be agents that corrupt human nature.

### GUIDE FOR READING

**B** **Possible Response:** Thoreau feels part of nature, and he delights in all his sensations.

### Active Reading

**EVALUATING AUTHOR'S OBSERVATION**

**C** Have students evaluate Thoreau's thoughts on loneliness.

**Possible Responses:** He says that loneliness has nothing to do with physical separation from other people. What separates people is spiritual distance.

### Literary Analysis   NATURE WRITING

**D** Ask students what Thoreau learns from digging under the ice of the frozen pond.

**Possible Response:** He learns that life goes on beneath the ice. The fish are not disturbed by the storms of winter; Thoreau sees this as a model of heavenly bliss.

---

**A**

115    is. Its thin current slides away, but eternity remains. I would drink deeper; fish in the sky, whose bottom is pebbly with stars. I cannot count one. I know not the first letter of the alphabet. I have always been regretting that I was not as wise as the day I was born. The intellect is a cleaver; it discerns and rifts its way into the secret of things. I do not wish to be any more busy with

120    my hands than is necessary. My head is hands and feet. I feel all my best faculties concentrated in it. My instinct tells me that my head is an organ for burrowing, as some creatures use their snout and fore-paws, and with it I would mine and burrow my way through these hills. I think that the richest vein is some-

**1**

125    where hereabouts; so by the divining rod and thin rising vapors I judge; and here I will begin to mine.

**125 divining rod:** a forked stick that is believed to indicate the presence of underground water.

FROM *Solitude*

130    This is a delicious evening, when the whole body is one sense, and imbibes delight through every pore. I go and come with a strange liberty in Nature, a part of herself. As I walk along the stony shore of the pond in my shirt

135    sleeves, though it is cool as well as cloudy and windy, and I see nothing special to attract me, all the elements are unusually congenial to me. The bullfrogs trump to usher in the night, and the note of the whippoorwill is borne on the rippling wind from over the water. Sympathy with

140    the fluttering alder and poplar leaves almost takes away my breath; yet, like the lake, my serenity is rippled but not ruffled. These small waves raised by the evening wind are as remote from storm as the smooth reflecting surface. Though it is now dark, the wind still blows and roars in the wood, the waves still

145    dash, and some creatures lull the rest with their notes. The repose is never complete. The wildest animals do not repose, but seek their prey now; the fox, and skunk, and rabbit, now roam the fields and woods without fear. They are Nature's watch-men,—links which connect the days of animated life. . . .

**2**

**130–145** What does Thoreau say he is part of, and why does he feel as he does?

**B**

WORDS TO KNOW

**congenial** (kən-gēn′yəl) *adj.* suited to one's needs or nature; agreeable
**serenity** (sə-rĕn′ĭ-tē) *n.* a mental and spiritual calm; tranquillity

386

---

## Teaching Options

✓ Assessment   **Standardized Test Practice**

**MAKE INFERENCES AND DRAW CONCLUSIONS** For some standardized tests, students will be asked to read a passage and then make inferences and draw conclusions based on what they have read. To provide students with practice, read aloud or write on the chalkboard the following questions.

1. Which words best describe Thoreau's feelings throughout the section called "Solitude"?
   **A.** peaceful and content
   **B.** anxious and expectant
   **C.** lonely and wistful
   **D.** restless and eager
   **Answer:** A

2. What can you infer about Thoreau, based on the unconventional lifestyle he adopted?
   **A.** He is a person in search of excitement.
   **B.** He is unhappy that most people would reject his lifestyle.
   **C.** He would return to conventional society if he felt he could succeed there.
   **D.** He is not afraid to follow his own path, despite what society might think.

   **Answer:** D

   Help students through the process of choosing the correct answers. Their answers should be supported by information in the selection.

150 Men frequently say to me, "I should think you would feel lonesome down there, and want to be nearer to folks, rainy and snowy days and nights especially." I am tempted to reply to such,—This whole earth which we inhabit is but a point in space. How far apart, think you, dwell the two most distant
155 inhabitants of yonder star, the breadth of whose disk cannot be appreciated by our instruments? Why should I feel lonely? Is not our planet in the Milky Way? This which you put seems to me not to be the most important question. What sort of space is that which separates a man from his fellows and makes him
160 solitary? I have found that no exertion of the legs can bring two minds much nearer to one another. . . .

**153–160** Thoreau suggests that because we are all in this life together, the physical distance between us is insignificant.

FROM

# The Pond in Winter

Every winter the liquid and trembling surface of the pond, which was so sensitive to every breath, and reflected every light and shadow, becomes solid to the depth of a foot or a foot and a
165 half, so that it will support the heaviest teams, and perchance the snow covers it to an equal depth, and it is not to be distinguished from any level field. Like the marmots in the surrounding hills, it closes its eye-lids and becomes dormant for three months or more. Standing on the snow-covered plain, as if in a pasture
170 amid the hills, I cut my way first through a foot of snow, and then a foot of ice, and open a window under my feet, where, kneeling to drink, I look down into the quiet parlor of the fishes, pervaded by a
175 softened light as through a window of ground glass, with its bright sanded floor the same as in summer; there a perennial waveless
180 serenity reigns as in the amber twilight sky, corresponding to the cool and even temperament of the inhabitants. Heaven is
185 under our feet as well as over our heads. . . .

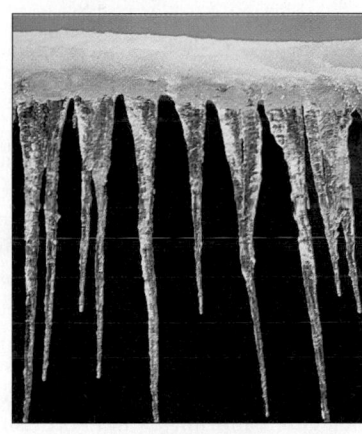

**167 marmots:** rodents that hibernate in the winter; groundhogs.

> WORDS
> TO
> KNOW    **perennial** (pə-rĕn′ē-əl) *adj.* lasting through the year or through many years; enduring

**387**

**Literary Analysis** NATURE WRITING

**A** What do the titles of this chapter and the previous chapter, "The Pond in Winter," suggest about Thoreau's writing?

**Possible Responses:** He was sensitive to nature and its rhythms of change; he used natural phenomena to gain insights and wisdom about life.

**Literary Analysis: IMAGERY**

**B** Ask students to note the pairs of opposites that Thoreau contrasts in order to heighten the drama of the coming of spring.

**Possible Responses:** "storm and winter"/"serene and mild weather"; "dark and sluggish hours"/"bright and elastic ones"; "clouds of winter"/"influx of light"; "cold gray ice"/"transparent pond . . . full of hope"

**GUIDE FOR READING**

**C** **Possible Response:** Thoreau left the woods because he had other lives to live, other things to experience. He implies that continuing to live in the woods could become as empty and routine as living in society.

**D** **Possible Response:** He is comparing life to a sailing voyage. He does not want to live his life like a passive "passenger," shut up below decks; he prefers to live like a member of the crew, out "on the deck of the world" and close to nature.

---

**A** FROM *Spring*

**1**

One attraction in coming to the woods to live was that I should have leisure and opportunity to see the spring come in. The ice
190 in the pond at length begins to be honey-combed, and I can set my heel in it as I walk. Fogs and rains and warmer suns are gradually melting the snow; the days have grown sensibly longer; and I see how I shall get through the winter without adding to my woodpile, for large fires are no longer necessary. I am on the alert for the first signs of spring, to hear the chance
195 note of some arriving bird, or the striped squirrel's chirp, for his stores must be now nearly exhausted, or see the woodchuck venture out of his winter quarters. . . .

The change from storm and winter to serene and mild weather, from dark and sluggish hours to bright and elastic ones, is a
200 memorable crisis which all things proclaim. It is seemingly instantaneous at last. Suddenly an influx of light filled my house, though the evening was at hand, and the clouds of winter still overhung it, and the eaves were dripping with sleety rain. I looked out the window, and lo! where yesterday was cold
205 gray ice there lay the transparent pond already calm and full of hope as in a summer evening, reflecting a summer evening sky in its bosom, though none was visible overhead, as if it had intelligence with some remote horizon. . . .

**B**

191 **sensibly:** noticeably.

200 **crisis:** turning point.

**2**
**3** FROM *Conclusion*

I left the woods for as good a reason as I went there. Perhaps it
210 seemed to me that I had several more lives to live, and could not spare any more time for that one. It is remarkable how easily and insensibly we fall into a particular route, and make a beaten track for ourselves. I had not lived there a week before my feet wore a path from my door to the pond-side; and though
215 it is five or six years since I trod it, it is still quite distinct. It is true, I fear that others may have fallen into it, and so helped to keep it open. The surface of the earth is soft and impressible by the feet of men; and so with the paths which the mind travels. How worn and dusty, then, must be the highways of the world,
220 how deep the ruts of tradition and conformity! I did not wish to take a cabin passage, but rather to go before the mast and on

209–211 Why does Thoreau leave the woods? **C**

220–223 On a sailing ship, passengers stayed in private compartments near the middle of the ship, while the crew shared living quarters at the front ("before the mast"). What is Thoreau comparing here? How does he want to live his life? **D**

388 UNIT THREE PART 1: CELEBRATIONS OF THE SELF

---

**Teaching Options**

 Mini Lesson **Grammar**

**MODIFIERS:** *GOOD* **AND** *WELL*
**Instruction** Students frequently confuse the words *good* and *well* in contexts in which *good* is an adjective and *well* is an adverb.
Incorrect: Thoreau uses imagery **good.** (An adjective does not modify a verb.)
Correct: Thoreau uses imagery **well.** (An adverb modifies a verb.)
Correct: Thoreau was a **good** carpenter. (An adjective modifies a noun.)
Students may also confuse comparative and superlative forms of *good* and *well.* Use the com-

parative form when comparing two things and the superlative for three or more things.

| Positive | Comparative | Superlative |
|---|---|---|
| good | better | best |
| well | better | best |

Use **Grammar Transparencies and Copymasters,** p. 136.

 Use McDougal Littell's *Language Network,* Chapter 7, for more instruction and practice in modifiers.

Photo by Ernst Haas. Copyright © Tony Stone Images

the deck of the world, for there I could best see the moonlight amid the mountains. I do not wish to go below now.

225     I learned this, at least, by my experiment; that if one advances confidently in the direction of his dreams, and endeavors to live the life which he has imagined, he will meet with a success unexpected in common hours. He will put some things behind, will pass an invisible boundary; new, universal, and more liberal laws will begin to establish themselves around and 230 within him; or the old laws be expanded, and interpreted in his favor in a more liberal sense, and he will live with the license of a higher order of beings. In proportion as he simplifies his life, the laws of the universe will appear less complex, and solitude will not be solitude, nor poverty poverty, nor weakness weak- 235 ness. If you have built castles in the air, your work need not be lost; that is where they should be. Now put the foundations under them. . . .

## Customizing Instruction

### Students Acquiring English
**1** Explain that *honey-combed* means "having the texture of a honeycomb." A honeycomb is a wax structure built by bees to store honey and house their offspring. Ask a volunteer who has seen a honeycomb to describe or draw it.

### Less Proficient Readers
**2** Ask students how the coming of winter and spring to Walden Pond affects Thoreau.
**Possible Responses:** He seems to find beauty in the details of both seasons. He seems fascinated and comfortable in both seasons. The pond's freezing in winter and then thawing in spring gave Thoreau new opportunities to study nature's beauties and gain new insights.

**Set a Purpose** Have students read the "Conclusion" to understand why Thoreau did not think money was important.

### Multiple Learning Styles
**Visual Learners**
**3** At this point in the reading, students who are visual learners might want to create drawings that suggest Thoreau's feelings toward Walden Pond. Their drawings can focus on a peaceful scene or on the changing seasons, reflecting the images Thoreau creates in his writing.

### Less Proficient Readers
**4** Ask a volunteer to explain what Thoreau means by "castles in the air" in line 235.
**Possible Responses:** Thoreau means unrealistic fantasies, dreams, daydreams.

**Cross Curricular Link**   **Social Studies**

**NATURE CONSERVATION** Since ancient times farming, grazing, and wood cutting have created problems in the natural environment. In the United States, concern about conserving natural resources began when European settlers realized the enormously destructive effects of their activities. Huge forests had been cleared for agriculture, which in turn depleted the soil, and animal species such as buffalo, deer, wolves, bears, and mountain lions had been nearly wiped out.

    In 1832 George Catlin, an artist and writer, suggested setting aside large areas in the western United States for wildlife. The federal government responded to the thinking of conservationists in 1864, when it gave Yosemite Valley to the state of California to be used as a public park and recreation area. In 1872 Yellowstone Park became the nation's first national park.

    The conservation movement today focuses on many issues. A greater understanding of ecology—the science that explores the complex relationships between living things and the environment—now guides public policies aimed at conservation.

**A** Possible Responses: to be an individual or nonconformist; to live one's life according to internal incentives rather than bow to external pressures from groups

**Active Reading**

> EVALUATING AUTHOR'S
> OBSERVATIONS

**B** Use these questions to help students evaluate Thoreau's ideas.

• What would the world be like if everyone took Thoreau's advice?

**Possible Responses:** People might be happier, less resentful, kinder, wiser; or they might be poorer and have less freedom.

• Is Thoreau's depiction of poverty realistic? Are the poor really more independent than the rich?

**Possible Response:** Thoreau discusses poverty in an idealized way. The poor may have more independence from the trappings of a materialistic society, but they are also less likely to have time for contemplation.

**GUIDE FOR READING**

**C** Possible Responses: Rich and poor alike can receive the same pleasures and lessons from nature; Thoreau suggests that poverty gives people a certain ability to accept hardship.

**D** Possible Response: The parable suggests that renewal or rebirth is a constant possibility in life.

---

Why should we be in such desperate haste to succeed, and in such desperate enterprises? If a man does not keep pace with his
240 companions, perhaps it is because he hears a different drummer. Let him step to the music which he hears, however measured or far away. It is not important that he should mature as soon as an appletree or an oak. Shall he turn his spring into summer? If the condition of things which we were made for is not yet, what
245 were any reality which we can substitute? We will not be shipwrecked on a vain reality. Shall we with pains erect a heaven of blue glass over ourselves, though when it is done we shall be sure to gaze still at the true ethereal heaven far above, as if the former were not? . . .
250 However mean your life is, meet it and live it; do not shun it and call it hard names. It is not so bad as you are. It looks poorest when you are richest. The fault-finder will find faults even in paradise. Love your life, poor as it is. You may perhaps have some pleasant, thrilling, glorious hours, even in a poorhouse.
255 The setting sun is reflected from the windows of the almshouse as brightly as from the rich man's abode; the snow melts before its door as early in the spring. I do not see but a quiet mind may live as contentedly there, and have as cheering thoughts, as in a palace. The town's poor seem to me often to live the most inde-
260 pendent lives of any. May be they are simply great enough to receive without <u>misgiving</u>. Most think that they are above being supported by the town; but it oftener happens that they are not above supporting themselves by dishonest means, which should be more <u>disreputable</u>. Cultivate poverty like a garden herb, like
265 sage. Do not trouble yourself much to get new things, whether clothes or friends. Turn the old; return to them. Things do not change; we change. Sell your clothes and keep your thoughts. God will see that you do not want society. If I were confined to a corner of a garret all my days, like a spider, the world would be
270 just as large to me while I had my thoughts about me. The philosopher said: "From an army of three divisions one can take away its general, and put it in disorder; from the man the most <u>abject</u> and <u>vulgar</u> one cannot take away his thought." Do not seek so anxiously to be developed, to subject yourself to many
275 influences to be played on; it is all <u>dissipation</u>. Humility like darkness reveals the heavenly lights. The shadows of poverty and meanness gather around us, "and lo! creation widens to our view." We are often reminded that if there were bestowed on us

239–242 This is one of the most famous passages in Thoreau's writings. The "different drummer" evolved from one of his journal entries describing an 1839 river voyage when he had fallen asleep to the sound of someone's beating a drum "alone in the silence and the dark." The phrase "marching to the beat of a different drummer" became popular in the nonconformist 1960s. What does it mean to hear a different drummer? **A**

255 **almshouse:** poorhouse.

255–260 What similarities between poverty and wealth does Thoreau find? What benefits of poverty does Thoreau see? **C**

|        | **misgiving** (mĭs-gĭv′ĭng) *n.* a feeling of doubt, mistrust, or uncertainty |
| WORDS  | **disreputable** (dĭs-rĕp′yə-tə-bəl) *adj.* lacking respectability of character or behavior |
| TO     | **abject** (ăb′jĕkt′) *adj.* low; contemptible; wretched |
| KNOW   | **vulgar** (vŭl′gər) *adj.* coarse; common |
|        | **dissipation** (dĭs′ə-pā′shən) *n.* a reckless waste of resources; wastefulness |

390

---

## Teaching Options

 **Mini Lesson** **Grammar**

**MODIFIERS: NOUNS AS ADJECTIVES**

**Instruction** Nouns are sometimes used as adjectives. For example, Thoreau uses the noun *garden* as an adjective in line 264: "Cultivate poverty like a *garden* herb." Students can determine how a word is used by examining the context. In the example, the sentence would not make sense if *garden* were a noun; its position indicates that it modifies *herb.*

**Exercises** In each of the following sentences, have students underline the noun used as an adjective and identify the noun or pronoun that it modifies.

1. Thoreau describes the perfect <u>summer</u> life of an insect. *(life)*

2. The <u>winter</u> sun warmed the writer's spirit. *(sun)*

3. A clean and airy light came though the <u>cabin</u> door. *(door)*

4. Thoreau became fascinated by <u>pond</u> life long before he lived at Walden. *(life)*

5. <u>Bird</u> sounds drifted through the branches year round. *(sounds)*

Use **Grammar Transparencies and Copymasters,** p. 69.

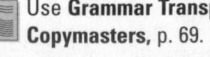 Use McDougal Littell's *Language Network,* "Parts of Speech," for more instruction and practice in parts of speech.

the wealth of Croesus, our aims must still be the same, and our means essentially the same. Moreover, if you are restricted in your range by poverty, if you cannot buy books and newspapers, for instance, you are but confined to the most significant and vital experiences; you are compelled to deal with the material which yields the most sugar and the most starch. It is life near the bone where it is sweetest. You are defended from being a trifler. No man loses ever on a lower level by <u>magnanimity</u> on a higher. Superfluous wealth can buy superfluities only. Money is not required to buy one necessary of the soul. . . .

The life in us is like the water in the river. It may rise this year higher than man has ever known it, and flood the parched uplands; even this may be the eventful year, which will drown out all our muskrats. It was not always dry land where we dwell. I see far inland the banks which the stream anciently washed, before science began to record its freshets. Every one has heard the story which has gone the rounds of New England, of a strong and beautiful bug which came out of the dry leaf of an old table of apple-tree wood, which had stood in a farmer's kitchen for sixty years, first in Connecticut, and afterward in Massachusetts,—from an egg deposited in the living tree many years earlier still, as appeared by counting the annual layers beyond it; which was heard gnawing out for several weeks, hatched perchance by the heat of an urn. Who does not feel his faith in a resurrection and immortality strengthened by hearing of this? Who knows what beautiful and winged life, whose egg has been buried for ages under many concentric layers of woodenness in the dead dry life of society, deposited at first in the alburnum of the green and living tree, which has been gradually converted into the semblance of its well-seasoned tomb,—heard perchance gnawing out now for years by the astonished family of man, as they sat round the festive board,—may unexpectedly come forth from amidst society's most trivial and handselled furniture, to enjoy its perfect summer life at last!

I do not say that John or Jonathan will realize all this; but such is the character of that morrow which mere lapse of time can never make to dawn. The light which puts out our eyes is darkness to us. Only that day dawns to which we are awake. There is more day to dawn. The sun is but a morning star. ❖

279 **Croesus** (krē′səs): a king of Lydia (now part of Turkey) in the sixth century B.C. who became legendary for his great wealth.

**299–317** What is the message of this famous parable of the "strong and beautiful bug"?  **D**

312 **alburnum** (ăl-bûr′nəm): the part of a tree's trunk through which sap flows.

316 **handselled:** cheap; discounted; bought from a traveling salesman.

318 **John or Jonathan:** the common man. Thoreau's use of familiar given names here is similar to that in the expression "every Tom, Dick, and Harry."

WORDS
TO
KNOW

**magnanimity** (măg′nə-nĭm′ĭ-tē) *n.* generosity

**391**

---

### Students Acquiring English

**1** Discuss with students Thoreau's use of the word *poverty,* a word that usually has negative associations. Thoreau believes that people should cultivate poverty as they would a plant in their garden. In this case, he considers poverty an alternative to being trapped in the materialistic world.

### Less Proficient Readers

**2** Ask students to explain why Thoreau did not think money was important.

**Possible Responses:** Truth and the inner meaning of life are available to rich and poor alike; the poor may have an advantage in finding them, however, since they are freed from the distractions that wealth brings.

### Gifted and Talented

Ask students to evaluate Thoreau's assumption that it was necessary to retreat to the woods to live simply and deliberately.

---

✓ **Assessment Informal Assessment**

**JOURNAL ENTRY** You can informally assess students' understanding of the essay by asking them to write a journal entry about the major themes expressed in *Walden.* Have students write the head "Where I Lived, and What I Lived For" at the top of a sheet of paper. Then have them assume Thoreau's voice and write a reflective piece that explains where he lived, why he chose to live there, and what he learned.

**RUBRIC**

**3 Full Accomplishment** Students show a full understanding of the setting of the selection, Thoreau's purpose for living at Walden Pond, and the insights about life that he gained.

**2 Substantial Accomplishment** Students have a basic understanding of *Walden*'s themes, but they leave out some details about Thoreau's activities and thoughts.

**1 Little or Partial Accomplishment** Students show little understanding of Thoreau's activities, goals, or ideas.

## GUIDING STUDENT RESPONSE

## Connect to the Literature

**1. What Do You Think?**
Possible Responses: It would be lonely, boring, and uncomfortable. It would be peaceful; there would be no hurry and no stress about grades, money, or fitting in.

**Comprehension Check**
- to "simplify," to live deliberately and to ignore material gain
- to embrace poverty because it allows one to concentrate on spiritual growth

 Use Selection Quiz in
**Unit Three Resource Book**, p. 25.

## Think Critically

**2.** Possible Response: Having learned a valuable lesson from his experience at Walden, Thoreau was ready for new experiences and new lessons.

**3.** Possible Response: that one can live a full life without material possessions.

**4.** Possible Responses: personal integrity, peace, solitude, writing

**5.** Remind students that an aphorism is a concise statement of a principle or truth.

## Literary Analysis

**Nature Writing** Possible Responses: In the excerpt from "Solitude," Thoreau feels intimate with the natural world. Rather than feeling lonely, he feels fulfilled, experiencing himself as a part of nature. Thoreau contrasts his feeling of intimacy with the loneliness of townspeople whose thinking separates them from one another.

**Figurative Language** Possible Response: "I do not let time rule my life and habits; I take whatever I can extract from the passing moments." Metaphor: "The intellect is a cleaver" (line 118); Simile: "Still we live meanly, like ants" (line 47). Personification includes "I look down into the quiet parlor of the fishes" (lines 172–174).

---

## Connect to the Literature

**1. What Do You Think?**
Would you like to live in a cabin in the woods as Thoreau did? Share your thoughts with a classmate.

**Comprehension Check**
- What does Thoreau advise people to do so that their lives will not be "frittered away by detail"?
- What is Thoreau's advice to the poor?

## Think Critically

**2.** How would you explain Thoreau's reasons for leaving Walden Pond?

 THINK ABOUT
- the meaning of the statement "I had several more lives to live"
- the parable of the bug in the apple-tree
- Thoreau's ideas about tradition, conformity, and success

**3.** What do you think is the most valuable lesson that Thoreau learned from his experience of living in the woods?

**4.** In these excerpts from *Walden,* Thoreau frequently discusses what is not important. What do you think *was* important to him?

**5.** **ACTIVE READING** **EVALUATING AUTHOR'S OBSERVATIONS**
Look over the aphorisms you copied into your
**READER'S NOTEBOOK** and your evaluations of them.
Which one comes closest to expressing one of your own views about life? Which one is most opposed to your views? Explain your answers.

## Extend Interpretations

**6. The Writer's Style** Thoreau is fond of **paradoxes,** statements that seem to contradict themselves but are nevertheless true. For example, he writes, "I did not wish to live what was not life" (page 383) and "We are determined to be starved before we are hungry" (page 384). Tell what you think he means by each of these statements. What other paradoxes can you find in these excerpts?

**7. Comparing Texts** What connections do you see between the ideas expressed in *Walden* and those expressed in "Civil Disobedience" or Emerson's "Self-Reliance"?

**8. Connect to Life** Consider the experiences that you identified for the Connect to Your Life activity on page 381. How do your desires compare with Thoreau's wish to live simply and deliberately in the woods?

**392** UNIT THREE    PART 1: CELEBRATIONS OF THE SELF

---

## Literary Analysis

**NATURE WRITING** **Nature writing** is a term for a type of essay in which the writer uses firsthand observations to explore the mysteries of the human relationship with nature. According to Frank Stewart in *A Natural History of Nature Writing,* nature writers are "moved by the joyous, wild, and dazzling beauty in the world." Thoreau, the father of American nature writing, was renowned for his understanding of nature's ways through patient, frequent, careful observations of his surroundings. He used richly poetic language to convey what he learned from his observations.

**Cooperative Learning Activity** Work with a small group to read aloud and discuss one or more passages from *Walden,* such as the excerpt "Solitude," on pages 386–387. Then discuss Thoreau's observations of nature and his insights about life. Finally, list two or three words you would use to describe Thoreau's relationship with nature.

**REVIEW** **FIGURATIVE LANGUAGE** Thoreau was a poet as well as an essayist, and in *Walden* he used striking figurative language to express abstract concepts. Consider the **metaphor** "Time is but the stream I go a-fishing in." Try to convey the same idea without using figurative language. Find other good examples of figurative language—**metaphor, simile,** and **personification**—in these excerpts from *Walden.*

---

## Extend Interpretations

**Writer's Style** In saying, "I did not wish to live what was not life," Thoreau criticizes the dry, unfulfilling lifestyles of civilized society and extols his rich, full life in nature. "We are determined to be starved before we are hungry" is Thoreau's way of ridiculing the human tendency to prepare for the worst eventuality—starving—and thereby miss so much present enjoyment. Another paradox occurs on page 386: "I have always been regretting that I was not as wise as the day I was born."

By this, Thoreau suggests that civilization erodes a child's innate wisdom and spiritual awareness.

**Comparing Texts** Emerson's ideas about originality and independence of mind inform these passages from *Walden.* Thoreau trusts himself, intending to live deliberately in the woods and to discover for himself whether life is mean or sublime.

**Connect to Life** Students should find evidence in the text to support their comparisons.

## Writing Options

**1. Letter from Walden Pond**
Imagine that you are Thoreau and that you have been living at Walden Pond for one month. Your parents have asked you to come back to town, get a real job, and settle down. Write a letter to them explaining why you want to continue living at Walden Pond.

**2. Interpretive Essay** One of the well-known quotations from *Walden* is "Our lives are frittered away by detail." Write an essay explaining what you think this quotation means. Use examples to elaborate your ideas.

**3. Nature Writing** Spend one hour alone closely observing nature. You might go to a forest preserve or sit in your own backyard. Draft an informal essay, modeled on *Walden*, to describe your thoughts and feelings.

## Activities & Explorations

**Photo Essay** Take a series of photographs of a pond or forest at different times of the day. Mount the photos on poster board. Try to convey the feeling of Thoreau's experience at Walden. Use quotations from Thoreau as captions for some of your photos. ~ **VIEWING AND REPRESENTING**

## Inquiry & Research

**Walden Today** Walden Pond is now a state reservation where thousands swim, fish, and hike each year. Some people believe that overuse is destroying Walden Pond and that the area should be made into a limited-use nature preserve. Others say that Walden should remain freely accessible to everyone. Research the current condition of Walden Pond and hold a debate on this issue.

 **More Online: Research Starter**
www.mcdougallittell.com

## Vocabulary in Action

**EXERCISE A: ASSESSMENT PRACTICE** For each group of words below, write the letter of the word that is an antonym of the boldfaced vocabulary word.

1. **vulgar:** (a) classy, (b) ordinary, (c) popular
2. **abject:** (a) appropriate, (b) accidental, (c) lofty
3. **disreputable:** (a) honorable, (b) famous, (c) noticeable
4. **mean:** (a) predictable, (b) superior, (c) basic
5. **congenial:** (a) illegal, (b) sophisticated, (c) incompatible
6. **magnanimity:** (a) selfishness, (b) rejection, (c) fragility
7. **sublime:** (a) exciting, (b) average, (c) excessive
8. **rudiment:** (a) completion, (b) estimation, (c) delicacy
9. **serenity:** (a) stupidity, (b) chaos, (c) peace
10. **dissipation:** (a) greed, (b) honesty, (c) thrift

**EXERCISE B: IDIOMS** Write the vocabulary word, not used in Exercise A, that is suggested by each set of familiar expressions.

1. That's the way the cookie crumbles. You can't fight city hall. Like it or lump it.
2. ants in your pants; on pins and needles; climbing the walls
3. Haste makes waste. Look before you leap. Wear your thinking cap.
4. year in, year out; for a month of Sundays; not a flash in the pan
5. smell a rat; think something's fishy; have second thoughts

### Building Vocabulary
Several Words to Know in this lesson have multiple meanings. For an in-depth lesson on choosing the right meaning, see page 630.

| WORDS TO KNOW | | | | |
|---|---|---|---|---|
| abject | disreputable | mean | perturbation | serenity |
| congenial | dissipation | misgiving | resignation | sublime |
| deliberately | magnanimity | perennial | rudiment | vulgar |

##  Grammar
**Mini Lesson**

**DOUBLE NEGATIVES** Using two negative words in the same clause to convey "no" or "not" is called a double negative. Only one negative word is necessary.

> Incorrect: Concord <u>didn't</u> have <u>no</u> rain for weeks.
> Correct: Concord had <u>no</u> rain for weeks.
> Correct: Concord <u>didn't</u> have <u>any</u> rain for weeks.

You can easily correct the sentence by dropping one negative word or by changing it to a positive word. Negative words include *no, not, neither, never, none, nothing, nobody, nowhere, hardly, scarcely, barely, without.* Positive words include *any, either, ever, anybody, anything,* and *anywhere.*

**Exercises** Ask students to correct the double negatives in the following sentences.

1. Thoreau <u>hardly had no</u> provisions when he decided to occupy the cabin. *(hardly had any)*
2. He <u>wouldn't let none</u> of his family's concerns deter him. *(wouldn't let any)*

 Use **Grammar Transparencies and Copymasters**, p. 137.

 Use McDougal Littell's *Language Network*, Chapter 7, for more instruction and practice in double negatives.

## Writing Options

**1. Letter from Walden Pond** Suggest that students list their reasons for remaining at Walden. After brainstorming on their own, students might review Thoreau's reasons and experiences. Remind students to consider the audience and ask themselves what tone would be appropriate and what arguments would be effective.

**2. Interpretive Essay** Remind students to plan an organized essay with a clearly stated interpretation supported by examples from Thoreau's essay and their own experience.

**3. Nature Writing** Student essays should reflect an organizational plan and contain descriptive details and figurative language. Observations about nature should suggest insights about life.

## Activities & Explorations

**Photo Essay** Encourage students to explain the connection between the selected photos and the quotations from *Walden.*

## Inquiry & Research

**Resource for STUDENTS:**

**The Walden Woods Project** is dedicated to preserving endangered sites in the Walden Woods ecosystem and to educating people on land-preservation issues. Address:

The Walden Woods Project
44 Baker Farm
Lincoln, MA 01773-3004
E-mail: www.project@walden.org
Phone: (800) 554-3569

## Vocabulary in Action

**Exercise A**

1. a
2. c
3. a
4. b
5. c
6. a
7. b
8. a
9. b
10. c

**Exercise B**

1. resignation
2. perturbation
3. deliberately
4. perennial
5. misgiving

# LEARNING the Language of Literature

## Form in Poetry

### The Shapes and Sounds of Poetry

All works of art have form, a particular organization of parts to make a whole. **Form, or structure,** in poetry refers to the way the words are arranged in lines, the way the lines are arranged in stanzas, and the way the units of sound are organized in rhythm and rhyme. In general, poetic forms fall into two categories: conventional form and organic form.

**CONVENTIONAL FORM** Poems in conventional form follow certain fixed rules: for example, they have a limited number of lines, a specified meter and rhyme scheme, and a definite structure. Such poems are also called **fixed form** poems, and include the **sonnet,** the **ballad,** the **epic,** the **elegy,** the **ode,** the **villanelle,** and **blank verse.** The great English poets before the 19th century, such as William Shakespeare and John Milton, used conventional poetic forms, as did American poets.

**ORGANIC FORM** The organic form of poetry, also known as **irregular form,** developed in the early 19th century. The English romantic poets wanted more flexible verse forms to fit the new content of their poetry. Unlike the conventional form that provides an ideal pattern for poems to follow, the **organic form** takes its shape and pattern from the content of the poem itself. That is, the form of a poem "grows" naturally out of what the poem says.

### Poetic Form in Action

One way to understand the difference between conventional and organic forms is to compare the poetry of Henry Wadsworth Longfellow and Emily Dickinson. Longfellow was somewhat conventional in most of his poems, as shown in the following stanza from "A Psalm of Life." You can hear the regular beat of the poem even without scanning its meter: stressed syllables alternate with unstressed

syllables four times in each line. This metrical pattern is called **trochaic tetrameter.** (See the chart on page 142.) The excerpted lines below have a regular meter (even the dash in the second line counts as an unstressed syllable). Longfellow's poems also have a predictable alternating rhyme scheme and punctuation.

*from* "A Psalm of Life"

| | |
|---|---|
| Tell me not, in mournful numbers, | a |
| Life is but an empty dream!— | b |
| For the soul is dead that slumbers, | a |
| And things are not what they seem. | b |

—Henry Wadsworth Longfellow

Now look at the first stanza of a poem by Emily Dickinson. The meter of her poem is also trochaic tetrameter, but notice the missing beat at the end of the second and fourth lines. This rhythmical variation—combined with the first line running on to the second, the unaccented dashes, and the simple rhyme scheme—gives the poem a forward acceleration, even a breathless quality, that fits perfectly with the speaker's feelings of joy and excitement.

*from* "Exultation is the going"

| | |
|---|---|
| Exultation is the going | a |
| Of an inland soul to sea, | b |
| Past the houses—past the headlands— | c |
| Into deep Eternity— | b |

—Emily Dickinson

---

## Teaching the Lesson

Students will be reading a variety of poetic forms. This lesson will give students the language for analyzing and understanding poetic form.

### Objectives

- understand the following literary terms:
  - form, conventional and organic
  - trochaic tetrameter
  - free verse
  - anaphora
- analyze the melodies of literary language, including the use of evocative rhythms
- connect literature to historical contexts and to the student's own experiences

### Introducing the Concept

As distinguished from prose, poetry communicates with readers in ways that are often more condensed, more suggestive, and more emotional. Part of this comes from poetry's form—the way its language is arranged in lines. Supported by elements such as rhythm and rhyme, the arrangement of lines helps make poetry the memorable— and memorizable—literature it is. However, the form can range from fixed and prescribed to free and irregular.

### Motivating the Students

Invite students to consider why they like some poems more than others. Ask them to name their favorite poem and to briefly state what they like about it. Suggest that our favorite poems tend to be poems that strike a chord of recognition: they make connections with how we see the world. Help students self-monitor their response to their chosen poem by having them consider the following questions:

1. What appealing imagery does the poet use?
2. What message does the poem convey?
3. How does the poem make me feel?
4. What techniques does the poet use to create the mood of the poem?

As they read each poem, students can write their reactions to these questions and keep their responses in their Working Portfolios.

### Presenting the Concepts

Read through the strategies aloud or project them on a transparency. Select one of the students' favorite poems and model how to use the strategies to analyze the poem.

## Free Verse

Free verse, also known by its French name *vers libre,* is different from conventional and other organic forms in its lack of regular meter and rhyme. The freedom of free verse extends only so far. Free verse still uses rhythm, although not in the regular patterns of meter. It also depends largely on other sound devices besides rhyme to achieve musical effects, such as various types of repetition.

The great master of free verse in American poetry is Walt Whitman. At a time when all American poetry (and most English poetry) sounded like Longfellow, Whitman created a new form of poetic song:

> *from* "I Hear America Singing"
>
> I hear America **singing**, the varied carols I hear,
> Those of mechanics, each one **singing** his as it
>    should be blithe and strong,
> The carpenter **singing** his as he measures his
>    plank or beam,
>
>             –Walt Whitman

Although Whitman's poem lacks meter, it has a recognizable cadence provided by the repetition of *singing* and the parallel phrasing of the lines themselves. Whitman also uses a related technique called **anaphora** in which the same word or phrase is repeated at the beginning of two or more lines, like this:

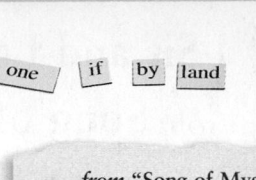

> *from* "Song of Myself"
>
> **Or** I guess the grass is itself a child, the
>    produced babe of the vegetation.
> **Or** I guess it is a uniform hieroglyphic,
>
>             –Walt Whitman

Ironically, repetitive devices such as parallelism and anaphora, like free verse itself, were developed very long ago. You can find evidence of them in the Twenty-third Psalm, for instance. Whitman's resurrection of these ancient devices freed future poets from the conventions that had been layered onto poetic expression for so many centuries and threatened to drain the life out of poetry.

Whitman's revolutionary poems were first published in 1855, but it took most English-language poets until the 20th century to catch up. This part of Unit Three includes poetry by Whitman and by some 20th-century poets who followed his lead.

**YOUR TURN** Now that you've explored two major poetic forms, do you prefer the conventional form or free verse poetry? Explain.

---

## Strategies for Reading: Understanding Poetic Form

1. Read each poem at least three times: first to get an overall sense of the meaning; then to clarify or deepen the meaning; and finally to study the form. Be sure to read the poem aloud, too.

2. For conventional and organic poems, scan for meter and identify the rhyme scheme. Review the Literary Analysis activities on meter (page 142) and on rhyme scheme (page 347).

3. For free verse poems, identify devices of repetition and parallelism that substitute for patterns of meter and rhyme.

4. **Monitor** your reading strategies and modify them when your understanding breaks down. Remember to use your Strategies for Active Reading: **predict, visualize, connect, question, clarify,** and **evaluate.**

---

## Making Connections

### Poetic Devices

Encourage students to explore the parallel phrasing and anaphora in the Twenty-third Psalm (King James version) reprinted here.

#### TWENTY-THIRD PSALM

The Lord is my shepherd; I shall not want.

He maketh me to lie down in green pastures: he leadeth me beside the still waters.

He restoreth my soul: he leadeth me in the paths of righteousness for his name's sake.

Yea, though I walk through the valley of the shadow of death, I will fear no evil: for thou art with me; thy rod and thy staff they comfort me.

Thou preparest a table before me in the presence of mine enemies: thou anointest my head with oil; my cup runneth over.

Surely goodness and mercy shall follow me all the days of my life: and I will dwell in the house of the Lord forever.

Anaphora can be found in the repetition of *He* at the beginnings of the second and third stanzas. Discuss how fragments of parallel structure ("He maketh/restoreth," "he leadeth," "I will fear," "I will dwell," "Thou preparest," and "thou anointest") and the simple grammatical setup of most clauses—subject, verb, and predicate—contribute to the soothing, reassuring rhythm.

# I Hear America Singing
# I Sit and Look Out
## *from* Song of Myself

*Poetry by* WALT WHITMAN

## OVERVIEW

 This selection is included in the **Grade 11 InterActive Reader.**

### Objectives

1. understand and appreciate three classic **poems** (**Literary Analysis**)
2. identify and understand **free verse** and Whitman's poetic devices for creating rhythm (**Literary Analysis**)
3. apply **strategies for reading free verse** (**Active Reading**)

### Summary

Written in free verse, these poems show Whitman's revolutionary approach to poetic form and content. The expansive lines in "I Hear America Singing," a joyful anthem to ordinary workers, encompass broad ranges of experience. "I Sit and Look Out" catalogs the miseries of the human condition. In the excerpts from the long poem "Song of Myself," the speaker revels in the eternal life-giving forces of nature.

### Thematic Link

Like the **transcendentalists,** Walt Whitman believed the physical world embodied the spirit. His poetry **celebrates** the union of **self** with nature.

---

### 5-Minute Warm-Up

***Daily***
***Language***
***SkillBuilder***

Have students **proofread** the display sentences on page 337j and write them correctly. The sentences also appear on Transparency 11 of **Grammar Transparencies and Copymasters.**

---

( **Connect to Your Life** )

**Images of America**  Many of Walt Whitman's poems contain vivid images of America in the mid-1800s. What images do you think capture the spirit and reality of America today? Share descriptions or sketches with a small group of classmates.

## Build Background

**A Revolution in Poetry**  Walt Whitman's first book of poems, *Leaves of Grass,* was so revolutionary in content and form that publishers would not publish it. After Whitman printed the book himself in 1855, many established poets and critics disparaged it. In 1856, the *Saturday Review* suggested that "if the *Leaves of Grass* should come into anybody's possession, our advice is to throw them instantly behind the fire."

Doubtless Whitman was shocked and hurt by such a reception, for he saw himself as capturing the spirit of his country and his times. In the preface to *Leaves of Grass* he wrote, "The United States themselves are essentially the greatest poem." Whitman's images encompass all of American life, including the common and "vulgar." His lines are long and rambling, like the vastly expanding country. His language reflects the vigor and tang of American speech, resounding with new, distinctively American, rhythms. Most of his poems are marked by optimism, vitality, and a love of nature, free expression, and democracy—values often associated with the America of his day.

## Focus Your Reading

**LITERARY ANALYSIS**  **FREE VERSE**  Walt Whitman is generally credited with bringing free verse to American poetry. **Free verse** is poetry without regular patterns of rhyme and meter. Whitman, however, does use the following poetic devices to create rhythm:

> **Catalog** There are frequent lists of people, things, and attributes.
> **Repetition** Words or phrases are repeated at the beginning of two or more lines.
> **Parallelism** Related ideas are phrased in similar ways.

**ACTIVE READING**  **STRATEGIES FOR READING FREE VERSE**
Use the following strategies as you read Whitman's free verse:

- Read the poems aloud, and listen to the rhythm of the lines.
- Notice where he uses the devices of catalog, repetition, and parallelism.
- Do not spend too much time on any one line; instead, appreciate the sweep of his images and ideas.
- The speaker can be identified with Whitman himself. Build a mental image of the speaker, particularly as you read "Song of Myself."

---

## LESSON RESOURCES

**UNIT THREE RESOURCE BOOK,** pp. 26–27

**ASSESSMENT RESOURCES**
**Formal Assessment,** pp. 73–74
**Teacher's Guide to Assessment and Portfolio Use**
**Test Generator**

**SKILLS TRANSPARENCIES AND COPYMASTERS**
**Literary Analysis**
- Poetic Devices, T12 (for Cooperative Learning Activity, p. 404)

**Reading and Critical Thinking**
- Compare and Contrast, T15 (for Extend Interpretations 7, p. 404)

**Grammar**
- Prepositional Phrases, C84 (for Mini Lessons, pp. 401 and 403)

**Vocabulary**
- Analogies, C48 (for Mini Lesson, p. 397)

**Writing**
- Critical Review, C26 (for Writing Option 1, p. 405)

**Communications**
- Nonverbal Strategies, T15 (for Activities & Explorations 2, p. 405)

**INTEGRATED TECHNOLOGY**

**Audio Library**
**LaserLinks**
- Biographical Connection: Walt Whitman. See **Teacher's SourceBook,** p. 41.

**Visit our website:**
www.mcdougallittell.com

# I Hear America Singing

## WALT WHITMAN

*I* hear America singing, the varied carols I hear,
Those of mechanics, each one singing his as it should be blithe[1] and
   strong,
The carpenter singing his as he measures his plank or beam,
The mason singing his as he makes ready for work, or leaves off work, | **1**
5  The boatman singing what belongs to him in his boat, the deckhand
   singing on the steamboat deck,
The shoemaker singing as he sits on his bench, the hatter singing as
   he stands,
The wood-cutter's song, the ploughboy's on his way in the morning, or | **2**
   at noon intermission or at sundown,
The delicious singing of the mother, or of the young wife at work, or
   of the girl sewing or washing,
Each singing what belongs to him or her and to none else,
10  The day what belongs to the day—at night the party of young fellows,
   robust, friendly,
Singing with open mouths their strong melodious songs.

---

1. **blithe** (blīth): carefree and lighthearted.

## TEACHING THE LITERATURE

### Customizing Instruction

**Less Proficient Readers**
This poem celebrates workers in a variety of occupations in the mid-1800s. Have students list workers that might appear in this poem if Whitman were writing it today.

**Set a Purpose** Have students read to see how the poet feels about his country and about himself.

**Students Acquiring English**
Introduce the poem by discussing the poet's purpose. Whitman writes to show the variety of workers that make up America and to emphasize their contributions to American life. Help students identify words that show the positive attitude of the poet toward his subjects.
**Possible Responses:** *singing, blithe, strong, delicious, robust, friendly, melodious*

  Use **Spanish Study Guide** for additional support, pp. 100–102.

**Gifted and Talented**
Ask students to interpret the connotative power of the word *singing* and consider how this word choice opens levels of meaning. Remind students that many voices blended in song create a harmony. Then ask students to state the theme of the poem.

**Students Acquiring English**
**1** Explain that a *mason* is someone who works with stone.

**2** Explain that a *ploughboy* is one who helps ready the fields for planting.

---

## Vocabulary Strategy

**UNDERSTANDING ANALOGIES** A word analogy is a statement that compares two pairs of words. The relationship between the two words in the first pair is the same as the relationship between the two words in the second pair. Give the following example.
advertising : selling :: reporting :
**A.** exploring
**B.** informing
**C.** destroying
Guide students to select B as the correct answer. Suggest that they state the relationship between each pair of words in a sentence: *Frail is the*

opposite of *robust. Oppression* is the opposite of *freedom.*
**Exercises** Have students choose the word from the list that best completes each analogy.
trench      cacophonous      quiet
happy      famine
**1.** water : drought :: food : *(famine)*
**2.** height : mountain :: depth : *(trench)*
**3.** dry : humid :: melodious : *(cacophonous)*

  Use **Vocabulary Transparencies and Copymasters**, pp. 39, 48.

A lesson on analogies appears on p. 254 in the Pupil's Edition.

## Reading and Analyzing

### Literary Analysis FREE VERSE

"I Hear America Singing" has neither meter nor rhyme. Ask students how the use of free verse affects the sound of the poem when it is read aloud. Ask why free verse suits the poem's topics and themes.

**Possible Responses:** Free verse sounds more like natural speech than does traditional verse; free verse adds to the spontaneous, conversational tone of the poem.

 Use **Unit Three Resource Book,** p. 27 for more practice.

### Active Reading:
**STRATEGIES FOR READING FREE VERSE**

Ask students to find a word that is repeated and to suggest some effects of its repetition.

**Possible Response:** The repetition of the word *singing* unifies the poem's imagery; it emphasizes the idea of the entire population singing together.

 Use **Unit Three Resource Book,** p. 26 for more practice.

### GUIDE FOR READING

Ⓐ **Possible Responses:** The catalog of sorrows might cause a reader to become saddened, depressed, or sympathetic.

## Thinking Through the Literature

1. **Comprehension Check** Possible Responses: mechanic, carpenter, mason, shoemaker, woodcutter, mother
2. **Possible Responses:** the optimistic spirit and vitality of American workers; the importance of manual labor to America's growth
3. **Possible Responses:** Whitman is illustrating the significance of a job done well for its own sake; he sees manual workers as the heart and soul of America.

## Thinking Through the Literature

1. **Comprehension Check** Name two of the people singing in "I Hear America Singing."
2. What do you think singing represents in this poem? Consider who the singers are and what they might be singing about.
3. Why do you think Whitman does not mention wealthy entrepreneurs, prominent leaders, or powerful politicians in this poem?

*Cliff Dwellers* (1913), George Bellows. Oil on canvas. 40 ³⁄₁₆″ × 42 ¹⁄₁₆″. Los Angeles County Museum of Art, Los Angeles County Fund. Copyright © 1995 Museum Associates, Los Angeles County Museum of Art, all rights reserved.

## Teaching Options

### BLOCK SCHEDULING: MANAGING TIME

**If your schedule requires that you cover the lesson objectives in a shorter time, use . . .**
- Preparing to Read, p. 396
- Thinking Through the Literature, p. 404

**If you want to take advantage of longer class time, use . . .**
- TE Teaching Options: Vocabulary Strategy, p. 397; Viewing and Representing, p. 399; Cross-Curricular Link, p. 400; Speaking and Listening, p. 402
- Choices & Challenges and Author Activity, p. 405

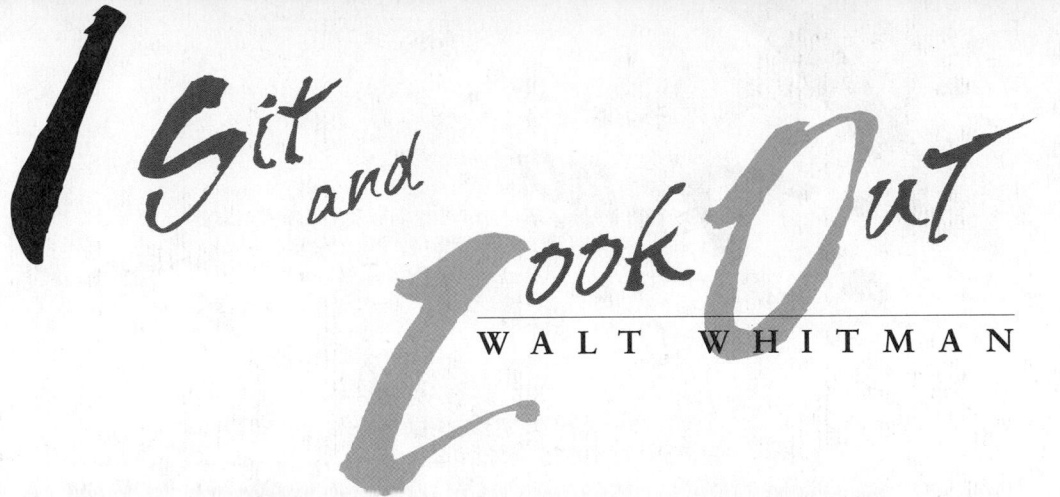

# I Sit and Look Out

## WALT WHITMAN

*I* sit and look out upon all the sorrows of the world, and
    upon all oppression and shame,
I hear secret convulsive sobs from young men at anguish
    with themselves, remorseful after deeds done,
I see in low life the mother misused by her children, dying,
    neglected, gaunt, desperate,
I see the wife misused by her husband, I see the
    treacherous seducer of young women,
5   I mark the ranklings of jealousy and unrequited love
    attempted to be hid, I see these sights on the earth,
I see the workings of battle, pestilence, tyranny, I see
    martyrs and prisoners,
I observe a famine at sea, I observe the sailors casting lots
    who shall be kill'd to preserve the lives of the rest,
I observe the slights and degradations cast by arrogant persons
    upon laborers, the poor, and upon negroes, and the like;
All these—all the meanness and agony without end I
    sitting look out upon,
10  See, hear, and am silent.

### GUIDE FOR READING

**2 convulsive:** intense and uncontrolled.

**2–8** Notice how many sorrows the speaker lists in this poem. What effect might this have on a reader? **A**

**3 low life:** the life of the lower classes.

**5 ranklings:** bitter feelings or resentments; **unrequited:** not returned.

**7 casting lots:** deciding by means of a random choice of objects (as in drawing straws).

## Thinking Through the Literature

1. **Comprehension Check** Name one of the social injustices described in this poem.
2. How do you evaluate the speaker's response to the sorrows of the world?

 **THINK ABOUT**
- what the speaker sees and hears
- why the speaker might respond with silence
- whether you think silence is the appropriate response

3. If Whitman were to write this poem today, do you think he would list the same sorrows or different ones? Explain your opinion.

I SIT AND LOOK OUT   **399**

---

---

## (Mini Lesson) Viewing and Representing

### *Cliff Dwellers* by George Bellows

**ART APPRECIATION** George Bellows is best known for his forceful sports paintings and spirited outdoor scenes of adults and children at play.
**Instruction** Draw students' attention to the predominant use of dark colors in this oil painting and the mood they create. Point out the building that dominates the background, and ask students what the artist suggests by placing the activity of the people against that backdrop.
**Possible Responses:** The darkness creates a somber mood. The building towers over the people and casts a shadow, which might symbolically suggest the difficulties of the people's lives.
**Application** Ask students to suggest reasons for the title of this painting.
**Possible Responses:** *Cliff Dwellers* might refer to the fact that the people in the painting live in high-rise apartment buildings. Perhaps their existence is as precarious as the existence of those who once lived in recesses or caves on cliffs. As in Whitman's poem, this painting depicts common people as busy and happy.

### GUIDE FOR READING

**A** **Possible Responses:** The speaker wants readers to accept him as a representative of humanity; to understand that this song of himself is also a song about them; to see that everyone is closely connected on a cosmic level.

**B** **Possible Response:** The poet uses five metaphors. Grass is: "the flag of my disposition," "the handkerchief of the Lord," "a child, the produced babe of the vegetation," "a uniform hieroglyphic," and "uncut hair of graves."

### Active Reading

> **STRATEGIES FOR READING FREE VERSE**

**C** Remind students that repetition is a device frequently used in free verse. Ask them why Whitman might have repeated the phrase *I guess* with each metaphor.

**Possible Responses:** It adds an informal, tentative tone to the comparisons, suggesting that the grass could be almost anything; it fits with the idea in line 15 that the speaker does not know what grass is; it shows that each of his metaphors is equally weighted in terms of importance.

### GUIDE FOR READING

**D** **Possible Response:** people of both sexes, all races, and all ages; young men, children, mothers, and old people

*from*

# Song of Myself

### WALT WHITMAN

## 1

I celebrate myself, and sing myself,
And what I assume you shall assume,
For every atom belonging to me as good belongs to you.

I loaf and invite my soul,
5  I lean and loaf at my ease observing a spear of summer grass.

My tongue, every atom of my blood, form'd from this soil, this air,
Born here of parents born here from parents the same, and their parents the same,
I, now thirty seven years old in perfect health begin,
Hoping to cease not till death.

10  Creeds and schools in abeyance,
Retiring back a while sufficed at what they are, but never forgotten,
I harbor for good or bad, I permit to speak at every hazard,
Nature without check with original energy.

**GUIDE FOR READING**

**1–3** Why do you think the speaker identifies the reader with himself at the very beginning of the poem? **A**

**10 in abeyance** (ə-bā′əns): temporarily set aside.

**11 sufficed at:** satisfied with.

400  UNIT THREE  PART 1: CELEBRATIONS OF THE SELF

## Teaching Options

**Cross Curricular Link**  **History**

**URBAN AND RURAL LIFE—1800s AND TODAY** In the United States of the early 1800s, most people lived in rural areas. Life for farmers was difficult, characterized by relentless labor, little leisure, and even less cash. A few wealthy farmers held the best land. Despite these conditions, urban areas remained comparatively underpopulated, accounting for only 15.3 percent of the total population by 1850. But cities were centers of wealth and influence, and urban residents were starting to demand and receive improvements to harbors, the police force, welfare programs, and other services. Again, though, in this "era of the common man," 50 percent of urban wealth was held by only 1 percent of the city residents.

By the latter part of the 20th century, only 1 person in 49 would be found living on a farm. Extraordinary improvements in farming methods as well as the lure of the city led to a concentration of 75 percent of the population in metropolitan areas by 1987. U.S. cities had undergone a metamorphosis from their 19th-century counterparts. Because of improved transportation and communication networks, suburbs were no longer thinly populated, but rather a booming part of the metropolis.

## 6

A child said *What is the grass?* fetching it to me with full
  hands,
15 How could I answer the child? I do not know what it is
  any more than he.
I guess it must be the flag of my disposition, out of hopeful
  green stuff woven.

C

Or I guess it is the handkerchief of the Lord,
A scented gift and remembrancer designedly dropt,
Bearing the owner's name someway in the corners, that we
  may see and remark, and say *Whose?*

20 Or I guess the grass is itself a child, the produced babe of
  the vegetation.
Or I guess it is a uniform hieroglyphic,
And it means, Sprouting alike in broad zones and narrow
  zones,
Growing among black folks as among white,
Kanuck, Tuckahoe, Congressman, Cuff, I give them the
  same, I receive them the same.

25 And now it seems to me the beautiful uncut hair of graves.
Tenderly will I use you curling grass,
It may be you transpire from the breasts of young men,
It may be if I had known them I would have loved them,
It may be you are from old people, or from offspring taken
  soon out of their mothers' laps,
30 And here you are the mothers' laps.

3

**16–25** What metaphors does the speaker use to describe what grass means to him?  **B**

**18 remembrancer designedly dropt:** a purposely dropped token of affection.

**21 hieroglyphic:** a system of symbols that represent meanings or speech sounds.

**24 Kanuck, Tuckahoe, . . . Cuff:** slang terms for various groups of people. A Kanuck (now spelled Canuck) is a Canadian, especially a French Canadian; a Tuckahoe is someone from the coast of Virginia; and a Cuff is an African American.

**25–33** The speaker presents the grass as "the uncut hair of graves." Who are the dead that he includes in this extended metaphor? **D**

**27 transpire:** emerge; ooze out.

## Customizing Instruction

### Students Acquiring English
**1** Define the following words for students to help them comprehend the poem.
- *loaf* (line 4): relax; behave in a lazy way
- *creeds* (line 10): formal religious beliefs
- *harbor* (line 12): provide a home for

### Less Proficient Readers
**2** Encourage students to reread this stanza several times and paraphrase the speaker's meaning.
**Possible Response:** I am putting my formal education aside for the moment, although I know that those ideas are valuable. I am allowing my natural thoughts and feelings to flow freely and take me wherever they might.

### Students Acquiring English
**3** Point out that in lines 14 through 21, the speaker uses the image of grass metaphorically to convey his thoughts about humanity and America. After reading each stanza, ask students to explain the comparison and the ideas it communicates.

 **Mini Lesson** **Grammar**

**PREPOSITIONAL PHRASES**

**Instruction** Explain that a prepositional phrase consists of a preposition, its object, and any modifiers of the object. A prepositional phrase acts as a modifier in a sentence. Write the following sentence on the chalkboard and point out the prepositional phrases.

In the preface to his volume of poems published in 1855, Walt Whitman wrote, "Of all nations the United States with veins full of poetical stuff most needs poets and will doubtless have the greatest and use them the greatest."

**Exercises** Ask students to identify the preposi-

tional phrases in each sentence.

1. After many years, Walt Whitman's work was accepted even by critics.
2. Because of Walt Whitman's varied jobs and travels, he could create vivid portraits of Americans as well as portraits of rural and urban life.
3. Until Walt Whitman's arrival on the poetic scene, free verse had not been accepted as a poetic form.

 Use **Grammar Transparencies and Copymasters,** p. 84.

Use McDougal Littell's *Language Network,* Chapter 2, for more instruction in prepositional phrases.

### GUIDE FOR READING

**A** **Possible Response:** that death is not an end but a change to something else; that there really is no death; that life and death are complementary forces—from death comes new life, such as the grass growing from graves

**B** **Possible Response:** Most people instinctively feel that it is bad to die, fearing an afterlife or simply regretting losing what they have in this life. Whitman's insights have persuaded him that dying can have much more positive consequences.

### Reading Skills and Strategies:
### MAKING INFERENCES

**C** Ask students what the speaker's description of his message as a "barbaric yawp" suggests about him.
**Possible Responses:** He is uncivilized; he is unafraid to express himself; he is natural and free.

What does it suggest about the free verse form of his message?
**Possible Responses:** The lack of regular rhythms and rhymes of formal poetry is natural, bold, and free, and perhaps seen as barbaric by contemporary readers.

### GUIDE FOR READING

**D** Death is waiting for everyone; no one can escape it.

This grass is very dark to be from the white heads of old
    mothers,
Darker than the colorless beards of old men,
Dark to come from under the faint red roofs of mouths.

O I perceive after all so many uttering tongues,
35 And I perceive they do not come from the roofs of mouths
    for nothing.

I wish I could translate the hints about the dead young
    men and women,
And the hints about old men and mothers, and the
    offspring taken soon out of their laps.

What do you think has become of the young and old men?
And what do you think has become of the women and
    children?

40 They are alive and well somewhere,
The smallest sprout shows there is really no death,
And if ever there was it led forward life, and does not wait
    at the end to arrest it,
And ceas'd the moment life appear'd.

All goes onward and outward, nothing collapses,
45 And to die is different from what any one supposed, and
    luckier.

**38–45** What concept of death does the speaker express in these lines?

**45** Why does the speaker think that to die is "luckier" than what people suppose?

## Teaching Options

**Mini Lesson** **Speaking and Listening**

**CHORAL READING** Reading aloud offers students an opportunity to use tone of voice, volume and tempo, expressions, and gestures to convey a poem's meaning. Choral reading is also a good way to express their understanding of a poem. Choose groups of students to select a Whitman poem and prepare a choral reading of it. Suggest that they decide how each line, depending on its meaning, should best be read—in a high or low voice, loudly or softly, and by an individual or by the group as a whole. Have them decide what gestures and facial expressions should accompany particular lines. Students should be able to justify their choices of verbal and nonverbal performance techniques by referring to their analysis of the poem.
**Present** Audience members should note their perceptions of subject, mood, and theme as they listen. Each presentation should be followed by a brief discussion of those three elements so that group members can evaluate their effectiveness.

**BLOCK SCHEDULING** This activity is particularly well-suited for longer class periods.

### 52

The spotted hawk swoops by and accuses me, he complains
    of my gab and my loitering.

I too am not a bit tamed, I too am untranslatable,
I sound my barbaric yawp over the roofs of the world.

The last scud of day holds back for me,
50  It flings my likeness after the rest and true as any on the
    shadow'd wilds,
It coaxes me to the vapor and the dusk.

I depart as air, I shake my white locks at the runaway sun,
I effuse my flesh in eddies, and drift it in lacy jags.

I bequeath myself to the dirt to grow from the grass I love,
55  If you want me again look for me under your boot-soles.

You will hardly know who I am or what I mean,
But I shall be good health to you nevertheless,
And filter and fibre your blood.

Failing to fetch me at first keep encouraged,
60  Missing me one place search another,
I stop somewhere waiting for you.

**48 yawp:** loud, rough speech.

**49 scud:** wind-blown cloud.

**53 effuse . . . eddies:** scatter my flesh in swirling currents.

**54 bequeath:** hand over, as if in a will.

**61** Why do you think the speaker says he's "waiting for you"?

SONG OF MYSELF **403**

## Customizing Instruction

### Multiple Learning Styles
**Bodily-Kinesthetic**

**1** Divide students into groups of three. Assign each group three or four consecutive lines of the poem from the section beginning with line 26 and ending with line 43. Tell each group to choose two members to interpret the poem through facial expressions and coordinated hand gestures and body movement, and one member to read the lines aloud. Allow a few minutes for preparation and then have the groups perform their passages in sequence.

### Less Proficient Readers

**2** Ask students to choose phrases that show the speaker's union with nature.
**Possible Responses:** "It coaxes me to the vapor and the dusk" (line 51); "I depart as air" (line 52); "I effuse my flesh in eddies" (line 53); "I bequeath myself to the dirt to grow from the grass I love" (line 54).

### Students Acquiring English

**3** Help students paraphrase the statement "I effuse my flesh in eddies" (line 53).
**Possible Responses:** My body is dissolving; I am changing my form, becoming one with the elements.

### Gifted and Talented
Tell students to think about the characteristics of Romanticism, the movement influencing writers, artists, and philosophers when Whitman lived. Ask students to decide whether Whitman is a Romantic, based on lines 46–61.

---

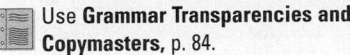 **Grammar**

**PLACEMENT OF PREPOSITIONAL PHRASES**
**Instruction** Explain that when a prepositional phrase modifies a noun or a pronoun, it acts as an adjective and is called an adjective phrase; when a prepositional phrase modifies a verb, an adjective, or an adverb, it acts as an adverb and is called an adverb phrase. An adjective phrase usually comes directly after the noun or pronoun it modifies. An adverb phrase that modifies a verb may appear anywhere in a sentence; an adverb phrase that modifies an adjective or another adverb usually appears near the word it modifies.
**Exercises** Ask students to insert the prepositional phrase in the correct place in each sentence.

1. Walt Whitman was originally thought to be "barbaric" and "noxious." (by critics)
   **Answer:** Walt Whitman was originally thought to be "barbaric" and "noxious" by critics.
2. The professor pointed out important passages to the students. (in the poems)
   **Answer:** The professor pointed out important passages in the poems to the students.

Use **Grammar Transparencies and Copymasters**, p. 84.

Use McDougal Littell's **Language Network**, Chapter 2, for more instruction and practice in prepositional phrases.

SONG OF MYSELF **403**

## GUIDING STUDENT RESPONSE

### Connect to the Literature

**1. What Do You Think?**
Students should support their choices of likes and dislikes with examples from the poem.

**Comprehension Check**

• The child asks the speaker what grass is.
• He compares himself to a spotted hawk.

### Think Critically

**2. Possible Responses:** The speaker is untamed, a nonconformist who is unafraid to express himself; he sees life and death as an endless cycle; he feels himself one with nature and all humanity.

**3. Possible Responses:** The grass is an image of hope, a reminder of God, an image of equality, or a symbol of the endless cycle of death and rebirth.

**4.** Some students may state that Whitman's poems seem more natural and conversational than traditional, metered poems.

**5. Possible Responses:** Romantics believed that the imagination was the source of ultimate truth. Romantics conceived of the spirit behind the natural world as the eternal life force, animating all beings on earth, and they emphasized the individual rather than society. In "Song of Myself," the speaker exuberantly embraces the energy of nature, seeking union with the life force emanating from the earth, the wind, and the clouds. Whitman suggests his ultimate union with this life force in the lines, "If you want me again look for me under your boot-soles" (line 55) and "I stop somewhere waiting for you (line 61).

### Literary Analysis

**Free Verse** Encourage students to highlight phrases or words that demand emphasis and to note the punctuation carefully. Students should practice reading the passages aloud from the marked copy and then find examples of repetition, parallelism, and catalog.

---

### Connect to the Literature

**1. What Do You Think?**
What do you like or dislike or wonder about "Song of Myself"? Share your responses with a partner.

**Comprehension Check**
• In section 6, what does a child ask the speaker to define?
• To what does the speaker compare himself at the beginning of section 52?

### Think Critically

**2.** Describe your impression of the speaker in this poem. Is he justified in celebrating himself?

 **THINK ABOUT**
- the speaker's view of himself
- the speaker's view of death
- the speaker's relationships with the reader and with others

**3.** What do you think grass **symbolizes,** or represents, in this poem?

**4.** **ACTIVE READING** **STRATEGIES FOR READING FREE VERSE**
Did you find Whitman's poems easier or more difficult to read than traditional, metered poems such as "A Psalm of Life"? Discuss the reading strategies you found most useful.

**5.** Review the characteristics of romanticism on page 341. What romantic qualities do you see in Whitman's poems? Cite lines as evidence.

### Extend Interpretations

**6.** **Critic's Corner** Ralph Waldo Emerson, one of Walt Whitman's few early supporters, described *Leaves of Grass* as "the most extraordinary piece of wit and wisdom that America has yet contributed." On the basis of what you know of Emerson from reading "Self-Reliance," what do you think he liked about Whitman's poems?

**7.** **Comparing Texts** "Ode to Walt Whitman" (pages 406–409) is a tribute to Whitman by the Chilean poet Pablo Neruda. What does Neruda celebrate about Whitman, and how does the style of Neruda's poem imitate Whitman's?

**8.** **Connect to Life** How would you compare Whitman's images of America in the mid-1800s with the images of today's America you described or sketched earlier?

---

### Literary Analysis

**FREE VERSE** Whitman is often considered the master of **free verse**—poetry without regular patterns of rhyme and meter. For example, consider lines 3 and 4 from "I Hear America Singing":

*The carpenter singing his as he
measures his plank or beam,
The mason singing his as he
makes ready for work, or
leaves off work,*

These lines flow more naturally than do rhymed, metrical lines and sound more like human speech—precisely the effect Whitman intended. Though free verse lacks meter, it does exhibit a variety of rhythmical devices. For example, in the quoted lines Whitman creates rhythm with **repetition** of the word *singing* and with **parallelism** in phrasing: "The carpenter singing his as he . . . / The mason singing his as he . . . ."

**Cooperative Learning Activity** With a few classmates, take turns reading aloud passages from "Song of Myself." Identify instances of repetition and parallelism, and of **catalog**—lists of people, things, or attributes. Discuss the appropriateness of free verse for a poem celebrating the self.

---

### Extend Interpretations

**Critic's Corner** Possible Responses: Whitman's unusual poetic topics and his use of free verse might have impressed Emerson, who valued nonconformity highly. Similarly, Whitman's willingness to speak out with conviction, even if it meant being inconsistent, would have met with Emerson's approval.

**Comparing Texts** Possible Responses: Neruda celebrates Whitman's strength, expansiveness, love for suffering people, and power to inspire. Like Whitman's verse, Neruda's ode has an organic, rather than a conventional, form. Instead of using traditional meter and rhyme, Neruda lets his thoughts and feelings flow, creating lines that vary in length and rhythm.

**Connect to Life** Students should cite specific lines in their comparisons.

## Writing Options

**1. Literary Review** Write a short review of the three Whitman poems, explaining whether you see consistency or contradiction in them. Read or display your review in class.

*"I Hear America Singing"*

*"I Sit and Look Out"*

*"Song of Myself"*

**2. Free-Verse Poem** Using Whitman's three poems as a model, write a free-verse poem about America today. As a starting point, you might develop one or more of the images you came up with for the Connect to Your Life activity on page 396. Share your poem with the class.

## Activities & Explorations

**1. Collage of Images** Using photos, drawings, or other images, create a collage that captures the spirit of one of the Whitman poems you have read. If you have a drawing program on your computer and access to a scanner, you can combine images you create with ones scanned from magazines or other sources. You might even include lines from the poem in your collage. Display your work in the classroom.
**~ VIEWING AND REPRESENTING**

**2. Interpretive Dance** Create and perform a dance interpretation of one of Whitman's poems. Let the movements of the dance suggest the mood and content of the poem. **~ PERFORMING**

---

## Walt Whitman
### 1819–1892

**Other Works**
*Democratic Vistas*
*Specimen Days*

**Early Experiences** "I am large. I contain multitudes," says Walt Whitman in "Song of Myself." It is a fitting description of a man whose writing touches on all aspects of life—the unique and the commonplace, the beautiful and the ugly. Whitman knew country life as well as city life, having grown up in rural Long Island and then in crowded Brooklyn. His varied work life included jobs as an office boy, a typesetter and printer, a school teacher, a carpenter, a newspaper editor and journalist, a nurse during the Civil War, and a government clerk in the Bureau of Indian Affairs.

**Revolutionary Poetry** His true life's work, however, was a book of poems called *Leaves of Grass*, which he began to work on in 1848. Whitman quit his job, moved in with his parents, and worked part-time as a carpenter while writing his poems. In 1855, unable to find a firm that would publish his 12-poem book, he had it printed at his own expense. Throughout his lifetime, Whitman rewrote, revised, and expanded *Leaves of Grass*; the ninth and final edition in 1891 contained nearly 400 poems.

**Literary Recognition** Many critics thought the poems in *Leaves of Grass* "barbaric" and "noxious." They were shocked by the poems' radical style and suspicious of the poems' subject matter, particularly the vivid sexual imagery. Other readers, most notably Ralph Waldo Emerson, praised Whitman. Gradually, the literary world recognized the brilliance of the book. By the time the fifth edition was published in 1871, many well-known writers in England and America were traveling to Whitman's home in Camden, New Jersey, to visit him. Today *Leaves of Grass* is often regarded as the greatest, most influential book of poetry in American literature.

## Author Activity

**Neruda's Whitman** Point out lines from the three Whitman poems that support Pablo Neruda's view of Whitman as a friend to the downtrodden and a promoter of "brotherhood on earth."

---

## Writing Options

**1. Literary Review To get students started on this assignment,** have them look at examples of book reviews in newspapers or periodicals. Instruct students that a review is not a summary but rather a highlighting of the significant aspects of the work to support the reviewer's perspective. Students also need to keep the reader of the review in mind. Urge students to quote lines from each poem to support their opinions. Encourage them to use biographical and historical details to bolster the points that they make.

**2. Free-Verse Poem To get students started on this assignment,** have them brainstorm additional images, decide on a theme, and list words and phrases that come immediately to mind. Remind students that repetition and catalog are effective poetic devices. Urge students to express their personal feelings as freely as Whitman does. **Musical learners** may find it helpful to set their words to background music to accompany an oral reading.

## Activities & Explorations

**1. Collage of Images** Encourage students to state the "spirit" of the poem they select. If possible, have students view published collections of collages to get ideas for techniques and materials.

**2. Interpretive Dance** Suggest that students work together beforehand to define the mood and content of the poem they select. Encourage students to share their ideas with a performance teacher or another adult familiar with modern dance styles.

---

## Author Background

Whitman spent most of his early career as a journalist. When he was barely 20, Whitman founded a weekly newspaper, the *Long Islander.* He went on to become an editor of the *Brooklyn Daily Eagle* from 1846 to 1848. After editing the *New Orleans Crescent* for six months in 1848, he returned to Brooklyn to edit another newspaper, the *Freeman.*

## Author Activity

**Neruda's Whitman** Answers will vary. Some students might cite lines from "I Sit and Look Out" in which Whitman describes the miseries of the downtrodden.

## Reading and Analyzing

**Literary Analysis: ALLUSION**

An allusion is an indirect reference to something, such as a person, event, thing, or literary work. In this ode, Pablo Neruda makes many allusions to the works of Walt Whitman. Challenge students to identify as many allusions as they can to the three Whitman poems they have just read.

**Possible Responses:** Lines 12–14 allude to "Song of Myself"—Whitman's use of the grass metaphor and his line "look for me under your boot-soles." Lines 65–67 allude to Whitman's theme of observing human suffering in "I Sit and Look Out." Lines 71–76 allude to Whitman's glorification of the common person, as in "I Hear America Singing."

**Literary Analysis: IMAGERY**

Have students note the images Neruda uses throughout this poem and compare them to the kinds of images that Whitman uses.

**Possible Response:** Neruda uses many images from nature, such as seagulls (lines 6–7), grass (lines 12–14), pine trees and prairies (lines 20–21), plains and mountains (lines 40–45), and alfalfa and poppies (lines 52–53). Whitman similarly uses many images from nature in "Song of Myself."

# Ode to Walt Whitman
### Pablo Neruda

*Walt Whitman's celebration of life reached beyond U.S. shores and inspired modern poets worldwide. Whitman's literary heirs include Pablo Neruda (1904–1973), the Nobel Prize–winning poet from Chile. In a speech delivered in 1972, Neruda expressed his gratitude to Whitman: "I was barely fifteen when I discovered Walt Whitman, my primary creditor. I stand among you today still owing this marvelous debt that has helped me live." The following poem by Neruda echoes Whitman's joyful poetic voice.*

*I* do not remember
at what age
nor where:
in the great damp South
5   or on the fearsome
coast, beneath the brief
cry of the seagulls,
I touched a hand and it was
the hand of Walt Whitman.
10   I trod the ground
with bare feet,
I walked on the grass,
on the firm dew
of Walt Whitman.

15  *D*uring
my entire
youth
I had the company of that hand,
that dew,
20   its firmness of patriarchal pine, its
prairie-like expanse,
and its mission of circulatory peace.

*N*ot
disdaining
the gifts
25  of the earth,
nor the copious
curving of the column's capital,[1]
nor the purple
initial
30  of wisdom,
you taught me
to be an American,
you raised
my eyes
35  to books,
towards
the treasure
of the grains:
broad,
40  in the clarity
of the plains,
you made me see
the high
tutelary[2]
45  mountain. From subterranean
echoes,
you gathered
for me
everything;
50  everything that came forth
was harvested by you,
galloping in the alfalfa,
picking poppies for me,
visiting
55  the rivers,
coming into the kitchens
in the afternoon.

*B*ut not only
soil
60  was brought to light
by your spade:
you unearthed
man,
and the
65  slave
who was humiliated
with you, balancing
the black dignity of his stature,
walked on, conquering
70  happiness.

*T*o the fireman
below,
in the stoke-hole,[3]
you sent
75  a little basket
of strawberries.
To every corner of your town
a verse
of yours arrived for a visit,
80  and it was like a piece
of clean body,
the verse that arrived,
like
your own fisherman beard
85  or the solemn tread of your acacia
legs.

---

1. **column's capital:** the ornamental top part of a column.
2. **tutelary** (tōōt'l-ĕr'ē): serving as a guardian or protector.
3. **fireman below in the stoke-hole:** On steamships, firemen are the workers who shovel coal to fuel the fires that heat the boilers; the rooms in which they work are called stokeholes.

## Reading and Analyzing

### Literary Analysis: STYLE

Ask students to compare and contrast Neruda's style in this ode to Whitman's style in the three poems they have just read.

**Possible Responses:** The poems are similar in that they are all written in free verse—they have no regular rhythm or rhyme—and they all express the strong, sincere emotions of the speaker or poet. Both Neruda and Whitman use alliteration to create a musical effect—for example, "its firmness of patriarchal pine, its/prairie-like expanse" (lines 20–21); "the copious/curving of the column's capital" (lines 26–27). Both use repetition of grammatical structures, as in lines 8–12: "I touched . . . I trod . . . I walked." The poems are different in that Neruda uses very short lines, whereas Whitman uses rather long ones.

### Literary Analysis: THEME

Have students compare the themes in Neruda's ode to those in Whitman's poems.

**Possible Response:** Both poets celebrate life in their poetry, especially as it is expressed in the natural world and in the lives of common people. Whitman's "I Hear America Singing" and "Song of Myself" express this theme directly by describing people and nature. Neruda's ode expresses the theme by celebrating Whitman's work.

*Y*our silhouette
passed among the soldiers:
the poet, the wound-dresser,
90    the night attendant
who knows
the sound
of breathing in mortal agony
and awaits with the dawn
95    the silent
return
of life.

*G*ood baker!
Elder first cousin
100   of my roots,
araucaria's
cupola,[4]
it is
now
105   a hundred
years
that over your grass
and its germinations,
the wind
110   passes
without wearing out your eyes

*N*ew
and cruel years in your Fatherland:
persecutions,
115   tears,
prisons,
poisoned weapons
and wrathful wars
have not crushed
120   the grass of your book;
the vital fountainhead
of its freshness.
And, alas!
those
125   who murdered
Lincoln
now
lie in his bed.
They felled
130   his seat of honor
made of fragrant wood,
and raised a throne
spattered
with misfortune and blood.

4. **araucaria's cupola** (ăr´ô-kăr´ē-əz kyōō´pə-lə): the projecting top of a South American evergreen tree.

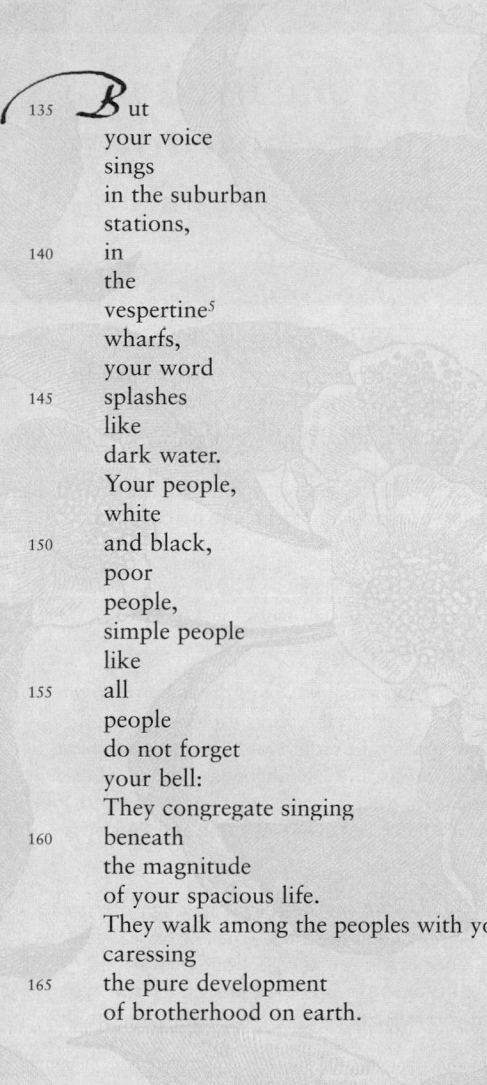

135 But
your voice
sings
in the suburban
stations,
140 in
the
vespertine[5]
wharfs,
your word
145 splashes
like
dark water.
Your people,
white
150 and black,
poor
people,
simple people
like
155 all
people
do not forget
your bell:
They congregate singing
160 beneath
the magnitude
of your spacious life.
They walk among the peoples with your love
caressing
165 the pure development
of brotherhood on earth.

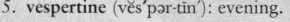

5. **vespertine** (věs′pər-tĭn′): evening.

## Customizing Instruction

### Students Acquiring English

Help students define the following words.

- *germination* (line 108): the sprouting of a seed
- *fountainhead* (line 121): source; origin
- *fragrant* (line 131): having a pleasant odor
- *congregate* (line 159): gather together; form a group
- *magnitude* (line 161): large size

### Gifted and Talented

Interested students can read more of Whitman and Neruda's poetry to analyze the influence Whitman had on Neruda. They might also write original odes celebrating a person, event, or work of art that has had a significant impact on their lives.

# OVERVIEW

## Objectives
1. understand and appreciate **experimental poetry** (Literary Analysis)
2. **make inferences** to understand poetry (**Active Reading**)

## Summary
Each of these poems by 20th-century experimental poets William Carlos Williams and E. E. Cummings brings an interesting twist to the romantic and transcendentalist traditions. "Danse Russe" uses concrete images to honor a private moment when the poet both confronts his essential aloneness and revels in his creative powers. In "anyone lived in a pretty how town," Cummings uses his trademark experimentation with grammar, punctuation, and other language conventions to create a tender love story between two unique characters who do not fit in.

## Thematic Link
These experimental poems **celebrate the self** and explore the breadth of its expression.

## 5-Minute Warm-Up

*Daily
Language
SkillBuilder*

Have students **proofread** the display sentences on page 337j and write them correctly. The sentences also appear on Transparency 11 of **Grammar Transparencies and Copymasters.**

# Danse Russe

*Poetry by* WILLIAM CARLOS WILLIAMS

# anyone lived in a pretty how town

*Poetry by* E. E. CUMMINGS

## Comparing Literature

### Traditions Across Time: Whitman's Heirs Express the Self

E. E. Cummings once remarked, "So far as I'm concerned, poetry and every other art was and is and forever will be strictly and distinctly a question of individuality." Like their literary forefather, Whitman, E. E. Cummings and fellow poet William Carlos Williams prized individuality and self-expression.

**Points of Comparison** As you read "Danse Russe" and "anyone lived in a pretty how town," notice how these poems, like Whitman's, spotlight the unique perceptions of individuals.

## Build Background

**Poetic Rebels** E. E. Cummings and William Carlos Williams defied many of the conventions of traditional poetry and ushered in innovative techniques and approaches. Both used the American idiom—our characteristic speech—in their poetry, rather than the formal diction of traditional poetry. Williams avoided symbolism and figurative language, instead concentrating on the use of specific concrete images to re-create experience. He wrote the poem "Danse Russe" in 1916, after seeing a performance of the Ballets Russes, a famous Russian ballet company that performed in New York that year. The company featured Vaslav Nijinsky, whose emotional expressiveness, perfect body control, and spectacular leaps led audiences to proclaim him a genius.

Cummings turned poetry upside down, inside out, and on its side. He created striking effects by violating rules of punctuation, spelling, grammar, and capitalization. His poem "anyone lived in a pretty how town," first published in the 1940 volume *50 Poems,* is actually a love story about two people.

## Focus Your Reading

**LITERARY ANALYSIS** **EXPERIMENTAL POETRY** Poetry of the kind you will read—in which the poets explore unusual subjects, invent new forms, order words in unexpected ways, or create striking effects through language—is often labeled **experimental poetry.** Keeping traditional poetry in mind, look for ways in which these poems by Williams and Cummings "break the rules."

**ACTIVE READING** **MAKING INFERENCES** Making inferences involves "reading between the lines"—making logical guesses based on evidence in the text to figure out what is not directly stated. Reading "anyone lived in a pretty how town" demands that you make many inferences. Consider the first stanza:

> *anyone lived in a pretty how town*
> *(with up so floating many bells down)*
> *spring summer autumn winter*
> *he sang his didn't he danced his did*

**READER'S NOTEBOOK** You might record your inferences, and the evidence on which you base them, in a chart like the one shown. Continue to do this as you read.

| Inferences | Evidence |
|---|---|
| "anyone" is a man | the words "he" and "his" in line 4 |
|  |  |
|  |  |

## LESSON RESOURCES

**UNIT THREE RESOURCE BOOK,** pp. 28–29

**ASSESSMENT RESOURCES**
**Formal Assessment,** pp. 75–76
**Teacher's Guide to Assessment and Portfolio Use**
**Test Generator**

**SKILLS TRANSPARENCIES AND COPYMASTERS**
**Literary Analysis**
• Style and Voice, T23 (for Literary Analysis, p. 410)
**Reading and Critical Thinking**
• Making Inferences, T7 (for Active Reading, p. 410)
**Writing**
• Point of View, T23 (for Writing Option 1, p. 415)

**INTEGRATED TECHNOLOGY**
**Audio Library**
**Visit our website:**
www.mcdougallittell.com

# danse russe

**William Carlos Williams**

If I when my wife is sleeping
and the baby and Kathleen[1]
are sleeping
and the sun is a flame-white disc
5   in silken mists
above shining trees,—
if I in my north room
dance naked, grotesquely
before my mirror
10  waving my shirt round my head
and singing softly to myself:
"I am lonely, lonely.
I was born to be lonely,
I am best so!"
15  If I admire my arms, my face,
my shoulders, flanks, buttocks
against the yellow drawn shades,—

Who shall say I am not
the happy genius of my household?

---

1. **Kathleen:** the nursemaid for the Williamses'
children.

## Thinking Through the Literature

1. What overall feeling do you get from the poem? Describe this feeling
   to your classmates.
2. Did the last two lines surprise you? Explain what you think they mean.
3. Why do you think the speaker dances and sings, "I am lonely"?
4. How well does the poem fit your ideas about loneliness?

DANSE RUSSE **411**

## TEACHING THE LITERATURE

### Customizing Instruction

**Less Proficient Readers**
Prepare students to read by telling
them that both poems have to do with
individuality and the lives that people
have apart from other people. Explain
that they will probably find "Danse
Russe" more accessible because the
writing style is more direct.

**Set a Purpose** Ask students to read to
find out what the speaker in "Danse
Russe" has in common with "anyone"
in the Cummings poem.

### Students Acquiring English

**1** Advise students to rely on context
to determine the meaning of the word
*grotesquely*. Lead them to understand
that in this context it means "odd" or
"unusual," not "ugly" or "abnormal."

Use **Spanish Study Guide** for
additional support, pp. 103–105.

**Gifted and Talented**
Ask students to list forms, techniques,
or other technical aspects of the poems
that are innovative or "experimental."
Discuss how the poets might have used
these forms to convey a message or
meaning.

## Thinking Through the Literature

1. Have students consider whether their
   feeling about the poem changed
   with the last two lines.
2. Possible Responses: Students might
   find the last two lines surprising,
   since the speaker says that he is
   both lonely and happy. Some
   students might suggest that the
   meaning of genius here is "the
   guiding spirit of a place."
3. Possible Response: The speaker is
   celebrating his individual selfhood:
   the poet recognizes that loneliness is
   an essential condition and takes joy
   in it.
4. Possible Responses: Since being
   lonely is usually viewed negatively,
   students might be surprised that the
   speaker thinks himself "best" when
   lonely.

Ask how line 14 of "Danse Russe" differs from the rhythm of the rest of the poem. Discuss its effect and how Williams uses rhythm experimentally.

**Possible Response:** Line 14 has four one-syllable words, each having equal stress. The effect is to emphasize this line of the poem, letting readers know that it contains an important idea.

Use **Unit Three Resource Book**, p. 29 for more practice.

**Active Reading**

MAKING INFERENCES

**A** Remind students to draw inferences such as conclusions, generalizations, and predictions and support them with textual evidence. Ask students what the poem's narrator thinks of the women and men of the town.

**Possible Response:** The women and men are thoughtless in the way they live and do not care as evidenced by phrases "both little and small" and "cared for anyone not at all."

**B** In lines 9–12, what does Cummings suggest happens to the children as they mature?

**Possible Response:** They lose their imaginativeness, intuition, and interest.

**C** Point out that Cummings reorders phrases and changes their meaning. What does it mean for "anyone" and "noone" to "dream their sleep" in line 30 while the "someones" and "everyones" "slept their dream" in line 20?

**Possible Response:** In line 30, "anyone" and "noone" are dead and seem to have transcended death, while the townspeople were never alive to life's possibilities.

Use **Unit Three Resource Book**, p. 28 for more practice.

# anyone lived in a pretty how town

## E. E. Cummings

**a**nyone lived in a pretty how town
(with up so floating many bells down)
spring summer autumn winter
he sang his didn't he danced his did.

**A** 5 Women and men(both little and small)
cared for anyone not at all
they sowed their isn't they reaped their
   same
sun moon stars rain

**B** 10 children guessed(but only a few
and down they forgot as up they grew
autumn winter spring summer)
that noone loved him more by more

**1** when by now and tree by leaf
15 she laughed his joy she cried his grief
bird by snow and stir by still
anyone's any was all to her

someones married their everyones
laughed their cryings and did their dance
(sleep wake hope and then)they
20 said their nevers they slept their dream

stars rain sun moon
(and only the snow can begin to explain
how children are apt to forget to remember
with up so floating many bells down)

25 one day anyone died i guess
(and noone stooped to kiss his face) **2**
busy folk buried them side by side
little by little and was by was

all by all and deep by deep
30 and more by more they dream their sleep **C**
noone and anyone earth by april
wish by spirit and if by yes.

Women and men(both dong and ding)
summer autumn winter spring
35 reaped their sowing and went their came
sun moon stars rain

## Teaching Options

**Mini Lesson** **Speaking and Listening**

**INTERPRETING POEMS**

**Prepare** Have students read "anyone lived in a pretty how town" to themselves in preparation for reading the poem aloud. Ask them to note how their emphasis on certain words is affected by their interpretation of the text.

**Present** Have students read the poem aloud and justify their choice of verbal performance techniques such as tone, speed, and emphasis by referring to their interpretations of the text. Ask listeners to evaluate how hearing the poem recited is different from reading the poem silently.

Remind them to think about what recitation techniques help present alternative interpretations of "anyone."

**BLOCK SCHEDULING** This activity is particularly well-suited for longer class periods.

Icarus (1947), Henri Matisse. Plate VIII from *Jazz*, École des Beaux Arts, Paris/Art Resource, New York. Copyright © 1995 Succession H. Matisse/Artists Rights Society (ARS), New York.

### Students Acquiring English
Explain to students that Cummings bends the rules of the English language, often putting words in an unexpected order or using words in unusual ways. Ask students to note the feelings that certain words—regardless of the order—create in them as they read both poems.

### Students Acquiring English
Before students begin reading, alert them to the fact that anyone and noone ("no one") are used as the names of characters in this poem. *Someones* and *everyones* (line 17) refer collectively to the other people who live in the town. Ask students to translate these words into their home languages and think about what message the poet might be sending by using these pronouns to refer to specific characters.

### Multiple Learning Styles
#### Interpersonal Learners
**1** Ask students to analyze "noone's" emotions and feelings toward "anyone" in lines 13–16.

**Possible Response:** She has a strong love for him, as evidenced by her emotional empathy with him (she laughs in his joy and cries in his grief).

### Less Proficient Readers
**2** What happens to "anyone" and to "noone"? Discuss interpretations of line 26, "(and noone stooped to kiss his face)."

**Possible Response:** They die. "Noone's" stooping to kiss "anyone's" face seems to be a metaphor for death. The poem never states outright that "noone" dies, but line 27 says that she and "anyone" were buried side by side.

---

**Mini Lesson** ## Viewing and Representing

### *Icarus* by Henri Matisse

**ART APPRECIATION** French painter Henri Matisse (1869–1954), one of the most influential artists of the 20th century, is best known for his use of intense color and lines to produce patterns and a sense of movement.

**Instruction** Point out that Matisse uses an abstract rather than a realistic style. Bold shapes represent objects and ideas and create emotional responses in the viewer. Ask students what objects are represented by the shapes in this painting, and what feelings the painting conveys.

**Possible Response:** The central figure is a person dancing, with his or her heart represented by the red dot. The blue background is the sky; the yellow bursts are stars. The painting creates an overall feeling of joy and oneness with the universe.

**Application** In what ways does the painting express the same ideas as "anyone lived in a pretty how town"?

**Possible Response:** The painting and poem both express the joy and "dance" of the individual life.

## GUIDING STUDENT RESPONSE

## Connect to the Literature

**1. What Do You Think?**
Students may have questions or comments about what happens in the poem, the contrast between "anyone"/"noone" and "some-ones"/"everyones," and about Cummings's use of experimental grammar.

**Comprehension Check**
• "Anyone" and "noone" are people who do not conform to the standards of their neighbors, who dance their own dance as individuals and are not regarded highly or remembered when they die.
• They lose their imaginativeness, intuition, and interest in others as they grow up.

## Think Critically

2. Possible Response: The people in town wanted nothing to do with "anyone," perhaps because he was different from them. The woman called "noone" came to love him; when "anyone" dies, they are buried together, united in death. The point of the story may be to urge people to escape the stultifying effect of small-town conformity and live more fully.
3. Students should cite specific lines to support their inferences.
4. Possible Response: The refrains are "sun moon stars rain" and the names of the seasons. These refrains suggest the passage of time and the inexorable workings of nature on people's lives.

## Connect to the Literature

**1. What Do You Think?**
Share with a classmate any questions or comments you have about "anyone lived in a pretty how town."

**Comprehension Check**
• Who are "anyone" and "noone"?
• How do the children in the town change when they grow up?

## Think Critically

2. Retell in your own words the story that unfolds in this poem. What, in your view, is the point of the story?

 **THINK ABOUT**
• how "anyone" compares with the other people who live in the town
• how you would describe the relationship between "anyone" and "noone"

3. **ACTIVE READING** **MAKING INFERENCES** On what evidence did you base some of the inferences you made as you read this poem? Review the chart you created in your **READER'S NOTEBOOK**. Compare your chart and interpretations with those of your classmates.

4. Notice the **refrains**—lines in which the same words are repeated—in this poem. What ideas do they suggest to you?

## Extend Interpretations

5. **Critic's Corner** Williams believed that the goal of a poem must be "to refine, to clarify, to intensify that eternal moment in which we alone live." Do you think "Danse Russe" clarifies a particular moment? Would Cummings agree with Williams's description of the goal of poetry? Defend your opinions.

6. **Connect to Life** Describe a real-life situation in which a person's individuality is stifled because of peer group pressure to conform. What advice do you think "anyone" in Cummings's poem would offer this person?

7. **Points of Comparison** Of "Danse Russe," "anyone lived in a pretty how town," "I Hear America Singing," and "Song of Myself"—which poem presents the most idealized view of individuality? Explain your opinion.

## Literary Analysis

**EXPERIMENTAL POETRY** Poetry described as **experimental** is often full of surprises—comic situations, conversational speech, playful use of words, descriptions of ordinary objects, and other distinctive elements not found in traditional verse forms.

William Carlos Williams belonged to a group of experimental poets known as the Imagists. Their poems contained sharp, clear images of striking beauty, such as the description of the sun above the trees in "Danse Russe." E. E. Cummings's "anyone lived in a pretty how town" reflects his poetic experiments, such as arranging words in scrambled order.

**Paired Activity** With a partner, choose about three stanzas of "anyone lived in a pretty how town" to rewrite, using standard capitalization, punctuation, diction and syntax (word order). Share your revision with the rest of the class. In your view, do Cummings's experiments with language and form add to or detract from the meaning of the poem?

## Extend Interpretations

**Critic's Corner** Possible Response: "Danse Russe" does clarify and immortalize one moment during a morning when the dancing poet celebrates his essential loneliness in life. Cummings probably wouldn't have placed as much importance on capturing a moment; he was more concerned with preserving human individuality, romance, and wonder in a world marked by mass movements, materialism, and mediocrity.

**Connect to Life** "anyone" would advise that people not give into peer pressure or try to conform and that they should follow their own inner rhythms.

**Points of Comparison** Students should be prepared to support their answer with textual evidence.

## Literary Analysis

**Experimental Poetry** Possible Response: Cummings's experiments with language and form add to the poem's theme of retaining individual uniqueness; the scrambled word order makes it so the reader can't take for granted what the poet is trying to say—the reader must "decode" the unique message.

# Choices & CHALLENGES

## Writing Options

**1. Diary Confession** Assume the identity of the speaker of "Danse Russe" and write a diary entry about the incident presented in the poem, making sure to explain why you are lonely.

**2. Headstone Inscription** In the style of E. E. Cummings, write an epitaph for the headstone of "anyone."

**3. Points of Comparison** Think about the unique personalities you read about in "I Hear America Singing," "Song of Myself," "Danse Russe," and "anyone lived in a pretty how town." Write a reflective essay giving your personal response to the varied ways that people in these poems express their individuality.

## Activities & Explorations

**Animation, Anyone?** Imagine you are planning an animated film based on "anyone lived in a pretty how town." Draw sketches to show how to visualize "anyone" and the world he lives in. Refer to details in the poem for ideas. ~ ART.

## William Carlos Williams

1883–1963
**Other Works**
*Paterson*
*In the American Grain*
*Spring and All*

**Poet and Physician** Williams was born in Rutherford, New Jersey, to an English father and a Puerto Rican mother. He received his medical degree in 1906 from the University of Pennsylvania, where he met the painter Charles Demuth and the poets H.D. and Ezra Pound. After completing his internship and spending a year in Europe, Williams established his medical practice in Rutherford in 1910.

**Keen Observer of the Ordinary** Williams wrote when he could, often jotting down ideas on prescription pads or composing poetry on a typewriter hidden in his desk. Convinced that poetry should be grounded in immediate reality, he wrote about the industrialized, urban world of northern New Jersey. Williams published more than 40 books during his lifetime, including poetry, plays, stories, novels, essays, and an autobiography. In 1963, he was posthumously awarded a Pulitzer Prize.

### Author Activity

**Williams on Video** View the videotape featuring William Carlos Williams from the *Voices and Visions* series, available at many public libraries.

## E. E. Cummings

1894–1962
**Other Works**
&
*1 x 1*
*95 Poems*

**Gifted Child** Edward Estlin Cummings, the son of a well-known Unitarian minister, was born in Cambridge, Massachusetts. Raised in a nurturing environment, Cummings began writing at age six and often illustrated his own stories.

**Bold Poet** During World War I, Cummings served as an ambulance driver in France. His surrealistic and savage account of his war experiences—*The Enormous Room*, published in 1922—propelled him into the public eye. The next year, his first volume of poetry, *Tulips and Chimneys*, was published. After the war, Cummings lived in Paris and then in New York's Greenwich Village, where he spent his days painting and writing. By the 1950s, Cummings's playful, innovative style had made him one of the most popular of American poets. His pioneering experiments with language remain a significant influence on poetry today.

### Author Activity

**Cummings's Voice** When Cummings read his poems aloud, he had a powerful effect on his listeners. Find and play audiotapes of his poems.

---

## Writing Options

**1. Diary Confession** Students' entries should include an interpretation of the events of the poem as well as language that exhibits their understanding of the emotions of the speaker. **To get students started on this project,** share with them the following statement that Williams once made regarding "Danse Russe": "The artist is way ahead of his age in his general thought. And so he's lonely, lonely. That's where the loneliness comes from." Suggest that they first reread the poem, picturing themselves as the speaker of the poem.

**2. Headstone Inscription To get students started on this assignment,** have them first write a short epitaph in normal prose style and then rewrite it in the style of Cummings. **To make this assignment easier,** have the whole class create a list of the experimental elements in the poem. Then have small groups each choose which elements to include in an epitaph and draft a group epitaph.

**3. Points of Comparison To adapt the assignment for visual learners,** have students construct an image such as a Venn diagram to compare the ways in which the people in the four poems express their individuality.

## Activities & Explorations

**Animation, Anyone? To adapt this project for auditory learners,** have students take sketches from other students and select types of musical accompaniment or specific musical pieces as a score for the film's animated scenes.

## Author Activity

**Video and Audiotape** Have students evaluate the effects of hearing a poem versus reading it silently. Which words do the poets emphasize? What sort of rhythms do you hear? Does the poet speak slowly or fast? How does hearing a poem aloud affect your interpretation of it?

---

## ✓ Assessment  Informal Assessment

**IDENTIFYING AND COMPARING THEMES** You can informally assess students' understanding of the poems' contents by asking them to compare the element of theme across "Danse Russe" and "anyone lived in a pretty how town." Have students write a paragraph that compares the themes of the two poems and how these themes are developed.

### RUBRIC

**3 Full Accomplishment** Paragraph clearly identifies themes of the poems and compares themes across the two poems, defending answers with examples.

**2 Substantial Accomplishment** Paragraph identifies themes from the two poems, but may not successfully compare them between poems or defend answers with examples.

**1 Little or Partial Accomplishment** Paragraph does not successfully identify themes of the poems and/or does not make comparisons between texts.

# OVERVIEW

## Objectives

1. understand and appreciate **poetry** that explores cultural and individual identity (**Literary Analysis**)
2. identify and understand the **speaker** (**Literary Analysis**)
3. understand **structure and form in poetry** (**Active Reading**)

## Summary

These two contemporary poems continue the theme of individuality derived from the romantic and transcendentalist traditions of the 19th century. "Ending Poem," co-written by mother and daughter poets Rosario Morales and Aurora Levins Morales, celebrates cultural identity—the individual as a product of diverse cultural strands. "Tía Chucha" by Luis Rodriguez, a Mexican-American poet, captures the individuality of a zany eccentric.

## Thematic Link

"Ending Poem" and "Tía Chucha" **celebrate the self,** both as an individual and as an embodiment of a cultural heritage.

### 5-Minute Warm-Up

*Daily*
*Language*
*SkillBuilder*

Have students **proofread** the display sentences on page 337j and write them correctly. The sentences also appear on Transparency 12 of **Grammar Transparencies and Copymasters.**

# Ending Poem
Poetry by AURORA LEVINS MORALES *and* ROSARIO MORALES

# Tía Chucha
Poetry by LUIS J. RODRIGUEZ

**Comparing Literature**

## Traditions Across Time: Whitman's Heirs Express the Self

In "Song of Myself," Whitman celebrates a distinct individual who also represents the nation at large. The poems you are about to read echo "Song of Myself" in that they too are celebrations of identity—either cultural or individual.

**Points of Comparison** As you read these poems, consider particular characteristics they have in common with Whitman's poetry.

## Build Background

**Celebrating Identity** "Ending Poem" was written by Aurora Levins Morales and her mother, Rosario Morales, poets of Puerto Rican ancestry. They created this poem to conclude a reading they did together in San Francisco. Rosario Morales explains: "We used lines from the poems we were performing to create a new whole that reflected . . . our differing yet clearly similar experiences as women, as immigrants and children of immigrants." She adds that the poem also reflects "our connection in spirit and community with the children of other migrations." This poem also appears at the end of a book the Moraleses co-authored, *Getting Home Alive.*

In "Tía Chucha," Luis J. Rodriguez celebrates individual identity rather than cultural identity. It is a portrait of the poet's eccentric aunt, who greatly influenced him when he was a child. *Tía* is Spanish for "aunt"; *chucha* is a Spanish nickname that may mean either "sweetheart" or "sly and foxy."

## Focus Your Reading

**LITERARY ANALYSIS SPEAKER** Similar to the narrator in fiction, the **speaker** of a poem is the voice that talks to the reader. In some poems, this voice may be the poet's; in other poems, the voice is that of someone or something other than the poet. Try to form a mental picture of the speaker when reading these two poems.

**ACTIVE READING STRUCTURE AND FORM IN POETRY**
The **structure** of a literary work is the way it is put together—the arrangement of its parts. **Form** is a structural term that refers to the arrangement of words and lines in poetry.

"Ending Poem" has an unusual form: notice that every other line is printed in italic type. It is a collaborative poem, with some lines contributed by Aurora and others by Rosario. According to the poets, the alternating typefaces do not signal whose line is whose but instead "blur origins and authorship," making the speaker a "new entity, a collective voice."

To get a sense of this collective voice, try reading the poem aloud, alternating lines with a partner. Also use the form of the second poem to help you focus on each different aspect of the speaker's Tía Chucha.

## LESSON RESOURCES

**UNIT THREE RESOURCE BOOK,** pp. 30–31

**ASSESSMENT RESOURCES**
**Formal Assessment,** pp. 77–78
**Teacher's Guide to Assessment and Portfolio Use**
**Test Generator**

**SKILLS TRANSPARENCIES AND COPYMASTERS**
**Literary Analysis**
• Form in Poetry: Structure, T11 (for Active Reading, p. 416)
**Reading and Critical Thinking**
• Compare and Contrast, T15 (for Writing Option 3, p. 422)

**Vocabulary**
• Using Reference Materials, C40 (for Mini Lesson, p. 417)
**Writing**
• The Uses of Dialogue, T24 (for Writing Option 1, p. 422)
• Compare-Contrast, C31 (for Writing Option 3, p. 422)
**Communications**
• Dramatic Reading, T12 (for Activities & Explorations 1, p. 422)
• Impromptu Speaking: Dialogue, Role-Play, Debate, T13 (for Activities & Explorations 2, p. 422)

• Verbal Strategies, T14 (for Activities & Explorations 1 and 2, p. 422)
• Nonverbal Strategies, T15 (for Activities & Explorations 1, p. 422)

**INTEGRATED TECHNOLOGY**

**Audio Library**
**Internet: Research Starter**
**Visit our website:**
www.mcdougallittell.com

# ending poem

**Aurora Levins Morales**

**and Rosario Morales**

*I* am what I am.
*A child of the Americas.*
A light-skinned mestiza[1] of the Caribbean.
*A child of many diaspora,[2] born into this continent at a crossroads.*

5   I am Puerto Rican. I am U.S. American.
*I am New York Manhattan and the Bronx.*
A mountain-born, country-bred, homegrown jíbara[3] child,
*up from the shtetl,[4] a California Puerto Rican Jew.*
A product of the New York ghettos I have never known.

10  *I am an immigrant*
and the daughter and granddaughter of immigrants.
*We didn't know our forbears'[5] names with a certainty.*
They aren't written anywhere.
*First names only, or mija, negra, ne,[6] honey, sugar, dear.*

15  I come from the dirt where the cane was grown.
*My people didn't go to dinner parties. They weren't invited.*
I am caribeña,[7] island grown.
*Spanish is in my flesh, ripples from my tongue, lodges in my hips,*
the language of garlic and mangoes.

20  *Boricua.[8] As Boricuas come from the isle of Manhattan.*
I am of latinoamerica, rooted in the history of my continent.
*I speak from that body. Just brown and pink and full of drums inside.*

Untitled [The Wedding Quilt] (1981), Rosario Morales.

---

1.  **mestiza** (měs-tē′sä) *Spanish:* a woman of mixed racial ancestry, especially one of mixed European and Native American ancestry.

2.  **diaspora** (dī-ăs′pər-ə): a migration or scattering of a group of people (here used as a plural).

3.  **jíbara** (hē′bä-rä) *Spanish:* a girl or woman of rural Puerto Rico, female peasant.

4.  **shtetl** (shtĕt′l): one of the small Jewish communities formerly found in Eastern Europe.

5.  **forbears:** ancestors (a variant spelling of *forebears*).

6.  **mija** (mē′hä), **negra** (nĕ′grä), **ne** (nĕ) *Spanish:* affectionate terms for girls or women.

7.  **caribeña** (kä-rē-bĕ′nyä) *Spanish:* a girl or woman of the Caribbean islands.

8.  **Boricua** (bô-rē′kwä) *Spanish:* Puerto Rican.

**Less Proficient Readers**
Discuss the concept of identity and emphasize that people derive a sense of identity from diverse sources, such as family, culture, religion, race, class, personality traits, likes, and dislikes.

**Set a Purpose** Have students read to find out what *identity* means to the speakers of the poems.
**Possible Response:** In "Ending Poem," the speakers view identity as the product of such influences as ancestry, race, class, and the places where they live and came from. In "Tía Chucha," the speaker sees identity as what a person does, how she interacts with people, and how true she is to herself.

**Students Acquiring English**
Tell students that the purpose of the poems is to explore personal identities and shaping influences. Point out that the poets use figurative language and symbols to explore this issue. Ask each student to find a figure of speech or a symbol in one of the poems and discuss its meaning as a class.

 Use **Spanish Study Guide** for additional support, pp. 106–108.

**Gifted and Talented**
As students read, ask them to consider the different types of identities explored in the poems—both individual and collective. In each poem, which type of identity is the focus? How does the form of each poem reflect this difference?

---

## Mini Lesson   Vocabulary Strategy

**USING REFERENCE MATERIALS** "Ending Poem" and "Tía Chucha" contain several Spanish words. Instruct students to use reference materials such as a Spanish-English dictionary to determine the exact meanings of these words. Point out that reference materials may not provide definitions for colloquial or slang terms. For example, have students look up the definition of *chucha* and compare it with the explanation of the word given on page 416.

**Activity** Have students look up the meanings of the Spanish words *poesía* ("poetry"), *ajo* ("garlic"), *raiz* ("root"), *regalos* ("presents"), and *cantar* ("to sing"). Then ask them to find these words in English in the poems and rewrite the lines substituting the Spanish words.

Use **Vocabulary Transparencies and Copymasters,** p. 40.

**Literary Analysis** SPEAKER

Ask students what the first line of "Ending Poem"—"I am what I am"—reveals about the speaker.

**Possible Responses:** The speaker accepts who she is; she is proud and makes no apologies for herself.

Use **Unit Three Resource Book,** p. 31 for more practice.

**Active Reading**

STRUCTURE AND FORM IN POETRY

Point out that line 10 of "Ending Poem" is shorter than those around it. Ask students to describe the effect that this line creates.

**Possible Response:** The line, which breaks up the rhythm of the longer lines, creates a dramatic effect.

Use **Unit Three Resource Book,** p. 30 for more practice.

**Literary Analysis: REPETITION**

**A** Ask students to identify the repeated element in these three stanzas and explain why they think the poets used repetition in this way.

**Possible Response:** Each stanza begins with the words *I am not.* The repetition emphasizes the fact that the speaker's cultural identity is diverse and hard to define. The speaker has roots in many cultures and does not wholly belong to a single one.

**Literary Analysis: FIGURATIVE LANGUAGE**

**B** What does the speaker mean when he says his aunt opened up the family like "an overripe avocado"?

**Possible Responses:** She opened up the family to emotional expression. She got past their tough exteriors to their messy, vulnerable insides.

I am not African.
*Africa waters the roots of my tree, but I cannot return.*

**A** 25 I am not Taína.[9]
*I am a late leaf of that ancient tree,*
and my roots reach into the soil of two Americas.
*Taíno is in me, but there is no way back.*

I am not European, though I have dreamt of those cities.
30 *Each plate is different,*
wood, clay, papier mâché, metal, basketry, a leaf, a coconut shell.
*Europe lives in me but I have no home there.*

The table has a cloth woven by one, dyed by another,
*embroidered by another still.*
35 I am a child of many mothers.
*They have kept it all going*
All the civilizations erected on their backs.
*All the dinner parties given with their labor.*

We are new.
40 *They gave us life, kept us going,*
brought us to where we are.
*Born at a crossroads.*
Come, lay that dishcloth down. Eat, dear, eat.
*History made us.*
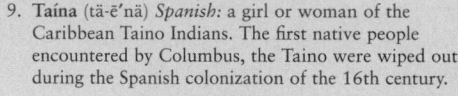 45 We will not eat ourselves up inside anymore.

*And we are whole.*

*In My Grandmother's Garden* (1982), Rosario Morales.

---

9. **Taína** (tä-ē′nä) *Spanish:* a girl or woman of the Caribbean Taino Indians. The first native people encountered by Columbus, the Taino were wiped out during the Spanish colonization of the 16th century.

## Thinking Through the Literature

1. Pick a line from this poem that you like or wonder about. Discuss this line with your classmates.
2. What do you think the **images** of roots, trees, and leaves in lines 24–28 might represent?
3. How do you interpret the last two lines of the poem?
4. Suggest a reason for the title "Ending Poem" other than the writers' use of the poem to end a poetry reading and a book.

## Thinking Through the Literature

1. Responses will vary.
2. These images compare the speaker's line of descent to a tree. Her ancestors are like the roots of the tree, and she herself is like a leaf on it.
3. Possible Responses: The poets no longer devour themselves with self-doubt or self-loathing about their backgrounds; they accept and love themselves as they are, as represented by sitting down at the table to which they once were not invited.
4. Possible Responses: The poets' old lives, in which they did not accept themselves fully, have ended; the time when they "weren't invited" has ended, too. This realization marks the ending of the old ways of thinking and acting.

*Woman with Turban* (1985), Gilberto Ruiz. Mixed media on fabric, 36″ × 52″, courtesy of Barbara Gillman Gallery, Miami Beach, Florida.

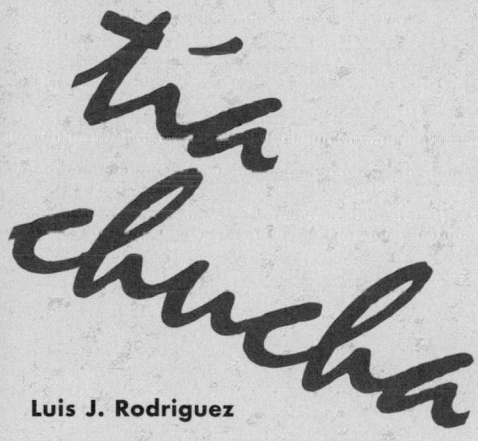

**Luis J. Rodriguez**

$E$very few years
Tía Chucha would visit the family
in a tornado of song
and open us up
5   as if we were an overripe avocado.
She was a dumpy, black-haired
creature of upheaval,
who often came unannounced
with a bag of presents
10  including home-made perfumes and colognes
that smelled something like
rotting fish
on a hot day at the tuna cannery.

TÍA CHUCHA **419**

## Mini Lesson  Viewing and Representing

*In My Grandmother's Garden*
**by Rosario Morales**

**ART APPRECIATION** Rosario Morales lived in Puerto Rico for 11 years. Her love for lizards and the island's wildlife inspired this crocheted wall hanging.

**Instruction** Explain that art can allow students to analyze ideas and cultures as represented in artistic media such as this crocheted wall hanging.

**Application** Ask students how the choice of subject matter, images, colors, and media (textile wall hanging) help to represent the ideas in "Ending Poem."

**Possible Response:** The lizard and the flowers represent the poets' appreciation of the natural beauty of their ancestors' home in Puerto Rico. The use of bright and varied colors represents the rich and varied cultures of the authors and the other immigrants for whom they speak. The textile wall hanging recalls the woven cloth mentioned in the poem that was the work of many hands, representing a cultural tradition and a contribution to civilization.

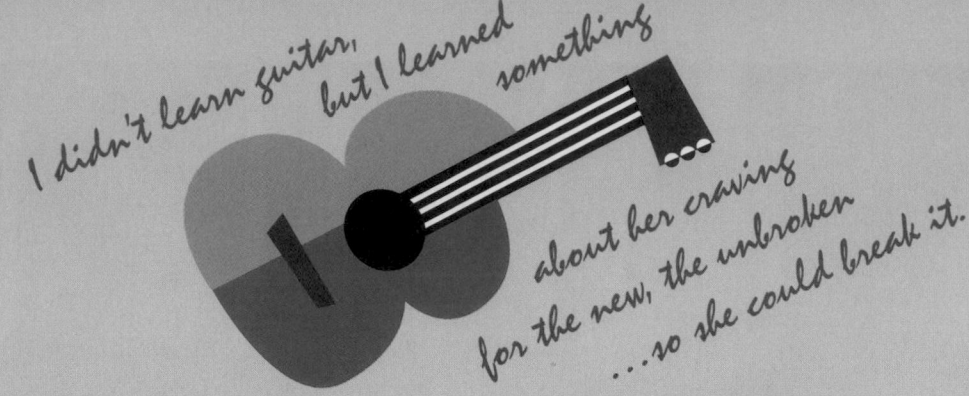

**A** Ask students which elements in these lines create a conversational tone.

**Possible Response:** The phrases *Oh sure* and *I mean* give the poem a conversational tone.

Have students discuss whether they think this tone works well in this poem.

**Possible Response:** A conversational tone is effective because it sounds like a young person's speech, and the speaker is recalling his childhood relationship with his aunt.

**Literary Analysis** SPEAKER

**B** What difference does it make here that the speaker is a relative of Tía Chucha?

**Possible Responses:** He is able to offer the reader insight on the family that he and Tía Chucha share. He presents his personal opinion that sometimes she is better off when she stays away from the family.

**Reading Skills and Strategies: CONNECT TO THE POETRY**

**C** Remind students that one way to interpret and appreciate literature is to connect it to their own experiences. Have students reread the last three stanzas of the poem and think of a person who has influenced them or someone they admire and would like to emulate. Ask students to write a short description of that person that includes a metaphor or simile, using the last three stanzas of this poem as a model.

---

They said she was crazy.
15 Oh sure, she once ran out naked
   to catch the postman
   with a letter that didn't belong to us.
   I mean, she had this annoying habit
   of boarding city buses
20 and singing at the top of her voice
   (one bus driver even refused to go on
   until she got off).
   But crazy?

   To me, she was the wisp
25 of the wind's freedom,
   a music-maker
   who once tried to teach me guitar
   but ended up singing
   and singing,
30 me listening,
   and her singing
   until I put the instrument down
   and watched the clock
   click the lesson time away.

35 I didn't learn guitar,
   but I learned something
   about her craving
   for the new, the unbroken
   . . . so she could break it.
40 Periodically she banished
   herself from the family
   and was the better for it.

I secretly admired Tía Chucha.
She was always quick with a story,
45 another *"Pepito"* joke,
   or a hand-written lyric
   that she would produce
   regardless of the occasion.

   She was a despot[1]
50 of desire;
   uncontainable
   as a splash of water
   on a varnished table.

   I wanted to remove
55 the layers
   of unnatural seeing
   the way Tía Chucha beheld
   the world, with first eyes,
   like an infant
60 who can discern
   the elixir[2]
   within milk.

   I wanted to be
   one of the prizes
65 she stuffed into
   her rumpled bag.

---

1. **despot** (dĕs′pət): a ruler with absolute power.
2. **elixir** (ĭ-lĭk′sər): a medicine believed to have the power to cure all ills.

---

## Teaching Options

 **Cross Curricular Link** **History**

**THE CHICANO MOVEMENT** For many Hispanic Americans, the struggle for equal rights has been a long and continuing battle. During the 1960s, in reaction to discrimination through such mechanisms as poll taxes, people began to voice their frustration and resentment and organize for action. As a result, the Chicano Movement of the 1960s was born. Mexican Americans especially played a strong role in this movement for ethnic pride, also called "brown power."

One of its leaders was Cesar Chavez, who organized California grape workers in the early 1960s. Chavez led a boycott to protest unhealthy and unfair treatment of Hispanic workers by the grape growers. Other leaders of the movement included Reies López Tijerina, who advocated for the descendants of families in New Mexico who had lost their lands. Since the 1960s, Hispanic Americans have made some progress in politics, professions, and education. Voter drives have improved the political participation of many Hispanic communities. Some Hispanic leaders today call for a change in focus from organizing within the political system to a renewed grassroots movement of Latino self-determination.

## Connect to the Literature

**1. What Do You Think?**
What are your impressions of Tía Chucha? Discuss them with your classmates.

> **Comprehension Check**
> Name one unusual thing that Tía Chucha does.

## Think Critically

**2.** Which lines of the poem do you think describe Tía Chucha most effectively?

**3.** Do you think you would appreciate or disapprove of a relative like Tía Chucha? Explain your answer.

> **THINK ABOUT**
> - how her visits affect the speaker's family
> - how others, such as the bus driver, view her
> - what happens when she tries to teach the speaker to play the guitar
> - the way she sees the world

**4.** As you learned from Build Background on page 416, the Spanish word *chucha* can mean either "sweetheart" or "sly and foxy." What connections can you make between this word's meanings and the speaker's aunt?

**5.** **ACTIVE READING   STRUCTURE AND FORM IN POETRY**
Think about the effect created by the arrangement of lines in "Tía Chucha." How would the effect have been different if Rodriguez had instead described his aunt in prose paragraphs?

## Extend Interpretations

**6. Connect to Life** It is sometimes said that people who are "crazy" see the world more clearly than do others. Do you agree or disagree? Explain your opinion, making reference to Tía Chucha and to someone else—for example, a character in a movie or TV show—who reminds you of her.

**7. Points of Comparison** What common characteristics do you see in "Ending Poem," "Tía Chucha," and "Song of Myself" (page 400)?

## Literary Analysis

**SPEAKER** The speaker of a poem, like the narrator of a story, is the voice that talks to the reader. In "Ending Poem," the speaker is a collective voice rather than an individual. The opening line "I am what I am" suggests the speaker's attitude toward herself. She accepts herself unconditionally, making no apologies for herself. In the rest of the poem, the speaker reveals the main source of her self-esteem: her embodiment of an African, European, and Taíno heritage.

**Cooperative Learning Activity** With a small group of classmates, reread "Tía Chucha." Discuss what you learn or can infer about the speaker. Try rewriting the poem, omitting the references to the speaker, and then decide what is lost or gained in the new version. Prepare a statement about why you think Rodriguez chose to make the speaker such a prominent part of the poem. Share your statement with other groups.

**REVIEW   TONE**   **Tone** is a writer's attitude toward his or her subject. A writer can communicate tone through **diction** (word choice), choice of details, and direct statements of his or her position. Compare the tone of "Ending Poem" with that of "Tía Chucha." In each poem, what attitude is expressed toward the subject? How intimately is the reader addressed?

---

## Writing Options

1. **Points of Comparison** Students' responses should include details that demonstrate understanding of the characters from the two poems.

2. **Autobiographical Sketch or Poem** Remind students that the tone of the sketch or poem should be one of self-acceptance and pride. **To get students started on this assignment,** tell them to list important people and events that have shaped their views.

3. **Contrast Essay** Students should use examples from "Tía Chucha" to explain the contrast. **To make this assignment easier,** have students complete the graphic organizer on page 422 to use as their prewriting notes.

## Activities & Explorations

1. **Paired Reading To make this assignment more challenging,** have students draft an "Artists' Statement" that justifies their choice of verbal and nonverbal performance techniques for their interpretation of the text. This statement could be printed and handed to the class or read to the class after the performance.

2. **Monologue** Encourage students to list Tía Chucha's traits and then to imagine her feelings about her life and family. Point out that they can talk about incidents in the poem and create new ones consistent with Tía Chucha's character.

3. **Self-Representation** To organize their ideas, students might draw the outline of a tree or a dinner table or use other motifs, such as a puzzle, a garden, or a museum exhibit.

## Art Connection

Possible Responses: The turban, sunglasses, and pose of the woman in the painting suggest that she, like Tía Chucha, is a cool, self-assured individual. The happy/sad faces suggest that she too is capable of dramatic flair. The ordered state of her bedroom and her fixed facial expression, however, suggest that she is unlike Tía Chucha, who is free-spirited and spontaneous.

## Writing Options

1. **Points of Comparison** Write a dialogue in which the speaker of "Song of Myself" and Tía Chucha exchange views about expressing individuality.

2. **Autobiographical Sketch or Poem** Define your own identity in an autobiographical sketch or poem titled "I Am What I Am." If you like, write a collaborative poem with a partner, modeled on "Ending Poem." Place this piece in your **Working Portfolio.**

3. **Contrast Essay** Consider again the ideas about viewing the world that you discussed for question 6. Then develop those ideas in an essay that contrasts the "crazy" and the so-called normal ways of seeing.

| Ways of Seeing | |
|----------------|-----------------|
| **Normal** | **Crazy** |
| indifferent | full of wonder |
| perceptive | imaginative |

## Activities & Explorations

1. **Paired Reading** With a partner, perform a dramatic reading of "Ending Poem" for the class. Include appropriate gestures or pantomimed scenes in your performance. If necessary, ask a Spanish-speaking classmate to help you with difficult pronunciations.
~ **SPEAKING AND LISTENING**

2. **Monologue** Assume the character of Tía Chucha and perform a monologue in which you express your feelings about your life and your family.
~ **PERFORMING**

3. **Self-Representation** In "Ending Poem," identity and heritage are described in terms of a tree and a dinner table. Create your own self-representation—perhaps a drawing or a collage of objects to show what contributes to your identity. ~ **ART**

## Art Connection

Look at the reproduction of Gilberto Ruiz's painting *Woman with Turban* below. What similarities do you see between the woman in the painting and Tía Chucha? What differences?

*Woman with Turban* (1985), Gilberto Ruiz. Mixed media on fabric, 36″ × 52″, courtesy of Barbara Gillman Gallery, Miami Beach, Florida.

## Inquiry & Research

**Puerto Rican History** Working with a small group of classmates, investigate the history of Puerto Rico. What events caused there to be so many different strains of ancestry among its people? What is the connection between Puerto Rico and New York City?

 **More Online: Research Starter**
www.mcdougallittell.com

## Teaching Options

### Mini Lesson — Speaking and Listening

**PRONOUNCING SPANISH WORDS**
**Prepare** Demonstrate some of the rules of pronunciation for Spanish words by pronouncing the word *hombre* ("man") or having a Spanish-speaking student volunteer to do it. The *h* is silent; the syllable *om* is pronounced with *o* as in *pot; bre* is pronounced like the English *bray*. The first syllable is stressed.

**Present** Have students practice the pronunciation of Spanish words and names from the poems, such as *mestiza, caribeña, Tía, latinoamerica, negra,* and *Pepito.* Students who speak Spanish can be paired with non-Spanish speakers for this activity. Or students can consult a Spanish dictionary, textbook, or information on the World Wide Web to learn how to pronounce the words.

## Aurora Levins Morales
1954–

## Rosario Morales
1930–

**A Blend of Cultures** Rosario Morales, a child of Puerto Rican immigrants, grew up in New York City. She married Richard Levins, a son of Jewish immigrants, and in 1951 returned to Puerto Rico with him to learn about the land she felt to be "both mine and not mine." In the early 1960s, she moved back to the U.S. mainland with her husband and her young daughter Aurora. Aurora Levins Morales was raised in New York and Chicago. She was influenced by the rich stories of her parents and her Puerto Rican and Jewish grandparents.

**Exploring Identity** Both Rosario and Aurora wrote as young children and were inspired to resume writing by the women's liberation movement of the early 1970s. In 1986 they co-authored *Getting Home Alive*, a dialogue in prose and poetry. This book explored their cultural, political, generational, and geographical identities. Aurora's recent books include *Medicine Stories, Writings on Cultural Activism*, and *Remedios*, which presents the history of the Atlantic world through the lives of Puerto Rican women.

## Luis J. Rodriguez
1954–

**Other Works**
*The Concrete River*
*America Is Her Name*
*Poems Across the Pavement*
*Trochemoche*

**Surviving the Streets** A son of Mexican immigrants, Luis J. Rodriguez was born in El Paso, Texas, and raised in Los Angeles, California. Growing up surrounded by violence, he barely escaped to reach adulthood and explore his creativity as a writer. In the 1960s and 1970s, Rodriguez became involved with Hispanic gangs in Los Angeles. In *Always Running: La Vida Loca— Gang Days in L.A.*, he describes how he eventually left gang life behind through the help of a counselor.

**Becoming a Creative Writer** After finishing high school, Rodriguez attended college and at various times worked as a school-bus driver, a truck driver, a factory worker, a carpenter, and a journalist. In addition to writing poetry and his memoirs, he has written articles, reviews, short stories, essays, and screenplays, including one of *Always Running*. Rodriguez told an interviewer, "Despite great odds, today I'm a poet and writer. . . . We all have the capabilities of great art and poetry. It's a matter of tapping into that creative reservoir we contain as human beings. Once tapped, this reservoir is inexhaustible." In 1989, Rodriguez founded Tía Chucha Press, named for his aunt, to publish the first works of emerging young poets.

## Inquiry & Research

**Puerto Rican History** The first known inhabitants of Puerto Rico were the Arawak Indians, most of whom died or were killed soon after the Spanish began to settle the island in 1508. Beginning in 1510, Africans were brought to the island to work on plantations and in mines. Although no full-blooded Native Americans are now known to live on Puerto Rico, some Puerto Ricans are descended from Arawaks and Africans who intermarried with Spanish settlers. In 1898, after the Spanish-American War, the United States took control of Puerto Rico; in 1952, the island became a self-governing commonwealth. During the 1950s, hundreds of thousands of Puerto Ricans migrated to the United States in search of jobs.

## Author Background

**Luis J. Rodriguez** In addition to poetry and his memoir, Luis Rodriguez has written a children's book, a collection of essays, short stories, and photojournalistic essays. The author sees writing as a "heroic and necessary task" that helps society achieve important changes.

---

 **Assessment  Standardized Test Practice**

**FIGURATIVE LANGUAGE** Some standardized tests include open-ended questions about literary elements such as figurative language. Instruct students to write a complete, concise essay to answer the following question:
Explain what the extended metaphor of the dinner table stands for in "Ending Poem." Support your answer with evidence from the poem.
**Possible Response:** The dinner table represents the speaker's cultural heritage. The first reference to a dinner occurs in line 16, when the speaker indicates that her people didn't go to dinner parties because they weren't invited. In other words, the speaker's ancestors were excluded from the dominant culture. As a symbol of the speaker's own cultural heritage, the dinner table is described in lines 30–31 as having many different kinds of plates, and in lines 33–35 as having a cloth created by the work of many hands. In line 43, the speaker invites a worker to eat at the table. The eating reflects her pride in her heritage and her willingness to share it with others.

## Objectives

1. understand and appreciate an **autobiographical story** (Literary Analysis)
2. identify examples of **humor** in the story (Literary Analysis)
3. consider the **purpose for reading** the story (Active Reading)

## Summary

In this autobiographical story, Keillor writes of his junior year in high school in a small town in Minnesota. He comically describes his participation in a school talent show organized by the love of his life, Dede Petersen. Keillor wants to be in the show, but Dede does not think he has any talent. After Keillor recites "O Captain! My Captain!" in front of his English class, however, his teacher tells Dede to put him in the show. To make the performance humorous, he practices reciting the poem with a British accent. The night of the talent show, Dede's ultra-cool boyfriend, Bill Swenson, is a hit, lip-synching Elvis's "All Shook Up." But when Bill tries to do another imitation, the audience starts to laugh. Keillor then changes the speed of the record to which Bill is lip-synching, and the audience howls with laughter. Bill slinks off the stage in disgrace. Keillor steps up to the microphone while the crowd is still jeering, but his humorous recitation is a resounding success.

## Thematic Link

In the story, Garrison Keillor matures from a boy who would not perform in front of others to a talented and confident entertainer, and his success at the school talent show is really a **celebration of the self.**

### 5-Minute Warm-Up

***Daily Language SkillBuilder***

Have students **proofread** the display sentences on page 337j and write them correctly. The sentences also appear on Transparency 12 of **Grammar Transparencies and Copymasters.**

---

# PREPARING to *Read*

*"I was an intense person, filled with powerful feelings."*

# Gary Keillor

*Autobiographical Story by* GARRISON KEILLOR

**Comparing Literature**

## Traditions Across Time: Whitman's Heirs Express the Self

Garrison Keillor is a popular radio host and writer. His story "Gary Keillor" is about a love-smitten teenager out to impress the girl of his dreams. Though this light story is a departure in style from the pieces in the first part of this subunit, it too celebrates the self.

**Points of Comparison**  Consider this story's message about individuality and self-expression. Try to connect Keillor's ideas to those of Whitman, Emerson, and Thoreau.

## Build Background

**Whitman's Elegy for Lincoln**  The assassination of Abraham Lincoln in 1865, shortly after the close of the Civil War, shocked and grieved the nation. To honor Lincoln's memory, Walt Whitman wrote "O Captain! My Captain!" In this poem Whitman compared Lincoln to a ship's captain who falls dead after guiding his ship safely through a horrific storm. Whitman's elegy figures prominently in the story you are about to read.

Like the main character in Keillor's story, generations of students have memorized Whitman's elegy for Lincoln. Some, like the students in the film *The Dead Poets' Society,* have even declaimed it to the delight of their peers. Here is the first stanza:

> *O Captain! my captain! our fearful trip is done,*
> *The ship has weathered every rack, the prize we sought is won.*
> *The port is near, the bells I hear, the people all exulting,*
> *While follow eyes the steady keel, the vessel grim and daring;*
> *    But O heart! heart! heart!*
> *      O the bleeding drops of red,*
> *        Where on the deck my Captain lies,*
> *        Fallen cold and dead.*

## Focus Your Reading

**LITERARY ANALYSIS** **HUMOR**  A literary work that is intended to induce laughter or amusement in the reader is said to be humorous. If you laugh while reading this story, think about why.

**ACTIVE READING** **PURPOSE FOR READING**
In school you are asked to read for a variety of purposes—to find out information, to understand a period in history, to interpret a theme, to take action on an issue, or to discover models for writing. This time your purpose is different. Read this story for enjoyment.

**READER'S NOTEBOOK**  After you finish the story, take a few minutes to make notes about the parts you found most entertaining.

---

## LESSON RESOURCES

**UNIT THREE RESOURCE BOOK,** pp. 32–36

**ASSESSMENT RESOURCES**
**Formal Assessment,** pp. 79–80
**Teacher's Guide to Assessment and Portfolio Use**
**Test Generator**

**SKILLS TRANSPARENCIES AND COPYMASTERS**
**Reading and Critical Thinking**
• Comparing Authors' Views, T23 (for Writing Option 1, p. 435)

**Grammar**
• Commas with Nonessential Elements, T55 (for Mini Lesson, p. 432)
• Appositives and Appositive Phrases, C85 (for Mini Lesson, p. 430)
• Commas with Parenthetical Expressions, C148 (for Mini Lesson, p. 432)

**Vocabulary**
• Idioms, C41 (for Mini Lesson, p. 426)

**Communications**
• Impromptu Speaking: Dialogue, Role-Play, Debate, T13 (for Mini Lesson, p. 429)

**INTEGRATED TECHNOLOGY**

**Visit our website:**
www.mcdougallittell.com

# gary keillor

Garrison Keillor

When I was sixteen years old, I stood six feet two inches tall and weighed a hundred and forty pounds. I was intense and had the metabolism[1] of a wolverine. I ate two or three lunches a day and three full dinners at night, as my family sat around the kitchen table and observed, and I cleaned off their plates too when they had poor appetites or were finicky. There was no food I disliked except muskmelon, which smelled rotten and loathsome. Everything else I ate. (It was Minnesota so we didn't have seafood, except fish sticks, of course.) I was a remarkable person. I was a junior in high school, Class of 1960. I was smart, so smart that poor grades didn't bother me in the slightest; I considered them no reflection on my intelligence. I read four books a week, and I sometimes walked home from school, all twelve miles, so I could relive favorite chapters out loud, stride along the shoulder of the highway past the potato farms, and say brilliant and outrageous things, and sing in a big throbbing voice great songs like "Til There Was You" and "Love Me Tender."

I had no wish to sing in front of an audience, songs were a private thing with me. I was an intense person, filled with powerful feelings, and I assumed that I would live alone for the rest of my life, perhaps in a monastery, silent, swishing around in a cassock,[2] my heart broken by a tragic love affair with someone like Natalie Wood,[3] my life dedicated to God.

I was a lucky boy. I had learned this two years before on a car trip to Colorado. My Uncle Earl and Aunt Myrna drove there that summer—he had been stationed in Colorado Springs during the war—along with my cousins Gordon and Mel, and I got to go too. I won that trip by dropping over to their house and being extremely nice. I'd say, "Here, let me wash those dishes." I'd say, "Boy, I'm sure in a mood to mow a lawn." And then she'd offer me a glass of nectar and a piece of angel food cake and I'd eat it and say, "Boy, I was looking at *National Geographic* the other night and they had a big article on Colorado. It was so interesting. Just the different rock formations and things. I don't see how people can look at those mountains and not know there's a God." And she'd smile at me, a good boy who mowed lawns and whose faith was pure, and I got to go. Of course my brothers and sisters were fit to be tied. "How come he gets to go? We never get to go. Oh no, we have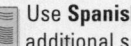

---

1. **metabolism** (mĭ-tăb′ə-lĭz′əm): the set of processes by which food is transformed into energy.

2. **cassock:** an ankle-length garment worn by clergymen.

3. **Natalie Wood:** a glamorous American movie star.

### Reading Skills and Strategies: PREVIEW

Have students choose partners and read "Gary Keillor" aloud to each other. Have them discuss their interpretations of it, their feelings about it, and any situations in their lives of which it reminds them.

### Literary Analysis    HUMOR

 Have students explain what is funny about Keillor's description of himself as a car passenger.

**Possible Response:** He says that he is a good passenger because he doesn't cause any problems for the adults—he behaves like a model teenager. This is humorous because it reveals Gary's understanding of what adults want from children. He is willing to act like a good boy in order to get what he wants from adults, but underneath his perfect behavior he is quite sly.

Use **Unit Three Resource Book**, p. 34 for more practice.

### Active Reading

PURPOSE FOR READING

Have students establish a purpose for reading this selection.

**Possible Response:** Keillor writes in a light-hearted, comic tone. The language is casual and conversational, and his descriptions of himself are funny. The reader knows from the beginning that this story is going to be entertaining.

Use **Unit Three Resource Book**, p. 33 for more practice.

---

to stay here all summer and work in the garden while he goes riding out to Colorado." They just didn't get it. Trips to Colorado don't fall in your lap. You've got to go out and earn Colorado.

    We took off on the trip, and I was a very good passenger. I sat in the favored front seat between my aunt and uncle, looking at the scenery for hours, no stains on my clothes, my face clean, a good strong bladder, never got carsick, and had a subtle sideways technique for picking my nose—you'd never see it even if you looked straight at me. Far off, the mountains appeared, shining on the horizon for almost a whole day, and then we rose up into them—snowcapped peaks, like the last scene in a western in which justice and romance prevail, and when we reached Denver (*EL.5280*, the sign said, exactly a mile), we ate dinner at a Chinese restaurant and my fortune cookie said: "You are enterprising⁴—take advantage of it." Well, there it was in a nutshell.

The mountains were startling in their whiteness and steepness, the valleys dark in the late afternoon, the peaks glittering in pure sunlight, beautiful stands of light gray-green aspen floating like fog, and my aunt took a picture of me with trees and mountains behind me. Just me, tall and intense. You would never guess I was from Minnesota. I thought, "This is my lucky picture. I'll keep it the rest of my life."

**M**y family lived in the country, along the Mississippi River between Minneapolis and Tryon, and I attended New Tryon High School, which was bulging under a tidal wave of children from new subdivisions on the other side of the river, places with names like Riverview Estates and Woodlawn and Forest Hills. Our side, South Tryon Township, along the West River Road, was still rural, truck farms, and scattered houses on big rolling tracts, and we West River Roaders were the cream of the school. The editor of the school paper, *The Beacon*, Elaine Eggert, was one of us; so were the stars of

the debate team and the speech team, three of the class officers, and the chairperson of the spring talent show, Dede Petersen, who rode on my bus.

I had been in love with Dede for two years, in an intense and secret way. She had bouncy blonde hair and wore soft sweaters, plaid skirts, penny loafers and knee socks. One winter day I wrote her a fourteen-page letter (single-spaced) saying that she was my ideal of womanhood, a person of pure taste, excellent judgment, stunning beauty, and natural intelligence, a woman to whom I could pledge myself in a spiritual friendship that would last forever no matter what. If the friendship should turn into physical love, good, and if not, fine. We would be friends for the rest of our lives, our souls communing⁵ over vast distances.

I did not, after long thought, give her the letter. I guessed that she might laugh at it and also that her boyfriend Bill Swenson might pound me into the ground. He was an intense person too.

One afternoon riding home on the bus, sitting behind her, I heard her complain to her pal Marcy about the miseries of planning the April talent show. Bill Swenson would be in it, lip-synching "All Shook Up," and he was terrific, but there wasn't much other talent around, nothing compared to last year, when all those guys sang "Bali Hai" with the coconuts on their chests,⁶ and the skit about school lunch when the kids pretended to vomit and out came green confetti, and of course last year there had been Barbara Lee. Barbara Lee was the most talented person ever to graduate from our school. She danced, she sang, she did the splits, she played

---

4. **enterprising:** willing to undertake new projects; ambitious.
5. **communing** (kə-myo͞o′nĭng): talking or meeting in close understanding.
6. **guys sang . . . chests:** In the musical *South Pacific*, sailors stationed on a remote island sing about women while wearing coconut shells (to imitate breasts) and grass skirts; later, a woman sings "Bali Hai," a song about a beautiful, magical island.

---

## Teaching Options

**USE CONTEXT TO DETERMINE MEANINGS OF IDIOMS**
Have students rely on context to determine the meanings of idiomatic phrases. An idiom is an expression that cannot be understood from the meanings of the individual words in the expression. Write the following sentence from page 426 on the chalkboard:

Well, there it was in a nutshell.

Have students read the previous lines and rely on context to determine the meaning of the idiomatic phrase *in a nutshell*.

 **Vocabulary Strategy**

**Possible Response:** What Keillor is saying is that his fortune cookie concisely describes his current situation. That he is enterprising is reflected in the fact that he found a way to get himself invited on the Colorado trip. *In a nutshell* means "summed up accurately in a few words."

**Application** Have students work in pairs to determine the meanings of the following idiomatic expressions: *West River Roaders were the cream of the school* (p. 426), *What burned my toast* (p. 427), and *Bill sort of went to pieces*

(p. 432). Have students read the paragraphs in which these idioms occur so that they can use context to determine their meanings.

Use **Vocabulary Transparencies and Copymasters**, p. 44.

A lesson on context clues appears on p. 326 in the Pupil's Edition.

Detail of *Play Within a Play* (1963), David Hockney. Oil on canvas and plexiglass, 72″ × 78″. Copyright © David Hockney.

**1  Less Proficient Readers**

• Ask students how Gary feels for Dede.
**Possible Response:** He has a crush on her.

• Have students discuss what is funny about the way he describes her.
**Possible Response:** He describes her as if she is an absolutely perfect woman, even though she is a teenager he does not know very well.

**Set a Purpose** Have students read on to find out if Gary continues to feel this way about Dede.

**Students Acquiring English**
Explain the following terms and expressions from pages 426–427.

• *EL. 5280*—"elevation 5,280 feet." Denver, Colorado, is known as the "Mile High City" because its elevation is one mile above sea level.

• *bulging under a tidal wave of children*—"becoming crowded due to the arrival of many new students." This is an example of figurative language (metaphor).

• *the splits*—"the act of lowering oneself to the ground with legs extended at right angles from the body." You might sketch a stick figure in this position to illustrate the point.

• *Broadway bound*—"headed for a career in theater." Broadway is a street in New York City where many famous theaters are located.

the marimba.[7] She was Broadway bound, no doubt about it.

I leaned forward and said, "Well, I think we have lots of talent." *Oh? like who, for example?* she said. I said, "Well, I could do something." *You?* she said. "Or I could get together with some other kids and we could do a skit." *Like what?* she said. I said, "Oh, I don't know. Something about the school burning down. It all depends."

"That doesn't sound funny to me," she said.

Marcy didn't think it was funny either.

What burned my toast was her saying *"You?"* when I volunteered to be in her talent show. I was only being helpful, I was not claiming to be another Barbara Lee. I had no interest in the stage at all until I heard her incredulity[8] and amusement—*"You?"*—and then I was interested

---

7. **marimba** (mə-rĭm′bə): a large wooden percussion instrument resembling a xylophone.

8. **incredulity** (ĭn′krĭ-dōō′lĭ-tē): disbelief.

GARY KEILLOR  **427**

---

*Play Within a Play* by David Hockney

**APPRECIATING ART** Since the beginning of his career, English artist David Hockney (1937– ) has been fascinated by the theater. In addition to designing sets for operas and plays, he uses the stage and stage curtains as metaphors in his canvases.

**Instruction** Have students describe the images they see in this painting.

**Possible Response:** There is a man standing behind plexiglass, with white patches on his hands, face, and jacket showing where he is pressing against it. He is dressed for a normal day at the office. In the background there are trees, two human forms, and a rainbow. There is an image of a head floating in the sky. The trees, people, and rainbow are reflected in a body of water.

**Application** Have students analyze ideas represented in the work. What types of feelings about performing on stage does this painting express? What might Hockney be saying about life?

**Possible Response:** This man fearfully presses his hands against the plexiglass. He is trapped. He is on stage and he wants to get off, but he can't. It is as if he is drowning, with thoughts of an audience swimming in his head. Hockney may be saying that life is a performance and we can never escape the watching eyes of other people.

### Literary Analysis: CHARACTERIZATION

**A** Point out that Keillor frequently uses the word *intense* to describe himself as a teenager. Have students discuss what readers learn about Keillor from his repetition of this word. Is there humor in his use of the word?

**Possible Response:** An intense person is usually someone who is very serious and concentrated, and this is how young Gary sees himself. However, his intensity leads him to have the rather ridiculous fantasy of joining a monastery after being rejected by Natalie Wood. The author finds it humorous to look back on his younger self and see how his intense feelings led him to overdramatize his life.

### Literary Analysis: IRONY

**B** What is humorous about the actions of Gary's mother in this scene? What is ironic, or unexpected, about Gary's reaction to her behavior?

**Possible Response:** Gary's mother is the kind of person who never speaks up or makes trouble, so her angry confrontation with the obnoxious truck driver is funny. It is ironic that Gary uses her example to justify his decision to enter show business, because his mother would never see the analogy between her situation and his.

### Active Reading

**PURPOSE FOR READING**

**C** How does Keillor's description of his actions help the reader enjoy the story?

**Possible Response:** He comically and realistically portrays a teenager's angst over his appearance and the lengths he will go to fix it. His description is both entertaining and true to life.

---

in being interested. A spiritual friendship with Dede was out of the question, if she thought I was the sort of guy you could say *"You?"* to.

No one in our family sang or performed for entertainment, only for the glory of God and only in groups, never solo. We were Christian people; we did not go in for show. But I was an intense young man. Intensity was my guiding principle. And when I thought about joining that monastery after Natalie Wood rejected me and spending my life in the woodshop making sturdy chairs and tables, I thought that perhaps I ought to get in the talent show at New Tryon High first, get a whiff of show business before I gave my life to God.

**2** It was one of those ugly and treacherous springs in the Midwest, when winter refuses to quit, like a big surly[9] drunk who heads for home and then staggers back for another round and a few more songs that everyone has heard before. It was cold and wet, and we sat day after day in dim airless classrooms, the fluorescent lights turned on at midday, the murky sky and bare trees filling the big classroom windows, pools of oil-slicked rain in the parking lot, the grass in front dead, the Stars and Stripes hanging limp and wet like laundry. In plane geometry, I was lost in the wilderness, had been lost since Christmas, and in history, we were slogging through World War I, and in English class, we were memorizing poems. "These are treasures you will carry with you forever," said Miss Rasmussen, a big woman in a blue knit suit. In her wanderings around the classroom as she talked about poetry and metaphor, she often stopped in the aisle and stood looming above me, her voice overhead, her hand resting on my desk, her puffy white hand and red knuckles and short ringless fingers. Her stopping there

> "Never give up on beauty," she said. "Never compromise your standards out of fear that someone may not understand." Teachers were full of useless advice like that.

indicated, I knew, her fondness for me. I was the only student of hers who wrote poems. She had even suggested that I memorize and recite one of my own poems. I declined. Part of the memorization assignment was reciting the poem in front of the class. My poems were far too intense and personal to be said out loud in front of people. I was memorizing Whitman's elegy[10] on the death of Abraham Lincoln, "O Captain! My Captain!" I walked home through the rain one cold day crying out, "O Captain! my Captain! our fearful trip is done,/The ship has weather'd every rack,[11] the prize we sought is won."

One day a fuel oil truck backed into our driveway and got stuck in the mud and the driver put it into forward gear and got dug in deeper. He gunned it in reverse and gunned it forward and rocked the truck loose and pulled forward and unwound his hose and started filling our fuel oil tank, but meanwhile he had left deep ruts in my mother's garden and the front yard. She was home alone, washing clothes. She heard the grinding and roaring from down in the laundry room and came outdoors to find her garden dug up and the tulips and irises destroyed, and the driver looked at her and said, "You ought to do something about your driveway." Not a word of apology, acted like it was the driveway's fault. My mother was the quietest, politest person ever, she felt that raising your voice indicated a flawed character, but she put her hands on her hips and said, "Mister, if

---

9. **surly:** bad-tempered; rude.
10. **elegy** (ĕl′ə-jē): a poem lamenting a person's death.
11. **rack:** buffeting (as by a storm).

---

## Teaching Options

### BLOCK SCHEDULING: MANAGING TIME

**If your schedule requires that you cover the lesson objectives in a shorter time, use . . .**
- Preparing to Read, p. 424
- Thinking Through the Literature, p. 434

**If you want to take advantage of longer class time, use . . .**
- TE Teaching Options: Vocabulary Strategy, p. 426; Viewing and Representing, p. 427; Speaking and Listening, p. 429; Cross-Curricular Link, p. 431; Informal Assessment, p. 433
- Choices & Challenges, p. 435

you can't figure out how to drive a truck, then they oughta find you a job you'd be able to handle." And she told him to get out and she would be sending the company a bill for the flower garden. And he did. And she did. And the company sent us a check and an apology from the general manager, a Harold L. Bergstrom.

It was the first time in my memory that my mother had fought back and raised her voice to a stranger, a watershed[12] moment for me. I heard the story from our neighbor, Mr. Couture, and I admired her so much for standing up to the jerk and defending our family's honor. Her principles had always told her to be quiet and polite and turn the other cheek and never make trouble, but there comes a time to let go of principle and do the right thing. To me, this seemed to open the door to show business.

nd then, about a week before the talent show, suddenly I was in. The real power behind the show wasn't Dede, it was Miss Rasmussen, my teacher, the adviser to the talent show, and the day I stood before the class and recited "O Captain! My Captain!" she told Dede to put me in the show. The next day, Miss Rasmussen had me stand up in class and recite it again. It was one of the finest pieces of oral interpretation she had ever seen, she said. She sat in a back corner of the room, her head bowed, her eyes closed, as I stood in front and with dry mouth launched the Captain's ship again, and she did not see the kids smirking and gagging and retching and pulling long invisible skeins of snot from their nostrils when my Captain died and I got to "O the bleeding drops of red,/Where on the deck my Captain lies,/Fallen cold and dead," they rolled their eyes and clutched at their hearts and died. Then, when she stood up, her eyes moist, and clapped, they all clapped too. "Wasn't that good!" she cried. "You really liked it, didn't you! Oh, I'm glad you did! He's going to recite it in the talent show, too! Won't that be nice!" A couple of boys in front clapped their hands over their mouths and pretended to lose

their lunch. They seemed to speak for most of the class.

So I was in the talent show, which I wanted to be, but with an inferior piece of material. I suggested to Miss Rasmussen that "O Captain! My Captain!" might not be right for the talent show audience, that maybe I could find a humorous poem, and she said, "Oh, it'll be just fine," not realizing the gravity[13] of the situation. "Never give up on beauty," she said. "Never compromise your standards out of fear that someone may not understand." Teachers were full of useless advice like that.

I tried not to think about "O Captain." I experimented with combing my hair a new way, with the part on the right. I was handsome at certain angles, I thought, and a right-hand part would emphasize a good angle. I stood at the bathroom mirror, a small mirror in my hand, and experimented holding my head cocked back and aimed up and to the right, a pose favored by seniors in their graduation pictures, which looked good from either side, and reciting "O Captain" with my head at that angle. I had good skin except when it flared up, which it did two days before the show, and it took a long time to repair the damage. There were six children in our family and only one bathroom, but I spent fifteen minutes behind a locked door doing surgery and applying alcohol and cold packs and skin-toned cream. The little kids stood banging on the door, pleading to use the toilet. I said, "Well, how bad do you have to go?" I was the one in show business, after all.

I worked on "O Captain" so that every line was set in my head. I recited it to myself in the mirror ("O Captain! O Captain! the fateful day is done,/Your blemishes have disappeared, the skin you sought is won") and for my mother, who said I was holding my head at an unnatural angle, and then, the Friday night before the

---

12. **watershed:** marking an important turning point.
13. **gravity:** seriousness or importance.

show, I recited it at a party at Elaine Eggert's house, and there my interpretation of "O Captain! My Captain!" took a sharp turn toward the English stage.

Miss Rasmussen loved a recording of Sir John Gielgud[14] reading "Favourites of English Poetry" and she played it once for our class, a whole hour of it, and from that day, all the boys in the class loved to do English accents. A little lisp,  endless dramatic pauses, inflections including shrill birdlike tones of wonderment, and instead of the vowel *o* that delicious English *aaooww,* a bleating sound not found anywhere in American speech. In the cafeteria, when my friend Ralph Moody came to the table where all of us West River Road rats sat, he stood holding his tray, peering down at us and the welter of milk cartons and comic books and ice cream wrappers and uneaten macaroni-cheese lunches, and after a long pause he cried "Aaaaooooowww," with a shudder, a great man forced to sit among savages. So at the party, surrounded by kids from the debate team and the newspaper, the cream of West River Road society, when Elaine had said for the sixth time, "Do the poem you're going to do on Monday," I reached back for Ralph's *Aaooww* and did "O Captain" as Sir John might have done it:

**A**

> Aoowww Cap-tin, myyyyy Cap-tin,
> aower _____ feeah-fool twip eez
>    done!
> Th' sheep has wethah'd _____ eviddy
>    rack!
> th' priiiiiiize we sot _____ eez won!
> But _____ aaaooooooooowwwww
> th' bleeeeeeeding drrrops _____ of
>    rrred _____
> wheahhhh _____
> on th' deck _____
> myyyy Captin liiiiiiiiies _____
> fallin _____
> caaaooooowwwld _____
> and _____ ded!

It was a good party poem. I recited it in the basement, and then everyone upstairs had to come down and hear it, and then Elaine had to call up a friend of hers in the city and I did it on the phone. It got better. "Miss Rasmussen is going to burst a blood vessel," said Elaine. She was a true rebel, despite the editorials she wrote extolling[15] the value of team play and school spirit. I was starting to see some of the virtues in her that I had previously imagined in Dede Petersen.

**b**ill Swenson had worked for weeks on "All Shook Up," and he looked cool and capable backstage before the curtain went up. His hair was slicked down, he wore heavy eye makeup, and he was dressed in a white suit with gold trim, without a single wrinkle in it. He stood, holding his arms out to the sides, avoiding wrinkling, and practiced moving his lips to "A-wella bless my soul, what'sa wrong with me? I'm itching like a man on a fuzzy tree." Dede knelt, shining his black shoes.

He pretended to be surprised to see me. "What are you doing here? You running the p.a. **2** or what?"

I told him I would be in the show, reciting a poem by Walt Whitman.

"Who? Twitman?" No. Whitman, I said.

"Well, I'm glad I don't have to follow that," he said, with heavy sarcasm. He glanced at my outfit, brown corduroy pants, a green plaid cotton shirt, a charcoal gray sweater vest, and said, "You better change into your stage clothes though."

"These are my stage clothes," I said.

"Oh," he said, his eyebrows raised. "Oh." He smiled. "Well, good luck." He did not know

---

14. **Sir John Gielgud:** a highly respected British actor and director.

15. **extolling** (ĭk-stō′lĭng): praising highly.

Illustration by Todd Schorr.

### Students Acquiring English

**1** Help students understand difficult terms to better appreciate the description of Sir John Gielgud's reading and the cafeteria scene. Explain that *shrill* means "high-pitched" or "piercing" and *bleating* means "a tremulous cry such as that made by a goat or sheep." Point out that *welter* means "confusion or upheaval."

**2** Explain that *p.a.* is an abbreviation for *public address.* A public-address system is equipment—such as microphones, amplifiers, and loudspeakers—that allows sound to be broadcast to a large audience.

### Less Proficient Readers

**3** Guide students' comprehension with the following questions.

• How does Bill think he will do in the talent show?

**Possible Response:** He has no doubt that he will be great.

• How does Dede help ensure his success?

**Possible Response:** She places his act after several serious acts so that the audience will be eager for a high-energy, fun performance.

**Set a Purpose** Have students read on to see how Bill does in the talent show.

how much luck I had. I had my lucky picture in my pocket, the one of me in the mountains.

Dede brushed his forehead with face powder and poofed up his hair. She gave him a light kiss on the lips. "You're going to be great," she said. He smiled. He had no doubt about that. She had put him high on the program, right after "America the Beautiful," a dramatic choral reading from *Antigone*,[16] a solo trumpet rendition of "Nobody Knows the Trouble I've Seen," and a medley of Rodgers and Hammerstein songs performed on the piano by Cheryl Ann Hansen. Then Bill would electrify the crowd with "All Shook Up," and then I would do "O Captain."

He was Mr. Cool. After Cheryl Ann Hansen's interminable[17] medley, which kids clapped and cheered for only because they knew that her mother had recently died of cancer, Bill grinned at Dede and bounced out on stage and yelled, "Hellllll-ooo baby!" in a Big Bopper[18] voice, and the audience clapped and yelled, "Helllooo baby!" and he yelled, "You knowwwwwwwww what I like!" and he was a big hit in the first five seconds. He said it again, "Hellllllllllooo baby!" and the audience yelled back, "Helllllllllooo baby!" And then Dede carefully set the phono-

---

16. *Antigone* (ăn-tĭg′ə-nē): an ancient Greek tragedy by Sophocles.
17. **interminable** (ĭn-tûr′mə-nə-bəl): endless.
18. **Big Bopper:** a popular singer of the late 1950s.

---

## Cross Curricular Link  Social Studies

**ORAL STORYTELLING** Before the invention of writing approximately 5,000 years ago, all stories were transmitted orally. Storytelling is an ancient art used to entertain and inspire people as well as educate them about their ancestors and history. Storytelling is also used to teach lessons about life and communicate the values of a particular culture.

Oral literature includes traditional songs, myths, legends, folk tales, riddles, and proverbs. Epics and sagas are other literary forms that derive from the oral tradition. The crucial aspect of oral storytelling is the fact that it is a live performance. The storyteller communicates as much with gestures, facial expressions, and vocal techniques as with the actu-al words. Audience reaction is another essential element. Because the text of an oral story is not committed to paper, each telling is slightly different, reflecting both the personality and talents of the storyteller and the reaction of a particular audience on a particular day. Formulaic elements can help storytellers remember very long stories—for example, the epics of Homer contain stock phrases and descriptive epithets that are repeated throughout the poems.

Have interested students listen to stories that older relatives tell about their own lives or about historical periods through which they lived. Invite students to retell these stories to classmates.

### Literary Analysis ▸ HUMOR

**A** What is funny about what Gary does to Bill, and why?

**Possible Response:** Gary really does not intend to help Bill by touching the record; he wants to embarrass Bill—and he succeeds. Bill is obviously not expecting to hear this change in the music, and although the audience is amused, he is not.

### Literary Analysis: IRONY

**B** What is ironic about Keillor's rendition of the poem "O Captain! My Captain!"?

**Possible Response:** The poem is serious and somber, and one would expect a serious reading. Instead, Keillor delivers the poem with an exaggerated English accent and an unexpected reference to Bill Swenson. His "straight" reading of the poem in English class got him into the talent show, but his performance is ultimately successful because he turns it into a comic act.

### Active Reading

**PURPOSE FOR READING**

**C** Writers generally try to end their stories with a satisfying conclusion. Ask students whether they find the ending of this story satisfying, and if so, what they enjoy about it.

**Possible Response:** Gary is able to participate in the talent show, use his sense of humor, get back at people who were mean to him, and make himself popular. Once his performance is over, the only remaining question is how Miss Rasmussen will react. Fortunately, she seems satisfied, believing that Gary forgot a line and changed his voice because he was nervous.

graph needle on the record of "All Shook Up" and Elvis's hoody voice blasted out in the auditorium and Bill started shimmying across the stage and tossing his head like a dustmop. "My friends say I'm acting queer as a bug, I'm in love—huh! I'm all shook up," and on the *huh* he stuck both arms in the air and threw his hip to the left, *huh,* and the audience sang along on the "hmm hmm hmm—oh—yeah yeah"—he was the star of the show right there. Dede ran to look out through a hole in the curtain, leaving me standing by the record player. She was so thrilled, she hopped up and down and squealed.

I could see part of him out there, his white suit hanging loose, the red socks flashing, him pulling out the red satin hanky and tossing it into the audience, *hmmm hmmm hmmm oh yeah yeah,* and at the end the whole auditorium stood up and screamed. He came off stage bright with sweat, grinning, and went back out and made three deep bows, and threw his hip, *huh,* and came off and Dede wiped his face with a towel and kissed him, and the audience was still screaming and whistling and yelling, "More! More!" and right then Bill made his fateful decision. He went out and did his other number.

It was "Vaya con Dios" by the Conquistadores.[19] Dede put the needle down and the guitars throbbed, and the audience clapped, but Bill hadn't worked as hard on "Vaya con Dios" as on "All Shook Up" and his lips didn't synch very well, but the main problem was that "Vaya con Dios" was "Vaya con Dios," and after "All Shook Up" it seemed like a joke, especially since the Conquistadores were a trio and Bill wasn't. Kids started to laugh, and Bill got mad— perhaps "Vaya con Dios" meant a lot to him personally—and his grim face and his clenched fists made "Vaya con Dios" seem even zanier.

> **"More! More!"**
> **and right then Bill**
> **made his fateful decision.**
> **He went out and**
> **did his other number.**

Dede ran to the hole in the curtain to see where the hooting and light booing were coming from, and there, standing by the record player, I thought I would help poor Bill out by lightly touching the record with my finger and making the music go flat and sour for a moment.

i t was miraculous, the effect this had, like pressing a laugh button. I touched the black vinyl rim and the music warbled, and fifty feet away, people erupted in fits of happiness. I did it again. How wonderful to hear people laugh! and to be able to give them this precious gift of laughter so easily. Then I discovered a speed control that let me slow it down and speed it up. The singers sounded demented,[20] in love one moment, carsick the next. The audience thought this was a stitch. But Bill sort of went to pieces. One prime qualification for a show business career, I would think, is the ability to improvise and go with the audience, but Bill Swenson did not have that ability. Here he was, rescued from his drippy encore, magically transformed into comedy, and he was too rigid to recognize what a hit he was. His lips stopped moving. He shook his fist at someone in the wings, perhaps me, and yelled a common vulgar expression at someone in the crowd, and wheeled around and walked off.

I didn't care to meet him, so I walked fast right past him onto the stage, and coming out of the bright light into the dark, he didn't see me until I

---

19. **"Vaya con Dios"** (vī′ä kôn dē′ôs) **by the Conquistadores:** A song (whose title is a Spanish expression of farewell, literally "Go with God") that was the biggest hit for this singing group of the 1950s and 1960s.

20. **demented:** mentally ill; insane.

---

## Teaching Options

### Mini Lesson  Grammar

**COMMAS WITH PARENTHETICAL EXPRESSIONS**
A parenthetical expression is a word or phrase inserted into a sentence as a comment or exclamation. Use commas to separate parenthetical expressions from the rest of a sentence. Write the following example on the chalkboard:

   Miss Rasmussen, I think, will like this poem.

Point out that in this case, *I think* is a parenthetical expression—it is set off by commas because the sentence is complete without it.

**Exercises** Have students insert commas in the following sentences as necessary to set off parenthetical expressions.

**1.** This story for example is both comical and entertaining.
   **Answer:** commas around *for example*

**2.** Bill Swenson I believe does not like Gary.
   **Answer:** commas around *I believe*

**3.** Of course Gary Keillor went on to become a famous storyteller.
   **Answer:** comma after *Of course*

 Use **Grammar Transparencies and Copymasters,** p. 148.

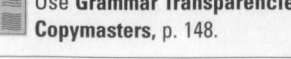 Use McDougal Littell's *Language Network.* Chapter 9, for more instruction and practice in the use of commas with parenthetical expressions.

was out of reach. There was still some heavy booing when I arrived at the microphone, and I made a deep English-actor type of bow, with princely flourishes and flutters, and they laughed, and then they were mine all the way. I held on to them for dear life for the next two minutes. I sailed into "O Captain," in my ripest accent, with roundhouse[21] gestures, outflung arms, hand clapped to the forehead _____ I cried:

> AOOWWW CAP-TIN, MYYYYY CAP-TIN,
> AOWER _____ FEEAH-FOOL
>    TWIP EEZ DONE!
> TH' SHEEP HAS WETHAH'D
>    _____ EVIDDY RACK!
> TH' PRIIIIIIIZE WE SOT _____
>    EEZ WON!
> BUT _____   _____
>    AAAAOOOOOOOWWWWW
> TH' BLLEEEEEEEDING DRRROPS
>
>    _____
> OF RRRED _____
> WHEAHH _____
> ON TH' DECK _____
> BEEEL SWEN-SON LIIIIIIIES
>
>    _____
> FALLIN _____
> CAAAOOOOWWWLD
>    _____ AND _____
>    _____ DED!

It wasn't a kind or generous thing to do, but it was successful, especially the *"AAAAAOOOOO OOWWWWW"* and also the part about Bill Swenson, and at the end there was shouting and whistling and pandemonium, and I left the stage with the audience wanting more, but I had witnessed the perils of success, and did not consider an encore. "Go out and take a bow," said Miss Rasmussen, and out I went, and came back off. Dede and Bill were gone. Dede was not feeling well, said Miss Rasmussen.

I watched the rest of the show standing at the back of the auditorium. The act after me was a girl from the wrong side of the river who did a humorous oral interpretation entitled "Granny on the Phone with Her Minister." The girl had painted big surprise eyebrows and a big red mouth on her so we would know it was comedy, and as the sketch went on, she shrieked to remind us that it was humorous. The joke was that Granny was hard-of-hearing and got the words wrong. Then came an accordionist, a plump young man named David Lee, Barbara's cousin, who was a little overambitious with "Lady of Spain" and should have left out two or three of the variations, and a tap dancer who tapped to a recording of "Nola" and who made the mistake of starting the number all over again after she had made a mistake. I enjoyed watching these dogs, strictly from a professional point of view. And then the choir returned to sing "Climb Every Mountain," and then Miss Rasmussen stood and spoke about the importance of encouraging those with talent and how lucky we should feel to have them in our midst to bring beauty and meaning to our lives. And then the lights came up, and my classmates piled into the aisles and headed for the door and saw me standing in back, modest me, looking off toward the stage. Almost every one of them said how good I was as they trooped past— clapped my shoulder, said, hey, you were great, you should've done more, that was funny—and I stood and patiently endured their attention until the auditorium was empty and then I went home.

"You changed the poem a little," Miss Rasmussen said the next day. "Did you forget the line?" "Yes," I said. "Your voice sounded funny," she said. I told her I was nervous. "Oh well," she said, "they seemed to like it anyway."

"Thank you," I said, "thank you very much." ❖

---

21. **roundhouse:** wide and sweeping.

**Customizing Instruction**

**Students Acquiring English**
**1** Help students visualize Bill's dancing by explaining that *shimmying* means "shaking and swaying." This simile suggests that when Bill danced, he tossed his head so forcefully that it looked like a dustmop being shaken out.

**Multiple Learning Styles**
**Visual Learners**
Ask students to visualize one of the acts in the talent show that Keillor describes and then draw it. Have students discuss ways in which they can depict the humor of the acts in their drawings.

---

✔ **Assessment Informal Assessment**

**JOURNAL ENTRIES** You can informally assess your students' understanding by asking them to retell the story of "Gary Keillor" in a series of brief journal entries. Tell them to assume Gary's voice and write five or six entries describing the events leading up to and including the talent show. Ask them to write a short statement at the beginning of their journals telling who Gary is, his age, and where he lives.

**RUBRIC**
**3** **Full Accomplishment** Entries cover all the major events of the story in the correct chronological order.

**2** **Substantial Accomplishment** Entries cover most of the major events but leave out some important facts or confuse the order of events slightly.

**1** **Little or Partial Accomplishment** Entries fail to cover the major events of the story and/or demonstrate serious confusion about the order of their occurrence.

## GUIDING STUDENT RESPONSE

### Connect to the Literature

**1. What Do You Think?**
Ask students if they were surprised by Miss Rasmussen's response.

**Comprehension Check**
- a photograph of himself, with trees and mountains behind him, taken by his aunt
- a comic recitation of Whitman's "O Captain"
- He changes the speed of the record to which Bill is lip-synching

 Use Selection Quiz
**Unit Three Resource Book,** p. 35.

### Think Critically

2. Most students probably enjoyed the talent show with Gary's prank on Bill Swenson and his comic rendering of Whitman's poem.

3. Possible Responses: She has unwittingly opened a way for Gary to express himself through humor and become popular. He may be—consciously or unconsciously—imitating a characteristic expression of Elvis Presley's.

4. Possible Responses: Before the talent show, Gary was not popular, considered himself untalented, did not express himself in public, and was in awe of Bill Swenson. After the talent show, Gary had gained the respect and admiration of other students, had a newfound sense of his own talent as a comedian, enjoyed the satisfaction and excitement of performing for an audience, and was no longer in awe of Bill Swenson.

5. Answers will vary. Some students may say that Dede Petersen influences Gary the most because his main reason for wanting to be in the talent show is to impress her; other students may state that without Miss Rasmussen's influence and support, Gary would have had neither the opportunity nor the confidence to perform in public; still other students will argue that Gary's mother influences him the most when she confronts the careless truckdriver, thereby going against her demure, ladylike upbringing and giving Gary an example of positive change.

6. Some students may say that Gary is a talented person who brought not beauty and meaning, but laughter, into people's lives.

### Connect to the Literature

**1. What Do You Think?**
What was your reaction to the outcome of the talent show? Share your comments with classmates.

**Comprehension Check**
- What is Gary Keillor's lucky picture?
- What is Gary's act in the talent show?
- What does Gary do to Bill Swenson at the talent show?

### Think Critically

2. **ACTIVE READING | PURPOSE FOR READING** What part or parts of this story did you enjoy the most, and why?

3. At the end of the story, why does Gary say to Miss Rasmussen, "Thank you, thank you very much"?

4. How would you describe the most important way in which Gary changes as a result of participating in the talent show?

 **THINK ABOUT**
- his description of himself as an "intense person" early in the story
- his popularity with other students before and after the talent show
- his attitude toward Bill Swenson

5. Consider the important female **characters** in Gary's life: Dede Petersen, Miss Rasmussen, and his mother. Which of them do you think influences him the most? Explain the reasons for your choice.

6. Miss Rasmussen says that talented people "bring beauty and meaning to our lives." Explain whether you agree with her opinion.

### Extend Interpretations

7. **What If?** Suppose Gary had recited Whitman's elegy in a serious way. Would his performance have been so successful? Why or why not?

8. **Connect to Life** How would you compare Gary's experiences of performing in front of the class with your own experiences?

9. **Points of Comparison** What connections do you see between Gary's conduct in this story and Emerson's ideas in the excerpt from "Self-Reliance"?

### Literary Analysis

**HUMOR** Humor is a term applied to a literary work whose purpose is to entertain and to evoke laughter. In literature there are three basic types of humor, all of which may involve exaggeration or irony. **Humor of situation** is derived from the plot of a work. It usually involves exaggerated events or situational irony, which occurs when something happens that is different from what was expected. **Humor of character** is often based on exaggerated personalities or on characters who fail to recognize their own flaws, a form of dramatic irony. **Humor of language** may include sarcasm, exaggeration, puns, or verbal irony, which occurs when what is said is not what is meant.

**Paired Activity** Get together with a partner and review your answers to question 2, about the parts of the story that you enjoyed the most. Then choose a passage that you find particularly funny. Reread the passage carefully and identify the source or sources of its humor: plot, character, or language. Then prepare an oral presentation of the passage for your class. As you practice reading the passage, keep in mind that the way the story is told is an important part of its humor. Record and then critique your presentation and those of your classmates.

### Literary Analysis

**Humor** To help students explore the types of humor, ask them to provide examples of each type from TV situation comedies or movies.

### Extend Interpretations

**What If?** Students may point out that after the hilarity caused by Bill Swenson's fiasco, the audience was primed to enjoy Gary's comic rendition.

**Connect to Life** Answers will vary. Some students may state that like Gary they have used humor to warm up an audience.

**Points of Comparison** Possible Response: Students may cite Emerson's dictum "Whoso would be a man, must be a nonconformist" and point out that Gary's conduct—his prank on Bill Swenson, his playful rendition of Whitman's elegy—shows that he too challenges convention.

## Writing Options

**1.** **Points of Comparison**

How do you imagine Whitman would have responded to Gary's comic recitation of his immortal poem? Write a dialogue between Whitman and Gary, showing Whitman's response. Be true to the ideas about individuality that Whitman expressed in his poetry.

**2. Story Sequel** Write a sequel to this story showing what happens when Gary and Dede Petersen or Bill Swenson meet the next time.

**3. Literary Review** In commenting on Lake Wobegon, Keillor's fictional home town, newspaper columnist Mary T. Schmich observed, "[It is] a town that lies not on any map but somewhere along the border of his imagination and his memory." Which elements in "Gary Keillor" might have been based on actual memories? Which might have been a product of Keillor's imagination? Write a review of the story, expressing your views.

## Activities & Explorations

**1. Drawn-Out Story** With a small group, paint or sketch a series of scenes that recapture the major incidents of the story. ~ ART

**2. Comic Recitation** Choose another poem that has become a classic, and perform a comic recitation of it for your classmates. ~ PERFORMING

## Art Connection

David Hockney's paintings use the stage and stage curtains as intriguing metaphors. Look again at *Detail of Play Within a Play* on page 427. What feelings about performing on stage does this painting suggest? How would you compare these feelings with Gary's in this story?

---

## Garrison Keillor

1942–

**Other Works**
*Lake Wobegon Days*
*Happy to Be Here*
*Leaving Home*
*We Are Still Married*
*WLT: A Radio Romance*

**A Lover of Language** The storyteller, writer, and radio-show host Garrison Keillor (kĕ′ lər) was born in Minnesota. He and his family were members of the Plymouth Brethren, a strict religious sect that frowned on dancing, card playing, and other forms of entertainment. As a child, however, Keillor fell in love with both the written and the spoken word. He enjoyed listening to religious parables and tales told by his relatives and other adults, and he developed a keen appetite for reading and writing. "When I was fourteen, I was happy to read all day every day and into the night." In the eighth grade, he submitted poems to the school paper under the name Garrison instead of his given name, Gary, "to hide behind a name that meant strength."

**Radio Career** In addition to reading and writing, Keillor's other childhood passion was listening to the radio. While attending the University of Minnesota, he worked for the campus radio station, and after graduating from college, he became the host of a classical music show on Minnesota Public Radio. In 1974, Keillor launched the immensely popular radio show *A Prairie Home Companion*, set in the mythical Midwestern town of Lake Wobegon.

**Celebrity and Writer** In addition to working as the host and writer of *A Prairie Home Companion*, Keillor has written several books. "Gary Keillor" is taken from his 1993 collection of stories, *The Book of Guys*.

## Author Activity

**Good Humor** Keillor is acclaimed for his storytelling skills. Listen to a recording of a humorous story he told on his radio show, *A Prairie Home Companion*. Compare the sources of humor in this oral performance with those in "Gary Keillor."

---

## Writing Options

1. **Points of Comparison** Students' dialogues should demonstrate an understanding of the meaning of Whitman's poem and Keillor's different interpretation of it. **To make this assignment more challenging,** have students read several literary interpretations or criticisms of Whitman's poem to get a sense of why it was written and how it was regarded at that time. Encourage students to keep their findings in mind as they write the dialogues.

2. **Story Sequel** Encourage students to review what Gary did to Bill while he was onstage. **To get students started on this assignment,** ask them to put themselves in Bill's or Dede's shoes. If they were Bill, would they be angry with Gary and strike back? If they were Dede, would they have a new admiration for Gary because he was funny, or would they resent Gary because of what he did to Bill?

3. **Literary Review To make this assignment easier for students,** select a particular episode from the story, such as the talent show, and discuss what might have really happened and what might have been embellished by Keillor's imagination.

## Activities & Explorations

1. **Drawn-Out Story** Students' scenes should reflect an understanding of the major incidents in the story. **To get students started on this assignment,** ask them to work with a partner and write down the most important scenes in the story before they draw them.

2. **Comic Recitation To get students started on this project,** bring in a tape of a popular comedian who makes fun of everyday life or serious events. Discuss the techniques the comedian uses to make the audience laugh. Encourage students to be original and not simply recite their poems with an English accent.

---

## Art Connection

Possible Responses: This painting suggests the performer's feelings of isolation and anxiety to win over the audience. When Gary enters the stage to a chorus of boos, he is in a comparable situation. He too is anxious to win over the audience. He does so through an exaggerated bow, "with princely flourishes and flutters."

## Author Activity

Many of Garrison Keillor's stories and radio programs are available on audio cassette. Students should be able to locate copies at their local library.

## PART 1 Reading the Prompt

Model the process of reading a prompt:

- Read through the prompt in its entirety.
- List key words and phrases of the assignment on the board ("summarize," "romantic view of the individual," "examples").
- Define each key word using the Strategies in Action to show how students can restate the prompt in their own words.

## PART 2 Planning a Synthesis Essay

- Evidence that students include in their charts might include quotations from the literature as well as their own thoughts about what these quotations mean or imply.
- Students can use freewriting to start their ideas flowing. Suggest that they freewrite about "Song of Myself," recording all the ideas and feelings that the poem brings to mind. Then they can read what they wrote and look for associations to the other pieces they have chosen.
- When they have completed their charts, students may select the best pieces of evidence to use in their essays. Remind them to keep the focus of the essay in mind as they select examples.

## PART 3 Drafting Your Essay

**Introduction** Students might briefly describe different ways in which individuals can relate to society—for example, assimilating, rebelling, actively participating, withdrawing.

**Organization** Have students carefully consider their organizational pattern before they begin writing.

**Conclusion** Students may conclude that all of the selections celebrate the individual and encourage people to express their unique talents and follow their own consciences.

**Revision** Students should proofread their quotations to make sure they match the original text and check for proper use of quotation marks, ellipsis points, and block quotations.

---

# Comparing Literature: Assessment Practice

Some assessment prompts ask you to synthesize, or pull together, information from several selections to make a generalization about a literary movement or genre. You will now practice writing an essay with this focus.

**PART 1** Reading the Prompt

Study the wording of the prompt carefully. Look for clues to help you identify the selections to examine and the basis on which you will examine them.

**Writing Prompt**

One issue important to 19th-century romantic writers—and to some 20th-century writers they inspired—was the relationship between the individual and society. Summarize the romantic **①** view of the individual, supporting your ideas with **②** examples from the works of Thoreau, Whitman, **③** and other writers you read in Unit 3, Part 1.

**STRATEGIES**
IN ACTION

**①** To **summarize** is to reduce something to its most important features.

**②** Notice the **concept** you will examine and summarize.

**③** Include **details** and **quotations** from selections to illustrate each feature of the concept.

**PART 2** Planning a Synthesis Essay

- Create a graphic to record examples.
- Identify lines and passages from romantic writers that relate to your concept—individuality.
- Look for connections among the examples. Determine what three or four features of the concept are suggested by the examples.
- Pull your examples together into a summary statement, or generalization, about the romantic view of the individual.

**Views of the Individual**

| "Civil Disobedience" | "Song of Myself" | | |
|---|---|---|---|
| | | | |
| ↓ | ↓ | ↓ | ↓ |

| **Romantic View of the Individual:** |
|---|
| |

**PART 3** Drafting Your Essay

**Introduction** State your thesis—your main point about the romantic view of the individual. Define "romantic" and name writers in this category.

**Organization** Present your ideas and examples in a logical way. You might begin with the earliest romantic writers and end with contemporary ones. Or you might discuss the idea about individuality shared by most of the writers and then go on to ideas linked only to one writer.

**Conclusion** Restate your main point, and leave the reader with a parting thought about the concept, perhaps about its relevance today.

**Revision** Allow time to review your work. Make sure it is clear, well-supported, and free from mistakes.

**Writing Handbook:** See page 1278: Order of Importance.

**436** UNIT THREE   PART 1: CELEBRATIONS OF THE SELF

---

**Mini Lesson** # Grammar

**PUNCTUATING QUOTATIONS IN A TEXT**

**Instruction** In a sentence, if quoted material is a complete sentence in the original text, or is the second half of a divided quote, then it is also separated by a comma preceding the words. (See examples 2 and 3 below.)

   If the quoted words do not begin with a capital letter and are not divided, then they are usually not preceded by a comma. (See examples 1 and 4 below.)

1. If "imitation is suicide," as Emerson states, then I say individuality is life.

2. "I celebrate myself," Whitman's speaker begins, "and sing myself."

3. The child asks the speaker what grass is, and the speaker thinks, "How could I answer the child?"

4. The speaker muses that grass may be God's "scented gift."

**Activity** Write the above sentences on the chalkboard with capital letters but without quotation marks and preceding commas. Then ask students to rewrite the sentences with proper punctuation.

## My First Summer in the Sierra

JOHN MUIR

In the tradition of the Romantics' reverence toward the natural world, John Muir (1838–1914) describes his experiences as a sheep herder in the Sierra Nevada Mountains. Muir—a famous naturalist, environmentalist, and writer—detailed the breathtaking scenery of this area, which later would become Yosemite National Park. Muir's book also contains several photographs and his own original sketches.

## Pilgrim at Tinker Creek

ANNIE DILLARD

In the same way that Thoreau closely observed Walden Pond, Dillard examines Tinker Creek in Virginia and the creatures that live there. This Pulitzer Prize-winning book is filled with striking descriptions of wildlife and unique insights about the wonders of nature.

## And Even *More* . . .

### Books
**The Enormous Room**
E. E. CUMMINGS
A savage and surrealistic account of Cummings's experiences in a French prisoner-of-war camp during World War I.

**Leaves of Grass**
WALT WHITMAN
Whitman's poetry collection, considered one of the most influential works in American literature.

**The Transcendentalists: An Anthology**
EDITED BY PERRY MILLER
A wide-ranging collection of works by representative writers of this literary movement.

### Other Media
**Voices & Visions: Walt Whitman**
A documentary about the poet, including dramatic readings of his works. Mystic Fire Video. (VIDEOCASSETTE)

**Garrison Keillor's Comedy Theater**
Witty monologues and songs from Keillor's live broadcasts that show his talent for self-expression. St. Paul, MN: High Bridge. (SOUND RECORDING)

**Gandhi**
Academy Award-winning film about India's celebrated leader who used civil disobedience to achieve independence from British rule. Columbia Home Video. (VIDEOCASSETTE)

### The Night Thoreau Spent in Jail

JEROME LAWRENCE AND ROBERT E. LEE

Issues of moral and civic responsibility take center stage in this play dramatizing the risks Thoreau took to follow his conscience. As the curtain rises, Thoreau is behind bars—his punishment for committing an act of civil disobedience. When Ralph Waldo Emerson, the famous transcendentalist, visits him, Thoreau challenges him to defy a government that fosters injustice.

The *Electronic Library* is a CD-ROM that contains additional fiction, nonfiction, poetry, and drama for each unit in The Language of Literature.

These are the additional selections found in Unit 3 of the *Electronic Library* that apply to Part 1.

Henry Wadsworth Longfellow
**The Tide Rises, the Tide Falls**

Washington Irving
**Rip Van Winkle**

William Cullen Bryant
**Thanatopsis**

Ralph Waldo Emerson
**Hymn at Concord Monument**
**Each and All**
**Days**

Henry David Thoreau
**Conclusion, *from* Walden**

Oliver Wendell Holmes
**The Chambered Nautilus**

James Russell Lowell
**Prelude to The Vision of Sir Launfal**

Walt Whitman
**Mannahatta**
**A Noiseless Patient Spider**

E. B. White
**Walden**

Have students choose one of the longer works mentioned to read silently with comprehension over a period of time.

## Objectives
- write a Reflective Essay
- use a written text as a model for writing
- revise a draft to avoid clichés
- form plurals and possessives correctly to insure clarity

## Introducing the Workshop

**A** **Reflective Essay** You might begin by collecting an assortment of columns from newspapers or magazines. Many of these columns are good examples of reflective essays. Like letters, reflective essays focus on the writer's responses to ordinary, everyday events. Students already communicate their experiences and responses through personal letters, e-mail messages, and phone calls.

Through writing a reflective essay, students will be able to share these experiences and their significance in a more formal way—with friends, family, classmates, magazines, or newspapers. In their essays, Thoreau and Emerson glean lessons from their own reflections and experiences. Brainstorm for ideas about the kinds of experiences that can lead to insights or lessons.

**Possible Responses:** The lesson may be quite simple, for example, the importance of getting to school on time or, as in the student model, the value of participating in sports.

### Basics in a Box
**B** **Using the Graphic** Like the ingredients in a milk shake or chemistry experiment, the elements in a reflective essay blend together to create something more than their individual parts. The graphic suggests how students might blend the ingredients of their experience to draft an effective essay.

**C** **Presenting the Rubric** Urge students to read and study the Standards for Writing a Successful Reflective Essay in order to better understand the assignment. Be sure students know that they should use these standards to assess their essays. You may also want to share with them the complete rubric, which describes several levels of proficiency.

---

# *Writing* Workshop — Reflective Essay

## Sharing your experience. . .

**A** **From Reading to Writing** In their essays, Emerson and Thoreau reflect on some basic truths about life that they derived from personal experience. Emerson's words, "Whoso would be a man, must be a nonconformist," still prod us to examine our lives today. Like Emerson and Thoreau, you too have personal experiences from which you learn important lessons. A **reflective essay** describes a personal experience and explores its significance. Autobiographies, letters, and memoirs often include reflective writing that gives insight into the writer's actions.

### For Your Portfolio
**WRITING PROMPT** Write an essay in which you reflect on an experience that taught you an important lesson.

**Purpose:** To share what the experience means to you

**Audience:** Your classmates, friends, or family

### Basics in a Box

**Reflective Essay at a Glance**

**B**

personal experience

thoughts observations connections

lesson learned

**C** **RUBRIC** Standards for Writing

**A successful reflective essay should**
- be written in the first person
- describe an important experience in your life or in the life of someone you admire
- use figurative language, dialogue, sensory details, or other techniques to re-create the experience for the reader
- explain the significance of the event
- make an observation about life based on the experience
- encourage readers to think about the significance of the experience in light of their own lives

---

## LESSON RESOURCES

### USING PRINT RESOURCES
**Unit Three Resource Book**
- Prewriting, p. 37
- Drafting and Elaboration, p. 38
- Peer Response, pp. 39–40
- Revising, Editing, and Proofreading, p. 41
- Student Models, pp. 42–47
- Rubrics, p. 48

### Writing Transparencies and Copymasters
- Writing Process Transparencies, pp. 1–4
- Writing Style Transparencies, p. 13
- Writing Template Copymasters, p. 28

### USING MEDIA RESOURCES
**Visit our website:**
www.mcdougallittell.com

# Analyzing a Student Model

**Stephanie Lauer**
**Bexley High School**

**Eternally Slow**

    <u>I am a slow cross-country runner.</u> Not a slow track runner, thank you very much, because anyone can be a slow track runner. After all, running around an oval twice in shorts split up to the waist can only last around five minutes. I'm talking about cross-country running. Over the river and through the woods. For 3.1 miles, and 3.1 miles isn't over in anything like five minutes, especially for those of us who start out with eight-minute miles and get progressively slower on good days.

    I will never be fast. But fortunately, I have fellow slow runners to keep me company. There is a special bond between us because we are so obviously not running for awards, or record-breaking times, or even to show off our unathletic legs. <u>We run simply because we love to run, and we love to be part of a team.</u> This love is what keeps us going through five-mile practices that we finish after everyone else has gone home, and through races we finish after the clock has been turned off because we got sick but we had to finish, just to finish. This love is what keeps us going when we start up our 6th hill as the guys are coming down their 15th. But we keep going, and <u>every year a few people who always considered themselves eternally slow discover they can charge up those hills just as fast as anyone else.</u>

    <u>Then they become runners with a purpose in addition to love.</u> They still cheer for me and my companions and make jokes about being slow, but they've moved up. They've become someday-varsity runners, the ones coaches look at when they talk about the future. These are the runners who talk about pasta and debate the merits of sports drinks. Exceed and Gatorade become the drinks of choice, replacing the trusty old H$_2$O preferred by the eternally slow. Someday-varsities are concerned with shoes. <u>The trusty Nikes left over from junior high don't have the gel pads or air capsules or heel counters needed when you're improving by leaps and bounds.</u> And times improve minute by minute as each race they push a little harder and find hidden reserves, allowing them to sprint just a little faster, to push up a hill a little stronger.

---

**RUBRIC**
IN ACTION

**❶** Immediately engages reader by making an unexpected statement

**❷** Begins to introduce the theme of the essay

**D**

**❸** Includes strong examples to show how important running is to the writer

**❹** Begins to explain what she learned from her years on the team

**❺** This writer uses precise language and images to describe the experiences of runners.
**Another Option:**
• Use dialogue.

---

 Use McDougal Littell's **Language Network,** Chapter 17, for more instruction on writing a reflective essay.

 To engage students visually, use **Power Presentation** 4, Reflective Essay.

---

## Teaching the Lesson

### Analyzing the Model
**"Eternally Slow"**

**D** The student model recounts the writer's experiences as a cross-country runner, one who is guided by highly personal motivations and standards for success.

    Cross-country courses might include a variety of natural features such as hills, creeks, sand, and uneven ground. Some courses may require runners to run on paved roads. Have students work in small groups to read the model and suggest qualities that cross-country runners might share.

**Possible Response:** Cross-country runners may be likely to be highly independent, enjoy privacy and the outdoors.

    In a larger group, discuss the student writer's humorous tone, especially in the opening paragraphs. Ask students to give an example of humor and suggest its effect on readers.

**Possible Response:** "especially for those of us who start out with eight-minute miles and get progressively slower on good days." Students may appreciate the candor of the writer and identify with her struggle to run for long distances.

    Have students identify the key words and phrases in the student model that correspond to the elements mentioned in the Rubric in Action.

1. The opening statement is unexpected because people don't often begin a personal description by acknowledging their limitations.

2. Note that in a reflective essay, the writer's feelings about the topic are central to effective writing. Readers need to know <u>why</u> this topic matters to the writer.

3. Ask students to name some of the examples the writer uses to show her love of running.
   **Possible Response:** finishing for the satisfaction of doing so, even when the race is over.

4. Here the writer hints at the overall lesson she will later state. Ask students to predict what that lesson might be.
   **Possible Response:** Long distance running offers unexpected benefits.

5. Have students suggest an alternative description based on the option listed.
   **Possible Response:** A group of runners, including someday-varsities, discusses how they progressed from slow runners and what the changes have meant to them.

**6.** Discuss how the writer makes her writing more authentic by acknowledging some of what she's missing as a slow runner.

**7.** Re-emphasize the importance of the writer's personal feelings in a reflective essay.

**8.** Have students compare the first and last sentences in the model. They will note that the writer began from the viewpoint of "I" and ended by including readers in "we." Discuss how this draws readers into the experience.

And eventually, the someday-varsities become varsities. They run to be good. Their races are what count for the team. When I watch them at the start with game faces on and toes to the line, I wonder what it would be like to be fast. I might even daydream about it a little, seeing myself pass one, then two, then three people in my sprint to the finish. But as I've grown older and my friends have become the varsity runners, I've realized that in a way, I'm lucky to be slow. Lucky because the coaches don't yell at me to pass another person when my legs are lead weights, even though I try anyway. Lucky because I don't cry before and/or after every race because I could/did let my team down.

**❻** Continues telling about her experiences as a runner

But don't get me wrong. The good probably does outweigh the bad for fast runners. I'll never know what it's like to cross the finish line with every other runner behind me. I'll never feel the complete exhaustion and euphoria coming after a championship. And I'll never be able to look at my time and think, "Man, am I good!"

But I don't love running any less. And I think I have a clearer perspective than most because I stay in one place as I watch the somedays become todays, and so-called slow runners become somedays. We all understand that running is about being the best. The best you can be with the body you have. Some of my friends, swimmers and basketball players, ask me why I compete if I never get better. <u>I always tell them it's because of the team and because I am accepted for being my best.</u> Slow runners, fast runners, and all the runners in between give unconditional support. <u>And we are all true cross-country runners—some of us just need a little extra time to get where we're going.</u>

**❼** States the lesson learned from the experience

**❽** Ends by making an observation about life based on the experience

First appeared in *Merlyn's Pen*.
Copyright © by Merlyn's Pen, Inc. All rights reserved.

 **Mini Lesson** **Viewing and Representing**

**PICTURING TEXT STRUCTURE**

**Instruction** Choosing an engaging experience to explore and a meaningful lesson to discuss are important parts of a reflective essay. However, organizing and structuring these elements and the details which support them is equally important in generating effective writing.

**Activity** Challenge students to analyze the structure of the student model. Have them create a graphic organizer or other visual representation

of that structure. Point out that the graphic organizer on page 438 suggests the key elements or ingredients of a reflective essay. Students' organizers should focus instead on how the writer of the model organized those elements in her essay. After reading the essay, students might talk with a partner about how each paragraph contributes to the overall effect.

A sample graphic is shown at the right.

# Writing Your Reflective Essay

## ❶ Prewriting

To find ideas for your essay, try listing some memorable experiences and think about why you remember them. You might look through **family photograph** albums to help jog your memory.

Here are some other approaches you may wish to try. Make a list of people who inspire you. What have these people done to earn your admiration? Jot down some notes about an incident from each person's life that shows his or her special qualities. See the **Idea Bank** in the margin for more suggestions. After you have selected your experience, follow the steps below.

### Planning Your Reflective Essay

▶ **1. Think about your experience.** Why do you remember this experience more clearly than others? What different emotions did you go through during the experience? Did your emotions change?

▶ **2. Explore the significance.** What is the significance of your experience? What is the most obvious meaning to you? What else did your experience teach you? Keep exploring to uncover as many levels of meaning as you can.

▶ **3. Decide on the scope of your essay.** Will you dwell on one example in depth or relate several events to create the impression you want?

▶ **4. Decide on the message you want to convey.** How can you encourage your readers to apply the meaning of the experience to their own lives?

## ❷ Drafting

> *A writer's material is what he cares about.*
> **John Gardner**

### Begin Writing

You might write about your experience as though you were writing a journal entry. Or, you may want to begin your draft by trying out a variety of ideas. Either way, keep writing and let your ideas flow even though you sense problems you'll need to address later.

### Organize Your Essay

You might start your paper with an account of your experience and then explain its significance. From that point, go on to discuss the larger lesson about life that the experience has taught you.

Or, you might begin with the larger lesson you want to share with your readers and then go on to describe the experience that helped you learn this lesson.

**IDEA**Bank

**1. Your Working Portfolio** 📁
Look for ideas in the **Writing Options** you completed earlier in this unit:

- **Personal Repsonse,** p. 348
- **Reflective Essay on Wealth,** p. 361
- **Personal Essay,** p. 368
- **Autobiographical Sketch or Poem,** p. 422

**2. Brainstorming Maxims**
Think about some of the maxims or lessons you learned about life. How did you learn each lesson? Choose one as the subject of your essay.

**3. Fables and Proverbs**
In a small group, think of all the proverbs and all the fable morals that you can. Discuss how the lessons taught by each might apply to your own experiences.

**Writer's Choice**

Will your essay focus on telling about the experience in detail, or will you briefly describe the experience and spend most of your essay reflecting upon its significance?

## Prewriting

### Choosing a Subject

If after reading the Idea Bank students are having difficulty choosing their subjects, suggest they try the following:

- Look at recent newspaper columns. What kinds of experiences are discussed? What lessons are shared? Why is a particular column engaging or dull?
- Flip through calendars or date books from recent years. Note memorable events.
- Study scrapbooks or collections of memorabilia.
- Talk with family and friends. Invite their recollections of challenging moments from the recent past.

📁 For more ideas, use the Writing Springboards in the LaserLinks.

### Planning the Reflective Essay

1. Have students work independently to list their initial ideas.
2. Suggest that auditory learners imagine they are recounting the experience for a friend.
3. Discuss the challenges of relating several events in a single essay. Clarify the expected length of the essay as well.
4. Have students write out 3-4 possible messages they feel arise from their experience. They can review these to determine which might be most engaging and relevant to readers.

## Drafting

### Organizing the Draft

The student model represents one approach to writing a reflective essay. Suggest that students begin their own writing by outlining their draft or creating a graphic organizer to visually represent their ideas. Emphasize that there is no one "right" choice.

introduce topic → link topic to theme of essay → introduce theme (lesson) formally → provide details and examples to support learning the lesson → acknowledge the complexity of the lesson and the experiences leading to it → state the lesson and present thought-provoking observation to close

## Elaborate on Ideas

Provide students with a thesaurus or computer word search tool in order to expand their options for precise, vivid language and details.

## Revising

### AVOIDING CLICHÉS

Explain that the change shown in the student model excerpt paints a much more specific image for readers, thus grabbing and holding their interest. To give students practice in avoiding clichés, invite pairs or groups to first brainstorm and then share with the class some examples of clichés. Write a selection of these on the board. Ask students to reword each posted example with more specific language in order to create an engaging and vivid description. Discuss how the revised descriptions compare in impact with the clichés.

## Editing and Proofreading

### POSSESSIVES AND PLURALS

Remind students that when they form possessives and plurals incorrectly, the result is confusion for readers. You might review the difference between common possessive pronouns (your, their) and contractions (you're, they're).

## Reflecting

 As students reflect on their writing efforts, urge them to recognize and evaluate their approaches to the assignment. For example, what was most—and least— useful about peer contributions? Have students add these self-evaluations to their working portfolios.

---

## Elaborate on Ideas

Precise, vivid language will help you convey the lesson about life you want to explain. Stephanie Lauer uses precise details about sports drinks and shoes and about coaches and daydreams to add spice to her essay.

After you write a rough draft of your whole essay, set it aside for a while before you go back to revise it. Taking a fresh look will help you see problems that you may have overlooked.

**Need revising help?**

Review the **Rubric**, p. 438.

Consider **peer reader** comments.

Check **Revising, Editing, and Proofreading**, p. 1269.

**Perplexed by possessives?**

See the **Grammar Handbook**, p. 1306.

### Publishing IDEAS

- Begin a collection of essays about your experiences in order to understand your feelings and give others insight into who you are.

- Submit the essay to your school newspaper or magazine.

**More Online: Publishing Options**
www.mcdougallittell.com

> **Ask Your Peer Reader**
>
> - How would you describe the main point of my essay?
> - Why is this experience important to me?
> - How does this experience relate to something you have thought about?
> - Is any part confusing? Which part?
> - If your interest lagged at some point, what could I do to make that part more interesting?

### ❸ Revising

**TARGET SKILL ▶ AVOIDING CLICHÉS** You have worked to use vivid language in your reflective essay. Now make sure that none of your images are clichés, expressions that were once fresh and powerful but have since been worn out through overuse.

> *talk about pasta and debate*
> *the merits of sports drinks.*
> These are the runners who ~~begin to think they know it all.~~
> ^

### ❹ Editing and Proofreading

**TARGET SKILL ▶ POSSESSIVES AND PLURALS** As you revise your reflective essay, be sure that you have formed plurals and possessives correctly. To form the possessive of a plural noun that ends in -s, add an apostrophe only. To form the possessive of a plural noun that does not end in -s, add both an apostrophe and an -s.

> They still cheer for our crowds turtle brigade and make jokes
> *their*
> about ~~they're~~ own slowness, but they've moved up. They've
> become someday-varsity runners, the ones in the coaches'
> plans for the future.

### ❺ Reflecting

**FOR YOUR WORKING PORTFOLIO** How did writing this essay influence your thinking about your experience? What went well as you were writing this piece? What problems did you encounter? Attach your answer to your finished work. Save your essay in your **Working Portfolio.**

**442** UNIT THREE   PART 1: CELEBRATIONS OF THE SELF

---

## Option

### Managing the Paper Load

For your first review, choose a narrow portion of the essays to address. For example, you might look only at opening or closing paragraphs. Select a classwide focus or let students choose one individually.

## Assessment Practice Revising & Editing

Read this paragraph from the first draft of a reflective essay. The underlined sections may include the following kinds of errors:

- **capitalization errors**
- **incorrect possessive forms**
- **incorrect plural forms**
- **verb tense errors**

For each underlined section, choose the revision that most improves the writing.

> It was after midnight when I <u>hear</u> Mr. Pinsky, my neighbor, start to play his
> <sub>(1)</sub>
> saxophone. After a few sweet saxophone cries, I recognized the tune of <u>"mood</u>
> <u>indigo."</u> This is my favorite of Duke Ellington's <u>melodies.</u> The familiar strains
> <sub>(2)</sub> <sub>(3)</sub>
> made me <u>forgot</u> my worries, and I fell asleep listening to the sad, lingering
> <sub>(4)</sub>
> tones. When I bumped into Mr. Pinsky the next day, I couldn't help myself. I
> raved about his playing and <u>had told</u> him I thought he was amazing. Then it
> <sub>(5)</sub>
> was <u>Mr. Pinskys</u> turn to amaze me: he offered to give me saxophone lessons!
> <sub>(6)</sub>

1. **A.** heared
   **B.** was hearing
   **C.** heard
   **D.** Correct as is

2. **A.** "Mood indigo"
   **B.** "Mood Indigo"
   **C.** "mood Indigo"
   **D.** Correct as is

3. **A.** melody
   **B.** melodyes
   **C.** melodys
   **D.** Correct as is

4. **A.** forgetting
   **B.** forget
   **C.** forgotten
   **D.** Correct as is

5. **A.** told
   **B.** was telling
   **C.** has told
   **D.** Correct as is

6. **A.** Mr. Pinskies
   **B.** Mr. Pinskys'
   **C.** Mr. Pinsky's
   **D.** Correct as is

### Assessment Practice

Using the first question as a model, guide students in evaluating the answer choices and choosing the correct response.

**A.** The first choice is misspelled, therefore it can't be correct.

**B.** This option incorrectly combines the verb "to hear" with the helping verb "was."

**C.** This choice correctly matches the tense of the verb "to hear" with that of "was" at the beginning of the sentence.

**D.** This verb is not in the same tense as the rest of the sentence.

**Need extra help?**

See the **Grammar Handbook**

Capitalization Chart, p. 1329

Possessive Nouns, p. 1306

Verb Tense, pp. 1310–1311

## Building Vocabulary

### Objectives

- research word origins as an aid to understanding meanings, derivations, and spellings
- apply meanings of word roots and affixes to determine the meanings of related words
- understand how to use word parts and word families to build vocabulary

### EXERCISE

1. *form.* **Possible Responses:** *formative* refers to something that shapes or molds; *formal* implies that a thing is taking a certain shape or following guidelines as to appearance.

2. *vid, vis.* **Possible Responses:** *visage* means "appearance"; *visionary* refers to one who has visions of what might be.

3. *anima.* **Possible Responses:** An *animator* is one who brings drawings to life; *animato* means "to sing or play music in a lively manner."

4. *div.* **Possible Responses:** *Division* refers to separating into parts; *divorce* means "to sever relationship with."

5. *phon.* **Possible Responses:** A *megaphone* is an instrument that makes a sound bigger; a *phonograph* reproduces sound from a recording.

## Enriching Your Vocabulary

Many modern English words you use daily are based on languages such as Latin and Greek that are thousands of years old. For example, look at the word *consistency* in the quotation to the right.

*Consistency*, which in this case refers to a steadfastness of thought over time, comes from the Latin root *sist*, meaning "to take a stand." A **root** is the core word part, to which other word parts can be added to create new words. Notice how the idea of

> A foolish consistency is the hobgoblin of little minds, adored by little statesmen and philosophers and divines.
> —Ralph Waldo Emerson, "Self-Reliance"

"taking a stand" or never veering from a particular path or vision is at the core of this meaning of *consistency*.

### Strategies for Building Vocabulary

Learning how to break up a word into its parts and recognizing the meanings of roots can help you enrich your vocabulary.

**❶ Break Up a Word into Parts** All complex words are ultimately built on roots. Prefixes (like *con-, de-, in-, un-*), and suffixes (such as *-ent, -en, -gy, -tion*) may also be added to a root to form new words. For example, the word *nonconformist* is made up of several word parts:

| Prefixes | Root | Suffix |
|---|---|---|
| non- + con- | + form | + -ist |
| (not)  (same) | (shape) | (person who believes in or does a certain thing) |

So, the literal meaning of *nonconformist* is "not-same-shape-person." At first this might look silly, but a closer look shows that a nonconformist is, indeed, someone whose behavior does not "fit in" with the accepted or popular look, custom, or way of thinking. Knowing the meaning of a word's root can often help you determine the meaning of the word.

**❷ Build Word Families** Words that derive from the same roots are known as a **word family.** It is useful to know that the meanings of words in a family are also related to the meaning of the root. For instance, using the information about the root of *nonconformist* in Strategy 1, what can you tell about the meaning of the words below?

uniform, deform, cuneiform, format, formulate

If you guessed that all five words derive from the Latin root *form* and that their meanings all have to do with "shape," you were right! The more roots

you know, the better you will be at deciphering unfamiliar words. Study the charts on this page to learn more about Greek and Latin roots.

| Greek Root | Meaning | Word Family |
|---|---|---|
| crat | power, strength | autocrat, bureaucrat |
| phil, philo | having a preference for, loving | philanthropic, philharmonic |
| phon | sound | phonetics, telephone |
| phys | nature | physics, physique |
| poli, polis | city | politics, politician, police |
| therm | heat | thermometer, thermal |

| Latin Root | Meaning | Word Family |
|---|---|---|
| anim | life, spirit, soul | animated, animosity |
| dict | say, speak | contradict, edict |
| domin | master | dominion, predominate |
| div | divide | dividend, indivisible |
| (s)pend, pens, pond | hang, weight | pendant, pensive, suspend, appendage |
| sent, sens | feel | sentiment, sensibility |
| vid, vis | see | evident, providence, visual |

**EXERCISE** Identify the common root for each word pair below. Then explain how the meaning of the root relates to the meaning of each word in the pair.

1. formative – formal
2. visage – visionary
3. animator – animato
4. division – divorce
5. megaphone – phonograph

## Grammar from Literature

Writers use adjectives in both prose and poetry for a variety of reasons.

- To make description more accurate and specific.
- To make writing more colorful and interesting.
- To describe and create characters and settings.

Notice how the adjectives in the following passage add detail and precision while creating a powerful image.

> There a perennial waveless serenity reigns as in the amber twilight sky, corresponding to the cool and even temperament of the inhabitants.
> —Henry David Thoreau, *Walden*

Phrases can also be used as adjectives. In the first example below, a prepositional phrase modifies the noun *waste*. In the second example, *at anguish* modifies *men*.

> I did not for a moment feel confined, and the walls
> *prepositional phrase*
> seemed a great waste of stone and mortar.
> —Thoreau, "Civil Disobedience"
> *prepositional phrases*
> I hear secret convulsive sobs from young men at anguish with themselves.
> —Walt Whitman, "I Sit and Look Out"

Adjectives also take the form of participles and participial phrases. You may recall that a participle is an *-ing* or *-ed* verb form used as an adjective. In the first example at the top of the next column, the participial phrase and the single-word participles modify *mother*. In the second example, the participial phrase modifies the pronoun *I*:

> *participial phrase*
> I see in low life the mother misused by her children,
> *single-word participles*
> dying, neglected, gaunt, desperate.
> —Whitman, "I Sit and Look Out"
> *participial phrase*
> Standing on the snow-covered plain, as if in a pasture amid the hills, I cut my way first through a foot of snow, and then a foot of ice.
> —Thoreau, *Walden*

**Using Adjectives in Your Writing** Look for opportunities in your writing to add precision by adding detail. Which modifiers will make the picture clearer for your reader? Which ones will make people and places more vivid and believable?

> Imagine a meadow of spring green and a glassy pond in the fading sunlight. The unbroken stillness gives way to the insistent call of a lovesick bullfrog.

**Usage Tip** To avoid confusion, place an adjective phrase close to the noun it modifies.

> CONFUSING
> Acting bravely, Whitman was inspired by Lincoln.
> CLEAR
> Acting bravely, Lincoln inspired Whitman.

**Punctuation Tip** Use a comma after an introductory adjective phrase if there is a chance of misreading.

> CONFUSING
> Written near a pond *Walden* is a famous book.
> CLEAR
> Written near a pond, *Walden* is a famous book.

**WRITING EXERCISE** Rewrite each sentence, adding an adjective or adjective phrase that modifies the underlined word. Use participle forms twice.

1. <u>Writers</u> such as Thoreau stress the importance of individual responsibility.
2. Thoreau describes how <u>people</u> make all of the government's decisions.
3. Sometimes <u>people</u> march off to war because they do not question the laws.
4. Thoreau's <u>book</u> has been an inspiration for many.
5. Thoreau got drinking water by chopping through the <u>ice</u>.

**GRAMMAR EXERCISE** Rewrite the following sentences, correcting any errors in usage.

1. Traveling across America, ordinary people inspired Walt Whitman.
2. Singing in the mill workers make their spirit heard.
3. Thoreau showed his opposition to government in a jail cell in Massachusetts.
4. Read by students throughout the world "I Hear America Singing" is a powerful expression of democracy.
5. Wishing not to get bogged down in the details of life, Walden was the answer for Thoreau.

## Sentence Crafting

### Objectives

- use adjectives in prose and poetry to add detail and precision to writing
- recognize how prepositional phrases, participles, and participial phrases can be used as adjectives
- revise drafts by using adjectives to make the writing clearer and more vivid
- practice proper placement of adjective phrases
- punctuate with commas after introductory adjective phrases

### WRITING EXERCISE

Answers will vary. Possible Responses are given.

1. <u>Concerned</u> writers such as Thoreau stress individual responsibility.
2. Thoreau describes how <u>few</u> people make all of the government's decisions.
3. Sometimes people, <u>acting like machines</u>, march off to war because they do not question the laws.
4. Thoreau's book <u>detailing his life at Walden Pond</u> has been an inspiration for many.
5. He got drinking water by chopping through the ice <u>on the frozen pond</u>.

### GRAMMAR EXERCISE

Answers for items 1 and 5 will vary. Possible Responses are given.

1. Traveling across America, Walt <u>Whitman gained inspiration from ordinary people</u>.
2. Singing in the <u>mill, workers</u> make their spirit heard.
3. <u>In a jail cell in Massachusetts,</u> Thoreau showed his opposition to government.
4. Read by students <u>worldwide, "I Hear America Singing"</u> is a powerful expression of democracy.
5. Wishing not to get bogged down in the details of life, <u>Thoreau found his answer at Walden</u>.

## OVERVIEW

### Introduction

This article places the selections in Part 2 of this unit in historical context by introducing students to the late 18th- and 19th-century Gothic tradition and its revival in the 20th century. The brief selections and quotations in **Voices from the Times** evoke the atmosphere of the Gothic literary tradition and help students understand the possible influences of historical contexts on literary works.

## Teaching Nonfiction

### Reading Skills and Strategies
### ESTABLISHING A PURPOSE FOR READING

Explain to students that this article introduces them to the Gothic literary tradition in America. Students are expected to read to understand the relationship between romanticism and the Gothic and to learn about the elements of Gothic literature.

### IDENTIFYING MAIN IDEAS AND SUMMARIZING

Point out to students that each paragraph in the article contains a main idea. Have students read the article one paragraph at a time, summarizing each main idea and the development of this idea through details.

### ANALYZING TEXT STRUCTURE

Ask students to analyze the text structure of this article. Ask them to note how the author has organized the information in the article and to determine how this influenced their understanding of the material.

# The Dark Side of Individualism

## American Gothic

**S**et in an ancient castle where strange and terrifying events take place, Horace Walpole's *The Castle of Otranto* (1765) spawned the Gothic tradition in English fiction. Eighteenth-century readers fell in love with the novel's weird setting and macabre plot, and over the next century, Gothic novels of varying literary quality poured from the presses. In them, some of the greatest creatures of all time were born—including the repulsive monster created from human body parts in Mary Shelley's *Frankenstein* (1818) and the dangerously attractive count in Bram Stoker's *Dracula* (1897). Today, Anne Rice's sexy vampire Lestat owes his immortal life to the Gothic tradition.

The spirit and imagery of the Gothic literary tradition came in part from the Gothic architecture of the Middle Ages. Cavernous Gothic cathedrals with their irregularly placed towers and their high stained-glass windows were intended to inspire awe and fear in religious worshipers. Gargoyles—those carvings of small deformed creatures squatting at the corners and crevices of Gothic cathedrals—were supposed to ward off evil spirits, but they often looked more like demonic spirits themselves. Think of a gargoyle—a grotesque creature—as the mascot of Gothic, and you will get a good idea of the kind of imaginative distortion of reality that Gothic represents.

Another force that gave rise to Gothic literature was the romantic movement. As you have already learned, romanticism developed as a reaction against the rationalism of the Age of Reason. Once the romantics freed the imagination from the lordship of reason, they could follow the imagination wherever it might lead them. For some romantic writers, the imagination led to the threshold of the unknown— that shadowy region where the fantastic, the demonic, and the insane reside. This is Gothic territory. Because of this perspective, the Gothic tradition can be called the dark side of individualism. When romantics looked at the individual, they saw hope (think of Longfellow's "A Psalm of Life"); but when Gothic

Gargoyles on the Cathedral of Notre Dame, Paris. Copyright © Van Phillips/Leo de Wys, Inc.

446

Bodiam Castle in East Sussex, England. Copyright © Penny Tweedie/Tony Stone Images.

writers looked at the individual, they saw potential evil (think of anything you've ever read by Edgar Allan Poe). While romantic writers were extolling the beauties of nature, the Gothic writers were peering into the darkness at the supernatural.

The Gothic tradition was firmly established in Europe before American writers had made names for themselves. By the 19th century, however, Edgar Allan Poe and Nathaniel Hawthorne, and to a lesser extent Washington Irving and Herman Melville, were using Gothic elements in their fiction.

Edgar Allan Poe, of course, was the master of the Gothic form in the United States. In many of his stories, dark medieval castles or decaying ancient estates provide the setting for weird and terrifying events. Many of Poe's male narrators are insane; his female characters, beautiful and dead (or dying). His plots involve extreme situations— not just murder, but live burials, physical and mental torture, and retribution from beyond the grave. For Poe, it was only in such extreme situations that people revealed their true natures. The Gothic dimension of his fictional world offered him a way to explore the human mind in these extreme situations and so arrive at an essential truth.

Hawthorne also used Gothic elements in his fiction to express what he felt were important truths. However, instead of looking at the mind and its functions (or dysfunctions) as Poe did, Hawthorne examined the human heart under various conditions of fear, greed, vanity, mistrust, and betrayal.

The door opened, and a figure glided in. The portmanteau dropped from my arms, and my heart's-blood was chilled. If an apparition of the dead were possible, and that possibility I could not deny, this was such an apparition. A hue, yellowish and livid; bones, uncovered with flesh; eyes, ghastly, hollow, woe-begone, and fixed in an agony of wonder upon me; and locks, matted and negligent, constituted the image which I now beheld.

**Charles Brockden Brown**
from *Arthur Mervyn*

Imagination is the queen of darkness; night the season of her despotism.

**James Kirke Paulding**
from *Westward Ho!*

The death . . . of a beautiful woman is, unquestionably, the most poetical topic in the world—and equally is it beyond doubt that the lips best suited for such topic are those of a bereaved lover.

**Edgar Allan Poe**
from "The Philosophy of Composition"

HISTORICAL BACKGROUND **447**

## Making Connections

### Literature
**A** The plethora of movies made about Frankenstein's monster illustrates the extent to which the Gothic tradition appeals to the popular imagination. The first Frankenstein film was produced by Thomas Edison in 1910. The classic Hollywood *Frankenstein* was released in 1931 and was followed by dozens of variations. Movies about vampires became popular again in the 1990s.

### Architecture
**B** The first association most people make with the word *Gothic* is probably Gothic cathedrals, such as Chartres and Notre Dame, but in 19th-century America, the Gothic style was seen in private homes as well. A. J. Downing, best known for designing the grounds of the White House and U.S. Capitol, popularized wooden Gothic cottages, which replaced the ordinary American house of the first quarter of the 19th century. Downing added pointed arches for doors and windows, steep roofs, picturesque irregularities, and other medieval trappings. One such house may be seen in the background of the famous 1930 Grant Wood painting *American Gothic*.

### Art
**C** American painters also extolled the beauties of nature, most notably the Hudson River School, which flourished from 1825 to 1870. Thomas Cole (1801–1848), its acknowledged leader, urged his followers to paint the wilderness in a passionate manner, the antithesis of the simplicity and unity emphasized by classicists.

### Literature
**D** In many ways, the truths regarding the human mind that Poe explored anticipated the work of great thinkers in psychology, such as Sigmund Freud. For example, Poe's "spirit of perverseness" (see "The Black Cat"), which he saw as a primitive inner impulse, is similar to Freud's death instinct. A chief reason for Poe's reputation is his concentration on the darker side of the human mind.

### History
**E** Hawthorne himself was certainly no Puritan, but one of his ancestors was a presiding judge at the Salem witch trials. Much of Hawthorne's writing reveals an obsession with his ancestors' sins, and many of his stories and novels may be viewed as attempts to atone for them.

### OUTLINING

Encourage students to use study strategies to better understand text. Ask them to outline the article as a study strategy. Remind them that the outline should contain the salient points of the essay.

### DISCUSSING

Because of the subject matter of the article, students will want to actively discuss it in class. Allow them to ask questions. As a starting point, ask the students to draw upon their own experiences with Gothic elements in movies, books, or computer games to provide a connection to the texts.

### EVALUATING

Ask student what elements of the Gothic literary tradition are contained in these passages.

**Possible Responses:** Brown and Hawthorne discuss the appearance of ghosts or apparitions from beyond the grave, a classic Gothic element; both Paulding and Hawthorne agree that the imagination flourishes at night; Brown, Hawthorne, and Lovecraft allude to fear; Brown, Poe, and Lovecraft all refer to death, the ultimate preoccupation of the Gothic novel.

### LaserLinks
### Historical Literary Connection: The Dark Side of Individualism

One offspring of the romantic movement was the Gothic movement, made up of writers who emphasized the fantastic and even the demonic. These portraits of great Gothic authors and of illustrations in the Gothic vein will familiarize students with the leaders of this movement and with the eerie style to which they aspired.

See Teacher's SourceBook p. 6 for bar codes.

---

## Voices from the Times

Moonlight, in a familiar room, falling so white upon the carpet, and showing all its figures so distinctly—making every object so minutely visible, yet so unlike a morning or noontide visibility— . . . [has created] a neutral territory, somewhere between the real world and fairyland, where the Actual and the Imaginary may meet, and each imbue itself with the nature of the other. Ghosts might enter here, without affrighting us.

**Nathaniel Hawthorne**
from *The Scarlet Letter*

The oldest and strongest emotion of mankind is fear, and the oldest and strongest kind of fear is fear of the unknown.

**H. P. Lovecraft**
from *Supernatural Horror in Literature*

---

## Traditions Across Time: Southern Gothic

After the real horrors of the Civil War, the popularity of Gothic writing waned in the United States. Realism replaced romanticism as the preferred American literary style. The Gothic spirit had to wait until the 20th century before it again found fertile ground for its particular brand of truth telling. That ground was the American South.

Modern Southern writers as diverse as William Faulkner, Carson McCullers, Truman Capote, and Flannery O'Connor are sometimes grouped together in the category of Southern Gothic because of the gloom and pessimism of their fiction. For William Faulkner, the crumbling medieval castle of 19th-century Gothic fiction became the decaying plantation, with its fallen aristocratic family isolated in time and place. Instead of ghostly figures stalking noble heroines, Faulkner gave us the ghost of the past hounding his not-so-noble characters to madness and death.

Coming after Faulkner, Flannery O'Connor saw the pressures of modern life making grotesques of us all. Like Hawthorne, O'Connor was interested in the human heart and its potential for evil. In her view, the old moral and religious order was crumbling. Criminals, con men, and fools—rather than ghosts and goblins—were unleashed upon the world.

Although this part of Unit Three focuses on the Gothic, you can see Gothic aspects in the work of writers in other units, such as Ambrose Bierce in Unit Four, Charlotte Perkins Gilman in Unit Five, and Sylvia Plath in Unit Six. Try identifying what's Gothic about the next horror movie you see or the next Stephen King or Anne Rice novel you read.

## American Gothic

### Objectives
- appreciate the craft of one of America's most renowned and influential writers
- interpret the possible influences of personal events in Poe's life on his literary works
- gain information on Poe's impact on the genres of poetry, short fiction, and the detective story

This Author Study offers a unique opportunity for students to focus on the work of a major writer. In addition, students can gather information about the life of Poe, gaining insight into the real person behind his famous poems and stories.

### Preview
#### Using Text Organizers
Have students preview the article noting the basic text organizers: title, subheads, images, captions, and time line. Ask students to describe the information they would expect to find in each section. Have students use the subheads to make an outline or graphic organizer. As they read, have them categorize information under the appropriate heading. Remind them to use text organizers to locate and categorize information as they do independent research.

---

**Author Study**

# EDGAR ALLAN POE

*"What a strange, though enormously talented writer, that Edgar Poe!"*

—Feodor Dostoyevsky

*Edgar A Poe*

**HIS LIFE**
**HIS TIMES**

## A Talented, Tormented Writer

*During a life marked by pain and loss, Edgar Allan Poe wrote haunting tales in which he explored the dark side of the human mind. A well-read man with a taste for literature, Poe was cursed with a morbidly sensitive nature and made his feelings of sadness and depression the basis of a distinctive body of literary work. Through this Author Study, you will explore the life and work of a mysterious American master.*

1809–1849

**"AMBITIOUS TO EXCEL"** Edgar Allan Poe was born in Boston, Massachusetts, in 1809, one of three children of a couple who toured the East as actors. Before he reached the age of three, however, his father abandoned the family and his mother died of tuberculosis.

John and Frances Allan, a well-to-do merchant and his wife who were both theater fans, took Poe into their Richmond, Virginia, home and became his foster parents. In 1815 the Allans moved to England. Poe's stay in England lasted only

| 1809 Is born in Boston on January 19 | 1811 Death of mother; taken in by the Allans |  Elizabeth Arnold Poe, mother | 1820 Returns from a five-year stay in England |
|---|---|---|---|

**1810**          **1815**          **1820**

| 1812 U.S. declares war on Great Britain. | 1819 Washington Irving publishes "Rip Van Winkle." |
|---|---|

450

five years. Mrs. Allan's ill health and the failure of the London branch of her husband's business forced the family to return to Richmond.

Poe continued his education in the United States, showing a flair for languages, particularly Latin and French. Schoolmates noted that he was "ambitious to excel." He started writing poems and by the time he was 16 had enough to fill a book.

**A Restless Spirit** In Poe's young adulthood, the pattern of his life became established: periods of personal difficulty would alternate with promises of a fresh start. In 1826 he began attending the University of Virginia, where his reckless spending habits led to heavy debts. Poe was forced to leave the school. He fled to Boston, attracted by the city's literary activity, and it was there that the anonymous *Tamerlane and Other Poems*, his first book, was published in 1827. Flat broke, the 18-year-old Poe enlisted in the army, but he continued to read widely and to experiment with poetry.

When Frances Allan died in 1829, the grief-stricken John Allan arranged for Poe's release from the army and secured him a place as a cadet in the U.S. Military Academy at West Point. Poe, however, found life at the academy confining and still had his eye on a writing career. By deliberately misbehaving, he managed to get himself expelled.

---

## LITERARY *Contributions*

Best known as a literary critic during his lifetime, today Poe is renowned for his poems and stories in the Gothic tradition (which is discussed in detail on pages 446–448).

**Poetic Pioneer** Poe regarded his poems as his greatest works. He believed that poetry should be musical, be expressive of beauty, and be composed logically. The following poems reflect Poe's strong views:

"The Raven" (1845)
"For Annie" (1849)
"Annabel Lee" (1849)

**Founder of the Short Story** Prior to Poe's time, short fiction consisted primarily of loose, rambling tales. It was Poe who insisted that a story or poem should create a single effect, containing no details or incidents that do not contribute to the effect—an idea that would have an enormous influence on subsequent writers. Among the stories in which he put his theory into practice are

"The Pit and the Pendulum" (1842)
"The Tell-Tale Heart" (1843)
"The Cask of Amontillado" (1846)

**Originator of the Detective Story** With the publication of "The Murders in the Rue Morgue" in 1841, Poe gave birth to a new genre: the detective story. His hero, who solves crimes solely by means of logic, has been the model for scores of later fictional detectives.

---

## LIFE AND TIMES

### Literature

**A** This observation of Poe is ironic, for it could be applied equally as well to Dostoyevsky. Dostoyevsky's fiction is humorless, mainly concerned with the psychology and dark complexity of the human soul. Of Poe's writing, Dostoyevsky further remarked that whatever seems fantastic and impossible is "presented to you so clearly that in the end you are apparently convinced of its possibility, though that event is . . . completely impossible. . . ."

### History

**B** Edgar Poe was never formally adopted by the Allans, and he kept his birth name throughout his life. Yet, he did recognize their importance to his life by taking their family name for his middle name.

### Literature

**C** Poe published this first collection under the anonymous "By a Bostonian." The title poem concerns Tamerlane, a 14th-century Mongolian conqueror, known also as Timur the Lame, who rose from modest origins to conquer much of Russia, Persia, India, and central Asia. The poem establishes the tone and subject matter for much of Poe's poetry to come: melancholy and the obsession with beauty and the tragedy of its loss (a dying Tamerlane returns home to find his beautiful childhood sweetheart already dead)

---

| 1825 A large inheritance restores John Allan's wealth. | 1826 Briefly attends the University of Virginia | 1827 Publishes *Tamerlane and Other Poems* | 1829 Frances Allan dies. | 1830 Enters West Point | 1831 Expelled from West Point; publishes *Poems* |

**1825**    **1830**

| 1821 Charles Baudelaire is born in France. | 1825 Erie Canal opens. | 1826 Thomas Jefferson and John Adams die on July 4. | 1828 Andrew Jackson is elected president. | 1830 Emily Dickinson is born. |

Charles Baudelaire

## Literature

**A** Poe described his own writing habits as "excessively slothful, and wonderfully industrious—by fits." Other accounts, however, describe Poe as a "fluent" and "driven" writer who, no matter the hour of night or day, could always be found at work. Poe's best works benefited from revision, resulting in finely polished manuscripts written in an unusual form: on half sheets of paper, pasted together at the ends to make one continuous sheet.

## Biography

**B** Maria Clemm was the sister of Edgar's father, and her daughter, Virginia, Poe's first cousin, was 13 at the time of their marriage. There is speculation that the couple was actually married in secret months earlier in Richmond. Poe frequently had to misrepresent her age, and their marriage certificate claims Virginia to be "of the full age of twenty-one years."

## Detective Fiction

**C** In "The Murders in the Rue Morgue" Poe introduced the first amateur detective, C. Auguste Dupin. By using his own skills of logic and analysis, Dupin leads the police to the solution of the crime. Poe called these types of stories "tales of ratiocination."

## Health

**D** In 1844 Edgar and Virginia moved to New York, but poverty and ill-health remained their constant companions. On December 15, 1846, a New York newspaper ran this paragraph under the headline "Illness of Edgar A. Poe":

> We regret to learn that this gentleman and his wife are both dangerously ill with the consumption, and that the hand of misfortune lies heavy upon their temporal affairs.

**A MAN OF LETTERS** Poe now began to embark on a literary career in earnest. In 1831, shortly after leaving West Point, he published *Poems,* then moved to Baltimore to live with his aunt Maria Clemm and her young daughter Virginia. There, he began writing **A** short stories, and in 1833 one of these, "MS. Found in a Bottle," won him a sorely needed $50 prize in a literary contest.

In 1834 John Allan died, leaving nothing to his foster son. The next year, Poe moved to Richmond to work for a periodical, the *Southern Literary Messenger.* The popularity of his book reviews in the *Messenger* led to a great increase in the magazine's circulation. In **C** May 1836, now editor of the *Messenger,* Poe **B** married his cousin Virginia; but before eight months had passed, a dispute with the magazine's publisher led him to resign his editorship and move his household to New York City. There, he published the short novel *The Narrative of Arthur Gordon Pym* before deciding to move again in search of work, this time to Philadelphia.

Poe's years in Philadelphia, though not without conflict, would be his most productive. In 1839, he became an editor of *Burton's* **D** *Gentleman's Magazine,* to which he contributed

both stories and reviews. The end of that year also saw the publication of the first collection of his short stories, called *Tales of the Grotesque and Arabesque.* Once again, Poe found himself at odds with his publisher, and he was fired from *Burton's* in mid-1840. In 1841, having failed in an attempt to start his own literary magazine, he accepted a job as editor of *Graham's Magazine,* for which he wrote the ground-breaking detective story "The Murders in the Rue Morgue."

**TROUBLES DILUTE SUCCESS** Poe's fame increased when a Philadelphia newspaper awarded him a $100 prize for "The Gold Bug" in 1843; and "The Raven," published in 1845, was an enormous success, bringing him the recognition as a poet he had long desired. But personal difficulties continued to dog Poe. Then, in early 1847, he was hit with a major blow: Virginia, who had been in poor health since 1842, died.

This is Poe's suggested design for the cover of *The Stylus,* his short-lived magazine.

| 1834 | 1835 | 1836 | | 1839 |
|---|---|---|---|---|
| Death of John Allan | Becomes editor of the *Southern Literary Messenger* | Marries Virginia Clemm | Virginia Clemm | Becomes an editor of *Burton's Gentleman's Magazine;* publishes *Tales of the Grotesque and Arabesque* |

**1835**     **1840**

| 1833 | 1836 | 1837 | 1838 | 1839 |
|---|---|---|---|---|
| Charles Dickens's first works are published in Britain. | Alamo falls; Texas becomes a republic. | Nathaniel Hawthorne publishes first series of *Twice-Told Tales.* | Cherokee driven west along the "Trail of Tears." | Daguerreotype (an early type of photograph) is invented. |

In the years following Virginia's death, Poe struggled with despair as well as with his own deteriorating health. In 1849 he became engaged to Elmira Royster Shelton, a widow who had been his boyhood sweetheart. Late that year, he left Richmond for Baltimore, where his health declined quickly. He collapsed on a Baltimore street and was taken to a hospital, where he died a few days later.

**POE'S REPUTATION** Poe's work generated |  strong responses: critics either loved him or hated him. Shortly after his death, a one-time friend published a biography that included harsh attacks on Poe's personal life. This work established the view of Poe as a gifted but socially unacceptable writer that would taint his reputation in America for many years. The French poet Charles Baudelaire, however, recognized and championed Poe's achievements, and eventually Baudelaire's favorable view began to influence thinking in the United States. Today, Poe is recognized as a master of poetry, a superb writer of short stories, and a profound explorer of the torments of the human soul

**More Online: Author Link**
www.mcdougallittell.com

## Poe's Death: The Mystery Continues  G

The exact reason for Poe's death in 1849 has never been established, although the most common theory is that he died from heart failure after consuming too much alcohol. In 1996, however, a Baltimore physician came up with a new solution of the mystery. A noted cardiologist and assistant professor of medicine, he was given a description of Poe's last four days but not told the patient's name. After careful study, the physician came up with his diagnosis—the victim, he said, was suffering from a classic case of rabies, caused by the bite of an infected animal. Poe's last days may never be unraveled to everyone's satisfaction, but if this theory is true, his reputation is cleared of at least one dark spot.

**Poe's grave in Baltimore, Maryland**

### Art and Music
**E** Response to Poe has been strong outside of literature. Edouard Manet, Odilon Redon, Paul Gauguin, Aubrey Beardsley, Henri Matisse, and Rene Magritte are among the major painters who illustrated or were inspired by Poe's writings. Composers as notable as Claude Debussy and Sergei Rachmaninoff have written instrumental works and operas influenced by Poe.

### Literature
**F** Poe's overwhelming influence on world literature comes from a relatively small amount of work. Poe wrote only a single (and short) novel, around 50 poems, and 70 short stories.

### Current Events
**G** Every year since 1949, in the early morning of January 19—Poe's birthday—a stranger visits Poe's grave at Westminster Church in Baltimore, placing a partial bottle of cognac and three roses. Dubbed the "Poe Toaster," the unknown visitor is witnessed each year from church windows by members of a Poe fan club. No one tries to uncover the man's identify, for, as it has been put, "the mystery has a charm no one wants to ruin." It is speculated that from 1949 through 1993 the same man was the visitor; since then two or three others appear to have shared the role. The three roses are thought to be left in memory of Poe, his wife, Virginia, and his mother-in-law, Maria Clemm.

| 1841 | 1845 | | 1847 | 1849 |
|------|------|--|------|------|
| Writes "The Murders in the Rue Morgue" | Becomes famous overnight after publication of "The Raven" | Poe lived in this house in New York City. | Death of Virginia | Dies in Baltimore on October 7 |

**1845**  **1850**

| 1841 | 1844 | 1846 | 1847 | 1848 | 1849 |
|------|------|------|------|------|------|
| A utopian community is established at Brook Farm. | Alexandre Dumas publishes *The Three Musketeers.* | U.S. goes to war with Mexico. | Frederick Douglass founds antislavery paper *The North Star.* | Women's rights convention is held in Seneca Falls, New York. | California gold rush begins. |

## OVERVIEW

 This selection is included in the **Grade 11 InterActive Reader.**

### Objectives

1. understand and appreciate a classic **short story** (Literary Analysis)
2. recognize and interpret **allegory** (Literary Analysis)
3. **clarify meaning** in a short story (Active Reading)

### Summary

To escape the Red Death, a disease that is ravaging the land, Prince Prospero and one thousand of his courtiers seal themselves in a walled abbey, where they indulge themselves in a life of pleasure. After many months of seclusion, the prince holds a lavish masquerade in seven rooms, each of a different color and design; the seventh room is decorated with black tapestry and deep red windows. The revelers suddenly notice a stranger who wears a ghastly costume designed to portray a victim of the Red Death. The hideous figure confronts Prospero, who falls dead. Others attempt to seize the stranger but grasp only empty garments. The ghostly figure has brought the feared Red Death, and one by one everyone dies.

### Thematic Link

In this **Gothic** horror story, Prospero and his party guests encounter the **dark side** of their fears and imagination and come face to face with the inevitability of death.

### 5-Minute Warm-Up

*Daily Language SkillBuilder*

Have students **proofread** the display sentences on page 337j and write them correctly. The sentences also appear on Transparency 13 of **Grammar Transparencies and Copymasters.**

**Mini Lesson** **Preteaching Vocabulary**

If you would like to preteach the WORDS TO KNOW for this selection, use the Mini Lesson, p. 456.

# The Masque of the Red Death

*Short Story by* EDGAR ALLAN POE

**Connect to Your Life**

**Facing an Epidemic** Imagine that your city or town has been struck by an epidemic of a deadly disease that seems to be incurable. The disease spreads rapidly but has not yet reached your neighborhood. How do you think you, other members of your family, and your neighbors would react? With a small group of classmates, discuss some actions that you could take in the crisis, both to protect yourself and to help other people.

## Build Background

**Plague** A deadly disease seems just the thing to inspire Poe's haunted imagination. Before the advances of 20th-century medicine, when people had no antibiotics and little knowledge about how diseases spread, an outbreak of disease could be a source of great terror. Poe's story may have been inspired by an outbreak of bubonic plague that killed about 25 million people in Europe (more than a quarter of the continent's population) in the mid-14th century. Victims experienced high fever, vomiting, pain, and swellings that oozed blood, and they were usually dead within three to five days. In "The Masque of the Red Death," Poe's characters try to find a place of refuge from a similar disease.

A depiction of the Great Plague of London. The Granger Collection, New York.

| WORDS TO KNOW | Vocabulary Preview | | | |
| --- | --- | --- | --- | --- |
| contagion | dauntless | impetuosity | pervade | tangible |
| courtier | grotesque | license | sagacious | untenanted |

## Focus Your Reading

**LITERARY ANALYSIS** **ALLEGORY** This story can be read as an **allegory,** a work with two layers of meaning. In an allegorical tale, most of the persons, objects, and events stand for abstract ideas or qualities. For example, a bird might represent freedom. As you read the story, take note of the characters, objects, and events that Poe describes. Think about what each might represent.

**ACTIVE READING** **CLARIFYING MEANING**

In "The Masque of the Red Death," Poe uses unusual, archaic vocabulary, partly to reinforce the story's setting in the past. The following strategies can help you **clarify** the meanings of particular words and passages:

- Use the Guide for Reading notes, which explain difficult words and passages.
- Reread difficult sentences or passages slowly and carefully. Try to **paraphrase** them—that is, to restate them in your own words.
- **Summarize** difficult passages.
- Use **context clues**—clues in the surrounding phrases—to help you figure out the meanings of unfamiliar words.

**READER'S NOTEBOOK** Record any questions you have about words or passages as you read the story.

## LESSON RESOURCES

**UNIT THREE RESOURCE BOOK,** pp. 51–55

**ASSESSMENT RESOURCES**
**Formal Assessment,** pp. 83–84
**Teacher's Guide to Assessment and Portfolio Use**
**Test Generator**

**SKILLS TRANSPARENCIES AND COPYMASTERS**
**Reading and Critical Thinking**
- Summarizing, T10 (for Active Reading, p. 454)

**Grammar**
- Participles and Participial Phrases, C86 (for Mini Lesson, p. 457)
- Past and Present Participles, C87 (for Mini Lesson, p. 463)

**Vocabulary**
- Meanings of Latin Roots, C42 (for Mini Lesson, p. 459)

**Writing**
- Opinion Statement, C34 (for Writing Option 1, p. 463)

**Communications**
- Impromptu Speaking: Dialogue, Role-Play, Debate, T13 (for Activities & Explorations, p. 463)

**INTEGRATED TECHNOLOGY**
**Audio Library**
**Net Activities**
**LaserLinks**
- Historical Connection: The Plague. See **Teacher's SourceBook,** p. 44.

**Internet: Research Starter**
**Visit our website:**
www.mcdougallittell.com

EDGAR ALLAN POE

# The Masque of the Red Death

*Il ridotto* [The foyer] (about 1757–1760), Pietro Longhi. Oil on canvas, 62.5 cm × 51 cm, Fondazione Scientifica Querini Stampaglia, Venice, Italy, Erich Lessing/Art Resource, New York.

THE "RED DEATH" HAD LONG DEVASTATED THE COUNTRY. NO PESTILENCE HAD EVER BEEN SO FATAL, OR SO HIDEOUS. BLOOD WAS ITS

2 **devastated** (dĕv′ə-stā′tĭd): laid waste to.

3 **pestilence** (pĕs′tə-ləns): a very destructive infectious disease.

## Reading Skills and Strategies: PREVIEW

Have students read the first two paragraphs, then reread lines 21–29 to clarify their understanding of the passage. Tell students that this passage introduces the basic plot of the story.

## Active Reading **CLARIFYING MEANING**

**A** Have students record their questions about unfamiliar words or difficult passages in their Reader's Notebooks. Remind students that paraphrasing is one strategy to help them clarify the meaning of a particular passage. Have students paraphrase the opening paragraph of the story.

Use **Unit Three Resource Book**, p. 52 for more practice.

## GUIDE FOR READING

**B** Possible Response: Outside the abbey, people are dying from the Red Death; inside the abbey, people are celebrating their escape from it.

## Literary Analysis **ALLEGORY**

**C** Ask students what the abbey represents.

Possible Responses: a fortress against or immunity from death

**D** Ask students what the huge black clock might represent.

Possible Responses: time running out; doom or death approaching

Use **Unit Three Resource Book**, p. 53 for more exercises.

## GUIDE FOR READING

**E** Possible Responses: The chimes remind the guests of the passage of time and the inevitability of death.

---

**A**

5　Avatar and its seal—the redness and horror of blood. There were sharp pains, and sudden dizziness, and then profuse bleeding at the pores, with dissolution. The scarlet stains upon the body, and especially upon the face of the victim, were the pest ban which shut him out from the aid and from the sympathy of his fellow

10　men. And the whole seizure, progress, and termination of the disease were the incidents of half an hour.

But the Prince Prospero was happy and <u>dauntless</u> and <u>sagacious</u>. When his dominions were half depopulated, he summoned to his presence a thousand hale and lighthearted friends

15　from among the knights and dames of his court, and with these retired to the deep seclusion of one of his castellated abbeys. This was an extensive and magnificent structure, the creation of the prince's own eccentric yet august taste. A strong and lofty wall girded it in. This wall had gates of iron. The <u>courtiers</u>, having

**C** 20　entered, brought furnaces and massy hammers and welded the bolts. They resolved to leave means neither of ingress or egress to the sudden impulses of despair or of frenzy from within. The abbey was amply provisioned. With such precautions the courtiers might bid defiance to <u>contagion</u>. The external world could take

25　care of itself. In the meantime it was folly to grieve, or to think. The prince had provided all the appliances of pleasure. There were buffoons, there were improvisatori, there were ballet-dancers, there were musicians, there was Beauty, there was wine. All these and security were within. Without was the "Red Death."

30　It was toward the close of the fifth or sixth month of his seclusion, and while the pestilence raged most furiously abroad, that the Prince Prospero entertained his thousand friends at a masked ball of the most unusual magnificence.

**1**

It was a voluptuous scene, that masquerade. But first let me tell

35　of the rooms in which it was held. There were seven—an imperial suite. In many palaces, however, such suites form a long and straight vista, while the folding doors slide back nearly to the walls on either hand, so that the view of the whole extent is scarcely impeded. Here the case was very different; as might have

40　been expected from the duke's love of the *bizarre*. The apartments were so irregularly disposed that the vision embraced but little more than one at a time. There was a sharp turn at every twenty or thirty yards, and at each turn a novel effect. To the right and left, in the middle of each wall, a tall and narrow Gothic window

45　looked out upon a closed corridor which pursued the windings of the suite. These windows were of stained glass whose color

WORDS TO KNOW

**dauntless** (dônt′lĭs) *adj.* fearless
**sagacious** (sə-gā′shəs) *adj.* wise
**courtier** (kôr′tē-ər) *n.* a member of a royal court
**contagion** (kən-tā′jən) *n.* the spreading of disease

456

---

**5 Avatar** (ăv′ə-tär′): an appearance in physical form of an unseen force.

**7 dissolution:** death.

**8 pest ban:** a proclamation announcing that a person is afflicted with the plague.

**1–29** How is life outside the abbey different from life inside?

**B**

**16 castellated abbey** (kăs′tə-lā′tĭd ăb′ē): a fortified building formerly used as, or built to resemble, a monastery.

**21 ingress** (ĭn′grĕs′) **or egress** (ē′grĕs′): entry or exit.

**23 provisioned:** provided with supplies.

**27 improvisatori** (ĭm-prŏv′ĭ-zə-tôr′ē): poets who recite verses that they make up as they go along.

**34–72** If you are having trouble visualizing the setting, try drawing a floor plan of the abbey's suite of seven rooms and labeling their colors. The arrangement of the rooms will be important later on.

**2**

---

## Teaching Options

 **Preteaching Vocabulary**

### USING CONTEXT CLUES

**Instruction** Write the following sentence on the chalkboard and ask a volunteer to summarize the meaning of the sentence:

> In the 14th century the deadly bubonic plague pervaded the population, quickly spreading from one person to another.

Have students use the meaning of the sentence to infer meanings for the word *pervade.*

**Exercises** Have students apply the strategy to figure out the meanings of underlined words in the following sentences.

1. The lack of restrictions at the academy allowed students the <u>license</u> to act according to their own judgment.
2. She felt the tiny hairs raise suddenly on the back of her neck, making her fear <u>tangible</u>.
3. Unafraid of the threat to his reputation, the <u>dauntless</u> <u>courtier</u> told the truth before other members of the royal court.

Use **Unit Three Resource Book**, pp. 54 for more exercises.

A lesson on using context clues appears on p. 326 in the Pupil's Edition.

varied in accordance with the prevailing hue of the decorations of the chamber into which it opened. That at the eastern extremity was hung, for example, in blue—and vividly blue were its win-
50 dows. The second chamber was purple in its ornaments and tapestries, and here the panes were purple. The third was green throughout, and so were the casements. The fourth was furnished and lighted with orange—the fifth with white—the sixth with vio-let. The seventh apartment was closely shrouded in black velvet
55 tapestries that hung all over the ceiling and down the walls, falling in heavy folds upon a carpet of the same material and hue. But in this chamber only, the color of the windows failed to cor-respond with the decorations. The panes here were scarlet—a deep blood color. Now in no one of the seven apartments were
60 there any lamp or candelabrum amid the profusion of golden ornaments that lay scattered to and fro or depended from the roof. There was no light of any kind emanating from lamp or can-dle within the suite of chambers. But in the corridors that followed the suite, there stood, opposite to each window, a heavy
65 tripod, bearing a brazier of fire that projected its rays through the tinted glass and so glaringly illumined the room. And thus were produced a multitude of gaudy and fantastic appearances. But in the western or black chamber the effect of the firelight that streamed upon the dark hangings through the blood-tinted panes,
70 was ghastly in the extreme, and produced so wild a look upon the countenances of those who entered, that there were few of the company bold enough to set foot within its precincts at all.

It was in this apartment, also, that there stood against the west-ern wall a gigantic clock of ebony. Its pendulum swung to and fro
**D** 75 with a dull, heavy, monotonous clang; and when the minute hand made the circuit of the face, and the hour was to be stricken, there came from the brazen lungs of the clock a sound which was clear and loud and deep and exceedingly musical, but of so peculiar a note and emphasis that, at each lapse of an hour, the musicians of
80 the orchestra were constrained to pause, momentarily, in their performance, to hearken to the sound; and thus the waltzers per-force ceased their evolutions; and there was a brief disconcert of the whole gay company; and, while the chimes of the clock yet rang, it was observed that the giddiest turned pale, and the more
85 aged and sedate passed their hands over their brows as if in con-fused reverie or meditation. But when the echoes had fully ceased, a light laughter at once <u>pervaded</u> the assembly; the musicians looked at each other and smiled as if at their own nervousness and folly, and made whispering vows, each to the other, that the

**65 brazier** (brā′zhər): metal pan for holding a fire.

**71 countenances** (koun′tə-nən-səz): faces.

**74 ebony** (ĕb′ə-nē): a hard, very dark wood.

**77 brazen:** brass.

**79–94** How do you explain the effect of the ebony clock's chimes on the assembled guests?

**82 evolutions:** intricate patterns of movement.

WORDS
TO **pervade** (pər-vād′) v. to spread throughout
KNOW

**457**

## Customizing Instruction

### Students Acquiring English
**1** Make sure students understand the meaning of the synonyms *masked ball* and *masquerade:* "a party at which people wear costumes."

**2** Pause at the beginning of this paragraph and point out that lines 35–94 contain a description of the rooms and important furnishings in the rooms where the masked ball will take place. Have students read this section and then collaborate on an oral description of the setting. Fill in any key elements that they miss.

### Gifted and Talented
Point out that Poe italicizes several words borrowed from languages other than English, such as *bizarre* (line 40), *decora* (line 97), and *fête* (line 103). Have them research the origins of these words to understand the mean-ings and to find out when they first entered American English.

 **Mini Lesson Grammar**

## PARTICIPLES AND PARTICIPIAL PHRASES
**Instruction** A participle is a verb form that can function as part of a verb phrase or as an adjec-tive. A participial phrase contains a participle plus any complements or modifiers. Write these sen-tences on the chalkboard:
The guests <u>had danced</u> all night.
The <u>dancing</u> guests swirled about the room.
We saw the guests <u>dancing at the abbey</u>.
Underline the participles as shown. Have students identify the participle that functions as part of a verb phrase (*had danced*), the participle that functions as an adjective (*dancing*—modifies

*guests*), and the participial phrase (*dancing at the abbey*—modifies *guests*).
**Exercises** Identify the participle or participial phrase and its function in each sentence.
1. We watched the courtiers securing the gates. (*securing the gates;* adjective modifying *courtiers*)
2. Prince Prospero had invited one thousand guests. (*had invited;* verb phrase)

Use **Grammar Transparencies and Copymasters**, p. 86.

Use McDougal Littell's ***Language Network***, Chapter 2, for more instruction in participles.

## Reading and Analyzing

### Literary Analysis: IRONY

**A** Remind students that in this context *mad* means "insane." What is ironic about the narrator's mention that "There are some who would have thought [Prospero] mad"?

**Possible Responses:** While appearing to admire his brilliance in the description of his tastes, the narrator casts doubt upon Prospero's sanity by indicating that even his followers need to reassure themselves that he is not mad.

### GUIDE FOR READING

**B Possible Response:** The images lend an unreal, dreamy quality to the setting, making it a place where anything can happen.

### Literary Analysis  ALLEGORY

**C** Ask students to think about the presence and behavior of dreams at Prospero's ball. What might dreams represent in this story?

**Possible Responses:** light-heartedness; the precariousness of life; self-delusion; ignorance of death

### Literary Analysis: SETTING

**D** Ask students which details about the seventh room make it grotesque in appearance. What mood is created by this setting?

**Possible Responses:** Details include the black drapery, blood-colored panes, sable carpets, and black clock. The mood may be described as creepy, somber, or horrible.

### GUIDE FOR READING

**E Possible Response:** The black room frightens them because the only light in it is the color of blood.

**F Possible Response:** The people are first surprised and then horrified.

---

90 next chiming of the clock should produce in them no similar emotion; and then, after the lapse of sixty minutes (which embrace three thousand and six hundred seconds of the Time that flies), there came yet another chiming of the clock, and then were the same disconcert and tremulousness and meditation as before.

95 But in spite of these things, it was a gay and magnificent revel. The tastes of the duke were peculiar. He had a fine eye for colors and effects. He disregarded the *decora* of mere fashion. His plans were bold and fiery, and his conceptions glowed with barbaric luster. There are some who would have thought him mad. His followers felt that he was not. It was necessary to hear and see and touch him to be *sure* that he was not.

He had directed, in great part, the movable embellishments of the seven chambers, upon occasion of this great *fête*; and it was his own guiding taste which had given character to the masqueraders. Be sure they were grotesque. There were much glare and glitter and piquancy and phantasm—much of what has been seen since in *Hernani*. There were arabesque figures with unsuited limbs and appointments. There were delirious fancies such as the madman fashions. There was much of the beautiful, much of the wanton, much of the *bizarre*, something of the terrible, and not a little of that which might have excited disgust. To and fro in the seven chambers there stalked, in fact, a multitude of dreams. And these—the dreams—writhed in and about, taking hue from the rooms, and causing the wild music of the orchestra to seem as the echo of their steps. And, anon, there strikes the ebony clock which stands in the hall of velvet. And then, for a moment, all is still, and all is silent save the voice of the clock. The dreams are stiff-frozen as they stand. But the echoes of the chime die away— they have endured but an instant—and a light, half-subdued laughter floats after them as they depart. And now again the music swells, and the dreams live, and writhe to and fro more merrily than ever, taking hue from the many-tinted windows through which stream the rays of the tripods. But to the chamber which lies most westwardly of the seven, there are now none of the maskers who venture; for the night is waning away; and there flows a ruddier light through the blood-colored panes; and the blackness of the sable drapery appalls; and to him whose foot falls upon the sable carpet, there comes from the near clock of ebony a muffled peal more solemnly emphatic than any which reaches *their* ears who indulge in the more remote gaieties of the other apartments.

But these other apartments were densely crowded, and in them

**94 disconcert:** confusion.

**97 *decora*:** fine things.

**102–123** Notice the comparison of the masqueraders to dreams, phantasms, and a madman's fancies. How do such comparisons **B** help you imagine the scene?

**107 *Hernani*** (ĕr'nä-nē): a play by Victor Hugo, first staged in 1830, notable for its use of color and spectacle; **arabesque** (ăr'ə-bĕsk'): characterized by complicated decorations.

**124–131** Why do you think none of the revellers venture into the **E** seventh room?

> WORDS
> TO
> KNOW   **grotesque** (grō-tĕsk') *adj.* having a bizarre, fantastic appearance

---

## Teaching Options

**If your schedule requires that you cover the lesson objectives in a shorter time, use . . .**
- Preparing to Read, p. 454
- Thinking Through the Literature, p. 462
- Vocabulary in Action, p. 462

**If you want to take advantage of longer class time, use . . .**
- TE Teaching Options: Viewing and Representing, p. 455; Preteaching Vocabulary, p. 456; Vocabulary Strategy, p. 459; Speaking and Listening, p. 460; Informal Assessment, p. 461
- Choices & Challenges, p. 463

beat feverishly the heart of life. And the revel went whirlingly on,
until at length there commenced the sounding of midnight upon
135 the clock. And then the music ceased, as I have told; and the evolutions of the waltzes were quieted; and there
was an uneasy cessation of all things as
before. But now there were twelve strokes
to be sounded by the bell of the clock;
140 and thus it happened, perhaps, that
more of thought crept, with more of
time, into the meditations of the
thoughtful among those
who reveled. And thus,
145 too, it happened, perhaps, that before the
last echoes of the last
chime had utterly
sunk into silence,
150 there were many indi-
viduals in the crowd
who had found leisure to
become aware of the
presence of a masked fig-
155 ure which had arrested the
attention of no single individual before. And the
rumor of this new presence
having spread itself whisper-
160 ingly around, there arose at
length from the whole company
a buzz, or murmur, expressive of
disapprobation and surprise—then,
finally of terror, of horror, and of
165 disgust.

In an assembly of phantasms such as I
have painted, it may well be supposed that no
ordinary appearance could have excited such
sensation. In truth the masquerade license
170 of the night was nearly unlimited; but the
figure in question had out-Heroded
Herod, and gone beyond the bounds of even the prince's indefinite decorum. There are chords in the hearts of the most reckless
which cannot be touched without emotion. Even with the utterly
175 lost, to whom life and death are equally jests, there are matters of

**144–165** What effect does the strange figure who appears at the stroke of midnight have on the revellers? **F**

Detail of *Adoration of the Magi: Lorenzo il Magnifico as Youngest of Magi* (1459), Benozzo Gozzoli. Palazzo Medici Riccardi, Florence, Italy, Erich Lessing/Art Resource, New York.

**171–172 out-Heroded Herod:** been more extreme than the biblical king Herod, who ordered the deaths of all male babies up to two years old in an effort to kill the infant Jesus. This expression is used in Shakespeare's *Hamlet.*

WORDS
TO     **license** (lī'səns) *n.* a lack of restrictions on behavior; freedom
KNOW

**459**

**Customizing Instruction**

**Students Acquiring English**
**1** Help students paraphrase the description, particularly the phrases *delirious fancies; much of the wanton, much of the bizarre;* and *not a little of that which might have excited disgust.*

**Less Proficient Readers**
**2** Be sure students understand the turning point of the plot by asking the following questions:
• What happens at the stroke of midnight?
**Possible Response:** The clock strikes, people stop dancing, and then they notice a stranger.

• What might the guests be thinking about at this moment?
**Possible Response:** the passage of time; their own deaths

**Set a Purpose** Have students read to find out who this stranger is and what he does.

**Multiple Learning Styles**
**Kinesthetic Learners**

**3** Have students work in small groups to use visual signs, gestures, or body language to illustrate how the guests respond to the appearance of the stranger.

---

**Mini Lesson** **Vocabulary Strategy**

**APPLYING MEANINGS OF LATIN ROOT WORDS**
**Instruction** Tell students that they can apply meanings of root words in order to comprehend meanings of other words based on these roots. The word *license,* for example, is based on the Latin root *licere,* which means "to be permitted." When the narrator describes the "masquerade license of the night" as "nearly unlimited," he is saying that there is virtually no restriction on or limit to the behavior allowed.
**Application** Other words in this story that have Latin roots are *contagion, dauntless, impetuosity,*

*pervade, sagacious,* and *tangible.* Have students work in pairs to research the word origins and find the roots of these words. Ask them to use each word in a sentence.

Use **Vocabulary Transparencies and Copymasters,** p. 42.

A lesson on Latin roots appears on p. 444 in the Pupil's Edition.

**Ⓐ** What does the masked figure represent?

**Possible Responses:** death; the Red Death

### GUIDE FOR READING

**Ⓑ Possible Responses:** Prospero has locked himself and his friends away to avoid the Red Death and is insulted by the reminder of it; he thinks someone is mocking their fear of the plague; the figure frightens his guests and spoils his party.

### Active Reading CLARIFYING MEANING

**Ⓒ** Ask students to summarize what happens after Prospero demands that the stranger be seized.

**Possible Response:** Some guests try to approach the stranger but cannot bring themselves to touch him. The stranger walks past Prospero and through all seven of the rooms. Prospero pursues him with a dagger into the seventh room, where the stranger confronts him and the prince falls dead. The stranger then disappears, leaving the guests behind to die one by one.

### GUIDE FOR READING

**Ⓓ Possible Responses:** Everyone is stunned; they are all afraid of the figure; they believe it is a supernatural presence; they want to witness a confrontation between the prince and the figure.

---

which no jest can be made. The whole company, indeed, seemed now deeply to feel that in the costume and bearing of the stranger neither wit nor propriety existed. The figure was tall and gaunt, and shrouded from head to foot in the habiliments of the grave.
180 The mask which concealed the visage was made so nearly to resemble the countenance of a stiffened corpse that the closest scrutiny must have difficulty in detecting the cheat. And yet all this might have been endured, if not approved, by the mad revellers around. But the mummer had gone so far as to assume the
185 type of the Red Death. His vesture was dabbed in *blood*—and his broad brow, with all the features of the face, was besprinkled with the scarlet horror.

When the eyes of Prince Prospero fell upon this spectral image (which with a slow and solemn movement, as if more fully to sustain its *role,* stalked to and fro among the waltzers), he was seen to
190 be convulsed, in the first moment with a strong shudder either of terror or distaste; but, in the next, his brow reddened with rage.

"Who dares?" he demanded hoarsely of the courtiers who stood near him—"who dares insult us with this blasphemous
195 mockery? Seize him and unmask him—that we may know whom we have to hang at sunrise, from the battlements!"

It was in the eastern or blue chamber in which stood the Prince Prospero as he uttered these words. They rang throughout the seven rooms loudly and clearly—for the prince was a bold and
200 robust man, and the music had become hushed at the waving of his hand.

It was in the blue room where stood the prince, with a group of pale courtiers by his side. At first, as he spoke, there was a slight rushing movement of this group in the direction of the
205 intruder, who at the moment was also near at hand, and now, with deliberate and stately step, made closer approach to the speaker. But from a certain nameless awe with which the mad assumptions of the mummer had inspired the whole party, there were found none who put forth a hand to seize him; so that,
210 unimpeded, he passed within a yard of the prince's person; and, while the vast assembly, as if with one impulse, shrank from the centers of the rooms to the walls, he made his way uninterruptedly, but with the same solemn and measured step which had distinguished him from the first, through the blue chamber to the
215 purple—through the purple to the green—through the green to the orange—through this again to the white—and even thence to the violet, ere a decided movement had been made to arrest him. It was then, however, that the Prince Prospero, maddening with rage and the shame of his own momentary cowardice, rushed
220 hurriedly through the six chambers while none followed him on

**179 habiliments** (hə-bĭl′ə-mənts): clothing.

**180 visage** (vĭz′ĭj): face.

**184 mummer:** a person dressed for a masquerade.

**188–196** Why does Prince Prospero get so mad? **Ⓑ**

**207–217** Why do you think the masked figure is allowed to walk the length of the rooms uninterrupted? **Ⓓ**

---

## Teaching Options

### Speaking and Listening

**NONVERBAL COMMUNICATION**

**Prepare** Ask students to present "The Masque of the Red Death" to the class using only nonverbal communication. Explain that the elements of nonverbal communication include eye contact, facial expressions, body language, gestures, and so on. Students can work in pairs or cooperative groups to discuss how emotion, meaning, and messages presented in the story can be conveyed using elements of nonverbal communication. Ask them to consider ways in which various nonverbal techniques will affect their presentation of the story.

**Present** Have students present their nonverbal interpretations of the story. Students should justify their choice of nonverbal performance techniques by referring to the narrative and to their interpretation of Prince Prospero's character. Audience members should evaluate how the performance enhances their understanding of the narrative.

**BLOCK SCHEDULING** This activity is particularly well-suited for longer class periods.

account of a deadly terror that had seized upon all. He bore aloft a drawn dagger, and had approached, in rapid impetuosity, to within three or four feet of the retreating figure, when the latter, having attained the extremity of the velvet apart-
225 ment, turned suddenly and confronted his pursuer. There was a sharp cry—and the dagger dropped gleaming upon the sable carpet, upon which, instantly after-wards, fell prostrate in death the
230 Prince Prospero. Then, summoning the wild courage of despair, a throng of the revellers at once threw themselves into the black apartment, and seizing the mum-
235 mer, whose tall figure stood erect and motionless within the shad-ow of the ebony clock, gasped in unutterable horror at finding the grave-cerements and corpselike
240 mask, which they handled with so violent a rudeness, untenanted by any tangible form.

**1** And now was acknowledged the presence of the Red Death. He
245 had come like a thief in the night. And one by one dropped the rev-ellers in the blood-bedewed halls of their revel, and died each in the despairing posture of his fall. And the life of the ebony
250 clock went out with that of the last of the gay. And the flames of the tripods expired.
**2** And Darkness and Decay and the Red Death held illimitable dominion over all. ❖

Skull (19th or 20th century), artist unknown. Carved and painted wood, 8⅞″ × 5⅜″ × 6½″, National Museum of American Art, gift of Herbert Waide Hemphill, Jr., and museum purchase made possible by Ralph Cross Johnson, Smithsonian Institution, Washington, D.C./Art Resource, New York.

**230–242** Poe's language is hard to understand here. Essentially, he says that when a group of revellers rip off the figure's costume, there is nothing underneath.

**239 cerements** (sĕr′ə-mənts): cloth wrappings for the dead.

**253 illimitable dominion** (ĭ-lĭm′ĭ-tə-bəl də-mĭn′yən): unlimited power.

| | |
|---|---|
| WORDS | **impetuosity** (ĭm-pĕch′ōō-ŏs′ĭ-tē) *n.* unthinking action |
| TO | **untenanted** (ŭn-tĕn′ən-tĭd) *adj.* not occupied |
| KNOW | **tangible** (tăn′jə-bəl) *adj.* able to be touched or felt |

**461**

## GUIDING STUDENT RESPONSE

### Connect to the Literature

**1. What Do You Think?**
Have students support their reactions with specific descriptions from the text.

**Comprehension Check**
- They close themselves off in the abbey to escape the disease called the Red Death.
- The figure is dressed to resemble a victim of the Red Death.
- They all die.

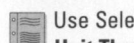 Use Selection Quiz
**Unit Three Resource Book**, p. 55.

### Think Critically

**2. Possible Response:** Poe wanted readers to feel a sense of horror or hopelessness at the end of the story. All details within the story are presented to create the effect of horror.

**3. Possible Response:** The passage sets up the contrast or conflict between the danger of disease outside the abbey and the effort to avoid the disease within the abbey.

**4. Possible Response:** The sound of the clock made the people think about passing time and approaching death; the clock reminded people of the seriousness of life in the midst of their effort to celebrate and to avoid thinking.

**5. Possible Responses:** Prince Prospero might be described as artistic, unbalanced, unfeeling for his subjects, selfish or self-indulgent, hot tempered, or bizarre. Prospero is deluded in thinking that it is possible to escape death. No matter how wealthy or powerful a person is or how elaborate the attempt to avoid death, humans cannot escape their own mortality. The macabre decorations of the rooms enforce the impression of Prince Prospero's eccentricity and possible madness. His response of anger toward the mysterious stranger may be the result of realizing his own mortality.

**6. Possible Response:** No one can run away from death. Death can strike at any time, eventually coming to all—even the rich and powerful.

### Connect to the Literature

**1. What Do You Think?**
How did you react to the masked figure's first appearance?

**Comprehension Check**
- Why does Prince Prospero close himself and his courtiers off in the abbey?
- Why does the masked figure's presence cause such a sensation?
- What happens to the prince and the revellers?

### Think Critically

**2.** What feeling do you think Poe wanted readers to have at the end of the story? Give reasons for your opinion.

**3.**  **ACTIVE READING  CLARIFYING MEANING** Refer to questions you may have recorded in your **READER'S NOTEBOOK** about words or passages. Look again at lines 21–29, and recall the techniques you used to clarify your understanding of this passage. How does the passage set up the basic plot of the story?

**4.** The ebony clock, when it chimes, has the ability to silence the revellers. What might their thoughts be during these still moments?

**5.** What are your impressions of Prince Prospero?

 **THINK ABOUT**
- his plan to escape the Red Death
- the decorated rooms of the party suite
- why he becomes angry

**6.** What message or messages do you see in this story?

**THINK ABOUT**
- what literally happens to the revellers
- what the Red Death might stand for

### Extend Interpretations

**7. Comparing Texts** Compare this story with "The Devil and Tom Walker" (page 349). Which story did you find more horrifying? Cite evidence to support your choice.

**8. Connect to Life** Recall your earlier discussion about what you might do when faced with an epidemic, and think about how people today react to epidemic diseases. Bearing these things in mind, give your opinion of Prospero's reactions.

### Literary Analysis

**ALLEGORY** "The Masque of the Red Death" can be read as an **allegory**, a literary work in which most of the people, objects, and events stand for abstract qualities. Here are some important things to know about allegories:

- An allegory usually has a second level of meaning in addition to its literal meaning.
- Some allegories are intended to teach moral lessons. In the fable of the tortoise and the hare, for example, the actions of the tortoise—the slow, focused, character—are shown as more admirable than those of the cunning but easily distracted hare.
- Stories that are not formal allegories may nevertheless contain some allegorical elements—some objects, people, or events that stand for abstract ideas or qualities.

**Paired Activity** Review the story to find elements that might have allegorical meanings. Explain what you think is the meaning of each element, as well as how Poe used the elements to convey a moral lesson. You might use a chart like this one to record your interpretations. Compare charts with a partner, and defend your interpretations.

| Person, Object, Event | Possible Meaning | Possible Lesson of Story |
|---|---|---|
| The prince | | |
| The abbey | | |
| The series of seven rooms | | |
| The clock | | |
| The stranger | | |

### Extend Interpretations

**Comparing Texts** Possible Responses: "The Masque of the Red Death" is more horrifying because it keeps a consistent tone of gloom and fear; "Tom Walker" is more terrifying because the dreary swamp is scarier than a decorated castle or because the story describes evil in an everyday setting.

**Connect to Life** Even though many students will know of irrational responses to modern diseases, they may agree that Prospero was irresponsible to abandon his subjects when the epidemic raged. Others may argue that because Prospero could do nothing to cure the Red Death, his retreat to save himself and his friends is acceptable.

### Literary Analysis

**Allegory** Students should also consider the allegorical role color plays in the story, with scarlet representing blood, the Red Death, a warning, and black representing death, doom, and mourning.

# Choices & CHALLENGES

## Writing Options

1. **Newspaper Editorial** Prospero and his friends escape to the abbey after half the people in his lands have died. Pretend that you are a newspaper editor in the prince's domain, and write an editorial giving your opinion of this action.

2. **Poetic Retelling** In a ballad or another type of narrative poem, retell the story of the prince and his friends. Make sure that you include all the key events.

3. **Archaeological Report** In the role of an archaeologist who has excavated the remains of Prospero's abbey, write a descriptive report about the remains you have found and the conclusions you have drawn from them.

## Activities & Explorations

1. **A Fantastic Set** Design the set for a television version of "The Masque of the Red Death." You can either make drawings or make a model of the set representing the suite of rooms.
~ ART

2. **Radio Drama** Work with a group of classmates to create a radio dramatization of the story. Figure out how you might turn some of the narration into dialogue. You might also include sound effects (chimes, the laughter of revellers) and music to make your dramatization more effective.
~ PERFORMING

## Inquiry & Research

**Medical Detective** Find out more about the great outbreak of plague in Europe during the mid-1300s. What caused it? What parts of Europe were affected? How did people try to contain it? Present your findings to the class in an oral report.

**More Online: Research Starter**
www.mcdougallittell.com

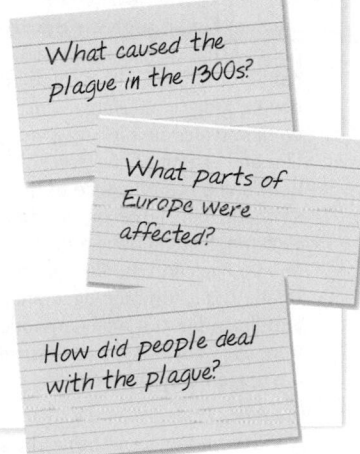

*What caused the plague in the 1300s?*

*What parts of Europe were affected?*

*How did people deal with the plague?*

## Vocabulary in Action

**EXERCISE A: WORD KNOWLEDGE** In the chart shown here, the Words to Know are grouped under headings that refer to elements in the story. Use each group of words to write two or more sentences about the person or thing named by its heading. You may also want to include in your sentences words that you looked up on your own.

| Red Death | Masked Ball | Prince Prospero |
|---|---|---|
| contagion | courtier | dauntless |
| pervade | grotesque | sagacious |
| untenanted | license | impetuosity |
| tangible | | |

**EXERCISE B** Work with classmates to act out some of the sentences you created for Exercise A.

### Building Vocabulary

Many of the Words to Know in this lesson are from French or Latin. For an in-depth lesson on word origins, see page 550.

| WORDS TO KNOW | | | | |
|---|---|---|---|---|
| contagion | grotesque | pervade | tangible |
| courtier | impetuosity | sagacious | untenanted |
| dauntless | license | | |

 **Mini Lesson** **Grammar**

### USING PAST AND PRESENT PARTICIPLES

**Instruction** Remind students that a participle is a verb form that can function as part of a verb phrase or as an adjective. Present tense participles always end in *-ing*. Past participles often end in *-ed;* however, they can take other forms as well. Write these sentences on the chalkboard:

The <u>dancing</u> guests felt safe from the Red Death.
The <u>enraged</u> Prince Prospero attacked the mysterious stranger.

Underline the participles as shown. Have students identify the present participle (*dancing*) and the past participle (*enraged*).

**Exercises** Have students identify the tense of each underlined participle.

1. The <u>invited</u> guests arrived in elaborate costumes. *(past participle)*
2. <u>Whispering</u> behind their masks, the guests wondered about the identity of the mysterious stranger. *(present participle)*

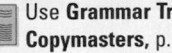 Use **Grammar Transparencies and Copymasters,** p. 87.

 Use McDougal Littell's *Language Network,* Chapter 2, for more instruction in participles.

## Writing Options

1. **Newspaper Editorial** Students' editorials should explain their opinions regarding the action taken by Prospero and his friends. Students should support their opinions with evidence from the text.
2. **Poetic Retelling** Students' retellings should demonstrate an understanding of the key events of the narrative. Have volunteers read their poems aloud to the rest of the class. You might ask students how the poetic form affects the drama of Poe's story.
3. **Archaeological Report** Students' reports should draw conclusions about the remains of the abbey based upon details from the story.

## Activities & Explorations

1. **A Fantastic Set** Students' drawings or models should draw upon descriptive details in the story.
2. **Radio Drama** A radio drama depends entirely upon sound to convey all elements of a narrative. Help students figure out how to turn narrative into dialogue and have them include sound effects.

## Inquiry & Research

**Medical Detective** Students' research should disclose some of the following facts:

Plague is caused by a bacteria called *Yersinia pestis,* which commonly infects rats. Humans catch the disease from fleas that have bitten infected rats. Most of western Europe suffered from plague in the middle of the 1300s. People sought to avoid the plague by staying out of houses where the disease had struck and by fleeing infected cities. Governments tried to impose quarantines on infected cities or to ban travelers from infected areas, but these measures failed to stop the spread of the disease. Because doctors believed that diseases spread by foul-smelling vapors, people used incense or bouquets of flowers to avoid catching the plague.

## Vocabulary in Action

**Sentences will vary.** Encourage students to write sentences that contain context clues so that someone unfamiliar with a word can figure out the meaning.

**464** UNIT THREE AUTHOR STUDY

## Teaching Nonfiction

### Build Background

Stephen King (b. 1947) is a popular novelist of science fiction and horror. He has captured millions of readers with his chilling stories, and many of them have been made into films.

In this excerpt, King discusses the role of the imagination in horror fiction and the "dancing partner" that the imagination seeks—death.

In 1981 King further wrote, "The best tales of terror deal with questions of memory and mortality, and the fact that they so often haunt us after the lights are out, laughing ominously in the dark with teeth grown wondrously sharp and long, only prove the truth and the practicality of their vision.

"This is not defense but warning: you must not come to tales such as these with your guard down. They will entertain you . . . but they will not comfort you."

### Skills and Strategies
#### IDENTIFYING MAIN IDEAS

Ask students to identify the sentence that they think expresses King's main idea about horror. Then have students identify the details King uses to support his main idea. Have students produce summaries of King's main idea.

**Possible Responses:** The main idea is expressed in the sentence "What's behind the door or lurking at the top of the stairs is never as frightening as the door or the staircase itself." The main idea is supported with various examples showing how the audience's (or character's) curiosity about the "closed door" is stronger than the fear of what might be lurking behind the door.

#### EVALUATING LITERARY TERMS

A paradox is a statement or situation that seems to contradict itself but is true. Ask students to explain the paradox that King claims lies behind horror stories.

**Possible Response:** An audience believes that the horror they are about to experience will come from learning the reality of something unknown and imagined as unimaginably terrifying— but the horror actually comes from within a person's own imagination and is bound to disappoint when reality doesn't match expectations.

---

## from Danse

*Essay by* STEPHEN KING

### Preparing to Read

## Build Background

Stephen King is probably the best-known writer of horror fiction since Poe. In 1981, after making a name for himself with a number of bestselling novels, King wrote *Danse Macabre,* a nonfiction work in which he discussed horror in literature and film and examined the psychology of terror. The book's title is a reference to the "Dance of Death," a symbolic representation of Death, in the form of a skeleton, leading people to their graves. In the Middle Ages and the Renaissance, the Dance of Death was a common decoration on cemetery walls and the subject of many artworks. In this excerpt from the book, King discusses the inner tensions that are triggered by spine-tingling tales.

I want to say something about imagination purely as a tool in the art and science of scaring people. The idea isn't original with me; I heard it expressed by William F. Nolan at the 1979 World Fantasy Convention. Nothing is so frightening as what's behind the closed door, Nolan said. You approach the door in the old, deserted house, and you hear something scratching at it. The audience holds its breath along with the protagonist as she or he (more often she) approaches that door. The protagonist throws it open, and there is a ten-foot-tall bug. The audience screams, but this particular scream has an oddly relieved sound to it. "A bug ten feet tall is pretty horrible," the audience thinks, "but I can deal with a ten-foot-tall bug. I was afraid it might be a *hundred* feet tall."...

Bill Nolan was speaking as a screenwriter when he offered the example of the big bug behind the door, but the point applies to all media. What's behind the door or lurking at the top of the stairs is never as frightening as the door or the staircase itself. And because of this, comes the paradox: the artistic work of horror is almost always a disappointment. It is the classic no-win situation. You can scare people with the unknown for a long, long time (the classic example, as Bill Nolan also pointed out, is the Jacques Tourneur film with Dana Andrews, *Curse of the Demon*), but sooner or later, as in poker, you have to turn your down cards up. You have to open the door and show the audience what's behind it. And if what happens to be behind it is a bug, not ten but a hundred feet tall, the audience heaves a sigh of relief (or utters a scream of relief) and thinks, "A bug a hundred feet tall is pretty horrible, but I can deal with that. I was afraid it might be a *thousand* feet tall."...

The danse macabre is a waltz with death. This is a truth we cannot afford to shy away from.

# Macabre

Like the rides in the amusement park which mimic violent death, the tale of horror is a chance to examine what's going on behind doors which we usually keep double-locked. Yet the human imagination is not content with locked doors. Somewhere there is another dancing partner, the imagination whispers in the night—a partner in a rotting ball gown, a partner with empty eyesockets, green mold growing on her elbow-length gloves, maggots squirming in the thin remains of her hair. To hold such a creature in our arms? Who, you ask me, would be so mad? Well . . . ?

"You will not want to open this door," Bluebeard tells his wife in that most horrible of all horror stories, "because your husband has forbidden it." But this, of course, only makes her all the more curious. . . . and at last, her curiosity is satisfied.

"You may go anywhere you wish in the castle," Count Dracula tells Jonathan Harker, "except where the doors are locked, where of course you will not wish to go." But Harker goes soon enough.

And so do we all. Perhaps we go to the forbidden door or window willingly because we understand that a time comes when we must go whether we want to or not . . . and not just to look, but to be pushed through. Forever.

## Thinking Through the Literature

1. How do you think King's ideas explain the appeal of Poe's work?

2. What do King's feelings seem to be about the "dancing partner" that the imagination seeks?

3. How might an audience react if a writer or filmmaker did not "open the door and show the audience what's behind it"?

DANSE MACABRE **465**

### Teaching Nonfiction

## Thinking Through the Literature

1. **Possible Responses:** Poe artfully builds up the anticipation of horror and makes a reader insatiably curious about the truth or outcome of a situation. In "The Masque of the Red Death," Poe creates horror by concealing the truth of the stranger until late in the story.

2. **Possible Response:** King describes a repellent figure, but he suggests that humans are fascinated and attracted by that deathly image.

3. **Possible Responses:** Even though expectations probably would not be met, an audience would be disappointed if the focus of tension is never revealed for what it is.

## OVERVIEW

### Objectives
1. understand and appreciate a classic narrative **poem (Literary Analysis)**
2. identify and analyze **sound devices** in a poem **(Literary Analysis)**
3. **draw conclusions** about the speaker in a poem **(Active Reading)**

### Summary
Alone in his study at midnight, trying to cope with his grief over the loss of his beloved Lenore, the speaker of this poem thinks he hears someone rapping at his door. He finds no one at his door, but when he opens the window shutter, a raven flies in and perches on a statue of the Greek goddess Athena. The speaker asks the raven its name, and the bird's response of "Nevermore" starts a chain of speculations in the speaker's mind. The speaker begs for forgetfulness, for relief from his suffering, for reassurance that Lenore and he someday will be reunited in Eden, but each time the raven croaks, "Nevermore." Finally, the speaker orders the bird to leave. Again, the raven croaks, "Nevermore."

### Thematic Link
In "The Raven," Edgar Allan Poe leads the reader into a **gothic** exploration of the mysterious depths of an individual soul. As the speaker in the poem describes his strange encounter, we experience with him the **dark side** of a mind haunted by grief, fear, anger, pain, and possibly madness.

---

### 5-Minute Warm-Up

***Daily Language SkillBuilder***

Have students **proofread** the display sentences on page 337k and write them correctly. The sentences also appear on Transparency 13 of **Grammar Transparencies and Copymasters.**

---

# The Raven
*Poetry by* EDGAR ALLAN POE

"*Take thy beak from out my heart, and take thy form from off my door!*"

### ( Connect to Your Life )

**The Pain of Loss** The speaker of "The Raven," one of the most famous poems in American literature, is a man grieving over the death of his beloved, Lenore. To understand the speaker's feelings, think about a time when you or someone you know lost a loved one—a person or a pet—through death or separation. Write a brief account of how you or the other person handled the loss.

## Build Background

**The Raven's Reputation** The raven that visits the poem's speaker lands on a bust of the ancient Greek goddess of wisdom, Athena. To the ancient Greeks, the raven was a bird of prophecy. In Western culture, ravens have long been associated with mystery, evil omens, and death. When writing his poem about loss, Poe first considered using an owl or a parrot as his mysterious visitor, but because of its cultural associations, the raven became his choice.

---

WORDS TO KNOW
**Vocabulary Preview**

| | |
|---|---|
| beguiling | implore |
| decorum | ominous |
| dirge | placid |
| discourse | respite |
| divining | tempest |

---

## Focus Your Reading

**LITERARY ANALYSIS** **SOUND DEVICES** One distinctive feature of "The Raven" is Poe's handling of **rhyme,** the repetition of similar sounds. Poe used rhymes in the following ways to produce musical effects in the poem:

- **End rhyme:** similar or identical sounds at the ends of lines
- **Internal rhyme:** rhymes within a line
- **Rhyme scheme:** the basic pattern of the end rhymes

Read "The Raven" aloud to better appreciate Poe's use of rhyme and other sound devices. As you read, notice how Poe maintains the rhyme scheme.

**ACTIVE READING** **DRAWING CONCLUSIONS** Readers **draw conclusions** by using their own knowledge and experiences to make logical guesses about characters and events in what they read. As you read "The Raven," try to draw conclusions about the speaker. Consider the following:

- the events he describes
- his physical condition when the events take place
- his intense sorrow about his loss

In your ▭ **READER'S NOTEBOOK,** list your conclusions about the speaker, and explain how you arrived at them.

---

## LESSON RESOURCES

**UNIT THREE RESOURCE BOOK,** pp. 56–60

**ASSESSMENT RESOURCES**
**Formal Assessment,** pp. 85–86
**Teacher's Guide to Assessment and Portfolio Use**
**Test Generator**

**SKILLS TRANSPARENCIES AND COPYMASTERS**
Literary Analysis
- Poetic Devices, T12 (for Cooperative Learning Activity, p. 471)

**Reading and Critical Thinking**
- Drawing Conclusions, T4 (for Active Reading, p. 466)

**Grammar**
- Comparison of Regular and Irregular Adjectives and Adverbs, T52 (for Mini Lesson, p. 472)
- Comparative Forms of Adjectives and Adverbs, C128 (for Mini Lesson, p. 472)

**Writing**
- Sensory Word List, T14 (for Writing Option 1, p. 472)

**Communications**
- Impromptu Speaking: Dialogue, Role-Play, Debate, T13 (for Activities & Explorations 1, p. 472)

**INTEGRATED TECHNOLOGY**
**Audio Library**
**Net Activities**
Visit our website:
www.mcdougallittell.com

# THE RAVEN

EDGAR

ALLAN

POE

*O*nce upon a midnight dreary, while I pondered, weak and weary,
Over many a quaint and curious volume of forgotten lore—
While I nodded, nearly napping, suddenly there came a tapping,
As of someone gently rapping, rapping at my chamber door.
5 "'Tis some visitor," I muttered, "tapping at my chamber door—
      Only this and nothing more."

Ah, distinctly I remember it was in the bleak December;
And each separate dying ember wrought its ghost upon the floor.
Eagerly I wished the morrow;—vainly I had sought to borrow
10 From my books surcease[1] of sorrow—sorrow for the lost Lenore—
For the rare and radiant maiden whom the angels name Lenore—
      Nameless *here* forevermore.

And the silken, sad, uncertain rustling of each purple curtain
Thrilled me—filled me with fantastic terrors never felt before;
15 So that now, to still the beating of my heart, I stood repeating
"'Tis some visitor entreating entrance at my chamber door;—
Some late visitor entreating entrance at my chamber door;—
      That it is and nothing more."

---

1. **surcease:** an end.

Have students read to find out how the speaker's attitude toward the raven changes over the course of the poem.

### Literary Analysis  SOUND DEVICES

 **A** Point out the evocative rhythms created by the repeated consonant sounds at the beginnings of words in these lines. Why do you think Poe used this repetition?

**Possible Response:** to make the poem more musical and dramatic; to enhance the poem's haunted, foreboding atmosphere; to emphasize the dark, eerie, or nightmarish nature of the speaker's experience

**B** Choose a student to read the stanza aloud. Ask students to identify the end words that rhyme.

**Answer:** *before, explore, explore, more*

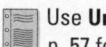 Use **Unit Three Resource Book,** p. 58 for more practice.

### Active Reading
DRAWING CONCLUSIONS

**C** Ask students how the speaker reacts to the bird's entrance.

**Answer:** He smiles, addresses the bird courteously, considers him "lordly," regards himself as blessed by the visit, refers to him as a friend, and worries that the bird will desert him.

Use this textual evidence to draw conclusions about the speaker.

**Possible Responses:** He is lonely; he is not superstitious or easily frightened; he is mentally unstable; he is deluded and hallucinating.

Use **Unit Three Resource Book,** p. 57 for more practice.

---

Presently my soul grew stronger; hesitating then no longer,
20  "Sir," said I, "or Madam, truly your forgiveness I <u>implore</u>;
But the fact is I was napping, and so gently you came rapping,
And so faintly you came tapping, tapping at my chamber door,
That I scarce was sure I heard you"—here I opened wide the door;—
            Darkness there and nothing more.

**A**  25  Deep into that darkness peering, long I stood there wondering, fearing,
Doubting, dreaming dreams no mortal ever dared to dream before;
But the silence was unbroken, and the stillness gave no token,
And the only word there spoken was the whispered word, "Lenore!"
This I whispered, and an echo murmured back the word "Lenore!"
30              Merely this and nothing more.

**B**  Back into the chamber turning, all my soul within me burning,
Soon again I heard a tapping somewhat louder than before.
"Surely," said I, "surely that is something at my window lattice;
Let me see, then, what thereat is, and this mystery explore—
35  Let my heart be still a moment and this mystery explore;—  **1**
            'Tis the wind and nothing more!"

Open here I flung the shutter, when, with many a flirt and flutter,
In there stepped a stately Raven of the saintly days of yore.[2]
Not the least obeisance[3] made he; not a minute stopped or stayed he;
40  But, with mien[4] of lord or lady, perched above my chamber door—
Perched upon a bust of Pallas[5] just above my chamber door—
**C**              Perched, and sat, and nothing more.

Then this ebony bird <u>beguiling</u> my sad fancy into smiling,
By the grave and stern <u>decorum</u> of the countenance it wore,
45  "Though thy crest be shorn and shaven, thou," I said, "art sure no craven,[6]
Ghastly grim and ancient Raven wandering from the Nightly shore—
Tell me what thy lordly name is on the Night's Plutonian[7] shore!"
            Quoth the Raven, "Nevermore."

---

2. **saintly days of yore:** sacred days of the past.

3. **obeisance** (ō-bā′səns): a polite gesture of respect, such as a bow.

4. **mien** (mēn): a way of carrying oneself; appearance.

5. **bust of Pallas:** statue of the head and shoulders of Athena, the Greek goddess of wisdom.

6. **craven:** cowardly person.

7. **Plutonian:** having to do with Pluto, the Roman god of the dead and ruler of the underworld.

| WORDS | **implore** (ĭm-plôr′) *v.* to beg; earnestly ask for |
|---|---|
| TO | **beguiling** (bĭ-gī′lĭng) *adj.* charming or delighting **beguile** *v.* |
| KNOW | **decorum** (dĭ-kôr′əm) *n.* proper and dignified behavior |

468

---

## Teaching Options

  ## **Speaking and Listening**

### DRAMATIC READING

**Prepare**  Help students prepare a dramatic presentation based on the poem. Have them work in cooperative groups to list the characteristics of the speaker that the narrative suggests. Students should consider the quality of the speaker's voice—its tone, pitch, and volume—and the speed with which he speaks. They should also consider the speaker's posture and gestures.

**Present**  Student groups can decide how to present the dramatic reading. Each group should select a student to read the poem. Other group members may prepare the setting, create props, or make sound effects.

**BLOCK SCHEDULING**  This activity is particularly well-suited for longer class periods.

Much I marveled this ungainly fowl to hear <u>discourse</u> so plainly,
Though its answer little meaning—little relevancy bore;
For we cannot help agreeing that no living human being
Ever yet was blessed with seeing bird above his chamber door—
Bird or beast upon the sculptured bust above his chamber door,
      With such name as "Nevermore."

55 But the Raven, sitting lonely on the <u>placid</u> bust, spoke only
That one word, as if his soul in that one word he did outpour.
Nothing farther then he uttered—not a feather then he fluttered—
Till I scarcely more than muttered "Other friends have flown before—
On the morrow *he* will leave me, as my hopes have flown before."
60       Then the bird said, "Nevermore."

Startled at the stillness broken by reply so aptly spoken,
"Doubtless," said I, "what it utters is its only stock and store
Caught from some unhappy master whom unmerciful Disaster
Followed fast and followed faster till his songs one burden bore—
65 Till the <u>dirges</u> of his Hope that melancholy burden bore
      Of 'Never—nevermore.'"

But the Raven still beguiling all my fancy into smiling,
Straight I wheeled a cushioned seat in front of bird and bust and door;
Then, upon the velvet sinking, I betook myself to linking
70 Fancy unto fancy, thinking what this <u>ominous</u> bird of yore—
What this grim, ungainly, ghastly, gaunt, and ominous bird of yore
      Meant in croaking, "Nevermore."

This I sat engaged in guessing, but no syllable expressing
To the fowl whose fiery eyes now burned into my bosom's core;
75 This and more I sat <u>divining</u>, with my head at ease reclining
On the cushion's velvet lining that the lamp-light gloated o'er,
But whose velvet violet lining with the lamp-light gloating o'er,
      *She* shall press, ah, nevermore!

WORDS
TO
KNOW

**discourse** (dĭ-skôrs′) *v.* to speak
**placid** (plăs′ĭd) *adj.* undisturbed; calm or quiet
**dirge** (dûrj) *n.* a slow, mournful piece of music; a funeral hymn
**ominous** (ŏm′ə-nəs) *adj.* threatening; menacing
**divining** (dĭ-vī′nĭng) *adj.* finding out through intuition; guessing from incomplete evidence **divine** *v.*

469

**A** Ask students to use the dialogue to clarify why the speaker thinks the raven was sent to his chamber.

**Possible Response:** He thinks God sent the bird to distract him from his grief.

## Reading Skills and Strategies:
### COMPARE AND CONTRAST

**B** Ask students to describe how the speaker views the bird.

**Possible Response:** At first the speaker welcomes the bird as a distraction from his misery, but later he becomes angry and calls the bird "ghastly," "ominous," and "a thing of evil."

## Literary Analysis | SOUND DEVICES |

**C** Ask students to find the internal rhymes in this stanza. *(parting, upstarting; token, spoken, unbroken).* Ask them what they think the use of evocative rhythms adds to the poem.

**Possible Responses:** makes it more compelling; makes it more memorable; creates tension because the rhymes interlock lines within stanzas very tightly

## Active Reading
| DRAWING CONCLUSIONS |

**D** Ask students to draw conclusions about the end of the poem: What happens to the raven? What kind of creature is the raven? What happens to the speaker?

**Possible Responses:** The raven remains perched on the bust of Pallas. Perhaps it is an immortal creature or a symbol of some eternal truth. The raven may also symbolize death or the permanence of the speaker's loss. The speaker seems either to die or to sink into endless despair at the end of the poem.

---

**A**

Then, methought, the air grew denser, perfumed from an unseen censer[8]
80 Swung by Seraphim[9] whose foot-falls tinkled on the tufted floor.
"Wretch," I cried, "thy God hath lent thee—by these angels he hath sent thee
Respite—respite and nepenthe[10] from thy memories of Lenore;
Quaff,[11] oh quaff this kind nepenthe and forget this lost Lenore!"
                      Quoth the Raven, "Nevermore."

**B**

85 "Prophet!" said I, "thing of evil!—prophet still, if bird or devil!—
Whether Tempter[12] sent, or whether tempest tossed thee here ashore,
Desolate yet all undaunted, on this desert land enchanted—
On this home by Horror haunted—tell me truly, I implore—
Is there—*is* there balm in Gilead?[13]—tell me—tell me, I implore!"
90                       Quoth the Raven, "Nevermore."

"Prophet!" said I, "thing of evil!—prophet still, if bird or devil!
By that Heaven that bends above us—by that God we both adore—
Tell this soul with sorrow laden if, within the distant Aidenn,[14]
It shall clasp a sainted maiden whom the angels name Lenore—
95 Clasp a rare and radiant maiden whom the angels name Lenore."
                      Quoth the Raven, "Nevermore."

**C**

"Be that word our sign of parting, bird or fiend!" I shrieked, upstarting—
"Get thee back into the tempest and the Night's Plutonian shore!
Leave no black plume as a token of that lie thy soul hath spoken!
100 Leave my loneliness unbroken!—quit the bust above my door!
Take thy beak from out my heart, and take thy form from off my door!"
                      Quoth the Raven, "Nevermore."

**D**

And the Raven, never flitting, still is sitting, *still* is sitting
On the pallid[15] bust of Pallas just above my chamber door;
105 And his eyes have all the seeming of a demon's that is dreaming,
And the lamp-light o'er him streaming throws his shadow on the floor;
And my soul from out that shadow that lies floating on the floor
                   Shall be lifted—nevermore!

---

8. **censer:** a container in which incense is burned, especially during religious services.
9. **Seraphim** (sĕr′ə-fĭm): angels of the highest rank.
10. **nepenthe** (nĭ-pĕn′thē): a drug that eases grief or sorrow by causing forgetfulness.
11. **quaff:** drink deeply.
12. **Tempter:** the Devil.
13. **balm** (bäm) **in Gilead** (gĭl′ē-əd): relief from suffering. The phrase comes from the Bible (Jeremiah 8:22) and refers to a soothing ointment from Gilead, a region of Palestine.
14. **Aidenn** (ād′n): heaven (from the Arabic form of the word *Eden*).
15. **pallid:** pale.

| WORDS TO KNOW | **respite** (rĕs′pĭt) *n.* a brief period of rest or relief from pain or labor<br>**tempest** (tĕm′pĭst) *n.* a violent storm |
|---|---|

---

# Teaching Options

## ✓ Assessment Informal Assessment

**EVALUATING THE SPEAKER** You can assess your students' understanding of the poem by asking them to complete the following activity. This activity allows students to make inferences and to support them with textual evidence and experience. On a scale of 1 to 10, with 1 being the least and 10 being the most, have students rate the speaker of "The Raven" in these five areas: sadness, intelligence, sense of humor, devotion, and sanity. Ask students to write a sentence to explain each of their ratings. Students might organize their thoughts in a chart and then compare their evaluations with their classmates' evaluations.

### RUBRIC

**3 Full Accomplishment** Student's ratings are based on the information in the poem, and the explanations are well developed and support the ratings.

**2 Substantial Accomplishment** Student's ratings are based on the information in the poem, but the explanations need more development.

**1 Little or Partial Accomplishment** Student's ratings are not supported by details in the poem, and the sentences do not explain them.

# *Thinking* through the LITERATURE

## Connect to the Literature

**1. What Do You Think?**
What three words would you use to describe the raven?

┌─────────────────────────────────────┐
**Comprehension Check**
- When do the events in the poem take place?
- Where does the speaker look to find the source of the sound he hears?
- What is the raven's response to all the speaker's questions?
└─────────────────────────────────────┘

## Think Critically

**2.** `ACTIVE READING` `DRAWING CONCLUSIONS` Refer to the **conclusions** about the **speaker** that you recorded in your 📖 READER'S NOTEBOOK. What conclusions did you draw about his mental state?

**3.** What meaning or meanings do you think the word *nevermore* has in the poem? What effect does the **repetition** of the word have on you?

**4.** How do you explain the raven and its visit?

┌─────┐
│THINK│ { • why the bird comes to the speaker
│ABOUT│ { • whether the bird is real or an illusion
└─────┘

## Extend Interpretations

**5. Critic's Corner** The poet James Russell Lowell wrote this couplet: "There comes Poe, with his raven, like Barnaby Rudge, / Three-fifths of him genius and two-fifths sheer fudge." (Barnaby Rudge is a character in a Charles Dickens novel who walks about with a pet raven on his back.) Do you agree with Lowell's view of Poe? Explain your opinion, referring to what you know about Poe's life and writings.

**6. Connect to Life** Recall your thoughts about the way in which you or someone you know handled a loss. What useful advice do you think you could give the speaker of "The Raven"?

| Stanza | Rhyme Scheme |
|--------|--------------|
| Stanza 1 | |
| Stanza 2 | |

## Literary Analysis

`SOUND DEVICES` Much of the musical quality of "The Raven" is produced by Poe's use of **rhyme**, the repetition of similar or identical sounds, to drive the poem's rhythm forward. Rhyme is employed by poets in various ways.

- **End rhyme** is the use of words with similar or identical sounds at the ends of lines:

  *. . . tapping at my chamber door—*
  *Only this and nothing more.*

- **Internal rhyme** is the use of rhyming words within a line:

  *Back into the chamber turning, all*
  *my soul within me burning*

- A **rhyme scheme** (pattern of end rhymes in a stanza or poem) can be identified by assigning a letter, starting with *a*, to each line, with lines that rhyme being given the same letter. Here is an example from Poe's poem "Annabel Lee":

  *It was many and many a year ago,*   a
  *In a kingdom by the sea.*   b
  *That a maiden there lived whom*
    *you may know*   a
  *By the name of Annabel Lee;—*   b

**Cooperative Learning Activity** Get together with a group of classmates, and have each member of the group record the rhyme scheme, along with any uses of internal rhyme, in a different stanza of "The Raven." Gather your information in a simple chart like the one shown here, and then compare findings. Does the rhyme scheme change from stanza to stanza, or does it stay the same? How does Poe's use of rhyme scheme affect the overall atmosphere of the poem?

THE RAVEN    **471**

---

## Extend Interpretations

**Critic's Corner** Students who agree with Lowell may feel that Poe wastes his genius by writing about events that are not solely based in reality. Students who disagree with Lowell are apt to point out Poe's use of vivid sensory imagery in his prose, his effective and original use of rhyme and rhythm in his poetry, and his gift for creating a compelling, mysterious atmosphere.

**Connect to Life** Some students may state that time will decrease the intensity of the speaker's loss. Others may say that the speaker should be among people instead of remaining solitary.

---

## Connect to the Literature

**1. What Do You Think?**
Possible Responses: gloomy, ominous, solemn, dark, grim, otherworldly

**Comprehension Check**
- in December, near midnight
- He first looks outside the door of his room, then outside the window.
- "Nevermore"

 Use Selection Quiz in **Unit Three Resource Book,** p. 60.

## Think Critically

**2.** Possible Responses: The speaker is deeply depressed; he's obsessed with his grief; he's deluded with moments of clarity; he's superstitious.

**3.** Possible Responses: The repetition suggests that the speaker will never cease to lament his loss, that he will never forget Lenore, or that he will never see Lenore again.

**4.** Possible Responses: Perhaps the raven is an illusion that the speaker creates as an image of his despair because he will never see Lenore again; the raven might be a real bird, and the speaker in his depressed state finds meaning in the bird's croaking.

## Literary Analysis

**Sound Devices** The rhyme scheme stays the same from stanza to stanza: *abcbbb*. The second, fourth, fifth, and sixth lines of all stanzas rhyme on the same sound, "ore." (The fifth line repeats the word that is in the fourth line, so it adds to the effect.) All the stanzas also have internal rhymes in the first and third lines, and the rhyming sound in the third line is reused in the middle of the fourth line. (Sometimes these are **slant rhymes,** as in stanza 6: "that is," "lattice," and "there-at is.") The effect of this complicated rhyme scheme is almost hypnotic or trancelike, which adds to the feeling of mystery and foreboding of the poem.

## Choices & Challenges

### Writing Options

1. **Prose Description** Students' descriptions should have the basic paragraph elements of topic sentence, body, and closing sentence. There should be several sensory details organized in a spatial order or in the order of importance.

2. **Speaker's Diary Entry** Students should make logical connections between the diary entry and the poem.

3. **Poetic Parody** Have students work in pairs to check each other's meter and rhyme. Ask for volunteers to read their parodies aloud.

### Activities & Explorations

1. **Dramatic Reading** The Speaking and Listening Mini-Lesson on page 468 will help students prepare for this activity. Students who are audience members can evaluate how well the performances increase their appreciation and understanding.

2. **Image of the Study** Encourage students to explain what they did to reflect the mood of the poem.

### Inquiry & Research

**Psychological View** Have students form cooperative groups for this activity. Students can brainstorm to develop a list of psychotic disorders and their symptoms. **To get students started on this activity,** provide a list of some disorders that students can research—for example, paranoia, schizophrenia, depression, and bipolar disorder.

### Vocabulary in Action

**EXERCISE A**

1. tempest
2. implore
3. respite
4. divining
5. decorum
6. ominous
7. dirge
8. placid
9. discourse
10. beguiling

**EXERCISE B**

Responses will vary. Be sure students are acting out the meanings of the words, not just the sounds of the syllables.

---

### Writing Options

1. **Prose Description** Write a prose description of the setting of "The Raven." Use words and phrases that evoke the same overall atmosphere as the poem itself.

2. **Speaker's Diary Entry** Writing as the speaker, compose a diary entry for a day one week after the events described in the poem. What does the speaker think and feel now? What has happened to the raven?

3. **Poetic Parody** A parody is an imitation (usually intended to be humorous) of a literary or artistic work. Write one or two stanzas of a parody of "The Raven." You might use another bird or animal in place of the raven, change the reason for the speaker's sorrow, or invent a new message for the intruder to utter. Whatever you change, try to follow Poe's meter and rhyme schemes so that your parody will be recognizable. Place the parody in your **Working Portfolio.**

### Activities & Explorations

1. **Dramatic Reading** With other members of your class, take turns performing dramatic readings of the poem. You might make video or audio recordings of the readings. ~ **PERFORMING**

2. **Image of the Study** Make an illustration of the speaker's study, including him and the raven. Try to capture the mood of Poe's poem through your use of details and color. ~ **ART**

### Inquiry & Research

**Psychological View** Modern psychology—the systematic study of human behavior—did not develop until several decades after Poe's death. In the 20th century, however, it became common for literary critics to discuss characters' actions in psychological terms. Find out some basic information about psychology—and in particular about psychotic disorders and psychotherapy. Then discuss the speaker of "The Raven" in terms of his possible psychological condition.

### Vocabulary in Action

**EXERCISE A: MEANING CLUES** Read each magazine article title below and write the vocabulary word you would expect to find in the article.

1. "Wild Weather: Protecting Yourself from the Elements"
2. "How to Ask for Forgiveness . . . and Get It"
3. "Vacation Spots for When You Really Need a Break"
4. "Psychics and Fortunetellers: Help or Hype?"
5. "Modern Manners for Modern Times"
6. "Flee or Fight? What to Do When You're in Danger"
7. "Avoiding the Wrong Music for Your Wedding"
8. "Tossing and Turning? You Too Can Sleep Like a Rock"
9. "How to Hold Up Your End of the Conversation"
10. "Putting That Certain Someone Under Your Spell"

**EXERCISE B** With a partner, take turns acting out the meanings of the words *implore, decorum, placid, ominous, divine,* and *respite.* (In some cases, you may be able to communicate the meaning with a single gesture.

| WORDS TO KNOW | | | | |
|---|---|---|---|---|
| beguiling | discourse | ominous | respite |
| decorum | divining | placid | tempest |
| dirge | implore | | |

**Building Vocabulary**
For an in-depth lesson on word connotation and denotation, see page 908.

---

### Mini Lesson: Grammar

**COMPARATIVE FORMS OF ADJECTIVES AND ADVERBS** The comparative degree of an adjective or adverb is used to compare two persons, places, groups, things, ideas, or actions; the superlative degree is used to compare three or more. The comparative and superlative degrees of one-syllable modifiers and most two-syllable adjectives are formed by adding -er and -est respectively. Most two-syllable adverbs, adverbs ending in -ly, and all three-syllable modifiers use *more* and *most* to form the comparative and superlative. Illustrate these points with examples such as the following.

| Positive | Comparative | Superlative |
|---|---|---|
| sad | sadder | saddest |
| brilliant | more brilliant | most brilliant |
| brilliantly | more brilliantly | most brilliantly |
| miserable | more miserable | most miserable |

 Use **Grammar Transparencies and Copymasters,** p. 128.

 Use McDougal Littell's *Language Network,* Chapter 7, for more instruction and practice in comparative adjectives and adverbs.

# PREPARING to *Read*

## The Fall of the House of Usher

*Short Story by* EDGAR ALLAN POE

*"I have . . . no abhorrence of danger, except in its absolute effect—in terror."*

### ( Connect to Your Life )

**Nothing to Fear but Fear** Roderick Usher, the main character in this story, claims that his greatest fear is that he will lose his life and sanity to fear. Many people have found that when fear takes over, it prevents them from reacting in an effective manner. Have you ever witnessed a situation in which someone showed fear? How did the fear seem to affect the person's judgment and ability to handle the situation? Jot down your thoughts.

## Build Background

**From Fear to Terror** "The Fall of the House of Usher" was written in 1839, when Poe was developing his literary theories. In "The Philosophy of Composition" (1846), he asserted that the writer of a literary work must plot the work out completely before beginning to write—an assertion at odds with the views of the literary community of his day. Poe crafted his works to achieve "unity of effect," with every part of each work, every detail, designed to contribute to a single overall feeling. Poe's particular genius was for exploring the strange and fantastic, conveying psychological terror through carefully chosen details and events.

> WORDS TO KNOW
> **Vocabulary Preview**
>
> affinity            insipid
> aghast             insoluble
> alleviation        interment
> annihilate         narrative
> deficiency         obstinate
> emaciated          terrestrial
> fitfully             vivacious
> futility

## Focus Your Reading

**LITERARY ANALYSIS  MOOD**  Throughout this story, Poe develops an atmosphere that plays a vivid role in the tale's development. **Mood** is the feeling or atmosphere that a writer conveys with his or her words. Here are three of Poe's mood-building techniques:

- detailed descriptions of settings though the use of imagery and figurative language
- precisely chosen words and phrases
- the use of a narrator who both observes and participates in the events recounted

As you read, notice how these features of the story work to create a mood. What effect does the mood have on you?

**ACTIVE READING  UNDERSTANDING COMPLEX SENTENCES**  In this story, Poe makes frequent use of **complex sentences,** piling detail upon detail to describe scenes or convey emotions. Use these techniques to help you understand a complex sentence:

- Look for the **main idea.** Locate the subject and the verb that form the basic kernel of the sentence.
- If the subject and verb are in inverted order, rearrange them.
- Temporarily disregard modifiers that do not seem crucial to the meaning.
- Read on. A confusing sentence might be followed by a sentence or two that clarifies it.

Take notes in your  📖 READER'S NOTEBOOK  about words or passages that you find especially difficult. After finishing the story, try applying a variety of strategies to clarify your understanding of those passages.

THE FALL OF THE HOUSE OF USHER  **473**

---

### Objectives

1. understand and appreciate a classic Gothic **short story (Literary Analysis)**
2. identify and understand **mood** in a short story **(Literary Analysis)**
3. **understand complex sentences (Active Reading)**

### Summary

"The Fall of the House of Usher" is narrated by a childhood friend of Roderick Usher. Invited by Usher to visit, the narrator arrives at the gloomy old family mansion and finds his boyhood friend greatly changed and depressed. Usher's twin sister, Madeline, who has been ill for a long time, dies during the narrator's visit. After burying her in the family vault, however, Usher grows increasingly agitated and is convinced she is still alive. The narrator tries to find rational causes for the sounds that he, too, begins to hear. Suddenly, Madeline appears, dressed in her bloody shroud. Usher and his sister fall dead into each other's arms; the narrator flees the house in horror. Upon looking back at the house, the narrator sees its walls collapse and sink into the adjacent lake.

### Thematic Link

"The Fall of the House of Usher" is a classic **Gothic** horror story. The narrator's rationalism contrasts sharply with Roderick Usher's **dark** and mystical frame of mind.

> ### 5-Minute Warm-Up
>
> *Daily*
> *Language*
> *SkillBuilder*
>
> Have students **proofread** the display sentences on page 337k and write them correctly. The sentences also appear on Transparency 13 of **Grammar Transparencies and Copymasters.**

 **Preteaching Vocabulary**

If you would like to preteach the WORDS TO KNOW for this selection, use the Mini Lesson p. 474.

**Reading Skills and Strategies:
PREVIEW**

Remind students that paraphrasing
complex sentences can help them
understand the main ideas.

**Literary Analysis** `MOOD`

 Have students analyze Poe's word
choice by reading the first sentence of
the story aloud. Ask students to identify
the sounds and words that evoke the
mood of the story.

**Possible Responses:** Words such as
*dull, dark, soundless, autumn, clouds,
oppressively, alone, dreary, shades,
evening,* and *melancholy* evoke a
somber, gloomy mood.

Use **Unit Three Resource Book,**
p. 63 for more practice.

**Active Reading**

`UNDERSTANDING
COMPLEX SENTENCES`

 Have students identify the main
idea of this sentence. What subject and
verb form the basic kernel of the sentence? Have students summarize the
sentence to clarify its meaning.

**Possible Responses:** The subject and
verb "I looked" form the basic kernel of
the sentence. The main idea is the narrator's observation and description of
the house and landscape. The sentence
can be summarized: The narrator
observed the house and landscape, the
details of which he found decayed,
bleak, and depressing.

Use **Unit Three Resource Book,**
p. 62 for more practice.

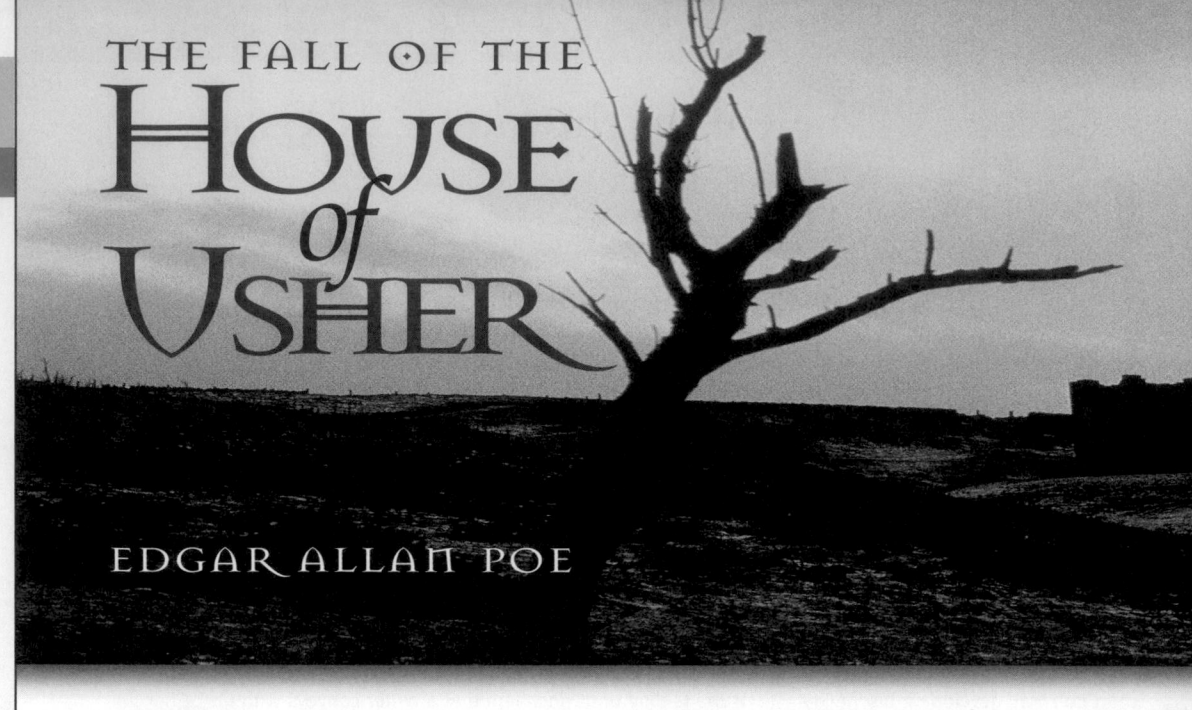

# THE FALL OF THE
# HOUSE
## *of*
# USHER

### EDGAR ALLAN POE

*Son coeur est un luth suspendu;
Sitôt qu'on le touche il résonne.*
—De Béranger

**(A)**

D uring the whole of a dull, dark, and soundless day in the
autumn of the year, when the clouds hung oppressively
low in the heavens, I had been passing alone, on horseback, through a singularly dreary tract of country, and
5    at length found myself, as the shades of the evening
drew on, within view of the melancholy House of Usher.
I know not how it was—but, with the first glimpse of
the building, a sense of insufferable gloom pervaded my
spirit. I say insufferable; for the feeling was unrelieved by any of
10 that half-pleasurable, because poetic, sentiment with which the
mind usually receives even the sternest natural images of the desolate or terrible. I looked upon the scene before me—upon the mere
house, and the simple landscape features of the domain—upon the
bleak walls—upon the vacant eye-like windows—upon a few rank

**(B)**

15 sedges—and upon a few white trunks of decayed trees—with an
utter depression of soul which I can compare to no earthly sensation more properly than to the after-dream of the reveller upon
opium—the bitter lapse into every-day life—the hideous dropping

**GUIDE FOR READING**

***Son coeur . . . résonne*** French: His
heart is a hanging lute; / As soon
as one touches it, it sounds (lines
from a poem by the 19th-century
French poet Pierre Jean de
Béranger).

## Teaching Options

 **Mini Lesson**   **Preteaching Vocabulary**

**USING CONTEXT CLUES** Call students' attention to
the list of WORDS TO KNOW. Tell them that sometimes they can rely on context to determine
meanings of unfamiliar words. One context clue
strategy is **restatement,** in which a difficult word
is rephrased in slightly easier language. Signal
words for restatement include *that is, in other
words,* and *or.* Dashes and commas sometimes
signal restatement, too. Use the model sentence
to demonstrate the strategy.

**Model Sentence**
The narrator wondered whether changing certain
details of the Usher landscape would destroy or
<u>annihilate</u> its gloom.

**Instruction**
• Write the model sentence on the chalkboard.
• Ask a volunteer to identify the signal word for
restatement. *(or)*
• Have students identify the word in the sentence
that restates the word *annihilate. (destroy)*
• Ask a volunteer to use *annihilate* in a sentence.

off of the veil. There was an iciness, a sinking, a sickening of the
20 heart—an unredeemed dreariness of thought which no goading of
the imagination could torture into aught of the sublime. What was
it—I paused to think—what was it that so unnerved me in the
contemplation of the House of Usher? It was a mystery all
<u>insoluble</u>; nor could I grapple with the shadowy fancies that
25 crowded upon me as I pondered. I was forced to fall back upon
the unsatisfactory conclusion, that while, beyond doubt, there *are*
combinations of very simple natural objects which have the power
of thus affecting us, still the analysis of this power lies among
considerations beyond our depth. It was possible, I reflected, that
30 a mere different arrangement of the particulars of the scene, of the
details of the picture, would be sufficient to modify, or perhaps to
<u>annihilate</u> its capacity for sorrowful impression; and, acting upon
this idea, I reined my horse to the precipitous brink of a black and
lurid tarn that lay in unruffled lustre by the dwelling, and gazed
35 down—but with a shudder even more thrilling than before—upon
the remodelled and inverted images of the gray sedge, and the
ghastly tree-stems, and the vacant and eye-like windows.

**34 tarn:** a small mountain lake.

| WORDS TO KNOW | **insoluble** (ĭn-sŏl′yə-bəl) *adj.* having no solution; unsolvable |
|---|---|
| | **annihilate** (ə-nī′ə-lāt′) *v.* to destroy completely; wipe out |

475

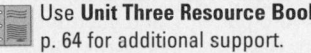

**A** Have students paraphrase the complex sentence in lines 46–55.

**Possible Response:** The writer described his troubling illness and his wish to see me. He hoped that my cheerful company would relieve his condition.

### Literary Analysis: POINT OF VIEW

**B** Ask students what characteristics are revealed about the narrator in this passage.

**Possible Response:** While cautious about the odd ("singular") invitation from Usher, the narrator is responsive to Usher's sincere request. The narrator is intelligent and perceptive, and also a caring friend.

### GUIDE FOR READING

**C** The narrator knows that the Ushers are an old family known for their artistic sensibility and charitable contributions. He also knows that there are no surviving cousins or other branches of the family; the Usher name was passed directly from father to son. Therefore, to the local people, the name of the family estate, "House of Usher," came to mean both the family and the house.

**D** **Possible Responses:** The narrator feels a sense of dread and an ominous cast over the House of Usher, but he also recognizes his feelings as superstitious and based on feelings of terror.

### Literary Analysis: FORESHADOWING

**E** Ask students what event the "barely perceptible fissure" might foreshadow.

**Possible Response:** the collapse or fall of the House of Usher

---

**1** evertheless, in this mansion of gloom I now proposed to myself a sojourn of some weeks. Its proprietor, Roderick Usher, had been one of my boon companions in boyhood; but many years had elapsed since our last meeting. A letter, however, had lately reached me in a distant part of the country—a letter from him—which, in its wildly importunate nature, had admitted of no other than a personal reply. The MS. gave evidence of nervous agitation. The writer spoke of acute bodily illness—of a mental disorder which oppressed him—and of an earnest desire to see me, as his best and indeed his only personal friend, with a view of attempting, by the cheerfulness of my society, some <u>alleviation</u> of his malady. It was the manner in which all this, and much more, was said—it was the apparent *heart* that went with his request—which allowed me no room for hesitation; and I accordingly obeyed forthwith what I still considered a very singular summons.

Although, as boys, we had been even intimate associates, yet I really knew little of my friend. His reserve had been always excessive and habitual. I was aware, however, that his very ancient family had been noted, time out of mind, for a peculiar sensibility of temperament, displaying itself, through long ages, in many works of exalted art, and manifested, of late, in repeated deeds of munificent yet unobtrusive charity, as well as in a passionate devotion to the intricacies, perhaps even more than to the orthodox and easily recognizable beauties, of musical science. I had learned, too, the very remarkable fact, that the stem of the Usher race, all time-honored as it was, had put forth, at no period, any enduring branch; in other words, that the entire family lay in the direct line of descent, and had always, with very trifling and very temporary variation, so lain. It was this <u>deficiency</u>, I considered, while running over in thought the perfect keeping of the character of the premises with the accredited character of the people, and while speculating upon the possible influence which the one, in the long lapse of centuries, might have exercised upon the other—it was this deficiency, perhaps, of collateral issue, and the consequent undeviating transmission, from sire to son, of the patrimony with the name, which had, at length, so identified the two as to merge the original title of the estate in the quaint and equivocal appellation of the "House of Usher"—an appellation which seemed to include, in the minds of the peasantry who used it, both the family and the family mansion.

I have said that the sole effect of my somewhat childish experiment—that of looking down within the tarn—had been to

*Line markers: 40, 45, 50, 55, 60, 65, 70, 75, 80*

**44 had admitted of no other than:** had required.

**45 MS.:** an abbreviation of *manuscript.*

**72 collateral** (kə-lăt′ər-əl) **issue:** relatives not in the direct line of descent.

**76 equivocal appellation** (ĭ-kwĭv′ə-kəl ăp′ə-lā′shən): ambiguous name.
**54–78** Summarize what the narrator already knows about Roderick Usher and his family estate.

---

WORDS
TO
KNOW

**alleviation** (ə-lē′vē-ā′shən) *n.* a decrease in severity; relief
**deficiency** (dĭ-fĭsh′ən-sē) *n.* a lack

476

---

## Teaching Options

## Speaking and Listening

**ORAL READING** Ask students to prepare an oral reading of the opening paragraph (lines 1–38). They can work in pairs or cooperative groups to identify and analyze the effect of aesthetic elements within the text, such as formal language, alliteration, repetition of phrases and word patterns, and interruptive punctuation (dashes). Have students discuss how the mood and meaning presented in the opening paragraph could be conveyed in an oral reading. Ask them to consider ways in which various elements of verbal communication—such as volume, pitch, enunciation, pace, stress, and tone—will affect their presentation of the story.

**Present** Have students present their oral interpretations. They should justify their choice of verbal performance techniques by referring to their interpretations of the story's narrator, setting, and mood. Audience members should evaluate how the performance enhances their understanding.

**BLOCK SCHEDULING** This activity is particularly well-suited for longer class periods.

deepen the first singular impression. There can be no doubt that the consciousness of the rapid increase of my superstition—for why should I not so term it?—served mainly to accelerate the increase itself. Such, I have long known, is the paradoxical law of all sentiments having terror as a basis. And it might have been for this reason only, that, when I again uplifted my eyes to the house itself, from its image in the pool, there grew in my mind a strange fancy—a fancy so ridiculous, indeed, that I but mention it to show the vivid force of the sensations which oppressed me. I had so worked upon my imagination as really to believe that about the whole mansion and domain there hung an atmosphere peculiar to themselves and their immediate vicinity—an atmosphere which had no <u>affinity</u> with the air of heaven, but which had reeked up from the decayed trees, and the gray wall, and the silent tarn—a pestilent and mystic vapor, dull, sluggish, faintly discernible, and leaden-hued.

   Shaking off from my spirit what *must* have been a dream, I scanned more narrowly the real aspect of the building. Its principal feature seemed to be that of an excessive antiquity. The discoloration of ages had been great. Minute fungi overspread the whole exterior, hanging in a fine tangled web-work from the eaves. Yet all this was apart from any extraordinary dilapidation. No portion of the masonry had fallen; and there appeared to be a wild inconsistency between its still perfect adaptation of parts, and the crumbling condition of the individual stones. In this there was much that reminded me of the specious totality of old woodwork which has rotted for long years in some neglected vault, with no disturbance from the breath of the external air. Beyond this indication of extensive decay, however, the fabric gave little token of instability. Perhaps the eye of a scrutinizing observer might have discovered a barely perceptible fissure, which, extending from the roof of the building in front, made its way down the wall in a zigzag direction, until it became lost in the sullen waters of the tarn.

   Noticing these things, I rode over a short causeway to the house. A servant in waiting took my horse, and I entered the Gothic archway of the hall. A valet, of stealthy step, thence conducted me, in silence, through many dark and intricate passages in my progress to the *studio* of his master. Much that I encountered on the way contributed, I know not how, to heighten the vague sentiments of which I have already spoken. While the objects around me—while the carvings of the ceilings, the sombre

**79–96** Consider the narrator's description of his first impressions of  the house. What are your impressions of the narrator?

**106 specious totality**
(spē'shəs tō-tăl'ĭ-tē): false appearance of soundness.

**E**

**117 Gothic** (gŏth'ĭk) **archway:** a doorway topped by an arch with a pointed peak, characteristic of Gothic architecture.

WORDS
TO
KNOW

**affinity** (ə-fĭn'ĭ-tē) *n.* a kinship or likeness

477

**Literary Analysis: GOTHIC SETTING**

**A** Ask students which details of the room help create the Gothic setting.
**Possible Responses:** large, lofty room; long, narrow, pointed windows; filtered window light; vaulted ceiling

**GUIDE FOR READING**

**B** The description of the room as dark, gloomy, and lacking any vitality emphasizes the foreboding mood of the story.

**Literary Analysis: CHARACTERIZATION**

**C** One method of characterization is the description of a character's physical appearance. Ask students the following questions.

• What does the description of Usher's face reveal about his character?
**Possible Response:** He is an eccentric, sensitive, and tormented man.

• What effect does Usher's appearance have on the narrator?
**Possible Response:** The narrator is shocked by Usher's appearance and responds with pity and awe.

**1**
125 tapestries of the walls, the ebon blackness of the floors, and the phantasmagoric armorial trophies which rattled as I strode, were but matters to which, or to such as which, I had been accustomed from my infancy—while I hesitated not to acknowledge how familiar was all this—I still wondered to find how unfamiliar were the fancies which ordinary images were stirring up. On one of the staircases, I met the physician of the family. His counte-
**2**
130 nance, I thought, wore a mingled expression of low cunning and perplexity. He accosted me with trepidation and passed on. The valet now threw open a door and ushered me into the presence of his master.

135 The room in which I found myself was very large and lofty. The windows were long, narrow, and pointed, and at so vast a distance from the black oaken floor as to be altogether inaccessible from within. Feeble gleams of encrimsoned light made their way through the trellissed panes, and served to render sufficiently distinct the more prominent objects around; the eye, however,
**A**
140 struggled in vain to reach the remoter angles of the chamber, or the recesses of the vaulted and fretted ceiling. Dark draperies hung upon the walls. The general furniture was profuse, comfortless, antique, and tattered. Many books and musical instruments lay scattered about, but failed to give any vitality to the scene. I
145 felt that I breathed an atmosphere of sorrow. An air of stern, deep, and irredeemable gloom hung over and pervaded all.

Upon my entrance, Usher arose from a sofa on which he had been lying at full length, and greeted me with a vivacious warmth which had much in it, I at first thought, of an overdone
150 cordiality—of the constrained effort of the *ennuyé* man of the world. A glance, however, at his countenance convinced me of his perfect sincerity. We sat down; and for some moments, while he spoke not, I gazed upon him with a feeling half of pity, half of awe. Surely, man had never before so terribly altered, in so brief
155 a period, as had Roderick Usher! It was with difficulty that I could bring myself to admit the identity of the wan being before me with the companion of my early boyhood. Yet the character of his face had been at all times remarkable. A cadaverousness of
**C**
complexion; an eye large, liquid, and luminous beyond compar-
160 ison; lips somewhat thin and very pallid, but of a surpassingly beautiful curve; a nose of a delicate Hebrew model, but with a breadth of nostril unusual in similar formations; a finely moulded chin, speaking, in its want of prominence, of a want of moral energy; hair of a more than web-like softness and tenuity;—these
165 features, with an inordinate expansion above the regions of the

**124 phantasmagoric armorial** (făn-tăz′mə-gôr′ĭk är-môr′ē-əl) **trophies:** looming wall decorations bearing coats of arms.

**134–146** How does the description of the room contribute to the mood **B** of the story?

**150 ennuyé** (äN-wē-ā′) *French:* bored.

**3**

**158 cadaverousness** (kə-dăv′ər-əs-nĭs): corpselike appearance.

WORDS
TO **vivacious** (vĭ-vā′shəs) *adj.* full of energy; lively
KNOW

478

**BLOCK SCHEDULING: MANAGING TIME**

**If your schedule requires that you cover the lesson objectives in a shorter time, use . . .**
• Preparing to Read, p. 473
• Thinking Through the Literature, p. 496
• Vocabulary in Action, p. 499

**If you want to take advantage of longer class time, use . . .**
• TE Teaching Options: Preteaching Vocabulary, p. 474; Viewing and Representing, pp. 479, 482; Speaking and Listening, pp. 476, 492; Cross-Curricular Links, pp. 477, 489; Standardized Test Practice, p. 484; Informal Assessment, p. 494
• Choices & Challenges, pp. 498–499

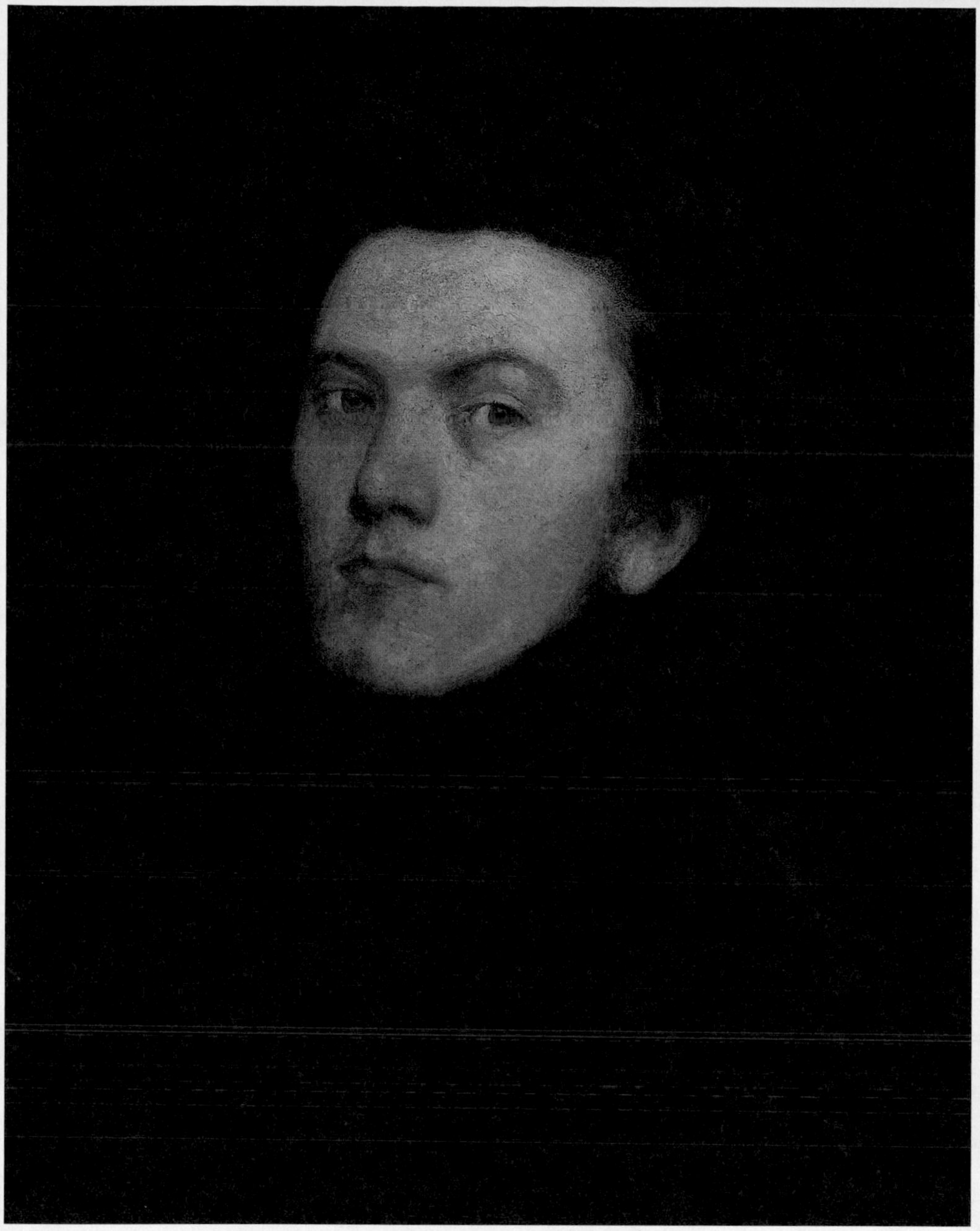

*Self-Portrait,* Bertalan Székely. Hungarian National Gallery, Budapest. Photo by Mester Tibor Foto, Budapest.



## Customizing Instruction

### Less Proficient Readers

**1** Ask students why the interior of the house is familiar to the narrator.

**Possible Response:** He used to visit the house when he was a boy.

**2** Tell students that *countenance* means "face."

### Gifted and Talented

**3** Ask students which details in Usher's appearance seem paradoxical. Have them discuss how his characterization is an allegory for his entire family.

**Possible Responses:** Usher is alive, yet his complexion is described as having a corpselike appearance. Repulsive features, such as his large, liquid eye, appear next to beautiful and delicate features, such as the curve of his lip and his nose. Certain features are paradoxes in and of themselves: a chin that is finely molded, and yet lacking in prominence; a nose that is delicate, and yet with unusual nostrils. Roderick Usher is a symbol of his family, of which he is the last heir—aristocratic, refined, beautiful, yet rapidly declining.

## Mini Lesson Viewing and Representing

*Self Portrait*
**by Bertalan Székely**

**ART APPRECIATION** Explain that the painting is a self-portrait of the artist.

**Instruction** Have students analyze the colors and composition of the painting.

**Possible Response:** The colors surrounding the artist's face are dark and somber, in contrast to the artist's pale, serious face. The artist's face is the focus of the composition.

**Application** Have students interpret the artist's view of himself, using elements of the painting to support their interpretations.

**Possible Response:** The artist has purposely focused the work on his own face, an indication, perhaps, of self-awareness or of defiance regarding the close scrutiny; the artist tilts his chin upward, yet turns his eyes away from the viewer. Some of the artist's features are striking—his pale, broad forehead and nicely arched eyebrows; others are blunt—the rounded nose, the too-large ears, the slight underbite.

- Ask students how Roderick Usher might portray himself in a painting. What colors would he use? How would he compose the self-portrait? On what features would he focus?

### Active Reading

**UNDERSTANDING COMPLEX SENTENCES**

Ⓐ Various techniques can help students understand complex sentences.

- Point out the use of inverted word order. Write this clause on the chalkboard: "In the manner of my friend I was at once struck with an incoherence—an inconsistency." Underline the subject or main idea of the clause: I was at once struck with an incoherence—an inconsistency. Then rearrange the syntax to make it more understandable: "I was at once struck with an incoherence—an inconsistency —in the manner of my friend."
- Ask students to reread the entire complex sentence and paraphrase it.

**Possible Response:** I was struck by my friend's inconsistent manner, which seemed to arise from his struggle to overcome his nervousness.

### Literary Analysis: CHARACTERIZATION

Ⓑ Have students explain the maladies from which Roderick Usher suffers.

**Possible Response:** He suffers from an acute sensitivity of taste, touch, smell, and sight. His sense of sound is less sensitive, but only to particular sounds, such as that from stringed instruments. He also suffers deeply from depression over his sister's severe illness.

### GUIDE FOR READING

Ⓒ **Possible Response:** Usher is so shaken by fear and terror that he is certain he will go insane and die.

Ⓓ **Possible Response:** He sees Usher as being a prisoner of his own superstitions.

Ⓔ **Possible Response:** He is startled because Madeline's appearance has drastically changed from her long, mysterious illness.

---

temple, made up altogether a countenance not easily to be forgotten. And now in the mere exaggeration of the prevailing character of these features, and of the expression they were wont to convey, lay so much of change that I doubted to whom I spoke.
170 The now ghastly pallor of the skin, and the now miraculous lustre of the eye, above all things startled and even awed me. The silken hair, too, had been suffered to grow all unheeded, and as, in its wild gossamer texture, it floated rather than fell about the face, I could not, even with effort, connect its Arabesque expression
175 with any idea of simple humanity.

Ⓐ In the manner of my friend I was at once struck with an incoherence—an inconsistency; and I soon found this to arise from a series of feeble and futile struggles to overcome an habitual trepidancy—an excessive nervous agitation. For something of this
180 nature I had indeed been prepared, no less by his letter, than by reminiscences of certain boyish traits, and by conclusions deduced from his peculiar physical conformation and temperament. His action was alternately vivacious and sullen. His voice varied rapidly from a tremulous indecision (when the animal
185 spirits seemed utterly in abeyance) to that species of energetic concision—that abrupt, weighty, unhurried, and hollow-sounding enunciation—that leaden, self-balanced, and perfectly modulated guttural utterance, which may be observed in the lost drunkard, or the irreclaimable eater of opium, during the periods
190 of his most intense excitement.

It was thus that he spoke of the object of my visit, of his earnest desire to see me, and of the solace he expected me to afford him. He entered, at some length, into what he conceived to be the nature of his malady. It was, he said, a constitutional and a family evil,
195 and one for which he despaired to find a remedy—a mere nervous affection, he immediately added, which would undoubtedly soon pass off. It displayed itself in a host of unnatural sensations. Some of these, as he detailed them, interested and bewildered me; although, perhaps, the terms and the general manner of their narra-
200 tion had their weight. He suffered much from a morbid acuteness of the senses; the most insipid food was alone endurable; he could wear only garments of certain texture; the odors of all flowers were oppressive; his eyes were tortured by even a faint light; and there were but peculiar sounds, and these from stringed instruments, 1
205 which did not inspire him with horror.

Ⓑ To an anomalous species of terror I found him a bounden slave. "I shall perish," said he, "I *must* perish in this deplorable 2 folly. Thus, thus, and not otherwise, shall I be lost. I dread the

**174 Arabesque** (ăr′ə-bĕsk′): intricately interwoven (like the design on an Oriental carpet).

**186 concision** (kən-sĭzh′ən): briefness of communication; terseness.

**1**
**204 but peculiar:** only certain.

**2**

| WORDS TO KNOW | **insipid** (ĭn-sĭp′ĭd) *adj.* lacking in flavor; bland |

480

---

## Teaching Options

**Mini Lesson** ## Vocabulary Strategy

**UNDERSTANDING PREFIXES:** *in-*
Students can expand their vocabulary by applying meanings of prefixes in order to comprehend unfamiliar words. A prefix is a letter or group of letters added to the beginning of a base word or root. Sometimes, a prefix completely changes the meaning of a word or root. Write this prefix and root on the chalkboard:

   in + sufferable

Tell students that the prefix *in-* means "not." Knowing that the word *sufferable* means "capable of being endured," ask students how the prefix *in-* changes the word's meaning.

**Application** Have students explain how the prefix *in-* affects the meaning of each base word or root in the words *insoluble* and *insipid.*

**Possible Responses:** *Insoluble* is formed from the Latin word *solvere,* which means "to solve"; the prefix *in-* changes the meaning to "unsolvable." *Insipid* is formed from the Latin word *sapere,* which means "to taste"; the prefix *in-* changes the meaning to "lacking in flavor."

Use **Vocabulary Transparencies and Copymasters**, p. 44.

A lesson on prefixes appears on p. 1130 in the Pupil's Edition.

events of the future, not in themselves, but in their results. I
shudder at the thought of any, even the most trivial, incident,
which may operate upon this intolerable agitation of soul. I have,
indeed, no abhorrence of danger, except in its absolute effect—in
terror. In this unnerved, in this pitiable, condition I feel that the
period will sooner or later arrive when I must abandon life and
reason together, in some struggle with the grim phantasm,
FEAR."

I learned, moreover, at intervals, and through broken and
equivocal hints, another singular feature of his mental condition.
He was enchained by certain superstitious impressions in regard
to the dwelling which he tenanted, and whence, for many years,
he had never ventured forth—in regard to an influence whose
supposititious force was conveyed in terms too shadowy here to
be re-stated—an influence which some peculiarities in the mere
form and substance of his family mansion had, by dint of long
sufferance, he said, obtained over his spirit—an effect which the
*physique* of the gray walls and turrets, and of the dim tarn into
which they all looked down, had, at length, brought about upon
the *morale* of his existence.

He admitted, however, although with hesitation, that much of
the peculiar gloom which thus afflicted him could be traced to a
more natural and far more palpable origin—to the severe and
long-continued illness—indeed to the evidently approaching
dissolution—of a tenderly beloved sister, his sole companion for
long years, his last and only relative on earth. "Her decease," he
said, with a bitterness which I can never forget, "would leave him
(him, the hopeless and the frail) the last of the ancient race of the
Ushers." While he spoke, the lady Madeline (for so was she
called) passed through a remote portion of the apartment, and,
without having noticed my presence, disappeared. I regarded her
with an utter astonishment not unmingled with dread; and yet I
found it impossible to account for such feelings. A sensation of
stupor oppressed me as my eyes followed her retreating steps.
When a door, at length, closed upon her, my glance sought
instinctively and eagerly the countenance of the brother; but he had
buried his face in his hands, and I could only perceive that a far
more than ordinary wanness had overspread the emaciated fingers
through which trickled many passionate tears.

The disease of the lady Madeline had long baffled the skill of
her physicians. A settled apathy, a gradual wasting away of the
person, and frequent although transient affections of a partially
cataleptical character were the unusual diagnosis. Hitherto she

**2**

**3** **207–216** In your own words, sum
up Usher's view of his situation. **C**

**222 supposititious**
(sə-pŏz′ĭ-tĭsh′əs): supposed. How
does the narrator seem to regard
Usher's condition? **D**

**224 dint:** force; power.

**237–241** Why do you think the
narrator's first glimpse at Madeline
Usher is so startling? **E**

**251 cataleptical** (kăt′l-ĕp′tĭ-kəl):
involving paralysis and
unconsciousness; trancelike.

**B**

## Customizing Instruction

### Gifted and Talented
**1** Have students use this description
of Roderick Usher's acute sensitivity to
clarify their interpretation of the epi-
graph at the beginning of the story.

### Less Proficient Readers
**2** Ask students to paraphrase lines
206–216 as simply as possible.
**Possible Response:** The narrator thinks
that Usher is a slave to terror. Usher
believes he will die in this tortured
state—afraid of terror. Usher tells the
narrator that at some point he will lose
his mind and his life in the struggle
with fear.

**3** Have students explain what it is
that Roderick Usher struggles against.
**Answer:** his own feelings of fear
Encourage them to work together to
find other places in the story where
Usher expresses his fear.

### Students Acquiring English
Defining the following words and
phrases will help students understand
the story:
Line 170: *lustre* means "glow or sheen"
Line 173: *gossamer* means "like a film
of cobwebs"
Line 194: *malady* means "disease"
Line 206: *anomalous species of terror*
means "an unusual kind of fear"
Line 215: *phantasm* means "ghost"
Line 226: *physique* means "form or
structure"
Line 232: *approaching dissolution*
refers to the upcoming death of
Usher's sister

WORDS
TO
KNOW      **emaciated** (ĭ-mā′shē-ā′tĭd) *adj.* excessively thin; wasted away **emaciate** *v.*

**481**

**A** Remind students that they can make more sense of a complex sentence by locating the main idea and restating the sentence in their own words. Ask a volunteer to restate the complex sentence that begins at the end of line 251 on page 481 and continues onto page 482.
**Possible Response:** Until recently, Madeline had endured her disease. Just before the narrator arrived at the house, however, she became deathly ill. The narrator does not expect to see her alive again.

**GUIDE FOR READING**

**B** She has probably taken to her bed.

**Literary Analysis: POINT OF VIEW**

**C** Ask students to summarize the narrator's feelings at this point in his visit.
**Possible Response:** The narrator senses the futility of trying to cheer up a man who is consumed by darkness and gloom.

**GUIDE FOR READING**

**D** **Possible Responses:** The narrator is observant and creative; he appreciates Roderick's art and its ideals; he is sensitive to Roderick and identifies with him.

**Literary Analysis** | MOOD |

**E** Ask students what this image describes. Have them describe the mood created by Usher's painting.
**Possible Response:** The image describes a burial crypt. The mood created is unnatural, creepy, frightening, and claustrophobic.

*Head of Ophelia,* study (about 1897), Edwin Austin Abbey. Oil on wood, 14" x 9⅜". Edwin Austin Abbey Memorial Collection, Yale University Art Gallery, New Haven, Connecticut.

**A** 255   had steadily borne up against the pressure of her malady, and had not betaken herself finally to bed; but on the closing in of the evening of my arrival at the house, she succumbed (as her brother told me at night with inexpressible agitation) to the prostrating power of the destroyer; and I learned that the glimpse I had obtained of her person would thus probably be the last I should obtain—that the lady, at least while living, would be seen by me no more.   **1**

259 Where, probably, is Madeline at this point?   **B**

---

## Teaching Options

 **Mini Lesson** **Viewing and Representing**

*Head of Ophelia*
**by Edwin Austin Abbey**

**ART APPRECIATION** The painting is the artist's interpretation of the character Ophelia from Shakespeare's play *Hamlet.* In the play, Ophelia despairs at Hamlet's thoughtless treatment of her and drowns herself.
**Instruction** Have students describe elements of the work, including color, line, shape, quality of brushstroke, and style.
**Possible Response:** The face of Ophelia is cast in a pale color, made all the more pale by the contrast of her long, unkempt locks of red hair. Her pale

blue eyes seem perfect circles in her oval face. The focus of the painting is on Ophelia's face, which is represented in somewhat realistic detail; away from Ophelia's face, the artist's brushstroke roughens and has a hurried or unfinished appearance.
**Application** Have students analyze the ideas and meaning represented in the work. How does the artist characterize Ophelia?
**Possible Response:** The work represents Ophelia's despair. Her wide-open eyes make her appear to be in a trance. She seems paralyzed by her state.

• Ask students to compare and contrast the representation of Ophelia in the painting with the description of Madeline in the text.

260 or several days ensuing, her name was unmentioned
by either Usher or myself; and during this period I was
busied in earnest endeavors to alleviate the melancholy of my friend. We painted and read together, or
I listened, as if in a dream, to the wild improvisations of his
265 speaking guitar. And thus, as a closer and still closer intimacy
admitted me more unreservedly into the recesses of his spirit, the
more bitterly did I perceive the futility of all attempt at cheering a
mind from which darkness, as if an inherent positive quality,
poured forth upon all objects of the moral and physical universe in
270 one unceasing radiation of gloom.

I shall ever bear about me a memory of the many solemn hours
I thus spent alone with the master of the House of Usher. Yet I
should fail in any attempt to convey an idea of the exact character of the studies, or of the occupations, in which he involved
275 me, or led me the way. An excited and highly distempered ideality
threw a sulphureous lustre over all. His long improvised dirges
will ring forever in my ears. Among other things, I hold painfully
in mind a certain singular perversion and amplification of the
wild air of the last waltz of Von Weber. From the paintings over
280 which his elaborate fancy brooded, and which grew, touch by
touch, into vagueness at which I shuddered the more thrillingly,
because I shuddered knowing not why—from these paintings
(vivid as their images now are before me) I would in vain
endeavor to educe more than a small portion which should lie
285 within the compass of merely written words. By the utter
simplicity, by the nakedness of his designs, he arrested and over-
awed attention. If ever mortal painted an ideal, that mortal was
Roderick Usher. For me at least, in the circumstances then
surrounding me, there arose out of the pure abstractions which
290 the hypochondriac contrived to throw upon his canvas, an intensity of intolerable awe, no shadow of which felt I ever yet in the
contemplation of the certainly glowing yet too concrete reveries
of Fuseli.

One of the phantasmagoric conceptions of my friend,
295 partaking not so rigidly of the spirit of abstraction, may be shad-
owed forth, although feebly, in words. A small picture presented
the interior of an immensely long and rectangular vault or tunnel,
with low walls, smooth, white, and without interruption or
device. Certain accessory points of the design served well to
300 convey the idea that this excavation lay at an exceeding depth
below the surface of the earth. No outlet was observed in any
portion of its vast extent, and no torch or other artificial source

**275 distempered ideality**
(ĭ'dē-ăl'ĭ-tē): diseased creativity.

**276 sulphureous** (sŭl-fyŏŏr'ē-əs)
**luster:** lurid glow; nightmarish
quality.

**279 Von Weber** (fôn vā'bər): the
German romantic composer Karl
Maria von Weber.

**288** What do the narrator's
observations about Roderick Usher
reveal about his own personality?

**293 Fuseli** (fyŏŏ'zə-lē'): the Swiss-
born British painter Henry Fuseli,
many of whose works feature
fantastic or gruesome elements.

| WORDS TO KNOW | **futility** (fyŏŏ-tĭl'ĭ-tē) *n.* uselessness |
|---|---|

483

## Customizing Instruction

### Students Acquiring English
**1** Help students translate the archaic
verbs that Poe uses into modern
English.
Line 252: *had steadily borne up* means
that Madeline had steadily endured or
suffered the disease
Line 253: *betaken* means "taken"

### Multiple Learning Styles
**Auditory Learners**
**2** Ask students to imagine the
sounds of Roderick Usher's "wild
improvisations of his speaking guitar."
Have them describe what feelings or
mood these sounds might evoke. Invite
students to create the sound on an
instrument of their choice, defending
their interpretation of the sound with
evidence from the text.

### Less Proficient Readers
**3** Ask students to paraphrase lines
288–292 as simply as possible.
**Possible Response:** For me, the
abstract paintings that Usher created
had an intensity I hadn't felt since looking at Fuseli's paintings.

### GUIDE FOR READING

**A** **Possible Response:** The picture suggests an underground tomb with no way out; the light seems supernatural and foreboding.

### Reading Skills and Strategies: DRAWING INFERENCES

**B** Ask students what inference they can draw regarding the significance of "The Haunted Palace."

**Possible Response:** The true subject of the poem is the House of Usher. The verses recall a time long ago when the "palace" was a beautiful place inhabited by "good angels." In the fifth stanza, the poem bitterly recalls the arrival of "evil things, in robes of sorrow."

### GUIDE FOR READING

**C** The poem contributes to the mood of foreboding and doom by describing the ominous fall of a once-vibrant and happy palace that mirrors the evil disintegration of the House of Usher.

### Reading Skills and Strategies: CLARIFYING MEANING

**D** Ask students to summarize Usher's opinion described in this paragraph.

**Possible Response:** He believes that all growing things have consciousness and feeling. Furthermore, he believes that things such as the stones of the house are alive. As evidence he cites the atmosphere that surrounds the house and tarn, and he says that the place has had an evil effect on his family.

---

of light was discernible; yet a flood of intense rays rolled throughout, and bathed the whole in a ghastly and inappropriate splendor.

I have just spoken of that morbid condition of the auditory nerve which rendered all music intolerable to the sufferer, with the exception of certain effects of stringed instruments. It was, perhaps, the narrow limits to which he thus confined himself upon the guitar which gave birth, in great measure, to the fantastic character of his performances. But the fervid *facility* of his *impromptus* could not be so accounted for. They must have been, and were, in the notes, as well as in the words of his wild fantasias (for he not unfrequently accompanied himself with rhymed verbal improvisations), the result of that intense mental collectedness and concentration to which I have previously alluded as observable only in particular moments of the highest artificial excitement. The words of one of these rhapsodies I have easily remembered. I was, perhaps, the more forcibly impressed with it as he gave it, because, in the under or mystic current of its meaning, I fancied that I perceived, and for the first time, a full consciousness on the part of Usher of the tottering of his lofty reason upon her throne. The verses, which were entitled "The Haunted Palace," ran very nearly, if not accurately, thus:—

**I.**

In the greenest of our valleys,
    By good angels tenanted,
Once a fair and stately palace—
    Radiant palace—reared its head.
In the monarch Thought's dominion—
    It stood there!
Never seraph spread a pinion
    Over fabric half so fair.

**II.**

Banners yellow, glorious, golden,
    On its roof did float and flow
(This—all this—was in the olden
    Time long ago);
And every gentle air that dallied,
    In that sweet day,
Along the ramparts plumed and pallid,
    A winged odor went away.

**III.**

Wanderers in that happy valley
    Through two luminous windows saw

**296–305** What does this picture suggest to you?

**312** *impromptus* (ăN-prôNp-tü′) *French:* musical pieces made up as they are played.

**332–333 Never seraph** (sĕr′əf) . . . **half so fair:** No angel ever spread its wing over half as beautiful a structure.

---

## Teaching Options

### ✓ Assessment **Standardized Test Practice**

**DESCRIBING PLOT, SETTING, CHARACTER, AND MOOD** For some standardized tests, students will be asked to describe the narrative elements of a passage. Students will select the best answer from a series of multiple-choice items. To provide students with practice, write the following questions on the chalkboard and read aloud or have students reread the opening passage of the story.

**1.** Which word best describes the mood of this passage?
   **A.** apathetic
   **B.** gloomy
   **C.** lonely
   **D.** hopeful

**2.** The author of this passage conveys mood through
   **A.** a third-person narrator.
   **B.** precisely chosen words and phrases.
   **C.** the use of modifiers.
   **D.** simple sentences.

Spirits moving musically
    To a lute's well-tunèd law;
Round about a throne, where sitting
    (Porphyrogene!)
350  In state his glory well befitting,
    The ruler of the realm was seen.

### IV.

And all with pearl and ruby glowing
    Was the fair palace door,
355  Through which came flowing, flowing, flowing
    And sparkling evermore,
A troop of Echoes whose sweet duty
    Was but to sing,
In voices of surpassing beauty,
360    The wit and wisdom of their king.

### V.

But evil things, in robes of sorrow,
    Assailed the monarch's high estate;
(Ah, let us mourn, for never morrow
365    Shall dawn upon him, desolate!)
And, round about his home, the glory
    That blushed and bloomed
Is but a dim-remembered story
    Of the old time entombed.

### VI.

370  And travellers now within that valley,
    Through the red-litten windows see
Vast forms that move fantastically
    To a discordant melody;
375  While, like a rapid ghastly river,
    Through the pale door;
A hideous throng rush out forever,
    And laugh—but smile no more.

    I well remember that suggestions arising from this ballad led us
380 into a train of thought wherein there became manifest an opinion
of Usher's which I mention not so much on account of its novelty
(for other men have thought thus), as on account of the pertinacity with which he maintained it. This opinion, in its general
form, was that of the sentience of all vegetable things. But, in his
385 disordered fancy, the idea had assumed a more daring character,
and trespassed, under certain conditions, upon the kingdom of
inorganization. I lack words to express the full extent, or the
earnest *abandon* of his persuasion. The belief, however, was
connected (as I have previously hinted) with the gray stones of the

**349 porphyrogene** (pôr-fîr′ə-jēn′): a son born to a ruling king.

**326–378** How does the poem contribute to the story's mood? **C**

**382–383 pertinacity** (pûr′tn-ăs′ĭ-tē): stubbornness.

**384 sentience** (sĕn′shəns) **of all vegetable things:** consciousness of all growing things.

**A** Possible Response: He is mentally ill. His thoughts, which are becoming more and more disorganized, reveal symptoms of dementia.

**Literary Analysis: POINT OF VIEW**

**B** Ask students how the narrator now sees Usher.
Possible Response: The narrator now understands that Usher is mentally ill.

**Literary Analysis** MOOD

**C** Ask students to analyze the mood evoked in this passage. Ask what precisely chosen words and phrases convey this mood.
Possible Responses: The mood evoked is one of claustrophobia. The mood is conveyed by words and phrases such as "smothered," "oppressive atmosphere," and "small, damp, and entirely without means of admission for light."

**Literary Analysis: FORESHADOWING**

**D** Ask students what they think the location of the donjonkeep beneath the narrator's room might foreshadow. What feeling does this detail create in them as readers?
Possible Responses: The narrator might hear or experience the effects of something that happens in the donjonkeep. This detail creates a feeling of foreboding and suspense.

---

390 home of his forefathers. The conditions of the sentence had been here, he imagined, fulfilled in the method of collocation of these stones—in the order of their arrangement, as well as in that of the many *fungi* which overspread them, and of the decayed trees which stood around—above all, in the long undisturbed

395 endurance of this arrangement, and in its reduplication in the still waters of the tarn. Its evidence—the evidence of the sentience—was to be seen, he said (and I here started as he spoke), in the gradual yet certain condensation of an atmosphere of their own about the waters and the walls. The result was discoverable, he

400 added, in that silent yet importunate and terrible influence which for centuries had moulded the destinies of his family, and which made *him* what I now saw him—what he was. Such opinions need no comment, and I will make none.

Our books—the books which, for years, had formed no small

405 portion of the mental existence of the invalid—were, as might be supposed, in strict keeping with this character of phantasm. We pored together over such works as the "Ververt et Chartreuse" of Gresset; the "Belphegor" of Machiavelli; the "Heaven and Hell" of Swedenborg; the "Subterranean Voyage of Nicholas Klimm"

410 of Holberg; the "Chiromancy" of Robert Flud, of Jean D'Indaginé, and of Dela Chambre; the "Journey into the Blue Distance" of Tieck; and the "City of the Sun" of Campanella. One favorite volume was a small octavo edition of the "Directorium Inquisitorium," by the Dominican Eymeric de

415 Gironne; and there were passages in Pomponius Mela, about the old African Satyrs and Aegipans, over which Usher would sit dreaming for hours. His chief delight, however, was found in the perusal of an exceedingly rare and curious book in quarto Gothic—the manual of a forgotten church—the *Vigiliae*

420 *Mortuorum secundum Chorum Ecclesiae Maguntinae.*

I could not help thinking of the wild ritual of this work, and of its probable influence upon the hypochondriac, when, one evening, having informed me abruptly that the lady Madeline was no more, he stated his intention of preserving her corpse for a fort-

425 night (previously to its final <u>interment</u>), in one of the numerous vaults within the main walls of the building. The worldly reason, however, assigned for this singular proceeding, was one which I did not feel at liberty to dispute. The brother had been led to his resolution (so he told me) by consideration of the unusual char-

430 acter of the malady of the deceased, of certain obtrusive and eager inquiries on the part of her medical men, and of the remote and exposed situation of the burial-ground of the family. I will not

**379–403** What comment would you **A** make about Usher's opinion?

**407–415** "Ververt et Chartreuse" . . . **Pomponius Mela:** extravagantly imaginative works of fiction, theology, philosophy, and geography.

**419–420** *Vigiliae Mortuorum secundum Chorum Ecclesiae Maguntinae* (wĭ-gĭlʹē-ī môr-tōō-ôrʹo͝om sĕ-ko͝onʹdo͝om kôrʹo͝om ĕ-klāʹsē-ī mä-go͝on-tēʹnĭ) *Latin:* Wakes for the Dead, in the Manner **3** of the Choir of the Church of Mainz.

WORDS
TO     **interment** (ĭn-tûrʹmənt) *n.* burial
KNOW

486

---

**Teaching Options**

 **Grammar**

**COMPARISONS OF IRREGULAR ADJECTIVES AND ADVERBS** Most adjectives and adverbs have two forms of comparison: comparative and superlative. The comparative form shows two things being compared. The superlative form compares three or more things. Display the following example:
**Positive:** gloomy
**Comparative:** gloomier
**Superlative:** gloomiest

A few adjectives and adverbs have irregular forms of comparison.

**Positive  Comparative  Superlative**
good better best
well better best
bad worse worst
badly worse worst
ill worse worst
far (distance) farther farthest
far (degree, time) further furthest
little (amount) less least
many more most
much more most

**Gifted and Talented**

**1** Ask students to draw an inference about Usher's character from the text's detailed listing of books.

**Possible Response:** Usher is finding solace, even delight in books that are eccentric, rare, extravagantly imaginative, and forgotten—qualities that also describe his character.

**Less Proficient Readers**

**2** Help students understand this passage by asking the following questions:

• What does Usher tell the narrator?

**Possible Response:** that Madeline has died

• What does Usher plan to do with Madeline's body?

**Possible Response:** keep it in a vault for two weeks before burying it

• What causes Usher to make these unusual arrangements?

**Possible Response:** the nature of her disease and the overly curious doctors who wish to examine the body

**Students Acquiring English**

**3** Tell students that the phrase *was no more* means that the lady Madeline has died. Also tell students that *fortnight* means "two weeks."

**Gifted and Talented**

**4** Throughout the story Poe uses language that evokes the theme of physical decay. Have students identify such language in this passage and throughout the story.

deny that when I called to mind the sinister countenance of the person whom I met upon the staircase, on the day of my arrival at the house, I had no desire to oppose what I regarded as at best but a harmless, and by no means an unnatural, precaution.

At the request of Usher, I personally aided him in the arrangements for the temporary entombment. The body having been encoffined, we two alone bore it to its rest. The vault in which we placed it (and which had been so long unopened that our torches, half smothered in its oppressive atmosphere, gave us little opportunity for investigation) was small, damp, and entirely without means of admission for light; lying, at great depth, immediately beneath that portion of the building in which was my own sleeping apartment. It had been used, apparently, in remote feudal times, for the worst purpose of a donjonkeep, and, in later days, as a place of deposit for powder, or some other highly combustible substance, as a portion of its floor, and the whole interior of a long archway through which we reached it, were carefully sheathed with copper. The door, of massive iron, had

**D**

**446 donjonkeep** (dŏn′jən-kēp′): dungeon.

**Exercises** Complete each of the following sentences with the correct form of the modifier in parentheses.

**1.** Madeline's condition is _____ today than it was yesterday. (bad) *(Answer: worse)*

**2.** The _____ view of all could be seen from the tarn. (good) *(Answer: best)*

**3.** Roderick Usher spent _____ hours brooding than the narrator did. (many) *(Answer: more)*

**4.** As the days passed, Usher became _____ communicative. (little) *(Answer: less)*

**5.** The narrator had to run _____ than he had thought to escape the horrible house. (far) *(Answer: farther)*

Use **Grammar Transparencies and Copymasters**, p.129.

Use McDougal Littell's **Language Network**, Chapter 7, for more instruction and practice in irregular adjectives and adverbs.

**A** Ask what precisely chosen words and phrases in this passage help convey an eerie mood. Have students summarize the effect of these details.

**Possible Response:** Words and phrases that describe live features on Madeline's corpse—the blush and the lingering smile on her face—create an eerie mood. The effect of these details is to suggest that she is not really dead.

**Literary Analysis: FORESHADOWING**

**B** Have students refer back to lines 258–260 on page 482. What do these lines, combined with the description of how Madeline looks after she dies, foreshadow?

**Possible Responses:** She is not truly dead; the narrator will see her come back from the dead.

**GUIDE FOR READING**

**C** Possible Response: Usher has grown even more insane in his grief.

**Literary Analysis: FIRST-PERSON NARRATOR**

**D** Have students analyze what effect the narrator's experience has upon the reader.

**Possible Response:** The narrator's experience is significant because the reader identifies with the narrator's rational, reasonable point of view. The mood of fear or terror is heightened for the reader when even the calm narrator becomes frightened.

**GUIDE FOR READING**

**E** Possible Response: witnessing the decline of Usher

---

been, also, similarly protected. Its immense weight caused an unusually sharp, grating sound, as it moved upon its hinges.

Having deposited our mournful burden upon tressels within this region of horror, we partially turned aside the yet unscrewed
455 lid of the coffin, and looked upon the face of the tenant. A striking similitude between the brother and sister now first arrested my attention; and Usher, divining, perhaps, my thoughts, murmured out some few words from which I learned that the deceased and himself had been twins, and that sympathies of a
460 scarcely intelligible nature had always existed between them. Our glances, however, rested not long upon the dead—for we could not regard her unawed. The disease which had thus entombed the lady in the maturity of youth, had left, as usual in all maladies of a strictly cataleptical character, the mockery of a faint blush upon
465 the bosom and the face, and that suspiciously lingering smile upon the lip which is so terrible in death. We replaced and screwed down the lid, and, having secured the door of iron, made our way, with toil, into the scarcely less gloomy apartments of the upper portion of the house.

 nd now, some days of bitter grief having elapsed, an
470 observable change came over the features of the mental disorder of my friend. His ordinary manner had vanished. His ordinary occupations were neglected or forgotten. He roamed from chamber to chamber with hurried,
475 unequal, and objectless step. The pallor of his countenance had assumed, if possible, a more ghastly hue—but the luminousness of his eye had utterly gone out. The once occasional huskiness of his tone was heard no more; and a tremulous quaver, as if of extreme terror, habitually characterized his utterance. There were
480 times, indeed, when I thought his unceasingly agitated mind was laboring with some oppressive secret, to divulge which he struggled for the necessary courage. At times, again, I was obliged to resolve all into the mere inexplicable vagaries of madness, for I beheld him gazing upon vacancy for long hours, in
485 an attitude of the profoundest attention, as if listening to some imaginary sound. It was no wonder that his condition terrified—that it infected me. I felt creeping upon me, by slow yet certain degrees, the wild influences of his own fantastic yet impressive superstitions.
490 It was, especially, upon retiring to bed late in the night of the seventh or eighth day after the placing of the lady Madeline within the donjon, that I experienced the full power of such feelings. Sleep came not near my couch—while the hours waned and waned away. I struggled to reason off the nervousness which had

**1**

**470–489** What do you infer about the changes in Usher's behavior? **C**

**2**
**493 couch:** bed.

---

**Mini Lesson** ## Vocabulary Strategy

**UNDERSTANDING FIGURATIVE LANGUAGE**
**Instruction** Figurative language is language that communicates meaning beyond the literal meaning of the words. Authors such as Poe use figurative language to emphasize ideas and evoke emotions. Write the following sentence from the story (lines 453–455) on the chalkboard and underline the phrases shown.

Having deposited our mournful burden upon tressels within this region of horror, we partially turned aside the yet unscrewed lid of the coffin, and looked upon the face of the tenant.

Tell students that they can rely on context to determine the meaning of figurative language in a work. For example, students can use context clues to figure out that the "mournful burden" Usher and the narrator carry is the body of Madeline; they can also use context clues to figure out that "region of horror" refers to the underground burial vault. Poe uses figurative language, in this case, to evoke the emotions of grief and fear.

dominion over me. I endeavored to believe that much, if not all
of what I felt, was due to the bewildering influence of the gloomy
furniture of the room—of the dark and tattered draperies, which,
tortured into motion by the breath of a rising tempest, swayed
fitfully to and fro upon the walls, and rustled uneasily about the
decorations of the bed. But my efforts were fruitless. An irrepressible tremor gradually pervaded my frame; and, at length,
there sat upon my very heart an incubus of utterly causeless
alarm. Shaking this off with a gasp and a struggle, I uplifted
myself upon the pillows, and, peering earnestly within the intense
darkness of the chamber, hearkened—I know not why, except
that an instinctive spirit prompted me—to certain low and indefinite sounds which came, through the pauses of the storm, at
long intervals, I knew not whence. Overpowered by an intense
sentiment of horror, unaccountable yet unendurable, I threw on
my clothes with haste (for I felt that I should sleep no more
during the night), and endeavored to arouse myself from the
pitiable condition into which I had fallen, by pacing rapidly to
and fro through the apartment.

I had taken but few turns in this manner, when a light step on
an adjoining staircase arrested my attention. I presently recognized it as that of Usher. In an instant afterward he rapped, with
a gentle touch, at my door, and entered, bearing a lamp. His
countenance was, as usual, cadaverously wan—but, moreover,
there was a species of mad hilarity in his eyes—an evidently
restrained *hysteria* in his whole demeanor. His air appalled me—
but any thing was preferable to the solitude which I had so long
endured, and I even welcomed his presence as a relief.

"And you have not seen it?" he said abruptly, after having
stared about him for some moments in silence—"you have not
then seen it?—but, stay! you shall." Thus speaking, and having
carefully shaded his lamp, he hurried to one of the casements, and
threw it freely open to the storm.

The impetuous fury of the entering gust nearly lifted us from
our feet. It was, indeed, a tempestuous yet sternly beautiful night,
and one wildly singular in its terror and its beauty. A whirlwind
had apparently collected its force in our vicinity; for there were
frequent and violent alterations in the direction of the wind; and
the exceeding density of the clouds (which hung so low as to press
upon the turrets of the house) did not prevent our perceiving the
life-like velocity with which they flew careering from all points
against each other, without passing away into the distance. I say
that even their exceeding density did not prevent our perceiving

495–500 Which of the narrator's
experiences in the Usher mansion
might have led to his conclusion?

502 **incubus** (ĭn'kyə-bəs): burden.

525 **stay:** wait.

3

| WORDS |
| TO |
| KNOW |

**fitfully** (fĭt'fə-lē) *adv.* in an irregular way; unsteadily

489

---

**Cross Curricular Link** **Psychology**

**TWINS** After burying Madeline, Roderick Usher
reveals to the narrator that he and his sister had
been twins. The genetic phenomenon of twins—
nature's clones—has fascinated geneticists, neurosci-
entists, psychologists, and twins and their families
for years. Identical twins come from the same fertil-
ized egg and are, therefore, genetically identical.
Fraternal twins, however, are created by the fertiliza-
tion of two different eggs and share only 50 percent
of their genes (the same amount as any siblings).
The bond that exists between identical twins has
been described by twins themselves as "telepathic,"
"totally connected," and "bound together forever."

One fairly new field of study is twin bereave-
ment or loss. Research shows that surviving twins,
particularly identical twins, feel their loss acutely.
Many surviving twins grow more isolated and
become intensely lonely later in life. One surviving
twin described the death of his brother as like
watching himself die. Another twin described her
life after the death of her twin as resembling exile.
In the case of identical twins, many surviving
twins knew of the death of their counterpart
before they were told of the event.

**Reading Skills and Strategies:**
**SUMMARIZING**

Ⓐ Have students summarize the narrator's purpose in reading to Usher.
**Possible Response:** The narrator hopes that hearing a story read aloud will calm Usher's nerves.

**Reading Skills and Strategies:**
**PREDICTING**

Ⓑ Ask students to predict whether the narrator's chance selection of a book to read aloud will be significant, and why.
**Possible Response:** Poe does not include any insignificant details in his stories—everything has meaning. The "Mad Trist" will probably prove to have some relation to Usher's state of mind or to what happens next in the story.

**GUIDE FOR READING**

Ⓒ **Possible Responses:** eerie, foreboding

**1**

this—yet we had no glimpse of the moon or stars, nor was there any flashing forth of the lightning. But the under surfaces of the huge masses of agitated vapor, as well as all <u>terrestrial</u> objects immediately around us, were glowing in the unnatural light of a faintly luminous and distinctly visible gaseous exhalation which hung about and enshrouded the mansion.

"You must not—you shall not behold this!" said I, shuddering, to Usher, as I led him, with a gentle violence, from the window to a seat. "These appearances, which bewilder you, are merely electrical phenomena not uncommon—or it may be that they have their ghastly origin in the rank miasma of the tarn. Let us close this casement;—the air is chilling and dangerous to your frame. Here is one of your favorite romances. I will read, and you shall listen:—and so we will pass away this terrible night together."

**548 miasma** (mī-ăz′mə): poisonous vapors.

The antique volume which I had taken up was the "Mad Trist" of Sir Launcelot Canning; but I had called it a favorite of Usher's more in sad jest than in earnest; for, in truth, there is little in its uncouth and unimaginative prolixity which could have had interest for the lofty and spiritual ideality of my friend. It was, however, the only book immediately at hand; and I indulged a vague hope that the excitement which now agitated the hypochondriac, might find relief (for the history of mental disorder is full of similar anomalies) even in the extremeness of the folly which I should read. Could I have judged, indeed, by the wild overstrained air of vivacity with which he hearkened, or apparently hearkened, to the words of the tale, I might well have congratulated myself upon the success of my design.

**555 prolixity** (prō-lĭk′sĭ-tē): tedious length; wordiness.

Ⓐ

Ⓑ

I had arrived at that well-known portion of the story where Ethelred, the hero of the Trist, having sought in vain for peaceable admission into the dwelling of the hermit, proceeds to make good an entrance by force. Here, it will be remembered, the words of the narrative run thus:

"And Ethelred, who was by nature of a doughty heart, and who was now mighty withal, on account of the powerfulness of the wine which he had drunken, waited no longer to hold parley with the hermit, who, in sooth, was of an <u>obstinate</u> and maliceful turn, but, feeling the rain upon his shoulders, and fearing the rising of the tempest, uplifted his mace outright, and, with blows, made quickly room in the plankings of the door for his gauntleted hand; and now pulling therewith sturdily, he so cracked, and ripped, and tore all asunder, that the noise of the dry and hollow-sounding wood alarumed and reverberated throughout the forest."

**572 hold parley** (pär′lē) **with:** converse with.

**573 in sooth:** truly.

WORDS
TO
KNOW

**terrestrial** (tə-rĕs′trē-əl) *adj.* on the ground; earthly
**obstinate** (ŏb′stə-nĭt) *adj.* stubborn

490

---

 **Mini Lesson** ## Grammar

**APOSTROPHES: POSSESSIVE COMPOUNDS** One of the functions of an apostrophe is to show the possessive case. When you need to show the possessive case for a compound noun or word group, add the apostrophe and *s* only to the last word.
the great-grandfather'<u>s</u> will
the medical doctor'<u>s</u> prognosis
Roderick Usher'<u>s</u> letter
If both share the possession, then only add *'s* to the last noun:
Madeline and Roderick'<u>s</u> family

But if both do not share possession, add *'s* to both nouns:
Madeline'<u>s</u> and Roderick'<u>s</u> hands

**Exercises** Have students rewrite the following sentences, using apostrophes correctly.
1. The (heir apparent) family home contained a small fissure in the wall.
   **Answer:** The heir apparent's family home contained a small fissure in the wall.

**Multiple Learning Styles**
**Visual Learners**
**1** Ask students to visualize the scene outside the window based on descriptions in the text. Then have students create their own illustration, sketch, or painting of this scene.

**Students Acquiring English**
Defining these words and phrases will help students understand the story.
Line 549: *casement* means "window"
Line 570: *doughty* means "courageous"
Line 571: *mighty withal* means "also very strong"
Line 578: *asunder* means "apart"
Line 579: *alarumed* means "alarmed"; *reverberated* means "echoed"

**Less Proficient Readers**
**2** Ask students to summarize lines 580–586.
**Possible Response:** The narrator paused while reading because he thought he heard a sound in the mansion similar to the cracking and ripping sound described in "Mad Trist." The narrator believes it is the coincidence that strikes him, because the other sounds of the storm do not disturb him.

580     At the termination of this sentence I started and, for a moment, paused; for it appeared to me (although I at once concluded that my excited fancy had deceived me)—it appeared to me that, from some very remote portion of the mansion, there came, indistinctly, to my ears, what might have been, in its exact similarity
585 of character, the echo (but a stifled and dull one certainly) of the very cracking and ripping sound which Sir Launcelot had so particularly described. It was, beyond doubt, the coincidence alone which had arrested my attention; for, amid the rattling of the sashes of the casements, and the ordinary commingled noises
590 of the still increasing storm, the sound, in itself, had nothing, surely, which should have interested or disturbed me. I continued the story:

    "But the good champion Ethelred, now entering within the door, was sore enraged and amazed to perceive no signal of the
595 maliceful hermit; but, in the stead thereof, a dragon of a scaly and prodigious demeanor, and of a fiery tongue, which sate in guard before a palace of gold, with a floor of silver; and upon the wall there hung a shield of shining brass with this legend enwritten—

    *Who entereth herein, a conqueror hath bin;*
600     *Who slayeth the dragon, the shield he shall win.*

**591** How would you describe the mood of the story at this point? **C**

THE FALL OF THE HOUSE OF USHER     **491**

---

2. Usher was tormented by (his twin sister) illness.
**Answer:** Usher was tormented by his twin sister's illness.
3. (The House of Usher) legacy was ill-fated.
**Answer:** The House of Usher's legacy was ill-fated.
4. (The black and lurid tarn) surface remained unrippled.
**Answer:** The black and lurid tarn's surface remained unrippled.

5. Reading from the "Mad Trist" did little to soothe (Roderick and the narrator) nerves.
**Answer:** Reading from the "Mad Trist" did little to soothe Roderick's and the narrator's nerves.

 Use **Grammar Transparencies and Copymasters,** p. 160.

Use McDougal Littell's *Language Network,* Chapter 10, for more instruction and practice in possessives.

**A** Possible Response: They increase the tension and horror in the story.

**Literary Analysis: POINT OF VIEW**

**B** Ask students to analyze the narrator's state of mind, using elements of the passage to defend their interpretation.

Possible Response: The narrator is becoming a bit unnerved himself by the "coincidental" sounds he hears. His unnerved state is supported by the overly sensitive description he gives of the sound: "a low and apparently distant, but harsh, protracted, and most unusual screaming or grating sound—."

**Literary Analysis** MOOD

**C** Ask students how the narrator's state of mind influences the mood created in this passage. Ask students to describe that mood.

Possible Response: The narrator's own unnerved state heightens the mood of increasing fear and anxiety.

**Reading Skills and Strategies: DRAWING INFERENCES**

**D** Have students draw inferences about Roderick Usher's response, using elements of the passage to defend their interpretation.

Possible Response: He responds with complete terror to the appearance of Madeline. His terror is shown through the repetition of phrases ("I dared not"), the hysterical interruptions ("–ha ha!"), and the series of questions ("whither shall I fly?"; "Will she not be here anon?"; "Is she not hurrying to upbraid me for my haste?").

---

And Ethelred uplifted his mace, and struck upon the head of the dragon, which fell before him, and gave up his pesty breath, with a shriek so horrid and harsh, and withal so piercing, that 605 Ethelred had fain to close his ears with his hands against the dreadful noise of it, the like whereof was never before heard."

Here again I paused abruptly, and now with a feeling of wild amazement—for there could be no doubt whatever that, in this instance, I did actually hear (although from what direction it proceeded I found it impossible to say) a low and apparently 610 distant, but harsh, protracted, and most unusual screaming or grating sound—the exact counterpart of what my fancy had already conjured up for the dragon's unnatural shriek as described by the romancer.

Oppressed, as I certainly was, upon the occurrence of this second 615 and most extraordinary coincidence, by a thousand conflicting sensations, in which wonder and extreme terror were predominant, I still retained sufficient presence of mind to avoid exciting, by any observation, the sensitive nervousness of my companion. I was by no means certain that he had noticed the sounds in question; although, 620 assuredly, a strange alteration had, during the last few minutes, taken place in his demeanor. From a position fronting my own, he had gradually brought round his chair, so as to sit with his face to the door of the chamber; and thus I could but partially perceive his features, although I saw that his lips trembled as if he were murmuring 625 inaudibly. His head had dropped upon his breast—yet I knew that he was not asleep, from the wide and rigid opening of the eye as I caught a glance of it in profile. The motion of his body, too, was at variance with this idea—for he rocked from side to side with a gentle yet constant and uniform sway. Having rapidly taken notice of all this, I 630 resumed the <u>narrative</u> of Sir Launcelot, which thus proceeded:

"And now, the champion, having escaped from the terrible fury of the dragon, bethinking himself of the brazen shield, and of the breaking up of the enchantment which was upon it, removed the carcass from out of the way before him, and 635 approached valorously over the silver pavement of the castle to where the shield was upon the wall; which in sooth tarried not for his full coming, but fell down at his feet upon the silver floor, with a mighty great and terrible ringing sound."

No sooner had these syllables passed my lips, than—as if a 640 shield of brass had indeed, at the moment, fallen heavily upon a floor of silver—I became aware of a distinct, hollow, metallic, and clangorous, yet apparently muffled, reverberation. Completely unnerved, I leaped to my feet; but the measured rocking move-

**602 pesty:** poisonous.

**613 romancer:** storyteller.

**614** What effect do the passages from the "Mad Trist" have on the events of the story? **A**

**631–638** What do you predict will happen?

WORDS
TO      **narrative** (năr′ə-tĭv) *n.* a story
KNOW

492

---

### Mini Lesson **Speaking and Listening**

**DRAMATIC READING** Ask students to present to the class a dramatic reading of the passage containing Roderick Usher's response to the noises he hears (lines 652–669). Explain that they will need to make valid interpretations of the text. Students can work in cooperative groups to discuss possible characteristics of Usher (unnerved, terrorized, insane) and how these characteristics will influence their choices of verbal and nonverbal performance techniques (tone, volume, gestures, and so on). Remind students that Usher is speaking directly to the narrator in this passage.

**Present** Have students present their dramatic reading. Students should be able to justify their choice of verbal and nonverbal performance techniques by referring to the narrative passage and to their interpretation of Usher's character. Audience members should evaluate how the performance increases their understanding of the story and character.

**BLOCK SCHEDULING** This activity is particularly well-suited for longer class periods.

ment of Usher was undisturbed. I rushed to the chair in which he
sat. His eyes were bent fixedly before him, and throughout his
whole countenance there reigned a stony rigidity. But, as I placed
my hand upon his shoulder, there came a strong shudder over his
whole person; a sickly smile quivered about his lips; and I saw
that he spoke in a low, hurried, and gibbering murmur, as if
unconscious of my presence. Bending closely over him, I at length
drank in the hideous import of his words.

   "Not hear it?—yes, I hear it, and *have* heard it. Long—long—
long—many minutes, many hours, many days, have I heard it—
yet I dared not—oh, pity me, miserable wretch that I am!—I
dared not—I *dared* not speak! *We have put her living in the
tomb!* Said I not that my senses were acute? I *now* tell you that I
heard her first feeble movements in the hollow coffin. I heard
them—many, many days ago—yet I dared not—*I dared not
speak!* And now—to-night—Ethelred—ha ha!—the breaking of
the hermit's door, and the death-cry of the dragon, and the
clangor of the shield—say, rather, the rending of her coffin, and
the grating of the iron hinges of her prison, and her struggles
within the coppered archway of the vault! Oh! whither shall I fly?
Will she not be here anon? Is she not hurrying to upbraid me for
my haste? Have I not heard her footstep on the stair? Do I not
distinguish that heavy and horrible beating of her heart?
Madman!"—here he sprang furiously to his feet, and shrieked
out his syllables, as if in the effort he were giving up his soul—
*"Madman! I tell you that she now stands without the door!"*

   As if in the superhuman energy of his utterance there had been
found the potency of a spell, the huge antique panels to which the
speaker pointed threw slowly back, upon the instant, their
ponderous and ebony jaws. It was the work of the rushing gust—
but then without those doors there *did* stand the lofty and
enshrouded figure of the lady Madeline of Usher. There was
blood upon her white robes, and the evidence of some bitter
struggle upon every portion of her emaciated frame. For a
moment she remained trembling and reeling to and fro upon the
threshold—then, with a low moaning cry, fell heavily inward
upon the person of her brother, and in her violent and now final
death-agonies, bore him to the floor a corpse, and a victim to the
terrors he had anticipated.

   From that chamber, and from that mansion, I fled <u>aghast</u>. The
storm was still abroad in all its wrath as I found myself crossing
the old causeway. Suddenly there shot along the path a wild light,
and I turned to see whence a gleam so unusual could have issued;

**D**

**652–669** On the basis of what
Usher is saying, what do you
expect to happen next?

**3**

WORDS
TO      **aghast** (ə-găst') *adj.* overcome with fear; terrified
KNOW

**493**

**Customizing Instruction**

**Less Proficient Readers**
**1** Have students locate the main idea
of this complex sentence. Remind them
to disregard temporarily any modifiers
that do not seem essential to the
meaning of the sentence.
**Possible Response:** I did hear a
screaming or grating sound.

**Gifted and Talented**
**2** Have students read to discover the
ironic humor in this passage.
**Possible Response:** While the narrator
has avoided exciting Usher by his
observations, he has, through his
detailed observations, excited and
unnerved his readers.

**Students Acquiring English**
Help students translate Poe's archaic
language into modern English.
Line 663: *whither shall I fly?* means
"where shall I go?"
Line 664: *Will she not be here anon?*
means "Won't she be here soon?"
Line 669: *without the door* means "outside the door"

**Multiple Learning Styles**
**Visual Learners**
**3** Ask students to close their eyes as
you read aloud this passage of the story
so that they can create a mental picture
of what the narrator and Usher see as
the door opens. Ask students what feelings or emotions the image creates.
**Possible Response:** feelings of horror
or terror

### Literary Analysis  MOOD

**A** Ask students to identify details from the text that help create a sense of suspense in this description. Have them defend their interpretation by referring to details in the text.

**Possible Response:** Suspense is created by details such as the wild light of the blood-red moon, which indicate that something really horrible is about to happen.

### Active Reading

#### UNDERSTANDING COMPLEX SENTENCES

**B** Have students identify the emotion conveyed in the final, complex sentence of the story.

**Possible Response:** horror or terror

### Reading Skills and Strategies: COMPARING AND CONTRASTING

Have students compare and contrast "Spleen LXXXI" with "The Fall of the House of Usher" in terms of subject, form, and mood.

**Possible Responses:** The subject of this poem, like Poe's story, is the triumph of despair and death over joy and life. The form is different—poetic verse as opposed to prose fiction—but the mood created by Baudelaire is strikingly similar to the mood of "The Fall of the House of Usher." It creates feelings of sadness, hopelessness, fear, and dread.

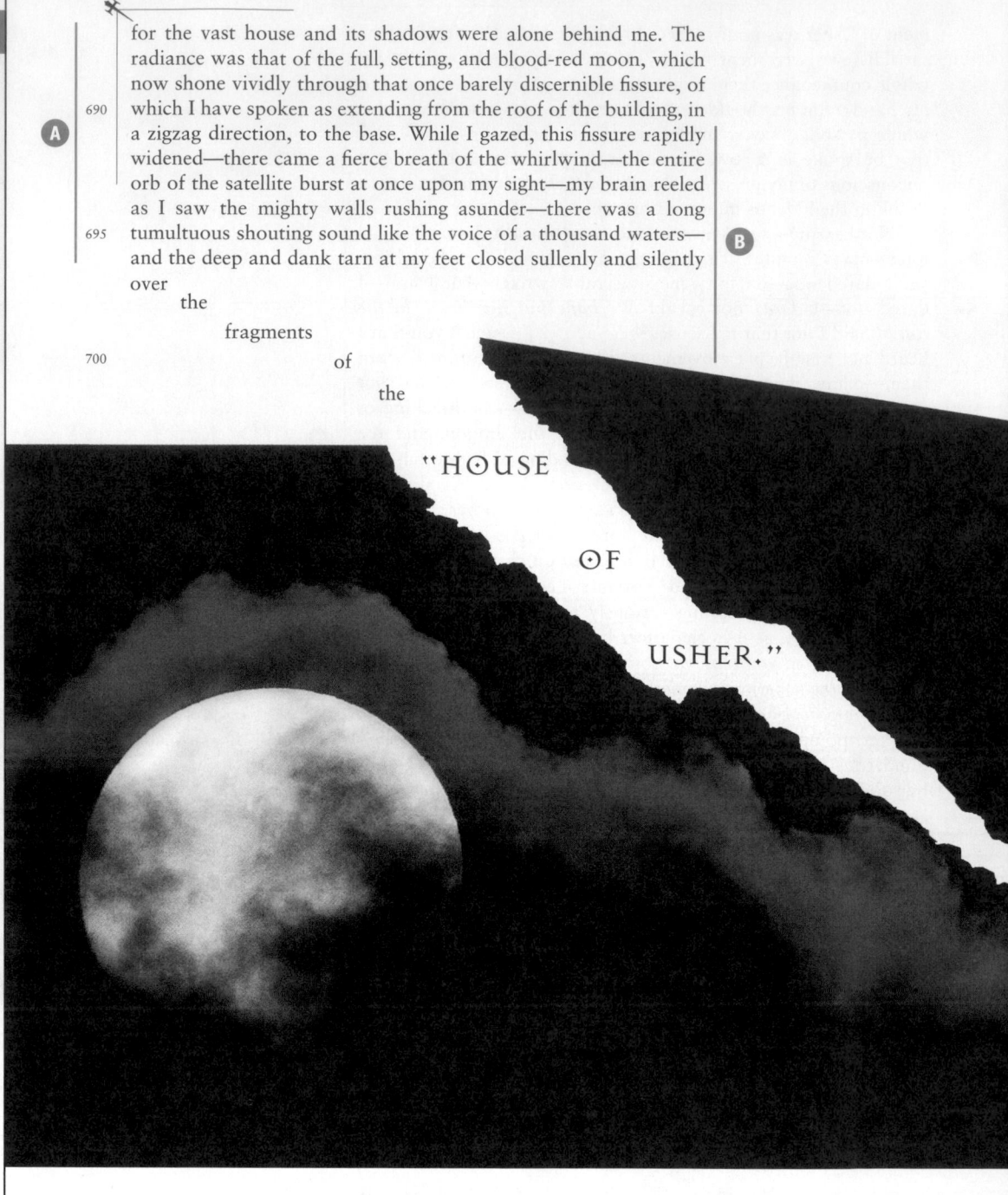

**A** for the vast house and its shadows were alone behind me. The radiance was that of the full, setting, and blood-red moon, which now shone vividly through that once barely discernible fissure, of which I have spoken as extending from the roof of the building, in a zigzag direction, to the base. While I gazed, this fissure rapidly widened—there came a fierce breath of the whirlwind—the entire orb of the satellite burst at once upon my sight—my brain reeled as I saw the mighty walls rushing asunder—there was a long tumultuous shouting sound like the voice of a thousand waters— **B** and the deep and dank tarn at my feet closed sullenly and silently over the fragments of the

"HOUSE OF USHER."

690

695

700

**494**   UNIT THREE   **AUTHOR STUDY:** EDGAR ALLAN POE

## Teaching Options

## Informal Assessment

**JOURNAL ENTRY** You can informally assess your students' understanding of the story by asking them to respond to the following scenario. This activity allows students to draw inferences and support them with textual evidence and experience as well as to describe setting, character, and mood.

*Imagine you are the narrator of "The Fall of the House of Usher." Since fleeing the scene of the house crashing into the tarn, you are still troubled by your experience and are having trouble sleeping at night. Write a journal entry describing your experience at the House of Usher and its overall effect on you. Be sure to include your feelings about the setting, Roderick and Madeline Usher, and the strange events of your stay there.*

# Spleen

### Charles Baudelaire

*The renowned French poet Charles Baudelaire (1821–1867) found a soul mate in Edgar Allan Poe. In translating Poe's short stories and poems, Baudelaire discovered the artistic bonds they shared: "The first time I opened a book of his I saw, with horror and delight, not just subjects I had dreamt of, but sentences I had thought of, and written by him twenty years before." The first stanza of "Spleen LXXXI" mirrors the first sentence of "The Fall of the House of Usher" (page 474).*

## LXXXI

When the low heavy sky weighs like a lid
Upon the spirit aching for the light
And all the wide horizon's line is hid
By a black day sadder than any night;

5 When the changed earth is but a dungeon
    dank
Where batlike Hope goes blindly fluttering
And, striking wall and roof and moldered
    plank,
Bruises his tender head and timid wing;

When like grim prison bars stretch down
    the thin,
10 Straight, rigid pillars of the endless rain,
And the dumb throngs of infamous
    spiders spin
Their meshes in the caverns of the brain,

Suddenly, bells leap forth into the air,
Hurling a hideous uproar to the sky
15 As 'twere a band of homeless spirits who fare
Through the strange heavens, wailing
    stubbornly.

And hearses, without drum or instrument,
File slowly through my soul; crushed,
    sorrowful
Weeps Hope, and Grief, fierce and
    omnipotent,
20 Plants his black banner on my drooping skull.

*—Translated by Sir John Squire*

**Less Proficient Readers**

**1** Have students paraphrase lines 695–700 as simply as possible.

**Possible Response:** As I watched, the crack widened and the walls of the House of Usher crashed into the lake.

**RUBRIC**

**3 Full Accomplishment** Response comments on key events and their effect of terror or horror upon the narrator, conveys the setting's Gothic atmosphere, and interprets the characters of Roderick and Madeline Usher.

**2 Substantial Accomplishment** Response shows some understanding of the story and acknowledges its effect on the narrator, comments briefly on the setting and characters.

**1 Little or Partial Accomplishment** Response does not accurately convey the events of the story or their effect on the narrator.

## GUIDING STUDENT RESPONSE

### Connect to the Literature

**1. What Do You Think?**
Possible Response: Particularly vivid images near the end of the story include the luminous landscape during the storm, the death of Roderick in the arms of his thought-to-be-dead sister, Madeline, and the collapse of the house in the moonlight.

**Comprehension Check**
• because Roderick asked him to come; because he wants to help his friend recover from his illness
• to put the body of Roderick's sister, who was thought to be dead, in the vault for two weeks before burying her
• The house splits in two and tumbles into the neighboring lake.

 Use Selection Quiz in **Unit Three Resource Book,** p. 65.

### Think Critically

**2.** Possible Responses: How did Madeline escape from the sealed coffin and open the iron door? Why did the house collapse when Roderick and his sister died? Why didn't Roderick release Madeline from her coffin days earlier, when he realized that she was still alive?

**3.** The sentence means that Roderick Usher has no living uncles, aunts, cousins, or other relations outside of his immediate family—he and his sister are the last members of the family of Usher. This makes the connection between them and the physical house stronger.

**4.** Possible Responses: anxious, worried, gloomy, overly depressed, sophisticated, solitary, burdened by the past

**5.** Students who think Usher's mood greatly influenced the narrator might point to lines 486–488 as evidence. Students who disagree might point out that the narrator senses strangeness about the house even before he encounters Usher.

### Literary Analysis

**Mood** Ask students to find out the following:
• What overall feeling or effect is conveyed in the collective details of the story?
• Are certain details repeated to heighten an effect? What mood do those details convey?

**496** UNIT THREE AUTHOR STUDY

---

### Connect to the Literature

**1. What Do You Think?**
After you finished the story, what image in it remained most vivid in your mind?

**Comprehension Check**
• Why does the narrator visit the House of Usher?
• Why do the narrator and his friend go to a vault below the mansion?
• What happens to the house at the end of the story?

### Think Critically

**2.** What thoughts or unanswered questions about what took place at the House of Usher still linger in your mind?

**3.**  **ACTIVE READING** | **UNDERSTANDING COMPLEX SENTENCES**
Review your **READER'S NOTEBOOK** notes about difficult passages in the story. Then read the sentence in lines 62–67 (page 476). Explain what the sentence means and what useful information it gives you about the Usher family.

**4.** What are your impressions of Roderick Usher?

**THINK ABOUT** { • his family background • his condition when the narrator arrives • his final revelations

**5.** How deeply do you think Roderick Usher's state of mind influences the **narrator's**? Give reasons for your answer.

### Extend Interpretations

**6. Comparing Texts** Compare the first stanza of Baudelaire's poem "Spleen LXXXI" with the opening lines of "The Fall of the House of Usher." What similarities and differences do you see?

**7. Critic's Corner** In his critical commentary *Danse Macabre,* Stephen King states, "The tale of horror is a chance to examine what's going on behind doors which we usually keep double-locked." On the basis of the works you've read in this Author Study, how well do you think Edgar Allan Poe understood what goes on behind the locked doors of the human mind? Cite evidence from the works to support your views.

**8. Connect to Life** Recall the important points in your earlier discussion about fear. Then think about the role fear plays in each of the Poe selections. Choose one of Poe's characters, and tell what chance he or she might have had to overcome fear before a situation became worse.

**496** UNIT THREE AUTHOR STUDY: EDGAR ALLAN POE

---

### Literary Analysis

**MOOD** One of the most prominent features of this story is its **mood,** the feeling or atmosphere that the writer's words convey to the reader. In this classic tale of horror, Poe developed a gloomy and frightening mood in a variety of ways:
• His detailed descriptions of the setting through the use of **imagery,** or words or phrases that re-create sensory experiences—"vacant eye-like windows," "black and lurid tarn," "decayed trees"—help build up an impression of a place where it is impossible for happiness to exist.
• His precisely chosen words and phrases—"dreary," "bleak," "rank," "extensive decay"—create a gloomy, oppressive picture.
• His choice of a narrator who takes part in the events heightens the sense of fear by allowing the narrator to present his immediate reactions, as when he speaks of "a strange fancy" growing in his mind.

**Paired Activity** With another student, fill in a chart like the one shown, listing the **moods** conveyed by specific details in the story. Then review the information about Poe's theory of "unity of effect" under Build Background on page 473. Referring to your chart, try to identify the overall feeling and effect Poe may have wanted to convey in "The Fall of the House of Usher."

| Descriptive Detail | Effect of Description |
|---|---|
| "clouds hung oppressively low" | depression, dread |
| | |
| | |

---

### Extend Interpretations

**Comparing Texts** Both describe a day of low clouds and convey a mood of sadness. "Spleen LXXXI" mentions the speaker's desire for light, while "The Fall of the House of Usher" gives more emphasis to the narrator's destination and to the appearance of the countryside.

**Critic's Corner** Some students will agree that Poe knew the secrets of the human mind—particularly sadness and fear—very well. Others may feel that Poe is more intent on creating a gloomy sensation than in examining human secrets.

**Connect to Life** The speaker of "The Raven" might have considered other explanations of the raven before he accepted it as a prophet of his hopeless future. Roderick Usher might have sought experiences that would help him overcome his fears rather than brooding over books and music.

# THE AUTHOR'S STYLE
## Poe's Painstaking Prose

Style is the particular way that a writer expresses himself or herself. A writer's style involves such characteristics as diction, or word choice; sentence length and construction; the presence or absence of figurative language; and tone. Edgar Allan Poe's style has delighted—and frightened—readers for over a century.

### Key Aspects of Poe's Style

- a use of dashes or other interrupters in sentences to suggest hurried or excited speech
- a strong rhythm (even in prose works), produced by a repetition of phrases and word patterns
- a frequent use of figurative language, particularly similes and metaphors
- formal language that is suited to upper-class settings or intellectual characters

## Analysis of Style

On the right are passages from three other stories by Poe. Study the chart above, and read each passage carefully. Then complete the following activities:

**A** • Find several examples of each stylistic feature in the three passages. Decide what Poe was trying to achieve stylistically.

**B** • Find at least two additional stylistic features in the passages. Describe them and give examples of each.

**C** • Look again at the Poe stories in the Author Study. With a partner, find and list examples of some of their stylistic features.

## Applications

**1. Comparing Points of View** "The Masque of the Red Death" is told from the third person point of view; "The Fall of the House of Usher," from a first-person point of view. How does the point of view affect each story's emotional intensity?

**2. Style in Action** Choose a story, not by Poe, that you have read in this book. Rewrite a passage of it in an imitation of Poe's style. How does your retelling change the nature of the story?

**3. Speaking and Listening** With a group of classmates, read aloud passages chosen from the selections in this Author Study. What differences in the passages reflect differences in the works' purposes? What similarities are regular characteristics of Poe's style?

---

*from* "The Imp of the Perverse"

We have a task before us which must be speedily performed. We know that it will be ruinous to make delay. The most important crisis of our life calls, trumpet-tongued, for immediate energy and action. We glow, we are consumed with eagerness to commence the work, with the anticipation of whose glorious result our whole souls are on fire. It must, it shall be undertaken today, and yet we put it off until tomorrow; and why? There is no answer, except that we feel *perverse*. . . .

I have said thus much, that in some measure I may answer your question—that I may explain to you why I am here. . . . Had I not been thus prolix, you might either have misunderstood me altogether, or, with the rabble, have fancied me mad.

---

*from* "William Wilson"

But the house!—how quaint an old building was this!—to me how veritably a palace of enchantment! There was really no end to its windings—to its incomprehensible subdivisions. It was difficult, at any given time, to say with certainty upon which of its two stories one happened to be.

---

*from* "Ligeia"

I trembled not—I stirred not—for a crowd of unutterable fancies connected with the air, the stature, the demeanor, of the figure, rushing hurriedly through my brain, had paralyzed—had chilled me into stone. I stirred not—but gazed upon the apparition. There was a mad disorder in my thoughts—a tumult unappeasable.

---

## The Author's Style

Poe's style is easily recognizable through the mood or feeling it creates in readers. His finished work is seamless, but he achieves his effects through thoughtful use of certain literary techniques. Students will be made aware of stylistic elements through the "Key Aspects of Poe's Style" chart. They will then find examples of the four elements in the excerpts in the right margin.

## Analysis of Style

**A** First activity

**dashes and other interrupters:** All three excerpts use dashes; those from "William Wilson" and "Ligeia" most suggest excited speech. The phrase "how quaint an old building was this!" in "William Wilson" is an interrupter.

**strong rhythm:** "The Imp of the Perverse": "We have." "We know," "We glow, we are consumed," "we feel"; "William Wilson": "how quaint . . . how veritably"; "Ligeia": "I trembled not—I stirred not"

**figurative language:** "The Imp of the Perverse": the crisis "calls, trumpet-tongued"; "our whole souls are on fire"

**formal language:** The diction and syntax of all three excerpts are very formal. Many sentences are long and complex.

**B** Second activity

**rhetorical question:** "The Imp of the Perverse": "why? There is no answer, except that we feel *perverse.*"

**first-person narrator:** It is used in all three excerpts to make the horror more personal and real to the reader.

**C** Third activity

There are many examples of the **key aspects** of Poe's style throughout the selections in this unit. For example, Poe's repetition of "nothing more" and "nevermore" at the end of each stanza in "The Raven" creates a strong rhythm and contributes to the gloomy tone of the poem.

---

## Applications

**1. Comparing Points of View** Students should comment on whether they identified with the narrator of "The Fall of the House of Usher" and how this affected their experience of the story.

**2. Style in Action** Students should attempt to employ the stylistic elements listed in the Key Aspects box.

**3. Speaking and Listening** Before students select passages to read aloud, they might form small groups to discuss the purpose of each selection. Suggest that they consider the themes and overall mood of each work.

## Writing Options

1. **Roderick Usher's Letter** The language of the letter should convey a persuasive, emotional charge, such as nervousness or agitation, that reflects Usher's emotional state.

2. **Comparing Ushers** Student comparisons should include some of the following: both are ill, each twin shares a unique sympathy for the other, both are the last of the Ushers. Differences: Madeline is physically ill; Roderick is mentally ill. Students may suggest that Poe, in making the brother and sister twins, split the mental and physical states of one being into two.

3. **Madeline's Retelling** Suggest to students that they make vivid use of sensory details to bring alive Madeline's experience of awakening in the vault.

## Activities & Explorations

1. **Eerie Pantomime** Suggest to students that they quickly outline the key events of the story and the emotional charge or mood conveyed by each event. Encourage students to discuss how to use nonverbal techniques to convey specific emotions and moods.

2. **Usher Poster** **To get students started on this activity,** have them brainstorm a list of the most memorable scenes or images in the story.

3. **Charting Usher Events** Students' flow charts might include the following events: the narrator finds his friend much changed; the narrator tries to cheer his friend; Usher creates strange paintings and musical pieces; Madeline "dies" and the two men bury her; Usher and the narrator hear strange sounds; Madeline awakens in the vault and appears before Usher and the narrator; the house collapses into the lake.

## Inquiry & Research

**Science** Students can locate appropriate print information using a periodical guide or a computerized library database. Periodicals containing recent information about twins include *Health* and *Psychology Today*.

## Writing Options

1. **Roderick Usher's Letter** The narrator of "The Fall of the House of Usher" tells of the persuasive letter that Usher wrote, inviting him to the house. Write your own version of that letter. Be sure to convey Usher's emotional state.

2. **Comparing Ushers** In a comparison-contrast essay, discuss Roderick Usher and his ancestral home. In what ways are the two similar? Alternatively, compare Roderick and Madeline Usher. Why do you think Poe made the brother and sister twins?

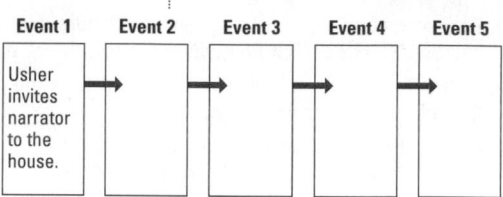

**Writing Handbook**
See page 1281: Compare and Contrast.

3. **Madeline's Retelling** In a few paragraphs, briefly retell the story as it might be told by Madeline after she awakens in the vault. Try using Poe's style. Put your story in your **Working Portfolio.**

## Activities & Explorations

1. **Eerie Pantomime** Join with other members of your class to create and perform a pantomime or an interpretive dance that tells the story of the House of Usher without the use of words.
~ **PERFORMING**

2. **Usher Poster** Imagine that you're part of a team that is making a movie version of the story. Create a poster to attract a new generation of Poe fans.
~ **ART**

3. **Charting Usher Events** To clarify the plot of the story, make a flow chart that shows the sequence of events in it. You can use the following chart as a model.
~ **VIEWING AND REPRESENTING**

| Event 1 | Event 2 | Event 3 | Event 4 | Event 5 |
|---|---|---|---|---|
| Usher invites narrator to the house. | | | | |

## Inquiry & Research

**Science** Usher tells the narrator that he and his sister were twins who shared "sympathies of a scarcely intelligible nature." Psychologists have conducted interesting research into twins and the characteristics they share. Look into popular magazines and psychology textbooks to find out what psychologists have learned, and report your findings to the class.

## Teaching Options

**Mini Lesson** **Grammar**

**DASHES** A dash is a punctuation mark used to set off a sudden break in thought, an interruption in dialogue, a series or list of items, or a parenthetical element. The following examples are taken from Poe's "The House of Usher."

**a sudden break in thought**
What was it—I paused to think—what was it that so unnerved me in the contemplation of the House of Usher?

**an interruption in dialogue**
"you have not then seen it?—but, stay! you shall."

**a series or list**
I looked upon the scene before me—upon the mere house, and the simple landscape features of the domain—upon the bleak walls—upon the vacant eye-like windows. . . .

**clarifying parenthetical remark**
I have said that the sole effect of my somewhat childish experiment—that of looking down within the tarn—had been to deepen the first singular impression.

**Exercises** Rewrite the following sentences correctly, adding dashes where they are needed.

1. The narrator was unnerved by his first glimpse of the House of Usher of the gloomy house, the dark tarn, and the bleak landscape.

**Answer:** The narrator was unnerved by his first glimpse of the House of Usher—of the gloomy

## Vocabulary in Action

**EXERCISE A: CONTEXT CLUES** Read the following sentences, and decide which Word to Know would best replace the underlined word or phrase.

1. People in the 1800s must have been horribly <u>shocked</u> at the events depicted in "The Fall of the House of Usher."

2. Many must have slept <u>badly, waking up often</u>, after reading the story.

3. In the days when there were few drugs for the <u>reduction</u> of physical pain, Poe's descriptions of disease and suffering probably struck a responsive chord.

4. In this <u>tale</u> Poe exploits people's anxieties about death and decay.

5. In Poe's time there was widespread fear about the <u>laying to rest</u> of people who were not really dead.

**EXERCISE B: MEANING CLUES** On your paper write the Word to Know that best matches each description.

1. two objects or people alike in many ways
2. a diet that lacks enough nutrients
3. a hurricane that leaves an entire town in ruins
4. unsuccessful efforts to accomplish something
5. a dog whose ribs are showing
6. a bird that can't fly, such as an ostrich
7. a cheerleader with a lot of spirit
8. a plain, boring meal
9. a mule that will not budge
10. problems without answers

| WORDS TO KNOW | | | |
|---|---|---|---|
| | affinity | emaciated | interment |
| | aghast | fitfully | narrative |
| | alleviation | futility | obstinate |
| | annihilate | insipid | terrestrial |
| | deficiency | insoluble | vivacious |

**Building Vocabulary**
For an in-depth lesson on context clues, see page 326.

---

# Edgar Allan Poe

## Author Study Project
### A CRITICAL SCRAPBOOK ON POE

Edgar Allan Poe's reputation as a writer has varied greatly. During his lifetime, some critics condemned him for his strange tales, but Poe had his champions as well. In the decades since his death, critics have continued a fierce debate about Poe's writing ability. Working alone or with a group, create a scrapbook of critical and popular views of Poe's work. You might also include critical reviews of Poe by your classmates. The following are some sources you might uses in your research.

**Books and Periodicals** Look for opinions about Poe's writings in reviews and critical biographies. Be sure to note whose opinions they are and when they were expressed. Find out whether any of the opinions were motivated by nonliterary considerations. Focus especially on the opinions of well-known writers who were Poe's contemporaries, such as James Russell Lowell, Ralph Waldo Emerson, and Elizabeth Barrett Browning.

**Computer Resources** See if you can find any CD-ROMs that contain comments about Poe. Look for Poe newsgroups and Web sites on the Internet.

**Survey** Devise a set of questions that you can use to interview students, friends, and family members about their views of Poe. You might want to bring along some samples of Poe's work for them to look over before you ask your questions. Present your results in a graph or chart.

**More Online: Research Starter**
www.mcdougallittell.com

---

## Vocabulary in Action

**EXERCISE A**

1. aghast
2. fitfully
3. alleviation
4. narrative
5. interment

**EXERCISE B**

1. affinity
2. deficiency
3. annihilate
4. futility
5. emaciated
6. terrestrial
7. vivacious
8. insipid
9. obstinate
10. insoluble

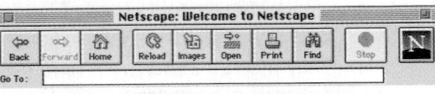

## Author Study Project
### A CRITICAL SCRAPBOOK ON POE

Encourage students to formulate their own list of criteria for literary criticism before they investigate what others have said and written about Poe's works. They should ask themselves what they look for in a book or story, such as an exciting plot, well-drawn characters, situations that they can relate to personally, beautiful prose, interesting ideas about life or human nature, and so on. When they read critical essays or remarks about Poe, they should consider their own criteria and evaluate whether the criticism aligns with their own views.

**Secondary Print Sources**
Suggest the following sources to students. Arthur Hobson Quinn's classic *Edgar Allan Poe: A Critical Biography* (Johns Hopkins University Press, 1998) is available in paperback. Students might also consult the following collections of critical essays: *The Tales of Poe,* edited and with an introduction by Harold Bloom (Chelsea House Publishers, 1987) and *New Essays on Poe's Major Tales,* edited by Kenneth Silverman (Cambridge University Press, 1993).

**MULTIMEDIA PROJECT**
Students can turn their work into multimedia projects by videotaping a round-table discussion among four or five of Poe's critics. Students can assume the identities of literary critics whose comments they have read, or they can simply share their own views. Student groups should represent varied opinions about the value of Poe's work so that the discussion will be a lively debate on the topic. One student may serve as moderator of the discussion.

---

house, the dark tarn, and the bleak landscape.

2. Inside the house, he observed the objects around him the carved ceilings, tapestries, and armor.
**Answer:** Inside the house, he observed the objects around him—the carved ceilings, tapestries, and armor.

3. Madeline her face paler than the color of death stared at Roderick.
**Answer:** Madeline—her face paler than the color of death—stared at Roderick.

4. "The storm will not harm us Roderick, what in the world?"
**Answer:** "The storm will not harm us—Roderick, what in the world?"

5. Madeline suddenly appeared before them in her shroud her burial gown now covered with blood.
**Answer:** Madeline suddenly appeared before them in her shroud—her burial gown—now covered with blood.

 Use McDougal Littell's *Language Network,* Chapter 10, for more instruction and practice in dashes.

This selection is included in the **Grade 11 InterActive Reader.**

### Objectives

1. understand and appreciate a classic **short story** that explores a Gothic theme **(Literary Analysis)**
2. identify and understand **foreshadowing (Literary Analysis)**
3. **interpret** the story as an **allegory (Active Reading)**

### Summary

Dr. Heidegger invites four elderly friends to his study to participate in an experiment. They include a merchant who has lost his money in speculation, a colonel who has wasted his life in pursuit of pleasure, and a ruined politician. All three men had been suitors of the fourth guest, a woman who has led a scandalous life. Dr. Heidegger has a vase containing water that he says is from the Fountain of Youth. As proof of the water's virtues, Dr. Heidegger shows how a dried rose blooms again after being placed in it. He then offers the liquid to his guests, warning them to be models of virtue and to set a good example if they become young again. The first glass that the four guests drink brightens their faces; the second glass brings them into middle age; the third glass returns them to the prime of their youth. Now they mock old Heidegger, and the three men immediately renew their rivalry over the widow. In the resulting fight, the water is spilled, and quickly the four grow old again. At the end Dr. Heidegger says that he has learned from the experiment that he doesn't want to be young again. Meanwhile his four guests make plans to look for the Fountain of Youth.

### Thematic Link

Dr. Heidegger's experiment leads his guests back into their youths and provides a glimpse at **the dark side of individualism**. Dr. Heidegger, as the interested observer, gains insight into the human heart.

### 5-Minute Warm-Up

***Daily Language SkillBuilder***

Have students **proofread** the display sentences on page 337k and write them correctly. The sentences also appear on Transparency 14 of **Grammar Transparencies and Copymasters.**

---

## PREPARING to *Read*

# Dr. Heidegger's Experiment

*Short Story by* NATHANIEL HAWTHORNE

**Connect to Your Life**

**Aging Gracefully** What do you like most about being the age you are right now? What aspects of growing older do you look forward to? What aspects of growing older are undesirable to you? Do you think youth and age should be measured by the years a person has lived or by a person's behavior and outlook? With a small group of classmates, discuss these questions about youth and aging.

## Build Background

**Forever Young** You may have heard about the Spanish explorer Ponce de León (pŏns′ də lē-ōn′) and his travels throughout Florida in search of the Fountain of Youth. People believed that water from this fountain would make old people young again. Although the fountain was a myth, the belief in a magic liquid that could bring the dead to life or that could confer immortality has a long history. During the Middle Ages, alchemists (early chemists who combined science and magic) sought the "elixir of life," a substance they believed would prolong life indefinitely. Nathaniel Hawthorne was fascinated by the concept of immortality, and in several stories—including "Dr. Heidegger's Experiment"—he wrote about men who possessed the secret elixir of life.

> WORDS TO KNOW
> **Vocabulary Preview**
>
> decrepit    exultingly
> deferential    stigma
> dispute    transient
> efface    tremulous
> exhilaration    venerable

## Focus Your Reading

**LITERARY ANALYSIS** **FORESHADOWING** While watching a movie or television show, have you ever accurately guessed other events that were going to happen? A writer's use of hints or clues to indicate events that will occur later in a story is called **foreshadowing.** Foreshadowing creates suspense and at the same time prepares the reader for what is to come. As you read "Dr. Heidegger's Experiment," look for clues that might help you guess how the story will unfold.

**ACTIVE READING** **INTERPRETING ALLEGORY** As you recall, an **allegory** is a work of literature in which people, objects, and events stand for abstract qualities, such as evil, compassion, or greed. For example, the four guests in "Dr. Heidegger's Experiment" are not realistic, fully developed characters. Instead, they seem more like representations of ideas. Allegories are written not only to entertain but also to teach lessons or moral principles.

**READER'S NOTEBOOK** Draw a chart like the one below, and complete it as you read the story or right after you finish reading it. Identify an abstract quality or idea that each of the four guests in the story might represent.

| Character | What he or she loses or wastes | What happens when he or she is given a second youth | What he or she might represent |
|---|---|---|---|
| Mr. Medbourne | wealth | schemes to make money again | greed |
| Col. Killigrew | | | |
| Mr. Gascoigne | | | |
| Widow Wycherly | | | |

---

## LESSON RESOURCES

**UNIT THREE RESOURCE BOOK,** pp. 66–70

**ASSESSMENT RESOURCES**
**Formal Assessment,** pp. 89–90
**Teacher's Guide to Assessment and Portfolio Use**
**Test Generator**

**SKILLS TRANSPARENCIES AND COPYMASTERS**
**Reading and Critical Thinking**
• Predicting Outcomes, T2 (for Extend Interpretations, item 5, p. 514)

**Grammar**
• Comparison of Regular and Irregular Adjectives and Adverbs, T52 (for Mini Lesson, p. 502)
**Vocabulary**
• Suffixes, C46 (for Mini Lesson, p. 507)
**Writing**
• Short Story, C29 (for Writing Option 3, p. 515)
**Communications**
• Nonverbal Strategies, T15 (for Mini Lesson, p. 508)

**INTEGRATED TECHNOLOGY**

**Audio Library**
**Visit our website:**
www.mcdougallittell.com

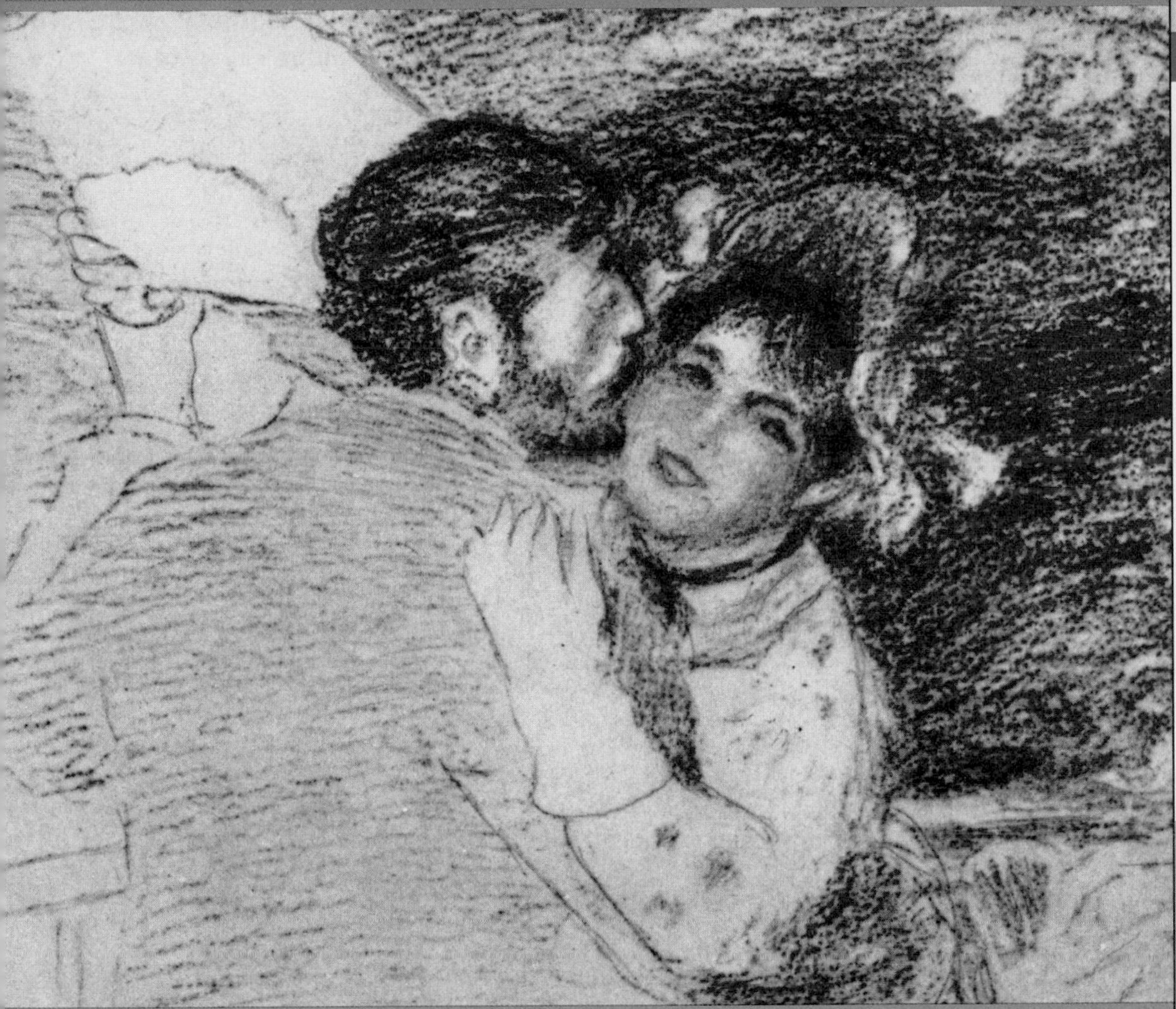

# Dr. Heidegger's Experiment

NATHANIEL HAWTHORNE

501

## Customizing Instruction

### Less Proficient Readers

Tell students that they will meet five characters who have gathered for a rather unusual experiment. Have students establish a purpose for reading—to find out who these characters are and why they are meeting.

### Students Acquiring English

Explain to students that Nathaniel Hawthorne wrote in the 1800s. As a result, his vocabulary is more formal than that commonly used today. Encourage them to use context clues to define unfamiliar words.

Use **Spanish Study Guide** for additional support, pp. 121–123.

### Gifted and Talented

Tell students that Hawthorne often chooses a point of view that allows ambiguity to enter the narration. Have students focus on how the narrator's interpretations of the events affect their understanding of the theme of the story.

## Mini Lesson Preteaching Vocabulary

**USING CONTEXT CLUES** Call students' attention to the list of WORDS TO KNOW. Remind them that they can rely on context to determine the denotation of words. Sometimes they can determine the meaning of an unfamiliar word by examining another word in the sentence that has a similar meaning. This similarity is often indicated by the conjunction *and.* Use the following model to demonstrate the strategy.

**Model Sentence**

The guests exclaimed <u>exultingly</u> and danced joyfully around the room.

**Instruction**

- Write the model sentence on the board.
- Ask a volunteer to locate the synonym for *exultingly* by its placement in the sentence.

**Possible Response:** *Joyfully* modifies *danced* just as *exultingly* modifies *exclaimed.*

- Based on this similarity in meaning, have students define *exultingly*.
- Ask a volunteer to use *exultingly* in an original sentence.

Use **Unit Three Resource Book,** p. 69 for exercises.

**A lesson on context clues appears on p. 326 in the Pupil's Edition.**

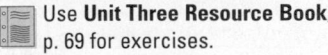

**Reading Skills and Strategies:**
**PREVIEW**

Tell students to pause in their reading from time to time to predict what will happen in the story.

**Literary Analysis** [FORESHADOWING]

Explain that foreshadowing is a technique with which the writer hints at events that will occur later in the story. The guests' past rivalry for the Widow Wycherly foreshadows the rivalry that erupts later in the story.

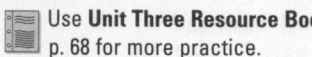 Use **Unit Three Resource Book**, p. 68 for more practice.

**Active Reading**
[INTERPRETING ALLEGORY]

Explain that an allegory is literary work in which characters, objects, and events represent abstract qualities and ideas. In other words, one thing stands for another. Ask students to consider the allegorical qualities each character represents.

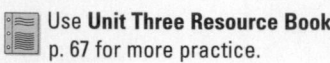 Use **Unit Three Resource Book**, p. 67 for more practice.

**GUIDE FOR READING**

**A** **Possible Response:** Mr. Medbourne has lost his money; Colonel Killigrew has lost his health; Mr. Gascoigne has lost his reputation; Widow Wycherly has lost her beauty and good name.

**B** **Possible Response:** The men were all rivals for the woman's affection.

**C** **Possible Responses:** mysterious, spooky, magical

---

That very singular man, old Dr. Heidegger, once invited four <u>venerable</u> friends to meet him in his study. There were three white-bearded gentlemen, Mr. Medbourne, Colonel Killigrew, and Mr. Gascoigne, and a withered gentlewoman, whose name was the Widow Wycherly. They were all melancholy old creatures, who had been unfortunate in life, and whose greatest misfortune it was, that they were not long ago in their graves. Mr. Medbourne, in the vigor of his age, had been a prosperous merchant, but had lost his all by a frantic speculation, and was now little better than a
15  mendicant. Colonel Killigrew had wasted his best years, and his health and substance, in the pursuit of sinful pleasures, which had given birth to a brood of pains, such as the gout, and divers other torments of soul and body. Mr. Gascoigne was a ruined politician, a man of evil fame, or at least had been so, till time
20  had buried him from the knowledge of the present generation, and made him obscure instead of infamous. As for the Widow Wycherly, tradition tells us that she was a great beauty in her day; but, for a long while past, she had lived in deep seclusion, on account of certain scandalous stories, which had prejudiced
25  the gentry of the town against her. It is a circumstance worth mentioning, that each of these three old gentlemen, Mr. Medbourne, Colonel Killigrew, and Mr. Gascoigne, were early lovers of the Widow Wycherly, and had once been on the point of cutting each other's throats for her sake. And, before pro-
30  ceeding farther, I will merely hint, that Dr. Heidegger and all his four guests were sometimes thought to be a little beside themselves; as is not unfrequently the case with old people, when worried either by present troubles or woeful recollections.

"My dear old friends," said Dr. Heidegger, motioning them to
35  be seated, "I am desirous of your assistance in one of those little experiments with which I amuse myself here in my study."

If all stories were true, Dr. Heidegger's study must have been a very curious place. It was a dim, old-fashioned chamber, festooned with cobwebs, and besprinkled with antique dust.
40  Around the walls stood several oaken book-cases, the lower shelves of which were filled with rows of gigantic folios, and black-letter quartos, and the upper with little parchment covered duodecimos. Over the central book-case was a bronze bust of

WORDS
TO
KNOW    **venerable** (věn'ər-ə-bəl) *adj.* worthy of respect because of age, dignity, or character

502

**A** **12–25** What has each of these four characters wasted or lost?

**15 mendicant** (měn'dĭ-kənt): beggar.

**17 gout:** a painful disease of the joints, once thought to be caused by eating too much rich food.

**21 obscure instead of infamous** (ĭn'fə-məs): little known rather than well-known for wickedness.

**25 gentry:** respectable or socially high-ranking people.

**B** **25–28** What relationship did the four guests have in their youth?

**C** **37–60** Notice the details included in this Gothic description of Dr. Heidegger's study. What mood is established by this description?

**39 festooned:** decorated in draping curves.

**41–43 folios . . . quartos . . . duodecimos:** books of different sizes.

---

## Teaching Options

 **Mini Lesson** **Grammar**

**COMPARATIVES**

**Instruction** Remind students that the comparative degree of an adjective or adverb is used to compare two persons, places, groups, things, ideas, or actions. The comparative degree of shorter adjectives and a few adverbs is formed by adding the suffix *-er*. Longer adjectives and most adverbs use the word *more* or *less* to form the comparative degree. A few adjectives and adverbs have irregular comparatives.

Write the following sentences on the chalkboard and have students identify the comparative form

of the adjective in parentheses:

Dr. Heidegger has a (wise) attitude towards old age than his four friends. (*wiser*)

The guests drink the potion to become (decrepit) than they are. (*less decrepit*)

**Exercises** Ask students to write the appropriate comparative form of each adjective or adverb in parentheses.

1. Widow Wycherly was (beautiful) in her youth than in old age. (*more beautiful*)

2. Of the two men, it was difficult to say whose behavior was (bad). (*worse*)

Hippocrates, with which, according to some authorities, Dr.
45 Heidegger was accustomed to hold consultations, in all difficult
cases of his practice. In the obscurest corner of the room stood a
tall and narrow oaken closet, with its door ajar, within which
doubtfully appeared a skeleton. Between two of the book-cases
hung a looking-glass, presenting its high and dusty plate within a
50 tarnished gilt frame. Among many wonderful stories related of
this mirror, it was fabled that the spirits of all the doctor's
deceased patients dwelt within its verge, and would stare him in
the face whenever he looked thitherward. The opposite side of the
chamber was ornamented with the full length portrait of a young
55 lady, arrayed in the faded magnificence of silk, satin, and bro-
cade, and with a visage as faded as her dress. Above half a century ago, Dr. Heidegger had been on the point of marriage with
this young lady; but, being affected with some slight disorder, she
had swallowed one of her lover's prescriptions, and died on the
60 bridal evening.

> "I am desirous of your assistance in one of those little experiments with which I amuse myself here in my study."

The greatest curiosity of the study remains to be mentioned: it
was a ponderous folio volume, bound in black leather, with massive silver clasps. There were no letters on the back, and nobody
could tell the title of the book. But it was well known to be a
65 book of magic; and once, when a chambermaid had lifted it,
merely to brush away the dust, the skeleton had rattled in its
closet, the picture of the young lady had stepped one foot upon
the floor, and several ghastly faces had peeped forth from the mirror; while the brazen head of Hippocrates frowned, and
70 said—"Forbear!"
Such was Dr. Heidegger's study. On the summer afternoon of
our tale, a small round table, as black as ebony, stood in the center of the room, sustaining a cut-glass vase, of beautiful form and
elaborate workmanship. The sunshine came through the window,
75 between the heavy festoons of two faded damask curtains, and
fell directly across this vase; so that a mild splendor was reflected

**44** Hippocrates (hĭ-pŏk′rə-tēz′): a Greek physician, considered to be the father of medicine.

**48–50** This is no ordinary mirror. Watch what it reveals as the story continues.

**52** verge: border.

**53** thitherward: in that direction.

**56** visage (vĭz′ĭj): face.

**70** forbear: stop; cease.

**3.** The previous story had (few) examples of symbolism than this one. (*fewer*)
**4.** Each alchemist believed that his formula was (good) than anyone else's. (*better*)

 Use McDougal Littell's *Language Network,* Chapter 7, for more instruction and practice in comparatives.

**A** Ask students to interpret what the rose might represent.

**Possible Responses:** The rose might represent love, youth, and the beauty, decay, and death that are part of nature.

### Literary Analysis
FORESHADOWING

**B** Ask students how Widow Wycherly's comment might hint at what is to come.

**Possible Responses:** Her face will become smooth; all the old people will become younger.

---

from it on the ashen visages of the five old people who sat around. Four champagne glasses were also on the table.

"My dear old friends," repeated Dr. Heidegger, "may I reckon
80 on your aid in performing an exceedingly curious experiment?"

Now Dr. Heidegger was a very strange old gentleman, whose eccentricity had become the nucleus for a thousand fantastic stories. Some of these fables, to my shame be it spoken, might possibly be traced back to mine own veracious self; and if any
85 passages of the present tale should startle the reader's faith, I must be content to bear the <u>stigma</u> of a fiction-monger.

When the doctor's four guests heard him talk of his proposed experiment, they anticipated nothing more wonderful than the murder of a mouse in an air-pump, or the examination of a cob-
90 web by the microscope, or some similar nonsense, with which he was constantly in the habit of pestering his intimates. But without waiting for a reply, Dr. Heidegger hobbled across the chamber, and returned with the same ponderous folio, bound in black leather, which common report affirmed to be a book of magic.
95 Undoing the silver clasps, he opened the volume, and took from among its black-letter pages a rose, or what was once a rose, though now the green leaves and crimson petals had assumed one brownish hue, and the ancient flower seemed ready to crumble to dust in the doctor's hands.

100 "This rose," said Dr. Heidegger, with a sigh, "this same withered and crumbling flower, blossomed five-and-fifty years ago. It was given me by Sylvia Ward, whose portrait hangs yonder; and I meant to wear it in my bosom at our wedding. Five-and-fifty years it has been treasured between the leaves of this old volume.
105 Now, would you deem it possible that this rose of half a century could ever bloom again?"

"Nonsense!" said the Widow Wycherly, with a peevish toss of her head. "You might as well ask whether an old woman's wrinkled face could ever bloom again."

110 "See!" answered Dr. Heidegger.

He uncovered the vase, and threw the faded rose into the water which it contained. At first, it lay lightly on the surface of the fluid, appearing to imbibe none of its moisture. Soon, however, a singular change began to be visible. The crushed and dried petals
115 stirred, and assumed a deepening tinge of crimson, as if the flower were reviving from a death-like slumber; the slender stalk and twigs of foliage became green; and there was the rose of half a century, looking as fresh as when Sylvia Ward had first given it to her lover. It was scarcely full-blown; for some of its delicate

**83–86** The narrator admits to having told fables about Dr. Heidegger in the past.

**84 veracious:** truthful.

**86 fiction-monger:** liar.

**107 peevish:** irritable.

**113 imbibe:** absorb.

**119 full-blown:** completely open.

WORDS
TO
KNOW    **stigma** (stǐg'mə) *n.* a mark of disgrace

504

---

### BLOCK SCHEDULING: MANAGING TIME

**If your schedule requires that you cover the lesson objectives in a shorter time, use . . .**
- Preparing to Read, p. 500
- Thinking Through the Literature, p. 514
- Vocabulary in Action, p. 515

**If you want to take advantage of longer class time, use . . .**
- TE Teaching Options: Preteaching Vocabulary, p. 501; Viewing and Representing, pp. 505, 510–511; Cross-Curricular Link, p. 506; Speaking and Listening, p. 508; Informal Assessment, p. 513; Standardized Test Practice, p. 512
- Choices & Challenges, p. 515

*Déjeuner* [Luncheon] (1876), Gustave Caillebotte. Oil on canvas, 52 cm × 75 cm, private collection.

The crushed and dried petals stirred, . . . as if the

flower were reviving from a death-like slumber.

DR. HEIDEGGER'S EXPERIMENT     **505**

## Customizing Instruction

**Less Proficient Readers**

**1** Ask students to describe in their own words what happens to the rose when it is placed in the water.

**Gifted and Talented**

Allow students to copy the following quotation from Henry James's review of Hawthorne's *The Scarlet Letter*: "The faults of the book are, to my sense, a want of reality and an abuse of the fanciful element of a certain superficial symbolism. The people strike me not as characters, but as representatives, very picturesquely arranged, of a single state of mind; and the interest of the story lies, not in them, but in the situation, which is insistently kept before us, with little progression. . . . "

Remind students of the definition of allegory. Ask them if they think the underlined statement could apply to "Dr. Heidegger's Experiment." Have them use elements of the text to defend or refute James's interpretation.

### Mini Lesson **Viewing and Representing**

*Déjeuner* [Luncheon] **by Gustave Caillebotte**

**ART APPRECIATION** This 1876 painting by the French Impressionist artist Gustave Caillebotte (1848–1894) shows the dining room of the painter's family home. Pictured are Caillebotte's mother, his brother René, and the family butler. Notice that a third place is set in the foreground.

**Instruction** Explain that the darkness of this scene makes this an atypical Impressionist work; most Impressionist canvases are flooded with light. Ask students what mood is created by the darkness of the scene. Also have students examine the placement of the figures. Ask what inference they might make about the relationship between mother and son.

**Possible Responses:** The darkness creates a somber, formal, and heavy mood. The mother and son are separated physically, which might represent an emotional distance. Also, each seems more intent upon the food than upon the other person at the table.

### GUIDE FOR READING

**A** **Possible Responses:** sensible, because he has no desire to relive the perils of youth and he appreciates the gifts of old age.

**B** **Possible Response:** He reminds them that they should avoid the mistakes they made when they were young.

### Literary Analysis

FORESHADOWING

**C** Ask students what they think Dr. Heidegger's warning to his guests foreshadows.

**Possible Responses:** The guests will repeat their mistakes; they will make new mistakes; they will forget what they learned as they grew older.

### GUIDE FOR READING

**D** **Possible Responses:** Yes, they will be looking at the situation with the benefit of much experience. No, they don't know whether they will lose their memories along with their years.

**E** **Possible Responses:** to see whether people can become young again; to see how people behave if given a second chance; to prove that people can't change.

red leaves curled modestly around its moist bosom, within which two or three dewdrops were sparkling.

"That is certainly a very pretty deception," said the doctor's friends; carelessly, however, for they had witnessed greater miracles at a conjurer's show: "pray how was it effected?"

"Did you never hear of the 'Fountain of Youth,'" asked Dr. Heidegger, "which Ponce De Leon, the Spanish adventurer, went in search of, two or three centuries ago?"

"But did Ponce De Leon ever find it?" said the Widow Wycherly.

"No," answered Dr. Heidegger, "for he never sought it in the right place. The famous Fountain of Youth, if I am rightly informed, is situated in the southern part of the Floridian peninsula, not far from Lake Macaco. Its source is overshadowed by several gigantic magnolias, which, though numberless centuries old, have been kept as fresh as violets, by the virtues of this wonderful water. An acquaintance of mine, knowing my curiosity in such matters, has sent me what you see in the vase."

"Ahem!" said Colonel Killigrew, who believed not a word of the doctor's story: "and what may be the effect of this fluid on the human frame?"

"You shall judge for yourself, my dear colonel," replied Dr. Heidegger; "and all of you, my respected friends, are welcome to so much of this admirable fluid, as may restore to you the bloom of youth. For my own part, having had much trouble in growing old, I am in no hurry to grow young again. With your permission, therefore, I will merely watch the progress of the experiment."

While he spoke, Dr. Heidegger had been filling the four champagne glasses with the water of the Fountain of Youth. It was apparently impregnated with an effervescent gas, for little bubbles were continually ascending from the depths of the glasses, and bursting in silvery spray at the surface. As the liquor diffused a pleasant perfume, the old people doubted not that it possessed cordial and comfortable properties; and, though utter skeptics as to its rejuvenescent power, they were inclined to swallow it at once. But Dr. Heidegger besought them to stay a moment.

"Before you drink, my respectable old friends," said he, "it would be well that, with the experience of a life-time to direct you, you should draw up a few general rules for your guidance, in passing a second time through the perils of youth. Think what a sin and shame it would be, if, with your peculiar advantages,

**128 conjurer's:** magician's.

**148–149** What do you think of Dr. Heidegger's reason for not wanting to be young again? **A**

**152–153 was apparently . . . gas:** seemed to have a bubbling gas dissolved in it.

**157 cordial** (kôr′jəl): stimulating.

**158 rejuvenescent** (rĭ-jōō′və-nĕs′ənt): producing renewed youth.

**159 besought them to stay:** begged them to wait.

**160–166** What warning does Dr. Heidegger give his guests? **B**

**Cross Curricular Link** **History**

**PONCE DE LEÓN AND THE FOUNTAIN OF YOUTH**
Ponce de León (c. 1460–1521) may have heard tales of the "Fountain of Youth" while accompanying Columbus on his second voyage to the Americas. The fountain was supposedly located on the island of Bimini. Ponce de León searched for the island from 1513 until 1521, when he was killed by a native tribe in Florida. Interestingly, according to medieval legend, the fountain or spring was the Water of Life in the Garden of Eden, thought to be located in the Far East. As students may recall, the early Spanish explorers thought America was the Far East.

165 you should not become patterns of virtue and wisdom to all the young people of the age!"

The doctor's four venerable friends made him no answer, except by a feeble and <u>tremulous</u> laugh; so very ridiculous was the idea, that, knowing how closely repentance treads behind the
170 steps of error, they should ever go astray again.

"Drink, then," said the doctor, bowing: "I rejoice that I have so well selected the subjects of my experiment."

With palsied hands, they raised the glasses to their lips. The liquor, if it really possessed such virtues as Dr. Heidegger
175 imputed to it, could not have been bestowed on four human beings who needed it more woefully. They looked as if they had never known what youth or pleasure was, but had been the off-spring of Nature's dotage, and always the gray, <u>decrepit</u>, sapless, miserable creatures, who now sat stooping round the doctor's
180 table, without life enough in their souls or bodies to be animated even by the prospect of growing young again. They drank off the water, and replaced their glasses on the table.

Assuredly there was an almost immediate improvement in the aspect of the party, not unlike what might have been produced by
185 a glass of generous wine, together with a sudden glow of cheerful sunshine, brightening over all their visages at once. There was a healthful suffusion on their cheeks, instead of the ashen hue that had made them look so corpselike. They gazed at one another, and fancied that some magic power had really begun to smooth
190 away the deep and sad inscriptions which Father Time had been so long engraving on their brows. The Widow Wycherly adjusted her cap, for she felt almost like a woman again.

> "Drink, then," said the doctor, bowing: "I rejoice that I have so well selected the subjects of my experiment."

"Give us more of this wondrous water!" cried they, eagerly. "We are younger—but we are still too old! Quick!—give us more!"
195 "Patience, patience!" quoth Dr. Heidegger, who sat watching the experiment, with philosophic coolness. "You have been a long

**167–170** Should the guests feel so confident that they will not repeat the errors of the past? **D**

**171–172** What do you think is the purpose of Dr. Heidegger's experiment? **E**

**173 palsied:** trembling.

**175 imputed:** attributed; credited.

**178 dotage** (dō′tĭj): feebleness due to old age.

**184 aspect:** appearance.

**187 healthful suffusion:** rosy glow of health.

| WORDS TO KNOW | |
|---|---|
| **tremulous** (trĕm′yə-ləs) *adj.* marked by trembling, quivering, or shaking | |
| **decrepit** (dĭ-krĕp′ĭt) *adj.* weakened, worn out, or broken down by old age or hard use | |

**507**

## GUIDE FOR READING

**(A)** **Possible Responses:** physical, given the altered appearance of the rose and the guests; psychological, because the narrator drops clues that the water may not really possess the virtues attributed to it and that the characters only imagine the change that comes over them

## Literary Analysis: SIMILE

**(B)** Remind students that a simile is a figure of speech that compares two things that have something in common. A simile uses the word *like* or *as*. Ask students what is being compared in the simile in lines 217 and 218.

**Possible Response:** Widow Wycherly's rejuvenation is compared to darkness that gives way to day.

## GUIDE FOR READING

**(C)** **Possible Response:** They begin to behave just as they had in their prime.

## Active Reading

| INTERPRETING ALLEGORY |

Ask students to consider what Dr. Heidegger might represent allegorically.

**Possible Response:** Dr. Heidegger is associated with many symbols of learning and wisdom. Therefore he might represent the wisdom that is acquired by the passage of time.

time growing old. Surely, you might be content to grow young in half an hour! But the water is at your service."

Again he filled their glasses with the liquor of youth, enough of which still remained in the vase to turn half the old people in the city to the age of their own grand-children. While the bubbles were yet sparkling on the brim, the doctor's four guests snatched their glasses from the

210 table, and swallowed the contents at a single gulp. Was it delusion? Even while the draught was passing down their throats, it seemed to have wrought a change on their whole systems. Their eyes grew clear and bright; a dark shade deepened among their silvery locks; they sat around the table, three gentlemen of middle

215 age, and a woman, hardly beyond her buxom prime.

"My dear widow, you are charming!" cried Colonel Killigrew, whose eyes had been fixed upon her face, while the shadows of age were flitting from it like darkness from the crimson day-break.

The fair widow knew, of old, that Colonel Killigrew's compli-
220 ments were not always measured by sober truth; so she started up and ran to the mirror, still dreading that the ugly visage of an old woman would meet her gaze. Meanwhile, the three gentlemen behaved in such a manner, as proved that the water of the Fountain of Youth possessed some intoxicating qualities; unless,

225 indeed, their <u>exhilaration</u> of spirits were merely a lightsome dizziness, caused by the sudden removal of the weight of years. Mr. Gascoigne's mind seemed to run on political topics, but whether relating to the past, present, or future, could not easily be determined, since the same ideas and phrases have been in vogue these

230 fifty years. Now he rattled forth full-throated sentences about patriotism, national glory, and the people's right; now he muttered some perilous stuff or other, in a sly and doubtful whisper, so cautiously that even his own conscience could scarcely catch the secret; and now, again, he spoke in measured accents, and a

**1** 235 deeply <u>deferential</u> tone, as if a royal ear were listening to his well-turned periods. Colonel Killigrew all this time had been trolling forth a jolly bottle-song, and ringing his glass in symphony with the chorus, while his eyes wandered towards the buxom figure of the Widow Wycherly. On the other side of the

**207–215** Is the effect of the water physical or psychological? Watch how the narrator blurs the line between what is real and what is an illusion throughout the story. **(A)**

**219–257** How do the guests begin to behave as soon as their youth is restored? **(C)**

WORDS
TO
KNOW

**exhilaration** (ĭg-zĭl'ə-rā'shən) *n.* a lively delight
**deferential** (dĕf'ə-rĕn'shəl) *adj.* extremely respectful

508

---

 **Mini Lesson** **Speaking and Listening**

**INTERPRETING CHARACTER** Ask students to choose one of the characters and tell the story of his or her earlier years from that character's perspective. Students may work in groups to prepare each character's version of the events that led him or her to this end. Students must justify their choice of verbal performance techniques by referring to their analysis of the text. Have students list what is known about the character's personality and background from Hawthorne's story before they evolve their account in the character's own words. The choice of vocabulary and the tone of the explanation should be consistent with Hawthorne's portrait.

**Present** Students may tell the story with different speakers indicating different phases of the character's life. Students who are audience members should evaluate the logic of the account and the consistency of the performance in relation to the original text.

**BLOCK SCHEDULING** This activity is particularly well-suited for longer class periods.

table, Mr. Medbourne was involved in a calculation of dollars and cents, with which was strangely intermingled a project for supplying the East Indies with ice, by harnessing a team of whales to the polar icebergs.

As for the Widow Wycherly, she stood before the mirror, curtseying and simpering to her own image, and greeting it as the friend whom she loved better than all the world beside. She thrust her face close to the glass, to see whether some long-remembered wrinkle or crow's-foot had indeed vanished. She examined whether the snow had so entirely melted from her hair, that the venerable cap could be safely thrown aside. At last, turning briskly away, she came with a sort of dancing step to the table.

"My dear old doctor," cried she, "pray favor me with another glass!"

"Certainly, my dear madam, certainly!" replied the complaisant doctor; "See! I have already filled the glasses."

There, in fact, stood the four glasses, brim full of this wonderful water, the delicate spray of which, as it effervesced from the surface, resembled the tremulous glitter of diamonds. It was now so nearly sunset, that the chamber had grown duskier than ever; but a mild and moon-like splendor gleamed from within the vase, and rested alike on the four guests, and on the doctor's venerable figure. He sat in a high-backed, elaborately-carved, oaken armchair, with a gray dignity of aspect that might have well befitted

**245 simpering:** smiling in a silly, self-conscious way.

**254-255 complaisant** (kəm-plā'sənt): willing to please.

**2**

The doctor's four guests snatched their glasses from the table, and swallowed the contents at a single gulp.

that very Father Time, whose power had never been disputed, save by this fortunate company. Even while quaffing the third draught of the Fountain of Youth, they were almost awed by the expression of his mysterious visage.

But, the next moment, the exhilarating gush of young life shot through their veins. They were now in the happy prime of youth. Age, with its miserable train of cares, and sorrows, and diseases, was remembered only as the trouble of a dream, from which they

**266 quaffing** (kwŏf'ĭng): drinking heartily.

WORDS
TO
KNOW

**dispute** (dĭ-spyōōt') v. to question or doubt

**509**

**Less Proficient Readers**
Help students summarize the nature of the experiment and its outcome. Then have them establish a purpose by reading to find out how the four react to being young again.

**Possible Response:** Dr. Heidegger's four friends drink water that supposedly comes from the Fountain of Youth. They appear to feel and look younger.

**Students Acquiring English**
**1** Explain that the phrase *royal ear . . . listening to his well-turned periods* means that Gasciogne spoke politely and eloquently, as if his audience were a king or queen.

**Gifted and Talented**
**2** Have students analyze the characteristics of word choice in Hawthorne's use of *diamonds* in this sentence. Ask them to determine why it might be appropriate.

### Literary Analysis: METAPHOR

**(A)** Ask students to what the narrator is comparing the "world's successive scenes." What view of experience does this metaphor express?

**Possible Response:** a gallery of faded pictures. Once youth is gone, experiences become pale; as one ages, remembered experiences seem unreal or removed from life.

### GUIDE FOR READING

**(B) Possible Responses:** Each makes people seem more like one another; each erases the individualizing characteristics of middle-aged people.

**(C) Possible Responses:** old age; because they are becoming young again, they can make fun of what they were

### Reading Skills and Strategies: EVALUATING

**(D)** Ask students if they think the behavior described in lines 304–311 is realistic.

**Possible Responses:** Yes, the four guests have become youths, and youths are exuberant; no, they would have learned from their experiences and they would behave more cautiously.

### GUIDE FOR READING

**(E) Possible Responses:** The narrator wants the reader to decide. The characters may indeed have grown outwardly young, while the mirror reflects their inner selves, which haven't changed; the characters may believe their outward appearance has changed, but the mirror reflects the truth—that they are still old.

---

**1**

**A**

had joyously awoke. The fresh gloss of the soul, so early lost, and without which the world's successive scenes had been but a gallery of faded pictures, again threw its enchantment over all 275 their prospects. They felt like new-created beings, in a new-created universe.

"We are young! We are young!" they cried, <u>exultingly</u>.

Youth, like the extremity of age, had <u>effaced</u> the strongly marked characteristics of middle life, and mutually assimilated 280 them all. They were a group of merry youngsters, almost maddened with the exuberant frolicksomeness of their years. The most singular effect of their gayety was an impulse to mock the infirmity and decrepitude of which they had so lately been the victims. They laughed loudly at their old-fashioned attire, the wide-285 skirted coats and flapped waistcoats of the young men, and the ancient cap and gown of the blooming girl. One limped across the floor, like a gouty grandfather; one set a pair of spectacles astride of his nose, and pretended to pore over the black-letter pages of the book of magic; a third seated himself in an arm-chair, and strove to 290 imitate the venerable dignity of Dr. Heidegger. Then all shouted mirthfully, and leaped about the room. The Widow Wycherly—if so fresh a damsel could be called a widow—tripped up to the doctor's chair, with a mischievous merriment in her rosy face.

"Doctor, you dear old soul," cried she, "get up and dance with 295 me!" And then the four young people laughed louder than ever, to think what a queer figure the poor old doctor would cut.

**2**

"Pray excuse me," answered the doctor, quietly. "I am old and rheumatic, and my dancing days were over long ago. But either of these gay young gentlemen will be glad of so pretty a partner." 300 "Dance with me, Clara!" cried Colonel Killigrew.

"No, no, I will be her partner!" shouted Mr. Gascoigne.

"She promised me her hand, fifty years ago!" exclaimed Mr. Medbourne.

They all gathered round her. One caught both her hands in his 305 passionate grasp—another threw his arm about her waist—the third buried his hand among the glossy curls that clustered beneath the widow's cap. Blushing, panting, struggling, chiding, laughing, her warm breath fanning each of their faces by turns,

**D**

she strove to disengage herself, yet still remained in their triple 310 embrace. Never was there a livelier picture of youthful rivalship, with bewitching beauty for the prize. Yet, by a strange deception, owing to the duskiness of the chamber, and the antique dresses

**3**

which they still wore, the tall mirror is said to have reflected the figures of the three old, gray, withered grand-sires, ridiculously 315 contending for the skinny ugliness of a shrivelled grand-dam.

**278–280** How does the narrator **B** say youth and old age are alike?

**279 assimilated:** absorbed.

**281–296** Whom or what are the **C** guests mocking, and why?

**291 mirthfully:** joyfully.

**298 rheumatic** (rŏŏ-măt'ĭk): made stiff by a condition such as arthritis.

**309 strove to disengage herself:** struggled to free herself.

**311–315** The narrator is unclear about whether the reflection is real or an illusion. Why? What **E** does the image in the mirror reveal?

**314–315 grand-sires . . . grand-dam:** old men . . . old woman.

> WORDS
> TO
> KNOW
>
> **exultingly** (ĭg-zŭl'tĭng-lē) *adv.* in a joyful and triumphant way
> **efface** (ĭ-fās') *v.* to rub or wipe out; erase

**510**

---

## Teaching Options

### Viewing and Representing

*La Danse à la Campagne* [*The country dance*] **by Pierre Auguste Renoir**

**ART APPRECIATION** A leader of the French Impressionist movement, Renoir (1841–1919) was perhaps its most popular painter. His work is especially noted for its motion and beautiful use of color. The drawing on p. 511 is a typical example of a Renoir portrait, including his use of two friends as models.

**Instruction** Explain to students the following principles of viewing a work of art.

- Look at the picture to get an overall impression.
- Notice to which part of the picture your eye is drawn.
- Ask yourself what draws your eye to a certain place. Is it the color? the shading? the lines?
- Think about whether the artwork reminds you of others you have seen. If so, is it because the artists use similar styles, or is it because the subject matter is similar?
- Think about your emotional response to the art. For example, does the picture make you feel sad, happy, or lonely?

Age, with its miserable train of cares, and sorrows, and diseases, was remembered only as the trouble of a dream, from which they had joyously awoke.

DR. HEIDEGGER'S EXPERIMENT    **511**

**Ⓐ Possible Response:** Their behavior is the same. Earlier, the narrator said that in their youth they would have "cut each other's throats" over the widow, and now they are "grappling fiercely at one another's throats."

**Ⓑ Possible Response:** He believes that old age is as valuable as youth, since he says he loves the withered rose just as much as the fresh one.

**Ⓒ Possible Responses:** that youth is a "delirium"; that people do not learn from their mistakes; that it is unwise to try to regain the past; that people do not acquire any lasting wisdom from a life-time of living; that death is inevitable

### Reading Skills and Strategies: SPECULATING

Ask students to draw inferences about what would have happened had the liquid not been spilled.

**Possible Responses:** Someone would have been hurt or killed; they would have fought over who should be allowed to drink the rest of the liquid; they would have grown old anyway and realized that their youthful appearance was just an illusion.

---

But they were young: their burning passions proved them so. Inflamed to madness by the coquetry of the girl-widow, who neither granted nor quite withheld her favors, the three rivals began to interchange threatening glances. Still keeping hold of the fair prize, they grappled fiercely at one another's throats.

As they struggled to and fro, the table was overturned, and the vase dashed into a thousand fragments. The precious Water of Youth flowed in a 330 bright stream across the floor, moistening the wings of a butter-fly, which, grown old in the decline of summer, had alighted there to die. The insect fluttered lightly through the chamber, and set-tled on the snowy head of Dr. Heidegger.

"Come, come, gentlemen!—come, Madam Wycherly," ex-335 claimed the doctor, "I really must protest against this riot."

They stood still, and shivered; for it seemed as if gray Time were calling them back from their sunny youth, far down into the chill and darksome vale of years. They looked at old Dr. Heidegger, who sat in his carved arm-chair, holding the rose of 340 half a century, which he had rescued from among the fragments of the shattered vase. At the motion of his hand, the four rioters resumed their seats; the more readily, because their violent exer-tions had wearied them, youthful though they were.

"My poor Sylvia's rose!" ejaculated Dr. Heidegger, holding it 345 in the light of the sunset clouds: "it appears to be fading again."

And so it was. Even while the party were looking at it, the flower continued to shrivel up, till it became as dry and fragile as when the doctor had first thrown it into the vase. He shook off the few drops of moisture which clung to its petals.

350 "I love it as well thus, as in its dewy freshness," observed he, pressing the withered rose to his withered lips. While he spoke, the butterfly fluttered down from the doctor's snowy head, and fell upon the floor.

His guests shivered again. A strange chillness, whether of the 355 body or spirit they could not tell, was creeping gradually over them all. They gazed at one another, and fancied that each fleet-ing moment snatched away a charm, and left a deepening furrow where none had been before. Was it an illusion? Had the changes of a life-time been crowded into so brief a space, and were they

**319 coquetry** (kō′kǐ-trē): flirtatious behavior.

**318–329** How does the characters' behavior in this scene compare with that of their youth? **Ⓐ**

**338 vale:** valley.

**344 ejaculated:** exclaimed.

**350–353** Can you infer how Dr. Heidegger feels about old age from the way he regards the rose? **Ⓑ**

---

## Teaching Options

### ✓ Assessment **Standardized Test Practice**

**CHOOSING THE BEST SUMMARY** For some standardized tests, students will be asked to choose the best summary of a passage. To provide students with some help in choosing the best summary, read aloud or write on the chalkboard the following question.

Which of the following statements best summarizes the guests' reactions to the effects of Dr. Heidegger's potion?

**A.** They don't believe that the potion can truly make them younger.

**B.** The four characters feel younger and more sprightly as the potion takes effect.

**C.** After drinking the potion, the four deride old age, and the three men rekindle their rivalry over the widow.

Lead students through the process of choosing the best summary. Consider each choice. Point out that, while all of the statements contain accurate information, the best summary should include the most complete information. For that reason, C is the best choice.

now four aged people, sitting with their old friend, Dr.
360 Heidegger?

"Are we grown old again, so soon!" cried they, dolefully.

In truth, they had. The Water of Youth possessed merely a
virtue more <u>transient</u> than that of wine. The delirium which it cre-
365 ated had effervesced away. Yes! they were old again. With a shuddering impulse, that showed her a woman still, the widow clasped
her skinny hands before her face, and wished that the coffin-lid
were over it, since it could be no longer beautiful.

"Yes, friends, ye are old again," said Dr. Heidegger; "and lo!
370 the Water of Youth is all lavished on the ground. Well—I bemoan
it not; for if the fountain gushed at my very doorstep, I would not
stoop to bathe my lips in it—no, though its delirium were for
years instead of moments. Such is the lesson ye have taught me!"

But the doctor's four friends had taught no such lesson to
375 themselves. They resolved forthwith to make a pilgrimage to
Florida, and quaff at morning, noon, and night, from the
Fountain of Youth. ❖

**364 delirium:** a temporary state of
mental confusion and clouded
consciousness.

**369-373** What lesson has Dr.
Heidegger learned?

---

## LITERARY LINK

# 𝔐ONODY
### (Elegy for Nathaniel Hawthorne)

### HERMAN MELVILLE

*Herman Melville (1819–1891),
best known for his famous sea
story* Moby-Dick, *became friends
with Nathaniel Hawthorne around
1850. Though their relationship
grew strained, Melville's admiration
for Hawthorne was enduring.
In "Monody" the speaker of the
poem mourns Hawthorne's death.*

To have known him, to have loved him
    After loneness long;
And then to be estranged in life,
    And neither in the wrong;
And now for death to set his seal—
5    Ease me, a little ease, my song!
By wintry hills his hermit-mound[1]
    The sheeted snow-drifts drape,
And houseless there the snow-bird flits
    Beneath the fir-trees' crape;[2]
10 Glazed now with ice the cloistral[3] vine
    That hid the shyest grape.

---

1. **hermit-mound:** the burial mound where the dead
   man rests in isolation, like a hermit.
2. **crape:** a black cloth used in funeral decorations.
3. **cloistral** (kloi'strəl): secluded.

WORDS
TO
KNOW    **transient** (trăn'shənt) *adj.* lasting or existing for only a short time

**513**

---

---

✓ Assessment **Informal Assessment**

**CHANGING POINT OF VIEW** Remind students that
this story was told from the point of view of a
third-person narrator who was not one of the
characters. Ask students to choose a character to
be the first-person narrator and to explain how
the different point of view affects the story in at
least four places. Have students consider the feelings and motivations of their character before they
begin writing.

**RUBRIC**

1 **Full Accomplishment** The student clearly
   shows the impact of the changed point of
   view in four well-chosen examples. The com-

ments and feelings revealed are consistent
with the character.

2 **Substantial Accomplishment** The student
   shows the impact of the changed point of
   view in fewer examples, and most comments
   and feelings are consistent with the character.

3 **Little or Partial Accomplishment** The student
   has difficulty identifying any examples that
   would be affected by the change in point of
   view and does not capture the character of
   the narrator.

## GUIDING STUDENT RESPONSE

## Connect to the Literature

**1. What Do You Think?**
Students should be able to explain why the ending is consistent with the events and the characters in the story.

**Comprehension Check**
• to assist him in an experiment with "youth-giving" water
• He tells them to use their experience to pass along virtue and wisdom to young people.
• to find the Fountain of Youth so they can drink from it morning, noon, and night

 Use Selection Quiz
**Unit Three Resource Book**, p. 70.

## Think Critically

**2. Possible Responses:** Hawthorne may have intended to teach that evil ways are difficult to overcome or that people tend to repeat the same mistakes according to their nature.

**3. Possible Responses:** Some students may mention the disregard shown senior citizens in society at large. They may compare this attitude with the four friends' mockery of old age when they have recovered their youth.

**4. Possible Responses:** Yes, because the rose changed and they could see the changes in each other; no, because the mirror still reflected old people.

## Literary Analysis

**Foreshadowing** Hawthorne uses foreshadowing to alert the reader to the outcome—that all is not going to turn out well for the guests. The reader is prepared when the men once again fight for the hand of the Widow Wycherly. Other examples of foreshadowing are the blooming and fading of the rose, the mirror reflecting the people as old, and the doctor's warning to his friends about their behavior.

**Review Mood** Details in the setting help to create a mysterious atmosphere. By contrast, the mood of "The Fall of the House of Usher" is one of unrelieved gloom.

---

## Connect to the Literature

**1. What Do You Think?**
What are your thoughts about the ending of this story?

**Comprehension Check**
• Why does Dr. Heidegger invite his friends to his chamber?
• What warning does the doctor give his guests?
• What do the four guests resolve to do at the end of the story?

## Think Critically

**2.**  **ACTIVE READING** **INTERPRETING ALLEGORY**
Look over the **character** chart you made in your **READER'S NOTEBOOK**. What lesson or lessons do you think Hawthorne intended this story to teach?

 **THINK ABOUT**
• what qualities the characters might represent
• what Dr. Heidegger is testing
• why Dr. Heidegger says he would not drink from the Fountain of Youth

**3.** Compare your attitudes toward youth and aging with those expressed by the **characters** in this story.

**THINK ABOUT**
• Dr. Heidegger's comments about the withered rose (page 512)
• the guests' behavior when restored to youth
• the guests' desire to find the Fountain of Youth

**4.** The narrator is deliberately unclear about whether the guests are actually restored to youth. What do you think? Support your answer.

## Extend Interpretations

**5. What If?** What do you think would have happened if the Water of Youth had not spilled?

**6. Different Perspectives** A year before his death at the age of 59, Hawthorne wrote, "Everything is beautiful in youth—all things are allowed it." How do you think each of the characters in "Dr. Heidegger's Experiment" would respond to this viewpoint?

**7. Comparing Texts** Reread Melville's poem "Monody" on page 513. Compare the speaker's regrets with the characters' regrets in "Dr. Heidegger's Experiment."

**8. Connect to Life** If people could regain their youth again, do you think they would make the same mistakes? Explain.

---

## Literary Analysis

**FORESHADOWING**

**Foreshadowing** is a writer's use of hints or clues to indicate events that will occur later in a story. For example, the former rivalry for the Widow Wycherly that is mentioned on page 502 foreshadows the rivalry that occurs later in Dr. Heidegger's study (page 510). Foreshadowing is a technique that helps build suspense and arouse the reader's curiosity.

**Paired Activity** Working with a partner, scan the story for two other examples of foreshadowing. Did Hawthorne's use of foreshadowing add to or detract from your enjoyment of the story? Share your response with classmates.

COMMENT or EVENT →foreshadows→ COMMENT or EVENT

**REVIEW** **MOOD** How would you describe the **mood** of this story, or the atmosphere conveyed to the reader? What elements make the mood similar to or different from the mood of "The Fall of the House of Usher"?

---

## Extend Interpretations

**What If?** Students' responses should be based on the events that have already transpired in the story and should take into account the histories of the characters.

**Different Perspectives** Possible Responses: The four friends would endorse Hawthorne's opinion; Dr. Heidegger, himself, would challenge it for he has observed the violence and folly that can characterize this stage of life.

**Comparing Texts** Possible Responses: The speaker in "Monody" regrets a failed relationship, his estrangement from Hawthorne that death has made eternal; the characters in the story have selfish regrets over losing something personally valued, such as money, health, reputation, or beauty.

**Connect to Life** Some students may say that people often tend to repeat their mistakes if the promise of money, power, beauty, or love is involved, in spite of past experiences. However, other students may feel that people learn from past mistakes and would lead a different life if given a second chance.

# *Choices & Challenges*

## Writing Options

**1. Warning Label** Hazardous products carry labels that caution consumers about their use. Write a warning label that might appear on a bottle of water from the Fountain of Youth.

**2. Science News** Write a summary of Dr. Heidegger's experiment for a popular scientific or medical journal.

**3. Story Ending** If you could be ten years old again, knowing what you know now, would you turn back the clock? Give your answer as the concluding paragraphs of a story about a teenager who chooses to become ten years old again. Save your writing in your **Working Portfolio**.

## Activities & Explorations

**Product Chart** Look for magazine and TV ads promising people that they can look and feel younger. Then, in a chart, record the names of the products or services advertised and what they claim to do. How do these products or services compare to the Water of Youth? What advice would you give a consumer? ~ **VIEWING AND REPRESENTING**

## Vocabulary in Action

**EXERCISE: ASSESSMENT PRACTICE** Write the letter of the word that is an antonym of the boldfaced word.

1. **efface:** (a) mock, (b) preserve, (c) disguise
2. **stigma:** (a) award, (b) beauty, (c) hero
3. **decrepit:** (a) large, (b) fashionable, (c) sturdy
4. **venerable:** (a) dishonorable, (b) famous, (c) pale
5. **transient:** (a) wealthy, (b) permanent, (c) feeble
6. **deferential:** (a) similar, (b) accepting, (c) contemptuous
7. **exhilaration:** (a) gloom, (b) delay, (c) anticipation
8. **dispute:** (a) accept, (b) challenge, (c) admire
9. **tremulous:** (a) tired, (b) steady, (c) tiny
10. **exultingly:** (a) quietly, (b) arrogantly, (c) sadly

## Nathaniel Hawthorne
### 1804–1864

**Other Works**
*The Scarlet Letter*
*The House of the Seven Gables*
"The Minister's Black Veil"
"Rappaccini's Daughter"

**The Sorrows of Youth** Nathaniel Hawthorne was born in Salem, Massachusetts. His childhood was not especially happy. His father, a sea captain, died when Hawthorne was four years old, and his grieving mother became reclusive. After graduating from Bowdoin College in Maine, where one of his classmates was Henry Wadsworth Longfellow, Hawthorne secluded himself at his mother's home in Salem for 12 years. He dedicated himself to writing and reading, hoping to develop his craft.

**A Flair for Writing** Hawthorne, a descendant of a prominent Massachusetts Bay Colony settler and of a Salem witch trial judge, was fascinated by the society of his Puritan ancestors and studied colonial New England history during his long seclusion. Many of Hawthorne's stories are drawn from the darker aspects of his Puritan heritage. In 1837, Hawthorne published his first collection of short stories, *Twice-Told Tales*. In 1842, he married and settled in Concord, Massachusetts. In 1850, with the publication of *The Scarlet Letter*, Hawthorne gained acclaim as a writer. Despite his success, he made little money.

**An Unhappy Ending** Eventually, Hawthorne became despondent over money, his poor health, and his inability to write. Hawthorne died in 1864 while visiting New Hampshire with his old friend, the former U.S. president Franklin Pierce. Among the pallbearers at Hawthorne's funeral were Longfellow, Ralph Waldo Emerson, Oliver Wendell Holmes, and James Russell Lowell.

## Writing Options

**1. Warning Label To get students started on this assignment,** have them consider what Dr. Heidegger and his guests learned before they write their warning label.

**2. Science News To get students started on this assignment,** have them think of their audience. They should emphasize the scientific rather than the sociological aspects of the experiment. Another approach would be to have students pair up and tape an interview in which one student is the interviewer and the other is Dr. Heidegger being interviewed for a scientific or medical program.

**3. Story Ending To get students started on this assignment,** ask them to brainstorm the events in the life of a ten-year-old and the feelings of a ten-year-old. **Visual learners** might create a series of cartoons depicting the events that led to the teenager's decision after experiencing life as a ten-year-old.

## Activities & Explorations

**Product Chart To get students started on this assignment,** have them work in small groups to make a list of sources for the advertisements. Students can choose a source from the list and bring in examples. Students might even record television commercials. After students have pooled their information, they can discuss how to advise consumers.

## Vocabulary in Action

| | | | |
|---|---|---|---|
| 1. b | 4. a | 7. a | 10. c |
| 2. a | 5. b | 8. a | |
| 3. c | 6. c | 9. b | |

---

 **Grammar**

### AVOIDING ILLOGICAL COMPARISONS

**Instruction** Tell students that a comparison can be confusing if words are missing or the construction is illogical. Give the following example and explain the illogical comparison that is made. Mr. Gascoigne's political reputation was more infamous than anyone's.

(Since Mr. Gascoigne's reputation cannot be more infamous than his own, *anyone's* must be changed to *anyone else's* to exclude him from the comparison.)

**Exercises** Ask students to correct the illogical comparisons in each of the following sentences.

1. As a young woman, Widow Wycherly may have believed that she was more attractive to men than any woman. (*any other woman*)
2. By the end of the story, Colonel Killigrew's appearance was as elderly as Dr. Heidegger. (*Dr. Heidegger's appearance*)
3. Nathaniel Hawthorne writes more insightfully than all authors. (*all other authors*)
4. Dr. Heidegger was calmer than anyone in the room. (*anyone else*)

Use **Grammar Transparencies and Copymasters**, p. 133.

 Use McDougal Littell's *Language Network,* Chapter 7, for more instruction and practice in avoiding illogical comparisons.

# A Rose for Emily

*Short Story by* WILLIAM FAULKNER

**Comparing Literature**

## Traditions Across Time: Southern Gothic

Critics often place William Faulkner, along with writers such as Flannery O'Connor and Truman Capote, in the literary tradition known as Southern Gothic. The elements of Gothic fiction include disturbed or unbalanced characters, strange or terrifying events, and gloomy or rundown settings. Faulkner's story "A Rose for Emily" is particularly interesting to compare with Edgar Allan Poe's 19th-century Gothic tale, "The Fall of the House of Usher."

**Points of Comparison** As you read, compare the two stories in terms of their settings and other Gothic elements noted above.

## Build Background

**Art Imitates Life** The first-person narrator of "A Rose for Emily" speaks for an entire community—the fictional town of Jefferson, Mississippi. Jefferson is the county seat of William Faulkner's fictional Yoknapatawpha (yŏk'nə-pə-tô'fə) County. Over a span of more than 30 years, Faulkner wrote novels and short stories about the land and the people of Jefferson and Yoknapatawpha County, creating a complete world that was patterned after his own home of Oxford. Many of the inhabitants of Faulkner's fictional world are based on real people.

Faulkner's writing preserves the manners of Southern life at an earlier time; be warned that the narrator refers to African Americans with a term that is offensive to contemporary readers.

| WORDS TO KNOW | Vocabulary Preview | |
|---|---|---|
| circumvent | edict | profoundly |
| coquettish | encroach | tedious |
| dank | obliterate | temerity |
| diffident | obscure | thwart |
| divulge | pallid | virulent |

## Focus Your Reading

**LITERARY ANALYSIS** **CHARACTERIZATION** The methods a writer uses to portray a **character** are called **characterization.** For example, one technique that Faulkner uses to acquaint you with Miss Emily is to show her behavior over the course of her lifetime. As you read, note what her actions reveal about her.

**ACTIVE READING** **SEQUENCING EVENTS** Faulkner often used **flashbacks** in his stories, shuffling the order of events. His unusual approach to **sequencing events** was based on his notion of the fluidity of time, in which the past and the future seem to merge. Sentences beginning with the words *when, after,* and *during* help the reader note any time shifts.

**READER'S NOTEBOOK** As you read, keep a time line showing the sequence of events in Miss Emily's life. After you finish reading each section, jot down the important moments in chronological order. The sample timeline below lists two events from the first section.

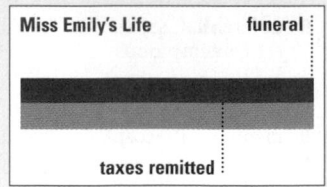

Miss Emily's Life — funeral

taxes remitted

# A ROSE for EMILY

## William Faulkner

### I

When Miss Emily Grierson died, our whole town went to her funeral: the men through a sort of respectful affection for a fallen monument, the women mostly out of curiosity to see the inside of her house, which no one save an old manservant—a combined gardener and cook—had seen in at least ten years.

It was a big, squarish frame house that had once been white, decorated with cupolas and spires and scrolled balconies in the heavily lightsome style of the seventies,[1] set on what had once been our most select street. But garages and cotton gins had encroached and obliterated even the august names of that neighborhood; only Miss Emily's house was left, lifting its stubborn and coquettish decay above the cotton wagons and the gasoline pumps—an eyesore among eyesores. And now Miss Emily had gone to join the representatives of those august names where they lay in the cedar-bemused[2] cemetery among the ranked and anonymous graves of Union and Confederate soldiers who fell at the battle of Jefferson.

Alive, Miss Emily had been a tradition, a duty, and a care; a sort of hereditary obligation upon the town, dating from that day in 1894 when Colonel Sartoris, the mayor—he who fathered the edict that no Negro woman should appear on the streets without an apron—remitted her taxes, the dispensation dating from the death of her father on into perpetuity.[3] Not that Miss Emily would have accepted charity. Colonel Sartoris invented an involved tale to the effect that Miss Emily's father had loaned money to the town, which the town, as a matter of business, preferred this way of repaying. Only a man of Colonel Sartoris' generation and thought could have invented it, and only a woman could have believed it.

When the next generation, with its more modern ideas, became mayors and aldermen, this arrangement created some little dissatisfaction. On the first of the year they mailed her a tax notice. February came, and there was no reply. They wrote her a formal letter, asking her to call at the sheriff's office at her convenience. A week

---

1. **the seventies:** the 1870s.
2. **cedar-bemused:** almost lost in cedar trees (literally, confused by cedars).
3. **remitted . . . perpetuity:** released her from paying taxes forever after the time of her father's death.

WORDS
TO
KNOW

**encroach** (ĕn-krōch') *v.* to advance beyond original limits; intrude
**obliterate** (ə-blĭt'ə-rāt') *v.* to wipe out, leaving no trace
**coquettish** (kō-kĕt'ĭsh) *adj.* flirtatious
**edict** (ē'dĭkt') *n.* an order put out by a person in authority

517

**Active Reading**  SEQUENCING EVENTS

Remind students that they're expected to analyze the characteristics of clearly written texts, including patterns of organization. Faulkner relates events not in chronological order, but in the order in which he wishes to reveal certain facts about Miss Emily. This pattern of organization contributes to the mystery he creates about her character. Have students construct a time line to help them sort out the chronological sequence of events in Miss Emily's life.

 Use **Unit Three Resource Book**, p. 72 for more practice.

**Literary Analysis**  CHARACTERIZATION

**A** Ask students to determine what this "tableau" tells us about the character of Emily's father. Point out that in Miss Emily's era, the horsewhip was the preferred weapon for fathers chasing away unwelcome suitors.

**Possible Responses:** He was fiercely protective of Emily, as his clutching the horsewhip suggests; his figure dominates the scene as he dominated her life; from his appearance in silhouette, one could interpret that he was not a man easy to know.

 Use **Unit Three Resource Book**, p. 73 for more practice.

---

later the mayor wrote her himself, offering to call or to send his car for her, and received in reply a note on paper of an archaic shape, in a thin, flowing calligraphy[4] in faded ink, to the effect that she no longer went out at all. The tax notice was also enclosed, without comment.

They called a special meeting of the Board of Aldermen. A deputation[5] waited upon her, knocked at the door through which no visitor had passed since she ceased giving china-painting lessons eight or ten years earlier. They were admitted by the old Negro into a dim hall from which a stairway mounted into still more shadow. It smelled of dust and disuse—a close, <u>dank</u> smell. The Negro led them into the parlor. It was furnished in heavy, leather-covered furniture. When the Negro opened the blinds of one window, they could see that the leather was cracked; and when they sat down, a faint dust rose sluggishly about their thighs, spinning with slow motes[6] in the single sun-ray. On a tarnished gilt easel before the fireplace stood a crayon portrait of Miss Emily's father.

They rose when she entered—a small, fat woman in black, with a thin gold chain descending to her waist and vanishing into her belt, leaning on an ebony cane with a tarnished gold head. Her skeleton was small and spare; perhaps that was why what would have been merely plumpness in another was obesity in her. She looked bloated, like a body long submerged in motionless water, and of that <u>pallid</u> hue. Her eyes, lost in the fatty ridges of her face, looked like two small pieces of coal pressed into a lump of dough as they moved from one face to another while the visitors stated their errand.

She did not ask them to sit. She just stood in the door and listened quietly until the spokesman

*German Teapot* (1994), Charles Warren Mundy. Oil on canvas, 14″ × 18″.

came to a stumbling halt. Then they could hear the invisible watch ticking at the end of the gold chain.

Her voice was dry and cold. "I have no taxes in Jefferson. Colonel Sartoris explained it to me. Perhaps one of you can gain access to the city records and satisfy yourselves."

"But we have. We are the city authorities, Miss Emily. Didn't you get a notice from the sheriff, signed by him?"

"I received a paper, yes," Miss Emily said. "Perhaps he considers himself the sheriff . . . I have no taxes in Jefferson."

"But there is nothing on the books to show that, you see. We must go by the—"

"See Colonel Sartoris. I have no taxes in Jefferson."

"But, Miss Emily—"

"See Colonel Sartoris." (Colonel Sartoris had been dead almost ten years.) "I have no taxes in Jefferson. Tobe!" The Negro appeared. "Show these gentlemen out."

---

4. **calligraphy:** beautiful handwriting.
5. **deputation:** a small group representing a larger one.
6. **motes:** specks.

WORDS TO KNOW

**dank** (dăngk) *adj.* unpleasantly damp; moist and chilly
**pallid** (păl′ĭd) *adj.* abnormally pale

518

---

 **Viewing and Representing**

*German Teapot* **by Charles Warren Mundy**

**ART APPRECIATION** At first glance, the work of Charles Warren Mundy (1945– ) seems anachronistic because it remains representational in an era when abstraction rules. This oil painting demonstrates why Mundy is one of the main figures of modern realism.

**Instruction** Explain that while the subject of *German Teapot* may be delicate—a porcelain pot, vase, and pink carnation on a silver, mirrored tray—Mundy's brush technique is not. He creates tension by rendering his subject in bold, decisive strokes.

**Application** Have students view the painting first at arm's length and then close up. Ask students to evaluate how Mundy's use of brush strokes affects their perception of the painting.

**Possible Response:** From a distance it looks very "polished" in the way light reflects from the surfaces, but on closer inspection, thick, abrupt strokes seem to suggest that the artist was in a hurry. If you look too closely at the flower, it loses its form and fades into a nondescript patch of color.

# II

So she vanquished them, horse and foot, just as she had vanquished their fathers thirty years before about the smell. That was two years after her father's death and a short time after her sweetheart—the one we believed would marry her—had deserted her. After her father's death she went out very little; after her sweetheart went away, people hardly saw her at all. A few of the ladies had the <u>temerity</u> to call, but were not received, and the only sign of life about the place was the Negro man—a young man then—going in and out with a market basket.

"Just as if a man—any man—could keep a kitchen properly," the ladies said; so they were not surprised when the smell developed. It was another link between the gross, teeming world and the high and mighty Griersons.

A neighbor, a woman, complained to the mayor, Judge Stevens, eighty years old.

"But what will you have me do about it, madam?" he said.

"Why, send her word to stop it," the woman said. "Isn't there a law?"

"I'm sure that won't be necessary," Judge Stevens said. "It's probably just a snake or a rat that nigger of hers killed in the yard. I'll speak to him about it."

The next day he received two more complaints, one from a man who came in <u>diffident</u> deprecation.[7] "We really must do something about it, Judge. I'd be the last one in the world to bother Miss Emily, but we've got to do something." That night the Board of Aldermen met—three graybeards and one younger man, a member of the rising generation.

"It's simple enough," he said. "Send her word to have her place cleaned up. Give her a certain time to do it in, and if she don't . . ."

"Dammit, sir," Judge Stevens said, "will you accuse a lady to her face of smelling bad?"

So the next night, after midnight, four men crossed Miss Emily's lawn and slunk about the house like burglars, sniffing along the base of the brickwork and at the cellar openings while one of them performed a regular sowing motion with his hand out of a sack slung from his shoulder. They broke open the cellar door and sprinkled lime there, and in all the outbuildings. As they recrossed the lawn, a window that had been dark was lighted and Miss Emily sat in it, the light behind her, and her upright torso motionless as

> "We really must do something about it, Judge. I'd be the last one in the world to bother Miss Emily, but we've got to do something."

that of an idol. They crept quietly across the lawn and into the shadow of the locusts that lined the street. After a week or two the smell went away.

That was when people had begun to feel really sorry for her. People in our town, remembering how old lady Wyatt, her great-aunt, had gone completely crazy at last, believed that the Griersons held themselves a little too high for what they really were. None of the young men were quite good enough for Miss Emily and such. We had long thought of them as a tableau,[8] Miss Emily a slender figure in white in the background, her father a spraddled silhouette in

---

7. **deprecation:** disapproval.
8. **tableau** (tăb′lō′): dramatic scene or picture.

---

| WORDS TO KNOW | **temerity** (tə-mĕr′ĭ-tē) *n.* foolish boldness |
| | **diffident** (dĭf′ĭ-dənt) *adj.* shy and timid; lacking self-confidence |

519

## Reading and Analyzing

### Reading Skills and Strategies: MAKING INFERENCES

**A** Remind students that they are expected to draw inferences and support them with textual evidence and experience. Ask what they can infer about the social status of most townspeople based on their response to Miss Emily's poverty after her father's death.

**Possible Response:** Most folks are just getting by financially, and a family like the Griersons assumed a higher social standing because of its wealth. There is a distinct separation between the classes in this society, and people in lower classes resent the wealthy at the same time that they are fascinated by them and yearn to connect with them.

### Literary Analysis: SETTING

In the 1880s, when Miss Emily was seeing Homer, it would have been socially unacceptable for a Southern "lady" to associate with a "Yankee." It wasn't just the Mason–Dixon line that divided Homer and Emily; there was also the class divide. It was believed that a woman from a prominent family, no matter how impoverished by circumstances, should not become involved with a working-class man.

### Literary Analysis
#### CHARACTERIZATION

**B** Have students compare this description of Miss Emily to the one on page 518. Ask them why the narrator compares Emily's face to that of a lighthouse-keeper.

**Possible Responses:** Her face appears drawn and intense from years of waiting for something to happen; she lives in isolation as a lighthouse stands alone.

---

the foreground, his back to her and clutching a horsewhip, the two of them framed by the back-flung front door. So when she got to be thirty and was still single, we were not pleased exactly, but vindicated; even with insanity in the family she wouldn't have turned down all of her chances if they had really materialized.

**A**

**1**  When her father died, it got about that the house was all that was left to her; and in a way, people were glad. At last they could pity Miss Emily. Being left alone, and a pauper, she had become humanized. Now she too would know the old thrill and the old despair of a penny more or less.

The day after his death all the ladies prepared to call at the house and offer condolence and aid, as is our custom. Miss Emily met them at the door, dressed as usual and with no trace of grief on her face. She told them that her father was not dead. She did that for three days, with the ministers calling on her, and the doctors, trying to persuade her to let them dispose of the body. Just as they were about to resort to law and force, she broke down, and they buried her father quickly.

We did not say she was crazy then. We believed she had to do that. We remembered all the young men her father had driven away, and we knew that with nothing left, she would have to cling to that which had robbed her, as people will.

### III

She was sick for a long time. When we saw her again, her hair was cut short, making her look like a girl, with a vague resemblance to those angels in colored church windows—sort of tragic and serene.

White frame house in Holly Springs, Mississippi

The town had just let the contracts for paving the sidewalks, and in the summer after her father's death they began the work. The construction company came with niggers and mules and machinery, and a foreman named Homer Barron, a Yankee—a big, dark, ready man, with a big voice and eyes lighter than his face. The little boys would follow in groups to hear him cuss the niggers, and the niggers singing in time to the rise and fall of picks. Pretty soon he knew everybody in town. Whenever you heard a lot of laughing anywhere about the square, Homer Barron would be in the center of the group.

**520**  UNIT THREE  PART 2: THE DARK SIDE OF INDIVIDUALISM

---

## Teaching Options

### BLOCK SCHEDULING: MANAGING TIME

**If your schedule requires that you cover the lesson objectives in a shorter time, use . . .**
- Preparing to Read, p. 516
- Thinking Through the Literature, p. 525
- Vocabulary in Action, p. 527

**If you want to take advantage of longer class time, use . . .**
- TE Teaching Options: Preteaching Vocabulary, p. 517; Workplace Link, p. 519; Vocabulary Strategy, p. 523; Viewing and Representing, pp. 518, 524; Informal Assessment, p. 522; Speaking and Listening, p. 526
- Choices & Challenges, pp. 526–527

**520**  UNIT THREE  PART 2

Presently we began to see him and Miss Emily on Sunday afternoons driving in the yellow-wheeled buggy and the matched team of bays from the livery stable.

At first we were glad that Miss Emily would have an interest, because the ladies all said, "Of course a Grierson would not think seriously of a Northerner, a day laborer." But there were still others, older people, who said that even grief could not cause a real lady to forget *noblesse oblige*[9]—without calling it *noblesse oblige*. They just said, "Poor Emily. Her kinsfolk should come to her." She had some kin in Alabama; but years ago her father had fallen out with them over the estate of old lady Wyatt, the crazy woman, and  there was no communication between the two families. They had not even been represented at the funeral.

And as soon as the old people said, "Poor Emily," the whispering began. "Do you suppose it's really so?" they said to one another. "Of course it is. What else could . . ." This behind their hands; rustling of craned[10] silk and satin behind jalousies[11] closed upon the sun of Sunday afternoon as the thin, swift clop-clop-clop of the matched team passed: "Poor Emily."

She carried her head high enough—even when we believed that she was fallen. It was as if she demanded more than ever the recognition of her dignity as the last Grierson; as if it had wanted

that touch of earthiness to reaffirm her imperviousness. Like when she bought the rat poison, the arsenic. That was over a year after they had begun to say "Poor Emily," and while the two female cousins were visiting her.

"I want some poison," she said to the druggist. She was over thirty then, still a slight woman, though thinner than usual, with cold, haughty black eyes in a face the flesh of which was strained across the temples and about the eye-sockets as you imagine a lighthouse-keeper's face ought to look. "I want some poison," she said.

"Yes, Miss Emily. What kind? For rats and such? I'd recom—"

"I want the best you have. I don't care what kind."

The druggist named several. "They'll kill anything up to an elephant. But what you want is—"

"Arsenic," Miss Emily said. "Is that a good one?"

"Is . . . arsenic? Yes, ma'am. But what you want—"

"I want arsenic."

The druggist looked down at her. She looked back at him, erect, her face like a strained flag. "Why, of course," the druggist said. "If that's what you want. But the law requires you to tell what you are going to use it for."

Miss Emily just stared at him, her head tilted back in order to look him eye for eye, until he looked away and went and got the arsenic and wrapped it up. The Negro delivery boy brought her the package; the druggist didn't come back. When she opened the package at home there was written on the box, under the skull and bones: "For rats."

---

9. ***noblesse oblige*** (nō-blĕs′ ō-blēzh′): the responsibility of people of high social position to behave in a noble fashion.

10. **craned:** stretched.

11. **jalousies** (jăl′ə-sēz): doors or windows containing overlapping slats that can be opened or closed.

B

3

## Customizing Instruction

### Students Acquiring English
**1** Help students paraphrase this sentence.

**Possible Response:** Like the other people in the town, Emily would now feel excited when she had a little money to spend and sad when she had none.

### Less Proficient Readers
**2** Make sure that students understand the deferential treatment Miss Emily continues to receive. Ask students to explain why the druggist does not press her to answer his question.

**Possible Responses:** He has too much respect for her status in the town; she intimidates him by sheer force of character.

### Gifted and Talented
**3** Point out that Miss Emily fails to comply with the law when she refuses to tell the druggist her reason for wanting to buy the arsenic. Have students discuss what they can infer from this detail or what event it might foreshadow.

---

**Mini Lesson** ## Grammar

**SUPERLATIVES**

**Instruction** Adjectives have three forms, or degrees: the positive degree (*nice*), the comparative degree (*nicer*), and the superlative degree (*nicest*). The comparative degree is used to compare one person, place, thing, or idea with another one. The superlative degree is used to compare three or more persons, places, groups, things, ideas, or actions.

**Exercises** Have students choose the correct adjective in each sentence.

1. Which writer do you think is better/best, Faulkner or Poe?

2. That summer was the warmer/<u>warmest</u> of all.

3. Some instructions are <u>less helpful</u>/least helpful than others.

4. There were four bedrooms to choose from, and she chose the larger/<u>largest</u> one.

5. You think your joke is bad; mine is <u>worse</u>/worst!

6. It was the crazier/<u>craziest</u> feeling—I'd never felt that way before.

> **Language Network** Use McDougal Littell's *Language Network*, Chapter 7, for more instruction and practice in superlatives.

## Active Reading [SEQUENCING EVENTS]

Remind students that they're expected to construct images such as graphic organizers based on text structure. Have them create a chart to follow the sequence of events in the story. The chart can compare the order in which major events in the story occur with the order in which the narrator presents them.

| Order in which narrator reveals events | Order in which events occur |
|---|---|
| 1. Miss Emily dies. | 8 |
| 2. The aldermen visit about taxes. | 7 |
| 3. Miss Emily gives painting lessons. | 6 |
| 4. Her father dies. | 1 |
| 5. Homer Barron disappears. | 4 |
| 6. The aldermen apply lime around her house. | 5 |
| 7. Homer Barron arrives in town. | 2 |
| 8. Miss Emily asks the druggist for poison. | 3 |
| 9. Townspeople discover the bridal tomb. | 9 |

## Literary Analysis: POINT OF VIEW

Point out that the narrator uses a first-person plural voice. Ask students to consider why the story is told from this point of view.

**Possible Responses:** The narrator speaks for the townspeople, as the all-seeing spirit of the town or the register of town gossip and consensus; the point of view is inclusive: the plural form draws the reader into the story.

## IV

So the next day we all said, "She will kill herself"; and we said it would be the best thing. When she had first begun to be seen with Homer Barron, we had said, "She will marry him." Then we said, "She will persuade him yet," because Homer himself had remarked—he liked men, and it was known that he drank with the younger men in the Elks' Club—that he was not a marrying man. Later we said, "Poor Emily" behind the jalousies as they passed on Sunday afternoon in the glittering buggy, Miss Emily with her head high and Homer Barron with his hat cocked and a cigar in his teeth, reins and whip in a yellow glove.

Then some of the ladies began to say that it was a disgrace to the town and a bad example to the young people. The men did not want to interfere, but at last the ladies forced the Baptist minister—Miss Emily's people were Episcopal—to call upon her. He would never <u>divulge</u> what happened during that interview, but he refused to go back again. The next Sunday they again drove about the streets, and the following day the minister's wife wrote to Miss Emily's relations in Alabama.

So she had blood-kin under her roof again and we sat back to watch developments. At first nothing happened. Then we were sure that they were to be married. We learned that Miss Emily had been to the jeweler's and ordered a man's toilet set in silver, with the letters H. B. on each piece. Two days later we learned that she had bought a complete outfit of men's clothing, including a nightshirt, and we said, "They are married." We were really glad. We were glad because the two female cousins were even more Grierson than Miss Emily had ever been.

So we were not surprised when Homer Barron—the streets had been finished some time since—was gone. We were a little disappointed that there was not a public blowing-off,[12] but we believed that he had gone on to prepare for Miss Emily's coming, or to give her a chance to get rid of the cousins. (By that time it was a cabal,[13] and we were all Miss Emily's allies to help <u>circumvent</u> the cousins.) Sure enough, after another week they departed. And, as we had expected all along, within three days Homer Barron was back in town. A neighbor saw the

> We learned that Miss Emily had been to the jeweler's and ordered a man's toilet set in silver, with the letters H. B. on each piece.

Negro man admit him at the kitchen door at dusk one evening.

And that was the last we saw of Homer Barron. And of Miss Emily for some time. The Negro man went in and out with the market basket, but the front door remained closed. Now and then we would see her at a window for a moment, as the men did that night when they sprinkled the lime, but for almost six months she did not appear on the streets. Then we knew that this was to be expected too; as if that quality of her father which had <u>thwarted</u> her woman's life

---

12. **blowing-off:** celebration.
13. **cabal** (kə-băl′): a group united in a secret plot.

| WORDS TO KNOW | **divulge** (dĭ-vŭlj′) v. to make known something private |
|---|---|
| | **circumvent** (sûr′kəm-věnt′) v. to avoid or get around by clever maneuvering |
| | **thwart** (thwôrt) v. to block or hinder; prevent the fulfillment of |

522

## Teaching Options

### ✓ Assessment Informal Assessment

**NEWS REPORT** You can informally assess students' understanding of the story's events and the sequence by having them prepare a news report on the murder of Homer Barron. Ask them to present the story in a chronological sequence of events and to take into account motivations for the crime and the extent of its cover-up.

**RUBRIC**

**3** **Full Accomplishment** The report is polished, takes character motivation into account, and presents an accurate sequence of events.

**2** **Substantial Accomplishment** The report is consistent with character motivation and describes the sequence of events, but seems less polished.

**1** **Little or Partial Accomplishment** The report is disjointed, and the facts are not consistent with the story.

so many times had been too <u>virulent</u> and too furious to die.

When we next saw Miss Emily, she had grown fat and her hair was turning gray. During the next few years it grew grayer and grayer until it attained an even pepper-and-salt iron-gray, when it ceased turning. Up to the day of her death at seventy-four it was still that vigorous iron-gray, like the hair of an active man.

From that time on her front door remained closed, save for a period of six or seven years, when she was about forty, during which she gave lessons in china-painting. She fitted up a studio in one of the downstairs rooms, where the daughters and granddaughters of Colonel Sartoris' contemporaries were sent to her with the same regularity and in the same spirit that they were sent to church on Sundays with a twenty-five-cent piece for the collection plate. Meanwhile her taxes had been remitted.

Then the newer generation became the backbone and the spirit of the town, and the painting pupils grew up and fell away and did not send their children to her with boxes of color and <u>tedious</u> brushes and pictures cut from the ladies' magazines. The front door closed upon the last one and remained closed for good. When the town got free postal delivery, Miss Emily alone refused to let them fasten the metal numbers above her door and attach a mailbox to it. She would not listen to them.

Daily, monthly, yearly we watched the Negro grow grayer and more stooped, going in and out with the market basket. Each December we sent her a tax notice, which would be returned by the post office a week later, unclaimed. Now and then we would see her in one of the downstairs windows—she had evidently shut up the top floor of the house—like the carven torso of an idol in a niche,[14] looking or not looking at us, we could never tell which. Thus she passed from generation to generation—dear, inescapable, impervious, tranquil, and perverse.

And so she died. Fell ill in the house filled with dust and shadows, with only a doddering Negro man to wait on her. We did not even know she was sick; we had long since given up trying to get any information from the Negro. He talked to no one, probably not even to her, for his voice had grown harsh and rusty, as if from disuse.

She died in one of the downstairs rooms, in a heavy walnut bed with a curtain, her gray head propped on a pillow yellow and moldy with age and lack of sunlight.

## V

The Negro met the first of the ladies at the front door and let them in, with their hushed, sibilant[15] voices and their quick, curious glances, and then he disappeared. He walked right through the house and out the back and was not seen again.

The two female cousins came at once. They held the funeral on the second day, with the town coming to look at Miss Emily beneath a mass of bought flowers, with the crayon face of her father musing <u>profoundly</u> above the bier[16] and the ladies sibilant and macabre; and the very old men—some in their brushed Confederate uniforms—on the porch and the lawn, talking of Miss Emily as if she had been a contemporary of theirs, believing that they had danced with her and courted her perhaps, confusing time with its mathematical progression, as the old do, to whom all the past is not a diminishing road but, instead, a huge meadow which no winter ever quite

---

14. **niche** (nĭch): an indented space in a wall.
15. **sibilant** (sĭb'ə-lənt): making a hissing sound.
16. **bier** (bîr): a platform for a coffin.

| WORDS | **virulent** (vîr'yə-lənt) *adj.* extremely poisonous or harmful |
| TO | **tedious** (tē'dē-əs) *adj.* boring because of dullness |
| KNOW | **profoundly** (prə-found'lē) *adv.* deeply; intensely |

 **Vocabulary Strategy**

### CONNOTATION

**Instruction** Remind students that when reading literature, they are expected to interpret the connotative power of words. The connotations of a word can vary because they are what the word suggests, the ideas or feelings associated with it. The denotation of a word does not vary, because it is the explicit and recognized dictionary definition.

Point out that Faulkner describes Miss Emily in her later years as having a "pallid hue" (page 518). The denotation of *pallid* is "pale" or "colorless," but the word also carries the connotation of death.

**Application** Have students work in groups to consider the different connotations of the following pairs of synonyms: *eat/devour; collect/hoard; decay/putrefy.*

Use **Vocabulary Transparencies and Copymasters**, p. 48.

A lesson on connotation appears on p. 908 in the Pupil's Edition.

**Reading Skills and Strategies:**
**MAKING INFERENCES**

**(A)** Remind students that they're expected to draw inferences and support them with textual evidence and experience. Ask them what they can infer about the room from the manner in which its door was opened.

**Possible Response:** It must have been sealed shut—opening the door required breaking it down.

**(B)** Ask students to infer from details in the text what Miss Emily had intended the upstairs room to be.

**Possible Response:** She had intended the room to be her marriage suite, a master bedroom for her and Homer.

**Active Reading**

**SEQUENCING EVENTS**

**(C)** Ask students how there could have been a gray hair on the pillow if no one had seen the room in forty years.

**Possible Response:** Although no one else in town had seen the room for forty years, it's still possible that Miss Emily had access to it. Of course, Miss Emily's hair had turned gray several months after Homer's disappearance—about forty years before the funeral.

**(A)** touches, divided from them now by the narrow bottle-neck of the most recent decade of years.

Already we knew that there was one room in that region above stairs which no one had seen in forty years, and which would have to be forced. They waited until Miss Emily was decently in the ground before they opened it.

The violence of breaking down the door seemed to fill this room with pervading dust. A thin, acrid pall[17] as of the tomb seemed to lie everywhere upon this room decked and furnished as for a bridal:[18] upon the valance curtains of faded rose color, upon the rose-shaded lights, upon the dressing table, upon **(B)** the delicate array of crystal and the man's toilet things backed with tarnished silver, silver so tarnished that the monogram was <u>obscured</u>. Among them lay a collar and tie, as if they had just been removed, which, lifted, left upon the surface a pale crescent in the dust. Upon a chair hung the suit, carefully folded; beneath it the two mute shoes and the discarded socks.

The man himself lay in the bed.

For a long while we just stood there, looking down at the profound and fleshless grin. The body had apparently once lain in the attitude of an embrace, but now the long sleep that outlasts love, that conquers even the grimace of love, had cuckolded him.[19] What was left of him, rotted beneath what was left of the nightshirt, had become inextricable from the bed in which he lay;

*Woman in Distress* (1882), James Ensor. Musée d'Orsay, Paris, Giraudon/Art Resource. Copyright © Estate of James Ensor/VAGA, New York.

and upon him and upon the pillow beside him lay that even coating of the patient and biding dust.

Then we noticed that in the second pillow was the indentation of a head. One of us lifted something from it, and leaning forward, that faint and invisible dust dry and acrid in the nostrils, we saw a long strand of iron-gray hair. ❖ **(C)**

---

17. **acrid pall** (ăk′rĭd pôl′): bitter-smelling covering.
18. **bridal:** wedding.
19. **cuckolded him:** made his wife or lover unfaithful to him.

WORDS
TO     **obscure** (ŏb-skyŏŏr′) *v.* to cover over; hide
KNOW

524

---

**Mini Lesson** ## Viewing and Representing

*Woman in Distress* **by James Ensor**

**ART APPRECIATION** James Ensor (1860–1949) was considered a herald of modern expressionist art. A Belgian painter, Ensor used gloomy colors and heavily textured surfaces to paint interiors, seascapes, and towns. He was known for his preoccupation with the themes of death and hypocrisy. Later, he produced works featuring fantastic or macabre subjects—carnival masks, skeletons, and grotesque figures. He is seen as one of the forerunners of the surrealist art movement.

**Instruction** Although *Woman in Distress* is one of Ensor's earliest works, one can detect in the paint-

ing the young artist's disregard for traditional rules of form. Point out the painting's distorted images, muted palette, and textured surfaces.

**Application** Ask students to describe the atmosphere or mood that Ensor creates through his use of color, his treatment of the drapes, and the pose of the woman.

**Possible Response:** The mood is one of resignation and despair. The atmosphere is depressing, cluttered. It's difficult to discern the body of the woman lying on the bed. She has drawn the curtains by her bed so she can't see out and the daylight can't reach her. Still, the light-filled window to the left suggests a ray of hope.

## Connect to the Literature

**1. What Do You Think?**
Were you surprised by the ending of this story? Talk about your reaction.

> **Comprehension Check**
> • How did Emily's father treat young men who wanted to date her?
> • What is the reason Homer Barron disappears?

## Think Critically

**2.** What do you think motivates Miss Emily to commit murder?

> **THINK ABOUT**
> • her father's reaction to her previous suitors
> • what Homer Barron's intentions toward Miss Emily might have been
> • what Miss Emily's deepest feelings and hidden longings might have been
> • the appearance of the upstairs room and the bed when discovered

**3.** How would you judge the way the community responds to Miss Emily throughout her life? Support your opinion.

**4.** How much responsibility, if any, do you think the community bears for Miss Emily's crime?

**5.** **ACTIVE READING** **SEQUENCING EVENTS** Use the time line you made in your **READER'S NOTEBOOK** to retell the story to another student. Do you think relating the events in strict chronological order weakens or improves the story?

## Extend Interpretations

**6. Different Perspectives** What might the servant, Tobe, say if he were the telling the story?

**7. Critic's Corner** The critic Cleanth Brooks stated, "Miss Emily's story constitutes a warning against the sin of pride. heroic isolation pushed too far ends in homicidal madness." Do you agree with his summary? Explain why or why not. What other possible meanings can you draw from Miss Emily's story?

**8. Connect to Life** How do you think Miss Emily compares with people who have committed shocking crimes in recent years?

**9. Points of Comparison** What are the similarities between Miss Emily's home and the mansion in "The Fall of the House of Usher?" How do each of these places set the stage for the events that occur?

---

## Literary Analysis

**CHARACTERIZATION**

**Characterization** refers to the techniques a writer uses to develop characters. A writer may reveal a character through one or more of the following ways:
• the character's physical description
• the character's actions, words, and feelings
• a narrator's direct comments about the character's nature
• other characters' actions, words, and feelings

**Paired Activity** Which techniques does Faulkner use most effectively to reveal the character of Miss Emily? With a partner, find at least three specific examples of characterization that help you learn more about her. Then compare your examples with those of other groups.

**REVIEW** **FORESHADOWING**

**Foreshadowing** is the writer's use of hints or clues that prepare the readers for events that occur later in the story. For example, Emily's denial of her father's death and her refusal to bury him foreshadows her response to Homer Barron's death. What other instances of foreshadowing are there in this story? Find details that give clues about events to come.

---

## Connect to the Literature

**1. What Do You Think?**
Students should go back through the story to search for clues that hint at the surprise ending.

**Comprehension Check**
• He chased her suitors away.
• Homer disappears because Emily has poisoned him.

 Use Selection Quiz in **Unit Three Resource Book,** p. 75.

## Think Critically

**2.** Possible Responses: She feels Homer Barron has wronged her because he apparently does not want to marry her; she wants to keep Homer from ever leaving her; she would rather have him dead than have him reject her.

**3.** Possible Responses: The community's response to Miss Emily vacillates: the townspeople respect her, and yet hold her in disdain; they support her, and then they have it in for her; at times they envy her; at other times, they pity her.

**4.** Possible Responses: none—Miss Emily couldn't accept rejection; a great deal—with friends to support her, Miss Emily might have been able to bear Homer's desertion.

**5.** Possible Response: Telling the story in chronological order weakens it because the shocking revelation—the discovery of Homer's skeleton and a strand of Miss Emily's hair—no longer comes at the end.

## Literary Analysis

**Foreshadowing** Possible Responses: the bad smell and the sowing of lime suggest that a dead animal or a dead body is in the house, unburied; the purchase of poison suggests that Miss Emily was responsible for this death.

---

## Extend Interpretations

**Different Perspectives** If Tobe were telling the story, he might reveal his motives for concealing Miss Emily's crime from the townspeople.

**Critic's Corner** Possible Responses: Yes, Miss Emily's pride was hurt when Homer Barron was planning to leave her, and she could not face the outside world. No, many people who are reclusive would never consider killing someone. Other meanings might be the tragedy of being unloved or overprotected; the ruthlessness of a proud, isolated person; or the mysteriousness of human behavior.

**Connect to Life** In pointing out comparisons, students may mention examples of crimes committed by young people.

**Points of Comparison** Possible Responses: Both Miss Emily's home and the mansion in "The Fall of the House of Usher" are gloomy and decaying. They symbolize the main character's declining fortune. By creating an atmosphere of melancholy and foreboding, these settings set the stage for the eerie events that occur.

## Writing Options

1. **Obituary for Miss Emily** Bring in the obituary page from a newspaper so that students can identify the information typically presented in an obituary. Student responses should contain accurate details from the story.

2. **Secret Diary** Remind students that she would be writing for her own eyes only and would thus be free to express herself in any way she chose.

3. **Points of Comparison** Students' reports should present factual information, such as the doctor's diagnosis of Madeline's condition and the exchange between Miss Emily and the druggist.

4. **Points of Comparison** Possible Responses: All three stories contain elements of decay. "The Masque of the Red Death" focuses on the plague. "Dr. Heidegger's Experiment" portrays the old people in decline, and "A Rose for Emily" contains a decaying corpse.

## Activities & Explorations

1. **Short Story Video** Encourage students to decide what criteria to apply in evaluating the film adaptation. Students may state that in Faulkner's story Emily ages into a bloated old woman, but in the film she remains slim.

2. **Theatrical Performance** Students can approach the dramatic scene as a scripted performance or as an improvisational activity.

## Inquiry & Research

**The "New South"** Have students work in small groups to do their research, using electronic resources and reference books.

## Art Connection

**Southern Mansion** Students should refer to the description of Miss Emily's house on page 517.

---

## Writing Options

1. **Obituary for Miss Emily** Drawing on details in the story, write Miss Emily's obituary for the *Jefferson Enquirer*. Use examples of newspaper obituaries as models.

2. **Secret Diary** Suppose that Miss Emily's diary were found in the locked room after her death. Write three entries that might be found in the diary, describing Miss Emily's feelings about her courtship by Homer Barron, her father's death, her encounter with the aldermen, or her decision to buy arsenic.

3. **Points of Comparison** Imagine you are a detective investigating the deaths of Madeline in "The Fall of the House of Usher" and Homer Barron in a "A Rose for Emily." Write a set of police reports summarizing the circumstances surrounding each death.

4. **Points of Comparison** What specifically does "A Rose for Emily" have in common with other Gothic works you read in this part of Unit Three? Would you say that Faulkner is closer in spirit to Hawthorne or Poe? Write your responses to these two questions as lecture notes to deliver to the class. Include details from the stories to support your views.

## Activities & Explorations

1. **Short Story Video** View the video of "A Rose for Emily" provided with the program. Did the characters and the setting in the video match your mental picture of what they would be like? Discuss this question with a small group of classmates. ~ **VIEWING AND REPRESENTING**

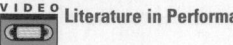 Literature in Performance

2. **Theatrical Performance** With a partner, rehearse a dramatic scene showing what might have happened the night Homer Barron was last seen entering Miss Emily's kitchen. What did Homer and Miss Emily say to each other? Perform your scene for classmates. ~ **PERFORMING**

## Inquiry & Research

**The "New South"** While Miss Emily resists change and clings to the traditions of the "Old South"— the South before the Civil War—her town takes strides to become more modern. Toward the end of the 1800s, a "New South," built on the foundation of business and industry, was emerging. Locate more information about this shift and the clashing values between the "Old South" and the "New South." Summarize your findings.

## Art Connection

**Southern Mansion** The house pictured on pages 520–521 is near Faulkner's hometown of Oxford, Mississippi, and exemplifies the kind of house he was familiar with. How closely does this house match your mental image of Miss Emily's house?

---

### (Mini Lesson) Speaking and Listening

**DRAMATIC PERFORMANCE**

**Instruction** Have students enact a final confrontation between Homer and Emily. Although students must imagine what might have taken place, suggest that they justify their choice of verbal and nonverbal performance techniques by referring to their analysis and interpretation of the story. Remind students that their performances should convey the characters' motivations. Each character has a hidden agenda and/or harbors a truth nearly unbearable to the self or to the other. Homer must convey his ambivalence without being direct. Yes, he likes being with Miss Emily as her paramour, but no, he doesn't want to marry her. Miss Emily is ready to murder what she cherishes most.

**Prepare** Have students work in groups to discuss how best to portray these characters as they grapple with their conflict of needs.

**Present** Have pairs of student actors take turns interpreting the scene. Let students discuss what techniques work best to convey the tension between the couple.

**BLOCK SCHEDULING** This activity is particularly well-suited for longer class periods.

## Vocabulary in Action

**EXERCISE: CONTEXT CLUES** Write the vocabulary word that best completes each sentence.

1. Miss Emily's life held little interest—it consisted merely of one _____ day after another.

2. The mayor had issued a foolish _____ that Miss Emily would not have to pay taxes.

3. Instead of directly offering financial help to her, he took another route by making up an involved story to _____ the problem.

4. When a new administration tried to make her pay, the obstructions created by her stubbornness made her able to _____ every attempt.

5. When Miss Emily insisted on something, no one in town had the _____ to argue with her.

6. Closed shutters and moist air gave her house an unpleasantly _____ atmosphere.

7. Miss Emily never sunned, and her complexion became _____.

8. Perhaps the judge was normally bold, but he reacted to the foul smell from Miss Emily's house with _____ hesitation.

9. The townspeople thought that sprinkling lime might destroy, or _____, the source of the smell.

10. Miss Emily had always been a no-nonsense kind of woman, not the type to behave in a _____ fashion toward any man.

11. Although the town realized that she kept company with Homer Barron, no one knew just how _____ in love she had been.

12. Only after her death did anyone dare to _____ on the privacy of the upstairs room.

13. Enough tarnish had formed on the silver of the men's toilet things to _____ the monogram.

14. Was it Homer's plans to leave town that made Miss Emily react in such a _____ fashion?

15. Did she know that a clue on the pillow would _____ her closely kept secret?

**Building Vocabulary**

For an in-depth lesson on context clues, see page 326.

| WORDS TO KNOW | | | | |
|---|---|---|---|---|
| encroach | edict | temerity | circumvent | tedious |
| obliterate | dank | diffident | thwart | profoundly |
| coquettish | pallid | divulge | virulent | obscure |

## William Faulkner
### 1897–1962

**Other Works**
*As I Lay Dying*
*The Sound and the Fury*
*Intruder in the Dust*

**Aimless Youth** William Faulkner, the great-grandson of a colorful Civil War hero, was nurtured on legends of the honor and gallantry of his Mississippi ancestors. Though a high school dropout, Faulkner read widely. For years, he drifted aimlessly. He traveled, did odd jobs, and attended the University of Mississippi for one year as a special student.

**Focus on Writing** By the late 1920s, Faulkner had published his first two novels. In 1929, his writing career blossomed. In a 13-year period, he published 15 books—novels and collections of short stories—including his masterworks *Light in August* (1932) and *Absalom, Absalom!* (1936). Faulkner focused his considerable talents on the land and people of northern Mississippi. His challenging experiments with stream of consciousness and fractured chronology cost him a wide audience, however. To earn a living, he worked as a Hollywood screenwriter during the 1930s and 1940s.

**Prestige and Fame** After World War II, Faulkner's critical reputation and popularity grew, and in 1949 he won the Nobel Prize in literature. By the time he died, Faulkner was widely regarded as one of America's greatest writers.

## Vocabulary in Action

1. tedious
2. edict
3. circumvent
4. thwart
5. temerity
6. dank
7. pallid
8. diffident
9. obliterate
10. coquettish
11. profoundly
12. encroach
13. obscure
14. virulent
15. divulge

## Author Background

Despite winning two Pulitzer Prizes and the Nobel Prize for literature, Faulkner considered himself first a farmer and only secondarily a writer. He stated: "My life is farmland and horses and the raising of grain and feed. I took up writing simply because I liked it. . . . I look after my farm and my horses and then when there is time I write, or if I have something I want to write, I will find time to write it, but just to be a writer is not my life."

---

**Mini Lesson** **Grammar**

**MODIFIERS: ILLOGICAL COMPARISONS**

**Instruction** Tell students that they can correct many illogical comparisons by adding the word *other* or *else* to the sentence. Write the following example on the chalkboard.

The Griersons had more respect than any family in the community.

This sentence implies that the Griersons were not a family in the community. Help students understand the difference in meaning when the sentence is revised to read, "The Griersons had more respect than any other family in the community."

**Exercises** Have students revise the following illogical comparisons by adding the word *other* or *else*.

1. Homer came closer to marrying Emily than anyone. *(revise to read "than anyone else")*

2. Emily's insanity was less obvious than that of any Gothic protagonist. *(revise to read "than that of any other Gothic protagonist")*

3. Emily's desire to possess Homer was stronger than everything in her life. *(revise to read "than everything else")*

 Use McDougal Littell's *Language Network,* Chapter 7, for more instruction and practice in modifiers.

### Objectives
1. understand and appreciate a Southern Gothic **short story** (Literary Analysis)
2. identify and examine **irony** (Literary Analysis)
3. **draw conclusions about characters** (Active Reading)

### Summary
In the rural Alabama twilight a one-armed vagabond approaches the desolate farmhouse of Lucynell Crater and her deaf, disturbed adult daughter of the same name. The vagabond, Tom T. Shiftlet, agrees to perform much-needed repairs on the farm in exchange for food and accommodations. Shiftlet easily gains Mrs. Crater's confidence, and she suggests that he marry her daughter and remain at the farm. Shiftlet, who seems more interested in Mrs. Crater's old Ford than in her daughter, agrees to the marriage on the condition that Mrs. Crater finance repairs to the car and a honeymoon trip to Mobile. After a brief civil ceremony, Shiftlet departs with his bride, but he soon abandons her at a roadside cafe and heads on toward Mobile.

### Thematic Link
O'Connor's characters assume an almost comic absurdity, but their insincerity and base motivations evoke the **dark side** of human nature. Although it's difficult for the reader to identify with these unsympathetic characters whose **individualism** consists of a bizarre assortment of peculiarities, they somehow call to mind our own idiosyncrasies and imperfections.

---

### 5-Minute Warm-Up

***Daily Language SkillBuilder***

Have students **proofread** the display sentences on page 337k and write them correctly. The sentences also appear on Transparency 15 of **Grammar Transparencies and Copymasters.**

---

## PREPARING to *Read*

*"Nothing is like it used to be, lady,' he said. 'The world is almost rotten.'"*

# The Life You Save May Be Your Own

*Short Story by* FLANNERY O'CONNOR

### Comparing Literature

### Traditions Across Time: Southern Gothic

Influenced by Edgar Allan Poe and Nathaniel Hawthorne, Flannery O'Connor wrote stories filled with sinister characters and bizarre situations. Like these two earlier writers of Gothic literature, she vividly portrays the experiences of isolated, self-absorbed people set against the backdrop of a grotesque world.

**Points of Comparison** As you read "The Life You Save May Be Your Own," compare the characters with those in Poe's and Hawthorne's stories.

### Build Background

**Southern Sideshow** As a child, Flannery O'Connor had a pet chicken that could either walk backward or forward, and some news reporters came to photograph the animal. This experience, she later said, marked her for life, for it began her preoccupation with the grotesque—a fascination she shares with other writers of her region who are often classified as belonging to the literary tradition known as Southern Gothic. "Southern writers are fond of 'writing about freaks,' " she remarked, "because we are still able to recognize one." O'Connor's fictional world—the 1940s and 1950s South—is populated with misfits, fanatics, and con artists. O'Connor believed that "distortion was the only way to make people see." In twisting reality, she used elements of the grotesque to convey a message about the need for spiritual renewal.

> WORDS TO KNOW
> **Vocabulary Preview**
> composed    morose
> gaunt       rue
> list

### Focus Your Reading

**LITERARY ANALYSIS** **IRONY** Irony is a contrast between what is expected and what actually exists or happens. In literature, **situational irony** is a contrast between what a character expects to happen and what actually happens. **Dramatic irony** occurs when readers know more about a situation in a story than the characters do. Look for examples of irony in this story.

**ACTIVE READING** **DRAWING CONCLUSIONS ABOUT CHARACTERS**

O'Connor never tells the reader directly whether her **characters** are good or evil. Instead, she allows the reader to **draw conclusions** about characters based on clues, such as the characters' thoughts, words, and actions. The names O'Connor gives characters and the **imagery** she uses to describe them also provide hints about characters and their moral conduct.

**READER'S NOTEBOOK** To help you draw conclusions about the characters, use the reading-strategy questions inserted throughout the selection. Write your responses in your notebook.

**528**   UNIT THREE   PART 2: THE DARK SIDE OF INDIVIDUALISM

---

## LESSON RESOURCES

**UNIT THREE RESOURCE BOOK,** pp. 76–81

**ASSESSMENT RESOURCES**
**Formal Assessment,** pp. 93–94
**Teacher's Guide to Assessment and Portfolio Use**
**Test Generator**

**SKILLS TRANSPARENCIES AND COPYMASTERS**
**Literary Analysis**
• Irony, T21 (for Paired Activity, p. 539)

**Reading and Critical Thinking**
• Drawing Conclusions, T4 (for Active Reading, p. 528)

**Grammar**
• Double Negatives, T53 (for Mini Lesson, p. 540)
• Double Negatives, C137 (for Mini Lesson, p. 540)

**Vocabulary**
• Analogies, C48 (for Mini Lesson, p. 538)

**Writing**
• Compare-Contrast, C31 (for Writing Option 3, p. 540)
• Opinion Statement, C34 (for Writing Option 1, p. 540)

**Communications**
• Evaluating Roles in Groups, T8 (for Mini Lesson, p. 536)

**INTEGRATED TECHNOLOGY**

**Audio Library**
**Visit our website:**
www.mcdougallittell.com

# YOUR OWN
# MAY BE
# YOU SAVE
# THE LIFE

## FLANNERY O'CONNOR

## TEACHING THE LITERATURE

### Customizing Instruction

**Less Proficient Readers**
Tell students that this story begins when a tramp arrives at the run-down farm where Mrs. Crater lives with her daughter.

**Set a Purpose** Ask students to consider these questions as they read the story:
• What kind of a person is Mrs. Crater?
• What kind of a person is Mr. Shiftlet?
• Does what the characters say reflect their true feelings?

**Students Acquiring English**
This short story contains dialect, American idioms, colloquial sayings, and figurative language that some students may find difficult to understand. Have these students work in pairs with native speakers who can read confusing passages aloud to aid comprehension.

 Use **Spanish Study Guide** for additional support, pp. 127–129.

**Gifted and Talented**
Have small groups discuss what aspects of this story make it appropriate for inclusion in a group of Southern Gothic works. Ask them to write brief essays based on their discussions that contain reasons why it belongs or does not belong in the Southern Gothic tradition.

The old woman and her daughter were sitting on their porch when Mr. Shiftlet came up their road for the first time. The old woman slid to the edge of her chair and leaned forward, shading her eyes from the piercing sunset with her hand. The daughter could not see far in front of her and continued to play with her fingers. Although the old woman lived in this desolate spot with only her daughter and she had never seen Mr. Shiftlet before, she could tell, even from a distance, that he was a tramp and no one to be afraid of. His left coat sleeve was folded up to show there was only half an arm in it, and his <u>gaunt</u> figure <u>listed</u> slightly to the side as if the breeze were pushing him. He had on a black town suit and a brown felt hat that was turned up in the front and down in the back and he carried a tin toolbox by a handle. He came on, at an amble, up her road, his face turned toward the sun which appeared to be balancing itself on the peak of a small mountain.

The old woman didn't change her position until he was almost into her yard; then she rose with one hand fisted on her hip. The daughter, a large girl in a short blue organdy dress, saw him all at once and jumped up and began to stamp and point and make excited speechless sounds.

Mr. Shiftlet stopped just inside the yard and set his box on the ground and tipped his hat at her as if she were not in the least afflicted; then he turned toward the old woman and swung the hat all the way off. He had long black slick hair that hung flat from a part in the middle to beyond the tips of his ears on either side. His face descended in forehead for more than half its length and ended suddenly with his features just balanced over a jutting steel-trap jaw. He seemed to be a young man but he had a look of <u>composed</u>

| WORDS TO KNOW | **gaunt** (gônt) *adj.* thin and bony<br>**list** (lĭst) *v.* to lean or tilt to one side<br>**composed** (kəm-pōzd′) *adj.* calm; cool and collected |
| --- | --- |

**529**

---

 **Mini Lesson** ## Preteaching Vocabulary

**USING CONTEXT CLUES** Sometimes students can determine the meaning of an unfamiliar word by analyzing a cause-and-effect relationship in the text. Write the following sentence on the chalkboard and ask a volunteer to explain the cause-and-effect relationship implied in it.
Part of the shed's foundation had collapsed, so the structure <u>listed</u> to one side.

**Possible Response:** Because the foundation had partially fallen, the shed leaned to one side.

**Exercises** Have students apply the strategy to figure out the meanings of underlined words in the following sentences.

1. The stranger hadn't eaten in days and looked <u>gaunt</u>.
2. She became so upset by his story that he <u>rued</u> telling it.
3. Having studied for weeks, Ellen felt quite <u>composed</u> on the day of the exam.
4. Tom appeared <u>morose</u> after his employer scolded him in front of his fellow workers.

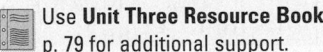 Use **Unit Three Resource Book,** p. 79 for additional support.

**A lesson on using context clues appears on p. 326 in the Pupil's Edition.**

**Reading Skills and Strategies:**
**PREVIEW**

Have students pay close attention to the disparities between characters' spoken dialogue, thoughts, and actions.

**Literary Analysis** | IRONY |

Remind students that situational irony is when something happens that is the opposite of what someone expects. Have them look for examples of irony as they continue reading, paying attention to what characters expect as well as to what they as readers expect.

📖 Use **Unit Three Resource Book**, p. 78 for more practice.

**Active Reading**

| DRAWING CONCLUSIONS |
| ABOUT CHARACTERS |

Ask students to draw conclusions about characters and support them with textual evidence and experience. Have them comment on any unusual aspects of Mr. Shiftlet's behavior and speech. Ask them to find clues that allow them to draw conclusions about his personality. Does Mrs. Crater draw similar conclusions?

**Possible Response:** Shiftlet's lengthy, grandiose pose while viewing the sunset seems somewhat peculiar. In conversation, he avoids answering several direct questions, and his anecdote about the heart seems distinctly odd. Mrs. Crater, however, appears to relate to Mr. Shiftlet, accepting his behavior as perfectly natural and agreeing matter-of-factly with his comments.

📖 Use **Unit Three Resource Book**, p. 77 for more practice.

dissatisfaction as if he understood life thoroughly.

"Good evening," the old woman said. She was about the size of a cedar fence post and she had a man's gray hat pulled down low over her head.

 The tramp stood looking at her and didn't answer. He turned his back and faced the sunset. He swung both his whole and his short arm up slowly so that they indicated an expanse of sky and his figure formed a crooked cross. The old woman watched him with her arms folded across her chest as if she were the owner of the sun, and the daughter watched, her head thrust forward and her fat helpless hands hanging at the wrists. She had long pink-gold hair and eyes as blue as a peacock's neck.

He held the pose for almost fifty seconds and then he picked up his box and came on to the porch and dropped down on the bottom step. "Lady," he said in a firm nasal voice, "I'd give a fortune to live where I could see me a sun do that every evening."

"Does it every evening," the old woman said and sat back down. The daughter sat down too and watched him with a cautious, sly look as if he were a bird that had come up very close. He leaned to one side, rooting in his pants pocket, and in a second he brought out a package of chewing gum and offered her a piece. She took it and unpeeled it and began to chew without taking her eyes off him. He offered the old woman a piece but she only raised her upper lip to indicate she had no teeth.

Mr. Shiftlet's pale, sharp glance had already passed over everything in the yard—the pump near the corner of the house and the big fig tree that three or four chickens were preparing to roost in—and had moved to a shed where he saw the square rusted back of an automobile. "You ladies drive?" he asked.

"That car ain't run in fifteen year," the old woman said. "The day my husband died, it quit running."

"Nothing is like it used to be, lady," he said. "The world is almost rotten."

"That's right," the old woman said. "You from around here?"

"Name Tom T. Shiftlet," he murmured, looking at the tires.

"I'm pleased to meet you," the old woman said. "Name Lucynell Crater and daughter Lucynell Crater. What you doing around here, Mr. Shiftlet?"

He judged the car to be about a 1928 or '29 Ford. "Lady," he said, and turned and gave her his full attention, "lemme tell you something. There's one of these doctors in Atlanta that's taken a knife and cut the human heart—the human heart," he repeated, leaning forward, "out of a man's chest and held it in his hand," and he held his hand out, palm up, as if it were slightly weighted with the human heart, "and studied it like it was a day-old chicken, and lady," he said, allowing a long significant pause in which his head slid forward and his clay-colored eyes brightened, "he don't know no more about it than you or me."

"That's right," the old woman said.

"Why, if he was to take that knife and cut into every corner of it, he still wouldn't know no more than you or me. What you want to bet?"

"Nothing," the old woman said wisely. "Where you come from, Mr. Shiftlet?"

He didn't answer. He reached into his pocket and brought out a sack of tobacco and a package of cigarette papers and rolled himself a cigarette, expertly with one hand, and attached it in a hanging position to his upper lip. Then he took a box of wooden matches from his pocket and struck one on his shoe. He held the burning match as if he were studying the mystery of flame while it traveled dangerously toward his skin. The daughter began to make loud noises and to point to his hand and shake her finger at him, but when the flame was just before touching him, he leaned down with his hand cupped over it as if he were going to set fire to his nose and lit the cigarette.

He flipped away the dead match and blew a stream of gray into the evening. A sly look came

## Teaching Options

### BLOCK SCHEDULING: MANAGING TIME

**If your schedule requires that you cover the lesson objectives in a shorter time, use . . .**
- Preparing to Read, p. 528
- Thinking Through the Literature, p. 539
- Vocabulary in Action, p. 541

**If you want to take advantage of longer class time, use . . .**
- TE Teaching Options: Preteaching Vocabulary, p. 529; Viewing and Representing, pp. 531, 535, 537; Speaking and Listening, p. 536; Cross-Curricular Link, p. 532; Standardized Test Practice, p. 534; Informal Assessment, p. 541
- Choices & Challenges and Author Activity, pp. 540–541

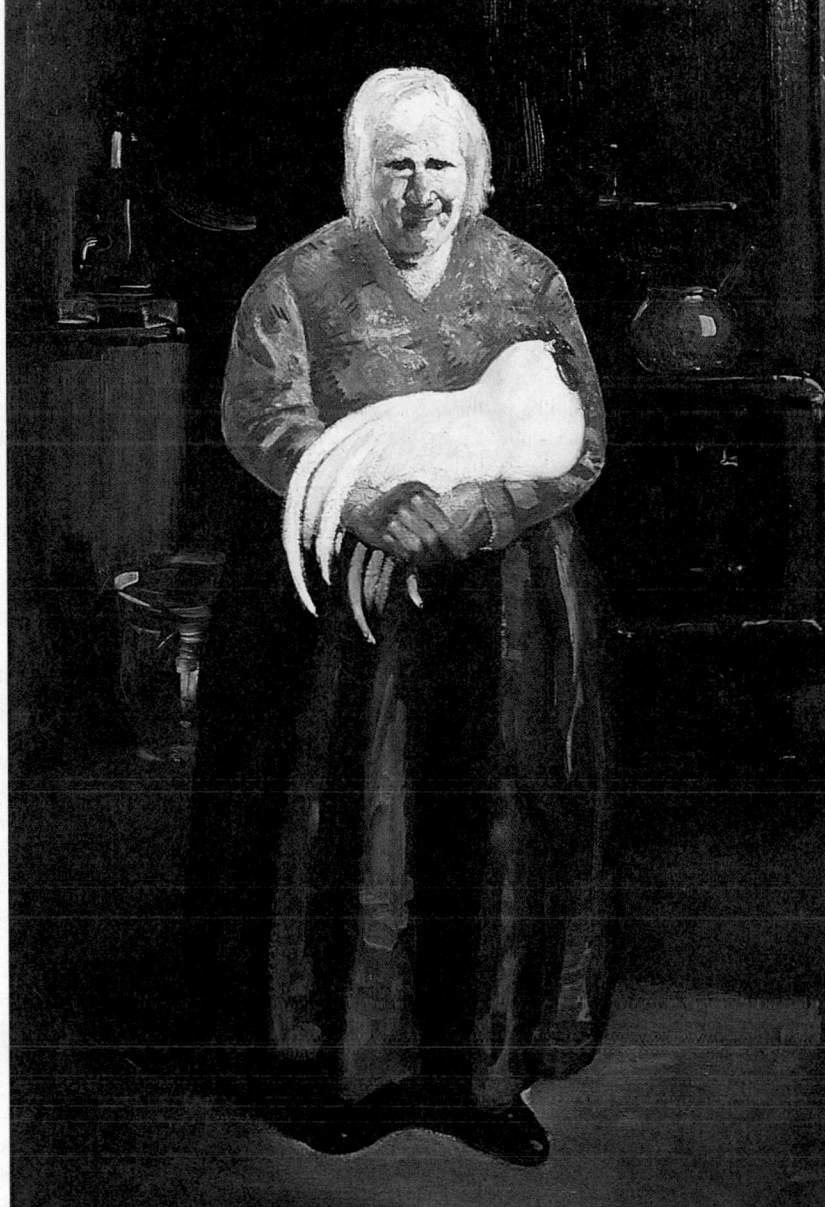

*Mrs. Gamely* (1930), George Luks. Oil on canvas, 66″ × 48″, collection of Whitney Museum of American Art, purchase (31.289). Copyright © 1995 Whitney Museum of American Art.

### Less Proficient Readers

Point out how Mr. Shiftlet and Mrs. Crater frequently change the subject of their conversation. Ask if these conversational shifts provide clues to the characters' personalities.

**Possible Response:** While Mrs. Crater concentrates on practical matters, Mr. Shiftlet seems concerned with larger issues, such as the state of the world and what people can know of the human heart.

### Students Acquiring English

**1** Explain to students that a tramp is a person traveling aimlessly, often looking for odd jobs or begging.

**2** Point out that for many cultures, the heart symbolically represents the seat of human emotions.

### Gifted and Talented

**3** Have students analyze Mr. Shiftlet's diatribe against the physician in Atlanta. Is it an appropriate response to Mrs. Crater's question? Does Shiftlet actually believe that he and Mrs. Crater understand the heart's physiology as well as does a physician who has studied and dissected the organ? To what else might Shiftlet be alluding?

### Multiple Learning Styles
#### Kinesthetic Learners

**4** Shiftlet's dexterity in the complex task of rolling and lighting his cigarette with one hand indicates that the injury to his arm is not a recent one. Have students perform simple two-handed tasks with one hand (e.g., folding paper, tying shoes, etc.) to appreciate the skill necessary to accomplish them.

 **Viewing and Representing**

### *Mrs. Gamely* by George Luks

**ART APPRECIATION** After working as a newspaper artist and recording scenes of fighting in the Spanish-American War, Luks became a social realist painter, depicting scenes of the everyday life of common people. His landlady, Mrs. Gamely, served as the subject of several of his paintings.

**Instruction** Ask students to examine the use of light in the painting, particularly the highlighting applied to the kitchen objects in the background. Ask how the highlights influence our perception of the subject's environment.

**Possible Response:** The highlights bring a sense of cleanliness and orderliness to the surroundings. The well-maintained, functional objects—stove, pot, pump, and coal scuttle—reflect the dignity of everyday life.

**Application** Ask students to describe how meanings are communicated through elements of design. Have them study the figure in the foreground and determine the artist's attitude toward his subject. Have them provide evidence to support their opinions, and suggest that they focus on the artist's use of light.

**Possible Response:** Although her features are coarse and her expression ambiguous, Mrs. Gamely projects an aura of goodness and decency, which the artist enhances by bathing her head in light.

**A** Dramatic irony occurs when the reader is aware of a reality of which a character is ignorant. O'Connor employs irony both in her description and in her characters' dialogue. Ask students to explain the irony of Shiftlet's statement that he served in the "Arm Service."
**Possible Response:** His misuse of the term *armed services* is ironic in light of the fact that he has lost his arm.

**B** Irony contrasts what we expect to what actually exists. Point out the double meaning in the statement "I would give her up for nothing on earth."

### ACTIVE READING

**C** **EVALUATE** Possible Response: To help students with characterization, have them consider what the characters say, what they do, how they look, and what the author tells us about them.

### ACTIVE READING

**D** **CLARIFY** Ask students to point out hints that suggest what Mrs. Crater has on her mind.
**Possible Response:** When Mrs. Crater sees Shiftlet teach Lucynell one word (which, apparently, is more than she has ever done), she assumes that he is interested in her daughter. Mrs. Crater probably believes that if Shiftlet teaches her to say the term of endearment (*sugarpie*), the romantic connection between the two will grow stronger.

---

over his face. "Lady," he said, "nowadays, people'll do anything anyways. I can tell you my name is Tom T. Shiftlet and I come from Tarwater, Tennessee, but you never have seen me before: how you know I ain't lying? How you know my name ain't Aaron Sparks, lady, and I come from Singleberry, Georgia, or how you know it's not George Speeds and I come from Lucy, Alabama, or how you know I ain't Thompson Bright from Toolafalls, Mississippi?"

"I don't know nothing about you," the old woman muttered, irked.

"Lady," he said, "people don't care how they lie. Maybe the best I can tell you is, I'm a man; but listen lady," he said and paused and made his tone more ominous still, "what is a man?"

The old woman began to gum a seed. "What you carry in that tin box, Mr. Shiftlet?" she asked.

"Tools," he said, put back. "I'm a carpenter."

"Well, if you come out here to work, I'll be able to feed you and give you a place to sleep but I can't pay. I'll tell you that before you begin," she said.

**1** There was no answer at once and no particular expression on his face. He leaned back against the two-by-four that helped support the porch roof. "Lady," he said slowly, "there's some men that some things mean more to them than money." The old woman rocked without comment and the daughter watched the trigger that moved up and down in his neck. He told the old woman then that all most people were interested in was money, but he asked what a man was made for. He asked her if a man was made for money, or what. He asked her what she thought she was made for but she didn't answer, she only sat rocking and wondered if a one-armed man could put a new roof on her garden house. He asked a lot of questions that she didn't answer. He told her that he was twenty-eight years old and had lived a varied life. He had been a gospel singer, a foreman on the railroad, an assistant in an undertaking parlor, and he come over the **2** radio for three months with Uncle Roy and his Red Creek Wranglers. He said he had fought and

bled in the Arm Service of his country and visited every foreign land and that everywhere he had seen people that didn't care if they did a thing one way or another. He said he hadn't been raised thataway.

A fat yellow moon appeared in the branches of the fig tree as if it were going to roost there with the chickens. He said that a man had to escape to the country to see the world whole and that he wished he lived in a desolate place like this where he could see the sun go down every evening like God made it to do.

"Are you married or are you single?" the old woman asked.

There was a long silence. "Lady," he asked finally, "where would you find you an innocent woman today? I wouldn't have any of this trash I could just pick up."

The daughter was leaning very far down, hanging her head almost between her knees watching him through a triangular door she had made in her overturned hair; and she suddenly fell in a heap on the floor and began to whimper. Mr. Shiftlet straightened her out and helped her get back in the chair.

"Is she your baby girl?" he asked.

"My only," the old woman said, "and she's the sweetest girl in the world. I would give her up for nothing on earth. She's smart too. She can sweep the floor, cook, wash, feed the chickens, and hoe. I wouldn't give her up for a casket of jewels."

"No," he said kindly, "don't ever let any man take her away from you."

"Any man come after her," the old woman said, " 'll have to stay around the place."

Mr. Shiftlet's eye in the darkness was focused on a part of the automobile bumper that glittered in the distance. "Lady," he said, jerking his short arm up as if he could point with it to her house and yard and pump, "there ain't a broken thing on this plantation that I couldn't fix for you, one-arm jackleg[1] or not. I'm a

---

1. **jackleg:** someone who does work he or she has not been trained to do.

---

# Teaching Options

## Cross Curricular Link **History**

**HENRY FORD** Born in Michigan in 1863, Henry Ford showed an early talent for mechanics. While working as an engineer for a Detroit lighting company in the 1880s, Ford began to develop plans for an engine-powered carriage. He produced his first gasoline-powered vehicle in 1896 and started his own automobile manufacturing factory in 1903. Soon his Model T was the most popular car in the country.

Ford's success stemmed from two basic concepts: the assembly line and standardization of product. The assembly line, which he implemented in 1913, allowed him to cut the price of his cars in half. By making huge quantities of identical cars, he was able to simplify the process even further. In fact, it was not until 1927 that Ford produced a car in another color than black.

man," he said with a sullen dignity, "even if I ain't a whole one. I got," he said, tapping his knuckles on the floor to emphasize the immensity of what he was going to say, "a moral intelligence!" and his face pierced out of the darkness into a shaft of door light and he stared at her as if he were astonished himself at this impossible truth.

**ACTIVE READING**

**C** **EVALUATE** How would you characterize Mr. Shiftlet? Mrs. Crater? her daughter, Lucynell?

The old woman was not impressed with the phrase. "I told you you could hang around and work for food," she said, "if you don't mind sleeping in that car yonder."

"Why listen, lady," he said with a grin of delight, "the monks of old slept in their coffins!"

"They wasn't as advanced as we are," the old woman said.

The next morning he began on the roof of the garden house while Lucynell, the daughter, sat on a rock and watched him work. He had not been around a week before the change he had made in the place was apparent. He had patched the front and back steps, built a new hog pen, restored a fence, and taught Lucynell, who was completely deaf and had never said a word in her life, to say the word bird. The big rosy-faced girl followed him everywhere, saying "Burrttddt ddbirrrttdt," and clapping her hands. The old woman watched from a distance, secretly pleased. She was ravenous for a son-in-law.

Mr. Shiftlet slept on the hard narrow back seat of the car with his feet out the side window. He had his razor and a can of water on a crate that served him as a bedside table and he put up a piece of mirror against the back glass and kept his coat neatly on a hanger that he hung over one of the windows.

In the evenings he sat on the steps and talked while the old woman and Lucynell rocked violently in their chairs on either side of him.

The old woman's three mountains were black against the dark blue sky and were visited off and on by various planets and by the moon after it had left the chickens. Mr. Shiftlet pointed out that the reason he had improved this plantation was because he had taken a personal interest in it. He said he was even going to make the automobile run.

He had raised the hood and studied the mechanism, and he said he could tell that the car had been built in the days when cars were really built. You take now, he said, one man puts in one bolt and another man puts in another bolt and another man puts in another bolt so that it's a man for a bolt. That's why you have to pay so much for a car: you're paying all those men. Now if you didn't have to pay but one man, you could get you a cheaper car and one that had had a personal interest taken in it, and it would be a better car. The old woman agreed with him that this was so.

Mr. Shiftlet said that the trouble with the world was that nobody cared, or stopped and took any trouble. He said he never would have been able to teach Lucynell to say a word if he hadn't cared and stopped long enough.

"Teach her to say something else," the old woman said.

"What you want her to say next?" Mr. Shiftlet asked.

The old woman's smile was broad and toothless and suggestive. "Teach her to say 'sugarpie,'" she said.

**ACTIVE READING**

**D** **CLARIFY** What do you think is on the old woman's mind?

Mr. Shiftlet already knew what was on her mind.

The next day he began to tinker with the automobile, and that evening he told her that if she would buy a fan belt, he would be able to make the car run.

The old woman said she would give him the money. "You see that girl yonder?" she asked, pointing to Lucynell who was sitting on the floor a foot away, watching him, her eyes blue even in the dark. "If it was ever a man wanted to take

## Customizing Instruction

### Students Acquiring English
**1** Point out that a *two-by-four* is a piece of lumber two inches thick and four inches wide.

**2** Explain that Shiftlet is claiming to have performed on radio broadcasts with a country-and-western band.

### Gifted and Talented
**3** Have students evaluate Shiftlet's comments about the way Mrs. Crater's car was built. Ask them to decide if they agree or disagree with his remarks and to provide evidence to support their opinions.

**Possible Response:** Shiftlet is obviously misinformed about the "'28 or '29 Ford." Fords had been built on assembly lines since 1914, and the assembly-line process was responsible for greatly reducing the cost of automobiles.

### Students Acquiring English
**4** Explain that the phrase *what was on her mind* means "what she was thinking about."

DRAWING CONCLUSIONS
ABOUT CHARACTERS

**A** Have students evaluate Mrs. Crater's statement and note the humor embedded therein. Then ask them to explain why she'd insist that Lucynell and her husband remain at home with her.

**Possible Response:** Mrs. Crater is lazy. Lucynell currently performs most household chores, and she expects that her future son-in-law would work on her plantation, too.

**Literary Analysis: SIMILE**

**B** Remind students that a simile is a directly stated comparison between two things that are essentially different. Similes usually contain the word *like* or *as*. Ask students to identify the simile in the passage and to name the two things that it compares.

**Possible Response:** The simile compares Mrs. Crater's words with a group of buzzards.

Ask students to suggest why the author chose the image of buzzards in a tree to complete the simile.

**Possible Response:** Buzzards, or vultures, generally lurk near carrion or creatures close to death. Traditionally their presence signifies ominous portents.

---

her away, I would say, 'No man on earth is going to take that sweet girl of mine away from me!' but if he was to say, 'Lady, I don't want to take her away, I want her right here,' I would say, 'Mister, I don't blame you none. I wouldn't pass up a chance to live in a permanent place and get the sweetest girl in the world myself. You ain't no fool,' I would say."

"How old is she?" Mr. Shiftlet asked casually.

"Fifteen, sixteen," the old woman said. The girl was nearly thirty but because of her innocence it was impossible to guess.

"It would be a good idea to paint it too," Mr. Shiftlet remarked. "You don't want it to rust out."

"We'll see about that later," the old woman said.

The next day he walked into town and returned with the parts he needed and a can of gasoline. Late in the afternoon, terrible noises issued from the shed and the old woman rushed out of the house, thinking Lucynell was somewhere having a fit. Lucynell was sitting on a chicken crate, stamping her feet and screaming, "Burrddttt! bddurrddtttt!" but her fuss was **[1]** drowned out by the car. With a volley of blasts it emerged from the shed, moving in a fierce and stately way. Mr. Shiftlet was in the driver's seat, sitting very erect. He had an expression of serious modesty on his face as if he had just raised the dead.

That night, rocking on the porch, the old woman began her business, at once. "You want you an innocent woman, don't you?" she asked sympathetically. "You don't want none of this trash."

"No'm, I don't," Mr. Shiftlet said.

"One that can't talk," she continued, "can't **[2]** sass you back or use foul language. That's the kind for you to have. Right there," and she pointed to Lucynell sitting cross-legged in her chair, holding both feet in her hands.

"That's right," he admitted. "She wouldn't give me any trouble."

"Saturday," the old woman said, "you and her and me can drive into town and get married." **A**

Mr. Shiftlet eased his position on the steps.

"I can't get married right now," he said. "Everything you want to do takes money and I ain't got any."

"What you need with money?" she asked.

"It takes money," he said. "Some people'll do anything anyhow these days, but the way I think, I wouldn't marry no woman that I couldn't take on a trip like she was somebody. I mean take her to a hotel and treat her. I wouldn't marry the Duchesser Windsor," he said firmly, "unless I **[3]** could take her to a hotel and giver something good to eat.

"I was raised thataway and there ain't a thing I can do about it. My old mother taught me how to do."

"Lucynell don't even know what a hotel is," the old woman muttered. "Listen here, Mr. Shiftlet," she said, sliding forward in her chair, "you'd be getting a permanent house and a deep well and the most innocent girl in the world. You don't need no money. Lemme tell you something: there ain't any place in the world for a poor, disabled, friendless drifting man."

The ugly words settled in Mr. Shiftlet's head like a group of buzzards in the top of a tree. He didn't answer at once. He rolled himself a cigarette and lit it and then he said in an even voice, "Lady, a man is divided into two parts, body and spirit." **B**

The old woman clamped her gums together.

"A body and a spirit," he repeated. "The body, lady, is like a house: it don't go anywhere; but the spirit, lady, is like a automobile: always on the move, always . . ."

"Listen, Mr. Shiftlet," she said, "my well never goes dry and my house is always warm in the winter and there's no mortgage on a thing about this place. You can go to the courthouse and see for yourself. And yonder under that shed **[4]** is a fine automobile." She laid the bait carefully. "You can have it painted by Saturday. I'll pay for the paint."

---

## Teaching Options

☑ Assessment **Standardized Test Practice**

**MAKING INFERENCES** Certain test situations require students to infer information from the context of a passage. To practice this process, write the following on the chalkboard:
Why does Mrs. Crater suggest that Shiftlet visit the courthouse?

**A.** Shiftlet and Lucynell's wedding ceremony would take place in the courthouse.

**B.** Shiftlet could examine the mortgage records filed at the courthouse.

**C.** Shiftlet could register the Ford and obtain license plates.

Have students read the last paragraph on page 534. Then lead them through the process of inferring information. Explain that while statements A and C might be true, the information provided in the context allows us to infer only statement B.

The Interloper (1958), Billy Morrow Jackson. Collection of Mrs. Virginia Penofsky.

THE LIFE YOU SAVE MAY BE YOUR OWN    **535**

## Customizing Instruction

### Students Acquiring English

**1** Explain that the idiom *drowned out* means "overcame a quieter sound." The car made so much noise that it rendered Lucynell's screaming inaudible.

**2** Point out that the phrase *sass you back* means "to answer disrespectfully or scornfully."

### Less Proficient Readers

**3** Point out that "Duchesser Windsor" refers to Wallis Simpson, the Duchess of Windsor, for whom King Edward VII abdicated his throne in order to wed.

**4** Ask students to discuss the sentence "She laid the bait carefully." What is the bait? What does Mrs. Crater hope to catch?

**Possible Response:** The bait is the automobile. Mrs. Crater hopes to use it to catch a son-in-law.

---

**Mini Lesson** **Viewing and Representing**

### The Interloper by Billy Morrow Jackson

**ART APPRECIATION** Born in 1926, Billy Morrow Jackson taught art at the University of Illinois until his retirement in 1987. Painted in 1958, *The Interloper* is divided into two sections: a landscape that features a withered corn field after harvest, and a portrait of a young man posed in front of the remnants of an outbuilding.

**Instruction** Ask students to note the varied use of texture in the painting—the thick, palette-knife application in the middle-distance cornfield, the mottled look of the weathered boards, and the intricate, cross-hatched weave of the man's jacket. Explain that the varied textures work together to create the illusion of depth.

**Application** Ask students to study the subject of *The Interloper* (which means "the intruder"). Have them suggest differences or similarities between the man in the painting and their visualization of Mr. Shiftlet. What does the man in the painting seem to have in mind? What feeling does this situation create in viewers?

**Possible Response:** The man in the painting has a smug, shifty look about him, just as Mr. Shiftlet would have. The painting suggests that the interloper intends to prey upon the inhabitants of the farmhouse in the distance, creating an uncomfortable, foreboding feeling.

THE LIFE YOU SAVE    **535**

**A** Ask students to explain what this passage reveals about Mr. Shiftlet. Why does O'Connor compare his smile to a snake? What does she mean by saying "he recalled himself"?

**Possible Response:** The simile suggests Mr. Shiftlet's evil intentions. Shiftlet soon hides the smile to better maintain his subterfuge.

**ACTIVE READING**

**B** **CONCLUDE** Have students consider what Shiftlet's priorities seem to be.

**Literary Analysis:** IRONY

**C** Situational irony contrasts what a character expects with what actually happens. Have students explain the differences between expectations and the reality of "The Hot Spot."

**Possible Response:** One would expect a café with such a name to be a lively gathering place, but it's empty, and Lucynell falls asleep at the counter soon after she arrives.

**Literary Analysis: SOUTHERN GOTHIC**

Like other Southern Gothic writers, O'Connor's work reflects socio-cultural decay and evokes a brooding sense of evil. Point out similarities that the story shares with other Southern Gothic works. Then ask students to consider what makes the story different from these other works.

**Possible Response:** O'Connor is quite funny, and the humor in her work often outweighs the gloom. She creates a sense of absurdity that's quite unlike the unremitting malevolence of a traditional Gothic short story.

---

**A** In the darkness, Mr. Shiftlet's smile stretched like a weary snake waking up by a fire. After a second he recalled himself and said, "I'm only saying a man's spirit means more to him than anything else. I would have to take my wife off for the weekend without no regards at all for cost. I got to follow where my spirit says to go."

"I'll give you fifteen dollars for a weekend trip," the old woman said in a crabbed voice. "That's the best I can do."

"That wouldn't hardly pay for more than the gas and the hotel," he said. "It wouldn't feed her."

**1** "Seventeen-fifty," the old woman said. "That's all I got so it isn't any use you trying to milk me. You can take a lunch."

Mr. Shiftlet was deeply hurt by the word *milk*. He didn't doubt that she had more money sewed

**ACTIVE READING**

**B** **CONCLUDE** What can you conclude about Mr. Shiftlet's intentions from these negotiations?

up in her mattress, but he had already told her he was not interested in her money. "I'll make that do," he said and rose and walked off without treating[2] with her further.

On Saturday the three of them drove into town in the car that the paint had barely dried on, and Mr. Shiftlet and Lucynell were married in the Ordinary's[3] office while the old woman witnessed. As they came out of the courthouse, Mr. Shiftlet began twisting his neck in his collar. He looked <u>morose</u> and bitter as if he had been insulted while someone held him. "That didn't satisfy me none," he said. "That was just something a woman in an office did, nothing but paperwork and blood tests. What do they know about my blood? If they was to take my heart and cut it out," he said, "they wouldn't know a thing about me. It didn't satisfy me at all."

"It satisfied the law," the old woman said sharply.

"The law," Mr. Shiftlet said and spit. "It's the law that don't satisfy me."

He had painted the car dark green with a yellow band around it just under the windows. The three of them climbed in the front seat and the old woman said, "Don't Lucynell look pretty? Looks like a baby doll." Lucynell was dressed up in a white dress that her mother had uprooted from a trunk and there was a Panama hat on her head with a bunch of red wooden cherries on the brim. Every now and then her placid expression was changed by a sly isolated little thought like a shoot of green in the desert. "You got a prize!" the old woman said.

Mr. Shiftlet didn't even look at her.

They drove back to the house to let the old woman off and pick up the lunch. When they were ready to leave, she stood staring in the window of the car, with her fingers clenched around the glass. Tears began to seep sideways out of her eyes and run along the dirty creases in her face. "I ain't ever been parted with her for two days before," she said.

Mr. Shiftlet started the motor.

"And I wouldn't let no man have her but you because I seen you would do right. Goodbye, Sugarbaby," she said, clutching at the sleeve of the white dress. Lucynell looked straight at her and didn't seem to see her there at all. Mr. Shiftlet eased the car forward so that she had to move her hands.

The early afternoon was clear and open and surrounded by pale blue sky. Although the car would go only thirty miles an hour, Mr. Shiftlet imagined a terrific climb and dip and swerve that went entirely to his head so that he forgot his morning bitterness. He had always wanted an automobile, but he had never been able to afford one before. He drove very fast because he wanted to make Mobile by nightfall.

---

2. **treating:** discussing terms; negotiating.
3. **Ordinary's:** judge's.

WORDS TO KNOW **morose** (mə-rōs') *adj.* gloomy and ill-tempered

536

---

## Speaking and Listening

**DRAMATIC PRESENTATION**

**Prepare** Have groups of three students prepare, organize, plan, and present a dramatic presentation of a scene from "The Life You Save May Be Your Own." Have the groups work cooperatively to select a scene that they'd like to present. Have each student select a character and make a list of personal characteristics and individual behaviors. Have them work on the dialect and mannerisms that their character will employ.

**Present** Student groups can decide how they'll stage and present the scene. Audience members

should evaluate verbal and nonverbal performance techniques by referring to the analysis and interpretation of the text.

**BLOCK SCHEDULING** This activity is particularly well-suited for longer class periods.

Occasionally he stopped his thoughts long enough to look at Lucynell in the seat beside him. She had eaten the lunch as soon as they were out of the yard and now she was pulling the cherries off the hat one by one and throwing them out the window. He became depressed in spite of the car. He had driven about a hundred miles when he decided that she must be hungry again and at the next small town they came to, he stopped in front of an aluminum-painted eating place called The Hot Spot and took her in and ordered her a plate of ham and grits. The ride had made her sleepy and as soon as she got up on the stool, she rested her head on the counter and shut her eyes. There was no one in The Hot Spot but Mr. Shiftlet and the boy behind the counter, a pale youth with a greasy rag hung over his shoulder. Before he could dish up the food, she was snoring gently.

"Give it to her when she wakes up," Mr. Shiftlet said. "I'll pay for it now."

The boy bent over her and stared at the long pink-gold hair and the half-shut sleeping eyes. Then he looked up and stared at Mr. Shiftlet. "She looks like an angel of Gawd," he murmured.

"Hitchhiker," Mr. Shiftlet explained. "I can't wait. I got to make Tuscaloosa."

The boy bent over again and very carefully touched his finger to a strand of the golden hair, and Mr. Shiftlet left.

*Road to Rhome* (1938), Alexander Hogue. Private collection.

THE LIFE YOU SAVE MAY BE YOUR OWN **537**

---

## Reading and Analyzing

### ACTIVE READING

**A** **QUESTION** Have students consider his insistence on marrying an innocent woman, and his conversations with Mrs. Crater.

### Literary Analysis IRONY

**B** Ask students what is ironic about Shiftlet's reason for looking for a hitchhiker.

**Possible Response:** He tells himself that now that he owns a car, he has a responsibility to others. In order to get the car, however, he callously abandoned his responsibility toward Lucynell.

### Literary Analysis: STORY TITLE

**C** Ask students to interpret the story's title.

**Possible Response:** The road sign appeals to people's desire for self-preservation, which is what motivates Shiftlet's actions throughout the story.

### ACTIVE READING

**D** **EVALUATE** Have students consider the example of motherhood provided by Mrs. Crater and the fact that Shiftlet has abandoned Lucynell. Also, note that he repeats the phrase spoken by the cook in The Hot Spot.

### Active Reading

DRAWING CONCLUSIONS
ABOUT CHARACTERS

**E** Ask students to explain why Shiftlet's comments might have upset the boy. Have them use textual evidence to support their opinions.

**Possible Response:** The child's appearance indicated "that he had left somewhere for good," and he becomes uncomfortable at the mention of mothers. He probably ran away from home after a disagreement with his mother.

### ACTIVE READING

**A** **QUESTION** Why do you think Mr. Shiftlet feels "more depressed than ever"?

**B**

**C**

He was more depressed than ever as he drove on by himself. The late afternoon had grown hot and sultry and the country had flattened out. Deep in the sky a storm was preparing very slowly and without thunder as if it meant to drain every drop of air from the earth before it broke. There were times when Mr. Shiftlet preferred not to be alone. He felt too that a man with a car had a responsibility to others, and he kept his eye out for a hitchhiker. Occasionally he saw a sign that warned: "Drive carefully. The life you save may be your own."

The narrow road dropped off on either side into dry fields, and here and there a shack or a filling station stood in a clearing. The sun began to set directly in front of the automobile. It was a reddening ball that through his windshield was slightly flat on the bottom and top. He saw a boy in overalls and a gray hat standing on the edge of the road and he slowed the car down and stopped in front of him. The boy didn't have his hand raised to thumb the ride, he was only standing there, but he had a small cardboard suitcase and his hat was set on his head in a way to indicate that he had left somewhere for good. "Son," Mr. Shiftlet said, "I see you want a ride."

The boy didn't say he did or he didn't but he opened the door of the car and got in, and Mr. Shiftlet started driving again. The child held the suitcase on his lap and folded his arms on top of it. He turned his head and looked out the window away from Mr. Shiftlet. Mr. Shiftlet felt oppressed. "Son," he said after a minute, "I got the best old mother in the world so I reckon you only got the second best."

The boy gave him a quick dark glance and then turned his face back out the window.

"It's nothing so sweet," Mr. Shiftlet continued, "as a boy's mother. She taught him his first prayers at her knee, she give him love when no other would, she told him what was right and what wasn't, and she seen that he done the right thing. Son," he said, "I never <u>rued</u> a day in my life like the one I rued when I left that old mother of mine."

The boy shifted in his seat but he didn't look at Mr. Shiftlet. He unfolded his arms and put one hand on the door handle.

"My mother was a angel of Gawd," Mr. Shiftlet said in a very strained voice. "He took her from heaven and giver to me and I left her."

### ACTIVE READING

**D** **QUESTION** Why do you think Mr. Shiftlet is speaking this way to the hitchhiker?

His eyes were instantly clouded over with a mist of tears. The car was barely moving.

The boy turned angrily in the seat. "You go to the devil!" he cried. "My old woman is a fleabag and yours is a stinking polecat!" and with that he flung the door open and jumped out with his suitcase into the ditch.

Mr. Shiftlet was so shocked that for about a hundred feet he drove along slowly with the door still open. A cloud, the exact color of the boy's hat and shaped like a turnip, had descended over the sun, and another, worse looking, crouched behind the car. Mr. Shiftlet felt that the rottenness of the world was about to engulf him. He raised his arm and let it fall again to his breast. "Oh Lord!" he prayed. "Break forth and wash the slime from this earth!"

The turnip continued slowly to descend. After a few minutes there was a guffawing peal of thunder from behind and fantastic raindrops, like tin-can tops, crashed over the rear of Mr. Shiftlet's car. Very quickly he stepped on the gas, and with his stump sticking out the window, he raced the galloping shower into Mobile. ❖

**E**

WORDS
TO
KNOW

**rue** (rōō) v. to regret

538

## Teaching Options

 **Mini Lesson** ## Vocabulary Strategy

**ANALOGIES** Remind students that they are expected to read and understand analogies. Explain that analogies are drawn from two words that are related in some way. Students need to focus on the relationship, not the individual words, to understand the analogy. Write the following analogy on the chalkboard.

mountain : height :: ocean : depth

Explain that this analogy focuses on the relationship between item (*mountain*) and characteristic (*height*).

**Application** Have students copy the following pairs of words: *farm : corn; restaurant : cook; pencil : writing;* and *car : driver.* For each pair, ask them to create an analogy, or add two words that express a similar relationship.

**Possible Responses:** *factory : automobile; theater : actor; brush : painting; airplane : pilot*

Use **Vocabulary Transparencies and Copymasters**, p. 49.

A lesson on analogies appears on p. 254 in the Pupil's Edition.

# *Thinking* through the LITERATURE

## Connect to the Literature

**1. What Do You Think?**
What is your opinion of Mr. Shiftlet? Jot down your feelings and share them with the class.

> **Comprehension Check**
> • What are Lucynell's disabilities?
> • What does Mr. Shiftlet do while living on the farm?
> • Why do the three main characters go to town together?

## Think Critically

**2.** Do you blame Mrs. Crater for what happens to Lucynell? Why or why not?

**3.** At what point did you first suspect Mr. Shiftlet of manipulating Mrs. Crater? Why do you think he is successful?

**4.** How do you interpret the story's title?

> • the road sign Mr. Shiftlet sees
> • whose life needs to be saved
> • who is a potential savior

**5.** **ACTIVE READING** **DRAWING CONCLUSIONS ABOUT CHARACTERS** Review your responses to the reading-strategy questions that you jotted down in your **READER'S NOTEBOOK.** What did you find the most striking about each of the three main characters? What conclusions can you draw about their sense of morality?

## Extend Interpretations

**6. What If?** Suppose the story ended right after Mr. Shiftlet leaves The Hot Spot and before he meets the hitchhiker. How might your perceptions of him be different?

**7. Critic's Corner** The critic Dorothy Walters notes that "the grotesque, in many of its forms, relies for effect upon a balance between the two contrary impulses of the terrible and the comic." What in O'Connor's story do you see as terrible, and what do you see as comic? Does O'Connor achieve a satisfactory balance to you?

**8. Connect to Life** In what ways does Mr. Shiftlet resemble real-life con artists you know about?

**9.** **Points of Comparison** Think about the stories by Hawthorne and Poe that you read earlier. Which character most reminds you of Mr. Shiftlet?

THE LIFE YOU SAVE MAY BE YOUR OWN **539**

## Literary Analysis

**IRONY**  As you have learned, **irony** is the contrast between what is expected and what actually exists or happens. In "The Life You Save May Be Your Own," O'Connor skillfully uses **situational irony** to emphasize the startling gap between her characters' expectations and the events that actually unfold. For example, at the end of this story, Mr. Shiftlet prays that the world's rottenness—slime—be washed away, and a rain shower soon chases *him.* **Dramatic irony** occurs when readers learn information that remains unknown to certain characters. For example, readers detect what the counter boy at The Hot Spot does not—that Lucynell, the "angel of Gawd," will be a major problem when she wakes up.

**Paired Activity** Working with a partner, find other examples of each kind of irony in the story. What view of the world does O'Connor suggest with these ironies?

**REVIEW** **CHARACTERIZATION**
Which techniques of characterization does O'Connor use most effectively in this story—physical description; presentation of a character's actions, words, or feelings; direct comments by the narrator; or the reactions of other characters? Support your answer with examples.

---

## Writing Options

1. **Letter of Opinion** A slightly different approach can be taken by having students use either today's date or a date in 1957 on their letters. Depending on the date, students should consider the appropriateness of the TV ending.

2. **Sequel: The Saga Continues** If students choose to focus on Lucynell, they need to consider her difficulty in communicating. If they focus on Shiftlet, they might want to reform him or have him begin a new deception.

3. **Points of Comparison** Draw students' attention to the surnames O'Connor gives her characters: Shiftlet—Shifty, or deceitful; shiftless. Crater—a hole created by an impact; emptiness.

## Activities & Explorations

1. **Wanted Poster** Students who like to draw might team with students who like to write in order to design a wanted poster. Remind students that there is a physical description of Shiftlet on page 529. On their posters, students might also include the kinds of people who should be particularly on the lookout for Shiftlet. Allot classroom space for students to display their posters.

2. **Points of Comparison** **To get students started on this assignment,** have them brainstorm adjectives to describe the characters they choose to portray.

## Inquiry & Research

Students should use appropriate print and nonprint resources to do their research.

---

# Choices & CHALLENGES

## Writing Options

1. **Letter of Opinion** In 1957, an adaptation of this story was broadcast on television. In the TV version, the ending was changed, according to O'Connor, "by having Shiftlet suddenly get a conscience and come back for the girl." Write a letter to the network that presented the show, either protesting or supporting this change. Give reasons for your opinion.

2. **Sequel: The Saga Continues** Extend the story by writing a brief episode revealing what happens to Lucynell after Mr. Shiftlet leaves her at The Hot Spot or what Mr. Shiftlet encounters when he reaches Mobile. Save your writing in your **Working Portfolio.**

3. **Points of Comparison** "Dr. Heidegger's Experiment" is an **allegory,** a work of literature in which people, objects, and events stand for abstract qualities, such as evil, compassion, or greed. Do you think that "The Life You Save May Be Your Own" can also be thought of as an allegory? Write your response in a comparison-and-contrast essay.

**Writing Handbook**
See page 1281: Compare and Contrast.

## Activities & Explorations

1. **Wanted Poster** By hand or with the help of a computer, improve this wanted poster for Mr. Shiftlet. Include comments on his appearance, behavior, and manipulative techniques. ~ **ART**

2. **Points of Comparison** Sketch caricatures to depict the grotesqueness of the characters in Gothic tales. Choose characters from "The Life You Save May Be Your Own" and from one of Poe's or Hawthorne's short stories in this unit. Are there similarities in your portrayals? ~ **ART**

## Inquiry & Research

1. **Con Artists** Locate information about real-life con artists and the manipulative techniques they use to dupe people. Summarize your findings in a brief report.

2. **Antisocial Personalities** Find out more about the personality traits of misfits, such as Mr. Shiftlet, in a psychology textbook and other sources. Write a case study, based on your research, that profiles the behavior of an antisocial individual.

WANTED

$$$$ REWARD $$$$
$$$$ REWARD $$$$

**MR. SHIFTLET**
For Abandoning The Daughter of Ms. Lucynell Crater. Was Last Seen Driving A Dark Green Ford.

**$$ REWARD $$**

---

# Teaching Options

## Mini Lesson Grammar

**MODIFIERS: DOUBLE NEGATIVES** **Instruction** A modifier describes or qualifies another word or phrase. Using two negative modifiers to express a single negation actually creates a meaning opposite to what the writer intends. To illustrate this point, write the following sentences on the chalkboard and have students compare their meanings.
I <u>don't</u> want <u>no</u> money for my work.
I <u>don't</u> want money for my work.
**Exercises** Ask students to identify double negatives (if any) in the following sentences. Ask them to revise the sentences by deleting one of the negative modifiers.

1. That doctor wouldn't know no more about the heart than you or me. *(wouldn't, no)*

2. I looked, but I didn't see nothing. *(didn't, nothing)*

3. I would give her up for nothing on earth. *(no double negative)*

 Use **Grammar Transparencies and Copymasters,** p. 137.

 Use McDougal Littell's **Language Network,** Chapter 7, for more instruction and practice in modifiers.

## Vocabulary in Action

**EXERCISE: ASSESSMENT PRACTICE** Write the letter of the word pair that expresses a relationship similar to that expressed by the capitalized pair.

1. LIST : TOPPLE :: (a) need : want, (b) damage : ruin, (c) laugh : cry, (d) irritate : annoy
2. GAUNT : SKELETON :: (a) tall : giant, (b) timid : lion, (c) bold : villain, (d) mountainous : hill
3. COMPOSED : EXCITED :: (a) proud : arrogant, (b) hesitant : foolish, (c) careful : skillful, (d) cowardly : brave
4. MOROSE : PARTY POOPER :: (a) sassy : smart aleck, (b) clumsy : athlete, (c) rich : hero, (d) lazy : student
5. RUE : SORROW :: (a) admire : scorn, (b) yearn : superiority, (c) trust : confidence, (d) appreciate : adoration

### Building Vocabulary

For an in-depth lesson on analogies, see page 254.

| WORDS TO KNOW | composed gaunt list | morose rue |
| --- | --- | --- |

## Flannery O'Connor
### 1925–1964

**Other Works**
*Everything That Rises Must Converge*
*A Good Man Is Hard to Find*
*The Violent Bear It Away*
*The Habit of Being: Letters*

**A Flair for Writing** Flannery O'Connor lived a short, brilliant life. Born in Savannah, Georgia, O'Connor began drawing cartoons and writing as a young girl. In her high school yearbook, she wrote that her chief hobby was "collecting rejection slips." After high school, O'Connor attended college in Georgia and the Writers' Workshop at the University of Iowa.

**Personal Triumphs** In 1950, while completing her first novel, *Wise Blood*, O'Connor learned that she was suffering from lupus, the degenerative disease that had killed her father when she was 15. O'Connor returned to Milledgeville, Georgia, to live with her mother on a farm for the last 14 years of her life. Despite her debilitating illness and the specter of an early death, O'Connor continued to write, producing two acclaimed volumes of short stories and a second novel.

**Biting Humor** As a writer, O'Connor is noted for her intense Catholic faith and her comic portrayal of grotesque characters obsessed with sin and salvation. O'Connor's grim humor is at once her writing's most disturbing feature and its strength, allowing the reader to acknowledge the severe human faults of her characters while at the same time extending them sympathy. O'Connor herself commented, "I like [my stories] better than anybody and read them over and over and laugh and laugh."

## Author Activity

**The Writer's Eye** Read O'Connor's views about writing in her book, *The Habit of Being: Letters*. Based on her comments, write the script for an interview, using a question-and-answer format. Working with a partner, create an audiotape of the interview to present to the class.

## Vocabulary in Action

1. b
2. a
3. d
4. a
5. c

## Author Activity

Have students work in pairs to create an interview script. You might suggest that students not write the interview out verbatim but instead put notes on index cards, so their interview will sound more natural on audiotape.

## Informal Assessment

**STORYBOARD** You can informally assess students' comprehension of the main events of the story and the order in which they occurred by having them create storyboards or cartoon strips that summarize the story. Students may illustrate their storyboards with sketches of key events, but all storyboards should include text or captions as well.

**RUBRIC**

3 **Full Accomplishment** Storyboard successfully focuses on key events, leaving out none that are crucial to the plot, and arranges them in the proper sequence.

2 **Substantial Accomplishment** Storyboard includes most of the key events but may leave out one or two or may confuse the order slightly.

1 **Little or Partial Accomplishment** Storyboard does not capture most key events, or it places them in the wrong sequence.

## PART 1 Reading the Prompt

Model the process of reading a prompt:

• Read through the entire prompt.

• List key words of the assignment on the board. ("analysis," "relationship between setting and characters")

• Define key words and phrases using the Strategies in Action to show how students can restate the prompt in their own words.

## PART 2 Planning an Analytical Essay

• Suggest that students begin by selecting their favorite Gothic story from each century. Encourage them to select the major character in each story who is most colorful.

• To generate ideas about how character and setting interacts, have students explain why a cheerful, ordinary person would seem out of place in a Gothic story.

• In their charts, students might note sensory details, dialogue, descriptions, and words that suggest mood.

## PART 3 Drafting Your Essay

**Introduction** Suggest that students begin by explaining what Gothic tales are. Then they can state their opinions about the relationship between the setting and characters in both works.

**Organization** Review the two common patterns for organizing an essay that compares: a subject-by-subject pattern, in which the features of one story are discussed and then those of the other story; and a feature-by-feature pattern, in which one feature of both stories is discussed and then another feature.

**Conclusion** Students may conclude that the horror in these stories comes from the decay and destruction that are reflected in both the setting and characters.

**Revision** Remind students to be sure they have clarified which story each piece of supporting evidence comes from.

## Comparing Literature: Assessment Practice

In writing assessments, you will often be asked to analyze a story in order to clarify its meaning. You are now going to practice writing an analytical essay in which you investigate the connections between two literary elements.

### PART 1 Reading the Prompt

Often you will be asked to write in response to a prompt like the one below. First, read the entire prompt carefully. Then read through it again, looking for key words that help you identify the purpose of the essay and decide how to approach it.

**Writing Prompt**

Choose a 19th-century Gothic tale and another 20th-century Gothic tale from this unit. Write a literary ~~analysis~~ that explores the relationship ❶ between the setting and the characters in both ❷ works. How do the settings reflect or shape the characters?

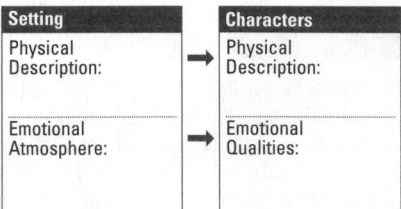

STRATEGIES
IN ACTION

❶ **Analysis** involves looking at parts in relation to a whole.

❷ Notice the two **elements** you will relate—setting and character.

### PART 2 Planning an Analytical Essay

• Pick two Gothic tales to analyze. For each story, create a diagram to organize details.

• Make notes about relevant story elements. Write physical descriptions of the setting and main character(s) in each story, and identify emotional qualities suggested by the descriptions.

• Look for connections between the elements you are analyzing.

| Setting | | Characters |
|---|---|---|
| Physical Description: | → | Physical Description: |
| Emotional Atmosphere: | → | Emotional Qualities: |

### PART 3 Drafting Your Essay

**Introduction** Begin by explaining the focus of your analysis—the relationship between setting and character in two Gothic tales. Identify the stories.

**Organization** In the body of your paper, point out resemblances between the setting and characters in one story. Then discuss setting and characters in the other story.

**Conclusion** Make a comparison between the two stories. If possible, end with a generalization about the relationship between character and setting in Gothic stories.

**Revision** Allow time to review your work for mistakes and unclear wording.

**Writing Handbook**
See page 1283: Analysis

## Billy Budd

HERMAN MELVILLE

Good and evil collide in this allegorical tale, set on the battleship *Indomitable*. Melville's short novel centers on the relationship of three men serving in the British Navy. Billy Budd, the angelic "Handsome Sailor," is pitted against the diabolical Claggart, a petty officer, who falsely accuses him of plotting a mutiny. Following a violent confrontation between these two men, Captain Vere, the commander, must uphold the truth and administer justice.

## Intruder in the Dust

WILLIAM FAULKNER

Race relations in the deep South form the backdrop of Faulkner's novel, set in his mythical Yoknapatawpha County. Lucas Beauchamp, an elderly African-American farmer, is framed for the shooting death of a white man. After his arrest, a mob gathers at the jail house, hoping for a lynching. Charles ("Chick") Mallison, a white teenager, rises to Lucas's defense and helps unravel this chilling murder mystery.

## And Even *More* . . .

### Books

**The Fall of the House of Usher and Other Stories**
EDGAR ALLAN POE
More tales of bizarre and extraordinary events.

**The Complete Stories**
FLANNERY O'CONNOR
A collection of short stories in the Southern Gothic literary tradition.

**Selected Writings of Truman Capote**
TRUMAN CAPOTE
A sampling of the critically acclaimed author's literary works, including his Gothic tale "Miriam."

### Other Media

**Rappaccini's Daughter**
Film adaptation of Hawthorne's eerie tale about an exotically beautiful young woman and the fatal flowers that bloom in her father's garden. PBS *The American Short Story* video series. (VIDEOCASSETTE)

**Intruder in the Dust**
Film adaptation of Faulkner's novel. MGM/UA Home Video. (VIDEOCASSETTE)

**The Haunting**
Film adaptation of Shirley Jackson's Gothic novel *The Haunting of Hill House*. MGM/UA Home Video. (VIDEOCASSETTE)

### American Gothic Tales

EDITED BY JOYCE CAROL OATES

Oates's anthology of haunting tales shows the far reaches of the Gothic imagination in American literature. This collection includes the short stories of nearly 50 writers from the past two

The *Electronic Library* is a CD-ROM that contains additional fiction, nonfiction, poetry, and drama for each unit in *The Language of Literature*.

These are the additional selections found in Unit 3 of the *Electronic Library* that apply to Part 2.

Edgar Allan Poe
**Hop-Frog**

Nathaniel Hawthorne
**The Minister's Black Veil**

Herman Melville
**Bartleby, the Scrivener**

Encourage students to select one of the longer selections as an opportunity to read silently with comprehension over a period of time.

## Objectives
- write a short story
- use a written text as a model for writing
- use dialogue to reveal character
- punctuate dialogue correctly

## Introducing the Workshop

**A** **Short Story** Make a three-column chart on the chalkboard and label the columns *Suspense, Humor,* and *Surprise.* Encourage students to list familiar titles and authors of short stories under each heading. Invite students to give a brief summary of their favorite short stories.

Remind students that a short story can usually be read in one sitting. While it has only one main conflict, a short story still includes the same elements as a novel—character, setting, plot, and theme. Briefly review these terms with students.

Point out that through writing a short story, students will be able to think creatively and entertain their audiences. Some students may want to consider submitting their short stories for publication, either to a commercial magazine or one that publishes student writing.

## Basics in a Box

**B** **Using the Graphic** There are three basic parts to a short story—the introduction, the body, and the conclusion. Since space is limited, it is important to establish the characters and the setting quickly, then introduce the conflict. The graphic offers suggestions for sections that students can use to draft an effective short story.

**C** **Presenting the Rubric** To better understand the assignment, students can refer to the Standards for Writing a Successful Short Story. Be sure students understand that their own short stories will be evaluated using these standards. You may also want to share with them the complete rubric, which describes several levels of proficiency.

---

# *Writing* Workshop

## Short Story

## Creating your own story. . .

**A** **From Reading to Writing** Stories such as "The Masque of the Red Death" may horrify you, while other stories delight you with humor, suspense, or surprises. You not only have the opportunity to read the stories of others, but you can also create stories of your own that will affect others. A **short story** uses characters, action, and setting to explore a conflict and create an experience that engages readers. Like all literary works worth reading, short stories entertain us and touch our feelings at the same time they teach us something worth remembering.

### For Your Portfolio

**WRITING PROMPT** Write a short story. You might choose to use a surprise ending or twist.

**Purpose:** To engage and entertain readers

**Audience:** Your classmates, friends, family, or a wider audience

### Basics in a Box

#### Short Story at a Glance

| Introduction | Body | Conclusion |
|---|---|---|
| **Sets the stage by** | **Develops the plot by** | **Finishes the story by** |
| • introducing the **characters** | • introducing the **conflict** | • resolving the **conflict** |
| • describing the **setting** | • telling a sequence of **events** | • telling the **last event** |
| | • developing **main characters** | |
| | • building toward a **climax** | |

**B**

**C** **RUBRIC** **Standards for Writing**

**A successful short story should**
- use the elements of character, setting, and plot to create a convincing world
- use techniques such as vivid sensory language, concrete details, and dialogue to create believable characters and setting
- develop and resolve a central conflict
- present a clear sequence of events
- maintain a consistent point of view

**544**    UNIT THREE    PART 2: THE DARK SIDE OF INDIVIDUALISM

---

## LESSON RESOURCES

**USING PRINT RESOURCES**
**Unit Three Resource Book**
- Prewriting, p. 82
- Drafting and Elaboration, p. 83
- Peer Response, pp. 84–85
- Revising, Editing, and Proofreading, p. 86
- Student Models, pp. 87–92
- Rubrics, p. 93

**Writing Transparencies and Copymasters**
- Writing Process Transparencies, pp. 3, 4
- Writing Style Transparencies, pp. 22, 24
- Writing Template Copymasters, p. 29

**USING MEDIA RESOURCES**
**Visit our website:**
www.mcdougallittell.com

# Analyzing a Student Model

**Sarah Mossberger
North Posey High School**

## Reunited

"You missed the turn," said Mom.

"How do you know?" Dad asked.

"Well, the sign back there said, 'Turn here for Gettysburg, 5 miles.' I'd say that was a pretty subtle hint."

We were on our way to Gettysburg and had been driving all day. Dad had taken the "scenic route." Mom was in a bad mood. Well, we all were. I was probably in the worst mood. Going to some stupid old battlefield wasn't exactly my idea of the perfect summer vacation.

⁎ ⁎ ⁎

"Come on," said Dad, "let's all stretch our legs a while. We can go to the museum first. Then we'll go on the car tour later. I want to get some fresh air before we have to get back into that car again."

We went through the museum for an hour or so. It wasn't all that bad. In fact, I learned some things from the displays. A museum attendant dressed in a Civil War-era business suit told us that several Civil War battles would be reenacted on the battlefields around the museum.

After lunch, we got back into the car to drive around the grounds. A one-way road led us to different battlefields, look-out towers, and memorials. There were areas by the sides of the road where we could park our car, get out, and walk around. From these places we watched some of the battle reenactments. . . .

About mid-afternoon, Dad pulled over for what seemed like the umpteenth time, and we got out of the car. I wandered off by myself. All of a sudden, I looked up. Standing in front of me was a boy, probably fourteen or fifteen years old. He was dressed in North colors, blue. He had on a jacket, and it was buttoned up the front. His outfit looked really old, like it was an actual soldier's uniform. It was in really good condition, and he even had a gun with him. He didn't have on a hat, so I could see his blondish-brown hair. He had bright blue eyes and was just a little taller than I am.

"Hi," I said softly, and I felt myself blush. He was kind of cute.

"Hi," he said just as softly.

"Are you working here for the summer?" I asked.

"Well, not exactly," he answered slowly.

"My name's Sarah Williams."

"Mine's Seth Roberts, and I'm looking for my brother Caleb."

"Is he dressed as a soldier too?"

"Sarah, come on," said my mom. "We're ready!"

"Coming!" I hollered. "Well, I hope you find your brother. Good luck."

"Thank you. Maybe I'll see you again."

---

## RUBRIC
### IN ACTION

**❶** This writer begins with dialogue to introduce the characters and setting.

**Other Options:**
- Start the story with the central conflict.
- Start with the first event.

**D**

**❷** Introduces a character with detailed description

**❸** Uses dialogue to introduce the story's conflict

---

## Teaching the Lesson

### Analyzing the Model

**D** **"Reunited"** The student model is a story about a high school girl's trip with her parents to the Civil War battlefields in Gettysburg, Pennsylvania. The girl meets two interesting, and somewhat mysterious, young boys.

Explain that Gettysburg is located in southern Pennsylvania, near the Maryland border. It was the site of the Battle of Gettysburg on July 1–3, 1863, which turned the outcome of the Civil War in favor of the Union. This battle was one of the bloodiest battles of the Civil War.

You may also want to mention that although it was unusual, some families, especially those in border states, had relatives fighting in both the Union and Confederate armies.

Have students read the model, then discuss the Rubric in Action. Point out the key words and phrases in the student model that correspond to the elements mentioned in the Rubric in Action.

1. Have students suggest an alternate opening based on the other options listed.

   **Possible Response:** I was standing on a slight rise, looking out at the peaceful, rolling green landscape in front of me, when all of a sudden I heard someone yelling. "Get out of here quickly!" a boy of about fourteen, dressed in North colors shouted. "Don't you know this is a battlefield?"

2. Point out to students that if their stories are historical fiction, they will have to do some research to make sure their details are accurate.

3. Ask students what the dialogue reveals about the characters.

   **Possible Response:** Both characters were shy. Seth did not answer Sarah's question directly.

---

Use McDougal Littell's **Language Network**, Chapter 22, for more instruction on writing a short story.

To engage students visually, use **Power Presentation** 5, Short Story.

**4.** Ask students to explain the reference to Casper. How is this a foreshadowing?

**Possible Response:** Casper is a friendly ghost of television and movie fame. Later in the story the narrator realizes that both boys are ghosts.

**6.** Point out that Little Round Top was the site of one of the pivotal battles that took place during the three days of fighting at Gettysburg. At Little Round Top, Joshua L. Chamberlain led his Union soldiers as they successfully held off the invading Confederates.

Ask students to summarize the plot twist in the model.

**Possible Response:** The twins were fighting on opposite sides. Caleb shot and killed Seth. Now that they have found each other, their spirits can both rest in peace.

**7.** Remind students that the conflict has to be resolved.

---

"I hope so," I said.

"Listen, if you see my brother, tell him to meet me at . . . the bottom of Little Round Top around 5:00, okay?"

"Sure, anything to help," I said, "but how will I know your brother when I see him?"

"Trust me, you'll know. We're twins," he answered.

\* \* \*

"Mom," I said as I caught up with my parents, "couldn't you see I was in the middle of a conversation?"

"You were?" asked my mom. "With who? Casper?"

"Funny, Mom. Didn't you see the boy?"

"No."

"Honestly?"

"Yes. I'm sorry if I embarrassed you."

We got back into the car and continued the tour. At every stop I watched for Seth. Later in the afternoon, I thought I saw Seth again, but this time he was wearing grey, the South's colors. I realized it must be his brother Caleb, so I walked over to him. "Are you by chance Caleb Roberts?" I asked.

"Yes! Yes, I am. Why?" he asked.

"I sort of know your brother. He wants you to meet him."

"Okay," he said. "Where?"

"At the bottom of Little Round Top at 5:00."

"Thank you," he said, his eyes shining. "I've been looking for him. Good-bye."

"Bye," I said as he walked off.

\* \* \*

At about 4:45 my family and I were at Little Round Top, and there was Seth, waiting. I looked down at my watch. It was 5:00 when Caleb walked up.

"Oh Seth, it's you! I'm so sorry! I didn't mean to shoot you. I didn't mean to kill you. And then I got hit, too. But I think that was for the best. I knew I wouldn't have been able to live with what I'd done." Seth embraced Caleb.

"Shhh, it's okay, Caleb. I know you didn't mean it. That's why I've kept looking for you. I love you, Caleb."

What did Caleb mean? He'd killed Seth and then been killed himself? How could they be dead? They were standing right there. Then it hit me—my mother hadn't seen Seth.

"Thank you, Sarah," cried Caleb.

"Yeah, thank you," said Seth. "Without you, I couldn't have found him. Thank you again. Good-bye."

"Good-bye," I said. I felt a lump in my throat. A ray of light fell onto them. As if they were floating on the beam, they slowly faded away. I began to cry, not because I was sad, but out of happiness for Seth. He had finally found his brother.

**❹** Foreshadows story twist

**❺** Maintains a consistent point of view with narrator relating the events

**❻** Spells out story twist

**❼** This writer resolves the conflict between fantastic and real with Sarah's explanation.

**Other Options:**
• End with the climax.
• Describe the setting to suggest the character's feelings.

# Writing Your Short Story

## ❶ Prewriting

*To imagine yourself inside another person . . . is what a story writer does in every piece of work . . . .*   **Eudora Welty**

As you look for ideas for your story, you might try listing interesting settings, characters, and conflicts. Then mix and match them, or ask yourself what story each might lead to. Other possible sources of writing ideas include your daydreams, news stories, or experiences from your life. See the **Idea Bank** in the margin for additional ideas. After you have chosen your story idea, follow the steps below.

### Planning Your Short Story

▶ **1. Imagine the characters and setting.** Who will be in the story and how will you show their personality traits? What setting will you use?

beginning → event 1 → event 2 → event 3 → final event/resolution

▶ **2. Think through the plot.** What are the main events? What is the conflict? Will the conflict be resolved? If so, how? You might make a sequence chart like this one to help you organize your ideas.

▶ **3. Choose a narrator.** Who will tell your story? Will the story be told from the first-person or third-person point of view?

▶ **4. Create a mood.** Will your story be frightening? humorous? mysterious?

▶ **5. Identify your goals and audience.** Are you writing for children, your peers, or a general audience?

## ❷ Drafting

Begin your story wherever you like: at the beginning, the conclusion, or the incident that triggers the conflict. You can rearrange the sections later. Many good stories begin in the middle and then go back to the beginning to provide more information. Remember, however, that the order of events must be clear.

**Flesh Out the Characters** Use **description**, **dialogue**, and **action** to make your characters real.

- Describe a character's physical appearance, habits, or talents.
- Tell what the character says and how the words are spoken.
- Show the character's actions. How does the character react to other people and events?

**Use Description to Show Rather Than Tell Your Story** For instance, instead of telling the readers that Seth and Caleb disappeared, the writer uses description to show them disappearing: "A ray of light fell onto them. As if they were floating on the beam, they slowly faded away."

## IDEA Bank

**1. Your Working Portfolio** 🗂
Build on one of the **Writing Options** you completed earlier in this unit:

- **Madeline's Retelling,** p. 498
- **Story Ending,** p. 515
- **Sequel: The Saga Continues,** p. 540

**2. A Picture Tells 1,000 Words**
Look at paintings or photographs and ask yourself what story a picture is telling or might tell.

**3. What If?**
Set your imagination free by asking "What if?" questions. What if time travel were possible? What if guns magically disappeared?

**Have a question?**

See the **Writing Handbook**

Narrative Writing, pp. 1279–1280

---

# Guiding Student Writing

## Prewriting

### Choosing a Story Idea
If after reading the Idea Bank students are having difficulty choosing a story idea, suggest they try the following:

- Think about an event that really happened. Consider questions such as the following: What if the event ended differently? How would the event change if it happened in the past or in the future?
- Read several newspaper headlines. Brainstorm ideas for stories that could fit the headlines.
- Think of a favorite book or story character. Brainstorm other settings and events for that character.

### Planning the Short Story
**2.** You may want to have students write the beginning, the resolution, and each event on a separate index card.

**3.** Review the different points of view if necessary.

**4.** Have students brainstorm a list of possible moods, then choose one. Students can then make another list of words relating to the mood they choose. These words may be used in the story.

### Drafting
Before students begin their drafts, encourage them to try out several different arrangements of the section index cards they made previously.

### Flesh Out Characters
Have pairs of students write detailed descriptions of someone they know to practice describing a character. Encourage students to become more observant of the appearances, mannerisms, and words of the people around them.

### Use Description to Show Rather Than Tell Your Story
Suggest that students read through favorite short stories and novels to find examples of showing instead of telling. You may want to invite students to copy good examples on index cards, cite the source, and display the cards on a bulletin board.

## Drafting

### Organize the Events

Point out that although there is no one right way to organize a story, the events must be arranged in a way that makes sense to the reader. For example, the writer of the student model could have begun with a flashback instead of relating the events in chronological order. She could have started at the end, where she describes the boys fading away, then written about the experience of meeting them. Have students suggest how using a flashback would change the effect of the student model.

## Revising

### USING DIALOGUE

Remind students that dialogue—what a character says and how he or she says it—will reveal something about their characters. Ask students what the dialogue between the mother and daughter might reveal about each.

## Editing and Proofreading

### PUNCTUATING DIALOGUE

Remind students that certain punctuation rules apply when writing dialogue. Tell students to start a new paragraph every time the speaker changes. The first word in the sentence begins with a capital letter. End punctuation is used in the same way as with sentences that are not in the dialogue. See the Grammar Mini Lesson on T549 for more information on using quotation marks with dialogue.

Errors in the example include the following:

- A new paragraph is needed after the word *asked* because the speaker changes from the narrator to the narrator's mother.

- The word *No* is used as a complete sentence and must be followed by a period. The word *what* should be capitalized since it begins the next sentence.

- Since the narrator is quoting the boy within her own speech, single quotation marks are needed to set off the boy's words.

## Reflecting

 Have students write a brief note describing and assessing their writing experience. They can clip their assessment to their short story and place both in their working portfolios.

UNIT THREE   PART 2

---

**Need revising help?**

Review the **Rubric,** p. 544

Consider **peer reader** comments

Check **Revision Guidelines,** p. 1269

**Daunted by punctuating dialogue?**

See the **Grammar Handbook,** p. 1327

**Publishing IDEAS**

- Submit your story to the school literary magazine. or a popular magazine for teens.

- Adapt your story to make a reader's theater script and present it with the help of classmates.

**More Online: Publishing Options** www.mcdougallittell.com

---

**Organize the Events** A natural way to organize events in a story is to use **chronological order**—the order in which the events occur. Another choice is to use **flashback**—a recalling of past events After the flashback, return to the present and continue telling the story. Just be sure that the sequence of events and the connections between ideas are clear.

**Ask Your Peer Reader**

- What is the central conflict in my story?
- How would you describe the main character?
- When and where does the story take place?
- Was there any part that was hard to follow? What would make it clearer?

### ❸ Revising

**TARGET SKILL ▶ USING DIALOGUE** Dialogue can add suspense to your story and help readers get to know your characters. Good dialogue shows the most important things characters say to each other. Notice how the writer sometimes avoided direct responses, such as "yes" and "no," to keep the dialogue moving.

> "Mom," I said as I caught up with my parents, "couldn't you see I was in the middle of a conversation?"
>
> You were? asked
> "~~No,~~" ~~said~~ my mom. "With who? Casper?"
>
> Funny Mom
> "~~No.~~ Didn't you see the boy?"

### ❹ Editing and Proofreading

**TARGET SKILL ▶ PUNCTUATING DIALOGUE** In writing dialogue, remember to start a new paragraph each time the speaker changes. Also, use single quotation marks to indicate a quote within a quote. Here is how the writer above used this technique in her story:

> "Didn't you see the boy?" I asked. ¶My mother looked puzzled, too.
>
> "No, what did he say?"
>
> "He wants me to find his brother. He said, 'Tell him to meet me at the bottom of Little Round Top around 5:00.'"

### ❺ Reflecting

**FOR YOUR WORKING PORTFOLIO** How did you decide to end your story? What other endings did you consider, and why did you pick the one you did? Attach your answers to your finished work. Save your short story in your **Working Portfolio.**

Read this passage from the first draft of a short story. The underlined sections may include the following kinds of errors:

- **lack of pronoun-antecedent agreement**
- **correctly written sentences that should be combined**
- **punctuation errors**
- **misplaced modifiers**

For each underlined section, choose the revision that most improves the writing.

---

Ms. Padrone ran her hardware store like a prison ward. <u>Their</u> rules were
(1)
strict and unbending. "One sale item per customer," read one sign. "No

layaways," read another. <u>"No exceptions," said Ms. Padrone</u>
(2)

<u>"Nate, said Dad, one windy autumn day, "we</u> need two new rakes. Please
(3)
run down to Padrone's and buy a couple." <u>I tried to get out of it. I couldn't get</u>
(4)
out of it.

<u>So there I stood asking for two rakes in front of the counter.</u> Just my luck,
(5)
rakes were on sale.

"You want TWO rakes?" Ms. Padrone snapped. "Well, you can't have <u>it!</u> The
(6)
sign says only one per customer and that's final."

---

**1. A.** Its
   **B.** His
   **C.** Her
   **D.** Correct as is

**2. A.** "No exceptions", said
   **B.** "No exceptions" said
   **C.** "No exceptions, said
   **D.** Correct as is

**3. A.** "Nate," said Dad, one windy autumn day, "we
   **B.** "Nate said Dad, one windy autumn day, "we
   **C.** "Nate", said Dad, one windy autumn day, we
   **D.** Correct as is

**4. A.** I tried to get out of it, but I couldn't.
   **B.** I tried to get out of it, I couldn't get out of it.
   **C.** I tried to get out of it, I couldn't.
   **D.** Correct as is

**5. A.** So asking for two rakes there, I stood in front of the counter.
   **B.** So there I stood, in front of the counter, asking for two rakes.
   **C.** So I asked for two rakes in front of the counter, and there I stood.
   **D.** Correct as is

**6. A.** theirs.
   **B.** this!
   **C.** them!
   **D.** Correct as is

**Need extra help?**

See the **Grammar Handbook:**

Pronoun Agreement, p. 1307

Punctuation Chart, p. 1327

Writing Complete Sentences, p. 1323

Using Modifiers Correctly, p. 1313

---

**Assessment Practice**
Guide students in choosing the correct answers by showing them how to eliminate incorrect choices for the first question.

A. The pronoun *Its* refers back to the proper noun Mrs. Padrone in the previous sentence. Since Mrs. Padrone is feminine, the neutral pronoun *its* is incorrect.

B. Mrs. Padrone is feminine, so the masculine pronoun *his* is incorrect.

D. The plural pronoun *their* is incorrect.

C. This choice is correct. *Her* is a singular feminine pronoun and agrees with its antecedent, Mrs. Padrone.

**Answers:**
**1.** C; **2.** D; **3.** A; **4.** A; **5.** B; **6.** C

---

 **Grammar**

### PUNCTUATING QUOTATIONS

**Instruction** Quotation marks are used at the beginning and end of a direct quotation.

- If a direct quotation is separated by explanatory words, begin the second part of the quotation with a lower case letter. If the second part of the quotation is a sentence, capitalize the first letter.
- Single quotation marks are used to indicate a quote within a quote.

**Activity** Write these sentences on the chalkboard. Invite volunteers to add quotation marks

and any other punctuation or capitalization that is needed.

I don't know where the car keys are, said my brother, do you?

I think Mom said, they're on the counter in the kitchen, I yelled from upstairs.

**Correct:** "I don't know where the car keys are," said my brother. "Do you?"

**Correct:** "I think Mom said, 'They're on the counter in the kitchen,'" I yelled from upstairs.

 Use McDougal Littell's *Language Network*, Chapter 10, for more instruction and practice in punctuating quotations.

## Objectives

- research word origins as an aid to understanding meanings
- apply meanings of word roots and affixes to determine the meanings of related words
- understand how to use word parts and word families to build vocabulary
- research word origins as an aid to understanding derivations
- research word origins as an aid to spelling

## EXERCISE

1. *Venerable* derives from Latin *venerārī*, "to worship or reverence" (and includes the suffix *-able*, "worthy of"), and something that is venerable is worthy of reverence or admiring deference.

2. *Shrouded* derives from Old English *scrūd*, "garment," and something that is shrouded is covered or veiled, as a body is by a garment.

3. *Disconcert* derives from French *des-*, "do the opposite of," and *concerter*, "to bring into agreement," and to disconcert a person or thing is to throw the person or thing into a state of disorder or confusion.

4. *Termination* derives from Latin *termināre*, "end" (and includes the suffix *-ation*, "action or process"), and termination is an ending or the conclusion of something.

5. *Magnificence* derives from Latin *magnificentia*, "nobility or greatness of character" (itself deriving from *magnus*, "great"), and magnificence is a greatness or splendor, especially of surroundings or dress.

6. *Divulge* derives from Latin *dis-*, "completely" and *vulgāre*, "to make known," and to divulge is to make public.

7. *Transient* derives from Latin *trāns-*, "across," and *īre*, "to go," and something that is transient passes by or goes away quickly.

8. *Dispute* derives from Latin *disputāre*, "to discuss" (itself deriving from *dis-*, "apart," and *putāre*, "to think or calculate"), and to dispute is to discuss in an argumentative way.

9. *Virulent* derives from Latin *vīrulentus*, "poisonous" (itself deriving from *vīrus*, "poison"), and something that is virulent is poisonous or bitterly harmful like a poison.

10. *Circumvent* derives from Latin *circum-*, "around," and *venīre*, "to come," and to circumvent something is to go around it or avoid it.

## *Finding the Sources of Words*

Exploring word histories can help you remember words' meanings and expand your understanding of the English language. For example, in the excerpt on the right, Edgar Allan Poe used the word *grotesque* to mean "having a bizarre, fantastic appearance," and the history of the word sheds a good deal of light on how it came to have that meaning.

The adjective *grotesque* has been part of the English language for about 400 years. During the Renaissance, when ancient Roman buildings were being excavated in Italy, the Italians used the word *grotte*, meaning "caves," to refer to the subterranean chambers they uncovered. The fanciful wall paintings that were found in the chambers were called *pitture grottesche* (literally "cave paintings") and the adjective came to be applied to a similarly fanciful style of contemporary art. The word passed into French in the form *grotesque* and thence into English, gradually acquiring the extended senses of "distorting natural forms in an absurd or ugly way" and "exotic or bizarre in appearance."

> He had directed, in great part, the movable embellishments of the seven chambers, upon occasion of this great *fête;* and it was his own guiding taste which had given character to the masqueraders. Be sure they were grotesque. —Edgar Allan Poe, "The Masque of the Red Death"

## Strategies for Building Vocabulary

The strategies that follow can help you use information about words' etymology—their origin and history—as a tool for inferring meanings, enriching vocabulary, and improving spelling.

❶ **Word Parts** Learning the meanings of word parts such as affixes and roots can give you insights into words' meanings. When trying to determine the meaning of a word, first break the word into its parts, then combine the meanings of the parts to produce a possible definition, as in this example:

embellishment
word parts
em + bellish + ment
Latin origins
in- + bellus + -mentum
meanings of parts
"to cause to be" + "beautiful" + "a means of"
definition
**something that beautifies**

❷ **Word Families** Words derived from a single linguistic "ancestor" form what is known as a word family. If you know the meaning of one word in such a family, you can often figure out the meanings of other words in the family. For example, the word *tangible* contains the root of the Latin word *tangere*, "to touch." The following list shows some other members of the *tangere* family.

**Words Derived from Latin *Tangere***

| English Word | Meaning |
|---|---|
| tangent | touching at a single point |
| tangible | able to be perceived by the sense of touch |
| tact | skill and grace in dealing with others |
| tactile | relating to the sense of touch |
| contact | a coming together or touching |
| contagious | communicable by contact |

❸ **Spelling** In many cases, a knowledge of word families can help you spell more accurately. The word *perspiration*, for example, contains *spir*, the root of the Latin verb *spīrāre*, "to blow or breathe." This root is also found in *spirit*, *transpire*, *inspire*, *respiration*, and *inspiration*. Notice that the root's spelling is the same in all of the words, even though its pronunciation varies.

**EXERCISE** Use a dictionary to trace the origin of each of these words. Then explain how the word's etymology relates to its meaning.

1. venerable
2. shrouded
3. disconcert
4. termination
5. magnificence
6. divulge
7. transient
8. dispute
9. virulent
10. circumvent

## Grammar from Literature

Adverbs provide a way to improve precision in your writing. They describe, clarify, and qualify. Notice how Edgar Allan Poe uses adverbs both to add rhythm to his writing and to tell how and when actions occur.

> adverb       adverb
> **While I nodded, nearly napping, suddenly there came a tapping,**
> adverb
> **As of someone gently rapping, rapping on my chamber door.**
> —Edgar Allan Poe, "The Raven"

Adverbs modify not only verbs; they can be used to qualify adjectives and other adverbs. By carefully choosing adverbs, Flannery O'Conner is able to make her description very exact.

> adverbs
> **The daughter was leaning very far down, hanging her**
> adverb
> **head almost between her knees.**
> —Flannery O'Connor, "The Life You Save May Be Your Own"

Adverbs can take the form of prepositional phrases. The following sentence contains a pair of prepositional phrases that tell where Miss Emily died.

> prepositional phrases
> **She died in one of the downstairs rooms, in a heavy walnut bed with a curtain.**
> —William Faulkner, "A Rose for Emily"

Infinitive phrases can also function as adverbs. In the sentence below, an infinitive phrase modifies the verb *invited*.

> **That very singular man, old Dr. Heidegger, once**
> infinitive phrase
> **invited four venerable friends to meet him in his study.**
> —Nathaniel Hawthorne, "Dr. Heidegger's Experiment"

**Using Adverbs in Your Writing** When you revise, examine your verbs and modifiers. Would the addition of an adverb that tells *how, when,* or *where* make your writing more precise or accurate? Notice the difference adverbs make in this portion of a synopsis of "A Rose for Emily."

> LACKING DETAIL
> **Emily was poor. She was seeing a burly construction foreman. Rumors began. No one could have guessed the truth.**
>
> REVISED USING ADVERBS
> **After her father's death, Emily was somewhat poor. Soon, she was regularly seeing a rather burly construction foreman. In no time, rumors began to fly around town about their relationship. No one, however, could have ever guessed the truth.**

**Usage Tip** Remember, only adverbs can modify adjectives and other adverbs. Confusion about this fact can lead to errors in usage.

> INCORRECT       adjective
> **Poe is a master at creating real scary stories.**
> CORRECT       adverb
> **Poe is a master at creating really scary stories.**

**WRITING EXERCISE** Rewrite these sentences, adding adverbs and adverb phrases that modify the underlined words. Follow the directions in parentheses.

1. The cut-glass vase <u>stands</u> in the sunlight. (Tell where it stands.)
2. Dr. Heidegger <u>pours</u> the magical water. (Add two adverb elements. Tell how and where he pours the water.)
3. Dr. Heidegger nods as his guests <u>leap</u> energetically. (Add two adverb elements. Tell how he nods and where the guests leap.)
4. The ancient rose is <u>dry</u> and <u>faded.</u> (Add three adverb elements. Tell when and how the rose is dry and how it is faded.)
5. Now that they are old again, the guests are <u>anxious.</u> (Add an infinitive phrase that tells how or for what the guests are anxious.)

**PROOFREADING EXERCISE** Rewrite these sentences, correcting errors in usage. If a sentence contains no error, write *Correct.*

1. Hawthorne explores some real interesting aspects of human nature.
2. The revelers were near exhausted by the end of the ball.
3. The guests found the guest who resembled a victim of the Red Death awful frightening.
4. Gothic writers certainly achieve a mood of gloom.
5. If you haven't read "The Fall of the House of Usher," you sure should.

### Objectives

- use adverbs to add rhythm to writing and to create exact descriptions
- recognize how prepositional phrases and infinitive phrases can function as adverbs
- revise drafts by examining verbs and modifiers to make writing more precise and accurate
- use adverbs to modify adjectives and other adverbs

### WRITING EXERCISE

Answers will vary. **Possible Responses** are given.

1. The cut-glass vase stands in the sunlight <u>on a small round table</u>.
2. Dr. Heidegger <u>slowly</u> pours the magical water <u>into the glass</u>.
3. Dr. Heidegger nods <u>sadly</u> as his guests leap energetically <u>about his study</u>.
4. The ancient rose is <u>once again</u> dry <u>to the touch</u> and faded <u>with age</u>.
5. Now that they are old again, the guests are anxious <u>to begin their journey</u>.

### PROOFREADING EXERCISE

1. Hawthorne explores some <u>really</u> interesting aspects of human nature.
2. The revelers were <u>nearly</u> exhausted by the end of the ball.
3. The guests found the guest who resembled a victim of the Red Death <u>awfully</u> frightening.
4. Correct
5. If you haven't read "The Fall of the House of Usher," you <u>surely</u> should.

## Objectives

- reflect on and assess understanding of the unit
- demonstrate an understanding of the American philosophy of individualism
- demonstrate an understanding of form in poetry
- assess and build portfolios

## Reflecting on the Unit

| OPTION 1 |

To get students started, have them review the selections and take notes on the characteristics of romantic and transcendentalist characters versus Gothic characters. Students should consider both internal and external characteristics. Placing their character in a setting will enhance their descriptions or portraits.

| OPTION 2 |

A successful response will

- include writers from both centuries and from both parts of the unit.
- accurately represent the views of each writer.
- accurately interpret Thoreau's views.

| OPTION 3 |

A successful response will

- make reasonable generalizations about the views of romantic and transcendentalist writers and the views of Gothic writers
- compare and contrast students' own beliefs with those of the romantic and transcendentalist writers and the Gothic writers.
- take a stand about good and evil and support it with examples from literature and real life.

## Self Assessment

Ask students to support their matching of authors with characteristics of American individualism. Students should provide relevant examples from each writer's work.

---

# The Spirit of Individualism

Do you feel you have gained a deeper understanding of the American philosophy of individualism as it developed in the 19th century? Has reading 19th-century literature sharpened your reading skills? To explore what you've learned from the selections in this unit, choose one or more of the options in each of the following sections.

Detail of *The Wanderer* (1818), Caspar David Friedrich, Kunsthalle, Hamburg, Germany, Bridgeman/Art Resource, New York.

## Reflecting on the Unit

| OPTION 1 |

**The Concept of the Individual** The selections in this unit reflect two different concepts of the individual. To illustrate the difference, create two portraits of individuals—one representing the romantic and transcendentalist view, the other representing the Gothic view. Choose your own medium for the portrait: an illustration, an oral description, a written character sketch, or any combination of these.

| OPTION 2 |

**Roundtable Discussion** Reread the quotation from Thoreau that begins this unit (page 336). Do you think the other writers in this unit—especially the 20th-century writers—would agree with Thoreau? Get together with a group of five classmates, with each student choosing a writer from the unit to role-play. Make sure your group represents writers from both centuries and from both parts of the unit. Then participate in a group discussion about individual freedom, evaluating Thoreau's statement from the point of view of the writer you are playing. During the discussion, pay attention to the writers' different attitudes toward individual freedom.

| OPTION 3 |

**Visions of Good and Evil** Compare and contrast the portrayals of human nature in the two parts of the unit: "Celebrations of the Self" and "The Dark Side of Individualism." What generalizations about the views of romantic and transcendentalist writers can you infer from the selections in Part 1? Compile a list of them, then come up with a similar list for the Gothic writers in Part 2. Write a few paragraphs explaining which vision of human nature you agree with more.

**552**   UNIT THREE   THE SPIRIT OF INDIVIDUALISM

## Self ASSESSMENT

**READER'S NOTEBOOK**

To show how your understanding has deepened as you have read this unit, create a cluster diagram or list in which you identify about five key characteristics of American individualism. For each characteristic, indicate which of the writers represented in the unit would consider it admirable.

## Reviewing Literary Concepts

OPTION 1

**Analyzing Imagery** The 19th-century writers represented in this unit used imagery for a variety of purposes: to illustrate ideas; to enhance descriptions of character and setting; to create moods; to reflect psychological realities—the inner workings of characters' minds. Go back through the selections in the unit and identify, in a chart like the one shown, which of these purposes each writer's imagery primarily serves.

| Selection | Primary Use of Imagery | Example of Imagery |
|-----------|------------------------|--------------------|
| "A Psalm of Life" | to illustrate ideas | "Footprints on the sands of time" (line 28) |
| "The Devil and Tom Walker" | to enhance description and to create mood | "The swamp was thickly grown with great gloomy pines and hemlocks . . ." (pp. 351-352) |

OPTION 2

**Understanding Form in Poetry** With a partner, review all the poems in the unit (including the Literary Links and Links Across Cultures) and classify them. Which are traditional in form, written in stanzas with a regular meter and rhyme scheme? Which are nontraditional in form? Of the nontraditional poems, which are written in free verse? Which would you label *experimental,* and why? After you classify the poems, draw conclusions about the strengths and weaknesses of traditional and nontraditional forms. What is gained or lost by using each form? Which form do you prefer?

## Building Your Portfolio

- **Writing Options** Many of the Writing Options in this unit asked you to give your personal response to a writer's ideas. Choose the two responses which you believe were the most thorough and interesting examinations of a writer's ideas. Write a cover note explaining your choices, and place these pieces in your **Presentation Portfolio.**

- **Writing Workshops** In this unit you wrote a Reflective Essay about a learning experience. You also wrote a Short Story. Which do you think was a more successful piece of writing, and why? Attach a note explaining your evaluation, and put the work in your **Presentation Portfolio.**

- **Additional Activities** Review the assignments you completed under **Activities & Explorations** and **Inquiry & Research.** Keep a record in your portfolio of any assignments that you think are worthy of expanding into a larger project.

### Self ASSESSMENT

**READER'S NOTEBOOK**

From the following list of literary terms discussed in this unit, select the ones that you think you need to know more about. Jot down those terms and their definitions. Refer to the **Glossary of Literary Terms** (page 1342).

| | |
|---|---|
| narrator | Gothic |
| omniscient narrator | allegory |
| aphorism | end rhyme |
| essay | internal rhyme |
| paradox | mood |
| nature writing | foreshadowing |
| catalog | characterization |
| repetition | flashback |
| parallelism | situational irony |
| speaker | dramatic irony |
| humor | |

### Self ASSESSMENT

Look over the pieces you have added to your **Presentation Portfolio** so far. Is there enough variety in the writing and activities you've selected? Make a note of ways to add more diversity as the year goes on.

### Setting GOALS

Jot down ideas or issues that you'd like to explore further as you read literature from the second half of the 19th century in the next unit.

---

## Reviewing Literary Concepts

OPTION 1

Use the Unit Three Resource Book p. 96 to provide students with a ready made, full depth chart for analyzing imagery.

OPTION 2

A successful response will

- correctly classify all poems in the unit as traditional or nontraditional.
- correctly identify which poems are written in free verse.
- identify those poems the student feels are experimental and why.
- decide the strengths and weaknesses of traditional and nontraditional forms.
- develop and discuss opinions about the nature of the forms and explain personal preference, if any, for either form.

## Building Your Portfolio

Students will use their Presentation Portfolios to file what they consider their highest quality work—the very best projects and activities from their Working Portfolios

For more information on using and assessing portfolios, see the *Teacher's Guide to Assessment and Portfolio Use* p. 53.

## Conflict and Expansion

The selections in Unit Four explore two great conflicts that greatly affected the American character: the conflict over slavery that culminated in our nation's bloodiest war, and the conflict between white settlers moving westward and the peoples they would dispossess. The unit is divided into two parts to better represent the dramatic conflicts of the era.

### Part 1

**A House Divided** The literature in this part of the unit explores the realities of slavery and the terrors of the Civil War. The selections in the **Traditions Across Time** section show how the civil rights movement unfolded from the events of more than a hundred years before.

### Part 2

**Tricksters and Trailblazers** The works in this section show how westward expansion occasioned a shift in focus to new problems and future challenges. An **Author Study** on Mark Twain examines his contributions to American literature. The other selections focus on the enormous changes of post-Civil War America—changes in the lives of Native Americans, settlers, pioneers, and women. The selections in **Traditions Across Time** showcase 20th-century literature of the West.

# CONFLICT and EXPANSION

**W**e all declare for liberty; but in using the same word we do not mean the same thing.

Abraham Lincoln
*16th president
of the
United States*

**I**f the Indians had tried to make the whites live like them, the whites would have resisted, and it was the same way with many Indians.

Wamditanka
*(Big Eagle)
Santee Sioux*

554

 **Mini Lesson** ## Viewing and Representing

*Pictorial quilt*
**by Harriet Powers**

**ART APPRECIATION**

**Instruction** Quilting is one of the oldest art forms. Ancient Chinese and Russians wore quilted garments for protection and warmth; the Saracens wore quilted clothing as armor in the Crusades. English and Dutch settlers brought the art of quilting to America. Because of a scarcity of sewing materials and the lack of other means of artistic expression, pioneer women turned to quilting to create art. They produced lavish and inventive designs. As late as 1883, nearly 75 percent of the beds in the United States were covered with handmade quilts.

American quilters often told stories in their quilts, using colors, shapes, forms, and texture as their tools.

Pictorial quilt (1895–1898), Harriet Powers. Pieced and appliquéd cotton embroidered with plain and metallic yarns, 69″ × 105″, bequest of Maxim Karolik, courtesy of Museum of Fine Arts, Boston.

555

## Making Connections

To help students explore connections among the art, the quotation, and the unit theme, have them consider the following questions.

**Ask: Compare the two quotations. What does each quotation reveal about the importance of point of view?**

**Possible Response:** The quotations complement each other because both point out that every group looks at an issue from its own point of view, which is influenced by self-interest and experience.

**Ask: Do you think American life is a "melting pot" or a "glorious quilt" like the one on this page?**

**Possible Responses:** It is like a melting pot because each generation loses more of its distinct cultural characteristics and gains those that are unique to the United States. It is like a quilt because each person's heritage remains separate, yet we are all stitched together by the common thread of American life.

**Ask: How do the quotations fit in with the unit theme as defined by the unit title?**

**Possible Response:** Both quotations suggest that a root cause of 19th-century conflicts was differing points of view. The quote by Wamditanka gives a Native American point of view on the conflicts that resulted from westward expansion of white settlements.

---

Use the following questions to help develop students' visual literacy.

**Identify some of the shapes in the quilt—what objects do they represent?**

**Possible Responses:** people, animals, celestial bodies such as sun, moon, and stars

**Ask them to identify some of the Biblical stories represented in the work.**

**Possible Responses:** the story of Jonah, the story of the Garden of Eden, the story of Noah's Ark, the Crucifixion, the Nativity

| Features and Selections | Literary Analysis | Reading and Critical Thinking | Writing Opportunities | | |
|---|---|---|---|---|---|
| **Conflict and Expansion**<br>**Time Line**<br>**Historical Background/**<br>**A House Divided** | | Voices from the Times, 559, 633<br>Choosing Quotations, 622 | | | |
| SLAVE NARRATIVE<br>*from* Narrative of the Life of Frederick Douglass, an American Slave | Autobiography and Style, 562, 571 | Author's Purpose, 562, 571<br><br>Informal Assess., 569<br>CCL: History, 570 | Closing Statement, 572<br>Antislavery Editorial, 572<br>Comparison, 572<br>Autobiographical Sketch | | |
| POETRY<br>Stanzas on Freedom<br>Free Labor | Symbol, 574, 578 | Protest Poetry, 574, 578<br><br>Informal Assess., 577 | New Stanza, 579<br><br>Protest Poem, 579 | | |
| SHORT STORY<br>An Occurrence at Owl Creek Bridge<br><br>Literary Link<br>Letter to Sarah Ballou | Point of View, 580, 591 | Analyzing Structure, 580, 591<br>Self-Assess., 589 | Evaluation of Bierce, 592<br><br>Comparison Essay, 592 | | |
| SHORT STORY<br>A Mystery of Heroism | Naturalism, 593, 602<br><br>Review: Irony, 602 | Visualizing, 593, 602<br><br>Author Activity, 604<br>Test Practice, 604 | Letter Home, 603<br>Literary Analysis, 603<br><br>Different Ending, 603 | | |
| SPEECH<br>The Gettysburg Address | Style, 605, 607 | Interpreting Historical Context, 605, 607 | Modern Paraphrase, 608<br>Letter to Lincoln, 608 | | |
| AUTOBIOGRAPHY<br>**Comparing Literature**<br>*from* Coming of Age in Mississippi<br><br>Literary Link<br>Frederick Douglass | Eyewitness Report, 609, 616 | Chronological Order, 609, 616<br>Author Activity, 617<br>Informal Assess., 614 | Mother's Letter, 617<br><br>Points of Comparison, 617<br>Eyewitness Account, 617 | | |
| POETRY<br>Ballad of Birmingham | Ballads, 618, 620<br><br>Test Practice, 619 | Narrative Poetry, 618, 620<br><br>Author Activity, 621 | Original Ballad, 621<br>Points of Comparison, 621 | | |
| Comparing Literature<br>**Assessment Practice** | Compare and Contrast Literary Selections, 622 | Reading the Prompt, 622 | Comparison-Contrast Essay, 622 | | |
| Writing Workshop: Literary<br>  **Interpretation**<br>**Assessment Practice**<br>**Building Vocabulary**<br>**Sentence Crafting** | Analyzing a Student Model, 625 | | Literary Interpretation, 624 | | |

| | | | | | |
|---|---|---|---|---|---|
| **Learning the Language of Literature**<br>Setting in Regional Literature | Setting in Regional Literature, 636 | Strategies for Reading, 637 | | | |
| FOLK TALE<br>The Indian and the Hundred Cows / El indito de las cien vacas | Cuento, 638, 643 | Theme, 638, 643<br>Informal Assess., 642 | Sermon on Charity, 644<br><br>Comic Tale, 644 | | |

LEGEND    **DLS – Daily Language SkillBuilder**<br>               **CCL – Cross Curricular Link**        **Green type – Teacher's Edition**

| Features and Selections | Literary Analysis | Reading and Critical Thinking | Writing Opportunities | |
|---|---|---|---|---|
| **FOLK TALE** <br> High Horse's Courting <br> *from* Black Elk Speaks <br><br> **Literary Link** <br> I Will Fight No More | Oral Literature, 645, 652 | Identifying Author's Purpose, 645, 652 <br> Test Practice, 653 | Modernizing a Story, 653 | |
| **AUTHOR STUDY** <br> **Mark Twain** | | | | |
| **AUTOBIOGRAPHY** <br> *from* The Autobiography of Mark Twain | Irony, 658, 667 | Predicting, 658, 667 <br><br> Informal Assess., 665 | Screenplay Script, 668 <br><br> Instruction Manual, 668 <br> Newspaper Report, 668 | |
| **MEMOIR** <br> *from* Life on the Mississippi | Description, 669, 676 | Visualizing, 669, 676 <br> Workplace Link, 672 <br> Informal Assess., 675 | Diary Entry, 677 <br><br> Magazine Article, 677 | |
| **SHORT STORY** <br> The Notorious Jumping Frog of Calaveras County <br> **NEWSPAPER ARTICLE** <br> The First Jumping Frog | Tall Tale, 679, 685 | Understanding Dialect, 679, 685 | Stranger's Tale, 687 <br> Local Storytelling, 687 <br> Dialects Today, 687 <br> Performance Review, 687 | |
| **Author's Style** <br> Author Study Project | Analysis of Style, 686 | | Imitating Style, 686 <br> Changing Style, 686 | |
| **SHORT STORY** <br> A Wagner Matinee <br><br> **Related Reading** <br> Letters of a Woman Homesteader | Setting, 688, 697 <br><br> Primary Source, 700 | Conclusions About Character, 688, 697 <br> Informal Assess., 696 <br> Evaluating an Argument, 700 | Cause / Effect Analysis, 698 <br> Telegram from Boston, 698 <br> Interview, 698 | |
| **Comparing Literature** <br> The Legend of Gregorio Cortez | Legend, 702, 718 | Judgments About Text, 702, 718 <br> Informal Assess., 717 | Farewell Letter, 719 <br><br> Points of Comparison, 719 <br> Workplace Link, 716 | |
| **Comparing Literature** <br> **Assessment Practice** | Evaluate a Literary Work, 720 | Reading the Prompt, 720 | Evaluative Essay, 720 | |
| **Communication Workshop:** <br> **Storytelling** <br> **Assessment Practice** <br> **Building Vocabulary** <br> **Sentence Crafting** | | Analyze a Storytelling Script, 724 | | |
| **Reflect and Assess** <br> **Conflict and Expansion** | Reviewing Literary Concepts, 731 | What Is Liberty? 730 | Irrepressible Conflicts, 730 | |
| **Reading and Writing for Assessment** | Test-Taking Strategies, 732–737 | | | |

LEGEND    DLS – Daily Language SkillBuilder <br>          CCL – Cross Curricular Link         Green type – Teacher's Edition

# UNIT FOUR
# RESOURCE MANAGEMENT GUIDE
## PART 1

To introduce the theme/literary period of this unit, use Fine Art Transparencies T26–28 in the Communications Transparencies and Copymasters.

| | Unit Resource Book | Assessment | Integrated Technology and Media | **Additional Support**<br>Literary Analysis Transparencies |
|---|---|---|---|---|
| *from* **Narrative of the Life of Frederick Douglass, an American Slave**<br>*pp. 562–573* | • Summary p. 4<br>• Active Reading p. 5<br>• Literary Analysis p. 6<br>• Words to Know p. 7<br>• Selection Quiz p. 8 | • Selection Test, Formal Assessment pp. 105–106<br>⊙ Test Generator | ◯ Audio Library<br><br>◔ Research Starter www.mcdougallittell.com | • Style, Voice T23 |
| **Stanzas on Freedom**<br>**Free Labor**<br>*pp. 574–579* | • Active Reading p. 9<br>• Literary Analysis p. 10 | • Selection Test, Formal Assessment pp. 107–108<br>⊙ Test Generator | ◯ Audio Library | |
| **An Occurrence at Owl Creek Bridge**<br>*pp. 580–592* | • Summary p. 11<br>• Active Reading p. 12<br>• Literary Analysis p. 13<br>• Words to Know p. 14<br>• Selection Quiz p. 15 | • Selection Test, Formal Assessment pp. 109–110<br>⊙ Test Generator | ◯ Audio Library | • Point of View T20 |
| **A Mystery of Heroism**<br>*pp. 593–604* | • Summary p. 16<br>• Active Reading p. 17<br>• Literary Analysis p. 18<br>• Words to Know p. 19<br>• Selection Quiz p. 20 | • Selection Test, Formal Assessment pp. 111–112<br>⊙ Test Generator | ◯ Audio Library<br>◔ Research Starter www.mcdougallittell.com | |
| **The Gettysburg Address**<br>*pp. 605–608* | • Summary p. 21<br>• Active Reading p. 22<br>• Literary Analysis p. 23<br>• Words to Know p. 24<br>• Selection Quiz p. 25 | • Selection Test, Formal Assessment pp. 113–114<br>⊙ Test Generator | ◯ Audio Library | • Style, Voice T23 |
| *from* **Coming of Age in Mississippi (1968)**<br>*pp. 609–617* | • Summary p. 26<br>• Active Reading p. 27<br>• Literary Analysis p. 28<br>• Selection Quiz p. 29 | • Selection Test, Formal Assessment pp. 115–116<br>⊙ Test Generator | | • Compare/Contrast Themes and Conflicts T16 |
| **Ballad of Birmingham (1969)**<br>*pp. 618–621* | • Active Reading p. 30<br>• Literary Analysis p. 31<br>• Comparing Literature p. 32 | • Selection Test, Formal Assessment p. 117<br>⊙ Test Generator | ◯ Audio Library | |

## Writing Workshop: Literary Interpretation

| | | Unit Assessment | Unit Technology | |
|---|---|---|---|---|
| **Unit Four Resource Book**<br>• Prewriting p. 33<br>• Drafting and Elaboration p. 34<br>• Peer Response Guide pp. 35–36<br>• Revising, Editing, and Proofreading p. 37<br>• Student Models pp. 38–43<br>• Rubric for Evaluation p. 44 | ⊙ **Power Presentations CD-ROM**<br>**Writing Transparencies and Copymasters** T11, T20, C30<br>**Teacher's Guide to Assessment and Portfolio Use** | • Unit Four, Part 1 Test, Formal Assessment pp. 119–120<br>⊙ Test Generator<br>• Unit Four Integrated Test, Integrated Assessment pp. 31–38 | ◔ ClassZone www.mcdougallittell.com<br>⊙ EasyPlanner CD-ROM<br>⊙ Electronic Library | |

| Reading and Critical Thinking Transparencies | Grammar Transparencies and Copymasters | Vocabulary Transparencies and Copymasters | Writing Transparencies and Copymasters | Communications Transparencies and Copymasters |
|---|---|---|---|---|
| • Determining Author's Purpose and Bias T19 | • Daily Language SkillBuilder T15<br>• Identifying Independent and Subordinate Clauses C88 | • Denotation and Connotation C49 | • Compare-Contrast C32<br>• Autobiographical Incident C35 | • Evaluating Roles in Groups T8<br>• Dramatic Reading T12 |
| | • Daily Language SkillBuilder T15<br>• Distinguishing a Clause from a Phrase C90 | • Figurative Language C50 | • Figurative Language and Sound Devices T15 | |
| • Evaluating Story Elements T6<br>• Analyzing Text Structure T17 | • Daily Language SkillBuilder T16<br>• Using *That* and *Which* T44<br>• Essential and Nonessential Clauses C91<br>• Punctuating Nonessential Clauses C149 | • Prefixes C51 | • Critical Review C26<br>• Compare-Contrast C32 | |
| • Visualizing T8 | • Daily Language SkillBuilder T16<br>• Adjective Clauses C92<br>• Commas in Names and Titles C150 | • Meanings of Roots C52 | • Literary Interpretation C30 | • Appreciative Listening T2<br>• Interviewing T9<br>• Impromptu Speaking: Dialogue, Role-Play, Debate T13 |
| • Paraphrasing and Summarizing T41 | • Daily Language SkillBuilder T17<br>• Using *That* and *Which* T44<br>• Adjective and Relative Clauses C95 | | • Research Report C33 | |
| • Analyzing Text Structure T17<br>• Sequence Chain T49 | • Daily Language SkillBuilder T17<br>• Adverb Clauses C96<br>• Punctuating Adverb Clauses C151 | • Sensory Details C53 | • Eyewitness Report C25 | • Interviewing T9<br>• Impromptu Speaking: Dialogue, Role-Play, Debate T13 |
| • Making Judgments T5 | • Daily Language SkillBuilder T17<br>• Introduction to Noun Clauses C101 | | • Compare-Contrast C32 | • Dramatic Reading T12<br>• Verbal Strategies T14 |

## STUDENTS ACQUIRING ENGLISH

The **Spanish Study Guide,** pp. 130–153, includes language support for the following pages:
• Family and Community Involvement (per unit)

• Selection Summaries and Vocabulary
• Active Reading
• Literary Analysis

UNIT FOUR
# RESOURCE MANAGEMENT GUIDE
## PART 2

To introduce the theme/literary period of this unit, use Fine Art Transparencies T26–28 in the Communications Transparencies and Copymasters.

| | Unit Resource Book | Assessment | Integrated Technology and Media | Additional Support<br>Literary Analysis Transparencies |
|---|---|---|---|---|
| **The Indian and the Hundred Cows/El Indito de las Cien Vacas**<br>*pp. 638–644* | • Summary p. 47<br>• Active Reading p. 48<br>• Literary Analysis p. 49<br>• Selection Quiz p. 50 | • Selection Test, Formal Assessment p. 121<br>⊙ Test Generator | ◯ Audio Library | • Legends, Myths, and Folk Tales T24 |
| **High Horse's Courting**<br>*pp. 645–653* | • Summary p. 51<br>• Active Reading p. 52<br>• Literary Analysis p. 53<br>• Selection Quiz p. 54 | • Selection Test, Formal Assessment p. 123<br>⊙ Test Generator | ◯ Audio Library | |
| *from* **The Autobiography of Mark Twain**<br>*pp. 658–668* | • Summary p. 55<br>• Active Reading p. 56<br>• Literary Analysis p. 57<br>• Words to Know p. 58<br>• Selection Quiz p. 59 | • Selection Test, Formal Assessment pp. 125–126<br>⊙ Test Generator | ◯ Audio Library<br><br>ⓘ Research Starter www.mcdougallittell.com<br>⊙ NetActivities | |
| *from* **Life on the Mississippi**<br>*pp. 669–677* | • Summary p. 60<br>• Active Reading p. 61<br>• Literary Analysis p. 62<br>• Selection Quiz p. 63 | • Selection Test, Formal Assessment pp. 127–128<br>⊙ Test Generator | ◯ Audio Library<br>▭ Video: Literature in Performance, Video Resource Book pp. 15–20<br>ⓘ Research Starter www.mcdougallittell.com<br>⊙ NetActivities | |
| **The Notorious Jumping Frog of Calveras County**<br>*pp. 679–687* | • Summary p. 64<br>• Active Reading p. 65<br>• Literary Analysis p. 66<br>• Words to Know p. 67<br>• Selection Quiz p. 68 | • Selection Test, Formal Assessment pp. 129–130<br>⊙ Test Generator | ◯ Audio Library<br>⊙ NetActivities | |
| **A Wagner Matinee**<br>*pp. 688–699* | • Summary p. 69<br>• Active Reading p. 70<br>• Literary Analysis p. 71<br>• Words to Know p. 72<br>• Selection Quiz p. 73 | • Selection Test, Formal Assessment pp. 131–132<br>⊙ Test Generator | ◯ Audio Library | • Setting T13 |
| **The Legend of Gregorio Cortez**<br>*pp. 702–719* | • Summary p. 74<br>• Active Reading p. 75<br>• Literary Analysis p. 76<br>• Selection Quiz p. 77<br>• Comparing Literature p. 78 | • Selection Test, Formal Assessment pp. 133–134<br>⊙ Test Generator | ◯ Audio Library | • Legends, Myths, and Folk Tales T24 |

## Writing Workshop: Storytelling

| | Unit Assessment | Unit Technology | |
|---|---|---|---|
| **Unit Four Resource Book** ⊙ **Power Presentations CD-ROM**<br>• Planning Your Performance p. 79<br>• Preparing, Practicing, and Presenting p. 80<br>• Peer Response Guide pp. 81–82<br>• Refining p. 83<br>• Student Models p. 84<br>• Standards for Evaluation p. 85 | • Unit Four, Part 2 Test, Formal Assessment pp. 135–136<br>⊙ Test Generator<br>• Unit Four Integrated Test, Integrated Assessment pp. 31–38 | ⓘ ClassZone www.mcdougallittell.com<br>⊙ EasyPlanner CD-ROM<br>⊙ Electronic Library | |

| Reading and Critical Thinking Transparencies | Grammar Transparencies and Copymasters | Vocabulary Transparencies and Copymasters | Writing Transparencies and Copymasters | Communications Transparencies and Copymasters |
|---|---|---|---|---|
| | • Daily Language SkillBuilder T18<br>• Independent and Subordinate Clauses C89 | • Using a Dictionary C54 | • Short Story C29 | |
| • Determining Author's Purpose and Audience T19 | • Daily Language SkillBuilder T18<br>• Distinguishing a Clause from a Phrase C90 | • Using Specified Dictionaries C55 | • Short Story C29 | • Interviewing T9<br>• Impromptu Speaking: Dialogue, Role-Play, Debate T13 |
| • Predicting Outcomes T2 | • Daily Language SkillBuilder T19<br>• Essential and Nonessential Clauses C91<br>• Punctuating a Series of Clauses C156 | • Synonyms and Antonyms C56 | • The Uses of Dialogue T24<br>• Eyewitness Report T25 | |
| • Visualizing T8 | • Daily Language SkillBuilder T19<br>• Using *That* and *Which* T44<br>• Adjective Clauses: Common Introductory Words C94<br>• Commas in Names and Titles C150 | • Analogies C57 | • Reflective Essay C28 | • Evaluation Matrix: Film/Video T7 |
| | • Daily Language SkillBuilder T19<br>• Using *That* and *Which* T44<br>• Use of *That* and *Which* in Adjective Clauses C93 | • Meanings of Roots C58 | • Short Story C29 | • Impromptu Speaking: Dialogue, Role-Play, Debate T13 |
| • Cause and Effect T1<br>• Drawing Conclusions T4<br>• Interviewing T39 | • Daily Language SkillBuilder T20<br>• Introductory Adverbial Clauses C98<br>• Punctuating Introductory Adverbial Clauses C152 | • Meanings of Roots C59 | | • Appreciative Listening T2 |
| • Making Judgments T5 | • Daily Language SkillBuilder T20<br>• Using *That* and *Which* T44<br>• Noun Clauses: Common Introductory Words C104 | • Word History C60<br>• English from Spanish C61 | | • Interviewing T9<br>• Impromptu Speaking: Dialogue, Role-Play, Debate T13 |

## STUDENTS ACQUIRING ENGLISH

The **Spanish Study Guide,** pp. 154–174, includes language support for the following pages:
• Family and Community Involvement (per unit)

• Selection Summaries and Vocabulary
• Active Reading
• Literary Analysis

| Selection | SkillBuilder Sentences | Suggested Answers |
|---|---|---|
| *from* Narrative of the Life of Frederick Douglass, an American Slave | **1.** slave owners usualy tried to prevent there slaves from learning to read and write.<br><br>**2.** Educated slaves were thoght to be a threat to the sistem of slavery because slaves who could earn there own living would be not so dependant on their owners. | **1.** **S**lave owners **usually** tried to prevent **their** slaves from learning to read and write.<br><br>**2.** Educated slaves were **thought** to be a threat to the **system** of slavery because slaves who could earn **their** own living would be **less dependent** on their owners. |
| Stanzas on Freedom<br>Free Labor | **1.** Abolitionists efforts tryed to focus the publics' attention on the plight of slaves.<br><br>**2.** Newspapers poems novels slave narratives— all of which were used to further the fight against slavery. | **1.** Abolitionists' efforts **tried** to focus the public**'s** attention on the plight of slaves.<br><br>**2.** Newspapers, poems, novels, **and** slave narratives—**all were** used to further the fight against slavery. |
| An Occurrence at Owl Creek Bridge | **1.** The civil war is a dark episode in our History the teacher told Henry and I.<br><br>**2.** Their's no way that we can imagine the pain that soldiers and civilians must of felt. | **1.** "The **C**ivil **W**ar is a dark episode in our **h**istory," the teacher told Henry and **me**.<br><br>**2.** **There's** no way that we can imagine the pain that soldiers and civilians must **have** felt. |
| A Mystery of Heroism | **1.** The meadow was a peaceful place until the battles ferocity destroyed it.<br><br>**2.** They should have sat the bucket down carefully than nothing could of happened to it. | **1.** The meadow **had been** a peaceful place until the battle**'s** ferocity destroyed it.<br><br>**2.** They should have **set** the bucket down carefully. **Then** nothing could **have** happened to it. |
| The Gettysburg Address | **1.** I wunder, "how many people actually herd president Lincoln give The gettysburg address?" said Maura.<br><br>**2.** "Well there was 15000 people at the dedication ceremoney that day said Lee. | **1.** "I **wonder** how many people actually **heard** **P**resident Lincoln give the **G**ettysburg **A**ddress," said Maura.<br><br>**2.** "Well, there **were** 15,000 people at the dedication **ceremony** that day," said Lee. |

| Selection | SkillBuilder Sentences | Suggested Answers |
|---|---|---|
| *from* Coming of Age in Mississippi | 1. Several representative from the naacp and core will attends the rally. | 1. Several **representatives** from the **NAACP** and **CORE** will **attend** the rally. |
| | 2. We would like to be served here Anne Moody said firmly. | 2. "We would like to be served here," Anne Moody said firmly. |
| Ballad of Birmingham | 1. Narrative poetry which was often sang to the accompaniment of musical instruments was one of the earlier forms of poetry sayed the professor. | 1. "Narrative poetry, which was often **sung** to the accompaniment of musical instruments, was one of the **earliest** forms of poetry," **said** the professor. |
| | 2. For the people of centuries ago, the telling of stories in poetic form was comparable to today's television and movies as a result the storyteller was a highly respected member of the community. | 2. For the people of centuries ago, the telling of stories in poetic form was comparable to today's television and movies. **As** a result, the storyteller was a highly respected member of the community. |
| The Indian and the Hundred Cows/El Indito de las Cien Vacas | 1. Although cuentos were originally passed down oral in the southwest José Griego y Maestas adapted them into written tails. | 1. Although cuentos were originally passed down **orally** in the **S**outhwest, José Griego y Maestas adapted them into written **tales**. |
| | 2. The History teacher said, The Indian and the Hundred Cows provides a humerous look at the clash between a Native American culture and christianity. | 2. The **h**istory teacher said, " 'The Indian and the Hundred Cows' provides a hum**o**rous look at the clash between a Native American culture and **C**hristianity." |
| High Horse's Courting *from* Black Elk Speaks | 1. In the story High Horse's Courting the young man desperate with love for a girl makes no less than four attempts to win it. | 1. In the story "High Horse's Courting," the young man, desperate with love for a girl, makes no **fewer** than four attempts to win **her**. |
| | 2. Black Elk's story is an invalueable piece of sioux folk heritage being recorded in the book Black Elk Speaks by John G Neihardt saved it for future generations. | 2. Black Elk's story is an **invaluable** piece of **S**ioux folk heritage. **B**eing recorded in the book **Black Elk Speaks** by John G. Neihardt saved **the story** for future generations. |
| *from* The Autobiography of Mark Twain | 1. Mark Twains name was samuel clemens and he lived his early years in hannibal missouri. | 1. Mark Twain's **given** name was **S**amuel **C**lemens. **H**e lived his early years in **H**annibal, **M**issouri. |
| | 2. The autobiography of mark twain re-create the atmosphere of small town life in the 1800s. | 2. **The Autobiography of Mark Twain** re-create**s** the atmosphere of small town life in the 1800s. |

| Selection | SkillBuilder Sentences | Suggested Answers |
|---|---|---|
| *from* Life on the Mississippi | 1. Mark Twain recounts with humor what happens to mr. bixby and he during his training. | 1. Mark Twain recounts with humor what happens to **M**r. **B**ixby and **him** during his training. |
| | 2. Mark Twains descriptive gifts bringing the experiences of a steam boat pilot to life said the reviewer. | 2. "Mark Twain**'s** descriptive gifts **bring** the experiences of a **steamboat** pilot to life**,**" said the reviewer. |
| The Notorious Jumping Frog of Calaveras County | 1. Neither this story or the three others in the book is what I remember. | 1. Neither this story **nor** the three others in the book **are** what I remember. |
| | 2. He knew what would happen when he excepted the task but he felt that he couldn't hardly refuse after all his friend had did for him. | 2. He knew what would happen when he **accepted** the task**,** but he felt that he **could** hardly refuse after all his friend had **done** for him. |
| A Wagner Matinee | 1. Exhausted by the train trek she collapsed as soon as she sees the bed. | 1. Exhausted by the train trek**,** she collapsed as soon as she **saw** the bed. |
| | 2. Wagners music like so many operas are very moving. | 2. Wagner**'s** music**,** like **that of** so many operas**,** **is** very moving. |
| The Legend of Gregorio Cortez | 1. "One of these days they warned him, "your going to put out your eye" | 1. "One of these days**,**" they warned him, "**you're** going to put out your eye**.**" |
| | 2. You cant blame him for wanting to seek vengeance whose going to object to that. | 2. You can**'**t blame him for wanting to seek vengeance**.** **Who's** going to object to that**?** |

| Grammar Focus by Unit | Unit One | Unit Two | Unit Three | Unit Four | Unit Five | Unit Six | Unit Seven |
|---|---|---|---|---|---|---|---|
| | Parts of a Sentence | Verbs | Phrases | Clauses, Part I | Clauses, Part II | Special Sentence Structures, Part I | Special Sentence Structures, Part II |

*The Language of Literature* offers several options for integrating grammar instruction and literature.

- Each literature unit has a grammar focus. The Teacher's Edition includes Mini Lessons for each selection that help develop the grammar focus for the unit and spring from the content of the specific literature.
- The Pupil Edition includes several full-page lessons on Sentence Crafting. These lessons are related to both the literature and the grammar focus for the unit and help students use grammar in their own writing.
- Daily Language SkillBuilders in the Teacher's Edition provide students with ongoing proofreading practice and reinforce punctuation, spelling, grammar and usage, and capitalization.
- Grammar Copymasters and Transparencies, which may be used to complement or extend lessons in the Teacher's Edition, present grammar in a traditional, systematic sequence. References to appropriate copymasters or transparencies are included at point of use in the Teacher's Edition Mini Lessons.

TE Mini Lessons shown in green
PE instruction shown in black

## Part 1

**Using Clauses**
**Identifying Clauses: Independent and Subordinate**
from *Narrative of the Life of Frederick Douglass, an American Slave,* p. 572
**Clause vs. Phrase**
"Stanzas on Freedom," "Free Labor," p. 579
**Clauses: Essential vs. Nonessential**
"An Occurrence at Owl Creek Bridge," p. 590
**Adjective Clauses**
"A Mystery of Heroism," p. 598
**Relative Adjective Clauses: Correct Use of *that* and *which***
The Gettysburg Address, p. 608
**Adverb Clauses**
from *Coming of Age in Mississippi,* p. 611
**Noun Clauses**
"Ballad of Birmingham," p. 621
**Sentence Fragments**
Writing Workshop, p. 629
**Structure: Compound Sentences**
**Clauses In Compound Sentences**
Sentence Crafting, p. 631

**Verb Usage**
**Verb Tenses**
Writing Workshop, p. 629

**End Marks and Commas**
**Punctuation for Clauses**
"An Occurrence at Owl Creek Bridge," p. 592
from *Coming of Age in Mississippi,* p. 617
**Commas: Names and Titles**
"A Mystery of Heroism," p. 603
**Commas: Introductory Adverb Clause**
from *Coming of Age in Mississippi,* p. 617
**Unnecessary Commas**
Writing Workshop, p. 629

**Other Punctuation**
**Semicolons: In Place of the Period**
Sentence Crafting, p. 631

**Style**
**Creating Compound Sentences**
Sentence Crafting, p. 631

## Part 2

**Using Clauses**
**Identifying Clauses: Independent and Subordinate**
"The Indian and the Hundred Cows," p. 644
**Clause vs. Phrase**
"High Horse's Courting," pp. 648–649
**Clauses: Essential vs. Nonessential**
from *The Autobiography of Mark Twain,* p. 663
**Adjective Clauses**
Sentence Crafting, p. 729
**Relative Adjective Clauses: Correct Use of *that* and *which***
from *Life on the Mississippi,* p. 671
"The Notorious Jumping Frog of Calaveras County," p. 681
**Relative Adjective Clauses: Relative Pronouns**
**Adjective Clauses: Relative Adverbs**
from *Life on the Mississippi,* p. 671
**Adverb Clauses**
"A Wagner Matinee," p. 694
Sentence Crafting, p. 729
**Noun Clauses: Common Introductory Words**
"The Legend of Gregorio Cortez," pp. 704–705
**Sentence Fragments**
Communication Workshop, p. 727
**Complex Sentences**
Sentence Crafting, p. 729

**Verb Usage**
**Verb Tenses**
Communication Workshop, p. 727

**End Marks and Commas**
**Punctuation for Clauses**
from *The Autobiography of Mark Twain,* p. 666
**Commas: Names and Titles**
from *Life on the Mississippi,* p. 677
**Commas: Introductory Adverb Clause**
"A Wagner Matinee," p. 698
Sentence Crafting, p. 729

**Style**
**Creating Complex Sentences**
Sentence Crafting, p. 729

# TIME LINE 1850–1900

# CONFLICT and EXPANSION

This time line shows major dates and events in United States and world history from the mid-1850s to 1900. Help students recognize that this fifty-year period was characterized worldwide by conflict and territorial expansion.

## Literature: 1852

**A** In one year, *Uncle Tom's Cabin* sold over 300,000 copies. Abolitionists hailed it as a true portrayal of slavery, while Southerners denounced it as a pack of lies.

## World: 1857

**B** On the morning of May 10, 1857, Indian soldiers stormed the imperial palace at Delhi. They killed the English men and women living there and persuaded Bahadur Shah II, the aged Mughal monarch who had been living under the rule of the British, to lead a rebellion against the British. In Kanpur on the Ganges River, almost the entire British community was killed by rebelling Indian soldiers. Only four out of the 568 British residents of Kanpur survived. The British subdued the rebellion, but relations between the two groups changed drastically as the British set about "civilizing" their Indian subjects.

## United States: 1863

**C** Although personally opposed to slavery, Lincoln was convinced that it was his first duty to preserve the Union, not to free the slaves. He wrote, "If I could save the Union without freeing any slave, I would do it; and if I could save it by freeing all the slaves, I would do it; and if I could do it by freeing some and leaving others alone, I would also do that."

## EVENTS IN AMERICAN LITERATURE

### 1850          1860          1870

**1851** Herman Melville's *Moby-Dick* is published

**A** **1852** Harriet Beecher Stowe publishes *Uncle Tom's Cabin*, increasing tension between proslavery and antislavery forces

**1863** Abraham Lincoln delivers Gettysburg Address

**1876** Mark Twain publishes *The Adventures of Tom Sawyer* and begins writing *The Adventures of Huckleberry Finn*

## EVENTS IN THE UNITED STATES

### 1850          1860          1870

**1851** Former slave Sojourner Truth speaks at women's rights convention

**1857** Supreme Court's Dred Scott decision declares slaves and former slaves are not U.S. citizens and thus not entitled to basic rights

**1859** Abolitionist John Brown is hanged for treason after leading raid on federal arsenal at Harpers Ferry

**1860** Abraham Lincoln is elected president; in response, South Carolina secedes from Union, followed eventually by ten other Southern states

**C** **1863** Lincoln signs Emancipation Proclamation

**1865** Civil War ends; Lincoln is assassinated; 13th Amendment to Constitution abolishes slavery

**D** **1868** Congress passes 14th Amendment to Constitution, prohibiting discrimination against African Americans

**1873** Colt's Manufacturing Company introduces Peacemaker revolver, most famous sidearm of West

**1874** Joseph F. Glidden patents barbed wire, key development in settlement of West

**1876** At Battle of Little Bighorn, several thousand Sioux and Cheyenne warriors defeat and kill about 200 U.S. Army troops commanded by Lieutenant George Armstrong Custer

**1877** Chief Joseph of Nez Perce tribe surrenders to U.S. Army

## EVENTS IN THE WORLD

### 1850          1860          1870

**1852** David Livingstone explores Zambezi River in central Africa

**B** **1857** Sepoys rebel against British rule in India

**1861** Czar Alexander II of Russia frees serfs

**1867** Alfred Nobel invents dynamite; Meiji era in Japan begins period of modernization

**E** **1869** Suez Canal is completed in Egypt

**1870** Italy is unified

**1871** Franco-Prussian War ends; Germany is unified

**1872** Critics coin term *impressionism* after Claude Monet's painting "Impression: Sunrise"

**556** UNIT FOUR   CONFLICT AND EXPANSION

## United States: 1868

**D** The 14th Amendment gave citizenship to freedmen and guaranteed them basic rights, including due process of law. The language of the amendment later served as a powerful support for the civil rights movement.

## World: 1869

**E** The Suez Canal through Egypt shortened the sea distance between Britain and India by 4,000 miles, yet the British were opposed to its construction. Apparently, they feared that other European nations would use this direct Mediterranean Sea to Indian Ocean route to threaten their near monopoly on trade with Asia.

# PERIOD PIECES

Confederate money

Steam engine

Decorative carriage
clock from 1870

1880 — 1890 — 1900

**1882** Frederick Douglass completes autobiography

**F** **1891** Ambrose Bierce publishes "An Occurrence at Owl Creek Bridge"

**1883** Twain's *Life on the Mississippi* is published

**1895** Stephen Crane's fictional account of the Civil War, *The Red Badge of Courage*, is published

**1897** In Pittsburgh, Willa Cather hears
**G** her first Wagnerian opera and becomes passionate fan of the German composer

1880 — 1890 — 1900

**1883** "Buffalo Bill" Cody organizes Wild West show and begins touring United States and Europe

**1890** At Wounded Knee Creek, South Dakota, U.S. soldiers kill more than 200 Sioux in last battle of Indian Wars

**1893** Henry Ford develops gasoline-powered automobile

**1896** Supreme Court upholds "separate but equal" doctrine of Jim Crow laws, widely used to discriminate against African Americans

**1898** Spanish-American War results in
**H** United States gaining control of Guam, Puerto Rico, and the Philippines

1880 — 1890 — 1900

**1885** At Berlin Conference, 14 European nations lay down rules for division of Africa

**1893** France takes over Indochina

**1895** Japanese defeat Chinese in Sino-Japanese War

**1896** Menelik II maintains Ethiopian independence after victory over Italians at Battle of Adowa

**1900** Boxer Rebellion protests foreign
**J** influence in China

TIME LINE **557**

## Literature: 1891

**F** Ambrose Bierce (1842–c. 1914) was a leading member of the Western literary circle that included, for a time, Mark Twain and Joaquin Miller. In the early years of the 20th century, Bierce became disillusioned with life in the United States and moved to Mexico where he disappeared during its civil war. When and how he died are questions that are still unanswered.

## Literature: 1897

**G** After 17 years of writing stories for various magazines, Willa Cather (1873–1947) published her first novel, *Alexander's Bridge*, in 1912. For the next several years she wrote novels set in the American West, where she grew up. In 1922, she won the Pulitzer Prize for *One of Ours*, the story of a boy from the Western plains who is killed while fighting in Europe during World War I.

## United States: 1898

**H** Two serious hindrances to the military during the Spanish-American War—cumbersome travel and yellow fever—led to an engineering marvel and a medical victory. In 1914, the Panama Canal opened to vessels sailing from the Caribbean Sea to the Pacific Ocean, and in 1937 a vaccine protected future generations from yellow fever.

## DECORATIVE CARRIAGE CLOCK

**I** A carriage clock is designed for display. It can be carried by its gold handle and appears attractive when viewed from any side. Such clocks were bought and shown off by the "carriage trade," wealthy store patrons who did their shopping by carriage rather than on foot.

## World: 1900

**J** The Boxer Rebellion of 1900, so called because it was led by the Righteous and Harmonious Fists, was a mass movement which targeted for destruction all foreigners, machines, and Christianity. The Boxers and their supporters rebelled against foreign intrusion and technological advances, which they blamed for weakening the efficacy of their empire.

## OVERVIEW

### Introduction

This essay places the selections in Part 1 of this unit in historical context by giving students an overview of slavery, the Civil War, and the 20th-century civil rights movement in the United States. The selections in **Voices from the Times** address the central issues of the era. This essay will help students interpret the possible influences of historical contexts on literary works.

## Teaching Nonfiction

### Reading Skills and Strategies
### ESTABLISHING A PURPOSE FOR READING

Explain to students that this essay introduces them to the Civil War and the conflicts over the rights of black Americans. Have students review the article and establish a purpose for reading (to find out).

Remind them to adjust their purposes as they encounter difficult or unexpected material.

### USING TEXT ORGANIZERS

Have students preview the article noting the basic text organizers: title, subheads, images and captions, and sidebar commentary. Ask them to predict what information they expect to locate in each section of the text. After they have completed the article, have students use the heads to categorize information under the appropriate heading. Encourage students to include information in the correct category as they read the selection in the unit.

# A House Divided

## Slavery and the Civil War

By the time of Abraham Lincoln's inauguration as President in March of 1861, seven states—South Carolina, Mississippi, Florida, Alabama, Georgia, Louisiana, and Texas—had seceded from the Union and formed the Confederate States of America, with Jefferson Davis as President. A month later, Confederate troops opened fire on Northern troops attempting to resupply Fort Sumter, a federal installation in the Charleston, South Carolina, harbor. Three days later, Lincoln ordered additional troops to enforce the law. In response, Virginia, Arkansas, North Carolina, and Tennessee joined the Confederacy. The Civil War had begun.

When the war ended on April 9, 1865, with General Robert E. Lee's surrender to General Ulysses S. Grant at Appomattox Court House, Virginia, more than 620,000 men had been killed—nearly as many as have died in all other wars that the United States has fought—and at least that many more had been wounded. Much of the South lay in ruins, scarred by gutted plantation houses, burned bridges, and uprooted railroad lines. However, the Union had been preserved, and nearly 4 million slaves had gained their freedom.

UNION GENERAL

Ulysses S. Grant

Before the Civil War, *United States* had been a plural noun. People were used to saying "The United States *are* . . . ," with the emphasis on the individual *states* more than the *united* interests of all. However, a strong belief in states' rights ultimately threatened the union itself and allowed the institution of slavery a longer history in the Southern states than in the Northern states and in most of Latin America and Europe as well. "A house divided against itself cannot stand," maintained Abraham Lincoln. "I believe this government cannot endure permanently half slave and half free." After the Civil War, the United States had become irrevocably one country. People began saying "The United States *is* . . ."

In the years before the war, slavery was a major subject engaging a large number of writers. Public lectures were a forum by which many writers supported themselves. Henry David Thoreau, as active in the political and social world as he was in the literary, lectured on the individual's responsibility to take action against unjust laws. His lecture, published as the essay "Civil Disobedience" (page 369) in 1849, has since become famous, providing some of the basis for the American tradition of nonviolent protest that took hold about 100 years later during the civil rights movement.

This crucial time period also generated some of the first important literature by African Americans. Frances Ellen Watkins Harper became the first popular African-American poet, as she traveled throughout the North lecturing to substantial audiences in favor of abolition and punctuating her lectures with recitations of her poems. Most eloquent of all, however, was Frederick Douglass, the escaped slave who taught himself to read and write and later became a champion of the abolitionist cause and woman suffrage. Douglass's

CONFEDERATE GENERAL

Robert E. Lee

**D** I know this well, that if one thousand, if one hundred, if ten men whom I could name—if ten *honest* men only—ay, if *one* HONEST man, in this State of Massachusetts, *ceasing to hold slaves*, were actually to withdraw from this copartnership [with government by refusing to pay taxes], and be locked up in the county jail therefor, it would be the abolition of slavery in America. For it matters not how small the beginning may seem to be: what is once well done is done forever.

**Henry David Thoreau**
from "Civil Disobedience"

The South, in my opinion, has been aggrieved by the acts of the North, as you say. I feel the aggression, and am willing to take every proper step for redress. . . . As an American citizen, I take great pride in my country, her prosperity and institutions, and would defend any State, if her rights were invaded. But I can anticipate no greater calamity for the country than a dissolution of the Union. It would be an accumulation of all the evils we complain of, and I am willing to sacrifice everything but honor for its preservation.

**Robert E. Lee**
from a letter to his son
three months before the war

This Southern Confederacy must be supported now by calm determination and cool brains. We have risked all and we must play our best, for the stake is life or death.

**Mary Boykin Chesnut**
from her diary

Mary Chesnut

HISTORICAL BACKGROUND **559**

**History**

**A** The Battle of Antietam, one of the Civil War's deadliest conflicts, occurred in Maryland on September 17, 1862. Because it resulted in over 24,000 casualties, the event was labeled a Pyrrhic victory. The Battle of Shiloh in Tennessee also cost both sides heavy losses.

**Literature**

**B** Some of the most vivid scenes of the violence of slavery and the Civil War appear in fiction. *Uncle Tom's Cabin, The Red Badge of Courage,* and the Pulitzer Prize-winning *Gone with the Wind* are among the best selling and most popular of all American novels. Stowe's novel outsold everything except the Bible at one time, and Mitchell's saga of Scarlett O'Hara has never gone out of print.

**Statistics**

**C** Historians estimate that 10 to 20 million slaves were transported to the Americas. Of these, nearly half died of disease, brutality, or execution. The importation of slaves to the United States was outlawed in 1808, but black-market sales continued. Some entrepreneurs specialized in breeding slaves with certified qualities, listed like the pedigrees of racehorses.

**History**

**D** One poignant result of the Civil War was the confiscation by the government of General Robert E. Lee's family home in Arlington, Virginia, just outside of the capital city. The extensive grounds of the mansion were turned into a cemetery for the war dead—a gesture intended to ensure that Lee would never be able to live there again. The Lee estate is now Arlington National Cemetery.

**VOICES FROM THE TIMES**

**Ask: How realistic does Thoreau's challenge seem to you?**

**Possible Response:** Expecting everyone to stop paying taxes was unrealistic, but he probably hoped that he could inspire a small group to follow him.

**Ask: What can you infer about Robert E. Lee's feelings toward secession and Civil War from his letter to his son?**

**Possible Responses:** His support for the South during the Civil War became a matter of honor;

secession from the Union was probably not a decision reached easily by the southern states; Lee knew the catastrophe that would follow secession.

**Ask: What does Mary B. Chesnut mean when she states that the situation is life or death?**

**Possible Responses:** She could be referring to the lives of the men and boys who went off to fight, or to the life of the old plantation system in the South that would perish if the Union army won.

## Teaching Nonfiction

**DRAWING INFERENCES**

This essay discusses how slavery and the Civil War provided material for many writers during this period. Ask students to consider how personal experiences in the life of a writer and crucial events in the life of a nation can influence literature. Have them draw inferences from the essay and support them with textual evidence.

**SUMMARIZING**

Ask students to summarize the text in their own words. Ask them to include in their summaries an identification of the main ideas of the essay as well as supporting details.

**VOICES FROM THE TIMES**

**Ask: How does Lincoln's statement reveal which side of the Civil War he was on?**

**Possible Response:** His statement lays blame for the war on the South. The nation is described as a living being that will either "survive" or "perish." The South aggressively "made" war in an effort to kill the nation; the North reluctantly "accepted" war because it wanted to save the nation's life.

**Ask: How does Clara Barton's statement echo that of General Sherman and Walt Whitman?**

**Possible Responses:** All three realize the waste and suffering of the war; all three see the war as a tragedy and a catastrophe.

Voices
*from the* TIMES

Both parties deprecated war, but one of them would make war rather than let the nation survive, and the other would accept war rather than let it perish. And the war came.

**Abraham Lincoln**
from *Second Inaugural Address*

Clara Barton

I saw, crowded into one old sunken hotel, lying upon its bare, wet, bloody floors, 500 fainting men hold up their cold, bloodless, dingy hands as I passed, and beg me in Heaven's name for a cracker to keep them from starving (and I had none); or to give them a cup that they might have something to drink water from, if they could get it (and I had no cup and could get none).

**Clara Barton**
on wounded soldiers awaiting
transfer to hospitals

War is hell.
**William Tecumseh Sherman**

Look down fair moon and bathe this
    scene,
Pour softly down night's nimbus floods
    on faces ghastly, swollen, purple,
On the dead on their backs with arms
    toss'd wide,
Pour down your unstinted nimbus
    sacred moon.

**Walt Whitman**
"Look Down Fair Moon"

autobiography remains one of the most moving, authentic accounts we have of the bitter history of slavery.

As always during periods of great change, it is the experience of individuals caught up in large historical forces that finally gives life to events and makes them real. Walt Whitman worked as an army nurse in New York and Washington and on the front lines during the first three years of the war. Many of his poems written at this time are painfully personal. His famous elegies for Abraham Lincoln, "When Lilacs Last in the Dooryard Bloom'd" and "O Captain! My Captain!" express the grief of a nation still mourning the losses of the Civil War. Ambrose Bierce's story "An Occurrence at Owl Creek Bridge" has its origins in his own experience as a foot soldier in the war. The strange twists of that story, like others he wrote, prefigure his own mysterious disappearance years later in Mexico. Stephen Crane's story "A Mystery of Heroism" describes the forces—external and internal—that impel a soldier in battle.

## Traditions Across Time: The Civil Rights Movement

Though the horrors of slavery cannot be minimized, its end turned out to be only the first step in a long, arduous struggle for equal rights for African Americans. With publications and speeches by Martin Luther King, Jr., Malcolm X, and others, the civil rights movement of the 1950s and 1960s generated some of the most memorable work. Included in this part of Unit Four is Anne Moody's graphic and vivid account of one of the first sit-ins in Mississippi. Also, in the tradition of James Russell Lowell, Frances Ellen Watkins Harper, and other abolitionist poets, Robert Hayden and Dudley Randall address the struggle in historical as well as personal terms.

## Slavery and the Civil War

**561**

## Objectives

1. understand and appreciate a **slave narrative** (Literary Analysis)
2. examine **autobiography and style** (Literary Analysis)
3. analyze **author's purpose** (Active Reading)

## Summary

In this excerpt from his autobiography, former slave Frederick Douglass describes his experiences when his owner sent him to work for Mr. Covey, a man with a reputation as a slave breaker. Douglass relates how his harsh treatment at Covey's hands during the first six months breaks him "in body, soul, and spirit." Fearing for his life, Douglass pleads with his owner for protection but is forced to return to Covey. When Covey attempts to tie him up and beat him, Douglass fights him off. Douglass marks this incident as a turning point—one that restores his manhood and self-confidence and makes him again determined to seek his freedom.

## Thematic Link

The United States was truly **"a house divided"** by **slavery** when Frederick Douglass published his autobiography in 1845. First-person accounts such as Douglass's raised people's consciousness of what life was like for enslaved people and gave impetus to the abolitionist movement.

### 5-Minute Warm-Up

*Daily Language SkillBuilder*

Have students **proofread** the display sentences on page 555i and write them correctly. The sentences also appear on Transparency 15 of **Grammar Transparencies and Copymasters.**

**EDITOR'S NOTE:** This selection was excerpted from a larger work; material was deleted to shorten and focus the selection.

Detail of *A Load of Brush* (1912), Louis Paul Dessar.

# PREPARING to *Read*

## *from* Narrative of the Life of Frederick Douglass, an American Slave

*Slave Narrative by* FREDERICK DOUGLASS

### Connect to Your Life

**Land of the Free?** What do you know about slavery in the United States? Get together with a group of classmates and share what you have learned from slave narratives such as the one by Olaudah Equiano (page 94), from movies such as *Amistad,* from TV programs, or from history books. Record your group's knowledge about slavery in a word web.

## Build Background

**From Slave to Hero** After escaping from slavery in 1838, Frederick Douglass gave public lectures about his experiences. To convince skeptics who doubted that such an eloquent speaker could have ever been a slave, Douglass decided to write his autobiography, *Narrative of the Life of Frederick Douglass.* The book became one of the most famous slave narratives ever. As a boy, Douglass was a servant in the home of Hugh Auld of Baltimore, where Mrs. Auld taught Douglass the alphabet and some simple spelling. After Mr. Auld commanded his wife to stop educating the boy, Douglass taught himself to read with the help of white playmates. When Douglass was 16, he was sent back to his first home to live with Hugh Auld's brother, Thomas. Thomas Auld believed that Douglass had been too spoiled as a house slave to be useful on a plantation and decided it was necessary to break the young man's spirit. Auld rented Douglass for a year to Edward Covey, who had a reputation as a slave breaker. This excerpt from Douglass's narrative covers the time that Douglass spent with Covey.

> **WORDS TO KNOW**
> **Vocabulary Preview**
> faculty   intimate   sundry
> interpose   languish

## Focus Your Reading

**LITERARY ANALYSIS   AUTOBIOGRAPHY AND STYLE**

As you recall, an **autobiography** is the story of a person's life, written by that person. The style of an autobiography is as individual as its author. **Style** is not what is said but how it is said. For example, style can be described as formal or conversational, concise or elaborate, objective (matter-of-fact) or subjective (personal and emotional). Among the elements contributing to style are word choice, sentence length, tone, figurative language, and use of dialogue. Notice such elements as you read Douglass's narrative, and think about how you would describe his style.

**ACTIVE READING   AUTHOR'S PURPOSE**   Authors may write for any number of reasons, such as to inform, to entertain, or simply to express themselves. Frederick Douglass published his autobiography in 1845 primarily as a protest of slavery, with the hope that those who read his book would support the cause of freedom. Consider how readers of the time might have responded to this excerpt.

**READER'S NOTEBOOK**   Divide a page from your notebook into the areas shown. As you read, note your reactions to the slaves and masters presented in the selection. Primarily, you will be reacting to Douglass himself and to Covey, but also jot down your thoughts about Sandy, Bill, and Master Thomas.

| Slaves | Masters |
|---|---|
| Douglass | Covey |
| Sandy | Master Thomas |
| Bill | |

## LESSON RESOURCES

**UNIT FOUR RESOURCE BOOK,** pp. 4–8

**ASSESSMENT RESOURCES**
**Formal Assessment,** pp. 105–106
**Teacher's Guide to Assessment and Portfolio Use**
**Test Generator**

**SKILLS TRANSPARENCIES AND COPYMASTERS**
**Literary Analysis**
• Style, Voice, T23 (for Cooperative Learning Activity, p. 571)

**Reading and Critical Thinking**
• Determining Author's Purpose and Bias, T19 (for Active Reading, p. 562)
**Grammar**
• Identifying Independent and Subordinate Clauses, C88 (for Mini Lesson, p. 572)
**Vocabulary**
• Denotation and Connotation, C49 (for Mini Lesson, p. 564)
**Writing**
• Compare-Contrast, C32 (for Writing Option 3, p. 572)
• Autobiographical Incident, C35 (for Writing Option 4, p. 572)

**Communications**
• Evaluating Roles in Groups, T8 (for Mini Lesson, p. 568)
• Dramatic Reading, T12 (for Mini Lesson, p. 568)

**INTEGRATED TECHNOLOGY**
**Audio Library**
**LaserLinks**
• Historical Connection: An American Slave. See **Teacher's SourceBook,** p. 48.
**Internet: Research Starter**
**Visit our website:**
www.mcdougallittell.com

# from Narrative of the Life of Frederick Douglass

### Frederick Douglass

I left Master Thomas's house, and went to live with Mr. Covey, on the 1st of January, 1833. I was now, for the first time in my life, a field hand. In my new employment, I found myself even more awkward than a country boy appeared to be in a large city. I had been at my new home but one week before Mr. Covey gave me a very severe whipping, cutting my back, causing the blood to run, and raising ridges on my flesh as large as my little finger. The details of this affair are as follows: Mr. Covey sent me, very early in the morning of one of our coldest days in the month of January, to the woods, to get a load of wood. He gave me a team of unbroken oxen. He told me which was the in-hand ox, and which the off-hand[1] one. He then tied the end of a large rope around the horns of the in-hand ox, and gave me the other end of it, and told me, if the oxen started to run, that I must hold on upon the rope. I had never driven oxen before, and of course I was very awkward. I, however, succeeded in getting to the edge of the woods with little difficulty; but I had got a very few rods into the woods, when the oxen took fright, and started full tilt, carrying the cart against trees, and over stumps, in the most frightful manner. I expected every moment that my brains would be dashed out against the trees. After running thus for a considerable distance, they finally upset the cart, dashing it with great force against a tree, and threw themselves into a dense thicket.

How I escaped death, I do not know. There I was, entirely alone, in a thick wood, in a place new to me. My cart was upset and shattered, my oxen were entangled among the young trees, and there was none to help me. After a long spell of effort, I succeeded in getting my cart righted, my oxen disentangled, and again yoked to the cart. I now proceeded with my team to the place where I had, the day before, been chopping wood, and loaded my cart pretty heavily, thinking in this way to tame my oxen. I then proceeded on my way home. I had now consumed one half of the day. I got out of the woods safely, and now felt out of danger. I stopped my oxen to open the woods gate; and just as I did so, before I could get hold of my ox rope, the oxen again started, rushed through the gate, catching it between the wheel and the body of the cart, tearing it to pieces, and coming within a few inches of crushing me against the gate-post. Thus twice, in one short day, I escaped death by the merest chance. On my return, I told Mr. Covey what had happened, and how it happened. He ordered me to return to the woods again immediately. I did so, and he followed on after me. Just as I got into the

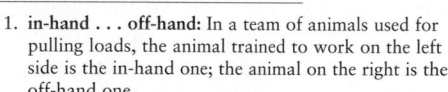

**1**

---

1. **in-hand . . . off-hand:** In a team of animals used for pulling loads, the animal trained to work on the left side is the in-hand one; the animal on the right is the off-hand one.

## TEACHING THE LITERATURE

### Customizing Instruction

**Less Proficient Readers**
Prepare students to read by telling them that, as a house slave, Douglass was not used to the manual labor required of a field slave.

**Set a Purpose** Have students read to find out how Douglass's inexperience gets him into trouble.

### Students Acquiring English

Students might be challenged by the long sentences and difficult syntax used by Douglass. You may wish to read certain passages aloud to make sure students understand them.

Use **Spanish Study Guide** for additional support, pp. 133–135.

### Gifted and Talented

Read to students the following remark by Richard Whately: "It is observed by Homer that a man loses half his virtue the day he becomes a slave; he might have added, with truth, that he is likely to lose more than half when he becomes a slavemaster."

**Set a Purpose** Have students, as they read, think about how this remark applies to this selection.

### Less Proficient Readers

**1** Have students predict how Mr. Covey will react to the news that his cart has been destroyed and support their predictions with textual evidence.

---

**Mini Lesson** **Preteaching Vocabulary**

**USING CONTEXT CLUES**
**Instruction** Write the following sentence on the chalkboard and ask a volunteer to rely on context to determine the meaning of the underlined word.

> Keesha didn't want Jake to be disappointed, so she tried to <u>intimate</u> to Jake that he might not be suited to the job.

Tell students that when they encounter an unfamiliar word, they can try to substitute a known word (in this case, *hint*) that makes sense in the context of the sentence.

**Exercises** Ask students to rely on context to determine the meanings of the underlined terms in the following sentences.
1. Jake is timid and small and would seem to have no <u>faculty</u> for working with large, aggressive bulls.
2. Lee decided to <u>interpose</u> on Jake's behalf by praising his determination and intelligence.
3. "Don't worry," said Jake, "If I don't get the job, I won't <u>languish</u> and fade away."
4. "There are varied and <u>sundry</u> options open to me," he said.

Use **Unit Four Resource Book,** p. 7 for more exercises.

**A lesson on context clues appears on p. 326 in the Pupil's Edition.**

Have students review Build Background on page 562. Remind them that when Douglass's autobiography was published in 1845, slavery was still widespread and Douglass risked his freedom by writing his *Narrative*.

### Literary Analysis

**AUTOBIOGRAPHY AND STYLE**

Ask students to describe Frederick Douglass's style of writing. Have them consider whether it is formal or informal, concise or elaborate, objective or subjective.

**Possible Response:** His style is formal, elaborate, and objective. His long, complex sentences, detailed descriptions, and matter-of-fact tone contribute to this style.

 Use **Unit Four Resource Book**, p. 6 for more practice.

### Active Reading | AUTHOR'S PURPOSE

**A** Ask students how this subjective passage might relate to the author's purpose for writing this autobiography. How does his motivation affect his credibility?

**Possible Response:** Douglass's vivid description of the emotional and physical toll of slavery personalizes the experience in a way that both informs and persuades the reader that slavery is an evil institution that must be eradicated. His writing is very credible because he has firsthand experience of slavery.

 Use **Unit Four Resource Book**, p. 5 for more practice.

---

*A Load of Brush* (1912), Louis Paul Dessar. Oil on canvas, 28 ¼″ × 36 ¼″, National Museum of American Art, gift of John Gellatly, Smithsonian Institution, Washington, D.C./Art Resource, New York.

woods, he came up and told me to stop my cart, and that he would teach me how to trifle away my time, and break gates. He then went to a large gum-tree, and with his axe cut three large switches, and, after trimming them up neatly with his pocket-knife, he ordered me to take off my clothes. I made him no answer, but stood with my clothes on. He repeated his order. I still made him no answer, nor did I move to strip myself. Upon this he rushed at me with the fierceness of a tiger, tore off my clothes, and lashed me till he had worn out his switches, cutting me so savagely as to leave the marks visible for a long time after. This whipping was the first of a number just like it, and **1** for similar offenses.

I lived with Mr. Covey one year. During the first six months, of that year, scarce a week passed without his whipping me. I was seldom free from a sore back. My awkwardness was almost always his excuse for whipping me. We were worked fully up to the point of endurance. Long before day we were up, our horses fed, and by the first approach of day we were off to the field with our hoes and ploughing teams. Mr. Covey gave us enough to eat, but scarce time to eat it. We were often less than five minutes taking our meals. We were often in the field from the first approach of day till its last lingering ray had left us; and at saving-fodder time, midnight often caught us in the field binding blades.[2]

Covey would be out with us. The way he used to stand it, was this. He would spend the most of his afternoons in bed. He would then come out fresh in the evening, ready to urge us on with his words, example, and frequently with the whip. Mr. Covey was one of the few slaveholders who could and did work with his hands. He was a hard-working man. He knew by himself just what a man or a boy could do. There was no deceiving him. His work went on in his absence almost as well as in his presence; and he had the <u>faculty</u> of making us feel that he was ever present with us. This he did by surprising us. He seldom approached the spot where we were at work openly, if he could do it secretly. He always aimed at taking us by surprise. Such was his cunning, that we used to call him, among ourselves, "the snake." When we were at work in

---

2. **saving-fodder . . . binding blades:** They are gathering and bundling ("binding") corn-plant leaves ("blades") to use as food for livestock ("fodder").

WORDS
TO
KNOW

**faculty** (făk′əl-tē) *n.* a natural power or ability

564

---

## Teaching Options

### Mini Lesson | **Vocabulary Strategy**

**CONNOTATION/DENOTATION**

**Instruction** The dictionary definition of a word is called its *denotation;* the emotional attitude conveyed by a word is called its *connotation.* While Douglass's description of Covey seems objective, some words in his description have negative connotations.

**Application** Have students write the denotations and connotations of the words listed in the chart. Then ask students to find synonyms for the words. Discuss how substituting the synonyms might change the reader's impression. Remind students that the context of a word can sometimes give it a negative connotation (e.g., *coiled up/snake*).

| Words Douglass uses | Denotation | Connotation | Synonym |
|---|---|---|---|
| cunning | skill | slyness; skill in deception | cleverness |
| scream out | give a loud, high, piercing cry | yell in anger | shout |
| coiled up | gathered in a circular form | like a snake | sitting |
| crawl | go on hands and knees | like a snake | creep |

the cornfield, he would sometimes crawl on his hands and knees to avoid detection, and all at once he would rise nearly in our midst, and scream out, "Ha, ha! Come, come! Dash on, dash on!" This being his mode of attack, it was never safe to stop a single minute. His comings were like a thief in the night. He appeared to us as being ever at hand. He was under every tree, behind every stump, in every bush, and at every window, on the plantation. He would sometimes mount his horse, as if bound to St. Michael's, a distance of seven miles, and in half an hour afterwards you would see him coiled up in the corner of the wood-fence, watching every motion of the slaves. He would, for this purpose, leave his horse tied up in the woods. Again, he would sometimes walk up to us, and give us orders as though he was upon the point of starting on a long journey, turn his back upon us, and make as though he was going to the house to get ready; and, before he would get half way thither, he would turn short and crawl into a fence-corner, or behind some tree, and there watch us till the going down of the sun. . . .

**If** at any one time of my life more than another, I was made to drink the bitterest dregs of slavery, that time was during the first six months of my stay with Mr. Covey. We were worked in all weathers. It was never too hot or too cold; it could never rain, blow, hail, or snow, too hard for us to work in the field. Work,

*My awkwardness was almost always his excuse for whipping me.*

work, work, was scarcely more the order of the day than of the night. The longest days were too short for him, and the shortest nights too long for him. I was somewhat unmanageable when I first went there, but a few months of this discipline tamed me. Mr. Covey succeeded in breaking me. I was broken in body, soul, and spirit. My natural elasticity was crushed, my intellect languished, the disposition to read departed, the cheerful spark that lingered about my eye died; the dark night of slavery closed in upon me; and behold a man transformed into a brute!

Sunday was my only leisure time. I spent this in a sort of beast-like stupor, between sleep and wake, under some large tree. At times I would rise up, a flash of energetic freedom would dart through my soul, accompanied with a faint beam of hope, that flickered for a moment, and then vanished. I sank down again, mourning over my wretched condition. I was sometimes prompted to take my life, and that of Covey, but was prevented by a combination of hope and fear. My sufferings on this plantation seem now like a dream rather than a stern reality. . . .

I have already <u>intimated</u> that my condition was much worse, during the first six months of my stay at Mr. Covey's, than in the last six. The circumstances leading to the change in Mr. Covey's course toward me form an epoch in my humble history. You have seen how a man was made a slave; you shall see how a slave was made a man. On one of the hottest days of the month of August, 1833, Bill Smith, William Hughes, a slave named Eli, and myself, were engaged in

WORDS TO KNOW  **languish** (lăng'gwĭsh) v. to become weak
**intimate** (ĭn'tə-māt) v. to make known indirectly; hint

**565**

## Customizing Instruction

### Less Proficient Readers

**1** Ask how Douglass's inexperience in the fields caused him trouble.
**Possible Response:** He did not know how to control the oxen, the cart crashed, and Mr. Covey whipped him for his "carelessness."
**Set a Purpose** Ask students to read to find out how Douglass copes with the challenges of his new situation.

### Multiple Learning Styles
**Spatial or Graphic Learners**

**2** If the subject were not so serious, the description of Covey would be comical. Suggest that after students read the description of Covey's actions, they quickly sketch a cartoon that captures his essence. After students have finished reading the selection, they can share their cartoons with the class.

### Students Acquiring English

**3** This sentence contains some difficult vocabulary. Divide the sentence into clauses as follows: *My natural elasticity was crushed,/my intellect languished,/the disposition to read departed,* and so forth. Assign each clause to a different group of students and have them come up with their own brief paraphrase of it. Then ask the groups to share their findings as you work with them to determine the meaning of the entire sentence.

Use **Vocabulary Transparencies and Copymasters,** p. 50.

**A lesson on connotation and denotation appears on p. 908 in the Pupil's Edition.**

### Literary Analysis | AUTOBIOGRAPHY AND STYLE |

**A** Ask students to give examples of factual and subjective description in this passage. Discuss the effect that Douglass achieves by using both types of description.
**Possible Responses:** Factual—"the work was simple, requiring strength rather than intellect"; "my strength failed me." Subjective—"I nerved myself up, feeling it would never do to stop work"; "[I] felt as if held down by an immense weight." Factual descriptions lend credibility to the account, while subjective details make the autobiography more personal and emotionally engaging.

### Reading Skills and Strategies: MAKING JUDGMENTS

**B** Ask students to consider the historical context and their own experiences to decide whether they think it's a good idea for Douglass to complain to Thomas about Covey. Have students give reasons for their responses.
**Possible Responses:** Yes—Thomas might take pity on him and take him back into the household. No—he could be punished by Thomas or by Covey for running away from Covey's farm.

### Literary Analysis: CHARACTERIZATION

**C** Ask students what Douglass's seven-mile walk reveals about him.
**Possible Responses:** He is determined, strong, brave, persistent, hopeful.

**A** **1** fanning wheat.[3] Hughes was clearing the fanned wheat from before the fan. Eli was turning, Smith was feeding, and I was carrying wheat to the fan. The work was simple, requiring strength rather than intellect; yet, to one entirely unused to such work, it came very hard. About three o'clock of that day, I broke down; my strength failed me; I was seized with a violent aching of the head, attended with extreme dizziness; I trembled in every limb. Finding what was coming, I nerved myself up, feeling it would never do to stop work. I stood as long as I could stagger to the hopper[4] with grain. When I could stand no longer, I fell, and felt as if held down by an immense weight. The fan of course stopped; every one had his own work to do; and no one could do the work of the other, and have his own go on at the same time.

**Mr.** Covey was at the house, about one hundred yards from the treading-yard where we were fanning. On hearing the fan stop, he left immediately, and came to the spot where we were. He hastily inquired what the matter was. Bill answered that I was sick, and there was no one to bring wheat to the fan. I had by this time crawled away under the side of the post and rail-fence by which the yard was enclosed, hoping to find relief by getting out of the sun. He then asked where I was. He was told by one of the hands. He came to the spot, and, after looking at me awhile, asked me what was the matter. I told him as well as I could, for I scarce had strength to speak. He then gave me a savage kick in the side, and told me to get up. I tried to do so, but fell back in the attempt. He gave me another kick, and again told me to rise. I again tried, and succeeded in gaining my feet; but, stooping to get the tub with which I was feeding the fan, I again staggered and fell. While down in this situation, Mr. Covey took up the hickory slat with which Hughes had been striking off the half-bushel measure, and with it gave me a

heavy blow upon the head, making a large wound, and the blood ran freely; and with this again told me to get up. I made no effort to comply, having now made up my mind to let him do his worst. In a short time after receiving this blow, my head grew better. Mr. Covey had now left me to my fate. At this moment I resolved, for the first time, to go to my master, enter a complaint, and ask his protection. In order to do this, I must that afternoon walk seven miles; and this, under the circumstances, was truly a severe undertaking. I was exceedingly feeble; made so as much by the kicks and blows which I received, as by the severe fit of sickness to which I had been subjected. I, however, watched my chance, while Covey was looking in an opposite direction, and started for St. Michael's. I succeeded in getting a considerable distance on my way to the woods, when Covey discovered me, and called after me to come back, threatening what he would do if I did not come. I disregarded both his calls and his threats, and made my way to the woods as fast as my feeble state would allow; and thinking I might be overhauled by him if I kept the road, I walked through the woods, keeping far enough from the road to avoid detection, and near enough to prevent losing my way. I had not gone far before my little strength again failed me. I could go no farther. I fell down, and lay for a considerable time. The blood was yet oozing from the wound on my head. For a time I thought I should bleed to death; and think now that I should have done so, but that the blood so matted my hair as to stop the wound. After lying there about three quarters of an hour, I nerved myself up again, and started on my way, through bogs and briers, barefooted and bareheaded, tearing my feet sometimes at nearly every step; and after a journey of about seven miles, occupying some five hours to perform it, I arrived at master's

---

3. **fanning wheat:** using a machine that blows air to separate grains of wheat from the unusable husks.
4. **hopper:** a funnel-shaped container for storing grain.

## Teaching Options

### BLOCK SCHEDULING: MANAGING TIME

**If your schedule requires that you cover the lesson objectives in a shorter time, use . . .**
- Preparing to Read, p. 562
- Thinking Through the Literature, p. 571
- Vocabulary in Action, p. 573

**If you want to take advantage of longer class time, use . . .**
- TE Teaching Options: Preteaching Vocabulary, p. 563; Vocabulary Strategy, p. 564; Viewing and Representing, p. 567; Speaking and Listening, p. 568; Informal Assessment, p. 569; Cross-Curricular Link, p. 570
- Choices & Challenges and Author Activity, pp. 572–573

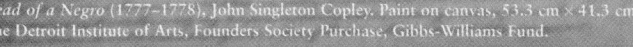

*Head of a Negro* (1777–1778), John Singleton Copley. Paint on canvas, 53.3 cm × 41.3 cm. The Detroit Institute of Arts, Founders Society Purchase, Gibbs-Williams Fund.

## Customizing Instruction

### Students Acquiring English

**1** Explain that *attended with* means "along with" or "accompanied by."

### Less Proficient Readers

**2** Ask students to summarize the events that led up to Douglass's decision to go to his former master. Suggest that they identify main ideas in the text to produce their summaries. **Possible Response:** Douglass became ill and had to stop working. Covey found him and beat him until he bled.

### Multiple Learning Styles
**Logical-Mathematical Learners**

**3** Douglass says it took him about five hours to walk seven miles. If an average person can walk one mile in 15 to 20 minutes, ask students how long it should take someone to walk seven miles. *(between 1 hour and 45 minutes and 2 hours and 20 minutes)* Is the narrator's pace above or below average? *(below average)* What are some possible reasons for the slowness of his pace? *(his wounds, exhaustion, difficult terrain)*

 **Viewing and Representing**

*Head of a Negro* **by John Singleton Copley**

**ART APPRECIATION** As a young man, John Singleton Copley (1738–1815) worked as a professional painter and engraver. The subject for *Head of a Negro* may have been a young servant in the Copley household.

**Instruction** Explain that when wealthy people had their portraits painted, they would wear expensive, ornate clothing that the artist would render in great detail. Copley was known for creating luxurious settings for his subjects. Ask students to examine this painting and consider the most striking aspect of it. What artistic elements contribute to this focus?

**Possible Response:** The man's clothing is suggested by a few rough strokes, and there is no background to the painting at all. Only the man's face is painted in detail, which leads viewers to focus on his face and expression.

**Application** Have students discuss the following questions:

• Is the style of this portrait realistic? Explain why or why not.

• How would you describe the young man's expression? What can you tell about his personality?

### Literary Analysis: CHARACTERIZATION

**(A)** Ask students what they can infer about Thomas from his actions and words and from Douglass's description of him in this passage.

**Possible Responses:** Thomas is disturbed by Douglass's appearance and by what Douglass told him but is not alarmed enough to do anything about it; money means more to him than his slave's life; he isn't above using threats to get what he wants.

### Literary Analysis AUTOBIOGRAPHY AND STYLE

**(B)** Some of what the narrator describes is based on fact, and some of it on feeling. Ask students to give examples of fact and feeling in the passage.

**Possible Responses:** Fact—Douglass seized Covey by the throat; the two held on to each other. Feeling—Douglass was resolved to fight; resistance was unexpected; Covey was taken aback.

### Reading Skills and Strategies: MAKING INFERENCES

**(C)** Ask students to infer why Covey says he would not have whipped Douglass half so much. Remind them to support their inferences with textual evidence.

**Possible Responses:** Covey wants to maintain the fiction that he still has the upper hand; he refuses to believe that he did not win out over his slave; he thinks slaves are stupid and will believe whatever he says.

---

store. I then presented an appearance enough to affect any but a heart of iron. From the crown of my head to my feet, I was covered with blood. My hair was all clotted with dust and blood; my shirt was stiff with blood. My legs and feet were torn in <u>sundry</u> places with briers and thorns, and were also covered with blood. I suppose I looked like a man who had escaped a den of wild beasts, and barely escaped them. In this state I appeared before my master, humbly entreating him to <u>interpose</u> his authority for my protection. I told him all the circumstances as well as I could, and it seemed, as I spoke, at times to affect him. He would then walk the floor, and seek to justify Covey by saying he expected I deserved it. He asked me what I wanted. I told him, to let me get a new home; that as sure as I lived with Mr. Covey again, I should live with but to die with him; that Covey would surely kill me; he was in a fair way for it. Master Thomas ridiculed the idea that there was any danger of Mr. Covey's killing me, and said that he knew Mr. Covey; that he was a good man, and that he could not think of taking me from him; that, should he do so, he would lose the whole year's wages; that I belonged to Mr. Covey for one year, and that I must go back to him, come what might; and that I must not trouble him with any more stories, or that he would himself *get hold of me*. After threatening me thus, he gave me a very large dose of salts,[5] telling me that I might remain in St. Michael's that night, (it being quite late,) but that I must be off back to Mr. Covey's early in the morning; and that if I did not, he would *get hold of me*,

> *I resolved to fight; and, suiting my action to the resolution, I seized Covey hard by the throat.*

which meant that he would whip me. I remained all night, and, according to his orders, I started off to Covey's in the morning, (Saturday morning,) wearied in body and broken in spirit. I got no supper that night, or breakfast that morning. I reached Covey's about nine o'clock; and just as I was getting over the fence that divided Mrs. Kemp's fields from ours, out ran Covey with his cowskin, to give me another whipping. Before he could reach me, I succeeded in getting to the cornfield; and as the corn was very high, it afforded me the means of hiding. He seemed very angry, and searched for me a long time. My behavior was altogether unaccountable. He finally gave up the chase, thinking, I suppose, that I must come home for something to eat; he would give himself no further trouble in looking for me. I spent that day mostly in the woods, having the alternative before me,—to go home and be whipped to death, or stay in the woods and be starved to death. That night, I fell in with Sandy Jenkins, a slave with whom I was somewhat acquainted. Sandy had a free wife who lived about four miles from Mr. Covey's; and it being Saturday, he was on his way to see her. I told him my circumstances, and he very kindly invited me to go home with him. I went home with him, and talked this whole matter over, and got his advice as to what course it was best for me to pursue. I found Sandy an old adviser. He told

---

5. **salts:** mineral salts used to relieve faintness and headache or reduce swelling.

WORDS TO KNOW

**sundry** (sŭn′drē) *adj.* various; miscellaneous
**interpose** (ĭn′tər-pōz′) *v.* to interfere in order to help; intervene

568

---

## Teaching Options

 **Mini Lesson** ## Speaking and Listening

**PERSUASIVE SPEECH**

**Prepare** Help students prepare a short speech similar to one that Douglass might have presented to an anti-slavery society. Have students work in cooperative groups to define the message of the speech and to organize evidence to support their position. Encourage students to use details from the selection to illustrate the points they want to make.

**Present** One student from each group can present the speech. Have the groups hold several practice sessions in order to critique and refine the presen-

tation. Have students refer to the criteria for evaluating a persuasive speech in the Communications Handbook. The entire class will be the audience for the final presentations. After the speech, have the presenter, in the persona of Douglass, respond to questions from the audience. If the presenter cannot answer a question, invite other audience members to respond.

**BLOCK SCHEDULING** This activity is especially well-suited for longer class periods.

me, with great solemnity, I must go back to Covey; but that before I went, I must go with him into another part of the woods, where there was a certain *root*, which, if I would take some of it with me, carrying it *always on my right side*, would render it impossible for Mr. Covey, or any other white man, to whip me. He said he had carried it for years; and since he had done so, he had never received a blow, and never expected to while he carried it. I at first rejected the idea, that the simple carrying of a root in my pocket would have any such effect as he had said, and was not disposed to take it; but Sandy impressed the necessity with much earnestness, telling me it could do no harm, if it did no good. To please him, I at length took the root, and, according to his direction, carried it upon my right side. This was Sunday morning. I immediately started for home; and upon entering the yard gate, out came Mr. Covey on his way to meeting.[6] He spoke to me very kindly, bade me drive the pigs from a lot near by, and passed on towards the church. Now, this singular conduct of Mr. Covey really made me begin to think that there was something in the *root* which Sandy had given me; and had it been on any other day than Sunday, I could have attributed the conduct to no other cause than the influence of that root; and as it was, I was half inclined to think the *root* to be something more than I at first had taken it to be. All went well till Monday morning. On this morning, the virtue of the *root* was fully tested. Long before daylight, I was called to go and rub, curry, and feed, the horses. I obeyed, and was glad to obey. But whilst thus engaged, whilst in the act of throwing down some blades from the loft, Mr. Covey entered the stable with a long rope; and just as I was half out of the loft, he caught hold of my legs, and was about tying me. As soon as I found what he was up to, I gave a sudden spring, and as I did so, he holding to my legs, I was brought sprawling on the stable floor. Mr. Covey seemed now to think he had me, and could do what he pleased; but at

this moment—from whence came the spirit I don't know—I resolved to fight; and, suiting my action to the resolution, I seized Covey hard by the throat; and as I did so, I rose. He held on to me, and I to him. My resistance was so entirely unexpected, that Covey seemed taken all aback.[7]  He trembled like a leaf. This gave me assurance, and I held him uneasy, causing the blood to run where I touched him with the ends of my fingers. Mr. Covey soon called out to Hughes for help. Hughes came, and, while Covey held me, attempted to tie my right hand. While he was in the act of doing so, I watched my chance, and gave him a heavy kick close under the ribs. This kick fairly sickened Hughes, so that he left me in the hands of Mr. Covey. This kick had the effect of not only weakening Hughes, but Covey also. When he saw Hughes bending over with pain, his courage quailed. He asked me if I meant to persist in my resistance. I told him I did, come what might; that he had used me like a brute for six months, and that I was determined to be used so no longer. With that, he strove to drag me to a stick that was lying just out of the stable door. He meant to knock me down. But just as he was leaning over to get the stick, I seized him with both hands by his collar, and brought him by a sudden snatch to the ground. By this time, Bill came. Covey called upon him for assistance. Bill wanted to know what he could do. Covey said, "Take hold of him, take hold of him!" Bill said his master hired him out to work, and not to help to whip me; so he left Covey and myself to fight our own battle out. We were at it for nearly two hours. Covey at length let me go, puffing and blowing at a great rate, saying that if I had not resisted, he would not have whipped me half so much. The truth was, that he had not whipped me at all. I considered him as getting entirely the worst end of the bargain; for he had drawn no

---

6. **meeting:** church service.

7. **taken all aback:** so surprised as to be unable to move or respond.

## Customizing Instruction

### Students Acquiring English

**1** Explain that *but* means "only" and *he was in a fair way for it* means "he was inclined toward it; he wanted to do it."

### Less Proficient Readers

**2** Ask students why Douglass tries to get help. Have them explain whether Douglass is successful.

**Possible Responses:** He seeks help because he fears for his life. His master does not help him, though; instead he threatens him and sends him back to Covey.

**Set a Purpose** Have students read to find out what happens when Douglass returns to Covey's farm.

### Gifted and Talented

**3** Have students discuss their thoughts about how Richard Whately's idea—that a slave master loses more than half his virtue—applies to Douglass's narrative. Encourage students to read additional sections of Douglass's autobiography, noting the role of virtue in the actions of Douglass and his masters.

---

✓ **Assessment** **Informal Assessment**

**SUMMARIZING** Have students work in small groups to prepare a student who has not done the reading (in pretense or actuality) for a test on this selection. Each "teacher" has only three minutes to speak to the unprepared student and therefore should coordinate a presentation that covers the main events and ideas. Have group members first work together to identify and organize the material. Then they can divide the main events and ideas to be covered into three-minute chunks.

**RUBRIC**

**3** **Full Accomplishment** The main events and ideas are well developed and presented in chronological order.

**2** **Substantial Accomplishment** The main events and ideas are in order, but one or two need elaboration.

**1** **Little or Partial Accomplishment** Some main events and/or ideas are missing, and organization is lacking.

### Active Reading | AUTHOR'S PURPOSE |

**A** Ask students to speculate about how readers in Douglass's time might have felt reading the description of his "glorious resurrection." Have them especially consider readers who themselves owned slaves.

**Possible Response:** Most readers would have been moved by this description of Douglass's newfound optimism and self-confidence. Readers who owned slaves would have found their beliefs about Africans—that they were somehow less "human" than Europeans—challenged by Douglass's description of how his spirit was transformed.

### Literary Analysis

| AUTOBIOGRAPHY AND STYLE |

Ask students to describe how the author's feelings about himself change throughout the selection. What does Douglass learn about himself, and what does the reader learn about slavery? Have students cite details in the text to defend their interpretations.

**Possible Response:** At the beginning, Douglass was frustrated and rebellious about the treatment he received at the hands of Covey. Then the harsh discipline broke his spirit and he became depressed. Finally, when his very life seemed to be on the line, he rallied and stood up to Covey, asserting his dignity and resolving to no longer think of himself as a slave. Douglass learns that he is capable of great strength and fortitude and that by keeping freedom in his heart he will one day achieve it in actuality. The reader learns about the terrible effects of slavery on both the oppressed and the oppressor.

blood from me, but I had from him. The whole six months afterwards, that I spent with Mr. Covey, he never laid the weight of his finger upon me in anger. He would occasionally say, he didn't want to get hold of me again. "No," thought I, "you need not; for you will come off worse than you did before."

This battle with Mr. Covey was the turning-point in my career as a slave. It rekindled the few expiring embers of freedom, and revived within me a sense of my own manhood. It recalled the departed self-confidence, and inspired me again with a determination to be free. The gratification afforded by the triumph was a full compensation for whatever else might follow, even death itself. He only can understand the deep satisfaction which I experienced, who has himself repelled by force the bloody arm of slavery. I felt as I never felt before. It was a glorious resurrection, from the tomb of slavery, to the heaven of freedom. My long-crushed spirit rose, cowardice departed, bold defiance took its place; and I now resolved that, however long I might remain a slave in form, the day had passed forever when I could be a slave in fact. I did not hesitate to let it be known of me, that the white man who expected to succeed in whipping, must also succeed in killing me.

**A**

From this time I was never again what might be called fairly whipped, though I remained a slave four years afterwards. I had several fights, but was never whipped. ❖

## Teaching Options

**C**ross
Curricular Link   **History**

In 1963, one hundred years after Abraham Lincoln signed the Emancipation Proclamation freeing the slaves in the Confederate states, Martin Luther King, Jr., stood on the steps of the Lincoln Memorial and spoke of his dream of freedom for African Americans. Have students listen to a recording of that famous speech. Ask them to consider what King meant when he said, "We must face the tragic fact that the Negro is still not free." Ask students to reread the last two paragraphs of the selection, in which Frederick Douglass speaks of his determination to be free. Invite them to compare Douglass's dream of freedom with King's dream.

## Connect to the Literature

**1. What Do You Think?**
What are your impressions of Frederick Douglass?

**Comprehension Check**
• What was Covey's first reason for beating Douglass?
• How did Master Thomas respond when Douglass asked for protection from Covey?
• How did Douglass keep Covey from beating him again?

## Think Critically

**2.** Explain what you think Douglass means when he states, "However long I might remain a slave in form, the day had passed forever when I could be a slave in fact" (page 570).

**3.** What do Douglass's choices reveal to you about his character?

THINK ABOUT
{ • his resolve to ask Master Thomas for protection
  • his agreeing to take the root from Sandy
  • his decision to fight Covey

**4.** What would you say freedom means to Douglass?

**5.** ACTIVE READING  AUTHOR'S PURPOSE  Think about your reactions to Douglass and his fellow slaves, on the one hand, and to Covey and Master Thomas on the other. How does Douglass's writing make his **audience** feel about slavery? Explain.

**6.** What do the **conflicts** between Douglass and Covey reveal about slavery's effects on both slaves and masters?

## Extend Interpretations

**7. Comparing Texts**  Reread the next-to-last paragraph, in which Douglass describes his feelings of freedom and manhood after resisting Covey's brutality. Cite specific examples to compare Douglass's ideas with Emerson's philosophy in the excerpt from "Self-Reliance" on page 364.

**8. Connect to Life**  In what situations today might a person be inspired by Douglass's life story?

## Literary Analysis

AUTOBIOGRAPHY AND STYLE

The **style** of a literary work is the distinctive way in which it was written. Douglass's style in this autobiography is formal and elegant. Often his diction, or choice of words, is elevated ("whilst thus engaged"). His tone is restrained, as opposed to furious. He uses little direct dialogue. What other features of his style did you notice?

Critics often comment that Douglass is surprisingly **objective**—he can be quite factual and unemotional, given the brutality he describes. Consider this example:

*We were worked fully up to the point of endurance. . . . Mr. Covey gave us enough to eat, but scarce time to eat it.*

Yet at times Douglass can also be **subjective,** describing his personal feelings in emotionally charged words and figurative expressions:

*It was a glorious resurrection, from the tomb of slavery, to the heaven of freedom.*

**Cooperative Learning Activity**
With a group of classmates, choose three passages that you think give an especially telling picture of slavery. Decide whether the passages are primarily objective, subjective, or a combination of both. Discuss how Douglass's style might suit his **purpose** of convincing a largely white audience to abolish slavery.

## Extend Interpretations

**Comparing Texts** By citing specific examples, students should conclude that Douglass's ideas mainly support Emerson's philosophy.
**Connect to Life** Students will probably cite examples of individuals who are struggling to overcome oppression and adversity.

## Literary Analysis

**Autobiography and Style** Have students discuss whether they think objective, subjective, or a combination of both is most effective as a strategy for convincing Douglass's audience to abolish slavery. Have them support their opinions with the passages they select. If there is time, have students present their selected passages and decide as a class which is the most persuasive passage and why.

## Connect to the Literature

**1. What Do You Think?**
Possible Responses: strong-willed, educated, eloquent, proud

**Comprehension Check**
• Covey accused Douglass of trifling away time and breaking gates.
• He dismissed Douglass's fears about Covey and threatened to whip Douglass himself if he didn't return to Covey; Master Thomas was more worried about losing a year's wages than Douglass's life.
• He fought back and beat Covey.

 Use Selection Quiz
**Unit Four Resource Book**, p. 8.

## Think Critically

**2.** Possible Response: Although physically enslaved, his soul would be free.
**3.** Possible Responses: He is determined because he can no longer accept his lot as a slave; he recognizes injustice and wants to do something about it; he is grateful for the help that Sandy gives him.
**4.** Possible Responses: having the ability to choose; being able to learn and read freely. He believes that manhood depends on freedom.
**5.** Possible Response: Mr. Covey and Master Thomas are portrayed as cruel, heartless men; Douglass and his fellow slaves are portrayed as real people who are oppressed and treated brutally. Douglass's writing shows both the humanity of African Americans and the inhumanity of slavery.
**6.** Possible Response: They are dehumanizing to both. Masters can become monsters of power; and slaves can become exhausted, robotic, desperate, or violent.

## Writing Options

1. **Closing Statement** Students' statements should have a clear purpose, and both the objective and subjective elements should support that purpose.

2. **Antislavery Editorial** Point out to students that the purpose of an editorial is to formally and publicly state one's position on a current event or topic of debate. Students can defend their positions with facts and opinions.

3. **Comparison of Slave Narratives** Suggest that students compare and contrast not only the physical and emotional experiences of the authors, but also how they interpreted their slavery experiences after attaining freedom. **To extend this assignment,** have students compare Douglass's view of the African-American experience with the views of Julius Lester in *To Be a Slave,* Richard Wright in *American Hunger,* and James Baldwin in *Notes of a Native Son.*

4. **Autobiographical Sketch** Remind students that they should not only describe the experience, but should explain why it was a turning point for them. Some students might say that their lives have not yet had a turning point. Suggest that those students write about an event in their lives that they think was significant in some way.

## Activities & Explorations

1. **Living to Tell** Review with students the purpose (to retell an episode) and audience (Anti-Slavery Society) of this speech. Discuss how retelling the episode to a friendly audience might affect the way students deliver their message. See the mini lesson on page 568 for tips on presenting the speech.

2. **Story in Pictures** To help students get started, suggest that they divide the selection into small units and decide which scenes they will depict. The final product should be loyal to the original text.

3. **Discussion of Covey** To get students started on this activity, have them brainstorm a character cluster for Covey.

## Writing Options

1. **Closing Statement** Imagine that Covey had Douglass arrested for fighting him. As Douglass's attorney, write a closing statement for the trial. Use both objective evidence and subjective language to persuade a jury that Douglass was right to defend himself.

**Writing Handbook**
See page 1283: Analysis.

2. **Antislavery Editorial** Douglass founded an antislavery newspaper, the *North Star.* Based on your reading of this excerpt, write an outline for an editorial about slavery that you would write for his paper.

3. **Comparison of Slave Narratives** In an essay, compare and contrast the excerpts from the narratives of Douglass and Olaudah Equiano (page 94). Focus on the content, style, theme, and purpose of each selection.

**Writing Handbook**
See page 1281: Compare and Contrast.

|  | Douglass | Equiano |
|---|---|---|
| Content |  |  |
| Style |  |  |
| Theme |  |  |
| Purpose |  |  |

4. **Autobiographical Sketch** Douglass's fight with Covey was a turning point for him. Think of an incident from your own life that you would describe as a turning point.

Write about this incident in a short autobiographical sketch, explaining why it changed your life.

## Activities & Explorations

1. **Living to Tell** As Douglass, retell an episode from this selection as a short speech to the Anti-Slavery Society. ~ PERFORMING

2. **Story in Pictures** Collaborate with several classmates on a picture book for young readers. Recount Douglass's time with Covey, simplifying the language and illustrating important scenes. Then share the picture book with younger readers at home or in your school. ~ ART

3. **Discussion of Covey** Gather in a small group to discuss why Covey never again whipped Douglass. Speculate about why Covey did not tell authorities about Douglass's resistance and have him punished. Draw on your own experiences with bullies to come up with reasons. Share notes from your discussion with the rest of the class. ~ SPEAKING AND LISTENING

## Inquiry & Research

1. **Another View** Find another slave narrative, such as *Incidents in the Life of a Slave Girl,* by Harriet Jacobs, or *The History of Mary Prince, a West Indian Slave.* How does the writer's experience of slavery compare to Frederick Douglass's experience? Make comparisons in an oral presentation.

2. **Slave Laws** States where slavery was legal had special laws restricting the activities of slaves. Research these laws, using published or electronic sources, and hang a poster in your classroom that lists ten of the harshest laws.

 **More Online: Research Starter** www.mcdougallittell.com

## Art Connection

The 18th-century portrait on page 567 does not depict Frederick Douglass but an unnamed man, perhaps a servant of the artist, John Singleton Copley. Realistic portraits of African Americans were rare during the 18th and 19th centuries. What seems to be this man's state of mind? If you had to pull out a line from the Frederick Douglass selection to go with this painting, which line would you choose, and why?

*Head of a Negro* (1777–1778), John Singleton Copley. Paint on canvas, 53.3 cm × 41.3 cm. The Detroit Institute of Arts, Founders Society Purchase, Gibbs-Williams Fund.

 **Mini Lesson** **Grammar**

### IDENTIFYING CLAUSES: INDEPENDENT AND SUBORDINATE

**Instruction** A clause is a group of words that contains a verb and its subject. An independent clause expresses a complete thought and can stand alone. A subordinate clause cannot stand alone because it does not express a complete thought. Write the following sentence on the chalkboard and have students identify the independent and subordinate clauses.

Because he was a house slave, young Frederick Douglass was able to educate himself.

Point out that subordinate clauses often begin with an introductory word such as *because, when,* or *while.*

**Exercises** Have students underline the independent clauses and put brackets around the dependent clauses.

1. [When Mrs. Auld taught young Frederick Douglass the alphabet], Mr. Auld objected.

2. People read Douglass's autobiography and they flocked to his lectures.

3. [While Douglass was on tour in Europe], his friends raised money to buy his freedom.

## Vocabulary in Action

**EXERCISE A: MEANING CLUES** Read each magazine article title below and write the vocabulary word that you would expect to find in that article.

1. "Sibling Rivalry: When to Step In"
2. "Making the Most of Your Natural Talents"
3. "Energy Boosters: Some Perfect Pick-Me-Ups"
4. "How to Get What You Want Without Having to Ask"
5. "Too Much Junk? How to Have a Successful Garage Sale"

**Building Vocabulary**

Some of the Words to Know have more than one meaning. For an in-depth lesson on words with multiple meanings, see page 630.

**EXERCISE B:** Team up with a partner to write a sentence that uses as many of the Words to Know as possible. Describing a humorous or unlikely situation is fine, as long as the words are used accurately. Then either act out this sentence as someone reads it to the class, or draw an illustration of it to show to your classmates.

| WORDS TO KNOW | faculty interpose | intimate languish | sundry |
|---|---|---|---|

## Frederick Douglass
### 1817?–1895

**Other Works**
*My Bondage and My Freedom*
*The Life and Times of Frederick Douglass*
"What to the Slave Is the Fourth of July?"
"The Color Line"

**Lecturing to the World** After having grown up in slavery in Maryland, Frederick Douglass escaped when he was 21 and fled to New York City disguised as a sailor. Three years later, Douglass spoke so eloquently to the Massachusetts Anti-Slavery Society that they hired him to lecture about his experiences. Soon after that he became one of the country's most prominent antislavery speakers, devoting his life to fighting for abolition, suffrage and civil rights. The publication of his autobiography, *Narrative of the Life of Frederick Douglass, an American Slave* (1845), resulted in widespread publicity and the possibility of recapture by his former owner. To remove himself from this dangerous situation, Douglass embarked on a two-year speaking tour in England, Scotland, Wales and Ireland.

**Publisher and Statesman** During Douglass's trip abroad, two friends raised the money to purchase his freedom. After returning to America in 1847 as a free man, Douglass settled in Rochester, New York, and founded an antislavery newspaper called the *North Star.* He continued lecturing against slavery and in 1848 addressed the first Women's Rights Convention in Seneca Falls, New York. As the Civil War began, Douglass was instrumental in recruiting the first African-American troops— including his own sons—for the 54th Massachusetts Volunteers. During the war, he advised President Abraham Lincoln. Douglass held several government positions after the war, including the post of Minister to Haiti. Throughout his life, Douglass continued to champion civil rights for African Americans and for women.

## Author Activity

**Poetic Tribute** Read Robert Hayden's poem "Frederick Douglass" on page 615. Is Hayden justified in his praise of Douglass? Use evidence from Douglass's life and autobiography to support your answer.

## Vocabulary in Action

**Exercise A**
1. interpose
2. faculty
3. languish
4. intimate
5. sundry

## Author Activity

**Poetic Tribute** Accept all reasonable responses that students support with evidence from the selection or from other sources of information about Douglass's life. Students might argue that the very fact that Douglass's words are still being read more than 100 years after his death shows that Hayden's praise was justified.

 Use **Grammar Transparencies and Copymasters,** p. 88.

 Use McDougal Littell's *Language Network,* Chapter 3, for more instruction and practice in clauses.

## OVERVIEW

### Objectives

1. understand and appreciate **protest poems** (Literary Analysis)
2. identify and appreciate **symbols** in a poem (Literary Analysis)
3. apply **strategies for reading protest poetry** (Active Reading)

### Summary

James Russell Lowell, a lifelong abolitionist, published "Stanzas on Freedom" in 1843. The poem challenges free men and women to work on behalf of their enslaved brothers and sisters, declaring that one is not free if others are held in bondage. In "Free Labor," published in 1857 by Frances Ellen Watkins Harper, the speaker describes the conditions of slavery by referring to her clothing—an "easy garment" that was not the product of slave labor. The poem poignantly depicts the slaves' lives of relentless toil. The speaker's conscience is clear by virtue of not having purchased goods ultimately derived from the labor of slaves.

### Thematic Link

Feelings against **slavery** escalated in the decades before the **Civil War.** The fires of opposition were fanned by writers such as Lowell and Harper, whose protest poems called for the abolition of slavery.

### 5-Minute Warm-Up

*Daily*
*Language*
*SkillBuilder*

Have students **proofread** the display sentences on page 555i and write them correctly. The sentences also appear on Transparency 15 of **Grammar Transparencies and Copymasters.**

# Stanzas on Freedom

*Poetry by* JAMES RUSSELL LOWELL

# Free Labor

*Poetry by* FRANCES ELLEN WATKINS HARPER

*Methods of Protest*

*writing a letter to the editor*

*staging a benefit concert*

*circulating a petition*

( **Connect to Your Life** )

**Standing for Justice** Name a current social or political situation you think should be protested. How would you attempt to generate public interest in solving this problem? With a group of classmates, brainstorm ten ways to publicize issues, adding to the list shown here. Then rate the effectiveness of the methods you listed on a scale of 1 to 10, with 10 being the most effective.

## Build Background

**Demand for Change** These two poems were written before the Civil War to protest slavery. In the United States, public opposition to slavery began in the 1680s when Quakers criticized slavery on religious grounds. Although the antislavery movement grew steadily in the 1700s, it gained momentum in the decades prior to the Civil War. By 1840, there were more than 2,000 antislavery societies and at least a dozen abolitionist newspapers. At the height of the movement, abolitionists in the North not only gave public lectures that denounced slavery but also published antislavery almanacs, magazines, and pamphlets. These publications often featured antislavery poems. In 1843, poet James Russell Lowell, a lifelong abolitionist, published "Stanzas on Freedom." Frances Ellen Watkins Harper, an antislavery lecturer and the most popular African-American poet of her time, published "Free Labor" in 1857.

## Focus Your Reading

**LITERARY ANALYSIS  SYMBOL**  A **symbol** is a person, place, object, or activity that has a concrete meaning but also stands for something beyond itself. Familiar symbols include a heart (symbolizing love), a dove (symbolizing peace), and a handshake (symbolizing friendship). The symbols in a poem are usually more original and complex; interpreting them is essential to understanding and enjoying the work. Look for words used as symbols in "Stanzas on Freedom" and "Free Labor."

**ACTIVE READING  STRATEGIES FOR READING PROTEST POETRY**
These works are examples of **protest poetry,** written less to express personal feelings than to persuade readers to support a certain cause. You might approach these poems as you approached the political speeches, letters, and essays in the second part of Unit Two, "The Right to Be Free."

- **First reading** Get a sense of the general ideas and overall feeling of each poem.
- **Second reading** Be more analytical. Determine the intended audience.
- **Third reading** Analyze what the poet wants readers to feel. Pay attention to your emotional reactions and the symbols, images, or devices that trigger them.

**READER'S NOTEBOOK** Begin to take notes as you first read the poem, and add to your notes as you read a second and a third time.

## LESSON RESOURCES

**UNIT FOUR RESOURCE BOOK,**
pp. 9–10

**ASSESSMENT RESOURCES**
**Formal Assessment,**
pp. 107–108
**Teacher's Guide to Assessment and Portfolio Use**
**Test Generator**

**SKILLS TRANSPARENCIES AND COPYMASTERS**
**Grammar**
- Distinguishing a Clause from a Phrase, C90 (for Mini Lesson, p. 579)

**Vocabulary**
- Figurative Language, C50 (for Mini Lesson, p. 576)

**Writing**
- Figurative Language and Sound Devices, T15 (for Writing Options 1 and 2, p. 579)

**INTEGRATED TECHNOLOGY**
**Audio Library**
**LaserLinks**
- Historical Connection: The Anti-Slavery Movement. See **Teacher's SourceBook,** p. 49.

**Visit our website:**
www.mcdougallittell.com

# Stanzas on Freedom

### JAMES RUSSELL LOWELL

Men! whose boast it is that ye
Come of fathers brave and free,
If there breathe on earth a slave,
Are ye truly free and brave?
5 If ye do not feel the chain,
When it works a brother's pain,
Are ye not base[1] slaves indeed,
Slaves unworthy to be freed?

Women! who shall one day bear
10 Sons to breathe New England air,
If ye hear, without a blush,
Deeds to make the roused blood rush
Like red lava through your veins,
For your sisters now in chains,—
15 Answer! are ye fit to be
Mothers of the brave and free?

Is true Freedom but to break
Fetters[2] for our own dear sake,
And, with leathern hearts, forget
20 That we owe mankind a debt?
No! true freedom is to share
All the chains our brothers wear,
And, with heart and hand, to be
Earnest to make others free!

25 They are slaves who fear to speak
For the fallen and the weak;
They are slaves who will not choose
Hatred, scoffing, and abuse,
Rather than in silence shrink
30 From the truth they needs must think;
They are slaves who dare not be
In the right with two or three.

---

1. **base:** having little or no honor, courage, or decency; low or inferior.
2. **fetters:** chains or other bonds.

## Thinking Through the Literature

1. **Comprehension Check** What does Lowell call those who are afraid to speak?

2. Judging from this poem, how do you think Lowell would define *freedom* and *slavery*?

   **THINK ABOUT**
   • his view of the "free" men and women he addresses in the first and second stanzas
   • his definition of "true freedom" in the third stanza
   • whom he describes as slaves in the last stanza

3. **ACTIVE READING** | **PROTEST POETRY** What kind of people do you believe Lowell is speaking to in this poem, and what does he want them to do?

4. Think again about the way Lowell uses the term *slaves* in the last stanza. Who in present-day America might Lowell view as slaves in this sense?

STANZAS ON FREEDOM **575**

## Mini Lesson  Speaking and Listening

**DRAMATIC READING** These two poems are particularly appropriate for dramatic readings because they espouse a cause. Share with students these tips for dramatic readings:
• Identify with the feelings of the speaker.
• Read the poem several times so you know the language, rhyme, and rhythm.
• Read the poem naturally, emphasizing important words and phrases.

• Pause at the end of each complete thought, not necessarily at the ends of lines. Look for end punctuation to help you.
• Practice reading aloud, using a tape recorder if possible.
**Present** Have students work in small groups to prepare a dramatic reading of each poem. Suggest that they divide the poems up according to stanzas and work together to make the presentation of each stanza as effective as

possible, marking words to emphasize and places to pause. Students should be able to justify their verbal performance techniques by referring to their interpretations of the texts. Audience members should evaluate how the performance increases their understanding of each poem's message.

**BLOCK SCHEDULING** This activity is particularly well suited for longer class periods.

Tell students that reading the poems aloud will help them identify the main ideas and experience the emotional impact.

**Active Reading** STRATEGIES FOR READING PROTEST POETRY

The first reading of a protest poem should leave readers with a strong impression of its main idea. Both Lowell and Harper introduce their main ideas in the first few lines of their poems. Ask students to identify the lines that tell readers what each poem will be about.

**Possible Responses:** In its first four lines, "Stanzas on Freedom" introduces the idea that no one is free while any-one else is enslaved. The first stanza of "Free Labor" informs readers that the poem is about people's implicit support of slavery by wearing garments made of cotton picked by slaves.

 Use **Unit Four Resource Book**, p. 9 for more practice.

**Literary Analysis** SYMBOL

**A** Remind students that writers some-times use words to stand for something else. Ask them to explain what a "wreath of household love" might represent.

**Possible Response:** A wreath is circu-lar, so it might stand for the family that surrounds a woman—in this case, the slave family that was "rudely torn apart" as its members were sold off.

 Use **Unit Four Resource Book**, p. 10 for more practice.

# Free Labor

## FRANCES ELLEN WATKINS HARPER

I wear an easy garment,
   O'er it no toiling slave
Wept tears of hopeless anguish,
   In his passage to the grave.

**1**

5  And from its ample folds
   Shall rise no cry to God,
Upon its warp and woof[1] shall be
   No stain of tears and blood.

Oh, lightly shall it press my form,
10   Unladened[2] with a sigh,
I shall not 'mid its rustling hear,
   Some sad despairing cry.

This fabric is too light to bear
   The weight of bondsmen's[3] tears,
15 I shall not in its texture trace
   The agony of years.

Too light to bear a smother'd sigh,
   From some lorn[4] woman's heart,
**A** Whose only wreath of household love
20   Is rudely torn apart.

Then lightly shall it press my form,
   Unburden'd by a sigh;
And from its seams and folds shall rise,
   No voice to pierce the sky,

25 And witness at the throne of God,
   In language deep and strong,
That I have nerv'd[5] Oppression's hand,
   For deeds of guilt and wrong.

---

1. **warp and woof:** In weaving cloth, the lengthwise threads ("warp") pass over and under the crosswise threads ("woof").
2. **unladened:** unburdened.
3. **bondsmen's:** slaves'.
4. **lorn:** forlorn; lonely and unhappy.
5. **nerv'd:** strengthened.

Collection of The New York Historical Society.

576

576   UNIT FOUR   PART 1

## Teaching Options

 **Mini Lesson** ## Vocabulary Strategy

**FIGURATIVE LANGUAGE**

**Instruction** Remind students that they can rely on context to determine the meaning of figurative language. Students should first identify the main idea and feelings conveyed by the passage in which the figurative language is found. Then they can infer the meaning of the figurative word or phrase.

In "Stanzas on Freedom," for example, the phrase "leathern hearts" is found in a stanza that pro-claims the callousness of those who, secure in their own well-being, forget about the hardships of others. Therefore, "leathern hearts" means unfeeling hearts, unmoved by the plight of those who suffer. The poet compares the hearts to leather because leather is a tough, dead material.

**Application** Ask students to work in small groups to identify figurative language in both poems. Students should keep in mind the main ideas and the feelings conveyed by each poem to determine the meanings of the words and phrases they extract.

 Use **Vocabulary Transparencies and Copymasters**, p. 50.

A lesson on context clues appears on p. 326 in the Pupil's Edition.

From the collections of the Library of Congress.

**Less Proficient Readers**
Have students summarize the main ideas of each poem.

**Possible Responses:** In "Stanzas on Freedom," the speaker wants people to realize that no one is truly free as long as anyone else is in slavery. In "Free Labor," the speaker explains that she will not support slavery by wearing clothes that ultimately derive from the labor of slaves.

**Students Acquiring English**

**1** Help students understand what the speaker's garment will not cry out and why it is free from stain.

✓ Assessment **Informal Assessment**

**CONTRASTING ACROSS TEXTS** You can informally assess your students' understanding of poetic style by asking them to contrast several elements of "Stanzas on Freedom" with those of "Free Labor." Although both poems fall under the genre of protest poetry, the poets use rhyme, rhythm, repetition, and alliteration in different ways.

**RUBRIC**

**3** **Full Accomplishment** Students characterize each poet's use of all four devices, giving an example of each.

**2** **Substantial Accomplishment** Students analyze the effect of three devices and can recognize examples of each.

**1** **Little or Partial Accomplishment** Students have difficulty in seeing how the poets employ the devices and in finding examples.

## GUIDING STUDENT RESPONSE

## Connect to the Literature

**1. What Do You Think?**
Possible Responses: Phrases such as "tears of hopeless anguish" and "stain of tears and blood" create images of the cruelty of slavery.

**Comprehension Check**
• The speaker will not wear garments made by slaves.
• The toiling slave's voice would cry to God that the wearer had strengthened oppression.

## Think Critically

2. Possible Responses: The speaker explains that no slave was involved in producing his or her garment. The speaker implies that readers should avoid products that derive from slave labor.

3. Possible Responses: Students should be able to draw conclusions about the speaker and support them with text evidence and experience. The speaker stands up for a belief and is not afraid to take action against injustice. The speaker may have personally experienced oppression.

4. Students should defend their choices by referring to the language of the lines and the emotional impact.

## Literary Analysis

**Symbol** Remind students that a symbol stands for something beyond itself. As they discuss the possible symbolic meanings, they should first identify the literal meanings of *chains* and *garment*. Possible Responses: *chains,* literal—"a connected, flexible series of links"; symbolic—"slavery" or "the inability to be in charge of one's own fate"; *garment,* literal—"an article of clothing"; symbolic—"antislavery" or "freedom to work"

**Cooperative Learning Activity** You might suggest that students divide up the responsibilities of paraphrasing the poems, checking for accuracy, writing the speech, and presenting it to the class. Audience members should evaluate the effectiveness of the speeches in comparison to the poems. A class discussion of the advantages of using symbols should follow the presentation of all the speeches.

---

## Connect to the Literature

**1. What Do You Think?**
Describe the images that the poem "Free Labor" creates in your mind.

**Comprehension Check**
• What kind of garment won't the speaker wear?
• Whose voice would rise from this garment, and what would it say to God?

## Think Critically

2.  **ACTIVE READING  PROTEST POETRY** In your own words, explain how "Free Labor" protests slavery.

**THINK ABOUT**
• what the **title** might mean
• what makes the speaker's garment "easy" and "light"
• what it means to "have nerv'd Oppression's hand"
• what specific action the poet might want her audience to take

3. What kind of person might the speaker in this poem be? What would you guess about the speaker's past?

4. Which do you think are the most effective lines in this poem? Explain your choice.

## Extend Interpretations

5. **Comparing Texts** If both "Stanzas on Freedom" and "Free Labor" had been read widely before the Civil War, which one do you think would be more likely to stir people to take a stand against slavery? Why?

6. **Connect to Life** What examples of art today do you think are comparable to the antislavery poems of the 19th century?

---

## Literary Analysis

**SYMBOL** As you know, a **symbol** has a concrete meaning in itself while also standing for something else, such as an idea or a feeling. In the story "Dr. Heidegger's Experiment," for example, the blooming and fading rose symbolizes human life. What do you think the chains in "Stanzas on Freedom" symbolize? In "Free Labor," what might the garment stand for?

**Cooperative Learning Activity** Work as a small group to paraphrase each of these poems as a short speech. Instead of using symbols, spell out what Lowell and Harper mean in literal terms. Read the speeches aloud to the class. Are they as effective as the poems? What are some advantages of using symbols to express ideas?

| Symbol | Ideas |
|--------|-------|
| Chains | |
| | |
| | |
| | |
| Garment | |
| | |
| | |

---

## Extend Interpretations

**Comparing Texts** Possible Responses: "Stanzas on Freedom" because it appeals to reason; "Free Labor" because it appeals to emotion
**Connect to Life** Students might cite photographs, cartoons, video clips, or documentaries as art forms that can stir strong emotions about the plight of the oppressed.

## Writing Options

**1. New Stanza** The first and second stanzas of "Stanzas on Freedom" begin "Men!" and "Women!" Imagine that the next stanza begins "Youths!" Complete such a stanza, writing what you believe would reflect a teenager's situation in those times. Read your stanza to classmates.

**2. Protest Poem** Write a protest poem to influence people to take a stand on some contemporary issue, perhaps the one you named in the Connect to Your Life activity on page 574.

## Activities & Explorations

**Political Poster** Create a poster to persuade people in the 1850s to take a stand against slavery. As an alternative, create a poster urging people today to take a stand against a modern injustice.
~ **ART**

## Writing Options

1. **New Stanza To get students started on this assignment,** have them brainstorm the special contributions that young people could make to the antislavery movement. Also ask them to note the rhyme scheme and rhythm of the first two stanzas so that theirs is consistent with the original.

2. **Protest Poem To get students started on this assignment,** have them review the contemporary issues that they jotted down for the Connect to Your Life activity on page 574. Making a quick outline might help students focus their thoughts before beginning to write.

## Activities & Explorations

**Political Poster** Students might like to work with partners to create posters. **To get students started on this assignment,** have them agree on a topic, create a succinct written message, and determine visual images they wish to use. They can develop their own artwork, use material from magazines, or generate visuals on the computer.

## James Russell Lowell
### 1819–1891

**Other Works**
*Poems*
*A Fable for Critics*
*My Study Windows*
*Under the Willows*

**Literary Activist** James Russell Lowell, a member of a prominent Massachusetts family, had achieved fame for his poetry and essays by the time he was 30. A well-known abolitionist, he wrote editorials for the antislavery newspaper, the *Pennsylvania Freeman*, and also contributed to the *National Anti-Slavery Standard* and other periodicals. In addition to "Stanzas on Freedom," Lowell also wrote other antislavery poems, including "On the Capture of Fugitive Slaves Near Washington," and dealt with this subject in The Biglow Papers, a collection of poetic letters attributed to the fictional Hosea Biglow.

**Tragedy and Achievement** While Lowell's literary reputation grew, his life took a tragic turn when his wife and three of his four children died within six years of one another. In 1856 he became professor of modern languages at Harvard, succeeding Henry Wadsworth Longfellow in that post. A year later, he accepted the editorship of the newly founded magazine *Atlantic Monthly*, and he remarried. In 1877 Lowell was appointed U.S. Minister to Spain and took a similar post in England three years later. After the death of his second wife in 1885, Lowell returned home, where he remained for the rest of his life.

## Frances Ellen Watkins Harper
### 1825–1911

**Other Works**
"The Slave Mother"
*Poems on Miscellaneous Subjects*
*Iola Leroy*

**A Gifted Orphan** Later known as the "Bronze Muse," poet, novelist, lecturer, and social reformer Frances Ellen Watkins Harper was born free in the slave city of Baltimore, Maryland. Orphaned at the age of three, she was raised by her aunt and uncle and attended her uncle's private school until she was 13. Harper then began working as a housekeeper. Because the family for whom she worked owned a bookstore, Harper was able to read books in her spare time. When she was fourteen, she began to write poems and essays.

**On Freedom's Road** In 1850, Harper moved to Ohio and became a teacher, but she soon decided to devote herself to the abolitionist cause. She traveled throughout the North and the Midwest giving lectures on the evils of slavery. Harper, who combined her artistic and political lives by reciting her poems during her speeches, wrote to a friend: "You would be amused to hear some of the remarks which my lectures call forth. 'She is a man,' again 'She is not colored, she is white. She is painted.'" After marrying in 1860, Harper settled on a farm in Ohio. Following her husband's death in 1864, she began lecturing on the topic of equal rights for the newly freed.

 **Mini Lesson** Grammar

**CLAUSES VS. PHRASES Instruction** A phrase is a group of related words that does not contain a verb and its subject and that functions as a single part of speech. A clause is a group of words that does contain a verb and its subject. An independent clause can stand alone as a sentence; a subordinate clause cannot. Display the following sentences to give examples of phrases and clauses:
<u>When a poet uses symbols</u>, the layers of meaning are multiplied. (subordinate clause; verb—*uses*, subject—*poet*)

<u>A single poem might offer a reader much food for thought</u>. (independent clause; verb—*might offer*, subject—*poem*)
James Russell Lowell's middle years were filled <u>with personal tragedy and professional triumph</u>. (phrase)
**Exercises** Ask students to identify the underlined segments of each sentence as phrases, independent clauses, or subordinate clauses.
1. Those <u>who spoke out against slavery</u> were often subjected to hostile acts. (*subordinate clause*)

2. Lowell's direct address <u>of men and women</u> in his poem does not allow any adult to escape his message. (*phrase*)

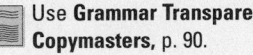 Use **Grammar Transparencies and Copymasters,** p. 90.

 Use McDougal Littell's *Language Network,* Chapters 2 and 3, for more instruction and practice.

# OVERVIEW

 This selection is included in the **Grade 11 InterActive Reader.**

## Objectives

1. appreciate a **short story** (Literary Analysis)
2. identify and examine **point of view** (Literary Analysis)
3. **analyze structure** in a short story (Active Reading)

## Summary

Peyton Farquhar, a Southern planter, is about to be hanged by Union soldiers as punishment for his attempt to set fire to a railroad bridge across Owl Creek. He focuses his last thoughts on his wife and children. When the signal is given, Farquhar falls through the bridge. As he plunges toward the water, the rope apparently breaks, giving him a chance to escape. Struggling with the rushing current, Farquhar manages to untie his hands and dodge bullets from soldiers on the bridge. He makes his way downstream and finally arrives safely on shore. After a nightmarish journey through the forest, Farquhar reaches his plantation at dawn and sees his wife waiting to greet him. At that moment he feels a stunning blow at the back of his neck; then all is dark and silent. Farquhar hangs dead from the Owl Creek Bridge. His heroic escape proves to have been a fantasy.

## Thematic Link

Peyton Farquhar sacrifices his life in the war that unified **"a house divided."** Trying to preserve the South as he believes it should be, he suffers the fate of many patriots in the **Civil War.**

## 5-Minute Warm-Up

*Daily*
*Language*
*SkillBuilder*

Have students **proofread** the display sentences on page 555i and write them correctly. The sentences also appear on Transparency 16 of **Grammar Transparencies and Copymasters.**

# An Occurrence at Owl Creek Bridge

*Short Story by* AMBROSE BIERCE

### Connect to Your Life

**Final Thoughts** This story is about a man who is facing death. It is often said that when people have a close brush with death, their life flashes before their eyes. What do you think might be the last thoughts of someone about to die? Would such a person think about the meaning of life, the loved ones left behind, or the immediate situation? Discuss the possibilities with a group of your classmates.

## Build Background

**Writing What He Knew** Ambrose Bierce enlisted in the Union Army at 18 and fought bravely in several major battles of the Civil War. After the war, he moved to San Francisco and began an equally distinguished career as a journalist. In this story, Bierce fictionalizes a real hanging that took place in 1862 during the bloody battle of Shiloh in Tennessee. Bierce's firsthand knowledge of the war and his training as a reporter can be seen in the opening two paragraphs of the story, in which he objectively describes the setting for a hanging that is about to occur.

> WORDS TO KNOW
> **Vocabulary Preview**
>
> apprise     ludicrous
> evade     perceptibly
> inaccessible     interminable
> preternaturally     subordinate
> ineffable     summarily

## Focus Your Reading

**LITERARY ANALYSIS | POINT OF VIEW** The **point of view** in a story is the narrative perspective from which it is told. In the **first-person** point of view, the narrator is a character in the work who describes events using the pronouns *I, me,* and *my.* In the **third-person** point of view, events are related by a voice outside the action, who uses such pronouns as *he, she,* and *they.* The third-person point of view may be **omniscient** (aware of all characters' thoughts) or **limited** (focused on one character's thoughts). Try to identify the point of view in Bierce's story.

**ACTIVE READING | ANALYZING STRUCTURE** The **structure** of a literary work is the arrangement of its parts. This story is arranged in three numbered sections. A change of section signals a change in time. To ensure your understanding as you read, be aware of when the events in each section take place.

**READER'S NOTEBOOK** To help you follow the sequence of events and clarify what happens in each section, use the reading strategy questions inserted throughout the story. Write down answers to the questions in your Reader's Notebook. Also, jot down other ideas that come to you, especially those relating to the main character's last thoughts.

# LESSON RESOURCES

**UNIT FOUR RESOURCE BOOK,** pp. 11–15

**ASSESSMENT RESOURCES**
**Formal Assessment,** pp. 109–110
**Teacher's Guide to Assessment and Portfolio Use**
**Test Generator**

**SKILLS TRANSPARENCIES AND COPYMASTERS**
**Literary Analysis**
• Point of View, T20 (for Paired Activity, p. 591)

**Reading and Critical Thinking**
• Evaluating Story Elements, T6 (for Writing Option 1, p. 592)

**Grammar**
• Using *That* and *Which,* T44 (for Mini Lesson, p. 590)
• Essential and Nonessential Clauses, C91 (for Mini Lesson, p. 590)
• Punctuating Nonessential Clauses, C149 (for Mini Lesson, p. 592)

**Vocabulary**
• Prefixes, C51 (for Mini Lesson, p. 584)

**Writing**
• Critical Review, C26 (for Writing Option 1, p. 592)
• Compare-Contrast, C32 (for Writing Option 2, p. 592)

**INTEGRATED TECHNOLOGY**
**Audio Library**
**LaserLinks**
• Historical Connection: Life of a Civil War Soldier. See **Teacher's SourceBook,** p. 50.
**Visit our website:**
www.mcdougallittell.com

# An Occurrence at Owl Creek Bridge

Ambrose Bierce

## I

A man stood upon a railroad bridge in northern Alabama, looking down into the swift water twenty feet below. The man's hands were behind his back, the wrists bound with a cord. A rope closely encircled his neck. It was attached to a stout cross-timber above his head and the slack fell to the level of his knees. Some loose boards laid upon the sleepers[1] supporting the metals of the railway supplied a footing for him and his executioners—two private soldiers of the Federal army, directed by a sergeant who in civil life may have been a deputy sheriff. At a short remove upon the same temporary platform was an officer in the uniform of his rank, armed. He was a captain. A sentinel at each end of the bridge stood with his rifle in the position known as "support," that is to say, vertical in front of the left shoulder, the hammer resting on the forearm thrown straight across the chest—a formal and unnatural position, enforcing an erect carriage of the body. It did not appear to be the duty of these two men to know what was occurring at the center of the bridge; they merely blockaded the two ends of the foot planking that traversed it.

Beyond one of the sentinels nobody was in sight; the railroad ran straight away into a forest for a hundred yards, then, curving, was lost to view. Doubtless there was an outpost farther along. The other bank of the stream was open ground—a gentle acclivity topped with a stockade of vertical tree trunks, loopholed for rifles, with a single embrasure through which protruded the muzzle of a brass cannon commanding the

---

1. **sleepers:** railroad ties.

---

### Customizing Instruction

**Less Proficient Readers**
Tell students that in Section I of the story they will meet Peyton Farquhar, a man waiting to be hanged.
**Set a Purpose** Have students read to find out what he is thinking and feeling as he faces death.

**Students Acquiring English**
Explain that hanging was a common method of executing soldiers during the Civil War. Prepare students for the sequence of events by explaining that the story is told using flashbacks.

 Use **Spanish Study Guide** for additional support, pp. 139–141.

**Gifted and Talented**
Ask students to decide by the end of the story whether the author deceives the reader or whether clues within the text help a careful reader anticipate the ending. Students should be prepared to defend their responses using elements of the text.

---

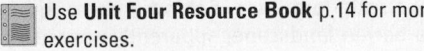

### Mini Lesson — Preteaching Vocabulary

**USING CONTEXT CLUES**
**Instruction** Students can expand their vocabularies by relying on context to determine the meanings of unfamiliar words.
**Exercises** Have students apply the strategy to figure out the meanings of underlined words in the following sentences.

1. Although it might seem <u>ludicrous</u> to people in the 1990s who have safeguards protecting their rights, prompt execution of traitors and others was a reality during the Civil War.
2. The sentinels were <u>subordinate</u> to the captain and awaited his orders.
3. Do one's senses become <u>preternaturally</u> alert just before the moment of death?
4. During a war, military tactics must often be decided <u>summarily</u> and without the benefit of lengthy deliberation.
5. In order to lead effectively, the captain of the troop must be <u>apprised</u> of all new developments as soon as they happen.

 Use **Unit Four Resource Book** p.14 for more exercises.
**A lesson on context clues appears on p. 326 in the Pupil's Edition.**

**Literary Analysis** POINT OF VIEW

Ask students to identify the point of view used in the beginning of the story. Have them analyze the effect created by this point of view.

**Possible Response:** The point of view is third-person. The objectivity imparted by this choice adds to the grimness of the scene and directs attention to the physical details of the bridge and the soldiers' placement instead of involving the reader's emotions.

Use **Unit Four Resource Book**, p. 13 for more practice.

**Active Reading**

ANALYZING STRUCTURE

Remind students to analyze the text structure for how it influences their understanding of the order of events in the story. Ask students what impact the scene in the story's first paragraph (page 581) is meant to have on readers and why the author might have chosen to open in this way.

**Possible Responses:** The first paragraph creates suspense by making readers wonder what the condemned man has done to invite this fate.

Use **Unit Four Resource Book**, p. 12 for more practice.

ACTIVE READING

**A QUESTION** **Possible Response:** those of the man who is about to be hanged

ACTIVE READING

**B CLARIFY** **Possible Response:** It is the signal for the sergeant to step aside so that the plank will tilt, allowing the victim to be hanged.

Union soldiers. From the collections of the Library of Congress.

bridge. Midway of the slope between bridge and fort were the spectators—a single company of infantry in line, at "parade rest," the butts of the rifles on the ground, the barrels inclining slightly backward against the right shoulder, the hands crossed upon the stock. A lieutenant stood at the right of the line, the point of his sword upon the ground, his left hand resting upon his right. Excepting the group of four at the center of the bridge, not a man moved. The company faced the bridge, staring stonily, motionless. The sentinels, facing the banks of the stream, might have been statues to adorn the bridge. The captain stood with folded arms, silent, observing the work of his subordinates, but making no sign. Death is a dignitary who when he comes announced is to be received with formal manifestations of respect, even by those most familiar with him. In the code of military etiquette silence and fixity are forms of deference.

The man who was engaged in being hanged was apparently about thirty-five years of age. He was a civilian, if one might judge from his habit, which was that of a planter. His features were good—a straight nose, firm mouth, broad forehead, from which his long, dark hair was combed straight back, falling behind his ears to the collar of his well-fitting frock-coat. He wore a mustache and pointed beard, but no whiskers; his eyes were large and dark gray, and had a kindly expression which one would hardly have expected in one whose neck was in the hemp. Evidently this was no vulgar assassin. The liberal military code makes provision for hanging many kinds of persons, and gentlemen are not excluded.

The preparations being complete, the two private soldiers stepped aside and each drew away the plank upon which he had been standing. The sergeant turned to the captain, saluted and placed himself immediately behind that officer, who in turn moved apart one pace. These movements left the condemned man and the sergeant standing on the two ends of the same plank, which spanned three of the cross-ties of the bridge. The end upon which the civilian stood almost, but not quite, reached a fourth. This plank had been held in place by the weight of the captain; it was now held by that of the sergeant. At a signal from the former the latter would step aside, the plank would tilt and the condemned man go down between two ties. The arrangement commended itself to his judgment as simple and effective. His face

WORDS
TO
KNOW   **subordinate** (sə-bôr′dn-ĭt) *n.* one who is lower in rank

582

 **Viewing and Representing**

*Union Soldiers,* anonymous

**APPRECIATING ART** The Civil War is very well documented in photographs. The photographic process at the time involved imprinting the image on a glass plate, rather than on film.
**Instruction** Have students examine the photograph closely and point out details.
**Possible Responses:** The three Union soldiers are leaning against a large tree. Behind and around them is a barren landscape, apparently scarred by battles. One soldier appears to be reading a letter, while the others gaze off into space. Their uniforms appear to be in good repair.

**Application** Ask students to analyze the ideas and impressions conveyed by the photograph. Have them consider the poses of the soldiers and the mood conveyed by these poses.
**Possible Responses:** The soldiers appear relaxed, perhaps waiting for further orders or enjoying a rest from travel and conflict. The mood is one of peace or inactivity, which contrasts with images of battle and destruction evoked by the landscape.

had not been covered nor his eyes bandaged. He looked a moment at his "unsteadfast footing,"

**ACTIVE READING**

**A** **QUESTION** Whose thoughts and feelings does the narrator relate?

then let his gaze wander to the swirling water of the stream racing madly beneath his feet. A piece of dancing driftwood caught his attention and his eyes followed it down the current. How slowly it appeared to move! What a sluggish stream!

He closed his eyes in order to fix his last thoughts upon his wife and children. The water, touched to gold by the early sun, the brooding mists under the banks at some distance down the stream, the fort, the soldiers, the piece of drift— all had distracted him. And now he became conscious of a new disturbance. Striking through the thought of his dear ones was a sound which he could neither ignore nor understand, a sharp, distinct, metallic percussion like the stroke of a blacksmith's hammer upon the anvil; it had the same ringing quality. He wondered what it was, and whether immeasurably distant or near by— it seemed both. Its recurrence was regular, but as slow as the tolling of a death knell.[2] He awaited each stroke with impatience and—he knew not why—apprehension. The intervals of silence grew progressively longer; the delays became maddening. With their greater infrequency the sounds increased in strength and sharpness. They hurt his ear like the thrust of a knife; he feared he would shriek. What he heard was the ticking of his watch.

He unclosed his eyes and saw again the water below him. "If I could free my hands," he thought, "I might throw off the noose and spring into the stream. By diving I could <u>evade</u> the bullets and, swimming vigorously, reach the bank, take to the woods and get away home. My home, thank God, is as yet outside their lines; my wife and little ones are still beyond the invader's **3** farthest advance."

As these thoughts, which have here to be set down in words, were flashed into the doomed man's brain rather than evolved from it the

**ACTIVE READING**

**B** **CLARIFY** What does the captain's nod mean?

captain nodded to the sergeant. The sergeant stepped aside.

---

## II

Peyton Farquhar was a well-to-do planter, of an old and highly respected Alabama family. Being a slave owner and like other slave owners a politician he was naturally an original secessionist[3] and ardently devoted to the Southern cause. Circumstances of an imperious nature, which it is unnecessary to relate here, had prevented him from taking service with the gallant army that had fought the disastrous campaigns ending with the fall of Corinth,[4] and he chafed under the inglorious restraint, longing for the release of his energies, the larger life of the soldier, the opportunity for distinction. That opportunity, he felt, would come, as it comes to all in war time. Meanwhile he did what he could. No service was too humble for him to perform in aid of the South, no adventure too perilous for him to undertake if consistent with the character of a civilian who was at heart a soldier, and who in good faith and without too much qualification assented to at least a part of the frankly villainous dictum that all is fair in love and war.

One evening while Farquhar and his wife were sitting on a rustic bench near the entrance to his grounds, a gray-clad soldier rode up to the gate and asked for a drink of water. Mrs. Farquhar

---

2. **tolling of a death knell:** the slow, steady ringing of a bell at a funeral or to indicate death.

3. **secessionist** (sĭ-sĕsh′ə-nĭst): one who supported the withdrawal of Southern states from the Union.

4. **Corinth:** a town in Mississippi that was the site of a Civil War battle in 1862.

WORDS
TO
KNOW **evade** (ĭ-vād′) v. to escape or avoid

**583**

## Customizing Instruction

### Students Acquiring English

**1** Explain that the word *habit* in this case refers to the way the man is dressed.

### Less Proficient Readers

**2** Ask students to note the description of the man about to be hanged and to explain what is meant by "Evidently this was no vulgar assassin."

**Possible Response:** Peyton Farquhar is a gentleman, not a common criminal. His refined features, good grooming, and kind expression reveal this fact.

**3** Ask students to summarize the last thoughts and feelings of the man about to be hanged. Focus their attention on his escape theories.

**Possible Responses:** The character thinks about his wife and family, reacts to the ticking of his watch, and works out an escape plan consisting of freeing his hands, throwing off his noose, swimming to the bank while evading bullets, and arriving at home.

**Set a Purpose** Have students read to find out the background of Peyton Farquhar, why he is about to be hanged, and what happens as the execution goes forward.

### Gifted and Talented

Ask students to pick out examples of foreshadowing.

## BLOCK SCHEDULING: MANAGING TIME

**If your schedule requires that you cover the lesson objectives in a shorter time, use . . .**
- Preparing to Read, p. 580
- Thinking Through the Literature, p. 591
- Vocabulary in Action, p. 592

**If you want to take advantage of longer class time, use . . .**
- TE Teaching Options: Preteaching Vocabulary, p. 581; Viewing and Representing, pp. 582, 587; Vocabulary Strategy, pp. 584–585; Speaking and Listening, p. 586; Cross-Curricular Link, p. 588; Self-Assessment, p. 589
- Choices & Challenges, p. 592

Tell students that careful reading should enable them to determine why Farquhar is being hanged. Ask them to look for clues in the text and piece them together to find an explanation.

**Possible Response:** Farquhar is devoted to the secessionist cause and does what he can to help the South. The "gray-clad soldier" says that hanging is the penalty for sabotaging the bridge, and he also emphasizes the importance of the bridge to the North. Farquhar shows great interest in this information, so readers can infer that he was caught while trying to destroy the bridge.

### ACTIVE READING

**Ⓐ ANALYZE** **Possible Response:** These events occur before the events in Section I and explain why Farquhar is about to be hanged.

**Reading Skills and Strategies:**
**CLARIFYING**

**Ⓑ** Ask students to explain the significance of this paragraph.

**Possible Response:** The Confederate soldier who gave Peyton Farquhar the information about the bridge was actually a Union spy who set a trap for Farquhar.

### ACTIVE READING

**Ⓒ EVALUATE** **Possible Response:** Students might refer back to what they wrote in Connect to Your Life on page 580. The fact that Peyton Farquhar has been calm throughout his ordeal might make these thoughts very convincing.

---

was only too happy to serve him with her own white hands. While she was fetching the water her husband approached the dusty horseman and inquired eagerly for news from the front.

"The Yanks are repairing the railroads," said the man, "and are getting ready for another advance. They have reached the Owl Creek bridge, put it in order and built a stockade on the north bank. The commandant has issued an order, which is posted everywhere, declaring that any civilian caught interfering with the railroad, its bridges, tunnels or trains will be <u>summarily</u> hanged. I saw the order."

"How far is it to the Owl Creek bridge?" Farquhar asked.

"About thirty miles."

"Is there no force on this side the creek?"

"Only a picket post[5] half a mile out, on the railroad, and a single sentinel at this end of the bridge."

"Suppose a man—a civilian and student of hanging—should elude the picket post and perhaps get the better of the sentinel," said Farquhar, smiling, "what could he accomplish?"

The soldier reflected. "I was there a month ago," he replied. "I observed that the flood of last winter had lodged a great quantity of driftwood against the wooden pier at this end of the bridge. It is now dry and would burn like tow."[6]

The lady had now brought the water, which the soldier drank. He thanked her ceremoniously, bowed to her husband and rode away. An hour later, after nightfall, he repassed the plantation, going northward in the direction from which he had come. He was a Federal scout.

### ACTIVE READING

**Ⓐ ANALYZE** When do these events occur and what do they explain?

**Ⓑ**

---

— III —

As Peyton Farquhar fell straight downward through the bridge he lost consciousness and was as one already dead. From this state he was awakened—ages later, it seemed to him—by the pain of a sharp pressure upon his throat, followed by a sense of suffocation. Keen, poignant[7] agonies seemed to shoot from his neck downward through every fiber of his body and limbs. These pains appeared to flash along well-defined lines of ramification[8] and to beat with an inconceivably rapid periodicity. They seemed like streams of pulsating fire heating him to an intolerable temperature. As to his head, he was conscious of nothing but a feeling of fullness—of congestion. These sensations were unaccompanied by thought. The intellectual part of his nature was already effaced; he had power only to feel, and feeling

**1**

---

5. **picket post:** the camp of soldiers who are assigned to guard against a surprise attack.

6. **tow:** coarse, dry fiber.

7. **poignant** (poin′yənt): physically painful.

8. **flash . . . ramification:** spread out rapidly along branches from a central point.

WORDS
TO
KNOW
**summarily** (sə-mĕr′ə-lē) *adv.* in a way that is quick and bypasses usual procedures

---

**Mini Lesson** **Vocabulary Strategy**

**PREFIXES**

**Instruction** Remind students that applying the meanings of prefixes can help them determine the meanings of unfamiliar words. A prefix is a letter or letters added to the beginning of a word to change its meaning. Give students some examples of common prefixes and their meanings.

| Prefix | Meaning |
|---|---|
| anti- | against or opposite |
| circum- | around |
| com-, co- | with or together |
| contra-, counter- | against or opposite |
| de- | down or away from |
| ex-, e-, ef- | out or away from |
| in- | not or without |
| re- | again or back |
| sub- | under or from below |
| un- | not, reverse of |

was torment. He was conscious of motion. Encompassed in a luminous cloud, of which he was now merely the fiery heart, without material substance, he swung through unthinkable arcs of oscillation, like a vast pendulum. Then all at once, with terrible suddenness, the light about him shot upward with the noise of a loud plash; a frightful roaring was in his ears, and all was cold and dark. The power of thought was restored; he knew that the rope had broken and he had fallen into the stream. There was no additional strangulation; the noose about his neck was already suffocating him and kept the water from his lungs. To die of hanging at the bottom of a river!—the idea seemed to him <u>ludicrous</u>. He opened his eyes in the darkness and saw above him a gleam of light, but how distant, how <u>inaccessible</u>! He was still sinking, for the light became fainter and fainter until it was a mere glimmer. Then it began to grow and brighten, and he knew that he was rising toward the surface—knew it with reluctance, for he was now very comfortable. "To be hanged and drowned," he thought, "that is not so bad; but I do not wish to be shot. No; I will not be shot; that is not fair."

**ACTIVE READING**

**C** EVALUATE Would these be the thoughts of a man on the brink of death?

He was not conscious of an effort, but a sharp pain in his wrist <u>apprised</u> him that he was trying to free his hands. He gave the struggle his attention, as an idler might observe the feat of a juggler, without interest in the outcome. What splendid effort!—what magnificent, what superhuman strength! Ah, that was a fine endeavor! Bravo! The cord fell away; his arms parted and floated upward, the hands dimly seen on each side in the growing light. He watched them with a new interest as first one and then the other pounced upon the noose at his neck. They tore it

away and thrust it fiercely aside, its undulations resembling those of a water-snake. "Put it back, put it back!" He thought he shouted these words to his hands, for the undoing of the noose had been succeeded by the direst pang that he had yet experienced. His neck ached horribly; his brain was on fire; his heart, which had been fluttering faintly, gave a great leap, trying to force itself out at his mouth. His whole body was racked and wrenched with an insupportable anguish![9] But his disobedient hands gave no heed to the command. They beat the water vigorously with quick, downward strokes, forcing him to the surface. He felt his head emerge; his eyes were blinded by the sunlight; his chest expanded convulsively, and with a supreme and crowning agony his lungs engulfed a great draught of air, which instantly he expelled in a shriek!

He was now in full possession of his physical senses. They were, indeed, <u>preternaturally</u> keen and alert. Something in the awful disturbance of his organic system had so exalted and refined them that they made record of things never before perceived. He felt the ripples upon his face and heard their separate sounds as they struck. He looked at the forest on the bank of the stream, saw the individual trees, the leaves and the veining of each leaf—saw the very insects upon them: the locusts, the brilliant-bodied flies, the gray spiders stretching their webs from twig to twig. He noted the prismatic colors in all the dewdrops upon a million blades of grass. The humming of the gnats that danced above the eddies of the stream, the beating of the dragon-flies' wings, the strokes of the water-spiders' legs, like oars which had lifted their boat—all these made audible music. A fish slid along beneath his eyes and he heard the rush of its body parting the water.

---

9. **racked . . . anguish:** stretched and twisted with unendurable physical pain.

---

WORDS TO KNOW

**ludicrous** (lōō′dĭ-krəs) *adj.* laughably absurd; ridiculous
**inaccessible** (ĭn′ăk-sĕs′ə-bəl) *adj.* not obtained easily, if at all; unreachable
**apprise** (ə-prīz′) *v.* to give notice to; inform
**preternaturally** (prē′tər-năch′ər-əl-ē) *adv.* more than naturally; extraordinarily

585

---

## Customizing Instruction

### Students Acquiring English
Help students define the following words and idioms found on pages 584–585.
- *Yanks*—members of the Federal or Union army; Northerners
- *get the better of*—overcome, defeat, or trick
- *suffocation*—being unable to breathe
- *idler*—person who watches without taking part
- *undulations*—wavelike motions
- *gave no heed*—paid no attention; ignored

### Gifted and Talented
**1** Ask students to note Bierce's choice of verbs in the first paragraph of Section III and to think about what they may imply.

### Less Proficient Readers
Use the following questions to guide students' understanding:
- What is Peyton Farquhar's background, and why is he being executed?

**Possible Response:** Peyton Farquhar is a Southern plantation owner who tried to burn Owl Creek Bridge.

- Ask students what happens when the execution takes place.

**Possible Response:** The rope that was to hang Farquhar apparently breaks. He fights for his life, escaping the way that he imagined while he was standing on the bridge.

**Set a Purpose** Have students read to find out whether Farquhar makes it home to his family.

---

**Exercises** Ask students to match words on the left with their definitions on the right.

| | |
|---|---|
| **1.** counterswirl | a. to wipe out |
| **2.** deflected | b. to meddle or come between |
| **3.** commingled | c. reverse current |
| **4.** interminable | d. not constant or firm |
| **5.** monotonous | e. turned away from |
| **6.** circumstances | f. mixed together |
| **7.** subordinate | g. in a single tone |
| **8.** interfere | h. not ending or terminating |
| **9.** unsteadfast | i. surroundings of an event |
| **10.** efface | j. one who is under another in rank |

**Answers:** 1. d; 2. f; 3. g; 4. i; 5. h; 6. j; 7. k; 8. c; 9. e; 10. a

 Use **Vocabulary Transparencies and Copymasters**, p. 52.

**A lesson on prefixes appears on p. 1130 in the Pupil's Edition.**

## Reading and Analyzing

### Reading Skills and Strategies: HYPOTHESIZING

**A** Ask students what causes the movements to be "grotesque and horrible, their forms gigantic."

**Possible Responses:** They are the enemies of the condemned man, and so he perceives them as threatening; his perception of reality is distorted; perhaps he is dreaming and so their forms are nightmarish.

### Literary Analysis POINT OF VIEW

**B** Ask whose thoughts and sensations are focused on exclusively here.

**Answer:** Peyton Farquhar's

What is unusual or strange about his ability to see the gray eye of the man on the bridge?

**Possible Responses:** unlikely that he could see it; adds to dreamlike, surreal quality

### Literary Analysis: ALLITERATION

**C** Ask what effect this use of alliteration creates.

**Possible Response:** The repetition of the *d* sound seems to emphasize the slow deliberation of the soldiers' actions and the inevitability of the gunshots that are to follow.

---

He had come to the surface facing down the stream; in a moment the visible world seemed to wheel slowly round, himself the pivotal point, and he saw the bridge, the fort, the soldiers upon the bridge, the captain, the sergeant, the two privates, his executioners. They were in silhouette against the blue sky. They shouted and gesticulated, pointing at him. The captain had drawn his pistol, but did not fire; the others were unarmed. **A** Their movements were grotesque and horrible, their forms gigantic.

**B** **1** Suddenly he heard a sharp report and something struck the water smartly within a few inches of his head, spattering his face with spray. He heard a second report, and saw one of the sentinels with his rifle at his shoulder, a light cloud of blue smoke rising from the muzzle. The man in the water saw the eye of the man on the bridge gazing into his own through the sights of the rifle. He observed that it was a gray eye and remembered having read that gray eyes were keenest, and that all famous marksmen had them. Nevertheless, this one had missed.

A counter-swirl had caught Farquhar and turned him half round; he was again looking into the forest on the bank opposite the fort. The sound of a clear, high voice in a monotonous singsong now rang out behind him and came across the water with a distinctness that pierced and subdued all other sounds, even the beating of the ripples in his ears. Although no soldier, he had frequented camps enough to know the dread significance of that **C** deliberate, drawling, aspirated chant; the lieutenant on shore was taking a part in the morning's work. How coldly and pitilessly—with what an even, calm intonation, presaging,[10] and enforcing tranquillity in the men—with what accurately measured intervals fell those cruel words:

"Attention, company! . . . Shoulder arms! . . . Ready! . . . Aim! . . . Fire!"

Farquhar dived—dived as deeply as he could. The water roared in his ears like the voice of **2** Niagara, yet he heard the dulled thunder of the

volley and, rising again toward the surface, met shining bits of metal, singularly flattened, oscillating slowly downward. Some of them touched him on the face and hands, then fell away, continuing their descent. One lodged between his collar and neck; it was uncomfortably warm and he snatched it out.

As he rose to the surface, gasping for breath, he saw that he had been a long time under water; he was <u>perceptibly</u> farther down stream— nearer to safety. The soldiers had almost finished reloading; the metal ramrods flashed all at once in the sunshine as they were drawn from the barrels, turned in the air, and thrust into their sockets. The two sentinels fired again, independently and ineffectually.

The hunted man saw all this over his shoulder; he was now swimming vigorously with the current. His brain was as energetic as his arms and legs; he thought with the rapidity of lightning.

"The officer," he reasoned, "will not make that martinet's[11] error a second time. It is as easy to dodge a volley as a single shot. He has probably already given the command to fire at will. God help me, I cannot dodge them all!"

An appalling plash within two yards of him was followed by a loud, rushing sound, *diminuendo,*[12] which seemed to travel back through the air to the fort and died in an explosion which stirred the very river to its deeps! A rising sheet of water curved over him, fell down upon him, blinded him, strangled him! The cannon had taken a hand in the game. As he shook his head free from the commotion of the smitten water he heard the deflected shot humming through the air ahead, and in an

---

10. **presaging** (prĕs′ĭj-ĭng): predicting.
11. **martinet** (mär′tn-ĕt′): strict disciplinarian; one who demands that regulations be followed exactly.
12. *diminuendo* (dĭ-mĭn′yōō-ĕn′dō) *Italian:* gradually decreasing in loudness.

WORDS TO KNOW

**perceptibly** (pər-sĕp′tə-blē) *adv.* in a way that can be perceived by the senses or the mind; noticeably

586

---

## Teaching Options

## Speaking and Listening

**REALISTIC DIALOGUE**

**Prepare** Ask students to imagine the conversation that might have ensued when Peyton Farquhar told his wife that he was thinking about trying to burn down the bridge. Students should keep in mind what can be learned from Section II about the characters of both Farquhar and his wife in order to determine their feelings and words. Tell students that their dialogue must move toward Farquhar's ultimate decision to attempt the sabotage. Divide students into pairs and ask them to write their version of the dialogue and practice with the appropriate gestures and facial expressions.

**Present** After students have practiced their dialogues, they should perform their scenarios in class. They should be able to justify their choice of verbal and nonverbal performance techniques by referring to their interpretations of the characters and the language used by Bierce. Audience members should evaluate how plausible the language and content of each dialogue is and how well it furthers understanding of character and motive.

**BLOCK SCHEDULING** This activity is especially well suited for longer class periods.

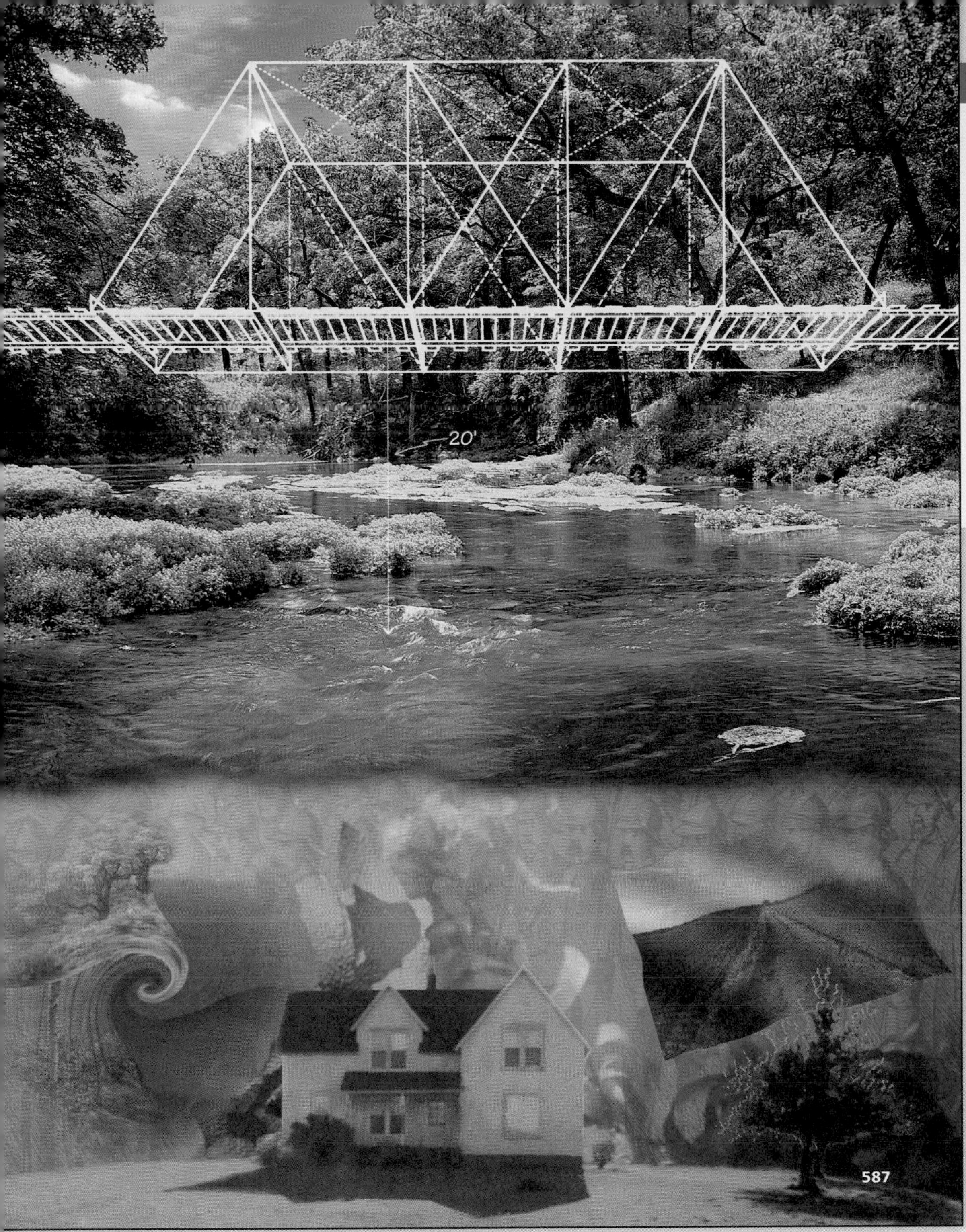


## Customizing Instruction

### Students Acquiring English

**1** Help students use context clues to understand these multiple-meaning words.

- *smartly*—in a sharp, vigorous manner
- *report*—the sound of a gunshot

**2** Make sure students understand this reference to Niagara Falls, a large waterfall on the border between New York State and Ontario, Canada.

### Multiple Learning Styles

**Visual Learners**

**3** Interested students might paint or sketch this dreamlike scene in which Farquhar sees shiny scraps of metal rain down through the water.

## Mini Lesson Viewing and Representing

**Instruction** Some students have a tendency to read the text and ignore the illustrations. Point out that the illustrations that accompany a story can serve several important functions.

- They can help readers visualize characters and setting, including the time period.
- They can help readers understand concepts, especially if diagrams or charts are included.
- They can give readers clues as to what can be expected to happen.

**Application** Have students work in small groups to study the details of the illustrations on pages 581, 584, and 587 and then to discuss the function of each one in this story. Encourage students to analyze at length the complex illustration on page 587.

**Possible Responses:** The photo on page 581 shows what real Union soldiers, like the ones who are executing Farquhar, looked like. The illustration on page 584 shows what Farquhar hoped to accomplish—the destruction of a railroad bridge. The illustration on page 587 could serve as a clue that Farquhar's experience was a fantasy—the places that he sees in the story's last section are shown hazily under water.

**A** People who have had near-death experiences often report having seen a bright light. After students have finished the story, ask how these details foreshadow the ending.
**Possible Response:** The light and the æolian harps making heavenly music might make a careful reader suspect that Farquhar is near death now.

**ACTIVE READING**

**B EVALUATE Possible Response:** It may be that since Farquhar narrowly escaped death, his surroundings seem all the more precious to him, or the changes in the surroundings might indicate that this is a fantasy.

**Reading Skills and Strategies: VISUALIZING**

**C** Ask students how Bierce enables the reader to see the state in which Farquhar is at this point in his journey.
**Possible Responses:** Bierce's imagery paints a vivid picture of Farquhar as he nears his home. His neck is "horribly swollen" and has "a circle of black." "His tongue was swollen with thirst. . . ."

**ACTIVE READING**

**D CLARIFY Possible Response:** Farquhar is hanged; he had never escaped.

---

instant it was cracking and smashing the branches in the forest beyond.

"They will not do that again," he thought; "the next time they will use a charge of grape.[13] I must keep my eye upon the gun; the smoke will apprise me—the report arrives too late; it lags behind the missile. That is a good gun."

Suddenly he felt himself whirled round and round—spinning like a top. The water, the banks, the forests, the now distant bridge, fort and men—all were commingled and blurred. Objects were represented by their colors only; circular horizontal streaks of color—that was all he saw. He had been caught in a vortex and was being whirled on with a velocity of advance and gyration that made him giddy and sick. In a few moments he was flung upon the gravel at the foot of the left bank of the stream—the southern bank—and behind a projecting point which concealed him from his enemies. The sudden arrest of his motion, the abrasion of one of his hands on the gravel, restored him, and he wept with delight. He dug his fingers into the sand, threw it over himself in handfuls and audibly blessed it. It looked like diamonds, rubies, emeralds; he could think of nothing beautiful which it did not resemble. The trees upon the bank were giant garden plants; he noted a definite order in their arrangement, inhaled the fragrance of their blooms. A strange, roseate light shone through the spaces among their **A** trunks and the wind made in their branches the music of æolian harps.[14] He had no wish to perfect his escape—was content to remain in that enchanting spot until retaken.

A whiz and rattle of grapeshot among the branches high above his head roused him from his dream. The baffled cannoneer had fired him a random farewell. He sprang to his feet, rushed up the sloping bank, and plunged into the forest.

All that day he traveled, laying his course by the rounding sun. The forest seemed <u>interminable</u>; nowhere did he discover a break

in it, not even a woodman's road. He had not known that he lived in so wild a region. There was something uncanny in the revelation.

By night fall he was fatigued, footsore, famishing. The thought of his wife and children urged him on. At last he found a road which led him in what he knew to be the right direction. It was as wide and straight as a city street, yet it seemed untraveled. No fields bordered it, no dwelling anywhere. Not so much as the barking of a dog suggested human habitation. The black bodies of the trees formed a straight wall on both sides, terminating on the horizon in a point, like a diagram in a lesson in perspective. Overhead, as he looked up through this rift in the wood, shone great golden stars looking unfamiliar and grouped in strange constellations. He was sure they were arranged in some order

**ACTIVE READING**

**EVALUATE** Can you account for the changes in the surroundings? **B**

which had a secret and malign[15] significance. The wood on either side was full of singular noises, among which—once, twice, and again, he distinctly heard whispers in an unknown tongue.

His neck was in pain and lifting his hand to it he found it horribly swollen. He knew that it had a circle of black where the rope had bruised it. His eyes felt congested; he could no longer close them. His tongue was swollen with thirst; he relieved its fever by thrusting it forward from between his teeth into the cold air. How softly the turf had carpeted the untraveled avenue—he could no longer feel the roadway beneath his feet!

Doubtless, despite his suffering, he had fallen asleep while walking, for now he sees another scene—perhaps he has merely recovered from a

**1**

**C**

---

13. **grape:** short for *grapeshot,* a cluster of several small iron balls fired in one shot from a cannon.

14. **music of æolian** (ē-ō′lē-ən) **harps:** heavenly, or unearthly, music.

15. **malign** (mə-līn′): evil; harmful; threatening harm or evil.

WORDS TO KNOW **interminable** (ĭn-tûr′mə-nə-bəl) *adj.* endless

---

## Teaching Options

**Cross Curricular Link History**

**THE 54TH REGIMENT** Although African American men clamored to join the war effort from the moment the Civil War was declared, it was not until January 1, 1863, with the issuing of the Emancipation Proclamation, that they were allowed to do so. The 54th Massachusetts Infantry was born soon after, when Governor Andrew of Massachusetts received permission to recruit black troops. On May 28, 1863, just a few short months after its inception, the 54th Massachusetts Infantry was ordered to report to Hilton Head, South Carolina.

Although officials were nervous about reactions to the troops, the soldiers marched through Boston

to their ship in the harbor to an uproarious reception. Henry Wadsworth Longfellow was moved to write in his diary, "Saw the first regiment of blacks march through Beacon Street. An imposing sight, with something wild and strange about it, like a dream. At last the North consents to let the Negro fight for freedom."

The courageous deeds of the 54th Massachusetts Infantry in some of the most crucial and bloody battles of the Civil War ended most opposition to black soldiers. When they finally returned home at war's end, they were given a welcome that paid homage to their heroism and great sacrifices during the war. They became known as the Glory Regiment.

Copyright © Ed Simpson/Tony Stone Images.

delirium.[16] He stands at the gate of his own home. All is as he left it, and all bright and beautiful in the morning sunshine. He must have traveled the entire night. As he pushes open the gate and passes up the wide white walk, he sees a flutter of female garments; his wife, looking fresh and cool and sweet, steps down from the veranda to meet him. At the bottom of the steps she stands waiting, with a smile of <u>ineffable</u> joy, an attitude of matchless grace and dignity. Ah, how beautiful she is! He springs forward with extended arms. As he is about to clasp her he feels a stunning blow

upon the back of the neck; a blinding white light blazes all about him with a sound like the shock of a cannon—then all is darkness and silence!

Peyton Farquhar was dead; his body, with a broken neck, swung gently from side to side beneath the timbers of the Owl Creek bridge. ❖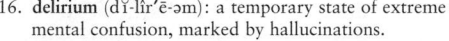

**ACTIVE READING**

**CLARIFY** What kills Farquhar? **D**

---

16. **delirium** (dĭ-lîr′ē-əm): a temporary state of extreme mental confusion, marked by hallucinations.

WORDS
TO
KNOW

**ineffable** (ĭn-ĕf′ə-bəl) *adj.* unable to be expressed in words

**589**

### Reading Skills and Strategies: MAKING INFERENCES

Have students look for clues in the text and make an inference about which side of the war Sullivan Ballou is on.

**Possible Response:** He is a Union soldier; he is in the 2nd Rhode Island regiment and he writes, "I know how strongly American Civilization now leans on the triumph of the Government."

### Literary Analysis: COMPARING SUBJECTS AND THEMES

Ask students to compare the subject and theme of this letter to the subject and theme of "An Occurrence at Owl Creek Bridge."

**Possible Responses:** The subject of both works is a person's last thoughts before dying, and both Sullivan Ballou and Peyton Farquhar turn their thoughts to their families. The themes of hope, faith, courage, and devotion to a cause are present in both pieces.

---

**LITERARY LINK**

# Letter to Sarah Ballou

### SULLIVAN BALLOU

*Major Sullivan Ballou of the 2nd Rhode Island regiment wrote the following letter to his wife on July 14, 1861. He was killed about a week later at the first battle of Bull Run.*

My very dear Sarah:

The indications are very strong that we shall move in a few days—perhaps tomorrow. Lest I should not be able to write again, I feel impelled to write a few lines that may fall under your eye when I shall be no more. . . .

I have no misgivings about, or lack of confidence in the cause in which I am engaged, and my courage does not halt or falter. I know how strongly American Civilization now leans on the triumph of the Government, and how great a debt we owe to those who went before us through the blood and sufferings of the Revolution. And I am willing—perfectly willing—to lay down all my joys in this life, to help maintain this Government, and to pay that debt. . . .

Sarah my love for you is deathless, it seems to bind me with mighty cables that nothing but Omnipotence could break; and yet my love of Country comes over me like a strong wind and bears me unresistibly on with all these chains to the battle field.

The memories of the blissful moments I have spent with you come creeping over me, and I feel most gratified to God and to you that I have enjoyed them so long. And hard it is for me to give them up and burn to ashes the hopes of future years, when, God willing, we might still have lived and loved together, and seen our sons grown up to honorable manhood, around us. I have, I know, but few and small claims upon Divine Providence, but something whispers to me—perhaps it is the wafted prayer of my little Edgar, that I shall return to my loved ones unharmed. If I do not my dear Sarah, never forget how much I love you, and when my last breath escapes me on the battle field, it will whisper your name. Forgive my many faults, and the many pains I have caused you. How thoughtless and foolish I have often times been! How gladly would I wash out with my tears every little spot upon your happiness. . . .

But, O Sarah! if the dead can come back to this earth and flit unseen around those they loved, I shall always be near you; in the gladdest days and in the darkest nights . . . *always, always,* and if there be a soft breeze upon your cheek, it shall be my breath, as the cool air fans your throbbing temple, it shall be my spirit passing by. Sarah do not mourn me dead; think I am gone and wait for thee, for we shall meet again. . . .

---

**Mini Lesson**

## Grammar

### ESSENTIAL VS. NONESSENTIAL CLAUSES

**Instruction** An essential adjective clause is one that must be included to make the meaning of a sentence complete. A nonessential clause is one that adds extra information. Display the following sentences to illustrate the difference.

The story <u>that we read on Tuesday</u> was very suspenseful.

The story "An Occurrence at Owl Creek Bridge," <u>which we read on Tuesday</u>, was very suspenseful.

**Exercises** Ask students to identify the underlined clause as essential or nonessential.

1. The noose <u>that was pulled so tightly around his neck</u> almost choked him. *(essential)*
2. The current of the river, <u>which had flooded three years previously</u>, held him mercilessly in its grip. *(nonessential)*
3. Ambrose Bierce, <u>whose writing is often compared to Edgar Allan Poe's</u>, disappeared in Mexico at age seventy-one. *(nonessential)*

 Use **Grammar Transparencies and Copymasters**, p. 91.

 Use McDougal Littell's *Language Network* for more instruction and practice in clauses.

# *Thinking* through the LITERATURE

## Connect to the Literature

1. **What Do You Think?**
Did you like the ending of this story, or dislike it? Share your reaction with classmates.

**Comprehension Check**
- What is Peyton Farquhar's background?
- What does Farquhar do after he falls through the bridge?
- How does Farquhar die?

## Think Critically

2. How did the ending change the way you interpreted events in the story?

3. Why do you think Peyton Farquhar has the last thoughts he does before he dies?

4. What is the Union soldiers' reason for hanging Farquhar? Cite evidence from section II to support your view.

5. **ACTIVE READING  ANALYZING STRUCTURE** Tell when the events in each numbered section take place. How would changing the order of the three sections affect the story and your understanding of events?

6. Judging from this story, how do you think the author, Ambrose Bierce, views war?

 **THINK ABOUT**
- the statement about hanging and "the liberal military code" (page 582)
- Farquhar's sentiments about the Southern cause, and the result of these sentiments
- the action of the Federal scout who visits Farquhar

## Extend Interpretations

7. **Comparing Texts** Read the letter from Sullivan Ballou, an actual Civil War soldier, on page 590. Compare his thoughts to Farquhar's as he faces death.

8. **Connect to Life** Were the thoughts of Farquhar and Ballou similar to those you imagined a person would have when facing death?

## Literary Analysis

 **POINT OF VIEW** The perspective from which events in a story are narrated is called **point of view.** Notice that the first three paragraphs of this story are told from a **third-person omniscient,** or all-knowing, point of view, as though the narrator is an objective observer of the entire scene. Then, in the fourth paragraph, the perspective subtly shifts to focus on Peyton Farquhar's personal thoughts and sensations. This focus on one character's inner life is called **third-person limited** point of view.

**Paired Activity** With a partner, analyze the point of view in sections II and III of the story. Where does the point of view shift? How do the shifts affect the level of suspense? Discuss possible reasons why Bierce did not write the story entirely from the third-person omniscient point of view or entirely from the third-person limited point of view.

---

## GUIDING STUDENT RESPONSE

### Connect to the Literature

1. **What Do You Think?**
Some students may find the ending disappointing if they were hoping that Farquhar would be reunited with his wife.

**Comprehension Check**
- Peyton Farquhar is a well-to-do planter from an old and highly respected Alabama family.
- Farquhar fantasizes that he escapes.
- Farquhar is hanged.

Use Selection Quiz
**Unit Four Resource Book,** p. 15.

### Think Critically

2. Responses will vary. Students should include the idea that Section III is a fantasy. They might say that in hindsight they can identify foreshadowing or other clues to the ending.

3. Possible Responses: He loves his wife and family and does not want to leave them; what is happening is so horrible that he blocks it out with the fantasy.

4. Possible Responses: He attempted to interfere with the railroad bridge; the Federal scout entrapped him by telling him the defenses were minimal; Farquhar's desire to help the South is made very evident.

5. Possible Responses: The scout tells Farquhar of the bridge; Farquhar attempts to destroy it and is captured; he awaits execution; he drops from the bridge; he fantasizes an escape; he dies. Remind students that the text structure influences their understanding of the story. Changing the order of the sections would lessen the suspense. The suspense builds after the captain nods at the end of Section I, and the background is related in Section II. The reader is waiting to see what happens when Farquhar falls.

6. Possible Response: He seems to view war as a futile game: Farquhar is set up by a Federal soldier and defends the Southern cause with a doomed act of sabotage.

---

## Extend Interpretations

**Comparing Texts** Possible Response: Both men are consumed with thoughts of their families and love for their wives; however, both remain committed to the causes they serve.

**Connect to Life** Some students may state that they imagine a person facing death would think of loved ones.

## Literary Analysis

**Point of View** Both Section II and Section III contain examples of third-person omniscient and third-person limited point of view. Section II opens with the omniscient narrator but then switches to limited when the feelings of Farquhar are related. The detail about the Union scout comes from outside Farquhar's awareness, however. The third section is almost entirely limited as the story of Farquhar's fantasy is told. The final paragraph shifts back to omniscient narrator. The shifts in point of view increase suspense. Students may offer several reasons for Bierce's variation of narrator. He maintains suspense at the beginning but yet allows insight into Farquhar's thoughts by shifting to third-person limited. His choice of point of view also maintains the surprise ending, as many readers do not realize that the main character is fantasizing his escape.

## Writing Options

1. **Evaluation of Bierce To get students started on the assignment,** suggest that they divide their paper into three columns, each corresponding to one of the issues to be covered.

2. **Comparison Essay** Possible Responses: Similarities include the use of suspense and vivid, sensory, surreal descriptions. "An Occurrence at Owl Creek Bridge," however, places a realistic character in a realistic situation from which he escapes temporarily into a fantasy. In Poe's work, characters and situations are more grotesque; fantasy is intertwined with, rather than sharply separated from, reality.

## Vocabulary in Action

**EXERCISE A**

1. c
2. d
3. e
4. a
5. b

---

# Choices & CHALLENGES

## Writing Options

**1. Evaluation of Bierce** Draft an evaluation of Ambrose Bierce as a storyteller, based on "An Occurrence at Owl Creek Bridge." Consider how convincing you find his description of Farquhar's last thoughts, how you feel about the ending, and what meaning you draw from the story. Place your writing in your **Working Portfolio.**

**Writing Handbook**
See page 1283: Analysis.

**2. Comparison Essay** Ambrose Bierce is thought to have been influenced by Edgar Allan Poe. In a brief essay, explore similarities and differences you see in their styles and concerns.

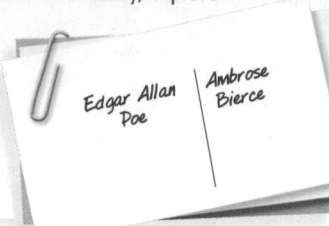

Edgar Allan Poe | Ambrose Bierce

## Vocabulary in Action

**EXERCISE A: SYNONYMS** For each phrase in the first column, write the letter of the synonymous phrase from the second column.

1. dodge the servant    a. apprise the spies
2. favored the ludicrous    b. wager on the major
3. interminable noise    c. evade the maid
4. notify the secret agents    d. preferred the absurd
5. bet on the general's subordinate    e. ceaseless peacelessness

**EXERCISE B:** Draw cartoons that illustrate the meaning of the following vocabulary words: *ineffable, inaccessible, preternaturally, perceptibly, summarily.*

**Building Vocabulary**
Several of the Words to Know contain prefixes and suffixes. For an in-depth study of affixes, see page 1130.

## Ambrose Bierce
1842–1914?

**Other Works**
*Black Beetles in Amber*
*Can Such Things Be?*
*The Devil's Dictionary*

**In the Line of Fire** Ambrose Bierce was born into a large, poor, intensely religious family and spent his early years on an Indiana farm. After a miserable childhood, he left home for good at 15 and landed a job at a newspaper setting type. Three years later he enlisted in the Union Army, and received several citations for bravery after fighting in some of the war's fiercest battles. After the war, Bierce worked as a surveyor in the West. He moved to San Francisco in 1866, where he worked for a newspaper and published some of his short stories. He married in 1872 and lived in London for several years with his wife. He earned the nickname "Bitter Bierce" for his cynical humor and cruel wit. His finest stories, such as "An Occurrence at Owl Creek Bridge," published in *Tales of Soldiers and Civilians* in 1891, concern the ironic futility of war.

**Vanished** During the latter part of his life, Bierce continued to publish short stories, essays, and poems and to work as a political reporter and columnist for the San Francisco *Examiner.* At 71, Bierce revisited Civil War battle sites where he had fought and then went to Mexico to report on the Mexican Revolution as an observer with Pancho Villa's rebel army. He never returned to the United States, and all trace of him disappeared. Before he left, he wrote to a niece, "If you hear of my being stood up against a Mexican stone wall and shot to rags, please know that I think that a pretty good way to depart this life. It beats old age, disease or falling down the cellar stairs."

---

## Teaching Options

 **Mini Lesson** **Grammar**

### PUNCTUATION FOR CLAUSES

**Instruction** Commas are used to set off nonessential or nonrestrictive clauses. The use of commas indicates that a clause could be omitted without affecting the meaning of the sentence. Essential clauses are necessary to the meaning of the sentence and should not be set off with commas. Display the following sentences :

   The man who had tried to sabotage the bridge was hanged.

   Peyton Farquhar, who had tried to sabotage the bridge, was hanged.

**Exercises** Have students punctuate the following sentences correctly.

1. The soldier who was standing on the other end of the plank stepped aside. *(no commas needed)*

2. The flashback section without which the story would make no sense was my favorite part. *(commas around "without which the story would make no sense")*

 Use **Grammar Transparencies and Copymasters,** p. 149.

> Use McDougal Littell's *Language Network* for more instruction and practice in punctuating clauses.

# A Mystery of Heroism

*Short Story by* STEPHEN CRANE

*"He was an intruder in the land of fine deeds."*

**Connect to Your Life**

**Heroes and Fine Deeds** What does the term *heroism* mean to you? With a small group of classmates, brainstorm a list of personal heroes and heroic actions. Then try to agree on a definition of the term.

## Build Background

**Civil War Tales** Following the remarkable success of his Civil War novel, *The Red Badge of Courage,* Stephen Crane wrote a series of sketches about battles in the Civil War. He did careful research, interviewing veterans and visiting the site where a battle had been fought in Virginia. "A Mystery of Heroism" appeared in *The Little Regiment and Other Episodes of the American Civil War* in 1896. Set on a battlefield, this short story focuses on the motives and actions of Fred Collins, a Union soldier. In this story, Crane uses **dialect** ("Dern yeh! I ain't afraid t' go.") to reflect how soldiers might actually speak and, like an impressionistic painter, provides vivid details to capture the soldiers' sensations in the heat of battle.

WORDS TO KNOW
**Vocabulary Preview**

| | |
|---|---|
| eloquence | tousled |
| furtive | provisional |
| futile | retraction |
| genial | stupendous |
| incessant | sullenly |

## Focus Your Reading

**LITERARY ANALYSIS** **NATURALISM** Stephen Crane represents a literary movement known as **naturalism,** an offshoot of realism. Like realistic writers, naturalists sought to portray common people and ordinary life accurately. The naturalists, however, also sought to describe the effect of natural and social forces—such as instinct and environment—on the individual. Consider how these forces affect Fred Collins in this story.

**ACTIVE READING** **VISUALIZING** **Visualizing** is the process of forming mental pictures as you read. Good readers use the details supplied by writers to picture characters, settings, and events in their mind. For example, notice how Crane's details in this passage help you experience what a soldier under fire might hear, see, and smell:

*There was the blaring thunder of a shell. Crimson light shone through the swift-boiling smoke and made a pink reflection on part of the wall of the well.*

**READER'S NOTEBOOK** As you read, use Crane's descriptive details to visualize the setting, the characters, and the events. Create a chart like this one to record your impressions.

| Impressions | | |
|---|---|---|
| Setting | Characters | Events |
| | | |

# LESSON RESOURCES

**UNIT FOUR RESOURCE BOOK,** pp. 16–20

**ASSESSMENT RESOURCES**
**Formal Assessment,** pp. 111–112
**Teacher's Guide to Assessment and Portfolio Use**
**Test Generator**

**SKILLS TRANSPARENCIES AND COPYMASTERS**
**Reading and Critical Thinking**
• Visualizing, T8 (for Active Reading, p. 593)

**Grammar**
• Adjective Clauses, C92 (for Mini Lesson, p. 598)
• Commas in Names and Titles, C150 (for Mini Lesson, p. 603)
**Vocabulary**
• Meanings of Roots, C52 (for Mini Lesson, p. 600)
**Writing**
• Literary Interpretation, C30 (for Writing Option 2, p. 603)
**Communications**
• Appreciative Listening, T2 (for Activities & Explorations 2, p. 603)

• Interviewing, T9 (for Activities & Explorations 3, p. 603)
• Impromptu Speaking: Dialogue, Role-Play, Debate, T13 (for Activities & Explorations 3, p. 603)

**INTEGRATED TECHNOLOGY**

**Audio Library**
**Internet: Research Starter**
**Visit our website:**
www.mcdougallittell.com

## OVERVIEW

**Objectives**
1. understand and appreciate a **short story** (Literary Analysis)
2. identify characteristics of **naturalism** (Literary Analysis)
3. **visualize** setting, characters, and events (**Active Reading**)

**Summary**
In the midst of an intense battle Fred Collins of A Company feels thirsty. The only source of water—a well across the meadow in front of his company—had once been an oasis of peace; now it is a prime target. Collins's comrades shame him into attempting to obtain water. He crosses the field, wondering whether his action qualifies him as a hero. When he looks into the well, he suddenly feels paralyzed with terror. He seizes the bucket, awkwardly fills it, and scampers back across the meadow. A dying officer in his path pleads for water, and although Collins at first refuses to stop, he returns to give the officer a drink. Finally Collins rejoins his regiment. Two lieutenants playfully argue over the bucket, causing the water to spill to the ground.

**Thematic Link**
The **Civil War** tested the mettle of all involved in the conflict. Fred Collins, too, must take the measure of himself.

**5-Minute Warm-Up**

*Daily Language SkillBuilder*

Have students **proofread** the display sentences on page 555i and write them correctly. The sentences also appear on Transparency 16 of **Grammar Transparencies and Copymasters.**

 **Mini Lesson** **Preteaching Vocabulary**
If you would like to preteach the WORDS TO KNOW for this selection, use the Mini Lesson p. 595.

**Reading Skills and Strategies:**
**PREVIEW**

Have students read the Preparing to Read page and look at the art work on page 594. Tell them to recall battle scenes from war movies to stimulate their imaginations as they read.

**Literary Analysis** 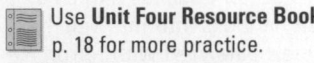 NATURALISM

Explain that naturalism views humans simply as creatures in the natural world. They react to external environmental forces and internal stresses and motivations over which they have little control or understanding.

Use **Unit Four Resource Book,** p. 18 for more practice.

**Active Reading** VISUALIZING

Remind students that they're expected to analyze the melodies of literary language including the use of evocative words. Tell students to look for words and phrases that build pictures of the setting and action. Ask students to identify examples of such words and phrases in the opening paragraph.

**Possible Responses:** "the incessant wrestling of the two armies," "a battery was arguing in tremendous roars," "a red streak as round as a log flashed low in the heavens, like a monstrous bolt of lightning."

Use **Unit Four Resource Book,** p. 17 for more exercises.

*Battle of Chancellorsville,* unknown artist. Corbis-Bettmann.

594

## Teaching Options

 **Mini Lesson** **Viewing and Representing**

*The Battle of Chancellorsville*

**ART APPRECIATION** This lithograph captures the tumult of soldiers caught up in the heat and swirl of battle.
**Instruction** Explain that the focus of *The Battle of Chancellorsville* is a broken line of soldiers reeling under attack. Like Crane, the artist provides many details to convey the horror of war.

**Application** Have students view the painting and then describe their impressions of the battle. Students should identify the details that affect them most strongly.
**Possible Response:** Like the soldiers in Crane's short story, those in the painting strike a variety of unheroic poses. Details such as the slain soldiers in the foreground, the galloping, riderless horse, and the hatless soldier holding his ears suggest the horror and chaos of war. The enemy is a blur of figures partially shrouded by clouds of smoke.

# A Mystery of Heroism

★ ★ ★ ★ ★ ★ ★ ★ ★ ★ ★

## Stephen Crane

★ ★ ★ ★ ★ ★ ★ ★ ★ ★ ★ ★ ★ ★ ★ ★ ★ ★ ★ ★ ★ ★ ★ ★ ★

The dark uniforms of the men were so coated with dust from the <u>incessant</u> wrestling of the two armies that the regiment almost seemed a part of the clay bank which shielded them from the shells. On the top of the hill a battery[1] was arguing in tremendous roars with some other guns and to the eye of the infantry, the artillerymen, the guns, the caissons,[2] the horses, were distinctly outlined upon the blue sky. When a piece was fired a red streak as round as a log flashed low in the heavens, like a monstrous bolt of lightning. The men of the battery wore white duck trousers, which somehow emphasized their legs, and when they ran and crowded in little groups at the bidding of the shouting officers, it was more impressive than usual to the infantry.

---

1. **battery:** group of cannons.
2. **caissons** (kā'sŏnz'): horse-drawn wagons used to carry ammunition.

WORDS
TO
KNOW

**incessant** (ĭn-sĕs'ənt) *adj.* ceaseless; continual

**595**

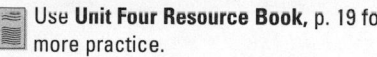

**Literary Analysis** NATURALISM

Ask students to explain why Crane's portrayal of Fred Collins is naturalistic.

**Possible Response:** He is an ordinary character who speaks in the dialect of the lower middle class of the time. His desire for a drink at this moment shows that his physical needs take precedence over all other concerns.

**Reading Skills and Strategies: EVALUATING**

**A** Ask students why Crane introduces the wounded lieutenant at this point.

**Possible Responses:** The lieutenant provides a contrast to Fred Collins. He has been wounded in combat while Fred's greatest worry seems to be his thirst.

**Reading Skills and Strategies: PREDICTING**

**B** Ask students to predict Fred Collins's actions.

**Possible Response:** Fred Collins will try to get a drink of water no matter what the risk.

**Active Reading** VISUALIZING

**C** Ask students what the imagery in this paragraph suggests about Crane's vision of war. Ask them to analyze the details that contribute to this vision.

**Possible Response:** Crane shows the grim horror of war. Such details as the gunners dying on the ground and the suffering of the horses—innocent spectators of the battle—add to the horror of the scene.

F red Collins of A Company was saying: "Thunder, I wisht I had a drink. Ain't there any water round here?" Then somebody yelled: "There goes th'bugler!"

As the eyes of half of the regiment swept in one machine-like movement there was an instant's picture of a horse in a great convulsive leap of a death wound and a rider leaning back with a crooked arm and spread fingers before his face. On the ground was the crimson terror of an exploding shell, with fibres of flame that seemed like lances. A glittering bugle swung clear of the rider's back as fell headlong the horse and the man. In the air was an odor as from a conflagration.[3]

Sometimes they of the infantry looked down at a fair little meadow which spread at their feet. Its long, green grass was rippling gently in a breeze. Beyond it was the grey form of a house half torn to pieces by shells and by the busy axes of soldiers who had pursued firewood. The line of an old fence was now dimly marked by long weeds and by an occasional post. A shell had blown the well-house to fragments. Little lines of grey smoke ribboning upward from some embers indicated the place where had stood the barn.

From beyond a curtain of green woods there came the sound of some stupendous scuffle as if two animals of the size of islands were fighting. At a distance there were occasional appearances of swift-moving men, horses, batteries, flags, and, with the crashing of infantry volleys were heard, often, wild and frenzied cheers. In the midst of it all, Smith and Ferguson, two privates of A Company, were engaged in a heated discussion, which involved the greatest questions of the national existence.

**1** The battery on the hill presently engaged in a frightful duel. The white legs of the gunners scampered this way and that way and the officers redoubled their shouts. The guns, with their demeanors of stolidity and courage, were typical of something infinitely self-possessed in this clamor of death that swirled around the hill.

One of a "swing" team was suddenly smitten **2** quivering to the ground and his maddened brethren dragged his torn body in their struggle to escape from this turmoil and danger. A young soldier astride one of the leaders swore and fumed in his saddle and furiously jerked at the bridle. An officer screamed out an order so violently that his voice broke and ended the sentence in a falsetto[4] shriek.

The leading company of the infantry regiment was somewhat exposed and the colonel ordered it moved more fully under the shelter of the hill. There was the clank of steel against steel.

A lieutenant of the battery rode down and passed them, holding his right arm carefully in his left hand. And it was as if this arm was not at all a part of him, but belonged to another man. His sober and reflective charger[5] went slowly. The officer's face was grimy and perspiring and his uniform was tousled as if he had been in direct grapple with an enemy. He smiled grimly when the men stared at him. He turned his horse toward the meadow. **A**

Collins of A Company said: "I wisht I had a drink. I bet there's water in that there ol' well yonder!" **B**

"Yes; but how you goin' to git it?"

For the little meadow which intervened was now suffering a terrible onslaught of shells. Its green and beautiful calm had vanished utterly. Brown earth was being flung in monstrous handfuls. And there was a massacre of the young blades of grass. They were being torn, burned, obliterated. Some curious fortune of the battle had made this gentle little meadow the object of the red hate of the shells and each one as it

---

3. **conflagration** (kŏn′flə-grā′shən): huge fire.
4. **falsetto:** at a pitch higher than the normal vocal range.
5. **charger:** warhorse.

WORDS TO KNOW  **stupendous** (stoō-pĕn′dəs) *adj.* of amazing size; enormous
**tousled** (tou′zəld) *adj.* messy; rumpled **tousle** *v.*

596

## Teaching Options

### BLOCK SCHEDULING: MANAGING TIME

**If your schedule requires that you cover the lesson objectives in a shorter time, use . . .**
• Preparing to Read, p. 593
• Thinking Through the Literature, p. 602
• Vocabulary in Action, p. 604

**If you want to take advantage of longer class time, use . . .**
• TE Teaching Options: Preteaching Vocabulary, p. 595; Viewing and Representing, p. 594; Cross-Curricular Link, p. 597; Vocabulary Strategy, pp. 600–01 Standardized Test Practice, p. 604
• Choices & Challenges, p. 603

exploded seemed like an imprecation[6] in the face of a maiden.

The wounded officer who was riding across this expanse said to himself: "Why, they couldn't shoot any harder if the whole army was massed here!"

A shell struck the grey ruins of the house and as, after the roar, the shattered wall fell in fragments, there was a noise which resembled the flapping of shutters during a wild gale of winter. Indeed the infantry paused in the shelter of the bank, appeared as men standing upon a shore contemplating a madness of the sea. The angel of calamity had under its glance the battery upon the hill. Fewer white-legged men labored about the guns. A shell had smitten one of the pieces and after the flare, the smoke, the dust, the wrath of this blow was gone, it was possible to see white legs stretched horizontally upon the ground. And at that interval to the rear, where it is the business of battery horses to stand with their noses to the fight awaiting the command to drag their guns out of the destruction or into it or wheresoever these incomprehensible humans demanded with whip and spur—in this line of passive and dumb spectators, whose fluttering hearts yet would not let them forget the iron laws of man's control of them—in this rank of brute-soldiers there had been relentless and hideous carnage. From the ruck[7] of bleeding and prostrate horses, the men of the infantry could see one animal raising its stricken body with its fore-legs and turning its nose with mystic and profound eloquence toward the sky.

Some comrades joked Collins about his thirst. "Well, if yeh want a drink so bad, why don't yeh go git it?"

"Well, I will in a minnet if yeh don't shut up."

A lieutenant of artillery floundered his horse straight down the hill with as great concern as if it were level ground. As he galloped past the colonel of the infantry, he threw up his hand in swift salute. "We've got to get out of that," he roared angrily. He was a black-bearded officer, and his eyes, which resembled beads, sparkled like those of an insane man. His jumping horse sped along the column of infantry.

The fat major standing carelessly with his sword held horizontally behind him and with his legs far apart, looked after the receding horseman and laughed. "He wants to get back with orders pretty quick or there'll be no batt'ry left," he observed.

The wise young captain of the second company hazarded[8] to the lieutenant colonel that the enemy's infantry would probably soon attack the hill, and the lieutenant colonel snubbed him.

A private in one of the rear companies looked out over the meadow and then turned to a companion and said: "Look there, Jim." It was the wounded officer from the battery, who some time before had started to ride across the meadow, supporting his right arm carefully with his left hand. This man had encountered a shell apparently at a time when no one perceived him and he could now be seen lying face downward with a stirruped foot stretched across the body of his dead horse. A leg of the charger extended slantingly upward precisely as stiff as a stake. Around this motionless pair the shells still howled.

---

6. **imprecation** (ĭm′prĭ-kā′shən): curse; oath.
7. **ruck**: crowd; jumble.
8. **hazarded**: ventured a guess.

WORDS
TO
KNOW

**eloquence** (ĕl′ə-kwəns) *n.* expressiveness

**597**

## Cross Curricular Link **History**

**NATURALIST MOVEMENTS IN OTHER CULTURES**

Émile Zola, who might be called the father of the naturalist movement, influenced writers in many other countries. German literature began to manifest naturalistic characteristics in 1884, with the publication of the poetry anthology *Dichtercharaktere,* which focused on the theme of urban life. This book was followed by Arno Holz's *Book of the Times*, which made him the foremost naturalist poet in Germany. His later works concerned themselves with the depiction of the most minute elements of everyday life. Developments in the 20th century made the scientific objectivity of German naturalism too narrow for new writers.

In Korea, the influences of naturalism on literature were not felt until the 1920s. Yom Sangsop, one of the first writers to introduce elements of naturalism into his writing, defined it as "an expression of awakened individuality." He believed that the purpose of naturalism was to expose the base side of life and the disillusionment that occurs when one's heroes are toppled. Korean naturalistic writers often used the first-person point of view to make themselves the subjects of analytical dissection, and because of their friction with society, writers often turned to nature in their works.

Naturalists believe that people's lives are affected by natural and social forces. Ask students what social force prompts Fred Collins to make the decision that he does.

**Possible Responses:** Collins is influenced by his peers, who attack his courage and wound his pride through their remarks.

**Reading Skills and Strategies: MAKING INFERENCES**

**A** Have students describe how Collins must feel right now.

**Possible Responses:** Collins may have been hoping that the officers would deny him permission, thereby allowing him to save face among his comrades. He may be wondering how he got himself into this situation or may be marshaling his courage to fulfill his task.

**Reading Skills and Strategies: CLARIFYING**

**B** Explain the quotation "Say, he must be a desperate cuss." Identify the tone that the speaker might be using.

**Possible Responses:** Collins might be desperate for water or for approval; *cuss* suggests that he is stubborn. This remark could be made in a tone of admiration or ridicule.

**Reading Skills and Strategies: EVALUATING**

**C** Ask students for Collins's definition of a hero. Have students consider whether they agree with this definition.

**Answer:** men who do not feel fear when in danger

---

here was a quarrel in A Company. Collins was shaking his fist in the faces of some laughing comrades. "Dern yeh! I ain't afraid t' go. If yeh say much, I will go!"

"Of course, yeh will! Yeh'll run through that there medder, won't yeh?"

Collins said, in a terrible voice: "You see, now!" At this ominous threat his comrades broke into renewed jeers.

Collins gave them a dark scowl and went to find his captain. The latter was conversing with the colonel of the regiment.

"Captain," said Collins, saluting and standing at attention. In those days all trousers bagged at the knees. "Captain, I want t' git permission to go git some water from that there well over yonder!"

The colonel and the captain swung about simultaneously and stared across the meadow. The captain laughed. "You must be pretty thirsty, Collins?"

"Yes, sir; I am."

"Well—ah," said the captain. After a moment he asked: "Can't you wait?"

"No, sir."

The colonel was watching Collins's face. "Look here, my lad," he said, in a pious[9] sort of a voice. "Look here, my lad." Collins was not a lad. "Don't you think that's taking pretty big risks for a little drink of water?"

"I dunno," said Collins, uncomfortably. Some of the resentment toward his companions, which perhaps had forced him into this affair, was beginning to fade. "I dunno wether 'tis."

The colonel and the captain contemplated him for a time.

"Well," said the captain finally.

"Well," said the colonel, "if you want to go, why go."

Collins saluted. "Much obliged t' yeh."

As he moved away the colonel called after him. "Take some of the other boys' canteens with you an' hurry back now."

"Yes, sir. I will."

The colonel and the captain looked at each other then, for it had suddenly occurred that they could not for the life of them tell whether Collins wanted to go or whether he did not.

They turned to regard Collins and as they perceived him surrounded by gesticulating[10] comrades the colonel said: "Well, by thunder! I guess he's going."

Collins appeared as a man dreaming. In the midst of the questions, the advice, the warnings, all the excited talk of his company mates, he maintained a curious silence.

They were very busy in preparing him for his ordeal. When they inspected him carefully it was somewhat like the examination that grooms give a horse before a race; and they were amazed, staggered by the whole affair. Their astonishment found vent in strange repetitions.

"Are yeh sure a-goin'?" they demanded again and again.

"Certainly I am," cried Collins, at last furiously.

He strode <u>sullenly</u> away from them. He was swinging five or six canteens by their cords. It seemed that his cap would not remain firmly on his head, and often he reached and pulled it down over his brow.

There was a general movement in the compact column. The long animal-like thing moved slightly. Its four hundred eyes were turned upon the figure of Collins.

"Well, sir, if that ain't th' derndest thing. I never thought Fred Collins had the blood in him for that kind of business."

---

9. **pious** (pī'əs): high-minded; solemn.
10. **gesticulating** (jĕ-stĭk'yə-lā'tĭng): gesturing.

WORDS
TO
KNOW

**sullenly** (sŭl'ən-lē) *adv.* resentfully; sulkily

598

---

 **Mini Lesson** **Grammar**

**INTRODUCTION TO ADJECTIVE CLAUSES**

**Instruction** Adjective clauses are subordinate clauses used as adjectives to modify nouns or pronouns. Usually the adjective clause immediately follows the noun or pronoun it modifies. Most often it is introduced by the relative pronouns *who, whom, whose, which,* and *that.* Display the following sentence:
The well, <u>which was across the meadow</u>, became his destination.
Explain that the adjective clause modifies *well.*

**Exercises** Rewrite the following sentences, replacing the underlined words or phrases with adjective clauses.
1. His <u>loose</u> cap distracted him from his mission.
2. The lieutenant <u>with the wounds</u> begged him for a drink of water.
3. He was surrounded by <u>flaming red</u> flying arrows.
4. The <u>cheering</u> soldiers welcomed him back into their midst.

"What's he goin' to do, anyhow?"

"He's goin' to that well there after water."

"We ain't dyin' of thirst, are we? That's foolishness."

"Well, somebody put him up to it an' he's doin' it."

"Say, he must be a desperate cuss."

When Collins faced the meadow and walked away from the regiment he was vaguely conscious that a chasm, the deep valley of all prides, was suddenly between him and his comrades. It was <u>provisional</u>, but the provision was that he return as a victor. He had blindly been led by quaint emotions and laid himself under an obligation to walk squarely up to the face of death.

But he was not sure that he wished to make a <u>retraction</u> even if he could do so without shame. As a matter of truth he was sure of very little. He was mainly surprised.

It seemed to him supernaturally strange that he had allowed his mind to maneuver his body into such a situation. He understood that it might be called dramatically great.

However, he had no full appreciation of anything excepting that he was actually conscious of being dazed. He could feel his dulled mind groping after the form and color of this incident.

Too, he wondered why he did not feel some keen agony of fear cutting his sense like a knife. He wondered at this because human expression had said loudly for centuries that men should feel afraid of certain things and that all men who did not feel this fear were phenomena,[11] heroes.

He was then a hero. He suffered that disappointment which we would all have if we discovered that we were ourselves capable of

those deeds which we most admire in history and legend. This, then, was a hero. After all, heroes were not much.

No, it could not be true. He was not a hero. Heroes had no shames in their lives and, as for him, he remembered borrowing fifteen dollars from a friend and promising to pay it back the next day, and then avoiding that friend for ten months. When at home his mother had aroused him for the early labor of his life on the farm, it had often been his fashion to be irritable, childish, diabolical, and his mother had died since he had come to the war.

He saw that in this matter of the well, the canteens, the shells, he was an intruder in the land of fine deeds.

He was now about thirty paces from his comrades. The regiment had just turned its many faces toward him.

From the forest of terrific noises there suddenly emerged a little uneven line of men. They fired fiercely and rapidly at distant foliage on which appeared little puffs of white smoke. The spatter of skirmish firing was added to the thunder of the guns on the hill. The little line of men ran forward. A color-sergeant[12] fell flat with his flag as if he had slipped on ice. There was hoarse cheering from this distant field.

Collins suddenly felt that two demon fingers were pressed into his ears. He could see nothing but flying arrows, flaming red. He lurched from the shock of this explosion, but he made a mad rush for the house, which he viewed as a man

### ★ ★ ★ ★ ★ ★ ★ ★ ★ ★

## "Don't you think that's taking pretty big risks for a little drink of water?"

### ★ ★ ★ ★ ★ ★ ★ ★ ★ ★

---

11. **phenomena** (fĭ-nŏm′ə-nə): exceptional or remarkable people.

12. **color-sergeant:** a soldier who carries a military unit's flag, or "colors," into battle.

| WORDS TO KNOW | **provisional** (prə-vĭzh′ə-nəl) *adj.* temporary |
| | **retraction** (rĭ-trăk′shən) *n.* a taking back of something said |

599

## Customizing Instruction

### Less Proficient Readers

**1** Ask students to explain what motivates Fred Collins to go for the water.

**Possible Response:** It becomes clear that Fred Collins has placed himself in the position of having to go for water because his friends have challenged his courage and ability to do so. Since he first thought of the idea, the meadow has become a battlefield, but his pride will not let him back down now.

Tell students that they are expected to adjust their purpose for reading to find out what happens when Collins crosses the meadow to the well.

### Students Acquiring English

**2** Explain that the idiom *look here* is synonymous with "understand" or "please consider."

**3** Point out that the phrase *blood in him* means "courage" or "nerve."

### Multiple Learning Styles
**Interpersonal Learners**

Some students might empathize with Fred Collins as he contemplates the action he is about to undertake. Ask students if there was a time in their lives when they found themselves in a similar situation, unwilling or unable to back down, yet not happy about going ahead.

### Gifted and Talented

**4** Ask students to define and discuss the following metaphor: "he was an intruder in the land of fine deeds."

**Possible Responses:**

1. His cap, which was loose, distracted him from his mission.

2. The lieutenant who was wounded begged him for a drink of water.

3. He was surrounded by flying arrows that were flaming red.

4. The soldiers, who were cheering, welcomed him back into their midst.

Use **Grammar Transparencies and Copymasters**, p. 92.

Use McDougal Littell's *Language Network*, Chapter 3, for more instruction and practice in adjective clauses.

**A** Ask students to analyze the effect Crane creates by piling one sensory detail upon another in these paragraphs.
**Possible Response:** The many details allow the reader to experience the chaos and tumult of sounds and sensations around Fred Collins. Some are distinguishable; others merge into a crescendo.

**Reading Skills and Strategies: ANALYZING**
**B** Ask students to analyze the significance of Collins's action in turning back to give the lieutenant some water.
**Possible Response:** This action can be viewed as truly heroic. He risks his life to comfort another human being.

**Literary Analysis: THEME**
Ask students what Crane is suggesting by having his character give the officer a drink.
**Possible Response:** Ordinary people have the ability to reach beyond themselves and act heroically.

**Literary Analysis: IRONY**
**C** Have students explain the irony of the ending and ask them to suggest why Crane ended the story in this way.
**Possible Responses:** After Collins's great effort to get the water, it spills. Collins's so-called heroic act, which almost costs him his life, actually benefits no one. He himself never even tastes the water he craves.

---

**A** submerged to the neck in a boiling surf might view the shore. In the air, little pieces of shell howled and the earthquake explosions drove him insane with the menace of their roar. As he ran the canteens knocked together with a rhythmical tinkling.

As he neared the house each detail of the scene became vivid to him. He was aware of some bricks of the vanished chimney lying on the sod. There was a door which hung by one hinge.

**1** Rifle bullets called forth by the insistent skirmishers came from the far-off bank of foliage. They mingled with the shells and the pieces of shells until the air was torn in all directions by hootings, yells, howls. The sky was full of fiends who directed all their wild rage at his head.

When he came to the well he flung himself face downward and peered into its darkness. There were <u>furtive</u> silver glintings some feet from

the surface. He grabbed one of the canteens and, unfastening its cap, swung it down by the cord. The water flowed slowly in with an indolent gurgle.

And now as he lay with his face turned away he was suddenly smitten with the terror. It came upon his heart like the grasp of claws. All the power faded from his muscles. For an instant he was no more than a dead man.

The canteen filled with a maddening slowness in the manner of all bottles. Presently he recovered his strength and addressed a screaming oath to it. He leaned over until it seemed as if he intended to try to push water into it with his hands. His eyes as he gazed down into the well shone like two pieces of metal and in their expression was a great appeal and a great curse. The stupid water derided[13] him.

There was the blaring thunder of a shell. Crimson light shone through the swift-boiling smoke and made a pink reflection on part of the wall of the well. Collins jerked out his arm and canteen with the same motion that a man would use in withdrawing his head from a furnace.

He scrambled erect and glared and hesitated. On the ground near him lay the old well bucket, with a length of rusty chain. He lowered it swiftly into the well. The bucket struck the water and then turning lazily over, sank. When, with hand reaching tremblingly over hand, he hauled it out, it knocked often against the walls of the well and spilled some of its contents.

In running with a filled bucket, a man can adopt but one kind of gait. So through this terrible field over which screamed practical[14] angels of death Collins ran in the manner of a farmer chased out of a dairy by a bull.

---

13. **derided:** mocked.
14. **practical:** virtual.

**furtive** (fûr′tĭv) *adj.* secret; sneaky

---

## Teaching Options

**Mini Lesson** **Vocabulary Strategy**

**ROOT WORDS**
**Instruction** Remind students that they're expected to apply meanings of prefixes, roots, and suffixes in order to comprehend unfamiliar words. Explain that root words are the base words that contain a word's meaning. Give students the definitions of some common roots.

| Root | Meaning |
|---|---|
| anima | spirit, breath |
| ced, ceed, cess | to go, to move, or to yield |
| chron | time |
| gen | kind or sort |
| ject, jet | to throw |
| locu, loqu | to speak |
| spec, spect | to look at, observe |
| tract | to pull or draw |

is face went staring white with anticipation—anticipation of a blow that would whirl him around and down. He would fall as he had seen other men fall, the life knocked out of them so suddenly that their knees were no more quick to touch the ground than their heads. He saw the long blue line of the regiment, but his comrades were standing looking at him from the edge of an impossible star. He was aware of some deep wheel ruts and hoof prints in the sod beneath his feet.

The artillery officer who had fallen in this meadow had been making groans in the teeth of the tempest of sound. These <u>futile</u> cries, wrenched from him by his agony, were heard only by shells, bullets. When wild-eyed Collins came running, this officer raised himself. His face contorted and blanched[15] from pain, he was about to utter some great beseeching cry. But suddenly his face straightened and he called: "Say, young man, give me a drink of water, will you?"

Collins had no room amid his emotions for surprise. He was mad from the threats of destruction.

"I can't," he screamed, and in this reply was a full description of his quaking apprehension. His cap was gone and his hair was riotous. His clothes made it appear that he had been dragged over the ground by the heels. He ran on.

The officer's head sank down and one elbow crooked. His foot in its brass-bound stirrup still stretched over the body of his horse and the other leg was under the steed.

But Collins turned. He came dashing back. His face had now turned grey and in his eyes was all terror. "Here it is! Here it is!"

The officer was as a man gone in drink. His arm bended like a twig. His head drooped as if his neck was of willow. He was sinking to the ground, to lie face downward.

Collins grabbed him by the shoulder. "Here it is. Here's your drink. Turn over! Turn over, man, for God's sake!"

With Collins hauling at his shoulder, the officer twisted his body and fell with his face turned toward that region where lived the unspeakable noises of the swirling missiles. There was the faintest shadow of a smile on his lips as he looked at Collins. He gave a sigh, a little primitive breath like that from a child.

Collins tried to hold the bucket steadily, but his shaking hands caused the water to splash all over the face of the dying man. Then he jerked it away and ran on.

The regiment gave him a welcoming roar. The grimed faces were wrinkled in laughter.

His captain waved the bucket away. "Give it to the men!"

The two <u>genial</u>, sky-larking[16] young lieutenants were the first to gain possession of it. They played over it in their fashion.

When one tried to drink the other teasingly knocked his elbow. "Don't, Billie! You'll make me spill it," said the one. The other laughed.

Suddenly there was an oath, the thud of wood on the ground, and a swift murmur of astonishment from the ranks. The two lieutenants glared at each other. The bucket lay on the ground empty. ❖

---

★ ★ ★ ★ ★ ★ ★ ★ ★ ★

## His face went staring white with anticipation— anticipation of a blow that would whirl him around and down.

★ ★ ★ ★ ★ ★ ★ ★ ★ ★

---

15. **blanched:** turned white.
16. **sky-larking:** playful; fun-loving.

WORDS TO KNOW
**futile** (fyōōt′l) *adj.* useless
**genial** (jēn′yəl) *adj.* having a friendly disposition

601

## Customizing Instruction

### Students Acquiring English

**1** Point out that the "fiends" are the personification of bullets and shells flying overhead.

**2** Explain that the regiment who are in a safe place seem to Collins as distant as an "impossible star."

### Less Proficient Readers
Remind students that they're expected to produce summaries of texts by identifying main ideas and supporting details. Ask students to summarize Collin's trip to and from the well.

**Possible Response:** Fred Collins makes it to the well safely. Once there, he feels terrified. After he fills the bucket, he runs as quickly as he can back to the regiment. On the way the wounded lieutenant begs him for a drink of water. Although he at first refuses, he then goes back and gives him a drink. Collins makes it back safely.

**Application** Have students form groups to think of words that contain these roots. Students should try to define the words by applying the meaning of the root and then use a dictionary to check their definitions. Some of the WORDS TO KNOW contain the roots listed above, as well as some of the other words associated with this selection (*eloquence, genial, incessant, rejected, retraction, spectators*).

Use **Vocabulary Transparencies and Copymasters,** p. 53.

A lesson on root words appears on p. 326 in the Pupil's Edition.

## GUIDING STUDENT RESPONSE

### Connect to the Literature

**1. What Do You Think?**
Some students may state that the ending suggests that Collins risked his life in vain.

**Comprehension Check**
• The other soldiers consider Collins foolish.
• The wounded lieutenant lying in the meadow asks for a drink.
• The bucket of water spills.

 Use Selection Quiz
**Unit Four Resource Book**, p. 20.

### Think Critically

**2. Possible Response:** This omission underscores the insignificance of Collins's actions in the story.

**3. Responses will vary.** Students may suggest Collins gains a new perspective on heroism and war. He learns that heroes are ordinary and flawed, not superhuman and virtuous. He no longer glorifies war but realizes its brutality.

**4. Responses will vary.** Some students might say Collins acts heroically by risking his life to get water and then by sharing it with the dying officer. Other students might say that Collins acted foolishly, risking his life unnecessarily to save face with his regiment.

**5. Responses will vary.** Good responses will include descriptive language that evokes vivid images of war scenes. The picture of war is anything but grand and heroic, emphasizing the insignificance of officers and ordinary soldiers.

**6. Possible Response:** The nature of heroism is complex and puzzling. Evidence might include the following: Collins's spontaneous decision to help a wounded soldier is more heroic than his deliberate attempt to get water.

### Literary Analysis

**Naturalism** Students' evaluations of Collins's degree of freedom will vary. Students, however, should note that Collins himself is not sure how his mind finagled his body into such danger.
**Review: Irony** Possible Response: Collins's deeds do no good. They help neither himself nor his regiment.

---

### Connect to the Literature

**1. What Do You Think?**
How did you react to the ending of this story?

**Comprehension Check**
• How do the other soldiers feel about Collins's attempt to get water?
• Who asks Collins for a drink of water on his way back from the well?
• What happens to the bucket of water at the end of the story?

### Think Critically

**2.** Why do you think Fred Collins is not mentioned in the last three paragraphs of this story? Explain your answer.

**3.** How would you explain what Collins learns from his brush with death?

**4.** Do you consider Collins a hero? Cite evidence to support your answer.

 THINK ABOUT
  • the risks he takes and why he takes them
  • his emotions in the heat of battle
  • how he treats the dying artillery officer

**5.** **ACTIVE READING** **VISUALIZING** Review the details you listed in your **READER'S NOTEBOOK.** What words would you use to describe the picture of war that you formed in your imagination?

**6.** How would you explain the **title** of this story?

### Extend Interpretations

**7. The Writer's Style** Often Crane uses figurative language— **similes, metaphors,** and **personification**—to describe a soldier's sensations. Which figures of speech in the story strike you as especially vivid?

**8. What If?** If Collins had been killed, how would the effect of this story be different?

**9. Comparing Texts** Which **character** do you think shows more courage, Collins in Crane's story or Peyton Farquhar in "An Occurrence at Owl Creek Bridge," on page 581? Explain the reasons for your choice.

**10. Connect to Life** How do Collins and his deeds compare with the heroes and heroic actions you listed for the Connect to Your Life activity on page 593?

**602** UNIT FOUR PART 1: A HOUSE DIVIDED

### Literary Analysis

**NATURALISM** As a literary movement, **naturalism** originated in France in the late 1800s with the grisly, extreme realism of novelist Émile Zola. Naturalistic writers sought not only to render common people and ordinary life accurately but also to describe how instinct and environment affect human behavior.

Many of the naturalists' ideas reflected intellectual trends emerging in Europe in biology, economics, and psychology. For example, the writings of Charles Darwin strongly influenced naturalistic thought. In *The Origin of Species* (1859), Darwin proposed his theory that species evolve through a process of natural selection, whereby only those with the most favorable traits adapt and survive. The naturalists, too, tended to believe that the fate of humans, like that of any other species in nature, was determined by forces beyond individual control.

**Cooperative Learning Activity** With a small group of classmates, debate to what extent Collins's actions are determined by forces beyond his control. Cite passages to support your opinion. On a scale like the one below, place a mark to record your group's view about his degree of freedom. Then compare your scale with other groups' scales.

**Collins's Actions**

| | |
|---|---|
| Totally Free | Totally Predetermined |

**REVIEW** **IRONY** **Irony** refers to a contrast between what is expected and what actually exists or happens. What do you find ironic about Collins's deeds? Explain your answer.

---

### Extend Interpretations

**The Writer's Style** Responses will vary. Examples include the description of troops as "animal-like" and "machine-like."
**What If?** Possible Response: The story would be less cynical and more conventional. Collins's act of sacrificing his life might make him seem like a conventional hero, rather than a questionable one.

**Comparing Texts** Responses will vary. Some students may say that Collins is more heroic because he does return to try to give the wounded lieutenant a drink of water. Other students may say that Peyton Farquhar is more heroic because he gave up his home, his family, and his life to support the Confederacy.
**Connect to Life** Some students may say that the heroes they listed have nobler motives then Collins does.

## Writing Options

**1. Letter Home** As Collins, write a letter to a friend or a relative in civilian life. Explain your views about war, your relationship with your comrades, your act of "heroism," and what you learned from your brush with death.

| Characteristics of Naturalism | Present? |
|---|---|
| 1. | ☐ |
| 2. | ☐ |
| 3. | ☐ |

**2. Literary Analysis** To what extent is "The Mystery of Heroism" a good example of naturalistic fiction? Using what you learned about **naturalism** on pages 593 and 602, write a brief critique of this story. As a prewriting task, look again at the scale you created for the Literary Analysis activity. Place your critique in your **Working Portfolio.**

**3. Different Ending** What are some other ways that this story might have ended? Draft an alternative ending to the story, and read it aloud to classmates.

**Writing Handbook**
See page 1279: Narrative Writing.

## Activities & Explorations

**1. Combat Sketch** Using details from your Active Reading chart, draw a sketch to accompany the story. ~ **ART**

**2. War Songs** Find and listen to a recording of Civil War songs, such as "Tenting on the Old Camp Ground" or "The Old Union Wagon." What aspects of war do the song lyrics address? Choose a song that you think fits the mood and events of Crane's story, play the recording for your classmates, and then point out the connections you see. ~ **MUSIC**

**3. Interview with Collins** With a partner, role-play a journalist interviewing Collins about his conduct on the battlefield. In the interview, be faithful to Collins's perspective on events and try to imitate his dialect. ~ **SPEAKING AND LISTENING**

## Inquiry & Research

**Photo Gallery** Crane himself never served in the Civil War. He relied on resources such as newspaper and magazine accounts, veterans' tales, and combat photographs to re-create the grim reality of battle. Crane was impressed by the riveting photographs taken by Mathew B. Brady, a photographer who had traveled with the Union army. Find reproductions of Brady's photographs in history books and biographies such as *Mr. Lincoln's Camera Man* by Roy Meredith and *Mathew Brady* by Barry Pritzker. With a group of classmates, prepare an exhibit of these photographs. Then present a guided tour of the exhibit, explaining what each photo reveals.

**More Online: Research Starter**
www.mcdougallittell.com

Mathew Brady in the field with his darkroom wagon.

## Writing Options

1. **Letter Home** To make their letters convincing, students need to think about how articulate Fred Collins is and whether letter writing would come easily to him. **To make the assignment more challenging,** have students imitate the dialect Crane uses in this story.
2. **Literary Analysis To get students started on this assignment,** have them list the characteristics of naturalistic fiction as the model indicates, check whether the characteristic is present, and note the page number or example from the story.
3. **Different Ending To get students started on this assignment,** ask them first to work in groups to brainstorm ideas for different endings. Students should then choose an alternative ending that is meaningful and consistent with the plot of the story.

## Activities & Explorations

1. **Combat Sketch** An alternative to original art might be to create a collage or to generate images on the computer as a slide show which would offer several illustrations for the story's actions.
2. **War Songs Auditory learners** might create their own lyrics and music to fit the mood and events of the story.
3. **Interview with Collins To get students started on this assignment,** have each of the partners prepare five to ten questions. The interviewer should choose the best questions to write on index cards. Interviewers should also follow up promising responses with impromptu questions.

## Inquiry & Research

**Photo Gallery** Linguistic learners might prepare catalogues of the exhibit with the information printed under the reproduction of each photograph or prepare an audio tape with appropriate cues so that viewers can tour the exhibit on their own.

---

**(Mini Lesson)** ## Grammar

### COMMAS IN NAMES AND TITLES

**Instruction** Explain that commas are used to set off titles that follow personal names and to set off abbreviations such as *Inc.* and *Ltd.* Show students how the comma separates the title from the name in the following model sentence. They crisply saluted Robert Martinez, Sergeant-at-Arms.

**Exercises** Ask students to rewrite the following sentences with the correct punctuation.
1. After the Civil War, James Mele M.D. went into private practice. (*James Mele, M.D.,*)
2. Harriet Brown Attorney joined the company of Lesoto, McKenzie Inc. established in 1965. (*Harriet Brown, Attorney, . . . McKenzie, Inc.,*)
3. Paper Supplies Ltd. announced the company would be setting up a branch here. (*Paper Supplies, Ltd.,*)
4. Officially she is known as Tamara Robinson Ph.D. but she rarely uses her full title. (*Robinson, Ph.D.,*)

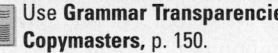 Use **Grammar Transparencies and Copymasters,** p. 150.

 Use McDougal Littell's *Language Network,* Chapter 9, for more instruction and practice in commas.

## Vocabulary in Action

**EXERCISE**

1. stupendous
2. tousled
3. eloquence
4. incessant
5. sullenly
6. genial
7. provisional
8. retraction
9. futile
10. furtive

## Author Activity

Possible Response: Both the novel and the short story depict war as an ignoble, not a heroic, activity. Crane emphasizes human insignificance.

**To get students started on this activity,** have them create a chart similar to the one they used to record their impressions and ideas while reading "A Mystery of Heroism." **Auditory learners** might find that listening to a recording of *The Red Badge of Courage* will deepen their appreciation of the novel and help them compare it with the short story.

---

## Vocabulary in Action

**EXERCISE: MEANING CLUES** On your paper, write the Word to Know whose meaning is suggested by each sentence.

1. The battle resulted in a tremendous number of deaths.
2. The soldiers looked as if they had been swept up by a tornado.
3. The two armies did not need to exchange words; the cannons expressed their feelings very well.
4. The army had to endure continual fire from enemy artillery.
5. Many men, forced to charge the enemy, obeyed orders unwillingly.
6. Several sergeants relieved their stress by joking around with one another.
7. The major came up with a plan to use until he got new orders.
8. The soldier who asked to be allowed to go to the well knew that it was too late to change his mind.
9. It was useless to try to save the badly wounded man.
10. Both sides sent scouts to spy on the enemy.

| WORDS TO KNOW | eloquence<br>furtive<br>futile<br>genial | incessant<br>provisional<br>retraction | stupendous<br>sullenly<br>tousled |
|---|---|---|---|

### Stephen Crane
### 1871–1900

**Other Works**
*The Red Badge of Courage*
"The Bride Comes to Yellow Sky"
"The Open Boat"

**Naturalistic Writer** As both a resident of the urban slums and a newspaper reporter, Crane walked the mean streets of New York City, recording the struggles and hopelessness of the people who lived there. His first novel, *Maggie: A Girl of the Streets* (1893), was rejected by publishers for its shocking depiction of the degradation and immorality of slum life. Crane had to borrow money to have the novel published independently. Later hailed by critics and writers alike, *Maggie* has been called America's "first truly naturalistic novel." Crane's second naturalistic novel, *The Red Badge of Courage* (1895), exposed American readers, for the first time, to a brutally realistic account of a young soldier's experiences in the Civil War. These and other works broke new ground in choice of subject, point of view, and style.

**Foreign Correspondent** In his short lifetime, Crane undertook a series of far-flung writing assignments. In 1895, under contract with a newspaper syndicate, he toured Mexico and the American West, settings for "The Blue Hotel" and "The Bride Comes to Yellow Sky." Later, as a war correspondent, he covered the Spanish-American War in Cuba and Puerto Rico and the Greco-Turkish War in Greece. These experiences affected his health.

**Early Death** By the age of 25, Crane was a star reporter and literary phenomenon. Settling in London in 1897, he came to know Joseph Conrad, Henry James, H. G. Wells, and other writers. However, as he wrote feverishly to pay off debts, his health steadily deteriorated. At the age of 28, Crane died of tuberculosis in Germany.

## Author Activity

**War Stories** Read Crane's masterpiece, *The Red Badge of Courage*. Then compare the picture of war in the novel with that in "A Mystery of Heroism."

**604** UNIT FOUR PART 1: A HOUSE DIVIDED

---

## Teaching Options

✓ **Assessment Standardized Test Practice**

**IDENTIFYING SUPPORTING IDEAS** For some standardized tests, students will be given a choice of details and asked to choose the one that best completes the statement about the text. They can test the validity of their choice by carefully reading the relevant passage. Often the questions follow the chronological pattern of the reading. Although other choices may look correct, only one answer can be supported by the text. Work with students in choosing the best answer to complete the following statements.

1. The infantry is positioned
   a. on a hill.
   b. across a meadow.
   c. under the shelter of a clay bank.
2. When Fred Collins first spies the well, it is
   a. in a heavy area of fighting.
   b. across a peaceful field.
   c. in the hands of the enemy.
3. The officers tell Fred Collins
   a. that he cannot get water.
   b. that he should bring water back for the others.
   c. that he will die.

**Answers:** 1. c; 2. b; 3. b

*"... that government of the people, by the people, for the people, shall not perish from the earth."*

# The Gettysburg Address

*Speech by* ABRAHAM LINCOLN

### Connect to Your Life

**President Lincoln** What words come to mind when you think of Abraham Lincoln? With classmates, discuss what you know about Lincoln, creating a word web like the one started here. List words and phrases that you associate with Lincoln's early life, his presidency, his appearance, his character, his leadership during the Civil War, and his death.

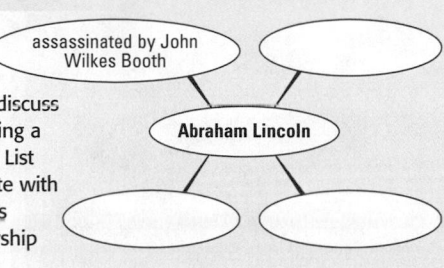

assassinated by John Wilkes Booth

Abraham Lincoln

## Build Background

**Gettysburg** The Battle of Gettysburg, the turning point of the Civil War, began over shoes. The advancing Confederate army needed shoes; to get them, some Confederate soldiers were sent to nearby Gettysburg, Pennsylvania, where they accidentally encountered Union soldiers. Soon, two huge forces began to maneuver for battle—the 75,000 Confederate troops of General Robert E. Lee and the 90,000 Union army troops under General George Meade. For three days—July 1–3, 1863—the two sides fought a horrendous battle. In the end, the Union won, but the losses on both sides were staggering—28,000 Confederate soldiers and 23,000 Union soldiers killed or wounded. On November 19, 1863, President Lincoln spoke at the dedication of the National Soldiers' Cemetery at the Gettysburg battlefield. Though Lincoln spoke for little more than two minutes, his words still echo through the ages.

WORDS TO KNOW
**Vocabulary Preview**

conceive          devotion
consecrate        resolve
detract

## Focus Your Reading

**LITERARY ANALYSIS** **STYLE** As you recall, the distinctive way in which a work of literature is written is its **style.** One technique of style is **repetition,** or the recurrence of words, phrases, or lines. For example, Patrick Henry used repetition for emphasis in his speech on pages 263–266:

> The war is inevitable—and *let it come! I repeat it, sir, let it come!*

Notice repetition and other features of Lincoln's style in the address.

**ACTIVE READING** **INTERPRETING HISTORICAL CONTEXT** When you read a speech, keep in mind the **historical context**—the occasion, the audience, and the purpose of the speech. Lincoln delivered this speech shortly after the Battle of Gettysburg. At a solemn dedication ceremony held at the battle site, a crowd of some 15,000 mourners listened to the eloquent main speaker, Edward Everett, deliver a two-hour speech. Then Lincoln, barely glancing at his handwritten address, spoke for roughly two minutes.

Try to imagine yourself in the audience as you read this speech. Lincoln does not explain things that he assumes his listeners already know. For example, "Four score and seven years ago" means 87 years before, in 1776, when the Declaration of Independence was signed.

📖 **READER'S NOTEBOOK** As you go through each paragraph, fill in the blanks, so to speak. What has occurred recently? What is happening as Lincoln speaks? Define any terms or references that a person unfamiliar with American history would not understand.

THE GETTYSBURG ADDRESS **605**

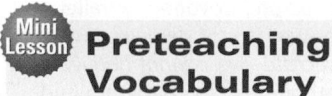

## Reading and Analyzing

### Active Reading | INTERPRETING HISTORICAL CONTEXT

Remind students that they're expected to interpret the possible influences of historical context. Ask them to consider the thoughts and emotions of Lincoln's audience when he gave his address. Many of his listeners had lost loved ones, and some were questioning the wisdom of pursuing the war. As students read, have them record the possible responses of those who attended the dedication of the National Soldier's Cemetery.

| Notes About the Speech | Possible Thoughts of Listeners |
|---|---|
|  |  |
|  |  |
|  |  |

 Use **Unit Four Resource Book** p. 22 for more practice.

### Literary Analysis | STYLE

Have students identify and analyze the characteristics of clearly written text including word choice and syntax. Remind them to consider the effect of aesthetic elements in the speech, particularly Lincoln's use of repetition and parallel structure. Ask them to read examples aloud and discuss why these techniques are so often used in speeches.

**Possible Response:** repetition—*dedicate, consecrate, devotion;* parallel structure—*we cannot dedicate—we cannot consecrate—we cannot hallow.* These techniques create rhythm and dramatic cadence, heightening the impact of the message.

 Use **Unit Four Resource Book** p. 23 for more practice..

# ABRAHAM LINCOLN
# THE GETTYSBURG ADDRESS

**FOUR SCORE AND SEVEN YEARS AGO**[1]
our fathers brought forth on this continent a new nation, <u>conceived</u> in liberty, and dedicated to the proposition that all men are created equal. Now we are engaged in a great civil war, testing whether that nation, or any nation so conceived and so dedicated, can long endure. We are met on a great battlefield of that war. We have come to dedicate a portion of that field as a final resting place for those who here gave their lives that that nation might live. It is altogether fitting and proper that we should do this. But, in a larger sense, we cannot dedicate—we cannot <u>consecrate</u>—we cannot hallow[2] —this ground. The brave men, living and dead, who struggled here have consecrated it far above our poor power to add or <u>detract</u>. The world will little note nor long remember what we say here, but it can never forget what they did here. It is for us, the living, rather, to be dedicated here to the unfinished work which they who fought here have thus far so nobly advanced. It is rather for us to be here dedicated to the great task remaining before us— that from these honored dead we take increased devotion to that cause for which they gave the last full measure of <u>devotion</u>; that we here highly <u>resolve</u> that these dead shall not have died in vain; that this nation, under God, shall have a new birth of freedom; and that government of the people, by the people, for the people, shall not perish from the earth.

Gettysburg on the day that Lincoln spoke.

---

1. **four score and seven years ago:** 87 years ago—that is, in 1776. (*Score* means "a group of twenty.")
2. **hallow:** set apart as holy.

WORDS
TO
KNOW

**conceived** (kən-sēvd') *adj.* originated **conceive** *v.*
**consecrate** (kŏn'sĭ-krāt') *v.* to declare sacred
**detract** (dĭ-trăkt') *v.* to take away; diminish
**devotion** (dĭ-vō'shən) *n.* earnest dedication
**resolve** (rĭ-zŏlv') *v.* to make a firm decision

606

## Teaching Options

 **Mini Lesson** **Preteaching Vocabulary**

**USING CONTEXT CLUES**
Students can often understand the meaning of an unfamiliar word by examining the context in which the word is used. Have students use the context to infer the meaning of *devotion.*

 No one can question the *devotion* of those who give their lives to protect their loved ones.

**Exercises** Ask students to use context clues to determine the meanings of the underlined terms.

1. A ceremony was held to <u>consecrate</u> the war memorial in honor of all those who had given their lives in the cause of freedom.

2. A handful of rowdy protesters tried to <u>detract</u> from the solemnity of the occasion.

3. A nation <u>conceived</u> in liberty must acknowledge the birth rights of citizens to express their opinions.

4. We must <u>resolve</u> to honor their memories by following their example.

 Use **Unit Four Resource Book** p. 24 for more practice.

**A lesson on context clues appears on p. 326 in the Pupil's Edition.**

## Connect to the Literature

**1. What Do You Think?**
What words, phrases, or sentences stand out most in your mind? Share your choices with a partner.

**Comprehension Check**
- According to Lincoln, to which proposition is the nation dedicated?
- For what cause does Lincoln say the soldiers died?

## Think Critically

**2.** **ACTIVE READING** **INTERPRETING HISTORICAL CONTEXT** Given what you know about the historical context of the speech, define the "unfinished work" left for the living to complete. Pretend you are explaining it to a foreign friend who has never studied American history.

**3.** What kind of person do you think Lincoln was? Use evidence from this speech to explain your opinion.

**THINK ABOUT**
- the emotions his speech stirs
- his attitude toward those who fought at Gettysburg
- the goals he sets for his audience
- his vision of the nation

**4.** Lincoln was mistaken when he said "The world will little note, nor long remember what we say here. . . ." Why do you think the world still remembers this speech?

## Extend Interpretations

**5. What If?** How would your reaction to this speech be different if Lincoln had mentioned the Confederate forces as the enemy?

**6. Critic's Corner** Edward Everett, the main speaker at Gettysburg, later sent Lincoln this note: "I should be glad if I could flatter myself that I had come as near to the central idea of the occasion in two hours as you did in two minutes." How would you express "the central idea of the occasion" that Lincoln's speech captured?

**7. Connect to Life** Of what value to Americans today are the ideas Lincoln expressed at Gettysburg? In explaining your opinion, cite lines from Lincoln's speech.

## Literary Analysis

**STYLE** **Style** is the distinctive way in which a work of literature is written. Several elements contribute to style, such as word choice, sentence length, tone, and imagery, as well as particular techniques such as **repetition.** In the Gettysburg Address, Lincoln repeats words such as *dedicate, consecrate, devotion,* and *people* to emphasize key ideas. Sometimes he combines this technique with **parallelism**—the use of the same grammatical form to express ideas of equal importance—as in this sentence:

*But, in a larger sense, we cannot dedicate—we cannot consecrate—we cannot hallow—this ground.*

The parallel phrases "we cannot dedicate," "we cannot consecrate," "we cannot hallow" give the sentence a rhythmic cadence and drive home the point.

**Cooperative Learning Activity** In a small group, reread Lincoln's speech, looking for more examples of repetition and parallelism. Discuss the effect that these techniques create. To appreciate the effect, try rewriting a sentence without using the technique, and then compare your version with Lincoln's. For example, what happens to the last sentence if you remove the parallel structure?

---

## GUIDING STUDENT RESPONSE

### Connect to the Literature

**1. What Do You Think?**
Students' examples may include moving lines showing Lincoln's use of repetition, parallel structure, or comparisons.

**Comprehension Check**
- All men are created equal.
- The soldiers died for freedom, democracy, and equality.

📋 Use Selection Quiz
**Unit Four Resource Book,** p. 25.

### Think Critically

**2.** Responses will vary. Students may say that the unfinished work includes preserving the Union, ending the war, abolishing slavery, healing the nation's wounds, and building a stronger democracy.

**3.** Possible Response: Students may say that Lincoln was a compassionate, inspirational leader who was devoted to the American people and democratic principles.

**4.** Responses will vary. Reasons that account for the speech's enduring fame might include the following: the dignified wording, its almost biblical tone, its evident sincerity, and the wisdom of its message.

### Literary Analysis

Style Possible Response: The last sentence loses its resonance, cadence, and power.

---

## Extend Interpretations

**What If?** Responses will vary. Some students may say that they would have reacted less favorably to the speech if Lincoln had stirred up hostile feelings toward the South, rather than focusing on saving the Union. Others may say they would have reacted more strongly to the speech if Lincoln had blamed the Southern states for seceding from the Union.

**Critic's Corner** Possible Response: Lincoln summed up the grief and hope of a great nation caught up in a tragic, divisive war.

**Connect to Life** Accept all reasonable, well-supported responses. Many students may say that the address speaks to the struggles for liberty and equality today and that it offers inspiration to nations torn by civil war.

# Choices & CHALLENGES

## Writing Options

1. **Modern Paraphrase** Student responses will vary, but all should include Lincoln's main ideas. **To extend this activity,** use the paraphrases as the basis for an exploration of diction. Students can compare their paraphrases with Lincoln's formal language, tone, and word choice. Have students discuss which style is more suited to the audience and to the occasion.

2. **Letter to Lincoln** Student letters should refer to specific points made in the speech and should reflect an accurate interpretation of the historical context.

## Inquiry & Research

**Battle Report** Students should research the Battle of Gettysburg in a variety of print and nonprint resources.

## Vocabulary in Action

1. correct
2. correct
3. incorrect
4. correct
5. incorrect

---

## Writing Options

1. **Modern Paraphrase** Write a paraphrase of the Gettysburg Address in modern language. To prepare, you might review the definitions you wrote for an uninformed audience in your  **READER'S NOTEBOOK.**

2. **Letter to Lincoln** Imagine that you are a parent who has lost a son at Gettysburg, fighting for either the Union or the Confederate army. Write a letter to Lincoln in response to his speech.

## Inquiry & Research

**Battle Report** With a group of classmates, research the Battle of Gettysburg and its significance in the Civil War. Gather information from encyclopedias, Civil War history books, and electronic sources. Share your findings in a report.

**More Online: Research Starter**
www.mcdougallittell.com

## Vocabulary in Action

**EXERCISE: CONTEXT CLUES** Decide whether the boldfaced vocabulary word is used correctly or incorrectly in each sentence. Write *correct* or *incorrect* on your paper.

1. The federal government decided to **consecrate** the ground at Gettysburg by making it a cemetery for the men who had died there.
2. Lincoln asked the audience to imitate the soldiers' **devotion** to the cause of liberty.
3. The president gazed out upon the **detract** where the battle had been fought.
4. He wanted to ensure that a nation **conceived** in liberty would endure.
5. The Union Army had tried to **resolve** the Confederate Army.

**Building Vocabulary**
For an in-depth lesson on context clues, see page 326.

---

# Abraham Lincoln
1809–1865

**Humble Origin** Abraham Lincoln rose from a simple beginning to become president of the United States. The son of illiterate parents, he was born in a log cabin and raised on the Kentucky and Indiana frontier. Young Lincoln had almost no formal schooling; he educated himself by diligent study of the few books available to him. Encouraged by his stepmother, Lincoln read and reread the Bible, John Bunyan's *Pilgrim's Progress,* Aesop's *Fables,* and Daniel Defoe's *Robinson Crusoe,* as well as history books and biographies.

**President of the United States** Lincoln's election as president coincided with the first secessions of Southern states from the Union. During his first term in office, he led the nation through its most divisive period—the Civil War. Despite strong opposition, he issued the historic Emancipation Proclamation in 1863, freeing the slaves in Confederate-held territory. The letters and speeches of Lincoln's presidency are characterized by a simple, touching eloquence. "In times like the present," Lincoln told a wartime Congress, "men should utter nothing for which they would not willingly be responsible through time and in eternity."

**Assassination** A few weeks into Lincoln's second term, and five days after General Robert E. Lee surrendered to General Ulysses S. Grant at Appomattox, Lincoln was shot and killed by John Wilkes Booth while attending a theatrical performance in Washington.

---

## Teaching Options

### Mini Lesson Grammar

**ADJECTIVE AND RELATIVE CLAUSES**

**Instruction** An adjective clause is a subordinate clause that modifies a noun or a pronoun. An adjective clause that begins with a relative pronoun (*who, whom, whose, that,* or *which*) is called a relative clause. There are two types of adjective clauses, essential and nonessential. An essential clause is necessary to complete the meaning of the sentence; a nonessential clause simply adds extra information to a sentence. In formal writing, we use *that* to begin essential adjective clauses and *which* to begin nonessential adjective clauses.

**Exercises** Have students underline the correct introductory word for each relative clause.

1. It is not Edward Everett's two-hour oration <u>that</u>/which people remember most from that day.
2. When President Lincoln spoke, he barely glanced at his notes, that/<u>which</u> he had written on the train.

 Use **Grammar Transparencies and Copymasters,** p. 95.

  Use McDougal Littell's *Language Network,* Chapter 3, for more instruction and practice in clauses.

# *from* Coming of Age in Mississippi

*Autobiography by* ANNE MOODY

**Comparing Literature**

## Traditions Across Time: The Civil Rights Movement

Though the Thirteenth Amendment officially abolished slavery in 1865, new "Jim Crow" laws that discriminated against African Americans were eventually established by whites in many Southern states. Such laws denied African Americans the right to vote, the right to attend state universities, even the right to use public facilities like swimming pools, restrooms, and lunch counters. This firsthand account by civil-rights activist Anne Moody describes an attempt to overturn Jim Crow laws a hundred years after the Civil War.

**Points of Comparison**  As you read, compare the social climate of Moody's time with the climate that produced Frederick Douglass and the protest poets James Russell Lowell and Frances E. W. Harper. Also compare the writers' purposes for writing.

## Build Background

**Uniting for Change**  *Coming of Age in Mississippi* is Anne Moody's true account of her experiences as a college student in the civil rights movement of the 1960s. During this time, volunteers in the South registered African-American voters at risk of their lives; "freedom riders" braved beatings and killings to desegregate Interstate buses and bus stations; and protesters took part in sit-ins to integrate lunch counters, parks, and theaters. The result of the movement was the Civil Rights Act of 1964, the most far-reaching civil rights legislation in American history.

## Focus Your Reading

**LITERARY ANALYSIS  EYEWITNESS REPORT**  This selection is an account of a 1963 sit-in at a lunch counter in Jackson, Mississippi. A newspaper article of the time might have reported: "Today three Negro college students sat down at a segregated Woolworth's lunch counter and were attacked by an angry white mob." Notice how much more you learn from this **eyewitness report** by Moody, a participant in the sit-in.

**ACTIVE READING  CHRONOLOGICAL ORDER**  Eyewitness reports are usually narrated in **chronological order,** or time order. (The ancient Greek word *chronos* means "time.") A chronological pattern of organization, or text structure, helps put the reader in the writer's place, experiencing events as they unfold.

**READER'S NOTEBOOK**  To help you understand and recall what happens from the time the sit-in begins until it ends, create a sequence chain like the one begun here. In the boxes, summarize significant events in the order that they occur.

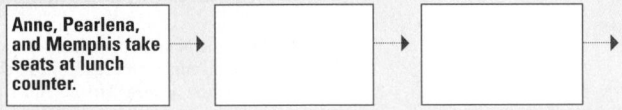

Anne, Pearlena, and Memphis take seats at lunch counter. →   →   →

## OVERVIEW

### Objectives
1. understand an **eyewitness report** (Literary Analysis)
2. understand **chronological order** (Active Reading)

### Summary
College student Anne Moody participates in a 1963 sit-in at a Woolworth's lunch counter in Jackson, Mississippi, as part of an ongoing movement to desegregate public facilities. Moody and two classmates sit at a counter reserved for whites and ask to be served. They are denied service but remain seated. The press arrives and questions the protesters and onlookers. Then a group of high school students arrives, chanting racist slogans and taunting the demonstrators. Violence breaks out; Moody is slapped and thrown to the floor, and a companion is beaten. The demonstrators return to their seats, and others join their protest. After three hours, the demonstrators agree to leave. At a rally that evening, Moody recognizes the growing solidarity among African Americans, but she also recognizes the intractable hatred of the segregationists.

### Thematic Link
A century after the **Civil War** turned the nation into **a house divided,** racial division continued to spark conflict. Dedicated people in the civil rights movement struggled to complete the work begun by early abolitionists.

**5-Minute Warm-Up**

*Daily Language SkillBuilder*

Have students **proofread** the display sentences on page 555j and write them correctly. The sentences also appear on Transparency 17 of **Grammar Transparencies and Copymasters.**

## Reading Skills and Strategies: PREVIEW

Have students review the information in Preparing to Read to familiarize themselves with the context of this eyewitness report.

## Literary Analysis

### EYEWITNESS REPORT

Eyewitness accounts are classified as primary sources because they offer direct, firsthand knowledge of an event. As they read Anne Moody's eyewitness report, ask students to consider how it may differ from a secondary account of the civil rights movement.

**Possible Response:** Moody's account makes the event come to life for the reader. It lets us know what it felt like to participate in a demonstration.

Use **Unit Four Resource Book**, p. 28 for more practice.

## Active Reading

### CHRONOLOGICAL ORDER

**A** Direct students' attention to the chronological organization of the paragraph. Have students note specific words and phrases that indicate the chronological sequence, and ask them to explain how this method of organization contributes to the presentation.

**Possible Response:** Words and phrases include *before, as soon as,* and specific times. In addition to adding specificity, the organization allows the reader to follow the sequence of events more closely.

Use **Unit Four Resource Book**, p. 27 for more exercises.

FROM

# Coming of Age

had counted on graduating in the spring of 1963, but as it turned out, I couldn't because some of my credits still had to be cleared with Natchez College. A year before, this would have seemed like a terrible disaster, but now I hardly even felt disappointed. I had a good excuse to stay on campus for the summer and work with the Movement, and this was what I really wanted to do. I couldn't go home again anyway, and I couldn't go to New Orleans—I didn't have money enough for bus fare.

During my senior year at Tougaloo, my family hadn't sent me one penny. I had only the small amount of money I had earned at Maple Hill. I couldn't afford to eat at school or live in the dorms, so I had gotten permission to move off campus. I had to prove that I could finish school, even if I had to go hungry every day. I knew Raymond and Miss Pearl were just waiting to see me drop out. But something happened to me as I got more and more involved in the Movement. It no longer seemed important to prove anything. I had found something outside myself that gave meaning to my life.

I had become very friendly with my social science professor, John Salter, who was in charge of NAACP[1] activities on campus. All during the year, while the NAACP conducted a boycott of the downtown stores in Jackson, I had been one of Salter's most faithful

---

1. **NAACP:** the National Association for the Advancement of Colored People, an organization that works to end discrimination against African Americans and other minority groups.

## Teaching Options

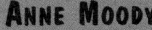
# in Mississippi

ANNE MOODY

canvassers[2] and church speakers. During the last week of school, he told me that sit-in demonstrations were about to start in Jackson and that he wanted me to be the spokesman for a team that would sit-in at Woolworth's lunch counter. The two other demonstrators would be classmates of mine, Memphis and Pearlena. Pearlena was a dedicated NAACP worker, but Memphis had not been very involved in the Movement on campus. It seemed that the organization had had a rough time finding students who were in a position to go to jail. I had nothing to lose one way or the other. Around ten o'clock the morning of the demonstrations, NAACP headquarters alerted the news services. As a result, the police department was also informed, but neither the policemen nor the newsmen knew exactly where or when the demonstrations would start. They stationed themselves along Capitol Street and waited.

To divert attention from the sit-in at Woolworth's, the picketing started at J. C. Penney's a good fifteen minutes before. The pickets were allowed to walk up and down in front of the store three or four times before they were arrested. At exactly 11 A.M., Pearlena, Memphis, and I entered Woolworth's from the rear entrance. We separated as soon as we stepped into the store, and made small purchases from various counters. Pearlena had given Memphis her watch. He was to let us know when it was 11:14. At 11:14 we were to join him near the lunch counter and at exactly 11:15 we were to take seats at it.

Seconds before 11:15 we were occupying three seats at the previously segregated Woolworth's lunch counter. In the beginning the waitresses seemed to ignore us, as if they really didn't know what was going on. Our waitress walked past us a couple of times before she noticed we had started to write our own orders down and realized we wanted service. She asked us what we wanted. We began to read to her from our order slips. She told us that we would be served at the back counter, which was for Negroes.

"We would like to be served here," I said.

---

2. **canvassers:** people who canvass, or go door to door to get support for a cause or gather opinions on an issue.

---

## Mini Lesson  Grammar

### ADVERB CLAUSES
**Instruction** Explain that adverb clauses beginning with such words as *after, as, before, since, until, when,* and *while* can be used to show relationships or changes over time. They are subordinate clauses that can modify verbs, adjectives, or adverbs. Write the following sentence on the chalkboard:

<u>Before the sit-in</u>, Anne had always hated white Mississippians.

Ask students to identify the word and part of speech that the underlined adverb clause modifies.

**Answer:** *hated;* verb

**Exercises** For each sentence, have students identify the adverb clause and the word it modifies.
1. Everyone felt stronger after they heard Medgar Evers's speech. *(after they heard Medgar Evers's speech; stronger)*
2. Ann decided to work for the Movement while she attended college. *(while she attended college; to work)*

Use **Grammar Transparencies and Copymasters**, p. 96.

Use McDougal Littell's *Language Network,* Chapter 3, for more instruction and practice in adverb clauses.

**A** Have students summarize Moody's role at the sit-in and the initial reaction at the lunch counter.

**Possible Response:** Moody was spokesperson for the group. The waitress fled; white people at the counter left; one woman expressed sympathy; news reporters asked questions.

### Active Reading
**CHRONOLOGICAL ORDER**

Remind students to identify the main ideas in their summaries of the events in the sequence charts in their Reader's Notebooks. They might include such events as the following:

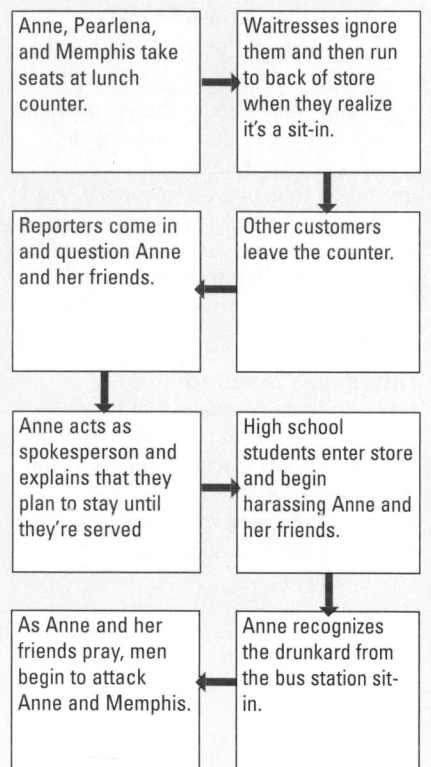

| | |
|---|---|
| Anne, Pearlena, and Memphis take seats at lunch counter. | Waitresses ignore them and then run to back of store when they realize it's a sit-in. |
| Reporters come in and question Anne and her friends. | Other customers leave the counter. |
| Anne acts as spokesperson and explains that they plan to stay until they're served | High school students enter store and begin harassing Anne and her friends. |
| As Anne and her friends pray, men begin to attack Anne and Memphis. | Anne recognizes the drunkard from the bus station sit-in. |

**1** **A** The waitress started to repeat what she had said, then stopped in the middle of the sentence. She turned the lights out behind the counter, and she and the other waitresses almost ran to the back of the store, deserting all their white customers. I guess they thought that violence would start immediately after the whites at the counter realized what was going on. There were five or six other people at the counter. A couple of them just got up and walked away. A girl sitting next to me finished her banana split before leaving. A middle-aged white woman who had not yet been served rose from her seat and came over to us. "I'd like to stay here with you," she said, "but my husband is waiting."

The newsmen came in just as she was leaving. They must have discovered what was going on shortly after some of the people began to leave the store. One of the newsmen ran behind the woman who spoke to us and asked her to identify herself. She refused to give her name, but said she was a native of Vicksburg and a former resident of California. When asked why she had said what she had said to us, she replied, "I am in sympathy with the Negro movement." By this time a crowd of cameramen and reporters had gathered around us taking pictures and asking questions, such as Where were we from? Why did we sit-in? What organization sponsored it? Were we students? From what school? How were we classified?

I told them that we were all students at Tougaloo College, that we were represented by no particular organization, and that we planned to stay there even after the store closed.

"All we want is service," was my reply to one of them. After they had finished probing for about twenty minutes, they were almost ready to leave.

At noon, students from a nearby white high school started pouring in to Woolworth's. When they first saw us they were sort of surprised. They didn't know how to react. A few started to heckle and the newsmen became interested again. Then the white students started chanting all kinds of anti-Negro slogans. We were called a little bit of everything. The rest of the seats except the three we were occupying had been roped off to prevent others from sitting down. A couple of the boys took one end of the rope and made it into a hangman's noose. Several attempts were made to put it around our necks. The crowds grew as more students and adults came in for lunch.

We kept our eyes straight forward and did not look at the crowd except for occasional glances to see what was going on. All of a sudden I saw a face I remembered—the drunkard from the bus **2** station sit-in. My eyes lingered on him just long enough for us to recognize each other. Today he was drunk too, so I don't think he remembered where he had seen me before. He took out a knife, opened it, put it in his pocket, and then began to pace the floor. At this point, I told Memphis and Pearlena what was going on. Memphis suggested that we pray. We bowed our heads, and all hell broke loose. A man rushed forward, threw Memphis from his seat, and slapped my face. Then another man who worked in the store threw me against an adjoining counter.

**Down** on my knees on the floor, I saw Memphis lying near the lunch counter with blood running out of the corners of his mouth. As he tried to protect his face, the man who'd thrown him down kept kicking him against the head. If he had worn hard-soled shoes instead of sneakers, the first kick probably would have killed Memphis. Finally a man dressed in plain clothes identified himself as a police officer and arrested Memphis and his attacker.

### **Mini Lesson** Vocabulary Strategy

**SENSORY DETAILS**

**Instruction** Sensory details appeal to the senses of sight, smell, taste, touch, and hearing. Encourage students to enhance their writing by using details that refer to things we can experience with our senses. Write the model sentences on the chalkboard. Ask a volunteer to identify the sensory detail and to explain how it improves the sentence.

**Model Sentences**

I looked at Memphis, and I could see that he was hurt.

I looked at Memphis, and I could see blood running from the corners of his mouth.

**Possible Response:** Detail: "blood running from the corners of his mouth." It creates an image for the reader and helps him or her better understand the idea.

**Exercises** Have students revise the following sentences by replacing modifiers with sensory details.

1. The sunset looked beautiful.
2. This medicine tastes bad.
3. The shortstop's throw was bad.
4. From the collision came a terrible sound.

Use **Vocabulary Transparencies and Copymasters**, p. 54.

On May 23, 1963, Anne Moody (right), John R. Salter (left), and Joan Trumpauer (middle) are harassed during a sit-in demonstration at a lunch counter in Jackson, Mississippi. AP/Wide World Photos.

Pearlena had been thrown to the floor. She and I got back on our stools after Memphis was arrested. There were some white Tougaloo teachers in the crowd. They asked Pearlena and me if we wanted to leave. They said that things were getting too rough. We didn't know what to do. While we were trying to make up our minds, we were joined by Joan Trumpauer. Now there were three of us and we were integrated. The crowd began to chant, "Communists, Communists, Communists." Some old man in the crowd ordered the students to take us off the stools.

"Which one should I get first?" a big husky boy said.

"That white nigger," the old man said.

The boy lifted Joan from the counter by her waist and carried her out of the store. Simultaneously, I was snatched from my stool by two high school students. I was dragged about thirty feet toward the door by my hair when someone made them turn me loose. As I was getting up off the floor, I saw Joan coming back inside. We started back to the center of the counter to join Pearlena. Lois Chaffee, a white Tougaloo faculty member, was now sitting next to her. So Joan and I just climbed across the rope at the front end of the counter and sat down. There were now four of us, two whites and two Negroes, all women. The mob started smearing us with ketchup, mustard, sugar, pies, and everything on the counter. Soon Joan and I were joined by John Salter, but the moment he sat down he was hit on the jaw with what appeared to be brass knuckles. Blood gushed from his face and someone threw salt into the open wound. Ed King, Tougaloo's chaplain, rushed to him.

## Mini Lesson  Viewing and Representing

**PHOTOGRAPH**

**Instruction** Have each student examine the effect of media on constructing his or her own perception of reality. Ask students to identify the position of the camera when this photograph was taken.

**Possible Response:** The photographer is behind the lunch counter several feet to the right of his subjects. This position provides a depth of field that allows us to view a variety of facial expressions. It also places Moody, the only African American visible, at the center of everyone's attention.

**Application** Ask students to contrast the expressions of the people in the photo. Have them discuss why the photo is a powerful image of the civil rights movement and how it affects their perception of reality.

**Possible Response:** The contrast between Moody's weary sadness and the alternately gleeful, callous, and hate-filled expressions of her tormentors says much about the long struggle for equality. It helps us better understand the difficulties that people in the movement faced.

### Literary Analysis
**EYEWITNESS REPORT**

**A** Ask students to focus on Moody's description of the high school student who joins her at the counter. How is this description characteristic of her report?

**Possible Response:** Moody describes the boy's action matter-of-factly, as if she takes for granted the courage he needed to face the angry mob.

**B** Have students discuss how the events Moody describes have changed her attitude towards racists.

**Possible Response:** Prior to the sit-in, she hated the racists; now she realizes that they suffer from a sickness. She is calm, confident, and pragmatic about the situation.

### Reading Skills and Strategies:
**COMPARING ACROSS TEXTS**

Students should be able to compare literary elements such as theme across texts. After they have read "Frederick Douglass" on page 615, ask students to create a theme statement that applies to both Hayden's poem and Moody's autobiographical account.

**Possible Responses:** The fight for equality requires a person to take great risks, but the results are worth it. Freedom and equality are so essential to human life that people will fight for them no matter what the cost.

Have students identify adjectives Hayden uses to describe freedom. Ask them to decide which adjective is most applicable to Moody's report.

**Possible Responses:** *terrible,* because battling racism is difficult; *beautiful,* because freedom is worth any risk to achieve it.

---

At the other end of the counter, Lois and Pearlena were joined by George Raymond, a CORE[3] field worker and a student from Jackson State College. Then a Negro high school boy sat down next to me. The mob took spray paint from the counter and sprayed it on the new demonstrators. The high school student had on a white shirt; the word "nigger" was written on his back with red spray paint.

We sat there for three hours taking a beating when the manager decided to close the store because the mob had begun to go wild with stuff from other counters. He begged and begged everyone to leave. But even after fifteen minutes of begging, no one budged. They would not leave until we did. Then Dr. Beittel, the president of Tougaloo College, came running in. He said he had just heard what was happening.

About ninety policemen were standing outside the store; they had been watching the whole thing through the windows, but had not come in to stop the mob or do anything. President Beittel went outside and asked Captain Ray to come and escort us out. The captain refused, stating the manager had to invite him in before he could enter the premises, so Dr. Beittel himself brought us out. He had told the police that they had better protect us after we were outside the store. When we got outside, the policemen formed a single line that blocked the mob from us. However, they were allowed to throw at us everything they had collected. Within ten minutes, we were picked up by Reverend King in his station wagon and taken to the NAACP headquarters on Lynch Street.

After the sit-in, all I could think of

was how sick Mississippi whites were. They believed so much in the segregated Southern way of life, they would kill to preserve it. I sat there in the NAACP office and thought of how many times they had killed when this way of life was threatened. I knew that the killing had just begun. "Many more will die before it is over with," I thought. Before the sit-in, I had always hated the whites in Mississippi. Now I knew it was impossible for me to hate sickness. The whites had a disease, an incurable disease in its final stage. What were our chances against such a disease? I thought of the students, the young Negroes who had just begun to protest, as young interns.[4] When these young interns got older, I thought, they would be the best doctors in the world for social problems.

**Before** we were taken back to campus, I wanted to get my hair washed. It was stiff with dried mustard, ketchup and sugar. I stopped in at a beauty shop across the street from the NAACP office. I didn't have on any shoes because I had lost them when I was dragged across the floor at Woolworth's. My stockings were sticking to my legs from the mustard that had dried on them. The hairdresser took one look at me and said, "My land, you were in the sit-in, huh?"

"Yes," I answered. "Do you have time to wash my hair and style it?"

"Right away," she said, and she meant right away. There were three other ladies already waiting, but they seemed glad to let me go ahead of them. The hairdresser was real nice. She even took my stockings off and washed my legs while my hair was drying.

There was a mass rally that night at the Pearl Street Church in Jackson, and the place was packed. People were standing two abreast in the aisles. Before the speakers began, all the sit-inners

---

3. **CORE:** the Congress of Racial Equality, a civil rights organization that coordinated marches and demonstrations in the 1960s.

4. **interns:** students or recent graduates who are undergoing practical training, particularly medical training.

---

## Teaching Options

✓ **Assessment** **Informal Assessment**

**LITERARY RESPONSE** Have students use elements of the text to defend, clarify, and negotiate their responses to the selection. Ask individual students to select a passage from the selection that particularly moved or intrigued them, and then write a paragraph about that passage and their response to it. Have students sit in a circle and share their passages and responses. Encourage students to question and interact with each other.

**RUBRIC**

**3** **Full Accomplishment** Response reflects a full understanding of a telling passage, and the student interacts meaningfully with peers.

**2** **Substantial Accomplishment** Response reflects thoughtful consideration of a passage, but the student interacts minimally with peers.

**1** **Little or Partial Accomplishment** Response reflects little consideration or understanding, and the student exhibits little interaction.

walked out on the stage and were introduced by Medgar Evers.[5] People stood and applauded for what seemed like thirty minutes or more. Medgar told the audience that this was just the beginning of such demonstrations. He asked them to pledge themselves to unite in a massive offensive against segregation in Jackson, and throughout the state. The rally ended with "We Shall Overcome" and sent home hundreds of determined people. It seemed as though Mississippi Negroes were about to get together at last.

Before I demonstrated, I had written Mama. She wrote me back a letter, begging me not to take part in the sit-in. She even sent ten dollars for bus fare to New Orleans. I didn't have one penny, so I kept the money. Mama's letter made me mad. I had to live my life as I saw fit. I had made that decision when I left home. But it hurt to have my family prove to me how scared they were. It hurt me more than anything else—I knew the whites had already started the threats and intimidations. I was the first Negro from my hometown who had openly demonstrated, worked with the NAACP, or anything. When Negroes threatened to do anything in Centreville, they were either shot like Samuel O'Quinn or run out of town, like Reverend Dupree.

I didn't answer Mama's letter. Even if I had written one, she wouldn't have received it before she saw the news on TV or heard it on the radio. I waited to hear from her again. And I waited to hear in the news that someone in Centreville had been murdered. If so, I knew it would be a member of my family. ❖

---

5. **Medgar Evers:** a civil rights leader and major organizer and supervisor for the NAACP in Mississippi from 1954 until he was killed by a sniper in 1963.

## LITERARY LINK

# FREDERICK DOUGLASS
### Robert Hayden

When it is finally ours, this freedom, this liberty, this beautiful
and terrible thing, needful to man as air,
usable as earth; when it belongs at last to all,
when it is truly instinct, brain matter, diastole, systole,[1]
5  reflex action; when it is finally won; when it is more
than the gaudy mumbo jumbo of politicians:
this man, this Douglass, this former slave, this Negro
beaten to his knees, exiled, visioning a world
where none is lonely, none hunted, alien,
10  this man, superb in love and logic, this man
shall be remembered. Oh, not with statues' rhetoric,
not with legends and poems and wreaths of bronze alone,
but with the lives grown out of his life, the lives
fleshing his dream of the beautiful, needful thing.

---

1. **diastole** (dī-ăs′tə-lē), **systole** (sĭs′tə-lē): The heart pumps blood in two steps. Diastole refers to the heart's enlargement when it fills with blood; systole refers to the heart's contraction when the blood pumps out.

Frederick Douglass (about 1850), unknown photographer. Daguerreotype, 3⅛″ × 2¼″, National Portrait Gallery, Smithsonian Institution/Art Resource, New York.

FREDERICK DOUGLASS **615**

### ⌒Cross Curricular Link  History

**MEDGAR EVERS** Born in Decatur, Mississippi, in 1925, Medgar Wiley Evers served in the U.S. Army during World War II and then returned to Mississippi to attend college. After graduation, he worked as an insurance agent. He joined the NAACP in 1952 and was appointed the organization's field secretary for Mississippi in 1954. For more than a decade, Evers worked tirelessly to improve living conditions of African Americans in the state. On June 12, 1963, an assassin shot and killed Evers outside his Jackson home as he returned from a local rally. Byron De La Beckwith, a white supremacist, was accused of the murder, but two trials in 1964 ended with the juries deadlocked. Thirty years later, in 1994, a Jackson jury finally convicted Beckwith of the crime.

## Customizing Instruction

**Students Acquiring English**

**1** Point out that "We Shall Overcome" is a spiritual hymn that became the anthem of the civil rights movement.

**Multiple Learning Styles**
**Musical Learners**

Have students research songs of the civil rights movement, such as "We Shall Overcome" and "Ain't Gonna Let Nobody Turn Me Around." Suggest that they locate recordings by such artists as Joan Baez, Bob Dylan, Mahalia Jackson, Odetta, and Pete Seeger. Encourage them to find performances that they feel are particularly moving and share them with the class.

## GUIDING STUDENT RESPONSE

## Connect to the Literature

**1. What Do You Think?**
Responses will vary. Some students may state that Anne Moody's actions show great courage, determination, and self-restraint.

## Comprehension Check
• They were participating in a sit-in.
• They were refused service, heckled, attacked, and smeared with food.
• Their action united people.

 Use Selection Quiz
**Unit Four Resource Book**, p. 29.

## Think Critically

**2.** Emphasize how detailed notes and summaries that identify main ideas and supporting details can aid in understanding the sequence of events and why they happened.

**3.** Possible Responses: The store manager cares more about his merchandise than about the demonstrators. The police only half-heartedly protected the demonstrators; they probably shared the crowd's racism. The manager was just trying to protect his store from damage; the police kept order as best they could.

**4.** Possible Responses: Yes, because racism infects people with hate; no, because it is a state of mind and not an illness.

**5.** Possible Response: She is a serious, determined person who shows bravery in the face of adversity.

**6.** Responses will vary. Some students may state that for a noble cause they too would take great risks despite the consequences.

---

## Connect to the Literature

**1. What Do You Think?**
What is your opinion of Anne Moody's actions? Discuss your thoughts with classmates.

**Comprehension Check**
• Why were Anne Moody and her fellow students sitting at the Woolworth's lunch counter?
• Name one of the things that happened to them after they sat down.
• What positive effect did their action have on African Americans in Mississippi?

## Think Critically

**2.** **ACTIVE READING** **CHRONOLOGICAL ORDER**
Using the sequence chain you created in your **READER'S NOTEBOOK**, summarize what happens during the sit-in. How clearly did you understand what was happening?

**3.** How do you explain the behavior of the store manager and the police during the sit-in?

**4.** Moody describes Mississippi whites' racism as "an incurable disease in its final stage" and the protesters as "interns." Do you think these are good metaphors? Explain your answer.

**5.** How would you describe Moody to someone who has not read this selection?

**6.** Do you think you would have been able to take such a risk as Moody did?

 THINK ABOUT
{
• the cause for which she is protesting
• the violence she witnesses and endures
• her belief that someone in her family could be murdered
}

## Extend Interpretations

**7.** **Connect to Life** What forms does the fight against racism presently take in this country? Tell whether you believe this fight is closer to being won today than it was when Anne Moody was writing. Support your opinion.

**8.** **Points of Comparison** How would you compare Anne Moody with Frederick Douglass? Think about how he is portrayed in his autobiography and also in the poem by Robert Hayden on page 615.

---

## Literary Analysis

**EYEWITNESS REPORT** This excerpt from Anne Moody's autobiography recounts an actual historical event: a sit-in at a Woolworth's lunch counter in 1963. An **eyewitness report** is a firsthand account of an event written by someone who directly observed it or participated in it. (As such, an eyewitness account is a primary source.) Eyewitness reports are narrated from the first-person point of view; this single point of view is maintained throughout. Eyewitness reports almost always include:
• objective **facts** about an event (the 5 W's: *who, what, when, where,* and *why*)
• a **chronological** (time-order) pattern of organization or text structure
• vivid **sensory details** that bring the scene to life
• **direct quotations** from people who were present
• description of the writer's **subjective feelings** and interpretations

**Cooperative Learning Activity**
Gather in small groups and, on a chart, record examples from the selection that show these characteristics of eyewitness reports. After you have compiled your chart, imagine that the group is researching student participation in civil rights protests of the 1960s. What would Moody's eyewitness report tell you? What wouldn't it tell you? Discuss these questions.

---

## Extend Interpretations

**Connect to Life** Possible Responses: challenging inequities in housing, jobs, health care, and education; countering negative stereotypes in the media; fighting the miscarriage of justice.
**Points of Comparison** Possible Responses: Students may compare Moody's and Douglass's courage in standing up for their cause, dignity in the face of adversity, and the purpose of their autobiographies. They may contrast Moody's passive resistance to violence versus Douglass's retaliation against Mr. Covey.

## Literary Analysis

**Eyewitness Report** Responses will vary. Some students may state that Moody's report documents the courage and dedication of the students participating in the civil rights protests of the 1960s. The report does not describe the ultimate impact on segregation that the protests achieved.

## Writing Options

**1. Mother's Letter, Anne's Reply**
Write the letter that you think Anne Moody's mother sent to her. Then write the reply Anne might have written.

**2. Points of Comparison**
In an analytical essay, point out connections you see between Anne Moody and the antislavery writers you read earlier in Unit 4. You might explore their purposes for writing and the social climates in which they wrote.

**Writing Handbook**
See page 1283: Analysis.

**3. Eyewitness Account** Attend a political rally, sporting event, or performance and write an eyewitness account of the event. Include relevant facts and vivid sensory details that will help your readers share your experiences. As an experiment, you and another classmate might attend the same event and compare your accounts. Do your facts and details match?

**Writing Handbook**
See page 1280: Chronological Order.

## Activities & Explorations

**On the Scene** With several classmates, videotape imaginary interviews for a documentary about the sit-in. Explore the viewpoints and motivations of participants, bystanders, and authorities. Share your videotape.
~ SPEAKING AND LISTENING

## Art Connection

**Under Siege** What does the photo of the sit-in on page 613 reveal that Moody's description of the same scene does not?

---

## Anne Moody
1940–

**Other Works**
*Mr. Death: Four Stories*

**Burning Memory** When Anne Moody was growing up as the daughter of poor sharecroppers in rural Mississippi, she saw a neighboring family killed when their house was set on fire. The violence was brought about by a white citizens' guild, an organization dedicated to intimidating African Americans who in some way threatened whites' power. Moody's mother advised her, "Just act like you don't know nothing." Moody slowly came to realize that her mother's advice might be the safest course, but it was one that Anne herself could not follow.

**Student Activist** In her teens, Moody spent summers working in a factory, carefully saving money to make her dream of college a reality. She earned a basketball scholarship to Natchez Junior College but transferred to Tougaloo College, where she became involved with the civil rights

movement. She was a volunteer for the Congress of Racial Equality (CORE) and a civil rights coordinator at Cornell University—a position in which she faced constant threats to her life. She worked for voting rights, on literacy projects, and for an end to segregated public facilities. Her experiences in the civil rights movement became the basis for a book that is widely considered to be a masterpiece of the movement, *Coming of Age in Mississippi*, from which this selection is taken.

**Lasting Creed** Although Moody eventually left the civil rights movement, her heart has never deserted the battle for human rights. She explains, "I realized that the universal fight for human rights, dignity, justice, equality, and freedom is . . . the right of every ethnic and racial minority, every suppressed and exploited person, every one of the millions who daily suffer one or another of the indignities of the powerless and voiceless masses."

## Author Activity

Read more of *Coming of Age in Mississippi*. Find out what other protests Anne took part in and how they compare to the sit-in.

---

 **Mini Lesson** ## Grammar

**PUNCTUATION OF ADVERB CLAUSES**

**Instruction** When an adverb clause introduces a sentence, it requires a comma. No comma is necessary when the clause appears at the end of a sentence. Display the following sentences as a model:

> Before the sit-in, there was a picket line to distract people's attention.
>
> There was a picket line to distract people's attention before the sit-in.

**Exercises** Have students underline the adverb clause in each sentence and add commas as necessary.

1. Anne saw the need to fight for civil rights more clearly than the rest of her family did. *(no comma needed)*

2. When they sensed that the crowd was becoming violent the protesters decided to pray. *(comma needed after "violent")*

3. After she had finished her business at the NAACP office Anne went to have her hair washed. *(comma needed after "office")*

 Use **Grammar Transparencies and Copymasters**, p. 151.

---

## Writing Options

1. **Mother's Letter, Anne's Reply** For the mother's letter, encourage students to consider the following: She begged Moody not to participate in the sit-in; she included $10 bus fare to New Orleans; she let Anne know that the family was frightened. For the reply, suggest that students consider Moody's reaction: She was angry; it hurt her to see how scared her family was.

2. **Points of Comparison** Essays should contain arguments that are well supported by examples from *Coming of Age in Mississippi* and the antislavery selections.

3. **Eyewitness Account To get students started on this assignment,** have them check a local newspaper for a listing of upcoming events.

## Activities & Explorations

**On the Scene** Encourage students to assign different roles to group members: a director, participants in the sit-in, onlookers, researchers, news writers, narrators, and a camera operator. Suggest that students view televised documentaries to see how they are organized and what is involved.

## Art Connection

**Under Siege** Possible Responses: The photo reveals details such as facial expressions, the size of the crowd, and specific actions.

## Author Activity

Anne Moody eventually left the civil rights movement. Even though she did not originally think of herself as a writer, but rather "first and foremost an activist," ironically it was her writing that caused her to leave the movement. She explains, "I came to see through my writing that no matter how hard we in the movement worked, nothing seemed to change." She also became discouraged when the movement "began to splinter and get more narrowly nationalistic in its thinking."

 Use McDougal Littell's *Language Network,* Chapter 3, for more instruction and practice in adverb clauses.

## OVERVIEW

### Objectives

1. understand and appreciate a **ballad** commemorating a tragic event (**Literary Analysis**)
2. identify and appreciate the characteristics of **ballads** (**Literary Analysis**)
3. apply **strategies for reading narrative poetry** (**Active Reading**)

### Summary

"Ballad of Birmingham" tells of a little girl killed in the bombing of the 16th Street Baptist Church in 1963. Randall employs the ballad technique to present the story of a mother who refuses her daughter's request to participate in a civil rights march. Instead, the mother sends her to church, where she believes her daughter will be safe. A third-person speaker then tells of the subsequent explosion in the church and the mother's frantic search through the rubble to find her daughter. As the ballad ends, the mother finds her missing daughter's shoe.

## Reading and Analyzing

### Active Reading

READING NARRATIVE POETRY

Ask students to evaluate the effectiveness of typical ballad characteristics used in this poem, such as different speakers and repetition.

**Possible Responses:** Because the poem gives voices to the mother and the daughter, the tragedy of the loss is felt more intimately. Repetition of the mother's refusal to let her child participate in the march makes the irony of the child's death more powerful.

 Use **Unit Four Resource Book,** p. 30 for more practice.

### Literary Analysis  | BALLADS |

Ask students to explain the subject of this ballad in their own words.

**Possible Response:** A mother loses her daughter in the bombing of a church.

 Use **Unit Four Resource Book,** p. 31 for more practice.

### 5-Minute Warm-Up

*Daily Language SkillBuilder*

Have students **proofread** the display sentences on page 555j and write them correctly. The sentences also appear on Transparency 17 of **Grammar Transparencies and Copymasters.**

---

*"She raced through the streets of Birmingham / calling for her child."*

# Ballad of Birmingham

*Poetry by* DUDLEY RANDALL

### Comparing Literature

## Traditions Across Time: The Civil Rights Movement

Earlier in this part of Unit 4 you read poems that protested slavery. The following selection, Dudley Randall's "Ballad of Birmingham," is also a protest poem. Inspired by an actual historical event—the 1963 bombing of the 16th Street Baptist Church in Birmingham—this poem protests the violence inflicted on participants in the civil rights movement.

**Points of Comparison**   As you read, think again how poetry can be an instrument of political change. Try to see connections between Randall's poem and the antislavery poems by Harper and Lowell.

## Build Background

### City of "Bombingham"

Birmingham is Alabama's largest city. In the spring of 1963, Dr. Martin Luther King, Jr., led a huge demonstration to protest racial discrimination in Birmingham, which was then considered one of the most segregated cities of the South. Police dogs and fire hoses were used against the peaceful protesters, including children. Later that year, four young African-American girls were killed when the 16th Street Baptist Church was bombed. A white supremacist, Robert Chambliss, was finally convicted of the murders in 1977.

## Focus Your Reading

| LITERARY ANALYSIS | BALLADS |   A **ballad** is a narrative poem that was originally meant to be sung. Traditional folk ballads are forms of oral literature, composed anonymously and passed down through performance. Early ballads often commemorated tragedies—ill-fated love affairs, wars, shipwrecks, and murders. Literary ballads imitate the style of folk ballads but are composed by one individual and written down as they are created. "Ballad of Birmingham" is a literary ballad. Notice how it resembles a song, and consider how it might make a tragic event live on in memory.

| ACTIVE READING | READING NARRATIVE POETRY |   A **narrative poem** is one that tells a story. Like a work of fiction it has characters, setting, and plot. However, a narrative poem, particularly a ballad, tells a story in a much more condensed form, without many of the details that aid a reader. You will have to make inferences as you read. The following strategies will help you get the most from the "Ballad of Birmingham."

- Read the poem aloud to appreciate its patterns of rhythm and rhyme.
- Infer who is speaking. Often ballads are structured as a conversation between two people.
- Watch for abrupt shifts in time. In ballads there are often no transitions to indicate that time has passed.
- Bring your background knowledge to the poem. The poet assumes his readers already know what happened in Birmingham.

**READER'S NOTEBOOK**   If, after reading, you have questions about the events or references in the poem, write them down in your notebook.

---

## LESSON RESOURCES

**UNIT FOUR RESOURCE BOOK,** pp. 30–32

**ASSESSMENT RESOURCES**
**Formal Assessment,** p. 117
**Teacher's Guide to Assessment and Portfolio Use**
**Test Generator**

**SKILLS TRANSPARENCIES AND COPYMASTERS**
**Reading and Critical Thinking**
- Making Judgments, T5 (for Writing Option 2, p. 621)

**Grammar**
- Introduction to Noun Clauses, C101 (for Mini Lesson, p. 621)

**Writing**
- Compare-Contrast, C32 (for Writing Option 2, p. 621)

**Communications**
- Dramatic Reading, T12 (for Activities & Explorations 1, p. 621)
- Verbal Strategies, T14 (for Activities & Explorations 1, p. 621)

**INTEGRATED TECHNOLOGY**
**Audio Library**
**Visit our website:**
www.mcdougallittell.com

# Ballad of Birmingham

DUDLEY RANDALL

"Mother dear, may I go downtown
instead of out to play,
and march the streets of Birmingham
in a freedom march today?"

5   "No, baby, no, you may not go,
for the dogs are fierce and wild,
and clubs and hoses, guns and jails
ain't good for a little child."

"But, mother, I won't be alone.
10  Other children will go with me,
and march the streets of Birmingham
to make our country free."

"No, baby, no, you may not go,
for I fear those guns will fire.
15  But you may go to church instead,
and sing in the children's choir."

She has combed and brushed her nightdark hair,
and bathed rose petal sweet,
and drawn white gloves on her small brown hands,
20  and white shoes on her feet.

The mother smiled to know her child
was in the sacred place,
but that smile was the last smile
to come upon her face.

25  For when she heard the explosion,
her eyes grew wet and wild.
She raced through the streets of Birmingham
calling for her child.

She clawed through bits of glass and brick,
30  then lifted out a shoe.
"O, here's the shoe my baby wore,
but, baby, where are you?"

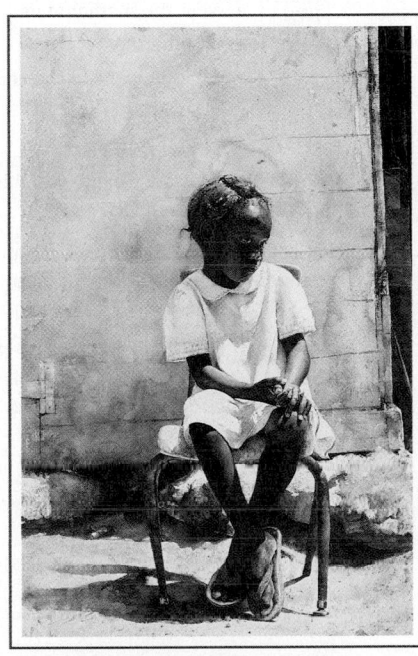

*Flip Flops and Lace* (1991), Stephen Scott Young.
Copyright © Stephen Scott Young. Courtesy of
John H. Surovek Gallery, Palm Beach, Florida.

BALLAD OF BIRMINGHAM   **619**

**Students Acquiring English**

**1** Point out that "dogs . . . and clubs and hoses, guns and jail" refer to weapons used by Birmingham law-enforcement officers to intimidate and subdue civil-rights protesters.

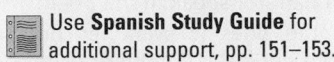 Use **Spanish Study Guide** for additional support, pp. 151–153.

**Less Proficient Readers**
Explain that the first four stanzas of the poem present a conversation between a mother and her daughter. Then a third-person speaker narrates the events that follow.

**Set a Purpose** Have students read to find out the story narrated by the poem.

**Gifted and Talented**
Have students locate other sources—literary works, newspaper reports, documentary films—that deal with the 1963 bombing of the 16th Street Baptist Church. Have them compare and contrast each source with this ballad in terms of what it teaches about the incident. What are the strengths and weaknesses of each source?

---

✓ **Assessment** **Standardized Test Practice**

**IDENTIFYING THEME** For some tests, students will be asked to infer possible themes of a work based on their analyses of plot and character. To help students prepare for this type of question, display or read aloud the following example.
Which one of the following statements could <u>not</u> be a theme of "Ballad of Birmingham?"

**A.** Hatred destroys the innocent.
**B.** No place is truly safe from the threat of violent people.
**C.** Children should never go anywhere unaccompanied.
**D.** The fight for justice demands much sacrifice.
Students should see that there is no justification for C as the theme. All the others are possible interpretations of Randall's poem.

## GUIDING STUDENT RESPONSE

### Connect to the Literature

**1. What Do You Think?**
Students might have been shocked, saddened, horrified.

**Comprehension Check**
• The mother, her child, and a third-person narrator speak in the poem.
• The mother does not want her child to march but instead to go to church.
• The church has been bombed and the child's shoe is found.

### Think Critically

2. Possible Response: The poem does not say how the mother knew it was the church that was bombed, nor is the death of the child explicitly stated.

3. Possible Responses: Students might question why this happened, what the repercussions were, and how people outside of Birmingham reacted.

4. Possible Responses:
• The child would rather march for freedom than play a child's game.
• The mother fears harm will come to the child in the march, so she sends her child to church.
• The mother smiles to think that her child is in a sacred place, untouched by violence. In fact, the church is the target of violence.
• The child, so young and innocent, ends up dying by violent means.

### Literary Analysis

**Ballads** Students should find that Randall's "Ballad in Birmingham" reflects the listed characteristics of ballads. Their examples of each characteristic should be specific.

**To get students started on their own ballad stanzas,** have them first brainstorm true events as possible subjects and decide on one. Then students might choose the speakers for their poems, and write the first stanza as the first speaker addressing the other.

---

### Connect to the Literature

**1. What Do You Think?**
What was the first emotion you felt after reading the poem?

**Comprehension Check**
• Who is speaking in the poem?
• What do the speakers disagree about?
• What has happened at the end of the poem?

### Think Critically

2. **ACTIVE READING** **READING NARRATIVE POETRY** What details did you have to infer because they were not directly explained in the poem?

3. What questions do you still have about the events in the poem?

4. What **ironies** do you see in the poem?

**THINK ABOUT**
• what the child would rather do than play
• what the mother fears
• why the mother smiles
• what happens to the child

### Extend Interpretations

5. **The Writer's Style** How well do you think the traditional **style** of the poem fits its subject?

6. **Connect to Life** Why should the tragedy in Birmingham still be remembered today? Name a recent tragedy that you think will be remembered 40 years from now.

7. **Points of Comparison** Compare Randall's **purpose** and **audience** with the purpose and audience for "Stanzas on Freedom" (page 575) and "Free Labor" (page 576).

### Literary Analysis

**BALLADS** As you recall, a **ballad** is a narrative poem that was originally meant to be sung. "Barbara Allan" and "John Henry" are traditional folk ballads. A literary ballad you may have studied is Longfellow's "The Wreck of the Hesperus," about a young woman killed in a shipwreck. A ballad typically has the following characteristics:

• It focuses on a single incident, beginning in the middle of a crisis and proceeding directly to the resolution, with only the sketchiest background information, character development, or descriptive detail.
• It consists of four-line stanzas, or **quatrains,** with **end rhyme** in the second and fourth lines.
• Each stanza has a regular **meter,** usually with four stressed syllables in the first and third lines and three stressed syllables in the second and fourth lines.
• Action is developed through **dialogue.**
• There is often **repetition** of words, phrases, and lines to emphasize ideas and to create suspense.

**Paired Activity** With a partner, go through the "Ballad of Birmingham" and note which of these ballad characteristics it shows. Be prepared to give examples. Then collaborate in writing your own ballad stanza, on any subject you choose. Share your stanza with the class.

---

## Extend Interpretations

**The Writer's Style** Possible Response: The regular rhyme and song-like rhythms give the poem an air of innocence, which sharply contrasts with the horror of the violence that kills an innocent child and destroys a sacred place.

**Connect to Life** Possible Responses: Students might indicate the need to remember the past in order to appreciate the sacrifices of those who helped bring about reform; the past can serve as a warning to people living in the present. Students might mention any tragedies brought about by gratuitous violence, such as the Oklahoma City bombing or recent terrorist attacks.

**Points of Comparison** Students should be able to compare elements of purpose and audience across texts. Possible Response: Randall's purpose is to communicate the horror that marked a specific event in the civil rights struggle of the 1960s. His audience is anyone who may not have grasped the human dimension of the tragedy and the terrible anguish of the bereaved. Both "Stanzas on Freedom" and "Free Labor" were written to promote the cause of abolition. The intended audience was anyone opposed to slavery who had not acted on his or her convictions.

## Writing Options

**1. Original Ballad** Using what you have learned about the ballad form, write your own ballad to commemorate a true event. You might finish the ballad you began for the Literary Analysis activity.

**2. Points of Comparison** Evaluate "Ballad of Birmingham" against either "Stanzas on Freedom" or "Free Labor." In a critical essay, tell which you believe is a more effective protest poem, and why.

**Writing Handbook**
See page 1281: Compare and Contrast

## Activities & Explorations

**1. Learned by Heart** Memorize "Ballad of Birmingham" and perform it for an audience who has never heard it. Monitor yourself as you prepare. What makes the poem easy to memorize? What lines do you want to emphasize for dramatic effect? ~ **SPEAKING AND LISTENING**

**2. Sorrowful Song** Set "Ballad of Birmingham" to music, either composing your own melody or adapting an existing one. Perform your song for the class. ~ **MUSIC**

**3. Ballads of Today** What contemporary rock, rap, or pop songs qualify as ballads? Bring in a recording of one such song, and in a lecture-demonstration, explain what elements make it a ballad. ~ **MUSIC**

## Inquiry and Research

Find out more about the bombing of the 16th Street Baptist Church and the events in Birmingham that led up to and followed it. Spike Lee's 1997 documentary "Four Little Girls" is an excellent source of information. You might also consult Martin Luther King's "Letter from Birmingham Jail" (page 1136).

## Dudley Randall
1914-

**Other Works**
*A Litany of Friends*
*After the Killing*
*Broadside Memories: Poets I Have Known*

**Poet of All Trades** Dudley Randall, the first poet laureate of Detroit, Michigan, wrote his earliest poem when he was four years old. His first published poems appeared in the *Detroit Free Press* when he was only 13. Randall, who received his education at Wayne University (now Wayne State University), the University of Michigan, and the University of Ghana, worked for many years at different jobs before becoming a book publisher and an editor. He was employed as a foundry worker for 5 years, a mail carrier for 13 years, and a librarian for 24 years.

**Four Little Girls** "Ballad of Birmingham" was Randall's response to the 1963 church bombing that killed four young girls in that city. This poem eventually led to the birth of Broadside Press,

which Randall founded and operated until 1977. As he explains, "Folk singer Jerry Moore of New York had it ["Ballad of Birmingham"] set to music, and I wanted to protect the rights to the poem by getting it copyrighted." After Randall learned that leaflets could be copyrighted, he printed his poem on a single sheet of paper called a broadside. "Ballad of Birmingham" was the first title published by Broadside Press.

**Publishing for the People** As a publisher, Randall provided an important forum for numerous African-American poets. Under Randall's direction, Broadside published nearly sixty books by such distinguished writers as Gwendolyn Brooks, Sonia Sanchez, Nikki Giovanni, Haki Madhubuti (Don L. Lee), and Etheridge Knight.

## Author Activity

If you can, obtain some books published by Broadside Press. What do the concerns and styles of the authors tell you about the period in which Randall was publishing?

BALLAD OF BIRMINGHAM **621**

---

## Writing Options

1. **Original Ballad To get students started on this assignment,** ask them to make a flow chart of what is to be covered in each stanza so that their direction is clear before they begin.
2. **Points of Comparison To get students started on this assignment,** have them set up a chart on which to note theme, purpose, audience, style, tone, mood, and form.

## Activities & Explorations

1. **Learned by Heart** Have students practice in pairs, with each student taking turns at the role of prompter. Students might improve their performances by taping themselves and listening to their recordings, noting areas to be improved. Students might first perform their poetic interpretations of their memorized poems in front of their own class and then in front of younger students so that they feel less nervous initially.
2. **Sorrowful Song Auditory learners** could be paired with those students not as skilled in the area of music to help them with this activity.
3. **Ballads of Today To get students started on this assignment,** review the elements of the ballad and think of popular songs that might show these characteristics.

## Inquiry & Research

Students should locate appropriate print and nonprint information using text and technical resources, including the library database and the Internet under related headings, such as *Civil Rights Movement, Martin Luther King, Jr.* Students might check web sites on the Internet that offer the perspectives of witnesses to the event.

---

 **Mini Lesson** **Grammar**

**INTRODUCTION TO NOUN CLAUSES**
**Instruction** Tell students that noun clauses are subordinate clauses that function as nouns in sentences. Noun clauses might be introduced by a variety of words, including the following: *who, whom, whose, which, that, whoever, whomever, what, whatever, how, that, when, where, whether,* and *why*. The best way to identify noun clauses is to determine the function of the clause in the sentence.

<u>Whoever is writing the ballad</u> should note the important characteristics of the ballad form. *(subject)*

**Exercises** Ask students to underline the noun clauses and identify their function.

**1.** The irony is <u>that the mother's worry was misplaced.</u> *(predicate nominative)*
**2.** <u>What she saw that day</u> would scar her for the rest of her life. *(subject)*
**3.** The mother's question of <u>when the suffering would end</u> expressed the despair of so many. *(object of the preposition)*

 Use **Grammar Transparencies and Copymasters**, p. 101.

Use McDougal Littell's *Language Network,* Chapter 3, for more instruction and practice in clauses.

**PART 1 Reading the Prompt**
Model the process of reading a prompt:
• Read through the prompt in its entirety.
• List the key words from the assignment on the board ("compare and contrast," "Douglass, Lowell, and Harper, and later works by Moody and Randall," "purpose, audience, theme, tone, and style," "conclusion").
• Define each key word using the Strategies in Action to show how students can restate the prompt in their own words.

**PART 2 Planning a Comparison-Contrast Essay**
• Students might wish to make their charts large enough so that they can jot down supporting evidence. Encourage students to skim or review each selection as they fill in the chart.
• To make organizing easier, encourage students to use the word *same* to identify similar elements. Dissimilar ones will require more detailed notes.

**PART 3 Drafting Your Essay**
**Introduction** Students may wish to write a sentence or two about each movement. Then they can state their opinions about the literature.
**Organization** In order to compare and contrast the two movements, students will need to make generalizations about each. They can then include evidence that supports those generalizations.
**Conclusion** Students must decide whether the differences or the similarities are more important.
**Revision** Remind students to use double quotation marks around direct quotations and the titles of stories and poems. Book titles should be underlined or set in italic type.

---

## Comparing Literature: Assessment Practice

Some assessment prompts ask you to compare and contrast different literary selections. You will now practice writing an essay with a comparison-contrast focus.

### PART 1   Reading the Prompt

Often you will be asked to write in response to a prompt like the one below. First, read the entire prompt carefully. Then read through it again, looking for key words that help you identify the purpose of the essay and what it must include.

> **Writing Prompt**
>
> Compare and contrast literature of the 19th-century antislavery movement with literature of the 1960s civil rights movement. Point out important similarities and differences you see between works by Douglass, Lowell, and Harper, and later works by Moody and Randall. Concentrate on purpose, audience, theme, tone, and style. Draw a conclusion about which is more significant—the parallels or the divergences between the movements.

**STRATEGIES IN ACTION**

❶ **Compare and contrast** literature from two different periods, stating how it is alike and different.

❷ Cite **examples** from the selections named.

❸ Focus on five **literary elements**.

❹ **Conclude,** or make a decision supported by evidence

### PART 2   Planning a Comparison-Contrast Essay

• Create a chart with a row for each literary element you will discuss.

• For each selection, make notes related to these literary elements. (Recall your answers to relevant discussion questions.)

• Identify and mark similarities and differences among selections.

• Decide which seem more important, the similarities or the differences.

|  | Antislavery | | | Civil Rights | |
| --- | --- | --- | --- | --- | --- |
|  | Douglass | Lowell | Harper | Moody | Randall |
| Purpose |  |  |  |  |  |
| Audience |  |  |  |  |  |
| Theme |  |  |  |  |  |
| Tone |  |  |  |  |  |
| Style |  |  |  |  |  |

### PART 3   Drafting Your Essay

**Introduction** Begin by stating your purpose—to compare and contrast antislavery and civil rights literature.

**Organization** Summarize characteristics of antislavery literature, giving examples to support your ideas. Show how selections from the civil rights movement resemble antislavery works, then show how they differ.

**Conclusion** End your essay by stating an opinion about the relative importance of the resemblances and differences. Be sure your points lead to this conclusion.

**Revision** Allow time to review your work. Make sure it is clear, well-supported, and free from mistakes.

**Writing Handbook**
See page 1281: Compare and Contrast

---

 **Mini Lesson**   ## Choosing Quotations

**SUPPORTING EVIDENCE**
**Instruction** Common facts do not need to be treated as quotations, but words or ideas taken directly from another writer should be credited. Also, if the writer's word choice, language, or phrasing is important, it should be quoted directly.
    Read each sentence aloud and ask students how they would treat it.
• The Emancipation Proclamation was signed in 1863. (no quotes needed; common fact)

• What a variety of misbeliefs the audience held: she was a man, for instance, or she was a white person who had been painted. (should be quoted; phrasing is important)
**Application** Facts and quotations are two types of evidence that students might use to support their conclusions. Remind them to consider whether quoting is appropriate in each case.

## LITERATURE CONNECTIONS

### Jubilee
MARGARET WALKER

**These thematically related readings are provided along with *Jubilee*:**

**Come Up from the Fields Father**
WALT WHITMAN

**The Sheriff's Children**
CHARLES WADDELL CHESTNUTT

**Traveling the Long Road to Freedom**
DONOVAN WEBSTER

**To the University of Cambridge, in New England**
PHILLIS WHEATLEY

**To Phillis Wheatley**
LISA CLAYTON

**Virginia Portrait**
STERLING A. BROWN

*from* **Incidents in the Life of a Slave Girl**
HARRIET A. JACOBS

**Raise a Ruckus Tonight**
**Many Thousand Gone**
TWO SLAVE SONGS

### The Souls of Black Folk
W. E. B. DU BOIS

**These thematically related readings are provided along with *The Souls of Black Folk*:**

**Atlanta Exposition Address**
BOOKER T. WASHINGTON

**Booker T. and W. E. B.**
DUDLEY RANDALL

**Address to the 4th International Convention of the Negro Peoples of the World**
MARCUS GARVEY

*from* **Coming of Age in Mississippi**
ANNE MOODY

*from* **Warriors Don't Cry**
MELBA PATILLO BEALS

**After Dreaming of President Johnson**
HOWARD GORDON

**Communication and Reality**
MALCOLM X

*from* **Sushi and Grits: Ethnic Identity and Conflict in a Newly Multicultural America**
ITABARI NJERI

## And Even *More . . .*

### Books
**The Red Badge of Courage**
STEPHEN CRANE
A gripping novel about a young Civil War soldier's initiation into battle.

**Battle Cry of Freedom**
JAMES M. MCPHERSON
A Pulitzer Prize-winning book on the history of the Civil War.

**Lincoln at Gettysburg**
GARRY WILLS
A critically acclaimed book examining the impact of the Gettysburg Address on America's democratic ideals.

### Other Media
**Frederick Douglass: When the Lion Wrote History**
Three-part documentary about the eloquent speaker and writer whose words shaped people's views on slavery and the rights of African Americans. WETA/ROJA Productions (VIDEOCASSETTE)

**The Civil War**
A compelling six-part documentary produced by Ken Burns. PBS. (VIDEOCASSETTE)

**Walt Whitman's Civil War**
Dramatic readings of the renowned poet's war literature are intertwined with combat scenes from movies. Churchill. (VIDEOCASSETTE)

### Civil War Women
EDITED BY FRANK D. MCSHERRY, CHARLES G. WAUGH, AND MARTIN HARRY GREENBERG
The varied roles women played during the Civil War come to life in this collection of short stories by distinguished women writers. Among the contributors are Louisa May Alcott, Kate Chopin, and Eudora Welty.

The *Electronic Library* is a CD-ROM that contains additional fiction, nonfiction, poetry, and drama for each unit in *The Language of Literature*.

These are the additional selections found in Unit 4 of the *Electronic Library* that apply to Part 1.

Negro Spiritual
**Go Down, Moses**
**Swing Low, Sweet Chariot**

Robert E. Lee
**Letters to His Family: To His Wife, To His Son**
**Farewell to His Army**

Walt Whitman
**O Captain! My Captain!**

Have students choose one long or several smaller selections to read silently with comprehension over a period of time.

## Objectives
- write a Literary Interpretation
- use a written text as a model
- revise a draft to draw conclusions
- use the historical present tense to write about a literary work

## Introducing the Workshop

**A Literary Interpretation** Establish some criteria for what makes a literary work worth interpreting. By analyzing the elements of a work of literature, students will better understand the work and may find it more interesting. Remind students that they will probably be asked to interpret a work of literature in school. Having a procedure to follow will make the task much easier.

### Basics in a Box
**B Using the Graphic** The items in a literary interpretation work together in a specific order to create the overall piece. The introduction acquaints the reader with the literary work and the writer's interpretation of it. In the body of the paper, the image of the book shown in the graphic illustrates the importance of basing the literary interpretation on specific evidence from the literature. The conclusion wraps up important points made earlier in the paper.

**C Presenting the Rubric** To better understand the assignment, students can refer to the Standards for Writing a Successful Literary Interpretation. You may also want to share with them the complete rubric, which describes several levels of proficiency. Let students know that their literary interpretations will be assessed according to this rubric.

---

# *Writing* Workshop — Literary Interpretation

## Finding meaning . . .

Ⓐ **From Reading to Writing** After reading a powerful work of literature like Ambrose Bierce's "An Occurrence at Owl Creek Bridge" or Stephen Crane's "A Mystery of Heroism," you may be filled with questions about its meaning. Writing a **literary interpretation** is a good way to explore your own ideas about the meaning of a literary work and to analyze the elements in the work that communicate the meaning.

### For Your Portfolio

**WRITING PROMPT** Write an interpretation of a literary work in which you explain its meaning.

**Purpose:** To explain your interpretation
**Audience:** Others who are familiar with the work

---

## Basics in a Box

**Literary Interpretation at a Glance**

Ⓑ

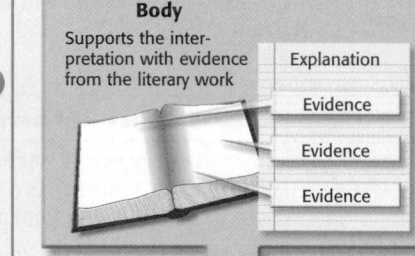

**Introduction**
Introduces the literary work and includes a clear thesis statement that introduces the interpretation

**Body**
Supports the interpretation with evidence from the literary work

- Explanation
- Evidence
- Evidence
- Evidence

**Conclusion**
Summarizes the interpretation

### Ⓒ RUBRIC Standards for Writing

**A successful literary interpretation should**

- clearly identify the title and author of the literary work
- give a clearly stated interpretation at or near the beginning of the essay
- present evidence and quotations from the text to support the interpretation
- take into account other interpretations and contradictory evidence

**624** UNIT FOUR PART 1: A HOUSE DIVIDED

---

Use McDougal Littell's *Language Network,* Chapter 19, for more instruction on writing a literary interpretation.

To engage students visually, use **Power Presentation** 6, Literary Interpretation.

## LESSON RESOURCES

### USING PRINT RESOURCES
**Unit Four Resource Book**
- Prewriting, p. 33
- Drafting and Elaboration, p. 34
- Peer Response, pp. 35–36
- Revising, Editing, and Proofreading, p. 37
- Student Models, pp. 38–43
- Rubric, p. 44

**Writing Transparencies and Copymasters**
- Writing Process Transparencies
- Writing Style Transparencies
- Writing Template Copymasters

### USING MEDIA RESOURCES
**Visit our website:**
www.mcdougallittell.com

# Analyzing a Student Model

**Molly Ball**
**Cherry Creek High School**

### The Red Badge of Courage

Stephen Crane's *The Red Badge of Courage* (1895) owes many of its ideas to the Naturalist movement of the late 19th century; likewise, a good understanding of the ideas of Naturalism can be drawn from the ideas in *The Red Badge of Courage*. Crane uses the setting of the American Civil War to illustrate two important naturalistic concepts: that the natural world is indifferent to the affairs of its creatures, including humans, and that humans and their struggles are therefore insignificant.

*The Red Badge of Courage* rejects the Romantic idea that nature is a sympathetic mirror of human emotion. Instead, the natural world, as presented in the book, is completely indifferent to human struggles. Henry, upon viewing a battle scene, is surprised "that Nature had gone tranquilly on with her golden process in the midst of so much devilment." He expects something dark, cloudy, and appropriately sinister to reflect the evil he sees because he is still too naive to understand that Nature is more than just a backdrop for human affairs. He does not realize that Nature is a force much larger than he or his species, a machine whose mysterious workings will continue regardless of the squabbles in its midst. As Henry matures, he comes to understand this. Pondering his own actions, he comforts himself with the knowledge that "the sky would forget. . . . The imperturbable sun shines on insult and worship." Nature, Crane shows us, cannot be truthfully personified. In reality, it is wholly impassive to humankind. It is not sensitive to us, and it cannot be affected by us.

Logically, a natural world so completely indifferent must cherish (or not cherish) all of its creatures equally; thus, man cannot justify feeling superior to any other species. Crane implies this when Henry sees the dead soldier, "black ants swarming greedily upon the gray face." If we are disgusted by the image of the ants, we must be more disgusted by the battle scenes, in which humans swarm upon each other with no regard for the

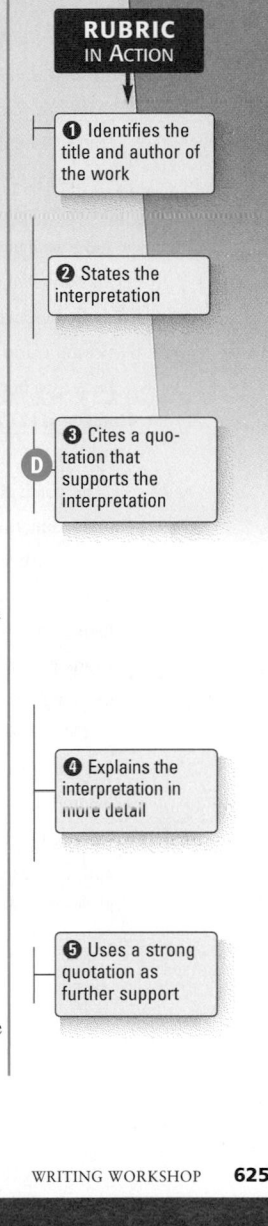

### RUBRIC
### IN ACTION

**❶** Identifies the title and author of the work

**❷** States the interpretation

**❸** Cites a quotation that supports the interpretation

**❹** Explains the interpretation in more detail

**❺** Uses a strong quotation as further support

---

## Mini Lesson — Viewing and Representing

### PICTURING TEXT STRUCTURE

**Instruction** While word choice and ideas are important, a literary interpretation also needs structure in order to be effective. A careful approach to writing will make the finished piece easier to follow.

**Activity** Have students analyze the text structure of the student model by constructing an image such as a graphic organizer. The graphic students construct should reflect how the student writer has organized her piece. Students might first use different-colored self-adhesive notes to label the components of the student sample. A sample organizer is shown.

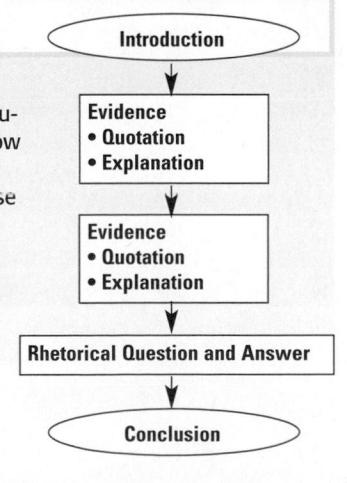

Introduction

↓

Evidence
• Quotation
• Explanation

↓

Evidence
• Quotation
• Explanation

↓

Rhetorical Question and Answer

↓

Conclusion

---

## Teaching the Lesson

### Analyzing the Model
#### *The Red Badge of Courage*

**❹** The student model introduces the reader to a literary interpretation of the novel *The Red Badge of Courage.*

Explain that *The Red Badge of Courage* was written in 1894 by Stephen Crane. It was first published as a serial in a Philadelphia newspaper. In 1895 it was released as a book. The story is set during the Civil War, and centers around Henry Fleming, a young Union soldier.

Have students read the model aloud. Then ask them to share anything they know about the Naturalist movement.

**Possible Response:** The Naturalist movement in literature started with 19th century French author Émile Zola. The naturalist writers used a form of scientific observation to depict human character. Naturalists believed people were shaped by heredity, environment, and circumstances beyond their control. American writers who reflect this view include Theodore Dreiser, Jack London, and Upton Sinclair.

Have students read the student model and then discuss the Rubric in Action. Point out the key words and phrases in the student model that correspond to the elements mentioned in the Rubric in Action.

2. Ask students to restate the interpretation in their own words.
   **Possible Response:** Nature doesn't care about humans or their meaningless struggles.

3. Ask students how the quotation supports the interpretation.
   **Possible Response:** The quotation shows that although the battle scene is chaotic, with loud guns booming and men screaming and shouting, the sun continues to shine. The natural world is indifferent to war.

5. Point out that the quotations from the novel are followed by the student writer's interpretation of them.

6. Remind students that any conclusions they draw must be logical and supported by evidence from the novel.

7. Explain that a rhetorical question is one that is asked only for effect, not for information. Ask students what effect the rhetorical question has in the student model.

**Possible Response:** The student writer uses the rhetorical question to expand on her interpretation of the naturalistic concepts in the novel.

death or life of their prey. The parallel between the soldiers and the ants is striking, and it shows that human behavior is no more sophisticated than that of insects. This natural equality also is apparent when Henry enters battle: "Into the youth's eyes there came a look that one can see in the orbs of a jaded horse." If man is no more noble than any other animal, it makes sense that Henry's fear should take the same form as that of a horse. By showing the similarities between human and animal action, Crane illustrates his naturalistic view that all species are basically equal in significance.

So here we find Henry, in the middle of a struggle for his very existence; yet the world around him will continue whether he lives or dies, just as if he were a horse or an ant. What, then, can this struggle amount to? Not much, says Crane. Ultimately, human effort, especially war, is futile; even the lives of men who strive toward lofty goals are fleeting and insignificant. "The youth could not tell from the battle flags flying like crimson foam in many directions which color of cloth was winning." But what difference can it make when all that is at stake are pieces of cloth? The battle begins to seem absurd and silly, much like the silliness of the image of the lunging men being "bandied about like light toys between the contending forces." Crane presents a picture of human effort as ultimately futile and meaningless, and of humankind as insignificant on any objective scale.

Clearly, Stephen Crane presents his interpretation of Naturalism in *The Red Badge of Courage* by displaying a man in a setting and context where he is undeniably an unimportant part of something much larger. Through this lens, the human race seems tiny in the vastness of nature and time, as do all other creatures. Ultimately, human actions are altogether inconsequential.

**❻** Draws a conclusion from quoted evidence to support the interpretation

**❼** Reinforces her interpretation by asking a rhetorical question and answering it as she believes the author would

**❽** This writer concludes by restating the interpretation.
**Other Options:**
· End with a summary of the evidence.
· End with a quotation from the text.

# Writing Your Literary Interpretation

## ❶ Prewriting

Begin by choosing a work of literature to write about. You might select a work that you especially liked or one you had problems with in some way. See the **Idea Bank** in the margin for more suggestions. Then follow the steps below.

### Planning Your Literary Interpretation

▶ **1. Develop an interpretation.** Read the story more than once, taking notes in your Reader's Notebook. Freewrite about the literary elements in the work. What are the main character's most significant thoughts or actions? What is the central conflict? What is the theme? Write your interpretation of the story as a tentative thesis statement.

▶ **2. Gather evidence to support your interpretation.** Use a chart to list significant passages from the text and how they support your interpretation.

| Evidence from the text | How it supports interpretation |
|---|---|
|  |  |
|  |  |
|  |  |

▶ **3. Test your interpretation.** Does the evidence support your interpretation? What contradictory evidence did you find? How can you revise your interpretation to account for more of the evidence?

## ❷ Drafting

*If everybody is thinking alike then somebody isn't thinking.*
**General George S. Patton, U.S. Army**

Try out your interpretation by just writing down your ideas. A good way to start is to try to get through an entire first draft without stopping. When you get stuck, leave a blank or write yourself a note but keep going. You can revise form and style later. Eventually, you should organize your writing into the following parts:

- **Introduction**—identifies the author and title of the work and briefly states the main point of the interpretation
- **Body**—presents evidence from the text to support the interpretation
- **Conclusion**—restates the interpretation and summarizes the evidence

### Ask Your Peer Reader

- What is the main point of my interpretation?
- What evidence did I present for my interpretation?
- Are you convinced that my interpretation is reasonable? Why or why not?
- What other points should I include to clarify my interpretation?

---

### IDEABank

**1. Your Working Portfolio**
Build on one of the **Writing Options** you completed earlier in this unit:
- **Evaluation of Bierce,** p. 592
- **Literary Analysis,** p. 603

**2. Favorite Authors**
Make a list of your favorite authors. Go to the library and look for new, different, or unfamiliar selections by these authors.

**3. Freewriting**
Look through the Table of Contents of your literature book and consider two or three possible selections to interpret. Then freewrite on these pieces to help you decide which one you want to continue working with.

---

## Prewriting

### Choosing a Literary Work
If after reading the Idea Bank students are having difficulty choosing a literary work, suggest they try the following:

- Sign on to one of the literary discussion groups on the Internet. There are several that specialize in young adult literature.
- Work with a few classmates and brainstorm a list of books you have read. You might each choose one from the list.
- Several organizations publish lists of favorite young adult books. These should be available at the library or through your teacher.

### Planning the Literary Interpretation

1. As students reread the text they have chosen, have them record their questions and critical responses in their Reader's Notebook. Encourage them to write down passages from the text that strike them as significant. You might then pair students who are writing interpretations of the same book. Allow time for them to discuss their notes and key passages from the text before they write a tentative thesis statement.

2. Have students list all the evidence they can think of that supports their thesis.

3. Remind students that they must be able to support their interpretation with evidence from the novel. Encourage students to write down any evidence that disproves their view. Have them think about how they can revise their thesis statement to fit any conflicting evidence.

## Drafting

### Organizing the Draft
Remind students that they should include a brief summary of the text in their literary interpretation.

Point out that students can follow the basic organization of introduction, body, and conclusion for this type of writing. However, they can make some changes from the model within this structure. For example, the writer of the student model could have started with a quotation that supports her interpretation, and introduced the title and author of the work later on. Ask students how this would change the effect of the student model.

## Revising

### CONCLUSIONS

Remind students that a conclusion must follow logically from the material presented in the paper. In the example on this page, the writer has introduced a new interpretation instead of drawing a conclusion about the statements she made in the body of the paper. Introducing a new idea at this point only confuses the reader.

## Editing and Proofreading

### VERB TENSE

Remind students that verb tenses show the time of an action or state of being. The three most common tenses are the present, past, and future. The past tense is usually formed by adding -d or -ed to the present: *looked, skated.* Irregular verbs have a spelling change: *swim, swam; eat, ate.* The future tense is formed by using the words *shall* or *will* with the present: *shall eat, will skate.* Students need to understand the different tenses so they can write their interpretations in the historical present tense. Students should check their use of tense so they produce an error-free final draft.

Point out that the sample shows the use of the past tense instead of the historical present. The last sentence is a direct quote from the book and should be kept in the past tense as it was originally written.

## Reflecting

Have students write a brief note evaluating the way in which they approached the writing assignment. You might also ask them to consider how satisfied they are with their final draft. Would they make any further changes if they were to revise their writing again? Have them attach these self-evaluations to their literary interpretations and place both in their working portfolios.

628   UNIT FOUR   PART 1

---

**Need revising help?**

Review the **Rubric,** p. 624.

Consider **peer reader** comments.

Check **Revising, Editing, and Proofreading** p. 1269.

**Stumped by verb tenses?**

See the **Grammar Handbook,** p. 1396.

## Publishing
### IDEAS

- Read your interpretation aloud, preferably to an audience that has read the story.
- Collect interpretations of works by a particular author in one book. Keep it as a classroom reference source.

**More Online: Publishing Options** www.mcdougallittell.com

## ❸ Revising

**TARGET SKILL ▶ CONCLUSIONS** A good conclusion in a literary interpretation summarizes what was presented in the body of the paper, does not introduce anything new, and leaves the reader with a sense of closure and something to think about.

> *Clearly, Stephen Crane presents his interpretation of Naturalism*
> ~~In~~ *The Red Badge of Courage* ~~Stephen Crane offers a psychological study~~
> ~~of fear all the more remarkable because he had never actually seen a battle~~
> ~~at the time. He also wants to display~~ *by displaying a* man in ~~his~~ *a* setting and context where
> he is undeniably an unimportant part of something much larger. Through
> this lens, the human race seems tiny in the vastness of nature and time, as
> do all other creatures. *Ultimately, human actions are altogether inconsequential.*

## ❹ Editing and Proofreading

**TARGET SKILL ▶ VERB TENSE** When writing about a literary work, use the present tense (called the historical present); that is, write about a past action as if it were happening now. However, keep the verbs in quotations in the tense in which they were written.

> What, then, *can* ~~could~~ this struggle amount to? Not much, *says* ~~said~~ Crane.
> Ultimately, human effort especially war *is* ~~was~~ futile; even the lives of men
> who *strive* ~~strove~~ toward lofty goals *are* ~~were~~ fleeting and insignificant. "The youth
> could not tell from the battle flags flying like crimson foam in many
> directions which color of cloth was winning."

## ❺ Reflecting

**FOR YOUR WORKING PORTFOLIO** What helped you the most in developing your literary interpretation? How did your interpretation change as you wrote? Attach your answers to your finished work. Save your literary interpretation in your **Working Portfolio.**

Read this opening from the first draft of a literary analysis. The underlined sections may include the following kinds of errors:

- **lack of parallel structure**
- **verb tenses errors**
- **sentence fragments**
- **comma errors**

For each underlined section, choose the revision that most improves the writing.

---

"Flowers for Algernon," written by Daniel Keyes, questions the relationship between <u>intelligent and happiness</u>. As the story <u>began</u>, Charlie Gordon is an
(1)                              (2)
eager and happy worker with a limited intellect. After an experimental operation, Charlie's intelligence triples. <u>He develops many new insights. Which are often disturbing to him.</u> Charlie becomes less <u>optimistic, as he</u> learns more
(3)                                         (4)
about the world. <u>When Charlie's new intelligence finally fades, he returns to his earlier life.</u> By the end of the story, Charlie's previous happiness <u>vanished</u> as
(5)                                                (6)
well.

---

1. **A.** can you be intelligent and happiness
   **B.** intelligence and being happy
   **C.** intelligence and happiness
   **D.** Correct as is

2. **A.** begins
   **B.** begun
   **C.** has begun
   **D.** Correct as is

3. **A.** He develops many new insights, which are often disturbing to him.
   **B.** He develops many new insights which disturbing him.
   **C.** He develops many new insights are often disturbing to him.
   **D.** Correct as is

4. **A.** optimistic as he,
   **B.** optimistic as, he
   **C.** optimistic as he
   **D.** Correct as is

5. **A.** When Charlie's new intelligence finally fades he, then, returns to his earlier life.
   **B.** When Charlie's new intelligence finally fades. He returns to his earlier life.
   **C.** When Charlie's new intelligence finally fades he returns to his earlier life.
   **D.** Correct as is

6. **A.** was vanished
   **B.** has vanished
   **C.** did vanish
   **D.** Correct as is

**Need extra help?**

See the **Grammar Handbook**:

Verb Tense, p. 1310

Correcting Fragments, p. 1323

Punctuation Chart, pp. 1327–1328

---

## Assessment Practice
Demonstrate how students can eliminate incorrect choices for the first question.

**A.** The structure here is not parallel. *Be intelligent* is a phrase, while *happiness* is a noun.

**B.** The structure here is not parallel. *Intelligence* is a noun, while *being happy* is a phrase.

**D.** This sentence lacks parallel structure because *intelligent* is an adjective and *happiness* is a noun.

**C.** This choice is correct. Since the words *intelligence* and *happiness* are both nouns, the structure is parallel.

**Answers**
**1.** C; **2.** A; **3.** A; **4.** C; **5.** D; **6.** B

## Objectives

- use context clues to determine the most suitable meaning of a word with multiple meanings
- use a dictionary to determine precise usage and the most suitable definition

## EXERCISE

1. *habit:* a distinctive dress or costume
2. *distinction:* being singled out for accolades and honors
3. *remove:* distance or separation
4. *report:* an explosive noise
5. *stock:* the rear wooden or metal handle or part of a rifle, pistol, or automatic weapon

## Finding the Right Meaning

The English language is huge and diverse. The *Oxford English Dictionary* lists about 500,000 words, and another half-million technical and scientific terms have not yet been added to the dictionary. Despite this wealth of words, a single word often has multiple meanings, making it difficult, sometimes, to determine which meaning is intended in a particular context.

Consider the use of the words *works* and *base* in the excerpt on the right. The word *work* has more than 20 meanings. In this excerpt, *works* means "steadily increasing influence." If you were to look up

*base* in a dictionary, you would find two entries, each with several meanings, such as "a foundation," "a headquarters," or "morally bad." The meaning for *base* used in this excerpt can be found in the second entry—the word means "low and inferior."

> If ye do not feel the chain,
> When it works a brother's pain,
> Are ye not base slaves indeed,
> Slaves unworthy to be freed?
> —James Russell Lowell, "Stanzas on Freedom"

## Strategies for Building Vocabulary

Because many words have multiple meanings, it is important to know how to determine which meaning a writer intends. Here are two methods for doing this.

**❶ Determine Meaning from Context** First try to figure out the meaning of the word from the context. Consider the word *light* in this excerpt from "Free Labor."

> This fabric is too light to bear
>     The weight of bondsmen's tears,
> I shall not in its texture trace
>     The agony of years.
> —Frances Ellen Watkins Harper, "Free Labor"

Do you think *light* means "having little weight" or "electromagnetic radiation"? Since in this context *light* is used as an adjective describing fabric, and fabric is more likely to be lightweight than to glow in the dark, the context helps you infer that *light* means "having little weight."

**❷ Consider Dictionary Meanings** When context clues don't help with meaning, consult a dictionary. For example, in "An Occurrence at Owl Creek Bridge," the narrator states, "Some loose boards laid upon the sleepers supporting the metals of the railway supplied a footing for him and his executioners." If you look up *sleeper* in a dictionary,

you'll find several meanings. At first glance, a definition like "a sleeping car on a railroad train" might seem to be relevant.

However, a train car would most likely *not* be "supporting the metals of the railway," so that meaning makes no sense. If you read on, you will find a definition like "a heavy beam used as a support for rails in a railroad track." Given the context, this definition seems to make the most sense.

Always read *all* the definitions for a word before deciding which meaning is intended. If you have trouble deciding which definition is correct, try choosing the one you think works best and reading it aloud in the sentence in place of the unfamiliar word.

**EXERCISE** Use a dictionary to define each underlined word in these excerpts from "Occurrence at Owl Creek Bridge."

1. He was a civilian, if one might judge from his <u>habit</u>, which was that of a planter.
2. He chafed under the inglorious restraint, longing for the release of his energies, the larger life of the soldier, the opportunity for <u>distinction</u>.
3. At a short <u>remove</u> upon the same temporary platform was an officer.
4. Suddenly he heard a sharp <u>report</u> and something struck the water smartly within a few inches of his head.
5. A single company of infantry [were] in line, at "parade rest," the butts of the rifles on the ground, . . . the hands crossed upon the <u>stock</u>.

## Grammar from Literature

A compound sentence is a sentence that consists of two or more independent clauses. Look at the sentence below. Notice that independent clauses can stand alone as sentences.

> independent clause      independent clause
> You have seen how a man was made a slave; **you shall see how a slave was made a man.**
> —*Narrative of the Life of Frederick Douglass, an African Slave*

Compound sentences can show a number of types of relationships between ideas. Here are some examples from " An Occurrence at Owl Creek Bridge."

> SEQUENCE OF EVENTS
> This plank had been held in place by the weight of the captain; **it was now held by that of the sergeant.**
>
> SIMULTANEOUS EVENTS
> The intervals of silence grew progressively longer; **the delays became maddening.**
>
> EXPLANATION
> The hunted man saw all this over his shoulder; **he was now swimming vigorously with the current.**

Notice that in each of the preceding examples the independent clauses are linked by a semicolon. Independent clauses can also be linked by a comma and a coordinating conjunction, such as *and, or, nor, but, yet, for,* or *so.*

> CAUSE AND EFFECT
> There was a mass rally that night at the Pearl Street Church in Jackson, **and the place was packed.**
> —Anne Moody, *Coming of Age in Mississippi*

**Using Compound Sentences in Your Writing** Showing connections between ideas is a key element of effective writing. As you revise your writing, look for related ideas and consider combining them in compound sentences. By doing so, you may also eliminate repetition and wordiness. If you use coordinating conjunctions, be sure to choose ones that clearly express the relationships between the ideas.

> RELATED IDEAS
> **Ambrose Bierce was a journalist. He had a reporter's eye for detail.**
>
> COMPOUND SENTENCE
> **Ambrose Bierce was a journalist,** so **he had a reporter's eye for detail.**

**Usage Tip** When a pronoun in the second clause of a compound sentence refers to a noun in the first clause, be sure there is no confusion about which noun the pronoun replaces.

> UNCLEAR
>    noun        noun     pronoun
> **The captain nods to the sergeant, and** he **steps aside.**

Note that in this sentence it is not clear whether the captain or the sergeant steps aside. There are several ways in which the sentence can be rewritten to clarify its meaning. Here are two possibilities:

> CLEAR
> **The captain nods to the sergeant, and** the sergeant **steps aside.**
>
> CLEAR
> **The captain nods to the sergeant,** who **steps aside.**

**WRITING EXERCISE** For items 1 and 2, join the sentences to form compound sentences. For items 3–5, make each simple sentence into a compound sentence by adding another independent clause. Use *and* as a connector only once.
1. The executioners stand quietly. They are deeply affected by the gravity of the situation.
2. Farquhar stands on one end of a plank. A sergeant stands on the other.
3. A sentinel stands on each end of the bridge.
4. The prisoner feels pressure on his throat.
5. At first he imagines his body is sinking into the river.

**GRAMMAR EXERCISE** Rewrite the sentences so that it is clear which noun the pronoun replaces.
1. Farquhar welcomes the scout; he is in disguise.
2. The increasing number of desertions resulted in more frequent hangings, yet they didn't seem to solve anything.
3. Farquhar's escape begins at the bridge, but it is only imaginary.
4. Bierce provides readers with believable characters and interesting plot twists, and they are held in keen suspense.
5. Farquhar travels a lonely road to his home; it grows stranger and stranger.

---

### Objectives
- use compound sentences to show relationships between ideas
- use the correct punctuation when linking independent clauses in a compound sentence
- revise drafts for effective writing by combining related ideas in compound sentences
- practice using pronouns and antecedents in a compound sentence

### WRITING EXERCISE
Responses will vary.
1. The executioners stand quietly, yet they are deeply affected by the gravity of the situation.
2. Farquhar stands on one end of a plank; a sergeant stands on the other.
3. A sentinel stands on each end of the bridge, and a company of infantry watches from a hillside.
4. The prisoner feels pressure on his throat; pain shoots through his body.
5. At first he imagines his body is sinking into the river, but then he feels it rising to the surface.

### GRAMMAR EXERCISE
1. **Possible Response:** Farquhar welcomes the scout, <u>who</u> is in disguise.
2. The increasing number of desertions resulted in more frequent hangings, yet <u>the hangings</u> didn't seem to solve anything.
3. Farquhar's escape begins at the bridge, but <u>the escape</u> is only imaginary.
4. Bierce provides readers with believable characters and interesting plot twists, and <u>readers</u> are held in keen suspense.
5. **Possible Response:** Farquhar travels a lonely road to his home; <u>the road</u> grows stranger and stranger.

### OVERVIEW

**Introduction**

This essay provides historical background for the selections in Part 2 of this unit, which focus on life in the West in the late 1800s and into the 1900s. The selections in Voices from the Times give insight into some of the concerns and issues of westward expansion. This essay will help students interpret the possible influences of historical contexts on a literary work.

## Teaching Nonfiction

**Reading Skills and Strategies**

**ESTABLISHING A PURPOSE FOR READING**

Explain to students that this essay will help them understand the lure of the West. Have the students review the article and establish a purpose for reading (to find out).

**MONITORING AND MODIFYING READING STRATEGIES**

Ask students to read through the article silently. Have them monitor their comprehension of the material and, if necessary, modify their reading strategies when understanding breaks down. Encourage students to ask questions about the article as a way of increasing comprehension.

**ANALYZING TEXT STRUCTURE**

Ask students to analyze the text structure of the essay for how it influences their understanding of the issues surrounding westward expansion. Have students note how the author has organized material in the essay and how this organization influences their understanding of the material.

# Tricksters and Trailblazers

## The Vanishing Frontier

**B**efore white settlers in large numbers had pushed west of the Mississippi, the vast frontier was populated by many tribes of Native Americans. The Sioux (soō), the Cheyenne (shī-ĕn′), the Arapaho (ə-răp′e-hō′), the Kiowa (kī′ə-wô′), and the Comanche (kə-măn′chē) on the Great Plains had developed a way of life that depended almost exclusively on the large herds of buffalo, estimated at 15 million head in 1865. In the Southwest, the Apache had fought against the Spanish for 250 years; but other southwestern tribes, such as the Navajo, had adopted Spanish ways and were raising sheep and goats and cultivating crops. The Nez Perce (nĕz′ pûrs′) of the Pacific Northwest had coexisted peacefully with white traders and trappers since Lewis and Clark first explored their vast territory in 1805.

(A) In 1841 the first caravan of covered wagons brought pioneers across the Great Plains, heading for fertile territories in California and Oregon. Within two years, more than 1,000 people had made the journey. During the California gold rush of 1849, the dream of riches lured thousands of miners west. Within 30 years of that first discov-

632

A 19th-centry artist's rendition of a Native American chief's refusal to allow a wagon train to pass through his country.

ery, gold or silver had been found in every Western state and territory.

By the 1860s, the plains themselves began to be settled. The free land granted by the Homestead Act of 1862 attracted thousands of settlers west. Newly constructed railroads transported more than 8 million settlers in two decades alone.

**B**

**C**

This relatively rapid settlement of the West doomed the Native American way of life. White settlers believed that they were bringing civilization to the wilderness, and few considered the Indians as having any legitimate claim to the land. One by one the tribes of the Northwest and of the Great Plains were forced—either through armed conflict or signed treaties—to give up their territories to the U.S. government. The tribes were often relocated onto cramped reservations, on land so poor that no white settlers wanted it.

**D**

This part of Unit Four includes a variety of selections to give you an idea of what was lost and gained during this dramatic episode in

---

# Voices
## *from the* TIMES

No white person or persons shall be permitted to settle upon or occupy any portion of the territory, or without the consent of the Indians to pass through the same.

**Treaty of 1868**

Our land here is the dearest thing on earth to us. Men take up land and get rich on it, and it is very important for us Indians to keep it.

**White Thunder**
48th U.S. Congress, 1st session
Senate Report 283

I did not know then how much was ended. When I look back now from this high hill of my old age, I can still see the butchered women and children lying heaped and scattered all along the crooked gulch as plain as when I saw them with eyes still young. And I can see that something else died there in the bloody mud, and was buried in the blizzard. A people's dream died there. It was a beautiful dream.

**Black Elk**
recalling the Battle of Wounded Knee
in *Black Elk Speaks*

HISTORICAL BACKGROUND    **633**

---

## Making Connections

### History

**A** The canvas-topped Conestoga wagon, manufactured in Lancaster County, Pennsylvania, remained in steady use from 1750 until the completion of the railroad in the mid-1850s. Even after the railroad was completed, however, poor settlers continued to travel in the swaying wooden vehicles, which were usually hitched to four or six horses or oxen.

### Literature

**B** Among the sodbusters were women who kept journals and wrote letters home. They recorded their experiences fording streams, observing the beauty of the Rocky Mountains, and having to move on with the wagon train without children who had wandered off or been killed by animals. They also recorded their day-to-day struggles to find dry fuel, to cook under their wagons during rainstorms, and to endure floods, swarming insects, accidents, and disease.

### Sociology

**C** Former slaves, disillusioned by the failure of Reconstruction in the South, were among the thousands of pioneers who looked to the Great Plains for a better life. These African-American pioneers, known as Exodusters, homesteaded primarily in Kansas.

### History

**D** One of the most destructive experiments concerning Native Americans was conducted by Captain R. H. Pratt in the 1880s. He took Native American children away from their families and sent them to a training school in Carlisle, Pennsylvania, to teach them to live in the white world. The graves on the school grounds testify to the difficulties the Sioux, Apache, Ponca, Cheyenne, and others had in acclimatizing themselves to white culture, religion, and language.

---

**VOICES FROM THE TIMES**

**Ask: What do these quotations say about the role of the land in the lives of Native Americans?**

**Possible Responses:** that it is a source of power and authority and that it is crucial to their survival as a people and as a culture

**Ask: What do you think is the dream referred to by Black Elk?**

**Possible Responses:** the dream of the Native Americans to live peacefully on their own land and under their traditional laws; the dream of the

people to co-exist with white settlers; the dream of Native Americans to pass their culture and their land on to their children

**Ask: What do these quotations suggest about conflicts between Native Americans and whites?**

**Possible Responses:** that Native Americans tried valiantly to keep their land, even going through the white man's system of government to do so; that regardless of treaties, Native Americans could not keep white settlers from taking their land; that Native Americans were repeatedly wronged

**OUTLINING**

Have students create an outline of the article as a study strategy to better understand the text. Remind students to note the main ideas and supporting details of the text.

**DISCUSSING**

Encourage students to discuss this text as a class. Have them draw upon their own backgrounds to provide connection to the essay whenever possible by asking them to respond to specific issues (i.e., the forcing of Native American tribes off their territories).

**LaserLinks**
**Historical Literary Connection:**
**Tricksters and Trailblazers**
See Teacher's SourceBook p. 52 for bar codes.

---

VOICES *from the* TIMES

The dead man lay stretched out on the pool table, right in the middle of the saloon/courtroom. The grizzled old judge walked around the body as if he were measuring it for size. No one knew the dead man's name, so the judge searched his pockets for identification. He found out the man's name was O'Brien. He also found $40 and a six-shooter.

The judge stepped back and thumbed his old dusty law book, the *Revised Statutes of Texas* for 1879. After thinking about the situation for a while, he turned to the coroner's jury and the other men hanging around the saloon.

"Gentlemen," he said, "that man fell from the bridge and that's all there is about it. But there is one thing that is not so plain, and that is what was he doing with that gun? Of course he's dead and can't explain, but that ain't the fault of the law; it's his own misfortune. Justice is justice, and law is law, and as he can't offer no satisfactory explanation of the matter I shall be obliged to fine him forty dollars for carrying a concealed weapon."

Welcome to the court of Judge Roy Bean, the Law West of the Pecos. Not to mention the coroner and the best saloonkeeper. For 20 years, Roy Bean was a legend throughout the Southwest. Texas Rangers, Mexican shepherds, and New York tourists came to his combination courtroom and saloon for justice, whiskey, and entertainment. The justice and whiskey were a little on the shady side, but the entertainment was first rate.

**Paul Robert Walker**
from *Judge Roy Bean:*
*Law West of the Pecos*

634

---

American history. You'll recognize the Native American trickster tradition in the two tales "The Indian and the Hundred Cows" and "High Horse's Courting." You'll also see tricksters in the humorous excerpt from Mark Twain's autobiography and in the tale "The Notorious Jumping Frog of Calaveras County." On a more serious note, Willa Cather takes a very unromantic view of life on the plains in her story of hardship and longing, "A Wagner Matinee."

After the Civil War and by the time the West was being settled, American literature was also changing. Realism replaced romanticism as the dominant literary style, in part because people wanted to read more truthful accounts of ordinary life rather than the sentimentality of much romantic fiction. The new regional diversity that sprang up among the mining camps, cattle ranches, farming communities, and frontier towns in the West gave rise to new regional literature called local-color realism. Mark Twain, who once lived in a mining camp, was foremost among the local-color realists. Later in the century, Willa Cather carried on the spirit of local-color realism with increasing sophistication. When you read Twain and Cather, think about the difference between their writing and the writing of Poe, Hawthorne, and Thoreau, who wrote earlier in the century, and you'll understand the direction American literature was going.

## Traditions Across Time: Writing of the New West

America's unique relationship with the frontier has continued to influence our literature and character, engaging our writers and thinkers to the present day. Although the days of the "Wild West" are gone, its mythic lure of freedom remains a powerful force. Américo Paredes incorporates the trickster tradition into his modern retelling of a Mexican-American folk song, "The Legend of Gregorio Cortez."

---

**VOICES FROM THE TIMES**

**Ask: What does the anecdote about Judge Roy Bean suggest about life in the wild west?**

**Possible Responses:** that a powerful man could bend the law to suit his own purposes; that life was rough and dangerous

## The Vanishing Frontier

635

## Objectives

- understand the following literary terms:

  Regional literature

  Setting

  Local color realism

  Dialect
- analyze the relevance of setting and time frame to text's meaning
- appreciate a writer's craft
- recognize distinctive characteristics of cultures through reading

## Teaching the Lesson

In this section, students will be introduced to the role of setting in regional literature through various selections from American literature. This lesson will help students recognize the significant elements of setting and teach them how to create effective settings in their own work.

### Introducing the Concepts

Writers of regional literature throughout history have made the setting and plot of their works inseparable. They have placed their readers in the midst of their works by providing details about the location and time period, which enables the reader to visualize where the action is occurring. Authors have also used setting to convey mood to the reader. As students read the selections in this unit, have them consider the following questions:

Where and when does the story take place?

What atmosphere is created by the setting?

What is the relationship between the characters and their setting?

What stories do you know in which setting is crucial to plot? Consider films, books, and plays.

As they finish reading the selections, students can write their reactions to these questions and keep their responses in their Working Portfolios.

# LEARNING the Language of Literature

# Setting in Regional Literature

## Pride of Place

Sports fans scream for the home team; people wave flags and wear T-shirts proclaiming their allegiance to specific localities and schools. Almost everybody today exhibits some kind of pride in a specific region of the country. The same enthusiasm for place can be found in the regional writing that sprang up in the United States during the second half of the 19th century and has continued to the present day.

## The Growth of Regional Literature

**Regional literature** arose from an effort to represent accurately the speech, manners, habits, history, folklore, and beliefs of people in specific geographical areas. Regionalism has been part of American literature from the beginning. Washington Irving's tales of Dutch New York and Nathaniel Hawthorne's stories of Puritan New England are just two examples. After the Civil War, however, when realism became the dominant literary movement, writers began to focus on the lives of ordinary people and to avoid the supernaturalism and sentimentality found in much of the work of Irving, Hawthorne, and Poe.

A factor that contributed to the growth of regional writing was the boom in publishing in the late 1800s. Popular magazines started up all over the United States to meet the demand for news about the rest of the country. Mark Twain's "The Notorious Jumping Frog of Calaveras County" was first published in a New York magazine and became an immediate sensation.

## The Importance of Setting

The effectiveness of regional writing depends to a large extent on the depiction of setting. Setting—

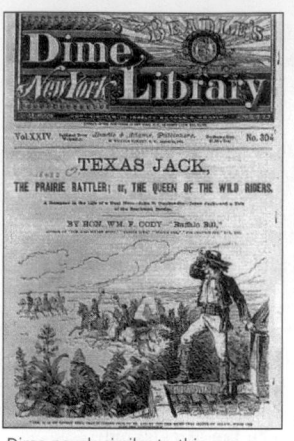

Dime novels similar to this one became popular in the late 1800s.

basically, the time and place in which a story's events occur—includes several key elements:

- Geographical location and physical features—such as a river, a camp, a house, or a car (Remember how important the car is in Flannery O'Connor's "The Life You Save May Be Your Own"?)
- The time in which the events are embedded—a season of the year or a historical period (What would *The Crucible* be without its historical setting?)
- The jobs and daily activities of the characters (In Faulkner's "A Rose for

## Local Color Realism

In 1868, a popular story about the California gold rush—Bret Harte's "The Luck of Roaring Camp"—launched a specific form of regional writing called **local color realism.** Mark Twain, with his memorable

*The Jolly Flatboatmen in Port,* (1857), George Caleb Bingham.

characters, was a master of local color. Other local color realists at this time include Joel Chandler Harris in the South and Sarah Orne Jewett in New England. Later regional writers, such as Willa Cather, William Faulkner, and Flannery O'Connor, developed sophisticated ways of making universal statements about the human condition while focusing on the local and the particular.

### Presenting the Concepts

Read through the strategies aloud or project them on a transparency. Select a popular film and model how to use the strategies to analyze the work. Ask students how they would analyze the relationship between the setting and the meaning of a text.

Emily," the disappearance of students for Miss Emily's china-painting lessons tells a lot about the changing lives of Southern women after the Civil War.)

- The culture of the characters, including their religious and moral beliefs and the social and economic conditions in which they live (Think about the cultural differences between the characters in Hawthorne's "Dr. Heidegger's Experiment" and those in "The Life You Save May Be Your Own.")

## A Closer Look

Two means of conveying setting that are commonly found in regional literature are (1) dialects—distinctive forms of language spoken in particular areas or by particular groups of people—and (2) detailed descriptions of location. Take a look at the beginning of Simon Wheeler's rambling tale in Twain's "The Notorious Jumping Frog of Calaveras County":

> "Rev. Leonidas W. H'm, Reverend Le— Well, there was a feller here once by the name of Jim Smiley, in the winter of '49—or maybe it was the spring of '50—I don't recollect exactly, somehow, though what makes me think it was one or the other is because I remember the big flume warn't finished when he first come to the camp. . . ."
>
> —Mark Twain, "The Notorious Jumping Frog of Calaveras County"

The pronunciations indicated by the spellings *feller* and *warn't*, the expression "I don't recollect," and the use of *come* rather than *came* all contribute to the regional flavor of the piece.

**YOUR TURN** Rewrite the passage in the dialect of another region or in the sort of language you speak with your friends. How does the change in dialect alter the story?

Now look at this description from Cather's "A Wagner Matinee," in which the narrator recalls the Nebraska farm where he grew up:

> I saw again the tall, naked house on the prairie, black and grim as a wooden fortress; the black pond where I had learned to swim, its margin pitted with sun-dried cattle tracks; the rain gullied clay banks about the naked house, the four dwarf ash seedlings where the dish-cloths were always hung to dry before the kitchen door.
>
> —Willa Cather, "A Wagner Matinee"

Notice the lack of color and the harshness of the setting described: both the landscape and the evidences of human habitation are black, pitted, and bare.

**YOUR TURN** What feeling about life on the frontier do you get from the description? How could you rewrite the passage to change that feeling?

## Strategies for Reading: Regional Literature

1. Determine what the details of **setting** reveal about the particular region and time period.
2. Notice how the **characters** exemplify the values of their particular culture or time period.
3. Think about why the story was created in the first place. What was the writer aiming at?
4. **Monitor** your reading strategies and modify them when your understanding breaks down. Remember to use the Strategies for Active Reading: **predict, visualize, connect, question, clarify,** and **evaluate.**

SETTING IN REGIONAL LITERATURE **637**

### Regional Literature Across Cultures

Writers from cultures throughout the world have produced works of literature that represent the people and characteristics of their particular region. Ask students to compare the examples below with the selections of American literature that they will be reading in this part of the unit.

### *Jude the Obscure* by Thomas Hardy (England, 1895)

During his career as a novelist and later as a poet, Hardy created an imaginary geographical area, which he called Wessex, out of his native area of Dorset in England. *Jude the Obscure* is a truly regional novel whose setting is essential to its plot and its characters. The opening scene of the novel takes place in Marygreen, a thinly disguised version of the real town of Fawley. In this case, the surname of the title character is Fawley. The novel, which was so criticized for its perceived immorality that Hardy resolved never to write fiction again, centers around the futile efforts of a poor young man to educate himself and the consequences of his common-law marriage. The time period—the 19th century—is a subtheme of the novel, as Hardy laments the disintegration of the countryside.

### *Is There Nowhere Else Where We Can Meet?* by Nadine Gordimer (South Africa, 1950)

Nadine Gordimer's two-page story about an encounter between a white woman and a black man in South Africa contains detailed descriptions of the color of the sky, the texture of the grass, the background sounds that the female character hears as she walks along, and the appearance of indigenous plants. Gordimer describes the morning as "cool" and "gray" and has her female character wear a coat with the collar turned up, setting both the season and the atmosphere. The impact of this story is heightened by the author's emphasis on the physical features of the landscape and her implicit use of the political situation in South Africa as a background for her two characters.

## OVERVIEW

### Objectives

1. understand and appreciate a *cuento*, or a **folk tale** (Literary Analysis)
2. identify characteristics of **cuentos** (Literary Analysis)
3. **determine the theme** of a *cuento* (Active Reading)

### Summary

An Indian who is a devout churchgoer hears a priest say in his sermon that if you give to God, God will return your gift a hundredfold. Taking the words literally, the Indian gives the priest his cow, expecting to receive 100 cows in return. He goes in search of them, and, finding some near the church, drives them home to his corral. Two cattle herders tell him that the cows belong to the priest, but the Indian insists that they are his. The infuriated priest confronts the Indian for taking his cows, but the Indian defends his new property with a bow and arrow, reminding the priest of the promise made in his sermon. The priest leaves, resolving to be more careful in the future about what he says in his sermons.

### Thematic Link

This folk tale, which combines elements of the Native American **trickster** tale with details about life on the **vanishing frontier**, presents a conflict that arises because of cultural differences.

### 5-Minute Warm-Up

*Daily Language SkillBuilder*

Have students **proofread** the display sentences on page 555j and write them correctly. The sentences also appear on Transparency 18 of **Grammar Transparencies and Copymasters.**

---

*"You know when you make a donation to God, He returns it a hundredfold."*

# The Indian and the Hundred Cows / El indito de las cien vacas

*Folk Tale retold by* JOSÉ GRIEGO Y MAESTAS
(hô-sě′ grě-yě′gô ē mä-ěs′täs)

*Translated by* RUDOLFO A. ANAYA (rōō-dôl′fô ä-nä′yä)

### Connect to Your Life

**Communication Breakdown** Think of a time when you misunderstood or misinterpreted something that someone told you. What do you think caused this breakdown in communication? What was the result of the misunderstanding? Jot down your thoughts about this experience.

## Build Background

**Cultural Contact** Since the earliest Spanish settlements, the Native American and Mexican populations in the Southwest had come into close contact. Before Mexico won its independence in 1821, Spain's system of Roman Catholic missions in California, New Mexico, and Colorado was staffed with Franciscan priests who tried to convert Native Americans to Catholicism and settle them on mission lands.

A conflict erupts between a fictional priest and a Native American member of his congregation in "The Indian and the Hundred Cows," published in *Cuentos: Tales from the Hispanic Southwest.* The tales in this collection were selected and adapted in Spanish by the scholar José Griego y Maestas and were translated into English by the novelist Rudolfo A. Anaya. The English version of the tale appears on page 639; the Spanish version, on page 641. Anaya wrote: "My English variations of these old, old *cuentos* are my versions. . . . I started with José Griego's adaptations from the literal transcriptions originally compiled by Juan B. Rael, and I worked from Spanish into English to suit my own rhythm."

## Focus Your Reading

**LITERARY ANALYSIS** **CUENTO** As you know, a **folk tale** is a short, simple story that is handed down, usually by word of mouth, from generation to generation. "The Indian and the Hundred Cows" is a *cuento,* a traditional folk tale that comes from the oral tradition of New Mexico and southern Colorado. Early settlers and their descendants told *cuentos* to entertain, to reinforce cultural values, and to teach traditional customs and beliefs to their children.

**ACTIVE READING** **DETERMINING THEME** Theme is the central idea or ideas that the writer wishes to share with the reader. In simple stories, such as folk tales and fables, the theme is called the **moral**—a lesson about life or about people and their actions. Sometimes the moral is directly stated at the end of the story, while in others the moral is implied. Making inferences about the significance of plot events and characters' actions can help you figure out the theme or moral.

**READER'S NOTEBOOK** In "The Indian and the Hundred Cows," you can infer the moral based on what the main characters learn when they resolve a problem. To help you discover the central theme of the story, create a diagram like the one shown, and fill it in as you read.

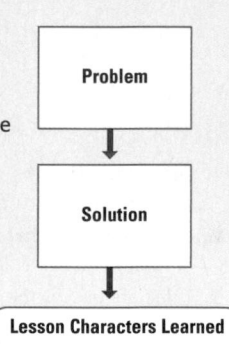

Problem

↓

Solution

↓

Lesson Characters Learned

---

## LESSON RESOURCES

**UNIT FOUR RESOURCE BOOK,** pp. 47–50

**ASSESSMENT RESOURCES**
**Formal Assessment,** p. 121
**Teacher's Guide to Assessment and Portfolio Use**
**Test Generator**

**SKILLS TRANSPARENCIES AND COPYMASTERS**
**Literary Analysis**
• Legends, Myths, and Folk Tales, T24 (for Cooperative Learning Activity, p. 643)

**Grammar**
• Independent and Subordinate Clauses, C89 (for Mini Lesson, p. 644)

**Vocabulary**
• Using a Dictionary, C54 (for Mini Lesson, p. 639)

**Writing**
• Short Story, C29 (for Writing Option 2, p. 644)

**INTEGRATED TECHNOLOGY**
**Audio Library**
**Visit our website:**
www.mcdougallittell.com

# The Indian and the Hundred Cows

translated by
rudolfo a. anaya

*In a small pueblo there once lived an Indian who was so devoted to the church he never missed mass on Sunday. One Sunday, during his homily,[1] the priest said:*

"Have charity, my children. Give alms[2] to the poor. If you expect God's help it is necessary that you also help the church. You know that when you make a donation to God, He returns it a hundredfold."

The Indian, who was listening carefully, decided to give a cow that he had to the priest. That afternoon he brought his cow to the church and told the priest, "Padre,[3] I have brought you my cow so that God will give me a hundred cows."

"Yes, yes, my son," the priest answered. "Have faith in God and He will repay your gift." Then the priest took the cow and added it to his own herd.

The Indian returned home very satisfied and he began to build a large corral where he could keep his hundred cows when they arrived. When he finished his corral he sat down to wait for the cows. He waited some time and then thought, "Perhaps the cows don't come on their own, maybe I should go for them." So he set out to look for his promised hundred cows. Near the church he came upon a large herd which he drove home and locked securely in his corral.

Later that afternoon the two *vaqueros*[4] who took care of the priest's herd rode to the Indian's home.

"Why do you have these cattle locked up?" they asked gruffly. "Have they done some damage?"

"No, they haven't done any damage," the Indian answered. "I have them locked up because they're mine. I gave the priest a cow and he promised me God would give me a hundred, and here they are!"

"These are the priest's cattle, not yours," the cowboys answered.

"No, these are mine because he promised me a hundred for one!" the Indian insisted.

The cowboys returned to tell the priest what had happened. When he heard the news the

---

1. **homily** (hŏm′ə-lē): sermon.
2. **alms:** money or goods given as charity to the poor.
3. **Padre** (pä′drĕ) *Spanish:* Father; used as a form of address for a priest.
4. **vaqueros** (vä-kĕ′rôs) *Spanish:* cowboys.

**Literary Analysis** CUENTO

What clues in the Indian's behavior suggest that this story is a folk tale?

**Possible Response:** The Indian believes that a magical event will happen (that he will receive 100 cows from God) and has prepared for it by building the corral. Magical events often occur in folk tales, and the characters often believe in magic.

 Use **Unit Four Resource Book,** p. 49 for additional support.

**Active Reading** DETERMINING THEME

**A** Remind students that a moral is a lesson about life or about people and their actions. Ask students to draw inferences about the moral of the story from this exchange between the priest and the Indian.

**Possible Response:** Both believe they are right, but the Indian has a defense for his actions—that the priest promised something in church and therefore it must be so. The moral might be to be careful about word choice—the listener might interpret literally expressions used figuratively.

**B** Have students analyze the last sentence. What does the priest do and think? Have students summarize the moral of the story.

**Possible Response:** The priest admits defeat and goes home. He realizes that the Indian got the better of him, and he knows that his own words were to blame. The moral is to be careful what you promise because you will be held to it.

 Use **Unit Four Resource Book,** p. 48 for additional support.

*Castle Mission,* John Runne. Copyright © John Runne, Evergreen Art Company, Evergeen, Colorado.

priest became very angry. He got on his mule and the three rode to the Indian's home. When they arrived at the corral the Indian was sitting by the gate, his bow and quiver of arrows ready.

"Why have you locked up my cattle in your corral!" the priest shouted. "Is this the way you show your gratitude?"

"But these are my cows," the Indian answered.

"And who gave them to you?"

**A** "You did. You said at mass whoever gave one cow would get a hundred in return!"

**1** "That's not what I meant, you thief!" the priest cried angrily. "You are a thief and you must turn my cattle loose." He got down from his mule to open the gate but stopped when he **2** saw the Indian put an arrow to his bow.

"Padre, if you dare touch the lock I will stick this arrow into your heart. Then the devils in hell will give you a hundred more."

The priest backed away. He realized the Indian meant to make him keep the promise he had made in church, and there was nothing he could do. So he got on his mule and quietly rode **B** home, reminding himself to be more careful with what he said in his sermons. ❖

## Teaching Options

 **Mini Lesson** **Speaking and Listening**

**TELLING STORIES: Prepare** Have students give group storytelling performances of "The Indian and the Hundred Cows." Each group should work together to decide how to divide up the storytelling. For example, students could divide the story into speaking parts: the Indian, the priest, the vaqueros, and the narrator. Instruct them to focus on tone of voice, volume, and effective pacing—not too fast, not too slow—when speaking. Also, speaking distinctly, staying in character, using pauses for emphasis, and addressing the audience directly are important storytelling skills. As a class,

draw up evaluative criteria and draft a checklist for students to use in assessing other groups' performances.

**Present** Have students practice presenting their interpretations of the story. Individual members can evaluate each other's performance. Then have the groups give their performances. Finally, have the class evaluate each group's performances, identifying strong points and areas for improvement.

 **BLOCK SCHEDULING** This activity is particularly well-suited for longer class periods.

# EL INDITO de LAS CIEN VACAS

## iNTERPRETADO POR JOSÉ GRIEGO Y MAESTAS

*Habia un indio del pueblo muy devoto que no faltaba a misa nunca. Y un domingo en el sermón que les echó el padre, les dijo:*

"Hagan caridades, hijos. Den limosna. Miren que para que Dios les ayude, es menester que ustedes también le den a la iglesia, porque han de saber que el que le hace una donación a Dios, Dios le devuelve ciento por uno."

El indito, que estaba escuchando, de una vez intentó traerle al padre una vaquita que tenía. En la tarde le trujo la vaquita y le dijo, "Tata padre, aquí te traigo esta vaquita para que Dios me de cien por una vaquita."

"Sí, sí, hijo. Ten fe en que Dios te va a recompensar esta limosna."

El indito se volvió a su casa muy satisfecho y empezó a hacer un corral grande para cuando le vinieran las cien vacas. Acabó su corral y se puso a esperar las vacas. El miraba para todos rumbos a ver por donde venían y viendo que no venían, ya se puso en camino a buscarlas. Pensó, "Quizás las vacas no venir solas. Quizás yo ir por ellas." Pues el primer hatajo de vacas que encontró lo arreó para su corral y lo encerró y atrincó bien la puerta.

EL INDITO DE LAS CIEN VACAS **641**

**Literary Analysis** CUENTO

Ask your students how, even if they cannot read and interpret the Spanish version, they might infer that it is a folk tale or *cuento*.

**Possible Response:** The length is short. Also, the last paragraph, which is brief and set off from the rest of the story, might state the moral.

**Reading Skills and Strategies: COMPARING**

Direct students' attention to the last sentence on page 641. Tell them that the word *vaca* means "cow." Then ask them to find the corresponding sentence in the English version and to infer the meaning of *hatajo*. Then ask any Spanish speakers to translate the sentence and point out any differences between the two versions.

**Possible Response:** *Hatajo* must mean "herd." The corresponding sentence is the following: "Near the church he came upon a large herd which he drove home and locked securely in his corral" (page 639). The Spanish version can be translated literally as "He drove home the first herd of cattle that he found, enclosed them, and locked the door well." The Spanish version does not state that the Indian was near the church.

Detail of *Castle Mission*, John Runne.

Más tarde cayeron los que cuidaban las vacas y eran de tata padre las vacas y le dijeron al indio:

"¿Por qué tienes estas vacas encerradas? ¿Qué te hicieron daño?"

"No, no me hicieron daño, pero yo le di a tata padre mi vaquita y él me prometió que Dios me daría cien, y estas son."

"Estas son del padre y no tuyas," le decían los vaqueros.

"No son. Estas son mías porque él me prometió darme el ciento por uno."

Los vaqueros se fueron a avisarle al padre. Luego el padre se enojó, montó en su mula y se fueron los tres junto. Cuando llegaron al corral de las vacas, ya el indito estaba allí en la puerta con su arco y su carcaje.

"Pero, indio grosero, ¿por qué tienes mis vacas encerradas aquí?"

"Porque estas son mías, tata padre."

"¿Quién te las dio?"

"Tú me las distes. Tú decir allá en misa que el que te diera una vaca, tú le dabas cien."

"Pero indio embustero, tú eres un ladrón y estas vacas voy a echarlas." El padre se apeó a abrir la puerta y el indito puso una flecha en su arco.

"Tata padre, si tú mueves una tranca, te ensarto esta flecha en el mero corazón."

"No, no, hijo, con las armas no se juega. Si así quieres, está bien."

**Pues** le dejó el padre las vacas al indio y se fue el padre muy callado a su casa, recordando que en otra ocasión, valía más escoger sus palabras con cuidado. ❖

# Teaching Options

✓ **Assessment** Informal Assessment

**MAKING A JUDGMENT** Students can informally assess their own understanding of the folk tale by pretending to be a judge who must decide the case between the priest and the Indian. Students should write out their judgments, deciding who should get the cows based on their understanding of the theme (moral) and purpose of the *cuento*. Students should include details from the *cuento* to support their judgments.

**RUBRIC**

**3** **Full Accomplishment** Response includes a carefully written judgment that reflects the *cuento*'s theme, or moral, and is supported by a retelling of the events from a neutral party's point of view.

**2** **Substantial Accomplishment** Response includes a judgment that somewhat reflects the theme or moral of the *cuento* and provides some supporting details.

**1** **Little or Partial Accomplishment** Response states a judgment that either does not reflect the theme of the *cuento* or does not provide relevant details from the *cuento*.

# *Thinking* through the LITERATURE

## Connect to the Literature

**1. What Do You Think?**
Did you enjoy this *cuento*? Share your opinion with classmates.

> **Comprehension Check**
> • What misunderstanding arises between the priest and the Indian?
> • What does the Indian do when a hundred cows don't show up?
> • What does the Indian threaten to do if the priest opens up the gate?

## Think Critically

**2.** Should the priest have let the Indian keep the hundred cows? Give reasons for your answer.

**3.** Why do you think the Indian and the priest misunderstand one another?

 **THINK ABOUT**
> • what the priest means when he tells the churchgoers that God returns gifts a hundredfold
> • what makes the Indian believe he can take the cows

**4.** **ACTIVE READING** **DETERMINING THEME** Review the diagram you made earlier that showed how plot events point to the theme. What do you think is the moral, or **theme,** of this *cuento*? Is the moral a guiding principle that might apply to most people's lives? Why or why not?

## Extend Interpretations

**5. Comparing Texts** The two Native American Coyote stories you read in Unit One were trickster tales. Would you say that "The Indian and the Hundred Cows" is a trickster tale in the same way that the Coyote stories are? Explain your opinion.

**6. The Writer's Style** Rudolfo A. Anaya, the translator of this tale, retold the *cuentos* in written form and then translated them into English to suit his own "rhythm." What do you think might be gained or lost through this process? If you know some Spanish, evaluate how Anaya's English version of "The Indian and the Hundred Cows" differs from the Spanish.

**7. Connect to Life** At the heart of this *cuento* is a misunderstanding that arises because of differences between cultures. What cultural differences might cause misunderstandings among people who live in your community? Was the misunderstanding you described in the Connect to Your Life activity on page 638 the result of cultural differences?

## Literary Analysis

**CUENTO**  Folk tales, such as this *cuento,* often serve to teach family obligations or societal values. First brought to the southwestern part of the United States by Spanish and Mexican settlers, *cuentos* were further shaped and influenced by the landscape and by Native American cultures in this area. By reading *cuentos* such as "The Indian and the Hundred Cows," you can learn about the culture of this region.

**Cooperative Learning Activity** Meet with a small group and hold a panel discussion in which you address these questions about "The Indian and the Hundred Cows":
• What did you learn about the frontier Southwest, where the tale originated?
• What values do you think this tale might teach?
• Are there tales that reveal the ways of living or the values of your community?

---

## Connect to the Literature

**1. What Do You Think?**
Have students cite specific lines to support their opinion.

**Comprehension Check**
• The Indian literally interprets the priest's homily about getting one hundredfold for whatever you give.
• He goes looking for them and finds the priest's herd.
• He threatens to shoot an arrow into the priest's heart.

> Use Selection Quiz
> **Unit Four Resource Book,** p. 50.

## Think Critically

**2.** Possible Responses: Yes, he should have kept his word; no, he should have given the Indian back his own cow because the others rightfully belonged to the priest.

**3.** Possible Responses: The Indian is accustomed to taking what people say literally; he respects the priest as an authoritative interpreter of his faith; the priest is only speaking figuratively.

**4.** Possible Responses: Be careful what you say; be sure that people keep their word; be fair in your dealings. The moral has universal application.

## Literary Analysis

**Cuento** Possible Responses: The Southwest frontier was a challenging environment both physically and socially; the tale teaches the values of honesty, courage, and justice; responses to the last question will vary. Suggest that students share tales from their neighbors, families, or friends and think about what they reveal about the way of life or values of their community.

---

## Extend Interpretations

**Comparing Texts** Some students may argue that the Indian in this *cuento* does not deliberately intend to trick anyone. He is not devious, but devout and trusting.

**Writer's Style** Invite students to speculate about what is lost and gained in retelling stories in general. They may suggest that details may be lost or changed, but that frequently the story gains the unique style of the particular teller. Even students who have not studied Spanish may learn from a comparative reading of the two versions—for example, the second paragraph has changed little, while the last paragraph is considerably changed.

**Connect to Life** Students should support their answers with specific examples.

## Writing Options

1. **Sermon on Charity** Encourage students to match the tone and style of the priest's original homily. Their speeches may reflect what the priest has learned about values such as honesty as well as about the understanding of figurative language. **To make this assignment more challenging,** have students deliver their sermons to the class, reminding them to model their tone, volume, and speaking style according to their interpretation of the priest's character. They should be able to justify their choice of verbal and nonverbal performance techniques by referring to their interpretations of the text.

2. **Comic Tale** Remind students to write a simple story with dramatic events, interesting characters, and effective dialogue. Encourage students to use the folk tale as a model of handling humor; it is often effective to present a humorous story in a straight-forward way. **To get students started on this activity,** have them work in groups to list examples of figurative speech and how each could be misconstrued.

## Inquiry & Research

**Translation from Spanish To make this assignment easier,** have students work in groups, and assign each group different paragraphs. Then, as a class, compile a list of words that share a Latin root.

## Writing Options

1. **Sermon on Charity** Imagine that the priest again speaks to churchgoers about the importance of charity when he delivers his next homily, on the Sunday after the incident in the story. Write part of the sermon he might give that day.

2. **Comic Tale** Draft a humorous folk tale in which a figurative statement is taken literally. If the misunderstanding you described in the Connect to Your Life activity on page 638 is applicable here, you might use it as the basis for your folk tale. Place your story in your **Working Portfolio.**

## Activities & Explorations

**Mural Art** Working with a small group, create a mural, a traditional Mexican art form, that depicts a scene from this *cuento.* Paint the images on oversized sheets of paper. Tape the completed mural to a wall in the classroom.

## Inquiry & Research

**Translations from Spanish** Some words in English are similar to Spanish words. These words—such as *Indian* and *indio, deity* and *Dios*—often have common roots that are based on words with Latin origins.

Choose five words from the Spanish version of "The Indian and the Hundred Cows," and use an English-Spanish dictionary to translate them. Then make a chart showing each Spanish word and its English equivalent. If you can think of any related English words that seem to share a common Latin root with the Spanish word, add them to the chart, as in the example shown.

| Spanish Word | English Equivalent | From Common Root |
|---|---|---|
| ciento | hundred | cent, century, centennial |

**Building Vocabulary**
For an in-depth lesson on root words, see page 444.

## Rudolfo A. Anaya
1937–

**Other Works**
*Bless Me, Ultima*
*Heart of Aztlán*
*Tortuga*
*Alburquerque*

**Celebrating the Past** Rudolfo A. Anaya, one of the most widely read Mexican-American writers in the United States, was born, raised, and educated in New Mexico. In his novels, short stories, plays, and poetry, he draws on the rich culture and history of his native Southwest and on the myths and legends of the Spanish *cuentos.* As Anaya has observed, "each community has art to offer, and now we've come to a place in American history where we celebrate that." Until his retirement in 1993, Anaya taught creative writing and literature at the University of New Mexico.

## José Griego y Maestas

**An Ear for Language** José Griego y Maestas adapted "The Indian and the Hundred Cows" from the original Spanish version gathered by Juan B. Rael from Southwestern storytellers. Griego, who received his master's degree in Spanish literature from the University of New Mexico, has taught at the College of Santa Fe. An expert in the field of bilingual education, he has directed and administered New Mexico's bilingual education program. Griego has also served as the director of the Guadalupe Historic Foundation in Santa Fe.

## Teaching Options

**Mini Lesson** ## Grammar

**INDEPENDENT AND SUBORDINATE CLAUSES**
**Instruction** Remind students that a clause contains a subject and a verb. There are two types of clauses, independent and subordinate. An independent clause can stand alone as a sentence, and a subordinate clause cannot. Display the following sentence and have students identify the subordinate and independent clauses.

While the Indian listened carefully, the priest preached his sermon. (subordinate—*While*

the Indian listened carefully; independent—*the priest preached his sermon*)
**Exercises** In each sentence, have students identify each clause as subordinate or independent.

1. In the story, the Indian takes the priest's words literally because he has great faith.
   **Answer:** independent—*the Indian takes the priest's words literally;* subordinate—*because he has great faith*

2. When a story is told orally over generations, it changes.
   **Answer:** independent—*it changes;* subordinate—*When a story is told orally over generations*

 Use **Grammar Transparencies and Copymasters,** p. 89.

Use McDougal Littell's *Language Network,* Chapter 3, for more instruction and practice in clauses.

# High Horse's Courting *from* Black Elk Speaks

*Folk Tale by* BLACK ELK, *told through* JOHN G. NEIHARDT

**Connect to Your Life**

**For Richer or for Poorer** In a small group, share ideas about how important wealth or earning ability is in courtship. Do you believe money should be an important consideration in deciding whom to marry? Do you think some parents would have different ideas than you and your classmates have? Share your group's ideas with the rest of the class.

## Build Background

**Sioux Courtship** Black Elk was an Oglala Sioux medicine man who was born in the 19th century, before his people were driven from their lands in the northern Great Plains onto reservations. "High Horse's Courting" is a story that Black Elk learned from Watanye, an older member of his tribe, and later passed on to Nebraska writer John G. Neihardt, who preserved it in the book *Black Elk Speaks.* The story deals with courtship in the context of traditional Sioux beliefs and customs. Usually, before marrying, a Sioux man had to prove himself in war or hunting. Having many horses increased a man's status, and a man's offer of horses to a woman's family signaled a marriage proposal. If the horses were accepted, the wedding would take place a few days later.

## Focus Your Reading

**LITERARY ANALYSIS** **ORAL LITERATURE** Folk tales, fables, myths, legends, chants, and oral histories are examples of **oral literature**— literature that is passed from one generation to another by performance or word of mouth. As you read "High Horse's Courting" from *Black Elk Speaks,* notice words and phrases that sound like conversational speech. By giving voice to their cultural heritage, storytellers like Black Elk keep the past alive.

**ACTIVE READING** **IDENTIFYING AUTHOR'S PURPOSE** Black Elk explained one of his purposes in telling his oral stories to John G. Neihardt: "There is so much to teach you. What I know was given to me for men and it is true and it is beautiful." When speakers and writers communicate, they have different **purposes,** or goals, in mind—for example, to inform, to entertain, to persuade, or to express feelings. A reading selection, such as Black Elk's story, may have more than one purpose.

**READER'S NOTEBOOK** To help identify the various purposes of "High Horse's Courting," fill in a questionnaire like the following as you read. Jot down reasons to support your responses.

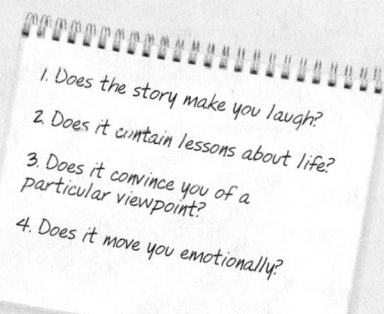

1. Does the story make you laugh?
2. Does it contain lessons about life?
3. Does it convince you of a particular viewpoint?
4. Does it move you emotionally?

**Objectives**
1. appreciate a Sioux **folk tale (Literary Analysis)**
2. understand and appreciate **oral literature (Literary Analysis)**
3. identify author's purpose (Active Reading)

**Summary**
Black Elk begins by describing love and courtship among members of his tribe. He then tells the story of High Horse, a young man who is lovesick over a beautiful girl. High Horse offers the girl's father two horses, then four horses, in exchange for his daughter, but the father refuses. High Horse then makes two attempts to steal the girl from her tepee at night, but both attempts fail. Dejected, High Horse leaves with his friend to go on the warpath together, and they steal an entire herd of horses from a Crow camp. With this herd of horses as proof of his manhood, High Horse is allowed to marry the girl.

**Thematic Link**
The folk tale recalls rituals of courtship and marriage in the Sioux tradition and culture, which **vanished** as white settlers pushed the **frontier** through Native American lands. This written record of Black Elk's oral story incorporates **trickster** humor as a young man attempts to steal the girl he loves.

### 5-Minute Warm-Up

*Daily Language SkillBuilder*

Have students **proofread** the display sentences on page 555j and write them correctly. The sentences also appear on Transparency 18 of **Grammar Transparencies and Copymasters.**

## LESSON RESOURCES

## Reading and Analyzing

### Active Reading
**IDENTIFYING AUTHOR'S PURPOSE**

 Remind students that folk stories commonly serve multiple purposes—especially to entertain and to inform and instruct. Have students analyze the opening line of the story and discuss what purpose(s) it reveals for Black Elk to tell the story.

**Possible Response:** The first line of the story, "You know, in the old days," indicates that Black Elk wants to inform listeners about times past, and to instruct by passing down lessons learned from the past. His purpose is also to record the way of life of the Sioux, which he saw was disappearing forever.

Use **Unit Four Resource Book** p. 52 for more practice.

### Literary Analysis  ORAL LITERATURE

 Have students analyze the paragraph to find words, phrases, sentence structures, and other aspects that indicate that the story has been spoken.

**Possible Response:** Black Elk's run-on sentences and use of the present tense to describe his feelings create a loose, conversational tone. It seems that Black Elk is stringing together ideas as they come to him, which is typical of conversation.

Use **Unit Four Resource Book** p. 53 for more practice.

# HIGH HORSE'S COURTING

## Teaching Options

### BLOCK SCHEDULING: MANAGING TIME

**If your schedule requires that you cover the lesson objectives in a shorter time, use . . .**
- Preparing to Read, p. 645
- Thinking Through the Literature, p. 652

**If you want to take advantage of longer class time, use . . .**
- TE Teaching Options: Vocabulary Strategy, p. 647; Viewing and Representing, p. 650, Cross-Curricular Link, p. 651; Standardized Test Practice, p. 653
- Choices & Challenges, p. 653

**Black Elk told through John C. Neihardt**

**YOU** KNOW, IN THE OLD DAYS, IT WAS NOT SO VERY EASY TO GET A GIRL WHEN

you wanted to be married. Sometimes it was hard work for a young man and he had to stand a great deal. Say I am a young man and I have seen a young girl who looks so beautiful to me that I feel all sick when I think about her. I cannot just go and tell her about it and then get married if she is willing. I have to be a very sneaky fellow to talk to her at all, and after I have managed to talk to her, that is only the beginning.

Probably for a long time I have been feeling sick about a certain girl because I love her so much, but she will not even look at me, and her parents keep a good watch over her. But I keep feeling worse and worse all the time; so maybe I sneak up to her tepee in the dark and wait until she comes out. Maybe I just wait there all night and don't get any sleep at all and she does not come out. Then I feel sicker than ever about her.

Maybe I hide in the brush by a spring where she sometimes goes to get water, and when she comes by, if nobody is looking, then I jump out and hold her and just make her listen to me. If she likes me too, I can tell that from the way she acts, for she is very bashful and maybe will not say a word or even look at me the first time. So I let her go, and then maybe I sneak around until I can see her father alone, and I tell him how many horses I can give him for his beautiful girl, and by now I am feeling so sick that maybe I would give him all the horses in the world if I had them.

Well, this young man I am telling about was called High Horse, and there was a girl in the village who looked so beautiful to him that he was just sick all over from thinking about her so much and he was getting sicker all the time. The girl was very shy, and her parents thought a great deal of her because they were not young anymore and this was the only child they had. So they watched her all day long, and they fixed it so that she would be safe at night, too, when they were asleep. They thought so much of her that they had made a rawhide bed for her to sleep in, and after they knew that High Horse was sneaking around after her, they took rawhide thongs and tied the girl in bed at night so that nobody could steal her when they were asleep, for they were not sure but that their girl might really want to be stolen.

*Wild Horses of Nevada* (1927), Maynard Dixon. Oil, 44″ × 50″, courtesy of the William A. Karges Family Trust.

HIGH HORSE'S COURTING  **647**

## Customizing Instruction

### Students Acquiring English
Discuss with students the meaning of the word *courting* in the title of the story. Explain that *courting* means "doing things in order to win someone's affection and love." A more particular meaning is "seeking to win a pledge of marriage from someone," as in this story. Have students give examples of courting customs from their home cultures.

Use **Spanish Study Guide** for additional support, pp. 157–159.

### Less Proficient Readers
Tell students that one way folk stories affect their audiences is by addressing universal problems and feelings, so that the listener or reader can identify with the characters.

**Set a Purpose** Have students read to find descriptions of feelings that are universal, such as the lovesickness, confusion, and awkwardness of someone who is courting. Have them think about how these descriptions affect their response to the story.

### Gifted and Talented
Have students discuss how this story would be different if narrated by one of its characters, rather than by an outside observer.

### Students Acquiring English
**1** Be sure students know that *rawhide* is untanned leather made from the skin of animals and that *thongs* are narrow strips of leather like shoelaces.

---

 **Vocabulary Strategy**

**USING REFERENCE MATERIALS: SPECIALIZED DICTIONARIES Instruction** Being able to use reference materials such as specialized dictionaries helps students determine precise word meanings and usage as well as understand historical references in literature. Specialized dictionaries include subject area dictionaries, specialized language dictionaries (for such things as slang and clichés) and foreign language dictionaries.

**Application** Have students use a specialized dictionary to look up information about the two other Native American tribes mentioned in the story, Crows and Lakotas. Ask them to report on what kinds of information the dictionary provides, as well as what they learn about the two tribes and their relationships.

Use **Vocabulary Transparencies and Copymasters**, p. 56.

**A** Oral literature is passed from one generation to another by performance or word of mouth. Ask students to give examples of words or phrases that seem to indicate that the narrator is speaking out loud to an audience.

**Possible Response:** The interjection *well* and the phrase *of course* indicate direct speaking to an audience.

**Reading Skills and Strategies: EVALUATE**

**B** Ask students to evaluate whether they think the description of High Horse is realistic or exaggerated and to support their answers with textual evidence and personal experience. How do they think the description helps the storyteller achieve his purpose?

**Possible Response:** The description is exaggerated. High Horse is described as walking "with his head hanging down as though he might just fall down and die any time." This is not a realistic response from someone, even if he is lovesick. The exaggeration helps to entertain with humor and to capture the reader's interest through empathy with the character's misery.

**Literary Analysis: CHARACTERIZATION**

**C** Point out the repetition of High Horse's words each time his friend has a new plan. How does this technique serve to characterize High Horse?

**Possible Response:** The repetition of an idea or thought is common in folk tales and reinforces the actions and attributes of a character so that readers will remember him or her. In this case, High Horse's refrain emphasizes that he is fixated on a single goal and that he is willing to do anything to achieve it.

---

**A** Well, after High Horse had been sneaking around a good while and hiding and waiting for the girl and getting sicker all the time, he finally caught her alone and made her talk to him. Then he found out that she liked him maybe a little. Of course this did not make him feel well. It made him sicker than ever, but now he felt as brave as a bison bull, and so he went right to her father and said he loved the girl so much that he would give two good horses for her—one of them young and the other one not so very old.

**1** But the old man just waved his hand, meaning for High Horse to go away and quit talking foolishness like that.

High Horse was feeling sicker than ever about it; but there was another young fellow who said he would loan High Horse two ponies and when he got some more horses, why, he could just give them back for the ones he had borrowed.

Then High Horse went back to the old man and said he would give four horses for the girl—two of them young and the other two not hardly old at all. But the old man just waved his hand and would not say anything.

So High Horse sneaked around until he could talk to the girl again, and he asked her to run away with him. He told her he thought he would just fall over and die if she did not. But she said she would not do that; she wanted to be bought like a fine woman. You see she thought a great deal of herself too.

**B** That made High Horse feel so very sick that he could not eat a bite, and he went around with his head hanging down as though he might just fall down and die any time.

Red Deer was another young fellow, and he and High Horse were great comrades, always doing things together. Red Deer saw how High Horse was acting, and he said: "Cousin, what is the matter? Are you sick in the belly? You look as though you were going to die."

Then High Horse told Red Deer how it was, and said he thought he could not stay alive much longer if he could not marry the girl pretty quick.

Red Deer thought awhile about it, and then he said: "Cousin, I have a plan, and if you are man enough to do as I tell you, then everything will be all right. She will not run away with you; her old man will not take four horses; and four horses are all you can get. You must steal her and run away with her. Then afterwhile you can come back and the old man cannot do anything because she will be your woman. Probably she wants you to steal her anyway." **2**

**SO** THEY PLANNED WHAT HIGH HORSE HAD TO DO, AND HE SAID HE loved the girl so much that he was man enough to do anything Red Deer or anybody else could think up.

So this is what they did.

That night late they sneaked up to the girl's tepee and waited until it sounded inside as though the old man and the old woman and the girl were sound asleep. Then High Horse crawled under the tepee with a knife. He had to cut the rawhide thongs first, and then Red Deer, who was pulling up the stakes around that side of the tepee, was going to help drag the girl outside and gag her. After that, High Horse could put her across his pony in front of him and hurry out of there and be happy all the rest of his life.

When High Horse had crawled inside, he felt so nervous that he could hear his heart drumming, and it seemed so loud he felt sure it would 'waken the old folks. But it did not, and afterwhile he began cutting the thongs. Every time he cut one it made a pop and nearly scared him to death. But he was getting along all right and all the thongs were cut down as far as the girl's thighs, when he became so nervous that his knife slipped and stuck the girl. She gave a big, loud yell. Then the old folks jumped up and yelled too. By this time High Horse was outside, and he and Red Deer were running away like antelope. The old man and some other people chased the young men but they got away in the dark and nobody knew who it was. **3**

Well, if you ever wanted a beautiful girl you will know how sick High Horse was now. It was very bad the way he felt, and it looked as though

---

**Teaching Options**

**Mini Lesson** Grammar

**PHRASES AND CLAUSES Instruction** Phrases and clauses are both grammatical structures in which words function in groups, instead of just individually. Clauses contain a verb and its subject, while phrases do not contain both these elements. Phrases can act as adjectives and adverbs, modifying a noun; they can also act as nouns and verbs. Clauses can be either independent or subordinate; independent clauses can stand alone as sentences, while subordinate clauses cannot. Help students practice identifying phrases and clauses with the following example:

When High Horse crawled in the tepee, he was nervous.

Explain that the sentence contains two clauses: subordinate (*When High Horse crawled in the tepee*) and independent (*he was nervous*). It also contains a phrase, *in the tepee*.

**Exercises** Have students identify phrases and clauses in the following sentences:

**1.** In matters of the heart, people often act desperately.

**Answer:** phrase—*In matters of the heart;* clause (independent)—*people often act desperately*

he would starve even if he did not drop over dead sometime.

Red Deer kept thinking about this, and after a few days he went to High Horse and said: "Cousin, take courage! I have another plan, and I am sure, if you are man enough, we can steal her this time." And High Horse said: "I am man enough to do anything anybody can think up, if I can only get that girl."

So this is what they did.

They went away from the village alone, and Red Deer made High Horse strip naked. Then he painted High Horse solid white all over, and after that he painted black stripes all over the white and put black rings around High Horse's eyes. High Horse looked terrible. He looked so terrible that when Red Deer was through painting and took a good look at what he had done, he said it scared even him a little.

"Now," Red Deer said, "if you get caught again, everybody will be so scared they will think you are a bad spirit and will be afraid to chase you."

So when the night was getting old and everybody was sound asleep, they sneaked back to the girl's tepee. High Horse crawled in with his knife, as before, and Red Deer waited outside, ready to drag the girl out and gag her when High Horse had all the thongs cut.

High Horse crept up by the girl's bed and began cutting at the thongs. But he kept thinking, "If they see me they will shoot me because I look so terrible." The girl was restless and kept squirming around in bed, and when a thong was cut, it popped. So High Horse worked very slowly and carefully.

But he must have made some noise, for suddenly the old woman awoke and said to her old man: "Old Man, wake up! There is somebody in this tepee!" But the old man was sleepy and didn't want to be bothered. He said: "Of course there is somebody in this tepee. Go to sleep and don't bother me." Then he snored some more.

But High Horse was so scared by now that he lay very still and as flat to the ground as he could. Now, you see, he had not been sleeping very well for a long time because he was so sick about the girl. And while he was lying there waiting for the old woman to snore, he just forgot everything, even how beautiful the girl was. Red Deer, who was lying outside ready to do his part, wondered and wondered what had happened in there, but he did not dare call out to High Horse.

Afterwhile the day began to break and Red Deer had to leave with the two ponies he had staked there for his comrade and girl, or somebody would see him.

So he left.

*Home Is the Hunter* (1994), Gary Kapp. Oil, 34″ × 46″.

## Customizing Instruction

### Multiple Learning Styles
**Kinesthetic Learners**
**1** Have students read the sentence to the class while pantomiming the old man's movements.

### Students Acquiring English
**2** Explain that "to be man enough" means to be manly enough—to have the strength, courage, and other manly attributes needed to take a certain course of action. Ask students if they see any humor or irony in this statement by High Horse. Have them use the phrase in a sentence.

### Less Proficient Readers
**3** Assist students in describing the development of the plot. Draw a flow chart on the board and ask students to identify the sequence of events in the paragraph.
**Possible Response:**

### Initiating Event
**Event 1:** High Horse crawls into the tent.
**Event 2:** He cuts the thongs.
**Event 3:** He becomes nervous and sticks the girl with the knife.
**Event 4:** The girl yells.
**Event 5:** The old folks jump up and yell.
**Event 6:** High Horse and Red Deer run away.

### Final Outcome
**Event 7:** The old man and other people chase them, but they get away.

2. Black Elk's story, both entertaining and informative, describes a lost way of life.
   **Answer:** phrase—*both entertaining and informative;* clause (independent)—*Black Elk's story describes a lost way of life*
3. Tired from the loss of his people, Chief Joseph surrendered.
   **Answer:** phrase—*Tired from the loss of his people;* clause (independent)—*Chief Joseph surrendered*
4. When Black Elk describes people breaking camp to move away from an area, he paints a historically accurate picture.

**Answer:** phrase—*to move away from an area;* clauses—(subordinate) *When Black Elk describes people breaking camp to move away from an area;* (independent) *he paints a historically accurate picture*

 Use **Grammar Transparencies and Copymasters,** p. 90.

 Use McDougal Littell's *Language Network,* Chapters 2 and 3, for more instruction in phrases and clauses.

**A** Ask students what they think is the purpose of this part of Black Elk's story.

**Possible Response:** Black Elk describes the beliefs of some of the Sioux villagers about sacred beings and their powers.

### Literary Analysis ORAL LITERATURE

**B** Ask students how this passage might affect today's listener differently than it did a young Sioux listener in the 1840s. Tell students that they can recognize distinctive characteristics of cultures through reading.

**Possible Response:** The actions of High Horse and Red Deer would have impressed a Sioux audience much more than a modern audience, who might not see the valor or honor of killing the horse guard. Explain that these actions were not uncommon among warring Native American tribes and that they represented courage and skill.

### Reading Skills and Strategies: CONTRASTING

**C** Students will notice immediately that Chief Joseph's speech is a very different kind of text than "High Horse's Courting." Ask them to identify specific differences in purpose, style, and tone.

**Possible Responses:** Chief Joseph's purpose is to end a battle; his style is that of a somber speech; and his tone is resigned, heartsick, and sad. Black Elk's purposes are to entertain and to pass along cultural information; his style is that of a humorous folk tale; and his tone is light.

---

Now when it was getting light in the tepee, the girl awoke and the first thing she saw was a terrible animal, all white with black stripes on it, lying asleep beside her bed. So she screamed, and then the old woman screamed and the old man yelled. High Horse jumped up, scared almost to death, and he nearly knocked the tepee down getting out of there.

People were coming running from all over the village with guns and bows and axes, and everybody was yelling.

By now High Horse was running so fast that he hardly touched the ground at all, and he looked so terrible that the people fled from him and let him run. Some braves wanted to shoot at him, but the others said he might be some sacred being and it would bring bad trouble to kill him.

High Horse made for the river that was near, and in among the brush he found a hollow tree and dived into it. Afterwhile some braves came there and he could hear them saying that it was some bad spirit that had come out of the water and gone back in again.

That morning the people were ordered to break camp and move away from there. So they did, while High Horse was hiding in his hollow tree.

Now Red Deer had been watching all this from his own tepee and trying to look as though he were as much surprised and scared as all the others. So when the camp moved, he sneaked back to where he had seen his comrade disappear. When he was down there in the brush, he called, and High Horse answered, because he knew his friend's voice. They washed off the paint from High Horse and sat down on the river bank to talk about their troubles.

**1** High Horse said he never would go back to the village as long as he lived and he did not

*Night Horse* (1992), C. J. Wells. Oil, 70″ × 60″, courtesy of Joan Marcus Fine Art.

care what happened to him now. He said he was going to go on the war-path all by himself. Red Deer said: "No, cousin, you are not going on the war-path alone, because I am going with you."

So Red Deer got everything ready, and at night they started out on the war-path all alone. After several days they came to a Crow camp just about sundown, and when it was dark they sneaked up to where the Crow horses were grazing, killed the horse guard, who was not thinking about enemies because he thought all the Lakotas were far away, and drove off about a hundred horses.

They got a big start because all the Crow horses stampeded and it was probably morning before the Crow warriors could catch any horses to ride. Red Deer and High Horse fled with their herd three days and nights before they reached the village of their people. Then they drove the

---

## Teaching Options

 **Viewing and Representing**

*Night Horse* **by C. J. Wells**

**ART APPRECIATION** Tell students that C. J. Wells, a native of New Mexico, was raised by her grandmother after being abandoned by her parents. Part Arikara Indian, Wells is known for her fierce independence and sharp sense of humor.

**Instruction** Have students note the size of the oil painting, the positioning of the figures, and the effect the use of dark colors has on the mood. Focus student attention on the stars and horse on the cloak, and the leather horse whip in the Native American man's hair.

**Application** Have students discuss whether the horse is part of a ceremonial costume that the man is wearing or is a manifestation of the man's vision. Ask students to describe the emotional impact that Wells's painting has for them.

**Possible Responses:** Student interpretations will vary, but should incorporate elements from the painting. Students may view the horse as a symbol of the strong connection to the natural world in Native American religion and beliefs. Students may feel sadness or anger at the loss of Native American peoples and their cultures, or they may feel moved by the painting's beauty and depth.

whole herd right into the village and up in front of the girl's tepee. The old man was there, and High Horse called out to him and asked if he thought maybe that would be enough horses for his girl. The old man did not wave him away that time. It was not the horses that he wanted. What he wanted was a son who was a real man and good for something.

So High Horse got his girl after all, and I think he deserved her. ❖

# I Will Fight No More Forever

## Chief Joseph

*Below is the famous surrender speech made in 1877 by Chief Joseph of the Nez Perce (nĕz' pûrs'). In that year, Chief Joseph and his people, after being forced from their traditional lands in northeastern Oregon, had won several battles with U.S. Army forces led by General Oliver O. Howard. However, their only recourse lay in retreat. Chief Joseph and his remaining group of 750 traveled more than 1,000 miles and were only 40 miles from the Canadian border when they were surrounded by more U.S. troops. Following a five-day siege in which several chieftains were killed, including his own brother, Chief Joseph handed over his rifle.*

Tell General Howard I know his heart. What he told me before I have in my heart. I am tired of fighting. Our chiefs are killed. Looking Glass is dead. Toohoolhoolzote is dead. The old men are all dead. It is the young men who say yes or no. He who led on the young men is dead. It is cold and we have no blankets. The little children are freezing to death. My people, some of them, have run away to the hills, and have no blankets, no food; no one knows where they are—perhaps freezing to death. I want to have time to look for my children and see how many of them I can find. Maybe I shall find them among the dead. Hear me, my chiefs! I am tired; my heart is sick and sad. From where the sun now stands I will fight no more forever.

Chief Joseph. Courtesy of the Heye Foundation, National Museum of the American Indian, Smithsonian Institution (33738).

I WILL FIGHT NO MORE FOREVER **651**

---

---

**Cross Curricular Link** **History**

**THE VANISHING FRONTIER** The 1870s and 1880s were a bitter, painful time for the tribes of the Plains, as white settlers pushed westward into tribal territories. Below are some of the pivotal events in the conflict between Native Americans and the federal government.

**Key Events: 1876–1887**

- June 1876—Lieutenant Colonel George Custer and his troops are wiped out by the Sioux at the Battle of Little Bighorn in Montana.
- Autumn 1876—Overwhelmed by the full force of the U.S. Army, many Sioux surrender and agree to live on reservations; others flee to Canada.
- 1877—The Nez Perce lead a brilliant but losing campaign against federal troops, crossing 1,000 miles before Chief Joseph surrenders in Montana.
- 1887—The Dawes Act breaks up traditional Native American organizations; only those Native Americans accepting reservation land are allowed to become U.S. citizens.

## Connect to the Literature

**1. What Do You Think?**
Have students refer to their Reader's Notebooks to guide their reactions.

**Comprehension Check**
- He accidentally stabs her while cutting the thongs that bind her.
- He and Red Deer steal 100 horses from a Crow camp; his bravery impresses the girl's father.

 Use Selection Quiz
**Unit Four Resource Book,** p. 54.

## Think Critically

**2. Possible Response:** He did deserve her because he loved her enough to make many efforts to win her.

**3. Possible Responses:** The girl might have resented him for causing her to lose her self-respect, since she had wanted to be bought according to custom. Her parents and others might have seen High Horse as a proud and selfish man who acted in disregard of social standards.

**4.** Accept well-supported answers.

**5. Possible Responses:** determination, persistence, the necessity of proving oneself

## Literary Analysis

**Oral Literature** Explain to students that they do not need to memorize the words of the story, just the events they will cover in their assigned portion. Tell students to retell the story in their own words, use gestures, and vary their tone of voice. Students might find it helpful to visualize or sketch their segment of the story. Listeners should evaluate in what ways the story changed from the original to the storytelling performance.

---

## Connect to the Literature

**1. What Do You Think?**
What thoughts came to mind as you read this tale of courtship? Share your reaction with a partner.

**Comprehension Check**
- What goes wrong the first time High Horse tries to steal the girl?
- How does High Horse finally win the girl?

## Think Critically

**2.** Do you think High Horse deserved to marry the girl he loved? Give reasons for your answer.

**3.** How might things have worked out if High Horse had just stolen the girl, as he had first planned to do?

 **THINK ABOUT**
- how he and the girl might have felt about each other afterward
- how the girl's parents and others might have viewed him

**4.** **ACTIVE READING** **IDENTIFYING AUTHOR'S PURPOSE**
Based on the questionnaire you made in your **READER'S NOTEBOOK**, what do you think were Black Elk's two most important purposes for telling this story? Cite evidence to support your answer.

**5.** "He was always teaching me things," Black Elk said of Watanye, who told him this story. In your opinion, what values does "High Horse's Courting" teach?

## Extend Interpretations

**6.** **Comparing Texts** In one section of *Black Elk Speaks,* Black Elk mourns what the Sioux lost after the massacre at Wounded Knee (see quotation on page 633), much as Chief Joseph, on page 651, mourns what the Nez Perce lost in their final battle with U.S. Army forces. If you were a spiritual leader of a group, as these men were, how would you help your people survive such a defeat?

**7.** **The Writer's Style** What makes this story sound as if it were being told to someone, instead of read from a book? Support your answer with examples.

**8.** **Connect to Life** Compare and contrast the courtship customs of the Sioux with those praticed among your own circle of friends and family.

---

## Literary Analysis

**ORAL LITERATURE** "High Horse's Courting" is an example of **oral literature,** literature that is passed from one generation to another by performance or word of mouth. *Black Elk Speaks* was written primarily to record the traditional Sioux way of life that was destroyed with the coming of whites. Stories that are communicated orally are alive in a way that written stories are not. When a story is committed to paper it becomes fixed—it is set in print. In contrast, oral stories change because they are often retold in slightly different ways, depending on who the speaker is, what he or she remembers about the story, and the words he or she chooses in the retelling.

**Cooperative Learning Activity**
Divide this tale among the members of a small group of classmates. Have each group member retell a portion of the tale in his or her own words. Use gestures and vary the tone of voice to make the story come alive. How was the story altered during the performance?

---

## Extend Interpretations

**Comparing Texts** Accept all reasonable responses.
**The Writer's Style** The conversational style with its repetitions, interjections, and exaggerations.
**Connect to Life** Remind students that one way to structure a comparison-and-contrast essay is to deal fully with each subject in turn. For example, first write about the roles of the suitor, young woman, and parents in Sioux courtship customs, and then deal with corresponding roles in the writer's own cultural courtship traditions. Another approach is to interweave the two subjects. The student could first compare and contrast the suitor's role between the two cultures, then the young woman's role, then the parents' roles.

# *Choices* & CHALLENGES

## Writing Options

**Modernizing a Story** Write a story outline that adapts this tale to a modern setting. What obstacles might a young person today have to overcome to win his or her love? What would he or she offer instead of horses? Save your outline in your **Working Portfolio.**

## Activities & Explorations

**Talk Show** Act out a talk-show interview with High Horse, the girl he loved, the girl's father, and Red Deer. The audience should ask questions about the characters' reasons for acting and feeling as they did at specific points in the tale. ~ **SPEAKING AND LISTENING**

## Inquiry & Research

**Sioux Culture** Find out more about traditional Sioux (Lakota) courtship and marriage customs or research any other aspects of Sioux culture that interest you, such as bison hunting or spirituality. Share your knowledge in an oral presentation.

### Black Elk
1863–1950

**Other Works**
*The Sacred Pipe*

**A Boyhood Vision** At age 9, Black Elk had a vision in which he was given the power to help his fellow Oglala Sioux. He later interpreted his vision to mean that he should help his people survive the coming of white settlers—a belief that grew stronger as he witnessed the defeat of General George Custer's troops at the Battle of Little Bighorn.

**Betrayal and Violence** In his 20s, Black Elk joined Buffalo Bill's Wild West Show, hoping to learn from the whites something that would benefit his people. In 1889, after touring Europe with the show, he returned home to find that a new treaty had deprived his tribe of half its land. Tensions between the Sioux and the U.S. Army led, in the following year, to the Battle of Wounded Knee, in which soldiers massacred nearly 300 unarmed Sioux men, women, and children.

**Reflections of the Past** For the rest of his life, Black Elk lived on the Pine Ridge Reservation in South Dakota, saddened that he had failed to save his people. In 1931 he told the story of his life and visions to John G. Neihardt, who helped him write his life story, *Black Elk Speaks.*

### John G. Neihardt
1881–1973

**Other Works**
*Collected Poems*
*Indian Tales and Others*
*When the Tree Flowered*

**The Stamp of the Frontier** John G. Neihardt grew up in the frontier town of Wayne, Nebraska. From 1901 to 1907, he lived near the Omaha Indian Reservation. His experiences with the Omaha and other tribes that lived on the Great Plains influenced his poetry and fiction.

**Literary Achievements** Between 1915 and 1941, Neihardt published a five-part epic poem, *The Cycle of the West,* about the displacement of Native Americans by white settlers in the 1800s. While doing research for the final part of this epic—*The Song of the Messiah*—he met with Black Elk. The result of their talks was Neihardt's most popular book, *Black Elk Speaks.*

**Career Highlights** From 1943 to 1948, Neihardt served with the Bureau of Indian Affairs. In earlier years, he had worked as the literary editor of the *Minneapolis Journal* and the *St. Louis Post-Dispatch.* He also taught poetry at the University of Nebraska and at the University of Missouri. Neihardt was named Nebraska's poet laureate in 1921.

HIGH HORSE'S COURTING **653**

## Writing Options

**Modernizing a Story** Students' outlines should demonstrate an understanding of the courtship struggle in "High Horse's Courting" and the ability to recognize shared characteristics of cultures. **To get students started on this assignment,** have them work with a partner to brainstorm examples of modern struggles to win someone's love and the courtship customs involved.

## Activities & Explorations

**Talk Show** Students should collaborate on a plan to determine who assumes which roles and also which type of talk show format they will follow. The talk show host will be responsible for ensuring that group members take turns speaking. The host should ask for questions from the studio audience about the characters' actions and feelings in the story. **To make this assignment easier,** break the class into five groups. Each group should choose a character, assign one person to represent the character in the talk show, and then write questions that explore the character's actions and feelings in more detail. Questions should assist students in exploring the themes of the story and developing the characters more fully.

## Inquiry & Research

**Sioux Culture** You may want to provide the following books for students to use in their research: *Blackfoot Lodge Tales* by George Bird Grinnell (Lincoln: University of Nebraska Press, 1971); *The American Indian: Past and Present* by Roger I. Nichols (New York: McGraw Hill, 1985).

---

 **Assessment** **Standardized Test Practice**

**PREDICTING OUTCOMES** For some standardized tests, students will be asked to answer open-ended questions that test their ability to predict outcomes and perceive cause-and-effect relationships. Have students answer the following questions:

1. When he went on the war-path, did you expect High Horse to come back and get the girl? Support your answer with evidence from the text.

2. Do you think that High Horse's disappointment and defeat played a role in making him a real man? Support your answer with evidence from the text.

3. What kind of relationship do you think High Horse will have with his father-in-law? Support your answer with evidence from the text.

Students' responses should demonstrate their ability to analyze and critically evaluate the text, and to provide well-supported answers to the questions. Emphasize that making predictions about outcomes and characters requires making inferences, or reading between the lines, as they read a selection.

HIGH HORSE'S COURTING **653**

## Objectives
- appreciate the writings of one of America's most recognizable authors
- understand the impact of Mark Twain's writings on America's national identity
- learn about Samuel Clemens's life by reading nonfiction

## Presenting the Author
This Author Study offers students the opportunity to concentrate on the works of a major writer. Students can also learn about the life of Samuel Clemens, the real man behind the legendary Mark Twain.

## Monitoring and Modifying Reading Strategies
When you introduce this Author Study to students, encourage them to monitor and modify their reading strategies as they read. The different types of information included on these four pages may require them to modify their strategies. For example, they might summarize paragraphs in the running text and then simply list details from the sidebar columns. Developing a repertoire of strategies will help students become flexible and responsive readers.

# Author Study
# Mark Twain

### OVERVIEW

> *"The human race has one really effective weapon, and that is laughter."*
>
> —*Mark Twain*

*Mark Twain* [signature]

HIS LIFE
HIS TIMES

## An American Legend

*For generations of readers, Mark Twain has embodied the spirit of America. A poor boy who worked his way to international fame, Twain used his comic genius to comment on human nature and the pretensions of his day. Read more about this American spokesman who made people laugh even as he made them think about themselves and their society.*

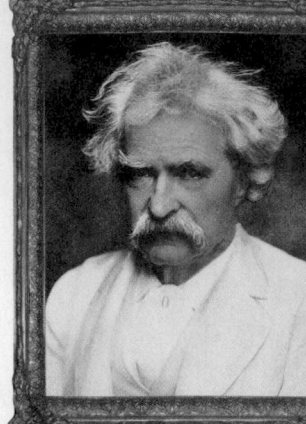

1835–1910

"THE FASCINATION OF RIVER LIFE" On November 30, 1835, Mark Twain was born as Samuel Langhorne Clemens in Florida, Missouri. When Clemens was four years old, his family moved some 30 miles to the Mississippi River town of Hannibal, a bustling port of about 500 people. When he was 11, his father died of pneumonia. To help support the family, Clemens took jobs as a grocery clerk and delivery boy. When he was 13, a local print shop hired him as an apprentice, and a few years

| 1835 | 1839 | 1846 |
|---|---|---|
| Is born Nov. 30 as Samuel Langhorne Clemens in Florida, Missouri | Moves with family to Hannibal, Missouri | Clemens's father dies |

| **1830** | | | **1840** | |
|---|---|---|---|---|

| 1835 | 1836 | 1838 | 1848 |
|---|---|---|---|
| Halley's comet appears. | Martin Van Buren is elected president. | Native Americans walk the Trail of Tears. | Gold is discovered in California. |

**A**

654

later, he became a pressman at his brother Orion's newspaper. Before long, he was writing comic sketches 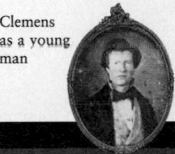 for the newspaper and itching to travel.

Clemens left Hannibal at the age of 18. Four years later, he decided to seek his fortune in South America. He boarded a Mississippi River steamboat for New Orleans, but along the way, he made a life-changing decision. Horace Bixby, a veteran steamboat pilot whom Clemens met on the voyage, taught him "how to steer the boat and thus made the fascination of river life more potent than ever" for Clemens. Under Bixby's stern guidance, Clemens became a licensed riverboat pilot. He reveled in a job that suited his love of freedom. And he got an education. Clemens wrote later, "When I find a well-drawn character in fiction or biography I generally take a warm personal interest in him, for the reason that I have known him before—met him on the river."

The steamboat caught the imagination of young Sam Clemens.

## LITERARY Contributions

Many writers and critics hail Mark Twain as an author whose work has had a lasting effect on 20th-century fiction. One of them, Ernest Hemingway, remarked that "all modern American literature comes from one book by Mark Twain, called *Huckleberry Finn*." Twain's ability to bring ordinary American voices into the realm of art is demonstrated in these major works:

**Novels**
*The Gilded Age* (1873)
*The Adventures of Tom Sawyer* (1876)
*The Prince and the Pauper* (1881)
*The Adventures of Huckleberry Finn* (1884)

**Tales and Sketches**
*The Celebrated Jumping Frog of Calaveras County, and Other Sketches* (1867)
*Mark Twain's Sketches, New and Old* (1875)
*The Stolen White Elephant and Other Stories* (1882)

**Travel Sketches**
*The Innocents Abroad* (1869)

**Other Works**
*Roughing It* (1872)
*Life on the Mississippi* (1883)
*How to Tell a Story and Other Essays* (1897)
*Mark Twain's Autobiography* (incomplete at his death; published posthumously in 1924)

## LIFE AND TIMES

### Astronomy
**A** The presence of Halley's comet in the sky at the time of Samuel Clemens's birth was considered by his family and friends to be a lucky omen. His family were literate people, but, for them and many others of their time, luck and superstition still took precedence over science. Halley's comet, with a return period of approximately 76 years, is the only comet visible to the unaided eye that returns during a single lifetime. According to historians, this comet was also seen during the Norman Conquest of England in 1066 and was incorporated into the Bayeux Tapestry of that time.

### Career
**B** Samuel Clemens claimed that he realized his true calling as a writer when he apprenticed at the print shop. One day he happened to read a page being printed about Joan of Arc. Unfamiliar with the story of the saint, he asked his brother Henry, the family scholar, about her. He was astounded to find out that she was a historical figure and even more stunned when he realized the amazing truths revealed by books. From that time on he avidly read books on history and literature. By starting his career in a print shop, Samuel Clemens followed in the footsteps of other great writers, including Benjamin Franklin.

### Architecture
**C** Clemens spent eight months in the northeast, living first in New York City and then in Philadelphia. He wrote about the cities and his life for his brother's paper in Iowa. In February 1854, he wrote about his visit to Washington, D. C. He described the public buildings as "fine specimens of architecture" that would suit a city such as New York, but in Washington they looked like "so many palaces in a Hottentot village." The other buildings of the city, he noted, were very poor and built haphazardly as if "they might have been emptied out of a sack. . . "

**C 1851** Takes job at his brother Orion's newspaper

Clemens as a young man

**1859** Becomes Mississippi riverboat pilot

**1863** Starts using the pen name Mark Twain

**1865** Earns national fame with "The Notorious Jumping Frog of Calaveras County"

**1869** Publishes *The Innocents Abroad,* based on his travels

**1850**　　　　**1860**

**1852** Harriet Beecher Stowe publishes *Uncle Tom's Cabin.*

**1860** Abraham Lincoln is elected president.

**1861** The Civil War begins.

**1863** Lincoln issues the Emancipation Proclamation.

**1865** The Confederacy surrenders at Appomattox; Lincoln is assassinated.

**1868** President Johnson is impeached; Grant is elected president.

## History

**A** Throughout the buildup to the Civil War, Clemens remained steadfastly apolitical, refusing to commit himself to either side. He had hoped to be able to continue working as a pilot on the Mississippi River, but the era of the steamboat ended when the river became a point of violent conflict. Clemens had to decide whether to limit his piloting to the southern route and choose the Confederacy, or give up his career on the Mississippi and return home. Two years after he started his career as a steamboat pilot, Clemens returned to St. Louis, refusing to fight on either side.

## World Culture

**B** Clemens, writing as Mark Twain, gave Americans a different view of the wonders of Europe. He challenged the myths that surrounded his European ports of call and relayed to his readers the realities of travel in Europe and the Middle East. His judgments were not based on the history and charm of Europe but on such areas as the cleanliness of the people, the competence of his guides, and whether a particular hotel had soap.

## Literature

**C** The inspiration for Twain's characters Tom Sawyer and Huck Finn came from Clemens's childhood experiences. When he was a child, Clemens spent his summers on a family farm in Florida, Missouri. He re-created the freedom of these summers with the character of Tom Sawyer. Huck Finn was based on Clemens's friend Tom Blankenship, older by four years and a member of a large, boisterous family. Together, he and young Sam Clemens, who climbed out his bedroom window at night, scoured Hannibal for adventures that Clemens later wrote about as Mark Twain.

**A** **"A PICNIC ON A GRAND SCALE"** In 1861, when the Civil War halted shipping on the Mississippi, 26-year-old Clemens traveled west to Nevada with his brother. At first, he tried mining and prospecting for gold and silver—a dismal failure that turned him back to writing. In 1862, he took a $25-a-week job as a journalist for the Virginia City *Territorial Enterprise*. In 1863, he published his first article under the pen name "Mark Twain," riverboat jargon for water two fathoms, or 12 feet, deep—water just deep enough to keep a steamboat safely afloat. By the time Twain left the West three years later, his star was rising. He debuted as a stage performer, riveting audiences with his entertaining stories. Even more important, he had won national fame with his humorous tale "The Notorious Jumping Frog of Calaveras County."

Twain sailed to Europe and the Middle East in 1867, enjoying "a picnic on a grand scale," as he put it. Along the way, he supplied **B** irreverent newspaper articles about his fellow travelers and foreign manners to papers in California and New York City. Later, Twain expanded the articles into his first and highly successful book, *The Innocents Abroad*. But the trip had another important consequence, too. Aboard ship, Twain met Charley Langdon, the 18-year-old son of a wealthy New York coal merchant. One day Charley showed Twain a picture of his handsome older sister, Olivia, and from that moment, Twain was charmed.

Twain and Olivia Langdon were married in 1870, and the couple settled in Hartford, Connecticut. Over the next two decades, Twain focused his talents and energies on serious writing, producing his greatest works. Among the most important were *The* **C** *Adventures of Tom Sawyer* (1876), *Life on the Mississippi* (1883), and his masterpiece, *The Adventures of Huckleberry Finn* (1885). It was also during these years that Twain matured into America's first celebrity author.

As America developed a national identity, people looked to writers like Twain to create true-to-life images of Americans. Twain's characters reflected the reality of a new nation that was growing rapidly. His realism, his truthful imitation of real life, won him national favor. All over the country, people felt they knew this shaggy-haired, drawling

**1870**
**Marries Olivia Langdon**

**1876**
**Publishes *The Adventures of Tom Sawyer***

**1884**
**Launches a publishing company**

**1885**
**Publishes *The Adventures of Huckleberry Finn***

**1870**

**1880**

**1876**
**George Custer is killed at Little Bighorn.**

**1879**
**F. W. Woolworth opens his five-and-ten-cent store.**

**1880**
**John D. Rockefeller's Standard Oil Company of Ohio controls U.S. refining business.**

**1886**
**Statue of Liberty is dedicated.**

character who made a splash in his trademark white suit.

**"A VAST EMPTINESS"** In the last decades of his life, Twain suffered one painful loss after another. A publishing business he began in the 1880s failed in 1894, forcing him to declare bankruptcy. For several years, Twain wrote and lectured abroad at a grueling pace in order to repay his debts and rebuild his fortune. Between 1896 and 1910, the loss of his cherished Hartford mansion and the death of his wife and two of his daughters plunged him into despair. Twain wrote intensely during this painful period, but his humor grew more biting. After the death of his daughter Jean on Christmas Eve, 1909, Twain fell ill. Feeling lost in "a vast emptiness," he died a few months later, on April 21.

**More Online: Author Link**
www.mcdougallittell.com

# The Gilded Age

The last three decades of the 19th century were characterized by an explosive growth in technology, which was accompanied by a growth in corruption in politics, business, and society. Between 1870 and 1890, the **D** gap between the rich and the poor grew wider than ever before. For example, on one side of New York City, elegant and ornate hotels and mansions flourished, yet many people in the city were living in shanty towns or tenements. Mark Twain dubbed this period "the Gilded Age"—a satirical commentary on the extravagant displays of the wealthy.

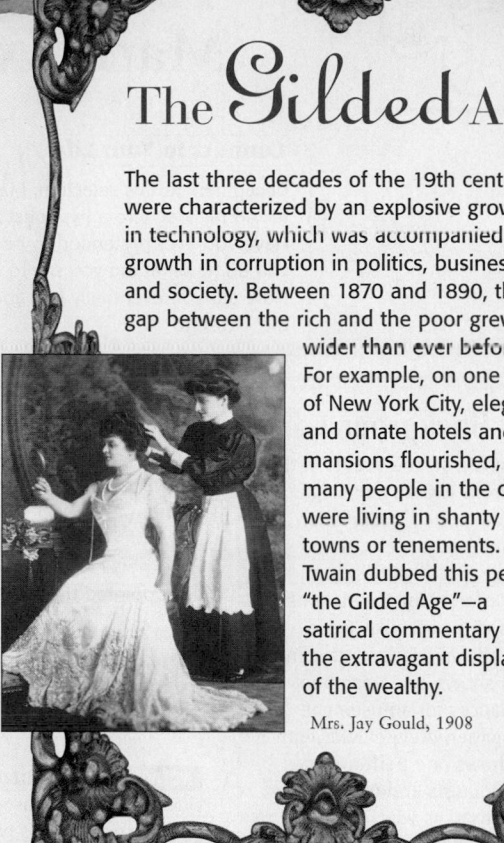
Mrs. Jay Gould, 1908

## World Politics

**D** In the late 1890s, Twain and his family spent time in Vienna, Austria. By this time Twain, through his lecturing, had become an unofficial ambassador for American culture abroad. While in Vienna, he became involved in an international peace movement headquartered there. When Czar Nicholas II of Russia called for international disarmament and offered to disarm if other powers would also, Twain regarded this as political naiveté. Rather, he believed that only a balance of terror could promote worldwide peace.

## Twain

**E** On the night Mark Twain died, Halley's Comet was again visible in the sky for the first time since his birth 75 years earlier. Thousands of friends and admirers crowded Twain's funeral in New York City, while hundreds more lined the streets. He is buried in Elmira, New York, next to his wife Olivia and their daughters Susy and Jean.

**1894**
Publishing company goes bankrupt

**1895**
Begins overseas lecture tour to raise money

**1901**
Death of Olivia on June 5

**1910**
Dies April 21 at Redding, Connecticut **E**

**1890**

**1900**

**1910**

**1890**
Immigration to America by Europeans soars.

**1903**
W. E. B. Du Bois publishes *The Souls of Black Folk.*

**1904**
Theodore Roosevelt is elected president.

**1909**
National Association for the Advancement of Colored People forms.

**1910**
Halley's comet returns.

## OVERVIEW

### Objectives

1. appreciate an excerpt from an **autobiography (Literary Analysis)**
2. identify and understand **irony (Literary Analysis)**
3. **predict** events in an autobiography **(Active Reading)**

### Summary

Twain recounts the visit of a mesmerizer to his hometown. During the first nights of the show, several people in the audience are hypnotized and, reacting to the mesmerizer's suggestions, they perform such antics as fleeing from imaginary snakes and viewing invisible sunsets. The young Mark Twain fails to be hypnotized for three nights and finally decides to pretend. His acting ability and imagination soon make him the favorite subject of the hypnotist and the audience. In one part of the act, he is supposed to follow the mesmerizer's unspoken command. He is at first worried that this challenge will expose him as a fraud. However, the mesmerizer endorses everything that Twain does. When the mesmerizer leaves town, Twain is the only one who disbelieves in hypnotism. Years later he confesses his deception to his mother, but his performance had been so impressive that she refuses to believe him. Twain concludes that lies can live a long time.

### Thematic Link

In this excerpt from his autobiography, Mark Twain shows that he is as much of a **trickster** as some of the characters he created. He describes how he pretended to be mesmerized by a traveling hypnotist, who arrived in the small towns that grew as the **frontier vanished.** Ironically, his deception outlives many of the people who witnessed it.

### 5-Minute Warm-Up

*Daily Language SkillBuilder*

Have students **proofread** the display sentences on page 555j and write them correctly. The sentences also appear on Transparency 19 of **Grammar Transparencies and Copymasters.**

# *from* The Autobiography of Mark Twain

**Connect to Your Life**

**Deception!** In this selection, Mark Twain describes how he once talked his way into a hypnotist's act and pretended to be hypnotized. Have you ever pretended to be something you're not? If so, why did you do it? What did you say to convince other people to believe you? How did you eventually feel about deceiving other people? Jot down the incident.

## Build Background

**The Mesmerizer** The events in this excerpt from Twain's autobiography take place around 1850, when Americans had no televisions, radios, computer games, compact discs, or movies for entertainment. Small-town people like Twain turned to local talent or traveling minstrel shows and steamboat performances for amusement. The showmen drew crowds with magic shows and performances by ventriloquists and mesmerizers, or hypnotists. As you probably know, a hypnotist places a person in a suggestible, trancelike state; the hypnotist then may order the person to perform antics.

WORDS TO KNOW
**Vocabulary Preview**

| | |
|---|---|
| collusion | implacable |
| confederate | odious |
| credulity | rapt |
| dissemble | unassailable |
| gullible | usurping |

## Focus Your Reading

**LITERARY ANALYSIS** **IRONY** One element that adds tension and humor to Twain's story is **irony,** the contrast between appearance and actuality. At the mesmerizer's show, the young Twain, already a ham, is eager to show off his imagination and intellect by pretending to be hypnotized. He expects to relish the success of his exploits but is instead disappointed by the deception and trickery of hypnotism:

*The truth is I did not have to wait long to get tired of my triumphs. . . . The glory which is built upon a lie soon becomes a most unpleasant incumbrance.*

Watch for other examples of irony as you read Twain's story.

**ACTIVE READING** **PREDICTING** **Predicting** is the process of using text clues to make a reasonable guess about what will happen in a story. Sometimes a story's twist will surprise you; sometimes your predictions will hit the mark. Either way, watching for text clues can help you to find the irony in Twain's story. For example, what clues in the passage below could help you predict what will happen next?

*When I saw the "subjects" perform their foolish antics on the platform and make the people laugh and shout and admire I had a burning desire to be a subject myself.*

**READER'S NOTEBOOK** As you read, use a chart like this one to record your predictions and the clues from the text that led you to make an educated guess. Here's an example:

| Predictions | Text Clues |
|---|---|
| I predict he'll find a way to get involved. | Twain says he can't resist the temptation to be a subject. |
| | |

**658** UNIT FOUR AUTHOR STUDY: MARK TWAIN

## LESSON RESOURCES

**UNIT FOUR RESOURCE BOOK,** pp. 55–59

**ASSESSMENT RESOURCES**
**Formal Assessment,** pp. 125–126
**Teacher's Guide to Assessment and Portfolio Use**
**Test Generator**

**SKILLS TRANSPARENCIES AND COPYMASTERS**
**Reading and Critical Thinking**
• Predicting Outcomes, T2 (for Active Reading, p. 658)

**Grammar**
• Essential and Nonessential Clauses, C91 (for Mini Lesson, p. 663)
• Punctuating a Series of Clauses, C156 (for Mini Lesson, p. 666)

**Vocabulary**
• Synonyms and Antonyms, C56 (for Mini Lesson, p. 664)

**Writing**
• The Uses of Dialogue, T24 (for Writing Option 1, p. 668)
• Eyewitness Report, T25 (for Writing Option 3, p. 668)

**INTEGRATED TECHNOLOGY**

**Audio Library**
**Net Activities**
**Internet: Research Starter**
**Visit our website:**
www.mcdougallittell.com

# from THE AUTOBIOGRAPHY OF MARK TWAIN

## MARK TWAIN

### TEACHING THE LITERATURE
#### Customizing Instruction

**Less Proficient Readers**
Tell students that the selection concerns the consequences of deception. Ask them to think about the possible effects of deceiving others. Have them imagine how they would react if they found out someone had deceived them for an extended period of time.

**Set a Purpose** Have students read to find out when Twain begins to deceive people and his reason for doing so.

**Students Acquiring English**
Write the word *hypnosis* on the board and ask volunteers to explain its meaning. Use mock demonstrations to help students understand the term.

Use **Spanish Study Guide** for additional support, pp. 160–162.

**Gifted and Talented**
Ask students to think about how the content and tone of this narrative would differ if it were told by one of the audience members.

**An** exciting event in our village was the arrival of the mesmerizer.[1] I think the year was 1850. As to that I am not sure but I know the month—it was May; that detail has survived the wear of fifty years. A pair of connected little incidents of that month have served to keep the memory of it green for me all this time; incidents of no consequence and not worth embalming, yet my memory has preserved them carefully and flung away things of real value to give them space and make them comfortable. The truth is, a person's memory has no more sense than his conscience and no appreciation whatever of values and proportions. However, never mind those trifling incidents; my subject is the mesmerizer now.

He advertised his show and promised marvels. Admission as usual: 25 cents, children half price. The village had heard of mesmerism in a general way but had not encountered it yet. Not many people attended the first night but next day they had so many wonders to tell that everybody's curiosity was fired and after that for a fortnight the magician had prosperous times. I was fourteen or fifteen years old, the age at which a boy is willing to endure all things, suffer all things short of death by fire, if thereby he may be conspicuous and show off before the public; and so, when I saw the "subjects" perform their foolish antics on the platform and make the

people laugh and shout and admire I had a burning desire to be a subject myself.

Every night for three nights I sat in the row of candidates on the platform and held the magic disk[2] in the palm of my hand and gazed at it and tried to get sleepy, but it was a failure; I remained wide awake and had to retire defeated, like the majority. Also, I had to sit there and be gnawed with envy of Hicks, our journeyman;[3] I had to sit there and see him scamper and jump when Simmons the enchanter exclaimed, "See the snake! See the snake!" and hear him say, "My, how beautiful!" in response to the suggestion that he was observing a splendid sunset; and so on—the whole insane business. I couldn't laugh, I couldn't applaud; it filled me with bitterness to have others do it and to have people make a hero of Hicks and crowd around him when the show was over and ask him for  more and more particulars of the wonders he had seen in his visions and manifest in many ways that they were proud to be acquainted

---

1. **mesmerizer** (mĕz'mə-rī´zər): hypnotist; from the name of an Austrian physician, Franz Anton Mesmer, who popularized hypnotism in the 1770s.

2. **magic disk:** object used by the mesmerizer to focus a subject's attention, helping him or her to achieve the hypnotic state.

3. **journeyman:** sound and experienced, but not brilliant, craftsman or performer.

---

## **Mini Lesson** Preteaching Vocabulary

**USING CONTEXT CLUES** **Instruction** Remind students that they can expand their vocabulary through wide reading and the use of context clues to determine the meanings of unfamiliar words. One way of using context clues is by analyzing text for a cause-and-effect relationship, directly stated or implied. Demonstrate the strategy by writing the following model on the board.

**Model Sentence**

Because he was <u>gullible</u>, his <u>confederate</u> in the venture, who was <u>unscrupulous</u>, led them both into grave legal difficulties.

**Practice** Ask students to determine the cause-and-effect relationship implied in the sentence. Then have volunteers apply this understanding by guessing the meanings of *gullible* and *confederate* and using each word in a sentence.

 Use **Unit Four Resource Book,** p. 58 for additional support.

A lesson on context clues appears on p. 326 in the **Pupil's Edition.**

### Reading Skills and Strategies:
### PREVIEW

Prepare students for this selection by having them look at the picture on page 662 and explain what they think is happening. Then have students predict what this selection might be about.

### Literary Analysis | IRONY

Dramatic irony occurs when the reader knows something that the characters in a literary work do not. Ask students to identify the dramatic irony of Twain's description of the fourth night and to explain what this dramatic irony contributes to Twain's account.

**Possible Response:** We know that Mark Twain is not really under the hypnotist's power, but those witnessing the show believe he has been hypnotized. This discrepancy adds suspense, because we don't know if his deception will succeed, and it intensifies the humor, because we can enjoy the audience's gullibility.

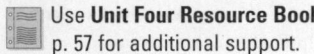 Use **Unit Four Resource Book**, p. 57 for additional support.

### Active Reading | PREDICTING

Ask students what they think will happen after Mark Twain makes up an act.

**Possible Responses:** He will be exposed as a fraud and retire in shame; his act will be a success.

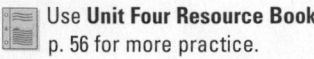 Use **Unit Four Resource Book**, p. 56 for more practice.

with him. Hicks—the idea! I couldn't stand it; I was getting boiled to death in my own bile.[4]

**1** On the fourth night temptation came and I was not strong enough to resist. When I had gazed at the disk a while I pretended to be sleepy and began to nod. Straightway came the professor and made passes over my head and down my body and legs and arms, finishing each pass with a snap of his fingers in the air to discharge the surplus electricity;[5] then he began to "draw" me with the disk, holding it in his fingers and telling me I could not take my eyes off it, try as I might; so I rose slowly, bent and gazing, and followed that disk all over the place, just as I had seen the others do. Then I was put through the other paces. Upon suggestion I fled from snakes, passed buckets at a fire, became excited over hot steamboat-races, made love to imaginary girls and kissed them, fished from the platform and landed mud cats[6] that outweighed me—and so on, all the customary marvels. But not in the customary way. I was cautious at first and watchful, being afraid the professor would discover that I was an impostor and drive me from the platform in disgrace; but as soon as I realized that I was not in danger, I set myself the task of terminating Hicks's usefulness as a subject and of <u>usurping</u> his place.

It was a sufficiently easy task. Hicks was born honest, I without that incumbrance[7]—so some people said. Hicks saw what he saw and reported accordingly, I saw more than was visible and added to it such details as could help. Hicks had no imagination; I had a double supply. He was born calm, I was born excited. No vision could start a rapture in him and he was constipated as to language, anyway; but if I saw a vision I emptied the dictionary onto it and lost the remnant of my mind into the bargain.

At the end of my first half-hour Hicks was a thing of the past, a fallen hero, a broken idol, and I knew it and was glad and said in my heart, "Success to crime!" Hicks could never have been mesmerized to the point where he could kiss an imaginary girl in public or a real one either, but I was competent. Whatever Hicks had failed in, I made it a point to succeed in, let the cost be what it might, physically or morally. He had shown several bad defects and I had made a note of them. For instance, if the magician asked, "What do you see?" and left him to invent a vision for himself, Hicks was dumb and blind, he couldn't see a thing nor say a word, whereas the magician soon found out that when it came to seeing visions of a stunning and marketable sort I could get along better without his help than with it.

**Then** there was another thing: Hicks wasn't worth a tallow dip[8] on mute mental suggestion. Whenever Simmons stood behind him and gazed at the back of

---

4. **bile** (bīl): bitterness; ill humor.
5. **discharge . . . electricity:** It was once believed, wrongly, that hypnosis was linked to electricity and magnetism.
6. **mud cats:** catfish.
7. **incumbrance:** burden; obligation.
8. **wasn't worth a tallow dip:** wasn't any good. A tallow dip was an inexpensive candle.

WORDS TO KNOW    **usurping** (yōō-sûr′pǐng) *n.* taking another's place wrongfully **usurp** *v.*

660

his skull and tried to drive a mental suggestion into it, Hicks sat with vacant face and never suspected. If he had been noticing he could have seen by the rapt faces of the audience that something was going on behind his back that required a response. Inasmuch as I was an impostor I dreaded to have this test put upon me, for I knew the professor would be "willing" me to do something, and as I couldn't know what it was, I should be exposed and denounced. However, when my time came, I took my chance. I perceived by the tense and expectant faces of the people that Simmons was behind me willing me with all his might. I tried my best to imagine what he wanted but nothing suggested itself. I felt ashamed and miserable then. I believed that the hour of my disgrace was come and that in another moment I should go out of that place disgraced. I ought to be ashamed to confess it but my next thought was not how I could win the compassion of kindly hearts by going out humbly and in sorrow for my misdoings, but how I could go out most sensationally and spectacularly.

There was a rusty and empty old revolver lying on the table among the "properties"[9] employed in the performances. On May Day two or three weeks before there had been a celebration by the schools and I had had a quarrel with a big boy who was the school bully and I had not come out of it with credit.[10] That boy was now seated in the middle of the house, halfway down the main aisle. I crept stealthily and impressively toward the table, with a dark and murderous scowl on my face, copied from a popular romance, seized the revolver suddenly, flourished it, shouted the bully's name, jumped off the platform and made a rush for him and chased him out of the house before the paralyzed people could interfere to save him. There was a storm of applause, and the magician, addressing the house, said, most impressively—

"That you may know how really remarkable this is and how wonderfully developed a subject we have in this boy, I assure you that without a single spoken word to guide him he has carried out what I mentally commanded him to do, to the minutest detail. I could have stopped him at a moment in his vengeful career by a mere exertion of my will, therefore the poor fellow who has escaped was at no time in danger."

So I was not in disgrace. I returned to the platform a hero and happier than I have ever been in this world since. As regards mental suggestion, my fears of it were gone. I judged that in case I failed to guess what the professor might be willing me to do, I could count on putting up something that would answer just as well. I was right, and exhibitions of unspoken suggestion became a favorite with the public. Whenever I perceived that I was being willed to do something I got up and did something—anything that occurred to me—and the magician, not being a fool, always ratified it.

**Hicks had no IMAGINATION; I HAD A DOUBLE SUPPLY. HE WAS BORN CALM, I WAS BORN EXCITED.**

---

9. **"properties"**: articles, other than costumes and scenery, that are used on the stage during a dramatic performance.

10. **credit**: honor or distinction.

WORDS TO KNOW **rapt** (răpt) *adj.* deeply moved, delighted, or absorbed

661

## Mini Lesson: Speaking and Listening

**STORYTELLING Prepare** Remind students that they're expected to present valid interpretations in different ways such as by telling stories. Read a passage from the autobiography aloud to emphasize the storytelling qualities of Mark Twain's prose. Discuss how the tone of voice of the reader is dictated by the incident and how literary devices add excitement and vividness to the account. Ask students to write about an incident from their lives in a similar style. Their stories should be no longer than one paragraph, but each should contain a beginning, supporting details, and a conclusion.

**Present** Have students exchange their paragraphs with a partner for critique. Then they can practice reading their stories with the appropriate tone of voice. Ask them to justify their choice of verbal performance techniques by referring to Twain's style. Suggest that they present their stories while sitting on a chair and allow the story to unfold so that the audience can visualize the action. Invite audience members to evaluate the effectiveness of storytelling methods and to assess how closely the presenters followed Twain's model.

**BLOCK SCHEDULING** This activity is particularly well-suited for longer class periods.

# Reading and Analyzing

**Reading Skills and Strategies:**
**CONNECTING**

**Ⓐ** Twain is making an observation about human nature. Explain that each student is expected to connect literature to his or her own experiences. Have students judge the truth of this statement from their own vantage points.

**Reading Skills and Strategies:**
**HYPOTHESIZING**

**Ⓑ** Ask students why they think the mesmerizer did not try to protect Twain if, as Twain suspected, he was not fooled by Twain's performance.
**Possible Responses:** He didn't care about Twain's comfort; he knew Twain wouldn't give himself away; he was willing to let Twain suffer in order to gain more popularity for his show and, ultimately, more money for himself.

**Literary Analysis** | IRONY |

**Ⓒ** Ask students to explain the situational irony in Twain's reaction to the skeptics in the community.
**Possible Responses:** He says he is as hurt as if he were not deceiving them, yet they are right to be skeptical because he is a fraud.

**Active Reading** | PREDICTING |

**Ⓓ** Ask students to predict how Mark Twain will handle his success and fame.
**Possible Responses:** Twain will revel in it; Twain will start to feel guilty.

THE MESMERIZER

662   UNIT FOUR   AUTHOR STUDY: MARK TWAIN

---

# Teaching Options

## Untitled

Franz Mesmer (1734–1815), the Austrian physician that gave his name to "mesmerizing," is considered a pioneer in the scientific study of hypnotism. Mesmer developed a theory called "animal magnetism" that suggested that magnetic force governs human health by acting upon an invisible fluid in the body.
**Instruction** Focus students' attention on the

## Ⓜ Viewing and Representing

colors, shapes, and lines in this poster. This poster attempts to stir up interest in the mesmerizer's act, so the artist's techniques must attract attention quickly and convey an intriguing idea of what will be seen in the show.
**Application** Ask students to determine which elements are the most attention-getting in the poster.
**Possible Response:** The colors and shapes are psychedelic and eye-catching.

Ask students how the artist's use of lines and angles gives an impression of the mesmerizer's power.
**Possible Responses:** The stance of the mesmerizer shows him exerting control over the subject. The mesmerizer holds the other man suspended at an angle. The suspended man apparently cannot change his position, as suggested by his hands at his side and his wide staring eyes.

When people asked me, "How *can* you tell what he is willing you to do?" I said, "It's just as easy," and they always said admiringly, "Well, it beats *me* how you can do it."

Hicks was weak in another detail. When the professor made passes over him and said "his whole body is without sensation now—come forward and test him, ladies and gentlemen," the ladies and gentlemen always complied eagerly and stuck pins into Hicks, and if they went deep Hicks was sure to wince, then that poor professor would have to explain that Hicks "wasn't sufficiently under the influence." But I didn't wince; I only suffered and shed tears on the inside. The miseries that a conceited boy will endure to keep up his "reputation"! And so will a conceited man; I know it in my own person and have seen it in a hundred thousand others. That professor ought to have protected me and I often hoped he would, when the tests were unusually severe, but he didn't. It may be that he was deceived as well as the others, though I did not believe it nor think it possible. Those were dear good people but they must have carried simplicity and <u>credulity</u> to the limit. They would stick a pin in my arm and bear on it until they drove it a third of its length in, and then be lost in wonder that by a mere exercise of will power the professor could turn my arm to iron and make it insensible to pain. Whereas it was not insensible at all; I was suffering agonies of pain.

 that fourth night, that proud night, that triumphant night, I was the only subject. Simmons invited no more candidates to the platform. I performed alone every night the rest of the fortnight. Up to that time a dozen wise old heads, the intellectual aristocracy of the town, had held out as <u>implacable</u> unbelievers. I was as hurt by this as if I were engaged in some honest occupation.

There is nothing surprising about this. Human beings feel dishonor the most, sometimes, when they most deserve it. That handful of overwise old gentlemen kept on shaking their heads all the first week and saying they had seen no marvels there that could not have been produced by <u>collusion</u>; and they were pretty vain of their unbelief too and liked to show it and air it and be superior to the ignorant and the <u>gullible</u>. Particularly old Dr. Peake, who was the ringleader of the irreconcilables and very formidable; for he was an F.F.V.,[11] he was learned, white-haired and venerable, nobly and richly clad in the fashions of an earlier and a courtlier day, he was large and stately, and he not only seemed wise but was what he seemed in that regard. He had great influence and his opinion upon any matter was worth much more than that of any other person in the community. When I conquered him at last, I knew I was undisputed master of the field; and now after more than fifty years I acknowledge with a few dry old tears that I rejoiced without shame.

In 1847 we were living in a large white house on the corner of Hill and Main Streets—a house that still stands but isn't large now although it hasn't lost a plank; I saw it a year ago and noticed that shrinkage. My father died in it in March of the year mentioned but our family did not move out of it until some months afterward. Ours was not the only family in the house; there was another, Dr. Grant's. One day Dr. Grant and Dr. Reyburn argued a matter on the street with sword canes and Grant was brought home

---

11. **F.F.V.:** First Family of Virginia. Dr. Peake has high social status because his ancestors were among the first settlers of Virginia.

---

WORDS TO KNOW

**credulity** (krĭ-dōō′lĭ-tē) *n.* an inclination to believe too readily
**implacable** (ĭm-plăk′ə-bəl) *adj.* impossible to satisfy
**collusion** (kə-lōō′zhən) *n.* a secret agreement for a deceitful purpose
**gullible** (gŭl′ə-bəl) *adj.* easily deceived or tricked

**663**

---

## Customizing Instruction

### Students Acquiring English
**1** Explain that the idiomatic phrase *it beats me* means "I can't understand it."

### Less Proficient Readers
Point out the extremes to which Mark Twain goes in order to conceal his deception. He allows audience members to push pins into his arms and conceals his pain.

**Set a Purpose** Have students read to find out how Twain deceives even the most stubborn unbelievers.

**2** Read this passage aloud and then invite students to suggest words or phrases of their own to describe old Dr. Peake. Write the students' words on the board and help them compile a description of the old man.

### Multiple Learning Styles
**Kinesthetic Learners**

Invite students to work with partners to act out their own renditions of Twain's performances under hypnosis. They should read over the text carefully and choose a scene with visual appeal and humor. After they have practiced, have the students perform their scenes for the class.

---

 **Grammar**
Mini Lesson

**ESSENTIAL VS. NONESSENTIAL CLAUSES**
**Instruction** An essential adjective clause makes the meaning of a sentence complete. A nonessential adjective clause adds extra information to a sentence the intended meaning of which is already complete and clear. Display the following sentences to show the difference.
Mark Twain, <u>whose later work became pessimistic and bitter in tone</u>, is hailed as the creator of the "great American novel," *The Adventures of Huckleberry Finn.* (nonessential—the meaning remains the same if the clause is eliminated)

Huck Finn might be considered an American hero because he embodies those qualities <u>that reflect the country's ideals</u>. (essential—the meaning would be changed if the clause were omitted)
The show continued after the audience members stopped puncturing his arm with the pins, which seemed to be feet long instead of inches. (*which . . . inches; nonessential*)

Use **Grammar Transparencies and Copymasters**, p. 91.

Use McDougal Littell's ***Language Network,*** Chapter 3, for more instruction and practice with clauses.

**A** Have students identify the sensory words and phrases that help them visualize this scene. Then ask them to describe the atmosphere that these sensory details create.

**Possible Responses:** "black smoke rolling and tumbling"; "flames burst . . . and turn red"; "the shrieks of the despairing"; "faces at the window"; "veiling smoke." These words create a horrifying, nightmarish atmosphere.

### Literary Analysis: STYLE

**B** Explain that local color realism is a style of writing that truthfully imitates ordinary life and brings a particular region alive by portraying the dialects, dress, mannerisms, customs, and character types. Remind students that they're expected to analyze the relevance of setting and time frame to the text's meaning. Ask what details in this passage reveal Dr. Peake's position in the society of the time.

**Possible Responses:** Dr. Peake's ruffled shirt, wristbands, and gold-headed cane; the deference other townsmen show him as the head of an aristocratic old family; Twain's reference to him as "the great chief"

### Literary Analysis | IRONY |

**C** Note the dramatic irony in Dr. Peake's response. Ask students what the reader knows that Dr. Peake doesn't.

**Possible Responses:** Twain is deceiving the audience; Twain heard the information from Dr. Peake himself.

---

multifariously punctured. Old Dr. Peake caulked the leaks and came every day for a while to look after him.

The Grants were Virginians, like Peake, and one day when Grant was getting well enough to be on his feet and sit around in the parlor and talk, the conversation fell upon Virginia and old times. I was present but the group were probably unconscious of me, I being only a lad and a negligible quantity.[12] Two of the group— Dr. Peake and Mrs. Crawford, Mrs. Grant's mother—had been of the audience when the Richmond theater burned down thirty-six years before, and they talked over the frightful details of that memorable tragedy. These were eye-witnesses, and with their eyes I **(A)** saw it all with an intolerable vividness: I saw the black smoke rolling and tumbling toward the sky, I saw the flames burst through it and turn red, I heard the shrieks of the despairing, I glimpsed their faces at the windows, caught fitfully through the veiling smoke, I saw them jump to their death or to mutilation worse than death. The picture is before me yet and can never fade.

In due course they talked of the colonial mansion of the Peakes, with its stately columns and its spacious grounds, and by odds and ends I picked up a clearly defined idea of the place. I was strongly interested, for I had not before heard of such palatial things from the lips of people who had seen them with their own eyes. One detail, casually dropped, hit my imagination hard. In the wall by the great front door there

was a round hole as big as a saucer—a British cannon ball had made it in the war of the Revolution. It was breathtaking; it made history real; history had never been real to me before.

Very well, three or four years later, as already mentioned, I was king bee and sole "subject" in the mesmeric show; it was the beginning of the second week; the performance was half over; just then the majestic Dr. Peake with his ruffled bosom and wrist-bands and his gold-headed cane entered, and a deferential citizen vacated his seat beside the Grants and made the great chief take it. This happened while I was trying to invent something fresh in the way of vision, in response to the professor's remark— "Concentrate your powers. Look—look attentively. There—don't you see something? Concentrate—concentrate! Now then—describe it."

Without suspecting it, Dr. Peake, by entering the place, had reminded me of the talk of three years before. He had also furnished me capital and was become my <u>confederate</u>, an accomplice in my frauds. I began on a vision, a vague and dim one (that was part of the game at the beginning of a vision; it isn't best to see it too clearly at first, it might look as if you had come loaded with it). The vision developed by degrees and gathered swing, momentum, energy. It was the Richmond fire. Dr. Peake was cold at first and his fine face had a trace of polite scorn in it; but when he began to recognize that fire, that

**B**

**C**

THE GLORY WHICH IS BUILT UPON A LIE SOON BECOMES A MOST UNPLEASANT INCUMBRANCE.

---

12. **negligible quantity:** something insignificant or unimportant; nothing.

| WORDS TO KNOW | **confederate** (kən-fĕd′ər-ĭt) *n.* one who assists in a plot; associate |
| --- | --- |

664

---

 **Mini Lesson** ## Vocabulary Strategy

### IDENTIFYING SYNONYMS AND ANTONYMS

**Instruction** Remind students that it is important to discriminate between the denotative and connotative meanings of words. A word has both denotations, or dictionary definitions, and connotations, or emotional overtones and associations. Both the denotation and connotation of a word must be taken into account when choosing the most precise synonym and antonym for the word. For example, *gullible* means "easily deceived or tricked." The word *gullible* has a negative connotation, suggesting that one is foolishly trusting. Thus the word *innocent* would not be an exact syn-

onym, since it does not have similar connotations. A better synonym would be *credulous*. Antonyms for *gullible*, which would suggest a wise or calculating quality, include *shrewd* or *astute*.

**Application** Ask students to choose antonyms and synonyms for each of the following words: *credulity, implacable, usurp, odious, rapt.* Tell students that their synonyms should take into account the connotation of each word as it is used in the selection.

Use **Vocabulary Transparencies and Copymasters**, p. 56.

---

expression changed and his eyes began to light up. As soon as I saw that, I threw the valves wide open and turned on all the steam and gave those people a supper of fire and horrors that was calculated to last them one while! They couldn't gasp when I got through—they were petrified. Dr. Peake had risen and was standing—and breathing hard. He said, in a great voice:

"My doubts are ended. No collusion could produce that miracle. It was totally impossible for him to know those details, yet he has described them with the clarity of an eyewitness—and with what <u>unassailable</u> truthfulness God knows I know!"

I saved the colonial mansion for the last night and solidified and perpetuated Dr. Peake's conversion with the cannon-ball hole. He explained to the house that I could never have heard of that small detail, which differentiated this mansion from all other Virginian mansions and perfectly identified it, therefore the fact stood proven that I had *seen* it in my vision. Lawks![13]

It is curious. When the magician's engagement closed there was but one person in the village who did not believe in mesmerism and I was the one. All the others were converted but I was to remain an implacable and unpersuadable disbeliever in mesmerism and hypnotism for close upon fifty years. This was because I never would examine them, in after life. I couldn't. The subject revolted me. Perhaps it brought back to me a passage in my life which for pride's sake I wished to forget; though I thought, or persuaded myself I thought, I should never come across a "proof" which wasn't thin and cheap and probably had a fraud like me behind it.

The truth is I did not have to wait long to get tired of my triumphs. Not thirty days, I think. The glory which is built upon a lie soon becomes a most unpleasant incumbrance. No doubt for a while I enjoyed having my exploits told and retold and told again in my presence and wondered over and exclaimed about, but I quite

distinctly remember that there presently came a time when the subject was wearisome and <u>odious</u> to me and I could not endure the disgusting discomfort of it. I am well aware that the world-glorified doer of a deed of great and real splendor has just my experience; I know that he deliciously enjoys hearing about it for three or four weeks and that pretty soon after that he begins to dread the mention of it and by and by wishes he had been with the damned before he ever thought of doing that deed. I remember how General Sherman[14] used to rage and swear over "While we were marching through Georgia," which was played at him and sung at him everywhere he went; still, I think I suffered a shade more than the legitimate hero does, he being privileged to soften his misery with the reflection that his glory was at any rate golden and reproachless[15] in its origin, whereas I had no such privilege, there being no possible way to make mine respectable.

**How** easy it is to make people believe a lie and how hard it is to undo that work again! Thirty-five years after those evil exploits of mine I visited my old mother, whom I had not seen for ten years; and being moved by what seemed to me a rather noble and perhaps heroic impulse, I thought I would humble myself and confess my ancient fault. It cost me a great effort to make up my mind; I dreaded the sorrow that would rise in her face and the shame that would look out of her eyes; but after long and troubled reflection, the sacrifice seemed due and

---

13. **Lawks!:** an expression of wonder or amusement, shortened from "Lord, have mercy!"

14. **General Sherman:** William Tecumseh Sherman, the Union commander who led a destructive march from Atlanta, Georgia, to the Atlantic Ocean, cutting the Confederacy in two.

15. **reproachless:** so good and upright as to make any criticism impossible.

WORDS TO KNOW
**unassailable** (ŭn'ə-sā'lə-bəl) *adj.* impossible to dispute or disprove; undeniable
**odious** (ō'dē-əs) *adj.* arousing, or worthy of, strong dislike

665

---

### Literary Analysis | IRONY |

**A** Ask students to explain the situational irony that underlies Twain's statement.

**Possible Response:** Twain did such a good job of deceiving his mother that she offers as proof of his honesty the very proof he used to deceive her.

Have students consider the situational irony in the consequences of Twain's deception. Ask students to cite some of these consequences.

**Possible Responses:** He lost his faith in hypnotists and for fifty years believed that there must be a fraud behind instances he witnessed; his firsthand experience with hypnotism led him to be revolted by it; his fraud converted the entire town into believers; although prompted by the desire for attention, he soon became disgusted by the renown his deceit engendered; when he rallies himself to disappoint his mother by telling her the truth, she doesn't believe him.

### Literary Analysis: POINT OF VIEW

Ask students to evaluate how the first-person point of view contributes to dramatic and situational irony.

**Possible Responses:** Students should recognize that first-person point of view creates the dramatic irony because the reader knows the truth of Twain's actions. The underlying dramatic irony enables the reader to comprehend the situational irony and to appreciate the humor of the examples.

---

right and I gathered my resolution together and made the confession.

To my astonishment there were no sentimentalities, no dramatics, no George Washington effects; she was not moved in the least degree; she simply did not believe me and said so! I was not merely disappointed, I was nettled[16] to have my costly truthfulness flung out of the market in this placid and confident way when I was expecting to get a profit out of it. I asserted and reasserted, with rising heat, my statement that every single thing I had done on those long-vanished nights was a lie and a swindle; and when she shook her head tranquilly and said she knew better, I put up my hand and *swore* to it—adding a triumphant, "*Now* what do you say?"

It did not affect her at all; it did not budge her the fraction of an inch from her position. If this was hard for me to endure, it did not begin with the blister she put upon the raw[17] when she began to put my sworn oath out of court with *arguments* to prove that I was under a delusion and did not know what I was talking about. Arguments! Arguments to show that a person on a man's outside can know better what is on his inside than he does himself. I had cherished some contempt for arguments before, I have not enlarged my respect for them since. She refused to believe that I had invented my visions myself; she said it was folly: that I was only a child at the time and could not have done it. She cited the Richmond fire and the colonial mansion and said they were quite beyond my capacities. Then I saw my chance! I said she was right—I didn't invent those; I got them from Dr. Peake. Even this great shot did not damage. She said Dr. Peake's evidence was better than mine, and he had said in plain words that it was impossible **A** for me to have heard about those things. Dear, dear, what a grotesque and unthinkable situation: a confessed swindler convicted of honesty and condemned to acquittal by circum-

stantial evidence furnished by the swindled! **A**

I realized with shame and with impotent vexation that I was defeated all along the line. I had but one card left but it was a formidable one. I played it and stood from under. It seemed ignoble to demolish her fortress after she had defended it so valiantly but the defeated know not mercy. I played that master card. It was the pin-sticking. I said solemnly—

"I give you my honor, a pin was never stuck into me without causing me cruel pain."

She only said—

"It is thirty-five years. I believe you do think that now but I was there and I know better. You never winced."

She was so calm! and I was so far from it, so nearly frantic.

"Oh, my goodness!" I said, "let me *show* you that I am speaking the truth. Here is my arm; drive a pin into it—drive it to the head—I shall not wince."

She only shook her gray head and said with simplicity and conviction—

"You are a man now and could <u>dissemble</u> the hurt; but you were only a child then and could not have done it."

**And** so the lie which I played upon her in my youth remained with her as an unchallengeable truth to the day of her death. Carlyle[18] said "a lie cannot live." It shows that he did not know how to tell them. If I had taken out a life policy on this one the premiums would have bankrupted me ages ago. ❖

---

16. **nettled:** irritated; annoyed.
17. **the blister . . . raw:** a bad thing made even worse.
18. **Carlyle:** Thomas Carlyle, a British historian and essayist.

WORDS
TO **dissemble** (dĭ-sĕm′bəl) *v.* to disguise or conceal behind a false appearance
KNOW

666

---

## Teaching Options

### 🔴 Mini Lesson  Grammar

**PUNCTUATING CLAUSES IN A SERIES Instruction**
Commas can help make the meaning of a sentence clearer and help readers understand the relation of its parts. Commas also separate items in a series. Several clauses in a series require commas unless all clauses are joined by *and, or,* or *nor.* Display the following sentence to illustrate comma placement with serial clauses. Have students underline the clauses.
Mark Twain felt <u>that he could do a better job than Hicks</u>, <u>that the audience would enjoy his performance more</u>, and <u>that he could escape detection</u>.

**Exercise** Have students rewrite the following sentence with commas correctly placed.
Whatever actions he took or whatever visions he saw or whatever words he spoke were all endorsed by the mesmerizer. *(Whatever actions he took, whatever visions he saw, or whatever words he spoke were all endorsed by the mesmerizer.)*

 Use **Grammar Transparencies and Copymasters**, p. 156.

Use McDougal Littell's *Language Network*, Chapter 9, for more instruction and practice in punctuating clauses.

# *Thinking* through the LITERATURE

## Connect to the Literature

**1. What Do You Think?**
What did you find humorous about this selection? Explain.

> **Comprehension Check**
> - What prompted Twain to become a subject?
> - What weaknesses made Hicks a bad subject?
> - Why did Twain's feelings change after the mesmerizer left town?

## Think Critically

**2.** How would you describe Twain's attitude toward himself as a boy and toward the people in his hometown?

**3.** Do you think it was wrong for young Twain to deceive people by pretending to be mesmerized? Explain your opinion.

 THINK ABOUT
- why Twain decides to deceive people
- how he feels about deceiving
- his later failure to make his mother believe the truth

**4.** Do you agree with the statements Twain makes about human nature in the story? Consider Carlyle's statement that "a lie cannot live" and Twain's opposing viewpoint. Give reasons for your opinion.

**5.** ACTIVE READING PREDICTING Review your list of **predictions** and **clues.** Were you able to predict everything that happened? Or were you surprised by how some aspects of the story developed? Support your answer with evidence from the story.

## Extend Interpretations

**6. Critic's Corner** Elmer J. Joseph, a member of our student advisory board, complained about this selection: "Much is left unsaid about what happened to the mesmerizer and whether he knew how much of an impostor the narrator was." Do you think the mesmerizer knew the young Twain was faking? Share your conclusions with other students, giving reasons for your views.

**7. Connect to Life** Twain wrote that the incidents in his autobiography "must interest the average human being because [these incidents] are of a sort which he is familiar with in his own life." Can you easily relate this story to your own life? Consider what you wrote for the Connect to Your Life.

## Literary Analysis

 **IRONY** **Irony** is the contrast between what we expect and what actually happens. In ironic situations, appearances are often deceiving and outcomes are usually surprising. The ugly duckling turns into a beautiful swan. The trusted friend turns out to be a phony.

In this selection, Twain relies on situational irony to poke fun at society and himself. In a story that uses **situational irony,** things turn out to be the opposite of what we expect, and characters are surprised by what actually happens.

Twain expects to enjoy the thrill of celebrity but soon finds his victory is hollow and worthless:

> *No doubt for a while I enjoyed having my exploits told and retold and told again in my presence . . . but . . . there presently came a time when the subject was wearisome and odious to me and I could not endure the disgusting discomfort of it.*

**Paired Activity** Work with a partner to identify two or three other examples of situational irony in this story. Discuss what makes each example both ironic and humorous. You might use a chart like this one to organize your information.

| Twain's Situational Irony ||
|---|---|
| **What Twain Expects** | **What Happens** |
| To enjoy the thrill of being the subject of hypnotism. | He is the only one in town who is not interested in hypnotism. |

---

## Extend Interpretations

**Critic's Corner** Encourage students to consider how the mesmerizer reacted to young Twain's enthusiastic response to his methods, and have students analyze Twain's perceptions of the hypnotist. Remind them to support their conclusions with text evidence.

**Connect to Life** Tell students that their experiences do not have to be elaborate deceptions like Mark Twain's hoax. Students might recall instances when a deception was short-lived, but made them feel what Mark Twain feels.

---

## Connect to the Literature

**1. What Do You Think?**
Students should cite specific examples from the text and be able to explain the humor.

**Comprehension Check**
- Twain was prompted by his envy of Hicks and his desire to be in the limelight.
- According to Twain, Hicks had no imagination, he was calm, and he described only what he saw.
- Twain grew tired of hearing his exploits described.

Use Selection Quiz
**Unit Four Resource Book,** p. 59.

## Think Critically

**2. Possible Responses:** He is vain; he's impressed with his own abilities; he's proud; he looks down on the unimaginative Hicks; he respects the pompous Dr. Peake; he views his audience as naive and gullible.

**3.** Students should defend their opinions with details about Twain's own feelings and the consequences of his acts.

**4.** Students' should support their responses with examples from their experiences.

**5.** Accept all well-supported responses.

## Literary Analysis

**Irony Possible Responses:** Twain expects to be unmasked as an impostor by the hypnotist; instead the hypnotist uses his dissembling to boost the popularity of his show. Twain is upset that some do not believe in him; he is so convincing at the end of the two weeks that not even his mother will believe he was acting. He expects that his mother will be upset at him for lying all those years ago. Instead she thinks he is deceiving her now.

## Writing Options

1. **Screenplay Script** Have students read the passage aloud to appreciate the vividness of Twain's description and then compose a brief outline listing the details to include in their scripts.

2. **Instruction Manual** Have students assign the following roles: recorder, who makes notes of the group's ideas; director, who poses questions and keeps the discussion on track; options-generator, who prompts the group to consider other approaches.

3. **Newspaper Report** Remind students that space is limited in a newspaper article. The answers to the *who, what, when, where,* and *why* questions must appear within the first sentences of a newspaper report.

## Activities & Explorations

1. **Stage Directions** Have students simulate the movements of the mesmerizer and Twain so that their actions can be translated into stage directions. Students may choose to create a computer-generated diagram.

2. **Advertising Flyer** Have students look at flyers for current movies, concerts, speeches, or other special events to use as models. Encourage them to use a variety of typefaces and type sizes so that the lettering adds to the impact of their messages.

## Inquiry & Research

**Science** Have students consult indexes before using other resources (see the Inquiry and Research Mini Lesson at the bottom of this page). Also remind them that a preliminary outline of the topics to investigate will help focus their research.

## Vocabulary in Action

| | |
|---|---|
| 1. a | 6. c |
| 2. c | 7. c |
| 3. b | 8. b |
| 4. b | 9. a |
| 5. a | 10. b |

---

## Writing Options

1. **Screenplay Script** If you were writing a screenplay of this excerpt, how would you have Twain tell the story of the Richmond Theater fire? Analyze Twain's account of hearing the story. Then write the lines that Twain would deliver. Put your script in your **Working Portfolio.**

2. **Instruction Manual** Working in a small group, put together tips for an instruction manual called *How to Be a Good Mesmerizer.* Base your tips on the practices of Simmons (the mesmerizer) and his model "subject," the young Mark Twain.

3. **Newspaper Report** Imagine you're a reporter for the *Hannibal Chronicle* in 1850. Last night you saw the mesmerizer's show and watched Twain perform under hypnosis. You were so amazed that you couldn't wait to describe the events. Write an engaging article about the performance that captivated the audience.

## Activities & Explorations

1. **Stage Directions** How would you stage a performance of the mesmerist and Twain's convincing performance? Pick one dramatic scene from the selection and write stage directions for it. Use the diagram below to show how the action progresses. ~ **VIEWING AND REPRESENTING**

2. **Advertising Flyer** Pretend that Twain goes on the road with the mesmerizer. Design a flyer advertising an upcoming performance in another Mississippi River town. ~ **ART**

## Inquiry & Research

**Science** Twain pretended to be hypnotized by the mesmerizer. But could he have really been hypnotized? Find out more about hypnosis using scientific journals, psychology journals, encyclopedias, and on-line resources. What is hypnosis? Does it really work? How is someone hypnotized? Is it dangerous? Report what you find to the class.

**More Online: Research Starter** www.mcdougallittell.com

| Wings (off-stage) | Upstage Right | Upstage Center | Upstage Left | Wings (off-stage) |
|---|---|---|---|---|
| | Right | Center | Left | |
| | Downstage Right | Downstage Center | Downstage Left | |

**AUDIENCE**

## Vocabulary in Action

**EXERCISE: ASSESSMENT PRACTICE** For each group of words below, write the letter of the word that is the best synonym for the boldfaced word.

1. **usurping** (a) seizing, (b) defeating, (c) borrowing
2. **rapt** (a) hidden, (b) casual, (c) spellbound
3. **unassailable** (a) leaky, (b) unquestionable, (c) mistaken
4. **gullible** (a) doubtful, (b) overtrusting, (c) excitable
5. **collusion** (a) conspiracy, (b) mixture, (c) idea
6. **dissemble** (a) feel, (b) disconnect, (c) hide
7. **implacable** (a) quiet, (b) indecisive, (c) unyielding
8. **credulity** (a) payment, (b) trust, (c) respect
9. **odious** (a) disgusting, (b) secretive, (c) humble
10. **confederate** (a) falsity, (b) accomplice, (c) team

| WORDS TO KNOW | | | | | |
|---|---|---|---|---|---|
| | collusion | credulity | gullible | odious | unassailable |
| | confederate | dissemble | implacable | rapt | usurping |

**Building Vocabulary**
Several Words to Know in this lesson contain prefixes and suffixes. For an in-depth study of word parts, see page 1130.

---

 **Inquiry and Research**

**USING INDEXES Instruction** Using indexes will help students locate appropriate print and non-print resources in which to find information about a topic. Indexes are reference books or on-line resources that provide alphabetized listings of names, places, subjects, titles, or authors of works or first names of works. Each listing in an index is followed by the titles of works that contain information on the subject. Indexes such as *The Readers' Guide to Periodical Literature* and *The New York Times Index* can help students locate information in newspapers, magazines, journals, and books. Remind students not to overlook the indexes to encyclopedias, which often suggest related topics to investigate.

**Application** Have students consult an index to begin their research on hypnosis, the subject of the Inquiry and Research activity. Ask students to submit a 4 x 6 card that lists the name of the index used, bibliographical information about it, its format (whether an on-line resource, a CD-ROM, or a reference book), and the title of a book or an article about hypnosis that the index identifies. Encourage students to consult the reference librarian for help in locating or using indexes.

# PREPARING to *Read*

*"The face of the water, in time, became a wonderful book."*

## from Life on the Mississippi

*Memoir by* MARK TWAIN

### Connect to Your Life

**A Change of Heart** In this excerpt, Twain recalls how his view of the Mississippi River changed as he became a riverboat pilot. Have you ever experienced a change of heart as you learned more about a person, an activity, a place, or a subject? What characteristics fascinated you in the beginning? Why? How did your feelings change as you became more knowledgeable? Describe such a situation with a group of classmates.

## Build Background

**Dangerous Expedition!** In Twain's day, piloting a paddle steamboat was tricky because the Mississippi was constantly changing. South of St. Louis, Missouri, the huge brown river meanders, curving and looping back on itself, looking like "a long, pliant apple paring," as Twain put it. The powerful current would move from one side to the other, changing course often. Along this twisting course lurked hidden sandbars and submerged wrecks. Depending on the season, low water or floods added more dangers. Riverboat pilots constantly swapped precious information about the changing river as they sailed its perilous length.

## Focus Your Reading

**LITERARY ANALYSIS** **DESCRIPTION** Twain brings the Mississippi River to life by using **description**—writing that helps a reader picture scenes, events, and people. By using colorful comparisons and vivid details, Twain helps us see the river as he did. Many of the details Twain uses appeal to our senses, like those in his description of sunset on the river.

> *A broad expanse of the river was turned to blood; in the middle distance the red hue brightened into gold. . . .*

Watch for more examples of descriptive details and comparisons as you read.

**ACTIVE READING** **VISUALIZING** When writers skillfully describe a scene or a character, they help readers **visualize,** or form a mental picture based on their written descriptions. The more precise the **details** a writer supplies about a person, setting, or event, the more vivid the picture you can form in your mind's eye. For example, what details make it so easy to visualize the part of the river described in this passage?

> *High above the forest wall a clean-stemmed dead tree waved a single leafy bough that glowed like a flame. . . .*

**READER'S NOTEBOOK** As you read, record the details and comparisons that help you to clearly visualize the Mississippi. Here's an example:

| Mississippi Descriptions | |
|---|---|
| **Details** | **Comparison** |
| the red hue brightened into gold | leafy bough glows like a flame |
| | |

## OVERVIEW

 This selection is included in the **Grade 11 InterActive Reader.**

### Objectives
1. appreciate a selection from a classic **memoir (Literary Analysis)**
2. appreciate and examine **description (Literary Analysis)**
3. **visualize** details in a memoir **(Active Reading)**

### Summary
Mark Twain recounts how he lightly undertook the challenge of becoming a riverboat pilot and learning twelve or thirteen hundred miles of the Mississippi. He thought that because the river was so wide, it would be an easy task to steer the boat down the middle of it. However, Mr. Bixby teaches him otherwise over the next few weeks. Twain learns to hug the bank on upstream runs, is taught the various points of the river, and is hauled out of a comfortable bed in the middle of the night to take his watch. He soon realizes that the job of a steamboat pilot is more real and "worklike" than romantic. After filling a notebook full of facts and journeying eight hundred miles up the river, Twain understands that the river's placid surface hides an entire world, invisible to those who cannot read the water. The river still fascinates him now that he can read its subtle signals, but he laments that fact that he can no longer appreciate a sunset on the river purely for its beauty.

### Thematic Link
Twain discovers that the steamboat pilots of the Mississippi are true **trailblazers** as he learns to navigate its waters. He must watch for clues and landmarks as carefully as any scout penetrating the wilderness of a new **frontier.**

### 5-Minute Warm-Up

*Daily Language SkillBuilder*

Have students **proofread** the display sentences on page 555k and write them correctly. The sentences also appear on Transparency 19 of **Grammar Transparencies and Copymasters.**

## LESSON RESOURCES

**UNIT FOUR RESOURCE BOOK,** pp. 60–63

**ASSESSMENT RESOURCES**
**Formal Assessment,**
  pp. 127–128
**Teacher's Guide to Assessment and Portfolio Use**
**Test Generator**

**SKILLS TRANSPARENCIES AND COPYMASTERS**
**Reading and Critical Thinking**
• Visualizing, T8 (for Active Reading, p. 669)

**Grammar**
• Using *That* and *Which,* T44 (for Mini Lesson, p. 671)
• Adjective Clauses: Common Introductory Words, C94 (for Mini Lesson, p. 671)
• Commas in Names and Titles, C150 (for Mini Lesson, p. 677)
**Vocabulary**
• Analogies, C57 (for Mini Lesson, p. 673)
**Writing**
• Reflective Essay, C28 (for Writing Option 2, p. 677)

**Communications**
• Evaluation Matrix: Film/Video, T7 (for Activities & Explorations 2, p. 677)

**INTEGRATED TECHNOLOGY**

**Audio Library**
**Net Activities**
**Video: Literature in Performance**
• *Life on the Mississippi,* a film adaptation. See **Video Resource Book,** pp. 15–20.
**Internet: Research Starter**
**Visit our website:**
www.mcdougallittell.com

## Reading and Analyzing

**Reading Skills and Strategies:
PREVIEW**

Discuss the Build Background of the
selection to help students get a sense
of the difficult challenge the young
Twain faces on the Mississippi.

**Literary Analysis** DESCRIPTION

 An analogy is a comparison between
two dissimilar things in order to clarify
the less familiar of the two. Twain uses
colorful comparisons to make his experiences on the river vivid even to those far
removed from his time and place. Ask
students to explain why the analogy Mr.
Bixby gives in his directions is effective.

**Possible Responses:** Everyone has
peeled an apple or watched someone
else peel one, so immediately it is clear
how close to the other boats Bixby
wants Twain to steer. The trick is to
avoid contact with the other boats but
stay as close as possible.

Use **Unit Four Resource Book**,
p. 62 for more practice.

**Active Reading** VISUALIZING

 Remind students that an author's
choice of verbs is important in creating
mental pictures for the reader. Ask students what "flaying" means and why
Twain uses this verb metaphorically to
describe Mr. Bixby's response to his
steering.

**Possible Response:** *Flaying* means
"stripping the skin from," and it
metaphorically conveys how severe Mr.
Bixby's criticism felt to Twain.

Use **Unit Four Resource Book**,
p. 61 for more practice.

*from* LIFE ON THE

# Mississippi

MARK TWAIN

A
CUB-PILOT'S
EXPERIENCE

What with lying on the rocks four days at
Louisville, and some other delays, the poor old
*Paul Jones* fooled away about two weeks in making the
voyage from Cincinnati to New Orleans. This gave me a
chance to get acquainted with one of the pilots, and he
taught me how to steer the boat, and thus made the
fascination of river life more potent than ever for me. . . .

I soon discovered two things. One was that a
vessel would not be likely to sail for the mouth
of the Amazon under ten or twelve years; and
the other was that the nine or ten dollars still left
in my pocket would not suffice for so impossible
an exploration as I had planned, even if I could
afford to wait for a ship. Therefore it followed
that I must contrive a new career. The *Paul Jones*
was now bound for St. Louis. I planned a siege
against my pilot, and at the end of three hard
days he surrendered. He agreed to teach me the

Mississippi River from New Orleans to St. Louis
for five hundred dollars, payable out of the first
wages I should receive after graduating. I entered
upon the small enterprise of "learning" twelve or
thirteen hundred miles of the great Mississippi
River with the easy confidence of my time of life.
If I had really known what I was about to
require of my faculties,[1] I should not have had
the courage to begin. I supposed that all a pilot

---

1. **faculties:** abilities.

## Teaching Options

### BLOCK SCHEDULING: MANAGING TIME

**If your schedule requires that you
cover the lesson objectives in a
shorter time, use . . .**
• Preparing to Read, p. 669
• Thinking Through the Literature,
p. 676

**If you want to take advantage of
longer class time, use . . .**
• TE Teaching Options: Workplace
Link, p. 672; Vocabulary Strategy,
p. 673; Speaking and Listening,
p. 674; Informal Assessment, p. 675
• Choices & Challenges, p. 677

had to do was to keep his boat in the river, and I did not consider that that could be much of a trick, since it was so wide.

The boat backed out from New Orleans at four in the afternoon, and it was "our watch" until eight. Mr. Bixby, my chief, "straightened her up," plowed her along past the sterns of the other boats that lay at the Levee,[2] and then said,  "Here, take her; shave those steamships as close as you'd peel an apple." I took the wheel, and my heartbeat fluttered up into the hundreds; for it seemed to me that we were about to scrape the side off every ship in the line, we were so close. I held my breath and began to claw the boat away from the danger; and I had my own opinion of the pilot who had known no better than to get us into such peril, but I was too wise to express it. In half a minute I had a wide margin of safety intervening between the *Paul Jones* and the ships; and within ten seconds more I was set

aside in disgrace, and Mr. Bixby was going into danger again and flaying me alive with abuse of my cowardice.  I was stung, but I was obliged to admire the easy confidence with which my chief loafed from side to side of his wheel, and trimmed the ships so closely that disaster seemed ceaselessly imminent.[3] When he had cooled a little he told me that the easy water was close ashore and the current outside, and therefore we must hug the bank, upstream, to get the benefit of the former, and stay well out, downstream, to take advantage of the latter. In my own mind I resolved to be a downstream pilot and leave the upstreaming to people dead to prudence.[4]

---

2. **Levee** (lĕv′ē): a landing place for boats on a river.

3. **imminent** (ĭm′ə-nənt): about to happen.

4. **dead to prudence:** lacking good judgment.

## Customizing Instruction

### Less Proficient Readers
Tell students that this selection is Mark Twain's account of how he learned to be a steamboat pilot. Explain that the pilot had to navigate the boat both upstream against the current of the river as well as downstream.
**Set a Purpose** Have students read to understand the discrepancy between Twain's original idea of a river pilot's task and the reality.

### Students Acquiring English
Show students a map that locates the Mississippi River so that they are aware of its great length. Tell students that steamboats on the Mississippi River were essential for transportation of people and cargo until the latter part of the 19th century. Remind students that Mark Twain is looking back at this portion of his life from a perspective of many years later.

Use **Spanish Study Guide** for additional support, pp. 163–165.

### Gifted and Talented
Suggest to students that a journey on water is often seen as a metaphor for one's journey through life. Ask students as they read to consider the metaphorical implications of Twain's initiation into the mysteries of riverboat piloting.

---

 ## Mini Lesson  Grammar

**INTRODUCTORY WORDS FOR ADJECTIVE CLAUSES**
**Instruction** Adjective clauses are subordinate clauses that modify a noun or pronoun. Adjective clauses may be introduced by relative pronouns or relative adverbs. Relative pronouns include *who, whom, whose, that,* and *which*. Relative adverbs include *after, before, since, when, where,* and *why*. Display the following sentences. Point out each introductory word and explain the function that it fulfills.

Mark Twain grew up in the era *when* riverboats ruled the Mississippi. (*The adjective clause*

*modifies* era; *the relative adverb* when *introduces the clause and modifies* ruled.)
After several lessons, *which* included scolding and instruction, Mark Twain felt more confident about his skills. (*The adjective clause modifies* lessons; *the relative pronoun* which *introduces the clause and acts as the subject of* included.)

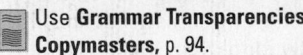 Use **Grammar Transparencies and Copymasters**, p. 94.

Use McDougal Littell's *Language Network,* Chapter 3, for more instruction and practice in adjective clauses.

### Literary Analysis: CHARACTERIZATION

Ask students to draw inferences about Mark Twain's young self from his reactions to Mr. Bixby's information and to his wake-up call in the middle of the night. Have them consider why Twain portrays his character in this way.

**Possible Responses:** He seems naïve, rather lazy, and slow to comprehend the significance and seriousness of what he is being told. This portrayal adds humor to his narrative, emphasizes the patience of Mr. Bixby in taking him on, shows by contrast how skilled Mr. Bixby is, and reveals how different the life of a riverboat pilot is from most ordinary occupations.

### Literary Analysis   DESCRIPTION

**A** Ask students to find the analogy that Twain uses to describe Bixby's agitation at his ignorance.

**Answer:** "he shuffled from one side of his wheel to the other as if the floor was hot."

### Active Reading   VISUALIZING

**B** Call students' attention to the metaphorical description of Mr. Bixby's wrath. Then ask them to listen to the following: "Mr. Bixby would mutter to himself awhile, and then get angrier and yell at me again." Ask students to decide which version enables them to gain a clearer picture of what Mr. Bixby is feeling and doing.

Mark Twain at age fifteen.

yawed[5] too far from shore, and so dropped back into disgrace again and got abused.

The watch was ended at last, and we took supper and went to bed. At midnight the glare of a lantern shone in my eyes, and the night watchman said, "Come, turn out!" And then he left. I could not understand this extraordinary procedure; so I presently gave up trying to, and dozed off to sleep. Pretty soon the watchman was back again, and this time he was gruff. I was annoyed. I said,

"What do you want to come bothering around here in the middle of the night for? Now, as like as not, I'll not get to sleep again to-night."

The watchman said, "Well, if this ain't good, I'm blessed."

HELLO, WATCHMAN! AIN'T THE NEW CUB TURNED OUT YET?

**1** Now and then Mr. Bixby called my attention to certain things. Said he, "This is Six-Mile Point." I assented. It was pleasant enough information, but I could not see the bearing of it. I was not conscious that it was a matter of any interest to me. Another time he said, "This is Nine-Mile Point." Later he said, "This is Twelve-Mile Point." They were all about level with the water's edge; they all looked about alike to me; they were monotonously unpicturesque. I hoped Mr. Bixby would change the subject. But no; he would crowd up around a point, hugging the shore with affection, and then say: "The slack water ends here, abreast this bunch of China trees; now we cross over." So he crossed over. He gave me the wheel once or twice, but I had no luck. I either came near chipping off the edge of a sugar plantation, or I

The "offwatch" was just turning in, and I heard some brutal laughter from them, and such remarks as "Hello, watchman! ain't the new cub turned out yet? He's delicate, likely. Give him some sugar in a rag, and send for the chambermaid to sing 'Rock-a-by Baby' to him." **2**

About this time Mr. Bixby appeared on the scene. Something like a minute later I was climbing the pilothouse steps with some of my

---

5. **yawed:** swerved.

---

## Teaching Options

### Workplace Link **Contracts**

**STARTING A NEW JOB Instruction** Mark Twain obviously felt that once he was accepted as a cub-pilot, the hard part was over—but he soon realizes that it was just beginning. Mr. Bixby had certain expectations and assumed that Twain knew something about the job. Although Twain overcame these first obstacles to eventually become a full-fledged pilot, he could have started his career more smoothly by following some guidelines for new employees. New employees should remember the following:

• Show initiative.

• Start early and stay late.

• Learn from your mistakes.

• Ask questions and take notes.

• Check understanding of instructions by restating them in your own words.

**Application** Ask students to point out occasions when Twain could have implemented these guidelines. Have them think of questions that he should have asked Mr. Bixby during his first training sessions. Then ask students to create a brief training manual for a cub-pilot that Bixby could have handed out before Twain began to work. The training manual should outline the duties and hours of the job and should describe ways that a new employee can make a good impression.

clothes on and the rest in my arms. Mr. Bixby was close behind, commenting. Here was something fresh[6]—this thing of getting up in the middle of the night to go to work. It was a detail in piloting that had never occurred to me at all. I knew that boats ran all night, but somehow I had never happened to reflect that somebody had to get up out of a warm bed to run them. I began to fear that piloting was not quite so romantic as I had imagined it was; there was something very real and worklike about this new phase of it. . . .

Mr. Bixby made for the shore and soon was scraping it, just the same as if it had been daylight. And not only that, but singing:

Father in heaven, the day is declining, etc.

It seemed to me that I had put my life in the keeping of a peculiarly reckless outcast. Presently he turned on me and said, "What's the name of the first point above New Orleans?"

I was gratified to be able to answer promptly, and I did. I said I didn't know.

"Don't *know*?"

This manner jolted me. I was down at the foot[7] again, in a moment. But I had to say just what I had said before.

"Well, you're a smart one!" said Mr. Bixby. "What's the name of the *next* point?"

Once more I didn't know.

"Well, this beats anything. Tell me the name of *any* point or place I told you."

I studied awhile and decided that I couldn't.

"Look here! What do you start out from, above Twelve Mile Point, to cross over?"

"I—I—don't know."

"You—you—don't know?" mimicking my drawling manner of speech. "What *do* you know?"

"I—I—nothing, for certain."

"By the great Caesar's ghost, I believe you! You're the stupidest dunderhead I ever saw or ever heard of, so help me Moses! The idea of

*you* being a pilot—you! Why, you don't know enough to pilot a cow down a lane."

Oh, but his wrath was up! He was a nervous man, and he shuffled from one side of his wheel to the other as if the floor was hot. He would boil awhile to himself, and then overflow and scald me again.

"Look here! What do you suppose I told you the names of those points for?"

I tremblingly considered a moment, and then the devil of temptation provoked me to say, "Well to—to—be entertaining, I thought."

This was a red rag to the bull. He raged and stormed so (he was crossing the river at the time) that I judged it made him blind, because he ran over the steering oar of a trading scow.[8] Of course the traders sent up a volley of red-hot profanity. Never was a man so grateful as Mr. Bixby was, because he was brimful, and here were subjects who could *talk back*. He threw open a window, thrust his head out, and such an irruption followed as I never had heard before. The fainter and farther away the scowmen's curses drifted, the higher Mr. Bixby lifted his voice and the weightier his adjectives grew. When he closed the window he was empty. You could have drawn a seine[9] through his system and not caught curses enough to disturb your mother with. Presently he said to me in the gentlest way, "My boy, you must get a little memorandum book; and every time I tell you a thing, put it down right away. There's only one way to be a pilot, and that is to get this entire river by heart. You have to know it just like A B C."

That was a dismal revelation to me, for my memory was never loaded with anything but blank cartridges. However, I did not feel discouraged long. I judged that it was best to

---

6. **fresh:** new.
7. **down at the foot:** at the bottom of the class.
8. **scow:** a flat-bottomed boat used chiefly to transport freight.
9. **seine** (sān): large fishing net.

**Customizing Instruction**

**Less Proficient Readers**
Ask students to contrast Twain's original perception of a riverboat pilot's job with the reality.
**Possible Responses:** It is much harder than he thought it would be and much less romantic. He thought that a pilot merely had to keep the boat in the middle of the river; instead a pilot must navigate through many obstacles during the day and at night.
**Set a Purpose** Have students adjust their purpose for reading to find out whether Twain makes any progress in his training and how his feelings about the river change.

**Students Acquiring English**
1 Explain that Mr. Bixby is giving Twain information about the river that will help him to navigate. Ask students what Twain thinks about Mr. Bixby's topics of conversation.
**Possible Responses:** Twain thinks Mr. Bixby is boring and wishes he would change the subject. Twain is oblivious to the importance of the landmarks.
2 Point out that the men of the "offwatch" mockingly suggest that Twain should be coddled like a baby.

**Multiple Learning Styles**
**Visual Learners**
Students may find the construction of a spider map helpful to clarify both the methods used to characterize Twain in this selection and the information conveyed through each method. They should create categories for methods of characterization such as what Twain does, what he says, what he thinks, and what Mr. Bixby says and does, and list examples of the words, thoughts, or actions that give insight into the character of Mark Twain.

## (Mini Lesson) Vocabulary Strategy

**UNDERSTANDING ANALOGIES Instruction** Remind students that reading and understanding analogies is a way to expand their vocabulary. An analogy consists of two pairs of words that are related to each other in the same way. Write the following analogy on the board:
SIEGE : ATTACK :: odyssey : journey
Ask students to determine how *siege* and *attack* are related to each other. Have a volunteer state the relationship in a sentence such as "A siege is a prolonged attack." Students should see the similarity of relationship in the second pair; an odyssey is a prolonged or extended journey.

**Exercises**
1. PROFANITY : WRATH :: laughter :
   (A) scorn (B) excitement (C) amusement
   (D) grief *(C)*
2. MONOTONOUS : DIVERSE :: succinct :
   (A) vapid (B) jovial (C) laconic (D) discursive *(D)*
3. RAPTURE : SATISFACTION :: obsequious :
   (A) polite (B) heavy (C) abrupt (D) sad *(A)*

Use **Vocabulary Transparencies and Copymasters**, p. 57.

**A lesson on analogies appears on p. 254 in the Pupil's Edition.**

**A** Explain that Twain employs an extended analogy that compares the river to a book. Earlier, Mr. Bixby tells Twain that he must learn the river "just like A B C." Ask students to trace the details that help develop this analogy.
**Possible Responses:** "a dead language to the uneducated passenger"; "had a new story to tell every day"; "never a page that was void of interest"

### Literary Analysis: CHARACTERIZATION

**B** Ask students what change in Mark Twain is revealed through his description of how he views a sunset after learning the lore of the river. Have them contrast his tone in this passage with the tone at the beginning of his narrative.
**Possible Responses:** Twain no longer sees the beautiful surface of the river; he has gained a wisdom about what lies beneath the surface and can no longer take the river for granted. He feels the weight of the responsibility of being a pilot. His tone is more serious.

### Literary Analysis | DESCRIPTION |

**C** The selection ends with an implied analogy between a riverboat pilot and a doctor. Ask students what similarities Twain sees between himself and a doctor.
**Possible Responses:** Twain can no longer appreciate the superficial beauty of the river. He now knows what danger lurks beneath the surface. He believes a doctor cannot look at someone as beautiful, but must interpret outward charms as manifestations of hidden disease and decay.

---

make some allowances, for doubtless Mr. Bixby was "stretching."[10] . . .

**1** By the time we had gone seven or eight hundred miles up the river, I had learned to be a tolerably plucky upstream steersman, in daylight; and before we reached St. Louis I had made a trifle of progress in night work, but only a trifle. I had a notebook that fairly bristled with the names of towns, "points," bars, islands, bends, reaches, etc.; but the information was to be found only in the notebook—none of it was in my head. It made my heart ache to think I had only got half of the river set down; for as our watch was four hours off and four hours on, day and night, there was a long four-hour gap in my book for every time I had slept since the voyage began. . . .

＊＊＊

**A** . . . The face of the water, in time, became a wonderful book—a book that was a dead language to the uneducated passenger, but which told its mind to me without reserve, delivering its most cherished secrets as clearly as if it uttered them with a voice. And it was not a book to be read once and thrown aside, for it had a new story to tell every day. Throughout the long twelve hundred miles there was never a page that was void of interest, never one that you could leave unread without loss, never one that you would want to skip, thinking you could find higher enjoyment in some other thing. There never was so wonderful a book written by man; never one whose interest was so absorbing, so unflagging, so sparklingly renewed with every reperusal.[11] The passenger who could not read it was charmed with a peculiar sort of faint dimple on its surface (on the rare occasions when he did not overlook it altogether); but to the pilot that was an *italicized* passage; indeed, it was more than that, it was a legend of the largest capitals,[12] with a string of shouting exclamation points at the end of it, for it meant that a wreck or a rock was buried there that could tear the life out of the strongest vessel that ever floated. It

is the faintest and simplest expression the water ever makes, and the most hideous to a pilot's eye. In truth, the passenger who could not read this book saw nothing but all manner of pretty pictures in it, painted by the sun and shaded by the clouds, whereas to the trained eye these were not pictures at all, but the grimmest and most dead earnest of reading matter.

Now when I had mastered the language of this water, and had come to know every trifling feature that bordered the great river as familiarly as I knew the letters of the alphabet, I had made a valuable acquisition. But I had lost something, too. I had lost something which could never be restored to me while I lived. All the grace, the beauty, the poetry, had gone out of the majestic river! I still kept in mind a certain wonderful sunset which I witnessed when steamboating was new to me. A broad expanse of the river was turned to blood; in the middle distance the red hue brightened into gold, through which a solitary log came floating, black and conspicuous; in one place a long, slanting mark lay sparkling upon the water; in another the surface was broken by boiling, tumbling rings, that were as many-tinted as an opal; where the ruddy flush was faintest, was a smooth spot that was covered with graceful circles and radiating lines, ever so delicately traced; the shore on our left was densely wooded, and the somber shadow that fell from this forest was broken in one place by a long, ruffled trail that shone like silver; and high above the forest wall a clean-stemmed dead tree waved a single leafy bough that glowed like a flame in the unobstructed splendor that was flowing from the sun. There were graceful curves, reflected images, woody heights, soft distances; and over the whole scene, far and near, the dissolving lights drifted steadily,

---

10. **"stretching":** exaggerating.

11. **reperusal** (rē′pə-rōō′zəl): rereading.

12. **a legend of the largest capitals:** an inscription in large capital letters.

---

## Teaching Options

 **Speaking and Listening**

**PERSUADING Prepare** Ask students to review characteristics of Mark Twain as he appears at the beginning of the excerpt and of Mr. Bixby. Then have students work in pairs to develop arguments that they think Twain might have used to persuade Bixby to take him on as an apprentice. Students should also incorporate the counterarguments with which Bixby might have responded. Arguments and responses should reflect what students know about the characters' personalities. Student dialogues should present adequate and organized evidence to support their arguments, and mean-

ing should be reinforced by appropriate nonverbal techniques such as gestures and facial expressions.
**Present** Students should role-play their dialogues in front of the class. Audience members should assess the effectiveness of the arguments presented, the realism and relevance of the responses, and the success of the nonverbal techniques. They should also evaluate how consistent the performance is with the characters as they are presented in the text.

**BLOCK SCHEDULING** This activity is particularly well-suited to longer class periods.

enriching it every passing moment with new marvels of coloring.

I stood like one bewitched. I drank it in, in a speechless rapture. The world was new to me, and I had never seen anything like this at home. But as I have said, a day came when I began to cease from noting the glories and the charms which the moon and the sun and the twilight wrought upon the river's face; another day came when I ceased altogether to note them. Then, if that sunset scene had been repeated, I should have looked upon it without rapture, and should have commented upon it, inwardly, after this fashion: "This sun means that we are going to have wind tomorrow; that floating log means that the river is rising, small thanks to it; that slanting mark on the water refers to a bluff reef[13] which is going to kill somebody's steamboat one of these nights, if it keeps on stretching out like that; those tumbling 'boils' show a dissolving bar and a changing channel there; the lines and circles in the slick water over yonder are a warning that that troublesome place is shoaling up[14] dangerously; that silver streak in the shadow of the forest is the 'break' from a new snag, and he has located himself in the very best place he could have found to fish for steamboats; that tall dead tree, with a single living branch, is not going to last long, and then how is a body ever going to get through this blind place at night without the friendly old landmark?"

No, the romance and beauty were all gone from the river. All the value any feature of it had for me now was the amount of usefulness it could furnish toward compassing the safe

Pilot's certificate issued to Mark Twain in 1859.

THE WORLD WAS NEW TO ME, AND I HAD NEVER SEEN ANYTHING LIKE THIS AT HOME.

piloting of a steamboat. Since those days, I have pitied doctors from my heart. What does the lovely flush in a beauty's cheek mean to a doctor but a "break" that ripples above some deadly disease? Are not all her visible charms sown thick with what are to him the signs and symbols of hidden decay? Does he ever see her beauty at all, or doesn't he simply view her professionally, and comment upon her unwholesome condition all to himself? And doesn't he sometimes wonder whether he has gained most or lost most by learning his trade? ❖

---

13. **bluff reef:** an underwater ridge of rock.
14. **shoaling up:** becoming too shallow for safe navigation, because of a buildup of sand or silt in the riverbed.

---

## GUIDING STUDENT RESPONSE

## Connect to the Literature

**1. What Do You Think?**
Students might see Twain as a person able to laugh at himself, as a person with skills other than ability to write, or as someone who thinks about his experiences and draws conclusions about them.

**Comprehension Check**
• the riverboat on which Twain began his training as a riverboat pilot
• Bixby had been telling Twain crucial landmarks along the river and Twain had not paid attention to the information.
• Twain as a riverboat pilot learned to understand the significance of marks on the water, so he now sees the river as a source of vital information, not a picture of beauty and romance.

 Use Selection Quiz
**Unit Four Resource Book,** p. 63.

## Think Critically

**2.** Students should recognize that the job is more difficult than Twain expected it to be, that it requires extensive knowledge and skill, and that it demands an unusual sleep schedule.

**3.** Students who think Twain makes this point convincingly may refer to his comments about the life-and-death significance of the information a pilot gleans from the "book" of the river. Students who disagree might argue that the "book" is fascinating only for practical reasons, not because it is really interesting or enjoyable.

**4.** Twain's descriptions of the beauty of the river or his interpretations of the meaning of various sights might alter some students' impressions of the river.

## Connect to the Literature

**1. What Do You Think?**
What opinion of Mark Twain do you form from this selection? Support your opinion.

**Comprehension Check**
• What is the *Paul Jones?*
• Why did Bixby think Twain was "the stupidest dunderhead"?
• Why does Twain fear that the romance of the river is gone for him?

## Think Critically

**2.** What are your impressions of the job of a riverboat pilot?

 THINK ABOUT

• Twain's first impressions of piloting on the river
• what changes Twain had to make in his everyday habits
• the kinds of things Twain had to memorize and use on the job
• the nature of the river

**3.** Do you think Twain convincingly explains how the Mississippi was like a book that one could never tire of reading? Defend your answer.

**4.** **ACTIVE READING** **VISUALIZING** Review your **READER'S NOTEBOOK** record of the details and comparisons that helped you **visualize** the Mississippi. Which details or comparisons changed or affirmed your previous impression of the river?

## Extend Interpretations

**5.** **Comparing Texts** In his *Autobiography* and in *Life on the Mississippi,* Twain retells different episodes of his life. Which work do you prefer? Discuss your preferences in a small group. Cite evidence to support your opinion.

**6.** **What If?** Imagine that Twain gave up the idea of riverboat piloting after the first trip with Mr. Bixby. How might his view of the river have been different?

**7.** **Connect to Life** Recall your discussion, in the Connect to Your Life activity on page 669, about your own experiences with a change of heart. Do you think what you learned outweighed any sense of loss you felt? Explain.

## Literary Analysis

**DESCRIPTION** **Description** is the process by which a writer creates a picture in words of a scene, an event, or a character. Two descriptive devices include:

• **Imagery,** or descriptive words and phrases a writer uses to re-create sensory experience. Sensory details appeal to the reader's senses of sight, hearing, smell, taste, and touch. For example, Twain uses the image of a jewel to help readers visualize the restless river:

*In another [place] the surface was broken by boiling, tumbling rings, that were as many-tinted as an opal. . . .*

• **Analogies,** which show the similarities between two things that are otherwise unlike each other. To help readers understand his fascination with the Mississippi, Twain compared the river to a book:

*The face of the water, in time, became a wonderful book—a book that was a dead language to the uneducated passenger, but which told its mind to me without reserve, delivering its most cherished secrets. . . .*

**Paired Activity** With a partner, look for additional examples of these descriptive devices in the selection. Use a chart like the one below to identify each example as imagery or analogy, and record the effects of each example on you as a reader.

| Twain's Descriptions | | |
|---|---|---|
| Detail | Descriptive Device | Effect |
| | | |

## Extend Interpretations

**Comparing Texts** Students who prefer the *Autobiography* excerpt might praise its portrait of a spirited young man or its descriptions of a traveling show. Those who prefer the *Life on the Mississippi* excerpt might emphasize its descriptions of how demanding the job of riverboat pilot was.

**What If?** Twain probably would not have been able to recognize many of the danger signs in the river if he had given up piloting; he might retain his ability to see the river as a beautiful scene.

**Connect to Life** Many students may agree with Twain that learning a skill entails an unavoidable loss of a sense of wonder.

## Literary Analysis

**Description** Many of Twain's analogies are humorous: comparing his request for pilot training to a siege (page 670), Bixby's scolding to being skinned alive (page 671), his own ignorant reply to waving a red flag at a bull (page 673). Others are thought provoking, such as comparing a woman's complexion to a danger sign on the river's surface (page 675). His imagery in the passage beginning "But I had lost something" (page 674) mainly creates a picture of the river as seen by an untrained eye.

# Choices & Challenges

## Writing Options

**1. Diary Entry** Twain says he would not have had the courage to learn the duties of a riverboat pilot had he known at the start what would be required of him. Write a diary entry describing the chores, routines, responsibilities—and rewards—of a pilot as Twain presents them in his memoir.

**2. Magazine Article** In October 1874, Twain wrote to the *Atlantic Monthly's* editor, William Dean Howells, about an idea he had for a series in the magazine, capturing the "old Mississippi days of steamboating glory and grandeur as I saw them." Pretend that you are Twain, and write a short article about your life on the Mississippi. Include details about the scenery along the riverbanks, the crowds of people you met, and the adventures you encountered.

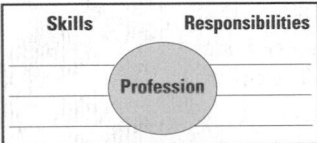

Writer
Mark Twain.

## Activities & Explorations

**1. Occupational Outlook** Twain agreed to pay Mr. Bixby $500 for his apprenticeship. Today, most people learn the specific tasks and responsibilities of their professions while on the job. On a diagram like this one, identify another profession that would require on-the-job training. Be sure to include specific skills and responsibilities that an apprentice would gain. Present your diagram to the class.
~ **SPEAKING AND LISTENING**

Skills          Responsibilities

**Profession**

**2. Video Adaptation** View the videotaped excerpt of *Life on the Mississippi* provided as a part of this program. Focus on the interaction between Twain and Mr. Bixby. How is it similar to or different from their interaction in Twain's memoir? Does it realistically depict the actions in the memoir? In a class discussion, compare the videotape portrayals with those in the selection.
~ **VIEWING AND REPRESENTING**

 **Literature in Performance**

## Inquiry & Research

A view of downtown , Hannibal, Missouri, on the Mississipi River, hometown of writer Mark Twain.

**Geography** Write a brief report on the Mississippi River as it is today. What effect does the river have on the people who live near it? Does it continue to be a thriving avenue of commerce, or has it been replaced? How has the river's physical appearance changed over the years?

 **More Online: Research Starter**
www.mcdougallittell.com

## Writing Options

**1. Diary Entry To get students started on this assignment,** have them organize their details in columns under the headings of chores, routines, responsibilities, rewards. Remind students that because it is a diary entry, they should include personal reflections on the various aspects of their day and night consistent with what Mark Twain reveals about his feelings.

**2. Magazine Article** Review with students some specific facts about the culture, customs, and people of the states bordering the Mississippi in the post–Civil War era. Encourage students to refer to Mark Twain's other writings for descriptive passages of what they might see along the river. **Visual learners** might illustrate their articles.

## Activities & Explorations

**1. Occupational Outlook** Ask students to think about part-time jobs they may have had and what they learned once they were actually doing the job. Students might fill in a sample diagram using their part-time experiences. Students might also interview employees in occupations that have extensive on-the-job training to find out the skills that are taught and the responsibilities that are acquired through the actual work experience.

**2. Video Adaptation To get students started on this assignment,** have them review what was revealed about Mark Twain's relationship with Mr. Bixby in the text. Students should record evidence from the text that leads them to these inferences. Then have students view the video, and defend the videotape portrayals or refute the accuracy of them.

## Inquiry & Research

**Geography** Students might check an encyclopedia for general information on the Mississippi River first. Then they might locate more specific print information through the use of the library database and the Internet. The Chambers of Commerce for the states that border the Mississippi might also be a source of current and comparative information.

LIFE ON THE MISSISSIPPI **677**

---

##  Grammar

**COMMAS IN NAMES AND TITLES Instruction** The use of commas in sentences helps to eliminate confusion. One of the functions of a comma is to set off a title following a personal name. Abbreviations such as *Inc.* and *Ltd.* are also set off with commas. Display the following sentence to illustrate the placement of the comma:

> After she graduated from law school, she could sign her name as Sylvia Robinson, Esquire.

**Exercises** Ask students to rewrite the following sentences with the correct punctuation.

**1.** His name appeared on the program as Kyle Elias State Senator. *(Kyle Elias, State Senator)*

**2.** Although we called her Sister Jeanne, her formal title was Jeanne Kelly S.M. *(Jeanne Kelly, S.M.)*

 Use **Grammar Transparencies and Copymasters,** p. 150.

 Use McDougal Littell's *Language Network,* Chapter 9, for more instruction and practice in commas.

LIFE ON THE MISSISSIPPI **677**

## Reading and Analyzing

### Literary Analysis: EPIGRAMS

Tell students that an epigram is a brief, clever, and usually memorable statement. Epigrams might offer advice or an insight into human nature. Ask students to choose an epigram on this page that they feel relates to Mark Twain's experience as a cub-pilot.

**Possible Responses:** "Man is the only animal that blushes. Or needs to." "Courage is resistance to fear, mastery of fear—not absence of fear." "Good breeding consists in concealing how much we think of ourselves and how little we think of the other person." "There are several good protections against temptations, but the surest is cowardice."

### Active Reading | VISUALIZING |

**A** Twain uses very concrete images to represent more abstract ideas. Have students look at the epigram that states, "Put all your eggs in one basket, and—watch the basket." Ask students what Twain is advising in this epigram and how the image conveys his meaning clearly.

**Possible Responses:** Twain is saying that if you invest all your time, energy, hope, or money in one project or goal, then you have a responsibility to be vigilant to safeguard your investment. The image of eggs is a good one because if the basket is taken, the eggs are gone. Any sensible person would watch the basket. People need to be as sensible in taking care of more significant possessions.

### Literary Analysis | DESCRIPTION |

Ask students to find epigrams that use analogies to convey their meaning.

**Possible Responses:** the first, ninth, fourteenth, and sixteenth

---

# EPIGRAMS
## MARK TWAIN

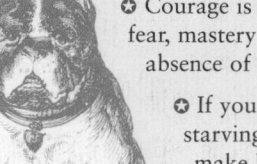

✪ Don't, like the cat, try to get more out of an experience than there is in it. The cat, having sat upon a hot stove lid, will not sit upon a hot stove lid again. Nor upon a cold stove lid.

✪ It is by the goodness of God that in our country we have those three unspeakably precious things: freedom of speech, freedom of conscience, and the prudence never to practice either of them.

✪ Man is the only animal that blushes. Or needs to.

✪ I am an old man and have known a great many troubles, but most of them have never happened.

✪ Nothing so needs reforming as other people's habits.

✪ When I was a boy of fourteen, my father was so ignorant I could hardly stand to have the old man around. But when I got to be twenty-one, I was astonished at how much the old man had learned in seven years.

✪ There are several good protections against temptations, but the surest is cowardice.

✪ Courage is resistance to fear, mastery of fear—not absence of fear.

✪ If you pick up a starving dog and make him prosperous, he will not bite you. This is the principal difference between a dog and a man.

✪ Put all your eggs in one basket, and—watch the basket.

✪ Good breeding consists in concealing how much we think of ourselves and how little we think of the other person.

✪ To promise not to do a thing is the surest way in the world to make a body want to go and do that very thing.

✪ Habit is habit, and not to be flung out of the window by any man, but coaxed downstairs a step at a time.

✪ One of the most striking differences between a cat and a lie is that a cat only has nine lives.

✪ Each person is born to one possession which outvalues all the others—his last breath.

✪ Everyone is a moon, and has a dark side which he never shows to anybody.

*"Well, there was a feller here once by the name of Jim Smiley . . ."*

# The Notorious Jumping Frog of Calaveras County

*Short Story by* MARK TWAIN

## Connect to Your Life

**Telling Tales** The narrator of this story asks an old Westerner if he knows anything about a man named Smiley. The old man corners him and tells him an incredible tale about a wager on a jumping frog. Think about a situation in which you heard someone tell an outlandish story that others believed. What made the tale so convincing? Discuss this situation with a group of classmates.

## Build Background

**Western Humor** Twain got the idea for this story in the gold hills outside San Francisco in 1865. While there, he mined for gold and spent time listening to local storytellers, who told this tale and others without ever cracking a smile. From these storytellers, Twain learned two truths about humor writing that he used for the rest of his life: one, the manner in which a person tells a story is what makes it funny; and two, a successful humorist should always pretend to be dead serious.

WORDS TO KNOW
**Vocabulary Preview**

| | |
|---|---|
| cavorting | infamous |
| commission | lattice |
| dilapidated | recommence |
| enterprising | tranquil |
| inclination | vagabond |

## Focus Your Reading

**LITERARY ANALYSIS** **TALL TALE** This story by Twain is an example of a **tall tale**, a distinctively American form of humorous story that features exaggeration. Much of a tall tale's rich humor comes from its use of **local color**, or writing that truthfully imitates ordinary life and brings a region alive by portraying its typical dress, mannerisms, customs, character types, and **dialects.** In Twain's tale, dialect, or local language, plays a crucial role, as seen in this passage:

*Smiley was monstrous proud of his frog, and well he might be for fellers that had traveled and been everywheres all said he laid over any frog that ever they see.*

As you read, be on the lookout for the characteristics of a tall tale.

**ACTIVE READING** **UNDERSTANDING DIALECT** Sometimes **dialects** are so different from familiar language that they can be hard to understand. Moreover, writers often reproduce the sound of words in a dialect by using unconventional spellings. As you read Twain's tale, use these techniques to decode difficult passages of dialect:

- Read slowly. Listen to the words as if someone were speaking them. You might try reading the story aloud to help you recognize unusual words as you pronounce them.
- Use **context clues** to figure out the meaning of unfamiliar words. For example, Twain writes, "You'd see that frog whirling in the air like a doughnut—see him turn one summerset. . . ." Twain restates the meaning of the unfamiliar word *summerset.* He uses the phrase "whirling in the air like a doughnut" to indicate that *summerset* must be the word *somersault.*

**READER'S NOTEBOOK** As you read, jot down unfamiliar words and expressions and what you think they mean. Here's an example:

| DIALECT | |
|---|---|
| Well, thish-yer Smiley had rat terriers | Thish-yer = this here |

---

# OVERVIEW

## Objectives
1. understand and appreciate a classic **short story (Literary Analysis)**
2. identify characteristics of a **tall tale (Literary Analysis)**
3. **understand** Twain's use of **dialect (Active Reading)**

## Summary
The narrator of this frame story locates a man named Simon Wheeler in a mining camp and inquires if he knows a Leonidas W. Smiley. Wheeler does not, but he begins a rambling reminiscence about a gambler named *Jim* Smiley. According to Wheeler, Smiley would bet on horse races, dog or cat fights, the success of revivalists at camp meetings, the likelihood of death for ailing people, anything. He was remarkably successful in his gambling career, but Smiley's downfall came when he initiated a frog jumping contest with a stranger. While Smiley went to the swamp to get the stranger a frog, the stranger filled Smiley's frog, Dan'l Webster, full of quail shot. When Smiley returned and the contest started, Dan'l Webster couldn't move from his spot. Only after the stranger left did Smiley realize he had been cheated. The narrator makes his escape just as Wheeler starts into a story about Smiley's one-eyed cow with no tail.

## Thematic Link
Twain's travels in the West brought him into contact with **tricksters and trailblazers,** who taught him lessons about humor.

### 5-Minute Warm-Up

*Daily Language SkillBuilder*

Have students **proofread** the display sentences on page 555k and write them correctly. The sentences also appear on Transparency 19 of **Grammar Transparencies and Copymasters.**

### Mini Lesson — Preteaching Vocabulary
If you would like to preteach the WORDS TO KNOW for this selection, use the Mini Lesson, p. 680.

---

## LESSON RESOURCES

**UNIT FOUR RESOURCE BOOK,** pp. 64–68

**ASSESSMENT RESOURCES**
**Formal Assessment,** pp. 129–130
**Teacher's Guide to Assessment and Portfolio Use**
**Test Generator**

**SKILLS TRANSPARENCIES AND COPYMASTERS**
**Grammar**
- Using *That* and *Which*, T44 (for Mini Lesson, p. 681)

- Use of *That* and *Which* in Adjective Clauses, C93 (for Mini Lesson, p. 681)
**Vocabulary**
- Meanings of Roots, C58 (for Mini Lesson, p. 683)
**Writing**
- Short Story, C29 (for Writing Option 1, p. 687)
**Communications**
- Impromptu Speaking: Dialogue, Role-Play, Debate, 113 (for Mini Lesson, p. 684)

**INTEGRATED TECHNOLOGY**
**Audio Library**
**Net Activities**
**Visit our website:**
www.mcdougallittell.com

**Literary Analysis** | TALL TALE |

A tall tale is a humorous story with exaggerated characters and impossible events. Twain uses a framing device so that readers initially meet a first-person narrator who provides the context for the tall tale told by Simon Wheeler. Ask students to contrast these two narrators.

**Possible Response:** The narrator's language is formal, and his diction is lofty. Simon Wheeler speaks in dialect. The narrator is skeptical of the tales told about Jim Smiley; Wheeler believes in them wholeheartedly. The narrator's tone is ironic; Wheeler's is earnest and sincere.

 Use **Unit Four Resource Book** p. 66 for additional practice.

**Active Reading**

| UNDERSTANDING DIALECT |

**A** Read aloud this passage of dialogue to give students a sense of how Simon Wheeler sounds. Then ask them to review the passage, identify examples of dialect, and define them using context clues.

**Possible Responses:** *Laying for a chance* means "waiting for an opportunity"; *solit'ry* means "solitary"; *feller'd* means "fellow would"; *ary side* means "any side"; *reg'lar* means "regularly."

Ask students what the use of dialect contributes to the story.

**Possible Responses:** It captures the atmosphere of the setting and makes the tale seem authentic. It also adds humor.

 Use **Unit 4 Resource Book** p. 65 for more practice.

---

# The NOTORIOUS Jumping Frog of CALAVERAS COUNTY

## Mark Twain

In compliance with the request of a friend of mine who wrote me from the East, I called on good-natured, garrulous[1] old Simon Wheeler and inquired after my friend's friend, Leonidas W. Smiley, as requested to do, and I hereunto append[2] the result. I have a lurking suspicion that *Leonidas W. Smiley* is a myth, that my friend never knew such a personage, and that he only conjectured that if I asked old Wheeler about him, it would remind him of his <u>infamous</u> *Jim* Smiley and he would go to work and bore me to death with some exasperating reminiscence of him as long and as tedious as it should be useless to me. If that was the design, it succeeded.

I found Simon Wheeler dozing comfortably by the barroom stove of the <u>dilapidated</u> tavern in the decayed mining camp of Angel's, and I noticed that he was fat and baldheaded and had an expression of winning gentleness and simplicity upon his <u>tranquil</u> countenance. He roused up and gave me good day. I told him that a friend of mine had <u>commissioned</u> me to make some inquiries about a cherished companion of his boyhood named *Leonidas W. Smiley—Rev. Leonidas W. Smiley*, a young minister of the Gospel, who he had heard was at one time a resident of Angel's Camp. I added that if Mr. Wheeler could tell me anything about this Rev. Leonidas W. Smiley, I would feel under many obligations to him.

Simon Wheeler backed me into a corner and blockaded me there with his chair, and then sat down and reeled off the monotonous narrative which follows this paragraph. He never smiled, he never frowned, he never changed his voice from the gentle-flowing key to which he tuned his initial sentence, he never betrayed the slightest suspicion of enthusiasm, but all through the interminable[3] narrative there ran a vein of impressive earnestness and sincerity which showed me plainly that, so far from his imagining that there was anything ridiculous or funny about his story, he regarded it as a really important matter and admired its two heroes as men of transcendent genius in finesse.[4] I let him go on in his own way and never interrupted him once.

"Rev. Leonidas W. H'm, Reverend Le—Well, there was a feller here once by the name of *Jim* Smiley, in the winter of '49—or maybe it was the spring of '50—I don't recollect exactly, somehow, though what makes me think it was one or the other is because I remember the big flume[5] warn't finished when he first come to the camp; but anyway, he was the curiousest man about always betting on anything that turned up you ever see, if he could get anybody to bet on the other side, and if he couldn't he'd change sides. Any way that

---

1. **garrulous** (găr'ə-ləs): extremely talkative.
2. **hereunto append**: add to this document.
3. **interminable** (ĭn-tûr'mə-nə bəl): seemingly endless.
4. **men of . . . finesse** (fə-něs'): exceptionally brilliant men.
5. **flume**: a wooden trough built as a channel for running water—used in gold mining to separate particles of gold.

| WORDS TO KNOW | **infamous** (ĭn'fə-məs) *adj.* notorious<br>**dilapidated** (dĭ-lăp'ĭ-dā'tĭd) *adj.* in a state of disrepair; rundown<br>**tranquil** (trăng'kwəl) *adj.* undisturbed; peaceful<br>**commission** (kə-mĭsh'ən) *v.* to assign a task or duty to |
| --- | --- |

**680**

---

## Teaching Options

 **Mini Lesson** ## Preteaching Vocabulary

**USING CONTEXT CLUES** **Instruction** Students can expand their vocabulary through wide reading and by using the context to figure out the meanings of words. One type of context clue to look for is a synonym in the surrounding text. Write the following sentence on the chalkboard. Ask a volunteer to find the synonym for *latticed* in the sentence. Have students define *latticed*.

The <u>latticed</u> box allowed the pet to breathe through large spaces formed by <u>crisscrossed</u> strips of wood.

**Exercises** Have students apply the strategy to figure out the meanings of underlined words.

1. The narrator had no <u>inclination</u> to visit Simon Wheeler, nor did he desire a lengthy conversation with him.

2. Many of the miners were quite <u>enterprising</u> and thought of imaginative ways to make money when gold proved to be elusive.

3. The life of miners who led a <u>vagabond</u> existence, drifting from place to place, did not appeal to the young writer.

 Use **Unit Four Resource Book** p. 67 for more exercises.

**A lesson on context clues appears on p. 326 in the Pupil's Edition.**

suited the other man would suit *him*—any way just so's he got a bet, *he* was satisfied. But still he was lucky, uncommon lucky; he most always come out winner. He was always ready and laying for a chance; there couldn't be no solit'ry thing mentioned but that feller'd offer to bet on it and take ary side you please, as I was just telling you. If there was a horse race, you'd find him flush or you'd find him busted at the end of it; if there was a dogfight, he'd bet on it; if there was a cat fight, he'd bet on it; if there was a chicken fight, he'd bet on it; why, if there was two birds setting on a fence, he would bet you which one would fly first; or if there was a camp meeting, he would be there reg'lar to bet on Parson Walker, which he judged to be the best exhorter about here, and so he was too, and a good man. If he even see a straddlebug start to go anywheres, he would bet you how long it would take him to get to—to wherever he was going to, and if you took him up, he would foller that straddlebug to Mexico but what he would find out where he was bound for and how long he was on the road. Lots of the boys here has seen that Smiley and can tell you about him. Why, it never made no difference to *him*—he'd bet on *any* thing—the dangdest feller. Parson Walker's wife laid very sick once for a good while, and it seemed as if they warn't going to save her; but one morning he come in and Smiley up and asked him how she was, and he said she was considerable better—thank the Lord for his inf'nite mercy—and coming on so smart that with the blessing of Prov'dence she'd get well yet; and Smiley, before he thought, says, 'Well, I'll resk two-and-a-half she don't anyway.'

"Thish-yer Smiley had a mare—the boys called her the fifteen-minute nag but that was only in fun, you know, because of course she was faster than that—and he used to win money on that horse, for all she was so slow and always had the asthma, or the distemper, or the consumption,[6] or something of that kind. They used to give her two or three hundred yards' start and then pass her underway, but always at the fag end of the race she'd get excited and desperatelike, and come <u>cavorting</u> and straddling up and scattering her legs around limber, sometimes in the air and sometimes out to one side among the fences, and kicking up m-o-r-e dust and raising m-o-r-e racket with her coughing and sneezing and blowing her nose—and always fetch up at the stand just about a neck ahead, as near as you could cipher it down.[7]

**A** "And he had a little small bull-pup, that to look at him you'd think he warn't worth a cent but to set around and look ornery and lay for a chance to steal something. But as soon as money was up on him he was a different dog; his underjaw'd begin to stick out like the fo'castle[8] of a steamboat and his teeth would uncover and shine like the furnaces. And a dog might tackle him and bullyrag[9] him, and bite him and throw him over his shoulder two or three times, and Andrew Jackson—which was the name of the pup—Andrew Jackson would never let on but what *he* was satisfied and hadn't expected nothing else—and the bets being doubled and doubled on the other side all the time, till the money was all up; and then all of a sudden he would grab that other dog jest by the j'int of his hind leg and freeze to it—not chaw, you understand, but only just grip and hang on till they throwed up the sponge,[10] if it

 1

*He was always ready and laying for a chance.*

---

6. **distemper . . . consumption:** diseases of mammals.

7. **cipher** (sī'fər) **it down:** calculate it; figure it.

8. **fo'castle** (fōk'səl): forecastle—the part of a steamboat in front of the superstructure.

9. **bullyrag:** harass.

10. **throwed up the sponge:** gave up.

WORDS
TO
KNOW

**cavorting** (kə-vôr'tĭng) *adj.* prancing about; capering **cavort** *v.*

## Customizing Instruction

**Less Proficient Readers**
Introduce the story-within-a-story format and give a quick overview so that students are prepared for what they read. Encourage students not to get stuck on the first paragraph, which uses exaggeratedly formal language. In essence, the narrator looks up a man named Simon Wheeler as a favor to a friend. Wheeler then tells him a long and rambling story about Jim Smiley, a gambler who loved to bet on anything. The narrator wonders if his friend set him up for this tedious tale.

**Set a Purpose** Have students read to find out what happens to Jim Smiley's dog, Andrew Jackson, and his frog, Dan'l Webster.

**Students Acquiring English**
Remind students that this story is set in a mining camp in the West in the 1800s and that the language reflects the setting. Before discussion of each segment of the story, define the words and expressions that students have recorded in their Reader's Notebooks.

**1** To clarify understanding before moving on, ask questions such as the following:
- Why are people so surprised when Smiley's horse wins a race?
  **Answer:** She appears very sickly yet applies a burst of speed at the end.
- What is his dog's strategy for winning dogfights?
  **Answer:** He clamps his jaws onto his opponent's hind leg.

Use **Spanish Study Guide** for additional support, pp. 166–168.

---

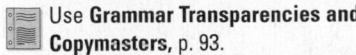

### Mini Lesson Grammar

**USE OF *THAT* AND *WHICH* IN ADJECTIVE CLAUSES**
**Instruction** An adjective clause is a subordinate clause that modifies a noun or pronoun. Often the adjective clause is introduced by a relative pronoun such as *who, that,* or *which.* Tell students *which* generally introduces nonessential clauses and *that* generally introduces essential clauses. Display the following sentences as examples.

> The narrator's interest, which had never been strong, flagged by the end of the story. (nonessential)

> He saved the errand <u>that he had promised to do for his friend</u> until the end of the day. (*essential*)

**Exercises** Ask students to rewrite the following sentences, inserting essential or nonessential clauses as indicated and using the correct relative pronouns and punctuation.

1. Jim Smiley's cow (Simon Wheeler mentioned it) was quite an intriguing sight. (*Jim Smiley's cow, which Simon Wheeler mentioned, was quite an intriguing sight.*)
2. The stranger (he deceived Jim Smiley) probably never visited the Angel Camp again. (*The stranger who deceived Jim Smiley probably never visited the Angel camp again.*)

Use **Grammar Transparencies and Copymasters**, p. 93.

Use McDougal Littell's *Language Network*, Chapter 3, for more instruction and practice in adjective clauses.

682

**Active Reading**

| UNDERSTANDING DIALECT |

**A** One way to understand unfamiliar dialect is to use context clues. Have students use this strategy to translate "he got shucked out bad."

**Possible Response:** Andrew Jackson became discouraged and didn't try to win; the quotation means that he lost the fight badly.

**Literary Analysis** | TALL TALE |

**B** Ask students to pick out examples of exaggeration in the feats of Andrew Jackson and Dan'l Webster.

**Possible Responses:** Andrew Jackson would wait to fight back until the bets were doubled; he always won; he gave Smiley a look that said his heart was broken. Smiley taught Dan'l Webster to catch a fly every time he saw one, no matter how far away it was; the stranger poured five pounds of quail shot into Dan'l Webster.

**Reading Skills and Strategies: CLARIFYING MEANING**

**C** Ask students what the brackets indicate.

**Possible Response:** The brackets indicate an interruption in the narrative, an aside from the first-person narrator that is not part of Simon Wheeler's tale.

**Active Reading**

| UNDERSTANDING DIALECT |

**D** Ask students to render this passage into standard English.

**Possible Response:** Smiley had a yellow cow with one eye and a short stump for a tail that looked like a banana.

---

was a year. Smiley always come out winner on that pup till he harnessed a dog once that didn't have no hind legs, because they'd been sawed off in a circular saw, and when the thing had gone along far enough and the money was all up and he come to make a snatch for his pet holt,[11] he see in a minute how he'd been imposed on and how the other dog had him in the door, so to speak, and he 'peared surprised, and then he looked sorter discouragedlike and didn't try no more to win the fight, and so he got shucked out bad. He give Smiley a look, as much as to say his heart was broke, and it was *his* fault for putting up a dog that hadn't no hind legs for him to take holt of, which was his main dependence in a fight, and then he limped off a piece and laid down and died. It was a good pup, was that Andrew Jackson, and would have made a name for hisself if he'd lived, for the stuff was in him and he had genius—I know it, because he hadn't no opportunities to speak of, and it don't stand to reason that a dog could make such a fight as he could under them circumstances if he hadn't no talent. It always makes me feel sorry when I think of that last fight of his'n and the way it turned out.

"Well, thish-yer Smiley had rat terriers, and chicken cocks, and tomcats and all them kind of things till you couldn't rest, and you couldn't fetch nothing for him to bet on but he'd match you. He ketched a frog one day and took him home, and said he cal'lated[12] to educate him; and so he never done nothing for three months but set in his back yard and learn that frog to jump. And you bet you he *did* learn him, too. He'd give him a little punch behind, and the next minute you'd see that frog whirling in the air like a doughnut—see him turn one summerset, or maybe a couple if he got a good start, and come down flatfooted and all right, like a cat. He got him up so in the matter of ketching flies, and kep' him in practice so constant, that he'd nail a fly every time as fur as he could see

him. Smiley said all a frog wanted was education and he could do 'most anything—and I believe him. Why, I've seen him set Dan'l Webster down here on this floor—Dan'l Webster was the name of the frog—and sing out, 'Flies, Dan'l, flies!' and quicker'n you could wink he'd spring straight up and snake a fly off'n the counter there, and flop down on the floor ag'in as solid as a gob of mud, and fall to scratching the side of his head with his hind foot as indifferent as if he hadn't no idea he'd been doin' any more'n any frog might do. You never see a frog so modest and straight-for'ard as he was, for all he was so gifted. And when it come to fair and square jumping on a deadlevel, he could get over more ground at one straddle than any animal of his breed you ever see. Jumping on a dead level was his strong suit, you understand; and when it come to that, Smiley would ante up money on him as long as he had a red.[13] Smiley was monstrous proud of his frog, and well he might be for fellers that had traveled and been everywheres all said he laid over any frog that ever *they* see.

"Well, Smiley kep' the beast in a little lattice box, and he used to fetch him downtown sometimes and lay for a bet. One day a feller—a stranger in the camp, he was—come acrost him with his box and says:

"'What might it be that you've got in the box?'

"And Smiley says, sorter indifferentlike, 'It might be a parrot, or it might be a canary, maybe, but it ain't—it's only just a frog.'

"And the feller took it and looked at it careful, and turned it round this way and that, and says, 'H'm—so 'tis. Well, what's *he* good for?'

"'Well,' Smiley says, easy and careless, 'he's good enough for *one* thing, I should judge—he can outjump any frog in Calaveras County.'

"The feller took the box again and took another long, particular look, and give it back to Smiley

---

11. **pet holt:** favorite grip.
12. **cal'lated** (kăl′lā′tĭd): calculated; intended.
13. **red:** red cent (slang for a penny).

WORDS
TO
KNOW

**lattice** (lăt′ĭs) *n.* an open framework made of spaced, crisscrossed strips

682

---

## Teaching Options

| BLOCK SCHEDULING: MANAGING TIME |

**If your schedule requires that you cover the lesson objectives in a shorter time, use . . .**
• Preparing to Read, p. 679
• Thinking Through the Literature, p. 685
• Vocabulary in Action, p. 687

**If you want to take advantage of longer class time, use . . .**
• TE Teaching Options: Preteaching Vocabulary, p. 680; Speaking and Listening, p. 684; Vocabulary Strategy, p. 683
• The Author's Style and Choices & Challenges, pp. 686–687

and says, very deliberate, 'Well,' he says, 'I don't see no p'ints[14] about that frog that's any better'n any other frog.'

"'Maybe you don't,' Smiley says. 'Maybe you understand frogs and maybe you don't understand 'em; maybe you've had experience and maybe you ain't only a amature, as it were. Anyways, I've got *my* opinion, and I'll resk forty dollars that he can outjump any frog in Calaveras County.'

"And the feller studied a minute and then says, kinder sadlike, 'Well, I'm only a stranger here and I ain't got no frog; but if I had a frog, I'd bet you."

"And then Smiley says, 'That's all right—that's all right—if you'll hold my box a minute, I'll go and get you a frog.' And so the feller took the box and put up his forty dollars along with Smiley's, and set down to wait.

"So he set there a good while thinking and thinking to himself, and then he got the frog out and prized his mouth open and took a teaspoon and filled him full of quail shot[15]—filled him pretty near up to his chin—and set him on the floor. Smiley he went to the swamp and slopped around in the mud for a long time, and finally he ketched a frog and fetched him in and give him to this feller, and says:

"'Now, if you're ready, set him alongside of Dan'l, with his forepaws just even with Dan'l's, and I'll give the word.' Then he says, 'One—two—three—*git!*' and him and the feller touched up the frogs from behind, and the new frog hopped off lively, but Dan'l give a heave and hysted up his shoulders—so—like a Frenchman, but it warn't no use—he couldn't budge; he was planted as solid as a church, and he couldn't no more stir than if he was anchored out. Smiley was a good deal surprised, and he was disgusted too, but he didn't have no idea what the matter was, of course.

"The feller took the money and started away, and when he was going out at the door, he sorter jerked his thumb over his shoulder—so—at Dan'l and says again, very deliberate, 'Well,' he says, 'I

don't see no p'ints about that frog that's any better'n any other frog.'

"Smiley he stood scratching his head and looking down at Dan'l a long time, and at last he says, 'I do wonder what in the nation that frog throw'd off for—I wonder if there ain't something the matter with him—he 'pears to look mighty baggy, somehow.' And he ketched Dan'l by the nap of the neck and hefted him, and says, 'Why, blame my cats if he don't weigh five pound!' and turned him upside down and he belched out a double handful of shot. And then he see how it was, and he was the maddest man—he set the frog down and took out after that feller, but he never ketched him. And—"

[Here Simon Wheeler heard his name called from the front yard and got up to see what was wanted.] And turning to me as he moved away, he said: "Just set where you are, stranger, and rest easy—I ain't going to be gone a second."

But, by your leave, I did not think that a continuation of the history of the <u>enterprising</u> <u>vagabond</u> *Jim* Smiley would be likely to afford me much information concerning the Rev. *Leonidas W.* Smiley and so I started away.

At the door I met the sociable Wheeler returning, and he buttonholed[16] me and <u>recommenced</u>:

**1** "Well, thish-yer Smiley had a yaller one-eyed cow that didn't have no tail, only just a short stump like a bannanner, and—"

However, lacking both time and <u>inclination</u>, I did not wait to hear about the afflicted cow but took my leave.

---

14. **p'ints:** points.
15. **quail shot:** small lead pellets for firing from a shotgun.
16. **buttonholed:** detained for conversation.

WORDS TO KNOW
**enterprising** (ĕn′tər-prī′zĭng) *adj.* possessing imagination and initiative
**vagabond** (văg′ə-bŏnd′) *n.* a wanderer; drifter
**recommence** (rē′kə-mĕns′) *v.* to begin again
**inclination** (ĭn′klə-nā′shən) *n.* a favorable disposition; desire

**683**

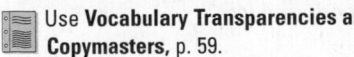

## Teaching the Literature

### Build Background

The story of the frog loaded with shot was in circulation for years before Twain first heard it during a brief gold-mining excursion. Because of heavy rains, the miners spent most of their time gathered around a warm stove swapping stories. Twain was struck by the story of the frog and the deadpan manner in which it was told. He later submitted his version to a New York publisher, and it appeared in the *Saturday Press* on November 18, 1865. Instantly popular, the story was reprinted in many other papers and made Twain famous. Rather than enjoying this fame, however, Twain was irritated that the frog story received more attention than his other work. It became the title story of his first book, *The Celebrated Jumping Frog of Calaveras County, and Other Sketches* (1867).

### Teaching Nonfiction:
### Skills and Strategies
### EXAMINING AUTHOR'S PURPOSE

An author's purpose in writing may be to inform, to influence, to express opinions, or to entertain. Although one purpose is usually the most important, a writer can have two or more.

After students read the excerpt from the *Herald,* have them identify the journalist's purpose for writing this article.

**Possible Responses:** The journalist wanted to entertain his or her readers; the journalist wanted to point out problems with gambling.

### COMPARING TEXTS

This newspaper article provides another version of the frog story that students can compare to Twain's version. Although it is believed that Twain heard the story of the frog long after this article was published, both presentations share certain details. Ask students to identify details the stories have in common, and then have them cite stylistic elements that Twain uses that do not appear in the article.

You might also have students discuss whether this story would be likely to appear in a newspaper today, and whether people today would find it as entertaining as people in Twain's era.

**Possible Responses:** Common details: the Yankee boasts about his toad, he wins the contest by filling the frog with shot. Stylistic differences: dialect, imagery, analogy, similes, contrast, exaggeration.

---

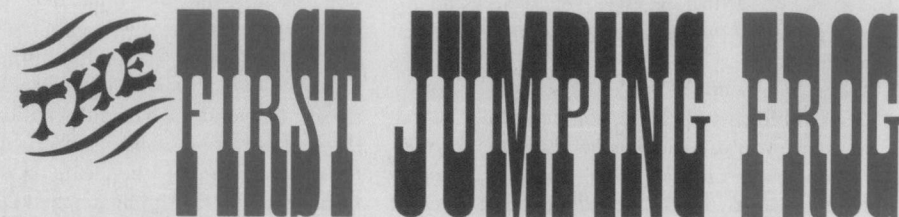

# THE FIRST JUMPING FROG

## Build Background

Ever wonder where Mark Twain came up with the idea for his famous "The Notorious Jumping Frog of Calaveras County"? Here's an article that appeared in the Sonora, California, *Herald* on June 11, 1853—fourteen years before Twain wrote his short story.

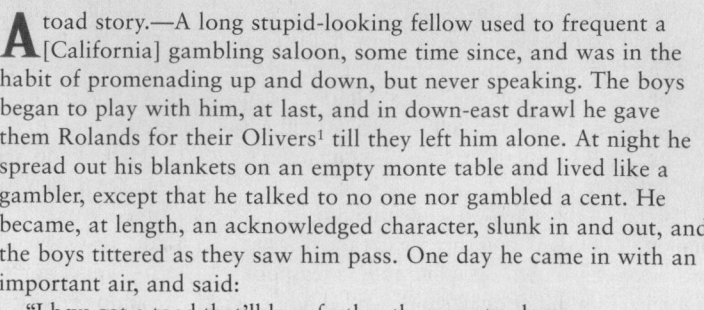

Twain on his frog, colored caricature by Frederick Waddy (1872)

A toad story.—A long stupid-looking fellow used to frequent a [California] gambling saloon, some time since, and was in the habit of promenading up and down, but never speaking. The boys began to play with him, at last, and in down-east drawl he gave them Rolands for their Olivers[1] till they left him alone. At night he spread out his blankets on an empty monte table and lived like a gambler, except that he talked to no one nor gambled a cent. He became, at length, an acknowledged character, slunk in and out, and the boys tittered as they saw him pass. One day he came in with an important air, and said:

"I have got a toad that'll leap further than any toad you can scare up."

They soon surrounded him, and roared and laughed.

"Yes," says he, "I'll bet money on it. Barkeeper, give me a cigar box to hold my toad in."

The fun was great, and the oddity was the talk of all hands. A gambler, in the evening, happened to come across a big frog, fetched him to the gambling house, and offered to jump him against the Yankee's toad.

"Well," says Yank, "I'll bet liquors on it." A chalk line was made and the toad put down. They struck the boards behind the toad and he leaped six feet, then the frog jumped seven. Yank paid the liquors; but, next morning, he says aloud:

"My toad waren't beat. No man's toad can leap with my toad. I have two ounces and two double eagles, and all of them I bet on my toad." The boys bet with him again, and his toad leaped six feet, but the frog leaped only two feet.

"The best two out of three," said the gamblers.

"Very well," says Yank. But still the frog could not go over two feet. Yank pocketed the bets.

"My frog is darn heavy this morning," says the gambler.

"I reckoned it would be, stranger," says the Yankee, "for I rolled a pound of shot into him last night."

---

1. **Gave them Rolands for their Olivers:** gave them punch for punch.

---

## Teaching Options  Mini Lesson Speaking and Listening

**TELLING A HUMOROUS ANECDOTE** **Prepare** Mark Twain believed that the manner in which a story is told adds to its humor and that the more serious the delivery, the stronger the humor. Ask students to choose a humorous anecdote to present to the class. The anecdote need not be original, but students must become familiar enough with the story to tell it from memory. Students should practice telling their stories with seriousness, appropriate facial expressions, clear enunciation, effective pauses, and strong delivery of the climax. These criteria can also help the audience evaluate the performances.

**Present** Have students work in groups of five or six, taking turns presenting their anecdotes. Audience members should evaluate the effectiveness of the humorous delivery. After all students in the group have performed, they should discuss ways in which to improve their own performances and those of others through adjustments in tone, facial expressions, enunciation, pauses, and delivery of the climax.

**BLOCK SCHEDULING** This activity is particularly well suited for longer class periods.

## Connect to the Literature

**1. What Do You Think?**
Do you think the narrator of this story had a good sense of humor? Explain your opinion.

> **Comprehension Check**
> - How did the narrator get involved with Simon Wheeler?
> - Why did Wheeler refer to Smiley as "the curiousest man"?
> - Why did Smiley lose his bet on Dan'l Webster?

## Think Critically

**2.** **ACTIVE READING** **UNDERSTANDING DIALECT** Review your notes in your  **READER'S NOTEBOOK** on unusual words and expressions in Twain's story. What does Wheeler's **dialect** tell you about his character? Cite examples from the story to support your conclusion.

**3.** What sort of person is Jim Smiley?

> **THINK ABOUT** { • his relationship with his animals
> • how he deals with the loss of his wager

**4.** How did Twain's use of **exaggeration** make this tale amusing? Use examples from the story to support your views.

## Extend Interpretations

**5. Critic's Corner** According to writer John Gerber, Twain's organization of this tale "seems wholly directionless," yet "actually, it is carefully molded for climax." Do you agree that Wheeler seems to tell a rambling tale when in fact it carefully builds to a climax? Use examples from the story to support your ideas.

**6. Comparing Texts** Twain believed that good humor writing depended more on how a story was told than on the subject matter of the story. Based on your reading of both jumping frog versions, do you agree? Support your ideas with examples from both versions of the jumping frog story.

**7. Connect to Life** Refer to your notes and review the situation in which you observed someone fooling other people with an outrageous tale. Did the storyteller in the situation you observed use any of the same techniques that Twain did in his tale about the frog? Describe any similarities and differences between the two tales.

## Literary Analysis

**TALL TALE** A **tall tale** is a distinctively American type of humorous story characterized by **exaggeration.** Tall tales and practical jokes have a similar kind of humor. In both, someone gets fooled, to the amusement of the person or persons who know the truth. In this tall tale, Twain uses both exaggeration and **dialect** for comic effect.

- **Exaggeration** involves stretching the truth to an unrealistic extent. Here, Twain exaggerates the lengths to which Smiley would go to make a bet:

*He would foller that straddlebug to Mexico but what he would find out where he was bound for and how long he was on the road.*

- **Dialect** is the distinct form of a language spoken in one geographic area by a particular social or ethnic group. A group's dialect is reflected in its characteristic pronunciation, vocabulary, expressions, and grammatical constructions. Throughout the story of the jumping frog, Twain reproduces the dialect spoken in California around the time of the Civil War, as seen here:

*And he had a little small bull-pup, that to look at him you'd think he warn't worth a cent but to set around and look ornery and lay for a chance to steal something.*

**Paired Activity** Find in this story three or four examples of Twain's combining dialect and exaggeration. Then share your examples with a partner, explaining how you think the combination of dialect and exaggeration creates a humorous effect.

---

## Connect to the Literature

**1. What Do You Think?**
Students who think the narrator lacks a sense of humor can point to his description of Wheeler's story as exasperating, tedious, and interminable. Those who think he has a sense of humor might point to the humor in the story and the narrator's comment that Wheeler seemed not to recognize that anything was ridiculous or funny about his story.

**Comprehension Check**
- The narrator asked Simon Wheeler about the friend of a friend, Reverend Leonidas W. Smiley.
- Wheeler thought Smiley's habit of betting on anything was odd.
- The stranger fed Smiley's frog quail shot so he would be too heavy to jump far.

 Use Selection Quiz
**Unit Four Resource Book,** p. 68.

## Think Critically

**2.** Some students may point out that Wheeler is folksy, talkative, simple, relaxed, and sensitive toward animals.

**3.** Possible Responses: Smiley, who is obsessed with betting, views his animals primarily as sources of revenue in helping him con the unwary. Though tricky and persistent, he is also naive in trusting his prized frog to a total stranger while traipsing through the swamps looking for a frog to oppose Dan'l. He explodes with anger when the stranger cons him at his own game.

**4.** Exaggerations include the description of the bull-pup with a jaw like the front of a steamboat, characterizing the dog as having "genius" and the frog as being "gifted," and describing the lead-shot-filled frog as being "planted as solid as a church."

## Literary Analysis

**Tall Tale** Possible Responses: "Smiley always come out winner on that pup till he harnessed a dog once . . . so he got shucked out bad." "Smiley was monstrous proud of his frog . . . *they* see." " 'Why, blame my cats if he don't weigh five pound!' " Students will find a variety of examples of dialect combined with exaggeration.

---

## Extend Interpretations

**Critic's Corner** Students may agree that the story develops systematically from general description of Smiley's eagerness to gamble, through particular animals he kept and his training of the frog, to the detailed description of the conversation with the stranger and the jumping contest.

**Comparing Texts** Many students will agree that "The Notorious Jumping Frog . . ." is funnier than the newspaper account because of the way it is told—the victimized narrator, Wheeler's speech rhythms, and the strange stories about Smiley's other animals add humor to the basic tale of the frog jumping contest. Some students may prefer the newspaper account for moving quickly to the punch line.

**Connect to Life** Students' experiences with other storytellers will vary. Students might consider the manner of telling the story (both Wheeler and the narrator use a sincere tone to tell a bizarre story), and the use of exaggeration, dialogue, and figures of speech.

## The Author's Style

Mark Twain's style is distinctively witty and personal, and he re-creates for the modern reader a sense of the United States in which he lived. Students will be made aware of Twain's style through the "Key Aspects of Twain's Style" chart and then find examples of the points in the excerpts in the right margin.

## Analysis of Style

**A First activity**

**comic exaggeration:** "Smiley said all a frog wanted was education and he could do 'most anything . . .'" "[the ant] is the hardest working creature in the world . . .'"

**humorous subject:** teaching a frog to jump in *The Notorious Jumping Frog of Calaveras County;* the working habits of an ant in *A Tramp Abroad*

**rambling and indirect narratives:** "The mammoth grandstand was clothed in flags, streamers, and rich tapestries and packed with several acres of small-fry tributary kings, their suites, and the British aristocracy"; "He'd give him a little punch behind, and the next minute you'd see that frog whirling in the air like a doughnut—see him turn one summerset, or maybe a couple if he got a good start . . ."

**offbeat figurative language:** Simile: ". . . frog whirling in the air like a doughnut . . ."; Metaphor: "every individual a flashing prism of gaudy silks and velvets . . ."; Irony: "dragging his worthless property to the top—which is as bright a thing to do as . . ."

**analogies:** "and he does climb it, dragging his worthless property to the top—which is as bright a thing to do as it would be for me to carry a sack of flour from Heidelberg to Paris by way of Strasburg."

**dialect and idioms:** "He ketched a frog one day . . ."; "And you bet you he did learn him, too."

**B Second activity**

**Other examples:** Personification: ". . . I never saw anything to begin with it but a fight between an Upper Mississippi sunset and the aurora borealis"; Hyperbole: "Smiley said all a frog wanted was education and he could do 'most anything . . .'"; Rhetorical question: "He goes out foraging, he makes a capture, and then what does he do? Go home? No . . ."

**C Third activity**

The Twain selections should provide students with numerous examples of his stylistic devices.

# THE AUTHOR'S STYLE
## Twain's Witty Writing

**Style** is the distinctive way in which a work of literature is written. Style refers not so much to what is said but to how it is said. Word choice, imagery, sentence structure, and tone all contribute to a writer's style. Twain masterfully employed witty devices that contributed to his lively personal style.

### Key Aspects of Twain's Style

- comic exaggeration
- humorous and entertaining subject matter
- rambling and indirect narratives, often involving the use of more words than necessary to express an idea
- offbeat **similes, metaphors,** and **irony**
- use of **analogies** to deepen meaning and understanding
- use of **dialect** and **idioms**—the vocabulary of the ordinary person

## Analysis of Style

At the right are excerpts from three of Twain's stories. Study the list above, then read each excerpt carefully. Complete the following activities:

**A** • Find examples of Twain's key stylistic devices in the excerpts. Think about the effect that is created by each device.

**B** • Find examples of other devices you see at work in the excerpts.

**C** • Review the other reading selections in this Author Study. Choose one, and discuss with others the stylistic devices that Twain has used in it.

## Applications

**1. Imitating the Style** Choose one excerpt, and write another paragraph for the story using Twain's style. Share your work by reading it to the class.

**2. Changing the Style** Choose one excerpt, and rewrite it in your own humorous style. Then, with a partner, read your versions and the originals aloud, and compare them.

**3. Speaking and Listening** In small groups, take turns reading each excerpt aloud to hear the unique American voices Twain brought to literature. What **character** do you imagine telling each story? What **mood** does each excerpt convey? Discuss the differences you hear in each of these oral interpretations.

### from A Connecticut Yankee in King Arthur's Court

Vast as the show-grounds were, there were no vacant spaces in them. . . . The mammoth grandstand was clothed in flags, streamers, and rich tapestries and packed with several acres of small-fry tributary kings, their suites, and the British aristocracy; with our own royal gang in the chief place, and each and every individual a flashing prism of gaudy silks and velvets—well, I never saw anything to begin with it but a fight between an Upper Mississippi sunset and the aurora borealis.

### from The Notorious Jumping Frog of Calaveras County

He ketched a frog one day and took him home, and said he cal'lated to educate him; and so he never done nothing for three months but set in his back yard and learn that frog to jump. And you bet you he *did* learn him, too. He'd give him a little punch behind, and the next minute you'd see that frog whirling in the air like a doughnut—see him turn one summerset, or maybe a couple if he got a good start. . . . Smiley said all a frog wanted was education and he could do 'most anything—and I believe him.

### from A Tramp Abroad

I am persuaded that the average ant is a sham . . . ; he is the hardest working creature in the world,—when anybody is looking,— but his leather-headedness is the point I make against him. He goes out foraging, he makes a capture, and then what does he do? Go home? No,—he goes anywhere but home. . . . He makes his capture, as I have said; . . . comes to a weed; it never occurs to him to go around it; no, he must climb it; and he does climb it, dragging his worthless property to the top—which is as bright a thing to do as it would be for me to carry a sack of flour from Heidelberg to Paris by way of Strasburg steeple.

## Applications

**1. Imitating the Style** Remind students to revisit the Key Aspects box on the page before beginning their creations.

**2. Changing the Style** Have students go through the entire writing process for this activity—prewriting, drafting, editing, and publishing. Encourage them to choose manageable sections of no more than 20 lines.

**3. Speaking and Listening** Have students use the following criteria to critique oral interpretation. The student

- makes and supports a valid interpretation of how the character might voice those lines
- uses voice (volume and tone) to establish mood and convey meaning
- uses movement and gestures to establish mood and convey meaning
- uses facial expressions to establish mood and convey meaning

# *Choices & CHALLENGES*

## Writing Options

**1. The Stranger's Tale** Rewrite part of "The Notorious Jumping Frog of Calaveras County" as if you were the stranger who outwitted Jim Smiley. Try to use local color and dialect. Place your writing in your **Working Portfolio.**

**2. Local Storytelling** Obtain a copy of Twain's sketches and tales, and choose a tale to rewrite for a younger audience.

**3. Dialects Today** Find out more about dialects spoken in the United States today. What are some major dialects? Where are they spoken? Write a brief report of your findings.

## Vocabulary in Action

**EXERCISE A: MEANING CLUES** For each sentence, write *T* or *F* to indicate whether the statement is true or false.

1. An **enterprising** character would know how to help his frog jump highest.
2. An **infamous** person usually has a good reputation.
3. If you **recommence** telling a story, you are starting over from the beginning.
4. A **dilapidated** mining office is in excellent condition.
5. **Lattice** is a good source of several vitamins.

**EXERCISE B: WORD KNOWLEDGE** Design a crossword puzzle, using all of the Words to Know below, plus other words if you wish. Then exchange puzzles with a classmate and solve his or her puzzle.

commission    tranquil    inclination
cavorting     vagabond

| WORDS TO KNOW | cavorting | inclination | recommence |
|---|---|---|---|
| | commission | infamous | tranquil |
| | dilapidated | lattice | vagabond |
| | enterprising | | |

---

**Netscape: Welcome to Netscape**

## Mark Twain
### Author Study Project
CREATING A MULTIMEDIA BIOGRAPHY

Work with a small group, a partner, or alone to create a multimedia biography of Mark Twain, emphasizing his gifts as a humorist. To focus your work, think about some aspect of Twain's travels, jobs, performances, or personal life that fascinates you. Then choose a form you'd like your biography to take. You might tell a tall tale, make a video or a Web page, stage an interview or a talk show, or combine any of these possibilities. The following suggestions will help you with your research:

**Films and Impersonations** Several videos look at aspects of Twain's life and the America of his day. Hal Holbrook, an actor well known for his impersonations of Mark Twain, has filmed *Mark Twain Gives an Interview.* Watch the performance and pay attention to Holbrook's portrayal of Mark Twain.

**Books and Periodicals** Search these materials for images of Twain, his family, his homes in Hannibal and Hartford, documents and publications related to his life, and the changing society around him. Many biographies of Twain provide a rich store of anecdotes and quotations. An especially useful book is *Mark Twain and His World* by Justin Kaplan.

**Computer Resources** Search for nonprint materials for your presentation. Use CD-ROMs and the Internet as resources. Contact museums in Hannibal and Hartford as well as organizations like the Mark Twain Association of New York.

**More Online: Research Starter**
www.mcdougallittell.com

---

## Writing Options

1. **The Stranger's Tale To get students started on this assignment,** ask them to reread the section in which the stranger appears. Have students list what the stranger does and says before and after the contest. Students might conclude that the idea to fill Smiley's frog with quail shot wasn't premeditated but just occurred to him while waiting for Smiley to return. Students should also note how quickly the stranger leaves and his last comment. To give a pretext for the story from the stranger's perspective, students might have the stranger boast about his victory to a friend.

2. **Local Storytelling To get students started on this assignment,** have them look at several of Mark Twain's sketches. They should choose one that is likely to appeal to younger students with an emphasis on plot and obvious humor. Possibilities include "Story of the Bad Little Boy" or "The Siamese Twins." When rewriting, students should be careful not to omit anything central to understanding the story. **Linguistic learners** might volunteer to tell their stories at a local elementary school.

3. **Dialects Today To get students started on this assignment,** have them first consult a very general source for facts about the major dialects and the geographical location in which they are commonly spoken.

## Vocabulary in Action

1. T      3. T      5. F
2. F      4. F

**Netscape: Welcome to Netscape**

## Author Study Project

Encourage students to think about which kind of media would be best for the aspect of Twain's life they choose to highlight. For example, a Web page is a good way to organize and provide links between brief anecdotes or sayings. An interview or talk show is appropriate for presenting Twain's mannerisms and quick wit. Remind students that their presentations will need to be based on solid research into the facts of Twain's life and personality.

---

## Mini Lesson  Speaking and Listening

**ANALYZING A PERFORMANCE REVIEW**

**Instruction** Show students the filmed performance by Hal Holbrook entitled *Mark Twain Gives an Interview.* Have them write a review of the performance.

**Prepare** Tell students the following criteria may be used to write their review of a performance.

- identifies its subject at the beginning
- opens with a general opinion
- includes enough facts, examples, and specifics to support the general opinion

- displays logical organization
- quickly establishes a tone

**Present** Pair students and have them share their reviews with their partners. Together the students may analyze the written reviews using the above criteria. Then have them compare their partner's review with their own responses.

# OVERVIEW

 This selection is included in the **Grade 11 InterActive Reader.**

## Objectives

1. understand and appreciate a **short story** (Literary Analysis)
2. identify and understand **setting** (Literary Analysis)
3. **draw conclusions about character** in a short story (**Active Reading**)

## Summary

An impending visit from his Aunt Georgiana sparks Clark's memories of her caring for him during his boyhood in rural Nebraska. Thirty years earlier, Georgiana was a music teacher at the Boston Conservatory. She eloped to Nebraska, where she and her new husband homesteaded in the most primitive of conditions. Clark, who now lives in Boston, plans to treat his aunt to an afternoon concert. Georgiana seems so preoccupied with unfinished chores back at the farm that Clark wonders if he should have planned the concert visit. Once in the concert hall, however, Georgiana comes alive. Wagner's emotionally charged music moves her to tears. When the concert is over and the rest of the audience has left, Georgiana suddenly cries out that she doesn't want to go. For her, stepping outside the concert hall means a return to the harsh, barren life of a Nebraska farm.

## Thematic Link

Aunt Georgiana represents one of the many quiet **trailblazers** who turned the American **frontier** into farmland.

---

### 5-Minute Warm-Up

*Daily Language SkillBuilder*

Have students **proofread** the display sentences on page 555k and write them correctly. The sentences also appear on Transparency 20 of **Grammar Transparencies and Copymasters.**

---

### Mini Lesson — **Preteaching Vocabulary**

If you would like to preteach the WORDS TO KNOW for this selection, use the Mini Lesson p. 690.

---

# A Wagner Matinee

*Short Story by* WILLA CATHER

### Connect to Your Life

**Turning Points** Recall a time when you had to choose between two things that were very important to you. What were your choices? What factors did you weigh in making your decision? Looking back, do you think you made the right choice?

## Build Background

**Cultural Backdrop** The story you are about to read is set in Boston around 1900. At that time, many city dwellers were able to enjoy cultural opportunities, such as art museums and concerts featuring music by great European composers. In contrast, Easterners who made the choice to go west, like Aunt Georgiana in this story, left such worldly pleasures behind. Instead, these homesteaders faced long hours of strenuous labor and endured natural disasters such as drought, flood, and prairie fires.

This story contains several references to operas by the German composer Richard Wagner (väg'nər). It also mentions other operas and composers as well as musical terms such as *prelude, motive, overture, solo,* and *chorus.* It is not necessary to be familiar with these musical references to understand the story. However, if you do have a knowledge of classical music, you might briefly describe Wagner's operas and explain the musical terms to other students before they read.

---

| WORDS TO KNOW **Vocabulary Preview** | | |
| --- | --- | --- |
| callow | pathetic | sordid |
| conjecture | pious | superficially |
| excruciatingly | reproach | trepidation |
| inexplicable | | |

---

## Focus Your Reading

**LITERARY ANALYSIS** **SETTING** The setting of a story refers to the time and place in which the action occurs. In some stories, setting may greatly influence plot events and shape the characters' lives. For example, in "A Wagner Matinee," the contrasting settings of turn-of-the-century Boston and the Nebraska frontier have a strong impact on both the narrator of the story and his aunt. As you read, note the details of each location.

**ACTIVE READING** **DRAWING CONCLUSIONS ABOUT CHARACTER** Understanding a character in a story is often like getting to know a real person. You **draw conclusions,** or make logical decisions, about the person by combining the impressions you have already formed with new facts you have discovered. To become better acquainted with Aunt Georgiana, the main character in "A Wagner Matinee," look closely at the details as you read the story, note what they suggest about the kind of person she is, and then draw conclusions that are solidly based on evidence.

**READER'S NOTEBOOK** To help you gather evidence as you read, create a chart like the one below, and fill it in with details about Aunt Georgiana. Then consider the evidence as you draw conclusions.

| Observations | What They Reveal |
| --- | --- |
| Physical appearance | |
| Major decisions | |
| Actions and reactions | |

---

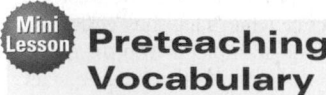

## LESSON RESOURCES

**UNIT FOUR RESOURCE BOOK,** pp. 69–73

**ASSESSMENT RESOURCES**
**Formal Assessment,** pp. 131–132
**Teacher's Guide to Assessment and Portfolio Use**
**Test Generator**

**SKILLS TRANSPARENCIES AND COPYMASTERS**
**Literary Analysis**
• Setting, T13 (for Activity, p. 697)

**Reading and Critical Thinking**
• Cause and Effect, T1 (for Writing Option 1, p. 698)

**Grammar**
• Introductory Adverbial Clauses, C98 (for Mini Lesson, p. 694)
• Punctuating Introductory Adverbial Clauses, C152 (for Mini Lesson, p. 698)

**Vocabulary**
• Meanings of Roots, C59 (for Mini Lesson, p. 690)

**Communications**
• Appreciative Listening, T2 (for Inquiry & Research, p. 698)

**INTEGRATED TECHNOLOGY**

**Audio Library**
**LaserLinks**
• Cultural Connection: East and West
• Music Connection: At the Opera. See **Teacher's SourceBook,** pp. 56–57.

**Visit our website:**
www.mcdougallittell.com

# A Wagner Matinee

*Willa Cather*

I received one morning a letter, written in pale ink on glassy, blue-lined note-paper, and bearing the postmark of a little Nebraska village. This communication, worn and rubbed, looking as though it had been carried for some days in a coat pocket that was none too clean, was from my Uncle Howard and informed me that his wife had been left a small legacy by a bachelor relative who had recently died, and that it would be necessary for her to go to Boston to attend to the settling of the estate. He requested me to meet her at the station and render her whatever services might be necessary. On examining the date indicated as that of her arrival, I found it no later than tomorrow. He had characteristically delayed writing until, had I been away from home for a day, I must have missed the good woman altogether.

The name of my Aunt Georgiana called up not alone her own figure, at once <u>pathetic</u> and grotesque, but opened before my feet a gulf of recollection so wide and deep, that, as the letter dropped from my hand, I felt suddenly a stranger to all the present conditions of my existence, wholly ill at ease and out of place amid the

WORDS
TO
KNOW

**pathetic** (pə-thĕt′ĭk) *adj.* arousing pity or compassion

689

## TEACHING THE LITERATURE
### Customizing Instruction

**Students Acquiring English**
Review the meaning of the title. Explain that Richard Wagner (1813–1883) was a German opera composer and that a matinee is a theatrical performance or concert that takes place during the afternoon.

Use **Spanish Study Guide,** pp. 169–171, for additional support.

**Less Proficient Readers**
Explain that this story is about a woman who left her life in a bustling city to homestead on the Nebraska prairie. Ask students to share what they know about homesteading and to think about how they would feel if they had made such a drastic move.

**1** Ask students to explain why Aunt Georgiana is on her way to Boston.
**Answer:** to settle the estate of a relative who has left her money

**Set a Purpose** Have students read to find out more about Aunt Georgiana's life.

**Gifted and Talented**
Ask students to study Cather's literary style in this story. Have them point out and analyze examples of imagery, detailed description, and poetic language in favorite passages.

**Cross Curricular Link  History**

**PIONEER FAMILIES** The Homestead Act of 1862, also known as the "log-cabin legislation," encouraged many families to head west. From 1860 to 1870, Nebraska's population burgeoned from fewer than 30,000 to more than 122,000 people. The Homestead Act gave families title to 160 acres of land for a small fee. In order to lay claim to the land, however, settlers had to occupy and work it for five years—a formidable challenge indeed. In addition to the loneliness and backbreaking work, families faced terrible hardships and the most severe conditions: threats of attack, first from Indians and then from the cattlemen competing for land; and natural calamities such as blizzards,

droughts, prairie fires, and insects. Between 1874 and 1877, huge swarms of crop-destroying grasshoppers invaded Nebraska. For all the settlers who gave up and returned east, thousands of others took their place. Some farming families pushed farther west. It was not uncommon for a pioneer family to resettle six or seven times. For pioneer women, life consisted of backbreaking labor in a harsh environment. Aunt Georgiana had six children—a moderate number. More children in a family meant more workers on the field. By the age of forty years, many woman looked as though they'd seen sixty.

**A** Ask students what conclusions they can draw about Aunt Georgiana's character based on the narrator's description of her physical appearance, his comments, and his landlady's response to her. What is their impression of her, and what details contribute to this impression?

**Possible Responses:** She has endured many hardships; however "misshapen," she must have a strong constitution both physically and mentally. The narrator's "awe and respect" and his comparison of her to explorers suggest that she is courageous and hardworking, a pioneer worthy of admiration. Her history as a music teacher suggests a "classier" background than one might expect from looking at her.

📖 Use **Unit Four Resource Book** p. 70 for more practice.

**Literary Analysis**  SETTING

 **B** Ask students to summarize their impressions of Aunt Georgiana's homestead. How does this setting contrast with the Boston setting of her youth?

**Possible Response:** The homestead is a harsh and uncivilized place to live. Georgiana and Howard had to make their first home in a cavelike dugout, and they were always in danger from Indian attack. The place was isolated, and opportunities for travel were few. In contrast, Georgiana must have had a culturally and socially stimulating life as a teacher at the Boston Conservatory, and she would have enjoyed all the amenities of city life.

📖 Use **Unit Four Resource Book** p. 71 for more practice.

---

familiar surroundings of my study. I became, in short, the gangling farmer-boy my aunt had known, scourged with chilblains[1] and bashfulness, my hands cracked and sore from the corn husking. I felt the knuckles of my thumb tentatively, as though they were raw again. I sat again before her parlor organ, fumbling the scales with my stiff, red hands, while she, beside me, made canvas mittens for the huskers.[2]

The next morning, after preparing my landlady somewhat, I set out for the station. When the train arrived I had some difficulty in finding my aunt. She was the last of the passengers to alight, and it was not until I got her into the carriage that she seemed really to recognize me. She had come all the way in a day coach; her linen duster had become black with soot and her black bonnet grey with dust during the journey. When we arrived at my boarding-house the landlady put her to bed at once and I did not see her again until the next morning.

Whatever shock Mrs. Springer experienced at my aunt's appearance, she considerately concealed. As for myself, I saw my aunt's misshapen figure with that feeling of awe and respect with which we behold explorers who have left their  ears and fingers north of Franz-Josef-Land,[3] or their health somewhere along the Upper Congo.[4] My Aunt Georgiana had been a music teacher at the Boston Conservatory, somewhere back in the latter sixties. One summer, while visiting in the little village among the Green Mountains where her ancestors had dwelt for generations, she had kindled the callow fancy of the most idle and shiftless of all the village lads, and had conceived for this Howard Carpenter one of those extrava-

gant passions which a handsome country boy of twenty-one sometimes inspires in an angular, spectacled woman of thirty. When she returned to her duties in Boston, Howard followed her, and the upshot of this inexplicable infatuation was that she eloped with him, eluding the reproaches of her family and the criticisms of her friends by going with him to the Nebraska frontier. Carpenter, who, of course, had no money, had taken a homestead in Red Willow County, fifty miles from the railroad. There they had measured off their quarter section themselves by driving across the prairie in a wagon, to the wheel of which they had tied a red cotton handkerchief, and counting off its revolutions. They built a dugout in the red hillside, one of those cave dwellings whose inmates so often reverted to primitive conditions. Their water they got from the lagoons where the buffalo drank, and their slender stock of provisions was always at the mercy of bands of roving Indians. For thirty years my aunt had not been further than fifty miles from the homestead.

But Mrs. Springer knew nothing of all this, and must have been considerably shocked at what was left of my kinswoman. Beneath the soiled linen duster which, on her arrival, was the most conspicuous

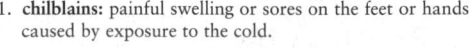

For thirty years my aunt had not been further than fifty miles from the homestead.

---

1. **chilblains:** painful swelling or sores on the feet or hands, caused by exposure to the cold.
2. **huskers:** farm workers who remove cornhusks by hand.
3. **Franz-Josef-Land:** a group of small, mostly ice-covered islands in the Arctic Ocean north of Russia.
4. **Upper Congo:** river in central Africa, now called the Zaire (zä-îr') River.

WORDS
TO
KNOW
**callow** (kăl′ō) *adj.* lacking adult maturity or experience; immature
**inexplicable** (ĭn-ĕk′splĭ-kə-bəl) *adj.* difficult or impossible to explain
**reproach** (rĭ-prōch′) *n.* an expression of blame or disapproval

690

---

## Teaching Options

**Mini Lesson**  ## Preteaching Vocabulary

**APPLYING MEANINGS OF ROOTS Instruction**
Students can extend their vocabulary through systematic word study. Use the chart on page 691 to show students how to apply meanings of Latin, Greek, and Anglo-Saxon roots in order to comprehend unfamiliar words. The English language borrows words from many other languages. Many English words come from Old German through Old English. Many others derive ultimately from Latin, the language of the ancient Roman empire, or from Greek. Use the word *matinee* from the title to show how a word descends from Latin. In

French, it is spelled *matinée* and means "morning." The Latin word for "morning" is *matutinus,* which comes from *Matuta,* Goddess of the Dawn. Another related word in English is *matutinal,* which means "occurring in the morning" or "early."
**Application** Use the first two columns in the chart to analyze word roots with students. Then have volunteers provide words for the third column. Another option is to fill in the first column on the chalkboard and then have students work in small groups, each with a dictionary, to complete the second and third columns.

feature of her costume, she wore a black stuff dress, whose ornamentation showed that she had surrendered herself unquestioningly into the hands of a country dressmaker. My poor aunt's figure, however, would have presented astonishing difficulties to any dressmaker. Originally stooped, her shoulders were now almost bent together over her sunken chest. She wore no stays, and her gown, which trailed unevenly behind, rose in a sort of peak over her abdomen. She wore ill-fitting false teeth, and her skin was as yellow as a Mongolian's from constant exposure to a pitiless wind and to the alkaline water which hardens the most transparent cuticle into a sort of flexible leather.

I owed to this woman most of the good that ever came my way in my boyhood, and had a reverential affection for her. During the years when I was riding herd for my uncle, my aunt, after cooking the three meals—the first of which was ready at six o'clock in the morning—and putting the six children to bed, would often stand until midnight at her ironing-board with me at the kitchen table beside her, hearing me recite Latin declensions and conjugations, gently shaking me when my drowsy head sank down over a page of irregular verbs. It was to her, at her ironing or mending, that I read my first Shakespeare, and her old text-book on mythology was the first that ever came into my empty hands. She taught me my scales and exercises, too—on the little parlor organ, which her husband had bought her after fifteen years,

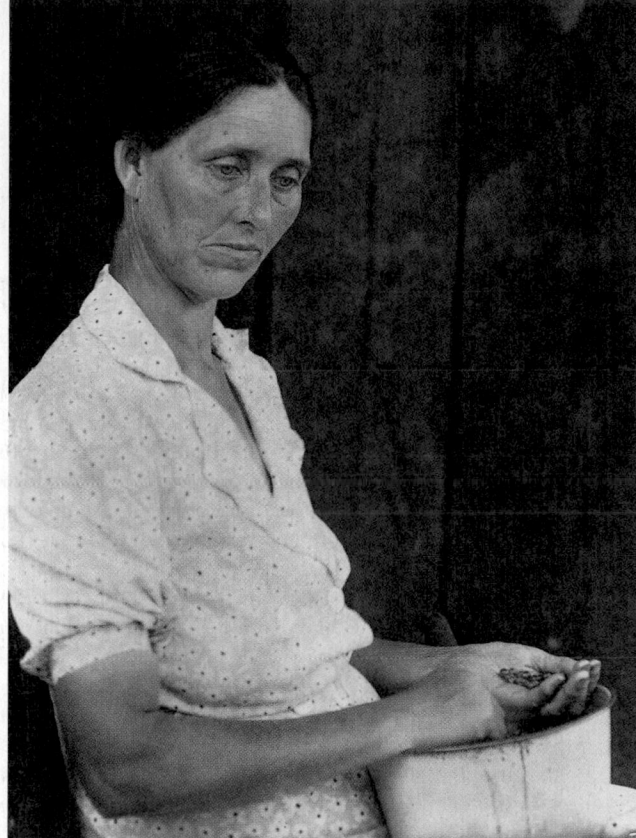

*Mrs. Stewart, Housewife and Singer, Brasstown, North Carolina*, Doris Ulmann. Doris Ulmann Collection, #635, Special Collections, University of Oregon Library.

during which she had not so much as seen any instrument, but an accordion that belonged to one of the Norwegian farmhands. She would sit beside me by the hour, darning and counting while I struggled with the "Joyous Farmer," but she seldom talked to me about music, and I understood why. She was a pious woman; she had the consolations of religion and, to her at least, her martyrdom was not wholly sordid. Once when I had been doggedly beating out some easy passages from an old score of

WORDS TO KNOW

**pious** (pī′əs) *adj.* having or showing reverence for God
**sordid** (sôr′dĭd) *adj.* wretched; dirty; morally degraded

691

| Word | Latin Roots | Other words with same root |
|------|-------------|----------------------------|
| **conjecture** | *con-*, together + *jacere*, to throw (*jectum* is the past participle) | projection, eject |
| **excruciatingly** | *ex-*, completely + *cruciare*, to torment | crucify |
| **inexplicable** | *in-*, not + *ex-* (reversal) + *plicare*, to fold | implicate |
| **pious** | *pius*, devoted, dutiful | impious, piety |
| **reproach** | *re-*, back + *prope*, near | approach |
| **superficially** | *superficies*, surface *super-*, above + *facies*, face, form, shape | supercilious artificial |

| Word | Greek Root | Other words with same root |
|------|-----------|----------------------------|
| **pathetic** | *pathos*, passion, suffering | apathy |
| | Old English Root (Anglo-Saxon) | |
| **callow** | *calu*, bare, bald (like a fledgling, hence inexperienced) | |

Use **Unit Four Resource Book** p. 72 for more practice.

## Active Reading DRAWING
### CONCLUSIONS ABOUT CHARACTER

**Ⓐ** Ask students what Aunt Georgiana's words in this passage reveal about her character.

**Possible Responses:** She regrets having sacrificed music; she is discontent with her life; she wants to spare her nephew from experiencing the same sorrow and regret.

**Ⓑ** Ask students to describe how Georgiana has changed since leaving Boston, based on how she acts when Clark suggests they visit the Common.

**Possible Responses:** Whereas once she felt comfortable and at home in the city, now she seems timid, old-fashioned, unworldly, and preoccupied with the farm.

## Literary Analysis SETTING

**Ⓒ** Ask students to point out sensory details in Clark's description that help them envision the concert hall.

**Possible Responses:** veritable hanging gardens, brilliant as tulip beds; one lost the contour of faces and figures; there was only the color of bodices past counting; shimmer of fabrics soft and firm, silky and sheer; all the colors that an impressionist finds in a sunlit landscape

Ask students what atmosphere these details evoke.

**Possible Responses:** lush; colorful; warm; crowded; glowing; vital; diverse; soft

---

**Ⓐ** *Euryanthe*[5] I had found among her music books, she came up to me and, putting her hands over my eyes, gently drew my head back upon her shoulder, saying tremulously, "Don't love it so well, Clark, or it may be taken from you. Oh! dear boy, pray that whatever your sacrifice may be, it be not that."

When my aunt appeared on the morning after her arrival, she was still in a semi-somnambulant state. She seemed not to realize that she was in the city where she had spent her youth, the place longed for hungrily half a lifetime. She had been so wretchedly train-sick throughout the journey that she had no recollection of anything but her discomfort, and, to all intents and purposes, there were but a few hours of nightmare between the farm in Red Willow County and my study on Newbury Street. I had planned a little pleasure for her that afternoon, to repay her for some of the glorious moments she had given me when we used to milk together in the straw-thatched cowshed and she, because I was more than usually tired, or because her husband had spoken sharply to me, would tell me of the splendid performance of the *Huguenots*[6] she had seen in Paris, in her youth. At two o'clock the Symphony Orchestra was to give a Wagner program, and I intended to take my aunt; though, as I conversed with her, I grew doubtful about her enjoyment of it. Indeed, for her own sake, I could only wish her taste for such things quite dead, and the long struggle mercifully ended at last. I suggested our visiting the Conservatory and the Common[7] before lunch, but she seemed altogether too timid to wish to venture out. She questioned me absently about **Ⓑ** various changes in the city, but she was chiefly concerned that she had forgotten to leave instructions about feeding half-skimmed milk to a certain weakling calf, "old Maggie's calf, you know, Clark," she explained, evidently having forgotten how long I had been away. She was further troubled because she had neglected to

tell her daughter about the freshly-opened kit of mackerel in the cellar, which would spoil if it were not used directly.

**Ⓑ** I asked her whether she had ever heard any of the Wagnerian operas,[8] and found that she had not, though she was perfectly familiar with their respective situations, and had once possessed the piano score of *The Flying Dutchman*. I began to think it would have been best to get her back to Red Willow County without waking her, and regretted having suggested the concert.

From the time we entered the concert hall, however, she was a trifle less passive and inert, and for the first time seemed to perceive her surroundings. I had felt some <u>trepidation</u> lest she might become aware of the absurdities of her attire, or might experience some painful embarrassment at stepping suddenly into the world to which she had been dead for a quarter of a century. But, again, I found how <u>superficially</u> I had judged her. She sat looking about her with eyes as impersonal, almost as stony, as those with which the granite Rameses[9] in a museum watches the froth and fret that ebbs and flows[10] about his pedestal—separated from it by the lonely stretch of centuries. I have seen this same aloofness in old miners who drift into the Brown hotel at Denver, their pockets full of bullion,[11] their linen soiled, their haggard faces unshaven; standing in the thronged corridors

---

5. *Euryanthe* (yōō′rē-ăn′thē): an opera by the German composer Carl Maria von Weber.

6. *Huguenots* (hyōō′gə-nŏts′): an opera by the German composer Giacomo Meyerbeer.

7. **the Common:** Boston Common, a public park.

8. **Wagnerian operas:** The orchestra will play selections from several operas composed by Wagner, including *The Flying Dutchman, Tannhauser, Tristan and Isolde*, and a cycle of four operas called *The Ring of the Nibelung*.

9. **Rameses** (răm′sēz′): one of the ancient kings of Egypt of that name.

10. **froth . . . flows:** happiness and sadness that comes and goes.

11. **bullion:** gold.

---

WORDS TO KNOW

**trepidation** (trĕp′ĭ-dā′shən) *n.* fearful uncertainty or worry

**superficially** (sōō′pər-fĭsh′ə-lē) *adv.* in a shallow way; concerned with only what is obvious

---

## Teaching Options

### BLOCK SCHEDULING: MANAGING TIME

**If your schedule requires that you cover the lesson objectives in a shorter time, use . . .**
- Preparing to Read, p. 688
- Thinking Through the Literature, p. 697
- Vocabulary in Action, p. 699

**If you want to take advantage of longer class time, use . . .**
- TE Teaching Options: Cross-Curricular Links, pp. 689, 699; Preteaching Vocabulary, p. 690; Viewing and Representing, p. 693; Informal Assessment, p. 696
- Choices & Challenges and Author Activity, pp. 698–699

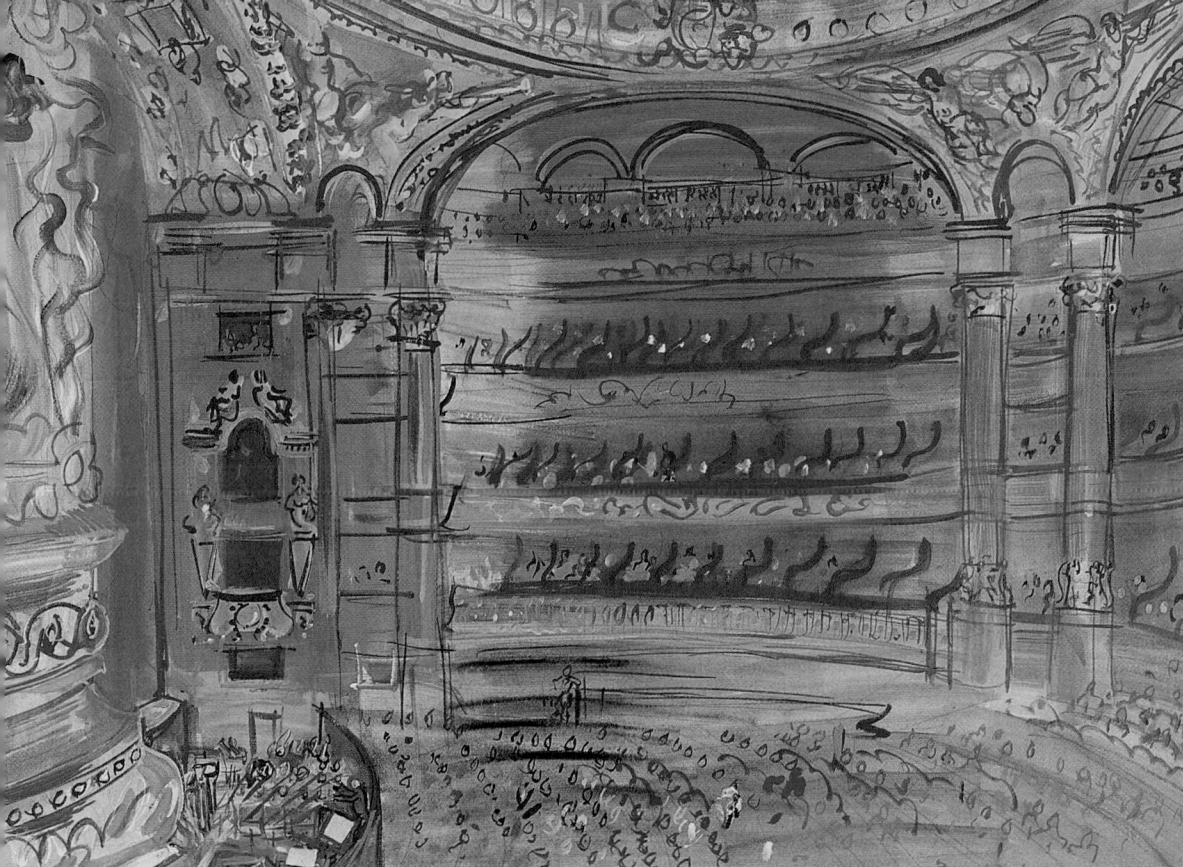

*The Opera, Paris* (about 1924), Raoul Dufy. Watercolor and gouache on paper, 19″ × 25″, The Phillips Collection, Washington, D.C.

**1**

as solitary as though they were still in a frozen camp on the Yukon,[12] conscious that certain experiences have isolated them from their fellows by a gulf no haberdasher could bridge.

**C**

We sat at the extreme left of the first balcony, facing the arc of our own and the balcony above us, veritable hanging gardens, brilliant as tulip beds. The matinée audience was made up chiefly of women. One lost the contour of faces and figures, indeed any effect of line whatever, and there was only the color of bodices past counting, the shimmer of fabrics soft and firm, silky and sheer; red, mauve, pink, blue, lilac, purple, ecru, rose, yellow, cream, and white, all

the colors that an impressionist[13] finds in a sunlit landscape, with here and there the dead shadow of a frock coat. My Aunt Georgiana regarded them as though they had been so many daubs of tube-paint on a palette.

When the musicians came out and took their places, she gave a little stir of anticipation and looked with quickening interest down over the rail at that invariable grouping, perhaps the first

**C**

---

12. **Yukon** (yōō′kŏn′): a river in the Yukon Territory, in northwest Canada.

13. **impressionist:** member of a movement in French painting that emphasized the play of light and color.

A WAGNER MATINEE **693**

---

 **Viewing and Representing**

*Mrs. Stewart, Housewife and Singer, Brasstown, North Carolina* **by Doris Ulmann**

*The Opera, Paris* **by Raoul Dufy**

**ART APPRECIATION** The painter Raoul Dufy (1877–1953) and the photographer Doris Ulmann (1882–1934) were contemporaries of Willa Cather (1873–1947). Ulmann, like Cather, was a noted realist. Her photograph *Mrs. Stewart* (page 691) is an example of documentary photography from the Great Depression. Dufy contributed to a movement away from romanticism.

**Instruction** Have students compare and contrast the visual effects of two media: the impressionist painting *The Opera, Paris,* and the documentary photograph *Mrs. Stewart.* Ask them to describe how shape, line, color, and texture communicate meaning and to consider how different visual techniques convey messages.

**Possible Responses:** The black-and-white photograph has the same bleak yet poignant quality evoked in Cather's description of Aunt Georgiana, including the detail of the rough-hewn clapboards in the background. It could

be a portrait of her. In the painting, all is suggested; the only clear lines are ones that stress the architectural features or heads in the audience, but the swaths of color capture Cather's description of the audience as well as the elegance, splendor, and vibrancy of a concert hall.

A WAGNER MATINEE **693**

**A** Ask students what sensory details help them visualize the homestead.

**Possible Responses:** "tall, naked house"; "black and grim as a wooden fortress"; "black pond"; "pitted with sun-dried cattle tracks"; "rain gullied clay banks"; "flat world"

Ask students to compare the atmosphere of this setting with that of the concert hall.

**Possible Responses:** The concert hall is warm, colorful, and crowded, and its atmosphere is full of creative and social energy; the homestead is stark, harsh, and lonely, and its atmosphere is epitomized by dishrags hung to dry from seedlings.

### Literary Analysis: TONE

**B** Discuss the tone of the question and what it suggests about her attitude.

**Possible Responses:** She's wistful, chagrined, sad, nostalgic, self-pitying, envious.

### Reading Skills and Strategies: MAKING INFERENCES

**C** Clark admits that he is unable to gauge how much of Aunt Georgiana's appreciation of music survives. Ask students to give their opinions about this and cite evidence from the text.

**Possible Response:** The fact that she weeps throughout the second half of the program suggests that her emotional appreciation of music has survived intact. Perhaps she would no longer be able to analyze the music as thoroughly on an intellectual level (suggested by her "dim eyes"), but her soul responds eagerly to it.

---

wholly familiar thing that had greeted her eye since she had left old Maggie and her weakling calf. I could feel how all those details sank into her soul, for I had not forgotten how they had sunk into mine when I came fresh from ploughing forever and forever between green aisles of corn, where, as in a treadmill, one might walk from daybreak to dusk without perceiving a shadow of change. The clean profiles of the musicians, the gloss of their linen, the dull black of their coats, the beloved shapes of the instruments, the patches of yellow light thrown by the green shaded lamps on the smooth, varnished bellies of the 'cellos and the bass viols in the rear, the restless, wind-tossed forest of fiddle necks and bows—I recalled how, in the first orchestra I had ever heard, those long bow strokes seemed to draw the heart out of me, as a conjurer's stick reels out yards of paper ribbon from a hat.

The first number was the *Tannhauser* overture. When the horns drew out the first strain of the Pilgrim's chorus, my Aunt Georgiana clutched my coat sleeve. Then it was I first realized that for her this broke a silence of thirty years; the inconceivable silence of the plains. With the battle between the two motives, with the frenzy of the Venusberg theme and its ripping of strings, there came to me an overwhelming sense of the waste and wear we are so powerless to combat; and I saw again the tall, naked house on the prairie, black and grim as a wooden fortress; the black pond where I had learned to swim, its margin pitted with sun-dried cattle tracks; the rain gullied clay banks about the naked house, the four dwarf ash seedlings where the dish-cloths were always hung to dry before the kitchen door.

She sat staring at the orchestra through a dullness of thirty years

The world there was the flat world of the ancients; to the east, a cornfield that stretched to daybreak; to the west, a corral that reached to sunset; between, the conquests of peace, dearer bought than those of war.

The overture closed, my aunt released my coat sleeve, but she said nothing. She sat staring at the orchestra through a dullness of thirty years, through the films made little by little by each of the three hundred and sixty-five days in every one of them. What, I wondered, did she get from it? She had been a good pianist in her day I knew, and her musical education had been broader than that of most music teachers of a quarter of a century ago. She had often told me of Mozart's operas and Meyerbeer's, and I could remember hearing her sing, years ago, certain melodies of Verdi's. When I had fallen ill with a fever in her house she used to sit by my cot in the evening—when the cool, night wind blew in through the faded mosquito netting tacked over the window and I lay watching a certain bright star that burned red above the cornfield—and sing "Home to our mountains, O, let us return!" in a way fit to break the heart of a Vermont boy near dead of homesickness already.

I watched her closely through the prelude to *Tristan and Isolde*, trying vainly to <u>conjecture</u> what that seething turmoil of strings and winds might mean to her, but she sat mutely staring at the violin bows that drove obliquely downward, like the pelting streaks of rain in a summer shower. Had this music any message for her? Had she enough left to at all comprehend this power which had kindled the world since she

WORDS
TO
KNOW    **conjecture** (kən-jĕk'chər) *v.* to make a judgment on the basis of uncertain evidence; guess

694

---

### Mini Lesson — Grammar

**INTRODUCTORY ADVERBIAL CLAUSES Instruction**
Unlike a phrase, a **clause** is a group of words that contain a verb and its subject. An **adverbial clause** is a subordinate clause; it cannot stand alone as a complete sentence. Adverbial clauses are often introduced by words such as *when, while, before, after, as soon as, since,* and *as.* An **introductory adverbial clause** is one that is found at the beginning of a sentence. Within a sentence, it functions as an adverb modifying the main verb. Write the following sentence on the board.

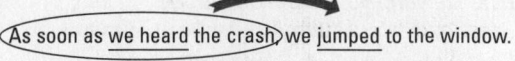

As soon as we heard the crash, we jumped to the window.

- Say the main (independent) clause out loud: "we jumped to the window." Ask students if it can stand alone as a sentence. *(yes)* Then say the adverbial clause aloud: "As soon as we heard the crash." Ask students if the clause can stand alone as a sentence. *(no)* Does it express a complete thought? *(no)*

had left it? I was in a fever of curiosity, but Aunt Georgiana sat silent upon her peak in Darien.[14] She preserved this utter immobility throughout the number from *The Flying Dutchman*, though her fingers worked mechanically upon her black dress, as though, of themselves, they were recalling the piano score they had once played. Poor old hands! They had been stretched and twisted into mere tentacles to hold and lift and knead with; the palms unduly swollen, the fingers bent and knotted—on one of them a thin, worn band that had once been a wedding ring. As I pressed and gently quieted one of those groping hands, I remembered with quivering eyelids their services for me in other days.

Soon after the tenor began the "Prize Song," I heard a quick drawn breath and turned to my aunt. Her eyes were closed, but the tears were glistening on her cheeks, and I think, in a moment more, they were in my eyes as well. It never really died, then—the soul that can suffer so <u>excruciatingly</u> and so interminably; it withers to the outward eye only; like that strange moss which can lie on a dusty shelf half a century and yet, if placed in water, grows green again. She wept so throughout the development and elaboration of the melody.

During the intermission before the second half of the concert, I questioned my aunt and found that the "Prize Song" was not new to her. Some years before there had drifted to the farm in Red Willow County a young German, a tramp cow puncher, who had sung the chorus at Bayreuth,[15] when he was a boy, along with the other peasant boys and girls. Of a Sunday morning he used to sit on his gingham-sheeted bed in the hands' bedroom which opened off the kitchen, cleaning the leather of his boots and saddle, singing the "Prize Song," while my aunt went about her work in the kitchen. She had hovered about him until she had prevailed upon him to join the country church, though his sole fitness for this step, in so far as I could gather, lay in his boyish

face and his possession of this divine melody. Shortly afterward he had gone to town on the Fourth of July, been drunk for several days, lost his money at a faro[16] table, ridden a saddled Texas steer on a bet, and disappeared with a fractured collar-bone. All this my aunt told me huskily, wanderingly, as though she were talking in the weak lapses of illness.

"Well, we have come to better things than the old *Trovatore*[17] at any rate, Aunt Georgie?" I queried, with a well meant effort at jocularity.

Her lip quivered and she hastily put her handkerchief up to her mouth. From behind it she murmured, "And you have been hearing this ever since you left me, Clark?" Her question was the gentlest and saddest of reproaches. **B**

The second half of the program consisted of four numbers from the *Ring*, and closed with Siegfried's funeral march. My aunt wept quietly, but almost continuously, as a shallow vessel overflows in a rainstorm. From time to time her dim eyes looked up at the lights which studded the ceiling, burning softly under their dull glass globes; doubtless they were stars in truth to her. I was still perplexed as to what measure of musical comprehension was left to her, she who had heard nothing but the singing of Gospel Hymns at Methodist services in the square frame school-house on Section Thirteen for so many years. I was wholly unable to gauge how much of it had been dissolved in soapsuds, or worked into bread, or milked into the bottom of a pail. **C**

---

14. **peak in Darien** (dâr´ē-ĕn´): an allusion to a poem by the English poet John Keats, in which Keats describes Spanish explorers on a mountain in Darien, a region that is now Panama. The Spaniards stand silent and amazed as they become the first Europeans to view the Pacific Ocean.

15. **Bayreuth** (bī-roit´): the Bayreuth Festival, an annual international music festival in Germany that presents Wagner's operas.

16. **faro:** a gambling game.

17. *Trovatore* (trô´vä-tô´rĕ): *Il Trovatore* is an opera by the Italian composer Giuseppe Verdi.

WORDS TO KNOW  **excruciatingly** (ĭk-skrōō´shē-ā´tĭng-lə) *adv.* in a way that causes great pain or distress

**695**

**Customizing Instruction**

**Less Proficient Readers**

**1** Help students appreciate figurative language by having them reread and paraphrase this passage. Ask them to explain what Clark means here.

**Possible Response:** He's describing what it was like for him the first time he heard an orchestra. The music seemed to reach into his soul and bring forth something magical and wonderful.

**Set a Purpose** Have students read to find out what happens to Clark and Aunt Georgiana by the end of the story.

**Students Acquiring English**

**2** Help students appreciate figurative language. Point out this passage and explain that the phrase *strings and winds* refers to the musical instruments. The violin is an example of a string instrument; the oboe or flute, a wind instrument. Have them describe how watching a section of violin bows moving downward together could be like watching a rain shower.

**Gifted and Talented**

Have students discuss what might have happened to Georgiana had she stayed in Boston rather than eloped.

• Circle "As soon as we heard the crash." Underline the subject and verb ("we heard") in the clause. Point out that this is an adverbial clause. Draw an arrow from the circled clause to the main verb. Explain that the entire clause modifies the verb "jumped" by telling when the action occurred.

**Exercises** For each of the following sentences, have students circle the adverbial clause and underline its subject and verb.

1. While she washed dishes, he practiced playing the organ. (*While <u>she washed</u> dishes*)

2. Since the concert was free that day, everyone wanted to go. (*Since <u>the concert was</u> free that day*)

3. Before the conductor continued, the violinist took a bow. (*Before <u>the conductor continued</u>*)

4. When the concert ended, they were both sad. (*When <u>the concert ended</u>*)

5. As it was time to go, we could not sit there any longer. (*As <u>it was</u> time to go*)

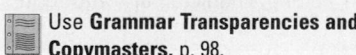 Use **Grammar Transparencies and Copymasters**, p. 98.

 Use McDougal Littell's *Language Network*, Chapter 3, for more instruction in adverbial clauses.

## Reading and Analyzing

*House in Winter* (1941), Wright Morris. Photo taken near Lincoln, Nebraska.

The deluge of sound poured on and on; I never knew what she found in the shining current of it; I never knew how far it bore her, or past what happy islands. From the trembling of her face I could well believe that before the last numbers she had been carried out where the myriad graves are, into the grey, nameless burying grounds of the sea; or into some world of death vaster yet, where, from the beginning of the world, hope has lain down with hope and dream with dream and, renouncing,[18] slept.

The concert was over; the people filed out of the hall chattering and laughing, glad to relax and find the living level again, but my kinswoman made no effort to rise. The harpist slipped its green felt cover over his instrument; the flute-players shook the water from their mouthpieces; the men of the orchestra went out one by one, leaving the stage to the chairs and music stands, empty as a winter cornfield.

I spoke to my aunt. She burst into tears and sobbed pleadingly. "I don't want to go, Clark, I don't want to go!"  **A**

I understood. For her, just outside the door of the concert hall, lay the black pond with the cattle-tracked bluffs; the tall, unpainted house, with weather-curled boards; naked as a tower, the crook-backed ash seedlings where the dishcloths hung to dry; the gaunt, molting turkeys picking up refuse about the kitchen door. ❖  **B**

---

18. **renouncing:** giving up.

## Teaching Options

# *Thinking* through the LITERATURE

## Connect to the Literature

**1. What Do You Think?**
What thoughts do you have about Aunt Georgiana? Discuss them with a classmate.

> **Comprehension Check**
> - Why is Aunt Georgiana on her way to Boston?
> - Why is Clark grateful to his aunt?
> - How does Clark expect his aunt to react to the concert?

## Think Critically

**2.** Do you think that Aunt Georgiana will be tempted to stay in Boston and not return to her home in Nebraska? Why?

**3.** In your opinion, was it a good idea for Clark to take Aunt Georgiana to the concert? Defend your view.

**4.** **ACTIVE READING** **DRAWING CONCLUSIONS ABOUT CHARACTER**
Based on the diagram you made about Aunt Georgiana in your  **READER'S NOTEBOOK**, what details from the story present the strongest evidence about the kind of person she is? From the choices that Aunt Georgiana has made in her life, what conclusions can you draw about her character?

> **THINK ABOUT**
> - the circumstances of her elopement
> - how she feels about life on the farm
> - how she treated Clark as a child in her home
> - your own insights into making difficult choices

**5.** What new insights do you think Clark gains over the course of the story? Explain your answer.

## Extend Interpretations

**6. Different Perspectives** If the events were described by Aunt Georgiana rather than Clark, how might the story differ?

**7. Critic's Corner** "A Wagner Matinee" created a stir when it appeared in *Everybody's Magazine* in 1904. Cather's family objected to the fictional portrait of her real-life aunt Franc. One of her friends criticized the writer's portrayal of Nebraska: "The stranger to this state will associate Nebraska with the aunt's wretched figure, her ill-fitting false teeth, her skin yellowed by the weather." Is Cather's portrait of Aunt Georgiana too unflattering? Do you think her portrayal of Nebraska is too harsh? Support your answers with details.

**8. Connect to Life** What do you think Aunt Georgiana would say to a young person who believed love could overcome all problems in a marriage? Explain your answer.

## Literary Analysis

**SETTING** As you recall, the **setting** of a story refers to the time and place in which the action occurs. In "A Wagner Matinee," Cather sharply distinguishes between two places—a Nebraska homestead and the Boston concert hall—that have a profound effect on Aunt Georgiana. The elegance and vibrancy of the concert hall are contrasted with the barrenness of Red Willow County and the "tall, naked house on the prairie, black and grim as a wooden fortress." How do the descriptions of the two settings highlight the sacrifices Aunt Georgiana made when she chose to marry?

**Activity** Go back through the story and record details describing the Nebraska farm and the Boston concert hall. Then, acting as a set designer for a movie, TV program, or play based on the story, sketch the two settings described. Compare your depictions with those of other students.

---

## Extend Interpretations

**Different Perspectives** Some students may point out the literary value gained by having an outside observer gradually discover the main character's thoughts. Some may say that Georgiana would be less capable than Clark of interpreting her emotions at the concert; for example, she may not have described her soul in terms of the moss simile (p. 695). Others may say that Clark's point of view deprives the reader of fuller insight into his aunt's feelings.

**Critic's Corner** Answers will vary. Accept all reasonable, well-supported responses.

**Connect to Life** Possible Responses: Aunt Georgiana's advice might be practical, warning that romantic love, though rosy and passionate, is short-lived. Moreover, it can temporarily overshadow other important concerns and prompt hasty decisions (such as elopement). Love is necessary in a marriage, but shared values and interests are also important.

---

## GUIDING STUDENT RESPONSE

### Connect to the Literature

**1. What Do You Think?**
Students should use text evidence to support their opinions.

**Comprehension Check**
- to settle the estate of a recently deceased relative
- He is grateful for the kindness and guidance she gave him as a boy, introducing him to music and the classics.
- At first he expects she may be embarrassed about the way she is dressed; he even suspects that life on the farm may have impaired her ability to respond to music.

 Use Selection Quiz
**Unit Four Resource Book,** p. 73.

### Think Critically

**2.** Possible Responses: Based on her reaction at the end of the concert, she may be tempted to stay in Boston just to have access to such cultural events and be spared the harshness of life in Nebraska. On the other hand, she has spent thirty years in Nebraska tending the farm and raising her children, and she might feel compelled to return.

**3.** Possible Responses: no, because it has reminded her of what she gave up when she left Boston; yes, because she will be able to enjoy memories of the concert and the experience has strengthened her bond with her nephew.

**4.** Accept all reasonable, well-supported opinions.

**5.** Possible Response: Clark comes to appreciate the extent of his aunt's sacrifice in choosing the pioneer life, and he realizes her heroism—the very tenacity that helped her raise a family on the frontier also enabled her to preserve her passion for music. Clark realizes, also, that his aunt's love for music became his own legacy.

### Literary Analysis

**Setting** Possible Responses: The setting descriptions highlight her sacrifices by providing before-and-after images of her life. Before marriage, her life was filled with people, color, and music; after, her life was lonely, colorless, and culturally barren.

## Writing Options

**1. Cause-and-Effect Analysis** Possible causes of Aunt Georgiana's choice include romantic love, a desire for adventure, and a desire to escape her family; effects include a life of hard work on the frontier and the loss of the cultural enrichment that she loved.

**2. Telegram from Boston** Student responses will vary but should express Clark's understanding of how the concert affected his aunt.

**3. Interview: Personal Sacrifices** Student interviews should explore the reasons why the sacrifice was so difficult.

## Explorations & Activities

**1. Real Estate Ad** Students may draw on examples from newspapers, brochures, or magazines. Some student responses may be satirical propaganda.

**2. Opera Poster** This is an excellent opportunity for **visual and auditory learners.** Some students may find it inspiring to listen to recordings of Wagner's music while creating their posters. Accept abstract drawings.

## Inquiry & Research

**Music Appreciation** Encourage students to listen to the pieces by Wagner mentioned in the story, especially *Tristan and Isolde, The Flying Dutchman,* and Siegfried's funeral march from the *Ring.* Students can use them as mood setters to imagine the tastes and emotions of the characters. Ask them to listen for the musical passages that resonate the most.

---

# Choices & CHALLENGES

## Writing Options

**1. Cause-and-Effect Analysis** Draft a short cause-and-effect analysis, explaining why Aunt Georgiana chose to marry and move to the Nebraska frontier and what impact this choice had on her life.

**2. Telegram from Boston** Imagine that you are Clark. Write a telegram to be sent to your uncle, Howard Carpenter, explaining what has happened to Aunt Georgiana during her visit to Boston.

**3. Interview: Personal Sacrifices** Aunt Georgiana gave up a life of music that she loved. Ask a friend or family member to reveal to you his or her feelings about something he or she has given up in life. Then write up your interview with that person.

## Explorations & Activities

**1. Real Estate Ad** Create a real estate advertisement to "sell" the virtues of life on the frontier, using details from your reading of "A Wagner Matinee." As an alternative, you may want to create an ad discouraging people from moving to the frontier.

**2. Opera Poster** Using music reference books and recordings, research the music of Richard Wagner. Use what you learn to create a poster advertising the performance that Clark and Aunt Georgiana attend.

## Inquiry & Research

**Music Appreciation** Find recordings of operas by Richard Wagner. Then play one or two of the excerpts that Aunt Georgiana hears performed at the concert in Boston, and explain how you think she may have reacted to each piece of music. You may also want to find and play music by other composers mentioned in the story, such as Mozart and Verdi.

## Vocabulary in Action

**EXERCISE A: CONTEXT CLUES** Write the vocabulary word that best completes each sentence.

1. If you think of Wagner as the composer of operas featuring large blonds wearing helmets with horns sticking out of them, you might _____ that his music is not relevant to your life.

2. However, bear in mind that it is easy to dismiss or ridicule things that we look at only _____, without considering them in depth.

3. In reacting to opera, to literature, or to art, a person who is scornful of what he or she is unfamiliar with deserves _____.

4. Wagner's music is filled with familiar emotions; one whole opera was composed while he was hopelessly and _____ in love with a woman who could never be his.

5. Brilliant as he was, Wagner was a careless student with childish attitudes who showed many signs of being _____.

6. His continuing financial irresponsibility makes it difficult to pity him and view his money troubles as _____.

7. Puzzled by his music, which was far ahead of its time, many opera lovers at first found his work _____.

8. Financial problems and a lack of quick success may well have filled Wagner with a sense of _____ about the future.

9. Although some musical dramas, called oratorios, involve biblical characters, Wagner's work does not have these _____ connections.

10. Even if the theme of his work is not religiously spiritual, listening to it can lift one out of the petty, mean, and _____ events of the world and provide a glimpse of purity and beauty.

**EXERCISE B** Try acting out the Words to Know by using only a facial expression and gestures.

| WORDS TO KNOW | callow conjecture excruciatingly inexplicable | pathetic pious reproach | sordid superficially trepidation |
|---|---|---|---|

**Building Vocabulary**
For an in-depth lesson on context clues, see page 326.

---

## Teaching Options

### (Mini Lesson) Grammar

**PUNCTUATING INTRODUCTORY ADVERBIAL CLAUSES Instruction** Use a comma to set off an introductory adverbial clause. Write the following sentence on the chalkboard:

> After she spent the day working so hard I wanted to treat her to a concert.

Ask a volunteer to underline the introductory adverbial clause and read the sentence aloud. The other students should detect a pause after the word *hard.* Explain that adding a comma after *hard* sets off the introductory adverbial clause, makes the structure of the sentence more apparent, and reflects a pause in natural speech.

**Exercises** Have students underline each introductory adverbial clause and punctuate each sentence correctly.

1. While the violins were playing tears began to fall.
   *(comma after "While the violins were playing")*

2. As soon as they got home she fell asleep.
   *(comma after "As soon as they got home")*

3. Before the concert started the lights went out.
   *(comma after "Before the concert started")*

 Use **Grammar Transparencies and Copymasters** p. 152.

 Use McDougal Littell's *Language Network,* Chapter 3, for more instruction in adverbial clauses.

## Willa Cather
### 1873–1947

**Other Works**
*Death Comes for the Archbishop*
*One of Ours*
*The Song of the Lark*

**The Making of a Writer** Willa Cather believed that "the most basic material a writer works with is acquired before the age of fifteen. . . . Those years determine whether one's work will be poor and thin or rich and fine." Born in Back Creek Valley, Virginia, Cather moved to the prairies of Nebraska when she was nine years old. The land there—and the pioneers who lived on it—gave Cather her distinctive voice. Her acclaimed novels *O Pioneers!* and *My Àntonia* are set on her beloved prairie.

**Cultural Influences** As a child, Cather enjoyed a rich cultural life despite the limitations of growing up in the young frontier town of Red Cloud. She had fine books in her home and excellent teachers at school. Among her Nebraska neighbors were educated European immigrants who introduced her to French and German literature, taught her to read classical Latin and Greek, and taught her the history and appreciation of classical music and opera. The railroad brought traveling stock companies to the opera house in Red Cloud, where Cather saw plays and light operas; she herself wrote, staged, and performed in amateur plays.

**Career Path** After studying journalism at the University of Nebraska, Cather went to Pittsburgh, where she worked as a magazine editor, a critic, and a teacher. From 1906 on, far from the wild Nebraska frontier of her childhood, Cather lived in New York City, supporting herself as a novelist.

## Author Activity

Read another short story from her collection *Youth and the Bright Medusa* or *Obscure Destinies*. Prepare a comparison chart in which you show the realistic details of setting and characters in the story you chose and in "A Wagner Matinee."

## Vocabulary in Action

1. conjecture
2. superficially
3. reproach
4. excruciatingly
5. callow
6. pathetic
7. inexplicable
8. trepidation
9. pious
10. sordid

## Author Background

The land gave Willa Cather her voice. Few other writers have written of the American Midwest with such passion and such truth. She had the power to ennoble the ordinary details of prairie life with her rich prose. For example, to her the brilliant color of a wild prairie rose was "a dye made of sunlight and morning and moisture, so intense that it could not possibly last."

*My Antonia* (1918), a poignant and memorable novel, chronicles the lives of an immigrant pioneer family. *One of Ours* (1922), which is about a young man's quest for freedom and identity on the eve of WWI, won the Pulitzer Prize for fiction in 1923. Encourage your students to read these excellent novels.

A WAGNER MATINEE **699**

## Humanities

**MUSIC APPRECIATION** Richard Wagner (1813–1883) was a world-renowned German composer. His interest in theater led him to integrate drama with music in revolutionary ways. Wagner believed opera should be a "total work of art," combining poetic, dramatic, and musical elements to create a whole greater than the sum of its parts. To that end, he made extensive use of *leitmotif* ("leading motive")—a thematic musical passage in which the harmonic, melodic, or rhythmic pattern was associated with a specific character, feeling, idea, or situation. This technique reached its highest development in the *Ring* cycle, mentioned in this selection. In the last of its four operas, *Gotterdämmerung* ("Twilight of the Gods"), the technique had evolved into a complex network of music that functioned as a conceptual language.

Primary Source

## Objectives

- read and analyze letters
- read to be informed about life as a homesteader
- construct images such as graphic organizers based on text structure

## Further Background

"Letters of a Woman Homesteader" is a first-hand account of life as a homesteader. Elinore Pruitt arrived in Burnt Fork, Wyoming, in April 1909, and went to work as a housekeeper for Clyde Stewart, a prosperous Scottish rancher. She had previously been married to Harry Rupert, whom she divorced before leaving Native American territory. Six weeks after arriving in Wyoming, she married Stewart "between planting oats and other work that must be done." The Stewarts had three sons: Jamie, who died in infancy; Henry Clyde; and Calvin.

## Reading for Information

As you read through this selection with students, have them use the material in the right-hand column as a guide to reading letters. The following are possible responses to the four questions.

## Evaluating An Argument

1. She is writing to a friend who sent a Christmas package. Her apologetic tone suggests that the letter is a belated thank-you for the package.

2. **Analyzing the Evidence** Possible entries to the chart are provided below.

| Homesteading | |
|---|---|
| Pros | Cons |
| job security | hard work |
| no rent | coyotes |
| beauty of nature | loneliness |
| independence | no physician |
| plenty to eat | |
| home of one's own | |

---

*from*
# LETTERS OF A WOMAN HOMESTEADER
## Elinore Pruitt Stewart

*In 1909, Elinore Pruitt Stewart (formerly Rupert) left Denver and became a homesteader, a person who received public land free of charge under the Homestead Act of 1862. She moved to Burnt Fork, Wyoming, and wrote the following letter about her new life.*

January 23, 1913

Dear Mrs. Coney,—

❶ I am afraid all my friends think I am very forgetful and that you think I am ungrateful as well, but I am going to plead not guilty. Right after Christmas Mr. Stewart came down with *la grippe*[1] and was so miserable that it kept me busy trying to relieve him. Out here where we can get no physician we have to dope ourselves, so that I had to be housekeeper, nurse, doctor, and general overseer. That explains my long silence.

And now I want to thank you for your kind thought in prolonging our Christmas. The magazines were much appreciated. They relieved some weary night-watches, and the box did Jerrine more good than the medicine I was having to give her for *la grippe*. She was content to stay in bed and enjoy the contents of her box.

When I read of the hard times among the Denver poor, I feel like urging them every one to get out and file on land. I am very enthusiastic about women homesteading. It really requires less strength and labor to raise plenty to satisfy a large family than it does to go out to wash, with the added satisfaction of knowing that their job will not be lost to them if they care to keep it. Even if improving the place does go slowly, it is that ❷ much done to stay done. Whatever is raised is the homesteader's own, and there is no house-rent to pay. This year Jerrine cut and dropped enough potatoes to raise a ton of fine potatoes. She wanted to try, so we let her, and you will remember that she is but six years old. We had a man to break the ground and

---

1. *la grippe* (lä-grēp′) *French:* the flu; influenza.

## Reading for Information

Have you ever received a letter or an e-mail from a friend who has moved away? Like Stewart, did he or she attempt to justify the new circumstances by explaining how much better his or her life is now than before? Letters are more than just personal correspondence; they are also primary sources that reveal details and personal observations of the life and times of the writer.

### EVALUATING AN ARGUMENT

In her letter, Stewart discusses the benefits of homesteading and gives reasons to support those opinions. Use the questions and activities below to help you evaluate her argument.

❶ In the beginning of the letter, Stewart explains why she hasn't written. To whom is she writing? What does her **tone** suggest about the purpose of the letter?

❷ **Analyzing the Evidence** Stewart describes aspects of homesteading that she likes, such as "Whatever is raised is the homesteader's own." She also tells of things she dislikes. Make a chart similar to the one below and list Stewart's pros and cons of homesteading.

| HOMESTEADING | |
|---|---|
| Pros | Cons |
| no rent | loneliness |

cover the potatoes for her and the man irrigated them once. That was all that was done until digging time, when they were ploughed out and Jerrine picked them up. Any woman strong enough to go out by the day could have done every bit of the work and put in two or three times that much, and it would have been so much more pleasant than to work so hard in the city and then be on starvation rations in the winter.

**❸** To me, homesteading is the solution of all poverty's problems, but I realize that temperament has much to do with success in any undertaking, and persons afraid of coyotes and work and loneliness had better let ranching alone. At the same time, any woman who can stand her own company, can see the beauty of the sunset, loves growing things, and is willing to put in as much time at careful labor as she does over the washtub, will certainly succeed; will have independence, plenty to eat all the time, and a home of her own in the end.

Experimenting need cost the homesteader no more than the work, because by applying to the Department of Agriculture at Washington he can get enough of any seed and as many kinds as he wants to make a thorough trial, and it doesn't even cost postage. Also one can always get bulletins from there and from the Experiment Station of one's own State concerning any problem or as many problems as may come up. I would not, for anything, allow Mr. Stewart to do anything toward improving my place, for I want the fun and the experience myself. And I want to be able to speak from experience when I tell others what they can do. Theories are very beautiful, but facts are what must be had, and what I intend to give some time.

**❹** Here I am boring you to death with things that cannot interest you! You'd think I wanted you to homestead, wouldn't you? But I am only thinking of the troops of tired, worried women, sometimes even cold and hungry, scared to death of losing their places to work, who could have plenty to eat, who could have good fires by gathering the wood, and comfortable homes of their own, if they but had the courage and determination to get them.

I must stop right now before you get so tired you will not answer. With much love to you from Jerrine and myself, I am

Yours affectionately,

*Elinore Rupert Stewart*

*Westly Potato Camp, Edison, California,* Dorothea Lange (1895–1965). Copyright © 1982. The Dorothea Lange Collection, The Oakland Museum of California, The City of Oakland, gift of Paul S. Taylor.

**❸** Stewart states that "temperament has much to do with success in any undertaking." What do you think she means? She then describes the qualities of a person who she thinks will dislike homesteading and those of a person she thinks will like it. How do these descriptions support her overall argument that homesteading is better than city life?

**❹ Concluding the Letter** Reread the next-to last paragraph of the letter, and explain whether you think this conclusion effectively ends her argument in favor of homesteading.

**Evaluating** You've analyzed the pros and cons of homesteading and learned Stewart's reasons for leaving Denver. If you had been living in that city in 1913 and read this letter, would it move you to take up homesteading? Explain.

3. Stewart means that attitude can determine whether one succeeds or fails in much of life. She describes the kind of person who would like homesteading (independent, appreciative of nature, hardworking) and the kind of person who would not like it (fearful, lazy, needy). Stewart seems to contend that homesteading attracts hard-working, self-reliant people and can also transform a lazy person into a hard-working farmer.

4. **Concluding the Letter** Her conclusion is effective since it leaves the reader with a reinforced image of the suffering and deprivation Stewart associates with city life.

### Evaluating

**Possible Responses:** Yes, if I were poor and living in the city in 1913, this letter might motivate me to become a home-steader because Stewart's descriptions of the freedom and beauty of the plains is inviting and makes poverty seem less dire. No, this letter alone would not inspire me to become a homesteader because it is simply one person's opinion. I would need to research the idea more and get opinions from other homesteaders before I would make that decision.

Encourage students who are interested to read more about conditions in Denver in 1913. Have them consider the information to decide if they would act to become homesteaders. Ask students to write a letter explaining their decision.

### Objectives

1. appreciate a prose retelling of a traditional **ballad (Literary Analysis)**
2. understand and appreciate a **legend (Literary Analysis)**
3. **make judgments about text (Active Reading)**

### Summary

Gregorio Cortez is remembered in song for his honor, his values, and his skills as a cowboy and farmer. When his brother Román tricks an American by exchanging a lame horse for a sorrel mare, Cortez and Román are confronted by the man and a sheriff. The sheriff shoots the unarmed Román and then shoots at Gregorio Cortez, who kills the sheriff. Cortez takes flight on the sorrel mare and eludes hundreds of Texas Rangers and sheriffs, killing a few along the way. Finally, a man named El Teco, greedy for the reward money, betrays Cortez, who surrenders to spare his family from further persecution. There are several trials to convict Cortez; at all of them he defends himself so eloquently that he wins his freedom. In the end, he is tried and convicted for horse stealing. Later, the (fictional) daughter of President Lincoln arranges for his release from prison. Before he leaves, however, enemies give Cortez a slow-working poison that kills him within the year.

### Thematic Link

In this retelling of the *corrido,* Cortez is a **trailblazer,** both culturally and literally.

### 5-Minute Warm-Up

***Daily***
***Language***
***SkillBuilder***

Have students **proofread** the display sentences on page 555k and write them correctly. The sentences also appear on Transparency 20 of **Grammar Transparencies and Copymasters.**

---

## PREPARING to *Read*

# The Legend of Gregorio Cortez

*Fiction by* AMÉRICO PAREDES

**Comparing Literature**

### Traditions Across Time: Writing of the New West

The *cuento* "The Indian and the Hundred Cows" teaches important cultural values of the Southwestern frontier, while Black Elk's retelling of "High Horse's Courting" portrays distinctive customs and beliefs of the Sioux who lived in the northern Great Plains. "The Legend of Gregorio Cortez," a modern prose retelling of an old ballad, gives some clues about the ideals of Mexican Americans living in the Texas border region during the early 1900s.

**Points of Comparison**   As you read, compare the cultural values revealed in this legend with those evident in the *cuento* and the Sioux tale.

### Build Background

**The Man Behind the Legend** "The Legend of Gregorio Cortez" is a prose retelling of a *corrido,* a fast-paced ballad from the Mexican oral tradition. Both the original *corrido* and this retelling are based on the life of Gregorio Cortez, who was born in Mexico in 1875. On June 12, 1901, while Cortez was living in Karnes County, Texas, he shot and killed Sheriff Brack Morris just after the

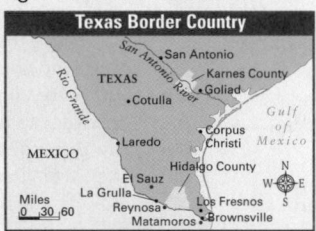

**Texas Border Country**

sheriff shot Cortez's brother. In his flight to the border, Cortez walked more than 100 miles and rode another 400 miles. On the way, he killed another sheriff and eluded several posses, some with as many as 300 men. He was finally captured—out of ammunition and on foot—near the border town of Laredo. After a three-year legal battle, Cortez was acquitted of killing the first sheriff but sentenced to life for killing the second. He spent about 12 years in prison before being pardoned by the governor of Texas in 1913. Cortez died three years later of unknown causes.

### Focus Your Reading

**LITERARY ANALYSIS   LEGEND**   A **legend** is a story passed down orally from generation to generation and popularly believed to have a historical basis. Many legends, such as "The Legend of Gregorio Cortez," feature a **cultural hero**—a larger-than-life figure who reflects the values of a people. The cultural hero's role is to provide a noble image that will inspire and guide the actions of all who share that culture.

**ACTIVE READING   MAKING JUDGMENTS ABOUT TEXT**   Like many legends, this retelling of the *corrido* about Gregorio Cortez mixes fact, exaggeration, and fiction, much as a tall tale does, to create an unforgettable hero. To determine how much this legend stretches the truth, **make judgments** about, or evaluate, the accuracy of the details and situations as you read.

**READER'S NOTEBOOK**   Make judgments as to which details and situations in "The Legend of Gregorio Cortez" are factual, exaggerated, or fictional. Use a diagram like the one shown to record your judgments.

```
            Details and Events
        ┌─────────┼─────────┐
    Factual   Exaggerated  Fictional
```

---

## LESSON RESOURCES

**UNIT FOUR RESOURCE BOOK,** pp. 74–78

**ASSESSMENT RESOURCES**
**Formal Assessment,** pp. 133–134
**Teacher's Guide to Assessment and Portfolio Use**
**Test Generator**

**SKILLS TRANSPARENCIES AND COPYMASTERS**
**Literary Analysis**
• Legends, Myths, and Folk Tales, T24 (for Cooperative Learning Activity, p. 718)

**Reading and Critical Thinking**
• Making Judgments, T5 (for Active Reading, p. 702)

**Grammar**
• Using *That* and *Which,* T44 (for Mini Lesson, p. 704)
• Noun Clauses: Common Introductory Words, C104 (for Mini Lesson, p. 704)

**Vocabulary**
• Word History, C60 (for Mini Lesson, p. 707)
• English from Spanish, C61 (for Mini Lesson, p. 710)

**Communications**
• Interviewing, T9 (for Activities & Explorations 2, p. 719)
• Impromptu Speaking: Dialogue, Role-Play, Debate, T13 (for Activities & Explorations 2, p. 719)

**INTEGRATED TECHNOLOGY**
**Audio Library**
**LaserLinks**
• Cultural Connection: Mexican Rural Life. See **Teacher's SourceBook,** p. 57.

**Visit our website:**
www.mcdougallittell.com

# The Legend of
# Gregorio Cortez

### Américo Paredes

**THEY** still sing of him—in the *cantinas*[1] and the country stores, in the ranches when men gather at night to talk in the cool dark, sitting in a circle, smoking and listening to the old songs and the tales of other days. Then the *guitarreros*[2] sing of the border raids and the skirmishes, of the men who lived by the phrase, "I will break before I bend."

They sing with deadly-serious faces, throwing out the words of the song like a challenge, tearing savagely with their stiff, callused fingers at the strings of the guitars.

And that is how, in the dark quiet of the ranches, in the lighted noise of the saloons, they sing of Gregorio Cortez.

After the song is sung there is a lull. Then the old men, who have lived long and seen almost everything, tell their stories. And when they tell about Gregorio Cortez, the telling goes like this:

---

1. *cantinas* (kän-tē′näs) *Spanish:* taverns or bars.
2. *guitarreros* (gē-tä-rĕ′rôs) *Spanish:* guitar players.

THE LEGEND OF GREGORIO CORTEZ **703**

**Reading Skills and Strategies: PREVIEW**

Briefly summarize the events of the selection for students. Remind them that this legend was originally a *corrido*, or ballad.

**Literary Analysis** LEGEND

Explain that a legend is a story passed down from one generation to the next. Unlike a myth, a legend is popularly believed to have a historical basis. Many legends are based on real people or events but contain a great deal of exaggeration and fictional filler. Ask students what elements make this a legend.

**Possible Responses:** It is based on historical fact and on an actual person; it is loaded with exaggerated feats that a superhero is capable of performing. It has been passed for generations in the form of a ballad.

Use **Unit Four Resource Book**, p. 76 for additional support.

**Active Reading** MAKING JUDGMENTS

Remind students that they're expected to evaluate the credibility of information sources. As they read, have them make judgments about the accuracy of the narrator's account and determine whether details in the legend are fact, exaggeration, or fiction. Have them consider the narrator's motive to decide if he is a credible source.

**Possible Responses:** You have to read with some level of skepticism. When feats become superhuman, factual accounts turn to fiction. The narrator's motive is to bolster the heroic status of Gregorio Cortez.

Use **Unit Four Resource Book**, p. 75 for additional support.

## How Gregorio Cortez Came to Be in the County of El Carmen

That was good singing, and a good song; give the man a drink. Not like these pachucos[3] nowadays, mumbling damn-foolishness into a microphone; it is not done that way. Men should sing with their heads thrown back, with their mouths wide open and their eyes shut. Fill your lungs, so they can hear you at the pasture's farther end. And when you sing, sing songs like *El Corrido de Gregorio Cortez*. There's a song that makes the hackles rise. You can almost see him there—Gregorio Cortez, with his pistol in his hand.

He was a man, a Border man. What did he look like? Well, that is hard to tell. Some say he was short and some say he was tall; some say he was Indian brown and some say he was blond like a newborn cockroach. But I'd say he was not too dark and not too fair, not too thin and not too fat, not too short and not too tall; and he looked just a little bit like me. But does it matter so much what he looked like? He was a man, very much of a man; and he was a Border man. Some say he was born in Matamoros; some say Reynosa; some say Hidalgo county on the other side. And I guess others will say other things. But Matamoros, or Reynosa, or Hidalgo, it's all the same Border; and short or tall, dark or fair, it's the man that counts. And that's what he was, a man.

Not a gunman, no, not a bravo. He never came out of a cantina wanting to drink up the sea at one gulp. Not that kind of man, if you can call that kind a man. No, that wasn't Gregorio Cortez at all. He was a peaceful man, a hardworking man like you and me.

He could shoot. Forty-four and thirty-thirty, they were the same to him. He could put five bullets into a piece of board and not make but one hole, and quicker than you could draw a good deep breath. Yes, he could shoot. But he could also work.

He was a vaquero,[4] and a better one there has not ever been from Laredo to the mouth. He could talk to horses, and they would understand. They would follow him around, like dogs, and no man knew a good horse better then Gregorio Cortez. As for cattle, he could set up school for your best caporal.[5] And if an animal was lost, and nobody could pick up a trail, they would send for Gregorio Cortez. He could always find a trail. There was no better tracker in all the Border country, nor a man who could hide his tracks better if he wanted to. That was Gregorio Cortez, the best vaquero and range man that there ever was.

But that is not all. You farmers, do you think that Gregorio Cortez did not know your business too? You could have told him nothing about cotton or beans or corn. He knew it all. He could look into the sky of a morning and smell it, sniff it the way a dog sniffs, and tell you what kind of weather there was going to be. And he would take a piece of dirt in his hands and rub it back and forth between his fingers—to see if the land had reached its point—and you would say he was looking into it. And perhaps he was, for Gregorio Cortez was the seventh son of a seventh son.[6]

You piddling modern farmers, vain of yourselves when you make a bale! You should have seen the crops raised by Gregorio Cortez. And when harvesting came, he was in there with the rest. Was it shucking corn? All you could see was the shucks fly and the pile grow, until you didn't know there was a man behind the pile. But he was even better at cotton-picking time. He would bend down and never raise his head till he came out the other end, and he would

---

3. **pachucos** (pä-chōō′kōs) *Spanish:* young toughs.
4. **vaquero** (vä-kě′rō) *Spanish:* cowboy.
5. **caporal** (kä-pô-räl′) *Spanish:* boss of a ranch.
6. **seventh son of a seventh son:** According to the folklore of several cultures, the seventh son of a seventh son is always lucky and may be gifted with certain supernatural powers.

---

 **Grammar**

**INTRODUCTORY WORDS FOR NOUN CLAUSES**

Remind students that a noun clause is a subordinate clause that is used as a noun in a sentence. A noun clause can serve as the subject, the direct object, the indirect object, the predicate nominative, or as the object of a preposition. The introductory word in a noun clause can be a pronoun or a subordinating conjunction.

Display the following chart for students to copy:

| Words Introducing Noun Clauses | |
|---|---|
| Pronouns | who, whom, whose, which, whoever, whomever, what, whatever |
| Subordinating Conjunctions | how, that, whether, when, where, why |

Point out that some of the words that introduce noun clauses also introduce adjective and adverb clauses. Students must study the sentence to determine the clause's function.

be halfway through another row before the next man was through with his. And don't think the row he went through wasn't clean. No flags, no streamers, nothing left behind, nothing but clean, empty burrs where he had passed. It was the same when clearing land. There were men who went ahead of him, cutting fast along their strip in the early morning, but by noontime the man ahead was always Gregorio Cortez, working at his own pace, talking little and not singing very much, and never acting up.

FOR Gregorio Cortez was not of your noisy, hell-raising type. That was not his way. He always spoke low, and he was always polite, whoever he was speaking to. And when he spoke to men older than himself he took off his hat and held it over his heart. A man who never raised his voice to parent or elder brother, and never disobeyed. That was Gregorio Cortez, and that was the way men were in this country along the river. That was the way they were before these modern times came, and God went away.

He should have stayed on the Border; he should not have gone up above, into the North. But it was going to be that way, and that was the way it was. Each man has a certain lot in life, and no other thing but that will be his share. People were always coming down from places in the North, from Dallas and San Antonio and Corpus and Foro West. And they would say, "Gregorio Cortez, why don't you go north? There is much money to be made. Stop eating

*New Mexico Peon* (1945), Ernest L. Blumenschein. Oil on canvas, 40" × 25", collection of Kathleen and Gerald Peters, Santa Fe, New Mexico.

beans and tortillas and that rubbery jerked beef. One of these days you're going to put out one of your eyes, pull and pull with your teeth on that stuff and it suddenly lets go. It's a wonder all you Border people are not one-eyed. Come up above with us, where you can eat white bread and ham."

Use McDougal Littell's *Language Network*, Chapter 3, for more instruction in noun clauses.

## Customizing Instruction

### Students Acquiring English

**1** Explain that *hackles* refers to the short hairs on the back of an animal's neck that stand up straight when the animal is annoyed, angry, or alarmed. Something that makes the hackles rise is something that makes you angry.

**2** Tell students that *piddling* means "beneath consideration." For the narrator, modern farmers aren't even worth mentioning, and they certainly don't belong in the same story as the hero of this legend.

### Gifted and Talented

**3** Have students consider what this passage reveals about the narrator. Ask them to discuss the belief that "God went away" and to decide if this attitude is more representative of an older than of a younger person.

### Less Proficient Readers

**4** Read this passage aloud to help students understand that the narrator believes that fate controls people's lives. Have them decide what the narrator means by saying "each man has a certain lot in life." Ask if they share the narrator's belief that everyone has a destiny—an inevitable fate.

**Set a Purpose** Have students read to discover other points that demonstrate the belief that each person is destined to live a predetermined course of events.

---

Write these three sentences and underline the subordinate clauses as shown.
**1.** Here is the tree <u>where he tied the horse</u>.
**2.** <u>Whoever helped him</u> was put in jail.
**3.** Knowing <u>where his mother was</u> disturbed him.
Ask students which sentences contain a noun clause. (*2,3*)
The clause in the first sentence acts as an adjective; it modifies the noun *tree*; the noun clause in the second sentence acts as a subject; the noun clause in the third sentence acts as the direct object of the gerund *Knowing*.

**Exercises** In each sentence, have students underline the clause; identify the introductory word, and the clause's function.
**1.** <u>Why he decided to surrender</u> is an amazing story. (*why; subject*)
**2.** The tragedy was <u>how Román died</u>. (*how; predicate nominative*)
**3.** The old men sang to <u>whomever gathered in the cantina</u>. (*whomever; indirect object*)
**4.** No one knew <u>whether he would make it out alive</u>. (*whether; direct object*)

 Use **Grammar Transparencies and Copymasters**, p. 104.

**Reading Skills and Strategies:**
**CONNECT**

Have each student draw upon his/her own background to provide connection to texts. Ask students to think of legends that they know—stories either passed down in their family or community—and the elements that make them memorable.

**Active Reading** | MAKING JUDGMENTS |

**A** Ask students to describe their impressions of Román. What is his role in the legend?
**Possible Responses:** He serves as a contrast to Gregorio; he is a character with flaws; he represents traits that the culture views as problematic.

**Literary Analysis** | LEGEND |

**B** Ask students to explain how Gregorio's premonition enhances the characterization of him as a cultural hero.
**Possible Responses:** It makes him seem wise and all-knowing, and it suggests he has superhuman power.

# Román was just like the young men of today,...

But Gregorio Cortez would only smile, because he was a peaceful man and did not take offense. He did not like white bread and ham; it makes people flatulent and dull. And he liked it where he was. So he always said, "I like this country. I will stay here."

But Gregorio Cortez had a brother, a younger brother named Román. Now Román was just like the young men of today, loud-mouthed and discontented. He was never happy where he was, and to make it worse he loved a joke more than any other thing. He would think nothing of playing a joke on a person twice his age. He had no respect for anyone, and that is why he ended like he did. But that is yet to tell.

Román talked to Gregorio and begged him that they should move away from the river and go up above, where there was much money to be made. And he talked and begged so, that finally Gregorio Cortez said he would go with his brother Román, and they saddled their horses and rode north.

Well, they did not grow rich, though things went well with them because they were good workers. Sometimes they picked cotton; sometimes they were vaqueros, and sometimes they cleared land for the Germans. Finally they came to a place called El Carmen, and there they settled down and farmed. And that was how Gregorio Cortez came to be in the county of El Carmen, where the tragedy took place.

### Román's Horse Trade and What Came of It

Román owned two horses, two beautiful sorrels[7] that were just alike, the same color, the same markings, and the same size. You could not have told them apart, except that one of them was lame. There was an American who owned a little sorrel mare. This man was dying to get Román's sorrel—the good one—and every time they met he would offer to swap the mare for the horse. But Román did not think much of the mare. He did not like it when the American kept trying to make him trade.

"I wonder what this Gringo[8] thinks," Román said to himself. "He takes me for a fool. But I'm going to make him such a trade that he will remember me forever."

And Román laughed a big-mouthed laugh. He thought it would be a fine joke, besides being a good trade. There were mornings when the American went to town in his buggy along a narrow road. So Román saddled the lame sorrel, led him a little way along the road, and stopped under a big mesquite[9] that bordered on the fence. He fixed it so the spavined[10] side was against the mesquite. Román waited a little while, and soon he heard the buggy coming along the road. Then he got in the saddle and began picking mesquites off the tree and eating them. When the American came around the bend, there was Román on his sorrel horse. The American stopped his buggy beside Román and looked at the horse with much admiration.

---

7. **sorrels:** horses of a light reddish brown.

8. **gringo** (grēng′gô) *Spanish:* slang term for a foreigner, especially someone from the United States.

9. **mesquite** (mĕ-skēt′): thorny, shrublike tree with sweet seeds.

10. **spavined** (spăv′ĭnd): afflicted with spavin, a disease in which a horse's hind leg joint becomes enlarged, resulting in lameness.

## Teaching Options

### Cross Curricular Link **History**

**TEXAS GERMANS** Toward the end of the 1800s, many German immigrants settled in Texas, especially in the area north of San Antonio, where they were lured by inexpensive, fertile farmland. They established cultural enclaves and towns with such names as New Braunfels, Fredericksburg, and Bergheim, communities that today attest to Texas's German heritage.

It was a fine animal, exactly like the other one, but the American could not see the spavined leg.

"Changed your mind?" the American said.

Román stopped chewing on a mesquite and said, "Changed my mind about what?"

"About trading that horse for my mare."

"You're dead set on trading your mare for this horse of mine?" Román said.

"You know I am," the American said. "Are you ready to come round?"

"I'm in a trading mood," said Román. "With just a little arguing you might convince me to trade this horse for that worthless mare of yours. But I don't know; you might go back on the deal later on."

**1** "I never go back on my word," the American said. "What do you think I am, a Mexican?"

"We'll see, we'll see," said Román. "How much are you willing to give in hand?"

"Enough to give you the first square meal you've had in your life," the American said.

**2** ROMÁN just laughed, and it was all he could do to keep from guffawing. He knew who was getting the best of things.

So they made the deal, with Román still sitting on his spavined horse under the tree, chewing on mesquites.

"Where's the mare?" Román said.

"She's in my yard," said the American, "hung to a tree. You go get her and leave the horse there for me because I'm in a hurry to get to town."

That was how Román had figured it, so he said, "All right, I'll do it, but when I finish with these mesquites."

"Be sure you do, then," the American said.

"Sure, sure," said Román. "No hurry about it, is there?"

"All right," the American said, "take your time." And he drove off leaving Román still sitting on his horse under the mesquite, and as he drove off the American said, "Now isn't that just like a Mexican. He takes his time."

Román waited until the American was gone, and then he stopped eating mesquites. He got off and led the horse down the road to the American's yard and left him there in place of the little sorrel mare. On the way home Román almost fell off his saddle a couple of times, just laughing and laughing to think of the sort of face the American would pull when he came home that night.

The next morning, when Gregorio Cortez got up he said to his brother Román, "Something is going to happen today."

"Why do you say that?" asked Román.

**B** "I don't know," said Gregorio Cortez. "I just know that something is going to happen today. I feel it. Last night my wife began to sigh for no reason at all. She kept sighing and sighing half the night, and she didn't know why. Her heart was telling her something, and I know some unlucky thing will happen to us today."

But Román just laughed, and Gregorio went inside the house to shave. Román followed him into the house and stood at the door while Gregorio shaved. It was a door made in two sections; the upper part was open and Román was leaning on the lower part, like a man leaning out of a window or over a fence. Román began to tell Gregorio about the horse trade he had made the day before, and he laughed pretty loud about it, because he thought it was a good

**Customizing Instruction**

**Less Proficient Readers**
Ask students to describe Gregorio's main traits. Then have them compare Román to his brother.

**Possible Responses:** Gregorio's hard-working, polite, and perfect in all he does. Román doesn't seem to share his brother's ideals; he is tricky; he doesn't take anything seriously.

**Students Acquiring English**

**1** Point out that to *give your word* means "to make a promise," and that to *go back on your word* means "to break a promise." Ask students to share similar phrases from their first language and to try to explain how the phrases translate literally.

**Multiple Learning Styles**
**Interpersonal Learners**

**2** Ask students to explain the strategy Román uses to handle the American's insult toward Mexicans.

**Possible Response:** He doesn't let the insult upset him; he deflects the insult to the American and proves the American to be the greater fool.

## ...loud-mouthed and discontented.

THE LEGEND OF GREGORIO CORTEZ **707**

## Vocabulary Strategy

**WORD HISTORY Instruction** Remind students that they're expected to research word origins to understand meanings and extend their vocabulary. Explain that many English and Spanish words come originally from Latin. Researching the history, or etymology, of the word *legend* will help them retain its meaning and learn new related words. Explain that in Middle English, spoken five to eight hundred years ago, *legend* meant "the story of a saint's life." It came from the Old French and Medieval Latin word *legenda,* which means "things for reading." Other words have trickled

down from the Latin verb *legere,* which means "to collect, gather, or read": *legal, legacy, collect, lecture, elect, dialect.* Point out to students the common Latin word root *leg* or *lect* in these words.

**Application** As they read, have students use reference materials to research and record the word origins of at least five words from the selection. Where applicable, they should list words related with a common root.

Use **Vocabulary Transparencies and Copymasters,** p. 60.

**A** Ask students to decide if they share the narrator's view of gunfights.

**Possible Response:** No, the narrator presents a romanticized view that minimizes the ugliness and suffering of such violence.

**Literary Concept: CULTURAL HERO**

**B** How does Gregorio's behavior after he kills the sheriff show him to be heroic?

**Possible Response:** Although he knows he should flee as soon as possible, his priority is to take his wounded brother to their mother's house in town, an act that risks his life.

**Literary Analysis** | LEGEND

**C** Have students decide if the description of the Americans' fear of Cortez is exaggerated or not. How does exaggeration, an element of legend, enhance Cortez as a cultural hero?

**Possible Response:** It makes him seem unconquerable.

---

joke. Gregorio Cortez just shaved, and he didn't say anything.

When what should pull in at the gate but a buggy, and the American got down, and the Major Sheriff of the county of El Carmen got down too. They came into the yard and up to where Román was leaning over the door, looking out.

The American had a very serious face. "I came for the mare you stole yesterday morning," he said.

Román laughed a big-mouthed laugh. "What did I tell you, Gregorio?" he said. "This Gringo . . . has backed down on me." . . .

Just as the word "Gringo . . ." came out of Román's mouth, the sheriff whipped out his pistol and shot Román. He shot Román as he stood there with his head thrown back, laughing at his joke. The sheriff shot him in the face, right in the open mouth, and Román fell away from the door, at the Major Sheriff's feet.

**A** AND then Gregorio Cortez stood at the door, where his brother had stood, with his pistol in his hand. Now he and the Major Sheriff met, each one pistol in hand, as men should meet when they fight for what is right. For it is a pretty thing to see, when two men stand up for their right, with their pistols in their hands, front to front and without fear. And so it was, for the Major Sheriff also was a man.

**1** Yes, the Major Sheriff was a man; he was a gamecock[11] that had won in many pits, but in Gregorio Cortez he met a cockerel[12] that pecked his comb. The Major Sheriff shot first, and he missed; and Gregorio Cortez shot next, and he didn't miss. Three times did they shoot, three times did the Major Sheriff miss, and three times did Gregorio Cortez shoot the sheriff of El Carmen. The Major Sheriff fell dead at the feet of Gregorio Cortez, and it was in this way that Gregorio Cortez killed the first sheriff of many that he was to kill.

When the Major Sheriff fell, Gregorio Cortez

looked up, and the other American said, "Don't kill me; I am unarmed."

"I will not kill you," said Gregorio Cortez. "But you'd better go away."

So the American went away. He ran into the brush and kept on running until he came to town and told all the other sheriffs that the Major Sheriff was dead.

Meanwhile, Gregorio Cortez knew that he too must go away. He was not afraid of the law; he knew the law, and he knew that he had the right. But if he stayed, the Rangers[13] would come, and the Rangers have no regard for law. You know what kind of men they are. When the Governor of the State wants a new Ranger, he asks his sheriffs, "Bring all the criminals to me." And from the murderers he chooses the Ranger, because no one can be a Ranger who has not killed a man. So Gregorio Cortez knew that the best thing for him was to go away, and his first thought was of the Border, where he had been born. But first he must take care of his brother, so he put Román in the buggy and drove into town, where his mother lived. **B**

Now there was a lot of excitement in town. All the Americans were saddling up and **2** loading rifles and pistols, because they were going out to kill Cortez. When all of a sudden, what should come rolling into town but the buggy, driven by Gregorio Cortez. They met him on the edge of town, armed to the teeth, on horseback and afoot, and he on the buggy, holding the reins lightly in his hands. Román was in the back, shot in the mouth. He could neither speak nor move, but just lay there like one who is dead.

They asked him, "Who are you?"

And he said to them, "I am Gregorio Cortez."

They all looked at him and were afraid of **C** him, because they were only twenty or twenty-

---

11. **gamecock:** rooster trained for fighting.
12. **cockerel:** young rooster.
13. **Rangers:** mounted riflemen organized to protect Anglo ranchers and settlers in Texas.

---

## Teaching Options

**Multicultural Link**   **History**

**OUTLAW HEROES** Heroes appear in many of the world's cultures as friends of the poor and fighters against injustice. Many heroes, however, began as criminals. In Mexico Francisco "Pancho" Villa (1878–1923), a daring bandit who became a leader of a revolutionary movement, gained wide admiration. In the United States, Charles Arthur "Pretty Boy" Floyd (1901–1934) was an Oklahoma outlaw of the Dust Bowl years. According to Woody Guthrie's ballad "Pretty Boy Floyd," Floyd defended his wife's honor against a verbally abusive deputy sheriff, killing the gun-toting lawman

with a chain. The ballad also depicts Floyd sending Christmas dinners to poor families. The most famous outlaw-hero in Anglo-Saxon culture—the subject of over 40 English and Scottish ballads—is Robin Hood, the legendary 12th-century English archer who robbed from the rich and gave to the poor. Operating out of Sherwood Forest with his band of merry men, including Friar Tuck and Little John, Robin remained loyal to the king while fighting the wicked Sheriff of Nottingham.

Chama Running Red (1925), John Sloan. Courtesy of The Anschutz Collection. Photo by James O. Milmoe.

five, and they knew that they were not enough. So they stepped aside and let him pass and stood talking among themselves what would be the best thing to do. But Gregorio Cortez just drove ahead, slowly, without seeming to care about the men he left behind. He came to his mother's house, and there he took down his brother and carried him in the house. He stayed there until dawn, and during the night groups of armed men would go by the house and say, "He's in there. He's in there." But none of them ever went in.

At dawn Gregorio Cortez came out of his mother's house. There were armed men outside, but they made no move against him. They just watched as he went down the street, his hands resting on his belt. He went along as if he was taking a walk, and they stood there watching until he reached the brush and he jumped into it and disappeared. And then they started shooting at him with rifles, now that he was out of pistol range.

"I must get me a rifle," said Gregorio Cortez, "a rifle and a horse."

They gathered in a big bunch and started after him in the brush. But they could not catch Gregorio Cortez. No man was ever as good as

THE LEGEND OF GREGORIO CORTEZ **709**

---

### Gifted and Talented

**1** Ask students to consider why the narrator reinforces the idea that the sheriff was "a man." Have them define the narrator's idea of masculinity and decide if they agree with it.

**Possible Response:** The narrator seems to define manhood by one's willingness to fight and kill to settle a dispute, and he continues with an extended metaphor on cockfighting, which can be seen as an example of mindless cruelty. Rather, a true "man" resolves conflicts through more peaceful means.

### Students Acquiring English

**2** Explain that the phrase *saddling up* means the Americans were preparing their horses for a journey.

---

### Cross Curricular Link  History

**TEXAS RANGERS** The Texas Rangers were originally ten men hired by Stephen F. Austin to protect settlers from Indian attacks. In 1835, the year before the Republic of Texas was born, the rangers became an official paid force defending the frontier. A plainclothes mounted police force, they were said to "ride like Mexicans, shoot like Tennesseans, and fight like the very devil." Ten years later, when the United States annexed Texas, the rangers lost their job to federal agents but regrouped as a volunteer militia. During the Mexican War (1846–1848), they served as scouts and guerrilla fighters, and they won acclaim for their skill and bravery in battle. After that war, they fought against the Comanches. During the Civil War, rangers fought as guerrillas for the Confederate cause. After the war, the rangers policed cattle rustling, quelled riots, suppressed feuds and range wars, and captured train robbers. In 1935 the rangers became part of the Texas Department of Public Safety and merged with the highway patrol.

**Literary Analysis: CULTURAL HERO**

**A** Ask students to identify the new aspect of Gregorio Cortez that makes him an even more impressive, larger-than-life hero.

**Possible Response:** He leaves no trail as he travels.

**Literary Analysis** | LEGEND |

**B** Ask students what the Mexican's response to Gregorio Cortez tells them about Cortez.

**Possible Response:** The Mexican idolizes Cortez; Cortez has become a living legend; he's already a cultural hero; Cortez's reputation precedes him.

**Active Reading** | MAKING JUDGMENTS |

**C** Ask students if they think that the description of Cortez's escape from 300 men is exaggerated.

**Possible Response:** Most students will answer in the affirmative.

# They'll never catch me like that,...

him in hiding his own tracks, and he soon had them going around in circles, while he doubled back and headed for home to get himself a rifle and a horse.

### How Gregorio Cortez Rode the Little Sorrel Mare All of Five Hundred Miles

He went in and got his thirty-thirty, and then he looked around for the best horse he had. It is a long way from El Carmen to the Border, all of five hundred miles. The first thing he saw in the corral was the little sorrel mare. Gregorio Cortez took a good look at her, and he knew she was no ordinary mare.

"You're worth a dozen horses," said Gregorio Cortez, and he saddled the little mare.

**1** But by then the whole wasp's nest was beginning to buzz. The President of the United States offered a thousand dollars for him, and many men went out to get Gregorio Cortez. The Major Sheriffs of the counties and all their sheriffs were out. There were Rangers from the **2** counties, armed to the teeth, and the King Ranch Rangers from the Capital, the meanest of them all, all armed and looking for Cortez. Every road was blocked and every bridge guarded. There were trackers out with those dogs they call hounds, that can follow a track better than the best tracker. They had railroad cars loaded with guns and ammunition and with men, moving up and down trying to head him off. The women and children stayed in the houses, behind locked doors, such was the fear they all had of Gregorio Cortez. Every town from the Capital to the Border was watching out for him. The brush and the fields were full of men, trying to pick up his trail. And Gregorio Cortez rode out for the

Border, through brush and fields and barbed wire fences, on his little sorrel mare.

He rode and rode until he came to a great broad plain, and he started to ride across. But just as he did, one of the sheriffs saw him. The sheriff saw him, but he hid behind a bush, because he was afraid to take him on alone. So he called the other sheriffs together and all the Rangers he could find, and they went off after Gregorio Cortez just as he came out upon the plain.

Gregorio Cortez looked back and saw them coming. There were three hundred of them.

"We'll run them a little race," said Gregorio Cortez.

Away went the mare, as if she had been shot from a gun, and behind her came the sheriffs and the Rangers, all shooting and riding hard. And so they rode across the plain, until one by one their horses foundered and fell to the ground and died. But still the little mare ran on, as fresh as a **3** lettuce leaf, and pretty soon she was running all alone.

"They'll never catch me like that," said Gregorio Cortez, "not even with those dogs called hounds."

Another big bunch of sheriffs rode up, and they chased him to the edge of the plain, and into the brush went Cortez, with the trackers after him, but they did not chase him long. One moment there was a trail to follow, and next moment there was none. And the dogs called **A** hounds sat down and howled, and the men scratched their heads and went about in circles looking for the trail. And Gregorio Cortez went on, leaving no trail, so that people thought he was riding through the air.

There were armed men everywhere, and he could not stop to eat or drink, because wherever

## Vocabulary Strategy

**ENGLISH FROM SPANISH** Remind students that languages influence each other. Many everyday English words come from Spanish. Review the following terms with the class. Point out that the word *peon*, an unskilled laborer or farm worker, is a Spanish term adopted by English speakers. It comes from the Latin word for foot-soldier, *pedo*. *Guitar* comes from the Spanish word *guitarra*, adapted from the Arabic *qitar*, from the Greek word for a lyre, *kithara*. The Moors were an Arabic people who settled in Spain during the eighth century. Originally from Northern Africa, they

would have had close ties to ancient Greece and its language.

*Corral* is another Spanish word used in English. There is some speculation that it came originally from a Hottentot word, *kraal*. The Hottentots are the Bantu people of southern Africa. Some of them may have been enslaved and sent with Spaniards who settled what is now Mexico and the southwestern United States. The Spanish settlers of South and Central America introduced the concept of "cowboy" and its practices to North America, so it makes sense that the language

he tried to stop armed men were there before him. So he had to ride on and on. Now they saw him, now they lost him, and so the chase went on. Many more horses foundered, but the mare still ran, and Gregorio Cortez rode on and on, pursued by hundreds and fighting hundreds every place he went.

"So many mounted Rangers," said Gregorio Cortez, "to catch just one Mexican."

It was from the big bunches that he ran. Now and again he would run into little ones of ten or a dozen men, and they were so scared of him that they would let him pass. Then, when he was out of range they would shoot at him, and he would shoot back at them once or twice, so they could go back and say, "We met up with Gregorio Cortez, and we traded shots with him." But from the big ones he had to run. And it was the little sorrel mare that took him safe away, over the open spaces and into the brush, and once in the brush, they might as well have been following a star.

**So** it went for a day, and when night fell Cortez arrived at a place named Los Fresnos and called at a Mexican house. When the man of the house came out, Cortez told him, "I am Gregorio Cortez."

**B**

That was all he had to say. He was given to eat and drink, and the man of the house offered Gregorio Cortez his own horse and his rifle and his saddle. But Cortez would not take them. He thanked the man, but he would not give up his little sorrel mare. Cortez was sitting there, drinking a cup of coffee, when the Major Sheriff of Los Fresnos came up with his three hundred men. All the other people ran out of the house

and hid, and no one was left in the house, only Gregorio Cortez, with his pistol in his hand.

Then the Major Sheriff called out, in a weepy voice, as the corrido says. He sounded as if he wanted to cry, but it was all done to deceive Gregorio Cortez.

"Cortez," the Major Sheriff said, "hand over your weapons. I did not come to kill you. I am your friend."

"If you come as my friend," said Gregorio Cortez, "why did you bring three hundred men? Why have you made me a corral?"

The Major Sheriff knew that he had been caught in a lie, and the fighting began. He killed the Major Sheriff and the second sheriff under him, and he killed many sheriffs more. Some of the sheriffs got weak in the knees, and many ran away.

"Don't go away," said Gregorio Cortez. "I am the man you are looking for. I am Gregorio Cortez."

They were more than three hundred, but he jumped their corral, and he rode away again, and those three hundred did not chase him any more.

**C**

He rode on and on, until he came to a river called the San Antonio. It is not much of a river, but the banks are steep and high, and he could not find a ford. So he rode to a ranch house nearby, where they were holding a *baile*[14] because the youngest child of the house had been baptized that day, and he asked the man of the house about a ford.

"There are only two fords," the man said. "One is seven miles upstream and the other is seven miles down."

---

14. *baile* (bäy′lĕ) *Spanish:* dance.

# ...not even with those dogs called hounds.

—

THE LEGEND OF GREGORIO CORTEZ **711**

---

---

### Literary Analysis: CULTURAL HERO

**A** What qualities in this passage make Cortez seem heroic or superhuman?

**Possible Responses:** He can talk to his horse; he is capable of incredible and brave physical feats.

### Literary Analysis: MOOD

**B** Ask students to define the mood, or atmosphere, that this scene creates.

**Possible Response:** excitement; suspense; humor

"I will take another look at the river," said Gregorio Cortez. He left the baile and rode slowly to the river. It was steep, and far below he could see the water flowing; he could barely see it because it was so dark. He stood there thinking, trying to figure out a way, when he heard the music at the baile stop.

He knew the Rangers were at the baile now. So he leaned over in his saddle and whispered in the mare's ear. He talked to her, and she understood. She came to the edge of the bank, with soft little steps, because she was afraid. But Gregorio Cortez kept talking to her and talking to her, and finally she jumped. She jumped far out and into the dark water below, she and Gregorio Cortez.

The other bank was not so high, but it was just as steep. Gregorio Cortez took out his reata,[15] and he lassoed a stump high on the bank. He climbed up the rope and got a stick, and with the stick he worked on the bank as fast as he could, for he could hear the racket of the dogs. The ground was soft, and he knocked off part of the top, until he made something like a slope. Then he pulled and talked until the mare struggled up the bank to where he was. After that they rested up a bit and waited for the Rangers. Up they came with their dogs, to the spot where the mare had jumped. When they came up to the river's edge, Cortez fired a shot in the air and yelled at them, "I am Gregorio Cortez!"

Then he rode away, leaving them standing there on the other side, because none of them

*Cliffs Beyond Abiquiu, Dry Waterfall* (1943), Georgia O'Keeffe. Oil on canvas, 76.2 cm × 40.6 cm, The Cleveland (Ohio) Museum of Art, bequest of Georgia O'Keeffe (87.141). Copyright © 1996 The Georgia O'Keeffe Foundation/Artists Rights Society (ARS), New York. Photo Copyright © The Cleveland Museum of Art.

was brave enough to do what Cortez had done.

He rode on and on, and sometimes they chased him and sometimes he stood and fought. And every time he fought he would kill them a Ranger or two. They chased him across the Arroyo del Cíbolo and into an oak grove, and there they made him a corral. Then they sent the dogs away and sat down to wait, for they wanted to catch him asleep. Gregorio Cortez thought for a little while what he should do. Then he made his mare lie down on the ground, so she would not be hurt. After that Gregorio Cortez began talking to himself and answering himself in different voices, as if he had many men. This made the Rangers say to one another, "There is a whole army of men with Gregorio Cortez." So they broke up their corral and went away, because they did not think there were enough of them to fight Gregorio Cortez and all the men he had. And Gregorio Cortez rode away, laughing to himself.

He kept riding on and on, by day and by night, and if he slept the mare stood guard and she would wake him up when she heard a noise. He had no food or cigarettes, and his ammunition was running low. He was going along a narrow trail with a high barbed wire fence on one side and a nopal[16] thicket on the other, and right before he hit a turn he heard **1**

---

15. **reata** (rĕ-ä′tä) *Spanish:* lasso or lariat.
16. **nopal** (nô-päl′) *Spanish:* kind of cactus.

---

### Mini Lesson · Viewing and Representing

*Chama Running Red* **by John Sloan**

*Cliffs Beyond Abiquiu, Dry Waterfall* **by Georgia O'Keeffe**

**ART APPRECIATION** American painter John Sloan (1871–1951) was a member of The Eight, a group of artists who believed that artists should reveal the ongoing life of real people. Georgia O'Keeffe (1887–1986) used the landscape, bones, and flowers to create strong, often symbolic, organic forms.

**Instruction** Have students compare and contrast their impressions of the mood of the two landscape paintings, on this page and page 709. What do the shape, lines, and colors communicate? What sort of visual technique does each artist use to convey the mood?

**Possible Responses:** Sloan's painting is wide open and liberating. It projects a sense of forward movement, with the river and road. O'Keeffe's painting is claustrophobic. The dead-end canyon wall with a tiny pocket of blue sky at the very top suggests no hope of escape. The colors in Sloan's painting are sharp, rich, intense; O'Keeffe's colors reinforce the concept of an inhospitable landscape.

horses ahead. The first man that came around the turn ran into Gregorio Cortez, with his pistol in his hand. There was a whole line of others behind the first, all armed with rifles, but they had to put the rifles away. Then Gregorio Cortez knocked over a tall nopal plant with his stirrup and made just enough room for his mare to back into while the Rangers filed by. He stopped the last one and took away his tobacco, matches, and ammunition. And then he rode away.

He rode on to La Grulla, and he was very thirsty, because he had not had water in a long time, and the mare was thirsty too. Near La Grulla there was a dam where the vaqueros watered their stock. But when Gregorio Cortez got there, he saw twenty armed men resting under the trees that grew close to the water. Gregorio Cortez stopped and thought what he could do. Then he went back into the brush and **2** began rounding up cattle, for this was cattle country and steers were everywhere. Pretty soon he had two hundred head, and he drove them to water and while the cattle drank he and the mare drank too. After he had finished, some of the Rangers that were resting under the trees came over and helped him get the herd together again, and Gregorio Cortez rode off with the herd, laughing to himself.

HE rode on and on, and by now he knew that the Rio Grande was near. He rode till he came to Cotulla, and there he was chased again. The little mare was tired, and now she began to limp. She had cut her leg and it was swelling up. Gregorio Cortez rode her into a thicket, and the Rangers made him a corral. But once in the brush, Gregorio Cortez led the mare to a *coma*[17] tree and tied her there. He unsaddled her and hung the saddle to the tree, and he patted her and talked to her for a long while. Then he slipped out of the thicket, and the Rangers didn't see him because they were waiting for him to ride out. They waited for three days and finally they crept in and found only the mare and the saddle.

### How El Teco Sold Gregorio Cortez for a Morral[18] Full of Silver Dollars

Gregorio Cortez was gone. While all the armed men were guarding the thicket where the mare was tied, he walked into Cotulla itself. He walked into town and mixed with the Mexicans there. He sat on the station platform and listened to other men while they talked of all the things that Gregorio Cortez had done. Then he went to a store and bought himself new clothes and walked out of the town. He went to the river and took a bath and then swam across, because the bridge was guarded. That sort of man was Gregorio Cortez. They don't make them like him any more.

He had only three cartridges left, one for one pistol and two for the other, and he had left his rifle with the mare. But he was very near the Rio Grande, and he expected to cross it soon. Still he needed ammunition, so he walked into El Sauz and tried to buy some, but they did not sell cartridges in that town. Then he thought of trying some of the houses, and chose one in which there was a pretty girl at the door because he knew it would be easier if he talked to a girl. There was not a woman that did not like Gregorio Cortez.

The girl was alone, and she invited him into the house. When he asked for ammunition, she told him she had none.

"My father has taken it all," she said. "He is out looking for a man named Gregorio Cortez."

Gregorio Cortez was embarrassed because he could see that the girl knew who he was. But she did not let on and neither did he. He stayed at **3** the house for a while, and when he left she told him how to get to the Rio Grande by the quickest way.

---

17. *coma* (kô'mä) *Spanish:* kind of thorn tree.
18. *morral* (mô-räl') *Spanish:* large bag or pouch.

THE LEGEND OF GREGORIO CORTEZ   **713**

### Customizing Instruction

**Students Acquiring English**

**1** Explain that the phrase *hit a turn* means that Cortez "reached a bend" in the trail.

**2** Point out that the phrase *rounding up* means "gathering" or "bringing together."

**3** Explain that the idiom *let on* means "acknowledge" or "disclose."

**Multiple Learning Styles**
**Visual Learners**

Have students use a map to trace Gregorio Cortez's escape route. Have them use maps to answer the following questions: How many miles did he travel before surrendering? How many rivers did Cortez have to cross to get from El Carmen back to Mexico? Have students locate the cities, towns, and rivers mentioned in the story.

---

**Cross Curricular Link** **Geography**

**TEXAS GEOGRAPHY** "The Legend of Gregorio Cortez," set amid the varied landscape of Texas, mentions a variety of features and locations. The Rio Grande, which forms the border between Texas and Mexico, begins in the San Juan Mountains of Colorado and flows southeasterly for 1,885 miles before it empties into the Gulf of Mexico near Brownsville, Texas, and Matamoros, Mexico. In Mexico, people call the river Río Bravo del Norte. Laredo is a border town on the Rio Grande; it's about 200 miles northwest of Brownsville. Another scene tales place in Cotulla, a small town in La Salle County, about halfway between San Antonio and Laredo. It lies near the Nueces River—over fifty miles from the Rio Grande. The town of Goliad, in Goliad County, lies about 75 miles southeast of San Antonio, and more than 100 miles east of Cotulla.

**Literary Analysis** ⬛ LEGEND

**A** Ask students to explain how the narrator's reference to Judas further enhances the legend of Gregorio Cortez.

**Possible Response:** By referring to El Teco as Judas, the narrator links the betrayal of Cortez to the betrayal of Jesus.

**Literary Analysis: CULTURAL HERO**

**B** Have students discuss Cortez's response to El Teco's betrayal. Ask them to decide if this response makes him seem more heroic to the audience.

**Possible Responses:** Cortez's forgiveness of his enemy is an extraordinary Christian gesture and, given the circumstances, it embodies a cultural virtue that many aspire to attain.

Now all the people along the river knew that Gregorio Cortez was on the Border, and that he would soon cross, but no one told the sheriffs what they knew. And Gregorio Cortez walked on, in his new clothes, with his pistols in a morral, looking like an ordinary man, but the people he met knew that he was Gregorio Cortez. And he began to talk to people along the way.

SOON he met a man who told him, "You'll be on the other side of the river tonight, Gregorio Cortez."

"I think I will," he said.

"You'll be all right then," said the man.

"I guess so," said Gregorio Cortez.

"But your brother won't," the man said. "He died in the jail last night."

"He was badly wounded," said Gregorio Cortez. "It was his lot to die, but I have avenged his death."

"They beat him before he died," the man said. "The Rangers came to the jail and beat him to make him talk."

This was the first news that Gregorio Cortez had heard, and it made him thoughtful.

He walked on, and he met another man who said, "Your mother is in the jail, Gregorio Cortez."

"Why?" said Gregorio Cortez. "Why should the sheriffs do that to her?"

"Because she is your mother," the man said. "That's why. Your wife is there too, and so are your little sons."

Gregorio Cortez thought this over, and he walked on. Pretty soon he met another man who said, "Gregorio Cortez, your own people are suffering, and all because of you."

"Why should my own people suffer?" said Cortez. "What have I done to them?"

"You have killed many sheriffs, Gregorio Cortez," said the man. "The Rangers cannot catch you, so they take it out on other people like you. Every man that's given you a glass of water has been beaten and thrown in jail. Every man who has fed you has been hanged from a tree branch, up and down, up and down, to make him tell where you went, and some have died rather than tell. Lots of people have been shot and beaten because they were your people. But you will be safe, Gregorio Cortez; you will cross the river tonight."

"I did not know these things," said Gregorio Cortez.

And he decided to turn back, and to give himself up to the Governor of the State so that his own people would not suffer because of him.

He turned and walked back until he came to a place called Goliad, where he met eleven Mexicans, and among them there was one that called himself his friend. This man was a vaquero named El Teco, but Judas should have been his name. Gregorio Cortez was thirsty, and he came up to the eleven Mexicans to ask for water, and when El Teco saw Gregorio Cortez he thought how good it would be if he could get the thousand-dollar reward. So he walked up to Cortez and shook his hand and told the others, "Get some water for my friend Gregorio Cortez."

Then El Teco asked Gregorio Cortez to let him see the pistols he had, and that he would get him some ammunition. Gregorio Cortez smiled, because he knew. But he handed over the guns to El Teco, and El Teco looked at them and put them in his own morral. Then El Teco called the sheriffs to come and get Gregorio Cortez.

**A**

# Every man that's given you a glass of water...

 **Multicultural Link**   **History**

**DRAWING FROM THE BIBLE** According to Christian Scripture, Judas Iscariot betrayed Jesus of Nazareth to the Romans for thirty pieces of silver. Jesus foretold of his betrayal while sharing a Passover meal with his disciples. That night, after this Last Supper, Judas led a group of Roman soldiers to the garden at Gethsemane, and he identified Jesus to them by greeting Jesus with a kiss.

# ...has been beaten and thrown in jail.

**B**

When Gregorio Cortez saw what El Teco had done, he smiled again and said to him, "Teco, a man can only be what God made him. May you enjoy your reward."

But El Teco did not enjoy the reward, though the sheriffs gave him the money, one thousand dollars in silver, more than a morral could hold. He did not enjoy it because he could not spend it anywhere. If he went to buy a taco at the market place, the taco vender would tell him that tacos were worth two thousand dollars gold that day. People cursed him in the streets and wished that he would be killed or die. So El Teco became very much afraid. He buried the money and never spent it, and he never knew peace until he died.

## How Gregorio Cortez Went to Prison, but Not for Killing the Sheriffs

When the sheriffs came to arrest Gregorio Cortez, he spoke to them and said, "I am not your prisoner yet. I will be the prisoner only of the Governor of the State. I was going to the Capital to give myself up, and that is where I'll go."

The sheriffs saw that he was in the right, so they went with him all the way to the Capital, and Cortez surrendered himself to the Governor of the State.

Then they put Cortez in jail, and all the Americans were glad, because they no longer were afraid. They got together, and they tried to **1** lynch him. Three times they tried, but they could not lynch Gregorio Cortez.

And pretty soon all the people began to see that Gregorio Cortez was in the right, and they did not

want to lynch him any more. They brought him gifts to the jail, and one day one of the judges came and shook the hand of Gregorio Cortez and said to him, "I would have done the same."

But Gregorio Cortez had many enemies, for he had killed many men, and they wanted to see him hanged. So they brought him to trial for killing the Major Sheriff of the county of El Carmen. The lawyer that was against him got up and told the judges that Cortez should die, because he had killed a man. Then Gregorio Cortez got up, and he spoke to them.

"Self-defense is allowed to any man," said Gregorio Cortez. "It is in your own law, and by your own law do I defend myself. I killed the sheriff, and I am not sorry, for he killed my brother. He spilled my brother's blood, which was also my blood. And he tried to kill me too. I killed the Major Sheriff defending my right."

And Gregorio Cortez talked for a long time to the judges, telling them about their own law. When he finished even the lawyer who was against him at the start was now for him. And all the judges came down from their benches and shook hands with Gregorio Cortez.

The judges said, "We cannot kill this man."

They took Gregorio Cortez all over the State, from town to town, and in each town he was tried before the court for the killing of a man. But in every court it was the same. Gregorio Cortez spoke to the judges, and he told them about the law, and he proved that he had the right. And each time the judges said, "This man was defending his right. Tell the sheriffs to set him free."

THE LEGEND OF GREGORIO CORTEZ **715**

**Less Proficient Readers**
Remind students that they're expected to produce summaries of texts by identifying the main idea and supporting details. Have volunteers help construct a summary of the events that led up to Cortez's capture. Elicit information by asking who betrayed Cortez, and why. Then have students explain what happened to the reward money.

**Possible Response:** El Teco betrayed Cortez because he wanted the reward money. El Teco's reward money, however, proved worthless. He couldn't spend it anywhere because shopkeepers—angry at him for betraying Cortez—charged him absurd amounts. El Teco ended up burying the reward money because it only brought him misery.

**Set a Purpose** Ask students to adjust their purpose for reading to find out what will happen to Cortez now that he has been captured and put on trial.

**Students Acquiring English**

**1** Help students determine the meaning of the verb *lynch*. Ask students to use context clues, prior knowledge, and a dictionary to define the word.

**Possible Response:** To hang an accused criminal without a trial.

---

**Cross Curricular Link** **Government**

**CONSTITUTIONAL LAW** The Fifth Amendment to the U.S. Constitution prohibits courts from trying a person twice for the same crime, a practice known as "double jeopardy." Cortez's repeated trials might have been for the killings of his various pursuers. The Sixth Amendment provides the accused with the right to counsel and a right to be tried by a jury—rights of which Cortez did not avail himself.

**Active Reading** | MAKING JUDGMENTS

Ⓐ Ask students if they think that the sentence Cortez received was a fair one.

**Possible Responses:** Yes, because he killed so many of people; no, because horse stealing was a trumped-up charge; a life sentence is too harsh a punishment for stealing a horse; furthermore, the horse belonged to his brother, even if the trade was unfair.

**Literary Analysis** | LEGEND

Ⓑ Point out the narrator's comment about Cortez's burial place. Ask them how this comment might contribute to Cortez's status as a legendary figure.

**Possible Response:** The mystery of his burial place makes Cortez seem like a more mythic figure.

**Active Reading** | MAKING JUDGMENTS

Ⓒ Ask students if they believe that the corrido was actually forbidden in the United States.

**Possible Response:** Although forbidding the song would have been illegal, it's conceivable that local American authorities might have tried to repress such a right to free speech. Such unconstitutional censorship could have existed in the early 1900s, when civil liberties were not as strongly protected as they are today.

And so it was that Gregorio Cortez was not found guilty of any wrong because of the sheriffs he had killed. And he killed many of them, there is no room for doubt. No man has killed more sheriffs than did Gregorio Cortez, and he always fought alone. For that is the way the real men fight, always on their own. There are young men around here today, who think that they are brave. Dangerous men they call themselves, and it takes five or six of them to jump a fellow and slash him in the arm. Or they hide in the brush and fill him full of buckshot as he goes by. They are not men. But that was not the way with Gregorio Cortez, for he was a real man.

Now the enemies of Gregorio Cortez got together and said to each other, "What are we going to do? This man is going free after killing so many of our friends. Shall we kill him ourselves? But we would have to catch him asleep, or shoot him in the back, because if we meet him face to face there will be few of us left."

Then one of them thought of the little sorrel mare, and there they had a plan to get Gregorio Cortez. They brought him back to court, and the lawyer who was against him asked, "Gregorio Cortez, do you recognize this mare?"

"I do," said Gregorio Cortez. "And a better little mare there never was."

Then the lawyer asked him, "Have you ridden this mare?"

And Gregorio Cortez answered, "She carried me all the way from El Carmen to the Border, a distance of five hundred miles."

**T**HEN the lawyer asked him, "Is this mare yours?"

And Gregorio Cortez saw that they had him, but there was nothing he could do, because he was an honest man and he felt that he must tell the truth. He said no, the mare did not belong to him.

Then the judges asked Gregorio Cortez, "Is this true, Gregorio Cortez? Did you take this mare that did not belong to you?"

And Gregorio Cortez had to say that the thing was true.

So they sentenced Gregorio Cortez, but not for killing the sheriffs, as some fools will tell you even now, when they ought to know better. No, not for killing the sheriffs but for stealing the little sorrel mare. The judge sentenced him to ninety-nine years and a day. And the enemies of Gregorio Cortez were happy then, because they thought Cortez would be in prison for the rest of his life.

Ⓐ

### How President Lincoln's Daughter Freed Gregorio Cortez, and How He Was Poisoned and Died

But Gregorio Cortez did not stay in prison long. Inside of a year he was free, and this is the way it came about. Every year at Christmastime, a pretty girl can come to the Governor of the State and ask him to give her a prisoner as a Christmas present. And the Governor then has to set the prisoner free and give him to the girl. So it happened to Cortez. One day President Lincoln's daughter visited the prison, and she saw Gregorio Cortez. As soon as she saw him she went up and spoke to him.

"I am in love with you, Gregorio Cortez," President Lincoln's daughter said, "and if you promise to marry me I will go to the Governor next Christmas and tell him to give you to me."

Gregorio Cortez looked at President Lincoln's daughter, and he saw how beautiful she was. It made him thoughtful, and he did not know what to say.

"I have many rich farms," President Lincoln's daughter said. "They are all my own. Marry me and we will farm together."

Gregorio Cortez thought about that. He could see himself already like a German, sitting on the gallery, full of ham and beer, and belching and breaking wind while a half-dozen little blond cockroaches played in the yard. And he was tempted. But then he said to himself, "I can't

### Workplace Link Contracts

**WRITING INSTRUCTIONS** Effective instructions are direct, logically organized, and written in simple language to convey information clearly. Often in the format of an outline, instructions spell out step-by-step procedures to follow. To be fully prepared for the workplace, students must learn to
• Organize ideas to ensure logical progression.
• Use writing to clarify ideas.
• Compile written ideas into appropriate formats.
**Instruction** Before sending a jury to deliberate a verdict, the judge provides a set of instructions explaining the applicable laws, rules of evidence, and burden of proof.

**Application** Gregorio Cortez pleaded self-defense to the charge of murder. Have student groups research the legal definition of self-defense in a law dictionary or other appropriate source and draw up a set of instructions to the jury on how to decide guilt or innocence.

marry a Gringo girl. We would not make a matching pair."

So he decided that President Lincoln's daughter was not the woman for him, and he told her, "I thank you very much, but I cannot marry you at all."

But President Lincoln's daughter would not take his no. She went to the Governor and said, "I would like to have a prisoner for Christmas."

And the Governor looked at her and saw she was a pretty girl, so he said, "Your wish is granted. What prisoner do you want?"

And President Lincoln's daughter said, "I want Gregorio Cortez."

The Governor thought for a little while and then he said, "That's a man you cannot have. He's the best prisoner I got."

But President Lincoln's daughter shook her head and said, "Don't forget that you gave your word."

"So I did," the Governor said, "and I cannot go back on it."

And that was how Gregorio Cortez got out of prison, where he had been sentenced to ninety-nine years and a day, not for killing the sheriffs, as some fools will tell you, but for stealing the little sorrel mare. Gregorio Cortez kept his word, and he did not marry President Lincoln's daughter, and when at last she lost her hopes she went away to the north.

Still, the enemies of Gregorio Cortez did not give up. When they heard that he was getting out of prison they were scared and angry, and they started thinking of ways to get revenge. They got a lot of money together and gave it to a man who worked in the prison, and this man gave Cortez a slow poison just before Gregorio Cortez got out of jail.

And that was how he came to die, within a year from the day he got out of jail. As soon as he came out and his friends saw him, they said to each other, "This man is sick. This man will not last the year."

And so it was. He did not last the year. He died of the slow poison they gave him just before he was let out, because his enemies did not want to see him free.

AND that was how Gregorio Cortez came to die. He's buried in Laredo some place, or maybe it's Brownsville, or Matamoros, or somewhere up above. To tell the truth, I don't know. I don't know the place where he is buried any more than the place where he was born. But he was born and lived and died, that I do know. And a lot of Rangers could also tell you that.

So does the corrido; it tells about Gregorio Cortez and who he was. They started singing the corrido soon after he went to jail, and there was a time when it was forbidden in all the United States, by order of the President himself. Men sometimes got killed or lost their jobs because they sang *El Corrido de Gregorio Cortez*. But everybody sang it just the same, because it spoke about things that were true.

Now it is all right to sing *El Corrido de Gregorio Cortez*, but not everybody knows it any more. And they don't sing it as it used to be sung. These new singers change all the old songs a lot. But even so, people still remember Gregorio Cortez. And when a good singer sings the song— good and loud and clear—you can feel your neck-feathers rise, and you can see him standing there, with his pistol in his hand. ❖

## GUIDING STUDENT RESPONSE

## Connect to the Literature

**1. What Do You Think?**
Have students support their opinions with text evidence.

**Comprehension Check**
- He shot and killed the Sheriff in self-defense, after the Sheriff shot his brother.
- El Teco wants the $1000 reward being offered for Cortez's capture.
- for stealing the horse he used for his escape

Use Selection Quiz
**Unit Four Resource Book,** p. 77.

## Think Critically

2. Possible Responses: honesty, stamina, resourcefulness, courage, loyalty

3. Possible Responses: The narration reveals deep conflicts between the two cultures—Anglo and Mexican. The sheriffs and rangers are portrayed as bullying racists so inept that hundreds of them cannot capture one man. The American horse trader spews demeaning stereotypes. Cortez is harassed and receives no justice in the U.S. courts.

4. If possible, elicit from students their own code of honor—the set of personal laws they live by.

5. Possible Responses: Realistic—the confrontation where the Sheriff shoots Román; the persecution of Cortez's family, friends, and supporters. Exaggerations—the number of sheriffs Cortez kills; hundreds of armed men afraid of him; his crossing of the San Antonio River; his trials in town after town; the marriage proposal from Lincoln's daughter.

## Literary Analysis

**Legend** Possible Responses: Outlandish details and remarkable events are more memorable. It's not enough to say, "This guy did something no one else could do, but something we all strive to do." Exaggeration and embellished facts all serve to dress an otherwise ordinary man capable of courageous acts as a death-defying superhero possessed with amazing powers.

---

## Connect to the Literature

**1. What Do You Think?**
Did you enjoy this retelling of the *corrido?* Discuss your opinions with classmates.

**Comprehension Check**
- Why is Cortez being pursued?
- Why does El Teco betray Cortez?
- For what crime is Cortez finally sentenced to prison?

## Think Critically

2. Which of Gregorio Cortez's personal qualities do you find most admirable? Why?

3. What do the comments and attitudes of the **speaker** in this retelling reveal about cultural conflicts between Anglos and Mexicans in the Texas border area during this time period?

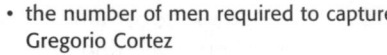
THINK ABOUT
- the portrayal of the sheriffs and the Texas Rangers
- the number of men required to capture Gregorio Cortez
- the conversation between Román and the American who owns the mare
- the treatment Cortez receives in U.S. courts

4. Do you think Gregorio Cortez was right to live by the code "I will break before I bend"? Defend your opinion.

5. **ACTIVE READING** **MAKING JUDGMENTS ABOUT TEXT** Refer to the diagram you made in your **READER'S NOTEBOOK.** Which details and events in this story seem especially realistic and which appear to be purely fictional?

## Extend Interpretations

6. **Critic's Corner** Some readers argue that because Gregorio Cortez kills many people, he is an inappropriate person to present as a hero. Argue for or against that position.

7. **Connect to Life** Think of other heroes you have encountered in movies, TV programs, books, cartoons, or newspaper and magazine articles. Which of them resemble Gregorio Cortez, and in what ways?

8. **Points of Comparison** What cultural values revealed in "The Legend of Gregorio Cortez" are also highly regarded in "The Indian and the Hundred Cows" and "High Horse's Courting"? Support your answer with examples from all three stories.

---

## Literary Analysis

**LEGEND** Like myths, fables, and folk tales, **legends** belong to the oral tradition of literature. A mix of both fact and fiction, "The Legend of Gregorio Cortez" centers on a **cultural hero,** who embodies the values of early 20th-century Mexican Americans from the Texas border region. This kind of hero is not the creation of a single writer, but rather evolves from communal tales—told orally or sung to musical accompaniment—that were passed down from one generation to the next.

**Cooperative Learning Activity**
Review the biographical information about Gregorio Cortez in the Build Background feature on page 702. Why do you think singers and storytellers might have exaggerated or invented certain events in Cortez's life? Share your response with a small group of classmates.

---

## Extend Interpretations

**Critic's Corner** Possible Responses: Inappropriate hero figure—no matter how pure his motive, Cortez's violence is excessive and should not be condoned or exemplified. Appropriate hero figure—given the culture and the time, Cortez's response is admirable; he does not seek to cause trouble, but combats it effectively; **or,** a hero figure upholding cultural values cannot be held to the same standards that dictate the lives of ordinary people; this is a legend, not a manual for dispute resolution—Cortez's violence represents the Mexican's struggle for respect and honor in Texas at the time.

**Connect to Life** Students should support their answers with specific evidence from the text.

**Points of Comparison** Make sure students include examples from all three stories. Possible Responses: courage, cunning, ingenuity

## Writing Options

**1. Farewell Letter** Write a farewell letter from Gregorio to his young sons in which he explains the reasons for his actions and gives them advice for living their lives.

**2. Points of Comparison** Imagine a meeting between Gregorio Cortez and High Horse, the lovesick young man in "High Horse's Courting." Write a fictional dialogue in which they discuss the ideals of manhood that are prized in each of their cultures. Both characters should explain how their behavior illustrates these ideals. Refer to the stories for examples.

## Activities & Explorations

**1. Map of the Setting** Copy and enlarge the map of the Texas border region on page 702 to locate some of the places mentioned in this story. Write a brief description explaining the importance of these sites. Then draw the escape route followed by Gregorio Cortez as he tried to elude the Texas Rangers and the sheriffs. How likely is it that the *real* Gregorio Cortez followed the route described in the story? ~ GEOGRAPHY

**2. TV Newscast** With a small group, report the story of Gregorio Cortez for a national evening news broadcast. Include spot interviews to make your report lively. ~ SPEAKING AND LISTENING

## Inquiry & Research

**Colorful Folk Songs** This story is a prose retelling of a Mexican folk song, "El Corrido de Gregorio Cortez." If possible, find recordings of *corridos* about Cortez or other heroes, such as Pancho Villa or José Mosqueda. Play your favorites for the class.

## Américo Paredes

1915–

**Other Works**
*Corridos and Calaveras*
*Between Two Worlds*
*The Hammon and the Beans and Other Stories*
*A Texas-Mexican Cancionero*

**Resounding Mexican Voices** Américo Paredes, the son of a rancher, grew up near Brownsville, Texas, along the Mexican border. During this time, he absorbed the colorful traditions, songs, and legends of the area. This early experience with these traditions shaped Paredes's lifework. In describing his fascination with Mexican *corridos* and other folk songs, he said, "I started 'collecting' these songs around 1920, when I first became aware of them on the lips of the *guitarreros* and other people of the ranchos and the towns."

**Scholarly Pursuits** After serving in the U.S. Army during World War II, Paredes attended the University of Texas, where he earned his bachelor's, master's, and doctoral degrees. In 1954 he joined the faculty at the university, where

he has served as the director of the Center for Intercultural Studies in Folklore and Oral History and of the Mexican-American Studies program.

**Impressive Credentials** While a professor of English and anthropology at the University of Texas, Paredes published numerous books documenting Mexican-American folk traditions. Among his best-known works are *"With His Pistol in His Hand": A Border Ballad and Its Hero* (1958), from which "The Legend of Gregorio Cortez" is taken, and *Folktales of Mexico* (1970). Paredes also has been the editor of the *Journal of American Folklore* and has edited many works on cultural anthropology. For his achievement in preserving the Mexican-American folk tradition, Paredes has received several important awards, among them the Order of the Aztec Eagle, Mexico's highest award to foreigners.

## Author Activity

**The Storyteller's Voice** Read a selection from *Folktales from Mexico* by Paredes, and perform it orally for the class. Use gestures and props to make the story come alive.

## Author Activity

**Other Works** Students might also read *Corridos and Calaveras, Between Two Worlds, The Hammon and the Beans and Other Stories,* and *A Texas-Mexican Cancionero*.

## Writing Options

**1. Farewell Letter** Students should write the letter in the first person. Encourage students to assume a style that would convey Cortez's character—his modesty in light of his heroism, his sense of family loyalty, his adherence to a code of honor, and his subtle sense of humor.

**2. Points of Comparison** Dialogues should clearly express each culture's ideal of manhood, reveal how each character reflects that ideal in his behavior, and refer to the two stories for examples.

## Activities & Explorations

**1. Map of the Setting** Students' maps should clearly mark Cortez's route, the Mexican border, the rivers and towns mentioned in the text: Rio Grande, San Antonio River, El Carmen, Brownsville, Matamoros, La Grulla, Cotulla, Laredo, Goliad, and the capital (Austin).

**2. TV Newscast** Ask students to describe their location. What do they want the viewer to see in the background during the interviews, what sort of scenes should they capture to dramatize Cortez's daring escape and his later ordeals at trial and in prison.

## Inquiry & Research

**Colorful Folk Songs** Traditional ballads about legendary heroes include "Casey Jones," "John Henry," and "Tom Dooley." Ballads composed by known individuals include Woody Guthrie's "Pretty Boy Floyd," Bob Dylan's "Hurricane" and "The Lonesome Death of Hattie Carroll," the Beatles' "The Ballad of John and Yoko" and "Rocky Raccoon," and Bob Marley's "I Shot the Sheriff." Encourage students to see if they can download musical excerpts from websites dedicated to folk songs or search on-line to find access to recordings at local libraries.

## PART 1 Reading the Prompt

Model the process of reading a prompt:
- Read the entire prompt aloud.
- List key words of the assignment on the board ("choose three of these pieces," "evaluate," "most entertaining," "evidence").
- Define key words using the Strategies in Action to show how students can restate the prompt for themselves.

## PART 2 Planning an Evaluative Essay

- Students should begin by choosing selections. Encourage them to choose at least one that they enjoyed.
- Students may wish to brainstorm possible criteria before selecting ones to use in their essays. Criteria might include characters, style of language, humorous events, exaggeration, irony, or tone.
- Students may find it helpful to jot down supporting evidence, such as examples and quotations, beside each chart.

## PART 3 Drafting Your Essay

**Introduction** Students might start with a brief discussion about the role of entertaining stories in the days before television was common.

**Organization** If students focus on one criterion at a time, they might arrange these by order of importance. If they focus on one story at a time, they might start with the least entertaining and build to the most. Encourage them to consider both methods before they write.

**Conclusion** Students might consider ending their essays with a humorous quotation from one of the selections.

**Revision** Remind students to pay close attention to capitalization when they write titles of works. You may wish to remind students that book titles are underlined or italicized, while story titles are written inside quotation marks.

---

In writing assessments, you will often be asked to evaluate the quality or merit of a literary work. You are now going to practice writing an essay with this kind of evaluative focus.

### PART 1   Reading the Prompt

Often you will be asked to write in response to a prompt like the one below. First, read the entire prompt carefully. Then read through it again, looking for key words that help you identify the purpose of the essay and decide how to approach it.

> **Writing Prompt**
>
> Many of the selections from Unit Four, Part Two are intended to entertain audiences. Choose three of these pieces to explore. In an essay, evaluate ❶ the three and decide which you found to be the most entertaining. Justify your ratings with ❷ evidence from the literary selections. ❸

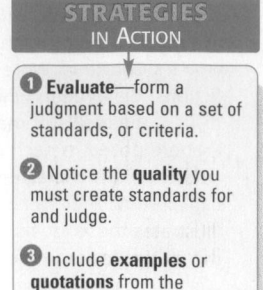

**STRATEGIES IN ACTION**

❶ **Evaluate**—form a judgment based on a set of standards, or criteria.

❷ Notice the **quality** you must create standards for and judge.

❸ Include **examples** or **quotations** from the selections.

### PART 2   Planning an Evaluative Essay

- Determine your criteria—the key literary elements and devices that make stories entertaining.

- For each selection, create an evaluation grid like the example shown.

- Rate your responses to each of the criteria by filling in where they fall on the continuum.

- Note which selection received the highest ratings and why.

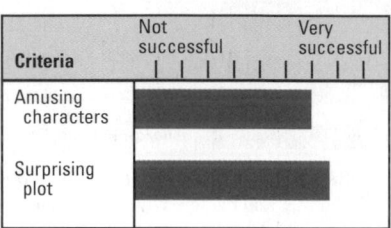

| Criteria | Not successful | | | | | | | | Very successful |
|---|---|---|---|---|---|---|---|---|---|
| Amusing characters | | | | | | | | | |
| Surprising plot | | | | | | | | | |

### PART 3   Drafting Your Essay

**Introduction** Begin by identifying the three selections you are judging. Then state your general opinion about which one is the most entertaining. Quickly summarize the criteria you used to make your decision.

**Organization** Evaluate each selection individually, or focus on one criterion at a time and apply it to all three selections. Remember to maintain the focus of your essay as you write. Support your judgments with examples, quotations, and details from the stories.

**Conclusion** Sum up your general impression of the most entertaining selection, and restate your key points.

**Revision** Allow time to review your work. Make sure it is clear, well-supported, and free from mistakes.

**Writing Handbook** See page 1283: Analysis

LITERATURE CONNECTIONS

## The Adventures of Huckleberry Finn

MARK TWAIN

These thematically related readings are provided along with *The Adventures of Huckleberry Finn:*

**Three Days of Forest, A River, Free**
RITA DOVE

**The Outlaws**
SELMA LAGERLÖF

*from* **Nine Pounds of Luggage**
MAUD PARRISH

**Freedom**
WILLIAM STAFFORD

*from* **Mississippi Solo**
EDDY HARRIS

*from* **Life on the Mississippi**
MARK TWAIN

**The Negro Speaks of Rivers**
LANGSTON HUGHES

**Narrative of Daniel Fisher**
DANIEL FISHER

## My Ántonia

WILLA CATHER

These thematically related readings are provided along with *My Ántonia:*

**Prairie Town**
WILLIAM STAFFORD

**If There Be Sorrow**
MARI EVANS

**On the Divide**
WILLA CATHER

*from* **The Quilters**
NORMA BRADLEY BUFERD

**Night on the Prairies**
WALT WHITMAN

**The Chrysanthemums**
JOHN STEINBECK

The *Electronic Library* is a CD-ROM that contains additional fiction, nonfiction, poetry, and drama for each unit in *The Language of Literature.*

These are the additional selections found in Unit 4 of the *Electronic Library* that apply to Part 2.

retold by Julius Lester
**Brer Rabbit and the Tar Baby**
**Brer Fox and Brer Rabbit Go Hunting**

Bret Harte
**The Outcasts of Poker Flat**

Stephen Crane
**The Open Boat**

Encourage students to choose one of these selections to enjoy in silent sustained reading.

## And Even *More* . . .

**Books**

**Giants in the Earth**
OLE EDVART RÖLVAAG
A heroic tale focusing on Norwegian pioneers who settled in South Dakota.

**Bury My Heart at Wounded Knee: An Indian History of the American West**
DEE BROWN
A powerful chronicle of the West from a Native American perspective.

**Remington and Russell: Artists of the West**
WILLIAM C. KETCHUM, JR.
Profiles of two artists best known for their creative depictions of the West.

**Other Media**

**Life on the Mississippi**
Television adaptation of Mark Twain's autobiographical work about his apprenticeship on a riverboat. Films Inc. (VIDEOCASSETTE)

**Shane**
A classic Western adapted from Jack Schaefer's novel about homesteaders and the heroic gunfighter who protects them. Paramount Home Video. (VIDEOCASSETTE)

### Mexican-American Folklore

JOHN O. WEST
This sweeping collection contains fascinating examples that reflect the rich culture of the American Southwest—legends, songs, festivals, proverbs, riddles, superstitions, crafts, tales of saints and revolutionaries, and more.

# Communication Workshop
## Storytelling

### Objectives
- select a written version of a story
- prepare a script to indicate how to tell the story
- practice and present the story
- evaluate interpretive choices

## Introducing the Workshop

**A Storytelling** Ask students if they have ever seen a storyteller perform. Invite them to discuss their experiences. Point out that through preparing a written version of a story and presenting that story, students will be able to use their creativity and introduce their audience to a long-popular form of entertainment.

Establish some criteria for what makes a good story, as well as an effective storyteller. Some students may be interested in retelling a traditional folk tale, while others may choose a more modern story, or may want to make up their own. They should observe that the storyteller needs enthusiasm, a sense of humor, and an ability to communicate with audiences.

### Basics in a Box
**B Using the Guidelines and Standards** Preparing for a storytelling presentation is a two-part process. The guidelines offer suggestions for successfully completing both parts of the process. Point out that students' scripts and performances will be evaluated according to these standards.

Use McDougal Littell's **Language Network,** Chapter 27, for more instruction on oral communication.

To engage students visually, use **Power Presentation** 7, Storytelling.

---

## Presenting an engaging tale . . .

**A** **From Reading to Presenting** Long ago, folk tales such as "The Indian and the Hundred Cows" were passed down by word of mouth through **storytelling.** Early storytellers combined music, dance, stories, and poetry to pass on important information. Today, many folk tales have been written down, but professional storytellers still perform these and other stories at schools, libraries, and festivals. Professional storytellers use costumes, props, gestures, and expressions to entertain their audiences. When you tell your friends about something exciting that happened to you, you are telling a story too.

### For Your Portfolio

**WRITING PROMPT** Prepare a script or notes in which you plan how to tell a story. Then tell the story.

**Purpose:** To entertain
**Audience:** Classmates, hospital patients or nursing home residents, listeners at a library story hour

### Basics in a Box

**B** **GUIDELINES & STANDARDS** Storytelling

**To prepare a useful script**
- select or prepare a written version of the story
- mark individual lines with appropriate gestures, movements, and tone of voice
- indicate changes in mood and scene
- include a description of the setting, props, and costumes

**To present a successful performance**
- memorize the story (though not necessarily word for word from the script)
- consider the needs and interests of the audience members and maintain eye contact with them
- speak clearly, varying your voice as necessary
- incorporate body movements, facial expressions, props, and costumes as needed

## LESSON RESOURCES

**USING PRINT RESOURCES**
**Unit Four Resource Book**
- Planning Your Performance, p. 79
- Preparing, Practicing, and Presenting, p. 80
- Peer Response, p. 81
- Refining Your Performance, p. 82
- Student Model, pp. 83–84
- Rubric, p. 85

**Speaking and Listening Transparencies**
- Reading Aloud, p. 11
- Dramatic Reading, p. 12
- Giving and Using Feedback to Improve Performance, p. 16

**USING MEDIA RESOURCES**
**Visit our website:**
www.mcdougallittell.com.

# A Storyteller in Action

- Storyteller begins speaking while sitting
- Tells story from memory
- Uses beads to create a simple costume that connects to story
- Uses gesture and voice to grab audience's interest immediately

**C**

- Moves to a standing position to shift the mood and maintain the audience's attention
- Makes dramatic movements and facial expressions to build tension

- Maintains eye contact to keep audience involved
- Performs specific actions to help the audience visualize the story

COMMUNICATION WORKSHOP **723**

## Analyzing the Visual Model

### "A Storyteller in Action"

**C** The student model introduces the students to the physical requirements of storytelling.

Explain that the pictures show a storyteller in action. In order to maintain the interest of the audience, it is necessary for the storyteller to develop a repertoire of movements and facial expressions.

Students can take turns reading aloud the captions under the photos. Point out the key words and phrases in the student model that correspond to the elements mentioned in the Guidelines & Standards.

Have students look at the picture in the upper left-hand corner. Ask them what kind of story the girl might be telling. What ideas for characters do they get from the beads?
**Possible Response:** She may be telling a Native American legend or a story involving a wealthy woman.

Have students look at the middle picture of the storyteller. Ask students what the standing posture and arm gestures might symbolize.
**Possible Response:** The storyteller appears to be looking at something off in the distance and pointing to it, or perhaps she is raising an arm to throw something.

Have students look at the picture at the far right. Call attention to the way the storyteller's eyes are focused straight ahead. Ask what the hand gestures might indicate.
**Possible Response:** The storyteller looks as though she is planting seeds or dropping something into a bag.

## Analyzing a Storytelling Script

### "The Warrior Maiden"

**D** The student model introduces the reader to a story script based on an old Native American folk tale. It includes stage directions and ideas for props.

You may want one student to read the entire story aloud first. Then have that student reread sections aloud as a second student gives stage directions and a third performs the gestures. Read and discuss the Guidelines in Action as students work through the storytelling activity.

1. Have students suggest an alternate costume and props.

   **Possible Response:** A beaded necklace of another color, moccasins, and brown clothes to look like deerskin would all work. If real branches and vines are not available, props could be drawn on construction paper or cardboard.

2. Invite several students to try the actions and use a menacing tone of voice.

3. Ask students what the gesture in the photo is showing. Then tell them to think about how the Oneida people felt, and try making gestures to show these feelings.

4. Demonstrate how to use your voice to change the mood. Repeat the last two sentences using different intonations and ask students to identify the mood.

---

# Analyzing a Storytelling Script

**The Warrior Maiden:**
**An Oneida Folk Tale**

> **GUIDELINES**
> IN ACTION

*Sit on stool; pause before beginning; make a wide, sweeping gesture with both arms*

Costume: purple and white beaded necklaces, black clothes; props: feathery branch to represent woodbine, vine to represent honeysuckle

**1** Describes the costume and props needed

Long ago, in the days before the white settlers came to this continent, the Oneida people were beset by their *menacingly* old enemies, the Mingoes. The invaders attacked the *Stand up* Oneida villages, stormed their palisades, set fire to their *Pretend to throw spear* longhouses, laid waste to the land, destroyed the cornfields, killed men and boys, and abducted the women *Motion of letting grains of sand fall from one hand to the other* and girls. There was no resisting the Mingoes, because their numbers were like grains of sand, like pebbles on a lake shore.

**2** Gives body movement and vocal cues

*sadly* The villages of the Oneida lay deserted, their fields untended, the ruins of their homes blackened. The men had taken the women, the old people, the young boys and girls into the deep forests, hiding them in secret places among rocks, in caves, and on desolate mountains. The Mingoes searched for victims, but could not find them. The Great Spirit himself helped the people to hide and shielded their places of refuge from the eyes of their enemies.

*Put hands on stomach to show hunger* Thus the Oneida people were safe in their inaccessible retreats, but they were also starving. Whatever food they *Hold out one palm* had been able to save was soon eaten up. They could *Hold out the other palm* either stay in their hideouts and starve, or leave them in search of food and be discovered by their enemies. The warrior chiefs and sachems met in council but could find no other way out.

**3** Uses gestures to act out story images

*Change to hopeful tone* Then a young girl stepped forward in the council and said that the good spirits had sent her a dream showing *Hands on hips* her how to save the Oneida. Her name was Aliquipiso *deliberately* and she was not afraid to give her life for her people. . . .

**4** Adjusts voice to change mood

# Preparing to Tell a Story

## ❶ Planning Your Performance

Choose a story you would love to tell. For instance, you might choose a favorite fable, folk tale, or legend. You also might choose to tell your own story about something that happened to you. Be sure to choose a story that strongly interests you. See the **Idea Bank** for other suggestions. After you select a story, follow the steps below.

### Developing Your Performance

▶ **1. Tighten the plot.** Outline your own story or work with a published one. Analyze the story for any subplots that you need to get rid of in order to concentrate on a single, clearly developed theme.

▶ **2. Learn your story.** You don't need to memorize every word in the story you plan to tell. However, you should read the story or your outline several times so you know it very well.

▶ **3. Think of the story as a series of movie scenes.** Like a movie director, you must interpret the characters and events in the story to make them come to life. Identify the opening scene, the middle scenes, and the ending scene. How does each scene look and sound? How might you change your voice to indicate different characters? What facial expressions and movements would enhance the story? What costumes and props could you use?

▶ **4. Signal the ending.** How can you make sure the audience recognizes the ending? You might change the tone of your voice or use a statement such as "The moral of this fable is . . ."

## ❷ Developing Your Script

After choosing a story to tell and planning how to shape it, you should prepare a script to guide your performance.

### Preparing the Script

▶ **1. Write out the story as a script.** After planning the story and making sure the plot is tightly focused, you need to prepare a script. Write out your own story or photocopy a published story. Leave large margins and extra space between the lines, if possible.

▶ **2. Give an overview of any props or costumes needed.** At the top of the script, describe any props or costumes you want to use.

▶ **3. Mark up the script.** Add directions for gestures, tone of voice, facial expressions, and movements to specific sections of the story.

**IDEABank**

**1. Your Working Portfolio**
Look for ideas in the **Writing Options** you completed earlier in this unit:
- **Comic tale,** p. 644
- **Modernizing a Story,** p. 653
- **Screenplay Script,** p. 668

**2. Observe a Storyteller**
Find out where a storyteller is performing in your area and arrange to watch the performance.

**3. Listen to Storytellers**
Check out audiotapes from your library that feature storytellers or short story readers.

## Preparing to Tell a Story

### Planning the Performance
If after reading the Idea Bank students are having difficulty choosing their stories, suggest they try the following:
- Check out collections of fairy tales or folk tales from the library. Read through them and find one to adapt.
- Look for books of short plays that you might be able to use for storytelling.
- Contact a local chapter of the Storytellers' Guild for information on storytellers and storytelling. Your public librarian or a performing arts center may have a telephone number.
- Explore one of the Internet links for storytellers. Use the keyword *Storyteller* to find them.

### Developing the Performance
1. Review with students how to identify the main plot and subplots in a story. You may want to have them draw a graphic organizer or make an outline of the story to help them identify and remove subplots.
2. Encourage students to tape record their stories. They can play the tape several times and try to tell the story along with it. Also suggest that they associate key words in the story with gestures.
3. Visual students may want to sketch the scenes. They may also find it helpful to have another student take several posed photographs of them dramatizing different scenes. Students could arrange the photos in order on a poster board and use it as a reference for future rehearsals.
4. Have students work in small groups to brainstorm several ways they might use to indicate the ending of their story.

### Developing the Script
Suggest that students either make several copies of the script, or use self-adhesive notes to mark their copy. Once they have made the final changes to their directions, they can write them on the script. Students may want to use a different colored ink for the directions, or highlight the directions after writing them.

## Practicing and Presenting

Remind students that actors rehearse their parts many times before giving a performance. Suggest that students make a checklist based on the guidelines for a performance and distribute a copy to each of the peer reviewers. The reviewers can make comments next to each of the guidelines. Then the storyteller can look over all of the comments, see which areas need the most improvement, and work first on those areas. You might arrange for students to perform their storytelling for a group of younger students.

## Refining Your Performance

**EVALUATING YOUR INTERPRETIVE CHOICES**

Remind students that pacing is very important. If the pace is too fast, the audience will not be able to follow the story. If the pace is too slow, the audience will lose interest. Suggest that students watch a video of a play or of a comedy stand-up routine and take notes on the actors' pacing. Students should be able to justify their interpretive choices, both verbal and nonverbal, by referring their techniques to their interpretation of the story.

## Reflecting

Encourage students to recognize and evaluate the way in which they approached the storytelling assignment. Which planning strategies were most helpful? Did they rehearse in front of a live audience, or did they videotape themselves? Was this rehearsal helpful? How did comments from their peer reviewers help them? Have students add these self-evaluations to their working portfolios.

---

**Practicing Tip**

You might have someone videotape your performance so you can check your movements and expressions, or you may audiotape it to check your voice.

**Publishing
IDEAS**

- Offer to tell your story during a story hour at the public library or at your school library.
- Ask someone to videotape you as you tell your story to your classmates.

**More Online:
Publishing Options**
www.mcdougallittell.com

---

## ❸ Practicing and Presenting

Practice reading your story aloud several times, possibly in front of a mirror. Change any words that sound awkward. Eventually, you should be able to tell your story without looking at your script. Your goal is not to memorize the story word for word, but to learn it so well that you can comfortably tell it to others. Then find a **practice audience** of one or two people and rehearse your story. Consider these guidelines for your performance.

- Use your body movement or position to get the audience's attention before you begin.
- Make eye contact with the audience.
- Speak clearly at a comfortable pace.
- Use a different voice for each character.
- Use props that are large enough to be seen from the back of the room.

> **Ask Your Peer Reviewers**
> - Which parts of the story interested you most?
> - Which voices, gestures, and facial expressions were most effective?
> - Were the characters real to you? Why or why not?
> - How did my pacing affect the story?

## ❹ Refining Your Performance

**TARGET SKILL ▶ EVALUATING YOUR INTERPRETIVE CHOICES**

Think about the choices you made as you performed your story. Do these choices make your interpretation work? Here are some items to consider.

- **Pacing.** Is the pace too fast? too slow? Should some parts be delivered more slowly than others? If so, which ones?
- **Volume.** Is your voice loud enough? too loud?
- **Props and costumes.** Do the props and costumes help your audience understand the story?
- **Movements and expression.** Are your body movements and facial expressions effective? Are there any others that might help make the story more enjoyable?

Now revise your performance to include any needed changes.

## ❺ Reflecting

**FOR YOUR WORKING PORTFOLIO** What did you discover about telling a story? How did telling the story help you understand it better? Attach your answers to your story script. Save your story script in your **Working Portfolio.**

Read this paragraph from the first draft of a story. The underlined sections may include the following kinds of errors:

- **comma errors**
- **correctly written sentences that should be combined**
- **sentence fragments**
- **verb-tense errors**

For each underlined section, choose the revision that most improves the writing.

> Many years ago, our town was the setting for a truly supernatural event. <u>The moon was full. It was shining. It was bright.</u> (1) <u>It is exactly midnight when</u> (2) a strange wind began to stir. <u>It blew strong and cold. The wind was like and icy fist.</u> (3) Then the noise started. At first it was a quiet hum, but it changed. <u>The single chord harmonic and beautiful grew louder and louder.</u> (4) The sound became almost overwhelming <u>and then, it suddenly stopped.</u> (5) <u>Although some people say that it was the wind in the trees.</u> (6) This is not true. Only I know the real story.

1. **A.** The moon was shining and full and bright.
   **B.** The moon was full and shining and bright.
   **C.** The full moon was shining brightly.
   **D.** Correct as is

2. **A.** It will be exactly midnight when
   **B.** It was exactly midnight when
   **C.** It had been exactly midnight when
   **D.** Correct as is

3. **A.** The wind blew strong and cold, like an icy fist.
   **B.** The wind blew strong and cold. The wind was like an icy fist.
   **C.** Strong and cold. The wind blew like an icy fist.
   **D.** Correct as is

4. **A.** The single chord harmonic and beautiful, grew louder and louder.
   **B.** The single chord, harmonic and beautiful, grew louder and louder.
   **C.** The single chord, harmonic and beautiful grew louder and louder.
   **D.** Correct as is

5. **A.** and then it suddenly, stopped.
   **B.** and, then it suddenly stopped.
   **C.** and then it suddenly stopped.
   **D.** Correct as is

6. **A.** Even though some people say that it was the wind in the trees.
   **B.** Although some people say that, it was the wind in the trees.
   **C.** Some people say that it was the wind in the trees.
   **D.** Correct as is

**Need extra help?**

See the **Grammar Handbook**

Correcting Fragments, p. 1323

Punctuation Chart, pp. 1327–1328

Verb Tense, p. 1310

**Assessment Practive**

Explain that students should read the entire paragraph before they answer the questions. Then demonstrate how students can eliminate incorrect choices for the first question.

**A.** Using the word *and* to link the ideas does not give the reader an indication of how the ideas are related.

**B.** Using the word *and* to link the ideas does not give the reader an indication of how the ideas are related.

**D.** These three sentences need to be combined.

**C.** This example correctly combines the three ideas. It relates the words *full* and *moon,* then describes the way the full moon looks.

**Answers:**
**1.** C; **2.** B; **3.** A; **4.** B; **5.** C; **6.** C

## Building Vocabulary

### Objectives

- research word origins as an aid to understanding meanings and derivations
- use a dictionary to determine precise usage and pronunciation
- practice classifying homophones, homonyms, and homographs

### EXERCISE

1. *Heard* (hûrd), the past tense of *hear*, derives from an inflected form of Old English *hFeren;* herd (hûrd), "a group of cattle or other animals," derives from Old English *heord;* homophones.

2. Both *invalid* (ĭn'və-lĭd), "a person incapacitated by illness," and *invalid* (ĭn-văl'ĭd), "not legally, factually, or logically valid," derives ultimately from Latin *invalidus;* homographs.

3. *Loom* (lōōm), "to come into view as if in a magnified form," is of uncertain (possibly Scandinavian) origin; *loom* (lōōm), "a device for weaving threads into cloth," derives from Old English *gellma;* homonyms.

4. *Pour* (Pôr), "to make flow from a container," derives from Latin *purAre; pore* (Pôr), "to read or study carefully," derives from Middle English *pouren;* homophones.

5. *Quiver* (kwĭv'ər), "to shake tremulously," derives from Middle English *quiveren; quiver* (kwĭv'ər), "a case for holding arrows," derives from Old French *cuivre;* homonyms.

## Words That Sound and Look Alike

Imagine you are listening to someone read the excerpt on the right. How might you misinterpret the word *rapt* if it were unfamiliar to you?

Might you momentarily think of the word *wrapped* and imagine the audience sitting with their heads covered up like mummies? In Twain's world anything is possible, but in this case the context helps you know that *wrapped* is incorrect. The actual word, *rapt*, means "deeply moved, delighted, or absorbed."

> Whenever Simmons stood behind him and gazed at the back of his skull and tried to drive a mental suggestion into it, Hicks sat with vacant face and never suspected. If he had been noticing he could have seen by the rapt faces of the audience that something was going on behind his back that required a response.
> —*The Autobiography of Mark Twain*

*Rapt* and *wrapped* are **homophones**, different words that sound the same.

## Strategies for Building Vocabulary

In addition to homophones, homonyms and homographs may cause confusion for English speakers and writers. Use the etymologies of these terms, which come from the Greek language, to help you remember their meanings.

**❶ Homophones** The term *homophone* comes from the Greek words *homos* ("same") and *phōnē* ("sound"). Homophones like *rapt* and *wrapped* can cause comprehension errors and spelling mistakes because they are pronounced the same but spelled differently. Learning sets of homophones can help you choose the correct word. The chart below provides some examples.

**Homophones**

| Alike in | Different in | Examples |
|---|---|---|
| pronunciation | meanings and spellings | *past/passed; weigh/way/whey; boarder/border* |

**❷ Homonyms** Words that have the same pronunciation and spelling but different meanings are called **homonyms.** The term comes from the Greek words *homos* ("same") and *onuma* ("name"). When, for example, the narrator of Willa Cather's "A Wagner Matinee" states, "The deluge of sound poured on and on; . . . I never knew how far it bore her, or past what happy islands," the reader must recognize that *bore* is the word meaning "carried" rather than, for example, the word meaning "to drill a hole."

Unlike multiple meanings of a single word, homonyms have separate entries in dictionaries because they have different derivations—their being spelled and pronounced alike is only coincidence.

*Bore,* the past tense of *bear,* comes from a form of the Old English word *beran,* whereas *bore* meaning "to drill a hole" comes from a different Old English word, *borian.* See the chart for more examples.

**Homonyms**

| Alike in | Different in | Examples |
|---|---|---|
| pronunciation and spelling | meaning | *story* (tale)/*story* (floor of a building) *lock* (length of hair)/*lock* (device for securing a door) |

**❸ Homographs** The term *homograph* comes from the Greek words *homos* and *graphē* ("writing"). **Homographs** are words with the same spelling but with different pronunciations and meanings, such as *present* (prĕz'ənt) and *present* (prĭ-zĕnt'). Practice can help you remember the different pronunciations and meanings. See the chart below for more examples.

**Homographs**

| Alike in | Different in | Examples |
|---|---|---|
| spelling | pronunciation and meaning | *wind* (wĭnd)/*wind* (wīnd); *incense* (ĭn'sĕns')/ *incense* (ĭn-sĕns') |

**EXERCISE** Use a dictionary to identify the meanings, pronunciations, and origins of the words in each pair. Then classify the words as homophones, homonyms, or homographs and use each in a sentence.

1. *heard* and *herd*    3. *loom* and *loom*    5. *quiver* and *quiver*
2. *invalid* and *invalid*    4. *pour* and *pore* (verb)

## Grammar from Literature

Writers use complex sentences when they want to link two or more ideas that are related but not of equal importance. Complex sentences consist of one independent clause and one or more subordinate clauses. The less important ideas are expressed in subordinate clauses, which cannot stand alone as sentences. Look at the examples below.

> adverb subordinate clause
> **When the horns drew out the first strain of the**
> independent clause
> **Pilgrim's chorus, my Aunt Georgiana clutched my coat sleeve.**
> —Willa Cather, "A Wagner Matinee"
>
> adverb clause
> **I was hurt by this as if I were engaged in some honest occupation.**
> —Mark Twain, *The Autobiography of Mark Twain*
>
> adjective clause
> **The Indian, who was listening carefully, decided to**
> adjective clause
> **give a cow that he had to the priest.**
> —"The Indian and the Hundred Cows,"
> translated by Rudolfo A. Anaya

Each subordinate clause functions as a single part of speech—in the examples as an adverb or adjective.

**Using Adjective and Adverb Clauses in Your Writing**
Examine your own writing for related ideas that could be more clearly expressed by using adjective or adverb clauses in complex sentences. Look for places where added detail is needed or where wording could be streamlined. Decide which idea you wish to

emphasize. Usually the less important idea is placed in the adjective or adverb clause. Notice the difference in emphasis in the examples below.

> adverb clauses
> **Samuel Clemens tried out the names Jefferson Snodgrass and simply Josh** before he settled on Mark Twain as a pen name.
>
> **Samuel Clemens settled on Mark Twain as a pen name** after he tried out the names Jefferson Snodgrass and simply Josh.

The first example focuses on names Clemens tried out; the second draws attention to the name Clemens chose.

**Usage Tip** Since a subordinate clause contains a subject and verb, you might mistakenly confuse it with a sentence. The introductory word in a subordinate clause, such as *although, after, because, if,* or *where,* causes the clause to be an incomplete thought. A subordinate clause is a fragment until it is joined to an independent clause.

> INCORRECT
> **When Clark received the letter.**
>
> CORRECT
> **When Clark received the letter, he realized his aunt was arriving in just one day.**

**Punctuation Tip** Use a comma to set off an adverbial clause at the beginning of a sentence.

> **When Aunt Georgiana arrived at the train station, her clothes were covered with dust.**
>
> **Aunt Georgiana's clothes were covered with dust when she arrived at the train station.**

---

**WRITING EXERCISE** Combine each pair of sentences in items 1–3 by expressing the less important idea as a subordinate clause. In sentences 4–5, add subordinate clauses as indicated in parentheses.

1. Aunt Georgiana was visiting relatives in the Green Mountains. She met Harold Carpenter.
2. Their homestead was lonely and primitive. The reason for this was that it lay fifty miles from the railroad.
3. The couple moved to Nebraska. Land was free and available there.
4. They built a dugout to live in. (Add an adverb clause at the start of the sentence.)

5. Boston seemed exciting to someone from the West. (Add an adjective clause describing Boston. Set the clause off in commas.)

**GRAMMAR EXERCISE** Both fragments and sentences are listed below. Rewrite the fragments as sentences. Correct errors in punctuation in the sentences.

1. If a young couple wanted adventure.
2. When the railroad was completed in 1850.
3. Travelers on wagon trains took time to regain their energy, after they had completed such long journeys.
4. Although the lure of gold drew many people.
5. When the concert ended Georgiana did not want to leave.

---

### Objectives
- use complex sentences to link two or more related ideas
- understand that subordinate clauses function as an adverb or adjective
- revise drafts by using adjective and adverb clauses in complex sentences to clearly express ideas, add detail, or streamline wording
- practice creating complex sentences by joining subordinate clauses—fragments—to an independent clause

### WRITING EXERCISE
Responses will vary.
1. Aunt Georgiana was visiting relatives in the Green Mountains <u>when she met Harold Carpenter.</u>
2. Their homestead was lonely and primitive <u>because it lay 50 miles from the railroad.</u>
3. The couple moved to Nebraska, <u>where land was free and available.</u>
4. <u>After they chose their land,</u> they built a dugout to live in.
5. Boston, <u>which teemed with night life and culture,</u> seemed exciting to someone from the West.

### GRAMMAR EXERCISE
Responses may vary.
1. If a young couple wanted adventure, <u>they might try homesteading.</u>
2. When the railroad was completed in 1850, <u>settlement in the West increased.</u>
3. Travelers on wagon trains took time to regain their <u>energy after</u> they had completed such long journeys.
4. Although the lure of gold drew many people, <u>only a few got rich.</u>
5. When the concert <u>ended, Georgiana</u> did not want to leave.

## Objectives

- reflect on and assess their understanding of the unit
- compare text events with his/her own and other readers' experiences
- understand such literary concepts as point of view and character
- assess and build their portfolios

## Reflecting on the Unit

### OPTION 1

A successful response will

- include how the student thinks each writer in the unit would've defined *liberty*.
- include an explanation of what *liberty* means to the student.

### OPTION 2

A successful response will

- describe the insights into the development of the West that these selections have given the students.
- choose three or four characters to include in a role-play.
- role-play a discussion about issues of settling the frontier.

### OPTION 3

Suggest that each student plan his or her writing by using the left side of a piece of paper to jot down notes on the nature of the selected conflict, its 19th-century resolution, and any aspects of it that are still unresolved. On the right side of the paper, the student can note his or her personal judgments and opinions. Encourage students to do additional reading to determine what action they would take.

## Self Assessment

Encourage students to consider not only what they have learned about the past but also how that knowledge has affected their understanding of the people and events of their own time.

# Conflict and Expansion

Did your assumptions about slavery, the Civil War, the civil rights movement, and the development of the West change as you read this unit? As you complete one or more of the options in each of the following sections, think about how your ideas have developed.

Detail of pictorial quilt (1895–1898), Harriet Powers. Pieced and appliquéd cotton embroidered with plain and metallic yarns, 69″ × 105″, bequest of Maxim Karolik, courtesy of Museum of Fine Arts, Boston.

## Reflecting on the Unit

### OPTION 1

**What Is Liberty?** Think about Abraham Lincoln's words on the first page of this unit: "We all declare for liberty; but in using the same word we do not all mean the same thing." How do you think the writers represented in this unit would define *liberty*? Write a series of statements describing what you think liberty means to each author. Then write what liberty means to you.

### OPTION 2

**Life in the West** The selections in Part 2 of this unit deal with the ways of life of different peoples in the American West—from Native Americans to Hispanic and Anglo settlers to people facing new conflicts and challenges in the 20th century. What insights into the development of the West have the selections given you? With a small group of classmates, role-play three or four characters from the selections and discuss what was gained and what was lost as the frontier was gradually settled.

### OPTION 3

**Irrepressible Conflicts** In the second half of the 19th century, the United States faced wrenching conflicts—over slavery, over preserving the Union, and over the settlement of the West. Some of these conflicts even spilled over into the 20th century. Write a few paragraphs about one of the major conflicts dealt with in this unit's selections, explaining your opinion of the way the conflict was resolved at the time and telling what further progress, if any, needs to be made.

**730** UNIT FOUR CONFLICT AND EXPANSION

## Self ASSESSMENT

### 📖 READER'S NOTEBOOK

Make a list of the selections in this unit that impressed you the most. Briefly explain how and why you were affected by each one. Which ones taught you something you didn't know before?

## Reviewing Literary Concepts

**Examining Point of View** Work with a partner—one of you listing the selections in this unit that are told from the first-person point of view, the other listing the selections that are told from the third-person point of view. Compare the lists, then discuss the following questions:

- Why do you think the author of each selection chose the point of view that he or she used?

- How would each selection be different if it were told from a different point of view?

**Analyzing Setting** The selections in this unit take place in a variety of settings, from a slave plantation in Maryland to the Texas-Mexico border early in the 20th century. Which selections gave you the most detailed picture of a particular time, place, and culture? Choose three or four selections in which you visualized the setting most clearly. For each one, write details you recall about setting in a chart like the one shown. What kinds of details make setting come alive?

| Time | Place | Culture |
| --- | --- | --- |
| | | |

### 📁 Building Your Portfolio

- **Writing Options** Several of the Writing Options asked you to imitate literary forms you read, such as the protest poem, ballad, or comic tale. Review your examples of creative writing and choose one that you think is particularly strong. Write a cover note describing what you like about the piece, and add both the note and the piece to your **Presentation Portfolio.** 📁

- **Writing and Communication Workshops** In this unit you wrote a Literary Interpretation in which you explained the meaning a work had for you. You also wrote a Storytelling Script with directions for performing a story. Which of these pieces is ready for an audience? Attach a cover letter with ideas for publishing or performing the piece, then add it to your **Presentation Portfolio.** 📁

- **Additional Activities** Reflect on the various assignments you completed under **Activities & Explorations** and **Inquiry & Research.** Which activity taught you the most? Write a note explaining your choice and add it to your portfolio.

### Self ASSESSMENT

📖 **READER'S NOTEBOOK**

In this unit, you have read autobiographies, folk tales, and works of local-color realism. Write down some distinguishing characteristics of each of these kinds of writing, then list a selection from the unit that is a good example of each kind.

### Self ASSESSMENT

At this point your **Presentation Portfolio** 📁 contains a substantial amount of your work. Review the work it contains and decide which pieces show your thinking and writing abilities best. What other kinds of writing would you like to try as the year goes on?

### Setting GOALS

Look back through your assignments and notebook to identify writing skills and thinking skills you would like to strengthen. Select three or four skills to improve as you study the next unit.

---

## Reviewing Literary Concepts

Remind students that each of them should discuss every selection, not just the ones on his or her own list. You may want to suggest that each pair of students choose one selection from each of their lists and rewrite a passage of it from a different point of view.

Use the Unit 4 Resource Book, p. 88, to provide students a ready-made, full-depth chart for examining setting. Be sure students discuss the relevance of the setting (place and time frame) to the text's meaning.

### 📁 Building Your Own Portfolio

Students will use their Presentation Portfolios to file what they consider their highest quality work—the very best projects and activities from their Working Portfolios.

📖 For more information on using writing and assessing portfolios, see the *Teacher's Guide to Assessment and Portfolio Use,* p. 53.

## OVERVIEW

The Reading and Writing for Assessment feature provides practice in taking standardized tests. As students work through this lesson, they will read a nonfiction passage and answer multiple-choice and essay questions. Boxed strategies located alongside the text will help guide students through the test. These strategies model processes students can use as they take standardized tests.

This feature is based on and will help to prepare students for state assessments, including end-of-course assessments. It will also prepare students for the reading comprehension questions used on such college board examinations as the SAT and the ACT.

### Objectives

• understand and apply strategies for reading a test selection
• recognize literary techniques in a test selection
• understand and apply strategies for answering multiple-choice questions about a test selection
• respond to a writing prompt and present ideas in a logical order
• understand and apply strategies for revising and proofreading a test response

---

# Reading&Writing   for Assessment

**W**hen you studied strategies for reading a test selection on pages 330–335, you practiced techniques for success on reading and writing assessments. These kinds of tests are often important end-of-course examinations. The following pages will give you more practice with test-taking strategies. Work through the models to practice applying each of the following strategies.

### PART 1   How to Read a Test Selection

Here are the basic strategies you studied earlier along with several new ones based on a different type of reading selection. By applying basic test-taking strategies, by taking notes, and by highlighting or underscoring passages as you read, you can focus on the key information you need to know.

> **STRATEGIES FOR READING A TEST SELECTION**
>
> ▸ **Before you begin reading, skim the questions that follow the passage.** These can help focus your reading.
>
> ▸ **Think about the title.** What does it suggest about the overall message and tone of the passage?
>
> ▸ **Use your active reading strategies, such as analyzing, predicting, and questioning.** Make notes in the margin to help you focus your reading. You may do this only if the test directions allow you to mark on the test itself.
>
> ▸ **Look for main ideas.** These are often stated at the beginnings or ends of paragraphs. Sometimes main ideas are implied, not stated. After reading each paragraph, ask "What was this passage about?"
>
> ▸ **Note the literary elements and techniques used by the writer.** You might consider the tone (writer's attitude toward the subject), the structure (how the writer organizes details into a single message), or the use of techniques like foreshadowing or depiction of people. Then ask yourself what effect the writer achieves with each choice.
>
> ▸ **Examine the sequence of ideas.** Are the ideas developed in chronological order, presented in order of importance, or organized in some other way? What does the sequence of ideas suggest about the writer's message?
>
> ▸ **Think about the message and writer's purpose.** What questions does the selection answer? What new questions does it imply? Can you make any generalizations?

732

## Reading Selection

### An English Foothold in North America

1   England's first significant attempt to carve out a colony of its
own in North America (after an earlier failed attempt at Roanoke)
nearly collapsed, as disease and starvation threatened the new
settlement. However, through the determination of its colonists
and the development of a marketable crop, ❶ England's first
permanent settlement in North America took shape.

2   **The Business of Colonization**  The rulers of England—
unlike the Spanish—decided not to fund the risky venture of
colonizing the Americas. Instead, King James I in 1606 granted
a charter, or official permit, to two joint-stock companies, the
Virginia companies of London and Plymouth. Numerous
investors had pooled their wealth in order to finance the trip to
North America. The Virginia Company of Plymouth soon
disbanded, leaving only the Virginia Company of London, later
simply called the Virginia Company.

3   ❷ The Virginia Company had lured financial supporters with
the chance of reaping wealth in the form of gold or silver for a
relatively small investment. England was to get something from
the expedition, too. The King's charter guaranteed that the
English monarch would receive one-fifth of all gold and silver
found by the colonists.

4   In April of 1607, nearly four months after the Virginia
Company's three ships—and nearly 150 passengers and crew
members—had pushed out of an English harbor, the North
American shore rose on the horizon. Reaching the coast of
Virginia, the vessels slipped into a broad coastal river and sailed
inland until they reached a small peninsula. There, the colonists
climbed off their ships and claimed the land as theirs. They
named the settlement Jamestown and the river the James, in
honor of their king.

5   **A Disastrous Start**  ❸ John Smith sensed trouble from the
beginning. Nearly all of the settlers seemed to be consumed by
one thought—the discovery of gold. Because the investors in the
colony demanded a quick return on their investment, the
colonists directed much of their energy toward searching the
land for riches. As Smith later put it, "There was no talk, no
hope, no work, but dig gold, wash gold, refine gold, load gold."
Smith warned of disaster, but few listened to the arrogant
captain, who had made few friends on the voyage over.

---

**❶ Read actively—
predict.**

**ONE STUDENT'S
THOUGHTS**

"This selection will
explain how England's
first permanent colony
in North America got
started."

**YOUR TURN**

Based on paragraph 1,
what topics can you
predict will become
main ideas in the rest of
the passage?

**❷ Read actively—
analyze.**

"For a small investment,
the Virginia Company
promised wealth. People
must have expected to
get rich easily. I wonder
how that will work out."

**❸ Note literary
elements such as tone
and foreshadowing.**

"Now the writer gives
us John Smith's point of
view."

**YOUR TURN**

Based on John Smith's
concerns, what kind of
future do you think lies
ahead for the colony?

---

## Teaching the Lesson

Begin by previewing the text. Note the
title and identify the subject of the
reading selection. Read through the
questions and prompts at the end of
the text. Ask students what they will
need to look for as they read.

1  Some test selections, like this one,
begin with a summary of main ideas.
Students can use this summary to
help predict what information will be
contained in this passage. This
particular selection also includes
subtitles, which can help students
identify main ideas.

**YOUR TURN** It will probably be about
the formation of England's first colony
in North America and the challenges
faced by the colonists.

### Customizing for Less Proficient Readers

2  Some students may have difficulty
understanding how the colony was
financed. Help them understand
terms such as *stock, investor,
finance,* and *investment.* Use the
following questions to help students
analyze paragraphs two and three.

• Who paid for the trip from England
to North America?

**Possible Response:** wealthy
investors in England

• What did the people who paid for
the trip hope to get in return?

**Possible Response:** They hoped to
get rich off gold and silver in North
America.

• What did the people who paid for
the trip have to do with the Virginia
Company?

**Possible Response:** They paid for
the trip by buying shares in the
Virginia Company, which means
they owned it.

3  Students should be alert to clues
that will help predict the content as
well as the tone of the selection. For
example, the word *disastrous* in the
subtitle before paragraph five is one
such hint.

**YOUR TURN** Food and shelter will
become a problem because the colonists
spend all their time searching for gold.

**4** In order to answer test questions about a selection's theme, students may have to look for clues in the writer's words and tone. For example, this writer states that colonists "refused" to plant crops. The word *refused* makes the colonists sound obstinate, lazy, and foolish.

**YOUR TURN** The colonists should have been more concerned with survival than getting rich. This writer seems to think the Jamestown colonists brought their predicament upon themselves.

**5** Students should realize that a quotation of this length probably warrants a test question. Students should ask themselves about the writer's purpose in including the quotation. Is it entertaining? Does it provide new information? Does it offer a different perspective on the subject?

**YOUR TURN** The quotation shows that the colonists spent too much time searching for gold instead of collecting food or building shelter.

**6** When a test question asks students the writer's opinion of a person or character, students can find the answer by examining everything the writer says about that person. Use the following questions to help students analyze the writer's portrayal of John Smith.

• What words does the writer use to describe Smith?

**Possible Responses:** arrogant, wins few friends, takes control, forces, seasoned soldier, flatters and negotiates

• How does the writer describe Smith's effect on the colony?

**Possible Response:** He saves the colony by forcing the colonists to work and by negotiating with the Powhatan. When he leaves, the colony falls apart.

• Is the writer's overall picture of John Smith positive or negative?

**Possible Response:** positive

**7** Understanding the sequence of ideas is important when students are tested on a historical selection. Students will not need to remember exact dates but should be able to remember the general time frame. Students should also be able to explain how events in the selection are related to each other, especially if the writer is demonstrating how one historical event caused another. Creating a time line of events can help students in this area.

---

6  Disease from infected river water struck first. Hunger soon followed. ❹ The colonists, many of whom were unaccustomed to a life of labor, had refused to clear fields, plant crops, or even gather shellfish from the river's edge. After several months, one settler described the terrifying predicament.

7     Thus we lived for the space of five months in this miserable distress...our men night and day groaning in every corner of the fort, most pitiful to hear. If there were any conscience in men, it would make their hearts to bleed to hear the pitiful murmurings and outcries of our sick men for relief, every night and day for the space of six weeks: ❺ some departing out of the World, many times three or four in a night; in the morning their bodies trailed out of their cabins like dogs, to be buried.

8  By the winter of 1607 only 38 colonists remained alive. Standing among them was John Smith, who took control of the settlement. ❻ "You see that power now rests wholly with me," he announced. "You must now obey this law,...he that will not work shall not eat." Smith held the colony together by forcing the colonists to farm. He also received food and support from nearby Powhatan peoples, who had watched warily as the English established their settlement. Smith, a seasoned soldier, knew the Powhatan easily could wipe out the settlement. So he flattered and negotiated his way into winning an uneasy friendship with the group's leader, Chief Powhatan.

9  Just as Jamestown began to look like a real village, tragedy struck. A stray spark ignited a gunpowder bag Smith was wearing and set him on fire. Badly burned, Smith headed back to England, leaving Jamestown to fend for itself.

10  In the spring of 1609, the Virginia Company dispatched another 600 colonists, including women and children, to Jamestown. The newcomers arrived to find a settlement of disorganized colonists who were being threatened by angry Powhatan. Fearing the growing English presence, the Powhatan killed much of the colonists' livestock and harassed those settlers who attempted to hunt or farm. ❼ By the winter of 1609, conditions in Jamestown had deteriorated to the point of famine. In what became known as the "starving time," colonists ate roots, rats, snakes, and even boiled shoe leather. Of the hundreds of settlers who began the winter, only about 60 survived to see the relief ship that arrived in the spring.

734

---

**STRATEGIES IN ACTION**

❹ **Think about the message or theme.**
"Even if the settlers found plenty of gold, it would do them no good unless they returned to England. You can't eat gold."

**YOUR TURN**
What larger lesson does the writer intend for readers to draw from this passage?

❺ **Look for main ideas.**
"Based on what this colonist said, it's amazing that anyone in Jamestown survived."

**YOUR TURN**
What main ideas of the selection are supported by this quotation?

❻ **Note the techniques the writer uses to portray character.**
"Here, the writer shows us Smith's character by providing the words Smith said, as well as telling us Smith's actions."

❼ **Examine the sequence of ideas.**
"This selection describes events dating from 1606–1609—the time it took for the English to develop a 'foothold in North America.'"

---

## Check Your Understanding

Have students use the following questions to test their own understanding of the selection before they answer the questions in their texts.

• What were the main ideas in the selection?
• What literary elements does the writer use? How does the writer encourage readers to care about the information presented?
• What structure does the writer use for the selection?
• Did the selection answer all your questions about the subject? If not, what questions remain unanswered?

Use the strategies in the box and notes in the side column to help you answer the questions below and on the following pages. Based on the selection you have just read, choose the best answer for each of the following questions.

1. Which of the following statements is a theme of this selection?

   A. Courage and a sense of adventure can overcome the harshest adversities.

   B. Soldiers make the best leaders.

   C. Success comes to those who work hard, not to those who are lazy.

   D. Greed is not a good motivation for action.

2. The settlers got into trouble because they

   A. were too sick to work.

   B. didn't plant crops for food.

   C. didn't have enough supplies.

   D. had poor leadership.

3. The tone of paragraphs 5-9 is mostly

   A. personal.

   B. angry.

   C. judgmental.

   D. objective.

4. What is the writer's opinion of John Smith?

   A. The writer admires Smith's leadership ability.

   B. The writer considers Smith to be overbearing.

   C. all of the above

   D. none of the above

5. The writer characterizes the Powhatan as

   A. indifferent.

   B. fearful.

   C. greedy.

   D. lacking in resources.

---

**STRATEGIES** FOR ANSWERING MULTIPLE-CHOICE QUESTIONS

▶ Ask questions that help you eliminate some of the choices.

▶ Pay attention to choices such as "all of the above" or "none of the above." To eliminate them, all you need to find is one answer that doesn't fit.

▶ **Skim your notes.** Details you noticed as you read may provide answers.

**STRATEGIES** IN ACTION

**Ask questions.** What kind of men were these settlers?

ONE STUDENT'S THOUGHTS

"The writer says in paragraph 5 that John Smith is arrogant. That doesn't sound very objective. So I can eliminate choice D."

YOUR TURN

What other choices do not accurately reflect the tone of the writer?

**Skim your notes.**

ONE STUDENT'S THOUGHTS

"The writer says the Powhatan killed the settlers' livestock. If they were greedy or lacking in resources, they would have taken the livestock for themselves. So I can eliminate choices C and D."

YOUR TURN

What other choice is not supported by the evidence in the selection?

---

## Guilding Student Response

### Multiple-Choice Questions

1. C
2. B
3. C

**YOUR TURN** Choices A and B do not accurately reflect the tone of the writer. Although the writer's tone reflects his or her own opinion, the writer does not offer a personal opinion or use accusatory, angry language.

4. C
5. B

**YOUR TURN** The writer describes the Powhatan as wary, uneasy, and angry—not indifferent. Choice A can be eliminated.

## Short-Answer Question

**Possible Response:** By using the quotation, the writer is able to capture the feeling of the situation. Unlike the selection as a whole, the quotation presents a personal viewpoint and allows the reader to fully understand the predicament of the colonists.

**YOUR TURN** The tone of the quotation is more personal and less objective than the selection.

## Essay Question

The writer seems to think that John Smith could have prevented "the starving time." The writer suggests that many of the colonists' problems were brought on by inexperience and a lack of leadership. For example, the writer says the colonists only wanted to mine gold and did not spend any time clearing fields, planting crops, or fishing.

John Smith was different from the rest of the colonists. The writer describes him as an intelligent, hard-working soldier who predicted trouble from the beginning and took control when things got out of hand. When Smith returned to England, the settlers could not keep up the peace with the Powhatan or even manage to keep farming. However, the writer leaves the reader wondering why John Smith didn't intervene earlier to prevent "the starving time."

**YOUR TURN** The writer says John Smith is arrogant and has a hard time making friends. However, the writer also describes John Smith as a "seasoned soldier" with common sense and leadership skills.

---

**PART 3** How to Respond in Writing

You may also be asked to write answers to questions about a reading passage. Short-answer questions usually ask you to answer in a sentence or two. Essay questions require a fully developed piece of writing.

### Short-Answer Question

**STRATEGIES FOR RESPONDING TO SHORT-ANSWER QUESTIONS**

▶ **Identify the key words** in the writing prompt that tell you the ideas to discuss. Make sure you know what is meant by each.
▶ **State your response directly** and to the point.
▶ **Support your ideas** by using evidence from the selection.
▶ **Use correct grammar.**

> **Sample Question**
>
> Answer the following question in one or two sentences.
>
> The factual information in the quotation from the Jamestown colonist could be summarized in a single sentence. Why is it more effective for the writer to use a quotation than to summarize the information it provides?

### Essay Question

**STRATEGIES FOR ANSWERING ESSAY QUESTIONS**

▶ **Look for direction words** in the writing prompt, such as *essay, analyze, describe,* or *compare and contrast* that tell you how to respond directly to the prompt.
▶ **List the points** you want to make before beginning to write.
▶ **Write an interesting introduction** that presents your main point.
▶ **Develop your ideas** by using evidence from the selection that supports the statements you make. Present the ideas in a logical order.
▶ **Write a conclusion** that summarizes your points.
▶ **Check your work** for correct grammar.

> **Sample Prompt**
>
> In the opinion of the writer, could John Smith have prevented "the starving time"? Write an essay in which you analyze the writer's characterization of John Smith's leadership skills.

---

**STRATEGIES IN ACTION**

Support your ideas by using evidence from the selection.

**ONE STUDENT'S THOUGHTS**

"The colonist expresses much more emotion than the writer does. For example, the colonist says the cries of the settlers would make your heart bleed."

**YOUR TURN**

How else is the tone of the quotation different from that of the selection?

---

Look for direction words.

**ONE STUDENT'S THOUGHTS**

"The important words are analyze, characterization, and leadership skills. My essay will have to use evidence from the selection about John Smith's character to argue that the writer thinks Smith could or could not have prevented 'the starving time.'"

**YOUR TURN**

What does the writer say about John Smith's character?

## PART 4

**How to Revise and Edit a Test Selection**

Here is a student's first draft in response to the writing prompt on page 736. Read it and answer the multiple-choice questions that follow.

| | |
|---|---|
| 1 | The writer seems to think that John Smith could indeed prevent |
| 2 | "the starving time." The writer creates the impression that many of |
| 3 | the colonists' problems were brought on by laziness and lack of |
| 4 | leadership. For example, the writer says the colonists did not spend |
| 5 | any time clearing fields, planting crops, or fishing. |
| 6 | The writer describes John Smith as an intelligent, hard- |
| 7 | working soldier who predicted trouble from the beginning. The |
| 8 | writer says that Smith's return to England was a tragedy for |
| 9 | Jamestown. Without Smith's leadership, the settlers could not |
| | even manage to keep farming. |

1. The BEST way to make it clear that "the starving time" occurred in the past, not in the future, would be to change the sentence in lines 1 and 2 ("The writer...'the starving time.'") in which of the following ways?

A. The writer seems to think that John Smith could indeed have prevented "the starving time."

B. The writer seems to think that John Smith would indeed prevent "the starving time."

C. The writer seems to think that John Smith did indeed prevent "the starving time."

D. Make no change.

2. The BEST way to make the connection between paragraphs clearer would be to add which of the following sentences to the beginning of line 6 ("The writer...from the beginning.")?

A. John Smith was different from the rest of the colonists.

B. Only a few colonists remained alive after the first winter.

C. The Powhatan could have wiped out the settlement.

D. Make no change.

3. The BEST way to summarize and conclude this essay would be to add which of the following sentences to the end of line 9 ("Without Smith's leadership...keep farming.")?

A. Only a few settlers survived "the starving time" and lived to see the spring relief ship.

B. During "the starving time," the colonists even ate boiled shoe leather.

C. The writer implies that with strong leadership, Jamestown could have avoided "the starving time."

D. Make no change.

**STRATEGIES** FOR REVISING, EDITING, AND PROOFREADING

▶ Read the passage carefully.
▶ Note the parts that are confusing or don't make sense. What kinds of errors would that signal?
▶ Look for errors in grammar, usage, spelling, and capitalization. Common errors include:
  • run-on sentences
  • sentence fragments
  • no subject-verb agreement
  • unclear pronoun antecedents
  • lack of transition words

Answers
1. A
2. A
3. C

**Check Your Understanding**
Have students re-read their own responses to the short-answer and essay questions. Then have students use the following questions to guide them as they revise and edit their work.

• Have I responded directly to the direction words in the writing prompt?
• Have I supported my ideas with evidence from the selection?
• Have I presented my ideas in a logical order?
• Have I included an introduction and a conclusion?
• Have I used correct grammar?

## The Changing Face of America

The selections in Unit Five explore the increasing diversity of American life and literature as more women began to write and as immigration and industrialization changed the way Americans lived. The unit is divided into two sections to represent the wide range of literary concerns that writers voiced in the 19th and 20th centuries.

### —————— Part 1 ——————

**Women's Voices, Women's Lives** This part of the unit traces the development of literature by women from Emily Dickinson to Julia Alvarez. From these selections, students can infer the growth of the women's movement and its expression in literature. Students will see how the prevailing attitudes of the past and present influenced the topics, themes, and content of women's writing. The Dickinson, Gilman, and Chopin selections place the literature in its historical context, probe the social concerns of the time, and examine the writers' techniques. **Traditions Across Time** presents contemporary writing of women from different cultural traditions, including Asian, Hispanic, and African American.

### —————— Part 2 ——————

**The American Dream** The works in this section explore how a diverse group of writers reacted to the rapid changes and sharp contrasts of the 19th and 20th centuries. The writers attempt to capture the richness and diversity of the American experience. **Traditions Across Time** probes the changing face of contemporary American society.

# THE CHANGING FACE OF AMERICA

If we

are to

achieve

a richer

culture,

rich in

contrasting

values,

we must

recognize

the whole

gamut of

human

potentialities.

**MARGARET MEAD**
*anthropologist*

*Mr. and Mrs. Isaac Newton Phelps Stokes* (1897), John Singer Sargent. Oil on canvas, 85¼" × 39¾", The Metropolitan Museum of Art, bequest of Edith Minturn Phelps Stokes (Mrs. I. N.), 1938. (38.104). Copyright © 1989 The Metropolitan Museum of Art.

738

 **Mini Lesson** Viewing and Representing

*Mr. and Mrs. Isaac Newton Phelps Stokes*
**by John Singer Sargent**

**ART APPRECIATION**
**Instruction** This painting from 1897 typifies the work of American portraitist John Singer Sargent (1856–1925). Originally Mrs. Stokes requested a formal portrait, but after four sittings, Sargent said, "I want to paint you as you are." He suggested a less-conventional pose alongside a Great Dane, but when the dog was unavailable, Sargent substituted her husband.

**Ask: What, if anything, seems ironic about the portrait and its title? Explain.**
**Possible Responses:** The portrait's title implies a portrait of equals—the same attention being given to the wife and husband. However, the confident appearance and forward position of the more brightly lit Mrs. Stokes clearly make her the focal point. Mr. Stokes's position in the shadowy background suggests that he may be less comfortable in the social world and may want his wife to get major attention.

739

## Making Connections

To help students explore connections among the art, the quotation, and the unit theme, have them consider the following questions.

**Ask: The quotation by Margaret Mead (1901–1978) explores the composition of American culture. How do you define this culture?**
**Possible Response:** American culture includes all aspects of the American experience, including literature, music, art, sports, television, movies, and radio.

**Ask: What do you think Mead means when she says that "we must recognize the whole gamut of human potentialities"?**
**Possible Response:** American culture is made up of many different voices, not just those of the majority. American culture is richer when all voices are heard, including those of women and minorities.

**Ask: What can you infer about the subjects of the Sargent painting on this page? What is interesting about the woman's clothing?**
**Possible Responses:** They are relatively young; their clothing marks them as being well-to-do. The woman is wearing a shirt and tie much like her husband's— and breaks out of the "feminine" mold.

**Ask: Study the art, quotation, and unit title. Based on these, how do you think American literature and life might be changing?**
**Possible Responses:** America's "face" is changing because it is increasingly multicultural and voices of both genders are heard; our literature reflects our increasing richness and diversity.

| Features and Selections | Literary Analysis | Reading and Critical Thinking | Writing Opportunities | |
|---|---|---|---|---|
| **The Changing Face of America**<br>**Time Line**<br>**Historical Background/**<br>**Women's Voices, Women's Lives** | | Voices from the Times, 743 | | |
| **AUTHOR STUDY**<br>**Emily Dickinson** | | | | |
| POETRY<br>Selected Poems<br><br>Letter to Thomas Wentworth<br>  Higginson | Figurative Language, 750, 760<br>Review: Paradox, 760 | Poetry, 750, 760<br><br>Informal Assess., 756<br>Test Practice, 759<br>Letter, 755 | Mini Poem, 762<br>Comparison-Contrast<br>  Essay, 762 | |
| Author's Style<br>Author Study Project | Analysis of Style, 761 | | Changing Style, 761<br>Imitation of Style, 761 | |
| Learning the Language of Literature<br>Social Themes in Fiction | Social Themes in Fiction, 763 | Strategies for Reading, 764 | | |
| SHORT STORY<br>The Yellow Wallpaper<br><br>**Related Reading**<br>*from* Complaints and Disorders | First-Person Narrator, 765, 779 | Inferences About Narrator, 765, 779<br>Informal Assess., 776<br>Test Practice, 778<br>Finding Evidence, 782 | Advertising Copy, 780<br><br>Letter to Editor, 780<br><br>Extend Story, 780 | |
| SHORT STORY<br>The Story of an Hour | Plot, 783, Surprise Ending, 786<br>Review: Irony, 786 | Predicting, 783, 786<br><br>Informal Assess., 785 | Husband's Monologue, 787<br><br>Wife's Epitaph, 787<br>Different Ending, 787<br>Essay About Marriage, 787 | |
| SHORT STORY<br>Comparing Literature<br>Seventeen Syllables | Coming of Age Story, 788, 800 | Understanding Conflicts, 788, 800<br>Workplace Link, 795<br>Test Practice, 796<br>Informal Assess., 799 | Points of Comparison, 801<br><br>Character Sketch, 801 | |
| POETRY<br>Comparing Literature<br>Adolescence—III | Imagery, 802, 804 | Visualizing, 802, 804 | Points of Comparison, 805<br><br>Rosie's Diary Entry, 805<br>Write A Review, 805 | |
| SHORT STORY<br>Comparing Literature<br>I Stand Here Ironing<br><br>**Literary Link**<br>Ironing Their Clothes | Interior Monologue, 806, 815<br>Review: Metaphor, 815 | Judgments About<br>  Character, 806, 815<br>Author Activity, 817<br>Informal Assess., 809<br>Test Practice, 817 | Points of Comparison, 816<br><br>Story Sequel, 816<br>Relationships, 816<br>Emily's Interview, 816 | |
| Comparing Literature<br>Assessment Practice | | Reading the Prompt, 818 | Synthesis Essay, 818 | |

LEGEND    DLS – Daily Language SkillBuilder
CCL – Cross Curricular Link          Green type – Teacher's Edition

| Features and Selections | Literary Analysis | Reading and Critical Thinking | Writing Opportunities | |
|---|---|---|---|---|
| **Historical Background/ The American Dream** | | Voices from the Times, 821, 822 | | |
| **POETRY** Chicago / Lucinda Matlock | Tone, 824, 828 <br> Review: Personification, 828 | Synthesizing Details, 824, 828 | Hometown Poems, 829 <br> Comparison-Contrast Essay, 829 | |
| **POETRY** Richard Cory / Miniver Cheevy | Characterization in Poetry, 830, 833 <br> Review: Rhyme and Meter, 833 | Evaluating Character, 830, 831, 833 <br> Test Practice, 832 | Miniver's Monologue, 834 <br> Farewell Note, 834 <br> Interview Questions, 834 | |
| **POETRY** We Wear the Mask / Sympathy | Symbol, 835, 838 <br> Review: Tone, 838 | Interpreting Symbols, 835, 838 | Narrative Sequel, 839 <br> Lyrics of a Songbird, 839 | |
| **SHORT STORY** Winter Dreams | Characters, 840, 860 <br> Review: Symbol, 860 | Evaluating Character, 840, 860 <br> Informal Assess., 849, 856 | Psychological Evaluation, 861 <br> Dexter's Resume, 861 <br> Personal Lecture, 861 | |
| **SHORT STORY** America and I <br> **Related Reading** The New Immigrants | Voice, 863, 873 | Understanding Analogies, 863, 873 <br><br> Test Practice, 869 <br> Comparing Text and Graphic, 875 | Tips for Newcomers, 874 <br> Letter to Russia, 874 <br> Memoir, 874 | |
| **SHORT STORY** **Comparing Literature** In the American Society <br> **Literary Link** My Father and the Figtree | Structure, 877, 892 <br> Review: Characters, 892 | Motivations, 877, 892 <br> Informal Assess., 887, 890 | Points of Comparison, 893 <br> Assimilation, 893 <br> Critical Review, 893 | |
| **POETRY** **Comparing Literature** Defining the Grateful Gesture <br> Refugee Ship <br> Assessment Practice | Theme and Title, 894, 898 <br><br><br> Literary Analysis, 900 | Conclusions About Theme, 894, 896, 898 <br> Test Practice, 897 <br><br> Reading the Prompt, 900 | Points of Comparison, 899 <br> Sapia's Language, 899 <br><br> Analytical Essay, 900 | |
| **Writing Workshop:** Comparison-and-Contrast Essay **Assessment Practice** **Building Vocabulary** **Sentence Crafting** | | Analyzing a Student Model, 903 | Comparison-and-Contrast Essay, 902 | |
| **Reflect and Assess** **The Changing Face of America** | Reviewing Literary Concepts, 911 | Woman's Proper Place, 910 | Portfolio Building, 911 | |

LEGEND  DLS – Daily Language SkillBuilder
CCL – Cross Curricular Link        Green type – Teacher's Edition

| Speaking and Listening Viewing and Representing | Inquiry and Research | Grammar, Usage, and Mechanics | Vocabulary |
|---|---|---|---|
| Art Appreciation, 825 | | DLS, 824<br><br>Noun Clauses, 829 | Connotative/Denotative Meanings, 827 |
| Musical Adaptation, 834<br><br>Author Activity, 834 | | DLS, 830<br><br>Noun Clause, 834 | Rely on Context Clues, 831 |
| Personal Mask, 839<br>Political Cartoon, 839<br>Author Activity, 839 | | DLS, 835<br><br>Appositive Clauses, 839 | Connotative Power of Words, 837 |
| Illustrated Calendar, 861<br>Art Connection, 861<br>Historical Recordings, 848<br>Art Appreciation, 853, 859<br><br>Dramatic Reading, 854 | Clothing Styles, 861<br>Using Indexes, 861 | DLS, 840<br><br>Semicolons, 846<br>Noun Clauses, 862 | Synonyms, 862<br>Using Context Clues, 842<br>Meanings of Root Words, 857 |
| Yiddish Words, 865<br>Photographs, 867<br>Workplace Link, 875 | | DLS, 863<br><br>Commas, 866<br>Noun Clauses, 874 | Using Context Clues, 864<br>Suffixes and Root Words, 870 |
| Art Appreciation, 881, 888<br>Mandarin, 883<br>Workplace Link, 885<br>Critical Review of Literature, 891 | | DLS, 877<br><br>Introductory Words, 884 | Assessment Practice, 893<br>Context Clues, 870<br>Word History, 882 |
| Art Appreciation, 895 | | DLS, 894<br><br>Pronouns in Comparison, 899 | Understanding Analogies, 896 |
| | | Parallel Construction/ Modifiers, 906<br>Revising and Editing, 907<br><br>Using Noun Clauses, 909 | Recognizing Denotations and Connotations, 908 |
| American Dream, 910 | | | |

# RESOURCE MANAGEMENT GUIDE
## PART 1

To introduce the theme/literary period of this unit, use Fine Art Transparencies T29–31 in the Communications Transparencies and Copymasters.

**Additional Support**

| | Unit Resource Book | Assessment | Integrated Technology and Media | Literary Analysis Transparencies |
|---|---|---|---|---|
| **Selected Poems by Emily Dickinson** pp. 750–762 | • Active Reading p. 4 <br> • Literary Analysis p. 5 | • Selection Test, Formal Assessment pp. 137–138 <br> ◉ Test Generator | ◠ Audio Library <br><br> ▭ Video: Literature in Performance, Video Resource Book pp. 21–26 <br> ◉ Research Starter www.mcdougallittell.com <br> ◉ NetActivities | |
| **The Yellow Wallpaper** pp. 765–781 | • Summary p. 6 <br> • Active Reading p. 7 <br> • Literary Analysis p. 8 <br> • Words to Know p. 9 <br> • Selection Quiz p. 10 | • Selection Test, Formal Assessment pp. 139–140 <br> ◉ Test Generator | ◠ Audio Library | • Point of View T20 |
| **The Story of an Hour** pp. 783–787 | • Summary p. 11 <br> • Active Reading p. 12 <br> • Literary Analysis p. 13 <br> • Selection Quiz p. 14 | • Selection Test, Formal Assessment pp. 141–142 <br> ◉ Test Generator | ◠ Audio Library <br><br> ▭ Video: Literature in Performance, Video Resource Book pp. 27–32 | |
| **Seventeen Syllables (1949)** pp. 788–801 | • Summary p. 15 <br> • Active Reading p. 16 <br> • Literary Analysis p. 17 <br> • Words to Know p. 18 <br> • Selection Quiz p. 19 | • Selection Test, Formal Assessment pp. 143–144 <br> ◉ Test Generator | ◠ Audio Library | |
| **Adolescence-III (1980)** pp. 802–805 | • Active Reading p. 20 <br> • Literary Analysis p. 21 | • Selection Test, Formal Assessment pp. 145–146 <br> ◉ Test Generator | ◠ Audio Library | |
| **I Stand Here Ironing (1956)** pp. 806–817 | • Summary p. 22 <br> • Active Reading p. 23 <br> • Literary Analysis p. 24 <br> • Words to Know p. 25 <br> • Selection Quiz p. 26 <br> • Comparing Literature p. 27 | • Selection Test, Formal Assessment pp. 147–148 <br> ◉ Test Generator | ◠ Audio Library <br><br> ◉ Research Starter www.mcdougallittell.com | • Point of View T20 |
| | | **Unit Assessment** | **Unit Technology** | |
| | | • Unit Five, Part 1 Test, Formal Assessment pp. 149–150 <br> ◉ Test Generator <br> • Unit Five Integrated Test, Integrated Assessment pp. 39–46 | ◉ ClassZone www.mcdougallittell.com <br> ◉ EasyPlanner CD-ROM <br> ◉ Electronic Library | |

| Reading and Critical Thinking Transparencies | Grammar Transparencies and Copymasters | Vocabulary Transparencies and Copymasters | Writing Transparencies and Copymasters | Communications Transparencies and Copymasters |
|---|---|---|---|---|
| • Venn Diagram T50 | • Daily Language SkillBuilder T21<br>• Adjective and Adverb Clauses C100 | • Denotation and Connotation C62 | • Effective Language T13<br>• Compare-Contrast C31 | • Evaluation Matrix: Film/Video T7<br>• Evaluating Roles in Groups T8<br>• Reading Aloud T11 |
| • Making Inferences T7 | • Daily Language SkillBuilder T21<br>• Agreement of Subject and Verb T47<br>• Sentence Fragments II C108<br>• Subject-Verb Agreement II C124 | • Word Origins C63 | • Critical Review C26<br>• Short Story C29 | • Interviewing T9<br>• Dramatic Reading T12<br>• Impromptu Speaking: Dialogue, Role-Play, Debate T13 |
| • Predicting Outcomes T2 | • Daily Language SkillBuilder T21<br>• Sentence Fragments T42<br>• Complete Sentences C73 | • Using Reference Materials C64 | • Persuasive Essay C27 | • Evaluation Matrix: Film/Video T7 |
|  | • Daily Language SkillBuilder T22<br>• Adverb Clauses: Subordinating Conjunctions C97<br>• Semicolons and Conjunctive Adverbs C157 | • Idioms C65 |  | • Impromptu Speaking: Dialogue, Role-Play, Debate T13 |
| • Visualizing T8 |  | • Word Origins C66 | • Compare-Contrast C31 | • Dramatic Reading T12<br>• Verbal Strategies T14 |
| • Making Judgments T5<br>• Compare and Contrast T15 | • Daily Language SkillBuilder T22<br>• Adverb Clauses with *Because* C99 | • Homonyms C67 | • Showing, Not Telling T22 | • Evaluating Roles in Groups T8<br>• Impromptu Speaking: Dialogue, Role-Play, Debate T13 |

## STUDENTS ACQUIRING ENGLISH

The **Spanish Study Guide,** pp. 175–196, includes language support for the following pages:
• Family and Community Involvement (per unit)
• Selection Summaries and Vocabulary
• Active Reading
• Literary Analysis

# RESOURCE MANAGEMENT GUIDE
## PART 2

To introduce the theme/literary period of this unit, use Fine Art Transparencies T29–31 in the Communications Transparencies and Copymasters.

| | Unit Resource Book | Assessment | Integrated Technology and Media | Additional Support — Literary Analysis Transparencies |
|---|---|---|---|---|
| **Chicago**<br>**Lucinda Matlock**<br>*pp. 824–829* | • Active Reading p. 28<br>• Literary Analysis p. 29 | • Selection Test, Formal Assessment pp. 151–152<br>🔘 Test Generator | 🎧 Audio Library | • Tone T19 |
| **Richard Cory**<br>**Miniver Cheevy**<br>*pp. 830–834* | • Active Reading p. 30<br>• Literary Analysis p. 31 | • Selection Test, Formal Assessment pp. 153–154<br>🔘 Test Generator | 🎧 Audio Library | • Characterization T6 |
| **We Wear the Mask**<br>*pp. 835–839* | • Active Reading p. 32<br>• Literary Analysis p. 33 | • Selection Test, Formal Assessment pp. 155–156<br>🔘 Test Generator | 🎧 Audio Library | • Tone T19 |
| **Winter Dreams**<br>*pp. 840–862* | • Summary p. 34<br>• Active Reading p. 35<br>• Literary Analysis p. 36<br>• Words to Know p. 37<br>• Selection Quiz p. 38 | • Selection Test, Formal Assessment pp. 157–158<br>🔘 Test Generator | 🎧 Audio Library | • Characterization T6 |
| **America and I**<br>*pp. 863–874* | • Summary p. 39<br>• Active Reading p. 40<br>• Literary Analysis p. 41<br>• Words to Know p. 42<br>• Selection Quiz p. 43 | • Selection Test, Formal Assessment pp. 159–160<br>🔘 Test Generator | 🎧 Audio Library | • Style, Voice T23 |
| **In the American Society**<br>**(1986)**<br>*pp. 877–893* | • Summary p. 44<br>• Active Reading p. 45<br>• Literary Analysis p. 46<br>• Words to Know p. 47<br>• Selection Quiz p. 48 | • Selection Test, Formal Assessment pp. 161–162<br>🔘 Test Generator | 🎧 Audio Library | • Character: Change and Motivation T7 |
| **Defining the Grateful**<br>**Gesture (1986)**<br>**Refugee Ship (1982)**<br>*pp. 894–899* | • Active Reading p. 49<br>• Literary Analysis p. 50<br>• Comparing Literature p. 51 | • Selection Test, Formal Assessment pp. 163–164<br>🔘 Test Generator | 🎧 Audio Library | |

## Writing Workshop: Comparison-and-Contrast Essay

| | | Unit Assessment | Unit Technology | |
|---|---|---|---|---|
| **Unit Five Resource Book**<br>• Prewriting p. 52<br>• Drafting and Elaboration p. 53<br>• Peer Response Guide pp. 54–55<br>• Revising, Editing, and Proofreading p. 56<br>• Student Models pp. 57–62<br>• Rubric for Evaluation p. 63 | 💿 **Power Presentations CD-ROM**<br>**Writing Transparencies and Copymasters** T11, T20, C30<br>**Teacher's Guide to Assessment and Portfolio Use** | • Unit Five, Part 2 Test, Formal Assessment pp. 165–166<br>🔘 Test Generator<br>• Unit Five Integrated Test, Integrated Assessment pp. 39–46 | ℹ️ ClassZone www.mcdougallittell.com<br>🔘 EasyPlanner CD-ROM<br>🔘 Electronic Library | |

| Reading and Critical Thinking Transparencies | Grammar Transparencies and Copymasters | Vocabulary Transparencies and Copymasters | Writing Transparencies and Copymasters | Communications Transparencies and Copymasters |
|---|---|---|---|---|
| • Reading for Details T16 | • Daily Language SkillBuilder T22<br>• Noun Clauses I C102 | • Denotation and Connotation C68 | • Compare-Contrast C32 | |
| • Compare and Contrast T15 | • Daily Language SkillBuilder T23<br>• Noun Clauses I C102 | • Idioms C69 | | • Appreciative Listening T2 |
| | • Daily Language SkillBuilder T23<br>• Appositive Clauses C105 | • The Connotative Power of Words C70 | | |
| • Evaluation Matrix T55 | • Daily Language SkillBuilder T23<br>• Noun Clauses II C103<br>• Semicolons C158 | • Meanings of Roots C71 | | |
| • Compare and Contrast T15 | • Daily Language SkillBuilder T24<br>• Noun Clauses: Common Introductory Words C104<br>• Commas: Introductory Words C153 | • Suffixes and Roots C72 | • Autobiographical Incident C35 | |
| • Making Inferences T7 | • Daily Language SkillBuilder T24<br>• Introductory Words for Noun Clauses—Who and Whom C106 | • Word History C73 | • Critical Review C26<br>• Persuasive Essay C27<br>• Compare-Contrast C31 | |
| • Drawing Conclusions T4<br>• Events and Consequences T57 | • Daily Language SkillBuilder T25<br>• Pronouns in Comparisons C126 | • Analogies C74 | • Interpretive Essay C36 | |

## STUDENTS ACQUIRING ENGLISH

The **Spanish Study Guide,** pp. 197–217, includes language support for the following pages:
• Family and Community Involvement (per unit)

• Selection Summaries and Vocabulary
• Active Reading
• Literary Analysis

| Selection | SkillBuilder Sentences | Suggested Answers |
|---|---|---|
| Selected Poems by Emily Dickinson | 1. Not all critics agrees about the interpretations of Emily Dickinsons poems; many of which are deceptively simple. | 1. Not all critics **agree** about the interpretations of Emily Dickinson**'s** poems, many of which are deceptively simple. |
| | 2. If she would of published them before she would of died, she might of been able to prevent the alterations to her poems. | 2. If she **had** published them before **she died**, she might **have** been able to prevent the alterations to her poems. |
| The Yellow Wallpaper | 1. Ben says hed like to live in the last century when the pace of life was more slow | 1. Ben says he'd like to **have lived** in the last century, when the pace of life was **slower than it is now.** |
| | 2. I think that in those day's life was to simple for women, they could'nt vote, they could'nt get jobs and there husbands treated them as children. | 2. I think that in those **days** life was **too** simple for women: they **couldn't** vote, they **couldn't** get jobs, and **their** husbands treated them **like** children. |
| The Story of an Hour | 1. Woman were supposed to be cared for by there husbands and in return they catered to they're husbands wishes. | 1. **Women** were supposed to be cared for by **their** husbands, and in return they catered to **their husbands'** wishes. |
| | 2. One student asked does the action take place in the time frame of a hour? | 2. One student asked, **"D**oes the action take place in the time frame of **an** hour?**"** |
| Seventeen Syllables | 1. In the story Rosie's mother and her friends write haiku looking for a creative outlet. | 1. In the story, Rosie's mother and her friends, **looking for a creative outlet**, write haiku. |
| | 2. Haiku poems, that were written in japanese, they have a diffrent number of syllables when their translated into english. | 2. Haiku poems that were written in **Japanese** have a **different** number of syllables when **they're** translated into **E**nglish. |

| Selection | SkillBuilder Sentences | Suggested Answers |
|---|---|---|
| I Stand Here Ironing | 1. I Stand Here Ironing is a story about how difficult it can be. Raising children alone. | 1. "I Stand Here Ironing" is a story about how difficult it can be **to raise** children alone. |
| | 2. Emily is a sad and lonely little girl; because of her mother does not give her enough attention. | 2. Emily is a sad and lonely little girl **because her** mother does not give her enough attention. |
| Chicago<br>Lucinda Matlock | 1. When I read two poems about a spacific time period i feel like I get a more better perspective on It. | 1. When I read two poems about a **specific** time period, **I feel as if** I get a **better** perspective on it. |
| | 2. Chicago in the early 1900s seem like a misrable place with their poverty hunger prostitution and back breaking labor. | 2. Chicago in the early 1900s **seems** like a **miserable** place, with **its** poverty, hunger, prostitution, and **back-breaking** labor. |
| Richard Cory<br>Miniver Cheevy | 1. Edwin Arlington Robinson growed up in Gardiner Maine. | 1. Edwin Arlington Robinson **grew** up in Gardiner, Maine. |
| | 2. Robinsons first collection The Torrent and The Night Before was suppose to be a surprise for his mother but she dyed a week before they were published. | 2. Robinson**'s** first collection, <u>**The Torrent and The Night Before**</u>, was **supposed** to be a surprise for his mother, but she **died** a week before **it was** published. |
| We Wear the Mask<br>Sympathy | 1. Have you read any've Dunbar novels or short stories. | 1. Have you read **any of** Dunbar**'s** novels or short stories**?** |
| | 2. African Americans where not treated respectfuly in the nineteen century. | 2. African Americans **were** not treated **respectfully i**n the **nineteenth** century. |

| Selection | SkillBuilder Sentences | Suggested Answers |
|---|---|---|
| Winter Dreams | 1. Dexter did'nt care for Spring but he loved the Fall. | 1. Dexter **didn't** care for **s**pring, but he loved the **f**all. |
| | 2. When dexter was twenty four he returned from New York. | 2. When **D**exter was **twenty-four,** he returned from New York. |
| America and I | 1. Immigrants often worked in sweetshops where the conditions were real dangerous. | 1. Immigrants often worked in **sweatshops** where the conditions were **really** dangerous. |
| | 2. Between 1870 and 1920, aproximately 20 million people came to america and looking for a better lives. | 2. Between 1870 and 1920, approximately 20 million people came to **A**merica looking for a better **life**. |
| In the American Society | 1. The Changs are an immagrent family who owns a pancake house from China. | 1. The Changs are an **immigrant** family **from China** who **own** a pancake house. |
| | 2. Callie the narrator is also Monas oldest sister. | 2. Callie, the narrator, is also Mona**'s older** sister. |
| Defining the Grateful Gesture Refugee Ship | 1. Us Americans should apreciate the ethnic diversity of our country, Americans have many diffrent customs and storys to share. | 1. **We** Americans should **appreciate** the ethnic diversity of our country. Americans have many **different** customs and **stories** to share. |

| Grammar Focus by Unit | Unit One | Unit Two | Unit Three | Unit Four | Unit Five | Unit Six | Unit Seven |
|---|---|---|---|---|---|---|---|
| | Parts of a Sentence | Verbs | Phrases | Clauses, Part I | Clauses, Part II | Special Sentence Structures, Part I | Special Sentence Structures, Part II |

*The Language of Literature* offers several options for integrating grammar instruction and literature.

- Each literature unit has a grammar focus. The Teacher's Edition includes Mini Lessons for each selection that help develop the grammar focus for the unit and spring from the content of the specific literature.

- The Pupil Edition includes several full-page lessons on Sentence Crafting. These lessons are related to both the literature and the grammar focus for the unit and help students use grammar in their own writing.

- Daily Language SkillBuilders in the Teacher's Edition provide students with ongoing proofreading practice and reinforce punctuation, spelling, grammar and usage, and capitalization.

- Grammar Copymasters and Transparencies, which may be used to complement or extend lessons in the Teacher's Edition, present grammar in a traditional, systematic sequence. References to appropriate copymasters or transparencies are included at point of use in the Teacher's Edition Mini Lessons.

TE Mini Lessons shown in green
PE instruction shown in black

## Part 1

**Parts of the Sentence**
**Complete Sentences**
"The Story of an Hour," p. 787

**Using Clauses**
**Adjective Clauses**
Dickinson poems, p. 757
**Adverb Clauses**
Dickinson poems, p. 757
"Seventeen Syllables," p. 792
"Adolescence—III," p. 805
**Adverbial Clauses: *because***
"I Stand Here Ironing," p. 816
**Sentence Fragments**
"The Yellow Wallpaper," pp. 780–781

**Subject-Verb Agreement**
"The Yellow Wallpaper," p. 769

**Other Punctuation**
**Semicolons: Independent Clauses Joined by Conjunctive Adverb or Transitional Expression**
"Seventeen Syllables," p. 801

## Part 2

**Using Clauses**
**Noun Clauses**
"Chicago," "Lucinda Matlock," p. 829
"Richard Cory," "Miniver Cheevy," p. 834
"Winter Dreams," p. 862
"In the American Society," p. 884
Sentence Crafting, p. 909
**Noun Clauses: Appositive Clauses**
"We Wear the Mask," "Sympathy," p. 839
**Noun Clauses: Common Introductory Words**
"America and I," p. 874
Sentence Crafting, p. 909
**Noun Clauses: *who* and *whom***
Sentence Crafting, p. 909
**Run-on Sentences**
Writing Workshop, p. 907

**Using Modifiers**
**Modifiers: Positive, Comparative, and Superlative Degrees**
Writing Workshop, p. 907
**Modifiers: Illogical Comparisons *than, as***
"Defining the Grateful Gesture," "Refugee Ship," p. 899

**Capitalization**
**Capitalizing Proper Nouns and Proper Adjectives**
Writing Workshop, p. 907

**End Marks and Commas**
**Commas After Introductory Words: *next, yes, no***
"America and I," p. 866

**Other Punctuation**
**Semicolons: Independent Clauses Joined by Conjunctive Adverb or Transitional Expression**
"Winter Dreams," p. 846

**Style**
**Parallel Series**
Writing Workshop, p. 907

This time line shows major dates and events in America and the world from the mid-1850s to 1925. Help students recognize that this period of seventy years was characterized worldwide by technological advances, the changing roles of women in society, and issues relating to immigration.

# THE CHANGING FACE OF AMERICA

## EVENTS IN AMERICAN LITERATURE

| 1855 | 1867 | 1879 |
|---|---|---|
| **A** **1856** *New York Tribune* publishes letters by Margaret Fuller about her travels in Europe, making her America's first woman foreign correspondent<br><br>**1862** Emily Dickinson writes 366 poems within the year | **1869** Louisa May Alcott completes writing of *Little Women* **D**<br><br>**1870** Bret Harte publishes story collection *The Luck of Roaring Camp, and Other Sketches* | **1883** Emma Lazarus writes sonnet "The New Colossus," dedicated to Statue of Liberty<br><br>**1890** Charlotte Perkins Gilman writes "The Yellow Wallpaper," which describes the emotional and intellectual decline of a young wife and mother |

### Literature: 1862

**A** By the time she was thirty years old, Emily Dickinson (1830–1886) had become almost a total recluse. She never left her father's house and garden, dressed only in white, and received few visitors. Her creative output, however, was remarkable. She wrote more than a thousand poems, of which only seven were published during her lifetime.

## EVENTS IN THE UNITED STATES

| 1855 | | 1879 |
|---|---|---|
| **B** **1857** Elizabeth Blackwell establishes New York Infirmary for women and children, the first medical clinic of its kind | **1870** John D. Rockefeller founds Standard Oil Company<br><br>**1872** Susan B. Anthony is arrested and fined for leading a group of women to test their right to vote<br><br>**1876** Alexander Graham Bell patents first telephone | **1879** Thomas Edison invents first practical light bulb<br><br>**1882** Congress passes Chinese Exclusion Act, suspending Chinese immigration for ten years<br><br>**1883** First metal-framed skyscraper, ten stories high, is built in Chicago<br><br>**1886** Statue of Liberty is dedicated in New York Harbor; trade unionists organize American Federation of Labor (AFL) |

### United States: 1857

**B** Although at first no medical school would admit her, Elizabeth Blackwell (1821–1910) was determined to become a doctor. Finally a medical school in Geneva, New York, relented and allowed her to attend classes. The decision inspired a storm of protest, but Blackwell persevered and graduated at the head of her class in 1849, thus becoming the first woman to receive a medical degree in the United States.

## EVENTS IN THE WORLD

| 1855 | 1867 | 1879 |
|---|---|---|
| **C** **1855** Florence Nightingale, British nurse, introduces hygienic standards into military hospitals during Crimean War<br><br>**1856** Two states of Australia introduce modern secret-voting procedure known as Australian ballot | **1868** Remains of Cro-Magnon man discovered in Europe **E**<br><br>**1870** After a troubled reign, Queen Isabella II of Spain abdicates throne in favor of her son, Alfonso XII | **1885** Karl Benz of Germany builds single-cylinder engine for motor car |

### World: 1855

**C** When Florence Nightingale (1820–1910), the founder of trained nursing as a profession for women, first arrived at the military hospitals in Turkey with her unit of 38 nurses, she encountered unspeakable conditions and hostility from the doctors. She and her nurses were initially forbidden to enter the wards, and they battled against rats and fleas in their own quarters. When the nurses were finally allowed to do their jobs, Florence Nightingale earned the title "Lady with the Lamp" because of her habit of prowling the wards at night to check on the wounded men.

**740** UNIT FIVE THE CHANGING FACE OF AMERICA (1855–1925)

### Literature: 1883

**D** Construction work began on the Statue of Liberty in France in 1875. Americans were to pay for the cost of the pedestal on which the statue would stand. To help raise this money, Lazarus wrote a poem "The New Colossus," the last five lines of which ("'Give me your tired, your poor/Your huddled masses . . .'") are inscribed on a bronze plaque found inside the pedestal.

### World: 1885

**E** Benz (1844–1929) is credited with building the first practical motor car, the *Motorwagen*. It had three wheels, but the rest of the vehicle had features still in use today: electric ignition, differential gears, and a water-cooled engine. His company made its first four-wheeled vehicle in 1893, and the Benz name survives today as part of Mercedes Benz.

## PERIOD PIECES

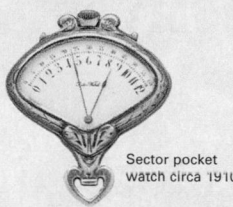

Sector pocket watch circa 1910

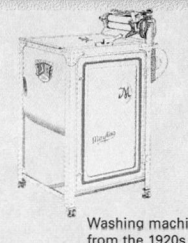

Washing machine from the 1920s

Charlie Chaplin popularizes silent movies.

**F**

---

**1891**      **1903**      **1915**

**1893** Paul Laurence Dunbar publishes first volume of poetry, *Oak and Ivy,* while working as elevator operator

**1897** Edward Arlington Robinson publishes "Richard Cory"

**1898** Henry James publishes *The Turn of the Screw*

**1899** Kate Chopin publishes her novel, *The Awakening*

**1911** Edith Wharton publishes the tragic novel *Ethan Frome*

**1914** Carl Sandburg writes the poem "Chicago," an energetic celebration of life early in the 20th century

**1915** Edgar Lee Masters writes "Lucinda Matlock," part of *Spoon River Anthology*

**1922** F. Scott Fitzgerald publishes short story "Winter Dreams"

**1925** Eugene O'Neill publishes *Desire Under the Elms,* a play based on a Greek tragedy that explores family conflicts

---

**1891**      **1903**      **1915**

**1892** Ellis Island in New York Harbor **G** becomes chief U.S. immigration station

**1898** Spanish-American War begins in the Caribbean

**1901** President McKinley is assassinated

**1903** Near Kitty Hawk, North Carolina, Orville and Wilbur Wright make first flight in engine-powered airplane

**1907** Japan limits emigration to U.S. in response to hostility toward Japanese laborers

**1913** Ford Motor Company puts first moving assembly line into place and is soon producing 1,000 Model T automobiles a day

**1920** Congress passes 19th Amendment, giving women right to vote

**1924** Ending centuries of nearly open admissions, Congress passes Immigration Act of 1924 that limits number of immigrants from outside of Western Hemisphere

---

**1891**      **1903**      **1915**

**1893** New Zealand becomes first country to grant women suffrage

**1896** Italian physicist Guglielmo Marconi creates first radio

**1898** Pierre and Marie Curie discover radium and polonium

**1901** After 64 years as ruler of Great Britain, Queen Victoria dies

**1903** Emmeline Pankhurst founds **H** Women's Social and Political Union in England to further woman suffrage

**1912** "Unsinkable" English ship *Titanic* sinks on maiden voyage, **I** killing 1,513; African National Congress formed in South Africa

**1914** World War I breaks out in Europe

**1915** Albert Einstein postulates **J** general theory of relativity

**1918** Women aged 30 and over gain suffrage in England

**1919** Gandhi becomes leader of Indian independence movement

TIME LINE    **741**

---

## PERIOD PIECES

**F** A sector-shaped pocket watch tells time in an arc, not a circle. This distinctive shape makes the time easy to see and the watch easy to handle.

### United States: 1892

**G** Named for its original owner—Samuel Ellis, an 18th-century farmer—Ellis Island closed in 1954. It reopened in 1990 as the Ellis Island Immigration Museum, part of the Statue of Liberty National Monument, which it is near.

### World: 1903

**H** Nearly a decade later, the WSPU, frustrated in attempts to secure voting rights for women, adopted militant tactics. Activists such as Emmeline Pankhurst were put in jail, where they went on hunger strikes. In 1913 the government passed the so-called "Cat and Mouse" Act, under which prisoners whose health was in danger because of hunger strikes were released and then rearrested when their health improved. Pankhurst was arrested 12 times in 1913 under this act.

### World: 1912

**I** The *Titanic* sinking is the ultimate ship disaster in the minds of nearly all Americans. However, the United States had its own incredible ship disaster, with a loss of life even greater than that of the *Titanic.* In 1865, within hours of John Wilkes Booth's being shot to death as Lincoln's assassin, the *Sultana,* a Mississippi River paddle steamer scandalously overcrowded with 2,400 Union soldiers returning north after the recently ended Civil War, exploded near Memphis and nearly 1,700 men lost their lives. A lack of publicity at the time, due to the assassination coverage, explains why the disaster never entered the consciousness of most Americans.

### World: 1915

**J** Einstein developed two theories of relativity. His 1905 special theory of relativity, among other things, showed that nothing can move faster than the speed of light and introduced the famous $E=mc^2$ energy-and-mass formula. His 1915 general theory of relativity concerned gravity and included the idea that any light, say of a star, that passes near the sun on its way to Earth is bent due to the sun's gravitational pull. These theories altered notions of the interrelationships of space, time, motion, mass, and gravitation.

#### OVERVIEW

## Introduction
This article places the selections in Part 1 of this unit in historical context by providing students with an overview of the women's movement of the 19th and 20th centuries. An **Author Study** of Emily Dickinson offers details of the first major American woman poet. The **Traditions Across Time** section updates the progress of the emancipation of women as reflected in the writings of a diversity of authors. The selection quoted in **Voices from the Times** gives insight into one of the issues involved in the women's fight for equality and rights. This article will enable students to interpret the possible influences of historical contexts on the literary works in this unit.

## Teaching Nonfiction

### Reading Skills and Strategies
### ESTABLISHING A PURPOSE FOR READING
Explain to students that this article will introduce them to the issue of women's rights and the role of literature in the women's rights movement of the late 19th and 20th centuries. Students should read to understand the complexities of the movement and learn about the major literary figures of the time.

### NOTETAKING
Encourage students to note unfamiliar words as they read this article. Students are expected to use reference material such as glossaries, dictionaries, and available technology to determine precise usages and definitions.

### DRAWING CONCLUSIONS
This article provides some indication of women's expectations and their acceptable role in 19th-century American society. Using the information provided, students are expected to draw conclusions about the lives that women led during this time and support these conclusions with textual evidence and experience.

# Women's Voices, Women's Lives

## A New Literature

"*The* power of a woman is in her refinement, gentleness and elegance; it is she who makes etiquette, and it is she who preserves the order and decency of society. Without women, men soon resume the savage state, and the comfort and the graces of the home are exchanged for the misery of the mining camp." So said a popular book of etiquette in 1880, voicing a widely

held notion about women's place in society. At the same time, however, the movement to give women the right to vote was reemerging after a period of inactivity in the years following the Civil War. Both before and after the war, however, the woman's suffrage movement was only the most public aspect of a growing force for women to have a voice in both politics and literature. Sojourner Truth's eloquent speech articulating the realities of women's lives, delivered at one women's rights convention (see Voices from the Times), resonated in the hearts of many 19th-century women.

**A**

One important factor in the growth of the women's movement was the spread of university education among women of the era, although popular newspapers of the time trumpeted the dangers: "Are We Destroying Woman's Beauty? The Startling Warning of a Great English Physician Against Higher Education of Women. How Intellectual Work Destroys Beauty" proclaimed a *New York Journal* headline in 1896.

**B**

**C**

A suffragist struggles with police in 1913 (above) and suffragists argue for the vote before a congressional committee in 1871 (below).

Emily Dickinson

The 1890s also saw the emergence of the poetry of Emily Dickinson—the first major American woman poet—although emergence may not be the right word to apply to a body of work that has become widely known only in the last 40 years. A near contemporary of Walt Whitman, and just as important in the development of a uniquely American literary voice, Dickinson was virtually unknown during her lifetime. Her anonymity was due in large part to the difficulties she would have experienced in trying to overcome prevailing attitudes about a woman's proper place. When Dickinson's sister published a collection of her poetry in 1890, after Dickinson's death, most critical reviews were negative, objecting especially to what was considered an odd poetic style, with its unusual imagery, untraditional meters, inexact rhymes, and grammatical errors. Nonetheless, a century later, Dickinson looms as one of our most important poets, not only of her time but of any time.

Around the same time, Charlotte Perkins Gilman—related on her father's side to a noted family of writers and social reformers that included Harriet Beecher Stowe, the author of *Uncle Tom's Cabin*—became one of the most noted advocates for women. Fleeing her own repressive marriage, she moved from the East Coast to California, where she wrote and spoke out on behalf of women's rights and against male domination.

Harriet Beecher Stowe

Kate Chopin's fiction articulates the frustrations of generations of women that were confined to a sort of extended childhood by the men in their lives. Her gentle stories depicting some of the most obvious of women's difficulties were extremely popular in the 1890s. Her 1899 novel *The Awakening*, however, stepped over the line in its portrayal of a woman's hidden passion, arousing a public protest so vigorous that Chopin ceased writing completely.

## Making Connections

### History

**A** In 1827 New York state abolished slavery, and Isabella Baumfree was one of the persons freed. Then, citing a vision prompting her to travel widely and preach God's message of love and brotherhood, Isabella left New York in 1843, changed her name to Sojourner Truth, and began lecturing widely. She was in the Midwest for the years 1850–1851, where she drew large crowds. In addition to speaking for abolitionist causes, she often appeared at suffrage gatherings. She raised money for her travels by dictating her life story to a printer and selling the pamphlet for 25¢.

### Education

**B** In 1870 Boston evangelist Henry Fowle Durant proposed an education for women equivalent to that offered to men. He founded Wellesley Female Seminary, which in 1875 became Wellesley College, a private institution for women. Today Wellesley's average enrollment is 2,200.

### History

**C** In spite of headlines such as these, there were female pioneers in academia. One example is Maria Mitchell (1818–1889), who became the first woman elected to the American Academy of Arts and Sciences. She taught astronomy at Vassar College after 1865 and was a leader in the daily photography of sunspots, one of her special areas of interest.

### Literature

**D** Thomas Wentworth Higginson reviewed Dickinson's work early in her career and pronounced her a "wholly new and original poetic genius." However, he felt that her poems were "odd . . . too delicate—not strong enough to publish."

### Literature

**E** Kate Chopin was particularly stung by criticism of her novel in her St. Louis hometown. Nearly all newspaper reviews were negative ("too strong for moral babes, and should be labeled 'poison.'"), some magazines refused to review it, St. Louis's libraries banned it, and the St. Louis Fine Arts Club refused to grant her a membership. It took more than 60 years for St. Louis's Mercantile Library, the oldest library west of the Mississippi, to put a copy of *The Awakening* on its shelves.

Have students identify the main idea of each paragraph in this article and note whether it is stated in a topic sentence or implied by details within the paragraph. Have students produce a summary of the article by tracing the development of the main ideas.

**DISCUSSING**

Allow students time to discuss this article as a class. Begin the discussion by asking specific questions to which students are expected to use elements of the text to clarify and defend their responses.

---

$V$oices
_from the_ $T$IMES

borne thirteen children, and seen most all sold off to slavery, and when I cried out with my mother's grief, none but Jesus heard me! And ain't I a woman?

Then they talk about this thing in the head; what's this they call it? ["Intellect," someone whispers.] That's it, honey. What's that got to do with women's rights or Negroes' rights? If my cup won't hold but a pint, and yours holds a quart, wouldn't you be mean not to let me have my little half-measure full?

Then that little man in black there, he says women can't have as much rights as men, 'cause Christ wasn't a woman! Where did your Christ come from? From God and a woman! Man had nothing to do with Him.

If the first woman God ever made was strong enough to turn the world upside down all alone, these women together ought to be able to turn it back, and get it right side up again! And now they is asking to do it, the men better let them.

Obliged to you for hearing me, and now old Sojourner hasn't got nothing more to say.

Sojourner Truth

---

## Traditions Across Time: A Diversity of Voices

In 1920 the 19th Amendment to the Constitution gave women the right to vote, but suffrage heralded no great revolution. Women did not unite at the polls to gain reforms for themselves; instead, many voted like their fathers or husbands or didn't vote at all. This political failure combined with the cultural changes rocking the 1920s—the rise of advertising, Hollywood glamour, and the flapper image of woman —to further inhibit women's intellectual and literary development. The playwright Lillian Hellman, one of the few American women writing successfully in the 1930s and 1940s, summed up her generation this way: "By the time I grew up, the fight for the emancipation of women, their rights under the law, in the office, in bed, was stale stuff. My generation didn't think much about the place or the problems of women."

Only after the eruption of the feminist movement in the late 1960s were large numbers of women again inspired to examine the quality of their lives and find voices of their own. With the renewed confidence of women came a desire to rediscover female writers of the more recent past. Hence Hisaye Yamamoto's "Seventeen Syllables" and Tillie Olsen's "I Stand Here Ironing"—both stories about women struggling with oppressive conditions—are more popular today than when they were written.

The legacy of 19th-century women writers lives on in the richness and diversity of contemporary women's writing. Women of all ages and ethnic groups are writing today, giving voice to a multitude of experiences and concerns. Julia Alvarez's poem "Ironing Their Clothes" expresses loving feelings associated with a household chore, while Rita Dove's poem "Adolescence—III" portrays a young girl on the verge of becoming a woman.

---

**VOICES FROM THE TIMES**

**Ask: What elements of Sojourner Truth's argument make it convincing?**

**Possible Responses:** It is based on personal experience; her speech is simple and her points are basic; she uses easily understandable images and allegories to make her point.

**Ask: How does Sojourner Truth rebut the argument that women need protection?**

**Possible Responses:** She points out several examples of the self-sufficient strength of women, especially black women, and their importance to the origin of Christ and humankind.

## A New Literature

745

## OVERVIEW

### Objectives
- appreciate the work of one of America's great poets
- interpret life in nineteenth-century America through the lens of her writing
- learn about Emily Dickinson's life by reading nonfiction

The Author Study offers students the opportunity to focus on the works of a major American poet. Students can learn about Emily Dickinson's life, helping them to interpret her poetry and place it in a historical context.

### Preview
Have students preview the article noting the basic text organizers: title, subheads, images and captions, and time line. Ask students to describe the information they would expect to locate in each section. Have students use the subheads to create an outline or a graphic organizer. As they read, have them categorize information from the article under the appropriate heading. Remind students that when they do independent research, they should also use text organizers to categorize information.

# Author Study
# Emily Dickinson

1830–1886

## OVERVIEW

*"If I read a book [and] it makes my whole body so cold no fire ever can warm me I know that is poetry."*

—Emily Dickinson

## A Life of Insight and Isolation

*Although she chose to withdraw from society, Emily Dickinson became one of the most prominent American poets. Her contribution of 1,775 poems was virtually unknown during her lifetime, which was partly due to her anonymity. She once wrote, "Publication—is the Auction / Of the Mind of Man—" and later asked that all her poems be burned upon her death. This startlingly innovative poet left the world pondering her untold secrets. As you read this Author Study, discover the fully realized life that Emily Dickinson's poetry reveals.*

**A** **"THE FAIREST HOME I EVER KNEW"** Emily Dickinson was born on December 10, 1830, in Amherst, Massachusetts. She spent her entire life in this small New England farming community, taking fewer than a dozen extended trips away from home. As a young girl, she enjoyed exploring the countryside, playing the piano, singing, and attending social gatherings with friends and relatives.

The center of Dickinson's existence was her family. Her father, Edward, was a prominent businessman and lawyer.

| 1830 Is born Dec. 10 in Amherst, Massachusetts | 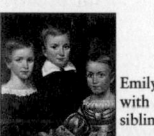 Emily with siblings | 1840 Enters Amherst Academy | 1847 Attends Mount Holyoke Female Seminary |  |
|---|---|---|---|---|

HER LIFE
HER TIMES

**1830** — **1840** — **1850**

| 1841 Utopian community Brook Farm is founded in Massachusetts. | 1845 Henry David Thoreau lives at Walden Pond. | 1848 Seneca Falls women's rights convention is held. |

746

Although he was stern and aloof, Dickinson greatly admired his "pure and terrible" heart. On the other hand, she criticized her mother, Emily Norcross Dickinson, and once bitterly observed that she never had a mother. Dickinson and her mother developed a more intimate relationship after Mrs. Dickinson suffered a paralyzing stroke.

Dickinson felt particularly close to her older brother, Austin, and her younger sister, Lavinia, or Vinnie. With Austin, who moved next door after his marriage, she shared a quick-witted sense of humor and a passion for learning. Like Emily, Vinnie remained unmarried and helped run the household. Devoted and loyal, Vinnie shared her sister's secrets and protected her privacy.

"SUCH ARE THE INLETS OF THE MIND" Dickinson's father frowned on books that might "joggle" his daughter's mind, but he encouraged her education. She attended Amherst Academy and then enrolled at Mount Holyoke Female Seminary in nearby South Hadley when she was 16.

While she was still a student, Dickinson experienced a religious crisis. Pressured to join a church, she wrestled with doubt.

Dickinson's home in Amherst, Massachusetts

## LITERARY Contributions

Emily Dickinson chose privacy over fame. During her lifetime she consented to one or two publications of her poems—others were published without her permission. It wasn't until after her death that numerous collections of her poems were published. The genius of her poetry—her innovative style, verbal precision, and sharp observations—has influenced generations of poets and delighted generations of readers.

**A Unique Voice** In 1890, the book *Poems by Emily Dickinson* was edited by Mabel Loomis Todd and T. W. Higginson. This first collection of Dickinson's poems was altered to make the poems, which the editors thought "too crude in form," more presentable.

**The Authoritative Version** Dickinson's talent was not widely recognized until a complete, unaltered edition of her poetry was published in 1955. Edited by Thomas H. Johnson, *The Poems of Emily Dickinson, Including Variant Readings Critically Compared With All Known Manuscripts* was the first book to eliminate the tamperings of earlier editors.

**Avid Correspondent** Dickinson wrote more than 1,000 letters to family and friends, which illustrate her original style and reveal the richness of her day-to-day life. *The Letters of Emily Dickinson,* edited by Thomas H. Johnson and Theodora Ward, appeared in 1958.

## LIFE AND TIMES

### History
**A** The small farming town of Amherst, settled in 1703 in west-central Massachusetts, held tenaciously to its Puritan past and the beliefs of the Founding Fathers in the years before the Civil War. Dickinson's grandfather helped establish local Amherst College, whose purpose was to train missionaries and reinforce Puritan values at a time when they seemed to be fading away. The founders of the college deliberately tried to recreate the religious fervor of John Winthrop and his generation.

### Literature
**B** Emily Dickinson maintained a complicated, idealized relationship with her father. Absent from home for much of her early life, he seemed to pay little attention to her when he was present. However, she remained devoted to him and idealized him in her poetry and writing. She portrayed him as a heroic figure, superior to others—images that do not fit with what we know about him from other sources.

### More About Dickinson
**C** Dickinson was obsessed with home. She declared it the "definition of God." Except for the years 1840–1855, when she lived nearby, Dickinson spent her entire life in the house in which she was born. Townspeople found the family strange, and gossip centered on Emily, considered "the climax of all the family oddity." Except for spending part of 1864–1865 in Boston for eye treatments, Dickinson, who by 1870 dressed only in white, is not known to have left her house the last 30 years of her life.

### Religion
**D** Because of her deep religious skepticism, Dickinson is not considered a religious poet. Yet religion formed a major theme in her poetry and played a significant role early in her life, when, according to one writer, she was "terrorized by old-fashioned sermons about damnation." Later she pulled away from religion, and her poetry expresses both her ambiguity about religion and her guilt over her inability to conform to the revival mania that gripped her family and friends.

| 1852 First poem is published in Springfield *Daily Republican* | | 1861 "I taste a liquor never brewed—" published | 1862 Begins correspondence with Thomas W. Higginson | 1864–1865 Visits Boston twice for eye treatments | |
|---|---|---|---|---|---|
| **1860** | | | | **1870** | |
| 1855 Walt Whitman publishes *Leaves of Grass.* | 1857 R. W. Emerson lectures at Amherst, visits Austin Dickinson. | 1860 Abraham Lincoln is elected president. | 1861 U.S. Civil War begins. | 1865 Thirteenth Amendment to U.S. Constitution abolishes slavery. | |

## Literature

**A** Seventy years after Emily Dickinson's death, the complete and accurate collection of her works was published. The task of dating the poems was daunting, since Dickinson left little evidence about her methods of writing. Poems she included with letters could be dated, but the dates of poems scribbled on recipes and the backs of old envelopes had to be determined by Dickinson's handwriting, which seemed to vary from year to year and could be matched with dated correspondence.

## American Culture

**B** The Victorian culture of nineteenth-century America encouraged contemplation of death, eternity and the "crossover" of the soul from earth to eternity. Daguerreotype impressions were often taken of the newly deceased and kept as mementos by grieving families. As her best friend died at fourteen, Emily was allowed to watch over her in her last hours—an experience that haunted her emotionally and spiritually. Dickinson's poetry and correspondence reveal her subsequent fascination with death and dying and the fate of the soul.

## Dickinson's Lifestyle

**C** Scholars have offered many reasons for Emily Dickinson's retreat into a life of seclusion. Her sister-in-law spread the story that Emily was heartbroken over her relationship with Charles Wadsworth, but historians feel that this is an inadequate and perhaps diversionary explanation. Other explanations have been suggested, including agoraphobia, a need to please her father, anorexia, and her creation of a private religion. Emily's sister Lavinia maintained that the seclusion "just happened" and was simply a choice that Emily made—an explanation that many regard as the most logical, although it seems too simplistic to contain the full story.

By her late 20s, she stopped attending church services altogether. Many of her poems reflect the conflict she experienced between her own convictions and those that surrounded her.

After one year at Mount Holyoke, Dickinson returned home. Although her formal schooling had ended, she continued to educate herself. During her late teens or early 20s, Dickinson found her calling—she began to write poetry. While doing household chores, she jotted down **A** her thoughts on scraps of paper, old recipes, and the backs of envelopes. She wrote late at night by **B** candlelight. Inspired by intense sufferings of loss, loneliness, and death, she composed a remarkable number of short, profound, gemlike poems.

### "THE SOUL SELECTS HER OWN SOCIETY"

The year 1862 marked a turning point in Dickinson's life. That year the Reverend Charles Wadsworth—an older, married man whom Dickinson admired and reportedly loved—took a position in California. In the same year, she wrote 366 poems. Perhaps as a consequence of grief over lost love or as a result of a new-found focus on her writing, Dickinson, now in her 30s, gradually withdrew from the world.

**C** By the time she reached middle age, Dickinson rarely ventured beyond her house and garden. Still, she maintained contact with **D** friends and family by means of a prolific correspondence. Furthermore, the self-imposed isolation did not prohibit her from forming an alliance with the neighborhood children. It was typical of her to lower, by a cord, small baskets of baked goods and fruit from her bedroom window.

### "THIS IS MY LETTER TO THE WORLD"

After living in seclusion for almost 20 years, Dickinson fell ill in 1884. She suffered from Bright's disease, a gradual failure of the kidneys, and died on May 15, 1886. A short time later Vinnie carried out her sister's wishes and burned nearly all of her correspondence from family and friends. Fortunately, Vinnie rescued a box full of poems bound neatly into homemade booklets that Emily had stored.

Of the 1,775 poems Dickinson wrote, only seven were published, anonymously, while she was alive. As a result of Vinnie's persistence, the first volume of Dickinson's poetry was published four years after her death. Even though she was reclusive, her poems, according to the 20th-century American poet Allen Tate, reveal a life that was "one of the richest and deepest ever lived on this continent."

 **More Online: Author Link**
www.mcdougallittell.com

**1874** Her father dies in Boston. In 1875, her mother dies. | Edward Dickinson

**1883** Her favorite nephew, Gilbert, dies of typhoid.

**1884** Suffers first attack of kidney disease

**1886** Dies in Amherst on May 15

**1890** Poems are published by Emily's sister

 Lavinia Dickinson

**1880**

**1890**

**1876** Alexander Graham Bell invents the telephone.

**1879** Edison invents the light bulb.

**1887** Interstate Commerce Act is passed.

## 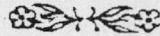 Dickinson's Legacy Today

The life of Emily Dickinson inspired several contemporary playwrights. *Alison's House* (1931), a Pulitzer Prize-winning play by Susan Glaspell, explores what happens to a poet's unpublished poems when her family discovers them after her death. William Luce's two-act play based on Dickinson's life, *The Belle of Amherst,* opened on Broadway on April 28, 1976. In the 1980 film version of the play, Julie Harris re-created the starring role that had earned her a Tony Award.

The following is a dramatization from *The Belle of Amherst* that captures Emily's thoughts and feelings about her neighbors, particularly Henrietta Sweetser:

> *Here in Amherst, I'm known as Squire Edward Dickinson's half-cracked daughter. Well, I am! The neighbors can't figure me out. I don't cross my father's ground to any house or town. I haven't left the house for years.*
>
> *The Soul selects her own society—then—shuts the door.*
>
> *Why should I socialize with village gossips?* (Emily turns to the window. . . .)
>
> *There goes one of them now—Henrietta Sweetser—everyone knows Henny. Look at her! She's strolling by the house, trying to catch a glimpse of me. Would you like that?*
>
> *So I give them something to talk about. I dress in white all year round, even in winter. "Bridal white," Henny calls it.*
>
> (She mimics back-fence gossips.)
>
> *"Dear, dear? Dresses in bridal white, she does, every day of the blessed year. Year in, year out. Disappointed in love as a girl, so I hear. Poor creature. All so very sad. And her sister, Lavinia, a spinster too. Didn't you know? Oh, yes. Stayed unmarried just to be at home and take care of Miss Emily. Two old maids in that big house. What a lonely life, to shut yourself away from good people like us."*
>
> *Indeed!*

Julie Harris as Emily Dickinson in *The Belle of Amherst*

### Literature

**D** Despite her seclusion, Dickinson maintained friendships with several leading literary figures. One of them was Helen Hunt Jackson (1830–1885), a childhood friend of Dickinson's from Amherst and one of those who actively urged Dickinson to publish. Jackson, an activist for the cause of Native Americans, published the novel *Ramona* in 1884 to bring awareness to the situation of Native Americans living on missions in California. An earlier novel, *Mercy Philbrick's Choice* (1876), is assumed to be a fictionalized account of Emily Dickinson's life.

### More About Dickinson

**E** When Emily Dickinson died at fifty-five, she had lived as a recluse for a quarter of a century. Few of her friends had seen her since she was thirty years old. She maintained her seclusion during her final illness. Even her personal physician was forced to diagnose her condition by watching her walk—fully dressed and with her face averted in shadows—past an open doorway. He was not allowed any closer.

### Music

**F** Dickinson's legacy is felt strongly in music. As early as 1896, a composer set one of her poems to music. Since then her poetry has served as inspiration for numerous song cycles, cantatas, and even a few operas. Of American writers, perhaps only the poetry of Whitman has inspired more musical settings than Dickinson's. The most performed of these works is Aaron Copland's *Twelve Poems of Emily Dickinson* for Soprano and Piano (1949–1950).

# OVERVIEW

Several poems from this lesson are included in the **Grade 11 InterActive Reader.**

## Objectives

1. understand and appreciate representative **poems** by Emily Dickinson (**Literary Analysis**)
2. identify and appreciate **figurative language** (**Literary Analysis**)
3. apply **strategies for reading poetry** (**Active Reading**)

## Summary

This sample of Emily Dickinson's work includes eight poems and a letter to Thomas Wentworth Higginson. "This is my letter to the World" expresses Dickinson's hope that her readers will judge her tenderly. "'Hope' is the thing with feathers" compares hope to a bird that continues to sing through the storms of life. "Success is counted sweetest" conveys the idea that success is truly understood only by the defeated. "Much Madness is divinest Sense" offers paradoxical definitions of madness and sanity that counter conventional views. In "My life closed twice," the speaker reflects on two overwhelming events that afforded some idea of heaven and a taste of hell. "After great pain, a formal feeling comes" depicts the numbing effect of intense grief. The last two poems examine death from a first-person perspective. "I heard a Fly buzz when I died" shows the speaker looking back at the moment of death. The last poem personifies death as a refined gentleman who escorts the speaker on a carriage ride into eternity.

## Thematic Link

From the perspective of her contemporaries, Emily Dickinson probably would have been seen as a very unlikely pioneer of a new literature. Her preference for a reclusive, genteel New England life, similar in its domestic routines to so many other women's lives at that time, belied the intense creative fervor of her inner life.

### 5-Minute Warm-Up

***Daily Language SkillBuilder***

Have students **proofread** the display sentences on page 739i and write them correctly. The sentences also appear on Transparency 21 of **Grammar Transparencies and Copymasters.**

---

# *Selected poems by* **Emily Dickinson**

## ( Connect to Your Life )

**Poetic Subjects** Emily Dickinson's poems are like diary entries in that they explore the private realm of thought, feeling, and imagination. The following poems convey fresh observations about some of life's timeless concerns: nature, hope, success, madness, pain, and death. Use a graphic like this one to explore the emotions such concepts trigger in you.

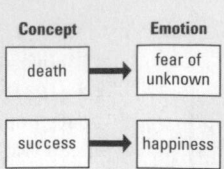

| Concept | | Emotion |
|---|---|---|
| death | → | fear of unknown |
| success | → | happiness |

## Build Background

**A Unique Style** Emily Dickinson's observations are as poignant and personal as her poetic style. One of the originators of modern American poetry, Dickinson departed from the poetic traditions of the 19th century in her inventive treatment of rhyme, punctuation, capitalization, and sentence structure. Dickinson's poems are also short, usually no longer than 20 lines. She wrote most of her poetry in dense **quatrains** (four-line stanzas) that echo the simple rhythms of the church hymns she knew and loved. However, she added a fresh twist with **slant rhymes,** or words that do not rhyme exactly, and used **dashes** to highlight important words and help break up the singsong rhythm of her poems.

## Focus Your Reading

**LITERARY ANALYSIS** **FIGURATIVE LANGUAGE** Dickinson used fresh and original **figurative language** to communicate ideas beyond the literal meaning of words, including the following:

**Simile:** a figure of speech that compares two things that have something in common, using *like* or *as*
   *The Nerves sit ceremonious, like Tombs—*

**Metaphor:** a figure of speech that directly states a comparison between two things
   *"Hope" is the thing with feathers—*

**Personification:** a figure of speech in which an object, animal, or idea is given human characteristics
   *The simple News that Nature told—*

**ACTIVE READING** **STRATEGIES FOR READING POETRY** The following suggestions can help you increase your understanding and enjoyment of Dickinson's poetry:

- Read each poem once for overall impression, then again for meaning. Then read it at least one more time, this time aloud, to appreciate Dickinson's unique **style, rhythm,** and **imagery.**
- Think about Dickinson's use of **figurative language.** Pay close attention to words that are capitalized for emphasis.
- Pause when you encounter dashes, just as you do when you come to commas or periods in a poem.

**READER'S NOTEBOOK** As you read, jot down any questions you may have about any poetic element or device at work within a poem.

---

## LESSON RESOURCES

**UNIT FIVE RESOURCE BOOK,** pp. 4–5

**ASSESSMENT RESOURCES**
**Formal Assessment,** pp. 137–138
**Teacher's Guide to Assessment and Portfolio Use**
**Test Generator**

**SKILLS TRANSPARENCIES AND COPYMASTERS**
**Reading and Critical Thinking**
- Venn Diagram, T50 (for Writing Option 2, p. 762)

**Grammar**
- Adjective and Adverb Clauses, C100 (for Mini Lesson, p. 757)

**Vocabulary**
- Denotation and Connotation, C62 (for Mini Lesson, p. 755)

**Writing**
- Effective Language, T13 (for Writing Option 1, p. 762)
- Compare-Contrast, C31 (for Writing Option 2, p. 762)

**Communications**
- Evaluation Matrix: Film/Video, T7 (for Activities & Explorations 2, p. 762)
- Evaluating Roles in Groups, T8 (for Author Study Project, p. 762)
- Reading Aloud, T11 (for Author Study Project, p. 762)

**INTEGRATED TECHNOLOGY**

**Audio Library**
**Net Activities**
**Video: Literature in Performance**
- *Finished Knowing.* See **Video Resource Book,** pp. 21–26.

**Internet: Research Starter**
**Visit our website:**
www.mcdougallittell.com

*Emily Dickinson*

# This is my letter to the World

This is my letter to the World
That never wrote to Me—
The simple News that Nature told—
With tender Majesty

5  Her Message is committed
To Hands I cannot see—
For love of Her—Sweet—countrymen—
Judge tenderly—of Me

## GUIDE FOR READING

**1 this:** Dickinson's poetry, or this particular poem.

**3** What might Nature's "simple  News" be?

**5 committed:** given over; entrusted.

**6** Whose might be the "Hands"  that the speaker cannot see?

## Thinking Through the Literature

1. What is your impression of the speaker of this poem?

2. Dickinson sees her poem as her "letter to the World." Based on your reading of the poem, what can you infer about the message she wants to share with others?

3. Dickinson says that her message is "The simple News that Nature told." What does this suggest about Dickinson's feelings for nature?

    **THINK ABOUT**
    • in line 4, the "tender Majesty" with which nature communicates
    • in line 7, the feeling she hopes her readers will have about nature

4. Most of Dickinson's poems were not published during her lifetime. Do you think she expected that other people would ever read them? What lines in this poem lead you to your conclusion?

# TEACHING THE LITERATURE

## Customizing Instruction

**Less Proficient Readers**
Remind students that they're expected to establish a purpose such as to find out what Dickinson asks for in her "letter" and how she envisions hope.

**Students Acquiring English**
Tell students that most of Dickinson's vocabulary is simple, but that her unusual use of capitalization and dashes may make her poetry seem difficult. Explain that these aspects of her style are her ways of emphasizing ideas in her writing.

Use **Spanish Study Guide** for additional support, pp. 178–81.

**Gifted and Talented**
Emily Dickinson pointed the way for many poets to follow. Amy Lowell, an Imagist poet, admired Dickinson and wrote this line about her in "The Sisters," a poem she published in 1925: "But Emily would set doors ajar and slam them/And love you for your speed of observation." Ask students to keep this quotation in mind as they read the following poems. They should then be prepared to use elements of text to defend their responses to this idea.

## GUIDE FOR READING

**1** **Possible Responses:** beauty, hope, mortality, immortality, love

**2** **Possible Responses:** her reader's; a lost lover's; God's; other people's in general

## Thinking Through the Literature

1. Some students may see the speaker as a solitary person who loves nature; others may see the speaker as a timid person who is concerned with the world's judgment.

2. Possible Responses: She wants to share her experiences with nature and the simple truths derived from them.

3. Possible Responses: She loves nature and is inspired by it; she prefers enjoying nature rather than spending time with other people.

4. Possible Responses: Yes, she believed others would read them because the first lines say that this is her letter to the world, and the last lines ask that her countrymen judge her tenderly. No, she did not expect others to read them because she did not publish many of them during her lifetime.

**Literary Analysis**

FIGURATIVE LANGUAGE

 **A** Ask students to identify the metaphor in line 1 and to decide if the metaphor is effective.

**Answer:** Hope is a bird. The metaphor is effective because it creates a concrete image of an abstract quality.

 Use **Unit Five Resource Book,** p. 5 for more practice.

### GUIDE FOR READING

**B** **Possible Responses:** Hope soars high and is lighthearted; hope is braver than it is intelligent; hope persists; hope is like music.

**Active Reading**

STRATEGIES FOR READING POETRY

After their first reading of "Success is counted sweetest," ask students to decide with whom the speaker identifies more, the winning army or the defeated soldier.

**Possible Response:** the defeated soldier

Use **Unit Five Resource Book,** p. 4 for more practice.

## Thinking Through the Literature

1. Sketches might include a perched, singing bird, a bird in a wind-tossed tree, an icy landscape, a stormy sea.
2. **Possible Responses:** Birds are light; they fly above the earth, and their song is cheerful; hope can lift people's spirits and, like a song, can cheer people through bad times.
3. **Possible Responses:** Hope is selfless and purely giving; it asks nothing in return from the person who hopes.

---

*Emily Dickinson*

# "Hope" is the thing with *feathers*

**A** "Hope" is the thing with feathers—
That perches in the soul—
And sings the tune without the words—
And never stops—at all—

5    And sweetest—in the Gale—is heard—
And sore must be the storm—
That could abash the little Bird
That kept so many warm—

I've heard it in the chillest land—
10   And on the strangest Sea—
Yet, never, in Extremity,
It asked a crumb—of Me.

### GUIDE FOR READING

**1–4** What qualities of hope are suggested by this image?    **B**

**6 sore:** severe.

**7 abash:** frustrate; baffle.

**11 Extremity:** greatest need or peril.

### Thinking Through the Literature

1. On a sheet of paper, sketch the images that came to you as you read the poem.
2. Why do you think Dickinson pictures hope as a bird?

   THINK ABOUT { • the qualities of a bird
   • the qualities of hope that are similar to those of a bird
3. How do you interpret the last two lines?

---

## Teaching Options

 **Cross Curricular Link** **Social Sciences**

**WOMEN'S EDUCATION IN THE 19TH CENTURY** By 1850 at least 50 percent of the nation's women could read and write—a sizable improvement over the previous century. From 1820 to 1860 the number of academies, or "seminaries," offering secondary education to girls from middle-class families increased. The goal of the schools was to go beyond the "ornamentals"—skills that enhanced girls' chances for marriage—and provide an education to equip women for their roles in society. Educators felt that secondary education would enable women to improve their housekeeping skills and spread their moral influence.

Many women were taught to teach, a role for which they were believed to have a particular aptitude. Emma Willard, founder of the first endowed institution for women, explained that "suitable instructions for young women . . . would be first, moral and religious; second, literary; third, domestic; and fourth, ornamental." Mount Holyoke Seminary, opened in 1837, held high academic standards, but students also performed domestic chores to prepare them for their later roles. The school, as Emily Dickinson found out, placed an extreme emphasis on piety and produced many missionaries and "self-denying female teachers."

*Emily Dickinson*

# Success is counted sweetest

Success is counted sweetest
By those who ne'er succeed.
To comprehend a nectar
Requires sorest need.

5    Not one of all the purple Host
Who took the Flag today
Can tell the definition
So clear of Victory

As he defeated—dying—
10    On whose forbidden ear
The distant strains of triumph
Burst agonized and clear!

**GUIDE FOR READING**

**2  ne'er:** never.

**1–2** Who prizes success most?  **2**

**3  comprehend:** fully appreciate;
**nectar:** a sweet beverage.

**5  Host:** army.

**6  took the Flag:** captured the
enemy's flag as a token of victory.

## Thinking Through the Literature

1. What were you thinking as you finished reading this poem?
2. How do you interpret lines 3 and 4? Explain how they relate to lines 1 and 2.
3. In this poem, Dickinson uses the image of a battlefield to make her point. Why might the defeated soldier be better able to appreciate victory than a winning soldier?

SUCCESS IS COUNTED SWEETEST    **753**

---

## Customizing Instruction

### Students Acquiring English

**1** Help students to use the marginal notes to understand that this unusually elevated (for Dickinson) language means "to fully appreciate a sweet drink, one must be really thirsty."

### GUIDE FOR READING

**2** **Answer:** The person who does not succeed prizes success the most.

### Multiple Learning Styles
**Auditory/Musical Learners**

Ask students to select instrumental music that matches the tone and theme of each poem. Have students read the poems against the background of the music.

## Thinking Through the Literature

1. Students may think of the agony of listening to an enemy's triumph, of how success is clearest to those who fail, or of personal experiences that relate to Dickinson's point about appreciating success.
2. Possible Responses: To fully understand the value of a drink, one must be extremely thirsty. To fully appreciate success, one must have been denied it.
3. Possible Responses: Winners might take victory for granted; people focus more on what they want or need than on what they have.

---

## BLOCK SCHEDULING: MANAGING TIME

**If your schedule requires that you cover the  lesson objectives in a shorter time, use . . .**
- Preparing to Read, p. 750
- Thinking Through the Literature, p. 760

**If you want to take advantage of longer class time, use . . .**
- TE Teaching Options: Cross-Curricular Link, p. 752; Vocabulary Strategy, p. 755; Informal Assessment, p. 756; Standardized Test Practice, p. 759
- Author's Style, p. 761; Choices & Challenges, p. 762

## Reading and Analyzing

### Literary Analysis: PARADOX

A paradox is a seemingly contradictory or absurd statement that may nonetheless suggest an important truth. Ask students to locate the paradoxical statements found in "Much Madness is divinest Sense." Have them justify these statements in light of the rest of the poem.

**Possible Responses:** "Much Madness is divinest Sense . . . Much Sense—the starkest Madness"; The majority sets the standard; if someone deviates from that standard that person will be seen as mad. If one wishes to be accepted, he or she must go along with the majority.

### Active Reading

| STRATEGIES FOR READING POETRY |
| --- |

Invite a student to read "Much Madness is divinest Sense" aloud, pausing appropriately at the dashes. Ask students to analyze the function of each dash—whether it represents a mark of punctuation such as a period or substitutes for a verb or is meant to convey a tone.

### GUIDE FOR READING

**A Possible Responses:** To the speaker, what society regards as madness is actually good sense; conversely, what society regards as sensible is utter insanity.

### Literary Analysis: PARADOX

**B** Ask students to explain the first sentence in the second paragraph.

**Possible Responses:** Because she has written the poems, she is too close to them to be able to see any flaws in them. She finds it difficult to distance herself from her poems to attain the objectivity to evaluate them.

---

*Emily Dickinson*

# Much Madness is divinest Sense

Much Madness is divinest Sense
To a discerning Eye—
Much Sense—the starkest Madness—
'Tis the Majority
5  In this, as All, prevail—
Assent—and you are sane—
Demur—you're straightway dangerous—
And handled with a Chain—

### GUIDE FOR READING

**2 discerning:** having keen insight and good judgment.

**4 Majority:** the community at large; the society.

**1–4** According to the speaker, what are the meanings of madness and sense? **A**

**6 assent:** agree.

**7 demur** (dĭ-mûr'): voice opposition; object.

**8 handled with a Chain:** In the 19th century, those who were considered insane were often kept chained in asylums.

---

## Thinking Through the Literature

1. What impact did this poem have on you? Jot down some thoughts.
2. What might Dickinson have been feeling when she wrote this poem?

   | THINK ABOUT |
   | --- |
   • the speaker's own views about madness and sense
   • the meanings of madness and sense in the larger society
3. Do you agree with the speaker's attitudes about madness and sense? Support your opinion, citing examples from your own observations and experiences.

---

## Thinking Through the Literature

1. The poem will have a different impact on different students. Some may think of personal experiences that support or challenge Dickinson's paradox; some may think about conflicts between individuals and the majority.

2. Possible Responses: She might have been reflecting on the mistreatment accorded to some nonconformists; she might have felt that her own values set her apart from others in her society.

3. Students who agree with the speaker might point to government reactions to dissenters. Those who disagree might emphasize that people generally tolerate differences in clothing, values, and life styles.

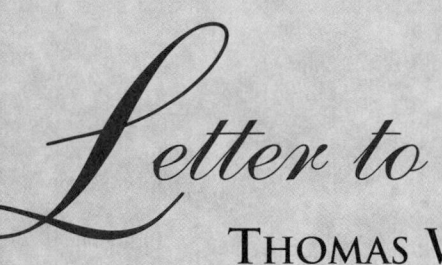

# Letter to
## THOMAS WENTWORTH HIGGINSON

*Emily Dickinson*

## Teaching the Literature

### Build Background
According to *American Authors, 1600–1900*, Dickinson "was too much for Higginson, the friend of young aspiring writers; he was kindly, he patronized her, he understood her not at all. She kept him as a friend, but she never made the same mistake again"—the "mistake" being the attempt to get her poems published. In 1890 Higginson helped edit the posthumous edition of Dickinson's poems. His editing style, however, corrupted her work. Not until Thomas Johnson's 1955 edition of the complete Dickinson poems did the literary world see her poetry the way it was originally written.

## Preparing to Read

### Build Background
In April 1862 critic and literary editor Thomas Wentworth Higginson published an essay, "Letter to a Young Contributor," in the *Atlantic Monthly*. He offered practical advice to beginning writers on how to break into print, urging them, "Charge your style with life." One young writer who responded to Higginson's essay was Emily Dickinson, who was 32 years old at the time. She submitted four poems along with the following unsigned letter. Characteristically, she broke with tradition, enclosing a signed calling card in its own envelope in place of a signature.

Unfortunately, Higginson's reply to Dickinson's letter no longer exists. Apparently, he offered criticism of her poems —which she referred to as "surgery"—and asked about her education, her family and friends, and books she had read. Although Dickinson's letter sparked an important literary correspondence that lasted more than 20 years, she steadfastly ignored Higginson's advice on how to improve her poems.

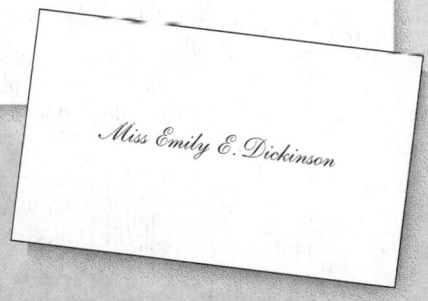

*Letter to Mr. T. W. Higginson*
*April 15, 1862*

*Mr. Higginson,*

*Are you too deeply occupied to say if my verse is alive?*

*The Mind is so near itself—it cannot see, distinctly—and I have none to ask. Should you think it breathed—and had you the leisure to tell me, I should feel quick gratitude—* **B**

*If I make the mistake—that you dared to tell me— would give me sincerer honor toward you—*

*I enclosed my name—asking you, if you please— Sir—to tell me what is true? That you will not betray me—it is needless to ask—since honor is its own pawn—*

*Miss Emily E. Dickinson*

## Teaching Nonfiction

### Skills and Strategies
### PARAPHRASING
Have students paraphrase Dickinson's letter.

**Possible Response:** I hope that you are not too busy to evaluate my poetry. Because I have written the poems, I am too close to them to be able to see any flaws. If you think the poems are good, I would be grateful if you would tell me so. If you do not like them, I would respect your honest criticism. I have enclosed my name so that you may respond to me with your answer, and I know that you will do so as a matter of honor.

## Vocabulary Strategy

**DENOTATIVE AND CONNOTATIVE MEANINGS**
**Instruction** Remind students that the denotation of a word is its dictionary definition and that the connotations of a word are its associated attitudes or emotions. A poet such as Emily Dickinson, whose writing is so condensed, must choose each word with great care. Its denotation must be exact, and its connotations must evoke the desired associations as well. The word *nectar*, for example, means "a sweet

beverage," but it also conjures up something associated with the gods, something divinely delicious. Therefore to substitute a synonym such as *cordial* or *punch* takes away an association that deepens Dickinson's theme.
**Application** Have students work in groups to define the underlined word in each of the following quotations. Then have them analyze how substituting the word given in parentheses alters the meaning of the line.

1. "Her Message is <u>committed</u>/To Hands I cannot see—" (delivered)
2. "If Immortality <u>unveil</u>/A third event to me" (disclose)

Use **Vocabulary Transparencies and Copymasters**, p. 62.

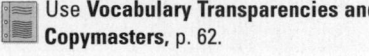

## Reading and Analyzing

### GUIDE FOR READING

**A** **Possible Responses:** It is an unthinkable loss.

### Literary Analysis

**FIGURATIVE LANGUAGE**

**B** Ask students to explain the simile in line 2 of "After great pain, a formal feeling comes."
**Possible Responses:** After an experience of great pain such as the death of a loved one, the nerves are deadened like the inanimate marble of tombs; the immobility is itself a reminder of the event that transpired; the bereaved endure a kind of walking death.

### Literary Analysis: MOOD

Have students analyze the use of evocative rhythm and words in "After great pain. . ." Ask them to decide what mood Dickinson creates by the end of the poem.
**Possible Responses:** somber; calm; heavy; hopeless

## Thinking Through the Literature

1. **Possible Responses:** parting from a loved one who has died
2. **Possible Responses:** Dickinson's attitude toward death is complex. She ascribes to immortality the quality of unveiling or revealing events to the deceased. She wonders whether those events will be as overwhelming and inconceivable as the two losses she experienced in this life.
3. Students who think the poem would be disturbing might state that it explores the experience of loss in all its agony and uncertainty; students who think the poem would be comforting might state that the speaker hints at a belief in immortality.

---

*Emily Dickinson*

# My life closed twice before its close

My life closed twice before its close—
It yet remains to see
If Immortality unveil
A third event to me

5   So huge, so hopeless to conceive
As these that twice befell.
Parting is all we know of heaven,
And all we need of hell.

**GUIDE FOR READING**

**6 befell** (bĭ-fĕl'): happened.
**5–8** How does the speaker feel about the loss of a loved one? **A**

## Thinking Through the Literature

1. What kind of "parting" might Dickinson be referring to in the last two lines of the poem?
2. What does this poem reveal about Dickinson's attitude toward death?

   **THINK ABOUT**
   - the human quality she gives to immortality (line 3)
   - the use of the descriptive phrases "so huge" and "so hopeless to conceive," and what they describe
3. Would a reader who has recently experienced the loss of a loved one be disturbed or comforted by this poem? Explain your answer.

756   UNIT FIVE   AUTHOR STUDY: EMILY DICKINSON

---

## Teaching Options

 Assessment **Informal Assessment**

**RECOGNIZING POETIC FORM** You may informally assess students' understanding of poetic form and techniques by having them identify rhyme scheme, meter, slant rhyme, personification, and metaphor in the first three poems. Ask students to work with partners to create a chart to be filled in for each poem.

**RUBRIC**

**3 Full Accomplishment** Students correctly identify the rhyme scheme, meter, and slant rhyme in each poem. They also recognize all instances of personification and metaphor.

**2 Substantial Accomplishment** Students have few errors in rhyme scheme, meter, and slant rhyme. They recognize some instances of personification and metaphor.

**1 Little or Partial Accomplishment** Students struggle with the concepts of rhyme scheme, meter, and slant rhyme, and fail to detect personification or metaphor.

*Emily Dickinson*

# After great pain, a formal feeling comes

**B**  After great pain, a formal feeling comes—
The Nerves sit ceremonious, like Tombs—
The stiff Heart questions was it He, that bore,
And Yesterday, or Centuries before?

5  The Feet, mechanical, go round—
Of Ground, or Air, or Ought—
A Wooden way
Regardless grown,
A Quartz contentment, like a stone—

10  This is the Hour of Lead—
Remembered, if outlived,
As Freezing persons, recollect the Snow—
First—Chill—then Stupor—then the letting go—

### GUIDE FOR READING

**3  He, that bore:** the heart that felt the pain.

**6  Ought:** anywhere.

**8  regardless:** unmindful.

**1–9** What different responses to mental anguish are described in these lines? **1**

**10–13** How is someone who experiences emotional pain similar to "Freezing persons"? **2**

## Thinking Through the Literature

1. What emotions do you think the speaker is trying to convey? Jot down your impressions.

2. In this poem, Dickinson uses **metaphors** that leave an image of the "formal feeling" that follows pain. How do the metaphors reveal this formal feeling of loss?

3. Why do you think the speaker focuses on the numbed feelings after a loss rather than on the agony and pain?

## Mini Lesson: Grammar

**ADJECTIVE AND ADVERB CLAUSES** An adjective clause is a subordinate clause that functions as an adjective to modify a noun or a pronoun. An adverb clause is a subordinate clause that functions as an adverb to modify a verb, an adjective, or another adverb, and answers *where, when, why, how, to what extent,* or *under what circumstances.* Adjective and adverb clauses can sometimes be introduced by the same words, so it is important to recognize how the clause functions. Display the following sentences as examples:

Many people never realized the intensity of Dickinson's experiences <u>because she lived as a recluse.</u> (adverb clause modifying *realized*)

Emily Dickinson asked Higginson to critique the poems <u>that she enclosed with her letter.</u> (adjective clause modifying *poems*)

**Exercises** Classify the clauses as adjective or adverb and identify the word or words that each clause modifies.

1. Her modesty is shown by the fact <u>that she had no desire for public adulation.</u> (*adjective clause; fact*)

2. Emily Dickinson acted <u>as if she wanted Higginson's suggestions</u>. (*adverb clause; acted*)

Use **Grammar Transparencies and Copymasters**, p. 100.

 Use McDougal Littell's *Language Network,* Chapter 3, for more instruction and practice in clauses.

**758** UNIT FIVE AUTHOR STUDY

## Reading and Analyzing

### Literary Analysis

**FIGURATIVE LANGUAGE**

**A** Ask students to explain the simile Dickinson uses in lines 2–4.

**Possible Responses:** The speaker rests in a moment of peace, poised between the fervor of life and the trauma of death, just as those in the eye of a storm await the next onslaught; the people around the deathbed have exhausted their first grief and now await the final moment or next part of the storm.

### Active Reading

**STRATEGIES FOR READING POETRY**

**B** Ask students why so many words are capitalized in the second quatrain of "I heard a Fly buzz."

**Possible Responses:** Capitals emphasize the significance of the moment for those witnessing this event of death.

### GUIDE FOR READING

**C** **Possible Responses:** The speaker hears a fly buzzing and sees it between herself and the window. Then she loses light and sight, conscious only of the fly's buzzing at the moment of her death.

### Literary Analysis

**FIGURATIVE LANGUAGE**

**D** Point out that this poem is based upon the personification of death. Ask students to explain the character traits ascribed to Death.

**Possible Responses:** dignity, kindness, gentleness, courtesy, patience

---

*Emily Dickinson*

# I heard a Fly buzz when I died

**A**
*I* heard a Fly buzz—when I died—
The Stillness in the Room
Was like the Stillness in the Air—
Between the Heaves of Storm—

**B**
5   The Eyes around—had wrung them dry—
And Breaths were gathering firm
For that last Onset—when the King
Be witnessed—in the Room—

I willed my Keepsakes—Signed away
10   What portion of me be
Assignable—and then it was
There interposed a Fly—

With Blue—uncertain stumbling Buzz—
Between the light—and me—
15   And then the Windows failed—and then
I could not see to see—

**GUIDE FOR READING**

**4 Heaves:** risings and fallings.

**7 the King:** God.

**5–8** In the 19th century, people usually died at home in the presence of friends and family.

**12 interposed:** came between.

**13–16** What are the dying person's last sensations? **C**

---

### Thinking Through the Literature

1. What is your reaction to the way the poem ends? Briefly describe your reactions to a classmate.

2. How would you describe the view of death presented in the poem?

   **THINK ABOUT**
   • the moments just before death described in the first and last stanzas
   • the meaning of lines 5–8

3. Look closely at Dickinson's last stanza. What does she do to make the portrayal of death a realistic one?

---

## Thinking Through the Literature

1. Some students may find the dimming light a believable image of what dying is like; some may find the last line awkward.

2. The speaker presents death in terms of physical sensations such as silence, fading light, and the buzzing of a fly; the speaker signs a will before dying; the speaker dies surrounded by mourners.

3. Some students will think that the emotionless description of the gradually fading light and the buzzing sound makes the portrayal realistic; some students may think the fading of light symbolizes the fading of life.

# Because I could not stop for Death

**D**

Because I could not stop for Death—
He kindly stopped for me—
The Carriage held but just Ourselves—
And Immortality.

5　We slowly drove—He knew no haste
And I had put away
My labor and my leisure too,
For His Civility—

We passed the School, where Children strove
10　At Recess—in the Ring—
We passed the Fields of Gazing Grain—
We passed the Setting Sun—

Or rather—He passed Us—
The Dews drew quivering and chill—
15　For only Gossamer, my Gown—
My Tippet—only Tulle—

We paused before a House that seemed
A Swelling of the Ground—
The Roof was scarcely visible—
20　The Cornice—in the Ground—

Since then—'tis Centuries—and yet
Feels shorter than the Day
I first surmised the Horses' Heads
Were toward Eternity—

## GUIDE FOR READING

**8 Civility:** politeness.

**1–8** How is Death portrayed in these lines? **1**

**11 Gazing Grain:** grain leaning toward the sun.

**15 Gossamer:** a thin, light cloth.

**16 Tippet:** shawl; **Tulle** (to̅o̅l): fine netting.

**20 Cornice** (kôr′ nĭs): the molding around the top of a building.

**17–20** What do you think this house represents? **2**

**21–24** How does the speaker seem to feel about the length of time that has passed? **3**

## Customizing Instruction

**Less Proficient Readers**
Ask students to describe Dickinson's portrayal of death in each poem.
**Possible Responses:** In "I heard a Fly buzz" the deathbed scene is calm, and the dying speaker is distracted by the buzzing of a fly. In "Because I could not stop for Death," death is personified as a kindly gentleman who stops by to escort his passenger on a carriage ride toward eternity.

### GUIDE FOR READING

**1** **Possible Responses:** Death is portrayed as a suitor or a kindly gentleman who drives slowly.

**2** **Possible Responses:** a grave; a tomb; a coffin

**3** **Possible Responses:** calm and accepting; slightly surprised

---

## ✓ Assessment **Standardized Test Practice**

**MAKING INFERENCES** For some standardized tests, students will be asked to make inferences based on what they have read in the passage. To provide students with some help in making correct inferences, read aloud or write on the board the following question:
Which word best describes the speaker's tone toward dying in "Because I could not stop for Death"?
**A.** disillusioned
**B.** ironic
**C.** lighthearted

Lead students through the process of considering each choice. The correct choice will describe the tone heard throughout the poem, not just in one or two stanzas. Initially, **C** seems the word that best describes the tone. However, in stanza 4, the speaker feels a chill as the setting sun passes the carriage, and the journey seems destined to end in the ground. Answer **A** does not fit the first two stanzas. Therefore, **B** is the best choice. Emily Dickinson reverses expectations of death by portraying it as a kindly gentleman, but instead of taking his passenger to a glorious destination, they end at a house in the ground, for all eternity.

## GUIDING STUDENT RESPONSE

### Connect to the Literature

1. **What Do You Think?**
   Possible Response: Death is kind, unhurried, courteous.

**Comprehension Check**

• The speaker has died.
• Death's carriage holds Death, the speaker, and Immortality.
• Time passes, but even centuries feel shorter than the day the speaker first realized where the carriage was heading.

### Think Critically

2. Possible Responses: These objects symbolize aspects of life—childhood, adulthood, old age; growth, productive work, decline.

3. Possible Responses: The house is a grave or a tomb. Strategies might include paying attention to the capitalized words, pausing at dashes, or using the context to infer what house death would pause at.

4. Many students will agree that Dickinson's poems are letters in the sense that they share her personal insights about life and death.

5. Possible Responses: The poems show an intelligent, reflective woman who leads an intense life even though she has isolated herself from the world; she does not fear death; she has an active mind that draws poetic inspiration from all facets of life.

### Literary Analysis

**Figurative Language** Have students list some ideas associated with the abstract concept before they begin composing their definitions. Encourage students to brainstorm possible figures of speech. After they have finished, students should share their definitions and note how figurative language creates a richer experience of the concept than a simple definition can.

### Connect to the Literature

1. **What Do You Think?**
   What image of death do you get from "Because I could not stop for Death—"?

   **Comprehension Check**
   • What has happened to the speaker?
   • What does Death's carriage hold?
   • What has happened to time?

### Think Critically

2. In the third stanza of "Because I could not stop for Death—" the carriage passes the school, fields of grain, and the setting sun. What might these objects **symbolize?**

3. **ACTIVE READING** **STRATEGIES FOR READING POETRY** Reread lines 17–20. What does the house in this stanza represent? Refer to your **READER'S NOTEBOOK** to review any questions or reactions that you may have recorded about the stanza. Explain what strategy you used to help you arrive at this meaning.

4. In "This is my letter to the World" Dickinson, in effect, states that the poem is her letter. Do you think the other poems are additional "letters" from Dickinson? Consider the evidence.

    **THINK ABOUT**
   • what you can conclude about her personality
   • what the poems suggest about what she values
   • what the poems suggest about her view of the world

5. Based on the eight poems you've read, what are your impressions of Emily Dickinson as a person? Give reasons for your answer.

### Extend Interpretations

6. **Critic's Corner** Read Dickinson's quotation on the definition of poetry (page 746). In your opinion, do the poems in this Author Study meet the standards expressed by this definition? Explain.

7. **Connect to Life** How did discovering Dickinson's observations about nature, hope, success, and death affect your feelings about these topics that you recorded for the graphic shown on page 750?

### Literary Analysis

**FIGURATIVE LANGUAGE**

**Figurative language** consists of groups of words that express ideas beyond the literal meaning of the words. Dickinson's poetry features some common figures of speech.

**Similes** compare two unlike things that have something in common, using *like* or *as*. The following lines from "I heard a Fly buzz—when I died—" compare the tense atmosphere of a death to the short periods of calm that occur in the midst of a violent storm:

*The Stillness in the Room*
*Was like the Stillness in the Air—*

A **metaphor** directly compares two unlike things. An **extended metaphor** compares two things at some length and in several ways. The extended metaphor in "'Hope' is the thing with feathers—" compares hope to a bird.

**Personification** is a figure of speech in which an object, animal, or idea is given human characteristics. In "Because I could not stop for Death—" death is personified as a kind gentleman.

**Cooperative Learning Activity** In small groups, choose an abstract concept (such as victory or truth) and compose your own definition by using figures of speech. Determine what is being compared. What ideas does the comparison bring out?

**REVIEW** **PARADOX** A **paradox** is a statement that seems to contradict itself but may suggest the truth. Note the paradox here:

*Success is counted sweetest*
*By those who ne'er succeed.*

### Extend Interpretations

**Critic's Corner** Possible Response: Dickinson suggests that real poetry evokes response in the reader's whole being. Opinions will vary as to whether all the poems evoke such a response, or just certain ones. Ask students to support their opinions with specific details from the poems.

**Connect to Life** Possible Responses: Ask students to form small groups to share their original feelings about the concepts. Then have students share their changed perceptions, citing lines from the poems to indicate why their feelings altered.

# THE AUTHOR'S STYLE
## Dickinson's Stylistic Experiments

Emily Dickinson's style is as unique and personal as her observations about the world. In her inventive treatment of rhyme, punctuation, capitalization, and sentence structure, she rebelled against the poetic traditions of the 1800s.

### Key Aspects of Dickinson's Style

- short, untitled lyric poems, usually no longer than 20 lines
- dense **quatrains,** or four-line stanzas, that echo the simple rhythms of church hymns
- **slant rhymes,** or words that do not rhyme exactly
- dashes used to highlight important words and to break up the singsong rhythm of her poems
- unconventional capitalization and inverted syntax to emphasize words
- omission of conjunctions, pronouns, prepositions, or articles to heighten the effect of compression

## Analysis of Style

At the right are **quatrains** of three well-known Dickinson poems. Study the chart above, and then complete the following activities:

**A** • Find examples of **slant rhyme,** inverted syntax, and omission of different parts of speech.

**B** • Find at least two or three additional stylistic devices that you see at work in any of the three examples. What effect do they create?

**C** • Look again at the eight poems in this Author Study. Choose one, and discuss with other readers the stylistic devices you see at work.

## Applications

**1. Changing Style** Until 1955, volumes of Dickinson's poetry consisted of "corrected" versions of her poems. Acting as a 19th-century editor, rewrite one of Dickinson's poems, using standard punctuation and capitalization. Share your version with the class.

**2. Imitation of Style** Write a **quatrain** (four-line stanza) on any subject, imitating Dickinson's style. Copy your quatrain onto a page with the opening quatrains of other poems by Dickinson, and see if your classmates or your teacher can pick yours out.

**3. Speaking and Listening** Obtain a copy of *The Complete Poems of Emily Dickinson* edited by Thomas H. Johnson. In a small group, share a reading of Dickinson's poems. Discuss the strengths and weaknesses of each.

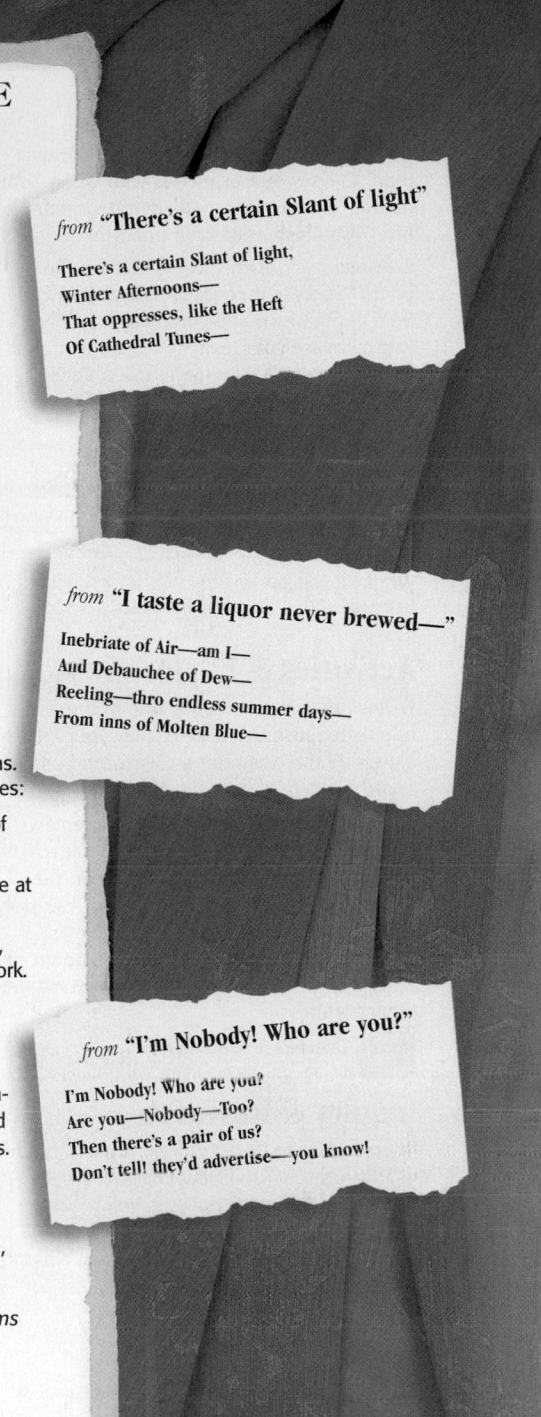

*from* **"There's a certain Slant of light"**

There's a certain Slant of light,
Winter Afternoons—
That oppresses, like the Heft
Of Cathedral Tunes—

*from* **"I taste a liquor never brewed—"**

Inebriate of Air—am I—
And Debauchee of Dew—
Reeling—thro endless summer days—
From inns of Molten Blue—

*from* **"I'm Nobody! Who are you?"**

I'm Nobody! Who are you?
Are you—Nobody—Too?
Then there's a pair of us?
Don't tell! they'd advertise—you know!

761

Emily Dickinson's remarkable insights on nature, human emotions, and death take on greater meaning because of her distinctive style.

## Analysis of Style

**A** First activity
**slant rhyme:** too/know
**inverted syntax:** "Inebriate of Air—am I"
**omission of different parts of speech:** preposition—"There's a certain Slant of light,/ . . . Winter Afternoons"; article— "Inebriate of . . . Air" "And Debauchee of . . . Dew"

**B** Second activity
**alliteration:** "Debauchee of Dew"; the alliteration emphasizes this phrase.
**metaphor:** "From inns of Molten Blue"; this metaphor provides an image of the blue skies as the purveyor of the intoxicants of air and dew.
**simile:** "There's a certain Slant of light . . . That oppresses, like the Heft of Cathedral Tunes—"; this simile creates a solemn effect, comparing the effect of the light to the dirges emanating from an organ in a cathedral.

**C** Third activity
Ask students to form groups. Assign each group a different poem to analyze. Then have each group present the analysis. Students should find several devices in each poem.

## Applications

1. **Changing Style** Discuss with students the differences that editing the poem produced.
2. **Imitation of Style** Remind them of the meter favored by Dickinson (iambic tetrameter in the first and third lines, iambic trimeter in the second and fourth) and her use of slant rhyme, dashes, and capitalization.
3. **Speaking and Listening** Ask students to choose one or two favorites and to practice them before reading them aloud. Encourage them to have specific examples of each strength or weakness that they detect; do not allow general criticism. To make this assignment more challenging, have students find criticisms on a few of Emily Dickinson's most widely read poems. Have them analyze these written literature reviews and compare them to their own responses. Students should choose the critic's view that they support. Hold an informal debate in which the students defend their critic's view against other perspectives. Students should be able to cite examples from the poem to support the interpretation that they have chosen.

## Author Study Project
### PRESENTING A POETRY SLAM

Student readers should practice reading their poems aloud many times before the poetry slam. They might work with partners or in front of a mirror, and they should concentrate on how they can use their voice to enhance the meaning of a poem or to emphasize certain words. Students should justify their choice of verbal performance techniques by referring to their interpretation of the poem. Two or more students might read the same poem with different vocal techniques, allowing the audience to decide which technique is best for that poem.

### Secondary Print Sources
Students will probably want to research Dickinson's poems and letters beyond the ones included in their textbook. The following collections are good sources: *The Complete Poems of Emily Dickinson,* edited by Thomas H. Johnson (Little Brown, 1976); *Emily Dickinson: Selected Letters,* edited by Thomas Johnson (Belknap Press, 1985); *The Master Letters of Emily Dickinson,* edited by R. W. Franklin (Amherst College Press, 1986).

### MULTIMEDIA PROJECT
Students can preserve a record of their poetry slam in the form of a multimedia presentation. For example, they might create a book with copies of the poems that were read, the judges' ratings and comments, and photos or illustrations of the readers. A videotape of the poetry slam would complete the presentation. Another possibility is to create a Web site with text, graphics, and sound documenting the event and encouraging students in other schools to share in the experience via the Internet.

## Writing Options

**1. Mini Poem** Create a short poem of fewer than 20 lines that expresses your views about nature, success, loss, pain, death, or hope. After you finish, read your poem to the class.

**2. Comparison-Contrast Essay** Reread the poem "Success is counted sweetest." Write a brief comparison-and-contrast essay in which you compare your own views about success with Dickinson's. You might use a Venn diagram like this one. Place your essay in your **Working Portfolio.**

My definition of success — similarities — Dickinson's definition of success

**Writing Handbook**
See page 1281: Compare and Contrast.

## Activities & Explorations

**1. Illustrated Poem** Choose one of these poems to illustrate. Then display your art alongside the poem on a classroom bulletin board. ~ **ART**

**2. Video Adaptation** View the documentary *Finished Knowing,* included on the video provided with this program. Focus on the filmmaker's message as she threads her story with lines from Emily Dickinson's works. Compare this film with Dickinson's poem "This is my letter to the World." ~ **VIEWING AND REPRESENTING**

 **VIDEO** Literature in Performance

## Inquiry & Research

**Historical Connection** Find out more about life in 19th-century rural New England. What values and beliefs did people hold? What kinds of challenges did they face? Then present a brief oral report with visual aids.

 **More Online: Research Starter**
www.mcdougallittell.com

Since the 1990s, poetry slams have become a popular form of entertainment in schools and cafés and on college campuses. With your classmates, plan a reading of Dickinson's poems and letters. The following suggestions can help you launch a successful event:

**Plan the Event** First, choose several Dickinson poems or letters to read aloud. Next, determine the order in which the poems and letters will be read. For example, you may want to present the works in chronological order, or you may group them by theme. To heighten the dramatic effect, consider using props, sound effects, or music to accompany the reading.

**Create a Program Guide** Use a computer to create a program guide. Include the following:
- a brief biographical sketch about Dickinson's life and work
- titles of poems in the appropriate order
- the names of the readers
- illustrations of Emily Dickinson

**Include the Ingredients** In addition to readers, you will need the following:
- **MC.** A master of ceremonies to introduce readers and engage the audience.
- **Audience.** A group of people who cheer, boo, weep, laugh, or make clever remarks—depending on the quality of the presentations.
- **Judges.** A panel of three or four people who rate the readers on a scale of 1 to 10. The rating is determined partly by audience reaction.

**Hold the Reading** Presenters should read slowly and clearly, make eye contact with the audience, and pace the reading according to the punctuation of the material. You may want to videotape the reading for future audiences.

# LEARNING the Language of *Literature*

## Social Themes in Fiction

### Issues for Us All

Social issues are issues that affect groups of people trying to live together peacefully, in a nation, for example, or in a religious community, a geographical region, or a neighborhood. Today, crime is a social issue; so are all forms of discrimination.

American writers have always shown an interest in how society is organized. The dynamics of Puritan society, for instance—with its strictly enforced rules and punishments—have inspired great literary works from Nathaniel Hawthorne's *The Scarlet Letter* (1850) to Arthur Miller's *The Crucible* (1953). Although both of these works focus on the Puritans, Hawthorne explored the effects of Puritan morality on individual lives, whereas Miller, by exposing wrongs committed in the name of righteousness during the Salem witch trials, sought to suggest parallels to events of his own time.

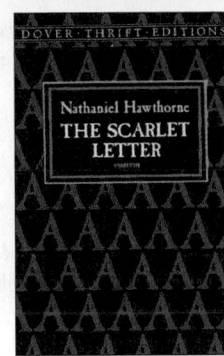

Nathaniel Hawthorne's
*The Scarlet Letter* (1850)

novel *Uncle Tom's Cabin* and the poetry of James Russell Lowell and Frances Ellen Watkins Harper.

As the nation expanded westward after the Civil War, another social issue gained prominence: Native Americans' presence on lands coveted by white settlers. Unlike the issue of slavery, however, the conflict between white settlement and the Native American way of life did not become the focus of a large body of American literature— although the tension simmering below the surface is evident in folk tales such as "The Indian and the Hundred Cows." That tale has a basically social theme, dealing as it does with the interaction between Native Americans and European settlers. You can infer from the tale that even Christianity, which promised to bind the two cultures together in common faith, was ironically a source of conflict. This simple folk tale demonstrates how effectively fiction can illuminate a large social problem by dramatizing conflicts between characters.

### Dramatizing Social Issues

One issue that pervaded American life in the 19th century was slavery. Strong antislavery themes appear in such works as Harriet Beecher Stowe's

### Identifying Social Themes

A social issue that emerged in the second half of the 19th century is the role of women in society. All of the selections in this part of Unit Five

---

## The *Spark* that *Ignited* the Fire

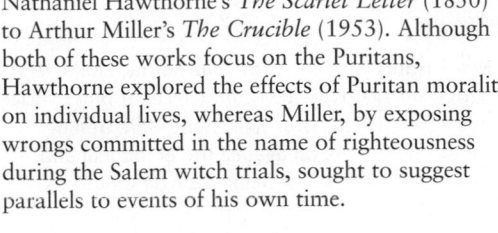

Harriet Beecher Stowe's *Uncle Tom's Cabin* (1852)

Perhaps the most famous American novel with a social theme is Harriet Beecher Stowe's *Uncle Tom's Cabin,* published in 1852. Intending to expose slavery's evil effects on society as a whole, Stowe portrayed not only the suffering of the enslaved characters but also the moral degradation of the slaveholder. More than a million copies of Stowe's powerful novel had been sold by the end of 1853, and it helped convince many Northerners that slavery had to end. Years later, when Stowe visited the White House during the Civil War, President Abraham Lincoln greeted her by saying, "So this is the little lady who made the big war."

SOCIAL THEMES IN FICTION **763**

---

### Presenting the Concepts

Read through the strategies aloud or project them on a transparency. The excerpts from the two selections that follow—"The Yellow Wallpaper" and "The Story of an Hour"—should set students up to be receptive to their social messages.

---

### Objectives
- understand theme
- identify conflicts and how they are addressed
- identify social themes in works of literature
- analyze the relevance of setting and time frame to text's meaning
- connect literature to historical contexts, current events, and his/her own experiences
- increase knowledge of American culture by studying literature that focuses on social conflict and social issues throughout the history of the United States

## Teaching the Lesson

Students will be reading literary works with the social issue of women's role in society as the central theme. This lesson will give them some background on the significance and use of social themes in American literature. Remind students to interpret the influences of historical context on the literary works they read.

### Introducing the Concepts

Since the early days of American literature, writers have used all genres of literature to bring social issues to the attention of the reading public. In the 19th and early 20th centuries, in particular, novels with a contemporary social theme, such as the role of women in society, were likely to generate reaction and create public debate of the central issue. As students read the selections in this unit, have them consider the following questions:

What is the central theme of each selection?

In what ways are today's social issues brought to the attention of the public?

As they read the following selections, students can write their reactions to these questions and keep their responses in their Working Portfolios.

The public debate over women's rights and their role in society in England and America inspired writers, some from other cultures, to focus their attention on what became known as the Woman Question. This social issue preoccupied writers of many nationalities during the late 19th century and, evolving with time, inspired the feminist writers who emerged in the early 20th century. Ask students to compare the examples below with the American literature in this part of the unit.

### From Norway: Henrik Ibsen

In 1879 Norwegian playwright Henrik Ibsen published *A Doll's House*. The play caused great scandal and remained a subject of discussion and debate for years after its initial appearance.

Nora Helmer, whose husband calls her his "little songbird," forged her dead father's signature in order to raise money to take her sick husband Torvald abroad. She is found out and blackmailed. Unable to meet the blackmailer's demands, Nora is forced to confess her crime to her husband. He becomes very angry and, convinced she has ruined him and his career, accuses her of immorality, indecency, and other "disgusting values." When the blackmailer relents, Torvald attempts to return matters to their original state by telling Nora he has forgiven her and that, as always, he will guide and counsel her.

Nora's unprecedented and shocking response is to refuse to submit to her husband. She realizes that she has lived "like a beggar" in her own house, surviving by performing for her husband like a doll or a pet. She decides to leave her life in the sheltered cage. In the final scene, she slams the door on her husband and their three children.

### From England: George Gissing

George Gissing's 1893 novel *The Odd Women* centers around three sisters left destitute by their father's death. Two of them attempt to make ends meet by doing the work deemed acceptable for genteel ladies. The third sister marries a man she does not love and begins a grim and brutal existence. The "odd women" of the title refer to Victorian women who were unmarried and, as such, were seen as leading "useless, lost, futile lives."

address this issue in one way or another. As you read them, look for the following characteristics to help you identify social themes:

- Works that address social issues often focus on people who have few, if any, rights and privileges in society. The first-person narrator of "The Yellow Wallpaper," although comfortably middle-class, has no control over her life. Early in the story, she explains her complete submission to her doctor and her husband.

> So I take phosphates . . . and tonics, and journeys, and air, and exercise, and am absolutely forbidden to "work" until I am well again.
>
> Personally, I disagree with their ideas.
>
> Personally, I believe that congenial work, with excitement and change, would do me good.
>
> But what is one to do?
>
> —Charlotte Perkins Gilman, "The Yellow Wallpaper"

**YOUR TURN** What would you do if you found yourself in disagreement with your doctor and your spouse?

- Some works dealing with social themes contain direct statements that are clues to their themes. In "The Story of an Hour," the main character, after hearing that her husband is dead, reflects on the control he has exercised over her.

> There would be no powerful will bending hers in that blind persistence with which men and women believe they have a right to impose a private will upon a fellow creature.
>
> —Kate Chopin, "The Story of an Hour"

**YOUR TURN** How is this character's attitude different from that expressed in the passage from "The Yellow Wallpaper"?

- Many works with social themes portray characters struggling against poverty, prejudice, or other social obstacles. The narrator of "I Stand Here Ironing," for example, runs up against the emotional and financial limitations of being a single mother.

### Strategies for Reading: Social Themes in Literature

1. Look for characters who have little power and ask yourself what social factors contribute to their situations.
2. Clarify the conflicts in the story and determine to what extent they are caused by forces beyond the characters' control.
3. Evaluate direct statements of the characters' opinions to see whether they provide clues to a theme.
4. Think about the author's reason for writing the story. What was he or she trying to achieve?
5. **Monitor** your reading strategies and modify them when your understanding breaks down. Remember to use the Strategies for Active Reading: **predict, visualize, connect, question, clarify,** and **evaluate.**

# The Yellow Wallpaper

*Short Story by* CHARLOTTE PERKINS GILMAN

## Connect to Your Life

**Medical Practices** This is a story about a woman who undergoes medical treatment for a "nervous condition" more than a hundred years ago. In a small group, discuss some medical treatments of the past that are no longer prescribed. List them on a word web like the one shown.

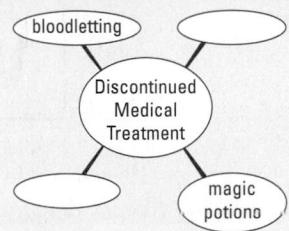

bloodletting

Discontinued Medical Treatment

magic potions

## Build Background

**"Women's Disorders"** This story was written in 1890, when many women—especially nonworking middle-class and upper-class women—suffered from a variety of physical and mental disorders, such as fatigue and depression. If they sought medical treatment and no organic cause could be determined, their ills were often diagnosed as vague, trivial "nervous conditions," curable through isolation and prolonged rest. Although today it is believed that some of these disorders may have been caused by the stress of living within the rigid social roles to which women were confined, doctors in the late 1800s typically felt that the root of many women's illnesses was their gender. They assumed that women were weak and emotionally unstable, and thus by their very nature predisposed to illness.

> **WORDS TO KNOW**
> **Vocabulary Preview**
>
> | | | |
> |---|---|---|
> | atrocious | impertinence | querulous |
> | basely | inanimate | undulating |
> | derision | patent | |
> | felicity | perseverance | |

## Focus Your Reading

**LITERARY ANALYSIS** **FIRST-PERSON NARRATOR** The **narrator** of a story is the character or voice that relates the story's events to the reader. When a story is told from the first-person point of view, the narrator is a character in the story. "The Yellow Wallpaper" is told from the first-person point of view, and the narrator is an unnamed woman diagnosed with a nervous condition.

**ACTIVE READING** **MAKING INFERENCES ABOUT THE NARRATOR** The narrator in this story writes journal entries about her experiences. Much of what happens seems distorted or is unexplained; to understand the events, therefore, you must make **inferences,** or logical guesses, based on the details the narrator provides and what you know about life. As you read, allow yourself to perceive things as the narrator does. Occasionally, though, stand back from her to examine her perceptions and actions with a critical eye.

**READER'S NOTEBOOK** Record your responses to the questions inserted throughout this story. Also jot down other inferences you make about the narrator and the evidence on which you base your inferences.

---

### OVERVIEW

 This selection is included in the **Grade 11 InterActive Reader.**

**Objectives**
1. understand and appreciate a classic **short story (Literary Analysis)**
2. examine **first-person narrator** in a short story **(Literary Analysis)**
3. **make inferences about the narrator (Active Reading)**

**Summary**
The narrator and her husband rent an old mansion that has long stood empty. The woman suffers from a nervous condition, and her husband, who is a doctor, recommends that she recuperate in solitude. He has forbidden her to write because he says it is too taxing, and so she writes her account in secret. She sleeps in a large old nursery at the top of the house, which contains a bed that is fastened to the floor, barred windows, and yellow wallpaper. The woman slowly becomes obsessed with the pattern in the wallpaper. She spends an increasing amount of time examining the wallpaper and decides that it depicts a woman trapped behind bars. Finally she locks herself in the room and starts to peel it off the wall. When she is finished, she crawls in a circle around the room, believing that she herself has escaped from the wallpaper pattern and is free to creep around.

**Thematic Link**
"The Yellow Wallpaper" is an example of the **new literature** that began to emerge in the late 1800s, in which long-repressed **women's voices** began to be heard. **Women's lives** were ruled by their husbands and by their perceived place in society.

### 5-Minute Warm-Up

*Daily Language SkillBuilder*

Have students **proofread** the display sentences on page 739i and write them correctly. The sentences also appear on Transparency 21 of **Grammar Transparencies and Copymasters.**

### Preteaching Vocabulary

If you would like to preteach the WORDS TO KNOW for this selection, use the Mini Lesson p. 766.

THE YELLOW WALLPAPER **765**

---

## LESSON RESOURCES

**UNIT FIVE RESOURCE BOOK,** pp. 6–10

**ASSESSMENT RESOURCES**
**Formal Assessment,** pp. 139–140
**Teacher's Guide to Assessment and Portfolio Use**
**Test Generator**

**SKILLS TRANSPARENCIES AND COPYMASTERS**
**Literary Analysis**
• Point of View, T20 (for Literary Analysis, p. 779)
**Reading and Critical Thinking**
• Making Inferences, T7 (for Active Reading, p. 765)

**Grammar**
• Agreement of Subject and Verb, T47 (for Mini Lesson, p. 769)
• Sentence Fragments II, C108 (for Mini Lesson, p. 780)
• Subject-Verb Agreement II, C124 (for Mini Lesson, p. 769)
**Vocabulary**
• Word Origins, C63 (for Mini Lesson, p. 772)
**Writing**
• Critical Review, C26 (for Writing Option 2, p. 780)
• Short Story, C29 (for Writing Option 3, p. 780)
**Communications**
• Interviewing, T9 (for Activities and Explorations 3, p. 780)

• Dramatic Reading, T12 (for Mini Lesson, p. 770)
• Impromptu Speaking: Dialogue, Role-Play, Debate, T13 (for Mini Lesson, p. 774)

**INTEGRATED TECHNOLOGY**
**Audio Library**
**LaserLinks**
• Historical Connection: "Nervous Conditions"
• Author Background: Charlotte Perkins Gilman. See **Teacher's SourceBook,** p. 61.
**Visit our website:**
www.mcdougallittell.com

**Reading Skills and Strategies:**
**PREVIEW**

Briefly summarize the events of the story, and discuss the context of the story, as outlined in Preparing to Read.

**Literary Analysis**

FIRST-PERSON NARRATOR

Ask students what the advantages and limitations of first-person narration are.
**Possible Responses:** Advantages—In first-person narration, the reader is pulled into the story through the narrator's thoughts, feelings, and emotions. Limitations—The reader learns only what the narrator sees and hears about events and other characters.

 Use **Unit Five Resource Book,** p. 8 for more practice.

**Active Reading** | MAKING INFERENCES ABOUT THE NARRATOR

**A** Ask students what they can infer about the narrator and her ideas about marriage from this remark.
**Possible Response:** The narrator does not expect a husband to take his wife's ideas seriously. She is observant and sees the ways in which her marriage is flawed, but she is also pragmatic and accepts that most men in her society would not behave any better.

 Use **Unit Five Resource Book,** p. 7 for more practice.

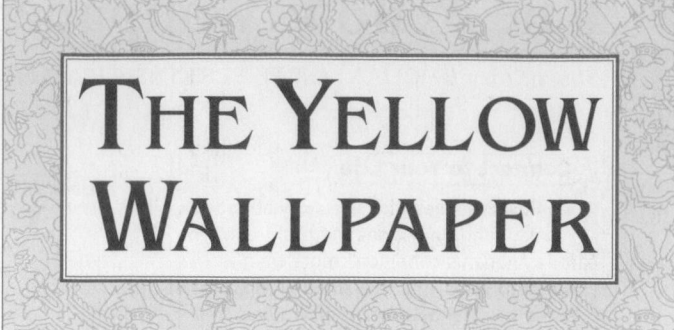

# THE YELLOW WALLPAPER

## CHARLOTTE PERKINS GILMAN

**It** is very seldom that mere ordinary people like John and myself secure ancestral halls for the summer.

A colonial mansion, a hereditary estate, I would say a haunted house, and reach the height of romantic felicity—but that would be asking too much of fate!

Still I will proudly declare that there is something queer about it.

Else, why should it be let so cheaply? And why have stood so long untenanted?

**A** John laughs at me, of course, but one expects that in marriage.

John is practical in the extreme. He has no patience with faith, an intense horror of superstition, and he scoffs openly at any talk of things not to be felt and seen and put down in figures.

John is a physician, and *perhaps*—(I would not say it to a living soul, of course, but this is dead paper and a great relief to my *mind*)—*perhaps* that is one reason I do not get well faster.

You see he does not believe I am sick!

And what can one do?

If a physician of high standing, and one's own husband, assures friends and relatives that there is really nothing the matter with one but temporary nervous depression—a slight hysterical[1] tendency—what is one to do?

My brother is also a physician, and also of high standing, and he says the same thing.

So I take phosphates or phosphites—whichever it is, and tonics, and journeys, and air, and exercise, and am absolutely forbidden to "work" until I am well again.

Personally, I disagree with their ideas.

---

1. **hysterical:** Hysteria is the presence of a physical ailment with no underlying physical cause.

WORDS TO KNOW    **felicity** (fĭ-lĭs′ĭ-tē) *n.* happiness; bliss

---

## Teaching Options

 **Preteaching Vocabulary**

**USING CONTEXT CLUES** Call students' attention to the list of WORDS TO KNOW. Remind them that sometimes they can determine the meaning of an unfamiliar word by relying on context clues in the surrounding text.
**Instruction** Write the following model sentence on the chalkboard and ask a volunteer to use the context to determine the meaning of *atrocious.*

Dave had such atrocious taste in clothing that he made the "worst dressed" list three years in a row.

**Exercises** Ask students to rely on context to determine the meanings of underlined terms in the following sentences:

1. Amy behaved basely and intolerably toward Luis when she unjustly accused him of cheating.
2. The long, undulating road climbed over hills and descended into valleys for many miles.
3. The derision of the audience was unmistakable as the performers were booed off the stage.

 Use **Unit Five Resource Book,** p. 9 for more exercises.

**A lesson on using context clues appears on p. 326 in the Pupil's Edition.**

A Woman Sewing in an Interior (about 1900), Wilhelm Hammershøi. Christie's, London, Bridgeman/Art Resource, New York.

767

## Customizing Instruction

**Less Proficient Readers**

**Set a Purpose** Ask students to read the first section of the story to grasp the situation and to make inferences about the narrator.

**Students Acquiring English**

Explain that everything that happens in the story is described through the eyes of the narrator. Point out that as the story progresses, her narration becomes harder to follow. Suggest that students read aloud in pairs and use questioning and rereading strategies to decipher events when their understanding breaks down.

Use **Spanish Study Guide** for additional support, pp. 182–84.

**Gifted and Talented**

Invite students to take "diagnostic" notes as they read, imagining that they are physicians or psychologists. Ask them to confer with you as a group after they have finished reading the story and present their diagnoses with supporting notes based on what they read. Invite them to critique the treatment the woman received.

## Mini Lesson — Viewing and Representing

*A Woman Sewing in an Interior* **by Wilhelm Hammershøi**

**ART APPRECIATION** In this work by Danish painter Hammershøi (1864–1916), a woman in a floor-length dress sits sewing next to a window illuminated by sunlight.

**Instruction** Point out the use of light and darkness in the painting. Ask: Where is your eye drawn when you look at this painting?

**Possible Response:** The window is light and bright and draws the eye away from the room and from the woman.

**Application** Ask students how they would describe the mood of the painting. What connection can students make between the art and the story?

**Possible Response:** The darkness of the room makes it seem claustrophobic, dull, and uninviting, like the lives of women who were confined to restricted roles in life. The brightness of the window makes the outdoors seem inviting even though there is no scenery visible.

Personally, I believe that congenial work, with excitement and change, would do me good.

But what is one to do?

I did write for a while in spite of them; but it *does* exhaust me a good deal—having to be so sly about it, or else meet with heavy opposition.

**ACTIVE READING**

**A CLARIFY** Why is the narrator writing in secret?

I sometimes fancy that in my condition if I had less opposition and more society and stimulus—but John says the very worst thing I can do is to think about my condition, and I confess it always makes me feel bad.

So I will let it alone and talk about the house.

The most beautiful place! It is quite alone, standing well back from the road, quite three miles from the village. It makes me think of English places that you read about, for there are hedges and walls and gates that lock, and lots of separate little houses for the gardeners and people.

There is a *delicious* garden! I never saw such a garden—large and shady, full of box-bordered paths, and lined with long grape-covered arbors with seats under them.

There were greenhouses, too, but they are all broken now.

There was some legal trouble, I believe, something about the heirs and coheirs; anyhow, the place has been empty for years.

That spoils my ghostliness, I am afraid, but I don't care—there is something strange about the house—I can feel it.

I even said so to John one moonlight evening, but he said what I felt was a draft, and shut the window.

I get unreasonably angry with John sometimes. I'm sure I never used to be so sensitive. I think it is due to this nervous condition.

But John says if I feel so, I shall neglect proper self-control; so I take pains to control myself— before him, at least, and that makes me very tired.

I don't like our room a bit. I wanted one downstairs that opened on the piazza and had roses all over the window, and such pretty old-fashioned chintz hangings! but John would not hear of it.

He said there was only one window and not room for two beds, and no near room for him if he took another.

He is very careful and loving, and hardly lets me stir without special direction.

I have a schedule prescription for each hour in the day; he takes all care from me, and so I feel basely ungrateful not to value it more.

He said we came here solely on my account, that I was to have perfect rest and all the air I could get. "Your exercise depends on your strength, my dear," said he, "and your food somewhat on your appetite; but air you can absorb all the time." So we took the nursery at the top of the house.

**ACTIVE READING**

**B EVALUATE** Describe the relationship between the narrator and her husband.

It is a big, airy room, the whole floor nearly, with windows that look all ways, and air and sunshine galore. It was nursery first and then playroom and gymnasium, I should judge; for the windows are barred for little children, and there are rings and things in the walls.

The paint and paper look as if a boys' school had used it. It is stripped off—the paper—in great patches all around the head of my bed, about as far as I can reach, and in a great place on the other side of the room low down. I never saw a worse paper in my life.

One of those sprawling flamboyant patterns committing every artistic sin.

It is dull enough to confuse the eye in following, pronounced enough to constantly irritate and provoke study, and when you follow the lame uncertain curves for a little distance they suddenly commit suicide—plunge off at outrageous angles, destroy themselves in unheard of contradictions.

WORDS
TO
KNOW

**basely** (bās'lē) *adv.* dishonorably; meanly

The color is repellent, almost revolting; a smouldering unclean yellow, strangely faded by the slow-turning sunlight.

It is a dull yet lurid orange in some places, a sickly sulphur tint in others.

No wonder the children hated it! I should hate it myself if I had to live in this room long.

There comes John, and I must put this away,—he hates to have me write a word.

We have been here two weeks, and I haven't felt like writing before, since that first day.

I am sitting by the window now, up in this atrocious nursery, and there is nothing to hinder my writing as much as I please, save lack of strength.

John is away all day, and even some nights when his cases are serious.

I am glad my case is not serious!

But these nervous troubles are dreadfully depressing.

John does not know how much I really suffer. He knows there is no *reason* to suffer, and that satisfies him.

Of course it is only nervousness. It does weigh on me so not to do my duty in any way!

I meant to be such a help to John, such a real rest and comfort, and here I am a comparative burden already!

Nobody would believe what an effort it is to do what little I am able,—to dress and entertain, and order things.

It is fortunate Mary is so good with the baby. Such a dear baby!

And yet I *cannot* be with him, it makes me so nervous.

I suppose John never was nervous in his life. He laughs at me so about this wallpaper!

At first he meant to repaper the room, but afterwards he said that I was letting it get the better of me, and that nothing was worse for a nervous patient than to give way to such fancies.

He said that after the wallpaper was changed

**ACTIVE READING**

 **CONNECT** What do the details about the room suggest about its function?

it would be the heavy bedstead, and then the barred windows, and then that gate at the head of the stairs, and so on.

"You know the place is doing you good," he said, "and really, dear, I don't care to renovate the house just for a three months' rental."

"Then do let us go downstairs," I said, "there are such pretty rooms there."

Then he took me in his arms and called me a blessed little goose, and said he would go down to the cellar, if I wished, and have it white-washed into the bargain.

But he is right enough about the beds and windows and things.

It is an airy and comfortable room as any one need wish, and, of course, I would not be so silly as to make him uncomfortable just for a whim.

I'm really getting quite fond of the big room, all but that horrid paper.

Out of one window I can see the garden, those mysterious deepshaded arbors, the riotous old-fashioned flowers, and bushes and gnarly trees.

Out of another I get a lovely view of the bay and a little private wharf belonging to the estate. There is a beautiful shaded lane that runs down there from the house. I always fancy I see people walking in these numerous paths and arbors, but John has cautioned me not to give way to fancy in the least. He says that with my imaginative power and habit of story-making, a nervous weakness like mine is sure to lead to all manner of excited fancies, and that I ought to use my will and good sense to check the tendency. So I try.

I think sometimes that if I were only well enough to write a little it would relieve the press of ideas and rest me.

But I find I get pretty tired when I try.

It is so discouraging not to have any advice and companionship about my work. When I get really well, John says we will ask Cousin Henry and

| WORDS TO KNOW | **atrocious** (ə-trō′shəs) *adj.* shockingly bad or lacking in taste; awful |
| --- | --- |

**769**

## Customizing Instruction

### Students Acquiring English

**1** Help students understand the meaning of archaic terms. Point out that *on my account* means "for my sake."

### Multiple Learning Styles
**Visual Learners**

**2** Ask students to close their eyes while you read aloud the description of the nursery. Ask them what words and phrases help them visualize the room.

**Possible Responses:** "windows are barred"; "rings . . . in the walls"; "stripped off . . . paper—in great patches"; "lame uncertain curves"; "outrageous angles"; "smouldering unclean yellow"; "sickly sulphur tint"

Ask students what atmosphere is created by these evocative words describing the nursery.

**Possible Responses:** depressing, like a jail, ugly, menacing

### Students Acquiring English

**3** Explain that, in this context, *save* means "except for." You might paraphrase the last part of this sentence for students: "there is nothing to prevent me from writing as much as I want to, except that I don't feel strong enough to do it."

### Less Proficient Readers

**4** Have students explain who Mary and the baby might be and why the narrator cannot be with the baby.

**Possible Responses:** The baby is the narrator's; Mary is probably the nursemaid. The narrator may be kept from seeing the baby because it makes her too nervous.

 **Grammar**
Mini Lesson

**SUBJECT-VERB AGREEMENT** Remind students that a singular verb is used with a singular subject and a plural verb is used with a plural subject. Words that come between a subject and its verb do not affect subject-verb agreement. Write the sentence on the chalkboard:

The mansion, unlike other homes in the area, was uninhabited for many years.

**Instruction** Underline the subject and verb as shown. Point out that the word *homes* is part of a parenthetical phrase set off by commas and should not be confused with the subject of the sentence. Review that a compound subject joined

by *and* takes a plural verb; a compound subject preceded by *each, every,* or *many a* takes a singular verb; and a compound subject joined by *or* or *nor* uses a verb that agrees with the subject nearer to the verb. Indefinite pronouns may be either singular or plural, depending on how they are used in the sentence.

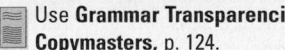 Use **Grammar Transparencies and Copymasters,** p. 124.

Use McDougal Littell's *Language Network,* Chapter 5, for more instruction in subject-verb agreement.

Julia down for a long visit; but he says he would as soon put fireworks in my pillowcase as to let me have those stimulating people about now.

I wish I could get well faster.

But I must not think about that. This paper looks to me as if it knew what a vicious influence it had!

There is a recurrent spot where the pattern lolls like a broken neck and two bulbous eyes stare at you upside down.

I get positively angry with the <u>impertinence</u> of it and the everlastingness. Up and down and sideways they crawl, and those absurd, unblinking eyes are everywhere. There is one place where two breadths didn't match, and the eyes go all up and down the line, one a little higher than the other.

**A** I never saw so much expression in an <u>inanimate</u> thing before, and we all know how much expression they have! I used to lie awake as a child and get more entertainment and terror out of blank walls and plain furniture than most children could find in a toystore.

I remember what a kindly wink the knobs of our big, old bureau used to have, and there was one chair that always seemed like a strong friend.

I used to feel that if any of the other things looked too fierce I could always hop into that chair and be safe.

The furniture in this room is no worse than inharmonious, however, for we had to bring it all from downstairs. I suppose when this was used as a playroom they had to take the nursery things out, and no wonder! I never saw such ravages as the children have made here.

**B** The wallpaper, as I said before, is torn off in spots, and it sticketh closer than a brother—they must have had <u>perseverance</u> as well as hatred.

Then the floor is scratched and gouged and splintered, the plaster itself is dug out here and there, and this great heavy bed which is all we found in the room, looks as if it had been through the wars.

But I don't mind it a bit—only the paper.

There comes John's sister. Such a dear girl as she is, and so careful of me! I must not let her find me writing.

She is a perfect and enthusiastic housekeeper, and hopes for no better profession. I verily believe she thinks it is the writing which made me sick!

But I can write when she is out, and see her a long way off from these windows.

There is one that commands the road, a lovely shaded winding road, and one that just looks off over the country. A lovely country, too, full of great elms and velvet meadows.

This wallpaper has a kind of sub-pattern in a different shade, a particularly irritating one, for you can only see it in certain lights, and not clearly then.

But in the places where it isn't faded and where the sun is just so—I can see a strange, provoking, formless sort of figure, that seems to skulk about behind that silly and conspicuous front design.

### ACTIVE READING

**CLARIFY** Describe the **C** effect the wallpaper is having on the narrator.

There's sister on the stairs!

Well, the Fourth of July is over! The people are all gone and I am tired out. John thought it might do me good to see a little company, so we just had mother and Nellie and the children down for a week.

Of course I didn't do a thing. Jennie sees to everything now.

But it tired me all the same.

John says if I don't pick up faster he shall send me to Weir Mitchell[2] in the fall.

---

2. **Weir Mitchell:** Dr. Silas Weir Mitchell, famous for his "rest cure" for nervous diseases, which is no longer considered effective.

WORDS TO KNOW
**impertinence** (ĭm-pûr'tn-əns) *n.* improper boldness; rudeness
**inanimate** (ĭn-ăn'ə-mĭt) *adj.* not alive; lifeless
**perseverance** (pûr'sə-vîr'əns) *n.* persistence in the face of difficulty; determination

770

---

*Stairway* (1949), Edward Hopper. Oil on wood, 16″ × 11 ⅞″, Collection of Whitney Museum of American Art, New York, Josephine N. Hopper Bequest (70.1265). Copyright © 1995 Whitney Museum of American Art. Photo by Geoffrey Clements.

771

## Customizing Instruction

### Students Acquiring English

**1** Be sure that second-language students understand what is meant by the reference to "fireworks in my pillowcase." Ask students to describe the image that the expression creates and have them explain how it relates to entertaining visitors.

**Possible Response:** Fireworks in her pillowcase conveys the image of a sleeping, relaxed narrator being suddenly awakened by loud, jarring, confusing, even frightening, sounds and sights. John's use of the fireworks image could indicate that he believes that whatever level of calm and relaxation his wife has achieved will be destroyed by contact with other people.

### Less Proficient Readers

**2** Ask volunteers to summarize the story so far and to share their inferences. Ask: What do you think the narrator's real problem is?

**Possible Responses:** The narrator is being haunted by malevolent spirits connected with the house; she is suffering from depression and is slipping into dementia.

**Set a Purpose** Encourage students to keep reading between the lines to look for additional signs of the narrator's deterioration.

## (Mini Lesson) Viewing and Representing

**Stairway by Edward Hopper**

**ART APPRECIATION** Edward Hopper (1882–1967) is generally considered the foremost American realistic painter of the 20th century. Sparsely furnished interiors and stark exteriors, solitary figures, or groups of figures who are isolated from one another are common in his work.

**Instruction** In *Stairway,* the viewer looks down from a banistered staircase at yellow walls and an open white door, beyond which lie dark green hills. Explain that mood is the feeling created by a work of literature or art. Have students discuss the mood they sense in this picture.

**Possible Responses:** loneliness, fear of the outside/unknown, hope

**Application** Ask students whether the picture expresses feelings similar to those in the story.

**Possible Responses:** Yes, because the unknown is a powerful presence in the picture, just as it is in the story. No, because the story is chaotic and confusing, while the picture is very ordered and realistic.

## Reading and Analyzing

### Active Reading | MAKING INFERENCES ABOUT THE NARRATOR

**A** Ask students to use text evidence and their own experience to draw inferences about what the narrator means when she says Dr. Mitchell is "just like John and my brother, only more so!"

**Possible Responses:** He is paternalistic, arrogant, too sure of himself; he doesn't understand the narrator's wants or needs.

**B** Ask what the narrator means by saying she is fond of the room both in spite of and because of the wallpaper.

**Possible Response:** The wallpaper fascinates and repulses her at the same time.

### Literary Analysis | FIRST-PERSON NARRATOR

**C** Ask students to speculate how the description of this scene would have been different if John were narrating the story.

**Possible Response:** John would not have described the conversation as a "real earnest reasonable talk." He would have focused on the narrator's tears and his own view of her psychological state. His account would seem very rational but would ignore the feelings of the narrator.

### ACTIVE READING

**D** **EVALUATE** If students need help, share the following thought processes with them. **Think-Aloud Model:** *The "dim shape" that the narrator senses in the wallpaper pattern has now taken on a clearer shape–that of a woman stooping and creeping about. This makes me think that the narrator is beginning to hallucinate.*

---

**A** But I don't want to go there at all. I had a friend who was in his hands once, and she says he is just like John and my brother, only more so!

Besides, it is such an undertaking to go so far.

I don't feel as if it was worth while to turn my hand over for anything, and I'm getting dreadfully fretful and querulous.

I cry at nothing, and cry most of the time.

Of course I don't when John is here, or anybody else, but when I am alone.

And I am alone a good deal just now. John is kept in town very often by serious cases, and Jennie is good and lets me alone when I want her to.

So I walk a little in the garden or down that lovely lane, sit on the porch under the roses, and lie down up here a good deal.

**B** I'm getting really fond of the room in spite of the wallpaper. Perhaps *because* of the wallpaper.

It dwells in my mind so!

I lie here on this great immovable bed—it is nailed down, I believe—and follow that pattern about by the hour. It is as good as gymnastics, I assure you. I start, we'll say, at the bottom, down in the corner over there where it has not been touched, and I determine for the thousandth time that I *will* follow that pointless pattern to some sort of a conclusion.

I know a little of the principle of design, and I know this thing was not arranged on any laws of radiation, or alternation, or repetition, or symmetry, or anything else that I ever heard of.

It is repeated, of course, by the breadths, but not otherwise.

Looked at in one way each breadth stands alone, the bloated curves and flourishes—a kind of "debased Romanesque"[3] with *delirium tremens*[4]—go waddling up and down in isolated columns of fatuity.[5]

But, on the other hand, they connect diagonally, and the sprawling outlines run off in great slanting waves of optic horror, like a lot of wallowing seaweeds in full chase.

The whole thing goes horizontally, too, at least it seems so, and I exhaust myself in trying to distinguish the order of its going in that direction.

They have used a horizontal breadth for a frieze, and that adds wonderfully to the confusion.

There is one end of the room where it is almost intact, and there, when the crosslights fade and the low sun shines directly upon it, I can almost fancy radiation after all,—the interminable grotesques seem to form around a common center and rush off in headlong plunges of equal distraction.

It makes me tired to follow it. I will take a nap I guess.

I don't know why I should write this.

I don't want to.

I don't feel able.

And I know John would think it absurd. But I *must* say what I feel and think in some way—it is such a relief!

But the effort is getting to be greater than the relief.

Half the time now I am awfully lazy, and lie down ever so much.

John says I mustn't lose my strength, and has me take cod liver oil and lots of tonics and things, to say nothing of ale and wine and rare meat.

Dear John! He loves me very dearly, and hates to have me sick. I tried to have a real earnest reasonable talk with him the other day, and tell him how I wish he would let me go and make a visit to Cousin Henry and Julia.

But he said I wasn't able to go, nor able to stand it after I got there; and I did not make out a very good case for myself, for I was crying before I had finished.

It is getting to be a great effort for me to think straight. Just this nervous weakness I suppose.

And dear John gathered me up in his arms, and

**C**

---

3. **Romanesque:** an artistic style characterized by simple ornamentation.

4. *delirium tremens:* violent trembling and hallucinations caused by excessive drinking.

5. **fatuity** (fə-tōō′ĭ-tē): foolishness; smug stupidity.

---

WORDS
TO
KNOW

**querulous** (kwĕr′ə-ləs) *adj.* given to complaining

772

---

## Teaching Options

 **Mini Lesson** ## Vocabulary Strategy

### WORD ORIGINS

**Instruction** Tell students that researching word origins can help them recognize related words and aid in understanding meanings and can also uncover interesting or surprising information that will help them remember a new word. For example, explain that the word *hysterical* (page 766) is derived from the Greek word *hystera,* meaning *uterus.* The ancient notion was that emotional excitability was caused by a disturbance of the womb.

**Application** Have students create a chart to record etymologies for the following words from the selection. Encourage students to add to the chart as they read.

| Word | Etymology | Definition |
|------|-----------|------------|
| discouraging (p. 769) | (*dis,* meaning "away" + *corage* [Old French] meaning "heart, spirit") | (depriving of confidence, or spirit) |
| flamboyant (p. 768) | ([Old French] *flambe,* meaning "flame") | (characterized by waving curves suggesting flames; ornate) |
| distraction (p. 772) | (*dis,* meaning "away" + *trahere* [Latin], meaning "to draw") | (drawn in different directions; mental confusion) |

just carried me upstairs and laid me on the bed, and sat by me and read to me till it tired my head.

He said I was his darling and his comfort and all he had, and that I must take care of myself for his sake, and keep well.

He says no one but myself can help me out of it, that I must use my will and self-control and not let any silly fancies run away with me.

There's one comfort, the baby is well and happy, and does not have to occupy this nursery with the horrid wallpaper.

If we had not used it, that blessed child would have! What a fortunate escape! Why, I wouldn't have a child of mine, an impressionable little thing, live in such a room for worlds.

I never thought of it before, but it is lucky that John kept me here after all, I can stand it so much easier than a baby, you see.

Of course I never mention it to them any more—I am too wise,—but I keep watch of it all the same.

There are things in that paper that nobody knows but me, or ever will.

Behind that outside pattern the dim shapes get clearer every day.

It is always the same shape, only very numerous.

And it is like a woman stooping down and creeping about behind that pattern. I don't like

### ACTIVE READING

**EVALUATE** How do you explain the figure beginning to appear in the wallpaper?

it a bit. I wonder—I begin to think—I wish John would take me away from here!

It is so hard to talk with John about my case, because he is so wise, and because he loves me so.

But I tried it last night.

It was moonlight. The moon shines in all around just as the sun does.

I hate to see it sometimes, it creeps so slowly, and always comes in by one window or another.

John was asleep and I hated to waken him, so I kept still and watched the moonlight on that undulating wallpaper till I felt creepy.

The faint figure behind seemed to shake the pattern, just as if she wanted to get out.

I got up softly and went to feel and see if the paper *did* move, and when I came back John was awake.

"What is it, little girl?" he said. "Don't go walking about like that—you'll get cold."

I thought it was a good time to talk, so I told him that I really was not gaining here, and that I wished he would take me away.

"Why darling!" said he, "our lease will be up in three weeks, and I can't see how to leave before.

"The repairs are not done at home, and I can not possibly leave town just now. Of course if you were in any danger, I could and would, but you really are better, dear, whether you can see it or not. I am a doctor, dear, and I know. You are gaining flesh and color, your appetite is better, I feel really much easier about you."

"I don't weigh a bit more," said I, "nor as much; and my appetite may be better in the evening when you are here, but it is worse in the morning when you are away!"

"Bless her little heart!" said he with a big hug, "she shall be as sick as she pleases! But now let's improve the shining hours[6] by going to sleep, and talk about it in the morning!"

"And you won't go away?" I asked gloomily.

"Why, how can I, dear? It is only three weeks more and then we will take a nice little trip of a few days while Jennie is getting the house ready. Really dear you are better!"

"Better in body perhaps—" I began, and stopped short, for he sat up straight and looked at me with such a stern, reproachful look that I could not say another word.

---

6. **improve the shining hours:** make good use of time (an allusion to the poem "Against Idleness and Mischief" by Isaac Watts: "How doth the little busy bee / Improve each shining hour, / And gather honey all the day / From every opening flower!").

---

WORDS
TO
KNOW     **undulating** (ŭn'jə-lā'tĭng) *adj.* moving with a wavelike motion **undulate** *v.*

773

## Customizing Instruction

### Less Proficient Readers

Use the following questions to guide students to understand the narrator's state of mind and her husband's treatment of her disorder.

- How does the narrator spend her time?

  **Possible Response:** She spends most of her time alone  crying, resting, writing, and obsessing about the wallpaper.

- What does the narrator think would help her recuperate?

  **Possible Response:** having company or visiting relatives

- Why does John think that she would not be able to stand a visit?

  **Possible Response:** She was wrought up and crying when she made the request, so she does not seem well enough to travel.

**1** Ask students to pause at this point and discuss changes in the narrator as a result of the rest cure.

**Possible Responses:** She is getting worse; she has difficulty thinking straight and talking; she cries a lot and seems more dependent on her husband.

### Multiple Learning Styles
#### Interpersonal Learners

**2** Have students discuss the tone that the narrator's husband takes with her. What does he seem to think about her illness? Ask students to hypothesize about why the narrator has hidden her obsession with the wallpaper from him.

**Possible Responses:** The tone he has taken with her seems to be one of gentle but firm admonishment; he seems to think that all she needs is self-control to overcome her illness. She may hide her obsession with the wallpaper because she doesn't want John to know that she has really lost control.

| Word | Etymology | Definition |
|------|-----------|------------|
| grotesques (p. 772) | (from *pittura grotesesca* ([Old Italian], meaning "cave painting") | (a style of art characterized by fantastic human and animal forms often interwoven with foliage) |
| renovate (p. 769) | (*re*, meaning "again" + *novare* [Latin], meaning "to make new") | (to restore to a former, better state) |

Use **Vocabulary Transparencies and Copymasters**, p. 63.

**A lesson on word origins appears on p. 550 in the Pupil's Edition.**

## Reading and Analyzing

"My darling," said he, "I beg of you, for my sake and for our child's sake, as well as for your own, that you will never for one instant let that idea enter your mind! There is nothing so dangerous, so fascinating, to a temperament like yours. It is a false and foolish fancy. Can you not trust me as a physician when I tell you so?"

### ACTIVE READING

**A** **INFER** What is the "idea" that John says the narrator should not "let . . . enter your mind"?

So of course I said no more on that score, and we went to sleep before long. He thought I was asleep first, but I wasn't, and lay there for hours trying to decide whether that front pattern and the back pattern really did move together or separately.

**On** a pattern like this, by daylight, there is a lack of sequence, a defiance of law, that is a constant irritant to a normal mind.

The color is hideous enough, and unreliable enough, and infuriating enough, but the pattern is torturing.

You think you have mastered it, but just as you get well underway in following, it turns a back-somersault and there you are. It slaps you in the face, knocks you down, and tramples upon you. It is like a bad dream.

The outside pattern is a florid arabesque,[7] reminding one of a fungus. If you can imagine a toadstool in joints, an interminable string of toadstools, budding and sprouting in endless convolutions—why, that is something like it.

That is, sometimes!

There is one marked peculiarity about this paper, a thing nobody seems to notice but myself, and that is that it changes as the light changes.

When the sun shoots in through the east window—I always watch for that first long, straight ray—it changes so quickly that I never can quite believe it.

That is why I watch it always.

By moonlight—the moon shines in all night when there is a moon—I wouldn't know it was the same paper.

At night in any kind of light, in twilight, candle light, lamplight, and worst of all by moonlight, it becomes bars! The outside pattern I mean, and the woman behind it is as plain as can be.

I didn't realize for a long time what the thing was that showed behind, that dim sub-pattern, but now I am quite sure it is a woman.

By daylight she is subdued, quiet. I fancy it is the pattern that keeps her so still. It is so puzzling. It keeps me quiet by the hour.

I lie down ever so much now. John says it is good for me, and to sleep all I can.

Indeed he started the habit by making me lie down for an hour after each meal.

It is a very bad habit I am convinced, for you see I don't sleep.

And that cultivates deceit, for I don't tell them I'm awake—O no!

The fact is I am getting a little afraid of John.

He seems very queer sometimes, and even Jennie has an inexplicable look.

It strikes me occasionally, just as a scientific hypothesis,—that perhaps it is the paper!

I have watched John when he did not know I was looking, and come into the room suddenly on the most innocent excuses, and I've caught him several times *looking at the paper!* And Jennie too. I caught Jennie with her hand on it once.

She didn't know I was in the room, and when I asked her in a quiet, a very quiet voice, with the most restrained manner possible, what she was doing with the paper—she turned around as if she had been caught stealing, and looked quite angry—asked me why I should frighten her so!

Then she said that the paper stained everything it touched, that she had found yellow smooches[8] on all my clothes and John's, and she wished we would be more careful!

Did not that sound innocent? But I know she was studying that pattern, and I am determined that nobody shall find it out but myself!

---

7. **florid arabesque:** an elaborate interwoven pattern.
8. **smooches:** dirty marks or spots; smudges.

## Teaching Options

 **Mini Lesson** **Speaking and Listening**

### ROLE-PLAYING

**Prepare** Role-playing gives students the opportunity to explore literary characters and their conflicts more deeply by imagining themselves as those characters. Through role-playing, students can extend and improvise upon story lines, testing the development and outcome of a story against their own sense of reality. Encourage students to reread the literary work that is their point of departure, to read the characters' dialogue aloud more than once in order to "hear" the characters' voices, and to discuss the work with other members of their group.

**Present** Invite groups of three to role-play the narrator, John, and Jennie. Encourage groups to use their creativity to interpret the characters' views of themselves and one another and to decide at what point in the story their performance should be set. Invite a succession of groups to perform, giving the class an opportunity to consider several interpretations.

**BLOCK SCHEDULING** This activity is particularly well-suited for longer class periods.

**Life** is very much more exciting now than it used to be. You see I have something more to expect, to look forward to, to watch. I really do eat better, and am more quiet than I was.

John is so pleased to see me improve! He laughed a little the other day, and said I seemed to be flourishing in spite of my wallpaper.

I turned it off with a laugh. I had no intention of telling him it was *because* of the wallpaper—he would make fun of me. He might even want to take me away.

**ACTIVE READING**

**PREDICT** The narrator's attitude seems to have changed. Do you think she will get better?

I don't want to leave now until I have found it out. There is a week more, and I think that will be enough.

**I'm** feeling ever so much better! I don't sleep much at night, for it is so interesting to watch developments; but I sleep a good deal in the daytime.

In the daytime it is tiresome and perplexing.

There are always new shoots on the fungus, and new shades of yellow all over it. I cannot keep count of them, though I have tried conscientiously.

It is the strangest yellow, that wallpaper! It makes me think of all the yellow things I ever saw—not beautiful ones like buttercups, but old foul, bad yellow things.

But there is something else about that paper—the smell! I noticed it the moment we came into the room, but with so much air and sun it was not bad. Now we have had a week of fog and rain, and whether the windows are open or not, the smell is here.

It creeps all over the house.

I find it hovering in the dining room, skulking in the parlor, hiding in the hall, lying in wait for me on the stairs.

It gets into my hair.

Even when I go to ride, if I turn my head suddenly and surprise it—there is that smell!

Such a peculiar odor, too! I have spent hours in trying to analyze it, to find what it smelled like.

It is not bad—at first, and very gentle, but quite the subtlest, most enduring odor I ever met.

In this damp weather it is awful, I wake up in the night and find it hanging over me.

It used to disturb me at first. I thought seriously of burning the house—to reach the smell.

But now I am used to it. The only thing I can think of that it is like is the *color* of the paper! A yellow smell.

There is a very funny mark on this wall, low down, near the mopboard. A streak that runs round the room. It goes behind every piece of furniture, except the bed, a long, straight, even *smooch*, as if it had been rubbed over and over.

I wonder how it was done and who did it, and what they did it for. Round and round and round—round and round and round—it makes me dizzy!

**I really** have discovered something at last.

Through watching so much at night, when it changes so, I have finally found out.

The front pattern *does* move—and no wonder! The woman behind shakes it!

Sometimes I think there are a great many women behind, and sometimes only one, and she crawls around fast, and her crawling shakes it all over.

Then in the very bright spots she keeps still, and in the very shady spots she just takes hold of the bars and shakes them hard.

And she is all the time trying to climb through. But nobody could climb through that pattern—it strangles so; I think that is why it has so many heads.

They get through, and then the pattern strangles them off and turns them upside down, and makes their eyes white!

If those heads were covered or taken off it would not be half so bad.

**I think** that woman gets out in the daytime!

And I'll tell you why—privately—I've seen her! I can see her out of every one of my windows!

---

### Less Proficient Readers

**1** Ask students to share their views of the narrator's changing mental condition, based on inferences they have made about her narrative. What does the fact that she is concerned about whether the two patterns on the wallpaper are moving together or separately suggest about her mental state?

**Possible Responses:** She no longer questions that it is moving, only in what direction; she is losing touch with reality.

**Set a Purpose** Encourage students to predict what will happen and ask them to read to see whether their predictions come to pass.

### Multiple Learning Styles
**Linguistic Learners**

**2** Read aloud this passage and ask students to pay attention to the figurative language. What images does the narrator use and what do those images say about how the wallpaper is affecting her?

**Possible Responses:** The narrator compares the wallpaper to a torturing, bullying person and to a fungus growing out of control. Her perceptions are getting increasingly distorted and violent. She views the wallpaper as a cunning adversary that tortures and assaults her.

### Gifted and Talented

**3** Ask students what they think the woman in the wallpaper represents.

**Possible Response:** The woman stands for the narrator's view of herself or of the plight of all women—trapped and trying to climb through the pattern or role that society has defined for them.

---

**Cross Curricular Link  Psychology**

**DEPRESSION** Clinical depression affects 10 million Americans a year, in all age groups, including up to 5 percent of the teen population. Signs of clinical depression include feelings of sadness, emptiness, or hopelessness; inability to concentrate or make decisions; loss of energy; sleep and appetite disturbances; and changes in behavior.

*Postpartum depression* affects one in ten new mothers. Symptoms can range from mild to severe and can appear up to a year after giving birth. Symptoms include anxiety, nervousness, exhaustion, lack of interest in the baby, and uncontrollable crying. About one in one thousand women suffer from *postpartum psychosis,* in which symptoms such as insomnia, hallucinations, and bizarre feelings and behavior are very exaggerated.

Although mild cases of postpartum depression usually disappear on their own, most types of depression should be treated by a competent medical professional. Treatment may consist of medications, psychological therapy, or a combination of the two.

## Reading and Analyzing

---

It is the same woman, I know, for she is always creeping, and most women do not creep by daylight.

I see her on that long road under the trees, creeping along, and when a carriage comes she hides under the blackberry vines.

I don't blame her a bit. It must be very humiliating to be caught creeping by daylight!

**1** I always lock the door when I creep by daylight. I can't do it at night, for I know John would suspect something at once.

**A** And John is so queer now, that I don't want to irritate him. I wish he would take another room! Besides, I don't want anybody to get that woman out at night but myself.

I often wonder if I could see her out of all the windows at once.

But, turn as fast as I can, I can only see out of one at one time.

And though I always see her, she may be able to creep faster than I can turn!

I have watched her sometimes away off in the open country, creeping as fast as a cloud shadow in a high wind.

ACTIVE READING

**B** EVALUATE What is the narrator's condition?

If only that top pattern could be gotten off from the under one! I mean to try it, little by little.

I have found out another funny thing, but I shan't tell it this time! It does not do to trust people too much.

There are only two more days to get this paper off, and I believe John is beginning to notice. I don't like the look in his eyes.

And I heard him ask Jennie a lot of professional questions about me. She had a very good report to give.

She said I slept a good deal in the daytime.

John knows I don't sleep very well at night, for all I'm so quiet!

He asked me all sorts of questions, too, and pretended to be very loving and kind.

**C** As if I couldn't see through him!

Still, I don't wonder he acts so, sleeping under this paper for three months.

It only interests me, but I feel sure John and Jennie are secretly affected by it.

**Hurrah!** This is the last day, but it is enough. John to stay in town over night, and won't be out until this evening.

Jennie wanted to sleep with me—the sly thing! but I told her I should undoubtedly rest better for a night all alone.

That was clever, for really I wasn't alone a bit! As soon as it was moonlight and that poor thing began to crawl and shake the pattern, I got up and ran to help her.

I pulled and she shook, I shook and she pulled, and before morning we had peeled off yards of that paper.

A strip about as high as my head and half around the room.

And then when the sun came and that awful pattern began to laugh at me, I declared I would finish it today!

We go away tomorrow, and they are moving all my furniture down again to leave things as they were before.

Jennie looked at the wall in amazement, but I told her merrily that I did it out of pure spite at the vicious thing.

She laughed and said she wouldn't mind doing it herself, but I must not get tired.

How she betrayed herself that time!

But I am here, and no person touches this paper but me,—not *alive*!

**D** She tried to get me out of the room—it was too patent! But I said it was so quiet and empty and clean now that I believed I would lie down again and sleep all I could; and not to wake me even for dinner—I would call when I woke.

So now she is gone, and the servants are gone, and the things are gone, and there is nothing left but that great bedstead nailed down, with the canvas mattress we found on it.

We shall sleep downstairs tonight, and take the boat home tomorrow.

WORDS TO KNOW | **patent** (păt'nt) *adj.* obvious; apparent

776

---

## Teaching Options

### ✓ Assessment **Informal Assessment**

### Less Proficient Readers

**1** To help students understand the extent of the narrator's deterioration, ask the following questions:

• What is the significance of the narrator's statement that she always locks the door when she creeps by daylight?

**Possible Response:** It reveals that the narrator is spending her days creeping around the room.

• What does the narrator think John will suspect if she creeps by daylight?

**Possible Responses:** He will suspect that she wants to escape from him; that she has lost control; that she is mad.

**A** **CLARIFY** Possible Responses:
She believes that she has freed all the women in the wallpaper; she believes she has escaped from the wallpaper herself.

**Reading Skills and Strategies:**
**EVALUATE**

**B** Ask students to describe the narrator's state at the end of the story and to predict what might happen to her afterward.

• What is the narrator doing?
  **Answer:** She is crawling around the room.

• Why does her husband faint?
  **Possible Response:** He is shocked by her condition.

• Can she still be helped? Why or why not?
  **Possible Responses:** Yes, if she gets away from her controlling husband and gets proper treatment for her disorder. No, her condition seems too far gone.

---

I quite enjoy the room, now it is bare again. How those children did tear about here! This bedstead is fairly gnawed!

But I must get to work.

I have locked the door and thrown the key down into the front path.

I don't want to go out, and I don't want to have anybody come in, till John comes.

I want to astonish him.

I've got a rope up here that even Jennie did not find. If that woman does get out, and tries to get away, I can tie her!

But I forgot I could not reach far without anything to stand on!

This bed will *not* move!

I tried to lift and push it until I was lame, and then I got so angry I bit off a little piece at one corner—but it hurt my teeth.

Then I peeled off all the paper I could reach standing on the floor. It sticks horribly and the pattern just enjoys it! All those strangled heads and bulbous eyes and waddling fungus growths just shriek with <u>derision</u>!

I am getting angry enough to do something desperate. To jump out of the window would be admirable exercise, but the bars are too strong even to try.

Besides I wouldn't do it. Of course not. I know well enough that a step like that is improper and might be misconstrued.

I don't like to *look* out of the windows even— there are so many of those creeping women, and they creep so fast.

**A** | **CLARIFY** What does the narrator now believe?

I wonder if they all come out of that wallpaper as I did?

But I am securely fastened now by my well-hidden rope—you don't get *me* out in the road there!

I suppose I shall have to get back behind the pattern when it comes night, and that is hard!

It is so pleasant to be out in this great room and creep around as I please!

I don't want to go outside. I won't, even if Jennie asks me to.

For outside you have to creep on the ground, and everything is green instead of yellow.

But here I can creep smoothly on the floor, and my shoulder just fits in that long smooch around the wall, so I cannot lose my way.

Why there's John at the door!

It is no use, young man, you can't open it! How he does call and pound!

Now he's crying for an axe.

It would be a shame to break down that beautiful door!

"John dear!" said I in the gentlest voice, "the key is down by the front steps, under a plantain leaf!"

That silenced him for a few moments.

Then he said—very quietly indeed, "Open the door, my darling!"

"I can't," said I. "The key is down by the front door under a plantain leaf!"

And then I said it again, several times, very gently and slowly, and said it so often that he had to go and see, and he got it of course, and came in. He stopped short by the door.

"What is the matter?" he cried. "What are you doing!"

I kept on creeping just the same, but I looked at him over my shoulder.

"I've got out at last," said I, "in spite of you and Jane.[9] And I've pulled off most of the paper, so you can't put me back!"

Now why should that man have fainted? But he did, and right across my path by the wall, so that I had to creep over him every time! ❖

**B**

---

9. **in spite of you and Jane:** This reference to a previously unmentioned Jane is a point of debate. It could be an error made by the original printer for the name of the sister-housekeeper Jennie or Cousin Julia. It is also possible, however, that Jane is the narrator, here freeing herself from both her husband and her commonplace, wifely "Jane" self.

| WORDS TO KNOW | **derision** (dĭ-rĭzh′ən) *n.* harsh ridicule or mockery; scorn |
|---|---|

---

# Teaching Options

## ✓ Assessment **Standardized Test Practice**

**SENTENCE COMPLETION** Explain that a sentence-completion question contains a sentence with words missing. The student's job is to read the sentence and select the word or words that best complete it. Copy the following example on the board and go through the process of solving it aloud with the class.

Charlotte Perkins Gilman was able to write convincingly about a woman's mental breakdown because she had _____ the experience. *(d)*

(a) researched
(b) heard about
(c) read about
(d) lived

**Application** Ask students to compose a sentence-completion question about "The Yellow Wallpaper" on a slip of paper, with the answer circled. Ask them to fold their papers and place them in a container at the front of the room. Read each question aloud. Students will record their answers and grade themselves at the end.

## Connect to the Literature

1. **What Do You Think?**
What unanswered questions do you have about this story?

### Comprehension Check
- What treatment has been prescribed for the narrator?
- What is unusual about the yellow wallpaper?
- What is the narrator doing at the end of the story?

## Think Critically

2.  **ACTIVE READING** **MAKING INFERENCES ABOUT THE NARRATOR** Review the **inferences** about the narrator that you listed in your **READER'S NOTEBOOK**. Based on these inferences, how do you explain the narrator's behavior at the end of the story?

3. Why do you think the **narrator** becomes so obsessed with the wallpaper?

> **THINK ABOUT**
> - the descriptions of the patterns and colors
> - the amount of time she spends in the room
> - the changes the narrator finds in the wallpaper

## Extend Interpretations

4. **Critic's Corner** Over the years, "The Yellow Wallpaper" has been interpreted in different ways: as a Gothic horror tale like those of Edgar Allan Poe, as a semiautobiographical account of a mental breakdown (see the writer's biography on page 781), and as a symbolic presentation of the effects of social and economic oppression on women. What aspects of the story do you think prompted each of these interpretations? State which interpretation you favor, and explain your reasons.

5. **Comparing Texts** From reading the excerpt from *Complaints and Disorders* on page 782, do you think Dr. S. Weir Mitchell would have found the narrator of this story to be an ideal patient? Explain.

6. **The Writer's Style** As the story progresses, the narrator's paragraphs become increasingly short, sometimes consisting of just a single sentence or sentence fragment. What reason might Gilman have had for using this curt, choppy style? What effect does the style have on you as a reader?

7. **Connect to Life** Which of the narrator's traits would be considered normal in a woman today?

## Literary Analysis

**FIRST PERSON NARRATOR** The **narrator** relates a story's events to the reader and, in the first-person point of view, is a character in the story. A first-person narrator engages the reader, communicating a sense of immediacy and personal concern. The reader may even identify with such a narrator. Sometimes, however, the credibility, or the trustworthiness, of the narrator is open to question. In Poe's "The Fall of the House of Usher," for example, the reader is not quite sure about the narrator's credibility. Did the events he described really happen, or are they mere figments of his imagination?

In "The Yellow Wallpaper," the first-person narrator begins to see **images** in the wallpaper: bars, bulbous eyes, a creeping woman, and more. If the wallpaper reflects the narrator's psychological state, you can use it as evidence to draw conclusions about her feelings and preoccupations.

**Cooperative Learning Activity**
Working with a small group of classmates, go back through the story and list the images that describe the wallpaper. Try to interpret each image, associating it with some aspect of the narrator's life. (There are no definite answers.) What general statement can your group make about the narrator's problem? What are the advantages and disadvantages of using a first-person narrator to tell this story, especially in light of the narrator's condition?

## GUIDING STUDENT RESPONSE

## Connect to the Literature

1. **What Do You Think?**
Students will probably have questions relating to the fantasy elements of the story. Remind them that the narrator is probably suffering from some sort of depression, as described in the Cross-Curricular Link on p. 775.

### Comprehension Check
- a "rest cure," with no work whatsoever
- The narrator sees a woman trapped behind the designs in the wallpaper.
- crawling on her hands and knees around the room

 Use Selection Quiz
**Unit Five Resource Book**, p. 10.

## Think Critically

2. Some students may see the story as a ghost story, with the ghost in the wallpaper driving the narrator insane. Others may interpret the story as an allegory of the plight of women at the time, with the restrictions of her "rest cure" driving the narrator insane.

3. Some students may say that because the woman is denied meaningful activity and is forced to endure isolation, she has little to think about but the wallpaper. Others may say that the wallpaper does indeed contain a trapped woman or ghost that only the narrator can see.

## Literary Analysis

**First-Person Narrative** Have students trace the narrator's descent into madness in terms of her descriptions of the yellow wallpaper. How does her perception of the wallpaper change? How does her perception of her husband and Jennie change?

## Extend Interpretations

**Critic's Corner** Possible Responses: Gothic horror tale—the trapped woman in the wallpaper who drives the narrator insane; semiautobiographical—the narrator's descent into madness corresponds to the symptoms of clinical depression; the author suffered from a similiar illness; symbolic presentation—women's social and economic oppression drives them into insanity; the "cures" make the situation even worse.

**Comparing Texts** Possible Response: Yes, she fits the profile of the upper-middle-class "ideal" patient.

**Writer's Style** Gilman was probably trying to convey the narrator's feeling of tension, anxiety, and moment-by-moment introspection. Some students may find short paragraphs readable; others may find them jarring. Invite students to rewrite passages from the story by combining several short paragraphs into one longer one. Discuss the altered effect. Encourage students to experiment with different paragraph lengths in their own fiction writing.

**Connect to Life** Possible Responses: her imagination and creativity; her desire to write and work; her postpartum depression; her feelings of isolation and frustration

## Writing Options

1. **Advertising Copy** Encourage students to read newspaper or magazine ads for books to prepare for writing their ads. **To make this assignment more challenging,** have students create ads in 19th-century style.

2. **Letter to Editor** Students' letters should follow the correct format for a business letter. Tell students to express their honest opinions and to avoid making sweeping generalizations.

3. **Extend the Story** Students may work in small groups for this activity. Suggest that they begin by first listing what they know about the characters from the story; then they can make logical extensions into the past or future. A prequel might include some foreshadowing of the events in the selection; a sequel might include a flashback.

## Activities & Explorations

1. **Dramatic Scene** Remind students to stay in character as they perform their scene.

2. **Wallpaper Design** Hold a class art exhibit to display and prompt a discussion of the variety of students' visions of the wallpaper.

3. **Top Story** Suggest that students set a time limit for presenting their news stories, just as would be done for a real newscast. Students can outline their news stories to make sure that they cover the key points, and they can practice their timing, cutting the news story as necessary.

## Vocabulary in Action

**Exercise A**
1. sassy
2. gross
3. whining
4. evident
5. sneer
6. stick-to-itiveness
7. jumping fish
8. shining rock
9. smile
10. critical

## Writing Options

1. **Advertising Copy** Write a few sentences of advertising copy that you think would intrigue people enough to make them want to read this story.

2. **Letter to Editor** When Gilman first tried to get "The Yellow Wallpaper" published, she sent the story to the famous author William Dean Howells, who passed it along to H. E. Scudder, editor of the *Atlantic Monthly.* In rejecting Gilman's story, Scudder wrote her this response: "Mr. Howells has handed me this story. I could not forgive myself if I made others as miserable as I have made myself. " Do you agree that this story makes readers miserable? Would you recommend it to your friends? Write a letter to the editor, expressing your views.

3. **Extend the Story** Write a sequel to the story, showing what will happen to the narrator and her husband, or a prequel, describing what their courtship was like. Save your story in your **Working Portfolio.**

## Activities & Explorations

1. **Dramatic Scene** With a partner, improvise a dramatic scene in which the narrator and her husband discuss her illness and treatment. In your scene, have the narrator attempt to explain how she feels and what she needs in order to recover, and have her husband explain to her why his treatment is the preferred therapy. ~ **PERFORMING**

2. **Wallpaper Design** Re-create the infamous yellow wallpaper. Go back through the story to pinpoint some of its specific characteristics, but also base your work on the narrator's impressions of it. Use markers, paints, or crayons—or any combination—on oversized paper or poster board. ~ **ART**

3. **Top Story** How might a television station cover the final scene as a sensationalized news story? Write and perform a newscast of the events, including interviews with John, Jennie, Cousin Henry and Julia, and the narrator herself. ~ **SPEAKING AND LISTENING**

## Inquiry & Research

**Depression** A modern clinician might say that after the birth of her child, the narrator of this story experiences a postpartum depression that later develops into postpartum psychosis. Find out more about these illnesses. What causes them? What are their symptoms, and which of the symptoms does the narrator exhibit? How are the conditions treated today?

## Vocabulary in Action

**EXERCISE A: MEANING CLUES** Review the Words to Know in the boxes at the bottom of the selection pages. Answer the following questions.

1. Would a child show **impertinence** by being sleepy, by being sassy, or by being shy?

2. Which would most likely be described as **atrocious**—something gross, something elegant, or something amusing?

3. Would a **querulous** person be likely to respond to an unpleasant situation by whining, by suffering in silence, or by making the best of it?

4. Is a **patent** lie one that is unnecessary, one that is highly creative, or one that is evident?

5. Which facial expression communicates **derision**—a wink, a sneer, or a yawn?

6. Does a person who has **perseverance** possess the quality of stick-to-itiveness, of quick-wittedness, or of open-mindedness?

7. Would you see the water in a lake **undulating** as a result of freezing weather, of a jumping fish, or of serious pollution?

8. Which is **inanimate**—a sleeping person, a barking dog, or a shining rock?

9. Would someone experiencing **felicity** be most likely to smile, to glare, or to sob?

10. If you thought someone had behaved **basely**, would you feel critical, jealous, or respectful?

**EXERCISE B** Working with a partner, act out the meaning of these vocabulary words—*felicity, impertinence, perseverance,* and *derision*—while another pair of students tries to guess them.

**Building Vocabulary**
For an in-depth lesson on word connotation and denotation, see page 908.

## Mini Lesson Grammar

**SENTENCE FRAGMENTS**

**Instruction** To be complete, a sentence must have a subject and a verb and express a complete thought. A sentence fragment is only part of a sentence: it may be missing the subject, the verb, or both. In "The Yellow Wallpaper," Charlotte Perkins Gilman uses sentence fragments deliberately in order to show the fragmentation of the narrator's thought process. Write this sentence fragment from the story (p. 776) on the chalkboard:

A strip about as high as my head and half around the room.

Ask students what would be needed to make this a sentence. (*The fragment could serve as a noun phrase; a verb would make it a complete sentence.*)

**Exercises** Have students rewrite the fragments in the following list as complete sentences.

1. A terrible smell in the room. (*There was a terrible smell in the room.*)

2. The house a colonial mansion, but old and decrepit. (*The house was a colonial mansion, but it was old and decrepit.*)

# Charlotte Perkins Gilman
1860–1935

**Other Works**
*Herland*
*The Living of Charlotte Perkins Gilman: An Autobiography*

**Mental Illness** After reading "The Yellow Wallpaper," a doctor wrote to Charlotte Perkins Gilman, praising the story's "detailed account of incipient insanity." Of course, he assumed she had not herself experienced what she had written about. Unfortunately, she had. After the birth of her daughter in 1885, Gilman suffered from severe depression, a condition known today as postpartum depression. She consulted the noted neurologist Dr. S. Weir Mitchell, who advised her: "Live as domestic a life as possible. Have your child with you all the time. . . . Lie down an hour after each meal. Have but two hours' intellectual life a day. And never touch pen, brush or pencil as long as you live." By following Mitchell's orders, Gilman became even more depressed.

**Triumph** Eventually, Gilman saved herself from a total mental breakdown by ignoring her doctor's advice. Gilman wrote "The Yellow Wallpaper" in 1890 to protest doctors' "rest cures" for women. Learning that Dr. Mitchell had changed his treatment after reading her story, Gilman said, "If that is a fact, I have not lived in vain." In 1894 she divorced her first husband, Charles Stetson, and sent her daughter to live with him and his new wife. An artist and art teacher, she resumed painting and teaching. She gave lectures about women's issues, started a magazine, *The Forerunner,* and began publishing poems and articles. Within a ten-year period, Gilman wrote her best-known work of nonfiction, *Women and Economics* (1898), as well as *Concerning Children* (1900), *The Home: Its Work and Influence* (1903), and *Human Work* (1904).

**Final Years** At the age of 72, Gilman was diagnosed with incurable cancer. She continued writing for three more years; but when the pain of the disease began to prevent her from working, she committed suicide.

---

**3.** Two things bothered me about the room. The bed and the wallpaper. *(Two things bothered me about the room—the bed and the wallpaper.)*

**4.** Went for a walk in the garden. *(She went for a walk in the garden.)*

**5.** John a respected physician. *(John was a respected physician.)*

**6.** Too nervous to be around the baby. *(She was too nervous to be around the baby.)*

 Use **Grammar Transparencies and Copymasters,** p. 108.

 Use McDougal Littell's *Language Network,* Chapter 3, for more instruction in sentence fragments.

## Objectives

- To read and analyze statistics, primary sources, and quotations
- To evaluate evidence and validate conclusions
- To find out about medical attitudes towards women in the 1880s–1900

# Connecting to the Literature

Students who wonder whether the physician husband in the story "The Yellow Wallpaper" was typical of his time can look for answers in nonfiction sources such as *Complaints and Disorders: The Sexual Politics of Sickness.* In this excerpt, students will read factual information about medical treatment of women in the 1880s.

# Reading for Information

Tell students that the excerpt presents a particular viewpoint about medical care for women. As you go through the excerpt with students, have them use the material in the right-hand column as a guide to finding evidence about a topic.

❶ Students should evaluate the credibility of information sources including how the writer's motivation may affect credibility. The authors provide statistics and quotations from a primary source to support their claims. Some students may say that the evidence seems strong and convincing; others may say that they would like to see more evidence from other sources, because these authors have a bias.

❷ The writers' choice of subject indicates that they are interested in women's rights, and their comments indicate that they feel women have been unfairly and improperly treated by the medical establishment.

# Comparing Texts

Possible Responses: Dr. S. Weir Mitchell would not have found the narrator to be an ideal patient because she secretly defied her doctor's orders. On the other hand, Dr. Mitchell might have found the narrator to be an ideal patient because her husband seemed prosperous and able to pay for a long period of treatment.

---

*from*

## Complaints and Disorders

### by Barbara Ehrenreich and Deirdre English

In 1900 there were 173 doctors (engaged in primary patient care) per 100,000 population, compared to 50 per 100,000 today. So, it was in the interests of doctors to cultivate the illnesses of their patients with frequent home visits and drawn-out "treatments." A few dozen well-heeled lady customers were all that a doctor needed for a successful urban practice. Women—at least, women whose husbands could pay the bills—became a natural "client caste"[1] to the developing medical profession.

❶ In many ways, the upper-middle-class woman was the ideal patient: her illnesses—and her husband's bank account—seemed almost inexhaustible. Furthermore, she was usually submissive and obedient to the 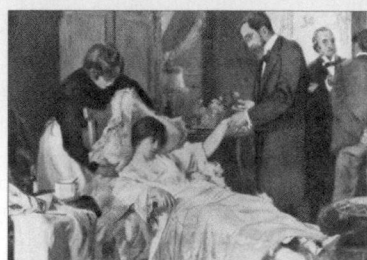 "doctor's orders." The famous Philadelphia doctor S. Weir Mitchell expressed his profession's deep appreciation of the female invalid in 1888:

> With all her weakness, her unstable emotionality, her tendency to morally warp when long nervously ill, she is then far easier to deal with, far more amenable to reason, far more sure to be comfortable as a patient, than the man who is relatively in a like position. The reasons for this are too obvious to delay me here, and physicians accustomed to deal with both sexes as sick people will be apt to justify my position.

❷ In Mitchell's mind women were not only easier to relate to, but sickness was the very key to femininity: "The man who does not know sick women does not know women."

---

1. **caste** (kăst): a group or class of people.

---

# Reading for Information

In the 20th century, women have asserted their rights at home, in the workplace, and even in the field of medicine, but conditions were very different in the 19th century. The story "The Yellow Wallpaper" provides a glimpse of the way in which female patients were treated at that time. How do you think this treatment reflected the limitations of women's role in society? This excerpt can help you support your opinion.

## FINDING EVIDENCE

When you research a topic, it is helpful to keep in mind the questions you are trying to answer or the conclusions you are trying to prove or validate. Then, as you read, you can look for statistics, primary sources, and quotations that tell you what you need to know. Use the activities below to examine the evidence in this article.

❶ **Evaluating Evidence** The writers explain why "the upper-middle-class woman was the ideal patient." What evidence do they use to support this claim? What is your reaction to their evidence?

❷ What can you infer about the writers by their choice of subject and the nature of their comments?

**Comparing Texts** Do you think Dr. S. Weir Mitchell would have found the narrator of "The Yellow Wallpaper" to be an ideal patient? Explain your opinion.

# The Story of an Hour

*Short Story by* KATE CHOPIN

( **Connect to Your Life** )

**Marriage Guidelines** "The Story of an Hour" reveals a young woman's private thoughts about her life and marriage. What kind of relationship do you expect to have with a spouse? What are some guidelines for a good marriage? With a small group of classmates, discuss your thoughts about and expectations of marriage.

## Build Background

**Status of Women** This story takes place about 100 years ago, near the turn of the century, when the status of women was very different from what it is today. Both custom and law severely limited women's actions and their control over their own lives. Because women could not vote, they had almost no political or legal power; and because they could not own property and their educational and employment opportunities were limited, they had little or no financial independence. Few careers were open to middle-class and upper-class single women, and even fewer to married women—like Mrs. Mallard in this story—who were expected to be supported by their husbands. Those who did work had to turn their wages over to their fathers or their husbands. In most American marriages of the time, the husband was the undisputed head of the household and made all the important decisions.

## Focus Your Reading

**LITERARY ANALYSIS** **PLOT** The **plot** of a literary work is the sequence of actions and events. Generally, plots are built around a **conflict**—a problem or a struggle between two or more opposing forces. The plot of this story is built around Mrs. Mallard's inner conflict. Notice the opposing forces within her.

**ACTIVE READING** **PREDICTING** Using what you already know to figure out what might happen is called **predicting.** To make a prediction, you gather clues as you read and then use them to make reasonable guesses about what will occur in the story. For example, the first sentence of this story provides a detail about Mrs. Mallard's health and an unexpected piece of news. Use these clues and others to make predictions as you read. Feel free to revise your predictions as you come upon new clues.

**READER'S NOTEBOOK** On a chart like the one shown, jot down the clues you find and the predictions you make.

| Clues | Predictions |
| --- | --- |
|  |  |

## OVERVIEW

**Objectives**
1. understand and appreciate a **short story (Literary Analysis)**
2. identify and examine **plot (Literary Analysis)**
3. use clues in the story to make **predictions (Active Reading)**

**Summary**
Because Mrs. Mallard suffers from heart trouble, the news of her husband Brently's death in a railroad disaster is broken to her gently. After an outburst of grief, she retreats to her room. As the reality of her husband's death sinks in, she whispers the words "free, free, free." She welcomes the chance to live for herself. Responding to her sister's pleas, Mrs. Mallard finally emerges from her room and goes downstairs. At the same moment, someone opens the front door. Brently Mallard, who was actually far from the scene of the accident, has arrived home. On seeing her husband enter, Mrs. Mallard falls to the floor dead.

**Thematic Link**
In "The Story of an Hour" Kate Chopin reveals the innermost thoughts of a woman who is told that her husband has suddenly been killed. Her thoughts and feelings about her new-found freedom give insight about women's lives at the end of the nineteenth century.

**5-Minute Warm-Up**

*Daily Language SkillBuilder*

Have students **proofread** the display sentences on page 739i and write them correctly. The sentences also appear on Transparency 21 of **Grammar Transparencies and Copymasters.**

## LESSON RESOURCES

**UNIT FIVE RESOURCE BOOK,** pp. 11–14

**ASSESSMENT RESOURCES**
**Formal Assessment,** pp. 141–142
**Teacher's Guide to Assessment and Portfolio Use**
**Test Generator**

**SKILLS TRANSPARENCIES AND COPYMASTERS**
**Reading and Critical Thinking**
• Predicting Outcomes, T2 (for Active Reading, p. 783)

**Grammar**
• Sentence Fragments, T42 (for Mini Lesson, p. 787)
• Complete Sentences, C73 (for Mini Lesson, p. 784)
**Vocabulary**
• Using Reference Materials, C64 (for Mini Lesson, p. 784)
**Writing**
• Persuasive Essay, C27 (for Writing Option 4, p. 787)
**Communications**
• Evaluation Matrix: Film/Video, T7 (for Activities & Explorations, p. 787)

**INTEGRATED TECHNOLOGY**
**Audio Library**
**LaserLinks**
• Historical Connection: Women's Lives: Late 1800s. See **Teacher's SourceBook,** p. 62.
**Video: Literature in Performance**
• *The Story of an Hour.* See **Video Resource Book,** pp. 27–32.
**Visit our website:** www.mcdougallittell.com

**Active Reading** PREDICTING

 Ask students to consider the first paragraph of the story and to make predictions about what might happen to Mrs. Mallard and how she might react to the news of her husband's death.

**Possible Responses:** Mrs. Mallard might collapse upon hearing the bad news; she will feel terrible that she is still alive but that her husband is dead; she will not wish to go on living without him.

Use **Unit Five Resource Book,** p. 12 for additional support.

**Literary Analysis** PLOT

**B** Remind students that conflict is a struggle between two opposing forces. Ask students to identify Mrs. Mallard's conflict and to tell how it is resolved.

**Possible Response:** Mrs. Mallard's conflict is internal. She is trying to repress certain feelings or thoughts. Her conflict is resolved when she allows those thoughts to enter her mind.

Use **Unit Five Resource Book,** p. 13 for additional support.

**Literary Analysis: IRONY**

**C** Point out the dramatic irony in Josephine's worries about Mrs. Mallard. Ask students what the reader knows that she does not.

**Answer:** Mrs. Mallard feels joyous and strong, not ill with grief.

**D** Ask students what is ironic about the doctors' diagnosis.

**Possible Response:** Mrs. Mallard died not from joy, but from grief at her impending loss of freedom.

---

# THE STORY OF AN HOUR

### Kate Chopin

 Knowing that Mrs. Mallard was afflicted with a heart trouble, great care was taken to break to her as gently as possible the news of her husband's death.

It was her sister Josephine who told her, in broken sentences; veiled hints that revealed in half concealing. Her husband's friend Richards was there, too, near her. It was he who had been in the newspaper office when intelligence of the railroad disaster was received, with Brently Mallard's name leading the list of "killed." He had only taken the time to assure himself of its truth by a second telegram, and had hastened to forestall any less careful, less tender friend in bearing the sad message.

She did not hear the story as many women have heard the same, with a paralyzed inability to accept its significance. She wept at once, with sudden, wild abandonment, in her sister's arms. When the storm of grief had spent itself she went away to her room alone. She would have no one follow her.

There stood, facing the open window, a comfortable, roomy armchair. Into this she sank, pressed down by a physical exhaustion that haunted her body and seemed to reach into her soul.

She could see in the open square before her house the tops of trees that were all aquiver with the new spring life. The delicious breath of rain was in the air. In the street below a peddler was crying his wares. The notes of a distant song which someone was singing reached her faintly, and countless sparrows were twittering in the eaves.

There were patches of blue sky showing here and there through the clouds that had met and piled one above the other in the west facing her window.

She sat with her head thrown back upon the cushion of the chair, quite motionless, except when a sob came up into her throat and shook her, as a child who has cried itself to sleep continues to sob in its dreams.

She was young, with a fair, calm face, whose lines bespoke repression and even a certain strength. But now there was a dull stare in her eyes, whose gaze was fixed away off yonder on one of those patches of blue sky. It was not a glance of reflection, but rather indicated a suspension of intelligent thought.

There was something coming to her and she was waiting for it, fearfully. What was it? She did not know; it was too subtle and elusive to name. But she felt it, creeping out of the sky, reaching toward her through the sounds, the scents, the color that filled the air.

Now her bosom rose and fell tumultuously. She was beginning to recognize this thing that was approaching to possess her, and she was striving to beat it back with her will—as powerless as her two white slender hands would have been.

When she abandoned herself, a little whispered word escaped her slightly parted lips. She said it over and over under her breath: "free, free, free!" The vacant stare and the look of terror that had followed it went from her eyes. They stayed keen

> What could love, the unsolved mystery, count for in face of this possession of self-assertion which she suddenly recognized as the strongest impulse of her being!

**B**

---

## Teaching Options

### USING REFERENCE SOURCES Instruction

Reference materials such as a dictionary and a thesaurus can help students determine the precise usage of words. A dictionary is used to find the denotation of a word. In considering the choices of synonyms offered by a thesaurus, students must determine the connotations of each before making their selection. Looking up the definition of a possible synonym in the dictionary will assist in this decision.

**Exercises** Have students use a dictionary and a thesaurus as needed to decide which synonym best replaces the underlined word in each sentence.

## Mini Lesson — Vocabulary Strategy

1. Richards rushes to the house with <u>intelligence</u> of the accident. (inspiration, perspicuity, <u>knowledge</u>)

2. She has an <u>exalted</u> perception of the meaning of life after hearing the news. (glorified, <u>heightened</u>, dignified)

3. Her sister's <u>intelligence</u> made her indispensable in a crisis. (shrewdness, comprehension, <u>levelheadedness</u>)

4. People might <u>exalt</u> the attributes of a dead person as the passage of years takes away negative memories. (<u>magnify</u>, intensify, elate)

Use **Vocabulary Transparencies and Copymasters,** p. 64.

and bright. Her pulses beat fast, and the coursing blood warmed and relaxed every inch of her body.

She did not stop to ask if it were or were not a monstrous joy that held her. A clear and exalted perception enabled her to dismiss the suggestion as trivial.

She knew that she would weep again when she saw the kind, tender hands folded in death; the face that had never looked save with love upon her, fixed and gray and dead. But she saw beyond that bitter moment a long procession of years to come that would belong to her absolutely. And she opened and spread her arms out to them in welcome.

There would be no one to live for her during those coming years; she would live for herself. There would be no powerful will bending hers in that blind persistence with which men and women believe they have a right to impose a private will upon a fellow creature. A kind intention or a cruel intention made the act seem no less a crime as she looked upon it in that brief moment of illumination.

And yet she had loved him—sometimes. Often she had not. What did it matter! What could love, the unsolved mystery, count for in face of this possession of self-assertion which she suddenly recognized as the strongest impulse of her being!

"Free! Body and soul free!" she kept whispering.

 Josephine was kneeling before the closed door with her lips to the keyhole, imploring for admission. "Louise, open the door! I beg; open the door—you will make yourself ill. What are

Morning Glories (1873), Winslow Homer. Private Collection.

you doing, Louise? For heaven's sake open the door."

"Go away. I am not making myself ill." No; she was drinking in a very elixir of life[1] through that open window.

 Her fancy was running riot along those days ahead of her. Spring days, and summer days, and all sorts of days that would be her own. She breathed a quick prayer that life might be long. It was only yesterday she had thought with a shudder that life might be long.

She arose at length and opened the door to her sister's importunities. There was a feverish triumph in her eyes, and she carried herself unwittingly like a goddess of Victory. She clasped her sister's waist, and together they descended the stairs. Richards stood waiting for them at the bottom.

Someone was opening the front door with a latchkey. It was Brently Mallard who entered, a little travel-stained, composedly carrying his grip-sack[2] and umbrella. He had been far from the scene of accident, and did not know there had been one. He stood amazed at Josephine's piercing cry; at Richards's quick motion to screen him from the view of his wife.

But Richards was too late.

When the doctors came they said she had died of heart disease—of joy that kills. ❖

---

1. **elixir of life:** a medicine that restores vigor or the essence of life.

2. **grip-sack:** a small traveling bag or satchel.

## GUIDING STUDENT RESPONSE

### Connect to the Literature

**1. What Do You Think?**
Possible Responses: surprised, shocked

**Comprehension Check**
• heart disease
• She is informed that her husband has died; at first, she bursts into tears but soon looks forward to the freedom that will be hers.
• Her husband is alive.

 Use Selection Quiz
**Unit Five Resource Book,** p.14.

### Think Critically

**2.** Some students may state that they used the detail about Mrs. Mallard's heart condition as a clue to predict her death at the end of the story.

**3.** Possible Responses: the shock of seeing her husband alive; grief at realizing that freedom had been snatched away from her; a series of shocks to a weak heart

**4.** Possible Responses: She has been sheltered in a confining social role; she feels relieved at her husband's death; she longs for freedom but is too passive to fight for it; she is physically weak.

**5.** Possible Responses: stifling; conventional; placid on the surface

### Literary Analysis

**Plot and Surprise Ending** Key events, in sequence, include the news of Brently's death, Mrs. Mallard's weeping, her going upstairs and gradual realization of her freedom, her sister's plea to open the door, Mrs. Mallard's refusal, her opening the door and descending the stairs, Brently's return, and Mrs. Mallard's death. Students should support their opinions about the surprise ending with specific reasons.

**Review: Irony** Dramatic irony occurs in that the reader—but not the other characters—learns about Mrs. Mallard's joy at the thought of her freedom. Examples of situational irony include the following: Richards, in his concern to spare Mrs. Mallard by breaking the sad news gently to her first, unwittingly sets her up to be shocked; Mrs. Mallard wishes for a long life, but her life is cut short; she dies from grief but not from the grief her sister and friend feared might kill her.

### Connect to the Literature

**1. What Do You Think?**
How did you react to the ending of this story?

**Comprehension Check**
• What disease afflicts Mrs. Mallard?
• What news does Mrs. Mallard receive at the beginning of the story, and how does she react?
• What does Mrs. Mallard learn at the end of the story?

### Think Critically

**2.** [ACTIVE READING] [PREDICTING] What **predictions** did you make as you read, and what clues did you use to make them? Refer to the chart you made in your [📖 READER'S NOTEBOOK]. Tell whether your predictions were accurate.

**3.** How would you explain the cause of Mrs. Mallard's death?

**4.** What are your impressions of Mrs. Mallard?

 **THINK ABOUT**
• how Richards and Josephine treat her
• her initial reaction to the news of her husband's death
• why she says under her breath "free, free, free!"
• how she reacts when her husband arrives

**5.** How would you describe Mrs. Mallard's relationship with her husband?

### Extend Interpretations

**6. What If?** What might the future have been like for the Mallards if Mrs. Mallard had lived?

**7. The Writer's Style** Reread the fifth and sixth paragraphs of the story, which describe what Mrs. Mallard sees and hears from her open window after learning of her husband's death. What do you think the **imagery** in these paragraphs contributes to the story?

**8. Comparing Texts** Both "The Story of an Hour" and "The Yellow Wallpaper" were written in the 1890s. How would you compare the **themes** of the two stories? Which story do you prefer, and why?

**9. Connect to Life** How would you compare Mrs. Mallard's view of marriage with your own?

### Literary Analysis

[PLOT AND SURPRISE ENDING]
In "The Story of an Hour," the **plot,** or the sequence of events, focuses on Mrs. Mallard's inner conflict. Though she feels deep grief over her husband's death, she cannot help looking forward to the freedom that widowhood will bring. The plot begins with a surprise announcement—the death of Mr. Mallard—and then builds toward a **surprise ending**—Mr. Mallard's return and Mrs. Mallard's sudden death. A surprise ending is an unexpected plot twist at the conclusion of a story.

**Cooperative Learning Activity** In this story the events of the plot occur within the span of an hour. With a group of classmates, draw the outline of a clock. Note the events in the order in which they occur and Mrs. Mallard's feelings about them. Then discuss the surprise ending. Do you find it clever and fitting? a masterstroke of irony? a cheap trick? Share your conclusions with other groups.

[REVIEW] [IRONY] Surprise endings, almost by definition, are ironic. Mr. Mallard's return and Mrs. Mallard's death are examples of situational irony. What other examples of situational irony or dramatic irony do you see in this story? Discuss them in class.

### Extend Interpretations

**What If?** Possible Responses: Mrs. Mallard may have been unhappy in her marriage after tasting the possibility of freedom; she may have left her husband because she could not settle for marriage again; she may have resumed her old routine.

**Writer's Style** Possible Responses: She sees trees "aquiver with the new spring of life," hears sparrows "twittering," and notices patches of blue sky—joyous images that hint at her new sense of life and freedom and that contrast with the death of her husband.

**Comparing Texts** Possible Responses: Chopin's story is shorter than Gilman's, but its sentences tend to be longer. Its narrator is objective and uses the third-person point of view, as opposed to the highly subjective first-person point of view in "The Yellow Wallpaper." Both stories show upper-middle-class married women of the 1890s trapped in confining roles and escaping through tragedy—death in one case, insanity in the other. Have students explain their preferences.

**Connect to Life** Accept all reasonable responses.

# Choices & CHALLENGES

## Writing Options

**1. Husband's Monologue** What feelings do you think Brently Mallard will have about his wife's sudden death? Will his feelings be similar to or different from her feelings about his supposed death? Write a monologue expressing his feelings.

**2. Wife's Epitaph** Write an appropriate epitaph for Mrs. Mallard, commenting on her life or the circumstances of her death. Remember to draw on your knowledge of her private thoughts.

**3. Different Ending** Imagine that Brently Mallard indeed dies in the train wreck. Write a brief summary of an alternative ending for the story, and share it with your classmates.

**4. Essay About Marriage** Alexis de Tocqueville wrote, "In America, the independence of woman is irrecoverably lost in the bonds of matrimony." Write a persuasive essay, supporting or challenging this opinion. Use details from "The Story of an Hour" in your essay.

**Writing Handbook**
See page 1285: Persuasive Writing

## Activities & Explorations

**Story and Video** View the video of "The Story of an Hour," provided with this program. Which version—the oral interpretation or the dramatization—impressed you more, and why? What changes did you notice between the original story and the dramatization? Why do you think the director chose to make those changes? ~ **VIEWING AND REPRESENTING**

 **Literature in Performance**

## Kate Chopin
### 1851–1904

**Other Works**
*At Fault*
*Bayou Folk*
*A Night in Acadie*

**Early Years** Kate Chopin was born Catherine O'Flaherty in St. Louis, Missouri. When she was five years old, her father was killed in a railroad disaster similar to the one described in "The Story of an Hour," leaving her mother a 27-year-old widow. As a student at Sacred Heart Academy, Chopin exhibited "gifts as a teller of marvelous stories," and as a young woman she was a belle of St. Louis society. In 1870 she married Oscar Chopin, a Creole businessman, and settled with him in New Orleans.

**Family and Work** In 1879 financial problems forced the Chopins and their five young sons to move to rural Louisiana, where their sixth child, a daughter, was born. In 1882 Oscar Chopin died of malaria,

leaving his family in debt. Before she returned home to St. Louis in 1884, Chopin raised her children alone and managed her husband's business.

**Moments of Inspiration** In 1889 Chopin's first poem and first story were published. Over the next ten years, she published two novels, more than a hundred short stories, and many reviews and poems. According to her son Felix, Chopin would "go weeks and weeks without an idea, then suddenly grab her pencil and old lapboard . . . , and in a couple of hours her story was complete and off to the publisher."

**Literary Concerns** Chopin's local-color stories about the Creoles, Cajuns, African Americans, and Indians whom she had known in Louisiana won her acclaim, but her stories about women seeking to be free often aroused protest. Severe criticism was directed at her second novel, *The Awakening* (1899), for its depiction of a woman's adulterous affair. That novel and Chopin's other works dealing with women's issues have since received greater appreciation.

 **Mini Lesson** ## Grammar

### REVIEWING COMPLETE SENTENCES

**Instruction** Remind students that a sentence must contain a subject and a predicate and must express a complete thought. Display the sentence to illustrate these components of a complete sentence:

> After her husband's death, the intrepid Kate Chopin raised her children, managed her husband's business, and found time to write.

Complete Subject—"the intrepid Kate Chopin"
Complete Predicate—"raised her children, managed her husband's business, and found time to write after her husband's death"

**Exercises** Ask students to determine which part is missing from each fragment and to add either

the subject or predicate. Sentences should have subject-verb agreement and logical meaning.

1. Took place within the time frame of an hour (subject)
2. Although her first reaction was grief, Mrs. Mallard later (predicate)
3. Detects the irony that her sister's concern is misplaced (subject)

 Use **Grammar Transparencies and Copymasters**, p. 73.

 Use McDougal Littell's *Language Network*, Chapter 1, for more instruction in complete sentences.

## Writing Options

1. **Husband's Monologue To get students started on this assignment,** have them brainstorm Brently Mallard's possible emotions. Then have students write the monologue using the first-person point of view. **Kinesthetic learners** might read their monologues aloud with appropriate gestures and movement.

2. **Wife's Epitaph To get students started on this assignment,** remind them that an epitaph is an inscription placed on a tomb or monument to honor the memory of the person buried there. Some students may want to compose epitaphs in poetic form, using rhyme, rhythm, and/or meter.

3. **Different Ending To get students started on this assignment,** have them think about what Mrs. Mallard's life as a widow might be like and how much freedom she would actually have. Encourage them to brainstorm ideas in groups of three before writing independently.

4. **Essay About Marriage To get students started on this assignment,** remind them that persuasive writing must appeal to the reader's reason and emotions. Have students choose a viewpoint and list reasons for their belief. Then they should extract details from the story that support or challenge those reasons. Remind students to arrange their paragraphs in the order of importance, with the strongest argument last. **To make this assignment more challenging,** have students compare the truth of this statement in the 1890s and in the 1990s.

## Activities & Explorations

Students should notice that the setting of Chopin's short story is an American home in the late 1800s. In the dramatization, the setting is a British home in the late 1900s. In the recitation, the setting is a simple backdrop. The modern setting in the dramatization gives new meaning to the "freedom" that Mrs. Mallard anticipates.

## Objectives

1. appreciate a Japanese-American **short story** (Literary Analysis)
2. examine a **coming-of-age story** (Literary Analysis)
3. understand **conflicts** (Active Reading)

## Summary

Rosie is the teenage daughter of Japanese-American parents who have a farm in California. As the story opens, Rosie's mother has a newfound passion for writing haiku, which Rosie's father resents. He curtails a visit with a family friend because his wife is conversing with the husband about haiku. Meanwhile, Rosie has discovered that she has romantic feelings for a boy, Jesus, who helps her family on their farm. One day a publisher comes to present Rosie's mother with a prize she has won in a haiku contest. The father angrily takes the prize, a painting, outside and destroys it. Inside the house, Rosie's mother tells her for the first time that her marriage to Rosie's father was an arranged marriage and done solely out of desperation—she wanted to escape Japan, where she was stigmatized by a failed love affair that had resulted in a stillborn illegitimate son. While the memory of a recent encounter with Jesus lingers in Rosie's mind, her mother demands that she promise never to marry.

## Thematic Link

This story explores the oppression existent in Japanese-American **women's lives** in the 1930s and one woman's struggle to find her **voice** through writing poetry.

### 5-Minute Warm-Up

***Daily Language SkillBuilder***

Have students **proofread** the display sentences on page 739i and write them correctly. The sentences also appear on Transparency 22 of **Grammar Transparencies and Copymasters.**

**Mini Lesson**

## Preteaching Vocabulary

If you would like to preteach the WORDS TO KNOW for this selection, use the Mini Lesson, p. 790.

---

# PREPARING to *Read*

# Seventeen Syllables

*Short Story by* HISAYE YAMAMOTO (hē-sa′yĕ ya′ma-mō′tō)

**Comparing Literature**

## Traditions Across Time: A Diversity of Voices

"Seventeen Syllables" is a modern short story by a Japanese-American writer. Set in California in the 1930s, this story explores conflicts between a Japanese-born husband and wife and between them and Rosie, their American-born daughter. Like the stories you read in the first part of this section, this story describes a married woman's struggles to reach her potential.

**Points of Comparison**   Compare the husband-and-wife relationship in this story with the one in "The Yellow Wallpaper."

## Build Background

**Japanese Immigrants** Early Japanese immigrants were mostly single men, who, after settling in America, often sought to get married. In accordance with Japanese custom, family members arranged marriages for them with Japanese women, who then immigrated. While facing the challenges of adjusting to a radically different culture, these couples also struggled to bridge the cultural differences that separated them from their American-born children.

After coming to the United States, many Japanese immigrants maintained an interest in Japanese literature. Groups were formed to write and study traditional forms of Japanese poetry, and numerous Japanese-language anthologies and magazines were devoted to this literature. In this story, the main character's mother writes haiku—poems with only 17 syllables.

| WORDS TO KNOW | **Vocabulary Preview** | |
|---|---|---|
| adamant | irrevocable | unobtrusive |
| delectable | preoccupied | untoward |
| dubious | repercussion | vacillating |
| indiscretion | | |

## Focus Your Reading

**LITERARY ANALYSIS   COMING-OF-AGE STORY**   A **coming-of-age story** portrays an adolescent in the process of growing up. The main character faces conflicts, makes difficult decisions, and gains new awareness of self and others. In "Seventeen Syllables," Rosie matures as she faces conflicts and struggles to understand them.

**ACTIVE READING   UNDERSTANDING CONFLICTS**
Understanding Rosie's conflicts is critical to understanding this story. Use these strategies:

- Review the definition of **conflict.** (See Glossary of Literary Terms, page 1247.)
- As you read, write down conflicts (internal and external) involving Rosie and also conflicts between her parents.
- Ask these questions about each conflict: How does it affect Rosie? How is it resolved?

**READER'S NOTEBOOK**  In your notebook, record the conflicts you identify, their effects on Rosie, and their resolutions (if resolved).

---

# LESSON RESOURCES

**UNIT FIVE RESOURCE BOOK,** pp. 15–19

**ASSESSMENT RESOURCES**
**Formal Assessment,** pp. 143–144
**Teacher's Guide to Assessment and Portfolio Use**
**Test Generator**

**SKILLS TRANSPARENCIES AND COPYMASTERS**
**Grammar**
- Adverb Clauses: Subordinating Conjunctions, C97 (for Mini Lesson, p. 792)

- Semicolons and Conjunctive Adverbs, C157 (for Mini Lesson, p. 801)
**Vocabulary**
- Idioms, C65 (for Mini Lesson, p. 798)
**Communications**
- Impromptu Speaking: Dialogue, Role-Play, Debate, T13 (for Mini Lesson, p. 794)

**INTEGRATED TECHNOLOGY**
**Audio Library**
**LaserLinks**
- Background Connection: Farm Workers in California, 1930s.
- Art Gallery: Japanese Art. See **Teacher's SourceBook,** pp. 63–64.
**Visit our website:**
www.mcdougallittell.com

# SEVENTEEN SYLLABLES

● Hisaye Yamamoto

*Consolation* (1961), Ruth Gikow. 30″ × 18″, collection of Dr. Violet Friedman.

The first Rosie knew that her mother had taken to writing poems was one evening when she finished one and read it aloud for her daughter's approval. It was about cats, and Rosie pretended to understand it thoroughly and appreciate it no end, partly because she hesitated to disillusion her mother about the quantity and quality of Japanese she had learned in all the years now that she had been going to Japanese school every Saturday (and Wednesday, too, in the summer). Even so, her mother must have been skeptical about

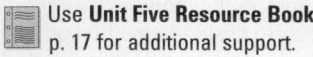
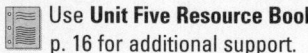
the depth of Rosie's understanding, because she explained afterwards about the kind of poem she was trying to write.

See, Rosie, she said, it was a *haiku*, a poem in which she must pack all her meaning into seventeen syllables only, which were divided into three lines of five, seven, and five syllables. In the one she had just read, she had tried to capture the charm of a kitten, as well as comment on the superstition that owning a cat of three colors meant good luck.

"Yes, yes, I understand. How utterly lovely," Rosie said, and her mother, either satisfied or seeing through the deception and resigned, went back to composing.

> • It was a *haiku*, a poem in which she must pack all her meaning into seventeen syllables only.

The truth was that Rosie was lazy; English lay ready on the tongue but Japanese had to be searched for and examined, and even then put forth tentatively (probably to meet with laughter). It was so much easier to say yes, yes, even when one meant no, no. Besides, this was what was in her mind to say: I was looking through one of your magazines from Japan last night, Mother, and towards the back I found some *haiku* in English that delighted me. There was one that made me giggle off and on until I fell asleep—

*It is morning, and lo!*
*I lie awake, comme il faut,[1]*
*sighing for some dough.*

Now, how to reach her mother, how to communicate the melancholy song? Rosie knew

formal Japanese by fits and starts, her mother had even less English, no French. It was much more possible to say yes, yes.

It developed that her mother was writing the *haiku* for a daily newspaper, the *Mainichi Shimbun*,[2] that was published in San Francisco. Los Angeles, to be sure, was closer to the farming community in which the Hayashi[3] family lived and several Japanese vernaculars[4] were printed there, but Rosie's parents said they preferred the tone of the northern paper. Once a week, the *Mainichi* would have a section devoted to *haiku*, and her mother became an extravagant contributor, taking for herself the blossoming pen name, Ume Hanazono.[5]

So Rosie and her father lived for awhile with two women, her mother and Ume Hanazono. Her mother (Tome Hayashi by name) kept house, cooked, washed, and, along with her husband and the Carrascos, the Mexican family hired for the harvest, did her ample share of picking tomatoes out in the sweltering fields and boxing them in tidy strata in the cool packing shed. Ume Hanazono, who came to life after the dinner dishes were done, was an earnest, muttering stranger who often neglected speaking when spoken to and stayed busy at the parlor table as late as midnight scribbling with pencil on scratch paper or

---

1. *comme il faut* (kôm′ ēl fō′) *French:* as is proper; as usual.
2. *Mainichi Shimbun* (mī-nē′chē shēm′bŏŏn).
3. **Hayashi** (hä-yä′shē).
4. **Japanese vernaculars:** newspapers in the Japanese language.
5. **Ume Hanazono** (ŏŏ′mĕ hä′nä-zō′nō).

 **Mini Lesson** ## Preteaching Vocabulary

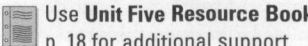

carefully copying characters on good paper with her fat, pale green Parker.

The new interest had some repercussions on the household routine. Before, Rosie had been accustomed to her parents and herself taking their hot baths early and going to bed almost immediately afterwards, unless her parents challenged each other to a game of flower cards or unless company dropped in. Now if her father wanted to play cards, he had to resort to solitaire (at which he always cheated fearlessly), and if a group of friends came over, it was bound to contain someone who was also writing *haiku*, and the small assemblage would be split in two, her father entertaining the non-literary members and her mother comparing ecstatic notes with the visiting poet.

If they went out, it was more of the same thing. But Ume Hanazono's life span, even for a poet's, was very brief—perhaps three months at most.

**One** night they went over to see the Hayano family in the neighboring town to the west, an adventure both painful and attractive to Rosie. It was attractive because there were four Hayano girls, all lovely and each one named after a season of the year (Haru, Natsu, Aki, Fuyu),[6] painful because something had been wrong with Mrs. Hayano ever since the birth of her first child. Rosie would sometimes watch Mrs. Hayano, reputed to have been the belle of her native village, making her way about a room, stooped, slowly shuffling, violently trembling (*always* trembling), and she would be reminded that this woman, in this same condition, had carried and given issue to three babies. She would look wonderingly at Mr. Hayano, handsome, tall, and strong, and she would look at her four pretty friends. But it was not a matter she could come to any decision about.

On this visit, however, Mrs. Hayano sat all evening in the rocker, as motionless and unobtrusive as it was possible for her to be, and Rosie found the greater part of the evening practically anaesthetic.[7] Too, Rosie spent most of it in the girls' room, because Haru, the garrulous[8] one, said almost as soon as the bows and other greetings were over, "Oh, you must see my new coat!"

It was a pale plaid of grey, sand, and blue, with an enormous collar, and Rosie, seeing nothing special in it, said, "Gee, how nice."

"Nice?" said Haru, indignantly. "Is that all you can say about it? It's gorgeous! And so cheap, too. Only seventeen-ninety-eight, because it was a sale. The saleslady said it was twenty-five dollars regular."

"Gee," said Rosie. Natsu, who never said much and when she said anything said it shyly, fingered the coat covetously and Haru pulled it away.

"Mine," she said, putting it on. She minced in the aisle between the two large beds and smiled happily. "Let's see how your mother likes it."

She broke into the front room and the adult conversation and went to stand in front of Rosie's mother, while the rest watched from the door. Rosie's mother was properly envious. "May I inherit it when you're through with it?"

Haru, pleased, giggled and said yes, she could, but Natsu reminded gravely from the door, "You promised me, Haru."

Everyone laughed but Natsu, who shame-facedly retreated into the bedroom. Haru came in laughing, taking off the coat. "We were only kidding, Natsu," she said. "Here, you try it on now."

After Natsu buttoned herself into the coat, inspected herself solemnly in the bureau mirror,

---

6. **Haru** (hä´rōō), **Natsu** (nät´sōō), **Aki** (ä´kē), **Fuyu** (fōō´yōō): the Japanese words for spring, summer, autumn, and winter, respectively.

7. **anaesthetic:** causing sleep; boring.

8. **garrulous** (găr´ə-ləs): talkative.

---

WORDS TO KNOW

**repercussion** (rē´pər-kŭsh´ən) *n.* a far-reaching effect
**unobtrusive** (ŭn´əb-trōō´sĭv) *adj.* not noticeable; not calling attention to oneself

791

### Active Reading

**UNDERSTANDING CONFLICTS**

**A** What does Rosie notice that her parents are doing?

**Possible Response:** Her mother is talking about haikus with Mr. Hayano, and her father is looking through magazines and failing at conversing with Mrs. Hayano.

**What conclusions can you draw about conflicts in her parents' relationship?**

**Possible Response:** Her mother's interest in haiku is coming between them.

**B** Until now, readers have had to make inferences about the conflict between Mr. and Mrs. Hayashi. However, Mr. Hayashi's actions and his conversation with his wife now bring it out into the open. Have students identify and summarize the conflict.

**Possible Response:** Mr. Hayashi is jealous, resentful, and unhappy that Mrs. Hayashi is so involved with the haiku, in which he has no interest. She is challenging his control over the family by having an activity of her own, which is threatening to him.

### Literary Analysis

**COMING-OF-AGE STORY**

**C** Ask students how Rosie handles her feelings about the conflict. How do her thoughts indicate that she has conflicting emotions?

**Possible Response:** Rosie daydreams about ways to escape the conflict: she imagines them all dying in a car crash, and then she wishes her father would laugh. She is caught between her desire to destroy her family and her desire to heal it.

---

and reluctantly shed it, Rosie, Aki, and Fuyu got their turns, and Fuyu, who was eight, drowned in it while her sisters and Rosie doubled up in amusement. They all went into the front room later, because Haru's mother quaveringly called to her to fix the tea and rice cakes and open a can of sliced peaches for everybody. Rosie noticed that her mother and Mr. Hayano were talking together at the little table—they were discussing a *haiku* that Mr. Hayano was planning to send to the *Mainichi*, while her father was sitting at one end of the sofa looking through a copy of *Life*, the new picture magazine. Occasionally, her father would comment on a photograph, holding it toward Mrs. Hayano and speaking to her as he always did—loudly, as though he thought someone such as she must surely be at least a trifle deaf also.

The five girls had their refreshments at the kitchen table, and it was while Rosie was showing the sisters her trick of swallowing peach slices without chewing (she chased each slippery crescent down with a swig of tea) that her father brought his empty teacup and untouched saucer to the sink and said, "Come on, Rosie, we're going home now."

"Already?" asked Rosie.

"Work tomorrow," he said.

He sounded irritated, and Rosie, puzzled, gulped one last yellow slice and stood up to go, while the sisters began protesting, as was their wont.

"We have to get up at five-thirty," he told them, going into the front room quickly, so that they did not have their usual chance to hang onto his hands and plead for an extension of time.

Rosie, following, saw that her mother and Mr. Hayano were sipping tea and still talking together, while Mrs. Hayano concentrated, quivering, on raising the handleless Japanese cup to her lips with both her hands and lowering it back to her lap. Her father, saying nothing, went out the door, onto the bright porch, and down

the steps. Her mother looked up and asked, "Where is he going?"

"Where is he going?" Rosie said. "He said we were going home now."

"Going home?" Her mother looked with embarrassment at Mr. Hayano and his absorbed wife and then forced a smile. "He must be tired," she said.

Haru was not giving up yet. "May Rosie stay overnight?" she asked, and Natsu, Aki, and Fuyu came to reinforce their sister's plea by helping her make a circle around Rosie's mother. Rosie, for once having no desire to stay, was relieved when her mother, apologizing to the perturbed Mr. and Mrs. Hayano for her father's abruptness at the same time, managed to shake her head no at the quartet, kindly but <u>adamant</u>, so that they broke their circle and let her go.

Rosie's father looked ahead into the windshield as the two joined him. "I'm sorry," her mother said. "You must be tired." Her father, stepping on the starter, said nothing. "You know how I get when it's *haiku*," she continued, "I forget what time it is." He only grunted.

As they rode homeward silently, Rosie, sitting between, felt a rush of hate for both—for her mother for begging, for her father for denying her mother. I wish this old Ford would crash, right now, she thought, then immediately, no, no, I wish my father would laugh, but it was too late: already the vision had passed through her mind of the green pick-up crumpled in the dark against one of the mighty eucalyptus trees they were just riding past, of the three contorted, bleeding bodies, one of them hers.

Rosie ran between two patches of tomatoes, her heart working more rambunctiously than she had ever known it to. How lucky it was that Aunt Taka and Uncle Gimpachi[9] had come tonight, though, how very lucky. Otherwise she

---

9. **Aunt Taka** (tä'kä) . . . **Uncle Gimpachi** (gēm-pä'chē).

WORDS
TO
KNOW

**adamant** (ăd'ə-mənt) *adj.* stubborn; not giving in

---

## Teaching Options

### Mini Lesson Grammar

**ADVERB CLAUSES: SUBORDINATING CONJUNCTIONS** An adverb clause is a type of subordinate clause that modifies a verb, adjective, or other adverb. Generally, adverb clauses answer the questions *How?*, *Why?*, *When?*, and *Where?* Adverb clauses are usually introduced by subordinating conjunctions such as *because, as, when, than, in order that, as if, where, after, before, if, although, unless,* and *so that.* Illustrate these grammatical structures with the following model sentences:

She was running after she was kissed.

She was more nervous than she wanted to be.

| Adverb clause | Subordinating conjunction | Word Modified/ part of speech | Question the clause answers |
|---|---|---|---|
| after she was kissed | after | running/verb | When was she running? |
| than she wanted to be | than | nervous/ adjective | To what extent was she nervous? |

Use **Grammar Transparencies and Copymasters**, p. 97.

Use McDougal Littell's ***Language Network***, Chapter 3, for more instruction in adverb clauses.

Japanese-American family in the 1930s. Photo by Russell Lee. Underwood Photo Archives, San Francisco.

might not have really kept her half-promise to meet Jesus Carrasco. Jesus was going to be a senior in September at the same school she went to, and his parents were the ones helping with the tomatoes this year. She and Jesus, who hardly remembered seeing each other at Cleveland High where there were so many other people and two whole grades between them, had become great friends this summer—he always had a joke for her when he periodically drove the loaded pick-up up from the fields to the shed where she was usually sorting while her mother and father did the packing, and they laughed a great deal together over infinitesimal repartee[10] during the afternoon break for chilled watermelon or ice cream in the shade of the shed.

What she enjoyed most was racing him to see which could finish picking a double row first. He, who could work faster, would tease her by slowing down until she thought she would surely pass him this time, then speeding up furiously to leave her several sprawling vines behind. Once he had made her screech hideously by crossing over, while her back was turned, to place atop the tomatoes in her green-stained bucket a truly monstrous, pale green worm (it had looked more like an infant snake). And it was when they had finished a contest this morning, after she had

 **1**
 **2**

---

10. **infinitesimal repartee** (ĭn′fĭ-nĭ-tĕs′ə-məl rĕp′ər-tē′): an attempt at witty conversation about trivial matters (a humorous exaggeration of the term *small talk*).

SEVENTEEN SYLLABLES **793**

SEVENTEEN SYLLABLES **793**

COMING-OF-AGE STORY

**A** Remind students that conflicts can also be internal, meaning that they take place within a character's mind. Coming-of-age stories often deal with the internal conflicts of adolescent characters. Have students identify what Rosie's internal conflict is.

**Possible Response:** Her internal conflict is over whether or not to keep the appointment with Jesus. She senses, but has not admitted to herself, that he has romantic feelings about her, and she is unsure of her feelings for him.

**B** Ask students to describe Rosie's reaction to Jesus's kiss and then to explain why they think she responds that way.

**Possible Response:** She enjoys the kiss at first but then feels overwhelmed. She also seems frightened, either by her own sexual feelings or by the suddenness of events.

### Active Reading

UNDERSTANDING CONFLICTS

**C** Mr. Hayashi's abrupt, impolite response to Rosie's request marks a continuation of family conflict. Invite students to suggest why her father is upset.

**Possible Response:** He may have gone to the bathhouse to escape a conversation about haiku, an issue that has been a continuing source of tension in the family.

---

pantingly pointed a green finger at the immature tomatoes evident in the lugs[11] at the end of his row and he had returned the accusation (with justice), that he had startlingly brought up the matter of their possibly meeting outside the range of both their parents' *dubious* eyes.

"What for?" she had asked.

"I've got a secret I want to tell you," he said.

"Tell me now," she demanded.

"It won't be ready till tonight," he said. She laughed. "Tell me tomorrow then."

"It'll be gone tomorrow," he threatened.

"Well, for seven hakes,[12] what is it?" she had asked, more than twice, and when he had suggested that the packing shed would be an appropriate place to find out, she had cautiously answered maybe. She had not been certain she was going to keep the appointment until the arrival of mother's sister and her husband. Their coming seemed a sort of signal of permission, of grace, and she had definitely made up her mind to lie and leave as she was bowing them welcome.

**1**
**A**
So as soon as everyone appeared settled back for the evening, she announced loudly that she was going to the privy outside, "I'm going to the *benjo!*" and slipped out the door. And now that she was actually on her way, her heart pumped in such an undisciplined way that she could hear it with her ears. It's because I'm running, she told herself, slowing to a walk. The shed was up ahead, one more patch away, in the middle of the fields. Its bulk, looming in the dimness, took on a sinisterness that was funny when Rosie reminded herself that it was only a wooden frame with a canvas roof and three canvas walls that made a slapping noise on breezy days.

Jesus was sitting on the narrow plank that was the sorting platform and she went around to the other side and jumped backwards to seat herself on the rim of a packing stand. "Well, tell me," she said without greeting, thinking her voice

---

• *All that remained intact now was*

*yes*

*and*

*no*

*and*

*oh,*

*and even these few sounds would not easily out.*

---

sounded reassuringly familiar.

"I saw you coming out the door," Jesus said. "I heard you running part of the way, too."

"Uh-huh," Rosie said. "Now tell me the secret."

"I was afraid you wouldn't come," he said.

Rosie delved around on the chicken-wire bottom of the stall for number two tomatoes, ripe, which she was sitting beside, and came up with a left-over that felt edible. She bit into it and began sucking out the pulp and seeds. "I'm here," she pointed out.

"Rosie, are you sorry you came?"

"Sorry? What for?" she said. "You said you were going to tell me something."

---

11. **lugs:** shallow boxes in which fruit is shipped.

12. **for seven hakes:** a play on the phrase "for heaven's sake."

---

WORDS
TO
KNOW

**dubious** (dōō′bē-əs) *adj.* doubtful; suspicious

794

---

 **Mini Lesson** **Speaking and Listening**

**PROBLEM SOLVING BY ROLE-PLAYING**

**Prepare** Role-playing is a method of conflict resolution. Review the major conflicts of the story with students, and have them work in small groups to role play these conflicts.

**Present** Have students take on the roles of Mr. and Mrs. Hayashi and Rosie in order to discuss the conflicts between them. One student might want

to act as a moderator in case the characters come to an impasse. After their role-playing, students should record what conflicts they were able to resolve and the ways in which they were resolved. Finally, students should evaluate each other's communication skills using praise and concrete suggestions for improvement.

"I will, I will," Jesus said, but his voice contained disappointment, and Rosie fleetingly felt the older of the two, realizing a brand-new power which vanished without category under her recognition.

"I have to go back in a minute," she said. "My aunt and uncle are here from Wintersburg. I told them I was going to the privy."

Jesus laughed. "You funny thing," he said. "You slay me!"

"Just because you have a bathroom *inside,*" Rosie said. "Come on, tell me."

Chuckling, Jesus came around to lean on the stand facing her. They still could not see each other very clearly, but Rosie noticed that Jesus became very sober again as he took the hollow tomato from her hand and dropped it back into the stall. When he took hold of her empty hand, she could find no words to protest; her vocabulary had become distressingly constricted and she thought desperately that all that remained intact now was yes and no and oh, and even these few sounds would not easily out. Thus, kissed by Jesus, Rosie fell for the first time entirely victim to a helplessness <u>delectable</u> beyond speech. But the terrible, beautiful sensation lasted no more than a second, and the reality of Jesus' lips and tongue and teeth and hands made her pull away with such strength that she nearly tumbled.

Rosie stopped running as she approached the lights from the windows of home. How long since she had left? She could not guess, but gasping yet, she went to the privy in back and locked herself in. Her own breathing deafened her in the dark, close space, and she sat and waited until she could hear at last the nightly calling of the frogs and crickets. Even then, all she could think to say was oh, my, and the pressure of Jesus' face against her face would not leave.

No one had missed her in the parlor, however, and Rosie walked in and through quickly, announcing that she was next going to take a bath. "Your father's in the bathhouse," her mother said, and Rosie, in her room, recalled that she had not seen him when she entered. There had been only Aunt Taka and Uncle Gimpachi with her mother at the table, drinking tea. She got her robe and straw sandals and crossed the parlor again to go outside. Her mother was telling them about the *haiku* competition in the *Mainichi* and the poem she had entered.

Rosie met her father coming out of the bathhouse. "Are you through, Father?" she asked. "I was going to ask you to scrub my back."

"Scrub your own back," he said shortly, going toward the main house.

"What have I done now?" she yelled after him. She suddenly felt like doing a lot of yelling. But he did not answer, and she went into the bathhouse. Turning on the dangling light, she removed her denims and T-shirt and threw them in the big carton for dirty clothes standing next to the washing machine. Her other things she took with her into the bath compartment to wash after her bath. After she had scooped a basin of hot water from the square wooden tub, she sat on the grey cement of the floor and soaped herself at exaggerated leisure, singing "Red Sails in the Sunset" at the top of her voice and using da-da-da where she suspected her words. Then, standing up, still singing, for she was possessed by the notion that any attempt now to analyze would result in spoilage and she believed that the larger her volume the less she would be able to hear herself think, she obtained more hot water and poured it on until she was free of lather. Only then did she allow herself to step into the steaming vat, one leg first, then the remainder of her body inch by inch until the water no longer stung and she could move around at will.

She took a long time soaking, afterwards remembering to go around outside to stoke the embers of the tin-lined fireplace beneath the tub

---

---

| WORDS TO KNOW | **delectable** (dĭ-lĕk′tə-bəl) *adj.* highly pleasing; delightful |
|---|---|

**795**

---

### Students Acquiring English

**1** Explain that privy means "outhouse" or "outdoor toilet." It comes from the same Latin root as the word private.

### Gifted and Talented

**2** Ask students to make inferences about what Rosie's "brand-new power" might be.

**Possible Response:** She has been implying to Jesus that she does not know why he has asked her there. When she sees his disappointment, something in her "fleetingly" recognizes his vulnerability. The reader might infer that her new power is her ability to attract a member of the opposite sex.

### Less Proficient Readers

**3** Help students understand the events and emotions of this passage by asking them the following questions.

• What happens to Rosie when Jesus takes the tomato from her hands?

**Possible Response:** She cannot speak.

• Why do you think she describes the kiss as a "terrible, beautiful sensation"—how can it be both terrible and beautiful?

**Possible Response:** Her shock or embarrassment at the event and its suddenness might have made it terrible, yet it felt beautiful because she really likes Jesus.

• What does Rosie do after he kisses her?

**Possible Response:** She breaks away and hides in the privy until she calms down.

**Set a Purpose** Have students read to find evidence about Rosie's emotions regarding Jesus and their encounter.

---

## Workplace Link  Contracts

### READING MAPS

**Instruction** Reading maps is directly important for those working in occupations that involve travel—such as sales, tourism, or the military—or that involve land use, such as geology, agriculture, and real estate development. Map reading also helps develop skills of graphic literacy that are important in computers and other fields.

**Application** The Hayashi farm is on the way from San Francisco to Los Angeles, perhaps in the San Joaquin Valley, one of California's major agricultural areas. Ask students to use a map of California to plot a route from San Francisco to Los Angeles through the San Joaquin Valley, without using any interstate highways. (The interstate highway system did not exist at the time the story takes place.) Invite students to calculate their mileage and the probable amount of time the trip would take if the driver averaged 40 miles per hour—the approximate speed a driver would have gone during the 1930s.

**A** Have students offer two recent details about Rosie's father's behavior and draw a conclusion about what is troubling him.

**Possible Response:** Detail 1: Rosie's father yells at Rosie for no reason. Detail 2: Rosie's father disappears while her mother talks about haiku with Rosie's aunt and uncle. Conclusion: Rosie's father is still upset at the changes in his wife's behavior and her new absorbing interest in haiku.

**Reading Skills and Strategies:
MAKING A CONNECTION**

**B** Remind students that drawing upon their own backgrounds provides them with connection to texts and gives literature more meaning. Ask them to think of instances in their own lives when they acted as Rosie does when she hides in the outhouse to watch Jesus. Do they think the author has created a realistic portrait of a young person?

**Possible Response:** Students should draw upon their experiences to relate to the literature. Responses should reflect an understanding of Rosie's adolescent confusion and a criticism of the author's ability to create a realistic character.

**Reading Skills and Strategies:
MAKING INFERENCES**

**C** Ask what the revelation that Mrs. Hayashi has won first prize in the poetry contest suggests.

**Possible Response:** She has real talent. Her obsession with writing may not be a passing fancy.

---

**A** and to throw on a few more sticks so that the water might keep its heat for her mother, and when she finally returned to the parlor, she found her mother still talking *haiku* with her aunt and uncle, the three of them on another round of tea. Her father was nowhere in sight.

At Japanese school the next day (Wednesday, it was), Rosie was grave and giddy by turns. Preoccupied at her desk in the row for students on Book Eight, she made up for it at recess by performing wild mimicry for the benefit of her friend Chizuko.[13] She held her nose and whined a witticism or two in what she considered was the manner of Fred Allen; she assumed intoxication and a British accent to go over the climax of the Rudy Vallee recording of the pub conversation about William Ewart Gladstone; she was the child Shirley Temple piping, "On the Good Ship Lollipop"; she was the gentleman soprano of the Four Inkspots trilling, "If I Didn't Care."[14] And she felt reasonably satisfied when Chizuko wept and gasped, "Oh, Rosie, you ought to be in the movies!"

Her father came after her at noon, bringing her sandwiches of minced ham and two nectarines to eat while she rode, so that she could **1** pitch right into the sorting when they got home. The lugs were piling up, he said, and the ripe tomatoes in them would probably have to be taken to the cannery tomorrow if they were not ready for the produce haulers tonight. "This heat's not doing them any good. And we've got no time for a break today."

It was hot, probably the hottest day of the year, and Rosie's blouse stuck damply to her back even under the protection of the canvas. But she worked as efficiently as a flawless machine and kept the stalls heaped, with one part of her mind listening in to the parental murmuring about the heat and the tomatoes and with another part planning the exact words she would say to Jesus when he drove up with the

---

first load of the afternoon. But when at last she saw that the pick-up was coming, her hands went berserk and the tomatoes started falling in the wrong stalls, and her father said, "Hey, hey! Rosie, watch what you're doing!"

"Well, I have to go to the *benjo*," she said, hiding panic.

"Go in the weeds over there," he said, only half-joking.

"Oh, Father!" she protested.

"Oh, go on home," her mother said. "We'll make out for awhile."

In the privy Rosie peered through a knothole toward the fields, watching as much as she could of Jesus. Happily she thought she saw him look in the direction of the house from time to time before he finished unloading and went back toward the patch where his mother and father worked. As she was heading for the shed, a very presentable black car purred up the dirt driveway to the house and its driver motioned to her. Was this the Hayashi home, he wanted to know. She nodded. Was she a Hayashi? Yes, she said, thinking that he was a good-looking man. He got out of the car with a huge, flat package and she saw that he warmly wore a business suit. "I have something here for your mother then," he said, in a more elegant Japanese than she was used to.

She told him where her mother was and he came along with her, patting his face with an immaculate white handkerchief and saying something about the coolness of San Francisco. To her surprised mother and father, he bowed and introduced himself as, among other things,

**B**

**2**

---

13. **Chizuko** (chē-zo͞o′kō).

14. **Fred Allen . . . "If I Didn't Care":** The comedian Fred Allen had a radio show during the 1930s and 1940s. Rudy Vallee was a singer popular during the 1920s and 1930s, who performed a comedy routine featuring a conversation about Gladstone, a 19th-century British prime minister. Shirley Temple was a famous child star of the 1930s. "If I Didn't Care" was a hit record for the Four Inkspots, a popular African-American singing group, in 1939.

WORDS
TO
KNOW    **preoccupied** (prē-ŏk′yə-pīd′) *adj.* lost in thought; intensely concerned

---

**Teaching Options**

✓ Assessment **Standardized Test Practice**

**ARRANGING EVENTS IN SEQUENCE** For some standardized tests, students will be asked to answer multiple-choice questions that test their understanding of the sequence of events. Have students read from "No one had missed her in the parlor" on page 795 to the bottom of page 796. Then have them answer the following questions:

1. What did Rosie do after returning home from meeting Jesus?
   **A.** She mimicked for her friends.
   **B.** She took a bath.
   **C.** She drank tea with her aunt and uncle.
   **D.** She looked at Jesus from the privy.
   **Answer:** B

2. Rosie mimicked at recess, took a bath, and spied on Jesus. Which choice indicates the correct order of these activities?
   **A.** First, second, third
   **B.** Second, first, third
   **C.** Third, second, first
   **D.** First, third, second
   **Answer:** B

*Returning Sails to Gyotoku* (about 1837–1838) Ichiryusai Hiroshige. From the series *Eight Views of the Edo Suburbs*, woodblock print, 23.5 cm × 36 cm., Edo Period, Japan. The Art Institute of Chicago, Clarence Buckingham Collection (1943.708). Photo Copyright © 1995 The Art Institute of Chicago, all rights reserved.

the *haiku* editor of the *Mainichi Shimbun*, saying that since he had been coming as far as Los Angeles anyway, he had decided to bring her the first prize she had won in the recent contest.

"First prize?" her mother echoed, believing and not believing, pleased and overwhelmed. Handed the package with a bow, she bobbed her head up and down numerous times to express her utter gratitude.

"It is nothing much," he added, "but I hope it will serve as a token of our great appreciation for your contributions and our great admiration of your considerable talent."

"I am not worthy," she said, falling easily into his style. "It is I who should make some sign of my humble thanks for being permitted to contribute."

"No, no, to the contrary," he said, bowing again.

But Rosie's mother insisted, and then saying that she knew she was being unorthodox, she asked if she might open the package because her curiosity was so great. Certainly she might. In fact, he would like her reaction to it, for personally, it was one of his favorite Hiroshiges.[15]

Rosie thought it was a pleasant picture, which looked to have been sketched with delicate quickness. There were pink clouds, containing some graceful calligraphy, and a sea that was a pale blue except at the edges, containing four sampans[16] with indications of people in them.

---

15. **Hiroshiges** (hē′rō-shē′gĕz): works by Hiroshige, master designer of color prints, considered one of Japan's most important artists. (See art on this page.)

16. **sampans:** small boats, used in Japan, that can be either sailed or rowed.

---

## Mini Lesson  Viewing and Representing

*Returning Sails to Gyotoku*
**by Ichiyusai Hiroshige**

**ART APPRECIATION** One of Japan's best-known artists, Hiroshige (1797–1858) has influenced generations of Western artists. Returning Sails to Gyotoku is one of a series of eight prints, each of which includes a poem.

**Instruction** Point out to students that lines are very important in this painting, the horizontal lines of the land contrasting with the vertical lines of the sails. Ask students what effect or mood those lines create in the painting.

**Possible Response:** The lines create a mood of order and tranquillity. The sails are straight up, so there must be little wind.

**Application** Ask students to analyze the painting and evaluate how the artist feels about the place and activity he is depicting. What elements of design does he use to accomplish this?

**Possible Response:** Overall, the artist has produced a very pleasing depiction of this scene in Japan. His use of warm, beautiful colors, as well as the natural shading of colors, indicates that he considers it a beautiful place. The lines give a sense of order and peace to the work of the people on the boats. He seems to respect the culture.

## Customizing Instruction

**Students Acquiring English**

**1** Explain to students that the phrase *pitch right into the sorting* contains the idiom to *pitch in*, which means "to help," usually eagerly and energetically. The phrase implies that there was a serious labor shortage and they were counting on her to get a lot of sorting done. Ask students to use the idiom in a sentence of their own.

**Multiple Learning Styles**
**Visual Learners**

**2** Enhance visual learners' understanding of the events of the story by having them create a diagram of the setting where much of the activity takes place, showing the Hayashis' house, the fields, the privy, and the shed. Have them share their drawings with other students to compare and contrast how they each imagined the setting.

### Literary Analysis

**COMING-OF-AGE STORY**

**A** One characteristic of a coming-of-age story is that the adolescent character gains awareness about another person and about himself or herself. Discuss why Rosie might feel that the truth about her parents' marriage would "level her life, her world to the very ground."

**Possible Response:** Rosie anticipates that she will learn things that will permanently change the way she feels about her parents and that her sense of hope for the future will be destroyed.

### Reading Skills and Strategies:
### MAKING INFERENCES

**B** Ask students to infer why Mrs. Hayashi tells the story of her marriage and then makes Rosie promise never to marry.

**Possible Response:** She wants to save Rosie from a fate like her own.

### Active Reading

**UNDERSTANDING CONFLICTS**

**C** What does Rosie's mother's face convey to her about the central nature of the conflict between them?

**Possible Response:** Their conflict is that they do not understand each other; Rosie only gives "glib agreement" to her mother.

What conclusion does Rosie draw from the fact that her mother's embrace and consolations are delayed?

**Possible Response:** Her mother has given up on helping her in some ways—that her mother knows and disapproves of the course Rosie will take.

---

Pines edged the water and on the far-off beach there was a cluster of thatched huts towered over by pine-dotted mountains of grey and blue. The frame was scalloped and gilt.

After Rosie's mother pronounced it without peer and somewhat prodded her father into nodding agreement, she said Mr. Kuroda[17] must at least have a cup of tea after coming all this way, and although Mr. Kuroda did not want to impose, he soon agreed that a cup of tea would be refreshing and went along with her to the house, carrying the picture for her.

"Ha, your mother's crazy!" Rosie's father said, and Rosie laughed uneasily as she resumed judgment on the tomatoes. She had emptied six lugs when he broke into an imaginary conversation with Jesus to tell her to go and remind her mother of the tomatoes, and she went slowly.

• *"Do you know why I married your father?"* ...

*"No,* said Rosie.... *Don't tell me now, she wanted to say, tell me tomorrow, tell me next week, don't tell me today.*

Mr. Kuroda was in his shirtsleeves expounding some *haiku* theory as he munched a rice cake, and her mother was rapt. Abashed in the great man's presence, Rosie stood next to her mother's chair until her mother looked up inquiringly, and then she started to whisper the message, but her mother pushed her gently away and reproached, "You are not being very polite to our guest."

"Father says the tomatoes . . ." Rosie said aloud, smiling foolishly.

"Tell him I shall only be a minute," her mother said, speaking the language of Mr. Kuroda.

When Rosie carried the reply to her father, he did not seem to hear and she said again, "Mother says she'll be back in a minute."

"All right, all right," he nodded, and they worked again in silence. But suddenly, her father uttered an incredible noise, exactly like the cork of a bottle popping, and the next Rosie knew, he was stalking angrily toward the house, almost running in fact, and she chased after him crying, "Father! Father! What are you going to do?"

He stopped long enough to order her back to the shed. "Never mind!" he shouted. "Get on with the sorting!"

And from the place in the fields where she stood, frightened and <u>vacillating</u>, Rosie saw her father enter the house. Soon Mr. Kuroda came out alone, putting on his coat. Mr. Kuroda got into his car and backed out down the driveway onto the highway. Next her father emerged, also alone, something in his arms (it was the picture, she realized), and, going over to the bathhouse woodpile, he threw the picture on the ground and picked up the axe. Smashing the picture, glass and all (she heard the explosion faintly), he reached over for the kerosene that was used to encourage the bath fire and poured it over the wreckage. I am dreaming, Rosie said to herself, I am dreaming, but her father, having made sure that his act of cremation was <u>irrevocable</u>, was even then returning to the fields.

---

17. **Kuroda** (kōō-rō′dä).

---

| WORDS<br>TO<br>KNOW | **vacillating** (văs′ə-lā′tĭng) *adj.* swinging from one course of action or opinion to another; indecisive **vacillate** *v.*<br>**irrevocable** (ĭ-rĕv′ə-kə-bəl) *adj.* impossible to take back or undo |
|---|---|

**798**

---

## Teaching Options

### (Mini Lesson) Vocabulary Strategy

**USING CONTEXT TO UNDERSTAND IDIOMS**

**Instruction** An idiom is an expression that cannot be understood from the meanings of its individual words. Idioms are often particular to a region or culture and are therefore difficult for non-native speakers to understand. Students should practice relying on context to determine the meanings of idioms. Demonstrate that the phrase *came after* on page 796 does not make sense from analyzing its individual words ("after" seems to imply a time sequence). However, by reading the sentence further, it is obvious that her father came to collect or pick up his daughter.

**Application** Have students work cooperatively with a partner to determine the meanings of the idioms in *she chased each slippery crescent down* (p. 792) and *I shall only be a minute* (p. 798). Advise students to summarize the activity of the sentence first and then use the context to guess the meaning of the idioms.

Use **Vocabulary Transparencies and Copymasters**, p. 65.

Rosie ran past him and toward the house. What had become of her mother? She burst into the parlor and found her mother at the back window watching the dying fire. They watched together until there remained only a feeble smoke under the blazing sun. Her mother was very calm.

"Do you know why I married your father?" she said without turning.

"No," said Rosie. It was the most frightening question she had ever been called upon to answer. Don't tell me now, she wanted to say, tell me tomorrow, tell me next week, don't tell me today. But she knew she would be told now, that the telling would combine with the other violence of the hot afternoon to level her life, her world to the very ground.

It was like a story out of the magazines illustrated in sepia,[18] which she had consumed so greedily for a period until the information had somehow reached her that those wretchedly unhappy autobiographies, offered to her as the testimonials of living men and women, were largely inventions: Her mother, at nineteen, had come to America and married her father as an alternative to suicide.

At eighteen she had been in love with the first son of one of the well-to-do families in her village. The two had met whenever and wherever they could, secretly, because it would not have done for his family to see him favor her—her father had no money; he was a drunkard and a gambler besides. She had learned she was with child; an excellent match had already been arranged for her lover. Despised by her family, she had given premature birth to a stillborn son, who would be seventeen now. Her family did not turn her out, but she could no longer project herself in any direction without refreshing in them the memory of her indiscretion. She wrote to Aunt Taka, her favorite sister in America, threatening to kill herself if Aunt Taka would

not send for her. Aunt Taka hastily arranged a marriage with a young man of whom she knew, but lately arrived from Japan, a young man of simple mind, it was said, but of kindly heart. The young man was never told why his unseen betrothed was so eager to hasten the day of meeting.

The story was told perfectly, with neither groping for words nor untoward passion. It was as though her mother had memorized it by heart, reciting it to herself so many times over that its nagging vileness had long since gone.

"I had a brother then?" Rosie asked, for this was what seemed to matter now; she would think about the other later, she assured herself, pushing back the illumination which threatened all that darkness that had hitherto been merely mysterious or even glamorous. "A half-brother?"

"Yes."

"I would have liked a brother," she said.

Suddenly, her mother knelt on the floor and took her by the wrists. "Rosie," she said urgently, "promise me you will never marry!" Shocked more by the request than the revelation, Rosie stared at her mother's face. Jesus, Jesus, she called silently, not certain whether she was invoking the help of the son of the Carrascos or of God, until there returned sweetly the memory of Jesus' hand, how it had touched her and where. Still her mother waited for an answer, holding her wrists so tightly that her hands were going numb. She tried to pull free. Promise, her mother whispered fiercely, promise. Yes, yes, I promise, Rosie said. But for an instant she turned away, and her mother, hearing the familiar glib agreement, released her. Oh, you, you, you, her eyes and twisted mouth said, you fool. Rosie, covering her face, began at last to cry, and the embrace and consoling hand came much later than she expected. ❖

---

18. **sepia** (sē′pē-ə): a dark, reddish-brown color.

799

---

## GUIDING STUDENT RESPONSE

## Connect to the Literature

**1. What Do You Think?**
Possible Responses: Rosie, because she is destined to disappoint her mother simply by wanting to get married; Mrs. Hayashi, because she is in an unhappy marriage and will no longer write haiku

**Comprehension Check**
• He picks tomatoes at her parents' farm.
• Rosie's father burns it.
• She makes her promise not to marry.

 Use Selection Quiz
**Unit Five Resource Book**, p. 19.

## Think Critically

**2.** Possible Response: Mrs. Hayashi's advice not to marry grows out of the conflicts between her husband and herself; the conflict between Rosie and Mrs. Hayashi during the conversation also grows out of previous conflicts; Rosie's response to her mother grows out of her own inner conflicts.

**3.** Most students will probably answer that Rosie will not follow her mother's advice, basing their opinion on her newfound interest in Jesus.

**4.** Possible Response: She feels a combination of physical attraction, fear, and embarrassment.

**5.** Possible Responses: He does not understand poetry; he wants a more traditional wife; he is jealous that because of the poetry she talks to other men and spends less time with him.

**6.** Possible Responses: Yes, she could try to explain how important her haiku is to her to make her husband understand; no, the nature of their marriage means that she will always have to sacrifice her desires to her husband's needs.

## Connect to the Literature

**1. What Do You Think?**
What character were you most concerned about as you finished reading the story?

**Comprehension Check**
• In what circumstances do Rosie and Jesus Carrasco become friends?
• What happens to the prize Rosie's mother receives for writing haiku?
• What does Rosie's mother make Rosie promise at the end of the story?

## Think Critically

**2.** **ACTIVE READING** **UNDERSTANDING CONFLICTS** Think about the conversation between Rosie and her mother after the burning of the picture. How does this conversation relate to the other **conflicts** in the story? Refer to the conflict you listed in your  **READER'S NOTEBOOK**.

**3.** Do you think Rosie is more likely to follow her mother's advice not to marry or to follow her own way? Cite evidence from the story to support your opinion.

**4.** How would you describe Rosie's feelings after Jesus Carrasco kisses her?

**5.** Why does Rosie's father's react as he does to his wife's writing?

**THINK ABOUT**
{
• the changes in the family's routine and social life
• the intensity of the farm work
• the prize awarded Mrs. Hayashi
}

**6.** Can Mrs. Hayashi do anything to resolve the **conflict** between her husband's needs and her own desires? Explain your answer.

## Extend Interpretations

**7. What If?** How would the effect of the story be different if the visit to the Hayano family were not included?

**8. Connect to Life** Like Mrs. Hayashi in this story, many women today are torn between family obligations and creative work. What advice would you give to someone trying to meet her obligations and still achieve her potential?

**9.** **Points of Comparison** What similarities and differences do you see between Mrs. Hayashi's situation and that of the unnamed narrator in "The Yellow Wallpaper"?

## Literary Analysis

**COMING-OF-AGE STORY**
A coming-of-age story is a story about growing up. The **plot** describes a rite of passage, or the experiences that lead the main character to a new level of maturity. In "Seventeen Syllables," two related plot lines operate simultaneously. The development of Rosie's relationship with Jesus Carrasco forms one plot line. In this part of the story, Yamamoto explores the conflicting emotions that often surround such a relationship. The second plot line involves Mrs. Hayashi's haiku writing and the **conflicts** she and her husband experience because of it.

**Paired Activity** With a partner, create two time lines, one above the other. Indicate events related to Rosie's romance with Jesus Carrasco on the top line and events connected with Mrs. Hayashi's haiku writing on the bottom one. Circle points on the time lines where the two plots overlap at crucial points. Then write a statement that answers this question: What does Yamamoto communicate about Rosie and her adolescent awakening? Share your time line and thematic statement with other pairs of students.

## Extend Interpretations

**What If?** The visit to the Hayano family is a pivotal dramatic scene where the conflict between Mr. Hayashi and Mrs. Hayashi becomes glaringly apparent.
**Connect to Life** Accept all reasonable responses.
**Points of Comparison** Possible Response: Both women are confined by their roles as wives and mothers and find it impossible to combine their obligations as women with their desire to express themselves creatively; both women are described as "crazy" by their husbands for wanting to pursue a writing career.

## Literary Analysis

**Coming-of-Age Story** Students should acknowledge the connection between Rosie's awakening as a woman and the conflict she witnesses between her parents when her mother asserts her independence through her haiku writing.

# *Choices & CHALLENGES*

## Writing Options

1. **Points of Comparison** Write a dialogue in which Mrs. Hayashi and the narrator of "The Yellow Wallpaper" exchange views about writing as a tool for self-expression. For your prewriting notes, list some of the points you discussed in answering question 9.

2. **Character Sketch** Imagine that a book of haiku by Mrs. Hayashi—under her pen name Ume Hanazono—is soon to be published. Write a biographical note about the author that might appear on the book's cover.

## Vocabulary in Action

**EXERCISE: CONTEXT CLUES** Write the word that best completes each of the following sentences.

1. In the early 1800s, European paintings tended to be quite realistic, showing gorgeous flowers and _____ fruit.

2. Japanese prints were quite detailed but more subtle and _____ than European works.

3. The arrival of some of these prints in Europe had a surprising impact, with long-lasting _____.

4. The impressionists abandoned classic Western painting styles, becoming _____ with some of the Japanese techniques.

5. Skeptical critics were _____ about paintings that depicted "impressions" of reality.

6. Still, the course the impressionists took was not a _____ one; it remained focused and steady.

7. Unswayed by criticism, the impressionists were _____ in their attempts to convey the effects of light and shadow and capture fleeting moments.

8. One critic scorned Renoir's paintings for what he considered an _____ use of color.

9. This critic ridiculed Renoir for his _____ as an artist.

10. The influence of the impressionists and the Japanese printmakers who inspired them proved _____, persisting even today.

### Building Vocabulary
For an in-depth lesson on context clues, see page 326.

| WORDS TO KNOW | adamant<br>delectable<br>dubious<br>indiscretion | irrevocable<br>preoccupied<br>repercussion<br>unobtrusive | untoward<br>vacillating |
|---|---|---|---|

## Hisaye Yamamoto
### 1921–

**Other Works**
"Yoneko's Earthquake"
"Wilshire Bus"

**Japanese-American Writer** The daughter of Japanese immigrants, like her character Rosie, Yamamoto was born in Redondo Beach, California. Along with many other Japanese Americans, she was interned by the U.S. government during World War II. While she was in the detention camp, the interest in writing that she had developed as a teenager led her to write a column for the camp newspaper and to publish a serialized mystery. For three years after the war, she worked as a columnist for the *Los Angeles Tribune*, an African-American weekly. Later, she received a John Hay Whitney Foundation Opportunity Fellowship that allowed her to write fiction full time for a year.

**Literary Focus** Yamamoto has had a relatively small literary output. She has published only one collection in the United States—*Seventeen Syllables and Other Stories*—yet she continues to receive critical acclaim. In 1986 she received a lifetime achievement award from the Before Columbus Foundation. Her work, which features Japanese-American protagonists, often focuses on encounters between representatives of different races and cultures. Using irony and realistic detail, Yamamoto shows the oppression caused by racism and sexism.

**Mother's Influence** "Seventeen Syllables," which was first published in 1949, was inspired by the life of Yamamoto's mother, who had published senryu, a traditional form of Japanese poetry, in Japanese-language newspapers. According to Yamamoto, her mother, like most women, did not have a chance to fulfill her potential. "She had us kids to look after, on top of all the housework and working alongside my father in the fields."

## Writing Options

1. **Points of Comparison** To get students started on this assignment, have them create lists of character attributes for both the narrator of "The Yellow Wallpaper" and Mrs. Hayashi. Their dialogues should take into account the cultural and class differences between the two women as well as their similar struggles to write and their husbands' perception of them as "crazy."

2. **Character Sketch** To get students started on this assignment, have them read several examples of author biographies and outline the kinds of information they include.

## Vocabulary in Action

1. delectable
2. unobtrusive
3. repercussion
4. preoccupied
5. dubious
6. vacillating
7. adamant
8. untoward
9. indiscretion
10. irrevocable

---

 **Grammar**

**SEMICOLONS AND CONJUNCTIVE ADVERBS** Use a semicolon before a conjunctive adverb that joins the clauses of a compound sentence. Remind students that conjunctive adverbs are followed by a comma. Write the following sentence on the board, underlining the conjunctive adverb:
Mrs. Hayashi wanted to write haiku; <u>however</u>, her husband did not approve.

**Exercises** Have students copy the following sentences and put in the correct punctuation, using semicolons.

1. Rosie liked Jesus, at the same time she felt nervous around him. (*Rosie liked Jesus; at the same time, she felt nervous around him.*)

2. Mrs. Hayashi was talented at writing haiku. Indeed she won a prize for one of her poems. (*Mrs. Hayashi was talented at writing haiku; indeed, she won a prize for one of her poems.*)

 Use **Grammar Transparencies and Copymasters**, p. 157.

 Use McDougal Littell's *Language Network*, Chapter 10, for more instruction in semicolons and conjunctive adverbs.

### Objectives

1. understand and appreciate a modern **poem** (Literary Analysis)
2. identify and appreciate **imagery** (Literary Analysis)
3. **visualize** the images in a poem (Active Reading)

### Summary

The speaker in "Adolescence—III" lives, in a sense, in two different worlds. In the real world, the speaker's daily life consists of manual labor, poverty, scabbed knees, and a bleak window view of clay soil and chicken manure. In the speaker's fantasy world, however, love comes to her, and her beloved's touch magically makes her scabs "fall away." The speaker's daydreams show the power of her imagination and of her yearning to become a woman.

## Reading and Analyzing

### Literary Analysis  IMAGERY

**A** Have students analyze Dove's use of imagery by reading the first stanza of the poem, paying attention to which words and phrases help them see, hear, feel, taste, and/or smell what is being described.

**Possible Response:** Words and phrases such as "glowed orange in sunlight," "rotted in shadow," "grew orange and softer," "swelling out," and "starched cotton slips" help the reader experience the speaker's comparison of herself to ripening tomatoes.

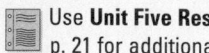 Use **Unit Five Resource Book,** p. 21 for additional support.

### Active Reading  VISUALIZING

**B** Have students close their eyes while you read aloud the second stanza. Ask students to let the words and phrases form pictures in their minds as you read. After reading the stanza, ask: What picture or image lingers most clearly in your mind?

**Possible Responses:** the row of lipstick stubs on the windowsill, the scarred knees wrapped in big-band dresses

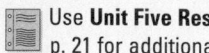 Use **Unit Five Resource Book,** p. 20 for additional support.

---

## PREPARING to *Read*

*"I have loved you in my dreams."*

# Adolescence—III

*Poetry by* RITA DOVE

**Comparing Literature**

### Traditions Across Time: A Diversity of Voices

The speaker of "Adolescence—III," a modern poem by an African-American writer, is at an awkward age. She is not yet a woman, but no longer a child. Still, she has a distinct personality and a rich inner life. She may bring to mind the unnamed narrator in "The Yellow Wallpaper," the main character in "The Story of an Hour," and the speakers in Emily Dickinson's poems. As you read this poem, consider connections between the speaker and these selections.

## Build Background

### Rita Dove's Poetry

"Adolescence—III" is the third in a series of three poems about being young that Rita Dove wrote for *The Yellow House on the Corner,* her first volume of poetry. Dove often gives public readings of her poems and intends them to be read aloud. Her language is restrained and concise, and she lets the images in her poems speak for themselves. She often creates speakers who are displaced—living, as she puts it, in "two different worlds."

## Focus Your Reading

**LITERARY ANALYSIS  IMAGERY**  **Imagery** is language that represents sensory experience. To help bring the poem inside the reader, poets choose words that help readers see, hear, feel, taste, and smell what's being described. For example, in the opening lines of this poem, Dove uses this image to describe rows of tomatoes: "they glowed orange in sunlight / And rotted in shadow."

**ACTIVE READING  VISUALIZING**  **Visualizing** is the process of forming mental pictures from a written description. Use these tips as you read Dove's poem:

- Let the words and phrases conjure up pictures and sensations in your imagination.
- Relate these pictures and sensations to your own experiences and feelings.
- Look for contrasting images. Some images describe things in the real world; others describe things in the speaker's dreams.

**READER'S NOTEBOOK**  As you read, list the images you visualize on a chart like the one below. Classify them according to what they describe.

| Images | |
| --- | --- |
| **Real World** | **Speaker's Dreams** |
| | |
| | |
| | |

---

## LESSON RESOURCES

**UNIT FIVE RESOURCE BOOK,** pp. 20–21

**ASSESSMENT RESOURCES**
**Formal Assessment,** pp. 145–146
**Teacher's Guide to Assessment and Portfolio Use**
**Test Generator**

**SKILLS TRANSPARENCIES AND COPYMASTERS**
**Reading and Critical Thinking**
- Visualizing, T8 (for Active Reading, p. 802)
**Vocabulary**
- Word Origins, C66 (for Mini Lesson, p. 803)
**Writing**
- Compare-Contrast, C31 (for Writing Option 1, p. 805)

**Communications**
- Dramatic Reading, T12 (for Activities & Explorations, p. 805)
- Verbal Strategies, T14 (for Activities & Explorations, p. 805)

**INTEGRATED TECHNOLOGY**
**Audio Library**
**Visit our website:**
www.mcdougallittell.com

Theresa (1987),
Romare
Bearden/Licensed by
VAGA, New York.
Watercolor and
collage, 8½″ × 11¼″,
courtesy of the Estate
of Romare Bearden.

# ADOLESCENCE — III

## RITA DOVE

**A**

With Dad gone, Mom and I worked
The dusky rows of tomatoes.
As they glowed orange in sunlight
And rotted in shadow, I too
5   Grew orange and softer, swelling out
Starched cotton slips.

**B**

The texture of twilight made me think of
Lengths of Dotted Swiss.[1] In my room
I wrapped scarred knees in dresses
10   That once went to big-band dances;
I baptized my earlobes with rosewater.
Along the window-sill, the lipstick stubs
Glittered in their steel shells.

Looking out at the rows of clay
15   And chicken manure, I dreamed how it would happen:
He would meet me by the blue spruce,
A carnation over his heart, saying,
"I have come for you, Madam;
I have loved you in my dreams."
20   At his touch, the scabs would fall away.
Over his shoulder, I see my father coming toward us:
He carries his tears in a bowl,
And blood hangs in the pine-soaked air.

---

1. **Dotted Swiss:** a crisp, sheer cotton fabric decorated with raised dots.

ADOLESCENCE—III   **803**

## Customizing Instruction

### Less Proficient Readers
Tell students that this poem describes one young woman's experiences as a teenager. Ask them to think of the feelings and hopes they have experienced during their teenage years. Tell students to draw upon their own experiences as a way to connect with the poem.

**Set a Purpose** Have students read to understand the speaker's daydreams about becoming a woman.

### Students Acquiring English
Tell students that "Adolescence—III" is told from the point of view of a young girl on the verge of adulthood. To help students understand the speaker's character, have them construct a web diagram of the "facts" of the speaker's life, based on details from the poem.

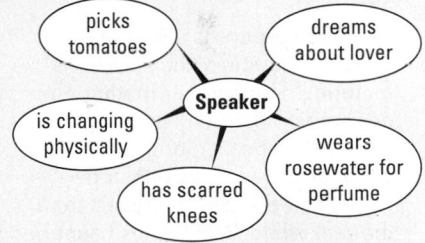

Use **Spanish Study Guide** for additional support, pp. 191–193.

---

## Vocabulary Strategy

**RESEARCHING WORD ORIGINS:** *adolescence*
**Instruction** The word *adolescence* is derived from the Latin root *alere,* which means "to nourish." The dreams and yearnings expressed by the speaker in the poem "Adolescence—III" reflect the state, or condition, of being an adolescent. Other words derived from this root include *adolescent, alible, aliment, alimony, alumnus,* and *coalesce.*
**Activity** Have students work in pairs to look up the definitions of *adolescent, alible, aliment, alimony, alumnus,* and *coalesce.* Ask students to use each word in a sentence. Have them also

describe how their knowledge of the root *alere* can help them recall the meanings of these words.

Use **Vocabulary Transparencies and Copymasters,** p. 66.

**A lesson on word origins appears on p. 550 in the Pupil's Edition.**

## GUIDING STUDENT RESPONSE

## Connect to the Literature

**1. What Do You Think?**
Students should support their reactions with textual evidence.

**Comprehension Check**
• They work in a tomato field.
• The man of her dreams will come to take her away.

## Think Critically

**2.** The speaker's father, mentioned in the first line of the poem, returns in the speaker's dream. The father may feel remorse for having injured the speaker and may now seek reconciliation. The blood may represent a violent act he has committed or will commit or the ties of kinship uniting his daughter and him.

**3.** Possible Responses: Like the ripening tomatoes, the speaker is maturing. She and her mother now do the work formerly done by her father. The speaker longs to become a woman, dresses as one in her room, and escapes in dreams from the real world. Two figures haunt her dreams: a lover, who may represent the magical possibilities of the future, and her father, who may represent the harsh realities of the past.

**4.** Images such as "dusky rows of tomatoes" and "the rows of clay and chicken manure" depict the real world as harsh and unappealing; the world of the speaker's dreams, by contrast, is vivid, fulfilling, and miraculous.

## Literary Analysis

**Imagery** The images listed on students' charts will vary. For example, the image "rows of clay and chicken manure" appeals to the senses of sight and smell, suggesting the offensive and harsh aspects of the real world.

---

## Connect to the Literature

**1. What Do You Think?**
What is your reaction to the speaker of this poem?

**Comprehension Check**
• What task do the speaker and her mother do?
• What does the speaker dream will happen to her?

## Think Critically

**2.** What do the last two lines of this poem mean to you?

**3.** What conclusions can you draw about the speaker?

 **THINK ABOUT**
• her comparison of herself to the tomatoes
• her feelings about her absent father
• how she dresses up in her room
• the figures in her dreams

**4.** **ACTIVE READING** **VISUALIZING** Based on the **images** you listed in your **READER'S NOTEBOOK**, how would you describe the contrast between the "two different worlds" the speaker lives in—the real world and that of her dreams?

## Extend Interpretations

**5. Critic's Corner** In commenting on her poetry, Dove has stated, "Obviously, as a black woman, I am concerned with race. . . . But certainly not every poem of mine mentions the fact of being black. They are poems about humanity, and sometimes humanity happens to be black. I cannot run from, I won't run from any kind of truth." How would you describe the truths about adolescence that this poem conveys?

**6.** **Points of Comparison** Compare the **speaker** of this poem with a **speaker, narrator,** or **character** from any selection in the first part of this subunit. Support the comparison with evidence from both works.

---

## Literary Analysis

**IMAGERY** **Imagery** refers to the words and phrases that re-create sensory experiences for the reader. Though the majority of images are visual, stimulating pictures in the reader's mind, images can appeal to any of the other senses—hearing, smell, taste, and touch. For example, in the first stanza, the speaker uses this image to describe herself: "swelling out / Starched cotton slips." This image appeals to the senses of sight and touch. It suggests growth and maturity.

**Paired Activity** With a partner, make a chart like the one shown. List two or more images that you find especially vivid in this poem. For each one, identify the sense or senses appealed to and tell what the image suggests to you. Share your chart with other pairs of students.

| Image | Appeals to... | Suggests |
|---|---|---|
| | | |
| | | |
| | | |

---

## Extend Interpretations

**Critic's Corner** Like many adolescents, the speaker longs for adulthood and sometimes lives in an imaginary world.

**Points of Comparison** Besides the comparison with Rosie in "Seventeen Syllables," which students can explore under Writing Options on page 805, students might compare the speaker with Mrs. Mallard in "The Story of an Hour." Both feel trapped by circumstances, dream of escape, and long for fulfillment.

## Writing Options

**1. Points of Comparison** In an essay, compare and contrast the imagery in this poem with that in an Emily Dickinson poem, such as "Success is counted sweetest" (page 753). Use the chart you made for the Literary Analysis activity on page 804 to help you get started.

**Writing Handbook**
See page 1281: Compare and Contrast.

**2. Rosie's Diary Entry** Both Rosie in "Seventeen Syllables" (page 789) and the speaker in this poem are on the threshold of adulthood. Moreover, they both work in tomato fields and have troubled feelings about their fathers. Imagine that Rosie has just read this poem. Write a diary entry from her point of view, relating the speaker's situation to her own.

**3. Write a Review** Dove says that in her poems she tries "very hard to create characters who are seen as individuals—not only as Blacks or as women, or whatever, but as a Black woman with her own particular problems. Does the speaker in "Adolescence—III" come across as an individual or as a typical teenager? Write a review, explaining your views.

*Dear Diary,*
*Today I read*
*a poem about*
*a girl like me.*

## Activities & Explorations

**1. Sketch** Make sketches of the speaker, the figure in her dreams, and the different settings for a book jacket of Rita Dove's poems. Refer to the images you listed in your
📖 **READER'S NOTEBOOK.** **~ ART**

**2. Oral Interpretation** With a partner read the poem aloud to the class. Decide on the method for your oral reading, such as alternating stanzas, alternating lines, or alternating readings of the entire poem. Vary the pitch and volume of your voices and the pace of the reading to express the speaker's emotions.
**~ SPEAKING AND LISTENING**

## Rita Dove
### 1952–

**Other Works**
*Fifth Sunday*
*Grace Notes*
*Museum*
*Through the Ivory Gate*
*Mother Love*

**Poet Laureate** Rita Dove has said, "Poetry is language at its most distilled and most powerful. It's like a bouillon cube: you carry it around and then it nourishes you when you need it." In October 1993 she became the seventh poet laureate of the United States—the youngest person and the first African American so honored. Serving as poet laureate until 1995, she used this post to cultivate a wider appreciation of poetry, especially among children and teenagers.

**A Lover of Books** Dove grew up in Akron, Ohio, where her father was the first African-American chemist at the Goodyear Tire and Rubber Company. As a child, she wrote plays and stories, created a comic book with her brother, took cello lessons, and listened to music every day with her family. Although her parents restricted her television viewing, they allowed her to visit the library as often as she wished. She would "rush into the local public library with the same eagerness other children reserved for the candy store, thrilled at the prospect of finding many and varied worlds waiting between the covers of all those books."

**Professor and Poet** Educated at Miami University in Ohio and the University of Iowa, Dove also studied drama and poetry in Germany as a Fulbright scholar. She taught English at Arizona State University for eight years and is currently the Commonwealth Professor of English at the University of Virginia. In 1987 Dove won a Pulitzer Prize for *Thomas and Beulah* (1986), a book of poems based on the lives of her maternal grandparents.

## Writing Options

1. **Points of Comparison** To help students focus their thinking, suggest that they create a Venn diagram, listing similarities and differences between the images in Dove's poem and in one of Dickinson's.
2. **Rosie's Diary Entry** Have students review "Seventeen Syllables" to gather details about Rosie and her perspective. **To make this assignment more challenging,** have them create a dialogue between Rosie and the speaker of "Adolescence—III."
3. **Write a Review** Students first should explain their understanding of the term "typical teenager." Their reviews should contain conclusions about the speaker based on details from the poem.

## Activities & Explorations

**Sketch** Encourage students to explain why they rendered the speaker, her dreams, and the settings as they did. **To make this assignment more challenging,** have students present their illustrations in a multimedia format.

**Oral Interpretation** Encourage students to explain why they chose certain verbal and nonverbal communication techniques to express the speaker's emotions.

---

## Mini Lesson Grammar

**ADVERB CLAUSES** An adverb clause is a subordinate clause that modifies a verb, an adjective, or an adverb. Adverb clauses answer *Where? When? Why? How? To what extent? Under what circumstances?* Adverb clauses are usually introduced by subordinating conjunctions, which show the relationship between ideas. Some common subordinating conjunctions are shown in the following chart.

Use **Grammar Transparencies and Copymasters,** p. 96.

| Relationship Shown | Subordinating Conjunctions |
|---|---|
| Time | as, soon as, after, before, since, until, when, whenever, while |
| Cause | because, since |
| Comparison | as, as much as, than |
| Condition | if, although, as long as, though, unless, provided that |
| Purpose | so that, in order that |
| Manner | as, as if, as though |
| Place | where, wherever |

 Use McDougal Littell's *Language Network,* Chapter 3, for more instruction in adverb clauses.

### Objectives

1. understand and appreciate a **short story** (Literary Analysis)
2. understand **interior monologue** (Literary Analysis)
3. make **judgments** about **character** (Active Reading)

### Summary

In this interior monologue, a mother reviews her relationship with her oldest daughter while ironing a dress. The review is prompted by a request from a concerned teacher who thinks that the daughter, Emily, needs help. The mother recalls that Emily's father left the family during the Great Depression before Emily was a year old. Emily's mother, only 19, had to work and so sent her daughter to live with relatives. Emily was thin and sickly, and as she grew up she worried about her looks. In school, she was considered slow. After her mother remarried and had other children, Emily had to help out with the chores. She grew to resent her younger sister, who was prettier and outgoing. Recently, Emily's talent for performing comedy routines has blossomed. The mother wants Emily to realize she can shape her own life and that she is not helpless like the dress on the ironing board.

### Thematic Link

Told through a **woman's voice,** this story examines a mother's struggle to raise her family alone during the Depression and World War II. Her monologue provides insights about **women's lives** at that period in history.

### 5-Minute Warm-Up

***Daily Language SkillBuilder***

Have students **proofread** the display sentences on page 739j and write them correctly. The sentences also appear on Transparency 22 of **Grammar Transparencies and Copymasters.**

---

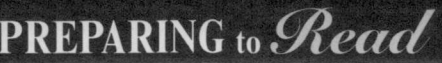

# PREPARING to *Read*

# I Stand Here Ironing

*Short Story by* TILLIE OLSEN

### Comparing Literature

## Traditions Across Time: A Diversity of Voices

"I Stand Here Ironing" is a story about a mother-and-daughter relationship. While ironing, the narrator recalls the events that helped shape her daughter Emily's personality and her own struggles to support her family during and after the Great Depression. Like the stories in the first part of this subunit, this story reflects the circumstances shared by countless women at a specific period in history.

**Points of Comparison** As you read, consider the narrator's struggles. Contrast them with those of the narrator in "The Yellow Wallpaper."

## Build Background

**Hard Times** During the Great Depression of the 1930s and World War II and its aftermath in the 1940s, many parents had to struggle to raise their families. After the stock market crashed in 1929 and the American economy collapsed, millions were left without jobs. Work was so scarce that Secretary of Labor Frances Perkins urged women to give up their jobs so that more men could be employed. Working mothers who kept their jobs often relied on government-supported nurseries for child care or on relatives.

As industry expanded to manufacture the equipment needed to fight World War II, thousands of workers found jobs. Even in the new prosperity, however, families faced problems. With their husbands serving in the armed forces, many women had to care for their children alone. At the same time, the wartime demand for workers brought about 6 million women into the work force. The government built large daycare centers to care for children while their mothers worked. Families now had money to spend, but the war brought shortages of meat, sugar, and other important goods.

**WORDS TO KNOW**
**Vocabulary Preview**

| | |
|---|---|
| anonymity | dredge |
| articulate | laceration |
| coherent | preening |
| compound | prestige |
| denunciation | ravaged |

## Focus Your Reading

**LITERARY ANALYSIS** | **INTERIOR MONOLOGUE** **Interior monologue** refers to the direct presentation of a character's thoughts in a short story or a poem. "I Stand Here Ironing" is an example of an interior monologue. As the narrator relates anecdotes and observations about her daughter Emily's childhood, her mind moves between the past and the present.

**ACTIVE READING** | **MAKING JUDGMENTS ABOUT CHARACTER** One way to understand the narrator better is to make judgments about her character and support them with reasons.

- Set up standards, for judging her as a parent.
- Gather evidence about how she treats her daughter.
- Measure the narrator's conduct against the standards and state your final judgment about her as a parent.

**READER'S NOTEBOOK** On a chart like the one shown, list the qualities of a good parent, examples of the narrator's conduct, and your judgment about her character.

| Qualities of a Good Parent | Narrator's Treatment of Emily |
|---|---|
| | |
| | |

Judgment _____

## LESSON RESOURCES

**UNIT FIVE RESOURCE BOOK,** pp. 22–27

**ASSESSMENT RESOURCES**
**Formal Assessment,** pp. 147–148
**Teacher's Guide to Assessment and Portfolio Use**
**Test Generator**

**SKILLS TRANSPARENCIES AND COPYMASTERS**
**Literary Analysis**
- Point of View, T20 (for Cooperative Learning Activity, p. 815)

**Reading and Critical Thinking**
- Making Judgments, T5 (for Active Reading, p. 806)

**Grammar**
- Adverb Clauses with *Because,* C99 (for Mini Lesson, p. 816)

**Vocabulary**
- Homonyms, C67 (for Mini Lesson, p. 811)

**Writing**
- Showing, Not Telling, T22 (for Writing Option 2, p. 816)

**Communications**
- Evaluating Roles in Groups, T8 (for Activities & Explorations 2, p. 816)

- Impromptu Speaking: Dialogue, Role-Play, Debate, T13 (for Activities & Explorations 3, p. 816)

**INTEGRATED TECHNOLOGY**
**Audio Library**
**LaserLinks**
- Historical Connection: Working Women, 1930s–1940s
- Author Background: Tillie Olsen
- Film Connection: Excerpt from "I Stand Here Ironing." See **Teacher's SourceBook,** pp. 65–66.
**Internet: Research Starter**
**Visit our website:**
www.mcdougallittell.com

# I Stand Here Ironing

Tillie Olsen

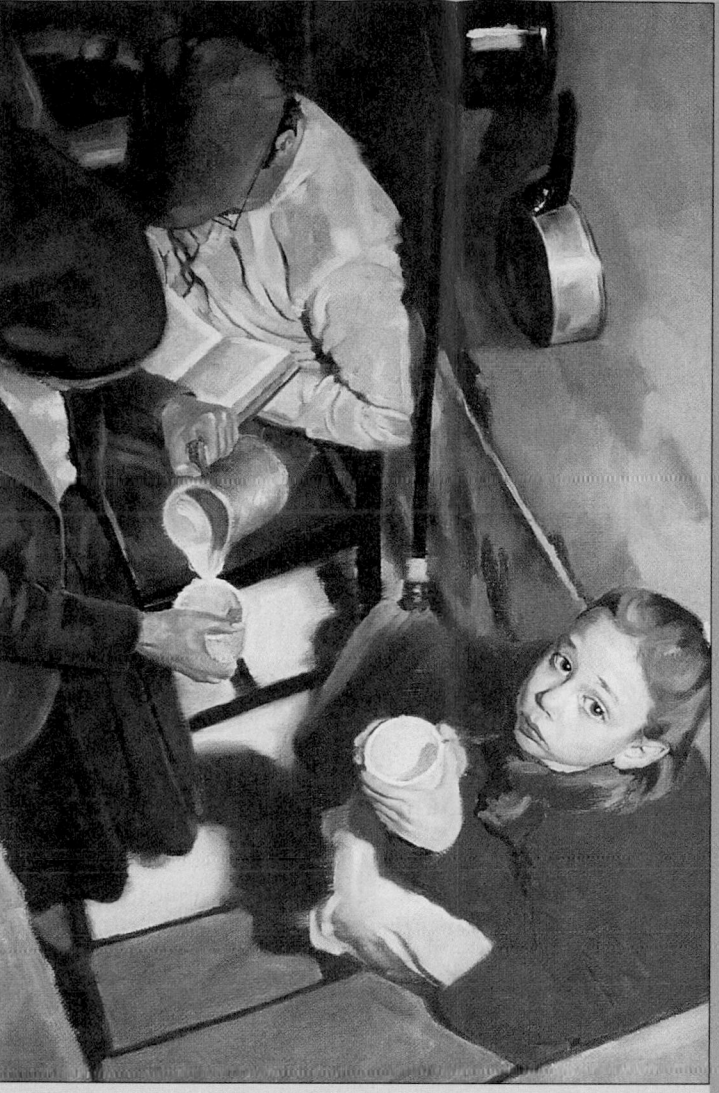

Illustration by Mike Dooling from *Mary McLean and the St. Patrick's Day Parade* by Steven Kroll. Illustration Copyright © 1990 by Mike Dooling, reprinted by permission of Scholastic Inc.

**I stand here ironing,** and what you asked me moves tormented back and forth with the iron.

"I wish you would manage the time to come in and talk with me about your daughter. I'm sure you can help me understand her. She's a youngster who needs help and whom I'm deeply interested in helping."

---

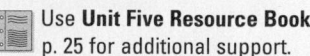

Tell students that this entire story takes place in the narrator's mind as she irons clothes. As students read, they should look for shifts between the present and the past.

### Literary Analysis

INTERIOR MONOLOGUE

 This paragraph could describe the process of interior monologue, a direct presentation of a character's unspoken thoughts. Ask students what has triggered thoughts about her daughter in the narrator's mind.

> **Answer:** a request for a conference about her daughter

Use **Unit Five Resource Book,** p. 24 for additional support.

### Active Reading   MAKING JUDGMENTS ABOUT CHARACTER

Ask students to review the choices Emily's mother makes on page 808 and to consider what they suggest about her character.

**Possible Responses:** Her choices include leaving Emily with her husband's family because she could not afford to raise her, putting Emily in a nursery school so she could work, and leaving Emily at the school even though she cried and hated going to school. These choices show that the mother believed in working for a living and that she had to toughen herself in order to endure the hardships of being a single parent.

Use **Unit Five Resource Book,** p. 23 for additional support.

---

"Who needs help." . . . Even if I came, what good would it do? You think because I am her mother I have a key, or that in some way you could use me as a key? She has lived for nineteen years. There is all that life that has happened outside of me, beyond me.

 And when is there time to remember, to sift, to weigh, to estimate, to total? I will start and there will be an interruption and I will have to gather it all together again. Or I will become engulfed with all I did or did not do, with what should have been and what cannot be helped.

She was a beautiful baby. The first and only one of our five that was beautiful at birth. You do not guess how new and uneasy her tenancy[1] in her now-loveliness. You did not know her all those years she was thought homely, or see her poring over her baby pictures, making me tell her over and over how beautiful she had been—and would be, I would tell her—and was now, to the seeing eye. But the seeing eyes were few or nonexistent. Including mine.

I nursed her. They feel that's important nowadays. I nursed all the children, but with her, with all the fierce rigidity of first motherhood, I did like the books then said. Though her cries battered me to trembling and my breasts ached with swollenness, I waited till the clock decreed.

Why do I put that first? I do not even know if it matters, or if it explains anything.

She was a beautiful baby. She blew shining bubbles of sound. She loved motion, loved light, loved color and music and textures. She would lie on the floor in her blue overalls patting the surface so hard in ecstasy her hands and feet would blur. She was a miracle to me, but when she was eight months old I had to leave her daytimes with the woman downstairs to whom she was no miracle at all, for I worked or looked for work and for Emily's father, who "could no longer endure" (he wrote in his good-bye note) "sharing want with us."

I was nineteen. It was the pre-relief, pre-WPA[2]

world of the depression. I would start running as soon as I got off the streetcar, running up the stairs, the place smelling sour, and awake or asleep to startle awake, when she saw me she would break into a clogged weeping that could not be comforted, a weeping I can hear yet.

After a while I found a job hashing[3] at night so I could be with her days, and it was better. But it came to where I had to bring her to his family and leave her.

It took a long time to raise the money for her fare back. Then she got chicken pox and I had to wait longer. When she finally came, I hardly knew her, walking quick and nervous like her father, looking like her father, thin, and dressed in a shoddy red that yellowed her skin and glared at the pockmarks. All the baby loveliness gone.

She was two. Old enough for nursery school they said, and I did not know then what I know now—the fatigue of the long day, and the lacerations of group life in the kinds of nurseries that are only parking places for children.

Except that it would have made no difference if I had known. It was the only place there was. It was the only way we could be together, the only way I could hold a job.

And even without knowing, I knew. I knew the teacher that was evil because all these years it has curdled into my memory, the little boy hunched in the corner, her rasp, "why aren't you outside, because Alvin hits you? that's no reason, go out, scaredy." I knew Emily hated it even if she did not clutch and implore "don't go Mommy" like the other children, mornings.

---

1. **tenancy** (tĕn'ən-sē): residence.
2. **pre-relief, pre-WPA:** preceding the creation of the welfare and employment programs—such as the Works Progress Administration (WPA)—by which the U.S. government tried to ease the effects of the Great Depression.
3. **hashing:** a slang term for working as a waitress, especially at a diner.

WORDS
TO
KNOW   **laceration** (lăs'ə-rā'shən) *n.* a physical, mental, or emotional wound

808

---

 **Cross Curricular Link  History**

**WORKING WOMEN DURING THE DEPRESSION** In 1932, during the Great Depression, nearly 13 million Americans were out of work. Many unemployed men felt humiliated because they were unable to support their families. Women who needed work faced the same shortage of jobs, and their hardships were compounded by discrimination in hiring. Married women were simply barred from many jobs because their husbands were expected to support them. Many school districts, for example, refused to hire married women and even fired female teachers who got married. It was frowned upon for a woman to take a job that a man might fill, although low-paying occupations traditionally regarded as "women's work" were still available, including domestic work and waitressing. It was not until the early 1940s, when the United States entered World War II, that the urgent need for factory workers opened a broader range of jobs for women.

She always had a reason why we should stay home. Momma, you look sick. Momma, I feel sick. Momma, the teachers aren't there today, they're sick. Momma, we can't go, there was a fire there last night. Momma, it's a holiday today, no school, they told me.

But never a direct protest, never rebellion. I think of our others in their three-, four-year-oldness—the explosions, the tempers, the denunciations, the demands—and I feel suddenly ill. I put the iron down. What in me demanded that goodness in her? And what was the cost, the cost to her of such goodness?

The old man living in the back once said in his gentle way: "You should smile at Emily more when you look at her." What *was* in my face when I looked at her? I loved her. There were all the acts of love.

It was only with the others I remembered what he said, and it was the face of joy, and not of care or tightness or worry I turned to them—too late for Emily. She does not smile easily, let alone almost always as her brothers and sisters do. Her face is closed and somber, but when she wants, how fluid. You must have seen it in her pantomimes, you spoke of her rare gift for comedy on the stage that rouses a laughter out of the audience so dear they applaud and applaud and do not want to let her go.

Where does it come from, that comedy? There was none of it in her when she came back to me that second time, after I had had to send her away again. She had a new daddy now to learn to love, and I think perhaps it was a better time.

Except when we left her alone nights, telling ourselves she was old enough.

"Can't you go some other time, Mommy, like tomorrow?" she would ask. "Will it be just a little while you'll be gone? Do you promise?"

The time we came back, the front door open, the clock on the floor in the hall. She rigid awake. "It wasn't just a little while. I didn't cry.

Three times I called you, just three times, and then I ran downstairs to open the door so you could come faster. The clock talked loud. I threw it away, it scared me what it talked."

She said the clock talked loud again that night I went to the hospital to have Susan. She was delirious with the fever that comes before red measles, but she was fully conscious all the week I was gone and the week after we were home when she could not come near the new baby or me.

She did not get well. She stayed skeleton thin, not wanting to eat, and night after night she had nightmares. She would call for me, and I would rouse from exhaustion to sleepily call back: "You're all right, darling, go to sleep, it's just a dream," and if she still called, in a sterner voice, "now go to sleep, Emily, there's nothing to hurt you." Twice, only twice, when I had to get up for Susan anyhow, I went in to sit with her.

Now when it is too late (as if she would let me hold and comfort her like I do the others) I get up and go to her at once at her moan or restless stirring. "Are you awake, Emily? Can I get you something?" And the answer is always the same: "No, I'm all right, go back to sleep, Mother."

They persuaded me at the clinic to send her away to a convalescent home in the country where "she can have the kind of food and care you can't manage for her, and you'll be free to concentrate on the new baby." They still send children to that place. I see pictures on the society page of sleek young women planning affairs to raise money for it, or dancing at the affairs, or decorating Easter eggs or filling Christmas stockings for the children.

They never have a picture of the children so I do not know if the girls still wear those gigantic red bows and the ravaged looks on the every other Sunday when parents can come to visit "unless otherwise notified"—as we were notified the first six weeks.

| WORDS TO KNOW | **denunciation** (dĭ-nŭn′sē-ā′shən) *n.* an act of condemning or accusing another; accusation |
| | **ravaged** (răv′ĭjd) *adj.* devastated; ruined **ravage** *v.* |

809

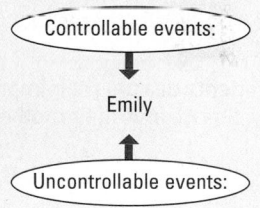

## Reading and Analyzing

*Girl Skipping Rope* (1943), Ben Shahn. Tempera on board, 15¼″ × 23½″, gift of the Stephen and Sybil Stone Foundation, Museum of Fine Arts, Boston (1971.702). Copyright © 1996 Estate of Ben Shahn/Licensed by VAGA, New York.

Oh she had physical

lightness and brightness...

bouncing like a ball

up and down up and down

over the jump rope...

but these were

momentary.

**(A)** **1** Oh it is a handsome place, green lawns and tall trees and fluted flower beds. High up on the balconies of each cottage the children stand, the girls in their red bows and white dresses, the boys in white suits and giant red ties. The parents stand below shrieking up to be heard and the children shriek down to be heard, and between them the invisible wall "Not to Be Contaminated by Parental Germs or Physical Affection."

**2** There was a tiny girl who always stood hand in hand with Emily. Her parents never came. One visit she was gone. "They moved her to Rose Cottage," Emily shouted in explanation. "They don't like you to love anybody here."

She wrote once a week, the labored writing of a seven-year-old. "I am fine. How is the baby. If I write my leter nicly I will have a star. Love."

There never was a star. We wrote every other day, letters she could never hold or keep but only hear read—once. "We simply do not have room for children to keep any personal possessions," they patiently explained when we pieced one Sunday's shrieking together to plead how much it would mean to Emily, who loved so to keep things, to be allowed to keep her letters and cards.

Each visit she looked frailer. "She isn't eating," they told us.

(They had runny eggs for breakfast or mush with lumps, Emily said later, I'd hold it in my mouth and not swallow. Nothing ever tasted good, just when they had chicken.)

It took us eight months to get her released home, and only the fact that she gained back so little of her seven lost pounds convinced the social worker.

I used to try to hold and love her after she came back, but her body would stay stiff, and after a while she'd push away. She ate little. Food sickened her, and I think much of life too. Oh she had physical lightness and brightness, twinkling by on skates, bouncing like a ball up and down up and down over the jump rope, skimming over the hill; but these were momentary.

She fretted about her appearance, thin and dark and foreign-looking at a time when every little girl was supposed to look or thought she should look a chubby blonde replica of Shirley Temple.[4] The doorbell sometimes rang for her, but no one seemed to come and play in the house or be a best friend. Maybe because we moved so much.

There was a boy she loved painfully through two school semesters. Months later she told me how she had taken pennies from my purse to buy him candy. "Licorice was his favorite and I brought him some every day, but he still liked Jennifer better'n me. Why, Mommy?" The kind of question for which there is no answer.

School was a worry to her. She was not glib or quick in a world where glibness and quickness were easily confused with ability to learn. To her overworked and exasperated teachers she was an overconscientious "slow learner" who kept trying to catch up and was absent entirely too often.

I let her be absent, though sometimes the illness was imaginary. How different from my now-strictness about attendance with the others. I wasn't working. We had a new baby, I was home anyhow. Sometimes, after Susan grew old enough, I would keep her home from school, too, to have them all together.

Mostly Emily had asthma, and her breathing, harsh and labored, would fill the house with a curiously tranquil sound. I would bring the two old dresser mirrors and her boxes of collections to her bed. She would select beads and single earrings, bottle tops and shells, dried flowers and pebbles, old postcards and scraps, all sorts of oddments; then she and Susan would play Kingdom, setting up landscapes and furniture, peopling them with action.

Those were the only times of peaceful companionship between her and Susan. I have edged away from it, that poisonous feeling between them, that terrible balancing of hurts and needs I had to do between the two, and did so badly, those earlier years.

Oh there are conflicts between the others too, each one human, needing, demanding, hurting, taking—but only between Emily and Susan, no, Emily toward Susan that corroding resentment. It seems so obvious on the surface, yet it is not obvious. Susan, the second child, Susan, golden- and curly-haired and chubby, quick and articulate and assured, everything in appearance and manner. Emily was not; Susan, not able to resist Emily's precious things, losing or sometimes clumsily breaking them; Susan telling jokes and riddles to company for applause while Emily sat silent (to say to me later: that was *my* riddle, Mother, I told it to Susan); Susan,

---

4. **Shirley Temple:** a famous child star of the 1930s.

| WORDS TO KNOW | **articulate** (är-tĭk′yə-lĭt) *adj.* clear and effective in speech |

**811**

## Customizing Instruction

### Less Proficient Readers
Use the following questions to help students understand Emily's early childhood experiences.

**1** Why did the parents and children have to "shriek" at each other? What was the purpose of this arrangement?
**Possible Response:** The children stood on balconies, and their parents stood on the ground far below them. This arrangement prevented parents from showing their children any physical affection.

**2** Why was the little girl who held hands with Emily moved?
**Possible Response:** Children in the home were not allowed to form close friendships.

### Students Acquiring English
**3** Define *fretted* as "worried."

**4** Explain to students that *glib* means "able to speak easily but perhaps insincerely" and that, in this context, *quick* means "thinking, understanding, or responding rapidly or easily."

### Less Proficient Readers
**5** Ask students to summarize Emily's relationship with her sister Susan by listing adjectives to describe it.
**Possible Responses:** resentful, hostile, bitter, competitive

**Set a Purpose** Have students read to find out what kind of person Emily becomes when she gets older.

### Gifted and Talented
Have students prepare a report on the early stages of child development. Their reports might include an analysis of how Emily's experiences might have affected her.

## Mini Lesson Vocabulary Strategy

**HOMONYMS Instruction** Homonyms are two or more words that have the same sound and often the same spelling, but differ in meaning. Share the following definitions and word origins for the word *mean*.
1. **to have in mind; intend; propose**—from Old English *maenan*, "to mean, tell, complain"
2. **low in value; poor; inferior; stingy; miserly; bad-tempered**—from Old English *maene*, "plentiful, common"
3. **halfway between extremes; medium; average**—from Latin *medius*, "middle"

**Application** Ask students to look up the various origins and meanings of the following words: *light, bear, arm, fast.* Ask students to use the homonyms in separate sentences to illustrate the different meanings. Then ask students to locate, list, and define homonyms in the story.
**Possible Responses:** *rare, seal*

Use **Vocabulary Transparencies and Copymasters,** p. 67.

**A lesson on homonyms appears on p. 728 in the Pupil's Edition.**

**A** Ask students how Ronnie's interruption causes the mother to evaluate her own present life.

**Possible Response:** She thinks, "That time of motherhood is almost behind me. . . ."

How does she handle Ronnie differently from Emily?

**Possible Response:** She pauses from her work long enough to cuddle Ronnie.

Who is the "she" who has left her seal on the family?

**Possible Response:** Emily—"In this and other ways she leaves her seal" refers to Ronnie's use of Emily's made-up word for comfort, *shoogily*.

### Literary Analysis: METAPHOR

**B** Ask what the narrator means by "imprisoned in her difference."

**Possible Responses:** Extremely talented people sometimes experience difficulty being accepted by other people; being a comedienne is only part of Emily's character, and her audience may refuse to look at other sides of her.

### Active Reading   MAKING JUDGMENTS ABOUT CHARACTER

**C** Encourage students to add to the charts in their Reader's Notebooks and make final judgments about the character of the narrator. In particular, have them consider the statement about human potential that she makes in the last paragraph.

---

who for all the five years' difference in age was just a year behind Emily in developing physically.

I am glad for that slow physical development that widened the difference between her and her contemporaries, though she suffered over it. She was too vulnerable for that terrible world of youthful competition, of <u>preening</u> and parading, of constant measuring of yourself against every other, of envy, "If I had that copper hair," "If I had that skin. . . ." She tormented herself enough about not looking like the others, there was enough of the unsureness, the having to be conscious of words before you speak, the constant caring—what are they thinking of me? without having it all magnified by the merciless physical drives.

R onnie is calling. He is wet and I change him. It is rare there is such a cry now. That time of motherhood is almost behind me when the ear is not one's own but must always be racked and listening for the child cry, the child call. We sit for a while and I hold him, looking out over the city spread in charcoal with its soft aisles of light. *"Shoogily,"* he breathes and curls closer. I carry him back to bed, asleep. *Shoogily.* A funny word, a family word, inherited from Emily, invented by her to say: *comfort.*

**A** In this and other ways she leaves her seal, I say aloud. And startle at my saying it. What do I mean? What did I start to gather together, to try and make <u>coherent</u>? I was at the terrible, growing years. War years. I do not remember them well. I was working, there were four smaller ones now, there was not time for her. She had to help be a mother, and housekeeper, and shopper. She had to set her seal. Mornings of crisis and near hysteria trying to get lunches packed, hair combed, coats and shoes found, everyone to school or Child Care on time, the baby ready for transportation. And always the paper scribbled on by a smaller one, the book looked at by Susan then mislaid,

the homework not done. Running out to that huge school where she was one, she was lost, she was a drop; suffering over the unpreparedness, stammering and unsure in her classes.

There was so little time left at night after the kids were bedded down. She would struggle over books, always eating (it was in those years she developed her enormous appetite that is legendary in our family) and I would be ironing, or preparing food for the next day, or writing V-mail[5] to Bill, or tending the baby. Sometimes, to make me laugh, or out of her despair, she would imitate happenings or types at school.

I think I said once: "Why don't you do something like this in the school amateur show?" One morning she phoned me at work, hardly understandable through the weeping: "Mother, I did it. I won, I won; they gave me first prize; they clapped and clapped and wouldn't let me go."

**B** Now suddenly she was Somebody, and as imprisoned in her difference as she had been in <u>anonymity</u>.

She began to be asked to perform at other high schools, even in colleges, then at city and statewide affairs. The first one we went to, I only recognized her that first moment when thin, shy, she almost drowned herself into the curtains. Then: Was this Emily? The control, the command, the convulsing and deadly clowning, the spell, then the roaring, stamping audience, unwilling to let this rare and precious laughter out of their lives.

Afterwards: You ought to do something about her with a gift like that—but without money or knowing how, what does one do? We have left it all to her, and the gift has as often eddied[6] inside,

---

5. **V-mail:** letters sent to and by soldiers in World War II. The mail was photographed on microfilm to make it easier to transport; enlarged prints were made for reading by the recipients.

6. **eddied:** whirled in circles, without progressing forward.

WORDS
TO
KNOW

**preening** (prē'nĭng) *n.* dressing and grooming oneself with excessive care; primping **preen** *v.*
**coherent** (kō-hîr'ənt) *adj.* understandable; logically consistent
**anonymity** (ăn'ə-nĭm'ĭ-tē) *n.* a state of being unknown or unrecognized, without special or distinguishing qualities

---

## Teaching Options

### BLOCK SCHEDULING: MANAGING TIME

**If your schedule requires that you cover the lesson objectives in a shorter time, use . . .**
- Preparing to Read, p. 806
- Thinking Through the Literature, p. 815
- Vocabulary in Action, p. 817

**If you want to take advantage of longer class time, use . . .**
- TE Teaching Options: Preteaching Vocabulary, p. 807; Viewing and Representing, pp. 810, 813; Vocabulary Strategy, p. 811; Speaking and Listening, p. 814; Cross-Curricular Link, p. 808; Informal Assessment, p. 809; Standardized Test Practice, p. 817
- Choices & Challenges and Author Activity, pp. 816–817

clogged and clotted, as been used and growing.

She is coming. She runs up the stairs two at a time with her light graceful step, and I know she is happy tonight. Whatever it was that occasioned your call did not happen today.

"Aren't you ever going to finish the ironing, Mother? Whistler[7] painted his mother in a rocker. I'd have to paint mine standing over an ironing board." This is one of her communicative nights and she tells me everything and nothing as she fixes herself a plate of food out of the icebox.

She is so lovely. Why did you want me to come in at all? Why were you concerned? She will find her way.

She starts up the stairs to bed. "Don't get me up with the rest in the morning." "But I thought you were having midterms." "Oh, those," she comes back in, kisses me, and says quite lightly, "in a couple of years when we'll all be atom-dead they won't matter a bit."

She has said it before. She *believes* it. But because I have been <u>dredging</u> the past, and all that <u>compounds</u> a human being is so heavy and meaningful in me, I cannot endure it tonight.

I will never total it all. I will never come in to say: She was a child seldom smiled at. Her father left me before she was a year old. I had to work her first six years when there was work, or I sent her home and to his relatives. There were years she had care she hated. She was dark and thin and foreign-looking in a world where the <u>prestige</u> went to blondeness and curly hair and dimples, she was slow where glibness was prized. She was a child of anxious, not proud, love. We were poor and could not afford for her the soil of easy growth. I was a young mother, I was a distracted mother. There were the other children pushing up, demanding. Her younger sister seemed all that she was not. There were years she did not want me to touch her. She kept too much in herself, her life was such she had to

*The Brown Sweater* (1952), Raphael Soyer. Oil on canvas, 50″ × 34″, Collection of Whitney Museum of American Art, New York, purchase and gift of Gertrude Vanderbilt Whitney by exchange (53.53). Copyright © 1995 Whitney Museum of American Art. Photo by Geoffrey Clements.

keep too much in herself. My wisdom came too late. She has much to her and probably nothing will come of it. She is a child of her age, of depression, of war, of fear.

Let her be. So all that is in her will not bloom —but in how many does it? There is still enough left to live by. Only help her to know—help make it so there is cause for her to know—that she is more than this dress on the ironing board, helpless before the iron. ❖

7. **Whistler:** James Abbot McNeill Whistler, a 19th-century American painter and etcher. His best-known painting is a portrait of his mother in her chair.

| WORDS<br>TO<br>KNOW | **dredge** (drĕj) *v.* to dig into; unearth<br>**compound** (kŏm-pound′) *v.* to form or make up; compose<br>**prestige** (prĕ-stēzh′) *n.* honor; admiration |
| --- | --- |

813

## Viewing and Representing

### *The Brown Sweater* by Raphael Soyer

**ART APPRECIATION** Raphael Soyer (1899–1987) was born in Russia and came to the United States in 1912. He quickly learned to observe the world of the Jewish ghetto around him. His subdued, realistic paintings are known for their sympathy with urban dwellers.

**Instruction** Point out the muted colors in the work and the relaxed face and posture of the central figure. Ask students to describe what is communicated through these techniques.

**Possible Response:** The colors give a somber feel to the piece. The serene, sad character in the middle contrasts with the active figures in the background—a mother trying awkwardly to contain two small children.

## Reading and Analyzing

**Reading Skills and Strategies:**
**COMPARE/CONTRAST**

In order to help understanding, have students compare and contrast the narrative point of view in "Ironing Their Clothes" with that of "I Stand Here Ironing."

**Possible Response:** Both the poem and the short story are written in the first-person point of view. A daughter narrates "Ironing Their Clothes" while a mother narrates "I Stand Here Ironing." In both works, ironing is used as a metaphor.

How are the daughters in these selections alike? How are they different?

**Possible Response:** They both want affection from their families. The daughter in "Ironing Their Clothes" substitutes the imagined closeness she feels while ironing her family's clothes for the real closeness she misses when with family members. The daughter in "I Stand Here Ironing" gets the attention she craves by performing comic routines for her family and other audiences.

**Reading Skills and Strategies:**
**EVALUATING**

Have students discuss their answers to the following questions: Which selection did you find more enjoyable? Why? Which one did you find more meaningful or true-to-life? Why?

# Ironing Their Clothes

**Julia Alvarez**

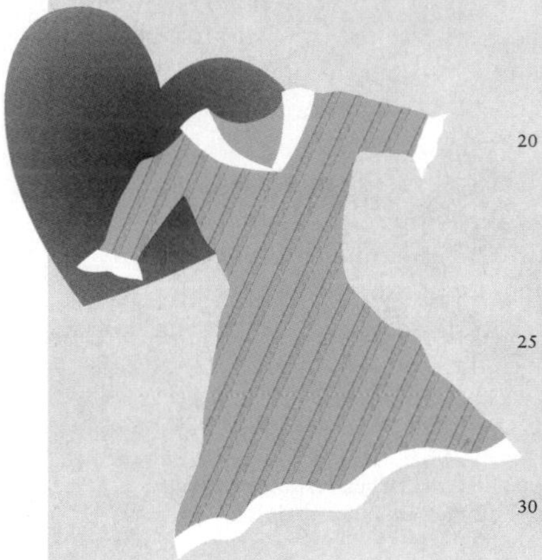

With a hot glide up, then down, his shirts,
I ironed out my father's back, cramped
and worried with work. I stroked the yoke,
the breast pocket, collar and cuffs,
5   until the rumpled heap relaxed into the shape
of my father's broad chest, the shoulders shrugged off
the world, the collapsed arms spread for a hug.
And if there'd been a face above the buttondown neck,
I would have pressed the forehead out, I would
10   have made a boy again out of that tired man!

If I clung to her skirt as she sorted the wash
or put out a line, my mother frowned,
a crease down each side of her mouth.
*This is no time for love!* But here
15   I could linger over her wrinkled bedjacket,
kiss at the damp puckers of her wrists
with the hot tip. Here I caressed complications
of darts, scallops, ties, pleats which made
her outfits test of the patience of my passion.
20   Here I could lay my dreaming iron on her lap. . . .

The smell of baked cotton rose from the board
and blew with a breeze out the window
to the family wardrobe drying on the clothesline,
all needing a touch of my iron. Here I could tickle
25   the underarms of my big sister's petticoat
or secretly pat the backside of her pajamas.
For she too would have warned me not to muss
her fresh blouses, starched jumpers, and smocks,
all that my careful hand had ironed out,
30   forced to express my excess love on cloth.

## Teaching Options

 **Mini Lesson** ## Speaking and Listening

**INTERVIEWS Prepare** By listening critically to interviews with public figures, students can make up their own minds about issues. Before an interview, the listener might examine his or her preconceptions about the subject, the speaker, and the context and establish criteria for evaluating the interview. During the interview, the listener should analyze appeals to emotion, look for errors in logic, and form questions mentally. After the interview, the listener may review and analyze the speaker's points.

**Present** The narrator's interior monologue is prompted by a question about Emily. Invite students to imagine that they are the person who asked the question and that they have heard the monologue. Ask students to jot down notes about their preconceptions and responses, including follow-up questions they would like to ask. Invite students to read their notes aloud. Discuss possible answers to students' questions.

**BLOCK SCHEDULING** This activity is particularly well suited for longer class periods.

## Connect to the Literature

1. **What Do You Think?**
   What mental picture do you have of the narrator of this story?

   **Comprehension Check**
   • Why is Emily separated from her family?
   • What talent does Emily develop?

## Think Critically

2. Who is the "you" the **narrator** addresses, and why has that person asked for her help in understanding Emily? Speculate about what Emily might have said or done to prompt the person's call.

3. What problems do you think Emily might have, and how might her past experiences have contributed to them?

   **THINK ABOUT**
   • her stiffness when her mother would try to hold her
   • her resentment toward her sister Susan
   • her differences from others her age
   • the summary in the next-to-last paragraph

4. What events in Emily's life might have contributed to her talent for performance?

5. **ACTIVE READING | MAKING JUDGMENTS ABOUT CHARACTER**
   How do you **evaluate** Emily's mother as a parent? Explain the reasons for your answer. Refer to the chart in your **READER'S NOTEBOOK**.

## Extend Interpretations

6. **Critic's Corner** One critic has pointed out that Olsen writes about people who are victims of harsh social, economic, familial, and political conditions. How well does "I Stand Here Ironing" fit this description? Who are the victims in the story? What conditions have oppressed them?

7. **Connect to Life** Do you think an individual's personality is mostly inborn, or mostly determined by parents and environment? Explain your answer, taking into consideration Emily's personality as well as those of people you know.

8. **Points of Comparison** Who do you think struggles against greater obstacles, the narrator in this story or the one in "The Yellow Wallpaper"? Cite examples in your answer.

## Literary Analysis

**INTERIOR MONOLOGUE** In a drama, the speech of a character who is alone on stage, voicing his or her thoughts, is known as a soliloquy or a monologue. In a short story or novel, the direct presentation of a character's unspoken thoughts is called an **interior monologue.** An interior monologue may jump back and forth between past and present, displaying thoughts, memories, and impressions just as they might occur to a person's mind. Events follow one another because of the way they fit together in the character's mind, not necessarily because they happened in that order.

**Cooperative Learning Activity** With a small group of students, discuss these questions: What does the interior monologue reveal about the driving forces in the narrator's life? Why is it significant that the narrator tells this story while ironing? How would the effect have been different if the events were told from the third-person point of view and in chronological order, beginning with Emily's birth? Choose one member to write a brief summary of the group's discussion. Share the summary with other groups.

**REVIEW METAPHOR** What does the mother mean when she says, in the last sentence of the story, "Only help her [Emily] to know . . . that she is more than this dress on the ironing board, helpless before the iron"? What is being compared to the iron? How appropriate is the comparison?

## Extend Interpretations

**Critic's Corner** Possible Response: In the story, both mother and daughter are victims of economic and familial hardships.

**Connect to Life** Students should support their opinions with textual evidence and with their own experience.

**Points of Comparison** Answers will vary. Students should note that the narrator in this story struggles against obstacles primarily caused by the economic turmoil of the period; the narrator in "The Yellow Wallpaper" struggles against obstacles caused by society's ingrained attitude toward women.

## Connect to the Literature

1. **What Do You Think?**
   Students should support their answers with text evidence.

**Comprehension Check**
• Emily is sent to a convalescent home after contracting measles.
• Emily develops a talent for comedic acting.

 Use Selection Quiz
**Unit Five Resource Book,** p. 26.

## Think Critically

2. Possible Responses: a teacher or counselor from school; the call is in response to problems with Emily's schoolwork.

3. Some students might point out that Emily might have problems with self-esteem caused by her past experiences.

4. Possible Response: Loneliness in the convalescent home and lack of attention at home may have made her more observant, sensitive to comic types and situations, and in need of an outlet.

5. Some students will say she did the best she could under the circumstances; others may find her lacking in understanding.

## Literary Analysis

**Interior Monologue** The event that sparks the narrator's interior monologue is the request by a teacher or counselor for her help in understanding Emily. The interior monologue reveals numerous conflicts between the narrator and Emily, as well as many facts about the difficulties of their lives. Student opinions about the effect of a third-person, chronological narrative will differ: Some may feel it would be more easily understandable; others may say it would lack the story's rich texture, tone, and emotional nuances.

**Review Metaphor** Difficult circumstances of life are compared to the iron; the daughter is compared to the dress. However, the metaphor emphasizes a contrast: Unlike the dress being ironed, a child is not passive and inert but can shape herself.

# Choices & CHALLENGES

## Writing Options

### 1. Points of Comparison
Students' essays should consider the different social and economic conditions of each narrator. However, they should recognize that both women love their children but are unable to care for them because of circumstances beyond their control.

### 2. Story Sequel
Remind students to remember the ages of Emily and her mother when considering what they will be like in ten years.

### 3. Response to Relationships
Encourage students to write about how these selections make them feel and how they think the characters should have treated each other.

### 4. Emily's Interview
Encourage students to place themselves in Emily's position and to think about where they agree or disagree with the mother's views.

## Activities & Explorations

### 1. Guidelines for Parents
Suggest that they organize a poster with columns for both good and bad qualities.

### 2. Informal Discussion
Suggest that students refer to the Historical Connection videodisc and Build Background, p. 806.

### 3. Role-Play
Divide students into "Walden" and "Ironing" groups. Ask them to make a list of observations about poverty from their selections.

## Art Connection
Explanations for the girl's sadness in the first painting might include poverty, loneliness, or distress about her family life. In the second painting, the building may have been bombed or demolished. In the third painting, the woman in the foreground seems to be lost in her own world and oblivious to the struggles of the mother in the background.

## Inquiry & Research

**Sibling Rivalry** In addition to magazine articles, you might suggest that students read the relevant chapters of textbooks on family psychology.

---

## Writing Options

### 1.  Points of Comparison
Both this story and "The Yellow Wallpaper" are told from the first-person point of view. Write an essay comparing these first-person narrators. Fill in a chart like this one for your prewriting notes.

|  | narrator of "I Stand Here Ironing" | narrator of "The Yellow Wallpaper" |
|---|---|---|
| circumstances in life |  |  |
| challenges faced |  |  |
| qualities shown |  |  |

### 2. Story Sequel
What do you think will happen next to Emily? What will the mother and daughter be like ten years later? Write a sequel to this story in the form of an interior monologue by Emily or her mother.

### 3. Response to Relationships
Write a personal response to the family relationships described in this story, in "Seventeen Syllables" (page 789), and in the poem "Ironing Their Clothes" (page 814).

### 4. Emily's Interview
Imagine that Emily has become a star comedienne and that a reporter for a fan magazine has said to her, "Tell me about your mother. How has she influenced your life?" Write Emily's response as part of an interview. Save your writing in your **Working Portfolio.**

## Activities & Explorations

### 1. Guidelines for Parents
Design a poster to display guidelines for good parenting. Refer to the qualities you listed. ~ ART

### 2. Informal Discussion
In what ways has Emily suffered because of the period in United States history in which she was born? Explore this question with a small group of classmates and record your conclusions. ~ SPEAKING AND LISTENING

### 3. Role-Play
In *Walden,* Henry David Thoreau makes some observations about poverty (page 390, lines 255–257), including that "the setting sun is reflected from the windows of the almshouse as brightly as from the rich man's abode." Role-play a conversation in which Thoreau and the narrator of "I Stand Here Ironing" debate the advantages of poverty. ~ PERFORMING

## Art Connection
Look again at the paintings shown on pages 807, 810, and 813. What stories do you read into these paintings? Why does the child in the first painting look so sad? What has happened to the red building in the second painting? In the third painting, what is the relationship between the girl in the foreground and the people in the background? Finally, how would you relate these artworks to the story "I Stand Here Ironing"?

## Inquiry & Research

### 1. Sibling Rivalry
Emily resents her younger sister Susan. Is this a common attitude? Find out what child-development experts say about sibling rivalry—conflicts among brothers and sisters. You might search a computer database for current magazine articles on the topic. What contributes to sibling rivalry? What can parents do to lessen it? Report your findings to the class.

### 2. Oral History
Interview a person who lived through the Great Depression or World War II, asking what family life was like at that time. Were any of the person's experiences similar to Emily's and her mother's? If possible, tape-record the interview and play the tape for the class.

 **More Online: Research Starter**
www.mcdougallittell.com

Illustration by Mike Dooling from *Mary McLean and the St. Patrick's Day Parade* by Steven Krull.

---

## Mini Lesson Grammar

**ADVERBIAL CLAUSES WITH *BECAUSE* Instruction** An adverbial clause is a subordinate clause that is used as an adverb to modify a verb, an adjective, or an adverb. It answers *Where? When? Why? How? To what extent?* or *Under what circumstances?* Subordinating conjunctions such as *because* usually introduce adverbial clauses. Write this sentence on the chalkboard.

We started early because traffic was heavy.

Ask students to identify the adverbial clause, its subordinating conjunction, and the question it answers.

**Answer:** *because traffic was heavy* is the adverbial clause; *because* is the conjunction; it answers the question *why?*

**Exercises** Have students underline the adverbial clause and tell what word it modifies in each sentence.

1. Because Emily was not gaining any weight, she was finally allowed to leave the convalescent home. (modifies *allowed*)

2. The narrator feels hopeful because Emily has turned out to be beautiful and talented. (modifies *hopeful*)

 Use **Grammar Transparencies and Copymasters,** p. 99.

 Use McDougal Littell's *Language Network,* Chapter 3, for more instruction in adverbial clauses.

## Vocabulary in Action

**EXERCISE: MEANING CLUES** Write the word described by each clue below.

1. A whip can cause this; so can a cruel comment.
2. You may do this to buried treasure or to almost-forgotten memories.
3. A mirror isn't required for this activity, but it is helpful.
4. The President has a lot of this; so does a Nobel Prize winner.
5. If a building's design is this, you can probably find your way around in it.
6. Warfare, plague, or famine can cause a nation to be described as this.
7. A secret agent wants and needs this quality; a person seeking fame does not.
8. It is almost impossible to be this if you try to talk with a mouth full of mashed potatoes.
9. One common response to this is "I did not!"; another is "Oh, yeah? Prove it!"
10. Dirt and water do this with respect to mud.

**Building Vocabulary**

Several of the Words to Know have Greek or Latin roots. For an in-depth lesson on root words, see page 444.

| WORDS TO KNOW | | | | |
|---|---|---|---|---|
| anonymity | coherent | denunciation | laceration | prestige |
| articulate | compound | dredge | preening | ravaged |

## Tillie Olsen
### 1913–

**Other Works**
*Yonnondio: From the Thirties*

**Working Mother** Tillie Olsen began writing as a teenager in the 1930s, during the Great Depression, but stopped to marry and raise a family. A mother of four daughters, she helped support her family by working as a waitress and a secretary, all the time carrying the desire to write "within her" while riding the bus, doing household chores, and working long hours at a job. She has explained, "It is no accident that the first work I considered publishable began: 'I stand here ironing, and what you asked me moves tormented back and forth with the iron.'"

**A Writer at Last** For years hampered in her efforts to write by the struggle to earn a living, Olsen resumed her career only after receiving a fellowship from Stanford University in 1956. She was in her late 40s before she was able to publish *Tell Me a Riddle* (1961), a collection of short stories. Immediately acclaimed, Olsen's book

earned her fellowships and university teaching assignments. A high school dropout in the 11th grade, Olsen has nevertheless taught at various schools, including the University of Massachusetts, Stanford University, Amherst College, and the Massachusetts Institute of Technology.

**Literary Concerns** Olsen writes of people who have known economic hardships and whose lives are lived for others. In *Silences* (1978), a book of essays, she explores some of the social, political, and economic conditions that have adversely affected writers—especially women—and the creation of literature throughout history. Through her own personal experiences, Olsen has gained insight into the "thwarting of what struggles to come into being but cannot." Through her writing, she has given voice to those who might otherwise be silent.

## Author Activity

According to Olson, her method of writing involves "trying to be inside the people whom I am writing about." To what extent do you think Olsen succeeded in getting inside Emily's mother in "I Stand Here Ironing"?

## Vocabulary in Action

1. laceration
2. dredge
3. preening
4. prestige
5. coherent
6. ravaged
7. anonymity
8. articulate
9. denunciation
10. compound

## Author Activity

Answers will vary. Some students may state that Olsen succeeds markedly in getting inside Emily's mother. This narrator is honest about her shortcomings and failures. At times, she seems to be addressing her inner self.

---

**Assessment  Standardized Test Practice**

**CHOOSING THE BEST SUMMARY** Many standardized tests require students to select the best summary statement for a passage. You can give students practice in this skill by asking them to discuss which of the following statements is the best summary of "I Stand Here Ironing."

**A.** "I Stand Here Ironing" is a mother's review of her mistakes in raising her first daughter and the child's resulting problems as a teenager.

**B.** "I Stand Here Ironing" is a story about a young mother and her daughter, who becomes a comedienne.

**C.** "I Stand Here Ironing" is a story about what it was like to raise children in the United States during the 1930s and 1940s.

Lead students through the process of choosing the best summary. Consider each choice. Point out that, while all the statements contain accurate information about the story, the best summary includes the most important information. For that reason, **A** is the best choice.

## PART 1 Reading the Prompt
Model the process of reading a prompt:
- Read the entire prompt aloud.
- On the board, list the assignment's key words. ("relate," "overall perspective on female self-fulfillment," "evidence")
- Define key words using the Strategies in Action to show how students can restate the prompt for themselves.

## PART 2 Planning a Synthesis Essay
- Point out that students might prefer to select a different group of stories from that shown in the example.
- To create charts, suggest that students fold a sheet of paper in thirds, like a letter, and then turn it sideways. This will provide ample space for them to note such details as events, dialogue, and observations.
- Before students fill in their charts, have them discuss the contrast between the lives of men and the lives of women in these stories. This may guide their search for supporting details.

## PART 3 Drafting Your Essay
**Introduction** Suggest that students begin with a statement that summarizes the similarities among all the female characters' lives. Then they can relate this to the topic of self-fulfillment.

**Organization** Have students consider several organizational patterns. For example, they might deal with the stories chronologically or organize their reasons by order of importance.

**Conclusion** Students may conclude that women's lives were controlled by their husbands and offered little chance for self-fulfillment. Their reasons might include the social structure that approved of this.

**Revision** Since the main characters are all female, have students check for incorrect pronoun forms or unclear pronoun referents.

---

Some assessment prompts ask you to synthesize information from two or more works of literature to discover a new perspective. You are now going to practice writing a synthesis essay.

### PART 1  Reading the Prompt

Read the writing prompt carefully, more than once. Look for key words that help you identify the purpose of the essay and decide how to approach it.

> **Writing Prompt**
>
> In Unit Five, Part 1, several works deal with the issue of self-fulfillment for women. In an essay, (relate) the ideas about women's self-fulfillment presented in three selections you have read—from both the 19th and 20th centuries. What overall perspective on female self-fulfillment do these selections suggest? Cite (evidence) to support your ideas.

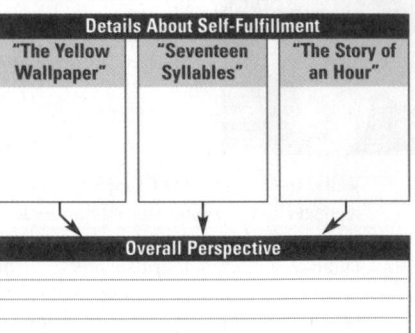

**STRATEGIES IN ACTION**

① Bring together, or **synthesize,** ideas from three selections.

② State a new idea—a **generalization** applying to all three selections.

③ Gather relevant **details** from the selections.

### PART 2  Planning a Synthesis Essay

- Choose three selections to examine: for example, "The Yellow Wallpaper," "The Story of an Hour," and "Seventeen Syllables."

- Create a diagram like the one shown.

- Jot down details about women's self-fulfillment in these selections.

- Identify patterns among these details.

- Based on these patterns, make a broad statement about self-fulfillment in women.

| Details About Self-Fulfillment | | |
|---|---|---|
| "The Yellow Wallpaper" | "Seventeen Syllables" | "The Story of an Hour" |
|  |  |  |

**Overall Perspective**

### PART 3  Drafting Your Essay

**Introduction** Begin by stating the thesis of your essay—the perspective on women's self-fulfillment that the selections share.

**Organization** Present the evidence in a logical way. For example, in each middle paragraph, you might state a supporting idea and then explain it with details.

**Conclusion** Restate your thesis and state a final thought.

**Revision** Allow time to review your work. Make sure it is clear, well-supported, and free from mistakes.

**Writing Handbook**
See page 1281: Explanatory Writing.

### LITERATURE CONNECTIONS

## Ethan Frome

EDITH WHARTON

**These thematically related readings are provided along with *Ethan Frome*:**

**The Snow Man**
WALLACE STEVENS

**Confessions of a Hypochondriac**
BARBARA GRAHAM

**Adventure**
SHERWOOD ANDERSON

**The Painted Door**
SINCLAIR ROSS

**Mirage**
CHRISTINA ROSSETTI

**Desert Places**
ROBERT FROST

**Dreams**
MARIE G. LEE

## The Awakening

KATE CHOPIN

This ground-breaking novel dramatizes the artistic and emotional awakening of Edna Pontellier, a 28-year-old woman who feels trapped by marriage and motherhood. Her true identity lies beyond the roles that society has imposed on her. In her quest for self-discovery, Edna willingly defies convention and takes enormous risks.

## And Even *More* . . .

### Books
**Mother Love**
RITA DOVE
A book of poems exploring mother-daughter relationships.

**The Madwoman in the Attic: The Woman Writer and the Nineteenth-Century Literary Imagination**
SANDRA M. GILBERT
Insightful study of notable women writers, including Emily Dickinson.

**A History of Women in America**
CAROLYN HYMOWITZ AND MICHAELE WEISSMAN
Overview of the shifting roles of women in American society.

### Other Media
**Cross Creek**
Feature film about writer Marjorie Kinnan Rawlings and her search for self-discovery in the backwoods of Florida.
(VIDEOCASSETTE)

**Ethan Frome**
Film adaptation of the novel, starring Liam Neeson. Touchstone Home Video.
(VIDEOCASSETTE)

**The Belle of Amherst**
Televised version of William Luce's play about Emily Dickinson. International Film Exchange. (VIDEOCASSETTE)

### Reena and Other Stories

PAULE MARSHALL
Marshall's collection of stories feature women and their relationships. Tillie Olsen highly praised this work, commending Marshall for her rare gift of creating "characters with such passionate understanding and radiant art that they remain with us permanently."

The *Electronic Library* is a CD-ROM that contains additional fiction, nonfiction, poetry, and drama for each unit in *The Language of Literature*.

These are the additional selections found in Unit 5 of the *Electronic Library* that apply to Part 1.

Emily Dickinson
**I taste a liquor never brewed**

Lucy Stone
**Disappointment Is the Lot of Women**

Have students select one of these books to read silently with comprehension over a period of time.

### Introduction

This article places the selections in Part 2 of this unit in historical context by providing students with an overview of the issues and concerns that dominated life in the late 19th and early 20th centuries. The **Traditions Across Time** section looks at how these issues reemerged in the mid-20th century. From the quotations in **Voices from the Times** students can infer the attitudes of a cross section of the American people regarding the American dream. This article will help students to interpret the possible influences of historical contexts on literary works.

## Teaching Nonfiction

### Reading Skills and Strategies
### ESTABLISHING A PURPOSE FOR READING

Explain to students that they are expected to read this article to understand the myth of the American dream and to learn about those people who pursued it.

### MONITORING AND MODIFYING READING STRATEGIES

Have students read the article silently and thoroughly. Ask them to monitor their comprehension of the information and, if necessary, modify their strategies when understanding breaks down. Suggest rereading and using additional resources such as dictionaries and glossaries as ways to increase comprehension.

### COMPARING AND CONTRASTING

Explain to students that they are expected to analyze text structures for how they influence understanding. Point out to students that the author of this article signals in the opening paragraph that this period of American history was a time of contrasts. Ask students to identify these contrasts and analyze how this structure influences their understanding of the material.

# The American Dream

## Illusion or Reality?

In the United States, the closing decades of the 19th century were a time of rapid change and sharp contrasts. Great entrepreneurs—such as Andrew Carnegie, J. P. Morgan, John D. Rockefeller, and Cornelius Vanderbilt—amassed vast fortunes by exploiting cheap labor in the cities and creating giant companies that controlled entire industries. Urban manufacturing centers swelled with the influx of immigrants from Europe and people from rural areas in search of work. Almost half of the U.S. population was crowded in about a dozen cities, and the majority of all U.S. workers were industrial laborers sweating in factories.

As the new century dawned, the belief in America as a unique place where work and merit, rather than social privilege, determined one's fate remained a powerful ideal. Everyone knew of Abraham Lincoln's rise from his early life in a simple log cabin in rural Illinois. Many also knew that the millionaire newspaperman Joseph Pulitzer had come to America as a poor young German-speaking immigrant, recruited to fight in the Civil War. Stories of people who had risen, through their own efforts, from humble beginnings to achieve fabulous success were told and retold.

For many writers, however, the underside of this ideal—the flaws hidden beneath its optimistic simplicity—became a preoccupation. In the novel *Sister Carrie*, Theodore Dreiser challenged the notion of self-improvement by depicting a heroine crushed by forces she cannot control. In *The Jungle,*

## Voices from the TIMES

Upton Sinclair exposed the appalling working conditions of immigrants in the Chicago stockyards. The poet and folksinger Carl Sandburg presented the seamy side of urban industrialization—the poverty, the crime, the corruption—even as he celebrated the courage and resilience of everyday men and women in the face of these blights.

In their poetry, Edgar Lee Masters and Edwin Arlington Robinson turned their gaze away from the cities to look at the changes surging through rural areas at this time. Each investigated, in a different way, the currents of discontent running beneath the surface stability of small-town life. Paul Laurence Dunbar, the first African American to earn his living solely by his writing, made his own sharp points in America's picturesque veneer by exposing the truth behind popular racial stereotypes of the day.

The American dream of material success was nowhere so minutely explored as in the stories and novels of F. Scott Fitzgerald. Nearly all of his works concern the tension between the very wealthy and those—like him—who were attracted to them. In following the lives of characters whose fates are determined by their responses to wealth and to those who possess it, he gave us intimate insights into the American preoccupation with money.

For the more than 20 million immigrants who came to America in the years between 1870 and 1920, the American dream was not just a compelling ideal but a last chance at survival. Many found work

The republic is a dream
Nothing happens unless first a dream.
**Carl Sandburg**
from "Washington Monument by Night"

The love of wealth is therefore to be traced, as either a principal or accessory motive, at the bottom of all that the Americans do; this gives to all their passions a sort of family likeness. . . . It may be said that it is the vehemence of their desires that makes the Americans so methodical; it perturbs their minds, but it disciplines their lives.
**Alexis de Tocqueville**
from *Democracy in America*

God gave me my money. I believe the power to make money is a gift from God . . . to be developed and used to the best of our ability for the good of mankind.
**John D. Rockefeller**

The business of America is business.
**Calvin Coolidge**

In your rocking chair by your window shall you dream such happiness as you may never feel.
**Theodore Dreiser**
from *Sister Carrie*

## Making Connections

**History**

**A** In 1890 the United States led the world in production of steel, largely because of Carnegie Steel Company. Scottish immigrant Andrew Carnegie, who began his career as a bobbin boy in a cotton mill earning $1.20 a week, amassed a fortune of hundreds of millions of dollars. Carnegie devoted much of his money to the endowment of libraries and to other philanthropic endeavors. He financed the construction of Carnegie Hall, which opened in 1891 and is famous for its glorious acoustics.

**History**

**B** Joseph Pulitzer's bequest of $2 million established the journalism school at Columbia University in New York City and launched an annual prize honoring educators, public servants, playwrights, composers, novelists, and poets. Recipients of the Pulitzer Prize for literature and drama include Willa Cather, William Faulkner, John Steinbeck, Edith Wharton, and Tennessee Williams.

**Health**

**C** In addition to exposing horrible working conditions, *The Jungle* (1906) also provoked public outrage at the conditions under which animals were slaughtered and meat and meat byproducts were packaged and sold. Pressure produced the Pure Food and Drug Act, which began efforts to guarantee consumers clean, edible food as well as drugs that have been tested before mass marketings.

**Literature**

**D** Robinson, although writing within traditional verse forms, produced a new kind of poetry for a new century. It was somber at times, psychological, and ironic. Masters, echoing Walt Whitman, called for an "American poetry, plain as the prairie, level as the quiet sea."

**Literature**

**E** Dunbar knew as early as his 27th year that he was suffering from an incurable disease. In the remaining six years of his life, he wrote substantially, publishing three volumes of poetry. His early death robbed America of a writer who could have become as well known as any in the first quarter of the 20th century. His complete poetry was published posthumously in one volume in 1913.

**VOICES FROM THE TIMES**

**Ask: According to Alexis de Tocqueville, what is the relationship between Americans and wealth?**

**Possible Responses:** He sees it as the prime motivator for all that Americans do; it is a passion for Americans; it is a disciplinary force.

**Ask: Both the Sandburg and Dreiser quotations talk about dreaming. Compare and contrast these two quotations.**

**Possible Response:** Sandburg implies the potential of dreaming and all that it can achieve; Dreiser dwells on the distance between dreaming and real life and implies that the two may never come together.

### OUTLINING

Have students create an outline of the article as a study strategy to better understand the text. Ask students to note the main ideas of the text as well as supporting details.

### DISCUSSING

Allow students time to discuss the article as a class. A possible starting point is a discussion on their definitions of the American Dream and its relevance to their lives.

**LaserLinks**
**Historical Literary Connection: The American Dream: Illusion or Reality?**

Many of the selections in Part 2 focus on a duality in American society—the coexistence of tremendous wealth and grinding poverty. This video presentation explores the "work-hard-enough-and-you-will-succeed" philosophy that has been so important for many newcomers to the United States.

See Teacher's SourceBook p. 67 for bar codes.

---

### Voices from the TIMES

Yuh don't belong, get me! Look at me, why don't youse dare? I belong, dat's me! *(pointing to a skyscraper across the street which is in process of construction—with bravado)* See dat building goin' up dere? See de steel work? Steel, dat's me! Youse guys live on it and tink yuh're somep'n. But I'm in it, see! I'm de hoistin' engine dat makes it go up! I'm it—de inside and bottom of it! Sure! I'm steel and steam and smoke and de rest of it! It moves—speed—twenty-five stories up—and me at de top and bottom—movin'! Youse simps don't move. Yuh're on'y dolls I winds up to see 'm spin.

**Eugene O'Neill**
from *The Hairy Ape*

"Give me your tired, your poor,
Your huddled masses yearning to
    breathe free,
The wretched refuse of your teeming
    shore.
Send these, the homeless, tempest-
    tossed to me:
I lift my lamp beside the golden door!"

**Emma Lazarus**
from "The New Colossus,"
inscribed at the base
of the Statue of Liberty

America is God's Crucible, the great Melting-Pot where all the races of Europe are melting and re-forming!

**Israel Zangwill**
from *The Melting Pot*

**822** UNIT FIVE   PART 2: THE AMERICAN DREAM

---

building skyscrapers, bridges, subways, and trolley lines in the growing cities. Anzia Yezierska's moving account of disillusion and persistence in her story "America and I" provides a glimpse of what life was like for immigrants in the sweatshops of New York City's garment district.

### Traditions Across Time: Dreams Lost and Found

Although the great waves of immigrants from Europe subsided during the 1920s—after the passage of restrictive quota laws—and during the Great Depression of the 1930s, the United States continued to be a "land of opportunity" for those in need. In the 1960s quotas based on nationality were lifted, and another wave of immigration began. The immigrants came mainly from Asia and the West Indies rather than from Europe.

These new immigrants came for the same reason as their predecessors a century before—to make a better life for themselves and their families—but some were also escaping homelands scarred by war and political persecution. Gish Jen's story "In the American Society" and Naomi Shihab Nye's poem "My Father and the Figtree" treat the immigrant experience with humor. Yvonne Sapia's poem "Defining the Grateful Gesture" and Lorna Dee Cervantes' poem "Refugee Ship" look at generational differences in immigrant families.

---

**VOICES FROM THE TIMES**
**Ask: What aspect of America do the quotations from "The New Colossus" and *The Melting Pot* epitomize?**
**Possible Responses:** tolerance; welcome; opportunity; equality; integration

**Ask: What aspect of American life does the O'Neill excerpt represent?**
**Possible Response:** the view of the worker conflicting perhaps with that of wealthy people or management

## Illusion or Reality?

## OVERVIEW

### Objectives

1. appreciate two classic **poems** (Literary Analysis)
2. identify and examine **tone** (Literary Analysis)
3. synthesize details in poetry (Active Reading)

### Summary

"Chicago" characterizes life in Chicago in the early 1900s. In the poem, Carl Sandburg personifies the city and explores its glories and strengths—as an ode to the working class of the city—as well as its crime, corruption, and poverty. "Lucinda Matlock" explores the character of the American rural life that began to decline during the Industrial Revolution. Edgar Lee Masters's poem is narrated by a deceased woman who chronicles her life in the fictional town of Spoon River, Illinois.

### Thematic Link

"Chicago" explores the **reality** of industrial life in early 20th-century Chicago, where so many immigrants and farm workers went to find **the American Dream.** "Lucinda Matlock" reaffirms the work ethic behind the American Dream and decries the **illusion** that happiness can be achieved without hard work.

### 5-Minute Warm-Up

***Daily Language SkillBuilder***

Have students **proofread** the display sentences on page 739j and write them correctly. The sentences also appear on Transparency 22 of **Grammar Transparencies and Copymasters.**

# Chicago

*Poetry by* CARL SANDBURG

# Lucinda Matlock

*Poetry by* EDGAR LEE MASTERS

### Connect to Your Life

**Ideal Settings** Where would you prefer to live—the city or the country? Why? Which environment do you think would let you live your life to the fullest? List some positive and negative features of city life and of country life. Then, as you read these poems, compare your own ideas with those of the speakers.

## Build Background

**The American Spirit** Carl Sandburg and Edgar Lee Masters wrote poetry that captured the vitality of America in the early 20th century. What Sandburg found when he moved to Chicago in 1913 was a metropolis of bustling industry and appalling slums, cultural achievements and criminal activity. From the ruins of a devastating 1871 fire, Chicago had risen to become the railroad hub of the nation and a center of meatpacking and manufacturing. At the same time, the city's population had increased explosively as people moved there from small towns in the Midwest and the South to find work. Written in 1914, "Chicago" catalogs both the negative and the positive aspects of the city, reflecting the energy and enthusiasm of its citizens in the early 1900s.

"Lucinda Matlock" is from Masters's *Spoon River Anthology,* a collection of 244 free-verse monologues spoken by deceased inhabitants of the fictional rural town of Spoon River. They disclose the joys and tragedies of their lives as they speak from the grave. Masters patterned these characters on the people he had observed while growing up in Lewistown, near the Spoon River of central Illinois. His model for Lucinda Matlock was his grandmother Lucinda, who died in 1910 at the age of 96.

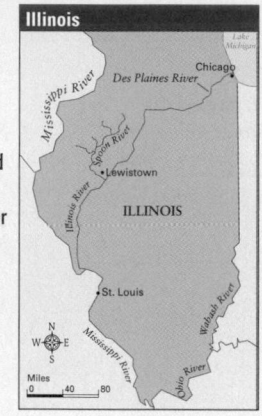

## Focus Your Reading

**LITERARY ANALYSIS  TONE  Tone** is the attitude a writer takes toward his or her subject. A writer can communicate tone through diction (word choice) and choice of details. Read these two poems aloud to help you identify the tone. The emotions conveyed in your voice should provide you with clues that hint at the tone.

**ACTIVE READING  SYNTHESIZING DETAILS**

"Chicago" catalogs, or lists, the attributes of a city, while "Lucinda Matlock" sums up the key moments of a woman's life. To bring these details into focus, synthesize the information. **Synthesizing** involves putting together clues, facts, and details to form an overall picture of a person, place, or event.

**READER'S NOTEBOOK** For each poem, use a spider diagram, like the example shown, to help you gather details as you read. Then note recurring patterns or relationships among the details you collected.

## LESSON RESOURCES

**UNIT FIVE RESOURCE BOOK,** pp. 28–29

**ASSESSMENT RESOURCES**
**Formal Assessment,** pp. 151–152
**Teacher's Guide to Assessment and Portfolio Use**
**Test Generator**

**SKILLS TRANSPARENCIES AND COPYMASTERS**
**Literary Analysis**
• Tone, T19 (for Paired Activity, p. 828)

**Reading and Critical Thinking**
• Reading for Details, T16 (for Active Reading, p. 824)
**Grammar**
• Noun Clauses I, C102 (for Mini Lesson, p. 829)
**Vocabulary**
• Denotation and Connotation, C68 (for Mini Lesson, p. 827)
**Writing**
• Compare-Contrast, C32 (for Writing Option 2, p. 829)

**INTEGRATED TECHNOLOGY**
**Audio Library**
**LaserLinks**
• Historical Connection: Urban and Rural Life in the Early 1900s
• Author Background: Carl Sandburg
• Author Background: Edgar Lee Masters. See **Teacher's SourceBook,** pp. 68–70.
**Visit our website:**
www.mcdougallittell.com

City Building (1930), Thomas Hart Benton. From *America Today*, distemper and egg tempera on gessoed linen with oil glaze, 92″ × 117″. Copyright © The Equitable Life Assurance Society of the United States. Copyright © 1996 T.H. Benton & R.P. Benton Testamentary Trusts/Licensed by VAGA, New York. Photo Copyright © 1988 Dorothy Zeidman.

# CHICAGO

## Carl Sandburg

$H$og Butcher for the World,
Tool Maker, Stacker of Wheat,
Player with Railroads and the Nation's Freight Handler;
Stormy, husky, brawling,
5   City of the Big Shoulders:

They tell me you are wicked and I believe them, for I have seen your
    painted women under the gas lamps luring the farm boys.

CHICAGO   **825**

## Mini Lesson   Viewing and Representing

*City Building* and *Country Dance* **by Thomas Hart Benton**

**ART APPRECIATION** Born in Neosho, Missouri, Benton (1889–1975) was the best-known American muralist of the 1930s and 1940s. Unlike his European contemporaries, Benton created art that is marked by realism rather than abstraction.
**Instruction** Knowing that the artist used realism in his paintings, viewers assume that the paintings convey what life was really like in America in the 1930s and 1940s. Point out the power of art to influence people's perceptions of reality.
**Application** Have students consider which parts

of reality the artist chooses to portray. How does the artist influence people's perceptions of reality about city and country life?
**Possible Responses:** The images in *City Building* show people hard at work, in natural rhythms of work, with clean clothing and great strength. The artist portrays a positive image of the hard labor of working people that helped to build American cities. He does not depict any misery or lack of privilege experienced by workers. Similarly, *Country Dance* shows an idyllic scene of country life and leaves viewers with a perception of the happiness and joy marked by a country dance.

CHICAGO / LUCINDA MATLOCK   **825**

Have students silently read the poems a few times to familiarize themselves with the poems, then have a volunteer read aloud.

**Active Reading**

SYNTHESIZING DETAILS

Have students discuss how Sandburg presents details in the first stanza of "Chicago." Ask them what overall impression they get about the city from these details.

**Possible Response:** Sandburg lists epithets and adjectives to describe the city. They give the impression that Chicago is a mighty, productive city, a center of trade and industry for the country.

Use **Unit Five Resource Book,** p. 28 for more practice.

**Literary Analysis** TONE

**A** Ask students to analyze how the author's choice of words reveals his tone. How would they describe the tone in lines 8–9?

**Possible Response:** The author's choice of words such as sneer and this my city creates a tone that is defiant, angry, and defensive about the hard work and life of the city.

Use **Unit Five Resource Book,** p. 29 for more practice.

 And they tell me you are crooked and I answer: Yes, it is true I have seen the gunman kill and go free to kill again.
 And they tell me you are brutal and my reply is: On the faces of women and children I have seen the marks of wanton hunger.
 And having answered so I turn once more to those who sneer at this my city, and I give them back the sneer and say to them:
10  Come and show me another city with lifted head singing so proud to be alive and coarse and strong and cunning.
Flinging magnetic curses amid the toil of piling job on job, here is a tall bold slugger set vivid against the little soft cities;
Fierce as a dog with tongue lapping for action, cunning as a savage pitted against the wilderness,
Bareheaded,
Shoveling,
15  Wrecking,
Planning,
Building, breaking, rebuilding,
Under the smoke, dust all over his mouth, laughing with white teeth,
Under the terrible burden of destiny laughing as a young man laughs,
20  Laughing even as an ignorant fighter laughs who has never lost a battle,
Bragging and laughing that under his wrist is the pulse, and under his ribs the heart of the people,
                                        Laughing!
Laughing the stormy, husky, brawling laughter of Youth, half-naked, sweating, proud to be Hog Butcher, Tool Maker, Stacker of Wheat, Player with Railroads and Freight Handler to the Nation.

## Thinking Through the Literature

1. Would you like to live in a city like the one depicted in this poem? Share your ideas with a classmate.

2. In your opinion, what are the best and worst aspects of the Chicago presented in the poem?

3. How well do you think Sandburg's poetic **style** suits his subject?

THINK ABOUT
- how you would characterize his use of rhythm
- the effectiveness of descriptive names like "Tool Maker" in helping you picture Chicago
- how the repetition in the last three lines affects your impression of the city
- how the city would seem different if described in formal, rhymed stanzas

4. ACTIVE READING SYNTHESIZING DETAILS Review the spider diagram you created in your READER'S NOTEBOOK. Based on these details, what is the overall picture of Chicago presented in this poem?

## Thinking Through the Literature

1. Some students may state that the strength and vitality of Chicago make it a city they would like to live in.

2. Possible Responses: Positive aspects include people working together as a community, the pride of the citizens, and the laughter of the workers; negative aspects include prostitution, injustice, and hunger.

3. Possible Responses: The style mirrors the city's freedom and ability to reinvent itself; it encapsulates attributes of the city and reinforces those images at the poem's end.

4. Students' responses should reflect a use of clues and details to form an overall picture of Chicago.

# Lucinda Matlock

Edgar Lee Masters

*Country Dance* (1928), Thomas Hart Benton. Oil on panel, 30″ × 25″, private collection. Copyright © 1996 T.H. Benton & R.P. Benton Testamentary Trusts/Licenses by VAGA, New York.

*I* went to the dances at Chandlerville,
And played snap-out at Winchester.
One time we changed partners,
Driving home in the moonlight of middle June,
5   And then I found Davis.
We were married and lived together for seventy years,
Enjoying, working, raising the twelve children,
Eight of whom we lost
Ere I had reached the age of sixty.
10   I spun, I wove, I kept the house, I nursed the sick,
I made the garden, and for holiday
Rambled over the fields where sang the larks,
And by Spoon River gathering many a shell,
And many a flower and medicinal weed—
15   Shouting to the wooded hills, singing to the green valleys.
At ninety-six I had lived enough, that is all,
And passed to a sweet repose.
What is this I hear of sorrow and weariness,
Anger, discontent and drooping hopes?
20   Degenerate sons and daughters,
Life is too strong for you—
It takes life to love Life.

**2 snap-out:** a game—similar to crack the whip—in which players join hands in a line, then run about trying to shake off those at the end of the line.

**17 repose:** rest (here the reference is to death, viewed as a quiet, serene sleep).

**20 degenerate** (dĭ-jĕn′ər-ĭt): showing a decline in vigor or moral strength.

## Customizing Instruction

### Students Acquiring English
Help students understand the meanings of the following words and phrases:

**1** The word *crooked* is a figurative word meaning "corrupt" or "unjust."

**2** The word *wanton* in this context means "merciless and limitless."

**3** *Ere* is an archaic term meaning "before."

### Gifted and Talented

**4** Have students offer interpretations of the last two lines of the poem. What do they think the narrator is saying about rural living?

---

### Mini Lesson  **Vocabulary Strategy**

**DISCRIMINATING BETWEEN CONNOTATIVE AND DENOTATIVE MEANINGS**

**Instruction** Being able to discriminate between connotative and denotative meanings helps students to appreciate the subtlety of word meanings and expand their vocabularies. Denotation is the literal meaning of a word, or dictionary definition. Connotation is the associated attitudes or emotions. Ask students which of the following is the connotative meaning of the word butcher used in the first line of "Chicago"— "a dealer in meat" or "harsh; rough; strong."

  **Answer:** "harsh; rough; strong"

**Application** Have students work in pairs to locate the words stormy, sneer, and bareheaded in the poem "Chicago" and write both their denotative and connotative meanings. Have a class discussion to compare students' answers. Ask students to defend their interpretations of connotative meanings by referring to the context of the poem and their own experiences.

Use **Vocabulary Transparencies and Copymasters,** p. 68.

A lesson on connotation and denotation appears on p. 908 in the Pupil's Edition.

### GUIDING STUDENT RESPONSE

## Connect to the Literature

**1. What Do You Think?**

Responses will vary. Some students may state that she is a vibrant women who worked hard, suffered very mucy, enjoyed simple pleasures, and loved life.

**Comprehension Check**

• She meets her husband on the way home from a dance.

• Most of her children died before she was 60.

## Think Critically

**2.** Possible Response: Sources of joy include love of husband and children, pride in caring for others and creating beauty, and success in meeting challenges. Sources of pain include hardship, overwork, and loss of loved ones.

**3.** Possible Response: Lucinda takes the good experiences along with the bad and makes the most of every situation; she has no sympathy for people who complain or grow depressed.

**4.** Possible Responses: She is fair because her own life has been difficult and she does not complain about it; she unjustly lumps a whole group together as "degenerate" without knowing their whole story.

**5.** Responses will vary. Some students may state that small-town life nurtured strong women who loved their families and triumphed over misfortune.

## Literary Analysis

**Tone** Possible Response: Her tone shifts at line 18, where she asks "What is this I hear of sorrow and weariness,/ Anger, discontent and drooping hopes?" and she becomes accusatory, reprimanding the "degenerate sons and daughters" for their lack of strength and fortitude.

**Personification** The personification of Chicago as a proud man emphasizes the city's strength and vitality as well as its complexity of good and bad traits. Suggest to students that personifications of cities do not necessarily have to be male.

## Connect to the Literature

**1. What Do You Think?**
What is your opinion of Lucinda Matlock's life?

**Comprehension Check**
• How did Lucinda Matlock meet her husband?
• What happened to most of her children?

## Think Critically

**2.**  **ACTIVE READING** **SYNTHESIZING DETAILS**  Refer to the details in the spider diagram from your **READER'S NOTEBOOK**. What were the sources of both joy and pain in her life?

**3.** How would you describe Lucinda Matlock's approach to life?

**4.** Do you think Lucinda is fair in her judgment of the "degenerate sons and daughters"? Explain your opinion.

**THINK ABOUT**
• the attitudes she attributes to them in lines 18–19
• what she might mean by her statements in lines 21–22

**5.** What portrait of small-town life do you get from this poem? Explain.

## Extend Interpretations

**6. Comparing Texts** How is Lucinda Matlock similar to and different from the people that the speaker of "Chicago" admires? Support your answer.

**7. Critic's Corner** In a review of *Spoon River Anthology,* Carl Sandburg wrote, "The people whose faces look out from the pages of the book are the people of life itself, each trait of them as plain or as mysterious as in the old home valley where the writer came from." Do you think his remark accurately describes Lucinda Matlock, as she is characterized in the poem? Explain.

**8. Connect to Life** Would you rather live in Sandburg's Chicago or Lucinda Matlock's Spoon River? Consider the positive and negative aspects of country and city life you recorded for the Connect to Your Life activity on page 824.

## Literary Analysis

**TONE**  Like tone of voice, the **tone** of a poem may reveal the speaker's feelings or the poet's attitude toward the subject of the poem. Tone often relies on the poet's choice of words and selection of details. For example, the tone of "Chicago" might be described as brash and spirited. Calling Chicago "Hog Butcher of the World" and "Tool Maker, Stacker of Wheat" suggests the energetic tone that the speaker is trying to convey. The words *shouting* and *singing* in line 15 of "Lucinda Matlock" suggest the speaker's deep and joyful relationship with the natural world.

**Paired Activity**  Reread "Lucinda Matlock" aloud to a partner, and discuss how the speaker's tone shifts toward the end of the poem. Cite words and details that reveal a change in the speaker's feelings.

**REVIEW** **PERSONIFICATION**

**Personification** is a figure of speech in which an object, animal, place, or idea is given human characteristics. For example, starting at line 10 in "Chicago," Sandburg personifies the city as a proud man. If you were to personify your own city or town, what kind of person would it be?

## Extend Interpretations

**Comparing Texts** Possible Responses: Lucinda lives in a rural area with tasks quite different from those of urban workers; however, like the Chicagoans, Lucinda attacks life with energy and vitality.

**Critic's Corner** Responses will vary. Some students may agree with Sandburg's opinion, stating that Lucinda Matlock's strength of spirit is an easily discernible trait.

**Connect to Life** Responses should include both pros and cons of life in the city and life in the country.

# Choices & CHALLENGES

## Writing Options

**1. Hometown Poems** Write a poem about your own city or town. You might imitate the style of "Chicago," using epithets, or descriptive names, and personification to depict the town. You might prefer to present the town indirectly, through a character sketch of a typical resident, as in "Lucinda Matlock." Gather the class's poems into a booklet of poems about communities.

**2. Comparison-Contrast Essay** Draft an essay in which you compare and contrast city life and country life. Place this piece in your **Working Portfolio.**

**Writing Handbook**
See page 1281: Compare and Contrast

## Carl Sandburg
### 1878–1967

**Other Works**
*The People, Yes*
*Always the Young Strangers*

**The Winding Road to Success** The renowned poet, award-winning historian, and popular folk musician Carl Sandburg was born in Galesburg, Illinois. Forced to leave school when he was 13 in order to find work, he roamed the Midwest as a youth, working at various jobs—including house painting and brick making. Eventually, he turned to journalism. After moving to Chicago in 1913, he became a reporter, editorial writer, and columnist for the *Chicago Daily News.*

**The People's Poet** The poem "Chicago" was one of Sandburg's earliest literary successes. His verse collections *Chicago Poems, Cornhuskers,* and *Smoke and Steel* established his fame as a poet of the people. Because he gave popular public readings around the country, it has been said that no other American writer was so widely read and heard at the same time.

**Literary Prizes** Sandburg won a number of awards and honors, including the 1951 Pulitzer Prize for poetry for *Complete Poems* and the 1939 Pulitzer Prize for history for *Abraham Lincoln: The War Years,* the last four volumes of a six-volume biography.

## Edgar Lee Masters
### 1868?–1950

**Other Works**
*Poems of People*
*Illinois Poems*
*Across Spoon River: An Autobiography*

**Bridging Two Centuries** Born with one foot in the nineteenth century and one foot in the twentieth, Edgar Lee Masters seemed at ease with both the old and the new. His poetry reflects his ties to small-town traditions and his awareness of the changing face of American culture in the early 1900s.

**The Birth of a Masterpiece** Edgar Lee Masters had already published 12 books of poetry, essays, and plays before he began writing his masterpiece, *Spoon River Anthology,* which he originally conceived as a work of prose. For the names of the poems' characters, Masters drew on "both the Spoon river and the Sangamon river neighborhoods, combining first names here with surnames there, and taking some also from the constitutions and State papers of Illinois."

**Critical Acclaim** The publication of *Spoon River Anthology* in 1915 immediately established Masters as an important American poet. In 1920, Masters gave up the Chicago law practice at which he had worked for 30 years and moved to New York City to write full time. He wrote more than 50 books, but none of his later works achieved the critical and popular success of *Spoon River Anthology.*

CHICAGO/LUCINDA MATLOCK **829**

---

## Writing Options

1. **Hometown Poems** To make this assignment more challenging, have students interview people in their towns as resources for their poems.
2. **Comparison-Contrast Essay** Students' responses should reveal their ability to draw inferences from the poems and support them with their own experiences. **To get students started on this assignment,** have them list attributes of city and country life in a chart.

---

## Grammar

**NOUN CLAUSES**

**Instruction** Noun clauses are subordinate clauses that function as nouns in sentences. To distinguish a noun clause from other types, students should evaluate how the clause is being used in the sentence. Ask students to identify the noun clause in the following sentence:

The poem addresses <u>whoever would criticize the city for its corruption</u>.

**Exercises** Ask students to identify the noun clause in each sentence.

1. The question is <u>whether they were proud or merely oppressed</u>.

2. <u>Whoever says that they were happy</u> is oversimplifying.

3. People in the country learn to live with <u>whatever nature gives them</u>.

4. The narrator would give <u>whoever despaired of life</u> a piece of her mind.

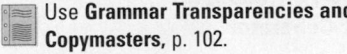 Use **Grammar Transparencies and Copymasters,** p. 102.

 Use McDougal Littell's *Language Network,* Chapter 3, for more instruction in noun clauses.

CHICAGO / LUCINDA MATLOCK **829**

## OVERVIEW

### Objectives
1. appreciate two **narrative poems** (Literary Analysis)
2. understand **characterization in narrative poetry** (Literary Analysis)
3. **evaluate character** in poetry (Active Reading)

### Summary
The poem "Richard Cory" shows that appearances can be deceiving. The title character is a man whom everyone in town admires for his sophistication and wealth—qualities that society would expect to make any person happy. Accordingly, all the people wish they were in his place, except Richard Cory himself. "Miniver Cheevy" is a poem about a man who longs for eras past and all the romance he imagines they contained. Miniver Cheevy would rather have lived during the time of Camelot or the Medicis, when valor, honor, and patronage reigned. Miniver uses his longings as an escape from his present life and an excuse for his excessive drinking and his lack of personal accomplishments.

### Thematic Link
"Richard Cory" reveals that the **reality** of **the American Dream** as most people define it does not necessarily bring happiness. "Miniver Cheevy" is an example of a person chasing after the **illusion** of romance in a past he does not know, in order to avoid having to create or deal with his own reality.

### 5-Minute Warm-Up

*Daily*
*Language*
*SkillBuilder*

Have students **proofread** the display sentences on page 739j and write them correctly. The sentences also appear on Transparency 23 of **Grammar Transparencies and Copymasters.**

# Richard Cory
# Miniver Cheevy

*Poetry by* EDWIN ARLINGTON ROBINSON

### Connect to Your Life

**Life's Disappointments** What do you think causes some people to feel regretful about their lives? How might they try to escape their unhappiness? With a small group of classmates, discuss these questions. Brainstorm a list of both positive and negative ways of coping with disappointing experiences.

## Build Background

**Tilbury Town** Edwin Arlington Robinson's "Richard Cory" and "Miniver Cheevy" are from a famous series of poems depicting the inner lives of imaginary residents in Tilbury Town, a fictional community modeled on Robinson's hometown of Gardiner, Maine. Tilbury Town, a typical small town in New England at the turn of the century, is a place where individuality and creativity are stifled. Though some members of this community chase after the American dream, it remains out of their reach. In most of his Tilbury Town poems, Robinson paints a complex psychological portrait of isolated individuals—often misfits and failures. "The failures are much more interesting," Robinson said. Along with his fascination with failed lives, Robinson also explores how his characters try to overcome their personal defeats and shortcomings.

## Focus Your Reading

**LITERARY ANALYSIS** **CHARACTERIZATION IN NARRATIVE POETRY**
**Narrative poetry** tells a story using elements of character, setting, and plot to develop a theme. To portray characters in narrative poems, poets may adapt the methods of **characterization** typically used in fiction:

- physical description
- the character's own actions, words, thoughts, and feelings
- other characters' actions, words, thoughts, and feelings
- the speaker's own direct comments

As you read "Richard Cory" and "Miniver Cheevy," note how you get to know the characters.

**ACTIVE READING** **EVALUATING CHARACTER** Robinson does not directly state how to view the characters in his poems. Are they good or bad? weak or strong? likable or unlikable? He leaves these **evaluations,** or judgments, up to the reader. Robinson provides you with clues that will shape your impressions of the characters' personalities and behavior.

**READER'S NOTEBOOK** To form valid opinions about Richard Cory and Miniver Cheevy, note the descriptive details Robinson uses to portray them. As you read each poem, jot down details you learned about the characters. Use a chart like the one shown.

| | Richard Cory | Miniver Cheevy |
|---|---|---|
| Traits | | |
| Behavior | | |
| Outlook on Life | | |

## LESSON RESOURCES

**UNIT FIVE RESOURCE BOOK,** pp. 30–31

**ASSESSMENT RESOURCES**
**Formal Assessment,** pp. 153–154
**Teacher's Guide to Assessment and Portfolio Use**
**Test Generator**

**SKILLS TRANSPARENCIES AND COPYMASTERS**
**Literary Analysis**
- Characterization, T6 (for Activity, p. 833)

**Reading and Critical Thinking**
- Compare and Contrast, T15 (for Extend Interpretations, item 6, p. 833)

**Grammar**
- Noun Clauses I, C102 (for Mini Lesson, p. 834)

**Vocabulary**
- Idioms, C69 (for Mini Lesson, p. 831)

**Communications**
- Appreciative Listening, T2 (for Activities & Explorations, p. 834)

**INTEGRATED TECHNOLOGY**

**Audio Library**
**Visit our website:**
www.mcdougallittell.com

# Richard Cory

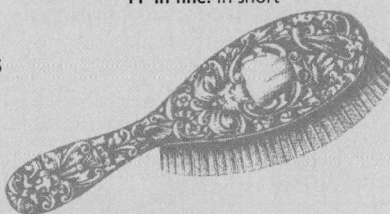

Edwin
Arlington
Robinson

Whenever Richard Cory went down town,
We people on the pavement looked at him:
He was a gentleman from sole to crown,
Clean favored, and imperially slim.

5  And he was always quietly arrayed,
And he was always human when he talked;
But still he fluttered pulses when he said,
"Good-morning," and he glittered when he walked.

And he was rich—yes, richer than a king—
10 And admirably schooled in every grace:
In fine, we thought that he was everything
To make us wish that we were in his place.

So on we worked, and waited for the light,
And went without the meat, and cursed the bread;
15 And Richard Cory, one calm summer night,
Went home and put a bullet through his head.

**4 clean favored:** having a tidy appearance; **imperially:** majestically; royally.

**5 arrayed:** dressed.

**10 schooled in every grace:** extremely well-mannered and cultured.

**11 In fine:** in short

## Thinking Through the Literature

1. What is your reaction to the ending of "Richard Cory"?
2. How do the townspeople seem to feel about Richard Cory? Support your ideas with details from the poem.
3. **ACTIVE READING** **EVALUATING CHARACTER** Review the chart in your **READER'S NOTEBOOK.** What is your opinion of Richard Cory?

   **THINK ABOUT** {
   • his physical appearance and other traits
   • his speech and behavior toward the townspeople
   • his apparent outlook on life

4. Why do you think Richard Cory kills himself?
5. What would you say is the **theme** of this poem?

---

---

 **Mini Lesson** Vocabulary Strategy

**RELY ON CONTEXT CLUES**

**Instruction** An idiomatic phrase is one whose meaning is not immediately apparent from the meanings of its individual words. Sometimes looking up the individual words in an idiomatic phrase can help students understand it, however, because the dictionary may list meanings for those words that students were not aware of. Write the following line on the chalkboard:

He was a gentleman from sole to crown.

*Sole* and *crown* have several meanings in the dictionary. From the context of the sentence, have students determine that sole means "the bottom of a person's foot" and crown means "the top part of the skull." In other words, Richard Cory was a complete gentleman, from head to foot. The context of the poem, in which the speaker describes people's absolute admiration of this man, provides a further clue to the meaning of the idiom.

Use **Vocabulary Transparencies and Copymasters,** p. 69.

## Reading and Analyzing

### Literary Analysis

**CHARACTERIZATION IN NARRATIVE POETRY**

 Have students look at the first six stanzas and describe ways in which the speaker characterizes Miniver Cheevy.

**Possible Response:** Miniver Cheevy is a somewhat bitter man who is unhappy with the times he lives in. He thinks that people in the past were able to achieve greatness, and he thinks that greatness is unachievable in his time.

Use **Unit Five Resource Book,** p. 31 for more practice.

### Active Reading

**EVALUATING CHARACTER**

 Have students evaluate the character of Miniver Cheevy. Is he rightly disenchanted, or is his discontent an excuse for his lack of accomplishments?

**Possible Response:** Miniver Cheevy lets his longing for a time past stand in the way of his happiness. He uses his discontent with the present as an excuse to drink and not do anything worthwhile, telling himself that modern times afford no opportunity for great, romantic deeds.

Use **Unit Five Resource Book,** p. 30 for more practice.

---

# Miniver Cheevy

### Edwin Arlington Robinson

**A** Miniver Cheevy, child of scorn,
　Grew lean while he assailed the seasons;
He wept that he was ever born,
　And he had reasons.

5　Miniver loved the days of old
　When swords were bright and steeds
　were prancing;
The vision of a warrior bold
　Would set him dancing.

Miniver sighed for what was not,
10　And dreamed, and rested from his labors;
He dreamed of Thebes and Camelot,
　And Priam's neighbors.

Miniver mourned the ripe renown
　That made so many a name so fragrant;
15　He mourned Romance, now on the town,
　And Art, a vagrant.

Miniver loved the Medici,
　Albeit he had never seen one;
He would have sinned incessantly
20　Could he have been one.

Miniver cursed the commonplace
　And eyed a khaki suit with loathing;
He missed the medieval grace
　Of iron clothing.

25　Miniver scorned the gold he sought,
　But sore annoyed was he without it;
Miniver thought, and thought, and thought,
　And thought about it.

Miniver Cheevy, born too late,
30　Scratched his head and kept on thinking;
**B** Miniver coughed, and called it fate,
　And kept on drinking.

**11 Thebes** (thēbz): a city of ancient Greece, the setting of many famous legends; **Camelot:** King Arthur's legendary castle.

**12 Priam's** (prī′əmz) **neighbors:** the participants in the Trojan War (during which Priam was king of Troy).

**17 Medici** (mĕd′ə-chē′): a powerful Italian noble family, among whose members were several cruel and immoral rulers of Florence during the Renaissance.

**18 albeit** (ôl-bē′ĭt): even though.

832　UNIT FIVE　PART 2: THE AMERICAN DREAM

---

## Teaching Options

### ✓ Assessment　Standardized Test Practice

**IDENTIFYING THE BEST SUMMARY**

Many standardized tests include items that require students to identify the best summary statement for a passage they have read. You can give students practice in this skill by writing the following statements on the chalkboard and asking them to discuss which is the best summary of "Miniver Cheevy."

**A.** Miniver Cheevy has been treated unfairly by life and therefore must drink to cope with his unjust circumstances.

**B.** Miniver Cheevy was born in the wrong time; he would have been a successful warrior had he been born in the past.

**C.** Miniver Cheevy uses the fact that he was not born in a more "romantic" era as an excuse for why he has not accomplished much.

During the discussion, point out that although **A** and **B** describe how Miniver himself might summarize his plight, the best summary statement is **C** because it is based on a more objective view of Miniver's situation.

## Connect to the Literature

1. **What Do You Think?**
   What is your impression of Miniver Cheevy? Share your thoughts with a classmate.

   **Comprehension Check**
   • What is Miniver Cheevy's position in society?
   • What does Miniver Cheevy daydream about?
   • How does Miniver Cheevy respond to the disappointments in his life?

## Think Critically

2. How would you describe Miniver Cheevy's view of the past? Why do you think he holds this view?

   **THINK ABOUT**
   { • the content of his daydreams
   • why he is disappointed with his own life
   • how he deals with his "fate"

3. How do you think the speaker of the poem feels about Miniver Cheevy? Cite lines from poem that suggest the speaker's attitude.

4. How does the final stanza of the poem influence your opinion of Miniver Cheevy?

5. **ACTIVE READING** **EVALUATING CHARACTER** Review the chart you made in your **READER'S NOTEBOOK**. Do you think Miniver Cheevy is a sympathetic or an unsympathetic character? Defend your view.

## Extend Interpretations

6. **Comparing Texts** How would you relate "Richard Cory" and "Miniver Cheevy" to the idea of the American dream?

7. **What If?** If Miniver Cheevy had lived during medieval times, do you think he would have found happiness? Why or why not?

8. **Connect to Life** Both Miniver Cheevy and Richard Cory solve their problems in self-destructive ways. In your opinion, what are some positive ways of coping with life's disappointments? Think about your discussion with classmates in the Connect to Your Life activity on page 830.

## Literary Analysis

**CHARACTERIZATION IN NARRATIVE POETRY** Like a short story or novel, **narrative poetry,** such as "Richard Cory" and "Miniver Cheevy," relies on literary elements, such as character, setting, plot, and point of view, to tell a story. Robinson adapts techniques of **characterization** to create compelling portraits of imaginary townspeople. For example, the speaker in "Richard Cory" and "Miniver Cheevy" acts as a narrator who reports information about the main character. The speaker in each of these poems provides you with a glimpse of the character's actions, appearance, feelings, and ideas.

**Activity** Create personality profiles of Richard Cory and Miniver Cheevy based on the specific details revealed about them in the poems. Use a format like the one shown.

> Character's Name:
> Physical Description
> Actions:
> Feelings:
> Thoughts:

**REVIEW** **RHYME AND METER**
**Rhyme** is the occurrence of a similar or identical sound at the ends of words. **Meter** is the pattern of stressed and unstressed syllables in each line. How do you think the arrangement of rhyming lines and the meter of "Miniver Cheevy" contribute to the overall effect of the poem?

RICHARD CORY / MINIVER CHEEVY **833**

### Connect to the Literature

1. **What Do You Think?**
   Responses will vary. Some students may find Miniver Cheevy a comic figure, who dreams much but does little.

**Comprehension Check**
• He is living on the fringes of society.
• He dreams of being a warrior or leader in the romantic "days of old."
• by drinking

### Think Critically

2. Possible Responses: He romanticizes the past based on heroic tales of old; he has no concept of the reality of everyday life in the past. He feels that he has not achieved anything notable because he is living in common times.
3. Possible Response: The speaker's tone is humorous and mildly critical of Miniver Cheevy, "child of scorn."
4. Responses will vary. The final stanza reveals that Miniver's longing for the past and criticism of modern life are merely a drunkard's dreams.
5. Responses will vary. Some students may state that Miniver's vivid imagination makes him somewhat sympathetic.

### Literary Analysis

**Characterization in Narrative Poetry** To further refine their personality profiles, students can also give descriptions of each man in terms of how the character sees himself, how others see him, and how the narrator views him.

**Rhyme and Meter** Have students tap out the meter as one student reads the poem aloud to help them get a sense of the overall effect.

## Extend Interpretations

**Comparing Texts** Possible Response: Both poems illustrate the failure of the "American dream": Richard Cory seems to be the embodiment of that dream, yet he chooses to kill himself; Miniver Cheevy rejects the idea of an American dream, focusing instead on an idealized past to justify his own failures.

**What If?** Possible Response: Miniver Cheevy is a dreamer, not a doer or an adventurer; in the medieval past he would have found another excuse to justify his failures. Miniver is unhappy because he thinks he has been treated unfairly by life. However, his true unhappiness seems to come from his own inadequacies, which have nothing to do with the era in which he was born.

**Connect to Life** Responses will vary. Some students may state that one way to cope with life's disappointment is to try to do something to help someone else instead of brooding over one's own troubles.

## Writing Options

1. **Miniver's Monologue** Monologues should reflect a longing for and idealization of the past. **To make this assignment more challenging,** have students deliver their monologues to the class.

2. **Farewell Note** Notes will vary. **To get students started on this activity,** have them discuss why the townspeople think Richard Cory is happy. Ask students whether money, success, and appearance are all that is needed to make a person happy, or whether other qualities and circumstances are needed.

3. **Interview Questions** Questions may touch upon what Cory thinks Tilbury residents think of him or what Miniver Cheevy thinks the Tilbury residents want for their lives. **To make this assignment more challenging,** have students break into pairs and either perform their interview for the class or tape it.

## Activities & Explorations

**Musical Adaptation** Students' musical variations will vary but should reflect the depressing tone of the poem. **To make this assignment easier,** first discuss with students what popular music group of today would best capture the tone of this poem. Students can then model their songs on this group's music.

## Author Activity

Students may want to compare the inhabitants of Robinson's Tilbury Town with those in Edgar Lee Master's Spoon River. Does the depiction of the American dream differ in these two poets' work?

---

# *Choices & CHALLENGES*

## Writing Options

**1. Miniver's Monologue** Write a monologue from Miniver Cheevy's point of view in which he glorifies moments from the past. Refer to images from the poem for ideas.

**2. Farewell Note** Compose a note that Richard Cory might have left, expressing his view of the townspeople and explaining why he took his life.

**3. Interview Questions** Imagine you are reporter who writes a news column profiling Tilbury Town residents. Write a list of ten interview questions you would ask either Richard Cory or Miniver Cheevy.

## Activities & Explorations

**Musical Adaptation** Listen to the song "Richard Cory" on Simon and Garfunkel's 1966 album *Sounds of Silence.* Compare the depiction of Richard Cory in the song with that in Robinson's poem. Which do you prefer? Why? Then create your own musical version of "Miniver Cheevy," composing original lyrics and music or setting the words of the poem to the tune of a familiar song that captures the poem's mood.
~ **MUSIC**

## Edwin Arlington Robinson
### 1869–1935

**Other Works**
*Tristram; Merlins; The Selected Poems of Edwin Arlington Robinson*

**New England Poet** A descendant of Anne Bradstreet, New England's first colonial poet, Edwin Arlington Robinson grew up in the river town of Gardiner, Maine. He began writing poetry when he was 11 and had already started to publish poems and translations before he entered Harvard in 1891. In 1893, after the death of his father, he returned to Gardiner, where he worked as a freelance writer, farmed, and worked on poems. His first collection, *The Torrent and The Night Before,* was privately printed in 1896. Although Robinson had intended the book to be a surprise for his mother, she died a week before the book was published.

**Life of Poverty** Following his mother's death, Robinson later moved to Greenwich Village in New York City, where he worked at a variety of menial jobs. Although living in poverty and obscurity, Robinson nevertheless continued to pursue his literary ambitions.

**President's Praise** Fortunately, Robinson's second volume of poems, the self-published *The Children of the Night,* came to the attention of President Theodore Roosevelt, who admired the book so much that he lent the struggling poet a hand by offering him a position as a clerk in the New York Customs House. Robinson gratefully accepted, working there from 1905 until 1909, when he was finally able to begin writing full time.

**Recognition and Rewards** Concentrating on his craft, Robinson slowly began to earn a living as a writer. His financial worries were eased by a small inheritance and a trust fund set up by an anonymous group of friends. As he became more able to devote himself to his poetry, Robinson gained a reputation as one of the country's most accomplished narrative poets. He was ultimately rewarded with a popular following and Pulitzer Prizes for *Collected Poems* (1921), *The Man Who Died Twice* (1924), and the best-selling *Tristram* (1927).

## Author Activity

Locate other Tilbury Town poems in a volume of Robinson's work or in a poetry anthology. Working with a small group, create an illustrated booklet of his poems. Group members should select about six poems and add accompanying illustrations, such as portraits of characters or a map of Maine.

---

## Teaching Options

**Mini Lesson** ## Grammar

### NOUN CLAUSE

**Instruction** A noun clause is a subordinate clause that is used as a noun in a sentence—as a subject, a direct object, an indirect object, a predicate nominative, or the object of a preposition. Write the following sentence on the chalkboard.

> <u>What she said</u> shocked me.

Underline the noun clause and have students determine that it functions as the subject.

**Exercises** In each sentence, have students underline the noun clause and identify its function in the sentence.

1. Robinson writes about <u>how appearances can</u> <u>be deceiving.</u> *(object of preposition)*

2. <u>Why Richard Cory is unhappy</u> is not told to the reader. *(subject)*

3. Miniver Cheevy knew <u>why the past was better</u>. *(direct object)*

4. The townspeople give <u>whoever is rich</u> a silent ovation. *(indirect object)*

 Use **Grammar Transparencies and Copymasters,** p. 102.

 Use McDougal Littell's *Language Network,* Chapter 3, for more instruction in noun clauses.

# PREPARING to *Read*

*"I know why the caged bird sings!"*

# We Wear the Mask
# Sympathy

*Poetry by* PAUL LAURENCE DUNBAR

**Connect to Your Life**

**Social Barriers** What social barriers sometimes keep people from becoming or showing who they really are? What happens to individuals who are prevented from realizing their potential? Discuss these questions with classmates.

## Build Background

**Turn-of-the-Century Race Relations** "We Wear the Mask" and "Sympathy" reflect the climate of racial prejudice that existed during Paul Laurence Dunbar's time. At the turn of the 19th century, African Americans faced legal discrimination, such as voting restrictions and segregation in schools and transportation. African Americans were also compelled to follow informal rules and customs, called racial etiquette, that reinforced their status as second-class citizens. For example, most white people never shook hands with African Americans, a gesture that would imply equality.

In "We Wear the Mask," the speaker reveals the pain that racial stereotyping caused African Americans. This poem was composed in the 1890s when a popular form of entertainment was the minstrel show, in which white men with blackened faces performed comedy and variety acts. In an exaggerated mimicry of African-American speech and behavior, blackface minstrels danced and sang sentimental songs while playing banjos, violins, and tambourines.

In "Sympathy," also composed in the 1890s, the speaker's attention is on a caged bird. The situation is perhaps reminiscent of Dunbar's own experiences of operating an elevator cage, the only job he could find after graduating high school. He was denied positions in business and journalism because of his race.

## Focus Your Reading

**LITERARY ANALYSIS** **SYMBOL** A **symbol** is a person, place, or object that has a concrete meaning in itself and also stands for something beyond itself, such as an idea or feeling. For example, a dove is not only a kind of bird but also a symbol of peace. Look for the central symbol in "We Wear the Mask" and "Sympathy." Note recurring descriptions of a person, place, or object that seems to have broader meanings within the context of the poem.

**ACTIVE READING** **INTERPRETING SYMBOLS** Interpreting symbols involves discovering what they might represent. On your second reading of "We Wear the Mask" and "Sympathy," follow these strategies to help you figure out the symbolic meanings in the poems:

- Identify a possible symbol.
- Consider the qualities of the symbolic object.
- Note the ideas or feelings the poet associates with the symbol.
- Consider the associations the symbol seems to trigger in you.
- Make a guess about what the symbol might represent.

**READER'S NOTEBOOK** To help you organize your thoughts about symbols as you reread the poems, create a chart like the one shown and fill it in.

| | Object | Qualities | Symbol of . . . |
|---|---|---|---|
| "We Wear the Mask" | | | |
| "Sympathy" | | | |

WE WEAR THE MASK / SYMPATHY **835**

# OVERVIEW

 This selection is included in the **Grade 11 InterActive Reader.**

**Objectives**

1. understand and appreciate two **poems (Literary Analysis)**
2. identify and examine **symbol** in poetry **(Literary Analysis)**
3. **interpret symbols** in poetry **(Active Reading)**

**Summary**

"We Wear the Mask" expresses the pain African Americans felt at the turn of the nineteenth century. African Americans were treated as secondary citizens, and they hid their true feelings of pain and sorrow behind a "happy" face that they showed to white people. "Sympathy" is another poem that powerfully expresses the feelings of an African American during this time. In this poem, the speaker likens himself to a caged bird who yearns to be free. The speaker feels all that a caged bird must—trapped, wounded, and desperate.

**Thematic Link**

"We Wear the Mask" and "Sympathy" both demonstrate that **the American dream** is not a **reality** for all Americans. People who can achieve the dream may have the **illusion** that it is open to everyone, but those whose dreams are caged like a bird have a different perspective.

## 5-Minute Warm-Up

*Daily Language SkillBuilder*

Have students **proofread** the display sentences on page 739j and write them correctly. The sentences also appear on Transparency 23 of **Grammar Transparencies and Copymasters.**

## LESSON RESOURCES

**UNIT FIVE RESOURCE BOOK,** pp. 32–33

**ASSESSMENT RESOURCES**
**Formal Assessment,** pp. 155–156
**Teacher's Guide to Assessment and Portfolio Use**
**Test Generator**

**SKILLS TRANSPARENCIES AND COPYMASTERS**
**Literary Analysis**
- Tone, T19 (for Review, p. 838)

**Grammar**
- Appositive Clauses, C105 (for Mini Lesson, p. 839)

**Vocabulary**
- The Connotative Power of Words, C70 (for Mini Lesson, p. 837)

**Writing**
- Elaboration, T10 (for Writing Option 1, p. 839)

**INTEGRATED TECHNOLOGY**

**Audio Library**
**Visit our website:**
www.mcdougallittell.com

## TEACHING THE LITERATURE

**Literary Analysis** [SYMBOL]

Have students identify the major symbol in each poem.

**Answers:** The symbol in "We Wear the Mask" is the mask. In "Sympathy," the symbol is the caged bird.

 Use **Unit Five Resource Book,** p. 33 for additional support.

**Active Reading**

[INTERPRETING SYMBOLS]

Ask students to interpret what the mask and the caged bird represent. Have students refer to specific lines that support their interpretation.

**Possible Response:** In "We Wear the Mask," the mask represents hiding one's true feelings to maintain one's dignity while suffering internally ("hides our cheeks"; "bleeding hearts"). The mask could represent the role all African Americans felt pressured by white society to fulfill ("why should the world be overwise") during the time of segregation. In "Sympathy," the caged bird represents an African American. The caged bird just wants to be free ("fain would be on the bough a-swing"), and it hurts itself trying to get out of the cage ("beats his wing"). African Americans may have felt like caged birds during segregation.

 Use **Unit Five Resource Book,** p. 32 for additional support.

---

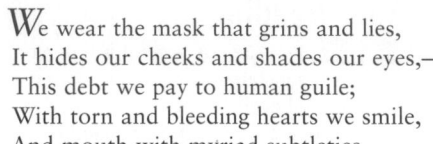

# WE WEAR THE MASK

### Paul Laurence Dunbar

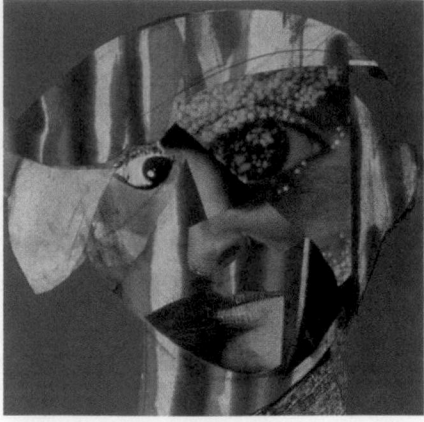

Detail of *Three Folk Musicians* (1967), Romare Bearden. Collage on canvas on board, 50″ × 60″. Copyright © Romare Bearden/VAGA, New York.

We wear the mask that grins and lies,
It hides our cheeks and shades our eyes,—
This debt we pay to human guile;
With torn and bleeding hearts we smile,
5   And mouth with myriad subtleties.

Why should the world be overwise,
In counting all our tears and sighs?
Nay, let them only see us, while
    We wear the mask.

10  We smile, but, O great Christ, our cries
To Thee from tortured souls arise.
We sing, but oh, the clay is vile
Beneath our feet, and long the mile;
But let the world dream otherwise,
15      We wear the mask.

**3 guile:** slyness and craftiness in dealing with others.

**5 myriad subtleties:** countless artful statements.

**12 vile:** disgusting or objectionable.

### Thinking Through the Literature

1. **Comprehension Check** Who is the speaker of the poem?
2. [ACTIVE READING] [INTERPRETING SYMBOLS]
   Review the chart you made in your  **READER'S NOTEBOOK.** In your own words, explain what wearing a mask represents in the poem.

   [THINK ABOUT] { • the description of wearing the mask as a "debt we pay to human guile"
   • who is wearing the mask and why
   • the feelings that the mask hides
3. Is "We Wear the Mask" relevant to people other than African Americans? Why or why not?

---

## Thinking Through the Literature

**1.** An African American
**2.** Possible Response: Wearing the mask means hiding one's feelings and pride and shielding oneself at the cost of continuing internal suffering; the speaker deceives himself as well as the whites—by pretending to be happy, the speaker is also denying his or her own pain.
**3.** Responses will vary. Some students may state that most people hide their real feelings to some extent.

# Sympathy

**Paul Laurence Dunbar**

I know what the caged bird feels, alas!
    When the sun is bright on the upland slopes;
When the wind stirs soft through the springing grass,
And the river flows like a stream of glass;
5      When the first bird sings and the first bud opes,
And the faint perfume from its chalice steals—
I know what the caged bird feels!

I know why the caged bird beats his wing
    Till its blood is red on the cruel bars;
10  For he must fly back to his perch and cling
When he fain would be on the bough a-swing;
    And a pain still throbs in the old, old scars
And they pulse again with a keener sting—
I know why he beats his wing!

15  I know why the caged bird sings, ah me,
    When his wing is bruised and his bosom sore,—
When he beats his bars and he would be free;
It is not a carol of joy or glee,
    But a prayer that he sends from his heart's deep core,
20  But a plea, that upward to Heaven he flings—
I know why the caged bird sings!

## Customizing Instruction

### Less Proficient Readers
Remind students that at the turn of the 19th century, segregation was rampant, and African Americans did not enjoy the basic rights and privileges that white people did.

**Set a Purpose** Have students read both poems to find evidence of how African Americans felt during this time of inequality.

### Students Acquiring English
- Point out that simple sentences in English usually follow the subject-verb-object structure, but in line 3 of "We Wear the Mask," the object ("this debt") precedes the verb ("pay").
- Help students understand difficult vocabulary in "Sympathy."
  Line 5: *opes* means "opens"
  Line 6: *chalice* means "a drinking cup or goblet" and refers figuratively to a budding flower
  Line 11: *fain* means "gladly" and *bough* means "limb of a tree"

 Use **Spanish Study Guide** for additional support, pp. 203–205.

### Gifted and Talented
Have students write a poem that reflects the theme of appearance versus reality in their own lives. Or, have them write a poem in which they compare themselves to an animal or object that they feel best describes them in their current situation.

##  Mini Lesson Vocabulary Strategy

**INTERPRET CONNOTATIVE POWER OF WORDS**
**Instruction** Connotation is the associated attitudes or emotions that a word evokes. In the poem "We Wear the Mask," the word grins connotes more than its literal meaning (denotation). In the context of this poem, grins means more than a broad smile. It connotes a forced, fake smile through clenched teeth.

**Application** Have students rely on the context of the poem to interpret the connotative power of words. Have them work in pairs to first determine the literal meanings and then the connotations that the following words evoke: *mask, throbs, pulse, keener, and core.* Ask students to use the words in sentences, emphasizing the connotations of the words.

 Use **Vocabulary Transparencies and Copymasters,** p. 70.

**A lesson on connotation appears on p. 908 in the Pupil's Edition.**

## GUIDING STUDENT RESPONSE

## Connect to the Literature

**1. What Do You Think?**
Responses will vary. Most students will empathize with the caged bird that longs to be free.

**Comprehension Check**
• springtime in nature
• on the bough of a tree
• a prayer or plea to be released

## Think Critically

2. Possible Response: The speaker longs to be free from the bars of segregation and prejudice that hold his people back.

3. Possible Response: The speaker sympathizes with the plight of the caged bird because he, too, is unable to be free in American society.

4. Students should describe how this structure influences their under-standing of the poem. The first stanza illustrates the blissful outdoors where the bird naturally belongs; the second stanza describes the bird's harsh imprisonment and struggle to be free; the final stanza explains that the bird's song is a plea to be released to his natural state, not a song of joy as humans might interpret it. The repetition in the first and last line of each stanza connects the speaker metaphorically to the plight of the caged bird.

5. Students should use specific lines from the text as well as interpretations of the poem to support their answer.

## Literary Analysis

**Symbol** To get students started, have them brainstorm as a group words that symbolize imprisonment or conceal-ment.

**Tone** To help students with this activity, have one or more volunteers read each poem aloud to get a sense of the tone. As a group, have students choose words that struck them as they lis-tened, then have students describe what tone these words suggest.

## Connect to the Literature

**1. What Do You Think?**
What was your reaction to the bird's plight?

**Comprehension Check**
• What is the season and the scene described in the first stanza of the poem?
• Where would the caged bird rather be perched?
• What kind of song does the caged bird finally sing?

## Think Critically

2. What do you think the poem reveals about the speaker's inner longings?

3. What do you think is the significance of the title?

4. How would you explain the progression of ideas in the poem?

 **THINK ABOUT**
• the situation described in each stanza
• what central ideas the speaker builds on
• the first and last line of each stanza

5. **ACTIVE READING** **INTERPRETING SYMBOLS** Refer to your the chart you made in your **READER'S NOTEBOOK**. What do you think the caged bird symbolizes? Support your interpretation with evidence.

## Extend Interpretations

6. **Comparing Texts** How did the historical information presented in the Build Background section on page 835 influence your interpretation of both "We Wear the Mask" and "Sympathy"? In what ways do these poems reflect turn-of-the-century race relations in the United States?

7. **Different Perspectives** In 1895, Booker T. Washington, one of the most prominent African-American leaders of his day, remarked, "No race can prosper till it learns that there is as much dignity in tilling a field as in writing a poem. It is at the bottom of life we must begin, and not at the top." Do you think the speaker in "Sympathy" would agree with this statement? Why or why not?

8. **Writer's Style** "Sympathy" is a **lyric poem,** or short poem in which a single speaker expresses thoughts and feelings in intensely emotional language. Which descriptive details from the poem did you find the most deeply moving? Why?

9. **Connect to Life** What oppressed groups around the world might identify with the bird's plight in "Sympathy"?

## Literary Analysis

**SYMBOL** A **symbol** is a person, place, or object that represents something beyond itself. Symbols in literature generally have several possible interpretations, rather than one precise meaning, and often communicate complex, abstract ideas. For example, a symbolic mask is more meaningful than an ordinary mask; a symbolic bird is more meaningful than an ordinary bird. Clues to the meaning of a particular symbol are usually found within the work itself.

**Activity** Think of other symbols besides the mask and the caged bird that could represent a similar idea in these poems. For example, Dunbar might have described camouflage, rather than a mask, or a prisoner, rather than a caged bird. Share your symbols with the class and then discuss whether any of them would work as well as the ones Dunbar used in his poems.

**REVIEW** **TONE** Describe the **tone** of these poems—the attitude expressed toward the subject. Point out words that suggest the tone you describe. How similar are the poems in tone?

## Extend Interpretations

**Comparing Texts** Possible Response: Students should interpret the possible influences of the his-torical context on these literary selections. The his-torical information provides context, or a lens through which to view the poems. Both poems offer an inside glimpse of what it was like to be an African American trying to live with discrimina-tion, prejudice, and segregation.

**Different Perspectives** Possible Response: No, the speaker in "Sympathy" wants to be free to soar, to express his thoughts and live his life without cruel restrictions based on race.

**Writer's Style** Responses will vary. Some students may mention the detail about the bird's blood on the bars of the cage.
**Connect to Life** Responses will vary. Students may mention victims of poverty, persecution, or totali-tarian regimes.

# Choices & CHALLENGES

## Writing Options

**1. Narrative Sequel** Imagine that the bird in "Sympathy" is released from its cage. Write a narrative sequel to the poem titled "I Know What the Freed Bird Feels," describing the bird's emotions after its long captivity. You might want to connect the bird's liberation to the freedoms gained by African Americans after the civil rights movement.

**Writing Handbook**
See page 1279: Narrative Writing

**2. Lyrics of a Songbird** Write the lyrics to the plea that the bird sings in the final stanza of the poem. Share your lyrics with classmates.

## Activities & Explorations

**1. Personal Mask** Create your own mask, designing it to reflect the role that you think society, your friends, or your family

expects you to play. Display your mask in the classroom. ~ **ART**

**2. Political Cartoon** Draw a political cartoon that illustrates Dunbar's view of racism as reflected in "We Wear the Mask" or "Sympathy." Consider using phrases from the poem as captions and labels. Study cartoons from newspaper editorial pages as models.
~ **VIEWING AND REPRESENTING**

---

## Paul Laurence Dunbar
### 1872–1906

**Other Works**
*Lyrics of Lowly Life*
*Poems of Cabin and Field*
*Lyrics of Sunshine and Shadow*

**Literary Beginnings** The son of former slaves, Paul Laurence Dunbar was born in Dayton, Ohio, and began to write when he was 12 years old. While in high school, he became editor of the school newspaper and contributed to a newspaper published by one of the Wright brothers, who later invented the airplane. Considered the class poet, he also published his first poems in the *Dayton Herald*.

**Budding Career** After high school, Dunbar took a job as an elevator operator, the only work he could find. His literary career was launched when a former teacher asked him to read a poem before a writers' convention. Dunbar published his first volume of poetry, *Oak and Ivy*, in 1893. The publication of his second volume, *Majors and Minors*, in 1896 attracted the attention of the noted writer William Dean Howells, whose favorable review helped establish Dunbar's career.

**Bittersweet Success** Despite earning critical acclaim, Dunbar felt disappointed that his serious

lyric poems were not as popular as his African-American dialect poems. He told a friend, "I didn't start with dialect, but dialect is what [white] people want. They won't let me do anything else, no matter how much I try. I've got to write dialect if I want them to listen."

**Failing Health** While his popularity continued to grow, Dunbar's health began to deteriorate. Following several bouts of pneumonia, Dunbar died from tuberculosis at the age of 33. By the time of his death, he had written four novels, four collections of short stories, more than ten volumes of poetry, and several musicals. He unfortunately did not live to see his lyric poems, such as "We Wear the Mask" and "Sympathy," win lasting respect.

## Author Activity

**The Music of Poetry** Excerpts from the following poems by Dunbar—"Twell de Night Is Pas'," "When I Gits Home," "An Antebellum Sermon," and "Ode to Ethiopia"—were used as the prologues to *Afro-American Symphony* by composer William Grant Still. Read these four poems, and then listen to a sound recording of Still's symphony, available at many libraries. How does the music capture the spirit of the poems?

WE WEAR THE MASK / SYMPATHY   **839**

---

## Writing Options

**1. Narrative Sequel** Students' narratives should reflect an understanding of the differences in situation between African Americans today and African Americans of Dunbar's time. **To get students started on this activity,** discuss the civil rights movement and make a list of the gains that African Americans have made in the last 100 years. Discuss emotions aside from happiness that a freed "bird" might feel, such as fear and doubt.

**2. Lyrics of a Songbird** Students' lyrics should demonstrate a desperate, longing tone.

## Activities & Explorations

**1. Personal Mask** Students' masks will vary. **To make this assignment easier,** have students first discuss whether all people wear masks of one form or another. They may feel that they wear different masks for their friends than they do for their family. Ask students to create one of the masks they wear, and have volunteers explain their masks to the class.

**2. Political Cartoon** Cartoons will vary. Point out that students' cartoons may be serious, satiric, or funny—all valid techniques to get their point across to the reader. Encourage students to explain why they chose the technique they did.

---

 **Grammar**

### APPOSITIVE CLAUSES

**Instruction** An appositive clause is a noun clause that identifies or explains a noun or pronoun. Write the following sentence on the chalkboard:

The runner's goal that he will win the state championship would almost certainly be accomplished.

Have students identify the appositive clause and understand that it explains the noun goal.

**Exercises** In each sentence, have students identify the appositive clause.

1. Dunbar's dream that his lyric poems would become as popular as his dialect poems came true after his death.

2. Dunbar's idea that his soul was like a caged bird inspired the title of Maya Angelou's autobiography.

3. Do you get the impression that Dunbar saw a bird in a cage and felt inspired to write about it?

   Use **Grammar Transparencies and Copymasters,** p. 105.

 Use McDougal Littell's *Language Network,* Chapter 3, for more instruction in appositive clauses.

### Objectives

1. understand and appreciate a **short story** (Literary Analysis)
2. analyze **characters** (Literary Analysis)
3. evaluate character (Active Reading)

### Summary

In Minnesota young Dexter Green quits his job as a caddy when asked to carry the clubs of a spoiled 11-year-old girl. His dreams of wealth and an upper-class lifestyle lead him first to an Ivy League university and then to financial success. At a country club one summer evening, Dexter meets and becomes infatuated with Judy Jones, the girl who'd caused him to quit his job many years before. They begin a romantic relationship, but Judy treats Dexter badly, frequently leaving him to date other men. After Dexter becomes engaged to another woman, Judy rekindles their relationship, but she soon abandons him once again. Years later, Dexter learns that an unhappily married Judy has lost her good looks. He realizes that something within himself has been lost.

### Thematic Link

Fitzgerald's work reflects the **changing face of America** in the 1920s. His characters pursue the **American dream** of wealth and social status.

---

### 5-Minute Warm-Up

***Daily Language SkillBuilder***

Have students **proofread** the display sentences on page 739k and write them correctly. The sentences also appear on Transparency 23 of **Grammar Transparencies and Copymasters.**

---

# PREPARING to *Read*

# Winter Dreams

*Short Story by* F. SCOTT FITZGERALD

### Connect to Your Life

**Dream Keepers** This story involves a young man from a small Midwestern town who pursues his dreams. What are your own aspirations? List some of them as labels on a bar graph like the one shown. Then draw bars to indicate, on a rising scale of 0 to 10, the importance you attach to achieving each aspiration.

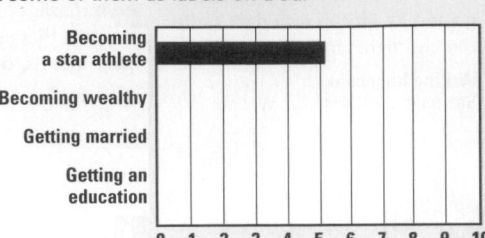

## Build Background

**Reckless Youth** F. Scott Fitzgerald coined the term *Jazz Age* to convey the glitter and glamour of the 1920s, when many Americans threw themselves into the pursuit of fun, excitement, money, and social status. Fitzgerald and his wife, Zelda, themselves enjoyed the high life, moving among fashionable hotels and resorts in the United States and Europe, giving and attending lavish parties, and engaging in reckless stunts, such as riding on the hoods of taxicabs and jumping into fountains. First published in 1922, "Winter Dreams" provides a glimpse of the wealthy in the United States around the time of World War I. The Minnesota setting is drawn from Fitzgerald's adolescence and early adulthood among the country-club set of St. Paul.

> **WORDS TO KNOW Vocabulary Preview**
>
> | | | |
> |---|---|---|
> | blatantly | malicious | precarious |
> | grimace | petulance | sully |
> | incorrigible | poignant | surfeit |
> | ingenuous | | |

## Focus Your Reading

**LITERARY ANALYSIS** **CHARACTERS** **Characters** are the people—and sometimes animals or creatures—who take part in the action of a story or a novel. **Static** characters remain unchanged by their experiences as the story progresses, while **dynamic** characters change. As the plot of "Winter Dreams" unfolds, note whether or not the two main characters—Dexter Green and Judy Jones—mature and develop as individuals.

**ACTIVE READING** **EVALUATING CHARACTER** The characters introduced in the first section of this story are people you will have to **evaluate,** or make judgments about, as the plot unfolds. When the story begins, Dexter Green is a teenager and Judy Jones is an 11-year-old girl. As you read, decide what you like and what you dislike about them. Also, try to figure out why they act as they do. Pay particular attention to the dreams Dexter Green has for his life, forming your own opinions about his aspirations.

**READER'S NOTEBOOK** To help you evaluate the characters, use the reading-strategy questions inserted throughout the selection. Write your responses in your notebook.

## LESSON RESOURCES

**UNIT FIVE RESOURCE BOOK,** pp. 34–38

**ASSESSMENT RESOURCES**
**Formal Assessment,** pp. 157–158
**Teacher's Guide to Assessment and Portfolio Use**
**Test Generator**

**SKILLS TRANSPARENCIES AND COPYMASTERS**
**Literary Analysis**
• Characterization, T6 (for Paired Activity, p. 860)

**Reading and Critical Thinking**
• Evaluation Matrix, T55 (for Active Reading, p. 840)

**Grammar**
• Noun Clauses II, C103 (for Mini Lesson, p. 862)
• Semicolons, C158 (for Mini Lesson, p. 846)

**Vocabulary**
• Meanings of Roots, C71 (for Mini Lesson, p. 857)

**INTEGRATED TECHNOLOGY**

**Audio Library**
**LaserLinks**
• Author Background: F. Scott Fitzgerald
• Art Gallery: Art Deco. See **Teacher's SourceBook,** pp. 70–72.
**Visit our website:**
www.mcdougallittell.com

# F. SCOTT FITZGERALD

## Winter Dreams

Some of the caddies were poor as sin and lived in one-room houses with a neurasthenic[1] cow in the front yard, but Dexter Green's father owned the second best grocery-store in Black Bear—the best one was "The Hub," patronized by the wealthy people from Sherry Island—and Dexter caddied only for pocket-money.

In the fall when the days became crisp and gray, and the long Minnesota winter shut down like the white lid of a box, Dexter's skis moved over the snow that hid the fairways of the golf course. At these times the country gave him a feeling of profound melancholy—it offended him that the links should lie in enforced fallowness,[2] haunted by ragged sparrows for the long season. It was dreary, too, that on the tees where the gay colors fluttered in summer there were now only the desolate sand-boxes knee-deep in crusted ice. When he crossed the hills the wind blew cold as misery, and if the sun was out he tramped with his eyes squinted up against the hard dimensionless glare.

In April the winter ceased abruptly. The snow ran down into Black Bear Lake scarcely tarrying for the early golfers to brave the season with red and black balls. Without elation, without an interval of moist glory, the cold was gone.

Dexter knew that there was something dismal about this Northern spring, just as he knew there was something gorgeous about the fall. Fall made him clinch his hands and tremble and repeat idiotic sentences to himself, and make brisk abrupt gestures of command to imaginary audiences and armies. October filled him with hope which November raised to a sort of ecstatic triumph, and in this mood the fleeting brilliant impressions of the summer at Sherry Island were ready grist to his mill.[3] He became a golf champion and defeated Mr. T. A. Hedrick in a marvelous match played a hundred times over the fairways of his imagination, a match each detail of which he changed about untiringly—

---

1. **neurasthenic** (nŏŏr´əs-thĕn´ĭk): weak and lacking in vigor.
2. **fallowness:** disuse.
3. **grist to his mill:** something that he could make good use of.

### Reading Skills and Strategies: PREVIEW

Tell students that this story is about the relationship between the main character and the girl of his dreams. As students read, they should consider what the girl represents to him.

### Literary Analysis  CHARACTERS

Explain that **static** characters remain unchanged by their experiences as the story progresses, while **dynamic** characters change. As students read the first section of "Winter Dreams," have them consider their first impressions of Dexter Green and Judy Jones.

 Use **Unit Five Resource Book**, p. 36 for additional support.

### Active Reading

**EVALUATING CHARACTER**

**A** Point out that Dexter seems quite impressed with the wealthy Mr. Mortimer Jones. Ask students to decide whether they agree with young Dexter's evaluation.

**Possible Response:** No, Mr. Jones seems to be a rather coarse individual, as his speech reveals, and one suspects that he imbibes more frequently than he should.

 Use **Unit Five Resource Book**, p. 35 for additional support.

**ACTIVE READING**

**B CLARIFY** Judy's imperious nature makes Dexter feel inferior, and he doesn't want to feel socially inferior to someone he's attracted to.

Illustration Copyright © 1995 Bart Forbes.

**S**ometimes he won

with almost

laughable ease,

sometimes he came

up magnificently

from behind.

sometimes he won with almost laughable ease, sometimes he came up magnificently from behind. Again, stepping from a Pierce-Arrow[4] automobile, like Mr. Mortimer Jones, he strolled frigidly into the lounge of the Sherry Island Golf Club—or perhaps, surrounded by an admiring crowd, he gave an exhibition of fancy diving from the spring-board of the club raft. . . . Among those who watched him in open-mouthed wonder was Mr. Mortimer Jones.

And one day it came to pass that Mr. Jones—himself and not his ghost—came up to Dexter with tears in his eyes and said that Dexter was the — — best caddy in the club, and wouldn't he decide not to quit if Mr. Jones made it worth his while, because every other — — caddy in the club lost one ball a hole for him— regularly—

"No, sir," said Dexter decisively, "I don't want to caddy any more." Then, after a pause, "I'm too old."

"You're not more than fourteen. Why the devil did you decide just this morning that you wanted to quit? You promised that next week you'd go over to the State tournament with me."

"I decided I was too old."

Dexter handed in his "A Class" badge, collected what money was due him from the caddy-master, and walked home to Black Bear Village.

"The best — — caddy I ever saw," shouted Mr. Mortimer Jones over a drink that afternoon. "Never lost a ball! Willing! Intelligent! Quiet! Honest! Grateful!"

---

4. **Pierce-Arrow:** a luxury automobile of the day.

**842**    UNIT FIVE    PART 2: THE AMERICAN DREAM

---

###  **Mini Lesson** Preteaching Vocabulary

**USING CONTEXT CLUES**

**Instruction** Call students' attention to the list of WORDS TO KNOW. Remind them that they can often figure out the meaning of an unfamiliar word by examining the context in which the word appears. Use the model sentence to demonstrate this strategy.

**Model Sentence**
Unable to hide her emotions, Judy smiled <u>blatantly.</u>

**Activity**
• Write the model sentence on the chalkboard.
• Ask a volunteer to summarize the meaning of the sentence.
• Have students use the meaning of the sentence to infer meanings for the word *blatantly*.
• Ask volunteers to use *blatantly* in sentences.

**Practice** Have students apply the strategy to determine the meanings of underlined words in the following sentences.

1. Wracked with pain, the golfer contorted his face into an ugly <u>grimace</u>.

The little girl who had done this was eleven—beautifully ugly as little girls are apt to be who are destined after a few years to be inexpressibly lovely and bring no end of misery to a great number of men. The spark, however, was perceptible. There was a general ungodliness in the way her lips twisted down at the corners when she smiled, and in the—Heaven help us!—in the almost passionate quality of her eyes. Vitality is born early in such women. It was utterly in evidence now, shining through her thin frame in a sort of glow.

**B**

**ACTIVE READING**

**CLARIFY** How does the little girl make Dexter quit?

**2** She had come eagerly out onto the course at nine o'clock with a white linen nurse and five small new golf-clubs in a white canvas bag which the nurse was carrying. When Dexter first saw her she was standing by the caddy house, rather ill at ease and trying to conceal the fact by engaging her nurse in an obviously unnatural conversation graced by startling and irrelevant grimaces from herself.

"Well, it's certainly a nice day, Hilda," Dexter heard her say. She drew down the corners of her mouth, smiled, and glanced furtively around, her eyes in transit falling for an instant on Dexter.

Then to the nurse:

"Well, I guess there aren't very many people out here this morning, are there?"

The smile again—radiant, blatantly artificial—convincing.

"I don't know what we're supposed to do now," said the nurse, looking nowhere in particular.

"Oh, that's all right. I'll fix it up."

Dexter stood perfectly still, his mouth slightly ajar. He knew that if he moved forward a step his stare would be in her line of vision—if he moved backward he would lose his full view of her face. For a moment he had not realized how young she was. Now he remembered having seen her several times the year before—in bloomers.[5]

Suddenly, involuntarily, he laughed, a short abrupt laugh—then, startled by himself, he turned and began to walk quickly away.

"Boy!"

Dexter stopped.

"Boy—"

Beyond question he was addressed. Not only that, but he was treated to that absurd smile, that preposterous smile—the memory of which at least a dozen men were to carry into middle age.

"Boy, do you know where the golf teacher is?"

"He's giving a lesson."

"Well, do you know where the caddy-master is?"

"He isn't here yet this morning."

"Oh." For a moment this baffled her. She stood alternately on her right and left foot.

"We'd like to get a caddy," said the nurse. "Mrs. Mortimer Jones sent us out to play golf, and we don't know how without we get a caddy."

Here she was stopped by an ominous glance from Miss Jones, followed immediately by the smile.

"There aren't any caddies here except me," said Dexter to the nurse, "and I got to stay here in charge until the caddy-master gets here."

"Oh."

Miss Jones and her retinue[6] now withdrew, and at a proper distance from Dexter became involved in a heated conversation, which was concluded by Miss Jones taking one of the clubs and hitting it on the ground with violence. For further emphasis she raised it again and was about to bring it down smartly upon the nurse's bosom, when the nurse seized the club and twisted it from her hands.

**3**

---

5. **bloomers:** baggy pants that end just below the knee, formerly worn by young girls.

6. **retinue** (rĕt'n-ōō'): a group of attendants or followers; entourage.

---

WORDS TO KNOW

**grimace** (grĭm'ĭs) *n.* a twisting or distortion of the face
**blatantly** (blāt'nt-lē) *adv.* in an extremely obvious way; conspicuously

**843**

## Customizing Instruction

### Less Proficient Readers

**1** Ask students to describe Dexter's aspirations, based on the content of his daydreams.

**Possible Responses:** He yearns for acceptance as a member of the upper class. He aspires to become a champion golfer or diver because he wants the country club members to admire him.

### Students Acquiring English

**2** Point out that the phrase "white linen nurse" refers to the attire of the girl's caretaker. Explain that wealthy families often employed nurses (or nursemaids or nannies) to care for their children. The presence here of a nurse is a sign of the girl's youth, not of her poor health.

### Multiple Learning Styles
**Interpersonal Learners**

**3** Ask students to discuss how Dexter must feel when the girl calls him "boy."

**Possible Response:** He might feel embarrassed, humiliated, or insulted. The girl's remark probably precipitated his decision to quit his job.

2. Dexter had hoped Judy's behavior would change, but she remained set in her ways and proved to be <u>incorrigible</u>.

3. Although she was fully aware of the problems her carelessness had caused, Judy managed to appear <u>ingenuous</u>.

4. There was nothing <u>malicious</u> in her motivations; she had no idea of the pain her actions had caused.

5. Nothing Dexter could do pleased her. She snapped with <u>petulance</u> at his every attempt at conversation.

6. The third act of the play, which was particularly <u>poignant</u>, moved the audience to tears.

7. The climber stood on a narrow ledge midway up the cliff's rocky face. He maintained this <u>precarious</u> balance while planning his next step.

8. The golf course lay under a pure white blanket of new-fallen snow, which was <u>sullied</u> only by the tracks of Dexter's skis.

9. Because of his excellent qualifications, he received a <u>surfeit</u> of offers for employment.

 Use **Unit Five Resource Book,** p. 37 for additional support.

**A lesson on context clues appears on p. 326 in the Pupil's Edition.**

### Active Reading

**EVALUATING CHARACTER**

**A** Ask students to decide what Judy's behavior reveals about her character. Then have them decide if they agree with Dexter's response to her attempt to beat the nurse.

**Possible Responses:** She's spoiled, childish, irrational, bold, violent. Though strongly attracted to the girl, Dexter has no reason to condone such behavior.

### Literary Analysis: NARRATION

Explain that Fitzgerald's narrator adopts a **third-person limited** point of view. The narrator has complete access to Dexter's thoughts and feelings but not to those of any other character.

**ACTIVE READING**

**B** **CLARIFY** **Possible Responses:** Dexter quits in order to rebel against the girl's arrogance; to escape his conflicting emotions—anger, humiliation, and desire; to maintain his pride and dignity; to uphold his self-image as defined by his daydreams.

---

**(A)** "You damn little mean old *thing!*" cried Miss Jones wildly.

Another argument ensued. Realizing that the elements of comedy were implied in the scene, Dexter several times began to laugh, but each time restrained the laugh before it reached audibility. He could not resist the monstrous conviction that the little girl was justified in beating the nurse.

The situation was resolved by the fortuitous appearance of the caddy-master, who was appealed to immediately by the nurse.

"Miss Jones is to have a little caddy, and this one says he can't go."

"Mr. McKenna said I was to wait here till you came," said Dexter quickly.

"Well, he's here now." Miss Jones smiled cheerfully at the caddy-master. Then she dropped her bag and set off at a haughty mince[7] toward the first tee.

"Well?" The caddy-master turned to Dexter. "What you standing there like a dummy for? Go pick up the young lady's clubs."

"I don't think I'll go out today," said Dexter.

"You don't—"

"I think I'll quit."

The enormity of his decision frightened him. He was a favorite caddy, and the thirty dollars a month he earned through the summer were not to be made elsewhere around the lake. But he had received a strong emotional shock, and his perturbation required a violent and immediate outlet.

**ACTIVE READING**

**B** **CLARIFY** Why does Dexter quit caddying?

It is not so simple as that, either. As so frequently would be the case in the future, Dexter was unconsciously dictated to by his winter dreams.

---

Now, of course, the quality and the seasonability of these winter dreams varied, but the stuff of them remained. They persuaded Dexter several years later to pass up a business course at the State university—his father, prospering now, would have paid his way—for the <u>precarious</u> advantage of attending an older and more famous university in the East, where he was bothered by his scanty funds. But do not get the impression, because his winter dreams happened to be concerned at first with musings on the rich, that there was anything merely snobbish in the boy. He wanted not association with glittering things and glittering people—he wanted the glittering things themselves. Often he reached out for the best without knowing why he wanted it—and sometimes he ran up against the mysterious denials and prohibitions in which life indulges. It is with one of those denials and not with his career as a whole that this story deals.

**1**

He made money. It was rather amazing. After college he went to the city from which Black Bear Lake draws its wealthy patrons. When he was only twenty-three and had been there not quite two years, there were already people who liked to say: "Now *there's* a boy—" All about him rich men's sons were peddling bonds precariously, or investing patrimonies[8] precariously, or plodding through the two dozen volumes of the "George Washington Commercial Course," but Dexter borrowed a thousand dollars on his college degree and his confident mouth, and bought a partnership in a laundry.

It was a small laundry when he went into it but Dexter made a specialty of learning how the

---

7. **mince:** an artificial, dainty way of walking with short steps.

8. **patrimonies:** estates or money inherited from ancestors.

---

WORDS
TO
KNOW    **precarious** (prĭ-kâr′ē-əs) *adj.* risky; uncertain

---

## Teaching Options

### BLOCK SCHEDULING: MANAGING TIME

**If your schedule requires that you cover the lesson objectives in a shorter time, use . . .**
- Preparing to Read, p. 840
- Thinking Through the Literature, p. 860
- Vocabulary in Action, p. 862

**If you want to take advantage of longer class time, use . . .**
- TE Teaching Options: Preteaching Vocabulary, pp. 842–43; Viewing and Representing, pp. 853, 859; Speaking and Listening, pp. 848, 854; Cross-Curricular Link, pp. 851, 855, 858; Informal Assessment, pp. 849, 856; Inquiry and Research, p. 861
- Choices & Challenges, pp. 861–62

Illustration by Todd Leonardo.

## Customizing Instruction

### Less Proficient Readers

Ask the following questions to make sure that students understand how Dexter pursues his dreams.

Why does Dexter choose to attend school in the East?
**Possible Response:** He wants the prestige that attending a famous university brings.

What does he sacrifice by attending that college?
**Possible Response:** He loses the money his father would have given him for the state university.

What does Dexter do after college?
**Possible Response:** He buys an interest in a laundry business.

Remind students that they're expected to adjust their purpose for reading to find out what happens when Dexter next meets Judy Jones.

### Students Acquiring English

**1** Explain that the idiomatic phrase *ran up against* means "came upon as an obstacle."

### Gifted and Talented

Point out that Dexter, like many Americans, seems to define social class in terms of money. Have students discuss their own attitudes toward class distinction and list other factors that might influence one's social status. As they read, ask them to consider whether social class is as important in their lives as it seems to be in Dexter's.

## Active Reading

**EVALUATING CHARACTER**

**A** Point out the young woman's reaction to hitting Mr. Hedrick with her golf ball ("I hit something."). Ask them to explain what this reaction suggests about her character.

**Possible Responses:** She's self-absorbed and self-centered; she's unconcerned with other people's well-being and their opinions of her.

**ACTIVE READING**

**B EVALUATE** **Possible Responses:** She's attractive, self-absorbed, conceited, thoughtless, careless, and insincere.

## Literary Analysis: FIGURATIVE LANGUAGE

**C** Remind students that they're expected to read to appreciate a writer's craft. Read this passage aloud to demonstrate Fitzgerald's skill in creating an image and a mood. Ask students to identify a metaphor and an example of personification.

**Possible Responses:** metaphor: waves described as "silver molasses"; personification: "moon held a finger to her lips."

## Literary Analysis | CHARACTERS

**D** Point out that five years before, when Dexter heard the same music, he was a spectator. Now that he is part of the life he aspired to, the music takes on new meaning. Have students describe in their own words Dexter's mood as he listens to the music.

**Possible Response:** When he hears the piano, he has a sense of ecstasy, excited expectation, and the serene satisfaction of having realized his dream.

---

English washed fine woolen golf-stockings without shrinking them, and within a year he was catering to the trade that wore knickerbockers.[9] Men were insisting that their Shetland hose and sweaters go to his laundry just as they had insisted on a caddy who could find golf-balls. A little later he was doing their wives' lingerie as well—and running five branches in different parts of the city. Before he was twenty-seven he owned the largest string of laundries in his section of the country. It was then that he sold out and went to New York. But the part of his story that concerns us goes back to the days when he was making his first big success.

When he was twenty-three Mr. Hart—one of the gray-haired men who liked to say "Now there's a boy"—gave him a guest card to the Sherry Island Golf Club for a weekend. So he signed his name one day on the register, and that afternoon played golf in a foursome with Mr. Hart and Mr. Sandwood and Mr. T. A. Hedrick. He did not consider it necessary to remark that **1** he had once carried Mr. Hart's bag over this same links, and that he knew every trap and gully with his eyes shut—but he found himself glancing at the four caddies who trailed them, trying to catch a gleam or gesture that would remind him of himself, that would lessen the gap which lay between his present and his past.

It was a curious day, slashed abruptly with fleeting, familiar impressions. One minute he had the sense of being a trespasser—in the next he was impressed by the tremendous superiority he felt toward Mr. T. A. Hedrick, who was a bore and not even a good golfer any more.

Then, because of a ball Mr. Hart lost near the fifteenth green, an enormous thing happened. **2** While they were searching the stiff grasses of the rough there was a clear call of "Fore!" from behind a hill in their rear. And as they all turned abruptly from their search a bright new ball sliced abruptly over the hill and caught Mr. T. A. Hedrick in the abdomen.

"By Gad!" cried Mr. T. A. Hedrick, "they ought to put some of these crazy women off the course. It's getting to be outrageous."

A head and a voice came up together over the hill:

"Do you mind if we go through?"

"You hit me in the stomach!" declared Mr. Hedrick wildly.

"Did I?" The girl approached the group of men. "I'm sorry. I yelled 'Fore!'"

Her glance fell casually on each of the men—then scanned the fairway for her ball.

"Did I bounce into the rough?"

It was impossible to determine whether this question was <u>ingenuous</u> or <u>malicious</u>. In a moment, however, she left no doubt, for as her partner came up over the hill she called cheerfully:

"Here I am! I'd have gone on the green except that I hit something."

As she took her stance for a short mashie[10] shot, Dexter looked at her closely. She wore a blue gingham dress, rimmed at throat and shoulders with a white edging that accentuated her tan. The quality of exaggeration, of thinness, which had made her passionate eyes and down-turning mouth absurd at eleven, was gone now. She was arrestingly beautiful. The color in her cheeks was centered like the color in a picture—it was not a "high" color, but a sort of fluctuating and feverish warmth, so shaded that it seemed at any moment it would recede and disappear. This color and the mobility of her mouth gave a continual impression of flux,[11] of intense life, of passionate vitality—balanced only partially by the sad luxury of her eyes.

---

9. **knickerbockers:** loose pants that end in a gathering just below the knee and are worn with long socks—formerly popular as golf wear.
10. **mashie:** an old name for the golf club now known as a five iron.
11. **flux:** change.

---

WORDS
TO
KNOW

**ingenuous** (ĭn-jĕn′yo͞o-əs) *adj.* innocent; naive
**malicious** (mə-lĭsh′əs) *adj.* wicked; spiteful

---

**Mini Lesson** **Grammar**

**PUNCTUATION: SEMICOLONS**

**Instruction** Remind students that sometimes they can use semicolons in place of periods to separate independent clauses. A semicolon indicates a more definite break than a comma or a conjunction does, but not as decisive a break as does a period. Display the following sentences to demonstrate the subtle shift in emphasis:

Fitzgerald gained popular success. His stories sold for thousand of dollars.

Fitzgerald gained popular success; his stories sold for thousand of dollars.

**Exercises** Have students rewrite the following sentences using semicolons.

1. The sound seemed beautiful to Dexter. He lay still and listened. *(The sound seemed beautiful to Dexter; he lay still and listened.)*
2. <u>The Great Gatsby</u> is more than a tale of the twenties. It is a timeless novel. *(The Great Gatsby is more than a tale of the twenties; it is a timeless novel. )*
3. Judy was born to wealth, but Dexter was not. *(Judy was born to wealth; Dexter was not.)*

She swung her mashie impatiently and without interest, pitching the ball into a sand-pit on the other side of the green. With a quick, insincere smile and a careless "Thank you!" she went on after it.

"That Judy Jones!" remarked Mr. Hedrick on the next tee, as they waited—some moments—for her to play on ahead. "All she needs is to be turned up and spanked for six months and then to be married off to an old-fashioned cavalry captain."

"My God, she's good-looking!" said Mr. Sandwood, who was just over thirty.

"Good-looking!" cried Mr. Hedrick contemptuously, "she always looks as if she wanted to be kissed! Turning those big cow-eyes on every calf in town!"

It was doubtful if Mr. Hedrick intended a reference to the maternal instinct.

"She'd play pretty good golf if she'd try," said Mr. Sandwood.

"She has no form," said Mr. Hedrick solemnly.

### ACTIVE READING

**EVALUATE** What is your opinion of Judy Jones?

"She has a nice figure," said Mr. Sandwood.

"Better thank the Lord she doesn't drive a swifter ball," said Mr. Hart, winking at Dexter.

Later in the afternoon the sun went down with a riotous swirl of gold and varying blues and scarlets, and left the dry, rustling night of Western summer. Dexter watched from the veranda of the Golf Club, watched the even overlap of the waters in the little wind, silver molasses under the harvest-moon. Then the moon held a finger to her lips and the lake became a clear pool, pale and quiet. Dexter put on his bathing-suit and swam out to the farthest raft, where he stretched dripping on the wet canvas of the springboard.

There was a fish jumping and a star shining and the lights around the lake were gleaming. Over on a dark peninsula a piano was playing the songs of last summer and of summers before that—songs from "Chin-Chin" and "The Count of Luxemburg" and "The Chocolate Soldier"[12]—and because the sound of a piano over a stretch

of water had always seemed beautiful to Dexter he lay perfectly quiet and listened.

The tune the piano was playing at that moment had been gay and new five years before when Dexter was a sophomore at college. They had played it at a prom once when he could not afford the luxury of proms, and he had stood outside the gymnasium and listened. The sound of the tune precipitated in him a sort of ecstasy and it was with that ecstasy he viewed what happened to him now. It was a mood of intense appreciation, a sense that, for once, he was magnificently attuned to life and that everything about him was radiating a brightness and a glamour he might never know again.

A low, pale oblong detached itself suddenly from the darkness of the Island, spitting forth the reverberated sound of a racing motor-boat. Two white streamers of cleft water rolled themselves out behind it and almost immediately the boat was beside him, drowning out the hot tinkle of the piano in the drone of its spray. Dexter raising himself on his arms was aware of a figure standing at the wheel, of two dark eyes regarding him over the lengthening space of water—then the boat had gone by and was sweeping in an immense and purposeless circle of spray round and round in the middle of the lake. With equal eccentricity one of the circles flattened out and headed back toward the raft.

"Who's that?" she called, shutting off her motor. She was so near now that Dexter could see her bathing-suit, which consisted apparently of pink rompers.[13]

The nose of the boat bumped the raft, and as the latter tilted rakishly he was precipitated toward her. With different degrees of interest they recognized each other.

---

12. **"Chin-Chin" . . . "The Chocolate Soldier":** three popular Broadway musicals, first performed in 1914, 1912, and 1909 respectively.

13. **rompers:** a loose-fitting one-piece garment with bloomerlike pants.

## Customizing Instruction

### Gifted and Talented

**1** Ask students to consider why Dexter doesn't tell his golfing partners that he once caddied at Sherry Island. **Possible Response:** He's embarrassed by his working-class origins.

### Students Acquiring English

**2** Point out that the word *fore* is a call golfers use to warn people who might be in the path of the ball they have hit.

### Less Proficient Readers

**3** Make students understand that Dexter immediately recognizes this interloper as the young girl he encountered on the golf course nine years earlier. She made a lasting impression on him.

### Students Acquiring English

**4** Explain that *calf* is used as slang for "young man" and that *cow eyes* is a slang expression that describes large eyes that have a gentle, beckoning look.

4. The public tired of Fitzgerald's wealthy characters. The Great Depression tarnished their glitter. (*The public tired of Fitzgerald's wealthy characters; the Great Depression tarnished their glitter.*)

5. The 30s brought more problems for the Fitzgeralds. Zelda suffered a breakdown, and Scott succumbed to alcoholism. (*The 30s brought more problems for the Fitzgeralds; Zelda suffered a breakdown, and Scott succumbed to alcoholism.*)

 Use **Grammar Transparencies and Copymasters**, p. 158.

 Use McDougal Littell's *Language Network*, Chapter 10, for more instruction and practice in semicolons.

### Literary Analysis | CHARACTERS

**A** Have students explain what Judy's treatment of this suitor reveals about her personality. Ask them to cite any evidence that shows her to be either a static or a dynamic character.

**Possible Responses:** She doesn't notice or care about the results of her behavior; she pulls back from people who pursue her. She hasn't changed— she's the same spoiled girl Dexter first encountered on the golf course.

### Literary Analysis: THEME

**B** Ask students to recall Judy Jones's last "casual whim," which prompted Dexter to quit his job. Have them explain how this new direction differs from the last one.

**Possible Responses:** The last time, Judy provoked anger and confusion, but this time, Dexter believes he loves her; this time his reaction draws him toward Judy rather than away from her.

### Active Reading | EVALUATING CHARACTER

**C** Ask students to explain why Dexter claims to be from Keeble rather than Black Bear Village.

**Possible Responses:** He's a snob, and he doesn't want to be grouped among the townspeople whom the wealthy patrons of Black Bear Village regard as their servants and inferiors; Keeble is less well-known than Black Bear Village, so the rich have no knowledge of its people and their social standing.

### ACTIVE READING

**D** **PREDICT** **Possible Responses:** They'll break up because Judy is too egotistical; their relationship will last because Dexter can bring the stability that Judy needs.

---

"Aren't you one of those men we played through this afternoon?" she demanded.

He was.

"Well, do you know how to drive a motor-boat? Because if you do I wish you'd drive this one so I can ride on the surf-board behind. My name is Judy Jones"—she favored him with an absurd smirk—rather, what tried to be a smirk, for, twist her mouth as she might, it was not grotesque, it was merely beautiful—"and I live in a house over there on the Island, and in that house there is a man waiting for me. When he **A** drove up at the door I drove out of the dock because he says I'm his ideal."

There was a fish jumping and a star shining and the lights around the lake were gleaming. Dexter sat beside Judy Jones and she explained how her boat was driven. Then she was in the water, swimming to the floating surf-board with a sinuous crawl. Watching her was without effort to the eye, watching a branch waving or a sea-gull flying. Her arms, burned to butternut, moved sinuously among the dull platinum ripples, elbow appearing first, casting the forearm back with a cadence of falling water, then reaching out and down, stabbing a path ahead.

They moved out into the lake; turning, Dexter saw that she was kneeling on the low rear of the now uptilted surf-board.

"Go faster," she called, "fast as it'll go."

Obediently he jammed the lever forward and the white spray mounted at the bow. When he looked around again the girl was standing up on the rushing board, her arms spread wide, her eyes lifted toward the moon.

"It's awful cold," she shouted. "What's your name?"

He told her.

"Well, why don't you come to dinner tomorrow night?"

His heart turned over like the fly-wheel of the boat, and, for the second time, her casual **B** whim gave a new direction to his life.

---

Next evening while he waited for her to come downstairs, Dexter peopled the soft deep summer room and the sun-porch that opened from it with the men who had already loved Judy Jones. He knew the sort of men they were—the men who when he first went to college had entered from the great prep schools with graceful clothes and the deep tan of healthy summers. He had seen that, in one sense, he was better than these men. He was newer and stronger. Yet in acknowledging to himself that he wished his children to be like them he was admitting that he was but the rough, strong stuff from which they eternally sprang.

When the time had come for him to wear good clothes, he had known who were the best tailors in America, and the best tailors in America had made him the suit he wore this evening. He had acquired that particular reserve peculiar to his university, that set it off from other universities. He recognized the value to him of such a mannerism and he had adopted it; he knew that to be careless in dress and manner required more confidence than to be careful. But carelessness was for his children. His mother's name had been Krimslich. She was a Bohemian of the peasant class and she had talked broken English to the end of her days. Her son must keep to the set patterns.

At a little after seven Judy Jones came downstairs. She wore a blue silk afternoon dress, and he was disappointed at first that she had not put on something more elaborate. This feeling was accentuated when, after a brief greeting, she went to the door of a butler's pantry and pushing it open called: "You can serve dinner, Martha." He had rather expected that a

---

## Teaching Options

**Mini Lesson** ## Speaking and Listening

### HISTORICAL RECORDINGS

**Instruction** Remind students that they're expected to demonstrate proficiency in each aspect of the listening process, such as focusing attention, interpreting, and responding. Explain that music is such a part of everyday life that listening to songs of another era can help them appreciate the difference between today's world and that described in a literary work.

**Application** On page 847, the narrator speaks of songs that make Dexter feel ecstatic. Fitzgerald

wrote this story in the 1920s, a period known as the Jazz Age. Have students research music from this era and bring recordings to share with the class. After they listen to several recordings, ask students to respond to the music by explaining how it might relate to the way the characters approach life in "Winter Dreams."

**BLOCK SCHEDULING** This activity is particularly well suited for longer class periods.

butler would announce dinner, that there would be a cocktail. Then he put these thoughts behind him as they sat down side by side on a lounge and looked at each other.

"Father and mother won't be here," she said thoughtfully.

He remembered the last time he had seen her father, and he was glad the parents were not to be here tonight—they might wonder who he was. He had been born in Keeble, a Minnesota village fifty miles farther north, and he always gave Keeble as his home instead of Black Bear Village. Country towns were well enough to come from if they weren't inconveniently in sight and used as footstools by fashionable lakes.

They talked of his university, which she had visited frequently during the past two years, and of the near-by city which supplied Sherry Island with its patrons, and whither Dexter would return next day to his prospering laundries.

During dinner she slipped into a moody depression which gave Dexter a feeling of uneasiness. Whatever petulance she uttered in her throaty voice worried him. Whatever she smiled at—at him, at a chicken liver, at nothing—it disturbed him that her smile could have no root in mirth, or even in amusement. When the scarlet corners of her lips curved down, it was less a smile than an invitation to a kiss.

Then, after dinner, she led him out on the dark sun-porch and deliberately changed the atmosphere.

"Do you mind if I weep a little?" she said.

"I'm afraid I'm boring you," he responded quickly.

"You're not. I like you. But I've just had a terrible afternoon. There was a man I cared about, and this afternoon he told me out of a clear sky that he was poor as a church-mouse. He'd never even hinted it before. Does this sound horribly mundane?"

"Perhaps he was afraid to tell you."

"Suppose he was," she answered. "He didn't start right. You see, if I'd thought of him as poor—well, I've been mad about loads of poor men, and fully intended to marry them all. But in this case, I hadn't thought of him that way, and my interest in him wasn't strong enough to survive the shock. As if a girl calmly informed her fiancé that she was a widow. He might not object to widows, but—

"Let's start right," she interrupted herself suddenly. "Who are you, anyhow?"

For a moment Dexter hesitated. Then:

"I'm nobody," he announced. "My career is largely a matter of futures."

"Are you poor?"

"No," he said frankly, "I'm probably making more money than any man my age in the Northwest. I know that's an obnoxious remark, but you advised me to start right."

There was a pause. Then she smiled and the corners of her mouth drooped and an almost imperceptible sway brought her closer to him, looking up into his eyes. A lump rose in Dexter's throat, and he waited breathless for the experiment, facing the unpredictable compound that would form mysteriously from the elements of their lips. Then he saw—she communicated her excitement to him, lavishly, deeply, with kisses that were not a promise but a fulfillment. They aroused in him not hunger demanding renewal but surfeit that would demand more surfeit . . . kisses that were like charity, creating want by holding back nothing at all.

It did not take him many hours to decide that he had wanted Judy Jones ever since he was a proud, desirous little boy.

**ACTIVE READING**

**PREDICT** Will Dexter and Judy have a lasting relationship?

WORDS TO KNOW
**petulance** (pĕch'ə-ləns) *n.* ill temper; annoyance
**surfeit** (sûr'fĭt) *n.* a fullness beyond the point of satisfaction

849

**A** Point out that although Dexter recognizes deficiencies in Judy's "unprincipled personality," he has "no desire to change her." Ask students to explain what this might reveal about Dexter's own personality.

**Possible Response:** He's somewhat shallow and weak-willed; he's controlled by passion and youthful ideals.

**Literary Analysis** | CHARACTERS |

**B** Remind students that a character's thoughts reveal much about his or her personality. Ask students to explain what Dexter's reaction to Judy's lie reveals about his attitude.

**Possible Responses:** He's so desperate that he interprets her lie as a sign of affection; he's willing to grasp at any basis for hope, no matter how flimsy.

| ACTIVE READING |

**C** **CONNECT** Remind each student to compare text events with his/her own and other readers' experiences.

**Possible Response:** Responses will vary; selfishness, insecurity, hedonism

**Literary Analysis: THEME**

**D** Have students compare Dexter's response to this autumn with his response to autumn at the beginning of the story.

**Possible Response:** As a boy, the season brought hope, but now he feels hopeless; as a boy, he noticed the subtleties of the seasons, but now "it had come and gone again" without notice; as a boy he envisioned his ideals, but now he realizes their falseness.

**4**

**A** It began like that—and continued, with varying shades of intensity, on such a note right up to the dénouement.[14] Dexter surrendered a part of himself to the most direct and unprincipled personality with which he had ever come in contact. Whatever Judy wanted, she went after with the full pressure of her charm. There was no divergence of method, no jockeying for position or premeditation of effects—there was a very little mental side to any of her affairs. She simply made men conscious to the highest degree of her physical loveliness. Dexter had no desire to change her. Her deficiencies were knit up with a passionate energy that transcended and justified them.

When, as Judy's head lay against his shoulder that first night, she whispered, "I don't know what's the matter with me. Last night I thought I was in love with a man and tonight I think I'm in love with you—"—it seemed to him a beautiful and romantic thing to say. It was the exquisite excitability that for the moment he controlled and owned. But a week later he was compelled to view this same quality in a different light. She took him in her roadster[15] to a picnic supper, and after supper she disappeared, likewise in her roadster, with another man. Dexter became enormously upset and was scarcely able to be decently civil to the other people present.

**B** When she assured him that she had not kissed the other man, he knew she was lying—yet he was glad that she had taken the trouble to lie to him.

He was, as he found before the summer ended, one of a varying dozen who circulated about her. Each of them had at one time been favored above all others—about half of them still basked in the solace of occasional sentimental revivals. Whenever one showed signs of dropping out through long neglect, she granted him a brief honeyed hour, which encouraged him to tag along for a year or so longer. Judy made these forays[16] upon the helpless and defeated without

malice, indeed half unconscious that there was anything mischievous in what she did.

When a new man came to town every one dropped out—dates were automatically canceled.

The helpless part of trying to do anything about it was that she did it all herself. She was not a girl who could be "won" in the kinetic[17] sense—she was proof against cleverness, she was proof against charm; if any of these assailed her too strongly she would immediately resolve the affair to a physical basis, and under the magic of her physical splendor the strong as well as the brilliant played her game and not their own. She was entertained only by the gratification of her desires and by the direct exercise of her own charm. Perhaps from so much youthful love, so many youthful lovers, she had come, in self-defense, to nourish herself wholly from within.

Succeeding Dexter's first exhilaration came restlessness and dissatisfaction. The helpless ecstasy of losing himself in her was opiate rather than tonic.[18] It was fortunate for his work during the winter that those moments of ecstasy came infrequently. Early in their acquaintance it had seemed for a while that there was a deep and spontaneous mutual attraction—that first August, for example—three days of long evenings on her dusky veranda, of strange wan[19] kisses through the late afternoon, in shadowy alcoves or behind the protecting trellises of the garden arbors, of mornings when she was fresh as a dream and almost shy at meeting him in the clarity of the rising day. There was all the ecstasy of an engagement about it, sharpened by his realization that there was no engagement. It was

**1**

---

14. **dénouement** (dā′nōō-mäN′): the resolution of the conflicts in a story's plot; a final outcome.

15. **roadster:** a sporty, two-seat open automobile.

16. **forays:** sudden attacks or raids.

17. **kinetic:** involving action.

18. **opiate . . . tonic:** deadening rather than stimulating.

19. **wan** (wŏn): weary or melancholy.

during those three days that, for the first time, he had asked her to marry him. She said "maybe some day," she said "kiss me," she said "I'd like to marry you," she said "I love you"—she said—nothing.

The three days were interrupted by the arrival of a New York man who visited at her house for half September. To Dexter's agony, rumor engaged them. The man was the son of the president of a great trust company. But at the end of a month it was reported that Judy was yawning. At a dance one night she sat all evening in a motor-boat with a local beau, while the New Yorker searched the club for her frantically. She told the local beau that she was bored with her visitor, and two days later he left. She was seen with him at the station, and it was reported that he looked very mournful indeed.

On this note the summer ended. Dexter was twenty-four, and he found himself increasingly in a position to do as he wished. He joined two clubs in the city and lived at one of them. Though he was by no means an integral part of the stag-lines at these clubs, he managed to be on hand at dances where Judy Jones was likely to appear. He could have gone out socially as much as he liked—he was an eligible young man, now, and popular with downtown fathers. His confessed devotion to Judy Jones had rather solidified his position. But he had no social aspirations and rather despised the dancing men who were always on tap for the Thursday or Saturday parties and who filled in at dinners with the younger married set. Already he was playing with the idea of going East to New York. He wanted to take Judy Jones with him. No disillusion as to the world in which she had grown up could cure his illusion as to her desirability.

**ACTIVE READING**

**CONNECT** Do you know anyone like Judy? What motivates her behavior?

Remember that—for only in the light of it can what he did for her be understood.

Eighteen months after he first met Judy Jones he became engaged to another girl. Her name was Irene Scheerer, and her father was one of the men who had always believed in Dexter. Irene was light-haired and sweet and honorable, and a little stout, and she had two suitors whom she pleasantly relinquished when Dexter formally asked her to marry him.

Summer, fall, winter, spring, another summer, another fall—so much he had given of his active life to the incorrigible lips of Judy Jones. She had treated him with interest, with encouragement, with malice, with indifference, with contempt. She had inflicted on him the innumerable little slights and indignities possible in such a case—as if in revenge for having ever cared for him at all. She had beckoned him and yawned at him and beckoned him again and he had responded often with bitterness and narrowed eyes. She had brought him ecstatic happiness and intolerable agony of spirit. She had caused him untold inconvenience and not a little trouble. She had insulted him, and she had ridden over him, and she had played his interest in her against his interest in his work—for fun. She had done everything to him except to criticize him—this she had not done—it seemed to him only because it might have sullied the utter indifference she manifested and sincerely felt toward him.

When autumn had come and gone again it occurred to him that he could not have Judy Jones. He had to beat this into his mind but he convinced himself at last. He lay awake at night for a while and argued it over. He told himself the trouble and the pain she had caused him, he enumerated her glaring deficiencies as a wife. Then he said to himself that he loved her, and after a while he fell asleep. For a week, lest he

WORDS TO KNOW

**incorrigible** (ĭn-kôr′ĭ-jə-bəl) *adj.* impossible to correct or reform; uncontrollable
**sully** (sŭl′ē) *v.* to spoil; tarnish

851

## Customizing Instruction

### Less Proficient Readers

**1** Discuss with students Judy's ability to "nourish herself wholly from within." She enjoys manipulating and exciting men by "the direct exercise of her own charm." She needs no affection and forms no deep attachments, so her type of emotional fulfillment remains "within."

### Students Acquiring English

**2** Explain that the word *stag* refers to a man who attends a dance or party alone, without a date. At the time, it was common practice for such men to "cut in" and dance with escorted ladies. Point out that Dexter is so desperate that he resorts to such stratagems in hopes of encountering Judy.

## Teaching Options

**Cross Curricular Link** **Music**

**ROOTS OF JAZZ** When military bands broke up after the end of the Spanish American War, hundreds of inexpensive used instruments flooded shops in New Orleans. The city was already home to a rich musical diversity. African and Caribbean rhythms, blues and gospel, ragtime, and European classical music swirled through an African-American and Creole community that highly val-ued musical education. These streams converged into jazz. Legend lists the Buddy Bolden Band as its first practitioner, but soon dozens of bands filled the red-light district of Storyville. When the navy insisted that Storyville's establishments be closed during World War I, these bands carried their new sound to the world.

**A** **EVALUATE** Possible Response: No, because he doesn't love her and is still infatuated with Judy; yes, because he needs to forget Judy and get on with his life.

**Reading Skills and Strategies: QUESTIONING**

**B** Have students question Dexter's motivation in deciding to marry Irene. Have them offer an explanation of his decision, given that he remains obsessed with Judy Jones.
Possible Responses: Irene makes him feel better about himself and helps him achieve "a certain tranquillity of spirit"; he might believe that marriage to Irene will make him forget Judy.

**Literary Analysis: FIGURATIVE LANGUAGE**

**C** Ask students to identify the things to which Dexter compares his future bride and to tell what these metaphors suggest about his feelings toward her.
Possible Responses: "a curtain spread behind him, a hand moving among the gleaming teacups, a voice calling to children." He sees her as part of the backdrop of domesticity. He refers to her as a series of parts, rather than as a whole person.

imagine her husky voice over the telephone or her eyes opposite him at lunch, he worked hard and late, and at night he went to his office and plotted out his years.

At the end of a week he went to a dance and cut in on her once. For almost the first time since they had met he did not ask her to sit out with him or tell her that she was lovely. It hurt him **1** that she did not miss these things—that was all. He was not jealous when he saw that there was a new man tonight. He had been hardened against jealousy long before.

He stayed late at the dance. He sat for an hour with Irene Scheerer and talked about books and about music. He knew very little about either. But he was beginning to be master of his own time now, and he had a rather priggish[20] notion that he—the young and already fabulously successful Dexter Green—should know more about such things.

That was in October, when he was twenty-five. In January, Dexter and Irene became engaged. It was to be announced in June, and they were to be married three months later.

**A** **EVALUATE** Do you approve of Dexter's decision to marry Irene?

The Minnesota winter prolonged itself interminably, and it was almost May when the winds came soft and the snow ran down into Black Bear Lake at last. For the first time in over a year Dexter was enjoying a certain tranquillity of spirit. Judy Jones had been in Florida, and afterward in Hot Springs, and somewhere she had been engaged, and somewhere she had broken it off. At first, when **B** Dexter had definitely given her up, it had made him sad that people still linked them together and asked for news of her, but when he began to be placed at dinner next to Irene Scheerer people didn't ask him about her any more—they told him about her. He ceased to be an authority on her.

May at last. Dexter walked the streets at night when the darkness was damp as rain, wondering that so soon, with so little done, so much of ecstasy had gone from him. May one year back had been marked by Judy's poignant, unforgivable, yet forgiven turbulence—it had been one of those rare times when he fancied she had grown to care for him. That old penny's worth of happiness he had spent for this bushel of content. He knew that Irene would be no more than a curtain spread behind him, a hand moving among gleaming tea-cups, a voice calling to children . . . fire and loveliness were gone, the magic of nights and the wonder of the varying hours and seasons . . . slender lips, downturning, dropping to his lips and bearing him up into a heaven of eyes. . . . The thing was deep in him. He was too strong and alive for it to die lightly.

**2**

**C**

In the middle of May when the weather balanced for a few days on the thin bridge that led to deep summer he turned in one night at Irene's house. Their engagement was to be announced in a week now—no one would be surprised at it. And tonight they would sit together on the lounge at the University Club and look on for an hour at the dancers. It gave him a sense of solidity to go with her—she was so sturdily popular, so intensely "great."

He mounted the steps of the brownstone house and stepped inside.

"Irene," he called.

Mrs. Scheerer came out of the living-room to meet him.

"Dexter," she said, "Irene's gone upstairs with a splitting headache. She wanted to go with you but I made her go to bed."

"Nothing serious, I—"

"Oh, no. She's going to play golf with you in the morning. You can spare her for just one night, can't you, Dexter?"

---

20. **priggish:** smug; conceited.

**852**

**poignant** (poin'yənt) *adj.* emotionally touching or moving

Autoportrait (about 1925), Tamara de Lempicka. Oil on wood, 35 × 26 cm, private collection.
Copyright © SPADEM/Kizette de Lempicka Foxhall.

WINTER DREAMS **853**

### Students Acquiring English

**1** Point out that been *hardened against* means "became immune to" or "conditioned to withstand." Ask students to use this definition to paraphrase the sentence.

**Possible Response:** He was no longer troubled by feelings of jealousy.

**2** Explain the meaning of Fitzgerald's "that old penny's worth of happiness . . . spent for this bushel of content." He means that by leaving Judy for Irene, Dexter would be exchanging fleeting moments of ecstasy for lengthy periods of contentment.

## Teaching Options

**Mini Lesson** ## Viewing and Representing

### *Autoportrait* **by Tamara de Lempicka**

**ART APPRECIATION** This poster-like oil painting is typical of Lempicka's aggressive, dramatic style. The sleek lines, rakish angles, and muted, metallic hues of the work reflect the Art Deco style that emerged in Paris in the mid-1920s and remained influential throughout the 30s. The style shows the influence of and infatuation with "modern" technology.

**Instruction** Point out the pun in the painting's title. *Autoportrait*, which can be interpreted as meaning "self-portrait," prominently features an auto. Explain that the portrait depicts the elegance and assurance many people enjoyed before the stock-market crash of 1929.

**Application** Remind students that they're expected to analyze relationships, ideas, and cultures as represented in various media. Ask students to describe what the subject's facial expression reveals about her attitude.

**Possible Responses:** Her calm, composed mouth and lidded, languid eyes reflect a sense of coolness and contentment; she seems self-assured and somewhat bored.

Her smile was kind. She and Dexter liked each other. In the living-room he talked for a moment before he said good night.

Returning to the University Club, where he had rooms, he stood in the doorway for a moment and watched the dancers. He leaned against the door-post, nodded at a man or two—yawned.

"Hello, darling."

The familiar voice at his elbow startled him. Judy Jones had left a man and crossed the room to him—Judy Jones, a slender enameled doll in cloth of gold: gold in a band at her head, gold in two slipper points at her dress's hem. The fragile glow of her face seemed to blossom as she smiled at him. A breeze of warmth and light blew through the room. His hands in the pockets of his dinner-jacket tightened spasmodically. He was filled with a sudden excitement.

"When did you get back?" he asked casually.

"Come here and I'll tell you about it."

She turned and he followed her. She had been away—he could have wept at the wonder of her return. She had passed through enchanted streets, doing things that were like provocative music. All mysterious happenings, all fresh and quickening hopes, had gone away with her, come back with her now.

She turned in the doorway.

"Have you a car here? If you haven't, I have."

"I have a coupé."

In then, with a rustle of golden cloth. He slammed the door. Into so many cars she had stepped—like this—like that—her back against the leather, so—her elbow resting on the door—waiting. She would have been soiled long since had there been anything to soil her—except herself—but this was her own self-outpouring.

With an effort he forced himself to start the car and back into the street. This was nothing, he must remember. She had done this before, and he had put her behind him, as he would have crossed a bad account from his books.

He drove slowly downtown and, affecting abstraction,[21] traversed the deserted streets of the business section, peopled here and there where a movie was giving out its crowd or where consumptive or pugilistic[22] youth lounged in front of pool halls. The clink of glasses and the slap of hands on the bars issued from saloons, cloisters[23] of glazed glass and dirty yellow light.

She was watching him closely and the silence was embarrassing, yet in this crisis he could find no casual word with which to profane the hour. At a convenient turning he began to zigzag back toward the University Club.

"Have you missed me?" she asked suddenly.

"Everybody missed you."

He wondered if she knew of Irene Scheerer. She had been back only a day—her absence had been almost contemporaneous with his engagement.

"What a remark!" Judy laughed sadly—without sadness. She looked at him searchingly. He became absorbed in the dashboard.

A perfect wave of emotion washed over him, carrying off with it a sediment of wisdom, of convention, of doubt, of honor.

---

21. **affecting abstraction:** pretending to be lost in thought.
22. **consumptive or pugilistic** (pyo͞o′jə-lĭs′tĭk): sickly or aggressive.
23. **cloisters:** places of religious retreat, such as convents and monasteries (here used metaphorically to refer to places of escape from life's problems).

"You're handsomer than you used to be," she said thoughtfully. "Dexter, you have the most remarkable eyes."

He could have laughed at this, but he did not laugh. It was the sort of thing that was said to sophomores. Yet it stabbed at him.

"I'm awfully tired of everything, darling." She called every one darling, endowing the endearment with careless, individual camaraderie. "I wish you'd marry me."

The directness of this confused him. He should have told her now that he was going to marry another girl, but he could not tell her. He could as easily have sworn that he had never loved her.

"I think we'd get along," she continued, on the same note, "unless probably you've forgotten me and fallen in love with another girl."

Her confidence was obviously enormous. She had said, in effect, that she found such a thing impossible to believe, that if it were true he had merely committed a childish indiscretion—and probably to show off. She would forgive him, because it was not a matter of any moment but rather something to be brushed aside lightly.

"Of course you could never love anybody but me," she continued, "I like the way you love me. Oh, Dexter, have you forgotten last year?"

"No, I haven't forgotten."

"Neither have I!"

Was she sincerely moved—or was she carried along by the wave of her own acting?

"I wish we could be like that again," she said, and he forced himself to answer:

"I don't think we can."

"I suppose not. . . . I hear you're giving Irene Scheerer a violent rush."

There was not the faintest emphasis on the name, yet Dexter was suddenly ashamed.

"Oh, take me home," cried Judy suddenly; "I don't want to go back to that idiotic dance—with those children."

Then, as he turned up the street that led to the residence district, Judy began to cry quietly to herself. He had never seen her cry before.

The dark street lightened, the dwellings of the rich loomed up around them, he stopped his coupé in front of the great white bulk of the Mortimer Joneses' house, somnolent, gorgeous, drenched with the splendor of the damp moonlight. Its solidity startled him. The strong walls, the steel of the girders, the breadth and beam and pomp of it were there only to bring out the contrast with the young beauty beside him. It was sturdy to accentuate her slightness—as if to show what a breeze could be generated by a butterfly's wing.

He sat perfectly quiet, his nerves in wild clamor, afraid that if he moved he would find her irresistibly in his arms. Two tears had rolled down her wet face and trembled on her upper lip.

"I'm more beautiful than anybody else," she said brokenly, "why can't I be happy?" Her moist eyes tore at his stability—her mouth turned slowly downward with an exquisite sadness: "I'd like to marry you if you'll have me, Dexter. I suppose you think I'm not worth having, but I'll be so beautiful for you, Dexter."

A million phrases of anger, pride, passion, hatred, tenderness fought on his lips. Then a perfect wave of emotion washed over him, carrying off with it a sediment of wisdom, of convention, of doubt, of honor. This was his girl who was speaking, his own, his beautiful, his pride.

"Won't you come in?" He heard her draw in her breath sharply.

Waiting.

"All right," his voice was trembling, "I'll come in."

ACTIVE READING

B EVALUATE How sincere does Judy seem?

2

3

C

## Customizing Instruction

### Gifted and Talented

1 Ask students to identify details that describe the landscape through which Dexter and Judy drive. Have students describe the impressions these details create and explain why Fitzgerald might want to create such impressions.

**Possible Responses:** Details: deserted, consumptive or pugilistic youth, lounged, clink of glasses, slap of hands on bars, glazed glass, dirty yellow light. Fitzgerald creates an impression of a tawdry, disreputable environment. By placing Dexter and Judy in such a locale, Fitzgerald accentuates the shabby, dishonest nature of their past relationship.

### Students Acquiring English

2 Help students paraphrase this figurative description. Suggest that strong emotion, like a powerful surf, overwhelms Dexter's better judgment and carries common sense away.

### Multiple Learning Styles
#### Interpersonal Learners

3 Have students offer advice to Dexter as he considers Judy's invitation. Ask them to recall similar incidents when they've been tempted to go against their better judgment.

## Cross Curricular Link **History**

**WOMEN AFTER WORLD WAR I** Before the Great War, women's lives had been strictly proscribed. Women faced arrest for such infractions as wearing improper clothing, for failing to wear stockings at the beach, for using profanity or smoking in public, and even for driving a car without a man beside them. Such arrests ceased after the war. The longevity rate, which had favored men, abruptly changed to favor women, and the decimation of a generation of young European men further enhanced women's role in society. In the United States, women made up 20 percent of the post-war workforce, and in 1919 the Nineteenth Amendment giving women the right to vote was submitted for states' approval. Four years later, The National Women's Party, formed in 1916, campaigned for an equal rights amendment.

## Reading and Analyzing

**Literary Analysis** CHARACTERS

**A** Based on these two paragraphs, ask students if they can detect a change in Dexter's character.

**Possible Responses:** He seems to recognize that he has become insensitive and self-absorbed. He no longer values popular opinion.

ACTIVE READING

**B EVALUATE Possible Responses:** He seems to be numbing himself against further pain; he might be deceiving himself about being beyond pain.

ACTIVE READING

**C QUESTION Possible Responses:** Perhaps she responded to the idea that he was madly in love with her; perhaps she simply obeyed a whim.

**5**

It was strange that neither when it was over nor a long time afterward did he regret that night. Looking at it from the perspective of ten years, the fact that Judy's flare for him endured just one month seemed of little importance. Nor did it matter that by his yielding he subjected himself to a deeper agony in the end and gave serious hurt to Irene Scheerer and to Irene's parents, who had befriended him. There was nothing sufficiently pictorial about Irene's grief to stamp itself on his mind.

**1**

**A** Dexter was at bottom hard-minded. The attitude of the city on his action was of no importance to him, not because he was going to leave the city, but because any outside attitude on the situation seemed superficial. He was completely indifferent to popular opinion. Nor, when he had seen that it was no use, that he did not possess in himself the power to move fundamentally or to hold Judy Jones, did he bear any malice toward her. He loved her, and he would love her until the day he was too old for loving—but he could not have her. So he tasted the deep pain that is reserved only for the strong, just as he had tasted for a little while the deep happiness.

Even the ultimate falsity of the grounds upon which Judy terminated the engagement—that she did not want to "take him away" from Irene—Judy, who had wanted nothing else—did not revolt him. He was beyond any revulsion or any amusement.

ACTIVE READING

EVALUATE What do you think of Dexter's response to Judy's betrayal? **B**

He went East in February with the intention of selling out his laundries and settling in New York—but the war came to America in March and changed his plans. He returned to the West, handed over the management of the business to his partner, and went into the first officers' training-camp in late April. He was one of those young thousands who greeted the war with a certain amount of relief, welcoming the liberation from webs of tangled emotion.

Illustration by Joseph Lyendecker. Courtesy of Cluett, Peabody & Co., Inc.

**H**e tasted the deep pain

that is reserved

only for the strong,

just as he had tasted

for a little while

the deep happiness.

## Teaching Options

✓ **Assessment** **Informal Assessment**

**ALTERNATIVE ENDING** You can informally assess students' understanding of the selection by having them create an alternative ending in which Dexter and Judy eventually reconcile and marry. Students could convey this information by having Devlin describe his observations of their relationship to a third party.

**RUBRIC**

3 **Full Accomplishment** Response reflects a full understanding of the characters and their personality traits.

2 **Substantial Accomplishment** Response reflects a general understanding of the characters but omits some of their personality traits.

1 **Little or Partial Accomplishment** Response shows little understanding of the characters or their individual personality traits.

This story is not his biography, remember, although things creep into it which have nothing to do with those dreams he had when he was young. We are almost done with them and with him now. There is only one more incident to be related here, and it happens seven years farther on.

It took place in New York, where he had done well—so well that there were no barriers too high for him. He was thirty-two years old, and, except for one flying trip immediately after the war, he had not been West in seven years. A man named Devlin from Detroit came into his office to see him in a business way, and then and there this incident occurred, and closed out, so to speak, this particular side of his life.

"So you're from the Middle West," said the man Devlin with careless curiosity. "That's funny—I thought men like you were probably born and raised on Wall Street. You know—wife of one of my best friends in Detroit came from your city. I was an usher at the wedding."

Dexter waited with no apprehension of what was coming.

"Judy Simms," said Devlin with no particular interest; "Judy Jones she was once."

"Yes, I knew her." A dull impatience spread over him. He had heard, of course, that she was married—perhaps deliberately he had heard no more.

"Awfully nice girl," brooded Devlin meaninglessly, "I'm sort of sorry for her."

"Why?" Something in Dexter was alert, receptive, at once.

"Oh, Lud Simms has gone to pieces in a way. I don't mean he ill-uses her, but he drinks and runs around—"

"Doesn't she run around?"

"No. Stays at home with her kids."

"Oh."

"She's a little too old for him," said Devlin.

"Too old!" cried Dexter. "Why, man, she's only twenty-seven."

He was possessed with a wild notion of rushing out into the streets and taking a train to Detroit. He rose to his feet spasmodically.

"I guess you're busy," Devlin apologized quickly. "I didn't realize—"

"No, I'm not busy," said Dexter, steadying his voice. "I'm not busy at all. Not busy at all. Did you say she was—twenty-seven? No, I said she was twenty-seven."

"Yes, you did," agreed Devlin dryly.

"Go on, then. Go on."

"What do you mean?"

"About Judy Jones."

Devlin looked at him helplessly.

 "Well, that's—I told you all there is to it. He treats her like the devil. Oh, they're not going to get divorced or anything. When he's particularly outrageous she forgives him. In fact, I'm inclined to think she loves him. She was a pretty girl when she first came to Detroit."

A pretty girl! The phrase struck Dexter as ludicrous.

"Isn't she—a pretty girl, any more?"

"Oh, she's all right."

"Look here," said Dexter, sitting down suddenly. "I don't understand. You say she was a 'pretty girl' and now you say she's 'all right.' I don't understand what you mean—Judy Jones wasn't a pretty girl, at all. She was a great beauty. Why, I knew her, I knew her. She was—"

Devlin laughed pleasantly.

"I'm not trying to start a row,[24]" he said. "I think Judy's a nice girl and I like her. I can't understand how a man like Lud Simms could fall madly in love with her, but he did." Then he added: "Most of the women like her."

Dexter looked closely at Devlin, thinking wildly that there must be a reason for this, some insensitivity in the man or some private malice.

**ACTIVE READING**

**QUESTION** Why do you think Judy married Lud Simms?

---

24. **row** (rou): a noisy argument or dispute.

---

**Customizing Instruction**

**Students Acquiring English**

**1** Help students paraphrase this sentence. Suggest that it means that Dexter is inflexible, refusing to consider any views other than his own.

**Less Proficient Readers**

**2** Ask students to identify Judy's husband and to characterize their marriage.
**Possible Response:** Judy married Lud Simms, who abuses alcohol and is unfaithful; Judy cares for their children and remains faithful to Lud.

---

## Vocabulary Strategy

**Mini Lesson**

### ROOT WORDS

**Instruction** Explain that a root is a word part that cannot stand alone and to which a prefix or suffix may be added. Roots, which often derive from Greek or Latin words, carry the base meaning of a word. Remind students that they are expected to apply meanings of prefixes, roots, and suffixes in order to comprehend words. To illustrate, explain that the word biography combines two Greek roots: bio, which means "life," and graphia, which means "write."

**Application** List the following root words: *poly*, meaning "many"; *vis/vid*, meaning "see"; and *stat*, meaning "stand." Have students work in pairs to choose one of the root words, create a list of words that contain it, and define those words.

Use **Vocabulary Transparencies and Copymasters**, p. 71.

**A lesson on root words appears on p. 444 in the Pupil's Edition.**

**Literary Analysis** CHARACTERS

Have students use Devlin's description of Judy to identify changes in Judy's character and to infer what might have caused them.

**Possible Response:** Devlin describes her as a drab, dutiful housewife who cares for her children and readily forgives her errant husband. Perhaps Simms is a kindred spirit, who treats her much as she used to treat her suitors. Her own past behavior might make her more willing to condone his errant ways.

---

ACTIVE READING

**A** **CLARIFY** **Possible Responses:**
He has lost his dreams and has nothing left to believe in or strive for. The Judy he once loved no longer exists. The things she represented—beauty, wealth, social status, romance, excitement—meant more to him than her actual being. He realizes now that he has lost his capacity to dream.

**Active Reading**

EVALUATING CHARACTER

Ask students to explain the role that dreams played in Dexter's life and the way that the loss of these dreams changed him.

**Possible Responses:** Dexter's dreams are unattainable illusions; without dreams to strive for, Dexter feels empty and doesn't care about life; Dexter was happier while he naively believed in false ideals and strove for them; Dexter can never achieve the same fullness of life he felt while he believed in ideals.

---

**1**    "Lots of women fade just like *that*," Devlin snapped his fingers. "You must have seen it happen. Perhaps I've forgotten how pretty she was at her wedding. I've seen her so much since then, you see. She has nice eyes."

A sort of dullness settled down upon Dexter. For the first time in his life he felt like getting very drunk. He knew that he was laughing loudly at something Devlin had said, but he did not know what it was or why it was funny. When, in a few minutes, Devlin went he lay down on his lounge and looked out the window at the New York sky-line into which the sun was sinking in dull lovely shades of pink and gold.

He had thought that having nothing else to lose he was invulnerable at last—but he knew that he had just lost something more, as surely as if he had married Judy Jones and seen her fade away before his eyes.

The dream was gone. Something had been taken from him. In a sort of panic he pushed the palms of his hands into his eyes and tried to bring up a picture of the waters lapping on Sherry Island and the moonlit veranda, and gingham on the golf-links and the dry sun and the gold color of her neck's soft down. And her mouth damp to his kisses and her eyes plaintive with melancholy and her freshness like new fine linen in the morning. Why, these things were no longer in the world! They had existed and they existed no longer.

For the first time in years the tears were streaming down his face. But they were for himself now. He did not care about mouth and eyes and moving hands. He wanted to care, and he could not care. For he had gone away and he could never go back any more. The gates were closed, the sun was gone down, and there was no beauty but the gray beauty of steel that withstands all time. Even the grief he could have borne was left behind in the country of illusion, of youth, of the richness of life, where his winter dreams had flourished.

ACTIVE READING

**CLARIFY** What makes Dexter so sad? **A**

"Long ago," he said, "long ago, there was something in me, but now that thing is gone. Now that thing is gone, that thing is gone. I cannot cry. I cannot care. That thing will come back no more." ❖

**T**he gates were closed, the sun was gone down, and there was no beauty but the **gray beauty** of **steel** that withstands all time.

---

## Teaching Options

**Cross Curricular Link** **Social Studies**

**THE AFTERMATH OF WORLD WAR I** The Great War, which resulted in wholesale slaughter unprecedented in history, fundamentally changed the way people viewed the world. It undermined Victorian values and engendered the dramatic shift in attitude witnessed during the 20s. Social historians have suggested that the wild parties characteristic of the Jazz Age stemmed not from exuberance, but from a sense of dismay. The literature of the time almost invariably expressed pessimism and alienation. In fact, Fitzgerald's closing paragraphs of "Winter Dreams" can be read as the lament of a generation that has lost its way in circumstances far more tragic than those of a failed romance with Judy Jones.

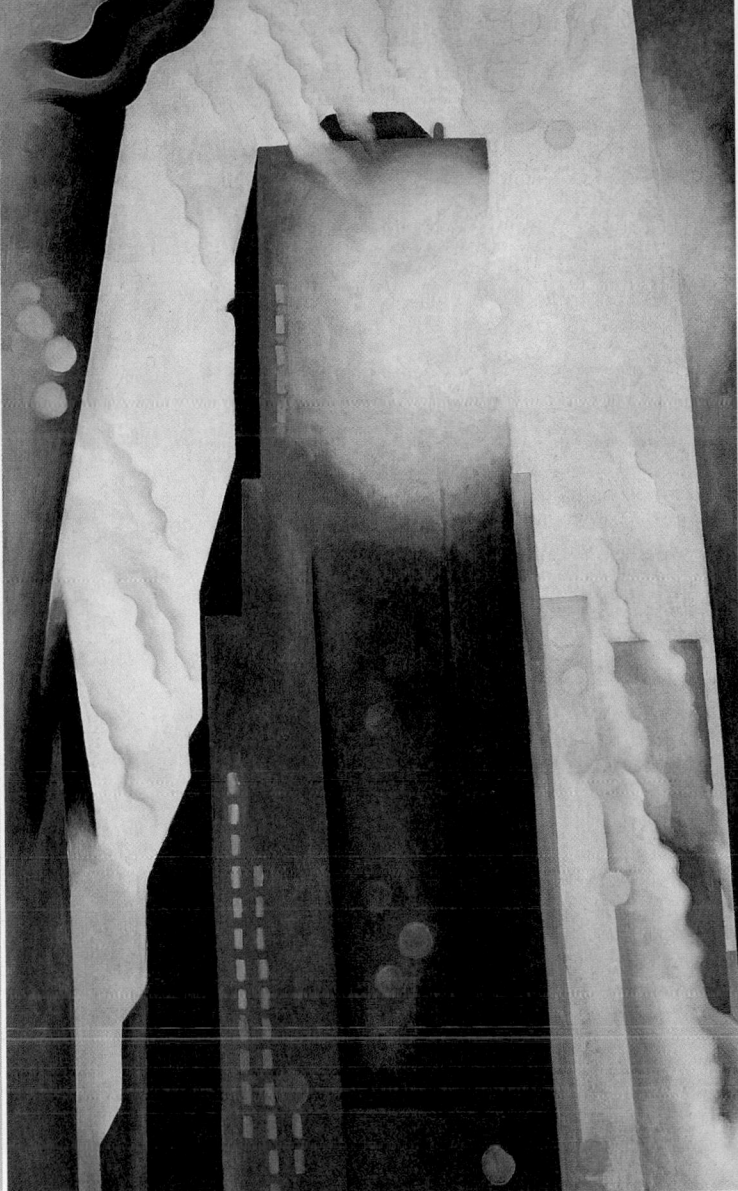

*The Shelton with Sunspots* (1926), Georgia O'Keeffe. Oil on canvas, 123.1 cm × 76.8 cm, The Art Institute of Chicago, gift of Leigh B. Block (1985.206). Photo Copyright © 1994 The Art Institute of Chicago, all rights reserved.

## Customizing Instruction

### Students Acquiring English

**1** Point out that Devlin's phrase **like that** means "instantly" or "immediately."

### Gifted and Talented

Have students discuss the role one's social background plays in interpersonal relationships. Have them decide whether the conflict between Dexter and Judy can serve as a metaphor for class conflict in America.

 **Mini Lesson** Viewing and Representing

*The Shelton with Sunspots* **by Georgia O'Keeffe**

**ART APPRECIATION** Early in her career, Georgia O'Keeffe (1887–1986) painted many views of New York City. Born in Wisconsin, she is most closely associated with the American Southwest, the setting for her most important paintings.

**Instruction** Have students research information about Georgia O'Keeffe and why she painted this painting. Some students should find O'Keeffe's account of the creation of The Shelton with Sunspots: "I went out one morning to look at [the Shelton] before I started to work and there was the optical illusion of a bite out of one side of the tower made by the sun, with sunspots against the building and against the sky. I made that painting beginning at the upper left and went off at the lower right without going back."

**Application** Remind students that they're expected to describe how meanings are communicated through elements of design. Ask them to note the details that identify the painting as a cityscape and to note elements that suggest a sense of dynamism and motion.

**Possible Responses:** rectangular, staggered blocks, rows of windows; rising smoke or steam, refracted light, sunspots

## GUIDING STUDENT RESPONSE

## Connect to the Literature

**1. What Do You Think?**
Responses will vary. Some students may state that they felt sorry for Dexter who has lost his capacity to dream.

**Comprehension Check**
• Dexter first meets Judy on the golf course.
• Irene is popular and makes him feel calm inside.
• Judy has lost her beauty and charm.

Use Selection Quiz
**Unit Five Resource Book**, p. 38.

## Think Critically

**2.** Responses will vary. Some students may state that only Dexter, who has idealized Judy, could feel so disconsolate at the news of her lost beauty.

**3.** Possible Responses: Dexter is drawn to her beauty and remains attracted to her because of the games she plays; for Dexter, winning Judy means attaining his dreams, for she symbolizes the wealth and social status he desires; Judy simply enjoys attracting men and exercising the power of her charm over them.

**4.** Students should notice that both Dexter and Judy use other people. Dexter plays with Irene's feelings for him, leaving her when Judy comes back to him. Judy likes to entice men to fall in love with her.

**5.** Students should consider Dexter's professional dreams—which he did realize—as well as his frustrated dreams about Judy.

## Literary Analysis

**Characters** Some students may argue that both Dexter Green and Judy Jones are dynamic characters. Dexter loses the dreams that gave meaning to his young life; Judy loses her appeal and settles for an unfaithful husband and a comfortable domesticity.

**Symbol** The setting sun is a traditional symbol for death. At the end of the story, the setting sun symbolizes the loss of Dexter's capacity to dream.

## Connect to the Literature

**1. What Do You Think?**
Describe how you felt about Dexter Green as you finished reading the story.

**Comprehension Check**
• Where does Dexter first meet Judy?
• Why does Dexter become engaged to Irene?
• What does Dexter learn about Judy some years later?

## Think Critically

**2.** Are your feelings about what has happened to Judy Jones the same as Dexter's? Explain your answer.

**3.** How do you account for Dexter and Judy's attraction?

**4.**  **ACTIVE READING** **EVALUATING CHARACTER** Review your responses to the reading-strategy questions that you jotted down in your ▢ **READER'S NOTEBOOK**. Do you approve or disapprove of the way Judy Jones and Dexter Green treat other people? What else do you like or dislike about them? Defend your views.

**5.** How worthwhile do you find Dexter's "winter dreams"?

**THINK ABOUT**
• what the dreams are
• what he gains from the dreams
• what he loses because of the dreams

## Extend Interpretations

**6. Critic's Corner** In the essay, "Scott Fitzgerald: The Apprentice Fiction," literary critic Marius Bewley notes, "Fitzgerald's ultimate subject is the character of the American Dream in which, in their respective ways, his principal heroes are all trapped." How well do you think this statement applies to "Winter Dreams"? Use examples from the story to support your opinion.

**7. What If?** If Dexter and Judy had married, what do you think their life together would have been like?

**8. The Writer's Style** Fitzgerald is admired for his use of **figurative language**—language (such as metaphors, similes, and personification) that communicates ideas or feelings beyond the literal meaning of the words. Find some examples of figurative language in the story, and explain what ideas or feelings you think each conveys.

**9. Connect to Life** How do the dreams you listed for the Connect to Your Life activity on page 840 compare with Dexter Green's "winter dreams"?

## Literary Analysis

**CHARACTERS** **Characters**—the imaginary people or creatures who inhabit the world of fiction—may be classified as either static or dynamic. **Static characters** tend to stay in a fixed position over the course of the story. They do not experience life-altering moments and seem to act the same, even though their situation changes. In contrast, **dynamic characters** evolve as individuals. They learn from their experiences and grow emotionally.

**Paired Activity** Working with a partner, classify Dexter Green and Judy Jones as either a static character or a dynamic character. To help you make a judgment, discuss the following questions:
• What were they like in the beginning of the story?
• Do they cling to the same behavior patterns as they become adults?
• How do they respond to the mistakes they have made in their lives?

**REVIEW** **SYMBOL** As you recall, a **symbol** is a person, place, or object that represents something beyond itself. What does the setting sun seem to symbolize at the end of "Winter Dreams"?

## Extend Interpretations

**Critic's Corner** Point out that in order to answer this question, students need to define Dexter's notion of the American Dream. After they've supported their opinion with details, invite them to compare their own conceptions of the American Dream with Dexter's.

**What If?** Students should consider what would have happened to their marriage if Judy had lost her beauty and charm.

**The Writer's Style** Figurative language evokes a certain sense beyond the meaning of the words. For example, the phrase "the country of illusion, of youth, of the richness of life" is a figurative expression comparing the early stage of life to a wondrous but unreal place.

**Connect to Life** Students may recognize that Dexter's dreams, though centered on one person, are common to young people.

## Writing Options

**1. Psychological Evaluation**
Pretend that you are a relationship counselor. Write a brief evaluation of Dexter and Judy's relationship.

**2. Dexter's Résumé** Write a draft of Dexter Green's résumé. Summarize his work experience, beginning with his job as a caddy.

**Writing Handbook**
See page 1294: Résumé.

**3. Personal Lecture** If you could offer advice to Dexter at the end of the story, what would you tell him? Outline the lecture that you would give him.

## Activities & Explorations

**Illustrated Calendar** Work with a small group of classmates to create a "Winter Dreams" illustrated calendar of the seasons. On the calendar, indicate what feelings Dexter associates with each season and what happens to him during the seasons. Use the calendar to help you investigate Fitzgerald's use of seasonal imagery in the story. What do winter and summer seem to represent? ~ **ART**

## Inquiry & Research

**Clothing Styles** Locate information about fashions of the period around World War I. Then sketch costume designs for a movie version of the story and display them in class. Alternatively, put on a fashion show with some of your classmates, modeling clothing of the time. Play popular music from this era in the background.

Experience
Caddy–Sherry
Island Golf
Club

## Art Connection

The self-portrait by the European artist Tamara de Lempicka shown on page 853 is representative of the Art Deco style of the 1920s and 1930s—consciously "modern" with its angularity, streamlined forms, and glorification of machines and technology. The automobile is an important element in this painting, as the punning title *Autoportrait* suggests. In what ways does the artwork remind you of Judy Jones in "Winter Dreams"?

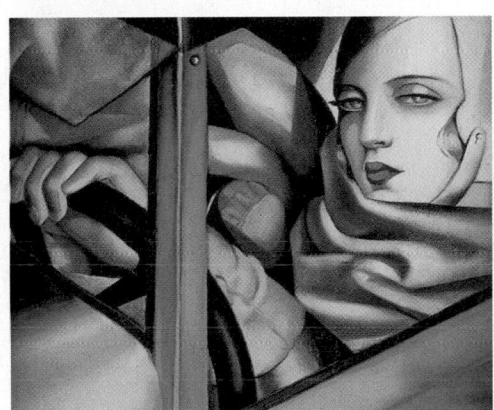

Detail of *Autoportrait* (about 1925), Tamara de Lempicka. Oil on wood, 35 cm x 26 cm, private collection. Copyright © SPADEM/Kizette de Lempicka Foxhall.

---

### Mini Lesson **Inquiry and Research**

**USING INDEXES** Tell students that indexes are valuable reference tools that list sources for information about a variety of subjects.

**Instruction** Remind students that they're expected to locate appropriate print and non-print information using text and technical resources, including databases and the Internet. Point out that they can learn what material is available on a topic by consulting such indexes as the *Reader's Guide to Periodical Literature, The Humanities Index,* and the *New York Times Index.* Many of these indexes are currently available on CD-ROM

and on-line services, as well as in bound volumes.

**Application** Have students work in small groups to research fashions and/or popular music of the World War I period. Students should consult as many indexes as possible to determine and list the available books and articles for their topic. The class might want to compile their reports to create a bibliographical reference for other students to use when doing related projects.

---

## Writing Options

1. **Psychological Evaluation** Students should account for the development, demise, and repeated rekindling of the failed relationship.
2. **Dexter's Résumé** Encourage students to find a proper form for a résumé. They may also speculate on the type of job Dexter might seek and tailor the résumé accordingly.
3. **Personal Lecture** Have students identify key ingredients for a meaningful relationship.

## Activities & Explorations

**Illustrated Calendar** Suggest that students make a calendar that charts the four seasons. Students should divide the story into sections that correspond to each season. Group members with artistic abilities may illustrate the calendar; visual and mathematical learners may design the layout, and linguistic learners can find quotations that suggest each season's effect on Dexter.

## Inquiry & Research

**Clothing Styles** Encourage students to use the library and/or on-line resources to complete their background research. For the fashion show, many everyday clothes can be easily adapted to mimic the style of the early 1900s. For example, tucking baggy pants into argyle socks gives the feel of what knickers were like.

## Art Connection

Point out that at the time this self-portrait was painted, it was unusual for a woman subject to stare directly out of the canvas. This unusual pose suggests extreme personal confidence and perhaps even arrogance, so apparent in Judy's aggressive behavior.

## Vocabulary in Action

**Exercise A**
1. f
2. a
3. e
4. i
5. g
6. b
7. c
8. j
9. d
10. h

**Exercise B**
You might want to conduct this activity in a "game show" format by counting the elapsed time required for students to identify the vocabulary word and scoring the response accordingly.

---

## Vocabulary in Action

**EXERCISE A: SYNONYMS** For each phrase in the first column, write the letter of the synonymous phrase in the second column.

1. a surfeit of change
2. mar the ravine
3. fool the ingenuous
4. comically hazardous
5. blatantly wishing
6. pathetic pig sounds
7. incorrigible filthiness
8. grimace during hugs
9. wary and evil
10. petulance and poor muscle tone

a. sully the gully
b. poignant oinking
c. hopeless soaplessness
d. suspicious and malicious
e. deceive the naive
f. too many pennies
g. openly hoping
h. crabbiness and flabbiness
i. hilariously precarious
j. make faces at embraces

| WORDS TO KNOW | blatantly | incorrigible | malicious | poignant | sully |
|---|---|---|---|---|---|
| | grimace | ingenuous | petulance | precarious | surfeit |

**EXERCISE B** See how quickly you can communicate some of the vocabulary words to a partner by saying things—other than synonyms—that call the words to mind. For *poignant,* for example, you might say "a hungry child; a sad song; Mother's Day cards; tearjerker movies; a puppy's whimper; nostalgic memories . . . ," continuing until the correct word is guessed.

**Building Vocabulary**
For an in-depth lesson on word connotation and denotation, see page 908.

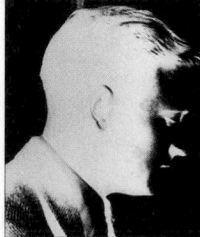

## F. Scott Fitzgerald
### 1896–1940

**Other Works**
*All the Sad Young Men*
*Tales of the Jazz Age*
*The Great Gatsby*
*Tender Is the Night*

**Stormy Romance** Francis Scott Key Fitzgerald experienced, and depicted in his fiction, the material success and eventual disillusionment that characterized the decade he dubbed the *Jazz Age.* While in army training in Alabama, he fell in love with Zelda Sayre, the beautiful and high-spirited daughter of an Alabama Supreme Court judge. They had a tumultuous courtship, with Zelda refusing to marry the aspiring writer until he was financially secure. Fortunately, his first novel, *This Side of Paradise* (1920), met with immediate success, and the couple were married within a week of the book's publication.

**Whirlwind Success** In the decade that followed, Fitzgerald's career flourished as he published two more novels, three short story collections, and a play. His 1925 novel of overindulgent lives, *The Great Gatsby*—of which "Winter Dreams" was a sort of rough draft—became famous. By 1929 he was selling stories for as much as $3,600 each. Then everything seemed to go wrong.

**A Turn of Fortune** In 1930, at the onset of the Great Depression, Zelda suffered the first of a number of mental breakdowns that would keep her hospitalized for much of the remainder of her life. At the same time, Fitzgerald was battling alcoholism, which, along with his need to earn money for Zelda's care, caused him to produce poor, hastily written fiction. Readers now rejected his subject matter, the lives of the wealthy, and by 1940 he was no longer a major writer. He died that year in Hollywood, leaving a "comeback" novel—*The Last Tycoon*—unfinished.

**Redeemed Reputation** After World War II, though, prosperity brought nostalgia for the 1920s and new respect for Fitzgerald's work. Today he is considered a major 20th-century writer whose stories make the Jazz Age come alive.

---

## Teaching Options

 **Grammar**

### NOUN CLAUSES

**Instruction** Explain that a noun clause is a subordinate clause that functions as a noun in a sentence. Point out that the introductory word in a noun clause can be a pronoun or a subordinating conjunction.

**Exercises** Have students identify the noun clause and its function in the following sentences.

1. Where Judy had gone was a mystery to Dexter. (*Where Judy had gone; subject*)
2. Dexter often speculated about whom Judy would marry. (*whom Judy would marry; object of a preposition*)
3. The annoying thing was that she abandoned Dexter at parties. (*that she abandoned Dexter at parties; predicate nominative*)
4. Mr. Devlin knew exactly where Judy had gone. (*where Judy had gone; direct object*)
5. Judy seemed to give whoever dated her endless grief. (*whoever dated her; indirect object*)

 Use **Grammar Transparencies and Copymasters**, p. 103.

 Use McDougal Littell's *Language Network,* Chapter 3, for more instruction and practice in noun clauses.

# America and I

*Short Story by* ANZIA YEZIERSKA (ənz-yä′ yĭ-zyĭr′skə)

### Connect to Your Life

**Life in a New Land** How do you think people who emigrate from their homelands feel? What challenges and opportunities await them in their new countries? Why do you think immigrants come to America? Share your thoughts about immigration with a small group of classmates. Then, as you read this story, compare your group's ideas with those of the narrator.

## Build Background

**A Wave of Immigrants** The Jewish narrator of "America and I" emigrates from Russia to the United States in the late 1800s. Between 1870 and 1920, millions of immigrants from around the world entered the United States. Although their countries of origin might have differed, these immigrants shared a great deal in terms of experience. Many had left their homelands to escape wars, religious persecution, poverty, and, in some cases, starvation. After arriving in the United States, they had to face the challenges of learning English and finding housing and work. Many settled in ethnic neighborhoods in cities, where they lived in dark, crowded tenements with inadequate sanitation. Those immigrants who were uneducated, unskilled, and poor often had to work under dangerous conditions in sweatshops, toiling long hours for low wages.

WORDS TO KNOW
**Vocabulary Preview**

| | |
|---|---|
| avid | pestilence |
| delve | simper |
| Indomitable | |

## Focus Your Reading

**LITERARY ANALYSIS** **VOICE** The term *voice* refers to a writer's unique use of language that allows a reader to "hear" a human personality in the writing. The elements of style that determine a writer's voice include diction, sentence structure, and tone. The term can be applied not only to the writer of a selection but also to the narrator of a story. As you read "America and I," try to hear the first-person narrator's voice and form an image of this young immigrant woman.

**ACTIVE READING** **UNDERSTANDING ANALOGIES** An **analogy** is an extended, point-by-point comparison of two things that have certain similarities. Its purpose is usually to make the less familiar of the two things more comprehensible. For example, the narrator of "America and I" draws an analogy between her experiences in America and those of the Pilgrims. As you read the analogy, note the points of comparison.

**READER'S NOTEBOOK** To help you grasp the meaning of the narrator's analogy on page 872, read it a second time. Create a chart like the one shown, and fill it as you reread.

| | Narrator's Experiences | Pilgrims' Experiences |
|---|---|---|
| Ocean voyage | | |
| View of America | | |
| Cross-cultural encounters | | |
| Expectations | | |

### Objectives
1. understand and appreciate a **short story** (Literary Analysis)
2. identify **voice** (Literary Analysis)
3. **understand analogies** (Active Reading)

### Summary
In this story an immigrant from Russia describes her disillusionment with the American dream. Having come to the United States excited about finding a fulfilling job, she at first is happy to work as a servant for an American family. After working hard every day for a month, however, she is told that she won't be getting any wages, just room and board. She begins a different job in a sewing factory; the pay is low and she only sees other immigrants, but she has her evenings free. Eventually she gets a better job and learns English, but she is still unfulfilled. After reading American history books, she learns that new Americans traditionally persevere despite difficulties. Inspired, she tries to bridge the gap between Americans and new immigrants by writing about immigrant life, finally finding work she loves. She concludes with the hope that future Americans will appreciate the gifts that new immigrants have to offer.

### Thematic Link
An immigrant woman pursues the **American dream** with hopes of instant fulfillment, only to find that she must be persistent and have patience.

### 5-Minute Warm-Up

***Daily Language SkillBuilder***

Have students **proofread** the display sentences on page 739k and write them correctly. The sentences also appear on Transparency 24 of **Grammar Transparencies and Copymasters.**

---

## LESSON RESOURCES

**UNIT FIVE RESOURCE BOOK,** pp. 39–43

**ASSESSMENT RESOURCES**
**Formal Assessment,** pp. 159–160
**Teacher's Guide to Assessment and Portfolio Use**
**Test Generator**

**SKILLS TRANSPARENCIES AND COPYMASTERS**
**Literary Analysis**
• Style, Voice, T23 (for Activity, p. 873)
**Reading and Critical Thinking**
• Compare and Contrast, T15

(for Extend Interpretations, item 7, p. 873)

**Grammar**
• Noun Clauses: Common Introductory Words, C104 (for Mini Lesson, p. 874)
• Commas: Introductory Words, C153 (for Mini Lesson, p. 866)
**Vocabulary**
• Suffixes and Roots, C72 (for Mini Lesson, p. 870)
**Writing**
• Autobiographical Incident, C35 (for Writing Option 3, p. 874)

**INTEGRATED TECHNOLOGY**

**Audio Library**
**LaserLinks**
• Historical Connection: Immigration and Workers
• Historical Connection: The Newest Immigrants. See **Teacher's SourceBook,** pp. 72–73.

**Visit our website:**
www.mcdougallittell.com

### Reading and Analyzing

**Reading Skills and Strategies: PREVIEW**

Tell students that this story is told by a young immigrant woman who feels like an outsider in the United States. As students read, tell them to consider her decisions and identify her personality traits.

**Literary Analysis** VOICE

 Remind students that the term *voice* refers to the use of language that allows a reader to "hear" a human personality in the writing. Ask students to describe the personality of the narrator that they hear in the opening paragraph.

**Possible Responses:** The narrator is assertive and passionate. She views herself as the speaker for millions of frustrated immigrants who cannot express their need for understanding.

Use **Unit Five Resource Book,** p. 41 for more practice.

**Active Reading**

UNDERSTANDING ANALOGIES

 When the narrator states that the prospect of coming to America makes her think of "wings" for her spirit, sunlight, singing, and beautiful music, what is she comparing her life in Russia to? Why?

**Possible Responses:** She is comparing her life in Russia to imprisonment, silence, darkness, and disharmony. Having found life in Russia bleak and oppressive, she expects life in America to be the exact opposite.

Use **Unit Five Resource Book,** p. 40 for additional support.

AMERICA AND I

★ ★ ★ ★

I was in America,

among the Americans,

but not of them.

Anzia Yezierska

**As** one of the dumb, voiceless ones I speak. One of the millions of immigrants beating, beating out their hearts at your gates for a breath of understanding.

Ach! America! From the other end of the earth from where I came, America was a land of living hope, woven of dreams, aflame with longing and desire.

Choked for ages in the airless oppression of Russia, the Promised Land rose up—wings for my stifled spirit—sunlight burning through my darkness—freedom singing to me in my prison—deathless songs tuning prison-bars into strings of a beautiful violin.

I arrived in America. My young, strong body, my heart and soul pregnant with the unlived lives of generations clamoring for expression.

What my mother and father and their mother and father never had a chance to give out in Russia, I would give out in America. The hidden sap of centuries would find release; colors that never saw light—songs that died unvoiced—romance that never had a chance to blossom in the black life of the Old World.

**864** UNIT FIVE PART 2: THE AMERICAN DREAM

## Teaching Options

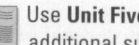 **Preteaching Vocabulary**

**USING CONTEXT CLUES**

**Instruction** When students encounter an unfamiliar word while reading, they can often use the context to try to figure out the word's meaning.

**Activity** Display the following sentence and ask a volunteer to summarize its meaning.

The explorers were reluctant to <u>delve</u> into the mystery of the sacred tomb.

Have students use the meaning of the sentence to suggest a meaning for the word *delve.* Then ask a volunteer to use the word in a new sentence.

**Application** Have students work in pairs and use context clues to figure out the meanings of the

underlined terms.

1. I am an <u>avid</u> reader; my nose is always in a book.

2. Despite personal injury and bad weather, the runner showed <u>indomitable</u> effort, finishing far ahead of the others.

3. I broke a vase in an antique shop and, with a sheepish <u>simper</u> on my face, handed the clerk my credit card.

Use **Unit Five Resource Book,** p. 42 for additional support.

A lesson on context clues appears on p. 326 in the Pupil's Edition.

In the golden land of flowing opportunity I was to find my work that was denied me in the sterile village of my forefathers. Here I was to be free from the dead drudgery for bread that held me down in Russia. For the first time in America, I'd cease to be a slave of the belly. I'd be a creator, a giver, a human being! My work would be the living joy of fullest self-expression.

But from my high visions, my golden hopes, I had to put my feet down on earth. I had to have food and shelter. I had to have the money to pay for it.

I was in America, among the Americans, but not of them. No speech, no common language, no way to win a smile of understanding from them, only my young, strong body and my untried faith. Only my eager, empty hands, and my full heart shining from my eyes!

God from the world! Here I was with so much richness in me, but my mind was not wanted without the language. And my body, unskilled, untrained, was not even wanted in the factory. Only one of two chances was left open to me: the kitchen, or minding babies.

My first job was as a servant in an American-ized family. Once, long ago, they came from the same village from where I came. But they were so well-dressed, so well-fed, so successful in America, that they were ashamed to remember their mother tongue.

"What were to be my wages?" I ventured timidly, as I looked up to the well-fed, well-dressed "American" man and woman.

They looked at me with a sudden coldness. What have I said to draw away from me their warmth? Was it so low from me to talk of wages? I shrank back into myself like a low-down bargainer. Maybe they're so high up in well-being they can't any more understand my low thoughts for money.

From his rich height the man preached down to me that I must not be so grabbing for wages. Only just landed from the ship and already thinking about money when I should be thankful to associate with "Americans."

The woman, out of her smooth, smiling fatness assured me that this was my chance for a summer vacation in the country with her two lovely children. My great chance to learn to be a civilized being, to become an American by living with them.

So, made to feel that I was in the hands of American friends, invited to share with them their home, their plenty, their happiness, I pushed out from my head the worry for wages. Here was my first chance to begin my life in the sunshine, after my long darkness. My laugh was all over my face as I said to them: "I'll trust myself to you. What I'm worth you'll give me." And I entered their house like a child by the hand.

The best of me I gave them. Their house cares were my house cares. I got up early. I worked till late. All that my soul hungered to give I put into the passion with which I scrubbed floors, scoured pots, and washed clothes. I was so grateful to mingle with the American people, to hear the music of the American language, that I never knew tiredness.

There was such a freshness in my brains and such a willingness in my heart that I could go on and on—not only with the work of the house, but work with my head—learning new words from the children, the grocer, the butcher, the iceman. I was not even afraid to ask for words from the policeman on the street. And every new word made me see new American things with American eyes. I felt like a Columbus, finding new worlds through every new word.

But words alone were only for the inside of me. The outside of me still branded me for a steerage[1] immigrant. I had to have clothes to forget myself that I'm a stranger yet. And so I had to have money to buy these clothes.

The month was up. I was so happy! Now I'd have money. *My own, earned* money. Money to buy a new shirt on my back—shoes on my feet. Maybe yet an American dress and hat!

Ach! How high rose my dreams! How plainly

---

1. **steerage:** the section of a passenger ship containing the cheapest accommodations.

**Less Proficient Readers**
Anzia Yezierska has a melodramatic, metaphorical style that may be hard for some students to follow. Listening to part of the selection on the audio tape may motivate students to read the rest of the selection independently.

**Set a Purpose** Have students read to find out whether the narrator is happy with her first job in America.

**Students Acquiring English**
Recent immigrants may identify with the narrator's sense of disillusionment and her search for respect and accep-tance in a new country. However, these students may be reluctant to discuss such feelings in class, so be sensitive about focusing attention on them.

 Use **Spanish Study Guide** for additional support, pp. 209–11.

**Gifted and Talented**
Have students note each decision the narrator makes and consider what they might have done in her place. Then have them choose one decision and improvise a scene showing what might have happened if the narrator had made a different choice. Invite them to present their scene for the class. As an alternative, have students research the experiences faced by another ethnic group upon arriving in America. Encourage students to create their own fictional first-person narrative about one immigrant's adjustment to American life.

 **Mini Lesson** ## Speaking and Listening

**YIDDISH WORDS**
**Instruction** Tell students that Yiddish is a language that resulted from the fusion of elements from German, Hebrew, Aramaic, Slavic, Old French, and Old Italian. This language, which was originally written in Hebrew characters, is spoken by Jews of Eastern and Central Europe. Some Yiddish words, like *bagel* and *chutzpah,* have entered English through Jewish popular culture.

**Application** Have interested students learn more about the Yiddish language and Jewish culture by researching the subjects in a library or on the Internet. They may write brief dialogues in Yiddish to be performed for the class. Suggest that they locate a speaker of Yiddish to coach them on pro-nunciation before their presentations.

**A** Ask students what the narrator compares herself to as she waits to get her wages.

**Possible Responses:** a prisoner, a hungry cat, a beggar

**Reading Skills and Strategies: MAKING JUDGMENTS**

**B** Ask students if the American family was intentionally taking advantage of the narrator. Then ask if they know of any similar situations that immigrants face today.

**Possible Responses:** The family may truly have believed that the narrator was lucky to work for room and board, but common sense says that it is unfair not to offer wages for full-time work. Many immigrants who work as nannies, gardeners, housekeepers, or farm workers today are not paid fairly.

**Literary Analysis** | VOICE |

**C** Have students identify words and phrases that help them "hear" the narrator's personality. Then ask them to describe the characteristics she shows in leaving her job.

**Possible Responses:** pride, courage, integrity, strength

**Active Reading**

| UNDERSTANDING ANALOGIES |

**D** When the narrator describes herself as being lost in a wilderness, what does she seem to be comparing herself to? Why?

**Possible Responses:** She compares herself to an explorer searching for a special place or to a child trying to find her way home. This comparison suggests that the real America is not what she envisioned.

---

I saw all that I would do with my visionary wages shining like a light over my head!

In my imagination I already walked in my new American clothes. How beautiful I looked as I saw myself like a picture before my eyes! I saw how I would throw away my immigrant rags tied up in my immigrant shawl. With money to buy—free money in my hands—I'd show them that I could look like an American in a day.

Like a prisoner in his last night in prison, counting the seconds that will free him from his chains, I trembled breathlessly for the minute I'd get the wages in my hand.

Before dawn I rose.

I shined up the house like a jewel-box.

I prepared breakfast and waited with my heart in my mouth for my lady and gentleman to rise. At last I heard them stirring. My eyes were jumping out of my head to them when I saw them coming in and seating themselves by the table.

Like a hungry cat rubbing up to its boss for meat, so I edged and <u>simpered</u> around them as I passed them the food. Without my will, like a beggar, my hand reached out to them.

The breakfast was over. And no word yet from my wages.

"*Gottuniu!*"[2] I thought to myself. "Maybe they're so busy with their own things they forgot it's the day for my wages. Could they who have everything know what I was to do with my first American dollars? How could they, soaking in plenty, how could they feel the longing and the fierce hunger in me, pressing up through each visionary dollar? How could they know the gnawing ache of my <u>avid</u> fingers for the feel of my own, earned dollars? *My* dollars that I could spend like a free person. *My* dollars that would make me feel with everybody alike!

Breakfast was long past.

Lunch came. Lunch past.

*Oi-i weh!*[3] Not a word yet about my money.

It was near dinner. And not a word yet about my wages.

---

I began to set the table. But my head—it swam away from me. I broke a glass. The silver dropped from my nervous fingers. I couldn't stand it any longer. I dropped everything and rushed over to my American lady and gentleman.

"*Oi weh!* The money—my money—my wages!" I cried breathlessly.

Four cold eyes turned on me.

"Wages? Money?" The four eyes turned into hard stone as they looked me up and down. "Haven't you a comfortable bed to sleep, and three good meals a day? You're only a month here. Just came to America. And you already think about money. Wait till you're worth any money. What use are you without knowing English? You should be glad we keep you here. It's like a vacation for you. Other girls pay money yet to be in the country."

It went black for my eyes. I was so choked no words came to my lips. Even the tears went dry in my throat.

I left. Not a dollar for all my work.

**F**or a long, long time my heart ached and ached like a sore wound. If murderers would have robbed me and killed me it wouldn't have hurt me so much. I couldn't think through my pain. The minute I'd see before me how they looked at me, the words they said to me—then everything began to bleed in me. And I was helpless.

For a long, long time the thought of ever working in an "American" family made me tremble with fear, like the fear of wild wolves. No—never again would I trust myself to an "American" family, no matter how fine their language and how sweet their smile.

It was blotted out in me all trust in friendship from "Americans." But the life in me still burned to live. The hope in me still craved to hope. In

---

2. *Gottuniu!* (gôt′ŏŏn-yōō) *Yiddish:* Oh, my God!

3. *Oi-i weh!* (oi′ vā′) *Yiddish:* Oh, woe! (a common expression of dismay or resignation).

---

WORDS
TO
KNOW
**simper** (sĭm′pər) *v.* to smile in a shy or self-conscious way
**avid** (ăv′ĭd) *adj.* having an intense desire or craving

866

---

## Teaching Options

 **Mini Lesson**  **Grammar**

**COMMAS: INTRODUCTORY WORDS**

**Instruction** Remind students that a comma should follow common introductory words such as *first, nevertheless, next, yes,* and *no.* Write the following sentence on the chalkboard and have a volunteer insert the comma.

No she would never trust herself to another "American" family.

Note that the comma helps make the meaning of the sentence clear.

**Application** Have students work in pairs to write five sentences about the selection using introductory words followed by commas. Each pair should write one sentence on the chalkboard to provide examples for discussion.

Use **Grammar Transparencies and Copymasters**, p. 153.

Use McDougal Littell's *Language Network,* Chapter 9, for more instruction and practice in commas.

"Where is America?
Is there an America?
What is this wilderness
in which I'm lost?"

**Students Acquiring English**

**1** Explain that the idiom *with my heart in my mouth* means "with a feeling of nervous expectation."

**Less Proficient Readers**

**2** Have students explain why the narrator leaves her first job as a housekeeper and nanny.

**Possible Responses:** After a month of hard work, the family refuses to pay her.

**Set a Purpose** Have students read on to find out how the narrator's next job turns out.

**Students Acquiring English**

**3** Make sure students understand the idiom *talk out my heart,* which means "say all the things that matter most to me."

darkness, in dirt, in hunger and want, but only to live on!

There had been no end to my day—working for the "American" family.

Now rejecting false friendships from higher-ups in America, I turned back to the Ghetto,[4] I worked on a hard bench with my own kind on either side of me. I knew before I began what my wages were to be. I knew what my hours were to be. And I knew the feeling of the end of the day.

From the outside my second job seemed worse than the first. It was in a sweatshop of a Delancey Street basement, kept up by an old, wrinkled woman that looked like a black witch of greed. My work was sewing on buttons. While the morning was still dark I walked into a dark basement. And darkness met me when I turned out of the basement.

Day after day, week after week, all the contact I got with America was handling dead buttons. The money I earned was hardly enough to pay for bread and rent. I didn't have a room to myself. I didn't even have a bed. I slept on a mattress on the floor in a rat-hole of a room occupied by a dozen other immigrants. I was always hungry—oh, so hungry! The scant meals I could afford only sharpened my appetite for real food. But I felt myself better off than working in the "American" family, where I had three good meals a day and a bed to myself. With all the hunger and darkness of the sweatshop, I had at least the evening to myself. And all night was mine. When all were asleep, I used to creep up on the roof of the tenement and talk out my heart in [3] silence to the stars in the sky.

"Who am I? What am I? What do I want with my life? Where is America? Is there an America? What is this wilderness in which I'm lost?" **D**

I'd hurl my questions and then think and think. And I could not tear it out of me, the feeling that America must be somewhere,

---

4. **Ghetto:** the part of New York City where Jewish immigrants lived and worked.

AMERICA AND I  **867**

---

 **Viewing and Representing**

**PHOTOGRAPHS** The photographs in this selection were most likely taken for journalistic rather than artistic purposes. They capture and convey details about immigrant life of the time.

**Instruction** Explain that students can use the photographs as primary sources to learn more about the conditions in which urban immigrants lived and worked. Studying the photographs will also enhance their appreciation of the story. Have students discuss what the photographs convey about tenement and ghetto life.

**Possible Responses:** The photos show overcrowding, hard labor, and poor conditions in sweatshops.

**Application** Ask students to point out details in the photographs that convey information about the lives of their subjects.

**Possible Responses:** hair, clothing, and architectural styles; items in the street; skyline details

**Literary Analysis: METAPHOR**

**A** Ask students why the narrator compares her self-assertion to a light in the darkness.

**Possible Response:** She is working in a dark basement; her self-assertion helps her find a better job and, therefore, a way out of the darkness.

**Reading Skills and Strategies: MAKING JUDGMENTS**

**B** Ask students how they feel about the narrator's leaving another job. Do they think she is brave? stupid? unrealistic? too picky? Have them give reasons for their answers.

**Literary Analysis** VOICE

**C** Have students notice the unusual syntax and ungrammatical usage that reflect the narrator's distinctive way of speaking. Ask students why the narrator is dissatisfied even after finding a much better job.

**Possible Response:** She wants to use her mind, not just her hands.

somehow—only I couldn't find it—*my America*, where I would work for love and not for a living. I was like a thing following blindly after something far off in the dark!

"*Oi weh!*" I'd stretch out my hand up in the air. "My head is so lost in America! What's the use of all my working if I'm not in it? Dead buttons is not me."

Then the busy season started in the shop. The mounds of buttons grew and grew. The long day stretched out longer. I had to begin with the buttons earlier and stay with them till later in the night. The old witch turned into a huge greedy maw for wanting more and more buttons.

For a glass of tea, for a slice of herring over black bread, she would buy us up to stay

another and another hour, till there seemed no end to her demands.

One day, the light of self-assertion broke into my cellar darkness.

"I don't want the tea. I don't want your herring," I said with terrible boldness. "I only want to go home. I only want the evening to myself!"

"You fresh mouth, you!" cried the old witch. "You learned already too much in America. I want no clock-watchers in my shop. Out you go!"

I was driven out to cold and hunger. I could no longer pay for my mattress on the floor. I no longer could buy the bite in the mouth. I walked the streets. I knew what it is to be alone in a strange city, among strangers.

But I laughed through my tears. So I learned

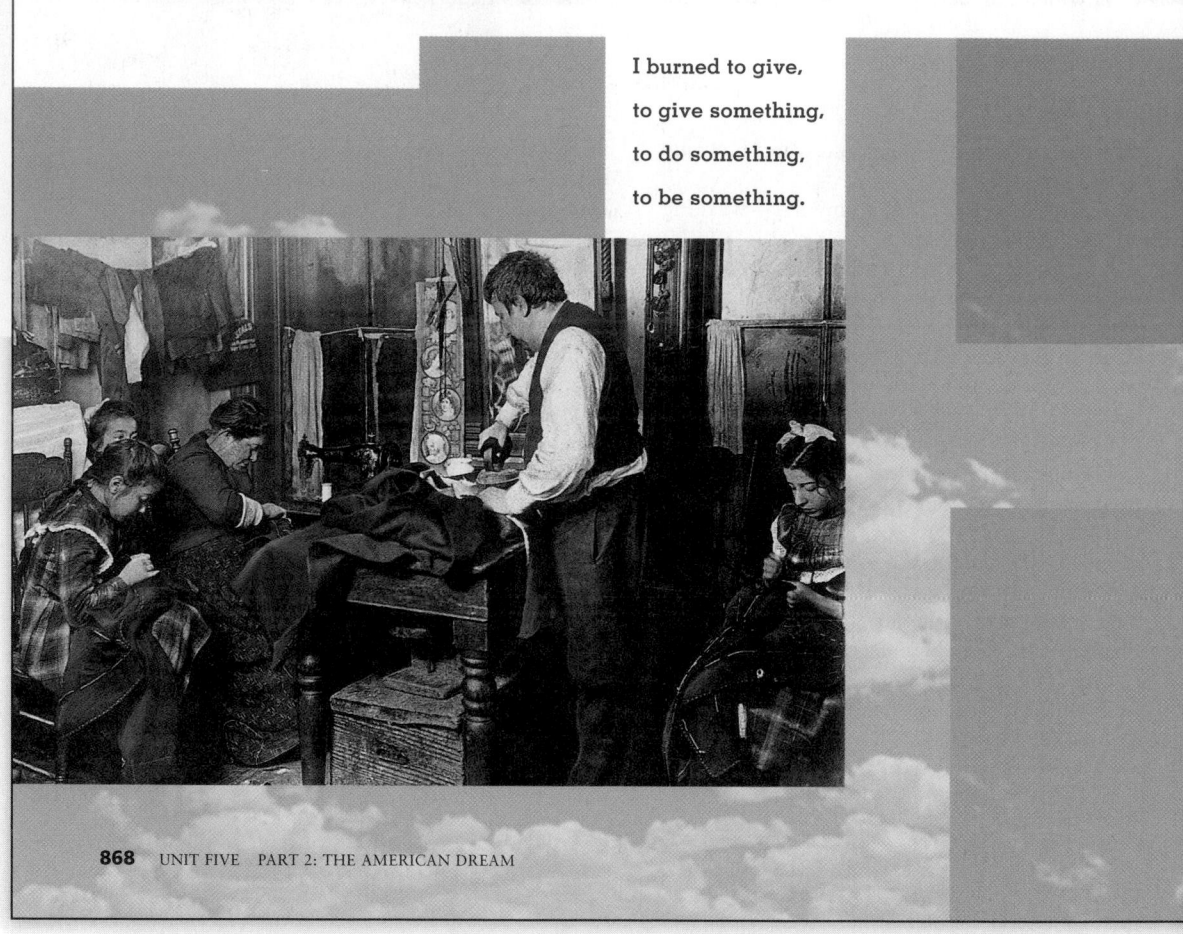

I burned to give,
to give something,
to do something,
to be something.

868    UNIT FIVE    PART 2: THE AMERICAN DREAM

## Teaching Options

### BLOCK SCHEDULING: MANAGING TIME

**If your schedule requires that you cover the lesson objectives in a shorter time, use . . .**
- Preparing to Read, p. 863
- Thinking Through the Literature, p. 873
- Vocabulary in Action, p. 874

**If you want to take advantage of longer class times, use . . .**
- TE Teaching Options: Preteaching Vocabulary, p. 864; Speaking and Listening, p. 865; Viewing and Representing, p. 867; Standardized Test Practice, p. 869; Vocabulary Strategy, pp. 870–71; Cross-Curricular Link, p. 872
- Choices & Challenges, p. 874

too much already in America because I wanted the whole evening to myself? Well America has yet to teach me still more: how to get not only the whole evening to myself, but a whole day a week like the American workers.

That sweatshop was a bitter memory but a good school. It fitted me for a regular factory. I could walk in boldly and say I could work at something, even if it was only sewing on buttons.

**G**radually, I became a trained worker. I worked in a light, airy factory, only eight hours a day. My boss was no longer a sweater and a blood-squeezer. The first freshness of the morning was mine. And the whole evening was mine. All day Sunday was mine.

Now I had better food to eat. I slept on a better bed. Now, I even looked dressed up like the American-born. But inside of me I knew that I was not yet an American. I choked with longing when I met an American-born, and I could say nothing.

Something cried dumb in me. I couldn't help it. I didn't know what it was I wanted. I only knew I wanted. I wanted. Like the hunger in the heart that never gets food.

An English class for foreigners started in our factory. The teacher had such a good, friendly face, her eyes looked so understanding, as if she could see right into my heart. So I went to her one day for an advice:

"I don't know what is with me the matter," I began. "I have no rest in me. I never yet done what I want."

"What is it you want to do, child?" she asked me.

"I want to do something with my head, my feelings. All day long, only with my hands I work."

"First you must learn English." She patted me as if I was not yet grown up. "Put your mind on that, and then we'll see."

So for a time I learned the language. I could almost begin to think with English words in my head. But in my heart the emptiness still hurt. I burned to give, to give something, to do some-

thing, to be something. The dead work with my hands was killing me. My work left only hard stones on my heart.

Again I went to our factory teacher and cried out to her: "I know already to read and write the English language, but I can't put it into words what I want. What is it in me so different that can't come out?"

She smiled at me down from her calmness as if I were a little bit out of my head. "What do *you want* to do?"

"I feel. I see. I hear. And I want to think it out. But I'm like dumb in me. I only feel I'm different—different from everybody."

She looked at me close and said nothing for a minute. "You ought to join one of the social clubs of the Women's Association," she advised.

"What's the Women's Association?" I implored greedily.

"A group of American women who are trying to help the working-girl find herself. They have a special department for immigrant girls like you."

I joined the Women's Association. On my first evening there they announced a lecture: "The Happy Worker and His Work," by the Welfare director of the United Mills Corporation.

"Is there such a thing as a happy worker at his work?" I wondered. "Happiness is only by working at what you love. And what poor girl can ever find it to work at what she loves? My old dreams about my America rushed through my mind. Once I thought that in America everybody works for love. Nobody has to worry for a living. Maybe this welfare man came to show me the *real* America that till now I sought in vain.

With a lot of polite words the head lady of the Women's Association introduced a higher-up that looked like the king of kings of business. Never before in my life did I ever see a man with such a sureness in his step, such power in his face, such friendly positiveness in his eye as when he smiled upon us.

"Efficiency is the new religion of business," he began. "In big business houses, even in up-to-date factories, they no longer take the first comer and

AMERICA AND I  **869**

---

## Customizing Instruction

### Students Acquiring English

**1** Tell students that a *maw* is the mouth of a meat-eating animal.

**2** Tell students that *fresh* is a slang term used to criticize people who speak too boldly, showing no respect.

### Less Proficient Readers

**3** Make sure students understand that the narrator's second job was sewing buttons on clothing and that she worked in the dark basement of a tenement.

• Why did the narrator prefer her second job to her first?

**Possible Response:** She had her evenings and nights free.

• Why was her second job "a bitter memory but a good school"?

**Possible Response:** It was an unpleasant experience, but it gave her the skills and experience that enabled her to get a better job in a factory.

**Set a Purpose** Have students read on to find out how the narrator seeks happiness in America.

---

✓ **Assessment Standardized Test Practice**

**CHOOSING THE BEST SUMMARY** Many standardized tests require students to select the best summary statement for a passage. You can give students practice in this skill by asking them to discuss which of the following is the best summary of "America and I."

**A.** "America and I" is about a Russian woman who comes to America and is mistreated by her employers.

**B.** "America and I" is about the poor conditions immigrants face in ghettos and sweatshops.

**C.** "America and I" is about the difficulties faced by a Russian immigrant in America before she discovered fulfilling work.

During the discussion, point out that all three statements contain true information about the selection, but statement **C** is the best summary because it describes the whole story, not just part of it.

give him any job that happens to stand empty. Efficiency begins at the employment office. Experts are hired for the one purpose, to find out how best to fit the worker to his work. It's economy for the boss to make the worker happy." And then he talked a lot more on efficiency in educated language that was over my head.

I didn't know exactly what it meant—efficiency—but if it was to make the worker happy at his work, then that's what I had been looking for since I came to America. I only felt from watching him that he was happy by his job. And as I looked on this clean, well-dressed, successful one, who wasn't ashamed to say he rose from an office-boy, it made me feel that I, too, could lift myself up for a person.

He finished his lecture, telling us about the Vocational Guidance Center that the Women's Association started.

**The** very next evening I was at the Vocational Guidance Center. There I found a young, college-looking woman. Smartness and health shining from her eyes! She, too, looked as if she knew her way in America. I could tell at the first glance: here is a person that is happy by what she does.

**A** "I feel you'll understand me," I said right away.

She leaned over with pleasure in her face: "I hope I can."

"I want to work by what's in me. Only, I don't know what's in me. I only feel I'm different."

She gave me a quick, puzzled look from the corner of her eyes. "What are you doing now?"

"I'm the quickest shirtwaist[5] hand on the floor. But my heart wastes away by such work. I think and think, and my thoughts can't come out."

"Why don't you think out your thoughts in shirtwaists? You could learn to be a designer. Earn more money."

"I don't want to look on waists. If my hands are sick from waists, how could my head learn to put beauty into them?"

"But you must earn your living at what you

know, and rise slowly from job to job."

I looked at her office sign: "Vocational Guidance." "What's your vocational guidance?" I asked. "How to rise from job to job—how to earn more money?"

The smile went out from her eyes. But she tried to be kind yet. "What *do* you want?" she asked, with a sigh of last patience.

"I want America to want me."

She fell back in her chair, thunderstruck with my boldness. But yet, in a low voice of educated self-control, she tried to reason with me:

"You have to *show* that you have something special for America before America has need of you."

"But I never had a chance to find out what's in me, because I always had to work for a living. Only, I feel it's efficiency for America to find out what's in me so different, so I could give it out by my work."

Her eyes half closed as they bored through me. Her mouth opened to speak, but no words came from her lips. So I flamed up with all that was choking in me like a house on fire:

"America gives free bread and rent to criminals in prison. They got grand houses with sunshine, fresh air, doctors and teachers, even for the crazy ones. Why don't they have free boarding-schools for immigrants—strong people—willing people? Here you see us burning up with something different, and America turns her head away from us."

Her brows lifted and dropped down. She shrugged her shoulders away from me with the look of pity we give to cripples and hopeless lunatics.

"America is no Utopia.[6] First you must become efficient in earning a living before you can indulge in your poetic dreams."

I went away from the vocational guidance

---

5. **shirtwaist:** a tailored blouse, usually with a collar and cuffs.

6. **Utopia:** an ideal place of perfect justice and social harmony.

## Vocabulary Strategy

**SUFFIXES AND ROOT WORDS**

**Instruction** Point out that students can build their vocabularies by learning the meanings of common suffixes and root words. A suffix is a word part that is added to the end of another word or word part. Noun suffixes, which make nouns out of other parts of speech, include: *-ance, -ity, -archy, -ent,* and *-ist.* Adjective suffixes, which make adjectives out of other parts of speech, include: *-able, -most, -ous,* and *-ical.*

A root is a word part, often of Greek or Latin origin, to which a prefix and/or a suffix may be added. Roots cannot stand alone. For example, the word *geology* consists of two roots—*geo,* which means "earth," and *logy,* which means "study of."

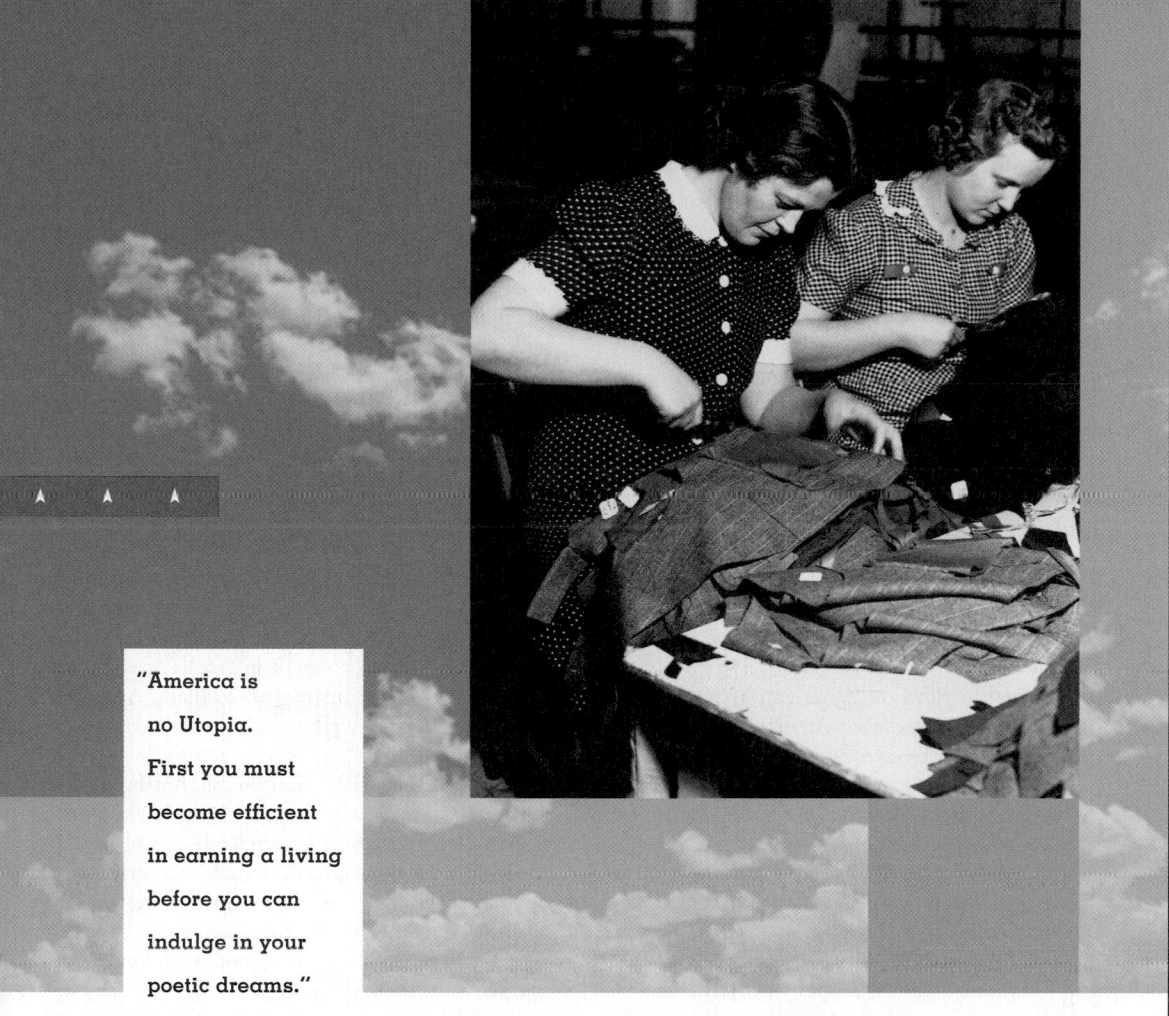

"America is no Utopia. First you must become efficient in earning a living before you can indulge in your poetic dreams."

office with all the air out of my lungs. All the light out of my eyes. My feet dragged after me like dead wood.

Till now there had always lingered a rosy veil of hope over my emptiness, a hope that a miracle would happen. I would open up my eyes some day and suddenly find the America of my dreams. As a young girl hungry for love sees always before her eyes the picture of lover's arms around her, so I saw always in my heart the vision of Utopian America.

But now I felt that the America of my dreams never was and never could be. Reality had hit me on the head as with a club. I felt that the America that I sought was nothing but a shadow—an echo —a chimera[7] of lunatics and crazy immigrants.

---

7. **chimera** (kĭ-mîr′ə): an illusion of the mind; fantasy.

---

## Active Reading

### UNDERSTANDING ANALOGIES

**A** Point out that this analogy restates the "wilderness" comparison on page 867. Ask students what similarities the narrator sees between her working conditions and a desert.

**Possible Responses:** Enduring drudgery is like crawling through a wilderness of sand. It is hard work, with no "water" or relief or understanding in sight. A person lost in a desert sees no end to it and no way out.

## Reading Skills and Strategies: ANALYZING

**B** Ask students to identify errors and misconceptions in the narrator's ideas about American history.

**Possible Response:** She stereotypes both the Pilgrims and the Native Americans. The Pilgrims are described as noble, good people who are surrounded by "savages" and who overcome all odds to create America. In the narrator's mind, the Pilgrims are shining examples of the spirit that made America, while the Native Americans are the evil forces that opposed them.

## Reading Skills and Strategies: MAKING GENERALIZATIONS

**C** Ask students to state the narrator's main idea about America.

**Possible Response:** America is a dream in the making, and every person can contribute to making this ideal a reality.

---

**A** Stripped of all illusion, I looked about me. The long desert of wasting days of drudgery stared me in the face. The drudgery that I had lived through, and the endless drudgery still ahead of me rose over me like a withering wilderness of sand. In vain were all my cryings, in vain were all frantic efforts of my spirit to find the living waters of understanding for my perishing lips. Sand, sand was everywhere. With every seeking, every reaching out I only lost myself deeper and deeper in a vast sea of sand.

I knew now the American language. And I knew now, if I talked to the Americans from morning till night, they could not understand what the Russian soul of me wanted. They could not understand *me* any more than if I talked to them in Chinese. Between my soul and the American soul were worlds of difference that no words could bridge over. What was that difference? What made the Americans so far apart from me?

I began to read the American history. I found from the first pages that America started with a band of Courageous Pilgrims. They had left their native country as I had left mine. They had crossed an unknown ocean and landed in an unknown country, as I.

But the great difference between the first Pilgrims and me was that they expected to make America, build America, create their own world of liberty. I wanted to find it ready made.

I read on. I <u>delved</u> deeper down into the American history. I saw how the Pilgrim Fathers came to a rocky desert country, surrounded by Indian savages on all sides. But undaunted, they **B** pressed on—through danger—through famine, <u>pestilence</u>, and want—they pressed on. They did not ask the Indians for sympathy, for understanding. They made no demands on anybody, but on their own <u>indomitable</u> spirit of persistence.

And I—I was forever begging a crumb of sympathy, a gleam of understanding from strangers who could not sympathize, who could not understand.

I, when I encountered a few savage Indian scalpers, like the old witch of the sweatshop, like my "Americanized" countryman, who cheated me of my wages—I, when I found myself on the lonely, untrodden path through which all seekers of the new world must pass, I lost heart and said: "There is no America!"

Then came a light—a great revelation! I saw America—a big idea—a deathless hope—a world still in the making. I saw that it was the glory of America that it was not yet finished. And I, the **C** last comer, had her share to give, small or great, to the making of America, like those Pilgrims who came in the *Mayflower*.

Fired up by this revealing light, I began to build a bridge of understanding between the American-born and myself. Since their life was shut out from such as me, I began to open up my life and the lives of my people to them. And life draws life. In only writing about the Ghetto I found America.

Great chances have come to me. But in my heart is always a deep sadness. I feel like a man who is sitting down to a secret table of plenty, while his near ones and dear ones are perishing before his eyes. My very joy in doing the work I love hurts me like secret guilt, because all about me I see so many with my longings, my burning eagerness, to do and to be, wasting their days in drudgery they hate, merely to buy bread and pay rent. And America is losing all that richness of the soul.

**The Americans** of to-morrow, the America that is every day nearer coming to be, will be too wise, too open-hearted, too friendly-handed, to let the least last-comer at their gates knock in vain with his gifts unwanted. ❖

---

| WORDS | **delve** (dĕlv) *v.* to conduct an investigation; search |
| TO | **pestilence** (pĕs'tə-ləns) *n.* any epidemic disease that is usually fatal |
| KNOW | **indomitable** (ĭn-dŏm'ĭ-tə-bəl) *adj.* not easily discouraged or defeated |

---

## Teaching Options

**Cross Curricular Link  History**

**TRIANGLE SHIRTWAIST COMPANY** By the early 1900s, New York City had many clothing factories in which immigrants were overworked and underpaid. The factories were crowded, dirty, and often very dangerous, with poor ventilation and many fire hazards. The Triangle Shirtwaist Company was one such factory. Most of its employees were immigrant women and girls from Russia, Italy, and Eastern Europe. They made a popular style of women's blouses, called shirtwaists, from fine cotton material. The factory owners, who put profit ahead of the safety of their workers, allowed flammable machine oil, fabric, and shirt patterns to be kept close together in an overcrowded room.

Workers were even allowed to smoke nearby. Fire drills were not conducted, and the building had only one fire escape, which ended two floors above ground level.

On Saturday, March 25, 1911, a fire began on the factory's eighth floor. In less than 30 minutes, 146 workers died, most from fire and smoke inhalation, some from jumping from windows to escape the blaze. Despite the careless use of hazardous materials, the lack of adequate fire escapes, and the locked factory doors, the factory owners were found not guilty of negligence because their building met the legal safety requirements.

## Connect to the Literature

**1. What Do You Think**
Describe the narrator and your attitude toward her.

**Comprehension Check**
- Why does the narrator leave her first job as a housekeeper and nanny?
- What kind of work does the narrator do in the sweatshop?

## Think Critically

**2.** What is your reaction to the **narrator's** ideas about America?

**THINK ABOUT**
- how she hopes immigrants will be treated in the future
- her "revelation" that America is still being made
- her understanding of American history
- what she expects America to provide for her

**3.** What do you think the narrator learns from her encounters with employers, teachers, and advisers?

**4.** In your opinion, what is the most important step the narrator takes in learning to live in America?

**5.** Do you think the American dream is an illusion or a reality for the narrator of this story? Explain.

**6.** **ACTIVE READING** **UNDERSTANDING ANALOGIES** Review the chart you made in your **READER'S NOTEBOOK**. What similarities does the narrator see between herself and the Pilgrims? What conclusion does she reach on the basis of her **analogy?**

## Extend Interpretations

**7.** **Comparing Texts** How does the narrator's account of the Pilgrims (page 872) compare with William Bradford's account of the Pilgrims' arrival in America (page 82)? Do you think the narrator's analogy between her experience and that of the Pilgrims is a valid one? Cite evidence to support your answer.

**8.** **Different Perspectives** In "What Is an American?" (page 290), de Crèvecoeur offers this vision of America: "Here individuals of all nations are melted into a new race of men, whose labors and posterity will one day cause great change in the world." Do you think the narrator of "America and I" shares this view? Why or why not?

**9.** **Connect to Life** How might a social worker have evaluated the narrator's progress in making a satisfying life for herself in America?

## Literary Analysis

**VOICE** **Voice** is the writer's stamp of originality—the distinctive way he or she uses language. Anzia Yezierska gives voice to her immigrant experience by writing about a character like herself who adapts to an alien culture. The conversational language of the first-person narrator in "America and I" contributes to her "stage presence." For example, the way the narrator tells anecdotes about her jobs almost sounds as though she is delivering a monologue to an audience. The narrator's melodramatic tone in recounting moments in her life further heightens the story's theatrical quality—another stylistic element that characterizes the voice of the piece.

**Activity** Reread the story and find examples of the following stylistic elements that characterize the narrator's voice:
- speech that reflects the narrator's immigrant background
- vivid anecdotes
- diction, or choice of words, that is intensely emotional

Share your examples with the class.

## Extend Interpretations

**Comparing Texts** Possible Responses: Both describe the hardships the Pilgrims endured, although the narrator blends the Pilgrims into other stages of American history. The narrator portrays Native Americans only as enemies and claims the Pilgrims had no one to help them. Bradford's account, however, describes how Squanto helped the Pilgrims survive in their new environment. Opinions about the validity of the analogy will vary. Have students give evidence to support their ideas.

**Different Perspectives** Possible Responses: She might agree that American immigrants are new people who act on new principles and are more open to new ideas and beliefs, but she might feel that Crèvecoeur exaggerates the benefits America has to offer, or she might argue that those benefits have changed over time. She might also feel that he emphasizes economic advantages more than personal fulfillment.

**Connect to Life** Students might create a two-column chart for the report, putting events of the narrator's life in America in the first column and the social worker's evaluations in the second. Encourage students to brainstorm, possibly with partners, about their evaluations of the narrator.

## Connect to the Literature

**1. What Do You Think?**
Responses will vary. Some students may state that they admire the narrator for her determination to find fulfilling work.

**Comprehension Check**
- Her employer refuses to pay her wages; she is only to be compensated with room and board.
- She sews buttons on clothing.

 Use **Unit Five Resource Book,** p. 43 for additional support.

## Think Critically

**2.** Possible Responses: Her original expectations are unrealistic, but she reaches a more mature understanding; she remains idealistic about the future of America.

**3.** Possible Responses: how to speak up for herself; not to expect always to be treated fairly; not to expect other people to rescue her

**4.** Possible Responses: learning English; learning history; getting job experience; learning to assert herself; writing

**5.** Possible Response: It seems an illusion at first, but she finds a way to do the work she loves—writing about the experiences of immigrants.

**6.** Possible Response: The narrator and the Pilgrims left distant homelands and faced many hardships in the new land. They had to press on with determination and very little help. The narrator decides that she must be more like the Pilgrims and help to build America.

## Literary Analysis

**Voice** The annotations on pages 866, 868, and 870 identify passages that help to create the narrator's voice.

## Vocabulary in Action

1. pestilence
2. delve
3. simper
4. indomitable
5. avid

## Writing Options

1. **Tips for Newcomers** To compile their tips, students can analyze the narrator's experiences and what she learns from each one.
2. **Letter to Russia** Suggest that students consider whether or not the narrator would encourage her friend to come to America.
3. **Looking Back: A Memoir** Have students brainstorm experiences with a partner and discuss what they learned from each one.

## Vocabulary in Action

**EXERCISE: CONTEXT CLUES** Write the vocabulary word that best completes each sentence below.

1. Is greed contagious—a _____ like smallpox or the plague?
2. Yezierska wondered this as she tried to _____ into what it meant to be an American.
3. Not content to _____ with pretended gratitude for food and a bed, she pursued her dream, even sacrificing security for independence.
4. Although she was disheartened, her desire for fulfillment remained _____ and could not be crushed.
5. Today, _____ scholars of Yezierska's life and writings labor excitedly to bring her works to wide attention.

| WORDS TO KNOW | avid | pestilence |
|---|---|---|
| | delve | simper |
| | indomitable | |

## Anzia Yezierska
1885?–1970

**Other Works**
*Bread Givers*
*Children of Loneliness*

**New Beginnings** Born, like the narrator of "America and I," in a village of Russian Poland, Anzia Yezierska migrated with her family to the United States in the late 1800s. The family settled in a tenement in New York City's Lower East Side, where Yezierska briefly attended public school until she was old enough to work to help support her family. She later worked as a cook, a servant, a waitress, and a needle-worker, sewing on buttons in a sweatshop.

**Lofty Ambitions** Although Jewish tradition discouraged the education of women, Yezierska rebelled against her family and went to college. Supporting herself by working at a laundry before and after classes, she began attending Columbia University in 1904. Her studies were designed to make a cooking teacher of her, but she decided to be a writer instead.

## Writing Options

1. **Tips for Newcomers** Think about the narrator's positive and negative experiences in this story. Write at least five tips to help recent immigrants adjust to life in America.
2. **Letter to Russia** Imagine that the narrator receives a letter from a friend back in Russia. Write the narrator's reply, answering questions about America, explaining what has happened to her since she arrived, and describing her feelings about her experiences.
3. **Looking Back: A Memoir** Compose a passage for a memoir you might someday write, describing an experience that was "a bitter memory but a good school" for you. Be sure to tell what you learned from it.

**Building Vocabulary**
For an in-depth lesson on context clues, see page 326.

**The Lure of Hollywood** In 1920 Yezierska published her first short story collection, *Hungry Hearts.* Paying her $10,000 for the film rights and hiring her to write the script, the Hollywood producer Samuel Goldwyn turned the book into a silent film. Called "the sweat-shop Cinderella," Yezierska instantly became famous. She moved to Hollywood, intending to become a screenwriter, but found herself unable to write so far away from the colorful New York neighborhoods that had first inspired her.

**Literary Achievements** Within a year Yezierska returned to New York, and in 1922 she published her first novel, *Salome of the Tenements,* which was followed, over the next 10 years, by three more novels and a second book of short stories. In 1950, after a silence of 18 years, she published the autobiographical novel *Red Ribbon on a White Horse* to critical acclaim. However, it failed to regain for her the fame and success she had experienced in the 1920s, and she spent the last years of her life in obscurity.

## Teaching Options

 **Mini Lesson** ## Grammar

**NOUN CLAUSES: COMMON INTRODUCTORY WORDS**
**Instruction** A noun clause is a subordinate clause that acts as a noun. A noun clause may function as a subject, direct object, indirect object, predicate nominative, or the object of a preposition. Noun clauses are introduced by a pronoun or a subordinating conjunction.

| Pronouns | Subordinating Conjunctions |
|---|---|
| who, whom, whose, which, that, whoever, whomever, what, whatever | how, that, when, where, whether, why |

Some of the words that introduce noun clauses also introduce adjective and adverb clauses. To determine the type of clause, students must examine how it functions in the sentence. Display the following sentence:

Learning *what America really had to offer* disappointed the woman. (Learn *what?* The clause is a direct object of the gerund *learning* and is therefore a noun clause.)

**Application** Have students write five sentences that have noun clauses.

 Use **Grammar Transparencies and Copymasters,** p. 104.

 Use McDougal Littell's *Language Network,* Chapter 3, for more instruction and practice in noun clauses.

## The New Immigrants

❶ Millions of immigrants entered the United States in the late 19th and early 20th centuries because they were lured by the promise of a better life. Some of these immigrants sought to escape difficult conditions—such as poverty, famine, land shortages, or religious or political persecution—in their native countries. Others, known as "birds of passage," intended to immigrate temporarily in order to make money and then return to their homelands.

❷ **Immigrants from Europe** Between 1870 and 1920, approximately 20 million Europeans arrived in the United States. Before 1890, most immigrants came from countries in western and northern Europe, including Great Britain, Ireland, and Germany. Beginning in the 1890s, however, increasing numbers came from southern and eastern Europe, especially Italy, Austria-Hungary, and Russia. In 1905 alone, nearly a million people arrived from these countries to the land of opportunity.

Many of these new immigrants left their homelands to escape religious persecution. Whole villages of Jews—businesspeople, intellectuals, workers, and farmers—were driven out of Russia by pogroms. These were organized anti-Semitic campaigns that led to the massacre of Jews during the early 1880s and early 1900s.

Other Europeans left because of rising population. Between 1800 and 1900, the population in Europe more than doubled to 432 million. This population explosion resulted in a lack of land available for farming. Farmers as well as laborers often found themselves competing for too few industrial jobs. Some emigrated to the United States, where jobs were supposedly plentiful.

### Where They Came From and Where They Settled, 1900

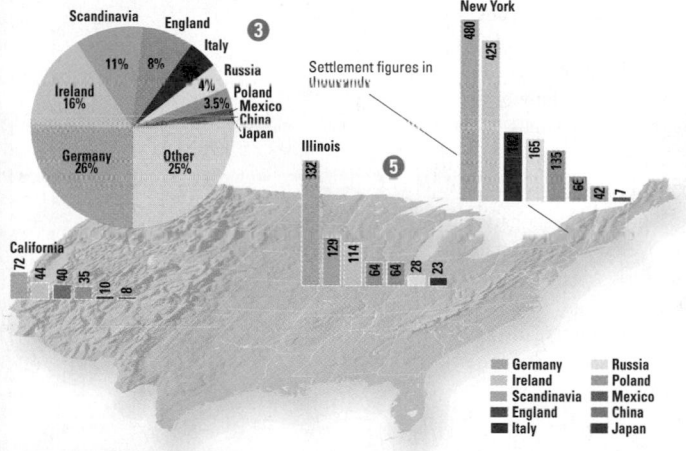

### Reading for Information

Think about how long your family has been in the United States. Were your ancestors' reasons for coming to America similar to those of the people this article describes?

#### COMPARING TEXT AND GRAPHIC INFORMATION

Historical articles contain an array of facts, figures, and information. Certain kinds of information are best presented in written text. Other kinds are easier to grasp when presented visually. Use the questions and activities below to examine two different forms of presentation.

❶ Try using a graphic device like this one to convey the information presented in this paragraph. What information cannot be included?

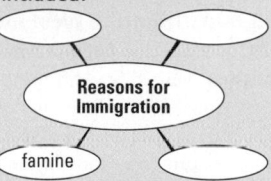

❷ This paragraph explains that millions of Europeans came to the United States during a 50-year period. What additional details do the bar graphs on this page provide about immigration during that period?

❸ Graphic devices can be combined to show how groups of data are related. Here, a pie graph (at the left) is combined with several small bar graphs and a map.

### Objectives
- read and analyze written materials
- recognize distinct characteristics of cultures through reading
- learn how to organize ideas through the use of graphs
- learn more about immigrants entering the United States in the late 19th and early 20th centuries

### Connecting to the Literature
"The New Immigrants" is the type of nonfiction article that can help students relate "America and I" to its historical context. The article provides information about the larger movement of which the story's fictional narrator was a part. The article also provides a link to mathematics, allowing students to understand the history of immigration through charts and statistics.

## Reading for Information
As you go through the article with students, have them use the material in the right-hand column as a guide to reading a nonfiction article and analyzing graphic information.

#### COMPARING TEXT AND GRAPHIC INFORMATION
1. **Possible Response:** This particular graphic cannot include information about the numbers of immigrants and when they arrived in the United States. Numbers and dates may be better suited for another type of chart, such as a bar graph or a line graph.
2. **Possible Response:** The bar graphs also tell the numbers of immigrants from several countries and the states where they settled as of 1900.

---

## Workplace Link — Reaching a Compromise

**Instruction** Tell students that *to negotiate* means to talk with others seeking to reach an agreement that may involve exchanging specific resources or resolving divergent interests. Workers and employers often negotiate to determine what work will be done, what hours employees will work, and how much payment they will receive. In her work situations, the narrator of "America and I" is powerless to negotiate better working conditions because she is unskilled, she doesn't speak

English, and immigrant labor is plentiful. In other work situations, though, workers can negotiate with employers to reach a compromise.

**Application** Have pairs of students think of work that a teenager might do. Have them act out a negotiation between employer and employee about pay, hours, and responsibilities. Then have the class discuss effective negotiating techniques.

3. **Possible Response:** The pie graph shows, in percentages, how many people had come to America from specific countries by 1900. The bar graphs tell, in actual numbers, how many immigrants settled in three states: California, Illinois, and New York. The map provides a visual that shows what regions of America had larger immigrant populations.

4. **Creating a Graphic Device**
   **Possible Response:** Most students will probably create a simple line graph, with vertical numbers for 5, 10, and 15 in thousands running up the left side, and the spread-out years 1895, 1900, 1905, 1910, 1915, and 1920 running horizontally at the bottom. The line would then start near the bottom in 1895 and gradually climb to 10,000 by 1900 and go straight across until reaching 1920. The 20 years at about 10,000 immigrants a year give the total of more than 200,000 by 1920. Many students might decide that the information in this case works equally well in graphic or textual presentations.

5. **Possible Response:** Among groups shown, Illinois was a more attractive destination only for Scandinavian immigrants. Except for Mexican immigrants, much of this had to do with immigrants settling near their port of entry, New York. Scandinavian immigrants possibly moved west to search for farmable land. Both media convey clear and useful information. A paragraph might be preferred by people who are linguistic learners and will also provide an outlet for writing interpretations. Some people prefer the visual information a graph provides. Graphs are a good way to provide much information in a concise package.

## Comparing Texts

The article is effective by itself, but the graphic devices make it more interesting and emphasize the statistics, which are the main concern of the article. By reading the article *and* studying the graphs, the reader is more likely to retain the information.

Finally, there was a spirit of reform and revolt in Europe, especially after the political disturbances in France, Germany, Italy, and elsewhere in the late 1840s. Many young European men and women were still influenced by the spirit of these movements and sought to start independent lives in the United States.

**Immigrants from China and Japan** While waves of Europeans arrived on the shores of the East Coast, Chinese immigrants came to the West Coast in smaller numbers. Between 1851 and 1883, about 200,000 Chinese arrived. Many came to seek their fortunes after the discovery of gold in 1848 sparked the California gold rush. The Chinese helped build the nation's first transcontinental railroad as well as other railroads in the West. When the railroads were completed, they turned to farming, mining, and domestic service. Chinese immigration was sharply limited by a congressional act in 1882.

❹ In 1884, the Japanese government allowed Hawaiian planters to recruit Japanese workers, and a Japanese emigration boom began. When the United States annexed Hawaii in 1898, Japanese emigration to the West Coast increased. As word of comparatively high American wages spread in Japan, the number of Japanese who entered the United States each year reached about 10,000. By 1920, more than 200,000 Japanese lived on the West Coast.

**Immigrants from the West Indies and Mexico** Between 1880 and 1920, about 260,000 immigrants arrived in the eastern and southeastern United States from the West Indies. They came from Jamaica, Cuba, Puerto Rico, and other islands. Many West Indians left their homelands because jobs were scarce.

The Mexican population in the United States also increased. Unlike the Europeans, Asians, and West Indians, however, some Mexicans became U.S. residents without even leaving home. As a result of the statehood of Texas in 1845 and the end of the Mexican War in 1848, the United States acquired vast territories from Mexico. Many of the residents of these territories chose to become American citizens.

Other Mexicans immigrated to the United States to find work or to flee political turmoil. As a result of the 1902 National Reclamation Act (also known as the Newlands Act), which encouraged the irrigation of arid land, new farmland was created in many Western states, including Texas, Arizona, and California. This farmland drew Mexican farm workers northward to seek jobs. After 1910, political and social upheavals in Mexico prompted even more immigration. Nearly a million people—7 percent of the population of Mexico at the time—came to the United States over the next 20 years.

876

What general information is presented in each of these graphic devices?

❹ **Creating a Graphic Device** Create a graphic device—such as a bar graph, a line graph, or a table—that presents the numerical information in this paragraph. Which presentation of the information—graphic or textual—do you find more understandable? Explain your opinion.

❺ Look at the bar graphs on the previous page for Illinois and New York. Write a paragraph explaining the 1900 immigration statistics for these states. Then compare your paragraph with the bar graphs. Which medium provides a better way of presenting the information?

**Comparing Texts** Review the article and the graphic devices. How effective would the article be without the graphic devices? How do the graphic devices contribute to your understanding of the article?

# In the American Society

*Short Story by* GISH JEN

**Comparing Literature**

### Traditions Across Time: Dreams Lost and Found

In this short story, a Chinese-American girl describes her immigrant parents' struggles to adjust to American society. Each of her parents clings to secret ambitions and personal dreams—like Dexter Green in "Winter Dreams" and the narrator of "America and I."

**Points of Comparison** As you read, think about how the challenges that the narrator's family faces contrast with those faced by the narrator of "America and I."

## Build Background

**Chinese Immigrants in American Society** Chinese immigrants have often had difficulty being accepted in American society. In the mid-1800s, large numbers of Chinese men came to California to work in the gold mines and on the Central Pacific railroad. When an economic depression struck in the 1870s, Americans who viewed Chinese workers as unfair, lower-paid competitors for jobs raised such an outcry that in 1882 Congress passed the Chinese Exclusion Act, prohibiting immigration from China to the United States.

The lifting of this ban in 1943 led to a new wave of Chinese immigration after World War II. Many Chinese came to the United States in the late 1940s to escape the bitter civil war between the Communists and the Nationalists in their homeland. After the Communists took over mainland China in 1949, Chinese immigrants—like the character Booker in this story—came mainly from Nationalist China on the island of Taiwan. The family in the story discovers, however, that even though the immigration policy has changed, Chinese Americans still face more subtle forms of prejudice.

**WORDS TO KNOW Vocabulary Preview**

| | | | | |
|---|---|---|---|---|
| amicably | contrite | intercede | largesse | recalcitrant |
| cajole | forte | jubilant | panache | scrutinize |

## Focus Your Reading

**LITERARY ANALYSIS** **STRUCTURE** The **structure** of a work of literature is the way in which it is put together—the arrangement of its parts. "In the American Society" is divided into two sections. Consider why the author structured the story this way.

**ACTIVE READING** **MAKING INFERENCES ABOUT MOTIVATIONS** A character's **motivations** are the reasons why he or she acts, feels, or thinks in a certain way. Often you must make inferences—logical guesses or conclusions based on the evidence you find in a story—to determine those reasons. For example, while reading "In the American Society," think about the characters' actions in the story. Then combine clues from the story with what you already know from your experiences to infer the reasons for those actions.

**READER'S NOTEBOOK** For each of the narrator's parents, make a chart like the one shown. List several of the character's actions, the motivations you infer, and the clues you used to make your inferences.

| Actions | Motivations | Clues |
|---|---|---|
| | | |
| | | |

## OVERVIEW

### Objectives
1. appreciate a contemporary **short story** (Literary Analysis)
2. identify and examine **structure** (Literary Analysis)
3. **make inferences about motivations** (Active Reading)

### Summary
The narrator, Callie, describes her Chinese father's problems adjusting to life in America. The Chang family owns a prosperous pancake house, but her father expects employees to work as servants would in China—to do personal favors for extra money—a practice they begrudge. He hires several illegal Chinese aliens who are then arrested by immigration authorities. Callie's father posts their bail, only to have them run away. Meanwhile, Mrs. Chang—who longs to join the local country club—is invited to a party. She buys a suit for Mr. Chang, who insists on keeping the price tag attached. At the party, Mr. Chang is accosted by the drunk guest of honor, who taunts him about the price tag. Mr. Chang throws the jacket defiantly into the swimming pool and abruptly leads his family from the party, only to realize that his car keys are still in the jacket pocket.

### Thematic Link
In this story, one immigrant family aspires to their version of **the American Dream.** Their **illusions** that material success will guarantee social privilege are dashed by a suburban society whose **reality** is inherently racist.

### 5-Minute Warm-Up

*Daily Language SkillBuilder*

Have students **proofread** the display sentences on page 739k and write them correctly. The sentences also appear on Transparency 24 of **Grammar Transparencies and Copymasters.**

---

## LESSON RESOURCES

**UNIT FIVE RESOURCE BOOK,** pp. 44–48

**ASSESSMENT RESOURCES**

**Formal Assessment,** pp. 161–162

**Teacher's Guide to Assessment and Portfolio Use**

**Test Generator**

**SKILLS TRANSPARENCIES AND COPYMASTERS**

**Literary Analysis**
• Character: Change and Motivation, T7 (for Review, p. 892)

**Reading and Critical Thinking**
• Making Inferences, T7 (for Active Reading, p. 877)

**Grammar**
• Introductory Words for Noun Clauses—*Who* and *Whom*, C106 (for Mini Lesson, p. 884)

**Vocabulary**
• Word History, C73 (for Mini Lesson, p. 882)

**Writing**
• Critical Review, C26 (for Writing Option 3, p. 893)
• Persuasive Essay, C27 (for Writing Option 2, p. 893)
• Compare-Contrast, C31 (for Writing Option 1, p. 893)

**INTEGRATED TECHNOLOGY**

**Audio Library**
**LaserLinks**
• Historical Connection: The Chinese in American Society
• Historical Connection: Chinese Immigration to the U.S. See **Teacher's SourceBook,** pp. 74–75.

**Visit our website:**
www.mcdougallittell.com

**Reading Skills and Strategies: PREVIEW**

Tell students to look for incidents that illustrate the conflicts the narrator's parents face in a new country.

**Literary Analysis** STRUCTURE

Have students preview the titles of the two sections of this story, "His Own Society" and "In the American Society." After reading the first two paragraphs, ask them to speculate what the titles suggest about the structure of the story.
**Possible Response:** The two sections might set up a contrast between the father's actions or feelings in the "society" of his own business and in the broader American society.

 Use **Unit Five Resource Book**, p. 46 for additional support.

**Active Reading** MAKING INFERENCES ABOUT MOTIVATIONS

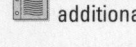 Ask students why the mother wants to join the country club despite all the problems she sees in doing so.
**Possible Responses:** She sees acceptance into the club as a symbol of social success; she wants the privilege of status and well-to-do friends.

 Use **Unit Five Resource Book**, p. 45 for additional support.

# IN THE AMERICAN SOCIETY

### GISH JEN

## I. HIS OWN SOCIETY

**1** When my father took over the pancake house, it was to send my little sister Mona and me to college. We were only in junior high at the time, but my father believed in getting a jump on things. "Those Americans always saying it," he told us. "Smart guys thinking in advance." My mother elaborated, explaining that businesses took bringing up, like children. They could take years to get going, she said, years.

In this case, though, we got rich right away. At two months we were breaking even, and at four, those same hotcakes that could barely withstand the weight of butter and syrup were supporting our family with ease. My mother bought a station wagon with air conditioning, my father an oversized, red vinyl recliner for the back room; and as time went on and the business continued to thrive, my father started to talk about his grandfather and the village he had reigned over in China—things my father had never talked about when he worked for other people. He told us about the bags of rice his family would give out to the poor at New Year's, and about the people who came to beg, on their hands and knees, for his grandfather to <u>intercede</u> for the more wayward of their relatives. "Like that Godfather in the movie," he would tell us as, his feet up, he distributed paychecks. Sometimes an employee would get two green envelopes instead of one, which meant that Jimmy needed a tooth pulled, say, or that Tiffany's husband was in the clinker again.

"It's nothing, nothing," he would insist, sinking back into his chair. "Who else is going to take care of you people?"

My mother would mostly just sigh about it.

WORDS TO KNOW **intercede** (ĭn'tər-sēd') v. to plead on behalf of another or mediate in a dispute

**878**

---

## Teaching Options

 **Mini Lesson** **Preteaching Vocabulary**

**CONTEXT CLUES**

**Instruction** Students can rely on context to determine the meanings of unfamiliar words. Write the following sentence on the board and ask a volunteer to summarize the meaning of the sentence. Then ask another student to offer a definition for the word *intercede.*

> Lila generally encouraged her children to work out their own problems, but she decided to <u>intercede</u> for her youngest child in her quarrel with her sisters.

**Application** Call students' attention to the list of WORDS TO KNOW on page 877. Have students work in pairs to review the definitions of these words in footnotes throughout the selection. Pairs should then write sentences using the words correctly. Encourage them to be creative—for example, they might use the words to create a "short short story" in ten sentences. Have the teams share their sentences and compare the contexts in which the words appear.

 Use **Unit Five Resource Book**, p. 47 for additional support.

A lesson on context clues appears on p. 326 in the Pupil's Edition.

"Your father thinks this is China," she would say, and then she would go back to her mending. Once in a while, though, when my father had given away a particularly large sum, she would exclaim, outraged, "But this here is the U—S—of—A!"—this apparently having been what she used to tell immigrant stock boys when they came in late.

She didn't work at the supermarket anymore; but she had made it to the rank of manager before she left, and this had given her not only new words and phrases, but new ideas about herself, and about America, and about what was what in general. She had opinions, now, on how downtown should be zoned; she could pump her own gas and check her own oil; and for all she used to chide Mona and me for being "copycats," she herself was now interested in espadrilles,[1] and wallpaper, and most recently, the town country club.

"So join already," said Mona, flicking a fly off her knee.

My mother enumerated the problems as she sliced up a quarter round of watermelon: There was the cost. There was the waiting list. There was the fact that no one in our family played either tennis or golf.

"So what?" said Mona.

"It would be waste," said my mother.

"Me and Callie can swim in the pool."

"Plus you need that recommendation letter from a member."

"Come on," said Mona. "Annie's mom'd write you a letter in sec."

My mother's knife glinted in the early summer sun. I spread some more newspaper on the picnic table.

"Plus you have to eat there twice a month. You know what that means." My mother cut another, enormous slice of fruit.

"No, I don't know what that means," said Mona.

"It means Dad would have to wear a jacket, dummy," I said.

"Oh! Oh! Oh!" said Mona, clasping her hand to her breast. "Oh! Oh! Oh! Oh! Oh!"

We all laughed: my father had no use for nice clothes, and would wear only ten-year-old shirts, with grease-spotted pants, to show how little he cared what anyone thought.

"Your father doesn't believe in joining the American society," said my mother. "He wants to have his own society."

"So go to dinner without him." Mona shot her seeds out in long arcs over the lawn. "Who cares what he thinks?"

But of course we all did care, and knew my mother could not simply up and do as she pleased. For in my father's mind, a family owed its head a degree of loyalty that left no room for dissent. To embrace what he embraced was to love; and to embrace something else was to betray him.

---

1. **espadrilles** (ĕs′pə-drĭlz′): casual shoes with cloth uppers and soles of twisted rope.

FOR IN MY FATHER'S

MIND, A FAMILY OWED

ITS HEAD A DEGREE

OF LOYALTY THAT LEFT

NO ROOM FOR DISSENT.

TO EMBRACE WHAT HE EMBRACED WAS

TO LOVE;

AND TO EMBRACE

SOMETHING ELSE WAS

TO BETRAY HIM.

## Customizing Instruction

### Less Proficient Readers
Preview the story by explaining that it is about a Chinese immigrant, Mr. Chang, who is struggling to find a place in American society. Tell students that the narrator of the story is Mr. Chang's daughter Callie.

**Set a Purpose** Have students read to find out what ideas, beliefs, or customs cause Mr. Chang to have a hard time dealing with his American employees.

### Students Acquiring English

**1** Point out that Mr. Chang's spoken English is not as fluent as that of other members of the Chang family. For example, he often misuses the -ing form of verbs. Offer students the chance to rewrite these two sentences in standard English.

**Possible Responses:** "Those Americans are always saying it. Smart guys think in advance."

Use **Spanish Study Guide** for additional support, pp. 212–14.

**2** Ask students how Mrs. Chang's job as supermarket manager changed her.

**Possible Responses:** She feels more involved in American society; she has become more concerned about her appearance and social status.

### Gifted and Talented
Ask students why Mr. Chang feels so compelled to assume the role of boss in the way he does.

---

## BLOCK SCHEDULING: MANAGING TIME

**If your schedule requires that you cover the lesson objectives in a shorter time, use . . .**
- Preparing to Read, p. 877
- Thinking through the Literature, p. 892
- Vocabulary in Action, p. 893

**If you want to take advantage of longer class time, use . . .**
- TE Teaching Options: Preteaching Vocabulary, p. 878; Vocabulary Strategy, p. 882; Speaking and Listening, p. 883; Cross-Curricular Links, pp. 880, 886; Workplace Link, p. 885; Informal Assessment, pp. 887, 890; Viewing and Representing, pp. 881, 888–889
- Choices & Challenges, p. 893

**A** Ask students why the father blames his employees for leaving him.

**Possible Responses:** He is in denial about his own managerial inadequacies; he clings to the past—the way things were done in China—and cannot yet bear to realize that that system isn't working for him here.

**B** Ask students why the girls made anonymous suggestions. What did they hope to accomplish?

**Possible Responses:** They could not confront their father without embarrassing him; they wanted to persuade their father to take steps to improve deteriorating conditions at the pancake house.

### Literary Analysis: CHARACTERIZATION

**C** Ask students what they infer from this sentence. How did the father feel about firing Skip? What does Mr. Chang's reaction tell you about his character?

**Possible Responses:** He feels distressed and anxious; he feels a responsibility for the welfare of his employees that makes it hard for him to dismiss them.

**D** What image does the phrase "life had him pinned" create? What do this image and other details in this paragraph reveal about Booker?

**Possible Responses:** Life is like a wrestler holding him to the mat; he is defeated or beaten down; he's struggling with great difficulty and determination to hold his own.

---

He demanded a similar sort of loyalty of his workers, whom he treated more like servants than employees. Not in the beginning, of course. In the beginning all he wanted was for them to keep on doing what they used to do, and to that end he concentrated mostly on leaving them alone. As the months passed, though, he expected more and more of them, with the result that for all his largesse, he began to have trouble keeping help. The cooks and busboys complained that he asked them to fix radiators and trim hedges, not only at the restaurant, but at our house; the waitresses that he sent them on errands and made them chauffeur him around. Our head waitress, Gertrude, claimed that he once even asked her to scratch his back.

"It's not just the blacks don't believe in slavery," she said when she quit.

My father never quite registered her complaint, though, nor those of the others who left. Even after Eleanor quit, then Tiffany, then Gerald, and Jimmy, and even his best cook, Eureka Andy, for whom he had bought new glasses, he remained mostly convinced that the fault lay with them.

"All they understand is that assembly line," he lamented. "Robots, they are. They want to be robots."

There *were* occasions when the clear running truth seemed to eddy,[2] when he would pinch the vinyl of his chair up into little peaks and wonder if he were doing things right. But with time he would always smooth the peaks back down; and when business started to slide in the spring, he kept on like a horse in his ways.

By the summer our dishboy was overwhelmed with scraping. It was no longer just the hashbrowns that people were leaving for trash, and the service was as bad as the food. The waitresses served up French pancakes instead of German, apple juice instead of orange, spilt things on laps, on coats. On the Fourth of July some greenhorn[3] sent an entire side of fries slaloming[4] down a lady's *massif centrale*.[5]

Meanwhile in the back room, my father labored through articles on the economy.

"What is housing starts?"[6] he puzzled. "What is GNP?"[7]

Mona and I did what we could, filling in as busgirls and bookeepers and, one afternoon, stuffing the comments box that hung by the cashier's desk. That was Mona's idea. We rustled up a variety of pens and pencils, checked boxes for an hour, smeared the cards up with coffee and grease, and waited. It took a few days for my father to notice that the box was full, and he didn't say anything about it for a few days more. Finally, though, he started to complain of fatigue; and then he began to complain that the staff was not what it could be. We encouraged him in this—pointing out, for instance, how many dishes got chipped—but in the end all that happened was that, for the first time since we took over the restaurant, my father got it into his head to fire someone. Skip, a skinny busboy who was saving up for a sportscar, said nothing as my father mumbled on about the price of dishes. My father's hands shook as he wrote out the severance check;[8] and he spent the rest of the day napping in his chair once it was over.

As it was going on midsummer, Skip wasn't easy to replace. We hung a sign in the window

---

2. **eddy:** form a whirlpool.
3. **greenhorn:** beginner.
4. **slaloming:** skiing in a zigzag path.
5. ***massif centrale*** (mä-sēf′ sĕn-träl′) *French:* central mass (usually used to refer to the highest group of peaks in a mountain range).
6. **housing starts:** the number of new houses on which construction began during a given period.
7. **GNP:** gross national product—the value of all the goods and services produced in a country during a given period. (As a measure of the strength of the national economy, the U.S. government now uses gross domestic product, or GDP, which is based on a somewhat different set of calculations.)
8. **severance check:** payment given to an employee who is dismissed.

WORDS TO KNOW | **largesse** (lär-zhĕs′) *n.* generosity

880

---

## Teaching Options

**Cross Curricular Link** | **Religions in China**

Many Chinese have been influenced by all three major belief systems in traditional Chinese thought.

- **Confucianism** places great importance on benevolence and respect for one's ancestors. Based on the ideas of Chinese philosopher and teacher Confucius (c.551–479 B.C.E.), also known as Kung Fu-tse, it emphasizes order and obedience.
- **Taoism,** attributed to Laozi (or Lao-tse, 6th century B.C.E.), emphasizes inner balance,

withdrawing from everyday life, accepting life's inevitable changes, and living in harmony with nature. It is based primarily on the book *Tao Te Ching* (*The Way and Its Power*).
- **Buddhism** was founded by Siddhartha Gautama (or Buddha, 560–480 B.C.E.) in India and then spread into China where it was influenced by Confucianism and Taoism. Buddhists live by strict moral standards and believe in reincarnation.

*Diner Interior with Coffee Urns* (1984), Ralph Goings. Oil on canvas, 44″ × 66″, courtesy of O. K. Harris Works of Art, New York. Photo Copyright © 1985 D. James Dee.

and advertised in the paper, but no one called the first week, and the person who called the second didn't show up for his interview. The third week, my father phoned Skip to see if he would come back, but a friend of his had already sold him a Corvette for cheap.

Finally a Chinese guy named Booker turned up. He couldn't have been more than thirty, and was wearing a lighthearted seersucker suit, but he looked as though life had him pinned: his eyes were bloodshot and his chest sunken, and the muscles of his neck seemed to strain with the effort of holding his head up. In a single dry breath he told us that he had never bussed tables but was willing to learn, and that he was on the lam from the deportation authorities.[9]

"I do not want to lie to you," he kept saying.

He had come to the United States on a student visa, had run out of money, and was now in a bind. He was loath[10] to go back to Taiwan, as it happened—he looked up at this point, to be sure my father wasn't pro-KMT[11]—but all he had was a phony social security card and a willingness to absorb all blame, should anything untoward come to pass.

"I do not think, anyway, that it is against law to hire me, only to be me," he said, smiling faintly.

Anyone else would have examined him on

---

9. **on the lam from the deportation authorities:** running away from immigration officials with the power to send illegal immigrants back to their own countries.

10. **loath:** unwilling.

11. **pro-KMT:** on the side of the Kuomintang, or Nationalist Party, which controls the government of Taiwan.

## Mini Lesson  **Viewing and Representing**

*Diner Interior with Coffee Urns* **by Ralph Goings**

**ART APPRECIATION** Goings (1928– ) is a photo-realistic painter—that is, his paintings reproduce the details of a scene as realistically as a photograph. Goings often photographs his subject first and then paints from the photograph.

**Instruction** Tell students that both painters and photographers pay attention to composition and lines. The way objects and shapes are arranged can draw attention to certain details or help a viewer's eyes move freely around the work. Ask students to describe the composition of the painting and tell what effect it creates.

**Possible Response:** The lines in the painting—the edge of the counter and the row of stools—draw the viewer's eyes toward the people. The viewer's eyes can move through the work by following the countertop to the customers, crossing to the left across the row of windows, and returning across the chrome appliances to the coffee urns.

**Application** Ask students to discuss the photo-realistic style of this painting. Do they like it? Does it seem any more or less "artistic" than other styles of painting? What subjects would best be captured in this style?

## Reading and Analyzing

### Reading Skills and Strategies: CONNECT

Students can connect literature to their own life experience as well as to current events. Ask students to draw upon their own backgrounds to make meaningful connections with what they read.

- Does Booker's situation remind you of anything that's happened to you or to someone you know?
- Does it make you reconsider any current events concerning immigrants in the United States?

### Active Reading | MAKING INFERENCES ABOUT MOTIVATIONS

Tell students that this story takes place in the 1960s, when racism was a serious issue that the nation was just beginning to address. Many private country clubs denied admission to Jews or to anyone who wasn't white and preferably an Anglo-Saxon Protestant as well.

**A** Why has Mrs. Lardner kept this information about her father secret? Why would she share this secret with Mrs. Chang?

**Possible Responses:** She would keep it secret to avoid being discriminated against for her Jewish background; she would share it with Mrs. Chang to convince her she is an ally or to let Mrs. Chang know she sympathizes with her concerns about prejudice at the club.

Illustration Copyright © Darryl Zudeck.

**1** this, but my father conceived of laws as speed bumps rather than curbs. He wiped the counter with his sleeve, and told Booker to report the next morning.

"I will be good worker," said Booker.

"Good," said my father.

"Anything you want me to do, I will do."

My father nodded.

Booker seemed to sink into himself for a moment. "Thank you," he said finally. "I am appreciate your help. I am very, very appreciate for everything." He reached out to shake my father's hand.

My father looked at him. "Did you eat today?" he asked in Mandarin.

 Booker pulled at the hem of his jacket.

"Sit down," said my father. "Please, have a seat."

**M**y father didn't tell my mother about Booker, and my mother didn't tell my father about the country club. She would never have applied, except that Mona, while over at Annie's, had let it drop that our mother wanted to join. Mrs. Lardner came by the very next day. **3**

"Why, I'd be honored and delighted to write you people a letter," she said. Her skirt billowed around her.

"Thank you so much," said my mother. "But it's too much trouble for you, and also my husband is . . ."

"Oh, it's no trouble at all, no trouble at all. I tell you." She leaned forward so that her chest freckles showed. "I know just how it is. It's a secret of course, but you know, my natural father was Jewish. Can you see it? Just look at my skin." **A**

882    UNIT FIVE    PART 2: THE AMERICAN DREAM

## Teaching Options

### Mini Lesson | Vocabulary Strategy

**WORD HISTORY**

**Instruction** Tell students that researching the history of a word will help them remember how to spell it. Write the word *intercede* on the board and tell students that it means "to mediate in a dispute" or "to plead on the behalf of another" and that it comes from the Latin *inter*, "between," + *cedere*, "to go." Suggest to students that if they are tempted to spell the word *i-n-t-e-r-c-e-e-d*, it will help them to remember the Latin verb.

**Application** Point out to students that several vocabulary words in this story come from Latin. Have students work in small groups to look up the history of the following words.

- *amicably*—see the late Latin word *amicabilis*
- *jubilant*—it ends *a-n-t*, not *e-n-t*, and comes from the Latin verb *jubilare*
- *recalcitrant*—it ends *a-n-t*, not *e-n-t*, and comes from the Latin verb *recalcitrare*
- *scrutinize*—the Latin spelling *scrutinium* reinforces the fact that there are no *a*'s, though when pronounced, the word might sound as if it has an *a*

 Use **Vocabulary Transparencies and Copymasters**, p. 73.

A lesson on word origins appears on p. 550 in the Pupil's Edition.

"My husband," said my mother.

"I'd be honored and delighted," said Mrs. Lardner with a little wave of her hands. "Just honored and delighted."

Mona was triumphant. "See, Mom," she said, waltzing around the kitchen when Mrs. Lardner left. "What did I tell you? 'I'm just honored and delighted, just honored and delighted.'" She waved her hands in the air.

"You know, the Chinese have a saying," said my mother. "To do nothing is better than to overdo. You mean well, but you tell me now what will happen."

"I'll talk Dad into it," said Mona, still waltzing. "Or I bet Callie can. He'll do anything Callie says."

"I can try, anyway," I said.

"Did you hear what I said?" said my mother. Mona bumped into the broom closet door. "You're not going to talk anything; you've already made enough trouble." She started on the dishes with a clatter.

Mona poked diffidently at a mop.

I sponged off the counter. "Anyway," I ventured. "I bet our name'll never even come up."

"That's if we're lucky," said my mother.

"There's all these people waiting," I said.

"Good," she said. She started on a pot.

I looked over at Mona, who was still cowering in the broom closet. "In fact, there's some black family's been waiting so long, they're going to sue," I said.

My mother turned off the water. "Where'd you hear that?"

"Patty told me."

She turned the water back on, started to wash a dish, then put it back down and shut the faucet.

"I'm sorry," said Mona.

"Forget it," said my mother. "Just forget it."

Booker turned out to be a model worker, whose boundless gratitude translated into a willingness to do anything. As he also learned quickly, he soon knew not only how to bus, but how to cook, and how to wait table, and how to keep the books. He fixed the walk-in door so that it stayed shut, reupholstered the torn seats in the dining room, and devised a system for tracking inventory. The only stone in the rice was that he tended to be sickly; but, reliable even in illness, he would always send a friend to take his place. In this way we got to know Ronald, Lynn, Dirk, and Cedric, all of whom, like Booker, had problems with their legal status and were anxious to please. They weren't all as capable as Booker, though, with the exception of Cedric, whom my father often hired even when Booker was well. A round wag of a man who called Mona and me *shou hou*—skinny monkeys—he was a professed nonsmoker who was nevertheless always begging drags off of other people's cigarettes. This last habit drove our head cook, Fernando, crazy, especially since, when refused a hit, Cedric would occasionally snitch one. Winking impishly at Mona and me, he would steal up to an ashtray, take a quick puff, and then break out laughing so that the smoke came rolling out of his mouth in a great incriminatory cloud. Fernando accused him of stealing fresh cigarettes too, even whole packs.

"Why else do you think he's weaseling around in the back of the store all the time," he said. His face was blotchy with anger. "The man is a thief."

Other members of the staff supported him in this contention and joined in on an "Operation Identification," which involved numbering and initialing their cigarettes—even though what they seemed to fear for wasn't so much their cigarettes as their jobs. Then one of the cooks quit; and rather than promote someone, my father hired Cedric for the position. Rumors flew that he was taking only half the normal salary, that Alex had been pressured to resign, and that my father was looking for a position with which

## Customizing Instruction

### Students Acquiring English

**1** Help students appreciate the figurative language in this passage. Ask students what two dissimilar things are being compared in the simile.

**Possible Response:** laws and speed bumps

Then ask what the narrator means by "my father conceived of laws as speed bumps rather than curbs"?

**Possible Responses:** He thought of laws as things that might slow you down, but not as barriers to action; just as speed bumps are less effective than curbs at stopping a car, no law could stop Mr. Chang's course of action.

### Multiple Learning Styles
**Interpersonal and Kinesthetic Learners**

**2** Ask volunteers to mime Booker's reaction. Why does he respond this way? What does his body language tell you?

**Possible Responses:** He feels humiliated and must preserve his dignity. Obviously, he hasn't eaten; he is in a pancake house and very hungry, but he is too proud to ask for food.

### Less Proficient Readers

**3** Help students make inferences about motivation by asking the following questions: Why doesn't the father tell the mother about Booker? And why doesn't she tell him about the country club?

**Possible Response:** Each suspects that the other might protest.

**Set a Purpose** Have students read on to find out what sort of conflicts arise at the restaurant.

## Mini Lesson — Speaking and Listening

**MANDARIN**

**Instruction** Tell students that China has many dialects and that these dialects differ so much in pronunciation that they are almost like separate languages. Of the seven major dialects—there are more than fifty—Mandarin is the official language and the most widely spoken language in China. Two-thirds of the population speak Mandarin. However, in Hong Kong, the main dialect is Yue, or Cantonese, and in Shanghai it is Wu.

The largest Chinese dictionary contains 50,000 characters; however, only 3,000 to 4,000 are used in everyday conversation. Each Chinese character is pronounced as a single syllable. *Shou hou,* or "skinny monkey," is pronounced like *show hoe* with an emphasis on the s in *show*—almost like saying *sew* with a heavy lisp. In Chinese, a certain cluster of consonant and vowel sounds becomes a different word when it is pronounced with a different tone. In English, by contrast, inflection does not change the word's denotation, only its connotation.

to placate Booker, who had been bypassed because of his health.

The result was that Fernando categorically refused to work with Cedric.

"The only way I'll cook with that piece of slime," he said, shaking his huge tattooed fist, "is if he's frying on the grill."

My father <u>cajoled</u> and cajoled, to no avail, and in the end was simply forced to put them on different schedules.

The next week Fernando got caught stealing a carton of minute steaks. My father would not tell even Mona and me how he knew to be standing by the back door when Fernando was on his way out, but everyone suspected Booker. Everyone but Fernando, that is, who was sure Cedric had been the tip-off. My father held a staff meeting in which he tried to reassure everyone that Alex had left on his own, and that he had no intention of firing anyone. But though he was careful not to mention Fernando, everyone was so amazed that he was being allowed to stay that Fernando was incensed nonetheless.

"Don't you all be putting your bug eyes on me," he said. "*He's* the crook." He grabbed Cedric by the collar.

Cedric raised an eyebrow. "Cook, you mean," he said.

At this Fernando punched Cedric in the mouth; and the words he had just uttered notwithstanding, my father fired him on the spot.

**W**ith everything that was happening, Mona and I were ready to be getting out of the restaurant. It was almost time: the days were still stuffy with summer, but our window shade had started flapping in the evening as if gearing up to go out. That year the breezes were full of salt, as they sometimes were when they came in from the East, and they blew anchors and docks through my mind like so many tumbleweeds, filling my dreams with wherries[12] and lobsters and grainy-

faced men who squinted, day in and day out, at the sky.

It was time for a change, you could feel it; and yet the pancake house was the same as ever. The day before school started my father came home with bad news.

"Fernando called police," he said, wiping his hand on his pant leg.

My mother naturally wanted to know what police; and so with much coughing and hawing, the long story began, the latest installment of which had the police calling immigration, and immigration sending an investigator. My mother sat stiff as whalebone as my father described how the man summarily refused lunch on the house and how my father had admitted, under pressure, that he knew there were "things" about his workers.

"So now what happens?"

My father didn't know. "Booker and Cedric went with him to the jail," he said. "But me, here I am." He laughed uncomfortably.

The next day my father posted bail for "his boys" and waited apprehensively for something to happen. The day after that he waited again, and the day after that he called our neighbor's law student son, who suggested my father call the immigration department under an alias. My father took his advice; and it was thus that he discovered that Booker was right: it was illegal for aliens to work, but it wasn't to hire them.[13]

In the happy interval that ensued, my father apologized to my mother, who in turn confessed about the country club, for which my father had no choice but to forgive her. Then he turned his attention back to "his boys."

My mother didn't see that there was anything to do.

---

12. **wherries:** light rowboats.

13. **it wasn't to hire them:** Although this statement was true at the time, U.S. law now prohibits the hiring of illegal aliens.

WORDS TO KNOW | **cajole** (kə-jōl´) *v.* to persuade by pleasant words or flattery; coax

---

## Teaching Options

### Grammar
*Mini Lesson*

**INTRODUCTORY WORDS FOR NOUN CLAUSES—*WHO* AND *WHOM***

**Instructions** A noun clause is a subordinate clause that is used as a noun in a sentence. The relative pronouns *who* and *whom* can introduce a noun clause. To find out whether to use *who* or *whom*, students should look at how the pronoun functions in the noun clause. Use *who* when the pronoun is the subject. Use *whom* when the pronoun is the direct or indirect object of the verb in the clause.

**Model** Write the following sentences on the board, circle the relative pronouns, and underline the noun clause. Have students explain how the relative pronoun is used in the clause.

They want to know <u>who is on the committee</u>. *(subject)*

They want to know <u>whom I elected</u>. *(direct object)*

Use **Grammar Transparencies and Copymasters,** p. 106.

Use McDougal Littell's *Language Network,* Chapter 3, for more instruction and practice in noun clauses.

WITH EVERYTHING THAT WAS HAPPENING, MONA AND I WERE READY TO BE GETTING OUT OF THE RESTAURANT. IT WAS ALMOST TIME: THE DAYS WERE STILL STUFFY WITH SUMMER, BUT OUR WINDOW SHADE HAD STARTED FLAPPING IN THE EVENING AS IF GEARING UP TO GO OUT.

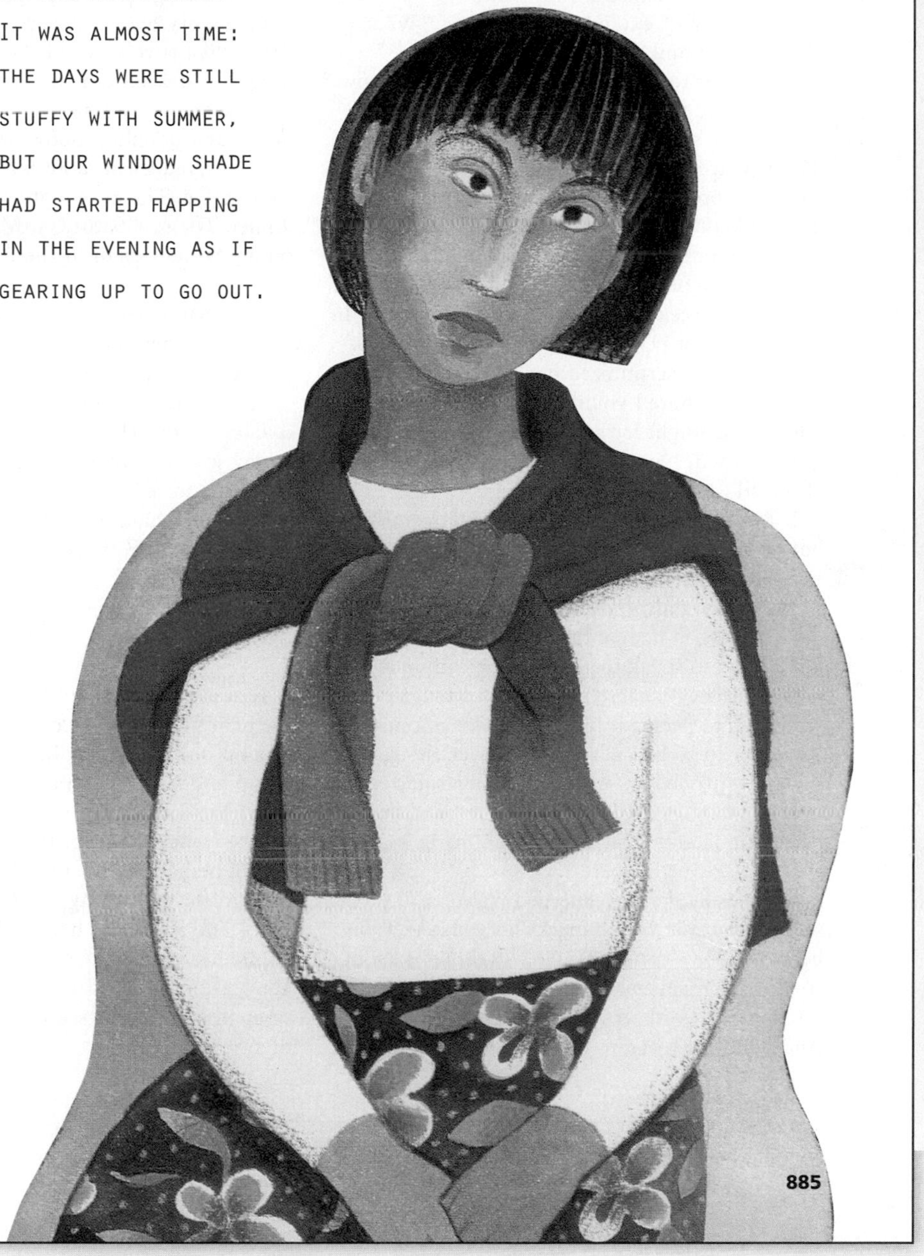

885

## Customizing Instruction

### Students Acquiring English

**1** Ask students why the narrator might describe the window shade flapping "as if gearing up to go out."
**Possible Responses:** It reflects the narrator's desire to get out of the restaurant. You can sense her own longing to be outside as you picture her during long evenings at the restaurant, gazing at the shade flapping in the wind.

**2** Help students understand what it means to "post bail." Explain that bail is a sum of money deposited with a court in exchange for the release of an arrested person. The money represents an assurance that the arrested person will reappear for his or her trial. If the accused person does not appear in court on the scheduled day, the bail money will not be refunded. Thus, if Booker and Cedric appear for their trial, the money will be returned to Mr. Chang.

### Less Proficient Readers

**3** Guide students to understand the events of the plot by asking these questions:

- What does Mr. Chang catch Fernando doing?
  **Answer:** stealing steaks.
- Why does Mr. Chang fire Fernando?
  **Answer:** because he punches Cedric in the mouth
- How do Booker and Cedric end up in jail?

**Possible Response:** Fernando tells police that illegal aliens are working at the restaurant.

**Set a Purpose** Have students predict how Booker and Cedric will repay Mr. Chang for his help. Have them read to find out what happens.

Cross Curricular Link **Workplace Link**

**PARTICIPATING AS A MEMBER OF A TEAM**

**Instruction** Explain to students that people need to work cooperatively and to contribute ideas, suggestions, and effort. For example, the cooks, waiter, and busboys in Mr. Chang's restaurant need to work together smoothly for service to be prompt and food to be well prepared. Without teamwork, the restaurant would fail.

**Application** Divide students into groups of four or five. They are to have a staff meeting to discuss problems and to offer suggestions to improve relationships among the staff at the pancake house. They need to develop a plan with at least three steps and with clear standards of evaluation. They can assume the roles of employees in Mr. Chang's restaurant.

**Literary Analysis: CHARACTERIZATION**

**A** Have students discuss their impressions of Mr. Chang based on his interaction with his wife.

**Possible Responses:** He has a strong sense of duty and responsibility to the community—in this case, the restaurant; he's empathic because of his own experience; he manages to hold onto his own beliefs despite a lack of active support from those closest to him.

**Active Reading** | MAKING INFERENCES ABOUT MOTIVATIONS

**B** What is Mr. Chang implying here?

**Possible Responses:** He feels outnumbered by females and believes that a son would support him no matter what; he believes that a son is more fearless than a daughter.

**Literary Analysis** | STRUCTURE

**C** Point out the title of the second section in the story. Ask students why the author might have divided the story into two parts.

**Possible Response:** to contrast the father's dealings with his employees with his dealings outside his business

**Active Reading** | MAKING INFERENCES ABOUT MOTIVATIONS

**D** Point out that the prefix *demi* means "half." Then ask why Mrs. Lardner referred to the girls as "*demi-guests*."

**Possible Responses:** because they are not full-fledged adults; because she invited them only to entertain her own daughter

"I like to talking to the judge," said my father.

"This is not China," said my mother.

"I'm only talking to him. I'm not give him money unless he wants it."

"You're going to land up in jail."

"So what else I should do?" My father threw up his hands. "Those are my boys."

"Your boys!" exploded my mother. "What about your family? What about your wife?"

My father took a long sip of tea. "You know," he said finally. "In the war my father sent our cook to the soldiers to use. He always said it— the province comes before the town, the town comes before the family."

"A restaurant is not a town," said my mother.

My father sipped at his tea again. "You know, when I first come to the United States, I also had to hide-and-seek with those deportation guys. If people did not helping me, I'm not here today."

My mother scrutinized her hem.

After a minute I volunteered that before seeing a judge, he might try a lawyer.

He turned. "Since when did you become so afraid like your mother?"

I started to say that it wasn't a matter of fear, but he cut me off.

"What I need today," he said, "is a son."

My father and I spent the better part of the next day standing in lines at the immigration office. He did not get to speak to a judge, but with much persistence he managed to speak to a judge's clerk, who tried to persuade him that it was not her place to extend him advice. My father, though, shamelessly plied her with compliments and offers of free pancakes until she finally conceded that she personally doubted anything would happen to either Cedric or Booker.

"Especially if they're 'needed workers,'" she said, rubbing at the red marks her glasses left on her nose. She yawned. "Have you thought about sponsoring them to become permanent residents?"

Could he do that? My father was overjoyed. And what if he saw to it right away? Would she perhaps put in a good word with the judge?

She yawned again, her nostrils flaring. "Don't worry," she said. "They'll get a fair hearing."

My father returned jubilant. Booker and Cedric hailed him as their savior, their Buddha incarnate. He was like a father to them, they said; and laughing and clapping, they made him tell the story over and over, sorting over the details like jewels. And how old was the assistant judge? And what did she say?

That evening my father tipped the paperboy a dollar and bought a pot of mums for my mother, who suffered them to be placed on the dining room table. The next night he took us all out to dinner. Then on Saturday, Mona found a letter on my father's chair at the restaurant.

Dear Mr. Chang,
You are the grat boss. But, we do not like to trial, so will runing away now. Plese to excus us. People saying the law in America is fears like dragon. Here is only $140. We hope some day we can pay back the rest bale. You will getting intrest, as you diserving, so grat a boss you are. Thank you for every thing. In next life you will be burn in rich family, with no more pancaks.

Yours truley,
Booker + Cedric

In the weeks that followed my father went to the pancake house for crises, but otherwise hung around our house, fiddling idly with the sump pump and boiler in an effort, he said, to get ready for winter. It was as though he had gone into retirement, except that instead of moving South, he had moved to the basement. He even took to showering my mother with little attentions, and to calling her "old girl," and when we finally heard that the club had entertained all the applications it could for the year, he was so sympathetic that he seemed more disappointed than my mother.

WORDS TO KNOW

**scrutinize** (skrōōt′n-īz′) *v.* to look over carefully; study
**jubilant** (jōō′bə-lənt) *adj.* joyful and triumphant

886

---

**Cross Curricular Link** **Government**

**IMMIGRATION LAW** The Illegal Immigration Reform and Immigrant Responsibility Act—passed in 1996—requires that anyone who wants to sponsor an immigrant relative be able to prove the financial ability to support that person at 125 percent of the poverty level, or about $22,000 per year for a family of four. According to the immigration service, under this new law one out of four Chinese Americans would not be able to sponsor a relative to come to the United States. In other changes in immigration laws, refugees seeking asylum are no longer granted the right to a hearing before an immigration judge; instead, any Immigration and Naturalization Service (INS) officer has the power to decide a refugee's fate by deporting him or her immediately or by barring entry to the country. Also, the status of legal immigrants is no longer secure; they can be deported if convicted of any one of a long list of crimes, including shoplifting. According to estimates, there are approximately 4 million illegal aliens currently living in the United States. Illegal aliens are often willing to work for lower wages than other workers are as long as they are paid in cash (which is untraceable).

C

Mrs. Lardner tempered the bad news with an invitation to a bon voyage[14] "bash" she was throwing for a friend of hers who was going to Greece for six months.

"Do come," she urged. "You'll meet everyone, and then, you know, if things open up in the spring . . ." She waved her hands.

My mother wondered if it would be appropriate to show up at a party for someone they didn't know, but "the honest truth" was that this was an annual affair. "If it's not Greece, it's Antibes," sighed Mrs. Lardner. "We really just do it because his wife left him and his daughter doesn't speak to him, and poor Jeremy just feels so *unloved*."

D

She also invited Mona and me to the goings on, as *"demi*-guests" to keep Annie out of the champagne. I wasn't too keen on the idea, but before I could say anything, she had already thanked us for so generously agreeing to honor her with our presence.

"A pair of little princesses, you are!" she told us. "A pair of princesses!"

The party was that Sunday. On Saturday, my mother took my father out shopping for a suit. As it was the end of September, she insisted that he buy a worsted rather than a seersucker, even though it was only ten, rather than fifty percent off. My father protested that it was as hot out as ever, which was true—a thick Indian summer had cozied murderously up to us—but to no avail. Summer clothes, said my mother, were not properly worn after Labor Day.

The suit was unfortunately as extravagant in length as it was in price, which posed an additional quandary, since the tailor wouldn't be in until Monday. The salesgirl, though, found a way of tacking it up temporarily.

"Maybe this suit not fit me," fretted my father.

"Just don't take your jacket off," said the salesgirl. He gave her a tip before they left, but when he got home refused to remove the price tag.

"I like to asking the tailor about the size," he insisted.

"You mean you're going to *wear* it and then return it?" Mona rolled her eyes.

"I didn't say I'm return it," said my father stiffly. "I like to asking the tailor, that's all."

3

**T**he party started off swimmingly, except that most people were wearing bermudas or wrap skirts. Still, my parents carried on, sharing with great feeling the complaints about the heat. Of course my father tried to eat a cracker full of shallots[15] and burnt himself in an attempt to help Mr. Lardner turn the coals of the barbeque; but on the whole he seemed to be doing all right. Not nearly so well as my mother, though, who had accepted an entire cupful of Mrs. Lardner's magic punch, and seemed indeed to be under some spell. As Mona and Annie skirmished over whether some boy in their class inhaled when he smoked, I watched my mother take off her shoes, laughing and laughing as a man with a beard regaled her with navy stories by the pool. Apparently he had been stationed in the Orient and remembered a few words of Chinese, which made my mother laugh still more. My father excused himself to go to the men's room then drifted back and weighed anchor at the hors d'oeuvres table, while my mother sailed on to a group of women, who tinkled at length over the clarity of her complexion. I dug out a book I had brought.

Just when I'd cracked the spine, though, Mrs. Lardner came by to bewail her shortage of servers. Her caterers were criminals, I agreed; and the next thing I knew I was handing out bits of marine life, making the rounds as <u>amicably</u> as I could.

"Here you go, Dad," I said when I got to the hors d'oeuvres table.

---

14. **bon voyage** (bôn´ vwä-yäzh´): a farewell to a traveler.
15. **shallots:** small garliclike onions.

| WORDS TO KNOW | **amicably** (ăm´ĭ-kə-blē) *adv.* in a friendly way |
|---|---|

887

## Customizing Instruction

**Students Acquiring English**

**1** Be sure students know that *savior* means a "person who rescues another person" and *incarnate* means "embodied in human form." Explain that Buddha—founder of Buddhism—taught his followers how to free themselves from worldly concerns.

**Less Proficient Readers**

**2** Ask students why Mr. Chang behaves as he does after Booker and Cedric leave.

**Possible Responses:** Booker and Cedric had confirmed the father's faith in the traditional Chinese system of doing business; now that they've let him down, he doesn't know what to believe. He is especially sympathetic with his wife when they are not admitted to the club because he is looking for a way to be close to her. Now that Booker and Cedric have abandoned him, he needs to feel close to his family.

**Set a Purpose** Have students read on to see what problems the Chang family faces in the next section of the story.

**Students Acquiring English**
Provide definitions for the following words.

• *seersucker*—a lightweight fabric that is usually puckered and striped
• *worsted*—a woolen fabric usually worn in winter
• *Indian summer*—a period of warm weather late in autumn
• *bermudas*—men's shorts, popular in the sixties, cut right above the knee

**3** Explain that *swimmingly* means "with great ease and success."

---

✓ **Assessment** **Informal Assessment**

**MISSING CHAPTER** You can informally assess students' understanding of the selection by having them write a missing chapter that describes the outcome of Booker and Cedric's trial. Do they think Booker and Cedric will be set free after their trial? Have them explain how Mr. Chang, and the rest of the family, will react to the results of the trial. Ask students to assume the voice of the narrator, Callie.

**RUBRIC**

**3 Full Accomplishment** Chapter reflects a thorough understanding of the characters' motivations and of circumstances surrounding the trial.

**2 Substantial Accomplishment** Chapter demonstrates a reasonable understanding of the characters' motivations and of the events leading up to the trial but lacks details.

**1 Little or Partial Accomplishment** Chapter shows a poor understanding of the characters' motivations and little awareness of events leading up to the trial.

**A** Ask students how they know that Jeremy is drunk.

**Possible Responses:** He "lurches"; he's carrying a bottle that he might have drunk himself and then recorked; his jaw hangs open.

### Active Reading | MAKING INFERENCES ABOUT MOTIVATIONS

**B** Why does Jeremy use words like *viticulture* and *forte* that most people would not use in casual conversation?

**Possible Responses:** He wants to confuse and embarrass Mr. Chang in front of the rest of the party guests; he's a pretentious boor who wants to show off his sophistication and who enjoys publicly humiliating other people.

**C** What makes Jeremy finally apologize to Mr. Chang? What do students think Mrs. Lardner whispered in his ear?

**Possible Responses:** Mrs. Lardner explains that she is trying to get the Changs into the country club and that Mr. Chang does not speak perfect English. Jeremy apologizes because he didn't realize Mr. Chang had a legitimate invitation or because he didn't know that Mr. Chang was not American-born and therefore could not engage in his style of witty conversation.

---

"Everything is fine," he said.

I hesitated to leave him alone; but then the man with the beard zeroed in on him, and though he talked of nothing but my mother, I thought it would be okay to get back to work. Just that moment, though, Jeremy Brothers **(A)** lurched our way, an empty, albeit corked, wine bottle in hand. He was a slim, well-proportioned man, with a Roman nose and small eyes and a nice manly jaw that he allowed to hang agape.

"Hello," he said drunkenly. "Pleased to meet you."

"Pleased to meeting you," said my father.

"Right," said Jeremy. "Right. Listen. I have this bottle here, this most <u>recalcitrant</u> bottle. You **1** see that it refuses to do my bidding. I bid it open sesame, please, and it does nothing." He pulled the cork out with his teeth, then turned the bottle upside down.

My father nodded.

"Would you have a word with it please?" said Jeremy. The man with the beard excused himself. "Would you please have a damned word with it?"

My father laughed uncomfortably.

"Ah!" Jeremy bowed a little. "Excuse me, excuse me, excuse me. You are not my man, not my man at all." He bowed again and started to **(B)** leave, but then circled back. "Viticulture[16] is not your <u>forte</u>, yes I can see that, see that plainly. But may I trouble you on another matter? Forget the damned bottle." He threw it into the pool, and winked at the people he splashed. "I have another matter. Do you speak Chinese?"

My father said he did not, but Jeremy pulled out a handkerchief with some characters on it anyway, saying that his daughter had sent it from Hong Kong and that he thought the characters might be some secret message.

"Long life," said my father.

"But you haven't looked at it yet."

"I know what it says without looking." My father winked at me.

"You do?"

"Yes, I do."

"You're making fun of me, aren't you?"

"No, no, no," said my father, winking again.

"Who are you anyway?" said Jeremy.

His smile fading, my father shrugged.

*"Who are you?"*

My father shrugged again.

Jeremy began to roar. "This is my party, *my party,* and I've never seen you before in my life." My father backed up as Jeremy came toward him. *"Who are you? WHO ARE YOU?"*

Just as my father was going to step back into the pool, Mrs. Lardner came running up. Jeremy **2** informed her that there was a man crashing his party.

"Nonsense," said Mrs. Lardner. "This is Ralph Chang, who I invited extra especially so he could meet you." She straightened the collar **C** of Jeremy's peach-colored polo shirt for him.

"Yes, well we've had a chance to chat," said Jeremy.

She whispered in his ear; he mumbled something; she whispered something more.

"I do apologize," he said finally.

My father didn't say anything.

"I do." Jeremy seemed genuinely <u>contrite</u>. "Doubtless you've seen drunks before, haven't you? You must have them in China."

"Okay," said my father.

As Mrs. Lardner glided off, Jeremy clapped his arm over my father's shoulders. "You know, I really am quite sorry, quite sorry."

My father nodded.

"What can I do, how can I make it up to you?"

"No thank you."

"No, tell me, tell me," wheedled Jeremy. "Tickets to casino night?" My father shook his head. "You don't gamble. Dinner at Bartholomew's?" My father shook his head again.

---

16. **viticulture:** the growing of grapevines.

---

| WORDS<br>TO<br>KNOW | **recalcitrant** (rĭ-kăl′sĭ-trənt) *adj.* stubborn; hard to deal with<br>**forte** (fôrt) *n.* something in which a person excels<br>**contrite** (kən-trīt′) *adj.* sorrowful for one's wrongdoing; repentant |
| --- | --- |

**888**

---

### Mini Lesson | Viewing and Representing

**The Splash by David Hockney**

**ART APPRECIATION** British-born artist David Hockney (1937– ) is well-known for his creative use of color and images. In *The Splash,* the image of a suburban house with swimming pool would be flat and trite if it weren't for the splash suggesting that something has just taken place.

**Instruction** Help students respond to aesthetic elements by having them compare and contrast *The Splash* with *Diner Interior with Coffee Urns* (page 881). The paintings depict very different scenes and have distinctly different styles. The

lines in *Diner Interior* draw the viewer's eyes toward the people. It's as if the viewer is sitting at the near end of the counter and glancing to the right. In *The Splash,* the spray of water breaks the painting's flat dimension with brush strokes that are nearly whimsical compared to the neat rendering of the rest of the suburban space. The paintings, however different, do share something in common. What is it?

**Possible Responses:** Each shares the perspective of an instant. In each painting the viewer is poised as a witness, and is almost part of the painting.

*The Splash* (1966), David Hockney. Acrylic on canvas, 72″ × 72″.
Copyright © David Hockney.

"WHO ARE YOU?

WHO ARE YOU?"

### Gifted and Talented

**1** Ask students to cite the literary source for the allusion "open sesame."
**Possible Response:** The source is "The History of Ali Baba and the Forty Thieves" from the *Tales of the Arabian Nights,* also known as *The Thousand and One Nights.* Ali Baba says the magic words "open sesame" to gain entry to the thieves' cave.

### Less Proficient Readers

**2** Make sure students understand why Jeremy is demanding to know who Mr. Chang is.
**Possible Response:** Jeremy has tried to engage Mr. Chang in conversation, but he wants to be in control. When Mr. Chang seems to be having a laugh at Jeremy's expense, Jeremy flies into a rage and accuses him of crashing his party, or coming to the party without an invitation.
**Set a Purpose** Ask students to evaluate Mr. Chang's ultimate response to this provocation.

### Students Acquiring English

Encourage students to use context clues to determine the meanings of the following words and terms: *zeroed in on, lurched, agape, do my bidding, wheedled.*

### Multiple Learning Styles
#### Musical Learners

Ask students to create a radio sound-track for this story. Have them think about what music they would select for Section I and for Section II. Encourage them to decide what sort of background noises would describe the pancake house, the Changs' kitchen at home, or the pool party.

---

In *Diner Interior,* the viewer seems to be sitting at the counter; in *The Splash,* the viewer seems to be approaching the diving board.
**Application** Have students discuss the paintings in terms of light and shadow. Why do they think these paintings were used to illustrate this story?
**Possible Responses:** Both paintings give a sense of light. In *Diner Interior,* it is crisp and clear, reflecting off all the surfaces; in *The Splash,* the light is intense and saturating; you can feel the glare of the sun, but there is also the sense of its absorption everywhere. The sun, like the cause of the splash, is out of the picture; you see only the effects. *Diner Interior* fits the setting of Section I of the story, while *The Splash* fits the setting of Section II. The splash might have been caused by the wine bottle that Jeremy throws into the pool.

## Literary Analysis: SYMBOLISM

**Ⓐ** Recall the narrator's comments on page 879 that her father chose to wear old clothes because of his values. Then ask students how to interpret Mr. Chang's action here.

**Possible Responses:** He may be trying to show Jeremy how little he cares for American values—in particular for money and clothes.

## Active Reading | MAKING INFERENCES ABOUT MOTIVATIONS

**Ⓑ** Why are the daughters proud of their father?

**Possible Responses:** He maintained his dignity and honor; he did not cater to the drunken man; he didn't let the man's comments embarrass him; his actions pleasantly surprised them.

## Reading Skills and Strategies: COMPARING TEXTS

Help students recognize the common elements and themes between Nye's poem and Jen's story by comparing across the texts. Use this outline to lead a class discussion:

• Generational differences in an immigrant family are played out between a father and his daughter.

• Tension exists between dreams or wishes and reality.

• Both fathers find ultimate success in a form of self-assertion. One stands his ground to declare his right to live in America as he wishes; the other finds the right land to plant a figtree.

---

"You don't eat." Jeremy scratched his chin. "You know, my wife was like you. Old Annabelle could never let me make things up—never, never, never, never, never."

My father wriggled out from under his arm.

"How about sport clothes? You are rather over-dressed, you know, excuse me for saying so. But here." He took off his polo shirt and folded it up. "You can have this with my most profound apologies." He ruffled his chest hairs with his free hand.

"No thank you," said my father.

"No, take it, take it. Accept my apologies." He thrust the shirt into my father's arms. "I'm so very sorry, so very sorry. Please, try it on."

Helplessly holding the shirt, my father searched the crowd for my mother.

"Here, I'll help you off with your coat."

My father froze.

Jeremy reached over and took his jacket off. "Milton's, one hundred twenty-five dollars reduced to one hundred twelve-fifty," he read. "What a bargain, what a bargain!"

"Please give it back," pleaded my father. "Please."

"Now for your shirt," ordered Jeremy.

Heads began to turn.

"Take off your shirt."

"I do not take orders like a servant," announced my father.

"Take off your shirt, or I'm going to throw this jacket right into the pool, just right into this little pool here." Jeremy held it over the water.

"Go ahead."

"One hundred twelve-fifty," taunted Jeremy. "One hundred twelve . . ."

My father flung the polo shirt into the water with such force that part of it bounced back up into the air like a fluorescent fountain. Then it settled into a soft heap on top of the water. My mother hurried up.

"You're a sport!" said Jeremy, suddenly breaking into a smile and slapping my father on the back. "You're a sport! I like that. A man with spirit, that's what you are. A man with panache. Allow me to return to you your jacket." He handed it back to my father. "Good value you got on that, good value."

My father hurled the coat into the pool too. "We're leaving," he said grimly. "Leaving!"

"Now, Ralphie," said Mrs. Lardner, bustling up; but my father was already stomping off.

"Get your sister," he told me. To my mother: "Get your shoes."

**"T**hat was *great,* Dad," said Mona as we walked down to the car. "You were *stupendous.*"

"Way to show 'em," I said.

"What?" said my father offhandedly.

Although it was only just dusk, we were in a gulch, which made it hard to see anything except the gleam of his white shirt moving up the hill ahead of us.

"It was all my fault," began my mother.

"Forget it," said my father grandly. Then he said, "The only trouble is I left those keys in my jacket pocket."

"Oh *no,*" said Mona.

"Oh no is right," said my mother.

"So we'll walk home," I said.

"But how're we going to get into the *house,*" said Mona.

The noise of the party churned through the silence.

"Someone has to going back," said my father.

"Let's go to the pancake house first," suggested my mother. "We can wait there until the party is finished, and then call Mrs. Lardner."

Having all agreed that that was a good plan, we started walking again.

"God, just think," said Mona. "We're going to have to *dive* for them."

My father stopped a moment. We waited.

"You girls are good swimmers," he said finally. "Not like me."

Then his shirt started moving again, and we trooped up the hill after it, into the dark. ❖

**Ⓐ**

**Ⓑ**

---

WORDS
TO
KNOW

**panache** (pə-năsh´) *n.* a sense of style; flair

**890**

---

## Teaching Options

✓ Assessment **Informal Assessment**

**NARRATOR'S VOICE** You can informally assess students' understanding of the selection by having them summarize the story and demonstrate their understanding of the author's point of view and purpose. Have students assume the identity of one of the characters in the story other than Callie. Then have them write a letter or diary entry, in the assumed voice, that describes their experiences and explains or interprets Mr. Chang's motivations.

**RUBRIC**

**3 Full Accomplishment** Writing fully reflects familiarity with Mr. Chang and offers sharp insight into his motivations.

**2 Substantial Accomplishment** Writing generally reflects familiarity with Mr. Chang and gives some insight, although limited, into his motivations.

**1 Little or Partial Accomplishment** Writing does not reflect sufficient familiarity with Mr. Chang; there is inadequate or no explanation of motivation.

# My Father and the Figtree

Naomi Shihab Nye

For other fruits my father was indifferent.
He'd point at the cherry trees and say,
"See those? I wish they were figs."
In the evenings he sat by my bed
weaving folktales like vivid little scarves.
They always involved a figtree.
Even when it didn't fit, he'd stick it in.
Once Joha was walking down the road and he saw a figtree.
Or, he tied his camel to a figtree and went to sleep.
Or, later when they caught and arrested him,
his pockets were full of figs.

At age six I ate a dried fig and shrugged.
"That's not what I'm talking about!" he said,
"I'm talking about a fig straight from the earth—
gift of Allah!—on a branch so heavy it touches the ground.
I'm talking about picking the largest fattest sweetest fig
in the world and putting it in my mouth."
(Here he'd stop and close his eyes.)

Years passed, we lived in many houses, none had figtrees.
We had lima beans, zucchini, parsley, beets.
"Plant one!" my mother said, but my father never did.
He tended garden half-heartedly, forgot to water, let the okra get too big.
"What a dreamer he is. Look how many things he starts
and doesn't finish."

The last time he moved, I got a phone call.
My father, in Arabic, chanting a song I'd never heard.
"What's that?"
"Wait till you see!"

He took me out to the new yard.
There, in the middle of Dallas, Texas,
a tree with the largest, fattest, sweetest figs in the world.
"It's a figtree song!" he said,
plucking his fruits like ripe tokens,
emblems, assurance
of a world that was always his own.

**Compare**
Suggest that students compare the characterization of the father in this poem to the characterization of Mr. Chang.

**Analyze**
Have students write a critical review of "In the American Society" by Gish Jen. The critical review of literature should meet the following criteria.
- identifies its subject at the beginning
- opens with a general opinion
- includes enough facts, examples, and specifics to support the general opinion
- displays logical organization
- quickly establishes a tone

Students should cover at least two literary elements of the story—such as characterization, theme, structure, or tone—and include at least one quotation from the selection.

After students have written their reviews, have them share their reviews with a group of classmates. Together the students should analyze the written reviews using the above criteria. Then have them compare their own responses with those of the other group members.

## GUIDING STUDENT RESPONSE

## Connect to the Literature

**1. What Do You Think?**
Responses will vary. Some students may say they admired the family for keeping their dignity at Mrs. Lardner's party.

**Comprehension Check**
• the local country club
• for being illegal aliens
• throws both of them into the pool

 Use **Unit Five Resource Book,** p. 48 for additional support.

## Think Critically

2. Students should explain that Mr. Chang wants to show his contempt for Jeremy's values.

3. Possible Responses: poorly—their behavior is too indirect to be truly helpful; with respect—they help him as well as they can without embarrassing him

4. Possible Responses: for Mr. Chang—to send his daughters to college, be the benevolent master of his employees, replicate Chinese business methods in the United States; for Mrs. Chang—to achieve class status and privilege by joining the country club, to wear the right clothes

5. Responses will vary. The society is exclusive, intolerant, and materialistic.

6. Possible Responses: In his own society—ineffective because he is a poor business manager and judge of character; effective because he acts according to his values. In American society—ineffective because he is socially inept; effective because he maintains his dignity

## Literary Analysis

**Structure** Remind students that analyzing the text structure can aid in their understanding of the selection. Possible Responses: Section I focuses on the father's problems at the pancake house. Section II focuses on Mrs. Chang's attempts to fit into American society. Together, the sections create a humorous view of American society, showing the foibles of people like Mr. Chang, who try to maintain their old practices in a new world, as well as the foibles of the country club set whose values prove flimsy.

---

## Connect to the Literature

**1. What Do You Think?** As you finished reading this story, what did you think of the Chang family? Share your comments with the class.

**Comprehension Check**
• What does the narrator's mother want to join?
• Why are Booker and Cedric arrested?
• What does the father do with Jeremy's shirt and his own jacket?

## Think Critically

2. **ACTIVE READING** **MAKING INFERENCES ABOUT MOTIVATIONS** How would you explain why Mr. Chang hurls his coat into the pool at Mrs. Lardner's party? Share some other inferences you made about the motivations for characters' behavior.

3. What is your opinion of the way the members of Mr. Chang's family treat him?

4. What does fitting into American society seem to mean to Mr. Chang? to Mrs. Chang?

5. How would you describe the American society that the Changs encounter?

6. In your view, is Mr. Chang more effective in his own society (Section I) or in the American society (Section II)?

 **THINK ABOUT**
• the way he treats his employees
• his efforts to help Booker and Cedric
• his encounter with Jeremy Brothers

## Extend Interpretations

7. **What If?** What do you think might have happened if Mr. Chang had returned to Mrs. Lardner's party to retrieve his keys?

8. **Connect to Life** For Mrs. Chang, joining the country club is an important sign of success in American society. What do you consider signs of success?

9. **Points of Comparison** How would you contrast the challenges that the Changs face in America with those faced by the narrator of "America and I" (page 864)?

## Extend Interpretations

**What If?** Responses will vary. Perhaps an altercation with Jeremy would have occurred.
**Connect to Life** Responses will vary. Some students may mention expensive cars or clothes or prestigious communities.

---

## Literary Analysis

**STRUCTURE** The **structure** of a work of literature is the way in which it is put together—the arrangement of its parts. Prose writing is most often structured either by idea or by incident. Gish Jen uses a two-part structure for her story, giving each section its own title: "I. His Own Society" and "II. In the American Society."

**Cooperative Learning Activity** With a small group of classmates, create a chart that lists similarities and differences between the two sections of this story. Then discuss these questions: What is the focus of each section? What do the sections tell together that neither tells alone? Share your chart with another group.

| | setting | characters | events | conflicts |
|---|---|---|---|---|
| Section I | | | | |
| Section II | | | | |

**REVIEW** **CHARACTERS** Earlier you learned that **static** characters remain the same over the course of a story, while **dynamic** characters learn and grow. Would you classify Mr. and Mrs. Chang as static or dynamic characters? Explain.

**Points of Comparison** Possible Responses: Both stories show that immigrants must struggle to be fully accepted in American society. The Changs are "fortunate" in their financial prosperity, while the narrator of "America and I" is poverty-stricken and must work harder just for survival. "In the American Society" focuses largely on the material aspects of American society, while "America and I" focuses more on the need for personal fulfillment.

## Writing Options

1. **Points of Comparison**

How would Mr. or Mrs. Chang define the American dream? Write an essay comparing his or her definition with Dexter Green's in "Winter Dreams" (page 841). Place this piece in your **Working Portfolio.**

**Writing Handbook**
See page 1281: Compare and Contrast

2. **Argument about Assimilation**
Outline an argument for or against assimilation—the process of adapting one's values and expectations in order to fit into the prevailing society. Keep in mind issues such as cultural identity, personal integrity, and economic necessity, and support your argument with reasons and examples drawn from this story and from the poem "My Father and the Figtree" (page 891).

3. **Critical Review** Did reading this story make you want to read another work by Gish Jen? In a draft of a critical review, discuss an aspect of the story—such as **tone, characterization,** or **theme**—that you particularly admired or disliked. Quote passages from the story to illustrate your ideas.

## Vocabulary in Action

**EXERCISE A: ASSESSMENT PRACTICE** For each group of words below, write the letter of the word that is a synonym of the boldfaced word.

1. **cajole:** (a) coax, (b) support, (c) control
2. **recalcitrant:** (a) ignorant, (b) unlucky, (c) headstrong
3. **forte:** (a) talent, (b) security, (c) sensitivity
4. **amicably:** (a) intensely, (b) pleasantly, (c) efficiently
5. **contrite:** (a) shallow, (b) clever, (c) apologetic

**EXERCISE B: MEANING CLUES** Write the vocabulary word, not used in Exercise A, that is suggested by each set of idioms.

1. walking on air, feeling one's heart sing, being A-OK
2. giving the shirt off one's back, being openhanded, showering blessings upon
3. take up the case of, be a go-between, pave the way
4. pore over, dig into, comb through
5. carry it off with style, show a lot of dash, strut one's stuff

**Building Vocabulary**
Most of the Words to Know in this lesson come from French. For an in-depth lesson on word origins, see page 550.

| WORDS TO KNOW | amicably | intercede | recalcitrant |
|---|---|---|---|
| | cajole | jubilant | scrutinize |
| | contrite | largesse | |
| | forte | panache | |

## Gish Jen
1956?–

**Other Works**
*Mona in the Promised Land*
"What Means Switch"
"The Water-Faucet Vision"

**Cultural Conflicts** Gish Jen, the daughter of Chinese immigrants, grew up in Scarsdale, New York, where hers was the only Asian family in the neighborhood. Like Ralph Chang's daughters in "In the American Society," Jen often felt ill at ease growing up in American society: "I'd learn all these manners from my parents . . . and then I found I didn't have the right manners for this society, and so I then had to learn this whole other set of right manners for this place where we were living."

**First Novel** In 1991 Jen published her first novel, *Typical American*, which was nominated for a National Book Critics Circle Award. The novel grew out of several short stories, including "In the American Society," as well as her experiences during a nine-month stay in China, when she taught English to coal-mining engineers.

## Writing Options

1. **Points of Comparison** Student essays will vary. **To get students started,** remind them that the essays must include a definition of the American Dream according to either Mr. Chang or Mrs. Chang and a comparison of that definition with Dexter Green's in "Winter Dreams."
2. **Argument about Assimilation To make this assignment easier,** precede this activity with a class discussion about alternatives to assimilation, such as the path followed by the Amish. Then explain to students that their primary tasks are analysis and evaluation. They need not use an outline form, but rather should list each idea followed by supporting reasons and examples. Encourage students to address at least two of the following issues: cultural identity, personal integrity, economic success.
3. **Critical Review To make this assignment easier,** suggest that students identify a friend from another class who has not read the story and write as if they were addressing that person. See page 891 for instructions about writing a critical review.

## Vocabulary in Action

**Exercise A**
1. a
2. c
3. a
4. b
5. c

**Exercise B**
1. jubilant
2. largesse
3. intercede
4. scrutinize
5. panache

## Author Note

**Other Works** Gish Jen's short story "Birthmates" is included in the anthology *The Best American Short Stories 1995.* Her second novel, *Mona in the Promised Land,* (1996) continues where *Typical American* left off. The year is 1968, Callie has (as Gish Jen did) gone off to Harvard-Radcliffe, and Mona is left alone with her parents in Scarshill, New York (Gish lived in Scarsdale). With affection and humor, the novel chronicles Mona's life from eighth grade to young motherhood.

## Objectives

1. understand and appreciate two contemporary **poems** (Literary Analysis)
2. understand how **theme and title** are related (Literary Analysis)
3. draw conclusions about theme (Active Reading)

## Summary

In "Defining the Grateful Gesture," an American-born speaker describes the difficulties of trying to honor the values and traditions of her mother, who was born in Puerto Rico. The speaker's mother lived a life much less affluent than that of her children, and she wants them to appreciate both their heritage and all the advantages they have. She tells stories of how hard she and her family worked and of the struggles faced by people in her community. The speaker feels both appreciation and guilt as she recognizes her mother's wishes and concerns, but at the same time feels distant from her mother's culture. The speaker in "Refugee Ship" describes how she is lost between two cultures. She feels "orphaned" from her Spanish name, or distant from the language of her heritage, which she never learned. At the same time, she feels her heritage will always be with her. Metaphorically, she is on a "ship that will never dock"—caught between two countries.

## Thematic Link

Both "Defining the Grateful Gesture" and "Refugee Ship" illustrate conflicts faced by individuals and families who have immigrated to the United States in search of **the American dream.** The **reality** of trying to adapt to a new culture while still honoring one's heritage presents many challenges.

### 5-Minute Warm-Up

*Daily Language SkillBuilder*

Have students **proofread** the display sentences on page 739k and write them correctly. The sentences also appear on Transparency 25 of **Grammar Transparencies and Copymasters.**

---

# PREPARING to *Read*

## Defining the Grateful Gesture

*Poetry by* YVONNE SAPIA

## Refugee Ship

*Poetry by* LORNA DEE CERVANTES

**Comparing Literature**

### Traditions Across Time: Dreams Lost and Found

"Defining the Grateful Gesture" and "Refugee Ship" are modern poems about the conflicts experienced in some immigrant families. The speakers in these poems are American-born children of immigrant parents. Like the narrator in "America and I," these speakers describe conflicts that are part of the process of adapting to a different culture.

**Points of Comparison**  As you read, think about the speakers' conflicts. How would you compare them with the narrator's in "America and I"?

## Build Background

**Hispanic Immigrants**  Many recent immigrants to the United States are from Spanish-speaking countries. Like immigrants of the past, they left their native lands for economic, social, or political reasons. In search of a better future in America, they have had to adjust to a new life and a different culture. Sometimes, this process can trigger family conflict. For example, immigrant parents may cling to their native languages, foods, and customs; their American-born children, on the other hand, may prefer American ways and feel distant from their parents' culture.

## Focus Your Reading

**LITERARY ANALYSIS  THEME AND TITLE**  The **theme** of a literary work is the central idea or ideas the writer wishes to share with the reader. Sometimes the **title** of a work may provide clues about the writer's message. Think about what the titles of these poems suggest about their messages.

**ACTIVE READING  DRAWING CONCLUSIONS ABOUT THEME**  In these poems, the **theme** is not stated directly. Instead, the reader must **draw conclusions** about the central idea based on evidence discovered in the poem. Use these tips to gather the evidence you need:

- Read the poem more than once, silently and aloud, without trying to figure out the central idea; instead, use your imagination to recreate the speaker's experiences, and try to relate them to your own.
- Note the details that impress you most.
- Describe the speaker's conflict in your own words.

**READER'S NOTEBOOK**  For each poem, fill in a chart listing connections between the speaker's experience and your own, key details, and a description of the speaker's conflict.

| Connections | Key Details | Speaker's Conflict |
|---|---|---|
|  |  |  |

---

# LESSON RESOURCES

**UNIT FIVE RESOURCE BOOK,** pp. 49–51

**ASSESSMENT RESOURCES**
**Formal Assessment,** pp. 163–164
**Teacher's Guide to Assessment and Portfolio Use**
**Test Generator**

**SKILLS TRANSPARENCIES AND COPYMASTERS**
**Reading and Critical Thinking**
- Drawing Conclusions, T4 (for Active Reading, p. 894)

**Grammar**
- Pronouns in Comparisons, C126 (for Mini Lesson, p. 899)

**Vocabulary**
- Analogies, C74 (for Mini Lesson, p. 896)

**Writing**
- Interpretive Essay, C36 (for Writing Option 2, p. 899)

**INTEGRATED TECHNOLOGY**
**Audio Library**
**Visit our website:**
www.mcdougallittell.com

# Defining the Grateful Gesture

Yvonne Sapia

*A*ccording to our mother,
when she was a child
what was placed before her
for dinner was not a feast,
5  but she would eat it
to gain back the strength
taken from her by long hot days
of working in her mother's house
and helping her father make
10  candy in the family kitchen.
No idle passenger
traveling through life was she.

And that's why she resolved
to tell stories about
15  the appreciation for satisfied hunger.
When we would sit down
for our evening meal
of arroz con pollo[1]
or frijoles negros con plátanos[2]

---

1. **arroz con pollo** (ä-rôs′ kôn pô′yô) *Spanish:* rice with chicken.
2. **frijoles negros con plátanos** (frē-hô′lĕs nĕ′grôs kôn plä′tä-nôs) *Spanish:* black beans with plantains (banana-like fruits).

*Analogía IV* (1972)), Victor Grippo.
59 cm × 76 cm × 94.5 cm, collection
of Jorge and Marion Helft.

DEFINING THE GRATEFUL GESTURE  **895**

## Reading and Analyzing

**Literary Analysis** THEME AND TITLE

 **A** Ask students to explain what conflict between the mother and her children the title illustrates.

**Possible Responses:** The mother does not want her children to take for granted what they have. She wants to be able to see that they are grateful, but they are unable to show their gratitude in a way that she appreciates.

 Use **Unit Five Resource Book**, p. 50 for additional support.

**Active Reading**

DRAWING CONCLUSIONS ABOUT THEME

**B** Ask students to explain the story of Mrs. Perez. Why do they think the speaker's mother tells this story? Ask them how the story relates to the poem's theme.

**Possible Response:** Mrs. Perez did not have enough money to feed her family, so she hunted for food in the neighborhood garbage. The mother tells this story to illustrate to her children the difference between their lives and her life in Puerto Rico. She wants them to realize that even though the Perez family was poor, the boys were healthy because of their mother's efforts and sacrifices.

Use **Unit Five Resource Book,** p. 49 for additional support.

## Thinking Through the Literature

**1.** went through neighbors' garbage

**2. Possible Responses:** She wants her children to appreciate what they have; she tells stories about her childhood in Puerto Rico to illustrate how grateful the Perez brothers were to have a meal.

**3. Possible Response:** Different generations experience conflicts as they adapt to American life.

---

**A**
20  she would expect us
to be reverent to the sources
of our undeserved nourishment,
and to strike a thankful pose
before each lift of the fork
25  or swirl of the spoon.

For the dishes she prepared
we were ungrateful,
she would say, and repeat
her archetypal³ tale about the Perez
30  brothers from her girlhood town of Ponce,⁴
who looked like ripe mangoes,
their cheeks rosed despite poverty.

**B**
My mother would then tell us about the day
she saw Mrs. Perez searching
35  the neighborhood garbage,
picking out with a missionary's care
the edible potato peels, the plantain skins,

the shafts of old celery to take
home to her muchachos⁵
40  who required more food
than she could afford. **B**

Although my brothers and I never
quite mastered the ritual
of obedience our mother craved,
45  and as supplicants failed
to feed her with our worthiness,
we'd sit like solemn loaves of bread,
sighing over the white plates
with a sense of realization, or relief,
50  guilty about possessing appetite.

---

3. **archetypal** (är′kĭ-tī′pəl): serving as an ideal example.
4. **Ponce** (pôn′sā): a seaport city of Puerto Rico.
5. **muchachos** (mōō-chä′chôs) *Spanish:* boys.

---

### Thinking Through the Literature

1. **Comprehension Check** What did Mrs. Perez do to get more food for her children?

2. How would you evaluate the speaker's mother?

{ • her attitude toward her children
• the values she tries to give them
• why she tells stories about her life in Puerto Rico

3. ACTIVE READING DRAWING CONCLUSIONS ABOUT THEME
How would you state the theme of this poem? Use the evidence you listed in your READER'S NOTEBOOK.

---

## Teaching Options

 **Mini Lesson** ## Vocabulary Strategy

**UNDERSTANDING ANALOGIES**

**Instruction** Explain that an analogy consists of two pairs of words related to each other in some way. Write this analogy on the chalkboard:

HUNGER : FOOD :: exhaustion : rest

Ask students to determine how *hunger* and *food* are related. Have a volunteer explain the relationship in a sentence, such as "food can cure hunger" and "rest can cure exhaustion."

**Exercises**

1. SHIP : WATER :: (A) travel : path (B) automobile : tire (C) airplane : passenger (D) train : rail

2. DESCENDANTS : FUTURE :: (A) leaders : founders (B) ancestors : past (C) history : heritage (D) past : prior

3. UNGRATEFUL : APPRECIATIVE :: (A) polite : honest (B) quiet : loud (C) thoughtful : reflective (D) careless : reckless

4. NOTES : MUSIC :: (A) opera : play (B) words : speech (C) work : job (D) race : runner

**Answers: 1.** D; **2.** B; **3.** B; **4.** B

Use **Vocabulary Transparencies and Copymasters**, p. 74.

A lesson on analogies appears on p. 254 in the Pupil's Edition.

# Refugee Ship

LORNA

DEE

CERVANTES

Like wet cornstarch, I slide
past my grandmother's eyes. Bible
at her side, she removes her glasses.
The pudding thickens.

5 Mama raised me without language.
I'm orphaned from my Spanish name.
The words are foreign, stumbling
on my tongue. I see in the mirror
my reflection: bronzed skin, black hair.

10 I feel I am a captive
aboard the refugee ship.
The ship that will never dock.
*El barco que nunca atraca.*[1]

---

1. *El barco que nunca atraca* (ĕl bär′kô kĕ
noon′ka a-tra-ka′): This is a translation,
in Spanish, of the previous line.

*Femme Violette*, Wifredo Lam. Photo courtesy of Sotheby's, New York.

## ✓ Assessment  Standardized Test Practice

## GUIDING STUDENT RESPONSE

### Connect to the Literature

**1. What Do You Think?**
Responses will vary. Some students may express sympathy for the speaker, who is lonely and without moorings.

**Comprehension Check**
• Spanish

### Think Critically

**2. Possible Response:** The Spanish translation of the line further emphasizes the speaker's longing for closer ties with her Hispanic culture.

**3. Possible Response:** The speaker feels orphaned from her Hispanic heritage, yet she feels trapped in that culture, unable to understand it or leave it.

**4. Possible Response:** She could learn Spanish and learn more about her heritage.

**5. Possible Response:** The speaker feels trapped in a culture she doesn't belong to. Like the speaker of "Defining the Grateful Gesture," she feels estranged from her parents' Hispanic culture; however, the speaker in "Refugee Ship" seems more conflicted about being poised between two cultures.

### Literary Analysis

**Theme and Title** Possible Responses: The title "Defining the Grateful Gesture" refers to the behavior the speaker's mother expects from her children, who listen to her stories about life in Puerto Rico but cannot imagine themselves in the place of those hungry children. The title "Refugee Ship" is a metaphor for how the speaker feels in American culture: she is a captive of her mother's culture and feels trapped on a refugee ship that will never dock on American shores.

---

### Connect to the Literature

**1. What Do You Think?**
What are your impressions of the speaker? Share them with your classmates.

**Comprehension Check**
• What language does the speaker use with difficulty?

### Think Critically

**2.** Why do you think the **speaker** ends this poem with the Spanish translation of the line "The ship that will never dock"?

**3.** How would you describe the speaker's situation?

 THINK ABOUT
 • her comparison of herself to a captive aboard a refugee ship
 • her attitude toward her Hispanic heritage

**4.** What, if anything, might the speaker do to improve her situation? Explain your answer.

**5.** **ACTIVE READING** **DRAWING CONCLUSIONS ABOUT THEME** How would you state the **theme** of this poem? Is the central idea similar to or different from the central idea of "Defining the Grateful Gesture"? Explain your answer by citing evidence listed in your **READER'S NOTEBOOK**.

### Extend Interpretations

**6. Connect to Life** Why is it important that children appreciate their ethnic heritage?

**7. Points of Comparison** How would you compare the speaker's conflicts with the narrator's in "America and I"? (page 864)

---

### Literary Analysis

**THEME AND TITLE** The **theme** is the central idea or message of a literary work. Theme should not be confused with subject—or what a work is about. Rather, theme is a perception about life or human nature, sometimes directly stated, but often only implied. At times, different readers may discover different themes in the same work.

The **title** of a work may suggest its theme. For example, "Winter Dreams," the title of F. Scott Fitzgerald's short story (page 841), emphasizes Dexter's dreams of youth rather than his later disillusionment. The title suggests that the theme of the story concerns the nature of youthful dreams.

**Cooperative Learning Activity** With a small group of classmates, discuss the appropriateness of the titles of these poems, "Defining the Grateful Gesture" and "Refugee Ship." Think about connections between title and theme, and brainstorm alternative titles for each poem. Then list two or more reasons why you think each poet chose the title she did. Share your list with other groups.

---

### Extend Interpretations

**Connect to Life** Possible Response: Your ethnic heritage is an integral part of who you are; knowing about your ethnic heritage connects you to your ancestors and helps you define your individual identity.

**Points of Comparison** Possible Response: The narrator in "America and I" is a new immigrant who wants to become an American but feels cut off from American society; the speaker in "Refugee Ship" has been raised in America and feels estranged from her family's culture but also tethered to it.

# Choices & CHALLENGES

## Writing Options

1. **Points of Comparison** The process of adapting to American life has consequences—both good and bad—for immigrants and their children. Describe these consequences in an essay, using examples from these poems and "America and I"

(page 864). Place this piece in your **Working Portfolio.**

**Writing Handbook**
See page 1281: Compare and Contrast

**2. Review of Sapia's Language**
Yvonne Sapia has described her goals as a poet: "In order to understand what is happening to all of us in a world we have become too busy to observe significantly, I try to convey the intense emotion of illuminating experience with sparse and carefully chosen language." Write a review about her choice of language in "Defining the Grateful Gesture." For example, you might describe the effects she creates by choosing words with religious connotations, such as "reverent," "ritual," "supplicants," and "solemn."

## Writing Options

1. **Points of Comparison To get students started on this assignment,** suggest that they review the poems and "America and I," making notes about key details that illustrate the experiences of immigrants and their children. To make this assignment easier, allow students to work in pairs to compare the selections.

2. **Review of Sapia's Language To get students started on this assignment,** suggest that they read the poem aloud to gain a deeper appreciation of the language. Ask them to note words and lines that they find particularly effective in conveying meaning.

## Yvonne Sapia
1946–

**Other Works**
*The Fertile Crescent*

**Writer and Teacher** Born in New York City, poet and novelist Yvonne Sapia received a bachelor's degree from Florida Atlantic University, a master's degree from the University of Florida, and a doctorate from Florida State University. She has worked as a reporter for the *Village Post* in Miami, taught at Florida state prisons, and conducted poetry workshops for gifted children and the elderly. She also has taught English at Lake City Community College in Florida.

**Literary Awards** Sapia received the Samuel French Morse Poetry Prize for her collection *Valentino's Hair,* which includes "Defining the Grateful Gesture." In 1991 she won the Charles H. and N. Mildred Nilon Excellence in Minority Fiction Award for her first novel, also entitled *Valentino's Hair.* The daughter of a Puerto Rican barber, Sapia was inspired by her father's real-life experience of cutting the hair of Rudolph Valentino, a silent-movie idol of the 1920s. Besides writing fiction and poetry, Sapia has also tried her hand at playwriting, finding plays "a way to free the voices of my characters."

## Lorna Dee Cervantes
1954–

**Other Works**
*From the Cables of Genocide: Poems on Love and Hunger*

**Cultural Background** Feminist poet and editor Lorna Dee Cervantes was born in San Francisco, California. Of Native American and Mexican ancestry, she grew up in a Mexican-American *barrio* in San Jose and was active in the Chicano movement in the 1970s. In poems such as "Refugee Ship," she addresses the conflict of cultures that many Americans of Mexican descent experience. She also founded a small press called Mango Publications to publish the work of Chicano writers.

**Literary Acclaim** Cervantes's first book of poetry, *Emplumada* (1981), won the American Book Award from the Before Columbus Foundation. Using bold, simple imagery, she traces her own life—from her experiences living in the *barrio* through her discovery of "books, those staunch, upright men." The recipient of two National Endowment for the Arts grants, Cervantes won the Paterson Poetry Prize for her second book, *From the Cables of Genocide: Poems on Love and Hunger* (1991).

DEFINING THE GRATEFUL GESTURE / REFUGEE SHIP  **899**

---

**Mini Lesson** ## Grammar

### PRONOUNS IN COMPARISON

**Instruction** A comparison can be made in a sentence by using a clause that begins with *than* or an *as . . . as* construction.
**Activity** Give students the following examples:
  Lena is better at reading poetry <u>than Jean is</u>.
  They have <u>as</u> many relatives in Mexico <u>as I have</u>.
Sometimes the final clause in a comparison is elliptical. In other words, some of its words are omitted. Give students the following examples:
  Lena is better at reading poetry <u>than she</u>.
  They have <u>as</u> many relatives in Mexico <u>as I</u>.
When words are omitted, it can be more difficult

to determine the correct pronoun to use in the clause. To decide which case of the pronoun to use in an elliptical clause, fill in the words that are not directly stated.
No one cares more about the family's heritage <u>than she (does)</u>.
I am <u>as</u> grateful <u>as he (is)</u>.

 Use **Grammar Transparencies and Copymasters,** p. 126.

 Use McDougal Littell's *Language Network,* Chapter 6, for more instruction and practice in pronouns in comparison.

## Comparing Literature
### ASSESSMENT PRACTICE

### PART 1 Reading the Prompt
Model the process of reading a prompt:
- First, read the entire prompt aloud.
- Then list key words of the assignment on the board. ("analyze," "support your ideas with evidence")
- Use the Strategies in Action to define each word or phrase and show how students can restate the prompt in their own words.

### PART 2 Planning an Analytical Essay
- Students might use freewriting to generate ideas about what the American dream is and why people seek it.
- Have students focus on one or two characters in each selection. Point out that they may have to infer some of the characters' goals and disappointments. They should make sure that evidence supports their inferences.
- After they have completed both charts, students should select the evidence that best supports their explanations.

### PART 3 Drafting Your Essay
**Introduction** Suggest that students begin by defining "the American dream" in their introductions. They can then state the focus of their essays and identify the authors, titles, and characters.

**Organization** Students should choose some logical method of organization. For example, they might contrast the impact of the American dream on different characters, or they could discuss first one selection and then another.

**Conclusion** Encourage students to provide a fresh perspective by offering an opinion, asking a rhetorical question, or making a prediction.

**Revision** Remind students to be sure that their subjects and verbs agree, especially in sentences that have prepositional phrases in the subject.

---

## Comparing Literature: Assessment Practice

In writing assessments, you will sometimes be asked to analyze a work of literature, or examine its parts. You are now going to practice writing an analytical essay in which you focus on one literary element.

### PART 1 Reading the Prompt

First, read the entire prompt carefully. Then read through it again, looking for key words and phrases that help you identify the purpose of the essay and ways to approach it.

**Writing Prompt**

Choose two selections from Unit 5, Part 2—one from the early 20th century and one from the late 20th century. Analyze how the characters are affected by the American dream of wealth and social success. Support your ideas with evidence.    ❶    ❷

**STRATEGIES IN ACTION**

❶ **To analyze** is to look at parts and relationships. You must identify different ways that characters are influenced by the American dream.

❷ Include **examples** and **quotations** from the selections.

### PART 2 Planning an Analytical Essay

- Pick two selections to analyze, and create a diagram for each main character.
- Look for descriptions of characters' responses to wealth and social success.
- Cite examples of goals, achievements, and disappointments that reflect the influence of the American dream.
- Link examples that illustrate the same point.

| How does American Dream Affect . . . | | |
|---|---|---|
| Goals? | Achievements? | Disappointments? |
| | | |

### PART 3 Drafting Your Essay

**Introduction** State the focus of your essay—how the American dream shapes the characters in the two selections you have chosen. Identify the authors and titles, and briefly present the characters you will analyze.

**Organization** Arrange the supporting evidence logically. Choose instances that most strongly illustrate your points.

**Conclusion** In the final paragraph, try to draw a conclusion about the overall impact of the American dream on the characters' lives.

**Revision** Make sure your work is clear, well-supported, and free of mistakes.

**Writing Handbook**
See page 1283: Analysis

### LITERATURE CONNECTIONS

## A Raisin in the Sun

LORRAINE HANSBERRY

**These thematically related readings are provided along with *A Raisin in the Sun*:**

**Queens, 1963**
JULIA ALVAREZ

**Everything That Rises Must Converge**
FLANNERY O'CONNOR

**Dreams**
LANGSTON HUGHES

**Judith's Fancy**
AUDRE LORDE

**Emerald City: Third & Pike**
CHARLOTTE WATSON SHERMAN

**Running from Racists**
SUZANNE SEIXAS

**The Beach Umbrella**
CYRUS COLTER

**What Is Africa to Me?—A Question of Identity**
PAULI MURRAY

## The Great Gatsby

F. SCOTT FITZGERALD

Fitzgerald's novel, set in New York during the 1920s, echoes the themes and motifs of his story "Winter Dreams." Though Jay Gatsby has achieved material success, his flighty dream girl, Daisy Buchanan, remains out of reach. Daisy, her brash husband Tom, and the other characters inhabit the glittering world of the Jazz Age, where wealth and glamour reign.

## And Even *More* . . .

**Books**

**Spoon River Anthology**
EDGAR LEE MASTERS
A collection of 244 free-verse monologues spoken by the deceased residents of a fictional town.

**American Dreams, Lost and Found**
STUDS TERKEL
The Pulitzer Prize-winning author's interviews with people who present their views of the American Dream.

**The Immigrant Experience: The Anguish of Becoming American**
EDITED BY THOMAS C. WHEELER
Nine first-person accounts of the immigrant experience.

**Other Media**

**Carl Sandburg Reading Cool Tombs and Other Poems**
Oral interpretations from the celebrated poet. Caedmon. (AUDIOCASSETTE)

**A Raisin in the Sun**
Film adaptation of Lorraine Hansberry's play, starring Sidney Poitier. Columbia Home Pictures Video. (VIDEOCASSETTE)

**The Women of Brewster Place**
Film adaptation of Gloria Naylor's novel about seven African-American women struggling to surmount the obstacles that thwart their hopes and dreams. Phoenix Entertainment Group, Inc. (VIDEOCASSETTE)

### Imagining America: Stories from the Promised Land

EDITED BY WESLEY BROWN AND AMY LING
In this anthology of short stories, the voices of 20th-century writers from diverse cultures share their visions of American society. Fictional immigrants and migrants struggle to adapt to alien cultures and to discover the meaning of their identities as Americans.

The *Electronic Library* is a CD-ROM that contains additional fiction, nonfiction, poetry, and drama for each unit in *The Language of Literature*.

These are the additional selections found in Unit 5 of the *Electronic Library* that apply to Part 2.

Edith Wharton
**Roman Fever**

Willa Cather
**Paul's Case**

Amy Lowell
**Patterns**

Edwin Arlington Robinson
**Mr. Flood's Party**

Encourage students to select one of these books as an opportunity to read silently with comprehension over a sustained period of time.

## Writing Workshop
### Comparison-and-Contrast Essay

**Objectives**
- write a Comparison-and-Contrast Essay
- use a written text as a model for writing
- revise a draft for parallel construction
- use comparative modifiers

## Introducing the Workshop

**A** **Comparison-and-Contrast Essay** Ask students to name a music group they like, then one they dislike. Have them do the same for a television or movie actor, then a kind of food. Point out that one thing that makes human beings interesting is that people have different likes and dislikes.

A good way to appreciate the similarities and differences between things is by comparing and contrasting them. As students work through the process of writing a comparison-and-contrast essay, they will discover how one thing differs from or is similar to another. In the process, the uniqueness of each becomes apparent.

**Basics in a Box**
**B** **Using the Graphic** A Venn diagram is an ideal tool for illustrating similarities and differences between two things. It allows writers to list characteristics of each individual subject, but it also highlights areas where the subjects have characteristics in common. The notes from such a diagram can form the skeleton of a comparison-and-contrast essay.

**C** **Presenting the Rubric** To better understand the assignment, students can refer to the Standards for Writing a Successful Comparison-and-Contrast Essay. You may also want to share with them the complete rubric, which describes several levels of proficiency. Let students know that you will be using the rubric to evaluate their Comparison-and-Contrast Essays.

 Use McDougal Littell's *Language Network*, Chapter 20, for more instruction on writing a comparison-and-contrast essay.

 To engage students visually, use **Power Presentation** 8, Comparison-and-Contrast Essay.

---

# Writing Workshop — Comparison-and-Contrast Essay

## Examining similarities and differences. . .

**A** **From Reading to Writing** In F. Scott Fitzgerald's story "Winter Dreams," the narrator observes, "Dexter Green's father owned the second best grocery-store in Black Bear—the best one was 'The Hub,' patronized by the wealthy people from Sherry Island." The comparisons in this passage help readers understand more about Dexter's life. You can use **comparison and contrast** any time you want to analyze the similarities and differences between objects, people, experiences, or effects.

**For Your Portfolio**

**WRITING PROMPT** Write a comparison-and-contrast essay in which you explore the similarities and differences between two or more subjects that interest you.

**Purpose:** To explain, illustrate, or clarify
**Audience:** People interested in the subjects being compared

### Basics in a Box

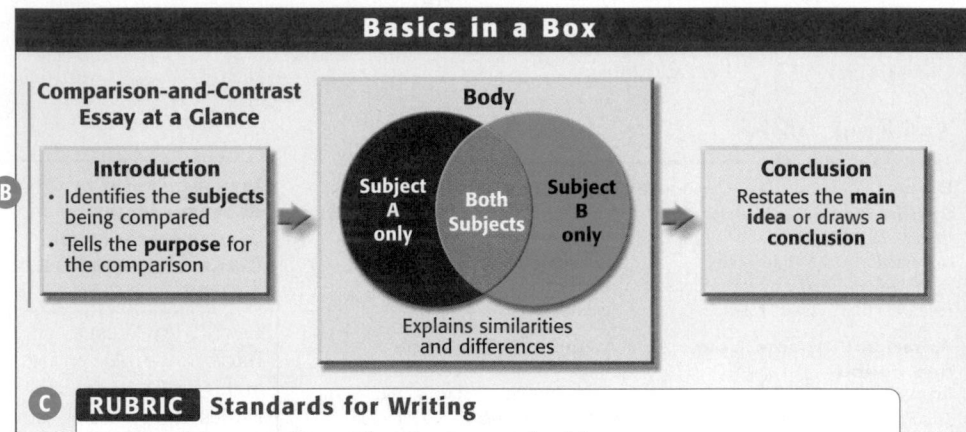

**Comparison-and-Contrast Essay at a Glance**

**B**

**Introduction**
- Identifies the **subjects** being compared
- Tells the **purpose** for the comparison

**Body**

Subject A only — Both Subjects — Subject B only

Explains similarities and differences

**Conclusion**
Restates the **main idea** or draws a **conclusion**

**C** **RUBRIC** **Standards for Writing**

**A successful comparison-and-contrast essay should**
- identify the subjects being compared
- establish a clear reason for the comparison
- include both similarities and differences and support them with specific examples and details
- follow a clear organizational pattern
- use transitional words and phrases to make the relationships among ideas clear
- summarize the comparison in the conclusion

---

## LESSON RESOURCES

**USING PRINT RESOURCES**
**Unit Five Resource Book**
- Prewriting, p. 52
- Drafting, p. 53
- Peer Response, p. 54
- Revising, Editing, and Proofreading, p. 55
- Student Models, pp. 56–62
- Rubric, p. 63

**Writing Transparencies and Copymasters**
- Writing Process Transparencies, pp. 1–4
- Writing Style Transparencies, pp. 17, 18
- Writing Template Copymasters, p. 31

**USING MEDIA RESOURCES**
**Visit our website:**
www.mcdougallittell.com

# Analyzing a Student Model

**Jillian Braithwaite**
**Evander Childs High School**

### Antigua: Almost Paradise

"Gad e cold!" was my first thought after going through Customs and walking outside. People were walking around the airport in shorts and tank tops and there I was, shivering in my borrowed coat. Making the transition from the weather in Antigua to the weather in New York was one experience I could have done without. Even though it was August, I was freezing.

I had been to New York a couple of times before, and it wasn't very dear to my heart. On one visit, my cousin and I were returning from the park one day, and as we were going into the elevator, a man got on with us. When the doors opened on the fifth floor, he snatched my chain. He was never caught. New York still owes me a 14-karat-gold necklace.

New York is a great city, but it's nowhere near as beautiful as Antigua, a small island in the Caribbean. My whole country could fit in the borough of Queens and there would still be room left over. But it has room for 365 beaches, one for every day of the year. (When it's a leap year, you take a shower on the extra day and repeat the process all over.)

The water in Antigua is a beautiful clear blue-green, and the sands are white and gold. When you walk, you feel the warmth right through your soul. So you walk more slowly. At New York beaches the water is much darker—it's so murky you can't even see your feet—and the sand is just a few shades lighter. It's more difficult to find a reason to linger.

I grew up in St. John's, Antigua's capital. Every Saturday morning I used to wake up early to go to market. When I arrived, I saw people coming off buses from all over the island to buy fruits, vegetables, meat, and fish. The market is like a huge kaleidoscope—reds of apples and beets; greens of okra, cabbage, fresh figs, and papaya; oranges of carrots, sweet potatoes, and pumpkins; and yellows of grapefruits, pineapples, and bananas.

The meat and fish market is in a separate building. Here you see butchers in their stalls chopping up whole cows, their once-white smocks all bloodstained. Sometimes you have to hold your nose. Other vendors sit with big baskets filled with doctor fish, angelfish, snappers, barracuda, shark, crab, shellfish, and all types of seafood.

In Antigua we use what Mother Nature provides as best we can and try not to waste anything. I used to have mango, coconut, lime, tangerine, orange, passion fruit, soursop, and pear trees right in my backyard.

I miss being able to go out back and pick a fruit, wash it, and then eat it. In New York I can only dream of doing things like that. The people in my building use the little yard at the back as a convenient garbage dump.

## RUBRIC
### IN ACTION

**❶** This writer begins with an anecdote.

**Another Option:**
- Begin with a statement of the reason for the comparison.

**❷** Introduces the two subjects being compared and contrasted: New York and Antigua

**❸** This writer examines the two subjects feature-by-feature.

**Other Options:**
- Discuss one subject completely, then the next.
- Discuss all the subjects' similarities first and then their differences (or vice versa).

**❹** Uses vivid sensory details to show the setting

**❺** Contrasts another feature of both places—backyards

---

## Teaching the Lesson

### Analyzing the Model
#### "Antigua: Almost Paradise"
**D** The student model compares and contrasts living in the Caribbean island country of Antigua with living in New York City. Direct students' attention to the title of the essay. Ask what the title suggests about the author's preferred place to live.

**Possible Response:** She probably prefers Antigua over New York City.

Have a volunteer read the quotation with which the writer begins the essay. Explain that the author is using a dialect, a regional variety, of English that is commonly spoken in Antigua. In standard English, these words probably are, "God, it's cold!" Ask what effect the writer's use of dialect in the opening statement has on the essay.

**Possible Response:** It both commands the reader's attention and establishes the author's affinity for her home country.

Have students read aloud the model, then discuss the Rubric in Action. Point out the key words and phrases in the student model that correspond to the elements mentioned in the Rubric in Action.

1. Have students suggest an alternate opening, using a statement of the reason for comparison.

   **Possible Response:** Moving from the tropical island of Antigua to the vast metropolis of New York City provides an extreme contrast in living conditions.

3. Point out that in the essay the writer compares several features of Antigua and New York City—here the writer begins with the beauty and size of Antigua in contrast to that of New York City.

5. The details of the contrast between Antigua and New York City lend themselves to visual imagery. Using the vivid descriptions in these paragraphs, readers can picture both places.

6. Transitional phrases help a writer effectively shift from one subject to another. Transitional words or phrases include the following: *similarly, both, likewise, however, on the other hand, yet, although, otherwise, still,* and *even though.*

7. Ask students which specific details bring into focus the differences between schools in Antigua and schools in New York City.

   **Possible Responses:** Students in Antigua would be hit with a belt if they insulted their teachers as students do in New York City. Students in Antigua wear uniforms while students in New York City do not. Students in Antigua are punished for minor infractions, such as an open top button on a uniform. Students in Antigua have to immediately stop what they are doing when the bell rings to end recess. They are not allowed to use the bathroom any time they want or to leave school to buy candy.

9. Explain that drawing a conclusion is the skill of adding up the details and then making a logical guess about their meaning. Note that the author of the model sees advantages and disadvantages to living in both places. Ask students to explain why the author prefers one place but is living in the other.

   **Possible Response:** The author prefers Antigua for its warmth and beauty, but she is living in New York City because of its opportunities, perhaps educational or economic.

---

But in some ways, life in New York is easier. Students here are always complaining about how unfair the school system is, that they can't do anything they want. But in comparison to the school system in Antigua, you people are living in the lap of luxury. Here I'll sit in class and watch students insult their teachers and think to myself, "They wouldn't last a day in Antigua. They'd have more welts on their backs than a tiger has stripes."

Teachers there don't take any lip from students. In my old school if you had so much as the top button of your uniform (that's right—uniform) open, you received one demerit. Three demerits equaled one detention and every Thursday at 4 P.M., that's where you'd find me.

In the primary school that I attended, two bells were rung after recess. At the sound of the first you were supposed to freeze, stop whatever you were doing. When the second bell rang you went back to class. No side trips to the bathroom, and—as I found out the hard way—no side trips to buy candy. The first and last time I tried doing that, the headmaster caught me and I got three lashes across my back with his infamous belt.

One reason I like New York is because if a teacher tried to do something like that, it would be the last time she raised her hand to anyone.

Parents in the United States are not as strict with their children as Antiguan parents either. American parents encourage their daughters' interest in boys. They allow them to wear makeup at 13 or 14 and let them bring their boyfriends home to meet the family.

If you're an Antiguan girl, you don't talk to your parents about makeup before 16 or, in some cases, 18, and you don't talk to them about boys ever.

For the last four years I've been living in the Bronx and I must admit, I do enjoy being able to do certain things that I wouldn't have dared to do in Antigua—like walking out of school anytime I want to without having to ask permission. But then I remember the things I miss most about Antigua—like all the open space. In New York all you see are big, ugly buildings and some garbage here and there to brighten the place up.

If Antigua had all the opportunities that New York has, I would be back there so fast that Superman would be the one asking if I was a bird or a plane.

**⑥** Uses a transitional phrase to signal a comparison

**⑦** Supports statements with specific examples

**⑧** Contrasts another feature of both places— parents

**⑨** This writer ends by drawing a conclusion from the comparison.
**Other Options:**
· Restate the main idea.
· Summarize the main points.

# Writing Your Comparison-and-Contrast Essay

## ❶ Prewriting

*Resemblances are the shadows of differences.
Different people see different similarities and differences.*
**Vladimir Nabokov, Russian novelist**

Think about why you might want to compare two things. Do you have a choice or decision to make? Do you want to convince someone that one thing is better than another? Maybe you and your friends disagree about the best running shoes, movies, or food. **List** ideas that come to mind. See the **Idea Bank** in the margin for more suggestions. After you choose your subjects, follow the steps below.

### Planning Your Comparison-and-Contrast Essay

▶ **1. Decide what features you will compare or contrast.** Think about the main idea of the essay. Focus on similarities and differences that are important to this main idea.

▶ **2. Choose an organizational pattern.** There are two basic patterns for organizing comparisons: subject-by-subject and feature-by-feature. The following chart shows the two patterns.

| Subject-by-Subject | Feature-by-Feature |
|---|---|
| Introduction | Introduction |
| Subject A | Feature 1 |
|    Feature 1 |    Subject A |
|    Feature 2 |    Subject B |
| Subject B | Feature 2 |
|    Feature 1 |    Subject A |
|    Feature 2 |    Subject B |
| Conclusion | Conclusion |

## ❷ Drafting

Begin writing by identifying the subjects you are comparing. You can work on creating a lively **introduction** now or you can do it during the revision stage. Stick to the **organizational pattern** you chose, and be sure to give the most specific and interesting examples and details to support your comparisons.

You can help your reader keep track of your ideas by using **transitional words and phrases,** such as *both, similarly, but, instead, in contrast,* and *however,* to indicate similarities and differences. Finally, write a **conclusion,** or brief summarizing paragraph.

### IDEABank

**1. Your Working Portfolio**
Look for ideas in the **Writing Options** you completed earlier in this unit:

- **Comparison-Contrast Essay,** p. 829
- **Points of Comparison,** pp. 893, 899

**2. Which Is Better?**
Think of topics such as sports teams or school activities that you and your friends disagree about. Choose two specific items to compare and contrast.

**3. Then and Now**
Skim magazines and newspapers. Look for a current event to compare with a past one or a new form of technology to compare with an older one.

**Need more help with comparison and contrast?**

See the **Writing Handbook,** pp. 1281-1282.

### Ask Your Peer Reader

- What is my reason for comparing and contrasting these subjects?
- What parts of my essay did you find most and least interesting? Why?
- What parts were confusing?

---

## Prewriting

### Choosing a Subject

If after reading the Idea Bank students are still having difficulty choosing their subjects, suggest that they try the following:

- Topics from other school subjects may make interesting comparisons. Here are some examples: Compare two animals—one living in its natural habitat with one living in captivity. Compare the style or subject matter of two artists. Compare two scientific discoveries or two types of space travel vehicles.
- Compare two political leaders, two people in the news, or two musicians in order to better understand each person.
- Compare two characters from the same book or play, or two characters from separate literary works.

### Planning the Comparison-and-Contrast Essay

1. Have students work with a partner to describe their ideas for their essay. Students should be sure that the topics chosen for comparison are related in some way and that they can find out enough information about each to have a solid comparison.

2. Point out that the writer of the student model used a feature-by-feature pattern in her essay. Ask how organizing her information subject-by-subject would have changed the essay.

   **Possible Response:** Some of the humor and power might have been lost because contrasts would not have been as direct.

## Drafting

### Organizing the Draft

Students may want to use an outline or other graphic organizer to order the subjects and features of their comparison-and-contrast essay.

Point out that neither pattern for organizing comparisons is superior to the other; students should choose a pattern of organization based on their topic. If students are comparing feature-by-feature, they might consider using their most powerful comparisons at the beginning or the end of the essay. Encourage students to decide whether some elements logically precede others, thus making transitions smoother.

## Revising
### PARALLEL CONSTRUCTION

Direct students' attention to the example. Before the sentences were corrected, the writer used the verbs *learned* and *stumbled* and the noun *discovering* in repeated sentence elements. Changing the verbs to the nouns *learning* and *stumbling* adds both balance and coherence to the sentence.

You may want to explain that in the example, the words *learning, discovering,* and *stumbling* are gerunds. A gerund is a verb form that ends in *-ing* and functions as a noun.

## Editing and Proofreading
### MODIFIERS

Students should produce final drafts that are error-free. The target skill for this workshop is using modifiers correctly. In general, shorter adjectives make the comparative form by adding the suffix *er* for comparisons, while longer adjectives use the word *more* before the adjective itself. In the example, *nice* and *quick* are shorter adjectives, and *desperate* is longer.

Most adverbs use the word *more* before the adverb to express comparison:

> I felt at home more quickly in London than I did in Paris.

## Reflecting

You might also have students consider the following questions as they reflect on their writing: Would the essay have read as smoothly if they had used the other organizational pattern? How did their peer readers' suggestions help them improve their comparison-and-contrast essays? Have students add these self-evaluations to their working portfolios.

**Need revising help?**

Review the **Rubric,** p. 902

Consider **peer reader** comments

Check **Revision Guidelines,** p. 1269

**Confused by comparative forms of modifiers?**

See the **Grammar Handbook,** p. 1313

## Publishing
### IDEAS

- If you compared two products, submit your essay to a consumer's guide.
- If you compared two movies, share your essay with others interested in the movies.

**More Online: Publishing Options** www.mcdougallittell.com

## ❸ Revising

**TARGET SKILL ▶ PARALLEL CONSTRUCTION** Writers often use parallel construction, or **parallelism**, to emphasize similarities and differences. They repeat similar grammatical structures or sentence patterns to link similar or contrasting ideas. The key is to make sure the repeated sentence elements are the same.

> Spending the summer in England gave me the opportunity to study a foreign language. ~~I learned~~ *Learning* new words for familiar things (tube for subway), discovering new words for familiar foods (biscuit for cracker), and ~~I stumbled~~ *stumbling* over odd pronunciations (I bet you can't pronounce Cholmondeley!) ~~These~~ were all part of my education.

## ❹ Editing and Proofreading

**TARGET SKILL ▶ MODIFIERS** Use comparative forms of modifiers to compare two people, places, ideas, or actions. Some modifiers add the suffix *-er* to make their comparative forms, and others use the word *more* with the basic form of the adjective or adverb. Be sure you use the proper form.

> I also learned that the English are ~~more nice~~ *nicer* than I had expected. Once, when I was lost and desperate *more* than usual, I found that Londoners were ~~more~~ quick*er* than most New Yorkers to help a puzzled tourist.

## ❺ Reflecting

**FOR YOUR WORKING PORTFOLIO** What did you learn about the two subjects you chose by analyzing their similarities and differences? What would you do differently the next time you compare and contrast two subjects? Attach your answers to your finished work. Save your comparison-and-contrast essay in your **Working Portfolio.**

Read this paragraph from the first draft of a student essay. The underlined sections may include the following kinds of errors:

- **lack of parallel structure**
- **capitalization errors**
- **incorrect comparative forms**
- **run-on sentences**

For each underlined section, choose the revision that most improves the writing.

> <u>Just because two women are sisters this doesn't mean they have a lot in</u>
> (1)
> <u>common.</u> Although Stella and Blanche are sisters in <u>Tennessee williams's play</u>
>                                                        (2)
> <u>a streetcar named Desire,</u> they are <u>different</u> than they are alike. <u>Stella is</u>
>                                          (3)                        (4)
> <u>satisfied and earthy, she has a realistic view of the world.</u> <u>Blanche is a dreamer</u>
>                                                                   (5)
> <u>and hopelessly romantic.</u> The sisters' desires tell the reader a lot about each
> character. Blanche aspires to a luxurious life. <u>She likes parties, music, and to</u>
>                                                    (6)
> <u>dance.</u> Stella, on the other hand, is content with her humble life.

1.  **A.** Just because two women are sisters. This doesn't mean they have a lot in common.
    **B.** Just because two women are sisters doesn't mean they have a lot in common.
    **C.** Just because two women are sisters, this doesn't mean they have a lot in common.
    **D.** Correct as is

2.  **A.** Tennessee Williams's play *a Streetcar Named Desire*
    **B.** Tennessee Williams's Play *A Streetcar named Desire*
    **C.** Tennessee Williams's play *A Streetcar Named Desire*
    **D.** Correct as is

3.  **A.** more different
    **B.** most different
    **C.** more differently
    **D.** Correct as is

4.  **A.** Stella is satisfied and earthy; She has a realistic view of the world.
    **B.** Stella is satisfied and earthy she has a realistic view of the world.
    **C.** Stella is satisfied and earthy. She has a realistic view of the world.
    **D.** Correct as is

5.  **A.** Blanche is a dreamer and a hopeless romantic.
    **B.** Blanche is a dreamer and hopeless.
    **C.** Blanche is a dreamer and a hopelessly romantic.
    **D.** Correct as is

6.  **A.** She likes parties, music, and to go dancing.
    **B.** She likes parties, music, and dancing.
    **C.** She likes parties, music, and dance.
    **D.** Correct as is

**Need extra help?**

See the **Grammar Handbook**

Capitalization Chart, p. 1329

Correcting Run-on Sentences, p. 1323

Regular Comparison, p. 1313

Remind students to carefully read all the choices before they answer each question. Then show students how to eliminate incorrect choices for the first question.

**A.** This choice splits the sentence into two sentences, but the first one is a fragment.

**C.** Adding a comma does not improve the sentence because the sentence still has the extraneous word *this*.

**D.** This sentence is incorrect because it has the extraneous word *this*.

**B.** This is the best choice because it eliminates the extraneous word *this*.

**Answers:**

1. B; **2.** C; **3.** A; **4.** C; **5.** A; **6.** B

## Building Vocabulary

### Objectives

- learn strategies for interpreting both the precise and implied meanings of a word
- discriminate between connotative and denotative meanings and interpret the connotative power of words
- identify the author's purpose and audience in order to choose the best word

### EXERCISE

Some **possible responses** follow.

1. *Retort:* Synonyms may include *comeback, reply,* and *counter.*
2. *Cajole:* Synonyms may include *coax* and *persuade.*
3. *Contrite:* Synonyms may include *sorry* and *repentant.*
4. *Ingenuous:* Synonyms may include *artless, naive,* and *innocent.*
5. *Malicious:* Synonyms may include *malevolent, spiteful,* and *harmful.*

---

## The Power of Words

Good writers recognize the power of language and choose words carefully for maximum impact. They consider both the **denotation,** or the precise meaning, of a word and its **connotations,** or implied meanings and overtones. For example, in his poem "Chicago," Carl Sandburg depends on the denotations and connotations of his chosen words to express both the negative and positive aspects of the city. Notice the word *cunning* in the lines on the right. What meanings does the word hold for you?

Although the word *cunning* has the denotation of "artfully clever," the word has negative connotations of slyness and craftiness often associated with predatory

> . . . here is a tall bold slugger set vivid
> against the little soft cities;
> Fierce as a dog with tongue lapping for
> action, cunning as a savage pitted against
> the wilderness.
>
> —Carl Sandburg, "Chicago"

creatures, such as foxes and wolves. On the other hand, it also carries the positive connotations of intelligence and a will to survive. If Sandburg had instead chosen a **synonym** (a word with a similar meaning) for *cunning,* such as *tricky* or *artful,* he would have lost the combined implications of intelligence, deceitful cleverness, and predation for the sake of survival that *cunning* connotes.

---

## Strategies for Building Vocabulary

Sensitivity to differences between denotation and connotation will enrich your understanding of literature and sharpen your powers of expression. The strategies that follow can help you become aware of the power of words.

❶ **Watch for Words with Impact** As you read, consider both the denotation and connotations of words. Ask yourself what associations a word brings to mind and what emotions it evokes. Look for meanings that are implied but not directly stated. For example, consider the different connotations of such similar words as *inexpensive, cheap,* and *bargain.*

❷ **Identify the Author's Purpose** Consider the author's purpose for writing and the audience for which the work is intended. What feelings is the author trying to convey? How does the choice of words affect the tone of the work? For example, in the excerpt below, the word *steel* is quite emotive, or charged with a number of associations. *Steel* implies a powerful strength and coldness, mirroring the feelings of Dexter.

> He wanted to care, and he could not care. . . .
> The gates were closed, the sun was gone down,
> and there was no beauty but the gray beauty of
> steel that withstands all time.
>
> —F. Scott Fitzgerald, "Winter Dreams"

❸ **Choose Words Carefully** When you write, remember that synonyms are not always interchangeable. For example, although *aspiration* and *illusion* are both synonyms for *dream,* the meaning of the phrase "the American dream" changes greatly when it becomes "the American aspiration" or "the American illusion." To test the power of connotation, think about the meanings that are implied by each synonym, as in the example that follows.

1. He is an intelligent individual.
   (*Intelligent* implies that the person has considerable mental ability.)
2. He is a brilliant individual.
   (*Brilliant* connotes that the person is exceptionally intelligent, perhaps even a genius.)
3. He is a knowing individual.
   (*Knowing* connotes that the person possesses intelligence and also a clever awareness of the world.)

---

**EXERCISE** Write a sentence for each word that follows. Then rewrite the sentence, substituting a synonym for the word. Explain how the meaning of the sentence changes when a synonym is used.

1. retort  3. contrite  5. malicious
2. cajole  4. ingenuous

## Grammar from Literature

Read the excerpts below from F. Scott Fitzgerald's "Winter Dreams." The blue passages in the examples below are subordinate clauses. They are functioning as nouns in the sentences.

> noun clauses as direct objects
> **He did not know** what it was **or** why it was funny.
>
> **The helpless part of trying to do anything about it**
> noun clause as predicate nominative
> **was** that she did it all herself.
>
> noun clause as object of preposition
> **Dexter waited with no apprehension of** what was coming.

A noun clause can function in the same ways that a single-word noun does—as subject, direct object, predicate nominative, indirect object, or object of a preposition.

A noun clause can be introduced by a pronoun (*who, whom, whose, which, that, whoever, whomever, what, whatever*) or by a subordinating conjunction (such as *how, that, when, where, whether, why*). Sometimes the introductory word *that* is understood rather than stated at the beginning of a noun clause.

> noun clause
> **She whispered, . . ."Last night I thought** I was in love with
> noun clause
> [another] man **and tonight I think** I'm in love with you."

**Using Noun Clauses in Your Writing** When you create a subordinate clause, you clarify and sometimes emphasize the relationship between or among ideas. Using noun clauses may also improve sentence variety.

**WRITING EXERCISE** Create a complex sentence by rewriting each pair of sentences below. Add introductory words if necessary, and rewrite the underlined portion as a noun clause. Eliminate words in italics.

1. A reader might wonder *about the outcome*. <u>Dexter will forget Judy and get on with his life.</u>
2. Social position was judged by *a number of things*. <u>Whom you married</u> counted and the <u>place you lived</u>.
3. Judy has a certain kind of behavior. *This* is quite acceptable to Dexter.
4. As you read, you must make decisions. <u>What do you like and dislike about the characters?</u>

In addition, using noun clauses sometimes eliminates awkward wording and improves the flow of your writing.

> ORIGINAL
> **Don't characters like Judy make you wonder about the motivations of people? Are some people just incapable of loyalty?**
>
> REWRITTEN
> **Don't characters like Judy make you wonder**
> noun clause as direct object
> whether some people are incapable of loyalty?
>
> ORIGINAL
> **The method the character will use to overcome his or her conflict is unknown. The information is not apparent until the denouement.**
>
> REWRITTEN        noun clause as subject
> **How the character will overcome his or her conflict is not apparent until the denouement.**

**Usage Tip** The choice about whether to use *who* or *whom* often causes confusion. The choice depends on how *who* or *whom* is functioning within a clause. *Who* is the nominative form of the pronoun and is used as a subject or predicate nominative. *Whom* is the objective form and is used as a direct object, indirect object, or object of prepositions.

> subject of the noun clause
> Who **loved Judy was no mystery.**
>
> direct object in a noun clause
> Whom **Judy loved was another matter altogether.**
>
>                        subject of the noun clause
> **Judy seemed capable of being attracted by** whoever **was passing.**
>
>                        direct object of the noun clause
> **Dexter was annoyed by** whomever **Judy chased.**

5. Make no mistake: Judy is aware *of something important*. <u>She has control over men.</u>

**GRAMMAR EXERCISE** Rewrite the sentences below, correcting any errors in pronoun usage. If there is no error, write *Correct*.

1. Who Judy hurt was of no importance to her.
2. At "cut-in" dances, a girl danced with whomever cut in.
3. Irene was the girl to whom Dexter was engaged.
4. He knew now who was speaking.
5. A friend of Fitzgerald's friend Ginevera King is who Fitzgerald used as an inspiration for the character Judy.

---

**Objectives**
- recognize that subordinate clauses can function as nouns in a sentence
- use noun clauses to improve sentence variety
- revise drafts by using subordinate clauses to emphasize or clarify the relationships among ideas
- practice creating complex sentences by linking noun clauses with an independent clause
- use *who* and *whom* correctly in a noun clause

**WRITING EXERCISE**

Answers will vary. Possible responses are shown.

1. A reader might wonder <u>whether Dexter will forget Judy and get on with his life</u>.
2. Social position was judged by <u>whom you married and where you lived</u>.
3. Judy has a certain kind of behavior <u>that</u> is quite acceptable to Dexter.
4. As you read, you must <u>decide what do you like and dislike about the characters</u>.
5. Make no mistake: Judy is aware <u>that she has control over men</u>.

**GRAMMAR EXERCISE**

1. <u>Whom</u> Judy hurt was of no importance to her.
2. At "cut-in" dances, a girl danced with <u>whoever</u> cut in.
3. Correct
4. Correct
5. A friend of Fitzgerald's friend Ginevera King is <u>whom</u> Fitzgerald used as an inspiration for the character Judy.

## Objectives

- reflect on and assess understanding of the unit
- demonstrate an understanding of the social position of American women of the past
- compare across texts elements of texts such as conflict and characterization
- reflect on and assess understanding of figurative language
- connect literature to historical contexts and current events
- assess and build portfolios

# Reflecting on the Unit

### OPTION 1

A successful response will

- select one character with whom the student identifies and explain why.
- select one character the student feels is unsympathetic and explain why.
- show an understanding of the struggles women faced in the selections in this unit.
- be written in clear, well-supported paragraphs that use information from the selections and from the student's life.

### OPTION 2

To get students started, have a class discussion on the American dream and the experiences the characters in this unit had while searching for it. List all of the main characters in this unit. Divide students into groups and allow them to decide which characters they will play. Each student will need to determine the viewpoint of his or her character in preparation for role-playing.

## Self Assessment

Ask students to connect the concerns they listed with selections they read in the unit. Have students explain why they feel the concerns they underlined are not relevant today.

# The Changing Face of America

What do you feel you've learned about the social position of American women in the past? What new thoughts do you have about the American dream? Choose one or more of the following options in each section and complete the activities to help determine what knowledge you've gained.

Detail of *Mr. and Mrs. Isaac Newton Phelps Stokes* (1897), John Singer Sargent. Oil on canvas, 85¼″ × 39¼″, The Metropolitan Museum of Art, bequest of Edith Minturn Phelps Stokes (Mrs. I. N.), 1938. (38.104). Copyright © 1989 The Metropolitan Museum of Art.

## Reflecting on the Unit

### OPTION 1

**A Woman's Proper Place** Many of the selections in the first part of this unit show American women's struggles with social constraints, stereotypes, and inequalities. Review the ways in which the female characters in these selections respond to oppression or limitation. Which character did you find it easiest to identify with? Which character did you find it most difficult to identify with? Jot down a couple of paragraphs explaining your choices.

### OPTION 2

**The American Dream** Think about the American dream in relation to the selections in the second part of this unit. Which characters would classify the American dream as an illusion? Which would view it as a reality? Form a group of four or five, with each member role-playing a different character. In a discussion of equality and economic opportunity in the United States, each student should classify the American dream as illusion or reality and defend that position according to the point of view of the character he or she is playing.

## Self ASSESSMENT

### READER'S NOTEBOOK

To illustrate what you've learned about the concerns that native-born and immigrant men and women had at the end of the 19th century, write down their concerns in a diagram like the one shown. Then underline any concerns that do not seem relevant today.

|  | Women | Men |
|---|---|---|
| Native born |  |  |
| Immigrants |  |  |

## Reviewing Literary Concepts

### OPTION 1

**Understanding Figurative Language** Many writers in this unit use figurative language—for example, simile, metaphor, and personification—to communicate ideas, feelings, character qualities, or states of mind. Select one example of figurative language from five different selections in the unit. Classify the type of figurative language used in each example and the primary idea or feeling conveyed.

| Selection | Example of Figurative Language | Type of Figurative Language | Idea, Feeling, or State of Mind Conveyed |
|---|---|---|---|
|  |  |  |  |
|  |  |  |  |

### OPTION 2

**Analyzing Social Themes** Social themes in fiction are insights or messages about large problems in society. Go back through the seven short stories you read in the unit, and list the social themes they deal with. How are these themes conveyed—are they expressed through direct statements or suggested through conflicts faced by characters? Which themes are the most obvious, and which are the most subtle? Which themes seem most relevant in today's American society?

## Portfolio Building

- **Writing Options** Several Writing Options in this unit involved writing from the perspective of a character. Which character did you come to understand most deeply in this way? Attach a cover note to the assignment explaining what you learned from assuming the role of a character. Place the assignment in your **Presentation Portfolio.**

- **Writing Workshop** In this unit you wrote a Comparison-Contrast Essay that explored similarities and differences between two subjects. Evaluate your essay. How interesting were the subjects you chose? How original were the comparisons and contrasts you made? Decide whether you want to add your essay to your **Presentation Portfolio.** If you do, attach a cover sheet telling what makes it worthy.

- **Additional Activities** Think about the various assignments you completed under **Activities & Explorations** and **Inquiry & Research.** Pick one that you felt was very challenging. Write a note explaining how the assignment challenged you and what you did to rise to the challenge. Add the note to your portfolio.

### Self ASSESSMENT

**READER'S NOTEBOOK.**
Copy the following list of literary terms. Place a check next to each item you were able to define. For those you couldn't define, look up the definition in the **Glossary of Literary Terms** (page 1244).

quatrains
slant rhyme
first-person narrator
plot
surprise ending
coming-of-age story
interior monologue
imagery

tone
narrative poetry
characterization
symbol
lyric poem
static and dynamic characters
voice
analogy

### Self ASSESSMENT

By now you should have quite a few pieces in your **Presentation Portfolio.** Are you satisfied with the pieces you've chosen so far? If so, why? Or would you like to replace some? If so, which ones, and why?

### Setting GOALS

After completing this unit's reading and writing activities, what topics would you like to continue learning about? Look back through the selections, your portfolios, and notebook. Jot down one or two topics you would like to read more about.

## Reviewing Literary Concepts

### OPTION 1

Use the Unit Five Resource Book p. 66, to provide students with a ready-made, full-depth chart for recording examples and explanations of figurative language.

### OPTION 2

A successful response will
- correctly list the social themes that each of the seven short stories in the unit deal with.
- decide how the themes are conveyed to readers—through direct statements or through suggestion by way of conflicts faced by characters.
- identify the more obvious themes and the more subtle ones.
- specify which themes are most relevant in today's society.

## Building Your Portfolio

Students will use their Presentation Portfolios to file what they consider their highest quality work—the very best projects and activities from their Working Portfolios.

For more information on using writing and assessing portfolios, see the *Teacher's Guide to Assessment and Portfolio Use* beginning on page 53.

## The Modern Age

The selections in Unit Six explore the development of new means of literary expression in the aftermath of World War I. The unit is divided into two sections to represent two different movements that contributed to the exciting literary innovations of this era: the Harlem Renaissance and Modernism.

—————— Part 1 ——————

**A New Cultural Identity** This part of the unit traces the development of a group of distinctive African-American literary voices during the 1920s. The unit includes the major Harlem Renaissance writers and explores their thoughts and feelings through poetry, fiction, essays, and letters. An **Author Study** on Langston Hughes gives the students an in-depth look at his contributions and accomplishments. Students will also discover the literary forms and techniques used by writers of the Harlem Renaissance. **Traditions Across Time** reaffirms the cultural identity of literature by African Americans with the writings of James Baldwin, Gwendolyn Brooks, and Toni Morrison.

—————— Part 2 ——————

**Alienation of the Individual** The works in this section explore how a diverse group of writers reacted to the sharp social and cultural changes of the post-World War I era. The writers represented here responded to the uncertainty and disillusionment of the war and the materialism of the age by forging bold new literary experiments such as free verse, stream-of-consciousness, and Imagism. An **Author Study** on Robert Frost will allow the students to study in-depth his writings and contributions. **Traditions Across Time** examines themes of alienation and rebellion in the works of Sylvia Plath and Anne Sexton.

# THE MOD**E**RN AGE

## make it new!

### Ezra Pound
*poet and critic*

*Rush Hour, New York* (1915), Max Weber. Oil on canvas, 36¼" × 30¼". National Gallery of Art, Washington, D.C., gift of the Avalon Foundation (1970.6.1 PA).

912

 **Viewing and Representing**

*Rush Hour, New York*
**by Max Weber**

**ART APPRECIATION**
**Instruction** Weber (1881–1961) is ranked as one of America's most skilled modern artists. Born in Bialystok, Russia (now Poland), Weber came to the United States with his family when he was ten years old. He received his formal art education at the Pratt Institute in Brooklyn and studied privately with a number of well-known painters. After a brief stint teaching school,

Weber traveled to Paris, where he lived from 1905 to 1909. It was there that Weber developed his distinctive style, influenced by primitive art and the aesthetics of Rousseau, Matisse, Picasso, and the Cubists and Futurists.

*Rush Hour, New York* exemplifies Weber's unique Cubist style, evident in the painting's angular fragmentation of images and planes, and in the dark green and brown palette. In its concern for industrialized life, modernity, and the energy of the city, the painting also shows the influence of Futurism.

913

To help students explore connections among the art, the quotation, and the unit theme, have them consider the following questions:

**Ask: What do you think of when you hear the word *modern*?**

Possible Responses: fashionable; current; up-to-date ideas, people, and things; trendy

**Ask: Ezra Pound called for writers to "Make it new!" How can writers make literature "new"?**

Possible Responses: by finding new and different ways of expressing their ideas; by using individual and historical experiences to interpret ideas and events

**Ask: Based on Pound's rallying cry to his fellow writers, what kind of literature would you expect to find in this unit?**

Possible Responses: literature that looks and sounds different from traditional writing, such as free verse in poetry and stream-of-consciousness in prose

**Ask: What does the painting on this page suggest about art in the modern age?**

Possible Response: Weber's departure from the traditional landscapes and portraits of the past suggest that modern art was as experimental as modern literature.

**Ask: What connection do you see between the painting and its title?**

Possible Response: The painting gives the impression of a series of images seen only for a second, similar to those seen from the window of a speeding subway or train as it passes in and out of tunnels.

**Ask: What are some of the recognizable images students can see in this painting.**

Possible Responses: the side of a building with windows; the image of a skyscraper in the upper left corner; the five points in the center of the painting, which could represent the crown of the Statue of Liberty; a glimpse of blue sky between buildings

| Features and Selections | Literary Analysis | Reading and Critical Thinking | Writing Opportunities | |
|---|---|---|---|---|
| **Unit Opener**<br>**Time Line**<br>**A New Cultural Identity: The Harlem Renaissance** | | | | |
| **AUTHOR STUDY**<br>**Langston Hughes** | | | | |
| POETRY<br>Selected Poems<br>**Links Across Cultures**<br>Flute Players,<br>*from* Love, Langston | Mood, 924, 928<br><br>Newspaper Article, 931 | Detecting Rhythm in<br> Poetry, 924, 928 | Congratulatory Letter, 929<br>Musical Poem, 929<br>Compare-Contrast Essay,<br> 929 | |
| ESSAY<br>When the Negro Was in Vogue | Tone, 932, 937 | Author's Perspective, 932,<br> 937<br>Informal Assess., 936 | Autobiographical Essay,<br> 939<br>Documentary Plan, 939 | |
| The Author's Style<br>Author Study Project | Analysis of Style, 938 | | Changing Style, 938<br>Imitation of Style, 938 | |
| POETRY<br>My City<br>Any Human to Another | Sonnet, 940, 943<br>Review: Figurative<br> Language, 943 | Determining Major Ideas in<br> a Poem, 940, 943 | Slogan About New York,<br> 944<br>Write a Review, 944 | |
| POETRY<br>If We Must Die<br>A Black Man Talks of Reaping | Extended Metaphor, 945,<br> 948<br>Review: Sonnet, 948 | Figurative and Literal<br> Meaning, 945, 948<br>Informal Assess., 947 | Problem-Solution Essay,<br> 949<br>Sonnet, 949 | |
| ESSAY<br>How It Feels to Be Colored Me | Autobiographical Essay,<br> 950, 957<br>Review: Tone | Author's Purpose, 950, 957 | Proposal, 958<br>Autobio. Essay, 958<br>Informal Assess., 955 | |
| OPEN LETTER<br>**Comparing Literature**<br>My Dungeon Shook: Letter to My<br> Nephew on the One Hundredth<br> Anniversary of the Emancipation | Open Letter, 959, 964<br><br>Review: Analogy, 964 | Analyzing Texts, 959, 964<br>Informal Assess., 965 | Points of Comparison, 965<br>Personal Response, 965<br>Compare-Contrast Essay,<br> 965 | |
| POETRY<br>**Comparing Literature**<br>Life for My Child Is Simple<br>Primer for Blacks | Style, 967, 971 | Comparing and Contrasting<br> Poems, 967, 971 | Points of Comparison, 972<br>Yearbook Biography, 972<br>Summary of Brooks's<br> Message, 972 | |
| LITERARY CRITICISM<br>**Comparing Literature**<br>Thoughts on the African-<br> American Novel | Literary Criticism, 973, 976 | Identifying Major Ideas,<br> 973, 976 | Letter to Toni Morrison, 977<br>Points of Comparison, 977<br>Essay about Art, 977<br>Informal Assess., 975 | |
| COMPARING LITERATURE<br>Assessment Practice | Compare and Contrast<br> Literary Works, 978 | | Comparison-Contrast<br> Essay, 978 | |
| Writing Workshop:<br> **Research Report**<br>**Assessment Practice**<br>**Building Vocabulary**<br>**Sentence Crafting** | | Analyzing a Student<br> Model, 981 | Research Report, 980<br><br><br><br>Details and Examples, 988 | |

LEGEND    **DLS – Daily Language SkillBuilder**
**CCL – Cross Curricular Link**       **Green type – Teacher's Edition**

| Features and Selections | Literary Analysis | Reading and Critical Thinking | Writing Opportunities | |
|---|---|---|---|---|
| **AUTHOR STUDY** **Robert Frost** | | | | |
| Life and Times | | Using Text Organizers, 996 | | |
| POETRY **Selected Poems** by Robert Frost | Mood in Poetry, 1000, 1005 | Analyzing Word Choice, 1000, 1005 Test Practice, 1004 | | |
| POETRY **The Death of the Hired Man** **In Praise of Robert Frost** (SPEECH) | Blank Verse, 1006, 1013 Speech, 1012 | Form in Poetry, 1006, 1013 | Neighborly Editorial, 1015 Informal Assess., 1011 | |
| The Author's Style Author Study Project | | Analysis of Style, 1014 | Imitating Style, 1014 Changing Style, 1014 | |
| **Learning the Language of Literature** Modernism | Modernism, 1016 | Strategies for Reading, 1017 | | |
| SHORT STORY **The End of Something** | Style, 1018, 1023 | Making Inferences, 1018, 1023 Informal Assess., 1021 | Personal Ad, 1024 Advice Letters, 1024 TV Script, 1024 | |
| POETRY **The Love Song of J. Alfred Prufrock** **Link Across Cultures** *from* The Diaries | Imagery, 1025, 1030 Diary, 1033 | Stream of Consciousness, 1025, 1030 Test Practice, 1031 | Letter to Prufrock, 1031 Partygoer's Narrative, 1031 Social Commentary, 1031 | |
| SHORT STORY **The Jilting of Granny Weatherall** | Stream of Consciousness, 1034, 1043 | Sequencing, 1034, 1043 Informal Assess., 1042 | Eulogy for Granny, 1044 Psychological Profile, 1044 | |
| SHORT STORY **The Man Who Was Almost a Man** | Point of View, 1045, 1055 Review: Irony, 1055 | Making Judgments, 1045, 1055 Test Practice, 1054 | Defining Adulthood, 1056 Letter Home, 1056 Editorial, 1056 Writing an Evaluation, 1052 | |
| POETRY **Comparing Literature** Mirror Self in 1958 | Speaker, 1057, 1061 | Linking Title and Theme, 1057, 1061 Test Practice, 1062 | Diary of a Housewife, 1062 Poetic Riddle, 1062 Points of Comparison, 1062 | |
| Comparing Literature **Assessment Practice** | Synthesize Information for Overall Picture, 1064 | Reading the Prompt, 1064 | Synthesis Essay, 1064 | |
| Reflect and Assess **The Modern Age** | Reviewing Literary Concepts, 1067 | | What's New? 1066 Building Your Portfolio, 1067 | |

LEGEND    **DLS – Daily Language SkillBuilder**
**CCL – Cross Curricular Link**      **Green type – Teacher's Edition**

| Speaking and Listening Viewing and Representing | Inquiry and Research | Grammar, Usage, and Mechanics | Vocabulary |
|---|---|---|---|
| | | DLS, 1000<br>Review: Adjectives, 1001 | Connotation and Denotation, 1003 |
| New England Collage, 1015<br>Communicating Ideas, 1010 | Farm Life, 1015 | DLS, 1006<br>Problems with Modifiers, 1012 | Using Context Clues / Statements, 1007<br>Connotations, 1009 |
| Speaking and Listening, 1014 | Living Museum Presentation, 1015 | | |
| Story Illustrations, 1024<br>Romantic Breakups, 1024<br><br>Art Appreciation, 1020 | | DLS, 1018<br>Modifiers, 1019<br>Commas, 1024 | Connotations, 1022 |
| Improvisational Scene, 1031<br>Prufrock's Caricature, 1031<br>Radio Talk Show, 1031<br>Broadway Smash Hit, 1032 | Michelangelo's Artistic Genius, 1031 | DLS, 1025<br>Inverted Subjects and Verbs, 1032 | Context Clues, 1026<br>Figurative Language, 1028 |
| Story Illustration, 1044<br>Tabloid Interview, 1044<br>Art Appreciation, 1036, 1041 | | DLS, 1034<br>Compound Subjects, 1038<br>Colon, 1044 | Analogies, 1044<br>Context Clues, 1035<br>Fig. Language and Idioms, 1039 |
| Dramatic Reading, 1056<br>Charting Expenses, 1056<br>Film Critics' Circle, 1056<br>Pronunciation of Dialect, 1047<br>Photographs, 1051 | | DLS, 1045<br>Complex Sentences, 1050<br>Quotation Marks , 1056 | Dictionaries and Slang, 1049 |
| Face-to-Face Conversation, 1062<br>A Doll's House, 1062 | Women's Roles, 1062<br>Confessional Poets, 1062 | Compound Sentences, 1060<br><br>Capitalizing Family Titles, 1063 | Word Origins: *Mirror*, 1059 |
| | | Ellipses, 1064 | |
| Respond to Prejudice, 1066<br>The Iceberg Principle, 1066 | | | |

UNIT SIX
# RESOURCE MANAGEMENT GUIDE
## PART 1

To introduce the theme/literary period of this unit, use Fine Art Transparencies T32–34 in the Communications Transparencies and Copymasters.

| | Unit Resource Book | Assessment | Integrated Technology and Media | Additional Support |
| | | | | Literary Analysis Transparencies |
| --- | --- | --- | --- | --- |
| **Selected Poems by Langston Hughes** *pp. 924–929* | • Active Reading p. 4<br>• Literary Analysis p. 5 | • Selection Test, Formal Assessment pp. 167–168<br>Test Generator | Audio Library<br><br>NetActivities | • Mood T18 |
| **When the Negro Was in Vogue** *pp. 932–939* | • Active Reading p. 6<br>• Literary Analysis p. 7 | • Selection Test, Formal Assessment pp. 169–170<br>Test Generator | Audio Library<br>Research Starter www.mcdougallittell.com | • Tone T19 |
| **My City Any Human to Another** *pp. 940–944* | • Active Reading p. 8<br>• Literary Analysis p. 9 | • Selection Test, Formal Assessment pp. 171–172<br>Test Generator | Audio Library | • Form in Poetry: Structure T11 |
| **If We Must Die A Black Man Talks of Reaping** *pp. 945–949* | • Active Reading p. 10<br>• Literary Analysis p. 11 | • Selection Test, Formal Assessment pp. 173–174<br>Test Generator | Audio Library | |
| **How It Feels to Be Colored Me** *pp. 950–958* | • Summary p. 12<br>• Active Reading p. 13<br>• Literary Analysis p. 14<br>• Words to Know p. 15<br>• Selection Quiz p. 16 | • Selection Test, Formal Assessment pp. 175–176<br>Test Generator | Audio Library | • Tone T19 |
| **My Dungeon Shook: Letter to My Nephew on the One Hundredth Anniversary of the Emancipation (1962)** *pp. 959–966* | • Summary p. 17<br>• Active Reading p. 18<br>• Literary Analysis p. 19<br>• Words to Know p. 20<br>• Selection Quiz p. 21 | • Selection Test, Formal Assessment pp. 177–178<br>Test Generator | Audio Library | • Theme in Nonfiction T22 |
| **Life for My Child Is Simple (1949) Primer for Blacks (1980)** *pp. 967–972* | • Active Reading p. 22<br>• Literary Analysis p. 23 | • Selection Test, Formal Assessment pp. 179–180<br>Test Generator | Audio Library | |
| **Thoughts on the African-American Novel (1984)** *pp. 973–977* | • Summary p. 24<br>• Active Reading p. 25<br>• Literary Analysis p. 26<br>• Selection Quiz p. 27<br>• Comparing Literature p. 28 | • Selection Test, Formal Assessment p. 181<br>Test Generator | Audio Library<br>Research Starter www.mcdougallittell.com | |

## Writing Workshop: Research Report

| | | Unit Assessment | Unit Technology | |
| --- | --- | --- | --- | --- |
| **Unit Six Resource Book**<br>• Prewriting p. 29<br>• Drafting and Elaboration p. 30<br>• Peer Response Guide pp. 31–32<br>• Revising, Editing, and Proofreading p. 33<br>• Student Models pp. 34–39<br>• Rubric for Evaluation p. 40 | **Power Presentations CD-ROM**<br><br>**Writing Transparencies and Copymasters** T11, T20, C33<br><br>**Teacher's Guide to Assessment and Portfolio Use** | • Unit Six, Part 1 Test, Formal Assessment pp. 183–184<br>Test Generator<br>• Unit Six Integrated Test, Integrated Assessment pp. 47–55 | ClassZone www.mcdougallittell.com<br>EasyPlanner CD-ROM<br>Electronic Library | |

| Reading and Critical Thinking Transparencies | Grammar Transparencies and Copymasters | Vocabulary Transparencies and Copymasters | Writing Transparencies and Copymasters | Communications Transparencies and Copymasters |
|---|---|---|---|---|
| | • Daily Language SkillBuilder T25<br>• Varying Sentence Structure C164 | • Syllabic Marks C75 | • Figurative Language and Sound Devices T15 | • Dramatic Reading T12<br>• Verbal Strategies T14<br>• Nonverbal Strategies T15 |
| • Drawing Conclusions T4<br>• Determining Author's Bias T22 | • Adverbial Elements C140 | • Using Context to Build Vocabulary C76 | • Reflective Essay C28 | • Appreciative Listening T2<br>• Evaluating Roles in Groups T8 |
| • Main Idea and Supporting Details T12<br>• Cluster Diagram T48 | • Comparative and Superlative Modifiers C132 | • Figurative Language C77 | • Literary Interpretation C30 | |
| • Comparing Authors' Views T23<br>• Problem-Solution Chart T56 | • Daily Language SkillBuilder T25<br>• Modifiers: Use of -er C135 | • Prefixes C78 | • Organizing Your Writing T11 | |
| • Drawing Conclusions T4<br>• Determining Author's Purpose and Audience T19 | • Daily Language SkillBuilder T26<br>• Distinguishing *Those* from *Them* C138 | • Figurative Language C79 | • Persuasive Essay C27<br>• Autobiographical Incident C35 | • Dramatic Reading T12 |
| • Compare and Contrast T15 | • Daily Language SkillBuilder T26<br>• Parallelism T57<br>• Parallel Compound Predicates C165 | • Denotation and Connotation C80 | • Compare-Contrast C31 | • Evaluating Roles in Groups T8<br>• Reading Aloud T11<br>• Impromptu Speaking: Dialogue, Role-Play, Debate T13 |
| • Compare and Contrast T15<br>• Paraphrasing and Summarizing T41 | • Daily Language SkillBuilder T27<br>• Punctuating Elements in a Series T54<br>• Parallelism T57<br>• Parallel Series C166 | • Prefixes C81 | • Achieving Conciseness T21 | • Dramatic Reading T12<br>• Impromptu Speaking: Dialogue, Role-Play, Debate T13 |
| • Main Idea and Supporting Details T12<br>• Organizational Chart: Horizontal T51<br>• Category Question Frame T60 | • Daily Language SkillBuilder T27<br>• Varying Sentence Openings C167 | • Greek and Latin Roots C82 | • Elaboration T10 | |

## STUDENTS ACQUIRING ENGLISH

The **Spanish Study Guide,** pp. 218–244, includes language support for the following pages:
• Family and Community Involvement (per unit)
• Selection Summaries and Vocabulary
• Active Reading
• Literary Analysis

UNIT SIX
# RESOURCE MANAGEMENT GUIDE
## PART 2

To introduce the theme/literary period of this unit, use Fine Art Transparencies T32–34 in the Communications Transparencies and Copymasters.

| | Unit Resource Book | Assessment | Integrated Technology and Media | Additional Support / Literary Analysis Transparencies |
|---|---|---|---|---|
| **Selected Poems by Robert Frost** *pp. 1000–1005* | • Active Reading p. 43<br>• Literary Analysis p. 44 | • Selection Test, Formal Assessment pp. 185–186<br>🖭 Test Generator | 🎧 Audio Library<br><br>💿 NetActivities | • Mood T18 |
| **The Death of the Hired Man** *pp. 1006–1015* | • Summary p. 45<br>• Active Reading p. 46<br>• Literary Analysis p. 47<br>• Words to Know p. 48<br>• Selection Quiz p. 49 | • Selection Test, Formal Assessment pp. 187–188<br>🖭 Test Generator | 🎧 Audio Library<br>ℹ️ Research Starter www.mcdougallittell.com | • Poetic Devices T12 |
| **The End of Something** *pp. 1018–1024* | • Summary p. 50<br>• Active Reading p. 51<br>• Literary Analysis p. 52<br>• Selection Quiz p. 53 | • Selection Test, Formal Assessment pp. 189–190<br>🖭 Test Generator | 🎧 Audio Library | • Modernist Literature T17 |
| **The Love Song of J. Alfred Prufrock** *pp. 1025–1032* | • Summary p. 54<br>• Active Reading p. 55<br>• Literary Analysis p. 56<br>• Words to Know p. 57<br>• Selection Quiz p. 58 | • Selection Test, Formal Assessment pp. 191–192<br>🖭 Test Generator | | • Modernist Literature T17 |
| **The Jilting of Granny Weatherall** *pp. 1034–1044* | • Summary p. 59<br>• Active Reading p. 60<br>• Literary Analysis p. 61<br>• Words to Know p. 62<br>• Selection Quiz p. 63 | • Selection Test, Formal Assessment pp. 193–194<br>🖭 Test Generator | 🎧 Audio Library | • Modernist Literature T17 |
| **The Man Who Was Almost a Man** *pp. 1045–1056* | • Summary p. 64<br>• Active Reading p. 65<br>• Literary Analysis p. 66<br>• Selection Quiz p. 67 | • Selection Test, Formal Assessment pp. 195–196<br>🖭 Test Generator | 🎧 Audio Library<br><br>📼 Video: Literature in Performance, Video Resource Book pp. 33–38 | • Point of View T20 |
| **Mirror (1963) Self in 1958 (1966)** *pp. 1057–1063* | • Active Reading p. 68<br>• Literary Analysis p. 69<br>• Comparing Literature p. 70 | • Selection Test, Formal Assessment pp. 197–198<br>🖭 Test Generator | 🎧 Audio Library | • Style, Voice T23 |
| | | ***Unit Assessment***<br>• Unit Six, Part 2 Test, Formal Assessment pp. 199–200<br>🖭 Test Generator<br>• Unit Six Integrated Test, Integrated Assessment pp. 47–55 | ***Unit Technology***<br>ℹ️ ClassZone www.mcdougallittell.com<br>💿 EasyPlanner CD-ROM<br>💿 Electronic Library | |

| Reading and Critical Thinking Transparencies | Grammar Transparencies and Copymasters | Vocabulary Transparencies and Copymasters | Writing Transparencies and Copymasters | Communications Transparencies and Copymasters |
|---|---|---|---|---|
| • Venn Diagram T50 | • Daily Language SkillBuilder T27<br>• Review: Adjective Elements C141 | • Denotation and Connotation C83 | | |
| • Generating Research Questions T26 | • Daily Language SkillBuilder T28<br>• Problems with *This, These; That, Those* C139 | • The Connotative Power of Words C84 | • Opinion Statement C34 | • Evaluating Roles in Groups T8<br>• Impromptu Speaking: Dialogue, Role-Play, Debate T13 |
| • Making Inferences T7 | • Daily Language SkillBuilder T28<br>• Punctuating Dialogue T56<br>• Illogical Comparisons C134<br>• Commas: Setting Off Quotations C154 | • Connotation C85 | • The Uses of Dialogue T24 | |
| • Noting Details T9 | • Daily Language SkillBuilder T29<br>• Inverted Subjects and Verbs C78 | • Figurative Language C86 | • Eyewitness Report C25 | • Interviewing T9<br>• Impromptu Speaking: Dialogue, Role-Play, Debate T13 |
| | • Daily Language SkillBuilder T29<br>• Parallelism T57<br>• Colons C159<br>• Parallel Compound Subjects C168 | • Figurative Language and Idioms C07 | | • Interviewing T9<br>• Impromptu Speaking: Dialogue, Role-Play, Debate T13 |
| • Making Judgments T5 | • Daily Language SkillBuilder T29<br>• Punctuating Dialogue T56<br>• Quotation Marks with Other Punctuation C162<br>• Creating Complex Sentences C169 | • Dictionaries and Slang C88 | • Literary Interpretation C30 | • Evaluation Matrix: Film/Video T7<br>• Impromptu Speaking: Dialogue, Role-Play, Debate T13<br>• Verbal Strategies T14 |
| • Cluster Diagram T48 | • Daily Language SkillBuilder T30<br>• Capitalizing Family Titles C143<br>• Creating Compound Sentences C170 | • Word Origins C89 | • Compare-Contrast C32 | • Impromptu Speaking: Dialogue, Role-Play, Debate T13 |

## STUDENTS ACQUIRING ENGLISH

The **Spanish Study Guide,** pp. 245–265, includes language support for the following pages:
• Family and Community Involvement (per unit)

• Selection Summaries and Vocabulary
• Active Reading
• Literary Analysis

| Selection | SkillBuilder Sentences | Suggested Answers |
|---|---|---|
| Selected Poems by Langston Hughes | 1. Manhattan is one of the largest cities in the World you can find all sorts of people their.<br><br>2. Has any of you ever heard the saying a joy shared is dubbled, and a burden shared is halfed. | 1. Manhattan is one of the largest cities in the **world; you** can find all sorts of people **there**.<br><br>2. **Have** any of you ever heard the saying **"A joy** shared is **doubled**, and a burden shared is **halved"?** |
| If We Must Die<br>A Black Man Talks of Reaping | 1. Whom do you think is the better poet of the two!<br><br>2. In the fight against tyrrany, one must remember to maintain their dignity. | 1. **Who** do you think is the better poet of the two**?**<br><br>2. In the fight against **tyranny**, one must remember to maintain **one's** dignity. |
| How It Feels to Be Colored Me | 1. This esay about a African-american girl's raceial identity.<br><br>2. She grown up in a town that was populated exclusivly by black people. | 1. This **essay is** about **an** African-**A**merican girl's **racial** identity.<br><br>2. She **grew** up in a town that was populated **exclusively** by black people. |
| My Dungeon Shook:<br>  Letter to My Nephew | 1. The occasion of Baldwins open letter was the 100th anniversery of the signing of the Emancipation proclamation.<br><br>2. Baldwin believed that a celebration was not ordered, because of African Americans was not yet free. | 1. The occasion of Baldwin**'s** open letter was the 100th **anniversary** of the signing of the Emancipation **P**roclamation.<br><br>2. Baldwin believed that a celebration was not **in order** because African Americans **were** not yet free. |

| Selection | SkillBuilder Sentences | Suggested Answers |
|---|---|---|
| Life for My Child Is Simple Primer for Blacks | 1. Annie Allen is fictional, and African American, mother. | 1. Annie Allen is **a fictional African-American** mother. |
| | 2. Gwendolyn Brooks, the first African American arthur to win a Pulitzer Prize. | 2. Gwendolyn Brooks **was** the first African-American **author** to win a Pulitzer Prize. |
| Thoughts on the African-American Novel | 1. Morrison notes, that the middle class did not exist, in front of the Industrial Revolution. | 1. Morrison notes that the middle class did not exist **before** the Industrial Revolution. |
| | 2. Some cultures did not develope the novel form on account of them telling stories orally. | 2. Some cultures did not **develop** the novel form **because they told** stories orally. |
| Selected Poems by Robert Frost | 1. In Frosts poem Mending Wall two people have different ideas about how neighbors should live they're lifes. | 1. In Frost**'s** poem "Mending Wall," two people have different ideas about how neighbors should live **their lives**. |
| | 2. "Good fences says one man make good neighbors," Do you agree with this here statement! | 2. "Good fences," says one man, "make good neighbors." Do you agree with **this statement?** |
| The Death of the Hired Man | 1. This poem is about a elderly farm hand who wants to desperately have a sense of home, belonging, and be proud. | 1. This poem is about **an** elderly farm hand who **desperately** wants **to** have a sense of home, belonging, and **pride**. |
| | 2. "Home is the place were, when you have to go their, they have to take you in, says Warren one of the poems speakers. | 2. "Home is the place **where**, when you have to go **there**, they have to take you in," says Warren**,** one of the poem**'s** speakers. |

| Selection | SkillBuilder Sentences | Suggested Answers |
|---|---|---|
| The End of Something | 1. The End of Something is one short story that feature Nick Adams he is also in many other short stories<br><br>2. Two of Hemingways most popular novels is The Sun also Rises and For whom the Bell Tolls. | 1. "The End of Something" is one short story that feature**s** Nick Adams. **H**e is also in many other short stories.<br><br>2. Two of Hemingway**'s** most popular novels **are** <u>The Sun **A**lso Rises</u> and <u>For **W**hom the Bell Tolls</u>. |
| The Love Song of J. Alfred Prufrock | 1. T. s. Eliot was a major figure in twenteith century Literature.<br><br>2. Ezra Pound thought Eliot's poem, 'The Love Song of J Alfred Prufrock' is the best he seen from an american. | 1. T. **S.** Eliot was a major figure in **twentieth- century** **l**iterature.<br><br>2. Ezra Pound thought Eliot's poem "The Love Song of J. Alfred Prufrock" **was** the best he **had** seen from an **A**merican. |
| The Jilting of Granny Weatherall | 1. Older woman might resent having to live in someone elses home.<br><br>2. Granny weatherall feels Cornelia does not keep her house up good. | 1. Older **women** might resent having to live in someone else's home.<br><br>2. Granny **W**eatherall feels Cornelia does not keep her house up **well**. |
| The Man Who Was Almost a Man | 1. This story tells about a young men and the gun he wish to by.<br><br>2. We know it take place in the South, but we don't no in which State. | 1. This story tells about a young **man** and the gun he **wishes** to **buy**.<br><br>2. We know it **takes** place in the South, but we don't **know** in which **s**tate. |
| Mirror<br>Self in 1958 | 1. Internal conflicts and being influenced by significant events shaped Sylvia Plaths poetry.<br><br>2. Anne Sexton about who much has been written, had a tragically short life. | 1. Internal conflicts and significant events shaped Sylvia Plath**'s** poetry.<br><br>2. Anne Sexton, about **whom** much has been written, had a tragically short life. |

| Grammar Focus by Unit | Unit One | Unit Two | Unit Three | Unit Four | Unit Five | Unit Six | Unit Seven |
|---|---|---|---|---|---|---|---|
| | Parts of a Sentence | Verbs | Phrases | Clauses, Part I | Clauses, Part II | Special Sentence Structures, Part I | Special Sentence Structures, Part II |

*The Language of Literature* offers several options for integrating grammar instruction and literature.

- Each literature unit has a grammar focus. The Teacher's Edition includes Mini Lessons for each selection that help develop the grammar focus for the unit and spring from the content of the specific literature.
- The Pupil Edition includes several full-page lessons on Sentence Crafting. These lessons are related to both the literature and the grammar focus for the unit and help students use grammar in their own writing.
- Daily Language SkillBuilders in the Teacher's Edition provide students with ongoing proofreading practice and reinforce punctuation, spelling, grammar and usage, and capitalization.
- Grammar Copymasters and Transparencies, which may be used to complement or extend lessons in the Teacher's Edition, present grammar in a traditional, systematic sequence. References to appropriate copymasters or transparencies are included at point of use in the Teacher's Edition Mini Lessons.

TE Mini Lessons shown in green
PE instruction shown in black

## Part 1

**Parts of Speech**
**Review: Parts of Speech**
**Distinguishing Plurals from Possessives**
Writing Workshop, p. 989

**Using Clauses**
**Adverb Clauses**
Hughes poems, pp. 938–939

**Verb Usage**
**Verb Tenses**
Writing Workshop, p. 989

**Using Modifiers**
**Comparisons of Regular Adjectives and Adverbs**
"If We Must Die," "A Black Man Talks of Reaping," p. 949
**Modifiers: Positive, Comparative, and Superlative Degrees**
"My City," "Any Human to Another," p. 944
**Problems with Modifiers: *those* and *them***
"How It Feels to Be Colored Me," p. 958

**End Marks and Commas**
**Commas, Interrupters: Parenthetical Expressions**
**Unnecessary Commas**
Writing Workshop, p. 989

**Style**
**The Need for Sentence Variety**
Hughes poems, p. 929
**Parallel Compound Predicates**
"My Dungeon Shook: Letter to My Nephew," p. 966
**Parallel Series**
"Life for My Child Is Simple," "Primer for Blacks," p. 972
Sentence Crafting, p. 991
**Sentences: Varying Beginnings**
"Thoughts on the African-American Novel," p. 977

## Part 2

**Parts of Speech**
**Review: Parts of Speech**
**Nouns and Pronouns as Adjectives**
Frost poems, p. 1001

**Parts of the Sentence**
**Unusually Placed Subjects**
"The Love Song of J. Alfred Prufrock," p. 1032

**Using Phrases**
**Prepositional Phrases**
Frost poems, p. 1001

**Using Clauses**
**Adjective Clauses**
Frost poems, p. 1001
**Structure: Compound Sentences**
"Mirror," "Self in 1958," p. 1060

**Using Modifiers**
**Using Modifiers**
Frost poems, p. 1012
**Modifiers: Illogical Comparisons *than, as***
"The End of Something," p. 1019

**Capitalization**
**Capitalizing Titles: Showing Family Relationships**
"Mirror," "Self in 1958," p. 1063

**End Marks and Commas**
**Commas: Setting Off Quotations**
"The End of Something," p. 1024

**Other Punctuation**
**Colon as a Sentence Connector**
"The Jilting of Granny Weatherall," p. 1044
**Quotation Marks with Other Punctuation**
"The Man Who Was Almost a Man," p. 1056

**Style**
**Parallel Compound Subjects**
"The Jilting of Granny Weatherall," p. 1038
**Creating Complex Sentences**
"The Man Who Was Almost a Man," p. 1050

This time line shows major dates and events in the United States and the world from 1910 to 1940. Help students recognize that these 30 years were characterized worldwide by experimentation and innovation in the arts, social upheaval, and political tensions marked by violence and war.

## American Literature: 1912

**A** Monroe's Chicago-based magazine published verse by Carl Sandburg, Vachel Lindsay, Robert Frost, Amy Lowell, H. D. (Hilda Doolittle), T. S. Eliot, and Ezra Pound, among others.

## American Literature: 1915

**B** T. S. Eliot's (1888–1965) best known work, *The Waste Land*, was published in 1922. Its style and pessimistic tone immediately provoked controversy, but eventually the poem came to be recognized as a defining text of modernism. Years later, Eliot was awarded the Nobel Prize in literature, among other honors, which acknowledged his role in defining and developing modern poetry.

## United States: 1909

**C** A professor of economics and later sociology, NAACP founder W. E. B. Du Bois (1868–1963), who pronounced his name to sound like "dew boys," was also a skilled essayist whose works include *The Souls of Black Folk* (1903).

## World: 1914

**D** World War I began after a Serbian nationalist assassinated the Austrian archduke Francis Ferdinand in Sarajevo.

## World: 1917

**E** Huge losses in World War I helped spur domestic unrest in Russia, where the czar was overthrown in the spring and the October Revolution brought the Communist Bolsheviks and their leader Lenin to power. The czar and his family were later executed by the Bolsheviks.

# THE MODERN AGE

## EVENTS IN AMERICAN LITERATURE

### 1910

**A** **1912** Harriet Monroe founds *Poetry* magazine, which would introduce many modernist poets

**B** **1915** Early poem by T. S. Eliot, "The Love Song of J. Alfred Prufrock," first appears in *Poetry*

**1916** Robert Frost's "The Road Not Taken" is published

**1917** The first collection of *The Cantos* by Ezra Pound is published in *Poetry*

**1919** Claude McKay writes "If We Must Die" during summer wave of violence against African Americans

### 1920

**1920s** Harlem Renaissance is in its heyday

**1922** Groundbreaking anthology, *The Book of American Negro Poetry*, is compiled by James Weldon Johnson

## EVENTS IN THE UNITED STATES

### 1910

**C** **1909** Sixty prominent black and white citizens found National Association for the Advancement of Colored People (NAACP) to end discrimination and prevent violence against black people

**1913** Armory Show in New York City exhibits modern art to large crowds and horrified critics

*Nude Descending a Staircase* by Marcel Duchamp

**1917** United States enters World War I, ensuring the Allied victory a year later

**1919** Congress ratifies 18th Amendment, which prohibits manufacture, transportation, and sale of alcoholic beverages, ushering in Prohibition

### 1920

**1920** U.S. Bureau of Census reports that for the first time the nation's rural population is less than half of total population

**F** **1921** First radio coverage of World Series demonstrates radio's growing popularity

**1922** Louis Armstrong joins King Oliver's Creole Jazz Band in Chicago, heralding Jazz Age

## EVENTS IN THE WORLD

### 1910

**1912** Qing Dynasty, in power in China since 1644, is overthrown by nationalist revolt in favor of a republic

**D** **1914** War erupts in Europe between Central Powers (Germany and Austria-Hungary) and Allies (Great Britain, France, and Russia)

**E** **1917** V. I. Lenin leads Bolshevik Revolution that topples Russian czar

**1918** The Allies, with U.S. help, defeat Central Powers, ending World War I; Bolsheviks become Russian Communist Party

**1919** The Treaty of Versailles is signed by Allies and Associated Powers and by Germany

### 1920

**1920** Hitler takes control of new National Socialist German Workers' (Nazi) Party

**1921** Mao Zedong co-founds China's Communist Party

**914**     UNIT SIX   THE MODERN AGE (1910–1940)

## United States: 1921

**F** Though many scientists helped to develop the radio, it was the Italian inventor Guglielmo Marconi (1874–1937) who ensured its practical application.

## PERIOD PIECES

The fashion of the 1920s

1936 Crosley Radio
Corporation's "Majestic"

Art deco wristwatch

### 1930

**1925** Countee Cullen publishes his first book of poetry, *Color*

**1926** Langston Hughes publishes *The Weary Blues*, depicting life in Harlem in the 1920s; Ernest Hemingway publishes his first novel, *The Sun Also Rises*

**1928** Zora Neale Hurston publishes "How It Feels to Be Colored Me"

**1930** Katherine Anne Porter's "The Jilting of Granny Weatherall" appears in collection titled *Flowering Judas*

**1931** Arna Bontemps's first novel, *God Sends Sunday*, is published

**1933** Gertrude Stein publishes *The Autobiography of Alice B. Toklas*

**1934** Dorothy West founds *Challenge*, a literary magazine for African-American writers

**1936** Dorothy Parker publishes *Collected Poems: Not So Deep as a Well*

### 1930

**1923** Performance of the Charleston in musical *Runnin' Wild* starts nationwide dance craze

**1927** Charles Lindbergh is first to fly solo across Atlantic, nonstop from New York to Paris; Babe Ruth hits season record of 60 home runs (since surpassed); first "talking" movie, *The Jazz Singer*, is released

**1929** Stock-market crash on Wall Street plunges nation into Great Depression

**1931** Empire State Building is completed, the world's then-tallest building at 102 stories

**1932** Franklin Delano Roosevelt is elected president at height of Depression, with nearly one-third of work force unemployed

**1938** Congress passes Fair Labor Standards Act, which establishes minimum wage and provides for adoption of 40-hour workweek

**1939** First regular television broadcasts begin

### 1930

**1928** Joseph Stalin becomes dictator of Communist Russia

**1930** Nationalists and Communists fight civil war in China

**1932** Saudi Arabia declares itself a single kingdom

**1933** Hitler and Nazis seize dictatorial control of Germany

**1937** Japan invades China

**1938** English prime minister claims "peace in our time" after ceding parts of Czechoslovakia to Hitler

**1939** Germany invades Poland and World War II begins

TIME LINE  **915**

---

### United States: 1923

**G** A fast-paced dance of African-American origin, the Charleston (named after the South Carolina city) was one of several dances that swept the United States during the Jazz Age, or Roaring Twenties.

### United States: 1927

**H** Babe Ruth's (1895–1948) record held up until 1961, when Roger Maris hit 61 home runs (Maris's record stood for 37 years until Mark McGwire hit 70 home runs in 1998). During the 1920s, Ruth sometimes hit more home runs in a year than entire teams. During his career, he averaged the phenomenal rate of one home run for every twelve times at bat.

### World: 1933

**I** The Great Depression brought to a head years of agitation by the militant Nazi party, whose leader, Adolf Hitler (1889–1945), granted himself dictatorial powers soon after becoming the country's chancellor.

---

### ART DECO WRISTWATCH

**J** Art deco, the dominant decorative and architectural style from about 1925 to 1940, was characterized by geometric designs, bold colors, and the use of glass and plastics. At the time, the synthetic substances known as plastics were still relatively new, having been in general production only since about 1900.

### American Literature: 1933

**K** Gertrude Stein (1874–1946) was a prolific writer. During her lifetime she produced over 500 literary works, including novels, plays, and articles. Much of her work was experimental and received mixed reviews for its eccentricities in style and punctuation. *The Autobiography of Alice B. Toklas* is the fictionalized account of Stein's own life from the viewpoint of her long-time companion, Alice Toklas.

## OVERVIEW

### Introduction
This article places the selections in Part 1 of this unit in historical context by providing students with background on the times and people of the Harlem Renaissance. The selections in **Voices from the Times** give students insight into African-American cultural identity during the first few decades of the 20th century. This essay will enable students to interpret the possible influences of historical contexts on the literary works in this unit.

## Teaching Nonfiction

### Reading Skills and Strategies:
#### ESTABLISHING A PURPOSE FOR READING
Explain to students that this article will introduce them to the significant figures and ideas of the Harlem Renaissance. Have students review the article and establish a purpose for reading (to find out).

### ACQUIRING VOCABULARY
Encourage students to write down any unfamiliar words they encounter in this article. Remind students that they are expected to use reference materials such as glossaries, dictionaries, and available technology to determine precise usage and meanings.

### DRAWING INFERENCES
This article gives some indications of the way in which African Americans were regarded in the early years of the 20th century. Using the information in the essay, ask students to draw inferences about the position of African Americans in society during this time. Remind students to support these inferences with textual evidence and experience.

# A New Cultural Identity

## The Harlem Renaissance

"The Harlem Renaissance was an unprecedented period of literary, musical, and artistic production among African Americans that reached its peak in the 1920s. This movement was centered in the Harlem section of Manhattan in New York City—a magnet for thousands of blacks migrating from the South, the Midwest, and even the West Indies. Southern blacks, in particular, were fleeing poverty and growing racial violence, hoping to find more economic and personal freedom in the North. Politically, the Renaissance years were an extremely difficult time for African Americans. During the "Red Summer" of 1919, there were bloody antiblack riots in 26 cities, including Chicago and Washington, D.C. In the 1920s, membership in the terrorist, white-supremacist Ku Klux Klan rose to more than 4 million nationwide.

Not only a magnet for blacks, Harlem drew whites as well—tourists flocked to nightspots such as the Cotton Club to hear the new jazz music played by Louis Armstrong and Duke Ellington. And white writers, publishers, and patrons of the arts developed a keen interest in Harlem residents and their culture.

For African Americans a new cultural identity crystallized during the Harlem Renaissance; it was the time of "The New Negro," in the words of philosopher Alain Locke, who first defined the movement. "New

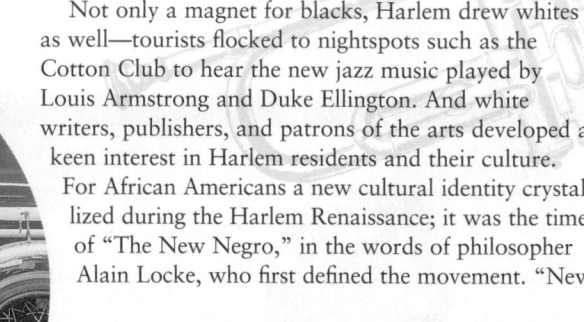

Harlem in the 1920s: a young couple out on the town (top), Lenox Avenue (below)

**916**

The Cotton Club

Negroes" rejected beastlike or sentimental stereotypes, claiming the right to define themselves and defend themselves against attack. "New Negroes" felt a collective identity—they had pride in their race and asserted its contributions to American culture. At the same time, they possessed an international consciousness, recognizing kinship among blacks in the United States, West Indies, and Africa. Such an international outlook was advocated by Marcus Garvey, a Jamaican immigrant whose popular back-to-Africa movement called on African Americans to leave the United States and form their own nation.

The writers of the Harlem Renaissance embodied these "New Negroes." Langston Hughes was one of the most original and important. In 1925, he published his first poetry collection, *The Weary Blues*, following it with dozens of volumes of poetry, fiction, plays, and essays over a career lasting into the 1960s. He praised blackness, embraced common people as subjects, and blended elements of blues and jazz into his work. The exuberant Zora Neale Hurston, raised in a small, all-black Florida town and trained in anthropology at Barnard College, also drew upon African-American folk traditions. Her stories, novels, essays, and folklore collections reflect a love of black language and manners. Hurston was one of the first writers to present African Americans as complete, multifaceted human beings. Other important Renaissance writers were James Weldon Johnson, Claude McKay, Countee Cullen, and Arna Bontemps, all of whom showed mastery of traditional literary forms and poured into them new expressions of individual and collective feeling. Yet another significant figure was Jean Toomer, whose experimental *Cane* (1923) blended poetry and prose to evoke the beautiful, terrible South of black experience.

## Voices from the TIMES

Lift every voice and sing
Till earth and heaven ring,
Ring with the harmonies of Liberty;
Let our rejoicing rise
High as the listening skies,
Let it resound loud as the rolling sea.
Sing a song full of the faith that the
    dark past has taught us,
Sing a song full of the hope that the
    present has brought us,
Facing the rising sun of our new day
    begun
Let us march on till victory is won.

> **James Weldon Johnson**
> "Lift Every Voice and Sing"
> (the "Negro national anthem,"
> first performed in 1900)

**C**

All art is propaganda and ever must be, despite the wailing of the purists. I stand in utter shamelessness and say that whatever art I have for writing has been used always for propaganda for gaining the right of black folk to love and enjoy.

> **W. E. B. Du Bois**
> from "Criteria of Negro Art"

I had an overwhelming desire to see Harlem. More than Paris, or the Shakespeare country, or Berlin, or the Alps, I wanted to see Harlem, the greatest Negro city in the world.

> **Langston Hughes**
> from *The Big Sea*

HISTORICAL BACKGROUND **917**

## Making Connections

### History
**A** Once the site of a Native American village, Harlem, in upper Manhattan, was settled in 1658 by Dutch farmers who called their settlement Nieuw Haarlem after the city of Haarlem in Holland. In 1672, African-American slaves built a wagon road connecting the area with lower Manhattan, but Harlem remained sparsely populated until the 19th century, when the New York and Harlem Railroad opened it for development.

Along the unattractive railroad tracks and elevated train lines in East Harlem, working-class and immigrant tenements sprang up. In West Harlem real estate speculators built elegant apartment buildings and row houses, anticipating an influx of middle-class residents. West Harlem became a mecca for more affluent and educated African Americans, although high rents also prompted apartment subdivision and overcrowding.

### Music
**B** In its syncopated rhythms, emphasis on self-expression and improvisation, and distortions in melody and harmony, jazz reflects the African, Caribbean, Spanish, and French influences in turn-of-the-century New Orleans, where it was born. From there, prompted by the demise of the Mississippi steamboats on which they worked, African-American jazz musicians migrated to the West Coast, the East Coast, and especially "up the river" to Chicago, where great talents like Louis Armstrong, King Oliver, and Earl "Fatha" Hines gathered to compose, perform, and record. By the end of the 1920s, composers such as the New York-based bandleader Duke Ellington were creating jazz compositions for larger groups, paving the way for the "big-band era" of the 1930s, while the earlier New Orleans style had become known as Dixieland.

### Literature
**C** Langston Hughes was working as a restaurant busboy in Washington, D. C., when the famous Midwestern poet Vachel Lindsay came in to dine. Hughes left some of his poems by Lindsay's plate, and, much impressed, Lindsay read some of them that night to an audience. The experience helped launch Hughes's career as a writer.

**VOICES FROM THE TIMES**
**Ask: What ideas or themes do these excerpts have in common?**
**Possible Responses:** All three of these excerpts infer a collective identity for African Americans; they all imply a shared past or a common present; the Johnson verse and the excerpt from Du Bois both touch on past oppression of African Americans and their fight to end it.

**Ask: What is the significance of Hughes's comparison of Harlem with the European places he cites?**
**Possible Response:** The European places are famous for their cultural significance or their awe-inspiring grandeur. By comparing Harlem to these places, Hughes raises Harlem beyond local importance and gives it stature equal to that of the great centers of European culture.

**SUMMARIZING**

Ask students to identify the main ideas and supporting details of this essay. Have them use their identification of these elements to summarize the essay in their own words.

**DISCUSSING**

Allow students time to discuss this essay as a class. Start the discussion by asking students to give examples of their collective identity based on their own experiences.

## Voices from the TIMES

Here in Manhattan is not merely the largest Negro community in the world, but the first concentration in history of so many diverse elements of Negro life. It has attracted the African, the West Indian, the Negro American; has brought together the Negro of the North and the Negro of the South; the man from the city and the man from the town and village; the peasant, the student, the business man, the professional man, artist, poet, musician, adventurer and worker, preacher and criminal, exploiter and social outcast. Each group has come with its own separate motives and for its own special ends, but their greatest experience has been the finding of one another.

**Alain Locke**
from *The New Negro*

Man, if you gotta ask you'll never know.
**Louis Armstrong**
when asked what jazz is

What American literature decidedly needs at the moment is color, music, gusto, the free expression of gay or desperate moods. If the Negroes are not in a position to contribute these items, I do not know what Americans are.
**Carl Van Doren**
from a speech to young African-American writers

Up you mighty race, you can accomplish what you will.
**Marcus Garvey**
(a rallying cry for his Universal Negro Improvement Association)

## Traditions Across Time: Reaffirming Cultural Identity

The Great Depression of the 1930s brought an end to the Harlem Renaissance, causing many of the writers who had gathered in Harlem to scatter and take other jobs to support themselves. But their work planted seeds that continue to generate important writing from the African-American experience.

In 1950, the poet Gwendolyn Brooks became the first African American to win a Pulitzer Prize. Throughout the 1950s and 1960s, James Baldwin, who left the United States and the racism he felt here to live in Paris, gave us some of the most important essays of the period, essays based on his experiences and struggles with racial identity. And in contemporary times, Toni Morrison has become one of the most accomplished American novelists, winning nearly every important literary award, including the Nobel Prize for literature. In her essay in this part of Unit Six, Morrison demonstrates the continuing effort to find and present the essentials of African-American life.

Toni Morrison accepting the 1993 Nobel Prize for literature in Stockholm, Sweden (above), and a close-up of the prize itself (at right)

**VOICES FROM THE TIMES**

**Ask: What does Locke focus on in his description of Harlem?**

**Possible Responses:** He focuses on the positive aspects of the community; he looks at the individuals who make up the community and emphasizes their diversity as well as their sense of unity.

**Ask: Why would Van Doren feel that African Americans were especially suited to fill a void in American literature at that time?**

**Possible Responses:** African-American writers were just becoming a recognized force in literature, and what they had to say was still new; their life experiences were different from those of most other writers, and their works reflected this.

## The Harlem Renaissance

919

## OVERVIEW

### Objectives
- appreciate the craft of one of the Harlem Renaissance's most renowned and influential writers
- interpret the possible influences of historical context on Hughes's poetry
- interpret the possible influences of personal events in Hughes's life on his literary works
- recognize distinctive and shared characteristics of cultures through Hughes's literary works
- be informed about the impact of Hughes's poems, plays, novels, and essays

This Author Study offers a unique opportunity for students to focus on the work of a major writer. In addition, students can gather information about the life of Langston Hughes, gaining insight into the person behind his powerful literary works.

### PREVIEW
### Using Text Organizers
Have students preview the article, noting the basic text organizers: title, subheads, images and captions, and time line. Ask students to describe the information they would expect to locate in each section. Have students use the subheads to create an outline or text organizer. As they read, have them categorize information from the article under the appropriate heading. Point out that students should use text organizers themselves to locate and categorize information as they do independent research.

---

# Langston Hughes

> "Life is a big sea full of many fish. I let down my nets and pull."
>
> —Langston Hughes

## Harlem's Poet Laureate

1902–1967

*A man who had worked as a busboy, a truck farmer, and a sailor, Langston Hughes understood and loved working class and poor African Americans. As a writer, Hughes vividly portrayed the lives of those people—whom literature had mostly ignored.*

*Hughes was one of the leading voices of the Harlem Renaissance in the 1920s. He never lost his emotional tie to Harlem. Through his poems, plays, novels, and essays, he brought that community to life for the world.*

**A WANDERING CHILDHOOD** James Mercer Langston Hughes was born on February 1, 1902, in Joplin, Missouri. Shortly afterward, his parents separated. His father emigrated to Mexico to escape racial discrimination in the United States and had little contact with Hughes for 11 years. His mother, a teacher, struggled to support herself and her son. She frequently moved in search of decent jobs,

---

**HIS LIFE**
**HIS TIMES**

**1900**

**1910**

1902
Is born on February 1 in Joplin, Missouri

1915
Reads his first poem at 8th-grade graduation

1903
W.E.B. Du Bois publishes *The Souls of Black Folk.*

*The Crisis* was a tool of expression for Hughes and other writers.

1909
NAACP is founded.

1914
World War I begins in Europe.

920

leaving Hughes in the care of relatives or family friends. From the ages of 7 to 12, Hughes lived in Lawrence, Kansas, with his maternal grandmother.

After his grandmother's death in 1915, Hughes rejoined his mother and her second husband in Lincoln, Illinois, where he completed grammar school. While Hughes was in seventh grade, his classmates elected him class poet, even though he had never written a poem in his life! Hughes took his duties seriously, composing multiple verses about his teachers and classmates.

The family moved again in 1916—this time to Cleveland, Ohio. There, Hughes attended Central High School. A popular student, he was elected to class offices, acted in school plays, and joined the track-and-field team. He also wrote dialect poems in the style of Paul Laurence Dunbar and free-verse poems in the style of Carl Sandburg.

WORLD TRAVELER  After graduating from high school, Hughes visited his father in Mexico and lived with him for a year. On the train trip there, Hughes observed the Mississippi River and composed what was ultimately to become one of his most famous poems, "The Negro Speaks of Rivers." Hughes had found his distinctive poetic voice and began to publish in magazines.

After convincing his father to send him to Columbia University, Hughes left for New York City in 1921. Unhappy at college, he dropped out after one year.

## LITERARY Contributions

During his life-long career as a writer, Hughes published over 40 books, including poetry, novels, fiction, nonfiction, autobiographies, and children's stories. He also wrote 30 plays and translated poetry by international poets. Hughes's versatility and his staggering output of literary work during his lifetime earned him the nickname "Harlem's Shakespeare."

### Poetry Collections
*The Weary Blues* (1926)
*Fine Clothes to the Jew* (1927)
*Shakespeare in Harlem* (1942)
*Fields of Wonder* (1947)
*One-Way Ticket* (1949)
*Montage of a Dream Deferred* (1951)
*Ask Your Mama: 12 Moods for Jazz* (1961)
*The Panther and the Lash: Poems of Our Times* (1967)

### Novels
*Not Without Laughter* (1930)
*Tambourines to Glory* (1958)

### Short Story Collections
*The Ways of White Folks* (1934)
*Laughing to Keep from Crying* (1952)
*Something in Common and Other Stories* (1963)

### Autobiographies
*The Big Sea* (1940)
*I Wonder As I Wander* (1956)

### Youth
**A** Langston Hughes's maternal grandmother, Mary Sampson Patterson Leary Langston, often read Hughes stories from the Bible, Grimm's fairy tales, or from newspapers and magazines. She also related to him heroic tales of brave men and women who had fought slavery and had striven for freedom.

One of those brave men was Lewis Sheridan Leary, her first husband. At the age of 24, Leary joined the men in John Brown's party and attacked the federal arsenal at Harpers Ferry. While trying to cross the Shenandoah River, Leary received numerous bullet wounds and died. A friend who survived the raid gave Leary's bloodstained shawl to his young widow. Fifty years after Leary's death, Hughes's grandmother still wore the shawl, sometimes using it as a blanket to cover her sleeping grandson.

### First Impressions
**B** On September 4, 1921, Langston Hughes first saw Manhattan. He described his response to the sight this way: "There is no thrill in all the world like entering, for the first time, New York harbor,—coming in from the flat monotony of the sea to this rise of dreams and beauty. New York is truly the dream city,—city of the towers near God, city of hopes and visions, of spires seeking in the windy air loveliness and perfection." Of Harlem, Hughes said, "I was in love with Harlem long before I got there."

### Publishing
**C** Harlem was the publishing headquarters for the most important African American magazines, including *Crisis, Messenger,* and *Opportunity.* W. E. B. Du Bois, the editor of *Crisis,* had predicted for years a cultural renaissance for African Americans.

| 1920 Finishes high school, and lives in Mexico with father | 1923 Works aboard a freighter bound for Africa | 1926 Publishes first collection of poetry, *The Weary Blues* | 1929 Graduates from Lincoln University in Pennsylvania | 1935 Receives Guggenheim Fellowship; play *Mulatto* is staged on Broadway | 1937 Reports on the Spanish Civil War |

**1920**  **1930**

| 1918 By end of World War I, thousands of African Americans move to northern cities. | 1922 The Harlem Renaissance begins. | 1929 The Great Depression begins; African-American artists start to leave Harlem. | 1934 *Jonah's Gourd Vine* by Zora Neale Hurston is published. | Zora Neale Hurston |

## Literary Innovation

**A** Hughes loved the blues. One night, in a little Harlem cabaret, Hughes expressed his reverence for the blues and his own sense of isolation by writing "The Weary Blues," a poem that included some of the blues lyrics he remembered from his childhood. The result was a fusion of early blues with the conventions of formal poetry. The blues had never before been honored in literature. Hughes worked on the poem's ending for two years before showing the poem.

## Business

**B** Hughes struggled most of his life to earn a living. The *Chicago Defender,* an African-American weekly, raised his salary to ten dollars per week only after he threatened to resign after discovering that he was making less than other staff writers. Hughes often thought of capitalizing on his popular character, Jesse B. Semple, by making a comic strip out of him. The owner of *Negro Digest* and *Ebony* wanted Hughes to create an illustrated, pocketsize volume featuring the character. Hughes liked the idea of a black publisher and illustrator, but when he requested a $100 advance to begin the project, nothing more was heard. Hughes also received royalties from an anthology of his poems translated into Dutch, Spanish, Portuguese, and Italian.

## The Simple Columns

**C** In 1942, Hughes began writing columns for the *Chicago Defender.* For the most part, Hughes's columns covered a variety of topics, including the blues, the evils of segregation, etc. Then on February 13, 1943, Hughes casually introduced the fictional character Jesse B. Semple as "My Simple Minded Friend." Semple, an African-American everyman, soon became the center of Hughes's column and a popular hit with readers. Arna Bontemps, another Harlem Renaissance writer, described Semple as "the only new humorous creation in black flesh in a very long time. . . the very hipped, race-conscious, fighting-back, city-bred great grandson of Uncle Remus." Hughes published five collections of short stories based on these columns.

Fascinated by the sights and sounds of Harlem, he remained in New York and supported himself as best he could.

In 1923 Hughes found work as a cabin boy on a freighter bound for Africa, a trip that moved him profoundly. He also sailed to Europe aboard another freighter and decided to remain there for awhile. In the fall of 1924, with only 25 cents in his pocket, Hughes returned to the United States to pursue his career as a writer.

**SUDDEN FAME** By winning a literary contest with "The Weary Blues" in 1925, Hughes won the support of a prominent critic. He also gained public notice through an encounter with Vachel Lindsay, a famous poet of the day. When Lindsay came to the hotel restaurant in Washington, D.C., where Hughes worked as a busboy, Hughes slipped three poems—including "The Weary Blues"—beside Lindsay's plate. The next morning the newspapers reported that Lindsay had "discovered" a busboy poet.

After receiving a scholarship, Hughes enrolled at Pennsylvania's Lincoln University in 1926, the same year in which his first collection of poems, *The Weary Blues,* was published. A second

collection, *Fine Clothes to the Jew,* appeared in 1927. In response to African-American critics who disliked Hughes's gritty depiction of the lives of ordinary working people, Hughes said, "I didn't know the upper-class Negroes well enough to write much about them. I knew only the people I had grown up with, and they weren't people whose shoes were always shined, who had been to Harvard, or who had heard of Bach. But they seemed to me good people, too."

**AN INFLUENTIAL CAREER** Hughes played a key role in the Harlem Renaissance. In his writing, he portrayed both the nightlife and the everyday experiences of Harlem. He championed the right of African-American artists to express their own culture. He also used his writing to protest racial discrimination, especially the form of legal segregation commonly known as Jim Crow laws.

The first African American to earn a living solely from writing, Hughes went on to publish more than 40 books. His efforts to re-create the structures and rhythms of blues and jazz music in poetic works, such as *Montage of a Dream Deferred* (1951), demonstrate his desire to use

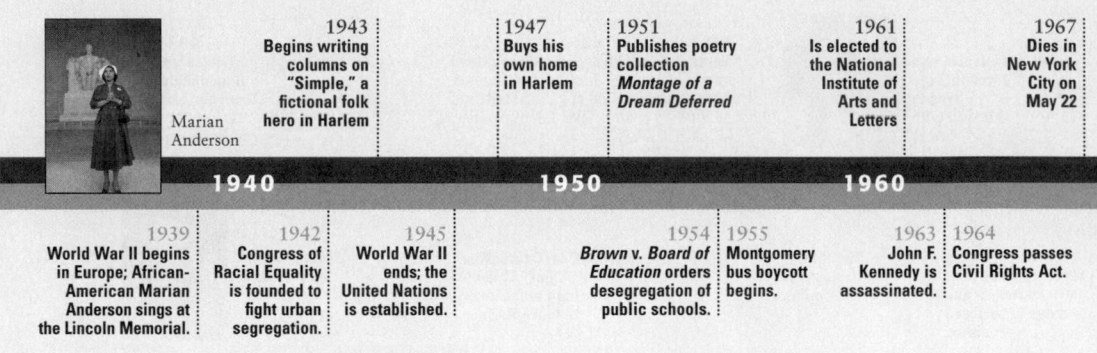

| | 1943 | 1947 | 1951 | 1961 | 1967 |
|---|---|---|---|---|---|
| Marian Anderson | Begins writing columns on "Simple," a fictional folk hero in Harlem | Buys his own home in Harlem | Publishes poetry collection *Montage of a Dream Deferred* | Is elected to the National Institute of Arts and Letters | Dies in New York City on May 22 |

**1940**　　　　　　　　　　**1950**　　　　　　　　　　**1960**

| 1939 | 1942 | 1945 | 1954 | 1955 | 1963 | 1964 |
|---|---|---|---|---|---|---|
| World War II begins in Europe; African-American Marian Anderson sings at the Lincoln Memorial. | Congress of Racial Equality is founded to fight urban segregation. | World War II ends; the United Nations is established. | *Brown* v. *Board of Education* orders desegregation of public schools. | Montgomery bus boycott begins. | John F. Kennedy is assassinated. | Congress passes Civil Rights Act. |

poetry to immortalize other African-American art forms. After a long and varied career, Hughes died in New York City in 1967.

Many have been encouraged by Hughes's poems of racial pride, such as the poets of the négritude movement—the French-speaking African poets who affirmed black culture. Succeeding generations of writers have been enormously influenced by Hughes, who has been called the "Poet Laureate of Harlem."

**More Online: Author Link**
www.mcdougallittell.com

## Goals of the Harlem Renaissance

In 1926 African-American journalist George S. Schuyler published "The Negro-Art Hokum," in which he ridiculed the idea of black and white cultural differences in the United States and argued that "any attempt on the part of the black American to aim at the production of any art distinctively Negro borders on self-deception." Responding to Schuyler, Hughes wrote "The Negro Artist and the Racial Mountain," an essay in which he laid out the goals of the writers and artists of the Harlem Renaissance. The final paragraph of the essay, which was published in *The Nation* in 1926, follows:

> *We younger Negro artists who create now intend to express our individual dark-skinned selves without fear or shame. If white people are pleased we are glad. If they are not, it doesn't matter. We know we are beautiful. And ugly too. The tom-tom cries and the tom-tom laughs. If colored people are pleased we are glad. If they are not, their displeasure doesn't matter either. We build our temples for tomorrow, strong as we know how, and we stand on top of the mountain, free within ourselves.*

*The Negro Looks Ahead* (1940), Richmond Barthe. Bronze, 16" × 10½" × 10½". Art & Artifacts Division, Schomburg Center for Research in Black Culture, The New York Public Library, Astor, Lenox, and Tilden Foundations. Photo by Manu Sassoonian.

### Home in Harlem
**D** From his arrival in Harlem in 1921, Hughes wanted a home of his own. In 1947, the success of the Broadway musical *Street Scene,* for which Hughes wrote the lyrics, allowed him finally to buy a home in Harlem. Referring to when he first arrived in Harlem, Hughes once said, "Had I been a rich young man, I would have bought a house in Harlem and built musical steps up to the front door, and installed chimes that at the press of a button played Ellington tunes."

### Music and Literature
**E** The fast, new sound of be-bop jazz, developed by musicians such as Dizzy Gillespie and Charlie Parker, turned away from the sweet music of swing, which was popular during World War II. In the poems published in Hughes's collection *Montage of a Dream Deferred,* he captured the fragmented, sometimes clashing images of Harlem life and unified them with words that represented the riffs and rhythms of "bop."

# Selected Poems

*by* LANGSTON HUGHES

## Objectives

1. understand and appreciate poems by Langston Hughes (**Literary Analysis**)
2. identify and appreciate **mood** (**Literary Analysis**)
3. detect **rhythm** in poetry (**Active Reading**)

## Summary

"I, Too" is a protest poem that asserts the place of "the darker brother" at the metaphoric "table" of American society. The poem also reveals the influence of Walt Whitman's poetry upon Hughes's work. In fact, Hughes once wrote that Whitman's *Leaves of Grass* "contains the greatest poetic statements of the real meaning of democracy ever made on our shores." The poem "Harlem" express-es the growing tension felt by many African Americans who have had to defer their dreams. The rhythms of the poem draw upon the 1940s music of bebop jazz. "The Weary Blues" expresses the poet's admiration for the musicians who play the blues, a form of music inspired by African-American spirituals and African-derived call-and-response work songs. In this poem, Hughes imitates the syncopated rhythm of blues music.

## Reading and Analyzing

### Literary Analysis [MOOD]

Read aloud the poem "I, Too." Ask students to describe the feeling, or mood, that the speaker creates. Have students use elements of the poem to defend their interpretation.

**Possible Response:** The straightfor-ward language creates a feeling of strength and confidence. The repetition of the word *I* suggests the speaker's own sense of personal strength.

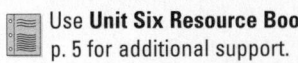 Use **Unit Six Resource Book,** p. 5 for additional support.

### Literary Analysis: FIGURATIVE LANGUAGE

**A** Ask students to interpret the metaphors of the kitchen and the din-ing room table.

**Possible Response:** The speaker is an African American who sees the division between the kitchen and the dining room table as symbolic of the segrega-tion in American society. One day, when this society is integrated, the speaker will no longer eat in the kitchen, but will "be at the table/When company comes."

---

### Connect to Your Life

**Gaining Recognition** Think about a time when you wanted to win recognition from a group or an individual. What accomplishment or quality were you hoping would be noticed? What strategies did you use to gain recognition? Use a cluster diagram like the one shown to explore the idea of gaining recognition. Then share your thoughts with a classmate.

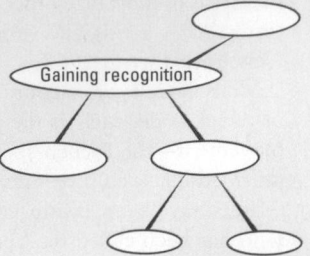

Gaining recognition

## Build Background

**Poet of Blues and Jazz** When Langston Hughes began to write, many African-American poets tried to sound like the white poets they had read in school. Instead of following that practice, Hughes incorporated the patterns of African-American speech and the rhythms of African-American music into his poetry. By doing so, Hughes hoped to gain recognition for the beauty of his culture. He also wrote protest poems, such as "I, Too," to expose the injustice of Jim Crow laws that imposed segregation upon African Americans.

Both "The Weary Blues" and "Harlem" are influenced by music. "The Weary Blues" draws on the blues, a style of music that African Americans developed in the late 19th century. Blues lyrics, which typically express sorrow or melancholy, often consist of three-line verses in which the second line repeats the first and the third expresses a response to the other two. "Harlem" draws on bebop jazz of the 1940s. Jazz evolved from ragtime and blues in the early 20th century. The music is characterized by syncopation, heavily accented rhythms, and improvisation on tunes and chord patterns. Bebop jazz has more complicated melodies and faster rhythmic changes than traditional jazz.

## Focus Your Reading

**LITERARY ANALYSIS** [MOOD] The **mood** of a poem is the emotional feeling or atmosphere that the poet creates for a reader. Poets create mood through their use of **imagery, figurative language, sound devices, rhythm,** and **description.** For example, the following line from "The Weary Blues" helps create a feeling of tiredness:

*By the pale dull pallor of an old gas light*

As you read each of the following poems, pay attention to the different moods that Hughes creates and the elements he uses to create them.

**ACTIVE READING** **DETECTING RHYTHM IN POETRY** Inspired by the blues and jazz he heard in Harlem nightclubs, Hughes tried to write poetry with the distinctive **rhythms** of these types of music. As you read the poems, try to detect the different rhythms that Hughes creates through his arrangement of stressed and unstressed syllables in a line. Use one or more of the following suggestions:

- Read the poems aloud, listening for the rhythm.
- Tap the rhythm out as you read the poems silently to yourself.
- Imagine how the poems would sound recited over a background of music, such as blues or jazz.

**READER'S NOTEBOOK** As you read the poems, copy lines whose rhythm appeals to you. Put accent marks over the syllables that you think should be stressed.

---

## LESSON RESOURCES

**UNIT SIX RESOURCE BOOK,** pp. 4–5

**ASSESSMENT RESOURCES**
**Formal Assessment,** pp. 167–168
**Teacher's Guide to Assessment and Portfolio Use**
**Test Generator**

**SKILLS TRANSPARENCIES AND COPYMASTERS**
**Literary Analysis**
- Mood, T18 (for Paired Activity, p. 928)

**Grammar**
- Varying Sentence Structure, C164 (for Mini Lesson, p. 929)

**Vocabulary**
- Syllabic Marks, C75 (for Mini Lesson, p. 925)

**Writing**
- Figurative Language and Sound Devices, T15 (for Writing Option 2, p. 929)

**Communications**
- Dramatic Reading, T12 (for Activities & Explorations 1, p. 929)
- Verbal Strategies, T14 (for Activities & Explorations 1, p. 929)

- Nonverbal Strategies, T15 (for Activities & Explorations 1, p. 929)

**INTEGRATED TECHNOLOGY**
**Audio Library**
**Net Activities**
**LaserLinks**
- Music Connection: Great Blues Musician
- Author Background: Langston Hughes. See **Teacher's SourceBook,** pp. 78–79.

**Visit our website:**
www.mcdougallittell.com

# I, Too

LANGSTON HUGHES

I, too, sing America.

I am the darker brother.
They send me to eat in the kitchen
When company comes,
5   But I laugh,
And eat well,
And grow strong.

Tomorrow,
I'll be at the table
10  When company comes.
**A**  Nobody'll dare
Say to me,
"Eat in the kitchen,"
Then.

15  Besides,
They'll see how beautiful I am
And be ashamed—

I, too, am America.

*Jim,* Selma Burke. Art and Artifacts
Division, Schomburg Center for
Research in Black Culture, The New
York Public Library, Astor, Lenox and
Tilden Foundations.

## Thinking Through the Literature

1. What is your opinion of the **speaker**? Share your thoughts with a classmate.
2. What do you believe the poem is saying about America?

 THINK ABOUT
   - the first and last lines
   - the identities of the speaker and the "they," in lines 3 and 16
   - what is meant by "when company comes," in line 4
   - what the speaker wants other people to recognize

3. How do you think the speaker expects to move from the "kitchen" to the "table"? How do you view his expectations?

**Less Proficient Readers**
Explain to students that the speaker of the poem uses the kitchen and the table as symbols to convey his message about discrimination.

**Set a Purpose** Have students read to find out what the speaker predicts for his future.

**Students Acquiring English**
Explain to students that the separation between the kitchen, where the speaker is sent to eat, and the table, where he is forbidden to eat, suggests the segregation in American life.

 Use **Spanish Study Guide** for additional support, pp. 221–223.

## Thinking Through the Literature

1. Possible Responses: The speaker is patient and confident; he respects himself; he expects to be treated as an equal.
2. Possible Response: Though America has traditionally excluded nonwhites, the speaker looks forward to a time when society will be inclusive rather than exclusive.
3. Possible Response: The speaker believes his strength and beauty will bring him to the table; he expects whites to become ashamed of the way they have treated him.

---

 **Mini Lesson** ## Vocabulary Strategy

**UNDERSTANDING SYLLABIC MARKS**
**Instruction** Understanding syllabic marks in a dictionary will help students determine the pronunciation and rhythm of a word's stressed and unstressed syllables. Write the following words on the chalkboard:

   mu•sic      to•mor•row

Tell students that the words listed in a dictionary are divided into syllables. A bullet, or a solid dot, indicates the division between syllables. For example, the word *music* has two syllables, and the word *tomorrow* has three.

**Exercises** For each word listed below, have students use a dictionary to rewrite the word, dividing it into syllables.

|   | Answers: |
|---|---|
| 1. beautiful | 1. beau•ti•ful |
| 2. renaissance | 2. ren•ais•sance |
| 3. America | 3. A•mer•i•ca |
| 4. integration | 4. in•te•gra•tion |
| 5. culture | 5. cul•ture |

 Use **Vocabulary Transparencies and Copymasters**, p. 75.

**Active Reading**

DETECTING RHYTHM IN POETRY

 Have students analyze the melodies of literary language, including Hughes's use of evocative rhythms, by reading lines 2–5 of the poem aloud, paying attention to which syllables naturally receive emphasis. Then have them copy lines 2–5 and mark the stressed and unstressed syllables.

Does it dry up
like a raisin in the sun?
Or fester like a sore—
And then run?

Ask students to describe this rhythm and the feelings it evokes. Also ask any students who marked the lines differently to explain their variations.

**Possible Responses:** The rhythm is disjointed and sounds syncopated or fast and abrupt. This rhythm evokes feelings of tension, dissatisfaction, anger, or anxiety.

Use **Unit Six Resource Book,** p. 4 for additional support.

**Active Reading**

DETECTING RHYTHM IN POETRY

**B** Point out to students that the word *syncopated* in the first line concerns rhythm. Ask one or more volunteers to read the first eight lines aloud. Then ask students to identify any patterns of rhythm that they heard.

**Possible Responses:** The passage contains long, flowing lines and short, emphatic ones; the repetition of line 6 is rhythmic.

**Literary Analysis** | MOOD |

**C** Ask students what mood or atmosphere the poem expresses.

**Possible Responses:** melancholy; bittersweet

# Harlem

LANGSTON HUGHES

**1** What happens to a dream deferred?

> **A** Does it dry up
> like a raisin in the sun?
> Or fester like a sore—
> 5 And then run?
> Does it stink like rotten meat?
> Or crust and sugar over—
> like a syrupy sweet?
>
> Maybe it just sags
> 10 like a heavy load.
>
> Or does it explode?

*Black Manhattan* 1969 Romare Bearden. Collage and Synthetic Polymer on board, 25 3/8" x 21". Schomburg Center for Research in Black Culture, Art & Artifacts Division, New York Public Library, Astor, Lenox and Tilden Foundations. Photo by Manu Sassoonian. Copyright @ Romare Bearden Foundation/Licensed by VAGA, New York.

## Thinking Through the Literature

1. What is your response to the last line? Share your reaction with a classmate.
2. What do you think is the poem's main message, or **theme**?

THINK ABOUT
- the **title**
- what the speaker's dream might be and why it might "explode"
- your own experiences of a dream that has been "deferred," or postponed

3. Do you agree or disagree with the speaker's opinion of what happens to a dream deferred? Explain your answer by citing details from the poem and from your own observations of life.

**926** UNIT SIX    AUTHOR STUDY: LANGSTON HUGHES

## Thinking Through the Literature

1. Responses will vary. Students may sense anger or threat; some may be surprised at the turn of thought.
2. The dream that has been put off or delayed may be a wish for prosperity, respect, equality, or security. The poem suggests that there may be serious consequences if dreams are denied.
3. Students may be able to identify how different people react to the loss or postponement of their dreams.

# The Weary Blues

## Langston Hughes

Droning a drowsy syncopated[1] tune,
Rocking back and forth to a mellow croon,[2]
   I heard a Negro play.
Down on Lenox Avenue the other night  **B**
5 By the pale dull pallor[3] of an old gas light
   He did a lazy sway. . . .
   He did a lazy sway. . . .
To the tune o' those Weary Blues.
With his ebony hands on each ivory key
10 He made that poor piano moan with melody. **C**
   O Blues!
Swaying to and fro on his rickety stool
He played that sad raggy tune like a musical <u>fool</u>. **2**
   Sweet Blues!
15 Coming from a black man's soul.
   O Blues!
In a deep song voice with a melancholy tone
I heard that Negro sing, that old piano moan—
   "Ain't got nobody in all this world,
20   Ain't got nobody but ma self.
   I's gwine to quit ma frownin'
   And put ma troubles on the shelf."
Thump, thump, thump, went his foot on the floor.
He played a few chords then he sang some more—
25   "I got the Weary Blues
   And I can't be satisfied.
   Got the Weary Blues
   And can't be satisfied—
   I ain't happy no mo'
30   And I wish that I had died."
And far into the night he crooned that tune.
The stars went out and so did the moon.
The singer stopped playing and went to bed
While the Weary Blues echoed through his head.
35 He slept like a rock or a man that's dead.

---

1. **syncopated** (sĭng′kɔ-pā′tĭd): characterized by a shifting of stresses from normally strong to normally weak beats.
2. **croon:** a soft humming or singing.
3. **pallor** (păl′ər): lack of color.

THE WEARY BLUES **927**

## Mini Lesson — Viewing and Representing

*Black Manhattan*
**by Romare Bearden**

**ART APPRECIATION**
The artist Romare Bearden was born in 1912 and grew up in Harlem, New York. One of the things Bearden remembered about growing up in Harlem was the ever-present sound of jazz music: "Not only was it on the radio and record players, but I often heard sounds of a piano from an open window, and in warm weather there were likely to be two or three musicians on a street corner playing for whatever onlookers might drop in the hat." It wasn't until the early 1960s, however, when Bearden was in his fifties, that he started working in the medium of collage. His collages met great and immediate success, and by 1969, the year in which Bearden created *Black Manhattan*, he was a celebrated artist.

**Instruction** Tell students that a collage is a combination of fragments of paper, images from newsprint or magazines, paint, and objects. Have students describe the use of color and the arrangement of images in this collage.

**Possible Response:** Blocks of color—red, blue, and cement gray—are broken up by altered images of African Americans sitting or looking out high-rise windows. The collage contains fragments of images of urban life—a face at the window, clothes hanging from the line, the repetition of the fire escapes, and so on.

## GUIDING STUDENT RESPONSE

## Connect to the Literature

**1. What Do You Think?**
Students may see the musician as old or young, ragged or smartly dressed, weary or energetic, expressing sadness or enjoying his music.

**Comprehension Check**
• the speaker and a musician
• a piano
• a blues song

## Think Critically

**2. Possible Responses:** The speaker admires the musician's enthusiasm (line 13) and feels compassion for his melancholy (lines 16–17, 35); he finds the music sad (line 13), soulful (line 15), and sweet (line 14).

**3.** Most students will agree that the shorter lines tend to have the heavily accented rhythms.

**4.** Students may identify such aspects as night life in Harlem, blues music, African-American speech patterns, or the rhythms of jazz music.

**5.** Some students may note that the blues verses have more regular rhythms than the other lines of the poem do; others may observe that the blues verses use dialect and the rest of the poem doesn't. Students may feel that the two styles are complementary.

**6.** Students may disagree. The optimism of "I, Too" may appeal to some; the message about the grave consequences of discrimination in "Harlem" may seem effective to others; the route of personal creativity in "The Weary Blues" offers another possible response.

## Connect to the Literature

**1. What Do You Think?** What vision of the musician did you develop as you read "The Weary Blues"? Describe your image of him.

**Comprehension Check**
• Who are the characters in "The Weary Blues"?
• What instrument does the singer play?
• What type of song does the singer sing?

## Think Critically

**2.** How does the **speaker** seem to feel about the musician and about blues music? Cite evidence from the poem.

**3.** **ACTIVE READING** **DETECTING RHYTHM IN POETRY** Which lines in "The Weary Blues" have the most heavily accented **rhythms**?

THINK ABOUT
{ • the rhythm of the lines that you copied into your 📖 READER'S NOTEBOOK
• how the rhythms of the long and the short lines differ

**4.** What aspects of African-American culture or African-American identity do you think Hughes wanted to gain recognition for in this poem? Explain.

**5.** What differences do you see between the two blues verses (lines 19–22 and 25–30) in "The Weary Blues" and the rest of the poem? How well do you think the two styles work together?

**6.** "The Weary Blues," "I, Too," and "Harlem" may be read as describing different ways of responding to discrimination. Which response do you think is more effective? Give reasons for your answer.

## Extend Interpretations

**7. Comparing Texts** How would you compare the vision of America suggested in "I, Too" with that in Walt Whitman's poem "I Hear America Singing" on page 397?

**8. Connect to Life** If Hughes were writing today, what features of contemporary African-American culture do you think he would portray in his poetry? Explain the aspects of African-American culture that Hughes might think deserve more recognition.

## Literary Analysis

MOOD In each of these poems, Hughes creates a certain **mood,** or emotional feeling or atmosphere. **Imagery, figurative language, description,** and **sound devices** contribute to the mood of each poem, as does the **rhythm** of the language Hughes uses. For example, in the poem "Harlem," the **similes** "fester like a sore" and "stink like rotten meat" convey a sense of disease and decay. This causes the reader to have negative feelings about the idea of deferring dreams.

**Paired Activity** Work with a partner to identify the mood of each of the three Hughes poems—"I, Too," "Harlem," and "The Weary Blues." Then list the elements—imagery, figurative language, sound devices, description, and rhythm—that contribute to the mood of each poem. Use a chart like the one shown to record your findings. Then share your perceptions in class.

| | Mood of Poem | Elements that Contribute to Mood |
|---|---|---|
| "I, Too" | | |
| "Harlem" | | |
| "The Weary Blues" | | |

## Extend Interpretations

**Comparing Texts** Possible Response: Whitman's subject is broader because by definition he encompasses all of American culture rather than a single group; Whitman is more exuberant, Hughes more gently melancholy and wryly humorous.
**Connect to Life** Responses will vary. Students might state that Hughes's interest in the lives of common people might lead him to portray struggling African Americans rather than prosperous ones.

## Literary Analysis

**Mood** Have students reread the three poems. As they read, have them think about the following questions:
• Which of the three speakers is the saddest? Which is most confident about the future? Which is most frustrated?
• What images, figurative expressions, sound devices, or rhythms impress you the most in each poem?
Possible Responses: "I, Too" is patient and self-assured; "Harlem" is frustrated and angry; "The Weary Blues" is resigned and melancholy.

## Writing Options

**1. Congratulatory Letter** "The Weary Blues," which Hughes referred to as his "lucky" poem, was the winning entry in a literary contest sponsored by *Opportunity* magazine. Draft a letter of congratulation to Hughes, telling him why his poem won first prize.

**2. Musical Poem** Begin writing a poem that in some way suggests a particular style of music you enjoy, as Hughes did in "I, Too," "Harlem," and "The Weary Blues." Have a classmate read it and guess what kind of music inspired you.

**3. Compare-Contrast Essay** Reread "I, Too," "Harlem," and "The Weary Blues." In an essay, compare and contrast the different responses to discrimination that are presented in these three poems. Before you begin, create a compare-and-contrast chart like this one to organize your ideas.

| Poem | Response to Discrimination |
|------|----------------------------|
| "I, Too" | |
| "Harlem" | |
| "The Weary Blues" | |

**Writing Handbook**
See page 1281: Compare and Contrast.

## Activities & Explorations

**1. Oral Readings** With a small group of classmates, plan an oral reading of one of the three poems by Hughes. Choose appropriate volumes, phrasings, pitches, and gestures. Decide whether the poem should be read by a single voice or by several voices and whether you will read with jazz accompaniment. Present your reading to the class. ~ **SPEAKING AND LISTENING/MUSIC**

**2. Poem Illustration** Create an illustration to accompany either "I, Too," "Harlem," or "The Weary Blues." Use images and colors that convey the mood of the poem. Then display your artwork in the classroom. ~ **ART**

**3. Map of Harlem** The blues singer in "The Weary Blues" and other African-American musicians played in clubs on Lenox Avenue in Harlem during the Harlem Renaissance. With a partner, use a map of New York City to locate Harlem and Lenox Avenue. Create an illustrated map of Harlem to accompany Hughes's poem. ~ **GEOGRAPHY**

**4. Blues Adaptation** Perform your own interpretation of the "weary blues," adapting or inventing a blues melody and making up additional lyrics. ~ **MUSIC**

## Inquiry & Research

**The Blues** In "The Weary Blues," Hughes incorporated the first blues lyrics he had ever heard when he was a child in Kansas. Find out more about the blues, using a print or on-line encyclopedia, a book about blues music, or the Internet. Look for answers to the following questions: What are the roots of blues music? Who are some well-known blues musicians? How has the blues influenced other popular forms of music? Answer these questions in a presentation to the class, accompanied by some recordings of blues music.

Blues musician Muddy Waters

 **More Online: Research Starter** www.mcdougallittell.com

## Writing Options

**1. Congratulatory Letter** Point out to students that the letter must concentrate on the reasons for the award. **To get students started on this activity,** suggest that they brainstorm a list of the elements in the poem that make it so powerful.

**2. Musical Poem** Students might play selections of the music that inspired them before reading aloud their poems.

**3. Compare-Contrast Essay** **To make this assignment less challenging,** have students compare and contrast the response to discrimination in two of the poems.

## Activities & Explorations

**1. Oral Readings** Encourage students to explain why they used certain techniques of nonverbal communication when reading the poems.

**2. Poem Illustration** Have students explain why they depicted the mood of the poem as they did.

**3. Map of Harlem** **To make this assignment more challenging,** have students research the names of clubs on Lenox Avenue during the height of the Harlem Renaissance.

## Inquiry & Research

**The Blues** Students can locate appropriate print information using a technical resource such as a library database and searching under the key words *blues; music, blues; musicians, blues.* For example, they might locate the *History of the Blues* (Hyperion, 1995), a companion volume to the PBS series of the same title; or *The Listener's Guide to the Blues* (Facts on File, 1982). Students can locate numerous on-line references by searching under the key word *blues.* Also, students can locate information about specific blues artists by searching under artists' names, such as Charley Patton, Robert Johnson, Ma Rainey, Bessie Smith, or Mississippi John Hurt.

---

**Mini Lesson** ## Grammar

### VARYING SENTENCE STRUCTURE

Remind students that there are four main sentence types: simple, compound, complex, and compound-complex. By using different combinations of independent and subordinates clauses, students can vary the structure of their sentences. Write the following sentences on the chalkboard and label each one.

**Simple Sentence** (one independent clause)
Many artists met at the clubs in Harlem.

**Compound Sentence** (two or more independent clauses)
Many artists met at the clubs in Harlem, and they listened to music until early morning.

**Complex Sentence** (one independent clause, one or more subordinate clauses)
Many artists who met at the clubs in Harlem listened to music until early morning.

**Compound-Complex Sentence** (two or more independent clauses, one or more subordinate clauses)
Many artists met at the clubs in Harlem, and they listened to music that stirred their own creativity.

 Use **Grammar Transparencies and Copymasters**, p. 164.

 Use McDougal Littell's *Language Network*, Chapter 3, for more instruction and practice in sentence structure.

## Literary Analysis MOOD

Ask volunteers to read "The Weary Blues" and "Flute Players" to the class. Then have pairs of students compare elements of the texts across texts, such as the moods in both poems. Have students consider the kinds of literary devices that Hughes and Rabéarivelo use to convey mood.

**Possible Responses:** Both poems convey a mood of sorrow, fatigue, and longing. Hughes uses a blues-influenced rhythm and repetition to help convey mood. Rabéarivelo primarily uses imagery to compare and contrast the music of the two flutes that express their sorrowful origins.

# FLUTE PLAYERS

### JEAN-JOSEPH RABÉARIVELO

*Jean-Joseph Rabéarivelo (1910–1937), from Madagascar, was one of the négritude poets inspired and championed by Langston Hughes. This poem, translated by Hughes, is close in spirit to "The Weary Blues."*

Your flute
  you carved from the shinbone of a mighty bull
  and polished it on barren hills beaten by sun.

His flute
  he carved from a reed trembling in the breeze
  and cut in it little holes beside a flowing brook
  drunk on dreams of moonlight.

Together
  you made music in the late afternoon
  as if to hold back the round boat
  sinking on the shores of the sky
  to save it from its fate:
  but are your plaintive incantations
  heeded by the gods of the wind,
  of the earth, of the forest, and the sand?

Your flute
  throws out a beat like the march of an angry bull
  toward the desert—
  but who comes back running,
  burned by thirst and hunger
  and defeated by weariness
  at the foot of a shadeless tree
  with neither leaves nor fruit.

His flute
  is like a reed that bends
  beneath the weight of a passing bird in flight—
  not a bird captured by a child
  whose feathers are caressed,
  but a bird lost from other birds
  who looks at his own shadow for solace
  in the flowing water.

Your flute and his
  regret their beginnings
  in the songs of both your sorrows.

Margrett Ann Duncan, Hughes's cousin

# from Love, Langston

*Newspaper Article*
*by* Dahleen Glanton

She was a homemaker from Joliet who had never ventured out of the Midwest. He was a world-renowned poet who had traveled around the globe five times before they ever met.

It was her search through the family's bloodline that in 1958 led Margrett Ann Duncan to Langston Hughes, her first cousin once removed. But it was their fondness and admiration for each other that kept them close for almost a decade.

She baked maple nut cakes and mailed them to him in an aluminum pan. The sweet token would be waiting for him at his East 127th Street apartment in Harlem when he returned from a trip to Paris or San Francisco or the West Indies. Afterward, he would return the pan filled with autographed books of his writings, candy for her four children, and always a friendly note expressing his gratitude.

On her birthday, Valentine's Day, and Christmas, the arrival of flowers, cards, or sometimes a singing telegram became an annual ritual that she cherished as much as his almost-monthly letters. On green-and-white stationery, Hughes shared almost every aspect of his life with the woman he fondly called his "No. 1 Coz." He wrote of his travels, his lectures, his performances, and the people he had met in faraway places. He spoke of his family, inquired about hers, and promised to visit as soon as he could. She pre-served every memento in a brown vinyl scrapbook kept locked away in a safe deposit box.

When his work brought him to Chicago, Hughes often stayed with Duncan and her husband in an 11-room home in Joliet she had inherited from her Aunt Jessie. Normally, Hughes would read poetry or perform readings to the accompaniment of a jazz quartet, but Duncan's favorite performance was when he appeared on stage in Chicago with gospel singer Mahalia Jackson. When her cousin was in town, the family partied into the early morning hours, then spent the rest of the day exchanging life stories. . . .

Duncan gave Hughes something he'd never had—knowledge about his father's family. His parents separated shortly after his birth, and he lived with his maternal grandmother in Lawrence, Kansas, until he was 12. When she died he moved to Lincoln, Illinois, with his mother and after high school lived a year with his father in Mexico. Among Duncan's vast collection of antiques and family heirlooms handed down from Aunt Jessie was a picture of Langston's grandfather, a man he had never seen. He borrowed the photograph from Duncan, she said, and never returned it. . . .

Duncan and her brother grew up much like their cousin. Their parents, too, separated when they were young. She and her brother clung to each other, and Langston Hughes clung to them.

---

---

## Preparing to Read

## Build Background

Imagine discovering that you have a celebrity in your family! That's what happened to Margrett Ann Duncan. For years, her Aunt Jessie had claimed to be related to Langston Hughes, but no one believed the elderly woman. Then after Aunt Jessie's death, Duncan discovered that she was indeed a cousin of Hughes. This article, printed in the *Chicago Tribune* on July 8, 1998, describes what happened after the two met—and how the celebrity benefited from the relationship as much as his stay-at-home cousin.

## OBJECTIVES

1. understand and appreciate an **essay** (Literary Analysis)
2. identify **tone** (Literary Analysis)
3. **draw conclusions about author's perspective** (Active Reading)

## Summary

In his essay "When the Negro Was in Vogue," Langston Hughes chronicles the key events and artists of the Harlem Renaissance, from its bright beginning with the musical revue *Shuffle Along* to its dissolution in 1929 with the advent of the Great Depression. Hughes lists the extraordinary African-American talents who rose to fame in the 1920s—including Eubie Blake, Bessie Smith, Ethel Waters, Paul Robeson, and Josephine Baker. Hughes also explains that beneath the sparkling surface of these times, however, was the ugly reality of Jim Crow laws. Unless they were performing celebrities, African Americans were barred from attending some Harlem clubs frequented by white patrons. In the essay, Hughes also notes that the renaissance movement neither benefited "ordinary" African Americans economically nor brought about racial equality.

## Reading and Analyzing

### Literary Analysis TONE

Tell students that the essay contains many different tones, reflecting Hughes's attitudes toward the different groups of people he describes. Have students read to identify these groups and Hughes's attitudes toward them.

 Use **Unit Six Resource Book,** p. 7 for additional support.

### Active Reading

DRAWING CONCLUSIONS ABOUT AUTHOR'S PERSPECTIVE

Ask students what conclusions they can draw about Hughes's perspective toward his subject, given that he experienced firsthand this extraordinary time period.

**Possible Responses:** Hughes's perspective is probably emotional and personal.

 Use **Unit Six Resource Book,** p. 6 for additional support.

---

# When the Negro Was in Vogue

*Essay by* LANGSTON HUGHES

### Connect to Your Life

**What's "In"?** Think about current fads that are popular with your classmates. What is the latest craze in fashion, music, or dance? Which celebrities—artists, authors, musicians, actors, and so on—are hot? Brainstorm with a small group of classmates and create a list of who and what is "in" at your school. As you read Hughes's essay, consider who and what were trendy in the 1920s during the Harlem Renaissance.

## Build Background

**Hughes in Harlem** Hughes first became acquainted with Harlem in 1921 while he was a student at Columbia University. Initially dazzled by Harlem's vibrant nightlife, Hughes later perceived the underlying economic and social problems that existed there. As an eyewitness to Harlem's renaissance, he captures the neighborhood's rich African-American cultural life as well as the hypocrisy and racism of the time in his essay "When the Negro Was in Vogue." The essay first appeared in the final section of Hughes's autobiography *The Big Sea* (1940).

## Focus Your Reading

LITERARY ANALYSIS TONE The **tone** of a literary work is an expression of a writer's attitude toward his or her subject. A writer conveys tone by *what* he or she says about a subject as well as *how* he or she says it. For example, in the following excerpt from "When the Negro Was in Vogue," Hughes displays a critical tone toward nightclub owners:

> *Some of the owners of Harlem clubs, delighted at the flood of white patronage, made the grievous error of barring their own race, after the manner of the famous Cotton Club.*

ACTIVE READING | DRAWING CONCLUSIONS ABOUT AUTHOR'S PERSPECTIVE To get the most out of reading a work of nonfiction, try to **draw conclusions** about the **author's perspective,** or view of the events and people described. Some authors adopt the perspective of an objective observer. Others identify emotionally with one or more of their subjects and try to express that person's point of view. To determine an author's perspective, pay attention to the facts that the author includes and to the emotions and opinions that the author expresses.

READER'S NOTEBOOK In your notebook, create a chart like the one shown. As you read the essay, record the facts that Hughes mentions and the emotions and opinions he expresses about each group of people.

|  | African-American Entertainers | Residents of Harlem | White Tourists |
|---|---|---|---|
| Facts |  |  |  |
| Opinions and Emotions |  |  |  |

---

## LESSON RESOURCES

**UNIT SIX RESOURCE BOOK,** pp. 6–7

**ASSESSMENT RESOURCES**
**Formal Assessment,** pp. 169–170
**Teacher's Guide to Assessment and Portfolio Use**
**Test Generator**

**SKILLS TRANSPARENCIES AND COPYMASTERS**
**Literary Analysis**
• Tone, T19 (for Cooperative Learning Activity, p. 937)

**Reading and Critical Thinking**
• Drawing Conclusions, T4 (for Active Reading, p. 932)

**Grammar**
• Adverbial Elements, C140 (for Mini Lesson, p. 938)

**Vocabulary**
• Using Context to Build Vocabulary, C76 (for Mini Lesson, p. 933)

**Writing**
• Reflective Essay, C28 (for Writing Option 1, p. 939)

**Communications**
• Appreciative Listening, T2 (for Activities & Explorations 1, p. 939)
• Evaluating Roles in Groups, T8 (for Inquiry & Research, p. 939)

**INTEGRATED TECHNOLOGY**

**Audio Library**
**Internet: Research Starter**
Visit our website:
www.mcdougallittell.com

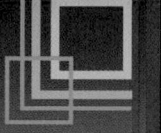

# When the Negro Was in Vogue

### LANGSTON  HUGHES

The 1920's were the years of Manhattan's black Renaissance. It began with *Shuffle Along, Running Wild,* and the Charleston. Perhaps some people would say even with *The Emperor Jones,* Charles Gilpin, and the tom-toms at the Provincetown. But certainly it was the musical revue, *Shuffle Along,* that gave a scintillating send-off to that Negro vogue in Manhattan, which reached its peak just before the crash of 1929, the crash that sent Negroes, white folks, and all rolling down the hill toward the Works Progress Administration.[1]

*Shuffle Along* was a honey of a show. Swift, bright, funny, rollicking, and gay, with a dozen danceable, singable tunes. Besides, look who were in it: The now famous choir director, Hall Johnson, and the composer, William Grant Still, were a part of the orchestra. Eubie Blake and Noble Sissle wrote the music and played and acted in the show. Miller and Lyles were the comics. Florence Mills skyrocketed to fame in the second act. Trixie Smith sang "He May Be Your Man But He Comes to See Me Sometimes." And Caterina Jarboro, now a European prima donna, and the internationally celebrated Josephine Baker were merely in the chorus. Everybody was in the audience—including me. People came back to see it innumerable times. It was always packed.

To see *Shuffle Along* was the main reason I wanted to go to Columbia. When I saw it, I was thrilled and delighted. From then on I was in the gallery of the Cort Theatre every time I got a chance. That year, too, I saw Katharine Cornell in *A Bill of Divorcement,* Margaret Wycherly in *The Verge,* Maugham's *The Circle* with Mrs. Leslie Carter, and the Theatre Gild production of Kaiser's *From Morn Till Midnight.* But I remember *Shuffle Along* best of all. It gave just the proper push—a pre-Charleston kick—to that Negro vogue of the 20's that spread to books, African sculpture, music, and dancing.

Put down the 1920's for the rise of Roland Hayes, who packed Carnegie Hall, the rise of Paul Robeson[2] in New York and London, of Florence Mills over two continents, of Rose McClendon in Broadway parts that never measured up to her, the booming voice of Bessie Smith and the low moan of Clara on thousands of records, and the rise of that grand comedienne of song, Ethel Waters, singing: "Charlie's elected now! He's in right for sure!" Put down the 1920's for Louis Armstrong and Gladys Bentley and Josephine Baker.[3]

White people began to come to Harlem in droves. For several years they packed the expensive Cotton Club on Lenox Avenue. But I was never there, because the Cotton Club was a Jim Crow[4] club for gangsters and monied whites. They were not cordial to Negro patronage, unless you were a celebrity like Bojangles. So Harlem Negroes did not like the Cotton Club and never appreciated its Jim Crow policy in the very heart of their dark community. Nor did ordinary Negroes like the growing influx of whites toward Harlem after sundown, flooding the little cabarets and bars where formerly only colored people laughed and sang, and where now

---

1. **Works Progress Administration:** an agency formed to help create jobs for the unemployed during the Depression.
2. **Paul Robeson** (rōb'sən): an actor, singer, and activist.
3. **Louis Armstrong . . . Josephine Baker:** Louis Armstrong was a pioneering jazz trumpeter; Gladys Bentley was a pianist and singer; and Josephine Baker was a singer, dancer, and movie actress.
4. **Jim Crow:** racially segregated.

## TEACHING THE LITERATURE

## Customizing Instruction

### Less Proficient Readers
Explain to students that the writer Langston Hughes experienced the Harlem Renaissance firsthand and observed many of the artists he mentions in this essay.

**Set a Purpose** Have students read to find out what the writer thinks about the Harlem Renaissance.

### Students Acquiring English
Explain to students that the word *vogue* means "style." The title of the essay means "when the Negro was in style" or "when the Negro was in fashion."

 Use **Spanish Study Guide** for additional support, pp. 224–226.

### Gifted and Talented Students
Encourage students to compare and contrast Hughes's interpretation of the positive and negative aspects of the Harlem Renaissance with that of another Harlem Renaissance writer, such as Countee Cullen.

---

## (Mini Lesson) Vocabulary Strategy

**USING CONTEXT TO BUILD VOCABULARY**
**Instruction** Tell students that they can use context to determine the meaning of words and to expand their vocabulary. Use the following model sentence to demonstrate the strategy:
   Nor did ordinary Negroes like the growing influx of whites toward Harlem after sundown, flooding the little cabarets.
Ask a volunteer to summarize the meaning of the sentence and to infer the meaning of the word *influx.* Then ask a volunteer to use the word *influx* in a sentence.

**Exercises** Ask students to use context clues to determine the meanings of the italicized words.
1. Some musicians and artists rose to *prominence* from lowly beginnings. (*importance, fame*)
2. For many African Americans, the *renaissance* brought a sense of renewal and rebirth. (*renewal, rebirth*)
3. The Harlem Renaissance was an *unprecedented* era of creativity among African Americans—never before did literary, musical, and artistic production reach such

a peak. (*without an earlier or similar example*)

 Use **Vocabulary Transparencies and Copymasters,** p. 76.

**A lesson on context clues appears on p. 326 in the Pupil's Edition.**

**Literary Analysis** TONE

**A** Have students compare and contrast Hughes's tone toward some owners of Harlem clubs and their white patrons with his tone toward the African-American musicians, such as Louis Armstrong and Bessie Smith, who perform in the clubs.

**Possible Response:** Hughes uses a sarcastic and critical tone toward the owners of the clubs. His tone toward the musicians, however, is one of celebration and delight.

**Active Reading**

```
DRAWING CONCLUSIONS ABOUT
AUTHOR'S PERSPECTIVE
```

**B** Ask students to draw a conclusion about Hughes's perspective toward other African-American writers during the Harlem Renaissance. Have students use elements of the text to defend their conclusions.

**Possible Response:** He is objective ("Maybe—since Negroes have writer-racketeers, as has any other race"), but also personal and appreciative ("I have known almost all of them," "the good ones have tried to be honest").

**Literary Analysis: DICTION AND SYNTAX**

**C** Tell students that **anaphora** is the repetition of a word or phrase at the beginning of successive clauses, sentences, or paragraphs. Have students analyze the syntax of the paragraph and identify an example of anaphora. Ask them to analyze the effect it creates.

**Possible Responses:** "It was a period when"; the anaphora creates a dramatic, musical, engaging effect.

---

the strangers were given the best ringside tables to sit and stare at the Negro customers—like amusing animals in a zoo.

The Negroes said: "We can't go downtown and sit and stare at you in your clubs. You won't even let us in your clubs." But they didn't say it out loud—for Negroes are practically never rude to white people. So thousands of whites came to Harlem night after night, thinking the Negroes loved to have them there, and firmly believing that all Harlemites left their houses at sundown to sing and dance in cabarets, because most of the whites saw nothing but the cabarets, not the houses.

Some of the owners of Harlem clubs, delighted at the flood of white patronage, made the grievous error of barring their own race, after the manner of the famous Cotton Club. But most of these quickly lost business and folded up, because they failed to realize that a large part of the Harlem attraction for downtown New Yorkers lay in simply watching the colored customers amuse themselves. And the smaller clubs, of course, had no big floor shows or a name band like the Cotton Club, where Duke Ellington[5] usually held forth, so, without black patronage, they were not amusing at all.

Some of the small clubs, however, had people like Gladys Bentley, who was something worth discovering in those days, before she got famous, acquired an accompanist, specially written material, and conscious vulgarity. But for two or three amazing years, Miss Bentley sat, and played a big piano all night long, literally all night, without stopping—singing songs like "The St. James Infirmary," from ten in the evening until dawn, with scarcely a break between the notes, sliding from one song to another, with a powerful and continuous underbeat of jungle rhythm. Miss Bentley was an amazing exhibition of musical energy—a large, dark, masculine lady, whose feet pounded the floor while her fingers pounded the keyboard—a perfect piece of African sculpture, animated by her own rhythm.

But when the place where she played became too well known, she began to sing with an accompanist, became a star, moved to a larger place, then downtown, and is now in Hollywood. The old magic of the woman and the piano and the night and the rhythm being one is gone. But everything goes, one way or another. The '20's are gone and lots of fine things in Harlem night life have disappeared like snow in the sun—since it became utterly commercial, planned for the downtown tourist trade, and therefore dull.

---

5. **Duke Ellington:** a gifted pianist, bandleader, and composer who helped advance jazz music.

ETHEL WATERS

LOUIS ARMSTRONG'S HOT FIVE

BESSIE SMI

934

---

**Mini Lesson** **Speaking and Listening**

**NONVERBAL COMMUNICATION**

**Instruction** In his essay, Hughes says that African Americans didn't express their frustration and anger at being barred from certain clubs. Ask: What gestures or facial expressions would convey feelings of frustration and anger?

**Possible Responses:** clenched fists, furrowed eyebrows, etc.

Tell students that elements of nonverbal communication include eye contact, facial expressions, arm and hand gestures, body posture, and proximity (distance from the audience). Each of these elements can effectively communicate emotions, such as anger, sadness, fear, disappointment, or frustration.

**Application** Have pairs or small groups of students select a passage from Hughes's essay and identify the emotions conveyed in the situation described. Then have them discuss how to communicate the situation and emotions using only elements of nonverbal communication. Have students practice presenting the passage as a nonverbal skit.

**Present** Invite pairs or small groups of students to present their skits to the rest of the class. Ask students to identify the expressions and gestures that conveyed specific emotions.

**BLOCK SCHEDULING** This activity is particularly well suited for longer class periods.

The lindy-hoppers at the Savoy[6] even began to practise acrobatic routines, and to do absurd things for the entertainment of the whites, that probably never would have entered their heads to attempt merely for their own effortless amusement. Some of the lindy-hoppers had cards printed with their names on them and became dance professors teaching the tourists. Then Harlem nights became show nights for the Nordics.

Some critics say that that is what happened to certain Negro writers, too—that they ceased to write to amuse themselves and began to write to amuse and entertain white people, and in so doing distorted and over-colored their material, and left out a great many things they thought would offend their American brothers of a lighter complexion. Maybe—since Negroes have writer-racketeers, as has any other race. But I have known almost all of them, and most of the good ones have tried to be honest, write honestly, and express their world as they saw it.

All of us know that the gay and sparkling life of the so-called Negro Renaissance of the '20's was not so gay and sparkling beneath the surface as it looked. Carl Van Vechten,[7] in the character of Byron in *Nigger Heaven,* captured some of the bitterness and frustration of literary Harlem that Wallace Thurman later so effectively poured into his *Infants of the Spring*—the only novel by a Negro about that fantastic period when Harlem was in vogue.

It was a period when, at almost every Harlem upper-crust dance or party, one would be introduced to various distinguished white celebrities there as guests. It was a period when almost any Harlem Negro of any social importance at all would be likely to say casually: "As I was remarking the other day to Heywood—," meaning Heywood Broun. Or: "As I said to George—," referring to George Gershwin.[8] It was a period when local and visiting royalty were not at all uncommon in Harlem. And when the parties of A'Lelia Walker, the Negro heiress, were filled with guests whose names would turn any Nordic social climber green with envy. It was a period when Harold Jackman, a handsome young Harlem school teacher of modest means, calmly announced one day that he was sailing for the Riviera for a fortnight, to attend Princess Murat's yachting party. It was a period when Charleston preachers opened up shouting churches as sideshows for

---

6. **lindy-hoppers at the Savoy:** people often did a popular 1920s dance, the lindy hop, at the Savoy, a famous Harlem ballroom.

7. **Carl Van Vechten** (văn vĕk'tən): Carl Van Vechten was a white photographer and writer who promoted and publicized the works of his African-American friends.

8. **Heywood . . . Gershwin:** Heywood Broun (hā'wood broōn) was a New York City newspaper columnist and social critic; George Gershwin was a famous composer.

JOSEPHINE BAKER

PAUL ROBESON

935

## Customizing Instruction

### Less Proficient Readers

1 Help readers understand that Hughes is criticizing the self-centered and insular view that "thousands of whites" held about people in Harlem.

### Students Acquiring English

2 Tell students that Hughes uses the word *Nordics* as a term for white people.

### Gifted and Talented

3 Invite students to read Thurman's *Infants of the Spring*, then give an oral report about the novel to the rest of the class.

### Multiple Learning Styles
**Visual Learners**

Have students analyze the photographs of some of the musicians and artists prominent during the Harlem Renaissance. Ask students to describe what characteristics of the period these images evoke.

## ⟨Cross Curricular Link⟩ Music

**RECORDINGS OF BLUES AND JAZZ** Many legendary recordings of blues and jazz music have been reissued on compact disc. The following list offers an introduction to some of the musicians Langston Hughes revered.

- **New Orleans, Chicago, New York** (BBC 3CD 821 3-CD set)
  One of the best overviews of jazz between 1917 and the beginning of swing, the set features selections by Jelly Roll Morton, Louis Armstrong, Ma Rainey, Fats Waller, and Cab Calloway.
- **The Best of Mississippi John Hurt** (Vanguard VCD-19/20)

Classics include "Salty Dog Blues," "Coffee Blues," and "Stagolee."
- **Louis Armstrong and the Blues Singers 1924–1930** (Affinity AFS 1018-6; 6-CD set) This collection includes Armstrong's sessions with the great blues singers Clara Smith and Ma Rainey.
- **Duke Ellington: Complete Edition Vol. 1 1924–1926** (Masters of Jazz MJCD 8 CD) and **Complete Edition Vol. 2 1926–1927** (Masters of Jazz MJCD 9 CD)
  These volumes highlight Ellington's musical legacy.

**Literary Analysis** TONE

(A) Ask students to describe Hughes's tone toward the intellectuals of the movement.
**Possible Response:** cynical

### Active Reading

**DRAWING CONCLUSIONS ABOUT AUTHOR'S PERSPECTIVE**

(B) How might Hughes characterize the intellectuals' way of thinking?
**Possible Responses:** as naive, too trusting of the white world

(C) Have students draw conclusions about the author's perspective on the house-rent parties. Ask:

• Why do you think he concludes the essay with a description of these parties?
**Possible Response:** In many ways the parties epitomize for Hughes the real, enduring renaissance—the one that took place among African Americans only, without the "vogue" element sparked by the whites' passing interest.

• Why do you think Hughes goes to these parties?
**Possible Response:** to hear the laughter and music of the real Harlem

white tourists. It was a period when at least one charming colored chorus girl, amber enough to pass for a Latin American, was living in a pent house, with all her bills paid by a gentleman whose name was banker's magic on Wall Street. It was a period when every season there was at least one hit play on Broadway acted by a Negro cast. And when books by Negro authors were being published with much greater frequency and much more publicity than ever before or since in history. It was a period when white writers wrote about Negroes more successfully (commercially speaking) than Negroes did about themselves. It was the period (God help us!) when Ethel Barrymore[9] appeared in blackface in *Scarlet Sister Mary!* It was the period when the Negro was in vogue.

I was there. I had a swell time while it lasted. But I thought it wouldn't last long. (I remember the vogue for things Russian, the season the Chauve-Souris[10] first came to town.) For how could a large and enthusiastic number of people be crazy about Negroes forever? But some Harlemites thought the millennium had come. They thought the race problem had at last been solved through Art plus Gladys Bentley. They were sure the New Negro would lead a new life from then on in green pastures of tolerance created by Countee Cullen, Ethel Waters, Claude McKay, Duke Ellington, Bojangles, and Alain Locke.[11]

(A)
(B) I don't know what made any Negroes think that—except that they were mostly intellectuals doing the thinking. The ordinary Negroes hadn't heard of the Negro Renaissance. And if they had, it hadn't raised their wages any. As for all those white folks in the speakeasies[12] and night clubs of Harlem—well, maybe a colored man could find *some* place to have a drink that the tourists hadn't yet discovered.

(C) Then it was that house-rent parties began to flourish—and not always to raise the rent either. But, as often as not, to have a get-together of one's own, where you could do the black-bottom[13] with no stranger behind you trying to

do it, too. Non-theatrical, non-intellectual Harlem was an unwilling victim of its own vogue. It didn't like to be stared at by white folks. But perhaps the downtowners never knew this—for the cabaret owners, the entertainers, and the speakeasy proprietors treated them fine—as long as they paid.

The Saturday night rent parties that I attended were often more amusing than any night club, in small apartments where God knows who lived—because the guests seldom did—but where the piano would often be augmented by a guitar, or an odd cornet, or somebody with a pair of drums walking in off the street. And where awful bootleg whiskey and good fried fish or steaming chitterling were sold at very low prices. And the dancing and singing and impromptu entertaining went on until dawn came in at the windows.

These parties, often termed whist parties or dances, were usually announced by brightly colored cards stuck in the grille of apartment house elevators. Some of the cards were highly entertaining in themselves.

Almost every Saturday night when I was in Harlem I went to a house-rent party. I wrote lots of poems about house-rent parties, and ate thereat many a fried fish and pig's foot—with liquid refreshments on the side. I met ladies' maids and truck drivers, laundry workers and shoe shine boys, seamstresses and porters. I can still hear their laughter in my ears, hear the soft slow music, and feel the floor shaking as the dancers danced. ❖

(C)

---

9. **Ethel Barrymore:** a famous American actress.

10. **Chauve-Souris** (shōv-sōō-rē′): a Paris-based cabaret act featuring actors who formerly lived in Russia.

11. **Countee Cullen . . . Alain Locke:** Countee Cullen was a leading poet; Ethel Waters was a popular singer and actress; Claude McKay was a best-selling author and political activist; Bill "Bojangles" Robinson was considered the greatest tap dancer of the era; Alain Locke (ä′lăn lŏk) was the editor of the anthology *The New Negro*.

12. **speakeasies:** illegal prohibition-era bars.

13. **the black-bottom:** an enormously popular 1920s dance.

✓ **Assessment** **Informal Assessment**

**SUMMARY** You can informally assess your students' understanding of Langston Hughes's essay "When the Negro Was in Vogue" by having them write a brief summary of it. Remind students that a summary highlights the most important ideas of a text, put in the reader's own words.

**RUBRIC**

**3 Full Accomplishment** The summary shows full understanding of the essay and the author's perspective toward the subject.

**2 Substantial Accomplishment** The summary shows basic understanding but omits some important ideas in the essay.

**1 Little or Partial Accomplishment** The summary shows little or no understanding of the essay and its main points.

# *Thinking* through the LITERATURE

## Connect to the Literature

1. **What Do You Think?**
   What impressions of Harlem in the 1920s did you get from reading this essay? Jot down words and phrases, or draw a sketch of Harlem.

   **Comprehension Check**
   • When did the Harlem Renaissance take place?
   • How did many blacks feel about whites who flocked to Harlem clubs?
   • Name two African-American celebrities to whom Hughes refers in his essay.

## Think Critically

2. Why do you think white America suddenly became fascinated by Harlem?

   **THINK ABOUT**
   {
   • the connotation of the word "vogue"
   • the different cultural attractions that Hughes describes
   • the reason Hughes gives for the closing of many Jim Crow clubs
   • the state of race relations in the 1920s
   }

3. What **irony** do you see in the situations described in this essay?

4. **ACTIVE READING** | **DRAWING CONCLUSIONS ABOUT AUTHOR'S PERSPECTIVE**

   Determine whether Hughes is objective in his writing or whether he seems sympathetic to any particular group. Support your conclusion with evidence from the chart you made in your **READER'S NOTEBOOK** and from the essay.

## Extend Interpretations

5. **What If?** How might the **perspective** of this essay be different if it had been written by one of the whites who "came to Harlem night after night" rather than by Hughes?

6. **Comparing Texts** How do you think the **speaker** of "We Wear the Mask" by Paul Laurence Dunbar (page 836) might react to this essay? Explain your answer.

7. **Connect to Life** In this essay, Hughes mentions some of the African-American cultural achievements and celebrities of the Harlem Renaissance. What specific cultural achievements or important celebrities might you include in an essay about African Americans today?

## Literary Analysis

**TONE** The **tone** of a work of literature reflects the attitude of the writer toward the subject he or she is writing about. For example, a writer's tone can be serious, comical, ironic, or bitter. A writer can communicate tone through his or her choice of words, choice of details, and direct statements of his or her position about a subject. For example, Hughes displays a sarcastic tone toward white tourists by listing wealthy people and gangsters together as equals:

*But I was never there, because the Cotton Club was a Jim Crow club for gangsters and monied whites.*

**Cooperative Learning Activity** With a small group of classmates, go back through the essay and identify Hughes's tone toward the different groups of people he describes, such as entertainers, nightclub owners, Harlem residents, and white tourists. For each group, list words and phrases that reveal Hughes's tone. When you have finished, share your findings with the class.

WHEN THE NEGRO WAS IN VOGUE    **937**

## Extend Interpretations

**What If?** Possible Responses: The essay might not express the concerns of the ordinary people of Harlem; it might focus more on the dancing and the music; it probably would not use the ironic tone that Hughes adopts.

**Comparing Texts** Possible Responses: The speaker of "We Wear the Mask" might agree with Hughes's comments about African Americans avoiding rudeness to white people and share Hughes's sympathy with ordinary Harlem residents; the speaker might also appreciate Hughes's use of an ironic tone in describing white people's fashionable appreciation of African-American culture.

**Connect to Life** Accept all reasonable responses. Students may cite a variety of African-American cultural achievements in the contemporary world.

Hughes brings alive the Harlem Renaissance with observations that are passionate, enthusiastic, critical, angry, sad, and deeply personal.

## Analysis of Style

Have students study the chart and apply the key aspects of Hughes's style to the excerpts at the right.

**(A)** First activity
**Possible Responses:**
**dialect:** "He played that sad raggy tune like a musical fool."
**passionate tone:** "Sweet Blues! / Coming from a black man's soul."
**irony, satire, paradox:** The title of the essay "When the Negro Was in Vogue" is itself satiric—the idea that a culture can be "in vogue" with people outside the culture.
**vivid imagery:** "With his ebony hands on each ivory key"
**rhythms:** "The Weary Blues" has a rhythm like blues music.

**(B)** Second activity
**Possible Responses:** His poems convey emotion, whereas his essay is more detached. The poems are rich with imagery, while the essay presents abstract thoughts.

**(C)** Third activity
There are many examples of the key aspects of Hughes's style throughout the selections in this unit. For example, "Harlem" is full of images describing what might happen to "a dream deferred."

## Applications

1. **Changing Style** Request that students prewrite, craft, edit, and publish.
2. **Imitation of Style** Remind students to revisit the Key Aspects box before beginning.
3. **Speaking and Listening** Have students use criteria to critique oral interpretation. Presenters should
• Make and support valid interpretations.
• Use volume, tone, movement, gestures, and facial expressions to establish mood and convey meaning.

---

# THE AUTHOR'S STYLE
### Hughes's Love Song to His People

When Langston Hughes's first book was published, one critic described him as "intensely subjective, passionate, keenly sensitive to beauty, and possessed of an unfaltering musical sense." Those qualities—as well as a great love for African-American culture—would characterize Hughes's style throughout his writing career. The following stylistic devices appear frequently in Hughes's work.

### Key Aspects of Hughes's Style

• use of dialect that is characteristic of African Americans in the urban North

• a passionate tone, often one of love, sympathy, or melancholy

• use of irony, satire, and paradox to expose racial problems and self-deceptions

• vivid imagery of the African-American experience, particularly life in Harlem

• rhythms that are taken from speech and music

## Analysis of Style

At the right are three excerpts from Hughes's work. Study the chart above, and then complete the following activities:

**(A)** Identify examples of different aspects of Hughes's style, such as his use of dialect, irony, or imagery.

**(B)** Compare the style of Hughes's poems with that of his essay.

**(C)** Go back through the selections in this Author Study, and find other examples of these key aspects of Hughes's style.

## Applications

**1. Changing Style** Working with a partner, rewrite a paragraph from "When the Negro Was in Vogue" in a more formal style. For example, change any dialect or slang to standard English. Discuss how the changes affect your feeling about the piece.

**2. Imitation of Style** Draft an original poem about discrimination and prejudice, using elements of Hughes's poetic style, such as irony or dialect.

**3. Speaking and Listening** With a small group of classmates, locate and read aloud another poem or piece of prose by Hughes. Discuss the stylistic devices that you hear in the work.

**938**   UNIT SIX   AUTHOR STUDY: LANGSTON HUGHES

---

*from* **"The Weary Blues"**

With his ebony hands on each ivory key
He made that poor piano moan with melody.
    O Blues!
Swaying to and fro on his rickety stool
He played that sad raggy tune like a musical fool.
    Sweet Blues!
Coming from a black man's soul.
    O Blues!

*from* **"Mother to Son"**

Well, son, I'll tell you:
Life for me ain't been no crystal stair.
It's had tacks in it,
And splinters,
And boards torn up,
And places with no carpet on the floor—
Bare.

*from* **"When the Negro Was in Vogue"**

I was there. I had a swell time while it lasted. But I thought it wouldn't last long. (I remember the vogue for things Russian, the season the Chauve-Souris first came to town.) For how could a large and enthusiastic number of people be crazy about Negroes forever? But some Harlemites thought the millennium had come. They thought the race problem had at last been solved through Art plus Gladys Bentley. They were sure the New Negro would lead a new life from then on in green pastures of tolerance created by Countee Cullen, Ethel Waters, Claude McKay, Duke Ellington, Bojangles, and Alain Locke.

---

## Teaching Options    Mini Lesson   **Grammar**

**ADVERBIAL ELEMENTS** Review adverbs and their usage with students.
An **adverb** is a part of speech used to modify a verb, an adjective, or another adverb. Adverbs tell *where, when, how,* or *to what extent* about the words they modify. Remind students that adverbs are often formed by adding *-ly* to adjectives.

He ran his fingers over the keyboard **lightly.**
(*Lightly* modifies the verb *ran.*)
He plays an **extremely** old piano. (*Extremely* modifies the adjective *old.*)

The musician plays **very** regularly at the club. (*Very* modifies the adverb *regularly.*)

An **adverb clause** is a subordinate clause that functions as an adverb to modify a verb, an adjective, or another adverb.

**After he made his first recording,** he celebrated with the other members of the band. (The adverb clause modifies the verb *celebrated* and tells when.)

The musicians were angry **because they couldn't enter the club except to perform.**

---

# Choices & CHALLENGES

## Writing Options

**1. Autobiographical Essay** Draft an auto-biographical essay, modeled on Hughes's, in which you express your opinions of a current trend.

**2. Documentary Plan** Imagine that you have been asked to produce a documentary about the Harlem Renaissance. Write notes about how you would cover the subject. List the film footage, photographs, and musical recordings you would need. Also, note which of the celebrities, tourists, and residents mentioned by Hughes you would like to interview. Place your notes in your **Working Portfolio.**

## Activities & Explorations

**1. Music of the 1920s** Find and listen to a recording of one of the musicians associated with the Harlem Renaissance, such as Duke Ellington, Louis Armstrong, Ethel Waters, or Bessie Smith. Then discuss with your classmates some of the qualities that you think made this music so popular in the 1920s. **~ MUSIC/SPEAKING AND LISTENING**

**2. Do the Lindy** Find out how to do the lindy hop, a popular Harlem dance that was named after the aviation hero Charles A. Lindbergh. With a partner, demonstrate the steps for the class. **~ DANCE**

## Inquiry & Research

**The Harlem Renaissance** Find out more about the literary and artistic movement called the Harlem Renaissance. Using literature anthologies, history books, and encyclopedias, investigate some of the important writers, artists, musicians, and performers who are associated with this movement. Then work with your classmates to create an informational bulletin board about the Harlem Renaissance.

## Langston Hughes
## Author Study Project
### CREATING A MULTIMEDIA TOUR

Working with a small group, create a multimedia tour of Harlem during the 1920s. You may wish to focus on the shows, the nightclubs, or the daily life of the area. Your guided tour might take the form of a video, a web page, a slide show, or some combination of these. Draw on the information you gathered during the Inquiry & Research activity to get started. Then use the following suggestions to complete your research.

**Photography of the Renaissance** Look in books and periodicals for photography of the era. You may want to investigate the work of famous photographers, such as James Van Der Zee. Try to find photographs of both celebrities and ordinary citizens of Harlem.

**Musical Recordings** Find recordings of the musical artists of the Harlem Renaissance. Since the Harlem Renaissance flourished during the early 20th century, you may want to locate records in public libraries or vintage record shops, as well as explore recordings reissued on CDs.

**Writings** Try to find other written descriptions of Harlem during the 1920s. You might want to try autobiographies, essays, newspaper articles, and collections of letters by famous individuals of the time. Check the Internet to see if there are web sites devoted to the Harlem Renaissance. Look for short, descriptive passages that can be used in your multimedia tour.

 **More Online: Research Starter**
www.mcdougallittell.com

## Author Study Project
### CREATING A MULTIMEDIA TOUR

Remind students that the print and nonprint materials they collect for their multimedia project need to be credited. For materials gathered from Web sites, students should cite the following information: author/ photographer/ artist, title of article, print publication in which material appeared previously (if applicable), and the Web address.

## Inquiry & Research

Many books have been written about the Harlem Renaissance: *The Portable Harlem Renaissance Reader,* edited by David L. Lewis (Penguin, 1995); *Voices from the Harlem Renaissance,* edited by Nathan Irving Huggins (Oxford University Press, 1995); *Rhapsodies in Black: Art of the Harlem Renaissance,* a collection of critical essays edited by Richard J. Powell (University of California Press, 1997); and *The Crisis Reader: Selections from Crisis Magazine,* by Sondra K. Wilson (Modern Library, 1999).

Students should also check nonprint resources, including Databases and the Internet, for information.

---

(The adverb clause modifies the adjective *angry* and tells why.)

**Exercises** Have students identify the adverbs and adverb clauses in each of the following sentences. Then tell which word the adverb or adverb clause modifies.

**1.** Whenever Hughes saw *Shuffle Along,* he delighted in the music.
**Answer:** Whenever Hughes saw *Shuffle Along;* modifies *delighted*

**2.** Hughes has a keenly personal view of the Harlem Renaissance.
**Answer:** *keenly;* modifies *personal*

 Use McDougal Littell's *Language Network,* Chapter 3, for more instruction and practice in adverbial elements.

## Objectives
1. understand and appreciate two **sonnets** (Literary Analysis)
2. determine major ideas in a poem (Active Reading)

## Summary
In "My City," poet James Weldon Johnson wonders what he'll miss most when he dies, and then realizes that it will be the city where he lives, Manhattan. In "Any Human to Another," poet Countee Cullen expresses a basic truth about the human condition: Sorrow is universal.

## Thematic Link
Harlem became the home of **a new cultural identity** for people of African descent, who contributed greatly to the urban vitality that "My City" celebrates. Cullen's "Any Human to Another" reiterates an ancient truth about sorrow, one that cannot be overlooked despite the promise of the **Harlem Renaissance.**

## Reading and Analyzing

### Active Reading

> DETERMINING MAJOR IDEAS IN A POEM

"My City" has two stanzas. What is the major idea expressed in the first stanza? in the second stanza?
**Possible Responses:** The first stanza asks what the speaker will miss most once he or she dies and lists a number of incorrect answers. The second stanza declares what it will be—Manhattan.

 Use **Unit Six Resource Book,** p. 8 for additional support.

### Literary Analysis  SONNET

Ask students to count the lines and note the rhyme scheme of "My City." How many lines are in the first stanza? How many in the second? What is the pattern of end rhymes in each stanza?
*Answers:* first stanza—8 lines, rhyme scheme *abbacddc;* second stanza— 6 lines, rhyme scheme *efefgg*

 Use **Unit Six Resource Book,** p. 9 for additional support.

---

# My City
*Poetry by* JAMES WELDON JOHNSON

# Any Human to Another
*Poetry by* COUNTEE CULLEN

### Connect to Your Life

**Impressions of New York** With a small group of classmates, brainstorm what you know about New York City. Use a cluster diagram to list your thoughts about and attitudes toward this city. Share them with the rest of the class.

## Build Background

**African-American Migration** New York City stirred strong feelings among the African Americans who migrated there in the early 20th century. To some, New York was a charismatic place, representing freedom and opportunities for self-fulfillment. To others, the harsh realities of urban living—such as overcrowding, prejudice, and unemployment—frustrated the expectations that originally had prompted their migration. In "My City," James Weldon Johnson expresses deep feelings about Manhattan, the New York City borough where Harlem is located.

During the Harlem Renaissance, many African-American writers focused on the racism and injustice that, they felt, denied them their rights and opportunities. Countee Cullen, however, believed that instead of restricting themselves to matters related to race, African-American writers should explore more deeply the human condition. In his poem "Any Human to Another," Cullen emphasizes the commonality of the human experience.

## Focus Your Reading

**LITERARY ANALYSIS  SONNET** A **sonnet** is a lyric poem of 14 lines. Some sonnets have a two-part structure: the first eight lines form one part, and the last six lines form another. Consider how the two parts of "My City" are related.

**ACTIVE READING  DETERMINING MAJOR IDEAS IN A POEM** Use these tips to identify the major ideas in "My City" and "Any Human to Another":
- Read the poems—silently and aloud—more than once.
- Remember that the end of a line may or may not signal the end of a complete thought. Look for periods, question marks, and exclamation points. These marks tell you that you have come to the end of a complete thought. Commas help you separate the different parts of a complete idea.
- Consider the **structure** of each poem. The way a poem is organized or divided gives a clue about where its **major ideas** reside. For example, the two-part structure of "My City" suggests that the poem has two "chunks" of meaning. "Any Human to Another," on the other hand, is divided into five stanzas, each of which conveys a major idea.
- For each part into which a poem is divided, first identify the **subject,** or the focus; then try to state the related major idea.

**READER'S NOTEBOOK** As you read "My City," fill in a chart like the one shown. Then for "Any Human to Another," create a different chart to list the major idea of each stanza.

| | Subject | Major Idea |
|---|---|---|
| lines 1–8 | | |
| lines 9–14 | | |

---

# LESSON RESOURCES

**UNIT SIX RESOURCE BOOK,** pp. 8–9

**ASSESSMENT RESOURCES**
**Formal Assessment,** pp. 171–172
**Teacher's Guide to Assessment and Portfolio Use**
**Test Generator**

**SKILLS TRANSPARENCIES AND COPYMASTERS**
**Literary Analysis**
- Form in Poetry: Structure, T11 (for Paired Activity, p. 943)

**Reading and Critical Thinking**
- Main Idea and Supporting Details, T12 (for Active Reading, p. 940)

**Grammar**
- Comparative and Superlative Modifiers, C132 (for Mini Lesson, p. 944)

**Vocabulary**
- Figurative Language, C77 (for Mini Lesson, p. 941)

**Writing**
- Literary Interpretation, C30 (for Writing Option 2, p. 944)

**INTEGRATED TECHNOLOGY**

**Audio Library**
**LaserLinks**
- Cultural Connection: New York City Through the Years
- Art Gallery: Art of the Harlem Renaissance. See **Teacher's SourceBook,** pp. 79–81.

**Visit our website:**
www.mcdougallittell.com

# My City

### JAMES WELDON JOHNSON

*New York Harbor/Paris* (about 1925),
Jan Matulka. Photo courtesy of Norfolk
Southern Corporation.

When I come down to sleep death's endless night,
The threshold of the unknown dark to cross,
What to me then will be the keenest loss,
When this bright world blurs on my fading sight?
5 Will it be that no more I shall see the trees
Or smell the flowers or hear the singing birds
Or watch the flashing streams or patient herds?
No, I am sure it will be none of these.

But, ah! Manhattan's sights and sounds, her smells,
10 Her crowds, her throbbing force, the thrill that comes
From being of her a part, her subtle spells,
Her shining towers, her avenues, her slums—
O God! the stark, unutterable pity,
To be dead, and never again behold my city!

## Thinking Through the Literature

1. **Comprehension Check** What is the one thing the speaker most regrets about death?
2. **ACTIVE READING** **DETERMINING MAJOR IDEAS IN A POEM** What relationship do you see between the main ideas in the two parts of this poem? Refer to the chart you made in your **READER'S NOTEBOOK**.
3. Is the speaker's description of New York City appealing? Is it accurate?

## Mini Lesson **Vocabulary Strategy**

**FIGURATIVE LANGUAGE**
**Instruction** Students can rely on context clues to determine the meanings of words and phrases used figuratively.
**Activity** Ask students to look at the phrase *subtle spells* in line 11 of "My City." Have them use context clues to interpret the meaning of this phrase.
**Possible Response:** The phrase occurs within a passage in which the city is personified as a woman. The poet is describing the ways in which the city charms him and makes him love "her." Thus, *subtle spells* refers to a magical effect that the city has on him.

**Application** In "Any Human to Another," have students use context clues to figure out the meanings of *marrow* (line 4: if it's "through the fat and past the bone," *marrow* must be a part of the body that it is within the bone) and *diverse* (line 11: the word *yet* indicates contrast, so if *diverse* can't "be fused and mingle," then it must be distinct).

Use **Vocabulary Transparencies and Copymasters**, p. 77.

Ask students to find examples of figurative language in "Any Human to Another." How does such language communicate ideas beyond the literal meaning of the words?

**Possible Responses:** Examples of figurative language include "Like an arrow, /Pierce to the marrow" and "Must intertwine/Like sea and river." Figurative language helps a reader create vivid impressions and make meaningful associations.

### Active Reading

> **DETERMINING MAJOR IDEAS IN A POEM**

 What is the main idea of the second stanza? Consider the simile that compares "Your grief and mine" with "sea and river."

**Possible Response:** Grief is common to all people; to try to separate one person's grief from that of all humanity would be like trying to separate the water of one river from the ocean into which it has flowed.

Use **Unit Six Resource Book**, p. 8 for more practice.

# Any Human to Another

COUNTEE CULLEN

The ills I sorrow at
Not me alone
Like an arrow,
Pierce to the marrow,
5   Through the fat
And past the bone.

Your grief and mine
Must intertwine
Like sea and river,
10   Be fused and mingle,
Diverse yet single,
Forever and forever.

Let no man be so proud
And confident,
15   To think he is allowed
A little tent
Pitched in a meadow
Of sun and shadow
All his little own.

20   Joy may be shy, unique,
Friendly to a few,
Sorrow never scorned to speak
To any who
Were false or true.

25   Your every grief
Like a blade
Shining and unsheathed[1]
Must strike me down.
Of bitter aloes[2] wreathed,
30   My sorrow must be laid
On your head like a crown.

---

1. **unsheathed:** removed from its protective case.

2. **bitter aloes** (ăl'ōz): a spiny-leaved plant from the juice of which a bad-tasting medicine is made.

*Shotgun, Third Ward #1* (1966), John T. Biggers. Oil on canvas, 76.2 × 121.9 cm, National Museum of American Art, Washington, D.C./Art Resource, New York.

942

## Teaching Options

### Mini Lesson — Speaking and Listening

**READING POETRY**

**Instruction** Share with students the following tips for reading poetry aloud:

- Be aware of natural breaks. Don't let line breaks trip you up; rely on the punctuation and the rhyme scheme to help you read smoothly. When you hit the end of one line, go immediately into the next one.
- Read the poem to yourself as many times as necessary to understand any unusual syntax or difficult phrasings. Having a thorough understanding of the poem's meaning will allow you to read it aloud with confidence.

**Model** Read aloud the first three lines of the second stanza in "Any Human to Another." Read it as one full sentence. Do not pause at the line breaks: "Your grief and mine must intertwine like sea and river."

**Application** Have students work in small groups to practice reading the poem aloud. They can alternate on stanzas or present personal interpretations through comparative readings. Ask them to listen for the melody of literary language, the tone and cadence that the rhyme scheme creates.

# *Thinking through the* LITERATURE

## Connect to the Literature

1. **What Do You Think?**
   What lines from "Any Human to Another" appeal to you the most, and why? Share your response with your classmates.

   **Comprehension Check**
   According to the speaker, which emotion—joy or sorrow—is more common?

## Think Critically

2. **ACTIVE READING  DETERMINING MAJOR IDEAS IN A POEM**
   How would you describe the major idea of each stanza in this poem? What **theme** do these ideas suggest? Refer to the chart in your ▯ **READER'S NOTEBOOK.**

3. What is your opinion of the speaker's ideas about sorrow and grief?

   **THINK ABOUT**
   - "Your grief and mine / Must intertwine..." (lines 7–8)
   - "Sorrow never scorned to speak / To any..." (lines 22–23)
   - "My sorrow must be laid / On your head like a crown" (lines 30–31)

4. How do the human qualities that the speaker attributes to joy and sorrow differ?

## Extend Interpretations

5. **What If?** How might you have responded to "Any Human to Another" if the speaker had expressed a defeatist attitude?

6. **Comparing Texts** Which poem do you think shows greater affection for other people—"My City" or "Any Human to Another"? Support your answer by citing lines from each poem.

7. **Connect to Life** What might individuals do to help make the speaker's dream for humanity in "Any Human to Another" come to pass?

## Literary Analysis

**SONNET**  A **sonnet** is a 14-line lyric poem that follows any of several rhyme schemes. One type of sonnet is the **Petrarchan** (pǐ-trär′kən) **sonnet** (named after Francesco Petrarch, 14th-century, the poet who perfected the form in Italian). It consists of two parts. The first eight lines, called the octave, usually have the rhyme scheme *abbaabba.* In the last six lines, called the sestet, the rhyme scheme may be *cdecde, cdcdcd,* or some other variation. Generally, the octave tells a story, introduces a situation, or raises a question. The sestet, in turn, comments on the story, situation, or question. Sonnets are commonly written in **iambic pentameter,** a metrical line of five feet, each of which is made up of two syllables, the first unstressed and the second stressed. By scanning the first line of "My City," you can see that the five feet are iambic:

When Ĭ | cŏme dówn | tŏ sléep
déath's énd | lĕss níght,

**Paired Activity**  With a partner, reread "My City" and then discuss the characteristics that make it a Petrarchan sonnet, charting the rhyme scheme and describing the relationship between the octave and the sestet.

**REVIEW  FIGURATIVE LANGUAGE**
Figurative language communicates ideas beyond the literal meaning of the words. Among the most common types of figurative language are **simile, metaphor,** and **personification.** Find examples of figurative language in "Any Human to Another."

---

# Writing Options

1. **Slogan About New York** Students may want to focus on Harlem or on Manhattan. Emphasize creating a catchy motto; *slogan* used to refer to the battle cry of a Scottish clan.

2. **Writing a Review** To get students started on this activity, have them meet in small groups to discuss definitions of the words *altruism*, *pity*, and *empathy*.

# Inquiry & Research

**Art** You might suggest the following titles to students:

The Institute of Visual Artists, Rhapsodies in Black: Art of the Harlem Renaissance (London: Hayward Gallery, Berkeley: University of California Press, 1997).

Abrams, Harry N., *Harlem Renaissance: Art of Black America* (New York: The Studio Museum in Harlem, 1987).

# Author Notes

**James Weldon Johnson** was a man of phenomenal accomplishment. Poet, lawyer, newspaper publisher, high school principal, composer of Broadway musicals, he also served as U.S. counsel to Venezuela from 1906 to 1909, and in Nicaragua, from 1909 to 1914.

**Countee Porter Cullen,** like Johnson, was born in the South. *The Medea and Some Poems* (1935) is another one of his notable works. He wrote one novel *One Way to Heaven* (1932) about life in Harlem. He was very influenced by the English Romantic poet John Keats.

---

## *Choices* & CHALLENGES

### Writing Options

1. **Slogan About New York** The speaker of "My City" has a strong reaction to New York City. Using the poem and the ideas you listed for the Connect to Your Life activity (page 940) as a basis, write a slogan that celebrates the city.

2. **Write a Review** Read the following quotation from Dr. Martin Luther King, Jr.: "True altruism is more than the capacity to pity; it is the capacity to empathize... Empathy is fellow feeling for the person in need—his pain, agony, and burdens." Write a review that relates this definition of altruism to the speaker's ideas in "Any Human to Another."

### Inquiry & Research

**Art** Find out about artists who were associated with the Harlem Renaissance, such as the sculptors Meta Warrick Fuller and Richmond Barthé, the painters Jacob Lawrence and Palmer C. Hayden, and the illustrator Aaron Douglas. Identify a particular work of art that you think suits "My City" or "Any Human to Another" in mood or images, and share it with the class.

---

## James Weldon Johnson

**1871–1938**
**Other Works**
*Autobiography of an Ex-Colored Man*
*Fifty Years and Other Poems*
*God's Trombones*

**Multitalented Leader** James Weldon Johnson was one of the most prominent African-American leaders of his time. Born into a middle-class family in Jacksonville, Florida, Johnson was a precocious child who read the books of Charles Dickens and Sir Walter Scott. After graduating from Atlanta University, he became a school principal, founded a daily newspaper, and became the first African-American lawyer to be admitted to the Florida bar. In 1902, after his newspaper folded and his school burned down, Johnson decided to go to New York, where he and his brother J. Rosamond became successful Broadway songwriters. Their song "Lift Every Voice and Sing" became known as the African-American "national anthem" (see page 917).

**Writer and Cultural Activist** During his writing career, Johnson published in all genres of literature. He also wrote *Black Manhattan*, a book about African-American history, and compiled the groundbreaking anthology *The Book of American Negro Poetry* (1922).

## Countee Cullen

**1903–1946**
**Other Works**
*The Ballad of the Brown Girl*
*The Black Christ and Other Poems*
*Copper Sun*

**Esteemed Poet** In 1925, while still an undergraduate at New York University, Countee Cullen published his first poetry collection, *Color,* which established his reputation as a poet. A superb student, he also won several poetry prizes. After graduating from college in 1925, Cullen went on to earn a master's degree at Harvard University.

**Literary Influences** Cullen was influenced by the English romantic poets, especially John Keats. In his introduction to the anthology *Caroling Dusk,* he stated his belief that African-American poets "may have more to gain from the rich background of English and American poetry than from any . . . yearnings towards an African inheritance." This philosophy is apparent in his own verse.

**Later Career** In the 1930s and 1940s, Cullen wrote a novel, *One Way to Heaven,* as well as children's books, translations, and (in collaboration with Arna Bontemps) a musical. He taught French at Frederick Douglass Junior High School until his death.

---

## Teaching Options

 **Mini Lesson** ## Grammar

**MODIFIERS: COMPARATIVE AND SUPERLATIVE**

**Instruction** Comparative modifiers compare two persons or things; superlative modifiers compare more than two persons or things. Put the following chart on the chalkboard.

| Adjective | Comparative | Superlative |
|---|---|---|
| good | better | best |
| happy | happier | happiest |
| skilled | more skilled | most skilled |

When comparing one person or thing to a group of similar people or things, use the comparative form plus the words *than* and *other* or *else*.

- That writer is more skilled than other writers.
- Cullen's first book of poems was better than anything else he wrote.

When using superlative modifiers, use the word *all,* not *any*:

- Langston Hughes became the most popular of *all* Harlem Renaissance writers.

 Use **Grammar Transparencies and Copymasters**, p. 132.

 Use McDougal Littell's *Language Network,* Chapter 7, for more instruction and practice in modifiers.

## If We Must Die

*Poetry by* CLAUDE McKAY

## A Black Man Talks of Reaping

*Poetry by* ARNA BONTEMPS (bôn-tän')

### Connect to Your Life

**Racial Injustice** In the early decades of the 20th century, African Americans suffered many injustices as a result of racial discrimination and prejudice. With a group of classmates, discuss a time when you witnessed someone being treated unfairly. Tell what you think provoked this treatment—was it race, age, gender, religion, income, or some other factor? How did the victim of injustice respond to the unfair treatment? Was the response, in your opinion, effective?

### Build Background

**Fighting Oppression** While still facing widespread discrimination and violence in the 1920s, some writers in Harlem denounced the injustices African Americans endured in a predominantly white society. Claude McKay wrote the poem "If We Must Die" in response to a wave of violence against African Americans during the so-called Red Summer of 1919, when escalating racial tension resulted in 26 bloody riots across the country. In "A Black Man Talks of Reaping," Arna Bontemps condemned the economic exploitation African Americans suffered even after the end of slavery.

### Focus Your Reading

**LITERARY ANALYSIS** **EXTENDED METAPHOR** An **extended metaphor** is a comparison between two things that is developed at some length and in several ways. In the poems you are about to read, notice the comparisons that describe the unfair treatment experienced by African Americans in the early 20th century.

**ACTIVE READING** **DISTINGUISHING FIGURATIVE AND LITERAL MEANING** **Figurative language** is language that communicates ideas beyond the literal meanings of words. The words in a figurative expression are not literally true; rather, they create impressions in the reader's mind. For example, in the first line of "My City," the poet uses the figurative expression "to sleep death's endless night." This expression compares the experience of death to a sleep that never ends, creating impressions such as peacefulness, darkness, and stillness. As you read "If We Must Die" and "A Black Man Talks of Reaping," use these tips to explore their figurative language:

- Read each poem once to grasp its overall meaning.
- Next reread the poems, noting important words and phrases.
- Ask questions about the comparisons you notice. For example, as you read "If We Must Die," ask yourself, Who are like hogs? What resembles being hunted and penned? As you read "A Black Man Talks of Reaping," ask yourself, What is comparable to *sowing* and *reaping*?

📖 **READER'S NOTEBOOK** On a chart similar to the one shown, list examples of figurative language in each poem, and describe the impressions created in your mind.

| Figurative Language | |
|---|---|
| Example | Impression |
| | |
| | |

**Objectives**
1. understand and appreciate two **poems** (Literary Analysis)
2. examine **extended metaphor** (Literary Analysis)
3. **distinguish figurative and literal meaning** (Active Reading)

**Summary**
"If We Must Die" is McKay's rallying cry against oppression. He warns his "kins-men" not to let themselves die like hogs hunted down by "mad and hungry dogs." He calls on them to fight bravely and to die nobly, since he believes they are going to die anyway. The final couplet of this Shakespearean sonnet states the speaker's resolve to die "fighting back." In "A Black Man Talks of Reaping," Bontemps compares the struggles of African Americans in a racist society to the efforts of a tenant farmer. The farmer sows, but when it's harvest time, he discovers that his "brother's sons" are reaping it all.

**Thematic Link**
Writing out of the severe social situations of their time, McKay and Bontemps helped create the **Harlem Renaissance.** Both writers were leaders in expressing **a new cultural identity.**

Have students read the Build Background and interpret the influences of the historical context on the work of these two poets.

### 5-Minute Warm-Up

**Daily Language SkillBuilder**

Have students **proofread** the display sentences on page 913i and write them correctly. The sentences also appear on Transparency 25 of **Grammar Transparencies and Copymasters.**

### LESSON RESOURCES

**UNIT SIX RESOURCE BOOK,** pp. 10–11

**ASSESSMENT RESOURCES**
**Formal Assessment,** pp. 173–174
**Teacher's Guide to Assessment and Portfolio Use**
**Test Generator**

**SKILLS TRANSPARENCIES AND COPYMASTERS**
**Reading and Critical Thinking**
- Comparing Authors' Views, T23 (for Extend Interpretations, item 6, p. 948)

**Grammar**
- Modifiers: Use of *-er,* C135 (for Mini Lesson, p. 949)

**Vocabulary**
- Prefixes, C78 (for Mini Lesson, p. 946)

**Writing**
- Organizing Your Writing, T11 (for Writing Option 1, p. 949)

**INTEGRATED TECHNOLOGY**

**Audio Library**
**LaserLinks**
- Historical Connection: Separate and Unequal. See **Teacher's SourceBook,** p. 82.

**Visit our website:**
www.mcdougallittell.com

## Reading and Analyzing

### Active Reading

**DISTINGUISHING FIGURATIVE
AND LITERAL MEANING**

 Ask students to explain the figurative meaning of "their thousand blows" in line 11.

**Possible Responses:** The phrase *their thousand blows* refers to the social wrongs and injustices that have been dealt against the speaker and his "kinsmen."

Use **Unit Six Resource Book**, p. 10 for additional support.

### Literary Analysis

**EXTENDED METAPHOR**

 Have students analyze the figurative language of the final stanza in "A Black Man Talks of Reaping."

**Possible Responses:** The *orchard* is the society in the United States; the *brother's sons* are the white majority; having to *glean* from the field is the status of being black in America; the *bitter fruit* is racial resentment.

Use **Unit Six Resource Book**, p. 11 for additional support.

## Thinking Through the Literature

1. McKay argues for a noble death, to die bravely while fighting back.
2. Possible Response: McKay is addressing other African Americans, who were suffering from oppression at the time the poem was written.
3. Responses will vary. Some students may mention the oppressors being compared to a pack of "mad and hungry dogs."

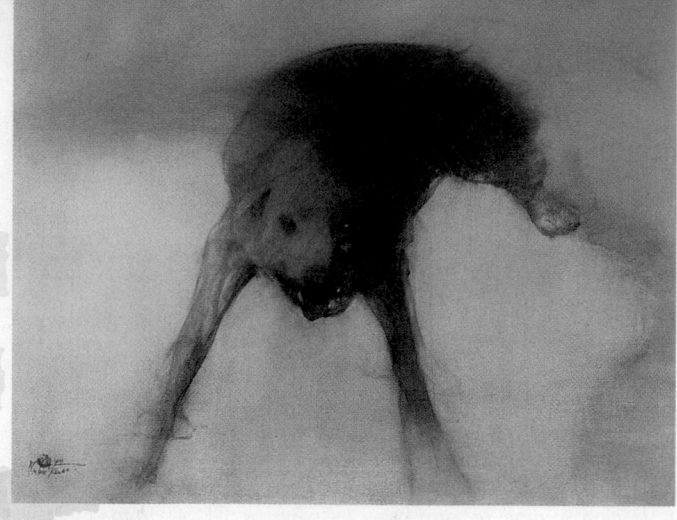

Copyright © Herbert Tauss.

## IF WE MUST DIE

**CLAUDE MCKAY**

If we must die, let it not be like hogs
Hunted and penned in an inglorious[1] spot,
While round us bark the mad and hungry dogs,
Making their mock at our accursed lot.
5 If we must die, O let us nobly die,
So that our precious blood may not be shed
In vain; then even the monsters we defy
Shall be constrained[2] to honor us though dead!
O kinsmen! we must meet the common foe!
10 Though far outnumbered let us show us brave,
And for their thousand blows deal one deathblow!
What though before us lies the open grave?
Like men we'll face the murderous, cowardly pack,
Pressed to the wall, dying, but fighting back!

1. **inglorious:** shameful; disgraceful.
2. **constrained:** forced.

## Thinking Through the Literature

1. **Comprehension Check** What type of death does the speaker argue for or against?
2. Whom is the speaker addressing? Support your answer.
3. **ACTIVE READING** **DISTINGUISHING FIGURATIVE AND LITERAL MEANING** Which figurative expressions created strong impressions in your mind? Refer to your chart.

## Teaching Options

 **Mini Lesson** Vocabulary Strategy

**PREFIXES *IN*- AND *OUT*-**

**Instruction** Students can apply the meanings of prefixes in order to comprehend new vocabulary. A prefix is a word part that comes at the beginning of a word and that changes the meaning of the base word. The prefix *in*- added to an adjective means "not," "lacking," or "without." The prefix *out*- with a verb means "surpassing" or "superior in degree." Write these two words from "If We Must Die" on the chalkboard. Underline the base words and circle the prefixes. Ask students to define the base words and describe how the prefixes change their meanings.

(in)glorious (line 2)    (out)numbered (line 10)

**Application** Have students work in small groups to brainstorm words with the prefix *in*- meaning "not," "lacking," or "without" and the prefix *out*- meaning "surpassing" or "superior in degree." Advise them to beware of words in which the prefix *in*- or *out* has a different meaning, such as *income* or *outboard*.

Use **Vocabulary Transparencies and Copymasters**, p. 78.

A lesson on prefixes appears on p. 1130 in the Pupil's Edition.

I have sown beside all waters in my day.
I planted deep, within my heart the fear
That wind or fowl would take the grain away.
I planted safe against this stark, lean year.

5 I scattered seed enough to plant the land
In rows from Canada to Mexico,
But for my reaping only what the hand
Can hold at once is all that I can show.

Yet what I sowed and what the orchard yields
10 My brother's sons are gathering stalk and root,
Small wonder then my children glean¹ in fields
They have not sown, and feed on bitter fruit.

---

1. **glean:** gather grain left behind by reapers.

Photo by Arthur Rothstein.
From the collections of the
Library of Congress.

A BLACK MAN TALKS OF REAPING **947**

## Customizing Instruction

**Students Acquiring English**
Encourage students to use context clues and a dictionary to define these phrases in "If We Must Die": *penned in, making their mock, accursed lot.*

**1** Ask students what the word *pack* in line 13 refers to.
   **Answer:** the dogs mentioned in line 3, as in *a pack of dogs*

**2** Ask students what it means to be *pressed to the wall* (line 14)
**Possible Responses:** You've been backing off and away from trouble until your back hits the wall behind you; now there's nowhere else to go.

Use **Spanish Study Guide** for additional support, pp. 230–232.

**Less Proficient Readers**
Suggest that students read "If We Must Die" four lines at a time, stopping to paraphrase what the speaker is saying in each section.

**Set a Purpose** Ask students to read both poems to find out how each speaker responds to oppression.

**Gifted and Talented**
Encourage students to research the political and social conditions for African Americans at the time Claude McKay wrote his poem. Ask them to share this historical context with the class.

---

✓ Assessment **Informal Assessment**

You can informally assess each student's understanding of the poems by having students invent two mottoes: one that summarizes the argument presented in "If We Must Die" and another that expresses the main idea of "A Black Man Talks of Reaping."

**RUBRIC**

**3** **Full Accomplishment** Student's mottoes convey a keen awareness of the ideas and feelings expressed in the two poems.

**2** **Substantial Accomplishment** Student's mottoes convey adequate awareness of the main ideas expressed in the two poems.

**1** **Little or Partial Accomplishment** Student's mottoes fail to convey the main message in either poem.

## GUIDING STUDENT RESPONSE

## Connect to the Literature

**1. What Do You Think?**
Some students may say that the poem gives them feelings of injustice and outrage.

**Comprehension Check**
He has reaped only as much as he can hold in his hand.

## Think Critically

**2.** Possible Responses: *sowing* might stand for the lifelong work of overcoming prejudice and resisting oppression; *reaping* might stand for the status one earns in society—"what the orchard yields"

**3.** Possible Response: The poem is about the struggle for a fair place in American society—a place where one's hard work is rewarded, a place where the harvest is not taken from the workers.

**4.** Possible Response: It feels as if McKay wrote "If We Must Die" with his back against the barricades. It is a war cry. It is meant to rally and to defeat the oppressor unto death. Bontemps's "A Black Man Talks of Reaping" also contends with the oppression of a racist society, but his response is to describe the plight of the exploited worker.

## Connect to the Literature

**1. What Do You Think?**
What feelings does "A Black Man Talks of Reaping" evoke in you?

**Comprehension Check**
• How much has the speaker reaped from all the seed he has scattered?

## Think Critically

**2.** **ACTIVE READING** **DISTINGUISHING FIGURATIVE AND LITERAL MEANING**
Interpret examples of figurative language you listed on the chart in your **READER'S NOTEBOOK**. What do you think *sowing* and *reaping* mean in this poem?

**3.** How would you state the **theme,** or the main message, of this poem?

**THINK ABOUT**
• the figurative meanings of "sown," "reaping," "my brother's sons," "glean," and "bitter fruit"
• the difference between reaping and gleaning
• why the speaker has reaped so little

**4.** How would you compare the wrongs the speakers face in these two poems and their responses to unfair treatment?

## Extend Interpretations

**5.** **Critic's Corner** When McKay's poem "If We Must Die" was published in 1919, it was read as a protest against white violence and a call for African Americans to resist oppression. After learning that a white American soldier who died in World War II had carried the poem with him, however, McKay said, "I felt assurance that 'If We Must Die' was just what I intended it to be, a universal poem." In your opinion, does this poem have a universal meaning? Explain your answer.

**6.** **Comparing Texts** How do you think Martin Luther King, Jr. (page 301) or Malcolm X (page 305) might respond to the ideas expressed by the speaker of "If We Must Die" or "A Black Man Talks of Reaping"?

**7.** **Connect to Life** Which of these poems do you think is more relevant to African Americans today, and why?

## Literary Analysis

**EXTENDED METAPHOR** A **metaphor** is a figure of speech that makes a comparison between two things that have something in common. An **extended metaphor** draws that comparison out and compares the two things in many ways. For example, an extended metaphor that compares life to a journey might be expressed in this way: Different ages in a person's life are signposts along life's journey, marked by high points such as graduation, marriage, and childbirth and by obstacles such as illness.

**Paired Activity** With a partner, reread "A Black Man Talks of Reaping." Then on a chart like the one shown, identify and interpret the parts of the extended metaphor comparing the African-American race to a farmer.

| Parts of the Metaphor | Interpretation |
|---|---|
|  |  |
|  |  |

**REVIEW** **SONNET** As you may recall, a **sonnet** is a 14-line lyric poem. "My City" (page 941) is an example of a Petrarchan sonnet. A second kind of sonnet, the **Shakespearean sonnet,** is divided into three quatrains (groups of four lines) and a couplet (two rhyming lines). Its rhyme scheme is *abab cdcd efef gg.* The couplet usually expresses a response to the important issue developed in the three quatrains. With a small group, explain how "If We Must Die" shows the features of a Shakespearean sonnet.

## Extend Interpretations

**Critic's Corner** Possible Response: The poem specifies no details about the hunted people—they might be any oppressed people in any place or time.

**Comparing Texts** Possible Responses: Both men would empathize with the feelings expressed in the poems. Malcolm X would be more likely to approve of the violent implications of "If We Must Die"; King would approve of both poems' message of defiance but would prefer the approach of "A Black Man Talks of Reaping."

**Connect to Life** Some students might say that "If We Must Die" still applies to the struggle African Americans face; other students might feel that "A Black Man Talks of Reaping" is still pertinent in light of the working man's continuing plight.

## Literary Analysis

**Extended Metaphor** Encourage pairs to share their charts with neighboring pairs.

**Sonnet** "If We Must Die" shows the form of the Shakespearean sonnet in its rhyme scheme and division into three quatrains and a couplet. It follows the rhyme scheme *abab cdcd efef gg.*

## Writing Options

**1. Problem-Solution Essay** What should a group do when it is a target of violence or economic exploitation by another group? Write an essay proposing and developing a solution, based on your interpretation of these poems and your personal philosophy or your knowledge of current events. Place this piece in your **Working Portfolio**.

**Writing Handbook**
See page 1283: Problem-Solution

**2. Write a Sonnet** Try writing a sonnet on any subject—perhaps the instance of unfair treatment you discussed for the Connect to Your Life activity on page 945. Use either the Shakespearean or the Petrarchan form, and remember that the end must somehow answer or comment on the beginning. Share a draft of your poem with a partner for comment.

## Activities & Explorations

**Activist Poster** With a small group of classmates, design a poster with print and art for each of the speakers of "If We Must Die" and "A Black Man Talks of Reaping." Each poster should feature a motto that expresses a goal, principle, or action advocated by the speaker for whom it is designed. ~ **VIEWING AND REPRESENTING**

## Claude McKay
### 1890?–1948

**Other Works**
*Banana Bottom*
*Banjo*
*Harlem: Negro Metropolis*
*A Long Way from Home*

**Harlem Renaissance Figure** Born and raised on the island of Jamaica, Claude McKay came to the United States in 1912. With the publication in 1922 of his major collection of poetry, *Harlem Shadows,* McKay helped launch the Harlem Renaissance.

**Militant Writer** Called "the poet of rebellion" by James Weldon Johnson, McKay protested racial injustice in both poetry and prose. His powerful sonnet "If We Must Die," first published in *The Liberator* in July 1919, is still one of the best-known African-American poems. The popularity of his novel *Home to Harlem*, about a soldier's life after World War 1, made McKay the first best-selling African-American novelist.

**Universal Themes** McKay spent most of the 1920s abroad, living for 12 years in the Soviet Union, France, Spain, and Morocco. He once said, "I have always felt that my gift of song was something bigger than the narrow confined limits of any one people and its problems."

## Arna Bontemps
### 1902–1973

**Other Works**
*The Old South*
*Personals*

**Inspired by Marcus Garvey** Through his poetry, novels, and plays, Arna Bontemps made a significant contribution to the development of African-American identity. Bontemps was born in Alexandria, Louisiana, the son of a teacher and a brick mason. While attending Pacific Union College, he heard the Jamaican social reformer Marcus Garvey speak in Los Angeles and learned about the flourishing Harlem Renaissance.

**At Work in Harlem** After graduating from college in 1923, Bontemps moved to Harlem to "see what all the excitement was about." What he discovered was "a foretaste of paradise." While earning a living by teaching, he concentrated as much as possible on his writing and within a year of his arrival in New York City began publishing poems in *Crisis* magazine. His first novel, *God Sends Sunday,* published in 1931, is considered by some to have been the final product of the Harlem Renaissance movement.

---

## Writing Options

1. **Problem-Solution Essay** Students' essays should propose concrete, specific solutions to the stated problem. Encourage students to include reasons why their solutions might work.

2. **Write a Sonnet** To get students started on this assignment, ask them to write a poem about how they deal with someone who is disrespecting them. Ask: What's the best way to respond when someone is putting you down?

## Activities & Explorations

**Activist Poster** Invite groups to explain how they decided to treat their posters graphically. What responses did they want the images to evoke?

## Author Notes

Claude McKay came to the United States to attend Tuskegee Institute. *The Liberator* was an avant-garde journal of politics and art. The brutality of racism in the States shocked McKay out of the comfortable conservatism he had grown up with in Jamaica.

---

## Mini Lesson  Grammar

**MODIFIERS: USE OF *er***

**Instruction** A modifier in the comparative degree compares one or two persons or things with a class of similar people or things. Examples of comparative degree modifiers include *better, finer,* and *more friendly* or *friendlier.* Point out that it is correct to say either *more friendly* or *friendlier,* but not *more friendlier.* The last phrase is redundant.

**Exercises** Say the following sentences aloud or have volunteers write them on the chalkboard. Have students decide whether each sentence is correct or incorrect, and ask them to fix any incorrect examples.

1. She was the *faster* runner of the two sisters. *(correct)*

2. There is a *more better* photograph than that one. *(Incorrect. Suggested answer: There is a better photograph than that one.)*

3. That flower is *more colorful* than the rest. *(correct. Make sure students don't think that colorfuller is an option.)*

 Use **Grammar Transparencies and Copymasters**, p. 135.

 Use McDougal Littell's *Language Network*, Chapter 7, for more instruction and practice in modifiers.

This selection is included in the **Grade 11 InterActive Reader.**

## Objectives

1. understand and appreciate an **autobiographical essay (Literary Analysis)**
2. **draw conclusions about author's purposes (Active Reading)**

## Summary

Zora Neale Hurston describes growing up in the all-black town of Eatonville, Florida, which gave her no experience of prejudice or racial discrimination. By the time she started high school in Jacksonville, Florida, her sense of herself was too well established to be impaired by racial prejudice. She describes how her awareness of her blackness depends on her circumstances and the people she is with. Sometimes she feels discriminated against, but rather than making her angry, it only astonishes her. She asks, "How *can* any deny themselves the pleasure of my company? It's beyond me." Above all, she sees herself as an individual filled with hopes, dreams, ambitions, memories, burdens, and fears.

## Thematic Link

A major voice of the **Harlem Renaissance,** Hurston explores her **cultural identity** in this autobiographical essay.

### 5-Minute Warm-Up

*Daily Language SkillBuilder*

Have students **proofread** the display sentences on page 913i and write them correctly. The sentences also appear on Transparency 26 of **Grammar Transparencies and Copymasters.**

---

# How It Feels to Be Colored Me

*Essay by* ZORA NEALE HURSTON

*"How can any deny themselves the pleasure of my company?"*

### Connect to Your Life

**Your Individuality** Imagine that you are filling out a college application and that one of the questions asks you to describe what makes you a unique individual. On a sheet of paper, list three or four qualities that you would attribute to yourself in such a description. Compare your list with a partner's.

## Build Background

**Flamboyant Personality** From the time she moved to Harlem in 1925 until her death in 1960, Zora Neale Hurston was the most prolific African-American woman writer. She was also a popular figure on the social scene during the Harlem Renaissance. According to her biographer Robert Hemenway, Hurston "acquired an instant reputation in New York for her high spirits and side-splitting tales of Eatonville," her Florida hometown. Like other writers of the Harlem Renaissance, such as Langston Hughes and Claude McKay, Hurston searched within herself for her identity rather than defining herself according to the racial stereotypes of her day. In this essay, first published in 1928, she uses several unique images to convey her individuality.

> **WORDS TO KNOW**
> **Vocabulary Preview**
> deplore     rend     veneer
> extenuating     specter

## Focus Your Reading

**LITERARY ANALYSIS** **AUTOBIOGRAPHICAL ESSAY** An essay is a short work of nonfiction that deals with a single subject. In an **autobiographical essay,** that subject is some aspect of the writer's life. The subject of Hurston's essay is her sense of herself as an individual and an African American.

**ACTIVE READING** **DRAWING CONCLUSIONS ABOUT AUTHOR'S PURPOSES** A writer usually writes for one or more **purposes**—to inform, to entertain, to express himself or herself, or to persuade readers to believe or do something. In this autobiographical essay, Hurston writes for multiple purposes. To **draw conclusions** about them, use these tips:

- Identify passages that affect you strongly.
- In these passages, consider the kinds of experiences she relates—for example, painful ones or generally happy ones—and the descriptive details she provides. Note especially her direct statements and comparisons.
- Ask yourself why she includes these passages, and state your own conclusions.

**READER'S NOTEBOOK** As you read, use a chart to gather data about selected passages from the beginning, middle, and end of this essay. Then state your conclusion about Hurston's purposes for writing each one.

**Hurston's Essay**

| Passages | Purposes |
|---|---|
| 1. Childhood in Eatonville | |
| 2. Experiencing Live Jazz | |
| 3. Comparison of People to Stuffed Bags | |

**950** UNIT SIX   PART 1: A NEW CULTURAL IDENTITY

---

## LESSON RESOURCES

**UNIT SIX RESOURCE BOOK,** pp. 12–16

**ASSESSMENT RESOURCES**
**Formal Assessment,** pp. 175–176
**Teacher's Guide to Assessment and Portfolio Use**
**Test Generator**

**SKILLS TRANSPARENCIES AND COPYMASTERS**
**Literary Analysis**
• Tone, T19 (for Review, p. 957)

**Reading and Critical Thinking**
• Drawing Conclusions, T4 (for Active Reading, p. 950)

**Grammar**
• Distinguishing *Those* from *Them,* C138 (for Mini Lesson, p. 958)

**Vocabulary**
• Figurative Language, C79 (for Mini Lesson, p. 953)

**Writing**
• Persuasive Essay, C27 (for Writing Option 1, p. 958)

• Autobiographical Incident, C35 (for Writing Option 2, p. 958)

**Communications**
• Dramatic Reading, T12 (for Author Activity, p. 958)

**INTEGRATED TECHNOLOGY**

**Audio Library**
**Visit our website:**
www.mcdougallittell.com

# How It Feels to Be Colored Me

**ZORA NEALE HURSTON**

I am colored but I offer nothing in the way of extenuating circumstances except the fact that I am the only Negro in the United States whose grandfather on the mother's side was *not* an Indian chief.

I remember the very day that I became colored. Up to my thirteenth year I lived in the little Negro town of Eatonville, Florida. It is exclusively a colored town. The only white people I knew passed through the town going to or coming from Orlando. The native whites rode dusty horses; the Northern tourists chugged down the sandy village road in automobiles. The town knew the Southerners and never stopped cane chewing when they passed. But the Northerners were something else again. They were peered at cautiously from behind curtains by the timid. The more venturesome would come out on the porch to watch them go past and got just as much pleasure out of the tourists as the tourists got out of the village.

The front porch might seem a daring place for the rest of the town, but it was a gallery seat for me. My favorite place was atop the gatepost. Proscenium box[1] for a born first-nighter.[2] Not only did I enjoy the show, but I didn't mind the actors knowing that I liked it. I usually spoke to them in passing. I'd wave at them and when they returned my salute, I would say something like this: "Howdy-do-well-I-thank-you-where-you-goin'?" Usually the automobile or the horse paused at this, and after a queer exchange of compliments, I would probably "go a piece of the way" with them, as we say in farthest Florida. If one of my family happened to come to the front in time to see me, of course negotiations would be rudely broken off. But even so, it is clear that I was the first "welcome-to-our-state" Floridian, and I hope the Miami Chamber of Commerce will please take notice.

During this period, white people differed from colored to me only in that they rode through town and never lived there. They liked to hear me "speak pieces" and sing and wanted to see me dance the parse-me-la, and gave me generously of their small silver for doing these things,

---

1. **proscenium** (prō-sē′nē-əm) **box:** a box seat near the stage.
2. **first-nighter:** a person who attends the opening performance of a play, an opera, or a similar show.

WORDS TO KNOW

**extenuating** (ĭk-stĕn′yōō-ā′tĭng) *adj.* lessening a fault by serving as a partial excuse **extenuate** *v.*

951

---

## TEACHING THE LITERATURE

### Customizing Instruction

**Students Acquiring English**
Hurston's figurative language may be difficult for students. Have them write down any phrases they do not understand as they read and ask about them during class discussion.

 Use **Spanish Study Guide** for additional support, pp. 233–235.

**Less Proficient Readers**
Ask students to read the opening paragraphs and visualize Hurston's native town. Have them summarize her impressions of her childhood in Eatonville.

**Set a Purpose** Have students read on to find out how adolescence changed her.

**Gifted and Talented**
Suggest that students write character sketches of themselves, employing vivid, figurative language similar to that used by Hurston.

---

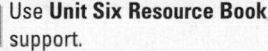

## Preteaching Vocabulary

**USING CONTEXT CLUES**

**Instruction** Remind students that sometimes they can figure out the meaning of an unfamiliar word by examining the context, or the surrounding words and phrases.

Display the following sentence and ask a volunteer to summarize its meaning.

I <u>deplore</u> rude behavior; I feel it's terrible to treat others without respect.

Have students use the meaning of the sentence to suggest meanings for the word *deplore*.

**Application** Have students use context clues to determine the meanings of the underlined terms.

1. The student failed the midterm exam. The only <u>extenuating</u> circumstance was his poor health.
2. This paper shredder can <u>rend</u> an entire book into small pieces in a matter of seconds.
3. The sight of the <u>specter</u> hovering in the doorway made me believe in the supernatural.
4. Behind a <u>veneer</u> of smiles, Jane was actually quite upset that her best friend was chosen over her for the lead role in the school play.

Use **Unit Six Resource Book**, p. 15 for additional support.

**A lesson on context clues appears on p. 326 in the Pupil's Edition.**

*Skipping Along,* Stephen Scott Young. Copyright © Stephen Scott Young. Photo courtesy of John H. Surovek Gallery, Palm Beach, Flordia.

which seemed strange to me, for I wanted to do them so much that I needed bribing to stop. Only they didn't know it. The colored people gave no dimes. They <u>deplored</u> any joyful tendencies in me, but I was their Zora nevertheless. I belonged to them, to the nearby hotels, to the county—everybody's Zora.

But changes came in the family when I was thirteen, and I was sent to school in Jacksonville. I left Eatonville, the town of the oleanders,[3] as Zora. When I disembarked from the riverboat at Jacksonville, she was no more. It seemed that I had suffered a sea change.[4] I was not Zora of Orange County any more, I was now a little colored girl. I found it out in certain ways. In my heart as well as in the mirror, I became a fast brown—warranted not to rub nor run.

# But I am not tragically colored.

There is no great sorrow dammed up in my soul, nor lurking behind my eyes. I do not mind at all. I do not belong to the sobbing school of Negrohood who hold that nature somehow has given them a lowdown dirty deal and whose feelings are all

hurt about it. Even in the helter-skelter skirmish that is my life, I have seen that the world is to the strong regardless of a little pigmentation[5] more or less. No, I do not weep at the world—I am too busy sharpening my oyster knife.[6]

Someone is always at my elbow reminding me that I am the granddaughter of slaves. It fails to register depression with me. Slavery is sixty years in the past. The operation was successful and the patient is doing well, thank you. The terrible struggle that made me an American out of a potential slave said, "On the line!" The Reconstruction said, "Get set!" and the generation before said, "Go!" I am off to a flying start and I must not halt in the stretch to look behind and weep. Slavery is the price I paid for civilization, and the choice was not with me. It is a bully[7] adventure and worth all that I have paid through my ancestors for it. No one on earth ever had a greater chance for glory. The world to be won and nothing to be lost. It is thrilling to think—to know that for any act of mine, I shall get twice as much praise or twice as much blame. It is quite exciting to hold the center of the national stage, with the spectators not knowing whether to laugh or to weep.

The position of my white neighbor is much more difficult. No brown <u>specter</u> pulls up a chair beside me when I sit down to eat. No dark ghost thrusts its leg against mine in bed. The game of keeping what one has is never so exciting as the game of getting.

---

3. **oleanders** (ō'lē-ăn'dərz): evergreen shrubs with fragrant flowers.
4. **sea change:** complete transformation.
5. **pigmentation:** darkness of skin coloration.
6. **oyster knife:** a reference to the saying "The world is my oyster," implying that the world contains treasure waiting to be taken, like the pearl in an oyster.
7. **bully:** excellent; splendid.

> WORDS TO KNOW
>
> **deplore** (dĭ-plôr') *v.* to feel strong disapproval of or deeply regret
> **specter** (spĕk'tər) *n.* a ghostly vision; phantom

952

---

I do not always feel colored. Even now I often achieve the unconscious Zora of Eatonville before the Hegira.[8] I feel most colored when I am thrown against a sharp white background.

For instance at Barnard.[9] "Beside the waters of the Hudson"[10] I feel my race. Among the thousand white persons, I am a dark rock surged upon, and overswept, but through it all, I remain myself. When covered by the waters, I am; and the ebb but reveals me again.

**Sometimes** it is the other way around. A white person is set down in our midst, but the contrast is just as sharp for me. For instance, when I sit in the drafty basement that is The New World Cabaret with a white person, my color comes. We enter chatting about any little nothing that we have in common and are seated by the jazz waiters. In the abrupt way that jazz orchestras have, this one plunges into a number. It loses no time in circumlocutions,[11] but gets right down to business. It constricts the thorax and splits the heart with its tempo and narcotic harmonies. This orchestra grows rambunctious, rears on its hind legs and attacks the tonal veil with primitive fury, rending it, clawing it until it breaks through to the jungle beyond. I follow those heathen—follow them exultingly. I dance wildly inside myself; I yell within, I whoop; I shake my assegai[12] above my head, I hurl it true to the mark yeeeeooww! I am in the jungle and living in the jungle way. My face is painted red and yellow and my body is painted blue. My pulse is throbbing like a war drum. I want to slaughter something—give pain, give death to what, I do not know. But the piece ends. The men of the orchestra wipe their lips and rest their fingers. I creep back slowly to the veneer we call civilization with the last tone and find the white friend sitting motionless in his seat, smoking calmly.

"Good music they have here," he remarks, drumming the table with his fingertips.

Music. The great blobs of purple and red emotion have not touched him. He has only heard what I felt. He is far away and I see him but dimly across the ocean and the continent that have fallen between us. He is so pale with his whiteness then and I am so colored.

**At** certain times I have no race. I am me. When I set my hat at a certain angle and saunter down Seventh Avenue, Harlem City, feeling as snooty as the lions in front of the Forty-Second Street Library, for instance. So far as my feelings are concerned, Peggy Hopkins Joyce on the Boule Mich with her gorgeous raiment, stately carriage,[13] knees knocking together in a most aristocratic manner, has nothing on me. The cosmic[14] Zora emerges. I belong to no race nor time. I am the eternal feminine with its string of beads.

I have no separate feeling about being an American citizen and colored. I am merely a fragment of the Great Soul that surges within the boundaries. My country, right or wrong.

Sometimes, I feel discriminated against, but it does not make me angry. It merely astonishes

---

8. **Hegira** (hĭ-jī′rə): journey (from the name given to Mohammed's journey from Mecca to Medina in 622).

9. **Barnard:** the college in New York City from which Hurston graduated in 1928.

10. **"Beside the waters of the Hudson":** a reference to the first line of Barnard's school song.

11. **circumlocutions** (sûr′kəm-lō-kyōō′shənz): unnecessary elaboration or "beating around the bush."

12. **assegai** (ăs′ə-gī′): a light spear, especially one with a short shaft and long blade, used in southern Africa.

13. **Peggy Hopkins Joyce . . . carriage:** one of the richest women of Hurston's day, walking along the Boulevard Saint-Michel in Paris, dressed in beautiful clothes, carrying herself like a queen.

14. **cosmic:** of or belonging to the universe.

---

WORDS TO KNOW

**rend** (rĕnd) v. to tear or split apart violently
**veneer** (və-nîr′) n. a thin surface layer that conceals what is below

**953**

*Bal Jeunesse* (about 1927), Palmer Hayden. Watercolor on paper, 14″ × 17″, collection of Meredith and Gail Wright Sirmans.

(A) me. How *can* any deny themselves the pleasure of my company? It's beyond me.

**[1]** (B) But in the main, I feel like a brown bag of miscellany propped against a wall. Against a wall in company with other bags, white, red, and yellow. Pour out the contents, and there is discovered a jumble of small things priceless and worthless. A first-water[15] diamond, an empty spool, bits of broken glass, lengths of string, a key to a door long since crumbled away, a rusty knife blade, old shoes saved for a road that never was and never will be, a nail bent under the weight of things too heavy for any nail, a dried flower or two still a little fragrant. In your hand is the brown bag. On the ground before you is the jumble it held—so much like the jumble in the bags, could they be emptied, that all might be dumped in a single heap and the bags refilled without altering the content of any greatly. A bit of colored glass more or less would not matter. Perhaps that is how the Great Stuffer of Bags **[2]** filled them in the first place—who knows? ❖ (C)

—————————————

15. **first-water:** of the highest quality or purity.

954    UNIT SIX    PART 1: A NEW CULTURAL IDENTITY

from

# Zora Neale Hurston: A Cautionary Tale and a Partisan View

### ALICE WALKER

*Novelist Alice Walker was responsible for rediscovering the writings of Zora Neale Hurston in the 1970s and bringing her to the attention of a new generation of readers. In the following excerpt from an essay on Hurston, Walker discusses the impact of Hurston's collection of black folktales,* Mules and Men, *first published in 1935.*

ZORA NEALE HURSTON
AUTHOR OF THEIR EYES WERE WATCHING GOD

MULES AND MEN

"Simply the most exciting book on black folklore and culture I have ever read."
—Roger D. Abrahams

. . . When I read *Mules and Men* I was delighted. Here was this perfect book! The "perfection" of which I immediately tested on my relatives, who are such typical black Americans they are useful for every sort of political, cultural, or economic survey. Very regular people from the South, rapidly forgetting their Southern cultural inheritance in the suburbs and ghettos of Boston and New York, they sat around reading the book themselves, listening to me read the book, listening to each other read the book, and a kind of paradise was regained. For what Zora's book did was this: it gave them back all the stories they had forgotten or of which they had grown ashamed (told to us years ago by our parents and grandparents—not one of whom could *not* tell a story to make you weep, or laugh) and showed how marvelous, and, indeed, priceless, they are. This is not exaggerated. No matter how they read the stories Zora had collected, no matter how much distance they tried to maintain between themselves, as new sophisticates, and the lives their parents and grandparents lived, no matter

ZORA NEALE HURSTON: A CAUTIONARY TALE AND A PARTISAN VIEW  **955**

**Reading Skills and Strategies:
COMPARING TEXTS**

Students are expected to compare and contrast elements across text, including purpose, style, and tone. Help students relate Alice Walker's essay to Zora Neale Hurston's with the following questions.

• Discuss the differences and similarities between these two selections.

**Possible Responses:** "How It Feels to Be Colored Me" is an autobiographical essay whose purpose is to share information about the author's life and express the author's opinions about race in America. Walker's piece is partly autobiographical, although its main purpose is to describe how African Americans respond to Hurston's work. "How It Feels to Be Colored Me" uses more informal language than Walker's essay does. The overall tone of both pieces is optimistic and celebratory.

• Compare and contrast your own reaction to the work of Zora Neale Hurston with Alice Walker's reaction.

• Is there a writer or public figure who is as important to you as Hurston is to Walker? Who is it, and why is this writer important to you?

how they tried to remain cool toward all Zora revealed, in the end they could not hold back the smiles, the laughter, the joy over who she was showing them to be: descendants of an inventive, joyous, courageous, and outrageous people; loving drama, appreciating wit, and, most of all, relishing the pleasure of each other's loquacious[1] and *bodacious*[2] company.

This was my first indication of the quality I feel is most characteristic of Zora's work: racial health; a sense of black people as complete, complex, *undiminished* human beings, a sense that is lacking in so much black writing and literature. (In my opinion, only Du Bois[3] showed an equally consistent delight in the beauty and spirit of black people, which is interesting when one considers that the angle of his vision was completely the opposite of Zora's.) Zora's pride in black people was so pronounced in the ersatz[4] black twenties that it made other blacks suspicious and perhaps uncomfortable (after all, *they* were still infatuated[5] with things European). Zora was interested in Africa, Haiti, Jamaica, and—for a little racial diversity (Indians)—Honduras. She also had a confidence in herself as an individual that few people (anyone?), black or white, understood. This was because Zora grew up in a community of black people who had enormous respect for themselves and for their ability to govern themselves. Her own father had written the Eatonville town laws. This community affirmed her right to exist, and loved her as an extension of its self. For how many other black Americans is this true? It certainly isn't true for any that I know. In her easy self-acceptance, Zora

was more like an uncolonized African than she was like her contemporary American blacks, most of whom believed, at least during their formative years, that their blackness was something wrong with them.

On the contrary, Zora's early work shows she grew up pitying whites because the ones she saw lacked "light" and soul. It is impossible to imagine Zora envying anyone (except tongue in cheek), and least of all a white person for being white. Which is, after all, if one is black, a clear and present calamity of the mind.

Condemned to a desert island for life, with an allotment of ten books to see me through, I would choose, unhesitatingly, two of Zora's: *Mules and Men,* because I would need to be able to pass on to younger generations the life of American blacks as legend and myth; and *Their Eyes Were Watching God,* because I would want to enjoy myself while identifying with the black heroine, Janie Crawford, as she acted out many roles in a variety of settings, and functioned (with spectacular results!) in romantic and sensual love. *There is no book more important to me than this one. . . .* ❖

---

1. **loquacious** (lō-kwā′shəs): very talkative.
2. *bodacious* (bō-dā′shəs): a Southern dialect term meaning "remarkable" or "spirited."
3. **Du Bois** (dōō bois′): the U.S. civil rights leader, editor, and author W. E. B. Du Bois (1868–1963).
4. **ersatz** (ĕr′zäts′): artificial; imitation.
5. **infatuated** (ĭn-făch′ōō-ā′tĭd): carried away by a foolish attraction.

## Connect to the Literature

1. **What Do You Think?**
If you had met Zora Neale Hurston, would you have liked her?

**Comprehension Check**
- What kind of community was Eatonville, Florida?
- What was the "sea change" Zora suffered at the age of 13?

## Think Critically

2. **ACTIVE READING** **DRAWING CONCLUSIONS ABOUT AUTHOR'S PURPOSES** What conclusions did you draw about Hurston's purposes for writing this essay? Refer to the chart in your 📖 **READER'S NOTEBOOK** to support your conclusions.

3. Why do you think Hurston concludes this essay by comparing people to stuffed bags?

4. What do you think Hurston's cultural identity meant to her?

**THINK ABOUT**
- her statement "I am not tragically colored"
- when she was aware of her color and when she forgot it
- her views of slavery, discrimination, and the United States
- her response to jazz

## Extend Interpretations

5. **Comparing Texts** In the Literary Link on page 955, Alice Walker identifies qualities she feels are characteristic of Hurston's writing. Which, if any, of these qualities do you detect in Hurston's essay? Explain your answer.

6. **Critic's Corner** Alice Walker, one of Hurston's greatest admirers, had this to say about Hurston's essay:

> *"How It Feels to Be Colored Me" is an excellent example of Zora Neale Hurston at her most exasperating. Published in 1928, near the beginning of Hurston's career, this essay presents two stereotypes: the "happy darky" who sings and dances for white folks, for money and for joy; and the educated black person who is, underneath the thin veneer of civilization, still a "heathen."*

Do you agree with Walker's views? Why or why not?

7. **Connect to Life** Which of the ideas expressed in Hurston's essay do you think might be controversial today?

## Literary Analysis

**AUTOBIOGRAPHICAL ESSAY** An **autobiographical essay** is a short work of nonfiction that focuses on an aspect of the writer's life. One of the challenges is to combine objective description with the expression of subjective feelings. For example, at the beginning of this essay, Hurston uses objective language to describe the white people passing through Eatonville: "The native whites rode dusty horses; the Northern tourists chugged down the sandy village road in automobiles." In contrast, when relating her own subjective feelings about watching these people, Hurston uses a figurative expression and emotionally charged words: "My favorite place was atop the gatepost. Proscenium box for a born first-nighter. Not only did I enjoy the show, but I didn't mind the actors knowing that I liked it."

**Activity** Reread the passage in which Hurston describes her reaction to jazz at The New World Cabaret. Then fill in a chart like the following, distinguishing the objective description from the subjective expression.

| Objective Description | Subjective Expression |
|---|---|
| | |
| | |

**REVIEW TONE** What **tone** is conveyed by Hurston's comparisons of life to a "show," a "game," and a "bully adventure"? Compare her attitude toward being African American with the attitudes of the other Harlem Renaissance writers you've read.

## Extend Interpretations

**Comparing Texts** Responses will vary. Some students may cite details from Hurston's essay to support Walker's view that her writing expresses a "delight in the beauty and spirit of black people."
**Critic's Corner** Students may agree or disagree but should present logical reasons for doing so. Walker might find parts of the essay disturbing because they imply that traditional African culture was uncivilized and because they extenuate the horrors of slavery.

**Connect to Life** Possible Responses: Hurston's implicit criticism of other African Americans' attitudes might be controversial, as well as her contention that slavery was the price she paid to become civilized. Some people might contend that nothing is worth the horrible price of slavery, and some might argue that white slave holders didn't civilize their slaves, because most slaves came from civilized African societies.

## Connect to the Literature

1. **What Do You Think?**
Students might cite one or more of Hurston's qualities, such as her self-confidence and enthusiasm, to support their response.

**Comprehension Check**
- Eatonville was an all-black community in Florida.
- Zora was no longer surrounded by others of her own race. She was now living among whites, and her race became an issue for the first time.

📖 Use Selection Quiz
**Unit Six Resource Book,** p. 16.

## Think Critically

2. Responses will vary. Some students may conclude that Hurston's primary purpose is to express her views about her identity in an entertaining way.

3. Possible Response: She was trying to convey the commonality of all human beings while retaining awareness of her heritage.

4. Responses will vary. Some students may say her identity meant a great deal to her in a positive sense; she did not dwell on the negative side of being black in the United States. Some may see this as a sign of individuality and strength of character. Others may feel that she underestimates the historical sufferings of African Americans and thereby slights those who have suffered.

## Literary Analysis

**Autobiographical Essay** Students' charts should distinguish subjective expressions from objective statements.
**Review Tone** Her comparisons of life to a show, a game, and an adventure suggest self-confidence and high spirits. Students' comparisons with other writers' attitudes will vary, but most will find that Hurston's attitude is markedly positive and casual.

## Writing Options

1. **Proposal for School Assembly**
Students may mention Hurston's sense of individuality and self-esteem as worthy of emulation.

2. **Autobiographical Essay To get students started on this activity,** remind them to use the first-person point of view. Since they are expressing their uniqueness, point out that their style and tone should be their own.

## Vocabulary in Action

1. a haunted house
2. insincere
3. ripping it
4. that the bus broke down ["that you thought it was Saturday" is also acceptable]
5. one that you find horrible

## Writing Options

1. **Proposal for School Assembly** Write a proposal to a committee planning a school assembly in honor of famous African Americans. In your proposal, present reasons why Hurston's essay should be read at the assembly.

**Writing Handbook**
See page 1285: Persuasive Writing.

2. **Autobiographical Essay** Imagine that an organization whose purpose is to foster racial or ethnic pride will award a scholarship to the applicant who best expresses an appreciation of his or her heritage. Draft an autobiographical essay, modeled after Hurston's, expressing your views about your heritage.

## Zora Neale Hurston
### 1891?–1960

**Other Works**
*Jonah's Gourd Vine*
*Moses, Man of the Mountain*
*Tell My Horse*
"Sweat"
"The Gilded Six-Bits"

**Arrival in Harlem** Born in the all-black town of Eatonville, Florida, Zora Neale Hurston took her mother's advice to "jump at de sun" and overcome poverty and prejudice. She entered Harlem society in 1925, arriving with "$1.50, no job, no friends, and a lot of hope." After she had won two second prizes—one for a short story and one for a play—in a literary contest sponsored by *Opportunity* magazine, Hurston came to the attention of the leaders of the Harlem Renaissance. In the New York City of the 1920s, Hurston soon became known for her flamboyant, theatrical personality as well as for her short stories.

**Folklorist** In 1928, after graduating from Barnard College, where she had studied with the renowned anthropologist Franz Boas, Hurston returned to her

## Vocabulary in Action

**EXERCISE: MEANING CLUES** Answer these questions.

1. What attraction at an amusement park would probably involve a **specter**—a roller coaster, a ring-toss game, or a haunted house?

2. If you said that someone had a **veneer** of friendliness, would you be suggesting that the person was eager, was hesitant, or was insincere?

3. If you were to **rend** a curtain, would you be closing it, ripping it, or hanging it?

4. Which would be an **extenuating** circumstance for being tardy for school—that you dawdled on the way, that the bus broke down, or that you thought it was Saturday?

5. Is an action that you **deplore** one that you find horrible, one that you find amusing, or one that you find boring?

**Building Vocabulary**
For an in-depth study of word connotation and denotation, see page 908.

native South to collect African-American folklore. "I had to go back, dress as they did, talk as they did, live their life," she said, "so I could get into my stories the world I knew as a child."

**Literary Success** Over the next two decades, Hurston built her reputation as the best African-American woman writer of her time with a steady stream of publications. Among her prominent works were the folklore collection *Mules and Men,* the novel *Their Eyes Were Watching God,* and her autobiography, *Dust Tracks on a Road.*

**Final Years** During the last 20 years of her life, Hurston struggled with financial and health problems. She died in poverty and was buried in an unmarked grave in Fort Pierce, Florida. Many readers have rediscovered Hurston in recent years, however—largely because of the African-American writer Alice Walker's efforts to publicize her life and work.

## Author Activity

Give a dramatic reading of one of the folktales in Hurston's *Mules and Men,* a book that Alice Walker said she would take with her to a desert island.

## Teaching Options

 **Mini Lesson** ## Grammar

**MODIFIERS: DISTINGUISHING *THOSE* FROM *THEM***
**Instruction** Modifiers are words used to limit, emphasize, or describe other words in a sentence. The word *those* can function as either a pronoun or an adjective (modifier). The word *them,* the objective form of the personal pronoun *they,* is always a pronoun, never an adjective.
Write these model sentences on the chalkboard.

Incorrect: Where did <u>them</u> Northerners say they were going?

Correct: Where did <u>those</u> Northerners say they were going? (adjective)
Correct: I follow <u>them</u> exultingly. (pronoun)
Correct: Where did you get <u>those</u>? (pronoun)

 Use **Grammar Transparencies and Copymasters,** p. 138.

 Use McDougal Littell's *Language Network,* Chapter 7, for more instruction and practice in modifiers.

# My Dungeon Shook:
Letter to My Nephew on the One Hundredth Anniversary
of the Emancipation

*Open Letter by* JAMES BALDWIN

### Comparing Literature

## Traditions Across Time: Reaffirming Cultural Identity

Like the writers of the Harlem Renaissance, James Baldwin explores African-American cultural identity. He wrote this essay as a letter to his nephew, advising him to discover for himself who he really is.

**Points of Comparison** Compare and contrast Baldwin's views about race relations with those of Harlem Renaissance writers.

## Build Background

**Effects of Racism** In this essay, written 100 years after Abraham Lincoln's Emancipation Proclamation, Baldwin refers to the harsh social conditions under which some African Americans lived, particularly the conditions he himself had witnessed while growing up in Harlem. The center of African-American culture in the 1920s, Harlem later became a bleak ghetto from which residents had little hope of escaping and which they had even less hope of improving. In the 1960s the sense of despair pervading decayed urban neighborhoods like Harlem fueled an atmosphere of violence. From 1964 to 1967, more than 100 race riots erupted in major cities across the United States.

| WORDS TO KNOW |
|---|
| **Vocabulary Preview** |

| | |
|---|---|
| aspire | monumental |
| constitute | paradox |
| devastation | perspective |
| impertinent | truculent |
| mediocrity | whence |

## Focus Your Reading

**LITERARY ANALYSIS** **OPEN LETTER** An **open letter** is addressed to a specific person but published for a wider readership. Consider the larger audience that Baldwin targets in "My Dungeon Shook."

**ACTIVE READING** **ANALYZING CHARACTERISTICS OF CLEARLY WRITTEN TEXTS** In this letter, Baldwin explores the complexity of race relations in the United States. Use these strategies to help you understand his ideas:

- Complex ideas sometimes require complex sentences. When you come upon these sentences, pay attention to the **syntax**—or the arrangement of the sentence parts. Identify the subject (the person, place, thing, or idea about which something is said) and the predicate (the part that tells or asks something about the subject).
- Watch for paradoxes and other thought-provoking statements. A **paradox** is a statement that appears to be a contradiction. For example, Baldwin writes, "It is the innocence which constitutes the crime." When you come upon such a statement, ask yourself what words signal a possible double meaning. Then try to figure out the underlying truth that the apparent contradiction conveys. In the paradox above, you probably associate innocence with the absence of wrongdoing. So in order to understand this sentence, you must determine what kind of innocence Baldwin means.

**READER'S NOTEBOOK** List and interpret thought-provoking statements in this letter, including the paradox discussed above.

**Objectives**
1. understand and appreciate an **open letter** (Literary Analysis)
2. analyze characteristics of **clearly written texts** (Active Reading)

**Summary**
In the open letter "My Dungeon Shook," James Baldwin encourages his nephew and namesake to learn to define himself in his own terms, not in those offered by the white world. He states that white people, out of inhumanity and fear, try to make African Americans believe in their inferiority. To Baldwin, the basic issue of integration is not whether whites accept blacks, but whether blacks accept whites. He counsels his nephew to accept the fact that American whites simply cannot understand who he is and where he comes from. Baldwin concludes by stating that the United States is celebrating the hundredth anniversary of the emancipation of its slaves (1863) one hundred years too soon. The reason is that blacks cannot be truly free until whites see reality. Once his nephew has armed himself with this truth about America, he can go on to do the work of making his country what it must become.

**Thematic Link**
"My Dungeon Shook" is an eloquent statement of one African American's search for **a new cultural identity**.

### 5-Minute Warm-Up

*Daily Language SkillBuilder*

Have students **proofread** the display sentences on page 913i and write them correctly. The sentences also appear on Transparency 26 of **Grammar Transparencies and Copymasters.**

## LESSON RESOURCES

## Reading and Analyzing

**Reading Skills and Strategies: PREVIEW**

Remind students that paraphrasing can help them understand the ideas in complex sentences.

**Active Reading**

**ANALYZING CHARACTERISTICS OF CLEARLY WRITTEN TEXTS**

**Ⓐ** Have students analyze the characteristics of Baldwin's text for its effect on the audience by exploring his word choice and diction. Suggest that they choose a difficult phrase or sentence and rephrase it using slang or some other type of varied diction.

As an example, write these two sentences on the chalkboard:
- Neither you nor your father exhibit any tendency towards holiness.
- Neither you nor your dad show any leaning towards being a saint.

Ask students to describe how the change in diction affects the audience. Then have them reflect on how a series of such diction choices determines the effect Baldwin's essay will have on the reader.

**Possible Responses:** The diction in the second sentence is informal and nearly humorous; it would make the audience relax and expect that the letter was going to be lighthearted. The serious diction that Baldwin chose suggests a wry comment on his brother and nephew without relaxing into light-heartedness. Such diction keeps the audience in a serious mood, alert to subtle irony.

 Use **Unit Six Resource Book,** p. 18 for additional support.

---

## MY DUNGEON SHOOK

## Letter to My Nephew on the One Hundredth Anniversary of the Emancipation

## James Baldwin

Dear James:
I have begun this letter five times and torn it up five times. I keep seeing your face, which is also the face of your father and my brother. Like him, you are tough, dark, vulnerable, moody—with a very definite tendency to sound truculent because you want no one to think you are soft. You may be like your grandfather in this, I don't know, but certainly both you and your father resemble him very much physically. Well, he is dead, he never saw you, and he had a terrible life; he was defeated long before he died because, at the bottom of his heart, he really believed what white people said about him. This is one of the reasons that he became so holy.[1] I am sure that your father has told you something about all that.

**Ⓐ** Neither you nor your father exhibit any tendency towards holiness: you really *are* of another era, part of what happened when the Negro left the land and came into what the late E. Franklin Frazier called "the cities of destruction." You can only be destroyed by believing that you really are what the white world calls a *nigger*. I tell you this because I love you, and please don't you ever forget it.

I have known both of you all your lives, have carried your Daddy in my arms and on my shoulders, kissed and spanked

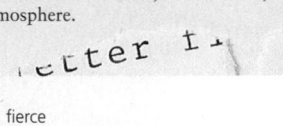

Copyright © Julian Allen.

him and watched him learn to walk. I don't know if you've known anybody from that far back; if you've loved anybody that long, first as an infant, then as a child, then as a man, you gain a strange perspective on time and human pain and effort. Other people cannot see what I see whenever I look into your father's face, for behind your father's face as it is today are all those other faces which were his. Let him laugh and I see a cellar your father does not remember and a house he does not remember and I hear in his present laughter his laughter as a child. Let him curse and I remember him falling down the cellar steps, and howling, and I remember, with pain, his tears, which my hand or your grandmother's so easily wiped away. But no one's hand can wipe away those tears he sheds invisibly today, which one hears in his laughter and in his speech and in his songs. I know what the world has done to my brother and how narrowly he has survived it. And I know, which is much worse, and this is the crime of which I accuse my country and my countrymen, and for which neither I nor time nor history will ever

---

1. **so holy:** Baldwin's stepfather was a minister who raised his children in a strict, conservative, religious atmosphere.

**WORDS TO KNOW**

**truculent** (trŭk′yə-lənt) *adj.* eager for a fight; fierce
**perspective** (pər-spĕk′tĭv) *n.* a mental view or outlook; point of view

960

---

## Teaching Options

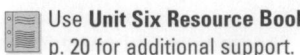

### Mini Lesson **Preteaching Vocabulary**

**USING CONTEXT TO DETERMINE CONNOTATIONS**
**Instruction** Remind students that connotation refers to the ideas or feelings that a word suggests. Substituting a synonym is a good way to explore a word's connotation.
**Exercises** Substitute an appropriate word from the list of WORDS TO KNOW for each underlined word or expression, then comment briefly on how the substituted word changes the effect.

1. Hope to be great! (*aspire;* suggests more possibility of success)
2. I don't like your bold attitude. (*impertinent;* suggests rudeness)

3. She believed that to watch television was to risk mental ruin. (*devastation;* suggests violent destruction)
4. I received an education that never rose above the average. (*mediocrity;* suggests something more inferior)
5. Two small wrongs add up to a serious wrong. (*constitute;* suggests more legal formality)

 Use **Unit Six Resource Book,** p. 20 for additional support.

A lesson on context clues appears on p. 326 in the Pupil's Edition.

forgive them, that they have destroyed and are destroying hundreds of thousands of lives and do not know it and do not want to know it. One can be, indeed one must strive to become, tough and philosophical concerning destruction and death, for this is what most of mankind has been best at since we have heard of man. (But remember: *most* of mankind is not *all* of mankind.) But it is not permissible that the authors of <u>devastation</u> should also be innocent. It is the innocence which <u>constitutes</u> the crime.

Now, my dear namesake, these innocent and well-meaning people, your countrymen, have caused you to be born under conditions not very far removed from those described for us by Charles Dickens in the London of more than a hundred years ago. (I hear the chorus of the innocents screaming, "No! This is not true! How *bitter* you are!"—but I am writing this letter to *you*, to try to tell you something about how to handle *them*, for most of them do not yet really know that you exist. I *know* the conditions under which you were born, for I was there. Your countrymen were *not* there, and haven't made it yet. Your grandmother was also there, and no one has ever accused her of being bitter. I suggest that the innocents check with her. She isn't hard to find. Your countrymen don't know that *she* exists, either, though she has been working for them all their lives.)

Well, you were born, here you came, something like fifteen years ago; and though your father and mother and grandmother, looking about the streets through which they were carrying you, staring at the walls into which

they brought you, had every reason to be heavyhearted, yet they were not. For here you were, Big James, named for me—you were a big baby, I was not—here you were: to be loved. To be loved, baby, hard, at once, and forever, to strengthen you against the loveless world. Remember that: I know how black it looks today, for you. It looked bad that day, too, yes, we were trembling. We have not stopped trembling yet, but if we had not loved each other none of us would have survived. And now you must survive because we love you, and for the sake of your children and your children's children.

This innocent country set you down in a ghetto in which, in fact, it intended that you should perish. Let me spell out precisely what I mean by that, for the heart of the matter is here, and the root of my dispute with my country. You were born where you were born and faced the future that you faced because you were black and *for no other reason*. The limits of your ambition were, thus, expected to be set forever. You were born into a society which spelled out with brutal clarity, and in as many ways as possible, that you were a worthless human being. You were not expected to <u>aspire</u> to excellence: you were expected to make peace with <u>mediocrity</u>. Wherever you have turned, James, in your short time on this earth, you have been told where you could go and what you could do (and *how* you could do it) and where you could live and whom you could marry. I know your countrymen do not agree with me about this, and I hear them saying, "You exaggerate." They do not know Harlem, and I do. So do you. Take no one's word for anything, including mine—but trust your experience.

> It is the innocence which constitutes the crime.

WORDS TO KNOW

**devastation** (dĕv′ə-stā′shən) *n.* complete destruction
**constitute** (kŏn′stĭ-tōōt′) *v.* to amount to; equal
**aspire** (ə-spīr′) *v.* to seek to achieve; strive
**mediocrity** (mē′dē-ŏk′rĭ-tē) *n.* a state of being only average in quality; moderate inferiority

961

## Reading and Analyzing

**Reading Skills and Strategies: QUESTIONING**

**A** Suggest that one way to monitor reading strategies and analyze difficult passages of a text is to formulate and answer questions about it. For example, in this passage, the reader might ask, How does knowing whence you came help remove limitations?

**Possible Response:** Knowledge of where you came from tells you what kinds of assumptions about yourself you may have grown up with. By recognizing the assumptions that limit you, you can change them.

**Literary Analysis: ANALOGY**

**B** Invite students to analyze the comparison in this passage.

**Possible Response:** For many white Americans of Baldwin's era, black self-assertion seemed as strange as if all the stars appeared during the daytime.

**Literary Analysis** `OPEN LETTER`

**C** Students are expected to read in varied sources, including letters. Ask students how the letter format differs from the essay format. Then have them reflect on how the difference in format affects the audience.

**Possible Responses:** The letter format allows writers to present their views in a more personal way because it includes references to the person addressed in the letter. An essay cannot do this. The audience of a letter will be more likely to identify with the writer because they can empathize with his or her relationship with the person to whom the letter is written.

 Use **Unit Six Resource Book,** p. 19 for additional support.

*My Brother* (1942), John Wilson. Oil on panel, 12″ × 10 ⅝″, Smith College Museum of Art, Northampton, Massachusetts, purchased 1943.

**962**

## Teaching Options

### Mini Lesson Viewing and Representing

*My Brother* **by John Wilson**

**ART APPRECIATION** Point out that when John Wilson (1922– ) painted this picture in 1942, he was just 20 years old. His own youthfulness may have helped him capture the poignancy of his brother's youth.

**Instruction** Suggest to students that artists can emphasize or minimize aspects of a subject's character depending on how he or she is portrayed. Ask students to think of four adjectives that capture the character or attitude of Wilson's brother, as shown in the painting.

**Possible Responses:** strong; silent; wounded; wondering

**Application** Have students describe how the meanings they saw in the painting are communicated through elements of design, including shape, line, color, and texture.

**Possible Responses:** Strength is shown by the large, blocky shapes of head and neck; silence is shown by the lines of the lips, which are closed and at rest; woundedness is shown by the lack of symmetry in the eyes, which are alert and aware, yet not wide; the attitude of wonder is shown again by the shape of the eyes.

*t*

Know <u>whence</u> you came. If you know whence you came, there is really no limit to where you can go. The details and symbols of your life have been deliberately constructed to make you believe what white people say about you. Please try to remember that what they believe, as well as what they do and cause you to endure, does not testify to your inferiority but to their inhumanity and fear. Please try to be clear, dear James, through the storm which rages about your youthful head today, about the reality which lies behind the words *acceptance* and *integration*. There is no reason for you to try to become like white people and there is no basis whatever for their <u>impertinent</u> assumption that *they* must accept *you*. The really terrible thing, old buddy, is that *you* must accept *them*. And I mean that very seriously. You must accept them and accept them with love. For these innocent people have no other hope. They are, in effect, still trapped in a history which they do not understand; and until they understand it, they cannot be released from it. They have had to believe for many years, and for innumerable reasons, that black men are inferior to white men. Many of them, indeed, know better, but, as you will discover, people find it very difficult to act on what they know. To act is to be committed, and to be committed is to be in danger. In this case, the danger, in the minds of most white Americans, is the loss of their identity. Try to imagine how you would feel if you woke up one morning to find the sun shining and all the stars aflame. You would be frightened because it is out of the order of nature. Any upheaval in the universe is terrifying because it so profoundly attacks one's sense of one's own reality. Well, the black man has functioned in the white man's world as a fixed star, as an immovable pillar: and as he moves out of his place, heaven and earth are shaken to their founda-

tions. You, don't be afraid. I said that it was intended that you should perish in the ghetto, perish by never being allowed to go behind the white man's definitions, by never being allowed to spell your proper name. You have, and many of us have, defeated this intention; and, by a terrible law, a terrible <u>paradox</u>, those innocents who believed that your imprisonment made them safe are losing their grasp of reality. But these men are your brothers —your lost, younger brothers. And if the word *integration* means anything, this is what it means: that we, with love, shall force our brothers to see themselves as they are, to cease fleeing from reality and begin to change it. For this is your home, my friend, do not be driven from it; great men have done great things here, and will again, and we can make America what America must become. It will be hard, James, but you come from sturdy, peasant stock, men who picked cotton and dammed rivers and built railroads, and, in the teeth of the most terrifying odds, achieved an unassailable and <u>monumental</u> dignity. You come from a long line of great poets, some of the greatest poets since Homer. One of them said, *The very time I thought I was lost, My dungeon shook and my chains fell off.*[2]

You know, and I know, that the country is celebrating one hundred years of freedom one hundred years too soon. We cannot be free until they are free. God bless you, James, and Godspeed.

Your uncle,
James

---

2. *The very time . . . fell off:* a quotation from the traditional spiritual "My Dungeon Shook." It contains an allusion to the biblical story of Paul and Silas (Acts 16), who were freed from an unjust imprisonment by an earthquake that broke their chains and opened the prison doors.

WORDS TO KNOW

**whence** (hwĕns) *adv.* from where
**impertinent** (ĭm-pûr′ tn ənt) *adj.* rude, ill-mannered
**paradox** (păr′ə-dŏks′) *n.* a seemingly contradictory statement that may nevertheless be true
**monumental** (mŏn′yə-mĕn′tl) *adj.* great and lasting

963

## Customizing Instruction

### Less Proficient Readers
Have less proficient readers work in pairs and take turns reading aloud. While one student reads aloud, the other can follow the text silently.

### Students Acquiring English
**1** Explain that Baldwin is interested in showing that words do not always mean what they seem to mean. Thus he suggests that *acceptance* does not mean that the majority (whites) should accept the minority (African Americans), but that the minority should accept the majority. Ask students to be alert to the possibility that Baldwin may be using words in unexpected ways.

### Multiple Intelligences
**Logical-Mathematical Learners**

Invite students to present the relationships among the essay's ideas in graphic form. They might accomplish this by noting key words—such as *innocence*, *integration*, *inhumanity*, *devastation*, *freedom*, *fear*, *blacks*, and *whites*—and using them to create a flowchart or word web showing how the ideas in the essay connect to one another.

### Less Proficient Readers
Make sure students understand the letter's main ideas.
- Ask students what limits Baldwin says society places on African Americans.
**Possible Response:** that they should be obedient and should believe in their own inferiority
- Ask students what advice Baldwin gives his nephew.
**Possible Responses:** to know whence he comes; to make whites understand their prejudice and thus end it

---

## Mini Lesson  Vocabulary Strategy

**DENOTATION AND CONNOTATION**
**Instruction** Understanding vocabulary requires discriminating between denotative and connotative meanings of words. Explain to students that a word's denotation is its dictionary meaning. Its connotation is made up of the attitudes and emotional overtones that the word also communicates.
**Application** Copy the following chart on the board, leaving out the answers in the second and third columns. Have students complete the chart.

| Word | Denotation | Connotation |
|---|---|---|
| innumerable | uncountable | not worthy of being numbered |
| upheaval | major change | violent upset, reversal of order |
| sturdy | strong | rugged, not easily harmed, tough |

Use **Vocabulary Transparencies and Copymasters**, p. 80.

A lesson on denotation and connotation appears on p. 908 in the Pupil's Edition.

## Connect to the Literature

**1. What Do You Think?**
If you were Baldwin's nephew, how would you feel about receiving this letter?

> **Comprehension Check**
> • According to Baldwin, what defeated James's grandfather?
> • What does Baldwin say *integration* means?

## Think Critically

**2.** What do you think Baldwin hoped his nephew would gain from the advice in the letter?

**3.** Do you believe that Baldwin was bitter, as he says his countrymen would claim?

**4.** | **ACTIVE READING** | **ANALYZING CHARACTERISTICS OF CLEARLY WRITTEN TEXTS** | Explain what you think Baldwin meant by "It is the innocence which constitutes the crime." Refer to the interpretation you wrote in your ▥ **READER'S NOTEBOOK**. Discuss your interpretations of other thought-provoking statements.

**5.** What ideas about cultural identity do you get from Baldwin's letter?

> **THINK ABOUT**
> • what he claims can destroy his nephew
> • what he attributes his family's survival to
> • what he says is the root of his dispute with his country
> • what he says white Americans fear and why he thinks they have those fears
> • what he says *integration* means
> • how he describes young James's ancestors

## Extend Interpretations

**6. Critic's Corner** In *Soul on Ice* (1968), the African-American activist Eldridge Cleaver wrote, "There is in James Baldwin's work the most grueling, agonizing, total hatred of the blacks, particularly of himself, and the most shameful, fanatical, fawning, sycophantic love of the whites that one can find in the writing of any black American writer of note in our time." Support or refute this opinion with evidence from the essay.

**7. Connect to Life** How do you think Baldwin would view racial attitudes in American society today?

**8.** **Points of Comparison** Compare and contrast Baldwin's views about race relations with the views expressed by any of the Harlem Renaissance writers you have read.

**964** UNIT SIX PART 1: A NEW CULTURAL IDENTITY

---

## Literary Analysis

> **OPEN LETTER** "My Dungeon Shook" is an **open letter,** addressed to a specific person but published for a wider readership. What in the letter suggests that Baldwin intended it not only for James but for the general public, particularly white Americans? How do you think he wanted them to respond?

**Cooperative Learning Activity**
With a small group of classmates, brainstorm responses that young James might have to his uncle's advice and ideas and the responses that a white American might have. Then draft two letters of response—one in James's voice and the other in the voice of a white American. Share your letters with other groups.

> **REVIEW** **ANALOGY** Baldwin draws an analogy between his nephew's probable reaction to seeing the stars shining while the sun is out and whites' reaction to blacks moving out of their fixed places. How does this analogy help you understand Baldwin's ideas about racism better? With a classmate, write your own analogy to illustrate your ideas about a social or political issue that is important to you.

---

# Choices & CHALLENGES

## Writing Options

**1.** **Points of Comparison**
Imagine that you are the host of a radio show featuring a panel discussion with Zora Neale Hurston and James Baldwin. With two other students, write some questions about race relations in the United States, as well as the comments that each writer might make in response. For your prewriting notes, use some of the ideas you discussed for question 8 on page 964. Re-create the panel discussion for the class.

**2. Personal Response** Write a personal response to Baldwin's letter, reacting to one or more of his paradoxical or thought-provoking statements.

*How can being innocent be criminal?*

**3. Compare-Contrast Essay**
How do you think the social conditions described in Baldwin's letter compare with the conditions under which African Americans live today? Using specific examples from the news and from your own observation, draft a comparison-contrast essay to answer this question. Place this piece in your **Working Portfolio.**

**Writing Handbook**
See page 1281: Compare and Contrast

## Activities & Explorations

**1. Commencement Address** Turn some of the ideas expressed by Baldwin in this letter into a commencement address that he might deliver at a high school graduation. Present the speech to the class. ~ **SPEAKING AND LISTENING**

**2. Photo Gallery of Harlem** Research photographs of Harlem in the 1960s. Choose several that you think best illustrate Baldwin's letter to his nephew, and show them to the class. ~ **VIEWING AND REPRESENTING**

**3. Group Discussion** In a small-group discussion, talk about a time when others' beliefs about you—either positive or negative—influenced your behavior or self-perception. Would you say that Baldwin's warning not to listen to negative messages from society applies more to young African-American men than to others? If you have a computer, extend the discussion through electronic mail, asking for opinions from friends or groups you belong to. ~ **SPEAKING AND LISTENING**

## Art Connection

An interesting aspect of John Wilson's painting *My Brother* (page 962) is that the face is painted in detail, whereas the background is barely sketched in. What do you think the artist achieves by this contrast? What is your impression of his brother?

Detail of *My Brother* (1942), John Wilson

## Inquiry & Research

**Music** Spirituals, such as the one Baldwin quotes at the end of his letter, express the pain caused by the oppression of slavery, as well as a hope for freedom. Find a recording of "My Dungeon Shook," the spiritual quoted by Baldwin, and play it for the class; or perform the song yourself, alone or with a group. Why do you think Baldwin alluded to the song in his title?

---

## ✓ Assessment Informal Assessment

**MAKING INFERENCES AND GENERALIZATIONS**
You can informally assess students' basic understanding of a written text and ability to analyze information in order to make inferences and generalizations by having them think about the following statement in Baldwin's letter:
*"My countrymen . . . have destroyed and are destroying hundreds of thousands of lives and do not know it and do not want to know it."*
Ask students to write a brief essay describing what Baldwin means by "destroying lives." Explain how this destruction takes place and what its results are.

**RUBRIC**
**3** **Full Accomplishment** Response describes and gives examples of several ways in which African Americans may be hampered in the pursuit of their goals.
**2** **Substantial Accomplishment** Response shows some understanding of the broad range of challenges faced by African Americans.
**1** **Little or Partial Accomplishment** Response does not demonstrate understanding of Baldwin's meaning and the challenges faced by African Americans.

---

## Writing Options

1. **Points of Comparison** Students' work should accurately reflect the views of Zora Neale Hurston and James Baldwin. **To get students started on this activity,** suggest that they reread selections by the writers and formulate questions.

2. **Personal Response** Students should choose one particular comment of Baldwin's and treat it directly in their responses. **To get students started on this activity,** encourage students to refer to the list of contradictory or thought-provoking statements they recorded in their Reader's Notebooks (see page 959).

3. **Compare-Contrast Essay** Students' opinions of today's social conditions will vary widely. Encourage them to develop examples through discussion with classmates as well as through research. **Sources of information** include newspapers, news magazines, and publications directed specifically at African Americans.

## Activities & Explorations

1. **Commencement Address** Remind students that a commencement address is primarily for the graduating class, but that parents and faculty members will also hear it. **To get students started on this activity,** have them read through Baldwin's letter searching out comments that would apply to young people who will soon be starting college or employment.

2. **Photo Gallery of Harlem** Photographs students present should be authentic. **Sources of information** include school, public, or college library collections. Encourage students to ask librarians for help.

3. **Group Discussion** Remind students that listening and speaking are equally important aspects of discussion. Students' opinions on the applicability of Baldwin's warning will vary with their life experience and knowledge.

# Art Connection

Possible Response: The artist emphasizes the dignity of an individual rather than the material status of his surroundings. Students might use words such as *serious, thoughtful,* or *sad.*

# Inquiry & Research

**Music** Baldwin may have alluded to the song both to express a hope for freedom in a time of crisis and to demonstrate the creative genius of African Americans. **To make this assignment more challenging,** encourage students to bring in other spirituals as well. You might recommend the recordings of African-American singers Paul Robeson, Marian Anderson, and Mahalia Jackson, all of whom are especially famous for singing spirituals.

# Vocabulary in Action

1. mediocrity
2. monumental
3. aspire
4. devastation
5. perspective
6. truculent
7. paradox
8. whence
9. constitute
10. impertinent

## Vocabulary in Action

**ACTIVITY: CONTEXT CLUES** Write the vocabulary word that best completes each sentence.

1. Abraham Lincoln has been praised by some and condemned by others, but virtually no one has accused him of _____

2. The Emancipation Proclamation he issued in 1863 had a _____ effect on the North's ability to win the Civil War.

3. Many Northerners thought that the nation should _____ to become a true "land of the free."

4. The South, fearing the _____ of its way of life, had seceded from the Union rather than risk losing the power to decide about slavery.

5. Lincoln thought slavery was wrong, but it was his _____ on the war—not on slavery—that caused him to issue the Emancipation Proclamation.

6. He knew that the border states, which were not fighting against the Union, could change their attitude toward the North to a _____ one if he declared that all slaves were free.

7. This concern resulted in the _____ that slaves were freed by the Union only in the areas outside any Union control.

8. To achieve freedom, then, a slave who reached Union lines would have to declare _____ he or she had come.

9. Lincoln's belief was that freeing Southern slaves and allowing them to enlist with Union forces could _____ a significant advantage for the North.

10. Does it show an _____ disrespect for Lincoln to suggest that his proclamation was too limited?

| WORDS TO KNOW | aspire | constitute | devastation | impertinent | mediocrity |
|---|---|---|---|---|---|
| | monumental | paradox | perspective | truculent | whence |

**Building Vocabulary**
For an in-depth study of context clues, see page 326.

## James Baldwin
### 1924–1987

**Other Works**
*Nobody Knows My Name*
*The Price of the Ticket*
*The Amen Corner*
*"Sonny's Blues"*

**Inspired Youth** Born and raised in Harlem, James Baldwin had to endure not only terrible poverty but harsh treatment by his stepfather and the burden of taking care of eight younger siblings while his mother worked. Baldwin realized later that "my teachers somehow made me believe that I could learn. And when I could scarcely see for myself any future at all, my teachers told me that the future was mine… everything was up to me."

**Preacher Turned Writer** When he was 14, Baldwin became a successful preacher, but he had quit preaching by the time he graduated from high school. Determined to become a writer, he moved to Greenwich Village in 1944.

**Settles in Paris** In 1948, tormented by the racial discrimination he saw around him, Baldwin moved to Paris, where he remained for most of his life.

**Critic of Society** Although Baldwin's fiction, especially the novel *Go Tell It on the Mountain,* was well received, it was his eloquent nonfiction—such as *Notes of a Native Son* and *The Fire Next Time*—that made him famous. In many of his essays, he took the role of "disturber of the peace," urging whites to face their racism and the damage it did. Baldwin never stopped challenging the country he loved to live up to its democratic ideals.

# Teaching Options

**Mini Lesson** **Grammar**

**PARALLEL COMPOUND PREDICATES**
**Instruction** Parallelism means using similar grammatical structures for ideas that are equal or similar. Compound predicates should refer to the same subject. In the case of a triple compound predicate, the subject either should appear just once or should occur three times.
**Exercises** In each sentence below, have students correct the structure so that it is parallel.

1. Your grandfather is dead, never saw you, and he had a terrible life.
**Possible Response:** Your grandfather is dead, he never saw you, and he had a terrible life.

2. I have carried your daddy in my arms, kiss him, and watching him learn to walk.
**Possible Response:** I have carried your daddy in my arms, kissed him, and watched him learn to walk.

 Use **Grammar Transparencies and Copymasters,** p. 165.

 Use McDougal Littell's *Language Network,* Chapter 15, for more instruction and practice in parallelism.

# Life for My Child Is Simple ❧ Primer for Blacks

*Poetry by* GWENDOLYN BROOKS

**Comparing Literature**

## Traditions Across Time: Reaffirming Cultural Identity

As a child, Gwendolyn Brooks met James Weldon Johnson and Langston Hughes, two of the distinguished poets of the Harlem Renaissance. Throughout her long career, Brooks's poetry has reflected the influence of this movement, particularly its affirmation of African-American cultural identity. The two poems you are about to read "Life for My Child Is Simple" and "Primer for Blacks"—explore the importance of self-esteem and racial pride, respectively.

**Points of Comparison** Consider how Brooks's ideas about African-American cultural identity compare with those of the other writers in this part of Unit Six.

## Build Background

**Thematic Shift** At the start of her career, Gwendolyn Brooks often wrote about the effects of racism and poverty on individuals' self-esteem. "Life for My Child Is Simple," from her Pulitzer Prize-winning collection *Annie Allen,* is one of a series of poems that trace the life of a fictitious African-American woman from infancy through motherhood and maturity. Although the speaker is Annie Allen, Brooks drew on her own experiences of raising her son, Henry, in writing this poem.

From 1967 on, Brooks became increasingly committed to political and social issues. Shifting her focus from the individual to African Americans in general, Brooks began to address, in poems such as "Primer for Blacks" and "To Those of My Sisters Who Kept Their Naturals," the lack of black unity and self-esteem that she perceived.

## Focus Your Reading

**LITERARY ANALYSIS** **STYLE** **Style** is the distinctive way in which a work of literature is written. Style refers not so much to what is said but how it is said. Two elements contributing to style are **diction** (word choice) and **tone** (writer's attitude). Consider ways in which these poems differ in style.

**ACTIVE READING** **COMPARING AND CONTRASTING POEMS**
Brooks wrote "Life for My Child Is Simple" early in her career and "Primer for Blacks" many years later. To determine the similarities and differences in the poems, try these tips:

- Ask yourself what is the focus or subject of each poem.
- List each speaker's main qualities.
- Describe each speaker's tone.
- Consider the diction in each poem. Are the words simple or difficult, common or unusual, concrete or abstract?
- Identify the theme of each poem—the approach to life it suggests.

**READER'S NOTEBOOK** On a compare/contrast matrix like the one shown, chart the attributes of these two poems.

| | "Life for My Child Is Simple" | "Primer for Blacks" |
|---|---|---|
| Subject | | |
| Speaker | | |
| Tone | | |
| Diction | | |
| Theme | | |

## Objectives
1. understand and appreciate two **poems (Literary Analysis)**
2. identify and examine **style** in poetry **(Literary Analysis)**
3. compare and contrast poems **(Active Reading)**

## Summary
"Life for My Child Is Simple" details some of the boisterous pleasures of a toddler, including throwing blocks out the window and pulling down curtains. Brooks suggests that although these pleasures are transient, naughty, and even dangerous, at least the child is reaching out toward the world and experience—a good instinct. "Primer for Blacks" encourages African Americans to appreciate their heritage and live out their pride in themselves.

## Thematic Link
Encourage students to note the distinctive characteristics of African-American culture in Brooks's poetry. Brooks bridges the **Harlem Renaissance** and the **Black Pride** movement of the 1960s. Like the poets and artists of the earlier time and the political activists of the later time, Brooks was working to forge **a new cultural identity** for African Americans.

### 5-Minute Warm-Up

*Daily Language SkillBuilder*

Have students **proofread** the display sentences on page 913j and write them correctly. The sentences also appear on Transparency 27 of **Grammar Transparencies and Copymasters.**

---

## LESSON RESOURCES

**UNIT SIX RESOURCE BOOK,** pp. 22–23

**ASSESSMENT RESOURCES**
**Formal Assessment,** pp. 179–180
**Teacher's Guide to Assessment and Portfolio Use**
**Test Generator**

**SKILLS TRANSPARENCIES AND COPYMASTERS**
**Literary Analysis**
- Style, Voice, T23 (for Cooperative Learning Activity, p. 971)

**Reading and Critical Thinking**
- Compare and Contrast, T15 (for Extend Interpretations, item 7, p. 971)

**Grammar**
- Punctuating Elements in a Series, T54 (for Mini Lesson, p. 972)
- Parallelism, T57 (for Mini Lesson, p. 972)
- Parallel Series, C166 (for Mini Lesson, p. 972)

**Vocabulary**
- Prefixes, C81 (for Mini Lesson, p. 969)

**Writing**
- Achieving Conciseness, T21 (for Writing Option 2, p. 972)

**Communications**
- Dramatic Reading, T12 (for Activities & Explorations 2, p. 972)
- Impromptu Speaking: Dialogue, Role-Play, Debate, T13 (for Mini Lesson, p. 970)

**INTEGRATED TECHNOLOGY**
**Audio Library**
**Visit our website:**
www.mcdougallittell.com

## Reading and Analyzing

### Literary Analysis | STYLE

Students are expected to analyze the characteristics of clearly written texts, including diction, a key aspect of style. To compare the diction of the two poems, ask students to find words in "Life for My Child Is Simple" that would be inappropriate in "Primer for Blacks," and vice versa.

**Possible Responses:** "Life": *slooshing sloppily*—line 13; "Primer": *geographic power*—line 17; *prime out-ride*—line 40; *ultimate Reality*—line 43

 Use **Unit Six Resource Book**, p. 23 for additional support.

### Active Reading

COMPARING AND
CONTRASTING POEMS

Point out the contrast between the two poems by asking the following questions:

• Which poem could have been written by someone of any race?
  **Answer:** "Life for My Child Is Simple"

• Which poem encourages people to reach for their potential?
  **Answer:** both

• Which poem celebrates the individual, and which celebrates the power of the group?
  **Answer:** "Life" celebrates the individual; "Primer" celebrates the group.

• Which poem uses anaphora (repetition at the beginning of a line)?
  **Answer:** both

 Use **Unit Six Resource Book**, p. 22 for additional support.

# Life for My Child Is Simple

## GWENDOLYN BROOKS

Life for my child is simple, and is good.
He knows his wish. Yes, but that is not all.
Because I know mine too.
And we both want joy of undeep and unabiding[1] things,
5   Like kicking over a chair or throwing blocks out of a window
Or tipping over an ice box pan
Or snatching down curtains or fingering an electric outlet
Or a journey or a friend or an illegal kiss.
No. There is more to it than that.
10  It is that he has never been afraid.
Rather, he reaches out and lo the chair falls with a beautiful crash,
And the blocks fall, down on the people's heads,
And the water comes slooshing sloppily out across the floor.
And so forth.
15  Not that success, for him, is sure, infallible.[2]
But never has he been afraid to reach.
His lesions are legion.[3]
But reaching is his rule.

---

1. **unabiding:** not lasting; continually changing.
2. **infallible** (ĭn-făl′ə-bəl): foolproof.
3. **His lesions are legion:** His injuries are many.

## Thinking Through the Literature

1. **Comprehension Check** Name one quality that the speaker admires about her son.
2. Why do you think the speaker's son is not "afraid to reach"?
3. What do you think "reaching" means to the speaker of this poem?
4. How would you describe the speaker's feelings for her child? Cite lines to support your answer.

## Thinking Through the Literature

1. **Comprehension Check** Possible Response: his courage to reach
2. Possible Responses: He is too young to have encountered experiences that would cause him fear; he has been raised in a positive spirit that encourages him to explore fearlessly.
3. Possible Responses: Literally, "reaching" means a child's reaching for objects—an important part of early learning. Figuratively, it means reaching or striving for anything in life that a human being might try to achieve or accomplish, such as equality or justice.
4. Possible Responses: The speaker clearly loves and admires her child. She may envy his simple view of life (line 1). She may also be somewhat bemused by his fearlessness and fearful of his future disillusionment (lines 15–18).

# Primer for Blacks

**GWENDOLYN BROOKS**

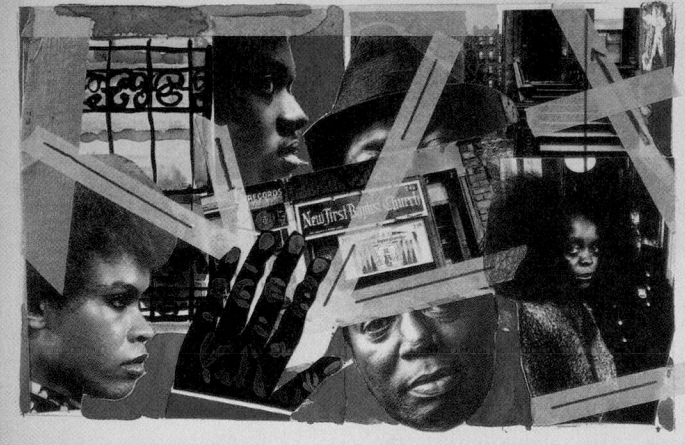

*110th Street*, Romare Bearden (1914–1988), Collage on paper, 14" × 22". Collection of Sam Shaw. Copyright © Romare Bearden Foundation/Licensed by VAGA, New York.

Blackness
is a title,
is a preoccupation,
is a commitment Blacks
5   are to comprehend—
and in which you are
to perceive your Glory.

The conscious shout
of all that is white is
10  "It's Great to be white."
The conscious shout
of the slack in Black is
"It's Great to be white."
Thus all that is white
15  has white strength and yours.

The word Black
has geographic power,
pulls everybody in:
Blacks here—
20  Blacks there—
Blacks wherever they may be.
And remember, you Blacks, what they told you—
remember your Education:
"one Drop—one Drop
25  maketh a brand new Black."

**3 preoccupation:** something that takes one's full attention.

**12 slack:** lack of force.

**24 one Drop:** Historically in the United States, a person has been considered black if he or she has only "one drop" of African blood.

PRIMER FOR BLACKS    **969**

## Customizing Instruction

### Less Proficient Readers
Both of Brooks's poems become much more readily understandable when read aloud. Stage a choral reading in which groups of students take turns reading aloud stanzas from "Primer for Blacks."

### Students Acquiring English
Discuss the following expressions in the two poems that might cause difficulty.
- *ice box pan* ("Life," line 6)—"a pan used to catch water from a melting block of ice in an old-fashioned ice box"
- *slooshing* ("Life," line 13)—an onomatopoetic word that means "splashing" or "flowing"
- *deep-brown middle-brown high-brown* ("Primer," line 36)—"varying shades of brown from deep brown to light brown"

 Use **Spanish Study Guide** for additional support, pp. 239–241.

### Gifted and Talented
Ask students to summarize the two poems and then to discuss or write about what each poem gains and loses by being retold in prose.

### Multiple Learning Styles
**Interpersonal Learners**

Have students exchange ideas about how to improve cultural self-esteem, based on their reading of "Primer for Blacks."

## Vocabulary Strategy

*(Mini Lesson)*

**PREFIXES Instruction** Being able to apply meanings of prefixes in order to comprehend vocabulary is a vital reading skill. Have students study the following chart of prefixes and word meanings.

| Word | Prefix | Stem | Meaning |
|---|---|---|---|
| unabiding | *un-*, "not" | *abide*, "wait" | "not remaining" |
| infallible | *in-*, "not" | *fallible*, "able to fail" | "not able to fail" |
| preoccupation | *pre-*, "before" | *occup-*, "busyness" | "a state of being already busied" |
| metamorphosis | *meta-*, "change" | *-morph-*, "form" | "a change in form" |

**Application** Copy the first two columns of the following chart on the chalkboard. Have students explain the meanings of the full words. Fill in their responses in the third column.

| Word | Stem | Meaning of full word |
|---|---|---|
| undauntable | *dauntable*, "able to be frightened" | "not capable of being frightened" |
| inarguable | *arguable*, "able to be argued" | "not capable of being argued against" |
| prejudice | *-jud-*, "judgment" | "a judgment before evidence is considered" |

Use **Vocabulary Transparencies and Copymasters**, p. 81.

A lesson on prefixes appears on p. 1130 in the Pupil's Edition.

## Literary Analysis: ANAPHORA

**A** Ask students to describe the effect of the repetition in lines 32–37.

**Possible Responses:** It gives equal weight to each shade of blackness; it emphasizes the sameness and unity of all types of blacks; it celebrates all types of blacks; it adds to the musicality of the lines.

## Reading Skills and Strategies: CLARIFYING

Suggest that one means of clarifying the text of a poem is to restate its message stanza by stanza. Have students clarify the text by restating the overall point of each stanza.

**Possible Responses:** Lines 1–7: blackness should be a focus for blacks; lines 8–15: whites are strong; lines 16–25: but blackness is strong, too, because it is widespread; lines 26–39: many partake of blackness and contribute to its strength; lines 40–47: blacks should dedicate themselves to being proud of their culture; lines 48–50: even blacks with low self-esteem should recognize that they are the backbone of black pride; lines 51–63: all blacks are included in blackness.

## Literary Analysis  STYLE

Ask students to compare the tone, or the writer's attitude toward her subject, in the two poems.

**Possible Response:** "Life" is written in a loving, joyous, infinitely patient tone; "Primer" is written in a rousing, no-nonsense, impatient tone.

---

Oh mighty Drop.
And because they have given us kindly
so many more of our people
Blackness
30    stretches over the land.
Blackness—
the Black of it,
the rust-red of it,
the milk and cream of it,
35    the tan and yellow-tan of it,
the deep-brown middle-brown high-brown of it,
the "olive" and ochre of it—
Blackness
marches on.

40    The huge, the pungent object of our prime out-ride
is to Comprehend,
to salute and to Love the fact that we are Black,
which *is* our "ultimate Reality,"
which is the lone ground
45    from which our meaningful metamorphosis,
from which our prosperous staccato,
group or individual, can rise.

Self-shriveled Blacks.
Begin with gaunt and marvelous concession:
50    YOU are our costume and our fundamental bone.

All of you—
you COLORED ones,
you NEGRO ones,
those of you who proudly cry
55    "I'm half INDian"—
those of you who proudly screech
"I'VE got the blood of George WASHington in MY veins"—
ALL of you—
you proper Blacks,
60    you half-Blacks,
you wish I weren't Blacks,
Niggeroes and Niggerenes.

You.

**37 ochre** (ō'kər): brownish orange-yellow.

**40 pungent** (pŭn'jənt): sharp and intense, like a powerful odor; **prime out-ride:** literally "principal riding out," perhaps here meaning "main effort."

**43 "ultimate Reality":** Here Brooks is quoting the activist Ron Karenga.

**46 staccato** (stə-kä'tō): the playing of musical notes in a crisp, disconnected way.

---

# Teaching Options

 **Mini Lesson** ## Speaking and Listening

### ROUNDTABLE DISCUSSION

**Prepare** Have students prepare for a roundtable discussion of "Primer for Blacks." Each student should write down three questions pertaining to the poem that he or she would like other students to help answer. Topics they should consider are the effect of the poem on black self-esteem; the effect of the poem on relations between the various races in the United States; the time frame in which the poem was written; the meanings of individual lines and stanzas in the poem. Divide students into groups of approximately six and have students seated so they face the center of

their discussion groups.

**Present** Students should take turns proposing their questions for discussion. For the first round or two, each student should have a chance to address each question in turn. You may want to assign a recorder in each group to note key words, phrases, or concepts that are shared. As the discussion concludes, revisit the results with the class as a whole, talking over the ideas raised in response to the more interesting questions.

**BLOCK SCHEDULING** This activity is particularly well-suited for longer class periods.

## Connect to the Literature

**1. What Do You Think?**
What emotions does "Primer for Blacks" stir in you? Share your response with your classmates.

**Comprehension Check**
• What does the speaker say should be the main effort of black people?

## Think Critically

**2.** Whom do you think the speaker is addressing at the end of the poem, and how do you think they are meant to feel?

**3.** What points about "Blackness" do you think the speaker makes in this poem?

> THINK ABOUT
> • the definitions in the first stanza
> • the comparison with whiteness in the second stanza
> • what "geographic power" might mean (line 17)
> • the different colors mentioned in lines 32–39
> • what can rise from "the fact that we are Black" (lines 42–47)
> • what the "concession" asked for in line 49 might be

**4.** Do you agree with the speaker's ideas about blackness?

**5.** ACTIVE READING COMPARING AND CONTRASTING POEMS
In your opinion, do "Life for My Child Is Simple" and "Primer for Blacks" suggest similar ways or different ways of approaching life? In explaining your response, refer to the compare/contrast matrix in your READER'S NOTEBOOK.

## Extend Interpretations

**6. Connect to Life** How important do you think it is to develop self-esteem and racial pride?

**7.** Points of Comparison Of the other writers represented in this part of Unit Six, whose ideas about African-American cultural identity are closest to Brooks's? Whose are farthest from hers? Support your views.

## Literary Analysis

**STYLE** **Style** is the way in which a piece of literature is written. Style refers not so much to what is said but how it is said. Many elements contribute to style—for example, tone, word choice, and imagery; sound devices such as repetition, rhyme, and alliteration; as well as the use of capitalization and punctuation. One type of repetition is **anaphora** (ə-năf'ər-ə), or the repetition of a word or words at the beginning of successive lines, clauses, or sentences.

In "Primer for Blacks," for example, notice the use of anaphora in lines 2–4: "is a title / is a preoccupation / is a commitment…" This repetition creates a cadence in which the definitions of "Blackness" build in importance—from a mere designation ("a title") to an abiding concern ("a preoccupation") to total devotion ("a commitment").

**Cooperative Learning Activity** On the basis of these two poems, in what ways would you say Brooks's style changed in the 30 years between "Life for My Child Is Simple" and "Primer for Blacks"? In what ways did it remain the same? In a small group, discuss these questions. Consider the forms of the poems; the use of sound devices such as repetition, rhyme, and alliteration; and the use of capitalization and punctuation. Record your findings on a chart, and share it with other groups.

## Connect to the Literature

**1. What Do You Think?**
Some students may feel new courage to acknowledge and be proud of their background, whatever it may be, as a result of reading the poem. Others may feel new sympathy for the struggles of African Americans and other minorities.

**Comprehension Check**
• To comprehend, salute, and love the fact that they are black

## Think Critically

**2. Possible Responses:** Some students may say she addresses African Americans who have not found a positive cultural identity. It is also possible that she addresses all blacks and wants them to realize the importance of black pride.

**3. Possible Responses:** Blackness is beautiful; it is a broad and powerful and preoccupying cultural identity; it includes many people of varied backgrounds, in different places, and of varied skin tones; it can give rise to great achievements through individual and group pride; it should not be slighted or used as a source of self-hate; it should recognize its own importance.

**4. Possible Responses:** Yes, cultivating cultural self-esteem is the first step in achieving selfhood and empowerment; no, the human individual is more important than any identification with the color of one's skin.

**5. Possible Response:** Yes; they stress the importance of living up to your full potential, of striving to be all you can be. Students should refer to the compare/contrast matrix they prepared in response to Reader's Notebook on page 967 when explaining their response.

## Extend Interpretations

**Connect to Life** Students should be able to discuss the importance of self-esteem; and even if they do not agree that racial pride is important, they should understand the negative consequences of failing to appreciate the value of one's heritage and the companionship of others of similar circumstances. **To get students started on this assignment,** ask them to list the consequences of self-esteem and racial pride.

**Points of Comparison** **To get students started on this assignment,** have them reread the earlier selections in Unit Six, taking notes on how cultural identity is represented and discussed in the different works.

## Literary Analysis

**Style** Ask students to identify other stylistic features of the two poems and to explain the effect they have on the reader.

## Writing Options

1. **Points of Comparison** Emphasize that students are only being asked to write a proposal, not an entire research paper. They should base their work closely on the ideas discussed previously. **To make this assignment more challenging,** ask students to undertake the research they have outlined in their proposals.

2. **Yearbook Biography** Some of the accomplishments such a boy might have might be sports-related or intellectually oriented, such as being a member of the math team or editor of the yearbook—any position that requires reaching toward a particular goal and attaining it. **To get students started on this activity,** discuss the kinds of personality profiles and accomplishments that are included in yearbooks. Ask them which of the accomplishments the boy in the poem might duplicate. List those activities and have them add more to the list.

3. **Summary of Brooks's Message** Students may reduce each stanza of the poem to one or two sentences in their summaries. Abstracts should be continuous, narrative-type summaries written in complete sentences. **To get students started on this activity,** review with them the results of the activity on clarifying on page 970 of the Teacher's Edition. Students can expand on those restatements to create their abstracts.

## Activities & Explorations

1. **T-shirt Emblem** Encourage students to use both text and graphics in their shirt designs. Students may wish to work in pairs or independently. You may wish to make this a joint project with the school art staff.

2. **Preach a Sermon** Sensitivity to racial stereotypes is important for this activity. You might suggest that students alter the ethnic identity of the speaker if they feel more comfortable doing so. **To make this activity easier,** ask students to write their sermons instead of giving them orally.

---

# Choices & Challenges

## Writing Options

1. [ **Points of Comparison** ] Write a proposal for a research paper based on the ideas you discussed for question 7 on page 971. Place this piece in your **Working Portfolio.**

**Writing Handbook**
See page 1287: Research Report Writing

2. **Yearbook Biography** What do you think the young boy described in "Life for My Child Is Simple" will be like as he grows older? Write a list of accomplishments to accompany his high school yearbook picture.

3. **Summary of Brooks's Message** Brooks calls "Primer for Blacks" a "preachment"—a statement intended to teach and to inspire to action. Write an abstract of the poem, summarizing the main points of the lesson that Brooks teaches.

## Activities & Explorations

1. **T-shirt Emblem** Design a T-shirt to illustrate the theme of "Life for My Child Is Simple" or "Primer for Blacks." If possible, actually make the T-shirt and wear it to class. ~ ART

2. **Preach a Sermon** Prepare a sermon based on "Primer for Blacks," and deliver it to the class. Try to reflect the speaker's tone in your delivery and to make each member of your audience feel as if you were speaking directly to him or her. ~ SPEAKING AND LISTENING

## Gwendolyn Brooks
### 1917–2000

**Other Works**
*Maud Martha*
*The Bean Eaters*
*To Disembark*
*The Near-Johannesburg Boy and Other Poems*

**Childhood Influences** Gwendolyn Brooks was born in Topeka, Kansas, but was taken as an infant to Chicago, which became her permanent home and a frequent setting for her poems. In her family's creative household, her early interest in writing poetry was nurtured by her mother, who told her that she would be the "lady Paul Laurence Dunbar" and took her to meet the Harlem Renaissance writers James Weldon Johnson and Langston Hughes. Her first published poem appeared in a children's magazine when she was 13.

**Early Works** After graduating from junior college, Brooks continued to write. In the early 1940s, she attended a poetry workshop taught by Inez Cunningham Stark, a socialite who was a reader for *Poetry* magazine, where Brooks was introduced to the work of such modernist poets as T. S. Eliot. She published her first poetry collection, *A Street in*

*Bronzeville,* in 1945, and with her second book, *Annie Allen,* she became the first African-American author to win a Pulitzer Prize.

**Watershed Event** A pivotal point in Brooks's career came in 1967, when she attended the Second Black Writers' Conference at Fisk University. After meeting younger, more militant African-American poets there, Brooks began responding in her poems to the social upheavals of the time, dealing with such subjects as Malcolm X, urban riots, and street-gang warfare. She has said, "Until 1967 my own blackness did not confront me with a shrill spelling of itself."

**Honored Poet** Among the honors Brooks has received are appointments as poet laureate of Illinois in 1968 and as poetry consultant to the Library of Congress in 1985. She has also received more than 50 honorary doctorates and in 1980 read her poetry at the White House.

## Author Activity

Read additional poems by Brooks—such as "Kitchenette Building," "One wants a Teller in a time like this," and "Horses Graze"—and analyze the style of each one.

---

## (Mini Lesson) Grammar

**PARALLEL SERIES** To use parallelism is to use a consistent structure in parts of a sentence that serve similar purposes. An element such as a preposition or an article should not appear in just two parts of a series of three; instead it should appear in all three. Write the following examples on the chalkboard:

Incorrect: Our object is to comprehend, salute, and to love blackness.

Correct: Our object is to comprehend, salute, and love blackness.

Correct: Our object is to comprehend, to salute, and to love blackness.

**Exercises** In the sentence below, have students revise the structure so that it is parallel.

His activities include throwing blocks, he tipped pans, snatching down curtains.

**Possible Response:** His activities include throwing blocks, tipping pans, and snatching down curtains.

 Use **Grammar Transparencies and Copymasters,** p. 166.

 Use McDougal Littell's *Language Network,* Chapter 15, for more instruction and practice in parallelism.

# PREPARING to *Read*

## Thoughts on the African-American Novel

*Literary Criticism by* TONI MORRISON

"What is
left out
is as
important
as what
is there."

**Comparing Literature**

### Traditions Across Time: Reaffirming Cultural Identity

During the Harlem Renaissance, writers, artists, and musicians depicted the realities of African-American life. Toni Morrison, a Nobel Prize winner, carries on this work in the late 20th century. In "Thoughts on the African-American Novel," she presents her views about African-American literature.

**Points of Comparison**  As you read, think about Morrison's views and consider how to apply them to other works in this part of Unit 6.

## Build Background

**Community and Language**
Toni Morrison grew up in an African-American community during the Depression. That community and its language—vivid, rhythmic, and magical—helped shape her writing: "I'm completely informed by that community, by my extended family, the language particularly. Not just the survival, but the way they spoke... this incredible merging of new language and Biblical language and sermonic language and street language and standard that created a third thing for me." In the selection you are about to read, Morrison describes the importance of oral language to the African-American novel.

## Focus Your Reading

**LITERARY ANALYSIS**  **LITERARY CRITICISM**  **Literary criticism** refers to a piece of writing—usually an essay—that focuses on a literary work or genre, describing some aspect of it, such as its origin, its characteristics, or its appeal. Consider what makes "Thoughts on the African-American Novel" a work of literary criticism.

**ACTIVE READING**  **IDENTIFYING MAJOR IDEAS**  In this piece, Toni Morrison discusses novels in general and the African-American novel in particular, describing its characteristics. Use these tips to identify the **major ideas,** or the ones that she considers important.

- First read the entire piece to get an overview of Morrison's ideas.
- Then reread each paragraph, and separate the major idea from the supporting details. The major idea is what the whole paragraph is about. The **supporting details** are the words, phrases, and sentences that tell something about the major idea.
- Remember that writers sometimes state the major idea as a topic sentence: other times, the major idea is implied, or suggested, by the details in the paragraph.

**READER'S NOTEBOOK**  As you read "Thoughts on the African-American Novel," use a chart like the one shown to list the major idea of each paragraph.

| Paragraph | Major Idea |
|-----------|-----------|
| 1 | |
| 2 | |
| 3 | |

**Objectives**
1. understand and appreciate an essay of **literary criticism** (Literary Analysis)
2. **identify major ideas** in an essay (Active Reading)

**Summary**
Toni Morrison explains the need for African-American novels and describes their characteristics. She traces the novel as an art form to the rise of the middle class. The novel taught the emerging middle class how to behave in the new conditions created by the Industrial Revolution. Now that black music has become part of the mainstream, African Americans need a new art form to express their values. Morrison argues that the novel best serves this purpose. She states that she deliberately infuses characteristics of black art into her own work. She emphasizes that African-American literature is like music and preaching in its power to elicit a participatory response in the audience.

**Thematic Link**
Like the writers of the **Harlem Renaissance,** Morrison is concerned about African-American **cultural identity**. She describes how a traditional genre, the novel, might express the values of black people.

### 5-Minute Warm-Up

*Daily Language SkillBuilder*

Have students **proofread** the display sentences on page 913j and write them correctly. The sentences also appear on Transparency 27 of **Grammar Transparencies and Copymasters.**

## LESSON RESOURCES

**UNIT SIX RESOURCE BOOK,** pp. 24–28

**ASSESSMENT RESOURCES**
**Formal Assessment,** p. 181
**Teacher's Guide to Assessment and Portfolio Use**
**Test Generator**

**SKILLS TRANSPARENCIES AND COPYMASTERS**
**Reading and Critical Thinking**
- Main Idea and Supporting Details, T12 (for Active Reading, p. 973)

**Grammar**
- Varying Sentence Openings, C167 (for Mini Lesson, p. 977)

**Vocabulary**
- Greek and Latin Roots, C82 (for Mini Lesson, p. 974)

**Writing**
- Elaboration, T10 (for Writing Option 3, p. 977)

**INTEGRATED TECHNOLOGY**

**Audio Library**
**Internet: Research Starter**
**Visit our website:**
www.mcdougallittell.com

**Reading Skills and Strategies:**
**PREVIEW**

Preview the selection by explaining that in this essay, the writer describes why English-language novels were written in the 1800s and what purpose she envisions for African-American novels today.

**Active Reading**

### IDENTIFYING MAJOR IDEAS

 **A** Help students identify main ideas and supporting details in the first paragraph of Morrison's essay.

**Possible Response:** The novel was an art form the middle class needed; the lower class did not need novels; nor did the upper class. Early novels were didactic in nature, teaching the new middle class how to act. Peasant cultures did not need the novel because their members understood the proper rules of behavior for their class.

Use **Unit Six Resource Book,** p. 25 for additional support.

**Literary Analysis**

### LITERARY CRITICISM

Students should be able to read to appreciate a writer's craft and connect literature to historical contexts. Point out that writers often set down their ideas about how writing is supposed to work in order to clarify their ideas and explain their methods to the public. Such essays fall under the category of literary criticism, or criticism (analysis) of literature. In this essay Morrison explains to her public her ideas about the novel.

Use **Unit Six Resource Book,** p. 26 for additional support.

# THOUGHTS ON THE African-American Novel

### TONI MORRISON

 **A** The label "novel" is useful in technical terms because I write prose that is longer than a short story. My sense of the novel is that it has always functioned for the class or the group that wrote it. The history of the novel as a form began when there was a new class, a middle class, to read it; it was an art form that they needed. The lower classes didn't need novels at that time because they had an art form already: they had songs, and dances, and ceremony, and gossip, and celebrations. The aristocracy didn't need it because they had the art that they had patronized,[1] they had their own pictures painted, their own houses built, and they made sure their art separated them from the rest of the world. But when the industrial revolution began, there emerged a new class of people who were neither peasants nor aristocrats. In large measure they had no art form to tell them how to behave in this new situation. So they produced an art form: we call it the novel of manners, an art form designed to tell people something they didn't know. That is, how to behave in this new world, how to distinguish between the good guys and the bad guys. How to get married. What a good living was. What would happen if you strayed from the fold. So that early works such as *Pamela,* by Samuel Richardson, and the Jane Austen material provided social rules and explained behavior, identified outlaws, identified the people, habits, and customs that one should approve of. They were didactic[2] in that sense. That, I think, is probably why the novel was not missed among the so-called peasant cultures. They didn't need it, because they were clear about what their responsibilities were and who and where was evil, and where was good.

But when the peasant class, or lower class, or what have you, confronts the middle class, the city, or the upper classes, they are thrown a little bit into disarray.[3] For a long time, the art form

that was healing for Black people was music. That music is no longer *exclusively* ours, we don't have exclusive rights to it. Other people sing it and play it; it is the mode of contemporary music everywhere. So another form has to take that place, and it seems to me that the novel is needed by African-Americans now in a way that it was not needed before—and it is following along the lines of the function of novels everywhere. We don't live in places where we can hear those stories anymore; parents don't sit around and tell their children those classical, mythological archetypal[4] stories that we heard years ago. But new information has got to get out, and there are several ways to do it. One is in the novel. I regard it as a way to accomplish certain very strong functions—one being the one I just described.

It should be beautiful, and powerful, but it should also *work*. It should have something in it that enlightens; something in it that opens the door and points the way. Something in it that suggests what the conflicts are, what the problems are. But it need not solve those problems because it is not a case study, it is not a recipe. There are things that I try to incorporate into my fiction that are directly and deliberately related to what I regard as the major characteristics of Black art, wherever it is. One of which is the ability to be both print and oral literature: to combine those two aspects so that the stories can be read in silence, of course, but one should be able to hear them as well. It should try deliberately to make you stand up and make you feel something profoundly in the same way that a

---

1. **patronized** (pā′trə-nīzd′): sponsored and supported.
2. **didactic** (dī-dăk′tĭk): intended to instruct.
3. **disarray** (dĭs′ə-rā′): disorder; confusion.
4. **archetypal** (är′kĭ-tī′pəl): serving as a pattern for later examples.

 **1**

**2**

---

## Teaching Options

 **Mini Lesson** ## Vocabulary Strategy

**GREEK AND LATIN ROOTS** **Instruction** Students are expected to apply the meanings of roots in order to comprehend words they encounter while reading. Remind students that many words in the English language derive from Greek or Latin. Copy this chart on the chalkboard.

| Word | Root | Word Meaning |
|------|------|--------------|
| patronize | Latin *pater,* "father" | "to support" |
| didactic | Greek *didaskein,* "to teach" | "intended to teach" |
| automobile | Greek *autos,* "self," and Latin *mobile,* "moving thing" | "a self-driven vehicle" |

**Application** Have students use the information from the chart to explain the meanings of the following words.
1. paternal *("fatherly")*
2. autodidact *("someone who is self-taught")*

Use **Vocabulary Transparencies and Copymasters,** p. 82.

A lesson on word roots appears on p. 444 in the Pupil's Edition.

Black preacher requires his congregation to speak, to join him in the sermon, to behave in a certain way, to stand up and to weep and to cry and to accede[5] or to change and to modify—to expand on the sermon that is being delivered. In the same way that a musician's music is enhanced when there is a response from the audience. Now in a book, which closes, after all—it's of some importance to me to try to make that connection—to try to make that happen also. And, having at my disposal only the letters of the alphabet and some punctuation, I have to provide the places and spaces so that the reader can participate. Because it is the affective[6] and participatory relationship between the artist or the speaker and the audience that is of primary importance, as it is in these other art forms that I have described.

To make the story appear oral, meandering, effortless, spoken—to have the reader *feel* the narrator without *identifying* that narrator, or hearing him or her knock about, and to have the reader work *with* the author in the construction of the book—is what's important. What is left out is as important as what is there. To describe sexual scenes in such a way that they are not clinical, not even explicit[7]—so that the reader brings his own sexuality to the scene and thereby participates in it in a very personal way. And owns it. To construct the dialogue so that it is heard. So that there are no adverbs attached to them: "loudly," "softly," "he said menacingly." The menace should be in the sentence. To use, even formally, a chorus. The real presence of a chorus. Meaning the community or the reader at large, commenting on the action as it goes ahead.

In the books that I have written, the chorus has changed but there has always been a choral note, whether it is the "I" narrator of *Bluest Eye,* or the town functioning as a character in *Sula,* or the neighborhood and the community

that responds in the two parts of town in *Solomon.* Or, as extreme as I've gotten, all of nature thinking and feeling and watching and responding to the action going on in *Tar Baby,* so that they are in the story: the trees hurt, fish are afraid, clouds report, and the bees are alarmed. Those are the ways in which I try to incorporate, into that traditional genre the novel, unorthodox novelistic characteristics— so that it is, in my view, Black, because it uses the characteristics of Black art. I am not suggesting that some of these devices have not been used before and elsewhere—only the reason why I do. I employ them as well as I can. And those are just some; I wish there were ways in which such things could be talked about in the criticism. My general disappointment in some of the criticism that my work has received has nothing to do with approval. It has something to do with the vocabulary used in order to describe these things. I don't like to find my books condemned as bad or praised as good, when that condemnation or that praise is based on criteria from other paradigms[8]. I would much prefer that they were dismissed or embraced based on the success of their accomplishment within the culture out of which I write.

I don't regard Black literature as simply books written *by* Black people, or simply as literature written *about* Black people, or simply as literature that uses a certain mode of language in which you just sort of drop *g*'s. There is something very special and very identifiable about it and it is my struggle to *find* that elusive but identifiable style in the books. My joy is when I think that I have approached it; my misery is when I think I can't get there. ❖

---

5. **accede** (ăk-sēd′): agree.

6. **affective:** emotional.

7. **not clinical, not even explicit:** not coldly impersonal or even clearly detailed.

8. **paradigms** (păr′ə-dīmz′): theoretical frameworks.

## GUIDING STUDENT RESPONSE

### Connect to the Literature

**1. What Do You Think?**
Students may state that Toni Morrison is deeply concerned about making her fiction engage her readers.

**Comprehension Check**
- the middle class
- music
- as stories in print and as oral literature

 Use Selection Quiz
**Unit Six Resource Book,** p. 27.

### Think Critically

**2. Possible Responses:** Morrison states that African Americans, like the middle class in the 18th century, need the novel to teach them how to live and to express their deepest values. African-American novels should have a strong oral element, making readers want to stand up and participate.

**3. Possible Response:** Readers should actually work with the author to construct the story and be given room to inject their own experiences.

**4. Possible Responses:** African-American literature derives from the tradition of oral storytelling. It reflects the heritage and values of black people and, like the arts of music and preaching, evokes a strong participatory response in the audience. A strong choral element is prominent in this literature.

**5. Responses will vary.** Some students may state that one characteristic of all great novels is the element of voice, or "the ability to be both print and oral literature."

**6. Possible Responses:** yes, because I like her writing in the essay and she seems to put her best effort into her work; no, because I don't agree with her essay's argument.

### Literary Analysis

**Literary Criticism** Responses will vary. Some students may choose Hurston's description of her emotional response while listening to jazz. Details such as "my pulse is throbbing like a war drum" help to pull the reader into her experience.

---

### Connect to the Literature

**1. What Do You Think?**
What are your impressions of Toni Morrison from this essay? Share your comments with your classmates.

**Comprehension Check**
- With what social class does Morrison associate the novel?
- According to Morrison, what art form reflected African-American life in the past?
- Morrison says that she intends her stories to work on two levels. Name these two levels.

### Think Critically

**2.** **ACTIVE READING** **IDENTIFYING MAJOR IDEAS**
Review the chart in your 📖 READER'S NOTEBOOK. Based on this chart, how would you summarize Morrison's ideas in this essay?

**3.** How would you describe the way Morrison views her relationship with her readers?

**4.** Based on this essay, how would you explain the major characteristics of African-American literature?

 **THINK ABOUT**
- Morrison's ideas about how novels function
- her comparisons of a writer to a preacher and a musician
- the statement "what is left out is as important as what is there"
- her views about dialogue

**5.** To what extent do you think Morrison's comments about the African-American novel might apply to other kinds of novels as well?

**6.** After reading her essay, would you be interested in reading Morrison's novels? Why or why not?

### Extend Interpretations

**7. Connect to Life** Morrison says that a novel should have "something in it that enlightens... that opens the door and points the way." Think about novels you have read or stories you have heard. Which one opened a door for you, and how?

**8.** **Points of Comparison** Based on her ideas about African-American literature, which of the selections in this part of Unit 6 do you think Morrison might praise the most? Explain your choice.

### Literary Analysis

**LITERARY CRITICISM** **Literary criticism** is a category of writing that focuses on a literary work or a genre, describing some aspect of it, such as its origin, its characteristics, or its effects. Works of literary criticism expand knowledge or enhance appreciation. Often, they put a literary work in a historical or a literary context and describe standards against which to measure its excellence.

**Cooperative Learning Activity**
According to Toni Morrison, an important standard for evaluating a work of African-American literature is whether or not the reader hears its language and responds to it personally. With a small group, choose two or three passages from Zora Neale Hurston's "How It Feels to Be Colored Me," on page 950, to read aloud. Then discuss whether each passage meets Morrison's standard. If so, identify the words, phrases, and sentences that pull you into it; if not, tell what you think the passage lacks. Then choose a member to give an oral interpretation of your favorite passage to the class.

---

### Extend Interpretations

**Connect to Life** Students should relate the novel to their own lives. They might focus on the theme, or the insight about life, that they derived from the work.

**Points of Comparison** Responses will vary. Some students may cite Claude McKay's poem "If We Must Die" for the strong emotional reaction it evokes from the audience.

# Choices & CHALLENGES

## Writing Options

**1. Letter to Toni Morrison** Write a letter to Toni Morrison responding to her ideas about African-American literature.

**2. Points of Comparison**
Create a dialogue in which Toni Morrison and a writer of your choice from Unit 6 share their views about African-American cultural identity.

**3. Essay About Art Form** In an essay modeled on Morrison's,

*Adventure Movies*
• *must take viewers away from ordinary life*

describe the function and the characteristics of a form of entertainment other than the novel—for example, adventure movies, musicals, cartoons, talk shows, interpretive dances, rock concerts, or situation comedies. Put this piece in your **Working Portfolio.** 

## Activities & Explorations

**Illustration** Design a poster to accompany Morrison's essay or an African-American novel of your choice. ~ **ART**

## Inquiry & Research

**Origin of the Novel** Morrison traces the novel to the rise of the middle class during the Industrial Revolution. With a small group, research the origins of the novel in the 18th century. Compile a list of the early novelists, and describe the characteristics of the first novels. Present an oral report to share your findings.

 **More Online: Research Starter**
www.mcdougallittell.com

---

## Toni Morrison
### 1931–

**Other Works**
*The Bluest Eye*
*Sula*
*Tar Baby*
*Jazz*
*Paradise*

**Literary Focus** Drawing on her childhood in the small town of Lorain, Ohio, Toni Morrison vividly re-creates the African American experience in her acclaimed novels. Much of her writing is set in fictional Midwestern African-American communities at various times in history. She has created several unforgettable characters—notably, African-American women who, like Pecola Breedlove in *The Bluest Eye*, suffer the effects of poverty, racism, and violence.

**Novelist, Educator, Editor** After receiving a bachelor's degree from Howard University and a master's degree from Cornell University, Morrison

taught college English for nine years. Then she worked for 20 years at Random House in New York City, editing works by such African Americans as Muhammad Ali, Toni Cade Bambara, Angela Davis, and Andrew Young. In 1989 she was appointed to the Robert F. Goheen Chair in the Council of the Humanities at Princeton University.

**Literary Acclaim** Morrison has won numerous awards and honors. In 1977 she won the prestigious National Book Critics Circle Award for her third novel, *Song of Solomon*, and she was awarded the 1988 Pulitzer Prize for *Beloved*. In 1993 she became the first African American to win the Nobel Prize in literature.

## Author Activity

Read one of Toni Morrison's novels, and then evaluate it according to her own standards for the African-American novel.

---

 **Mini Lesson**  **Grammar**

**VARYING SENTENCE BEGINNINGS Instruction** By varying the beginnings of sentences, students can emphasize different ideas and add interest to their writing. For example, instead of beginning a sentence with the subject, students might begin it with a subordinate clause or a prepositional phrase. Notice the different emphasis in the following sentences:

• Toni Morrison vividly explores the African-American experience in her acclaimed novels.
• In her acclaimed novels, Toni Morrison vividly explores the African-American experience.

The first sentence begins with the subject; the

second sentence begins with a prepositional phrase, giving more emphasis to the writer's "acclaimed novels."

**Application** Working in a small group, have students select a paragraph from Toni Morrison's essay to reread. Then have them list the different ways the sentences begin.

Use **Grammar Transparencies and Copymasters,** p. 167.

Use McDougal Littell's *Language Network,* Chapter 15, for more instruction and practice in sentence beginnings.

---

## Writing Options

1. **Letter to Toni Morrison** Student responses will vary but should reflect an understanding of Morrison's ideas about African-American literature, such as the strong oral element and the importance of the chorus.
2. **Points of Comparison** Students might consider creating a dialogue between Zora Neale Hurston and Toni Morrison.
3. **Essay about Art Form** Essays should present thoughtful, well-organized arguments that reflect understanding of their subject. **To get students started,** have them reread Morrison's essay, noting the sequence and logic of her argument. Suggest methods of prewriting, such as freewriting or making a rough outline or word web.

## Activities & Explorations

**Illustration** Posters should clearly reflect the content of the chosen work. **To get students started,** consult with them on obtaining materials they will need, including posterboard and drawing or painting materials. You may wish to do this activity in cooperation with the art staff in your school. You might also explore the possibility of using computer drawing programs to create the posters.

## Inquiry & Research

**Origin of the Novel** Reports should reflect thorough research into the origins of the novel in the 18th century. Suggest that students summarize the plots of the major novels they list. **To make this assignment more challenging,** have students choose one of the novels on their list to read; they then can discuss the values it taught the middle class in their oral reports.

## Author Activity

In their evaluations, students should identify the choral element in the novel and determine how Morrison attempts to elicit a participatory response in the reader.

## PART 1 Reading the Prompt
Model the process of reading a prompt:
- Read the entire prompt aloud.
- List the key words from the prompt on the board ("compare and contrast the theme about racial identity"; "consider the theme, the tone, and the use of figurative language"; "conclusion").
- Use the Strategies in Action to define key terms and to model how students can restate the prompt in their own words.

## PART 2 Planning a Comparison-Contrast Essay
- Remind students of the works they read by Martin Luther King, Jr., and Malcolm X in Unit 2. They may wish to use one of those modern works to compare and contrast.
- Before students evaluate the two works, have them briefly discuss what criteria they will use to judge whether a piece is effective or not.
- Point out, if necessary, that in this essay students are to consider only the theme about racial identity.

## PART 3 Drafting Your Essay
**Introduction** Students might begin with a general statement about changing attitudes about race during the past 50 years. They can use this to lead into their statement of purpose.

**Organization** Students may find it helpful to make an informal outline of the information that they are presenting. Encourage them to jot down the main points they want to make in the order in which they will present them. Then they can choose the supporting evidence that they will include.

**Conclusion** Students should explain not only which work they think is more effective but also why they made this decision.

**Revision** Remind students that if they use ideas or details from Alice Walker's review of Zora Neale Hurston, they must give her credit in their essays.

## Comparing Literature: Assessment Practice

In writing assessments you will sometimes be asked to compare and contrast two works in terms of certain literary elements. You are now going to practice writing a comparison-contrast essay that ends with an evaluation.

**PART 1** ## Reading the Prompt

To respond to a prompt like the one below, read it carefully more than once. Look for key words that help you identify the purpose of the essay and what you must do.

> **Writing Prompt**
>
> Throughout the 20th century, African-American writers have explored racial identity. In an essay, compare and contrast a work written during the Harlem Renaissance with one written later in the 20th century. Consider the theme, the tone, and the use of figurative language. In your conclusion, tell which work appeals to you more, and why.

**STRATEGIES**
IN ACTION

❶ **Compare and contrast,** or find similarities and differences in, a Harlem Renaissance work and a later work.

❷ Focus on three **literary elements.**

❸ **Conclude** with an opinion about which work is more appealing.

**PART 2** ## Planning a Comparison-Contrast Essay

- Choose two works to compare and contrast.
- Create a compare-and-contrast chart like the one shown.
- On this chart, jot down notes about the theme, tone, and figurative language in each work. Mark similarities and differences.
- Decide which work you prefer.

| | Harlem Renaissance Selection | Later Selection |
|---|---|---|
| Theme | | |
| Tone | | |
| Figurative Language | | |

**PART 3** ## Drafting Your Essay

**Introduction** State the purpose of your essay—to compare and contrast two works of African-American literature.

**Organization** Choose a logical method to present the information. For example, you might devote one paragraph to each literary element or you might cover all the elements in one work in the first part of the essay and all the elements in the other work in the second part.

**Conclusion** Briefly explain why you think one work is more appealing than the other. Be sure your earlier comparisons lead to this conclusion.

**Revision** Allow time to review your work. Make sure it is clear, well-supported, and free from mistakes.

**Writing Handbook**
See page 1281: Compare and Contrast

LITERATURE CONNECTIONS

## The Autobiography of Miss Jane Pittman

ERNEST J. GAINES

These thematically related readings are provided along with *The Autobiography of Miss Jane Pittman:*

**A Conspiracy of Grace**
ETHEL MORGAN SMITH

**Keeping the Thing Going While Things Are Stirring**
SOJOURNER TRUTH

**"It's Such a Pleasure to Learn"**
WALLACE TERRY

**To be of use**
MARGE PIERCY

**Booker T. and W. E. B.**
DUDLEY RANDALL

*from* **Having Our Say: The Delany Sisters' First Hundred years**
SARAH AND A. ELIZABETH DELANY WITH AMY HILL HEARTH

**The First Time I Sat in a Restaurant**
JO CARSON

**The Great White Myth**
ANNA QUINDLEN

**The Old Demon**
PEARL S. BUCK

## Go Tell It on the Mountain

JAMES BALDWIN

These thematically related readings are provided along with *Go Tell It on the Mountain:*

**Notes of a Native Son**
JAMES BALDWIN

**The Whipping**
ROBERT HAYDEN

**The Revelation**
JAMES WRIGHT

**Bright Thursdays**
OLIVE SENIOR

**The Man of Adamant**
NATHANIEL HAWTHORNE

**The Pot Maker**
MARITA BONNER

**Forgiveness in Families**
ALICE MUNRO

*from* **A Bintel Brief**
JEWISH DAILY FORWARD

**The Old Demon**
PEARL S. BUCK

The *Electronic Library* is a CD-ROM that contains additional fiction, nonfiction, poetry, and drama for each unit in *The Language of Literature.*

These are the additional selections found in Unit 6 of the *Electronic Library* that apply to Part 1.

Jean Toomer
**Beehive**
**November Cotton Flower**

Claude McKay
**The Tropics in New York**

Encourage students to select one of the longer works described as an opportunity to read silently with comprehension over a period of time.

## And Even *More* . . .

**Books**

**Selected Poems of Claude McKay**
CLAUDE MCKAY
A sampling of this Harlem Renaissance poet's works.

**Harlem Renaissance: Art of Black America**
EDITED BY DAVID C. DRISKELL
An overview of the artwork produced by painters and sculptors of this period.

**The Portable Harlem Renaissance Reader**
EDITED BY DAVID LEVERING LEWIS
Short stories, novel excerpts, essays, speeches, and other works by 45 Harlem Renaissance writers.

**Other Media**

**Against the Odds: The Artists of the Harlem Renaissance**
A documentary exploring this artistic and literary movement. PBS Video. (VIDEOCASSETTE)

**Go Tell It on the Mountain**
TV adaptation of Baldwin's novel, starring Paul Winfield and Alfre Woodard. Monterey Home Video. (VIDEOCASSETTE)

**Gwendolyn Brooks Reading Her Poetry**
Dramatic oral interpretations by this critically acclaimed poet. Caedmon. (SOUND RECORDING)

### Zora Neale Hurston: Folklore, Memoirs, and Other Writings

ZORA NEALE HURSTON

This compilation of Zora Neale Hurston's nonfiction features the original version of her autobiography *Dust Tracks on a Road,* as well as *Mules and Men,* her ground-breaking collection of African-American folklore. Also included are selected articles and Hurston's book on religious practices in the Americas.

## Objectives

- write a Research Report
- use a written text as a model for writing
- revise a draft to add details and examples
- use commas to clarify the relationship between ideas

## Introducing the Workshop

**A** **Research Report** Ask students in what, if anything, they consider themselves experts. Tell them that by writing research reports, they will become experts on their chosen topics.

Students may already know something about the Harlem Renaissance from previous class readings. The Harlem Renaissance was a fascinating period in African-American history, and much information is available on this topic. In doing a research report, students will focus on a specific aspect of this topic, do research to find out in-depth information about it, and present this information in a coherent, interesting written report.

Doing a research report enables students to gain control of information, and to share that information with others.

### Basics in a Box

**B** **Using the Graphic** The graphic analyzes the four main parts of a research report and briefly describes the function of each. Below the boxes representing the report proper is a box for research, which acts as the foundation upon which the report is built. Students can think of writing a research report as a two-step process, with researching representing the gathering of input, and writing representing the production of output.

**C** **Presenting the Rubric** To better understand the assignment, students can refer to the Standards for Writing a Successful Research Report. You may also want to share with them the complete rubric, which describes several levels of proficiency. Students should know that these standards will be used to assess their Research Reports.

---

# *Writing* Workshop — Research Report

## Researching the history of an era . . .

**A** **From Reading to Writing** We get a mere glimpse of the richness of the cultural scene during the Harlem Renaissance in this unit. It was a time when African Americans used a variety of means to show pride in their race and in the contributions they had made to American culture. This period offers a rich variety of choices for a **research report**—an academic paper that presents and interprets information collected through reading and other research. When you write a research report, you not only deepen your knowledge but you also sharpen your research skills.

**WRITING PROMPT** Write a historical research report about some aspect of the Harlem Renaissance or on another topic that your teacher has approved.

**Purpose:** To share information and to reach a conclusion about your topic

**Audience:** Your classmates, teacher, or anyone else interested in your topic

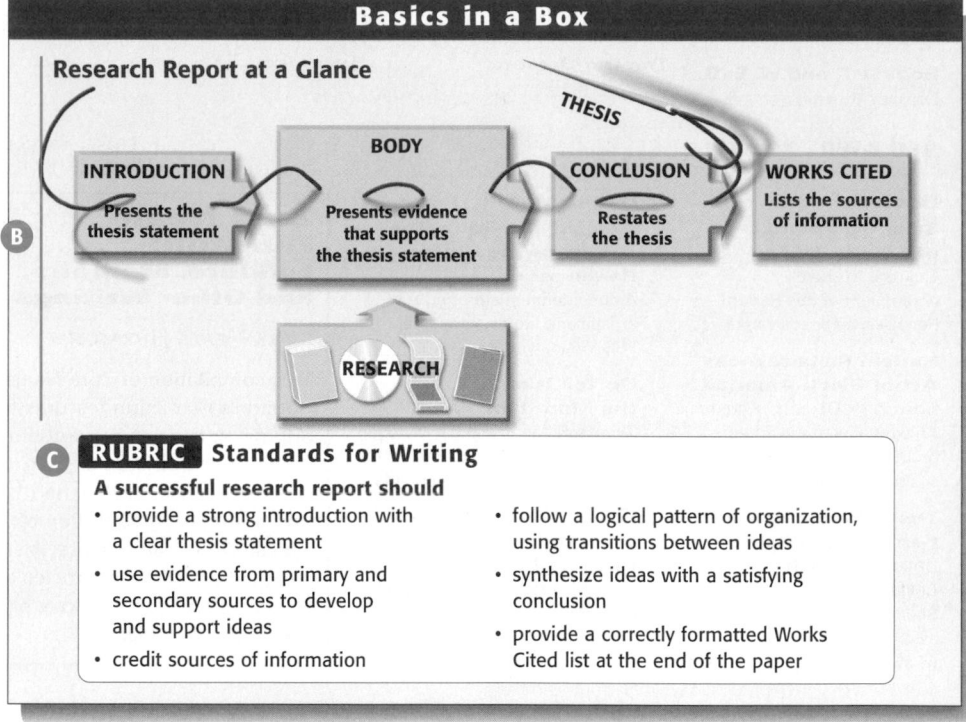

### Basics in a Box

**Research Report at a Glance**

THESIS

**B**

| INTRODUCTION | BODY | CONCLUSION | WORKS CITED |
|---|---|---|---|
| Presents the thesis statement | Presents evidence that supports the thesis statement | Restates the thesis | Lists the sources of information |

RESEARCH

**C** **RUBRIC** **Standards for Writing**

**A successful research report should**

- provide a strong introduction with a clear thesis statement
- use evidence from primary and secondary sources to develop and support ideas
- credit sources of information
- follow a logical pattern of organization, using transitions between ideas
- synthesize ideas with a satisfying conclusion
- provide a correctly formatted Works Cited list at the end of the paper

**980** UNIT SIX PART 1: A NEW CULTURAL IDENTITY

---

## LESSON RESOURCES

**USING PRINT RESOURCES**
**Unit Six Resource Book**
- Prewriting, p. 29
- Drafting and Elaboration, p. 30
- Peer Response, pp. 31–32
- Revising, Editing, and Proofreading, p. 33
- Student Models, pp. 34–39
- Rubric, p. 40

**Writing Transparencies and Copymasters**
- Writing Process Transparencies, pp. 3, 4
- Writing Template Copymasters, p. 33

**USING MEDIA RESOURCES**
**Visit our website:**
www.mcdougallittell.com

# Analyzing a Student Model

Izada Chan
Ms. VanVuren
English III
15 October

Chan 1

## Zora Neale Hurston

Zora Neale Hurston was a black writer who single-mindedly and eloquently spoke for her people and the black culture of the rural South. In reading about her, it is easy to get the impression that she was simply such an indomitable spirit that nothing could silence her or put her down. Basically, that is true, but the whole picture of her life is also much more complicated than that. In fact, she herself was so complicated that one writer titled an essay about her "Zora Neale Hurston: A Woman Half in Shadow" <u>Through an examination of Zora Neale Hurston's work, it will become evident that she was a talented and complex woman with conflicting sides to her personality.</u>

Hurston was a popular figure on the Harlem Renaissance scene from almost the first moment she moved to Harlem in 1925. She was so colorful that "for a long time she was remembered more as a *character* of the Renaissance than as one of the most serious and gifted artists to emerge during this period" <u>(Williams ix)</u>.

A prolific and gifted writer, she published her first story, "John Redding Goes to Sea," in 1921. By the time she died on January 28, 1960, she had written seven books—four novels, two books of folklore, and an autobiography—and over 50 shorter works including a dozen short stories, two plays, and many essays, articles, and newspaper columns. Yet, in spite of the fact that she won many prizes, including two Guggenheims and the Ainsfield-Wolf Book Award in Race Relations, and received much critical acclaim for her work, she died in poverty at the St. Lucie County Welfare Home in Fort Pierce, Florida. She was buried in an unmarked grave in the Garden of Heavenly Rest in Fort Pierce (Gates 289, 298, 311).

Hurston might well have remained unknown to most readers if it hadn't been for Alice Walker, a famous modern black writer. Walker fell in love with Hurston's work when she read *Mules and Men,* a collection of black folktales, Hurston's second book. Walker found Hurston's grave and put a marker on it in 1973. She published an article called "In Search of Zora Neale Hurston" in *Ms.* in 1975. That article led to a revival of interest in Hurston's work. According to Henry Louis Gates, "More people have read Hurston's works since 1975 than did between that date and the publication of her first novel, in 1934" (Gates 294).

**RUBRIC**
IN ACTION

❶ This writer begins with a pro-vocative statement to capture the reader's attention.
**Other Options:**
· Begin with a quotation.
· Relate an anecdote.

❷ Presents the thesis statement

❸ This writer supports a key idea with a direct quotation.
**Other Options:**
· Paraphrase a quotation.
· Summarize information.

❹ Credits sources using parenthetical documentation

❺ This writer presents information in a chronological order.
**Another Option:**
· Present informa-tion in a way that highlights causes and effects.

## Teaching the Lesson

### Analyzing the Model
**"Zora Neale Hurston"**

 The student model evaluates the life and writings of Zora Neale Hurston, a major talent of the Harlem Renaissance. Students may have already read information about Hurston in other selections in this unit; explain that a research paper presents more in-depth information than they have previously seen.

Have students read the model, then discuss the Rubric in Action. Point out the key words and phrases in the student model that correspond to the elements mentioned in the Rubric in Action.

1. As you discuss the other options, refer students to the Works Cited list on page 982. Ask them which sources might be likely places to find the information needed to write an alternate opening.
   **Possible Responses:** Either the Hurston autobiography or McKissack biography might be a good source for a quotation or an anecdote. More accessible information might be found in the Pierpont or Dickinson articles, or in the Walker or Williams forewords to books on or by Hurston.

2. Point out that the student writer used a lengthy sentence to express the complexity of the thesis statement. The writer prepares the reader for the report by saying that she will look at both Hurston's life and her work. She also prepares the reader for conflict within Hurston herself.

3. Remind students that paraphrasing is restating the material in their own words. Ask them to paraphrase the information in the quotation.
   **Possible Response:** During the Harlem Renaissance, Zora Neale Hurston distinguished herself as much for her original lifestyle as she did for her brilliant writing.

 Use McDougal Littell's *Language Network,* Chapter 24, for more instruction on writing a research report.

 To engage students visually, use **Power Presentation** 9, Research Report.

---

**Mini Lesson** ## Viewing and Representing

**PICTURING TEXT STRUCTURE**
**Instruction** A research report is generally a longer piece of writing than other assignments that students have worked on. The student model on pages 981-982 shows only the first part of the report by the student writer. The Works Cited section is included on page 982 so that students can see standard formatting for referencing sources.
**Activity** Have students create a graphic organizer or outline to analyze the text structure of the student model. Students' graphics should provide a breakdown of how the student writer organized

her piece, with the understanding that the entire piece has not been included. A sample outline is shown.

I. Introduction: Thesis Statement
II. Body
   A. Hurston part of Harlem Renaissance
      1. Accomplished writer; died unknown
      2. Rediscovered by Alice Walker
   B. Hurston's life
      1. Born in all-black town
      2. Effect of growing up in Eatonville

**6.** Point out how, in this paragraph, the student writer picks up the information about Eatonville and establishes the effect of living in such a town. Ask students what they think the writer will deal with next in this essay.

**Possible Responses:** The writer might tell how Hurston came to Harlem; the writer might discuss Hurston's education.

## WORKS CITED

A Works Cited section serves a dual function: It establishes the writer's credibility as a researcher, and it identifies sources of information for anyone wishing to read further on the topic. In this Works Cited section, the writer has followed MLA style, the style developed by the Modern Language Association.

Help students analyze the kinds of sources used by the student writer: works by a single author and by two authors; introduction, forewords, and afterword of books; an article from an encyclopedia; a magazine article; and an article found on a computer Website.

Chan 2

Hurston was born in 1891 in a small town called Eatonville, about five miles from Orlando, Florida. As Hurston put it, "Eatonville, Florida, is, and was at the time of my birth, a pure Negro town—charter, mayor, council, town marshall and all. It was not the first Negro community in America, but it was the first to be incorporated, the first attempt at organized self-government on the part of Negroes in America" (Hurston 1).

Growing up in Eatonville meant that Hurston not only was sheltered from much of the rampant racial prejudice of her day but also that she got to see African Americans in control of things, making up their own minds instead of waiting for white people to tell them what to do.

**❻** Uses a transitional phrase between paragraphs to connect ideas

Chan 13

**Works Cited**

Dickinson, Laurie. "Zora Neale Hurston." Voices from the Gaps: Women Writers of Color. Minneapolis: U of Minnesota. 15 June 1998. <http://www-engl.cla.umn.edu.//kd/vfg/Authors/ZoraNeale Hurston1>.

Gates, Henry Louis, Jr. Afterword. Tell My Horse: Voodoo and Life in Haiti and Jamaica. By Zora Neale Hurston. New York: Harper & Row, 1990. 289–311

"Harlem Renaissance." Grolier Multimedia Encyclopedia. 10th ed. CD-ROM. Danbury: Arolier, 1998.

McKissack, Patricia, and Fredrick McKissack. Zora Neale Hurston: Writer and Storyteller. Hillside: Enslow, 1992.

Hemenway, Robert E. Introduction. Dust Tracks on a Road: An Autobiography. By Zora Neale Hurston. Urbana: U of Illinois P, 1984. ix–xxxix.

Hurston, Zora Neale. Dust Tracks on a Road: An Autobiography. Urbana: U of Illinois P, 1984.

Pierpont, Claudia Roth. "A Society of One: Zora Neale Hurston, American Contrarian." The New Yorker 17 Feb. 1997: 80–91.

Walker, Alice. Foreword. Zora Neale Hurston: A Literary Biography. By Robert E. Hemenway. Urbana: U of Illinois P, 1977. xi–xviii.

Williams, Sherley Ann. Foreword. Their Eyes Were Watching God. By Zora Neale Hurston. Urbana: U of Illinois P, 1978. v–xv.

**Works Cited**

· Identifies sources of information used in researching the paper
· Alphabetizes entries by author's last name
· Lists complete publication information
· Punctuates entries correctly
· Double spaces entire list
· Follows a preferred style

**Need help with Works Cited?**

See pages 1290–1292 in the **Writing Handbook.**

# Writing a Research Report

*The important thing is not to stop questioning.*
**Albert Einstein**

## ❶ Prewriting and Exploring

If you are writing your research report on the Harlem Renaissance, you might begin by looking in the library for books or articles not only on the Harlem Renaissance, but also on the 1920s, on individuals whose works appear in this unit, on famous African Americans, on black history, on American jazz, or on American literature. See the **Idea Bank** in the margin for more suggestions on finding a subject. The steps below will also help you choose your subject and define your goal.

### Planning Your Research Report

► **1. Choose a topic.** What subjects really intrigue you? What would you like to learn about one of them? Make a list of ideas that appeal to you and then choose the topic that interests you most. You might also try making a word web like this one to generate ideas.

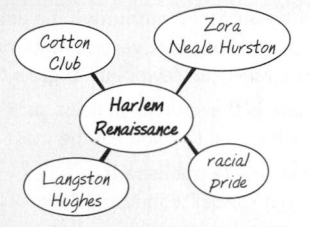

► **2. Narrow your topic.** Is your topic too broad for the research report you plan to write? Can it be divided into smaller parts? You could do some preliminary research in an encyclopedia, or look in the tables of contents and indexes of relevant books to see how they divide the subject into subtopics.

► **3. Decide on your goal.** What do you want to achieve with your report? Do you want to prove a point, draw a conclusion, or just learn and share information about the subject?

► **4. Consider your audience.** What do they already know about the subject? What extra background might they need?

► **5. Write a thesis statement.** Your thesis statement is a sentence that explains what your paper will be about. It will guide your research and help you sort out relevant and irrelevant information on your topic. Be flexible enough to consider reworking your thesis if your research leads you in new directions.

**IDEA** Bank

**1. Your Working Portfolio** 📁
Look for ideas in the **Writing Options** you completed earlier in the unit:

• **Documentary Plan** p. 939

• **Problem-Solution Essay** p. 949

• **Points of Comparison** p. 972

**2. Follow the News**
Look in the newspaper and on news broadcasts for issues, people, or events that intrigue you. Choose one to research and develop.

**3. Surf the Net**
Check out the Internet for ideas that interest you. Try a subject search using various search engines. Choose one topic and explore it further.

## Researching

### Primary and Secondary Sources

Review the examples of primary and secondary sources, and make sure that students understand the difference between them. Interviews are also considered a primary source, and may be applicable if a student is writing about a historical event or period.

Point out to students that literary works such as poetry and novels are not considered appropriate sources for a research report, since a research report relies on sources for facts.

### Evaluate Source Material

Have students share their proposed sources with a peer, and explain the value of each source to the report. Students can use the bulleted questions as criteria for accepting a source. When evaluating source materials, students should include an evaluation of the credibility of information, considering how the writer's motivation may affect credibility. Encourage students to resist the temptation to "pad" their Works Cited list with extraneous sources.

### Make Source Cards

Point out how each of the numbered source cards on this page can be found in the Works Cited list on page 982.

Some students may want to color code their source cards and note cards so that it is always clear which notes were found in which source.

**Research Tip**

Use primary sources when they are available and suit your purpose. Use secondary sources to explain difficult, hard-to-read, or hard-to-find material from primary sources.

**Be Wary on the Internet**

Evaluate information you find on the Internet the same way you would evaluate print material. Information from a government agency (.gov) or an educational institution (.edu) usually will be reputable. Material on someone's personal Web page may or may not be reliable.

**Research Tip**

For each note card you write, be sure to include a reference to the source and the page number where you found the information.

## ❷ Researching

Begin your research by making a list of relevant, interesting, and researchable questions. Use these questions to guide your review of reliable sources. You might look in general reference books, such as encyclopedias, and then examine books, periodicals, and on-line databases for more specific information.

| Source | Type of Information | Examples |
|---|---|---|
| Primary Sources | Direct, firsthand knowledge | letters, journals, diaries, original manuscripts |
| Secondary Sources | Secondhand information gathered from primary sources | encyclopedias, books, newspapers, magazines |

### Evaluate Your Source Material

These guidelines can help you evaluate your sources.

- **Is the author an unbiased authority?** The author's viewpoint may be influenced by his or her political position, gender, or ethnic background. Be sure to read material from a variety of viewpoints to get a balanced picture.

- **How up-to-date is the source?** In fields such as medicine or technology, rapid changes make it crucial that you get the most up-to-date information.

- **Where was the article published?** Newspapers that specialize in scandal or sensational stories, for example, are not reliable sources of information.

- **What is the intended audience?** Is the material written for a general audience? Some sources may provide oversimplified information, while other sources may be too technical.

### Make Source Cards

Make source cards to keep track of the information you find. Use index cards to record publishing information for each source you decide to use. Study the cards at the right and follow the format for each type of source card. Number each source card and refer to it when you take notes. You will then use these source cards to credit sources in your

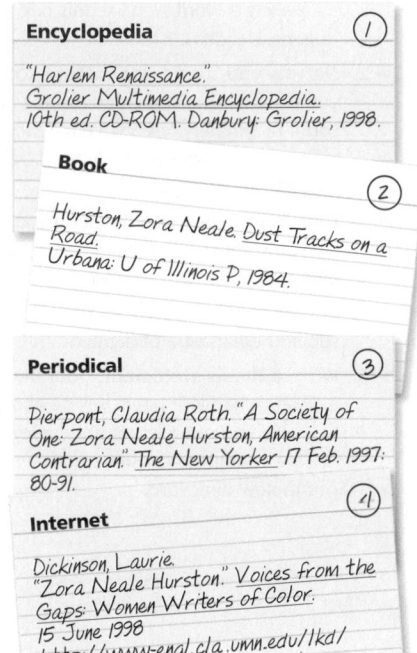

**Encyclopedia** ①

"Harlem Renaissance."
*Grolier Multimedia Encyclopedia.*
10th ed. CD-ROM. Danbury: Grolier, 1998.

**Book** ②

Hurston, Zora Neale. *Dust Tracks on a Road.*
Urbana: U of Illinois P, 1984.

**Periodical** ③

Pierpont, Claudia Roth. "A Society of One: Zora Neale Hurston, American Contrarian." *The New Yorker* 17 Feb. 1997: 80-91.

**Internet** ④

Dickinson, Laurie.
"Zora Neale Hurston." *Voices from the Gaps: Women Writers of Color.*
15 June 1998
http://www-engl.cla.umn.edu/lkd/vfg/Authors/ZoraNealeHurston.

report and to write your Works Cited list.

## Read Your Sources and Take Notes

As you read, keep your thesis statement and the questions you want answered in mind. Use a separate index card for each piece of information you record. Write the number of the source on each note card. Use the following techniques.

- **Paraphrase.** Restate the material in your own words.
- **Quotation.** Copy the original text word for word, including all punctuation marks. Use quotation marks to indicate the beginning and end of the quotation. Use this form to emphasize a point or when the author's words are well phrased.

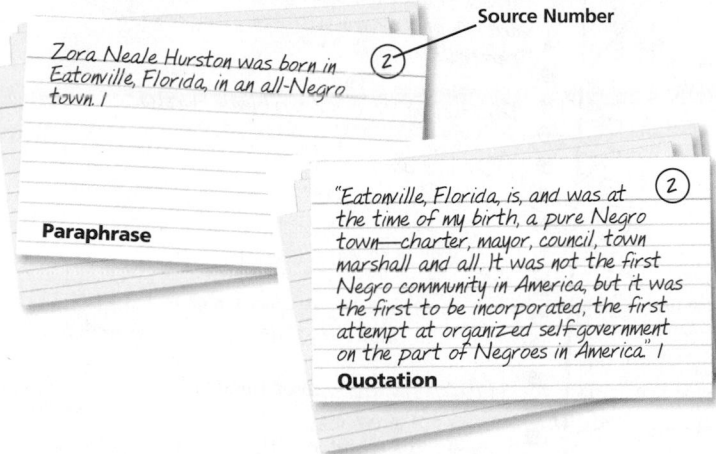

Source Number

Zora Neale Hurston was born in Eatonville, Florida, in an all-Negro town. 1

Paraphrase

"Eatonville, Florida, is, and was at the time of my birth, a pure Negro town—charter, mayor, council, town marshall and all. It was not the first Negro community in America, but it was the first to be incorporated, the first attempt at organized self-government on the part of Negroes in America." 1

Quotation

## Get Organized

Once you have gathered a quantity of material, begin to organize it. It is a good idea to make an outline that will provide the framework for the information you have collected.

Begin by grouping your note cards according to the main ideas on the cards. Then determine the best way to arrange those main ideas. You might want to use **chronological order, comparison-and-contrast order,** or **cause-and-effect order,** depending upon your subject. Now write your outline based on your arrangement of the main ideas and subpoints in your stacks of note cards. An example of a format you can follow is on the next page.

Need help documenting sources?

See the **Writing Handbook,** pp. 1290–1292

**More OnLine:**
**Research Starter**
www.mcdougallittell.com

## Read Sources and Take Notes

Encourage students to share informational articles with other students who are working on similar topics. Students who are having difficulty taking notes might work with a partner or use a laptop computer, if one is available to them. As students take notes on their source materials, suggest they use text organizers such as headings and graphic features to locate and categorize information.

The negative effects of careless notetaking cannot be overemphasized. Students might have a wonderful quotation on a note card, but have no idea who said it, or where they found it, or whether the statement is really a quotation or a paraphrase. Under such circumstances much time is taken up returning to the sources and searching out the precise references. To avoid such a waste of time, urge students to be exact when they take notes.

For instruction and practice in using ellipsis marks with quotations, see the bottom channel of this page.

## Get Organized

Stress to students the importance of an organizer such as an outline when writing a lengthy report. There is just too much information to rely on memory alone.

If students are using chronological order to organize their report, they might find it useful to note the year(s) covered on each note card.

 Mini Lesson

# Grammar

## USING AN ELLIPSIS MARK WITH QUOTATIONS

**Instruction** Use an ellipsis mark to quote only parts of a passage. An ellipsis mark consists of three spaced periods, signifying the omission of part of a quoted passage. When an ellipsis is used at the end of a passage, it is followed by a period to mark the end of the sentence. There will be four periods rather than three.

**Activity** Write these sentences on the board, then discuss why they are punctuated as shown:

Cary Wintz wrote, "Hurston did her best writing in the 1930s. . . ." (The last part of this sentence has been omitted.)

"While studying anthropology at Barnard College . . . Hurston began to publish her short stories and folklore in African-American periodicals." (The middle of this sentence has been omitted.)

## Using Note Cards to Create an Outline

Review with students the transformation from note cards to outline in the writing process. Point out how each note card on page 986 contributes to part of the outline.

Remind students of the three ways to organize a report, as presented on page 985. Ask them what kind of order the writer of this outline is following.
**Possible Response:** The writer is using a combination of ordering techniques—chronological under Roman numeral I, cause-and-effect under Roman numeral II, and comparison-and-contrast under Roman numeral III.

Point out that writers should make the outline work for them, and not adhere to any particular order at the expense of the fluidity of their report.

When students organize their note cards, they might want to write in the margin on each card which section of the outline that card deals with. If their note cards somehow become disordered, these notations facilitate reorganization.

# Using Note Cards to Create an Outline

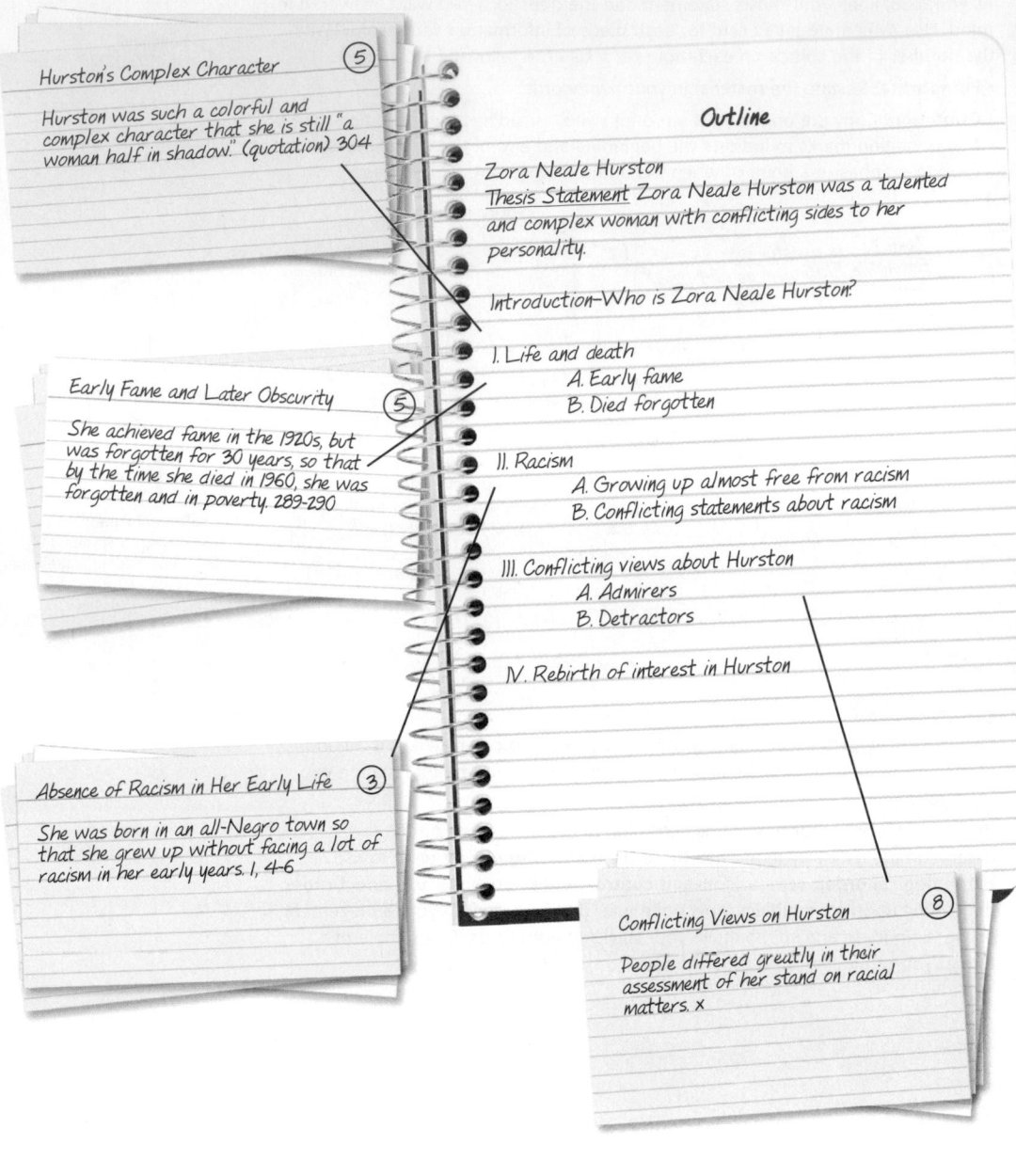

Hurston's Complex Character (5)

Hurston was such a colorful and complex character that she is still "a woman half in shadow." (quotation) 304

Early Fame and Later Obscurity (5)

She achieved fame in the 1920s, but was forgotten for 30 years, so that by the time she died in 1960, she was forgotten and in poverty. 289–290

Absence of Racism in Her Early Life (3)

She was born in an all-Negro town so that she grew up without facing a lot of racism in her early years. 1, 4–6

Conflicting Views on Hurston (8)

People differed greatly in their assessment of her stand on racial matters. x

Outline

Zora Neale Hurston
Thesis Statement Zora Neale Hurston was a talented and complex woman with conflicting sides to her personality.

Introduction—Who is Zora Neale Hurston?

I. Life and death
   A. Early fame
   B. Died forgotten

II. Racism
   A. Growing up almost free from racism
   B. Conflicting statements about racism

III. Conflicting views about Hurston
   A. Admirers
   B. Detractors

IV. Rebirth of interest in Hurston

## ❸ Drafting

Use your outline as a guide to begin writing. The first part of your report should state your main idea, or thesis. You will need to end with a conclusion that restates the thesis and summarizes your main points. The rest of your report should be organized according to your outline.

### Craft Your Thesis Statement

Now that you have researched your topic and written your outline, you should have a better understanding of what your report will accomplish. Shape your thesis statement to tell what your paper will prove.

### Stay Flexible As You Write Your Draft

In the drafting stage, concentrate on using clear, natural language to get your ideas on paper. Follow your outline and refer to your note cards as you write, but feel free to reorganize your material any time you collect new information or discover a different way of connecting ideas.

**Add Your Own Analysis.** Your report should not just be a collection of information from your sources. You must make inferences and interpret evidence to reach a conclusion. Use facts, quotations, statistics, and examples from your research to draw your own conclusions about your topic.

**Give Credit Where Credit Is Due.** If you do not credit the sources of information in your report, you are guilty of **plagiarism**—the unlawful use of another's words or ideas. To credit your sources, use parenthetical documentation. Within the text of the report, briefly identify the source. For example, after each quotation, paraphrase, or summary, list in parenthesis the author's name (or title, if no name is given) and the page number. Include a Works Cited list at the end of the report.

### Take Another Look

Take a break from your writing—a few days if possible. Then review your draft. Asking the following questions can help:

- How can I make my thesis statement clearer?
- What additional information would support my thesis statement?
- What information, if any, is irrelevant?
- How can I improve my organization?
- What facts and documentation do I need to check?

**? Ask Your Peer Reader**

- What did you like most about my report?
- What did you learn about my topic?
- Which ideas need more explanation?
- Does the order in which I've presented my ideas make sense? Would another type of organization work better?
- What impression were you left with when you read my conclusion?

**Need more help with parenthetical documentation?**

See the **Writing Handbook,** pp. 1290–1292.

## Drafting

### Organizing the Draft

Remind students of the different ways to organize a research report, as described on page 985. Point out that the student writer used all three methods. Students need to figure out what works best in their report. In addition, it is important to be flexible enough to change their organization if, while they are writing, they think of a structure that works better.

### Stay Flexible

Sometimes students are so intimidated by the writing process and the desire to produce a perfect first draft that they are unable to write at all. To avoid this difficulty, tell students that it is neither possible nor necessary to be perfect in the first draft. Encourage them to just write down their ideas at first, and to worry about the details later.

### Give Credit

Refer students to the student model on page 981. Have volunteers suggest why the writer used each citation, even when he did not use exact quotations. Be sure that students understand that even paraphrasing merits a citation, when the writer has leaned heavily on the source's ideas.

### Take Another Look

Students might find it helpful to make a checklist of the items they need to change. Some writers prefer to do the easy changes first, while other writers prefer the opposite approach. Suggest that students find the process that works best for them.

## Revising
### ELABORATING—DETAILS AND EXAMPLES

Help students analyze the changes made in the example to see how adding examples and details improved the writing. Ask students to justify the changes.

**Possible Response:** Being precise about the seven books and the shorter works that Hurston wrote gives the reader a better appreciation for the breadth and volume of Hurston's writing.

Have students read their reports, looking for places where details could be added to strengthen the draft and make the report more interesting. They may need to return to their note cards or even to the sources themselves.

## Editing and Proofreading
### USING COMMAS

Point out that adding detail often makes sentences longer and more complex. In the example, the sentence begins with a long dependent clause (ending with *for her work*). *She* is the simple subject of the clause, and *won* and *received* are the simple predicates. The noun *prizes* is modified by a gerund phrase, describing the prizes Hurston won. This phrase begins with *including* and ends with *Relations.* Because it is long and not essential to the meaning of the sentence, it is separated from the rest of the sentence by commas. By separating this phrase, the important elements of the sentence stand out, and its meaning is clearer. See the grammar lesson at the bottom of the TE 989 for more information on using commas with phrases.

Other errors include the following: The words *Book, Award, Race,* and *Relations* are capitalized because they are important words in the title of a prize. The word *acclaim* is misspelled. The words *County, Welfare,* and *Home* are capitalized because they are part of a proper noun. Students should check their punctuation and use of commas so they can produce an error-free final draft.

### Making a Works Cited List

Students should cross-reference their report and their Works Cited list to make sure that all works in the list are cited in the body of the paper. Suggest that they go through their reports and make a list of all citations. Then they can check off each citation on the Works Cited list.

---

**Need revising help?**

Review the **Rubric**, p. 980.

Consider **peer reader** comments.

Check **Revising, Editing, and Proofreading** p. 1269.

---

**Confused by commas?**

See the **Grammar Handbook:**

Clauses, p. 1331

Punctuation chart, pp. 1327–1328

---

## Publishing
### IDEAS

- Present your report to your class.
- Submit your paper to a student literary journal.

**More Online: Publishing Options** www.mcdougallittell.com

---

### ❹ Revising

**TARGET SKILL** ▶ **ELABORATING—DETAILS AND EXAMPLES** Your report will be more authorative and more interesting if you provide facts and statistics to support your point.

> *—four novels, two books of folklore, and an autobiography—*
> By the time she died on January 28, 1960, she had written seven books and over 50 shorter works such as essays, articles, and newspaper columns. *, including a dozen short stories, two plays, and many*

### ❺ Editing and Proofreading

**TARGET SKILL** ▶ **USING COMMAS** Reports include a great deal of information. The correct use of commas can help your readers better understand the relationship between ideas.

> Yet, in spite of the fact that she won many prizes, including two Guggenheims and the Ainsfield-Wolf book award in race relations, and received much critical acclaim for her work, she died in poverty at the St. Lucie county welfare home in Fort Pierce, Florida.

### ❻ Making a Works Cited List

When you have finished revising and editing your report, make a **Works Cited** list and attach it to the end of your paper. See pages 1290–1292 in the **Writing Handbook** for the correct format.

### ❼ Reflecting

**FOR YOUR WORKING PORTFOLIO** What new questions do you have about your topic? Create a list of relevant questions for study. Attach your questions to your research report and save your report in your **Working Portfolio.**

---

## Reflecting

Have students write a brief note addressing their writing experiences. They can clip their assessment to the research report and place both in their working portfolios.

# Assessment Practice Revising & Editing

Read this paragraph from the first draft of a research report. The underlined sections may include the following kinds of errors:

- **facts that need to be elaborated**
- **comma errors**
- **incorrect possessive forms**
- **verb tense errors**

For each underlined section, choose the revision that most improves the writing.

> Industrialization in the United States changed many <u>peoples</u> lives. Skilled
> (1)
> craftspeople could no longer compete with mass production, which required that
> each worker perform <u>one, small task over, and over.</u> Factory workers often <u>work</u>
> (2)                                                    (3)
> 10 to 15 hours a day. Industrialization also meant that the need for unskilled
> workers <u>is increasing</u> dramatically. Between 1877 and 1890, <u>6.3 million people</u>
> (4)                                                        (5)
> <u>mostly poor and unskilled came to the United States</u> from Europe. In 1840, the
> population of the United States was 17 million. <u>By 1900, it had jumped.</u>
> (6)

1. **A.** people's
   **B.** peoples's
   **C.** people
   **D.** Correct as is

2. **A.** one small task over and over
   **B.** one, small task over and over
   **C.** one small task over, and over
   **D.** Correct as is

3. **A.** working
   **B.** was working
   **C.** worked
   **D.** Correct as is

4. **A.** were increasing
   **B.** was increasing
   **C.** was increasingly
   **D.** Correct as is

5. **A.** 6.3 million people, mostly poor and unskilled came to the United States
   **B.** 6.3 million people mostly poor, and unskilled came to the United States
   **C.** 6.3 million people, mostly poor and unskilled, came to the United States
   **D.** Correct as is

6. **A.** By 1900, it was higher.
   **B.** By 1900, it had jumped higher.
   **C.** By 1900, it had jumped to over 76 million.
   **D.** Correct as is

**Need extra help?**

See the **Grammar Handbook**

Possessive Nouns, p. 1306

Verb Tense, p. 1310

Punctuation Chart, p. 1327–1328

**Assessment Practice**
Before students begin to identify errors in this passage, review the types of errors the passage contains. Remind students to carefully read the entire passage before correcting the errors.

Answers:
1. A; 2. A; 3. C; 4. B; 5. C; 6. C

## Grammar

**USING COMMAS TO SET OFF MODIFYING PHRASES**

**Instruction** If a modifying phrase is not essential to the meaning of a sentence, it should be set off from the rest of the sentence with commas.

**Activity:** Each sentence below has a phrase that modifies a noun or a pronoun. Write the sentences on the board. Have students decide on the correct placement of commas.

Zora Neale Hurston a gifted and prolific writer died forgotten and in poverty.

Reading the book *Mules and Men* she fell in love with Hurston's writing.

**Correct:**

Zora Neale Hurston, a gifted and prolific writer, died forgotten and in poverty.

Reading the book *Mules and Men,* she fell in love with Hurston's writing.

## Objectives

- recognize and appreciate nonstandard English found in regionalisms, slang and foreign terms, and archaic or obsolete words
- rely on context to determine the meaning of informal language
- use a dictionary to determine usage and meaning

## EXERCISE

1. Funky: slang; from Old French *fungier,* from Latin *fumigare*, to give off smoke; "relating to jazz or blues music," "earthy and uncomplicated," "unconventional or campy"

2. Grungy: slang; origin unknown; "dirty, rundown"

3. Carte Blanche: foreign; from French *carte*, ticket + *blanche*, blank; "unconditional authority"

4. Bummer: slang; probably from German *Bummler,* loafer; "a person, event, or experience that is disappointing," "a failure," also "an adverse reaction to drugs"

5. (Sit) a spell: informal; from Old English *spelian,* to substitute for; "a short time"

## It's Too Cool—or Is It Hot?

The dynamism of the English language is both a blessing and a curse. Wonderful nonstandard words and expressions enter the language every day, while others, once popular and widely used, disappear. For example, look at the once-common expressions highlighted on the right, in the excerpt from Zora Neale Hurston's essay "How It Feels to Be Colored Me."

The phrases "howdy do" and "go a piece" are **regionalisms**—that is, phrases you would most likely hear only in a certain area of a country. Informal language, slang terms, regionalisms, and foreign terms all begin their life outside of mainstream, standard

> I usually spoke to [Northern tourists] in passing. . . . I would say something like this: "Howdy-do-well-I-thank-you-where-you-goin'?" Usually the automobile or the horse paused at this, and after a queer exchange of compliments, I would probably "go a piece of the way" with them, as we say in farthest Florida.   —Zora Neale Hurston,
> "How It Feels to Be Colored Me"

English. Over time, however, many of these words become established in the language.

## Strategies for Building Vocabulary

Because English is so fertile and changeable, you are bound to encounter terms that are new to you. When you do, the strategies that follow can help you make sense of those words.

❶ **Consider the Big Picture** In her essay Hurston summarizes her life in this way: "It is a bully adventure and worth all I have paid through my ancestors for it." The slang term *bully* was very popular when Hurston wrote her essay, but it is probably not one with which you are familiar. From the context—Hurston's descriptions of her life and adventures—you might infer that *bully* means "exciting or great."

❷ **Look Up the Word** To check the accuracy of your inferences, look up the word in a dictionary. Read the different meanings of *bully* in the dictionary entry that follows, and choose the one you think Hurston intended.

> **bul·ly** (bo̅o̅l′ ē) *n., pl.* **-lies. 1.** A person who is habitually cruel to smaller or weaker people. **2.** A hired ruffian. **3.** *Archaic.* A fine person. **4.** *Archaic.* A sweetheart. **–bully** *v.* **-lied, -ly•ing, -lies. –tr.** To intimidate with superior size or strength. *–intr.* To behave like a bully. **–bully** *adj.* Excellent; splendid. **–bully** *interj.* Used to express approval: *Bully for you!* [Possibly from Middle Dutch *boele*, sweetheart.]

In this case, *bully* is an adjective meaning "excellent" or "splendid." Note that in most large,

comprehensive dictionaries, such as *The American Heritage Dictionary* or *The Oxford English Dictionary*, regional, slang, obsolete, or archaic usages appear after the standard definitions. You might also find information about a word in dictionaries of slang or other books that discuss the etymology of nonstandard words.

As you study the denotations and etymologies of words, you might find that some words, called **portmanteaus,** are formed by blending two or more existing words. For example, in her essay "Zora Neale Hurston: A Cautionary Tale and a Partisan View," Alice Walker describes her own ancestors as "relishing the pleasure of each other's loquacious and bodacious company."

*Bodacious,* meaning "intrepidly bold or daring," is a combination of *bold* and *audacious*. It began life as a regionalism and was popularized through the comic strip *Snuffy Smith.* Today the word is used throughout the United States. Perhaps in the future, if it survives, dictionaries will no longer label it a regionalism.

**EXERCISE** Use a dictionary to look up the words and phrases below. For each one, use your own words to write about its usage, origin, and meaning.

1. funky    3. carte blanche    5. (sit) a spell
2. grungy    4. bummer

**990**    UNIT SIX    PART 1: A NEW CULTURAL IDENTITY

## Grammar from Literature

Writers use parallel construction for a number of reasons:

- To group ideas of equal importance.
- To compare and contrast ideas.
- To create rhythm and a poetic effect.

Parallelism is the use of sentence parts that are similar in meaning and structure. One way to achieve parallelism is to use lists or series. The following example contains a series of prepositional phrases.

> **I belonged** to them, to the nearby hotels, to the country —everybody's Zora.
> —Zora Neale Hurston, "How It Feels to Be Colored Me"

Writers also use parallelism when making comparisons. In the following passage about African-American writers in the 1920s, Langston Hughes uses parallel infinitive phrases.

> **They ceased** to write to amuse themselves **and began** to write to amuse and entertain white people.
> —Langston Hughes, "When the Negro Was in Vogue"

**Using Parallelism in Your Writing** The use of parallelism is an effective tool for creating emphasis. In your writing, when you make a point or support an argument, look for places where parallel structures will capture your reader's attention. Use the rhythm of parallelism in both prose and poetry to add flow and grace to your writing. Look at the difference in the passages below.

> ORIGINAL
> **A number of elements contribute to the musical quality of poetry. Stressed syllables and repeated words create rhythm. Rhyming words and sound devices contribute to rhythm too.**

> REVISED USING PARALLELISM
> The rhythm of **repeated words,** the rhythm of **stressed syllables,** the rhythm of **rhyming words,** the rhythm of **sound devices**—all these make the music in poetry.

**Usage Tip** When you group sentence parts in a series, make sure the items in the series are all the same type of grammatical structure.

> INCORRECT
> **The Harlem Renaissance saw significant achievement** in literature, in fine art, **and** writing music.

In the example above, the first two items in the series are phrases composed of prepositions and objects. The last item is a gerund phrase. Changing the last item to a prepositional phrase makes the series parallel.

> CORRECT
> **The Harlem Renaissance saw significant achievement** in literature, in fine art, **and** in music.

---

**WRITING EXERCISE** Rewrite each of the items below creating a series. Be sure your structures are parallel.

1. Whites enjoyed the clubs. These were places where black owners welcomed them. Black performers entertained. Audience members might participate.
2. Gladys Bentley wowed audiences with her singing. She did a little foot stomping too. She played the piano.
3. Later, she began to sing with an accompanist. She started performing in larger clubs, and soon was enjoying her stardom.
4. The blues, one of the forms of music that originated in the Americas, and which was inspired by African-American spirituals, gave rise to jazz, rock, and soul music.
5. Langston Hughes criticizes some African Americans for trying to please whites by practicing acrobatics. He feels they wrote dishonestly and were responsible for segregating night clubs.

**GRAMMAR EXERCISE** Rewrite the sentences below, correcting any errors in parallelism. If a sentence contains no error, write *Correct.*

1. At rent parties Langston Hughes liked to hear people's laughter, enjoyed listening to the slow music, and relished feeling the floor shaking.
2. New York in the 1920s had many faces for African Americans: to some it held opportunities, to others it was a place of freedom, and to still more it was a place of self-fulfillment.
3. Rent parties offered lively entertainment, good food, and people who were interesting.
4. The literary devices Hughes uses in "When the Negro Was in Vogue" include satire, figurative language, and irony.
5. Many Harlem residents delighted in meeting celebrities, seeing black performers on Broadway, and they profited from the white tourists.

---

**Objectives**
- use parallelism—sentence parts that are similar in meaning and structure—in writing
- revise drafts by using a series of prepositional or infinitive phrases to add rhythm to writing and capture readers' attention
- practice creating series of phrases in parallel grammatical structure

**WRITING EXERCISE**

Responses will vary.

1. Whites enjoyed the clubs <u>where black owners welcomed them, where black performers entertained, and where audience members participated</u>.
2. Gladys Bentley wowed audiences <u>with her singing, foot stomping, and piano playing</u>.
3. Later, she began to sing with an accompanist, <u>to perform in larger clubs, and to enjoy her stardom</u>.
4. The blues, <u>which is one of the forms of music that originated in the Americas, and which was inspired by African-American spirituals, gave rise to jazz, rock, and soul music</u>.
5. Langston Hughes criticizes some African Americans for trying to please whites <u>by practicing acrobatics, writing dishonestly, and segregating nightclubs</u>.

**GRAMMAR EXERCISE**

1. At rent parties Langston Hughes <u>liked hearing</u> people's laughter, enjoyed listening to slow music, and relished feeling the floor shaking.
2. Correct
3. Rent parties <u>had lively entertainment, good food, and interesting people</u>.
4. Correct.
5. Many Harlem residents delighted in meeting celebrities, seeing black performers on Broadway, <u>and profiting from white tourists</u>.

## OVERVIEW

### Introduction

This article provides students with historical background for the selections in Part 2 of this unit by tracing the development of modernism as a response to the destruction caused by World War I and a reaction against the materialism of the 1920s. The selections in **Voices from the Times** give students insight into the attitudes and temperament of the modernist movement. This article will help students to interpret the possible influences of historical contexts on a literary work.

## Teaching Nonfiction

### Reading Skills and Strategies:
**ESTABLISHING A PURPOSE FOR READING**

Explain to students that this article will give them an overview of the years following World War I. Have the students establish a purpose for reading (to find out).

### MONITORING AND MODIFYING READING STRATEGIES

Ask students to read the article silently. Have them monitor their comprehension of the material and, if necessary, modify their reading strategies when understanding breaks down. Suggest that students reread the article more than once in order to increase comprehension.

### ANALYZING TEXT STRUCTURE

Ask students to analyze the text structure of the essay for how it influences their understanding of the modernist movement. Have students note how the author uses cause and effect and how this technique influenced their understanding of the essay.

# Alienation of the Individual

## Modernism

**W**orld War I remade the map of Europe, but that was only the most visible sign of a monumental change in the lives of nations and individuals. The four-year conflict, involving a total of 32 nations, devastated Europe. It was the first large-scale modern war, utilizing the savage new weapons of modern technology—poison gas, submarines, armored tanks, airplanes, and machine guns. By the time the war ended in 1918, nearly 10 million soldiers and almost as many civilians had been killed. Even though the United States did not enter the war until 1917, Americans shared the sense that civilization, as they had known it, was being destroyed. Uncertainty about what was to result from this political breakdown became a distinguishing characteristic of the age.

*Weeping Woman* (1937), Pablo Picasso. Tate Gallery, London/Art Resource, New York. Copyright © 1996 Artists Rights Society, (ARS), New York/SPA-DEM, Paris.

The end of the war signaled an end of idealism and ushered in an era marked by economic growth, technological advancement, and new ways to have fun. During the Roaring Twenties, as the decade of the 1920s is called, people had more money and more things to buy. An increasing number of radios carried the new strains of jazz into American homes. The availability of cars gave people more mobility and freedom. More people went out to nightclubs and to speakeasies, where illegal alcohol was plentiful. Movies became a popular form of entertainment. At the same time, political corruption was rampant;

**992**

gangsters flourished with the profits from the sale of illegal alcohol; and Americans, in general, grew distrustful of foreigners and intolerant of political dissent.

The literary movement known as modernism was a direct response to these social and cultural changes. Disillusioned by the war and appalled by the materialism of the age, the new generation of writers searched for different literary forms to express what they understood as the modern consciousness. "Make it new!" was the rallying cry that the poet and critic Ezra Pound inspired in these writers. And they did.

Although the writers in this part of the unit have their own individual styles, they share certain characteristics that have come to be identified with modernism. First of all, they felt that individuals, especially artists, were becoming increasingly threatened by and isolated amid the mass society that was developing at the time. Characters in modernist works are almost always alienated—withdrawn, unresponsive, hurt by unnamed forces.

A second characteristic shared by these modernist writers is experimentation. Katherine Anne Porter used stream-of-consciousness as a fictional technique to dramatize the interior life of her characters, especially their meandering patterns of thinking. In order to reflect the fragmentation of their experience, fiction writers such as Ernest Hemingway and Richard Wright composed short, fragmentary stories that didn't have traditional beginnings and endings. Poets such as Ezra Pound and T. S. Eliot created verse out of the fragments of modern experience—pieces of dreams, feelings, dialogue, images, and literary allusions. The great modern artists of the 20th century—Picasso, Matisse, and Duchamp, for example—visually captured this fragmentary nature of modern experience in their cubist designs, cutouts, and collages.

Finally, modernist writers are as notable for what they leave out of their writing as for what they put in. There is no narrative voice guiding the reader with explanations or details. The reader is left alone to figure

---

---

## Making Connections

### History
**A** Among the most famous of gangster horrors was the so-called St. Valentine's Day Massacre of February 14, 1929, in which members of Al Capone's gang—some dressed as policemen—shot down members of Bugs Moran's mob in a Chicago garage.

### Literature
**B** At loose ends after the war, many disillusioned Americans remained in Europe, often settling in the Left Bank district of Paris, where they were joined by a number of writers and artists. Ezra Pound, Ernest Hemingway, Gertrude Stein, F. Scott Fitzgerald, James Joyce, and George Orwell were just some of the many writers who lived for a time in Paris during the 1920s. The expatriate community was large enough to support Sylvia Beach's English-language bookstore, Shakespeare & Co., a popular Left Bank gathering place.

### Business
**C** New factory processes not only produced new materials—like rayon (1905) and cellophane (1912)—but also enabled mass production of goods at lower prices. A pioneer in this field was Henry Ford (1863–1947), who in 1913 introduced the assembly line. This innovation allowed his factory to produce cars more quickly and cheaply than ever before. As more goods were mass-produced, manufacturers saw a need to merchandise their products by creating an appetite for them in the public. Spurred by the introduction of the new medium of radio, the era of modern advertising began.

### Literature
**D** Living first in London and later in Paris and Rapallo, Italy, the Idaho-born poet Ezra Pound was among the leaders of modernism. Pound was a founder of the group of poets called imagists, who strove to convey ideas and feelings through the presentation of precise images rather than through direct statement. An example is his famous two-line poem "In a Station of the Metro." He also helped get many struggling writers' works published—such as T. S. Eliot's 1922 poem *The Waste Land,* a modernist landmark.

---

**VOICES OF THE TIMES**

**Ask: What contrasts does the imagery of Pound's poem convey?**
**Possible Responses:** individual vs. crowd; light vs. dark; beauty vs. dullness; life vs. death

**Ask: What did Eliot see as the mission of the modernist poet?**
**Possible Responses:** to use language in such a way as to force readers to pay attention to its real meaning; to avoid using easy language that dulls the senses of the readers

**Ask: How do the statements of Lewis and Eliot compare?**
**Possible Response:** Both men think that true writers should avoid the safety of conformity and take creative risks.

**Ask: What attitude towards life does Millay's famous quatrain express?**
**Possible Responses:** Better to live a full life than a long one; seize the day and forget tomorrow.

**NOTETAKING**

Explain to students that this essay contains numerous facts and discusses the essential elements of the modernist movement. Ask them to use note taking as study strategy to better understand the text and the information in it.

**SUMMARIZING**

Ask students to summarize the essay using their notes to help them. Remind students that summaries are written in their own words and do not include extraneous details.

**LaserLinks**
**Historical Literary Connection: Modernism**

The isolation and experimentation common to much modern writing can also be found in art. These works will get students thinking about the mood and tone present in many of the selections in Part 2.

See Teacher's SourceBook p. 84 for bar codes.

---

Voices *from the* TIMES

Four be the things I am wiser to know:
Idleness, sorrow, a friend, and a foe.
Four be the things I'd been better
   without:
Love, curiosity, freckles, and doubt.

**Dorothy Parker**
from "Inventory"

Which of us has known his brother? Which of us has looked into his father's heart? Which of us has not remained forever prison-pent? Which of us is not forever a stranger and alone?

**Thomas Wolfe**
from *Look Homeward, Angel*

Ernest Hemingway

The further you go in writing, the more alone you are.
**Ernest Hemingway**
from an interview

You are all a lost generation.
**Gertrude Stein**
spoken to Ernest Hemingway

There are people who eat the earth and eat all the people on it like in the Bible with the locusts. And other people who stand around and watch them eat it.

**Lillian Hellman**
from *The Little Foxes*

**994**   UNIT SIX

---

out what is going on in a story or a poem and what a character or speaker is feeling or thinking. These omissions place more demands on the reader to put together the pieces of the characters' experience.

## Traditions Across Time: The Lonely Self

Modernism dominated the arts and literature throughout the 20th century. The generation that came of age around World War II faced alienation similar to that experienced by the early modernists. Some of the great plays of Tennessee Williams and Arthur Miller feature characters—most notably, Blanche DuBois in *A Streetcar Named Desire* and Willy Loman in *Death of a Salesman*—who are trapped by their own inadequacies and pushed aside by stronger, more brutal forces in society. In the poems of Sylvia Plath and Anne Sexton in this part of the unit, you can see a hostile reaction to the pressures placed on women to conform to established roles during the 1950s and early 1960s.

A scene from the play *A Streetcar Named Desire*, starring Marlon Brando and Jessica Tandy. Copyright © Eileen Darby.

---

**VOICES FROM THE TIMES**

**Ask: What do you think Hemingway meant in this quotation?**

**Possible Responses:** The more creative a writer becomes, the more he reveals how he is different from others; pushing the creative boundaries results in isolation because creativity is essentially individual and cannot be understood by everyone.

**Ask: Why is Stein's "lost generation" appellation appropriate for those who came of age during and just after World War I?**

**Possible Responses:** because so many young men were killed during the war; because the war changed life so dramatically in the United States and in Europe and people felt lost without the traditions of the past; because that generation was so disillusioned by the mass destruction that resulted from the use of new technology in warfare

**Ask: Whom is Hellman talking about?**

**Possible Responses:** the powerful whom others fear; the rich who take advantage of the poor; the fascists who were taking over Europe while Western democracies just watched; those too cowardly to protect the weak

## Modernism

995

### Objectives
- appreciate the poetry of one of America's most popular and renowned poets
- interpret the influences of modernism on the themes and style of poems by Robert Frost
- understand Frost's influence on art and thought in the United States
- gain information about Frost by reading a speech written in his honor

This author study offers a unique opportunity for students to focus on the work of a major writer. In addition, students can gather information about the life of Robert Frost, gaining insight into the real person behind his now famous literary works.

## Author Study
# ROBERT FROST

*"Because of Robert Frost's life and work, . . . our hold on this planet has increased."*

*–John F. Kennedy*

*Robert Frost*

HIS LIFE
HIS TIMES

1874–1963

## A Simple but Resonant Voice

*Robert Frost is probably the most popular American poet; certainly he is one of America's very best. But in many ways he is a poet of surprises. Poems like "The Road Not Taken" have created a popular image of Frost as a writer of simple poems about country life. However, his work is filled with deep questions about modern society and the way we live. In this Author Study, you will learn more about the life and career of this great 20th-century poet.*

### "I WAS LOST WHEN I WROTE THAT FIRST POEM"
As a boy, Robert Frost was devoted to playing baseball. "I was so interested in baseball," he once recalled, "that my family was afraid I'd waste my life and be a pitcher. Later, they were afraid I'd waste my life and be a poet. . . . They were right."

| | | |
|---|---|---|
| **1874** Is born on March 26 in San Francisco | **1885** Moves with mother and sister to New England | **1895** Marries Elinor White |

**1870**     **1880**     **1890**

**1879** Thomas Edison invents the light bulb.

**1892** Ellis Island opens as immigrant entry point.

In popular imagination, Robert Frost is nearly always associated with rural New England. However, he was born in 1874 in San Francisco, California, and lived there for 11 years. It was not until after his father's death that Frost, his mother, and his sister moved east—eventually settling in Salem, New Hampshire.

At age 14, Frost began attending high school in the industrial community of Lawrence, Massachusetts, where his grandparents lived. In 1890, he wrote the ballad "La Noche Trist" ("The Sad Night"). To his delight, this first poem was published by the *Bulletin*, the school newspaper. The following year, Frost became editor himself and continued playing baseball and other sports. In his heart, Frost already knew his future. He would be a poet. As he would reveal years later, "I was lost when I wrote that first poem in ballad form."

LIFE ON DERRY FARM Frost's early manhood was filled with changes in direction. He enrolled at both Dartmouth College and Harvard University, but did not take a degree. For several years he drifted from occupation to occupation, working as a mill hand, a school teacher, and a reporter. In 1894 he sold a poem, "My Butterfly: An Elegy," to *The Independent*, a New York magazine. After this, he was able to sell a poem occasionally, mostly to local newspapers. During these

## LITERARY Contributions

After a shaky start, Robert Frost became one of America's best-known poets. However, he was not simply a grand-fatherly-looking poet of the people. In many ways he rebelled against his age and forged a new kind of distinctly American poetry.

**His Own Modernism** Some of Frost's contemporaries, such as T. S. Eliot and Ezra Pound, wrote dense, difficult poems, using experimental poetic forms and often treating obscure subject matter. Frost, however, preferred to write tightly structured poems about familiar, everyday topics. Yet much of his writing is serious and probing: families argue, accidents happen, people die. Frost used older poetic forms, such as blank verse, adapting them to the rhythms of everyday speech. No other poet can make conversation sound so natural within such a strict structure. His best-known poems include

"**The Death of the Hired Man**" (1914)
"**Mending Wall**" (1914)
"**The Road Not Taken**" (1914)
"**Stopping by Woods on a Snowy Evening**" (1923)
"'**Out, Out—**'" (1936)
"**The Gift Outright**" (1942)

**Poet of the Countryside** Many of Frost's poems are set in New England and give a sharp, generally unsentimental picture of rural American life. But the truths they tell about fear, isolation, and longing extend far beyond their limited setting.

## History

**A** During the 1870s, San Francisco was a crowded and wild metropolis. A booming silver mining industry attracted people searching for work and riches. Thousands of immigrants arrived in the city, creating an atmosphere of cultural diversity. Frost, whose mother taught him to read and write at home, had a great deal of free time to roam the busy streets and take odd jobs. When Frost and his family moved north of Boston in 1885, he found the transition to small, working-class New England towns difficult. He disliked the cold winters and attending regular school, and he felt that life in New England was much more rigid than life in San Francisco.

## School and Literature

**B** Although Frost always felt awkward and unpopular at Lawrence High School, academically he moved quickly to the head of his class. It was at this point in his life that he became captivated by reading and writing. He read books from a variety of subject areas, including botany, astronomy, and philosophy. He was especially drawn to the poetry of British Romantic poets Percy Shelley and John Keats, British Victorian writer Matthew Arnold, and American writer Edgar Allan Poe.

## Work Experiences

**C** Frost's experiences working at a variety of difficult jobs gave him life experience that is reflected in many of his later poems. He was able to empathize with many different kinds of struggling, working-class people, and he gained a broader knowledge of both city and rural life in New England.

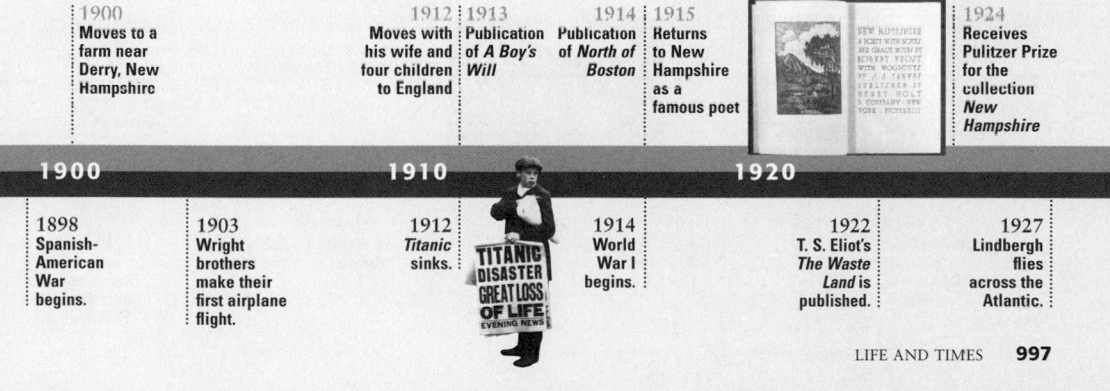

Edition of *New Hampshire*

| 1900 | 1912 | 1913 | 1914 | 1915 | | 1924 |
|------|------|------|------|------|---|------|
| Moves to a farm near Derry, New Hampshire | Moves with his wife and four children to England | Publication of *A Boy's Will* | Publication of *North of Boston* | Returns to New Hampshire as a famous poet | | Receives Pulitzer Prize for the collection *New Hampshire* |

**1900** · · · · · · · · · **1910** · · · · · · · · · **1920**

| 1898 | 1903 | 1912 | 1914 | 1922 | 1927 |
|------|------|------|------|------|------|
| Spanish-American War begins. | Wright brothers make their first airplane flight. | *Titanic* sinks. | World War I begins. | T. S. Eliot's *The Waste Land* is published. | Lindbergh flies across the Atlantic. |

TITANIC DISASTER GREAT LOSS OF LIFE EVENING NEWS

### Farming

**A** Farming in upper New England was not easy, even for experienced farmers. This area was plagued by thin soil, a rocky landscape, and cold winters. Many farmers at this time were giving up and moving closer to Boston. Frost, however, grew to love the land despite the fact that he was inexperienced with farm animals and disliked maintaining a regular schedule for chores. He often milked his cow at noon and midnight so he could sleep late in the morning. Between the years 1903 and 1905, Frost even sold several stories to two farm trade journals, *Eastern Poultryman* and *Farm-Poultry*. These stories were humorous tales of unfortunate farming experiences.

### World History

**B** With the outbreak of World War I in 1914, Frost decided to leave England. The physical danger of staying in Europe and the fact that war put a temporary stop to the poetry market left him with no choice. Frost was nervous, uncertain that he could find success as a poet in the United States. In 1915, the family left quietly at night, escorted by two British battleships. Frost traveled aboard the *St. Paul* in a convoy with the *Lusitania,* the famous ship that was sunk by a German submarine later that year. Frost would eventually write four poems about a close friend who was killed in the war.

## Author Study: ROBERT FROST

Frost in 1913

years, one stabilizing event in his life was his marriage to Elinor White, his high school sweetheart, whom he'd convinced to marry him in 1895.

In 1900, Frost's grandfather bought a farm for Frost and Elinor near Derry, New Hampshire. In this simple setting, during what was one of the richest periods of his life, Frost spent time with his growing family, taking walks, reading aloud great works of literature, and picnicking. He enjoyed encounters with other farmers, in which he absorbed the straightforward attitudes about life that would inspire his most important works. Frost worked the farm for 12 years but was unsuccessful. He began teaching **A** school in 1906 to help support his family. (The Frosts had six children, two of whom died in early childhood.)

In 1911, Frost figured out that 20 years of writing poems had earned him around $200. Determined to make a living from writing, he sold the farm and in 1912 moved his family to England, where it was reportedly cheaper to live. The move proved to be the turning point in his life.

RECOGNITION IN ENGLAND Less than two months after his arrival in England, Frost found a publisher for his first book of poems. *A Boy's Will* was published in 1913 and was well received. His second collection, *North of Boston* (1914), included "Mending Wall" and "After Apple-Picking," two poems that reflected his memories of farm life. The beginning of World War I forced the family **B** to return to the United States early in 1915, but Frost came home a famous man. Thanks to the U.S. publication of his two poetry collections, Frost found himself in demand for lectures and readings. His third book, *Mountain Interval* (1916), solidified his reputation. Frost bought a new farm at Franconia, New Hampshire, and began teaching at Amherst College in Massachusetts.

In 1924 his collection *New Hampshire* won the Pulitzer Prize, the first of four that Frost would receive. His position as one of America's leading writers was unmistakable.

"ACQUAINTED WITH THE NIGHT" Despite his public success, Frost was to face a series of personal tragedies. In 1934, his youngest daughter, Marjorie, died of a fever contracted in childbirth. Four years later, his wife died

| 1931 Receives Pulitzer Prize for *Collected Poems* | Frost's home in New Hampshire | 1937 Receives Pulitzer Prize for *A Further Range* | 1938 Death of Elinor Frost | 1943 Receives Pulitzer Prize for *A Witness Tree* |

**1930** — **1940**

| 1929 Stock market crashes; Great Depression begins. | 1932 Franklin Delano Roosevelt is elected president. | 1939 World War II begins. | 1941 U.S. enters World War II. | 1945 World War II ends; Harry S. Truman becomes president when Roosevelt dies. |

## The Best-Laid Plans

Reading his poem at John F. Kennedy's inauguration was a crowning moment of Frost's career. But things didn't go as planned. Frost had composed a new poem, "Dedication: For John F. Kennedy His Inauguration," and intended to read it aloud. But the day was extremely cold, and the sun was very bright. He began to read but could hardly see in the sun's glare; an unidentified official used his hat to try to create some shade. Frost finally gave up, saving an awkward moment by reciting "The Gift Outright," which he knew by heart. Later, Frost's friend Louis Untermeyer said of the Kennedy poem: "It was a good thing he couldn't read [it]; it was the worst thing he ever wrote."

Frost attempting to read at
President Kennedy's 1961 inauguration

suddenly of a heart attack. His only son, Carol, committed suicide in 1940. Understandably, Frost's 1942 collection *A Witness Tree* has a darkness of tone that reflects his anguish.

In the years after World War II, Frost wrote fewer poems and spent more time in his public role as a renowned writer. Sharing his standards for good poetry, Frost once said,

*A poem is never a put-up job, so to speak.
It begins as a lump in the throat, a sense of
wrong, a homesickness, a lovesickness. It
is never a thought to begin with. It is at its
best when it is a tantalizing vagueness. It
finds its thought and succeeds; or doesn't
find it and comes to nothing.*

One of Frost's final public appearances was at the inauguration of President John F. Kennedy in 1961, where he read his poem "The Gift Outright" before a national audience. It was one of the highest honors ever given to an American poet. Frost died in Boston in January 1963, at the age of 88.

**More Online: Author Link**
www.mcdougallittell.com

### Awards and Honors

**C** Frost was one of the most publicly recognized poets of all time. Over the course of his career he received honorary degrees from countless institutions. He also received many prestigious awards and honors, including four Pulitzer Prizes, the Gold Medal for Poetry, and others. Frost became the unofficial poet laureate of the United States and was honored on his 75th and 85th birthdays by the U. S. Senate. He celebrated his 80th birthday with a reception at the White House.

### Politics

**D** In Frost's later life, he became more interested in politics and world affairs and served as a type of cultural representative of the United States. In this capacity, Frost took several government-sponsored trips to countries such as Israel, Peru, Brazil, England, Ireland, and the Soviet Union. His trip to the Soviet Union was especially groundbreaking. Frost visited Moscow in 1962 as a guest of the Soviet government. While there he read the poem "Mending Wall" and met with Premier Nikita Khrushchev. Frost's mission was to bring American culture to the country and possibly try to smooth relations between Khrushchev and President Kennedy.

**C** **1950**
U.S. Senate passes resolution honoring Frost.

**1955**
State of Vermont names a mountain after Frost.

**1961**
Reads at President Kennedy's inauguration

**1962**
Receives the Congressional Medal of Honor

**1963**
Dies on January 29 in Boston

**1950**

**1960**

**1970**

**1955**
Bus boycott begins in Montgomery, Alabama.

**1957**
Soviet satellite *Sputnik* goes into orbit.

**D** **1962**
Cuban missile crisis increases U.S.-Soviet tensions.

**1963**
John F. Kennedy is assassinated.

### Objectives

1. understand and appreciate classic **poetry (Literary Analysis)**
2. identify **mood (Literary Analysis)**
3. **analyze word choice (Active Reading)**

### Summary

Each of these three Frost poems features a person who is either alone or separated from others in some way. In "Acquainted with the Night," a lone speaker expresses his isolation and unhappiness by describing a walk in the rain on a dark, empty street. "Mending Wall" is about the physical and spiritual walls people build between them. Each year the speaker and his neighbor come together to fix a stone wall separating their properties, despite the fact that there is no practical necessity for the wall. In "Out, Out," a young boy cutting wood accidentally lacerates his hand on a saw. The hand cannot be saved, and the boy knows instantly that his life will never be the same—that his injury separates him from other people. He dies of shock, slipping into the isolation of death as life continues to go on around him.

### Thematic Link

The Frost poems reflect the views of early 20th-century **modernism,** which centered on the idea of people becoming more and more isolated within a rapidly changing society. This **alienation of the individual** is shown in the three distinctly different scenarios.

---

#### 5-Minute Warm-Up

***Daily Language SkillBuilder***

Have students **proofread** the display sentences on page 913j and write them correctly. The sentences also appear on Transparency 27 of **Grammar Transparencies and Copymasters.**

---

## PREPARING to *Read*

# Selected Poems

*Poetry by* ROBERT FROST

> **Connect to Your Life**
>
> **Alone or Together?** The idea of being alone or somehow separated from others runs through many of Frost's poems. Yet often people choose to be alone. Think about times when you need companionship and times when you choose to be alone. What happens if you want other people around and no one chooses to be with you? Jot down your ideas. You may then discuss your ideas with a partner.

### Build Background

**Poetry of Frost** Robert Frost is perhaps the most widely read American poet of the 20th century. In many ways, he is a transitional figure between the 19th and 20th centuries. Like Emerson, Thoreau, and the other transcendentalists, Frost loved nature and wrote about the lone individual making choices about how to live. Like the modernists who were his contemporaries, Frost portrayed the forces in modern society that served to isolate people. Many of his poems portray tensions in relationships as well as the advantages and disadvantages of being alone.

### Focus Your Reading

**LITERARY ANALYSIS** **MOOD IN POETRY** **Mood** is the overall feeling or atmosphere that a writer creates for the reader. Frost uses a variety of devices to set the mood, including

- **imagery**—descriptive phrases that appeal to the senses
- **rhythm**—the pattern or flow of words and lines in a poem
- **repetition**—the repeated use of a word or phrase for emphasis

As you read each poem, decide what mood is communicated and what techniques Frost has used to get it across.

**ACTIVE READING** **ANALYZING WORD CHOICE** Be aware of the writer's **word choice.** Focus on the words and phrases that Frost uses to create **mood.** To increase your awareness, try these strategies:

- Read the poems aloud to help you notice mood-setting words or phrases.
- If a word catches your attention, stop and consider its meaning, your emotional response to it, and the effect it creates.

**READER'S NOTEBOOK** Fill in a chart like this one as you read each poem.

| "Acquainted with the Night" | |
|---|---|
| Word, phrase, or line | line 1 |
| Effect | loneliness, sadness |

---

## LESSON RESOURCES

**UNIT SIX RESOURCE BOOK,** pp. 43–44

**ASSESSMENT RESOURCES**
**Formal Assessment,** pp. 185–186
**Teacher's Guide to Assessment and Portfolio Use**
**Test Generator**

**SKILLS TRANSPARENCIES AND COPYMASTERS**
**Literary Analysis**
- Mood, T18 (for Activity, p. 1005)

**Reading and Critical Thinking**
- Venn Diagram, T50 (for Extend Interpretations 5, p. 1005)

**Grammar**
- Review: Adjective Elements, C141 (for Mini Lesson, p. 1001)

**Vocabulary**
- Denotation and Connotation, C83 (for Mini Lesson, p. 1003)

**INTEGRATED TECHNOLOGY**
**Audio Library**
**Net Activities**
**Visit our website:**
www.mcdougallittell.com

# Acquainted with the Night

### ROBERT FROST

I have been one acquainted with the night.
I have walked out in rain—and back in rain.
I have outwalked the furthest city light.

I have looked down the saddest city lane.
5  I have passed by the watchman on his beat
And dropped my eyes, unwilling to explain.

I have stood still and stopped the sound of feet
When far away an interrupted cry
Came over houses from another street,

10  But not to call me back or say good-by;
And further still at an unearthly height
One luminary[1] clock against the sky

Proclaimed the time was neither wrong nor right.
I have been one acquainted with the night.

---

1. **luminary:** giving off light.

Illustration © Litjiun Wong.

## Thinking Through the Literature

1. How would you describe the **speaker** of this poem? Write down a series of adjectives.

2. Do you feel sorry for the speaker? Explain why or why not.

3. How do you think the speaker feels about being alone at night? Cite phrases or lines from the poem that suggest his feelings.

4. Describe the mood of the poem. Cite words, phrases, and images that contribute to the **mood**.

 THINK ABOUT
- the expressiveness of words like *furthest, saddest,* and *unearthly*
- the effect of the very regular rhythm of the poem
- Frost's repetition of "I have . . ."

ACQUAINTED WITH THE NIGHT  **1001**

---

 Mini Lesson ## Grammar

### REVIEW: ADJECTIVE ELEMENTS
**Instruction** An adjective modifies a noun or a pronoun. Many different sentence elements can function as adjectives. Give students the following examples:

**Other Parts of Speech as Adjectives**
Nouns: *street* light, *city* lane
Pronouns: *my* footsteps, *his* beat
Participles: *interrupted* cry, *falling* rain
Articles: *a* clock, *the* sound, *an* idea
Infinitives: the one *to hear,* the way *to walk*

**Phrases and Clauses as Adjectives**
Prepositional Phrase: He saw a luminary clock *against the sky.*
Infinitive Phrase: That is one way *to walk home.*
Subordinate Clause: This is a street *that becomes dark and quiet at night.*

 Use McDougal Littell's **Language Network,** Chapter 7, for more instruction in adjectives.

# Mending Wall

### ROBERT FROST

**1**

Something there is that doesn't love a wall,
That sends the frozen-ground-swell under it
And spills the upper boulders in the sun,
And makes gaps even two can pass abreast.
5 The work of hunters is another thing:
I have come after them and made repair
Where they have left not one stone on a stone,
But they would have the rabbit out of hiding,
To please the yelping dogs. The gaps I mean,
10 No one has seen them made or heard them made,
But at spring mending-time we find them there.
I let my neighbor know beyond the hill;
And on a day we meet to walk the line
And set the wall between us once again.
15 We keep the wall between us as we go.
To each the boulders that have fallen to each.
And some are loaves and some so nearly balls

**2**

We have to use a spell to make them balance:

**GUIDE FOR READING**

**1–4** In some parts of New England, the farms are separated by low walls made of stones that are simply piled up, not mortared together. During the winter, moisture in the ground freezes and makes the earth expand, causing portions of the wall to topple.

**12–14** Notice that it is the speaker who lets the neighbor know it is time to mend the wall.

**1002**     UNIT SIX    AUTHOR STUDY: ROBERT FROST

"Stay where you are until our backs are turned!"
0  We wear our fingers rough with handling them.
   Oh, just another kind of outdoor game,
   One on a side. It comes to little more:
  There where it is we do not need the wall:
   He is all pine and I am apple orchard.
5  My apple trees will never get across
   And eat the cones under his pines, I tell him.
   He only says, "Good fences make good neighbors."
   Spring is the mischief in me, and I wonder
   If I could put a notion in his head:
0  "*Why* do they make good neighbors? Isn't it
   Where there are cows? But here there are no cows.
  Before I built a wall I'd ask to know
   What I was walling in or walling out,
   And to whom I was like to give offense.
35 Something there is that doesn't love a wall,
   That wants it down." I could say "Elves" to him,
   But it's not elves exactly, and I'd rather
   He said it for himself. I see him there,
   Bringing a stone grasped firmly by the top
40 In each hand, like an old-stone savage armed.
   He moves in darkness as it seems to me,
   Not of woods only and the shade of trees.
   He will not go behind his father's saying,
   And he likes having thought of it so well
45 He says again, "Good fences make good neighbors."

**23–26** According to the speaker, why is there no practical need for the wall? **B**

**27** What need does the neighbor see for the wall? **C**

**36–38** Notice the speaker's playful, teasing tone here.

**38–42** What is the speaker's opinion of his neighbor? **D**

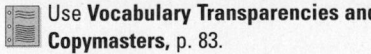

## Thinking Through the Literature

1. Which man in "Mending Wall" would you prefer as a neighbor? Why?

2. How do the **speaker** of the poem and his neighbor differ?

   THINK ABOUT
   { • how each feels about the wall and the job of rebuilding it
   { • the image the speaker has of his neighbor in lines 38–42

3. Explain what you think the wall represents in each of the following statements:

   THINK ABOUT
   { • "Something there is that doesn't love a wall."
   { • "We keep the wall between us as we go."
   { • "Before I built a wall I'd ask to know / What I was walling in or walling out."
   { • "He says again, 'Good fences make good neighbors.'"

4. Does the wall separate the neighbors or bring them closer together? Explain.

MENDING WALL   **1003**

## Customizing Instruction

### Students Acquiring English

**1** Since the first line is significant, rephrase it in usual word order to ensure that students understand its meaning.

**2** Point out that the speaker is not being literal; the rocks are shaped like balls and loaves of bread.

### Less Proficient Readers

**3** Ask students to explain the speaker's attitude toward the wall, as illustrated by the questions he asks.

**Possible Response:** He does not feel the wall is necessary. He wonders why someone would want a wall if there is no clear understanding of what is being walled in or walled out.

**Set a Purpose** Tell students to read "Out, Out—" to discover a very different kind of isolation.

## Thinking Through the Literature

1. Some might prefer the speaker for his conversation and his habit of inquiry; others might prefer a quiet, hardworking neighbor who prefers privacy.

2. Possible Response: The speaker does not like walls, wants to be friendly, and has an inquiring attitude about life; his neighbor likes walls because he is rigid and content to accept old ways without thinking for himself.

3. Possible Responses: first line—isolation; second line—emotional barrier; third line—protective barrier; fourth line—definitive boundaries

4. Possible Response: The wall separates the neighbors by marking the line between their properties, but it brings them together for the annual spring repairing.

## Vocabulary Strategy

Mini Lesson

### CONNOTATION AND DENOTATION

**Instruction** In addition to their literal meanings (denotations), words often evoke certain attitudes and emotions in readers (connotations). Poets are especially mindful of connotations, and they carefully choose words that will most accurately express their feelings and ideas. For example, in the poem "Acquainted with the Night," the word *night* does not refer only to a specific time of day. It also connotes negative feelings associated with the speaker's isolation.

**Application** Have students discriminate between the connotative and denotative meanings of the underlined words in the following lines from "Mending Wall."

• We keep the <u>wall</u> between us as we go (line 15)
• In each hand, like an old-stone <u>savage</u> armed (line 40)
• He moves in <u>darkness</u> as it seems to me (line 41)

Use **Vocabulary Transparencies and Copymasters,** p. 83.

**A lesson on connotation and denotation appears on p. 908 in the PE.**

**Literary Analysis: REPETITION**

**(A)** Ask students to describe the effect of the repetition of these words.

**Possible Response:** It imitates the unrelenting sound of the saw; it emphasizes the saw's brutality and insensitivity to the living things around it.

**Literary Analysis: STRUCTURE**

**(B)** Ask students to describe the effect created by the series of declarative sentences in these lines.

**Possible Response:** The sentences in lines 27–29 create a matter-of-fact and rather journalistic tone. The sentence in line 30 reflects the tension and disturbing nature of the situation.

**Active Reading**

**ANALYZING WORD CHOICE**

**(C)** Have students read the final lines of the poem aloud. Ask them what effect the poet's choice of words and phrases has.

**Possible Response:** The phrase "Little—less—nothing!" captures the diminishing sound of the boy's heartbeat. The last sentence matter-of-factly states the onlookers' emotional withdrawal from the dead boy.

# "Out, Out—"

## ROBERT FROST

The buzz saw snarled and rattled in the yard
And made dust and dropped stove-length sticks of wood,
Sweet-scented stuff when the breeze drew across it.
And from there those that lifted eyes could count
5   Five mountain ranges one behind the other
Under the sunset far into Vermont.
And the saw snarled and rattled, snarled and rattled,
As it ran light, or had to bear a load.
And nothing happened: day was all but done.
10  Call it a day, I wish they might have said
To please the boy by giving him the half hour
That a boy counts so much when saved from work.
His sister stood beside them in her apron
To tell them 'Supper.' At the word, the saw,
15  As if to prove saws knew what supper meant,
Leaped out at the boy's hand, or seemed to leap—
He must have given the hand. However it was,
Neither refused the meeting. But the hand!
The boy's first outcry was a rueful[1] laugh,
20  As he swung toward them holding up the hand
Half in appeal, but half as if to keep
The life from spilling. Then the boy saw all—
Since he was old enough to know, big boy
Doing a man's work, though a child at heart—
25  He saw all spoiled. 'Don't let him cut my hand off—
The doctor, when he comes. Don't let him, sister!'
So. But the hand was gone already.
The doctor put him in the dark of ether.
He lay and puffed his lips out with his breath.
30  And then—the watcher at his pulse took fright.
No one believed. They listened at his heart.
Little—less—nothing!—and that ended it.
No more to build on there. And they, since they
Were not the one dead, turned to their affairs.

---

1. **rueful** (rōō′fəl): expressing sorrow or regret.

## Teaching Options

**✓ Assessment  Standardized Test Practice**

**MAKE INFERENCES AND DRAW CONCLUSIONS** For some standardized tests, students will be asked to make inferences and draw conclusions about selections. To give students practice in answering these types of questions, ask them to respond to the following items:

1. In the first line of "Mending Wall," what is the something that Frost believes "doesn't love a wall"?

A. hunters

B. apple trees

C. nature

D. his neighbor

**Answer:** C

2. In "Out, Out—," what is Frost illustrating with his last sentence, "And they, since they/Were not the one dead, turned to their affairs"?

A. Witnessing death changes those people who are living.

B. People have trouble getting over the death of a loved one.

C. Death is a peaceful transition.

D. People are alone in death.

**Answer:** D

## Connect to the Literature

1. **What Do You Think?**
   What is your reaction to the accident in "'Out, Out—'"?

**Comprehension Check**
- What is the setting and time of day of the poem?
- How does the accident happen?
- What is the nature of the boy's injury?

## Think Critically

2.  **ACTIVE READING** **ANALYZING WORD CHOICE** **📖 READER'S NOTEBOOK** Briefly review the charts in your that you used to analyze **word choice** in each poem. Reread lines 19–22 of "'Out, Out—.'" What effect do they convey? What specific words and phrases help create this effect?

3. How does the **speaker** of the poem seem to feel about the boy's death?

   **THINK ABOUT**
   - the speaker's expression of personal feelings, as in lines 10–12
   - how the speaker describes the saw in lines 14–18
   - the speaker's comment in the last three lines

4. The title of this poem is an **allusion**, or indirect reference, to a famous speech in Shakespeare's *Macbeth* (Act Five, Scene 5). How do you think the following quotation from this play relates to the poem?

   *. . . Out, out, brief candle!*
   *Life's but a walking shadow, a poor player*
   *That struts and frets his hour upon the stage*
   *And then is heard no more.*

## Extend Interpretations

5. **Comparing Texts** Reread the poems, focusing on the speakers. Then draw and fill in a Venn diagram to compare and contrast the speakers' characteristics.

   Speaker 1   Speaker 2

6. **Connect to Life** In which poem is the portrayal of aloneness most closely related to an event or situation you yourself have experienced? Did reading the poem give you a new understanding of your reactions to the experience? Explain.

## Literary Analysis

**MOOD IN POETRY** **Mood** is the overall feeling or atmosphere that a writer creates. To create mood in his poems, Frost uses **imagery,** descriptive phrases that re-create sensory experiences for the reader. Imagery usually appeals to one of the five senses. In lines 39–40 of "Mending Wall," Frost creates a visual picture that helps the reader sense that the men are involved in more than a pleasant spring ritual.

Frost also uses **rhythm,** the pattern or flow of sound created by the arrangement of stressed and unstressed syllables in a line. He sometimes breaks the rhythm to introduce tension by inserting a dash, forcing the reader to pause briefly. A good example of this is in line 2 of "Acquainted with the Night."

**Repetition** is the repeated use of a word or phrase for emphasis and rhythmic effect. In "Acquainted with the Night," the repetition of the phrase "I have . . ." gives the poem a mood of growing despair.

**Activity** Imagery, rhythm, and repetition all contribute to the mood of Frost's poems. Create a chart like this one in which you list examples of these devices from all three poems.

| | "Acquainted with . . ." | "Mending Wall" | "'Out, Out—'" |
|---|---|---|---|
| Imagery | | | |
| Rhythm | | | |
| Repetition | | | |

This selection is included in the **Grade 11 InterActive Reader.**

### Objectives

1. understand and appreciate a **narrative poem (Literary Analysis)**
2. examine **blank verse (Literary Analysis)**
3. **understand form in poetry (Active Reading)**

### Summary

"The Death of the Hired Man" is a narrative poem that presents a conversation between a husband and a wife who own a farm. One winter night Mary tells her husband, Warren, that an elderly hired hand named Silas has returned to work at their farm. Warren does not find Silas to be useful or dependable and argues that Silas must go. In the past, Silas has deserted them for better-paying jobs during harvesting season, only to return in winter when work is scarce. Mary then attempts to explain the struggles faced by the man, who is reaching the end of his life and searching for a sense of comfort and self-respect. She argues that they must respect his need to feel useful and accepted. She urges Warren to visit the tired old man, who has fallen asleep in a chair by the stove, and listen seriously to his work plans. Warren goes, only to find that Silas has died.

### Thematic Link

"The Death of the Hired Man" reflects the **modernist** theme of **isolation** and the struggle to maintain human dignity in the modern world.

### 5-Minute Warm-Up

*Daily Language SkillBuilder*

Have students **proofread** the display sentences on page 913j and write them correctly. The sentences also appear on Transparency 28 of **Grammar Transparencies and Copymasters.**

**1006** UNIT SIX   AUTHOR STUDY

---

## PREPARING to *Read*

# The Death of the Hired Man

*Poetry by* ROBERT FROST

*"'It all depends on what you mean by home.'"*

### Connect to Your Life

**The Idea of Home** How would you define the idea of home? Do you think it is an actual physical place, or does it have more to do with the people at home and their attitudes toward you? How do you think your idea of home will change when you go to college or begin living on your own? Discuss your thoughts with a partner.

## Build Background

**A Hired Hand** You are about to read a **dramatic poem,** or a poem that tells a story. In this case, the story is about farmers who provide workers with temporary homes. In the first half of the 20th century, farming was a major source of employment in the United States. Since life on a farm is cyclical, based on the growing season, farmers needed to hire additional help at the busiest times, particularly the fall harvest. Workers generally saved their pay for the winter season, when there was no work to be done. In states where farming was an important industry (and particularly in New England and the South), a pool of itinerant labor existed. So important was the cycle of planting and harvesting—and having enough "hands" to help out—that the schedule of the school year was developed around it.

WORDS TO KNOW
**Vocabulary Preview**

| | |
|---|---|
| abide | harbor |
| assurance | taut |
| beholden | |

## Focus Your Reading

**LITERARY ANALYSIS  BLANK VERSE**  "The Death of the Hired Man" is written in a verse form known as blank verse. **Blank verse** is unrhymed poetry written in iambic pentameter. *Iambic* describes a basic pattern of an unstressed syllable (˘) followed by a stressed syllable (´): *the do˘ve.* *Pentameter* means that each line contains five such pairs of syllables:

*The do˘ve ta˘kes flı˘ght wı˘th gra˘ce tha˘t's e˘ffo˘rtle˘ss.*

As you read, try to recognize how the blank verse imitates the natural rhythms of English speech. Note also that sometimes Frost does not exactly follow this rhythmic pattern.

**ACTIVE READING  UNDERSTANDING FORM IN POETRY**  **Form** is the placement of a poem's lines on the page and the grouping of those lines into **stanzas.** The blank-verse **form** of "The Death of the Hired Man" may make it difficult for you to keep track of the **dialogue.** As you read, watch for devices that Frost has used to help you, including

- **quotation marks:** Double quotation marks indicate the beginning and end of each speech. Single quotation marks indicate quotations within a speech.
- **line breaks:** Frost generally leaves a blank line when the speaker changes and never presents Mary's and Warren's speeches on the same line.
- **point of view:** The narrator always speaks in the third person ("Mary sat," "Warren returned"); in the dialogue, first and second person are used.

**READER'S NOTEBOOK** Using a graphic like this one, record any part of the poem that causes you to pause to identify the speaker.

| Line(s) from Poem | Who I Think Is Speaking | Why I Think So |
|---|---|---|
| | | |
| | | |

**1006**   UNIT SIX   AUTHOR STUDY: ROBERT FROST

---

# The DEATH of the HIRED MAN

## ROBERT FROST

Philo Bound (about 1965), Billy Morrow Jackson. Oil on masonite. Illinois State Museum, Springfield.

Mary sat musing on the lamp-flame at the table,
Waiting for Warren. When she heard his step,
She ran on tiptoe down the darkened passage
To meet him in the doorway with the news
5   And put him on his guard. "Silas is back."
She pushed him outward with her through the door
And shut it after her. "Be kind," she said.
She took the market things from Warren's arms
And set them on the porch, then drew him down
10  To sit beside her on the wooden steps.

"When was I ever anything but kind to him?
But I'll not have the fellow back," he said.
"I told him so last haying, didn't I?
If he left then, I said, that ended it.
15  What good is he? Who else will <u>harbor</u> him
At his age for the little he can do?
What help he is there's no depending on.
Off he goes always when I need him most.
He thinks he ought to earn a little pay,
20  Enough at least to buy tobacco with,
So he won't have to beg and be <u>beholden</u>.
'All right,' I say, 'I can't afford to pay
Any fixed wages, though I wish I could.'
'Someone else can.' 'Then someone else will have to.'
25  I shouldn't mind his bettering himself
If that was what it was. You can be certain,
When he begins like that, there's someone at him

**1** Have students explain Silas's relationship to Mary and Warren. Ask students to describe Warren's apparent attitude toward Silas.

### GUIDE FOR READING
**1 musing on the lamp-flame:** looking thoughtfully at the flame of an oil lamp.

**13 haying:** the time of the year when hay is cut.

WORDS TO KNOW

**harbor** (här′bər) *v.* to shelter; protect
**beholden** (bǐ hōl′ dən) *adj.* obliged to feel grateful; indebted

**1007**

## TEACHING THE LITERATURE

### Customizing Instruction

**Students Acquiring English**
Explain to students that the poem consists mainly of dialogue between two speakers, Mary and Warren. Before students begin reading, work with them to scan the poem for colloquialisms and words related to farming that students might find challenging.

Use **Spanish Study Guide** for additional support, pp. 248–50.

**Less Proficient Readers**
Students might find some of the passages of dialogue difficult to follow. You might want to read the poem aloud first, making it clear who is speaking at what time.

**Set a Purpose** Have students read to learn how Mary's attitude toward Silas differs from Warren's attitude.

**Gifted and Talented**
As students read, ask them to think about how the character of Silas and the style and structure of this poem reflect modernist ideas.

**Less Proficient Readers**
**1** Have students explain Silas's relationship to Mary and Warren. Ask students to describe Warren's apparent attitude toward Silas.
**Possible Response:** Silas has worked for Mary and Warren on their farm. Warren feels he is useless and unreliable.

**2** Be sure students understand that Warren is recalling a conversation between Silas and himself in the past.

## Preteaching Vocabulary

**Mini Lesson**

**USING CONTEXT CLUES: SUMMARY STATEMENTS**
**Instruction** When students encounter an unfamiliar word, they should read further to see if the meaning of the word is summarized, or described. Write the following sentences on the chalkboard as an example:

The peacefulness of the library helped her to <u>muse</u> about possible ideas. After <u>an hour of silent</u> thought, she created a plan.

**Exercises** Ask students to figure out the meanings of the underlined terms.
1. Please pull the rope so that it is tight and firm

around the bundle. Once the rope is <u>taut,</u> throw the bundle into the back of the truck.
2. The plan seemed at first to be <u>daft,</u> but despite its apparent foolishness it worked.
3. His attitude began to <u>pique</u> my temper. Feeling provoked and angry, I went for a walk.

Use **Unit Six Resource Book,** p. 48 for additional support.

**A lesson on context clues appears on p. 326 in the Pupil's Edition.**

Explain to students that most of this narrative poem is a conversation between a husband and wife about an unreliable hired man. Have them consider the reactions the husband and wife have toward the hired man, Silas.

### Literary Analysis  BLANK VERSE

 Students should be able to analyze the melodies of literary language, especially the author's use of evocative rhythms. Ask them what Frost does to break the rhythm in this passage. Have them explain why he does this here.

**Possible Response:** He breaks the rhythm with a series of dashes. Mary was jarred by the sight of Silas sleeping against the barn door. In breaking the rhythm, the poet jars the readers too.

Use **Unit Six Resource Book,** p. 47 for additional support.

### Active Reading
UNDERSTANDING FORM IN POETRY

 Call students' attention to the way in which Frost indicates a change in speaker. Ask students to explain why Frost does not use "he said" and "she said."

**Possible Response:** This would be too repetitive and break up the rhythm of the poem. Frost's style allows readers to focus on what is being said.

Use **Unit Six Resource Book,** p. 46 for additional support.

### GUIDE FOR READING

**C** **Possible Response:** A college boy might have little respect for folk customs and unscientific ideas.

---

Trying to coax him off with pocket money—
In haying time, when any help is scarce.
30  In winter he comes back to us. I'm done."

**1**    "Sh! not so loud: he'll hear you," Mary said.

"I want him to: he'll have to soon or late."

32 **soon or late:** sooner or later; eventually.

"He's worn out. He's asleep beside the stove.
When I came up from Rowe's I found him here,
35  Huddled against the barn door fast asleep,
A miserable sight, and frightening, too—
You needn't smile—I didn't recognize him—
I wasn't looking for him—and he's changed.
Wait till you see."

            "Where did you say he'd been?"

**B**  40  "He didn't say. I dragged him to the house,
And gave him tea and tried to make him smoke.
I tried to make him talk about his travels.
Nothing would do: he just kept nodding off."

"What did he say? Did he say anything?"

45  "But little."

            "Anything? Mary, confess
He said he'd come to ditch the meadow for me."

46 **ditch:** plow.

"Warren!"

            "But did he? I just want to know."

"Of course he did. What would you have him say?
Surely you wouldn't grudge the poor old man
50  Some humble way to save his self-respect.
He added, if you really care to know,
He meant to clear the upper pasture, too.
That sounds like something you have heard before?
Warren, I wish you could have heard the way
55  He jumbled everything. I stopped to look
Two or three times—he made me feel so queer—
To see if he was talking in his sleep.
He ran on Harold Wilson—you remember—
The boy you had in haying four years since.
60  He's finished school, and teaching in his college.
Silas declares you'll have to get him back.
He says they two will make a team for work:

## Teaching Options

**2**

Between them they will lay this farm as smooth!
The way he mixed that in with other things.

65 He thinks young Wilson a likely lad, though daft
On education—you know how they fought
All through July under the blazing sun,
Silas up on the cart to build the load,
Harold along beside to pitch it on."

**3**  70 "Yes, I took care to keep well out of earshot."

"Well, those days trouble Silas like a dream.
You wouldn't think they would. How such things linger!
Harold's young college-boy's <u>assurance</u> piqued him.
After so many years he still keeps finding

75 Good arguments he sees he might have used.
I sympathize. I know just how it feels
To think of the right thing to say too late.
Harold's associated in his mind with Latin.
He asked me what I thought of Harold's saying

**4**  80 He studied Latin, like the violin,
Because he liked it—that an argument!
He said he couldn't make the boy believe
He could find water with a hazel prong—
Which showed how much good school had ever done him

85 He wanted to go over that. But most of all
He thinks if he could have another chance
To teach him how to build a load of hay—"

"I know, that's Silas' one accomplishment.
He bundles every forkful in its place.

90 And tags and numbers it for future reference,
So he can find and easily dislodge it
In the unloading. Silas does that well.
He takes it out in bunches like big birds' nests.
You never see him standing on the hay

95 He's trying to lift, straining to lift himself."
"He thinks if he could teach him that, he'd be
Some good perhaps to someone in the world.

**5** He hates to see a boy the fool of books.
Poor Silas, so concerned for other folk,

100 And nothing to look backward to with pride,
And nothing to look forward to with hope,
So now and never any different."

**65–66 daft on:** crazy about; obsessed with.

**73 piqued** (pēkt): aroused resentment in.

**83 find . . . prong:** refers to the practice of dowsing, in which a person uses a forked stick made of hazel wood to try to find underground water. Why do you think Harold might have rejected this method? **C**

WORDS
TO
KNOW  **assurance** (ə-shoor′əns) *n.* self-confidence

**1009**

### Multiple Learning Styles
**Bodily/Kinesthetic Learners**

**1** From this point to the end of the poem, have students act out the conversation between Mary and Warren. Students should think about what facial expressions and movements the speakers might use as they state their ideas.

### Students Acquiring English

**2** Tell students that "Between them they will lay this farm as smooth!" refers to Silas's belief that he and Harold Wilson will do an excellent job of haying in the coming season.

**3** Explain to students that "out of earshot" is an expression meaning "too far away to be heard." Ask them why they think Warren might have chosen not to listen to what Silas and Harold said to each other.

### Less Proficient Readers

**4** Ask students to explain the differences between Silas and Harold and why the days spent arguing with Harold now trouble Silas.

**Possible Responses:** Silas feels threatened by Harold's education and new ideas. He is troubled by the thought that Harold might not respect him or think he knows what he is doing. He also might have fatherly feelings toward Harold and want to steer him away from wasting his life on books.

### Students Acquiring English

**5** Tell students that "fool of books" refers to someone who is concerned with gaining knowledge from books but who is without life experience or common sense.

---

 **Mini Lesson** **Vocabulary Strategy**

**INTERPRET THE CONNOTATIVE POWER OF WORDS**
**Instruction** Remind students that connotation refers to the attitudes and emotions certain words evoke. Writers understand the power of connotation and use words that will have the strongest effect on readers. For example, when Mary describes finding Silas, she uses words such as *miserable* and *frightening* to describe his appearance. She also says she *dragged* him to the house. These words evoke strong feeling. Have students replace *miserable* with the word *unhappy,* or replace *dragged* with *brought.* Then have them explain how much more power the words chosen by Frost have.

**Application** Ask students to interpret the connotative power of the following words and phrases used in the poem.
- *worn out* (line 33)
- *old ma*n (line 49)
- *jumbled* (line 55)
- *blazing* (line 67)

Use **Vocabulary Transparencies and Copymasters,** p. 84.

**A lesson on connotation appears on p. 908 in the Pupil's Edition.**

**Active Reading**

**UNDERSTANDING FORM IN POETRY**

**B** Call students' attention to how Frost often follows a long passage by one speaker with a short response by the other speaker. Ask them how this mimics the real speech of people arguing different points.

**Possible Response:** One person tries to convince the other in a detailed explanation, and the other responds to what has been said quickly with his or her own thoughts.

**Literary Analysis: CHARACTERIZATION**

**C** Tell students that characterization is an author's use of literary techniques to create a character. One way writers help readers understand characters is by showing how they appear to other characters. Ask students to explain the picture they get of Silas through Mary's descriptions of him.

**Possible Response:** He is a sad, lonely, but proud individual who never accomplished much in his life.

---

Part of a moon was falling down the west,
Dragging the whole sky with it to the hills.
105   Its light poured softly in her lap. She saw it
And spread her apron to it. She put out her hand
Among the harplike morning-glory strings,
<u>Taut</u> with the dew from garden bed to eaves,
As if she played unheard some tenderness
110   That wrought on him beside her in the night.

**1**

"Warren," she said, "he has come home to die:
You needn't be afraid he'll leave you this time."

"Home," he mocked gently.

                "Yes, what else but home?
It all depends on what you mean by home.
115   Of course he's nothing to us, any more
Than was the hound that came a stranger to us
Out of the woods, worn out upon the trail."

"Home is the place where, when you have to go there,
They have to take you in."

                  "I should have called it
120   Something you somehow haven't to deserve."

**B**

Warren leaned out and took a step or two,
Picked up a little stick, and brought it back
And broke it in his hand and tossed it by.
"Silas has better claim on us you think
125   Than on his brother? Thirteen little miles
As the road winds would bring him to his door.
Silas has walked that far no doubt today.
Why doesn't he go there? His brother's rich,
A somebody—director in the bank."

130   "He never told us that."

                  "We know it, though."

"I think his brother ought to help, of course.
I'll see to that if there is need. He ought of right
To take him in, and might be willing to—
He may be better than appearances.

**110 wrought** (rôt) **on:** worked on.

**121–123** What words would you use to describe Warren's reaction? **A**

**134 better than appearances:** better than he looks.

> WORDS
> TO
> KNOW
>
> **taut** (tôt) *adj.* pulled tight; straight

**1010**

---

## Teaching Options

**Workplace Link** **Communicating Ideas**

**Instruction** In "The Death of the Hired Man," Mary describes Silas's recalling arguments with his coworker Harold Wilson with regret. She sympathizes with the experience of thinking of "the right thing to say too late." The ability to express ideas clearly and effectively is an important skill in both personal and professional situations. Before presenting an idea or a plan, students should spend time thinking carefully about details, issues people might raise, and effective ways to present information.

**Application** Ask each student to think of an idea he or she would like to present at school, at home, or in the community. This idea can concern a simple procedure or a larger issue that affects many people. Have each student then create a detailed and effective plan. Students should then present their ideas to the rest of the class. Students should show that they can defend their ideas and answer any questions presented by other students.

C

135　But have some pity on Silas. Do you think
　　　If he had any pride in claiming kin
　　　Or anything he looked for from his brother,
　　　He'd keep so still about him all this time?"

　　　"I wonder what's between them."

　　　　　　　　　　　　　　　　"I can tell you.

2

140　Silas is what he is—we wouldn't mind him—
　　　But just the kind that kinsfolk can't abide.
　　　He never did a thing so very bad.
　　　He don't know why he isn't quite as good
　　　As anybody. Worthless though he is,
145　He won't be made ashamed to please his brother."

　　　"I can't think Si ever hurt anyone."

　　　"No, but he hurt my heart the way he lay
　　　And rolled his old head on the sharp-edged chair-back.
　　　He wouldn't let me put him on the lounge.　　　　　　　**149 lounge:** couch
150　You must go in and see what you can do.
　　　I made the bed up for him there tonight.
　　　You'll be surprised at him—how much he's broken.
　　　His working days are done; I'm sure of it."

　　　"I'd not be in a hurry to say that."

155　"I haven't been. Go, look, see for yourself.
　　　But, Warren, please remember how it is:
　　　He's come to help you ditch the meadow.
　　　He has a plan. You mustn't laugh at him.
　　　He may not speak of it, and then he may.
160　I'll sit and see if that small sailing cloud
　　　Will hit or miss the moon."

　　　　　　　　　　　　　　It hit the moon.
　　　Then there were three there, making a dim row,
　　　The moon, the little silver cloud, and she.

　　　Warren returned—too soon, it seemed to her—
165　Slipped to her side, caught up her hand and waited.

　　　"Warren?" she questioned.
　　　　　　　　　　　　"Dead," was all he answered.

WORDS
TO
KNOW
　　　**abide** ((e-bīd') *v.* to put up with

1011

### Less Proficient Readers

**1** Have students explain the different views of home expressed by Mary and Warren. Ask them why Mary feels strongly that they should provide Silas with a final place to call home.

**Possible Response:** Warren calls a home a place where people are obligated to take you in when you need to go there. Mary calls home a place that you shouldn't have to deserve. She believes that Silas is entitled to a place to die peacefully.

**2** Ask students to explain how Silas is different from his brother. Why, according to Mary, will Silas not go to his brother?

**Possible Response:** The brother is wealthy and successful. Mary believes that going to his brother will make Silas feel shame.

### Students Acquiring English

Define the following words and phrases to help students comprehend the poem.

- *of right* (line 132)—according to standards of right and wrong
- *still* (line 138)—quiet, silent
- *abide* (line 141)—stand, put up with (Silas's family can't accept his personality, behavior, or lifestyle.)

✓ Assessment　**Informal Assessment**

**JOURNAL ENTRIES** You can informally assess your students' understanding of the poem by having them create two short journal entries, one from the point of view of Mary and one from the point of view of Warren. Each entry should express the speaker's point of view on the following ideas: Silas as a person and a worker; his or her responsibilities toward Silas; how he or she feels after Silas's death.

**RUBRIC**

**3 Full Accomplishment** Journal entries show a clear and complete understanding of ideas and attitudes presented in the poem.

**2 Substantial Accomplishment** Journal entries show some understanding of ideas and attitudes presented in the poem, but they are unclear or incomplete.

**1 Little or Partial Accomplishment** Journal entries are incomplete and do not show an adequate understanding of ideas and attitudes presented in the poem.

### Build Background

President Kennedy's (1917–1963) speech, given less than a month before he was assassinated, was inspired by his dedication to the arts and his knowledge of Frost as a person, poet, and teacher. The two shared a mutually supportive relationship. Before Kennedy became president, Frost was one of his strongest and most vocal political supporters. In 1962, Kennedy had the opportunity to present Frost with a Congressional Gold Medal in honor of his poetry and cultural work. In this speech, Kennedy focuses on Frost's accomplishments as both "an artist and an American."

### Teaching Nonfiction: Skills and Strategies

#### EXAMINING A SPEAKER'S PURPOSE

Speeches can be made to entertain, inspire, praise, instruct, inform, or persuade. Some speeches accomplish a variety of these purposes. The details and ideas presented, as well as the tone or attitude expressed in a speech, can lead audiences to understand a particular speaker's purpose.

Students know before they read that the primary purpose of Kennedy's speech is to praise Frost's literary accomplishments. Ask students to identify other purposes the speech serves.

**Possible Responses:** Kennedy's speech also supports the arts in the United States, outlining the importance of building a nation with spiritual strength as well as political strength. He warns his audience against becoming a nation that "disdains the mission of art." His speech also attempts to build national pride and optimism for the future.

#### IDENTIFYING MAIN IDEAS

Ask students to identify which line they believe expresses Kennedy's main idea about Frost's significance as an artist and thinker in the United States. Then ask what details Kennedy uses to both support and illustrate his main idea.

**Possible Responses:** The line that reads "he gave his age strength with which to overcome despair" expresses the main idea. Several statements illustrate how Frost gave the nation spiritual strength through art and his unique vision.

---

# *In Praise of*
# *Robert Frost*

*Speech by* JOHN F. KENNEDY

## Preparing to Read

### Build Background

**Frost and Kennedy** In January 1961, President-elect John F. Kennedy asked Robert Frost to read a poem at his inauguration. It was the first time such an invitation had ever been extended. Kennedy was a great admirer of Frost's poetry, and the two became friends. Frost died in January of 1963, and on October 27 of that year, Kennedy spoke at Amherst College at a ceremony honoring the poet and his literary achievement.

This day, devoted to the memory of Robert Frost, offers an opportunity for reflection which is prized by politicians as well as by others and even by poets. For Robert Frost was one of the granite figures of our time in America. He was supremely two things—an artist and an American.

A nation reveals itself not only by the men it produces but also by the men it honors, the men it remembers.

In America our heroes have customarily run to men of large accomplishments. But today this college and country honor a man whose contribution was not to our size but to our spirit; not to our political beliefs but to our insight; not to our self-esteem, but to our self-comprehension.

In honoring Robert Frost we therefore can pay honor to the deepest sources of our national strength. That strength takes many forms and the most obvious forms are not always the most significant.

The men who create power make an indispensable contribution to the nation's greatness. But the men who question power make a contribution just as indispensable, especially when that questioning is disinterested.

For they determine whether we use power or power uses us. Our national strength matters; but the spirit which informs and controls our strength matters just as much. This was the special significance of Robert Frost. . . .

"I have been," he wrote, "one acquainted with the night."

And because he knew the midnight as well as the high noon, because he understood the ordeal as well as the triumph of the human spirit, he gave his age strength with which to overcome despair. . . .

For art establishes the basic human truths which must serve as the touchstones of our judgment. The artist, however faithful to his personal vision of reality, becomes the last champion of the individual mind and sensibility against an intrusive society and an officious state.

The great artist is thus a solitary figure. He has, as Frost said, "a lover's quarrel with the world." In pursuing his perceptions of reality he must often sail against the currents of his time. This is not a popular role. . . .

In serving his vision of the truth the artist best serves his nation. And the nation which disdains the mission of art invites the fate of Robert Frost's hired man—the fate of having "nothing to look backward to with pride and nothing to look forward to with hope."

I look forward to a great future for America—a future in which our country will match its military strength with our moral restraint, its wealth with our wisdom, its power with our purpose. . . .

And I look forward to a world which will be safe not only for democracy and diversity but also for personal distinction.

Robert Frost was often skeptical about projects for human improvement. Yet I do not think he would disdain this hope.

---

## Teaching Options

 **Mini Lesson** ## Grammar

**MODIFIERS:** *THIS, THESE; THAT, THOSE*

**Instruction** *This* and *that* are adjectives that modify singular nouns; *these* and *those* are adjectives that modify plural nouns. Give students the following examples:

   Incorrect: *These* kind of nails is easier to use.
   Correct: *This* kind of nails is easier to use.
   Correct: *These* nails are easier to use.

**Exercises** Have students choose the correct modifier to complete each sentence.

1. (<u>Those</u>, That) methods of haying are organized and efficient.

2. We hoped to hire more of (those, <u>that</u>) type of worker.

3. (These, <u>This</u>) sort of problem occurs every harvest season.

4. Did you know (<u>those</u>, that) people cannot work together without arguing?

 Use **Grammar Transparencies and Copymasters**, p. 139.

 Use McDougal Littell's *Language Network*, Chapter 7, for more instruction in modifiers.

# *Thinking* through the LITERATURE

## Connect to the Literature

**1. What Do You Think?**
What reactions do you have to the poem's ending?

**Comprehension Check**
- Why is Warren angry at Silas?
- What does Harold Wilson represent to Silas?
- What changes Warren's mind about Silas's return?

## Think Critically

**2.** `ACTIVE READING` `UNDERSTANDING FORM IN POETRY`
In your 📖 READER'S NOTEBOOK, check any notes you made at points in the poem where you had to stop and think about who was speaking. What helped you figure out who the speaker was?

**3.** Whose position about Silas do you agree with, Mary's or Warren's? Why?

**4.** In lines 139–145, Mary explains Silas's relationship with his rich brother. What do you think she means by the last line?

**5.** Compare Warren's definition of home (lines 118–119) with Mary's (lines 119–120). How do you think each definition fits its speaker's personality?

## Extend Interpretations

**6. What If?** Suppose Silas had not died at the end of the poem. Do you think Mary would have been able to talk Warren into letting him stay? Why or why not?

**7. Critic's Corner** The poet Ezra Pound, reviewing Frost's second book of poetry, wrote, "I know more of farm life than I did before I had read his poems. That means I know more of 'Life.'" Think of the poems you've read in this Author Study. What do you think Pound meant by his statement? Do you agree with his praise of Frost's poetry?

**8. Connect to Life** Think about how you defined the idea of home in Connect to Your Life. How does your definition compare with the definitions Frost includes in "The Death of the Hired Man" (lines 118–120)? Is your idea of home closer to Warren's or to Mary's?

## Literary Analysis

`BLANK VERSE` Much of "The Death of the Hired Man" is written in **blank verse**, lines of unrhymed **iambic pentameter**. Blank verse, especially when handled by a master such as Frost, imitates the natural rhythms of English speech and thus sounds very much like the way people talk. A line of blank verse has five iambic feet, each consisting of an unstressed syllable followed by a stressed syllable. (*Penta-* comes from a Greek word meaning "five.")

> Some húmblĕ wáy tŏ sáve
> hĭs sélf-rĕspéct.

Good blank verse does not have a singsong quality; in fact, a reader may not even notice the use of the form. A period or comma within a line, by making the reader briefly pause, can help break up the regular rhythm and make the line sound more natural:

> *"He's worn out. He's asleep beside the stove."*

The use of common phrases and expressions also makes blank verse more closely resemble speech:

> *"He added, if you really care to know,"*

**Paired Activity** Review the text of "The Death of the Hired Man" one more time. Find lines in iambic pentameter that sound to you like natural speech and read them aloud to a partner. See if your partner agrees with your choices. Remember that not every line in the poem is in iambic pentameter.

## Extend Interpretations

**What If?** Students who think Warren would let Silas stay might point out that Warren does not object when Mary tells him she has made a bed for Silas, that Warren grows less hostile to Silas as Mary talks to him, or that Warren might accept taking care of Silas as a duty. Those who disagree might focus on Warren's practical nature and his resentment of Silas's leaving when he is most needed.

**Critic's Corner** Possible Response: Knowing more about particular ways of life helps a person better understand what living is about; learning about how people live contributes to a person's thinking about what it means to be human.

**Connect to Life** Those whose idea of home is closer to Mary's might focus on understanding and sympathy. Those closer to Warren's idea might feel that duty and doing what's right are more important than sympathy.

## GUIDING STUDENT RESPONSE

### Connect to the Literature

**1. What Do You Think?**
Students' reactions will vary. Some may think Silas's death is sad or tragic; others may think he was exhausted and his time had come.

**Comprehension Check**
- Silas left their farm when he was needed most.
- Silas thinks Harold learns only useless things at college.
- Mary asks him to be kind to Silas and tells him Silas is dying.

📄 Use Selection Quiz
**Unit Six Resource Book,** p. 49.

### Think Critically

**2.** Possible Responses: the quotation marks; the paragraph breaks that signal when the speaker changes.

**3.** Answers will vary. Students who share Mary's ideas might emphasize Silas's need for respect and a place to call home. Those who agree with Warren might insist that Silas, by leaving when he was most needed, did wrong to Warren and Mary.

**4.** Possible Responses: Silas would be ashamed to ask for help from his brother; if Silas asked for help, his brother would treat him in ways that would make Silas ashamed.

**5.** Possible Response: Mary sympathizes with Silas even though he doesn't deserve it; Warren sees taking care of Silas as a matter of duty—and feels that Silas's brother has a stronger duty to Silas than he and Mary do.

### Literary Analysis

**Blank Verse** Lines that students might select include "What help he is there's no depending on" (line 17), "Of course he did. What would you have him say?" (line 48), and "It all depends on what you mean by home" (line 114 ).

Robert Frost's distinct style helped make his words and ideas memorable and appealing to a variety of readers. Students can learn about specific aspects of Frost's style by reviewing the "Key Aspects of Frost's Style" chart and then finding examples of the five points in the excerpts in the right margin.

## Analysis of Style

**Ⓐ First activity**
**Possible Response:** The excerpt from "The Gift Outright" is closest to every-day speech patterns.

**Ⓑ Second activity**
The rhyming in the poems will probably appeal to most students, and the use of the word *land* in "The Gift Outright" could be confusing to some students. Students should articulate why certain words capture their attention and why they find certain word usages confusing.

**Ⓒ Third activity**
Images chosen by students might include the relationship between the land and people in "The Gift Outright," the long, two-pointed ladder sticking through an apple tree toward heaven in "After Apple Picking," images of the fleeting quality of nature in "Nothing Gold Can Stay," and the comparison of fire to desire in "Fire and Ice."

## Applications

1. **Imitating Style** Tell students that the subject matter of their poems need not be the same as in the excerpt they choose. Remind students to review the Key Aspects box on the page before rewriting the excerpts.

2. **Changing Style** Have students go through the entire writing process for this activity—prewriting, drafting, editing, and publishing.

3. **Speaking and Listening** Have students use the following criteria to critique oral interpretation. The student
   - makes and supports a valid interpretation of how the character might voice those lines.
   - uses voice (volume and tone) to establish mood and convey meaning.
   - uses movement and gestures to establish mood and convey meaning.
   - uses facial expressions to establish mood and convey meaning.

---

# THE AUTHOR'S STYLE
## Frost's Sly Simplicity

At a time when modern poetry was moving toward difficult, experimental writing, Robert Frost was able to create poems that still seem simple and natural to the reader. Yet complexity lies beneath the simple surface of his poems.

### Key Aspects of Frost's Style

- use of plain language to reflect the simple lives of New England farmers
- use of blank verse to achieve the natural rhythms of everyday speech
- use of metaphors that change commonplace ideas into experiences of deeper meaning
- use of repetition, dialogue, and dialect
- unusual word order for emphasis

## Analysis of Style

At the right are lines from four of Frost's poems. Study the chart above, and then read each excerpt carefully. Complete the following activities with a small group of classmates:

**Ⓐ** • Read the excerpts aloud, and discuss the rhythm of each. In which excerpt is the rhythm closest to the way you speak?

**Ⓑ** • Describe the word choice in the excerpts. What sort of words catch your eye? Are there any confusing word usages?

**Ⓒ** • Which excerpt do you think contains the most vivid image? What makes it easy to see what Frost is describing?

## Applications

**1. Imitating Style** Choose one of the four excerpts, and write a word-for-word imitation of its style: copy the grammatical structure of the original, replacing every noun with a noun, every verb with a verb, and so on. Compare your version with a partner's.

**2. Changing Style** Choose either "Nothing Gold Can Stay" or "Fire and Ice." Rewrite the excerpt as a short prose piece. Keep as many of Frost's original words as you can, but add words that fill in the meaning.

**3. Speaking and Listening** Decide who might be the speaker in "The Gift Outright," "After Apple-Picking," and "Fire and Ice." Then prepare a reading of each excerpt that reflects how you think the speaker might deliver the lines.

---

*from* **The Gift Outright**

The land was ours before we were the land's.
She was our land more than a hundred years
Before we were her people. . . .

*from* **After Apple-Picking**

My long two-pointed ladder's sticking
    through a tree
Toward heaven still,
And there's a barrel that I didn't fill
Beside it, and there may be two or three
Apples I didn't pick upon some bough.

*from* **Nothing Gold Can Stay**

Nature's first green is gold,
Her hardest hue to hold.
Her early leaf's a flower;
But only so an hour.

*from* **Fire and Ice**

Some say the world will end in fire,
Some say in ice.
From what I've tasted of desire
I hold with those who favor fire.

# Choices & CHALLENGES

## Writing Options

**Neighborly Editorial** Assume the role of either the narrator or the neighbor in "Mending Wall." Write an editorial for the local paper explaining why you agree or disagree with the statement "Good fences make good neighbors."

## Activities & Explorations

**New England Collage** Collect a series of pictures of the New England landscape. You should be able to get images from the tourist office of each state and from magazines and travel guides. Use these images to create a collage depicting the landscape that inspired Frost's poetry. ~ **ART**

## Inquiry & Research

**Farm Life** Research the changes technology has brought to farming in this century. Consider these questions: What was life on a farm like in 1900? What is it like today? When did the need for "hired men" begin to fade? Put your report in your **Working Portfolio.**

## Vocabulary in Action

**EXERCISE: SYNONYMS** Choose the Word to Know that best fits in each word group.

1. tolerate, endure, accept, _____
2. certainty, _____, poise, conviction
3. _____, obliged, indebted, obligated
4. rigid, stretched, tense, _____
5. secure, shield, _____, defend

| WORDS TO KNOW | abide | beholden | taut |
|---|---|---|---|
| | assurance | harbor | |

**Building Vocabulary**
Some of the Words to Know have more than one meaning. For an in-depth lesson on words with multiple meanings, see page 630.

## Robert Frost
### Author Study Project
LIVING MUSEUM PRESENTATION

In small groups, research and represent different stages of Frost's life. Either singly or in groups, actors will portray Frost and others from his world and dramatize a few events. Each group can focus on a different section below, or group members can each cover an area. For more details about Frost, refer to the Internet and to such other sources as biographies and letter collections. The goal is to get a well-rounded picture of Frost as a way of more fully appreciating his writing.

**Frost on the Farm** The farm in Derry was where Frost produced some of his earliest writing and where his children were born. What was family life like in the Frost household? What incidents became topics for poems?

**Frost in England** It was not until Frost moved his family to England in 1912 that his literary career began to take off. What happened there to make him a success? Who were some of the literary figures he met, and what influence did they have on his career?

**Frost on the Lecture Circuit** After he returned from England, Frost gave public presentations in which he talked about writing and read from his works. How was Frost received on the lecture circuit? What are some interesting statements he made about writing? about his fellow poets? about life?

 **More Online: Research Starter**
www.mcdougallittell.com

## Author Study Project
LIVING MUSEUM PRESENTATION

Encourage students to look for interesting details and experiences that truly show Frost in his different roles at different stages in his life. When students locate an event that they would like to dramatize, suggest that they first outline the basic facts of the event on paper. Then they can brainstorm to create appropriate dialogue based on their information.

### Secondary Print Sources
Students might consult some of the following sources: *Family Letters of Robert and Elinor Frost,* edited by Arnold Grade (State University of New York Press, 1972); *Robert Frost: A Biography,* by Jeffrey Meyers (Houghton Mifflin, 1996); *Robert Frost: A Pictorial Chronicle,* by Kathleen Morrison (Rinehart and Winston, 1974); *Selected Letters,* edited by Lawrence Thompson (Rinehart and Winston, 1964)

### MULTIMEDIA PROJECT
Students can turn their dramatizations into a multimedia project by producing their scenes in front of a video camera using simple sets and appropriate background music. Students should divide tasks related to producing the video among members of each group. Before each scene begins, a narrator can tell when each event is taking place and what significance the scene has in the life of Frost.

## Objectives
- understand the following literary terms:
  - Traditional narrative structure
  - Modernism
  - Protagonist
  - Irony
  - Understatement
  - Stream-of-consciousness technique
- connect literature to historical contexts and to the student's own experiences
- analyze text structures for how they influence understanding
- compare and contrast themes across texts

## Teaching the Lesson

In this section, students will be introduced to modernism through a comparison with traditional narrative structure. This lesson will present some of the defining features of modernist literature.

### Introducing the Concepts
The modernist poet Ezra Pound urged his literary colleagues to "make it new." Modernists are similar to other new generations in their need to reject the past in order to explore and understand the significance of their own experience and time. As students read the modernist literature in this unit, have them consider the following questions:

What central message or theme does the work convey?

Of what significance are the characters' actions, feelings, and thoughts?

What images or symbols linger in your mind?

What emotions or ideas do these images and symbols suggest?

As they read each short story and poem, students can write their reactions to these questions and keep their responses in their Working Portfolios.

### Presenting the Concepts
Read through the strategies aloud or project them on a transparency. Select one of the students' favorite modernist stories or poems and model how to use the strategies to analyze the work.

# LEARNING the Language of Literature

## Modernism

Imagine a world full of contradictions—a world of disillusion and hope, of crumbling traditions and explosive creative energy, of self-doubt and self-discovery. This is the modern world, the world that young European and American writers in the early decades of the century first struggled to come to terms with in their art.

*The Great Gatsby* (1925) captured the emptiness of modern life.

### Making It New
Ernest Hemingway, F. Scott Fitzgerald, William Faulkner, Katherine Anne Porter, T. S. Eliot, Ezra Pound, and William Carlos Williams were part of a generation of writers who created new ways of writing to respond to the new post-World War I realities. The loss of stability that was felt so strongly between 1914 and 1945 was reflected in the structure of their literature.

A comparison between Ernest Hemingway and Willa Cather can help you see the difference between a modernist work and a more traditionally structured one. Cather included in her works many modernist themes, such as the effects of alienation. But her method of storytelling is fairly traditional. For example, in "A Wagner Matinee" (page 688), the narrator directly explains the significance of his relationship with his aunt.

> I owed to this woman most of the good that ever came my way in my boyhood, and had a reverential affection for her. During the years when I was riding herd for my uncle, my aunt, after cooking three meals . . . and putting the six children to bed, would often stand until midnight at her ironing-board with me at the kitchen table beside her, hearing me recite Latin declensions and conjugations, gently shaking me when my drowsy head sank down over a page of irregular verbs.
>
> — Willa Cather, "A Wagner Matinee"

**YOUR TURN** What details explain Aunt Georgiana's character and the narrator's feelings about her?

The novels and short stories of Ernest Hemingway reflected Americans' shifting attitudes about the violence and upheaval of the modern world. His work is characterized by spare description and dialogue. In contrast to Willa Cather, Ernest Hemingway gives very little explanation about the relationship between his characters in "The End of Something" (page 1018). The story begins with a description of "a lumbering town" that was depleted of timber and thus abandoned by the lumber company. Into the description of the ruined lumber mill, Hemingway introduces his characters.

> The one-story bunk houses, the eating-house, the company store, the mill offices, and the big mill itself stood deserted in the acres of sawdust that covered the swampy meadow by the shore of the bay.
>
> Ten years later there was nothing of the mill left except the broken white limestone of its foundations showing through the swampy second growth as Nick and Marjorie rowed along the shore.
>
> — Ernest Hemingway, "The End of Something"

**YOUR TURN** What might be the connection between the ruined mill and Nick and Marjorie?

### The Defining Features of Modernism
Modernism comprises a vast diversity of individual styles. Yet there are some defining features of the literature that show a distinct break with the past.

- **A rejection of traditional themes and subject matter.** Instead of love, many modernists wrote of the inability to commit to, or even communicate with, others. Instead of marriage and the community, they often wrote of broken relationships and broken lives.

- **A focus on alienated individuals rather than "heroes" who stood for the values of the society.** The protagonist of T. S. Eliot's poem "The Love Song of J. Alfred Prufrock" (page 1025) is no heroic Gregorio Cortez but an insecure, lonely man who is consumed by self-doubt.

- **Frequent themes of impermanence and change.** For most modernists, nothing lasted—neither human institutions nor human attachments. Remember the loss of youthful dreams and beauty in F. Scott Fitzgerald's "Winter Dreams" (page 840).

- **The use of understatement and irony to reveal important emotions and ideas.** The modernists no longer felt confident to state universal truths directly in their works as the romantics and transcendentalists had before them. For example, Robert Frost ends "Out, Out—" (page 1004) with the acknowledgment that, essentially, life goes on. But instead of making a direct statement, he understates this truth by showing the bystanders calmly returning "to their affairs" because "they were not the one dead."

- **The use of symbols and images that suggest meanings rather than statements that explain meanings.** The speaker in Frost's "Acquainted with the Night" (page 1001) never admits that he's lonely or sad; the images in the poem tell you that.

- **The use of a stream-of-consciousness technique to show what's going on both inside and outside the characters.** Eliot's "The Love Song of J. Alfred Prufrock" and Porter's "The Jilting of Granny Weatherall" (pages 1025 and 1034) are both structured on the central characters' sometimes disconnected, but revealing, inner thoughts, feelings, and dreams.

## The Tip of the *Iceberg*

Although modernist writers often describe the characters' actions, feelings, and thoughts, they do not interpret the significance of these for the reader. Hemingway, for example, does not directly connect the mill to the main events of "The End of Something." He never explains why the characters speak to each other as they do. The reader is left to infer how they feel about each other from their actions and from what they do not say to each other as much as from what they do say. Hemingway once explained such omissions this way: "I always try to write on the principle of the iceberg. There is seven-eighths of it under water for every part that shows."

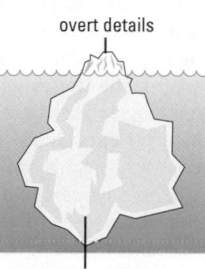

overt details

what must be inferred

## Strategies for Reading: Modernist Literature

1. Make inferences from detailed descriptions, especially of the setting, to understand the characters' feelings and attitudes.

2. Analyze how images relate to character and express complex emotions or ideas.

3. Watch for ironic situations that may point to larger themes.

4. In a stream-of-consciousness narrative, keep track of the twists and turns of a character's thoughts to understand what he or she is reacting to.

5. **Monitor** your reading strategies and modify them when your understanding breaks down. Remember to use your Strategies for Active Reading: **predict, visualize, connect, question, clarify,** and **evaluate.**

MODERNISM **1017**

## Literary Techniques: Stream-of-Consciousness

Coined by the American philosopher William James, the term stream-of-consciousness refers to the waking mind's flow of thoughts. James first used this phrase in his book *Principles of Psychology* (1890), but the term has come to have a literary meaning that describes a narrative technique adapted by many authors in the early 20th century. Stream-of-consciousness is supposed to show the mind at work by mimicking the mind's thought process. Writers use ungrammatical construction, snippets of incoherent thought, free associations of ideas, and images and words at the pre-speech level to illustrate this concept.

Students can read or listen to this famous example of stream-of-consciousness in Virginia Woolf's *Mrs. Dalloway*. Encourage them to look for elements of stream-of-consciousness mentioned above.

from *Mrs. Dalloway,* by Virginia Woolf

What a lark! What a plunge! For so it had always seemed to her, when, with a little squeak of the hinges, which she could hear now, she had burst open the French windows and plunged at Bourton into the open air. How fresh, how calm, stiller than this of course, the air was in the early morning; like the flap of a wave; the kiss of a wave; chill and sharp and yet (for a girl of eighteen as she then was) solemn, feeling as she did, standing there at the open window, that something awful was about to happen; looking at the flowers, at the trees with the smoke winding off them and the rooks rising, falling; standing and looking until Peter Walsh said, "Musing among the vegetables?"—was that it?—"I prefer men to cauliflowers"—was that it? He must have said it at breakfast one morning when she had gone out on to the terrace—Peter Walsh. He would be back from India one of these days, June or July, she forgot which, for his letters were awfully dull; it was his sayings one remembered; his eyes, his pocket-knife, his smile, his grumpiness and, when millions of things had utterly vanished—how strange it was!—a few sayings like this about cabbages.

## OVERVIEW

 This selection is included in the **Grade 11 InterActive Reader.**

### Objectives
1. understand a modernist **short story** (Literary Analysis)
2. examine **style** (Literary Analysis)
3. **make inferences** (Active Reading)

### Summary
This short story is set in Hortons Bay, Michigan—once known as a lumbering town. Nick and Marjorie, a young couple, approach the ruins of the lumber mill in their boat as they fish for trout. When they realize the fish are not biting, they set out two baited lines and go ashore to have a picnic supper. Nick comments that there is going to be a moon, and Marjorie replies, "I know it." This response irritates Nick because he says it reflects Marjorie's problem of "knowing everything." Marjorie senses that there is something more to Nick's irritation and probes further. Nick tells her that their relationship is no longer fun. Aware that Nick wants to end the relationship, Marjorie takes the boat away by herself. Bill, a friend who apparently knew Nick was going to break up with Marjorie, approaches Nick and asks how he feels. Nick abruptly sends him away.

### Thematic Link
The character Nick Adams epitomizes the literary movement known as **modernism.** He doesn't understand what has happened to his relationship with Marjorie or why he feels no joy in his life. His **alienation** from everyone around him makes him feel as if he is the only **individual** in the world.

### 5-Minute Warm-Up

***Daily Language SkillBuilder***

Have students **proofread** the display sentences on page 913k and write them correctly. The sentences also appear on Transparency 28 of **Grammar Transparencies and Copymasters.**

---

# PREPARING to *Read*

*" 'Isn't love any fun?' Marjorie said."*

# The End of Something

*Short Story by* ERNEST HEMINGWAY

> ### Connect to Your Life
>
> **Troubled Romance** This story depicts a young couple whose relationship is ending. Their troubles raise the question, Why do people fall out of love? In a small group, discuss various answers to this question and come up with a list of possible reasons. Share your list with those of other groups. Then, as you read the story, try to find out why the couple breaks up.

## Build Background

**The Nick Adams Stories** "The End of Something" is one of a series of Hemingway stories about the character Nick Adams. The stories, which are semiautobiographical, trace the life of this character through his youth in northern Michigan, his adolescence on the road, his days as a soldier in World War I, his postwar return to Michigan, and his married years in Europe. In this story, Nick is a young war veteran struggling to make sense of his life and the end of his love for a young woman. The story is set in Hortons Bay, a resort town on Lake Michigan, where Hemingway himself spent his childhood summers. Like Nick, Hemingway returned to the Hortons Bay area during the summer of 1919 to recover from his war wounds. Although the events of the story are fictional, Nick's pain, loneliness, and disillusionment with the world of adulthood were problems that Hemingway and other young men confronted upon returning from the war.

## Focus Your Reading

**LITERARY ANALYSIS** **STYLE** **Style** is the distinctive way in which a piece of literature is written. Style refers not so much to what is said but how it is said. Word choice, sentence length, tone, imagery, and the use of dialogue all contribute to a writer's style. One of the hallmarks of Hemingway's straightforward style is his simple, clipped dialogue. As you read "The End of Something," note the repetitions and omissions in the characters' speech that resemble real-life conversations.

**ACTIVE READING** **MAKING INFERENCES** The scenes in "The End of Something" consist almost entirely of **dialogue** between the main characters—Nick and Marjorie. As they speak, the narrator gives little direct information about how they feel or think. Hemingway's sparse style challenges readers to fill in the gaps. You will need to make **inferences,** or logical guesses, to discover the suggested meanings behind the characters' spoken words. Their remarks provide you with clues about their relationship.

**READER'S NOTEBOOK** To help you make inferences as you read, create a chart like the one shown and fill it in with moments of Nick and Marjorie's dialogue that seem meaningful. Then consider what their comments reveal.

| Dialogue Clues | What They Reveal |
|---|---|
| Nick's comments | |
| Marjorie's comments | |

---

## LESSON RESOURCES

**UNIT SIX RESOURCE BOOK,** pp. 50–53

**ASSESSMENT RESOURCES**
**Formal Assessment,** pp. 189–190
**Teacher's Guide to Assessment and Portfolio Use**
**Test Generator**

**SKILLS TRANSPARENCIES AND COPYMASTERS**
**Literary Analysis**
• Modernist Literature, T17 (for Cooperative Learning Activity, p. 1023)

**Reading and Critical Thinking**
• Making Inferences, T7 (for Active Reading, p. 1018)

**Grammar**
• Punctuating Dialogue, T56 (for Mini Lesson, p. 1024)
• Illogical Comparisons, C134 (for Mini Lesson, p. 1019)
• Commas: Setting Off Quotations, C154 (for Mini Lesson, p. 1024)

**Vocabulary**
• Connotation, C85 (for Mini Lesson, p. 1022)

**Writing**
• The Uses of Dialogue, T24 (for Writing Option 3, p. 1024)

**INTEGRATED TECHNOLOGY**
**Audio Library**
**Visit our website:** www.mcdougallittell.com

Illustration Copyright © D. J. McKay.

# The End of Something

### Ernest Hemingway

In the old days Hortons Bay was a lumbering town. No one who lived in it was out of sound of the big saws in the mill by the lake. Then one year  there were no more logs to make lumber. The lumber schooners came into the bay and were loaded with the cut of the mill that stood stacked in the yard. All the piles of lumber were carried away. The big mill building had all its machinery that was removable taken out and hoisted on board one of the schooners by the men who had worked in the mill. The schooner moved out of the bay toward the open lake carrying the two great saws, the travelling carriage that hurled the logs against the revolving, circular saws and all the rollers, wheels, belts, and iron piled on a hull-deep load of lumber. Its open hold covered with canvas and lashed tight, the sails of the schooner filled and it moved out into the open lake, carrying with it everything that had made the mill a mill and Hortons Bay a town.

The one-story bunk houses, the eating-house, the company store, the mill offices, and the big mill itself stood deserted in the acres of sawdust that covered the swampy meadow by the shore of the bay.

Ten years later there was nothing of the mill left except the broken white limestone of its foundations showing through the

**Reading Skills and Strategies:**

**PREVIEW**

Tell students that the story is told from the third-person point of view. Since the narrator does not explain what is happening, readers must use the characters' words and actions and the narrator's descriptions to make inferences.

**Active Reading** MAKING INFERENCES

 Students should be able to draw inferences and support them with textual evidence. Ask students to infer what Marjorie is like.

**Possible Responses:** Marjorie is romantic, imaginative, and positive. She compares a decaying mill to a castle. She seems to see the better side of things.

**B** Ask students what Hemingway is implying here. If there were another sentence at the end of the paragraph, what would they expect it to be?

**Possible Response:** "She loved Nick."

Use **Unit Six Resource Book,** p. 51 for additional support.

**Literary Analysis** STYLE

**C** Students should be able to analyze the characteristics of a clearly written text. Ask students to describe Hemingway's writing style in both the descriptive passages and the dialogue.

**Possible Response:** Hemingway is very matter-of-fact and to the point when he describes what Nick and Marjorie do on their fishing trip. The descriptive passages are direct and informative. The dialogue between the characters is concise and plain like everyday language.

Use **Unit Six Resource Book,** p. 52 for additional support.

*Canoe* (1957), David Park. Oil on canvas, 36″ × 48″, Thomas C. Woods Memorial Collection, Sheldon Memorial Art Gallery, University of Nebraska-Lincoln.

**1020** UNIT SIX PART 2: ALIENATION OF THE INDIVIDUAL

## Teaching Options

 **Viewing and Representing**

*Canoe* **by David Park**

**ART APPRECIATION** David Park (1911–1960) was born in Boston, Massachusetts. Throughout his career, Park was impressed with abstract art.
**Instruction** This painting shows a man and a woman rowing a canoe. Have students discuss the image and comment on the mood.
**Possible Responses:** Both the man and the woman have indistinct faces. The man's face does not have an eye, and the woman's face is almost gray. The lack of light in the painting—all the colors seem to be variations of green and gray—contributes to a depressing mood.

**Application** Have students analyze ideas represented in the work. Is this painting an accurate reflection of what Nick and Marjorie might look like?
**Possible Responses:** The work makes viewers wonder about the couple and creates the impression that they are unhappy or uncommunicative. *Canoe* could represent Nick and Marjorie because their relationship has disintegrated into habit and they no longer communicate.

swampy second growth as Nick and Marjorie rowed along the shore. They were trolling[1] along the edge of the channel-bank where the bottom dropped off suddenly from sandy shallows to twelve feet of dark water. They were trolling on their way to the point to set night lines for rainbow trout.

"There's our old ruin, Nick," Marjorie said.

Nick, rowing, looked at the white stone in the green trees.

"There it is," he said.

"Can you remember when it was a mill?" Marjorie asked.

"I can just remember," Nick said.

"It seems more like a castle," Marjorie said.

Nick said nothing. They rowed on out of sight of the mill, following the shore line. Then Nick cut across the bay.

"They aren't striking," he said.

"No," Marjorie said. She was intent on the rod all the time they trolled, even when she talked. She loved to fish. She loved to fish with Nick.

Close beside the boat a big trout broke the surface of the water. Nick pulled hard on one oar so the boat would turn and the bait spinning far behind would pass where the trout was feeding. As the trout's back came up out of the water the minnows jumped wildly. They sprinkled the surface like a handful of shot thrown into the water. Another trout broke water, feeding on the other side of the boat.

"They're feeding," Marjorie said.

"But they won't strike," Nick said.

He rowed the boat around to troll past both the feeding fish, then headed it for the point. Marjorie did not reel in until the boat touched the shore.

They pulled the boat up the beach and Nick lifted out a pail of live perch. The perch swam in the water in the pail. Nick caught three of them with his hands and cut their heads off and skinned them while Marjorie chased with her hands in the bucket, finally caught a perch, cut its head off and skinned it. Nick looked at her fish.

"You don't want to take the ventral fin[2] out," he said. "It'll be all right for bait but it's better with the ventral fin in."

He hooked each of the skinned perch through the tail. There were two hooks attached to a leader[3] on each rod. Then Marjorie rowed the boat out over the channel-bank, holding the line in her teeth, and looking toward Nick, who stood on the shore holding the rod and letting the line run out from the reel.

"That's about right," he called.

"Should I let it drop?" Marjorie called back, holding the line in her hand.

"Sure. Let it go." Marjorie dropped the line overboard and watched the baits go down through the water.

She came in with the boat and ran the second line out the same way. Each time Nick set a heavy slab of driftwood across the butt of the rod to hold it solid and propped it up at an angle with a small slab. He reeled in the slack line so the line ran taut out to where the bait rested on the sandy floor of the channel and set the click on the reel. When a trout, feeding on the bottom, took the bait it would run with it, taking line out of the reel in a rush and making the reel sing with the click on.

Marjorie rowed up the point a little way so she would not disturb the line. She pulled hard on the oars and the boat went way up the beach. Little waves came in with it. Marjorie stepped out of the boat and Nick pulled the boat high up the beach.

"What's the matter, Nick?" Marjorie asked.

"I don't know," Nick said, getting wood for a fire.

They made a fire with driftwood. Marjorie went to the boat and brought a blanket. The

---

1. **trolling:** a method of fishing in which a line and baited hook trail along behind a slow-moving boat.
2. **ventral fin:** fin on the underside of a fish.
3. **leader:** short length of line by which a hook is fastened to a fishing line.

---

**A** Ask students to discuss how the clipped, direct dialogue between characters adds to the mood of the scene.

**Possible Response:** The reader feels as if the two characters aren't connected and cannot express their true feelings to each other. The dialogue creates a feeling of tension and alienation—the reader can sense that this couple is not going to stay together.

### Active Reading

MAKING INFERENCES

**B** Point out Hemingway's omission of explanations and connections. Ask students to infer how Nick and Marjorie feel in this scene.

**Possible Response:** Nick has been unhappy in the relationship, but he cannot explain exactly why. Marjorie may have expected this breakup, but she is hurt and a bit embarrassed. She refuses to show her true feelings, and she acts angry to cover her hurt. Nick feels relieved and guilty at the same time. He is sad and wants to help Marjorie in some way, but Marjorie will not accept his help.

### Literary Analysis: CONFLICT

**C** Ask students to discuss what the true conflict of this story is.

**Possible Responses:** Nick versus himself—although Nick and Marjorie break up, it is because Nick is unhappy inside and cannot figure out his own feelings.

---

evening breeze blew the smoke toward the point, so Marjorie spread the blanket out between the fire and the lake.

Marjorie sat on the blanket with her back to the fire and waited for Nick. He came over and sat down beside her on the blanket. In back of them was the close second-growth timber[4] of the point and in front was the bay with the mouth of Hortons Creek. It was not quite dark. The fire-light went as far as the water. They could both see the two steel rods at an angle over the dark water. The fire glinted on the reels.

**A** Marjorie unpacked the basket of supper.

"I don't feel like eating," said Nick.

"Come on and eat, Nick."

"All right."

They ate without talking, and watched the two rods and the fire-light in the water.

"There's going to be a moon tonight," said Nick. He looked across the bay to the hills that were beginning to sharpen against the sky. Beyond the hills he knew the moon was coming up.

"I know it," Marjorie said happily.

"You know everything," Nick said.

"Oh, Nick, please cut it out! Please, please don't be that way!"

"I can't help it," Nick said. "You do. You know everything. That's the trouble. You know you do."

Marjorie did not say anything.

"I've taught you everything. You know you do. What don't you know, anyway?"

"Oh, shut up," Marjorie said. "There comes the moon."

They sat on the blanket without touching each other and watched the moon rise.

"You don't have to talk silly," Marjorie said. "What's really the matter?"

"I don't know."

"Of course you know."

"No I don't."

"Go on and say it."

Nick looked on at the moon, coming up over the hills.

"It isn't fun any more."

He was afraid to look at Marjorie. Then he looked at her. She sat there with her back toward him. He looked at her back. "It isn't fun any more. Not any of it."

She didn't say anything. He went on. "I feel as though everything was gone to hell inside of me. I don't know, Marge. I don't know what to say."

He looked on at her back.

"Isn't love any fun?" Marjorie said.

"No," Nick said. Marjorie stood up. Nick sat there his head in his hands.

"I'm going to take the boat," Marjorie called to him. "You can walk back around the point."

"All right," Nick said. "I'll push the boat off for you."

"You don't need to," she said. She was afloat in the boat on the water with the moonlight on it. Nick went back and lay down with his face in the blanket by the fire. He could hear Marjorie rowing on the water.

He lay there for a long time. He lay there while he heard Bill come into the clearing walking around through the woods. He felt Bill coming up to the fire. Bill didn't touch him, either.

"Did she go all right?" Bill said.

"Yes," Nick said, lying, his face on the blanket.

"Have a scene?"

"No, there wasn't any scene."

"How do you feel?"

"Oh, go away, Bill! Go away for a while."

Bill selected a sandwich from the lunch basket and walked over to have a look at the rods. ❖

---

4. **second-growth timber:** trees that cover an area after the original, "old growth" trees have been cut or burned.

---

## Teaching Options

 **Vocabulary Strategy**

### CONNOTATIONS

**Instruction** Students can rely on context to determine the connotations of words. Explain that all words have a literal meaning, or denotation. Many words also have connotations—additional, implied meanings—that evoke certain emotional responses in readers. Write the following sentence on the chalkboard:

Susie loved the apple pie; it was so <u>delectable</u> she could have eaten three pieces.

Have students rely on the context of the sentence to determine that *delectable* means "absolutely delicious." Point out that the connotation of the

word suggests that it was more than enjoyable—it suggests that the pie was very delicious.

**Application** Have students work in pairs to determine the connotations of the following words on page 1022: *silly, fun,* and *scene*. Point out to students that they know the denotations of these words, but must rely on the context to determine the connotation.

 Use **Vocabulary Transparencies and Copymasters**, p. 85.

*A lesson on connotation appears on p. 908 in the Pupil's Edition.*

# *Thinking through the* LITERATURE

## Connect to the Literature

1. **What Do You Think?**
   Which character do you feel the most sympathy for? Why? Share your thoughts with a classmate.

   **Comprehension Check**
   • How has Hortons Bay changed over the past ten years?
   • What do Nick and Marjorie do in the first part of the story?
   • Where does the final scene of the story occur?

## Think Critically

2. **ACTIVE READING** **MAKING INFERENCES** Review the chart you made in your **READER'S NOTEBOOK**. What lines of Nick and Marjorie's dialogue hint at the problems in their relationship? How would you describe the way they communicate to each other?

   **THINK ABOUT** { • what they say to each other
   • what they do not say to each other

3. Why do you think Nick wants to break up with Marjorie?

4. How do you think Nick feels at the end of the story?

   **THINK ABOUT** { • his actions after Marjorie leaves
   • his remark "Oh, go away, Bill! Go away for a while."

5. How would you describe Nick's attitude toward the natural environment in this story? Support your answer with evidence.

## Extend Interpretations

6. **Critic's Corner** In an article published in the *Kenyon Review,* critic George Hemphill wrote that Hemingway's story fails "because no necessary connection (other than biographical, perhaps) between the end of the boy and girl affair between Nick and Marjorie and the end of the old lumbering days in Michigan is suggested." What is your response to Hemphill's criticism? Do you think a connection between the Hortons Bay setting and Nick and Marjorie's relationship is implied or not? Discuss your ideas with your classmates.

7. **Different Perspectives** How did the information about Nick Adams presented in the Build Background feature on page 1018 influence your interpretation of the story? Do you think Nick's behavior can be attributed to his experiences as a young war veteran? Defend your view.

8. **Connect to Life** How does this ending of a relationship compare with breakups you have witnessed or experienced?

## Literary Analysis

**STYLE** Before becoming a novelist and short story writer, Hemingway earned his living as a journalist. "The End of Something" reflects the simple, direct **style** of a newspaper reporter—short sentences, close attention to detail, unadorned descriptions, precise language, detached point of view, and matter-of-fact tone. Note the conciseness of the following paragraph about Nick and Marjorie's breakup:

> *He was afraid to look at Marjorie. Then he looked at her. She sat there with her back toward him. He looked back at her. "It isn't fun any more. Not any of it."*

Hemingway's ear for authentic-sounding dialogue is also a keynote of his distinctive style.

**Cooperative Learning Activity** In a small group, rewrite a passage of the story and include Nick's feelings and thoughts. Share your rewrite with the class, and discuss differences between Hemingway's style and that of your rewrite. Do the additional details add or detract from the story?

## Extend Interpretations

**Critic's Corner** Possible Responses: Yes, the declining Hortons Bay is a symbol of their relationship; no, the setting does not seem symbolic because the story's tone is so realistic.

**Different Perspectives** Possible Response: The horrors of war have disillusioned Nick and alienated him from other people and even the natural landscape around him. He seems to have lost hope.

**Connect to Life** Students should relate details from the text to their personal experiences.

## Connect to the Literature

1. **What Do You Think?**
   Students should support their opinions with passages from the text.

**Comprehension Check**
• Hortons Bay was once a thriving lumber town; now the mill has shut down, and the town is practically deserted.
• fish from a boat
• on shore, by a campfire

 Use Selection Quiz
**Unit Six Resource Book**, p. 53.

## Think Critically

2. Possible Responses: When Nick answers "I don't know" to Marjorie's "What's the matter?"; the scene starting with "You know everything" on p. 1022. Their dialogue is terse and they seem on the verge of an argument.

3. Possible Responses: He no longer loves her; he is unhappy with himself but blames her for his problems.

4. Some students may note that Nick's holding "his head in his hands" and lying "with his face in the blanket" suggest that he feels miserable and lonely. Others may say he is frustrated and angry, since he tells Bill to go away. He cannot explain his feelings to anyone.

5. He seems removed from nature, barely noticing the things Marjorie points out and perfunctorily skinning the fish he catches.

## Literary Analysis

**Style** **To get students started,** have them form groups of five or six to do the rewrite. Students can discuss which of Nick's feelings and thoughts should be included and how. One or more volunteers might record the group's decisions and draft the actual copy. After sharing the rewrites with the class, students should indicate that Hemingway's version leaves much more to the reader's imagination than do the rewrites.

## Writing Options

**1. Personal Ad** Ads will vary. **To get students started on this assignment,** bring in several examples of personal ads from a local newspaper to review the form and discuss them. Then, have partners work together to list qualities that they think would be important to Nick and Marjorie based on their actions in the story.

**2. Advice Letters** Letters will vary. Encourage students to consult local newspapers for samples of letters printed in advice columns such as "Dear Abby." **To make this activity easier,** have students create a word web for how Marjorie feels about the breakup and about Nick. Then have students discuss the tone of the letter based on those feelings— angry, bitter, compassionate.

**3. TV Script** Students' scripts should stay as true to the actual story as possible. **To get students started on this assignment,** divide them into groups of five or six. Have one or two students write the script based on all members' ideas. Then, as some group members act out the script for the class, one member can direct them. Another member could be in charge of locating props, costumes, and background music.

## Activities & Explorations

**1. Story Illustrations** Students' drawings should accurately reflect the mood and the theme of the scene in the story. As an extension activity, ask students to explain to the class why they chose their scene and what artistic techniques they used to portray it accurately.

**2. Survey of Romantic Breakups** Encourage students to make sure their survey is fair by polling people of different ages and backgrounds. If they have trouble getting responses, they can write survey questions with multiple-choice answers. To make this assignment more challenging, assign an essay in which students analyze their findings and make several deductions about breakups— such as why, where, and when they occur.

## Writing Options

**1. Personal Ad** What do you think happens to Nick and Marjorie after the end of their relationship? Write a personal ad that either Marjorie or Nick might send to a local newspaper, describing the kind of person she or he would like to meet. Read your ad aloud to the class.

**2. Advice Letters** Write a letter from Marjorie to an advice columnist, asking for advice about how to deal with Nick and their crumbling relationship. Then write the columnist's response to Marjorie.

**3. TV Script** Imagine that you and a small group of your classmates are head writers for a TV soap opera called *Hortons Bay.* Write the script for an episode based on this story.

## Activities & Explorations

**1. Story Illustrations** Imagine that you have been asked to illustrate "The End of Something" for a collection of Hemingway's stories. Choose one scene from the story, and draw or paint it.
~ ART

**2. Survey of Romantic Breakups** What is the best way to end a relationship? Conduct an informal survey of ten males and ten females in your school or neighborhood. Record their responses, and report your findings to the class.
~ PSYCHOLOGY

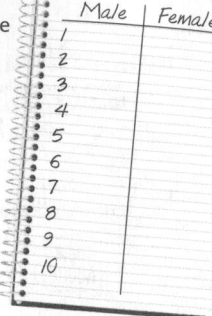

| | Male | Female |
|---|---|---|
| 1 | | |
| 2 | | |
| 3 | | |
| 4 | | |
| 5 | | |
| 6 | | |
| 7 | | |
| 8 | | |
| 9 | | |
| 10 | | |

# Ernest Hemingway
### 1899–1961

**Other Works**
*The Nick Adams Stories; A Farewell to Arms; Death in the Afternoon; The Sun Also Rises; For Whom the Bell Tolls; The Old Man and the Sea*

**The Faces of War** War punctuated Ernest Hemingway's life and career, from the World War I passages of *In Our Time*, his first book of short stories, to his journalistic accounts of chasing German U-boats with his yacht in the Caribbean during World War II. Hemingway found war the ultimate theater, where an artist could observe human nature and what he called "grace under pressure."

**On the Frontlines** At the age of 18, with the onset of World War I, Hemingway volunteered as a Red Cross ambulance driver, serving on the frontlines. After three weeks, he was severely wounded. He had a lengthy recovery in an Italian hospital and a love affair with an American nurse. What he experienced during that momentous year—the closeness of death, courage, physical and emotional pain, and romantic love—informs many of his novels and short stories.

**The Lure of Adventure** Other events of Hemingway's adventurous life also found their way into his fiction. In his highly acclaimed novel *The Sun Also Rises*, he depicted the members of what Gertrude Stein had dubbed the "lost generation"— young people, like himself, who were disillusioned by World War I and living a rather aimless life abroad in the 1920s. His desire for action led him to serve as a war correspondent during the Spanish civil war of the 1930s and during World War II. Out of these war experiences came a highly successful novel, *For Whom the Bell Tolls*, and a much criticized one, *Across the River and Into the Trees*. An avid sports enthusiast, Hemingway also wrote about bullfighting in Spain, big-game hunting in Africa, and deep-sea fishing in Florida.

**Tragic Ending** In 1953 Hemingway won the Pulitzer Prize for *The Old Man and the Sea*, and in 1954 he received the Nobel Prize in literature. However, the final years of his life were not happy. Suffering from the effects of alcoholism, injuries sustained in two plane crashes, and an emotional breakdown, he committed suicide in 1961.

## Teaching Options

**Mini Lesson** **Grammar**

**COMMAS: SETTING OFF QUOTATIONS**

**Instruction** A direct quotation is the exact words spoken by a person or character. Commas are used to set off a direct quotation from the rest of a sentence. Commas should not be used with indirect quotations. Place the following sentences on the chalkboard:

> Marjorie said, "I am leaving for Florida tomorrow."
> Marjorie said that she was leaving for Florida tomorrow.

Point out that a comma is used to set off Marjorie's direct quotation in the first sentence.

The second sentence is an example of an indirect quotation.

**Application** Have pairs of students extend the dialogue between Nick and Marjorie before Marjorie goes into the boat and rows away. Ask students to use both direct quotations set off by commas and indirect quotations in their writing.

 Use **Grammar Transparencies and Copymasters,** p. 154.

 Use McDougal Littell's *Language Network,* Chapter 9, for more instruction in setting off quotations.

# PREPARING to *Read*

## The Love Song of J. Alfred Prufrock

*Poetry by* T. S. ELIOT

### OVERVIEW

 This selection is included in the **Grade 11 InterActive Reader.**

**Objectives**
1. understand a classic modernist **poem (Literary Analysis)**
2. identify and appreciate **imagery (Literary Analysis)**
3. understand **stream of consciousness (Active Reading)**

**Summary**
In this stream-of-consciousness poem, J. Alfred Prufrock reveals his thoughts, feelings, and longings as he broods over whether to reach out to a woman and ask the "overwhelming question." Prufrock desires intimacy, but his fear of being misunderstood keeps him from taking risks. When he fails to ask his question, he relegates himself to an empty life and gives up the chance of fulfilling his dreams.

**Thematic Link**
Unable to take risks, Prufrock cannot have a meaningful relationship. This poem reflects his loneliness and **alienation** in the modern world.

**(Connect to Your Life)**

**Partygoer's Dilemma** In this poem, J. Alfred Prufrock, on his way to a party, is trying to decide what to say to a woman who will be there. Imagine that you are at a party and see someone you would like to get better acquainted with. You do not know how this person feels about you. Would you reach out to this person by starting a conversation, or would you hold back? Jot down the thoughts you might have as you try to decide what to do.

## Build Background

**Romantics Versus Modernists** In 1914 the poet Ezra Pound read "The Love Song of J. Alfred Prufrock" for the first time and enthusiastically wrote to Harriet Monroe, editor of *Poetry* magazine: "Eliot . . . has sent in the best poem I have yet had or seen from an American. . . . He has actually trained himself and modernized himself on his own." Modernist poets like Eliot and Pound sought to make a clear break with the poetic traditions of the past, especially 19th-century romanticism. Whereas romantic poets celebrated the individual and nature, Eliot portrayed the loneliness and alienation of the individual living in a dingy modern city. While romantic poets believed that poems should be written in everyday language for common people, Eliot used elevated diction and classical allusions to separate himself from the masses.

**WORDS TO KNOW**
**Vocabulary Preview**
digress
malinger
meticulous
obtuse
presume

## Focus Your Reading

**LITERARY ANALYSIS | IMAGERY** **Imagery** consists of words and phrases that appeal to any of the five senses and that help the reader imagine precisely what the writer is describing. The object of Eliot's modernist style in "The Love Song of J. Alfred Prufrock" is to create a verbal collage of society by weaving together the fragmentary images of the city, the tea party, and the beach. As Prufrock moves through each of these three scenes, note the scattered images that flood his mind.

**ACTIVE READING | UNDERSTANDING STREAM OF CONSCIOUSNESS**
**Stream of consciousness** is a technique developed by the modernists to present the flow of the seemingly unconnected thoughts, responses, and sensations as they occur in a character's mind. Eliot uses this technique to reveal the jumble of images, ideas, feelings, and daydreams that flow through Prufrock's mind. As the poem begins, Prufrock addresses a silent listener, perhaps someone who accompanies him to the party. Pretend you are the listener who hears Prufrock thinking aloud. As you read, pay attention to Prufrock's different associations and feelings about a decision he is trying to make.

**READER'S NOTEBOOK** To help you follow the structure of Prufrock's random train of thought about his decision, create a chart like the one shown, and fill it in with relevant details as you read.

| | |
|---|---|
| Part 1: Prufrock's musings about asking the "overwhelming question" (lines 1–83) | |
| Part 2: Prufrock's decision (lines 84–86) | |
| Part 3: Prufrock's justification for his decision (lines 87–110) | |

THE LOVE SONG OF J. ALFRED PRUFROCK **1025**

### 5-Minute Warm-Up

*Daily Language SkillBuilder*

Have students **proofread** the display sentences on page 913k and write them correctly. The sentences also appear on Transparency 29 of **Grammar Transparencies and Copymasters.**

 **Mini Lesson Preteaching Vocabulary**

If you would like to preteach the WORDS TO KNOW for this selection, use the Mini Lesson, p. 1026.

## LESSON RESOURCES

**UNIT SIX RESOURCE BOOK,** pp. 54–58

**ASSESSMENT RESOURCES**
**Formal Assessment,** pp. 191–192
**Teacher's Guide to Assessment and Portfolio Use**
**Test Generator**

**SKILLS TRANSPARENCIES AND COPYMASTERS**
**Literary Analysis**
• Modernist Literature, T17 (for Active Reading, p. 1025)

**Reading and Critical Thinking**
• Noting Details, T9 (for Active Reading, p. 1025)
**Grammar**
• Inverted Subjects and Verbs, C78 (for Mini Lesson, p. 1032)
**Vocabulary**
• Figurative Language, C86 (for Mini Lesson, p. 1028)
**Writing**
• Eyewitness Report, C25 (for Writing Option 2, p. 1031)

**Communications**
• Interviewing, T9 (for Activities & Explorations 3, p. 1031)
• Impromptu Speaking: Dialogue, Role-Play, Debate, T13 (for Activities & Explorations 3, p. 1031)

**INTEGRATED TECHNOLOGY**
**Visit our website:**
www.mcdougallittell.com

**Literary Analysis** IMAGERY

**A** This poem is full of descriptions that appeal to the senses. Which images especially evoke the feeling of a city at night?

**Possible Responses:** "half-deserted streets"; "one-night cheap hotels"; "sawdust restaurants with oyster-shells"

Use **Unit Six Resource Book,** p. 56 for additional support.

**Active Reading**

**UNDERSTANDING STREAM OF CONSCIOUSNESS**

**B** Point out that stream-of-consciousness writing generally lacks the "signposts" that unify language, such as transitions and conjunctions. Have students compare this to the technique often used in music videos.

Use **Unit Six Resource Book,** p. 55 for additional support.

**GUIDE FOR READING**

**C Possible Response:** The environment is unresponsive to events and emotions.

**D Possible Response:** They suggest a run-down neighborhood of shoddy restaurants and shady characters.

**E** trivial

**F Possible Response:** Wearing social masks, they are not sincere.

**G Possible Response:** ask the "overwhelming question"

---

# The Love Song of J. Alfred Prufrock

## T. S. ELIOT

S'io *credessi che mia risposta fosse*
*a persona che mai tornasse al mondo,*
*questa fiamma staria senza più scosse.*
*Ma per ciò che giammai di questo fondo*
*non tornò vivo alcun, s'i'odo il vero,*
*senza tema d'infamia ti rispondo.*

**A**

> Let us go then, you and I,
> When the evening is spread out against the sky
> Like a patient etherized upon a table;
> Let us go, through certain half-deserted streets,
> 5 The muttering retreats
> Of restless nights in one-night cheap hotels
> And sawdust restaurants with oyster-shells:
> Streets that follow like a tedious argument
> Of insidious intent
> 10 To lead you to an overwhelming question . . .

**B**

> Oh, do not ask, "What is it?"
> Let us go and make our visit.

> In the room the women come and go
> Talking of Michelangelo.

> 15 The yellow fog that rubs its back upon the window-panes,
> The yellow smoke that rubs its muzzle on the window-panes,
> Licked its tongue into the corners of the evening,
> Lingered upon the pools that stand in drains,
> Let fall upon its back the soot that falls from chimneys,
> 20 Slipped by the terrace, made a sudden leap,
> And seeing that it was a soft October night,
> Curled once about the house, and fell asleep.

**1026** UNIT SIX PART 2: ALIENATION OF THE INDIVIDUAL

**GUIDE FOR READING**

This is a quotation in Italian from Dante's *Inferno*. Speaking to a visitor in hell, one of the damned says that he will describe his torment only because the visitor cannot return alive to the world to repeat it.

**2–3** Ether was used to make a patient unconscious during an operation. How can an evening be like an etherized patient? **C**

**4–7** What do these lines suggest to you about this section of the city? **D**

**9 insidious** (ĭn-sĭd'ē-əs): more dangerous than it seems.

**10–12** Prufrock appears reluctant to say what his "overwhelming question" is.

**13–14** The women mentioned in these lines may be those at the party Prufrock is going to attend, or they may be women at other parties Prufrock has attended. Is Prufrock suggesting that their "talking of Michelangelo" at a party involves a serious or a trivial discussion of this great Renaissance artist? **E**

---

## Teaching Options

 ### Preteaching Vocabulary

**USING CONTEXT CLUES**

**Instruction** Students can rely on context to determine the meanings of unfamiliar words. Display the following sentence.

> He was <u>meticulous</u> in matters of dress; every item of clothing was chosen with care.

Ask a volunteer to determine the meaning of *meticulous* and identify the clues that suggest the meaning.

**Exercises** Ask students to use context clues to determine the meaning of each underlined word.

1. Do you <u>presume</u> to lie about me to my best friends? *("dare"; clue—"lie about me")*

2. I have a tendency to <u>digress</u>; my thoughts often travel down interesting by-paths. *("ramble"; clue—"travel down interesting by-paths")*

3. I wanted to <u>malinger</u> but decided I must finish what I had begun. *("avoid work"; clue—"finish what I had begun")*

4. I find I am <u>obtuse</u> when I try to think about complex lab reports in chemistry class. *("slow to learn"; clues—"try to think," "complex lab reports")*

Use **Unit Six Resource Book** p. 57 for additional support.

**A lesson on context clues appears on p. 326 in the Pupil's Edition.**

And indeed there will be time
For the yellow smoke that slides along the street
25  Rubbing its back upon the window-panes;
There will be time, there will be time
To prepare a face to meet the faces that you meet;
There will be time to murder and create,
And time for all the works and days of hands
30  That lift and drop a question on your plate;
Time for you and time for me,
And time yet for a hundred indecisions,
And for a hundred visions and revisions,
Before the taking of a toast and tea.

35  In the room the women come and go
Talking of Michelangelo.

And indeed there will be time
To wonder, "Do I dare?" and, "Do I dare?"
Time to turn back and descend the stair,
40  With a bald spot in the middle of my hair—
(They will say: "How his hair is growing thin!")
My morning coat, my collar mounting firmly to the chin,
My necktie rich and modest, but asserted by a simple pin—
(They will say: "But how his arms and legs are thin!")
45  Do I dare
Disturb the universe?
In a minute there is time
For decisions and revisions which a minute will reverse.

For I have known them all already, known them all—
50  Have known the evenings, mornings, afternoons,
I have measured out my life with coffee spoons;
I know the voices dying with a dying fall
Beneath the music from a farther room.
    So how should I <u>presume</u>?

55  And I have known the eyes already, known them all—
The eyes that fix you in a formulated phrase,
And when I am formulated, sprawling on a pin,
When I am pinned and wriggling on the wall,
Then how should I begin
60  To spit out all the butt-ends of my days and ways?
    And how should I presume?

<table>
<tr><td>WORDS<br>TO<br>KNOW</td><td>presume (prĭ-zōōm′) v. to act overconfidently; go beyond the proper<br>limits; dare</td></tr>
</table>

**1027**

---

23–34 This stanza reveals part of Prufrock's problem. Look for clues as you read.

26–27 What is Prufrock's idea of how people behave at parties or, perhaps, at any time? **F**

37–48 In this stanza, Prufrock seems to grow increasingly insecure. The repeated question "Do I dare?" suggests that he wants to do something extraordinary at the party. What do you think he wants to do? **G**

55–58 Prufrock recalls being scrutinized by women at other parties. The image of himself is one of a live insect that has been classified, labeled, and mounted for display.

56 **formulated:** reduced to a formula or prepared according to a formula.

---

---

## Reading and Analyzing

### GUIDE FOR READING

**A** **Possible Response:** While Prufrock is attracted to them and admires their beauty and grace, he is too intimidated by them to begin speaking.

**B** **Possible Response:** He feels that he too is one of the lonely men.

**C** **Possible Response:** His self-esteem is very low; he feels "pinned" under society's stare, and he "scuttles" to avoid notice in a hostile, silent world.

**D** **Possible Response:** death

**E** **Possible Responses:** humiliation; appearing foolish; being misunderstood

### Active Reading

**UNDERSTANDING STREAM OF CONSCIOUSNESS**

**F** Have students draw conclusions about Prufrock's character.

**Possible Responses:** Prufrock imagines what it would have been like had he dared to take a risk in this relationship. Such a change would have been tantamount to a resurrection, a stirring of emotional life.

### GUIDE FOR READING

**G** **Possible Response:** He feels lonely and isolated from life; therefore, expressing his feelings to another person—perhaps even declaring his love—would be like returning from the dead.

**H** **Possible Response:** the excitement and love that he dreams of

**I** **Possible Responses:** "We" might refer to those split by indecision; when "human voices" wake Prufrock from his dreams, he "drowns" in his fear of life.

---

And I have known the arms already, known them all—
Arms that are braceleted and white and bare
(But in the lamplight, downed with light brown hair!)
65 Is it perfume from a dress
That makes me so digress?
Arms that lie along a table, or wrap about a shawl.
  And should I then presume?
  And how should I begin?
  • • • • •
70 Shall I say, I have gone at dusk through narrow streets
And watched the smoke that rises from the pipes
Of lonely men in shirt-sleeves, leaning out of windows? . . .

I should have been a pair of ragged claws
Scuttling across the floors of silent seas.
  • • • • •
75 And the afternoon, the evening, sleeps so peacefully!
Smoothed by long fingers,
Asleep . . . tired . . . or it malingers,
Stretched on the floor, here beside you and me.
Should I, after tea and cakes and ices,
80 Have the strength to force the moment to its crisis?
But though I have wept and fasted, wept and prayed,
Though I have seen my head (grown slightly bald) brought in
  upon a platter,
I am no prophet—and here's no great matter;
I have seen the moment of my greatness flicker,
85 And I have seen the eternal Footman hold my coat, and snicker,
And in short, I was afraid.

And would it have been worth it, after all,
After the cups, the marmalade, the tea,
Among the porcelain, among some talk of you and me,
90 Would it have been worth while,
To have bitten off the matter with a smile,
To have squeezed the universe into a ball
To roll it towards some overwhelming question,
To say: "I am Lazarus, come from the dead,
95 Come back to tell you all, I shall tell you all"—
If one, settling a pillow by her head,
  Should say: "That is not what I meant at all.
  That is not it, at all."

**62–67** How would you describe Prufrock's attitude toward the women at the party? Notice that he wants to say something but doesn't know how. **A**

**70–72** Why do you think Prufrock wants to talk about "lonely men"? **B**

**73–74** Prufrock has presented an image of himself as an insect (lines 57–58) and, here, as a crab or lobster. What do these images suggest about Prufrock's self-esteem? **C**

**81–83** These lines allude to the biblical story of John the Baptist, who is imprisoned by King Herod (Matthew 14; Mark 6). To gratify his stepdaughter Salome, Herod orders the Baptist's head cut off and brought to him on a platter.

**85** Who or what do you think is "the eternal Footman"? **D**

**86** Who or what do you think Prufrock was afraid of? **E**

**87–110** In these two stanzas, Prufrock rationalizes his failure to ask the "overwhelming question."

**94 Lazarus:** In the biblical story (John 11:17–44), Lazarus lay dead in his tomb for four days before Jesus brought him back to life. Why do you think Prufrock compares himself to a character who returns from the dead? **G**

WORDS TO KNOW
**digress** (dĭ-grĕs′) v. to wander away from the main subject in a conversation or in writing; ramble
**malinger** (mə-lĭng′gər) v. to pretend illness in order to avoid duty or work

1028

---

## Teaching Options

 **Mini Lesson** ## Vocabulary Strategy

**UNDERSTANDING FIGURATIVE LANGUAGE**
**Instruction** Remind students that they can use context clues to determine the meaning of figurative language. Ask a volunteer to read lines 73–74 aloud. Then ask students the following questions.
• What does Prufrock mean when he says he "should have been a pair of ragged claws"? *(He is comparing himself to a lobster or a crab. This meaning can be understood from line 74: "Scuttling across the floors of silent seas.")*
• Why might a person say this of himself? *(Being a crab would relieve him of the responsibility to take risks and change his life.)*

**Activity** Ask students to form pairs and read lines 15–22 on p. 1026 aloud. Explain that the lines contain an extended metaphor. Ask in what ways the fog and the smoke are like a cat. Then ask students to make a list of all phrases that provide clues to that image. *("rubs its back"; "rubs its muzzle"; "licked its tongue"; "slipped by"; "made a sudden leap"; "curled . . . and fell asleep").*

Use **Vocabulary Transparencies and Copymasters,** p. 86.

**A lesson on context clues appears on p. 326 in the Pupil's Edition.**

And would it have been worth it, after all,
100  Would it have been worth while,
After the sunsets and the dooryards and the sprinkled streets,
After the novels, after the teacups, after the skirts that trail along
      the floor—
And this, and so much more?—
It is impossible to say just what I mean!
105  But as if a magic lantern threw the nerves in patterns on a
      screen:
Would it have been worth while
If one, settling a pillow or throwing off a shawl,
And turning toward the window, should say:
      "That is not it at all,
110  That is not what I meant, at all."

No! I am not Prince Hamlet, nor was meant to be;
Am an attendant lord, one that will do
To swell a progress, start a scene or two,
Advise the prince; no doubt, an easy tool,
115  Deferential, glad to be of use,
Politic, cautious, and meticulous;
Full of high sentence, but a bit obtuse;
At times, indeed, almost ridiculous—
Almost, at times, the Fool.

120  I grow old . . . I grow old . . .
I shall wear the bottoms of my trousers rolled.

Shall I part my hair behind? Do I dare to eat a peach?
I shall wear white flannel trousers, and walk upon the beach.
I have heard the mermaids singing, each to each.

125  I do not think that they will sing to me.

I have seen them riding seaward on the waves
Combing the white hair of the waves blown back
When the wind blows the water white and black.

We have lingered in the chambers of the sea
130  By sea-girls wreathed with seaweed red and brown
Till human voices wake us, and we drown.

**105** The magic lantern was a forerunner of the slide projector. In this image, the "nerves" may be Prufrock's inner self exposed for all to see.

**111–119** Notice that Prufrock resigns himself to playing a supporting role rather than a starring one in life.

**115 deferential** (dĕf′ə-rĕn′shəl): yielding to someone else's opinion.

**116 politic** (pŏl′ĭ-tĭk): skillful in dealing with others; diplomatic.

**124–128** In mythology, mermaids attract mortal men by their beauty and their singing, sometimes allowing men to live with them in the sea. What might the mermaids represent to Prufrock? **H**

**129–131** Whom do you think "we" refers to? What does the metaphor of waking and drowning suggest? **I**

WORDS
TO
KNOW
**meticulous** (mĭ-tĭk′yə-ləs) *adj.* extremely careful and precise about details
**obtuse** (ŏb-tōōs′) *adj.* slow to understand; dull

1029

**Cross Curricular Link  Humanities**

**MODERNISM** While T. S. Eliot was breaking new ground in poetry, visual artists and musicians were also trying out new techniques and using familiar materials in new ways. At the time Eliot wrote "The Love Song of J. Alfred Prufrock," artists Pablo Picasso (Spanish, 1881–1973) and Georges Braque (French, 1882–1963) were experimenting with cubism—painting and sculpture in which objects are broken down into geometric shapes. Musician Arnold Schönberg (Austrian, 1874–1951) was inventing atonal music—that is, music that doesn't depend on a particular key and in which all twelve tones of the scale are treated equally.

# *Thinking* through the LITERATURE

## GUIDING STUDENT RESPONSE

### Connect to the Literature

**1. What Do You Think?**
Responses will vary. Some students may state that Prufrock is a pitiable figure, cut off from his feelings and unable to act.

**Comprehension Check**
• to a patient etherized upon a table
• He is thin, balding, and middle-aged.
• mermaids

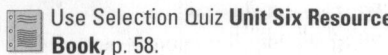 Use Selection Quiz **Unit Six Resource Book,** p. 58.

### Think Critically

**2.** Possible Responses: lonely; hopeless; powerless; insignificant

**3.** Possible Responses: He wanted to ask a woman out; he wanted to propose marriage; he wanted to ask about her feelings for him.

**4.** Possible Responses: Yes—he would rather worry than act; no—he would have had the satisfaction of having taken a risk.

**5.** Possible Response: They are shallow and judge people by appearances.

**6.** Responses will vary. Some students may believe that Prufrock is similar to most people. They may say that the "we" in the last line refers to all human beings, suggesting that Prufrock's plight represents a universal human condition. Others may say that most people are more confident than Prufrock.

### Literary Analysis

**Imagery** Possible Responses: Students might list the following as images Prufrock associates with himself: a man whose life has been a series of petty events (lines 49–54); an insect pinned to a board (lines 55–58); a sea creature with claws (lines 73–74); a man paralyzed by indecision (lines 75–80); a man relegated to playing a minor role in life (lines 111–119). Students might list the following as images that contrast with Prufrock: Lazarus (lines 90–95); Hamlet (line 111); mermaids singing (lines 124–131).

### Connect to the Literature

**1. What Do You Think?**
What are your impressions of Prufrock and his dilemma?

**Comprehension Check**
• In the beginning of the poem, to what does Prufrock compare the evening?
• What does Prufrock look like and about how old is he?
• What creatures will not sing to Prufrock?

### Think Critically

**2.** How do you think Prufrock feels at the end of the poem?

**3.** 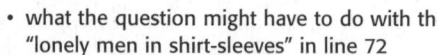 **ACTIVE READING** **UNDERSTANDING STREAM OF CONSCIOUSNESS** Review the chart you made in your **READER'S NOTEBOOK.** Based on Prufrock's meandering thoughts, what do you think his "overwhelming question" is? Why does Prufrock decide not to ask it?

**THINK ABOUT**
• what leads him to think about this question
• to whom the question might be directed
• why the question might "disturb the universe"
• what the question might have to do with the "lonely men in shirt-sleeves" in line 72
• the response he anticipates in lines 97–98 and 109–110

**4.** Do you think Prufrock makes the right decision in not asking his "overwhelming question"? Defend your view.

**5.** How would you judge the women at the tea party Prufrock attends? Support your opinion with evidence.

**6.** Do you think Prufrock is like or unlike most people?

### Extend Interpretations

**7. Comparing Texts** Read the excerpt from Kafka's *Diaries* on page 1033. In what ways do you think the bachelor described resembles Prufrock?

**8. Critic's Corner** Although now considered a classic modernist poem, "The Love Song of J. Alfred Prufrock" was not an immediate success. Several well-known American and British literary critics described the poem as dreadful and unpoetic. How would you respond to these critics?

**9. Connect to Life** Why do you think this poem is called a love song? How does it compare with love songs you know?

**1030** UNIT SIX   PART 2: ALIENATION OF THE INDIVIDUAL

### Literary Analysis

**IMAGERY** In keeping with other modernists, Eliot uses powerful **imagery—** vivid "word pictures"— to convey complex ideas and emotions. For example, the image of the evening as "a patient etherized upon a table" is richly suggestive of the general ill health and languor in Prufrock's world. The "yellow fog" depicted as an aimless alley cat is another striking image that conveys the atmosphere of Prufrock's city.

**Paired Activity** Most of the images in the poem are associated with Prufrock himself and reveal his fears, his self-consciousness, and his sustaining dreams. Meet with a partner to study these images. Create a chart like the one shown. In the first column, list images that Prufrock associates with himself, such as a man growing bald and skinny (lines 40–44). In the second column, list images that Prufrock uses in contrast to himself, such as the image of the prophet John the Baptist (lines 81–83). After you have charted several images of Prufrock, analyze what they tell you about him.

| Images that Describe Prufrock | Images that Contrast with Prufrock |
|---|---|
| A face to meet other faces (line 27) | 1. John the Baptist (lines 81–83) |
| 2. | 1. |
| 3. | 2. |

### Extend Interpretations

**Comparing Texts** Possible Responses: Both the bachelor and Prufrock are lonely men who present a false face to the world, who are overly concerned about their appearance, and whose lives are a series of petty events.

**Critic's Corner** Possible Responses: It is a very difficult and obscure poem; the language is very "poetic" and beautiful; it is not a poem one can fully comprehend on such a short acquaintance; it is rich enough to tempt one to reread it for better comprehension.

**Connect to Life** Possible Response: Prufrock's inaction makes the title of the poem ironic, for the poem becomes a song of love timidly unpursued rather than boldly sought.

## Writing Options

**1. Letter to Prufrock** If you were the person addressed in the poem, what advice would you give Prufrock? Write Prufrock a personal letter in which you counsel him.

> *He seems intelligent— not like the others here.*

**2. Partygoer's Narrative** Imagine you are a woman who has been watching Prufrock at the tea party. Draft a brief stream-of-consciousness narrative that presents the images, thoughts, and feelings that flow through your mind as you watch him. Save your writing in your **Working Portfolio.**

**3. Social Commentary** Write a newspaper commentary about the social scene at the party that Prufrock attends. Include details from the poem about the party guests, their conversations, the refreshments, and so on.

**Writing Handbook**
See page 1283: Analysis

## Activities & Explorations

**1. Improvisational Scene** With a partner, improvise a scene between Prufrock and the woman he wants to speak with. Add material of your own, but keep it consistent with Prufrock's character and the kind of woman he says will attend the party. **~ PERFORMING**

**2. Prufrock's Caricature** A caricature is a drawing of a person that exaggerates features to satirize that person or to highlight some aspect of his or her character. Draw a caricature of Prufrock based on details in the poem. Display your drawing for the class. **~ ART**

**3. Radio Talk Show** Imagine that you run a radio show on the arts and that T. S. Eliot will appear as your guest to publicize his new book, *Prufrock and Other Observations.* What questions would you ask him in order to help your listeners understand "The Love Song of J. Alfred Prufrock," and what might he answer? With a partner, prepare the interview and perform it for the class. **~ SPEAKING AND LISTENING**

## Inquiry & Research

**Michelangelo's Artistic Genius**
In "The Love Song of J. Alfred Prufrock," Eliot repeats the lines "In the room the women come and go / Talking of Michelangelo." Research Michelangelo's life and work. Then present your findings in a written report illustrated with pictures of some of Michelangelo's most important paintings and sculptures. Discuss with classmates why you think Eliot alludes to this great artist in his poem.

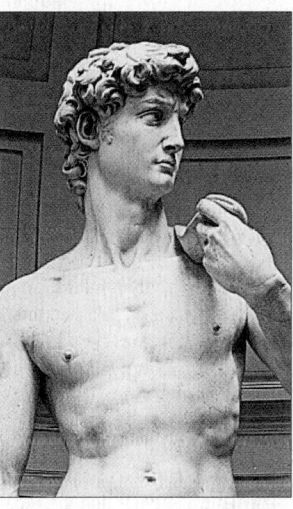

Michelangelo's *David*

## Writing Options

**1. Letter to Prufrock To make this assignment easier,** suggest that students think about the root of Prufrock's problem and what he could do to improve his lot.

**2. Partygoer's Narrative To get students started,** encourage them to check the poem to find information about Prufrock's appearance and demeanor at the party. Then suggest they put themselves in the character of the woman writing the narrative and jot down any thoughts, feelings, and images about Prufrock.

**3. Social Commentary To make this assignment more challenging,** ask students to research tea parties and include additional details in their commentaries.

## Activities & Explorations

**1. Improvisational Scene To get students started,** encourage them to first reread the poem to fix in their minds the question Prufrock might ask and how a woman at the party might respond to it.

**2. Prufrock's Caricature To get students started,** suggest that they use their charts from Literary Analysis on page 1030 to help in drawing the caricature.

**3. Radio Talk Show To get students started,** suggest that partners decide which aspects of the poem they will discuss in the interview. Students might also read the biography of T. S. Eliot on page 1032 and think of questions based on the information about his poetry.

## Inquiry & Research

**Michelangelo's Artistic Genius** Suggest that students work in small groups. Different members might research different aspects of Michelangelo's life and works. One or more members of the group might be responsible for obtaining pictures of the artist's works.

---

## ✓ Assessment **Standardized Test Practice**

**MAKING INFERENCES AND DRAWING CONCLUSIONS** For some standardized tests, students will be asked to demonstrate their understanding of a literary work by making inferences or drawing conclusions. Read the following three statements aloud and ask students which one best illustrates Prufrock's state of mind at the end of the poem.

**A.** He is pleased with his decision and looks forward to the rest of his life.

**B.** He has acknowledged that he does not lead a meaningful life, but he still looks forward to what will happen next.

**C.** He has accepted his small role in life and does not expect much from the future.

Lead students through the process of choosing the best conclusion. Have them consider each choice and try to find evidence to support each answer. Answer **A** does not appear to contain any correct conclusions; answer **B** starts off correctly, but there is no sign that the second half of the statement is true; answer **C** conforms most clearly with the final stanzas of the poem.

## Vocabulary in Action

### EXERCISE A: SYNONYMS
For each phrase in the first column, write the letter of the synonymous phrase from the second column.

1. meticulous yard work
2. to venture to eat
3. to scheme to malinger
4. as dull-witted as a fowl
5. to get way off track

A. as obtuse as a goose
B. to digress to excess
C. painstaking raking
D. to presume to consume
E. to plan faking some aching

| WORDS TO KNOW | digress malinger | meticulous obtuse | presume |
| --- | --- | --- | --- |

### EXERCISE B
Work with four other classmates to develop a short dramatic scene using five characters. Your scene can deal with any situation. The important thing is to portray each character in such a way that by the end of the scene, he or she has become associated with one of the five vocabulary words without anyone's having used that word in the scene. An association with the word can be developed through each character's actions and dialogue, as well as through other characters' actions toward, or dialogue about, him or her. Perform your dramatic scene for the rest of your classmates, and have them guess which vocabulary word is associated with each character.

**Building Vocabulary**
Several Words to Know come from Latin. For an in-depth lesson on word origins, see page 550.

## T. S. Eliot
### 1888–1965

**Other Works**
*The Waste Land*
"The Hollow Men"
*Murder in the Cathedral*
*Old Possum's Book of Practical Cats*

**Two National Identities** An American who transformed himself into an Englishman, Thomas Stearns Eliot was born in St. Louis, Missouri, and died in London, England, where he had become a British subject in 1927. Eliot's whole career shows a movement back and forth between what the United States and England each represented to him—the modern and the traditional, the popular and the elite, the secular and the religious, democracy and monarchy. Even his poetry is both learned and colloquial, highly sophisticated yet laced with slang.

**Breakthroughs in Poetry** Eliot's early poems, such as "The Love Song of J. Alfred Prufrock" and *The Waste Land*, were original, inventive, and irreverent depictions of the decay of civilization. Although Eliot proclaimed a firm belief in tradition, his poems

helped create a break with tradition and establish a new modernist poetic voice.

**Varied Professions** While his poems, plays, and critical essays were critically acclaimed, Eliot did not make enough money from his writing to live on. He worked in England as a teacher, a bank clerk, and an editor for a British publisher. As the founder and editor of *The Criterion*, a literary magazine, he was able to help younger writers, such as Marcel Proust, get a start in their careers.

**Critical Acclaim** Eliot won the Nobel Prize in literature in 1948. Two years after his death, Eliot was honored by a memorial tablet placed in the Poets' Corner of Westminster Abbey.

## Author Activity

**Broadway Smash Hit** Meet in a small group, and play cuts from a sound recording of *Cats,* Andrew Lloyd Webber's Broadway musical based on T. S. Eliot's *Old Possum's Book of Practical Cats.* As you listen closely to the lyrics, jot down your impressions.

---

### Sidebar (left column)

## Vocabulary in Action

**Exercise A**
1. C
2. D
3. E
4. A
5. B

## Author Activity

Students might compare the images in these lyrics with the images in "Prufrock."

## Teaching Options

---

## Grammar

**INVERTED SUBJECTS AND VERBS**

**Instruction** Every sentence contains a subject and a verb, usually in that order. Sometimes, especially in questions, the order is reversed. "The Love Song of J. Alfred Prufrock" is filled with such questions, though not all of them are signaled by a question mark. Write this sentence on the chalkboard.

There once <u>was</u> a <u>poet</u> by the name of T. S. Eliot. Underline the subject and verb as shown. Point out that the subject appears after the verb.

**Exercise** In each of the following sentences, ask students to underline the subject and verb and determine whether they are inverted or not. If they are inverted, ask students to rewrite the sen-

tence with the subject appearing before the verb. They may rewrite questions as statements.

1. In the room the <u>women</u> <u>come</u> and <u>go</u>, talking of Michelangelo. *(not inverted)*
2. <u>Dare</u> <u>I</u> disturb the universe? *(inverted—I dare disturb the universe.)*
3. <u>Would</u> <u>it</u> <u>have been</u> worthwhile? *(inverted—It would have been worthwhile.)*

Use **Grammar Transparencies and Copymasters**, p. 78.

Use McDougal Littell's *Language Network,* Chapter 1, for more instruction in unusually placed subjects.

*from*

# The Diaries

## Franz Kafka

*Czech-born writer Franz Kafka (1883–1924) shared T. S. Eliot's disillusionment with modern civilization in the 20th century. The characters in Kafka's imaginative stories and novels are plagued by anxiety, loneliness, alienation, and futility. In the following diary entry, Kafka profiles a bachelor who resembles J. Alfred Prufrock.*

The unhappiness of the bachelor, whether seeming or actual, is so easily guessed at by the world around him that he will curse his decision, at least if he has remained a bachelor because of the delight he takes in secrecy. He walks around with his coat buttoned, his hands in the upper pockets of his jacket, his arms akimbo,[1] his hat pulled down over his eyes, a false smile that has become natural to him is supposed to shield his mouth as his glasses do his eyes, his trousers are tighter than seem proper for his thin legs. But everyone knows his condition, can detail his sufferings. A cold breeze breathes upon him from within and he gazes inward with the even sadder half of his double face. He moves incessantly,[2] but with predictable regularity, from one apartment to another. The farther he moves away from the living, for whom he must still—and this is the worst mockery—work like a conscious slave who dare not express his consciousness, so much the smaller a space is considered sufficient for him. While it is death that must still strike down the others, though they may have spent all their lives in a sickbed—for even though they would have gone down by themselves long ago from their own weakness, they nevertheless hold fast to their loving, very healthy relatives by blood and marriage—he, this bachelor, still in the midst of life, apparently of his own free will resigns himself to an ever smaller space, and when he dies the coffin is exactly right for him.

---

1. **akimbo** (ə-kĭm′bō): with the elbows pointed outward.
2. **incessantly:** continually.

## OVERVIEW

 This selection is included in the **Grade 11 InterActive Reader.**

### Objectives

1. understand a modernist **short story** (**Literary Analysis**)
2. understand a **stream-of-consciousness** narrative (**Literary Analysis**)
3. use **sequencing** to order events (**Active Reading**)

### Summary

Ellen Weatherall is nearly eighty years old and lying in bed. She resists the efforts of Doctor Harry to examine her, insisting that she is well. The whispered voices of the doctor and her daughter Cornelia suggest otherwise, however. Granny Weatherall can hear them talking but cannot communicate with them, so she slips into her own private reverie, recalling some of the most prominent moments in her life. She has had a difficult but rewarding life, raising four children and running a farm after the premature death of her husband, John. She thanks God for all the blessings she has enjoyed, but she cannot prevent her thoughts from turning to the devastating event that has haunted her for sixty years: the day she was jilted by George. He took something from her that was never replaced, not even by the richness of her subsequent family experience. Granny dies, praying for a sign from God, and she feels jilted once again.

### Thematic Link

Porter's use of stream of consciousness illustrates a method of writing typical of **modernism.** On her deathbed, Granny Weatherall is **alienated** from present reality, traveling in circuitous routes through the last sixty years of her life.

### 5-Minute Warm-Up

*Daily Language SkillBuilder*

Have students **proofread** the display sentences on page 913k and write them correctly. The sentences also appear on Transparency 29 of **Grammar Transparencies and Copymasters.**

---

*"While she was rummaging around she felt death in her mind and it felt clammy and unfamiliar."*

# The Jilting of Granny Weatherall

*Short Story by* KATHERINE ANNE PORTER

### Connect to Your Life

**Haunting Memories** In the story you are about to read, Granny Weatherall is unable to shake the memory of an event that occurred 60 years earlier. Think about memories that replay again and again in your mind. Which of these do you recall so vividly that you can almost relive the moments? Discuss your responses with a small group of classmates.

## Build Background

**The Art of Storytelling** Katherine Anne Porter claimed to have thrown away trunkloads of manuscripts, allowing only her best work to be published. One of her early stories, "The Jilting of Granny Weatherall," shows Porter's masterly skill in capturing a character with a few concise details and creating a rich experience out of a central episode. The word *jilting* in the title of this story means "a desertion or betrayal, especially by a prospective bride or bridegroom shortly before a wedding." As the story begins, Granny Weatherall lies in bed as a doctor examines her. The second sentence plunges the reader into Granny's mind, where most of the story unfolds. Granny's mind readily moves from present to past and back again.

WORDS TO KNOW
**Vocabulary Preview**
embroidered    rummage
intently          tactful
plague

## Focus Your Reading

**LITERARY ANALYSIS** **STREAM OF CONSCIOUSNESS** **Stream of consciousness** is a literary technique that was developed by modernist writers to present the flow of a character's seemingly unconnected thoughts, responses, and sensations. A stream-of-consciousness narrative is not structured into a coherent, logical presentation of events. Rather, the connections are associative, with one impression suggesting another. Note Granny Weatherall's rambling patterns of thinking as she lies on her deathbed.

**ACTIVE READING** **SEQUENCING** In this stream-of-consciousness narrative, Porter shuffles the past and the present to show the distorted way that a dying person perceives the **sequence,** or time order, of events. The reader experiences Granny's sense of time as she imaginatively travels backward and forward through her life, re-creating dramatic moments. Look for time jumps in the story as you read.

**READER'S NOTEBOOK** Create a time line like the one shown to help you untangle the main events of Granny Weatherall's life. Jot down the key moments in chronological order. The sample timeline below lists two events.

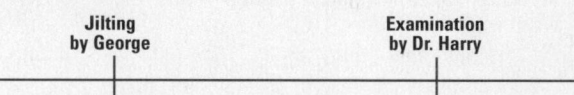

Jilting
by George

Examination
by Dr. Harry

---

### LESSON RESOURCES

**UNIT SIX RESOURCE BOOK,** pp. 59–63

**ASSESSMENT RESOURCES**
**Formal Assessment,** pp. 193–194
**Teacher's Guide to Assessment and Portfolio Use**
**Test Generator**

**SKILLS TRANSPARENCIES AND COPYMASTERS**
**Literary Analysis**
• Modernist Literature, T17 (for Literary Analysis, p. 1043)

**Grammar**
• Parallelism, T57 (for Mini Lesson, p. 1038)
• Colons, C159 (for Mini Lesson, p. 1044)
• Parallel Compound Subjects, C168 (for Mini Lesson, p. 1038)

**Vocabulary**
• Figurative Language and Idioms, C87 (for Mini Lesson, p. 1039)

**Communications**
• Interviewing, T9 (for Activities & Explorations 2, p. 1044)
• Impromptu Speaking: Dialogue, Role-Play, Debate, T13 (for Activities & Explorations 2, p. 1044)

**INTEGRATED TECHNOLOGY**

**Audio Library**
**Visit our website:**
www.mcdougallittell.com

# The JILTING of Granny Weatherall

**KATHERINE ANNE PORTER**

She flicked her wrist neatly out of Doctor Harry's pudgy careful fingers and pulled the sheet up to her chin. The brat ought to be in knee breeches.[1] Doctoring around the country with spectacles on his nose! "Get along now, take your schoolbooks and go. There's nothing wrong with me."

Doctor Harry spread a warm paw like a cushion on her forehead where the forked green vein danced and made her eyelids twitch. "Now, now, be a good girl, and we'll have you up in no time."

"That's no way to speak to a woman nearly eighty years old just because she's down. I'd have you respect your elders, young man."

"Well, Missy, excuse me." Doctor Harry patted her cheek. "But I've got to warn you, haven't I? You're a marvel, but you must be careful or you're going to be good and sorry."

"Don't tell me what I'm going to be. I'm on my feet now, morally speaking. It's Cornelia. I had to go to bed to get rid of her."

Her bones felt loose, and floated around in her skin, and Doctor Harry floated like a balloon around the foot of the bed. He floated and pulled down his waistcoat and swung

*La mere morte de l'artiste* [The artist's mother in death], James Ensor. Stedelijk Museum, Ostend, Belgium. Copyright © SABAM.

---

1. **knee breeches:** short pants or knickers worn by young boys.

1035

## TEACHING THE LITERATURE

### Customizing Instruction

**Less Proficient Readers**
Tell students that Granny Weatherall is nearly eighty years old. She is living with her daughter Cornelia, who has called a doctor to examine Granny. Ask students what impression they receive of Granny's character from the first few paragraphs of the story.
**Possible Responses:** opinionated; feisty; stubborn; ailing
**Set a Purpose** Have students read to find out what events in Granny's life stand out in her mind and how she feels about death.

### Students Acquiring English
Tell students that because of Granny Weatherall's illness, her mind slips in and out of the present. Prepare students for Granny's sudden transitions from present to past by telling them that the use of the past perfect tense will help signal this change. Clarify that John is Granny's dead husband and George is the man who jilted her (promised to marry her but did not show up at the wedding).

Use **Spanish Study Guide** for additional support, pp. 257–259.

### Gifted and Talented
Ask students what point of view Katherine Anne Porter chose for this story and why she might have chosen this point of view.

---

**Mini Lesson**  **Preteaching Vocabulary**

**USING CONTEXT CLUES**
**Instructions** Students can enrich their vocabulary by using context clues to determine the meanings of unfamiliar words. Sometimes students can define an unfamiliar word by finding a contrast in the sentence. Contrasts are indicated by words such as *but, although, not, however,* and *on the other hand.* Ask a volunteer to explain the contrast in the following sentence. Have students use their understanding of the contrast to define *intently.*

She tried to fix her eyes <u>intently</u> on the doctor to show her alertness, but instead her eyelids drooped and her focus blurred.

**Exercises** Have students apply the strategy to

determine the meanings of the underlined words.
1. Although she tried to be <u>tactful</u> to Cornelia, sometimes she was unknowingly rude.
2. The new medicine was supposed to be a <u>marvel</u>, but the results were a disappointment.
3. No moments of peace awaited her; instead she was <u>plagued</u> from morning until night with the demands of the children.

Use **Unit Six Resource Book**, p. 62 for more exercises.

**A lesson on context clues appears on p. 326 in the Pupil's Edition.**

### Reading Skills and Strategies: PREVIEW

Explain to students that because of Granny Weatherall's illness, her mind slips in and out of the present and moves by association rather than chronology.

### Literary Analysis
**STREAM OF CONSCIOUSNESS**

 Ask students to find the idea that triggers Granny's thoughts of death.
**Possible Response:** She was thinking about people looking at the letters in the attic after she died. This led her to the thought of death.

📖 Use **Unit Six Resource Book**, p. 61 for more practice.

### Active Reading | SEQUENCING |

 Ask students when the story about Granny's father and the hot toddy takes place and what clues indicate the sequence of events.
**Possible Responses:** Granny's father died sometime in the past—before we see Granny on her own deathbed. Clues include the use of the past perfect tense ("Her father *had lived* . . .") and Granny's mention of his "last birthday."

📖 Use **Unit Six Resource Book**, p. 60 for more practice.

*Portrait of Ambroise Vollard* (1909), Pablo Picasso. Pushkin Museum of Fine Arts, Moscow/Giraudon/Art Resource, New York. Copyright © Artist's Rights Society ARS), New York.

his glasses on a cord. "Well, stay where you are, it certainly can't hurt you."

"Get along and doctor your sick," said Granny Weatherall. "Leave a well woman alone. I'll call for you when I want you. . . . Where were you forty years ago when I pulled through milk-leg[2] and double pneumonia? You weren't even born. Don't let Cornelia lead you on," she shouted, because Doctor Harry appeared to float up to the ceiling and out. "I pay my own bills, and I don't throw my money away on nonsense!"

She meant to wave good-by, but it was too much trouble. Her eyes closed of themselves, it was like a dark curtain drawn around the bed. The pillow rose and floated under her, pleasant as a hammock in a light wind. She listened to the leaves rustling outside the window. No, somebody was swishing newspapers: no, Cornelia and Doctor Harry were whispering together. She leaped broad awake, thinking they whispered in her ear.

"She was never like this, *never* like this!" "Well, what can we expect?" "Yes, eighty years old. . . ."

Well, and what if she was? She still had ears. It was like Cornelia to whisper around doors. She always kept things secret in such a public way. She was always being <u>tactful</u> and kind. Cornelia was dutiful; that was the trouble with her. Dutiful and good: "So good and dutiful," said Granny, "that I'd like to spank her." She saw herself spanking Cornelia and making a fine job of it.

"What'd you say, Mother?"

Granny felt her face tying up in hard knots.

"Can't a body think, I'd like to know?"

"I thought you might want something."

"I do. I want a lot of things. First off, go away and don't whisper."

She lay and drowsed, hoping in her sleep that the children would keep out and let her rest a minute. It had been a long day. Not that she was tired. It was always pleasant to snatch a minute now and then. There was always so much to be done, let me see: tomorrow.

---

2. **milk-leg:** a painful swelling of the leg experienced by some women after giving birth.

WORDS TO KNOW
**tactful** (tăkt'fəl) *adj.* careful of others' feelings; considerate

1036

---

 **Viewing and Representing**

*Portrait of Ambroise Vollard* **by Pablo Picasso**

**ART APPRECIATION** This 1909 work was painted by Picasso (1881–1973) in a style known as Facet Cubism, which emphasized a disintegration of realistic images with the intersections of angles, facets, and planes composing the picture.

**Instruction** Although this painting is abstract, it is still recognizable as the head of a man. Ask students what effect the arrangement of colors has on the viewing of this painting and what the faceted cuts contribute to an analysis of the work.

**Possible Responses:** The brown focuses the attention of the viewer on the head. The darkness

of the green immediately around the head suggests an intensity of experiences or stimuli working on the man. The number of facets and the positioning create a movement.

**Application** Ask students why this abstract portrait is more relevant to Granny Weatherall's thoughts than a realistic portrait would be.

**Possible Responses:** Granny Weatherall's memories of both her husband and George have been filtered over sixty years. She has lost some facets of their characters, retained others, and probably created parts of them in her mind.

Tomorrow was far away and there was nothing to trouble about. Things were finished somehow when the time came; thank God there was always a little margin over for peace: then a person could spread out the plan of life and tuck in the edges orderly. It was good to have everything clean and folded away, with the hair brushes and tonic bottles sitting straight on the white embroidered linen: the day started without fuss and the pantry shelves laid out with rows of jelly glasses and brown jugs and white stone-china jars with blue whirligigs[3] and words painted on them: coffee, tea, sugar, ginger, cinnamon, allspice: and the bronze clock with the lion on top nicely dusted off. The dust that lion could collect in twenty-four hours! The box in the attic with all those letters tied up, well, she'd have to go through that tomorrow. All those letters—George's letters and John's letters and her letters to them both—lying around for the children to find afterwards made her uneasy. Yes, that would be tomorrow's business. No use to let them know how silly she had been once.

While she was rummaging around she found death in her mind and it felt clammy and unfamiliar. She had spent so much time preparing for death there was no need for bringing it up again. Let it take care of itself now. When she was sixty she had felt very old, finished, and went around making farewell trips to see her children and grandchildren, with a secret in her mind: This is the very last of your mother, children! Then she made her will and came down with a long fever. That was all just a notion like a lot of other things, but it was lucky too, for she had once for all got over the idea of dying for a long time. Now she couldn't be worried. She hoped she had better sense now. Her father had lived to be one hundred and two years old and had drunk a noggin of strong hot toddy[4] on his last birthday. He told the reporters it was his daily habit, and he owed his long life to that. He had made quite

a scandal and was very pleased about it. She believed she'd just plague Cornelia a little.

"Cornelia! Cornelia!" No footsteps, but a sudden hand on her cheek. "Bless you, where have you been?"

"Here, Mother."

"Well, Cornelia, I want a noggin of hot toddy."

"Are you cold, darling?"

"I'm chilly, Cornelia. Lying in bed stops the circulation. I must have told you that a thousand times."

Well, she could just hear Cornelia telling her husband that Mother was getting a little childish and they'd have to humor her. The thing that most annoyed her was that Cornelia thought she was deaf, dumb, and blind. Little hasty glances and tiny gestures tossed around her and over her head saying, "Don't cross her, let her have her way, she's eighty years old," and she sitting there as if she lived in a thin glass cage. Sometimes Granny almost made up her mind to pack up and move back to her own house where nobody could remind her every minute that she was old. Wait, wait, Cornelia, till your own children whisper behind your back!

In her day she had kept a better house and had got more work done. She wasn't too old yet for Lydia to be driving eighty miles for advice when one of the children jumped the track, and Jimmy still dropped in and talked things over: "Now, Mammy, you've a good business head, I want to know what you think of this? . . ." Old. Cornelia couldn't change the furniture around without asking. Little things, little things! They had been so sweet when they were little. Granny wished the old days were back again with the

---

3. **stone-china . . . whirligigs** (hwûr′lĭ-gĭgz′): jars made of thick pottery with blue spiral designs.

4. **noggin . . . toddy:** mug of a strong, hot alcoholic drink.

| WORDS TO KNOW | **embroidered** (ĕm-broi′dərd) *adj.* decorated with stitched designs **embroider** *v.*<br>**rummage** (rŭm′ĭj) *v.* to search through a confusion of objects<br>**plague** (plāg) *v.* to annoy; harass |
|---|---|

1037

**Students Acquiring English**
Explain to students that Doctor Harry and Cornelia's conversation takes place in the present.
**1** Ask students to explain what Granny means when she says about Cornelia, "She always kept things secret in such a public way."
**Possible Response:** Cornelia makes such a show of secrecy that nothing can stay secret.

**Less Proficient Readers**
**2** Ask students how Granny feels about death and why.
**Possible Response:** Granny feels she can be sensible about death because she prepared herself for it when she was sixty.
**Set a Purpose** Have students read to find out what hardships Granny endured in her life and what is happening to her in the present.

## BLOCK SCHEDULING: MANAGING TIME

**If your schedule requires that you cover the lesson objectives in a shorter time, use . . .**
- Preparing to Read, p. 1034
- Thinking Through the Literature, p. 1043
- Vocabulary in Action, p. 1044

**If you want to take advantage of longer class time, use . . .**
- TE Teaching Options: Preteaching Vocabulary, p. 1035; Viewing and Representing, pp. 1036, 1041; Vocabulary Strategy, p. 1039; Cross-Curricular Link, p. 1040; Informal Assessment, p. 1042
- Choices & Challenges, p. 1044

**A** Ask students what they think happened to Granny's husband, John.
**Possible Response:** He died young.

**Literary Analysis**
STREAM OF CONSCIOUSNESS

**B** Ask students to explain what leads Granny to think of the day she was jilted.
**Possible Responses:** She feels her pillow rising up around her shoulders and pressing upon her heart, causing the memory to be squeezed out. If she tries to hold the memory, she will suffocate.

Ask students to describe Granny's memory of that day.
**Possible Response:** When she thinks of the day, dark smoke covers the green fields where everything is planted in orderly rows.

Ask students what is the significance of the dark smoke covering the green, orderly fields.
**Possible Responses:** Granny has never really recovered from being jilted. The memory of that event still has the power to cast a blight over what she has made of her life.

**Active Reading** SEQUENCING

**C** Ask students when Granny was jilted and why she has prayed against remembering the man who did it.
**Possible Responses:** It happened sixty years ago. She feels that if she remembers, she will be filled with hatred.

---

children young and everything to be done over. It had been a hard pull, but not too much for her. When she thought of all the food she had cooked, and all the clothes she had cut and sewed, and all the gardens she had made—well, the children showed it. There they were, made out of her, and they couldn't get away from that. Sometimes she wanted to see John again and point to them and say, Well, I didn't do so badly, did I? But that would have to wait. That was for tomorrow. She used to think of him as a man, but now all the children were older than their father, and he would be a child beside her if she saw him now. It seemed strange and there was something wrong in the idea. Why, he couldn't possibly recognize her. She had fenced in a hundred acres once, digging the post holes herself and clamping the wires with just a negro boy to help. That changed a woman. John would be looking for a young woman with the peaked Spanish comb in her hair and the painted fan. Digging post holes changed a woman. Riding country roads in the winter when women had their babies was another thing: sitting up nights with sick horses and sick negroes and sick children and hardly ever losing one. John, I hardly ever lost one of them! John would see that in a minute, that would be something he could understand, she wouldn't have to explain anything!

It made her feel like rolling up her sleeves and putting the whole place to rights again. No matter if Cornelia was determined to be everywhere at once, there were a great many things left undone on this place. She would start tomorrow and do them. It was good to be strong enough for everything, even if all you made melted and changed and slipped under your hands, so that by the time you finished you almost forgot what you were working for. What was it I set out to do? she asked herself <u>intently</u>, but she could not remember. A fog rose over the valley, she saw it marching across the creek swallowing the trees and moving up the hill like an army of ghosts. Soon it would be at the near edge of the orchard, and then it was time to go in and light the lamps. Come in, children, don't stay out in the night air.

Lighting the lamps had been beautiful. The children huddled up to her and breathed like little calves waiting at the bars in the twilight. Their eyes followed the match and watched the flame rise and settle in a blue curve, then they moved away from her. The lamp was lit, they didn't have to be scared and hang on to mother any more. Never, never, never more. God, for all my life I thank Thee. Without Thee, my God, I could never have done it. Hail, Mary, full of grace.[5]

I want you to pick all the fruit this year and see that nothing is wasted. There's always someone who can use it. Don't let good things rot for want of using. You waste life when you waste good food. Don't let things get lost. It's bitter to lose things. Now, don't let me get to thinking, not when I am tired and taking a little nap before supper. . . .

The pillow rose about her shoulders and pressed against her heart and the memory was being squeezed out of it: oh, push down the pillow, somebody: it would smother her if she tried to hold it. Such a fresh breeze blowing and such a green day with no threats in it. But he had not come, just the same. What does a woman do when she has put on the white veil and set out the white cake for a man and he doesn't come? She tried to remember. No, I swear he never harmed me but in that. He never harmed me but in that. . .and what if he did? There was the day, the day, but a whirl of dark

---

5. **Hail . . . grace:** the beginning of a Roman Catholic prayer to the Virgin Mary.

---

WORDS
TO
KNOW

**intently** (ĭn-tĕnt′lē) *adv.* with concentrated attention

---

## Teaching Options

 **Mini Lesson** **Grammar**

**PARALLEL COMPOUND SUBJECTS**
**Instruction** Remind students that in lists, series, and compound elements of a sentence, parallel structure maintains balance and coherence. Grammatically equal elements should be treated in a parallel manner. Display the following sentences:

**Incorrect:** Granny Weatherall's <u>determination</u>, <u>fortitude</u>, and <u>being independent</u> helped her to survive.

**Correct:** Granny Weatherall's <u>determination</u>, <u>fortitude</u>, and <u>independence</u> helped her to survive.

**Exercises** Have students rewrite the sentences to create parallelism in the compound subjects.

1. Raising her children, management of the farm, and maintaining an orderly house were some of Granny's accomplishments. *(Raising her children, managing the farm, and maintaining an orderly house . . .)*

2. Canning, gardening, nursing, or house clean-up filled every waking minute. *(Canning, gardening, nursing, or housecleaning . . .)*

Use **Grammar Transparencies and Copymasters**, p. 168.

 Use McDougal Littell's *Language Network*, Chapter 15, for more instruction in parallelism.

smoke rose and covered it, crept up and over into the bright field where everything was planted so carefully in orderly rows. That was hell, she knew hell when she saw it. For sixty years she had prayed against remembering him and against losing her soul in the deep pit of hell, and now the two things were mingled in one and the thought of him was a smoky cloud from hell that moved and crept in her head when she had just got rid of Doctor Harry and was trying to rest a minute. Wounded vanity, Ellen, said a sharp voice in the top of her mind. Don't let your wounded vanity get the upper hand of you. Plenty of girls get jilted. You were jilted, weren't you? Then stand up to it. Her eyelids wavered and let in streamers of blue-gray light like tissue paper over her eyes. She must get up and pull the shades down or she'd never sleep. She was in bed again and the shades were not down. How could that happen? Better turn over, hide from the light, sleeping in the light gave you nightmares. "Mother, how do you feel now?" and a stinging wetness on her forehead. But I don't like having my face washed in cold water!

Hapsy? George? Lydia? Jimmy? No, Cornelia, and her features were swollen and full of little puddles. "They're coming, darling, they'll all be here soon." Go wash your face, child, you look funny.

Instead of obeying, Cornelia knelt down and put her head on the pillow. She seemed to be talking but there was no sound. "Well, are you tongue-tied? Whose birthday is it? Are you going to give a party?"

Cornelia's mouth moved urgently in strange shapes. "Don't do that, you bother me, daughter."

"Oh, no, Mother. Oh, no. . . ."

Nonsense. It was strange about children. They disputed your every word. "No what, Cornelia?"

"Here's Doctor Harry."

"I won't see that boy again. He just left five minutes ago."

"That was this morning, Mother. It's night now. Here's the nurse."

"This is Doctor Harry, Mrs. Weatherall. I never saw you look so young and happy!"

"Ah, I'll never be young again—but I'd be happy if they'd let me lie in peace and get rested."

She thought she spoke up loudly, but no one answered. A warm weight on her forehead, a warm bracelet on her wrist, and a breeze went on whispering, trying to tell her something. A shuffle of leaves in the everlasting hand of God, He blew on them and they danced and rattled. "Mother, don't mind, we're going to give you a little hypodermic."[6] "Look here, daughter, how do ants get in this bed? I saw sugar ants yesterday." Did you send for Hapsy too?

It was Hapsy she really wanted. She had to go a long way back through a great many rooms to find Hapsy standing with a baby on her arm, and the baby on Hapsy's arm was Hapsy and himself and herself, all at once, and there was no surprise in the meeting. Then Hapsy melted from within and turned flimsy as gray gauze and the baby was a gauzy shadow, and Hapsy came up close and said, "I thought you'd never come," and looked at her very searchingly and said, "You haven't changed a bit!" They leaned forward to kiss, when Cornelia began whispering

*Don't let your wounded vanity get the upper hand of you.*

---

6. **hypodermic** (hī′pə-dûr′mĭk): injection.

## Customizing Instruction

**Less Proficient Readers**
Ask students what hardships Granny endured in her past.
**Possible Responses:** Granny had to raise her children alone and do hard manual labor to keep the farm going. She tended anyone—human or animal—who was sick. She survived being jilted and the death of her husband.

Ask students what is happening to Granny in the present.
**Possible Responses:** Cornelia is putting a wet cloth on her head, the doctor is there to give her an injection, and her other children are coming.

**Set a Purpose** Have students read to find out Granny's last wishes before she dies.

### Students Acquiring English
**1** Ask students why John would be a child compared to his children.
**Possible Response:** He died at an age younger than his children are now.

### Gifted and Talented
**2** Have students consider what is revealed about Granny's character through the statement "Don't let good things rot for want of using." Ask students how she lived up to this quote in her own life.

### Students Acquiring English
**3** Tell students that an entire day has passed without Granny's realizing it. Doctor Harry is back with a nurse, and Granny's children have been summoned to her bedside. Ask students what Cornelia has been doing and why.
**Possible Response:** She has been crying because her mother is dying.

## Mini Lesson · Vocabulary Strategy

**FIGURATIVE LANGUAGE AND IDIOMS**
**Instruction** The meanings of figurative language and idioms can be determined through context. Ask students to find the phrase "the whole bottom dropped out of the world" on page 1040. Students should note that Granny is thinking of the day that she was jilted. The wedding cake was wasted; she was blind and sweating. These clues allow students to infer that the phrase means that she was shocked by the event and lost her orientation.
**Exercises** Have students find the following passages in the story and use context clues to determine the meanings of underlined phrases.

1. "when one of the children jumped the track" (p. 1037) *(got into trouble)*
2. "Granny felt her face tying up in hard knots." (p. 1036) *(frowning and tensing)*
3. "Cornelia's voice staggered and bumped like a cart in a bad road." (p. 1041) *(wavered and shook)*

 Use **Vocabulary Transparencies and Copymasters**, p. 87.

Ask students what three episodes in her past Granny relives on page 1040.

**Possible Responses:** the birth of her last child; the day she was supposed to marry George; comforting the children after a nightmare

### Literary Analysis
STREAM OF CONSCIOUSNESS

**Ⓐ** Ask students to trace the path that Granny's thoughts take to the memory of the birth of her child.

**Possible Responses:** Granny thinks about sending Cornelia to find George to tell him what she made of her life. She then wonders if a husband, children, and a home are enough to satisfy her. This doubt gives her pain, which leads her into reliving the pain of childbirth.

### Reading Skills and Strategies:
EVALUATING

**Ⓑ** Ask students what effect the jilting had on Granny.

**Possible Responses:** It was a defining moment in her life that has influenced everything she has felt and done. She did not forget the event or get over it.

---

from a long way off, "Oh, is there anything you want to tell me? Is there anything I can do for you?"

Yes, she had changed her mind after sixty years and she would like to see George. I want you to find George. Find him and be sure to tell him I forgot him. I want him to know I had my husband just the same and my children and my house like any other woman. A good house too and a good husband that I loved and fine children out of him. Better than I hoped for even. Tell him I was given back everything he took away and more. Oh, no, oh, God, no, there was something else besides the house and the man and the children. Oh, surely they were not all? What was it? Something not given back. . . . Her breath crowded down under her ribs and grew into a monstrous frightening shape with cutting edges; it bored up into her head, and the agony was unbelievable: Yes, John, get the Doctor now, no more talk, my time has come.

When this one was born it should be the last. The last. It should have been born first, for it was the one she had truly wanted. Everything came in good time. Nothing left out, left over. She was strong, in three days she would be as well as ever. Better. A woman needed milk in her to have her full health.

"Mother, do you hear me?"

"I've been telling you—"

"Mother, Father Connolly's here."

"I went to Holy Communion only last week. Tell him I'm not so sinful as all that."

"Father just wants to speak to you."

He could speak as much as he pleased. It was like him to drop in and inquire about her soul as if it were a teething baby, and then stay on for a cup of tea and a round of cards and gossip. He always had a funny story of some sort, usually

*Tell him I was given back eveything he took away and more.*

about an Irishman who made his little mistakes and confessed them, and the point lay in some absurd thing he would blurt out in the confessional showing his struggles between native piety and original sin. Granny felt easy about her soul. Cornelia, where are your manners? Give Father Connolly a chair. She had her secret comfortable understanding with a few favorite saints who cleared a straight road to God for her. All as surely signed and sealed as the papers for the new Forty Acres. Forever. . . . heirs and assigns[7] forever. Since the day the wedding cake was not cut, but thrown out and wasted. The whole bottom dropped out of the world, and there she was blind and sweating with nothing under her feet and the walls falling away. His hand had caught her under the breast, she had not fallen, there was the freshly polished floor with the green rug on it, just as before. He had cursed like a sailor's parrot and said, "I'll kill him for you." Don't lay a hand on him, for my sake leave something to God. "Now, Ellen, you must believe what I tell you. . . ."

So there was nothing, nothing to worry about any more, except sometimes in the night one of the children screamed in a nightmare, and they both hustled out shaking and hunting for the matches and calling, "There, wait a minute, here we are!" John, get the doctor now, Hapsy's time has come. But there was Hapsy standing by the bed in a white cap. "Cornelia, tell Hapsy to take off her cap. I can't see her plain."

Her eyes opened very wide and the room stood out like a picture she had seen somewhere.

---

7. **assigns:** people to whom property is transferred in a will or other legal document.

---

## Teaching Options

### Cross Curricular Link **Women's Studies**

**ROLE OF ANTEBELLUM SOUTHERN WOMEN**
Although the impression of southern women before the Civil War is one of delicate and beautiful ladies whiling away hours in conversation and genteel pursuits, the reality was quite different. Southern women, no matter what social class they occupied, had days filled with chores as well as the added responsibility of child rearing. Women in a lower social class might spend their days canning, sewing, tending to livestock, listening to their children say their lessons, cleaning the house, and tidying the yard before cooking and serving the evening meal. Women in a more secure economic situation also prepared meals, readied children for school, looked after the poultry, did the sewing, and received visitors. Plantation owners' wives had the most leisure, but that was only to be enjoyed after they finished making decisions on the running of the house, overseeing the slaves, caring for the children, and, in some cases, actually managing the plantation.

*Yvonne and Magdaleine Torn in Tatters* (1911), Marcel Duchamp. Oil on canvas, 23¼" × 28⅞". Philadelphia Museum of Art, Louise and Walter Arensberg Collection (1950-134-53).

Dark colors with the shadows rising towards the ceiling in long angles. The tall black dresser gleamed with nothing on it but John's picture, enlarged from a little one, with John's eyes very black when they should have been blue. You never saw him, so how do you know how he looked? But the man insisted the copy was perfect, it was very rich and handsome. For a picture, yes, but it's not my husband. The table by the bed had a linen cover and a candle and a crucifix.[8] The light was blue from Cornelia's silk lampshades. No sort of light at all, just frippery. You had to live forty years with kerosene lamps to appreciate honest electricity. She felt very strong and she saw Doctor Harry with a rosy nimbus[9] around him.

"You look like a saint, Doctor Harry, and I vow that's as near as you'll ever come to it."

"She's saying something."

"I heard you, Cornelia. What's all this carrying-on?"

"Father Connolly's saying—"

Cornelia's voice staggered and bumped like a cart in a bad road. It rounded corners and turned back again and arrived nowhere. Granny stepped up in the cart very lightly and reached for the reins, but a man sat beside her and she knew him by his hands, driving the cart. She did

---

8. **crucifix** (krōō′sə-fĭks′): a cross bearing a sculptured representation of the crucified Christ.

9. **nimbus:** halo of light.

THE JILTING OF GRANNY WEATHERALL **1041**

---

### Less Proficient Readers

**1** Ask students what Granny thinks about her soul.

**Possible Response:** She believes she is going straight to heaven.

**2** Granny believes it is Hapsy in the white cap. Ask students who it is.

**Possible Response:** It is the nurse whom Cornelia mentioned.

Have students list who is actually at Granny's bedside and why they are all there.

**Possible Responses:** Cornelia, Doctor Harry, the nurse, Father Connolly, Jimmy, Lydia (later); they are all there because she is so close to death.

Have students predict the ending of the story.

**Possible Response:** Granny Weatherall will die.

### Students Acquiring English

**3** Have students determine the meaning of *frippery* by using the context of the sentence.

**Possible Responses:** something frivolous; the light was more decorative than useful.

### Gifted and Talented

Students should read the story to appreciate the writer's craft. Remind students that although the stream of consciousness appears random in its direction, Katherine Anne Porter has subtly unified her story by the use of recurring images and symbols, some of which span past and present, some of which appear just in the present or the past. Ask students to pick out these unifying images and symbols.

---

**Mini Lesson**  # Viewing and Representing

*Yvonne and Magdaleine Torn in Tatters*
**by Marcel Duchamp**

**ART APPRECIATION** French painter Marcel Duchamp (1887–1968) began to experiment with Cubist techniques in 1911. His interest in this style was short-lived, but during this time, he painted several works that employed the device of "simultaneous aspects" in a way that was different from the method employed by other Cubists. He represented the same figures on different planes and in different attitudes to express more of the individual.

**Instruction** Ask students what images they can immediately pick out in this painting. *(two people in profile facing each other)* Ask students to describe what Duchamp then does with the profile shapes and what is suggested by his positioning of them.

**Possible Responses:** He repeats them behind the profile on the left. This might suggest thoughts about what is occurring between the two in the mind of one of the people involved.

## Literary Analysis: IRONY

**A** Have students explain the irony of Granny Weatherall's response to the imminence of her death.

**Possible Responses:** She is surprised, even though she contemplated it calmly earlier in the story. For all of her planning and putting things in order, she is not ready.

## Literary Analysis: THEME

**B** Ask students to state the theme of the story based on evidence from the last paragraph and from the story as a whole.

**Possible Responses:** Some sorrows cannot be forgotten or healed. Each life has one great disappointment or grief that overshadows all others. At the time of death, a person realizes what the most important or formative experience in his or her life has been. Life does not provide the answers or reassurances that people want, even at the moment before death.

---

not look in his face, for she knew without seeing, but looked instead down the road where the trees leaned over and bowed to each other and a thousand birds were singing a Mass. She felt like singing too, but she put her hand in the bosom of her dress and pulled out a rosary,[10] and Father Connolly murmured Latin in a very solemn voice and tickled her feet. My God, will you stop that nonsense? I'm a married woman. What if he did run away and leave me to face the priest by myself? I found another a whole world better. I wouldn't have exchanged my husband for anybody except St. Michael himself, and you may tell him that for me with a thank you in the bargain.

Light flashed on her closed eyelids, and a deep roaring shook her. Cornelia, is that lightning? I hear thunder. There's going to be a storm. Close all the windows. Call the children in. . . . "Mother, here we are, all of us." "Is that you, Hapsy?" "Oh, no, I'm Lydia. We drove as fast as we could." Their faces drifted above her, drifted away. The rosary fell out of her hands and Lydia put it back. Jimmy tried to help, their hands fumbled together, and Granny closed two fingers around Jimmy's thumb. Beads wouldn't do, it must be something alive. She was so amazed her thoughts ran round and round. So, my dear Lord, this is my death and I wasn't even thinking about it. My children have come to see me die. But I can't, it's not time. Oh, I always hated surprises. I wanted to give Cornelia the amethyst set—Cornelia, you're to have the amethyst set, but Hapsy's to wear it when she wants, and, Doctor Harry, do shut up. Nobody sent for you. Oh, my dear Lord, do wait a minute. I meant to do something about the Forty Acres, Jimmy doesn't need it and Lydia will later on, with that worthless husband of hers. I meant to finish the altar cloth and send six bottles of wine to Sister Borgia for her dyspepsia.[11] I want to send six bottles of wine to Sister Borgia, Father Connolly, now don't let me forget.

**A**

Cornelia's voice made short turns and tilted over and crashed. "Oh, Mother, oh, Mother, oh, Mother . . . ."

"I'm not going, Cornelia. I'm taken by surprise. I can't go."

You'll see Hapsy again. What about her? "I thought you'd never come." Granny made a long journey outward, looking for Hapsy. What if I don't find her? What then? Her heart sank down and down, there was no bottom to death, she couldn't come to the end of it. The blue light from Cornelia's lampshade drew into a tiny point in the center of her brain, it flickered and

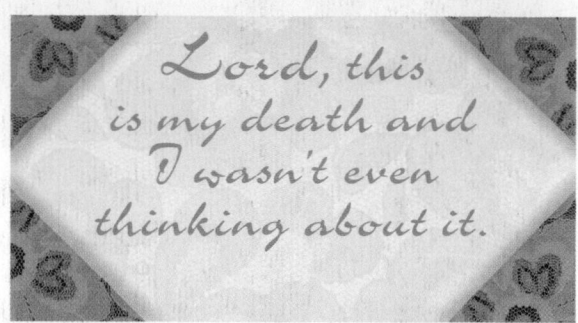

*Lord, this is my death and I wasn't even thinking about it.*

winked like an eye, quietly it fluttered and dwindled. Granny lay curled down within herself, amazed and watchful, staring at the point of light that was herself; her body was now only a deeper mass of shadow in an endless darkness and this darkness would curl around the light and swallow it up. God, give a sign!

For the second time there was no sign. Again no bridegroom and the priest in the house. She could not remember any other sorrow because this grief wiped them all away. Oh, no, there's nothing more cruel than this—I'll never forgive it. She stretched herself with a deep breath and blew out the light. ❖

**B**

---

10. **rosary** (rō′zə-rē): a string of beads used by Roman Catholics to count their prayers.

11. **dyspepsia** (dĭs-pĕp′shə): indigestion.

---

# Teaching Options

## Informal Assessment

**UNDERSTANDING CHARACTER** You can informally assess students' understanding of the character Granny Weatherall by asking them to create a preface to the story in which Granny is thinking about why she came to live with Cornelia. Prefaces should be written in the third-person limited point of view and should provide one or more plausible reasons, consistent with Granny's character, for her living with Cornelia. Students should try to incorporate a stream of consciousness technique to initiate Granny's reflections.

**RUBRIC**

**3**  **Full Accomplishment** Preface adheres to the third-person limited point of view, incorporates stream of consciousness, and advances reasons for Granny's decision.

**2**  **Substantial Accomplishment** Preface adheres to third-person limited point of view and includes one or two reasons that suit the character of Granny.

**1**  **Little or Partial Accomplishment** Preface is not narrated in third-person limited point of view, nor does it give solid reasons for Granny's residence with Cornelia.

## Connect to the Literature

**1. What Do You Think?**
What did you find the most memorable about Granny? Share your thoughts with a partner.

**Comprehension Check**
• Which characters mentioned in the story are mainly figures from Granny's past?
• What role did George play in Granny's life?
• Which of her daughters does Granny most want to see?

## Think Critically

**2.** ACTIVE READING | SEQUENCING EVENTS Use the time line you made in your  READER'S NOTEBOOK to retell the key events of Granny's life in chronological order. How do you picture her in the various stages of her life—young girl, wife and mother, and old widow?

**3.** Do you think Granny's moment of death—symbolized by her blowing out the light at the end of the story—is an act of resignation or an act of defiance? Explain your response.

**4.** How would you compare Granny's experience of death with her jilting by George 60 years before?

THINK ABOUT
• her expectations and surprises on each occasion
• her feelings about each experience
• her thoughts about God that relate to her jilting experience

**5.** Of all the relationships in her life, which one do you think means the most to Granny? Why?

**6.** What do you think Granny's rather unusual last name—Weatherall—suggests about her character?

## Extend Interpretations

**7. Critic's Corner** The writer Eudora Welty has remarked, "All the stories she [Porter] has written are moral stories about love and the hate that is love's twin. . . ." Do you think that assessment applies to this story? Explain.

**8. Comparing Texts** How would you compare the portrayal of death in this story with Emily Dickinson's portrayal of death in her poems "I heard a Fly buzz—when I died—" (page 758) and "Because I could not stop for Death—" (pages 759)?

**9. Connect to Life** Based on this story and your own experiences, how would you describe the power of memory in shaping people's lives?

THE JILTING OF GRANNY WEATHERALL **1043**

## Literary Analysis

STREAM OF CONSCIOUSNESS

The term *stream of consciousness* was coined by American psychologist William James to characterize the unbroken flow of thought that occurs in the waking mind. Later the term was adopted to describe a narrative method in modern works of literature. Porter uses stream of consciousness to dramatize Granny's interior life—her memories, secret longings, unsatisfied wishes. This approach allows the reader to develop an intimacy with Granny that would not be possible if the story dramatized only the external events that take place in the sickroom.

**Activity** Imitate Porter's fictional technique by writing a short stream-of-consciousness narrative in which George recalls jilting Granny Weatherall shortly before his own death. Include the random images, thoughts, and feelings he associates with this event. Share your narrative with classmates.

## GUIDING STUDENT RESPONSE

## Connect to the Literature

**1. What Do You Think?**
Students' responses should include examples from the text to support their observations. They may mention her strength of will, her attitude toward life, and her refusal to give up.

**Comprehension Check**
• John, George, Hapsy
• George jilted her on their wedding day.
• Hapsy

 Use Selection Quiz in **Unit Six Resource Book**, p. 63.

## Think Critically

**2. Possible Response:** As a young girl, carefree and happy until she was jilted; hardworking and satisfied with her life as a wife and mother; as an old widow, unhappy in losing her independence, haunted by memories from sixty years ago.

**3. Possible Responses:** resignation—she is still unsure and unready to die; defiance—she makes the choice to die.

**4.** There is a priest and no bridegroom at both the jilting and her death; both take her completely by surprise and fill her with dread and are something she can never forgive; there is no sign from God at the moment of her death.

**5. Possible Responses:** George, the man who jilted her and broke her heart—she is thinking about him on her deathbed; Hapsy, her favorite daughter whom she hopes to see in heaven.

**6. Possible Response:** She is hardy and self-sufficient—she can "weather all" storms.

## Extend Interpretations

**Critic's Corner** Students' responses should examine the passage in which Granny thinks of the deep pit of hell and the reason she has prayed not to remember George. Students should not overlook the times that Granny seems to see George and her feeling when she does so.

**Comparing Texts** In all three works, there is a sense of disappointment or anticlimax at the moment of death.

**Connect to Life** Possible Response: The memory of her jilting casts its shadow over Granny's life as she looks back. However, the fact remains that she went beyond that incident to build a life no matter how she views that life later.

## Literary Analysis

**Stream of Consciousness** Possible Responses: In forming their narratives, students should think about the differences in the jilting situation for George and Granny. George was in control of the situation; he chose not to show up. Also George was spared the humiliation of being left at the altar.

# Writing Options

1. **Eulogy for Granny** Remind students that a eulogy commemorates the life of the person who has died, emphasizing the positive aspects and recalling incidents that reveal the character of the deceased. Have students brainstorm the qualities of Granny that Cornelia would be likely to emphasize in her eulogy.

2. **Psychological Profile To get students started on this assignment,** the class might brainstorm qualities that they think would be found in strong elderly women. Then, after a discussion of these qualities, students should examine Granny Weatherall to determine how she fits the profile. **To make this assignment more challenging,** have students interview two or three elderly women about their lives and develop a comparison between the fictional Granny Weatherall and the real case studies.

# Activities & Explorations

1. **Story Illustration** Students might work in groups to illustrate the entire story. Encourage students who struggle with art to find illustrations that they think capture passages in the story.

2. **Tabloid Interview To get students started on this assignment,** ask each pair to think of reasons why George might have jilted Ellen Weatherall. Remind students that George might try to rationalize his actions to make himself look better.

# Vocabulary in Action

1. tactful
2. embroidered
3. intently
4. plague
5. rummage

---

## Writing Options

**1. Eulogy for Granny** Write a eulogy for Granny Weatherall that Cornelia might present to commemorate her mother. Include details from Granny's life that are mentioned in the story. Put your eulogy in your **Working Portfolio.**

**2. Psychological Profile** Write a psychological profile of strong elderly women. Use Granny Weatherall as a case study.

## Activities & Explorations

**1. Story Illustration** Sketch an illustration for this story. Choose a sentence or part of a sentence as a caption for your drawing. ~ **ART**

**2. Tabloid Interview** Working with a partner, role-play a reporter and George, the man who jilted Granny Weatherall. Conduct an interview with George for a tabloid article in which he reveals his motives for jilting Granny. ~ **SPEAKING AND LISTENING**

## Vocabulary in Action

**EXERCISE: ANALOGIES** On your paper, write the vocabulary word that best completes each analogy.

1. JUDGE : FAIR :: diplomat : _____
2. POTTERY : GLAZED :: cloth : _____
3. UNPLEASANTLY : HORRIBLY :: carefully : _____
4. HELP : HINDER :: comfort : _____
5. RETREAT : WITHDRAW :: sift : _____

**Building Vocabulary**
For an in-depth lesson on analogies, see page 254.

| WORDS TO KNOW | | |
|---|---|---|
| embroidered | plague | tactful |
| intently | rummage | |

## Katherine Anne Porter
### 1890–1980

**Other Works**
*Ship of Fools*
*Pale Horse, Pale Rider*
*The Never-Ending Wrong*

**Difficult Childhood** Katherine Anne Porter was born Callie Russell Porter in Indian Creek, Texas. The fourth of five children in a poor family, she later described herself as a "precocious, nervous, rebellious, unteachable" child. When she was two, her mother died. Porter was raised by her grandmother, who probably served as the model for Granny in "The Jilting of Granny Weatherall."

**Restless Years** Porter was educated at home and in various Catholic convent schools in the South. She always considered herself a "roving spirit." Porter remarked in an interview, "At sixteen I ran away and got married. And at twenty-one I bolted again, went to Chicago, got a newspaper job, and went into the movies." She later worked as a journalist in Chicago, Denver, and Fort Worth, Texas. When she went to Mexico in 1920 on assignment for a magazine, she arrived in the middle of a revolution. Porter's observations of this conflict later became the subject of several short stories in her highly praised first collection, *Flowering Judas* (1930), which launched her literary career.

**Emblems of Success** In the midst of three marriages, travel, and miscellaneous jobs, Porter produced the small body of work on which her reputation rests: five novellas, three volumes of short stories, and one long novel, *Ship of Fools* (1962), which took her 25 years to write. In 1966, she won the Pulitzer Prize and National Book Award for her *Collected Stories*.

---

## Teaching Options

**Mini Lesson** **Grammar**

**COLON AS SENTENCE CONNECTOR**

**Instructions** A colon signals that what follows is an explanation, an example, or a summation of what precedes it. A colon might be used between two independent clauses when the second clause explains the first. The first word of the second clause must be capitalized if it begins a formal statement. An informal statement does not require capitalization. Display the following sentence:

Doctor Harry pronounced his diagnosis: Granny Weatherall had only minutes to live.

**Exercises** Have students insert colons to complete the following sentences.

1. She felt that the birth of the other children was only a prelude to this one the birth of the last child was the one she had been awaiting.

2. The daughter she wanted was the daughter she couldn't have Hapsy was dead.

 Use **Grammar Transparencies and Copymasters,** p. 159.

 Use McDougal Littell's *Language Network,* Chapter 10, for more instruction in colons.

# The Man Who Was Almost a Man

*Short Story by* RICHARD WRIGHT

**( Connect to Your Life )**

**Coming of Age** The main character in this story, 17-year-old Dave Saunders, is on the threshold of adulthood. Think about the adults in your family, your school, or your community. What do you think it takes to be an adult? How do people display maturity in their attitudes and actions? With a partner, share your thoughts about what it means to be an adult.

## Build Background

**Rural Poverty in the Deep South** The abolishment of slavery in the South after the Civil War did not end the economic oppression of African Americans there. Landowners divided large plantations into smaller farms, which they rented to both white and black laborers who worked for a share of the earnings from the crop. Under the brutal systems of tenant farming and sharecropping, many African-American families—like the Saunders family in this story—endured a life of grinding poverty. Neither tenants nor sharecroppers earned enough money to escape a cycle of debt or to buy their own land and become economically independent.

Richard Wright's father was a cotton sharecropper in Mississippi in the early 1900s, about the time "The Man Who Was Almost a Man" takes place. In the story, young Dave works in the fields during the summer for his white employer, Mr. Hawkins, and earns a meager wage. Be warned that Dave occasionally uses offensive language, including a racist term for his fellow African Americans. Wright's intention is to lend realism to a character who is immature and lacking in awareness.

## Focus on Reading

**LITERARY ANALYSIS  POINT OF VIEW**   **Point of view** refers to the narrative perspective from which events in a story or novel are told. "The Man Who Was Almost a Man" is told from the **third-person limited point of view**—the narrator stands outside the action and focuses on one character's thoughts, observations, and feelings. Note how you see the story through two pairs of eyes—the narrator's and Dave's.

**ACTIVE READING  MAKING JUDGMENTS**   As the story opens, Dave is grumbling to himself about an earlier incident that occurred between him and the other field hands on the Hawkins plantation. The narrator reveals Dave's thoughts and feelings, but offers no opinions about his behavior. Wright expects the reader to **make judgments,** or evaluate, the character's conduct. As you read, evaluate the quality of Dave's decisions when he finds himself in difficult or frustrating situations.

**READER'S NOTEBOOK**   To help you make judgments about Dave's decisions, create a diagram like the one shown, and fill it in as you read the story. Evaluate the decisions as good or bad.

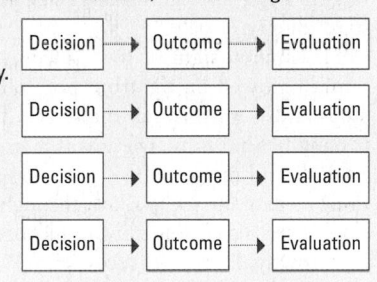

| Decision | → | Outcome | → | Evaluation |
| Decision | → | Outcome | → | Evaluation |
| Decision | → | Outcome | → | Evaluation |
| Decision | → | Outcome | → | Evaluation |

### Objectives
1. understand and appreciate a **short story (Literary Analysis)**
2. understand **point of view (Literary Analysis)**
3. **make judgments** about the main character's decisions **(Active Reading)**

### Summary
Dave, a poor boy in the South, desperately wants a gun, which a store owner offers to sell him for two dollars. Dave asks his mother for the money. She agrees to the purchase because Dave's father needs a gun. Dave buys the gun and is fascinated by it. Plowing the fields the next morning, he decides to shoot the gun. To his horror, he unintentionally shoots and kills the mule he is working with. Later that day a crowd gathers to bury the mule and investigate what happened. Dave tells the others that the mule died because it impaled itself on the point of the plow. It becomes clear that Dave shot the mule, and the crowd mocks him. Dave must pay for the mule with two years of free labor. That night, Dave hops a train out of town, taking the gun with him, telling himself that he is going somewhere where he can be a man.

### Thematic Link
On the threshold of adulthood, Dave feels **alienated** from others by the lack of respect shown him.

---

**5-Minute Warm-Up**

*Daily Language SkillBuilder*

Have students **proofread** the display sentences on page 913k and write them correctly. The sentences also appear on Transparency 29 of **Grammar Transparencies and Copymasters.**

---

**Editor's Note** This story contains some language that may be considered objectionable.

## LESSON RESOURCES

**Reading Skills and Strategies:
PREVIEW**

Have students refer to the Build
Background feature on page 1045 and
interpret the influences of the historical
context on Wright's story.

**Literary Analysis** | POINT OF VIEW |

Explain that the events of the story are
described through point of view. If students need more support in determining point of view, suggest that they
read aloud in pairs and use questioning
and rereading strategies when their
understanding breaks down.

Ask students to read the first sentence
of the story. Is the narrator speaking or
is Dave? How can they tell?

**Possible Response:** It is the narrator's
voice. The sentence mentions Dave by
name and tells about what he is doing
as if someone were watching him.

📖 Use **Unit Six Resource Book,**
p. 66 for more practice.

**Active Reading** | MAKING JUDGMENTS |

Ⓐ Dave reaches his first decision early
in the story. Ask students to complete
the first line in their Reader's Notebook
diagrams by listing Dave's decision to
buy a gun. Discuss whether they think
he has a legitimate reason for wanting
to own a gun.

**Possible Response:** No, he just wants
a gun so that he can feel like a man.

📖 Use **Unit Six Resource Book,**
p. 65 for more practice.

# THE MAN WHO WAS

D ave struck out across the fields, looking
homeward through paling light. Whut's
the use talkin wid em niggers in the
field? Anyhow, his mother was putting
supper on the table. Them niggers can't
understan nothing. One of these days he was
going to get a gun and practice shooting, then
they couldn't talk to him as though he were a
little boy. He slowed, looking at the ground.
Shucks, Ah ain scareda them even ef they are
biggern me! Aw, Ah know whut Ahma do. Ahm
going by ol Joe's sto n git that Sears Roebuck
catlog n look at them guns. Mebbe Ma will
lemme buy one when she gits mah pay from
ol man Hawkins. Ahma beg her t gimme some
money. Ahm ol ernough to hava gun. Ahm
seventeen. Almost a man. He strode, feeling
his long loose-jointed limbs. Shucks, a man
oughta hava little gun aftah he done worked
hard all day.

He came in sight of Joe's store. A yellow
lantern glowed on the front porch. He mounted
steps and went through the screen door, hearing
it bang behind him. There was a strong smell of
coal oil and mackerel fish. He felt very confident
until he saw fat Joe walk in through the rear
door, then his courage began to ooze.

"Howdy, Dave! Whutcha want?"

"How yuh, Mistah Joe? Aw, Ah don wanna
buy nothing. Ah jus wanted t see ef yuhd lemme
look at tha catlog erwhile."

"Sure! You wanna see it here?"

"Nawsuh. Ah wans t take it home wid me.
Ah'll bring it back termorrow when Ah come in
from the fiels."

"You plannin on buying something?"

"Yessuh."

"Your ma lettin you have your own money
now?"

"Shucks. Mistah Joe, Ahm gittin t be a man
like anybody else!"

Joe laughed and wiped his greasy white face
with a red bandanna.

"Whut you plannin on buyin?"

Dave looked at the floor, scratched his head,
scratched his thigh, and smiled. Then he looked
up shyly.

"Ah'll tell yuh, Mistah Joe, ef yuh promise
yuh won't tell."

"I promise."

"Waal, Ahma buy a gun."

"A gun? Whut you want with a gun?"

"Ah wanna keep it."

"You ain't nothing but a boy. You don't need
a gun."

"Aw, lemme have the catlog, Mistah Joe."

**1046**    UNIT SIX    PART 2: ALIENATION OF THE INDIVIDUAL

**BLOCK SCHEDULING: MANAGING TIME**

**If your schedule requires that you
cover the lesson objectives in a
shorter time, use . . .**
• Preparing to Read, p. 1045
• Thinking Through the Literature,
  p. 1055

**If you want to take advantage of
longer class time, use . . .**
• TE Teaching Options: Speaking and
  Listening, p. 1047; Cross-Curricular
  Links, pp. 1048, 1053; Vocabulary
  Strategy, p. 1049; Viewing and
  Representing, p. 1051; Workplace
  Link, p. 1052; Standardized Test
  Practice, p. 1054
• Choices & Challenges and Author
  Activity, p. 1056

# ALMOST A MAN RICHARD WRIGHT

Ah'll bring it back."

Joe walked through the rear door. Dave was elated.[1] He looked around at barrels of sugar and flour. He heard Joe coming back. He craned his neck to see if he were bringing the book. Yeah, he's got it. Gawddog, he's got it!

"Here, but be sure you bring it back. It's the only one I got."

"Sho, Mistah Joe."

"Say, if you wanna buy a gun, why don't you buy one from me? I gotta gun to sell."

"Will it shoot?"

"Sure it'll shoot."

"Whut kind is it?"

"Oh, it's kinda old . . . a left-hand Wheeler. A pistol. A big one."

"Is it got bullets in it?"

"It's loaded."

"Kin Ah see it?"

"Where's your money?"

"Whut yuh wan fer it?"

"I'll let you have it for two dollars."

"Just two dollahs? Shucks, Ah could buy tha when Ah git mah pay."

"I'll have it here when you want it."

"Awright, suh. Ah be in fer it."

He went through the door, hearing it slam again behind him. Ahma git some money from Ma n buy me a gun! Only two dollahs! He tucked the thick catalogue under his arm and hurried.

"Where yuh been, boy?" His mother held a steaming dish of black-eyed peas.

"Aw, Ma, Ah jus stopped down the road t talk wid the boys."

"Yuh know bettah t keep suppah waitin."

He sat down, resting the catalogue on the edge of the table.

"Yuh git up from there and git to the well n wash yosef! Ah ain feedin no hogs in mah house!"

She grabbed his shoulder and pushed him. He stumbled out of the room, then came back to get the catalogue.

"Whut this?"

"Aw, Ma, it's jusa catlog."

"Who yuh git it from?"

"From Joe, down at the sto."

"Waal, thas good. We kin use it in the outhouse."

"Naw, Ma." He grabbed for it. "Gimme ma catlog, Ma."

She held onto it and glared at him.

---
1. **elated:** proud and joyful.

 **Mini Lesson** ## Speaking and Listening

**PRONUNCIATION OF DIALECT**
**Instruction** Point out that dialect is a form of language that varies from the standard language in vocabulary, pronunciation, expressions, and grammatical constructions. Writers use dialect to add realism to stories, make characters richer and more specific, and convey a sense of the setting. Write the following sentence on the chalkboard: "Ah jus wanted t see ef yuhd lemme look at tha catlog erwhile." Point out that Wright replaces *I* with *Ah*, omits the *t* in *just*, and uses *lemme* instead of *let me*. He also omits several other letters and changes vowel sounds. Explain that

Wright uses dialect to convey how poor sharecroppers spoke in the early 20th-century South.
**Application** Working in small groups, have students choose a portion of the story that contains dialogue and take turns reading it aloud. Students should then discuss the differences between reading dialogue silently and reading or hearing it read aloud. Have each group present a brief oral report sharing its experiences.

**BLOCK SCHEDULING** This activity is particularly well suited for longer class periods.

"Quit hollerin at me! Whut's wrong wid yuh? Yuh crazy?"

"But Ma, please. It ain mine! It's Joe's! He tol me t bring it back t im termorrow."

She gave up the book. He stumbled down the back steps, hugging the thick book under his arm. When he had splashed water on his face and hands, he groped back to the kitchen and fumbled in a corner for the towel. He bumped into a chair; it clattered to the floor. The catalogue sprawled at his feet. When he had dried his eyes he snatched up the book and held it again under his arm. His mother stood watching him.

"Now, ef yuh gonna act a fool over that ol book, Ah'll take it n burn it up."

"Naw, Ma, please."

"Waal, set down n be still!"

He sat down and drew the oil lamp close. He thumbed page after page, unaware of the food his mother set on the table. His father came in. Then his small brother.

"Whutcha got there, Dave?" his father asked.

"Jusa catlog," he answered, not looking up.

"Yeah, here they is!" His eyes glowed at blue-and-black revolvers. He glanced up, feeling sudden guilt. His father was watching him. He eased the book under the table and rested it on his knees. After the blessing was asked, he ate. He scooped up peas and swallowed fat meat without chewing. Buttermilk helped to wash it down. He did not want to mention money before his father. He would do much better by cornering his mother when she was alone. He looked at his father uneasily out of the edge of his eye.

"Boy, how come yuh don quit foolin wid tha book n eat yo suppah?"

"Yessuh."

"How you n ol man Hawkins gitten erlong?"

"Suh?"

"Can't yuh hear? Why don yuh lissen? Ah ast yu how wuz yuh n ol man Hawkins gittin erlong?"

"Oh, swell, Pa. Ah plows mo lan than anybody over there."

"Waal, yuh oughta keep yo mind on whut yuh doin."

"Yessuh."

He poured his plate full of molasses and sopped it up slowly with a chunk of cornbread. When his father and brother had left the kitchen, he still sat and looked again at the guns in the catalogue, longing to muster courage enough to present his case to his mother. Lawd, ef Ah only had tha pretty one! He could almost feel the slickness of the weapon with his fingers. If he had a gun like that he would polish it and keep it shining so it would never rust. N Ah'd keep it loaded, by Gawd!

"Ma?" His voice was hesitant.

"Hunh?"

"Ol man Hawkins give yuh mah money yit?"

"Yeah, but ain no usa yuh thinking bout throwin nona it erway. Ahm keepin tha money sos yuh kin have cloes t go to school this winter."

He rose and went to her side with the open catalogue in his palms. She was washing dishes, her head bent low over a pan. Shyly he raised the book. When he spoke, his voice was husky, faint.

"Ma, Gawd knows Ah wans one of these."

"One of whut?" she asked, not raising her eyes.

"One of these," he said again, not daring even to point. She glanced up at the page, then at him with wide eyes.

"Nigger, is yuh gone plumb crazy?"

"Aw, Ma—"

"Git outta here! Don yuh talk t me bout no gun! Yuh a fool!"

"Ma, Ah kin buy one fer two dollahs."

"Not ef Ah knows it, yuh ain!"

"But yuh promised me one—"

# Teaching Options

## Cross Curricular Link  **U.S. History**

**1910** Wright's story is set around 1910. Some of the events of that year are listed below. Use this list as you plan lessons, assign research projects, or point out connections between the events and the literature.

### Key Events: 1910

• The National Urban League is formed by a group of social workers to help African Americans migrating to Northern cities from the South.

• **W. E. B. Du Bois** founds *The Crisis,* the most important African-American periodical of its time.

• As women gain the vote in several states, the National American Woman Suffrage Association receives half a million signatures on its petition for national woman suffrage.

• **Jack Johnson,** the first African-American heavyweight champion of the world, successfully defends his title in a bout with James L. Jeffries.

• The Supreme Court prohibits states from renting prisoners to private landowners and contractors for work in the fields.

"Ah don care whut Ah promised! Yuh ain nothing but a boy yit!"

"Ma, ef yuh lemme buy one Ah'll *never* ast yuh fer nothing no mo.'"

"Ah tol yuh t git outta here! Yuh ain gonna toucha penny of tha money fer no gun! Thas how come Ah has Mistah Hawkins t pay yo wages t me, cause Ah knows yuh ain got no sense."

"But, Ma, we needa gun. Pa ain got no gun. We needa gun in the house. Yuh kin never tell whut might happen."

"Now don yuh try to maka fool outta me, boy! Ef we did hava gun, yuh wouldn't have it!"

He laid the catalogue down and slipped his arm around her waist.

"Aw, Ma, Ah done worked hard alla summer n ain ast yuh fer nothin, is Ah, now?"

"Thas whut yuh spose t do!"

"But Ma, Ah wans a gun. Yuh kin lemme have two dollahs outta mah money. Please, Ma. I kin give it to Pa . . . Please, Ma! Ah loves yuh, Ma."

When she spoke her voice came soft and low.

"Whut yu wan wida gun, Dave? Yuh don need no gun. Yuh'll git in trouble. N ef yo pa jus thought Ah let yuh have money t buy a gun he'd hava fit."

"Ah'll hide it, Ma. It ain but two dollahs."

"Lawd, chil, whut's wrong wid yuh?"

"Ain nothin wrong, Ma. Ahm almos a man now. Ah wans a gun."

"Who gonna sell yuh a gun?"

"Ol Joe at the sto."

"N it don cos but two dollahs?"

"Thas all, Ma. Jus two dollahs. Please, Ma."

She was stacking the plates away; her hands moved slowly, reflectively. Dave kept an anxious silence. Finally, she turned to him.

"Ah'll let yuh git tha gun ef yuh promise me one thing."

"Whut's tha, Ma?"

"Yuh bring it straight back t me, yuh hear? It be fer Pa."

"Yessum! Lemme go now, Ma."

She stooped, turned slightly to one side, raised the hem of her dress, rolled down the top of her stocking, and came up with a slender wad of bills.

"Here," she said. "Lawd knows yuh don need no gun. But yer pa does. Yuh bring it right back t me, yuh hear? Ahma put it up. Now ef yuh don, Ahma have yuh pa lick yuh so hard yuh won fergit it."

"Yessum."

He took the money, ran down the steps, and across the yard.

"Dave! Yuuuuuh Daaaaave!"

He heard, but he was not going to stop now. "Naw, Lawd!"

The first movement he made the following morning was to reach under his pillow for the gun. In the gray light of dawn he held it loosely, feeling a sense of power. Could kill a man with a gun like this. Kill anybody, black or white. And if he were holding his gun in his hand, nobody could run over him; they would have to respect him. It was a big gun, with a long barrel and a heavy handle. He raised and lowered it in his hand, marveling at its weight.

He had not come straight home with it as his mother had asked; instead he had stayed out in the fields, holding the weapon in his hand, aiming it now and then at some imaginary foe. But he had not fired it; he had been afraid that his father might hear. Also he was not sure he knew how to fire it.

To avoid surrendering the pistol he had not come into the house until he knew that they were all asleep. When his mother had tiptoed to his bedside late that night and demanded the gun, he had first played possum; then he had told her that the gun was hidden outdoors, that he would bring it to her in the morning. Now he lay turning it slowly in his hands. He broke it,[2] took out the cartridges, felt them, and then put them back.

He slid out of bed, got a long strip of old flannel from a trunk, wrapped the gun in it, and

---

2. **broke it:** opened the cartridge chamber.

## Customizing Instruction

### Multiple Learning Styles
**Logical/Mathematical Learners**

**1** Explain to students that because of inflation, the value of a dollar in 1910 was much higher than it is today. One dollar in 1910 would be worth more than $40 in present buying power. For example, a steel walking plow listed at $7.15 in the 1910 Sears-Roebuck catalog would cost approximately $300 in today's money. Ask students to estimate how much Joe is asking for the gun by current values.

**Answer:** about $80

### Less Proficient Readers

**2** Make sure students understand the reasons Dave wants a gun so badly.

• How does Dave feel about himself?

**Possible Response:** He has low self-esteem and feels inferior to others.

• What does Dave believe will be the consequences of gun ownership?

**Possible Responses:** Other field hands won't talk to him as if he were a boy; he will be powerful; he will feel like a man.

**Set a Purpose** Have students read to find out whether Dave obeys his mother's instructions regarding the gun.

---

 **Vocabulary Strategy**

**DICTIONARIES AND SLANG**

**Instruction** Remind students that they can use dictionaries to determine precise word meanings. This story has numerous slang terms that add to the strong sense of place it conveys.
Read aloud the sentence "Shucks, Ah ain scareda them . . ." (p. 1046, column 1). Then, using a dictionary, read aloud the definitions of *shuck* and have the class notice that the form *shucks* is listed as an interjection that expresses mild disappointment, disgust, or annoyance.

**Application** Ask students to make a chart like the following and fill it in, using either an unabridged dictionary or a dictionary of slang.

| Location | Word (in context) | Story meaning | Other meanings | Source |
|----------|-------------------|---------------|----------------|--------|
| p. 1048, col. 2 | **plumb** crazy | | | |
| p. 1049, col. 2 | have yuh pa **lick** | | | |
| p. 1050, col. 1 | **fixin** t hitch up | | | |
| p. 1050, col. 1 | **Hot dog!** | | | |

Use **Vocabulary Transparencies and Copymasters**, p. 88.

## Reading and Analyzing

**Literary Analysis: DIALECT**

**(A)** Ask students to restate this passage of dialogue in standard English.

**Possible Response:** I didn't know I was getting up so early, Mister Hawkins. I was fixing (planning) to hitch up old Jenny and take her to the fields.

What effect does the change to standard English have?

**Possible Response:** The impact of the language is diluted. Anyone could be speaking, rather than someone from a specific place and time.

**Active Reading** | MAKING JUDGMENTS |

**(B)** Students should add Dave's decision to fire his gun to the diagrams in their Reader's Notebook. As they continue reading, have them consider whether this decision is a turning point in the story.

**Literary Analysis** | POINT OF VIEW |

**(C)** Ask students to analyze the effect of the shifts between the narrator's voice and Dave's voice. What does each voice provide that the other cannot? Is this an effective technique for telling this story? Why?

**Possible Response:** The narrator's voice provides objective details, while Dave's thoughts are raw and subjective. It is an effective technique because readers know they can trust the narrator to present the facts accurately, but they can also get inside Dave's mind and gain insight into his character through his thoughts, feelings, and reactions to events.

---

tied it to his naked thigh while it was still loaded. He did not go in to breakfast. Even though it was not yet daylight, he started for Jim Hawkins' plantation. Just as the sun was rising he reached the barns where the mules and plows were kept.

"Hey! That you, Dave?"

He turned. Jim Hawkins stood eying him suspiciously.

"What're yuh doing here so early?"

**(A)** "Ah didn't know Ah wuz gittin up so early, Mistah Hawkins. Ah wuz fixin t hitch up ol Jenny n take her t the fiels."

"Good. Since you're so early, how about plowing that stretch down by the woods?"

"Suits me, Mistah Hawkins."

"O.K. Go to it!"

He hitched Jenny to a plow and started across the fields. Hot dog! This was just what he wanted. If he could get down by the woods, he could shoot his gun and nobody would hear. He walked behind the plow, hearing the traces[3] creaking, feeling the gun tied tight to his thigh.

When he reached the woods, he plowed two whole rows before he decided to take out the gun. Finally, he stopped, looked in all directions, then untied the gun and held it in his hand. He turned to the mule and smiled.

"Know whut this is, Jenny? Naw, yuh wouldn know! Yuhs jusa ol mule! Anyhow, this is a gun, n it kin shoot, by Gawd!"

**(B)** He held the gun at arm's length. Whut t hell, Ahma shoot this thing! He looked at Jenny again.

"Lissen here, Jenny! When Ah pull this ol trigger, Ah don wan yuh t run n acka fool now!"

Jenny stood with head down, her short ears pricked straight. Dave walked off about twenty feet, held the gun far out from him at arm's length, and turned his head. Hell, he told himself, Ah ain afraid. The gun felt loose in his fingers; he waved it wildly for a moment. Then he shut his eyes and tightened his forefinger. Bloom! A report half deafened him and he thought his right hand was torn from his arm. He heard Jenny whinnying and galloping over the field, and he found himself on his knees, squeezing his fingers hard

between his legs. His hand was numb; he jammed it into his mouth, trying to warm it, trying to stop the pain. The gun lay at his feet. He did not quite know what had happened. He stood up and stared at the gun as though it were a living thing. He gritted his teeth and kicked the gun. Yuh almos broke mah arm! He turned to look for Jenny; she was far over the fields, tossing her head and kicking wildly.

"Hol on there, ol mule!"

When he caught up with her she stood trembling, walling[4] her big white eyes at him. The plow was far away; the traces had broken. Then Dave stopped short, looking, not believing. Jenny was bleeding. Her left side was red and wet with blood. He went closer. Lawd, have mercy! Wondah did Ah shoot this mule? He grabbed for Jenny's mane. She flinched, snorted, whirled, tossing her head.

"Hol on now! Hol on."

Then he saw the hole in Jenny's side, right between the ribs. It was round, wet, red. A crimson stream streaked down the front leg, flowing fast. Good Gawd! Ah wuzn't shootin at tha mule. He felt panic. He knew he had to stop that blood, or Jenny would bleed to death. He had never seen so much blood in all his life. He chased the mule for half a mile, trying to catch her. Finally she stopped, breathing hard, stumpy tail half arched. He caught her mane and led her back to where the plow and gun lay. Then he stooped and grabbed handfuls of damp black earth and tried to plug the bullet hole. Jenny shuddered, whinnied, and broke from him.

"Hol on! Hol on now!"

He tried to plug it again, but blood came anyhow. His fingers were hot and sticky. He rubbed dirt into his palms, trying to dry them. Then again he attempted to plug the bullet hole, but Jenny shied away, kicking her heels high. He stood helpless. He had to do something. He ran

**(C)**

---

3. **traces:** side straps or chains connecting the mule to the plow.
4. **walling:** rolling.

---

## Teaching Options

### CREATING COMPLEX SENTENCES

**Instruction** A complex sentence has one independent clause and one or more subordinate clauses. The information in the subordinate clause(s) elaborates on information in the independent clause.

**Practice** Write the following sentence on the chalkboard.

Before he went away, Dave worked as a field hand.

 **Mini Lesson** ## Grammar

Have students identify the independent clause (*Dave worked as a field hand*) and the subordinate clause (*Before he went away*).

**Exercise** For each exercise, students should put the separate sentences together to form one complex sentence. Possible responses are provided.

1. Dave borrowed a catalog from Mr. Joe. Mr. Joe owned a store. (*Dave borrowed a catalog from Mr. Joe, who owned a store.*)

2. He slept with the gun. He kept the gun under his pillow. (*He slept with the gun, which he kept under his pillow.*)

3. He had plowed two rows. He shot the gun off. (*After he had plowed two rows, he shot the gun off.*)

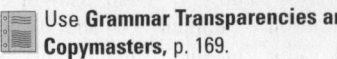 Use **Grammar Transparencies and Copymasters**, p. 169.

Use McDougal Littell's **Language Network**, Chapter 3, for more instruction in complex sentences.

Roy Stryker Collection, Photographic Archives, University
of Louisville, Kentucky, Negative 78.9.534.

THE MAN WHO WAS ALMOST A MAN     **1051**

## Customizing Instruction

### Less Proficient Readers
Page 1050 includes some of the most dramatic action of the story. Ask students to summarize what happens on this page.

**Possible Response:** Dave goes to the plantation early. Mr. Hawkins asks him to plow the stretch by the woods. Dave hitches Jenny the mule to the plow and starts plowing. He shoots the gun and Jenny runs off. He finds that he has shot Jenny. He chases her and tries to stop the bleeding

**Mini Lesson** ## Viewing and Representing

### Photographs

**Instruction** Tell students that the photographs in this selection constitute photojournalism—the documentation of history through photographs. Such photos are taken to record information, not for primarily artistic reasons. Photos are an important primary source for any researcher.

**Application** Have students examine the photographs in the selection and discuss what information they convey.

**Possible Responses:** They reveal details of clothing and setting; they illustrate the kind of work Dave does; they suggest great poverty.

THE MAN WHO WAS ALMOST A MAN     **1051**

**Literary Analysis: IMAGERY**

**A** Ask students to list the images used by the author to describe the dying mule. To what senses do these images appeal?

**Possible Responses:** hearing—low-pitched whinny; sight—sleepy, dreamy eyes; slopping in blood

**Reading Skills and Strategies: MAKING PREDICTIONS**

**B** Tell students that they can use textual evidence and experience to make predictions. Based on what they have read about Dave so far and what they know from their own experiences, what do they think Dave will do now?

**Possible Responses:** To save himself from punishment, he will lie about what has happened. He will tell the truth in hopes that people will go easier on him if he is honest.

**Literary Analysis: SITUATIONAL IRONY**

**C** Remind students that Dave hoped the gun would give him a feeling of control and power. Have them discuss the feelings he is experiencing now.

**Possible Response:** powerlessness; uselessness

**Active Reading** | **MAKING JUDGMENTS**

**D** Ask students to evaluate Dave's decision to lie about what has happened.

---

at Jenny; she dodged him. He watched a red stream of blood flow down Jenny's leg and form a bright pool at her feet.

"Jenny . . . Jenny," he called weakly.

His lips trembled. She's bleeding t death! He looked in the direction of home, wanting to go back, wanting to get help. But he saw the pistol lying in the damp black clay. He had a queer feeling that if he only did something, this would not be; Jenny would not be there bleeding to death.

**A** When he went to her this time, she did not move. She stood with sleepy, dreamy eyes; and when he touched her she gave a low-pitched whinny and knelt to the ground, her front knees slopping in blood.

"Jenny . . . Jenny . . ." he whispered.

**B** For a long time she held her neck erect; then her head sank, slowly. Her ribs swelled with a mighty heave and she went over.

**C** Dave's stomach felt empty, very empty. He picked up the gun and held it gingerly between his thumb and forefinger. He buried it at the foot of a tree. He took a stick and tried to cover the pool of blood with dirt—but what was the use? There was Jenny lying with her mouth open and her eyes walled and glassy. He could not tell Jim Hawkins he had shot his mule. But he had to tell something. Yeah, Ah'll tell em Jenny started gittin wil n fell on the point of the plow. . . . But that would hardly happen to a mule. He walked across the field slowly, head down.

It was sunset. Two of Jim Hawkins' men were over near the edge of the woods digging a hole in which to bury Jenny. Dave was surrounded by a knot of people, all of whom were looking down at the dead mule.

"I don't see how in the world it happened," said Jim Hawkins for the tenth time.

The crowd parted and Dave's mother, father, and small brother pushed into the center.

"Where Dave?" his mother called.

"There he is," said Jim Hawkins.

His mother grabbed him.

"Whut happened, Dave? Whut yuh done?"

"Nothin."

"C mon, boy, talk," his father said.

Dave took a deep breath and told the story he knew nobody believed.

"Waal," he drawled. "Ah brung ol Jenny down here sos Ah could do mah plowin. Ah plowed bout two rows, just like yuh see." He stopped and pointed at the long rows of up-turned earth. "Then somethin musta been wrong wid ol Jenny. She wouldn ack right a-tall. She started snortin n kickin her heels. Ah tried t hol her, but she pulled erway, rearin n goin in. Then when the point of the plow was stickin up in the air, she swung erroun n twisted herself back on it . . . She stuck herself n started t bleed. N fo Ah could do anything, she wuz dead." **D**

"Did you ever hear of anything like that in all your life?" asked Jim Hawkins.

There were white and black standing in the crowd. They murmured. Dave's mother came close to him and looked hard into his face. "Tell the truth, Dave," she said.

"Looks like a bullet hole to me," said one man.

"Dave, whut yuh do wid the gun?" his mother asked.

The crowd surged in, looking at him. He jammed his hands into his pockets, shook his head slowly from left to right, and backed away. His eyes were wide and painful.

"Did he hava gun?" asked Jim Hawkins.

"By Gawd, Ah tol yuh tha wuz a gun wound," said a man, slapping his thigh.

His father caught his shoulders and shook him till his teeth rattled.

"Tell whut happened, yuh rascal! Tell whut . . ."

Dave looked at Jenny's stiff legs and began to cry.

"Whut yuh do wid tha gun?" his mother asked.

"Whut wuz he doin wida gun?" his father asked.

"Come on and tell the truth," said Hawkins. "Ain't nobody going to hurt you . . ."

His mother crowded close to him.

"Did yuh shoot tha mule, Dave?"

---

## Teaching Options

### Mini Lesson **Workplace Link**

**WRITING AN EVALUATION**

**Instruction** Students with jobs may know that their job performance is evaluated periodically by a supervisor. This evaluation forms the basis for decisions about pay raises, promotions, layoffs, and firings. Employees are sometimes asked to rate their own performance as part of the evaluation process.

**Activity** Have students rate Dave's performance, based on information given in the story. They may choose to write it as a self-evaluation, that is, as if they were Dave, or they may write it from Mr. Hawkins's perspective. The evaluations should include strengths, areas for improvement, and a plan for future action. For the purposes of this exercise, students should write as if Dave were still available for work at the end of the story.

Roy Stryker Collection, Photographic Archives, University of Louisville, Kentucky, Negative 78.9.225.

Dave cried, seeing blurred white and black faces.

"Ahh ddinn gggo tt sshooot hher . . . Ah ssswear ffo Gawd Ah ddin. . . . Ah wuz a-tryin t sssee ef the old gggun would sshoot—"

"Where yuh git the gun from?" his father asked.

"Ah got it from Joe, at the sto."

"Where yuh git the money?"

"Ma give it t me."

"He kept worryin me, Bob. Ah had t. Ah tol im t bring the gun right back t me . . . It was fer yuh, the gun."

"But how yuh happen to shoot that mule?" asked Jim Hawkins.

"Ah wuzn shootin at the mule, Mistah Hawkins. The gun jumped when Ah pulled the trigger . . . N fo Ah knowed anythin Jenny was there a-bleedin."

Somebody in the crowd laughed. Jim Hawkins walked close to Dave and looked into his face.

"Well, looks like you have bought you a mule, Dave."

"Ah swear fo Gawd, Ah didn go t kill the mule, Mistah Hawkins!"

"But you killed her!"

All the crowd was laughing now. They stood on tiptoe and poked heads over one another's shoulders.

"Well, boy, looks like yuh done bought a dead mule! Hahaha!"

"Ain tha ershame."

"Hohohohoho."

Dave stood, head down, twisting his feet in the dirt.

"Well, you needn't worry about it, Bob," said Jim Hawkins to Dave's father. "Just let the boy keep on working and pay me two dollars a month."

"Whut yuh wan fer yo mule, Mistah Hawkins?"

Jim Hawkins screwed up his eyes.

"Fifty dollars."

"Whut yuh do wid tha gun?" Dave's father demanded.

Dave said nothing.

"Yuh wan me t take a tree n beat yuh till yuh talk!"

"Nawsuh!"

"Whut yuh do wid it?"

"Ah throwed it erway."

"Where?"

"Ah . . . Ah throwed it in the creek."

"Waal, c mon home. N firs thing in the mawnin git to tha creek n fin tha gun."

"Yessuh."

"What yuh pay fer it?"

"Two dollahs."

"Take tha gun n git yo money back n carry it t Mistah Hawkins, yuh hear? N don fergit Ahma lam you black bottom good fer this! Now march yosef on home, suh!"

Dave turned and walked slowly. He heard people laughing. Dave glared, his eyes welling with tears. Hot anger bubbled in him. Then he swallowed and stumbled on.

## Cross Curricular Link  Economics

**AFRICAN-AMERICAN SHARECROPPERS IN THE EARLY 20TH CENTURY** Between the time in which the story was set and the time in which it was written, much of the South remained a poverty-stricken, agrarian society. Income levels were much lower than in the North ($372 per capita in the South in 1929, for example, compared with $797 in the North). African-American sharecroppers were the lowest paid stratum of an already low-paid group. Because common crops such as cotton were overproduced, prices remained low, and farmers who did not own land could not earn enough to buy their own farms. Many farmers who had owned land went into debt and were forced into sharecropping. Between 1880 and 1930, the percentage of tenant farmers in the South increased from 36 percent to 55 percent.

### Literary Analysis: IMAGERY

**(A)** Ask students to examine the images in this final paragraph and decide whether the ending holds out any hope for Dave.

### Active Reading | MAKING JUDGMENTS

Have students add Dave's decision to leave home to the diagrams in their Reader's Notebook and explain why they think this decision was good or bad.

**Possible Responses:** It was a bad decision—he should have accepted responsibility for his actions. It was a good decision—he did not mean to kill the mule and was being punished unfairly.

Ask students to speculate about the outcome of Dave's decision.

---

That night Dave did not sleep. He was glad that he had gotten out of killing the mule so easily, but he was hurt. Something hot seemed to turn over inside him each time he remembered how they had laughed. He tossed on his bed, feeling his hard pillow. N Pa says he's gonna beat me . . . He remembered other beatings, and his back quivered. Naw, naw, Ah sho don wan im t beat me tha way no mo. Dam em all! Nobody ever gave him anything. All he did was work. They treat me like a mule, n then they beat me. He gritted his teeth. N Ma had t tell on me.

Well, if he had to, he would take old man Hawkins that two dollars. But that meant selling the gun. And he wanted to keep that gun. Fifty dollars for a dead mule.

He turned over, thinking how he had fired the gun. He had an itch to fire it again. Ef other men kin shoota gun, by Gawd, Ah kin! He was still, listening. Mebbe they all sleepin now. The house was still. He heard the soft breathing of his brother. Yes, now! He would go down and get that gun and see if he could fire it! He eased out of bed and slipped into overalls.

The moon was bright. He ran almost all the way to the edge of the woods. He stumbled over the ground, looking for the spot where he had buried the gun. Yeah, here it is. Like a hungry dog scratching for a bone, he pawed it up. He puffed his black cheeks and blew dirt from the trigger and barrel. He broke it and found four cartridges unshot. He looked around; the fields were filled with silence and moonlight. He clutched the gun stiff and hard in his fingers. But, as soon as he wanted to pull the trigger, he shut his eyes and turned his head. Naw, Ah can't shoot wid mah eyes closed n mah head turned. With effort he held his eyes open; then he

squeezed. *Blooooom!* He was stiff, not breathing. The gun was still in his hands. Dammit, he'd done it! He fired again. *Blooooom!* He smiled. *Blooooom! Blooooom! Click, click.* There! It was empty. If anybody could shoot a gun, he could. He put the gun into his hip pocket and started across the fields.

When he reached the top of a ridge he stood straight and proud in the moonlight, looking at Jim Hawkins' big white house, feeling the gun sagging in his pocket. Lawd, ef Ah had just one mo bullet Ah'd taka shot at tha house. Ah'd like t scare ol man Hawkins jusa little . . . Jusa enough t let im know Dave Saunders is a man.

To his left the road curved, running to the tracks of the Illinois Central. He jerked his head, listening. From far off came a faint *hoooof-hoooof; hoooof-hoooof; hoooof-hoooof. . . .* He stood rigid. Two dollahs a mont. Les see now . . . Tha means it'll take bout two years. Shucks! Ah'll be dam!

He started down the road, toward the tracks. Yeah, here she comes! He stood beside the track and held himself stiffly. Here she comes, erroun the ben . . . C mon, yuh slow poke! C mon! He had his hand on his gun; something quivered in his stomach. Then the train thundered past, the gray and brown box cars rumbling and clinking. He gripped the gun tightly; then he jerked his hand out of his pocket. Ah betcha Bill wouldn't do it! Ah betcha . . . The cars slid past, steel grinding upon steel. Ahm ridin yuh ternight, so hep me Gawd! He was hot all over. He hesitated just a moment; then he grabbed, pulled atop of a car, and lay flat. He felt his pocket; the gun was still there. Ahead the long rails were glinting in the moonlight, stretching away, away to somewhere, somewhere where he could be a man . . . . ❖

---

## Teaching Options

### ✓ Assessment  Standardized Test Practice

**PREDICTING WHAT HAPPENS NEXT** Standardized tests sometimes require students to demonstrate their understanding of literature by predicting what will happen next. Read the following three statements aloud and ask students which one expresses Dave's likeliest course of action.

**A.** Dave realizes he has made a foolish decision and returns to work off his debt to Mr. Hawkins.

**B.** Dave shows off his gun on the train and gets thrown off when the conductor hears of it.

**C.** Dave throws the gun away and goes to a city to find work.

Have students consider each choice and try to come up with evidence in each one's favor. **A** does not seem likely in light of Dave's recent decisions. It may be that Dave will head for a city for work as statement **C** suggests, but it seems unlikely that Dave will throw the gun away, given how important it is to him. **B** fits with what we know of Dave—he is still trying to use the gun to impress people.

# Connect to the Literature

**1. What Do You Think?** How did you respond to the ending of this story? Share your ideas with your classmates.

**Comprehension Check**
- How does Dave account for the accident with the mule?
- How does the crowd respond to Dave's mistake?
- What are Dave's reasons for getting out of town?

# Think Critically

**2.**  **ACTIVE READING** **MAKING JUDGMENTS** Review the diagram you made in your **READER'S NOTEBOOK**. How would you judge Dave's ability to make sound decisions? Does he behave like an adult? Support your judgments.

**3.** Does owning a gun give Dave what he wants? Explain.

> **THINK ABOUT**
> - why Dave wants to own a gun
> - how he handles the responsibility of a gun
> - how others treat him after he buys a gun
> - how he deals with consequences

**4.** Do you feel sorry for Dave? Explain why or why not. How do you think Richard Wright feels about him?

**5.** What do you predict might happen to Dave in the future?

# Extend Interpretations

**6. What If?** What would Dave's life have been like if he had not shot the mule?

**7. Different Perspectives** "Almos' A Man," an earlier version of "The Man Who Was Almost a Man," features an adult character with a wife and child. How would you view Dave's actions at the end of the story if he were a husband and father?

**8. Critic's Corner** Richard Wright is generally viewed as a protest writer. In this story, what do you think he is fighting for or against?

**9. Comparing Texts** Think about James Baldwin's advice in "My Dungeon Shook: Letter to My Nephew" on page 959. What advice might Baldwin have for Dave Saunders?

**10. Connect to Life** Discuss other cultural customs and practices that signify the passage of youth to maturity.

## Literary Analysis

**POINT OF VIEW** One reason that the reader gains insight into Dave's character is that the story is told from **third-person limited point of view,** a narrative perspective used by many modernist fiction writers. The narrator acts as a reporter with inside information. In "The Man Who Was Almost a Man," the narrator not only recounts the external events of the story but also gives voice to the inner workings of Dave's mind, expressed in **dialect.**

**Paired Activity** Reread the first paragraph of the story, and notice the way Richard Wright weaves dialect into the narration. Point out where the narration stops and Dave's thoughts begin. With a partner, read the first paragraph aloud, with one of you reading the narration and the other reading Dave's thoughts. What effect does Wright achieve by setting up his story this way? What if Dave's thoughts were not included in the story at all? Discuss these questions with your partner.

**REVIEW** **IRONY** **Irony** is a contrast between what is expected and what actually exists or happens. **Dramatic irony** occurs when readers know more about a situation in a story than the characters do. **Situational irony** is a contrast between what a character expects to happen and what actually happens. Discuss the many instances of situational irony in this story. For example, look at the ways in which owning a gun backfires, so to speak, on Dave.

## Extend Interpretations

**What If?** Possible Response: For a time Dave would have continued to work for Mr. Hawkins. But eventually he would have run off, seeking the respect denied him on the farm.

**Different Perspectives** Some students may state that if Dave were a husband and a father, he should stay on the farm to support his wife and child, no matter how great the sacrifice.

**Critic's Corner** Some students may say that Wright is fighting against the idea that guns provide real power or enhance masculinity. Others may say that he is protesting against the injustice of share cropping and the indignities suffered by tenant farmers.

**Comparing Texts** Students may say that Baldwin might urge Dave not to believe what others say about him and to try to build self-respect.

**Connect to Life** Some students may mention graduation from high school and obtaining a driver's license as cultural rites of passage. Responses might reflect a recognition of the distinctive and/or shared characteristics of different cultures represented by class members.

## Connect to the Literature

**1. What Do You Think?** Some students may feel relieved because Dave has taken the first step to create a new life for himself.

**Comprehension Check**
- He claims that the mule impaled herself on the point of the plow.
- The crowd jeers at him.
- He wants to avoid a beating from his father, to extricate himself from his debt to Mr. Hawkins, and to find a place where people will treat him as a man.

 Use Selection Quiz **Unit Six Resource Book,** p. 67.

## Think Critically

**2.** Possible Response: Dave's decisions are foolish because he never thinks about what to do or what might happen; he just reacts with excitement, panic, or another emotion.

**3.** Possible Response: No, buying the gun has put Dave heavily in debt, and he has acted so foolishly that everyone laughs at him.

**4.** Possible Response: Dave is a pathetic figure because he doesn't know how to act in a mature way.

**5.** Responses will vary. Some students may predict that Dave, who has worked hard for Mr. Hawkins, will find work in an urban area and do well at it. Others may predict that Dave's immaturity will spell trouble for him no matter where he goes.

## Literary Analysis

**Point of View** This narrative method allows the narrator not only to stand outside the action but also occasionally to show the reader Dave's innermost reactions rather than merely telling about them. This method creates an effect of immediacy, prompting the reader to identify with Dave.

**Review Irony** Students may note Dave's failure to stay and deal with the consequences of the accident as a lost opportunity to prove his manhood.

## Writing Options

1. **Defining Adulthood** Suggest that students get started by reviewing their initial thoughts on adulthood from Connect to Your Life on page 1045.

2. **Letter Home** Have students think about the way Wright renders Dave's speech and review the mini lesson on dialect (p. 1047). Encourage students to incorporate dialect into their letters. Students may want to reflect on Dave's feelings toward his family at the end of the selection and suggest how these feelings may change after he leaves home.

3. **Editorial: Dave's Situation To make this activity more challenging,** have students research life in the South for African Americans in the early part of this century and include pertinent information in their editorials.

## Activities & Explorations

1. **Dramatic Reading** Students should review the mini lesson on dialect. Encourage them to tape-record rehearsals and critique them as a means for improving their performances before presenting their dramatic readings to the class.

2. **Charting Expenses** Charts will vary based on local prices. Encourage interested students to do further research on the comparative cost of various articles at the time the story is set. In order to evaluate the relative economic status of sharecroppers, students may wish to find out the average salaries earned in 1910 by people in various jobs.

3. **Film Critics' Circle To make this activity more challenging,** ask students to list the story's scenes to determine whether any scenes were added to the film or left out of it. Which version makes for a tighter story?

## Author Activity

Students might create a Venn diagram to list similarities and differences between Bigger and Dave. Students might note that both Bigger and Dave struggle against poverty and feelings of hopelessness.

## Writing Options

1. **Defining Adulthood** What does it mean to be an adult? Write a definition of adulthood based on your reading of this story and on your own observations and experiences. Share your definition with the class.

2. **Letter Home** At the end of the story, Dave hops on a train to go "somewhere where he could be a man." Write the letter that Dave might eventually send to his family.

3. **Editorial: Dave's Situation** Write an editorial in which you agree or disagree with the following statement: Dave is merely a victim of circumstances. Support your position with evidence.

## Activities & Explorations

1. **Dramatic Reading** Wright uses dialect to capture the way his characters talk. To appreciate the sound of the characters' spoken words, work with a small group of classmates to plan and present a dramatic reading of this story. ~ **PERFORMING**

2. **Charting Expenses** Dave is paid $2.00 a month, roughly equivalent to $100.00 a month today. If Dave were a teenager today, how long would he have to work to buy the following items: a pair of sneakers, a CD or tape, a meal at a fast-food restaurant, a concert ticket? Record your findings in a chart or a graph. ~ **MATH AND ECONOMICS**

3. **Film Critics' Circle** View the video based on the story "The Man Who Was Almost a Man." How well do you think the film version succeeds in bringing the story to life? What moments did you find especially realistic? Discuss your responses. ~ **VIEWING AND REPRESENTING**

**VIDEO** Literature in Performance

| Item | Cost |
|---|---|
| Pair of sneakers | |
| CD or tape | |
| Fast food | |
| Concert ticket | |

## Richard Wright
### 1908–1960

**Other Works**
*Native Son*
*Lawd Today*
*Black Boy*
*White Man, Listen!*
*American Hunger*

**Barriers of Prejudice and Poverty** Richard Wright, the son of a poor sharecropper, was born in Mississippi. He endured a childhood marked by gnawing hunger, physical beatings, and an intense internal struggle against the religious and racial restrictions imposed on him by his family and his culture. To escape the poverty of the rural South, his father moved the family to Memphis, Tennessee. Unable to find work, however, Wright's frustrated father abandoned the family, and Wright was raised by his ailing mother and later by his stern grandmother. Often left alone while his relatives worked, Wright encountered the violence of the ghetto streets at age 6. He wrote later that it was only through books that he managed to stay alive, books that he got by borrowing a white man's library card.

**Literary Fame** Wright's first story was published in an African-American newspaper when he was 15. After winning first prize in a writing contest sponsored by *Story* magazine, he published his first collection of stories, *Uncle Tom's Children*. Two years later in 1940, Wright gained international fame for his novel *Native Son*. His fiction and his autobiographies, *Black Boy* and *American Hunger*, expose the brutal racism in American life.

## Author Activity

**The Creation of Characters** Read "How 'Bigger' Was Born," the introduction to *Native Son* in which Wright describes the real-life models for Bigger Thomas, the main character in the novel. Compare Dave to Wright's various portraits of Bigger.

## Teaching Options

### Mini Lesson Grammar

**QUOTATION MARKS WITH OTHER PUNCTUATION**

**Instruction** Remind students that there are special rules concerning quotation marks used with other marks of punctuation. Commas and periods are placed inside quotation marks. Semicolons and colons appear outside quotation marks. Question marks and exclamation points are placed inside quotation marks when they are part of the quotation. Otherwise, they go outside of the quotation marks. Write the following sentence on the chalkboard.

> Dave's mother said, "I'll never teach that boy how to be a man!"

The exclamation point is inside the quotation marks because it is part of the quotation.

**Exercise** Have students rewrite each sentence. Students do not need to change dialect to standard English.

1. Dave told Mr. Joe, "Ahma buy a gun". *(Dave told Mr. Joe, "Ahma buy a gun.")*

2. "Ah wanna keep it", Dave replied. *("Ah wanna keep it," Dave replied.)*

 Use **Grammar Transparencies and Copymasters**, p. 162.

Use McDougal Littell's *Language Network*, Chapter 10, for more instruction and practice in quotation marks.

# PREPARING to *Read*

## Mirror
*Poetry by* SYLVIA PLATH

## Self in 1958
*Poetry by* ANNE SEXTON

**Comparing Literature**

### Traditions Across Time: The Lonely Self

T.S. Eliot's "The Love Song of J. Alfred Prufrock," which was first published in 1915, features a character who is painfully aware of himself. This sort of modernist character reappears in "Mirror" and "Self in 1958." Both poems portray self-conscious women who fret over their identities.

**Points of Comparison** As you read, compare the modernist characters in all three of these poems, noting the troubling emotions that preoccupy their thoughts.

## Build Background

**True Confessions** Both Sylvia Plath and Anne Sexton broke new ground by writing openly and honestly about the reality of their lives in the 1950s and early 1960s. Like Charlotte Perkins Gilman and, to some extent, Kate Chopin before them, Plath and Sexton expressed turbulent and often violent emotions. Their poems read like confessions in which they expose their troubled lives in startling images that some readers still find shocking. "Mirror" begins very much like a riddle, asking the reader to figure out who is speaking, and then explores a woman's feelings about aging. Plath wrote the poem just four days before her 29th birthday and a few months before the birth of her second child. In "Self in 1958," Sexton expresses her feelings about her life two years after a suicide attempt and the first of several hospitalizations for psychiatric problems.

## Focus Your Reading

**LITERARY ANALYSIS** SPEAKER The **speaker** of a poem, like the narrator of a story, is the voice that talks to the reader. In "Mirror" and "Self in 1958," the speaker is someone or something other than the poet. In each of these poems, the speaker is a **persona,** a character of the poet's invention who likely acts as a disguise for some aspect of the poet's personality. Note that the speaker in Plath's poem is a mirror and in Sexton's poem, a doll.

**ACTIVE READING** LINKING TITLE AND THEME The **title** of a literary work often suggests its **theme,** or the main idea that explains the underlying meaning of the work. As you read "Mirror" and "Self in 1958," think about how these titles provide you with clues that hint at the central message expressed in the poems.

**READER'S NOTEBOOK** Create cluster diagrams like the ones shown and fill them in with details from the poems that seem to point to key ideas suggested by the titles.

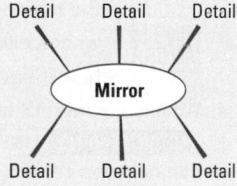

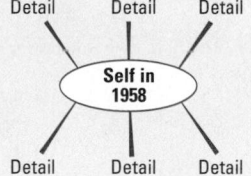

**Objectives**
1. understand and appreciate two confessional **poems** (Literary Analysis)
2. examine the **speaker** in poetry (Literary Analysis)
3. **link title and theme** (Active Reading)

**Summary**
In "Mirror" Sylvia Plath personifies a mirror that describes itself as silver, exact, and truthful. It tells of the various reflections that have appeared on its surface—the pink wall opposite, faces, darkness. A woman who has looked into the mirror since her youth pores over it, anguished by the signs of aging that she sees in her reflection. In Anne Sexton's "Self in 1958," the speaker compares herself to a plaster doll. She describes her appearance, her clothes, her house, and her life as synthetic, counterfeit; they are the accessories and setting that would be suitable for a doll. She cannot convey her real feelings to people, nor does she know if she still possesses feelings.

**Thematic Link**
The woman in "Mirror" struggles against the process of aging that moves her further into **alienation** from her youth. "Self in 1958" explores feelings of alienation so strong that the speaker feels like a plaster doll instead of a human being.

**5-Minute Warm-Up**

*Daily Language SkillBuilder*

Have students **proofread** the display sentences on page 913k and write them correctly. The sentences also appear on Transparency 30 of **Grammar Transparencies and Copymasters.**

---

## LESSON RESOURCES

**UNIT SIX RESOURCE BOOK,**
pp. 68–70

**ASSESSMENT RESOURCES**
**Formal Assessment,**
pp. 197–198
**Teacher's Guide to Assessment and Portfolio Use**
**Test Generator**

**SKILLS TRANSPARENCIES AND COPYMASTERS**
**Literary Analysis**
• Style, Voice, T23 (for Activity, p. 1061)

**Reading and Critical Thinking**
• Cluster Diagram, T48 (for Active Reading, p. 1057)
**Grammar**
• Capitalizing Family Titles, C143 (for Mini Lesson, p. 1063)
• Creating Compound Sentences, C170 (for Mini Lesson, p. 1060)
**Vocabulary**
• Word Origins, C89 (for Mini Lesson, p. 1059)
**Writing**
• Compare-Contrast, C32 (for Writing Option 3, p. 1062)

**Communications**
• Impromptu Speaking: Dialogue, Role-Play, Debate, T13 (for Activities & Explorations 1, p. 1062)

**INTEGRATED TECHNOLOGY**
**Audio Library**
**Visit our website:**
www.mcdougallittell.com

**Active Reading**

| LINKING TITLE AND THEME |

Before students read the poem, have them brainstorm their associations with mirrors. What do mirrors do? Is their role in people's daily lives important? Do people generally like what they see in mirrors? Then have students read the poem and consider how their associations relate to the poem's theme.

 Use **Unit Six Resource Book**, p. 68 for more practice.

**Literary Analysis** | SPEAKER |

Ask students to pick out details that describe the speaker.

**Possible Responses:** "silver and exact"; "unmisted by love or dislike"; "truthful"; "four-cornered"

 Use **Unit Six Resource Book**, p. 69 for more practice.

**Literary Analysis: PERSONIFICATION**

Ask students what Plath achieves by personifying the mirror.

**Possible Responses:** She provides a different perspective on a woman's self-image, honesty, vanity, and the process of aging. Personification helps the author to examine the way people look at themselves.

**GUIDE FOR READING**

**A** **Possible Responses:** She has a poor self-image; she dislikes herself and thinks of herself as more like a doll than a real person.

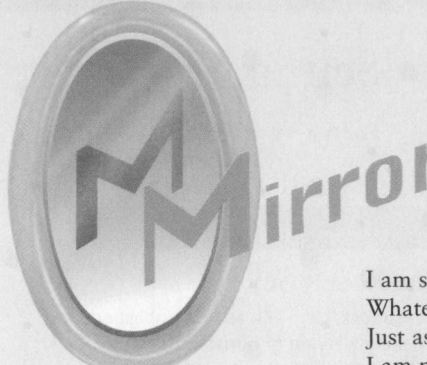

# Mirror

SYLVIA PLATH

I am silver and exact. I have no preconceptions.[1]
Whatever I see I swallow immediately
Just as it is, unmisted by love or dislike.
I am not cruel, only truthful—
5 The eye of a little god, four-cornered.
Most of the time I meditate on the opposite wall.
It is pink, with speckles. I have looked at it so long
I think it is a part of my heart. But it flickers.
Faces and darkness separate us over and over.

10 Now I am a lake. A woman bends over me,
Searching my reaches for what she really is.
Then she turns to those liars, the candles or the moon.
I see her back, and reflect it faithfully.
She rewards me with tears and an agitation of hands.
15 I am important to her. She comes and goes.
Each morning it is her face that replaces the darkness.
In me she has drowned a young girl, and in me an old woman
Rises toward her day after day, like a terrible fish.

---

1. **preconceptions:** opinions formed before adequate knowledge or understanding is achieved.

## Thinking Through the Literature

1. What images from the poem linger in your mind?

2. Why do you think the mirror is so important to the woman?

3. In your opinion, is the mirror "not cruel, only truthful"?

 THINK ABOUT
- the reality it reflects
- what feelings it has
- how it interprets the woman's reflection

4. What is the mirror's attitude toward the woman?

5. | ACTIVE READING | LINKING TITLE AND THEME | In what ways did the title help you zero in on the **theme?** Review the cluster diagram you made in your READER'S NOTEBOOK.

## Thinking Through the Literature

1. Responses will vary. Some students may mention the image of an old woman rising "like a terrible fish."

2. Possible Responses: She is interested in her appearance; she is vain; she measures her worth by what she sees; she dreads growing older.

3. Possible Responses: The mirror is inherently honest, simply reflecting an image; the mirror's language is cruel and harsh, particularly the description of "an old woman" rising "like a terrible fish."

4. Possible Responses: It looks down on her for not being objective; it is indifferent to her; it likes to watch her grow older.

5. Possible Responses: The title of the poem clues the reader into the speaker and the mirror's central place in reflecting the woman's image. The poem's theme is that women are defined by their image, and the woman in this poem feels alienated from the image of an aging face she finds reflected in the mirror.

SELF IN 1958

ANNE SEXTON

What is reality?
I am a plaster doll; I pose
with eyes that cut open without landfall or nightfall
upon some shellacked and grinning person,
5  eyes that open, blue, steel, and close.
Am I approximately an I. Magnin transplant?
I have hair, black angel,
black-angel-stuffing to comb,
nylon legs, luminous arms
10  and some advertised clothes.

**GUIDE FOR READING**

**6 I. Magnin:** a department store
that sells expensive clothing.

**1–10** What image of the speaker
do you form from these first ten
lines of the poem? How would you
describe her self-image?  **A**

---

## Customizing Instruction

### Less Proficient Readers
Remind students that this part of Unit Six is about alienation, or people's feeling of separation from other people or from reality. Ask students to speculate how a poem called "Mirror" might be related to alienation.

**Set a Purpose** Point out that both poems connect human beings with inanimate objects. Have students read to find out who is the speaker in each poem and what object each poem uses to express feelings of alienation.

### Students Acquiring English
Clarify the use of personification in "Mirror." To introduce "Self in 1958," students might benefit from a brief description of life for suburban homemakers in the 1950s. Then explain that Anne Sexton's poem draws from her own feelings. Approach analysis of the poem by stating the main idea of each stanza before looking at the individual lines.

 Use **Spanish Study Guide** for additional support, pp. 263–265.

### Gifted and Talented
Sylvia Plath wrote "Mirror" in 1961, and Anne Sexton's poem was written in 1958. Have students consider the portrayals of women in both poems—are they still relevant forty years later?

### Multiple Learning Styles
**Visual/Auditory Learners**

Read each poem aloud before discussion so that students can hear the rhythm and sound devices and can visualize the images created by the figurative language.

---

## Mini Lesson — Vocabulary Strategy

**RESEARCHING WORD ORIGINS: *MIRROR***
**Instruction** Remind students that they can research word origins as an aid to understanding the meanings of words. The word *mirror* is based upon the Latin root *mirari,* which means "to wonder at." *Miracle* and *mirage* are familiar words derived from the same root, but the word *mirror* itself is used to create many compound words including *mirror carp, mirror image,* and *mirror writing.*

**Application** Have students work in pairs to find the meanings of *mirage, mirror carp, mirror image,* and *mirror writing.* Ask them to use each word in a sentence. Then have students investigate other words that derive from the Latin root *mirari.*

 Use **Vocabulary Transparencies and Copymasters,** p. 89.

**A lesson on word origins appears on p. 550 in the Pupil's Edition.**

**A** Possible Responses: The doll house may be a crossroad because it is the center of the speaker's world; the speaker may be referring to this point of dissatisfaction in her life as a crossroad.

**B** Possible Responses: The speaker views her home as small, isolated, or limiting.

**Literary Analysis** SPEAKER

**C** Ask students to interpret the speaker's cry "They think I am me!"

Possible Responses: A doll is hollow, judged only by what is on the outside. The speaker might be referring to the fact that the people around her see only her exterior; they believe that her façade is her reality.

**GUIDE FOR READING**

**D** Possible Responses: The someone may refer to her husband or family, or to any and all the other people in her life; it may be a way of indicating that she does not feel involved in or in control of her own life.

**Active Reading**
LINKING TITLE AND THEME

Have students consider the theme of the poem and how the title relates to the theme.

Possible Response: The title may refer to the poet's own self in the year 1958. However, her description of the superficiality of life in the "doll's house" applies to the lives of many suburban women during the 1950s. The theme of the poem may be that the ideal woman's life depicted in 1950s advertising does not allow women to stay connected to their true selves.

---

I live in a doll's house
with four chairs,
a counterfeit table, a flat roof
and a big front door.
15  Many have come to such a small crossroad.
There is an iron bed,
(Life enlarges, life takes aim)
a cardboard floor,
windows that flash open on someone's city,
20  and little more.

Someone plays with me,
plants me in the all-electric kitchen,
Is this what Mrs. Rombauer said?
Someone pretends with me—
25  I am walled in solid by their noise—
or puts me upon their straight bed.
**C**  They think I am me!
Their warmth? Their warmth is not a friend!
They pry my mouth for their cups of gin
30  and their stale bread.

What is reality
to this synthetic doll
who should smile, who should shift gears,
should spring the doors open in a wholesome disorder,
35  and have no evidence of ruin or fears?
But I would cry,
rooted into the wall that
was once my mother,
if I could remember how
40  and if I had the tears.

1060

---

**15** *Crossroad* can refer to an intersection or to a crucial point. What is the crossroad referred to here?  **A**

**11–20** How does the speaker seem to feel about her home?  **B**

**23  Mrs. Rombauer:** Irma Rombauer, author of *The Joy of Cooking,* a classic cookbook containing advice and instruction as well as recipes.

**21–30** Who do you think is the "someone" (and the "they") that plays with and walls in the speaker?  **D**

---

**Teaching Options**

(Mini Lesson) **Grammar**

**COMPOUND SENTENCES**

**Instruction** A compound sentence has two or more independent clauses joined together. It is important not to confuse a compound sentence with a simple sentence that has compound subjects and/or compound predicates. Display the following sentences to illustrate this point.

Sylvia Plath and Anne Sexton struggled with their personal problems but created powerful poetry. *(simple sentence with compound subject and compound predicate)*

Sylvia Plath and Anne Sexton struggled with personal problems, but they both created powerful poetry. *(compound sentence—each independent clause has its own subject and verb)*

Use **Grammar Transparencies and Copymasters,** p. 170.

Use McDougal Littell's *Language Network,* Chapter 3, for more instruction in compound sentences.

## Connect to the Literature

**1. What Do You Think?**
What do you think
of the speaker's
description of
herself in "Self in
1958"?

**Comprehension Check**
- How would you describe the
  speaker's physical appearance?
- What keeps the speaker from
  crying?
- How is the speaker's home
  furnished?

## Think Critically

**2.** Why do you think the speaker describes herself as a doll?
Why can't she be herself?

**THINK ABOUT**
- how the speaker looks and acts
- the limitations of her existence in her house
- the expectations that others have of her
- the feelings she has but cannot express

**3.** Why do you think the speaker has lost the ability to cry?

**4.** The speaker questions the reality of her existence because
she feels so "synthetic," or fake. What might make her life
more authentic, or real?

**5.** **ACTIVE READING | LINKING TITLE AND THEME**
Review the cluster diagram you made in your
**READER'S NOTEBOOK**. Based on the details you
recorded, expand the title into a general statement that
explains the theme, or main idea, of the poem.

## Extend Interpretations

**6. Different Perspectives** Confessional poetry in general has
sometimes been attacked for its excessive emotional and
overly personal content. Do you find these flaws in "Self in
1958"? Why or why not? Defend your view.

**7. Critic's Corner** Anne Sexton once remarked that poetry
"should be a shock to the senses. It should also hurt." Do
you think this statement holds true for "Self in 1958"? Cite
phrases or lines from the poem to support your view.

**8. Connect to Life** Do you think "Self in 1958" expresses issues
that still concern women today? Support your response.

**9.** **Points of Comparison** What aspects of their lives do
Prufrock in "The Love Song of J. Alfred Prufrock," the woman
in "Mirror" and the speaker in "Self in 1958" find especially
disturbing? Which of these characters do you think is the
most self-conscious? Explain.

## Literary Analysis

**SPEAKER** *Persona* is a Latin
word meaning "actor's mask." In
each of these poems, the poet
invents a fictional character, or a
**persona,** to play the role of the
**speaker.** Surprisingly, the persona
in "Mirror" and "Self in 1958" is not
a human, but rather an inanimate
object, capable of speech and
thought. Plath and Sexton use a
persona in these poems to provide
a different and original perspective
on a woman's self-image.

**Activity** If the speakers of "Mirror"
and "Self in 1958" were women,
instead of inanimate objects, how
might the poems be different?
Rewrite a stanza from each of these
poems so that a woman is the
speaker. Then read aloud the
original stanzas and your revisions
to the class. Discuss which versions
are more inventive and surprising.

## Extend Interpretations

**Different Perspectives** Possible Responses: Yes, the
poem is too personal for others to relate to; no,
the themes of the poem are valid for many
women, even today.

**Critic's Corner** Possible Response: Yes. Most lines
from the poem could shock and hurt. "I am a
plaster doll"; "Someone pretends with me— / I am
walled in solid by their noise"; "Their warmth is
not a friend! / They pry my mouth for their cups
of gin"; "What is reality / to this synthetic doll";
"But I would cry, / rooted into the wall that / was
once my mother, / if I could remember how / and
if I had the tears."

**Connect to Life** Some students may think that
women have been liberated from this confining
role; others may say that women are still expected
to be perfect wives and mothers. Students should
cite lines from the text to support their opinion.

**Points of Comparison** Possible Response: All three
feel alienated by the masks they must wear, the
false selves they must present to the world.
Students may find any of the three characters to
be the most self-conscious; they should support
their opinion with lines from the text.

## Connect to the Literature

**1. What Do You Think?**
Possible Response: Although her
physical appearance seems attractive
and her existence materially comfortable, she emphasizes her synthetic
qualities and her emptiness.

**Comprehension Check**
- attractive; she has blue eyes, black
  hair, nice clothes
- She poses; her eyes open and close
  automatically; she is polished,
  grinning.
- counterfeit table; flat roof; big front
  door; iron bed; cardboard floors; all-
  electric kitchen

## Think Critically

**2.** Possible Responses: She doesn't feel
alive; she feels passive and
inanimate while other people
manipulate her; she doesn't feel that
she can express her emotions as a
person would.

**3.** Possible Responses: She no longer
experiences emotions strongly
enough to feel the need to cry;
crying is active, but the speaker feels
completely passive.

**4.** Possible Responses: She could
consult a therapist to help her deal
with her feelings of alienation; she
could turn to friends; she could
become involved in charity work.

**5.** Possible Responses: The idealized
role of the 1950s homemaker left
many feeling alienated and not real.

## Literary Analysis

**Speaker** Suggest that students review
"Mirror" for details that provide clues
into what the woman might say if she
were the speaker. For "Self in 1958"
students should focus on the main idea
of the stanza they choose and work on
communicating that idea without references to a doll or doll house.

## Writing Options

### 1. Diary of a Housewife
**To get students started,** have them note references to routines or activities in the poem and the speaker's attitude toward them. **Visual learners** might present a series of cartoons, using illustrations and captions to portray a week in the life of a housewife.

### 2. Poetic Riddle
**To get students started,** ask them to brainstorm possible objects that they could personify. Students should then list and organize the characteristics of this object.

### 3. Points of Comparison
**To get students started,** have them examine each poem for ideas about growing old. Students should copy quotations and examples that support each of their observations.

## Activities & Explorations

### 1. Face-to-Face Conversation
**S**uggest that partners review both poems and create a character sketch of each woman.

### 2. A Doll's House
Encourage students to avoid replicating the illustration on page 1059. Suggest that students experiment with other techniques besides literal representation to capture the feelings and self-image that the speaker expresses. Students might prefer to assemble images from magazines to create their illustrations.

---

## Writing Options

**1. Diary of a Housewife** Write a series of journal entries from the point of view of the speaker in "Self in 1958." Record her confessions about her daily life. Refer to the poem for ideas.

**2. Poetic Riddle** Using "Mirror" as a model, write a poem in the form of a riddle. Use the first-person "I" as you speak in the voice of an inanimate object. Include clues that will help the reader guess your identity. Save your poem in your **Working Portfolio.**

**3. Points of Comparison**
Write a brief essay in which you compare and contrast ideas about fears of growing old as expressed in "Mirror" and "The Love Song of J. Alfred Prufrock." Cite evidence from both poems to support your ideas.

**Writing Handbook**
See page 1281: Compare and Contrast

## Activities & Explorations

**1. Face-to-Face Conversation** With a partner, act out a conversation between the woman in "Mirror" and the speaker of "Self in 1958."
~ PERFORMING

**2. A Doll's House** Sketch a portrait of the speaker of "Self in 1958" in her house, based on details she provides in the poem. Share your portrait with the class.
~ ART

## Inquiry & Research

**1. Women's Roles** Both of these poems touch upon the reality of women's lives in the 1950s and early 1960s. Do research and interview women in your family or community to find out about women's roles at that time. Report your findings to the class.

**2. Confessional Poets** Find out what other poets are classified with Plath and Sexton as confessional poets. Read several poems by one of these poets, then choose one to present to the class. Discuss what the poem reveals about the poet's private life.

---

## Teaching Options

### ✓ Assessment Standardized Test Practice

**MAKING INFERENCES** For some standardized tests, students will be asked to make inferences based upon what they have read. Display the following sample questions. For each question, tell students to eliminate obviously wrong choices, review the poems for evidence that would support any of the remaining choices, and then choose the best answer.

In "Mirror" the reader can infer that the mirror is important to the woman because she
**A.** consults it often.
**B.** calls it a little god.
**C.** takes good care of it.
**D.** rewards it with tears.
**Answer:** A

In "Self in 1958" the reader can infer that the speaker
**A.** values her possessions.
**B.** takes comfort from her relationships with others.
**C.** is overwhelmed by her feelings.
**D.** feels trapped in her comfortable life.
**Answer:** D

## Sylvia Plath
### 1932–1963

**Other Works**
*The Colossus*
*Crossing the Water*
*Winter Trees*
*Ariel*

**Turbulent Emotions**  Sylvia Plath was described by the poet Robert Lowell, one of her teachers, as having an "air of maddening docility." Beneath that obedient surface, however, simmered the rage and rebellion that was to inform her best work—and that also triggered bouts of depression.

**Talented Coed**  When she was a junior at Smith College, Plath won *Mademoiselle's* fiction contest and was given a month's apprenticeship at the magazine's New York editorial offices. Shortly after her apprenticeship, she became seriously depressed and attempted suicide—an experience detailed in her only novel, *The Bell Jar.* After psychiatric treatment, Plath eventually returned to Smith and graduated with high honors.

**Poetic Outburst**  After graduation, Plath studied at Cambridge University in England, where she met and married the British poet Ted Hughes. Unfortunately, the marriage deteriorated, and in 1962 Plath left Hughes and took her two children to live in a London flat. As a result of the stress, Plath's buried anger rose to the surface, and she expressed her intense feelings in a frenzy of writing.

**Fatal Impulses**  In February 1963, Plath again experienced acute depression, and this time ended her life. Her last poems, considered her best work, were published in *Ariel* after her death. Plath was posthumously awarded a Pulitzer Prize for *Collected Poems.*

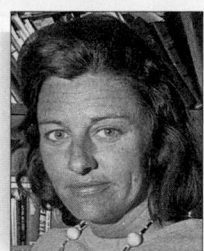

## Anne Sexton
### 1928–1974

**Other Works**
*All My Pretty Ones*
*The Awful Rowing Toward God*
*The Book of Folly*

**Buried Self**  Anne Sexton graduated from junior college, worked as a fashion model, married at 19, settled in a Boston suburb, and had two daughters. Despite the seeming normality of her life, Sexton suffered repeated mental breakdowns and was haunted by thoughts of suicide. "Until I was twenty-eight," she said, "I had a kind of buried self who didn't know she could do anything but make white sauce and diaper babies. I didn't know I had any creative depths. I was a victim of the American Dream, the bourgeois, middle-class dream. All I wanted was a little piece of life, to be married, to have children. I thought the nightmares, the visions, the demons would go away if there was enough love to put them down. . . . But one can't build little white picket fences to keep nightmares out."

**Poetry as Therapy**  At the suggestion of her psychiatrist, Sexton began writing poetry in her late 20s. In 1958 she attended Robert Lowell's poetry workshop at Boston University, where she and Sylvia Plath became friends. Sexton's first volume of poetry, *To Bedlam and Part Way Back,* details her initial mental breakdown, subsequent hospital stay, and attempt to reconcile with her family upon her return home. Struggling with depression all her life, Sexton still managed to publish ten books of poetry before her death from suicide just shy of her 46th birthday.

## Inquiry & Research

1. **Women's Roles** Students can form groups with each student pursuing a different research area, such as conducting interviews and oral histories; examining the depiction of women in advertisements, movies, television, and literature; and investigating facts about the economic status of women and their concentration in particular job types. To present their findings, groups may wish to create a multimedia presentation that includes pictures, posters, audio interviews, and video clips. **To make this assignment more challenging,** have students compare the roles of women in the 1950s and 1960s with women's roles today.

2. **Confessional Poets** **To get students started on this assignment,** have them locate appropriate print information using a library database and the Internet. Other confessional poets whose works students might explore include Robert Lowell and John Berryman.

---

 **Mini Lesson**   # Grammar

### CAPITALIZING FAMILY TITLES

**Instruction** Family titles are capitalized when they are used before a proper noun or in place of the person's name. Family titles are not capitalized when preceded by articles or possessive words. Display the following sentences:

> My brother received a graduation gift from Grandma Jones.
>
> My brother received a graduation gift from his grandmother.

**Exercises** Have students rewrite the following sentences with correct capitalization.

1. I asked mother for her opinion. *(Mother)*

2. After my brother Sam locked his keys in the car, aunt Carlotta gave him an extra key to keep in his wallet. *(Aunt Carlotta)*

3. She followed cousin Geraldine into the department store to buy a present for their grandfather. *(Cousin Geraldine)*

4. The letter from dad filled us in on his travels. *(Dad)*

 Use **Grammar Transparencies and Copymasters**, p. 143.

 Use McDougal Littell's *Language Network*, Chapter 8, for more instruction in capitalizing.

**PART 1 Reading the Prompt**
Model the process of reading a prompt:
- Read the entire prompt aloud.
- List key words of the assignment on the board ("Describe the plight of the modernist character"; "pulling together examples"; and "two selections by early modernists and one by a later modernist").
- Use the Strategies in Action to show how students can restate the prompt for themselves.

**PART 2 Planning a Synthesis Essay**
- Have students focus on one character in each selection.
- Suggest that they not only describe each character's situation, but also note events, actions, and other evidence that supports their descriptions.
- Students might jot down words and phrases that describe what is common to all the characters' situations. They can then create general definitions from those notes.

**PART 3 Drafting Your Essay**
**Introduction** Suggest that students include a brief explanation of modernism. For example, they might explain when and why the movement began.
**Organization** Students might also consider listing the elements that comprise their definitions and then organize those elements in order of importance. Students' examples might include concrete details from the selections, word choices, and tone.
**Conclusion** Students may mention any or all of the following as problems faced by modernist characters: confusion, indecision, self-consciousness, and unsureness about social roles.
**Revision** Students should check their essays to make sure they have punctuated ellipses correctly.

---

In writing assessments, you will sometimes be asked to synthesize, or put together, information from a variety of selections to form an overall picture. You are now going to practice writing an essay with this focus.

**PART 1** **Reading the Prompt**

Read the entire prompt carefully. Then read through it again, looking for key words that help you identify the purpose of the essay and decide how to approach it.

> **Writing Prompt**
>
> Many of the literary selections in Unit 6, Part 2, portray characters in despair. Describe the plight ❶ of the modernist character, pulling together examples from two selections by early modernists ❷ and one by a later modernist—Sexton or Plath.

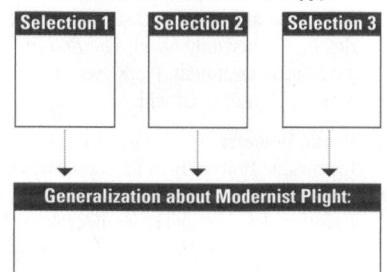

STRATEGIES
IN ACTION

❶ **Describe**, or name, important aspects of the modernist character's plight.

❷ Gather **details** about different characters' unhappy circumstances and find connections.

**PART 2** **Planning a Synthesis Essay**

- Choose three selections to explore.
- Create a diagram like the one shown and fill it in with details about the characters' unhappiness.
- Note recurring patterns.
- State a generalization about the modernist character's plight that covers the examples you have chosen.

**What Makes Characters Unhappy?**

| Selection 1 | Selection 2 | Selection 3 |
|---|---|---|
|  |  |  |

↓ ↓ ↓

**Generalization about Modernist Plight:**

**PART 3** **Drafting Your Essay**

**Introduction** Begin by stating your subject—the plight of the modernist character. Identify the authors and titles of the three selections you are exploring.

**Organization** Arrange the literary examples logically. For instance, you might first cite examples from the early modernist selections, followed by an example from the later modernist selection. Cite details that most strongly illustrate the characters' unhappiness.

**Conclusion** Bring the details you presented into focus by stating what the characters have in common.

**Revision** Allow time to review your work. Make sure it is clear, well-supported, and free from mistakes.

**Writing Handbook**
See page 1281: Explanatory Writing

**1064** UNIT SIX PART 2: ALIENATION OF THE INDIVIDUAL

---

 **Mini Lesson Punctuation**

**ELLIPSES**
**Instruction** For purposes of clarity or brevity, words, phrases, or longer sections may be left out of quoted material. Such an omission must be indicated with ellipsis points—a series of three spaced dots or periods.

The literary movement known as modernism resulted from all these societal changes.
The literary movement . . . resulted from all these societal changes.

Discuss the types of omissions that a writer might make. Examples include asides, unnecessary appositives, or irrelevant or misleading details.
**Application** The writing prompt asks students to provide examples from three selections. Direct quotations are one kind of example that they should include. Ellipses allow them to quote only the relevant sections of lengthy or complicated passages.

## The Nick Adams Stories

ERNEST HEMINGWAY

A boy goes on a camping trip with his father in Michigan. A young man is held hostage inside a cafe by two thugs. A soldier fights on the battlefields of World War I. A troubled veteran tries to heal his war wounds. These are just a sampling of Nick Adams's experiences depicted in the short stories from this collection, featuring one of the most memorable characters in American fiction.

## Invisible Man

RALPH ELLISON

The unnamed narrator, an African-American man, announces, "I am invisible, understand, simply because others refuse to see me." Ellison's critically acclaimed novel centers on the narrator's odyssey to discover who he is in a blind, uncaring world. His search for his identity is a complex quest, which takes him from the deep South to the North.

## And Even *More* . . .

### Books

**The Portable Dorothy Parker**
DOROTHY PARKER
A collection of literary works by this modernist writer, known for her biting wit.

**A Long Day's Journey into Night**
EUGENE O'NEILL
A drama about a troubled family and fractured relationships.

**A Streetcar Named Desire**
TENNESSEE WILLIAMS
A drama about a woman trapped by her own inadequacies.

### Other Media

**Tom and Viv**
Feature film about T. S. Eliot's marriage to his first wife, starring Willem Dafoe and Miranda Richardson. Miramax Films. (VIDEOCASSETTE)

**Black Boy**
A documentary exploring the life and literary career of Richard Wright. Mississippi Educational Television/BBC. (VIDEOCASSETTE)

**Voices & Visions: Sylvia Plath**
A documentary of the poet, including dramatic readings of her works. Mystic Fire Video. (VIDEOCASSETTE)

### The Heart Is a Lonely Hunter

CARSON McCULLERS

Four isolated people—a young aspiring composer, a would-be labor organizer, a cafe owner, and an African-American doctor—find comfort in their relationship with John Singer, who cannot hear or speak. This moving novel about loneliness is set in a small Southern community.

The *Electronic Library* is a CD-ROM that contains additional fiction, nonfiction, poetry, and drama for each unit in *The Language of Literature.*

These are the additional selections found in Unit 6 of the *Electronic Library* that apply to Part 2.

Robert Frost
**The Death of the Hired Man**

Sherwood Anderson
**Sophistication**

Katherine Anne Porter
**He**

Have students choose one of the selections mentioned to read silently with comprehension over a period of time.

## Objectives

- reflect on and assess their understanding of the unit
- compare text events with his/her own and other readers' experiences
- compare across texts elements of texts such as style, theme, mood, tone, conflict, and characterization
- assess and build portfolios

## Reflecting on the Unit

### OPTION 1

A successful response will

- identify examples of prejudice and mistreatment in the selections in Part 1 of this unit.
- identify how the characters responded to these prejudices and mistreatments.
- compare and contrast the characters' different responses.
- evaluate which responses to prejudice are most effective.

### OPTION 2

A successful response will

- compare and contrast the selections in this unit with those in previous units.
- consider literary techniques, content, writer's purpose, and writing style.
- explain which selection in this unit seems exceptionally original.

### OPTION 3

Have student groups brainstorm what they know and what they can infer about the characters in the selections and fill these insights in on their charts. Have each group display their charts to the class and have the groups compare and contrast them. Use the Unit 6 Resource Book, p. 71, to provide students a ready-made, full-depth chart for examining the iceberg principle.

### Self Assessment

Have students explain what they did and did not like about the writing styles in the unit. Ask them if they developed new opinions or changed old opinions about the genres they read. If so, what stories caused these changes?

# The Modern Age

How does the literature from the Harlem Renaissance writers and other modern writers differ from earlier American literature? What new challenges did this unit present to you as a reader and a writer? Explore these questions by completing one or more of the options below.

*Rush Hour, New York* (1915), Max Weber. Oil on canvas, 36¼″ × 30¼″. National Gallery of Art, Washington, D.C., gift of the Avalon Foundation (1970.6.1 PA).

## Reflecting on the Unit

### OPTION 1

**Ways to Respond to Prejudice**  Review the selections in Part 1, "A New Cultural Identity." What possible responses to prejudice and mistreatment do they suggest? Think about the range of responses to prejudice shown in the selections. Then, with a small group of classmates, discuss which responses to prejudice you think are the most effective.

### OPTION 2

**What's New?**  Recall the opening quotation of this unit: "Make it new!" What do you think the writers in this unit have done to make their writing different from earlier American literature? Jot down your ideas about each selection, and then, in a paragraph, explain which selection seems most innovative to you.

**THINK ABOUT**
- the use of rhyme and other techniques in the poetry selections
- the subject matter of all the selections
- the attitudes expressed
- the writers' styles

### OPTION 3

**The Iceberg Principle**  Recall Ernest Hemingway's comment that in his writing, seven-eighths of the story is concealed. Is that true for other selections in Part 2 of this unit? Working with a small group, create an iceberg chart for each selection, with a line dividing the iceberg into one-eighth above and seven-eighths below. Above the line, write what is stated or shown about the characters. Below the line, write what the reader must infer. Which selections require readers to make the most inferences?

**1066**    UNIT SIX   THE MODERN AGE

## Self ASSESSMENT

**READER'S NOTEBOOK**

To explore how your understanding of modern literature has developed over the course of the unit, jot down words and phrases that you associate with this literature. Then circle at least three words and phrases that you think describe modern literature most accurately. Pair up with a classmate and compare your list with your partner's, explaining your choices.

## Reviewing Literary Concepts

OPTION 1

**Modernist Characters and Techniques** What defines a modernist character? What are modernist literary techniques? For each selection from Part 2, identify modernist qualities of the main character(s) and/or modernist techniques used by the writer, such as understatement, irony, or stream of consciousness. Provide examples from the selections. Then write two paragraphs summarizing modernist character traits and literary techniques.

OPTION 2

**Comparing Poets' Styles** You have read several important American poets in this unit: Langston Hughes, Robert Frost, T. S. Eliot, and Gwendolyn Brooks. In fact, you have read more than one work by Hughes, Frost, and Brooks. What is distinctive about the styles of these four poets? Gather in a small group and list recognizable features of each poet's work in a chart. To test your knowledge, find another poem by one of these authors, circulate it without a title or author name, and see if your classmates can guess who wrote it.

## Building Your Portfolio

- **Writing Options** For several of the Writing Options in this unit, you either wrote a personal response to an author's ideas or imagined how two authors would respond to each other. Which of these assignments best demonstrates your understanding of an author? Explain in a cover letter and add the assignment to your **Presentation Portfolio.**

- **Writing Workshop** Earlier in the unit you wrote an Historical Research Report about the Harlem Renaissance or some other topic of interest. Evaluate your report—what was the most interesting discovery you made as you researched? What more would you like to find out? How clear is your presentation of facts? Answer these questions in an attached cover note and place your research report in your **Presentation Portfolio.**

- **Additional Activities** Review the assignments you completed under **Activities & Explorations** and **Inquiry & Research.** Keep a record in your portfolio of any you feel are representative of your best work.

### Self ASSESSMENT

**READER'S NOTEBOOK**

Thinking back over the literary concepts discussed in this unit, look for connections and distinctions between them. If you are unsure of any of these concepts, consult the **Glossary of Literary Terms** (page 1342) for definitions.

| | |
|---|---|
| rhythm | literary criticism |
| iambic pentameter | blank verse |
| | form |
| extended metaphor | stream of consciousness |
| figurative language | imagery |
| autobiographical essay | third-person limited point of view |
| open letter | dramatic irony |
| paradox | situational irony |
| analogy | speaker |
| diction | persona |

### Self ASSESSMENT

At this point your **Presentation Portfolio** probably has a considerable variety of your work. Think about what abilities you have developed since the beginning of the year and what kinds of writing or activities you would like to experiment with before the end of the year.

### Setting GOALS

As you read the selections in this unit, you might have wondered how economic, social, or historical events affected the way the literature was written. How can you use the knowledge you have gained from other subjects to broaden your understanding of the first four decades of the 20th century? Think of a few questions you would like to have answered.

---

## Reviewing Literary Concepts

OPTION 1

Have students create two-column charts to organize the information about each selection. Label the columns on one chart "character" and "modernist traits" and label the columns on the other chart "writer" and "modernist techniques." They can use details from their charts in their summaries.

OPTION 2

Students can create a cluster chart for each of the poets in which they identify distinctive characteristics. Ask students to consider style, theme, mood, and tone.

## Building Your Portfolio

Students will use their Presentation Portfolios to file what they consider their highest quality work—the very best projects and activities from their Working Portfolios.

For more information on using writing and assessing portfolios, see the Teacher's Guide to Assessment and Portfolio Use, p. 53.

## War Abroad and Conflict at Home

The selections in Unit Seven reflect the effects of World War II and the Vietnam War on the American psyche and highlight some of the issues of the postwar period, such as racial equality and the generation gap. The first part of the unit focuses on the diversity of people's reactions to World War II and the Vietnam War and the second part spotlights the tension between societal forces that bring people together and others that tear them apart.

### ——— Part 1 ———

**Remembering the Wars** The selections in this part of the unit explore Americans' reactions to World War II and the Vietnam War. From their reading, students will be able to compare and contrast people's responses to these two conflicts. **Traditions Across Time** analyzes moral, social, political, and personal aspects of the Vietnam War.

### ——— Part 2 ———

**Integration and Disintegration** The works in this part show how a diverse group of writers reacted to the upheavals and social changes that characterized postwar America. They reflect the emerging significance of minority cultures that resulted from the civil rights movement and the rebellion against conformity and authority that began in the 1960s. The selections in **Traditions Across Time** highlight the dramatic changes that have taken place in American society during the last two decades, emphasizing the issues of youth violence, immigration, and language.

# War ABROAD and Conflict

##  Mini Lesson — Viewing and Representing

*Ominous Omen*
**by Rupert Garcia**

**ART APPRECIATION**
**Instruction** Rupert Garcia (b. 1941) is one of the best known Chicano artists, first achieving prominence for his antiwar posters and drawings. His knowledge of the Vietnam War came from guarding airplanes and bombs at a secret base in the jungles of Thailand in the late 1960s. Later, back in the United States, he studied art in

San Francisco. Like his 1987 *Ominous Omen*, a huge canvas about 4′ × 11′, many of Garcia's canvases seem related to his experiences in Vietnam.

**Ask: What feelings do you think Garcia is trying to elicit from viewers?**
**Possible Response:** The artist is trying to create feelings of chaos, anger, confusion, fright, anxiety, desperation, and helplessness.

# War is a poor chisel
## to carve out tomorrows.

**MARTIN LUTHER KING, JR.**

MINISTER AND CIVIL RIGHTS LEADER

## at HOME

*Ominous Omen* (1987), Rupert Garcia. Chalk, linseed oil, oil paint on canvas, 47″ × 130″, courtesy of Rupert Garcia; Rena Bransten Gallery, San Francisco; and Galerie Claude Samuel, Paris. Copyright © Rupert Garcia.

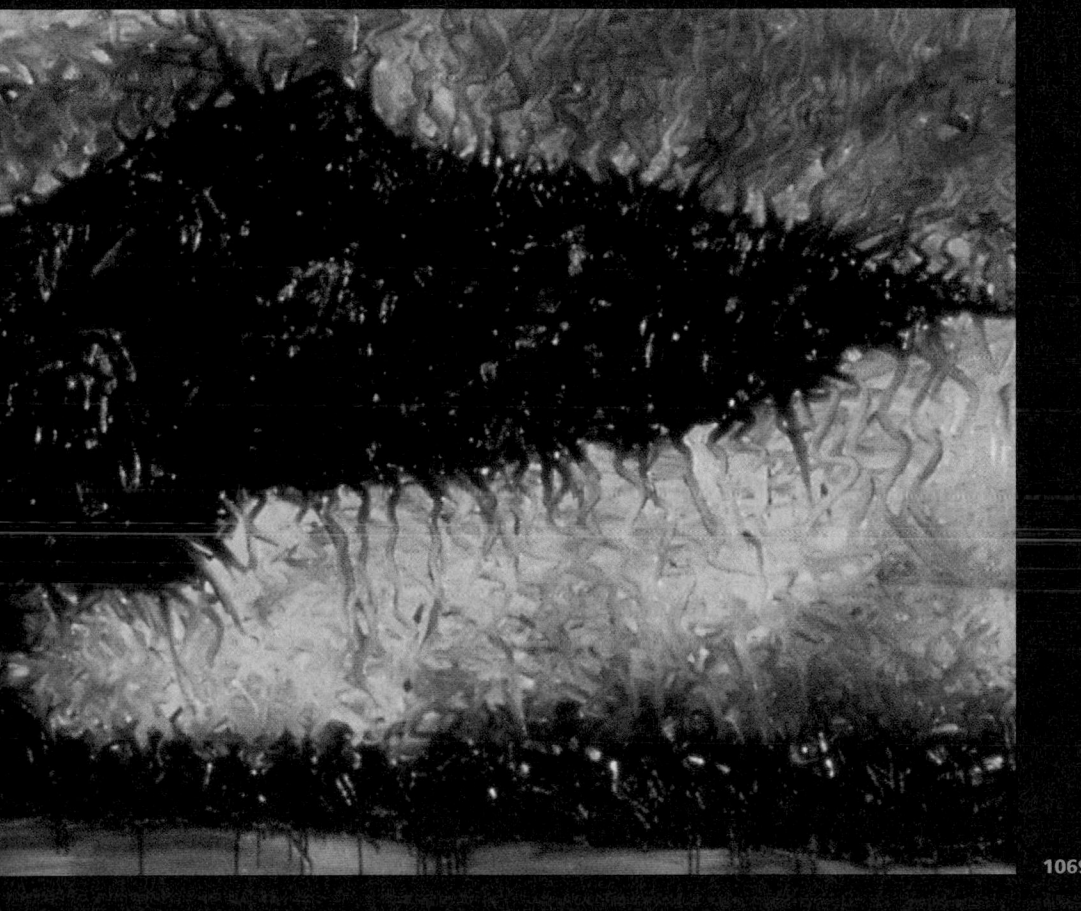

1069

| Features and Selections | Literary Analysis | Reading and Critical Thinking | Writing Opportunities | | |
|---|---|---|---|---|---|
| **War Abroad and Conflict at Home** <br> **Time Line** <br> **Historical Background/ Remembering the Wars** | | | | | |
| SHORT STORY <br> Armistice | Theme and Title, 1076, 1085 <br><br> Review: Point of View, 1085 | Conclusions about Character, 1076, 1085 <br> Informal Assess., 1084 | Analysis, 1086 <br> Letter to Editor, 1086 <br> Paragraph, 1086 <br> Presentation, 1086 | | |
| POETRY <br> The Death of the Ball Turret Gunner <br> ESSAY <br> Why Soldiers Won't Talk | Imagery and Tone, 1088, 1093 | Adjusting Reading Strategies, 1088, 1093 | Grave Inscriptions, 1094 <br> Personal Narrative, 1094 <br> Informal Assess, 1092 | | |
| ESSAY <br> Letter from Paradise, 21° 19′ N., 157° 52′ W. <br> POETRY <br> Related Reading <br> In Response to Executive Order 9066 | Mood, 1095, 1101 | Comparing Mood, 1095, 1101 <br><br> Analyzing an Issue, 1103 <br> Mood, 1099 | Memoir, 1102 | | |
| SHORT STORY <br> Comparing Literature <br> Ambush | Internal Conflict, 1105, 1109 <br> Review: Title, 1109 | Connecting to Experience, 1105, 1109 | Exhibit Proposal, 1110 <br> Points of Comparison, 1110 | | |
| POETRY <br> Comparing Literature <br> Camouflaging the Chimera <br> Deciding | Speaker in Poetry, 1111, 1117 | Structure in Poetry, 1111, 1117 | Points of Comparison, 1117 <br><br> Letter Writing, 1115 | | |
| POETRY <br> Comparing Literature <br> At the Justice Department, November 15, 1969 | Style, 1118, 1120 | Making Inferences, 1118, 1120 | TV Script, 1121 <br><br> Antiwar Storyboard, 1121 <br> Points of Comparison, 1121 <br> Summary, 1119 | | |
| Comparing Literature <br> Assessment Practice | Analyze Details, 1122 | Reading the Prompt, 1122 | Analytical Essay, 1122 | | |
| Communication Workshop: <br> Multimedia Exhibit <br> Assessment Practice <br> Building Vocabulary <br> Sentence Crafting | | | Multimedia Exhibit, 1126 | | |

| | | | | | |
|---|---|---|---|---|---|
| **Historical Background/ Integration and Disintegration** | | | | | |
| LETTER <br> Letter from Birmingham Jail | Allusion, 1136, 1146 | Logical Argument, 1136, 1146 <br> Test Practice, 1145 | Defining a Hero, 1147 <br> Editorial, 1147 <br> Compare-and-Contrast Essay, 1147 | | |
| Learning the Language of Literature <br> Tone in Contemporary Literature | | Reading Strategies, 1149 | | | |

LEGEND    **DLS – Daily Language SkillBuilder**
           **CCL – Cross Curricular Link**      **Green type – Teacher's Edition**

| Speaking and Listening Viewing and Representing | Inquiry and Research | Grammar, Usage, and Mechanics | Vocabulary |
|---|---|---|---|
| Art Appreciation, 1068 | | | |
| Readers Theater Performance, 1086 Memory Illustration, 1086 Art Appreciation, 1081 Role-Playing, 1082 | History of Anti-Semitism, 1086 German Victory, 1086 Conflicting Impressions, 1086 | DLS, 1076 Complements, 1087 | Context Clues, 1087 Context Clues, 1077 Prefixes, 1083 |
| Interview, 1091 Model Plane, 1094 Interview, 1091 | Shell Shock, 1094 | Rhythm, 1094 | Suffixes, 1090 |
| Contrasting Cartoons, 1102 Poem Recitation, 1100 | Japanese-American Internment, 1102 | DLS, 1095 Placement of Only, 1102 | Prefixes, 1097 |
| Movie Score, 1110 Art Appreciation, 1107 | Guerrilla Tactics, 1110 | DLS, 1105 Adverbs, 1110 | Context Clues, 1106 |
| Environmental Effects of War, 1117 | | DLS, 1111 Punctuation, 1117 | Context to Understand Figurative Language, 1112 |
| Opinion Poster, 1121 War Debate, 1121 | Impact of Antiwar Protests, 1121 | Varying Sentence Closers, 1121 | |
| | | | |
| | | Revising and Editing, 1129 Sentence Closers, 1131 | Analyzing Word Parts— Affixes, 1130 |
| | | | |
| Poster Design, 1147 Dramatic Skit, 1147 Photographs as Chronicles, 1140 Persuasive Speech, 1147 | Civil Rights Today, 1147 | DLS, 1136 Verbs, 1142 | Meaning Clues, 1147 Context Clues, 1138 Latin Roots, 1144 |
| | | | |

| Features and Selections | Literary Analysis | Reading and Critical Thinking | Writing Opportunities | | |
|---|---|---|---|---|---|
| **DRAMA** <br> Wandering | Tone and Dialogue, 1150, 1155 | Visualizing Stage Directions, 1150, 1155 <br> Informal Assess., 1152 | Drama Review, 1156 <br> Play Outline, 1156 | | |
| **SHORT STORY** <br> The Writer in the Family | Plot, 1157, 1166 | Drawing Conclusions, 1157, 1166 | Obituary, 1167 <br> Definition of Success, 1167 <br> Workplace Link, 1164 | | |
| **SHORT STORY** <br> Teenage Wasteland | Character, 1168, 1178 | Recognizing Details, 1168, 1178 <br> Informal Assess., 1177 | Rewritten Episode, 1179 <br> Persuasive Speech, 1179 | | |
| **SHORT STORY** <br> Separating | Dramatic Irony, 1180, 1191 <br><br> Review: Point of View, 1191 | Making Predictions, 1180, 1191 <br> Point of View, 1187 <br> Workplace Link, 1188 <br> Predictions, 1190 | Diary Entry, 1192 <br><br> Character Analysis, 1192 <br> Story Forecast, 1192 | | |
| **POETRY** <br> Mexicans Begin Jogging <br> Legal Alien | Tone, 1194, 1198 | Comparing Writers' Attitudes, 1198 | Editorial, 1199 | | |
| **SHORT STORY** <br> **Comparing Literature** <br> Hostage | Character, 1200, 1212 <br><br> Informal Assess., 1207 | Making Judgments, 1200, 1212 <br><br> Test Practice, 1211 | Character Sketch, 1213 <br><br> Expository Essay, 1213 <br><br> Literary Review, 1213 <br> Points of Comparison, 1213 | | |
| **ESSAY** <br> **Comparing Literature** <br> Mother Tongue | Personal Essay, 1215, 1221 | Main Ideas and Supporting Details, 1215, 1221 | Story Evaluation, 1222 <br> Points of Comparison, 1222 <br> Author Activity, 1222 <br> Letter, 1220 | | |
| **POETRY** <br> **Comparing Literature** <br> The Latin Deli: An Ars Poetica | Imagery, 1223, 1225 <br><br> Review: Title, 1225 | Analyzing Descriptive Details, 1223, 1225 | Description of a Place, 1226 <br> Grocery List, 1226 <br> Points of Comparison, 1226 | | |
| **ESSAY** <br> **Comparing Literature** <br> Staw into Gold: The Metamorphosis of the Everyday | Voice, 1227, 1232 | Analyzing Structure, 1227, 1232 | Letter of Advice, 1233 <br><br> Points of Comparison, 1233 | | |
| **Comparing Literature** <br> **Assessment Practice** | Evaluate Literary Work, 1234 | Reading the Prompt, 1234 | Evaluative Essay, 1234 | | |
| **Reflect and Assess** <br> **War Abroad and Conflict at Home** | Tone, 1237 <br> LinkingTitle and Theme, 1237 | Issues for Today and the Future, 1236 <br> Kinds of Courage, 1236 | Pictures of War, 1236 <br><br> Building Your Portfolio, 1237 | | |

To introduce the theme/literary period of this unit, use Fine Art Transparencies T35–37 in the Communications Transparencies and Copymasters.

|  | Unit Resource Book | Assessment | Integrated Technology and Media | Additional Support — Literary Analysis Transparencies |
|---|---|---|---|---|
| **Armistice** <br> *pp. 1076–1087* | • Summary p. 4 <br> • Active Reading p. 5 <br> • Literary Analysis p. 6 <br> • Words to Know p. 7 <br> • Selection Quiz p. 8 | • Selection Test, Formal Assessment pp. 201–202 <br> Test Generator | Audio Library <br><br> Research Starter www.mcdougallittell.com | • Point of View T20 |
| **The Death of the Ball Turret Gunner** <br> **Why Soldiers Won't Talk** <br> *pp. 1088–1094* | • Summary (Why Soldiers Won't Talk) p. 9 <br> • Active Reading p. 10 <br> • Literary Analysis p. 11 <br> • Selection Quiz (Why Soldiers Won't Talk) p. 12 | • Selection Test, Formal Assessment pp. 203–204 <br> Test Generator | Audio Library | • Tone T19 |
| **Letter from Paradise, 21° 19´N., 157° 52´W.** <br> **In Response to Executive Order 9066** <br> *pp. 1095–1102* | • Summary p. 13 <br> • Active Reading p. 14 <br> • Literary Analysis p. 15 <br> • Selection Quiz p. 16 | • Selection Test, Formal Assessment pp. 205–206 <br> Test Generator | Audio Library <br><br> Research Starter www.mcdougallittell.com | • Mood T18 |
| **Ambush (1990)** <br> *pp. 1105–1110* | • Summary p. 17 <br> • Active Reading p. 18 <br> • Literary Analysis p. 19 <br> • Selection Quiz p. 20 | • Selection Test, Formal Assessment pp. 207–208 <br> Test Generator | Audio Library <br><br> Research Starter www.mcdougallittell.com | • Multiple Conflicts/Themes T15 |
| **Camouflaging the Chimera (1988)** <br> **Deciding (1986)** <br> *pp. 1111–1117* | • Active Reading p. 21 <br> • Literary Analysis p. 22 | • Selection Test, Formal Assessment pp. 209–210 <br> Test Generator | Audio Library | |
| **At the Justice Department, November 15, 1969** <br> *pp. 1118–1121* | • Active Reading p. 23 <br> • Literary Analysis p. 24 <br> • Comparing Literature p. 25 | • Selection Test, Formal Assessment pp. 211–212 <br> Test Generator | Audio Library | • Style, Voice T23 |

| Communication Workshop: Multimedia Exhibit | *Unit Assessment* | *Unit Technology* | |
|---|---|---|---|
| **Unit Seven Resource Book** <br> • Planning Your Exhibit p. 26 <br> • Preparing Your Exhibit p. 27 <br> • Peer Response Guide pp. 28–29 <br> • Refining Your Exhibit p. 30 <br> • Standards for Evaluation p. 31 | • Unit Seven, Part 1 Test, Formal Assessment pp. 213–214 <br> Test Generator <br> • Unit Seven Integrated Test, Integrated Assessment pp. 57–72 | ClassZone www.mcdougallittell.com <br> EasyPlanner CD-ROM <br> Electronic Library | |

| Reading and Critical Thinking Transparencies | Grammar Transparencies and Copymasters | Vocabulary Transparencies and Copymasters | Writing Transparencies and Copymasters | Communications Transparencies and Copymasters |
|---|---|---|---|---|
| • Drawing Conclusions T4 | • Daily Language SkillBuilder T30<br>• Complements C79 | • Prefixes C90 | • Opinion Statement C34<br>• Interpretive Essay C36 | • Impromptu Speaking: Dialogue, Role-Play, Debate T13 |
| • Main Idea and Supporting Details T12<br>• Interviewing T39 | • Repetition vs. Redundancy C171 | • Suffixes C91 | • Autobiographical Incident C35 | • Interviewing T9<br>• Impromptu Speaking: Dialogue, Role-Play, Debate T13 |
| • Compare and Contrast T15 | • Daily Language SkillBuilder T31<br>• Compound Adjectives C70 | • Prefixes C90 | • Showing, Not Telling T22 | • Appreciative Listening T2 |
| • Noting Details T9<br>• Classification Tree T58 | • Daily Language SkillBuilder T31<br>• Adverb Qualifiers C71 | • Context Clues C92 | • Literary Interpretation C30 | • Appreciative Listening T2 |
| • Analyzing Text Structure T17<br>• Compare and Contrast T15 | • Daily Language SkillBuilder T31<br>• Capitalization II C145 | • Figurative Language C93 | • The Uses of Dialogue T24 | |
| • Making Inferences T7<br>• Using a Vertical Organizational Chart T52 | • Varying Sentence Closers C172 | | • Eyewitness Report C25 | • Impromptu Speaking: Dialogue, Role-Play, Debate T13 |

## STUDENTS ACQUIRING ENGLISH

The **Spanish Study Guide,** pp. 266–287, includes language support for the following pages:
• Family and Community Involvement (per unit)

• Selection Summaries and Vocabulary
• Active Reading
• Literary Analysis

To introduce the theme/literary period of this unit, use Fine Art Transparencies T35–37 in the Communications Transparencies and Copymasters.

| | Unit Resource Book | Assessment | Integrated Technology and Media | Additional Support — Literary Analysis Transparencies |
|---|---|---|---|---|
| **Letter from Birmingham Jail** *pp. 1136–1147* | • Summary p. 34<br>• Active Reading p. 35<br>• Literary Analysis p. 36<br>• Words to Know p. 37<br>• Selection Quiz p. 38 | • Selection Test, Formal Assessment pp. 215–216<br>◉ Test Generator | ◯ Audio Library | |
| **Wandering** *pp. 1150–1156* | • Summary p. 39<br>• Active Reading p. 40<br>• Literary Analysis p. 41<br>• Selection Quiz p. 42<br>• Comparing Literature p. 43 | • Selection Test, Formal Assessment pp. 217–218<br>◉ Test Generator | ◯ Audio Library | • Tone T19 |
| **The Writer in the Family** *pp. 1157–1167* | • Summary p. 44<br>• Active Reading p. 45<br>• Literary Analysis p. 46<br>• Words to Know p. 47<br>• Selection Quiz p. 48 | • Selection Test, Formal Assessment pp. 219–220<br>◉ Test Generator | ◯ Audio Library | • Multiple Conflicts/ Themes T15 |
| **Teenage Wasteland** *pp. 1168–1179* | • Summary p. 49<br>• Active Reading p. 50<br>• Literary Analysis p. 51<br>• Words to Know p. 52<br>• Selection Quiz p. 53 | • Selection Test, Formal Assessment pp. 221–222<br>◉ Test Generator | ◯ Audio Library | • Character: Change and Motivation T7 |
| **Separating** *pp. 1180–1193* | • Summary p. 54<br>• Active Reading p. 55<br>• Literary Analysis p. 56<br>• Words to Know p. 57<br>• Selection Quiz p. 58 | • Selection Test, Formal Assessment pp. 223–224<br>◉ Test Generator | ◯ Audio Library | |
| **Mexicans Begin Jogging Legal Alien** *pp. 1194–1199* | • Active Reading p. 59<br>• Literary Analysis p. 60 | • Selection Test, Formal Assessment pp. 225–226<br>◉ Test Generator | ◯ Audio Library | |
| **Hostage (1991)** *pp. 1200–1214* | • Summary p. 61<br>• Active Reading p. 62<br>• Literary Analysis p. 63<br>• Words to Know p. 64<br>• Selection Quiz p. 65 | • Selection Test, Formal Assessment pp. 227–228<br>◉ Test Generator | ◯ Audio Library<br>ⓘ Research Starter www.mcdougallittell.com | • Characterization T6 |
| **Mother Tongue (1990)** *pp. 1215–1222* | • Summary p. 66<br>• Active Reading p. 67<br>• Literary Analysis p. 68<br>• Words to Know p. 69<br>• Selection Quiz p. 70 | • Selection Test, Formal Assessment pp. 229–230<br>◉ Test Generator | ◯ Audio Library | |
| **The Latin Deli: An Ars Poetica (1991)** *pp. 1223–1226* | • Active Reading p. 71<br>• Literary Analysis p. 72 | • Selection Test, Formal Assessment pp. 231–232<br>◉ Test Generator | ◯ Audio Library | |
| **Straw into Gold: The Metamorphosis of the Everyday (1987)** *pp. 1227–1233* | • Summary p. 73<br>• Active Reading p. 74<br>• Literary Analysis p. 75<br>• Words to Know p. 76<br>• Selection Quiz p. 77<br>• Comparing Literature p. 78 | • Selection Test, Formal Assessment pp. 233–234<br>◉ Test Generator | | • Style, Voice T23 |
| | | **Unit Assessment**<br>• Unit Seven, Part 2 Test, Formal Assessment pp. 235–236<br>• End-of-Year Test, Formal Assessment pp. 237–248<br>◉ Test Generator<br>• Unit Seven Integrated Test, Integrated Assessment pp. 57–66<br>• End-of-Year Integrated Assessment pp. 67–86 | **Unit Technology**<br>ⓘ ClassZone www.mcdougallittell.com<br>◉ EasyPlanner CD-ROM<br>◉ Electronic Library | |

| Reading and Critical Thinking Transparencies | Grammar Transparencies and Copymasters | Vocabulary Transparencies and Copymasters | Writing Transparencies and Copymasters | Communications Transparencies and Copymasters |
|---|---|---|---|---|
| • Evaluating Argumentation II T21 | • Daily Language SkillBuilder T32<br>• Verbs: Voice and Mood C119 | • Latin Roots C94 | • Persuasive Essay C27<br>• Compare-Contrast C31 | • Evaluating Roles in Groups T8<br>• Impromptu Speaking: Dialogue, Role-Play, Debate T13 |
| • Visualizing T8 | • Daily Language SkillBuilder T32<br>• Proliferating Prepositional Phrases C173 | | • Critical Review C26 | • Dramatic Reading T12 |
| • Drawing Conclusions T4<br>• Dialoguing Frame T54 | • Daily Language SkillBuilder T32<br>• Verbs: Active and Passive Voice C68<br>• Unnecessary Commas C155 | • Context Clues C18 | • Topic Sentences and Thesis Statements T6 | |
| • Noting Details T9 | • Daily Language SkillBuilder T33<br>• Progressive and Emphatic Verb Forms C118 | • Synonyms and Antonyms C96 | • Persuasive Essay C27 | • Impromptu Speaking: Dialogue, Role-Play, Debate T13 |
| • Predicting Outcomes T2 | • Daily Language SkillBuilder T33<br>• Advanced Sentences: Sentence Openers C174<br>• Advanced Sentences: Periodic Sentences C175 | • Context Clues C18 | | • Verbal Strategies T14<br>• Nonverbal Strategies T15<br>• Interviewing T9 |
| • Comparing Authors' Views T23 | • Daily Language SkillBuilder T33<br>• Varying Types of Sentences C176 | • The Connotative Power of Words C95 | • Opinion Statement C34 | |
| • Making Judgments I5<br>• Events and Consequences T57<br>• Line Plots, Bar Graphs, Pie Charts T36-38 | • Daily Language SkillBuilder T34<br>• Interrupting Elements C177 | • Synonyms and Antonyms C96 | • Literary Interpretation C30 | • Impromptu Speaking: Dialogue, Role-Play, Debate T13 |
| • Spider Map T47<br>• Evaluation Matrix T55 | • Daily Language SkillBuilder T34<br>• Cohesion—Reader Expectation C178 | | • Critical Review C26 | • Appreciative Listening T2 |
| • Cluster Diagram T48<br>• Observation Chart T46<br>• Organizational Chart: Horizontal T51 | • Pronouns—Personal, Reflexive, and Intensive T39<br>• Indefinite Pronouns T40<br>• Types of Pronouns C65 | | • Sensory Word List T14<br>• Compare-Contrast C31 | • Impromptu Speaking: Dialogue, Role-Play, Debate T13 |
| • Compare and Contrast T15 | • Daily Language SkillBuilder T34<br>• Sentence Fragments T42<br>• Noun Phrases C179<br>• Style: Deliberate Fragments C180 | • Context Clues C18 | • Compare-Contrast T32 | |

## STUDENTS ACQUIRING ENGLISH

The **Spanish Study Guide,** pp. 288–317, includes language support for the following pages:
• Family and Community Involvement (per unit)
• Selection Summaries and Vocabulary
• Active Reading
• Literary Analysis

| Selection | SkillBuilder Sentences | Suggested Answers |
|---|---|---|
| Armistice | 1. The concern of Morris Lieberman were not for hisself but for Jews suffering from Nazi prosecution in Europe. | 1. The concern of Morris Lieberman **was** not for **himself** but for Jews suffering from Nazi **persecution** in Europe. |
| | 2. Staring Robert Redford, the novel, the natural, is one of Malamuds most wide known works because it was made into a movie. | 2. **The** novel **The Natural** is one of Malamud's most **widely** known works because it was made into a movie **starring** Robert Redford. |
| Letter from Paradise, 21° 19'N., 157° 52'W. In Response to Executive Order 9066 | 1. The japanese american speaker and Denise is best friends. | 1. The **Japanese-American** speaker and Denise **are** best friends. |
| | 2. Pearl Harbor in Oahu Hawaii was bombd on December 7 1941. | 2. Pearl Harbor in Oahu, Hawaii, was bomb**ed** on December 7, 1941. |
| Ambush | 1. Anyone who have been in active combat knows there is no triumf in war. | 1. Anyone who **has** been in active combat knows there is no **triumph** in war. |
| | 2. Conceled by the jungle brush along the trail he laid in wait to attack. | 2. **Concealed** by the jungle brush along the trail, he **lay** in wait to attack. |
| Camouflaging the Chimera Deciding | 1. The poets tran thi nga and yusef komunyakaa whom actually endured the war bring their experiences to the conscienceness of others'. | 1. The poets **Tran Thi Nga** and **Yusef Komunyakaa, who** actually endured the war, bring their experiences to the **consciousness** of **others**. |
| | 2. Whose gonna read the poems during the presentation asked the teacher. | 2. **"Who is going to** read the poems during the presentation?"** asked the teacher. |

| Selection | SkillBuilder Sentences | Suggested Answers |
| --- | --- | --- |
| Letter from Birmingham Jail | 1. He wrote this letter to emfasize the need for direct action, in it he sets fourth his guiding principals. | 1. He wrote this letter to **emphasize** the need for direct action. **In it**, he set **forth** his guiding **principles**. |
| Wandering | 1. The character name Him does'nt belive in war. | 1. The character **named** Him **doesn't believe** in war. |
|  | 2. The characters, She and He, wants Him to have the same ideals they do have. | 2. The characters She and He **want** Him to have the same ideals they **have**. |
| The Writer in the Family | 1. Its to bad that sometimes theres simple misunderstandings in a family that creates a lot of resentmint. | 1. It**'s too** bad that sometimes simple misunderstandings in a family **create lasting resentment**. |
|  | 2. If people talk to their familys honest and open a lot of divisivness might be avoided. | 2. If people **could** talk **honestly** and **openly with** their **families,** a lot of **divisiveness** might be avoided. |
| Teenage Wasteland | 1. Teenage wasteland and I stand here ironing is both about troubled families. | 1. "Teenage **W**asteland" and "I **S**tand **H**ere **I**roning" **are** both about troubled families. |
|  | 2. Rebellion is normal part of growing up it can go too far. | 2. Rebellion is **a** normal part of growing up, **but** it can go too far. |

| Selection | SkillBuilder Sentences | Suggested Answers |
|---|---|---|
| Separating | 1. The story, Seperating, depicts a painful episode in the lifes of the Maples an upper-middle-class family.<br><br>2. John Updike is quoted as saying, the moral of these stories are that all blessings are mixed. | 1. The story **"Separating"** depicts a painful episode in the **lives** of the Maples, an upper-middle-class family.<br><br>2. John Updike is quoted as saying, **"The** moral of these stories **is** that all blessings are mixed." |
| Mexicans Begin Jogging<br>Legal Alien | 1. Both poets has remembered his Mexican-American backgrounds.<br><br>2. There is irony, imagery, and metaphors in legal alien and Mexicans begin Jogging. | 1. Both poets **have** remembered **their** Mexican-American backgrounds.<br><br>2. There **are** irony, imagery, and metaphors in **"Legal A**lien" and "Mexicans **B**egin Jogging." |
| Hostage | 1. Joyce Carol Oates' is a prolific author who has wrote many novels short stories essays and poems. Averaging two books a year.<br><br>2. Oate's style is sometimes likened to Flannery O'Connors' both writers delve into the darker side of human nature. | 1. Joyce Carol **Oates** is a prolific author who has **written** many novels, short stories, essays, and poems. **She averages** two books a year.<br><br>2. **Oates's** style is sometimes likened to Flannery **O'Connor's because** both writers delve into the darker side of human nature. |
| Mother Tongue | 1. Its a kind of english she learnt at home.<br><br>2. Tans first book The Joy Luck Club was a huge success. | 1. It's a kind of **E**nglish she **learned** at home.<br><br>2. Tan's first book, **The Joy Luck Club**, was a huge success. |
| Straw into Gold: The Metamorphosis of the Everyday | 1. From Sandra Cisneros experiences comes the building blocks of her fiction and nonfiction proclaimed the publishers quotation.<br><br>2. She has did more than she ever would of thought possible her words in this essay gives encouragement to others. | 1. "From Sandra Cisneros**'s** experiences **come** the building blocks of her fiction and nonfiction," proclaimed the publisher**'s** quotation.<br><br>2. She has **done** more than she ever would **have** thought possible. **H**er words in this essay **give** encouragement to others. |

| Grammar Focus by Unit | Unit One | Unit Two | Unit Three | Unit Four | Unit Five | Unit Six | Unit Seven |
|---|---|---|---|---|---|---|---|
| | Parts of a Sentence | Verbs | Phrases | Clauses, Part I | Clauses, Part II | Special Sentence Structures, Part I | Special Sentence Structures, Part II |

*The Language of Literature* offers several options for integrating grammar instruction and literature.

- Each literature unit has a grammar focus. The Teacher's Edition includes Mini Lessons for each selection that help develop the grammar focus for the unit and spring from the content of the specific literature.
- The Pupil Edition includes several full-page lessons on Sentence Crafting. These lessons are related to both the literature and the grammar focus for the unit and help students use grammar in their own writing.
- Daily Language SkillBuilders in the Teacher's Edition provide students with ongoing proofreading practice and reinforce punctuation, spelling, grammar and usage, and capitalization.
- Grammar Copymasters and Transparencies, which may be used to complement or extend lessons in the Teacher's Edition, present grammar in a traditional, systematic sequence. References to appropriate copymasters or transparencies are included at point of use in the Teacher's Edition Mini Lessons.

TE Mini Lessons shown in green
**PE instruction shown in black**

## Part 1

**Parts of Speech**

**Adverbials: *only***
"Letter from Paradise, 21° 19′ N., 157° 52′ W.," "In Response to Executive Order 9066," p. 1102

**Adverbials: The Qualifiers**
"Ambush," p. 1110

**Parts of the Sentence**

**Complements**
"Armistice," p. 1087

**Using Clauses**

**Sentence Fragments**
Communication Workshop, p. 1129

**Subject-Verb Agreement**
Communication Workshop, p. 1129

**Capitalization**

**Capitalizing Proper Nouns and Proper Adjectives**
"Camouflaging the Chimera," "Deciding," p. 1117

**Other Punctuation**

**Punctuation: Dashes**
Sentence Crafting, p. 1131

**Style**

**Creating Complex Sentences**
Communication Workshop, p. 1129
**Rhythm: Repetition vs. Redundancy**
"The Death of the Ball Turret Gunner," "Why Soldiers Won't Talk," p. 1094

**Advanced Sentences: Sentence Closers**
"At the Justice Department, November 15, 1969," p. 1121
Sentence Crafting, p. 1131

## Part 2

**Parts of Speech**

**Pronouns**
"The Latin Deli: An Ars Poetica," p. 1226

**Using Phrases**

**Prepositional Phrases**
"Wandering," p. 1156

**Verb Usage**

**Verbs: Progressive and Emphatic Verb Forms**
"Teenage Wasteland," pp. 1174–1175

**Using Verbs: Voice and Mood**
"Letter from Birmingham Jail," pp. 1142–1143
"The Writer in the Family," pp. 1162–1163

**End Marks and Commas**

**Unnecessary Commas**
"The Writer in the Family," pp. 1160–1161

**Style**

**Advanced Sentences: Sentence Openers**
"Separating," p. 1183

**Advanced Sentences: Periodic Sentences**
"Separating," p. 1193

**Varying Types of Sentences**
"Mexicans Begin Jogging," "Legal Alien," p. 1199

**Interrupting Elements: Descriptions That Split Subject and Verb**
"Hostage," p. 1214

**Cohesion: Reader Expectation**
"Mother Tongue," p. 1222

**Noun Phrases**
"Straw into Gold: the Metamorphosis of the Everyday," p. 1231

**Style: Deliberate Fragments**
"Straw into Gold: the Metamorphosis of the Everyday," p. 1233

This time line shows major dates and events in America and the world from the 1940s to the late 1990s. Help students recognize that these six decades are characterized worldwide by war and by social and political revolution.

## United States: 1941

**A** The attack on Pearl Harbor began at 7:55 A.M. on December 7. By 9:45 A.M., 18 ships of the U.S. fleet had been sunk or critically disabled, about 190 planes had been destroyed or badly damaged, and some 2,400 people had been killed. This was more damage than had been inflicted on the U.S. Navy during the entire First World War. Yet just six months later, the U.S. Navy scored a major victory over Japanese forces at Midway, a strategic island in the middle of the Pacific Ocean, and the tide of war began shifting.

## World: 1940

**B** The outlook for Europe in 1940 was especially grim. By then, German forces had overrun Austria, Czechoslovakia, Poland, Norway, the Netherlands, Belgium, and finally France. Braced for a German invasion, Britain was the only major country in the region still resisting. CBS broadcaster Edward R. Murrow was on the scene in London, sending back to America grim accounts of the German bombardment of England during the Battle of Britain.

## World: 1948

**C** The Nazi persecution of Jews had greatly increased the flow of European Jews to Palestine, a historic region on the eastern banks of the Mediterranean Sea. This strained relations between Arabs and Jews there, and in 1947 the United Nations partitioned the region into separate Jewish and Arab states over the protests of neighboring Arab countries. When the State of Israel was officially proclaimed in 1948, Egypt, Jordan, Syria, Lebanon, and Iraq immediately declared war upon it.

## Literature: 1951

**D** A 1998 poll of writers and scholars ranked *The Catcher in the Rye* 64th

# War
### ABROAD and Conflict at HOME

## EVENTS IN AMERICAN LITERATURE

**1940**

**1940** John Steinbeck wins Pulitzer Prize in fiction for *The Grapes of Wrath*

**1945** Richard Wright details coming of age in *Black Boy*; Randall Jarrell publishes poem "The Death of the Ball Turret Gunner"

**1947** Tennessee Williams's *A Streetcar Named Desire* is first produced

**D 1951** J. D. Salinger's novel *Catcher in the Rye* is published

**1952** Bernard Malamud publishes baseball novel, *The Natural*

**1953** Arthur Miller's *The Crucible*, set during the Salem witch trials in 1692, explores contemporary events surrounding McCarthy hearings

**1960**

**F 1961** Joseph Heller's satirical war novel, *Catch-22*, is published

**1962** John Steinbeck wins Nobel Prize for literature

**1963** Joyce Carol Oates publishes her first book

**1969** Kurt Vonnegut publishes *Slaughterhouse-Five*; N. Scott Momaday's *House Made of Dawn* wins Pulitzer Prize

## EVENTS IN THE UNITED STATES

**1940**

**A 1941** The Japanese bomb Pearl Harbor, bringing United States into World War II

**1945** United States drops two atomic bombs on Japan, ending war in Pacific

**1950** Senator Joseph McCarthy claims Communist spies have infiltrated government bureaus; thousands of people are falsely accused of treasonous acts

**E 1953** Korean War ends after three years of fighting between Communist troops and UN-sponsored international forces.

**1954** Ruling in *Brown* v. *Board of Education*, Supreme Court declares segregated schools unconstitutional

**1960**

**1963** President John F. Kennedy is assassinated in Dallas

**1964** Congress passes Civil Rights Act of 1964

**1965** First U.S. combat forces land in Vietnam; Malcolm X is assassinated

**G 1967** Thurgood Marshall becomes first African-American justice on Supreme Court

**1968** Assassinations of Martin Luther King, Jr., and Robert F. Kennedy

## EVENTS IN THE WORLD

**1940**

**1940** German forces conquer **B** much of Europe

**1945** Germany surrenders to Allies

**1948** State of Israel is founded; **C** South African policy of apartheid begins

**1949** Communists gain control of China

**1957** Soviet Union launches *Sputnik*, first space satellite

**1960**

**1960** Seventeen African countries gain independence

**1966** Mao Zedong launches Cultural **H** Revolution in China (to 1976)

**1967** Six-Day War erupts between Israel and Arab nations

among the 100 best English-language novels. However, a student poll taken at the same time ranked the Salinger novel 2nd, just behind Fitzgerald's *The Great Gatsby*.

## United States: 1953

**E** The Korean War is sometimes called America's forgotten war. The U.S. government never actually declared war on North Korea; instead, U.S. troops fought alongside the South Koreans as part of a United Nations "police force."

## Literature: 1961

**F** Ranked 7th and 15th respectively by the 1998 polls, this novel introduced the phrase "catch-22" into the language. In this tale, an Air Force regulation states that a man is considered insane if he willingly flies dangerous combat missions. But, making the necessary request to be taken off such missions "proves" that the man is sane and therefore ineligible to be relieved. The self-defeating regulation is "catch-22."

# PERIOD PIECES

Console TV from 1948

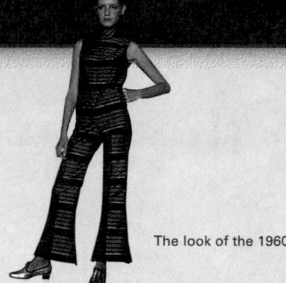

The look of the 1960s

Early digital watch

**I**

## 1980

**1970** Maya Angelou publishes autobiographical *I Know Why the Caged Bird Sings*

**1983** *The House on Mango Street* by Sandra Cisneros is published

**1985** Anne Tyler publishes *The Accidental Tourist*

**1989** Amy Tan's *The Joy Luck Club* is published

**1990** Tim O'Brien's *The Things They Carried* is published

**1993** Toni Morrison wins Nobel Prize for literature **L**

## 1980

**1969** U.S. astronauts land on moon

**1974** President Richard M. Nixon resigns to avoid impeachment over Watergate scandal **J**

**1975** First successful home VCR appears

**1977** First practical home computer, Apple II, hits market

**1981** First space shuttle, *Columbia*, is launched; Sandra Day O'Connor is first woman appointed to U.S. Supreme Court

**1989** Oil tanker *Exxon Valdez* runs aground, creating huge oil spill along Alaskan coast

**1991** Persian Gulf War breaks out, and United States leads Allied coalition against Iraq

**1995** Murrah Federal Building in Oklahoma City is bombed

**1996** Madeleine Albright becomes first woman secretary of state

**1997** Unmanned probe *Pathfinder* lands on Mars and sends back stunning pictures **M**

## 1980

**1975** South Vietnam surrenders as North Vietnamese troops occupy Saigon

**1979** Egypt's Anwar Sadat and Israel's Menachem Begin sign treaty ending war between Egypt and Israel; Soviet Union invades Afghanistan

**1985** Mikhail Gorbachev comes to power in Soviet Union and initiates reforms **K**

**1987** Palestinians begin *intifada* ("shaking off") against Israeli rule

**1989** Student demonstrators in China are killed in Tiananmen Square

**1991** Soviet Union breaks up into 15 republics; South Africa begins repeal of apartheid laws

**1992** Serbs begin war against Muslims and Croats in former Yugoslavia

**1994** Nelson Mandela is elected president of South Africa

TIME LINE **1071**

## Literature: 1993

**L** Morrison was the 11th U.S. writer to win the Nobel Prize for literature in the 92-year history of the award. She was also only the eighth woman, the second U.S. woman, and first African American to receive the prize.

## United States: 1997

**M** The *Pathfinder* probe was part of a renewed U.S. interest in space exploration in the late 1990s, which gained immeasurable public support when America's first human in space in 1962, John Glenn, went back to space as a 77-year-old in 1998.

## United States: 1967

**G** Marshall had served more than two decades as a lawyer for the NAACP, attacking racial discrimination in education, housing, and voting. He argued for the plaintiff in the case of *Brown* v. *the Board of Education* in which the Supreme Court declared school segregation unconstitutional.

## World: 1966

**H** Chinese leader Mao Zedong felt that the Soviet Union had betrayed the original principles of the communist revolution, and he launched a Cultural Revolution to stop China from following the Soviet model. To achieve the goals of the Revolution, Mao formed the Red Guards, made up of urban youths who attacked all things and people considered capitalist or bourgeois.

## PERIOD PIECES

**I** During the 1960s scientists and engineers made tremendous advances in microelectronics. Integrated circuits—tiny semiconductor chips containing interconnected transistors and other electronic devices—were developed.

## United States: 1974

**J** The scandal was named for an apartment complex in Washington, D.C. Five employees of Nixon's campaign committee were caught late at night breaking in to photograph documents and plant listening devices in the telephones of the Democratic National Committee headquarters housed there. When Nixon's role in trying to block the FBI's subsequent investigation was learned, he resigned.

## World: 1985

**K** Inadvertently, Gorbachev became one of the most important figures of the 20th century. His changes to the Soviet system—*glasnost, perestroika,* and other policies of political, economic, and social reform—ended up triggering the Soviet Union's breakup and by 1991 bringing the Cold War to an end.

## OVERVIEW

### Introduction

This article places the selections in Part 1 of this unit in historical context by providing students with a brief overview of World War II and the Vietnam War. The **Traditions Across Time** section puts the differences between the two wars into perspective. The accounts of World War II experiences quoted in **Voices from the Times** give students insight into the impact of the war on Americans. This article will enable students to interpret the possible influences of historical contexts on the literary works in this unit.

## Teaching Nonfiction

### Reading Skills and Strategies
### ESTABLISHING A PURPOSE FOR READING

Explain to students that this article will introduce them to the events leading up to World War II and America's involvement in the war and to the issues surrounding the Vietnam War. Students should read to understand the connection between the events of this period and the literature that resulted from these events.

### ACQUIRING VOCABULARY

This article contains a number of possibly unfamiliar words and historically significant terms. Ask students to note these words as they read the essay. Remind them that they are expected to use reference materials such as glossaries, dictionaries, and available technology to determine precise usage and meaning.

### NOTETAKING

Explain to students that this essay contains important dates and names. As they read, they can use notetaking as a study strategy to help them better understand the text.

# Remembering the Wars

## World War II

Images from World War II: U.S. troops roll through Europe (far right); a U.S. war propaganda poster (above); the yellow patch that European Jews were forced to wear (right); and the bombing of Pearl Harbor (below).

**World** War II was a catastrophe of epic dimensions. Never before had so many soldiers fought. Never before had such wholesale slaughter occurred. When the war finally ended in 1945, more than 78 million people had been killed or wounded. For the first time in history, more civilians than soldiers had died in a war. Adolf Hitler and the National Socialist German Workers' party, commonly called the Nazis, came to power in 1933, at the height of the Great Depression. Full of passionate intensity, Hitler set out to avenge Germany's defeat in World War I and to create a new German state called the Third Reich. He told his followers, "Close your eyes to pity! Act brutally!" Like a tidal wave, the German army overran Europe. By June 1940, British troops had retreated from Dunkirk across the English Channel.

As the Nazis surged across Europe, Hitler targeted certain groups for extermination—political dissenters, homosexuals, mental patients, Gypsies, Poles, Slavs, and especially Jews. Sometimes Jews were confined in squalid ghettoes, but most of the time they were herded into cattle cars for removal to concentration camps. By late 1942, the Nazis had set up six death camps in Poland, where thousands of Jews were gassed each day. In all, approximately 6 million Jews were systematically murdered in what became known as the Holocaust. Included in this part of the unit is Bernard Malamud's chilling story "Armistice." Set in New York City while the war rages in

Europe, the story reveals the roots of the kind of racial hatred that fueled the Holocaust. The armistice, or truce, between the two American characters at the end of the story seems unsatisfactory and temporary, just like the armistice signed by Germany and the allied European and U.S. forces at the end of World War I.

On December 7, 1941, Japanese bombers struck the American naval base at Pearl Harbor, Hawaii, killing approximately 2,000 sailors. This tragedy, which brought the United States into the war, is the occasion of Joan Didion's "Letter from Paradise." Didion describes her feelings as she visits Pearl Harbor a quarter of a century later, views the still-submerged battleships, and recalls the young men who died in the Sunday-morning sneak attack. Dwight Okita's poem "In Response to Executive Order 9066" recalls the reaction of the U.S. government to the fear engendered by Japanese aggression: the rounding up and banishing to internment camps of thousands of Japanese Americans.

The U.S. entry into the war turned the tide in favor of the Allies, but it was a long, hard fight. Two selections in this part of the unit deal with the experience of ordinary combat soldiers. Randall Jarrell's jolting poem "The Death of the Ball Turret Gunner" recalls the terror of aerial warfare, in which combatants felt painfully vulnerable under the fire of a faceless enemy. The prize-winning novelist John Steinbeck, whose work always speaks with sympathy for the common people, also reflects the point of view of the fighting soldier in his essay "Why Soldiers Won't Talk."

# Voices from the TIMES

*from*

### *"The Good War": An Oral History of World War Two*
by Studs Terkel

We were on our way to the movies on Sunday afternoon. I was twelve at the time. My dad loved Abbott and Costello. We were going to a matinee. We saw them all. On the way to the theater, the car radio was on. "Oh, my God!" my father said, "Pearl Harbor!" I said, "What's a Pearl Harbor?"

"We can't go to the movies," he said. He turned around right away. There was an outcry from the back seat: "We wanna see Abbott and Costello!" My two sisters were eight and six.

**Jean Bartlett**


On the morning of December 16, we were suddenly under a fantastic barrage. Every tank in Europe came over the hill, all the panzers in the world. We had no tanks at all. The weather was such that we had no air support. They went over our rifles like they weren't even there. We were completely cut off and surrounded. We ran through the hills, firing at anything. . . .

So there I am wandering around with the whole German army shooting at me, and all I've got is a .45 automatic. There were ample opportunities, however, because every place you went there were bodies and soldiers laying around. Mostly Americans. At one time or another, I think I had in my hands every weapon the United States Army manufactured. You'd run out of ammunition with that one, you'd throw it away and try to find something else. One time I had a submachine gun, first experience I ever had with one.

**Richard M. "Red" Prendergast**
remembering the Battle of the Bulge

# Making Connections

### Politics
**A** The Nazi secret police—the Gestapo—terrorized, arrested, tortured, and imprisoned all suspected enemies of the Nazi state. Hitler also established the elite, semiautonomous SS (Schutzstaffel), a well-trained, merciless security force that protected the Reich and supervised the concentration camps. The SS officer Dr. Josef Mengele became known as the Angel of Death for his work in selecting prisoners who were to be exterminated because they were unfit for work.

### History
**B** In areas under Nazi control, Jews—long a target of discrimination, random violence, and pogroms throughout Europe—were herded into restricted sections of cities. These areas were surrounded by barbed wire and policed by armed guards with vicious dogs.

### History
**C** Because mail service was erratic and letters were heavily censored to prevent useful information from falling into enemy hands, Americans were at times cut off from loved ones serving in the military or as doctors, journalists, and volunteers in refugee camps. Civilians made themselves useful at home by planting victory gardens and collecting tin, aluminum, used oil, and rubber for the war effort. Families of soldiers proudly displayed stars in their windows.

### History
**D** After the war, in November 1945, the United States, Britain, France, and Russia conducted an international tribunal to try Nazis for crimes against humanity. For 11 months, the Nuremberg trials brought to light details of atrocities and grisly medical experiments that shocked the world. Of the 22 defendants, 12 were sentenced to death for war crimes.

**VOICES FROM THE TIMES**
**Ask: Why might children have had a hard time understanding the significance of Pearl Harbor?**
**Possible Responses:** the unfamiliarity of the place; the distance of Hawaii from mainland United States; children's ignorance of the perils of a world war

**Ask: What feelings and images does this description of the Battle of the Bulge evoke?**
**Possible Responses:** feelings—confusion, terror, helplessness, desperation; images—smoke and flashes of gunfire; deafening noise; soldiers running around disorganized

**SUMMARIZING**

Ask students to write a summary of the article in their own words. The summary should identify the main idea and supporting details. Remind them to avoid inserting personal opinions and extraneous details. Encourage them to use their notes as guides for their summaries.

**DISCUSSING**

Allow students time to discuss the essay in class. A possible starting point could be a discussion of the students' perceptions of World War II and the Vietnam War and how their perceptions have been influenced by recent films and television programs.

---

# Voices from the TIMES

The only thing that kept you going was your faith in your buddies. It wasn't just a case of friendship. I never heard of self-inflicted wounds out there. Fellows from other services said they saw this in Europe. Oh, there were plenty of times when I wished I had a million-dollar wound. [Laughs softly.] Like maybe shootin' a toe off. What was worse than death was the indignation of your buddies. You couldn't let 'em down. It was stronger than flag and country.

With the Japanese, the battle was all night long. Infiltratin' the lines, slippin' up and throwin' in grenades. Or runnin' in with a bayonet or saber. They were active all night. Your buddy would try to get a little catnap and you'd stay on watch. Then you'd switch off. It went on, day in and day out. A matter of simple survival. The only way you could get it over with was to kill them off before they killed you. The war I knew was totally savage.

**E. B. "Sledgehammer" Sledge**
remembering the war in the Pacific

I first became aware of it when I was twelve or thirteen. It was one of the most important experiences of my life. In the school library, I was looking at photographs of the Holocaust. They were oversized books. I can still see the bindings and the mottled green cloth. It wasn't an assignment. Why was I doing this? It was a new library, new furniture, clean floors. The sun was coming through on the Appalachian hills. In contrast to the photographs, which were grainy, fuzzy. Parents wouldn't want their children to see these photographs.

In those grainy photos, you first think it's cords of wood piled up. You look again, it shows you human beings. You never get the picture out of your eye.

**Nora Watson**

**1074**   UNIT SEVEN

---

A U.S. soldier in Vietnam

## Traditions Across Time: War in Vietnam

Most Americans supported U.S. participation in World War II. Twenty years later, however, the Vietnam War split the American people into so-called hawks and doves—supporters and opponents of the war.

The United States intervened in South Vietnam to help that republic resist the Viet Cong—South Vietnamese Communist rebels—and the North Vietnamese army. The U.S. government wanted to stop the spread of communism in Southeast Asia, whereas the Vietnamese soldiers fighting U.S. troops wanted an independent nation free of foreign interference.

The war in Vietnam bred a degree of domestic conflict unseen since the Civil War. As the war dragged on and more U.S. soldiers died—approximately 58,000 in all—many Americans at home began to doubt the wisdom of continuing the U.S. presence in Vietnam. Indignant students, pacifists, and some returning Vietnam War veterans marched in the streets, calling for an end to the war. The literature of the time reflects the conflicts within the country, as well as within the ranks of the U.S. military. From Tim O'Brien's "Ambush," with its painful memory of an encounter with the enemy, to Denise Levertov's poem "At the Justice Department," a participant's account of an antiwar protest, these selections introduce the troublesome issues plaguing the people who were involved in the longest war in American history.

---

**VOICES FROM THE TIMES**

**Ask: Why was friendship so important to soldiers in World War II?**

**Possible Response:** In a savage and soul-destroying situation, a soldier's relationship with his buddies was a reminder that he was still human, that there was something to life beyond trying to kill the enemy.

**Ask: Why do you think looking at the book about the Holocaust was such a memorable experience for Nora Watson?**

**Possible Responses:** because the events recorded in the photos were such a contrast to her life and surroundings; because the photos were so stark and graphic; because this was her first exposure to Holocaust horrors

**1075**

# OVERVIEW

## Objectives
1. understand and appreciate a **short story** (Literary Analysis)
2. explore connections between **theme and title** (Literary Analysis)
3. draw conclusions about **character motivation** (Active Reading)

## Summary
It is 1940, and Morris Lieberman, a widower with a son, owns a small grocery story in Brooklyn. Morris was born in Russia, and one of his early memories is that of seeing a fellow Jew killed during a time of persecution. Morris has heard with dread the radio reports of the Nazi persecution of the Jews. France is about to surrender to Germany, and Morris had hoped that French military power would stop the Nazis and ensure the safety of the Jews. Every day his anxiety increases as he listens to the news broadcasts. Gus comes regularly to Morris's store to sell meat. Although sympathizing with the Nazis, he hasn't revealed his opinions because he wants to keep Morris's business. Morris's son, Leonard, has caused a rift between his father and Gus by noticing errors in Gus's bills. When the French surrender and sign an armistice, Morris and Gus argue: Morris says he wanted the French to win because they were protecting democracy, and Gus replies that Morris wanted them to win because they were protecting Jews. As Gus leaves the store, he asks himself why he should feel sympathy for Jews, and he drives away imagining himself as a Nazi soldier driving a tank triumphantly through Paris.

## Thematic Link
This short story recalls **World War II** by conveying a Jewish American's reaction to the Nazi conquest of Europe.

---

### 5-Minute Warm-Up

***Daily Language SkillBuilder***

Have students **proofread** the display sentences on page 1069i and write them correctly. The sentences also appear on Transparency 30 of **Grammar Transparencies and Copymasters.**

---

**Editor's Note** With the permission of the author or copyright holder, potentially offensive material has been deleted from the selection.

---

# Armistice

*Short Story by* BERNARD MALAMUD

### Connect to Your Life

**Preconceived Notions** Prejudice is the suspicion, dislike, or hatred of a particular group of people based on preconceived ideas about them. Think about a person you know who is prejudiced, however slightly, against a certain group. What is the group? Why do you think this person is prejudiced against this group? How does he or she demonstrate this prejudice? When is he or she most likely to show this prejudice? Discuss your thoughts with a classmate.

## Build Background

**Roots of Anti-Semitism** Anti-Semitism, prejudice against Jews, plays a major role in "Armistice," a story set during World War II before the United States entered the conflict. When Hitler came to power in Germany in 1933, he made anti-Semitism an official policy of the Nazi government, and during World War II, he instituted a program to exterminate all European Jews. As the Nazis conquered territories, as they did France in 1940, they rounded up the Jews of the area and sent them to concentration camps. Hitler carried anti-Semitism to a terrifying extreme, but the roots of anti-Semitism extend much further back in European history than the 1940s. Since ancient times both Christian and Muslim nations have persecuted and expelled Jews. Originally, Jews were persecuted for not following the dominant religion, but later they were also blamed for society's ills whenever economic or social conditions deteriorated.

WORDS TO KNOW **Vocabulary Preview**

| | | |
|---|---|---|
| contemptuously | inflict | pretense |
| derive | overwrought | |

## Focus Your Reading

**LITERARY ANALYSIS** **THEME AND TITLE** As you know, **theme** refers to the central idea that a writer wishes to share with a reader of a literary work. Most themes are not stated and must be figured out by the reader. One detail that can help suggest the theme of a story is its **title.** As you read "Armistice," consider what the title tells you about the story's theme.

**ACTIVE READING** **DRAWING CONCLUSIONS ABOUT CHARACTER MOTIVATION**

As you may recall, **motivation** refers to the forces impelling a **character's** actions. There are two main characters in this story: Morris, who is of Russian Jewish descent, and Gus, who is of German descent. As you read the story, think about why the two characters act as they do, particularly toward each other. Look for clues that will help you **draw conclusions** about their motivations and behaviors.

**READER'S NOTEBOOK** Being aware of characters' memories, dreams, and imaginings can provide clues to their motivations. Use a chart like the one shown to list the two main characters' memories, dreams, and imaginings.

| | Morris | Gus |
|---|---|---|
| Memories | | |
| Dreams | | |
| Imaginings | | |

---

## LESSON RESOURCES

**UNIT SEVEN RESOURCE BOOK,** pp. 4–8

**ASSESSMENT RESOURCES**
**Formal Assessment,** pp. 201–202
**Teacher's Guide to Assessment and Portfolio Use**
**Test Generator**

**SKILLS TRANSPARENCIES AND COPYMASTERS**
**Literary Analysis**
• Point of View, T20 (for Review, p. 1085)

**Reading and Critical Thinking**
• Drawing Conclusions, T4 (for Active Reading, p. 1076)

**Grammar**
• Complements, C79 (for Mini Lesson, p. 1087)

**Vocabulary**
• Prefixes, C90 (for Mini Lesson, p. 1083)

**Writing**
• Opinion Statement, C34 (for Writing Option 2, p. 1086)
• Interpretive Essay, C36 (for Writing Option 1, p. 1086)

**Communications**
• Impromptu Speaking: Dialogue, Role-Play, Debate, T13 (for Mini Lesson, p. 1082)

**INTEGRATED TECHNOLOGY**

**Audio Library**
**Internet: Research Starter**
**Visit our website:**
www.mcdougallittell.com

---

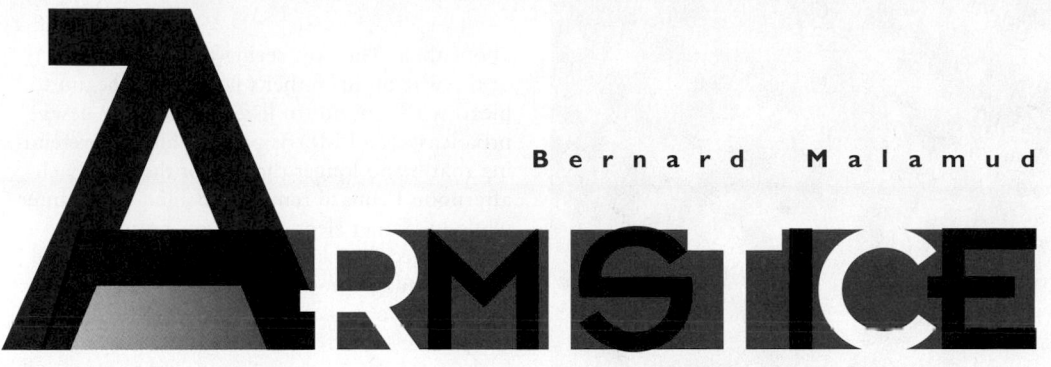

# Bernard Malamud
# ARMISTICE

When he was a boy, Morris Lieberman saw a burly Russian peasant seize a wagon wheel that was lying against the side of a blacksmith's shop, swing it around, and hurl it at a fleeing Jewish sexton.[1] The wheel caught the Jew in the back, crushing his spine. In speechless terror, he lay on the ground before his burning house, waiting to die.

Thirty years later Morris, a widower who owned a small grocery and delicatessen store in a Scandinavian neighborhood in Brooklyn, could recall the scene of the pogrom[2] with the twisting fright that he had felt at fifteen. He often experienced the same fear since the Nazis had come to power.

The reports of their persecution of the Jews that he heard over the radio filled him with dread, but he never stopped listening to them. His fourteen-year-old son, Leonard, a thin, studious boy, saw how <u>overwrought</u> his father became and tried to shut off the radio, but the grocer would not allow him to. He listened, and at night did not sleep, because in listening he shared the woes <u>inflicted</u> upon his race.

When the war began, Morris placed his hope for the salvation of the Jews in his trust of the French army. He lived close to his radio, listening to the bulletins and praying for a French victory in the conflict which he called "this righteous war."

On the May day in 1940 when the Germans ripped open the French lines at Sedan, his long-growing anxiety became intolerable. Between waiting on customers, or when he was preparing salads in the kitchen at the rear of the store, he switched on the radio and heard, with increasing dismay, the flood of reports which never seemed to contain any good news. The Belgians surrendered. The British retreated at Dunkerque,[3] and in mid-June, the Nazis, speeding toward Paris in their lorries,[4] were passing large herds of conquered Frenchmen resting in the fields.

Day after day, as the battle progressed, Morris sat on the edge of the cot in the kitchen listening to the additions to his sorrow, nodding his head the way the Jews do in mourning, then rousing himself to hope for the miracle that would save the French as it had saved the Jews in the wilderness. At three o'clock, he shut off the radio, because Leonard came home from school

---

1. **sexton:** caretaker of a synagogue or church.
2. **pogrom** (pə-grŏm′): organized persecution or massacre of a minority group, especially one conducted against Jews.
3. **Dunkerque** (dœn-kĕrk′): also spelled *Dunkirk;* a seaport in northern France. In 1940, more than 330,000 Allied troops, under enemy fire, were forced to evacuate the beaches there.
4. **lorries:** a British term for motor trucks.

| WORDS TO KNOW | |
|---|---|
| **overwrought** (ō′vər-rôt′) *adj.* excessively nervous or excited | |
| **inflict** (ĭn-flĭkt′) *v.* to cause to have or suffer; impose | |

**1077**

A butcher at a deli in New York City. Photo by Victor Laredo.

about then. The boy, seeing the harmful effect of the war on his father's health, had begun to plead with him not to listen to so many news broadcasts, and Morris pacified him by pretending that he no longer thought of the war. Each afternoon Leonard remained behind the counter while his father slept on the cot. From the dream-filled, raw sleep of these afternoons, the grocer managed to <u>derive</u> enough strength to endure the long day and his own bitter thoughts.

The salesmen from the wholesale grocery houses and the drivers who served Morris were amazed at the way he suffered. They told him that the war had nothing to do with America and that he was taking it too seriously. Some of the others made him the object of their ridicule outside the store. One of them, Gus Wagner, who delivered the delicatessen meats and provisions, was not afraid to laugh at Morris to his face.

Gus was a heavy man, with a strong, full head and a fleshy face. Although born in America, and a member of the AEF[5] in 1918, his imagination was fired by the Nazi conquests and he believed that they had the strength and power to conquer the world. He kept a scrapbook filled with clippings and pictures of the German army. He was deeply impressed by the Panzer divisions,[6] and when he read accounts of battles in which they tore through the enemy's lines, his mind glowed with excitement. He did not reveal his feelings directly because he considered his business first. As it was, he poked fun at the grocer for wanting the French to win.

Each afternoon, with his basket of liverwursts and bolognas on his arm, Gus strode into the store and swung the basket onto the table in the kitchen. The grocer as usual was sitting on the cot, listening to the radio.

---

5. **AEF:** American Expeditionary Forces; the 2 million U.S. soldiers sent overseas during World War I.

6. **Panzer divisions:** German armored forces, consisting largely of tanks.

WORDS TO KNOW    **derive** (dĭ-rīv′) v. to obtain; get; receive

**1078**

"Hello, Morris," Gus said, pretending surprise. "What does it say on the radio?" He sat down heavily and laughed.

When things were going especially well for the Germans, Gus dropped his attitude of *pretense* and said openly, "You better get used to it, Morris. The Germans will wipe out the Frenchmen."

Morris disliked these remarks, but he said nothing. He allowed Gus to talk as he did because he had known the meat man for nine years. Once they had nearly been friends. After the death of Morris's wife four years ago, Gus stayed longer than usual and joined Morris in a cup of coffee. Occasionally he repaired a hole in the screen door or fixed the plug for the electric slicing machine.

Leonard had driven them apart. The boy disliked the meat man and always tried to avoid him. He was nauseated by Gus's laughter, which he called a cackle, and he would not allow his father to do business with Gus in the kitchen when he was having his milk and crackers after school.

Gus knew how the boy felt about him and he was deeply annoyed. He was angered too when the boy added up the figures on the meat bills and found errors. Gus was careless in arithmetic, which often caused trouble. Once Morris mentioned a five-dollar prize that Leonard had won in mathematics and Gus said, "You better watch out, Morris. He's a skinny kid. If he studies too much, he'll get consumption."[7]

Morris was frightened. He felt that Gus was wishing harm upon Leonard. Their relations became cooler, and after that Gus spoke more freely about politics and the war, often expressing his contempt for the French.

The Germans took Paris and pushed on toward the west and south. Morris, drained of his energy, prayed that the ordeal would soon be over. Then the Reynaud cabinet fell. Marshal Pétain[8] addressed a request to the Germans for "peace with honor." In the dark Compiègne forest, Hitler sat in Marshal Foch's railroad car, listening to his terms being read to the French delegation.[9]

That night, after closing his store, Morris disconnected the radio and carried it upstairs. In his bedroom, the door shut tightly so Leonard would not be awakened, he tuned in softly to the midnight broadcast and learned that the French had accepted Hitler's terms and would sign the armistice tomorrow. Morris shut off the radio. An age-old weariness filled him. He wanted to sleep but he knew that he could not.

...the Germans ripped open the French lines at Sedan...

Morris turned out the lights, removed his shirt and shoes in the dark, and sat smoking in the large bedroom that had once belonged to him and his wife.

The door opened softly, and Leonard looked into the room. By the light of the street lamp which shone through the window, the boy could

---

7. **consumption:** tuberculosis.

8. **Reynaud** (rā-nō′) . . . **Marshal Pétain** (pā-tăn′): Reynaud was the premier of France at the time of its surrender to Germany in June 1940. After the Germans had occupied most of France, Pétain became premier of the unoccupied southern third of the nation. (Marshal is the highest rank in the French army.)

9. **In the dark Compiègne** (kôn-pyĕn′yə) **forest . . . delegation:** This meeting represents a cruel turnabout of Germany's surrender at the end of World War I. In 1918 a German delegation had heard the Allies' peace terms in a railroad car in this same forest. Leading the Allied delegation at that time was France's Marshal Ferdinand Foch (fôsh).

---

WORDS TO KNOW
**pretense** (prē′tĕns′) *n.* the act of pretending; a false appearance or action intended to deceive

1079

- 1940—Hungary, Rumania, and Slovakia join the Axis powers in November.
- 1941—Bulgaria joins Axis powers in March.
- 1941—Germany attacks Greece and Yugoslavia; Hitler abandons the Nonaggression Pact of 1939 and attacks the Soviet Union.
- 1941—Japan attacks Pearl Harbor in December and invades the Philippines, most of Southeast Asia and Burma, Indonesia, and many Pacific Ocean islands.
- 1941—United States enters the war against the Axis powers one day after the bombing of Pearl Harbor.
- 1942—The first Allied offensive begins with United States and British landings in North Africa.
- 1943—Fascist government in Italy is overthrown in September.
- 1944—D-Day invasion of Normandy by 156,000 Allied troops is successful.
- 1945—Germany is occupied; Hitler commits suicide on April 30th; German forces surrender on May 8.
- 1945—The war in the Pacific comes to an end after the atomic bombing of Hiroshima and Nagasaki in August.
- 1945—Japan formally surrenders on September 2.

**Literary Analysis: CHARACTER**

**A** Remind students that in addition to his knowledge of Jewish history, Morris himself endured persecution in Russia. He now fears the widespread destruction of the Jews in Europe. Ask students what Morris's repeated question suggests about his frame of mind.

**Possible Responses:** He identifies with his suffering people in Europe; haunted by the past, he doubts whether he and his son will escape persecution.

**Active Reading**

> **DRAWING CONCLUSIONS ABOUT CHARACTER MOTIVATION**

**B** Ask students what these words suggest about Gus's attitude toward Morris.

**Possible Responses:** He doesn't regard Morris as an individual but as a Jew; he stereotypes an entire group as sharing a particular attitude.

**Literary Analysis** | THEME AND TITLE |

**C** Ask students how the personal conflicts among Gus, Morris, and Leonard echo the larger conflict in Europe.

**Possible Responses:** The neighbors instinctively dislike one another but can get along until a catalyst impels them to active enmity; Gus's friendliness to Morris after the death of his wife shows some instinctive sympathy, which Leonard's behavior discourages. In the same way, individuals from hostile countries often find they have more in common than they have to fight about.

see his father in the chair. It made him think of the time when his mother was in the hospital and his father sat in the chair all night.

Leonard entered the bedroom in his bare feet. "Pa," he said, putting his arm around his father's shoulders, "go to sleep."

"I can't sleep, Leonard."

"Pa, you got to. You work sixteen hours."

"Oh, my son," cried Morris, with sudden emotion, putting his arms around Leonard, "what will become of us?"

The boy became afraid.

"Pa," he said, "go to sleep. Please, you got to."

"All right, I'll go," said Morris. He crushed his cigarette in the ashtray and got into bed. The boy watched him until he turned over on his right side, which was the side he slept on; then he returned to his room.

Later Morris rose and sat by the window, looking into the street. The night was cool. The breeze swayed the street lamp, which creaked and moved the circle of light that fell upon the street.

"What will become of us?" he muttered to himself. His mind went back to the days when he was a boy studying Jewish history. The Jews lived in an interminable exodus.[10] Long lines trudged forever with their bundles on their shoulders.

He dozed and dreamed that he had fled from Germany into France. The Nazis had found out where he lived in Paris. He sat in a chair in a dark room waiting for them to come. His hair had grown grayer. The moonlight fell on his sloping shoulders, then moved into the darkness. He rose and climbed out onto a ledge overlooking the lighted city of Paris. He fell. Something clumped to the sidewalk. Morris groaned and awoke. He heard the purring of a truck's motor and he knew that the driver was dropping the bundles of morning newspapers in front of the stationery store on the corner.

The dark was soft with gray. Morris crawled into bed and began to dream again. It was Sunday at suppertime. The store was crowded

with customers. Suddenly Gus was there. He waved a copy of *Social Justice* and cried out, "The Protocols of Zion![11] The Protocols of Zion!" The customers began to leave. "Gus," Morris pleaded, "the customers, the customers—"

He awoke shivering and lay awake until the alarm rang.

After he had dragged in the bread and milk boxes and had waited on the deaf man who always came early, Morris went to the corner for a paper. The armistice was signed. Morris looked around to see if the street had changed, but everything was the same, though he could hardly understand why. Leonard came down for his coffee and roll. He took fifty cents from the till and left for school.

The day was warm and Morris was tired. He grew uneasy when he thought of Gus. He knew that today he would have difficulty controlling himself if Gus made some of his remarks.

At three o'clock, when Morris was slicing small potatoes for potato salad, Gus strode into the store and swung his basket onto the table.

"Well, Morris"—he laughed—"why don't you turn the radio on? Let's hear the news."

Morris tried to control himself, but his bitterness overcame him. "I see you're happy today, Gus. What great cause has died?"

The meat man laughed, but he did not like that remark.

"Come on, Morris," he said, "let's do business before your skinny kid comes home and wants the bill signed by a certified public accountant."

"He looks out for my interests," answered Morris. "He's a good mathematics student," he added.

"That's the sixth time I heard that," said Gus.

---

10. **exodus:** a departure or emigration, usually of a large number of people.

11. **The Protocols of Zion:** anti-Jewish writings concerning an alleged conspiracy to establish a world government ruled by Jews (a notion that has been shown to be completely false). Zion is a name for Israel or the people of Israel, and *protocols*, here, means "agreements or treaties."

**BLOCK SCHEDULING: MANAGING TIME**

**If your schedule requires that you cover the lesson objectives in a shorter time, use . . .**
- Preparing to Read, p. 1076
- Thinking Through the Literature, p. 1085
- Vocabulary in Action, p. 1087

**If you want to take advantage of longer class time, use. . .**
- TE Teaching Options: Preteaching Vocabulary, p. 1077; Cross-Curricular Link, pp. 1078–1079; Viewing and Representing, p. 1081; Speaking and Listening, p. 1082; Informal Assessment, p. 1084
- Link Across Cultures, pp. 1083–1084
- Choices & Challenges, pp. 1086–1087

"You'll never hear it about your children."

Gus lost his temper. "What the hell's the matter with you Jews?" he asked. "Do you think you own all the brains in the world?"

"Gus," Morris cried, "you talk like a Nazi."

"I'm a hundred percent American. I fought in the war," answered Gus.

Leonard came into the store and heard the loud voices. He ran into the kitchen and saw the two men arguing. A feeling of shame and nausea overcame him.

"Pa," he begged, "don't fight."

Morris was still angry. "If you're not a Nazi," he said to Gus, "why are you so glad the French lost?"

"Who's glad?" asked Gus. Suddenly he felt proud and he said, "They deserved to lose, the way they starved the German people. Why the hell do you want them to win?"

"Pa," said Leonard again.

"I want them to win because they are fighting for democracy."

"Like hell," said Gus. "You want them to win because they're protecting the Jews—like that lousy Léon Blum."[12]

"You Nazi, you," Morris shouted angrily, coming from behind the table. "You Nazi! You don't deserve to live in America!"

"Papa," cried Leonard, holding him, "don't fight, please, please."

"Mind your own business, you little . . . ,"

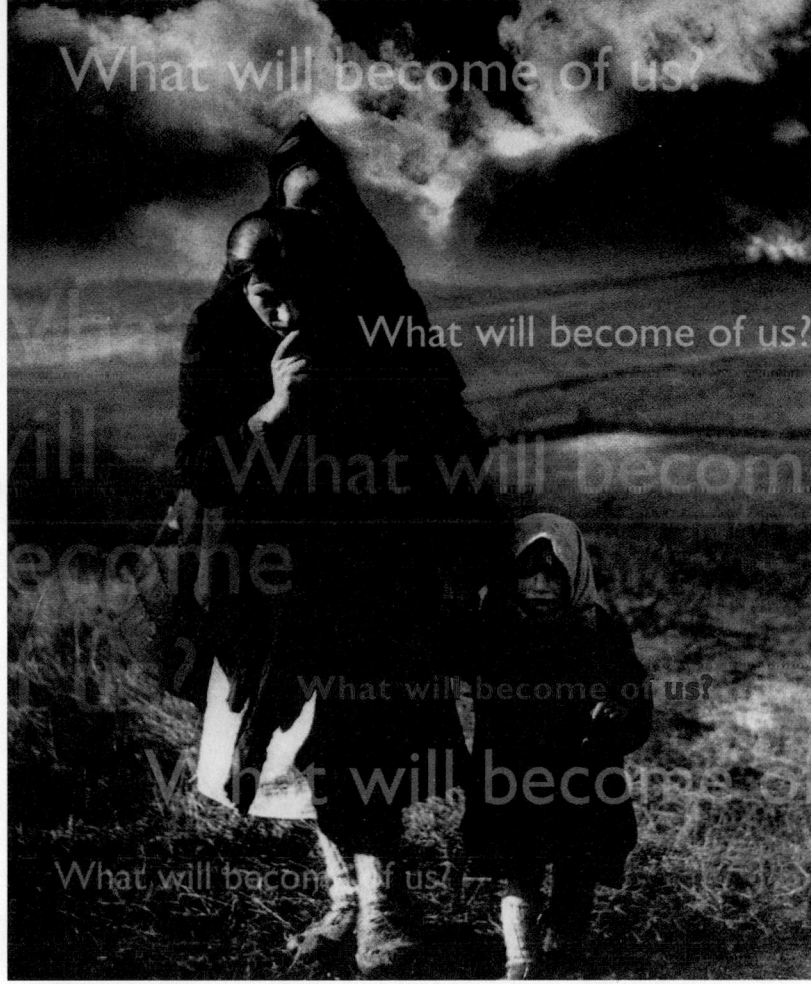

A mother and her children in Yugoslavia in 1943, three of the 10 million Europeans displaced by the war. Photo by George Skrigin.

said Gus, pushing Leonard away.

A sob broke from Leonard's throat. He began to cry.

Gus paused, seeing that he had gone too far.

Morris Lieberman's face was white. He put his

---

12. **Léon Blum** (blōōm): the first Socialist and the first Jew to become, in 1936, premier of France. His social reforms and opposition to the Nazis before and during the war led his enemies to adopt the slogan "Better Hitler than Blum."

 **Viewing and Representing**

### Photographs

**ART APPRECIATION** Skillful photographers leave no elements of their compositions to chance. The background that appears in a photograph enhances both impact and meaning.
**Instruction** Have students examine the backgrounds of the photographs on pages 1081 and 1082. Ask students to describe each background and to tell what it contributes to the message conveyed by the photograph.

**Possible Responses:** The refugees are pictured against a desolate field stretching into the distance with storm clouds behind and over them. These details suggest the length and hardship of their journey, the abandonment of their former lives, and the trials and storms that lie ahead. The Eiffel Tower, the symbol of France, appears behind Hitler and his advisors. The incongruity of German leaders in front of this French landmark emphasizes that the occupation of France is unnatural.

**Literary Analysis: PLOT**
Ask students whether the conflict between Morris and Gus is resolved.
**Possible Response:** No. Although they repress their hostility, Morris and Gus have irreconcilable differences.

**Active Reading**

> **DRAWING CONCLUSIONS ABOUT CHARACTER MOTIVATION**

Have students explain why Morris and Gus back off from pursuing open conflict.
**Possible Responses:** Morris stops fighting because of his son; he wants to protect Leonard from being upset or hurt through the fighting. Gus is afraid to lose Morris's business.

**(A)** Ask students what Gus's thoughts as he is driving away reveal about his character.
**Possible Response:** Gus is a bully. He identifies with a Nazi tank driver driving through conquered Paris.

**Literary Analysis** | TITLE AND THEME |
Ask students to explain the appropriateness of the title of the story.
**Possible Response:** In Europe, an armistice, or a cease-fire, is signed between France and Germany; in Brooklyn, Morris and Gus stop fighting yet remain inwardly hostile.

arm around the boy and kissed him again and again.

"No, no. No more, Leonard. Don't cry. I'm sorry. I give you my word. No more."

Gus looked on without speaking. His face was still red with anger, but he was afraid that he would lose Morris's business. He pulled two liverwursts and a bologna from his basket.

"The meat's on the table," he said. "Pay me tomorrow."

Gus glanced <u>contemptuously</u> at the grocer comforting his son, who was quiet now, and he walked out of the store. He threw the basket into his truck, got in, and drove off.

As he rode amid the cars on the avenue, he thought of the boy crying and his father holding him. It was always like that with the Jews. Tears and people holding each other. Why feel sorry for them?

 Gus sat up straight at the wheel, his face grim. He thought of the armistice and imagined that he was in Paris. His truck was a massive tank rumbling with the others through the wide boulevards. The French, on the sidewalks, were overpowered with fear.

He drove tensely, his eyes unsmiling. He knew that if he relaxed the picture would fade. ❖

Hitler and his advisors parade in Paris ten days after Nazi troops took the city. UPI/Bettmann.

> WORDS
> TO
> KNOW
>
> **contemptuously** (kən-tĕmp'chōō-əs-lē) *adv.* in a way that shows disdain or disgust; scornfully

---

## Teaching Options

**Mini Lesson** **Speaking and Listening**

**ROLE PLAYING**
**Prepare** Have students work in groups of three and choose a character—Gus, Morris, or Leonard—to role-play. Speaking as the character they have chosen, students should explain how they see the other two characters. Students assuming the role of Gus or Morris should recount the fight from that character's point of view, explaining his motives for engaging in the heated quarrel. Students playing Leonard should explain his attitude toward Gus and his feelings about the fight.

**Present** Have students present their characters' views to the class. Students should justify their choice of verbal and nonverbal performance techniques by referring to analysis of the text. Ask listeners to agree on valid criteria for evaluating the performances and apply their criteria to evaluate each portrayal. Encourage listeners to explain how the performance enhanced their understanding of each particular character's motivation.

 **BLOCK SCHEDULING** This activity is particularly well suited for longer class periods.

# *from* SURVIVAL IN AUSCHWITZ
### Primo Levi

*In Malamud's story "Armistice," the main character is alarmed by radio broadcasts about Nazi persecution of Jews. The following selection describes the true experiences of Primo Levi, an Italian chemist who survived the horrors of Auschwitz, a Nazi concentration camp in Poland.*

**1**

Today is working Sunday, *Arbeitssonntag:* we work until 1 P.M., then we return to camp for the shower, shave and general control for skin diseases and lice. And in the yards, everyone knew mysteriously that the selection would be today.

**2**

The news arrived, as always, surrounded by a halo of contradictory or suspect details: the selection in the infirmary took place this morning; the percentage was seven per cent of the whole camp, thirty, fifty per cent of the patients. At Birkenau,[1] the crematorium chimney has been smoking for ten days. Room has to be made for an enormous convoy arriving from the Poznan ghetto.[2] The young tell the young that all the old ones will be chosen. The healthy tell the healthy that only the ill will be chosen. Specialists will be excluded. German Jews will be excluded. Low Numbers[3] will be excluded. You will be chosen. I will be excluded.

At 1 P.M. exactly the yard empties in orderly fashion, and for two hours the gray unending army files past the two control stations where, as on every day, we are counted and recounted, and past the military band which for two hours without interruption plays, as on every day, those marches to which we must synchronize our steps at our entrance and our exit.

It seems like every day, the kitchen chimney smokes as usual, the distribution of the soup is already beginning. But then the bell is heard, and at that moment we realize that we have arrived.

Because this bell always sounds at dawn, when it means the reveille;[4] but if it sounds during the day, it means *"Blocksperre,"* enclosure in huts, and this happens when there is a selection to prevent anyone avoiding it, or when those selected leave for the gas, to prevent anyone seeing them leave.

Our *Blockältester*[5] knows his business. He has made sure that we have all entered, he has the door locked, he has given everyone his card with his number, name, profession, age and nationality and he has ordered everyone to undress completely, except for shoes. We wait like this, naked, with the card in our hands, for the commission to reach our hut. We are hut 48, but one can never tell if they

---

1. **Birkenau** (bîr′kə-nou′): Also known as Auschwitz II, this camp stood about two miles from an older camp, called Auschwitz I. Between 1 million and 4 million people were murdered at Auschwitz-Birkenau during the years 1942–1945.
2. **Poznan** (pôz′năn′) **ghetto:** the area of the Polish city of Poznan in which Jews were forced to live.
3. **Low Numbers:** prisoners with low identification numbers.
4. **reveille** (rĕv′ə-lē): a signal used to awaken people.
5. *Blockältester* (blôk′ĕl′tə-stər) *German:* block elder—a prisoner cooperating with the German guards by serving as the head of a block, or barracks.

---

---

 **Mini Lesson** ## Vocabulary Strategy

### APPLYING MEANINGS OF PREFIXES
**Instruction** Remind students that a prefix is a word part that is added to the beginning of another word or word part. Tell students that they can apply the meanings of common prefixes in order to comprehend unfamiliar words.

**Activity** Have students work in pairs to define the following words: *subaltern, irregularity, infirmary, synchronize, interminable, intolerable,* and *enclosure.* Students should refer to the prefix chart for help in writing their definitions and check them by referring to a dictionary.

| Prefix | Meaning |
|--------|---------|
| en- | to put or get into |
| ex- | apart; away; not |
| in-, ir- | not or without |
| re- | again or back |
| sub- | under or below |
| syn- | together |

Use **Vocabulary Transparencies and Copymasters**, p. 90.

A lesson on prefixes appears on p. 1130 in the Pupil's Edition.

### Literary Analysis: COMPARING TEXTS

Ask students to compare the sources of fear for Morris in "Armistice" and for the narrator in the excerpt from *Survival in Auschwitz*.

**Possible Responses:** Both feel a lack of control over their fate; although Morris is presently safe, he is uncertain of the future, and the narrator's future is very precarious; both are subjected to bullies.

Remind students that they're expected to compare elements of text across texts. Have them compare the characters of Gus and the SS man.

**Possible Response:** Gus and the SS man both make judgments on the basis of ethnic background and the physical appearance.

### Active Reading

> DRAWING CONCLUSIONS ABOUT
> CHARACTER MOTIVATION

 Ask students why the narrator walks as he does from the *Tagesraum* to the dormitory.

**Possible Response:** He is trying to look healthy and strong so he won't be selected for execution.

### Literary Analysis: TONE

Point out the calm, factual tone of the narrator. Have students consider how an emotional tone might have affected the narrative.

**Possible Responses:** An emotional tone might have obscured some of the details that the narrator conveys to the reader; also it might have made the events seem unusual rather than routine for the camp inmates.

---

are going to begin at hut 1 or hut 60. At any rate, we can rest quietly at least for an hour, and there is no reason why we should not get under the blankets on the bunk and keep warm.

Many are already drowsing when a barrage of orders, oaths and blows proclaims the imminent arrival of the commission. The *Blockältester* and his helpers, starting at the end of the dormitory, drive the crowd of frightened, naked people in front of them and cram them in the *Tagesraum* which is the Quartermaster's office.[6] The *Tagesraum* is a room seven yards by four: when the drive is over, a warm and compact human mass is jammed into the *Tagesraum*, perfectly filling all the corners, exercising such a pressure on the wooden walls as to make them creak. . . .

The *Blockältester* has closed the connecting-door and has opened the other two which lead from the dormitory and the *Tagesraum* outside. Here, in front of the two doors, stands the arbiter[7] of our fate, an SS subaltern.[8] On his right is the *Blockältester*, on his left, the quartermaster of the hut. Each one of us, as he comes naked out of the *Tagesraum* into the cold October air, has to run the few steps between the two doors, give the card to the SS man and enter the dormitory door. The SS man, in the fraction of a second between two successive crossings, with a glance at one's back and front, judges everyone's fate, and in turn gives the card to the man on his right or his left, and this is the life or death of each of us. In three or four minutes a hut of two hundred men is "done," as is the whole camp of twelve thousand men in the course of the afternoon.

 Jammed in the charnel-house[9] of the *Tagesraum*, I gradually felt the human pressure around me slacken, and in a short time it was my turn. Like everyone, I passed by with a brisk and elastic step, trying to hold my head high, my chest forward and my muscles contracted and conspicuous. With the corner of my eye I tried to look behind my shoulders, and my card seemed to end on the right.

As we gradually come back into the dormitory we are allowed to dress ourselves. Nobody yet knows with certainty his own fate, it has first of all to be established whether the condemned cards were those on the right or the left. By now there is no longer any point in sparing each other's feelings with superstitious scruples. Everybody crowds around the oldest, the most wasted-away, and most "muselmann";[10] if their cards went to the left, the left is certainly the side of the condemned.

Even before the selection is over, everybody knows that the left was effectively the "*schlechte Seite*," the bad side. There have naturally been some irregularities: René, for example, so young and robust, ended on the left; perhaps it was because he has glasses, perhaps because he walks a little stooped like a myope,[11] but more probably because of a simple mistake. . . .

There is nothing surprising about these mistakes: the examination is too quick and summary, and in any case, the important thing for the Lager[12] is not that the most useless prisoners be eliminated, but that free posts be quickly created, according to a certain percentage previously fixed.

---

6. **Quartermaster's office:** the office of the person who distributes food and clothing to the prisoners.

7. **arbiter** (är′bĭ-tər): judge; decider.

8. **SS subaltern:** a low-ranking officer in the Nazi special security force.

9. **charnel-house:** vault for the bones of the dead (here used figuratively).

10. **"muselmann"** (mo͞o′zəl-män′): concentration-camp slang for a person near death from starvation.

11. **myope** (mī′ōp′): nearsighted person.

12. **Lager** (lä′gər) *German:* camp.

---

## Teaching Options

### ✓ Assessment Informal Assessment

**UNDERSTANDING CHARACTER AND STYLE** Have students respond to the following scenario:

> *Morris has just heard the news that the Nazis have surrendered in World War II. He is so excited that he has difficulty falling asleep that evening. When he finally sleeps, this is what he dreams.*

Have students review the dream sequence on page 1080, then have them write their own dream sequence. Their paragraphs should reveal Morris's character and emotions, should include dream images, and should be written in a style consistent with Malamud's.

**RUBRIC**

**3  Full Accomplishment** Paragraphs thoroughly reveal Morris's character and emotions, include dream images, and are written in a style consistent with Malamud's.

**2  Substantial Accomplishment** Paragraphs reveal some aspects of Morris's character and emotions, include some relevant dream images, and are written in a style somewhat similar to Malamud's.

**1  Little or Partial Accomplishment** Paragraphs do not reveal aspects of Morris's character and emotions, do not clearly describe a dream sequence, or are not written in a style consistent with Malamud's.

## Connect to the Literature

1. **What Do You Think?**
   What was your reaction to Gus's daydream at the end of the story? Share your thoughts with classmates.

   **Comprehension Check**
   - Why does Gus make fun of Morris?
   - What event causes the argument between Gus and Morris at the end of the story?
   - After his fight with Morris, what does Gus imagine he is doing?

## Think Critically

2. Why do you think news of the war affects Morris as it does?

    **THINK ABOUT**
   - his memories of the pogrom in Russia
   - the two dreams he has

3. In your view, should Morris be as involved in the war as he is?

    **THINK ABOUT**
   - how his health is affected
   - what he might mean when he cries "What will become of us?"

4. **ACTIVE READING** | **DRAWING CONCLUSIONS ABOUT CHARACTER MOTIVATION** Look over the chart you created in your **READER'S NOTEBOOK**. How would you characterize Morris's memories and dreams? How would you describe Gus's imaginings? How do their different dreams and imaginings help explain their actions?

## Extend Interpretations

5. **Critic's Corner** Many critics have noted the focus on moral concerns in Bernard Malamud's writing. Evelyn Gross Avery writes: "Malamud defines Jewishness as a willingness to honor the Covenant by sacrificing and suffering for freedom and justice. A good Jew assumes responsibility for all the needy, but has a special obligation to his people. A good Jew awakens others to iniquities." How does Avery's comment affect your understanding of Morris Lieberman?

6. **Comparing Texts** Compare Morris Lieberman's impression of the Nazis and their treatment of Jews with Primo Levi's actual account of his experiences in a Nazi concentration camp in *Survival in Auschwitz* (page 1083). What descriptions of Levi's life in Auschwitz might surprise Morris? What descriptions would probably not surprise him?

7. **Connect to Life** How much anti-Semitism do you think exists in the United States today? Support your answer.

## Literary Analysis

**THEME AND TITLE** A story's **title** may provide clues to the work's **theme,** or message. In "Armistice," the title alludes to the armistice in Europe as well as to the one between Morris and Gus. The following passage describes Gus's thoughts and feelings after Morris promises his son that there will be no more fighting:

> *Gus looked on without speaking. His face was still red with anger, but he was afraid that he would lose Morris's business. He pulled two liverwursts and a bologna from his basket.*
>
> *"The meat's on the table," he said. "Pay me tomorrow."*
>
> *Gus glanced contemptuously at the grocer comforting his son, who was quiet now, and he walked out of the store. He threw the basket into his truck, got in, and drove off.*

How does the armistice in Europe mirror the one reached between Gus and Morris?

**Paired Activity** Get together with a classmate and discuss theme in "Armistice." What central idea do you think is suggested by the story's title? What other themes do you see in the story? Write out statements to express these themes, and then share them with other student pairs.

**REVIEW** | **POINT OF VIEW**
Malamud frequently uses the **third-person omniscient point of view,** in which the narrator reveals the thoughts of different characters. What do you think would have been lost if "Armistice" had been narrated only from Morris's viewpoint?

---

## Connect to the Literature

1. **What Do You Think?**
   Encourage students to articulate the reasons for their reactions and to recognize that the daydream is consistent with Gus's character as presented in the story.

   **Comprehension Check**
   - because Morris wants the French to defeat the Germans
   - the surrender of France to Germany
   - driving a German tank through Paris

    Use Selection Quiz
   **Unit Seven Resource Book,** p. 8.

## Think Critically

2. Possible Responses: Morris is Jewish and realizes he could be the one being persecuted; Morris is afraid that people will be swayed by their prejudices.

3. Possible Responses: yes, because his people are in danger; no, he is not personally threatened, and he is making himself sick with worry.

4. Possible Responses: Morris's memories and dreams are fearful and haunted. Gus's imaginings are arrogant and triumphant. Morris's dreams explain his terrible anxiety for the safety of his people, his son, and himself; Gus's imaginings explain his attempt to bully Morris and Leonard.

## Literary Analysis

**Theme and Title** The title "Armistice" suggests the central theme of the story. An armistice is a temporary cessation of fighting. Nations and people, too, might cease fighting, but often underlying hostilities remain. For example, Morris and Gus stop fighting not because they respect each other but for personal concerns: Morris, to comfort his son; Gus, to keep Morris's business.

**Review Point of View** Possible Responses: If the story had been written from Morris's point of view, the final scene would not have occurred, and the reader would have had to infer the extent of Gus's prejudice and contempt.

---

## Extend Interpretations

**Critic's Corner** Possible Responses: Morris Lieberman is living Malamud's philosophy; he feels an obligation to his people even though they are in Europe; he feels he cannot stand by and let Gus's prejudice go unchallenged.

**Comparing Texts** Possible Responses: The lack of compassion shown by the inmates toward those most likely to be killed—"the oldest, the most wasted away"—might surprise Morris. The brutality of the *Blockaltester* and the SS subaltern toward the imprisoned Jews would not surprise him.

**Connect to Life** Students might also suggest ways of combating this attitude, such as by remembering the victims of the Holocaust.

# Writing Options

1. **Dream Analysis** Remind students that dreams can be based loosely upon the day's events, or they can sometimes play out the dreamer's wishes or fears. Suggest that they list the images and events that occur in the dreams and analyze them. Their analysis should lead them to draw conclusions about Morris's state of mind.

2. **Letter to the Editor** Have students discuss the meanings of the phrase "a righteous war." Then have them choose the meaning that they prefer and draft their letters. Remind students that their letters must be logically organized and contain supporting reasons and examples.

3. **Eventful Paragraph** Let the class brainstorm various international events that had an impact on people in America. For example, the Vietnam War polarized the American public and seemed to make veterans scapegoats rather than heroes. After students have listed several examples, ask them to choose one and complete the assignment. **Interpersonal learners** might conduct interviews to help collect data about the effect of the event.

4. **World War II Presentation** Have students work in groups and delegate responsibility for each part of the exhibit to various group members. One student might research key events; another, important people; still another, social trends and recordings. A coordinator should then be responsible for facilitating the organization of the images and recordings into an effective outline.

# Activities & Explorations

1. **Readers Theater Performance** Remind students that a Readers Theater presentation involves making a script from the text. To do this, students do not need to rewrite the story but can add, delete, rearrange, or repeat where it seems appropriate. Encourage students to videotape their Readers Theater presentations.

2. **Memory Illustration** Students might include in their illustrations images from their own knowledge of prejudice and mistreatment.

---

## Choices & CHALLENGES

### Writing Options

**1. Dream Analysis** Write a dream interpretation analyzing the meaning of Morris's two dreams the night before his fight with Gus. Be sure to explain what you think certain actions symbolize and what the dreams reveal about Morris's state of mind.

**Writing Handbook**
See page 1283: Analysis.

**2. Letter to the Editor** Put yourself in Morris's place. Draft a letter to the editor of a newspaper explaining why you consider World War II a "righteous war."

**3. Eventful Paragraph** Write a paragraph about another event abroad that inflamed prejudices and affected how people perceived each other in the United States.

**4. World War II Presentation** Create an outline for a multimedia exhibit that captures the World War II era. Take notes on images that illustrate key events, people, and social trends during the war. Identify and list recordings of music that were popular at the time. Be sure to indicate how you would arrange and use these images and recordings in an exhibit. Place the outline in your **Working Portfolio.**

### Activities & Explorations

**1. Readers Theater Performance** Practice and present a Readers Theater performance of this story, with readers taking the parts of Morris, Gus, Leonard, and the narrator. You might use a few items of classroom furniture or some simple props to suggest the setting. ~ **VIEWING AND REPRESENTING/PERFORMING**

**2. Memory Illustration** Create an illustration, perhaps a painting or a collage, to depict Morris's memories of Jewish persecution and his fears for the future. ~ **ART**

### Inquiry & Research

**1. History of Anti-Semitism** Since ancient times, and in many countries, prejudice against Jews has resulted in discrimination and persecution. Investigate the history of anti-Semitism in Germany, Russia, France, Spain, or some other country, or research details about the Holocaust during World War II. In an oral report, share your knowledge with your classmates.

**2. German Victory** Find out more about the German victory over France during World War II, including how it was achieved and what resulted from it. Report your findings in class.

 **More Online: Research Starter** www.mcdougallittell.com

### Art Connection

**Conflicting Impressions** The photo on page 1081 shows a refugee family fleeing during World War II. The photo on page 1082 depicts Hitler and his entourage marching through Paris. What emotions and ideas do these pictures call to mind for you? How would you contrast the two processions in the photos?

---

# Inquiry & Research

**History of Anti-Semitism** Ask students to generate a list of relevant questions to focus their research. They might ask when evidence of anti-Semitism became apparent, what caused the feelings to surface, what actions were taken as a result, what the impact was upon the Jewish people then, what the long-term effect in the country has been, and whether it is still a problem. Encourage them to investigate a variety of nations and time periods so their reports, taken together, give a broad picture of anti-Semitism. Students can locate appropriate print and nonprint information using text resources including databases and the Internet. Remind them to use text organizers to locate and categorize information as they do independent research. Remind them to be careful about checking the validity of sources found on the Internet.

**German Victory** The German victory over France was, of course, a temporary one. As an alternative, students might research how France was liberated from the Germans.

# Art Connection

**Possible Response:** The photograph of Hitler and his entourage evokes fear, whereas the photograph of the refugees evokes compassion.

## Vocabulary in Action

**EXERCISE A: CONTEXT CLUES** Use a vocabulary word to complete each sentence.

1. We Americans can become _____ upon hearing about the tragic results of ethnic discrimination around the world while at the same time failing to recognize our own guilt in this area.

2. During World War II, Americans responded with horror to the Nazis' eagerness to _____ terrible misery on Jews and other minorities.

3. In the novel *Gentleman's Agreement,* published soon after World War II, a journalist uses the _____ that he is Jewish to explore how Jews are treated in the United States.

4. Used to being respected in his dealings with other people, the journalist is dismayed by how _____ he is often treated when he is thought to be Jewish.

5. The conclusions he is able to _____ from his experiment are that anti-Semitism is unfair, destructive, and shockingly widespread in the United States.

**EXERCISE B** Tell a "round robin" story in which one person begins a story and must keep talking until he or she has used one of the vocabulary words. Another person continues the story until he or she uses another word, and so on, until all the words are used.

| WORDS TO KNOW | | |
|---|---|---|
| contemptuously derive | inflict overwrought | pretense |

**Building Vocabulary**
For an in-depth lesson on context clues, see page 326

## Bernard Malamud
1914–1986

**Other Works**
*The Assistant*
*The Magic Barrel*
*A New Life*
*Pictures of Fidelman: An Exhibition*
*The Tenants*

**Impact of Early Experiences** Bernard Malamud grew up in a non-Jewish neighborhood in Brooklyn, New York, where his Russian Jewish immigrant parents owned a grocery store. Like Morris Lieberman in "Armistice," Malamud's father worked long hours just to make a meager living. Noting the close connection between his experience and his writing, Malamud said in an interview published in the *New York Times:* "People say I write so much about misery, but you write about what you write best. As you are grooved, so you are grieved. And the grieving is that no matter how much happiness or success you collect, you cannot obliterate your early experience."

**Teacher, Writer, Moralist** During his 12 years at Oregon State College, where he taught three days a week and wrote the other four, Malamud produced three novels and a collection of short stories. His first novel, *The Natural,* about a baseball player, was later made into a movie by the same name. In 1961 Malamud began teaching at Bennington College in Vermont. By 1967, when his novel *The Fixer* won both the Pulitzer Prize and the National Book Award, Malamud had become, according to one critic, "one of the foremost writers of moral fiction in America." Throughout his career, he wrote about the need for love, understanding, and responsibility and about the destructiveness of ignorance and hatred. Malamud wrote: "Literature, since it values man by describing him, tends toward morality."

### Author Activity

**Grave Pronouncement** The inscription on Malamud's grave reads: "Art celebrates life and gives us our measure." How do these words apply to "Armistice"?

## Vocabulary in Action

**Exercise A**
1. overwrought
2. inflict
3. pretense
4. contemptuously
5. derive

## Author Activity

Possible Response: Morris's empathy for the sufferings of the Jews in Europe celebrates the nobility of the human spirit.

 **Grammar**

**COMPLEMENTS**

**Instruction** A complement is one or more words that complete the meaning of the verb. There are four kinds of complements: *direct objects, indirect objects, objective complements,* and *subject complements.* A *direct object* is a word or group of words that receives the action of the verb. An *indirect object* is a word or group of words that comes before the direct object and answers the question *to whom, for whom, to what,* or *for what. Objective complements* follow a direct object

and identify or describe it. *Subject complements* are nouns, pronouns, or adjectives that follow a linking verb and identify or describe the subject.

**Activity** Display the following sentences to illustrate complements.

> Morris was <u>angry</u> with Gus for his blatant prejudice. (subject complement)
>
> Gus gave <u>himself</u> the <u>victory</u> in the argument. (*himself*: indirect object; *victory*: direct object)

The victory of the Germans made <u>them heroes</u>. (*them*: direct object; *heroes*: objective complement)

 Use **Grammar Transparencies and Copymasters,** p. 79.

 Use McDougal Littell's *Language Network,* Chapter 1, for more instruction in complements.

**1088** UNIT SEVEN PART 1

# OVERVIEW

## Objectives

1. appreciate a **poem** and an **essay** (Literary Analysis)
2. understand how **imagery** conveys **tone** (Literary Analysis)
3. **adjust reading strategies** for different genres (Active Reading)

## Summary

Randall Jarrell's poem "The Death of the Ball Turret Gunner" describes the nightmarish sensations of a soldier killed in aerial combat. In his essay "Why Soldiers Won't Talk," Steinbeck explains that former soldiers seem unwilling to talk about their experiences in battle because they do not actually remember them—and the more horrific the experience, the less they remember. While under fire, soldiers experience a mixture of fear, adrenaline flow, and fatigue. Both the mind and the body are disturbed and feverish. Everything begins to look unreal. The senses deaden, and soldiers are able to act in ways they normally could not. When the battle is over, the entire experience seems like a dream, and the soldiers' memories of it fade away.

## Thematic Link

Both Randall Jarrell and John Steinbeck **remember the wars** in these works— the horror of aerial warfare and the duress of soldiers in combat.

## Reading and Analyzing

### Literary Analysis

IMAGERY AND TONE

**A** Have students explain the image "my wet fur froze," and describe the tone it conveys. Then ask students to explain the image and describe the tone of the poem's last line.

**Possible Response:** Drops of sweat have frozen on the lining of clothing or hair. The image conveys a tone of nervousness and fear. The gunner is nervous and sweating, and his sweat has frozen. In the last line, after the gunner has been blown to bits, his remains are washed out of the turret with a hose. The tone of this line is brutal and matter-of-fact.

Use **Unit Seven Resource Book,** p. 11 for more practice.

---

# PREPARING to *Read*

# The Death of the Ball Turret Gunner
*Poetry by* RANDALL JARRELL

# Why Soldiers Won't Talk
*Essay by* JOHN STEINBECK

## Connect to Your Life

**Combat!** The following selections bring to life the old cliché "War is hell." Imagine for a moment, as best you can, what the experience of combat must be like. Visualize yourself as a soldier, suddenly thrust into the nightmare of battle. Then hypothesize an answer to the question John Steinbeck asks: Why do soldiers avoid talking about their combat experience? Share your thoughts with a small group of classmates.

## Build Background

**War Experiences** Both Randall Jarrell and John Steinbeck had war-related experiences during World War II. Jarrell served in the U.S. Army Air Force, teaching flight navigation in Arizona. He thus gained firsthand experience with fighter planes and gunners. A ball turret, mentioned in the title of his poem, was a Plexiglas bubble on the underside of certain planes. From it, a machine gunner fired at the enemy during combat. John Steinbeck gained combat experience while working as a news correspondent during World War II. To gather information for his dispatches, he spent time with a Flying Fortress unit in England, reported from North Africa, and accompanied frontline troops during the Allied invasion of Italy.

## Focus Your Reading

**LITERARY ANALYSIS** **IMAGERY AND TONE** As you may recall, **tone** is the attitude a writer takes toward a subject. Tone is communicated partly through **imagery,** that is, words and phrases that appeal to the senses. As you read the two selections, consider how imagery conveys tone.

**ACTIVE READING** **ADJUSTING READING STRATEGIES** When you read literary works from different genres, you need to make adjustments in your reading strategies. For example, when you read a poem, such as "The Death of the Ball Turret Gunner," you might use these strategies:

- Read the poem two or three times.
- Use footnotes and the dictionary to find the meanings of unfamiliar words or terms.
- Try to picture the poem's images and think about what they convey.

When you read Steinbeck's essay "Why Soldiers Won't Talk," follow these strategies:

- Identify the essay's main idea.
- Evaluate the reasons and opinions used to support the main idea.
- Determine your own position on the subject.

**READER'S NOTEBOOK** As you read, use these strategies and any others that work for you. Jot down notes about the poem's imagery and meaning and the development of the main idea in the essay.

1088   UNIT SEVEN   PART 1: REMEMBERING THE WARS

---

## LESSON RESOURCES

### UNIT SEVEN RESOURCE BOOK,
pp. 9–12

### ASSESSMENT RESOURCES
**Formal Assessment,**
pp. 203–204
**Teacher's Guide to Assessment and Portfolio Use**
**Test Generator**

### SKILLS TRANSPARENCIES AND COPYMASTERS
**Literary Analysis**
- Tone, T19 (for Paired Activity, p. 1093)

### Reading and Critical Thinking
- Interviewing, T39 (for Activities & Explorations 1, p. 1094)

**Grammar**
- Repetition vs. Redundancy, C171 (for Mini Lesson, p. 1094)

**Vocabulary**
- Suffixes, C91 (for Mini Lesson, p. 1090)

**Writing**
- Autobiographical Incident, C35 (for Writing Option 2, p. 1094)

### Communications
- Interviewing, T9 (for Mini Lesson, p. 1091)
- Impromptu Speaking: Dialogue, Role-Play, Debate, T13 (for Mini Lesson, p. 1091)

### INTEGRATED TECHNOLOGY
**Audio Library**
**LaserLinks**
- Personal Connection: A Soldier's Life. See **Teacher's SourceBook,** p. 95.

**Visit our website:**
www.mcdougallittell.com

# THE
DEATH
OF THE
BALL
TURRET
GUNNER

**RANDALL JARRELL**

A From my mother's sleep I fell into the State,
And I hunched in its belly till my wet fur froze.
Six miles from earth, loosed from its dream of life,
I woke to black flak[1] and the nightmare fighters.
5 When I died they washed me out of the turret with a hose.

---

1. **flak:** the fire of antiaircraft guns.

A.F.T.A.D. "Memphis Belle" B 17 (1943), Stow Wegenroth,
by permission of the Estate of Stow Wegenroth.

## Thinking Through the Literature

1. What is your reaction to the last line of this poem? Share your reaction with your classmates.

2. In reference to this poem, Randall Jarrell wrote that the gunner, who sat hunched up and revolved with the turret, looked like a fetus in the womb. With this **image** in mind, try to interpret the first four lines of the poem.

   THINK ABOUT { • what the phrase "fell into the State" might refer to
   • what sleeping, dreaming, and waking might mean

3. How would you describe the **speaker's** attitude toward his death?

4. What does this poem say to you about war and combat?

## TEACHING THE LITERATURE
### Customizing Instruction

**Less Proficient Readers**
Encourage students to form mental images of soldiers in fighter planes as they read. Explain that the speaker of the poem is the ball turret gunner and that he uses figurative language to describe his sensations while under attack.

**Set a Purpose** Remind students that they're expected to establish a purpose for reading, such as to understand the figurative language in this poem.

**Students Acquiring English**
Help students visualize the ball turret gunner and his situation. Jarrell described a ball turret as "a plexiglass sphere set into the belly of a B-17 or B-24 and inhabited by two .50-caliber machine guns and one man, a short, small man. When this gunner tracked with his machine guns a fighter attacking his bomber from below, he revolved with the turret; [he was] hunched upside down in this little sphere . . . . The fighters which attacked him were armed with cannon firing explosive shells." Explain that the "belly" of the plane refers to the bottom center of its fuselage and note the double meaning of the word.

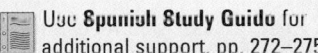 Use Spanish Study Guide for additional support, pp. 272–275.

**Gifted and Talented Students**
Remind students that Jarrell uses a dense, extended metaphor in his poem. Encourage students to work in pairs and write other metaphors to describe the ball turret gunner and his experiences.

## Thinking Through the Literature

1. Students should note that the statement in the last line is unemotional and matter-of-fact.

2. Possible Responses: Similar to a fetus awaiting birth, the gunner is in a state of nervous expectation. Crammed into the ball turret and wet, he's like a fetus in that he lives in another body (the plane) and is totally dependent on it. He's suspended above the earth and perhaps has been dreaming of a normal life. Like a fetus violently thrust into an unfamiliar world, he is awakened or called to action by the fire of guns.

3. Possible Responses: His death was simply a mess to be washed away; he expresses no feeling about his death, as if the event had happened to someone else.

4. Possible Responses: In war human beings are reduced to objects to be used and thrown away; war is dehumanizing.

**ADJUSTING READING STRATEGIES**

**A** Remind students that an essay generally presents a main point and provides supporting evidence. Ask students to identify and discuss the main point of this essay.

**Possible Response:** Soldiers do not speak about their painful memories in war because they have blocked them out and do not remember them.

 Use **Unit Seven Resource Book,** p. 10 for more practice.

### Reading Skills and Strategies: MAKING GENERALIZATIONS

**B** Ask students to make a generalization about what Steinbeck is saying about combat.

**Possible Responses:** The effects of war on a soldier are both internal and external; changes within the body enable a soldier not only to fight but to withstand the external bombardment of noise.

### Literary Analysis

**IMAGERY AND TONE**

**C** Ask students to identify the imagery in this passage and discuss the tone it conveys.

**Possible Responses:** "skin feels thick and insensitive"; "a salty taste in your mouth"; "painful knot is in your stomach"; The tone is direct, straightforward, and clinical.

# WHY SOLDIERS WON'T TALK

John Steinbeck

**D**uring the years between the last war and this one, I was always puzzled by the reticence[1] of ex-soldiers about their experiences in battle. If they had been reticent men it would have been different, but some of them were talkers and some were even boasters. They would discuss their experiences right up to the time of battle and then suddenly they wouldn't talk any more. This was considered heroic in them. It was thought that what they had seen or done was so horrible that they didn't want to bring it back to haunt them or their listeners. But many of these men had no such consideration in any other field.

 Only recently have I found what seems to be a reasonable explanation, and the answer is simple. They did not and do not remember—and the worse the battle was, the less they remember.

In all kinds of combat the whole body is battered by emotion. The ductless glands pour their fluids into the system to make it able to stand up to the great demand on it. Fear and ferocity are products of the same fluid. Fatigue toxins[2] poison the system. Hunger followed by wolfed food distorts the metabolic pattern already distorted by the adrenaline[3] and fatigue. The body and the mind so disturbed are really ill and fevered. But in addition to these ills, which come from the inside of a man and are given him so that he can temporarily withstand pressures beyond his ordinary ability, there is the further stress of explosion.

Under extended bombardment or bombing the nerve ends are literally beaten. The eardrums are tortured by blast and the eyes ache from the constant hammering.

This is how you feel after a few days of constant firing. Your skin feels thick and insensitive. There is a salty taste in your mouth. A hard, painful knot is in your stomach where

---

1. **reticence:** the tendency to be silent or say little.
2. **toxins:** poisons produced by the body that are capable of causing disease. Fatigue may be a symptom of a toxic infection.
3. **adrenaline** (ə-drĕn′ə-lĭn): a substance, also called epinephrine, secreted by the adrenal gland in response to stress. It speeds up the heartbeat and thereby increases bodily energy and resistance to fatigue.

## Teaching Options

**Mini Lesson** ## Vocabulary Strategy

**SUFFIXES**

**Instruction** Remind students that they're expected to apply meanings of suffixes in order to comprehend unfamiliar words. Explain that a suffix is a word part added to the end of a base word to form a new word. A suffix usually changes the part of speech of a word.

**Activity** Write the word *reasonable* on the chalkboard. Point out that the suffix -*able* means "capable of." One of the meanings of *reason* is "good judgment," so the word *reasonable* means "capable of good judgment."

**Exercise** Have students work in pairs to find out the meaning of the following words: *heroic, auditor, progressive, covetous,* and *validate.* Suggest that students separate the base word and the suffix, look up the meaning of the suffix in a dictionary, and then apply the meaning of the suffix to determine the meaning of the word.

 Use **Vocabulary Transparencies and Copymasters,** p. 91.

A lesson on suffixes appears on p. 1130 in the Pupil's Edition.

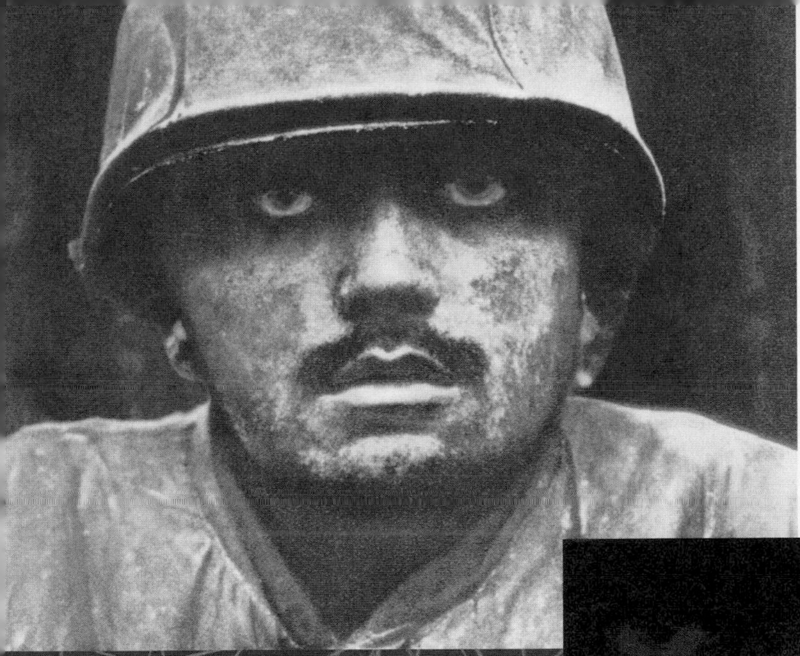

**Men in prolonged battle are not normal men. And when afterward they seem to be reticent—perhaps they don't remember very well.**

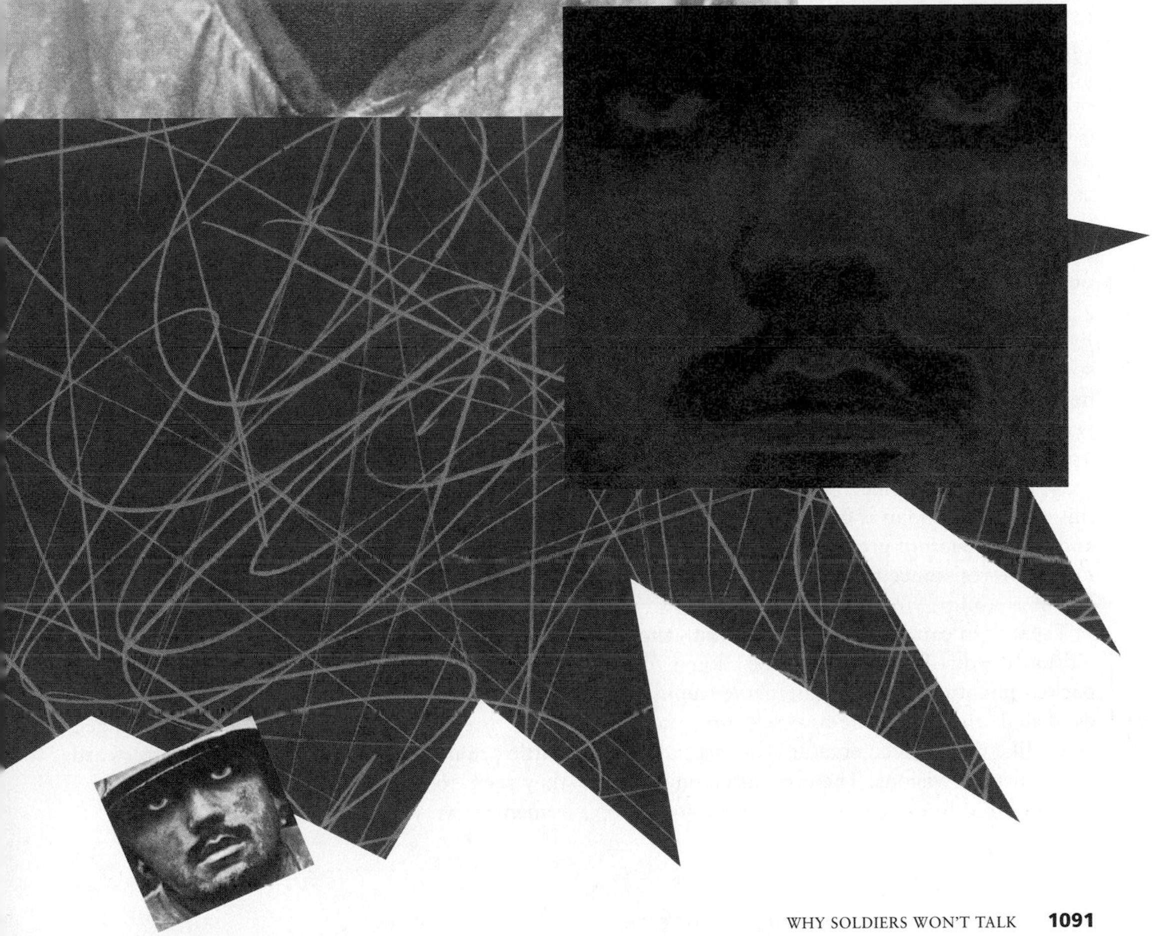



## Customizing Instruction

### Less Proficient Students

Explain to students that Steinbeck's essay is similar to Jarrell's poem in that it also concerns combat experience. Help students understand the time period of this essay. Clarify that Steinbeck is curious why soldiers in WWI, which ended in 1918, and soldiers of "this one" (WWII) do not tell about their experiences in combat. Point out that the United States entered WWII in 1941.

**Set a Purpose** Have students read to discover the physical symptoms a soldier suffers because of the stress of combat.

### Students Acquiring English

**1** Explain that the participle *wolfed* means "eaten quickly."

### Gifted and Talented

Point out that Steinbeck believes soldiers do not speak about their combat experiences because their memories have faded—as a coping mechanism for their survival. Ask students which they think is better—to remember a painful experience as part of the past and to deal with it as best they can, or to block it out and forget a part of their life forever.

## Mini Lesson Speaking and Listening

### INTERVIEW

**Instruction** Have students form pairs and take turns reading "The Death of the Ball Turret Gunner" and passages from "Why Soldiers Won't Talk" aloud. Ask them to pay attention to the details that convey the devastating effects of combat. Then, have them generate a list of ten questions to ask a soldier and develop reasonable answers to them. For example, they could explain what it feels like to be a ball turret gunner under fire or what the blasting sound does to one's ears.

**Prepare** Have pairs practice their interview, with one student assuming the role of soldier, the other that of interviewer. In this case, the soldier will be able to talk about his experience. Remind students that they're expected to justify the choice of verbal and nonverbal performance techniques by referring to the analysis of the text.

**Present** Students may decide how to present their interview to the class. Audience members should evaluate how the interview increases their appreciation for the works they've read and their empathy for the plight of a soldier.

**BLOCK SCHEDULING** This activity is particularly well suited for longer class periods.

**Reading Skills and Strategies:**
**CLARIFY**

**Ⓐ** Steinbeck uses fairly extensive physical descriptions to get his point across. Have students use elements of texts to clarify interpretations of what Steinbeck is saying about men who survive.

**Possible Responses:** Men who survive have deadened their senses. Those men who cannot will not be able to mentally survive war.

**Literary Analysis**

**IMAGERY AND TONE**

**Ⓑ** Have students locate the images in this passage and discuss what tone these images convey.

**Possible Responses:** "your whole body seems to be packed in cotton"; "main nerve trunks are deadened"; "out of the battered cortex curious dreamlike thoughts emerge." These images convey a grim, surreal tone. The soldier sleeps, and out of his battered brains come thoughts from the past, which are almost like visions quickly whisked away. These images help the reader understand how the soldier's experiences can fade into something he cannot recollect.

**Literary Analysis:**
**COMPARE AND CONTRAST**

Students are expected to compare and contrast elements of texts across texts. Ask them to list similarities and differences between the two selections.

**Possible Responses:** Similarities: Both tell about the horrors of war; both make reference to childbirth; both use vivid imagery. Differences: The poem focuses on a specific combat event, while the essay is about the body's physiological and psychological responses to combat.

---

the food is undigested. Your eyes do not pick up much detail and the sharp outlines of objects are slightly blurred. Everything looks a little unreal. When you walk, your feet hardly seem to touch the ground and there is a floaty feeling all over your body. Even the time sense seems to be changed. Men who are really moving at a normal pace seem to take forever to pass a given point. And when you move it seems to you that you are very much slowed down, although actually you are probably moving more quickly than you normally do.

**Ⓐ** Under the blast your eyeballs are so beaten that the earth and the air seem to shudder. At first your ears hurt, but then they become dull and all your other senses become dull, too. There are exceptions, of course. Some men cannot protect themselves this way and they break, and they are probably the ones we call shell-shock cases.

In the dullness all kinds of emphases change. Even the instinct for self-preservation is dulled so that a man may do things which are called heroic when actually his whole fabric of reaction is changed. The whole world becomes unreal. You laugh at things which are not ordinarily funny and you become enraged at trifles. During this time a kind man is capable of great cruelties and a timid man of great bravery, and nearly all men have resistance to stresses beyond their ordinary ability.

**Ⓑ** Then sleep can come without warning and like a drug. Gradually your whole body seems to be packed in cotton. All the main nerve trunks are deadened, and out of the battered cortex curious dreamlike thoughts emerge. It is at this time that many men see visions. The eyes fasten on a cloud and the tired brain makes a face of it, or an

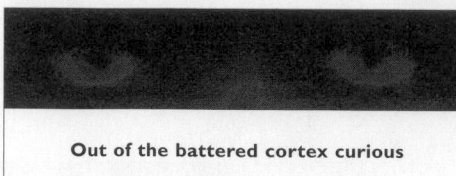

> Out of the battered cortex curious dreamlike thoughts emerge. It is at this time that many men see visions. The eyes fasten on a cloud and the tired brain makes a face of it, or an angel or a demon.

angel or a demon. And out of the hammered brain strange memories are jolted loose, scenes and words and people forgotten, but stored in the back of the brain. These may not be important things, but they come back with startling clarity into the awareness that is turning away from reality. And these memories are almost visions.

And then it is over. You can't hear, but there is a rushing sound in your ears. And you want sleep more than anything, but when you do sleep you are dream-ridden, your mind is uneasy and crowded with figures. The anesthesia your body has given you to protect you is beginning to wear off, and, as with most anesthesia, it is a little painful.

And when you wake up and think back to the things that happened they are already becoming dreamlike. Then it is not unusual that you are frightened and ill. You try to remember what it was like, and you can't quite manage it. The outlines in your memory are vague. The next day the memory slips farther, until very little is left at all. A woman is said to feel the same way when she tries to remember what childbirth was like. And fever leaves this same kind of vagueness on the mind. Perhaps all experience which is beyond bearing is that way. The system provides the shield and then removes the memory, so that a woman can have another child and a man can go into combat again.

It slips away so fast. Unless you made notes on the spot you could not remember how you felt or the way things looked. Men in prolonged battle are not normal men. And when afterward they seem to be reticent—perhaps they don't remember very well. ❖

---

## Teaching Options

✓ **Assessment** **Informal Assessment**

**WRITE A LETTER** You can informally assess students' understanding by asking them to respond to the following scenario. This activity allows students to draw inferences and support them with textual evidence and experience.

*Imagine that you are a friend of a soldier who has just arrived home from war. Family members are upset because they think something is wrong—the soldier will not talk to anybody about his experiences in battle. Write a letter to the family, mentioning some of the atrocities of combat, explaining why the soldier won't talk about his experiences and assuring them that he will recover.*

**RUBRIC**

**3 Full Accomplishment** The letter demonstrates an understanding of the horrors of war as well as the idea that soldiers don't speak because they don't remember—a perfectly natural occurrence.

**2 Substantial Accomplishment** The letter shows an understanding of the horrors of combat, but does not fully explain why the soldier will not speak to family members.

**1 Partial Accomplishment** The letter does not accurately convey either the horrors of combat or the reason why soldiers are silent.

# *Thinking* through the LITERATURE

## Connect to the Literature

**1. What Do You Think?**
Were you surprised at Steinbeck's explanation of why soldiers don't talk about their combat experiences?

> **Comprehension Check**
> • According to Steinbeck, why don't soldiers talk about combat?
> • What physical changes occur during combat?

## Think Critically

**2.** **ACTIVE READING** **ADJUSTING READING STRATEGIES** With a partner, discuss the notes you wrote down in your **READER'S NOTEBOOK** on the poem and essay. Which strategy was most valuable when you read "The Death of the Ball Turret Gunner"? Which was most helpful when you read "Why Soldiers Won't Talk"?

**3.** How are you affected by Steinbeck's use of the second-person "you" in his recounting of the physical effects of combat?

**4.** Steinbeck explains the physical experience of combat as a series of **causes** and **effects.** Do you think this is an effective method? Explain why or why not.

**5.** Does Steinbeck's explanation seem plausible to you?

**THINK ABOUT**
- the causes and effects he cites
- your own physical reactions to stress
- your own memory of stressful events
- other possible reasons why soldiers might not talk

## Extend Interpretations

**6. Comparing Texts** Do you think that Jarrell and Steinbeck offer consistent or conflicting accounts of what combat feels like? Explain your answer.

**7. Connect to Life** Think about the adjustments veterans must make when they return from combat. What does society do to help ease their transition back into civilian life? What else do you think could be done?

## Literary Analysis

**IMAGERY AND TONE** A writer sometimes conveys **tone,** his or her attitude toward a subject, through imagery. **Imagery** consists of the descriptive words and phrases used to re-create sensory experiences. In "The Death of the Ball Turret Gunner," notice the mental picture of a soldier created by the images "hunched in its belly" and "my wet fur froze." In "Why Soldiers Won't Talk," Steinbeck uses imagery to convey his attitude toward soldiers:

> *This is how you feel after a few days of constant firing. Your skin feels thick and insensitive. There is a salty taste in your mouth. A hard, painful knot is in your stomach where the food is undigested.*

**Paired Activity** Get together with a partner and discuss imagery in the two selections. List images from Jarrell's poem and Steinbeck's essay. From these images, what would you say is Jarrell's attitude toward the soldier? What is Steinbeck's attitude toward combat and its effect on soldiers? How would you characterize the tone in each piece? Do Jarrell and Steinbeck seem to have the same attitude toward war as a whole?

THE DEATH OF THE BALL TURRET GUNNER / WHY SOLDIERS WON'T TALK **1093**

## Extend Interpretations

**Comparing Texts** Many students are likely to feel that the authors offer consistent accounts because both describe the terrible toll that combat takes on soldiers. Others may feel that while Jarrell's poem is a condemnation of war, Steinbeck's essay does not condemn war itself.

**Connect to Life** Responses will vary. Students might mention the training and educational opportunities available to soldiers as well as the grants and loans available to veterans.

### Connect to the Literature

**1. What Do You Think?**
Some students may state that they thought soldiers deliberately repressed painful experiences.

**Comprehension Check**
• They don't remember what happened.
• The glands pour fluids into the system; adrenaline and fatigue disturb the mind and body.

Use Selection Quiz
**Unit Seven Resource Book,** p. 12.

### Think Critically

**2.** Some students may state that picturing the poem's images was most helpful in reading Jarrell's poem and that identifying Steinbeck's main idea gave them a framework for understanding his supporting reasons and details.

**3.** Possible Response: It created tension because it made it seem as if the events were really happening. It also made the essay more personal because Steinbeck spoke to the readers as if they were soldiers and knew exactly what he meant.

**4.** Students might point out that Steinbeck must explain why soldiers forget their combat experiences, and so explaining the causes of this condition is an effective method.

**5.** Possible Responses: yes, because people will often remember only the events before and after a particularly traumatic event; no, soldiers probably don't talk about their experience because they would have to relive it while they were talking, and they don't want to do that.

### Literary Analysis

**Imagery and Tone** Jarrell's tone is one of horror at the soldier's fate. He seems to condemn war for reducing people to objects. Steinbeck seems more intrigued about the various effects of combat than Jarrell is. Steinbeck stresses the physical responses to the pressures of war, which push the human body and psyche to their breaking point.

# Writing Options

1. **Grave Inscriptions** Have students discuss what difference there might be. For example, how well would the official know the gunner? Whose words would be more meaningful?

2. **Personal Narrative** Students' narratives should reflect an understanding of how emotional stress can cause physical symptoms. **To make this assignment easier for students,** brainstorm a list of fairly common stressful situations and their accompanying physical reactions.

# Activities & Explorations

1. **Interview with a Veteran** Students' interviews should reflect an understanding of the war in which the veteran fought, as well as some of the common symptoms soldiers exhibited during that war. **To get students started on this assignment,** have them work with a partner to come up with a list of questions to ask. Suggest that students explain Steinbeck's theory to the interviewee and ask whether he or she agrees.

2. **Model Plane** Students should consult reference books on WWII aircraft to get a better understanding of the makeup of the ball turret.

# Inquiry & Research

**Shell Shock** Encourage students to read about the condition from a soldier's point of view, rather than simply providing the technical, psychological definition. **To get students started,** divide the class into small groups to investigate some of the following questions as part of their research:

• When were the terms *shell shock* and *battle fatigue* first applied?

• Can civilians in a war suffer from the condition?

• Are these conditions ever found in people who are not at all involved in a war? If so, under what conditions is a person apt to develop the symptoms?

• Were the causes of battle fatigue in World War II the same as those in the Vietnam War? If not, explain how they differed.

---

## Writing Options

1. **Grave Inscriptions** Write two epitaphs—brief inscriptions on a tombstone—for the ball turret gunner. Write one that an official of "the State" might compose for him and one that the gunner might write for himself if he could.

2. **Personal Narrative** Write a personal narrative describing a situation in which you experienced extreme fear or stress. Focus on the physical reactions you had to the stress.

## Activities & Explorations

1. **Interview with a Veteran** Set up an interview with a combat veteran of Vietnam, Desert Storm, or any other world conflict. Does the veteran avoid talking in detail about actual battle experience? If permitted, tape-record your interview and share it with the class. ~ **SPEAKING AND LISTENING**

2. **Model Plane** Study the picture of the B-17 on page 1089, or any photograph of a B-17 or B-24 with a ball turret. Create a model of the plane with a gunner inside. Show your model to the class, sharing your own thoughts about what it would feel like to be inside such a plane. ~ **ART**

## Inquiry & Research

**Shell Shock** Investigate the condition known as *shell shock,* which is also called *battle fatigue* or *combat fatigue.* In an oral report, describe the symptoms of this condition to your classmates.

### Randall Jarrell
1914–1965

**Other Works**
*Losses*
*Pictures from an Institution*
*The Woman at the Washington Zoo*
*Complete Poems*

**Foremost WWII Poet** Randall Jarrell has been called "America's foremost poet of World War II." He drew upon his four years of army service and upon news dispatches from the war front in writing *Little Friend, Little Friend,* the collection in which some of his best-known poems appear. In praise of the collection, critic Suzanne Ferguson wrote, "The motif of the soldier as a child who barely learns the meaning of his life before he loses it, who lives and dies in a dream, . . . is developed in one striking poem after another."

**Life and Death** Born into a working-class family in Nashville, Tennessee, Jarrell spent much of his childhood in Long Beach, California. He earned a master's degree from Vanderbilt University in 1939 and went on to become a professor of creative writing and literature and a highly respected literary critic. A man who enjoyed playing tennis and driving sports cars, Jarrell died at the age of 51 after being struck by a car.

### John Steinbeck
1902–1968

**Other Works**
*Tortilla Flat*
*In Dubious Battle*
*Of Mice and Men*
*Cannery Row*
*East of Eden*

**The Writer's Charge** In 1962 John Steinbeck became the sixth American to win the Nobel Prize in literature. In his acceptance speech, he said: "Literature is as old as speech. It grew out of human need for it, and it has not changed except to become more needed. . . . The ancient commission of the writer has not changed. He is charged with exposing our many grievous faults and failures, with dredging up to the light our dark and dangerous dreams, for the purpose of improvement." In his classic novel *The Grapes of Wrath,* Steinbeck brought to light the suffering and exploitation of Depression-era migrant laborers.

**Living Simply** Steinbeck's life spanned both world wars, the Korean War, and the Vietnam War, in which one of his sons served. Steinbeck avoided publicity, preferring to live simply and casually. As a young man, he held jobs as a ranch hand, a factory worker, and a construction worker.

---

## Teaching Options  Grammar

**RHYTHM: REPETITION VS. REDUNDANCY**
**Instruction** Explain that redundancy is the needless use of words with similar meanings. Careful reading can help students spot and delete words that unnecessarily repeat an idea. Repetition occurs when a word or phrase is used more than once. Repetition that skillfully connects ideas can strengthen coherence and add to the rhythm of a sentence. Write the following sentence on the chalkboard:

**Model Sentence**

> Modern writers of today sometimes experiment with point of view.

Point out that the phrase *of today* unnecessarily repeats the idea expressed by the word *modern* and should be deleted.

> The soldiers' reticence could not be explained any other way; it was a reticence stemming from fear and pain.

The repetition here adds rhythm and coherence.

 Use **Grammar Transparencies and Copymasters,** p. 171.

 Use McDougal Littell's *Language Network,* Chapter 15, for more instruction in rhythm.

# Letter from Paradise, 21° 19′ N., 157° 52′ W.

*Essay by* JOAN DIDION

# In Response to Executive Order 9066

*Poetry by* DWIGHT OKITA

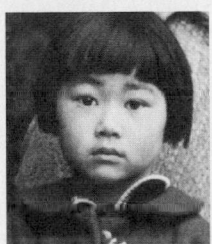

**Connect to Your Life**

**Acts of War** "Yesterday, December 7, 1941—a date which will live in infamy—the United States of America was suddenly and deliberately attacked by naval and air forces of the Empire of Japan." With those words, President Franklin D. Roosevelt, in response to the Japanese bombing of the U.S. naval base at Pearl Harbor in Oahu, Hawaii, began his request to Congress to declare war against Japan. What do you know about the attack on Pearl Harbor? What do you know about the later internment, or confinement, of Japanese Americans living on the West Coast of the United States? Brainstorm with a small group of classmates in order to share your knowledge.

## Build Background

**Effects of Pearl Harbor** When the first Japanese bombs struck Pearl Harbor shortly before eight in the morning, the American forces were utterly unprepared. Anchored ships, such as the *Nevada*, the *Utah*, and the *Arizona*, provided easy targets for bombs and torpedoes. Most American airplanes, parked in orderly rows, were destroyed on the ground. In the attack, 18 ships were sunk or damaged, nearly 200 planes were destroyed, and thousands of people were killed.

The attack spawned American hatred and fear of Japan—and of Japanese Americans. Fearing that Japanese Americans would cooperate with the enemy, people on the West Coast of the United States sought to have all persons of Japanese ancestry—citizens and noncitizens alike—removed from coastal areas. Such a removal was authorized by President Roosevelt in Executive Order 9066. During 1942 more than 110,000 Japanese Americans living along the West Coast were forcibly removed from their homes and sent to internment camps called "relocation centers."

Read Joan Didion's essay, which describes her visit to Pearl Harbor 25 years after the attack, and Dwight Okita's poem, which gives a Japanese-American girl's response to the relocation order, to gauge the repercussions of that "day of infamy" in 1941.

## Focus Your Reading

**LITERARY ANALYSIS** **MOOD** As you know, **mood** is the feeling or atmosphere that the writer creates for the reader. **Imagery, setting, dialogue,** and **figurative language** all contribute to the mood of a work, as do the sound and the **rhythm** of the language used. As you read the selections, think about the mood the writer conveys in each one.

**ACTIVE READING** **COMPARING MOOD** One way to compare two different selections is to compare the mood in each piece. As noted above, the images, dialogue, and figurative language in a literary work contribute to its mood.

**READER'S NOTEBOOK** As you read "Letter from Paradise," use a chart like the one shown to record the images, dialogue, and figurative language that contribute to the essay's mood. Create and fill out a similar chart for "In Response to Executive Order 9066."

| Images | Dialogue | Figurative Language |
|--------|----------|---------------------|
|        |          |                     |
|        |          |                     |

---

## OVERVIEW

**Objectives**
1. understand an **essay** and a **poem** (Literary Analysis)
2. understand **mood** (Literary Analysis)
3. compare **mood** in an essay and a poem (**Active Reading**)

**Summary**
In this essay, Didion describes her reactions to visiting Pearl Harbor, Hawaii, the naval base bombed by the Japanese on December 7, 1941. Twenty-five years after the bombing, she takes a tour boat to visit the sites where the American battleships were sunk. She finds herself overcome with grief. At a nearby cemetery, she is struck by the young ages of the soldiers buried there. She notices a couple placing flowers on the grave of a boy who was killed at age 19. She also notices men digging graves for soldiers recently killed in the Vietnam War. The speaker of Okita's poem "In Response to Executive Order 9066" is a 14-year-old Japanese-American girl who is preparing to go to an internment camp. Her favorite food is hot dogs, and her best friend is Denise—that is, until Denise hears that the speaker and her family are "trying to start a war."

**Thematic Link**
Both Didion and Okita are **remembering World War II** in their selections. Didion mourns the young soldiers who were killed and those who are dying in Vietnam. The speaker in Okita's poem recalls a different kind of war casualty—the internment of Japanese Americans.

**5-Minute Warm-Up**

*Daily Language SkillBuilder*

Have students **proofread** the display sentences on page 1069i and write them correctly. The sentences also appear on Transparency 31 of **Grammar Transparencies and Copymasters.**

---

## LESSON RESOURCES

**UNIT SEVEN RESOURCE BOOK,** pp. 13–16

**ASSESSMENT RESOURCES**
**Formal Assessment,** pp. 205–206
**Teacher's Guide to Assessment and Portfolio Use**
**Test Generator**

**SKILLS TRANSPARENCIES AND COPYMASTERS**
**Literary Analysis**
• Mood, T18 (for Activity, p. 1101)

**Reading and Critical Thinking**
• Compare and Contrast, T15 (for Active Reading, p. 1095)
**Grammar**
• Compound Adjectives, C70 (for Mini Lesson, p. 1102)
**Vocabulary**
• Prefixes, C90 (for Mini Lesson, p. 1097)
**Writing**
• Showing, Not Telling, T22 (for Writing Options, p. 1102)
**Communications**
• Appreciative Listening, T2 (for Mini Lesson, p. 1100)

**INTEGRATED TECHNOLOGY**
**Audio Library**
**LaserLinks**
• Geographical Connection: Pearl Harbor, Hawaii
• Historical Connection: Prejudice Against Japanese Americans
• Historical Connection: Japanese Americans During World War II. See **Teacher's SourceBook,** pp. 96–98.
**Internet: Research Starter**
**Visit our website:** www.mcdougallittell.com

## Reading and Analyzing

**Literary Analysis** [MOOD]

**A** Have students fill in a graphic organizer to list the images according to their sensory appeal in the first paragraph. Ask students to describe the mood this imagery creates.

**Possible Response:** The mood is festive and casual. Tourists sip drinks, toss coins at the swimming boys, and leaf through souvenir programs.

**B** Have students identify some images in this passage and explain the mood they convey.

**Possible Responses:** "water neither turquoise nor bright blue here but the grey of harbor waters everywhere"; "the rusted after-gun turret breaking the grey water"; "the flag at full mast." The mood is somber and mournful.

Use **Unit Seven Resource Book**, p. 15 for more practice.

**Active Reading** [COMPARING MOOD]

**C** Students are expected to compare and contrast moods within texts. Have students create another graphic organizer to record the images in this passage. Then ask them to contrast the mood of this passage with that at the beginning of the essay.

**Possible Responses:** "buried up there in the crater of an extinct volcano"; "APRIL 10 1928–MARCH 25 1945." The mood of this passage is tragic, depressing, and humbling; it contrasts with the cheaply festive atmosphere of the first paragraph.

Use **Unit Seven Resource Book**, p. 14 for more practice.

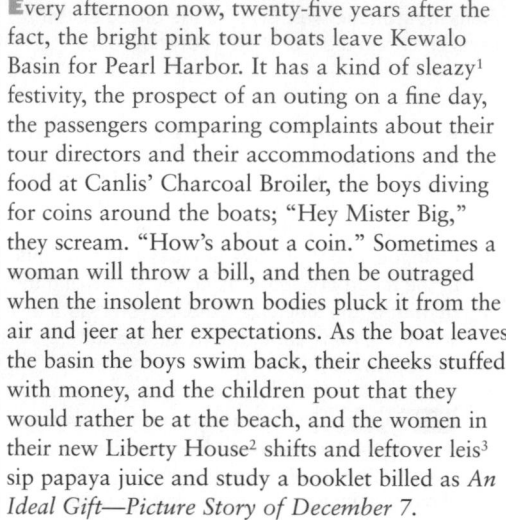

## Letter from Paradise, 21° 19' N., 157° 52' W.

### Joan Didion

**A** **E**very afternoon now, twenty-five years after the fact, the bright pink tour boats leave Kewalo Basin for Pearl Harbor. It has a kind of sleazy[1] festivity, the prospect of an outing on a fine day, the passengers comparing complaints about their tour directors and their accommodations and the food at Canlis' Charcoal Broiler, the boys diving for coins around the boats; "Hey Mister Big," they scream. "How's about a coin." Sometimes a woman will throw a bill, and then be outraged when the insolent brown bodies pluck it from the air and jeer at her expectations. As the boat leaves the basin the boys swim back, their cheeks stuffed with money, and the children pout that they would rather be at the beach, and the women in their new Liberty House[2] shifts and leftover leis[3] sip papaya juice and study a booklet billed as *An Ideal Gift—Picture Story of December 7*.

It is, after all, a familiar story that we have come to hear—familiar even to the children, for of course they have seen John Wayne and John Garfield at Pearl Harbor, have spent countless rainy afternoons watching Kirk Douglas and Spencer Tracy and Van Johnson[4] wonder out loud why Hickam[5] does not answer this morning —and no one listens very closely to the guide. Sugar cane now blows where the *Nevada* went **1** aground. An idle figure practices putting on Ford Island.[6] The concessionaire breaks out more papaya juice. It is hard to remember what we came to remember.

And then something happens. I took that bright pink boat to Pearl Harbor on two afternoons, but I still do not know what I went to find out, which is how other people respond a quarter of a century later. I do not know because there is a point at which I began to cry, and to notice no one else. I began to cry at the place where the *Utah* lies in fifty feet of water, water neither turquoise nor bright blue here but the grey of harbor waters everywhere, and I did not stop until after the pink boat had left the *Arizona,* or what is visible of the *Arizona*: the rusted after-gun turret[7] breaking the grey water, the flag at full mast because the Navy considers the *Arizona* still in commission, a full crew aboard, 1,102 men from forty-nine states. All I know about how other people respond is what I am told: that everyone is quiet at the *Arizona*.

**B**

---

1. **sleazy:** shabby; cheap; shoddy.
2. **Liberty House:** a major department store in Hawaii.
3. **leis** (lāz): wreaths made of large colorful flowers and worn around the neck.
4. **John Wayne . . . Van Johnson:** Hollywood actors who starred in films dramatizing the attack on Pearl Harbor.
5. **Hickam:** Hickam Air Force Base, near Pearl Harbor. It also was attacked on December 7.
6. **Ford Island:** an island within Pearl Harbor.
7. **after-gun turret:** a low, revolving gun mount located in the "aft," or rear part, of a ship.

**1096** UNIT SEVEN   PART 1: REMEMBERING THE WARS

## Teaching Options

### BLOCK SCHEDULING: MANAGING TIME

**If your schedule requires that you cover the lesson objectives in a shorter time, use . . .**
- Preparing to Read, p. 1095
- Thinking Through the Literature, pp. 1098, 1101

**If you want to take advantage of longer class time, use . . .**
- TE Teaching Options: Vocabulary Strategy, p. 1097; Informal Assessment, p. 1099; Speaking and Listening, p. 1100
- Choices & Challenges, p. 1102
- Related Reading, pp. 1103–1104

A few days ago someone just four years younger than I am told me that he did not see why a sunken ship should affect me so, that John Kennedy's assassination, not Pearl Harbor, was the single most indelible event of what he kept calling "our generation." I could tell him only that we belonged to different generations, and I did not tell him what I want to tell you, about a place in Honolulu that is quieter still than the *Arizona:* the National Memorial Cemetery of the Pacific. They all seem to be twenty years old, the boys buried up there in the crater of an extinct volcano named Punchbowl, twenty and nineteen and eighteen and sometimes not that old.

Copyright © 1991 P.J. Griffiths/Magnum Photos Inc.

"SAMUEL FOSTER HARMON," one stone reads. "PENNSYLVANIA. PVT 27 REPL DRAFT 5 MARINE DIV. WORLD WAR II. APRIL 10 1928—MARCH 25 1945." Samuel Foster Harmon died, at Iwo Jima,[8] fifteen days short of his seventeenth birthday. Some of them died on 7 December, and some of them died after the *Enola Gay* had

---

8. **Iwo Jima** (ē′wə jē′mə)ı Iwo Jima and Okinawa (ō′kĭ-nä′wə), mentioned later, are islands that lie several hundred miles south of Japan. They were the sites of the last two major World War II battles in the Pacific. In 1942 a battle on the island of Guadalcanal (gwŏd′l-ka-năl′), east of New Guinea, raged for six months. Together, the three battles produced more than 80,000 casualties.

The battleship *Arizona,* sunk in the Pearl Harbor attack. From the white platform (seen from the side in the photo above), observers look down at the submerged wreck. Copyright © 1991 H.K. Owen/Black Star.

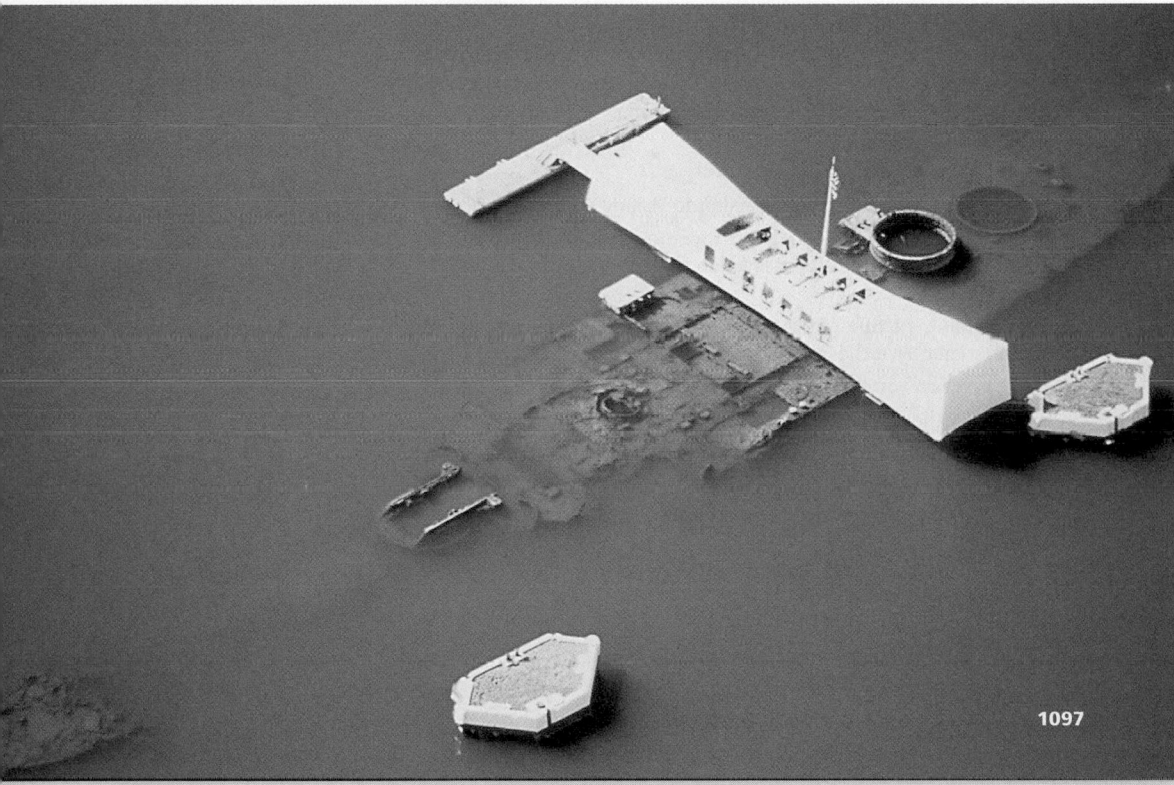

1097

**Literary Analysis** MOOD

(A) Have students describe the mood of this passage.

**Possible Responses:** somber—because a young boy died before ever getting the chance to live; sad—because the woman, probably his mother, still suffers terrible grief 21 years later

**Reading Skills and Strategies: VISUALIZE**

(B) Have students visualize what this graveyard looks like and ask them what details are especially striking. You might point out that Didion concludes her essay with matter-of-fact details about the cemetery: for example, the identification cards, streaked and splattered; the raw and trampled soil; the fast-growing grass in the moist climate.

---

already bombed Hiroshima, and some of them died on the dates of the landings at Okinawa and Iwo Jima and Guadalcanal, and one whole long row of them, I am told, died on the beach of an island we no longer remember. There are 19,000 graves in the vast sunken crater above Honolulu.

I would go up there quite a bit. If I walked to the rim of the crater, I could see the city, look down over Waikiki[9] and the harbor and the jammed arterials,[10] but up there it was quiet, and high enough into the rain forest so that a soft mist falls most of the day. One afternoon a couple came and left three plumeria[11] leis on the grave of a California boy who had been killed, at nineteen, in 1945. The leis were already wilting by the time the woman finally placed them on the grave, because for a long time she only stood there and twisted them in her hands. On the

whole I am able to take a very long view of death, but I think a great deal about what there is to remember, twenty-one years later, of a boy who died at nineteen. I saw no one else there but the men who cut the grass and the men who dig new graves, for they are bringing in bodies now from Vietnam. The graves filled last week and the week before that and even last month do not yet have stones, only plastic identification cards, streaked by the mist and splattered with mud. The earth is raw and trampled in that part of the crater, but the grass grows fast, up there in the rain cloud. ❖

---

9. **Waikiki** (wī′kĭ-kē′): a beach and resort district near Honolulu, on the Hawaiian island of Oahu.

10. **arterials:** major streets and highways.

11. **plumeria** (plōō-mîr′ē-ə): a tropical tree bearing large fragrant, colorful flowers.

## Thinking Through the Literature

1. **Comprehension Check** What does Didion see when she visits Pearl Harbor? when she visits the National Memorial Cemetery of the Pacific?

2. What **images** from this essay stay with you?

3. How do you explain Didion's reaction to visiting Pearl Harbor?

4. Didion first describes Pearl Harbor, then the National Memorial Cemetery of the Pacific. What links do you see between the two places?

5. Do you think the **title** of this essay is a good one? Offer reasons why Didion might have chosen it.

6. What point do you think Didion is making in this essay?

   THINK ABOUT { • the last lines of the selection
   • any **ironies** you see in the details she includes

7. If you have ever visited a war memorial, or any other memorial to the dead, how did your reaction compare with Didion's in this essay?

## Thinking Through the Literature

1. She sees the sunken battleships; she notices the gravestones of young soldiers.

2. Possible Responses: the rusted gun turret and the flag of the *Arizona,* the identification cards at the National Memorial Cemetery

3. Possible Responses: The magnitude of the event seemed to overwhelm her; adding to the pathos, perhaps, was the fact that new graves were being dug and filled with bodies from another war.

4. Possible Responses: Pearl Harbor marks the beginning of the war, and the cemetery signals the end for soldiers who were killed; at both places, nature persists—water covers the battleships at Pearl Harbor, and grass covers the graves in the cemetery.

5. Some students may notice that the word *Paradise* and the latitude and longitude readings in the title set up an ironical connection between it and the content of the essay.

6. Possible Responses: World War II cost a tremendous number of lives and now the United States was involved in a new war; we need to remember the human cost of war.

7. Students may say that visiting a war memorial stirs deep sadness and a profound sense of loss.

In Response to Executive Order 9066:

ALL AMERICANS OF JAPANESE DESCENT

MUST REPORT TO RELOCATION CENTERS

Dwight Okita

Dear Sirs:
    Of course I'll come. I've packed my galoshes
    and three packets of tomato seeds. Denise calls them
    love apples. My father says where we're going
5    they won't grow.

    I am a fourteen-year-old girl with bad spelling
    and a messy room. If it helps any, I will tell you
    I have always felt funny using chopsticks
    and my favorite food is hot dogs.
10    My best friend is a white girl named Denise—
    we look at boys together. She sat in front of me
    all through grade school because of our names:
    O'Connor, Ozawa. I know the back of Denise's head very
    well.

Clockwise from top: a woman and her children arriving at the relocation center in Manzanar, California; men in Manzanar; a young girl on evacuation day

1099

# Reading and Analyzing

## Literary Analysis MOOD

**A** Have students discuss how Denise's words affect the mood of the poem.

**Possible Responses:** Denise's words show that she is frightened and has "turned on" her friend; she's become suspicious and considers her former best friend the "Enemy." Cynicism and distrust have shattered Denise's innocence.

## Active Reading COMPARING MOOD

**B** Ask students what the tomato seeds might represent. Then have students contrast the mood in the last stanza with that in the first lines of the poem.

**Possible Responses:** The tomato seeds stand for the love and friendship the girls shared. The speaker is shocked and hurt by Denise's reaction, and the mood is one of sadness, confusion, and tenderness. In the first stanza, the tomato seeds represented her friend's love that the speaker wanted to take with her to the internment camp.

I tell her she's going bald. She tells me I copy on tests.
15  We're best friends.

I saw Denise today in Geography class.
She was sitting on the other side of the room.
**A** "You're trying to start a war," she said, "giving
      secrets
away to the Enemy, Why can't you keep your big
20  mouth shut?"

I didn't know what to say.
**B** I gave her a packet of tomato seeds
and asked her to plant them for me, told her
when the first tomato ripened
25  she'd miss me.

Clockwise from top: a car carrying a family to Manzanar; schoolgirls reciting the Pledge of Allegiance a few weeks before evacuation; a sign posted on the boundary of a relocation center; barracks at Manzanar

**1100**   UNIT SEVEN   PART 1: REMEMBERING THE WARS

# Teaching Options

##  Mini Lesson Speaking and Listening

### POEM RECITATION

**Instruction** Have students form small groups to analyze how the speaker in Okita's poem gets her points across without directly telling the reader how she feels. For example, to establish her American heritage, she describes what she likes to eat and who her best friend is. She also uses simple but symbolic details.

**Prepare** Have students select a meaningful event from their lives to retell to the class in a poem. Remind students that their poems need not

rhyme, but convey significant ideas or emotions. Point out that Okita often sets his poems to music and suggest that students find a piece of music to reflect the mood of the poem they will create and recite.

**Present** Students may decide how they will recite their poems. Audience members should evaluate how the recitation increases their appreciation for both the student's poem and Okita's.

**BLOCK SCHEDULING** This activity is particularly well-suited for longer class periods.

## Connect to the Literature

**1. What Do You Think?** What thoughts and feelings do you have about the speaker in Okita's poem?

> **Comprehension Check**
> • Who is the speaker's best friend?
> • What does the speaker give her friend?

## Think Critically

**2.** What do the details that the **speaker** mentions communicate to you about her?

**3.** If you had been in the speaker's situation, would your attitude toward the executive order have been similar to hers? Explain.

**4.** How do you interpret what the speaker's friend Denise says to her?

**5.** What do you think the tomato seeds might represent in the poem?

**THINK ABOUT**
> • what Denise calls them
> • where they will not grow
> • what the speaker says Denise will do when they ripen

**6.** **ACTIVE READING** **COMPARING MOOD** Use the charts you created in your **READER'S NOTEBOOK** to identify the overall **mood** of "Letter from Paradise" and "In Response to Executive Order 9066." Then compare the mood of Didion's essay with that of Okita's poem. Which piece do you think conveys mood more powerfully? Share your ideas with a classmate.

## Extend Interpretations

**7. The Writer's Style** Both Didion and Okita write in an understated style, not boldly offering their opinions but instead carefully piling up descriptive details. Which do you think are the most telling details included in each piece? Consider ones that are particularly informative or ironic. Explain your choice of details, telling what important ideas you believe the writer is suggesting with them.

**8. Connect to Life** Imagine that the United States was suddenly attacked by a foreign country. How do you suppose Americans would react? Would they support an immediate declaration of war? How would they treat citizens who had originally come from the attacking country, or whose relatives lived there?

## Literary Analysis

**MOOD** **Mood** is the feeling or atmosphere a writer creates for the reader. The mood within a literary work can change. In "Letter from Paradise," for example, notice the light, informal mood of this passage, which describes the tour boats that leave for Pearl Harbor:

> *It has a kind of sleazy festivity, the prospect of an outing on a fine day, the passengers comparing complaints about their tour directors and their accommodations and the food at Canlis' Charcoal Broiler, the boys diving for coins around the boats; "Hey Mister Big," they scream. "How's about a coin."*

Compare the boisterous mood in the above passage with the somber, contemplative mood conveyed by Didion's description of the setting of the National Memorial Cemetery:

> *If I walked to the rim of the crater, I could see the city, look down over Waikiki and the harbor and the jammed arterials, but up there it was quiet, and high enough into the rain forest so that a soft mist falls most of the day.*

**Activity** Answer these questions: How would you describe the mood Didion creates in the first paragraph of her essay? When does the mood change, and what changes it? Does it change again, or does it stay the same throughout the rest of the selection? What mood does Okita create in the first 15 lines of his poem? How does the mood change in the last 10 lines? Why do you think both authors chose to create different moods within their work?

---

## GUIDING STUDENT RESPONSE

## Connect to Literature

**1. What Do You Think?** Some students may express sadness at the breakup of a friendship.

**Comprehension Check**
• a white girl named Denise
• a packet of tomato seeds

 Use Selection Quiz in **Unit Seven Resource Book,** p. 18.

## Think Critically

**2.** Possible Responses: that she is strong and independent, able to speak ironically about going to the camp as if she's received an invitation; that she's determined and practical because she still wants her best friend to plant her tomato seeds

**3.** Some students may state that they would have been indignant at the executive order if they had been in the speaker's place.

**4.** Possible Responses: Denise is scared that she is losing her friend; Denise is repeating words she's heard from her parents, but she doesn't thoroughly understand them; Denise is now suspicious of her best friend because of what others have said; Denise doesn't want the speaker to know that she will miss her

**5.** Possible Responses: love; hope; friendship; peace

**6.** Both the poem and the essay begin in a casual, informal, albeit slightly ironic way and gradually become more serious. Didion's essay reflects the terrible loss and sadness inflicted by war. Okita's poem also reflects the sadness of a lost relationship.

---

## Extend Interpretations

**The Writer's Style** Students may mention Didion's detail that the Navy considers the sunken *Arizona* as still in commission. In Okita's poem, the detail that the tomato seeds will not grow in the internment camp suggests an arid, sunless place of captivity.

**Connect to Life** Some students may state that frightened people often look for scapegoats to punish and vent their anger on the innocent.

## Literary Analysis

**Mood** Possible Responses: In the first paragraph of the essay, the mood is festive. It changes when Didion describes how she cried when the tour boat reached the sunken ships. The mood never lightens again but grows more somber as she describes the cemetery and the grieving couple. At the end of the essay, Didion intensifies the sorrow by mentioning the dead soldiers brought from Vietnam and the rain cloud. In the first fifteen lines, Okita creates a mood of playfulness and innocence. The mood changes abruptly to one of fearful accusation and then wistful tenderness in the last 10 lines. In both works, the contrast in moods creates an ironic effect.

# Choices & CHALLENGES

## Writing Options

**Family Memoir** In her essay, Didion says, "I think a great deal about what there is to remember, twenty-one years later, of a boy who died at nineteen." In your mind, re-create this 19-year-old boy, giving him a name as well as physical and personal characteristics. Then write a short memoir detailing what a parent or a sister might remember most about him.

## Activities & Explorations

**Contrasting Cartoons** Make two cartoon sketches of the speaker in "In Response to Executive Order 9066." The first should depict her as she views herself, and the second should show her as she is perceived by other Americans after the attack on Pearl Harbor. Base your images on details and dialogue from the poem. ~ ART

## Inquiry & Research

**Japanese-American Internment** Find out more about the internment of Japanese Americans. What were some of the social and economic effects of imprisonment? Present your findings to the class. See the Related Reading on page 1103 for opposing views of the internment.

 **More Online: Research Starter**
www.mcdougallittell.com

---

## Joan Didion
1934–

**Other Works**
*Run River*
*Salvador*
*After Henry*
*Miami*

**A Distinctive Style** Joan Didion has received as much acclaim for her essays as she has for her best-selling novels. Critic Robert Towers describes her distinctive talent as "an instinct for details that continue to emit pulsations in the reader's memory and a style that is spare, subtly musical in its phrasing and exact." Like "Letter from Paradise," her essays tend to have a personal, confessional tone. In her collections *Slouching Towards Bethlehem* and *The White Album*, Didion deals with the themes of personal and cultural loss, disorder, and anxiety.

**Reasons for Writing** A screenwriter as well as a journalist and novelist, Didion was born and raised in California, where she has lived most of her life. She is married to the writer John Gregory Dunne, with whom she sometimes collaborates on screenplays. Of her writing, Didion says, "I write entirely to find out what I'm thinking, what I'm looking at, what I see and what it means. What I want and what I fear."

## Dwight Okita
1958–

**Other Works**
*Crossing with the Light*
*The Rainy Season*
*Salad Bowl Dance*

**Early Promise** A Japanese American and a native Chicagoan, Dwight Okita has been writing poetry since first grade. When given writing assignments in school, he had difficulty creating "linear compositions," and so he would add rhymed poems at the end of his assignments. His teachers started grading both his assigned compositions and his poems—giving him poor grades for the compositions but good grades for his poems. In high school, Okita took an interest in writing, acting, and music. Today, he combines these interests by giving dramatic readings of his poetry, which he often sets to music.

**Poetic Test** In writing "In Response to Executive Order 9066," Okita adopted the voice of his mother, who, as a youngster during World War II, was sent to an internment camp. He imagined how she might have said goodbye to her classmates before being taken away. Okita's play *Letters I Never Wrote* began as a spinoff of this poem.

---

## Teaching Options

### Writing Options

**Family Memoir To get students started on this activity,** have them review the few details given about the grieving couple. Encourage students to write a short description of the boy and his life before writing the memoir.

### Activities & Explorations

**Contrasting Cartoons** Students' cartoons should reflect the fact that the speaker views herself as a typical American teenage girl, while others view her as the enemy. **To make this assignment easier,** pair students who like to draw with those who don't. Partners can discuss design and layout, and both can contribute ideas.

### Inquiry & Research

**Japanese-American Internment** Encourage students to comment on what they've learned about discrimination and unfair persecution from researching the internment of Japanese Americans. For an extension activity, students might discuss similar events in history or in the present.

 **Mini Lesson** ## Grammar

### THE PLACEMENT OF *ONLY*

**Instruction** An adverb is a word used to modify a verb, an adjective, or another adverb. For clarity, an adverb should be placed as closely as possible to the word it modifies. For example, the adverb *only* should appear immediately before the word(s) it qualifies.

**Activity** Write the following sentences on the chalkboard.

> The speaker wants <u>only</u> to give her friend the tomato seeds. The speaker wants to give her friend <u>only</u> the tomato seeds.

The first sentence means that the speaker's sole desire is to give her friend the tomato seeds. The second sentence means that the speaker wants to give her friend the tomato seeds but nothing else.

**Exercise** Have students rewrite the sentences correctly.

1. The reason that only the Arizona sank was that the Japanese bombed it. (*The only reason*)
2. Denise is the one who could have only hurt the speaker so deeply. (*only one*)

 Use **Grammar Transparencies and Copymasters,** p. 70.

 Use McDougal Littell's *Language Network,* Chapter 7, for more instruction in adverbs.

# POINT / COUNTERPOINT:

## THE JAPANESE-AMERICAN INTERNMENT

*The Japanese bombing of Pearl Harbor in 1941 sparked war with the United States and spread fear that Japanese Americans would aid Japan during World War II. As a result, Executive Order 9066 was issued, and more than 110,000 Japanese Americans living on the West Coast of the United States were placed in internment camps. The following pieces present the arguments for and against internment.*

### JAPANESE-AMERICAN INTERNMENT WAS NECESSARY FOR NATIONAL DEFENSE.

❶ The United States was still reeling from the Japanese attack on Pearl Harbor that had brought it into World War II—a threat, some felt, to its very existence. Tom Clark, assistant to the commanding general of the U.S. Army's Western Defense Command and later associate justice of the Supreme Court, offered a justification for internment. "Soon after Pearl Harbor I was deluged by demands that, regardless of citizenship, every person of Japanese descent must be removed from the West Coast," he explained. "The threatening public attitude . . . would permit nothing less than total mass relocation."

❷ Chief Justice Earl Warren pointed out, on the other hand, that many Japanese Americans held dual citizenship and were educated in both Japan and the United States. "Their affiliation in time of war worried us," he explained.

War correspondent Walter Lippman offered more concrete reasons. "It is the fact that the Japanese navy has been reconnoitering[1] the Pacific Coast. . . . It is the fact that communication takes place between the enemy at sea and the enemy agents on land."

❸ Historians Donald Pike and Roger Olmsted observe that only Japan among the Axis nations had attacked the United States, and "suddenly the Japanese . . . threatened our very national existence."

---

1. **reconnoitering** (rē′kə-noi′ tər-ĭng): making a military inspection of an area.

## Reading for Information

At various points in American history, the threat of war has heightened feelings of suspicion and fear. Even ordinary citizens were viewed as threatening, particularly those who came from Japan, a nation that had attacked the United States at Pearl Harbor. What security measures— severe or relaxed—should a nation take under such circumstances? It's important to consider all sides before deciding which viewpoint seems more reasonable.

### ANALYZING AN ISSUE

An issue is a topic, policy, or action that is a matter of concern or debate. **Analyzing an issue** involves examining different points of view to evaluate each side of the argument and to make an informed judgment about the issue. Use the activities below to help you examine the issue of Japanese-American internment.

❶ **Position Statement**  Notice that the first argument begins with a position statement supporting the internment of Japanese Americans.

❷ Identify the reasons for interning Japanese Americans. What justifications did the U.S. government use for internment?

❸ **Analyzing Evidence**  Which reason supporting internment seems strongest to you? What evidence is provided to support that reason?

### Objectives

- read and analyze articles with opposing viewpoints
- evaluate arguments and make informed decisions
- connect literature to historical contexts
- determine why some people were for and others were against Japanese internment

### Connecting to the Literature

"Point/Counterpoint: The Japanese-American Internment" is the type of nonfiction article that can help students connect literature such as "In Response to Executive Order 9066" to actual historical events. The poem reflects a very controversial period in American history. Once students read this article, they will sympathize even more with the speaker of the poem and perhaps understand why other Americans felt internment was necessary.

### Reading for Information

Tell students that this article provides direct testimony from a military commander, legal personnel, a war correspondent, an internee, and several historians—all people intimately connected with World War II. As you read through this article with students, have them use the activities and questions in the right-hand column as a guide to analyzing an issue. The following are possible responses to the five questions and activities.

### ANALYZING AN ISSUE

1. **Position Statement**
   **Possible Response:** A position statement should clearly define the viewpoint of a particular speaker or group of speakers. The position statement is followed by concrete, convincing arguments as to why that position is the correct one.

2. **Possible Response:** The following are reasons for interning Japanese Americans: many Americans were demanding that every person of Japanese descent be interned; government officials were unsure of the loyalty of Japanese Americans who had dual citizenship; the Japanese navy had been inspecting the Pacific Coast and perhaps communicating with Japanese agents on land.

3. **Analyzing Evidence**
   **Possible Response:** The strongest reason supporting internment is the fact that many Americans were demanding that Japanese Americans be interned. In an atmosphere of panic, such people may have resorted to violence against citizens of Japanese ancestry. Internment was necessary to protect everyone involved. Evidence includes Clark's use of the words *deluged* and *threatening.*

**4. Possible Response:** An internee's comment makes the argument against internment less credible because he was a victim of the decision and might therefore be too close to the subject to provide a fair, objective analysis of the situation. However, his testimony increases the emotional appeal of the argument because he is a victim who suffered from the decision and the reader sympathizes with him.

**5. Possible Response:** The internment of Japanese Americans cannot be justified as a war measure because neither German Americans nor Italian Americans were interned. Furthermore, there is not one instance of Japanese-American disloyalty or sabotage during the war.

**Evaluating Arguments** Accept all reasonable, well-supported responses.

## JAPANESE-AMERICAN INTERNMENT WAS AN UNNECESSARY AND A RACIST ACT.

④ "Our unjust imprisonment was the result of two closely related emotions: racism and hysteria," says Edison Tomimaro Uno, a former internee. Uno says the claim that Japanese Americans were relocated for their own protection was "sheer hypocrisy" and denies that Japanese Americans posed a national security threat. Instead, he calls the relocation a crime attributable to "racism [and] economic and political opportunism."

"War makes for harsh measures," notes the historian Cary McWilliams, "but we cannot justify the evacuation even as a war measure. No such measure was taken against German or Italian nationals."[2]

⑤ Another historian, Henry Steele Commager, comments, "It is sobering to recall that the record does not disclose a single case of Japanese disloyalty or sabotage during the whole war." In fact, more than 25,000 Japanese Americans served in the armed forces during World War II, and the all-Japanese-American 442nd combat team inflicted more casualties and received more decorations than any other comparable army unit.

Relocation left many Americans with a legacy of shame. Chief Justice Earl Warren confessed in his autobiography that he "deeply regretted" his testimony in favor of internment. Tom Clark said, "It was a sad day in our constitutional history."

Japanese-American children wait for a train to take them to the Manzanar internment camp.

---

2. **German or Italian nationals:** people living in the United States who were born in Germany or Italy.

④ The second argument quotes Edison Tomimaro Uno, a Japanese-American internee, who states that the relocation was "attributable to 'racism [and] economic and political opportunism.'" What effect does including an internee's comment have on the **credibility** (believability) of the argument against internment? What effect do Uno's statements have on the "emotional appeal" of the argument?

⑤ What reasons are given to support the position that internment was an unnecessary and unjust act? What evidence is used to support those reasons?

**Evaluating Arguments** Which side of the debate over Japanese-American internment do you believe presents the most convincing case? Give reasons to support your opinion.

# Ambush

*Short Story by* TIM O'BRIEN

## Comparing Literature

### Traditions Across Time: War in Vietnam

The Vietnam War lasted nine years, claimed about 58,000 American lives, and left another 365,000 wounded. Night after night during that war, Americans at home watched footage of shocking combat scenes on the evening news programs. Like the soldiers described in John Steinbeck's essay, "Why Soldiers Won't Talk," the soldiers in Vietnam endured horrors—death, injury, physical hardship, and emotional trauma. In this story, Tim O'Brien recounts an incident in one soldier's combat experience and its effects on his life.

**Points of Comparison**  As you read, look for the similarities and differences in the ways war and its effects are portrayed in "Ambush" and in "Why Soldiers Won't Talk."

## Build Background

**Uncertainties of War**  During the Vietnam War, even though the American soldiers were better equipped and better trained than the enemy, they fought in a foreign land they did not understand and for a cause that became increasingly unpopular at home. The Vietnamese Communists were skilled at guerilla warfare, using small armies in surprise raids. Their knowledge of the land enabled them to disappear whenever the U.S. forces attacked. These tactics often created a climate of frustration and fear among American soldiers. Tim O'Brien, who served 14 months as an infantryman during the war, presents one soldier's response to the fear and confusion in Vietnam and the troubling memories that haunt him after the war.

## Focus Your Reading

**LITERARY ANALYSIS**  **INTERNAL CONFLICT**  **External conflict**—the struggle between a character and some outside force—is usually easy to identify in a work of fiction. **Internal conflict**—a struggle within a character—may be more subtle and complex. For example, an internal conflict may revolve around a decision a character has to make, or it may be reflected in behavior that is contradictory. As you read this story, watch for the development of internal conflicts in the main character.

**ACTIVE READING**  **CONNECTING TO EXPERIENCE**  Unlike many stories, this story presents a situation—a combat zone during the Vietnam War—that is unfamiliar to most readers. In order to enter into the experiences being related, you can use the following strategies:

- Pay attention to all the details the writer gives.
- Try to imagine what being a soldier in combat might be like.
- Call to mind any movies, books, or articles about the Vietnam War that give you some idea of what being in that war was like.
- Recall any situation involving extended conflict—living in a high-crime area, for example—that you have encountered or heard about. Think about what similarities are present in all conflicts.

**READER'S NOTEBOOK**  As you read, keep notes about which details in the story you can connect with in some way. Also note any aspects of the story with which you find it difficult to relate.

### Objectives
1. understand and appreciate a **short story** (Literary Analysis)
2. understand **internal conflict** (Literary Analysis)
3. **connect to experience** (Active Reading)

### Summary
In this story, O'Brien uses a first-person narrator to recount an incident of war. The narrator's nine-year-old daughter, knowing that her father writes war stories, asks him if he has ever killed anyone. The narrator says no but resolves to tell her the truth when she is grown. He then recalls how he killed a young man in Vietnam. He and another soldier were on patrol, taking turns sleeping and keeping watch. Out of the predawn fog, a young man approached, carrying a gun. Instinctively, the narrator pulled the pin on a grenade and threw it, wanting to make the man disappear, not to kill him. Then he describes seeing the man's corpse with a hole where an eye should be. The narrator realizes that he could have let the man pass unharmed and that there was no real danger. Years later, the incident still haunts him. Sometimes he can forgive himself, sometimes not.

### Thematic Link
**Remembering the wars** can bring to mind haunting experiences and unresolved conflicts.

### 5-Minute Warm-Up

*Daily Language SkillBuilder*

Have students **proofread** the display sentences on page 1069i and write them correctly. The sentences also appear on Transparency 31 of **Grammar Transparencies and Copymasters.**

## LESSON RESOURCES

**UNIT SEVEN RESOURCE BOOK,** pp. 17–20

**ASSESSMENT RESOURCES**
**Formal Assessment,** pp. 207–208
**Teacher's Guide to Assessment and Portfolio Use**
**Test Generator**

**SKILLS TRANSPARENCIES AND COPYMASTERS**
**Literary Analysis**
- Multiple Conflicts/Themes, T15 (for Paired Activity, p. 1109)

**Reading and Critical Thinking**
- Noting Details, T9 (for Active Reading, p. 1105)

**Grammar**
- Adverb Qualifiers, C71 (for Mini Lesson, p. 1110)

**Vocabulary**
- Context Clues, C92 (for Mini Lesson, p. 1106)

**Writing**
- Literary Interpretation, C30 (for Writing Option 2, p. 1110)

**Communications**
- Appreciative Listening, T2 (for Activities & Explorations, p. 1110)

**INTEGRATED TECHNOLOGY**
**Audio Library**
**LaserLinks**
- Historical Connection: U.S. Soldiers in Vietnam. See **Teacher's SourceBook,** p. 99.
**Internet: Research Starter**
**Visit our website:**
www.mcdougallittell.com

## Literary Analysis

**INTERNAL CONFLICT**

 Have students describe the narrator's internal conflict.

**Possible Response:** whether to tell his nine-year-old daughter, Kathleen, that he has killed someone

Ask students whether they agree with the narrator's decision not to tell Kathleen the truth until she is older.

**Possible Responses:** yes, because at age nine she might not understand about war, and she might reject her father for killing someone; no, because children can accept death, and it is better not to lie to them

Use **Unit Seven Resource Book,** p. 19 for more practice.

## Active Reading

**CONNECTING TO EXPERIENCE**

 Help students connect this story to their own experiences. Ask them if they have ever reacted to a situation automatically and then later wondered why they responded as they did. Was it helpful or hurtful that they were able to respond automatically? Did they regret their actions, or did they feel relieved? Students who have been trained to respond a certain way in a given situation—for example, as a lifeguard—will be able to share their experiences and insights.

Use **Unit Seven Resource Book,** p. 18 for more practice.

### TIM O'BRIEN

When she was nine, my daughter Kathleen asked if I had ever killed anyone. She knew about the war; she knew I'd been a soldier. "You keep writing these war stories," she said, "so I guess you must've killed somebody." It was a difficult moment, but I did what seemed right, which was to say, "Of course not," and then to take her onto my lap and hold her for a while. Someday, I hope, she'll ask again. But here I want to pretend she's a grown-up. I want to tell her exactly what happened, or what I remember happening, and then I want to say to her that as a little girl she was absolutely right. This is why I keep writing war stories:

He was a short, slender young man of about twenty. I was afraid of him—afraid of something—and as he passed me on the trail I threw a grenade that exploded at his feet and killed him.

Or to go back:

Shortly after midnight we moved into the ambush site outside My Khe.[1] The whole platoon was there, spread out in the dense brush along the trail, and for five hours nothing at all happened. We were working in two-man teams —one man on guard while the other slept, switching off every two hours —and I remember it was still dark when Kiowa shook me awake for the final watch. The night was foggy and hot. For the first few moments I felt lost, not sure about directions, groping for my helmet and weapon. I reached out and found three grenades and lined them up in front of me; the pins had

> "YOU KEEP
> WRITING
> THESE
> WAR STORIES
> SO I GUESS YOU
> MUST'VE KILLED
> SOMEBODY."

---

1. **My Khe** (mĭ'kĕ').

## Teaching Options

 **Vocabulary Strategy**

**CONTEXT CLUES Instruction** Remind students that they can rely on context—words and phrases in the surrounding text—to determine the meanings of unfamiliar words and technical vocabulary. Sometimes they may have to search for context clues in the sentences preceding and following the target word. Read aloud this sentence from page 1107. The target word is *muzzle.*

> He carried his weapon in one hand, <u>muzzle</u> down, moving without any hurry up the center of the trail.

Have students ask themselves where they have heard the word *muzzle* before. (*Possible Response: You put a muzzle over the nose and mouth of a vicious dog.*) Then ask them what else the word might mean. Lead

students to note the word *weapon* and to conclude that the muzzle must be a part of the weapon. Have them develop a definition for *muzzle* in this context. (*Possible Response: the discharging end of the firearm, or the "nose" of a rifle*)

**Activity** Have students use context clues to figure out the meaning of *platoon* (p. 1106), *lob* (p. 1107), *swiveling* (p. 1108), *peril* (p. 1108), *gape* (p. 1108).

 Use **Vocabulary Transparencies and Copymasters,** p. 92.

A lesson on context clues appears on p. 326 in the **Pupil's Edition.**

*Fenixes* (1984), Rupert Garcia. Pastel on paper, 40″ × 78¾″, courtesy of Rupert Garcia; Rena Bransten Gallery, San Francisco; and Galerie Claude Samuel, Paris. Copyright © Rupert Garcia.

already been straightened for quick throwing. And then for maybe half an hour I kneeled there and waited. Very gradually, in tiny slivers, dawn began to break through the fog, and from my position in the brush I could see ten or fifteen meters up the trail. The mosquitoes were fierce. I remember slapping at them, wondering if I should wake up Kiowa and ask for some repellent, then thinking it was a bad idea, then looking up and seeing the young man come out of the fog. He wore black clothing and rubber sandals and a gray ammunition belt. His shoulders were slightly stooped, his head cocked to the side as if listening for something. He seemed at ease. He carried his weapon in one hand, muzzle down, moving without any hurry up the center of the trail. There was no sound at all—none that I can remember. In a way, it seemed, he was part of the morning fog, or my own imagination, but there was also the reality of what was happening in my stomach. I had already pulled the pin on a grenade. I had come

up to a crouch. It was entirely automatic. I did not hate the young man; I did not see him as the enemy; I did not ponder issues of morality or politics or military duty. I crouched and kept my head low. I tried to swallow whatever was rising from my stomach, which tasted like lemonade, something fruity and sour. I was terrified. There were no thoughts about killing. The grenade was to make him go away—just evaporate—and I leaned back and felt my mind go empty and then felt it fill up again. I had already thrown the grenade before telling myself to throw it. The brush was thick and I had to lob it high, not aiming, and I remember the grenade seeming to freeze above me for an instant, as if a camera had clicked, and I remember ducking down and holding my breath and seeing little wisps of fog rise from the earth. The grenade bounced once and rolled across the trail. I did not hear it, but there must've been a sound, because the young man dropped his weapon and began to run, just two or three quick steps, then he hesitated,

AMBUSH **1107**

## Customizing Instruction

### Students Acquiring English
Make sure students understand the meanings of the word *ambush*. As a noun, it means "lying in wait to attack by surprise," "a hidden trap," or "a surprise attack." As a verb, the word means "to attack from a concealed position." To help them remember, explain the word's origin—it derives from the Latin word *imboscare*, meaning "to hide in the bushes."

Use **Spanish Study Guide** for additional support, pp. 279–281.

### Less Proficient Readers
Help students identify the source and symptoms of inner conflict by asking the following questions.
- How does the narrator respond when he sees the man with the rifle walking up the trail?
  **Possible Response:** Without even thinking, he pulls the pin from a grenade and throws it at him.
- How does he feel about tossing the grenade?
  **Possible Response:** It makes him feel sick to his stomach.
- Do you feel the narrator made the right decision when he threw the grenade? Why?
  **Possible Responses:** Yes, he threw it in self-defense; yes, he had no way of knowing the other man's intentions; no, he did not think about the situation but merely reacted in a panic; no, he didn't seem to be in any danger.

**Set a Purpose** Have students read on to find out how the narrator feels about this experience when looking back on it years later.

## Viewing and Representing

### *Fenixes* **by Rupert Garcia**

**ART APPRECIATION** Garcia was born in California in 1941. In this triptych—an art work divided into three panels—the center of attention lies in the bright panel to the left, where a figure appears to be caught on fire, as if from an explosion. The other two panels are closely related to the figure on the left, which has an almost photographic quality.
**Instruction** Tell students that historically a triptych was a piece of art consisting of three panels and telling a religious story.
**Application** Help students explain the thematic connection among the three panels. Ask them to

discuss what story this triptych tells.
**Possible Responses:** The theme here is warfare. On the left there is someone burning to death—the colors represent the conflagration of war. The middle panel looks like a swarm of helicopters skimming low to the ground at night—the cool blue is soothing in contrast to the orange and red on the left, and something about it is hopeful, suggesting rescue. The panel to the right depicts a soldier at arms in silhouette. The soldier's fuzzy outline and the dark, murky colors suggest a shroud of death. It might also be a ghostly reappearance of the soldier in the first panel.

## Literary Analysis INTERNAL CONFLICT

**(A)** What thought does the narrator express that lets you know he was in conflict about tossing the grenade from the very beginning?

**Possible Responses:** He says he wants to warn the man about the grenade. Even though he tosses it, he also wants the man somehow to escape the blast.

**(B)** How do you know that he hasn't "finished sorting it out"?

**Possible Responses:** He lies to his daughter, believing he is protecting her. Although she is astute enough to ask him directly if he killed anyone during the war, he is the one who cannot acknowledge the fact. Though he claims that he'll tell her the truth when she is older, he's really just buying time to come to terms with what he did. Even now, years later, he doesn't know whether to forgive himself. He is haunted by the image of the dead man.

## Reading Skills and Strategies: INTERPRETING

**(C)** Ask students what the young man's secret smile might mean.

**Possible Responses:** It is a mocking, vengeful smile, because the young man knows the narrator can never forgive himself for the killing; it is a smile of understanding, because the young man would have acted the same way in the narrator's place; it is a peaceful smile, because for the young man the incident is over, although it lives on in the narrator's mind.

EVEN NOW I HAVEN'T FINISHED SORTING IT OUT. SOMETIMES I FORGIVE MYSELF, OTHER TIMES I DON'T.

swiveling to his right, and he glanced down at the grenade and tried to cover his head but never did. It occurred to me then that he was about to **(A)** die. I wanted to warn him. The grenade made a popping noise—not soft but not loud either—not what I'd expected—and there was a puff of dust and smoke—a small white puff—and the young man seemed to jerk upward as if pulled by invisible wires. He fell on his back. His rubber sandals had been blown off. There was no wind. He lay at the center of the trail, his right leg bent beneath him, his one eye shut, his other eye a huge star-shaped hole.

It was not a matter of live or die. There was no real peril. Almost certainly the young man would have passed by. And it will always be that way.

Later, I remember, Kiowa tried to tell me that the man would've died anyway. He told me that it was a good kill, that I was a soldier and this was a war, that I should shape up and stop staring and ask myself what the dead man would've done if things were reversed.

None of it mattered. The words seemed far too complicated. All I could do was gape at the fact of the young man's body.

Even now I haven't finished sorting it out. **(B)** Sometimes I forgive myself, other times I don't. In the ordinary hours of life I try not to dwell on it, but now and then, when I'm reading a newspaper or just sitting alone in a room, I'll look up and see the young man coming out of the morning fog. I'll watch him walk toward me, his shoulders slightly stooped, his head cocked to the side, and he'll pass within a few yards of me and suddenly smile **(C)** at some secret thought and then continue up the trail to where it bends back into the fog. ❖

## Teaching Options

### BLOCK SCHEDULING: MANAGING TIME

**If your schedule requires that you cover the lesson objectives in a shorter time, use . . .**
- Preparing to Read, p. 1105
- Thinking Through the Literature, p. 1109

**If you want to take advantage of longer class time, use . . .**
- TE Teaching Options: Vocabulary Strategy, p. 1106; Viewing and Representing, p. 1107
- Choices & Challenges and Author Activity, p. 1110

## Connect to the Literature

**1. What Do You Think?**
What aspect of this story had the strongest impact on you?

**Comprehension Check**
- What was the young Vietnamese man doing before the narrator killed him?
- What does the dead soldier "do" when he "reappears" to the narrator?

## Think Critically

**2.** Why do you think the narrator kills the man?

THINK ABOUT
- the narrator's mental and physical state as the man nears
- Kiowa's remarks to the narrator
- the narrator's statement that "there was no real peril"

**3.** How would you describe the narrator's initial reactions after the killing?

**4.** Why do you think the narrator keeps writing war stories?

**5.** **ACTIVE READING** **CONNECTING TO EXPERIENCE** Look back at the notes you made in your **READER'S NOTEBOOK** about connecting to the experiences described in this story. What details drew you into the experiences the narrator relates? Were there any experiences that you could not relate to? Explain your answers.

## Extend Interpretations

**6. The Writer's Style** "Ambush" is a work of fiction, but the story reads like a nonfiction account of a true event. Why do you think O'Brien used this style? Do you think it is effective? Why or why not?

**7. Connect to Life** The fear and uncertainty of war can affect a person's ability to think clearly and make decisions. Think of other situations that might generate a level of anxiety and stress that would have similar consequences. Do you think decisions made under these circumstances should be judged in the same way as decisions made under ordinary circumstances? Explain your answer.

**8. Points of Comparison** "Ambush" and "Why Soldiers Won't Talk" both portray the effects of war on the soldiers who fight in them. Which of these selections seems most realistic and convincing to you? Support your answer with evidence from the selection.

## Literary Analysis

**INTERNAL CONFLICT**
An **external conflict** involves opposition with an outside force. The setting of "Ambush"—the Vietnam War—is a major external conflict between opposing nations and armies. Within that larger conflict the story focuses on the **internal conflicts**—the inner struggles—of the narrator. Internal conflicts may center on a decision a character must make or on problems that draw out contradictory behavior in the character. Internal conflicts often arise out of situations that are ambiguous—that can be interpreted in more than one way.

From the opening lines of the story, the narrator faces situations that generate internal conflicts for him. For example, when his daughter asks whether he has ever killed anyone, he does not know whether he should tell her the truth or not. He says, "It was a difficult moment, but I did what seemed right."

**Paired Activity** With a partner, identify another internal conflict the narrator experiences. Describe the conflict and the circumstances that lead to it. Tell whether you agree with the way the narrator tries to resolve the conflict.

**REVIEW** **TITLE**  The **title** of a work often carries more than one level of meaning. It may summarize a theme, raise a question, or make an ironic comment. Think about the meaning of the word *ambush*. Is more than one kind of ambush portrayed in this story? What is the main connection between the title and the story?

## Extend Interpretations

**Writer's Style** Responses will vary. Sound reasons for O'Brien's style follow: to make the story seem especially realistic and credible; to draw the reader into the action; to add to the story's suspense and shock value. Students' evaluation of the style should be well supported.

**Connect to Life** Many students will say that a different set of standards should be used to judge decisions made during extreme situations.

**Points of Comparison** Students who choose "Ambush" may say that the first-person narrator's impressions and vivid portrayal of combat make the story sound like an authentic eyewitness account. Students who choose "Why Soldiers Won't Talk" may cite the detailed descriptions of soldiers' physical and emotional reactions to battle conditions.

---

## Connect to the Literature

**1. What Do You Think?**
Some students may mention the ending in which the young man continues on the trail smiling and unharmed.

**Comprehension Check**
- He was walking along the trail. He had a gun with him, but he was not carrying it as if ready to fire.
- He comes walking out of the fog and smiles before walking away again.

Use Selection Quiz
**Unit Seven Resource Book**, p. 20.

## Think Critically

**2.** Sound reasons might include the following: The narrator, exhausted and terrified, automatically did what his training had taught him to do. Americans killed to save both their own and their fellow soldiers' lives because of the enormous threat from North Vietnam. As Kiowa believed, kill or be killed.

**3.** Possible Response: The American soldier felt so shocked and horrified no words could console him.

**4.** Some students might say that he is "confessing" to save his soul, while others might say he is trying to understand his actions in the war.

**5.** Students may list details about the setting, the narrator's reaction while tossing the grenade, or the explosion and its aftermath. Examples of engaging experiences will likely include compelling or highly dramatic moments, while unfamiliar experiences may include the narrator's complex emotional reactions.

## Literary Analysis

**Internal Conflict** Students may mention the narrator's conflict about whether to awaken Kiowa, to ask for mosquito repellent. Since the soldiers on patrol could sleep only in two-hour shifts, they must have been desperate for sleep; therefore, the narrator's decision not to disturb Kiowa is a compassionate one.

**Review Title** Possible Responses: One ambush is the actual attack that the narrator relates: how he lay in wait and killed an enemy soldier with a grenade. Another is the ambush of memory: how "in the ordinary hours of life" the narrator will "look up and see the young man coming out of the morning fog," reminding him of an event that happened years ago, lodged forever in his mind.

## Writing Options

1. **Exhibit Proposal** Encourage students to do the following: incorporate audio recordings of oral histories from men and women who served in Vietnam; include clippings from local newspapers covering the war; search the Internet and bookmark relevant sites; create their own memorial to the people who died in the war.

2. **Points of Comparison To get students started,** encourage them to find the thematic link between the two pieces. How do they think Steinbeck might respond if he were to read "Ambush"?

## Activities & Explorations

**Movie Score To get students started,** suggest that they listen to recordings of the scores to such war movies as *M\*A\*S\*H, Apocalypse Now,* and *Saving Private Ryan.*

## Inquiry & Research

**Guerrilla Tactics To make this assignment easier,** launch students into research by having them look up the dictionary definition of *guerilla.* Do not be surprised if students return from their research with gruesome details—booby traps were ubiquitous, creating a climate of fear and near paranoia. **To make this assignment more challenging,** suggest that students also look at international efforts to ban land mines.

## Author Activity

Students may mention that O'Brien describes the fear he felt in battle, contrasts fictional heroes with real ones, and explores the meaning of courage. He concludes that his resolve to do better next time in battle is a kind of courage.

---

# Choices & CHALLENGES

## Writing Options

1. **Exhibit Proposal** Draw up a proposal for a multimedia exhibit on Vietnam for your public library. Briefly describe the parts of the exhibit, including any technology components. Also include materials you think will be needed, a possible schedule for producing the exhibit, and a list of staff needs. Place the proposal in your **Working Portfolio.**

2. **Points of Comparison** Write a brief essay in which you analyze what happens in "Ambush" in terms of Steinbeck's ideas in "Why Soldiers Won't Talk." Consider how the two pieces might be considered to be in conflict as well as how Steinbeck's observations might help to explain what the narrator describes.

**Writing Handbook**
See page 1283: Analysis.

## Activities & Explorations

**Movie Score** Think about what episodes might go into a short movie based on "Ambush." Then look for pieces of music that would reflect the varying episodes and moods in such a movie. Put together the pieces in a sequence that could serve as a score for the film. If possible, get recordings of the works and play them for the class, explaining your choices. ~ MUSIC/SPEAKING AND LISTENING

## Inquiry & Research

**Guerrilla Tactics** Investigate the tactics used by the Vietcong guerrillas in the Vietnam War. Find out how their operations and attitudes created major obstacles for the American forces. Present your findings to the class, and discuss how the guerrilla tactics relate to what happens in "Ambush."

 **More Online: Research Starter**
www.mcdougallittell.com

---

# Tim O'Brien

**1946–**

**Other Works**
*If I Die in a Combat Zone, Box Me Up and Ship Me Home*
*Northern Lights*
*Going After Cacciato*
*The Nuclear Age*
*The Things They Carried*
*In the Lake of the Woods*

**War and Writing** In 1968, immediately after graduating from college with a bachelor's degree in political science, Tim O'Brien was drafted into the army. He was wounded in Vietnam, earning a Purple Heart. Discharged from the army as a sergeant, he accepted a full scholarship to Harvard University as a graduate student in government. While studying at Harvard, O'Brien wrote *If I Die in a Combat Zone, Box Me Up and Ship Me Home,* a book of memoirs about his combat experiences. He subsequently left Harvard to pursue writing as a full-time career.

**Major Awards** O'Brien's third book, *Going After Cacciato,* won the National Book Award in 1979.

Inspired by O'Brien's own struggle with the choice of whether to go to Vietnam or flee the country, the novel tells about a soldier who decides to escape from Vietnam and the army. *The Things They Carried,* O'Brien's fifth book, won the 1990 National Book Critics Circle Award as best novel of the year.

**Novelist's Focus** Although he writes about war, O'Brien does not consider himself a war novelist. The true concern of his writing, he says, is "the exploration of substantive, important human values." Regarding his most acclaimed novel, O'Brien said in an interview, "It's not really Vietnam that I was concerned about when I wrote *Cacciato;* rather, it was to have readers care about what's right and wrong and about the difficulty of doing right, the difficulty of saying no to a war."

## Author Activity

**Real-Life Experiences** Read some sections of O'Brien's memoirs, *If I Die in a Combat Zone, Box Me Up and Ship Me Home.* Share with the class any insights you gain into "Ambush" from O'Brien's reflections on his own experience.

---

# Teaching Options

**Mini Lesson** **Grammar**

**ADVERBS: QUALIFIERS Instruction** A qualifier is a word that limits or modifies the meaning of another word. Adverb qualifiers include *almost, completely, really, very, nearly,* and *quite.* Tell students that they can improve their writing by replacing a qualifying adverb and a weak adjective with one well-chosen adjective. Write the following sentence on the chalkboard. Ask students to think of a better adjective to replace *quite upset.* (*distraught; devastated; agitated*)

He was <u>quite upset.</u>

Lead students to realize that using fewer words leads to sharper writing and clearer thinking.

**Exercise** Have students underline the adverbial modifier in each sentence. Then have them identify at least one precise adjective that could replace the weak adverb/adjective pair.

1. The story was <u>really</u> interesting. (*intriguing; fascinating*)
2. He seemed <u>completely</u> confused by it all. (*bewildered; baffled; confounded*)
3. He felt <u>very</u> guilty for what happened. (*blameworthy; culpable*)

 Use **Grammar Transparencies and Copymasters,** p. 71.

 Use McDougal Littell's *Language Network,* Chapter 7, for more instruction in adverbs.

## Camouflaging the Chimera

*Poetry by* YUSEF KOMUNYAKAA
(yōō′sĕf kō′mōōn-yä′kä)

## Deciding

*Poetry by* WENDY WILDER LARSEN
*and* TRẤN THỊ NGA (drän thē nyä)

**Comparing Literature**

### Traditions Across Time: War in Vietnam

These poems present strong personal images of the Vietnam War from two perspectives—that of an American combat soldier and that of a Vietnamese civilian. Both pieces convey the upheaval of the war and bring to life its frightening realities.

**Points of Comparison** Compare the speaker in these poems with the characters and speakers in the World War II selections. Think about the turmoil and divisions experienced by people in both wars, and note similarities and differences in their attitudes toward war, life, and death.

## Build Background

**Evocative Titles** The word *chimera* in the title of the first poem has several meanings. It is the name of a mythical fire-breathing monster, a composite of a lion, a goat, and a serpent. The word also refers to a plant created from a mixture of cells of different species. In addition, *chimera* can mean a fantastic or terrible creation of the imagination.

The title of the second poem, "Deciding," refers to the difficult situation the speaker of the poem finds herself in. The speaker is a Vietnamese worker in an American office in Saigon who must decide whether to stay or flee after the United States has withdrawn its troops and the fall of South Vietnam appears imminent. She fears how she will be treated by the Communist victors from North Vietnam.

## Focus Your Reading

**LITERARY ANALYSIS  SPEAKER IN POETRY** The **speaker** of a poem, like the narrator of a story, is the voice that talks to the reader. In some poems, the speaker can be identified with the poet. However, in many poems, the speaker is someone or something other than the poet. As you read "Camouflaging the Chimera" and "Deciding," think about the role of the speaker in the two poems.

**ACTIVE READING  STRUCTURE IN POETRY** In poetry, **structure** refers to the arrangement of words, lines, and stanzas to produce a desired effect. The structure of a poem usually emphasizes important aspects of content and **mood.** In "Camouflaging the Chimera," for example, the staccato lines and brief, free verse stanzas help create a tense, wary mood.

**READER'S NOTEBOOK** As you read the poems, write down what you notice about the stanza structure in each one. Notice line length, the number of lines in each stanza, and the relationship between stanzas and the ends of sentences. Also, think about how the variety of stanza structure relates to the poem's mood and ideas.

### Objectives

1. understand and appreciate two **poems** about the Vietnam War (Literary Analysis)
2. understand the **speaker in poetry** (Literary Analysis)
3. examine **structure in poetry** (Active Reading)

### Summary

"Camouflaging the Chimera" is written from the viewpoint of a soldier fighting against the Viet Cong. The speaker describes the steps that the soldiers take to camouflage themselves so that they can lie in wait for the enemy. Their camouflaging is so successful that they become one with the countryside, invisible to the Viet Cong. In "Deciding," the speaker, a native Vietnamese, must decide whether to remain in Saigon or to flee before the communist onslaught. To remain is to risk capture and death; to flee is to abandon family, friends, and homeland forever.

### Thematic Link

In **remembering the Vietnam War**, the speakers of these poems present two perspectives—the soldier's and the civilian's.

## LESSON RESOURCES

**UNIT SEVEN RESOURCE BOOK,** pp. 21–22

**ASSESSMENT RESOURCES**
**Formal Assessment,** pp. 209–210
**Teacher's Guide to Assessment and Portfolio Use**
**Test Generator**

**SKILLS TRANSPARENCIES AND COPYMASTERS**
**Reading and Critical Thinking**
• Analyzing Text Structure, T17 (for Active Reading, p. 1111)

**Grammar**
• Capitalization II, C145 (for Mini Lesson, p. 1117)
**Vocabulary**
• Figurative Language, C93 (for Mini Lesson, p. 1112)
**Writing**
• The Uses of Dialogue, T24 (for Writing Options, p. 1117)

**INTEGRATED TECHNOLOGY**
**Audio Library**
**LaserLinks**
• Cultural Connection: Civilian Life in War-Torn Vietnam. See **Teacher's SourceBook,** pp. 99–100.
**Visit our website:**
www.mcdougallittell.com

**Literary Analysis** SPEAKER IN POETRY

Ask students to identify the speaker and the point of view. Then have them consider how the choice of speaker affects their experience of the poem.

**Possible Response:** The speaker is a soldier, and the point of view is first-person plural. The choice of speaker—a soldier in combat speaking for the entire platoon—heightens the immediacy of the experience and the intensity of the feelings conveyed.

 Use **Unit Seven Resource Book**, p. 22 for more practice.

**Active Reading**

STRUCTURE IN POETRY

Have students note that the sentences continue for more than one stanza. Ask students how this spilling over of ideas might reinforce the mood of the poem.

**Possible Responses:** The spilling over of ideas from stanza to stanza pushes the narrative forward, heightens the intensity, and reinforces the mood of anxiety.

 Use **Unit Seven Resource Book**, p. 21 for more practice.

### GUIDE FOR READING

**A** **Possible Response:** They are wearing camouflage made of nearby natural materials to blend in.

**B** **Possible Responses:** They are so still and look so much like the habitat that a bird might perch on them.

**C** **Possible Responses:** They are exhausted; they are remembering dead friends and past loves as they wait.

---

# Camouflaging the Chimera

### Yusef Komunyakaa

We tied branches to our helmets.
We painted our faces & rifles
with mud from a riverbank,

5   blades of grass hung from the pockets
of our tiger suits. We wove
ourselves into the terrain,
content to be a hummingbird's target.

We hugged bamboo & leaned
against a breeze off the river,
10  slow-dragging with ghosts

from Saigon to Bangkok,
with women left in doorways
reaching in from America.
We aimed at dark-hearted songbirds.

15  In our way station of shadows
rock apes tried to blow our cover,
throwing stones at the sunset. Chameleons

crawled our spines, changing from day
to night: green to gold,
20  gold to black. But we waited
till the moon touched metal,

till something almost broke
inside us. VC struggled
with the hillside, like black silk

25  wrestling iron through grass.
We weren't there. The river ran
through our bones. Small animals took refuge
against our bodies; we held our breath,

ready to spring the L-shaped
30  ambush, as a world revolved
under each man's eyelid.

### GUIDE FOR READING

**1–6** How do you visualize the soldiers from this description?

**5 tiger suits:** camouflage uniforms with black and green stripes.

**7** What might it mean to be "a hummingbird's target"?

**10–14** What is revealed about the soldiers' state of mind from their slow-dragging, or dancing, with ghosts and their aiming at songbirds?

**11 Saigon** (sī-gŏn'): formerly the capital of South Vietnam. **Bangkok** (băng'kŏk'): the capital of Thailand.

**15 way station:** a station between main stations, as on a railroad line. In what sense is the soldiers' position a "way station"?

**16 rock apes:** mountain-dwelling monkeys.

**16–21** Notice how the passage of time is suggested through these images of nature. In what ways are the soldiers like the chameleons?

**23–24 VC . . . silk:** The Viet Cong, Communist rebels who fought U.S. soldiers, typically wore black for camouflage during nighttime operations in the jungle.

**20–25** How were the American soldiers able to spot the VC?

**26–28** How well were the soldiers camouflaged?

---

## Teaching Options

 **Vocabulary Strategy**

**USING CONTEXT TO UNDERSTAND FIGURATIVE LANGUAGE**

**Instruction** Remind students that figurative language is one of the tools that poets use to suggest meaning. Explain that students should examine the context to help determine the meaning of figurative words and phrases. Write the following example on the board.

"We wove ourselves into the terrain . . ."

Point out that because this line appears in the context of the soldiers camouflaging themselves, it can be determined that they became one with the land, indistinguishable from the ground and foliage.

**Activity** Have students find the following examples of figurative language in the poem "Camouflaging the Chimera." Ask them to infer the meaning of the phrase from the context in which it appears.

1. "We hugged bamboo" (line 8)

2. "leaned against a breeze." (lines 8–9)

3. "But we waited / till the moon touched metal" (lines 20-21)

4. "like black silk / wrestling iron through grass." (lines 24-25)

**A lesson on context clues appears on p. 326 in the Pupil's Edition.**

Members of a long-range reconnaissance patrol unit in Vietnam. Photo by John Olson for *Life* Magazine. Copyright © Time Inc.

## Thinking Through the Literature

1. **Comprehension Check** What are the soldiers in the poem doing?

2. What did you think or feel as you visualized the **images** of the Vietnam War presented in this poem?

3. How do you interpret the last image in the poem?

4. What do you imagine the soldiers thought and felt in their "way station of shadows"? Support your answer with lines from the poem.

5. In line 26, how do you interpret the statement "We weren't there"?

6. Offer your explanation of the **title** "Camouflaging the Chimera."

THINK ABOUT
- which definition of chimera seems to best fit the poem (see page 1111)
- the visual image brought to your mind by the title

## Thinking Through the Literature

1. The soldiers are hiding and lying in wait to ambush the enemy.

2. Some students may state that visualizing the images made them feel tense and apprehensive.

3. Possible Responses: Each soldier sees his life pass before his eyes as he waits in ambush; the soldiers keep their individual worlds to themselves.

4. Possible Responses: Lines in the poem suggest they thought about the past and about women back home, and that the wait was tense and strained for them.

5. Possible Responses: They were so well camouflaged that they were invisible; they wished they were somewhere else.

6. Some students may say that the soldiers are the chimera, a violent and elemental force. Others may say that the chimera is the soldiers' own fear, which they hide from themselves.

## GUIDE FOR READING

**Ⓐ Possible Responses:** "We" are people working in the same office; they are Vietnamese people. They feel apprehension or numb dread.

**Literary Analysis** SPEAKER IN POETRY

**Ⓑ** Point out the change in the point of view in the second stanza to first-person singular. Ask students to explain the shift from plural to singular.

**Possible Response:** Although many people are in the same anxious and dangerous position, only the individual can make the decision to leave.

**Active Reading**
STRUCTURE IN POETRY

**Ⓒ** Have students explain the structure of this stanza.

**Possible Response:** The poet has used repetition and a series of questions with two statements inserted in the middle of the questions.

## GUIDE FOR READING

**Ⓓ Possible Responses:** "They" would be anyone in a position of authority in the new country. Her mother might not want to go because Vietnam is her country and she doesn't want to leave her family.

**Ⓔ Possible Responses:** She has decided to leave because she still has her childhood memories; she will not leave her country.

**Ⓕ Possible Responses:** It was happy and peaceful; soldiers were a part of life then too.

**Ⓖ Possible Responses:** terror; excitement; revulsion; sorrow.

# Deciding

Wendy Wilder Larsen and Tran Thi Nga

**W**e went to the office every day.
Though the situation was critical,
people at work said nothing.
Province Chiefs were running.
5   We told the Big Boss our country would be lost.
We told him we would blow ourselves up
if we could not leave.

Ⓑ I sat at my desk doing the financial report.
My thoughts went round and round.

10   Should I leave?
Should I go alone?
Should I take my mother?
She did not want to go.
She feared they wouldn't let her chew the betel.
15   Should I leave my children?
How would I make a living?
What would happen when the communists came?

When I made up my mind,
pictures of my childhood floated to the surface
20   as clear and strong as dreams.

**1** Our old house in Hadong.
The bamboo in the backyard.
We ate the shoots.
The soldiers made a fence from the stalks.
25   My sister and I painted the fence
first white, then blue, then her favorite yellow.
The small antigonon vine we planted
with its pink blossoms in spring.

## GUIDE FOR READING

**1–9** Who are "we"? What state of mind are these people in? Ⓐ

**12–14** Who are "they"? What are other reasons the mother might not want to leave? Ⓓ

**14 betel** (bēt'l): Many Asians chew nuts from the betel palm tree as a mild stimulant.

**18–20** Can you tell what the speaker has decided? Ⓔ

**21 Hadong** (hä'döng'): a town in North Vietnam.

**21–34** What can you tell about the speaker's childhood from these images? Ⓕ

**27 antigonon** (ăn-tĭ'gə-nän').

**1114**   UNIT SEVEN   PART 1: REMEMBERING THE WARS

## Teaching Options

### BLOCK SCHEDULING: MANAGING TIME

**If your schedule requires that you cover the lesson objectives in a shorter time, use . . .**
• Preparing to Read, p. 1111
• Thinking Through the Literature, p. 1116

**If you want to take advantage of longer class time, use . . .**
• TE Teaching Options: Informal Assessment, p. 1115
• Choices & Challenges, p. 1117

People running for a U.S. helicopter during the fall of Saigon in April 1975. Copyright © 1975 Nik Wheeler/Black Star.

## Customizing Instruction

### Less Proficient Readers
Ask students to identify the decision the speaker must make.
**Possible Responses:** She must decide whether or not to flee her country permanently.

### Students Acquiring English
**1** Make sure students understand that the sentence fragment at the beginning of the stanza introduces a flashback as the speaker thinks about her childhood and earlier life in Vietnam. The same device appears in line 29.

### Multiple Learning Styles
**Logical/Mathematical Learners**

Have students create a timeline of the events mentioned in this poem. Remind students that events will not appear in the same order in the timeline as they do in the poem.

Our ponds.
30 The many steps down
to the small bridge
where we'd sit hour after hour
letting our hands dip into the water
trying to catch the silver brown fish.

35 Airplanes bombing
running from our house
people dying, people calling from outside the walls
*don't take me. I'm not dead yet.*
The family hiding together in our house in Cholon
40 sunlight coming through the bullet holes.

**39 Cholon** (chō-lŏn'): the Chinese section of Saigon, in South Vietnam.

**35–40** What mood is created by these images?

DECIDING **1115**

---

## ✓ Assessment **Informal Assessment**

**LETTER WRITING** You can informally assess your students' understanding of the poem "Camouflaging the Chimera" by asking them to imagine that they are the speaker of the poem writing a letter home to a friend or family member. In this letter students should describe the maneuvers that have just taken place. Students should base the account on the poem and should reveal thoughts and feelings consistent with those of the speaker and capturing the experience for someone thousands of miles away.

**RUBRIC**

**3** **Full Accomplishment** Letters include accurate chronicling of the events in the poem, vivid description, and the unemotional yet insightful language of the speaker of the poem.

**2** **Substantial Accomplishment** Letters chronicle most of the events mentioned in the poem, offer some vivid description, and sound somewhat like the speaker of the poem.

**1** **Little or Partial Accomplishment** Letters do not convey a sense of what happens in the poem, are not descriptive, and do not echo the speaker's style.

### GUIDING STUDENT RESPONSE

## Connect to the Literature

### 1. What Do You Think?
Students should contrast reasons for staying with reasons for leaving Vietnam.

### Comprehension Check
• whether to flee Vietnam before the Communists take over
• memories of her peaceful childhood in Hadong; later memories of war in Cholon

## Think Critically

2. Students who believe the speaker decided to stay may say that her childhood memories convinced her that her homeland was worth staying in. Students who believe that the speaker, like the poet Nga, chose to flee may say that she realized her old, peaceful life was gone forever.
3. Some students may find it a hopeful image; others may find it represents the illusory nature of beauty; still others may say that the poet does not intend a specific message but wants each reader to draw his or her own inference.
4. Both American soldiers and Vietnamese civilians face the terror of the unknown. The soldiers cannot flee, but must repress their fears, remaining utterly still to ambush an unseen enemy. The civilians must wrestle with a terrible dilemma: whether to remain in their beloved country, risking capture and death, or to flee, abandoning their homeland forever.
5. In "Camouflaging the Chimera," the lines are short, with 3-line and 4-line stanzas alternating. The brief lines and stanzas reinforce a mood of tension and apprehension. In "Deciding," the stanzas vary in the number and length of lines. The short, staccato rhythm in the third stanza creates suspense and a mood of urgency. In stanza five, however, the longer lines ease the tension, supporting a mood of longing and nostalgia.

## Connect to the Literature

### 1. What Do You Think?
If you had been the speaker in "Deciding," would you have stayed or fled?

### Comprehension Check
• What does the speaker of "Deciding" have to decide?
• What memories does the speaker recall?

## Think Critically

2. How do you think the speaker's childhood memories influenced her decision?

3. What message do you draw from the final image of sunlight shining through bullet holes?

4. Judging only from these poems, whose experience of war do you think was worse, the American soldiers' or the Vietnamese civilians'?

 THINK ABOUT
{
• the soldiers' feelings as they wait in ambush and what you imagine the attack will be like
• the memories of the speaker in "Deciding" and the decision she is forced to make

5. **ACTIVE READING** **STRUCTURE IN POETRY** Review the notes you wrote down in your **READER'S NOTEBOOK**. What did you notice about the stanzas and line lengths in "Camouflaging the Chimera" and "Deciding"? How does the structure of each poem relate to the ideas and **mood** in each one?

## Extend Interpretations

6. **Connect to Life** Imagine that you are faced with the necessity of fleeing your country, possibly never to return. What images of your own life would fill your mind?

7. **Points of Comparison** "Deciding," "Armistice," and "Executive Order 9066" all deal with the turmoil and divisions experienced by civilians as a result of war. In what ways are the divisions described in the three pieces similar? In your opinion, which of the three situations described creates the most turmoil? Explain your answer.

## Literary Analysis

**SPEAKER IN POETRY** The **speaker** in a poem is sometimes a distant observer and at other times is intimately involved with the experiences and ideas being expressed. In both "Camouflaging the Chimera" and "Deciding," the use of first-person pronouns indicate that the speakers are active participants in the thoughts and actions described. In the following passage from "Camouflaging the Chimera," notice how the repeated use of the pronouns "we" and "our" emphasizes the speaker's identification with the group:

*We weren't there. The river ran through our bones. Small animals took refuge
against our bodies; we held our breath,...*

In "Deciding," the speaker also identifies with a group—"we"—which she distinguishes from another group—"they." The speaker reveals her own thoughts and memories but also refers throughout the poem to the words and feelings of others:

*Airplanes bombing
running from our house
people dying, people calling from outside the walls
don't take me. I'm not dead yet.*

**Cooperative Learning Activity** In a small group, discuss the speaker in each poem. Why do you think the poets made the speakers participants in the action? What would be lost if a detached observer had related a soldier's experience or a civilian's dilemma? What is the effect of each speaker's identification with his or her particular group?

## Extend Interpretations

**Connect to Life** Encourage students to visualize the situation briefly. Then invite them to begin by mentioning the first word, phrase, or sentence that enters their minds.

**Points of Comparison** The divisions are similar in that civilians—the Vietnamese people in Saigon, the Jewish people in Europe, and the Japanese-Americans bound for detention camps—are uprooted from the past and face an uncertain future. Opinions will vary as to which situation creates the most turmoil.

## Literary Analysis

**Speaker in Poetry** The choice of speaker affects the reader's emotional response to the poem and determines what kinds of details the reader is shown. By having the speakers participate in the action, the poets can provide details that are more immediate and vivid than those that a detached observer could furnish. "Camouflaging the Chimera" and the first stanza of "Deciding" use first-person plural speakers, an ideal choice for a poem on a shared public experience such as war.

# Choices & Challenges

## Writing Options

**Points of Comparison** Write a dialogue between the soldier in "The Death of the Ball Turret Gunner" and one of the soldiers on patrol in "Camouflaging the Chimera." Have the soldiers discuss their attitude toward war, death, and the enemy. Use images from the poems to develop their conversation.

## Inquiry & Research

**Environmental Effects of War** Both of these poems give a sense of Vietnam's unique physical environment. Investigate the effects of the war on the natural environment in Vietnam. Create an illustrated and annotated map of the country, detailing the environmental damage wrought.

### Wendy Wilder Larsen
1940–

**Encounter in Saigon** Born in Boston, Wendy Wilder Larsen lived in Saigon from 1970 to 1971 with her husband, who was head of the local bureau of *Time* magazine. While in Saigon, she taught English literature and met Tran Thi Nga, a Vietnamese bookkeeper in the *Time* office. In 1975 Larsen encountered Nga again, in New York, after Nga had fled from Saigon with three of her four children and a grandchild. Over lunch, Larsen began to learn about Nga's amazing life.

### Yusef Komunyakaa
1947–

**Other Works**
*Lost in the Bonewheel Factory*
*Copacetic*
*Thieves of Paradise*

**Portrait of a Poet** Born in Bogalusa, Louisiana, Yusef Komunyakaa entered the army at age 18, immediately after graduating from high school. After returning from Vietnam, where he earned a Bronze Star, Komunyakaa attended college in Colorado and eventually earned a master of fine arts degree in creative writing from the University of California at Irvine. He has lived in a number of countries for short periods, including Australia, Puerto Rico, and Japan. He is currently professor of English at Indiana University in Bloomington and travels across the United States and abroad to read his poetry. "Camouflaging the Chimera" is the first poem in his collection *Dien Cai Dau*, the title of which is Vietnamese slang for "crazy." Komunyakaa won the 1994 Pulitzer Prize for poetry for his book *Neon Vernacular: New and Selected Poems*.

### Tran Thi Nga
1927–

**Turbulent Times** Nga was born in China, where her Vietnamese father had been sent to teach. Her family returned to North Vietnam to live when she was still very young. During the Chinese occupation of North Vietnam, 18-year-old Nga married a Chinese general in order to save her father's life. Her husband died in battle, and Nga became the second wife of her sister's husband, who was the man she had originally loved. In 1954, when Vietnam was divided into North and South, Nga's family moved to Saigon. In 1975, as South Vietnam fell, Nga narrowly escaped with her family; they eventually settled in Connecticut.

**Verse Collaboration** Larsen and Nga decided to work together to write Nga's story, to be combined with the story of Larsen's experiences in Saigon. The result was a book in verse, *Shallow Graves: Two Women and Vietnam*, from which "Deciding" comes.

CAMOUFLAGING THE CHIMERA / DECIDING **1117**

## Writing Options

**Points of Comparison** To get students started, ask them to create a chart which lists the attitudes of each speaker towards war, death, and the enemy, along with the lines from the poem that support each inference. Have students use this evidence to build their dialogues. Students might find it helpful to work in pairs on this assignment. To adapt this assignment for interpersonal learners, have students prepare their dialogues and then present them as part of a talk show with a host who asks them to share their war experiences and views.

## Inquiry & Research

**Environmental Effects of War** To get students started, have them work in groups of three or four to research the topic and to create the map. Encourage students to divide their labor so that each member has an important and equal role to play. Invite students to ask the school librarian for help with research. Sources might include magazine and newspaper articles, books, and official documents. Remind students to use text organizers to locate and categorize information as they do independent research. **To make this assignment more challenging,** students could produce a documentary or slide show with before-and-after clips and commentary that detail the extent of the destruction. The images might be taken from photographs used with permission, from information downloaded from the Internet, or illustrations drawn by the students.

---

**Mini Lesson** ## Grammar

### PUNCTUATION: CAPITALIZATION

**Instruction** Remind students that proper nouns and proper adjectives must be capitalized. Several rules govern the capitalization of these words. Give students the following examples to illustrate some of these rules.

Tran Thi Nga (personal name)
Reverend Dr. Martin Luther King, Jr. (titles preceding name, personal name, and abbreviation as part of the name)
President of the United States (uniquely important position)

Aunt Michele (kinship name used before a proper noun)
Vietnamese (nationality)
Allah (name of a deity)

**Exercise** Ask students to rewrite the following sentences with the correct capitalization.

1. The chinese poet nga, with the help of her friend wendy wilder larsen, writes of her experiences during the vietnam war.
(Chinese, Nga, Wendy Wilder Larsen, Vietnam War)

2. Although english was not her native language, she picked up knowledge of the words by working as a bookkeeper for time magazine in saigon. (English, *Time*, Saigon)

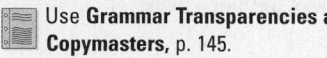 Use **Grammar Transparencies and Copymasters**, p. 145.

 Use McDougal Littell's *Language Network*, Chapter 8, for more instruction in capitalization.

# PREPARING to *Read*

# At the Justice Department, November 15, 1969

*Poetry by* DENISE LEVERTOV

### Comparing Literature

## Traditions Across Time: War in Vietnam

The Vietnam War created deep divisions between those Americans who supported the government's policy in Vietnam and those who felt that the war was wrong. "At the Justice Department, November 15, 1969" describes what happens when these two sides clash during an antiwar demonstration.

**Points of Comparison**  As you read the poem, compare the speaker's response to the Vietnam War with the public response to World War II described in "Armistice" and "Letter from Paradise."

## Build Background

**War Moratorium** Levertov's poem was written in response to a specific protest march. The New Mobilization to End the War in Vietnam, a coalition committee of antiwar groups, organized two major demonstrations called moratoriums in the fall of 1969. One of the moratoriums took place in Washington, D.C., on November 13–15. The protests were, for the most part, peaceful. On a Thursday, a single file of protesters formed a procession from Arlington National Cemetery, each carrying a candle and a poster with the name of an American killed in Vietnam or the name of a Vietnamese village destroyed by U.S. troops. Each paused at the White House to call out the name on his or her poster, then went on to the Capitol to deposit the poster in a coffin. Two days later, the largest group of protesters to have ever gathered in the nation's capital up to that point—crowd estimates varied from 200,000 to 800,000—assembled peacefully at the Washington Monument to demonstrate their opposition to the war. That evening, a group of a few thousand militants tried to raise the Viet Cong flag in front of the Justice Department. When the demonstration became violent, police used tear gas against the crowd.

## Focus Your Reading

LITERARY ANALYSIS  STYLE  **Style** is the particular way in which a piece of literature is written. Style refers not to what is said but how it is said. **Word choice, sentence length, rhythm,** and **imagery** all contribute to a writer's style. Notice the elements of style Levertov uses in her poem.

ACTIVE  MAKING INFERENCES  When you read a
READING  ABOUT MEANING  poem, you usually need to make **inferences** to figure out what is unstated yet implied. You can make inferences about the meaning of a poem by thinking about its descriptive details. Notice details related to the following categories:

- the description of the tear gas
- the speaker's description of the incident and what she would like it to be
- the relationship among the protesters
- the relationship between the protesters and the police

READER'S NOTEBOOK  List the poem's descriptive details as you read. Write down details related to the above categories as well as any other details that help you infer the poem's meaning.

# *A*t the *J*ustice *D*epartment, *N*ovember 15, 1969

Denise Levertov

**B**rown gas-fog, white
beneath the street lamps.
Cut off on three sides, all space filled
with our bodies.
5      Bodies that stumble
in brown airlessness, whitened
in light, a mildew glare,
      that stumble
hand in hand, blinded, retching.
10 Wanting it, wanting
to be here, the body believing it's
dying in its nausea, my head
clear in its despair, a kind of joy,
knowing this is by no means death,
15 is trivial, an incident, a
fragile instant.   Wanting it, wanting
      with all my hunger this anguish,
      this knowing in the body
the grim odds we're
20 up against, wanting it real.
Up that bank where gas
curled in the ivy, dragging each other
up, strangers, brothers
and sisters.   Nothing
25 will do but
to taste the bitter
taste. No life
other, apart from.

Antiwar demonstrators march to the Washington Monument
on Nov. 15, 1969. Photo by John Olson for *Life* Magazine.
Copyright © Time Inc.

## GUIDING STUDENT RESPONSE

## Connect to the Literature

**1. What Do You Think?**
Some students may state that the poem captures the intense sufferings the protesters sometimes endured.

**Comprehension Check**
• It makes her vomit, gives her nausea.
• She thinks that being tear-gassed is trivial. What's important is why they are there—to protest the war in Vietnam.

## Think Critically

**2.** Possible Responses: a feeling joy in sharing in the suffering of others; a commitment to persevere against any obstacles; a sense of solidarity with the other demonstrators

**3.** Possible Responses: To live a moral life, a person must share in the suffering of others; there is no life outside the peace movement.

**4.** Possible Responses: The tear gas represents the government's attempt to cover up and squelch the people's voice; the incident is "trivial" compared to the magnitude of suffering endured by the victims of the war; "wanting it real" means fully experiencing the struggle in which she is engaged.

## Literary Analysis

**Style** The repetition of the word wanting, which appears five times in lines 10–20, emphasizes how deeply the speaker yearns to share in the suffering of others. Levertov's style—the short choppy lines, the sudden shifts in image, the clipped phrases, the sentence fragments—creates the impression that she is writing about the experience as it actually happens, capturing all its violence and chaos. The poem has an immediate and intimate feel, like a "docu-poem."

## Connect to the Literature

**1. What Do You Think?**
How do the images in the poem compare with the images you have formed about antiwar marches in the 1960s?

**Comprehension Check**
• What is the speaker's physical response to the tear gas?
• What does the speaker think about when she's being tear-gassed?

## Think Critically

**2.** Describe the speaker's response to being tear-gassed. How do you explain her response?

THINK ABOUT { • what she says she wants
• what she calls the protesters

**3.** How do you interpret the last words of the poem: "No life other, apart from"?

**4.** ACTIVE READING  MAKING INFERENCES ABOUT MEANING
Look over the notes you wrote down in your READER'S NOTEBOOK. What can you infer about the poem's meaning? What might the tear gas represent? Why does the speaker call the incident "trivial"? What do you think she means by "wanting it real"?

## Extend Interpretations

**5. Different Perspectives** In the poem, the speaker doesn't mention the police officers who threw the tear gas into the crowd of antiwar protesters. How do you think the officers felt when they faced the protesters? Why do you think they felt compelled to tear-gas the demonstrators?

**6. Connect to Life** Think about a time you protested a policy or practice at home, at school, or in your community. What means did you use to express your dissatisfaction? Did your protest effect any change?

**7. Points of Comparison** Compare Morris's response to World War II in "Armistice" with the speaker's response to the Vietnam War. How does Morris's stand on the war affect his life? How does the speaker's stand affect her life? Who seems happier? Who suffers more? Why do you think that is?

## Literary Analysis

STYLE **Style** is the writer's uniquely individual way of communicating ideas. In Denise Levertov's "At the Justice Department, November 15, 1969," **word choice, sentence length, rhythm,** and **imagery** all help convey the poet's style. The style of the poem is also influenced by its subject and meaning. Notice the connection between style and subject in the following passage from the poem:

> *Bodies that stumble*
> *in brown airlessness, whitened*
> *in light, a mildew glare,*
>     *that stumble*
> *hand in hand, blinded, retching.*

The short, chaotic lines, choppy rhythm, and images of sightlessness help convey the experience of being tear-gassed.

**Paired Activity** With a partner, read aloud each sentence from the poem. Discuss what you notice about the word choice, sentence length, rhythm, and imagery in each one. You might want to use a chart like the one shown to list your ideas about these elements. Then answer these questions: How would you describe Levertov's style in the poem? What overall connection do you see between the style of the poem and its subject?

| Word Choice | Sentence Length | Rhythm | Imagery |
|---|---|---|---|
|  |  |  |  |

## Extend Interpretations

**Different Perspectives** Possible Responses: The officers felt threatened, perhaps angry. They were under orders to control the crowd and to use tear gas, if necessary; some may have regarded the protesters as an enemy to be curtailed and defeated.

**Connect to Life** Students should compare text events with their own experiences. Students might compare their degree of commitment with the speaker's in Levertov's poem.

**Points of Comparison** Some students may state that Morris's stand on the war exacts a terrible toll, physically and emotionally. He worries constantly about the Jewish people suffering in Europe, and even his sleep is haunted by nightmares. Though the speaker in Levertov's poem suffers physical pain and nausea, she also experiences a sense of exhilaration—"a kind of joy"—from belonging to the protest movement and suffering for a cause.

## Writing Options

**1. TV Script** Sketch out the script for a TV news report about the incident described in "At the Justice Department, November 15, 1969."

**2. Antiwar Storyboard** Create a storyboard chronicling the antiwar movement of the 1960s. Write a brief paragraph describing each image you use to tell the movement's story. Be sure to include images and notes about antiwar singers and their songs. Place the storyboard in your **Working Portfolio.**

**3. Points of Comparison** In Joan Didion's "Letter from Paradise," the author shows great compassion for American soldiers who died during World War II. In Levertov's poem, the speaker protests against the efforts of American soldiers. Write an exchange of letters between Didion and the poem's speaker in which both explain and defend their positions.

## Activities & Explorations

**1. Opinion Poster** Create a poster that could be carried by an antiwar protester or by a supporter of the war. Use slogans and images to express your opinion of the Vietnam War. ~ **ART**

**2. War Debate** Stage a debate between antiwar protesters and those who supported the war. Participants on both sides of the debate should research and prepare strong arguments to defend their positions. ~ **SPEAKING AND LISTENING**

## Inquiry & Research

**Impact of Antiwar Protests** Find out what impact the antiwar protests of the 1960s had on American policy in Vietnam. In particular, what effect did the protest demonstrations have on American troop withdrawal from Vietnam? Share your findings with your classmates.

---

## Denise Levertov
### 1923–1997

**Other Works**
*The Jacob's Ladder*
*O Taste and See*
*The Sorrow Dance*
*Relearning the Alphabet*
*Breathing the Water*
*Evening Train*

**Unusual Upbringing** Denise Levertov grew up in England, where she had an unusual home life. Her father, a Russian Jew who became an Anglican priest, trained Denise in religious philosophy and filled the house with theologians, booksellers, priests, and opera singers. Her mother, the daughter of a Welsh mystic, imparted to her a love of nature and spirituality.

**Young Poet** Although Levertov received no formal education—she was schooled at home by her mother—she never lacked the nerve or eloquence to speak out. Her poetic career began at age 5, when she declared she would become a poet. At age 12, she sent some poems to T. S. Eliot, who responded with two pages of criticism and encouragement.

**Passionate Activist** Never a passive observer, Levertov combined poetry and political activism to speak against social injustices. Some critics called her poetry preachy, while she criticized others for "mealy-mouthed" apathy in the face of social ills. In 1965, she cofounded the Writers and Artists Protest against the War in Vietnam. She participated in antiwar demonstrations in the 1960s and was jailed for protesting. In the 1980s she protested against U.S. involvement in civil wars in El Salvador, Honduras, and Nicaragua and spoke against nuclear armament and environmental abuse. According to her editor, Barbara Epler, "she was very 19th-century with her vision of what poetry was and how total a calling it was."

AT THE JUSTICE DEPARTMENT, NOVEMBER 15, 1969 **1121**

---

## (Mini Lesson) Grammar

**VARYING SENTENCE CLOSERS**

**Instruction** Tell students they can strengthen their writing by using sentence closers like the following:

**Appositive Phrases:** The protesters were silent, <u>a crowd of hazy figures, mimes in the tear-gas fog.</u>

**Present Participial Phrase:** Suddenly people ran, <u>scrambling up the hillside</u>.

**Past Participial Phrase:** I felt confident, <u>surrounded by people who cared</u>.

**Absolute Phrase:** The police left, <u>their fallen shields and tossed helmets a mound of debris</u>.

**Exercise** Have students write an appropriate closing for each simple sentence below.

1. Appositive phrase: The crowd was huge, . . .
2. Present participial phrase: We marched together, . . .
3. Past participial phrase: I wore an arm band, . . .

 Use **Grammar Transparencies and Copymasters**, p. 172.

 Use McDougal Littell's *Language Network*, Chapter 15, for more instruction in sentence closers.

---

## Writing Options

**1. TV Script To get students started on this assignment,** have them review factual material and events leading up to November 15, 1969. Students might research how the event was covered in contemporary newspapers and magazines. After comparing and contrasting the media coverage of the actual event, students can consider how their TV coverage will differ from that of newspapers and magazines.

**2. Antiwar Storyboard** Tell students that folk music was a big part of the peace movement in the 1960s. **To get students started on this assignment,** have them listen to recordings by folk musicians like Joan Baez and Arlo Guthrie.

**3. Points of Comparison** Students should notice that both Didion and Levertov are appalled at the tragedy of war. Didion's essay focuses on the terrible loss of young lives in World War II and in Vietnam; Levertov's poem describes the sacrifices activists endure to protest the Vietnam War.

## Activities & Exploration

**1. Opinion Poster To get students started on this assignment,** have them look through back issues of Life, Time, and Look magazines.

**2. War Debate To make this assignment more challenging,** have students consult the memoirs of Lyndon B. Johnson, Henry Kissinger, Richard Nixon, General Westmoreland, and Robert McNamara to identify key issues of the Vietnam era.

## Inquiry & Research

Have students work in pairs or small groups to research this question, using reference books, CD-ROMs, and Internet sites. This is an excellent topic for a research paper. Before beginning their research, students should generate relevant, interesting and researchable questions. Encourage them to use text organizers to locate and categorize information as they conduct independent research and draw conclusions from information gathered.

## PART 1 Reading the Prompt

Model the process of reading a prompt:

- First, read the prompt in its entirety.
- Then list key words and phrases of the assignment on the board. ("analyze," "topic: realities of life on the battlefield and their impact on soldiers")
- Use the Strategies in Action to define each word and show how students can restate the prompt in simpler language.

## PART 2 Planning an Analytical Essay

- Students might also try jotting down noteworthy details in random order and then categorizing them. Alternatively, they may create webs rather than charts.
- Students may find it easier to see patterns and relationships if they look at and discuss their notes with partners.
- After they have completed both charts, students should draw their conclusions and then select the evidence that best supports them.

## PART 3 Drafting Your Essay

**Introduction** Suggest that students begin by providing some background about the two wars that they will be writing about. They can then state their topic and selections.

**Organization** Students might compare the two selections in several other ways besides that mentioned in the text: chronologically, by selection, or by categories.

**Conclusion** Encourage students to spend time and thought on their conclusions. They might end their essays with quotations, predictions, or opinions.

**Revision** Students should produce an error-free final draft. Have them check their essays carefully for errors in capitalization. Remind them, if needed, that the names of historical events (such as wars) are capitalized, as are the names of countries and ethnic groups.

---

# Comparing Literature: Assessment Practice

In writing assessments you will sometimes be asked to analyze how the details in a work of literature are used to develop the main ideas. You are now going to practice writing an analytical essay with this kind of focus.

## PART 1 Reading the Prompt

Read the wording of the prompt carefully. Identify the selections you will be writing about, the type of writing you will be doing, and the topic of your essay.

> **Writing Prompt**
>
> Several of the selections in Unit Seven, Part 1, portray the experiences of soldiers in combat. Choose one of the selections from World War II and one from the Vietnam War. Analyze how the details described in each work reveal the difficult realities of life on the battlefield and the impact of those realities on the soldiers.

**STRATEGIES IN ACTION**

❶ To **analyze** is to look at parts in relation to a whole and to discover patterns, relationships, and recurring ideas.

❷ Notice the **topic** of your analysis—the realities of combat and their impact on soldiers.

## PART 2 Planning an Analytical Essay

- After choosing your two selections, think about ways to classify details that relate to your topic. For this essay, you might consider the different circumstances, people, actions, and attitudes experienced by a soldier in combat.

- For each selection, organize your details in a diagram. Note the realities and their effects.

- Look for patterns and relationships among the details.

- Draw conclusions from your analysis of the details.

| Types of Details | | | |
|---|---|---|---|
| Circumstances | People | Actions | Attitudes |
| | | | |
| | | | |

## PART 3 Drafting Your Essay

**Introduction** Begin by clearly stating your topic—for this essay, how details reveal the realities of combat and the impact of those realities on the soldiers. Identify the selections you will be analyzing.

**Organization** Present the evidence of your analysis in a clear, logical way. For example, you might choose the most forceful examples from each selection for each of the categories you are examining.

**Conclusion** In the final paragraph, state your conclusions. Tell the reader what you think the details in the two selections reveal about life on the battlefield and its effects on soldiers.

**Revision** Allow time to review your work. Make sure it is clear, well-supported, and free from mistakes.

**Writing Handbook** See page 1283: Analysis.

### LITERATURE CONNECTIONS

## Fallen Angels

WALTER DEAN MYERS

These thematically related readings are provided along with *Fallen Angels:*

**In the Forest at Night**
DUC THANH, TRANSLATED BY THANH T. NGUYEN AND BRUCE WEIGL

**What Were They Like?**
DENISE LEVERTOV

**look at this)**
E. E. CUMMINGS

**The Spoils of War**
LYNNE SHARON SCHWARTZ

*from* **Ghosts in the Wall**
KRIS HARDIN

**The Things They Carried**
TIM O'BRIEN

*from* **Dear America: Letters Home from Vietnam**
GEORGE OLSEN

## Farewell to Manzanar

JEANNE WAKATSUKI HOUSTON AND JAMES D. HOUSTON

These thematically related readings are provided along with *Farewell to Manzanar:*

*from* **Legends from Camp**
LAWSON FUSAO INADA

**Sleep in the Mojave Desert**
SYLVIA PLATH

**I Remember Pearl Harbor: Dealing with the "Problem Race"**
CHARLES SHIRO INOUYE

**Wilshire Bus**
HISAYE YAMAMOTO

**Trains at Night**
ALBERTO ALVARO RIOS

**Visiting Home**
KEVIN YOUNG

*from* **Unto the Sons**
GAY TALESE

**Lectures on How You Never Lived Back Home**
M. EVELINA GALANG

## And Even *More . . .*

**Books**

**Night**
ELIE WIESEL
A survivor's moving account of the Holocaust.

**A Rumor of War**
PHILIP CAPUTO
Considered among the best nonfiction accounts of the Vietnam War.

**Fire in the Lake: The Vietnamese and the Americans in Vietnam**
FRANCES FITZGERALD
A Pulitzer Prize–winning book about the U.S. military's role in Vietnam and Vietnamese cultural history.

**Other Media**

**Tora! Tora! Tora!**
Film about the attack of Pearl Harbor as seen from two viewpoints—American and Japanese. 20th Century-Fox. (VIDEOCASSETTE)

**The Best Years of Our Lives**
Academy Award-winning film about veterans adapting to civilian life after World War II. Embassy Home Entertainment. (VIDEOCASSETTE)

**No Time for Tears—The Women Who Served**
A documentary filled with personal accounts of women Vietnam veterans—nurses, doctors, and teachers. West End Films. (VIDEOCASSETTE)

### Writers on World War II

EDITED BY MORDECAI RICHER

This sweeping collection of nearly 150 writers, such as Randall Jarrell, John Cheever, and Primo Levi, documents the viewpoints of eyewitnesses and soldiers. Included are fictional excerpts, shocking observations, and poignant letters that convey the grim horror of World War II.

Encourage students to select and read one of the longer works described here as an opportunity to read silently with comprehension over a period of time.

## Objectives

- create a Multimedia Exhibit
- use a sample exhibit as a model
- refine an exhibit to make it more interesting, informative, and clear
- edit and proofread text for correct grammar and punctuation

## Introducing the Workshop

**A** **Multimedia Exhibit** Tell students that *multimedia* means "a combination of means of communication." Paintings, drawings, sculptures, photographs, video images, sound recordings, live performance, text, and artifacts are all means of communication (or *media*) that may be combined to create a multimedia exhibit. Ask students to describe some multimedia events they have experienced (these may include concerts or plays that employed video screens, and multimedia encyclopedia packages for computers). Ask them whether any particular media are well suited to multimedia presentations. Point out that a multimedia exhibit is an effective way to convey a variety of information in an entertaining, interesting way.

Inform students that although multimedia can, strictly speaking, be any combination of media, for the purposes of this project their multimedia exhibits must include, but are not limited to, text and visuals.

### Basics in a Box

**B** **Presenting the Guidelines & Standards** To better understand the assignment, students can refer to the Guidelines & Standards for a Successful Multimedia Exhibit. Remind them that their multimedia exhibits will be assessed according to these standards. You may wish to discuss each standard individually. These five guidelines will aid students in preparing effective multimedia exhibits.

Use McDougal Littell's **Language Network,** Chapter 29, for more instruction on creating media products.

To engage students visually, use **Power Presentation** 10, Multimedia Exhibit.

---

## Presenting text, sound, and images . . .

**From Reading to Exhibiting** In his story "Ambush," Tim O'Brien examines his experiences as a soldier during the Vietnam War and concludes, "Even now I haven't finished sorting it out. Sometimes I forgive myself. Other times I don't." It may be difficult to understand the strong feelings people have about war unless you know something about this emotional topic. One way to explore complex subjects is through **multimedia exhibits.** In such exhibits, video recordings, music, visuals, artifacts, and other media are used to engage viewers and teach them about particular topics.

### For Your Portfolio

**PROMPT** Create a multimedia exhibit about a topic that interests you.

**Purpose:** To describe and inform
**Audience:** Classmates, members of your community, people with similar interests

### Basics in a Box

#### GUIDELINES & STANDARDS Multimedia Exhibit

**A successful multimedia exhibit should**

- attract viewers' attention with appealing visuals, interesting artifacts, and clear text
- present information about a topic logically and clearly
- contain a variety of objects and materials appropriate to the subject
- include specific and accurate written information
- lead viewers along an easy-to-follow pathway, with clearly labeled beginning and ending points

## LESSON RESOURCES

**USING PRINT RESOURCES**
**Unit Seven Resource Book**
- Planning, p. 26
- Preparing, p. 27
- Peer Response, pp. 28–29
- Refining, p. 30
- Standards for Evaluation, p. 31

**USING MEDIA RESOURCES**
**Visit our website:**
www.mcdougallittell.com

# Analyzing a Multimedia Exhibit

## America at War

Large and engaging visuals capture viewers' attention.

A variety of appropriate materials—including photographs, text, a map, and military supply crates—teach viewers about the topic.

### Guidelines
### IN ACTION

An interactive computer display offers more information about the topic and involves viewers in the exhibit.

Text and visuals concerning specific events are arranged in a logical sequence.

Artifacts such as the protest buttons, dramatic magazine cover, and posters shown here engage viewers and bring the subject to life.

Captions and short descriptions give viewers background information about the items displayed.

COMMUNICATION WORKSHOP  **1125**

## Analyzing the Model

**C** **"America at War"**

The model shows a multimedia exhibit on the Vietnam War. The exhibit is comprised of visuals, text, artifacts, and a computer display.

Have students examine the model. Ask why the creator of the exhibit might have included artifacts, such as the buttons and magazine cover, rather than relying solely on text and visuals.
**Possible Response:** The visitor gets a much better idea of what the era was like by viewing actual items from it. Students can take turns reading aloud the Guidelines in Action. Point out key components of the model that correspond to the elements mentioned in the Guidelines in Action.

Explain that the exhibit begins with the text, visuals, and artifacts, and gradually leads the visitor to the interactive computer display. This prevents the visitor from getting caught up in the computer display at the beginning and overlooking the main part of the exhibit.

Remind students that in a multimedia exhibit, as in any other presentation, logical arrangement of materials is important. Arrangement may be chronological or by categories, as shown in the model.

Tell students that careful selection of artifacts is important to the success of a multimedia exhibit. Point out that the exhibit's creator was careful not to include artifacts that were from the correct era but unrelated to the Vietnam War. The result is a clear focus on the subject matter without distractions.

Tell students that in effective multimedia exhibits, text works to support visual information rather than to repeat it. The words add additional information that the visuals cannot express. Remind students that arrangement of materials for visibility is vital. If important visual or textual information is obscured, it is not contributing to the exhibit.

### Choosing a Topic

If after reading the Idea Bank students are having difficulty choosing their topics, suggest they try the following:

- Conduct a brainstorming session for each of the categories listed: historical periods, social movements, extraordinary people, scientific phenomena.

- Look through the index of an encyclopedia for some general topics that interest you. Choose one for your multimedia exhibit.

## Planning the Multimedia Exhibit

1. Have small groups of students work together to narrow their topics to the one or two most interesting elements. Have them examine those elements for the following qualities: Interesting to Others, Interesting to Me, Provides Interesting Materials.

2. Remind students that materials must be appropriate for a school project. Review questionable material for offensiveness.

3. The library may have volumes of older newspapers and magazines stored on microfilm. Students can ask the librarian to show them where to locate these materials as well as how to use them.

4. Before students sketch their own floor plans, you may wish to discuss the model floor plan shown on page 1127.

---

### IDEABank

**1. Your Working Portfolio**
Look for ideas in the **Writing Options** you completed earlier in this unit:

- **World War II Presentation,** p. 1086
- **Exhibit Proposal,** p. 1110
- **Antiwar Storyboard,** p. 1121

**2. Inspirational Exhibits**
Visit an art, science, or natural history museum and look for topic ideas in the exhibits you find there.

**3. Online Museums**
Visit a few museum Web sites to see what kinds of topics are covered there and to help you get ideas for your own exhibit.

### TECHTutor

Consider the following options when you are deciding which media to use in your exhibit:

- Audiotapes and CDs
- Posters, photos, slides, charts, maps, and graphs
- Videos
- Artifacts and other objects

---

# Creating Your Multimedia Exhibit

## ❶ Planning Your Exhibit

Since your exhibit will probably be a group effort, you might begin by brainstorming possible exhibit topics with a small group of your classmates. Try to come up with broad topics—such as sports, war, peace, and childhood—that you can later refine. See the **Idea Bank** in the margin for other suggestions. Then choose a topic that all group members are interested in. After you have selected a topic, follow the steps below.

### Planning Your Multimedia Exhibit

▶ **1. Narrow the focus of your subject.** You will need to break down your topic into more specific parts. Use a web to list various elements of your subject that you might cover, then pick one or two elements as your focus.

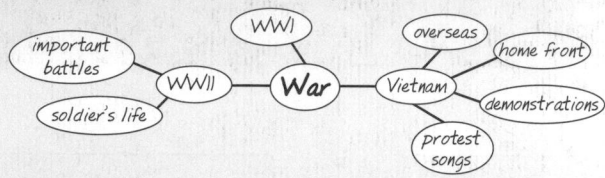

▶ **2. Brainstorm a list of materials.** What objects, materials, and media are most appropriate to your content and focus? Where will you find these things? Check the library and the Internet for books, photographs, audiotapes, and videos. Ask family members and friends for objects and artifacts that will fit in your exhibit. Are there any items you need that you will have to make yourself?

▶ **3. Conduct research.** Make some notes on what you already know about your topic and what you need to find out. Conduct library research to identify key ideas, dates, and facts that relate to your topic. As you research, consider what will interest your audience. What might they already know about this topic?

▶ **4. Sketch a rough floor plan.** Where will you set up your exhibit? Draw a sketch of the area and imagine how you might arrange items in it. Keep in mind the flow of traffic through your exhibit. To avoid traffic jams, make sure you put enough space between items in your exhibit. Also think about how many electrical outlets are available and where they are.

## ➋ Preparing Your Exhibit

After you have gathered all of your materials, use these steps to prepare your exhibit.

### Preparing Your Multimedia Exhibit

▶ **1. Revise your floor plan.** Depending on what materials you've gathered, you may need to revise your initial sketch. Will you group your materials chronologically? thematically? Which organization will offer the clearest and most interesting path through your exhibit?

▶ **2. Create visuals.** You may need to create charts, graphs, or maps for your exhibit. Make sure the visuals you create are neat, clear, and accurate. If necessary, conduct research to ensure accuracy. Also make sure your visuals are large enough.

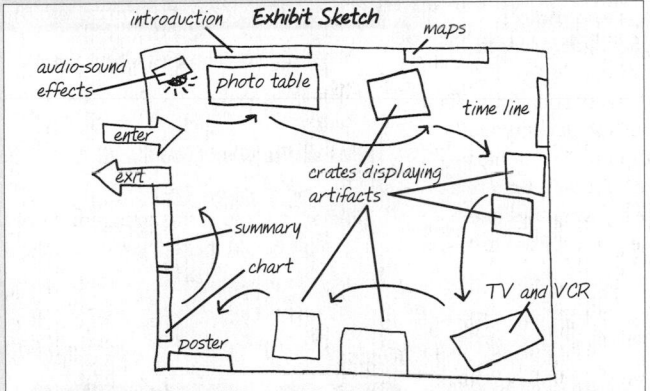

Exhibit Sketch

introduction · maps · audio-sound effects · photo table · enter · exit · time line · crates displaying artifacts · summary · chart · poster · TV and VCR

▶ **3. Write the text.** For the beginning point of your exhibit, create a sign that includes the title of the exhibit and a paragraph explaining what viewers are about to see or why you created the exhibit. Also create labels that identify the items in the exhibit, pointing out their important features and explaining their significance. Finally, write a paragraph for the end of your exhibit, summarizing what viewers have seen. Your text should be clear, specific, and accurate.

▶ **4. Proofread the text.** Although your exhibit may not include a lot of text, everything you write should be grammatically correct. Share the task of editing and proofreading with other group members. Refer to the **Grammar Handbook,** pages 1305–1341, to help you fix any grammatical errors.

▶ **5. Arrange your materials.** You may want to experiment with the layout, but use your final sketch to guide you in setting up your exhibit.

**Need help with your exhibit?**

See the **Communication Handbook**

Making Multimedia Presentations, p. 1304

Understanding Visual Messages, p. 1302

Using Visual Representations, p. 1303

## Preparing the Exhibit

1. Remind students that displays that absorb visitors' interest for long periods of time should be near the end of the exhibit. Careful planning will prevent traffic jams and ensure that visitors experience the whole exhibit.

2. Point out that while visuals should support text, they should not replace text. Encourage students to keep images simple and identifiable and to let text explain any complex ideas.

3. Remind students that although text should clarify things, it should be kept short. It should help visitors understand what they are seeing, not interpret or describe it for them.

4. Students should produce error-free final drafts. Suggest that they exchange texts for proofreading.

5. Remind students that the most important features of layout are logical arrangement of materials and traffic flow.

## Refining the Exhibit

Encourage students to make up questionnaires based on the questions in the Ask Your Peer Reviewers box. After the peer reviewers have walked through the exhibit and completed the questionnaire, students should analyze the reviewers' responses and decide which changes are realistic and would most improve the exhibit.

## Reflecting

Encourage each group to keep a notebook near the exit of the multimedia exhibit. Visitors can write comments about the exhibit. Ask exhibitors to comment on any suggestions or ideas they receive. Have students add these evaluations to their working portfolios.

**Need revising help?**

Review the **Guidelines & Standards,** p. 1124

Consider **peer reviewers'** comments

Check **Revision Guidelines,** p. 1269

**Unsure about visuals?**

See the **Communication Handbook**

Using Visual Representations, p. 1303

### Publishing IDEAS

- Invite other classes or families and friends to view your exhibit.
- Make a video of a group member proceeding through and explaining the exhibit.

**More Online: Publishing Options** www.mcdougallittell.com

### ❸ Refining Your Exhibit

After you have constructed your exhibit, ask several friends or classmates to walk through it and share their impressions. Use their feedback to make your exhibit as interesting, informative, and clear as possible. The following points can help you review your work:

- **Look at the exhibit as a whole.** Consider how well your materials work together. Does everything fit in the exhibit space? Does the order of the items make sense? Do any of the media you chose overpower other points of the exhibit?

- **Evaluate your information.** Have you presented enough information about the items? Have you presented too much? Are your facts accurate? Is the writing specific and clear?

- **Review your media choices.** Audiences often ignore lengthy text in favor of visuals. Do you have a good mix of sound, visuals, and text? Look for places where a visual would present your information more effectively than text. The example below shows one way to create a visual from text.

#### Ask Your Peer Reviewers

- What did you like best about the exhibit?
- What was confusing, unnecessary, or out of place?
- What else would you like to know about the topic?
- What changes in the arrangement of the exhibit would make it easier to follow?

**Original**
The United States began sending combat troops to Vietnam in 1965. By 1967, the troop strength was over 400,000. It remained at that level for two years, but began falling after 1969. In 1971, there were approximately 200,000 U.S. troops in Vietnam. All U.S. troops were withdrawn in 1973.

**Revised**

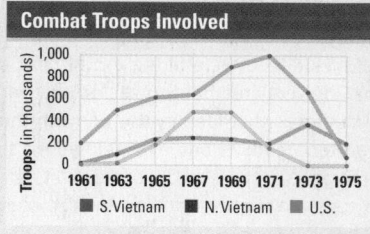

Combat Troops Involved

### ❹ Reflecting

**FOR YOUR WORKING PORTFOLIO** What did you discover about your topic while creating your exhibit? What did you learn about the strengths and weaknesses of the media themselves? Attach your reflections to any notes you made when preparing your exhibit. Save your notes in your **Working Portfolio.**

## Option
### Creating an Evaluation Form

Have students work on computers to create a "Multimedia Exhibit Evaluation Scale" based on the Guidelines & Standards for Designing a Multimedia Exhibit. The class should agree on percentages to be attached to each element. Have students state these percentages on their evaluation form. Have them print two copies, one to use for their evaluation of their multimedia exhibit and one for you to use.

## Assessment Practice Revising & Editing

Read this passage from the first draft of a multimedia exhibit brochure. The underlined sections may include the following kinds of errors:

- **incorrect verb forms**
- **incorrect possessive forms**
- **sentence fragments**
- **correctly written sentences that should be combined**

For each underlined section, choose the revision that most improves the writing.

> The new exhibit at the Lewiston Museum is called "The Watchful Eye." The exhibit showcases the work of Joanna Wing, an artist who <u>have contributed</u> a
> (1)
> great deal to the world of photography. <u>Here you will see her early photographs.</u>
> (2)
> <u>As well as samples of her recent work.</u> <u>You will see videos. You will hear sound</u>
> (3)
> <u>effects. She recorded them.</u>
>
> In a recent interview, Joanna explained that an important lesson she <u>have</u>
> (4)
> <u>learned</u> is to carry a camera at all times. She never knows when something will
> catch her eye. <u>A beautiful sunset or a sudden rainstorm.</u> <u>Joanna Wing's</u> work
> (5)          (6)
> will be on display during the month of October.

**1. A.** has contributed
   **B.** was contributed
   **C.** had contributed
   **D.** Correct as is

**2. A.** Here you will see her early photographs and samples of her recent work.
   **B.** Here you will see her early photographs, samples of her recent work.
   **C.** Here you will see her early photographs. Samples of her recent work, too.
   **D.** Correct as is

**3. A.** You will see videos, too. You will hear sound effects.
   **B.** You will see videos and hear sound effects that she recorded.
   **C.** She has made some videos. She has recorded a few sound effects.
   **D.** Correct as is

**4. A.** was learning
   **B.** will have learned
   **C.** has learned
   **D.** Correct as is

**5. A.** A beautiful sunset or a sudden rainstorm may inspire her to take a picture.
   **B.** Perhaps a beautiful sunset or a sudden rainstorm.
   **C.** Like a beautiful sunset or a rainstorm suddenly occurs.
   **D.** Correct as is

**6. A.** Joanna Wings'
   **B.** Joanna Wing
   **C.** Joanna Wings
   **D.** Correct as is

**Need extra help?**

See the **Grammar Handbook**

Correcting Fragments, p. 1323

Possessive Nouns, p. 1306

Verb Tense, p. 1310

---

**Assessment Practice**

Briefly review the kinds of errors that the passage may contain. Then show students how they can eliminate incorrect choices for the second question.

**B.** This choice is incorrect. The sentence has a comma between the items in a two-item list; a conjunction is required.

**C.** This choice is incorrect because it contains a sentence fragment.

**D.** The original is incorrect because it contains a sentence fragment.

**A.** This is the correct choice. The conjunction *and* joins the two nouns, *photographs* and *samples,* and corrects the fragment.

**Answers:**
**1.** A; **2.** A; **3.** B; **4.** C; **5.** A; **6.** D

## Building Vocabulary

### Objectives

- identify the two word parts: roots and affixes
- recognize word parts in order to decode unfamiliar words
- apply meanings of word roots and affixes in order to comprehend
- understand how to use word parts and word roots to build vocabulary
- use reference material such as a dictionary to determine precise meaning and usage

### EXERCISE

Students' sentences will vary.

1. *depopulate* (to remove or reduce population): *de-* (remove from) + *popul* (people) + *-ate* (to act upon)
2. *cataclysm* (a violent or sudden change in the earth such as a flood or earthquake): *cata-* (down) + *clysm* (to wash)
3. *interference* (act of getting in the way or between two things): *inter-* (between) + *fer* (to strike) + *-ence* (the act of)
4. *malform* (to shape poorly or abnormally): *mal-* (poorly) + *form* (shape)
5. *expunge* (drive out or remove completely): *ex-* (out of or drive out) + *punge* (to prick or puncture)

## Creating Words from Word Parts

**What's in a word?** While some words, called base words, cannot be further broken down, many English words are made up of two or more word parts. In the passage on the right, which words do you think are combinations of word parts?

Two examples are the nouns *assassination* and *generation.* They are formed by adding the word part *-ation* to a root derived from the Arabic *hassasin* and to the Latin root *gener.* Another word in the passage, the adjective *sunken,* is formed by adding the word part *-en* to the base word *sunk,* which is the past

> A few days ago someone just four years younger than I am told me that he did not see why a sunken ship should affect me so, that John Kennedy's assassination, not Pearl Harbor, was the single most indelible event of what he kept calling "our generation."
> —Joan Didion, "Letter from Paradise, 21° 19′ N., 157° 52′ W."

participle of the verb *sink.* Other examples include *younger, indelible,* and *calling.* Recognizing word parts and knowing their meanings can help you decode unfamiliar words.

---

## Strategies for Building Vocabulary

There are two types of word parts: roots and affixes. A **root** is a core word part that cannot stand alone, like *gener* or *onym.* The root, as the term implies, carries the fundamental meaning of the word. For example, *gener* means "birth" and *onym* means "name."

An **affix** is a word part that can be added to the beginning or end of a root or base word to change its meaning. An affix at the beginning of a word is called a **prefix,** while one at the end is called a **suffix.** The word *incessant,* for example, is made up of three word parts:

| Prefix | Root | Suffix |
|--------|------|--------|
| in- | cess | -ant |
| "not" | "to stop" | "in a state of" |

Together the parts mean "continuous" or "not ceasing."

❶ **Look for Prefixes** The prefix *in-* is part of many words in this subunit. For example, the word *inflict,* meaning "to deal out" or "to impose," is formed by adding the prefix *in-* ("on") to the Latin root *flict* ("to strike"). Note that the prefix *in-* can mean either "not" or "on." The chart on the right presents several common prefixes.

❷ **Identifying Suffixes** Adding a suffix to a base word often changes the word from one part of speech to another. For example, the suffix *-ation* changes the verb *generate* to the noun *generation.*

You can learn more about suffixes by studying the suffix chart below.

| Prefix | Meaning | Words |
|--------|---------|-------|
| cata- | in accordance with, down, against | catalogue, catastrophe |
| de- | to come down from, to remove from | derive, denounce |
| ex-, e-, ef- | out of, to drive out | exterminate, eject, effigy |
| inter- | between | intervene, intercede |
| mal- | badly, poorly | malnutrition, malevolent |
| prot-, proto- | first | protagonist, prototype |

| Suffix | Meaning | Words |
|--------|---------|-------|
| -ate | having, characterized by, resembling, to act upon | denigrate, radiate, laminate, subjugate |
| -en | made of, to make | silken, sunken |
| -ence | an action, the state or quality of | violence, belligerence |
| -fy | to make | simplify, notify |
| -ure | action, process, or condition | exposure, failure |

**EXERCISE** Identify the word parts that make up each word below. Use the meanings of the word parts to help define the word. Then use the word in a sentence. Use a dictionary to check your work.

1. depopulate   3. interference   5. expunge
2. cataclysm    4. malform

## Grammar from Literature

Experienced writers sometimes draw attention to details by adding modifying phrases or series of words to the ends of sentences. A sentence closer, as such a word group is called, may add information about the word immediately preceding it or may add information to the sentence as a whole. The examples below demonstrate the variety of structures that can be used as sentence closers.

> *adjective prepositional phrase*
> **Gus was a heavy man,** with a strong, full head and a fleshy face. —Bernard Malamud, "Armistice"
>
> *appositive phrase*
> **Here, in front of the two doors, stands the arbiter of our fate,** an SS subaltern. —Primo Levi, *Survival in Auschwitz*
>
> *participial phrases*
> **The graves filled last week . . . do not yet have stones, only plastic identification cards,** streaked by the mist and splattered with mud. —Joan Didion, "Letter from Paradise"

Subordinate clauses can also be used as closers, as in these examples:

> *adverb clause*
> **The next day the memory slips farther,** until very little is left at all. —John Steinbeck, "Why Soldiers Don't Talk"
>
> *adjective clauses*
> **The breeze swayed the street lamp,** which creaked and moved the circle of light that fell upon the street. —"Armistice"

A writer sometimes begins a sentence with an independent clause that is vague and follows it with a sentence closer that fills in the details. In this way, the writer generates interest by raising readers' curiosity as they read the sentence. Notice how Joan Didion does this in the following example.

> **They all seem to be twenty years old,** the boys buried up there in the crater of an extinct volcano named Punchbowl, twenty and nineteen and eighteen and sometimes not that old. —"Letter from Paradise"

**Using Sentence Closers in Your Writing** As you revise your writing, look for places where sentence closers could be used to add interesting details or vary your sentence structures. You can choose from a variety of structures that serve well as closers.

**Punctuation Tip** A sentence closer is usually separated from the rest of the sentence by a comma or a dash.

> ORIGINAL
> **Joan Didion establishes a mood by means of a number of images.**
>
> REVISED
> **Joan Didion establishes a mood by means of a number of images,** showing readers passengers and tour directors, bright pink tour boats, and boys diving for coins.

You may use a dash if the closer expresses a sudden, dramatic break in thought. Be careful, however, not to overuse dashes. If a phrase or clause simply adds information to the sentence, use a comma.

> **The grocer as usual was sitting on the cot,** listening to the radio. —"Armistice"
>
> **Some of the prisoners were not with us in the afternoon**—they had been taken to the gas chamber. —*Survival in Auschwitz*

---

**WRITING EXERCISE** Rewrite the sentences below, adding a correctly punctuated sentence closer to each. Try to use a variety of grammatical structures in your closers.

1. A great deal of suffering has been caused by prejudice.
2. Some soldiers are boasters.
3. An explosion rocked the building.
4. In 1942 the federal government forced thousands of Japanese Americans living on the West Coast into internment camps.
5. Many death-camp survivors are haunted by unspeakable memories.
6. The scene was one of total confusion.
7. It was truly unforgettable; he remembered all the details.
8. The Vietnam War spurred acts of protest that took many forms.
9. Beneath the memorial, the remains of the battleship *Arizona* lie in the water.
10. Soldiers returning from war must live not only with their deeds and memories but with the probing questions of their children.

---

## Sentence Crafting

**Objectives**
- vary sentence structure by adding modifying phrases or a series of words at the end
- revise drafts by using sentence closers to add detail and to vary sentence structure
- practice proper punctuation for sentence closers—commas and dashes
- practice using a variety of sentence closers: adjective prepositional phrases, appositive phrases, participial phrases, adverb and adjective clauses

**WRITING EXERCISE**
Possible responses are shown.

1. A great deal of suffering has been caused by prejudice, which takes the forms of suspicion, intolerance, and hatred based on differences.
2. Some soldiers are boasters, taking great pleasure in the details of their feats.
3. An explosion rocked the building, with debris flying in every direction for hundreds of feet.
4. In 1942 the federal government forced thousands of Japanese Americans living on the West Coast into internment camps, which were little more than outdoor prisons.
5. Many death-camp survivors are haunted by unspeakable memories, burned forever into their minds.
6. The scene was one of total confusion, with people pouring into the streets and screaming children looking for their parents.
7. It was truly unforgettable; he remembered all the details, whether significant or seemingly unimportant.
8. The Vietnam War spurred acts of protest that took many forms, some positive and some harmful.
9. Beneath the memorial the remains of the battleship *Arizona* lie in the water, a calm surface mocking the agitation and torment of death.
10. Soldiers returning from war must live not only with their deeds and memories but with the probing questions of their children, who will be unprepared for any answers they get.

### OVERVIEW

### Introduction

This article places the selections in Part 2 of this unit in an historical context by providing students with an overview of the social and cultural changes that swept America following World War II. The **Traditions Across Time** section sets the background for the final selections in this book. The short selections in **Voices from the Times** give insight into the attitudes and issues that pervaded the postwar decades. This article will help students to interpret the possible influences of the more recent historical contexts on literary works.

## Teaching Nonfiction

### Reading Skills and Strategies
**ESTABLISHING A PURPOSE FOR READING**

Explain to students that they are expected to read this article to learn about how American society changed during the middle years of this century and to understand why these changes happened.

### MONITORING AND MODIFYING READING STRATEGIES

Ask students to read through the article silently. Have them monitor their comprehension of the material and, if necessary, modify their reading strategies when understanding breaks down. Encourage students to use outside resources including glossaries, dictionaries, the Internet, and reference material as a way of increasing comprehension.

# Integration and Disintegration

## Postwar Society

*American* literature after World War II reflects the many changes that took place in society during that time. On the one hand, there were trends toward integration of African Americans, Latinos, women, and other groups previously excluded from political and cultural participation. On the other hand, there were trends toward the disintegration of structures and values that had been long upheld in the nation.

After the war, returning African-American veterans demanded the same rights and freedoms at home that they had fought to give to others abroad. In 1948 President Truman issued an executive order for integration of the armed forces and called for an end to discrimination in government hiring. Other civil rights advances followed, and in 1954 the Supreme Court's *Brown* v. *Board of Education* ruling struck down school segregation as unconstitutional. Martin Luther King, Jr., emerged as a civil rights leader during the 1955 Montgomery, Alabama, bus boycott, which ended segregation on city buses. In his 1963 "Letter from Birmingham Jail," he passionately defends the civil rights movement against critics who thought it was demanding too much, too soon.

The civil rights movement inspired other movements for justice. Mexican-American farmworkers and students, Native Americans, Asian Americans, feminists, the disabled, and many other Americans demanded basic rights and protested unfair laws, policies, and attitudes. Writers of literature called for inclusion and began to examine and celebrate their own particular cultural identities, as in Gary Soto's poem "Mexicans Begin Jogging" and Pat Mora's poem "Legal Alien."

**1132** UNIT SEVEN PART 2

As those barred from the mainstream demanded to join it, many within the mainstream wondered whether it was such a good place to be. American society in the 1950s was prosperous, consumerist, and conformist. Men striving to obtain "the good life" for their families were sometimes forced to suppress their individuality and desires as they worked for impersonal corporations. Works such as E. L. Doctorow's "The Writer in the Family," set in 1955, and Lanford Wilson's "Wandering" question the cost of such sacrifice.

In the 1960s, an influential youth counterculture arose, with the tenet, "Do your own thing." But as society became more permissive, the family as an institution seemed to weaken. Parents lost authority over children, and the divorce rate skyrocketed. Anne Tyler's "Teenage Wasteland," and John Updike's "Separating" are two stories that explore the breakup of a family.

Swearing-in ceremony of new U.S. citizens in New York City.

I have a dream that one day this nation will rise up and live out the true meaning of its creed, "We hold these truths to be self-evident; that all men are created equal." I have a dream that one day on the red hills of Georgia, sons of former slaves and the sons of former slave owners will be able to sit down together at the table of brotherhood. I have a dream that one day even the state of Mississippi, a state sweltering with the heat of injustice, sweltering with the heat of oppression, will be transformed into an oasis of freedom and justice. I have a dream that my four little children will one day live in a nation where they will not be judged by the color of their skin, but by the content of their character.

**Martin Luther King, Jr.**
from his "I Have a Dream" speech at
the 1963 March on Washington

For the first time in their history, women are becoming aware of an identity crisis in their own lives, a crisis which . . . has grown worse with each succeeding generation. . . . I think this is the crisis of women growing up—a turning point from an immaturity that has been called femininity to full human identity.

**Betty Friedan**
from *The Feminine Mystique*

They are the ones of our middle class who have left home, spiritually as well as physically, to take the vows of organization life . . .

**William H. Whyte, Jr.**
from *The Organization Man*

## Making Connections

### History

**A** In the 1960s, feminists began to call for a redefinition of women's place in society. The National Organization for Women (NOW), founded by Betty Friedan and other feminists in 1966, strove to ensure that women would share "equal rights in partnership with men." Soon a number of other women's organizations joined NOW in demanding opportunities for women to compete equally with men for high-paying jobs in construction, manufacturing, business, medicine, law, and politics.

### Literature

**B** Since the 1960s, publishing houses have printed increasing numbers of works by women and minority writers. Minority and female writers have also founded independent presses, magazines, and journals to explore their own experiences and concerns and to recover from the literature, songs, and diaries of past eras accounts that reflect their struggle for recognition.

### Society

**C** In 1946 Dr. Benjamin Spock (1903–1998) published the *Common Sense Book of Baby and Child Care*, which became the biggest-selling book in America after the Bible. Dr. Spock's name became a household word during the 1950s and 1960s as millions of parents relied on his advice to guide them through the experience of raising children. Unlike the experts who preceded him, Dr. Spock adapted Freudian theory to child-rearing and advised parents to raise their children with flexibility and understanding rather than punishment and rigidity. In the late 1960s, conservative critics of his methods accused him of encouraging permissiveness in parenting and, by implication, blamed him for much of the social upheaval of the time.

**VOICES FROM THE TIMES**
**Ask: What beliefs do the excerpts from Martin Luther King, Jr., and Betty Friedan have in common?**
Possible Responses: Both these excerpts demonstrate a belief that change will happen and that it will improve the lives of minorities or women. They share a belief that social change will allow minorities or women to be identified as people and Americans rather than identified only by their race or gender.

**Ask: What does the excerpt from William Whyte, Jr.'s book imply about America's middle class?**
Possible Responses: He implies that those Americans, usually men, who strive for the American dream by working for big business become totally removed from their families. Whyte's language implicitly compares this spiritual and physical commitment to work to taking religious vows.

**IDENTIFYING MAIN IDEAS AND DETAILS**

To help students comprehend the selection, suggest that they identify the main idea of each paragraph. They might use an outline format to take notes about the article, listing supporting details under each main idea.

**DISCUSSING**

Encourage students to discuss the article as a class. Start the discussion by asking students to evaluate the social significance of protest movements like the civil rights movement and the protests of the 1960s. Ask them to draw upon their own backgrounds in order to identify social or political issues today that could bring together different groups in a protest movement.

V o i c e s
*from the* T I M E S

Come mothers and fathers
Throughout the land,
And don't criticize
What you can't understand.
Your sons and your daughters
Are beyond your command.
Your old road is rapidly agin'.
Please get out of the new one
If you can't lend a hand,
For the times they are a-changin'.

> **Bob Dylan**
> from "The Times
> They Are A-Changin'"

We have allowed materialism to eclipse idealism, and overcompetitiveness to harm families and family values. Millions of people are in fear for the long-term security of their families, and a growing percentage is on the edge of poverty and despair.

> **Dr. Benjamin Spock**
> from *A Better World
> for Our Children*

My dream of America
is like dá bìn lòuh
with people of all persuasions and tastes
sitting down around a common pot
chopsticks and basket scoops here and
  there
some cooking squid and others beef
some tofu or watercress
all in one broth
like a stew that really isn't
as each one chooses what he wishes to eat
along with the good company
and the sweet soup
spooned out at the end of the meal.

> **Wing Tek Lum**
> "Chinese Hot Pot"

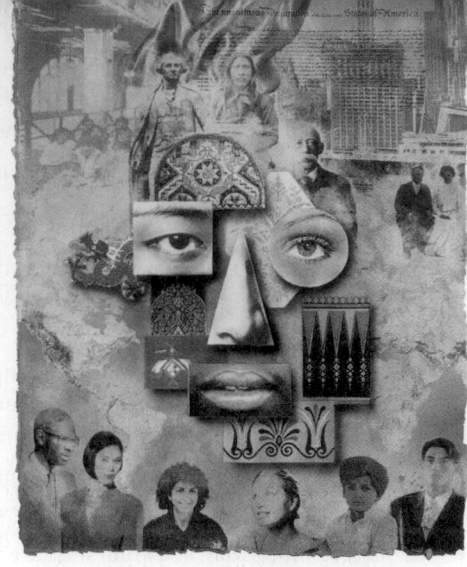

## Traditions Across Time: Continuing Transformation

Trends toward further integration and disintegration have continued since the 1980s. Violence, particularly youth violence, is an issue that tears at the heart of American society. Joyce Carol Oates's story "Hostage" and Garrett Hongo's poem "The Legend" show the ripple effects of sudden, inexplicable acts of violence. The nation also struggles with issues of immigration and language. In "Mother Tongue," Amy Tan reflects on the richness of her Chinese mother's "broken" English, and in "The Latin Deli," Judith Ortiz Cofer portrays Latin American immigrants who miss the comfort of spoken Spanish. The last selection in this book, "Straw into Gold," is an inspiring essay by Sandra Cisneros. In it she tells how being different from the norm helped her achieve a rewarding career as a writer, teacher, and lecturer. In many ways, her success exemplifies the dramatic social changes in America during the last half of the 20th century.

**VOICES FROM THE TIMES**

**Ask: What is the message of Bob Dylan's lyrics?**

**Possible Responses:** rebellion against tradition and authority; dominance of society by the young instead of the older generation; a deliberate distancing of generations

**Ask: What values does Wing Tek Lum's passage espouse?**

**Possible Responses:** appreciation of diversity; a spirit of cooperation; good will toward other people

## Postwar Society

1135

## OVERVIEW

This selection is included in the **Grade 11 InterActive Reader.**

### Objectives

1. understand a historic **letter** (Literary Analysis)
2. identify and examine **allusion** (Literary Analysis)
3. understand **logical argument: deduction and induction** (Active Reading)

### Summary

In this letter, Martin Luther King, Jr., justifies his involvement in leading direct action campaigns to end segregation in the South. He uses many biblical and political allusions to legitimize the movement's means and goals. Reminding his critics of conditions that precipitated the direct-action campaigns, he explains that their purpose is to bring about negotiation; that the majority of African Americans in the South continue to be denied the right to vote, and so have little legal redress; that the only way to gain civil rights is through legal and nonviolent pressure. He cites St. Thomas Aquinas, "any law that degrades human personality is unjust," to support his claim that "one has a moral responsibility to disobey unjust laws."

### Thematic Link

As a leader of the civil rights movement, King sought to **integrate** African Americans into the prosperous **postwar society** that most white Americans took for granted. With cogent arguments and powerful examples, he urges all Americans to fight the moral **disintegration** that allows prejudice and legal injustice to continue.

### 5-Minute Warm-Up

*Daily Language SkillBuilder*

Have students **proofread** the display sentences on page 1069j and write them correctly. The sentences also appear on Transparency 32 of **Grammar Transparencies and Copymasters.**

**Mini Lesson** **Preteaching Vocabulary**

If you would like to preteach the WORDS TO KNOW for this selection, use the Mini Lesson, p. 1138.

# *from* Letter from Birmingham Jail

*by* MARTIN LUTHER KING, JR.

### Connect to Your Life

**Personal Commitment** What issue do you feel strongly about? How far would you go to support your convictions? Would you speak out, write to Congress, march in a demonstration, or take even stronger measures?

## Build Background

**Defending Civil Disobedience** In 1963 the Reverend Martin Luther King, Jr., led a massive civil rights campaign in Birmingham, Alabama, involving drives for African-American voter registration and for desegregation in education and housing. During this nonviolent action, King was arrested and imprisoned several times. During one imprisonment, he wrote "Letter from Birmingham Jail," which has become a classic statement in support of civil disobedience. It was written in response to a published letter by eight local clergymen criticizing King's actions as "unwise and untimely." In the part of the letter that follows, King defends his actions by drawing upon the ideas of philosophers, religious scholars, biblical figures, and political thinkers with whom his audience, as clergymen, would have been familiar.

**WORDS TO KNOW**
**Vocabulary Preview**

| | |
|---|---|
| affiliate | latent |
| appraisal | provocation |
| cognizant | retaliating |
| diligently | segregated |
| estrangement | statute |

## Focus Your Reading

**LITERARY ANALYSIS** **ALLUSION** An **allusion** is a reference to a person, place, event, or literary work with which the author believes the reader will be familiar. In his letter, King mentions the Boston Tea Party, a well-known event in American history, in which a group of rebels dumped 15,000 pounds of tea into Boston's harbor to protest the British Tea Act of 1773. This allusion reminds the reader that civil disobedience is a time-honored means of resisting unjust laws. Note other allusions in this letter, and consider why King uses them.

**ACTIVE READING** **LOGICAL ARGUMENT: DEDUCTION AND INDUCTION** In your own persuasive essays, you likely have used these processes of reasoning:

- When you use **induction,** you begin with specific facts and then reach a general conclusion based on them.
- When you use **deduction,** you begin with a general statement and then infer specific statements from it.

In this letter, King uses induction in the second paragraph to explain why he is in Birmingham. He presents facts about his role in the Southern Christian Leadership Conference (SCLC) and then concludes with the general statement "I am here because I have organizational ties here."

King uses deduction, beginning with the third paragraph, to justify his presence in the city. He begins with the general statement that "Injustice anywhere is a threat to justice everywhere." Then in three subsequent paragraphs, he gives specific instances of injustices in Birmingham, such as unsolved bombings of African-American homes.

**READER'S NOTEBOOK** Select a passage that appeals to you and identify the process of reasoning used in it. Write notes about King's general and specific statements.

| | |
|---|---|
| **Induction:** specific ➡ general | **Deduction:** general ➡ specific |

## LESSON RESOURCES

**UNIT SEVEN RESOURCE BOOK,** pp. 34–38

**ASSESSMENT RESOURCES**
**Formal Assessment,** pp. 215–216
**Teacher's Guide to Assessment and Portfolio Use**
**Test Generator**

**SKILLS TRANSPARENCIES AND COPYMASTERS**
**Reading and Critical Thinking**
- Evaluating Argumentation II, T21 (for Active Reading, p. 1136)

**Grammar**
- Verbs: Voice and Mood, C119 (for Mini Lesson, p. 1142)

**Vocabulary**
- Latin Roots, C94 (for Mini Lesson, p. 1144)

**Writing**
- Persuasive Essay, C27 (for Writing Option 2, p. 1147)
- Compare-Contrast, C31 (for Writing Option 3, p. 1147)

**Communications**
- Evaluating Roles in Groups, T8 (for Activities & Explorations 3, p. 1147)

- Impromptu Speaking: Dialogue, Role-Play, Debate, T13 (for Activities & Explorations 2, p. 1147)

**INTEGRATED TECHNOLOGY**

**Audio Library**
**Visit our website:**
www.mcdougallittell.com

# from LETTER FROM BIRMINGHAM JAIL

Martin Luther King, Jr.

**APRIL 16, 1963**

King in a jail cell at the Jefferson County Courthouse in Birmingham.

**My Dear Fellow Clergymen:**

While confined here in the Birmingham city jail, I came across your recent statement calling my present activities "unwise and untimely." Seldom do I pause to answer criticism of my work and ideas. If I sought to answer all the criticisms that cross my desk, my secretaries would have little time for anything other than such correspondence in the course of the day, and I would have no time for constructive work. But since I feel that you are men of genuine goodwill and that your criticisms are sincerely set forth, I want to try to answer your statement in what I hope will be patient and reasonable terms.

I think I should indicate why I am here in Birmingham, since you have been influenced by the view which argues against "outsiders coming in." I have the honor of serving as president of the Southern Christian Leadership Conference, an organization operating in every Southern state, with headquarters in Atlanta, Georgia. We have some eighty-five affiliated organizations across the South, and one of them is the Alabama Christian Movement for Human Rights. Frequently we share staff, educational, and financial resources with our affiliates. Several months ago the affiliate here in Birmingham asked us to be on call to engage in a nonviolent direct-action program if such were deemed

necessary. We readily consented, and when the hour came, we lived up to our promise. So I, along with several members of my staff, am here because I was invited here. I am here because I have organizational ties here.

But more basically, I am in Birmingham because injustice is here. Just as the prophets of the eighth century B.C. left their villages and carried their "thus saith the Lord" far beyond the boundaries of their hometowns, and just as the Apostle Paul left his village of Tarsus and

**1137**

---

Have students read the Build Background Feature on p. 1136 and interpret the possible influences of the historical context on King's letter.

**Literary Analysis**  ALLUSION

 From the bottom of page 1137 to the top of page 1138, what sort of allusion is King making and why?

**Possible Response:** He is making a biblical allusion to Old Testament prophets and early leaders of the Christian church; this equates the movement for social justice and racial equality with the gospel, suggesting that it is inspired by divine revelation. King relies heavily on biblical allusions because they are part of the common language of Christian clergy.

📖 Use **Unit Seven Resource Book**, p. 36 for additional support.

**Active Reading**

> **LOGICAL ARGUMENT: DEDUCTION AND INDUCTION**

 In this paragraph, what generalization (or premise) does King begin his argument with? What deduction does he make about how this premise applies to the United States?

**Possible Responses:** Premise: "Injustice anywhere is a threat to justice everywhere." Deduction: "Anyone who lives inside the United States can never be considered an outsider anywhere within its bounds."

📖 Use **Unit Seven Resource Book**, p. 35 for more practice.

---

carried the gospel of Jesus Christ to the far corners of the Greco-Roman world, so am I compelled to carry the gospel of freedom beyond my own hometown. Like Paul, I must constantly respond to the Macedonian call for aid.[1]

**A** Moreover, I am cognizant of the interrelatedness of all communities and states. I cannot sit idly by in Atlanta and not be concerned about what happens in Birmingham. Injustice anywhere is a threat to justice everywhere. We are caught in an inescapable network of mutuality, tied in a single garment of destiny. Whatever affects one directly, affects all indirectly. Never again can we afford to live with the narrow, provincial "outside agitator" idea. Anyone who lives inside the United States can never be considered an outsider anywhere within its bounds.

**B**

 deplore the demonstrations taking place in Birmingham. But your statement, I am sorry to say, fails to express a similar concern for the conditions that brought about the demonstrations. I am sure that none of you would want to rest content with the superficial kind of social analysis that deals merely with effects and does not grapple with underlying causes. It is unfortunate that demonstrations are taking place in Birmingham, but it is even more unfortunate that the city's white power structure left the Negro community with no alternative.

In any nonviolent campaign there are four basic steps: collection of the facts to determine whether injustices exist; negotiation; self-purification; and direct action. We have gone through all these steps in Birmingham. There can be no gainsaying[2] the fact that racial injustice engulfs this community. Birmingham is probably the most thoroughly segregated city in the United States. Its ugly record of brutality is widely known. Negroes have experienced grossly unjust treatment in the courts. There have been more unsolved bombings of Negro homes and

churches in Birmingham than in any other city in the nation. These are the hard, brutal facts of the case. On the basis of these conditions, Negro leaders sought to negotiate with the city fathers. But the latter consistently refused to engage in good-faith negotiations.

Then, last September, came the opportunity to talk with leaders of Birmingham's economic community. In the course of the negotiations, certain promises were made by the merchants—for example, to remove the stores' humiliating racial signs.[3] On the basis of these promises, The Reverend Fred Shuttlesworth and the leaders of the Alabama Christian Movement for Human Rights agreed to a moratorium[4] on all demonstrations. As the weeks and months went by, we realized that we were the victims of a broken promise. A few signs, briefly removed, returned; the others remained.

As in so many past experiences, our hopes had been blasted, and the shadow of deep disappointment settled upon us. We had no alternative except to prepare for direct action, whereby we would present our very bodies as a means of laying our case before the conscience of the local and the national community. Mindful of the difficulties involved, we decided to undertake a process of self-purification. We began a series of workshops on nonviolence, and we repeatedly asked ourselves: "Are you able to accept blows without retaliating?" "Are you able to endure the ordeal of jail?" We decided to schedule our direct-action program for the Easter season, realizing that except for Christmas, this is the main shopping period

---

1. **Macedonian** (măs′ĭ-dō′nē-ən) **call for aid:** According to the Bible (Acts 16), a man appeared to the apostle Paul in a vision, calling him to preach in Macedonia (at that time a Roman province north of Greece).
2. **gainsaying:** denying.
3. **racial signs:** signs marking segregated buildings and other facilities.
4. **moratorium** (môr′ə-tôr′ē-əm): temporary stoppage.

WORDS TO KNOW
**cognizant** (kŏg′nĭ-zənt) *adj.* aware
**segregated** (sĕg′rĭ-gā′tĭd) *adj.* separated according to race **segregate** *v.*
**retaliating** (rĭ-tăl′ē-ā′tĭng) *n.* taking revenge **retaliate** *v.*

1138

---

## Teaching Options

### Mini Lesson  **Preteaching Vocabulary**

**USING CONTEXT CLUES**

**Instruction** Context clues provide inferences to word meaning. Tell students that to understand unfamiliar words, they should examine the context in which the word is used.

**Model Sentence**

The affiliate helping us coordinate the conference in Boston has long been associated with our organization.

• Write the model sentence on the chalkboard.
• Ask a volunteer to paraphrase the sentence.
• Have students use the meaning of the sentence to **infer** meanings for the word *affiliate*.

• Ask a volunteer to use *affiliate* in a sentence.

**Exercises** Ask students to use context clues to determine the meanings of underlined terms in the following sentences.

1. King was cognizant of the violent threats made against his life, but he never let that awareness turn to fear.

2. Can you imagine our class segregated according to hair color, with light-colored hair on one side and dark colored on the other, never allowing the two sides to mix?

3. It is difficult to keep from retaliating when someone has hurt you, because a part of you wants to get back at that person.

of the year. Knowing that a strong economic-withdrawal program would be the by-product of direct action, we felt that this would be the best time to bring pressure to bear on the merchants for the needed change.

Then it occurred to us that Birmingham's mayoral election was coming up in March, and we speedily decided to postpone action until after election day. When we discovered that the Commissioner of Public Safety, Eugene "Bull" Connor, had piled up enough votes to be in the runoff, we decided again to postpone action until the day after the runoff so that the demonstrations could not be used to cloud the issues. Like many others, we waited to see Mr. Connor defeated, and to this end we endured postponement after postponement. Having aided in this community need, we felt that our direct-action program could be delayed no longer.

You may well ask: "Why direct action? Why sit-ins,[5] marches, and so forth? Isn't negotiation a better path?" You are quite right in calling for negotiation. Indeed, this is the very purpose of direct action. Nonviolent direct action seeks to create such a crisis and foster such a tension that a community which has constantly refused to negotiate is forced to confront the issue. It seeks so to dramatize the issue that it can no longer be ignored. My citing the creation of tension as part of the work of the nonviolent-resister may sound rather shocking. But I must confess that I am not afraid of the word "tension." I have earnestly opposed violent tension, but there is a type of constructive, nonviolent tension which is necessary for growth. Just as Socrates[6] felt that it was necessary to create a tension in the mind so that individuals could rise from the bondage of myths and half-truths to the unfettered realm of creative analysis and objective appraisal, so must

Birmingham police turn fire hoses on civil rights demonstrators.

we see the need for nonviolent gadflies[7] to create the kind of tension in society that will help men rise from the dark depths of prejudice and racism to the majestic heights of understanding and brotherhood.

The purpose of our direct-action program is to create a situation so crisis-packed that it will inevitably open the door to negotiation. I therefore concur with you in your call for negotiation. Too long has our beloved Southland been bogged down in a tragic effort to live in monologue rather than dialogue.

One of the basic points in your statement is that the action that I and my associates have taken in Birmingham is untimely. Some have asked: "Why didn't you give the new city administration time to act?" The only answer that I can give to this query is that the new Birmingham administration must be prodded about as much as the outgoing one before it

---

5. **sit-ins:** peaceful demonstrations in which protesters occupied, and refused to leave, seats in segregated lunch counters and other places of business.

6. **Socrates** (sŏk′rə-tēz′): a Greek philosopher of the fifth century B.C.—one of the major influences in the development of Western thought.

7. **gadflies:** critics.

WORDS
TO
KNOW
**appraisal** (ə-prā′zəl) *n.* evaluation

1139

**Customizing Instruction**

### Students Acquiring English
Encourage students to use context clues, prior word knowledge, and a dictionary to learn the meanings of unfamiliar terms.
- *gospel*—religious teachings
- *sit idly by*—sit and do nothing
- *brutality*—cruel practices
- *conscience*—moral and ethical awareness
- *ordeal*—a difficult experience that tests one's character
- *query*—question
- *prodded*—urged to action through moral pressure

### Less Proficient Readers
Help students keep track of King's claims.

**1** What conditions does King refer to here?

**Possible Responses:** the brutality of racial injustice; the burning of homes and churches

### Gifted and Talented
**2** What does King mean by "a strong economic-withdrawal program"?
**Answer:** a boycott

### Less Proficient Readers
**3** What is the purpose of taking direct action?
**Possible Responses:** to negotiate with local lawmakers; to bring about civil rights for African Americans

**Set a Purpose** Have students read on to find out how King defines just and unjust laws.

4. King's own <u>appraisal</u> of the situation in Birmingham—when asked to evaluate it—was that the city had a dire need for direct action.

5. The people who <u>diligently</u> participated in nonviolent direct actions continually persevered under horrendous circumstances.

6. It is hard for us today to understand how such <u>statutes</u> existed—how such unjust laws could ever be passed.

7. King argued that people's <u>estrangement</u> from other people was as bad as alienation from God.

8. If people cannot vent their <u>latent</u> anxieties and fears, those emotions may eventually result in violent behavior.

9. A person must have tremendous resolve to withstand <u>provocation</u> so that it doesn't trigger an angry response.

Use **Unit Seven Resource Book,** p. 37 for additional support.

**A lesson on context clues appears on p. 326 in the Pupil's Edition.**

In 1968, civil-rights marchers in Memphis pass National Guard bayonets.

will act. . . . My friends, I must say to you that we have not made a single gain in civil rights without determined legal and nonviolent pressure. Lamentably, it is a historical fact that privileged groups seldom give up their privileges voluntarily. Individuals may see the moral light and voluntarily give up their unjust posture; but, as Reinhold Niebuhr[8] has reminded us, groups tend to be more immoral than individuals.

We know through painful experience that freedom is never voluntarily given by the oppressor; it must be demanded by the oppressed. Frankly, I have yet to engage in a direct-action campaign that was "well-timed" in the view of those who have not suffered unduly from the disease of segregation. For years now I have heard the word "Wait!" It rings in the ear of every Negro with piercing familiarity. This "Wait" has almost always meant "Never." We must come to see, with one of our distinguished jurists, that "justice too long delayed is justice denied."

We have waited for more than 340 years for our constitutional and God-given rights. The nations of Asia and Africa are moving with jetlike speed toward gaining political independence, but we still creep at horse-and-buggy pace toward gaining a cup of coffee at a lunch counter. Perhaps it is easy for those who

have never felt the stinging darts of segregation to say, "Wait." But when you have seen vicious mobs lynch your mothers and fathers at will and drown your sisters and brothers at whim; when you have seen hate-filled policemen curse, kick, and even kill your black brothers and sisters; when you see the vast majority of your twenty million Negro brothers smothering in an airtight cage of poverty in the midst of an affluent society; when you suddenly find your tongue twisted and your speech stammering as you seek to explain to your six-year-old daughter why she can't go to the public amusement park that has just been advertised on television, and see tears welling up in her eyes when she is told that Funtown is closed to colored children, and see ominous[9] clouds of inferiority beginning to form in her little mental sky, and see her beginning to distort her personality by developing an unconscious bitterness toward white people; when you have to concoct an answer for a five-year-old son who is asking: "Daddy, why do white people treat colored people so mean?"; when you take a cross-country drive and find it necessary to sleep night after night in the uncomfortable corners of your automobile because no motel will accept you; when you are humiliated day in and day out by nagging signs reading "white" and "colored"; when your first name becomes "nigger," your middle name becomes "boy" (however old you are) and your last name becomes "John," and your wife and mother are never given the respected title "Mrs."; when you are harried by day and haunted by night by the fact that you are a Negro, living constantly at tiptoe stance, never quite knowing what to expect next, and are

---

8. **Reinhold Niebuhr** (rīn'hōld' nē'boŏr'): a 20th-century American theologian whose writings deal mainly with moral and social problems.

9. **ominous** (ŏm'ə-nəs): threatening.

plagued with inner fears and outer resentments; when you are forever fighting a degenerating sense of "nobodiness"—then you will understand why we find it difficult to wait. There comes a time when the cup of endurance runs over, and men are no longer willing to be plunged into the abyss of despair. I hope, sirs, you can understand our legitimate and unavoidable impatience.

You express a great deal of anxiety over our willingness to break laws. This is certainly a legitimate concern. Since we so diligently urge people to obey the Supreme Court's decision of 1954 outlawing segregation in the public schools,[10] at first glance it may seem rather paradoxical[11] for us consciously to break laws. One may well ask: "How can you advocate breaking some laws and obeying others?" The answer lies in the fact that there are two types of laws: just and unjust. I would be the first to advocate obeying just laws. One has not only a legal but a moral responsibility to obey just laws. Conversely, one has a moral responsibility to disobey unjust laws. I would agree with St. Augustine[12] that "an unjust law is no law at all."

Now, what is the difference between the two? How does one determine whether a law is just or unjust? A just law is a man-made code that squares with the moral law or the law of God. An unjust law is a code that is out of harmony with the moral law. To put it in the terms of St. Thomas Aquinas:[13] An unjust law is a human law that is not rooted in eternal law and natural law. Any law that uplifts human personality is just. Any law that degrades human personality is unjust. All segregation statutes are unjust because segregation distorts the soul and damages the personality. It gives the segregator a false sense of superiority and the segregated a false sense of inferiority. Segregation, to use the terminology of the Jewish philosopher Martin Buber,[14] substitutes an "I-it" relationship for an "I-thou" relationship and ends up relegating

persons to the status of things. Hence segregation is not only politically, economically, and sociologically unsound, it is morally wrong and sinful. Paul Tillich[15] has said that sin is separation. Is not segregation an existential[16] expression of man's tragic separation, his awful estrangement, his terrible sinfulness? Thus it is that I can urge men to obey the 1954 decision of the Supreme Court, for it is morally right; and I can urge them to disobey segregation ordinances, for they are morally wrong.

**Let** us consider a more concrete example of just and unjust laws. An unjust law is a code that a numerical or power majority group compels a minority group to obey but does not make binding on itself. This is *difference* made legal. By the same token, a just law is a code that a majority compels a minority to follow and that it is willing to follow itself. This is *sameness* made legal.

Let me give another explanation. A law is unjust if it is inflicted on a minority that, as a result of being denied the right to vote, had no part in enacting or devising the law. Who can say that the legislature of Alabama which set up that state's segregation laws was democratically elected? Throughout Alabama all sorts of devious methods are used to prevent Negroes

---

10. **the Supreme Court's . . . public schools:** the U.S. Supreme Court's decision in the case *Brown v. Board of Education of Topeka, Kansas.*

11. **paradoxical** (păr′ə-dŏk′sĭ-kəl): self-contradictory.

12. **St. Augustine** (ô′gə-stēn′): a North African bishop of the fourth–fifth centuries, whose writings have been extremely influential throughout the history of Christianity.

13. **St. Thomas Aquinas** (ə-kwī′nəs): a noted medieval philosopher and theologian.

14. **Martin Buber** (bōō′bər): an influential 20th-century Jewish philosopher.

15. **Paul Tillich** (tĭl′ĭk): a German-born American theologian of the 20th century.

16. **existential** (ĕg′zĭ-stĕn′shəl): existing in the real world.

---

WORDS
TO
KNOW

**diligently** (dĭl′ə-jənt-lē) *adv.* in a persevering, painstaking manner
**statute** (stăch′ōōt) *n.* a law
**estrangement** (ĭ-strānj′mənt) *n.* separation; alienation

**1141**

## Customizing Instruction

### Students Acquiring English

Encourage students to use context clues, prior word knowledge, and a dictionary to learn the meanings of unfamiliar terms.

- *lamentably*—regrettably or sadly
- *at horse-and-buggy pace*—very slowly
- *lynch*—kill by hanging
- *at whim*—arbitrarily, on impulse
- *smothering*—suffocating
- *concoct*—to make up or contrive
- *harried*—harassed
- *at tiptoe stance*—cautiously
- *degenerating*—sinking or worsening
- *abyss of despair*—hell of hopelessness
- *just and unjust*—fair and wrong

### Gifted and Talented

**1** Ask students to cite examples from current or historical events that bolster Niebuhr's claim.

### Less Proficient Readers

Use the following questions to guide students' understanding of the text:

**2** To whom is King referring here?
**Answer:** white people

**3** What kind of law does King say should be disobeyed?
**Answer:** unjust laws

**4** What does King call segregation?
**Answer:** morally wrong and sinful

**Set a Purpose** Have students read on to find out what King has to say about nonviolent direct action.

## Cross Curricular Link **History**

**CIVIL RIGHTS MOVEMENT** While the civil rights movement peaked in the late fifties and early sixties, it had been centuries in the making. In 1787, when the Constitution was still being drafted, founders of our republic did not grant citizen status to enslaved people. It wasn't until after the Civil War, during Reconstruction and the drafting of the 13th–15th constitutional amendments (1865–1870), that African Americans were promised rights as citizens. In 1875 there was an attempt to legislate equal accommodations for blacks and whites in all public facilities except schools, but in 1883 the Supreme Court voided this Civil Rights Act. In another blow to racial justice, the Supreme Court (*Plessy v. Ferguson*, 1896) upheld "separate but equal" facilities for the races. By 1900, 18 states in the North and West had statutes forbidding racial discrimination, while "Jim Crow laws" further entrenched the South in segregation. It was not until after World War II that the armed forces were desegregated. During the late forties and early fifties, lawyers with the National Association for the Advancement of Colored People (NAACP) pressed for change through the courts. They won when the Supreme Court acknowledged that separate (and consistently inadequate) educational facilities for blacks were unconstitutional (*Brown v. Board of Education of Topeka, Kansas*, 1954).

**Active Reading**

> **LOGICAL ARGUMENT:**
> **DEDUCTION AND INDUCTION**

**Ⓐ** What method of reasoning does King use here?

**Answer:** deductive

• What is King's initial premise? What specific conclusion does he draw from it?

**Possible Response:** Premise: Laws can be applied unjustly. Conclusion: An ordinance requiring parade permits is unjust when it denies one's First Amendment right to peaceful assembly and protest.

**Literary Analysis** ┃ ALLUSION ┃

**Ⓑ** To what historical event does King indirectly refer here?

**Answer:** the Holocaust—Hitler's regime killed over 11 million people considered undesirable: Jews, Gypsies, gays, the disabled, and political dissenters.

**Active Reading**

> **LOGICAL ARGUMENT:**
> **DEDUCTION AND INDUCTION**

**Ⓒ** What sort of logical argument does this paragraph exemplify?

**Answer:** inductive reasoning

• What is King's general conclusion here?

**Possible Response:** "Shallow understanding from people of goodwill is more frustrating than absolute misunderstanding from people of ill will," or "Lukewarm acceptance is much more bewildering than outright rejection."

**Reading Skills and Strategies:**
**QUESTION**

**Ⓓ** What is the "hidden tension"?

**Possible Response:** racial prejudice and all its ugly consequences

from becoming registered voters, and there are some counties in which, even though Negroes constitute a majority of the population, not a single Negro is registered. Can any law enacted under such circumstances be considered democratically structured?

**Ⓐ** Sometimes a law is just on its face and unjust in its application. For instance, I have been arrested on a charge of parading without a permit. Now, there is nothing wrong in having an ordinance which requires a permit for a parade. But such an ordinance becomes unjust when it is used to maintain segregation and to deny citizens the First Amendment privilege of peaceful assembly and protest.

**[1]** I hope you are able to see the distinction I am trying to point out. In no sense do I advocate evading or defying the law, as would the rabid segregationist. That would lead to anarchy. One who breaks an unjust law must do so openly, lovingly, and with a willingness to accept the penalty. I submit that an individual who breaks a law that conscience tells him is unjust, and who willingly accepts the penalty of imprisonment in order to arouse the conscience of the community over its injustice, is in reality expressing the highest respect for law.

Of course, there is nothing new about this kind of civil disobedience. It was evidenced sublimely in the refusal of Shadrach, Meshach, and Abednego to obey the laws of Nebuchadnezzar,[17] on the ground that a higher moral law was at stake. It was practiced superbly by the early Christians, who were willing to face hungry lions and the excruciating pain of chopping blocks rather than submit to certain unjust laws of the Roman Empire. To a degree, academic freedom is a reality today because Socrates practiced civil disobedience. In our own nation, the Boston Tea Party represented a massive act of civil disobedience.

**Ⓑ** We should never forget that everything Adolf Hitler did in Germany was "legal" and everything the Hungarian freedom fighters[18]

did in Hungary was "illegal." It was "illegal" to aid and comfort a Jew in Hitler's Germany. Even so, I am sure that, had I lived in Germany at the time, I would have aided and comforted my Jewish brothers. If today I lived in a Communist country where certain principles dear to the Christian faith are suppressed, I would openly advocate disobeying that country's antireligious laws.

I must make two honest confessions to you, my Christian and Jewish brothers. First, I must confess that over the past few years I have been gravely disappointed with the white moderate. I have almost reached the regrettable conclusion that the Negro's great stumbling block in his stride toward freedom is not the White Citizen's Counciler or the Ku Klux Klanner,[19] but the white moderate, who is more devoted to "order" than to justice; who prefers a negative peace which is the absence of tension to a positive peace which is the presence of justice; who constantly says: "I agree with you in the goal you seek, but I cannot agree with your methods of direct action"; who paternalistically[20] believes he can set the timetable for another man's freedom; who lives by a mythical concept of time and who constantly advises the Negro to wait for a "more convenient season." Shallow understanding from people of goodwill is more frustrating than absolute misunderstanding from people of ill

---

17. **the refusal . . . Nebuchadnezzar** (nĕb′ə-kəd-nĕz′ər): In the Bible (Daniel 3), Shadrach (shăd′răk), Meshach (mē′shăk), and Abednego (ə-bĕd′nĭ-gō′) are three Hebrews condemned to death for refusing to worship an idol set up by Nebuchadnezzar, king of Babylon. When cast into a fiery furnace, they are miraculously protected from the fire and emerge unharmed.

18. **Hungarian freedom fighters:** Hungarians who participated in a 1956 rebellion against the Communist government of their homeland. (The uprising was crushed by troops sent into Hungary by the Soviet Union.)

19. **the White . . . Klanner:** the member of a group committed to the exclusion and persecution of African Americans and other minorities.

20. **paternalistically** (pə-tûr′nə-lĭs′tĭ-klē): in a manner that suggests a father's claim of protective authority over his children.

---

## Grammar

**VERBS: VOICE AND MOOD**

**Instruction** Mood is the way a verb expresses an idea. In English, there are three moods: indicative, imperative, and subjunctive. The indicative mood indicates a fact and is used in declarative, interrogative, and exclamatory sentences. The imperative mood gives a command or makes a request. The subjunctive mood can express (1) a wish or a condition contrary to fact or (2) a command or a request after the word *that*.

**Model** Write the following sentences on the board and discuss the mood of each underlined verb.

**Indicative (declaratory):** Eldridge Cleaver <u>was</u> another leader of the Civil Rights Movement.

**Indicative (interrogative):** <u>Was</u> Eldridge Cleaver another leader of the civil rights movement?

**Indicative (exclamatory):** I <u>forget</u>!

**Imperative:** <u>Protest</u> racial injustice now!

**Subjunctive (request):** The lawyers requested that the Supreme Court <u>rule</u> in favor of desegregation.

**Subjunctive (contrary to fact):** If segregation in the South <u>were</u> not fueled by racial injustice, there would not be such gross inequalities in the separate schools.

will. Lukewarm acceptance is much more bewildering than outright rejection.

I had hoped that the white moderate would understand that law and order exist for the purpose of establishing justice and that when they fail in this purpose, they become the dangerously structured dams that block the flow of social progress. I had hoped that the white moderate would understand that the present tension in the South is a necessary phase of the transition from an obnoxious negative peace, in which the Negro passively accepted his unjust plight, to a substantive and positive peace, in which all men will respect the dignity and worth of human personality. Actually, we who engage in nonviolent direct action are not the creators of tension. We merely bring to the surface the hidden tension that is already alive. We bring it out in the open, where it can be seen and dealt with. Like a boil that can never be cured so long as it is covered up but must be opened with all its ugliness to the natural medicines of air and light, injustice must be exposed, with all the tension its exposure creates, to the light of human conscience and the air of national opinion before it can be cured.

In your statement you assert that our actions, even though peaceful, must be condemned because they precipitate violence. But is this a logical assertion? Isn't this like condemning a robbed man because his possession of money precipitated[21] the evil act of robbery? Isn't this like condemning Socrates because his unswerving commitment to truth and his philosophical inquiries precipitated the act by the misguided populace in which they made him drink hemlock? Isn't this like condemning Jesus because his unique God-consciousness and never-ceasing devotion to God's will precipitated the evil act of crucifixion? We must come to see that, as the federal courts have consistently affirmed, it is wrong to urge an individual to cease his efforts to gain his basic constitutional rights because the quest may precipitate violence. Society must protect the robbed and punish the robber. . . .

Oppressed people cannot remain oppressed forever. The yearning for freedom eventually manifests itself, and that is what has happened to the American Negro. Something within has reminded him of his birthright of freedom, and something without has reminded him that it can be gained. Consciously or unconsciously, he has been caught up by the *Zeitgeist*,[22] and with his black brothers of Africa and his brown and yellow brothers of Asia, South America, and the Caribbean, the United States Negro is moving with a sense of great urgency toward the promised land of racial justice. If one recognizes this vital urge that has engulfed the Negro community, one should readily understand why public demonstrations are taking place. The Negro has many pent-up resentments and <u>latent</u> frustrations, and he must release them. So let him march; let him make prayer pilgrimages to the city hall; let him go on freedom rides—and try to understand why he must do so. If his repressed emotions are not released in nonviolent ways, they will seek expression through violence; this is not a threat but a fact of history. So I have not said to my people: "Get rid of your discontent." Rather, I have tried to say that this normal and healthy discontent can be channeled into the creative outlet of nonviolent direct action. And now this approach is being termed extremist.

*"Oppressed people cannot remain oppressed forever."*

---

21. **precipitated** (prĭ-sĭp'ĭ-tā'tĭd): brought about; caused.

22. **Zeitgeist** (tsīt'gīst') *German*: spirit of the time—the beliefs and attitudes shared by most of the people living in a particular period.

WORDS TO KNOW **latent** (lāt'nt) *adj.* existing in a hidden form

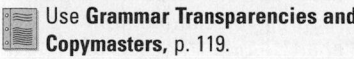

Ⓐ To whom does King indirectly refer here? Why does he use the word *disinherited*?

**Possible Responses:** He refers to the young African Americans, many of them students, who took part in the non-violent demonstrations and sit-ins. By using the word *disinherited*, King emphasizes that civil rights are the birthright of every American citizen, and that black Americans are unfairly denied these rights.

### Reading Skills and Strategies: COMPARING

Help students recognize the common elements between Giovanni's poem and King's letter. Consider using this outline to lead a class discussion.

### Theme
- Each one explores the tension between reality—the social conditions as they are—and expectation, what one aspires for.
- Each expresses the struggle to be free.

### Other Literary Elements
- Each work reveals a depth of intellect and sound reasoning as well as revolutionary zeal tempered by enlightenment.
- Both writers are African American.
- Each piece has an intimate style: King's is a letter, Giovanni's poem reads like an insight into a personal reflection.
- The tone in each is passionate as well as compassionate.

---

But though I was initially disappointed at being categorized as an extremist, as I continued to think about the matter, I gradually gained a measure of satisfaction from the label. Was not Jesus an extremist for love: "Love your enemies, bless them that curse you, do good to them that hate you, and pray for them which despitefully use you, and persecute you." Was not Amos[23] an extremist for justice: "Let justice roll down like waters and righteousness like an ever-flowing stream." Was not Paul an extremist for the Christian gospel: "I bear in my body the marks of the Lord Jesus." Was not Martin Luther[24] an extremist: "Here I stand; I cannot do otherwise, so help me God." And John Bunyan:[25] "I will stay in jail to the end of my days before I make a butchery of my conscience." And Abraham Lincoln: "This nation cannot survive half slave and half free." And Thomas Jefferson: "We hold these truths to be self-evident, that all men are created equal. . . ." So the question is not whether we will be extremists, but what kind of extremists we will be. Will we be extremists for hate or for love? Will we be extremists for the preservation of injustice or for the extension of justice? In that dramatic scene on Calvary's hill[26] three men were crucified. We must never forget that all three were crucified for the same crime—the crime of extremism. Two were extremists for immorality, and thus fell below their environment. The other, Jesus Christ, was an extremist for love, truth, and goodness, and thereby rose above his environment. Perhaps the South, the nation and the world are in dire need

James Meredith during his struggle to enter the University of Mississippi in 1962.

of creative extremists. . . .

I wish you had commended the Negro sit-inners and demonstrators of Birmingham for their sublime courage, their willingness to suffer, and their amazing discipline in the midst of great <u>provocation</u>. One day the South will recognize its real heroes. They will be the James Merediths,[27] with the noble sense of purpose that enables them to face jeering and hostile mobs, and with the agonizing loneliness that characterizes the life of the pioneer. They will be old, oppressed, battered Negro women, symbolized in a seventy-two-year-old woman in Montgomery, Alabama, who rose up with a sense of dignity and with her people decided not to ride segregated buses, and who responded with ungrammatical profundity to one who inquired about her weariness: "My feets is tired, but my soul is at rest." They will be the young high school and college students, the young ministers of the gospel and a host of their elders, courageously and nonviolently sitting in

---

23. **Amos:** a Hebrew prophet whose words are recorded in the Old Testament book bearing his name.

24. **Martin Luther:** a German monk who launched the Protestant Reformation with his condemnations of the wealth and corruption of the 16th-century Roman Catholic Church.

25. **John Bunyan:** a 17th-century English preacher and author of the famous religious allegory *The Pilgrim's Progress.* He was twice imprisoned for unlicensed preaching.

26. **Calvary's hill:** the site of Jesus's crucifixion.

27. **James Merediths:** people like James Meredith, who endured violent opposition from whites to become the first African American to attend the University of Mississippi.

---

WORDS
TO
KNOW

**provocation** (prŏv′ə-kā′shən) *n.* something that arouses anger

---

## Teaching Options

**Mini Lesson** ## Vocabulary Strategy

### LATIN ROOTS

**Instruction** To help students understand word meanings, they can use dictionaries to research word origins and learn the Latin roots of words. All the WORDS TO KNOW for this selection have Latin roots. Write the word *segregate* on the board; then read aloud the word's definition from a college dictionary: "to impose the separation of a race from the rest of society." Read the word's history: Latin *segregare*, "to separate from the flock" (from *se*, "apart" + *grex*, "flock").

**Application** Have students work in small groups with a dictionary; make sure the dictionary pro-

vides etymologies, or word histories. Student groups should research Latin roots for the WORDS TO KNOW: *affiliate* (*affiliare*, "to take to oneself as a son"), *appraisal* (*appretiare*, "to set a value on"), *cognizant* (*cognoscere*, "to learn"), *diligent* (*diligens*, "loving, attentive," from *diligere*, "to single out"), *estrangement* (*extraneus*, "strange, foreign"), *latent* (*latens*, from *latere*, "to lie hidden or concealed"), *provocation* (*provocare*, "to call forth, challenge"), *retaliating* (*retaliare*, "to repay in kind"), *statute* (*statutus*, past participle of *statuere*, "to set up, decree")

at lunch counters and willingly going to jail for conscience' sake. One day the South will know that when these disinherited children of God sat down at lunch counters, they were in reality standing up for what is best in the American dream and for the most sacred values in our Judaeo-Christian heritage, thereby bringing our nation back to those great wells of democracy which were dug deep by the founding fathers in their formulation of the Constitution and the Declaration of Independence.

Never before have I written so long a letter. I'm afraid it is much too long to take your precious time. I can assure you that it would have been much shorter if I had been writing from a comfortable desk, but what else can one do when he is alone in a narrow jail cell, other than write long letters, think long thoughts, and pray long prayers?

If I have said anything in this letter that overstates the truth and indicates an unreasonable impatience, I beg you to forgive me. If I have said anything that understates the truth and indicates my having a patience that allows me to settle for anything less than brotherhood, I beg God to forgive me.

I hope this letter finds you strong in the faith. I also hope that circumstances will soon make it possible for me to meet each of you, not as an integrationist or a civil-rights leader but as a fellow clergyman and a Christian brother. Let us all hope that the dark clouds of racial prejudice will soon pass away and the deep fog of misunderstanding will be lifted from our fear-drenched communities, and in some not too distant tomorrow the radiant stars of love and brotherhood will shine over our great nation with all their scintillating[28] beauty.

Yours for the cause of Peace and Brotherhood,

**Martin Luther King, Jr.**

---

28. **scintillating** (sĭn′tl-ā′tĭng): sparkling.

1

## LITERARY LINK

# REVOLUTIONARY DREAMS  Nikki Giovanni

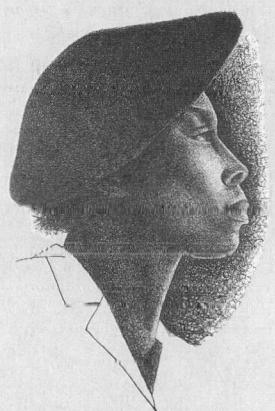

*On the Subway* (1986), Elizabeth Catlett. Courtesy of Isobel Neal Gallery, Chicago.

i used to dream militant
dreams of taking
over america to show
these white folks how it should be
5  done
i used to dream radical dreams
of blowing everyone away with my perceptive powers
of correct analysis
i even used to think i'd be the one
10  to stop the riot and negotiate the peace
then i awoke and dug
that if i dreamed natural
dreams of being a natural
woman doing what a woman
15  does when she's natural
i would have a revolution

---

### Less Proficient Readers

**1** Make sure students understand why King might need to apologize to the clergymen if he has exaggerated the situation of African Americans. Why would he beg forgiveness from God if he has been too patient?

**Possible Response:** If his response is too strong, then he may have offended the clergymen to whom he addresses his letter. If his response is not strong enough, then he must answer to God for lacking moral insight and courage. He is implying that he would rather err on the side of exaggerating.

### Students Acquiring English

Students can use context clues, prior word knowledge, and a dictionary to learn the meanings of unfamiliar terms. Encourage them to read the word histories.

• *extremist*—a radical; one who advocates or resorts to measures beyond the norm
• *in dire need*—desperate for; in urgent need
• *commended*—praised; represented as worthy
• *jeering*—taunting, mocking
• *profundity*—depth of meaning or intellect; wisdom, insight
• *disinherited*—deprived of a natural right or privilege
• *scintillating*—sparkling, glistening

### Gifted and Talented

Have students research and report on the activities of SNCC, the Student Nonviolent Coordinating Committee. Black college students launched the sit-in movement in Greensboro, North Carolina, in 1960. They strove to put in practice the nonviolent tactics used by Mohandas Gandhi to lead India out from British oppression.

---

## ✓ Assessment **Standardized Test Practice**

**CHOOSING THE BEST SUMMARY** Many standardized tests ask students to identify the best summary of a passage they have read. Ask students which of the following statements best summarizes the main idea of King's letter. Read them all aloud, and give students a chance to reflect on each statement.

**A.** We have a moral responsibility to disobey unjust laws.

**B.** We can gain civil rights only through persistent legal challenges and nonviolent civil disobedience.

**C.** We can change the unjust laws if we can get the local authorities to negotiate with us.

**D.** Any law that degrades a human being is unjust; segregation is degrading, and therefore is an unjust law.

Lead students through the process of selecting the best summary. Consider each choice. While all these statements contain nuggets of King's beliefs as expressed in the letter, **B** holds the most important information. After all, King had to persuade the clergy to accept his tactics as much as his goal.

## GUIDING STUDENT RESPONSE

### Connect to the Literature

**1. What Do You Think?**
Examples might include King's logic and determination, his description of southern African Americans' grief and anger, his comment about the unity of all people, and his hope for the future of brotherhood.

**Comprehension Check**
• unjust laws
• Jesus, Martin Luther, Abraham Lincoln, Thomas Jefferson

 Use Selection Quiz **Unit Seven Resource Book**, p. 38.

### Think Critically

**2.** Students may express the following viewpoints: The clergymen felt ashamed, since King's letter points out flaws in their thinking and implies their lack of depth in examining the issues. They admired the clarity and inspiration of King's writing. Their position on the demonstrations remained unchanged, despite King's eloquence.

**3.** Some students may reply that King's criticism was wise because he astutely recognized an important source contributing to segregation in the South. Others may say that King's criticism was unwise because he risked alienating white moderates and inadvertently provoked them into opposing civil rights activists.

**4.** Students who agree with King's methods may admire his advocacy of nonviolent action, his logical, four-step outline for achieving justice, and his courage in using direct action to protest unjust laws. Students who disagree with King's methods may admonish him for precipitating a crisis, oppose his distinction between justice and injustice, and object to his views on civil disobedience.

**5.** Students should point out how the use of deduction or induction helps King develop his argument logically and thus make his ideas and actions more convincing.

### Literary Analysis

**Allusion** Socrates dared to challenge tradition in his society, just as King dared to challenge the tradition of segregation in

### Connect to the Literature

**1. What Do You Think?**
What ideas and emotions in the letter had the greatest impact on you?

**Comprehension Check**
• According to King, it is morally right to disobey what kind of laws?
• Name a figure King admires as an extremist.

### Think Critically

**2.** How do you think the eight clergymen felt after reading King's letter? Point out specific passages that may have particularly influenced their reactions.

**3.** Explain whether you think King was wise to criticize the white moderate in his letter.

**4.** Do you agree with King's methods of standing up for his beliefs?

**THINK ABOUT**
• the four steps in a nonviolent campaign
• specific kinds of nonviolent direct action that he advocates
• his belief in the need to create "tension" to effect reform
• his distinction between just and unjust laws
• the measures you considered for the Connect to Your Life activity on page 1136

**5.** **ACTIVE READING** **LOGICAL ARGUMENT: DEDUCTION AND INDUCTION** Explain the process of reasoning King uses in one passage from this essay. Refer to the notes in your **READER'S NOTEBOOK**.

### Extend Interpretations

**6. The Writer's Style** King sometimes uses a technique known as **parallelism**—the use of the same grammatical forms to express equivalent thoughts. For example, he uses a series of *when* clauses beginning with "But *when* you have seen vicious mobs. . . ." Find other examples of this technique in the letter, and describe the effect.

**7. Comparing Texts** What might King have said about Nikki Giovanni's views of revolution in "Revolutionary Dreams" (page 1145)?

**8. Connect to Life** How realistic do you find the vision of America that King strives to bring about? Explain.

### Literary Analysis

**ALLUSION** An **allusion** is a reference to a historical or literary person, place, or event with which the reader is assumed to be familiar. Many works contain allusions to the Bible, classical mythology, Shakespeare's plays, or other works of literature. By using allusions, writers tap the knowledge and memory of the reader, drawing upon associations already in the reader's mind. For example, readers familiar with the Bible likely will recognize King's allusion to Shadrach, Meshach, and Abednego, the three Jews who risked death rather than worship an idol. By alluding to these biblical characters, King emphasizes the civil rights protesters' courage to die for their convictions.

**Cooperative Learning Activity** Work with three classmates to investigate King's allusions to these historical figures: Socrates, the Apostle Paul, Adolf Hitler, and James Meredith. Each member of the group should research one of these people in detail. After you have completed your research, write a note explaining the allusion and telling why you think King includes it in his argument. Pool your notes and share them with other groups.

the South. Hitler created a system of laws that not only segregated certain groups from the rest of German society—such as Jews, Gypsies, gays, disabled people, and political dissidents—but also murdered over 11 million of these people. The Apostle Paul traveled to foreign lands to spread the gospel, despite being persecuted for his Christian beliefs, just as King was criticized and even imprisoned for spreading the gospel of civil rights. James Meredith was the young man who insisted on being allowed access to the University of Mississippi; it took a court order to get him in, and once there he had to put up with daily assaults from other students and even professors.

### Extend Interpretations

**The Writer's Style** Possible Response: King uses a string of parallel phrases, shown in the following example, to emphasize points and to show patterns: "other than *write long letters, think long thoughts, and pray long prayers . . .*"

**Comparing Texts** Possible Response: In Giovanni's "Revolutionary Dreams," personal motives take priority over her political principles.

**Connect to Life** Some students may find King's vision of everyone living in love and brotherhood unattainable; others may find this vision achievable in small ways every day.

## Writing Options

**1. Defining a Hero** Near the end of his letter, King says, "One day the South will recognize its real heroes." What do you think are King's criteria for a hero? Write a review of the letter, supporting your answer.

**2. Editorial About King's Ideas** Write an editorial for your school newspaper in which you explain whether you find King's ideas and methods of standing up for his beliefs applicable today. Use both inductive and deductive reasoning to develop your argument.

**Writing Handbook**
See page 1285: Persuasive Writing.

**3. Compare-and-Contrast Essay** How would you compare King's methods of standing up for his beliefs with those described by Thoreau in "Civil Disobedience,"

on page 370? Write a compare-and-contrast essay to convey your ideas. Place this piece in your **Working Portfolio**.

## Activities & Explorations

**1. Poster Design** In this letter King uses several **aphorisms**—brief statements, usually one sentence long, that express a general principle or truth about life. Design a poster to represent the message that one of these aphorisms conveys. ~ **ART**

**2. Dramatic Skit** With a classmate, role-play a dialogue in which King and Thoreau comment on social conditions in their times and the use of civil disobedience as a means of opposing injustice. ~ **PERFORMING**

**3. Multimedia Presentation** With your classmates, plan and

present a multimedia program in memory of King. Use tape recordings of his speeches, slides or videotapes of his life, music, original poems, essays, or skits. Then share your presentation with other classes. ~ **VIEWING AND REPRESENTING**

## Inquiry & Research

**Civil Rights Today** With a small group of classmates, investigate some of the recent legislation—both state and federal—affecting civil rights. Some of the topics you might explore include fair housing laws, discrimination based on gender or age, rights of criminals, quotas in hiring practices, and harassment in the workplace. Present an oral report to the class to share your findings.

## Vocabulary in Action

**EXERCISE A: MEANING CLUES** On your paper, write the Word to Know whose meaning is suggested by each sentence.

1. Martin Luther King, Jr., was well acquainted with the political situation in Birmingham.
2. The city was divided along racial lines.
3. King's followers avoided fighting back violently.
4. There was a great deal of hidden frustration in the lives of African Americans.
5. The protesters in Birmingham strove to ignore any attempt to make them furious and lure them into violence.

**EXERCISE B: SYNONYMS** Write the Word to Know that is a synonym of each word below.

1. rule
2. isolation
3. assessment
4. associate
5. industriously

**Building Vocabulary**
Several Words to Know come from Latin. For an in-depth lesson on root words, see page 1130.

*See page 308 for the biography of Martin Luther King, Jr.*

| WORDS TO KNOW | affiliate appraisal | cognizant diligently | estrangement latent | provocation retaliating | segregated statute |
|---|---|---|---|---|---|

## Writing Options

**1. Defining a Hero** One criterion should be a commitment to nonviolence even when severely provoked.

**2. Editorial about King's Ideas** Advise students to be brief—no more than 250 words—and stick to one method of logical argument.

**3. Compare-and-Contrast Essay** **To get students started on this assignment,** have them scan both essays and list main ideas in their Reader's Notebooks under the headings "Compare" and "Contrast."

## Activities & Explorations

**1. Poster Design** Direct students to p. 1138, "Injustice anywhere is a threat to justice everywhere"; or p. 1142, "Shallow understanding from people of goodwill is more frustrating than absolute misunderstanding from people of ill will."

**2. Dramatic Skit** Suggest that students focus on abolition and civil rights.

**3. Multimedia Presentation** Have students divide into groups to concentrate on specific media: dramatic, visual, graphic, written, audio, and so on.

## Inquiry & Research

**Civil Rights Today** Hate crimes (or antibias) legislation is another important issue in many states and at the federal level.

## Vocabulary in Action

**Exercise A**
1. cognizant
2. segregated
3. retaliating
4. latent
5. provocation

**Exercise B**
1. statute
2. estrangement
3. appraisal
4. affiliate
5. diligently

---

## Mini Lesson Speaking and Listening

**PERSUASIVE SPEECH** What would King have said if he'd had a chance to respond to the clergy who criticized him by going on the radio? Have students write and deliver a speech that would persuade everyone listening to champion King's nonviolent campaign of civil disobedience to win civil rights.

**Prepare** Students may want to work in pairs. As they craft the speech, suggest that they use King's letter as a model of logical argument. Have them describe and rehearse the qualities of a presenta-

tion that would win new supporters and would compel people to take positive action in support of the civil rights movement. They should consider the appropriate tone and language for a radio audience.

**Present** Have students evaluate each radio speech for its effectiveness. Ask them to note what arguments or delivery techniques they found most persuasive.

**BLOCK SCHEDULING** This activity is particularly well-suited for longer class periods.

### Objectives
- understand the following literary terms:
  tone
  ironic humor
  implied social criticism
  anti-hero
- connect literature to historical contexts, current events, and to the student's own experiences
- understand literary terms appropriate to the selection such as protagonist
- draw inferences and support them with textual evidence and experience

## Teaching the Lesson

This lesson will give students the language for analyzing and understanding the distinguishing features of tone in contemporary literature.

### Introducing the Concepts
Invite students to name their favorite work of contemporary literature. Ask them to consider why they respond to this literary work more than others. Suggest that our favorite contemporary works tend to engage us with emotion, with ironic humor, with social awareness, or with a less-than-perfect protagonist who leads us to a new understanding. As students read the contemporary literature in this unit, have them consider the following questions:

What qualities or characteristics describe the protagonist?

Do you identify with the protagonist? Why or why not?

As they read each selection, students can write responses to these questions and keep them in their Working Portfolios.

### Presenting the Concepts
Have students preview the article, noting the basic text organizers: title, subheads, images and captions, and called out text. Ask them to describe what information they would expect to locate in each section. As they read, have students use the subheads to make an outline or graphic organizer. Have them categorize information from the article with the appropriate heading. Remind them to use similar text organizers to locate and categorize information when they are doing independent research.

# Tone in Contemporary Literature

War has a way of changing a nation's literature because it usually affects an entire generation. Realism had risen from the ashes of the Civil War, while modernism had defined its vision from the ruins of World War I. After the development of the cold war, with its threat of nuclear destruction, the human losses of the Vietnam War, and the civil violence of the 1960s, American literature began to change again. And no place is this change more evident than in the tone of the literature itself.

Women marching to celebrate the 50th anniversary of the passage of the 19th Amendment

## From Modern to Contemporary

**Tone** is the attitude that a writer takes toward a subject. For the modernist, the numbing effects of the early 20th century led to a detached, unemotional tone. For example, the pain that modernist characters feel—Prufrock's failure at the end of T. S. Eliot's poem (page 1025), Nick's silent suffering in Ernest Hemingway's "The End of Something" (page 1018), and Granny Weatherall's bitter disappointment in Katherine Anne Porter's story (page 1034)—is conveyed in a matter-of-fact tone that is sympathetic but distant.

Compare this modernist aloofness to Tim O'Brien's Vietnam story "Ambush" (page 1105). The tone of this contemporary story is one of engagement rather than detachment. From the narrator's opening exchange with his daughter to his conversation in flashback with his buddy after the killing and finally to his image of the dead soldier at the end, the story echoes with emotion. It even ends on a hopeful note, with the possibility of healing.

## Understanding Tone

Contemporary American writers are more diverse than ever before, so it is difficult to generalize about characteristics of their writing. As you read the selections in this part of Unit Seven, however, you'll notice differences in tone from modernist works. The chart and text that follow explore the distinguishing features of tone in contemporary literature.

| Differences in Tone | |
|---|---|
| **Modernist** | **Contemporary** |
| detached, unemotional | emotional |
| serious irony | humorous irony |
| concern with individual in isolation | concern with connections between people |
| no heroes | antiheroes |

**IRONIC HUMOR** Modernist literature is, as a rule, utterly humorless. Flannery O'Connor, writing in the 1950s, was one of the first to introduce a new kind of humor in American literature. Her characters, such as Mr. Shiftlet in "The Life You Save May Be Your Own" (page 528), are funny, not because they do funny things but because the reader can recognize the faults and weaknesses that the characters are blind to. O'Connor's humor thus comes from her ironic presentation of characters rather than from comic situations.

Instead of being defeated by irony as many modernist writers had been, contemporary writers look at irony, and absurd situations in general, as cause for subtle humor. The tone becomes something like, "If you can't fight it, you might as well laugh."

**IMPLIED SOCIAL CRITICISM** With a few exceptions, modernist writers usually stayed out of politics and were not very concerned about social injustices. After the 1960s, however, with the influence of the civil rights and the women's movements, the attitude toward the individual and society began to change—the individual was no longer seen in isolation but in relation to others.

It is this awareness of the larger social context that distinguishes contemporary voices from modernist ones. And it is more often an implied criticism of the barriers between people that colors contemporary literature. Read the following description taken from Joyce Carol Oates's story "Hostage" (page 1200). The narrator, a shy teenage girl, explains one of the barriers between her and the boy, Bruno, for whom she shows a strange fascination.

> I didn't know him. I didn't belong to his world. Though my family lived only a block or so from his family in a neighborhood of row houses . . . , my grandparents had emigrated from Budapest in the early 1900s and Bruno's parents had come from Lublin, a Polish city near the Russian border, in the early 1930s, and that made a considerable difference.
>
> —Joyce Carol Oates, "Hostage"

**YOUR TURN:** Is the tone of this passage matter-of-fact, bitter, or sarcastic?

**THE ANTI-HERO** An anti-hero is a protagonist who has the opposite qualities of a hero: he or she may be insecure, ineffective, cowardly, sometimes dishonest or dishonorable, most often a failure. The character from the play *Wandering* (p. 1150), called simply Him, who wants nothing out of life, is an anti-hero; so is the father following his own desires over his family's needs in John Updike's story "Separating" (page 1180).

The point of an anti-hero is not necessarily to incur praise or criticism but to help understanding. After all, a contemporary writer might ask, who can really be heroic in this world, where irony rules and things are not what they seem? The passage below is from Anne Tyler's story "Teenage Wasteland" (page 1168). Daisy, the anti-hero, is the mother of a boy who's caused trouble at school; the principal, Mr. Lanham, has called her to his office to detail her son's offenses.

**YOUR TURN:** Would you describe the tone of this passage as happy, angry, or dispirited?

> In the past, before her children were born, Daisy had been a fourth-grade teacher. It shamed her now to sit before this principal as a parent, a delinquent parent, a parent who struck Mr. Lanham, no doubt, as unseeing or uncaring.
>
> —Anne Tyler, "Teenage Wasteland"

## Strategies for Reading: Tone in Contemporary Literature

1. Identify the emotions conveyed in a work. Does the narrator express emotions, or does he or she seem detached from the action?

2. Notice any humor in the irony (both situational and dramatic).

3. Clarify what, if anything, is being criticized and what just needs to be understood and accepted.

4. **Monitor** your reading strategies and modify them when your understanding breaks down. Remember to use your Strategies for Active Reading: **predict, visualize, connect, question, clarify,** and **evaluate.**

TONE IN CONTEMPORARY LITERATURE **1149**

### Early Anti-Hero: *Don Quixote*

A fixture of contemporary literature, the anti-hero had its literary debut 400 years ago in Cervantes' novel *Don Quixote.* Its protagonist is Alonso Quijano, a gentle man devoted to the romantic tales of chivalry who changes his name to Don Quixote and sets out to undo the world's wrongs. To many of those he encounters along the way, Don Quixote is a laughable failure—a foolish man who mistakes miserable inns for castles and windmills for giants. The reader, however, identifies with his essential humanity, with his struggles in the materialistic world, and with his undaunted attempts (nearly all of them ineffective) to restore the chivalric code.

Share with students a section from Burton Raffel's 1995 translation of Cervantes' novel. In this excerpt from Volume, 1, Chapter 1, the inept Don Quixote makes preparations to leave home for his first expedition.

The first thing he did was polish up his great-grandfather's suit of armor, which for a century or so had been lying, thrown in a corner and forgotten, covered with mildew and quietly rusting away. He got it as clean and bright as he could, but saw that it had a major deficiency: the helmet was gone, and all that was left was a metal headpiece that would cover just the top of his skull. So he put together, ingeniously, a kind of half-helmet of cardboard that, fitted into the headpiece, looked very much like the real thing. True, when he wanted to test its strength and see if it could stand up under a slashing stroke, he pulled out his sword and gave it a couple of whacks, and the very first blow undid in a second what had taken him a week to put together. He couldn't help but think it a poor sign that he'd destroyed it so easily, so to safeguard himself against that risk he went back to work, lining the inside with iron bars until he was satisfied it was strong enough, after which, not wanting to make any further experiments, he declared it a perfect, finished helmet, ready for use.

As students read the contemporary literature in this unit, have them consider what each anti-hero helps them to understand about human beings and the world in which they live.

## OVERVIEW

### Objectives

1. understand and appreciate a one-act **drama** (Literary Analysis)
2. examine **tone and dialogue** (Literary Analysis)
3. **visualize stage directions** (Active Reading)

### Summary

The play, which is a series of interlocking dialogues, runs through the life of a character called Him. The first dialogue seems to be between Him and his parents. The parents say that he will learn discipline in the army. In subsequent pieces of dialogue, Him appears to be talking to a potential employer, a doctor or nurse, a recruitment officer, a girlfriend, and a psychologist. Him states that he doesn't believe in war or in killing people, and he declares that people don't really believe the principles they express, such as pride in country and in family. Then Him is conversing with his wife, who begs him to think of their children before stepping outside accepted norms of behavior. Next, Him, who appears to be working in an office, announces that he is sick. At what appears to be his funeral, someone recalls that Him was too radical and says that his wife is better off without him. The wife remarries. In a recap at the end, with characters repeating lines from earlier in the play, Him states disbelievingly, "That can't be the way people want to spend their lives."

### Thematic Link

Lanford Wilson's play is a commentary on the **disintegration** of common values in America's **postwar society.** The main character wants to live according to his own values but finds himself at odds with the beliefs and expectations of nearly everyone he encounters.

### 5-Minute Warm-Up

*Daily Language SkillBuilder*

Have students **proofread** the display sentences on page 1069j and write them correctly. The sentences also appear on Transparency 32 of **Grammar Transparencies and Copymasters.**

---

*She: Aren't you lost?*

*Him: I wasn't going anyplace in particular.*

# Wandering

*Drama by* LANFORD WILSON

### Connect to Your Life

**Biography: Fast-Forward** How would you present a person's life story in less than five minutes? Brainstorm with a small group to think of ways you could do this. Consider what events would be important to include and how you would show the passage of time. After your discussion, share your ideas with other groups

## Build Background

**Sixties Youth** *Wandering* is a very brief play sketching the life story of a man who questions the roles society expects him to assume. In the 1960s many young Americans began to reject long-accepted codes of behavior and values that they felt unnecessarily restricted people. For example, Many young men wondered why they should register for the draft, become soldiers in the Vietnam War, and then enter professions—duties that were expected of men in the United States. For a variety of reasons, some dodged the draft or tried to make themselves ineligible. Some declined to compete for job promotions or to work at all, because they did not want to be forced down conventional career paths. Young people of the time often expressed a wish to live freely, according to their own values and desires, rather than those of others. The main character in *Wandering* (called only Him) is such a person.

> WORDS TO KNOW
> **Vocabulary Preview**
> aggressor          regimentation
> compulsory        specimen
> indoctrination

## Focus Your Reading

LITERARY ANALYSIS TONE AND DIALOGUE In drama, **tone**—the attitude a writer takes towards a subject—is typically revealed through the **dialogue**—a conversation among characters. Note that in *Wandering*, the lines the characters deliver are often charged with emotional associations. Yet the playwright never states what those specific associations are. Instead, he leaves it to the reader to supply the viewpoint conveyed through the characters' spoken words.

ACTIVE READING VISUALIZING STAGE DIRECTIONS Imagine you are attending a theatrical production of *Wandering*. Seated in the audience, you await the curtains to rise. **Visualize,** or form a mental picture, of what you would see, based on the descriptive details given in the introductory **stage directions**—instructions for the director, actors, and stage crew. For example, try to picture the actors animated and gesturing when they are rapidly reciting their lines of dialogue and frozen at attention when they are not speaking.

READER'S NOTEBOOK After reading the stage directions, draw a rough floor plan, like the one below, to show what the stage might look like at the opening of the play. Include the placement of the furniture and the position of the actors. As you continue to read the play, refer to your floor plan to help you picture how scene changes and a 40-year time span might be presented with only three actors on a nearly barren stage.

| (standing) | | (seated) |
|---|---|---|
| **He** | **She** | x **Him** |
| x | x | |
| | | Bench |

---

## LESSON RESOURCES

**UNIT SEVEN RESOURCE BOOK,** pp. 39–43

**ASSESSMENT RESOURCES**
**Formal Assessment,** pp. 217–218
**Teacher's Guide to Assessment and Portfolio Use**
**Test Generator**

**SKILLS TRANSPARENCIES AND COPYMASTERS**
**Literary Analysis**
• Tone, T19 (for Cooperative Learning Activity, p. 1155)

**Reading and Critical Thinking**
• Visualizing, T8 (for Active Reading, p. 1150)

**Grammar**
• Proliferating Prepositional Phrases, C173 (for Mini Lesson, p. 1156)

**Writing**
• Critical Review, C26 (for Writing Option 1, p. 1156)

**Communications**
• Dramatic Reading, T12 (for Mini Lesson, p. 1154)

**INTEGRATED TECHNOLOGY**

**Audio Library**
**Visit our website:**
www.mcdougallittell.com

# Wandering

Lanford Wilson

He, She, *and* Him *are all about twenty-five. The stage, which can be very small, should have a bench to be used as chair, bed, couch, bench, whatever. He and She are standing at attention, side by side. Him enters and sits. The actors should retire to the attention position when not speaking. Actions and props should be pantomimed, and the play should be done very rapidly, without pause except toward the end, as indicated. The play runs through* Him's *life—a span of about forty years with several recaps[1] at the end. Actions and characterizations should be very simple.*

**She.** Where have you been?

**Him.** Wandering around.

**She.** Wandering around. I don't know why you can't be a man; you just wait till the army gets ahold of you, young man.

**He.** They'll make a man out of you.

**She.** Straighten you out.

**He.** A little <u>regimentation</u>.

**She.** Regulation.

**He.** Specification.

**She.** <u>Indoctrination</u>.

**He.** Boredom.

**She.** You'll get up and go to bed.

**He.** Drill, march.

**She.** Take orders.

**He.** Fight.

**She.** Do what they tell you.

**He.** Keep in step.

**She.** Do your part.

**He.** Kill a man.

**She.** You'll be a better person to live with, believe me. As a matter of fact your father and I are getting damn tired of having you around.

**He.** Looking after you.

**She.** Making your bed.

**He.** Keeping you out of trouble.

**She.** How old are you, anyway?

**Him.** Sixteen.

**He.** Sixteen, well, my God.

**She.** Shouldn't you be drafted before long?

**Him.** Two years.

**She.** You just better toe the mark.

**He.** How long at your present address?

**Him.** Six months.

**He.** Any previous experience as an apprentice?

**Him.** No sir.

**He.** Where did you live before that?

**Him.** I was just wandering around.

1. **recaps:** short for *recapitulations,* repetitions of the main point or points.

WORDS TO KNOW

**regimentation** (rĕj'ə-mən-tā'shən) *n.* the process of using discipline and control to organize into a rigid system

**indoctrination** (ĭn-dŏk'trə-nā'shən) *n.* the process of being taught fundamentals, especially of military customs and discipline

1151

## Reading and Analyzing

### Reading Skills and Strategies: PREVIEW

Explain to students that the characters He and She change throughout the play, representing different people. Also have them read carefully to keep track of shifts in dialogue, indicating a new stage in Him's life.

### Active Reading
#### VISUALIZING STAGE DIRECTIONS

Ask students to read the stage directions on page 1151. What mental picture do these directions create? Should there be more props/scenery/actors, or does minimalism work effectively here?

**Possible Responses:** The directions create a mental picture of a stage with only a bench and three actors present; more actors may have made the play less confusing; minimalism works well and keeps the play very precise and focused.

 Use **Unit Seven Resource Book,** p. 40 for more practice.

### Literary Analysis
#### TONE AND DIALOGUE

**A** Wilson uses dialogue rather than action or setting to establish changes in both scene and tone. Ask students if they can infer where and why this medical exam is taking place. Ask them to describe the tone of the scene based on She's dialogue.

**Possible Responses:** The scene is a draft board center where draftees are examined to see if they are fit for the military. She seems very serious and hurried. She is not interested in chatting or small talk.

 Use **Unit Seven Resource Book,** p. 41 for more practice.

---

**He.** Not good; draft status?

**Him.** Well, I haven't been called but—

**He.** We like fighters on our team, fellow.

**Him.** Well, actually I'm a conscientious—[2]

**(A) She.** Sit down. Roll up your sleeve. Take off your shirt. Stick out your tongue. Bend over, open your mouth, make a fist, read the top line. Cough. (*The boy coughs.*) Very good.

**Him.** Thank you.

**She.** Perfect specimen.

**Him.** I do a considerable amount of walking.

**He.** I don't follow you.

**Him.** I don't believe in war.

**He.** There's no danger of war. Our country is never an aggressor.

**Him.** But armies, see, I don't believe in it.

**He.** Do you love your country?

**Him.** No more than any other, the ones I've seen.

**He.** That's treason.

**Him.** I'm sorry.

**He.** Quite all right; we'll take you.

**Him.** I won't go.

**He.** Service is compulsory.

**Him.** It's my right.

**He.** You'll learn.

**Him.** I don't believe in killing people.

**He.** For freedom?

**Him.** No.

**He.** For love?

**Him.** No.

**He.** For money?

**Him.** No.

**He.** We'll teach you.

**Him.** I know, but I won't.

**He.** You'll learn.

**Him.** I won't!

**He.** You're going.

**Him.** I'm not.

**He.** You'll see.

**Him.** I'm sure.

**He.** You'll see.

**Him.** I'm flat-footed.

**He.** You'll do.

**Him.** I'm queer.

**He.** Get lost.

**She.** I'm lost.

**Him.** I'm sorry.

**She.** Aren't you lost?

**Him.** I wasn't going anyplace in particular.

**She.** That's unnatural.

**Him.** I was just wandering.

**She.** What will become of you?

**Him.** I hadn't thought of it.

**She.** You don't believe in anything.

**Him.** But you see, I do.

**He.** I see.

**Him.** It's just that no one else seems to believe—not really.

**He.** I see.

**Him.** Like this pride in country.

**He.** I see.

**Him.** And this pride in blood.

**He.** I see.

**Him.** It just seems that pride is such a pointless thing; I can't believe in killing someone for it.

**She.** Oh, my God, honey, it isn't killing, it's merely nudging out of the way . . .

---

2. **conscientious—** : The young man is interrupted in the middle of saying "conscientious objector." This is a person whose conscience does not permit taking an active part in any effort associated with the conduct of war.

WORDS TO KNOW
**specimen** (spĕs´ə-mən) *n.* an example of a group
**aggressor** (ə-grĕs´ər) *n.* one that begins an attack or a quarrel
**compulsory** (kəm-pŭl´sə-rē) *adj.* required without exception; mandatory

**1152**

---

## Teaching Options

### ✓ Assessment **Informal Assessment**

**SELF-ASSESSMENT** Students can assess their own understanding of the selection by responding to the following questions:

• Did you take sides in this story? Which side did you take and why?
• Did you have difficulty following the pace and character changes?
• What else do you wish you knew about the characters in the play?
• What do you think are the play's strengths and weaknesses?

**RUBRIC**

**3  Full Accomplishment** Responses reflect a full understanding of the events and characters and indicate a well-reasoned opinion.

**2  Substantial Accomplishment** Responses show a general understanding of the events, but may not fully reflect the characters or provide a well-reasoned opinion.

**1  Little or Partial Accomplishment** Responses show little understanding of the events and characters and do not indicate an informed opinion of the play.

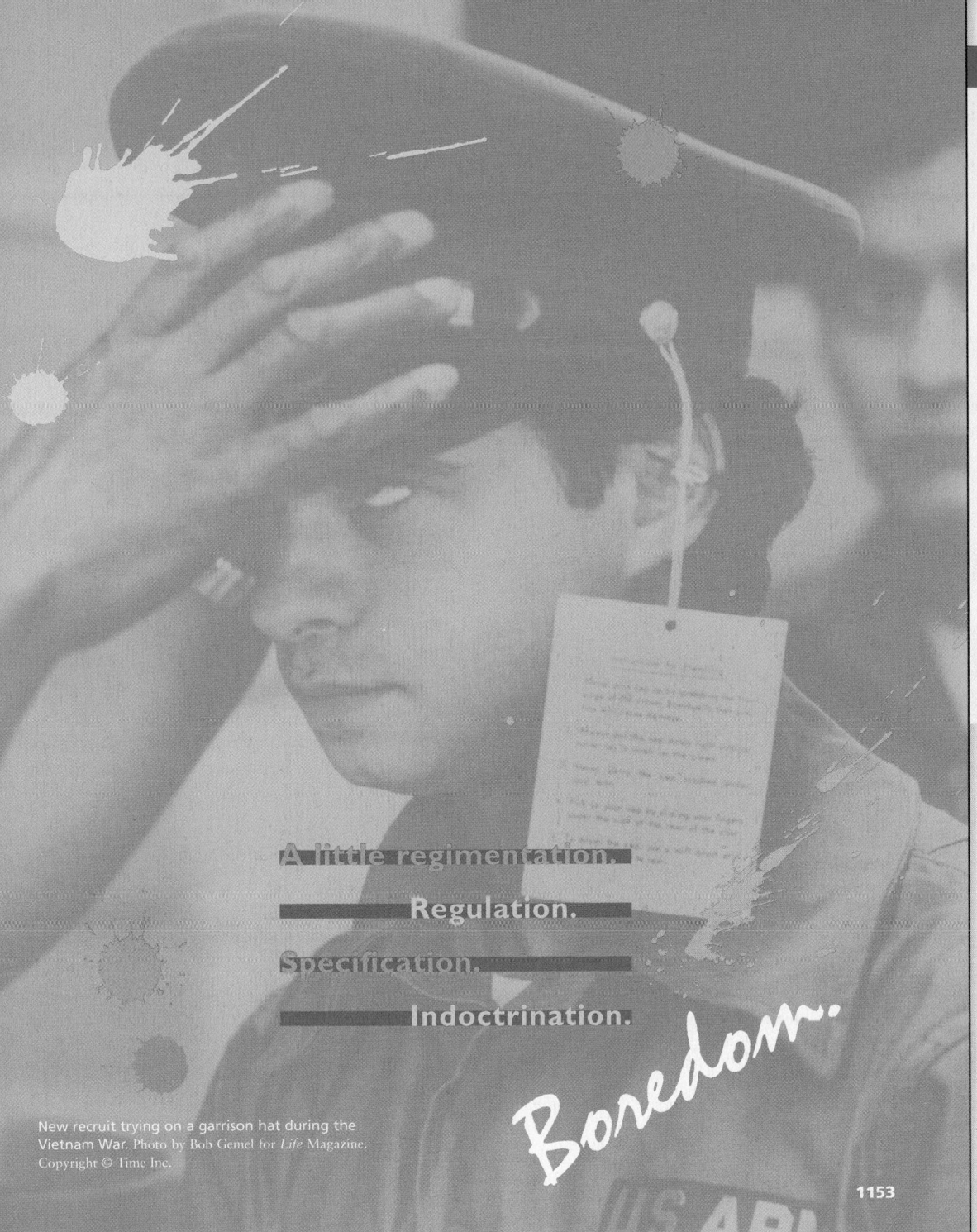

A little regimentation.

Regulation.

Specification.

Indoctrination.

Boredom.

New recruit trying on a garrison hat during the Vietnam War. Photo by Bob Gemel for *Life* Magazine. Copyright © Time Inc.

1153

## Customizing Instruction

### Less Proficient Readers
Have students skim through the play with you, pointing out the various identities assumed by He and She.

**Possible Responses:** On page 1151, He and She are Him's parents, and then He is a potential employer. On page 1152, She is a doctor or nurse examining Him for the draft; He is a draft official; She is a girlfriend or someone with whom Him has struck up a conversation; He is a psychologist; She is Him's wife. On page 1154, She is perhaps a doctor or nurse, and then a co-worker or secretary of Him's; He is a business associate; He and She are concerned friends or coworkers; She is Him's widow, attending Him's funeral with He; She becomes He's wife.

### Gifted and Talented
Have students share and discuss this play with an older friend or relative. Do older readers have stronger reactions to it than today's students do? Is the play outdated or is it still relevant?

**Cross Curricular Link** **History**

**A TIME OF UPHEAVAL AND PROTEST** Use the following information to make connections between the events and the literature of that time.

**Key Events: 1968**

- In January, the North Vietnamese launch a major offensive during Tet, their New Year's holiday. Americans are stunned.
- Antiwar Senator **Eugene McCarthy** decides to challenge President **Lyndon Johnson** for the Democratic nomination. Johnson decides not to seek reelection.
- **Martin Luther King, Jr.,** is assassinated in April, and Senator **Robert F. Kennedy** is killed in June.
- The Democratic National Convention in Chicago is the scene of violent street fights between antiwar demonstrators and police. The Democrats nominate **Hubert Humphrey,** who is defeated by **Richard Nixon** in November.

### Literary Analysis
#### TONE AND DIALOGUE

**A** Draw students' attention to the section of the play that seems to take place at Him's funeral. Ask students to analyze the attitude of She and He toward Him. How is their attitude toward Him different from the author's attitude, and how can readers tell?

**Possible Responses:** The dialogue conveys some tenderness and sadness at the death of Him, but She and He's true attitude, revealed at the end of this segment, is one of contempt and lack of understanding. The author, however, clearly considers Him to be a hero for refusing to conform to societal norms. Him is the only character who indicates that he is happy, and his statements show sincere moral reasoning rather than selfishness or ignorance.

### Literary Analysis: CLARIFY

**B** Point out that these words, used in wedding ceremonies, may suggest that Him's wife has married He after Him's death. Then discuss the fact that seeing a play performed is very different from reading one. Have students read the play silently and note parts that they find confusing. Then ask for volunteers to perform the play for the class. Finally, ask students if seeing the play performed helped clear any confusion.

---

**Him.** But we don't need it.

**She.** Think of our position, think of me, think of the children.

**Him.** I am.

**She.** You're shiftless, is what it is.

**Him.** I'm really quite happy; I don't know why.

**She.** Well, how do you think I feel?

**Him.** Not too well really.

**She.** Where does it hurt?

**Him.** Nothing to worry about.

**She.** Yes sir.

**Him.** Thank you.

**She.** And that's all for the morning; Mr. Trader is on line six.

**Him.** Thank you; send Wheeler in.

**He.** How are you, old boy?

**Him.** Not well, I'm afraid.

**She.** Don't be, it isn't serious.

**He.** Just been working too hard.

**She.** Why don't you lie down?

**He.** Best thing for you.

**She.** I know, but he was quite handsome; a gentle man.

**He.** Bit of a radical though; not good for the family.

**She.** I know.

**He.** You're better off.

**She.** I have a life of my own.     **He.** You have a life of your own.

**She.** He was such a lost lamb.

 **He.** Never agreed with anyone.

**She.** Arguments everywhere we went.

**He.** What kind of disposition is that?

**She.** I don't know what I ever saw in him.

**He.** You need someone who knows his way around.

**She.** I do.

**He.** I do.

(*A pause*)

---

**She.** I don't know why you can't be a man.

**He.** Keep in step.

**She.** Toe the mark.

**He.** Draft status?

**She.** Stick out your tongue.

**He.** You'll learn.

**She.** What'll become of you?

**He.** I see.

**She.** Think of the children.

**He.** Best thing for you.

**She.** I do.

(*A pause*)

**He.** I see.

**Him.** I mean, that can't be the way people want to spend their lives.

**She.** Trader on line six.

**Him.** Thank you.

**He.** Just been working too hard.

**She.** I do.

(*Pauses*)

**She.** Where?

**Him.** Wandering.

**He.** I see.

**Him.** They'll believe anything anyone tells them.

**He.** I see.

**Him.** I mean, that can't be the way people want to spend their lives.

**She.** That's all for the morning.

**Him.** Quite happy.

**He.** Best thing for you.

**She.** I do.

**He.** I do.

(*A pause*)

**She.** Where have you been?

(*A pause*)

**Him.** Can it?

*Blackout*

---

## Teaching Options

### Mini Lesson: Speaking and Listening

**DRAMA REENACTMENT** **Prepare** In groups of three or four (three actors and a director) have students prepare to perform a scene from this play for the class. To do this, students must interpret which lines cover a scene, where the scene takes place, exactly who the characters are, and how the line readings and gestures will convey what is going on. Have students consider tone, pitch, volume, and the speed with which the characters speak, as well as their posture and any props they might use. Help students divide the play into scenes and assign a scene to each group. Directors must understand the play and use interpersonal skills to facilitate preparation of the scene.

**Present** Student groups can decide how they will present the scene. Students who are audience members should evaluate how the performance increases their appreciation and understanding of the play. Performing students should justify their choice of verbal and nonverbal performance techniques by referring to their interpretation of the scene.

## Connect to the Literature

**1. What Do You Think?**
What questions do you want to ask about the characters and events in this play? Share them with a partner.

**Comprehension Check**
- How are stages of Him's life portrayed in the play?
- What is Him's view of military service?
- What happens to Him at the end of the play?

## Think Critically

**2.** 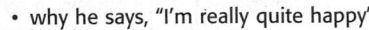 **ACTIVE READING** | **VISUALIZING STAGE DIRECTIONS** Which scene from the play were you able to picture most vividly? As you read the play, did you experience the impression of continuous action? Explain.

**3.** What different people do He and She portray in the course of the play? In general, how would you say this pair of characters perceives Him?

**4.** How would you evaluate Him's life?

 **THINK ABOUT**
- what he believes and what he does not believe
- why he says, "I'm really quite happy"
- how his life ends
- his final question, "That can't be the way people want to spend their lives. . . . Can it?"

**5.** What does the title of the play mean to you?

**6.** In what ways does Him remind you of anyone you know or have heard about?

## Extend Interpretations

**7. Comparing Texts** Compare and contrast Him, She, and He in *Wandering* to the characters "anyone," "noone," "someones," and "everyones" in E. E. Cummings poem "anyone lived in a pretty how town" (page 410). How do you think naming characters as pronouns contributes to the meaning in each of these works?

**8. The Writer's Style** In what ways would you consider Lanford Wilson's approach to writing plays experimental?

**9. Connect to Life** Could Him represent most young people of your generation, or is he strictly a child of the 1960s? Support your opinion.

## Literary Analysis

**TONE AND DIALOGUE**

**Dialogue**—written conversation between two or more characters—makes up most of the play's script. The dialogue in *Wandering* does not mimic ordinary conversation. It strings together clichéd, stock phrases in a highly rhythmic way. The lines are fragmentary and elliptical, forcing the audience to "fill in the blanks." Certain phrases are repeated, particularly in the recaps at the end. The style and topics of the dialogue reveal the play's **tone**—the writer's attitude toward the society of the time.

**Cooperative Learning Activity**
Listen for the tone revealed in the dialogue as you and two other students read the entire play rapidly, according to the playwright's stage directions. Then discuss the viewpoints that you think are conveyed through the dialogue.

---

## Extend Interpretations

**Comparing Texts** Possible Response: Using pronouns for characters' names allows them to stand in for many people.

**Writer's Style** Possible Responses: the names of the characters; the same characters playing different parts, representing different people in Him's life; the minimal setting; the compression of time; the interlocking dialogue.

**Connect to Life** Encourage students to debate this question, using evidence from their own life experience and reading.

## Literary Analysis

**Tone and Dialogue** Possible Responses: People mindlessly use clichés and stock phrases, merely repeating what they've heard everyone else say rather than expressing themselves in an original way. Likewise, Wilson would say that most people lead conventional lives, going along with the crowd instead of thinking for themselves.

---

### Connect to the Literature

**1. What Do You Think?**
Possible Responses: Where did Him go when he dodged the draft? Where did he work? How did Him meet his wife? How did he die?

**Comprehension Check**
- through his interactions with others, including his parents, an employer, a nurse, the draft board, a girlfriend, a psychologist, his wife, a secretary, a business associate, the wife's new husband
- Him is antiwar and is a conscientious objector.
- Him dies.

 Use Selection Quiz
**Unit Seven Resource Book**, p. 43.

### Think Critically

**2.** Have students support their choice with textual evidence. Possible Response: The interlocking dialogue gives a sense of continuous action from one stage of life to the next.

**3.** Possible Responses: Him's parents, an employer, a nurse, the draft board, a girlfriend, a psychologist, his wife, a secretary, a business associate, the wife's new husband; they disapprove of Him and consider Him selfish and irresponsible.

**4.** Some students may admire his desire for freedom and his courage to question social conventions; others may say that some conformity is necessary to build healthy families and orderly societies.

**5.** Possible Responses: The protagonist is "wandering" through his life, rather than staying on the "straight path" society has laid out for him. He considers wandering an adventure, but others consider it an irresponsible waste of time.

**6.** Have students support their comparisons with specific examples from the text.

## Writing Options

1. **Drama Review** To get students started, remind them to support their overall impressions of the play by evaluating specific aspects such as dialogue, characterization, shifts in time and place, and the lack of sets.
2. **Play Outline** To get students started, have the class brainstorm a list of current slang, clichés, and stock phrases to use in their outlines.

## Inquiry & Research

**Youth Counterculture** To help students get started and understand the rebellious spirit of the 1960s, they can locate recordings of music from that period that mirror the ideas expressed in Wilson's play. Possibilities include "Alice's Restaurant" by Arlo Guthrie, "The Fixin' to Die Rag" by Country Joe and the Fish, "Something's Happening Here" by Buffalo Springfield, and "The Times They Are a-Changing" by Bob Dylan. Have students compare and contrast the ideas and styles of the songs and the play.

## Vocabulary in Action

1. regimentation
2. specimen
3. aggressor
4. compulsory
5. indoctrination

## Writing Options

1. **Drama Review** In a review of *Wandering,* tell whether you like the play, what it would be like when performed on-stage, and what the play's intended meaning might be.
2. **Play Outline** Write an outline of a play presenting the life story of a person, male or female, from your own generation. What title would you give it? What key events would you include? What important phrases might you repeat?

## Inquiry & Research

**Youth Counterculture** Social changes in the 1960s spurred many of the nation's teenagers to defy mainstream culture. Find out how they expressed their new individuality through clothing styles and rock music. Report your findings in an oral report with audiovisual aids.

## Vocabulary in Action

**EXERCISE: CONTEXT CLUES** Write the Word to Know that best completes each sentence.

1. During the 1960s, many people rebelled against what they considered rigid and unnecessary _____ in life in the United States.
2. They felt that short hair and a starched shirt made a man a _____ of conformity.
3. Some believed that in the Vietnam War, the United States was not the victim but the _____.
4. During this war, some men burned their draft cards to protest _____ military service.
5. Some who were drafted fled the country rather than undergo the _____ involved in basic training and the betrayal of their own beliefs.

**Building Vocabulary**
For an in-depth lesson on context clues, see page 326.

| WORDS TO KNOW | aggressor compulsory indoctrination | regimentation specimen |
|---|---|---|

## Lanford Wilson
1937–

**Other Works**
*Lemon Sky*
*Fifth of July*
*Burn This*
*Redwood Curtain*
*Balm in Gilead*

**Surprise Vocation** Lanford Wilson began writing his first play during his lunch hour at the advertising agency where he was a graphic designer. He describes stumbling upon his vocation: "I was always very excited by theater. Growing up, I had no idea plays were written, for some reason. I started out writing stories, and then suddenly I realized something I was writing was a play. I thought, I don't know how to write a play. I don't even know what a play is."

**Starving Artist** In 1962 he moved to New York, where he lived in a rundown hotel. To gather material for his plays, he eavesdropped on conversations in all-night coffee shops. He produced his first play in 1963 at a coffeehouse theater that welcomed experimental works. To pay the rent, he worked as a complaint-department clerk, a hotel clerk, a dishwasher, and a waiter (he was fired after serving one meal). In 1966, when asked to contribute a two-minute play for a benefit evening, Wilson contributed a sketch he had written earlier. After the benefit, he felt "deprived of the challenge to write a two-minute play for a specific event." So he wrote *Wandering.*

**Theatrical Success Story** In 1969 Wilson cofounded the Circle Repertory Company, where he is still playwright-in-residence. More than 40 of his plays have been produced, and many enjoy frequent revivals. His plays depict real-life issues, yet they incorporate experimental presentational techniques. Wilson's awards include a Pulitzer Prize, two New York Drama Critics Circle Awards, an Emmy award nomination, and three Tony award nominations.

## Teaching Options

###  Grammar

**PROLIFERATING PREPOSITIONAL PHRASES**
A sentence with too many or poorly placed prepositional phrases can be confusing. Share the following examples with students:

**Unclear:** I ate in the restaurant next to the library by a window with a nice view of the beach before leaving for my physical.

**Clear:** Before leaving for my physical, I ate in the restaurant that's next to the library. I sat by a window with a nice view of the beach.

**Exercises** Have students rewrite the following sentence to clarify its meaning.

Him didn't believe in killing people for freedom, love, or money and in armies. *(Him didn't believe in armies or in killing people for freedom, love, or money.)*

 Use **Grammar Transparencies and Copymasters**, p. 173.

 Use McDougal Littell's *Language Network,* Chapter 2, for more instruction in prepositional phrases.

# The Writer in the Family

*Short Story by* E. L. DOCTOROW

*"Who was responsible for the fact that he had not lived up to anyone's expectations?"*

## Connect to Your Life

**The Meaning of Success** What is *success?* For some people, success means being able to "follow their bliss," regardless of financial rewards or considerations about social status. For others, it means finding a job that pays well and demands a lot of responsibility. In your eyes, what makes someone successful? Discuss this question with classmates.

## Build Background

**Portrait of the Writer as a Young Man**
"The Writer in the Family" appeared in E. L. Doctorow's only collection of short fiction to date, *Lives of the Poets* (1984). The collection's six loosely related stories and novella address the question of the writer's role in society. In essays and interviews, Doctorow has described the writer as a kind of witness, one whose biggest challenge is to understand his or her country as it really is and not as it wants to see itself. During most of the 1950s—the decade in which "The Writer in the Family" is set—the United States thought of itself as a place where anyone willing to work hard could achieve material comfort and personal success. Doctorow looks at this ideal through the eyes of Jonathan, the younger son of a "failure" named Jack.

### WORDS TO KNOW
**Vocabulary Preview**

| | |
|---|---|
| debilitated | robust |
| implicate | terminal |
| indestructible | |

## Focus Your Reading

**LITERARY ANALYSIS** **PLOT DEVELOPMENT** As you know, **plot** is the sequence of events in a literary work. Usually, these events center on a **conflict** that is present at the beginning of the story and that is developed through **characters'** actions. In this story, the seeds of conflict are planted in the first sentence:

*In 1955 my father died with his ancient mother still alive in a nursing home.*

Notice the chain of problems arising from this situation and how they are resolved.

**ACTIVE READING** **DRAWING CONCLUSIONS ABOUT CHARACTERS**
Although Jonathan's father, Jack, dies at the beginning of the story, you will still learn much about him through the comments of other characters. As you read, pull together these sometimes conflicting pieces of information, and draw your own conclusions about Jack's life.

**READER'S NOTEBOOK**
In a chart like this one, write down information you gain about Jack, under the name of the character who is the source of this information. After you finish the story, write what you believe is the truth about Jack's life.

| JACK | |
|---|---|
| Jonathan says: | Mother says: |
| Aunt Frances says: | Harold says: |
| I say: | |

## OVERVIEW

### Objectives
1. understand and appreciate a **short story** (Literary Analysis)
2. understand **plot development** (Literary Analysis)
3. **draw conclusions about characters** (Active Reading)

### Summary
Narrated by teenage Jonathan, the story is set in the Bronx in 1955. Jonathan's father, Jack, has died, and Jack's sisters have told their aged and infirm mother that Jack won't be visiting her anymore because he has moved to Arizona. To Grandma this means that her son has finally achieved success. Aunt Frances calls on Jonathan to write a fictitious letter from Jack to Grandma. Jonathan complies, and the letter is a great success. More requests for letters follow, and old family resentments begin to surface. Jonathan feels increasingly uneasy about writing the letters and is plagued by unsettling dreams about his father. He writes a final letter, as Jack, that displeases Aunt Frances.

### Thematic Link
In "The Writer in the Family" we see a microcosm of the **integration and disintegration** of **postwar society.** On the surface, the family appears to be functional, thriving, and happy, but underneath it is torn by petty prejudices, jealousy, and guilt.

### 5-Minute Warm-Up

*Daily Language SkillBuilder*

Have students **proofread** the display sentences on page 1069j and write them correctly. The sentences also appear on Transparency 32 of **Grammar Transparencies and Copymasters.**

## LESSON RESOURCES

**UNIT SEVEN RESOURCE BOOK,** pp. 44–48

**ASSESSMENT RESOURCES**
**Formal Assessment,** pp. 219–220
**Teacher's Guide to Assessment and Portfolio Use**
**Test Generator**

**SKILLS TRANSPARENCIES AND COPYMASTERS**
**Literary Analysis**
• Multiple Conflicts/Themes, T15 (for Literary Analysis, p. 1166)

**Reading and Critical Thinking**
• Drawing Conclusions, T4 (for Active Reading, p. 1157)

**Grammar**
• Verbs: Active and Passive Voice, C68 (for Mini Lesson, p. 1162)
• Unnecessary Commas, C155 (for Mini Lesson, p. 1160)

**Vocabulary**
• Context Clues, C18 (for Mini Lesson, p. 1158)

**Writing**
• Topic Sentences and Thesis Statements, T6 (for Writing Option 2, p. 1167)

**INTEGRATED TECHNOLOGY**
**Audio Library**
**Visit our website:**
www.mcdougallittell.com

**Reading Skills and Strategies:
PREVIEW**

As students read, have them look for signs of external and internal conflicts.

**Active Reading**

> DRAWING CONCLUSIONS
> ABOUT CHARACTERS

The characters in the story have conflicting opinions of each other and of Jack. Encourage students to gather textual evidence and to draw conclusions about the characters based on what they say about each other, what they do, and what they think. Students can construct graphic organizers to help them organize the information.

 Use **Unit Seven Resource Book,** p. 45 for more practice.

**Literary Analysis**

> PLOT DEVELOPMENT

Encourage students to analyze the plot of the story by having them construct a story map in their Reader's Notebooks. The organizer will help students compare and contrast the conflicts within the text. Students can fill in the story map as they read. After reading, students can use the story map as the basis for story retellings.

 Use **Unit Seven Resource Book,** p. 46 for more practice.

## The WRITER IN THE FAMILY

E.L. DOCTOROW

*In 1955* my father died with his ancient mother still alive in a nursing home. The old lady was ninety and hadn't even known he was ill. Thinking the shock might kill her, my aunts told her that he had moved to Arizona for his bronchitis. To the immigrant generation of my grandmother, Arizona was the American equivalent of the Alps, it was where you went for your health. More accurately, it was where you went if you had the money. Since my father had failed in all the business enterprises of his life, this was the aspect of the news my grandmother dwelled on, that he had finally had some success. And so it came about that as we mourned him at home in our stocking feet, my grandmother was bragging to her cronies about her son's new life in the dry air of the desert.

My aunts had decided on their course of action without consulting us. It meant neither my mother nor my brother nor I could visit Grandma because we were supposed to have moved west too, a family, after all. My brother Harold and I didn't mind—it was always a nightmare at the old people's home, where they all sat around staring at us while we tried to make conversation with Grandma. She looked terrible, had numbers of ailments, and her mind wandered. Not seeing her was no disappointment either for my mother, who had never gotten along with the old woman and did not visit when she could have. But what was disturbing was that my aunts had acted in the manner of that side of the family of making government on everyone's behalf, the true citizens by blood and the lesser citizens by marriage. It was exactly this attitude that had tormented my mother all her married life. She claimed Jack's family had never accepted her.

She had battled them for twenty-five years as an outsider.

A few weeks after the end of our ritual mourning my Aunt Frances phoned us from her home in Larchmont. Aunt Frances was the wealthier of my father's sisters. Her husband was a lawyer, and both her sons were at Amherst.[1] She had called to say that Grandma was asking why she didn't hear from Jack. I had answered the phone. "You're the writer in the family," my aunt said. "Your father had so much faith in you. Would you mind making up something? Send it to me and I'll read it to her. She won't know the difference."

*That evening,* at the kitchen table, I pushed my homework aside and composed a letter. I tried to imagine my father's response to his new life. He had never been west. He had never traveled anywhere. In his generation the great journey was from the working class to the professional class. He hadn't managed that either. But he loved New York, where he had been born and lived his life, and he was always discovering new things about it. He especially loved the old parts of the city below Canal Street, where he would find ships' chandlers[2] or firms that wholesaled in spices and teas. He was a salesman for an appliance jobber with accounts all over the city. He liked to bring home rare cheeses or exotic foreign vegetables that were sold only in certain neighborhoods. Once he brought home a barometer, another time an antique ship's telescope in a wooden case with a brass snap.

---

1. **Amherst:** A prestigious college in Massachusetts.
2. **ships' chandlers:** merchants dealing in nautical equipment.

## Teaching Options

 **Preteaching Vocabulary**

**USING CONTEXT CLUES   Instruction** Write the following sentence on the chalkboard and ask a volunteer to rely on the context to determine the meaning of the underlined word.

> Blessed with a healthy and <u>robust</u> physique, Sven walked 10 miles every day.

Tell students that when they encounter an unfamiliar word, they can try to substitute a known word (in this case, *strong*) that makes sense in the context of the sentence.

**Exercises** Have students determine the meanings of underlined terms in the following sentences:

1. Young people don't worry about health hazards; they think they're <u>indestructible</u>.

2. The tests on the sick children seemed to <u>implicate</u> a toxic substance in the well water they had been drinking.

3. Although the children were very ill, the illness wasn't <u>terminal</u>; they were expected to recover.

4. Because the children were very weak and <u>debilitated</u>, they were required to stay in bed for at least a week.

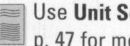 Use **Unit Seven Resource Book,** p. 47 for more exercises.

**A lesson on context clues appears on p. 326 in the Pupil's Edition.**

"Dear Mama," I wrote. "Arizona is beautiful. The sun shines all day and the air is warm and I feel better than I have in years. The desert is not as barren as you would expect, but filled with wildflowers and cactus plants and peculiar crooked trees that look like men holding their arms out. You can see great distances in whatever direction you turn and to the west is a range of mountains maybe fifty miles from here, but in the morning with the sun on them you can see the snow on their crests."

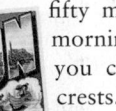

*My aunt* called some days later and told me it was when she read this letter aloud to the old lady that the full effect of Jack's death came over her. She had to excuse herself and went out in the parking lot to cry. "I wept so," she said. "I felt such terrible longing for him. You're so right, he loved to go places, he loved life, he loved everything."

We began trying to organize our lives. My father had borrowed money against his insurance and there was very little left. Some commissions were still due but it didn't look as if his firm would honor them. There were a couple of thousand dollars in a savings bank that had to be maintained there until the estate was settled. The lawyer involved was Aunt Frances' husband and he was very proper. "The estate!" my mother muttered, gesturing as if to pull out her hair. "The estate!" She applied for a job part-time in the admissions office of the hospital where my father's <u>terminal</u> illness had been diagnosed, and where he had spent some months until they had sent him home to die. She knew a lot of the doctors and staff and she had learned "from bitter experience," as she told them, about the hospital routine. She was hired.

I hated that hospital, it was dark and grim and full of tortured people. I thought it was masochistic of[3] my mother to seek out a job there, but did not tell her so.

We lived in an apartment on the corner of 175th Street and the Grand Concourse, one flight up. Three rooms. I shared the bedroom with my brother. It was jammed with furniture because when my father had required a hospital bed in the last weeks of his illness we had moved some of the living-room pieces into the bedroom and made over the living room for him. We had to navigate bookcases, beds, a gateleg table, bureaus, a record player and radio console, stacks of 78 albums,[4] my brother's trombone and music stand, and so on. My mother continued to sleep on the convertible sofa in the living room that had been their bed before his illness. The two rooms were connected by a narrow hall made even narrower by bookcases along the wall. Off the wall were a small kitchen and dinette and a bathroom. There were lots of appliances in the kitchen—broiler, toaster, pressure cooker, counter-top dishwasher, blender—that my father had gotten through his job, at cost. A treasured phrase in our house: *at cost.* But most of these fixtures went unused because my mother did not care for them. Chromium devices with timers or gauges that required the reading of elaborate instructions were not for her. They were in part responsible for the awful clutter of our lives and now she wanted to get rid of them. "We're being buried," she said. "Who needs them!"

So we agreed to throw out or sell anything inessential. While I found boxes for the appliances and my brother tied the boxes with twine, my mother opened my father's closet and took out his clothes. He had several suits because as a salesman he needed to look his best.

---

3. **was masochistic** (măs′ə-kĭs′tĭk) **of:** showed a desire for suffering on the part of.

4. **78 albums:** phonograph records of a type that became obsolete in the mid-20th century, played at a speed of 78 revolutions per minute.

WORDS
TO
KNOW
   **terminal** (tûr′mə-nəl) *adj.* final; fatal

**1159**

### Active Reading

**DRAWING CONCLUSIONS
ABOUT CHARACTERS**

**A** Ask: Why does Harold shout at his mother? Remind students to use evidence from the text as well as their own experience to draw conclusions about Harold's feelings.

**Possible Response:** Trying on Jack's clothing is an emotional experience for everyone because it emphasizes the permanence of his absence. When his mother starts to cry, Harold shouts to mask his own feelings of grief.

### Reading Skills and Strategies: ANALYZING

**B** Ask students what the boys' mother means when she says that a stake through the heart wouldn't kill the grandmother. What comparison is she making and what does that comparison say about how she views the grandmother?

**Possible Responses:** The mother is comparing the grandmother to a vampire, which, according to legend, can only be killed by driving a wooden stake through the heart. Vampires suck the blood out of their victims, so this comparison paints the grandmother as someone who is demanding and unsympathetic.

### Literary Analysis: CONFLICT

**C** Ask students to describe Ruth's conflict.

**Possible Response:** Ruth has an external conflict; it is with her husband's mother and sisters, who blame Ruth for Jack's failures. Ruth, however, believes that it is his mother who is responsible for Jack's failure to live up to expectations.

---

My mother wanted us to try on his suits to see which of them could be altered and used. My brother refused to try them on. I tried on one jacket which was too large for me. The lining inside the sleeves chilled my arms and the vaguest scent of my father's being came to me.

"This is way too big," I said.

"Don't worry," my mother said. "I had it cleaned. Would I let you wear it if I hadn't?"

It was the evening, the end of winter, and snow was coming down on the windowsill and melting as it settled. The ceiling bulb glared on a pile of my father's suits and trousers on hangers flung across the bed in the shape of a dead man. We refused to try on anything more, and my mother began to cry.

**A** "What are you crying for?" my brother shouted. "You wanted to get rid of things, didn't you?"

A few weeks later my aunt phoned again and said she thought it would be necessary to have another letter from Jack. Grandma had fallen out of her chair and bruised herself and was very depressed.

"How long does this go on?" my mother said.

"It's not so terrible," my aunt said, "for the little time left to make things easier for her."

My mother slammed down the phone. "He can't even die when he wants to!" she cried. "Even death comes second to Mama! What are they afraid of, the shock will kill her? Nothing **B** can kill her. She's <u>indestructible</u>! A stake through the heart couldn't kill her!"

When I sat down in the kitchen to write the letter I found it more difficult than the first one. "Don't watch me," I said to my brother. "It's hard enough."

"You don't have to do something just because someone wants you to," Harold said. He was two years older than me and had started at City College; but when my father became ill he had switched to night school and gotten a job in a record store.

"Dear Mama," I wrote. "I hope you're feeling well. We're all fit as a fiddle. The life here is good and the people are very friendly and informal. Nobody wears suits and ties here. Just a pair of slacks and a short-sleeved shirt. Perhaps a sweater in the evening. I have bought into a very successful radio and record business and I'm doing very well. You remember Jack's Electric, my old place on Forty-third Street? Well, now it's Jack's Arizona Electric and we have a line of television sets as well."

*I sent* that letter off to my Aunt Frances, and as we all knew she would, she phoned soon after. My brother held his hand over the mouthpiece. "It's Frances with her latest review," he said.

"Jonathan? You're a very talented young man. I just wanted to tell you what a blessing your letter was. Her whole face lit up when I read the part about Jack's store. That would be an excellent way to continue."

"Well, I hope I don't have to do this anymore, Aunt Frances. It's not very honest."

Her tone changed. "Is your mother there? Let me talk to her."

"She's not here," I said.

"Tell her not to worry," my aunt said. "A poor old lady who has never wished anything but the best for her will soon die."

I did not repeat this to my mother, for whom it would have been one more in the family anthology of unforgivable remarks. But then I had to suffer it myself for the possible truth it might embody. Each side defended its position with rhetoric,[5] but I, who wanted peace, rationalized the snubs and rebuffs each inflicted on the other, taking no stands, like my father himself.

---

5. **rhetoric** (rĕt′ər-ĭk): skillful talk.

> WORDS
> TO
> KNOW   **indestructible** (ĭn′dĭ-strŭk′tə-bəl) *adj.* impossible to destroy

**1160**

---

## Teaching Options

### Mini Lesson  Grammar

**UNNECESSARY COMMAS** Using too many commas can be confusing. A comma should be used only if a rule requires one or if the meaning is unclear without one. Write the sentence on the chalkboard and invite students to check the punctuation:

> In 1955, Jonathan's grandmother was in a nursing home.

Explain that although the comma is technically correct, the current style is to eliminate commas after short introductory phrases if there is no danger of misreading.

**Exercises** Have students rewrite each of the following sentences, adding or deleting commas as necessary. If a sentence is correct, students can write *C*.

1. Aunt Frances wanted to protect Grandma from the knowledge, of her son's death. (*Delete the comma.*)
2. Of Jack's sisters, Aunt Frances was the wealthier. (*C*)
3. Jonathan, Harold, and their mother, tried to organize their lives. (*Delete the comma after mother.*)

*Years ago* his life had fallen into a pattern of business failures and missed opportunities. The great debate between his family on the one side, and my mother Ruth on the other, was this: who was responsible for the fact that he had not lived up to anyone's expectations?

As to the prophecies, when spring came my mother's prevailed. Grandma was still alive.

One balmy Sunday my mother and brother and I took the bus to the Beth El cemetery in New Jersey to visit my father's grave. It was situated on a slight rise. We stood looking over rolling fields embedded with monuments. Here and there processions of black cars wound their way through the lanes, or clusters of people stood at open graves. My father's grave was planted with tiny shoots of evergreen but it lacked a headstone. We had chosen one and paid for it and then the stonecutters had gone on strike. Without a headstone my father did not seem to be honorably dead. He didn't seem to me properly buried.

My mother gazed at the plot beside his, reserved for her coffin. "They were always too fine for other people," she said. "Even in the old days on Stanton Street. They put on airs. Nobody was ever good enough for them. Finally Jack himself was not good enough for them. Except to get them things wholesale. Then he was good enough for them."

"Mom, please," my brother said.

"If I had known. Before I ever met him he was tied to his mama's apron strings. And Essie's apron strings were like chains, let me tell you. We had to live where we could be near them for the Sunday visits. Every Sunday, that was my life, a visit to mamaleh.[6] Whatever she knew I wanted, a better apartment, a stick of furniture, a summer camp for the boys, she spoke against it. You know your father, every decision had to be considered and reconsidered. And nothing changed. Nothing ever changed."

She began to cry. We sat her down on a nearby bench. My brother walked off and read the names on stones. I looked at my mother, who was crying, and I went off after my brother.

"Mom's still crying," I said. "Shouldn't we do something?"

"It's all right," he said. "It's what she came here for."

"Yes," I said, and then a sob escaped from my throat. "But I feel like crying too."

My brother Harold put his arm around me. "Look at this old black stone here," he said. "The way it's carved. You can see the changing fashion in monuments—just like everything else."

*Somewhere* in this time I began dreaming of my father. Not the <u>robust</u> father of my childhood, the handsome man with healthy pink skin and brown eyes and a mustache and the thinning hair parted in the middle. My dead father. We were taking him home from the hospital. It was understood that he had come back from death. This was amazing and joyous. On the other hand, he was terribly mysteriously damaged, or, more accurately, spoiled and unclean. He was very yellowed and <u>debilitated</u> by his death, and there were no guarantees that he wouldn't soon die again. He seemed aware of this and his entire personality was changed. He was angry and impatient with all of us. We were trying to help him in some way, struggling to get him home, but something prevented us, something we had to fix, a tattered suitcase that had sprung open, some mechanical thing: he had a car but it wouldn't start; or the car was made of wood; or his clothes, which had become too large for him, had caught in the door. In one version he was all bandaged and as we tried to lift him from his wheelchair into a taxi the bandage began to unroll and catch in the spokes

---

6. **mamaleh** (mä′mə-lə) *Yiddish:* mother.

| WORDS TO KNOW | **robust** (rō-bŭst′) *adj.* full of health and strength; vigorous<br>**debilitated** (dĭ-bĭl′ĭ-tā′tĭd) *adj.* weakened; enfeebled |

**1161**

Use **Grammar Transparencies and Copymasters**, p. 155.

4. Their apartment was small, and cluttered. *(Delete the comma.)*
5. Jack had enjoyed bringing home exotic things, like rare cheeses, and foreign vegetables. *(Delete the commas.)*
6. At the request of Aunt Frances Jonathan wrote fictitious letters to his grandmother. *(Insert a comma after* Frances.)

Use McDougal Littell's *Language Network*, Chapter 9, for more instruction and practice in commas.

## Customizing Instruction

**Less Proficient Readers**

**1** Use the following questions to guide students in identifying Jonathan's conflict:

- In what way does Aunt Frances's tone change when Jonathan says he thinks writing the letters is dishonest? Why does her tone change?
  **Possible Response:** Her tone becomes sharp and annoyed because she wants Jonathan to continue writing letters.

- What is the intent of Aunt Frances's message to Jonathan's mother? Why does Jonathan decide not to give the message to his mother?
  **Possible Response:** The message is meant to make his mother feel guilty because Aunt Frances knows that Jonathan's mother doesn't wish the best for her mother-in-law. Jonathan knows the message will annoy and upset his mother.

- What does Jonathan mean when he says "I had to suffer it myself for the possible truth it might embody"?
  **Possible Response:** Jonathan may feel that his grandmother's behavior toward his mother has been thoughtless and selfish, but not malicious, although his mother may perceive it as such.

- How does the conflict between the two sides of his family affect Jonathan?
  **Possible Response:** Jonathan tries to stay neutral, making excuses for each side in the conflict.

**Students Acquiring English**

**2** Help students rely on the context to understand the meanings of idioms. If necessary, explain that *put on airs* means to behave in an affected, superior manner.

of the wheelchair. This seemed to be some unreasonableness on his part. My mother looked on sadly and tried to get him to cooperate.

That was the dream. I shared it with no one. Once when I woke, crying out, my brother turned on the light. He wanted to know what I'd been dreaming but I pretended I didn't remember. The dream made me feel guilty. I felt guilty in the dream too because my enraged father knew we didn't want to live with him. The dream represented us taking him home, or trying to, but it was nevertheless understood by all of us that he was to live alone. He was this derelict[7] back from death, but what we were doing was taking him to some place where he would live by himself without help from anyone until he died again.

*Untitled (First Avenue)* (about 1945), Fairfield Porter. Oil on canvas, 32" × 26¼". The Parrish Art Museum, Southampton, New York. Gift of the Estate of Fairfield Porter (1980.10.16).

*At one* point I became so fearful of this dream that I tried not to go to sleep. I tried to think of good things about my father and to remember him before his illness. He used to call me "matey." "Hello, matey," he would say when he came home from work. He always wanted us to go someplace—to the store, to the park, to a ball game. He loved to walk. When I went walking with him he would say: "Hold your shoulders back, don't slump. Hold your head up and look at the world. Walk as if you meant it!" As he strode down the street his shoulders moved from side to side, as if he was hearing some kind of cakewalk.[8] He moved with a bounce. He was always eager to see what was around the corner.

The next request for a letter coincided with a special occasion in the house: My brother Harold had met a girl he liked and had gone out with her several times. Now she was coming to our house for dinner. We had prepared for this for days, cleaning everything in sight, giving the house a going-over, washing the dust of disuse from the glasses and good dishes. My mother came home early from work to get the dinner going. We opened the gateleg table in the living room and brought in the kitchen chairs. My mother spread the table with a laundered white cloth and put out her silver. It was the first family occasion since my father's illness.

I liked my brother's girlfriend a lot. She was a thin girl with very straight hair and she had a terrific smile. Her presence seemed to excite the air. It was amazing to have a living breathing girl in our house. She looked around and what she said was: "Oh, I've never seen so many books!" While she and my brother sat at the table my mother was in the kitchen putting the food into serving bowls and I was going from the kitchen to the living room, kidding around like a waiter, with a white cloth over my arm and a high style of service, placing the serving dish of green beans on the table with a flourish. In the kitchen my mother's eyes were sparkling. She looked at me and nodded and mimed the words: "She's adorable!"

---

7. **derelict:** a person rejected by society; tramp or vagrant.
8. **cakewalk:** music written to accompany a strutting dance.

**My brother** suffered himself to be waited on. He was wary of what we might say. He kept glancing at the girl—her name was Susan—to see if we met with her approval. She worked in an insurance office and was taking courses in accounting at City College. Harold was under a terrible strain but he was excited and happy too. He had bought a bottle of Concord-grape wine to go with the roast chicken. He held up his glass and proposed a toast. My mother said: "To good health and happiness," and we all drank, even I. At that moment the phone rang and I went into the bedroom to get it.

"Jonathan? This is your Aunt Frances. How is everyone?"

"Fine, thank you."

"I want to ask one last favor of you. I need a letter from Jack. Your grandma's very ill. Do you think you can?"

"Who is it?" my mother called from the living room.

"OK, Aunt Frances," I said quickly. "I have to go now, we're eating dinner." And I hung up the phone.

"It was my friend Louie," I said, sitting back down. "He didn't know the math pages to review." **C**

The dinner was very fine. Harold and Susan washed the dishes and by the time they were done my mother and I had folded up the gateleg table and put it back against the wall and I had swept the crumbs up with the carpet sweeper. We all sat and talked and listened to records for a while and then my brother took Susan home. The evening had gone very well.

Once when my mother wasn't home my brother had pointed out something: the letters from Jack weren't really necessary. "What is this ritual?" he said, holding his palms up. "Grandma is almost totally blind, she's half deaf and crippled. Does the situation really call for a literary composition? Does it need verisimilitude?[9]

Would the old lady know the difference if she was read the phone book?"

"Then why did Aunt Frances ask me?"

"That is the question, Jonathan. Why did she? After all, she could write the letter herself—what difference would it make? And if not Frances, why not Frances' sons, the Amherst students? They should have learned by now to write."

"But they're not Jack's sons," I said.

"That's exactly the point," my brother said. "The idea is *service*. Dad used to get them things wholesale, getting them deals on things. Frances of Westchester[10] really needed things at cost. And Aunt Molly. And Aunt Molly's husband, and Aunt Molly's ex-husband. Grandma, if she needed an errand done. He was always on the hook for something. They never thought his time was important. They never thought every favor he got was one he had to pay back. Appliances, records, watches, china, opera tickets, anything. Call Jack." **1**

"It was a matter of pride to him to be able to do things for them," I said. "To have connections."

"Yeah, I wonder why," my brother said. He looked out the window.

Then suddenly it dawned on me that I was being implicated.

"You should use your head more," my brother said. **2**

Yet I had agreed once again to write a letter from the desert and so I did. I mailed it off to Aunt Frances. A few days later, when I came home from school, I thought I saw her sitting in her car in front of our house. She drove a black Buick Roadmaster, a very large clean car with whitewall tires. It was Aunt Frances all right. She blew the horn when she saw me. I went over and leaned in at the window.

---

9. **verisimilitude** (vĕr′ə-sĭ-mĭl′ĭ-tōōd′): an appearance of reality; truth to life.

10. **Westchester:** an affluent county just north of New York City.

> WORDS
> TO
> KNOW    **implicate** (ĭm′plĭ-kāt′) v. to connect to an activity, especially one of an unsavory or criminal nature

**1163**

---

3. Aunt Frances needed another letter for Grandma. *(Another letter was needed for Grandma.)*

4. In the dream, it was understood by all that Jack was to live alone. *(In the dream, everyone understood that Jack was to live alone.)*

5. Jonathan was called "matey" by his father. *(Jonathan's father called him "matey.")*

6. Jonathan's letters were read to Grandma by Aunt Frances. *(Aunt Frances read Jonathan's letters to Grandma.)*

> Use **Grammar Transparencies and Copymasters**, p. 68.

> Use McDougal Littell's *Language Network*, Chapter 4, for more instruction in active and passive voice.

**A** Ask students to analyze the main conflict in the story by contrasting Aunt Frances's view of Jack's lack of accomplishment with Ruth's view. How do their theories reveal the way they feel about each other?

**Possible Response:** Aunt Frances blames Jack's devotion to his wife for his failure to succeed in life; Ruth blames Jack's devotion to his mother and sisters for his lack of success. They are jealous of each other and have always resented having to share Jack's attention and affection.

### Literary Analysis: SUSPENSE

**B** Jonathan doesn't reveal what he wrote in the letter. Ask how this increases suspense.

**Possible Response:** It leaves the reader wondering how Jonathan will resolve the conflict he feels about his father and whether the letter will make him feel even worse than he felt before.

### Reading Skills and Strategies: INTERPRETING

**C** Have students discuss Jonathan's judgment of himself. What did he write in the letter that would allow him to "soften" that judgment?

**Possible Response:** Jonathan is chagrined that he hadn't known of or guessed his father's love for the sea and dream of a naval career. However, in his last letter, he wrote that Jack wanted his ashes to be scattered in the ocean. Jonathan may think this shows that deep down, he really did understand his father's dream for his life, and that in some way he helped his father to fulfill that dream.

---

"Hello, Jonathan," she said. "I haven't long. Can you get in the car?"

"Mom's not home," I said. "She's working."

"I know that. I came to talk to you."

"Would you like to come upstairs?"

"I can't, I have to get back to Larchmont. Can you get in for a moment, please?"

*I got* in the car. My Aunt Frances was a very pretty white-haired woman, very elegant, and she wore tasteful clothes. I had always liked her and from the time I was a child she had enjoyed pointing out to everyone that I looked more like her son than Jack's. She wore white gloves and held the steering wheel and looked straight ahead as she talked, as if the car was in traffic and not sitting at the curb.

"Jonathan," she said, "there is your letter on the seat. Needless to say I didn't read it to Grandma. I'm giving it back to you and I won't ever say a word to anyone. This is just between us. I never expected cruelty from you. I never thought you were capable of doing something so deliberately cruel and perverse."

I said nothing.

"Your mother has very bitter feelings and now I see she has poisoned you with them. She has always resented the family. She is a very strong-willed, selfish person."

"No she isn't," I said.

"I wouldn't expect you to agree. She drove poor Jack crazy with her demands. She always had the highest aspirations and he could never fulfill them to her satisfaction. When he still had his store he kept your mother's brother, who drank, on salary. After the war when he began to make a little money he had to buy Ruth a mink jacket because she was so desperate to have one. He had debts to pay but she wanted a mink. He was a very special person, my brother, he should have accomplished something special, but he loved your mother and devoted his life to her. And all she ever thought about was keeping up with the Joneses."

I watched the traffic going up the Grand Concourse. A bunch of kids were waiting at the bus stop at the corner. They had put their books on the ground and were horsing around.

"I'm sorry I have to descend to this," Aunt Frances said. "I don't like talking about people this way. If I have nothing good to say about someone, I'd rather not say anything. How is Harold?"

"Fine."

"Did he help you write this marvelous letter?"

"No."

After a moment she said more softly: "How are you all getting along?"

"Fine."

"I would invite you up for Passover[11] if I thought your mother would accept."

I didn't answer.

She turned on the engine. "I'll say good-bye now, Jonathan. Take your letter. I hope you give some time to thinking about what you've done."

That evening when my mother came home from work I saw that she wasn't as pretty as my Aunt Frances. I usually thought my mother was a good-looking woman, but I saw now that she was too heavy and that her hair was undistinguished.

"Why are you looking at me?" she said.

"I'm not."

"I learned something interesting today," my mother said. "We may be eligible for a V.A. pension[12] because of the time your father spent in the Navy."

That took me by surprise. Nobody had ever told me my father was in the Navy.

"In World War I," she said, "he went to Webb's Naval Academy on the Harlem River. He was training to be an ensign. But the war ended and he never got his commission."

---

11. **Passover:** an important Jewish holiday, commemorating the Hebrew people's deliverance from slavery in Egypt.

12. **V.A. pension:** a pension paid by the Veterans Administration (now the Department of Veterans Affairs) to former members of the U.S. armed forces.

---

## Teaching Options

### Workplace Link  Writing a Business Letter

Jack was in the Navy during World War I and the family could be eligible for a pension if they can locate Jack's service records. Harold thinks that a duplicate of his father's service record might be filed in Washington. If Jack's wife were looking for those records today, she would need to send a request in writing to the National Personnel Records Center (NPRC). Her request would have to include some basic information in order to locate the service records: the veteran's complete name, service number or social security number, branch of service, dates of service, date and place of birth. The request must be signed and dated.

**Application** Have students assume the role of Jack's wife and tell them to write the request for Jack's service records. Students must be sure to include all of the basic information; they can make up dates, names, and locations as necessary. Students should use the form of a basic business letter. If students have access to the Internet, they can obtain the address of the NPRC by going to http://www.nara.gov/regional/stlouis.html. Encourage students to share any information they obtain from this source.

*After dinner* the three of us went through the closets looking for my father's papers, hoping to find some proof that could be filed with the Veterans Administration. We came up with two things, a Victory medal, which my brother said everyone got for being in the service during the Great War, and an astounding sepia photograph[13] of my father and his shipmates on the deck of a ship. They were dressed in bell-bottoms and T-shirts and armed with mops and pails, brooms and brushes.

"I never knew this," I found myself saying. "I never knew this."

"You just don't remember," my brother said.

I was able to pick out my father. He stood at the end of the row, a thin, handsome boy with a full head of hair, a mustache, and an intelligent smiling countenance.

"He had a joke," my mother said. "They called their training ship the *S.S. Constipation* because it never moved."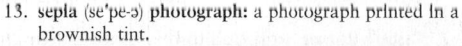

Neither the picture nor the medal was proof of anything, but my brother thought a duplicate of my father's service record had to be in Washington somewhere and that it was just a matter of learning how to go about finding it.

"The pension wouldn't amount to much," my mother said. "Twenty or thirty dollars. But it would certainly help."

I took the picture of my father and his shipmates and propped it against the lamp at my bedside. I looked into his youthful face and tried to relate it to the Father I knew. I looked at the picture a long time. Only gradually did my eye connect it to the set of Great Sea Novels in the bottom shelf of the bookcase a few feet away. My father had given that set to me: it was uniformly bound in green with gilt lettering and it included works by Melville, Conrad, Victor Hugo and Captain Marryat.[14] And lying across the top of the books, jammed in under the sagging shelf above, was his old ship's telescope in its wooden case with the brass snap.

I thought how stupid, and imperceptive, and self-centered I had been never to have understood while he was alive what my father's dream for his life had been.

On the other hand, I had written in my last letter from Arizona—the one that had so angered Aunt Frances—something that might allow me, the writer in the family, to soften my judgment of myself. I will conclude by giving the letter here in its entirety.

Dear Mama,

This will be my final letter to you since I have been told by the doctors that I am dying.

I have sold my store at a very fine profit and am sending Frances a check for five thousand dollars to be deposited in your account. My present to you, Mamaleh. Let Frances show you the passbook.

As for the nature of my ailment, the doctors haven't told me what it is, but I know that I am simply dying of the wrong life. I should never have come to the desert. It wasn't the place for me.

I have asked Ruth and the boys to have my body cremated and the ashes scattered in the ocean.
Your loving son,
Jack ❖

---

13. **sepia** (sē'pē-ə) **photograph:** a photograph printed in a brownish tint.

14. **Melville . . . Marryat** (măr'ē-ət): Herman Melville, an American writer who drew upon his experiences as a sailor in creating *Moby-Dick* and other novels; Joseph Conrad, a Polish-born English novelist (also a former sailor) whose works include *Lord Jim*; Victor Hugo, a French poet, novelist, and dramatist, among whose novels is the *Toilers of the Sea*; Captain Frederick Marryat, a British naval officer, an author of a number of novels dealing with life at sea.

## Customizing Instruction

**Students Acquiring English**
**1** Point out that the word *commission* has a different meaning here than on page 1159. Here, *commission* refers to an official certificate conferring military rank.

**Gifted and Talented**
**2** Have students use what they know about Jonathan and his family to write an alternate ending to the story. They might write a final letter with a different message. Challenge students to resolve conflicts in the story.

---

 **Assessment Informal Assessment**

**RETELLING** Ask pairs of students to retell the story in the first person, as Jonathan and Harold. Students can use their story maps as a guide for retelling the story. The retelling should summarize all the important points of the story and should convey each character's thoughts and feelings.

**RUBRIC**

**3** **Full Accomplishment** Retelling includes the key events of the plot in correct sequence, summarizes the characters' conflicts, and presents thoughts, feelings, and perceptions appropriate to Jonathan and Harold.

**2** **Substantial Accomplishment** Retelling omits one or two key events or presents them out of sequence, or it includes some thoughts and perceptions that do not correspond with Jonathan's and Harold's characters.

**1** **Little or Partial Accomplishment** Students have difficulty recalling the story's key events and/or depicting the characters.

## Connect to the Literature

**1. What Do You Think?**
Students will form an impression and judge the intentions of Jonathan's final letter.

**Comprehension Check**
- The aunts believe the news of Jack's death will be too shocking.
- Aunt Frances ask Jonathan to write letters impersonating his father.
- Jonathan learns that his father served in the Navy during World War I.

 Use Selection Quiz
**Unit Seven Resource Book**, p. 48.

## Think Critically

**2.** Students may say Jack's dream is business success, a good life for his family, or an adventure at sea. Other conclusions students may draw about Jack's life include that he acted courageously, felt deep concern for his loved ones, coped graciously with his career failures.

**3.** Possible Response: Aunt Frances views Jack's life as unfulfilled and financially unsuccessful, while Jonathan's mother views Jack's life as unchanging and disappointing.

**4.** Possible Responses: Family members have not come to terms with Jack's death; Jonathan's varied attempts to repair broken or defective things might represent his efforts to perpetuate his father's life by writing the letters.

**5.** Possible Response: Jonathan—sensitive, principled; his mother—truthful, discontented; Aunt Frances—scheming, manipulative; Harold—thoughtful, sensible.

## Literary Analysis

**Plot Development** Possible Responses: being kept away from his grandmother; his mother working in the hospital where her husband died; discarding his father's appliances, bought "at cost"; trying on his father's suits; visiting the cemetery; his dream; his brother's accusation that he is becoming just like his father; Aunt Frances's confrontation over the final letter; his realization that he didn't really know his father.

---

# *Thinking through the* LITERATURE

## Connect to the Literature

**1. What Do You Think?**
Share your reaction to Jonathan's last letter. Do you agree with Aunt Frances that it was cruel?

**Comprehension Check**
- Why do the aunts lie to the grandmother about Jack's death?
- What does Aunt Frances ask Jonathan to do for the grandmother?
- At the end of the story, what does Jonathan learn about his father's past?

## Think Critically

**2.** **ACTIVE READING   DRAWING CONCLUSIONS** What do you think was Jack's dream for his life? What other conclusions did you draw about his life? Look over the chart you made in your **READER'S NOTEBOOK**, and state the information on which you based your conclusions.

**3.** How does Jonathan's mother's view of Jack's life compare with Aunt Frances's view?

**4.** Tell how you interpret Jonathan's dream.

 **THINK ABOUT**
- his father's physical condition and attitude
- the obstacles that prevent the father from getting home
- the mother's attitude and actions
- Jonathan's feelings in the dream

**5.** Offer your final judgments of Jonathan, his mother, his Aunt Frances, and his brother Harold. Did these change from your earlier judgments?

## Extend Interpretations

**6. Different Perspectives** Why might someone classify "The Writer in the Family" as a coming-of-age story?

**7. Critic's Corner** Respond to this comment by critic Paul Levine:

*Jonathan's letters have a surprising effect on himself as well as others. To some family members, these fictions seem to make the dead man more real than when he was alive. To Jonathan, his constructions finally reveal something of his father's true nature which was hidden from him. The lies he creates disclose the truth about his own family situation.*

**8. Connect to Life** Name a real person or a fictional character who reminds you of Jonathan's father, and explain what they have in common.

---

## Literary Analysis

**PLOT DEVELOPMENT** As you recall, **plot** is based on **conflict**, a struggle between opposing forces. Conflict can be **external**, as when a character struggles with another character, a natural force, or a social circumstance. Conflict can also be **internal**, as when a character struggles with a moral dilemma. In "The Writer in the Family," external conflicts lead to internal conflicts for Jonathan. The letters that Aunt Frances requests create tension among the family members. As the plot develops, Jonathan must decide whether to keep writing. What other conflicts do you see in the story?

**Cooperative Learning Activity**
Working in a small group, create a diagram of the conflicts in this story. Show which characters are in conflict with other characters, and which characters are in conflict with themselves. Be prepared to tell what the conflicts are about. The most important conflicts in the story are internal ones faced by Jonathan. Discuss how his final letter resolves these conflicts.

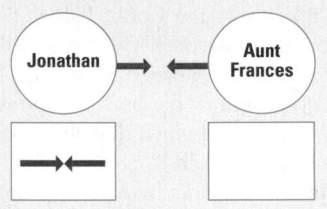

---

# Extend Interpretations

**Different Perspectives** Possible Response: Jonathan undergoes a personal transformation—a passage from youth to maturity.

**Critic's Corner** Possible Response: Writing the letters unwittingly becomes an act of self-discovery for Jonathan. His deceit is ironic because in the process he learns truths about his family members.

**Connect to Life** Good responses will mention an individual who parallels Jack's personality, ambitions, or circumstances in some evident way.

## Writing Options

**1. True Obituary** Write an obituary that tells the *real* truth about Jack's life instead of following the standard formula. Mention his background, accomplishments, disappointments, and family.

**2. Definition of Success** Define *a successful life*, drawing on the ideas you had about success both before and after you read the story. In your definition, make reference to at least one of the characters from the story as a positive or negative example.

## Inquiry & Research

**Mourning Rituals** When the story opens, Jonathan's family is observing *shiva*, the traditional seven-day period of mourning for Jews. Find out more or share what you already know about *shiva* rituals.

## Vocabulary in Action

**EXERCISE: CONTEXT CLUES** On your paper, write the Word to Know that best completes each sentence.

1. The boy's father suffered from a _____ illness.
2. The image of his sick father contrasted with the boy's memory of the healthy, _____ father of his childhood.
3. His father was quite _____ by his illness.
4. Aunt Frances _____ Jonathan in a plot to deceive his grandmother.
5. Sometimes we forget that people are not _____, that even the healthiest can die suddenly.

**Building Vocabulary**

For an in-depth study of context clues, see page 326.

| WORDS TO KNOW | debilitated | indestructible | terminal |
|---|---|---|---|
| | implicate | robust | |

## E(dgar) L(aurence) Doctorow
### 1931–

**Other Works**
*Ragtime*
*World's Fair*
*Billy Bathgate*

**Serious Novelist** E. L. Doctorow is one of the few bestselling American authors considered a "serious" writer by critics. Doctorow is known for the stylistic breadth of his fiction, which is alternately traditional and experimental, accessible and difficult. Many of his works blur the line separating fact from fiction. This strategy reflects Doctorow's belief, stated in the essay "False Documents," that "there is no fiction or nonfiction as we commonly understand the distinction: there is only narrative."

**Mixing History with Fiction** Such early novels as *The Book of Daniel* (1971) and *Ragtime* (1975) reimagine portions of this country's history, combining real-life events and figures with entirely fictitious ones. According to Doctorow, serious novelists use the power of the imagination to construct works of fiction "more valid, more real, more truthful than the 'true' documents of the politicians or the journalists or the psychologists." *The Book of Daniel*, for example, is based on the actual trial of Julius and Ethel Rosenberg, a communist couple executed for treason by the U.S. government during the Cold War period of the 1950s. Rather than merely dramatizing the facts of the case, Doctorow changes some facts and filters them through the highly subjective perspective of Daniel, the fictionalized couple's bitter and bewildered son.

**A More Personal Collection** When *Lives of the Poets* came out in 1984, its somewhat autobiographical flavor seemed like a departure for Doctorow, a writer who avoided drawing on his personal history in previous works of fiction. However, while this book is more personal than earlier works, it mixes fact and fiction in a similar way and displays the same fascination with the past.

THE WRITER IN THE FAMILY **1167**

## Writing Options

**1. True Obituary To help students get started,** tell them to refer to the character charts they created in their Reader's Notebooks. They can scan the story to look for details about Jack that they may have missed in their first reading. Like any essay, the obituary should have an opening statement, followed by paragraphs that develop the main points; it should finish with a few closing remarks.

**2. Definition of Success** Students' definitions should be clearly organized and should express strong opinions. Students should support their ideas with examples from the story or from their own lives.

## Vocabulary in Action

**EXERCISE**
1. terminal
2. robust
3. debilitated
4. implicate
5. indestructible

## Objectives

1. understand and appreciate a **short story** (Literary Analysis)
2. understand **protagonist and antagonist** (Literary Analysis)
3. **recognize important details** (Active Reading)

## Summary

Daisy Coble meets with the principal of the private high school that her son, Donny, attends, and the principal tells her that Donny is disruptive and not responsive in class. At the principal's suggestion, Daisy supervises Donny's homework. His grades improve slightly, but the school reports new behavior problems, including smoking and possibly drinking. A psychologist recommends a tutor, Cal Beadle, whom Donny meets with three times a week and grows to like. Cal says that Daisy and Matt, Donny's parents, are too controlling and accusatory. Although Daisy tries to be more positive with Donny, his behavior continues to deteriorate, and eventually he is expelled from school. Cal calls the expulsion unjust, but Daisy no longer trusts Cal. She enrolls Donny in a public school and stops the tutoring sessions. One day Donny runs away from home, and he does not return.

## Thematic Link

Daisy, who tries to help her teenage son Donny succeed in school, cannot prevent the **disintegration** of her family.

### 5-Minute Warm-Up

***Daily Language SkillBuilder***

Have students **proofread** the display sentences on page 1069j and write them correctly. The sentences also appear on Transparency 33 of **Grammar Transparencies and Copymasters.**

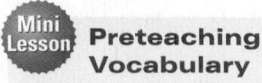
**Mini Lesson** **Preteaching Vocabulary**

If you would like to preteach the WORDS TO KNOW for this selection, use the Mini Lesson, p. 1170.

---

# PREPARING to *Read*

# Teenage Wasteland

*Short Story by* ANNE TYLER

"*I think this kid is hurting.*"

### ( Connect to Your Life )

**Troubled Teen** In this story, Daisy and Matt learn that their teenage son, Donny, is having trouble in school. What advice would you give to parents in this situation? With a small group of classmates, discuss things you would do or rules you might enforce to help a teenager improve in school.

## Build Background

**Academic Reform Debate** In keeping with other changes during the 1960s and 1970s, experimental theories of education were being tested in many U.S. schools and universities. Believing that teachers should act as assistants or helpers rather than as authority figures, supporters of "alternative schools" and "the open classroom" wanted to do away with traditional teaching methods. They wanted students to be free to discover their own learning styles, guide their own curriculum, and progress at their own pace. While quite successful in some schools, this academic reform movement met resistance from some educators and parents who felt that students, if left to themselves, would not be taught the basic skills of reading, writing, and arithmetic. In "Teenage Wasteland," Daisy and Matt, like many parents at the time, find themselves caught in the middle of this continuing debate. They receive conflicting advice from educators about how to help their son.

**WORDS TO KNOW**
**Vocabulary Preview**

| | |
|---|---|
| amiably | qualm |
| forlorn | shamble |
| looming | subdued |
| morass | temporize |
| punitive | vindictive |

## Focus Your Reading

**LITERARY ANALYSIS** **CHARACTER: PROTAGONIST AND ANTAGONIST** The **protagonist** is the central character in a short story, novel, or play. The **antagonist** is the character or force that the protagonist is pitted against. Decide who is the protagonist and who is the antagonist in this story.

**ACTIVE READING** **RECOGNIZING IMPORTANT DETAILS**

In "Teenage Wasteland," Tyler uses many **details**—or specific pieces of information—to create an experience for your imagination. All of these details contribute to the total effect of the story, and you should savor them as you read. For example, notice the following details that reveal how Daisy imagines the principal's perception of herself and her husband: "an overweight housewife in a cotton dress and a too-tall, too-thin insurance agent in a baggy, frayed suit." These details provide a strong clue about Daisy's self-image. Still, some details are more compelling than others and deserve special attention as you read. In this story about a troubled teen, one cluster of important details concerns the different pieces of advice that the parents receive about how to help their son.

**READER'S NOTEBOOK**

To help you track the different kinds of advice that Daisy and Matt receive, keep a list of that advice in your notebook. As you read, write down what the principal, the teachers, and the tutor say about how to help Donny. Put a check mark beside each piece of advice that Daisy and Matt follow.

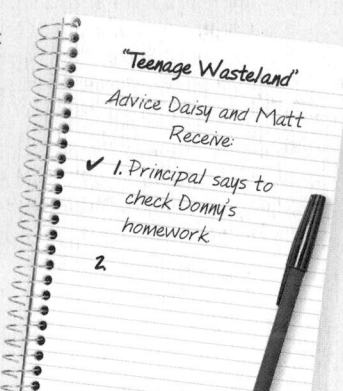

"*Teenage Wasteland*"
Advice Daisy and Matt Receive:
✔ 1. Principal says to check Donny's homework
2.

---

## LESSON RESOURCES

**UNIT SEVEN RESOURCE BOOK,** pp. 49–53

**ASSESSMENT RESOURCES**
**Formal Assessment,** pp. 221–222
**Teacher's Guide to Assessment and Portfolio Use**
**Test Generator**

**SKILLS TRANSPARENCIES AND COPYMASTERS**
**Literary Analysis**
• Character: Change and Motivation, T7 (for Cooperative Learning Activity, p. 1178)

**Reading and Critical Thinking**
• Noting Details, T9 (for Active Reading, p. 1168)

**Grammar**
• Progressive and Emphatic Verb Forms, C118 (for Mini Lesson, p. 1174)

**Vocabulary**
• Synonyms and Antonyms, C96 (for Mini Lesson, p. 1170)

**Writing**
• Persuasive Essay, C27 (for Writing Option 2, p. 1179)

**Communications**
• Impromptu Speaking: Dialogue, Role-Play, Debate, T13 (for Mini Lesson, p. 1176)

**INTEGRATED TECHNOLOGY**

**Audio Library**
**Visit our website:**
www.mcdougallittell.com

e used to have very blond hair—almost white—cut shorter than other children's so that on his crown a little cowlick always stood up to catch the light. But this was when he was small. As he grew older, his hair grew darker, and he wore it longer —past his collar even. It hung in lank, taffy colored ropes around his face, which was still an endearing face, fine-featured, the eyes an unusual aqua blue. But his cheeks, of course, were no longer round, and a sharp new Adam's apple jogged in his throat when he talked.

In October, they called from the private school he attended to request a conference with his parents. Daisy went alone; her husband was at work. Clutching her purse, she sat on the principal's couch and learned that Donny was noisy, lazy, and disruptive; always fooling around with his friends, and he wouldn't respond in class.

In the past, before her children were born, Daisy had been a fourth-grade teacher. It shamed her now to sit before this principal as a parent, a delinquent parent, a parent who struck Mr. Lanham, no doubt, as unseeing or uncaring. "It isn't that we're not concerned," she said. "Both of us are. And we've done what we could, whatever we could think of. We don't let him watch TV

# Teenage Wasteland

## Anne Tyler

*Table with Fruit* (1951–1952), David Park, Oil on canvas, 46″ × 35¼″, collection of Mr. and Mrs. R. Crosby Kemper. Photo by Edward B. Bigelow.

**1169**

### Reading Skills and Strategies: PREVIEW

As students read, tell them to think about whether they agree or not with the steps the adults take to help the teenager, Donny.

### Active Reading

**RECOGNIZING IMPORTANT DETAILS**

Readers can use details (textual evidence) provided by the author as well as their own experience to make inferences about characters and to make predictions about the outcome of the story. Encourage students to construct a cluster map for each main character and list important details on it.

 Use **Unit Seven Resource Book,** p. 50 for more practice.

### Literary Analysis

**CHARACTER: PROTAGONIST AND ANTAGONIST**

Explain that the protagonist is the character with whom the reader identifies and feels most sympathetic. The antagonist may be another character or a force of nature or society. The antagonist creates problems for the protagonist. Ask students to explain who is the protagonist and who is the antagonist in this story. What clues can they provide to support their responses?

**Possible Responses:** Daisy is the protagonist because she is the one who is trying to solve the problems created by Donny, the antagonist. Later in the story, Cal may be considered the antagonist, because he seems to obstruct Daisy's attempts to communicate with her son.

 Use **Unit Seven Resource Book,** p. 51 for additional support.

---

on school nights. We don't let him talk on the phone till he's finished his homework. But he tells us he doesn't *have* any homework or he did it all in study hall. How are we to know what to believe?"

From early October through November, at Mr. Lanham's suggestion, Daisy checked Donny's assignments every day. She sat next to him as he worked, trying to be encouraging, sagging inwardly as she saw the poor quality of everything he did—the sloppy mistakes in math, the illogical leaps in his English themes, the history questions left blank if they required any research.

Daisy was often late starting supper, and she couldn't give as much attention to Donny's younger sister. "You'll never guess what happened at . . ." Amanda would begin, and Daisy would have to tell her, "Not now, honey."

By the time her husband, Matt, came home, she'd be snappish. She would recite the day's hardships—the fuzzy instructions in English, the botched history map, the <u>morass</u> of unsolvable algebra equations. Matt would look surprised and confused, and Daisy would gradually wind down. There was no way, really, to convey how exhausting all this was.

In December, the school called again. This time, they wanted Matt to come as well. She and Matt had to sit on Mr. Lanham's couch like two bad children and listen to the news: Donny had improved only slightly, raising a D in history to a C, and a C in algebra to a B-minus. What was worse, he had developed new problems. He had cut classes on at least three occasions. Smoked in the furnace room. Helped Sonny Barnett break into a freshman's locker. And last week, during athletics, he and three friends had been seen off the school grounds; when they returned, the coach had smelled beer on their breath.

Daisy and Matt sat silent, shocked. Matt rubbed his forehead with his fingertips. Imagine, Daisy thought, how they must look to Mr. Lanham: an overweight housewife in a cotton dress and a too-tall, too-thin insurance agent in a baggy, frayed suit. Failures, both of them—the kind of people who are always hurrying to catch up, missing the point of things that everyone else grasps at once. She wished she'd worn nylons instead of knee socks.

It was arranged that Donny would visit a psychologist for testing. Mr. Lanham knew just the person. He would set this boy straight, he said.

When they stood to leave, Daisy held her stomach in and gave Mr. Lanham a firm, responsible handshake.

Donny said the psychologist was a jackass and the tests were really dumb; but he kept all three of his appointments, and when it was time for the follow-up conference with the psychologist and both parents, Donny combed his hair and seemed unusually sober and <u>subdued</u>. The psychologist said Donny had no serious emotional problems. He was merely going through a difficult period in his life. He required some academic help and a better sense of self-worth. For this reason, he was suggesting a man named Calvin Beadle, a tutor with considerable psychological training.

In the car going home, Donny said he'd be damned if he'd let them drag him to some stupid tutor. His father told him to watch his language in front of his mother.

That night, Daisy lay awake pondering the term "self-worth." She had always been free with her praise. She had always told Donny he had talent, was smart, was good with his hands. She had made a big to-do over every little gift he gave her. In fact, maybe she had gone too far, although, Lord knows, she had meant every word. Was that his trouble?

She remembered when Amanda was born. Donny had acted lost and bewildered. Daisy had been alert to that, of course, but still, a new baby keeps you so busy. Had she really done all she could have? She longed—she ached—for a time machine. Given one more chance, she'd do

| WORDS TO KNOW | **morass** (mə-răs′) *n.* a difficult, confused, or entangled state of affairs; puzzling mess |
| | **subdued** (səb-dōōd′) *adj.* made submissive; reduced in intensity; toned down |
| | **subdue** *v.* |

---

## Teaching Options

 **Mini Lesson** **Preteaching Vocabulary**

**SYNONYMS AND ANTONYMS Instruction** Remind students that synonyms are words with the same meaning and antonyms are words with opposite meanings.

**Activity** Have students, in groups or pairs, write brief definitions for each of the WORDS TO KNOW, using a dictionary if needed. Then have them brainstorm synonyms and antonyms for each word. Write each group's responses on the chalkboard. Use a thesaurus or dictionary to introduce additional synonyms or antonyms to the class. Have students use the WORDS TO KNOW in sentences.

Use **Unit Seven Resource Book,** p. 52 for more practice.

She longed—

she ached—

for a time machine.

Given one more chance,

she'd do it perfectly—

hug him more,

praise him more,

or perhaps

praise him less.

Oh, who can say . . .

## Mini Lesson  Viewing and Representing

*Girl Looking at Landscape*
**by Richard Diebenkorn**

**ART APPRECIATION** The muted colors of the foreground contrast with the vibrant, sunlit background of this painting.

**Instruction** Remind students that artists use light and color to convey meaning. Ask them what meanings are suggested by the contrast between the colors in the background and those in the foreground of this painting.

**Possible Response:** The rich, bright colors of the landscape outside the window suggest life and excitement. The drab colors of the girl's clothing and her indoor surroundings suggest boredom and fatigue.

**Application** How would you describe the feelings of the girl in this painting? Do you think the painting fits with the mood of the story?

**Possible Responses:** The girl seems to have a wistful attitude, as if longing to escape from her everyday life to something new and exciting. The painting fits the mood of quiet desperation that the story conveys.

## Reading and Analyzing

### Active Reading
**RECOGNIZING IMPORTANT DETAILS**

**(A)** Point out that the author introduces Cal with a physical description. Ask students what the physical details convey about him.

**Possible Responses:** He is a 1970s hippie; he dresses the same way Donny does, so maybe they will get along; his director's chair symbolizes his trait of being subtly controlling.

### Reading Skills and Strategies:
**EVALUATING**

**(B)** Ask students whether they think the sacrifices the family makes for Donny are worthwhile.

**Possible Responses:** Yes, a family should make every effort to help one of its members; no, others in the family should not have to suffer for one member's laziness and irresponsibility.

### Reading Skills and Strategies:
**MAKING JUDGMENTS**

**(C)** Ask students whether Donny's view of his parents seems accurate.

Possible Responses: Donny finds any restriction his parents place on him excessive; their demands are similar to those of other parents.

### Literary Analysis
**CHARACTER: PROTAGONIST AND ANTAGONIST**

**(D)** Ask students whom they see as the main character—the protagonist—at this point in the story.

**Possible Responses:** Daisy or Donny

Ask whom they see as the opposing character—the antagonist.

**Possible Responses:** Many students may see Cal as the antagonist because he is fueling Donny's self-destructive impulses.

## Teaching Options

---

**[1]** it perfectly—hug him more, praise him more, or perhaps praise him less. Oh, who can say . . .

The tutor told Donny to call him Cal. All his kids did, he said. Daisy thought for a second that he meant his own children, then realized her mistake. He seemed too young, anyhow, to be a family man. He wore a heavy brown handlebar mustache. His hair was as long and stringy as Donny's, and his jeans as faded. Wire-rimmed spectacles slid down his nose. He lounged in a canvas director's chair with his fingers laced across his chest, and he casually, <u>amiably</u> questioned Donny, who sat upright and glaring in an armchair.

"So they're getting on your back at school," said Cal. "Making a big deal about anything you do wrong."

"Right," said Donny.

"Any idea why that would be?"

"Oh, well, you know, stuff like homework and all," Donny said.

"You don't do your homework?"

**(A)** "Oh, well, I might do it sometimes but not just exactly like they want it." Donny sat forward and said, "It's like a prison there, you know? You've got to go to every class, you can never step off the school grounds."

"You cut classes sometimes?"

"Sometimes," Donny said, with a glance at his parents.

Cal didn't seem perturbed. "Well," he said, "I'll tell you what. Let's you and me try working together three nights a week. Think you could handle that? We'll see if we can show that school of yours a thing or two. Give it a month; then if you don't like it, we'll stop. If *I* don't like it, we'll stop. I mean, sometimes people just don't get along, right? What do you say to that?"

"Okay," Donny said. He seemed pleased.

"Make it seven o'clock till eight, Monday, Wednesday, and Friday," Cal told Matt and Daisy. They nodded. Cal <u>shambled</u> to his feet, gave them a little salute, and showed them to the door.

This was where he lived as well as worked, evidently. The interview had taken place in the dining room, which had been transformed into a kind of office. Passing the living room, Daisy winced at the rock music she had been hearing, without registering it, ever since she had entered the house. She looked in and saw a boy about Donny's age lying on a sofa with a book. Another boy and a girl were playing Ping-Pong in front of the fireplace. "You have several here together?" Daisy asked Cal.

"Oh, sometimes they stay on after their sessions, just to rap. They're a pretty sociable group, all in all. Plenty of goof-offs like young Donny here."

He cuffed Donny's shoulder playfully. Donny flushed and grinned.

Climbing into the car, Daisy asked Donny, "Well? What did you think?"

But Donny had returned to his old evasive self. He jerked his chin toward the garage. "Look," he said. "He's got a basketball net."

Now on Mondays, Wednesdays, and Fridays, they had supper early—the instant Matt came home. Sometimes, they had to leave before they were really finished. Amanda would still be eating her dessert. "Bye, honey. Sorry," Daisy would tell her.

Cal's first bill sent a flutter of panic through Daisy's chest, but it was worth it, of course. Just look at Donny's face when they picked him up: alight and full of interest. The principal telephoned Daisy to tell her how Donny had improved. "Of course, it hasn't shown up in his grades yet, but several of the teachers have noticed how his attitude's changed. Yes, sir, I think we're onto something here."

At home, Donny didn't act much different. He still seemed to have a low opinion of his parents. But Daisy supposed that was unavoidable—part of being fifteen. He said his parents were too "controlling"—a word that made Daisy give him a sudden look. He said they acted like wardens.

---

WORDS
TO
KNOW

**amiably** (āʹmē-ə-blē) *adv.* in a pleasant and friendly manner; good-naturedly
**shamble** (shămʹbəl) *v.* to walk or move awkwardly or clumsily

**1172**

---

### BLOCK SCHEDULING: MANAGING TIME

**If your schedule requires that you cover the lesson objectives in a shorter time, use . . .**
- Preparing to Read, p. 1168
- Thinking Through the Literature, p. 1178
- Vocabulary in Action, p. 1179

**If you want to take advantage of longer class time, use . . .**
- TE Teaching Options: Preteaching Vocabulary, p. 1170; Viewing and Representing, pp. 1169, 1171; Speaking and Listening, p. 1176; Informal Assessment, p. 1177
- Choices & Challenges, p. 1179

On weekends, they enforced a curfew. And any time he went to a party, they always telephoned first to see if adults would be supervising. "For God's sake!" he said. "Don't you trust me?"

"It isn't a matter of trust, honey . . . " But there was no explaining to him.

His tutor called one afternoon. "I get the sense," he said, "that this kid's feeling . . . underestimated, you know? Like you folks expect the worst of him. I'm thinking we ought to give him more rope."

"But see, he's still so suggestible," Daisy said. "When his friends suggest some mischief—smoking or drinking or such—why, he just finds it hard not to go along with them."

"Mrs. Coble," the tutor said, "I think this kid is hurting. You know? Here's a serious, sensitive kid, telling you he'd like to take on some grown-up challenges, and you're giving him the message that he can't be trusted. Don't you understand how that hurts?"

"Oh," said Daisy.

"It undermines his self-esteem—don't you realize that?"

"Well, I guess you're right," said Daisy. She saw Donny suddenly from a whole new angle: his pathetically poor posture, that slouch so <u>forlorn</u> that his shoulders seemed about to meet his chin . . . oh, wasn't it awful being young? She'd had a miserable adolescence herself and had always sworn no child of hers would ever be that unhappy.

They let Donny stay out later, they didn't call ahead to see if the parties were supervised, and they were careful not to grill him about his evening. The tutor had set down so many rules! They were not allowed any questions at all about any aspect of school, nor were they to speak with his teachers. If a teacher had some complaint, she should phone Cal. Only one teacher disobeyed—the history teacher, Miss Evans. She

called one morning in February. "I'm a little concerned about Donny, Mrs. Coble."

"Oh, I'm sorry, Miss Evans, but Donny's tutor handles these things now . . . "

"I always deal directly with the parents. You are the parent," Miss Evans said, speaking very slowly and distinctly. "Now, here is the problem. Back when you were helping Donny with his homework, his grades rose from a D to a C, but now they've slipped back, and they're closer to an F."

"They are?"

"I think you should start overseeing his homework again."

"But Donny's tutor says . . . "

"It's nice that Donny has a tutor, but you should still be in charge of his homework. With you, he learned it. Then he passed his tests. With the tutor, well, it seems the tutor is more of a crutch. 'Donny,' I say, 'a quiz is coming up on Friday. Hadn't you better be listening instead of talking?' 'That's okay, Miss Evans,' he says. 'I have a tutor now.' Like a talisman![1] I really think you ought to take over, Mrs. Coble."

"I see," said Daisy. "Well, I'll think about that. Thank you for calling."

Hanging up, she felt a rush of anger at Donny. A talisman! For a talisman, she'd given up all luxuries, all that time with her daughter, her evenings at home!

She dialed Cal's number. He sounded muzzy. "I'm sorry if I woke you," she told him, "but Donny's history teacher just called. She says he isn't doing well."

"She should have dealt with me."

"She wants me to start supervising his homework again. His grades are slipping."

"Yes," said the tutor, "but you and I both

---

1. **talisman** (tăl′ĭs-mən): a thing believed to possess magic power or to bring good luck.

| WORDS TO KNOW | **forlorn** (fər-lôrn′) *adj.* appearing sad or lonely |

**1173**

**Less Proficient Readers**

**1** Use the following questions to make sure students understand Donny's problems in school.

- Why does the principal ask Donny's parents for a conference?

  **Possible Responses:** Donny cuts class, smokes, and has a disruptive attitude.

- What does the school principal recommend?

  **Possible Response:** Donny should visit a psychologist for testing.

- What does the psychologist recommend?

  **Possible Response:** Donny needs a tutor.

**Set a Purpose** Have students read on to find out if the tutor is able to help Donny deal with his problems.

**Students Acquiring English**

**2** Have a volunteer explain that Ping-Pong, or table tennis, is a game for two or four players played on a dark green table with a net, paddles, and a small, hard ball. Ask the volunteer to pantomime the game. Explain that Ping-Pong is popular in the United States, China, and other countries.

**Students Acquiring English**

**3** Explain that in this context grill means "to question closely."

### Literary Analysis: CHARACTER

**A** Ask students what they can conclude about Daisy when she switches from agreeing with Miss Evans to becoming angry with her.

**Possible Responses:** Daisy is as suggestible as she says Donny is; she seems to agree with whoever was the last person to speak.

### Reading Skills and Strategies: SYNTHESIZING

**B** Ask what students can infer from the story's repeated use of the word *controlling*.

**Possible Responses:** Miriam may have picked up the word from Cal; the ways people control each other, and themselves, may be a theme of the story.

### Active Reading

RECOGNIZING IMPORTANT DETAILS

**C** Ask students to identify important details that help them evaluate Cal's students.

**Possible Responses:** They look like hoodlums; one was knifed in a tavern; another was sent to boarding school in midterm; other students have been with Cal for years.

### Literary Analysis: THIRD-PERSON LIMITED POINT OF VIEW

**D** Have students identify the point of view from which this story is told. Ask them to cite clues that indicate this point of view.

**Possible Responses:** The story is told from the third-person limited point of view, focusing on Daisy. Interior monologues reveal Daisy's troubled thoughts and feelings about Donny.

*Portrait of Richard Freeman* (1974), Fairfield Porter. Oil on panel, Bowdoin College Museum of Art, Brunswick, Maine, anonymous gift (1986,74.1).

"I care about

the *whole* child—

his happiness,

his self-esteem.

The grades will come.

Just give them time."

1174

## Teaching Options

 **Mini Lesson** **Grammar**

### VERBS: PROGRESSIVE AND EMPHATIC FORMS

**Instruction** In addition to the six basic tenses, verbs have other special forms, including the progressive and emphatic forms. The progressive forms show ongoing action. They are made by using a form of *be* with the present participle; they always end in *-ing*.

- I am walking (present progressive)
- I was walking (past progressive)
- I will (shall) be walking (future progressive)
- I have been walking (present perfect progressive)
- I had been walking (past perfect progressive)
- I will (shall) have been walking (future perfect progressive)

The present tense and the past tense have emphatic forms that give special force to the verb. To form the present emphatic, use the auxiliary verb *do* or *does* with the present form of the main verb. To form the past emphatic, use the auxiliary verb *did* with the present form of the main verb.

- Donny has emotional problems. (present)
- Donny does have emotional problems. (present emphatic)

know there's more to it than mere grades, don't we? I care about the *whole* child—his happiness, his self-esteem. The grades will come. Just give them time."

When she hung up, it was Miss Evans she was angry at. What a narrow woman!

It was Cal this, Cal that, Cal says this, Cal and I did that. Cal lent Donny an album by the Who.[2] He took Donny and two other pupils to a rock concert. In March, when Donny began to talk endlessly on the phone with a girl named Miriam, Cal even let Miriam come to one of the tutoring sessions. Daisy was touched that Cal would grow so involved in Donny's life, but she was also a little hurt, because she had offered to have Miriam to dinner and Donny had refused. Now he asked them to drive her to Cal's house without a qualm.

This Miriam was an unappealing girl with blurry lipstick and masses of rough red hair. She wore a short, bulky jacket that would not have been out of place on a motorcycle. During the trip to Cal's she was silent, but coming back, she was more talkative. "What a neat guy, and what a house! All those kids hanging out, like a club. And the stereo playing rock . . . gosh, he's not like grown-up at all! Married and divorced and everything, but you'd think he was our own age."

"Mr. Beadle was married?" Daisy asked.

"Yeah, to this really controlling lady. She didn't understand him a bit."

"No, I guess not," Daisy said.

Spring came, and the students who hung around at Cal's drifted out to the basketball net above the garage. Sometimes, when Daisy and Matt arrived to pick up Donny, they'd find him there with the others—spiky and excited, jittering on his toes beneath the backboard. It was staying light much longer now, and the neighboring fence cast narrow bars across the bright grass. Loud music would be spilling from Cal's windows. Once it was the Who, which Daisy recognized from the time that Donny had bor-

rowed the album. "Teenage Wasteland,"[3] she said aloud, identifying the song, and Matt gave a short, dry laugh. "It certainly is," he said. He'd misunderstood; he thought she was commenting on the scene spread before them. In fact, she might have been. The players looked like hoodlums, even her son. Why, one of Cal's students had recently been knifed in a tavern. One had been shipped off to boarding school in midterm; two had been withdrawn by their parents. On the other hand, Donny had mentioned someone who'd been studying with Cal for five years. "Five years!" said Daisy. "Doesn't anyone ever stop needing him?"

Donny looked at her. Lately, whatever she said about Cal was read as criticism. "You're just feeling competitive," he said. "And controlling."

She bit her lip and said no more.

In April, the principal called to tell her that Donny had been expelled. There had been a locker check, and in Donny's locker they found five cans of beer and half a pack of cigarettes. With Donny's previous record, this offense meant expulsion.

Daisy gripped the receiver tightly and said, "Well, where is he now?"

"We've sent him home," said Mr. Lanham. "He's packed up all his belongings, and he's coming home on foot."

Daisy wondered what she would say to him. She felt him looming closer and closer, bringing this brand-new situation that no one had prepared her to handle. What other place would take him? Could they enter him in public school? What were the rules? She stood at the living room window, waiting for him to show up. Gradually, she realized that he was taking too long. She checked the clock. She stared up the street again.

---

2. **the Who:** a British rock group formed in the early 1960s.

3. **"Teenage Wasteland":** The song is actually titled "Baba O'Riley" and can be found on the album *Who's Next* (1971).

| WORDS TO KNOW | **qualm** (kwäm) *n.* a disturbing uneasiness or doubt |
| | **looming** (lōō'mǐng) *adj.* appearing to the mind in a large and threatening form **loom** *v.* |

1175

**A**

**1**

**3**

**C**

**2**

**D**

## Customizing Instruction

### Students Acquiring English
**1** Because there are no quotation marks here, students may not realize that Daisy, in her thoughts, is paraphrasing Donny's incessant talk about Cal.

### Less Proficient Readers
**2** Ask the following questions to make sure students understand what happens to Donny after he starts seeing the tutor.
• What effect does going to a tutor have on Donny?
**Possible Response:** It has a negative effect: his attitude does not improve, and he is even more distant from his parents, who seem to lose all control over him.
• Why is Donny expelled?
**Possible Response:** Five cans of beer and cigarettes were found in his locker.

**Set a Purpose** Have students finish reading the story to find out what happens to Donny after his expulsion.

• Daisy tried to help her son. *(past)*
• Daisy did try to help her son. *(past emphatic)*
**Exercise** Have students identify each progressive or emphatic verb form in the following sentences and name its tense.
1. Cal has been practicing psychology for years. *(present perfect progressive)*
2. Not until Donny's principal called a conference did Daisy supervise her son's homework. *(past emphatic)*
3. Donny had been skipping classes for some

time. *(past perfect progressive)*
4. Often, school counselors do help students. *(present emphatic)*
5. Cal is working with Donny. *(present progressive)*

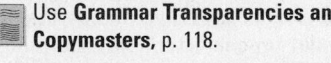 Use **Grammar Transparencies and Copymasters**, p. 118.

 Use McDougal Littell's *Language Network,* Chapter 4, for more instruction in verb forms.

**Reading Skills and Strategies: HYPOTHESIZING**

**A** Donny's father, Matt, plays almost no active role in the story. Invite students to theorize about his role in Donny's problems.

**Possible Response:** His apparent lack of involvement may be a partial cause of Donny's alienation.

**Reading Skills and Strategies: EVALUATING**

**B** Ask students what they think of Cal's handling of the situation.

**Possible Responses:** He is handling it well, giving Daisy time to cool off; he is exacerbating the problem by interfering; he should have called Daisy right away because, as Donny's parent, she should be handling the situation.

**Reading Skills and Strategies: MAKING JUDGMENTS**

**C** Ask students whether they believe Donny's version of events. Why or why not?

**Possible Responses:** No, Donny's refusal to name the boy makes his story seem untrue. Yes, Donny refuses to name the boy because he doesn't want to be a snitch.

**Literary Analysis**

> CHARACTER: PROTAGONIST
> AND ANTAGONIST

**D** Who is the "good guy" and who is the "bad guy" in the debate over Donny's schooling?

**Possible Response:** The author seems to intend Daisy to be the protagonist and Cal the antagonist.

**A** When an hour had passed, she phoned the school. Mr. Lanham's secretary answered and told her in a grave, sympathetic voice that yes, Donny Coble had most definitely gone home. Daisy called her husband. He was out of the office. She went back to the window and thought awhile, and then she called Donny's tutor.

"Donny's been expelled from school," she said, "and now I don't know where he's gone. I wonder if you've heard from him?"

There was a long silence. "Donny's with me, Mrs. Coble," he finally said.

"With you? How'd he get there?"

"He hailed a cab, and I paid the driver."

"Could I speak to him, please?"

There was another silence. "Maybe it'd be better if we had a conference," Cal said.

**B** "I don't *want* a conference. I've been standing at the window picturing him dead or kidnapped or something, and now you tell me you want a—"

"Donny is very, very upset. Understandably so," said Cal. "Believe me, Mrs. Coble, this is not what it seems. Have you asked Donny's side of the story?"

"Well, of course not, how could I? He went running off to you instead."

"Because he didn't feel he'd be listened to."

"But I haven't even—"

"Why don't you come out and talk? The three of us," said Cal, "will try to get this thing in perspective."

"Well, all right," Daisy said. But she wasn't as reluctant as she sounded. Already, she felt soothed by the calm way Cal was taking this.

Cal answered the doorbell at once. He said, "Hi, there," and led her into the dining room.

Donny sat slumped in a chair, chewing the knuckle of one thumb. "Hello, Donny," Daisy said. He flicked his eyes in her direction.

"Sit here, Mrs. Coble," said Cal, placing her opposite Donny. He himself remained standing, restlessly pacing. "So," he said.

Daisy stole a look at Donny. His lips were swollen, as if he'd been crying.

"You know," Cal told Daisy, "I kind of expected something like this. That's a very <u>punitive</u> school you've got him in—you realize that. And any half-decent lawyer will tell you they've violated his civil rights. Locker checks! Where's their search warrant?"

"But if the rule is—" Daisy said.

"Well, anyhow, let him tell you his side."

She looked at Donny. He said, "It wasn't my fault. I promise."

"They said your locker was full of beer."

"It was a put-up job! See, there's this guy that doesn't like me. He put all these beers in my locker and started a rumor going, so Mr. Lanham ordered a locker check."

"What was the boy's *name*?" Daisy asked.

"Huh?"

"Mrs. Coble, take my word, the situation is not so unusual," Cal said. "You can't imagine how <u>vindictive</u> kids can be sometimes."

"What was the boy's name," said Daisy, "so that I can ask Mr. Lanham if that's who suggested he run a locker check."

"You don't believe me," Donny said.

"And how'd this boy get your combination in the first place?"

"Frankly," said Cal, "I wouldn't be surprised to learn the school was in on it. Any kid that

> He did his assignments, and he earned average grades, but he gathered no friends, joined no clubs. There was something exhausted and defeated about him.

WORDS TO KNOW
**punitive** (pyōō′nĭ-tĭv) *adj.* punishing or having to do with punishment
**vindictive** (vĭn-dĭk′tĭv) *adj.* wanting revenge; bearing a grudge

1176

---

## Teaching Options

 **Mini Lesson** ## Speaking and Listening

**ROLE-PLAYING**

**Instruction** Students playing the roles of characters from a work of fiction should reread the work, taking notes that reflect their observations, interpretations, and questions about the characters. Their role-playing may include lines of dialogue from the work, as well as lines invented by the students that remain "in character." Brainstorming and rehearsing can greatly enhance the realism and effectiveness of the role-playing.

**Present** Invite groups of three to role-play the confrontation on pages 1176–1177 among Daisy, Donny, and Cal. Encourage students to bring out thoughts and emotions that they feel are under the surface of the characters. Students will need to make choices about verbal and nonverbal performance techniques, based on their interpretations of the text.

**BLOCK SCHEDULING** This activity is particularly well-suited for longer class periods.

marches to a different drummer,[4] why, they'd just love an excuse to get rid of him. The school is where I lay the blame."

"Doesn't *Donny* ever get blamed?"

"Now, Mrs. Coble, you heard what he—"

"Forget it," Donny told Cal. "You can see she doesn't trust me."

Daisy drew in a breath to say that of course she trusted him—a reflex. But she knew that bold-faced, wide-eyed look of Donny's. He had worn that look when he was small, denying some petty misdeed with the evidence plain as day all around him. Still, it was hard for her to accuse him outright. She temporized and said, "The only thing I'm sure of is that they've kicked you out of school, and now I don't know what we're going to do."

"We'll fight it," said Cal.

"We can't. Even you must see we can't."

"I could apply to Brantly," Donny said.

Cal stopped his pacing to beam down at him. "Brantly! Yes. They're really onto where a kid is coming from, at Brantly. Why, *I* could get you into Brantly. I work with a lot of their students."

Daisy had never heard of Brantly, but already she didn't like it. And she didn't like Cal's smile, which struck her now as feverish and avid—a smile of hunger.

On the fifteenth of April, they entered Donny in a public school, and they stopped his tutoring sessions. Donny fought both decisions bitterly. Cal, surprisingly enough, did not object. He admitted he'd made no headway with Donny and said it was because Donny was emotionally disturbed.

Donny went to his new school every morning, plodding off alone with his head down. He did his assignments, and he earned average grades, but he gathered no friends, joined no clubs. There was

something exhausted and defeated about him.

The first week in June, during final exams, Donny vanished. He simply didn't come home one afternoon, and no one at school remembered seeing him. The police were reassuring, and for the first few days, they worked hard. They combed Donny's sad, messy room for clues; they visited Miriam and Cal. But then they started talking about the number of kids who ran away every year. Hundreds, just in this city. "He'll show up, if he wants to," they said. "If he doesn't, he won't."

Evidently, Donny didn't want to.

It's been three months now and still no word. Matt and Daisy still look for him in every crowd of awkward, heartbreaking teenage boys. Every time the phone rings, they imagine it might be Donny. Both parents have aged. Donny's sister seems to be staying away from home as much as possible.

At night, Daisy lies awake and goes over Donny's life. She is trying to figure out what went wrong, where they made their first mistake. Often, she finds herself blaming Cal, although she knows he didn't begin it. Then at other times she excuses him, for without him, Donny might have left earlier. Who really knows? In the end, she can only sigh and search for a cooler spot on the pillow. As she falls asleep, she occasionally glimpses something in the corner of her vision. It's something fleet[5] and round, a ball—a basketball. It flies up, it sinks through the hoop, descends, lands in a yard littered with last year's leaves and striped with bars of sunlight as white as bones, bleached and parched and cleanly picked. ❖ [1]

---

4. **marches to a different drummer:** thinks and acts independently; a reference to Henry David Thoreau's famous quotation (page 390).

5. **fleet:** swiftly moving; fast.

WORDS TO KNOW
**temporize** (tĕm′pə-rīz′) *v.* to avoid immediate action or making a decision in order to gain time

1177

## Customizing Instruction

**Less Proficient Readers**
[1] Have students summarize what happened to Donny after he was expelled.
**Possible Response:** He was sent to a public school, and then he ran away from home.

**Gifted and Talented**
Invite students to write a short story based on the characters and events of "Teenage Wasteland," focusing on a character other than Daisy.

✓**Assessment** **Informal Assessment**

**SELF-ASSESSMENT** Students can assess their own understanding of the story by responding to the following questions.
• Did you take sides in this story? Which side did you take and why? Do you understand each character's perspective?
• Did you have difficulty following any of the events or ideas in the story?
• What else do you wish you knew about the characters and their lives?
• What do you think are the strengths and weaknesses of Anne Tyler's crafting of the story?

Do you think the ending diminishes or enhances her purpose for writing the story?
**RUBRIC**
**3 Full Accomplishment** Student feels confident answering all the questions and has definite opinions about and reactions to the story.
**2 Substantial Accomplishment** Student has something to say in response to each question, but some opinions are not well-reasoned.
**1 Little or Partial Accomplishment** Student has difficulty answering the questions and formulating opinions.

## Connect to the Literature

**1. What Do You Think?**
Responses will vary. Some students may find Donny's running away from home inevitable given his alienation from his family.

**Comprehension Check**
- She checks his assignments daily.
- Beer and cigarettes are found in his locker.
- He runs away from home.

 Use Selection Quiz
**Unit Seven Resource Book,** p. 53.

## Think Critically

**2.** Possible Responses: Donny will return home because he is too helpless to survive on his own; Donny will not return but will succumb to the perils of street life; Donny will establish an independent life that will force him to mature.

**3.** Possible Responses: Daisy and Matt for being spineless and ineffectual; Donny for being irresponsible and lazy; Cal for being a bad influence

**4.** Responses will vary. Some students may find Daisy sympathetic because she deeply wants to help her son but doesn't know how; other students may find Donny sympathetic because he desperately needs to find himself.

**5.** Responses will vary. Some students may say that Daisy and Matt should have trusted their own parental instincts in dealing with Donny.

**6.** Responses will vary. Some students may state that Donny seems to lack basic study skills—skills he might have acquired in a highly structured curriculum.

## Literary Analysis

**Protagonist and Antagonist** Students are likely to suggest Daisy as protagonist and Cal as antagonist; students may also suggest Donny as either protagonist or antagonist. Opinions will vary as to whether Daisy changes. Though she "fires" Cal, she still does not understand how she failed Donny.

---

## Connect to the Literature

**1. What Do You Think?**
How did you react to Donny's running away? Share your comments with your classmates.

**Comprehension Check**
- After the first conference with the principal, what does Daisy do at his suggestion?
- Why is Donny expelled from school?
- What does Donny do at the end of the story?

## Think Critically

**2.** What do you think will happen to Donny?

**3.** Who or what do you think is most responsible for Donny's running away?

 **THINK ABOUT**
- how Daisy tries to help him
- what Cal says and does
- Daisy's question, "Doesn't Donny ever get blamed?" (page 1177)

**4.** With whom do you sympathize more, Daisy or Donny? Explain why.

**5.** **ACTIVE READING** **RECOGNIZING IMPORTANT DETAILS**
Consider the pieces of advice that Daisy and Matt follow, as listed in your **READER'S NOTEBOOK.** Do you think that Daisy and Matt could have handled the situation better if they had done something differently? Explain your opinion.

**6.** From the **tone** of this story, do you think Anne Tyler takes sides in the academic reform debate? Support your opinion.

## Extend Interpretations

**7.** **Critic's Corner** Anne Tyler has said that she uses the family unit to show "how people manage to endure together—how they grate against each other, adjust, intrude, and protect themselves from intrusions, give up, and start all over again in the morning." How effectively do you think Tyler has portrayed the family in "Teenage Wasteland"?

**8.** **Comparing Texts** Compare "Teenage Wasteland" to another story of childhood troubles and parental guilt, "I Stand Here Ironing" (page 806). Which one do you think is sadder? Which mother do you think faces the greater difficulty in finding the right way to raise her child?

**9.** **Connect to Life** How would you describe a good parent?

---

## Literary Analysis

**PROTAGONIST AND ANTAGONIST** The **protagonist** is the main character in a narrative or drama, usually the one with whom the audience identifies. The **antagonist** is usually the principal character in opposition to the protagonist. The antagonist can also be a force of nature. Both of these characters are involved in a story's central conflict, and after the climax, the protagonist often has a change in feelings, personality, or outlook.

**Cooperative Learning Activity** With a small group of classmates, share your views about which character is the protagonist and which is the antagonist in "Teenage Wasteland." Give specific reasons for your answers. Discuss whether the protagonist changes by the end of the story. If so, how? If not, what prevents that character from changing? Share your opinions with other pairs of students.

---

## Extend Interpretations

**Critic's Corner** Responses will vary. Some students may state that Tyler has dealt honestly and realistically with family conflicts and the problems of communication.

**Comparing Texts** Responses will vary. Some students will find "Teenage Wasteland" the sadder story because Donny, unlike Emily, may never adjust to life. Donny's mother faces the greater difficulty because she is less mature and lacks confidence.

**Connect to Life** Responses will vary. Some students may state that a good parent helps children acquire a sense of responsibility for their own actions.

## Writing Options

**1. Rewritten Episode** Retell an episode from this story—such as the meeting between Donny and his mother after his expulsion from school—from Donny's point of view.

**2. Persuasive Speech** Draft a persuasive speech that could be delivered to the PTA, explaining how much control parents should exert over their teenage children. Use examples from the story and from your own experience as support. Place this piece in your **Working Portfolio**.

**Writing Handbook**
See page 1285: Persuasive Writing.

## Activities & Explorations

**Dramatic Scene** With a small group, act out one of the scenes from this story or imagine a related scene. For example, you might choose to show the first conversation between Daisy and the principal or Cal's interaction with his students. Stage your scene for your classmates.

## Vocabulary in Action

**EXERCISE: SYNONYMS AND ANTONYMS** Identify each pair of words by writing "Synonyms" or "Antonyms."

1. temporize–delay
2. punitive–forgiving
3. shamble–stride
4. forlorn–sad
5. qualm–confidence
6. morass–predicament
7. subdued–excited
8. amiably–agreeably
9. looming–menacing
10. vindictive–spiteful

**Building Vocabulary**
One of the Words to Know, *looming,* has two meanings. For an in-depth lesson on homophones, homographs, and homonyms, see page 728.

## Anne Tyler
### 1941–

**Other Works**
*Celestial Navigation*
*Earthly Possessions*
*Saint Maybe*
*Ladder of Years*
*Patchwork Planet*

**Nomadic Childhood** Shy, quiet, and keenly observant, Anne Tyler is the oldest of four children of Quaker parents. On a quest for the ideal community, her family moved frequently, living in several different Quaker communes throughout the Midwest and South. As Tyler later explained, this experience taught her to "look at the normal world with a certain amount of distance and surprise." This unusual point of view continues to influence her fiction.

**Popular Novelist** Tyler began writing while she was a student at Duke University, where she studied under the novelist Reynolds Price. In 1963 she married, and a few years later began both a family and a serious writing career. She did not receive national recognition until the publication of her sixth novel, *Searching for Caleb*, in 1976. Tyler first hit the bestseller list in 1982 with *Dinner at the Homesick Restaurant.* In 1988 another best-selling novel, *The Accidental Tourist,* was made into a movie, and a year later Tyler won a Pulitzer Prize for *Breathing Lessons.*

**Her Fictional Characters** In her more than 14 novels and 40 short stories, Tyler looks at the loneliness and isolation of middle-class family life. Many of her characters are comical and quirky—like the character who shelves her groceries in alphabetical order in *The Accidental Tourist.* Tyler portrays these characters with sympathy and gentle irony. She has said that the real heroes of her books are "first the ones who manage to endure and second the ones who are somehow able to grant other people the privacy of the space around them and yet still produce some warmth."

TEENAGE WASTELAND  **1179**

## Writing Options

**1. Rewritten Episode To help students get started,** have them form small groups to list details about Donny and about the particular episode they are rewriting.

**2. Persuasive Speech** Remind students to begin with an introduction that attracts listeners, such as a question, an anecdote, or a surprising statistic.

## Activities & Explorations

**Dramatic Scene** Students can work cooperatively, dividing up the responsibilities of writing, acting, and directing within their groups. Students should create an entertaining scene that is true to the characters and demonstrates a keen understanding of the story.

## Vocabulary in Action

1. Synonyms
2. Antonyms
3. Antonyms
4. Synonyms
5. Antonyms
6. Synonyms
7. Antonyms
8. Synonyms
9. Synonyms
10. Synonyms

---

## Mini Lesson  Speaking And Listening

**ANALYZING A PERFORMANCE REVIEW**
**Instruction** Working with several classmates, select a scene from Anne Tyler's short story "Teenage Wasteland." As the groups present their performance to the class, have the other class members write a review of the performance.
**Prepare** Tell students the following criteria may be used to analyze a written review of a performance.

- identifies its subject at the beginning
- opens with a general opinion
- includes enough facts, examples, and specifics to support the general opinion
- displays logical organization
- quickly establishes a tone

**Present** Have several students share their reviews with the class. Then have them compare their responses with the other reviewers'.

# Separating

*Short Story by* JOHN UPDIKE

## Objectives

1. understand and appreciate a **short story** (Literary Analysis)
2. understand **dramatic irony** (Literary Analysis)
3. **make predictions** (Active Reading)

## Summary

Joan and Richard Maple have decided to separate, and Joan insists they inform their four children individually when the whole family is home at the start of the summer. In the meantime, Richard spends his time doing repairs around the house, getting it ready for his departure. He and Joan have agreed they will inform the children after a dinner celebrating their daughter Judith's return from England. However, at the dinner Richard starts crying. When the children ask why, Joan tells them about the impending separation. Only John, the younger son, seems upset. When he and his father take a walk, John confides his unhappiness, not just with the separation, but with school as well. Richard, feeling selfish because he hadn't noticed John's misery, promises to help. He later tells his older son, Dickie, who was away at a concert. It becomes clear that Richard wants to marry someone else, although he has not told this to the children. Dickie asks why all this has happened, and Richard thinks that he really has forgotten why.

## Thematic Link

Richard and Joan Maple's decision to separate leads to **disintegration** of their family life.

### 5-Minute Warm-Up

**Daily
Language
SkillBuilder**

Have students **proofread** the display sentences on page 1069k and write them correctly. The sentences also appear on Transparency 33 of **Grammar Transparencies and Copymasters.**

## Connect to Your Life

**Breaking Ties** About half the marriages in the United States end in divorce. Before deciding to divorce, however, many married couples first agree to separate, or stop living together. What do you think are some reasons that married couples separate? How do you think a wife and husband feel once they have decided to separate? If they have children, how do you think the children feel? Jot down your responses to these questions, drawing from friends' experiences or your own.

## Build Background

**A Family Saga** You are about to read a story about marital separation by John Updike, one of America's most acclaimed authors. Much of his writing concerns upper-middle-class people caught in what Updike has called "the despair of the daily." These characters lose touch with one another and, in doing so, put a strain on their marriages and their families. "Separating" is one in a series of 17 stories the author wrote about Joan and Richard Maple, which appear in his collection *Too Far To Go* (published in 1979). The Maples stories, written over a period of 23 years, depict the couple's youthful marriage in the 1950s, the birth and growth of four children, their separation after 21 years of marriage, and their eventual divorce. Though the stories depict the breakup of a marriage, they still chronicle lives "in many ways happy," according to Updike. "That a marriage fails is less than ideal; but all things end under heaven. . . . The moral of these stories is that all blessings are mixed."

| WORDS TO KNOW Vocabulary Preview | | |
|---|---|---|
| congruous | minutiae | precipitous |
| diaphanous | mollified | stiltedly |
| dissolution | opulent | succulent |
| elemental | palpable | tersely |
| garrulously | permeable | tumultuous |

## Focus Your Reading

**LITERARY ANALYSIS** **DRAMATIC IRONY** A stylistic element in this story is the use of dramatic irony. **Dramatic irony** occurs when a reader knows more about a situation than the story's characters know. In the beginning of "Separating," note the information you learn about the Maples that is still kept hidden from their children.

**ACTIVE READING** **MAKING PREDICTIONS** **Making predictions** involves using clues in a story and prior knowledge about a situation to predict events that might occur. In "Separating," try to predict the characters' reactions as the plot unfolds.

**READER'S NOTEBOOK** Read pages 1181 to 1182 until the narrative break, indicated by extra space in the text. Then create a questionnaire form like the one shown, and fill it in. As you continue reading, revise your predictions as necessary.

1. What do you already know about the children of divorce?

2. What do you know about the Maples's children?

3. What is Joan and Richard's strategy for breaking the news of their decision?

4. What might happen as a result of their strategy?

## LESSON RESOURCES

**UNIT SEVEN RESOURCE BOOK,**
pp. 54–58

**ASSESSMENT RESOURCES**
**Formal Assessment,**
pp. 223–224
**Teacher's Guide to Assessment and Portfolio Use**
**Test Generator**

**SKILLS TRANSPARENCIES AND COPYMASTERS**
**Reading and Critical Thinking**
• Predicting Outcomes, T2 (for Active Reading, p. 1180)

**Grammar**
• Advanced Sentences: Sentence Openers, C174 (for Mini Lesson, p. 1183)
• Advanced Sentences: Periodic Sentences, C175 (for Mini Lesson, p. 1193)
**Vocabulary**
• Context Clues, C18 (for Mini Lesson, p. 1181)
**Communications**
• Verbal Strategies, T14 (for Mini Lesson, p. 1185)
• Nonverbal Strategies, T15 (for Mini Lesson, p. 1185)

**INTEGRATED TECHNOLOGY**
**Audio Library**
**Visit our website:**
www.mcdougallittell.com

# S E P A R A T I N G

J O H N   U P D I K E

*The* day was fair. Brilliant. All that June the weather had mocked the Maples' internal misery with solid sunlight—golden shafts and cascades of green in which their conversations had wormed unseeing, their sad murmuring selves the only stain in Nature. Usually by this time of the year they had acquired tans; but when they met their elder daughter's plane on her return from a year in England they were almost as pale as she, though Judith was too dazzled by the sunny <u>opulent</u> jumble of her native land to notice. They did not spoil her homecoming by telling her immediately. Wait a few days, let her recover from jet lag, had been one of their formulations, in that string of gray dialogues—over coffee, over cocktails, over Cointreau[1]—that had shaped the strategy of their <u>dissolution</u>, while the earth performed its annual stunt of renewal unnoticed beyond their closed windows. Richard had thought to leave at Easter; Joan had insisted they wait until the four children were at last assembled, with all exams passed and ceremonies attended, and the bauble[2] of summer to console them. So he had drudged away, in love, in dread, repairing screens, getting the mowers sharpened, rolling and patching their new tennis court.

The court, clay, had come through its first winter pitted and wind-swept bare of redcoat. Years ago the Maples had observed how often, among their friends, divorce followed a dramatic home improvement, as if the marriage were making one last effort to live; their own worst crisis had come amid the plaster dust and exposed plumbing of a kitchen renovation. Yet, a summer ago, as canary-yellow bulldozers gaily churned a grassy, daisy-dotted knoll into a muddy plateau, and a crew of pigtailed young men raked and tamped clay into a plane, this transformation did not strike them as ominous, but festive in its

---

1. **Cointreau** (kwăn-trō'): brand name of an expensive, orange-flavored, syrupy alcoholic beverage.
2. **bauble:** a bright, showy thing.

WORDS TO KNOW

**opulent** (ŏp'yo lont) *adj.* characterized by abundance, extravagance, or wealth
**dissolution** (dĭs'ə-lōō'shən) *n.* a breaking up; disintegration

**1181**

---

### Reading Skills and Strategies:
**PREVIEW**

Tell students that the main character in this story is a husband and father who must tell his children some bad news. As students read the story, tell them to consider what he says, does, and thinks.

### Active Reading
**MAKING PREDICTIONS**

 Ask students what they can predict Richard's state of mind will be when he tells the children about the separation.

**Possible Response:** He will find it difficult to remain calm and composed.

**B** Ask students what Joan's remark suggests about the real reason for their separation.

**Possible Response:** Perhaps Richard wants the separation so that he can have the freedom to see someone else.

Use **Unit Seven Resource Book**, p. 55 for more practice.

### Literary Analysis   **DRAMATIC IRONY**

Remind students that dramatic irony occurs when the reader knows more than one or more characters do. Ask students how the readers' knowledge of the impending separation affects their involvement in the story.

**Possible Responses:** Readers understand the deeper significance of Richard's actions; they share his dread of telling the children and his anticipation of their reactions to the news; they realize how the truth will shatter the children's innocence and trust.

Use **Unit Seven Resource Book**, p. 56 for more practice.

impudence; their marriage could rend the earth for fun. The next spring, waking each day at dawn to a sliding sensation as if the bed were being tipped, Richard found the barren tennis court—its net and tapes still rolled in the barn—an environment <u>congruous</u> with his mood of purposeful desolation, and the crumbling of handfuls of clay into cracks and holes (dogs had frolicked on the court in a thaw; rivulets had eroded trenches) an activity suitably <u>elemental</u> and interminable. In his sealed heart he hoped the day would never come.

Now it was here. A Friday. Judith was reacclimated; all four children were assembled, before jobs and camps and visits again scattered them. Joan thought they should be told one by one. Richard was for making an announcement at the table. She said, "I think just making an announcement is a cop-out. They'll start quarrelling and playing to each other instead of focusing. They're each individuals, you know, not just some corporate obstacle to your freedom."

"O.K., O.K. I agree." Joan's plan was exact. That evening, they were giving Judith a belated welcome-home dinner, of lobster and champagne. Then, the party over, they, the two of them, who nineteen years before would push her in a baby carriage along Fifth Avenue to Washington Square,[3] were to walk her out of the house, to the bridge across the salt creek, and tell her, swearing her to secrecy. Then Richard Jr., who was going directly from work to a rock concert in Boston, would be told, either late when he returned on the train or early Saturday morning before he went off to his job; he was seventeen and employed as one of a golf-course maintenance crew. Then the two younger children, John and Margaret, could, as the morning wore on, be informed.

"Mopped up, as it were," Richard said.

"Do you have any better plan? That leaves you the rest of Saturday to answer any questions, pack, and make your wonderful departure."

"No," he said, meaning he had no better plan, and agreed to hers, though to him it showed an edge of false order, a hidden plea for control, like Joan's long chore lists and financial accountings and, in the days when he first knew her, her too-copious lecture notes. Her plan turned one hurdle for him into four—four knife-sharp walls, each with a sheer blind drop on the other side.

All spring he had moved through a world of insides and outsides, of barriers and partitions. He and Joan stood as a thin barrier between the children and the truth. Each moment was a partition, with the past on one side and the future on the other, a future containing this unthinkable *now*. Beyond four knifelike walls a new life for him waited vaguely. His skull cupped a secret, a white face, a face both frightened and soothing, both strange and known, that he wanted to shield from tears, which he felt all about him, solid as the sunlight. So haunted, he had become obsessed with battening down the house against his absence, replacing screens and sash cords, hinges and latches—a Houdini[4] making things snug before his escape.

*The* lock. He had still to replace a lock on one of the doors of the screened porch. The task, like most such, proved more difficult than he had imagined. The old lock, aluminum frozen by corrosion, had been deliberately rendered obsolete by manufacturers. Three hardware stores had nothing that even approximately matched the mortised hole its removal (surprisingly easy) left. Another hole had to be gouged, with bits too small and saws too big, and the old hole fitted with a block of wood—the chisels dull, the saw rusty, his fingers thick with lack of sleep.

---

3. **Washington Square:** a fashionable area of Manhattan, in New York City.

4. **Houdini:** Harry Houdini (1874–1926), a famous American magician and escape artist.

| WORDS TO KNOW | |
|---|---|
| **congruous** (kŏng′grōō-əs) *adj.* fitting; suitable |
| **elemental** (ĕl′ə-mĕn′tl) *adj.* basic; like a natural force |

**1182**

### BLOCK SCHEDULING: MANAGING TIME

**If your schedule requires that you cover the lesson objectives in a shorter time, use . . .**
- Preparing to Read, p. 1180
- Thinking Through the Literature, p. 1191
- Vocabulary in Action, p. 1192

**If you want to take advantage of longer class time, use . . .**
- TE Teaching Options: Preteaching Vocabulary, p. 1181; Speaking and Listening, p. 1185; Viewing and Representing, p. 1186; Informal Assessment, p. 1187; Workplace Link, p. 1188; Standardized Test Practice, p. 1190.
- Choices & Challenges, p. 1192

Frank Wallace (1953),
Fairfield Porter. Oil on
canvas, 40″ × 30″,
Parrish Art Museum,
Southampton, New
York, gift of the Estate of
Fairfield Porter
(1980.10.59), photo
by Jim Strong.

*Each
moment
was a
partition,
with the
past on
one side
and the future on the other.*

**Less Proficient Readers**

**1** Help students speculate about what Richard's secret "white face" might represent.

**Possible Responses:** It might be the face of his lover for whom Richard is leaving his marriage. It might represent a part of his own spirit.

**Gifted and Talented**

Ask students to read the story to find descriptions that exemplify John Updike's concern for the "minutiae" of sensory perceptions. Have them discuss the effectiveness of these descriptions.

---

 **Grammar**
Mini Lesson

**ADVANCED SENTENCES: SENTENCE OPENERS**

**Instruction** Remind students that they're expected to compose increasingly more involved sentences. One method of varying sentences is to begin them in different ways: for example, with a subordinate clause, a single word modifier, or a phrase. Display the following examples:

• On Friday night at 1:00 AM, Richard planned to pick up his son and tell him the news. (*series of prepositional phrases*)

• When Richard thought of telling his children about the separation, he was filled with anxiety. (*subordinate clause*)

• Calmly, Joan explained the separation. (*single-word modifier*)

**Activity** Ask students to use these types of openers to vary the following sentences.

**1.** The tennis court, when it was first built, improved the estate.

**2.** Young laborers patiently tapped the clay into place.

**3.** Rain has eroded channels in the smoothness of the clay.

 Use **Grammar Transparencies and Copymasters,** p. 174.

 Use McDougal Littell's *Language Network,* Chapter 15, for more instruction in sentence composing.

## Reading and Analyzing

**Reading Skills and Strategies: ANALYZING**

**A** Have students discuss how crying shows Richard's "superior gift of strategy."

**Possible Responses:** By crying, he alerts the children that something is up. He is telling them all at once, as he had wanted to all along. His tears also make him seem more pathetic than Joan and might elicit sympathy from the children.

**Literary Analysis: POINT OF VIEW**

**B** Explain that the narration focuses on Richard's observations, thoughts, and feelings. Ask students what Richard's "twisted vision" of events in this passage reveals about his emotional state.

**Possible Responses:** He feels upset, mournful, guilty. He dreads his children's reactions. He's relieved to release the secret.

**Reading Skills and Strategies: CLARIFYING**

**C** Ask students what Richard's words reveal about what has happened to his marriage.

**Possible Responses:** Joan and he simply fell out of love. He doesn't mention any specific reason for the breakup.

**Active Reading**

**MAKING PREDICTIONS**

**D** Ask students to predict what John might do.

**Possible Response:** John, who is becoming very upset, might leave the dinner table abruptly or do something irrational.

---

The sun poured down, beyond the porch, on a world of neglect. The bushes already needed pruning, the windward side of the house was shedding flakes of paint, rain would get in when he was gone, insects, rot, death. His family, all those he would lose, filtered through the edges of his awareness as he struggled with screw holes, splinters, opaque instructions, <u>minutiae</u> of metal.

Judith sat on the porch, a princess returned from exile. She regaled them with stories of fuel shortages, of bomb scares in the Underground,[5] of Pakistani workmen loudly lusting after her as she walked past on her way to dance school. Joan came and went, in and out of the house, calmer than she should have been, praising his struggles with the lock as if this were one more and not the last of their long succession of shared chores. The younger of his sons for a few minutes held the rickety screen door while his father clumsily hammered and chiseled, each blow a kind of sob in Richard's ears. His younger daughter, having been at a slumber party, slept on the porch hammock through all the noise—heavy and pink, trusting and forsaken. Time, like the sunlight, continued relentlessly; the sunlight slowly slanted. Today was one of the longest days. The lock clicked, worked. He was through. He had a drink; he drank it on the porch, listening to his daughter. "It was so sweet," she was saying, "during the worst of it, how all the butchers and bakery shops kept open by candlelight. They're all so plucky and cute. From the papers, things sounded so much worse here—people shooting people in gas lines, and everybody freezing."

Richard asked her, "Do you still want to live in England forever?" *Forever*: the concept, now a reality upon him, pressed and scratched at the back of his throat.

"No," Judith confessed, turning her oval face to him, its eyes still childishly far apart, but the lips set as over something <u>succulent</u> and satisfactory. "I was anxious to come home. I'm an American." She was a woman. They had raised her; he and Joan had endured together to raise her, alone of the four. The others had still some raising left in them. Yet it was the thought of telling Judith—the image of her, their first baby, walking between them arm in arm to the bridge —that broke him. The partition between his face and the tears broke. Richard sat down to the celebratory meal with the back of his throat aching; the champagne, the lobster seemed phases of sunshine; he saw them and tasted them through tears. He blinked, swallowed, croakily joked about hay fever. The tears would not stop leaking through; they came not through a hole that could be plugged but through a <u>permeable</u> spot in a membrane, steadily, purely, endlessly, fruitfully. They became, his tears, a shield for himself against these others—their faces, the fact of their assembly, a last time as innocents, at a table where he sat the last time as head. Tears dropped from his nose as he broke the lobster's back; salt flavored his champagne as he sipped it; the raw clench at the back of his throat was delicious. He could not help himself.

His children tried to ignore his tears. Judith, on his right, lit a cigarette, gazed upward in the direction of her too energetic, too sophisticated exhalation; on her other side, John earnestly bent his face to the extraction of the last morsels— legs, tail segments—from the scarlet corpse. Joan, at the opposite end of the table, glanced at him surprised, her reproach displaced by a quick grimace, of forgiveness, or of salute to his superior gift of strategy. Between them, Margaret, no longer called Bean, thirteen and large for her age, gazed from the other side of his pane of tears as if into a shopwindow at something she coveted— at her father, a crystalline heap of splinters and

---

5. **the Underground:** London's subway system.

| WORDS | **minutiae** (mǐ-nōō′shē-ē′) *n.* tiny elements, details, or parts |
| TO | **succulent** (sŭk′yə-lənt) *adj.* tasty; delicious |
| KNOW | **permeable** (pûr′mē-ə-bəl) *adj.* able to be passed through |

memories. It was not she, however, but John who, in the kitchen, as they cleared the plates and carapaces[6] away, asked Joan the question: "*Why is Daddy crying?*"

Richard heard the question but not the murmured answer. Then he heard Bean cry, "Oh, no-oh!"—the faintly dramatized exclamation of one who had long expected it.

John returned to the table carrying a bowl of
1 salad. He nodded tersely at his father and his lips shaped the conspiratorial words "She told."

"Told what?" Richard asked aloud, insanely.

The boy sat down as if to rebuke his father's distraction with the example of his own good manners. He said quietly, "The separation."

Joan and Margaret returned; the child, in
3 Richard's twisted vision, seemed diminished in size, and relieved, relieved to have had the bogie-
2 man at last proved real. He called out to her—the distances at the table had grown immense—"You knew, you always knew," but the clenching at the back of his throat prevented him from making sense of it. From afar he heard Joan talking, levelly, sensibly, reciting what they had prepared: it was a separation for the summer, an experiment. She and Daddy both agreed it would be good for them; they needed space and time to think; they liked each other but did not make each other happy enough, somehow.

Judith, imitating her mother's factual tone, but in her youth off-key, too cool, said, "I think it's silly. You should either live together or get divorced."

Richard's crying, like a wave that has crested and crashed, had become tumultuous; but it was overtopped by another tumult, for John, who had been so reserved, now grew larger and larger at the table. Perhaps his younger sister's being credited with knowing set him off. "Why didn't you *tell* us?" he asked, in a large round voice quite unlike his own. "You should have *told* us you weren't getting along."

Richard was startled into attempting to force words through his tears. "We *do* get along, that's the trouble, so it doesn't show even to us—" C
*That we do not love each other* was the rest of the sentence; he couldn't finish it.

Joan finished for him, in her style. "And we've always, *especially,* loved our children."

John was not mollified. "What do you care about *us?*" he boomed. "We're just little things you *had.*" His sisters' laughing forced a laugh from him, which he turned hard and parodistic[7]: D

6. **carapaces** (kăr′ə-pā′səz): hard outer coverings or shells of animals such as lobsters.

7. **parodistic:** mocking.

*The Table* (1970), Fairfield Porter. Collection of Elizabeth Feld.

WORDS TO KNOW

**tersely** (tûrs′lē) *adv.* briefly

**tumultuous** (to͝o-mŭl′cho͞o-əs) *adj.* wild and disorderly

**mollified** (mŏl′ə-fīd′) *adj.* pacified; made calm **mollify** *v.*



## Customizing Instruction

### Less Proficient Readers

**1** Make sure students understand why Richard is crying and how his crying has forced the situation. Have students contrast how the Maples originally planned to tell their children about the separation with how they actually did inform them.

**Possible Response:** They planned to tell Judith first, then Dickie, and then John and Margaret the next morning. Instead, Joan breaks the news to Judith, John, and Margaret in the kitchen as they are clearing the plates after dinner.

**Set a Purpose** Have students adjust their purpose for reading, such as to understand how the Maples' children react to the news.

### Students Acquiring English

**2** Explain to students that a "bogieman" (or *bogeyman*) is an imaginary, evil being that causes terror in small children. The narrator uses the term here to represent Margaret's lingering fear—something Richard imagines she always had—that something was wrong between her parents.

## Mini Lesson Speaking and Listening

### PERFORMING A SCENE

**Prepare** Have students reread the segment of the story that describes what happens at dinner, from Richard's beginning to cry until his and John's leaving the table. Then organize students into groups of five—six if a director is desired—to act out this scene. Students first should create a script that fleshes out each character's lines and then should rehearse them, using appropriate gestures, facial expressions, movements, and tones. Remind students to justify the choice of verbal and nonverbal performance techniques by referring to their analysis and interpretations of the text.

**Present** Have groups of students perform their scene for the class. Audience members should evaluate how well the performance communicates Updike's portrayal of the family's dynamics at the dinner table.

**BLOCK SCHEDULING** This activity is particularly well suited for longer class periods.

## Reading and Analyzing

*Claire White* (1960), Fairfield Porter. Oil on canvas, 45 ½″ × 45″, collection of Stephen and Sheila Wald, Telluride, Colorado.

*Joan came and went, . . .
calmer than she should have been.*

## Teaching Options

 **Viewing and Representing**

*Frank Wallace* and *Claire White*
**by Fairfield Porter**

**ART APPRECIATION** Fairfield Porter (1907–1975) painted numerous portraits, seascapes, and landscapes. His work reflects the influence of the Impressionists.

**Instruction** Remind students that they're expected to describe how meanings are communicated through elements of design. Tell them that in a portrait, the subject's mood can be suggested by the position of the hands, feet, and shoulders and the tilting of the head. Ask students to examine both portraits and interpret each subject's mood.

**Possible Responses:** In *Frank Wallace*, the man appears to be waiting with an air of resignation and patience. His legs are crossed as he perches on a straight, small chair. One hand drapes over the other as if it is too much trouble to move them. His shoulders slump as though he lacks hope or energy. In *Claire White*, subtle differences in the subject's position create an impression of a woman resting, not waiting. She is sitting back in the chair, almost as if she has dropped into it from a standing position. Her arms are relaxed, and her bare feet, crossed, are informally positioned. Her repose suggests only an interlude between activities.

"Ha ha *ha*." Richard and Joan realized simultaneously that the child was drunk, on Judith's homecoming champagne. Feeling bound to keep the center of the stage, John took a cigarette from Judith's pack, poked it into his mouth, let it hang from his lower lip, and squinted like a gangster.

"You're not little things we had," Richard called to him. "You're the whole point. But you're grown. Or almost."

The boy was lighting matches. Instead of holding them to his cigarette (for they had never seen him smoke; being "good" had been his way of setting himself apart), he held them to his mother's face, closer and closer, for her to blow out. Then he lit the whole folder—a hiss and then a torch, held against his mother's face. Prismed by tears, the flame filled Richard's vision; he didn't know how it was extinguished. He heard Margaret say, "Oh stop showing off," and saw John, in response, break the cigarette in two and put the halves entirely into his mouth and chew, sticking out his tongue to display the shreds to his sister.

Joan talked to him, reasoning—a fountain of reason, unintelligible. "Talked about it for years . . . our children must help us . . . Daddy and I both want . . ." As the boy listened, he carefully wadded a paper napkin into the leaves of his salad, fashioned a ball of paper and lettuce, and popped it into his mouth, looking around the table for the expected laughter. None came. Judith said, "Be mature," and dismissed a plume of smoke.

Richard got up from this stifling table and led the boy outside. Though the house was in twilight, the outdoors still brimmed with light, the lovely waste light of high summer. Both laughing, he supervised John's spitting out the lettuce and paper and tobacco into the pachysandra.[8] He took him by the hand—a square gritty hand, but for its softness a man's. Yet, it held on. They ran together up into the field, past the tennis court. The raw banking left by the bulldozers was dotted with daisies. Past the court and a flat stretch where they used to play family baseball stood a soft green rise glorious in the sun, each weed and species of grass distinct as illumination on parchment. "I'm sorry, so sorry," Richard cried. "You were the only one who ever tried to help me with all the damn jobs around this place."

Sobbing, safe within his tears and the champagne, John explained, "It's not just the separation, it's the whole crummy year, I *hate* that school, you can't make any friends, the history teacher's a scud."

They sat on the crest of the rise, shaking and warm from their tears but easier in their voices, and Richard tried to focus on the child's sad year—the weekdays long with homework, the weekends spent in his room with model airplanes, while his parents murmured down below, nursing their separation. How selfish, how blind, Richard thought; his eyes felt scoured. He told his son, "We'll think about getting you transferred. Life's too short to be miserable."

They had said what they could, but did not want the moment to heal, and talked on, about the school, about the tennis court, whether it would ever again be as good as it had been that first summer. They walked to inspect it and pressed a few more tapes more firmly down. A little stiltedly, perhaps trying now to make too much of the moment, Richard led the boy to the spot in the field where the view was best, of the metallic blue river, the emerald marsh, the scattered islands velvety with shadow in the low light, the white bits of beach far away. "See," he said. "It goes on being beautiful. It'll be here tomorrow."

"I know," John answered, impatiently. The moment had closed.

Back in the house, the others had opened

---

8. **pachysandra** (păk´ĭ-săn´drə): small, low-growing, leafy plants used as ground cover.

| WORDS TO KNOW | **stiltedly** (stĭl´tĭd-lē) *adv.* in a stiffly dignified manner |

**1187**

## Customizing Instruction

### Students Acquiring English

**1** Encourage students to rely on context to determine the meaning of the word *scud*. Because it comes at the end of a string of complaints, students should infer that it is a negative word suggesting that the teacher is worthless or cruel.

**2** Explain that *scoured* means "scrubbed or flushed clean." Then ask how this term might apply to Richard's eyes.

**Possible Response:** His eyes feel hot and scraped, but also clean and clear so that he can see the truth of John's situation.

### Multiple Learning Styles
**Visual Learners**

Have students sketch a view of the Maples' property using the details described on this page. This sketch should help students appreciate the contrast between the serenity of the surroundings and the turmoil of the family members.

## ✓Assessment Informal Assessment

**ADAPTING POINT OF VIEW** You can informally assess your students' understanding of point of view by asking them to imagine that they are Judith observing the scene at the dinner table. Students should narrate the events and the other characters' reactions from Judith's perspective, using the third-person limited point of view. Their narratives should show what happens at dinner and should reveal the thoughts, feelings, and reactions that Judith hides beneath her mature and sophisticated pose.

**RUBRIC**

**3 Full Accomplishment** Students' narratives recount all the important events and reactions of the characters and provide many details about Judith's thoughts and feelings.

**2 Substantial Accomplishment** Students' narratives contain most of the important events and reactions of the characters and provide an overview of Judith's thoughts and feelings.

**1 Little or Partial Accomplishment** Students' narratives omit several important events, do not accurately describe the characters' reactions, and/or do not describe Judith's thoughts and feelings.

**Reading Skills and Strategies:
ANALYZING**

**A** Have students explain why Richard
feels both resentful and relieved that
the family dinner party went on without him.

**Possible Responses:** Since he is leaving the family, he is relieved that his
family can carry on without him; he is
vain enough, however, to want to feel
indispensable; he's hurt to realize that
they don't need him.

**Literary Analysis: SYMBOL**

**B** Have students discuss what the
image of the black mountain might
represent.

**Possible Responses:** the guilt Richard
feels about leaving his wife and family;
his dread of informing his son of the
separation; the uncertain reaction of his
older son to the news.

**Literary Analysis: SIMILE**

**C** Point out the way Richard compares himself to an assassin at a carnival who must go forward because there
is no turning back. Ask students to
explain what this simile reveals about
the way he feels.

**Possible Response:** The comparison
reveals that Richard knows his news
will hurt Dickie, and he feels regret that
he cannot turn back or undo what he
has begun.

**Literary Analysis: DRAMATIC IRONY**

**D** Ask students to suggest how their
own attitudes toward Dickie are affected by the fact that they already know
what he is about to learn.

**Possible Responses:** sympathize with
him; feel suspense about his reaction.

*Stephen and Kathy* (1965), Fairfield Porter. Oil on canvas.
Colby College Museum of Art, Waterville, Maine.

some white wine, the champagne being drunk,
and still sat at the table, the three females,
gossiping. Where Joan sat had become the
head. She turned, showing him a tearless face,
and asked, "All right?"

**A** "We're fine," he said, resenting it, though
relieved, that the party went on without him.

 *In* bed she explained, "I couldn't cry
I guess because I cried so much all spring. It
really wasn't fair. It's your idea, and you made
it look as though I was kicking you out."

"I'm sorry," he said. "I couldn't stop. I
wanted to but couldn't."

"You *didn't* want to. You loved it. You were
having your way, making a general announcement."

"I love having it over," he admitted. "God,

those kids were great. So brave and funny."
John, returned to the house, had settled to a
model airplane in his room, and kept shouting
down to them, "I'm O.K. No sweat." "And the
way," Richard went on, cozy in his relief, "they
never questioned the reasons we gave. No
thought of a third person. Not even Judith."

"That *was* touching," Joan said.

He gave her a hug. "You were great too. Very
reassuring to everybody. Thank you." Guiltily, he
realized he did not feel separated.

"You still have Dickie to do," she told him.
These words set before him a black mountain in
the darkness; its cold breath, its near weight
affected his chest. Of the four children, his elder
son was most nearly his conscience. Joan did not
need to add, "That's one piece of your dirty
work I won't do for you."

"I know. I'll do it. You go to sleep."

Within minutes, her breathing slowed, became
oblivious and deep. It was quarter to midnight.
Dickie's train from the concert would come in at
one-fourteen. Richard set the alarm for one. He
had slept atrociously for weeks. But whenever he
closed his lids some glimpse of the last hours
scorched them—Judith exhaling toward the
ceiling in a kind of aversion, Bean's mute staring,
the sunstruck growth in the field where he and
John had rested. The mountain before him
moved closer, moved within him; he was huge,
momentous. The ache at the back of his throat
felt stale. His wife slept as if slain beside him.
When, exasperated by his hot lids, his crowded
heart, he rose from bed and dressed, she awoke
enough to turn over. He told her then, "Joan, if
I could undo it all, I would."

"Where would you begin?" she asked. There
was no place. Giving him courage, she was
always giving him courage. He put on shoes
without socks in the dark. The children were
breathing in their rooms, the downstairs was
hollow. In their confusion they had left lights
burning. He turned off all but one, the kitchen
overhead. The car started. He had hoped it
wouldn't. He met only moonlight on the road; it

**Mini Lesson** ## Workplace Link

**PREPARING FOR PROJECTS**

**Instruction** One of Richard's chores is replacing
the lock on the screen door. Although he begins
this task believing it will be easy, it turns into a
complicated process that requires several stages
of work. Point out to students that they can do
projects at work, home, and school more efficiently by following a few simple steps:

• read directions, instructions, and requirements
carefully

• seek advice from people with experience

• list necessary tools and materials

• gather materials and tools and check them off
the list

• borrow or purchase any other necessary items

• create a time line that lists the amount of time
and the proposed deadline for each stage of the
project

• if others are involved, decide how to share
information with them

**Activity** Have students choose a project such as
running for a class office, organizing a car wash, or
painting a room. Ask them to write an outline of
the steps to take to prepare for the actual project.

seemed a <u>diaphanous</u> companion, flickering in the leaves along the roadside, haunting his rearview mirror like a pursuer, melting under his headlights. The center of town, not quite deserted, was eerie at this hour. A young cop in uniform kept company with a gang of T-shirted kids on the steps of the bank. Across from the railroad station, several bars kept open. Customers, mostly young, passed in and out of the warm night, savoring summer's novelty. Voices shouted from cars as they passed; an immense conversation seemed in progress. Richard parked and in his weariness put his head on the passenger seat, out of the commotion and wheeling lights. It was as when, in the movies, an assassin grimly carries his mission through the jostle of a carnival—except the movies cannot show the precipitous, <u>palpable</u> slope you cling to within. You cannot climb back down; you can only fall. The synthetic fabric of the car seat, warmed by his cheek, confided to him an ancient, distant scent of vanilla.

A train whistle caused him to lift his head. It was on time; he had hoped it would be late. The slender drawgates descended. The bell of approach tingled happily. The great metal body, horizontally fluted, rocked to a stop, and sleepy teen-agers disembarked, his son among them. Dickie did not show surprise that this father was meeting him at this terrible hour. He sauntered to the car with two friends, both taller than he. He said "Hi" to his father and took the passenger's seat with an exhausted promptness that expressed gratitude. The friends got in the back, and Richard was grateful; a few more minutes' postponement would be won by driving them home.

He asked, "How was the concert?"

"Groovy," one boy said from the back seat.

"It bit," the other said.

"It was O.K.," Dickie said, moderate by nature, so reasonable that in his childhood the unreason of the world had given him headaches, stomach aches, nausea. When the second friend had been dropped off at his dark house, the boy blurted, "Dad, my eyes are killing me with hay fever! I'm out there cutting that grass all day!"

"Do we still have those drops?"

"They didn't do any good last summer."

"They might this." Richard swung a U-turn on the empty street. The drive home took a few minutes. The mountain was here, in his throat. "Richard," he said, and felt the boy, slumped and rubbing his eyes, go tense at his tone, "I didn't come to meet you just to make your life easier. I came because your mother and I have some news for you, and you're a hard man to get ahold of these days. It's sad news."

"That's O.K." The reassurance came out soft, but quick, as if released from the tip of a spring.

Richard had feared that his tears would return and choke him, but the boy's manliness set an example, and his voice issued forth steady and dry. "It's sad news, but it needn't be tragic news, at least for you. It should have no practical effect on your life, though it's bound to have an emotional effect. You'll work at your job, and go back to school in September. Your mother and I are really proud of what you're making of your life; we don't want that to change at all."

"Yeah," the boy said lightly, on the intake of his breath, holding himself up. They turned the corner; the church they went to loomed like a gutted fort. The home of the woman Richard hoped to marry stood across the green. Her bedroom light burned.

"Your mother and I," he said, "have decided to separate. For the summer. Nothing legal, no divorce yet. We want to see how it feels. For some years now, we haven't been doing enough for each other, making each other as happy as we should be. Have you sensed that?"

"No," the boy said. It was an honest, unemotional answer: true or false in a quiz.

**1189**

### Reading Skills and Strategies: EVALUATING

**A** Have students evaluate Richard's character and decide if he accurately interprets John's reaction to news of the separation.

**Possible Responses:** Some students may feel that it seems unlikely that deep down the news of his parents' breakup did not upset John more than his troubles at school. Other students may feel that Richard is misinterpreting John's feelings in order to make himself feel less guilty. Still others may think John is too young to understand the impact that the separation will have on his life.

### Reading Skills and Strategies: INTERPRETING

**B** Ask students how they would interpret Richard's feelings after he has told Dickie the news.

**Possible Response:** Richard is relieved that Dickie did not react more dramatically. He feels that the worst is over now that he has told all the children. The burden of dealing with the separation now falls on them.

**C** Ask students why the gentle closing of the bedroom door sickens Richard.

**Possible Responses:** He realizes Dickie is in shock; he questions whether the children will even miss him. Although this impending separation has altered his life, perhaps it won't disturb their lives greatly.

**D** Ask students what they think Dickie's vague "Why?" really asks.

**Possible Responses:** Why are you doing this? Why don't you and Mom love each other any more? Why is something else more important than your family?

---

Glad for the factual basis, Richard pursued, even garrulously, the details. His apartment across town, his utter accessibility, the split vacation arrangements, the advantages to the children, the added mobility and variety of the summer. Dickie listened, absorbing. "Do the others know?"

"Yes."

"How did they take it?"

"The girls pretty calmly. John flipped out; he shouted and ate a cigarette and made a salad out of his napkin and told us how much he hated school."

His brother chuckled. "He did?"

**A** "Yeah. The school issue was more upsetting for him than Mom and me. He seemed to feel better for having exploded."

"He did?" The repetition was the first sign that he was stunned.

"Yes. Dickie, I want to tell you something. This last hour, waiting for your train to get in, has been about the worst of my life. I hate this. *Hate* it. My father would have died before doing it to me." He felt immensely lighter, saying this.
**B** He had dumped the mountain on the boy. They were home. Moving swiftly as a shadow, Dickie was out of the car, through the bright kitchen. Richard called after him, "Want a glass of milk or anything?"

"No thanks."

"Want us to call the course tomorrow and say you're too sick to work?"

"No, that's all right." The answer was faint, delivered at the door to his room; Richard listened for the slam that went with a tantrum. The door
**C** closed normally, gently. The sound was sickening.

*Joan* had sunk into that first deep trough of sleep and was slow to awake. Richard had to repeat, "I told him."

"What did he say?"

"Nothing much. Could you go say goodnight to him? Please."

She left their room, without putting on a bathrobe. He sluggishly changed back into his pajamas and walked down the hall. Dickie was already in bed, Joan was sitting beside him, and the boy's bedside clock radio was murmuring music. When she stood, an inexplicable light—the moon?—outlined her body through the nightie. Richard sat on the warm place she had indented on the child's narrow mattress. He asked him, "Do you want the radio on like that?"

"It always is."

"Doesn't it keep you awake? It would me."

"No."

"Are you sleepy?"

"Yeah."

"Good. Sure you want to get up and go to work? You've had a big night."

"I want to."

Away at school this winter he had learned for the first time that you can go short of sleep and live. As an infant he had slept with an immobile, sweating intensity that had alarmed his babysitters. In adolescence he had often been the first of the four children to go to bed. Even now, he would go slack in the middle of a television show, his sprawled legs hairy and brown. "O.K. Good boy. Dickie, listen. I love you so much, I never knew how much until now. No matter how this works out, I'll always be with you. Really."

Richard bent to kiss an averted face but his son, sinewy, turned and with wet cheeks embraced him and gave him a kiss, on the lips, passionate as a woman's. In his father's ear he moaned one word, the crucial, intelligent word: "*Why?*"
**D**

*Why.* It was a whistle of wind in a crack, a knife thrust, a window thrown open on emptiness. The white face was gone, the darkness was featureless. Richard had forgotten why. ❖

WORDS TO KNOW
**garrulously** (găr′ə-ləs-lē) *adv.* talking too much about trifles; talkative

1190

---

## Teaching Options

✓ Assessment **Standardized Test Practice**

**MAKING PREDICTIONS** For some standardized tests, students will be asked to make logical inferences about future actions based upon information in the text. To provide students with help in making predictions, read aloud or write on the board the following statement and choices.

You can tell from the story that Richard will most likely

**A.** dispute child support payments.

**B.** immediately try to build a relationship between his children and the other woman.

**C.** try to maintain a cordial relationship with Joan.

**D.** will find being separated as straightforward as his explanation to Dickie makes it seem.

Lead students through the process of choosing the best prediction based on what they know of Richard's character. Based on his feelings for his children, **A** seems an unlikely choice. Option **B** also seems unlikely, since he has concealed the identity of the other woman in his life. Since all the members of the family seem deeply hurt, Richard's rosy picture of a "straightforward" separation cited in option **D** is unrealistic. Therefore, **C** remains the only logical choice.

# *Thinking* through the LITERATURE

## Connect to the Literature

**1. What Do You Think?**
What was your reaction to the conversation that Richard and Dickie have in Dickie's bedroom?

> **Comprehension Check**
> - What question does Richard fear his children might ask about the cause of the separation?
> - How did John, Margaret, and Judith each react to the news of their parents' breakup?

## Think Critically

**2.**  **ACTIVE READING · MAKING PREDICTIONS** Review the questionnaire you filled out in your **READER'S NOTEBOOK**. Which of your predictions about what might happen in the story were accurate? What events, if any, in the story were a total surprise?

**3.** At the end of the story, did you feel sympathy for Richard? Point to things he says, does, or thinks that caused you to be sympathetic or not.

**4.** Think about Richard's and Joan's different plans for how to tell the children about the separation. What might Joan's plan reveal about her personality? What might Richard's plan reveal about his personality?

> **THINK ABOUT**
> - the explanations they offer their children
> - the "white face" in Richard's mind (pages 1182 and 1190)
> - Richard's remark, "Life's too short to be miserable" (page 1187)

**5.** Dickie asks his father, "Why?" and the narrator says, "Richard had forgotten why." What can you gather about why Richard and Joan are separating?

## Extend Interpretations

**6. The Writer's Style** To reinforce his themes, Updike often uses **symbols,** things that represent something beyond their concrete meanings. For instance, at the table Richard cracks the lobster's back, as he has cracked apart his family. What symbolism do you find in other objects in the story, such as the Maples' house and tennis court?

**7. Connect to Life** Do you think the behavior of the people in this story is true to life? Explain. Refer to your responses in the Connect to Your Life activity on page 1180.

---

## Literary Analysis

**DRAMATIC IRONY** Updike's use of **dramatic irony** in "Separating" establishes a relationship between the narrator and the reader from the very beginning of the story. The narrator of "Separating" confides that the Maples are going to separate. The reader holds privileged information, yet unknown to the characters who will most be affected by this decision—the children.

**Cooperative Learning Activity**
What do you think Updike's intentions were in sharing the news of the Maples' separation with the reader early in the story? What effect did this knowledge have on your involvement in the story? Meet with a small group to discuss these questions.

**REVIEW · POINT OF VIEW**
Although Richard is not the narrator of "Separating," the narration focuses on his point of view. This focus on one character's thoughts, observations, and feelings is called **third-person limited point of view.** How might your response to the story have changed if it had been told from the third-person omniscient point of view, in which the narrator reports different characters' thoughts and feelings?

SEPARATING **1191**

---

## Extend Interpretations

**Writer's Style** Students might note that by focusing on the deteriorating tennis court and fixtures of the house that need repair, Updike makes these objects symbols of the Maples' failed marriage. The obsolete, broken lock that Richard removes represents his broken marriage and his removal of himself from his family. The huge, black mountain represents the guilt, dread, and loss that Richard attempts to surmount.

**Connect to Life** Responses will vary. Students should compare text events with their own or others' experiences. Some students may say that the different reactions of the four children to the breakup are true to life. Other students may find Richard's displays of emotion excessive and therefore unbelievable.

---

SEPARATING **1191**

## Writing Options

1. **Diary Entry** Remind students that a diary entry would be written in the first person and might include events not mentioned in the story.
2. **Character Analysis** After students have listed behaviors and values, they should identify each as positive or negative.
3. **Story Forecast To get students started on this assignment,** discuss as a class what is known about the characters' future plans. For example, Joan and the children plan to stay in their house while Richard will move to an apartment across town. Remind students to take into consideration the personalities of each character as they predict their futures.

## Activities & Explorations

**Staging a Scene To get students started on this assignment**, help them to assign functions to each member of the group. One student can write dialogue for the scene, while another adds stage directions. Others can note details for costumes, scenery, and music. One student can act as the director to guide rehearsal of the scene.

## Vocabulary in Action

**Exercise A**
1. i
2. j
3. a
4. f
5. d
6. b
7. e
8. g
9. c
10. h

**Exercise B**
1. antonyms
2. antonyms
3. synonyms
4. synonyms
5. antonyms

---

## Writing Options

**1. Diary Entry** Write a diary entry from the perspective of a character in the story other than Richard—either Joan or one of the children.

**2. Character Analysis** Write a brief character analysis that examines Richard Maple's behavior and values. Make clear your final judgment of him.

**3. Story Forecast** Updike wrote three other stories about the Maples after "Separating." What do you think happens to Joan, Richard, and each of their four children in the stories to come? Write a narrative summarizing your predictions.

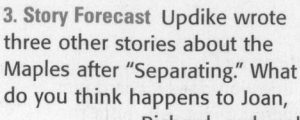

Richard Maple
behavior | values

## Activities & Exploration

**Staging a Scene** Imagine that you are making a TV movie of "Separating." With a small group of classmates, select a scene from this story and write stage directions explaining how the actors should speak their lines. Also write notes about the props, lighting, scenery, costumes, and music you would use to bring this scene to life. Perform the scene for the class. ~ **PERFORMING**

## Vocabulary in Action

**EXERCISE A: SYNONYMS** For each phrase in the first column, write the letter of the synonymous phrase from the second column.

1. a leaky depot
2. a primary need
3. luscious poultry
4. stiffly rejected
5. concisely discussing
6. a mollified minor
7. opulent quantities
8. makes dinky pieces
9. tumultuous water sports
10. garrulously complimenting

a. succulent duck
b. a soothed youth
c. chaotic aquatics
d. tersely conversing
e. bounteous amounts
f. stiltedly jilted
g. produces minutiae
h. chattily flattering
i. a permeable terminal
j. an elemental essential

**EXERCISE B: ASSESSMENT PRACTICE** Identify each pair of words as synonyms or antonyms.

1. diaphanous—solid
2. dissolution—union
3. palpable—concrete
4. congruous—appropriate
5. precipitous—flat

**Building Vocabulary**

Many of the Words to Know contain suffixes. For an in-depth lesson on word parts, see page 1130.

| WORDS TO KNOW | | | | | |
| --- | --- | --- | --- | --- | --- |
| congruous | elemental | mollified | permeable | succulent |
| diaphanous | garrulously | opulent | precipitous | tersely |
| dissolution | minutiae | palpable | stiltedly | tumultuous |

# John Updike
## 1932–

**Other Works**
*The Poorhouse Fair*
*Rabbit, Run*
*Pigeon Feathers and Other Stories*
*Couples*
*The Witches of Eastwick*
*Brazil*

**Boyhood Dreams** John Updike's birthplace, Shillington, Pennsylvania, inspired the small-town settings of many of his early novels. His father taught high school algebra, while his mother, "a very sensitive and witty woman," wrote several unpublished stories and novels. Her talents influenced Updike's career ambitions. As a teenager, John Updike aspired to become a cartoonist or a humorist and to write for the *New Yorker*. By his mid-twenties, he had achieved these goals.

**Literary Success** Since then Updike has earned the reputation as a critically acclaimed fiction writer, poet, and essayist who keenly observes the American scene. He won a National Book Award for his novel *The Centaur*, a Pulitzer Prize for his novels *Rabbit Is Rich* and *Rabbit at Rest*, and a National Book Critics Circle award for criticism for *Hugging the Shore*. Many of his novels and stories have been adapted as films, TV movies, and plays.

**Flair for High Drama** Much of Updike's work, like the short story "Separating," explores the tensions in middle-class American families. In an interview, he said, "I like middles. It is in middles that extremes clash, where ambiguity restlessly rules. . . . It seems to me that critics get increasingly querulous and impatient for madder music and stronger wine, when what we need is a greater respect for reality, its secrecy, its music."

---

 **Mini Lesson** ## Grammar

**ADVANCED SENTENCES: PERIODIC SENTENCES**

**Instruction** Explain that a loose sentence is one in which the main idea precedes the details or appended elements. A periodic sentence places the main idea at the end. Changing a loose sentence into a periodic sentence creates emphasis, and an occasional periodic sentence adds variety. Display the sentences below:

> John's behavior at the dinner table earned him some individual time with his father, although his sisters were scornful of his antics. (*loose sentence—the main idea is presented first*)

> By crying through much of the meal, Richard precipitated the announcement of the separation. (*periodic sentence—the main idea is at the end*)

**Exercise** Ask students to identify each of the following sentences as either loose or periodic.

1. Joan remained calm because, as she told Richard, her tears were spent. (*loose*)

2. After the three children are told about the separation, Richard feels temporary relief. (*periodic*)

3. Richard, after doing some repairs to the house, felt better. (*periodic*)

 Use **Grammar Transparencies and Copymasters,** p. 175.

 Use McDougal Littell's *Language Network* for more instruction and practice.

## OVERVIEW

This selection is included in the **Grade 11 InterActive Reader.**

### Objectives

1. understand and appreciate two contemporary **poems** (**Literary Analysis**)
2. examine **tone** in poetry (**Literary Analysis**)
3. compare writers' attitudes (**Active Reading**)

### Summary

Both poems present perspectives on the Mexican-American experience. The speaker of "Mexicans Begin Jogging," a factory worker and U.S. citizen, follows his boss's order to run when the border patrol arrives. He recognizes that it will take time for him and other citizens of foreign descent to be seen as Americans, but he accepts their prejudice without bitterness. "Legal Alien" portrays the dilemma of the speaker who has the advantages of knowing two languages fluently and belonging to two cultures, but who is accepted fully by neither the Mexicans nor the Americans. She remains on the outside of both groups because of her differences.

### Thematic Link

Gary Soto and Pat Mora highlight the difficulties of **integration** for Mexican Americans, who continue to be seen as outsiders in American **postwar society** because they differ from a preconceived notion of what an American should be.

### 5-Minute Warm-Up

*Daily Language SkillBuilder*

Have students **proofread** the display sentences on page 1069k and write them correctly. The sentences also appear on Transparency 33 of **Grammar Transparencies and Copymasters.**

---

# Mexicans Begin Jogging

*Poetry by* GARY SOTO

# Legal Alien

*Poetry by* PAT MORA

### Connect to Your Life

Both of the following poems explore what happens when someone is prejudged or is treated differently on the basis of a stereotype. Think of a time when someone judged you without first getting to know you. What was assumed about you, and why? What was your attitude about being prejudged in that way? With a small group of classmates, discuss the difficulties that prejudging creates, both for the person judging and the person being judged.

## Build Background

"Legal alien" is a term applied to an immigrant who has been granted legal permanent residence in the United States, even though he or she is not a U.S. citizen. The speaker in "Mexicans Begin Jogging" is a U.S. citizen who is mistakenly prejudged to be an "illegal alien"—an immigrant who enters the country illegally. An estimated 300,000 illegal aliens enter the United States each year. Many migrate north to cross the 1,952-mile-long border between the United States and Mexico. The Border Patrol, which was created in 1924, has thus far been unable to control illegal immigration from Mexico. Border Patrol activities include not only efforts to stop entry at the border but also searches to capture illegal immigrants in the United States in order to return them to their home countries.

## Focus Your Reading

**LITERARY ANALYSIS** **TONE** **Tone** refers to the attitude a writer takes toward the subject he or she is writing about. In these two poems, the speakers can be identified as the poets themselves. As you read, watch for clues that indicate each poet's attitude toward being prejudged. Is the poet angry? hurt? amused? Notice images and individual words—nouns, verbs, and adjectives—that convey how each poet feels.

**ACTIVE READING** **COMPARING WRITERS' ATTITUDES** These poems are paired because both are by Mexican-American writers and both are about being prejudged. You might find it interesting to compare the two works.

**READER'S NOTEBOOK** After you read the first poem, jot down one or two words to describe the writer's attitude, or tone. Then copy a word, phrase, or line that suggested this tone to you. As you read the second poem, compare or contrast its tone with that of the first poem. Again, copy a word, phrase, or line you found particularly revealing.

"Mexicans Begin Jogging"

Tone: _____

Suggested by: _____

---

## LESSON RESOURCES

**UNIT SEVEN RESOURCE BOOK,** pp. 59–60

**ASSESSMENT RESOURCES**
**Formal Assessment,** pp. 225–226
**Teacher's Guide to Assessment and Portfolio Use**
**Test Generator**

**SKILLS TRANSPARENCIES AND COPYMASTERS**
**Literary Analysis**
• Tone, T19 (for Paired Activity, p. 1198)

**Reading and Critical Thinking**
• Comparing Authors' Views, T23 (for Active Reading, p. 1194)

**Grammar**
• Varying Types of Sentences, C176 (for Mini Lesson, p. 1199)

**Vocabulary**
• The Connotative Power of Words, C95 (for Mini Lesson, p. 1195)

**Writing**
• Opinion Statement, C34 (for Writing Options, p. 1199)

**Communications**
• Interviewing, T9 (for Mini Lesson, p. 1197)

**INTEGRATED TECHNOLOGY**
**Audio Library**
**Visit our website:**
www.mcdougallittell.com

# MEXICANS BEGIN JOGGING

### GARY SOTO

**1**
At the factory I worked
In the fleck of rubber, under the press
Of an oven yellow with flame,
Until the border patrol opened
5   Their vans and my boss waved for us to run.
"Over the fence, Soto," he shouted,
And I shouted that I was American.
"No time for lies," he said, and pressed
A dollar in my palm, hurrying me
10   Through the back door.

**2**
Since I was on his time, I ran
And became the wag to a short tail of Mexicans—
Ran past the amazed crowds that lined
The street and blurred like photographs, in rain.
15   I ran from that industrial road to the soft
Houses where people paled at the turn of an autumn sky.
What could I do but yell *vivas*[1]
To baseball, milkshakes, and those sociologists
Who would clock me
20   As I jog into the next century
On the power of a great, silly grin.

---

1. *vivas* (vē'väs) *Spanish:* cheers.

Illegal immigrants scaling the wall along
the U.S.-Mexican border near Tijuana.
AP/Wide World Photos.

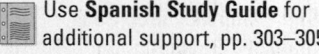

MEXICANS BEGIN JOGGING   **1195**

## Reading and Analyzing

**Literary Analysis** [TONE]

Ask students to define the tone Soto suggests by closing "Mexicans Begin Jogging" with the words "great, silly grin."

**Possible Responses:** bemused acceptance of the situation; optimism that he will in time be fully accepted as an American; confidence that his acceptance will be connected to maintaining good humor

 Use **Unit Seven Resource Book,** p. 60 for more practice.

**Active Reading**

[COMPARING WRITERS' ATTITUDES]

Have students identify phrases in "Legal Alien" that show a more serious attitude toward the problem of identity than that conveyed in "Mexicans Begin Jogging." Ask students to explain why Mora's attitude seems less optimistic or lighthearted than Soto's.

**Possible Responses:** "American but hyphenated"; "viewed by Anglos as . . . perhaps inferior"; "viewed by Mexicans as alien"; "a handy token"; "masking the discomfort." Mora cannot escape her problem of feeling like an outsider by running from it. The lack of acceptance undermines what she has to offer and who she really is. The speaker in "Mexicans Begin Jogging" realizes that he is judged on appearance; the speaker in "Legal Alien" is being judged even after her more intrinsic qualities have been revealed.

 Use **Unit Seven Resource Book,** p. 59 for more practice.

Looking through a hole in the border wall.
Copyright © Paul Fusco/Magnum Photos, Inc.

### Thinking Through the Literature

1. **Comprehension Check** Why does the boss want his workers to run?

2. Why do you think Soto runs even though he does not have to?

3. How would you describe Soto's apparent attitude toward being prejudged?

 THINK ABOUT
- his indicating that he is an American (line 7)
- the image he creates of the boss (lines 8–10)
- his cheering for baseball, milkshakes, and sociologists (lines 17–18)
- the image of himself in the last two lines

4. How do you interpret lines 15–16? Make inferences about the "soft / Houses where people paled at the turn of an autumn sky."

5. What does Soto suggest to you about the future direction of the United States in the line "As I jog into the next century"?

6. What **ironies** do you see in the **title** of this poem?

## Thinking Through the Literature

1. **Comprehension Check** Possible Response: There is a border patrol arriving to capture illegal aliens.

2. Possible Responses: His boss orders him to; he might get in trouble if he hangs around; he accepts it as one of the difficulties of being "different" from the mainstream United States culture.

3. Possible Responses: bemused but not bitter; cautiously optimistic that time will help change things; accepting of his ability to feel part of two different cultures.

4. Possible Response: middle-class suburban homes where white people live

5. Possible Responses: that Mexican Americans will seem less "strange" to other Americans as time goes on; that time is on his side; that any progress he makes will be steady but not rapid

6. Possible Responses: While the other workers, who are illegal, need to run from the authorities, Soto does not need to run; he can jog, like the pale suburbanites whose houses he runs by.

# LEGAL ALIEN

PAT MORA

1 Bi-lingual, Bi-cultural,
able to slip from "How's life?"
to *"Me'stan volviendo loca,"*[1]
able to sit in a paneled office
5 drafting memos in smooth English,
able to order in fluent Spanish
at a Mexican restaurant,
2 American but hyphenated,
viewed by Anglos as perhaps exotic,
10 perhaps inferior, definitely different,
viewed by Mexicans as alien,
(their eyes say, "You may speak
Spanish but you're not like me")
an American to Mexicans
15 a Mexican to Americans
a handy token
sliding back and forth
between the fringes of both worlds
by smiling
20 by masking the discomfort
of being pre-judged
Bi-laterally.[2]

---

1. *"Me'stan volviendo loca"* (mĕ-stän′
vôl-vē-ĕn′dô lô′kä) *Spanish:* "They're making
me crazy."

2. **Bi-laterally:** in a way that is undertaken by
two sides equally.

Illustration Copyright © Rob Colvin/Stock Illustration Source.

LEGAL ALIEN **1197**

## Mini Lesson · Inquiry and Research

**PREPARING FOR A FORMAL INTERVIEW**
**Instruction** Tell students that interviews can be an excellent source of information on various topics. Remind them that it is important to prepare carefully. Before the interview, interviewers should
• call to explain their purpose and make an appointment;
• read background information on the topic and/or on the person to be interviewed;
• generate a list of relevant questions that require more than a "yes" or "no" answer;
• prepare materials necessary for the interview.

During the interview, interviewers should
• listen carefully and take notes;
• ask questions to clarify points;
• follow up on interesting ideas;
• read over notes before terminating the interview.
Following the interview, interviewers should
• check spelling of difficult names or terms;
• send a thank-you note.

**Application** Have students do some background reading on the process of becoming a citizen. Then ask students to generate relevant, interesting, and researchable questions that they could use to elicit firsthand information on becoming a citizen during an interview with a new citizen.

---

## GUIDING STUDENT RESPONSE

### Connect to the Literature

**1. What Do You Think?**
Students should support their impressions with lines from the text.

**Comprehension Check**
• Anglos view her as exotic, perhaps inferior, and different. Mexicans view her as alien.

### Think Critically

**2.** Possible Response: It is a mixed blessing.

**3.** Possible Responses: conflicted, alienated, prejudged. Mora is more serious and less optimistic about her place in American society; Soto seems more optimistic about his future, and he also has a more sarcastic tone, gently mocking his boss and the white people who live in the nicer neighborhoods.

**4.** Possible Responses: The title implies that the poem has to do with legal immigrants; it has to do with people incorrectly perceived as "alien." The title also suggests that being a legal resident of the United States does not erase the differences that others perceive.

---

## Connect to the Literature

**1. What Do You Think?**
How do you visualize the writer of "Legal Alien"?

**Comprehension Check**
• How does the poet say she is viewed by Anglos? by Mexicans?

## Think Critically

**2.** How do you think the poet feels about being bilingual and bicultural?

 THINK ABOUT
• how she is viewed by Anglos
• how she is viewed by Mexicans
• her description of herself in lines 16–22

**3.** **ACTIVE READING** **COMPARING WRITERS' ATTITUDES** How did you describe the writer's attitude, or tone, in "Legal Alien" in your **READER'S NOTEBOOK**? Did you use the same word(s) to describe Gary Soto's attitude in "Mexicans Begin Jogging"? Explain how the tones are similar or different.

**4.** How do you interpret the **title** "Legal Alien"?

## Extend Interpretations

**5.** **Comparing Texts** How similar are the poets' experiences in "Mexicans Begin Jogging" and "Legal Alien"? Tell what the poems suggest to you about some difficulties of being Mexican American.

**6.** **Connect to Life** For the Connect to Your Life activity on page 1194, you were asked to recall a time when you were prejudged. Was your reaction closer to Gary Soto's or Pat Mora's in these poems?

---

## Literary Analysis

**TONE** As you know, **tone** is a writer's attitude toward a subject. A poet can communicate tone through **diction,** or choice of words. For example, elevated diction ("nerv'd Oppression's hand") and words with strong negative connotations ("toiling" and "anguish") help convey Frances E. W. Harper's serious, urgent tone in "Free Labor" (page 576). A poet can also state an attitude directly ("I celebrate myself, and sing myself"), as Walt Whitman does in "Song of Myself" (page 400). Often it is the **imagery** in a poem that suggests the writer's tone. In "Mexicans Begin Jogging," Gary Soto's amusement at being persistently and incorrectly prejudged is expressed through the humorous images of himself as "the wag to a short tail of Mexicans"; of himself cheering baseball, milkshakes, and sociologists; and of sociologists clocking him as he jogs, grinning, into the next century.

**Paired Activity** If someone were to tell you that Pat Mora's tone in "Legal Alien" was exactly the same as Gary Soto's in "Mexicans Begin Jogging," how would you prove this person wrong? What specific words and images would you point to in Mora's poem? Choose a classmate and convince him or her.

---

## Extend Interpretations

**Comparing Texts** Both poems deal with being Hispanic and thus "different" in the United States; both deal, more or less positively, with being of Mexican-American heritage. "Mexicans Begin Jogging" hints more at the real-world dangers of this situation; "Legal Alien" emphasizes the personal stress of being caught between two worlds.

**Connect to Life** Students' answers should reflect an understanding of the differences between the two poems' tone and the speakers' attitude.

## Literary Analysis

**Tone** Possible Responses: The tone of Soto's poem is more lighthearted, using the metaphor of being "the wag to a short tail of Mexicans" and describing a "great, silly grin." The speaker feels that one day society will be more accepting of Mexican Americans. Mora is much more conflicted about her bifurcated status in both the Mexican and American societies; she is viewed as "perhaps inferior" and "alien," and feels like a "handy token / sliding back and forth / between the fringes of both worlds."

# Choices & CHALLENGES

## Writing Options

**Guest Editorial** In both these poems, people are prejudged because they are Mexican Americans. To express your opinion about being prejudged in general or about your own experience with being prejudged, draft a guest column for a student magazine or newspaper. Save this piece in your **Working Portfolio.**

## Inquiry & Research

The title "Legal Alien" refers to a person who is authorized to live in the United States but is not a citizen of this country. In "Mexicans Begin Jogging" a worker is perceived to be an illegal alien, even though he is actually a U.S. citizen. Find out the different ways that a person can become a citizen of the United States. What requirements must someone meet?

## Art Connection

Look at the photographs of a wall along the U.S.-Mexican border on pages 1195 and 1196, and also look at the illustration on page 1197. What ideas do these pictures suggest to you, and how well do you think they fit the Soto and Mora poems? What other visuals can you think of to illustrate the poems?

## Gary Soto
### 1952–

**Other Works**
*Black Hair*
*The Tale of Sunlight*
*Where Sparrows Work Hard*
*Small Faces*

**Working-Class Roots** Gary Soto writes poetry that explores his childhood, his adolescence, and his ethnic identity. Growing up in a working-class Mexican-American family in the San Joaquin Valley in California, Soto worked as a migrant farm worker before entering college. When he encountered Donald Allen's anthology *The New American Poetry*, Soto decided to become a poet. "I discovered this poetry and thought, This is terrific; I'd like to do something like this."

**Early Books** Soto's first collection of poetry, *The Elements of San Joaquin*, is a bleak portrait of the lives of Mexican Americans. His prose memoirs include *Living up the Street*, which won an American Book Award.

**A Teacher's Advice** Soto has taught English and Chicano studies at the University of California, Berkeley. He has said that he wants his students "to understand how a writer puts things together, to see that it's not simply a mishmash of feelings."

## Pat Mora
### 1942–

**Other Works**
*Borders*
*Chants*
*Nepantla*
*House of Houses*

**Texas Treasure** A poet, essayist, and children's book author, Pat Mora was born in the border city of El Paso, Texas. She graduated from Texas Western College and received her master's degree from the University of Texas at El Paso. Mora taught college English for ten years and acted as the host of a radio show, *Voices: The Mexican-American in Perspective*.

**Awards and Anthologies** Mora has received many awards for her works, including awards from the Southwest Council of Latin American Studies and the National Association for Chicano Studies. Her work appears in the anthologies *New Worlds of Literature, Hispanics in the United States*, and *Woman of Her Word: Hispanic Women Write*.

**Why She Writes** In an interview, Mora identified the sources of her poetic inspiration. "I write, in part, because Hispanic perspectives need to be part of our literary heritage; I want to be part of that validation process. I also write because I am fascinated by the pleasure and power of words."

---

## Writing Options

**Guest Editorial To get students started on this assignment,** bring in some examples of guest columns from the opinion pages of newspapers to acquaint students with the range of tones, formats, and approaches they might use. Students can write in their own voices or they can adopt the voice of a character they have invented.

## Inquiry & Research

**To get students started on this assignment,** have them generate relevant, interesting, and researchable questions. Remind them to locate appropriate print and nonprint information by using civics textbooks, the library database, and the Internet and draw conclusions from information gathered. Students should use text organizers to locate and organize information as they conduct independent research. The U.S. Immigration and Naturalization Service can provide information about the process of becoming a citizen. **Interpersonal learners** could interview a new citizen about his or her experience. The Inquiry and Research Mini Lesson on page 1197 offers more in-depth information on interviewing.

## Art Connection

Remind students to think of the symbolism of a wall as well as its literal function. If the wall is interpreted symbolically, students should see more dimensions of the immigrants' experiences in these photographs. Visual learners might do a flip chart for "Mexicans Begin Jogging" to show the different stages of the speaker's journey.

---

## Mini Lesson  Grammar

**VARYING TYPES OF SENTENCES** Remind students that skillful writers use combinations of simple, compound, complex, and compound-complex sentences in their writing. Display the following sentences to illustrate these types of sentences:

- Gary Soto and Pat Mora both explore the Hispanic experience in their writing. (*simple sentence with one independent clause*)
- Gary Soto's writing is influenced by his Hispanic background, and Pat Mora's work has appeared in anthologies of Hispanic writing. (*compound sentence with two independent clauses*)
- Although both Gary Soto and Pat Mora write about the Hispanic experience, their works

possess universal meaning. (*complex sentence with an independent clause and a subordinate clause*)
- Although both Gary Soto and Pat Mora write about the Hispanic experience, their works possess universal meaning, and both writers reach a wide audience beyond the Hispanic community. (*compound-complex sentence with two independent clauses and a subordinate clause*)

 Use **Grammar Transparencies and Copymasters,** p. 176.

 Use McDougal Littell's **Language Network,** Chapter 15, for more instruction in sentence variety.

## Objectives

1. understand and appreciate a **short story** (Literary Analysis)
2. understand **character** (Literary Analysis)
3. **make judgments about character** (Active Reading)

## Summary

The narrator describes her fascination with Bruno Sokolov, a student who looks older than his 14 years, dresses strangely, and has a scar on his forehead. He is the leader of a neighborhood gang and the president of the ninth grade. On Saturdays the narrator visits the downtown library, where she sometimes sees Bruno. One Saturday a stranger grabs her, dragging her into the men's lavatory. Bruno rushes in, pummels the assailant, and stabs him repeatedly with his switchblade knife. For these actions, Bruno is given six months' probation and is required to undergo psychiatric treatment. Bruno's personality changes dramatically. At 16, he quits school; at 18, he joins the army and later dies in Korea.

## Thematic Link

Bruno Sokolov's **integration** into the society of his school is based on other students' fearful respect for him. His feelings of shame for having to undergo psychiatric treatment, however, lead to the **disintegration** of his personality.

### 5-Minute Warm-Up

***Daily Language SkillBuilder***

Have students **proofread** the display sentences on page 1069k and write them correctly. The sentences also appear on Transparency 34 of **Grammar Transparencies and Copymasters.**

### Preteaching Vocabulary

If you would like to preteach the WORDS TO KNOW for this selection, use the Mini Lesson, p. 1202.

---

*"He was famous for intimidating, or harassing, or actually beating up certain of his classmates."*

# Hostage

*Short Story by* JOYCE CAROL OATES

### Comparing Literature

## Traditions Across Time: Continuing Transformation

The narrator in "Hostage," by Joyce Carol Oates, is a ninth-grade girl who is strongly attracted to a boy at school. This boy, Bruno Sokolov, reputedly carries a switchblade in his pocket. Despite his aura of self-assurance, Bruno really is an outsider among his classmates.

**Points of Comparison**  As you read this story, think about the narrator's relationship with Bruno. Consider how you might compare and contrast Bruno with Donny, the troubled youth in "Teenage Wasteland."

## Build Background

**Oates's Fiction** Joyce Carol Oates frequently writes about ordinary people affected by violence. In response to a reviewer who criticized her preoccupation with violence, Oates defended her work in this way: "As Flannery O'Connor—another writer frequently attacked for the 'darkness and violence' of her work—has said, No writer is a pessimist; the very act of writing is an optimistic act." By writing about violence in our society, Oates does not intend merely to mirror today's headlines but to "bring about a change of heart."

**WORDS TO KNOW**
**Vocabulary Preview**

| | |
|---|---|
| abrasive | invest |
| affronted | lurid |
| antagonistic | obscure |
| aplomb | rakish |
| derisive | scrupulously |
| incongruously | sibilant |
| incredulously | subtle |
| infatuation | |

## Focus Your Reading

**LITERARY ANALYSIS**  **CHARACTER**  The **characters** are the people who take part in the action of a story. In some stories, the characters' actions and decisions seem to control what happens. In other stories, the characters seem rather to be victims of forces beyond their control. Consider to what extent the characters in "Hostage" control what happens to them.

**ACTIVE READING**  **MAKING JUDGMENTS ABOUT CHARACTER**  In "Hostage," Joyce Carol Oates provides plentiful details to help you visualize the narrator's classmate Bruno. One way to understand the story better and to enjoy it more is to make judgments about Bruno's character as you read about his actions. Try these tips:

- List Bruno's actions in the story.
- For each action, state your judgment of Bruno. For example, ask yourself whether you admire or disapprove of him for that particular action.
- State the criterion, or the standard you used to make your judgment.

For example, one of Bruno's actions is that he carries a switchblade. You may disapprove of him for doing so. Your criterion might be that anyone carrying such a weapon is a threat to others.

**READER'S NOTEBOOK**  On a chart like the one shown, list Bruno's actions, your judgments of him, and the criteria you used to make your judgments.

| Bruno's Actions | My Judgments of Bruno | Criteria |
|---|---|---|
| | | |

---

## LESSON RESOURCES

**UNIT SEVEN RESOURCE BOOK,** pp. 61–65

**ASSESSMENT RESOURCES**
**Formal Assessment,** pp. 227–228
**Teacher's Guide to Assessment and Portfolio Use**
**Test Generator**

**SKILLS TRANSPARENCIES AND COPYMASTERS**
**Literary Analysis**
• Characterization, T6 (for Cooperative Learning Activity, p. 1212)

**Reading and Critical Thinking**
• Making Judgments, T5 (for Active Reading, p. 1200)

**Grammar**
• Interrupting Elements, C177 (for Mini Lesson, p. 1214)

**Vocabulary**
• Synonyms and Antonyms, C96 (for Mini Lesson, p. 1208)

**Writing**
• Literary Interpretation, C30 (for Writing Option 2, p. 1213)

**Communications**
• Impromptu Speaking: Dialogue, Role-Play, Debate, T13 (for Activities & Explorations 1, p. 1213)

**INTEGRATED TECHNOLOGY**

**Audio Library**
**Internet: Research Starter**
**Visit our website:**
www.mcdougallittell.com

# Hostage

**Joyce Carol Oates**

BY the age of fourteen Bruno Sokolov had the heft and swagger of a near-grown man. His wide shoulders, sturdy neck, dark oily hair wetted and combed sleekly back from his forehead like a rooster's crest, above all his large head and the shrewd squint of his pebble-colored eyes gave him an air unnervingly adult, as if, in junior high school, in the company of children, he was in disguise, yet carelessly in disguise. He wore his older brothers' and even his father's cast-off clothing, <u>rakish</u> combinations that suited him, pin-striped shirts, sweater vests, suspenders, bulky tweed coats and corduroy trousers, cheap leather belts with enormous buckles, even, frequently, for there were always deaths in those big immigrant families, mourning bands around his upper arm that gave him a look both sinister and holy, to which none of our teachers could object. He was smart; he was tough; the natural leader of a neighborhood gang of boys; he carried a switchblade knife, or was believed to do so. He had a strangely scarred forehead—in one version of the story he'd overturned a pan of boiling water on himself as a small child, in another version his mother in a fit of emotion had overturned it on him. He spoke English with a strong accent, musical, yet mocking, as if these sounds were his own invention, these queer eliding vowels and diphthongs,[1] and he had remarkable self-confidence for a boy with his background, the son of Polish Russian immigrants—out of bravado he ran for, and actually won, our ninth-grade presidency, in a fluke of an election that pitted our teachers' choice, a "good" boy, against a boy whom most of the teachers mistrusted, or feared. Even when Bruno Sokolov spoke intelligently in class there was an overtone of <u>subtle</u> mockery, if not contempt, in his voice. His grades were erratic and he was often absent from school—"family reasons" the usual excuse—and he was famous for intimidating, or harassing, or actually beating up certain of his classmates. His play at football and basketball was that of a steer loosed happily among heifers, and when, as our class president, a black snap-on

---

1. **eliding vowels and diphthongs:** vowels that are omitted or slurred over and combinations of vowel sounds within single syllables (as in *soil*).

WORDS
TO
KNOW

**rakish** (rā′kǐsh) *adj.* dashingly or sportingly stylish; jaunty
**subtle** (sŭt′l) *adj.* so slight as to be difficult to detect

**1201**

Tell students that this story is about the narrator's fascination with a boy at her school. As students read, have them consider why the narrator is attracted to this particular boy.

**Literary Analysis** `CHARACTER`

 Ask students to summarize Bruno's distinctive traits.

**Possible Responses:** He has the physical build and confidence of a man; he wears unusual combinations of clothes with jauntiness; he is smart, tough, self-assured, and fearless.

Use **Unit Seven Resource Book**, p. 63 for more practice.

**Active Reading**

> **MAKING JUDGMENTS**
> **ABOUT CHARACTER**

 Ask students to describe their impressions of the narrator.

**Possible Responses:** She is bright but lacks confidence. She seems to be quiet and lonely. She is very modest, seeing nothing in herself that could interest someone like Bruno.

Use **Unit Seven Resource Book**, p. 62 for more practice.

**Literary Analysis: TRAGIC HERO**

A tragic hero is an exceptional character, often gifted, whose downfall is caused by a tragic flaw. Ask students what might be Bruno's tragic flaw.

**Possible Response:** his violent tendencies

Ask what the narrator's fantasy suggests about the future she envisions for Bruno.

**Possible Response:** exciting; larger than life; doomed; tragic

---

## Teaching Options

---

bow tie around his neck, he addressed the rowdy assemblage from the stage with the <u>aplomb</u> and drawling ease of a radio broadcaster or a politician, shrewd eyes glittering with a sense of his own power, we felt, aroused, laughing at his jokes, a shiver of certitude, rippling among even the dullest of us like a nervous reflex through a school of fish, that we were in the presence of someone distinctive; someone of whom, however we might dislike him, we might be proud.

I didn't know him. I didn't belong to his world. Though my family lived only a block or so from his family in a neighborhood of row houses built in the 1890s and hardly renovated since that time, my grandparents had emigrated from Budapest in the early 1900s and Bruno's parents had come from Lublin, a Polish city near the Russian border, in the early 1930s, and that made a considerable difference. And I was younger than Bruno, younger than most of my classmates—I had been skipped a grade in elementary school, a source of <u>obscure</u> pride and shame to me—so that if he happened to glance toward me, if his squinty amused stare drifted in my direction, there was nothing, it

## I didn't belong to his world.

seemed, on which it might snag. I was small, I was brainy, I was invisible. For my part I observed Bruno Sokolov <u>scrupulously</u>, in classes, in the school corridors, making his way down the stairs, pushing ahead in the cafeteria line, actions he seemed to perform without thinking, as if the very size of his body had to be accommodated, his needs and impulses immediately discharged. Even to be teased by Bruno Sokolov was an

honor of a kind but it was not an honor casually granted, for the Sokolovs, poor as they were, crowded into their shabby row house with its rear yard lifting to a railway embankment, nonetheless took themselves seriously; they were displaced tradesmen, not Polish peasants.

The immigrants' world retained its taxonomical[2] distinctions of class, money, power, "breeding." In America, you were hungry to move up but you had no intention of helping others, outside the family, to move up with you.

The places where imagination takes root . . . There was an oversized winter coat Bruno Sokolov wore in bad weather, Cossack-style, navy blue, with upturned collar, deep pockets, and frayed sleeves, the mere sight of which made me feel confused, light-headed, panicked. There was the back of Bruno's big head, observed slantwise from me in English class, the springy oily dark hair often separating in quills, falling about his ears, and every few weeks a fresh haircut, done at home, crude and brutal, shaved at the neck. There was the sound of his suddenly uplifted voice, ringing and <u>abrasive</u>, often drawling in mockery, the give-and-take, foulmouthed, of young adolescent boys, and my immediate sense of alarm when I heard it, but also my envy: a sharp stabbing envy that cut me like a knife: for of course Bruno Sokolov never spoke my name, even in derision. He gave no sign of knowing it.

The <u>infatuation</u> was hardly love, not even affection, for I often fantasized Bruno Sokolov dying, a violent cinematic death, and took a vengeful pleasure in it; but there was about my feeling for him that sense, common to love, of futility and wild optimism conjoined, a quicken-

1

---

2. **taxonomical:** having to do with the science of classification.

WORDS
TO
KNOW

**aplomb** (ə-plŏm′) *n.* self-confidence
**obscure** (ŏb-skyŏŏr′) *adj.* indistinct; not clearly understood
**scrupulously** (skrōō′pyə-ləs-lē) *adv.* in an extremely careful and thorough manner; conscientiously
**abrasive** (ə-brā′sĭv) *adj.* harsh and rough
**infatuation** (ĭn-făch′ōō-ā′shən) *n.* the state of being completely carried away by foolish or shallow love or affection

1202

---

 **Preteaching Vocabulary**

**USING CONTEXT CLUES**

**Instruction** Call students' attention to the list of WORDS TO KNOW. Remind students that they can use context clues to determine the meanings of unfamiliar words. One type of context clue is a cause-and-effect relationship, which may be stated directly or only implied. Demonstrate the strategy using the following model.

His <u>abrasive</u> personality discouraged some customers from frequenting his store.

**Activity**

- Write the model sentence on the board.
- Ask a volunteer to tell what cause-and-effect relationship can be seen in the sentence. (*As a result of the store owner's abrasive personality, he lost customers.*)
- Have students use their understanding of the cause-and-effect relationship to guess the meaning of *abrasive*.
- Ask a volunteer to create a new sentence using the word *abrasive*.

ing of the pulse even at the very instant that the quickening, the hope, is checked: *No. Don't.*

Midway in the school year when we were in ninth grade Bruno's father died a strange and much talked-of death and I waited for weeks to tell Bruno how sorry I was that it had happened, approaching him, one day, in the corridor outside our homeroom, with an aggressive sort of shyness, and Bruno stared down at me with a look of blank surprise as if a voice had sounded out of the very air beside him, a voice wrongly intimate and knowing. He was taller than I by more than a head, his height exaggerated by the springy thickness of his hair and the breadth of his shoulders. The shiny-smooth skin of his scar, disappearing under his hair, was serrated and would have been rough to the touch. His eyes were heavy-lidded from lack of sleep or grief and he stared at me for what seemed a long time before saying, with a shrug of his shoulders, "Yeah. Me too." And that was all.

My heart was beating rapidly, wildly. But that was all.

Even by the standards of our neighborhood Mr. Sokolov had died an unusual death. He was a large fleshy man with deep-set suspicious eyes and bushy but receding hair that gave him a perpetually <u>affronted</u> look; he dressed formally, in dark tight-fitting suits with old-fashioned wide lapels, starched white shirts, dark neckties. He and two brothers owned a small neighborhood grocery with a meat counter, a real butcher's shop as my mother spoke of it, and Mr. Sokolov so dominated the store, took such edgy excitable <u>antagonistic</u> pride in it, that many customers,

Illustration Copyright © Eric Dinyer.

including my mother, were offended by his manner. In Bruno's father Bruno's coarse sly charm was mere coarseness; he was in the habit of issuing commands, in Polish, to his brothers, in front of customers; the neighborhood belief was that he wasn't quite "right in the head"— and certainly the dislocations of language made for constant misunderstandings, and constant misunderstandings made for what is called, clinically, paranoia, that sense that the world's very tilt is in our disfavor, and that nothing, however accidental-seeming, is accidental. Mr. Sokolov's short temper led him into arguments and even into feuds with neighbors, customers, city authorities, local police; he was tyrannical

WORDS TO KNOW
**affronted** (ə-frŭn′tĭd) *adj.* intentionally insulted **affront** *v.*
**antagonistic** (ăn-tăg′ə-nĭs′tĭk) *adj.* openly hostile and aggressive toward another

1203

**Exercises** Have students apply the strategy to determine the meanings of the underlined words.

1. Her <u>infatuation</u> with Bruno made her shy and tongue-tied around him.

2. Because of Bruno's importance in her life, her memory <u>invests</u> him with mythical or heroic qualities.

3. The <u>lurid</u> details about Mr. Sokolov's death horrified even the most hardened members of the community.

4. His <u>rakish</u> manner and his <u>aplomb</u> made him seem unaffected by the hardships of his life.

5. The narrator was a <u>scrupulously</u> conscientious student; as a result, she was double-promoted.

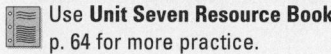 Use **Unit Seven Resource Book,** p. 64 for more practice.

A lesson on context clues appears on p. 326 in the Pupil's Edition.

**Reading Skills and Strategies:
SPECULATING**

**A** Ask students how the manner of his father's death might have affected Bruno.
**Possible Responses:** He might be shocked, angry, frightened, or vengeful.

**Literary Analysis: SYMBOL**

**B** Ask students what the library and the books might symbolize for the narrator.
**Possible Responses:** knowledge; the future; escape from a dreary life; change; the answer to the meaning of life

**Active Reading**

> **MAKING JUDGMENTS
> ABOUT CHARACTER**

**C** Ask students how Bruno's visits to the library influence their view of him.
**Possible Responses:** make him seem a more positive character; show him as someone who wants to learn; expose a more sensitive side of him

**Reading Skills and Strategies:
ANALYZING**

**D** Ask students what they think the narrator is referring to when she agrees with Bruno's comment about "stuff that scares you into thinking."
**Possible Response:** Bruno affects the narrator as reading the book *Dracula* might affect her. He gives her a glimpse of another world that is frightening but attractive and stimulating.

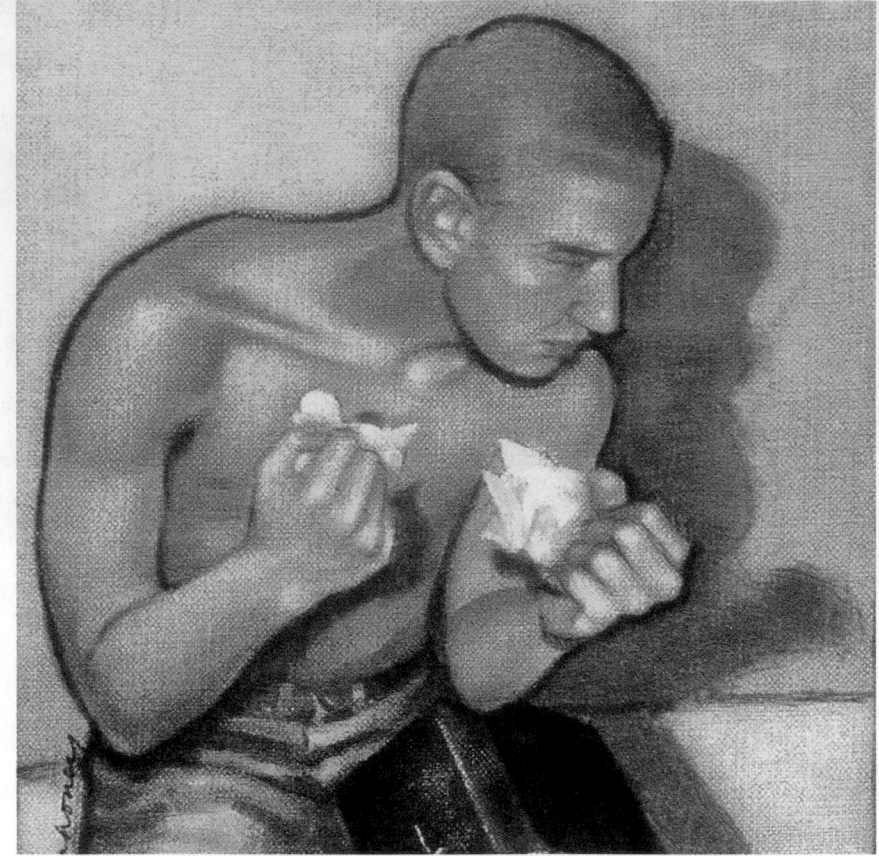

Illustration Copyright © 1987 Katherine Mahoney.

**1**  **A** with his family—three sons, two daughters, a wife who spoke virtually no English; he was driven to fits of rage when his store was vandalized, and burglarized, and police failed to arrest the criminals, or even to give the Sokolovs the satisfaction that they were trying to find them. (All this was "Mafia"-related. It was an open secret that the small neighborhood tradesmen were being extorted or were engaged in some elaborate process of attempting to resist extortion.) Mr. Sokolov died, in fact, defending his store: he was hiding at the rear when someone broke in, and he attacked the intruder with a meat cleaver, but was himself shot in the leg, and when the man ran limping and bleeding out into the alley Mr. Sokolov pursued him with the cleaver, limping and bleeding too, and shouting wildly in Polish . . . and somehow Mr. Sokolov and the other man both disappeared. A trail of their commingled blood drops led to an intersection close by, then stopped. Police theorized that a van had been parked there, and that Mr. Sokolov was taken away in it: he was missing for several days, the object of a much-publicized local search, then his body, or rather parts of his body, began to be discovered . . . floating in the canal, carelessly buried at the city dump, tossed into the weedy vacant lot behind St. John the Evangelist Church, to which the Sokolovs belonged. The murderer or murderers were

**1204**    UNIT SEVEN    PART 2: INTEGRATION AND DISINTEGRATION

---

## Teaching Options

 **Mini Lesson** **Viewing and Representing**

**ART APPRECIATION** This illustration by Katherine Mahoney conveys the tension and anger of its subject, the young man.
**Instruction** Ask students to analyze the ways in which the artist is able to convey the tense and angry mood of the figure.

**Possible Responses:** the grim profile; the hunched and powerful shoulders; the clenched fists with crumpled paper in them; the intense gaze; the book overturned on the young man's thigh, giving the impression that he was forced to stop reading because of sudden, strong emotion.

never found and twenty years later, long after Bruno Sokolov himself had died, in Korea, one of his cousins ran for mayor, and narrowly missed winning, on the strength of a passionate campaign against "organized crime" in the city.

**On** Saturday mornings in all but the worst winter weather I took two city buses downtown to the public library, where, in a windowless ground-floor room set aside for "young adult" readers I searched the shelves for books, especially novels, the search <u>invested</u> with a queer heart-stopping urgency as if the next book I chose, encased in its yellowing plastic cover, *YA* in tall black letters on its spine, might in some way change my life. I was of an age when any change at all seemed promising; I hadn't yet the temperament to conceive of change as fearful. I didn't doubt that *the* book, *the* revelation, awaited me, no matter that the books I actually did read were usually disappointing, too simplistically written and imagined, made up of characters too unswervingly good or bad to be believable. It was the search itself that excited me . . . the look and the feel of the books on their bracketed metal shelves, the smell of the room, a close, warm, stale mixture of floor wax, furniture polish, paper paste, the faint chemical scent of the middle-aged librarian's inky-black dyed hair. Sometimes the very approach to the library—my first glimpse of its Greek Revival portico and columns, its fanning stone steps—aroused me to a sickish apprehension, as if I understood beforehand that whatever I hoped to find there I would not find; or, by the act of finding it, making it my own, I would thereby lose it. The library was further invested with romance since every second or third Saturday I caught sight of Bruno Sokolov there too . . . and one day when I was sitting on the front steps, waiting for the bus, Bruno stooped over me unannounced to ask, in his oddly breezy, brotherly manner, what I'd checked out, and to show me what he had—adult science fiction by Heinlein, Bradbury, Asimov. Did he have a card for upstairs? for adult books? I asked, surprised, and Bruno said, "Sure." Another time he showed me a book with a dark <u>lurid</u> cover, a ghoulish face with red-gleaming eyes, Bram Stoker's *Dracula*—he hadn't checked it out of the library but had simply taken it from a shelf and slipped it inside his coat. Not stealing exactly, Bruno said, because he'd bring it back, probably. "The kind of stuff I like, it's things that make you think, y'know, the weirder the better," he said, smiling and showing big damp yellowed teeth, "—stuff that scares you into thinking, y'know what I mean?" His eyes were heavy-lidded, his lips rather thick, the lower lip in particular; the curious scar high on his forehead gleamed with reflected light. I saw with surprise his thick stubby battered-looking fingers clutching the book, dirt-edged nails, the knuckles nicked and raw, as if he hurt himself casually without knowing what he did, or caring. Or maybe his hands were roughened from work at the grocery. Or from fighting.

## I guessed he didn't know my name.

"Yes," I said, looking up at him, "—I know **D** what you mean."

I watched him walk away, my eyes pinching, following his tall figure in its forward-plunging impatient stride until he was out of sight. *Thief,* I thought. *I could turn you in.* It was only the second or third time we'd spoken together and it would be the final time. And I guessed he didn't know my name. Or even know that he didn't know.

It wasn't long afterward, on another Saturday

WORDS TO KNOW

**invest** (ĭn-vĕst′) *v.* to provide with a certain quality
**lurid** (lŏŏr′ĭd) *adj.* startling and sensational

**1205**

---

## Customizing Instruction

**Less Proficient Readers**
Ask students who killed Bruno's father.
**Possible Response:** criminals with possible ties to the Mafia

Have students explain what the narrator and Bruno have in common.
**Possible Response:** Both Bruno and the narrator love to read; the narrator goes to the library every Saturday and sometimes sees Bruno there.

**Set a Purpose** Have students read to find out whether the narrator ever sees Bruno in the library again.

**Students Acquiring English**
**1** Explain to students that *extortion* means "the act of getting money by threats." The *Mafia* refers to a network of loosely connected secret groups that hold power through violence and intimidation. Organized crime also makes money through control of gambling, narcotics sales, prostitution, and lending money at unlawful interest rates.

**Less Proficient Readers**
**2** Make sure students understand this reference to the Korean War (1950–1953), which was an outgrowth of the cold war between the United States and the Soviet Union. Point out that this detail provides a clue to the story's setting.

**Gifted and Talented**
Ask students to discuss what Bruno might symbolize for the narrator. Students should examine the character of the narrator, particularly as revealed in the library scene, to help them discover what Bruno represents to her.

### Literary Analysis  CHARACTER

**A** Ask students what the narrator's thoughts in this passage reveal about her personality.

**Possible Responses:** She seems shy; a daydreamer; agitated; thoughtful; confused by her feelings about boys.

Ask students whether the narrator appears to control the direction of her life or is acted upon by forces in her environment.

**Possible Responses:** She is acted upon by forces in her environment. She reacts to things that happen rather than taking action to shape what happens.

### Literary Analysis: CONFLICT

**B** Ask students how Oates makes it seem unlikely that the narrator can win this struggle against her assailant.

**Possible Responses:** He is about a hundred pounds heavier than she is; she is paralyzed with fear; he appears beyond reason and enraged.

### Active Reading

> MAKING JUDGMENTS
> ABOUT CHARACTER

**C** The narrator equates being mutilated, murdered, and held hostage with being shamed. Ask students why this reaction is consistent with her character.

**Possible Responses:** She is so shy and retiring that the prospect of being central in a drama is repugnant to her, even if the situation is not of her own making. She also feels that she should be fighting to save herself, not succumbing to the attacker's force.

---

morning, in late winter, in the library, downstairs, alone, emerging from the women's lavatory—that place of ancient toilets with chain-activated flushes, black-and-white-checked tile encrusted with decades of dirt, incongruously ornate plaster moldings—I heard someone say in a low insinuating voice, "Little girl? Eh? Little girl?—where're you going?" and was crudely awakened from my brooding trance, the usual spellbound state in which I walked about, when I was alone, in those days, dreaming not so much of Bruno Sokolov or one or another boy I knew as of the mysterious stab of emotions they aroused, the angry teasing hope they seemed to embody, and I'd just pushed through the heavy frosted-glass swinging door and saw, there, a few feet away, in the cavernous poorly lit corridor—this was in an alcove, not far from the young adults reading room—one of the hellish sights of my life: a man approaching me, smiling at me, intimate, <u>derisive</u>, accusatory. I had vaguely recalled this man following me down the stairs but I must have told myself, if I'd told myself anything, that he was simply headed for the men's lavatory. "Little girl—c'mon *here*," he said, less patiently. Did he know me? Was I expected to know him? I had seen him around the library and on the street outside, dressed shabbily yet flamboyantly in layers of mismatched clothing, overcoat, sweaters, shirt, filthy woolen scarf wound around his neck, unbuckled overshoes flapping on his feet; he was one of a number of oldish odd-looking and -behaving men who haunted the library, in cold weather especially, spending much of the day in the reference room, where they made a show of reading, or actually did read, the daily newspapers, turning the pages harshly, as if the world's events filled them with contempt. Sometimes they dozed, or muttered to themselves, or drank from pint bottles hidden in much-wrinkled paper bags, or forgot where they were,

the precariousness of their welcome, and addressed someone who didn't know them and who quickly edged away. If they caused much disruption one of the librarians, usually a stocky woman with pearl-framed glasses (whom I myself feared for her air of cold authority), ushered them outside, and shut the door behind them. Upon rare occasions police were called but I had never actually seen a policeman arrive.

But here, now, today, for no reason I could guess or would ever be explained to me, one of these men had followed me downstairs to the women's lavatory, speaking excitedly, scolding me, now walking straight at me as if he meant to run me down. He grabbed hold of my arm and wrestled me back against the wall, and the things I was carrying—my little beige leather army surplus purse, an armload of library books—went flying. I saw his coarse-veined face above me, and his white-rimmed rheumy mad eyes, felt his whiskers like wire brush against my skin, and must have screamed, though I don't remember screaming, and he panted, and cursed, and spoke to me with great urgency, now dragging me to the doorway of the men's lavatory, where, I suddenly knew, he would assault me, keep me hostage, kill me—there was no hope for me now. Had I not read of such horrors hinted in the newspaper, or heard of them, whispered, never fully articulated . . .

Yet I might have escaped my assailant, had I squirmed, ducked under his arm, twisted free. He outweighed me by more than one hundred pounds but I might have escaped him and run upstairs screaming for help except that I could not move; all the strength had drained from me. It was as if the mere touch of an adult, an adult's terrible authority, had paralyzed me.

But we were making noise, and the noises echoed in the high-ceilinged space. And then the frosted-glass window of the door to the lavatory shattered and fell in pieces around us. By now

| WORDS | **incongruously** (ĭn-kŏng′grōō-əs-lē) *adv.* in a manner that is not fitting, |
| TO | suitable, or in agreement; incompatibly |
| KNOW | **derisive** (dĭ-rī′sĭv) *adj.* mocking or ridiculing; scornful |

**1206**

---

## Teaching Options

 **Speaking and Listening**

### STORYTELLING

**Prepare** Have students imagine that they are the narrator thirty-four years after the incident, telling her daughter the story of what happened in the library to try to prepare her for the random violence she might encounter in the world. Students should base their accounts on textual evidence but should tell the story in the words that they imagine the narrator would use in an informal conversation with her teenage daughter. Stories should include the incident, her feelings, a

description of Bruno, and the lesson the narrator wants to convey to her daughter.

**Present** Ask students who are willing to tell their stories to small groups. Students' stories must be valid interpretations of the account but should also reflect the narrator's style. Listeners should evaluate the effectiveness of both the story and its lesson from their viewpoint as teenagers.

> BLOCK
> SCHEDULING This activity is particularly well-suited for longer class periods.

Illustration Copyright © Greg Spalenka.

### Less Proficient Readers
Ask students to summarize what happens to the narrator in the library.
**Possible Response:** A man whom she has seen around the library follows her downstairs to the lavatory, calls out to her, and takes her hostage.

**Set a Purpose** Have students read to find out how this conflict is resolved.

### Multiple Learning Styles
**Visual Learners**

Have students discuss the detailed description of the assailant's clothes and physical appearance. Ask what impression students have of his character from this description.
**Possible Responses:** He seems poor, unkempt, eccentric, unpredictable.

the librarian from the young adult room had emerged, and another woman was poking her head around a corner staring at us <u>incredulously</u>, and someone cried out for the madman to leave me alone, and the madman shouted back in a rage, and how many minutes passed in this way, or was it merely seconds, while I crouched unable to move yet trembling violently in a crook of a stranger's arm, breathing in the odors, the stench really, of his desperate being, a sharp smell of alcohol, and dirt-stiffened clothing, and I might have thought of praying, I might have thought of God, but all thoughts were struck from my brain, like shadows in a room blasted by light, and even the thought that I would be held hostage and mutilated and murdered and shamed before all **C**

WORDS
TO
KNOW

**incredulously** (ĭn-krĕj'ə-ləs-lē) *adv.* in a manner showing a lack of belief

**1207**

---

✓**Assessment** **Informal Assessment**

**UNDERSTANDING CHARACTER** You can informally assess your students' understanding of the selection and the characters by having them rewrite the scene outside the library between Bruno Sokolov and the narrator (page 1205) from Bruno's point of view. Have students write individually and then share their scenes in small groups.

**RUBRIC**

**3** **Full Accomplishment** Scenes reflect considerable insight into the two characters and their relationship and are consistent with the story's events.

**2** **Substantial Accomplishment** Scenes are true to the story's events but reflect limited insight into the characters and their relationship.

**1** **Little or Partial Accomplishment** Students omit events and/or have difficulty interpreting the characters.

### Active Reading

**MAKING JUDGMENTS ABOUT CHARACTER**

**A** The following questions can guide students to make judgments about Bruno.

- How do Bruno's actions contrast with those of the other onlookers?

  **Possible Responses:** Bruno is unhesitating; he moves swiftly without any attempt to reason; he relies on his physical force to settle this problem.

- What conclusions can you draw about Bruno from these actions?

  **Possible Responses:** He is bold, unafraid, courageous, impulsive, confident in his strength.

- Is Bruno a hero?

  **Possible Responses:** Yes, Bruno is a hero because he puts himself in danger to save someone else; no, Bruno is not a hero because he continues to attack the man long after the danger from him is past.

### Literary Analysis: INTERPRET

**B** Ask students what the narrator knows that others in her community don't.

**Possible Response:** She knows that Bruno kept attacking the man long after the man stopped attacking him.

### Literary Analysis  CHARACTER

**C** Ask students how Bruno changes after the incident and why.

**Possible Responses:** Bruno becomes withdrawn and sullen; he resigns his office, skips school, runs away from home, becomes an outsider. He is ashamed by the psychiatric treatment, which makes the differences that he reveled in seem abnormal.

---

the world had not the power to make me fight as I might have, and should have fought.

A number of people had gathered, but were shy of approaching us. The librarian with the pearl-framed glasses was trying to reason with my assailant, who, gripping me hard, with a kind of joy, kept saying, "No! No! No you don't—stay away!" His arm was crooked around my head, his elbow pinioning my neck, I half crouched in an awkward position, the side of my face against his coat, the rough material of his coat, and my hair bunched up fallen into my face; I did not think I was crying, for I had not the space or the breath for crying yet my face was wet with tears, my nose ran shamefully as a baby's—and all the while we swayed and lurched and staggered together, as in a comical dance, which, having begun, we could not end, for there was no way of ending, no way of escaping the corner we had backed into. Several times the word *police* was uttered and several times the madman threatened to "kill the little girl" if any police should so much as appear. Shouts and cries burst about us like birds' shrieks echoing in the passageway and then dipping abruptly to silence. My assailant had pulled me into the lavatory, the outer area of sinks and tall narrow mirrors and naked light bulbs, identical to the women's lavatory, it seemed, yet a forbidden space, and I was able to think clearly, for the first time since the madman had grabbed me, *He will have to kill me now to prove he can do it.*

And then the door was pushed open, and Bruno Sokolov appeared, crouched, unhesitating, moving swiftly—he had shoved his way  past the witnesses in the corridor, paying no attention to them, drawn by the excitement, the upset, the prospect of a fight, not knowing who I was until he saw me and perhaps not even knowing then, for there wasn't time to think; in **1** describing what happened I am trying to put into words quicksilver actions that took place within seconds, or split seconds: Bruno fierce and direct as on the basketball court when he deliberately ran down another player, pulling

the madman off me, yanking him away, the two of them screaming at each other, cursing, like men who know each other well, and there was Bruno of a height with my assailant fending off the man's frenzied windmill blows, the two of them now struggling by the sinks, Bruno punching, stabbing, kicking, a blade flashing in his right hand, and blood splashing on the floor, thick sinewy worms of red splashing on the tiled floor . . . Bruno had taken out his switchblade knife, and Bruno was using it, in wide sweeping furious strokes, cursing the man, saying repeatedly, "Die! Die! Die!" though the man had fallen to his knees shrieking in pain and terror, trying to shield his head with his arms. And there was Bruno in a pea-green army surplus jacket, bareheaded, sweating, crouched above him like a madman himself, his face so doughy-pale and distended in rage I would not have known it, eyes shining with moisture, "Die! *Die!*" with each stroke of the knife . . . but now I ran out of the lavatory and into the corridor, where someone caught me in her arms and walked me hurriedly down the hall to a cubicle of an office, the door shut, locked, a call placed to the emergency room of the closest hospital, the word *assault* uttered, and I saw it was the librarian with the pearl-framed glasses now as solicitous of me as a mother. And I knew I would be safe.

**My** assailant was a man of fifty-eight, an ex-mental patient now living on a disability pension from the U.S. Navy in a downtown hotel for transients. He did not die from Bruno Sokolov's attack but he was in critical condition for some weeks, semiconscious, and when conscious rarely coherent, unable to explain why he had assaulted me or even to recall that he had done so. Nor did he remember the junior high school boy who'd stabbed him with a wicked eight-inch switchblade knife, wounding him in the chest, belly, groin, arms, and face. His memories, such

---

## Teaching Options

 **Mini Lesson**  ## Vocabulary Strategy

### SYNONYMS AND ANTONYMS

**Instruction** Remind students that synonyms are words with similar meanings and that antonyms are words with opposite meanings. Explain to students that when choosing a synonym or an antonym for a word, they should distinguish between the denotative and connotative meanings of words.

**Exercise** Have students choose the best synonym for each underlined word.

1. The <u>stench</u> of his dirty clothes would remain in her memory always. (<u>stink</u>, aroma, smell)

2. Although he was far in front of her, she could

recognize him by his <u>swagger</u>. (stride, <u>strut</u>, walk)

3. The narrator ran to the librarian, who was <u>solicitous</u> of her after the upsetting incident. (eager, anxious, <u>considerate</u>)

4. The narrator defines her infatuation as combining feelings of futility and <u>optimism</u>. (brightness, <u>hopefulness</u>, enthusiasm)

**Application** Have students use a dictionary and/or thesaurus to determine an accurate antonym for each of the underlined words above.

Use **Vocabulary Transparencies and Copymasters**, p. 96.

as they were, were concentrated upon late childhood spent in a rural settlement in western Pennsylvania half a century ago.

# Following

this much-publicized incident things were never the same again for Bruno Sokolov. As a minor who had, in a sense, behaved heroically, he was not formally charged with any crime (possession of a deadly weapon, for instance, or "aggravated assault") and naturally witnesses testified in his behalf: he had rushed into the lavatory and thrown himself on the madman in order to save me, and then he had fought him, nearly killing him, in self-defense. (So I testified too. So I told everyone. Though I always knew that in the strictest sense it wasn't true.) But a juvenile-court judge placed him on six months' probation, during which time he was obliged to seek psychiatric therapy and to register as an outpatient at a state psychiatric facility, and the shame of that connection so qualified the glamour of Bruno's heroism, and what, literally, he had almost done—*killed a man! stabbed an adult man to death with a switchblade!*—that, in school, he became increasingly withdrawn and sullen, even among his pals, given to unpredictable displays of temper and childish violence, and his grades sharply declined, and he had to resign his class office, and there were intervals when he simply stayed away from school, and the psychiatric therapy was extended for another six months, and there were difficulties in the Sokolov family, and Bruno ran away, tried to enlist in the army, but failed, and came back home, working in the grocery after school and on Saturdays, and through the summer, and in the autumn, in high school; it could never have been the case that this hulking moody overgrown boy might have run for, let alone won, one of the class offices,

nor was he on any of the sports teams, hardly a schoolboy any longer but not a man either, bored, ironic, and truculent, out of scale in our classrooms and in our corridors, slamming his locker door shut as if he meant to break it . . . and should a textbook fall from his hand he'd be likely to give it a kick, but not out of clowning high spirits and not inviting you to laugh sharing a joke because there was no joke, only Bruno Sokolov's dangerous eyes shifting like water under wind, and then he'd be gone, no backward glance, hardly more than a tight ticlike grimace to acknowledge the tie, the bond, the secret between us, unspoken, that we were kin almost as blood relatives are kin who have virtually nothing to do with each other publicly and do not in a sense "know" each other at all, a phenomenon common with schoolchildren though perhaps not limited to them. *It's because of me*, I would think, staring after him, *what he is now—my fault*. Though at more sober moments I understood that what Bruno Sokolov had done had nothing to do with me, or no more to do with me than it had with the ex-mental patient he had nearly killed.

By sixteen Bruno Sokolov had quit school, by seventeen he had joined the army, by eighteen he'd been shipped overseas to die within a few months at the Battle of Taegu, Korea. Pvt. First Class Bruno J. Sokolov, his photograph, tough-jawed, squinty-eyed, hopeful, in the evening paper. And the other night I dreamt of him, a boy thirty-four years dead, remembering in the dream what I'd forgotten for years, that none of his friends had ever called him "Bruno" but always "Sokolov" or "Sokki"—"Sockie"—a harsh <u>sibilant</u> magical sound I had yearned to have the right to say, shouting it in the street as others did, and he would have turned, and he would have seen me, and he would have raised his hand in recognition. As if that might have made a difference. ❖

| WORDS TO KNOW | **sibilant** (sĭb′ə-lənt) *adj.* hissing |
|---|---|

**1209**

## Customizing Instruction

### Less Proficient Readers
Ask students how the conflict between the narrator and her assailant is resolved.
**Possible Response:** Bruno Sokolov attacks the assailant, severely wounding him.

Ask students whether they think Bruno's response was justified.

### Students Acquiring English
**1** Explain that *quicksilver* is another word for mercury, a silver-colored metallic element that is a liquid at room temperature. Mercury flows quickly; it is named after the swift-footed Roman messenger god. The narrator is saying that Bruno acted very swiftly, that the events in the men's lavatory happened so fast the narrator can hardly remember them all.

**2** Explain that a *minor* is a person under the age of 18, too young to be considered an adult by law. Also explain that *assault* means "attack," and that *aggravated assault* is a crime more serious than common assault. Bruno might have been charged with aggravated assault because of the viciousness of his attack and his use of the switchblade.

## Literary Analysis: CONFLICT

Tell students that they are often expected to compare elements of texts across texts. Ask students to compare the conflict in "The Legend" with that between the assailant and the narrator in "Hostage."

Possible Responses: Both conflicts claim random victims; both attacks are seemingly without motive.

## Literary Analysis   CHARACTER

Ask students to compare the narrator in "Hostage" with the speaker in "The Legend."

Possible Responses: Both feel ashamed. The narrator is ashamed because she didn't fight her way out of the situation before Bruno got involved, and the speaker is ashamed for feeling so distinct from the wounded man. Both characters feel compassion—the narrator for Bruno, the speaker for the dying man. Both will remember these incidents forever. Both are sensitive and thoughtful.

## Literary Analysis: IMAGERY

Ask students to locate evocative words and phrases that the poet uses to increase the poignancy of this man's death.

Possible Responses: "enjoys/the feel of warm laundry . . ./flannellike against his gloveless hands" (lines 6–8); "very skinny, dressed as one of the poor/ in rumpled suit pants and a plaid mackinaw,/dingy and too large" (lines 14–16); "a babbling no one understands" (line 31)

# The Legend

### Garrett Hongo

In Chicago, it is snowing softly
and a man has just done his wash for the week.
He steps into the twilight of early evening,
carrying a wrinkled shopping bag
5  full of neatly folded clothes,
and, for a moment, enjoys
the feel of warm laundry and crinkled paper,
flannellike against his gloveless hands.
There's a Rembrandt glow on his face,
10  a triangle of orange in the hollow of his cheek
as a last flash of sunset
blazes the storefronts and lit windows of the street.

He is Asian, Thai or Vietnamese,
and very skinny, dressed as one of the poor
15  in rumpled suit pants and a plaid mackinaw,
dingy and too large.
He negotiates the slick of ice
on the sidewalk by his car,
opens the Fairlane's back door,
20  leans to place the laundry in,
and turns, for an instant,
toward the flurry of footsteps
and cries of pedestrians
as a boy—that's all he was—
25  backs from the corner package store[1]
shooting a pistol, firing it,
once, at the dumbfounded man
who falls forward,
grabbing at his chest.

## Teaching Options

 **Mini Lesson**   ## Speaking and Listening

### INTERVIEWING

**Prepare** Have students think about interviews they have seen on television. Explain that the reporter usually prepares and asks questions that require more than a yes-or-no answer and listens carefully to the answers, sometimes using them as springboards to follow-up questions. Have the students work in pairs, with one student playing the role of a reporter and the other student the role of a witness to the shooting in "The Legend." Build on the details provided in the poem (time of day—sunset; time of year—winter; place—

section of town with a laundromat and a package store). Encourage students to continue the diction of the poem by trying to be as specific and colorful in their choice of language as the poet.

**Present** Have the reporter formulate and ask three well-thought-out questions. The witness's answers should reflect the poem's message about victimization and senseless violence. Each interview should be presented to the class, and listeners should evaluate how consistent the details are with the poem and how well the interviewer evokes appropriate responses from the witness.

**Less Proficient Readers**
Have students summarize the action of the poem.

**Possible Response:** An Asian man steps out of a laundromat on a cold winter day in Chicago. As he is putting his laundry in his car, a young man who has just robbed a liquor store shoots him to death.

Ask students to explain the significance of the last three lines of the poem.

**Possible Response:** The lines show the speaker's hope that the dead man, slain so brutally, will find peace and happiness in the next life.

30  A few sounds escape from his mouth,
a babbling no one understands
as people surround him
bewildered at his speech.
The noises he makes are nothing to them.
35  The boy has gone, lost
in the light array of foot traffic
dappling the snow with fresh prints.

Tonight, I read about Descartes'[2]
grand courage to doubt everything
40  except his own miraculous existence
and I feel so distinct
from the wounded man lying on the concrete
I am ashamed.

Let the night sky cover him as he dies.
45  Let the weaver girl cross the bridge of heaven[3]
and take up his cold hands.

                    In Memory of Jay Kashiwamura

---

1. **package store:** a liquor store.
2. **Descartes** (dā-kärt´): René Descartes, a French philosopher, scientist, and mathematician of the 1600s who believed that the proof of human existence was the ability to think. His most famous statement was "I think, therefore I am."
3. **weaver girl . . . heaven:** In Chinese legend, the weaver girl and her beloved are separated by the "river of Heaven"—the Milky Way. Once a year, magpies spread their wings to form a bridge that allows her to cross the river.

THE LEGEND  **1211**

---

✓ **Assessment Standardized Test Practice**

**CHOOSING THE BEST THEME** For some standardized tests, students will be asked to compare elements of two passages. Students can practice this skill by choosing the most accurate statement of a theme common to "Hostage" and "The Legend." Read aloud or write on the chalkboard the following question.

Which of the following statements best states the theme shared by the short story "Hostage" and the poem "The Legend"?

**A.** Life can be very difficult for immigrants and their children.

**B.** As long as a person is remembered, he is not dead.

**C.** Life is uncertain and fragile, vulnerable to the violence of the modern world.

Remind students that the theme is the central idea that the writer wishes to convey. Although the same work might suggest different themes to different readers, the best statement of theme will be the one supported by the development of the plot and the actions of the characters. For that reason, C is the best choice.

## GUIDING STUDENT RESPONSE

## Connect to the Literature

### Connect to the Literature

**1. What Do You Think?**
Some students may state that the violence is not gratuitous but consistent with Bruno's character.

**Comprehension Check**
- He is shot by an intruder and disappears, chasing him with a cleaver.
- in the basement of the public library by an ex-mental patient
- He resents the probation and psychiatric treatment; he becomes moody and withdrawn.

Use Selection Quiz in
**Unit Seven Resource Book,** p. 65.

## Think Critically

**2. Possible Responses:** She feels guilty over having been the catalyst for his action; she remains somewhat infatuated with him; she feels grateful to him for having saved her from harm.

**3. Responses will vary:** Some students may judge Bruno as excessively violent because he displays no self-control in subduing the narrator's assailant.

**4. Possible Responses:** Bruno withdraws from others because he is ashamed of his punishment; the psychiatric treatment and the violence he unleashed equate him with the assailant; the stabbing incident left him disturbed.

**5. Possible Responses:** Both Bruno and his father are physically strong but given to fits of rage. Faced with a crisis, both unleash their potential for violence.

## Literary Analysis

**Tragic Hero** Some students may say that Bruno doesn't fit the definition because the story doesn't say whether he is aware that he has contributed to his own downfall or because Bruno's downfall is less an error in judgment than an impulsive, uncontrollable outburst of anger and hate. Others may say that he does fit the definition because he brings about his own downfall, showing errors in judgment both in the violent way he stabs the vagrant and in his sullen behavior after the stabbing.

---

## Connect to the Literature

**1. What Do You Think?**
How did you react to the violence in this story? Share your comments with your classmates.

**Comprehension Check**
- How is Bruno's father killed?
- Where is the narrator attacked and by whom?
- How does Bruno's personality change after his fight with the ex-mental patient?

## Think Critically

**2.** How do you explain the narrator's feelings for Bruno at the end of the story?

**3.** **ACTIVE READING | MAKING JUDGMENTS ABOUT CHARACTER** What judgments did you make about Bruno's character while reading this story? State the criteria you used to make your judgments. Refer to the chart in your **READER'S NOTEBOOK.**

**4.** How do you account for the change in Bruno after the stabbing?

> **THINK ABOUT**
> - the emotional effects of his violent act
> - how the juvenile-court judge and others perceive him
> - the narrator's comment that Bruno's violent act had "no more to do with me than it had with the ex-mental patient he had nearly killed" (page 1209)

**5.** How would you compare Bruno with his father?

## Extend Interpretations

**6. Critic's Corner** One of our student board members, Katie McGuire, made this comment about the story: "At first, the author kept my interest by using a lot of description. . . . However, I think there was too much description. If the description was kept minimal, the story would have probably been more interesting." What do you think about the amount of description in Oates's story?

**7. Connect to Life** How would you explain why some people react violently in a threatening situation?

**8.** **Points of Comparison** Whom do you consider a more sympathetic character—Bruno in this story or Donny in "Teenage Wasteland"? Defend your answer.

---

## Extend Interpretations

**Critic's Corner** Have students point out specific passages that they feel contain too much description. Students could rewrite these passages, omitting some descriptive details, to evaluate the effectiveness of more straightforward language. If students feel the description enhances the story, ask them to highlight segments that they feel are most effective.

**Connect to Life** Responses will vary. Some students may state that a violent reaction may reflect deep feelings of insecurity.

**Points of Comparison** Responses will vary. Some students may find Bruno more sympathetic because he puts himself in danger to save someone else.

---

## Literary Analysis

**CHARACTER: TRAGIC HERO** One type of character sometimes found in drama and fiction is the tragic hero. Aristotle, an ancient Greek philosopher, was the first to define this character. According to Aristotle, a **tragic hero** is an exceptional character, often highly gifted. The hero's downfall is usually caused by a tragic flaw—an error in judgment or a defect in character—that leads to his or her destruction. Tragic heroes perceive how their own actions have brought about their ruin. The hero's fall arouses pity and fear in the audience—pity for the hero and fear for all humans, who share to some extent the hero's defects.

**Cooperative Learning Activity** Get together with a small group of classmates to discuss whether or not this definition of a tragic hero applies to Bruno. Then write a **summary** statement, stating your evaluation and supporting reasons. Share your statement with other groups.

## Writing Options

**1. Character Sketch** How do you believe Bruno's life would have turned out if he had not stabbed the ex-mental patient in the library? Write a profile of Bruno that might eventually have appeared in the local newspaper. Be prepared to explain your predictions for him.

**2. Expository Essay** Draft an expository essay in which you explore the causes and effects of Bruno's actions. Ask a partner to read your work and to make suggestions. Use a chart like the following to organize your prewriting notes.

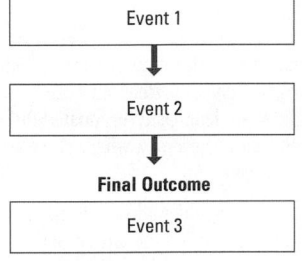

```
┌─────────────────────────┐
│        Event 1          │
└─────────────────────────┘
            ↓
┌─────────────────────────┐
│        Event 2          │
└─────────────────────────┘
            ↓
     Final Outcome
┌─────────────────────────┐
│        Event 3          │
└─────────────────────────┘
```

**Writing Handbook**
See page 1282: Cause and Effect

**3. Literary Review** In an interview, Joyce Carol Oates once argued that "all art is moral, educative, illustrative." To what extent do you think "Hostage" and Garrett Hongo's poem "The Legend" (page 1210) fit this description? What moral issues does each work raise? What does each work teach or show? Write a literary review to explore these questions. Place this piece in your **Working Portfolio.**

**4.** **Points of Comparison**
Write a dialogue in which the narrator of "Hostage" and Donny's mother in "Teenage Wasteland" (page 1169) exchange views about the needs of troubled youths.

## Activities & Explorations

**1. Role-Play** Gather in groups of five and role-play each of the following characters, telling how the character views Bruno Sokolov and why:
- the narrator
- the madman in the library
- the juvenile-court judge
- one of Bruno's teachers
- Bruno himself

~ PERFORMING

**2. Drawing** Review the many visual details that Oates uses to describe Bruno, such as his scarred forehead. Then sketch a portrait of him. ~ ART

**3. Debate** Was the sentence Bruno received from the juvenile-court judge justified? With a small group of classmates, have a debate. ~ SPEAKING AND LISTENING

## Inquiry & Research

**Crime Statistics** In "Hostage," both the narrator and Bruno are touched by violence. Find recent statistics on violent crime in the United States, and use them to answer the following questions and others that interest you: Has violent crime increased in recent years? What proportion of violent crime do teenagers commit? Has this proportion increased in recent years? You may also want to gather statistics for your own area from a local law-enforcement agency. Display your findings in line, bar, or pie graphs, and discuss with your classmates what these findings suggest about violence in this country.

**More Online: Research Starter**
www.mcdougallittell.com

---

**Mini Lesson**

## Reviewing Literature

**ANALYZING A LITERARY REVIEW**
**Instruction** Have students write a literary review comparing Joyce Carol Oates's short story "Hostages" and Garrett Hongo's poem "The Legend." They may use the suggested questions in the Writing Options, number 3, on page 1213.
**Prepare** Tell students the following criteria may be used to analyze a written review of literature.
- identifies the subject at the beginning

- opens with a general opinion
- includes enough facts, examples, and specifics to support the general opinion
- displays logical organization
- quickly establishes a tone

**Present** Have several students volunteer to share their reviews with the class. Then have them compare their responses with the other reviewers'.

---

## Writing Options

1. **Character Sketch To help students get started,** have them brainstorm a cause-and-effect chart to trace the development of Bruno's alternative life as they imagine it.
2. **Expository Essay To help students get started,** have them list and then rank in order of importance Bruno's actions for which they are going to explore the causes and effects.
3. **Literary Review** "Hostage" raises the following moral issues: Is violence justified? What is the moral line between self-defense and excessive cruelty, between heroism and brutality? "The Legend" raises such issues as the vulnerability of everyone to random acts of violence, the fragility of life, the unexpectedness of death.
4. **Points of Comparison** One of the issues students might raise is the importance of effective parenting. Daisy and Donny's father fail to make Donny accountable for his actions; Bruno's father dominates his children, venting his anger on them.

## Activities & Explorations

1. **Role-Play To get students started on this assignment,** have them go back to the section of the story in which Bruno is mentioned in relationship to the character. Students should brainstorm ideas about that character's attitude.
2. **Drawing To vary this assignment,** have some students draw a portrait of the narrator based on what she reveals about herself.
3. **Debate To make this assignment more challenging,** students might research the juvenile court system in their state. **Interpersonal learners** might take the role of moderator of the debate.

## Inquiry & Research

**Crime Statistics** Students can consult *Statistical Abstract of the United States, Uniform Crime Reports* (published by the F.B.I.), and annual reports produced by their state and local law enforcement departments.

## Vocabulary in Action

### EXERCISE A

1. antonyms
2. synonyms
3. antonyms
4. antonyms
5. synonyms
6. synonyms
7. antonyms
8. synonyms
9. antonyms
10. synonyms

### EXERCISE B

1. obscure
2. incongruously
3. derisive
4. aplomb
5. sibilant

## Author Activity

Possible Responses:  Both O'Connor and Oates write about violence and about unusual, misfit, disturbed, and disturbing characters; both present contemporary society as insensitive and unthinking. O'Connor's stories, however, usually include religious symbolism.

## Vocabulary in Action

**EXERCISE A: SYNONYMS AND ANTONYMS** Identify each pair of words as synonyms or antonyms. Afterward, choose a partner and take turns acting out the vocabulary word in each pair.

1. subtle—obvious
2. scrupulously—painstakingly
3. abrasive—soothing
4. rakish—drab
5. incredulously—doubtfully
6. infatuation—crush
7. antagonistic—agreeable
8. invest—supply
9. lurid—boring
10. affronted—offended

**EXERCISE B: CONTEXT CLUES** Choose one of these vocabulary words to complete each sentence: *aplomb, derisive, incongruously, obscure, sibilant.*

1. We often cannot know why people do the things they do; their motivations may be too _____ for anyone else to comprehend.
2. Sometimes the people whose behavior drives others away are those who are, _____, most in need of and eager for friends.
3. Similarly, those who are most _____ may be those who are most afraid of being made fun of.
4. Perhaps Bruno Sokolov was one of these people; perhaps his air of _____ masked deep doubts and insecurities.
5. When he boldly addressed the school assembly or spoke with seeming confidence in class, did he secretly fear _____ hisses of scorn from his listeners?

## Joyce Carol Oates

1938–

**Other Works**
*A Bloodsmoor Romance*
*Expensive People*
*The Time Traveler*
*Where Are You Going, Where Have You Been?*

**Prolific Writer**  Remarkable both for the quantity and the quality of her work, Joyce Carol Oates has published more than 25 novels, 15 volumes of short stories, and many collections of poems, essays, and plays. She has written an average of two books a year since she published her first collection of short stories, *By the North Gate*, when she was 25 years old. Many of her works hauntingly portray insanity and violence.

**Academic Excellence**  Oates was raised in a rural community outside Lockport, New York. Her father was a tool-and-die designer, and her mother was a housewife. Oates attended a one-room school, where her determination and studious habits set her apart

from her rowdy classmates. Her mother recalls, "She was always so hard-working, a perfectionist at everything." A brilliant student, Oates graduated Phi Beta Kappa from Syracuse University, where she was valedictorian of her class.

**Literary Aims**  After winning the National Book Award for *them*, Oates described the aim of her fiction. She said, "I have tried to give a shape to certain obsessions of mid-century Americans—a confusion of love and money, of categories of public and private experience, of . . . an urge to violence as the answer to all problems, an urge to self-annihilation, suicide, the ultimate experience and the ultimate surrender. The use of language is all we have to pit against death and silence."

## Author Activity

Oates often has been compared to Flannery O'Connor, author of "The Life You Save May Be Your Own" (page 529). In your view, what do the two writers have in common? How do they differ?

 **Mini Lesson** ## Grammar

**INTERRUPTING ELEMENTS: DESCRIPTIONS THAT SPLIT SUBJECT AND VERB**

**Instruction**  Interrupting elements include nonessential appositives, transitional and parenthetical expressions, and nonrestrictive modifiers. When these elements appear between the subject and verb in a sentence, they are set apart by commas. Display the sentence below as an example.

The story "Hostage," <u>in my opinion</u>, ranks among the best selections in the anthology.

**Exercise**  Ask students to rewrite the following sentences, incorporating the interrupting elements indicated in parentheses.

1. Joyce Carol Oates has earned a place for

herself in the literary world. (who grew up in a relatively humble household)
2. Bruno Sokolov remains in the narrator's heart after his death. (a symbol of a different and exciting world)
3. First-person point of view strongly contributes to the effectiveness of the story. (in fact)

 Use **Grammar Transparencies and Copymasters,** p. 177.

 Use McDougal Littell's *Language Network,* Chapter 9, for more instruction in interrupting elements.

# PREPARING to *Read*

# Mother Tongue

*Essay by* AMY TAN

## Comparing Literature

### Traditions Across Time: Continuing Transformation

The Mexican-American speaker of Pat Mora's poem "Legal Alien" is fluent in two languages—Spanish and English. In her essay "Mother Tongue," Amy Tan, a first generation Chinese American, describes her fluency in different kinds of "Englishes."

**Points of Comparison** As you read "Mother Tongue," compare Tan's examples of prejudgments based on language to the speaker's examples in "Legal Alien."

## Build Background

**Language, Family, and Culture** Amy Tan's image of herself as a writer transcends her ethnic background: "I don't see myself writing about culture and the immigrant experience," she contends. "That's just part of the tapestry. What I believe my books are about is relationships and family. I've had women come up to me and say they felt the same way about their mothers, and they weren't immigrants."

In "Mother Tongue," Amy Tan focuses on how the communication between her and her mother shapes their relationship. The essay was originally delivered as a speech entitled "Englishes: Whose English Is It Anyway?" that Tan gave as a member of a panel on bilingualism.

**WORDS TO KNOW**
**Vocabulary Preview**

diagnosis     quandary
disobedient    transcribe
impeccable

## Focus Your Reading

**LITERARY ANALYSIS**   **PERSONAL ESSAY**   A **personal essay** is a brief nonfiction work that expresses the writer's thoughts, feelings, and opinions on a subject. Often this type of essay provides an opportunity for a writer to explore the meaning of events and issues in his or her own life. Note Tan's insights about the power of language and the influence of her mother.

**ACTIVE READING**   **IDENTIFYING MAIN IDEAS AND SUPPORTING DETAILS**   Amy Tan's essay is organized into a series of paragraphs, each usually developing one **main idea,** or central point. The sentences in a paragraph that provide information, such as facts, descriptions, and examples, related to the main idea are called **supporting details.** To figure out a main idea that is not directly stated, summarize how the supporting details fit together.

**READER'S NOTEBOOK** Create a diagram like the one shown. Record the main idea and supporting details for each of the following topics discussed in "Mother Tongue":

❶ different kinds of "Englishes"
❷ mother's spoken English
❸ limitations of mother's English
❹ standardized tests
❺ Tan's envisioned reader for her fiction

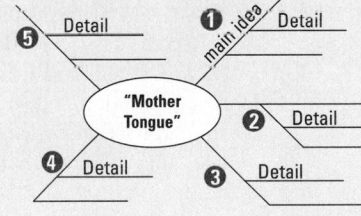

**Reading Skills and Strategies:
PREVIEW**

Preview this selection by giving an overview. This essay explores the different forms of language that the writer grew up with in her Chinese-American family and that she uses in her life and work.

**Literary Analysis** PERSONAL ESSAY

One of the issues Tan explores in this personal essay is the role that language plays in her life and in her mother's life. Suggest to students that as they read they chart the events Tan uses to explore the power and influence of language.

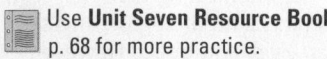 Use **Unit Seven Resource Book**, p. 68 for more practice.

**Active Reading**

**IDENTIFYING MAIN IDEAS AND SUPPORTING DETAILS**

**A** Have students identify the main idea of this paragraph.

**Possible Response:** As a writer, Tan loves language and recognizes its power.

Use **Unit Seven Resource Book**, p. 67 for more practice.

**Literary Analysis** PERSONAL ESSAY

**B** Ask students to summarize the significance of this event for Tan.

**Possible Response:** Having her mother in the audience made Tan keenly aware of the different "Englishes" she uses.

# MOTHER TONGUE
## 母 語
### AMY TAN

I am not a scholar of English or literature. I cannot give you much more than personal opinions on the English language and its variations in this country or others,

**A**   I am a writer. And by that definition, I am someone who has always loved language. I am fascinated by language in daily life. I spend a great deal of my time thinking about the power of language—the way it can evoke an emotion, a visual image, a complex idea, or a simple truth. Language is the tool of my trade. And I use them all—all the Englishes I grew up with.

**B**   Recently, I was made keenly aware of the different Englishes I do use. I was giving a talk to a large group of people, the same talk I had already given to half a dozen other groups. The nature of the talk was about my writing, my life, and my book, *The Joy Luck Club*. The talk was going along well enough, until I remembered one major difference that made the whole talk sound wrong. My mother was in the room. And it was perhaps the first time she had heard me give a lengthy speech, using the kind of English I have never used with her. I was

**1216**    UNIT SEVEN    PART 2: INTEGRATION AND DISINTEGRATION

---

## Teaching Options

 **Mini Lesson**   # Preteaching Vocabulary

**USING CONTEXT CLUES** One kind of context clue is an example that reveals the meaning of an unfamiliar word. Some signal words for examples are *such as, including, especially,* and *namely.* Write the following sentence on the chalkboard:

    There are several reasons why I can't <u>transcribe</u> the tape—for example, I don't have a cassette player, and I can't type.

Ask a volunteer to identify any signal words or surrounding text that help determine the meaning of the word *transcribe.*

**Possible Responses:** The phrase *for example* sets up the illustration; the example of the cassette player, followed by Tan's statement that she can't type,

suggest that *transcribe* means to make a copy of information.

**Exercises** Have students apply the strategy to figure out the meanings of the underlined words.

1. The <u>diagnosis</u> worried her, especially since the disease was identified in other family members.

2. Her use of standard English was <u>impeccable</u>, such as her carefully worded grammatical phrases.

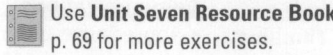 Use **Unit Seven Resource Book,** p. 69 for more exercises.

A lesson on context clues appears on p. 326 in the Pupil's Edition.

Amy Tan

saying things like, "The intersection of memory upon imagination" and "There is an aspect of my fiction that relates to thus-and-thus"—a speech filled with carefully wrought grammatical phrases, burdened, it suddenly seemed to me, with nominalized forms,[1] past perfect tenses, conditional phrases, all the forms of standard English that I had learned in school and through books, the forms of English I did not use at home with my mother.

Just last week, I was walking down the street with my mother, and I again found myself conscious of the English I was using, the English I do use with her. We were talking about the price of new and used furniture and I heard myself saying this: "Not waste money that way." My husband was with us as well, and he didn't notice any switch in my English. And then I realized why. It's because over the twenty years we've been together I've often used that same kind of English with him, and sometimes he even uses it with me. It has become our language of intimacy, a different sort of English that relates to family talk, the language I grew up with.

So you'll have some idea of what this family talk I heard sounds like, I'll quote what my mother said during a recent conversation which I videotaped and then <u>transcribed</u>. During this conversation, my mother was talking about a political gangster in Shanghai who had the same last name as her family's, Du, and how the gangster in his early years wanted to be adopted by her family, which was rich by comparison. Later, the gangster became more powerful, far richer than my mother's family, and one day showed up at my mother's wedding to

---

1. **nominalized** (nŏm′ə-nə-līzd′) **forms:** nouns formed from other parts of speech.

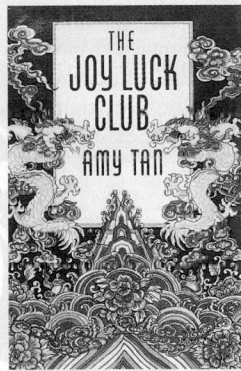

THE JOY LUCK CLUB
AMY TAN

WORDS TO KNOW

**transcribe** (trăn-skrīb′) v. to make a handwritten or typed copy of

1217

## Customizing Instruction

### Less Proficient Readers
Explain to students that the author is a first-generation Chinese American who grew up listening to her mother speak Chinese and "broken" English. In school, Tan learned and used standard English.

**Set a Purpose** Have students read to find out what the writer thinks about the power and influence of language.

**1** Ask students to summarize the significance of the English that Tan uses with her mother. What does Tan realize about the role this form of English has in her life?

**Possible Responses:** It has become a very personal kind of language; it is "family talk."

### Students Acquiring English
Point out to students the title of Tan's essay. Explain that the expression *mother tongue* refers to a person's native, or first, language. If appropriate, invite students to translate the expression into their own "mother tongues."

Use **Spanish Study Guide** for additional support pp. 309–311.

### Gifted and Talented
Encourage students to use elements of the text to negotiate interpretations of the essay's title. Have students complete a web diagram that illustrates the title's different meanings.

---

## BLOCK SCHEDULING: MANAGING TIME

**If your schedule requires that you cover the lesson objectives in a shorter time, use . . .**
- Preparing to Read, p. 1215
- Thinking Through the Literature, p. 1221
- Vocabulary in Action, p. 1222

**If you want to take advantage of longer class time, use . . .**
- TE Teaching Options: Preteaching Vocabulary, p. 1216; Speaking and Listening, p. 1218; Informal Assessment, p. 1220
- Choices & Challenges and Author Activity, p. 1222

## Reading and Analyzing

### Active Reading

**IDENTIFYING MAIN IDEAS AND SUPPORTING DETAILS**

**Ⓐ** Ask students to identify the details Tan uses to illustrate her mother's understanding of English. Have students explain the significance of the details.

**Possible Responses:** Details about Tan's mother (reads the *Forbes* report, listens to *Wall Street Week,* converses daily with her stockbroker, reads all of Shirley MacLaine's books) illustrate her ability to understand and speak the English language for her financial and personal interests. Details such as the *Forbes* report, which is difficult and specialized reading, show the depth of her understanding and intelligence.

### Literary Analysis   PERSONAL ESSAY

**Ⓑ** Ask students what insight Tan reveals about herself.

**Possible Responses:** When she was growing up, Tan was ashamed of her mother's English; like others, she was limited in her perceptions of her mother, feeling that "her English reflected the quality of what she had to say."

### Active Reading

**IDENTIFYING MAIN IDEAS AND SUPPORTING DETAILS**

**Ⓒ** Ask students to summarize the main idea of this paragraph and identify the supporting details.

**Possible Responses:** main idea—her mother's limited English skills negatively affects people's perceptions and treatment of her; supporting details—the hospital lost her CAT scan and does not apologize; the hospital will not provide her with more information; the hospital promises to find the CAT scan and apologizes for the ill treatment of Tan's mother only after the doctor speaks with Tan.

---

pay his respects. Here's what she said in part:

"Du Yusong having business like fruit stand. Like off the street kind. He is Du like Du Zong—but not Tsung-ming Island people. The local people call putong, the river east side, he belong to that side local people. That man want to ask Du Zong father take him in like become own family. Du Zong father wasn't look down on him, but didn't take seriously, until that man big like become a mafia. Now important person, very hard to inviting him. Chinese way, came only to show respect, don't stay for dinner. Respect for making big celebration, he shows up. Mean gives lots of respect. Chinese custom. Chinese social life that way. If too important won't have to stay too long. He come to my wedding. I didn't see, I heard it. I gone to boy's side, they have YMCA dinner. Chinese age I was nineteen."

**Ⓐ** You should know that my mother's expressive command of English belies[2] how much she actually understands. She reads the *Forbes* report, listens to *Wall Street Week,* converses daily with her stockbroker, reads all of Shirley MacLaine's books[3] with ease—all kinds of things I can't begin to understand. Yet some of my friends tell me they understand 50 percent of what my mother says. Some say they understand 80 to 90 percent. Some say they understand none of it, as if she were speaking pure Chinese. But to me, my mother's English is perfectly clear, perfectly natural. It's my mother tongue. Her language, as I hear it, is vivid, direct, full of observation and imagery. That was the language that helped shape the way I saw things, expressed things, made sense of the world.

Lately, I've been giving more thought to the kind of English my mother speaks. Like others, I have described it to people as "broken" or "fractured" English. But I wince when I say that. It has always bothered me that I can think of no way to describe it other than "broken," as if it were damaged and needed to be fixed, as if it

---

lacked a certain wholeness and soundness. I've heard other terms used, "limited English," for example. But they seem just as bad, as if everything is limited, including people's perceptions of the limited English speaker.

**Ⓑ** I know this for a fact, because when I was growing up, my mother's "limited" English limited my perception of her. I was ashamed of her English. I believed that her English reflected the quality of what she had to say. That is, because she expressed them imperfectly her thoughts were imperfect. And I had plenty of empirical[4] evidence to support me: the fact that people in department stores, at banks, and at restaurants did not take her seriously, did not give her good service, pretended not to understand her, or even acted as if they did not hear her.

**1** My mother has long realized the limitations of her English as well. When I was fifteen, she used to have me call people on the phone to pretend I was she. In this guise, I was forced to ask for information or even to complain and yell at people who had been rude to her. One time it was a call to her stockbroker in New York. She had cashed out her small portfolio[5] and it just so happened we were going to go to New York the next week, our very first trip outside California. I had to get on the phone and say in an adolescent voice that was not very convincing, "This is Mrs. Tan."

And my mother was standing in the back whispering loudly, "Why he don't send me check, already two weeks late. So mad he lie to me, losing me money."

And then I said in perfect English, "Yes, I'm getting rather concerned. You had agreed to send the check two weeks ago, but it hasn't arrived."

Then she began to talk more loudly. "What he want, I come to New York tell him front of his

---

2. **belies** (bǐ-līz′): gives a misleading picture of.

3. **Shirley MacLaine's books:** works by the American actress Shirley MacLaine, many of which deal with reincarnation, or rebirth after death.

4. **empirical** (ĕm-pîr′ĭ-kəl): based on observation.

5. **portfolio** (pôrt-fō′lē-ō′): group of investments.

---

## Teaching Options

### Mini Lesson   Speaking and Listening

**EFFECTIVE LISTENING SKILLS: ROLE-PLAY**

**Instruction** Amy Tan describes some of her mother's communication problems. For communication to occur, both the speaker and the listener must engage in the process.

Tell students that active listening skills include
- directing your attention to the speaker
- listening courteously
- paying attention to details
- taking notes, if appropriate
- asking questions to clarify
- keeping an open mind
- analyzing what you've heard

**Application** Have pairs of students role-play a listening situation. Have one student be the speaker, the other the listener. The speaker should explain a difficult process or complex situation. The listener should practice the skills for active listening. Then have students switch speaker/listener roles. Invite pairs of students to present their active listening role-play to the rest of the class.

 **BLOCK SCHEDULING** This activity is particularly well suited for longer class periods.

boss, you cheating me?" And I was trying to calm her down, make her be quiet, while telling the stockbroker, "I can't tolerate any more excuses. If I don't receive the check immediately, I am going to have to speak to your manager when I'm in New York next week." And sure enough, the following week there we were in front of this astonished stockbroker, and I was sitting there red-faced and quiet, and my mother, the real Mrs. Tan, was shouting at his boss in her impeccable broken English.

We used a similar routine just five days ago, for a situation that was far less humorous. My mother had gone to the hospital for an appointment, to find out about a benign[6] brain tumor a CAT scan[7] had revealed a month ago. She said she had spoken very good English, her best English, no mistakes. Still, she said, the hospital did not apologize when they said they had lost the CAT scan and she had come for nothing. She said they did not seem to have any sympathy when she told them she was anxious to know the exact diagnosis, since her husband and son had both died of brain tumors. She said they would not give her any more information until the next time and she would have to make another appointment for that. So she said she would not leave until the doctor called her daughter. She wouldn't budge. And when the doctor finally called her daughter, me, who spoke in perfect English—lo and behold—we had assurances the CAT scan would be found, promises that a conference call on Monday would be held, and apologies for any suffering my mother had gone through for a most regrettable mistake.

I think my mother's English almost had an effect on limiting my possibilities in life as well. Sociologists and linguists probably will tell you that a person's developing language skills are more influenced by peers. But I do think that the language spoken in the family, especially in immigrant families which are more insular, plays a large role in shaping the language of the child.

And I believe that it affected my results on achievement tests, IQ tests, and the SAT. While my English skills were never judged as poor, compared to math, English could not be considered my strong suit. In grade school I did moderately well, getting perhaps B's, sometimes B-pluses, in English and scoring perhaps in the sixtieth or seventieth percentile on achievement tests. But those scores were not good enough to override the opinion that my true abilities lay in math and science, because in those areas I achieved A's and scored in the ninetieth percentile or higher.

This was understandable. Math is precise; there is only one correct answer. Whereas, for me at least, the answers on English tests were always a judgment call, a matter of opinion and personal experience. Those tests were constructed around items like fill-in-the-blank sentence completion, such as, "Even though Tom was _____, Mary thought he was _____." And the correct answer always seemed to be the most bland combinations of thoughts, for example, "Even though Tom was shy, Mary thought he was charming," with the grammatical structure "even though" limiting the correct answer to some sort of semantic opposites,[8] so you wouldn't get answers like, "Even though Tom was foolish, Mary thought he was ridiculous." Well, according to my mother, there were very few limitations as to what Tom could have been and what Mary might have thought of him. So I never did well on tests like that.

The same was true with word analogies, pairs of words in which you were supposed to find some sort of logical, semantic relationship—for example, "*Sunset* is to *nightfall* as _____ is to _____." And here you would be presented

---

6. **benign** (bĭ-nīn′): not cancerous.
7. **CAT scan:** computerized axial tomography scan—a way of creating three-dimensional images of structures inside the human body.
8. **semantic** (sĭ-măn′tĭk) **opposites:** words opposite in meaning.

| WORDS TO KNOW | **impeccable** (ĭm-pĕk′ə-bəl) *adj.* flawless; perfect |
|---|---|
| | **diagnosis** (dī′əg-nō′sĭs) *n.* the identification of a physical disorder through an examination of its symptoms |

**1219**

## Customizing Instruction

### Less Proficient Readers
**1** Be sure students understand that in this situation the writer intervenes on her mother's behalf by pretending that she herself is her mother and speaking in clear, standard English. Ask students to explain why Tan needs to do this.

**Possible Responses:** Her mother is ignored or treated rudely because of her inability to speak standard English.

### Less Proficient Readers
**2** Remind students of the "routine" Tan used when speaking to her mother's stockbroker. How is this routine similar?

**Possible Response:** Tan must speak to the doctor herself, using standard English in order to receive appropriate practical action for her mother.

### Gifted and Talented
**3** Tell students that many minority groups have challenged the validity of standardized tests due to their bias towards conventions in standard English. Have students research data about standardized tests and evaluate their usefulness.

### Less Proficient Readers
**4** Help readers understand what an analogy is. Explain that an analogy is a statement that compares two pairs of words. The relationship between the two words in the first pair is the same as the relationship between the two words in the second pair. Write the following example on the chalkboard.

**cat : pet :: maple : tree** (cat is a kind of pet; maple is a kind of tree)

### Students Acquiring English
**5** Explain to students that the word *semantic* refers to "meaning in language."

**A** Have students infer from Tan's comments what she thinks about Asian-American students being steered away from careers in language arts.

**Possible Response:** She thinks it not only limits and prejudges the individual's ability, but, worse yet, limits the individual's own self-perception.

### Active Reading

#### IDENTIFYING MAIN IDEAS AND SUPPORTING DETAILS

**B** Ask students to identify the details Tan uses to support the main idea that she enjoys the challenge of disproving assumptions made about her.

**Possible Responses:** She became an English major; she began writing the week after her boss told her that writing was her worst skill.

### Literary Analysis PERSONAL ESSAY

**C** Ask students what Tan thinks about language ability tests.

**Possible Response:** Language tests offer only a limited assessment of ability; they cannot show or measure, among other things, the nature of an individual's thoughts.

### Reading Skills and Strategies: SUMMARIZING

Ask students what two factors Tan considers to be the major contributions to her success as a fiction writer.

**Possible Responses:** Tan's own rebellious nature and imagining her mother as her reader

---

with a list of four possible pairs, one of which showed the same kind of relationship: *red* is to *stoplight, bus* is to *arrival, chills* is to *fever, yawn* is to *boring.* Well, I could never think that way. I knew what the tests were asking, but I could not block out of my mind the images already created by the first pair, "sunset is to nightfall"—and I would see a burst of colors against a darkening sky, the moon rising, the lowering of a curtain of stars. And all the other pairs of words—red, bus, stoplight, boring—just threw up a mass of confusing images, making it impossible for me to sort out something as logical as saying: "A sunset precedes nightfall" is the same as "a chill precedes a fever." The only way I would have gotten that answer right would have been to imagine an associative[9] situation, for example, my being <u>disobedient</u> and staying out past sunset, catching a chill at night, which turns into feverish pneumonia as punishment, which indeed did happen to me.

**A** I have been thinking about all this lately, about my mother's English, about achievement tests. Because lately I've been asked, as a writer, why there are not more Asian Americans represented in American literature. Why are there few Asian Americans enrolled in creative writing programs? Why do so many Chinese students go into engineering? Well, these are broad sociological questions I can't begin to answer. But I have noticed in surveys—in fact, just last week—that Asian students, as a whole, always do significantly better on math achievement tests than in English. And this makes me think that there are other Asian-American students whose English spoken in the home might also be described as "broken" or "limited." And perhaps they also have teachers who are steering them away from writing and into math and science, which is what happened to me.

Fortunately, I happen to be rebellious in nature and enjoy the challenge of disproving assumptions made about me. I became an English major

**B** my first year in college, after being enrolled as pre-med. I started writing nonfiction as a freelancer the week after I was told by my former boss that writing was my worst skill and I should hone[10] my talents toward account management.

But it wasn't until 1985 that I finally began to write fiction. And at first I wrote using what I thought to be wittily crafted sentences, sentences that would finally prove I had mastery over the English language. Here's an example from the first draft of a story that later made its way into *The Joy Luck Club,* but without this line: "That was my mental <u>quandary</u> in its nascent[11] state." A terrible line, which I can barely pronounce.

Fortunately, for reasons I won't get into today, I later decided I should envision a reader for the stories I would write. And the reader I decided upon was my mother, because these were stories about mothers. So with this reader in mind—and in fact she did read my early drafts—I began to write stories using all the Englishes I grew up with: the English I spoke to my mother, which for lack of a better term might be described as "simple"; the English she used with me, which for lack of a better term might be described as "broken"; my translation of her Chinese, which could certainly be described as "watered down"; and what I imagined to be her translation of her Chinese if she could speak in perfect English, her internal language, and for that I sought to preserve the essence, but neither an English nor a Chinese structure. I wanted to capture what language ability tests can never reveal: her intent, her passion, her imagery, the rhythms of her speech and the nature of her thoughts.

**C** Apart from what any critic had to say about my writing, I knew I had succeeded where it counted when my mother finished reading my book and gave me her verdict: "So easy to read."

---

9. **associative:** based on mental connections.
10. **hone:** sharpen; focus.
11. **nascent:** (năs'ənt): emerging; beginning.

WORDS TO KNOW

**disobedient** (dĭs'ə-bē'dē-ənt) *adj.* not obeying instructions or orders
**quandary** (kwŏn'də-rē) *n.* a state of uncertainty

1220

---

## Teaching Options

**LETTER OF COMPLAINT** You can informally assess students' understanding of the essay by asking them to write a letter of complaint from Amy Tan to the director of the hospital. In the letter, students should express Tan's feelings about her mother's experience, about her mother's use of English, and why Tan believes her mother was treated in such a manner. This activity allows students to draw inferences and support them with textual evidence and experience.

### RUBRIC

**3 Full Accomplishment** The letter firmly conveys Tan's concern for her mother's health and expresses Tan's belief that her mother's unfair treatment was related to her use of English. The letter also includes details from the text to support conclusions.

**2 Substantial Accomplishment** The letter shows some understanding of the mother's experience and the causes of it, but it does not accurately draw conclusions from the text or offer details for support.

**1 Little or Partial Accomplishment** The letter does not convey an understanding of Tan's mother's experience or the causes of it. It does not include accurate conclusions drawn from the text or offer details for support.

# Thinking *through the* LITERATURE

## Connect to the Literature

**1. What Do You Think?**
What did you find most memorable about Amy Tan's mother? Share your thoughts with a partner.

> **Comprehension Check**
> • What are two kinds of "Englishes" that Amy Tan uses?
> • In general, how do people react to the way Tan's mother speaks English?

## Think Critically

2. How would you describe Tan's relationship with her mother?

3. How would you account for changes in Tan's attitude toward her mother's spoken English?

**THINK ABOUT**
- Tan's initial perceptions about her mother's "limited" English
- the qualities of the language Tan acquired from her mother
- the difference between her mother's understanding of English and her speaking ability
- Tan's identity as a writer

4. What do you consider the most important influences on Tan as a writer? Support your opinion.

5. Explain the significance of the title "Mother Tongue."

6. **ACTIVE READING IDENTIFYING MAIN IDEAS AND SUPPORTING DETAILS** Refer to the diagram you made in your **READER'S NOTEBOOK**. How would you summarize the main idea that Tan conveys about standardized tests and the details that she includes to support her point? What do you think is the main idea of the entire essay?

## Extend Interpretations

7. **Connect to Life** How would you compare Tan's various "Englishes" with the ones that you or your friends speak in informal and formal situations?

8. **Points of Comparison** In what ways are Amy Tan, her mother, and the speaker in Pat Mora's poem "Legal Alien" all prejudged because of their spoken language? Support your response with evidence from each selection.

## Literary Analysis

**PERSONAL ESSAY** The term **essay** is derived from the works of the 16th-century French writer Michel de Montaigne, who called his explorations of various subjects *essais,* the French word for "attempts." The essay writer does not presume to cover a subject completely. Following in this literary tradition, Amy Tan announces in the beginning of "Mother Tongue," "I am not a scholar of English or literature. I cannot give you much more than personal opinions on the English language. . . ." In this **personal essay,** Tan explores a topic that intrigues her and shares her own experiences and views. The reader, in turn, develops a more intimate awareness of what language means to Tan.

**Cooperative Learning Activity** With a small group of classmates, analyze Tan's personal essay. What do you think were Tan's main purposes for writing "Mother Tongue"? What issues and concerns does she raise? What is her attitude toward her subject? How would you describe the style of this essay? Create a chart like this one to record your thoughts and impressions.

### "Mother Tongue"

| Purpose | Theme | Tone | Style |
|---------|-------|------|-------|
|         |       |      |       |

MOTHER TONGUE **1221**

## Extend Interpretations

**Connect to Life** Students may mention that they use certain slang expressions when talking to friends and more formal English when presenting oral reports in school. Bilingual students may say that they may blend English with their native language in informal conversations with friends and family members with the same ethnic background.
**Points of Comparison** Possible Response: Amy Tan, her mother, and the speaker in Mora's poem are stereotyped based on their use of language.

## Literary Analysis

**Personal Essay** Have students complete the chart on page 1221, recording their thoughts about the purpose, theme, tone, and style of "Mother Tongue." Then have students share their charts with the rest of the class.

## GUIDING STUDENT RESPONSE

### Connect to the Literature

**1. What Do You Think?**
Students' answers should be supported with text evidence.

**Comprehension Check**
• Students may name two of the following: standard English, the English she speaks to her mother, her translation of her mother's Chinese.
• They generally do not take her seriously or give her good service and pretend not to understand or hear her.

Use Selection Quiz
**Unit Seven Resource Book,** p. 70.

### Think Critically

2. Responses will vary. Some students may say that Tan has a close but difficult relationship and that her mother's English embarrassed her when she was growing up. Others may point out Tan's mother enthusiastically supports her writing and that Tan acts protectively toward her mother.

3. Responses will vary. Some students may say that Tan gradually realized that her mother's spoken English did not reflect her breadth of comprehension. Moreover, Tan grew to appreciate the vividness and imagery of her mother's language.

4. Responses will vary. Important influences on Tan include her early awareness of language and the different "Englishes" spoken at home, her rebellious nature and competitive spirit, and her academic training.

5. Possible Response: The title points to the focus of the essay—the impact of Chinese, Tan's mother's native language (or "mother tongue"), and her mother's use of English (or her "mother's tongue.")

6. Responses will vary. The results of standardized tests tend to typecast Asian-American students as strong in math and weak in English. Possible responses for the main idea of the essay follow: Language shapes people's perceptions and their relationships with others; people form impressions and stereotypes based on the way someone speaks.

# Writing Options

1. **Story Evaluation To get students started on this activity,** suggest that they create a list of elements necessary for an effective short story.

2. **Points of Comparison** Tell students that their dialogues can be between the speakers as grown-ups or teenagers and should focus on the conflicts they faced growing up in two cultures.

# Author Activity

**Tan's Short Stories** Suggest that students consider in their reviews one or more of the following narrative elements: narrator, character, plot, conflict, setting, dialogue, and theme.

# Vocabulary in Action

1. grimace; diagnosis
2. evade; transcribe
3. despotic; impeccable
4. pallid; disobedient
5. surfeit; quandary

---

## Writing Options

**1. Story Evaluation** Tan states that she knew she had succeeded as a writer when her mother judged her work as "So easy to read." What criteria, or standards, do you use for evaluating a story? Write an evaluation of one of your favorite stories, explaining why you rate it so highly.

**Writing Handbook**
See page 1281: Explanatory Writing.

**2. Points of Comparison** Imagine a meeting between Amy Tan and the speaker of "Legal Alien." Write a dialogue in which they compare and contrast their views on how language shapes personal identity. Include details from the essay and the poem.

## Vocabulary in Action

**EXERCISE: CONTEXT CLUES** In each sentence, identify the word that is used incorrectly. Then, on your paper, write the Word to Know that should replace it.

1. Amy Tan's mother demanded to know the grimace of her illness.

2. The author taped an interview with her mother so that she could later evade the conversation.

3. As immigrants, the family members were aware that their English was not despotic.

4. Were you a well-behaved or a pallid child?

5. Amy Tan was in a surfeit because she wanted to be a writer but was expected to become a doctor.

**Building Vocabulary**
For an in-depth lesson on context clues, see page 326.

| WORDS TO KNOW | | |
|---|---|---|
| diagnosis | impeccable | transcribe |
| disobedient | quandary | |

---

## Amy Tan
### 1952–

**Other Works**
*The Joy Luck Club*
*The Kitchen God's Wife*
*The Hundred Secret Senses*

**Dual Identity** Amy Tan was born in Oakland, California, less than three years after her parents emigrated from China. At first, Tan turned away from her Chinese roots. "When I was growing up," Tan remarked, "I blamed everything on the fact that my mother was Chinese, while I thought of myself as totally American." After visiting China for the first time in 1987, she discovered another identity: "As soon as my feet touched China, I became Chinese."

**Résumé Highlights** Tan's parents had hoped that she would become a neurosurgeon or concert pianist, but she followed a different career path. Tan studied English and linguistics, then worked as a language development consultant for the disabled. She eventually became a business writer, preparing speeches for salespersons and corporate executives. Dissatisfied with business writing, Tan turned her talents to fiction writing.

**Tan's Greatest Hits** Tan's enormously successful novel, *The Joy Luck Club* (1989), appeared on *The New York Times* bestseller list for eight months and in 1993 was made into a feature film. She has since written two other popular novels as well as children's books. Tan has also performed with the "Rock Bottom Remainders"—a rock-and-roll band made up almost entirely of authors, including horror fiction writer Stephen King and humorist Dave Barry.

## Author Activity

**Tan's Short Stories** Read one of Amy Tan's short stories and write a brief review to share with the class.

---

# Teaching Options

 **Grammar**

**COHESION: READER EXPECTATION** Tell students that when they read a story, an essay, or any written work, they have certain expectations about how the text will flow. When ideas or events take an unexpected or awkward turn, readers' expectations are thwarted. Read aloud the first sentence of the following passage and ask students what expectation the sentence creates. Then read aloud the entire passage and ask students whether their expectations were met, and why.

> We must take a stand and show our outrage against this lethal disease! Instead of the usual bake sale fundraiser, we will hold a spaghetti dinner. The cost of the dinner will be $5.95, with half of the proceeds going to research.

**Exercise** Have students rewrite the second sentence so that it does not thwart reader expectations.

> Amy Tan credits her own rebellious nature as one of the reasons she became a fiction writer. In college she was enrolled as a premed student. *(She also credits her mother and all of the Englishes with which she grew up.)*

 Use **Grammar Transparencies and Copymasters**, p. 178.

 Use McDougal Littell's *Language Network,* Chapter 12, for more instruction on coherence.

# PREPARING to *Read*

## The Latin Deli: An Ars Poetica

*Poetry by* JUDITH ORTIZ COFER

**Comparing Literature**

### Traditions Across Time: Continuing Transformation

Like Pat Mora's poem "Legal Alien," Judith Ortiz Cofer's poem "The Latin Deli: An Ars Poetica" expresses the sentiments of people caught between two cultures. And like Amy Tan's essay "Mother Tongue," Ortiz Cofer's poem explores how the interplay between the cultures influences a person's self-image and identity.

**Points of Comparison**  As you read "The Latin Deli: An Ars Poetica" compare its portrayal of the bicultural experience with the other portrayals you have read.

## Build Background

**Between Two Worlds**  In the 1950s, Judith Ortiz Cofer emigrated to the United States from Puerto Rico. Her family moved back and forth between Paterson, New Jersey, and Puerto Rico according to her father's assignments in the U.S. Navy. These two places shaped her writing.

In Puerto Rico, Ortiz Cofer listened to her grandmother's stories in Spanish under a giant mango tree, surrounded by her extended family. There, she says, "I first began to feel the power of words." In Paterson, she spent much of her time alone, building up "an arsenal of [English] words by becoming an insatiable reader of books." Like the immigrants in her poem, "The Latin Deli: An Ars Poetica" (which means the "art of poetry" in Latin), Ortiz Cofer's family continued to follow certain Puerto Rican traditions and customs while living in New Jersey. For example, they spoke Spanish at home, shopped for Puerto Rican foods at the local *bodega,* and practiced strict Catholicism.

## Focus Your Reading

**LITERARY ANALYSIS  IMAGERY**  The descriptive words and phrases that a writer uses to re-create sensory experiences are called **imagery.** An image may appeal to one or more of the five senses: sight, sound, smell, taste, and touch. As you read "The Latin Deli: An Ars Poetica," note the sensory images and the impressions they leave on you as a reader.

**ACTIVE READING  ANALYZING DESCRIPTIVE DETAILS**  **Analyzing descriptive details** as you read involves recognizing the structure that a writer uses to bring the details of a description into sharper focus. The arrangement of the details helps you re-create in your own mind the people, places, objects, or events described. In "The Latin Deli: An Ars Poetica," Ortiz Cofer arranges the images in the order that someone would notice them. The "Patroness of Exiles"—the woman who runs the deli—is the focal point of the description.

**READER'S NOTEBOOK**  Create a word web like the one shown to help you analyze the descriptive details in the poem. As you read each stanza, add descriptive words and phrases that are associated with the deli owner. Use these details to visualize the "Patroness of Exiles" as she gradually comes into focus.

[word web diagram: center oval "Patroness of Exiles" connected to ovals labeled "a woman of no-age" and "descriptive detail" (×5)]

## LESSON RESOURCES

**UNIT SEVEN RESOURCE BOOK,** pp. 71–72

**ASSESSMENT RESOURCES**
**Formal Assessment,** pp. 231–232
**Teacher's Guide to Assessment and Portfolio Use**
**Test Generator**

**SKILLS TRANSPARENCIES AND COPYMASTERS**
**Reading and Critical Thinking**
• Cluster Diagram, T48 (for Active Reading, p. 1223)

**Grammar**
• Pronouns—Personal, Reflexive, and Intensive, T39 (for Mini Lesson, p. 1226)
• Indefinite Pronouns, T40 (for Mini Lesson, p. 1226)
• Types of Pronouns, C65 (for Mini Lesson, p. 1226)

**Writing**
• Sensory Word List, T14 (for Writing Option 1, p. 1226)
• Compare-Contrast, C31 (for Writing Option 3, p. 1226)

**Communications**
• Impromptu Speaking: Dialogue, Role-Play, Debate, T13 (for Activities & Explorations 1, p. 1226)

**INTEGRATED TECHNOLOGY**
**Audio Library**
**LaserLinks**
• Cultural Connection: Ethnic Festivals. See **Teacher's SourceBook,** p. 110.

**Visit our website:**
www.mcdougallittell.com

**Objectives**
1. understand and appreciate a **poem** about bicultural experience (Literary Analysis)
2. understand and appreciate **imagery** (Literary Analysis)
3. **analyze descriptive details** (Active Reading)

**Summary**
In this poem the speaker describes "the Patroness of Exiles," the owner of a Latin deli who sells native foods to her homesick customers and nurtures their spirits. To the Spanish-speaking immigrants who come to her store, she provides a warm setting, filled with foods and products from "places that now exist only in their hearts."

**Thematic Link**
Ortiz Cofer's poem suggests the longing and loneliness of Spanish-speaking immigrants undergoing the process of **integration** into American society.

## Customizing Instruction

**Less Proficient Readers**
• You might want to read the poem aloud with students, helping them to define Spanish words and to break down the long opening sentence. Discuss any phrases or images that students find challenging.
• As students read, ask them to think about why the deli is important to its customers.

**Students Acquiring English**
• You might ask students who have recently immigrated or who live with relatives who have recently immigrated to share their perspectives before they begin reading. Ask them to describe foods that remind them of their native culture.

 Use **Spanish Study Guide** for additional support, pp. 312–14.

## Reading and Analyzing

### Literary Analysis IMAGERY

 Ask students to list the sensory images in the opening lines of the poem. Have students identify images with religious associations. Ask students what these images suggests about the deli.

**Possible Responses:** Images such as "plastic Mother and Child" and "votive offerings" suggest that the deli is like a religious sanctuary, fulfilling deep spiritual needs for those who visit it.

Use **Unit Seven Resource Book**, p. 72 for more practice.

### Active Reading
ANALYZING DESCRIPTIVE DETAILS

 Ask students to notice the details that describe the deli owner. What picture of the deli owner do these details create for the reader's imagination?

**Possible Responses:** The details describing the deli owner create a picture of a woman who is like one of the family for her customers. "Her look of maternal interest" and her understanding smile suggest that she regards her customers like her own children.

Use **Unit Seven Resource Book**, p. 71 for more practice.

# The LATIN DELI: An Ars Poetica

## JUDITH ORTIZ COFER

Presiding over a formica counter,
plastic Mother and Child magnetized
to the top of an ancient register,
the heady mix of smells from the open bins
5    of dried codfish, the green plantains
hanging in stalks like votive offerings,
she is the Patroness of Exiles,
a woman of no-age who was never pretty,
who spends her days selling canned memories
10   while listening to the Puerto Ricans complain
that it would be cheaper to fly to San Juan
than to buy a pound of Bustelo coffee here,
and to Cubans perfecting their speech
of a "glorious return" to Havana—where no one
15   has been allowed to die and nothing to change until then;
to Mexicans who pass through, talking lyrically
of *dólares* to be made in El Norte—
                all wanting the comfort
of spoken Spanish, to gaze upon the family portrait
20   of her plain wide face, her ample bosom
resting on her plump arms, her look of maternal interest
as they speak to her and each other
of their dreams and their disillusions—
how she smiles understanding,
25   when they walk down the narrow aisles of her store
reading the labels of packages aloud, as if
they were the names of lost lovers: *Suspiros,
Merengues,* the stale candy of everyone's childhood.
                She spends her days
30   slicing *jamón y queso* and wrapping it in wax paper
tied with string: plain ham and cheese
that would cost less at the A&P, but it would not satisfy
the hunger of the fragile old man lost in the folds
of his winter coat, who brings her lists of items
35   that he reads to her like poetry, or the others,
whose needs she must divine, conjuring up products
from places that now exist only in their hearts—
closed ports she must trade with.

**2 Mother and Child:** statue of the Virgin Mary with the baby Jesus.

**5 plantains** (plăn′tənz): tropical fruits resembling bananas.

**6 votive** (vō′tĭv) **offerings:** gifts placed before religious shrines as signs of gratitude or prayer.

**11 San Juan** (săn wän′): the capital of Puerto Rico.

**14 Havana:** the capital of Cuba.

**17 *dólares*** (dô′lä-rĕs) *Spanish:* dollars; ***El Norte*** (ĕl nôr′tĕ): a name by which some Latin Americans refer to the United States (literally, "the North").

**30 *jamón y queso*** (hä-môn′ ē kĕ′sô) *Spanish:* ham and cheese.

**32 A&P:** a supermarket.

**36 divine:** guess.

## Teaching Options

### BLOCK SCHEDULING: MANAGING TIME

**If your schedule requires that you cover the lesson objectives in a shorter time, use . . .**
• Preparing to Read, p. 1223
• Thinking Through the Literature, p. 1225

**If you want to take advantage of longer class time, use . . .**
• Choices & Challenges and Author Activity, p. 1226

## Connect to the Literature

**1. What Do You Think?**
What do you find most striking about the deli described in this poem?

**Comprehension Check**
• What does the sales counter at the deli look like?
• What are some of the items sold?
• What countries are the immigrants in the poem from?

## Think Critically

**2.**  **ACTIVE READING** **ANALYZING DESCRIPTIVE DETAILS** Review the word web you made in your **READER'S NOTEBOOK**. What details about the "Patroness of Exiles," the deli owner, capture attention? How does the way of organizing details in the poem give a "you are there" quality to the description?

**3.** How do you think the customers in the deli would describe their homesickness for the native countries? Support your answer with evidence from the poem.

**4.** What do think most draws the people to shop at the deli—the food, the other customers, or the deli owner? Defend your view.

**5.** Why do you think the customers in the deli value language and communication so highly?

**THINK ABOUT**
• the topics of the customers' conversations
• how the customers read labels on packages
• how the deli owner listens to her customers
• "the fragile old man" reading his grocery list like poetry

## Extend Interpretations

**6. Critic's Corner** American poet Archibald Macleish writes in the opening line of his poem "Ars Poetica" that "a poem should be palpable," or easily perceived by the senses. Using this standard, how would you judge "The Latin Deli: An Ars Poetica"? Cite evidence from the poem as support.

**7. Connect to Life** What foods do you enjoy eating from your own ethnic or cultural heritage? What sorts of feelings or images do you associate with these foods?

**8. Points of Comparison** What similarities and differences do you see in the portrayals of the bicultural experience in "Legal Alien," "Mother Tongue," and "The Latin Deli: An Ars Poetica"?

## Literary Analysis

**IMAGERY** Images—vivid "word pictures"—have the power to convey emotion, mood, and the immediacy of experience. "The Latin Deli: An Ars Poetica" is full of sensory images charged with feeling. For example, the reader overhears snippets of conversations, smells the heady odor of codfish, and sees the wide-faced deli owner who presides over this colorful scene.

**Activity** Create a five-senses chart like the one below and fill it in with examples of imagery from the poem.

| Sense | Examples |
|-------|----------|
| Sight | |
| Sound | |
| Touch | |
| Smell | |
| Taste | |

**REVIEW** **TITLE** The title of a literary work may suggest its subject, convey its tone, or reflect its meaning. The title of this poem, for example, refers to its setting—a deli that is frequented by Latin Americans. Its subtitle comes from the Latin term *ars poetica*, which means "the art of poetry." Why do you think Ortiz Cofer chose this subtitle?

## Extend Interpretations

**Critic's Corner** Most students will say that the poem meets Macleish's standard because it is filled with vivid sensory images.

**Connect to Life** Ask students to describe the ingredients of their favorite ethnic foods and to name some family occasions on which they are served.

**Points of Comparison** Responses will vary: Students may point out that Soto's and Mora's poems focus on Hispanic speakers who contend with stereotypes and discrimination, while Ortiz Cofer's poem focuses on Spanish-speaking immigrants who long for their native cultures.

## Connect to the Literature

**1. What Do You Think?**
Responses will vary. Some students may mention the personal interest that the deli owner shows to her customers.

## Comprehension Check

• a plastic counter with an old cash register
• dried codfish, plantains, Bustelo coffee, canned goods, candy, and ham-and-cheese sandwiches
• Puerto Rico, Cuba, and Mexico

## Think Critically

**2.** Responses will vary. Students may mention details describing the deli owner's interaction with her customers. The way of organizing details creates a sense of immediacy, making readers feel as though they are scanning the store and its occupants.

**3.** Responses will vary. Descriptions of homesickness might include a longing for favorite foods, relatives, old friends, and the sounds of their native languages.

**4.** Responses will vary. Students who choose the food might say it provides comfort and triggers fond memories. Students who choose the customers might say they create a sense of community. Students who choose the deli owner might say she symbolizes a link to their cultural heritages.

**5.** Possible Response: For the customers, language and communication reaffirm their identities, represent important forms of self-expression, and foster cultural pride.

## Literary Analysis

**Imagery** Responses will vary. Examples of images include the following: Sight—"her plain wide face"; Sound—"talking lyrically / of *dólares*"; Touch—"the green plaintains / hanging in stalks"; Smell—"dried codfish"; Taste—"the stale candy."

**Review Title** Possible Responses: The phrase means "the art of poetry" and suggests that the deli owner's actions are essentially poetic.

# Choices & CHALLENGES

## Writing Options

**1. Description of a Place** **To get students started on this assignment,** have them sit quietly and try to imagine themselves in the location they will describe. Encourage them to recall vivid details about this place. Then have them freewrite, describing the images formed in their minds.

**3. Points of Comparison** Some students may notice that in Soto's poem the speaker looks forward to the "next century" when he will achieve full acceptance as an American. In Ortiz Cofer's poem, the people define their identity in terms of their native, not their adopted, country.

## Activities & Explorations

**1. Dramatic Skit** Encourage students to brainstorm topics that the "Patroness of Exiles" might discuss with her customers. Ask students to imagine what thoughts might be on the customers' minds as they move in and out of the store. Students can build a dialogue based on their ideas.

**2. Advertising Flyer** To get students started on this assignment, have them think about ads in newspapers and magazines. Ask them what techniques advertisers use to call attention to products.

## Inquiry & Research

**Latin American Cookbook** Students are expected to locate appropriate print and nonprint information. Students might want to illustrate their cookbooks or use lines from the poem to accompany certain recipes.

## Writing Options

**1. Description of a Place** Form a mental picture of an ethnic grocery, restaurant, or deli in your community and jot down your impressions of the foods, customers, and employees. Then write a vivid description with sensory details. If possible, visit this place before you begin to write.

**2. Grocery List** Like the "fragile old man" in the deli, write a grocery list and recite it aloud to the class, as though you were reading a beautiful poem.

**3. Points of Comparison** In a brief essay, contrast the ways the speaker in Gary Soto's poem "Mexicans Begin Jogging" and the people portrayed in "The Latin Deli: An Ars Poetica" define their personal and cultural identity.

**Writing Handbook**
See page 1281: Compare and Contrast

## Activities & Explorations

**1. Dramatic Skit** With a small group of classmates, perform a skit dramatizing a conversation that might occur among the "Patroness of Exiles" and a few of her customers in the deli.
**~ PERFORMING**

**2. Advertising Flyer** Create an illustrated advertising flyer that features different products on sale at the deli. Try to appeal to the emotions of your potential customers. ~ ART

## Inquiry & Research

**Latin American Cookbook** The deli in this poem carries traditional Latin American foods, such as plantains and dried codfish. Locate information about popular Latin American dishes, and find a recipe for one of them in an ethnic cookbook. Work with your classmates to compile your recipes into a Latin American cookbook. Identify the country of origin for each dish.

## Judith Ortiz Cofer
### 1952–

**Other Works**
*An Island Like You*
*Silent Dancing*
*The Line of the Sun*
*The Latin Deli*

**Bridging Differences** Judith Ortiz Cofer, an accomplished poet, essayist, and novelist, draws upon her memories of Puerto Rico in much of her work and often explores the immigrant experience. As a Puerto Rican-American writer, Ortiz Cofer remarks, "I believe my role as an artist is to build bridges. To unite us with the world and fellow beings."

**Education and Teaching** Ortiz Cofer earned a bachelor's degree from Augusta College in 1974 and received a master's degree from Florida Atlantic University in 1977. Before attending graduate school, she worked as a bilingual teacher at public schools in Florida. She has also taught at the University of Miami, Macon College, and the University of Georgia.

**Literary Career** In 1980 Ortiz Cofer published her first poetry collection, *Latin Women Pray*. She has since published several other books, including *The Latin Deli* (1993), a blending of prose and poetry; a collection of personal essays, *Silent Dancing: A Partial Remembrance of a Puerto Rican Childhood* (1990); and *An Island Like You: Stories of the Barrio* (1996). *The Line of the Sun* (1989), her semiautobiographical novel about a family caught between two cultures, was nominated for a Pulitzer Prize.

## Author Activity

**Poetry Slam** Read another poem from Ortiz Cofer's anthology *The Latin Deli,* and think of an inventive way to present an oral interpretation of it. As a class project, organize a poetry slam, in which students perform oral readings of Ortiz Cofer's poems and compete for prizes.

## Teaching Options

### Mini Lesson   Grammar

**TYPES OF PRONOUNS** Review the following types of pronouns. A **reflexive pronoun** is used as the direct object of a reflexive verb. An **intensive pronoun** is used in apposition to a noun or pronoun to increase its force. A **demonstrative pronoun** specifies the person or thing referred to. An **interrogative pronoun** asks a question. An **indefinite pronoun** does not refer to a specific person or thing and usually has no antecedent. A **relative pronoun** introduces a subordinate clause and always

has an antecedent. Display the examples shown.

**Reflexive:** Elena drove *herself* to the deli.
**Intensive:** The poet *herself* handed out books.
**Demonstrative:** *This* is the food that reminds me of home.
**Interrogative:** *Who* wanted the plantains?
**Indefinite:** *Someone* wanted dried codfish. *Most* of the food in the deli was delicious.
**Relative:** The Patroness of Exiles is a woman *who* nurtures her customers. (*woman* is the antecedent of *who*.)

**Application** Have students write a brief paragraph describing a supermarket and including different types of pronouns.

 Use **Grammar Transparencies and Copymasters**, p. 65.

 Use McDougal Littell's *Language Network*, Chapter 6, for more instruction in pronouns.

## Straw into Gold:
### The Metamorphosis of the Everyday

*Essay by* SANDRA CISNEROS

**Comparing Literature**

### Traditions Across Time: Continuing Transformation

In "Straw into Gold," Sandra Cisneros reviews the experiences that helped to shape her as a Latina writer. She chose to go her own way, defining herself instead of letting others define her.

**Points of Comparison**  As you read this essay, think about ways to compare Cisneros's self-examination with Martin Luther King, Jr.'s in "Letter from Birmingham Jail" (page 1136).

## Build Background

**The Title of This Essay** Sandra Cisneros is probably best known for *The House on Mango Street,* a book that has earned both popular and critical acclaim. She originally delivered the text of "Straw into Gold" as a speech. Her essay still retains some of the characteristics of an oral work—for example, a conversational tone and a distinctive voice. The phrase "Straw into Gold" refers to the challenge faced by the heroine in "Rumpelstiltskin." In this fairy tale, as you may recall, a miller's daughter will be put to death unless she can do the seemingly impossible—namely, spin gold out of mere straw. The word *metamorphosis* in the subtitle means "a change in form."

**WORDS TO KNOW**
**Vocabulary Preview**
| | |
|---|---|
| avalanche | intuitively |
| document | venture |
| edible | |

## Focus Your Reading

**LITERARY ANALYSIS**  **VOICE**  The term **voice** refers to a writer's unique use of language that allows a reader to "hear" a human personality in his or her writing. For example, in "Straw into Gold," Cisneros writes:

*I'd never seen anybody make corn tortillas. Ever.*

The use of a contraction, the everyday words, the short sentence followed by a single word, and the pauses before and after the word *ever*—all contribute to create Cisneros's voice in this essay: one that is personal, informal, almost conversational in its natural sound. Note other instances in this essay when you "hear" Cisneros behind her words.

**ACTIVE READING**  **ANALYZING STRUCTURE**  The structure of a literary work is the way in which it is put together—how its parts are organized. The structure of an essay is related to its purpose. For example, King's purpose in "Letter from Birmingham Jail" (page 1136) is to justify nonviolent resistance, so he builds his essay around the points supporting his argument. Cisneros's purpose in "Straw into Gold," on the other hand, is to share some of her formative experiences. She builds her essay around her recollections of growing up. Fittingly, she begins with an anecdote—a brief story that makes a point.

**READER'S NOTEBOOK**  Read the opening anecdote about making tortillas and write a summary of it. Continue to read, summarizing Cisneros's other recollections. Then write down the connections you see between the opening anecdote and the rest of the essay.

STRAW INTO GOLD: THE METAMORPHOSIS OF THE EVERYDAY  **1227**

# OVERVIEW

 This selection is included in the **Grade 11 InterActive Reader.**

**Objectives**
1. understand a **personal essay** (Literary Analysis)
2. understand and appreciate **voice** (Literary Analysis)
3. analyze structure (Active Reading)

**Summary**
In this personal essay, Sandra Cisneros weaves together her recollections of the events and people that have shaped her as a writer. She begins with an anecdote about her first attempt at making corn tortillas, a seemingly impossible task at which she succeeded. She reflects upon how much she has attained beyond her expectations and those of her family. Cisneros then describes how her relationships with various family members affected her life and career. As an author, a teacher, and a lecturer, Cisneros has traveled extensively—both literally and figuratively. Like the fairy-tale heroine, she has often spun straw into gold.

**Thematic Link**
By moving beyond cultural expectations for women and following her intuition, Cisneros has **integrated** her life and her art.

**5-Minute Warm-Up**

*Daily*
*Language*
*SkillBuilder*

Have students **proofread** the display sentences on page 1069k and write them correctly. The sentences also appear on Transparency 34 of **Grammar Transparencies and Copymasters.**

## LESSON RESOURCES

**UNIT SEVEN RESOURCE BOOK,**
pp. 73–78

**ASSESSMENT RESOURCES**
**Formal Assessment,**
pp. 233–234
**Teacher's Guide to Assessment and Portfolio Use**
**Test Generator**

**SKILLS TRANSPARENCIES AND COPYMASTERS**
**Literary Analysis**
• Style, Voice, T23 (for Cooperative Learning Activity, p. 1232)

**Reading and Critical Thinking**
• Compare and Contrast, T15 (for Extend Interpretations 8, p. 1232)
**Grammar**
• Sentence Fragments, T42 (for Mini Lesson, p. 1233)
• Noun Phrases, C179 (for Mini Lesson, p. 1231)
• Style: Deliberate Fragments, C180 (for Mini Lesson, p. 1233)

**Vocabulary**
• Context Clues, C18 (for Mini Lesson, p. 1228)
**Writing**
• Compare-Contrast (by Features), C32 (for Writing Option 2, p. 1233)

**INTEGRATED TECHNOLOGY**
**Visit our website:**
www.mcdougallittell.com

**Active Reading**

ANALYZING STRUCTURE

 Ask students to state the connection between the anecdote about making tortillas and Cisneros's completion of her MFA exam.

**Possible Response:** She considered both as seemingly impossible challenges, comparable to spinning gold from straw.

Use **Unit Seven Resource Book,** p. 74 for more practice.

**Literary Analysis** VOICE

 Ask students to locate phrases or sentences in which they "hear" Cisneros's personal voice.

**Possible Responses:** the Spanish words and phrases; "I had the same sick feeling . . ."; "I wanted to break down into tears"; "I'm glad my mama wasn't there"

Use **Unit Seven Resource Book,** p. 75 for more practice.

**Literary Analysis: ALLUSION**

**C** An allusion is an indirect reference to a person, place, event, or literary work with which the author believes the reader will be familiar. Cisneros alludes to "Rumpelstiltskin" in this passage. Have students compare literary elements across texts by asking them why she incorporates that allusion into her anecdote.

**Possible Response:** Like the miller's daughter in the fairy tale, Cisneros feels that she faces an impossible task.

Sandra Cisneros

# Straw into Gold: The Metamorphosis of the Everyday

**A B** When I was living in an artists' colony in the south of France, some fellow Latin-Americans who taught at the university in Aix-en-Provence invited me to share a home-cooked meal with them. I had been living abroad almost a year then on an NEA[1] grant, subsisting mainly on French bread and lentils so that my money could last longer. So when the invitation to dinner arrived, I accepted without hesitation. Especially since they had promised Mexican food.

What I didn't realize when they made this invitation was that I was supposed to be involved in preparing the meal. I guess they assumed I knew how to cook Mexican food because I am Mexican. They wanted specifically tortillas, though I'd never made a tortilla in my life.

It's true I had witnessed my mother rolling the little armies of dough into perfect circles, but my mother's family is from Guanajuato; they are *provincianos*, country folk. They only know how to make flour tortillas. My father's family, on the other hand, is *chilango*[2] from Mexico City. We ate corn tortillas but we didn't make them. Someone was sent to the corner tortilleria to buy some. I'd never seen anybody make corn tortillas. Ever.

Somehow my Latino hosts had gotten a hold of a packet of corn flour, and this is what they tossed my way with orders to produce tortillas. *Así como sea.* Any ol' way, they said and went back to their cooking.

**C** Why did I feel like the woman in the fairy tale who was locked in a room and ordered to spin straw into gold? I had the same sick feeling when I was required to write my critical essay for the MFA[3] exam—the only piece of noncreative writing necessary in order to get my graduate degree. How was I to start? There were rules involved here, unlike writing a poem or story, which I did intuitively. There was a step by step process needed and I had better know it. I felt as if making tortillas—or writing a critical paper, for that matter—were tasks so impossible I wanted to break down into tears.

Somehow though, I managed to make tortillas—crooked and burnt, but edible nonetheless. My hosts were absolutely ignorant when it came to Mexican food; they thought my tortillas were delicious. (I'm glad my mama wasn't there.) Thinking back and looking at an old photograph documenting the three of us consuming those lopsided circles I am amazed. Just as I am amazed I could finish my MFA exam.

I've managed to do a lot of things in my life I didn't think I was capable of and which many others didn't think I was capable of either. Especially because I am a woman, a Latina, an only daughter in a family of six men. My father would've liked to have seen me married long ago. In our culture men and women don't leave their father's house except by way of marriage. I crossed my father's threshold with nothing carrying me but my own two feet. A woman whom no one came for and no one chased away.

---

1. **NEA:** National Endowment for the Arts—a federal agency that funds artistic projects of organizations and individuals.
2. **chilango** (chē-län′gō) Mexican slang: native to Mexico City.
3. **MFA:** master of fine arts (an academic degree).

WORDS TO KNOW

**intuitively** (ĭn-tōō′ĭ-tĭv-lē) *adv.* without thinking; instinctively
**edible** (ĕd′ə-bəl) *adj.* fit to eat

1228

---

## Teaching Options

**USING CONTEXT CLUES**

**Instruction** One type of context clue contrasts an unknown word with something known. Signal words include *but, not, although, however,* and *on the other hand.*

**Activity** Write the following sentence on the chalkboard, and ask a volunteer to explain the contrast within the sentence. (*Writing is intuitive, not a consciously learned process.*) Have students use their understanding of the contrast to guess the meaning of *intuitive.*

Mini Lesson **Preteaching Vocabulary**

Sandra Cisneros describes her writing as an intuitive process, not something she consciously learned to do.

**Exercises** Have students apply the strategy to determine the meanings of the underlined words.

1. Although she <u>ventured</u> far beyond her given boundaries, she never forgot the neighborhoods where she grew up.
2. Fortunately the tortillas were <u>edible</u>, but some of the other food had to be discarded.

3. Cisneros uses her essay to <u>document</u> some of her formative experiences; however, she omitted some important events from this short piece.
4. To Cisneros, daily life offers an <u>avalanche</u> of raw material; however, some other people consider only a few experiences as worth recording.

 Use **Unit Seven Resource Book,** p. 76 for more practice.

A lesson on context clues appears on p. 326 in the Pupil's Edition.

*Olga* (1940),
Rufino Tamayo.
Private Collection.

o make matters worse, I left before any of my six brothers had <u>ventured</u> away from home. I broke a terrible taboo.[4] Somehow, looking back at photos of myself as a child, I wonder if I was aware of having begun already my own quiet war.

I like to think that somehow my family, my Mexicanness, my poverty, all had something to do with shaping me into a writer. I like to think my parents were preparing me all along for my life as an artist even though they didn't know it. From my father I inherited a love of wandering. He was born in Mexico City but as a young man he traveled into the U.S. vagabonding. He eventually was drafted and thus became a citizen. Some of the stories he has told about his first months in the U.S. with little or no English surface in my stories in *The House on Mango Street* as well as others I have in mind to write in the future. From him I inherited a sappy heart. (He still cries when he watches Mexican soaps—especially if they deal with children who have forsaken their parents.)

My mother was born like me—in Chicago but of Mexican descent. It would be her tough street-wise voice that would haunt all my stories and poems. An amazing woman who loves to draw and read books and can sing an opera. A smart cookie.

---

4. **taboo:** a strict cultural rule forbidding something.

WORDS
TO
KNOW
**venture** (vĕn'chər) v. to dare to go

1229

---

### *Olga* by Rufino Tamayo

**ART APPRECIATION**

**Instruction** Remind students that an artist conveys ideas through the choice of colors and shading, as well as the subject's posture, position, and expression. Ask students to analyze those elements of the Tamayo painting.

**Possible Responses:** The colors are muted, with gray predominating. One side of the woman's face is in shadow, as if turned from the light. She supports her tilted head with her hand and has a somber expression.

**Application** Ask students what connections they see between this painting and any of the ideas expressed in Cisneros's essay.

**Possible Responses:** Cisneros was expected to become a housewife. If she had, she might have felt trapped in a drab existence. Also, the subject in the painting looks as though she is faced with a seemingly impossible task. This painting might represent the "women who sat their sadness on an elbow," whose experiences Cisneros's writing would document.

---

### Less Proficient Readers
Tell students that this essay consists of Cisneros's recollections. It is organized according to themes or ideas, not chronologically. Ask students to state the main idea of the anecdote about making tortillas.

**Possible Response:** She tried and succeeded at something she considered impossible to do.

Guide students to see that recalling this occasion leads her to think about other tasks she has done that she didn't think she could. Ask students who else has been surprised by the extent of her achievements.

**Possible Responses:** her family; her father, in particular

**Set a Purpose** Have students read to find out what Cisneros believes made her a writer and what else she is proud of having accomplished.

### Students Acquiring English
Make sure students understand the title of the essay and its allusion to the "Rumpelstiltskin" story. Ask them in what sense writing about everyday events might be like turning straw into gold. Also have students note the Spanish words and phrases that Cisneros incorporates in her writing. Ask students why she might have chosen to use some Spanish words.

**Possible Responses:** They remind the reader of her Mexican heritage; they show how she still thinks in Spanish; sometimes there is no true English equivalent.

 Use **Spanish Study Guide** for additional support, pp. 315–317.

**Reading Skills and Strategies:**
**INFERRING**

**A** Ask students why they think Cisneros was afraid in school all the time.

**Possible Responses:** She didn't like rules, so she may have been in trouble frequently for breaking them; she reveals that her school record was poor, so she may have been afraid that she wouldn't know the right answer if she were called upon.

**Active Reading**
**ANALYZING STRUCTURE**

**B** Ask students to trace the connections that link Cisneros's recollections of her grandparents' home, her brothers, her years in school, and the move to their house. Ask students how this structure influences their understanding of the essay.

**Possible Responses:** All of these people, places, and events have affected her writing. The thematic organization reveals that the influences upon her as a writer is the main point of the essay. She has selected those memories and anecdotes that relate to her theme; she is not merely giving a litany of autobiographical details.

**Literary Analysis: ALLUSION**

**C** Ask students to complete the analogy to the fairy tale by identifying what the imagination corresponds to in the fairy tale.

**Possible Response:** magic

Ask students to connect the allusion to the subtitle of the essay.

**Possible Response:** Writing about experiences can transform them into something valuable or precious.

When I was a little girl we traveled to Mexico City so much I thought my grandparents' house on La Fortuna, number 12, was home. It was the only constant in our nomadic[5] ramblings from one Chicago flat to another. The house on Destiny Street, number 12, in the colonia Tepeyac would be perhaps the only home I knew, and that nostalgia[6] for a home would be a theme that would obsess me.

My brothers also figured greatly in my art. Especially the older two; I grew up in their shadows. Henry, the second oldest and my favorite, appears often in poems I have written and in stories which at times only borrow his nickname, Kiki. He played a major role in my childhood. We were bunk-bed mates. We were co-conspirators. We were pals. Until my oldest brother came back from studying in Mexico and left me odd woman out for always.

What would my teachers say if they knew I was a writer now? Who would've guessed it? I wasn't a very bright student. I didn't much like school because we moved so much and I was always new and funny looking. In my fifth-grade report card I have nothing but an <u>avalanche</u> of C's and D's, but I don't remember being that stupid. I was good at art and I read plenty of library books and Kiki laughed at all my jokes. At home I was fine, but at school I never opened my mouth except when the teacher called on me.

When I think of how I see myself it would have to be at age eleven. I know I'm thirty-two on the outside, but inside I'm eleven. I'm the girl in the picture with skinny arms and a crumpled skirt and crooked hair. I didn't like school because all they saw was the outside me. School was lots of rules and sitting with your hands folded and being very afraid all the time. I liked looking out the window and thinking. I liked staring at the girl across the way writing her name over and over again in red ink. I wondered why the boy with the dirty collar in front of me didn't have a mama who took better care of him.

I think my mama and papa did the best they could to keep us warm and clean and never hungry. We had birthday and graduation parties and things like that, but there was another hunger that had to be fed. There was a hunger I didn't even have a name for. Was this when I began writing?

In 1966 we moved into a house, a real one, our first real home. This meant we didn't have to change schools and be the new kids on the block every couple of years. We could make friends and not be afraid we'd have to say goodbye to them and start all over. My brothers and the flock of boys they brought home would become important characters eventually for my stories—Louie and his cousins, Meme Ortiz and his dog with two names, one in English and one in Spanish.

My mother flourished in her own home. She took books out of the library and taught herself to garden—to grow flowers so envied we had to put a lock on the gate to keep out the midnight flower thieves. My mother has never quit gardening.

This was the period in my life, that slippery age when you are both child and woman and neither, I was to record in *The House on Mango Street*. I was still shy. I was a girl who couldn't come out of her shell.

How was I to know I would be recording and <u>documenting</u> the women who sat their sadness on an elbow and stared out a window? It would be the city streets of Chicago I would later record, as seen through a child's eyes.

I've done all kinds of things I didn't think I could do since then. I've gone to a prestigious[7] university, studied with famous writers, and taken an MFA degree. I've taught poetry in schools in Illinois and Texas. I've gotten an NEA grant and run away with it as far as my courage would take

---

5. **nomadic:** moving from home to home; wandering.
6. **nostalgia** (nŏ-stăl'jə): a longing for things or people in the past.
7. **prestigious** (prĕ-stē'jəs): respected.

| WORDS TO KNOW | |
|---|---|
| **avalanche** (ăv'ə-lănch') *n.* an overwhelming amount |
| **document** (dŏk'yə-mənt) *v.* to provide a detailed account of |

### BLOCK SCHEDULING: MANAGING TIME

**If your schedule requires that you cover the lesson objectives in a shorter time, use . . .**
• Preparing to Read, p. 1227
• Thinking Through the Literature, p. 1232
• Vocabulary in Action, p. 1233

**If you want to take advantage of longer class time, use . . .**
• TE Teaching Options: Preteaching Vocabulary, p. 1228; Viewing and Representing, p. 1229
• Choices & Challenges, p. 1233

Street mural in a Latino neighborhood of Chicago

me. I've seen the bleached and bitter mountains of the Peloponnesus.[8] I've lived on an island. I've been to Venice twice. I've lived in Yugoslavia. I've been to the famous Nice[9] flower market behind the opera house. I've lived in a village in the pre-Alps and witnessed the daily parade of promenaders.

I've moved since Europe to the strange and wonderful country of Texas, land of polaroid-blue skies and big bugs. I met a mayor with my last name. I met famous Chicana and Chicano artists and writers and *políticos*.[10]

Texas is another chapter in my life. It brought with it the Dobie-Paisano Fellowship, a six-month residency on a 265-acre ranch. But most important, Texas brought Mexico back to me.

In the days when I would sit at my favorite people-watching spot, the snakey Woolworth's

counter across the street from the Alamo[11] (the Woolworth's which has since been torn down to make way for progress), I couldn't think of anything else I'd rather be than a writer. I've traveled and lectured from Cape Cod to San Francisco, to Spain, Yugoslavia, Greece, Mexico, France, Italy, and now today to Texas. Along the way there has been straw for the taking. With a little imagination, it can be spun into gold. ❖

---

8. **Peloponnesus** (pĕl'ə-pə-nē'səs): the peninsula forming the southern part of mainland Greece.

9. **Nice** (nēs): a port city in southern France.

10. **políticos** (pô-lē'tē-kôs) Spanish: politicians.

11. **Alamo:** a mission chapel in San Antonio, Texas—site of a famous battle in Texas's war for independence from Mexico.

## Customizing Instruction

**Less Proficient Readers**
Ask students to state what Cisneros believes contributed to her becoming a writer.
**Possible Responses:** her family; her nomadic existence; her trips to her grandparents' house; the move to their first permanent home

Ask students what else she is proud of having accomplished.
**Possible Responses:** going to a prestigious university; studying with famous writers; getting her graduate degree and obtaining grants and fellowships; teaching; traveling and living all over the world

 **Grammar**

**NOUN PHRASES**

**Instruction** Remind students that phrases are groups of words without subjects and predicates. A noun phrase, which consists of a noun and its modifiers functions as a noun would. Display the following examples:
- burnt, crooked tortillas
- her parents' expectations
- a rich and varied life

**Exercise** Have students identify the noun phrases in each of the following sentences.

1. Her favorite brother of all influenced her writing. *(Her favorite brother of all)*

2. The dislocated child in the family felt connected when she visited her grandparents' welcoming home. *(The dislocated child in the family; her grandparents' welcoming home)*

3. Cisneros's father's traditional Mexican beliefs shaped her young character. *(Cisneros's father's traditional Mexican beliefs; her young character)*

 Use **Grammar Transparencies and Copymasters**, p. 179.

Use McDougal Littell's *Language Network*, Chapter 2, for more instruction in noun phrases.

## GUIDING STUDENT RESPONSE

## Connect to the Literature

**1. What Do You Think?**
Some students may describe Cisneros's personality as sensitive, rebellious, and appreciative.

**Comprehension Check**
• make corn tortillas
• leaving home before her brothers
• Possible Responses: getting her graduate degree, grants, and fellowships; traveling and living all around the world; becoming a successful writer; teaching in schools; getting an NEA grant and other fellowships

 Use Selection Quiz in
**Unit Seven Resource Book**, p. 77.

## Think Critically

**2.** Possible Responses: She did not do what Mexican women were expected to do. She struck out on her own.

**3.** Responses will vary. Some students may mention that since Cisneros came from a close-knit, traditional household, defying her father's wishes was the greatest challenge she had to face.

**4.** Responses will vary. Some students may say that the anecdote reveals Cisneros's courage and determination to take on seemingly impossible challenges.

**5.** Possible Response: Cisneros takes everyday experience—the straw of her life—and turns it into gold, her prose and poetry. Like the daughter in the tale who had to accomplish an impossible task to save her life, Cisneros overcame difficult obstacles to become a successful writer.

## Literary Analysis

**Voice** Students might find it helpful to analyze the tortilla anecdote as a class before breaking into their small groups to analyze the additional selection. Assign each group a different selection to provide a comprehensive review. Have members of each group be responsible for one of the elements of the analysis with a group leader consolidating their findings.

## Connect to the Literature

**1. What Do You Think?**
How would you describe Cisneros's personality? Share your comments with your classmates.

**Comprehension Check**
• What do Cisneros's Latin American friends assume she can do?
• What family taboo does Cisneros break?
• Near the end of her essay, Cisneros says, "I've done all kinds of things I didn't think I could do." Name one of the achievements she lists.

## Think Critically

**2.** Why do you think Cisneros regards herself as a rebel?

**3.** What do you think was the greatest challenge Cisneros had to overcome to become a Latina writer?

 **THINK ABOUT**
• her poverty and rootlessness as a child
• her personal shyness
• her position as the only daughter in a male-dominated family
• her father's expectations of her

**4.** **ACTIVE READING** **ANALYZING STRUCTURE** Cisneros's essay begins with an anecdote about making tortillas. What connections do you see between this anecdote and her other recollections? Refer to what you wrote in your **READER'S NOTEBOOK**.

**5.** Why do you think Cisneros makes an **allusion** to the "Rumplestiltskin" tale in her essay?

## Extend Interpretations

**6.** **What If?** How would the effect of this essay have been different if Cisneros had not mentioned her weaknesses, such as her inability to come out of her shell?

**7.** **Connect to Life** Cisneros comments, "I managed to do a lot of things in my life I didn't think I was capable of." What can you gain by attempting to do the seemingly impossible? Explain your answer.

**8.** **Points of Comparison** How would you compare Cisneros and King as outsiders or rebels, based on this essay and the excerpt from "Letter from Birmingham Jail" (page 1136)?

## Literary Analysis

**VOICE** "Straw into Gold" reflects Cisneros's **voice,** or her unique way of using language to convey her personality in her writing. Among the elements that work together to create a writer's voice are sentence structure, diction, and tone.

For example, some writers rely on short, simple sentences, while others make use of long, complicated ones. Certain writers use concrete words; others prefer abstract terms. A writer's tone, or attitude toward the subject—for example, inviting, passionate, or sarcastic—also colors the voice.

Voice is similar to style, but not exactly the same. For instance, a textbook or manual might be written in a simple, direct style but might also lack a personal voice.

**Cooperative Learning Activity** With a small group of classmates, read aloud Cisneros's anecdote about making tortillas. Then analyze its sentence length, diction, and tone. Create a chart like the one shown to record your findings. Then choose a passage by another writer from the unit—analyze it, and jot down your findings on a second chart. Discuss how Cisneros's voice differs from this other writer's.

### Cisneros's Voice

| Sentence Length | Diction | Tone |
|---|---|---|
| | | |
| | | |

## Extend Interpretations

**What If?** Responses will vary. Some students may say that if Cisneros had not included her shortcomings, the essay would not be as inspirational. The reader would also lose perspective of her accomplishments.

**Connect to Life** Responses will vary. Many students might cite qualities such as self-confidence, self-respect, pride, and courage.

**Points of Comparison** Possible Response: Though both Cisneros and King willingly defy stereotypes and break rules, their motives and impact are different. Cisneros, as an aspiring writer, staged a more personal rebellion and may serve as a role model for other young artists who find themselves in a similar situation. King, as the great civil rights leader, staged a rebellion that ended many injustices.

## Writing Options

**1. Letter of Advice** What advice do you think Cisneros might give to an aspiring writer? Based on what you learned about her from reading this essay, create her letter of advice, and share it with your classmates. Place this piece in your **Working Portfolio.**

**2. Points of Comparison** Write a dialogue in which Cisneros and Martin Luther King, Jr., share their views about self-definition. Use the ideas you discussed for question 8 on page 1232 to get started.

## Art Connection

Look at the reproduction of the painting *Olga* by Rufino Tamayo on page 1229. What are your impressions of the woman in this painting? How would you compare them with your impressions of Cisneros?

## Vocabulary in Action

**EXERCISE: MEANING CLUES** For each sentence, write **Sense** or **Nonsense** on your paper to indicate whether the statement does or does not make sense.

1. The tortillas were quite edible; no one could eat them.
2. She was discouraged by an avalanche of criticism.
3. The two boys decided to venture away from home and never came back.
4. Cisneros draws a distinction between writing according to rules and writing intuitively.
5. She tried to document the lives of Latino immigrants, ignoring them completely.

**Building Vocabulary**
For an in-depth lesson on word connotation and denotation, see page 908.

# Sandra Cisneros
## 1954–

**Other Works**
*The House on Mango Street*
*Woman Hollering Creek and Other Stories*
*My Wicked Wicked Ways*

**Lonely Childhood** Born in Chicago, Sandra Cisneros was the only daughter of a Mexican father and a Mexican-American mother. Her family frequently moved between Mexico City and Chicago, so Cisneros seldom stayed long enough in one place to have close friends. To escape her loneliness, she turned to writing.

**Finding Her Voice** Cisneros wrote secretly at home, openly expressing her creativity only in high school where she edited a literary magazine. She took her first creative writing class in college. After completing college, Cisneros decided to attend graduate school. In the late 1970s, she enrolled in the Iowa Writers' Workshop at the University of Iowa. In these surroundings, she viewed herself as an outsider. "My classmates. . . had been bred as fine hothouse flowers," she has said. "I was a yellow weed among the city's cracks." Ironically, this realization was a blessing in disguise. It spurred Cisneros to write about her own experiences and to find her own voice: "I knew I was a Mexican woman. . . . My race, my gender, my class! That's when I decided I would write about something my classmates couldn't write about."

**Achieving Success** In 1984 Cisneros published *The House on Mango Street*, a series of 44 related prose vignettes narrated by Esperanza Cordero, a young girl growing up in a Latino neighborhood of Chicago. This book received the Before Columbus Foundation American Book Award in 1985. Since then, Cisneros has worked as a teacher to high school dropouts, a poet-in-residence at schools, and a visiting writer at colleges.

## Writing Options

**1. Letter of Advice To get students started on this assignment,** have them review the profile of Cisneros's personality that they created for What Do You Think? on page 1232. Also discuss with students the messages that her essay conveys to aspiring writers and people in general. Students should recognize that the tone of her letter of advice would be encouraging and would stress the importance of using everyday experiences to fuel one's writing.

**2. Points of Comparison To get students started,** have them identify the concept of self-definition. Then, as a class, chart each writer's views of self-definition with the supporting textual evidence to uphold that assessment. Finally, before students begin their dialogues, remind them that the voice heard in each selection should be echoed in the conversation.

## Art Connection

Responses will vary. Some students may state that the woman, like Cisneros and the miller's daughter in the fairy tale, seems to be faced with an insurmountable task.

## Vocabulary in Action

1. Nonsense
2. Sense
3. Sense
4. Sense
5. Nonsense

---

# Mini Lesson Grammar

## STYLE: DELIBERATE FRAGMENTS

**Instruction** Remind students that skillful writers have grammatical license to bend the rules for rhetorical effect. The sentence fragments that Sandra Cisneros employs in her essay contribute to her distinctive voice. Some of the fragments create a conversational tone, and others emphasize a point. Point out and discuss the following examples from page 1228.

• "So when the invitation to dinner arrived, I accepted without hesitation. <u>Especially since they had promised Mexican food.</u>"

Students should note that this fragment conveys her enthusiasm and adds a postscript of the type that might be heard in spoken conversation.

• "I'd never seen anybody make corn tortillas. <u>Ever.</u>" The one-word fragment emphasizes her lack of experience in making tortillas.

**Application** Divide students into groups and have them review Cisneros's essay to find examples of deliberate fragments. Have students explain what Cisneros gains by using each fragment.

Use **Grammar Transparencies and Copymasters,** p. 180.

## PART 1 Reading the Prompt

Model the process of reading a prompt:
- Read the entire prompt aloud.
- List key words and phrases of the assignment on the board. ("evaluate," "most important," "explain the reasons," "evidence")
- Define key words using the Strategies in Action to show how students can restate the prompt for themselves.

## PART 2 Planning an Evaluative Essay

- Students may wish to brainstorm additional criteria before deciding which they will use to judge the selections. Criteria might include timeliness, importance of issue, dramatic impact, relevance to a particular audience, or how memorable a work is.
- Students may find it helpful to limit their choices to their six favorite selections in this unit.

## PART 3 Drafting Your Essay

**Introduction** Students might start with a general statement that tells what the entire group of selections has in common—all the works deal with current issues.

**Organization** Before students organize their writing, they should consider how the two pieces that they selected are related. Then they can determine a logical method of organization. For instance, if each piece deals with different issues, students might use order of importance. If both pieces deal with a related issue, students might compare them point by point.

**Conclusion** Students may find it easier to write their conclusions if they first visualize a specific audience and imagine themselves talking to people in that audience.

**Revision** Students should produce final drafts that are error-free. Remind them to double-check possessive forms. Remind them that singular nouns, such as writers' names, take an apostrophe and s to show possession, even when the name ends with s.

## Comparing Literature: Assessment Practice

In writing assessments, you will often be asked to evaluate the quality or merit of a literary work. You are now going to practice writing an essay with an evaluative focus.

**PART 1** ## Reading the Prompt

First, read the entire prompt carefully. Then read through it again, looking for key words that help you identify the purpose of the essay and decide how to approach it.

> **Writing Prompt**
>
> The selections in Unit 7, Part 2, illuminate social issues of the 1960s and afterward. Evaluate these selections and choose the ❶ two that you would rate as the most ❷ important to be studied. In an essay, explain the reasons for your choice of ❸ selections. Justify your ratings with evidence. ❹

**STRATEGIES IN ACTION**

❶ **Evaluate**, or form a judgment.

❷ Create a set of standards, or **criteria**, for judging a work's importance—for example, lasting relevance, broad appeal, original insights, and artistic quality.

❸ **Explain**—tell how two selections fit your criteria.

❹ Provide **examples** from the selections.

**PART 2** ## Planning an Evaluative Essay

- Determine the key elements of important literary works, and use these elements as your criteria.

- For each selection, create an evaluation chart. If a criterion is applicable, mark the corresponding box and cite an example.

- Review your charts to see which two selections fit your criteria most closely. Flesh out the examples you noted.

| Criteria | Present? | Example |
|---|---|---|
| Lasting relevance | ☐ | _____ |
| _____ | ☐ | _____ |
| _____ | ☐ | _____ |
| _____ | ☐ | _____ |

**PART 3** ## Drafting Your Essay

**Introduction** State your purpose—to evaluate literary works—and identify the selections you rated as most important to study. Summarize your criteria for importance.

**Organization** Discuss each selection as a whole, or apply one criterion at a time to both selections. Maintain the focus of your essay as you write. Support your judgments with details from the selections.

**Conclusion** Sum up the literary and social value of the two works you examined, and restate the key points that reinforce your evaluation.

**Revision** Allow time to review your work. Make sure it is clear, well-supported, and free from mistakes.

**Writing Handbook** See page 1283: Analysis

LITERATURE CONNECTIONS

## Fahrenheit 451

RAY BRADBURY

These thematically related readings are provided along with *Fahrenheit 451*:

**"You Have Insulted Me"**
KURT VONNEGUT, JR.

**Burning a Book**
WILLIAM STAFFORD

**A Summer's Reading**
BERNARD MALAMUD

**Afterword to the Novel**
RAY BRADBURY

**The Portable Phonograph**
WALTER VAN TILBURG CLARK

**The Paterson Public Library**
JUDITH ORTIZ COFER

**The Phoenix**
SYLVIA TOWNSEND WARNER

## . . . And the Earth Did Not Devour Him

TOMÁS RIVERA

These thematically related readings are provided along with *. . . And the Earth Did Not Devour Him*:

*from* **Fields of Toil: A Migrant Family's Journey**
ISABEL VALLE

**Latin Women Pray**
JUDITH ORTIZ COFER

**Napa, California**
ANA CASTILLO

**The Plan of Delano**
NATIONAL FARM WORKERS ASSOCIATION

**The Whistle**
EUDORA WELTY

**First Confession**
FRANK O'CONNOR

**Fourth Grade Ukus (1952)**
MARIE HARA

**In Answer to Their Questions**
GIOVANNA (JANET) CAPONE

## And Even *More* . . .

**Books**

**Centaur**
JOHN UPDIKE
A novel about a father and son coming to terms with life and each other.

**What Manner of Man: A Biography of Martin Luther King, Jr.**
LERONE BENNETT, JR.
A compelling profile of the celebrated civil rights leader.

**The Disuniting of America: Reflections of a Multicultural Society**
ARTHUR M. SCHLESINGER, JR.
A thoughtful analysis by the Pulitzer Prize–winning historian about the fragmentation of American society stemming from cultural diversity.

**Other Media**

**Stand and Deliver**
Film about an inspirational high school teacher in a barrio of Los Angeles, starring Edward James Olmos. (VIDEOCASSETTE)

**The Accidental Tourist**
Film adaptation of Anne Tyler's novel about a travel writer coping with the loss of his son and the breakup of his marriage. (VIDEOCASSETTE)

**Eyes on the Prize**
Documentary series chronicling the U.S. civil rights movement. PBS Video. (VIDEOCASSETTE)

### Unsettling America: An Anthology of Contemporary Multicultural Poetry

EDITED BY MARIA MAZZIOTTI GILLAN AND JENNIFER GILLAN

A diverse chorus of poetic voices comment on ethnic pride and heritage, personal identity, and cultural stereotypes. Pat Mora, Lucille Clifton, Li Young Lee, Louise Erdrich, and Lawrence Ferlinghetti are among the notable poets included in this collection.

The *Electronic Library* is a CD-ROM that contains additional fiction, nonfiction, poetry, and drama for each unit in *The Language of Literature*.

These are the additional selections found in Unit 7 of the *Electronic Library*.

Gloria Steinem
**Ruth's Song (Because She Could Not Sing It)**

Betty Friedan
**The Problem That Has No Name, from The Feminine Mystique**

Encourage students to select one of the longer works described and use it as an opportunity to read silently with comprehension over a period of time.

## Objectives

- reflect on and assess understanding of the unit
- connect literature to experiences
- understand literary forms and terms as appropriate to the selections
- compare and contrast across texts elements such as theme and tone
- assess and build portfolios

# Reflecting on the Unit

### OPTION 1

A successful response will

- focus on one selection from the unit.
- indicate pictorially or in writing how the student was affected by the selection.
- convey that the selection had a powerful impact on the student.

### OPTION 2

A successful response will

- focus on two issues or problems raised in the unit.
- explain why those issues are important to the student.
- discuss the student's agreement or disagreement with how the issues were presented.
- report whether the student's opinion has changed as a result of his or her reading.

### OPTION 3

To get students started, ask them to make a list of different kinds of courage. They should keep the different possibilities in mind as they review the selections. Remind them that courage is not just seen in oversized heroic acts, but can also take the form of standing firm in a difficult situation or helping others when it is safer not to.

### Self Assessment

Ask students to describe their assumptions about people's thoughts and feelings during the period from World War II through the Vietnam War. If their preconceptions were confirmed, what specific information confirmed their thinking? If their preconceptions were contradicted, what was the new information they learned? Were they surprised by what they found?

# War Abroad and Conflict at Home

The selections in this unit look at personal experiences related to battles overseas and struggles at home. How did this unit affect your understanding of World War II, the Vietnam War, and postwar American society? Explore your ideas by completing one or more of the options in each section.

Detail of *Ominous Omen* (1987), Rupert Garcia. Chalk, linseed oil, oil paint on canvas, 47″ × 130″, courtesy of Rupert Garcia; Rena Bransten Gallery, San Francisco; and Galerie Claude Samuel, Paris. Copyright © Rupert Garcia.

## Reflecting on the Unit

### OPTION 1

**Pictures of War**  The selections in Part 1, "Remembering the Wars," deal with the effects of modern warfare on soldiers and civilians. For each selection you read, jot down a few phrases that describe the experiences it presents. Then choose the selection that presents war most vividly to you, and write a paragraph or draw a picture to show how that selection affected you.

### OPTION 2

**Issues for Today and the Future**  Review the selections in this unit, jotting down the social issues or problems they raise. Choose three or four issues that are most relevant to your own life and that you think will continue to be so in the future. Then do some freewriting about two of those issues. Explain why you think those issues are important to your life, whether you agree with how writers in this unit presented or interpreted the issues, and whether your opinions about the issues have changed as a result of reading the unit.

### OPTION 3

**Different Kinds of Courage**  How courageous are the characters and speakers presented in this unit? For each one that you can form an opinion about, assign a rating from 1 (very courageous) to 5 (not at all courageous) and describe in a few words the kind of courage shown. Then write a few paragraphs about a speaker or character who displays a kind of courage you admire.

### Self ASSESSMENT

**READER'S NOTEBOOK**
Make a list of the impressions you had before you read this unit about what people felt and thought during World War II, during the Vietnam War, and during the time between and after the wars. Then note whether your reading has confirmed your preconceptions or contradicted them.

# Reviewing Literary Concepts

### OPTION 1

**Describing Tone** Tone is the attitude that a writer takes toward a subject. Think back over the selections in Unit Seven, and describe the tone of each in a chart like the one begun here. In the third column, identify a feature of the content or style that helps convey this tone—for example, emphasis on emotions or personal relationships, an anti-hero as protagonist, comic irony, or implied social criticism.

| Selection | Tone | Feature |
|---|---|---|
| *Wandering* | cynical, critical | anti-hero opposed to war and conformity |

### OPTION 2

**Linking Title and Theme** Review the selections in this unit to determine the theme, or central idea, of each. Then choose four or five selections and jot down a few phrases to evaluate how the title of each selection connects to its theme. Discuss your opinions with a small group of classmates—different people often discover different themes in the same work.

## Self ASSESSMENT

**📖 READER'S NOTEBOOK**

Copy the following list of literary terms discussed in Unit Seven. Which are more useful in understanding poetry? Which are more useful in analyzing prose? Create a Venn diagram to classify these terms. Review those you are not sure about in the **Glossary of Literary Terms** (page 1342).

| | |
|---|---|
| point of view | plot development |
| imagery | protagonist |
| mood | antagonist |
| internal conflict | dramatic irony |
| speaker | tragic hero |
| style | personal essay |
| allusion | imagery |
| dialogue | voice |

poetry    both    prose

## 🔖 Building Your Portfolio

- **Writing Options** Several writing options in this unit asked you to express your opinion of characters, situations, issues, or artistic qualities reflected in the selections. Choose one of the pieces in which you think you offered the most compelling argument to support your viewpoint. Attach a cover note to the assignment explaining what you learned about presenting a convincing case to your audience, then put the assignment in your **Presentation Portfolio.** 🔖

- **Communication Workshop** In this unit you created a multimedia exhibit. Evaluate the quality of your exhibit, especially the print and audio-visual elements. Did the exhibit have a clear and unified focus? Did the media you included convey information in an interesting, creative way? Decide if you would like to keep your exhibit in your **Presentation Portfolio.** 🔖

- **Additional Activities** Review the assignments you completed under **Activities & Explorations** and **Inquiry & Research.** Which one did you think was the most successful? Save it in your portfolio with a cover note explaining what you wanted to accomplish with the activity and why it succeeded.

## Self ASSESSMENT

Look back over the work in your **Presentation Portfolio.** 🔖 Which piece or pieces are you most proud of? In what ways has your writing improved during this year? In what ways do you want to improve your writing further?

### Setting GOALS

You have read selections in this unit that raise important questions about political, cultural, social, and personal issues. Which of these issues would you like to learn more about? Consult with a librarian to help you compile a brief bibliography, and choose at least one title from your list to read on your own.

REFLECT AND ASSESS    **1237**

---

## Reviewing Literary Concepts

### OPTION 1

Use the Unit 7 Resource Book p.79 to provide students with a ready-made, full-depth chart for recording the tone of each selection.

### OPTION 2

If students need help getting started, suggest that they write a brief summary of each selection and see what theme emerges. As students confer, if they do differ in their ideas about a selection's theme, ask them to evaluate the different answers and decide whether any one has more merit than another. They should be sure to use information from the selection to back up their ideas. Remind them that they do not need to come to agreement; critics often disagree about works of art.

## 🔖 Building Your Portfolio

Students will use their Presentation Portfolios to file what they consider their highest quality work—the very best projects and activities from their Working Portfolios.

📄 For more information on using writing, and assessing portfolios, see the *Teacher's Guide to Assessment and Portfolio Use,* p. 53.

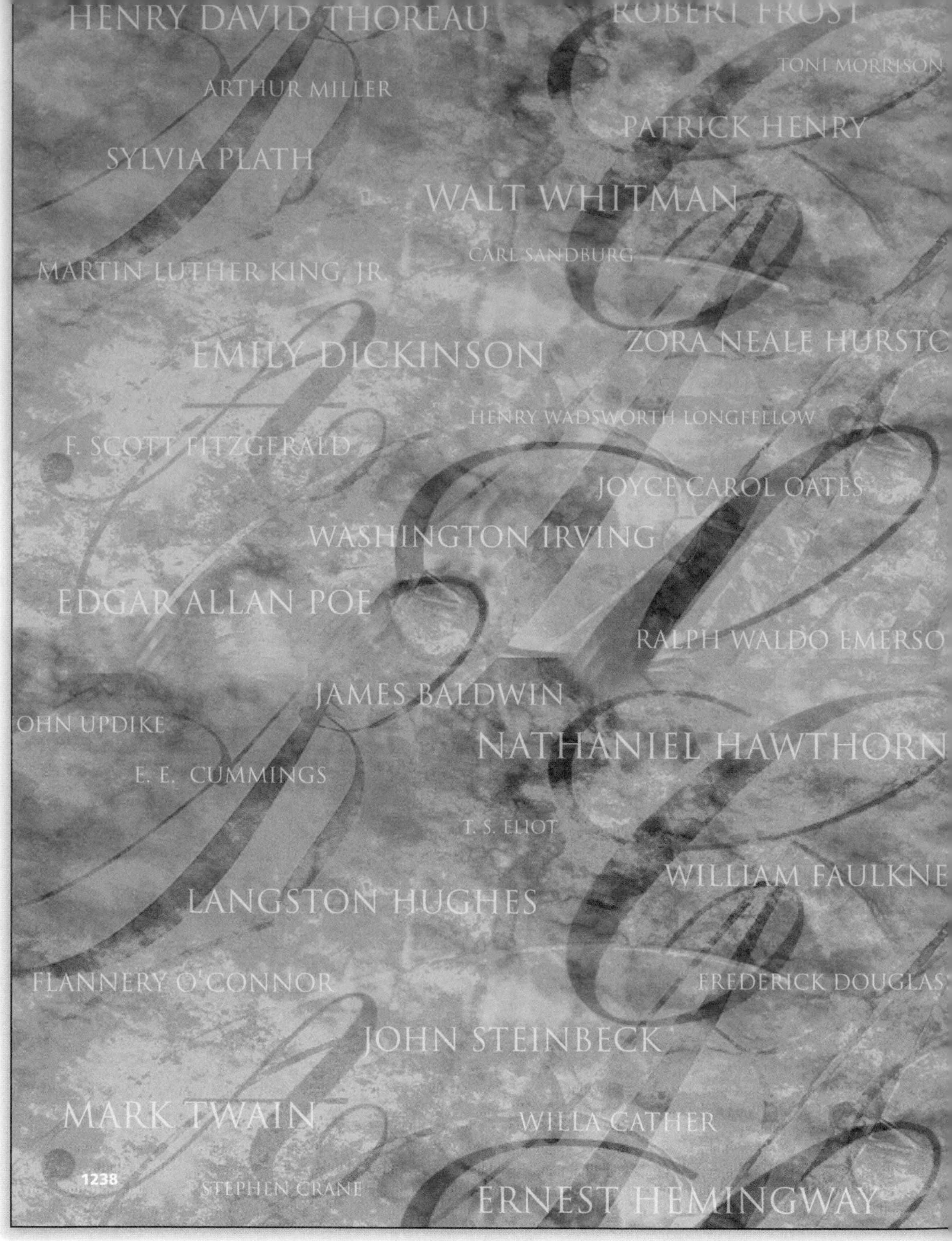

HENRY DAVID THOREAU

ROBERT FROST

TONI MORRISON

ARTHUR MILLER

PATRICK HENRY

SYLVIA PLATH

WALT WHITMAN

CARL SANDBURG

MARTIN LUTHER KING, JR.

ZORA NEALE HURSTON

EMILY DICKINSON

HENRY WADSWORTH LONGFELLOW

F. SCOTT FITZGERALD

JOYCE CAROL OATES

WASHINGTON IRVING

EDGAR ALLAN POE

RALPH WALDO EMERSON

JAMES BALDWIN

JOHN UPDIKE

NATHANIEL HAWTHORNE

E. E. CUMMINGS

T. S. ELIOT

WILLIAM FAULKNER

LANGSTON HUGHES

FLANNERY O'CONNOR

FREDERICK DOUGLASS

JOHN STEINBECK

MARK TWAIN

WILLA CATHER

STEPHEN CRANE

ERNEST HEMINGWAY

# Student *Resource Bank*

# Reading for Different Purposes

*You read for many different reasons. In a single day, you might read a short story for fun, a textbook for information to help you pass a test, and a weather map to find out if it will rain. For every type of reading, there are specific strategies that can help you understand and remember the material. This handbook will help you become a better reader in school, at home, and on the job.*

## Reading Literature

### Before Reading

- **Set a purpose** for reading. Are you reading as part of an assignment or for fun? What do you want to learn? Establishing a purpose will help you focus.
- **Preview** the work by looking at the title and any images and captions. Try to **predict** what the work will be about.
- Ask yourself if you can **connect** the subject matter with what you already know.

### During Reading

- **Check your understanding** of what you read. Can you restate the plot in your own words?
- Try to **connect** what you're reading to your own life. Have you experienced similar events or emotions?

- **Question** what's happening. You may wonder about events and characters' feelings.
- **Visualize,** or create a mental picture of, what the author describes.
- **Pause** from time to time to **predict** what will happen next.

### After Reading

- **Review** your predictions. Were they correct?
- Try to **summarize** the work, expressing the **main idea** or the basic plot.
- **Reflect on** and evaluate what you have read. Did the reading fulfill your purpose?
- To **clarify** your understanding, write down opinions or thoughts about the work, or discuss it with someone.

## Reading for Information

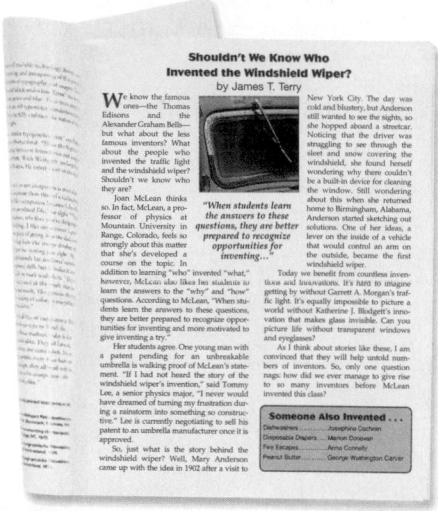

### Set a Purpose for Reading

- Decide why you are reading the material—to study for a test, to do research, or to find out more about a topic that interests you.
- Use your **purpose** to determine how detailed your **notes** will be.

### Look at Design Features

- Look at the **title** and **subheads** and at **boldfaced words** or phrases, **boxed text,** and any other text that is highlighted in some way.
- Use these **text organizers** for help in previewing the text and identifying the main ideas.
- Study photographs, maps, charts, and captions.

### Notice Text Structures and Patterns

- Does the text make **comparisons?** Does it describe **causes and effects?** Is there a **sequence** of events?
- Look for **signal words** such as *same, different, because, first,* and *then.* They can reveal the material's organizational pattern.

### Read Slowly and Carefully

- **Take notes** on the main ideas. State the information in your own words.
- Map the information by using a word web or another **graphic organizer.**
- Notice **unfamiliar words.** These are sometimes defined in the text.
- If there are **questions** accompanying the text, be sure that you can answer them.

### Evaluate the Information

- Think about what you have read. Does the text make sense? Is it complete?
- **Summarize** the information—state the main points in just a few words.

## Functional Reading

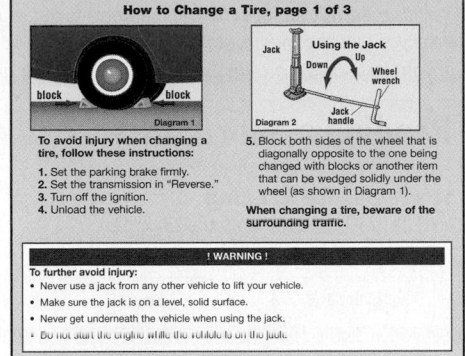

**How to Change a Tire, page 1 of 3**

**Diagram 1**

To avoid injury when changing a tire, follow these instructions:

1. Set the parking brake firmly.
2. Set the transmission in "Reverse."
3. Turn off the ignition.
4. Unload the vehicle.

**Using the Jack**

**Diagram 2**

5. Block both sides of the wheel that is diagonally opposite to the one being changed with blocks or another item that can be wedged solidly under the wheel (as shown in Diagram 1).

When changing a tire, beware of the surrounding traffic.

**! WARNING !**

To further avoid injury:
- Never use a jack from any other vehicle to lift your vehicle.
- Make sure the jack is on a level, solid surface.
- Never get underneath the vehicle when using the jack.
- Do not start the engine while the vehicle is on the jack.

### Identify the Audience, Source, and Purpose

- Look for clues that tell you whom the document is for. Is there an address or a title? Does the information in the document affect you?
- Look for clues that tell you who created the document. Is the source likely to be reliable?
- Think about the **purpose** of the document. Is it to show you how to do something? to warn you about something? to tell you about community events?

### Read Carefully

- Notice **headings** or **rules** that separate one section from another.
- Look for numbers or letters that signal steps in a **sequence.** If you are reading directions, read them all the way through at least once before performing the steps.
- Examine any charts, photographs, or other **visuals** and their captions.
- **Reread** complex instructions if necessary.

### Evaluate the Information

- Think about whether you have found the information you need.
- Look for telephone numbers, street addresses, or e-mail addresses of places where you could find more information.

# Reading Different Genres

*Reading an autobiography and reading a poem require different skills. Here are some tips to help you get the most out of the different genres, or types, of literature you read. The graphic organizers shown are just suggestions—use the note-taking method that works best for you.*

## Reading a Short Story

**Strategies for Reading**
- Keep track of events as they happen. Creating a chart like this one may help you.

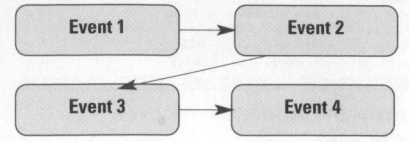

- From the details the writer provides, **visualize** the characters. **Predict** what they might do next.
- Look for specific adjectives that help you visualize the **setting**—the time and place in which events occur.

## Reading a Poem

**Strategies for Reading**
- Notice the **form** of the poem, or the number of its lines and their shape on the page.
- Read the poem aloud a few times. Listen for **rhymes** and **rhythms.**
- **Visualize** the images and comparisons.
- **Connect** with the poem by asking yourself what message the poet is trying to send.
- Create a word web or other **graphic organizer** to record your reactions and questions.

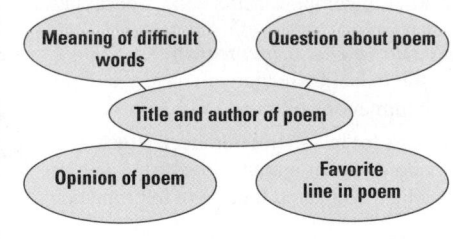

## Reading a Speech

**Strategies for Reading**
- Think about the **historical context**—the occasion, the audience, and the purpose—of the speech.
- You may need to **clarify** certain terms and names by looking them up in a dictionary, an encyclopedia, or a glossary.
- Try to **visualize** the speaker giving the speech and the audience reacting to it.
- Notice the **style** of the speech. Are certain words and phrases repeated for effect? Does the speaker use **rhetorical questions** (questions to which no answer is expected because the answer is obvious)?
- **Evaluate** the effectiveness of the speech. Is the speech clear? Is it persuasive?

## Reading Nonfiction

**Strategies for Reading**
- If you are reading a biography or autobiography, sketch a family tree or a word web to keep track of the people who are mentioned.
- When reading an essay, **evaluate** the writer's ideas and reasoning. Does the writer support opinions with facts and sound arguments?
- When reading an article or interview, **skim** it first to learn what its subject is. Look at any **headings** or **captions.** Then look for the **main idea.** Completing a chart like this one can help.

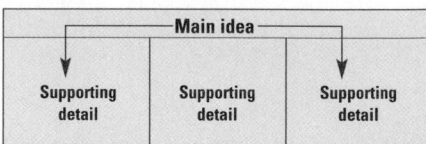

# Reading Different Formats

*These strategies will help you when you need to do research, learn about current events, or just find out more about a topic that interests you.*

## Reading Online Text

### Strategies for Reading

- Notice the page's **Web address,** sometimes called a URL. You may want to make a note of it if you will need to return to that page. Most Web addresses begin with the coding http://www.

- Read the **title** of the page to get a general idea of what topics the page covers.

- Notice **links** to related pages. Links are often "buttons" or underlined words. Clicking on a link will take you to a different page—one that may or may not have been created by the same person or organization.

- Look for a **menu bar** along the top, bottom, or side of the page. This gives you links to other parts of the Web site.

- Notice any **source citations.** Some sites tell you where their information is from, enabling you to judge its reliability.

- Write down **important ideas and details.** Try to restate the text in your own words. Then decide whether you need to check other sources.

## Reading a Newspaper or Magazine Article

### Strategies for Reading

- Read the **headline** and any **subheads** to learn what the article is about and how it is organized.

- Notice any photographs, charts, graphs, or other **visuals.** Read their **captions.** Be sure you understand how the visuals and the main text are related.

- Notice any **quotations.** Think about whether the people who are quoted are likely to be reliable authorities on the topic.

## Reading an Encyclopedia Article

### Strategies for Reading

- Read the **headline** and any **subheads** to make sure that the article covers the topic of interest to you.

- Look at **visuals** and read their **captions.** Some online or CD-ROM encyclopedias also include sound files, animated maps, and short movies.

- Pay attention to how the article is organized. You may want to **skim** the article, or read it quickly, as you look for **key words** related to your topic. Once you find the information you need, read slowly and carefully.

- Watch for a **"see also"** or **"related articles"** section or—if the encyclopedia is online—for highlighted links. These features direct you to additional articles that include information on your subject.

# Enriching Your Vocabulary

## Context Clues

One way to figure out the meaning of a word you don't know is by using context clues. The context of a word is made up of the punctuation marks, other words, sentences, and paragraphs that surround the word.

**General Context** Sometimes you need to read all the information in the sentence or paragraph in order to infer the meaning of an unfamiliar word. The underlined words below give clues to the meaning of the word in the boldface type.

> I told my parents that I wanted <u>to quit playing</u> the violin, but they encouraged me to **persevere** instead.

> Brad was not used to the **turbulent** motion of the waves, so he felt ill when <u>the boat moved too much</u>.

**Definition Clues** Often a difficult word will be followed its definition. Commas, dashes, or other punctuation marks may signal a definition.

> **Perennials**—<u>plants that live for more than two years</u>—make up only one-third of the garden's exhibit.

**Restatement Clues** Sometimes a writer restates a word or term in easier language. Commas, dashes, or other punctuation may signal restatement clues, as may expressions such as *that is, in other words,* and *or.*

> My sister is very **stingy;** that is, <u>she is unwilling to spend money</u>.

**Example Clues** Sometimes writers suggest the meaning of a word with one or two examples.

> Their new apartment was **arrayed** with many beautiful things, <u>such as a crystal lamp and a porcelain vase</u>.

**Comparison Clues** Sometimes a word's meaning is suggested by a comparison. *Like* and *as* are words that signal comparison clues.

> The prairie grasses **undulated** in the wind <u>like the waves of the ocean</u>.

**Contrast Clues** Sometimes writers point out differences between things or ideas. Contrast clues are often signaled by such words as *although, but, however, unlike,* and *in contrast to.*

> My dog is usually very calm, <u>unlike</u> our neighbor's dog, which is very **rowdy.**

**Idioms and Slang** An idiom is an expression whose overall meaning is different from the meaning of the individual words. Slang is informal language that comprises both made-up words and ordinary words that carry different meanings than in formal English. Use context clues to figure out the meaning of idioms and slang.

> If you're going to buy a house that has a garden, you'd better **have a green thumb!** (idiom)

> My parents **freaked out** when I told them that I went to the concert without their permission. (slang)

**TIP** One way to clarify your understanding of a word is to write a sentence using that word. Even better, use one of the context-clue strategies in your sentence. For example, include a restatement or definition clue.

*For more about context clues, see page 326.*

# Word Parts

If you know base words, roots, and affixes—that is, prefixes and suffixes—you can figure out the meanings of many new words.

**Base Words** A **base word** is a word that can stand alone. Other words or word parts can be added to base words to form new words.

**Roots** Many English words contain roots that come from older languages, such as Latin, Greek, and Old English. A **root** is a word part to which a prefix, a suffix, and/or another root must be added. Knowing the meaning of a word's root or roots can help you figure out the word's meaning.

| Root | Meaning | Examples |
|------|---------|----------|
| *agon* (Greek) | struggle, contest | antagonist, agony |
| *gon* (Greek) | figure having angles | pentagon, polygon |
| *circ* (Latin) | around | circle, circumference |
| *civ* (Latin) | citizen | civilian, civilization |
| *opt* (Latin) | eye | optical, optometrist |
| *hus* (Old English) | house | husband, husbandry |
| *mer(e)* (Old English) | sea, pool | mermaid, merman |

**Prefixes** A **prefix** is a word part that appears at the beginning of a base word or another word part. Attaching a prefix to an existing word usually changes the meaning of that word. Familiarizing yourself with the meanings of common prefixes can help you be prepared to figure out the meanings of unfamiliar words.

| Prefix | Meaning | Examples |
|--------|---------|----------|
| bi- | two | bicultural, bicycle |
| endo- | within | endoscope, endoskeleton |
| in- | not, without | inactive, insensitive |
| micro- | small | microbiology, microchip |
| pro- | before | proactive, prologue |
| trans- | over, across | transaction, transnational |

**Suffixes** A **suffix** is a word part attached to the end of a base word or another word part. Attaching a suffix to an existing word may alter the word's meaning. However, a suffix does not change a word's meaning when it is added as follows:

- to a noun to change the number
- to a verb to change the tense
- to an adjective to change the degree of comparison
- to an adverb to show how

| Suffix | Purpose | Examples |
|--------|---------|----------|
| -s, -es | to change the number of a noun | elephant + s, elephants |
| -ed, -ing | to change verb tense | whisper + ed, whispered<br>whisper + ing, whispering |
| -er, -est | to change the degree of comparison in modifiers | low + er, lower<br>low + est, lowest |
| -ly | to show how | joyful + ly, joyfully |

Other suffixes are added to a root or base word to change the word's meaning. These suffixes can also be used to change the word's part of speech.

| Suffix | Meaning | Examples |
|--------|---------|----------|
| -al | relating to | accidental, experimental |
| -ish | of, relating to, being | piggish, wolfish |
| -ize | to make | dramatize, philosophize |

To infer the meaning of an unfamiliar word from it parts, follow these steps.

- Divide the word into parts. Think of other words you know that share the same root(s) or base word.
- Ask, Do these other words all have the same or similar meanings?
- Consider the meanings of any prefixes or suffixes in the unfamiliar word.
- From the meaning of the word's parts, predict what the word means.
- Check the context and a dictionary or glossary to find out whether your prediction is correct.

*For more about roots, see page 444; for more about prefixes and suffixes, see page 1130.*

## Word Origins

When you study a word's origin and history, you find out when, where, and how the word came to be. A complete dictionary entry includes the word's history.

**dra•ma** (drä′mə) *n.* **1.** A work that is meant to be performed by actors. **2.** Theatrical works of a certain type or period in history. [Late Latin *drăma*, *drămat-*, from Greek *drān*, to do or perform.]

This entry shows you that the earliest form of the word *drama* was the Greek word *drān*.

**Word Families** Words that have the same root have related meanings. Such words make up a word family. The charts below show common Greek and Latin roots. Notice how the meanings of the English words are related to the meanings of their roots.

| Greek Root: | **soph,** wise |
|---|---|
| English: | **philosophy** "love of wisdom"; the study of logic and basic truths |
| | **sophisticated** worldly, refined, or complex |
| | **sophomore** "wise fool"; a student in the second year of high school or college |

| Latin Root: | **port,** to carry |
|---|---|
| English: | **import** to bring or carry in from an outside source |
| | **portable** carried or moved easily |
| | **portfolio** a portable case for holding materials |

| Latin Root: | **struct,** to build |
|---|---|
| English: | **construct** to build |
| | **destructive** wanting to ruin or eliminate something |
| | **structure** a building |

**TIP** Once you recognize a root in one English word, you will notice the same root in other words—members of the same word family. Because these words developed from the same root, they are similar in meaning.

**Foreign Words** Some foreign words that enter the English language keep their original form.

| Arabic | French | Japanese | Spanish |
|---|---|---|---|
| algebra | coupon | judo | bonanza |
| giraffe | gourmet | kimono | cargo |
| lime | memoir | ninja | guitar |
| mattress | rendezvous | samurai | patio |
| soda | sabotage | soy | stampede |
| zero | unique | tsunami | tuna |

*For more about word families and researching word origins, see page 206.*

## Synonyms and Antonyms

When you read, pay attention to the precise words a writer uses.

**Synonyms** A **synonym** is a word that has the same or almost the same meaning as another word. Read each set of synonyms listed below.

> attempt/try
> create/make
> help/assist
> labor/work
> pledge/vow
> occasionally/sometimes
> smart/intelligent
> wild/untamed

**TIP** You can find synonyms in a thesaurus or dictionary. In a dictionary, synonyms are often given following the definition of a word.

**Antonyms** An **antonym** is a word with a meaning opposite to that of another word. Read each set of antonyms listed below.

> arrive/depart
>
> cruel/kind
>
> different/similar
>
> fresh/stale
>
> noisy/silent
>
> polite/rude
>
> precede/follow
>
> timid/bold

Some antonyms are formed by adding one of the negative prefixes *anti-*, *in-*, and *un-* to a word, as in the chart below.

| Word | Prefix | Antonym |
|------|--------|---------|
| bacterial | anti- | antibacterial |
| climax | anti- | anticlimax |
| consistent | in- | inconsistent |
| definite | in- | indefinite |
| install | un- | uninstall |
| true | un- | untrue |

**TIP** You can find antonyms in dictionaries of synonyms and antonyms, as well as in some thesauruses.

**TIP** Some dictionaries contain notes that discuss synonyms and antonyms. These notes often include sentences that illustrate the relationships among the words.

## Denotative and Connotative Meaning

Good writers choose just the right word to communicate a specific meaning.

**Denotative Meaning** A word's dictionary meaning is called its **denotation.** The denotation of the word *thin*, for example, is "having little flesh; spare; lean."

**Connotative Meaning** The images or feelings you connect to a word are called **connotations.** Connotative meaning stretches beyond a word's dictionary definition. Writers rely on connotations of words to communicate shades of meaning, as well as positive or negative feelings. Examples of similar words with

| Positive Connotations | Negative Connotations |
|-----------------------|-----------------------|
| aroma | stench |
| bold | reckless |
| cloud | smog |
| delicate | weak |
| desire | envy |
| gaze | glare |
| inquisitive | nosy |
| plant | weed |
| reproduce | forge |
| slender | scrawny |

different connotations are listed below.

**TIP** Some dictionaries contain notes that discuss connotative meanings of the entry word and other related words.

For more information about denotative and connotative meanings, see page 908.

# Homonyms, Multiple-Meaning Words, and Homophones

Homonyms, multiple-meaning words, and homophones can be confusing to readers and can plague writers.

**Homonyms** Words that have the same spelling and pronunciation but different meanings and in most cases different origins are called **homonyms**. Consider this example:

> The **pitcher** on our baseball team drank an entire **pitcher** of lemonade after the game!

*Pitcher* can mean "the player who throws the ball from the mound to the batter in baseball," but it can also mean "a container for liquids."

**Words with Multiple Meanings** Multiple-meaning words are ones that have over time acquired additional meanings based on the original meaning. Consider these examples:

> James ran one **block** so he could catch the bus.

> Did that tall woman **block** your view of the movie screen?

*Block* clearly has multiple meanings, but all of the additional meanings have developed from the same original meaning. You will find all the meanings for *block* under one entry in the dictionary.

**Homophones** Words that sound alike but have different meanings and spellings are called **homophones**. Consider these examples:

> The **weather** is supposed to be good this weekend.

> Please let me know **whether** you want to go to see *Othello* or *Hamlet*.

Many common words with Anglo-Saxon origins have homophones *(there, their; write, right)*. Check your writing to make sure you have used the right word and not its homophone.

*For more about homonyms and homophones, see page 728; for more about multiple-meaning words, see page 630.*

# Analogies

**Analogy** An **analogy** is a comparison between two things that are similar in some way. Analogies often appear on tests, usually in a format like this:

TRACTOR : VEHICLE :: A) wrench : tool
B) lawnmower : lawn
C) farmer : farm
D) hay : barn
E) car : driver

To determine the correct answer, follow these steps:

- Read the part in capital letters as "*Tractor* is to *vehicle* as . . . "
- Read the answer choices as "*wrench* is to *tool*," "*lawnmower* is to *lawn*," "*farmer* is to *farm*," and so on.
- Ask yourself how the first two words, *tractor* and *vehicle,* are related. (A tractor is a kind of vehicle. So *tractor* is an item in the larger category of *vehicles.*)
- Then look for the answer that best shows the same relationship. (Of these possible answers, only item A shows the relationship of an item to a category.)

Here are some relationships that are often expressed in analogies:

| Relationship | Example |
|---|---|
| Part to whole | FINGER : HAND |
| Word to synonym | HARD : DIFFICULT |
| Word to antonym | RAINY : SUNNY |
| Degree of intensity | HAPPY : ECSTATIC |
| Item to category | LEMONADE : DRINK |
| Characteristic to object | STICKINESS : GLUE |

*For more about analogies, see page 254.*

## Specialized Vocabulary

Professionals who work in fields such as law, science, and sports use their own technical or specialized vocabulary. Use these strategies to help you figure out the meanings of specialized vocabulary.

**Use Context Clues** Often the surrounding text gives clues that help you infer the meaning of an unfamiliar term.

> After taxes are deducted you will **net** $680.

**Use Reference Tools** Textbooks often define a special term when it is first introduced. Look for definitions or restatements in parentheses. You may also find definitions in footnotes, a glossary, or a dictionary. If you need more information, refer to a specialized reference, such as one of the following:

- an encyclopedia
- a field guide
- an atlas
- a user's manual
- a technical dictionary

## Decoding Multisyllabic Words

Many words that are familiar to you when you speak them or hear them may be unfamiliar to you when you see them in print. When you come across a word unfamiliar in print, first try to pronounce it to see if you might recognize it. The following syllabication generalizations can help you figure out a word's pronunciation.

### Generalization 1: VCCV

When there are two consonants between two vowels, divide between the two consonants, unless they are a blend or a digraph.

> pic/ture    a/brupt    feath/er

### Generalization 2: VCCCV

When there are three consonants between two vowels, divide between the blend or the digraph and the other consonant.

> an/gler    mush/room    emp/tied

### Generalization 3: VCCV

When there are two consonants between two vowels, divide between the consonants, unless they are a blend or a digraph, the first syllable is a closed syllable, and the vowel is short.

> lath/er    ush/er    ten/der

### Generalization 4: Common Vowel Clusters

Do not split common vowel clusters, such as long vowel digraphs, *r*-controlled vowels, and vowel diphthongs.

> par/ty    poi/son    fea/ture

### Generalization 5: VCV

When you see a VCV pattern in the middle of a word, divide the word either before or after the consonant. If you divide the word after the consonant, the first vowel sound will be short. If you divide the word before the consonant, the first vowel sound will be long.

> box/ed    ro/bot    cra/zy

### Generalization 6: Compound Words

Divide compound words between the individual words.

> grape/vine    life/guard

### Generalization 7: Affixes

When a word includes an affix, divide between the base word and the affix.

> fast/er    rest/less

# Reading for Information

*Reading informational materials—such as textbooks, magazines, newspapers, and Web pages—requires the use of special strategies. For example, you need to study text organizers, such as headings and special type, to learn the main ideas, facts, terms, and names that are of importance. You also need to identify patterns of organization in the text. Using such strategies will help you to read informational materials with ease and quickly gain a clear understanding of their contents.*

## Reading a Textbook

Look for headings, large or dark type, pictures, and drawings. These special features, called **text organizers,** usually show the most important information on the page. Paying attention to them can help you understand and remember what you read.

### Strategies for Reading

**A** First, look at the **title** and any **subheads.** These will tell you the main ideas of the lesson.

**B** Many textbooks list one or more **objectives** or **key terms** at the beginning of each lesson. These identify the most important facts and details in the lesson.

**C** **Key terms** are often boldfaced or underlined where they first appear in the text. Be sure that you understand what they mean.

**D** Notice any **special features,** such as extended quotations or sidebar quotations, questions, or articles. These provide important information.

**E** Look at the **visuals**—illustrations, photographs, graphs, maps, time lines—and read their **captions.** Visuals often present information that is not in the main text.

SECTION 2

## **A** The Civil War Begins

| MAIN IDEA | WHY IT MATTERS NOW | **B** Terms & Names |
|---|---|---|
| Shortly after the nation's Southern states seceded from the Union, war began between the North and South. | The nation's identity was forged in part by the Civil War. Sectional divisions remain very strong today. | • Fort Sumter • Bull Run • Stonewall Jackson • Ulysses S. Grant • Robert E. Lee  • Antietam • Emancipation Proclamation • conscription • Clara Barton • income tax |

### One American's Story

On April 18, 1861, Major Robert Anderson was traveling by ship from Charleston, South Carolina, to New York City. That day, Anderson wrote a report to the secretary of war in which he described his most recent command.

**A Personal Voice** ROBERT ANDERSON

" Having defended Fort Sumter for thirty-four hours, until the quarters were entirely burned, the main gates destroyed by fire, . . . the magazine surrounded by flames, . . . four barrels and three cartridges of powder only being available, and no provisions but pork remaining, I accepted terms of evacuation . . . and marched out of the fort . . . with colors flying and drums beating . . . and saluting my flag with fifty guns. "

—quoted in *Fifty Basic Civil War Documents*

Major Robert Anderson observes the firing at Fort Sumter in 186

Months earlier, as soon as the Confederacy was formed, Confederate soldiers in each secessionist state began seizing federal installations—especially forts. By the time of Lincoln's inauguration on March 4, 1861, only four Southern forts remained in Union hands. The most important was **Fort Sumter,** on an island in Charleston harbor. **C**

Lincoln decided to neither abandon Fort Sumter nor reinforce it. He would merely send in "food for hungry men." At 4:30 A.M. on April 12, Confederate batteries began thundering away to the cheers of Charleston's citizens. The deadly struggle between North and South was under way.

### **A** Union and Confederate Forces Clash

News of Fort Sumter's fall united the North. When Lincoln called for volunteers, the response throughout the Northern states was overwhelming. However, Lincoln's call for troops provoked a very different reaction in the states of the

**168** CHAPTER 4  *The Union in Peril*

### More Strategies for Reading Textbooks

- Before you begin reading the text, read any **questions** that appear at the end of the lesson or chapter. These will help you focus your reading.

- Read slowly and carefully. If you see an unfamiliar word and can't find a definition in the text or in a marginal note, check the **glossary** or a dictionary. Look for **pronunciation guides** as you read.

- Take **notes** as you read. Doing this will help you understand new ideas and terms as well as remember what you are reading. Review your notes before a test to jog your memory.

- You may want to take notes in the form of a **graphic organizer,** such as a cause-and-effect chart or a comparison-and-contrast chart.

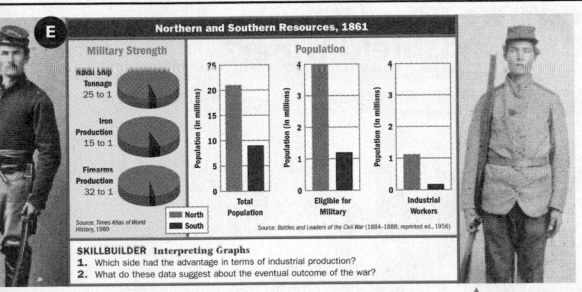

**E**

**Northern and Southern Resources, 1861**

**Military Strength**

Naval Ship Tonnage
25 to 1

Iron Production
15 to 1

Firearms Production
32 to 1

*Source: Times Atlas of World History, 1989*

**Population**

Population (in millions)

Total Population

Eligible for Military

Industrial Workers

North
South

*Source: Battles and Leaders of the Civil War (1884–1888; reprinted ed., 1956)*

**SKILLBUILDER** Interpreting Graphs
1. Which side had the advantage in terms of industrial production?
2. What do these data suggest about the eventual outcome of the war?

...ost Union troops saw the war as a struggle to preserve the Union.

**MAIN IDEA**

**D**

Making Inferences
Why were Northern factories and railroads so advantageous to the Union's war effort?

▲ Most Confederate soldiers fought to protect the South from Northern aggression.

upper South. In April and May, Virginia, Arkansas, North Carolina, and Tennessee seceded, bringing the number of Confederate states to eleven. The western counties of Virginia opposed slavery, so they seceded from Virginia and were admitted into the Union as West Virginia in 1863. The four remaining slave states—Maryland, Delaware, Kentucky, and Missouri—remained in the Union.

**STRENGTHS AND STRATEGIES** The Union and the Confederacy were unevenly matched. The Union enjoyed enormous advantages in resources over the South—more people, more factories, greater food production, and a more extensive railroad system. The Confederacy's advantages included "King Cotton," first-rate generals, and highly motivated soldiers. **A**

Both sides adopted military strategies suited to their objectives and resources. The Union, which had to conquer the South to win, devised a three-part plan:

- The navy would blockade Southern ports, so they could neither export cotton nor import much-needed manufactured goods.
- Union riverboats and armies would move down the Mississippi River and split the Confederacy in two.
- Union armies would capture the Confederate capital at Richmond, Virginia.

The Confederacy's strategy was mostly defensive, although Southern leaders encouraged their generals to attack the North if the opportunity arose.

**BULL RUN** The first bloodshed on the battlefield occurred about three months after Fort Sumter fell, near the little creek of **Bull Run,** just 25 miles from Washington, D.C. The battle was a seesaw affair. In the morning the Union army gained the upper hand, but the Confederates held firm, inspired by General Thomas J. Jackson. "There stands Jackson like a stone wall!" another general shouted, coining the nickname **Stonewall Jackson.** In the afternoon Confederate reinforcements helped win the first Southern victory. Fortunately for the Union, the Confederates were too exhausted to follow up their victory with an attack on Washington. Still, Confederate morale soared. Many Confederate soldiers, confident that the war was over, left the army and went home.

**UNION ARMIES IN THE WEST** Lincoln responded to the defeat at Bull Run by stepping up enlistments. He also appointed General George McClellan to lead the Union forces encamped near Washington. While McClellan drilled his troops, the Union forces in the west began the fight for control of the Mississippi River.

**REVIEW UNIT 169**

## Reading a Magazine Article

### Strategies for Reading

**A** Read the **title** and any other **headings** to get an idea of what the article is about and how it is organized.

**B** As you read the main text, notice any **quotations.** Who is quoted? Is the person a reliable authority on the subject?

**C** Notice text that is set off in some way, such as a passage in a **different typeface.** A quotation or statistic that sums up the article is sometimes presented in this way.

**D** Study **visuals,** such as photographs, graphs, charts, and maps. Make sure you know how they relate to the main text.

**A** # Shouldn't We Know Who Invented the Windshield Wiper?

by James T. Terry

We know the famous ones—the Thomas Edisons and the Alexander Graham Bells— but what about the less famous inventors? What about the people who invented the traffic light and the windshield wiper? Shouldn't we know who they are?

Joan McLean thinks so. In fact, McLean, a professor of physics at Mountain University in Range, Colorado, feels so strongly about this matter that she's developed a course on the topic. In addition to learning "who" invented "what," however, McLean also likes her students to learn the answers to the "why" and "how" questions. According to McLean, "When students learn the answers to these questions, they are better prepared to recognize opportunities for inventing and more motivated to give inventing a try."

Her students agree. One young man with a patent pending for an unbreakable umbrella is walking proof of McLean's statement. **B** "If I had not heard the story of the windshield wiper's invention," said Tommy Lee, a senior physics major, "I never would have dreamed of turning my frustration during a rainstorm into something so constructive." Lee is currently negotiating to sell his patent to an umbrella manufacturer once it is approved.

So, just what is the story behind the windshield wiper? Well, Mary Anderson came up with the idea in 1902 after a visit to

**C** *"When students learn the answers to these questions, they are better prepared to recognize opportunities for inventing...."*

New York City. The day was cold and blustery, but Anderson still wanted to see the sights, so she hopped aboard a streetcar. Noticing that the driver was struggling to see through the sleet and snow covering the windshield, she found herself wondering why there couldn't be a built-in device for cleaning the window. Still wondering about this when she returned home to Birmingham, Alabama, Anderson started sketching out solutions. One of her ideas, a lever on the inside of a vehicle that would control an arm on the outside, became the first windshield wiper.

Today we benefit from countless inventions and innovations. It's hard to imagine getting by without Garrett A. Morgan's traffic light. It's equally impossible to picture a world without Katherine J. Blodgett's innovation that makes glass invisible. Can you picture life without transparent windows and eyeglasses?

As I think about stories like these, I am convinced that they will help untold numbers of inventors. So, only one question nags: how did we ever manage to give rise to so many inventors before McLean invented this class?

**C**

### Someone Also Invented . . .

| | |
|---|---|
| Dishwashers | Josephine Cochran |
| Disposable Diapers | Marion Donovan |
| Fire Escapes | Anna Connelly |
| Peanut Butter | George Washington Carver |

## Reading a Web Page

### Strategies for Reading

**A** Look for the page's **Web address,** sometimes called a URL. If you think you will need to return to the page, write down the address or use the Web browser to "bookmark" the page or log it as a favorite site.

**B** Read the **title** of the page to find out what the page covers.

**C** Look for a **menu bar** along the top, bottom, or side of the page. This tells you about other parts of the site.

**D** Notice any **links** to related pages. Links are often "buttons" or underlined words.

**E** Some sites have **interactive areas** where you can make a comment. This site has a "Forum" area where experts answer questions on different topics.

## Patterns of Organization

Reading any type of writing is easier if you understand how it is organized. A writer organizes ideas in a sequence, or structure, that helps the reader see how the ideas are related. Five important structures are the following:

- main idea and supporting details
- chronological order
- comparison and contrast
- cause and effect
- problem-solution

This page contains an overview of the five structures, which you will learn about in more detail on pages *1255–1259*. Each type has been represented graphically to help you see how ideas are organized in it.

### Main Idea and Supporting Details

The main idea of a paragraph or a longer piece of writing is its most important point. Supporting details give more information about the main idea.

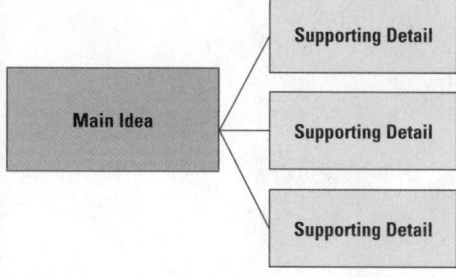

### Chronological Order

Writing that is organized in chronological order presents events in the order in which they occur.

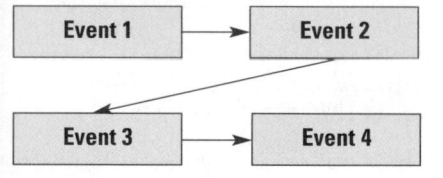

### Comparison and Contrast

Comparison-and-contrast writing explains how two or more subjects are similar and how they are different.

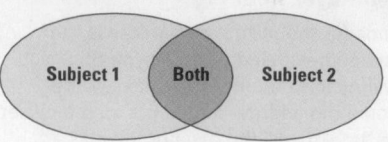

### Cause and Effect

Cause-and-effect writing explains the relationship between events. A cause is an event that gives rise to another event, or a condition, called an effect. A cause may have more than one effect, and an effect may have more than one cause.

**Single Cause with Multiple Effects**

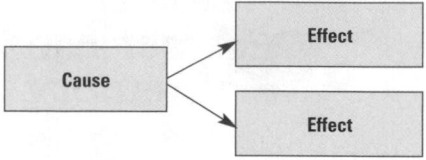

**Multiple Causes with Single Effect**

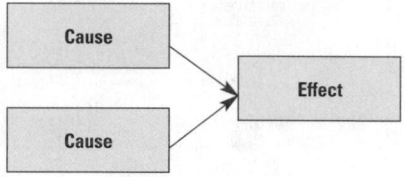

### Problem-Solution

This type of writing describes a difficult issue and suggests at least one way of dealing with it. The writer provides reasons to support his or her suggestion.

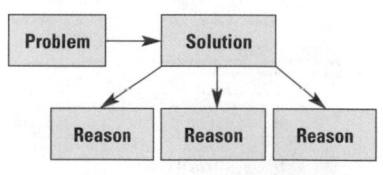

# Main Idea and Supporting Details

The **main idea** of a paragraph is the basic point the writer is making in that paragraph. The **supporting details** give you additional information about the main idea. A main idea may be stated directly, or it may be implied. If it is stated, it may appear anywhere in the paragraph. Often it appears in the first or the last sentence. An implied main idea is suggested through the details that are provided.

## Strategies for Reading

- To find the **main idea,** ask, What is this paragraph about?
- To find **supporting details,** ask, What else do I learn about the main idea?

MODEL

### Main Idea in the First Sentence

**Main idea** / **Supporting details**

More than one factor caused the farmland of the Great Plains to become a dust bowl in the 1930s. Overgrazing and overplowing stripped the fields bare of natural grasses whose roots kept the soil in place. When the rains stopped coming as frequently as they had, the soil dried out. The dry topsoil was easily carried off by the wind. Then blowing clouds of dirt worsened problems by blocking out sunlight, burying gardens and chicken coops, and covering train tracks and roads.

MODEL

### Main Idea in the Last Sentence

**Supporting details**

During the 1930s, many U.S. farmers needed help to survive. To aid them, Congress passed a soil-conservation act. This act allowed farmers to get government money for producing less of those crops that wear out the soil, such as cotton and wheat. Congress also created the Resettlement Administration, which loaned small farmers money to buy

**Main idea**

land. Many of Franklin D. Roosevelt's New Deal programs helped American farmers to recover from the economic and environmental crises of the 1930s.

MODEL

### Implied Main Idea

**Implied main idea:** Wind erosion reduces the productivity of farm fields in many ways.

When farm fields are dry and bare, wind easily erodes them. The first thing the wind carries away is their nutrient-rich topsoil, leaving the fields less fertile. Blowing grit may, in turn, harm whatever plants are standing, resulting in the production of fewer seeds. Dust clouds may also blot out sunlight, which is vital to plant growth. For this reason, too, wind erosion can result in reduced crop production.

## PRACTICE AND APPLY

During the 1930s, the Great Plains became a dust bowl of drifting dirt and sand. As a result, many Midwestern farmers lost, sold, or simply abandoned their land. After all, producing crops in such terrain was nearly impossible, and without crops to sell, most farmers could not afford to make their mortgage payments. So either farmers lost their farms when banks foreclosed on overdue mortgages or they sold their land at ridiculously low prices. Some farmers simply abandoned their land and went off to make better lives elsewhere.

Read the paragraph above and then do the following activities:

1. Identify the main idea of the paragraph and tell whether it is stated or implied.

2. List at least three details that support or expand on the main idea.

## PRACTICE AND APPLY ANSWERS

1. When the Great Plains became a Dust Bowl during the 1930s, many midwestern farmers lost, sold, or abandoned their land. Stated

2. Students should mention three of the following: producing crops in a Dust Bowl of drifting dirt and sand was nearly impossible; without crops to sell, most farmers could not afford to make their mortgage payments; farmers either lost their farms when banks foreclosed on overdue mortgages or they sold their land at ridiculously low prices; some farmers simply abandoned their land and went off to make better lives elsewhere.

# Chronological Order

**Chronological order,** also called time order, is the order in which events happen. It is also an order in which they may be presented. Historical events are usually presented in chronological order. Similarly, the steps of a process are often presented in the order in which they should happen.

## Strategies for Reading

- Look for the **individual events** or **steps in the sequence.**
- Look for words and phrases that identify **time,** such as *in 1871, within the year, by 1872, on that day, earlier,* and *later.*
- Look for words that signal **order,** such as *first, afterward, then, before, during, eventually,* and *next.*

MODEL

Time words and phrases / Event

In 1871, Alexander Graham Bell came to Boston for a few weeks to lecture on his father's system for teaching speech to the deaf. What he didn't know was that this brief trip would have a dramatic impact on his life. Bell's lectures amazed audiences, prompting other Bostonians to extend similar invitations to him. Within the year, the Scottish-born teacher and scientist found himself living in Boston—although he had moved with his parents from London, England, to Ontario, Canada, just a year before.

Order words

By 1872, Bell had opened a school in Boston for training teachers of the deaf. In 1873, he accepted a teaching position at Boston University as professor of vocal physiology.

During this period, Bell also met Thomas Watson, a young repair mechanic and model maker. Inspired by Bell's ideas and eager to help the inventor, Watson teamed up with Bell. For over two years the men worked together to create an apparatus for transmitting sound by electricity. Then, on April 6, 1875, Bell acquired a patent for a multiple telegraph. A

little less than a year later, on the heels of their first success, the two created the first telephone.

The first "telephonic communication" took place on March 10, 1876. On that day, Bell called to his assistant over a new transmitter he was trying out, "Mr. Watson! Come here! I want you!" and Mr. Watson heard him.

There was more work to do before others would have actual telephone service, of course. By 1915, however, coast-to-coast telephone communication was a reality.

By then, the two had also succeeded in inventing many other useful devices. In fact, although Bell is best known for inventing the telephone, he was also the father of many other equally amazing devices and scientific advancements.

## PRACTICE AND APPLY

Reread the model and then do the following activities:

1. List at least six words or phrases in the model that show time or order.

2. Draw a time line beginning with Bell's arrival in Ontario, Canada, in 1870 and ending with the availability of coast-to-coast phone service in 1915. Chart on the time line each major event described in the model.

---

## PRACTICE AND APPLY ANSWERS

1. Students may list any six of the following words or phrases categorized as indicated: time—in 1871; within the year; just a year; by 1872; in 1873; this period; for over two years; on April 6, 1875; a little less than a year later; on that day; by 1915; order—before, during, then, by then

2. Students should include the following events:
   1870: Bell moves from London, England, to Ontario, Canada, with his parents.
   1871: Bell gives lectures in Boston on his father's system for teaching speech to the deaf. More lectures soon follow.
   1872: Bell opens a school to train teachers of the deaf.
   1873: Bell accepts a teaching position at Boston University as professor of vocal physiology. He also meets and begins collaborating with Thomas Watson, a young repair mechanic and model maker.
   1875: On April 6, Bell acquires a patent for a multiple telegraph.
   1876: On March 10, Bell and Watson have the first "telephonic communication."
   1915: Coast-to-coast telephone service becomes available.

# Comparison and Contrast

**Comparison-and-contrast** writing explains how two subjects are alike and different. This type of writing is usually organized by subject or by feature. In **subject organization,** the writer discusses first one subject, then the other. In **feature organization,** the writer compares a feature of one subject with the same feature of the other, then compares another feature of both, and so on.

## Strategies for Reading

- Look for words and phrases that signal **comparison,** such as *like, alike, similarly, both,* and *in the same way.*

- Look for words and phrases that signal **contrast,** such as *unlike, in contrast, differ,* and *different.*

MODEL

**Subjects**

**Comparison words and phrases**

Booker T. Washington and W. E. B. Du Bois were alike in many ways. Both were devoted to helping their fellow African Americans attain equal rights. Both were educated black men with university teaching positions. Both also worked passionately toward their goal at the beginning of the 20th century. Nevertheless, they were not allies. Why? They had very different ideas about how blacks should go about attaining equal rights.

**Contrast words and phrases**

Washington believed that for black people to achieve equal status and power as citizens they needed to focus on learning crafts, farming, and industrial skills. He argued that by gaining such vocational skills and the economic security that would surely follow, black people would naturally earn the respect and acceptance of the white community. In Washington's opinion, however, to earn an education and economic security, black people would need to let go temporarily of the fight for civil rights and political power.

In contrast to Washington, W. E. B. Du Bois believed that black people could not afford to stop fighting for civil rights and political power. In his opinion, only agitation and protest would achieve social change. According to Du Bois, in the climate of extreme racism that existed in America at the time, Washington's approach would merely cause blacks to suffer even more oppression.

So although these two African-American contemporaries had the same goal, their different approaches to achieving this goal made them adversaries rather than allies.

## PRACTICE AND APPLY

Reread the model and then answer the following questions:

1. Is the model organized by subject or by feature?

2. In a sentence or two, summarize Washington's approach to attaining civil rights. Then summarize Du Bois's approach.

3. List three words or phrases that the writer uses to signal comparison or contrast.

PRACTICE AND APPLY ANSWERS

1. Subject
2. Washington believed that by becoming more educated and economically secure blacks would gain respect and equality with whites. However, to attain a vocational education, he proposed that blacks temporarily redirect their energy into improving themselves and their economic status rather than continuing to agitate and protest against discrimination. W.E.B. DuBois felt that the only way to achieve equal rights and political power in such a climate of extreme racism was to agitate and protest. He argued that Washington's approach would only increase the suffering of blacks.
3. Students may list any three of the following words or phrases categorized as indicated: comparison—alike, both, same; contrast—in contrast, different.

# Cause and Effect

A **cause** is an event, or something that happens. An **effect** is a result of an event. A cause-and-effect relationship exists when one event brings about, or causes, another event or a condition. When writers want to explain cause-and-effect relationships, they usually arrange the cause(s) and effect(s) in one of three ways:

1. as a description of the cause(s) followed by an explanation of the effect(s)

2. as a description of the effect(s) followed by an explanation of the cause(s)

3. as a chain of causes and effects

These patterns of organization are all examples of **cause-and-effect order.**

## Strategies for Reading

- To find the **effect(s),** ask, What happened?
- To find the **cause(s),** ask, Why did that happen?
- Look for **words and phrases that signal relationships between events,** such as *because, as a result, for that reason, so, consequently,* and *since.*

### MODEL

| | |
|---|---|
| **Cause** | In 1872 a group of tourists were awestruck by the deep canyons, dense pine forests, and refreshing rivers and waterfalls of Yellowstone, Montana. |
| **Effect that in turn becomes a cause** | They were so moved by the area's natural wonders, in fact, that they immediately wanted to protect them. |
| **Signal words and phrases** | So they trooped off to Washington, D.C., to demand that Yellowstone lands be set aside for public use. There, before Congress, with the help of breathtaking paintings and photographs by artists who had ventured to Yellowstone with government land surveyors, these passionate preservationists presented their case. |
| **Effect** | Dazzled, Congress responded to their pleas by creating the first national park, Yellowstone National Park. |

The next several national parks owe their establishment primarily to the enthusiasm and persuasive abilities of one nature lover, John Muir.

Muir took influential friends such as Ralph Waldo Emerson and Theodore Roosevelt on spectacular hikes through the Sierras. While on these hikes, he expressed his love of nature in passionate arguments for its preservation. In 1890, largely as a result of Muir's efforts, Yosemite, Sequoia, and General Grant national parks were established.

Interestingly, however, about 25 percent of today's national parks owe their preservation to looters—or rather, to a Congress roused into action by looters. In 1906, because Congress was concerned that widespread plundering of precious Southwestern archaeological sites was destroying important artifacts, it enacted a law to prevent such plundering. This law, called the Antiquities Act, authorized the president to set aside as national monuments extremely precious or threatened lands. Consequently, by calling on the powers granted to him under this law, President Theodore Roosevelt was able to put under government protection many sites that might otherwise have been destroyed. These sites would eventually earn national-park status.

## PRACTICE AND APPLY

Reread the model and then do the following activities:

1. In the cause-and-effect relationship of which they were a part, were looters a cause or an effect? On a cause-and-effect graphic organizer, show at least one cause-and-effect relationship in which looters were involved. To view samples of cause-and-effect graphic organizers, see page 1254 of this Reading Handbook.

2. List two cause-and-effect signal words or phrases that appear in the model.

## PRACTICE AND APPLY ANSWERS

1. Looters were a cause. Students' graphic organizers may illustrate one or more of the following cause-effect relationships:
   - cause—looting of archeological sites, effect—Congress becomes concerned about protecting land
   - causes—(1) concern over destruction of land by looters and (2) a desire to protect remaining land from looters, effect—Congress enacts Antiquities Act in 1906
   - cause—passage of Antiquities Act, effects—(1) president able to put under government protection many precious sites that might otherwise have been destroyed (2) president preserves as national monuments land that eventually earns national park status and makes up 25 percent of our present national parks

2. Students may list any two of the following words or phrases: so, responded, as a result of, because, consequently

# Problem-Solution

**Problem-solution** writing describes a difficult issue or problem and offers a solution for it. In such writing, the writer uses logical arguments to convince readers that the proposed solution will solve the problem. The writer may also explain how to carry out the solution.

## Strategies for Reading

- To find the **problem,** ask, What is this writing about?

- To find the **solution,** ask, What suggestion does the writer offer to remedy the problem?

- Look for the **reasons** the writer gives for choosing this solution. Is the thinking behind them logical? Is the evidence given to support them strong and convincing?

- Look for any **first steps** the writer recommends taking to carry out this solution. Ask, Are these steps clear and doable?

MODEL

**Problem**

You and some friends are interested in creating your own magazine. You also have several friends who want to start a band, and your sister wants to know more about Web-page design. You look in your textbooks for help, but you don't find the explanations you need. Frustrated, you and your friends find yourselves wondering how you can get the help you really need—the help of experts.

**Solution**

One solution is to establish a visiting-artists program at your school. A visiting-artists program is a formal means of getting visual and performing artists, poets and writers, computer-graphics experts, and other kinds of professional artists to visit your school. Once such a program is established, a school official could schedule and pay for visits by professional artists and arrange for interested students to attend the workshops and lectures given by them.

**Reasons**

Consequently, establishing such a program would enable you and your friends to get hands-on instruction from experts.

A good first step toward establishing such a program is to form a committee of students interested in getting the program adopted at your school. At the start, the committee would just conduct research to learn the following:

- which community organizations provide schools with names of artists who will come to visit
- which organizations provide money to support visiting-artists programs at schools, and what the procedure for applying for this money is
- how well visiting-artists programs have worked at other schools
- how many students would be interested in having such a program
- which teacher(s) would be willing to volunteer time to help run the program

A good second step toward establishing such a program is to draft a proposal that you can give to the school faculty and administrators. In this proposal, you would need to do the following:

- give school officials reasons for establishing the program
- show officials how the program could be implemented easily
- support your claims with research

Establishing a visiting-artists program may seem like a lot of trouble just to solve the problems you and your friends face. However, once the program is in place, you and others will be able to continue benefiting from it, exploring new interests and career options. For example, maybe next year you'll want to learn how to produce your own video, create special effects for movies, or become a makeup artist. With a visiting-artists program in place, you can learn about all those endeavors and more.

## PRACTICE AND APPLY

Reread the model and then answer the following questions:

1. What solution does the writer offer?
2. What reasons does she give for adopting it?
3. What steps does the writer suggest the students follow to enact this solution?

**PRACTICE AND APPLY ANSWERS**
1. The writer's solution is to establish a visiting artists program at your school.
2. Students may include some or all of the following reasons: You can get hands-on instruction from experts; You can get information you want that your textbooks don't contain; you and others can keep benefiting from it, exploring new interests and career options.
3. She recommends doing research as a good first step and drafting a proposal as a good second step.

# Functional Reading

*Functional reading is reading to discover such information as instruction in how to do something. When you read a map, a memo, or an instruction manual, you are engaged in functional reading. These guidelines show how you can improve your functional-reading skills.*

## Instruction Manual

### Strategies for Reading

**A** Look at the **title** on the page to discover what the text is about.

**B** Read the lists of **bulleted items** carefully. The bulleted points are usually the essential pieces of information.

**C** Be sure to read the text that immediately precedes a visual. This **lead-in text** can help you understand what the visual is intended to show.

**D** Pay attention to **captions** with pictures or drawings. These will help you interpret what you are seeing.

**E** Study **visuals** closely. These will help you interpret what you are reading and may even provide information not covered in the text.

---

**A** **Rules of the Road: Passing**

**Always use caution when passing another vehicle. When passing via the left lane on a two-lane highway, make sure that all of the following are true:**

- you can see the left lane clearly
- **B** the left lane is free of oncoming traffic for a distance great enough to allow you to pass
- you are sure that you will be able to return to your lane before you are within 200 feet of an oncoming vehicle

- you can see the car you have just passed in your rearview mirror before you re-enter the right-hand lane

**Do not pass via the left lane of a two-lane highway in any of the situations shown on the diagram below.**

**C** **In each of the following situations, the red car is breaking the law.**

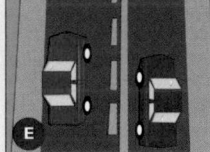   

**E** In a no passing zone    On a hill   **D**   Within 100 feet of a bridge, viaduct, tunnel, or railroad crossing    On a curve where you cannot see oncoming vehicles

25

---

## PRACTICE AND APPLY

Reread the page from the driving-instruction manual and then answer the following questions:

1. What essential piece of information does the lead-in text provide about the visual on this page?

2. What are the four driving situations described in which a driver should not pass another vehicle?

3. What do all of the bulleted items concern?

4. What information about lane markings can you gain from the visual that you do not learn from the text on this page?

---

**PRACTICE AND APPLY ANSWERS**

1. The lead-in text lets you know that, in each driving situation shown, the red car is breaking the law.

2. (1) in a no passing zone (2) on a hill (3) within 100 feet of a bridge, viaduct, tunnel, or railroad crossing (4) on a curve where you cannot see other vehicles

3. All of the bulleted items concern what you must make sure is true when passing via the left lane on a two-lane highway.

4. the lane markings that indicate a no passing zone

## Technical Manual

### Strategies for Reading

**(A)** Read the **title** to learn what material the page covers. This page, from a car owner's manual, explains how to operate the radio that comes with the car.

**(B)** Examine **pictures** or other **graphics.** Pictures can help you familiarize yourself with the various parts of an item or a process.

**(C)** Read any **labels** or **captions** that identify parts of the picture. These labels can help you locate buttons or other components.

**(D)** Check **numbered** or **lettered text** to see if it is linked by corresponding numbers or letters to parts of a diagram or illustration. If it is, refer to the picture as you read.

**(E)** Read the **text** carefully to learn how to perform particular tasks. If the manual presents the steps of a process in paragraph form, look for signal words such as *first, next, then,* and *finally* to learn the order in which you should follow the instructions.

### PRACTICE AND APPLY

Using the manual below, answer the questions.
1. How do you select scan-tuning mode? How do you deactivate this mode?
2. What steps must you follow to preset a station?

---

**(A) How to Operate the Radio**

The following diagram of your factory-installed radio shows the locations of its various features.

**(C)** 1. On/Off Knob and Volume Control    2. FM/AM Band Control Button    3. FM Band Selector Switch    8. Preset Station Number Display

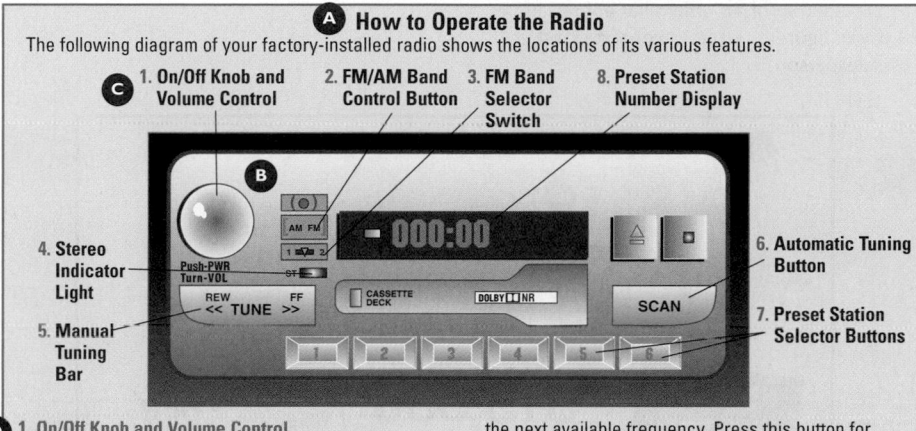

4. Stereo Indicator Light
5. Manual Tuning Bar
6. Automatic Tuning Button
7. Preset Station Selector Buttons

**(D)** **1. On/Off Knob and Volume Control**
Push this knob to turn the radio on or off. **(E)**

**2. FM/AM Band Control Button**
Press this button to select the AM band and a red light appears. Press this button a second time to deselect the AM band and tune in FM stations.

**3. FM Band Selector Switch**
Move this switch left to select FM band 1 or right to select FM band 2. *Note: This is inoperative when the AM band is selected.*

**4. Stereo Indicator Light (ST)**
When the radio receives an FM signal clear enough to produce in stereo, it does so and the light comes on.

**5. Manual Tuning Bar**
Press the left side of the button to select stations in descending order of frequency. Press the right side to select stations in ascending order.

**6. Automatic Tuning Button**
Press this button for less than 2 seconds to jump up to the next available frequency. Press this button for longer than 2 seconds to activate scan-tuning.

**In scan-tuning mode,** the radio jumps to the next station, remains there for 5 seconds, then jumps to the next station, remains there for 5 seconds, and so on, until the button is briefly pressed again.

**7. Preset Station Selector Buttons**
Use these buttons to preset 18 of your favorite radio stations (12 FM and 6 AM) by following these steps:

1. Select FM or AM with the FM/AM Band Control Button.
2. Select the station using manual tuning or scan-tuning.
3. Press and hold one of the preset station selector buttons until you hear a beep (about 3 seconds).

**To change a preset station,** repeat the steps above.

**8. Preset Station Number Display**
When a station or frequency is being broadcast, its number is displayed on this panel.

---

**PRACTICE AND APPLY ANSWERS**
1. Press the automatic tuning button for longer than 2 seconds. Briefly press the automatic tuning button again.
2. To preset a station, you must follow these steps: First, select FM or AM with the FM/AM Band Control Button. Next, select the station using manual tuning or scan-tuning. Third, press and hold one of the preset station selector buttons until you hear a beep (about 3 seconds).

**PRACTICE AND APPLY ANSWERS**

1. Students should list any four of the following: power steering, power brakes, power windows, leather seats, compact spare tire, halogen head-lights, air bags, 12.5-gallon fuel tank, floor mats, AM/FM radio
2. annual percentage rate
3. first-time buyers
4. tax, title, license, and $50.48 document fee
5. 3 days from publication

## Product Advertisement

### Strategies for Reading

**A** Read any **titles** or **subtitles** in the advertisement to find out what the product is and who is selling it.

**B** Study any **pictures** of the product. Does the product appear to fit your needs?

**C** Look for **essential information** such as price, features, and the location or phone number of the company selling the product.

**D** Make sure you understand any **abbreviations.** In the ad shown, *P/S, P/B,* and *P/W* stand for *power steering, power brakes,* and *power windows.* If there is no explanation of an unfamiliar abbreviation, try to figure it out from context or ask a salesperson.

**E** Look for **small print** in the advertisement. Small print often contains important information such as warnings, limitations, exclusions, end dates, and notice of extra fees.

### PRACTICE AND APPLY

Reread the advertisement and then answer the following questions:

1. List at least four features of the truck that is advertised.
2. What does the abbreviation *APR* stand for?
3. Who qualifies for the rebate?
4. What four fees must a buyer pay in addition to the $15,530 purchase price?
5. When does the offer expire?

## Product Manual

### Strategies for Reading

**(A)** Read the **title** to learn what material the page covers. This page is from the owner's manual of a car.

**(B)** Look for **numbered steps** or a **bulleted list** detailing how to perform a particular task.

**(C)** Notice any **subheads** that tell what a section of text is about. Also look for **labels,** such as *Diagram 1* or *Figure A*.

**(D)** Study any **pictures** or other **graphics** in the manual. If you are having trouble following the instructions, pictures can help you pinpoint where you are going wrong.

**(E)** Notice any **warning symbols,** such as exclamation points or stop signs. These symbols are meant to call your attention to special instructions that must be followed to complete the task safely and properly.

### PRACTICE AND APPLY

Reread the manual page and then answer the following questions:

1. What does this page explain how to do?

2. According to the instructions, what should you do to the tire diagonally opposite to the one being changed?

3. If you turned the wheel wrench clockwise, would the jack go up or down?

4. Why is it important to not start the engine while the vehicle is on the jack and to make sure the jack is on a level and solid surface?

**PRACTICE AND APPLY ANSWERS**
1. change a tire
2. block both sides of the wheel
3. up
4. to avoid personal injury

---

### (A) How to Change a Tire, page 1 of 3

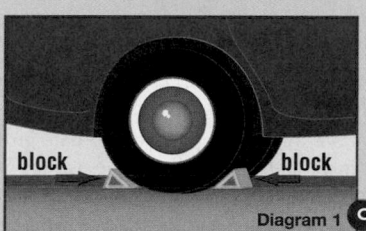

block        block

Diagram 1 **(C)**

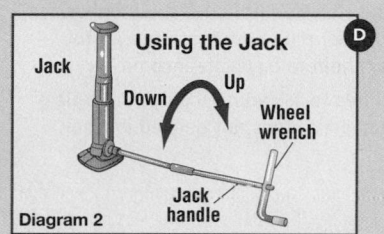

**Using the Jack**  **(D)**

Jack

Down — Up

Wheel wrench

Jack handle

Diagram 2

**To avoid injury when changing a tire, follow these instructions:**

**(B)**
1. Set the parking brake firmly.
2. Set the transmission in "Reverse."
3. Turn off the ignition.
4. Unload the vehicle.

5. Block both sides of the wheel that is diagonally opposite to the one being changed with blocks or other items that can be wedged solidly under the wheel (as shown in Diagram 1).

**When changing a tire, beware of the surrounding traffic.**

---

**! WARNING !** **(E)**

**To further avoid injury:**

- Never use a jack from any other vehicle to lift your vehicle.
- Make sure the jack is on a level, solid surface.
- Never get underneath the vehicle when using the jack.
- Do not start the engine while the vehicle is on the jack.

# Pay Stub

## Strategies for Reading

**A** Scan the entire pay stub to see whether the **personal information** and number of **hours** worked are correct. If anything is inaccurate, report it to your employer immediately.

**B** Look for explanations of **abbreviations** that are used on the stub. These may appear at the bottom of the stub or on the back. Some abbreviations are so commonly used, however, that they will probably not be defined in a key. These are

- *y.t.d.,* which means "year to date"—that is, up to the present date in this year

- *fed. ex.,* meaning "federal exemption," which is a number used to figure out how much of one's pay should be withheld to pay federal income tax

- *state ex.,* meaning "state exemption." The state exemption is the number used to determine how much money to withhold to pay state income tax

Feel free to ask your employer to explain any abbreviations not defined in a key.

**C** Pay particular attention to the **dollar amounts** listed as federal and state income-tax deductions, health-insurance deductions, and other **types of deductions.** If any of these strike you as excessive, feel free to ask how they were calculated.

**D** See the **net pay** figure to learn the actual amount of money you are taking home.

**E** If you wish to see how many **vacation days, sick days,** or **personal days** you have earned, look at the **accumulations section.**

### PRACTICE AND APPLY

Reread the pay stub and then answer the following questions:

1. According to this pay stub, how many hours did this employee work during this pay period?

2. What amount did she pay for union dues during this period?

3. For the entire year to the present date, how much money has been deducted from this employee's income?

4. What is this employee's net pay for this pay period?

5. What are this employee's year-to-date gross earnings? Is this figure the same as the employee's year-to-date taxable earnings?

**PRACTICE AND APPLY ANSWERS**
1. 80 hours
2. $4.05
3. $315.98
4. $623.94
5. $1,942.72; the same

| LOCATION | EMPLOYEE NAME | | SOC. SEC. NO. | | FED. EX. | STATE EX. | PAY PERIOD ENDING | CHECK NO. |
|---|---|---|---|---|---|---|---|---|
| Park #87 | Haley Allen Simpson | **A** | 987-65-4320 **B** | | S-000 | S-000 | 07/27/01 | 552573 |

*STATEMENT OF EARNINGS & LEAVE - NON-NEGOTIABLE*

| 987-65-4320 | | | DEDUCTIONS | | | | | | THIS IS A STATEMENT OF YOUR EARNINGS, DEDUCTIONS AND LEAVE. DETACH AND RETAIN FOR YOUR RECORDS | |
|---|---|---|---|---|---|---|---|---|---|---|
| TYPE | HOURS | AMOUNT | TYPE | AMOUNT | Y.T.D. | TYPE | AMOUNT | Y.T.D. | | |
| REG | 80.00 **A** | 747.20 | FIT | 96.79 **C** | 245.54 | | | | EARNINGS | 747.20 |
| | | | SIT | 22.42 | 58.29 | | | | **D** DEDUCTIONS | 123.26 |
| | | | DUE | 4.05 | 12.15 | | | | NET PAY | 623.94 |
| | | | | | | | | | Y.T.D. GROSS EARNINGS | 1942.72 |
| | | | | | | | | | Y.T.D. TAXABLE EARNINGS | 1942.72 |
| | | | | | | | | | Y.T.D. F.I.C.A. EARNINGS | |
| | | | | | | | | | ACCUMULATIONS | |
| | | | | | | | | | VACATION | 0.0001 |
| | | | | | | | | | **E** SICK/PERSONAL TIME | 0.0001 |
| | | | | | | TOTAL | 123.26 | 315.98 | | |
| TOTAL | 80.00 | 747.20 | | | | | | | EMPLOYEE # | 12329 |

| | | | | | |
|---|---|---|---|---|---|
| Union dues...............DUE | Medicare.....................MED | Garnishments...................GAR | State Tax Levy.......................STA |
| Park Pension ............PEN | Federal Witholdings............FIT | Child Support..................CHS | Federal Tax Levy...................FED |
| Municipal Pension ..............PEN | State Witholdings................SIT | Hospitalization-Dent. ..........DEN | Illinois Student Loan ..............STU |
| Laborers Pension ................PEN | Hamilton Insurance ..............HAM | Education Loan ....................EDU | Federal Student Loan ............FSL |
| Social Security.....................SOC | Equitable Life Ins. ..................EQU | Credit Union (Bank)................CRE | City Parking/Water.................PAR |

# Medicine Label

## Strategies for Reading

**A** Check the **Uses** section to make sure the medication can be used to treat your symptoms.

**B** Study the **directions,** which tell how much of the medication you should take and how often to take it.

**C** Always study the **warnings** and **drug-interaction precautions** on any medicine label. It is important to familiarize yourself with these sections in case there is any reason you should not take the medication or anything you should not do while taking the medication.

**D** Read the lists of both **active** and **inactive ingredients** to see whether the medication contains any ingredients to which you know you react unfavorably. Also check these lists if you are surprised by a negative reaction to the medicine. Doing so may help you to discover ingredients you should avoid in the future.

### PRACTICE AND APPLY

1. Name three symptoms that would be relieved by this product.

2. Should an 11-year-old child take this product to relieve hay-fever symptoms? Why or why not?

3. Name two active ingredients and two inactive ingredients. What are the purposes of the active ingredients you named?

4. What does the tampering warning say?

---

## No-Sneeze
### Allergy Sinus Tablets

**A** **Uses**
**No-Sneeze** can be used for the temporary relief of sinus congestion and pressure, sinus pain, nasal congestion, headache, runny nose, sneezing, itching of the nose or throat, itchy and watery eyes due to hay fever.

**B** **Directions**
**Adults & children 12 years of age and older:**
Take 2 tablets every 4–5 hours. Do not take more than 6 tablets in 24 hours except as directed by a doctor.

**Children under 12 years:**
Do not use this adult product in children under 12 years of age. This will provide more than the recommended dose (overdose) and could cause serious health problems.

**C** **Warnings**
**Do not exceed maximum specified in directions.** Do not take for pain for more than 7 days unless directed by a doctor. If pain or fever persists or worsens, if new symptoms develop, or if redness or swelling is present, consult a doctor. These could be signs of a serious condition. May cause excitability. If nervousness, dizziness, or sleeplessness occurs, discontinue use and consult a doctor. May cause drowsiness; alcohol, sedatives, and tranquilizers may increase the drowsiness effect. Avoid alcoholic beverages while taking this product. Do not take this product if you are taking sedatives or tranquilizers without first consulting your doctor. Use caution when driving a motor vehicle or operating machinery. Do not take this product, unless directed by a doctor, if you have a breathing problem such as emphysema or chronic bronchitis, or if you have glaucoma, or difficulty in urination due to enlargement of the prostate gland. Do not take this product if you have heart disease, high blood pressure, thyroid disease, or diabetes, unless directed by a doctor. As with any drug, if you are pregnant or nursing a baby, seek the advice of a health professional before using this product.

**Keep this and all drugs out of the reach of children.** In case of accidental overdose, contact a doctor or a Poison Control Center immediately. Prompt medical attention is critical for adults as well as children even if you do not notice any signs or symptoms of overdose.

**Drug Interaction Precautions** Do not use with other products containing acetaminophen. Do not use this product if you are now taking a prescription monoamine oxidase inhibitor (MAOI) (certain drugs for depression, psychiatric or emotional conditions, or Parkinson's disease), or for 2 weeks after stopping the MAOI drug. If you are uncertain whether your prescription drug contains an MAOI, consult a health professional before using this product.

**DO NOT USE IF CARTON IS OPEN, PROTECTIVE SEAL IS BROKEN, OR BLISTER UNIT IS BROKEN.**

**D** | **Active Ingredients:** (in each tablet) | **Purposes:** |
| --- | --- |
| Acetaminophen, 500 mg | Pain reliever |
| Chlorpheniramine maleate, 2 mg | Antihistamine |
| Pseudoephedrine HCl, 30 mg | Nasal decongestant |

**Inactive Ingredients:**
Benzyl Alcohol, Butylparaben, Castor Oil, Corn Starch, D&C Yellow #10, Edetate Calcium Disodium, FD&C Blue #1, Hydroxypropyl Methylcellulose, Magnesium Stearate, Methylparaben, Propylparaben, Sodium Lauryl Sulfate, Sodium Propionate, Sodium Starch Glycolate, Titanium Dioxide.

*Store at room temperature and avoid high humidity and excessive heat above 40°C (104°F).*
*See side panel for expiration date and lot number.*

---

**PRACTICE AND APPLY ANSWERS**
1. Students may list any three of the following symptoms: sinus congestion and pressure, sinus pain, nasal congestion, headache, runny nose, sneezing, itching of the nose or throat, itchy and watery eyes due to hay fever

2. No. This product will give a child under 12 years old more than the recommended dosage, and could cause serious health problems.

3. Students may list any two of the following active ingredients and the purposes noted in parentheses as well as any two of the following inactive ingredients: active ingredients—Acetaminophen (pain reliever), Chlorpheniramine maleate (antihistamine), Pseudoephedrine HCl (nasal decongestant); inactive ingredients—Benzyl Alcohol, Butylparaben, Castor Oil, Corn Starch, D&C Yellow #10, Edetate Calcium Disodium, FD&C Blue #1, Gelatin, Hydroxypropyl Methylcellulose, Magnesium Stearate, Methylparaben, Propylparaben, Sodium Lauryl Sulfate, Sodium Propionate, Sodium Starch Glycolate, Titanium Dioxide

4. Do not use if carton is open, protective seal is broken, or blister unit is broken.

# Passport Application

For most travel outside the United States, you must have a passport. Consequently, if you are a United States citizen, at some point you will likely need to fill out the passport application shown here. The instructions and other information on page 2 of this application will instruct you in how to do this. The strategies on the next page can also help.

UNITED STATES DEPARTMENT OF STATE
APPLICATION FOR ☐ PASSPORT ☐ REGISTRATION
(Type or print all capital letters in blue or black ink in white areas only)

**IMPORTANT PLEASE READ INSTRUCTIONS ON PAGE 2!**

1. NAME (First and Middle)
LAST

2. MAIL PASSPORT TO: STREET / RFD # OR P.O. BOX        APT. #
CITY        STATE
ZIP CODE        COUNTRY / IN CARE OF (if applicable)

☐ 5 Yr.  ☐ 10 Yr.  Issue Date
R    D    O    DP
End. #        Exp.

3. SEX ☐ M ☐ F
4. PLACE OF BIRTH (City & State or City & Country)
5. DATE OF BIRTH  Month Day Year
6. SOCIAL SECURITY NUMBER (SEE FEDERAL TAX LAW NOTICE ON PAGE 2)

7. HEIGHT Feet Inches
8. HAIR COLOR
9. EYE COLOR
10. HOME TELEPHONE ( )
11. BUSINESS TELEPHONE ( )
12. OCCUPATION

13. PERMANENT ADDRESS (DO NOT LIST P.O. BOX)  STREET/RFD #  CITY  STATE  ZIP CODE

14. FATHER'S FULL NAME Last First  BIRTHPLACE  BIRTHDATE  U.S. CITIZEN ☐ Yes ☐ No
15. MOTHER'S FULL MAIDEN NAME Last First  BIRTHPLACE  BIRTHDATE  U.S. CITIZEN ☐ Yes ☐ No

16. HAVE YOU EVER BEEN MARRIED? ☐ Yes ☐ No  SPOUSE'S OR FORMER SPOUSE'S FULL NAME AT BIRTH Last First  BIRTHPLACE  BIRTHDATE  U.S. CITIZEN ☐ Yes ☐ No

DATE OF MOST RECENT MARRIAGE Month Day Year  WIDOWED/DIVORCED? ☐ Yes Give Date ☐ No Month Day Year
17. OTHER NAMES YOU HAVE USED (1) (2)

18. HAVE YOU EVER BEEN ISSUED A U.S. PASSPORT? ☐ Yes ☐ No  IF YES, COMPLETE NEXT LINE AND SUBMIT PASSPORT IF AVAILABLE.  DISPOSITION
NAME IN WHICH ISSUED  MOST RECENT PASSPORT NUMBER  APPROXIMATE ISSUE DATE Month Day Year  ☐ Submitted ☐ Stolen ☐ Lost ☐ Other

It is necessary to submit a statement with an application for a new passport when a previous valid or potentially valid passport cannot be presented. The statement must set forth in detail why the previous passport cannot be presented. Use Form DSP-64.

STAPLE 1" TO  FROM 1" TO 1-3/8"  STAPLE
2 x 2  STAPLE  STAPLE
SUBMIT TWO RECENT IDENTICAL PHOTOS

19. EMERGENCY CONTACT. If you wish, you may supply the name, address and telephone number of a person not traveling with you to be contacted in case of emergency.
NAME
STREET
CITY  STATE  ZIP CODE
TELEPHONE ( )  RELATIONSHIP

20. TRAVEL PLANS (not mandatory)  Month Day Year
Date of Trip
Length of Trip
COUNTRIES TO BE VISITED

21. STOP. DO NOT SIGN APPLICATION UNTIL REQUESTED TO DO SO BY PERSON ADMINISTERING OATH. I have not, since acquiring United States citizenship, performed any of the acts listed under "Acts or Conditions" on the reverse of this application form (unless explanatory statement is attached). I solemnly swear (or affirm) that the statements made on this application are true and the photograph attached is a true likeness of me.

X _____  X _____
Parent's/Legal Guardian's Signature if identifying minor child  Applicant's Signature - age 13 or older

22. FOR ACCEPTANCE AGENT'S USE
Subscribed and sworn to (affirmed) before me  Month Day Year  (SEAL)
☐ Clerk of Court; Location
☐ PASSPORT Agent
☐ Postal Employee
☐ (Vice) Consul USA
(Signature of person authorized to accept application)

23. APPLICANT'S IDENTIFYING DOCUMENTS
☐ DRIVER'S LICENSE  ISSUE DATE: Month Day Year  EXPIRATION DATE: Month Day Year  ID No.
☐ PASSPORT
☐ OTHER (Specify) _____  PLACE OF ISSUE: _____  ISSUED IN THE NAME OF: _____

24. FOR ISSUING OFFICE USE ONLY (Applicant's evidence of citizenship)
☐ Birth Certificate  SR  CR  City  Filed/Issued:
☐ Passport  Bearer's Name:
☐ Report of Birth
☐ Naturalization/Citizenship Cert.  No.:  Issued:
☐ Other:
☐ Seen & Returned
☐ Attached
APPLICATION APPROVAL

25.
FEE _____  EXEC. _____  EF _____  OTHER _____

FORM DSP-11 (12-97)  (SEE INSTRUCTIONS ON PAGE 2)
Page 1
Form Approved OMB No. 1405-0004 (Exp. 5/31/2001) Estimated Burden - 20 Minutes*

## Strategies for Reading

**(A)** Beginning at the top, scan the entire application to see what the different sections are. Watch for **headings** that identify the sections and **lines** that divide one section from another.

**(B)** Notice **sections you should not or need not fill in.**

**(C)** Look for **difficult words** or **abbreviations**—such as *disposition* ("present location or status"), *mandatory* ("required, necessary"), *M* ("male"), and *F* ("female")—and determine what they mean.

**(D)** Notice **instructions** that tell you how to fill out particular sections of the application. Also notice instructions about **other materials you may need to provide.**

**(E)** Pay special attention to any part of the application that calls for your **signature.** Be sure to read all statements carefully before signing your name to them.

## PRACTICE AND APPLY

Reread the application and then answer the following questions:

1. When are you supposed to sign this application? If you are a minor child, who else must sign the form?

2. How many photos must you submit? What must each photograph show? What size must each be? How must you attach at least one of the photos?

3. What do all the areas of the application that you are not supposed to fill out have in common?

4. Which numbered item relates to travel plans? If you already have travel plans, do you have to include information about them?

5. If you had a valid passport before but cannot present it, what must you submit? On what form must you submit this?

## PRACTICE AND APPLY ANSWERS

1. You are supposed to sign it when requested to do so by the person administering oath; a parent or legal guardian

2. two; identical pictures of my face at least 1-3/8 inches long; the photos must be 2 inches by 2 inches; at least one must be stapled to the area shown on the application

3. They are all tinted tan.

4. 20; no—it's not mandatory

5. I must submit a statement that sets forth in detail why I cannot present my previous passport. I must submit this on Form DSP-64.

---

UNITED STATES DEPARTMENT OF STATE
### PASSPORT APPLICATION
#### HOW TO APPLY FOR A U.S. PASSPORT

**FOR INQUIRIES** (A fee is charged for this service.): National Passport Information Center, 1-900-225-5674, For TDD: 1-900-225-7778 **OR** For Credit Card Users: 1-888-362-8668, For TDD: 1-888-498-3648

U.S. passports are issued only to U.S. citizens or nationals. Each person must obtain his or her own passport. IF YOU ARE A FIRST-TIME APPLICANT, please complete and submit this application in person. (Applicants under 13 years of age usually need not appear in person unless requested. A parent or guardian may execute the application on the child's behalf.) Each application must be accompanied by (1) PROOF OF U.S. CITIZENSHIP, (2) PROOF OF IDENTITY, (3) TWO PHOTOGRAPHS, (4) FEES (as explained below) to one of the following acceptance agents: a clerk of any Federal or State court of record or a judge or clerk of any probate court accepting applications; a designated municipal or county official; a designated postal employee at an authorized post office; or an agent at a Passport Agency in Boston, Chicago, Honolulu, Houston, Los Angeles, Miami, New Orleans, New York, Philadelphia, San Francisco, Seattle, Stamford, or Washington, D.C.; or a U.S. consular official.

IF YOU HAVE HAD A PREVIOUS PASSPORT, inquire about eligibility to use Form DSP-82 (mail-in application). Address requests for passport amendment, extension of validity, or additional visa pages to a Passport Agency or a U.S. Consulate or Embassy abroad. Check visa requirements with consular officials of countries to be visited well in advance of your departure.

**(1) PROOF OF U.S. CITIZENSHIP.**
(a) APPLICANTS BORN IN THE UNITED STATES. Submit previous U.S. passport or **certified** birth certificate. A birth certificate must include your given name and surname, date and place of birth, date the birth record was filed, and seal or other certification of the official custodian of such records. A record filed more than 1 year after the birth is acceptable if it is supported by evidence described in the next paragraph.

IF NO BIRTH RECORD EXISTS, submit registrar's notice to that effect. Also submit an early baptismal or circumcision certificate, hospital birth record, early census, school, or family Bible records, newspaper or insurance files, or notarized affidavits of persons having knowledge of your birth (preferably with at least one record listed above). Evidence should include your given name and surname, date and place of birth, and seal or other certification of office (if customary) and signature of issuing official.

(b) APPLICANTS BORN OUTSIDE THE UNITED STATES. Submit previous U.S. passport or Certificate of Naturalization, or Certificate of Citizenship, or a Report of Birth Abroad, or evidence described below.

IF YOU CLAIM CITIZENSHIP THROUGH NATURALIZATION OF PARENT(S), submit the Certificate(s) of Naturalization of your parent(s), your foreign birth certificate, and proof of your admission to the United States for permanent residence.

IF YOU CLAIM CITIZENSHIP THROUGH BIRTH ABROAD TO U.S. CITIZEN PARENT(S), submit a Consular Report of Birth (Form FS-240) or Certification of Birth (Form DS-1350 or FS-545), or your foreign birth certificate, parents' marriage certificate, proof of citizenship of your parent(s), and affidavit of U.S. citizen parent(s) showing all periods and places of residence/physical presence in the United States and abroad before your birth.

**(2) PROOF OF IDENTITY.** If you are not personally known to the acceptance agent, you must establish your identity to the agent's satisfaction. You may submit items such as the following containing your signature AND physical description or photograph that is a good likeness of you: previous U.S. passport; Certificate of Naturalization or of Citizenship; driver's license (not temporary or learner's license); or government (Federal, State, municipal) identification card or pass. Temporary or altered documents are not acceptable.

IF YOU CANNOT PROVE YOUR IDENTITY as stated above, you must appear with an IDENTIFYING WITNESS who is a U.S. citizen or permanent resident alien who has known you for at least 2 years. Your witness must prove his or her identity and complete and sign an Affidavit of Identifying Witness (Form DSP-71) before the acceptance agent. You must also submit some identification of your own.

**(3) TWO PHOTOGRAPHS.** Submit two identical photographs of you alone, sufficiently recent to be a good likeness (normally taken within the last 6 months), 2 x 2 inches in size, with an image size from bottom of chin to top of head (including hair) of between 1 and 1-3/8 inches. Photographs must be clear, front view, full face, taken in normal street attire without a hat or dark glasses, and printed on thin paper with a plain light (white or off-white) background. They may be black and white or color. They must be capable of withstanding a mounting temperature of 225° Fahrenheit (107° Celsius). Photographs retouched so that your appearance is changed are unacceptable. Snapshots, most vending machine prints, and magazine or full-length photographs are unacceptable.

**(4) FEES.** Submit $60 if you are 16 years of age or older. The passport fee is $45. In addition, a fee of $15 is charged for the execution of the application. Your passport will be valid for 10 years from the date of issue except where limited by the Secretary of State to a shorter period. Submit $40 if you are 15 years of age or younger. The passport fee is $25 and the execution fee is $15. Your passport will be valid for 5 years from the date of issue, except where limited as above.

Expedited service is available only in the United States. Expedite requests will be processed in 3 workdays from receipt at a Passport Agency. This service is available only for early departure, generally with proof of travel. The additional fee is $35.

Pay the passport and execution fees in one of the following forms: Checks-personal, certified, traveler's; bank draft or cashier's check; money order-U.S. Postal, international, currency exchange; or if abroad, the foreign currency equivalent, or a check drawn on a U.S. bank.

Make passport and execution fees payable to Passport Services (except if applying at a designated acceptance facility, such as a State court or municipal office, pay execution fee as required) or the appropriate Embassy or Consulate, if abroad. Pay special postage if applicable.

An additional adjudication fee of $100 will be charged to previously undocumented passport customers who were born outside the United States and who have not been issued any of the following documents: a U.S. passport, a Consular Report of Birth Abroad, a Certification of Report of Birth, a Certificate of Naturalization or a Certificate of Citizenship.

An additional $15 fee will be charged when, upon request, the Department of State verifies issuance of a previous U.S. passport or Consular Report of Birth Abroad because the customer is unable to submit other evidence of U.S. citizenship.

No fee is charged to applicants with U.S. Government or military authorization for no-fee passports (except designated acceptance facilities may collect the execution fee).

**FEDERAL TAX LAW:**
26 U.S.C. 6039E (Internal Revenue Code) requires a passport applicant to provide his/her name and social security number. If you have not been issued a social security number...

# ❶ The Writing Process

*Different writers use different processes. Try out different strategies and figure out what works best for you. For some assignments, it is best to start by figuring out what you need to end up with, make a plan or outline, and stick to it. Other writing assignments may be more successful if you start by writing everything you know about the topic, allow things to get messy, and then reshape and revise the writing so it fits the assignment. Try both approaches and get to know yourself as a writer.*

*Also consider whether the assignment is high-stakes or low-stakes writing. When the success of the piece is very important, such as in a test, you might choose to focus on meeting the requirements or criteria of the assignment. When the purpose of the writing is to develop your ideas, there is more opportunity to experiment and take risks. Take into account the time factor as well. In a timed writing test, you may not have time to explore and revise.*

*Correct grammar and spelling are very important in your final product. You don't need to focus on these as you shape your ideas and draft your piece, but be sure you allow time for a careful edit before turning in your final piece.*

## ❶.❶ Prewriting

In the prewriting stage, you explore your ideas and discover what you want to write about.

### Finding Ideas for Writing
Try one or more of the following techniques to help you find a writing topic.

#### Personal Techniques
- Practice imaging, or trying to remember mainly sensory details about a subject—its look, sound, feel, taste, and smell.
- Complete a knowledge inventory to discover what you already know about a subject.
- Browse through magazines, newspapers, and on-line bulletin boards for ideas.
- Start a clip file of articles that you want to save for future reference. Be sure to label each clip with source information.

#### Sharing Techniques
- With a group, brainstorm a topic by trying to come up with as many ideas as you can without stopping to critique or examine them.
- Interview someone who knows a great deal about your topic.

#### Writing Techniques
- After freewriting on a topic, try looping, or choosing your best idea for more freewriting. Repeat the loop at least once.
- Make a list to help you organize ideas, examine them, or identify areas for further research.

#### Graphic Techniques
- Create a pro-and-con chart to compare the positive and negative aspects of an idea or a course of action.
- Use a cluster map or tree diagram to explore subordinate ideas that relate to your general topic or central idea.

### Determining Your Purpose
Your purpose for writing may be to express yourself, to entertain, to describe, to explain, to analyze, or to persuade. To clarify it, ask questions like these:

- Why did I choose to write about my topic?
- What aspects of the topic mean the most to me?
- What do I want others to think or feel after they read my writing?

**LINK TO LITERATURE** One purpose for writing is to clarify a subject. For example, Toni Morrison wrote "Thoughts on the African-American Novel," page 973, to explain why these novels need to be a unique form, incorporating art and oral tradition, and not be simply new stories by and about African Americans.

### Identifying Your Audience

Knowing who will read your writing can help you focus your topic and choose relevant details. As you think about your readers, ask yourself questions like these:

• What does my audience already know about my topic?

• What will they be most interested in?

• What language is most appropriate for this audience?

##  Drafting

In the drafting stage, you put your ideas on paper and allow them to develop and change as you write.

Two broad approaches in this stage are discovery drafting and planned drafting.

**Discovery drafting** is a good approach when you are not quite sure what you think about your subject. You just plunge into your draft and let your feelings and ideas lead you where they will. After finishing a discovery draft, you may decide to start another draft, do more prewriting, or revise your first draft.

**Planned drafting** may work better for research reports, critical reviews, and other kinds of formal writing. Try making a writing plan or a scratch outline before you begin drafting. Then, as you write, you can fill in the details.

LINK TO LITERATURE Some writers plan and outline; some write in a great flurry, without much previous planning as ideas occur to them. Of course, the ideas have been generating within them before they begin to write. Zora Neale Hurston who wrote "How It Feels to Be Colored Me," page 950, wrote her most popular novel, *Their Eyes Were Watching God,* "under internal pressure" in seven weeks. She says the story was "dammed up in me."

## 1.3 Revising, Editing, and Proofreading

The changes you make in your writing during this stage usually fall into three categories: revising for content, revising for structure, and proofreading to correct mistakes in mechanics.

Use the questions that follow to assess problems and determine what changes would improve your work.

### Revising for Content

• Does my writing have a main idea or central focus? Is my thesis clear?

• Have I incorporated adequate detail? Where might I include a telling detail, revealing statistic, or vivid example?

• Is any material unnecessary, irrelevant, or confusing?

WRITING TIP Be sure to consider the needs of your audience as you answer the questions under Revising for Content and Revising for Structure. For example, before you can determine whether any of your material is unnecessary or irrelevant, you need to identify what your audience already knows.

### Revising for Structure

• Is my writing unified? Do all ideas and supporting details pertain to my main idea or advance my thesis?

• Is my writing clear and coherent? Is the flow of sentences and paragraphs smooth and logical?

• Do I need to add transitional words, phrases, or sentences to make the relationships among ideas clearer?

• Are my sentences well constructed? What sentences might I combine to improve the grace and rhythm of my writing?

### Proofreading to Correct Mistakes in Grammar, Usage, and Mechanics

When you are satisfied with your revision, proofread your paper, looking for mistakes in grammar, usage, and mechanics. You may want to do this several times, looking for different types of mistakes each time. The following checklist may help.

### Sentence Structure and Agreement

- Are there any run-on sentences or sentence fragments?
- Do all verbs agree with their subjects?
- Do all pronouns agree with their antecedents?
- Are verb tenses correct and consistent?

### Forms of Words

- Do adverbs and adjectives modify the appropriate words?
- Are all forms of *be* and other irregular verbs used correctly?
- Are pronouns used correctly?
- Are comparative and superlative forms of adjectives correct?

### Capitalization, Punctuation, and Spelling

- Is any punctuation mark missing or not needed?
- Are all words spelled correctly?
- Are all proper nouns and all proper adjectives capitalized?

**WRITING TIP** For help identifying and correcting problems that are listed in the Proofreading Checklist, see the Grammar Handbook, pages 1305–1340.

You might wish to mark changes on your paper by using the proofreading symbols shown in the chart below.

---

**Proofreading Symbols**

| | | | |
|---|---|---|---|
| ^ | Add letters or words. | / | Make a capital letter lowercase. |
| ⊙ | Add a period. | ¶ | Begin a new paragraph. |
| ≡ | Capitalize a letter. | ↗ | Delete letters or words. |
| ⊂ | Close up space. | ∿ | Switch the positions of letters or words. |
| ↖ | Add a comma. | | |

---

## 1.4 Publishing and Reflecting

Always consider sharing your finished writing with a wider audience. Reflecting on your writing is another good way to bring closure to a project.

### Creative Publishing Ideas

Following are some ideas for publishing and sharing your writing.

- Post your writing on an electronic bulletin board or send it to others via e-mail.
- Create a multimedia presentation and share it with classmates.
- Publish your writing in a school newspaper or literary magazine.
- Present your work orally in a report, a speech, a reading, or a dramatic performance.
- Submit your writing to a local newspaper or a magazine that publishes student writing.
- Form a writing exchange group with other students.

**WRITING TIP** You might work with other students to publish an anthology of class writing. Then exchange your anthology with another class or another school. Reading the work of other student writers will help you get ideas for new writing projects and find ways to improve your work.

### Reflecting on Your Writing

Think about your writing process and whether you would like to add what you have written to your portfolio. You might attach a note in which you answer questions like these:

- What did I learn about myself and my subject through this writing project?
- Which parts of the writing process did I most and least enjoy?
- As I wrote, what was my biggest problem? How did I solve it?
- What did I learn that I can use the next time I write?

## 1.5 Using Peer Response

Peer response consists of the suggestions and comments your peers or classmates make about your writing.

You can ask a peer reader for help at any point in the writing process. For example, your peers can help you develop a topic, narrow your focus, discover confusing passages, or organize your writing.

### Questions for Your Peer Readers

You can help your peer readers provide you with the most useful kinds of feedback by following these guidelines:

- Tell readers where you are in the writing process. Are you still trying out ideas, or have you completed a draft?

- Ask questions that will help you get specific information about your writing. Open-ended questions that require more than yes-or-no answers are more likely to give you information you can use as you revise.

- Give your readers plenty of time to respond thoughtfully to your writing.

- Encourage your readers to be honest when they respond to your work. It's OK if you don't agree with them—you always get to decide which changes to make.

### Tips for Being a Peer Reader

Follow these guidelines when you respond to someone else's work:

- Respect the writer's feelings.

- Make sure you understand what kind of feedback the writer is looking for, and then respond accordingly.

- Use "I" statements, such as "I like . . . ," "I think . . . ," or "It would help me if . . . ." Remember that your impressions and opinions may not be the same as someone else's.

**WRITING TIP** Writers are better able to absorb criticism of their work if they first receive positive feedback. When you act as a peer reader, try to start your review by telling something you like about the piece.

The chart below explains different peer-response techniques to use when you are ready to share your work.

---

### Peer-Response Techniques

**Sharing** Use this when you are just exploring ideas or when you want to celebrate the completion of a piece of writing.

- *Will you please read or listen to my writing without criticizing or making suggestions afterward?*

**Summarizing** Use this when you want to know if your main idea or goals are clear.

- *What do you think I'm saying? What's my main idea or message?*

**Replying** Use this strategy when you want to make your writing richer by adding new ideas.

- *What are your ideas about my topic? What do you think about what I have said in my piece?*

**Responding to Specific Features** Use this when you want a quick overview of the strengths and weaknesses of your writing.

- *Are the ideas supported with enough examples? Did I persuade you? Is the organization clear enough for you to follow the ideas?*

**Telling** Use this to find out which parts of your writing are affecting readers the way you want and which parts are confusing.

- *What did you think or feel as you read my words? Would you show me which passage you were reading when you had that response?*

**Writing Handbook**

# ② Building Blocks of Good Writing

*Whatever your purpose in writing, you need to capture your readers' interest, organize your ideas well, and present your thoughts clearly. Giving special attention to some particular parts of a story or an essay can make your writing more enjoyable and more effective.*

## 2.1 Introductions

When you flip through a magazine trying to decide which articles to read, the opening paragraph is often critical. If it does not grab your attention, you are likely to turn the page.

### Kinds of Introductions

Here are some introduction techniques that can capture a reader's interest.

- Make a surprising statement
- Provide a description
- Pose a question
- Relate an anecdote
- Address the reader directly
- Begin with a thesis statement

**Make a Surprising Statement** Beginning with a startling statement or an interesting fact can capture your reader's curiosity about the subject, as in the model below.

> MODEL
> Although she wrote nearly 1,800 poems, Emily Dickinson probably did not want to publish any of them. Most of her poems were first published almost 100 years after they were written.

**Provide a Description** A vivid description sets a mood and brings a scene to life for your reader. Here, details about a horse's actions set the tone for an essay about horse training.

> MODEL
> Dust flew as the horse stomped the ground. The puffs of moisture blowing from his nostrils and the laid back ears let the spectators know the stomping was not some clever performance. As she approached cautiously, the trainer could see the wild look in the horse's eyes.

**Pose a Question** Beginning with a question can make your reader want to read on to find out the answer. The following introduction asks an important question about the fate of a well-known and respected writer.

> MODEL
> Zora Neale Hurston was one of the most successful writers of the Harlem Renaissance period. She wrote plays, novels, and essays that were enthusiastically received. How did it happen that such a talented and popular author died in poverty?

**Relate an Anecdote** Beginning with a brief anecdote, or story, can hook readers and help you make a point in a dramatic way. The anecdote below introduces an interview with a recently retired school teacher.

> MODEL
> "Down in the valley
> Where the green grass grows. . . ."
>
> The words and rhythm of the chanting children on the playground brought tears to Clara Jones's eyes. Though she could barely see the forms of the youngsters, she knew exactly the structure of the old jump-rope game they played.
>
> I began softly to ask her about her 55 years of teaching at Pleasant Hills Elementary School.

**Address the Reader Directly** Speaking directly to readers establishes a friendly, informal tone and involves them in your topic.

> MODEL
> Do you know how many trees will be cut down for the new shopping mall to be built? Do you know how many families will have to give up their homes so that some shoppers can have yet another department store that sells the same things as five others in our area?

**Begin with a Thesis Statement** A thesis statement expressing a paper's main idea may be woven into both the beginning and the end of nonfiction writing. The following is a thesis statement that introduces a literary analysis.

> MODEL
>
> In "Death of a Hired Man," Robert Frost uses the hushed conversation of a husband and wife to explore the meaning of a lonely person's life. The whole poem seems to take place in whispers, though the message is strong.

**WRITING TIP** In order to write the best introduction for your paper, you may want to try more than one of the methods and then decide which is the most effective for your purpose and audience.

##  Paragraphs

A paragraph is made up of sentences that work together to develop an idea or accomplish a purpose. Whether or not it contains a topic sentence stating the main idea, a good paragraph must have unity and coherence.

### Unity

A paragraph has unity when all the sentences support and develop one stated or implied idea. Use the following techniques to create unity in your paragraphs.

**Write a Topic Sentence** A topic sentence states the main ideas of the paragraph; all other sentences in the paragraph provide supporting details. A topic sentence is often the first sentence in a paragraph. However, it may also appear later in the paragraph or at the end, to summarize or reinforce the main idea, as shown in the model that follows.

> MODEL
>
> Cats purr when they are being stroked by humans. Cats purr when they cuddle up with other cats. Many cats purr when they are in the veterinarian's office. Some cats purr when they are frightened. Since cats seem to purr in situations of both joy and stress, the cause of purring is still a mystery to humans.

**Relate All Sentences to an Implied Main Idea** A paragraph can be unified without a topic sentence as long as every sentence supports the implied, or unstated, main idea. In the model below, all the sentences work together to create a unified impression of a frustrated writer trying to begin writing.

> MODEL
>
> He picked up his pencil at 9:27 and set it down purposefully on the tablet. A minute or so passed. Well, maybe he should sharpen the pencil. That took 30 seconds—now 9:29. He set his pencil down again. He readjusted his chair. He raked his left hand through his thick hair. Was there a spot of thinning hair? He got up to go look in the mirror. No, not yet. At 9:31 he sat down again and took up the pencil. This time he moved the tablet a little to the right.

### Coherence

A paragraph is coherent when all its sentences are related to one another and flow logically from one to the next. The following techniques will help you achieve coherence in paragraphs.

- Present your ideas in the most logical order.
- Use pronouns, synonyms, and repeated words to connect ideas.
- Use transitional devices to show the relationships among ideas.

In the model below, the writer used some of these techniques to create a unified paragraph.

> MODEL
>
> After you figure out how big to make the model ship for your film of a shipwreck, you will need to take some other factors into account as well. You will have to figure out how much to stir the water and what speed to set the film. Perhaps even more important is to be sure no real objects at full size can be seen by the camera. In other words, don't let your towels and soap dish sneak into the picture and be sure the cat is locked out of the bathroom.

## 2.3 Transitions

Transitions are words and phrases that show the connections between details. Clear transitions help show how your ideas relate to each other.

### Kinds of Transitions

Transitions can help readers understand several kinds of relationships:

- Time or sequence
- Spatial relationships
- Degree of importance
- Compare and contrast
- Cause and effect

**Time or Sequence** Some transitions help to clarify the sequence of events over time. When you are telling a story or describing a process, you can connect ideas with such transitional words as *first, second, always, then, next, later, soon, before, finally, after, earlier, afterward,* and *tomorrow.*

> MODEL
> Before a blood donation can be used, it must be processed carefully. First, a sample is tested for infectious diseases and identified by blood type. Next, preservatives are added. Finally, a blood cell separator breaks up the blood into its parts, such as red blood cells, platelets, and plasma.

**Spatial Relationships** Transitional words and phrases such as *in front, behind, next to, along, nearest, lowest, above, below, underneath, on the left,* and *in the middle* can help readers visualize a scene.

> MODEL
> Two rows of corn grew along the south side of the garden. In front of them stood the tomatoes climbing on wire enclosures and a couple of okra plants. In the middle rows were medium-height plants—bush beans, peas, potatoes, and a few peppers. Low-growing plants filled the front of the garden—radishes on the right, then rows of lettuce, spinach, and onions. On the left squash and cucumber vines spread over the ground.

**Degree of Importance** Transitional words such as *mainly, strongest, weakest, first, second, most important, least important, worst,* and *best* may be used to rank ideas or to show degree of importance.

> MODEL
> There are several reasons to eat plenty of fresh fruits and vegetables. The best reason is that they taste so good!

**Compare and Contrast** Words and phrases such as *similarly, likewise, also, like, as, neither . . . nor,* and *either . . . or* show similarity between details. *However, by contrast, yet, but, unlike, instead, whereas,* and *while* show difference. Note the use of both types of transitions in the model below.

> MODEL
> Although I like to shop in the big stores in the mall, when I'm really serious about buying something I go to a small store. Like big stores, many small stores carry a good selection of merchandise. But whereas the big stores may have lower prices, the small stores have more personal service and clerks who know about the products they sell.

**WRITING TIP** Both *but* and *however* may be used to join two independent clauses. When *but* is used as a coordinating conjunction, it is preceded by a comma. When *however* is used as a conjunctive adverb, it is preceded by a semicolon and followed by a comma.

**Cause and Effect** When you are writing about a cause-and-effect relationship, use transitional words and phrases such as *since, because, thus, therefore, so, due to, for this reason,* and *as a result* to help clarify that relationship and to make your writing coherent.

> MODEL
> As a result of the unusual amount of rain this summer, the grass is still lush and green even now in August.

## 2.4 Conclusions

A conclusion should leave readers with a strong final impression. Try any of these approaches.

### Kinds of Conclusions

Here are some effective methods for bringing your writing to a conclusion:

- Restate your thesis
- Ask a question
- Make a recommendation
- Make a prediction
- Summarize your information

**Restate Your Thesis** A good way to conclude an essay is by restating your thesis, or main idea, in different words. The conclusion below restates the thesis introduced on page 1273.

> MODEL
> In Robert Frost's "Death of a Hired Man," a sad human life unfolds in the whispered conversations between Mary and Warren. Quiet compassion is also evident and is the point of the poem.

**Ask a Question** Try asking a question that sums up what you have said and gives readers something new to think about. The question below concludes an appeal for preventing unwanted kittens and puppies.

> MODEL
> Considering how many kittens, puppies, cats, and dogs are put to sleep or die on the streets, don't you think it makes sense that all household pets should be neutered?

**Make a Recommendation** When you are persuading your audience to take a position on an issue, you can conclude by recommending a specific course of action.

> MODEL
> Help protect animals from careless humans. Volunteer at an animal shelter. Distribute literature around your neighborhood.

**Make a Prediction** Readers are concerned about matters that may affect them and therefore are moved by a conclusion that predicts the future.

> MODEL
> If the city council approves the new shopping mall, we will lose the woodlands that help make our neighborhood quiet and attractive. In their place, we will have traffic congestion, exhaust fumes, bright lights long into the night, and a source of danger to our children.

**Summarize Your Information** Summarizing reinforces the writer's main ideas, leaving a strong, lasting impression. The model below concludes with a statement that summarizes a review of a book.

> MODEL
> Patricia McKissack's biography gives a strong picture of W. E. B. Du Bois, who was a link between Frederick Douglass, whom he knew early in life, and Martin Luther King, Jr., whom he knew late in life.

## 2.5 Elaboration

Elaboration is the process of developing a writing idea by providing specific supporting details that are relevant and appropriate to the purpose and form of your writing.

- **Facts and Statistics** A fact is a statement that can be verified, while a statistic is a fact stated in numbers. Make sure the facts and statistics you supply are from a reliable, up-to-date source. As in the model below, the facts and statistics you use should strongly support the statements you make.

> MODEL
> A student who has an eye for beautiful gardens might consider a career in landscape architecture. The American Society of Landscape Architects has over 12,000 members, up 20 percent in the last five years. The average income of landscape architects is $52,886, which is higher than that of building architects.

Writing Handbook

- **Sensory Details** Details that show how something looks, sounds, tastes, smells, or feels can enliven a description, making readers feel they are actually experiencing what you are describing. Which senses does the writer appeal to in this paragraph?

MODEL

Sliding along on her cross-country skis, Sasha felt she was truly on top of the world. The action of the snow, skis, and sturdy boots massaged her feet. She opened her mouth to taste the sprinkles of snow. The view was a rainbow of color as snowflakes made tiny speckled prisms on her goggles.

- **Incidents** From our earliest years, we are interested in hearing "stories." One way to illustrate a point powerfully is to relate an incident or tell a story, as shown in the example below.

MODEL

The East India Company had a monopoly on supplying tea to the American Colonies. Tea shipments took on the symbolism of the increasing tyranny of the English government. On December 16, 1773, a group of about 150 colonists put burnt cork on their faces, dressed as Mohawk warriors, boarded the tea-carrying ships, and proceeded to dump the entire tea cargoes into Boston Harbor.

- **Examples** An example can help make an abstract or a complex idea concrete or can provide evidence to clarify a point for readers.

MODEL

Many of the stars and galaxies we see at night are showing us light from ancient times. Who knows where they really are today? For example, the light from the galaxy Andromeda started its light travel over two million years ago. That's how long it's taken the light to get here—over two million light years!

- **Quotations** Choose quotations that clearly support your points and be sure that you copy each quotation word for word. Remember always to credit the source.

MODEL

Do you know anyone who says "you all" to mean "the group of you"? "Have you all seen this movie?" McCrum, Cran, and MacNeil explain in *The Story of English* that this famous Southern expression comes from a Scots-Irish translation of the plural for you. They say the expression "is typical both of Ulster and of the (largely southern) states of America." Did you all know that?

## 2.6 Using Language Effectively

Effective use of language can help readers to recognize the significance of an issue, to visualize a scene, or to understand a character. The specific words and phrases that you use have everything to do with how effectively you communicate meaning. This is true of all kinds of writing, from novels to office memos. Keep these particular points in mind.

- **Specific Nouns** Nouns are specific when they refer to individual or particular things. If you refer to a *city*, you are being general. If you refer to *London*, you are being specific. Specific nouns help readers identify the *who, what,* and *where* of your message.

- **Specific Verbs** Verbs are the most powerful words in sentences. They convey the action, the movement, and sometimes the drama of thoughts and observations. Verbs such as *trudged, skipped,* and *sauntered* provide a more vivid picture of the action than the verb *walked*.

- **Specific Modifiers** Use modifiers sparingly, but when you use them, make them count. Is the building *big* or *towering*? Are your poodle's paws *small* or *petite*? Once again, it is the more specific word that carries the greater impact.

#  Descriptive Writing

*Descriptive writing allows you to paint word pictures about anything and everything in the world, from events of global importance to the most personal feelings. It is an essential part of almost every piece of writing, including essays, poems, letters, field notes, newspaper reports, and videos.*

---

**RUBRIC** **Standards for Writing**

**A successful description should**

- have a clear focus and sense of purpose.
- use sensory details and precise words to create a vivid image, establish a mood, or express emotion.
- present details in a logical order.

---

## 3.1 Key Techniques

**Consider Your Goals** What do you want to accomplish in writing your description? Do you want to show why something is important to you? Do you want to make a person or scene more memorable? Do you want to explain an event?

**Identify Your Audience** Who will read your description? How familiar are they with your subject? What background information will they need? Which details will they find most interesting?

**Think Figuratively** What figures of speech might help make your description vivid and interesting? What simile or metaphor comes to mind? What imaginative comparisons can you make? What living thing does an inanimate object remind you of?

> MODEL
>
> Into the room swooped the judge, black robe flapping like the ragged black feathers of a raven. With one menacing motion, he swished his robe and swirled the locks of his gray curly hair so that he could perch grimly behind the high bench of authority.

**Gather Sensory Details** Which sights, smells, tastes, sounds, and textures make your subject come alive? Which details stick in your mind when you observe or recall your subject? Which senses does it most strongly affect?

> MODEL
>
> At the first whiff of country air she was immediately transported to the scene of her grandmother's garden. Pungent tomato vines curled around splintery stakes, mushy tomatoes rotted on the ground in cheerful acknowledgment of plenty, and firm orangey fruit clung proudly to the vines soaking up the sweaty summer sun.

You might want to use a chart like the one shown here to collect sensory details about your subject.

| Sights | Sounds | Textures | Smells | Tastes |
|--------|--------|----------|--------|--------|
|        |        |          |        |        |

**Create a Mood** What feelings do you want to evoke in your readers? Do you want to soothe them with comforting images? Do you want to build tension with ominous details? Do you want to evoke sadness or joy?

> MODEL
>
> After the soft rain passed, raindrops sparkled on the leaves of trillium and jack-in-the-pulpit. Sun dappled the forest floor as a gentle breeze stirred the leaves overhead. Lush green moss nestled among the spreading roots of sturdy oaks, and bright colors flashed among the trees as songbirds fluttered through the mild, peaceful air.

## 3.2 Options for Organization

**Spatial Order** Choose one of these options to show the spatial order of a scene.

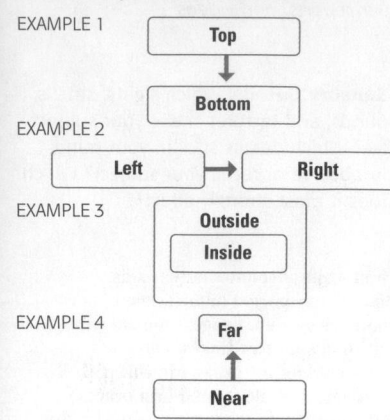

EXAMPLE 1

```
Top
  ↓
Bottom
```

EXAMPLE 2

```
Left → Right
```

EXAMPLE 3

```
Outside
Inside
```

EXAMPLE 4

```
Far
 ↑
Near
```

MODEL

Peering through the goggles, the diver surveyed the reef. To the left, a school of silvery fish swam near the surface. Below them, the reef was a rainbow of color. In the middle of the scene bright, tiny fish nosed along the reef. Below them on the sand a crab looked for food. Further right a cluster of fan coral waved its purple fronds in the gentle current. Beyond it lay the barnacle-encrusted shape of a ship's propeller.

**WRITING TIP** Use transitions that help the reader picture the relationship among the objects you describe. Some useful transitions for showing spatial relationships are *behind, below, here, in the distance, on the left, over,* and *on top.*

**Order of Impression** Order of impression is how you notice details.

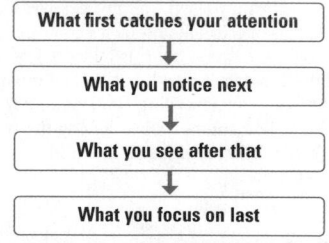

```
What first catches your attention
            ↓
What you notice next
            ↓
What you see after that
            ↓
What you focus on last
```

MODEL

Rain pelted against the windshield. Robbie narrowed his eyes to try to see the road in the brief clearing spasms between swipes of wiper blades. He could barely see that there was a little clearing far off in the horizon. Dark clouds made distinct shapes. Suddenly he noticed that against a small patch of lighter color was a swirling black cloud beginning to take the shape of a funnel.

**WRITING TIP** Use transitions that help readers understand the order of the impressions you are describing. Some useful transitions are *after, next, during, first, before, finally,* and *then.*

**Order of Importance** You might want to use order of importance as the organizing structure for your description.

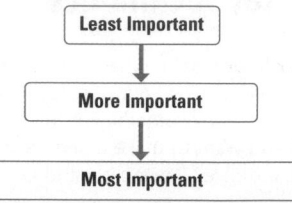

```
Least Important
       ↓
More Important
       ↓
Most Important
```

MODEL

I checked my backpack for the comforting essentials. Book? Yes. Journal and pencil? Yes. Water bottle? Yes. Tissues? Yes. Then I checked for the required essentials. Passport? Yes. Airline ticket? Yes. Map? Yes. Last of all, I checked the most important possession for this trip—a light heart and a sense of adventure. I was beginning my first real vacation in two years!

**WRITING TIP** Use transitions that help the reader understand the order of importance that you attach to the elements of your description. Some useful transitions are *first, second, mainly, more important, less important,* and *least important.*

# 4 Narrative Writing

*Narrative writing tells a story. If you write a story from your imagination, it is a fictional narrative. A true story about actual events is a nonfictional narrative. Narrative writing can be found in short stories, novels, news articles, and biographies.*

## RUBRIC  Standards for Writing

**A successful narrative should**

- include descriptive details and dialogue to develop the characters, setting, and plot.
- have a clear beginning, middle, and end.
- have a logical organization with clues and transitions to help the reader understand the order of events.
- maintain a consistent tone and point of view.
- use language that is appropriate for the audience.
- demonstrate the significance of events or ideas.

## 4.1  Key Techniques

**Identify the Main Events** What are the most important events in your narrative? Is each event part of the chain of events needed to tell the story? In a fictional narrative, this series of events is the story's plot.

MODEL

**Event 1** The actors practice with the props and check to see that the guns hold blanks instead of real bullets.

↓

**Event 2** The audience applauds the realistic action and dramatic plot.

↓

**Event 3** The climax occurs—the guns are fired, and both actors fall as expected.

↓

**Event 4** The curtain falls, but the actors who were shot cannot get up. Somehow tranquilizer darts have been used.

**Describe the Setting** When do the events occur? Where do they take place? How can you use setting to create mood and to set the stage for the characters and their actions?

MODEL

In the creaky old theater, the troupe of actors wander around working with their props. The air smells of phosphorus from the practice run of firing blank cartridges in the pistols.

**Depict Characters Vividly** What do your characters look like? What do they think and say? How do they act? What vivid details can show readers what the characters are like?

MODEL

A few minutes before curtain time, the stately actor who plays Norma opens and shuts her enormous pink and white umbrella as she takes short halting steps. The actors who play rivals Billy Jack and Spike work on spinning their pistols then crouching and aiming. Billy Jack adjusts his eye patch.

**WRITING TIP** Dialogue is an effective way of developing characters in a narrative. As you write dialogue, choose words that express your characters' personalities and show how the characters feel about one another and about the events in the plot.

MODEL

Norma strolls over to the poker table. "Hi, fellas," she says in a sultry voice.

"Hey, Norma," answers Billy Jack, first to respond. "Come right here. Bring me luck."

"Not so fast," complains Spike. "Come here, Norma. Or better yet, check out Billy Jack's hand on your way over."

Billy Jack shifts his right hand from his cards to the gun on his hip.

## 4.2 Options for Organization

**Option 1: Chronological Order** One way to organize a piece of narrative writing is to arrange the events in chronological order, as shown below.

MODEL

| | |
|---|---|
| **Introduction** *characters and setting* | A contemporary Navajo boy in New Mexico is nearing adulthood. His father wants him to learn the lore of his ancestors. His mother wants him to prepare for school instead. |
| **Event 1** | The boy wants to please both his parents. He goes into the mountains to seek wisdom. |
| **Event 2** | Animals visit the boy, representing both the old ways and the new. |
| **End** *perhaps show the significance of the events* | The boy finds that he does not have to disappoint either parent. He finds that he must work hardest on learning what he himself is best suited for. |

**Option 2: Flashback** It is also possible in narrative writing to arrange the order of events by starting with an event that happened before the beginning of the story.

**Flashback**
Begin with a key event that happened before the time in which the story takes place.

↓

Introduce characters and setting.

↓

Describe the events leading up to the conflict.

**Option 3: Focus on Conflict** When the telling of a fictional narrative focuses on a central conflict, the story's plot may follow the model shown below.

MODEL

| | |
|---|---|
| **Describe the main characters and setting** | The brothers arrive at the school gym long before the rest of the basketball team. Although the twins are physically identical, their personalities couldn't be more different. Mark is outgoing and impulsive, while Matt is thoughtful and shy. |
| **Present the conflict** | Matt realizes his brother is missing shots on purpose and believes they will lose the championship. |
| **Relate the events that make the conflict complex and cause the characters to change** | • Matt has a chance at a basketball scholarship if they win the championship.<br>• Mark needs money to buy a car.<br>• Matt and Mark have stood by each other no matter what. |
| **Present the resolution or outcome of the conflict** | Matt retells a family story in which their grandfather chose honor and integrity over easy money. Mark plays to win. |

#  Explanatory Writing

*Explanatory writing informs and explains. For example, you can use it to evaluate the effects of a new law, to compare two movies, to analyze a piece of literature, or to examine the problem of greenhouse gases in the atmosphere.*

## 5.1 Types of Explanatory Writing

There are many types of explanatory writing. Think about your topic and select the type that presents the information most clearly.

**Compare and Contrast** How are two or more subjects alike? How are they different?

MODEL
Leon and Father Paul have different beliefs about how to bury the dead, but they both have great affection for the old man who has died, Leon's grandfather. They both contribute their own rituals for the burial.

**Cause and Effect** How does one event cause something else to happen? Why do certain conditions exist? What are the results of an action or a condition?

MODEL
Because Leon and Ken did not ask for a funeral Mass for Teofilo, Father Paul did not think he should sprinkle holy water over the body.

**Analysis** How does something work? How can it be defined? What are its parts?

MODEL
The rituals of the Laguna people have strong cultural traditions. So also do the rituals of the Roman Catholic Church. Some groups of Native Americans believe deeply in both sets of rituals and find ways to incorporate both into their lives.

**Problem-Solution** How can you identify and state a problem? How would you analyze the problem and its causes? How can it be solved?

MODEL
Father Paul had to decide whether to go by the strict rules of his church or to help the family who wanted his help in a way that did not follow the rules.

## 5.2 Compare and Contrast

Compare-and-contrast writing examines the similarities and differences between two or more subjects. You might, for example, compare and contrast two short stories, the main characters in a novel, or two movies.

**RUBRIC** **Standards for Writing**

**Successful compare-and-contrast writing should**

- clearly identify the subjects that are being compared and contrasted.
- include specific, relevant details.
- follow a clear plan of organization dealing with the same features of both subjects under discussion.
- use language and details appropriate to the audience.
- use transitional words and phrases to clarify similarities and differences.

### Options for Organization

Compare-and-contrast writing can be organized in different ways. The examples that follow demonstrate feature-by-feature organization and subject-by-subject organization.

## Option 1: Feature-by-Feature Organization

**Feature 1**

MODEL

I. Different beliefs about burial practices.

    Subject A. Leon: traditional Laguna way.

    Subject B. Father Paul: Last Rites and a funeral Mass.

**Feature 2**

II. Both want a proper burial.

    Subject A. Leon: painted face, feather in hair, body to graveyard, corn meal and pollen.

    Subject B. Father Paul: decide whether to sprinkle holy water without full Catholic rites.

## Option 2: Subject-by-Subject Organization

**Subject A**

MODEL

I. Leon:

    Feature 1. Believes in traditional Laguna burial.

    Feature 2. Proper burial: painted face, feather in hair, body to graveyard, corn meal and pollen.

**Subject B**

II. Father Paul:

    Feature 1. Believes burial requires Last Rites and a funeral Mass.

    Feature 2. Must decide whether to sprinkle holy water without full Catholic rites.

**WRITING TIP** Remember your purpose for comparing and contrasting your subjects, and support your purpose with expressive language and specific details.

## 5.3 Cause and Effect

Cause-and-effect writing explains why something happened, why certain conditions exist, or what resulted from an action or a condition. You might use cause-and-effect writing to explain a character's actions, the progress of a disease, or the outcome of a war.

---

**RUBRIC** Standards for Writing

**Successful cause-and-effect writing should**

- clearly state the cause-and-effect relationship.
- show clear connections between causes and effects.
- present causes and effects in a logical order and use transitions effectively.
- use facts, examples, and other details to illustrate each cause and effect.
- use language and details appropriate to the audience.

### Options for Organization

Your organization will depend on your topic and purpose for writing.

- If you want to explain the causes of an event such as the closing of a factory, you might first state the effect and then examine its causes.

**Option 1: Effect to Cause Organization**

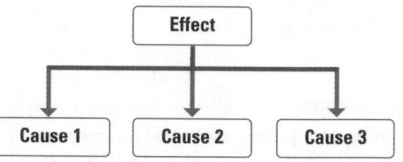

- If your focus is on explaining the effects of an event, such as the passage of a law, you might first state the cause and then explain the effects.

**Option 2: Cause to Effect Organization**

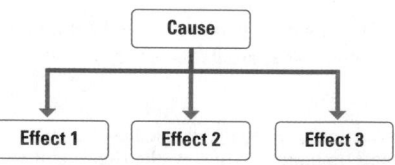

- Sometimes you'll want to describe a chain of cause-and-effect relationships to explore a topic such as the disappearance of tropical rain forests or the development of home computers.

## Option 3: Cause-and-Effect Chain Organization

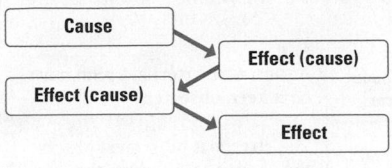

**WRITING TIP** Don't assume that a cause-and-effect relationship exists just because one event follows another. Look for evidence that the later event could not have happened if the first event had not caused it.

## 5.4 Problem-Solution

Problem-solution writing clearly states a problem, analyzes the problem, and proposes a solution to the problem. It can be used to identify and solve a conflict between characters, analyze a chemistry experiment, or explain why the home team keeps losing.

### RUBRIC  Standards for Writing

**Successful problem-solution writing should**
- identify the problem and help the reader understand the issues involved.
- analyze the causes and effects of the problem.
- integrate quotations, facts, and statistics into the text.
- explore possible solutions to the problem and recommend the best one(s).
- use language, tone, and details appropriate to the audience.

### Options for Organization

Your organization will depend on the goal of your problem-solution piece, your intended audience, and the specific problem you choose to address. The organizational methods that follow are effective for different kinds of problem-solution writing.

## Option 1: Simple Problem-Solution

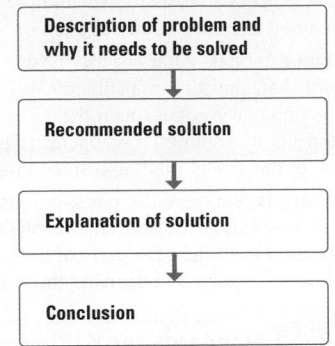

## Option 2: Deciding Between Solutions

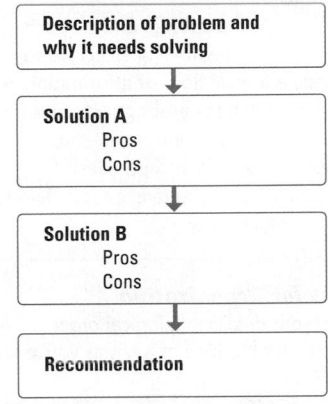

**WRITING TIP** Have a classmate read and respond to your problem-solution writing. Ask your peer reader: Is the problem clearly stated? Is the organization easy to follow? Do the proposed solutions seem logical?

## 5.5 Analysis

In writing an analysis, you explain how something works, how it is defined, or what its parts are. The details you include will depend upon the kind of analysis you write.

**Process Analysis** What are the major steps or stages in a process? What background information does the reader need to know—such as definitions of terms or a list of needed equipment—to understand the analysis? You might use process analysis to explain how Mark Twain learned to be a steamboat pilot.

**Definition Analysis** What are the most important characteristics of a subject? You might use definition analysis to explain the characteristics of a sonnet, the abilities of a physicist, or the skill of piloting a steamboat.

**Parts Analysis** What are the parts, groups, or types that make up a subject? Parts analysis could be used to explain the parts of the brain or the lessons learned by observing the river.

---

**RUBRIC** **Standards for Writing**

**A successful analysis should**

- hook the readers' attention with a strong introduction.
- clearly state the subject and its parts.
- use a specific organizing structure to provide a logical flow of information.
- show connections among facts and ideas through subordinate clauses and transitional words and phrases.
- use language and details appropriate for the audience.

---

## Options for Organization

Organize your details in a logical order appropriate for the kind of analysis you're writing.

**Option 1: Process Analysis** A process analysis is usually organized chronologically, with steps or stages in the order they occur.

MODEL

| | |
|---|---|
| Introduction | Navigating north from New Orleans |
| Background | Mark Twain follows this process for his first trip as a cub pilot. |
| Explain Steps | Step 1: Straighten out the boat. |
| | Step 2: Stay close to the moored boats. |
| | Step 3: Pass Six-Mile, Nine-Mile, and Twelve-Mile points. |
| | Step 4: Cross the river when the calm water ends. |

**Option 2: Definition Analysis** You can organize the details in a definition or parts analysis in order of importance or impression.

MODEL

| | |
|---|---|
| Introduce Term | A successful riverboat pilot must be a keen observer. |
| General Definition | The riverboat pilot must observe the surface of the river, the landmarks along the shore, and signs of nature. |
| Explain Qualities | Quality 1: The surface can tell of rising water or hidden hazards. |
| | Quality 2: Landmarks tell where the boat is; pilot must recall what dangers to avoid at that point. |
| | Quality 3: The sky can give hints about what weather may be coming. |

**Option 3: Parts Analysis** The following parts analysis explores three skills a riverboat pilot needs.

MODEL

| | |
|---|---|
| Introduce Subject | Piloting a riverboat required several skills. |
| Explain Parts | Part 1: recognize how weather might threaten the boat |
| | Part 2: observe floating objects that could show a rising river, see ripples in the water surface that could indicate a hazard |
| | Part 3: use landmarks to know where boat is and where dangers lie |

**WRITING TIP** Try to capture your readers' interest in your introduction. You might begin with a vivid description or an interesting fact, detail, or quotation. For example, an exciting excerpt from the narrative could open the process analysis.

An effective way to conclude an analysis is to return to your thesis and restate it in different words.

# ⑥ Persuasive Writing

*Persuasive writing allows you to use the power of language to inform and influence others. It can take many forms, including speeches, newspaper editorials, billboards, advertisements, and critical reviews.*

---

**RUBRIC** **Standards for Writing**

**Successful persuasion should**

- state the issue and the writer's position.
- give opinions and support them with facts or reasons.
- have a reasonable and respectful tone.
- answer opposing views.
- use sound logic and effective language.
- conclude by summing up reasons or calling for action.

---

## ⑥.1 Key Techniques

**Clarify Your Position** What do you believe about the issue? How can you express your opinion most clearly?

> MODEL
> Patients should not be so quick to request antibiotics for every sickness because the typical antibiotics are becoming less effective.

**Know Your Audience** Who will read your writing? What do they already know and believe about the issue? What objections to your position might they have? What additional information might they need? What tone and approach would be most effective?

> MODEL
> By overusing antibiotics, we are encouraging the development of microorganisms that can resist drugs. Sometimes it is best to let the body's natural defenses work on their own.

**Support Your Opinion** Why do you feel the way you do about the issue? What facts, statistics, examples, quotations, anecdotes, or opinions of authorities support your view? What reasons will convince your readers? What evidence can answer their objections?

> MODEL
> In explaining new research to combat microorganisms that cause dangerous diseases, authors of a *Business Week* article give this startling fact: "Killer microbes such as staph have evolved the ability to dice up penicillin and pump out tetracycline before either antibiotic has a chance to work."

| Ways to Support Your Argument | |
|---|---|
| **Statistics** | Facts that are stated in numbers |
| **Examples** | Specific instances that explain your point |
| **Observations** | Events or situations you yourself have seen |
| **Anecdotes** | Brief stories that illustrate your point |
| **Quotations** | Direct statements from authorities |

**Begin and End with a Bang** How can you hook your readers and make a lasting impression? What memorable quotation, anecdote, or statistic will catch their attention at the beginning or stick in their minds at the end? What strong summary or call to action can you conclude with?

> BEGINNING
> Stop before you call your doctor for medicine to cure that cold or ease that sore throat. You might be doing your body more harm than good by taking an antibiotic.

> CONCLUSION
> Listen to doctors when they suggest that antibiotics should be reserved for serious illness. Take the doctor's advice to drink lots of liquids and get bed rest instead of taking drugs for less serious illness. Maybe humanity can win the battle with microbes by slowing their evolution into supermicrobes that resist antibiotics.

## 6.2 Options for Organization

In a two-sided persuasive essay, you want to show the weaknesses of other opinions as you explain the strengths of your own.

The example below demonstrates one method of organizing your persuasive essay to convince your audience.

**Option 1: Reasons for Your Opinion**

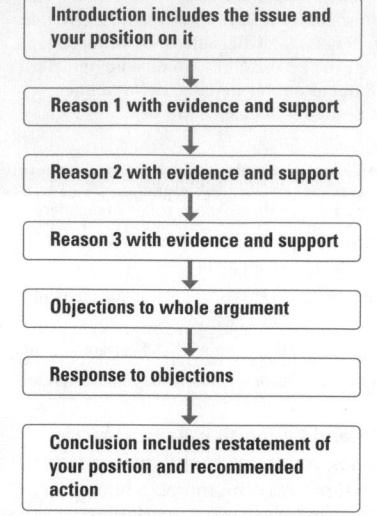

Introduction includes the issue and your position on it

⬇

Reason 1 with evidence and support

⬇

Reason 2 with evidence and support

⬇

Reason 3 with evidence and support

⬇

Objections to whole argument

⬇

Response to objections

⬇

Conclusion includes restatement of your position and recommended action

**Option 2: Point-by-Point Basis**

In the organization that follows, each reason and its objections are examined on a point-by-point basis.

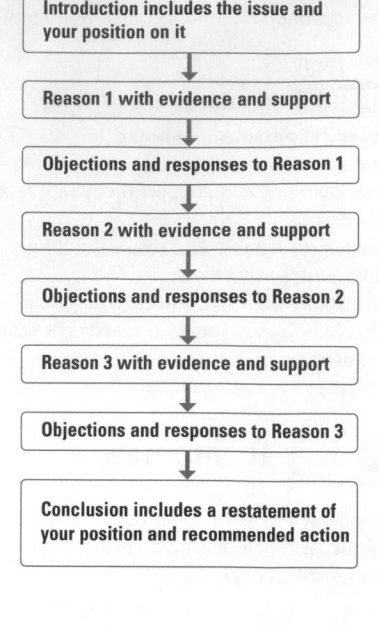

Introduction includes the issue and your position on it

⬇

Reason 1 with evidence and support

⬇

Objections and responses to Reason 1

⬇

Reason 2 with evidence and support

⬇

Objections and responses to Reason 2

⬇

Reason 3 with evidence and support

⬇

Objections and responses to Reason 3

⬇

Conclusion includes a restatement of your position and recommended action

**Beware of Illogical Arguments** Be careful about using illogical arguments. Opponents can easily attack your argument if you present illogical material.

**Circular reasoning**—trying to prove a statement by just repeating it in different words

> Antibiotics are being overused because people take them too often.

**Overgeneralization**—making a statement that is too broad to prove

> People are demanding antibiotics whenever they don't feel good.

**Either-or fallacy**—stating that there are only two alternatives when there are many

> If we don't set national limits on prescribing antibiotics, we will face worldwide epidemics caused by untreatable supermicrobes.

**Cause-and-effect fallacy**—falsely assuming that because one event follows another, the first event caused the second

> Supermicrobes are evolving because of the discovery of penicillin.

# 7 Research Report Writing

*A research report explores a topic in depth, incorporating information from a variety of sources.*

**RUBRIC  Standards for Writing**

**An effective research report should**
- clearly state the purpose of the report in a thesis statement.
- use evidence and details from a variety of sources to support the thesis.
- contain only accurate and relevant information.
- document sources correctly.
- develop the topic logically and include appropriate transitions.
- include a properly formatted Works Cited list.

## 7.1 Key Techniques

**Develop Relevant, Interesting, and Researchable Questions** Asking thoughtful questions is an ongoing part of research. Begin with a list of basic questions that are relevant to your topic. Focus on getting basic facts that answer the *who, what, where, when,* and *why* of your topic. If you were researching how Mark Twain's childhood experiences affected his attitudes, you might develop a set of questions similar to these.

> MODEL
> What was frontier life like in the early 1800s?
> Did frontier humor of the time resemble the humor in Twain's writing?
> What other famous people grew up in similar surroundings?

As you become more familiar with your topic, think of questions that might provide an interesting perspective that makes readers think.

> MODEL
> Did frontier life have similar effects on Mark Twain and Abraham Lincoln?

Check that your questions are researchable. Ask questions that will uncover facts, statistics, case studies, and other documentable evidence.

**Clarify Your Thesis** A thesis statement is one or two sentences clearly stating the main idea that you will develop in your report. A thesis may also indicate the organizational pattern you will follow and reflect your tone and point of view.

> MODEL
> Mark Twain was born in Missouri in 1835. Abraham Lincoln was born in rural Kentucky in 1809. A similar geography shaped both men as well as shaping their beliefs and temperaments.

**Document Your Sources** You need to document, or credit, the sources where you find your evidence. In the example below, the writer uses and documents a quotation from the introduction to a collection of Mark Twain's works.

> MODEL
> Bernard DeVoto quotes William Dean Howells as calling Mark Twain "the Lincoln of our literature" (DeVoto 5).

**Support Your Ideas** You should support your ideas with relevant evidence—facts, anecdotes, and statistics—from reliable sources. In the example below, the writer includes a fact about the style of both Twain and Lincoln.

> MODEL
> DeVoto points out that both men saw the humor in everyday life and used humor from their earliest years (5).

## 7.2 Gathering Information: Sources

You will use a range of sources to collect the information you need to develop your research paper. These will include both print and electronic resources.

**General Reference Works** To clarify your thesis and begin your research, consult reference works that give quick, general overviews on a subject. General reference works include encyclopedias, almanacs and yearbooks, atlases, and dictionaries.

**Specialized Reference Works** Once you have a good idea of your specific topic, you are ready to look for detailed information in specialized reference works. In the library's reference section, specialized dictionaries and encyclopedias can be found for almost any field. For example, in the field of literature, you will find specialized reference sources such as *Contemporary Authors* and *Twentieth-Century Literary Criticism.*

**Periodicals** Journals and periodicals are a good source for detailed, up-to-date information. Periodical indexes, found in print and on-line catalogs in the library, will help you find articles on a topic. The *Readers' Guide to Periodical Literature* indexes many popular magazines. More specialized indexes include the *Humanities Index* and the *Social Sciences Index.*

**Electronic Resources  Commercial information services** offer access to reference works such as dictionaries and encyclopedias, databases, and periodicals.

The **Internet** is a vast network of computer networks. News services, libraries, universities, researchers, organizations, and government agencies use the Internet to communicate and to distribute information. The Internet gives you access to the World Wide Web, which provides information on particular topics and links you to related topics and resources.

A **CD-ROM** is a research aid that stores information on a compact disk. Reference works on CD-ROMs may include text, sound, images, and video.

**Databases** are large collections of related information stored electronically. You can scan the information or search for specific facts.

RESEARCH TIP To find books on a specific topic, check the library's on-line catalog. Be sure to copy the correct call numbers of books that sound promising. Also look at books shelved nearby. They may relate to your topic.

## 7.3 Gathering Information: Validity of Sources

When you find source material, you must determine whether it is useful and accurate.

**Credibility of Authorship** Check whether an author has written several books or articles on the subject and has published in a well-respected newspaper or journal.

**Objectivity** Decide whether the information is fact, opinion, or propaganda. Reputable sources credit other sources of information.

**Currency** Check the publication date of the source to see whether the information is current.

**Credibility of Publisher** Seek information from a respected newspaper or journal, not from a tabloid newspaper or popular-interest magazine.

WEB TIP Be especially skeptical of information you locate on the Internet since virtually anyone can post anything there. Read the URL, or Internet address. Sites sponsored by a government agency (*.gov*) or an educational institution (*.edu*) are generally more reliable.

## 7.4 Taking Notes

As you find useful information, record the bibliographic information of each source on a separate index card. Then you are ready to take notes on your sources. You will probably use these three methods of note-taking.

**Paraphrase,** or restate in your own words, the main ideas and supporting details of the passage.

**Summarize,** or rephrase in fewer words, the original materials, trying to capture the key ideas.

**Quote,** or copy word for word, the original text, if you think the author's own words best clarify a particular point. Use quotation marks to signal the beginning and the end of the quotation.

For more details on making source cards and taking notes, see the Research Report Workshop on pages 980–988.

##  7.5 Options for Organization

Begin by reading over your note cards and sorting them into groups. The main-idea headings may help you find connections among the notes. Then arrange the groups of related note cards so that the ideas flow logically from one group to the next.

Like other forms of writing, research reports can be organized in several different ways. Some subjects may fit in chronological order. For other subjects, you may want to compare and contrast two topics. Other possibilities are a cause-and-effect organization or least-important to most-important evidence. If your material does not lend itself to any of the above organizations, try a general-to-specific approach.

Whatever your organizational pattern, making an outline can help guide the drafting process. The subtopics that you located in sorting your note cards will be the major topics of your outline, preceded by Roman numerals. Make sure that items of the same importance are parallel in form. For example, in the Option 1 Topic Outline below, topics I and II are both phrases. So are subtopics A and B.

A second kind of outline, shown below in Option 2, uses complete sentences instead of phrases for topics and subtopics.

### Option 1: Topic Outline

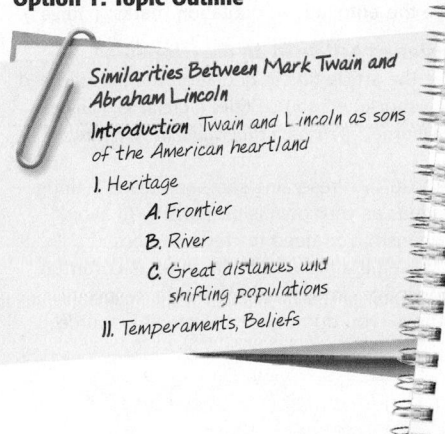

Similarities Between Mark Twain and Abraham Lincoln

**Introduction** Twain and Lincoln as sons of the American heartland

I. Heritage
  A. Frontier
  B. River
  C. Great distances and shifting populations

II. Temperaments, Beliefs

### Option 2: Sentence Outline

Similarities Between Mark Twain and Abraham Lincoln

**Introduction** Both Mark Twain and Abraham Lincoln were sons of the American heartland.

I. Twain and Lincoln were shaped by the places where they were born and raised.
  A. Both men lived in the frontier area of the nation.
  B. Both men were river men.
  C. The area in which they lived was characterized by great distances and shifting populations.

II. In addition to similarities in their geographic heritage, Twain and Lincoln shared certain traits and beliefs.

## 7.6 Documenting Sources

When you quote, paraphrase, or summarize information from a source, you need to credit that source. Parenthetical documentation is the accepted method for crediting sources. You may choose to name the author in parentheses following the information, along with the page number on which the information is found.

> MODEL
> *Innocents Abroad* was not just independent of European influence, it was indifferent to it (DeVoto 5).

In parenthetical documentation, you may also use the author's name in the sentence, along with the information. If so, enclose, in parentheses after the sentence, only the page number on which the information is found.

> MODEL
> According to DeVoto, Lincoln expressed a culture that had turned its gaze from Europe to the continent (3).

In either case, your reader can find out more about the source by turning to your Works Cited page, which lists complete bibliographical information for each source.

PUNCTUATION TIP When only the author and page number appear in parentheses, there is no punctuation between the two items. Also notice that the parenthetical citation comes after the closing quotation marks of a quotation, if there is one, and before the end punctuation of the sentence.

The examples above show citations for books with one author. The list that follows shows the correct way to write parenthetical citations for several kinds of sources.

### Guidelines for Parenthetical Documentation

**Work by One Author**
Put the author's last name and the page reference in parentheses: (DeVoto 34).

If you mention the author's name in the sentence, put only the page reference in parentheses: (34).

**Work by Two or Three Authors**
Put the authors' last names and the page reference in parentheses: (Baker and Gibson 84).

**Work by More Than Three Authors**
Give the first author's last name followed by *et al.* and the page reference: (Armento et al. 334-335).

**Work with No Author Given**
Give the title or a shortened version and (if appropriate) the page reference: ("Mark Twain's Portrait" 29).

**One of Two or More Works by Same Author**
Give the author's last name, the title or a shortened version, and the page reference: (Twain, Roughing It 47).

**Selection from a Book of Collected Essays**
Give the name of the author of the essay and the page reference: (Gerber 134).

**Dictionary Definition**
Give the entry title in quotation marks: ("jingo").

**Unsigned Article in an Encyclopedia**
Give the article title in quotation marks, followed by a shortened source title: ("Clemens, Samuel Langhorne," *Webster's Biographical Dictionary*)

WRITING TIP Presenting someone else's writing or ideas as your own is plagiarism. To avoid plagiarism, you need to credit sources. However, if a piece of information is common knowledge—information available in several sources—you do not need to credit a source.

## 7.7 Following MLA Manuscript Guidelines

The final copy of your report should follow the Modern Language Association (MLA) guidelines for manuscript preparation.

- The heading in the upper left-hand corner of the first page should include your name, your teacher's name, the course name, and the date, each on a separate line.

- Below the heading, center the title on the page.

- Number all the pages consecutively in the upper right-hand corner, one-half inch from the top. Also, include your last name before the page number.

- Double-space the entire paper.

- Except for the margins above the page numbers, leave one-inch margins on all sides of every page.

The Works Cited page at the end of your report is an alphabetized list of the sources you have used and documented. In each entry all lines after the first are indented an additional one-half inch.

**WRITING TIP** When your report includes a quotation that is longer than four lines, set it off from the rest of the text by indenting the entire quotation one inch from the left margin. In this case, you should not use quotation marks.

**Works Cited**

Models for Works Cited Entries

**Works Cited**

Armento, Beverly J., et al. <u>A More Perfect Union</u>. Boston: Houghton, 1991. 334–335.

Baker, Susan, and Curtis S. Gibson. "Lincoln." <u>Gore Vidal: A Critical Companion</u>. Westport: Greenwood, 1997. 87–92.

Gerber, John C. "Mark Twain's Use of the Comic Pose." <u>Critical Essays on Mark Twain, 1910–1980</u>. Ed. Louis J. Budd. Boston: Hall, 1983. 131–143.

Park, Clara Claiborne. "The River and the Road: Fashions in Forgiveness." <u>American Scholar</u> 66 (1997): 43–62.

Ravitch, Diane, ed. <u>The American Reader: Words That Moved a Nation</u>. New York: Harper, 1990.

Twain, Mark. <u>Early Tales and Sketches</u>. Ed. Edgar Marquess Branch and Robert H. Hirst. Berkeley: U of California P, 1979.

--- <u>Roughing It</u>. Ed. Harriet E. Smith and Edgar M. Branch. Berkeley: U of California P, 1993.

❶ Book with more than three authors; note that publishers' names are shortened

❷ Work with two authors

❸ Selection from a book of collected essays

❹ Article in scholarly journal

❺ Book with an editor but no single author

❻ Book with one author

❼ Second work by same author

## 7.8 MLA Documentation: Electronic Sources

As with print sources, information from electronic sources such as CD-ROMs or the Internet must be documented on your Works Cited page. You may find a reference to a source on the Internet and then use the print version of the article. If so, document it as you do other printed works. However, if you read or print out an article directly off the Internet, document it as shown below for an electronic source. Although electronic sources are shown separately below, they should be included on the Works Cited page with print sources.

**Internet Sources** Works Cited entries for Internet sources include the same kind of information as those for print sources. They also include the date you obtained the information and the electronic address of the source. Some of the information about the source may be unavailable. Include as much as you can. For more information on how to write Works Cited entries for Internet sources, see the MLA guidelines posted on the Internet or gain access to this document through the McDougal Littell website.

 **More Online: Style Guidelines**
www.mcdougallittell.com

**CD-ROMs** Entries for CD-ROMs include the publication medium (CD-ROM), the distributor, and the date of publication. Some of the information shown may not be always available. Include as much as you can.

---

> **Works Cited**
> Models for Works Cited entries for electronic sources

### Works Cited

Crisler, Vern. "The Comedy of Mark Twain." Home page. 12 Aug. 1998 <http://www.geocities.com/Athens/6208/comedy.html>.

❶ Home page; shows date you accessed it

"Lincoln, Abraham." Grolier Multimedia Encyclopedia. 1998 ed. CD-ROM. Danbury: Grolier Interactive.

❷ Encyclopedia article from CD-ROM version

"Mark Twain." Britannica Online. Vers. 98.2. Apr. 1998. Encyclopaedia Britannica. 22 Sept. 1998 <http://www.eb.com:180>.

❸ Encyclopedia article from online version

Newman, Rhoda. "Mark Twain, Internationalist." Foreign Service Journal Feb. 1996: 18–23. TwainWeb. Mark Twain Forum. 9 Sept. 1998 <http://web.mit.edu/linguistics/www/forum/filelist/intl01.html>.

❹ Article from a scholarly journal available on the Internet; includes page numbers and access date

Twain, Mark. "Correspondence with the San Francisco Alta California: 1867-1869." Mark Twain Quotations, Newspaper Collections, and Related Resources. Ed. Barbara Schmidt. Tarleton College. 9 Sept. 1998 <http://www.tarleton.edu/activities/pages/facultypages/schmidt/altaindex.html>.

❺ The complete text of the letters, available on the Internet; includes access date

VanSpanckeren, Kathryn. "The Rise of Realism: 1860–1914." Chap. 5 of An Outline of American Literature. U.S. Information Agency. 9 Sept. 1998 <http://odur.let.rug.nl/~usa/LIT/chap5.htm>.

# 8 Business Writing

*The ability to write clearly and succinctly is an essential skill in the business world. As you prepare to enter the job market, you will need to know how to create letters, memos, and résumés.*

## RUBRIC
### Standards for Writing

**Successful business writing should**

- have a tone and language geared to the appropriate audience.
- state the purpose clearly in the opening sentences or paragraph.
- use precise words and avoid jargon.
- present only essential information.
- present details in a logical order.
- conclude with a summary of important points.

## 8.1 Key Techniques

**Think About Your Purpose** Why are you doing this writing? Do you want to "sell" yourself to a college admissions committee or a job interviewer? Do you want to order or complain about a product? Do you want to set up a meeting or respond to someone's ideas?

**Identify Your Audience** Who will read your writing? What background information will they need? What questions might they have? What tone or language is appropriate?

**Support Your Points** What specific details clarify your ideas? What reasons do you have for your statements? What points most strongly support them?

**Finish Strongly** How can you best sum up your statements? What is your main point? What action do you want others to take?

## 8.2 Options

### Model 1: Letter

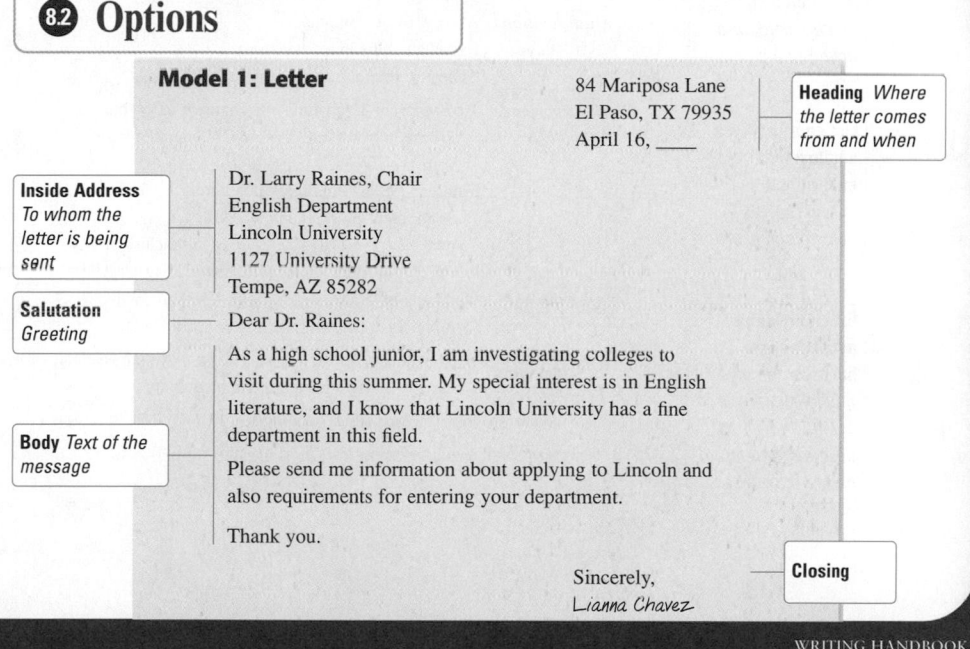

**Heading** *Where the letter comes from and when*

84 Mariposa Lane
El Paso, TX 79935
April 16, _____

**Inside Address** *To whom the letter is being sent*

Dr. Larry Raines, Chair
English Department
Lincoln University
1127 University Drive
Tempe, AZ 85282

**Salutation** *Greeting*

Dear Dr. Raines:

**Body** *Text of the message*

As a high school junior, I am investigating colleges to visit during this summer. My special interest is in English literature, and I know that Lincoln University has a fine department in this field.

Please send me information about applying to Lincoln and also requirements for entering your department.

Thank you.

Sincerely,

Lianna Chavez

**Closing**

## Model 2: Memo

**Heading** *Whom the memo is to and from, what it's about, and when it's being sent*

To: Jane Bakerman
From: Larry Raines
Re: Prospective Student
Date: 4/20/__

**Body**

Jane, attached is a copy of a letter from a high school junior who is interested in our program. Will you please send her the English Department flyer and then forward to the dean's office the request for a catalog? Thanks.

## Model 3: Résumé
A well-written résumé is invaluable when you apply for a part-time or full-time job or to college. It should highlight your skills, accomplishments, and experience. Proofread your résumé carefully to make sure it is clear and accurate and free of errors in grammar and spelling. It is a good idea to save a copy of your résumé on your computer or on a disk so that you can easily update it.

**State your purpose.** *This résumé is for a job application. A modified style can be used for a college application.*

**List your previous employment experience** *in reverse chronological order.*

**Extracurricular activities and hobbies** *can give a fuller picture of you and point out special job-related skills.*

**JOSEPH L. JASPER**
361 Alameda
Santa Fe, NM 87501

*Objective*   A summer position as a department store clerk

*Qualifications*   Ability to use computer
Excellent skills in mathematics
Cheerful, friendly disposition

*Work Experience*   1998–present—Part-time employment as cashier at college bookstore, Colorado College, Colorado Springs, CO
Summer 1998—Held clerk position at Drake's Department Store, Santa Fe, NM
Winter Vacation 1997, 1998—Part-time clerk at Big Four Drug Store, Colorado Springs, CO

*Education*   Our Lady of Light High School, Class of 1998
Completing freshman year at Colorado College

*Extracurricular Activities*   High School: Chorus, Math Club, first-string basketball
College: Chorus, Freshman Honor Society

*Hobbies*   Puzzles, basketball, reading

*References*   Available upon request

# ❶ Inquiry and Research

*In this age of seemingly unlimited information, the ability to locate and evaluate resources efficiently can spell the difference between success and failure—in both the academic and the business worlds. Make use of print and nonprint information sources.*

## ⓫ Finding Sources

Good research involves using the wealth of resources available to answer your questions and raise new questions. Knowing where to go and how to access information can lead you to interesting and valuable sources.

### Reference Works

Reference works are print and nonprint sources of information that provide quick access to both general overviews and specific facts about a subject. These include

**Dictionaries**—word definitions, pronunciations, and origins

**Thesauruses**—lists of synonyms and antonyms for each entry

**Glossaries**—collections of specialized terms, such as those pertaining to literature, with definitions

**Encyclopedias**—detailed information on nearly every subject, arranged alphabetically (*Encyclopaedia Britannica*). Specialized encyclopedias deal with specific subjects, such as music, economics, and science (*Encyclopedia of Economics*).

**Almanacs and Yearbooks**—current facts and statistics (*World Almanac, Statistical Abstract of the United States*)

**Atlases**—maps and information about weather, agricultural and industrial production, and other geographical topics (*National Geographic Atlas of the World*)

**Specialized Reference Works**—biographical data (*Who's Who, Current Biography*), literary information (*Contemporary Authors, Book Review Digest, Cyclopedia of Literary Characters, The Oxford Companion to English Literature*), and quotations (*Bartlett's Familiar Quotations*)

**Electronic Sources**—Many of these reference works and databases are available on CD-ROMs, which may include text, sound, photographs, and video. CD-ROMs can be used on a home or library computer. You can subscribe to services that offer access to these sources on-line.

### Periodicals and Indexes

One kind of specialized reference is a periodical.

- Some periodicals, such as *Atlantic Monthly* and *Psychology Today,* are intended for a general audience. They are indexed in the *Readers' Guide to Periodical Literature.*

- Many other periodicals, or journals, are intended for specialized or academic audiences. These include titles and subject matter as diverse as *American Psychologist* and *Studies in Short Fiction.* These are indexed in the *Humanities Index* and the *Social Sciences Index.* In addition, most fields have their own indexes. For example, articles on literature are indexed in the *MLA International Bibliography.*

- Many indexes are available in print, CD-ROM, and on-line forms.

### Internet

The Internet is a vast network of computers. News services, libraries, universities, researchers, organizations, and government agencies use the Internet to distribute information and to communicate. The Internet can provide links to library catalogs, newspapers, government sources, and many of the reference sources described above. The Internet includes two key features:

**World Wide Web**—source of information on specific subjects and links to related topics

**Electronic mail (e-mail)**—communications link to other e-mail users worldwide

### Other Resources

In addition to reference works found in the library and over the Internet, you can get information from the following sources: corporate publications, lectures, correspondence, and media such as films, television programs, and recordings. You can also observe directly, conduct your own interviews, and collect data from polls or questionnaires that you create yourself.

##  Evaluating Sources

Not all information is equal. You need to be a discriminating consumer of information and evaluate the credibility of the source, the reliability of the specific information included, and its value in answering your research needs.

### Credibility of Sources

You must determine the credibility and appropriateness of each source in order to write an effective report or speech. Ask yourself the following questions:

**Is the writer an authority?** A writer who has written several books on a subject or whose name is included in many bibliographies may be considered an authoritative source.

**Is the source reliable and unbiased?** What is the author's motivation? For example, a defense of an industry in which the author has a financial interest may be biased. A profile of a writer or scientist written by a close relative may also be biased.

**WEB TIP** Be especially skeptical of information you locate on the Internet, since virtually anyone can post anything there. Read the URL, or Internet address. Sites sponsored by a government agency (.gov) or an educational institution (.edu) are generally more reliable.

**Is the source up-to-date?** It is important to consult the most recent material, especially in fields such as medicine and technology that undergo constant research and development. Some authoritative sources have withstood the test of time, however, and should not be overlooked.

**Is the source appropriate?** What audience is the material written for? In general, look for information directed at the educated reader. Material geared to experts or to popular audiences may be too technical or too simplified and therefore not appropriate for most research projects.

### Distinguishing Fact from Opinion

As you gather information, it is important to recognize facts and opinions. A **fact** can be proven to be true or false. You could verify the statement "Congress rejected the bill" by checking newspapers, magazines, or the *Congressional Record.* An **opinion** is a judgment based on facts. The statement "Congress should not have rejected the bill" is an opinion. To evaluate an opinion, check for evidence presented logically and validly to support it.

### Recognizing Bias

A writer may have a particular bias. This does not automatically make his or her point of view unreliable. However, recognizing an author's bias can help you evaluate a source. Recognizing that the author of an article about immigration is a Chinese immigrant will help you understand that author's bias. In addition, an author may have a hidden agenda that makes him or her less than objective about a topic. To avoid relying on information that may be biased, check an author's background and gather a variety of viewpoints.

##  Collecting Information

People use a variety of techniques to collect information during the research process. Try out several of those suggested below and decide which ones work best for you.

### Paraphrasing and Summarizing

You can adapt material from other sources by quoting it directly or by paraphrasing or summarizing it. A paraphrase involves restating the information in your own words. It is often a simpler version but not necessarily a shorter version. A summary involves extracting the main ideas and supporting details and writing a shorter version of the information.

Remember to credit the source when you paraphrase or summarize. See the Writing Handbook—Research Report, pages 1287–1292.

| Strategies for Paraphrasing |
|---|
| 1. Select the portion of the article you want to record. |
| 2. Read it carefully and think about those ideas you find most interesting and useful to your research. Often these will be the main ideas. |
| 3. Retell the information in your own words. |

| Strategies for Summarizing |
|---|
| 1. Read the article carefully. Determine the main ideas. |
| 2. In your own words, write a shortened version of these main ideas. |

### Avoiding Plagiarism

Plagiarism is copying someone else's ideas or words and using them as if they were your own. This can happen inadvertently if you are sloppy about collecting information and documenting your sources. Plagiarism is intellectual stealing and can have serious consequences.

**How to Avoid Plagiarism**

1. When you paraphrase or summarize, be sure to change entirely the wording of the original by using your own words.

2. Both in notes and on your final report, enclose in quotation marks any material copied directly from other sources.

3. Indicate in your final report the sources of any ideas that are not general knowledge—including those in the visuals—that you have paraphrased or summarized.

4. Include a list of Works Cited with your finished report. See the Writing Handbook—Research Report, pages 1287–1292.

## ② Study Skills and Strategies

*As you read an assignment for the first time, review material for a test, or search for information for a research report, you use different methods of reading and studying.*

### 2.1 Skimming

When you run your eyes quickly over a text, paying attention to overviews, headings, topic sentences, highlighted words, and graphic features, you are skimming.

Skimming is a good technique for previewing material in a textbook or other source that you must read for an assignment. It is also useful when you are researching a self-selected topic. Skimming a source helps you determine whether it has pertinent information. For example, suppose you are writing a research report on Native American myths and legends. Skimming an essay or a book on myths and legends can help you quickly determine whether any part of it deals with your topic.

### 2.2 Scanning

To find a specific piece of information in a text, use scanning. To scan, place a card under the first line of a page and move it down slowly. Look for key words and phrases that signal the information you are looking for.

Scanning is useful in reviewing for a test or in finding a specific piece of information for a paper. Suppose you are looking for a discussion of the role of Coyote for your research report. You can scan a book chapter or an essay, looking for the key name *Coyote*.

## 2.3 In-Depth Reading

When you must thoroughly understand the material in a text, you use in-depth reading.

In-depth reading involves asking questions, taking notes, looking for main ideas, and drawing conclusions as you read slowly and carefully. For example, in researching your report on Native American myths and legends, you may find an essay on the common elements in tales of Coyote, the trickster, that are found in a number of Native American cultures. Since this is closely related to your topic, you will read it in depth and take notes. You also should use in-depth reading for reading textbooks and literary works.

## 2.4 Outlining

Outlining is an efficient way of organizing ideas and is useful in taking notes.

Outlining helps you retain information as you read in depth. For example, you might outline a chapter in a history textbook, listing the main subtopics and the ideas or details that support them. An outline can also be useful for taking notes for a research report or in reading a piece of literature. The following is an example of a topic outline that summarizes, in short phrases, part of a chapter.

MAIN IDEA: **Myths are concerned with fundamental issues.**
I. **The Cosmos**
    A. **Why things came to be**
    B. **How things work**
    C. **Power of nature**
II. **Past and Present**
    A. **Links historical events**
    B. **Builds hope**

## 2.5 Identifying Main Ideas

To understand and remember any material you read, identify its main idea.

In informative material, the main idea is often stated. The thesis statement of an essay or article and the topic sentence of each paragraph often state the main idea. In other material, especially literary works, the main idea is implied. After reading the piece carefully, analyze the important parts, such as characters and plot. Then try to sum up in one sentence the general point that the story makes.

## 2.6 Taking Notes

As you listen or read in depth, take notes to help you understand the material. Look and listen for key words that point to main ideas.

One way to help you summarize the main idea and supporting details is to take notes in modified outline form. In using a modified outline form, you do not need to use numerals and letters. Unlike a formal outline, a modified outline does not require two or more points under each heading, and headings do not need to be grammatically parallel. Yet, like a formal outline, a modified outline organizes a text's main ideas and related details. The following modified outline lists some Native American groups in western North America.

**Plains**
- **Cheyenne**
- **Comanche**
- **Sioux**

**Northwest Coast**
- **Chinook**

**California-Intermountain**
- **Nez Perce**
- **Paiute**
- **Shoshone**

**Southwest**
- **Apache**
- **Hopi**
- **Navajo**

Use abbreviations and symbols to make note taking more efficient. Following are some commonly used abbreviations for note taking.

| w/ | with | re | regarding |
|---|---|---|---|
| w/o | without | = | is, equals |
| # | number | * | important |
| &, + | and | def | definition |
| > | more than | Amer | America |
| < | less than | tho | although |

# ③ Critical Thinking

*Critical thinking includes the ability to analyze, evaluate, and synthesize ideas and information. Critical thinking goes beyond simply understanding something. It involves making informed judgments based on sound reasoning skills.*

## 3.1 Avoiding Faulty Reasoning

When you write or speak for a persuasive purpose, you must make sure your logic is valid. Avoid these mistakes in reasoning, called **logical fallacies.**

### Overgeneralization
Conclusions reached on the basis of too little evidence result in the fallacy called overgeneralization. A person who saw three cyclists riding bicycles without helmets might conclude, "Nobody wears bicycle helmets." That conclusion would be an overgeneralization.

### Circular Reasoning
When you support an opinion by simply repeating it in different terms, you are using circular reasoning. For example, "Sport utility vehicles are popular because more people buy them than any other category of new cars." This is an illogical statement because the second part of the sentence simply uses different words to restate the first part of the sentence.

### Either-Or Fallacy
Assuming that a complex question has only two possible answers is called the either-or fallacy. "Either we raise the legal driving age or accidents caused by teenage drivers will continue to increase" is an example of the either-or fallacy. The statement ignores other ways of decreasing the automobile accident rate of teenagers.

### Cause-and-Effect Fallacy
The cause-and-effect fallacy occurs when you say that event B was caused by event A just because event B occurred after event A.

A person might conclude that because a city's air quality worsened two months after a new factory began operation, the new factory caused the air pollution. However, this cause-and-effect relationship would have to be supported by more specific evidence.

## 3.2 Identifying Modes of Persuasion

Understanding persuasive techniques can help you evaluate information, make informed decisions, and avoid persuasive techniques intended to deceive you. Some modes of persuasion appeal to your various emotions.

### Loaded Language
Loaded language is words or phrases chosen to appeal to the emotions. It is often used in place of facts to shape opinion or to evoke a positive or negative reaction. For example, you might feel positive about a politician who has a *plan.* You might, however, feel negative about a politician who has a *scheme.*

### Bandwagon Appeal
Bandwagon taps into the human desire to belong. This technique suggests that "everybody" is doing it, or buying it, or believing it. Phrases such as "Don't be the only one . . ." and "Everybody is . . . " signal the bandwagon appeal.

### Testimonials
Testimonials present well-known people or satisfied customers who promote and endorse a product or idea. This technique taps into the appeal of celebrities or into people's need to identify with others just like themselves.

## 3.3 Logical Thinking

Persuasive writing and speaking require good reasoning skills. Two ways of creating logical arguments are deductive reasoning and inductive reasoning.

### Deductive Arguments

A deductive argument begins with a generalization, or premise, and then advances with facts and evidence that lead to a conclusion. The conclusion is the logical outcome of the premise. A false premise leads to a false conclusion; a valid premise leads to a valid conclusion provided that the specific facts are correct and the reasoning is correct.

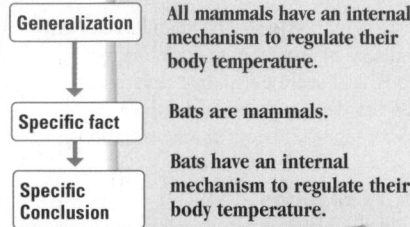

| | |
|---|---|
| **Generalization** | All mammals have an internal mechanism to regulate their body temperature. |
| **Specific fact** | Bats are mammals. |
| **Specific Conclusion** | Bats have an internal mechanism to regulate their body temperature. |

You may use deductive reasoning when writing a persuasive paper or speech. Your conclusion is the thesis of your paper. Facts in your paper supporting your premise should lead logically to that conclusion.

### Inductive Arguments

An inductive argument begins with specific evidence that leads to a general conclusion.

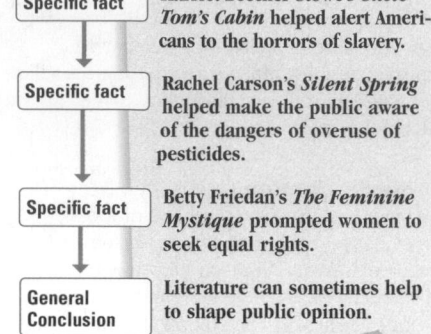

| | |
|---|---|
| **Specific fact** | Harriet Beecher Stowe's *Uncle Tom's Cabin* helped alert Americans to the horrors of slavery. |
| **Specific fact** | Rachel Carson's *Silent Spring* helped make the public aware of the dangers of overuse of pesticides. |
| **Specific fact** | Betty Friedan's *The Feminine Mystique* prompted women to seek equal rights. |
| **General Conclusion** | Literature can sometimes help to shape public opinion. |

The conclusion of an inductive argument often includes a qualifying term such as *some, often,* or *most.* This usage helps to avoid the fallacy of overgeneralization.

# 4 Speaking and Listening

*Good speakers and listeners do more than just talk and hear. They use specific techniques to present their ideas effectively, and they are attentive and critical listeners.*

## 4.1 Giving a Speech

In school, in business, and in community life, giving a speech is one of the most effective ways of communicating. Whether to persuade, to inform, or to entertain, you may often speak before an audience.

### Analyzing Audience and Purpose

In order to speak effectively, you need to know to whom you are speaking and why you are speaking. When preparing a speech, think about how much knowledge and interest your audience has in your subject. A speech has one of two main purposes: to inform or to persuade. A third purpose, to entertain, is often considered closely related to these two purposes.

A speech **to inform** gives the audience new information, provides a better understanding of information, or enables people to use information in a new way. An informative speech is presented in an objective way.

In a speech **to persuade,** a speaker tries to change the actions or beliefs of an audience.

### Preparing and Delivering a Speech

There are four main methods of preparing and delivering a speech:

**Manuscript** When you speak from **manuscript,** you prepare a complete script of your speech in advance and use it to deliver your speech.

**Memory** When you speak from **memory,** you prepare a written text in advance and then memorize it so you can deliver it word for word.

**Impromptu** When you speak **impromptu,** you speak on the spur of the moment without any special preparation.

**Extemporaneous** When you give an **extemporaneous** speech, you research and prepare your speech and then deliver it with the help of notes.

| Points for Effective Speech Delivery |
| --- |
| • Avoid speaking either too fast or too slow. Vary your **speaking rate** depending on your material. Slow down for difficult concepts. Speed up to convince your audience that you are knowledgeable about your subject. |
| • Speak loud enough to be heard clearly, but not so loud that your voice is overwhelming. |
| • Use a **conversational tone.** |
| • Use a change of **pitch,** or inflection, to help make your tone and meaning clear. |
| • Let your **facial expression** reflect your message. |
| • Make **eye contact** with as many audience members as possible. |
| • Use **gestures** to emphasize your words. Don't make your gestures too small to be seen. On the other hand, don't gesture too frequently or wildly. |
| • Use **good posture**—not too relaxed and not too rigid. Avoid nervous mannerisms. |

## 4.2 Analyzing, Evaluating and Critiquing a Speech

Evaluating speeches helps you make informed judgments about the ideas presented in a speech. It also helps you learn what makes an effective speech and delivery. Use these criteria to help you analyze, evaluate, and critique speeches.

---

**CRITERIA** **How to Evaluate a Persuasive Speech**

- Did the speaker have a clear goal or argument?
- Did the speaker take the audience's biases into account?
- Did the speaker support the argument with convincing facts?
- Did the speaker use sound logic in developing the argument?
- Did the speaker use voice, facial expression, gestures, and posture effectively?
- Did the speaker hold the audience's interest?

---

**CRITERIA** **How to Evaluate an Informative Speech**

- Did the speaker have a specific, clearly focused topic?
- Did the speaker take the audience's previous knowledge into consideration?
- Did the speaker cite sources for the information?
- Did the speaker communicate the information objectively?
- Did the speaker present the information in an organized manner?
- Did the speaker use visual aids effectively?
- Did the speaker use voice, facial expression, gestures, and posture effectively?

### 4.3 Using Active Listening Strategies

Listeners play an active part in the communication process. A listener has a responsibility just as a speaker does. Listening, unlike hearing, is a learned skill.

As you listen to a public speaker, use the following active listening strategies:

- Determine the **speaker's purpose.**
- Listen for the **main idea** of the message and not simply the individual details.
- **Anticipate the points** that will be made based on the speaker's purpose and main idea.
- Listen with an open mind, but **identify faulty logic, unsupported facts,** and **emotional appeals.**

### 4.4 Conducting Interviews

Conducting a personal interview can be an effective way to get information.

**Preparing for the Interview**
- Read any articles by or about the person you will interview. This background information will help you get to the point during the interview.
- Prepare a list of questions. Think of more questions than you will need. Include some yes/no questions and some open-ended questions. Order your questions from most important to least important.

**Participating in the Interview**
- Listen interactively. Be prepared to follow up on a response you find interesting.
- Avoid arguments. Be tactful and polite.

**Following Up on the Interview**
- Summarize your notes while they are still fresh in your mind.
- Send a thank-you note to the interviewee.

## 5 Viewing and Representing

*In our media-saturated world, we are immersed in visual messages that convey ideas, information, and attitudes. To understand and use visual representations effectively, you need to be aware of the techniques and the range of visuals that are commonly used.*

### 5.1 Understanding Visual Messages

Information is communicated not only with words but with graphic devices. A **graphic device** is a visual representation of data and ideas and the relations among them.

**Reading Charts and Graphs**
A chart organizes information by arranging it in rows and columns. It is helpful in showing complex information clearly. When interpreting a chart, first read the title. Then analyze how the information is presented. Charts can take many different forms. The following chart compares the transcendentalists and Gothic writers of the 1800s.

| A Comparison of Transcendentalists and Gothic Writers of the 1800s ||
|---|---|
| **Transcendentalists** | **Gothic Writers** |
| Optimists | Pessimists |
| Emphasis on nature | Emphasis on human frailty |
| Emphasis on human/universe connection | Emphasis on flawed universe |
| Emphasis on light | Emphasis on the dark |

There are several different types of **graphs,** visual aids that are often used to display numerical information.

- A **circle graph** shows proportions of the whole. The following circle graph shows the types of writing Zora Neale Hurston published.

**Types of Work Published by Zora Neale Hurston**

11% Books

25% Short Stories, Plays

64% Essays, Articles

Source: *Tell My Horse*, Harper, 1990.

- A **line graph** shows the change in data over a period of time. The following line graph shows the expansion of land used for raising crops between 1850 and 1900.

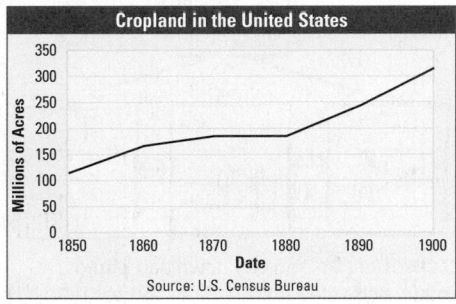

**Cropland in the United States**

Millions of Acres

350 300 250 200 150 100 50 0

1850 1860 1870 1880 1890 1900

Date

Source: U.S. Census Bureau

- A **bar graph** compares amounts.

### Interpreting Images

Speakers and writers often use visual aids to inform or persuade their audiences. These aids can be invaluable in helping you understand the information being communicated. However, you must interpret visual aids critically, as you do written material.

- **Examine photographs critically.** Does the camera angle or the background in the photo intentionally evoke a positive or negative response? Has the image been altered or manipulated?
- **Evaluate carefully the data presented in charts and graphs.** Some charts and graphs may exaggerate the facts. For example, a circle graph representing a sample of only ten people may be misleading if the speaker suggests that this data represents a trend.

## 5.2 Evaluating Visual Messages

When you view images, whether they are cartoons, advertising art, photographs, or paintings, there are certain elements to look for.

### CRITERIA How to Analyze Images

- Is color used realistically? Is it used to emphasize certain objects? To evoke a specific response?
- What tone is created by color and by light and dark in the picture?
- Do the background images intentionally evoke a positive or negative response?
- What is noticeable about the picture's composition, that is, the arrangement of lines, colors, and forms? Does the composition emphasize certain objects or elements in the picture?
- For graphs and charts, does the visual accurately represent the data?

## 5.3 Using Visual Representations

Tables, graphs, diagrams, pictures, and animations often communicate information more effectively than words alone do.

Use visuals with written reports to illustrate complex concepts and processes or to make a page look more interesting. Computer programs, CD-ROMs, and on-line services can help you generate

- **graphs** that present numerical information
- **charts** and **tables** that allow easy comparison of information
- **logos** and **graphic devices** that highlight important information
- **borders** and **tints** that signal different kinds of information
- **clip art** that adds useful pictures

- **interactive animations** that illustrate difficult concepts

You might want to explore ways of displaying data in more than one visual format before deciding which will work best for you.

## 5.4 Making Multimedia Presentations

A multimedia presentation is an electronically prepared combination of text, sound, and visuals such as photographs, videos, and animation. Your audience reads, hears, and sees your presentation at a computer, following different "paths" you create to lead the user through the information you have gathered.

### Planning Presentations

To create a multimedia presentation, first choose your topic and decide what you want to include. Then plan how you want your user to move through your presentation. For a multimedia presentation on the American Dream, you might include the following items:

- text discussing aspects of the American Dream

- taped reading from the Declaration of Independence

- tape of Martin Luther King's "I Have a Dream" speech

- chart showing "Dreams Won" and "Dreams to Be Fulfilled"

- video of immigrants at Ellis Island

- video interview with a scholar on what ideas and ideals have changed from decade to decade and what have remained the same

- photos of people who embody some aspect of the American Dream

You can choose one of the following ways to organize your presentation:

**a step-by-step,** with only one path, or order, in which the user can see and hear the information

**a branching path** that allows users to make some choices about what they will see and hear, and in what order

A flow chart can help you figure out the paths a user can take through your presentation. Each box in the flow chart that follows represents something about the American Dream for the user to read, see, or hear. The arrows on the flow chart show the possible paths the user can follow.

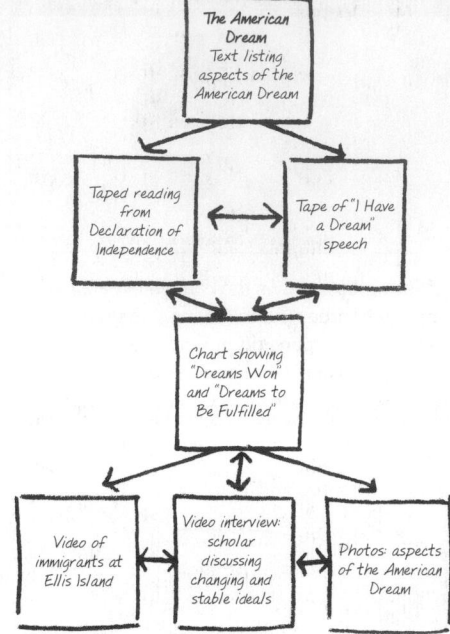

**TECHNOLOGY TIP** You can download photos, sound, and video from Internet sources onto your computer. This process allows you to add to your multimedia presentation various elements that would usually require complex editing equipment.

### Guiding Your User

Your user will need directions to follow the path you have planned for your multimedia presentation.

Most multimedia authoring programs allow you to create screens that include text or audio directions that guide the user from one part of your presentation to the next.

If you need help creating your multimedia presentation, ask your school's technology adviser. You may also be able to get help from your classmates or your software manual.

# Grammar Handbook

## ❶ Quick Reference: Parts of Speech

| Part of Speech | Definition | Examples |
|---|---|---|
| **Noun** | Names a person, place, thing, idea, quality, or action. | Silko, Rainy Mountain, churches, peace, honesty, hunting |
| **Pronoun** | Takes the place of a noun or another pronoun. | |
| Personal | Refers to the one speaking, spoken to, or spoken about. | I, me, my, mine, we, us, our, ours, you, your, yours, she, he, it, her, him, hers, his, its, they, them, their, theirs |
| Reflexive | Follows a verb or preposition and refers to a preceding noun or pronoun. | myself, yourself, herself, himself, itself, ourselves, yourselves, themselves |
| Intensive | Emphasizes a noun or another pronoun. | (Same as reflexives) |
| Demonstrative | Points to specific persons or things. | this, that, these, those |
| Interrogative | Signals questions. | who, whom, whose, which, what |
| Indefinite | Refers to person(s) or thing(s) not specifically mentioned. | both, all, most, many, anyone, everybody, several, none, some |
| Relative | Introduces subordinate clauses and relates them to words in the main clause. | who, whom, whose, which, that |
| **Verb** | Expresses action, condition, or state of being. | |
| Action | Tells what the subject does or did, physically or mentally. | run, reaches, listened, consider, decides, dreamt |
| Linking | Connects subjects to that which identifies or describes them. | am, is, are, was, were, sound, taste, appear, feel, become, remain, seem |
| Auxiliary | Precedes and introduces main verbs. | be, have, do, can, could, will, would, may, might |
| **Adjective** | Modifies nouns or pronouns. | **strong** women, **two** epics, **enough** time |
| **Adverb** | Modifies verbs, adjectives, or other adverbs. | walked **out, really** funny, **far** away |
| **Preposition** | Relates one word to another (following) word. | at, by, for, from, in, of, on, to, with |
| **Conjunction** | Joins words or word groups. | |
| Coordinating | Joins words or word groups used the same way. | and, but, or, for, so, yet, nor |
| Correlative | Join words or word groups used the same way and are used in pairs. | both . . . and, either . . . or, neither . . . nor |
| Subordinating | Joins word groups not used the same way. | although, after, as, before, because, when, if, unless |
| **Interjection** | Expresses emotion. | wow, ouch, hurrah |

## GRAMMAR PRACTICE ANSWERS

1. proper, concrete
2. common, concrete
3. common, concrete
4. common, abstract
5. proper, concrete
6. common, concrete; common, concrete
7. common, concrete
8. common, abstract
9. common, abstract
10. proper, concrete
11–15. compound: Rainy Mountain, grandmother, beadwork, Big Dipper; collective: group, herd, company
16. N. Scott Momaday's
17. Rainy Mountain's
18. buffalo's
19. companions'
20. cross's
21. gossip's
22. cousins'
23. people's
24. council's
25. grandmother's

## 2 Nouns

*A noun is a word used to name a person, place, thing, idea, quality, or action. Nouns can be classified in several ways. All nouns can be placed in at least two classifications. They are either common or proper. All are also either abstract or concrete. Some nouns can be classified as compound, collective, and possessive as well.*

**2.1 Common Nouns** are general names, common to an entire group.
EXAMPLES: *writer, song, bravery, hunter*

**2.2 Proper Nouns** name specific, one-of-a-kind things. (See Capitalization, page 1329.)
EXAMPLES: *Mourning Dove, Mississippi, Granny*

**2.3 Concrete Nouns** name things that can be perceived by the senses.
EXAMPLES: *windmill, turtle, clouds, canoe*

**2.4 Abstract Nouns** name things that cannot be observed by the senses.
EXAMPLES: *intelligence, fear, joy, loneliness*

|          | Common    | Proper            |
|----------|-----------|-------------------|
| Abstract | democracy | Age of Exploration |
| Concrete | woman     | Phoenix           |

**2.5 Compound Nouns** are formed from two or more words but express a single idea. They are written as single words, as separate words, or with hyphens. Use a dictionary to check the correct spelling of a compound noun.
EXAMPLES: *birthright, folk tale, Sky-World*

**2.6 Collective Nouns** are singular nouns that refer to groups of people or things. (See Collective Nouns as Subjects, page 1326.)
EXAMPLES: *army, flock, class, species*

**2.7 Possessive Nouns** show who or what owns something. Consult the chart below for the proper use of the possessive apostrophe.

| Category | Possessive Nouns | |
|----------|------|----------|
| | **Rule** | **Examples** |
| All singular nouns | Add apostrophe plus *-s* | Welty's, genius's, jury's, sister-in-law's |
| Plural nouns not ending in *-s* | Add apostrophe plus *-s* | children's women's people's |
| Plural nouns ending in *-s* | Add apostrophe only | witnesses' churches' males' Johnsons' |

### GRAMMAR PRACTICE

**A.** For each underlined noun, first tell whether it is common or proper. Then tell whether it is concrete or abstract.

1. My people named this knoll <u>Rainy Mountain</u>.
2. I returned there in July, just after my <u>grandmother</u> had died.
3. Grandmother used to sit by the window, crafting her <u>beadwork</u>.
4. The Kiowas surrendered before she was born, so my grandmother was spared the <u>humiliation</u> of imprisonment.
5. The <u>Kiowas</u> were on a long migration from the mountains.
6. Once a <u>group</u> of men had asked for one animal from the buffalo <u>herd</u>.
7. A <u>company</u> of soldiers carried out orders to disperse the tribe.
8. Born into the Sun Dance <u>culture</u>, my grandmother became a Christian in her later years.
9. Now I have her only in <u>memory</u>.
10. Kiowa legend tells how seven sisters became the stars of the <u>Big Dipper</u>.

**B. 11–15.** From the sentences above, write two compound nouns and three collective nouns.

**C.** Write the possessive form of the following nouns.

16. N. Scott Momaday
17. Kiowas
18. buffalo
19. companions
20. cross
21. gossip
22. cousins
23. people
24. council
25. grandmother

### ❸ Pronouns

*A pronoun is a word that is used in place of a noun or another pronoun. The word or word group to which the pronoun refers is called its antecedent.*

**3.1** **Personal Pronouns** are pronouns that change their form to express person, number, gender, and case. The forms of these pronouns are shown in the chart that follows.

| | Nominative | Objective | Possessive |
|---|---|---|---|
| **Singular** | | | |
| First Person | I | me | my, mine |
| Second Person | you | you | your, yours |
| Third Person | she, he, it | her, him, it | her, hers, his, its |
| **Plural** | | | |
| First Person | we | us | our, ours |
| Second Person | you | you | your, yours |
| Third Person | they | them | their, theirs |

**3.2** **Pronoun Agreement** Pronouns should agree with their antecedents in number and person. Singular pronouns are used to replace singular nouns. Plural pronouns are used to replace plural nouns. Pronouns must also match the gender (masculine, feminine, or neuter) of the nouns they replace.

**3.3** **Pronoun Case** Personal pronouns change form to show how they function in a sentence. This change of form is called *case*. The three cases are **nominative, objective,** and **possessive.**

**A nominative pronoun** is used as the subject or the predicate nominative of a sentence.

**An objective pronoun** is used as the direct or indirect object of a sentence or as the object of a preposition.

> SUBJECT    OBJECT
>
> *He will lead them to us.*
>
> OBJECT OF PREPOSITION

**A possessive pronoun** shows ownership. The pronouns *mine, yours, hers, his, its, ours,* and *theirs* can be used in place of nouns.

> **EXAMPLE:** *This horse is mine.*

The pronouns *my, your, her, his, its, our,* and *their* are used before nouns.

> **EXAMPLE:** *This is my horse.*

**USAGE TIP** To decide which pronoun to use in a comparison, such as *He tells better tales than (I or me),* fill in the missing words: *He tells better tales than I tell.*

**WATCH OUT!** Many spelling errors can be avoided if you watch out for *its* and *their.* Don't confuse the possessive pronoun *its* with the contraction *it's,* meaning *it is* or *it has.* The homonyms *they're* (contraction for *they are*) and *there* (a place or an expletive) are often mistakenly used for *their.*

**3.4** **Reflexive and Intensive Pronouns** These pronouns are formed by adding *-self* or *-selves* to certain personal pronouns. Their forms are the same, and they differ only in how they are used.

**Reflexive pronouns** follow verbs or prepositions and reflect back on an earlier noun or pronoun.

> **EXAMPLES:** *He likes himself too much. She is now herself again.*

**Intensive pronouns** intensify or emphasize the nouns or pronouns to which they refer.

> **EXAMPLES:** *They themselves will educate their children. You did it yourselves.*

| Singular | |
|---|---|
| First Person | myself |
| Second Person | yourself |
| Third Person | herself, himself, itself |

| Plural | |
|---|---|
| First Person | ourselves |
| Second Person | yourselves |
| Third Person | themselves |

**WATCH OUT!** Avoid using *hisself* or *theirselves.* Standard English does not include these forms.

> **NONSTANDARD:** *Did the pottery maker enjoy hisself?*
> **STANDARD:** *Did the pottery maker enjoy himself?*

**USAGE TIP** Reflexive and intensive pronouns should never be used without antecedents.

> **INCORRECT:** *Read a tale to my brother and myself.*
> **CORRECT:** *Read a tale to my brother and me.*

**3.5** **Demonstrative Pronouns** point out things and persons near and far.

| | Singular | Plural |
|---|---|---|
| **Near** | this | these |
| **Far** | that | those |

**WATCH OUT!** Avoid using the objective pronoun *them* in place of the demonstrative *those.*

> **INCORRECT:** *Let's dramatize one of them tales.*
> **CORRECT:** *Let's dramatize one of those tales.*

**3.6** **Indefinite Pronouns** do not refer to specific persons or things and usually have no antecedents. The chart shows some commonly used indefinite pronouns:

| Singular | Plural | Singular or Plural | |
|---|---|---|---|
| each | both | all | half |
| either | few | any | plenty |
| neither | many | more | none |
| another | several | most | some |

Here is another set of indefinite pronouns, all of which are singular. Notice that, with one exception, they are spelled as one word:

| anyone | everyone | no one | someone |
|---|---|---|---|
| anybody | everybody | nobody | somebody |
| anything | everything | nothing | something |

**USAGE TIP** Since all these are singular, pronouns referring to them should be singular.

> **INCORRECT:** *Did everybody play their part well?*
> **CORRECT:** *Did everybody play his or her part well?*

If the antecedent of the pronoun is both male and female, *his or her* may be used as an alternative, or the sentence may be recast:

> **EXAMPLES:** *Did everybody play his or her part well?*
> *Did all the students play their parts well?*

### GRAMMAR PRACTICE

Write the correct form of all incorrect pronouns in the sentences below.

1. Most cross-country travelers today confine theirselves to interstate highways.
2. William Least Heat-Moon preferred them highways that were colored in blue on maps.
3. Only by traveling these routes can someone find their way to small towns and interesting people like Kendrick Fritz.
4. This Hopi Indian hisself tells Heat-Moon some fascinating things about Hopi culture.
5. Did anyone notice that one of them two rules of the Spider Grandmother is similar to the Christian Golden Rule?

**3.7** **Interrogative Pronouns** tell a reader or listener that a question is coming. The interrogative pronouns are *who, whom, whose, which,* and *what.*

> **EXAMPLES:** *Who is going to rehearse with you?*
> *From whom did you receive the script?*

**USAGE TIP** *Who* is used for subjects, *whom* for objects. To find out which pronoun you need to use in a question, change the question to a statement:

> **QUESTION:** *(Who/Whom?) did you meet there?*
> **STATEMENT:** *You met ( ? ) there.*

**GRAMMAR PRACTICE ANSWERS**
1. theirselves = themselves
2. them = those
3. their = his or her
4. hisself = himself
5. them = those

Since the verb has a subject *(you)*, the needed word must be the object form, *whom.*

> **EXAMPLE:** *Whom did you meet there?*

**WATCH OUT!** A special problem arises when you use an interrupter such as *do you think* within a sentence:

> **EXAMPLE:** *(Who/Whom) do you think will win?*

If you eliminate the interrupter, it is clear that the word you need is *who.*

**3.8** **Relative Pronouns** relate, or connect, clauses to the words they modify in sentences. The noun or pronoun that the clause modifies is the antecedent of the relative pronoun. Here are the relative pronouns and their uses:

| Replacing: | Subject | Object | Possessive |
|---|---|---|---|
| **Persons** | who | whom | whose |
| **Things** | which | which | whose |
| **Things/Persons\*** | that | that | whose |

\* *That* generally will not replace specific names, such as *Mark Twain.*

Often short sentences with related ideas can be combined using relative pronouns to create a more effective sentence.

> **SHORT SENTENCE:** *Mark Twain may be America's greatest humorist.*
> **RELATED SENTENCE:** *Mark Twain wrote Huckleberry Finn.*
> **COMBINED SENTENCE:** *Mark Twain, who wrote Huckleberry Finn, may be America's greatest humorist.*

### GRAMMAR PRACTICE

Choose the appropriate interrogative or relative pronoun from the words in parentheses.

1. "The Notorious Jumping Frog" was written by Samuel Clemens, (who/whom) wrote under the pseudonym Mark Twain.
2. The story gained national fame for Mark Twain, (who/that) first published it in 1865.
3. (Who/Whom) do you think is funnier, Jim Smiley or the storyteller Simon Wheeler?
4. Twain was an engaging storyteller (who/whom) large audiences came to see.
5. Smiley spent months educating his frog, (which/whose) fame as a jumper spread throughout the gold camps.

## 4 Verbs

*A verb is a word that expresses an action, a condition, or a state of being. There are two main kinds of verbs: action and linking. Other verbs, called auxiliary verbs, are sometimes used with action verbs and linking verbs.*

**4.1** **Action Verbs** tell what action someone or something is performing, physically or mentally.

> **PHYSICAL ACTION:** *You hit the target.*
> **MENTAL ACTION:** *She dreamed of me.*

**4.2** **Linking Verbs** do not express action. Linking verbs link subjects to complements that identify or describe them. Linking verbs may be divided into two groups:

> **FORMS OF** *TO BE:* *She is our queen.*
> **VERBS THAT EXPRESS CONDITION:** *The writer looked thoughtful.*

**4.3** **Auxiliary Verbs,** sometimes called helping verbs, precede action or linking verbs and modify their meanings in special ways. The most commonly used auxiliary verbs are parts of the verbs *be, have,* and *do.*

> **Be:** *am, is, are, was, were, be, being, been*
> **Have:** *have, has, had*
> **Do:** *do, does, did*

Other common auxiliary verbs are *can, could, will, would, shall, should, may, might,* and *must.*

> **EXAMPLES:** *I always have admired her.*
> *You must listen to me.*

**4.4** **Transitive and Intransitive Verbs**
Action verbs can be either transitive or intransitive. A transitive verb directs the action towards someone or something. The transitive verb has an object. An intransitive verb does not direct the action towards someone or something. It does not have an object. Since linking verbs convey no action, they are always intransitive.

> **Transitive:** *The storm sank the ship.*
> **Intransitive:** *The ship sank.*

**GRAMMAR PRACTICE ANSWERS**
1. who
2. who
3. Who
4. whom
5. whose

**4.5** *Principal Parts* Action and linking verbs typically have four principal parts, which are used to form verb tenses. The principal parts are the *present*, the *present participle*, the *past*, and the *past participle*.

If the verb is a regular verb, the past and past participle are formed by adding the ending *-d* or *-ed* to the present part. Here is a chart showing four regular verbs:

| Present | Present Participle | Past | Past Participle |
|---------|--------------------|------|-----------------|
| risk | (is) risking | risked | (have) risked |
| solve | (is) solving | solved | (have) solved |
| drop | (is) dropping | dropped | (have) dropped |
| carry | (is) carrying | carried | (have) carried |

Note that the present participle and past participle forms are preceded by a form of *be* or *have*. These forms cannot be used alone as main verbs and always need an auxiliary verb.

EXAMPLES: *The actors were dressing themselves.*

*The playwright has stopped the rehearsal.*

The past and past participle of irregular verbs are not formed by adding *-d* or *-ed* to the present; they are formed in irregular ways.

| Present | Present Participle | Past | Past Participle |
|---------|--------------------|------|-----------------|
| begin | (is) beginning | began | (have) begun |
| break | (is) breaking | broke | (have) broken |
| bring | (is) bringing | brought | (have) brought |
| choose | (is) choosing | chose | (have) chosen |
| go | (is) going | went | (have) gone |
| lose | (is) losing | lost | (have) lost |
| see | (is) seeing | saw | (have) seen |
| swim | (is) swimming | swam | (have) swum |
| write | (is) writing | wrote | (have) written |

**4.6** *Verb Tense* The tense of a verb tells the time of the action or the state of being. An action or state of being can occur in the present, the past, or the future. There are six tenses, each expressing a different range of time.

**Present tense** expresses an action that is happening at the present time, occurs regularly, or is constant or generally true. Use the present part.

EXAMPLES
NOW: *That poet reads well.*
REGULAR: *I swim every day.*
GENERAL: *Time flies.*

**Past tense** expresses an action that began and ended in the past. Use the past part.

EXAMPLE: *The storyteller finished his tale.*

**Future tense** expresses an action (or state of being) that will occur. Use *shall* or *will* with the present part.

EXAMPLE: *They will attend the next festival.*

**Present perfect tense** expresses action (1) that was completed at an indefinite time in the past or (2) that began in the past and continues into the present. Use *have* or *has* with the past participle.

EXAMPLE: *Poetry has inspired readers throughout the ages.*

**Past perfect tense** shows an action in the past that came before another action in the past. Use *had* before the past participle.

EXAMPLE: *The witness had already testified before the defendant confessed.*

**Future perfect tense** shows an action in the future that will be completed before another action in the future. Use *shall have* or *will have* before the past participle.

EXAMPLE: *They will have finished the novel before seeing the movie version of the tale.*

**4.7** *Progressive Forms* The progressive forms of the six tenses show ongoing action. Use a form of *be* with the present participle of a verb.

PRESENT PROGRESSIVE: *She is rehearsing her lines.*
PAST PROGRESSIVE: *She was rehearsing her lines.*
FUTURE PROGRESSIVE: *She will be rehearsing her lines.*

**PRESENT PERFECT PROGRESSIVE:** *She has been rehearsing her lines.*
**PAST PERFECT PROGRESSIVE:** *She had been rehearsing her lines.*
**FUTURE PERFECT PROGRESSIVE:** *She will have been rehearsing her lines.*

**WATCH OUT!** Do not shift tense needlessly. Watch out for these special cases.

- In most compound sentences and in sentences with compound predicates, keep the tenses the same.

    **INCORRECT:** *Every morning they get up and went to work.*
    **CORRECT:** *Every morning they get up and go to work.*

- If one past action happens before another, do shift tenses—from the past to the past perfect:

    **INCORRECT:** *They wished they started earlier.*
    **CORRECT:** *They wished they had started earlier.*

#### GRAMMAR PRACTICE

Identify the tense of the verb(s) in each of the following sentences. If you find an unnecessary tense shift, correct it.

1. The setting of *The Crucible* is the late 17th century in Salem, Massachusetts.
2. Before the witch trials ended, people had lost their ability to make objective judgments.
3. Miller knew that the play pertains to his own time.
4. People will read it far into the future, and many will apply its message to their own time.
5. In the play some accuse others of being witches, even though they knew the accusation was false.

### 4.8 **Active and Passive Voice** The voice

of a verb tells whether the subject of a sentence performs or receives the action expressed by the verb. When the subject performs the action, the verb is in the active voice. When the subject is the receiver of the action, the verb is in the passive voice.

Compare these two sentences:

**ACTIVE:** *The Puritans did not celebrate Christmas.*
**PASSIVE:** *Christmas was not celebrated by the Puritans.*

To form the passive voice use a form of *be* with the past participle of the main verb.

**WATCH OUT!** Use the passive voice sparingly. It tends to make writing less forceful and less direct. It can also make the writing awkward.

**AWKWARD:** *The stories of hysterical witnesses were believed by gullible and fearful jurors.*
**CORRECT:** *Gullible and fearful jurors believed the stories of hysterical witnesses.*

There are occasions when you will choose to use the passive voice because

- you want to emphasize the receiver: *The king was shot.*
- the doer is unknown: *My books were stolen.*
- the doer is unimportant: *French is spoken here.*

### 4.9 **Mood** The mood identifies the manner in

which the verb expresses an idea. There are three moods.

**The indicative mood** states a fact or asks a question. You use this mood most often.

    **EXAMPLE:** *His trust was shattered by the betrayal.*

**The imperative mood** is used to give a command or make a request.

    **EXAMPLE:** *Be there by eight o'clock sharp.*

**The subjunctive mood** is used to express a wish or a condition that is contrary to fact.

    **EXAMPLE:** *If I were you, I wouldn't get my hopes up.*

#### GRAMMAR PRACTICE

For the first five items below, identify the boldfaced verb phrase as active or passive.

1. *The Crucible* **has played** in theaters throughout the world.
2. It **was written** by Arthur Miller, one of America's greatest dramatists.
3. Miller **did** not **approve** of Reverend Parris's greed for gold.
4. **Has** the reputation of the minister **been maligned?**
5. After the trials Parris **was voted** from office, and surviving victims **were awarded** compensation by the government.

### GRAMMAR PRACTICE ANSWERS
**Column 1**
1. is = present
2. ended = past
   had lost = past perfect
3. knew = past
   pertains = present
   pertains > pertained
4. will read = future
   will apply = future
5. accuse = present
   knew = past
   knew > know

**Column 2**
1. active
2. passive
3. active
4. passive
5. passive, passive

For the following items, identify the boldfaced verb as indicative or subjunctive in mood.

6. If Parris **were** alive today, would he tell his side of the story?

7. The jurors expressed their regret to all citizens who **had suffered.**

8. Many people at that time **were** devout Puritans.

9. Some of the farms belonging to the victims **were abandoned.**

10. If there **were** court-appointed lawyers at the time, would justice have been served?

### 5 Modifiers

*Modifiers are words or groups of words that change or limit the meanings of other words. The two kinds of modifiers are adjectives and adverbs.*

**5.1 Adjectives** An adjective is a word that modifies a noun or pronoun by telling *which one, what kind, how many,* or *how much.*

WHICH ONE: *this, that, these, those*
EXAMPLE: *Those actions were truly heroic.*

WHAT KIND: *large, beautiful, cowardly, innocent*
EXAMPLE: *Many innocent people suffered.*

HOW MANY: *ten, many, several, every*
EXAMPLE: *Every juror has to make up his or her own mind.*

HOW MUCH: *little, enough, less, abundant*
EXAMPLE: *Our farmers hope to have abundant rainfall this summer.*

The **articles** *a, an,* and *the* are usually classified as adjectives. These are the most common adjectives that you will use.

EXAMPLES: *The bridge was burned before the attack.*
*A group of peasants led the procession in the town.*

**5.2 Predicate Adjectives** Most adjectives come before the nouns they modify, as in the examples above. Predicate adjectives, however, follow linking verbs and describe the subject.

EXAMPLE: *My friends are very intelligent.*

Be especially careful to use adjectives (not adverbs) after such linking verbs as *look, feel, grow, taste,* and *smell.*

EXAMPLE: *The weather grows cold.*

**5.3 Adverbs** modify verbs, adjectives, or other adverbs by telling *where, when, how,* or *to what extent.*

WHERE: *The children played outside.*
WHEN: *The author spoke yesterday.*
HOW: *We walked slowly behind the leader.*
TO WHAT EXTENT: *He worked very hard.*

Unlike adjectives, adverbs tend to be mobile words; they may occur in many places in sentences.

EXAMPLES: *Suddenly the wind shifted. The wind suddenly shifted. The wind shifted suddenly.*

Changing the position of adverbs within sentences can vary the rhythm in your writing.

**5.4 Adjective or Adverb** Many adverbs are formed by adding *-ly* to adjectives.

EXAMPLES: *sweet, sweetly; gentle, gently*

However, *-ly* added to a noun will usually yield an adjective.

EXAMPLES: *friend, friendly; woman, womanly*

**5.5 Comparison of Modifiers** The form of an adjective or adverb indicates the degree of comparison that the modifier expresses. Both adjectives and adverbs have three forms, or degrees: the positive, comparative, and superlative.

**The positive form** is used to describe individual things, groups, or actions.

EXAMPLES: *Poe was a great writer. His descriptions are vivid.*

**The comparative form** is used to compare two things, groups, or actions.

EXAMPLES: *I think that Poe was a greater writer than Nathaniel Hawthorne. Poe's descriptions are more vivid.*

The **superlative form** is used to compare more than two things, groups, or actions.

**EXAMPLES:** *I think that Poe was the <u>greatest</u> short story writer of his century. Poe's descriptions are the <u>most vivid</u> I have ever read.*

**5.6** *Regular Comparisons* One-syllable and some two-syllable adjectives and adverbs form their comparative and superlative forms by adding *-er* or *-est*. All three-syllable and most two-syllable modifiers form their comparative and superlative by using *more* or *most*.

| Positive | Comparative | Superlative |
|---|---|---|
| small | smaller | smallest |
| thin | thinner | thinnest |
| sleepy | sleepier | sleepiest |
| useless | more useless | most useless |
| precisely | more precisely | most precisely |

**WATCH OUT!** Note that spelling changes must sometimes be made to form the comparative and superlative of modifiers.

**EXAMPLES:** *friendly, friendlier* (change *y* to *i* and add the ending)
*sad, sadder* (double the final consonant and add the ending)

**5.7** *Irregular Comparisons* Some commonly used modifiers have irregular comparative and superlative forms. You may wish to memorize them.

| Positive | Comparative | Superlative |
|---|---|---|
| good | better | best |
| bad | worse | worst |
| far | farther or further | farthest or furthest |
| little | less or lesser | least |
| many | more | most |
| well | better | best |
| much | more | most |

**5.8** *Using Modifiers Correctly* Study the tips that follow to avoid common mistakes.

***Farther*** and ***Further*** *Farther* is used for distances; use *further* for everything else.

**Avoiding double comparisons** You make a comparison by using *-er/-est* or by using *more/most*. Using *-er* with *more* or using *-est* with *most* is incorrect.

**INCORRECT:** *I like her <u>more better</u> than she likes me.*
**CORRECT:** *I like her <u>better</u> than she likes me.*

**Avoiding illogical comparisons** An illogical or confusing comparison results if two unrelated things are compared or if something is compared with itself. The word *other* or the word *else* should be used in a comparison of an individual member with the rest of the group.

**ILLOGICAL:** *"The Fall of the House of Usher" was as suspenseful as any Poe story.*
(Did Poe write "The Fall of the House of Usher"?)
**LOGICAL:** *"The Fall of the House of Usher" was as suspenseful as any <u>other</u> Poe story.*

***Bad*** vs. ***Badly*** *Bad,* always an adjective, is used before nouns or after linking verbs to describe the subject. *Badly,* always an adverb, never modifies a noun. Be sure to use the right form after a linking verb.

**INCORRECT:** *Ed felt <u>badly</u> after his team lost.*
**CORRECT:** *Ed felt <u>bad</u> after his team lost.*

***Good*** vs. ***Well*** *Good* is always an adjective. It is used before nouns or after a linking verb to modify the subject. *Well* is often an adverb meaning "expertly" or "properly." *Well* can also be used as an adjective after a linking verb, when it means "in good health."

**INCORRECT:** *Helen writes very <u>good.</u>*
**CORRECT:** *Helen writes very <u>well.</u>*
**CORRECT:** *Yesterday I felt <u>bad</u>; today I feel <u>well.</u>*

**Double negatives** If you add a negative word to a sentence that is already negative, the result will be an error known as a double negative. When using *not* or *-n't* with a verb, use "any-" words, such as *anybody* or *anything*, rather than "no-" words, such as *nobody* or *nothing*, later in the sentence.

> **INCORRECT:** *I don't have no money.*
> **CORRECT:** *I don't have any money.*
>
> **INCORRECT:** *We haven't seen nobody.*
> **CORRECT:** *We haven't seen anybody.*

Using *hardly, barely,* or *scarcely* after a negative word is also incorrect.

> **INCORRECT:** *They couldn't barely see two feet ahead.*
> **CORRECT:** *They could barely see two feet ahead.*

**Misplaced modifiers** A misplaced modifier is one placed so far away from the word it modifies that the intended meaning of the sentence is unclear. Place modifiers as close as possible to the words they modify.

> **MISPLACED:** *We found the child in the park who was missing.* (The child was missing, not the park.)
>
> **CLEARER:** *We found the child who was missing in the park.*

### GRAMMAR PRACTICE

Choose the correct word from each pair in parentheses.

1. Flannery O'Connor's story is (better/more better) than other stories I have read recently.
2. Mr. Shiftlet and Mrs. Crater (could/couldn't) hardly be less honest with each other.
3. Mr. Shiftlet says there isn't (any/no) broken thing on the farm that he can't fix.
4. He feels (good/well) about fixing the car.
5. Who do you think is the (stranger/strangest) person—Mr. Shiftlet or Mrs. Crater?
6. Mr. Shiftlet wouldn't have been able to hurt (anybody/nobody) if Mrs. Crater had not been so eager for Lucynell to get married.
7. As Mr. Shiftlet drove on alone he felt (depresseder/more depressed) than ever.
8. Shiftlet didn't feel very (well/good) about being alone, so he picked up a hitchhiker.

9. Shiftlet feels (bad/badly) about the rottenness of the world.
10. One wonders how many other great stories Flannery O'Connor would have written had she lived (longer/more longer).

---

### ❻ Prepositions, Conjunctions, and Interjections

**6.1** *Prepositions* A preposition is a word used to show the relationship between a noun or a pronoun and another word in the sentence.

| Commonly Used Prepositions | | | |
|---|---|---|---|
| above | down | near | through |
| at | for | of | to |
| before | from | on | up |
| below | in | out | with |
| by | into | over | without |

The preposition is always followed by a word or group of words that serves as its object. The preposition, its object, and modifiers of the object are called the **prepositional phrase.** In each example below, the prepositional phrase is underlined and the object of the preposition is in boldface type.

> **EXAMPLES**
> The future <u>of the entire **kingdom**</u> is uncertain.
> We searched <u>through the deepest **woods.**</u>

Prepositional phrases may be used as adjectives or as adverbs. The phrase in the first example is used as an adjective modifying the noun *future*. In the second example, the phrase is used as an adverb modifying the verb *searched*.

**WATCH OUT!** Prepositional phrases must be as close as possible to the word they modify.

> **MISPLACED:** *We have clothes for leisure wear of many colors.*
> **CLEARER:** *We have clothes of many colors for leisure wear.*

**GRAMMAR PRACTICE ANSWERS**
1. better
2. could
3. any
4. good
5. stranger
6. anybody
7. more depressed
8. good
9. bad
10. longer

**6.2** **Conjunctions** A conjunction is a word used to connect words, phrases, or sentences. There are three kinds of conjunctions: **coordinating conjunctions, correlative conjunctions,** and **subordinating conjunctions.**

**Coordinating conjunctions** connect words or word groups that have the same function in a sentence. These include *and, but, or, for, so, yet,* and *nor.*

Coordinating conjunctions can join nouns, pronouns, verbs, adjectives, adverbs, prepositional phrases, and clauses in a sentence.

These examples show coordinating conjunctions joining words of the same function:

**EXAMPLES**

*I have many friends <u>but</u> few enemies.* (two noun objects)

*We ran out the door <u>and</u> into the street.* (two prepositional phrases)

*They are pleasant <u>yet</u> seem aloof.* (two predicates)

*We have to go now, <u>or</u> we will be late.* (two clauses)

**Correlative conjunctions** are similar to coordinating conjunctions. However, correlative conjunctions are always used in pairs.

| Correlative Conjunctions | | |
|---|---|---|
| both . . . and | neither . . . nor | whether . . . or |
| either . . . or | not only . . . but also | |

**Subordinating conjunctions** introduce subordinate clauses—clauses that cannot stand by themselves as complete sentences. The subordinating conjunction shows how the subordinate clause relates to the rest of the sentence. The relationships include time, manner, place, cause, comparison, condition, and purpose.

**SUBORDINATING CONJUNCTIONS**

| | |
|---|---|
| TIME | *after, as, as long as, as soon as, before, since, until, when, whenever, while* |
| MANNER | *as, as if* |
| PLACE | *where, wherever* |
| CAUSE | *because, since* |
| COMPARISON | *as, as much as, than* |
| CONDITION | *although, as long as, even if, even though, if, provided that, though, unless, while* |
| PURPOSE | *in order that, so that, that* |

In the example below, the boldface word is the conjunction, and the underlined words are called a subordinate clause:

**EXAMPLE**: *Walt Whitman was a man of the people, **although** <u>many did not appreciate his poems.</u>*

*Walt Whitman was a man of the people* is an independent clause because it can stand alone as a complete sentence. *Although many did not appreciate his poems* cannot stand alone as a complete sentence; it is a subordinate clause.

**Conjunctive adverbs** are used to connect clauses that can stand by themselves as sentences. Conjunctive adverbs include *also, besides, finally, however, moreover, nevertheless, otherwise,* and *then.*

**EXAMPLE**: *She loved the fall; <u>however</u>, she also enjoyed winter.*

**6.3** **Interjections** are words used to show strong emotion, such as *wow* and *cool*. Often followed by an exclamation point, they have no grammatical relationship to the rest of a sentence.

**EXAMPLE**: *Thoreau lived in the woods by himself. <u>Amazing!</u>*

**GRAMMAR PRACTICE**

Label each of the boldface words as a preposition, conjunction, or interjection.

1. Thoreau's sojourn **at** Walden Pond lasted about two years, **yet** it made him famous.

2. Thoreau was determined that neither weather nor poverty would deter him, **since** his purpose was so important.

3. He lived just a few miles **from** Concord, **so** he was able to visit his friends and relatives frequently.

4. Thoreau left the woods **because** he thought **that** he might have other lives to live.

5. The cabin **in** which he lived has been re-created, **but** it is not **on** the site where he built it.

6. You're going to visit Walden Pond **with** us? **Great!**

**GRAMMAR PRACTICE ANSWERS**
1. preposition, conjunction
2. conjunction
3. preposition, conjunction
4. conjunction, conjunction
5. preposition, conjunction, preposition
6. preposition, interjection

# 7 Quick Reference: The Sentence and Its Parts

*The diagrams that follow will give you a brief review of the essentials of the sentence—subjects and predicates—and of some of its parts.*

Thoreau's original **cabin** | **cost** less than thirty dollars.

The **complete subject** includes all the words that identify the person, place, thing, or idea that the sentence is about.

The **complete predicate** includes all the words that tell or ask something about the subject.

**cabin** | **cost**

The **simple subject** tells exactly whom or what the sentence is about. It may be one word or a group of words, but it does not include modifiers.

The **simple predicate**, or **verb**, tells what the subject does or is. It may be one word or several, but it does not include modifiers.

**In *Walden*,** | Thoreau | **has offered** | readers his thoughts about living.

**subject**

A **prepositional phrase** consists of a preposition, its object, and any modifiers of the object. In this phrase, *in* is the preposition and *Walden* is its object.

Verbs often have more than one part. They may be made up of a **main verb**, like *offered*, and one or more **auxiliary**, or **helping**, **verbs**, like *has*.

A **direct object** is a word or group of words that tells who or what receives the action of the verb in the sentence.

An **indirect object** is a word or a group of words that tells *to whom* or *for whom* or *to what* or *for what* about the verb. A sentence can have an indirect object only if it has a direct object. The indirect object always comes before the direct object in a sentence.

## 8 The Sentence and Its Parts

*A sentence is a group of words used to express a complete thought. A complete sentence has a subject and predicate.*

**8.1 Kinds of Sentences** Sentences make statements, ask questions, give commands, and show feelings. There are four basic types of sentences.

| Type | Definition | Example |
|---|---|---|
| Declarative | states a fact, wish, intent, or feeling | I read Porter's story recently. |
| Interrogative | asks a question | Did you read her story? |
| Imperative | gives a command, request, or direction | Read the story carefully. |
| Exclamatory | expresses strong feeling or excitement | This writer is good! |

**WRITING TIP** One way to vary your writing is to employ a variety of different types of sentences. In the first example below, each sentence is declarative. Notice how much more interesting the revised paragraph is.

**SAMPLE PARAGRAPH:** *You have to see Niagara Falls in person. You can truly appreciate their awesome power in no other way. You should visit them on your next vacation. They are a spectacular sight.*

**REVISED PARAGRAPH:** *Have you ever seen Niagara Falls in person? You can truly appreciate their awesome power in no other way. Visit them on your next vacation. What a spectacular sight they are!*

**WATCH OUT!** Conversation frequently includes parts of sentences, or **fragments.** In formal writing, however, you need to be sure that every sentence is a complete thought and includes a subject and predicate. (See Correcting Fragments, page 1323.)

**8.2 Complete Subjects and Predicates**
A sentence has two parts: a subject and a predicate. The complete subject includes all the words that identify the person, place, thing, or idea that the sentence is about. The complete predicate includes all the words that tell what the subject did or what happened to the subject.

| Complete Subject | Complete Predicate |
|---|---|
| The poets of the time | wrote about nature. |
| This new approach | was extraordinary. |

**8.3 Simple Subjects and Predicates**
The simple subject is the key word in the complete subject. The simple predicate is the key word in the complete predicate. In the examples that follow, they are underlined.

| Simple Subject | Simple Predicate |
|---|---|
| The <u>poets</u> of the time | <u>wrote</u> about nature. |
| This new <u>approach</u> | <u>was</u> extraordinary. |

**8.4 Compound Subjects and Predicates** A compound subject consists of two or more subjects that share the same verb. They are typically joined by the coordinating conjunction *and* or *or.*

**EXAMPLE:** <u>Short story writers and poets</u> will read from their work.

A compound predicate consists of two or more predicates that share the same subject. They, too, are usually joined by the coordinating conjunction *and, but,* or *or.*

**EXAMPLE:** We <u>listened to the poets and discussed their work.</u>

**8.5 Subjects and Predicates in Questions** In many interrogative sentences, the subject may appear after the verb or between parts of a verb phrase.

**INTERROGATIVE:** <u>Was</u> the reading very interesting?
**INTERROGATIVE:** Why <u>were</u> those particular writers <u>invited</u>?

**GRAMMAR PRACTICE ANSWERS**

1. <u>Katherine Anne Porter</u> <u>published only six stories in her first collection</u>.
2. <u>"The Jilting of Granny Weatherall"</u> <u>was one of the six</u>.
3. <u>This story about a woman on her deathbed</u> <u>has been reprinted often</u>.
4. <u>Why is</u> <u>the main character</u> <u>called "Granny" rather than "Grandmother"?</u>
5. <u>Have</u> <u>you</u> <u>analyzed the symbolic meaning of her last name?</u>
6. <u>Both George and John</u> <u>probably died before Mrs. Weatherall.</u>
7. <u>There are</u> <u>memories of a former suitor that torment the dying woman.</u>
8. <u>The imagination of Katherine Anne Porter</u> <u>is evident in this portrait of an aged woman.</u>
9. <u>Five novelettes, three volumes of short stories, and only one novel</u> <u>comprise all of Miss Porter's works.</u>
10. <u>Her reputation</u> <u>is based on quality, not quantity.</u>

**8.6 Subjects and Predicates in Imperative Sentences** Imperative sentences give commands, requests, or directions. The subject of an imperative sentence is the person spoken to, or *you*. While it is not stated, it is understood to be *you*.

> **EXAMPLE:** *(You) Please tell me what you're thinking.*

**8.7 Subjects in Sentences That Begin with There and Here** When a sentence begins with *there* or *here*, the subject usually follows the verb. Remember that *there* and *here* are never the subjects of a sentence. The simple subjects in the example sentences are underlined.

> **EXAMPLES**
> *Here is the <u>solution</u> to the mystery.*
> *There is no <u>time</u> to waste now.*
> *There were too many <u>passengers</u> on the boat.*

---

**GRAMMAR PRACTICE**

Copy each of the following sentences. Then draw one line under the complete subject and two lines under the complete predicate.

1. Katherine Anne Porter published only six stories in her first collection.
2. "The Jilting of Granny Weatherall" was one of the six.
3. This story about a woman on her deathbed has been reprinted often.
4. Why is the main character called "Granny" rather than "Grandmother"?
5. Have you analyzed the symbolic meaning of her last name?
6. Both George and John probably died before Mrs. Weatherall.
7. There are memories of a former suitor that torment the dying woman.
8. The imagination of Katherine Anne Porter is evident in this portrait of an aged woman.
9. Five novelettes, three volumes of short stories, and only one novel comprise all of Miss Porter's works.
10. Her reputation is based on quality, not quantity.

**8.8 Complements** A complement is a word or group of words that completes the meaning of the sentence. Some sentences contain only a subject and a verb. Most sentences, however, require additional words placed after the verb to complete the meaning of the sentence. There are three kinds of complements: **direct objects, indirect objects,** and **subject complements.**

**Direct objects** are words or word groups that receive the action of action verbs. A direct object answers the question *what?* or *whom?* In the examples that follow, the direct objects are underlined.

> **EXAMPLES**
> *The students asked many <u>questions</u>.*
> (asked what?)
>
> *The teacher quickly answered <u>them</u>.*
> (answered what?)
>
> *The school accepted <u>girls and boys</u>.*
> (accepted whom?)

**Indirect objects** tell *to* or *for whom* or *what* the action of the verb is performed. Indirect objects come before direct objects. In the examples that follow, the indirect objects are underlined.

> **EXAMPLES**
> *My sister usually gave <u>her friends</u> good advice.* (gave to whom?)
>
> *Her brother sent the <u>post office</u> a heavy package.* (sent to what?)
>
> *His kind grandfather mailed <u>him</u> a new tie.* (mailed to whom?)

**Subject complements** come after linking verbs and identify or describe the subject. Subject complements that name or identify the subject of the sentence are called **predicate nominatives.** These include **predicate nouns** and **predicate pronouns.** In the examples that follow, the subject complements are underlined.

> **EXAMPLES**
> *My friends are very hard <u>workers</u>.*
> *The best writer in the class is <u>she</u>.*

Other subject complements describe the subject of the sentence. These are called **predicate adjectives.**

**EXAMPLE:** *The pianist appeared very energetic.*

Write all of the complements in the following sentences, and label them as direct objects, indirect objects, predicate nouns, or predicate adjectives.

1. In "Armistice," by Bernard Malamud, Morris had seen terrible persecution in Russia.

2. Morris felt sympathetic toward others of his race.

3. Because of his childhood memories, Morris feared the Nazis.

4. Seeing his father's anxiety, Leonard became concerned.

5. Gus delivered Morris delicatessen meats.

6. Delighted with military power, Gus was a Nazi sympathizer.

7. Laughing, Gus asked Morris questions about the German armies in France.

8. The main characters in Malamud's story create an armistice at the end.

9. Their truce is not permanent, however.

10. In spite of what Gus imagines, his delivery truck is not really a German tank.

## ❾ Phrases

*A phrase is a group of related words that does not have a subject and predicate and functions in a sentence as a single part of speech.*

**9.1** *Prepositional Phrases* A prepositional phrase is a phrase that consists of a preposition, its object, and any modifiers of the object. Prepositional phrases that modify nouns or pronouns are called **adjective phrases.** Prepositional phrases that modify a verb, an adjective, or another adverb are **adverb phrases.**

**ADJECTIVE PHRASE:** *The central character of the story is a wicked villain.*

**ADVERB PHRASE:** *He reveals his nature in the first scene.*

**9.2** *Appositives and Appositive Phrases* An appositive is a noun or pronoun that usually comes directly after another noun or pronoun and identifies or provides further information about that word. An appositive phrase includes the appositive and all its modifiers. In the following examples, the appositive phrases are underlined.

**EXAMPLES**

*We were discussing Edward Hopper, the painter.*

*Margaret Fuller, a well-known feminist, edited The Dial.*

Occasionally, an appositive phrase may precede the noun it tells about.

**EXAMPLE:** *A well-known feminist, Margaret Fuller edited The Dial.*

## ❿ Verbals and Verbal Phrases

*A verbal is a verb form that is used as a noun, an adjective, or an adverb. A verbal phrase consists of a verbal, all its modifiers, and all its complements. There are three kinds of verbals: infinitives, participles, and gerunds.*

**10.1** *Infinitives and Infinitive Phrases* An infinitive is a verb form that usually begins with *to* and functions as a noun, adjective, or adverb. The infinitive and its modifiers constitute an infinitive phrase. The examples that follow show several uses of infinitives and infinitive phrases. Each infinitive phrase is underlined.

**NOUN:** *To know her is my only desire.* (subject)

*I'm planning to walk with you.* (direct object)

*Her goal was to promote women's rights.* (predicate nominative)

**ADJECTIVE:** *We saw his need to be loved.* (adjective modifying *need*)

**ADVERB:** *She wrote to voice her opinions.* (adverb modifying *wrote*)

**GRAMMAR PRACTICE ANSWERS**

1. persecution—direct object
2. sympathetic—predicate adjective
3. Nazis—direct object
4. concerned—predicate adjective
5. Morris—indirect object
   meats—direct object
6. sympathizer—predicate noun
7. Morris—indirect object
   questions—direct object
8. armistice—direct object
9. permanent—predicate adjective
10. tank—predicate noun

Like verbs themselves, infinitives can take objects (*her* in the first noun example), be made passive (*to be loved* in the adjective example), and take modifiers (*with you* in the adverb example).

Because *to*, the sign of the infinitive, precedes infinitives, it is usually easy to recognize them. However, sometimes *to* may be omitted.

> **EXAMPLE:** *Let no one dare [to] <u>enter this shrine</u>.*

### 10.2 Participles and Participial Phrases

A participle is a verb form that functions as an adjective. Like adjectives, participles modify nouns and pronouns. Most participles use the present participle form, ending in *-ing*, or the past participle form, ending in *-ed* or *-en*. In the examples below, the participles are underlined.

> **MODIFYING A NOUN:** *The <u>dying</u> man had a smile on his face.*
> **MODIFYING A PRONOUN:** *<u>Frustrated</u>, everyone abandoned the cause.*

**Participial phrases** are participles with all their modifiers and complements.

> **MODIFYING A NOUN:** *The dogs <u>searching for survivors</u> are well trained.*
> **MODIFYING A PRONOUN:** *<u>Having approved your proposal</u>, we are ready to act.*

### 10.3 Dangling and Misplaced Participles

A participle or participial phrase should be placed as close as possible to the word that it modifies. Otherwise the meaning of the sentence may not be clear.

> **MISPLACED:** *The boys were looking for squirrels <u>searching the trees</u>.*
> **CLEARER:** *The boys <u>searching the trees</u> were looking for squirrels.*

A participle or participial phrase that does not clearly modify anything in a sentence is called a **dangling participle.** A dangling participle causes confusion because it appears to modify a word that it cannot sensibly modify.

Correct a dangling participle by providing a word for the participle to modify.

> **CONFUSING:** *Running like the wind, my hat fell off.* (The hat wasn't running.)
> **CLEARER:** *Running like the wind, I lost my hat.*

### 10.4 Gerunds and Gerund Phrases

A gerund is a verb form ending in *-ing* that functions as a noun. Gerunds may perform any function nouns perform.

> **SUBJECT:** *<u>Running</u> is my favorite pastime.*
> **DIRECT OBJECT:** *I truly love <u>running</u>.*
> **SUBJECT COMPLEMENT:** *My deepest passion is <u>running</u>.*
> **OBJECT OF PREPOSITION:** *Her love of <u>running</u> keeps her strong.*

**Gerund phrases** are gerunds with all their modifiers and complements. The gerund phrases are underlined in the following examples.

> **SUBJECT:** *<u>Wishing on a star</u> never got me far.*
> **OBJECT OF PREPOSITION:** *I will finish before <u>leaving the office</u>.*
> **APPOSITIVE:** *Her avocation, <u>flying airplanes</u>, finally led to full-time employment.*

---

### GRAMMAR PRACTICE

Identify the underlined phrases as appositive phrases, infinitive phrases, participial phrases, or gerund phrases.

1. In "The Masque of the Red Death," Poe uses allegory, <u>a device for representing abstract qualities.</u>
2. <u>To escape the plague,</u> Prince Prospero seals himself and his courtiers in a walled abbey.
3. <u>Feeling secure from the Red Death,</u> Prospero holds a lavish masquerade ball.
4. Every hour he heard the chimes <u>clanging mournfully.</u>
5. There suddenly appeared in the last room a masked figure, <u>the Red Death in a ghastly shroud.</u>
6. The Prince unsheathed his dagger <u>to kill the figure.</u>
7. <u>Killing the apparition</u> was impossible.

---

**GRAMMAR PRACTICE ANSWERS**

1. appositive phrase
2. infinitive phrase
3. participial phrase
4. participial phrase
5. appositive phrase
6. infinitive phrase
7. gerund phrase

# ⑪ Clauses

*A clause is a group of words that contains a subject and a verb. There are two kinds of clauses: independent clauses and subordinate clauses.*

## 11.1 *Independent and Subordinate Clauses*

An independent clause can stand alone as a sentence, as the word *independent* suggests.

**INDEPENDENT CLAUSE:** *Robert Hayden admired Frederick Douglass.*

A sentence may contain more than one independent clause.

**EXAMPLE:** *Robert Hayden admired Frederick Douglass, and he expressed his admiration in a poem.*

In the example above, the coordinating conjunction *and* joins the two independent clauses.

A subordinate clause cannot stand alone as a sentence. It is subordinate to, or dependent on, the main clause.

**EXAMPLE:** *Hayden did extensive research on Douglass before he wrote his poem.*

*Before he wrote his poem* depends on the independent clause. It cannot stand by itself.

## 11.2 *Adjective Clauses*

An adjective clause is a subordinate clause used as an adjective. It usually follows the noun or pronoun it modifies.

**EXAMPLE:** *The research that he did was very useful.*

Adjective clauses are typically introduced by the relative pronouns *who, whom, whose, which,* and *that* (see Relative Pronouns, page 1309). In the examples that follow, the adjective clauses are underlined.

**EXAMPLES**
*The autobiographer whom I liked best was Frederick Douglass.*

*He was a man who was determined to find freedom.*

*I read novels that let me escape from daily life.*

**WATCH OUT!** The relative pronouns *whom, which,* and *that* may sometimes be omitted when they are objects of their own clauses.

**EXAMPLE:** *The autobiographer [whom] I liked best was Frederick Douglass.*

## 11.3 *Adverb Clauses*

An adverb clause is a subordinate clause that is used as an adverb to modify a verb, an adjective, or another adverb. It is introduced by a subordinating conjunction (see Subordinating Conjunctions, page 1315).

Adverb clauses typically occur at the beginning or end of sentences. The clauses are underlined in these examples.

**MODIFYING A VERB:** *When we need you, we will call.*

**MODIFYING AN ADVERB:** *I'll stay here where there is shelter from the rain.*

**MODIFYING AN ADJECTIVE:** *Roman felt good when he finished his essay.*

## 11.4 *Noun Clauses*

A noun clause is a subordinate clause that is used in a sentence as a noun. A noun clause may be used as a subject, a direct object, an indirect object, a predicate nominative, or an object of a preposition. Noun clauses are often introduced by pronouns such as *that, what, who, whoever, which,* and *whose,* and by subordinating conjunctions, such as *how, when, where, why,* and *whether.* (See Subordinating Conjunctions, page 1315.)

**USAGE TIP** Because the same words may introduce adjective and noun clauses, you need to consider how the clause functions within its sentence.

To determine if a clause is a noun clause, try substituting *something* or *someone* for the clause. If you can do it, it is probably a noun clause.

**EXAMPLES:** *I know whose woods these are.* ("I know *something.*" The clause is a noun clause, direct object of the verb *know.*)

*Give a copy to whoever wants one.* ("Give a copy to *someone.*" The clause is a noun clause, object of the preposition *to.*)

**GRAMMAR PRACTICE ANSWERS**
1. noun clause
2. adverb clause
3. adjective clause
4. noun clause
5. adverb clause

Identify each underlined clause as an adjective clause, an adverb clause, or a noun clause.

1. Frederick Douglass's story illustrates <u>that a man can risk everything to be free.</u>
2. <u>When the slaves were working in the fields,</u> Covey often would sneak up on them.
3. Any man <u>who brutalizes others</u> is himself a brute.
4. Do you believe <u>that a slave breaker could be so mean?</u>
5. The institution of slavery brutalized slaves and masters <u>because it was so inhumane.</u>

## ⑫ The Structure of Sentences

*When classified by their structure, there are four kinds of sentences: simple, compound, complex, and compound-complex.*

**12.1 Simple Sentences** A simple sentence is a sentence that has one independent clause and no subordinate clauses. The fact that such sentences are called "simple" does not mean that they are uncomplicated. Various parts of simple sentences may be compound, and they may contain grammatical structures such as appositives and verbals.

**EXAMPLES**
*Ambrose Bierce and Stephen Crane, two great American writers, both wrote during the latter half of the 19th century.* (compound subject and an appositive)

*Crane, best known for writing fiction, also wrote great poetry.* (participial phrase containing a gerund phrase)

**12.2 Compound Sentences** A compound sentence has two or more independent clauses. The clauses are joined together with a comma and a coordinating conjunction (*and, but, or, nor, yet, for, so*), a semicolon, or a conjunctive adverb with a semicolon. Like simple sentences, compound sentences do not contain any dependent clauses.

**EXAMPLES**
*Walt Whitman was a great poet, yet he made very little money from his writing.*

*Emily Dickinson lived a relatively quiet life; however, that did not prevent her from writing great poems.*

**WATCH OUT!** Do not confuse compound sentences with simple sentences that have compound parts.

**EXAMPLE:** *A subcommittee drafted a document and immediately presented it to the entire group.* (here *and* signals a compound predicate, not a compound sentence)

**12.3 Complex Sentences** A complex sentence has one independent clause and one or more subordinate clauses. Each subordinate clause can be used as a noun or as a modifier. If it is used as a modifier, a subordinate clause usually modifies a word in the main clause and the main clause can stand alone. However, when a subordinate clause is a noun clause, it is a part of the independent clause; the two cannot be separated.

**MODIFIER:** *One should not complain, <u>unless she or he has a better solution.</u>*

**NOUN CLAUSE:** *We sketched pictures of <u>whomever we wished.</u>* (noun clause is the object of the preposition *of* and cannot be separated from the rest of the sentence)

**12.4 Compound-Complex Sentences** A compound-complex sentence has two or more independent clauses and one or more subordinate clauses. Compound-complex sentences are, simply, both compound and complex. If you start with a compound sentence, all you need to do to form a compound-complex sentence is add a subordinate clause.

**COMPOUND:** *All the students knew the answer, yet they were too shy to volunteer.*

**COMPOUND-COMPLEX:** *All the students knew the answer that their teacher expected, yet they were too shy to volunteer.*

## GRAMMAR PRACTICE

Tell whether each sentence is a simple sentence, a compound sentence, a complex sentence, or a compound-complex sentence.

1. Douglass first settled in Massachusetts with his wife, who was free.

2. He changed his original name, Frederick Bailey, to Frederick Douglass in order to avoid pursuit.

3. He taught himself to read and write, but his speaking skills, which made him famous, seemed to be innate.

4. The *Narrative of the Life of Frederick Douglass* contained a preface by William Lloyd Garrison and a prefatory letter by Wendell Phillips.

5. Garrison and Phillips were well known, and their names helped to sell the book.

---

## ⑬ Writing Complete Sentences

*A sentence is a group of words that expresses a complete thought. In writing that you wish to share with a reader, try to avoid both sentence fragments and run-on sentences.*

### 13.1 *Correcting Fragments*

A sentence fragment is a group of words that is only part of a sentence. It does not express a complete thought and may be confusing to the reader or the listener. A sentence fragment may be lacking a subject, a predicate, or both.

**FRAGMENT:** *waited for the boat to arrive* (no subject)
**CORRECTED:** *We waited for the boat to arrive.*
**FRAGMENT:** *people of various races, ages, and creeds* (no predicate)
**CORRECTED:** *People of various races, ages, and creeds gathered together.*
**FRAGMENT:** *near the old cottage* (neither subject nor predicate)
**CORRECTED:** *The burial ground is near the old cottage.*

In your own writing, fragments are usually the result of haste or incorrect punctuation. Sometimes fixing a fragment will be a matter of attaching it to a preceding or following sentence.

**FRAGMENT:** *We saw the two girls. Waiting for the bus to arrive.*
**CORRECTED:** *We saw the two girls waiting for the bus to arrive.*
**FRAGMENT:** *Newspapers appeal to a wide audience. Including people of various races, ages, and creeds.*
**CORRECTED:** *Newspapers appeal to a wide audience, including people of various races, ages, and creeds.*

### 13.2 *Correcting Run-on Sentences*

A run-on sentence is made up of two or more sentences written as though they were one. Some run-ons have no punctuation within them. Others may use only a comma where a conjunction or stronger punctuation is necessary. Use your judgment in correcting run-on sentences, as you have choices. You can make two sentences if the thoughts are not closely connected. If the thoughts are closely related, you can keep the run-on as one sentence by adding a semicolon or a conjunction.

**RUN-ON:** *We found a place by a small pond for the picnic it is three miles from the village.*
**MAKE TWO SENTENCES:** *We found a place by a small pond for the picnic. It is three miles from the village.*
**RUN-ON:** *We found a place by a small pond for the picnic it was perfect.*
**USE A SEMICOLON:** *We found a place by a small pond for the picnic; it was perfect.*
**ADD A CONJUNCTION:** *We found a place by a small pond for the picnic, and it was perfect.*

**WATCH OUT!** When you add a conjunction, make sure you use appropriate punctuation before it: a comma for a coordinating conjunction, a semicolon for a conjunctive adverb. (See Conjunctions, page 1315.) A very common mistake is to use a comma instead of a conjunction or an end mark. This error is called a **comma splice**.

**INCORRECT:** *He finished the apprenticeship, then he left the village.*
**CORRECT:** *He finished the apprenticeship, and then he left the village.*

## GRAMMAR PRACTICE ANSWERS

1. complex sentence
2. simple sentence
3. compound-complex sentence
4. simple sentence
5. compound sentence

**GRAMMAR PRACTICE ANSWERS**

The narrator in Charlotte Perkins Gilman's story "The Yellow Wallpaper" expects that her husband will laugh at her. That's an odd response, in my opinion. She could have lived more happily if the relationship between her and her husband were an equal partnership. We can acknowledge that men and women may be different in some ways without believing that they are as different as this story suggests. The male character acts practical and "strong"; the female character acts nervous and weak.

---

Rewrite the following paragraph, correcting all fragments and run-ons.

The narrator in Charlotte Perkins Gilman's story "The Yellow Wallpaper" expects that her husband will laugh at her, that's an odd response, in my opinion. She could have lived more happily. If the relationship between her and her husband were an equal partnership. We can acknowledge that men and women may be different in some ways. Without believing that they are as different as this story suggests. The male character acts practical and "strong," the female character acts nervous and weak.

## 14 Subject-Verb Agreement

*The subject and verb of a sentence must agree in number. Agreement means that when the subject is singular, the verb must be singular; when the subject is plural, the verb must be plural.*

**14.1 Basic Agreement** Fortunately, agreement between subject and verb in English is simple. Most verbs show the difference between singular and plural only in the third person present tense. The present tense of the third person singular ends in -s.

| Present Tense Verb Forms | |
|---|---|
| **Singular** | **Plural** |
| I sleep | we sleep |
| you sleep | you sleep |
| she, he, it sleeps | they sleep |

**14.2 Agreement with Be** The verb *be* presents special problems in agreement because this verb does not follow the usual verb patterns.

| Forms of *Be* | | | |
|---|---|---|---|
| **Present Tense** | | **Past Tense** | |
| **Singular** | **Plural** | **Singular** | **Plural** |
| I am | we are | I was | we were |
| you are | you are | you were | you were |
| she, he, it is | they are | she, he, it was | they were |

**14.3 Words Between Subject and Verb** A verb agrees only with its subject. When words come between a subject and its verb, ignore them when considering proper agreement. Identify the subject and make sure the verb agrees with it.

**EXAMPLES**
*A story in the newspapers tells about the 1890s.*

*Dad as well as Mom reads the paper daily.*

**14.4 Agreement with Compound Subjects** Use a plural verb with most compound subjects joined by the word *and*.

**EXAMPLE:** *My father and his friends (they) read the paper daily.*

You could substitute the plural pronoun *they* for *my father and his friends*. This shows that you need a plural verb.

If the compound subject is thought of as a unit, you use the singular verb. Test this by substituting the singular pronoun *it*.

**EXAMPLE:** *Peanut butter and jelly [it] is my brother's favorite sandwich.*

Use a singular verb with a compound subject that is preceded by *each, every,* or *many a*.

**EXAMPLE:** *Each novel and short story seems grounded in personal experience.*

With *or, nor,* and the correlative conjunctions *either . . . or* and *neither . . . nor*, make the verb agree with the noun or pronoun nearest the verb.

**EXAMPLES**
*Cookies or ice cream is my favorite dessert.*

*Either Cheryl or her friends are being invited.*

*Neither ice storms nor snow is predicted today.*

**14.5 Personal Pronouns as Subjects** When using a personal pronoun as a subject, make sure to match it with the correct form of the verb *be*. (See the chart in 14.2.) Note especially that the pronoun *you* takes the verbs *are* and *were*, regardless of whether it is referring to the singular *you* or to the plural *you*.

**WATCH OUT!** *You is* and *you was* are nonstandard forms and should be avoided in writing and speaking. *We was* and *they was* are also forms to be avoided.

**INCORRECT:** *You was wrong that time. They was friends at one time.*

**CORRECT:** *You were wrong that time. They were friends at one time.*

### 14.6 *Indefinite Pronouns as Subjects*

Some indefinite pronouns are always singular; some are always plural. Others may be either singular or plural.

| Singular Indefinite Pronouns | | | |
|---|---|---|---|
| another | either | neither | other |
| anybody | everybody | nobody | somebody |
| anyone | everyone | no one | someone |
| anything | everything | nothing | something |
| each | much | one | |

**EXAMPLES**

*Each* of the writers *was given* an award.
*Somebody* in the room upstairs *is sleeping*.

The indefinite pronouns that are always plural include *both, few, many*, and *several*. These take plural verbs.

**EXAMPLES**

*Many* of the books in our library *are* not in circulation.

*Few have been returned* recently.

Still other indefinite pronouns may be either singular or plural.

| Singular or Plural Indefinite Pronouns | | | |
|---|---|---|---|
| all | enough | most | plenty |
| any | more | none | some |

The number of the indefinite pronouns *any* and *none* depends on the intended meaning.

**EXAMPLES**

*Any* of these topics *has* potential for a good article. (any one topic)

*Any* of these topics *have* potential for a good article. (all of the many topics)

The indefinite pronouns *all, some, more, most,* and *none* are singular when they refer to a quantity or part of something. They are plural when they refer to a number of individual things. Context will usually give a clue.

**EXAMPLES**

*All of the flour is gone.* (referring to a quantity)

*All of the flowers are gone.* (referring to individual items)

### 14.7 *Inverted Sentences*

Problems in agreement often occur in inverted sentences beginning with *here* or *there*; in questions beginning with *why, where*, and *what*; and in inverted sentences beginning with a phrase. Identify the subject—wherever it is—before deciding on the verb.

**EXAMPLES**

*There clearly are far too many cooks in this kitchen.*

*What is the correct ingredient for this stew?*

*Far from the embroiled cooks stands the master chef.*

---

**GRAMMAR PRACTICE**

Locate the subject in each clause in the sentences below. Then choose the correct verb.

1. Many poets have written great poetry, but few (is/are) as talented as Emily Dickinson.

2. There (is/are) many lines in her work that all of her readers (treasures/treasure).

3. Some of her readers (appreciates/appreciate) her use of dashes, while others (finds/find) it confusing.

4. There (is/are) no question that she used unusual punctuation.

5. Each of the poems (presents/present) an idea to think about.

6. My favorite poems (was/were) "Much Madness is divinest Sense" and "Success is counted sweetest."

7. Neither of those poems (is/are) Felicia's favorite, though.

8. What (is/are) the dominant vowel sound in the last four lines of "Much Madness is divinest Sense"?

9. The consonant that prevails in the same poem (seems/seem) to be *s.*

10. I can't decide whether the sound or the ideas of the poems (is/are) more striking.

**GRAMMAR PRACTICE ANSWERS**
1. few > are
2. lines > are
   all > treasure
3. some > appreciate
   others > find
4. question > is
5. each > presents
6. poems > were
7. neither > is
8. sound > is
9. consonant > seems
10. sound or ideas > are

**GRAMMAR PRACTICE ANSWERS**

1. doesn't
2. has
3. were
4. don't
5. compares
6. wasn't
7. have
8. is
9. don't
10. seem

### 14.8 Sentences with Predicate Nominatives

When a predicate nominative serves as a complement in a sentence, use a verb that agrees with the subject, not the complement.

**EXAMPLES**

*The poems of Emily Dickinson are a portrait of a free spirit.* (*poems* is the subject—not *portrait*—and it takes the plural verb *are.*)

*A portrait of a free spirit is the poems of Emily Dickinson.* (Here, *portrait* is the subject, not the predicate nominative *poems.*)

### 14.9 Don't *and* Doesn't *as Auxiliary Verbs*

The auxiliary verb *doesn't* is used with singular subjects and with the personal pronouns *she, he*, and *it*. The auxiliary verb *don't* is used with plural subjects and with the personal pronouns *I, we, you*, and *they*.

**SINGULAR**

*Her <u>poetry doesn't</u> always rhyme precisely.*
*<u>She doesn't</u> always use rhyme in a stanza.*

**PLURAL**

*Her <u>lines don't</u> always rhyme exactly.*
*<u>They don't</u> always use regular rhythm either.*

### 14.10 Collective Nouns as Subjects

Collective nouns are singular nouns that name a group of persons or things. *Team*, for example, is the collective name of a group of individuals. A collective noun takes a singular verb when the group acts as a single unit. It takes a plural verb when the members of the group act separately.

**EXAMPLES**

*Our team usually wins.* (the team as a whole wins)

*Our team vote differently on most issues.* (the individual members vote)

### 14.11 Relative Pronouns as Subjects

When a relative pronoun is used as a subject of its clause—*who, which,* and *that* can serve as subjects—the verb of the clause must agree in number with the antecedent of the pronoun.

**SINGULAR**: *I didn't read the chapter on modern poets that was assigned.*

The antecedent of the relative pronoun *that* is the singular noun *chapter;* therefore, *that* is singular and must take the singular verb *was.*

**PLURAL**: *Emily Dickinson and Walt Whitman, who were 19th-century poets, are important poets in American literature.*

The antecedent of the relative pronoun *who* is the plural compound subject *Emily Dickinson and Walt Whitman.* Therefore, *who* is plural, and it takes the plural verb *were.*

---

**GRAMMAR PRACTICE**

Choose the correct verb for each of the following sentences.

1. Dickinson's daily life (don't/doesn't) seem to have been very exciting.
2. Her inner life, however, was a source of creativity that (have/has) amazed generations of readers.
3. Only a handful of her poems (were/was) published during her lifetime.
4. One wonders why more people (don't/doesn't) read her poetry today.
5. The speaker of one of the poems (compare/compares) hope to a bird.
6. A volume of her poems (weren't/wasn't) published until after her death.
7. A group of us (have/has) voted for our favorite Dickinson poem.
8. The poem about death as a gentleman caller, which we read two weeks ago, (are/is) my favorite.
9. We (don't/doesn't) agree that much madness is necessarily divinest sense.
10. Dickinson's letters to the world (seem/seems) largely to have gone unanswered.

# Quick Reference: Punctuation

| Punctuation | Function | Examples |
|---|---|---|
| **End Marks**<br>period,<br>question mark,<br>exclamation point | to end sentences | Fitzgerald wrote *The Great Gatsby*.<br>Was it the best novel of this century?<br>What a tremendous novel it is! |
| | initials and other abbreviations | Dr. Margaret Mead, R. E. Lee, General Motors Inc., P.M., A.D., ft., Blvd., Rd. |
| | items in outlines | I. Volcanoes<br>   A. Central-vent<br>      1. Shield |
| | **exception:** P.O. states | NE (Nebraska), NV (Nevada) |
| **Commas** | before conjunction in compound sentence | I have never disliked poetry, but now I really love it. |
| | items in a series | She is brave, loyal, and kind.<br>The slow, easy route is best. |
| | words of address | America, I love you.<br>We think of you often, Dad. |
| | parenthetical expressions | Well, just suppose that we can't?<br>Hard workers, as you know, don't quit.<br>I'm not a quitter, believe me. |
| | introductory phrases and clauses | In the beginning of the day, I feel fresh.<br>While she was out, I was here.<br>Having finished my chores, I went out. |
| | nonessential phrases and clauses | Ed Pawn, captain of the chess team, won.<br>Ed Pawn, who is the captain, won.<br>The two leading runners, sprinting toward the finish line, ended in a tie. |
| | in dates and addresses | Send it by July 15, 2001,<br>to Mercer Corporation, 12 Main Street, Minneapolis, Minnesota. |
| | in letter parts | Dear Jim,  Sincerely yours, |
| | for clarity, or to avoid confusion | By noon, time had run out.<br>What the minister does, does matter.<br>While cooking, Jim burned his hand. |
| **Semicolons** | in compound sentences that are not joined by coordinators *and,* etc. | The last shall be first; the first shall be last. I read the Bible; however, I have not memorized it. |
| | with items in series that contain commas | We invited my sister, Jan; her friend, Don; my uncle Jack; and Mary Dodd. |
| | in compound sentences that contain commas | After I ran out of money, I called my parents; but only my sister was home, unfortunately. |

| Punctuation | Function | Examples |
|---|---|---|
| **Colons** | to introduce lists | **Correct:** Those we wrote were the following: Dana, John, and Will. **Incorrect:** Those we wrote were: Dana, John, and Will. |
| | before a long quotation | Thomas Jefferson wrote: "We the people of the United States, in order to form a more perfect union . . . ." |
| | after the salutation of a business letter | Dear Ms. Williams: Dear Senator Willey: |
| | with certain numbers | 1:28 P.M., Genesis 2:5 |
| **Dashes** | to indicate an abrupt break in thought | I was thinking of my mother—who is arriving tomorrow—just as you walked in. |
| **Parentheses** | to enclose less important material | Our holiday (over the July 4 weekend) ended too soon. New York City (Have you ever been there?) really is a wonderful town. |
| **Hyphens** | with a compound adjective before nouns | A rectangle is a four-sided figure. |
| | in compounds with *all-, ex-, self-, -elect* | He's an ex-mayor but all-American. Our senator-elect is too self-important. |
| | in compound numbers (to *ninety-nine*) | Today, I turn twenty-one. |
| | in fractions used as adjectives | My cup is one-third full. |
| | between prefixes and words beginning with capital letters | Life may have seemed simpler in pre-Civil War days. It's very chilly for mid-June. |
| | when dividing words at the end of a line | Did you know that school segrega-tion has been illegal since 1954? |
| **Apostrophes** | to form possessives of nouns and indefinite pronouns | my friend's book, my friends' book, anyone's guess, somebody else's problem |
| | for omitted letters in contractions or numbers in dates | don't (omitted **o**); he'd (omitted **woul**) the class of '99 (omitted **19**) |
| | to form plurals of letters and numbers | I had two A's and no 2's on my report card. |
| **Quotation Marks** | to set off a speaker's exact words | Sara said, "I'm finally ready." "I'm ready," Sara said, "finally." Did Sara say, "I'm ready"? Sara said, "I'm ready!" |
| | for titles of stories, short poems, essays, songs, book chapters | I liked Oates's "Hostage," Steinem's "Sisterhood," and Plath's "Mirror." Chapter II is titled "Our Gang's Dark Oath." |
| **Ellipses** | for material omitted from a quotation | "We the people . . . in order to form a more perfect union . . . ." |
| **Italics** | for titles of books, plays, magazines, long poems, operas, films, TV series, recordings, names of ships | *The Scarlet Letter, The Crucible, Time, The Death of the Hired Man, West Side Story, Citizen Kane, The X-Files, The Spirit of St. Louis, The Best of Frank Sinatra, Lusitania* |

# Quick Reference: Capitalization

| Category/Rule | Examples |
|---|---|
| **People and Titles** | |
| Names and initials of people | Emily Dickinson, T. S. Eliot |
| Titles used with or in place of names | Professor Holmes, Senator Long, The President has arrived. |
| Deities and members of religious groups | Jesus, Allah, the Buddha, Zeus, Baptists, Roman Catholics |
| Names of ethnic and national groups | Hispanics, Jews, African Americans |
| **Geographical Names** | |
| Cities, states, countries, continents | New York, Maine, Haiti, Africa |
| Regions, bodies of water, mountains | the South, Lake Erie, Mount Katadin |
| Geographic features, parks | Great Plains, Everglades, Yellowstone |
| Streets and roads, planets | 55 East Ninety-fifth Street, Maple Lane, Venus, Jupiter |
| **Organizations and Events** | |
| Companies, organizations, teams | General Motors, Lions Club, Utah Jazz |
| Buildings, bridges, monuments | World Trade Towers, Golden Gate Bridge, Lincoln Memorial |
| Documents, awards | the Constitution, Nobel Prize |
| Special named events | Super Bowl, World Series |
| Governmental bodies, historical periods and events | the Supreme Court, the U.S. Senate, Harlem Renaissance, World War II |
| Days and months, holidays | Friday, May, Easter, Memorial Day |
| Specific cars, boats, trains, planes | Mustang, *Titanic*, *California Zephyr* |
| **Proper Adjectives** | |
| Adjectives formed from proper nouns | American League, French cooking, Emersonian period, Atlantic coast |
| **First Words and the Pronoun *I*** | |
| The first word in a sentence or quote | This is it. He said, "Let's go." |
| Complete sentence in parentheses | (Consult the previous chapter.) |
| Salutation and closing of letters | Dear Madam, Very truly yours, |
| First lines of most poetry<br>The personal pronoun *I* | Then am I<br>A happy fly<br>If I live<br>Or if I die. |
| First, last, and all important words in titles | *A Tale of Two Cities*, "The World Is Too Much with Us" |

# Little Rules That Make A Big Difference

## Sentences

**Avoid sentence fragments. Make sure all your sentences express complete thoughts.**

A sentence fragment is a group of words that does not express a grammatically complete thought. It may lack a subject, a predicate, or both. Fragments may be corrected by adding the missing element(s) or by changing the punctuation to make the fragment part of another sentence.

> **FRAGMENT:** *We admire Franklin Roosevelt. A man who prevailed over the serious handicap of polio.*
>
> **COMPLETE:** *We admire Franklin Roosevelt. He was a man who prevailed over the serious handicap of polio.* (adding a subject and a predicate verb)
>
> **COMPLETE:** *We admire Franklin Roosevelt, a man who prevailed over the serious handicap of polio.* (changing the punctuation)

**Avoid run-on sentences. Make sure all clauses in a sentence have the proper punctuation and/or conjunctions between them.**

A run-on sentence consists of two or more sentences written as though they were one or separated only by a comma. Correct run-ons by making two separate sentences, using a semicolon, adding a conjunction, or rewriting the sentence.

> **RUN-ON:** *James Galway is a great musician, he plays the flute.*
>
> **CORRECT:** *James Galway is a great musician. He plays the flute.*
>
> **CORRECT:** *James Galway is a great musician; he plays the flute.*
>
> **CORRECT:** *James Galway, who plays the flute, is a great musician.*

**Use end marks correctly.** Use a period, not a question mark, at the end of an indirect question.

An indirect question is a question that does not use the exact words of the original speaker. Note the difference between the following sentences, and observe that the second sentence ends in a period, not a question mark.

> **DIRECT:** *Lou asked, "What is that?"*
>
> **INDIRECT:** *Lou asked what it was.*

**Do not use quotation marks with indirect quotations within a sentence.**

A direct quotation uses the speaker's exact words. An indirect quotation puts the speaker's words in other words. Compare these sentences:

> **DIRECT:** *Jean said, "I'm going to be up all night writing my essay."* (quotation marks appropriate)
>
> **INDIRECT:** *Jean said that she was going to be up all night writing her essay.* (no quotation marks)

## Phrases

**Place participial and prepositional phrases as close as possible to the words they modify.** Participial and prepositional phrases are modifiers; that is, they tell about some other word in a sentence. To avoid confusion, they should be placed as close as possible to the word that they modify.

> **INCORRECT:** *Tiny microphones are planted by agents called bugs.*
>
> **CORRECT:** *Tiny microphones called bugs are planted by agents.*

**Avoid dangling participles. Make sure a participial phrase does modify a word in the sentence.**

> **INCORRECT:** *Disappointed in love, a hermit's life seemed attractive.* (Who was disappointed?)
>
> **CORRECT:** *Disappointed in love, the man became a hermit.*

## Clauses

**Use commas to set off nonessential adjective clauses.**

Do you need the clause in order to indicate precisely who or what is meant? If not, it is nonessential and should be set off by commas.

> **USE COMMAS:** *Maya Angelou, who is a great role model for youth, spoke at the inauguration.*
>
> **NO COMMAS:** *A poet who is a great role model for youth spoke at the inauguration.*

## Verbs

**Don't use past tense forms with an auxiliary verb or past participle forms without an auxiliary verb. (See Auxiliary Verbs, page 1309.)**

> **INCORRECT:** *I have saw her somewhere before.* (*saw* is past tense and shouldn't be used with *have*)
>
> **CORRECT:** *I have seen her somewhere before.*
>
> **INCORRECT:** *I seen her somewhere before.* (*seen* is a past participle and shouldn't be used without an auxiliary)

**Shift tense only when necessary.**

Usually, when you are writing in present tense, you should stay in present tense; when you are writing in past tense, you should stay in past tense.

> **INCORRECT:** *When Mark Twain tells stories, everybody listened.*
>
> **CORRECT:** *When Mark Twain told stories, everybody listened.*

Sometimes a shift in tense is necessary to show a logical sequence of actions or the relationship of one action to another.

> **CORRECT:** *After he had told his story, everybody went to sleep.*

## Subject-Verb Agreement

**Make sure subjects and verbs agree in number.**

> **INCORRECT:** *The history of civil wars are tragic.*
>
> **CORRECT:** *The history of civil wars is tragic.*
>
> **INCORRECT:** *Robert Frost, like many other poets, experiment with rhyme.*
>
> **CORRECT:** *Robert Frost, like many other poets, experiments with rhyme.*

**Use a singular verb with nouns that look plural but have singular meaning.**

Some nouns that end in *-s* are singular, even though they look plural. Examples are *measles, news, Wales,* and the names ending in *-ics* when they refer to a school subject, science, or general practice.

> **EXAMPLES:** *The United States is a great democracy.*
> *Physics was Albert Einstein's specialty.*

**Use a singular verb with titles.**

> **EXAMPLE:** The House of Seven Gables *was Hawthorne's second novel.*
> *"Revolutionary Dreams" is an ironic poem.*

**Use a singular verb with words of weight, time, and measure.**

> **EXAMPLES:** *Two weeks is the typical length of a vacation.*
> *Five dollars and two cents was the exact cost.*

## Pronouns

**Use personal pronouns correctly in compounds.**

Don't be confused about case when *and* joins a noun and a personal pronoun; the case of the pronoun still depends upon its function.

INCORRECT: *Her and her friends joined a book club.*

CORRECT: *She and her friends joined a book club.*

INCORRECT: *The librarian suggested two good books to John and I.*

CORRECT: *The librarian suggested two good books to John and me.*

INCORRECT: *The library lent John and they some books.*

CORRECT: *The library lent John and them some books.*

Usually, if you remove the noun and *and,* the correct pronoun will be obvious.

### Use *we* and *us* correctly with nouns.

When a noun directly follows *we* or *us,* the case of the pronoun depends upon its function.

INCORRECT: *Us readers really enjoy Frost's poetry.*

CORRECT: *We readers really enjoy Frost's poetry.* (*we* is the subject)

INCORRECT: *The drama coach assigned roles to we students.*

CORRECT: *The drama coach assigned roles to us students.* (*us* is the object of *to*)

### Avoid unclear pronoun reference.

The reference of a pronoun is ambiguous when the reader cannot tell which of two preceding nouns is its antecedent. The reference is indefinite when the idea to which the pronoun refers is only weakly or vaguely expressed.

AMBIGUOUS: *After Cal started tutoring Donny, Daisy worried that he* [who—Cal or Donny?] *wasn't doing what he should.*

CLEARER: *After Cal started tutoring Donny, Daisy worried that Donny wasn't doing what he should.*

INDEFINITE: *Some of our greatest writers have not been recognized as such during their lifetimes, which is a pity.*

CLEARER: *It is a pity that some of our greatest writers have not been recognized as such during their lifetimes.*

### Avoid change of person.

If you are writing in third person—using pronouns such as *she, he, it, they, them, his, her, its*—do not shift to second person—*you.*

INCORRECT: *The feudal laborer had to obey his lord, and you needed to obey the king as well.*

CORRECT: *The feudal laborer had to obey his lord, and he needed to obey the king as well.*

### Use correct pronouns in elliptical comparisons.

An elliptical comparison is a comparison from which words have been omitted. In order to choose the proper pronoun, fill in the missing words. Note the difference below:

EXAMPLES: *I agree with my parents more often than (I agree with) her.*
*I agree with my parents more often than she (agrees with them).*

### Don't confuse pronouns and contractions.

Personal pronouns are made possessive without the use of an apostrophe, as is the relative pronoun *whose.* Whenever you are unsure whether to write *it's* or *its, who's* or *whose,* ask if you mean *it is/has* or *who is/has.* If you do, write the contraction. Do the same for *you're* and *your, they're* and *their,* except that the contraction in this case is for the verb *are.*

### Modifiers

### Avoid double comparisons.

A double comparison is a comparison made twice. In general, if you use *-er* or *-est* on the end of a modifier, you would not also use *more* or *most* in front of it.

INCORRECT: *I like Miller's plays more better than Tennessee Williams's.*

CORRECT: *I like Miller's plays better than Tennessee Williams's.*

INCORRECT: *Hers was the most unkindest remark I have ever heard.*

CORRECT: *Hers was the most unkind remark I have ever heard.*

## Avoid illogical comparisons.

Can you tell what is wrong with the following sentence?

*Plays are more entertaining than any kind of performance art.*

This sentence is difficult to understand. To avoid such illogical comparisons, use *other* when comparing an individual member with the rest of the group.

*Plays are more entertaining than any other kind of performance art.*

To avoid another kind of illogical comparison, use *than* or *as* after the first member in a compound comparison.

**ILLOGICAL:** *Ramon wrote as many good poems if not more than Chidi. (Did Ramón write as many poems or as many good poems?)*

**CLEARER:** *Ramón wrote as many good poems as Chidi, if not more.*

## Avoid misplacing modifiers.

Modifiers of all kinds must be placed as close as possible to the words they modify. If you place them elsewhere, you risk being misunderstood.

**MISPLACED:** *Tourists can discover many famous historical sites walking in downtown Philadelphia.*

**CLEARER:** *Walking in downtown Philadelphia, tourists can discover many famous historical sites.*

---

### Words Not to Capitalize

**Do not capitalize *north, south, east,* and *west* when they are used to tell direction.**

**EXAMPLE:** *Chicago is north and west of Indianapolis.*

**EXAMPLE:** *Did you know that North Carolina and West Virginia are virtually neighboring states?* (North and West are part of the names of the states.)

---

**Do not capitalize *sun* and *moon,* and capitalize *earth* only when it is used with the names of other planets.**

**EXAMPLES:** *The sun and the moon are heavenly bodies in a solar system that includes Mars, Jupiter, and the Earth.*

*We now live on the earth, not in heaven.*

**Do not capitalize the names of seasons.**

**EXAMPLE:** *The summer will soon be over, and we'll return to school in the fall.*

**Do not capitalize the names of most school subjects.**

School subjects are capitalized only when they name a specific course, such as World History I. Otherwise, they are not capitalized.

**EXAMPLE:** *I'm taking physics, social studies, and a foreign language this year.*

Note: English and the names of other languages are always capitalized.

**EXAMPLE:** *Everybody takes English and either Spanish or French.*

---

### GRAMMAR PRACTICE

Rewrite each sentence correctly.

1. my favorite story by Mark Twain
2. The frog wouldn't jump for Smiley, filled with buckshot.
3. Most stories of the Wild West is full of adventure.
4. When Mark Twain publishes his stories, he became famous.
5. His attitude in his autobiography appeals to Rachel and I.
6. This year my hardest subjects are Chemistry, Electronics, and English.
7. Having read most of *Walden,* Thoreau is my favorite writer.
8. Chief Joseph's speech is the most saddest I have read in a long time.
9. *The Crucible* has important ideas for we people today.
10. Throwing a hysterical fit, Judge Hathorne thinks the girls are possessed.

---

### GRAMMAR PRACTICE ANSWERS

1. "From *Life on the Mississippi*" is my favorite story by Mark Twain.
2. Filled with buckshot, the frog wouldn't jump for Smiley.
3. Most stories of the Wild West are full of adventure.
4. When Mark Twain published his stories, he became famous.
5. His attitude in his autobiography appeals to Rachel and me.
6. This year my hardest subjects are chemistry, electronics, and English.
7. Having read most of *Walden,* I have decided that Thoreau is my favorite writer.
8. Chief Joseph's speech is the saddest I have read in a long time.
9. *The Crucible* has important ideas for us people today.
10. Throwing a hysterical fit, the girls make Judge Hathorne think that they are possessed.

# Commonly Confused Words

| | | |
|---|---|---|
| **accept/except** | The verb *accept* means "to receive or believe"; *except* is usually a preposition meaning "excluding." | Everyone except me had read *Beloved*. Toni Morrison accepted the Nobel Prize. |
| **advice/advise** | *Advise* is a verb; *advice* is a noun naming that which an *adviser* gives. | The doctor advised the narrator of "The Yellow Wallpaper" to stay in bed. Did he give her good advice? |
| **affect/effect** | As a verb, *affect* means "to influence." *Effect* as a verb means "to cause." If you want a noun, you will almost always want *effect*. | The Second World War affected the lives of millions. Do wars effect major changes? Their effects are unknown. |
| **all ready/already** | *All ready* is an adjective meaning "fully ready." *Already* is an adverb meaning "before or by this time." | The speaker in Gary Soto's poem is not all ready to run because he is already an American citizen. |
| **allusion/illusion** | An *allusion* is an indirect reference to something. An *illusion* is a false picture or idea. | Writers often make allusions to the Bible. He is under the illusion that he's a genius. |
| **among/between** | *Between* is used when you are speaking of only two things. *Among* is used for three or more. | There is no disagreement between you and me. "Adolescence—III" is among my favorite poems. |
| **bring/take** | *Bring* is used to denote motion toward a speaker or place. *Take* is used to denote motion away from such a person or place. | Bring the books over here, and I will take them to the library. |
| **fewer/less** | *Fewer* refers to the number of separate, countable units. *Less* refers to bulk quantity. | We have less literature and fewer selections in this year's curriculum. |
| **leave/let** | *Leave* means "to allow something to remain behind." *Let* means "to permit." | The librarian will leave some books on display but will not let us borrow any. |
| **lie/lay** | To *lie* is "to rest or recline." It does not take an object. To *lay* always takes an object. | Dogs love to lie in the sun. We always lay some bones next to him. |
| **loose/lose** | *Loose* (lo͞os) means "free, not restrained"; *lose* (lo͞oz) means "to misplace or fail to find." | Who turned the horses loose? I hope we won't lose any of them. |
| **precede/proceed** | *Precede* means "to go or come before." Use *proceed* for other meanings. | "A" precedes "b" in the alphabet. Everyone proceeded to the exit. |
| **than/then** | Use *than* in making comparisons; use *then* on all other occasions. | If you find Steinbeck's writing more vivid than Malamud's, then tell me. |
| **two/too/to** | *Two* is the number. *Too* is an adverb meaning "also" or "very." Use *to* before a verb or as a preposition. | Meg had to go to town, too. We had too much reading to do. Two chapters is too much. |

# Grammar Glossary

This glossary contains various terms you need to understand when you use the Grammar Handbook. Used as a reference source, this glossary will help you explore grammar concepts and the ways they relate to one another.

**A**

**Abbreviation** An abbreviation is a shortened form of a word or word group; it is often made up of initials. (B.C., A.M., *Maj.*)

**Active voice.** *See* **Voice.**

**Adjective** An adjective modifies, or describes, a noun or pronoun. (*happy* camper, she is *small*)

A *predicate adjective* follows a linking verb and describes the subject. (The day seemed *long.*)

A *proper adjective* is formed from a proper noun. (*Jewish* temple, *Alaskan* husky)

The *comparative* form of an adjective compares two things. (*more alert, thicker*)

The *superlative* form of an adjective compares more than two things. (*most abundant, weakest*)

| What Adjectives Tell | Examples |
|---|---|
| How many | *some* writers *much* joy |
| What kind | *grand* plans *wider* streets |
| Which one(s) | *these* flowers *that* star |

**Adjective phrase.** *See* **Phrase.**

**Adverb** An adverb modifies a verb, an adjective, or another adverb. (Clare sang *loudly.*)

The *comparative* form of an adverb compares two actions. (*more generously, faster*)

The *superlative* form of an adverb compares more than two actions. (*most sharply, closest*)

| What Adverbs Tell | Examples |
|---|---|
| How | climb *carefully* chuckle *merrily* |
| When | arrived *late* left *early* |
| Where | climbed *up* moved *away* |
| To what extent | *extremely* upset *hardly* visible |

**Adverb, conjunctive.** *See* **Conjunctive adverb.**

**Adverb phrase.** *See* **Phrase.**

**Agreement** Sentence parts that correspond with one another are said to be in agreement.

In *pronoun-antecedent agreement,* a pronoun and the word it refers to are the same in number, gender, and person. (*Bill* mailed *his* application. The *students* ate *their* lunches.)

In *subject-verb agreement,* the subject and verb in a sentence are the same in number. (A *child cries* for help. *They cry* aloud.)

**Ambiguous reference** An ambiguous reference occurs when a pronoun may refer to more than one word. (Bud asked his brother if *he* had any mail.)

**Antecedent** An antecedent is the noun or pronoun to which a pronoun refers. (If *Adam* forgets *his* raincoat, *he* will be late for school. *She* learned *her* lesson.)

**Appositive** An appositive is a noun or phrase that explains one or more words in a sentence. (Cary Grant, *an Englishman,* spent most of his adult life in America.)

An *essential appositive* is needed to make the sense of a sentence complete. (A comic strip inspired the musical *Annie.*)

A *nonessential appositive* is one that adds information to a sentence but is not necessary to its sense. (O. Henry, *a short-story writer,* spent time in prison.)

**Article** Articles are the special adjectives *a, an,* and *the.* (*the* day, *a* fly)

The *definite article* (the word *the*) is one that refers to a particular thing. (*the* cabin)

An *indefinite article* is used with a noun that is not unique but refers to one of many of its kind. (*a* dish, *an* otter)

**Auxiliary verb.** *See* **Verb.**

**C**

**Clause** A clause is a group of words that contains a verb and its subject. (*they slept*)

An *adjective clause* is a subordinate clause that modifies a noun or pronoun. (Hugh bought the sweater *that he had admired.*)

An *adverb clause* is a subordinate clause used to modify a verb, an adjective, or an adverb. (Ring the bell *when it is time for class to begin.*)

A *noun clause* is a subordinate clause that is used as a noun. (*Whatever you say* interests me.)

An *elliptical clause* is a clause from which a word or words have been omitted. (We are not as lucky as *they*.)

A *main (independent) clause* can stand by itself as a sentence. (*the flashlight flickered*)

A *subordinate (dependent) clause* does not express a complete thought and cannot stand by itself. (*while the nation watched*)

| Clause | Example |
|---|---|
| **Main** (independent) | The hurricane struck |
| **Subordinate** (dependent) | while we were preparing to leave. |

**Collective noun.** *See* **Noun.**

**Comma splice** A comma splice is an error caused when two sentences are separated with a comma instead of a correct end mark. (*The band played a medley of show tunes, everyone enjoyed the show.*)

**Common noun.** *See* **Noun.**

**Comparative.** *See* **Adjective; Adverb.**

**Complement** A complement is a word or group of words that completes the meaning of a verb. (The kitten finished the *milk*.) *See also* **Direct object; Indirect object.**

An *objective complement* is a word or a group of words that follows a direct object and renames or describes that object. (The parents of the rescued child declared Gus a *hero*.)

A *subject complement* follows a linking verb and renames or describes the subject. (The coach seemed *anxious*.) *See also* **Noun (predicate noun); Adjective, (predicate adjective).**

**Complete predicate** The complete predicate of a sentence consists of the main verb plus any words that modify or complete the verb's meaning. (The student *produces work of high caliber*.)

**Complete subject** The complete subject of a sentence consists of the simple subject plus any words that modify or describe the simple subject. (*Students of history* believe that wars can be avoided.)

| Sentence Part | Example |
|---|---|
| Complete subject | The man in the ten-gallon hat |
| Complete predicate | wore a pair of silver spurs. |

**Compound sentence part** A sentence element that consists of two or more subjects, verbs, objects, or other parts is compound. (*Lou* and *Jay* helped. Laura *makes* and *models* scarves. Jill sings *opera* and *popular music*.)

**Conjunction** A conjunction is a word that links other words or groups of words.

A *coordinating conjunction* connects related words, groups of words, or sentences. (*and, but, or*)

A *correlative conjunction* is one of a pair of conjunctions that work together to connect sentence parts. (*either . . . or, neither . . . nor, not only . . . but also, whether . . . or, both . . . and*)

A *subordinating conjunction* introduces a subordinate clause. (*after, although, as, as if, as long as, as though, because, before, if, in order that, since, so that, than, though, till, unless, until, whatever, when, where, while*)

**Conjunctive adverb** A conjunctive adverb joins the clauses of a compound sentence. (*however, therefore, yet*)

**Contraction** A contraction is formed by joining two words and substituting an apostrophe for a letter or letters left out of one of the words. (*didn't, we've*)

**Coordinating conjunction.** *See* **Conjunction.**

**Correlative conjunction.** *See* **Conjunction.**

 **D**

**Dangling modifier** A dangling modifier is one that does not clearly modify any word in the sentence. (*Dashing for the train, the barriers got in the way.*)

**Demonstrative pronoun.** *See* **Pronoun.**

**Dependent clause.** *See* **Clause.**

**Direct object** A direct object receives the action of a verb. Direct objects follow transitive verbs. (Jude planned the *party*.)

**Direct quotation.** *See* **Quotation.**

**Divided quotation.** *See* **Quotation.**

**Double negative** A double negative is the incorrect use of two negative words when only one is needed. (*Nobody didn't care.*)

 **E**

**End mark** An end mark is one of several punctuation marks that can end a sentence. See the punctuation chart on page 1327.

**F**

**Fragment.** *See* **Sentence fragment.**

**Future tense.** *See* **Verb tense.**

**G**

**Gender** The gender of a personal pronoun indicates whether the person or thing referred to is male, female, or neuter. (My cousin plays the tuba; *he* often performs in school concerts.)

**Gerund** A gerund is a verbal that ends in *-ing* and functions as a noun. (*Making* pottery takes patience.)

**H**

**Helping verb.** *See* **Verb (auxiliary verb).**

**I**

**Illogical comparison** An illogical comparison is a comparison that does not make sense because words are missing or illogical. (My computer is *newer than Kay.*)

**Indefinite pronoun.** *See* **Pronoun.**

**Indefinite reference** Indefinite reference occurs when a pronoun is used without a clear antecedent. (My aunt hugged me in front of my friends, and *it* was embarrassing.)

**Independent clause.** *See* **Clause.**

**Indirect object** An indirect object tells to whom or for whom (sometimes to what or for what) something is done. (Arthur wrote *Kerry* a letter.)

**Indirect question** An indirect question tells what someone asked without using the person's exact words. (My friend asked me if I could go with her to the dentist.)

**Indirect quotation.** *See* **Quotation.**

**Infinitive** An infinitive is a verbal beginning with *to* that functions as a noun, an adjective, or an adverb. (He wanted *to go* to the play.)

**Intensive pronoun.** *See* **Pronoun.**

**Interjection** An interjection is a word or phrase used to express strong feeling. (*Wow! Good grief!*)

**Interrogative pronoun.** *See* **Pronoun.**

**Intransitive verb.** *See* **Verb.**

**Inverted sentence** An inverted sentence is one in which the subject comes after the verb. (*How was the movie? Here come the clowns.*)

**Irregular verb.** *See* **Verb.**

**L**

**Linking verb.** *See* **Verb.**

**M**

**Main clause.** *See* **Clause.**

**Main verb.** *See* **Verb.**

**Modifier** A modifier makes another word more precise. Modifiers most often are adjectives or adverbs; they may also be phrases, verbals, or clauses that function as adjectives or adverbs. (*small* box, smiled *broadly*, house *by the sea*, dog *barking loudly*)

An *essential modifier* is one that is necessary to the meaning of a sentence. (Everybody *who has a free pass* should enter now. None *of the passengers* got on the train.)

A *nonessential modifier* is one that merely adds more information to a sentence that is clear without the addition. (We will use the new dishes, *which are stored in the closet.*)

**N**

**Noun** A noun names a person, a place, a thing, or an idea. (*auditor, shelf, book, goodness*)

An *abstract noun* names an idea, a quality, or a feeling. (*joy*)

A *collective noun* names a group of things. (*bevy*)

A *common noun* is a general name of a person, a place, a thing, or an idea. (*valet, hill, bread, amazement*)

A *compound noun* contains two or more words. (*hometown, pay-as-you-go, screen test*)

A *noun of direct address* is the name of a person being directly spoken to. (*Lee,* do you have the package? No, *Suki,* your letter did not arrive.)

A *possessive noun* shows who or what owns or is associated with something. (*Lil's* ring, a *day's* pay)

A *predicate noun* follows a linking verb and renames the subject. (Karen is a *writer.*)

A *proper noun* names a particular person, place, or thing. (*John Smith, Ohio, Sears Tower, Congress*)

**Number** A word is **singular** in number if it refers to just one person, place, thing, idea, or action, and **plural** in number if it refers to more than one person, place, thing, idea, or action. (The words *he, waiter,* and *is* are singular. The words *they, waiters,* and *are* are plural.)

**O**

**Object of a preposition** The object of a preposition is the noun or pronoun that follows a preposition. (The athletes cycled along the *route.* Jane baked a cake for *her.*)

**Object of a verb** The object of a verb receives the action of the verb. (Sid told *stories.*)

**Participle** A participle is often used as part of a verb phrase. (had *written*) It can also be used as a verbal that functions as an adjective. (the *leaping* deer, the medicine *taken* for a fever)

The *present participle* is formed by adding *-ing* to the present form of a verb. (*Walking* rapidly, we reached the general store.)

The *past participle* of a regular verb is formed by adding *-d* or *-ed* to the present form. The past participles of irregular verbs do not follow this pattern. (*Startled,* they ran from the house. *Spun* glass is delicate. A *broken* cup lay there.)

**Passive voice.** *See* **Voice.**

**Past tense.** *See* **Verb tense.**

**Perfect tenses.** *See* **Verb tense.**

**Person** Person is a means of classifying pronouns.

A *first-person* pronoun refers to the person speaking. (*We* came.)

A *second-person* pronoun refers to the person spoken to. (*You* ask.)

A *third-person* pronoun refers to some other person(s) or thing(s) being spoken of. (*They* played.)

**Personal pronoun.** *See* **Pronoun.**

**Phrase** A phrase is a group of related words that does not contain a verb and its subject. (*noticing everything, under a chair*)

An *adjective phrase* modifies a noun or a pronoun. (The label *on the bottle* has faded.)

An *adverb phrase* modifies a verb, an adjective, or an adverb. (Come *to the fair.*)

An *appositive phrase* explains one or more words in a sentence. (Mary, *a champion gymnast,* won gold medals at the Olympics.)

A *gerund phrase* consists of a gerund and its modifiers and complements. (*Fixing the leak* will take only a few minutes.)

An *infinitive phrase* consists of an infinitive, its modifiers, and its complements. (*To prepare for a test,* study in a quiet place.)

A *participial phrase* consists of a participle and its modifiers and complements. (*Straggling to the finish line,* the last runners arrived.)

A *prepositional phrase* consists of a preposition, its object, and the object's modifiers. (The Saint Bernard does rescue work *in the Swiss Alps.*)

A *verb phrase* consists of a main verb and one or more helping verbs. (*might have ordered*)

**Possessive** A noun or pronoun that is possessive shows ownership or relationship. (*Dan's* story, *my* doctor)

**Possessive noun.** *See* **Noun.**

**Possessive pronoun.** *See* **Pronoun.**

**Predicate** The predicate of a sentence tells what the subject is or does. (The van *runs well even in winter.* The job *seems too complicated.*) *See also* **Complete predicate; Simple predicate.**

**Predicate adjective.** *See* **Adjective.**

**Predicate nominative** A predicate nominative is a noun or pronoun that follows a linking verb and renames or explains the subject. (Joan is a computer *operator.* The winner of the prize was *he.*)

**Predicate pronoun.** *See* **Pronoun.**

**Preposition** A preposition is a word that relates its object to another part of the sentence or to the sentence as a whole. (Alfredo leaped *onto* the stage.)

**Prepositional phrase.** *See* **Phrase.**

**Present tense.** *See* **Verb tense.**

**Pronoun** A pronoun replaces a noun or another pronoun. Some pronouns allow a writer or speaker to avoid repeating a proper noun. Other pronouns let a writer refer to an unknown or unidentified person or thing.

A *demonstrative pronoun* singles out one or more persons or things. (*This* is the letter.)

An *indefinite pronoun* refers to an unidentified person or thing. (*Everyone* stayed home. Will you hire *anybody?*)

An *intensive pronoun* emphasizes a noun or pronoun. (The teacher *himself* sold tickets.)

An *interrogative pronoun* asks a question. (*What* happened to you?)

A *personal pronoun* shows a distinction of person. (*I* came. *You* see. *He* knows.)

A *possessive pronoun* shows ownership. (*My* spaghetti is always good. Are *your* parents coming to the play?)

A **predicate pronoun** follows a linking verb and renames the subject. (The owners of the store were *they*.)

A **reflexive pronoun** reflects an action back on the subject of the sentence. (Joe helped *himself*.)

A **relative pronoun** relates a subordinate clause to the word it modifies. (The draperies, *which* had been made by hand, were ruined in the fire.)

**Pronoun-antecedent agreement.** *See* **Agreement.**

**Pronoun forms**

The **subject form** of a pronoun is used when the pronoun is the subject of a sentence or follows a linking verb as a predicate pronoun. (*She* fell. The star was *she*.)

The **object form** of a pronoun is used when the pronoun is the direct or indirect object of a verb or verbal or the object of a preposition. (We sent *him* the bill. We ordered food for *them*.)

**Proper adjective.** *See* **Adjective.**

**Proper noun.** *See* **Noun.**

**Punctuation** Punctuation clarifies the structure of sentences. See the punctuation chart below.

**Quotation** A quotation consists of words from another speaker or writer.

A **direct quotation** is the exact words of a speaker or writer. (Martin said, *"The homecoming game has been postponed."*)

A **divided quotation** is a quotation separated by words that identify the speaker. (*"The homecoming game,"* said Martin, *"has been postponed."*)

An **indirect quotation** reports what a person said without giving the exact words. (*Martin said that the homecoming game had been postponed.*)

**Reflexive pronoun.** *See* **Pronoun.**

**Regular verb.** *See* **Verb.**

**Relative pronoun.** *See* **Pronoun.**

**Run-on sentence** A run-on sentence consists of two or more sentences written incorrectly as one. (*The sunset was beautiful its brilliant colors lasted only a short time.*)

**Sentence** A sentence expresses a complete thought. The chart at the top of the next page shows the four kinds of sentences.

A **complex sentence** contains one main clause and one or more subordinate clauses. (*Open the windows before you go to bed. If she falls, I'll help her up.*)

| Punctuation | Uses | Examples |
|---|---|---|
| Apostrophe (') | Shows possession | Lou's garage        Alva's script |
|  | Indicates a contraction | I'll help you.        The baby's tired. |
| Colon (:) | Introduces a list or quotation | three colors: red, green, and yellow |
|  | Divides some compound sentences | This was the problem: we had to find our own way home. |
| Comma (,) | Separates ideas | The glass broke, and the juice spilled all over. |
|  | Separates modifiers | The lively, talented cheerleaders energized the team. |
|  | Separates items in series | We visited London, Rome, and Paris. |
| Exclamation point (!) | Ends an exclamatory sentence | Have a wonderful time! |
| Hyphen (-) | Joins parts of some compound words | daughter-in-law, great-grandson |
| Period ( ) | Ends a declarative sentence | Swallows return to Capistrano in spring. |
|  | Indicates most abbreviations | min.    qt.    Blvd.    Gen.    Jan. |
| Question mark (?) | Ends an interrogative sentence | Where are you going? |
| Semicolon (;) | Divides some compound sentences | Marie is an expert dancer; she teaches a class in tap. |
|  | Separates items in series that contain commas | Jerry visited Syracuse, New York; Athens, Georgia; and Tampa, Florida. |

A **compound sentence** is made up of two or more independent clauses joined by a conjunction, a colon, or a semicolon. (*The ship finally docked, and the passengers quickly left.*)

A **simple sentence** consists of only one main clause. (*My friend volunteers at a nursing home.*)

| Kind of Sentence | Example |
|---|---|
| **Declarative** (statement) | Our team won. |
| **Exclamatory** (strong feeling) | I had a great time! |
| **Imperative** (request, command) | Take the next exit. |
| **Interrogative** (question) | Who owns the car? |

**Sentence fragment** A sentence fragment is a group of words that is only part of a sentence. (*When he arrived. Merrily yodeling.*)

**Simple predicate** A simple predicate is the verb in the predicate. (John *collects* foreign stamps.)

**Simple subject** A simple subject is the key noun or pronoun in the subject. (The new *house* is empty.)

**Split infinitive** A split infinitive occurs when a modifier is placed between the word *to* and the verb in an infinitive. (*to quickly speak*)

**Subject** The subject is the part of a sentence that tells whom or what the sentence is about. (*Lou* swam.) *See* **Complete subject; Simple subject.**

**Subject-verb agreement.** *See* **Agreement.**

**Subordinate clause.** *See* **Clause.**

**Subordinating conjunction.** *See* **Conjunction.**

**Superlative.** *See* **Adjective; Adverb.**

**Transitive verb.** *See* **Verb.**

**Unidentified reference** An unidentified reference usually occurs when the word *it, they, this, which,* or *that* is used. (In California *they* have good weather most of the time.)

**Verb** A verb expresses an action, a condition, or a state of being.

An **action verb** tells what the subject does, has done, or will do. The action may be physical or mental. (Susan *trains* guide dogs.)

An **auxiliary verb** is added to a main verb to express tense, add emphasis, or otherwise affect the meaning of the verb. Together the auxiliary and main verb make up a verb phrase. (*will* intend, *could have* gone)

A **linking verb** expresses a state of being or connects the subject with a word or words that describe the subject. (The ice *feels* cold.) Linking verbs include *appear, be* (*am, are, is, was, were, been, being*), *become, feel, grow, look, remain, seem, smell, sound,* and *taste.*

A **main verb** expresses action or state of being; it appears with one or more auxiliary verbs. (will be *staying*)

The **progressive form** of a verb shows continuing action. (She *is knitting.*)

The **past tense** and **past participle** of a **regular verb** are formed by adding *-d* or *-ed.* (*open, opened*) An **irregular verb** does not follow this pattern. (*throw, threw, thrown; shrink, shrank, shrunk*)

The action of a **transitive verb** is directed toward someone or something, called the object of the verb. (Leo *washed* the windows.) An **intransitive verb** has no object. (The leaves *scattered.*)

**Verb phrase.** *See* **Phrase.**

**Verb tense** Verb tense shows the time of an action or the time of a state of being.

The **present tense** places an action or condition in the present. (Jan *takes* piano lessons.)

The **past tense** places an action or condition in the past. (We *came* to the party.)

The **future tense** places an action or condition in the future. (You *will understand.*)

The **present perfect tense** describes an action in an indefinite past time or an action that began in the past and continues in the present. (*has called, have known*)

The **past perfect tense** describes one action that happened before another action in the past. (*had scattered, had mentioned*)

The **future perfect tense** describes an event that will be finished before another future action begins. (*will have taught, shall have appeared*)

**Verbal** A verbal is formed from a verb and acts as another part of speech, such as a noun, an adjective, or an adverb.

| Verbal | Example |
|---|---|
| **Gerund** (used as a noun) | Lamont enjoys *swimming*. |
| **Infinitive** (used as an adjective, an adverb, or a noun) | Everyone wants *to help*. |
| **Participle** (used as an adjective) | The leaves *covering the drive* made it slippery. |

**Voice** The voice of a verb depends on whether the subject performs or receives the action of the verb.

In the **active voice** the subject of the sentence performs the verb's action. (We *knew* the answer.)

In the **passive voice** the subject of the sentence receives the action of the verb. (The team *has been eliminated*.)

# Analyzing Text Features

## Reading a Magazine Article

A **magazine article** is designed to catch and hold your interest. Learning how to recognize the items on a magazine page will help you read even the most complicated articles. Look at the sample magazine article as you read each strategy below.

### Strategies for Reading

**A** Read the **title** and any other **headings** to get an idea of what the article is about. Frequently, the title presents the article's main topic.

**B** Study **visuals**—photos, pictures, or maps. Visuals help bring the topic to life and also help you understand the article.

**C** Notice any **quotations**. Who is quoted? Evaluate whether the person is a reliable authority on the subject.

**D** Stop and think about the author's **questions** while reading. These questions are used to introduce important topics.

**E** Look for **special features**, such as charts, tables, or graphs, that provide more detailed information on the topic.

### PRACTICE AND APPLY

Use the sample magazine page at right and the tips above to help you answer the following questions.

1. What is the article's main topic?
2. How is the quotation related to the title of the article?
3. Read the two quotations in the article. Why is the first speaker a reliable authority on the subject?
4. What question is used to introduce the story of how windshield wipers were invented?
5. What information appears in the shaded box?

---

**PRACTICE AND APPLY ANSWERS**

1. The main topic focus is the importance of less famous inventors and how their inventions influence people's lives.
2. The quotation answers the question posed in the title.
3. The first speaker is a professor who developed a course on inventors.
4. "So, just what is the story behind the windshield wiper?"
5. examples of inventions and the names of their creators

# Ⓐ Shouldn't We Know Who Invented the Windshield Wiper?

by James T. Terry

**W**e know the famous ones—the Thomas Edisons and the Alexander Graham Bells—but what about the less famous inventors? What about the people who invented the traffic light and the windshield wiper? Shouldn't we know who they are?

Joan McLean thinks so. In fact, McLean, a professor of physics at Mountain University in Range, Colorado, feels so strongly about this matter that she's developed a course on the topic. In addition to learning "who" invented "what," however, McLean also likes her students to learn the answers to the "why" and "how" questions. According to McLean, Ⓒ "When students learn the answers to these questions, they are better prepared to recognize opportunities for inventing and more motivated to give inventing a try."

Her students agree. One young man with a patent pending for an unbreakable umbrella is walking proof of McLean's statement. "If I had not heard the story of the windshield wiper's invention," said Tommy Lee, a senior physics major, "I never would have dreamed of turning my frustration during a rainstorm into something so constructive." Lee is currently negotiating to sell his patent to an umbrella manufacturer once it is approved.

Ⓓ So, just what is the story behind the windshield wiper? Well, Mary Anderson came up with the idea in 1902 after a visit to New York City. The day was cold and blustery, but

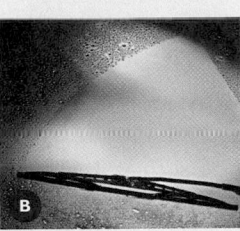

Ⓑ

*"When students learn the answers to these questions, they are better prepared to recognize opportunities for inventing...."* Ⓒ

Anderson still wanted to see the sights, so she hopped aboard a streetcar. Noticing that the driver was struggling to see through the sleet and snow covering the windshield, she found herself wondering why there couldn't be a built-in device for cleaning the window. Still wondering about this when she returned home to Birmingham, Alabama, Anderson started sketching out solutions. One of her ideas, a lever on the inside of a vehicle that would control an arm on the outside, became the first windshield wiper.

Today we benefit from countless inventions and innovations. It's hard to imagine getting by without Garrett A. Morgan's traffic light. It's equally impossible to picture a world without Katherine J. Blodgett's innovation that makes glass invisible. Can you picture life without transparent windows and eyeglasses?

As I think about stories like these, I am convinced that they will help untold numbers of inventors. So, only one question nags: how did we ever manage to give rise to so many inventors before McLean invented this class?

Ⓔ **Someone Also Invented . . .**

Dishwashers ................Josephine Cochran
Disposable Diapers.,.,,,,Marion Donovan
Fire Escapes ................Anna Connelly
Peanut Butter................George Washington Carver

## Reading a Textbook

The first page of a **textbook** lesson introduces you to a particular topic. The page also provides important information that will guide you through the rest of the lesson. Look at the sample textbook page as you read each strategy below.

### Strategies for Reading

**A** Preview the **title** and other **headings** to find out the lesson's main topic and related subtopics.

**B** Look for a list of terms or **vocabulary words**. These words will be identified and defined throughout the lesson.

**C** Read the **main idea**, **objectives**, or **focus**. These items summarize the lesson and establish a purpose for your reading.

**D** Find words set in special type, such as **italics** or **boldface.** Look for definitions or explanations before or after these terms.

**E** Notice any **special features** such as extended quotations or text placed in a tinted or colored box. For example, a **primary source** such as a **direct quotation** from a diary or interview is often used to provide firsthand information on a historical topic.

**F** Examine **visuals**, such as photos and drawings, and their captions. Visuals help bring the topic to life and enrich the text.

**PRACTICE AND APPLY ANSWERS**

1. The main topic is the beginning events of the Civil War.
2. Students should list "Fort Sumter".
3. Robert Anderson
4. Major Robert Anderson

### PRACTICE AND APPLY

Use the sample textbook page and the strategies above to help you answer the following questions.

1. What is the main topic of this lesson?
2. What vocabulary term is used on this page?
3. Who is quoted in the text?
4. In the picture, who is observing the fighting?

## SECTION 2

# The Civil War Begins

### MAIN IDEA

Shortly after the nation's Southern states seceded from the Union, war began between the North and South.

### WHY IT MATTERS NOW

The nation's identity was forged in part by the Civil War. Sectional divisions remain very strong today.

### Terms & Names

- Fort Sumter
- Bull Run
- Stonewall Jackson
- Ulysses S. Grant
- Robert E. Lee
- Antietam
- Emancipation Proclamation
- conscription
- Clara Barton
- income tax

**One American's Story**

On April 18, 1861, Major Robert Anderson was traveling by ship from Charleston, South Carolina, to New York City. That day, Anderson wrote a report to the secretary of war in which he described his most recent command.

### A PERSONAL VOICE ROBERT ANDERSON

"Having defended Fort Sumter for thirty-four hours, until the quarters were entirely burned, the main gates destroyed by fire, . . . the magazine surrounded by flames, . . . four barrels and three cartridges of powder only being available, and no provisions but pork remaining, I accepted terms of evacuation . . . and marched out of the fort . . . with colors flying and drums beating . . . and saluting my flag with fifty guns."

—quoted in *Fifty Basic Civil War Documents*

▲ Major Robert Anderson observes the firing at Fort Sumter in 1861.

Months earlier, as soon as the Confederacy was formed, Confederate soldiers in each secessionist state began seizing federal installations—especially forts. By the time of Lincoln's inauguration on March 4, 1861, only four Southern forts remained in Union hands. The most important was **Fort Sumter,** on an island in Charleston harbor.

Lincoln decided to neither abandon Fort Sumter nor reinforce it. He would merely send in "food for hungry men." At 4:30 A.M. on April 12, Confederate batteries began thundering away to the cheers of Charleston's citizens. The deadly struggle between North and South was under way.

## Union and Confederate Forces Clash

News of Fort Sumter's fall united the North. When Lincoln called for volunteers, the response throughout the Northern states was overwhelming. However, Lincoln's call for troops provoked a very different reaction in the states of the

# Understanding Visuals

## Reading a Chart

**Pie charts** can be used to show how parts relate to a whole and to each other. These tips can help you read a pie chart quickly and accurately. Look at the example as you read each strategy in this list.

### Strategies for Reading

**A** Read the **title** to find out the subject of the pie chart.

**B** Study the **labels** placed around the pie chart to identify the different parts of the total, or whole.

**C** Examine the **number** next to each label. Each number can be represented as a fraction of the total.

**D** Examine each part, or **sector**, of the pie chart. Each sector represents a fraction of the total.

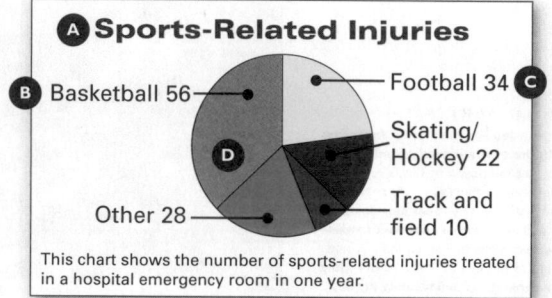

**A Sports-Related Injuries**

B Basketball 56

Football 34 C

Skating/Hockey 22

D

Track and field 10

Other 28

This chart shows the number of sports-related injuries treated in a hospital emergency room in one year.

### PRACTICE AND APPLY

Use the pie chart to answer the following questions.

1. What is the purpose of this pie chart?
2. Which sport is associated with the greatest number of injuries?
3. Which sport is associated with the least number of injuries?
4. Which sport is associated with approximately one third of all sports-related injuries?

**PRACTICE AND APPLY ANSWERS**

1. to compare the number of sports-related injuries among various sports
2. basketball
3. track and field
4. football

# Reading a Map

To read a **map** correctly, you have to identify and understand its elements. Look at the map below as you read each strategy in this list.

## Strategies for Reading

**A** Scan the **title** to understand the content of the map.

**B** Study the **legend**, or **key**, to find out what the symbols and colors on the map stand for.

**C** Study **geographic labels** to identify specific places on the map.

**D** Look at the **pointer**, or **compass rose**, to determine direction.

**E** Examine the **scale** to find out what each unit of measurement on the map is equal to in real-world distance.

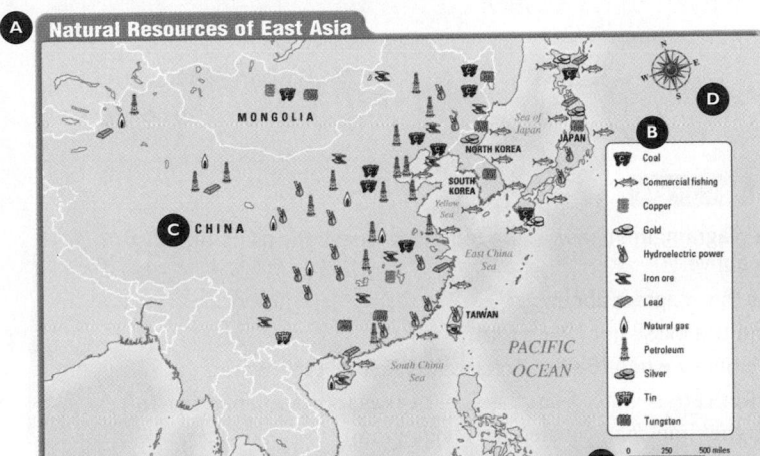

**A** Natural Resources of East Asia

## PRACTICE AND APPLY

Use the map to answer the following questions.

1. What is the purpose of this map?
2. Which country has the most resources in East Asia?
3. What are the main resources of the island of Taiwan?
4. What is the name of the large body of water that borders the coast of all of East Asia?

**PRACTICE AND APPLY ANSWERS**
1. to show the natural resources of East Asia
2. China
3. iron ore and hydroelectric power
4. the Pacific ocean

## Reading a Diagram

**Diagrams** combine pictures with a few words to provide a lot of information. Look at the example on the opposite page as you read each of the following strategies.

### *Strategies for Reading*

**A** Look at the **title** to get a quick idea of what the diagram is about.

**B** Study the **images** closely to understand each part of the diagram.

**C** Look at the **captions** and the **labels** for more information.

**PRACTICE AND APPLY**

Study the diagram, then answer the following questions using the strategies above.

**1.** What is this diagram about?

**2.** How did the Mississippi River form?

**3.** Approximately when did the Great Lakes first fill with water?

**4.** What river carries water from the Great Lakes to the Atlantic Ocean?

**5.** What is the time span covered in this diagram?

**PRACTICE AND APPLY ANSWERS**

1. The diagram explains how the Great Lakes were formed.
2. Ice sheets melted and draining meltwater ran south to form the Mississippi River.
3. 7,000 years ago
4. the St. Lawrence River
5. 14,000 years

## A Formation of the Great Lakes

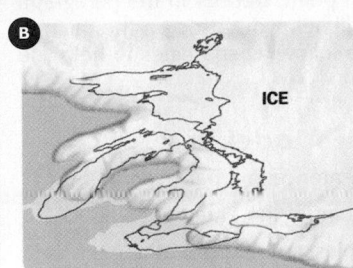

**B**

**14,000 YEARS AGO** Meltwater pools in front of the melting ice sheets. Rivers form, draining meltwater to the south into what will become the Mississippi. **C**

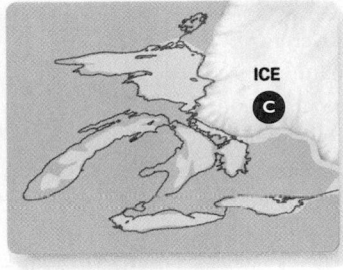

**C**

**7000 YEARS AGO** As the ice sheet melts and recedes, meltwater fills the lakes and drains westward to the Atlantic through the St. Lawrence River valley.

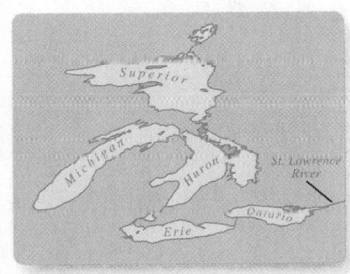

**TODAY** The Great Lakes drain into the Atlantic Ocean through the St. Lawrence River.

# Recognizing Text Structures

## Main Idea and Supporting Details

The **main idea** in a paragraph is its most important point. **Details** in the paragraph support the main idea. Identifying the main idea will help you focus on the main message the writer wants to communicate. Use the following strategies to help you identify a paragraph's main idea and supporting details.

### Strategies for Reading

- Look for the **main idea**, which is often the first sentence in a paragraph.
- Use the main idea to help you **summarize** the point of the paragraph.
- Identify specific **details**, including facts and examples, that **support** the main idea.

### The Dust Bowl

**Main Idea** — More than one factor caused the farmland of the Great Plains to become a dust bowl in the 1930s.

**Details** — Overgrazing and overplowing stripped the fields bare of natural grasses whose roots kept the soil in place. When the rains stopped coming as frequently as they had, the soil dried out. The dry topsoil was easily carried off by the wind. Then blowing clouds of dirt made matters worse by blocking out sunlight, burying gardens and chicken coops, and covering train tracks and roads.

#### PRACTICE AND APPLY

Read the following paragraph. Identify its main idea and list three supporting details.

During the 1930s, the Great Plains became a dust bowl. As a result, many Midwestern farmers lost, sold, or simply abandoned their land. After all, producing crops was nearly impossible, and without crops to sell, most farmers could not afford to make their mortgage payments. So either farmers lost their farms when banks foreclosed on overdue mortgages, or they sold their land at ridiculously low prices. Other farmers abandoned their land to seek better lives elsewhere.

**PRACTICE AND APPLY ANSWERS**
Main idea: many Mid-western farmers lost, sold, or simply abandoned their land. Students should list the three sentences that follow the main idea.

## Problem and Solution

Does the proposed **solution** to a **problem** make sense? In order to decide, you need to look at each part of the text. Use the following strategies to read the text below.

### Strategies for Reading

- Look at the beginning or middle of a paragraph to find the **statement of the problem**.
- Find **details** that explain the problem and tell why it is important.
- Look for the **proposed solution**.
- Identify the **supporting details** for the proposed solution.
- Think about whether the solution is a good one.

## Let's Hear from the Experts *by Chang Lee*

**Statement of problem**

In school, we study about famous painters, musicians, and writers of the past but learn little about artists in our own community today. Students in our high school want to learn more about the arts from the real experts—artists themselves.

**Explanation of problem**

Currently, we learn little about the types of work artists do. Because many of us will pursue careers in the arts, we can learn information about the issues and challenges that artists face—topics that are relevant to us. Also, all students find it more interesting to study current topics that relate directly to their lives.

For these reasons, a group of us have formed a committee to propose a visiting artists program. Our committee researched ten other schools in the state that run successful programs. We put this information in a proposal and presented it to school administrators. There is also a petition that is being circulated in the school. We are asking all students in the school to support our proposal and sign the petition today!

### PRACTICE AND APPLY

Read the text above. Then answer these questions.

1. What is the proposed solution in the third paragraph?
2. Identify at least one detail that supports the solution.
3. Do you think the solution is a good one? Explain why or why not.

**PRACTICE AND APPLY ANSWERS**

1. a visiting-artists program
2. Students should list either the second or third sentence in paragraph two.
3. Student answers will vary. (Sample answers are provided.) Reason why the solution is a good one: Students have researched other programs and therefore will design a meaningful program that addresses their specific needs. Reason why the solution is a poor one: The proposed program meets the needs of only a small minority of students.

# Sequence

It's important to understand the **sequence**, or order of events, in what you read. It helps you know what happens and why. Read the tips below to make sure a sequence is clear to you. Then look at the example on the opposite page.

### Strategies for Reading

- Read through the passage and think about what its **main steps**, or stages, are.
- Look for **words and phrases that signal time**: *today, in 1612, Friday, that morning, later,* or *at 3 o'clock.*
- Look for **words and phrases that signal order**: *first, second, now, during, after that,* or *finally.*

### PRACTICE AND APPLY

Read the article on the next page that describes the work of Alexander Graham Bell. Use the information from the article and the tips above to answer the questions.

1. List some words or phrases in the article that signal time.
2. List some phrases in the article that signal order.
3. A flow chart can help you understand a sequence of events. Use the information from the article to copy and complete this flow chart.

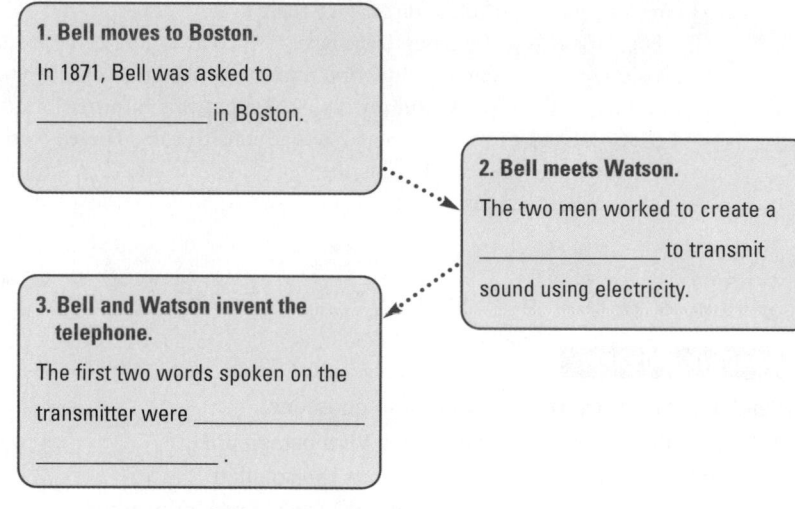

**1. Bell moves to Boston.**

In 1871, Bell was asked to

_____ in Boston.

**2. Bell meets Watson.**

The two men worked to create a

_____ to transmit sound using electricity.

**3. Bell and Watson invent the telephone.**

The first two words spoken on the transmitter were _____

_____ .

## PRACTICE AND APPLY ANSWERS

1. Students should list the following phrases: In 1871, a few weeks, two years, April 6, 1875, a little less than a year, By 1915.
2. Students should list the following words and phrases: Soon after, During this period, next, Finally, later, first, During, first, first, by then.
3. Lecture, machine, Mr. Watson

# The Work of Alexander Graham Bell

Alexander Graham Bell with a centennial telephone

In 1871, Alexander Graham Bell came to Boston for a few weeks to lecture on his father's system of teaching speech to the deaf. What he didn't know was that this brief trip would have a dramatic impact on his life. Bell's lectures amazed audiences. The Scottish-born teacher and scientist received so many invitations to speak that he decided to stay in the city.

Soon after, Bell opened a school in Boston for training teachers of the deaf. He also began teaching at Boston University. During this period, Bell met Thomas Watson, a young repair mechanic and model maker. For the next two years, the men worked together to create a machine for transmitting sound by electricity.

Finally, on April 6, 1875, Bell acquired a patent for a multiple telegraph, and a little less than a year later the two men created the first telephone. During the first "telephonic communication," Bell called to his partner over the new transmitter he was trying out. The first words he spoke were "Mr. Watson! Come here! I want you!" and Mr. Watson heard him. By 1915, coast-to-coast telephone communication was a reality.

Also by then, the two had succeeded in inventing many other useful devices. Although Bell is best known for inventing the telephone, he was also the father of many other equally amazing devices and scientific advancements. For example, Bell and others invented the "hydrodome," a hydrofoil boat that traveled above the water at high speeds.

# Cause and Effect

A **cause** is an event that brings about another event. An **effect** is something that happens as a result of the first event. Identifying causes and effects helps you understand how events are related. The tips below can help you find causes and effects in any reading.

## Strategies for Reading

- Look for an action or event that answers the question "What happened?" This is the **effect**.
- Look for an action or event that answers the question "Why did it happen?" This is the **cause**.
- Identify words or phrases that **signal** causes and effects, such as *because, as a result, therefore, thus, consequently, since,* and *led to.*

### PRACTICE AND APPLY

Read the cause-and-effect passage on the next page. Then answer the following questions. Notice that the first cause and effect in the passage are highlighted.

1. List any words in the passage that signal causes and effects. The first one is highlighted for you.

2. Because Congress was concerned about the effects of looters on the parks, what did it do?

3. Use two of the causes and effects in the first paragraph to copy and complete the following diagram.

**Cause:** *Tourists were moved by the area's wonders.* ┈┈▶ **Effect:**

**Cause:** ┈┈▶ **Effect:**

**PRACTICE AND APPLY ANSWERS**

1. Students should list the following words and phrases: Because, So, largely as a result, because, Consequently.
2. Congress created the Antiquities Act.
3. *Cause:* They were so moved by the area's wonders.
   *Effect:* They wanted to protect them.
   *Cause:* They presented their case before Congress in Washington.
   *Effect:* Congress created the first national park.

# The First National Parks

In 1872, a group of tourists was awestruck by the deep canyons, dense pine forests, and refreshing rivers and waterfalls of Yellowstone, Montana. Because the visitors were so moved by the area's natural wonders, they immediately wanted to protect them. So they trooped off to Washington, D.C., to demand that Yellowstone lands be set aside for public use. There, before Congress, with the help of breathtaking paintings and photographs by artists who had ventured to Yellowstone with government land surveyors, these passionate preservationists presented their case. Dazzled, Congress responded to their pleas by creating the first national park, Yellowstone National Park.

The next several national parks owe their establishment primarily to the enthusiasm and persuasive abilities of one nature lover, John Muir. Muir took influential friends such as Ralph Waldo Emerson and Theodore Roosevelt on spectacular hikes through the Sierras. While on these hikes, he expressed his love of nature in passionate arguments for its preservation. In 1890, largely as a result of Muir's efforts, Yosemite, Sequoia, and General Grant national parks were established.

Yosemite National Park

Interestingly, however, about 25 percent of today's national parks owe their preservation to looters— or rather, to a Congress roused into action by looters. In 1906, because Congress was concerned that widespread plundering of precious Southwestern archaeological sites was destroying important artifacts, it enacted a law to prevent such plundering. This law, called the Antiquities Act, authorized the president to set aside as national monuments extremely precious or threatened lands. Consequently, by calling on the powers granted to him under the law, President Theodore Roosevelt was able to put under government protection many sites that might otherwise have been destroyed. These sites would eventually earn national-park status.

# Comparison and Contrast

**Comparing** two things means showing how they are the same. **Contrasting** two things means showing how they are different. Comparisons and contrasts are often used in science and history books to make a subject clearer. Use these tips to help you understand comparison and contrast in reading assignments, such as the article on the opposite page.

## Strategies for Reading

- Look for **direct statements** of comparison and contrast: "These things are similar because . . ." or "One major difference is . . . ."
- Pay attention to **words and phrases that signal comparisons**, such as *also, both, is the same as,* and *in the same way.*
- Notice **words and phrases that signal contrasts**. Some of these are *however, still, but,* and *on the other hand.*

### PRACTICE AND APPLY

Read the essay on the opposite page. Then use the information from the article and the tips above to answer the questions.

1. List any words or phrases that signal comparisons. A sample has been highlighted for you.
2. List any words or phrases that signal contrasts. A sample has been highlighted for you.
3. A Venn diagram shows how two subjects are similar and how they are different. Copy this diagram, which uses information from the essay to compare and contrast Booker T. Washington and W.E.B. Du Bois. Add at least one similarity to the middle part of the diagram. Add at least one difference in each outer circle.

BOOKER T. WASHINGTON

believed in vocational training for African Americans

BOTH

promoted equality for African Americans

W.E.B. DU BOIS

believed in college education for African Americans

**PRACTICE AND APPLY ANSWERS**

1. Students should list the following words and phrases: alike, Both, Both, Both also, also, same.
2. Students should list the following words and phrases: Nevertheless, different, however, In contrast, although, different.
3. **Unique to Booker T. Washington:** Blacks must temporarily not engage in Civil Rights and political issues. **Unique to W.E.B. Dubois:** Blacks must actively protest for civil rights. **Both:** passionately worked towards goals, were college educated, and were African Americans.

# Less Than Allies

Comparison

Booker T. Washington and W.E.B. Du Bois were alike in many ways. Both were devoted to helping their fellow African Americans attain equal rights. Both were educated black men with university teaching positions. Both also worked passionately toward their goal at the beginning of the 20th century. Nevertheless, they were not allies. Why? They had very different ideas about how blacks should go about attaining equal rights.

W.E.B. Du Bois

Booker T. Washington

Washington believed that for black people to achieve equal status and power as citizens, they needed to focus on learning crafts, farming, and industrial skills. He argued that by gaining vocational skills and the economic security that would surely follow, black people would naturally earn the respect and acceptance of the white community. In Washington's opinion, however, to earn an education and economic security, black people would need to let go temporarily of the fight for civil rights and political power.

Contrast

In contrast to Washington, W.E.B. Du Bois said that social change would come by developing a small group of college-educated blacks he called the "Talented Tenth," those best and brightest 10 percent who would guide the black community. Du Bois also believed that black people could not afford to stop fighting for civil rights and political power. In his opinion, only agitation and protest would achieve social change. According to Du Bois, in the climate of extreme racism that existed in America at the time, Washington's approach would merely cause blacks to suffer even more oppression.

So although these two African American contemporaries had the same goal, their different approaches to achieving this goal made them adversaries rather than allies.

# Argument

An **argument** is an opinion backed up with reasons and facts. Examining an opinion and the reasons and facts that back it up will help you decide if the opinion makes sense. Look at the argument on the right as you read each of these tips.

## Strategies for Reading

- Look for words that **signal an opinion**: *I believe, I think, in my view, they claim, argue,* or *disagree.*

- Look for reasons, facts, or expert opinions that **support** the argument.

- Ask yourself if the argument and reasons **make sense**.

- Look for overgeneralizations or other **errors in reasoning** that may affect the argument.

### PRACTICE AND APPLY

Read the argument on the next page, and then answer the questions below.

1. LIst any words that signal an opinion.
2. List any words or phrases that give the writer's opinion.
3. The writer presents both sides of the argument. Copy and complete the chart below to show the two sides. One example has been provided for you.

| Reasons for | Reasons Against |
|---|---|
| 1. Students become aware of others' needs. | |

**PRACTICE AND APPLY ANSWERS**

1. Students should list the following words and phrases: claim, argue, believe, In my view, I don't believe, I think.

2. Students should list the following phrases: In my view, I don't believe, I think.

3. **Reasons for:** Students learn life skills; students explore careers.
   **Reasons against:** Students spend less time learning core subjects; community service violates the 13th amendment.

# A Fair Compromise

**By Jorge Romero**

The requirements for high school graduation have just changed in my community. As a result, all students must complete sixty hours of service learning, or they will not receive a diploma. Service learning is academic learning that also helps the community. Examples of service learning include cleaning up a polluted river, working in a soup kitchen, or tutoring a student. During a service experience, students must keep a journal and then write a report about what they have learned.

Supporters claim that there are many benefits of service learning. Perhaps most important, students are forced to think beyond their own interests and become aware of the needs of others. Students are also able to learn real-life skills that include responsibility, problem-solving, and working as part of a team. Finally, students can explore possible careers through service learning. For example, if a student wonders what teaching is like, he or she can choose to work in an elementary school classroom a few afternoons each month.

While there are many benefits, opponents point out problems with the new requirement. First, they argue that the

main reason students go to school is to learn core subjects and skills. Because service learning is time-consuming, students spend less time studying the core subjects. Second, they believe that forcing students to work without pay goes against the Thirteenth Amendment, which protects people from forced servitude, or slavery. By requiring service, the school takes away an individual's freedom to choose.

In my view, service learning is a great way to contribute to the community, learn new skills, and explore different careers. However, I don't believe you should force people to help others—the desire to help must come from the heart. I think the best solution is one that gives students choices: a student should be able to choose sixty hours of independent study or sixty hours of service. Choice encourages both freedom and responsibility, and as young adults we must learn to handle both wisely.

# Reading in the Content Areas

## Social Studies

**Social studies** class becomes easier when you understand how your textbook's words, pictures, and maps work together to give you information. Following these tips can make you a better reader of social studies lessons. As you read the tips, look at the sample lesson on the right-hand page.

### Strategies for Reading

**A** First, look at any **headings** or **subheads** on the page. These give you an idea of what each section covers.

**B** Make sure you know the meaning of any boldfaced or underlined **vocabulary terms**. These terms often appear on tests.

**C** Carefully read the text and think about **ways the information is organized**. Social studies books are often organized by chronological order, cause and effect, comparison and contrast, and geographic location.

**D** Look closely at **visuals** and **captions**. Think about how they relate to the text.

**E** Notice any **special features** such as extended quotations, sidebar questions, or text in a tinted box. For example, a **primary source** such as a **direct quotation** from a diary or interview is often used to provide information on a historical topic.

### PRACTICE AND APPLY

Carefully read the textbook page at right. Use the information from the page and from the tips above to answer these questions.

**1.** What is the main subject addressed on this page?

**2.** List and define the two vocabulary terms in the article.

**3.** List two major effects of World War I.

**4.** Who is both the speaker in the quotation and the subject of the photograph?

**PRACTICE AND APPLY ANSWERS**

1. American struggles with postwar issues

2. nativism: prejudice against foreign-born people
   Isolationism: a policy of pulling away from involvement in world affairs

3. Students should list the following sentences in the last paragraph: "A wave of nativism, or prejudice against foreign-born people, swept the nation" and "So, too, did a belief in isolationism, a policy of pulling away from involvement in world affairs."

4. Irving Fajans

## SECTION 1

# A Americans Struggle with Postwar Issues

| MAIN IDEA | WHY IT MATTERS NOW | Terms & Names |
|---|---|---|
| A desire for normality after the war and a fear of communism and "foreigners" led to postwar isolationism. | Americans today continue to debate political isolationism and immigration policy. | • nativism<br>• isolationism<br>• communism<br>• anarchists |
| | | • Sacco and Vanzetti<br>• quota system<br>• John L. Lewis |

### One American's Story

During the 1920s and 1930s, Irving Fajans, a department store sales clerk in New York City, tried to persuade fellow workers to join the Department Store Employees Union. He described some of the techniques union organizers used.

**E** **A PERSONAL VOICE** IRVING FAJANS

" If you were caught distributing . . . union literature around the job you were instantly fired. We thought up ways of passing leaflets without the boss being able to pin anybody down. . . . We . . . swiped the key to the toilet paper dispensers in the washroom, took out the paper, and substituted printed slips of just the right size! We got a lot of new members that way—It appealed to their sense of humor. "

—quoted in *The Jewish Americans*

During the war, workers' rights had been suppressed. In 1919, workers began to cry out for fair pay and better working conditions. Tensions arose between labor and management, and a rash of labor strikes broke out across the country. The public, however, was not supportive of striking workers. Many citizens longed to get back to normal, peaceful living—they felt resentful of anyone who caused unrest.

▲ Irving Fajans **D** organized department store workers in their efforts to gain better pay and working conditions during the 1920s.

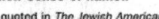

## Postwar Trends

**C** World War I had left much of the American public exhausted. The debate over the League of Nations had deeply divided America. Further, the Progressive Era had caused numerous wrenching changes in American life. The economy, too, was in a difficult state of adjustment. Returning soldiers faced unemployment or took their old jobs away from women and minorities. Also, the cost of living had doubled. Farmers and factory workers suffered as wartime orders diminished.

Many Americans responded to the stressful conditions by becoming fearful of outsiders. A wave of **nativism**, or prejudice against foreign-born people, swept the nation. So, too, did a belief in **isolationism**, a policy of pulling away from involvement in world affairs. **B**

## Science

Reading a **science** textbook becomes easier when you understand how the explanations, drawings, and special terms work together. Use the strategies below to help you better understand your science textbook. Look at the examples on the opposite page as you read each strategy in this list.

### Strategies for Reading

**A** Preview the **title** and **headings** on the page to see what scientific concepts will be addressed.

**B** Read the **key idea**, **objectives**, or **focus**. These items summarize the lesson purpose and establish a focus for your reading.

**C** Look for **boldfaced** and **italicized** words that appear in the text. Look for **definitions** of those words.

**D** Carefully examine any **pictures**, **diagrams**, or **charts**. Read the **titles** and **captions** and evaluate how the graphics help to illustrate and explain the text.

**E** Science textbooks discuss **scientific concepts** in terms of **everyday events** or **experiences**. Look for these places and consider how they improve your understanding.

### PRACTICE AND APPLY

Use the sample science page and the tips above to help you answer the following questions.

**1.** What important concept will be addressed in the lesson? Where on the page did you find this information?

**2.** What is the important question that is emphasized in italics?

**3.** What is the relative mass of a proton?

**4.** What is the purpose of the paper-cutting activity?

---

**PRACTICE AND APPLY ANSWERS**

**1.** Atomic structure. The concept is found in the title.

**2.** If all atoms are composed of these same components, why do different atoms have different chemical properties?

**3.** 1836

**4.** to use an everyday activity to help students imagine the width of an atom

## 3.6 Introduction to the Modern Concept of Atomic Structure

**Objective:** *To describe some important features of subatomic particles.*

In the years since Thomson and Rutherford, a great deal has been learned about atomic structure. The simplest view of the atom is that it consists of a tiny nucleus (about $10^{-13}$ cm in diameter) and electrons that move about the nucleus at an average distance of about $10^{-8}$ cm from it **(Figure 3.9).** To visualize how small the nucleus is compared with the size of the atom, consider that if the nucleus were the size of a grape, the electrons would be about one *mile* away on average. The nucleus contains protons, which have a positive charge equal in magnitude to the electrons' negative charge, and neutrons, which have almost the same mass as protons but no charge. The neutrons' function in the nucleus is not obvious. They may help hold the protons (which repel each other) together to form the nucleus, but we will not be concerned with that here. The relative masses and charges of the electron, proton, and neutron are shown in **Table 3.4.**

An important question arises at this point: *If all atoms are composed of these same components, why do different atoms have different chemical properties?* The answer lies in the number and arrangement of the electrons. The space in which the electrons move accounts for most of the atomic volume. The electrons are the parts of atoms that "intermingle" when atoms combine to form molecules. Therefore, the number of electrons a given atom possesses greatly affects the way it can interact with other atoms. As a result, atoms of different elements, which have different numbers of electrons, show different chemical behavior. Although the atoms of different elements also differ in their numbers of protons, it is the number of electrons that really determines chemical behavior. We will discuss how this happens in later chapters.

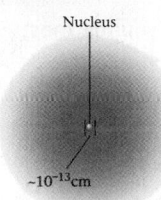

**Figure 3.9**
A nuclear atom viewed in cross section. (The symbol ~ means approximately.) This drawing does not show the actual scale. The nucleus is actually much smaller compared with the size of an atom.

**TABLE 3.4**
**The Mass and Charge of the Electron, Proton, and Neutron**

| Particle | Relative Mass* | Relative Charge |
|----------|----------------|-----------------|
| electron | 1 | 1− |
| proton | 1836 | 1+ |
| neutron | 1839 | none |

*The electron is arbitrarily assigned a mass of 1 for comparison.

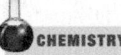

**CHEMISTRY**

In this model the atom is called a nuclear atom because the positive charge is localized in a small, compact structure (the nucleus) and not spread out uniformly, as in the plum pudding view.

**CHEMISTRY**

The *chemistry* of an atom arises from its electrons.

**WHAT IF?**

The average diameter of an atom is $1.3 \times 10^{-10}$ m.

What if the average diameter of an atom were 1 cm? How tall would you be?

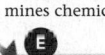

**CHEMISTRY in ACTION**

**How Big Is an Atom?**

1. Get a strip of paper 11" by 1".
2. Cut the paper in half. Discard one piece.
3. Repeat step 2 until you can no longer cut the paper. How many times could you cut it?
4. How many times would you need to cut the paper to have a piece of paper remaining that is the same width as an atom? (Average atom diameter = $1.3 \times 10^{-10}$ m.)

# Mathematics

Reading in **mathematics** is different from reading in history, literature, or science. Use the strategies below to help you better understand your **mathematics** textbook. Look at the examples on the opposite page as you read each strategy in the list.

## Strategies for Reading

**A** Preview the **title** and **headings** on the page to see what mathematics concepts will be covered.

**B** Find and read the **goals** or **objectives** for the lesson. These will tell you the most important points to know.

**C** Read **explanations** of the central concept carefully. Sometimes a concept is explained in more than one way to make sure you understand it.

**D** Study any **worked-out solutions** to sample problems. These are the key to understanding how to do the homework assignment.

### PRACTICE AND APPLY

Use the sample mathematics page and the strategies above to help you answer the following questions.

1. List the title of the lesson.
2. What is the first learning goal you should have for this lesson?
3. Explain how to write an equation for a line when given different types of information.
4. What does the sample problem show you how to do?
5. How can the formula for writing an equation of a line be applied to a real-life situation?

**PRACTICE AND APPLY ANSWERS**
1. Writing Equations of Lines
2. Writing linear equations
3. Use the slope-intercept form, the point-slope form, or the two points form.
4. Write an equation given the slope and y-intercept.
5. It can be used to create a model of the number of calories you burn while dancing.

# 2.4
## Writing Equations of Lines

### GOAL 1 WRITING LINEAR EQUATIONS

**What you should learn**

**GOAL 1** Write linear equations.

**GOAL 2** Write direct variation equations, as applied in **Example 7**.

**Why you should learn it**

▼ To model **real-life** quantities, such as the number of calories you burn while dancing in **Ex. 64**.

In Lesson 2.3 you learned to find the slope and y-intercept of a line whose equation is given. In this lesson you will study the reverse process. That is, you will learn to write an equation of a line using one of the following: the slope and y-intercept of the line, the slope and a point on the line, or two points on the line.

---

**CONCEPT SUMMARY**

**WRITING AN EQUATION OF A LINE**

**SLOPE-INTERCEPT FORM** Given the slope $m$ and the y-intercept $b$, use this equation:

$$y = mx + b$$

**POINT-SLOPE FORM** Given the slope $m$ and a point $(x_1, y_1)$, use this equation:

$$y - y_1 = m(x - x_1)$$

**TWO POINTS** Given two points $(x_1, y_1)$ and $(x_2, y_2)$, use the formula

$$m = \frac{y_2 - y_1}{x_2 - x_1}$$

to find the slope $m$. Then use the point-slope form with this slope and either of the given points to write an equation of the line.

---

Every nonvertical line has only one slope and one y-intercept, so the slope-intercept form is unique. The point-slope form, however, depends on the point that is used. Therefore, in this book equations of lines will be simplified to slope-intercept form so a unique solution may be given.

### EXAMPLE 1  *Writing an Equation Given the Slope and the y-intercept*

Write an equation of the line shown.

**SOLUTION**

From the graph you can see that the slope is $m = \frac{3}{2}$. You can also see that the line intersects the y-axis at the point $(0, -1)$, so the y-intercept is $b = -1$.

Because you know the slope and the y-intercept, you should use the slope-intercept form to write an equation of the line.

$y = mx + b$     **Use slope-intercept form.**

$y = \frac{3}{2}x - 1$     **Substitute $\frac{3}{2}$ for $m$ and $-1$ for $b$.**

▶ An equation of the line is $y = \frac{3}{2}x - 1$.

# Reading Beyond the Classroom

## Reading a Public Notice

**Public notices** can tell you about events in your community and give you valuable information about safety. When you read a public notice, follow these tips. Each tip relates to a specific part of the notice on the opposite page.

### Strategies for Reading

**A** Read the notice's **title**, if it has one. The title often gives the main idea or purpose of the notice.

**B** See if there is a logo, credit, or other way of telling **who created the notice**.

**C** Search for information that explains **who should read the notice**.

**D** Look for **instructions**—things the notice is asking or telling you to do.

**E** See if there are details that tell you how you can **find out more** about the topic.

**PRACTICE AND APPLY**

The notice on the opposite page is from a county government agency. Read it carefully and answer the questions below.

1. Who is the notice from?
2. Who is the notice for?
3. What special abilities are required for entry into the program?
4. Explain how to register for the program.
5. According to the notice, what must participants complete in order to receive a certificate?

**PRACTICE AND APPLY ANSWERS**
1. the Kalai Fire Department
2. boys and girls from 13 to 18
3. You must be able to run and swim 100 yards non-stop.
4. Call Renee Yamaguchi or Roger Amato
5. a 20-hour course

**(A)** *FOR IMMEDIATE RELEASE – JUNIOR LIFEGUARD PROGRAM AVAILABLE STARTING IN JUNE*

*COUNTY OF KALAI*
*KALAI FIRE DEPARTMENT*

May 9, 2002

**(B)** KALAI  The Ocean Safety Bureau of the Kalai Fire Department will be conducting its *Junior Lifeguard Program* at various sites between June 17 and July 20, 2002.

**(C)** Boys and girls between the ages of 13 and 18 are encouraged to participate in the program, which will teach lifesaving skills, including CPR, and provide extensive training in water safety. In order to participate, you must be able to run and swim 100 yards nonstop.

"Lifeguarding requires many skills that everyone should learn and practice," says County Lifeguard Elaine Ruates. "Knowing what to do, staying calm, and quickly and efficiently administering aid is the basis for successful lifesaving."

To receive a certificate, the participants must complete a 20-hour course at one of the following locations:

| | |
|---|---|
| Salt Marsh | June 17–21 |
| Papua | June 24–28 |
| Kalai | July 1–5 |
| Anaholo | July 8–12 |
| Hanale | July 15–19 |

**(D)** Classes are conducted Monday through Friday from 10:00 a.m. to 2:30 p.m. Participants should provide their own lunch and equipment (if available). There will be a final competition among the participants on Saturday, July 20, at Kalai Beach.

**(E)** To register, call Renee Yamaguchi at 555-5962 or Roger Amato at 555-7381.

## Reading a Web Page

If you need information for a report, project, or hobby, the World Wide Web can probably help you. The tips below will help you understand the **Web pages** you read. As you look at the tips, notice where they match up to the sample Web page on the right.

### Strategies for Reading

**A** Notice the page's **Web address**, or **URL**. You may want to write it down in case you need to access the same page at another time.

**B** Look for **menu bars** along the top, bottom, or side of the page. These guide you to other parts of the site that may be useful.

**C** Look for **links** to other parts of the site or to related pages. Links are often shown as underlined words.

**D** Use a **search** feature to quickly find out whether a certain kind of information is contained anywhere on the site.

**E** Many sites have a link that allows you to **contact** the creators with questions or feedback.

### PRACTICE AND APPLY

Read the Web site on the next page. Then use the information from the site and the tips above to answer the questions.

1. What is the Web address?

2. If you wanted to know whether the American History site contained any information about Henry David Thoreau, how could you go about finding out?

3. What link would direct you to historical events that occurred on today's date one hundred years ago?

4. If you were unable to find information at this site using the search feature, what link would allow you to ask for help?

5. In your own words, summarize the purpose and function of the American History site.

**PRACTICE AND APPLY ANSWERS**

1. http://www.amhistory.org
2. I would click the "search" link and type in "Henry David Thoreau".
3. "Today in History"
4. "Help and FAQs"
5. Answers will vary. Sample response: The American History site is a gateway to primary source materials relating to United States History and culture.

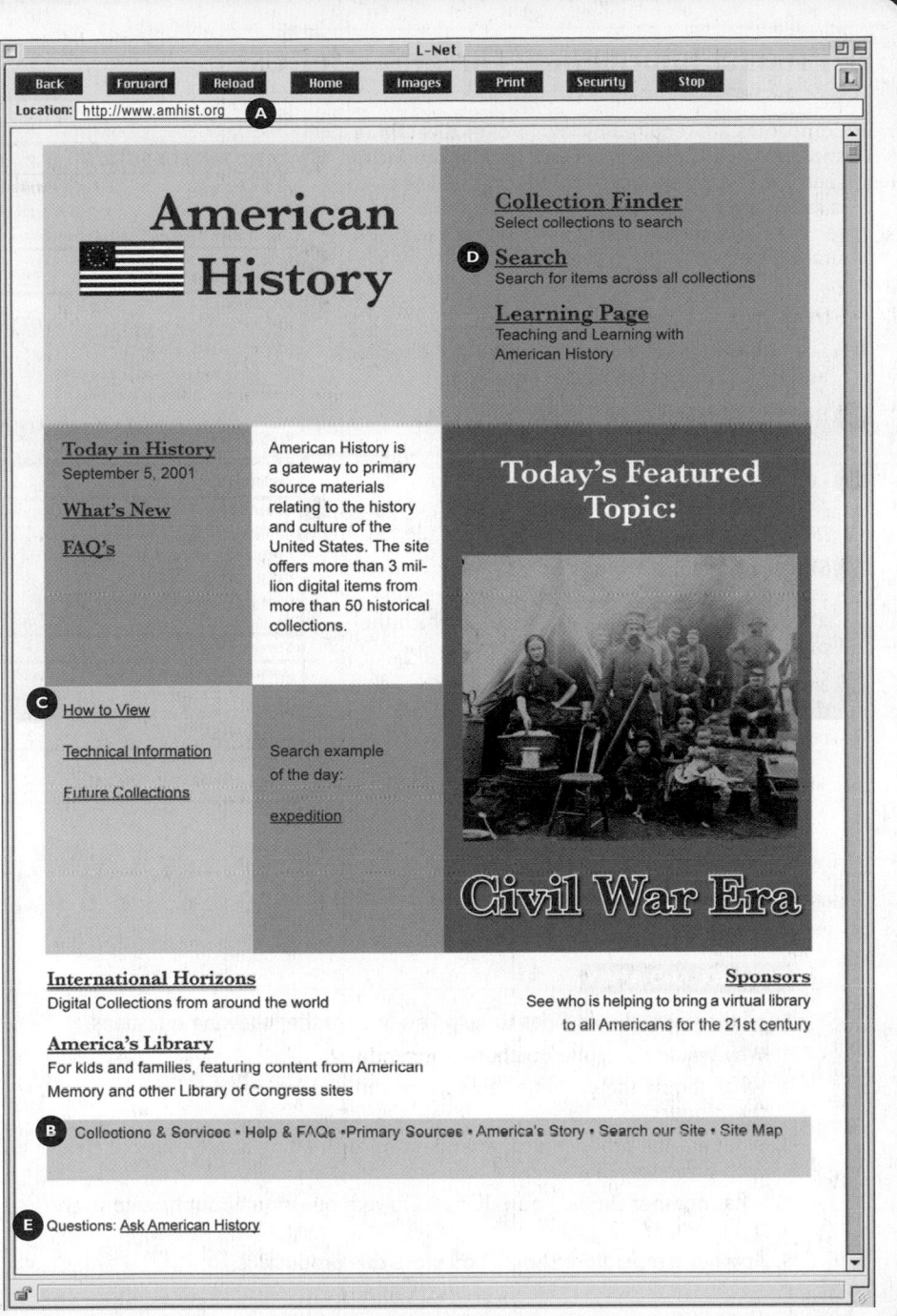

ACADEMIC READING HANDBOOK **1369**

## Product Information: Directions for Use

Companies are required by law to offer **directions** and warnings about the safe use of their products. Learning to read and follow product guidelines is important for your own safety. Look at the sample product information as you read each strategy below.

### Strategies for Reading

**A** Scan **headings** to understand important directions and other product topics that are covered.

**B** Read information on the **purpose**, or **uses**, for the product.

**C** Look closely at important **directions** and **recommendations** to ensure safe usage of the product.

**D** Study important **warnings** or other highlighted information that describe specific dangers, side effects, or important conditions under which the product must be used.

**E** Note **phone numbers** that are listed in the event that the consumer has a question or concern regarding the safe use of the product.

---

**A** **CALOSMOOTH LOTION**

| *Active Ingredient* | *Purpose* |
|---|---|
| Pramoxine HCl 1.01% | External analgesic |
| Zinc acetate 0.1% | Skin protectant |

**B** *Uses* Relieves itching and discomfort associated with poison ivy

**D** *Warnings*
- For external use only
- Avoid contact with eyes
- Stop use and ask doctor if condition worsens or itching persists more than 7 days

**Keep out of reach of children. If swallowed, get medical help or contact a Poison Control Center right away.**

**C** *Directions*
- Shake well
- Apply over affected area and blend into skin no more than 3 to 4 times daily
- For children under 2 years of age: ask a doctor

*Storage* 59°–77° F

*Inactive Ingredients* Alcohol USP, camphor, citric acid, diazolidinyl, urea, glycerin, fragrance, polysorbate 40, propylparaban, purified water

**E** **Questions** Call *1–800–555–1234* Monday–Friday, 9AM–5PM EST

---

**PRACTICE AND APPLY**

Read the product guidelines to help you answer the following questions.

1. Why would someone purchase this product?
2. What should the customer do if he or she accidentally swallows the product?
3. What are the product recommendations for treating a one-year-old child with poison ivy?
4. What number should you call if you have a question about how to use the product?
5. At what temperature should you store this product?

---

**PRACTICE AND APPLY ANSWERS**

1. to relieve itching and pain caused by poison ivy
2. get medical help or contact a Poison Control Center right away
3. ask a doctor
4. 1-800-555-1234
5. 59-77° F

## Reading a Recreation Schedule

Knowing how to read a **schedule** accurately will help you plan events and organize your time wisely. Look at the example as you read each strategy on this list.

### Strategies for Reading

**A** Scan the **title** and important **headings** to know what the schedule covers.

**B** Note the specific **locations** where different activities will occur.

**C** Look for **expressions of time** in terms of **dates** or **days of the week** and specific **hours and minutes** to help you understand how the weekly or daily schedule works.

**D** Look at specific **activities** to determine which ones occur at a given time and place.

| TFA Community Recreation Schedule: September 25–December 8 | | |
|---|---|---|
| Exterior doors to building close one-half hour prior to closing time. | | |
| **Facility** | **Days and Times** | **Activities** |
| **Eno Family Sports Center 555–4531** | | |
| Rosen Athletic Hall | M–S 10 AM–4 PM, Sun closed | Weight Training |
| Lockers and Showers | M–S 9 AM–5 PM, Sun closed | |
| Varsity Weight Room | Sat/Sun noon–4 PM | Weight Training |
| **Banks Recreation Pool 555–0721** | M–F 10 AM–2 PM, 6–7:30 PM | Adult Rec Swim |
| *Swimming, studying, etc., are not allowed in* | (Wed–Fri, 9/25–9/27 noon–2 PM only) | (must be over 16) |
| *the facility during non-rec hours.* | Sat/Sun 1–5 PM | Family swim—children OK |
| **Ford Center 555–3240** | M–F 9 AM–7 PM, Sat/Sun, 1–5 PM | Exercise Machines |
| | M/W/F 9 AM–2 PM, Sat 5–8 PM | Basketball Rec |
| | T/Th 11 AM–3 PM | Basketball Rec |
| | M/W/F 11 AM–3 PM, Sat noon–5 PM | Badminton Rec |
| | Sun noon–2 PM | Open Rec |

**PRACTICE AND APPLY**

Answer the following questions using the recreation schedule and the strategies on this page.

**1.** What time span is covered by this schedule?

**2.** What specific sports are played in the Ford Center?

**3.** If you are in weight training, on which day must you plan to shower at home?

**4.** What hours can adults swim if they go to the pool on the last Friday in September?

**PRACTICE AND APPLY ANSWERS**
1. September 25 – December 8
2. basketball and badminton
3. Sunday
4. noon – 2 P.M.

# Glossary of Literary Terms

**Act** An act is a major unit of action in a play, similar to a chapter in a book. Depending on their lengths, plays can have as many as five acts. Arthur Miller's play *The Crucible* has four acts.

*See also* **Drama; Scene.**

**Allegory** An allegory is a work of literature in which people, objects, and events stand for abstract qualities. In an allegory, a bird might represent freedom, for example, or a child might represent innocence.

***Example:*** Nathaniel Hawthorne's "Dr. Heidegger's Experiment" can be interpreted as an allegory with each of the characters representing an abstract quality—for instance, Mr. Medbourne might represent greed. In "The Masque of the Red Death," the main character Prospero, the sequence and the decorations of the rooms in the castle, and objects such as the ebony clock all have allegorical meaning.

*See pages 462, 500.*

**Alliteration** Alliteration is the repetition of consonant sounds at the beginnings of words. Poets use alliteration to impart a musical quality to their poems, to create mood, to reinforce meaning, to emphasize particular words, and to unify lines or stanzas. Note the examples of alliteration in the following line:

> Doubting, dreaming dreams no mortal ever dared to dream before.
> —Edgar Allan Poe, from "The Raven"

*See pages 467–469.*

**Allusion** An allusion is an indirect reference to a person, place, event, or literary work with which the author believes the reader will be familiar.

***Example:*** In "Speech in the Virginia Convention," Patrick Henry warns colonists not to be "betrayed with a kiss"—an allusion to the Apostle Judas, who betrayed Jesus by kissing him.

*See pages 267, 307, 1146.*

**Analogy** An analogy is a point by point comparison between two things for the purpose of clarifying the less familiar of the two subjects.

***Example:*** In "My Dungeon Shook," James Baldwin draws an analogy between his nephew's probable reaction to seeing the stars shining while the sun is out and white people's reaction to black people's moving out of their fixed places.

*See pages 676, 863, 964.*

**Anapest** *See* **Meter.**

**Anaphora** Anaphora is a repetition of a word or words at the beginning of successive lines, clauses, or sentences:

> Blackness
> is a title,
> is a preoccupation,
> is a commitment . . .
> —Gwendolyn Brooks, from "Primer for Blacks"

*See page 971.*
*See also* **Repetition.**

**Anecdote** An anecdote is a brief story that focuses on a single episode or event in a person's life and that is used to illustrate a particular point.

***Example:*** In "Straw into Gold," Sandra Cisneros provides an anecdote about the challenge she faced when ordered to make corn tortillas, a task she had never done before. This anecdote illustrates Cisneros's pluck in attempting the seemingly impossible.

*See page 1227.*

**Antagonist** An antagonist is usually the principal character in opposition to the **protagonist**, or hero of a narrative or drama. The antagonist can also be a force of nature.

*Example:* In Bernard Malamud's "Armistice," the antagonist is Gus Wagner, the meat man, who haggles about the Nazis' war tactics with the protagonist, Morris Lieberman.

See page 1178.
See also **Character; Protagonist.**

**Antihero** An antihero is a protagonist who has the qualities opposite to those of a hero; he or she may be insecure, ineffective, cowardly, sometimes dishonest or dishonorable, most often a failure. The character Him in Lanford Wilson's *Wandering* is an antihero. A popular antihero in contemporary culture is the cartoon character Homer Simpson.

**Aphorism** An aphorism is a brief statement, usually one sentence long, that expresses a general principle or truth about life.

*Example:* Ralph Waldo Emerson's "Self-Reliance" is sprinkled with such memorable aphorisms as "A foolish consistency is the hobgoblin of little minds."

See page 367.

**Assonance** Assonance is the repetition of vowel sounds within words. Both poets and prose writers use assonance to impart a musical quality to their works, to create mood, to reinforce meaning, to emphasize particular words, and to unify lines, stanzas, or passages. Note examples of assonance in the following lines:

> Along the window-sill, the lipstick stubs
> Glittered in their steel shells.
> — Rita Dove, from "Adolescence—III"

See also **Alliteration; Consonance; Rhyme.**

**Atmosphere** See **Mood.**

**Audience** Audience is the person or persons who are intended to read a piece of writing. The intended audience of a work determines its form, style, tone, and the details included. For example, Cabeza de Vaca's audience for *La Relación* was the king of Spain. Hence *La Relación* took the form of a formal report with a patriotic tone that included details of the explorers' hardship and determination. Had the work been addressed to Cabeza de Vaca's wife, it would likely have been less formal and probably would have included details about his personal feelings.

See pages 78, 98.

**Author's Purpose** A writer usually writes for one or more of these purposes: to inform, to entertain, to express himself or herself, or to persuade readers to believe or do something. For example, the purpose of a news report is to inform; the purpose of an editorial is to persuade the readers or audience to do or believe something.

*Example:* In *The Interesting Narrative of the Life of Olaudah Equiano,* the author's purpose is primarily to inform readers about the horrors that captured Africans endured in the holds of slave ships during the Middle Passage. Thoreau's purpose in "Civil Disobedience," on the other hand, is to persuade his audience to use nonviolent resistance to oppose unjust laws.

See pages 107, 116, 562, 645.

**Autobiographical Essay** See **Essay.**

**Autobiography** An autobiography is the story of a person's life written by that person. Generally written from the first-person point of view, autobiographies can vary in style from straightforward chronological accounts to impressionistic narratives.

*Example:* Both *Narrative of the Life of Frederick Douglass, an American Slave* and *Coming of Age in Mississippi* are autobiographies.

See pages 116, 571.

**Ballad** A ballad is a narrative poem that was originally meant to be sung. Ballads often contain dialogue and repetition and suggest more than they actually state. Traditional **folk ballads,** composed by unknown authors and handed down orally, are written in four-line stanzas with regular rhythm and rhyme. A **literary ballad** is one that is modeled on the folk ballads but written by a single author—for example, Dudley Randall's "Ballad of Birmingham."

*See page 620.*
*See also* **Narrative Poem; Rhyme; Rhythm.**

**Biography** A biography is a type of nonfiction in which a writer gives a factual account of someone else's life. Written in the third person, a biography may cover a person's entire life or focus on only an important part of it. The poet Carl Sandburg wrote an acclaimed six-volume biography of Abraham Lincoln. Modern biography includes a popular form called **fictionalized biography** in which writers use their imaginations to re-create past conversations and to elaborate on some incidents.

**Blank Verse** A poem written in blank verse consists of unrhymed lines of iambic pentameter. In other words, each line of blank verse has five pairs of syllables. In most pairs, an unstressed syllable is followed by a stressed syllable. The most versatile of poetic forms, blank verse imitates the natural rhythms of English speech, as in the following lines:

> Ĭ lét mў néighbŏr knŏw bĕyónd thĕ híll;
> Ănd ón á ă dáy wĕ méet tŏ wálk thĕ líne
> Ănd sét thĕ wáll bĕtwéen ŭs ónce ăgáin.
> —Robert Frost, from "Mending Wall"

*See also* **Meter; Rhythm.**
*See page 1013.*

**Caesura** (sĭ-zhŏŏr′ə) A caesura is a pause or a break in a line of poetry. Poets use a caesura to emphasize the word or phrase that precedes it or to vary the rhythmical effects. In the following line, a caesura follows the word *die:*

> If we must die, let it not be like hogs
> —Claude McKay, from "If We Must Die"

**Cast of Characters** The cast of characters is a list of all the characters in a play, usually in the order of appearance. This list is found at the beginning of a script.

*See page 165.*

**Catalog** A catalog is a list of people, things, or attributes. This technique, found in epics and in the Bible, also characterizes Whitman's style, as seen in the beginning of this line:

> Kanuck, Tuckahoe, Congressman, Cuff, I give them the same, I receive them the same.
> —Walt Whitman, from "Song of Myself"

*See page 396.*

**Character** Characters are the people, and sometimes animals or other beings, who take part in the action of a story or novel. Events center on the lives of one or more characters, referred to as **main characters.** The other characters, called **minor characters,** interact with the main characters and help move the story along. In Bernard Malamud's "Armistice," for example, Morris Lieberman and Gus Wagner are main characters, while Leonard, Morris's son, is a minor character.

Characters may also be classified as either static or dynamic. **Static characters** tend to stay in a fixed position over the course of the story. They do not experience life-altering moments and seem to act the same, even though their situations may change. In contrast, **dynamic characters** evolve as individuals, learning from their experiences and growing emotionally.

*See pages 860, 892, 1212.*
*See also* **Antagonist; Foil; Motivation; Protagonist.**

**Characterization** Characterization refers to the techniques a writer uses to develop characters. There are four basic methods of characterization:

1. A writer may use physical description. In F. Scott Fitzgerald's "Winter Dreams," Judy Jones is described as follows:

> She wore a blue gingham dress, rimmed at throat and shoulders with a white edging that accentuated her tan . . . She was arrestingly beautiful. The color in her cheeks was centered like the color in a picture—it was not a "high" color, but a sort of fluctuating and feverish warmth . . .

2. The character's own actions, words, thoughts, and feelings might be presented. In Fitzgerald's story, after Judy Jones tries to revive the romance between herself and Dexter, she cries and says, "I'm more beautiful than anybody else, . . . why can't I be happy?"

3. The actions, words, thoughts, and feelings of other characters provide another means of developing a character. Mr. Sandwood, in Fitzgerald's story, exclaims about Judy Jones: "My God, she's good-looking!" To which Mr. Hedrick replies: "Good looking! She always looks as if she wanted to be kissed! Turning those big cow-eyes on every calf in town!"

4. The narrator's own direct comments also serve to develop a character. The narrator of "Winter Dreams" says of Judy Jones:

> Whatever Judy wanted, she went after with the full pressure of her charm. There was no divergence of method, no jockeying for position or premeditation of effects—there was very little mental side to any of her affairs. She simply made men conscious to the highest degree of her physical loveliness.

*See pages 525, 539, 833.*
*See also* **Character; Narrator; Point of View.**

**Cliché** A cliché is an overused expression that has lost its freshness, force, and appeal. The phrase "happy as a lark" is an example of a cliché.

**Climax** In a plot structure, the climax, or **turning point,** is the moment when the reader's interest and emotional intensity reach a peak. The climax usually occurs toward the end of a story and often results in a change in the characters or a solution to the conflict.

**Example:** In Edgar Allan Poe's "The Masque of the Red Death," the climax occurs when the Red Death arrives at the masked ball and is confronted by Prince Prospero. Shortly afterward, Prospero and all of his guests die.

*See also* **Falling Action; Plot; Rising Action; Resolution.**

**Comedy** A comedy is a dramatic work that is light and often humorous in tone, usually ending happily with a peaceful resolution of the main conflict. A comedy differs from a **farce** by having a more believable plot, more realistic characters, and less boisterous behavior.

*See also* **Drama; Farce.**

**Coming-of-Age Story** In a coming-of-age story, the main character is an adolescent in the process of growing up. As the story unfolds, this character faces conflicts, makes difficult decisions, and gains new awareness of self and others. The **plot** describes a rite of passage, or the experiences that lead the main character to a new level of maturity.

**Example:** In "Seventeen Syllables," Rosie matures because of her relationship with Jesus Carrasco and her anguish over her parents' conflicts.

*See page 800.*

**Conceit** *See* **Extended Metaphor.**

**Conflict** A conflict is a struggle between opposing forces that is the basis of a story's plot. An **external conflict** pits a character against nature, society, or another character. An **internal conflict** is a conflict between opposing forces within a character.

**Example:** In "Coyote and the Buffalo," Coyote's struggle to keep Buffalo Bill from killing him is an external conflict, whereas Coyote's struggle to decide whether to kill and eat the buffalo cow is an internal conflict.

See pages 53, 88, 243, 1109, 1166.
See also **Antagonist; Plot.**

**Connotation** Connotation is the emotional response evoked by a word, in contrast to its **denotation,** which is its literal meaning. *Kitten,* for example, is defined as a "young cat." However, the word also suggests, or connotes, images of softness, warmth, and playfulness.

**Consonance** Consonance is the repetition of consonant sounds within and at the ends of words, as in the following line:

> Some late visitor entreating entrance at my chamber door.
>
> —Edgar Allan Poe, from "The Raven"

See also **Alliteration; Assonance.**

**Contrast** Contrast is a technique used to clarify something by showing it against its opposite. In "What Is an American?" for example, de Crèvecoeur contrasts America and Americans with Europe and Europeans.

**Corrido** A *corrido* is a fast-paced ballad that derives from the Mexican oral tradition. *Corridos* were first sung in Mexico in the mid-nineteenth century and soon spread to the border regions of South Texas. A *corrido* generally involves a cultural conflict.

**Example:** "The Legend of Gregorio Cortez," a prose retelling of a *corrido,* involves the struggle between Mexicans and Anglos in Texas at the beginning of the 20th century.

See also **Ballad; Narrative Poem.**

**Couplet** See **Sonnet.**

**Creation Myth** See **Myth.**

**Cuento** A *cuento* is a traditional folk tale that comes from the oral tradition of New Mexico and southern Colorado. First brought to the southwestern part of the United States by Spanish and Mexican settlers, *cuentos* were further influenced by Native American cultures in this area. Early settlers and their descendants told cuentos to entertain, reinforce cultural

values, and teach traditional customs and beliefs to their children. "The Indian and the Hundred Cows" is an example of a *cuento.*

See page 643.
See also **Folk Tale; Oral Literature.**

**Cultural Hero** A cultural hero is a larger-than-life figure who reflects the values of a people. Rather than being the creation of a single writer, this kind of hero evolves from the telling of folk tales from one generation to the next. The role of the cultural hero is to provide a noble image that will inspire and guide the actions of all who share that culture.

**Example:** Gregorio Cortez, a Mexican–American cultural hero, exhibits family loyalty when he shoots the sheriff who shot Cortez's brother, Román.

See page 718.

**Dactyl** See **Meter.**

**Denotation** See **Connotation.**

**Dénouement** The dénouement is the final unraveling or outcome of the plot in drama or fiction during which the complications of the plot are resolved, any mysteries are solved, and any secrets are explained.

**Example:** In "The Devil and Tom Walker," the dénouement explains what becomes of Tom's ill-gained wealth after his death.

**Description** Description is writing that helps a reader to picture scenes, events, and characters. Effective description usually relies on imagery, figurative language, and precise diction, as in the following passage;

> I saw again the naked house on the prairie, black and grim as a wooden fortress; the black pond where I had learned to swim, its margin pitted with sun-dried cattle tracks; the rain gullied clay banks about the naked house, the four dwarf ash seedlings where the dish-cloths were always hung to dry before the kitchen door.
>
> —Willa Cather, from "A Wagner Matinee"

See page 676.
See also **Diction; Figurative Language; Imagery.**

**Dialect** A dialect is the distinct form of a language as it is spoken in one geographical area or by a particular social or ethnic group. A group's dialect is reflected in characteristic pronunciations, vocabulary, idioms, and grammatical constructions. When trying to reproduce a given dialect, writers often use unconventional spellings to suggest the way words actually sound. Writers use dialect to establish setting, to provide local color, and to develop characters. In the following passage, the use of dialect captures the sound and tang of frontier speech:

> And he had a little small bull-pup, that to look at him you'd think he warn't worth a cent but to set around and look ornery and lay for a chance to steal something.
> —Mark Twain, from "The Notorious Jumping Frog of Calaveras County"

See pages 593, 637,685.
See also **Local Color Realism.**

**Dialogue** Dialogue is conversation between two or more characters in either fiction or nonfiction. In drama, the story is told almost exclusively through dialogue, which moves the plot forward and reveals character.

See pages 206, 1155.
See also **Drama.**

**Diary** A diary is a writer's personal day-to-day account of his or her experiences and impressions. Most diaries are private and not intended to be shared. Some, however, have been published because they are well written and provide useful perspectives on historical events or on the everyday life of particular eras. Two important American diaries, not included in this book, are Madame Sarah Kemble Knight's 18th-century diary of her journey on horseback from Boston to New York and Mary Boykin Chesnut's diary of the Civil War.

**Diction** A writer's or speaker's choice of words is called diction. Diction includes both vocabulary (individual words) and syntax (the order or arrangement of words). Diction can be formal or informal, technical or common, abstract or concrete. In the following complex sentence, the diction is formal:

> When, however, the mass movement repudiates violence while moving resolutely toward its goal, its opponents are revealed as the instigators and practitioners of violence if it occurs.
> —Martin Luther King, Jr., from *Stride Toward Freedom*

See pages 150, 1198.

**Drama** Drama is literature in which plot and character are developed through dialogue and action; in other words, drama is literature in play form. Dramas are meant to be performed by actors and actresses who appear on stage, before radio microphones, or in front of television or movie cameras.

Unlike other forms of literature, such as fiction or poetry, a work of drama requires the collaboration of many people in order to come to life. In an important sense, a drama in printed form is an incomplete work of art, a script that must be fleshed out by a director, actors, set designers, and others who interpret the work and stage a performance.

Most plays are divided into acts, with each act having an emotional peak, or climax, of its own. The acts sometimes are divided into scenes; each scene is limited to a single time and place. Most contemporary plays have two or three acts, although some have only one act.

See pages 101–102.
See also **Act; Dialogue; Scene; Stage Directions.**

**Dramatic Irony** See **Irony.**

**Elegy** An elegy is a poem written in tribute to a person, usually someone who has died recently. The tone of an elegy is usually formal and dignified. In "Gary Keillor," Gary gives a comic rendition of Walt Whitman's elegy for Abraham Lincoln, "O Captain! My Captain!"

**Epic Poem** An epic poem is a long narrative poem on a serious subject presented in an elevated or formal style. An epic traces the adventures of a hero whose actions consist of courageous, even superhuman deeds, which often represent the ideals and values of a group, nation, or race. *I Am Joaquín* is an epic poem.

*See page 316.*
*See also* **Narrative Poem.**

**Epithet** An epithet is a brief descriptive phrase that points out traits associated with a particular person or thing.

**Example:** Carl Sandburg's "Chicago" begins with a series of epithets, such as "Hog Butcher for the World."

**Essay** An essay is a short work of nonfiction that deals with a single subject. Essays are often informal, loosely structured, and highly personal. They can be descriptive, informative, persuasive, narrative, or any combination of these. Amy Tan's personal essay "Mother Tongue" combines all of these modes.

An **autobiographical essay** focuses on an aspect of a writer's life. Generally, writers of autobiographical essays use the first-person point of view, combining objective description with the expression of subjective feelings. Zora Neale Hurston's "How It Feels to Be Colored Me" is an example of an autobiographical essay.

*See pages 369, 957, 1221.*

**Exaggeration** *See* **Hyperbole.**

**Experimental Poetry** Poetry described as experimental is often full of surprises—comic situations, conversational speech, playful use of words, descriptions of ordinary objects, and other distinctive elements not found in traditional verse forms. William Carlos Williams belonged to a group of experimental poets known as the **Imagists.** Their poems contained sharp, clear images of striking beauty, similar to the ones found in haiku. E. E. Cummings's "anyone lived in pretty how town" reflects his

poetic experiments, such as altering the expected order of words.

*See page 414.*

**Exposition** Exposition is the part of a literary work that provides the background information necessary to understand characters and their actions. Typically found at the beginning of a work, the exposition introduces the characters, describes the setting, and summarizes significant events that took place before the action begins.

**Example:** In the exposition to "The Devil and Tom Walker," Washington Irving introduces the main characters—a miser and his wife—who dwell in a desolate house near a swamp and take wicked glee in hoarding things from each other.

*See also* **Plot; Rising Action.**

**Extended Metaphor** Like any metaphor, an extended metaphor is a comparison between two essentially unlike things that nevertheless have something in common. It does not contain the word *like* or *as*. An extended metaphor compares two things at some length and in various ways. Sometimes the comparison is carried throughout a paragraph, a stanza, or an entire selection. In the following stanza, notice the extended metaphor comparing hope to a bird:

> "Hope" is the thing with feathers—
> That perches in the soul—
> And sings the tune without the words—
> And never stops—at all— . . .
>
> —Emily Dickinson,
> from "'Hope' is the thing with feathers—"

Like an extended metaphor, a **conceit** compares two apparently dissimilar things in several ways. The word *conceit* usually implies a more elaborate, formal, and ingeniously clever comparison than the extended metaphor.

*See page 948.*

**External Conflict** *See* **Conflict.**

**Eyewitness Report** An eyewitness report is a firsthand account of an event written by someone who directly observed it or participated in it. (As such, an eyewitness account is a **primary source.**) Narrated from the first-person point of view, eyewitness reports almost always include the following:

- objective facts about an event
- a chronological (time-order) pattern of organization
- vivid sensory details
- quotations from people who were present
- description of the writer's feelings and interpretations.

The excerpt from Anne Moody's autobiography, *Coming of Age in Mississippi,* is an eyewitness report of a sit-in in 1963.

*See page 616.*
*See also* **Primary Source.**

**Fable** A fable is a brief tale that illustrates a clear, often directly stated, **moral,** or lesson. The characters in a fable are usually animals, but sometimes they are humans. The most well-known fables—for example, "The Fox and the Crow" and "The Tortoise and the Hare" are those of Aesop, a Greek slave who lived about 600 B.C. Traditionally, fables are handed down from generation to generation as oral literature.

*See also* **Oral Literature.**

**Falling Action** In a plot structure, the falling action, or **resolution,** occurs after the climax to reveal the final outcome of events and to tie up any loose ends.

**Example:** In Joyce Carol Oates's "Hostage," the falling action occurs after Bruno attacks the narrator's assailant, nearly killing him. We learn that Bruno is given six months' probation and psychiatric care. He withdraws from others, quits school, joins the army, and is shipped to Korea, where he dies in battle.

*See also* **Climax; Exposition; Plot; Rising Action.**

**Farce** A farce is a type of exaggerated comedy that features an absurd plot, ridiculous situations, and humorous dialogue. The main purpose of a farce is to keep an audience laughing. The characters are usually **stereotypes,** or simplified examples of different traits or qualities. Comic devices typically used in farces include mistaken identity, deception, wordplay—such as puns and double meanings—and exaggeration.

*See also* **Comedy; Stereotype.**

**Fiction** Fiction refers to works of prose that contain imaginary elements. Although fiction, like nonfiction, may be based on actual events and real people, it differs from nonfiction in that it is shaped primarily by the writer's imagination. For example, although Garrison Keillor's "Gary Keillor" is based on autobiographical experiences, it cannot be classified as nonfiction because it is imbued with imaginary events and exaggeration in order to hold the reader's interest. The two major types of fiction are novels and short stories. The four basic elements of a work of fiction are character, setting, plot, and theme.

*See also* **Novel; Short Story.**

**Figurative Language** Figurative language is language that communicates ideas beyond the literal meaning of words. Figurative language can make descriptions and unfamiliar or difficult ideas easier to understand. Note the figurative language in lines 3–5 below:

> Every few years
> Tía Chucha would visit the family
> in a tornado of song
> and open us up
> as if we were an overripe avocado.
> —Luis Rodriguez, from "Tía Chucha"

The most common types of figurative language, called **figures of speech,** are simile, metaphor, personification, and hyperbole.

*See pages 287, 293, 392, 760, 943.*
*See also* **Hyperbole; Metaphor; Personification; Simile.**

**Figures of Speech** *See* **Figurative Language.**

**First-Person Point of View** *See* **Point of View.**

**Flashback** A flashback is a scene that interrupts the action of a narrative to describe events that took place at an earlier time. It provides background helpful in understanding a character's present situation.

*Example:* William Faulkner's "A Rose for Emily" opens with Miss Emily's funeral, followed by a flashback that recounts how, when she was alive, Colonel Sartoris exempted her from paying taxes.

**Foil** A foil is a character whose traits contrast with those of another character. A writer might use a minor character as a foil to emphasize the positive traits of the main character.

*Example:* In "The Legend of Gregorio Cortez," the "loud-mouthed, discontented" Román is a foil for his heroic brother, Gregorio Cortez.

*See page 228.*
*See also* **Character.**

**Folk Tale** A folk tale is a short, simple story that is handed down, usually by word of mouth, from generation to generation. Folk tales include legends, fairy tales, myths, and fables. Folk tales often teach family obligations or societal values. "Coyote and the Buffalo" is an Okanogan folk tale and "The Indian and the Hundred Cows" is a Hispanic folk tale.

*See also* **Legend; Myth; Fable.**

**Foot** *See* **Meter.**

**Foreshadowing** Foreshadowing is a writer's use of hints or clues to indicate events that will occur in a story. Foreshadowing creates suspense and at the same time prepares the reader for what is to come.

*Example:* In Nathaniel Hawthorne's "Dr. Heidegger's Experiment," the former rivalry for the Widow Wycherly foreshadows the rivalry that occurs later in Dr. Heidegger's study.

*See pages 514, 525.*

**Form** At its simplest, form refers to the physical arrangement of words in a poem—the length and placement of the lines and the grouping of lines into stanzas. The term can also be used to refer to other types of patterning in poetry, anything from rhythm and other sound patterns to the design of a traditional poetic type, such as a sonnet or dramatic monologue. Finally, *form* can be used as a synonym for *genre*, which refers to literary categories, ranging from the broad (short story, novel) to the narrowly defined (sonnet).

*See also* **Genre, Stanza.**

**Free Verse** Free verse is poetry that does not have regular patterns of rhyme and meter. The lines in free verse often flow more naturally than do rhymed, metrical lines and thus achieve a rhythm more like that of everyday human speech. Walt Whitman is generally credited with bringing free verse to American poetry:

> I hear America singing, the varied carols I hear,
> Those of mechanics, each one singing his as it
>    should be blithe and strong,
> The carpenter singing his as he measures his
>    plank or beam,
> The mason singing his as he makes ready for
>    work, or leaves off work, . . .
>
> —Walt Whitman, from "I Hear America Singing"

*See page 395, 404.*
*See also* **Meter; Rhyme.**

**Genre** Genre refers to the distinct types into which literary works can be grouped. The four main literary genres are fiction, poetry, nonfiction, and drama.

**Gothic Literature** Gothic literature is characterized by grotesque characters, bizarre situations, and violent events. Originating in Europe, Gothic literature was a popular form of writing in the United States during the 19th century, especially in the hands of such notables as Edgar Allan Poe and Nathaniel Hawthorne. Interest in Gothic revived in the 20th century among southern writers such as William Faulkner and Flannery O'Connor.

*See pages 446–448.*

**Haiku** Haiku is a highly compressed form of Japanese poetry that creates a brief, clear picture in order to produce an emotional response. Haiku relies heavily on imagery, usually drawn from nature, and on the power of suggestion. When written in Japanese, a haiku has three lines of five, seven, and five syllables each. Here is a haiku written in English:

> Leaning out over
> The dreadful precipice,
> One contemptuous tree.
>
> —W. H. Auden

*See page 790.*

**Historical Context** The historical context of a literary work refers to the social conditions that inspired or influenced its creation. To understand and appreciate some works, the reader must relate them to particular events in history. For example, to understand fully Lincoln's "Gettysburg Address," the reader must imaginatively re-create the scene—Lincoln addressing a war-weary crowd on the very site where a horrific battle had recently been fought.

**Example:** Patrick Henry's "Speech in the Virginia Convention" was inspired by the British military buildup in America prior to the American Revolution; Martin Luther King's *Stride Toward Freedom* was inspired by the civil rights struggle of the 1950s to overturn segregation laws in the South.

*See pages 307, 369, 605.*

**Historical Narratives** Historical narratives are accounts of real-life historical experiences, given either by a person who experienced those events or by someone who has studied or observed them. Cabeza de Vaca's *La Relación,* William Bradford's *Of Plymouth Plantation,* and *The Interesting Narrative of the Life of Olaudah Equiano* all are historical narratives.

*See page 70.*
*See also* **Primary Sources; Secondary Sources.**

**Humor** is a term applied to a literary work whose purpose is to entertain and to evoke laughter—for example, Twain's "The Celebrated Jumping Frog of Calaveras County." In literature there are three basic types of humor, all of which may involve exaggeration or irony. **Humor of situation,** which is derived from the plot of a work, usually involves exaggerated events or situational irony. **Humor of character** is often based on exaggerated personalities or on characters who fail to recognize their own flaws, a form of dramatic irony. **Humor of language** may include sarcasm, exaggeration, puns, or verbal irony, which occurs when what is said is not what is meant.

*See pages 434, 679, 685.*
*See also* **Comedy; Farce; Irony.**

**Hyperbole** Hyperbole is a figure of speech in which the truth is exaggerated for emphasis or for humorous effect. The expression "I'm so hungry I could eat a horse" is a hyperbole.

**Example:** In Américo Paredes's "The Legend of Gregorio Cortez," the narrator, describing Cortez's abilities as a gunman, says, "He could put five bullets into a piece of board and not make but one hole, and quicker than you could draw a good deep breath."

*See also* **Understatement.**

**Iamb** *See* **Meter.**

**Iambic Pentameter** *See* **Blank Verse; Meter.**

**Imagery** The descriptive words and phrases that a writer uses to re-create sensory experiences are called imagery. By appealing to the five senses, imagery helps a reader imagine exactly what the characters and experiences being described are like. In the following passage, the imagery lets the reader experience the miserliness of the main character and his wife:

They lived in a forlorn-looking house that stood alone and had an air of starvation. A few straggling savin trees, emblems of sterility, grew near it; no smoke ever curled from its chimney . . . A miserable horse, whose ribs were as articulate as the bars of a gridiron, stalked about a field, where a thin carpet of moss . . . tantalized and balked his hunger.

—Washington Irving,
from "The Devil and Tom Walker"

The term **synesthesia** refers to imagery that appeals to one sense when another is being stimulated; for example, description of sounds in terms of colors, as in this passage:

Music. The great blobs of purple and red emotion have not touched him.

—Zora Neale Hurston,
from "How It Feels to Be Colored Me"

See pages 360, 496, 676, 779, 804, 1005, 1030, 1093, 1198, 1225.
See also **Description; Kinesthetic Imagery.**

**Imagists** See **Experimental Poetry; Style.**

**Impressionism** Impressionism refers to a technique of writing that reflects the ideals of a school of mid–19th-century French painters, including Manet, Monet, and Renoir. These painters believed that the artist should try to capture the impressions that an object makes rather than render it in precise, realistic detail. Impressionistic writers describe people, places, and events as they appear to an individual at a particular moment and from a particular angle of vision.

**Example:** In "A Mystery of Heroism," Crane uses an impressionistic technique to capture soldiers' sensations in battle.

**Interior Monologue** See **Monologue; Stream of Consciousness.**

**Internal Conflict** See **Conflict.**

**Inverted Syntax** Inverted syntax is a reversal in the expected order of words.

**Example:** In the first line of "Upon the Burning of Our House," Anne Bradstreet writes "when rest I took" rather than "when I took rest."

**Irony** Irony refers to a contrast between appearance and actuality. **Situational irony** is a contrast between what is expected to happen and what actually does happen, as in the poem "Richard Cory," when a gentleman who is admired and envied commits suicide. **Dramatic irony** occurs when readers know more about a situation or a character in a story than the characters do. In Flannery O'Connor's "The Life You Save May Be Your Own," for example, readers find out that Mr. Shiftlet is a scoundrel before the other characters do. **Verbal irony** occurs when someone states one thing and means another, as in the title of Stephen Crane's poem "Do Not Weep, Maiden, for War Is Kind."

See pages 539, 602, 667, 786, 1055, 1191.

**Kinesthetic Imagery** Kinesthetic imagery re-creates the tension felt through muscles, tendons, or joints in the body. In the following line, the phrase "the stiff Heart" creates a kinesthetic image:

The stiff Heart questions was it He, that bore,

—Emily Dickinson, from "After great pain, a formal feeling comes"

See also **Imagery.**

**Legend** A legend is a story passed down orally from generation to generation and popularly believed to have a historical basis. While some legends may be based on real people or situations, most of the events are either greatly exaggerated or fictitious. Like myths, legends may incorporate supernatural elements and magical deeds. But legends differ from myths in that they claim to be stories about real human beings and are often set in a particular time and place. "The Legend of Gregorio Cortez" is an example.

See page 718.

**Literary Criticism** Literary criticism refers to a piece of writing that focuses on a literary work or a genre, describing some aspect of it, such as its origin, its characteristics, or its effects. Toni Morrison's "Thoughts on the African-American Novel" is an example of literary criticism.

*See page 976.*

**Literary Letter** A literary letter is a letter that has been published and read by a wider audience because it was written by a well-known public figure or provides information about the period in which it was written. Abigail Adams's "Letter to John Adams" is an example of a literary letter.

*See page 282.*

**Loaded Language** Loaded language consists of words with strong connotations, or emotional associations. Writers and speakers use loaded language most often for persuasive purposes, as in this example:

> The God that holds you over the pit of hell, much as one holds a spider, or some loathsome insect over the fire, abhors you, and is dreadfully provoked.
>
> —Jonathan Edwards, from "Sinners in the Hands of an Angry God"

*See also* **Connotation.**

**Local Color Realism** Local color realism, especially popular in the late 18th century, is a style of writing that truthfully imitates ordinary life and brings a particular region alive by portraying the dialects, dress, mannerisms, customs, character types, and landscapes of that region. Mark Twain frequently uses local color realism in his writing for humorous effect.

*See pages 636, 679.*
*See also* **Dialect.**

**Lyric Poem** A lyric poem is a short poem in which a single speaker expresses thoughts and feelings in intensely emotional language. In a love lyric, a speaker expresses romantic love. In other lyrics, a speaker may meditate on nature or seek to resolve an emotional crisis. Anne Bradstreet's poem "To My Dear and Loving Husband" is a love lyric.

**Magical Realism** Magical realism is a style of writing that often includes exaggeration, unusual humor, magical and bizarre events, dreams that come true, and superstitions that prove warranted. Magical realism differs from pure fantasy in combining fantastic elements with realistic elements such as recognizable characters, believable dialogue, a true-to-life setting, a matter-of-fact tone, and a plot that sometimes contains historic events. This style characterizes some of the fiction of such influential South American writers as the late Jorge Luis Borges of Argentina and Gabriel Garcia Márquez of Colombia.

**Main Character** *See* **Character.**

**Memoir** A memoir is a form of auto-biographical writing in which a person recalls significant events in his or her life. Most memoirs share the following characteristics: (1) they usually are structured as narratives told by the writers themselves, using the first-person point of view; (2) although some names may be changed to protect privacy, memoirs are true accounts of actual events; (3) although basically personal, memoirs may deal with newsworthy events having a significance beyond the confines of the writer's life; (4) unlike strictly historical accounts, memoirs often include the writers' feelings and opinions about historical events, giving the reader insight into the impact of history on people's lives. Langston Hughes's "When the Negro Was in Vogue" is an example of a memoir.

**Metaphor** A metaphor is a figure of speech that compares two things that have something in common. Unlike similes, metaphors do not use the word *like* or *as*, but make comparisons directly.

**Example:** Abigail Adams's statement "our country is . . . the first and greatest parent" is a metaphor.

See pages 287, 347, 760, 815, 833.
See also **Figurative Language; Simile.**

**Meter** Meter is the repetition of a regular rhythmic unit in a line of poetry. Each unit, known as a **foot,** has one stressed syllable (indicated by a ′) and either one or two unstressed syllables (indicated by a ˘). The four basic types of metrical feet are the **iamb,** an unstressed syllable followed by a stressed syllable; the **trochee,** a stressed syllable followed by an unstressed syllable; the **anapest,** two unstressed syllables followed by a stressed syllable; and the **dactyl,** a stressed syllable followed by two unstressed syllables.

Two words are used to describe the meter of a line. The first word identifies the type of metrical foot—iambic, trochaic, anapestic, or dactylic—and the second word indicates the number of feet in a line: **monometer** (one foot), **dimeter** (two feet), **trimeter** (three feet), **tetrameter** (four feet), **pentameter** (five feet), **hexameter** (six feet), and so forth.

**Examples:** In "To My Dear and Loving Husband," the meter is **iambic pentameter,** the most common form of meter in English poetry.

> If ĕv | ĕr mán | wĕre lovéd | bў wífe | thĕn
> thée.

In the following lines from Henry Wadsworth Longfellow's "A Psalm of Life," the meter is trochaic tetrameter:

> Téll mĕ | nót, ĭn | móurnfŭl | númbĕrs,
> Lífe ĭs | bút ăn | émptў | dréam!—

See pages 142, 394.
See also **Rhythm; Scansion.**

**Minor Character** See **Character.**

**Modernism** Modernism was a literary movement that roughly spanned the time period between the two world wars, 1914–1945. Modernist works are characterized by a high degree of experimentation and spare, elliptical prose. Modernist characters are most often alienated people searching unsuccessfully for meaning and love in their lives. For example, in Hemingway's "The End of Something," Nick Adams feels alienated from his girlfriend but cannot explain why. The question of what's bothering Nick remains unanswered. Departing from the usual detailed narrative comments of his predecessors, Hemingway gives little direct information about the characters' feelings or thoughts. Instead, the reader has to infer the characters' inner thoughts from their words and actions and from the symbolism in the description of the setting.

See pages 992–994, 1016–1017.

**Monody** A lyric poem in which a single mourner expresses grief. Herman Melville's "Monody" laments the death of Nathaniel Hawthorne.

See page 513.
See also **Elegy.**

**Monologue** In a drama, the speech of a character who is alone on stage, voicing his or her thoughts, is known as a monologue, or a **soliloquy.** In a short story or a poem, the direct presentation of a character's unspoken thoughts is called an **interior monologue.** An interior monologue may jump back and forth between past and present, displaying thoughts, memories, and impressions just as they might occur in a person's mind. "I Stand Here Ironing" is an example of an interior monologue.

See pages 162, 815.
See also **Stream of Consciousness.**

**Mood** Mood is the feeling or atmosphere that a writer creates for the reader. The writer's use of connotation, imagery, figurative language, sound and rhythm, and descriptive details all contribute to the mood. These elements help create a creepy, threatening mood in the following passage:

> The swamp was thickly grown with great gloomy pines and hemlocks, . . . It was full of pits and quagmires, partly covered with weeds and mosses, where the green surface often betrayed the traveler into a gulf of black, smothering mud; . . .
>
> —Washington Irving, from "The Devil and Tom Walker"

See pages 496, 514, 928, 1005, 1101.
See also **Connotation; Description; Diction; Figurative Language; Imagery; Style.**

**Moral** See **Fable.**

**Motivation** Motivation is the stated or implied reason behind a character's behavior. The grounds for a character's action may not be obvious, but they should be comprehensible and consistent, in keeping with the character as developed by the writer.

**Example:** In Richard Wright's story "The Man Who Was Almost a Man," Dave's motivation for wanting to own a gun is to gain a sense of power and control.

See page 877.
See also **Character.**

**Myth** A myth is a traditional story, passed down through generations, that explains why the world is the way it is. Myths are essentially religious, because they present supernatural events and beings and articulate the values and beliefs of a cultural group. A **creation myth** is a particular kind of myth that explains how the universe, the earth, and life on earth began. "The World on the Turtle's Back" is an Iroquois creation myth.

See page 31.

**Narrative** A narrative is any type of writing that is primarily concerned with relating an event or a series of events. A narrative can be imaginary, as is a short story or novel, or factual, as is a newspaper account or a work of history. The word narration can be used interchangeably with narrative, which comes from the Latin word meaning "tell."

See also **Fiction; Nonfiction; Novel; Plot; Short Story.**

**Narrative Poem** A narrative poem is a poem that tells a story using elements of character, setting, and plot to develop a theme. Edgar Allan Poe's "The Raven" is a narrative poem, as is Dudley Randall's "Ballad of Birmingham."

See pages 618, 833.
See also **Ballad.**

**Narrator** The narrator of a story is the character or voice that relates the story's events to the reader.

**Example:** The narrator of Joyce Carol Oates's "Hostage" is one of the main characters, a girl in junior high school. The narrator of William Faulkner's "A Rose for Emily" is an unidentified citizen of Jefferson, Mississippi, Emily Grierson's hometown.

See pages 360, 779.

**Naturalism** An offshoot of realism, naturalism was a literary movement that originated in France in the late 1800s. Like the realists, the naturalists sought to render common people and ordinary life accurately. However, the naturalists emphasized how instinct and environment affect human behavior. Strongly influenced by Charles Darwin's ideas, the naturalists believed that the fate of humans is determined by forces beyond individual control. Stephen Crane's story "A Mystery of Heroism" is an example of naturalism.

See page 602.

**Nature Writing**  Nature writing refers to a type of essay in which the writer explores the relationship between humans and nature through firsthand observations. Henry David Thoreau, the father of American nature writing, was renowned for his patient, frequent, careful observations of Walden Pond and its environs. In *Walden,* he conveyed his observations and insights in richly poetic language.

*See page 392.*
*See also* **Essay.**

**Nonfiction**  Nonfiction is writing about real people, places, and events. Unlike fiction, nonfiction is largely concerned with factual information, although the writer shapes the information according to his or her purpose and viewpoint. Biography, autobiography, and newspaper articles are examples of nonfiction.

*See also* **Autobiography; Biography; Essay.**

**Novel**  A novel is an extended work of fiction. Like the short story, a novel is essentially the product of a writer's imagination. The most obvious difference between a novel and a short story is length. Because the novel is considerably longer, a novelist can develop a wider range of characters and a more complex plot.

**Octave**  *See* **Sonnet.**

**Off Rhyme**  *See* **Slant Rhyme.**

**Omniscient**  *See* **Point of View.**

**Onomatopoeia**  The word *onomatopoeia* literally means "name-making." It is the process of creating or using words that imitate sounds. The *buzz* of the bee, the *honk* of the car horn, the *peep* of the chick are all onomatopoetic, or echoic, words.

Onomatopoeia as a literary technique goes beyond the use of simple echoic words. Writers, particularly poets, choose words whose sounds suggest their denotative and connotative meanings: for example, *whisper, kick, gargle, gnash,* and *clatter.*

**Open Letter**  An open letter is addressed to a specific person but published for a wider readership.

*Example:* James Baldwin's "My Dungeon Shook" is an open letter addressed to his nephew, but intended for the general public, particularly white Americans.

*See page 964.*

**Oral Literature**  Oral literature is literature that is passed from one generation to another by performance or word of mouth. Folk tales, fables, myths, chants, and legends are part of the oral tradition of cultures throughout the world.

*See pages 20–22, 652.*
*See also* **Fable; Folk Tale; Legend; Myth.**

**Oxymoron**  *See* **Paradox.**

**Parable**  A parable is a brief story that is meant to teach a lesson or illustrate a moral truth. A parable is more than a simple story, however. Each detail of the parable corresponds to some aspect of the problem or moral dilemma to which it is directed. The story of the prodigal son in the Bible is a classic parable. In *Walden,* Thoreau's parable of the strong and beautiful bug that emerges from an old table is meant to show that, similarly, new life can awaken in human beings despite the deadness of society.

**Paradox**  A paradox is a statement that seems to contradict itself but may nevertheless suggest an important truth.

*Example:* In *Walden,* Henry David Thoreau writes the paradox "I am not as wise as the day I was born." The statement suggests that civilization erases a child's innate wisdom and spiritual awareness.

A special kind of paradox is the **oxymoron,** which brings together two contradictory terms, as in the phrases "wise fool" and "feather of lead."

*See pages 378, 392, 760, 959.*

**Parallelism** When a speaker or writer expresses ideas of equal worth with the same grammatical form, the technique is called parallelism, or parallel construction. Note that in the following example, each line or independent clause begins with the word *I* followed by a verb—*sit, hear, see* (and in the rest of the poem, *mark, observe*).

> I sit and look out upon all the sorrows of the world, and upon all oppression and shame,
>
> I hear secret convulsive sobs from young men at anguish with themselves, remorseful after deeds done,
>
> I see in low life the mother misused by her children, dying, neglected, gaunt, desperate,
>
> I see the wife misused by her husband, I see the treacherous seducer of young women . . .
>
> —Walt Whitman, from "I Sit and Look Out"

This parallel construction creates a rolling rhythm, emphasizes the role of the speaker, and conveys that the ideas all relate to the same theme—that the speaker observes "all the sorrows of the world."
*See pages 279, 404, 607.*

**Parody** Parody is writing that imitates either the style or the subject matter of a literary work for the purpose of criticism or humorous effect or for flattering tribute.

**Persona** *See* Speaker.

**Personal Essay** *See* Essay.

**Personification** Personification is a figure of speech in which an object, animal, or idea is given human characteristics.

**Example:** In Emily Dickinson's poem "Because I could not stop for Death," death is personified as a gentleman of kindness and civility
*See pages 750, 760, 828.*

**Persuasive Writing** Persuasive writing is intended to convince a reader to adopt a particular opinion or to perform a certain action. Effective persuasion usually appeals to both the reason and the emotions of an audience. Patrick Henry, Jonathan Edwards, Martin Luther King, Jr., and Malcolm X all use persuasion in their writing.
*See pages 158, 260–261.*

**Petrarchan Sonnet** *See* Sonnet.

**Plain Style** *See* Style.

**Plot** The plot is the sequence of actions and events in a literary work. Generally, plots are built around a **conflict**—a problem or struggle between two or more opposing forces. Plots usually progress through stages: exposition, rising action, climax, and falling action.

The **exposition** provides important background information and introduces the setting, characters, and conflict. During the **rising action,** the conflict becomes more intense and suspense builds as the main characters struggle to resolve their problem. The **climax** is the turning point in the plot when the outcome of the conflict becomes clear, usually resulting in a change in the characters or a solution to the conflict. After the climax, the **falling action** occurs and shows the effects of the climax. As the falling action begins, the suspense is over but the results of the decision or action that caused the climax are not yet fully worked out. The **resolution,** which often blends with the falling action, reveals the final outcome of events and ties up loose ends.

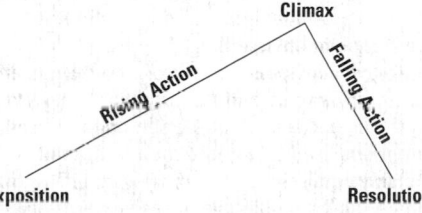

*See pages 243, 786, 1166.*
*See also* **Climax, Conflict, Exposition, Falling Action, Rising Action.**

**Poetry**  Poetry is language arranged in lines. Like other forms of literature, poetry attempts to re-create emotions and experiences. Poetry, however, is usually more condensed and suggestive than prose. Because poetry frequently does not include the kind of detail and explanation common to the short story or the novel, poetry tends to leave more to the reader's imagination. Poetry also may require more work on the part of the reader to unlock meaning.

Poems often are divided into stanzas, or paragraph-like groups of lines. The stanzas in a poem may contain the same number of lines or may vary in length. Some poems have definite patterns of meter and rhyme. Others rely more on the sounds of words and less on fixed rhythms and rhyme schemes. The use of figurative language is also common in poetry.

The form and content of a poem combine to convey meaning. The way that a poem is arranged on the page, the impact of the images, the sounds of the words and phrases, and all the other details that make up a poem work together to help the reader grasp its central idea.

*See pages 394–395, 1006.*
*See also* **Experimental Poetry; Form; Free Verse; Meter; Rhyme; Rhythm; Stanza.**

**Point of View**  Point of view refers to the narrative perspective from which events in a story or novel are told. In the **first-person** point of view, the narrator is a character in the work who tells everything in his or her own words and uses the pronouns *I, me, my.* Joyce Carol Oates's "Hostage" is narrated from the first-person point of view.

In the **third-person** point of view, events are related by a voice outside the action, not by one of the characters. A third-person narrator uses pronouns like *he, she,* and *they.* In the **third-person omniscient** point of view, the narrator is an all-knowing, objective observer who stands outside the action and reports what different characters are thinking. Flannery O'Connor's "The Life You Save May Be Your Own" is told from the third-person omniscient point of view. In the **third-person limited** point of view, the narrator stands outside the action and focuses on one character's thoughts, observations, and feelings. Richard Wright's "The Man Who Was Almost a Man" is told from the third-person limited point of view, focusing on Dave's thoughts, observations, and feelings.

In the **second-person** point of view, rarely used, the narrator addresses the reader intimately as *you.* Much of John Steinbeck's essay "Why Soldiers Don't Talk" is narrated from the second-person point of view.

*See pages 591, 1055, 1085, 1191.*

**Primary Sources**  Primary sources are those that offer direct, firsthand knowledge—such as diaries, memoirs, and personal histories. These sources often reveal the beliefs and motives of the people involved in a historical event, their ability to overcome obstacles, and the distinctive features of time and place in which they lived.

**Example:** *Of Plymouth Plantation* provides a glimpse of Plymouth colony through the eyes of William Bradford, its first governor and an eyewitness to the events he describes.

**Secondary sources,** on the other hand, offer indirect, secondhand knowledge—for example, "Women and Children First," which was written by a descendant of the Pilgrims more than 350 years after they landed.

*See pages 88, 98.*
*See also* **Eyewitness Report.**

**Prop**  Prop, an abbreviation of *property,* refers to a physical object that is used in a stage production.

**Example:** In Arthur Miller's *The Crucible,* an important prop is the small rag doll that Mary Warren brings from the court and gives to Elizabeth Proctor.

**Prose**  Generally, *prose* refers to all forms of written or spoken expression that are organized and that lack regular rhythmic patterns. Prose is characterized by logical order, continuity of thought, and individual style. Prose style varies from one writer to another, depending on such elements as word choice, sentence length and structure, use of figurative language, and tone.

**Examples:** Examples of the variety of prose styles can be seen in William Bradford's historical writing from the 17th century, Thomas Jefferson's political writing from the 18th century, Edgar Allan Poe's fiction from the 19th century, and Sandra Cisneros's fiction from the 20th century.

**Protagonist** The protagonist is the main character or hero in a narrative or drama, usually the one with whom the audience identifies.

**Example:** The young soldier, Fred Collins, is the protagonist of Stephen Crane's story "A Mystery of Heroism."

See page 1178.
See also **Antagonist; Character; Tragic Hero.**

**Protest Poetry** Protest poetry is poetry written primarily not to express personal feelings but to persuade readers to support a certain political cause or take a particular action.

**Example:** James Russell Lowell's "Stanzas on Freedom" and Frances Ellen Watkins Harper's "Free Labor" are both protest poems that speak out against slavery.

**Psalm** A psalm is a sacred song or hymn. Capitalized, the word refers to any of the sacred songs or hymns collected in the Old Testament *Book of Psalms.*

**Purpose** See **Author's Purpose.**

**Quatrain** A quatrain is a four-line stanza, as in the following example:

> This is my letter to the World
> That never wrote to Me—
> The simple News that Nature told—
> With tender Majesty
>
> —Emily Dickinson,
> from "This is my letter to the World"

See pages 750, 761.
See also **Poetry; Stanza.**

**Rationalism** Rationalism, a movement in 18th-century thought, emphasized the role of reason in human affairs. To the rationalists, the universe was a harmonious, carefully ordered place, in which each human being played a small role in the functioning of the whole—like a cog in a wheel. These thinkers also believed in human perfectibility, convinced that the exercise of reason would lead to scientific advances, better government, and eventually an ideal society. Thomas Jefferson's "Declaration of Independence," a masterpiece of political writing, reflects rationalist ideas about natural rights.

See pages 256–258, 270–276.

**Realism** In literature, realism has both a general and a special meaning. As a general term, *realism* refers to any effort to offer an accurate and detailed portrayal of actual life. Thus, critics talk about Shakespeare's realistic portrayals of his characters and praise the medieval poet Chaucer for his realistic descriptions of people from different social classes.

More specifically, realism also refers to a literary method developed in the 19th century. The realists based their writing on careful observations of contemporary life, often focusing on the middle or lower classes. They attempted to present life objectively and honestly, without the sentimentality or idealism that had colored earlier literature. Typically, realists developed their settings in great detail in an effort to re-create a specific time and place for the reader. Willa Cather, Kate Chopin, and Mark Twain are all considered realists.

See pages 636–637.
See also **Local Color Realism; Naturalism.**

**Refrain** In poetry, a refrain is part of a stanza, consisting of one or more lines that are repeated regularly, sometimes with changes, often at the ends of succeeding stanzas. For example, in "The Raven," the line "Quoth the Raven, 'Nevermore'" is a refrain. Refrains are often found in **ballads.**

**Repetition** Repetition is the recurrence of words, phrases, or lines. For example, the first line of "Song of the Sky Loom" is the same as the last line. Sometimes repetition is **incremental:** the structure of a line or stanza is repeated a certain number of times, with a slight variation in wording each time.

**Example:** The sequence "May the warp be . . . / May the weft be . . . / May the border be . . ." is an example of incremental repetition.

*See pages 37, 267, 404, 607, 1005.*
*See also* **Anaphora.**

**Resolution** *See* **Falling Action.**

**Rhetorical Question** A rhetorical question is a question to which no answer is expected because the answer is obvious. Rhetorical questions are often used in persuasive writing to emphasize a point or create an emotional effect.

**Example:** Patrick Henry asks this rhetorical question in his "Speech in the Virginia Convention": "Is life so dear, or peace so sweet, as to be purchased at the price of chains and slavery?"

*See page 262.*
*See also* **Persuasive Writing.**

**Rhyme** Rhyme is the similarity of sound between two words. Words rhyme when the sounds of their accented vowels, and all succeeding sounds, are identical, as in *tether* and *together.* For true rhyme, the consonants that precede the vowels must be different.

   Rhyme that occurs within a single line, as in the following example, is called **internal rhyme.**

> Ah, distinctly I <u>remember</u> it was in the bleak
> <u>December;</u>
>
> —Edgar Allan Poe, from "The Raven"

When rhyme comes at the end of a line of poetry, it is called **end rhyme.** The pattern of end rhyme in a poem is called the **rhyme scheme** and is charted by assigning a letter, beginning with the letter *a*, to each line. Lines that rhyme are given the same letter. The rhyme scheme of the following stanza is *aabbcc*:

> In silent night when rest I took          *a*
> For sorrow near I did not look           *a*
> I wakened was with thund'ring noise      *b*
> And piteous shrieks of dreadful voice.   *b*
> That fearful sound of "Fire!" and "Fire!" *c*
> Let no man know is my desire.            *c*
>
> —Anne Bradstreet,
> from "Upon the Burning of Our House"

*See pages 347, 471, 833.*
*See also* **Slant Rhyme.**

**Rhyme Scheme** *See* **Rhyme.**

**Rhythm** Rhythm refers to the pattern or flow of sound created by the arrangement of stressed and unstressed syllables in a line of poetry. Some poems follow a regular pattern, or **meter,** of accented and unaccented syllables. Poets use rhythm to bring out the musical quality of language, to emphasize ideas, to create mood, and to reinforce subject matter.

*See also* **Meter.**
*See pages 924, 1005.*

**Rising Action** In a plot structure, the rising action refers to events that lead to the climax by adding complications or expanding the conflict. Suspense usually builds during the rising action.

*See also* **Climax; Exposition; Falling Action; Plot; Suspense.**

**Romanticism** Romanticism was a movement in the arts that flourished in Europe and America throughout much of the 19th century. Romantic writers glorified nature and celebrated individuality. Their treatment of subject was emotional rather than rational, intuitive rather than analytic. Washington Irving and Henry Wadsworth Longfellow were popular American romantic writers.

*See pages 340–342.*

**Sarcasm** Sarcasm, a type of **verbal irony,** refers to a critical, contemptuous remark expressed in a statement in which literal meaning is the opposite of actual meaning. Sarcasm is mocking, and its intention is to hurt.

*See also* **Irony.**

**Satire** Satire is a literary technique in which foolish ideas or customs are ridiculed for the purpose of improving society. Satire may be gently witty, mildly abrasive, or bitterly critical. Short stories, poems, novels, essays, and plays all may be vehicles for satire.

**Example:** In the excerpt from *The Autobiography of Mark Twain,* Twain satirizes the gullibility of the people in his hometown who are easily duped by impostors, like the mesmerizer and himself.

**Scansion** The process of determining meter is known as scansion. When you scan a line of poetry, you mark its stressed and unstressed syllables in order to identify the rhythm.

*See also* **Meter.**

**Scene** A scene is a subdivision of an act in a drama. Each scene usually establishes a different time or place.

*See also* **Act; Drama.**

**Science Fiction** Science fiction is prose writing that presents the possibilities of the past or the future, using known scientific data and theories as well as the creative imagination of the writer. Most science fiction comments on present-day society through the writer's fictional conception of a past or future society. Ray Bradbury and Kurt Vonnegut, Jr., are two popular writers of science fiction.

**Secondary Sources** *See* **Primary Sources.**

**Sermon** A sermon is a form of religious persuasion in which a speaker exhorts the audience to behave in a more spiritual and moral fashion. "Sinners in the Hands of an Angry God" is a sermon.

**Setting** The setting of a literary work refers to the time and place in which the action occurs. A story can be set in an imaginary place, such as an enchanted castle, or a real place, such as New York City or Tombstone, Arizona. The time can be the past, the present, or the future.

**Example:** Willa Cather's story "A Wagner Matinee" is set in Boston around the turn of the 20th century.

*See pages 62, 78, 636–637, 697.*

**Sestet** *See* **Sonnet.**

**Short Story** A short story is a work of fiction that can be read in one sitting. It usually focuses on one or two major characters and one major conflict.

A short story must be unified; all the elements must work together to produce a total effect. This unity of effect is reinforced through an appropriate title and through the use of symbolism, irony, and other literary devices.

*See also* **Character; Conflict; Fiction; Novel; Plot; Setting; Theme.**

**Simile** A simile is a figure of speech that compares two things that have something in common, using a word such as *like* or *as.*

**Example:** Abigail Adams's statement "power and liberty are like heat and moisture" and Thoreau's statement "we live meanly, like ants" contain similes.

*See pages 287, 750, 760.*
*See also* **Figurative Language; Metaphor.**

**Situational Irony** *See* **Irony.**

**Slant Rhyme** Rhymes that are not exact but only approximate are known as slant rhymes, or **off rhymes:**

> "Hope" is the thing with feathers—
> That perches in the soul—
> And sings the tune without the words—
> And never stops—at all—
>
> —Emily Dickinson,
> from "'Hope' is the thing with feathers—"

*See page 750.*
*See also* **Rhyme.**

**Slave Narrative** A slave narrative is an autobiographical account written by someone who endured the miseries of slavery. Olaudah Equiano's and Frederick Douglass's autobiographies are examples of slave narratives. These writers often use sensory details to re-create their experiences. For example, to re-create the horror of confinement in the hold of a slave ship, Equiano gives the reader such details as "the galling of the chains" and "the groans of the dying."

*See page 98.*
*See also* **Autobiography.**

**Soliloquy** *See* **Monologue.**

**Sonnet** A sonnet is a 14-line lyric poem, commonly written in iambic pentameter. The **Petrarchan sonnet** consists of two parts. The first eight lines, called the **octave,** usually have the rhyme scheme *abbaabba.* In the last six lines, called the **sestet,** the rhyme scheme may be *cdecde, cdcdcd,* or another variation. The octave generally presents a problem or raises a question, and the sestet resolves or comments on the problem. James Weldon Johnson's "My City" is a Petrarchan sonnet. A **Shakespearean sonnet** is divided into three quatrains (groups of four lines) and a couplet (two rhyming lines). Its rhyme scheme is *abab cdcd efef gg.* The couplet usually expresses a response to the important issue developed in the three quatrains. Claude McKay's "If We Must Die" is a Shakespearean sonnet.

*See pages 943, 948.*
*See also* **Meter; Quatrain; Rhyme.**

**Sound Devices** *See* **Alliteration; Assonance; Consonance; Meter; Onomatopoeia; Repetition; Rhyme; Rhyme Scheme; Rhythm.**

**Speaker** The speaker of a poem, like the narrator of a story, is the voice that talks to the reader. In some poems, the speaker can be identified with the poet, as in the case of "Tía Chucha," Luis J. Rodriguez's tribute to his aunt. In other poems, the poet invents a fictional character, or a **persona,** to play the role of the speaker. *Persona* is a Latin word meaning "actor's mask." In Sylvia Plath's poem "Mirror," the persona is an inanimate object capable of speech and thought.

*See pages 421, 1061, 1116.*

**Stage Directions** Stage directions are the playwright's instructions for the director, performers, and stage crew. Usually set in italics, they are located at the beginning of and throughout a script. Stage directions usually tell the time and place of the action and explain how characters move and speak. They also describe scenery, props, lighting, costumes, music, or sound effects.

*See pages 162, 190.*
*See also* **Drama.**

**Stanza** A stanza is a group of lines that form a unit in a poem. A stanza is usually characterized by a common pattern of meter, rhyme, and number of lines. Longfellow's "A Psalm of Life" is written in four-line stanzas. During the 20th century, poets experimented more freely with stanza form than did earlier poets, sometimes writing poems without any stanza breaks.

*See page 347.*

**Stereotype** A stereotype is an over-simplified image of a person, group, or institution. Sweeping generalizations about "all Southerners" or "every used-car dealer" are stereotypes. Simplified or stock characters in literature are often called stereotypes. Such characters do not usually demonstrate the complexities of real people.

*Example:* In Washington Irving's "The Devil and Tom Walker," Tom Walker's wife is a stereotype of a greedy and shrewish wife.

**Stream of Consciousness** Stream of consciousness is a technique that was developed by modernist writers to present the flow of a character's seemingly unconnected thoughts, responses, and sensations. The term was coined by American psychologist William James to characterize the unbroken flow of thought that occurs in the waking mind.

*Example:* In "The Love Song of J. Alfred Prufrock," T. S. Eliot uses this technique to reveal the jumble of thoughts that flow through Prufrock's mind.

*See page 1043.*
*See also* **Modernism.**

**Structure**  The structure of a literary work is the way in which it is put together—the arrangement of its parts. In poetry, structure refers to the arrangement of words and lines to produce a desired effect. A common structural unit in poetry is the stanza, of which there are numerous types. In prose, structure is the arrangement of larger units or parts of a selection. Paragraphs, for example, are a basic unit in prose, as are chapters in novels and acts in plays. The structure of a poem, short story, novel, play, or nonfiction selection usually emphasizes certain important aspects of content.

*Examples:* F. Scott Fitzgerald's "Winter Dreams" is divided into six sections, each section reflecting another stage in Dexter Green's relationship with Judy Jones. Gish Jen's "In the American Society" is divided into two sections. The first section focuses on the father's own society, while the second section focuses on the American society into which the mother aspires to fit.

*See pages 580, 892.*
*See also* **Form; Stanza.**

**Style**  Style is the distinctive way in which a work of literature is written. Style refers not so much to what is said but how it is said. Word choice, sentence length, tone, imagery, and use of dialogue all contribute to a writer's style. A group of writers might exemplify common stylistic characteristics; for example, the Puritans who wrote in the **plain style**—a simple direct way of expressing ideas—or the **Imagists** whose poems are marked by compression and rich sensory images.

*Example:* E. E. Cummings's style is decidedly unconventional, breaking rules of capitalization, punctuation, diction, and syntax.

*See pages 497, 571, 606, 686, 761, 938, 971, 1014, 1023, 1120.*

**Surprise Ending**  A surprise ending is an unexpected plot twist at the end of a story.

*Example:* "Story of an Hour" ends with a surprise when Mrs. Mallard drops dead after her husband, presumed to be dead, reappears.

*See page 786.*
*See also* **Irony.**

**Surrealism**  Surrealism, a movement in art and literature, sought to express freely the creations of the imagination as revealed in dreams. This movement, which developed in France during the 1920s, reached the United States after World War II. The roots of this movement go back to Baudelaire, and it reflects Sigmund Freud's theories about the subconscious mind.

**Suspense**  Suspense is the excitement or tension that readers feel as they become involved in a story and eagerly await the outcome.

*Example:* In Ambrose Bierce's "An Occurrence at Owl Creek Bridge," the suspense builds as the reader awaits the outcome of Peyton Farquhar's attempted escape from hanging at the hands of Union troops.

*See page 514.*
*See also* **Rising Action.**

**Symbol**  A symbol is a person, place, or object that has a concrete meaning in itself and also stands for something beyond itself, such as an idea or feeling.

*Example:* In "Dr. Heidegger's Experiment," the blooming and fading rose symbolizes human mortality.

*See pages 578, 838, 860.*

**Synesthesia**  *See* **Imagery.**

**Tall Tale**  A tall tale is a distinctively American type of humorous story characterized by exaggeration. Tall tales and practical jokes have similar kinds of humor. In both, someone gets fooled, to the amusement of the person or persons who know the truth, as in Twain's "The Notorious Jumping Frog of Calaveras County."

*See page 685.*
*See also* **Humor; Hyperbole.**

**Theme** Theme is the central idea or ideas the writer intends to share with the reader. The idea may be a lesson about life or about people and their actions. Most themes are not obvious and must be inferred by the reader. At times, different readers discover different themes in the same work.

**Example:** One theme of "The Masque of the Red Death" could be stated, "No one, not even the wealthiest person, has the power to escape death."

*See pages 293, 298, 763–764, 898, 1085.*

**Third-Person Point of View** *See* **Point of View.**

**Title** The title of a literary work introduces readers to the piece and usually reveals something about its subject or theme. Often, a poet uses the title to provide information necessary for understanding a poem.

**Examples:** "A Worn Path," the title of Eudora Welty's short story, suggests the main character, Phoenix, herself: the path of her life is worn with age and struggle, and her life has centered on a single routine motivated by love. The title of Sylvia Plath's poem "Mirror" provides a necessary clue as to the identity of the speaker.

*See pages 898, 1085, 1109, 1225.*

**Tone** Tone is a writer's attitude toward his or her subject. A writer can communicate tone through **diction,** choice of details, and direct statements of his or her position. Unlike **mood,** which refers to the emotional response of the reader to a work, tone reflects the feelings of the writer. To identify the tone of a work of literature, you might find it helpful to read the work aloud, as if giving a dramatic reading before an audience. The emotions that you convey in an oral reading should give you hints as to the tone of the work.

**Examples:** Red Jacket's tone is serious and respectful in "Lecture to a Missionary"; Claude McKay's tone in "If We Must Die" is proud, defiant, and urgent.

*See pages 298, 421, 828, 838, 937, 957, 1093, 1148–1149, 1155, 1198.*

*See also* **Connotation; Diction; Mood; Style.**

**Tragedy** A tragedy is a dramatic work that presents the downfall of a dignified character who is involved in historically, morally, or socially significant events. The main character, or tragic hero, has a tragic flaw, a quality that leads to his or her destruction. The events in a tragic plot are set in motion by a decision that is often an error in judgment caused by the tragic flaw. Succeeding events are linked in a cause-and-effect relationship and lead inevitably to a disastrous conclusion, usually death. Arthur Miller's *The Crucible* could be classified as a tragedy.

**Tragic Hero** The ancient Greek philosopher Aristotle defined a tragic hero as a character whose basic goodness and superiority are marred by a tragic flaw that brings about or contributes to his or her downfall. The flaw may be poor judgment, pride, weakness, or an excess of an admirable quality. The tragic hero recognizes his or her own flaw and its consequences, but only after it is too late to change the course of events.

**Example:** Bruno, the hero of Joyce Carol Oates's "Hostage," might be considered a tragic hero because his excessively violent defense of a young girl leads to his ruin.

*See page 1212.*
*See also* **Character.**

**Transcendentalism** The philosophy of transcendentalism, an American offshoot of German romanticism, was based on a belief that "transcendent forms" of truth exist beyond reason and experience. Ralph Waldo Emerson, the leader of the movement, asserted that every individual is capable of discovering this higher truth through intuition. Henry David Thoreau and Walt Whitman are two well-known transcendentalist writers.

*See pages 341–342.*
*See also* **Romanticism.**

**Transcript** A transcript is a written record of words originally spoken aloud. For example, "The Examination of Sarah Good" provides the actual questions posed by the examiner and Sarah Good's responses to them during her interrogation for witchcraft in 1692.

*See page 148.*

**Trickster Tale** A trickster tale is a folk tale about an animal or person who engages in trickery, violence, and magic. Neither all good nor all bad, a trickster may be foolish yet clever, greedy yet helpful, immoral yet moral. "Coyote and the Buffalo" and "Fox and Coyote and Whale" are both trickster tales.

*See page 46.*
*See also* **Folk Tale.**

**Trochee** *See* **Meter.**

**Understatement** Understatement is a description of a person, an event, or an idea from a perspective that greatly plays down the importance of the subject, often to add humor or to make a point ironically.

**Example:** In "Letter to John Adams," Abigail Adams points out the tyranny of male power by gently saying, "I cannot say that I think you very generous to the ladies."

*See also* **Hyperbole.**

**Verbal Irony** *See* **Irony.**

**Voice** The term *voice* refers to a writer's unique use of language that allows a reader to "hear" a human personality in his or her writing. The elements of style that determine a writer's voice include sentence structure, diction, and tone. For example, some writers are noted for their reliance on short, simple sentences, while others make use of long, complicated ones. Certain writers use concrete words, such as *lake* or *cold,* which name things that you can see, hear, feel, taste, or smell. Others prefer abstract terms like *memory,* which name things that cannot be perceived with the senses. A writer's tone also leaves its imprint on his or her personal voice. The term can be applied to the narrator of a selection, as well as the writer.

In the following passage, the diction and tone help establish the narrator as a witty, sarcastic character:

> Tom's wife was a tall termagant, fierce of temper, loud of tongue, and strong of arm. Her voice was often heard in wordy warfare with her husband; and his face sometimes showed signs that their conflicts were not confined to words.
>
> —Washington Irving,
> "The Devil and Tom Walker"

*See pages 873, 1128.*
*See also* **Diction, Tone.**

**Word Choice** *See* **Diction.**

# Glossary of Words to Know
## In English and Spanish

## A

**abdicate** (ăb′dĭ-kāt′) *v.* to give up responsibility for
  **abdicar** *v.* renunciar a un cargo o responsabilidad

**abhor** (ăb-hôr′) *v.* to regard with disgust
  **aborrecer** *v.* odiar; tener aversión

**abide** (e-bīd′) *v.* to put up with
  **soportar** *v.* aguantar; tolerar

**abject** (ăb′jĕkt′) *adj.* low; contemptible; wretched
  **abyecto** *adj.* bajo; ruin; despreciable

**abode** (ə-bōd′) *n.* a dwelling place; home
  **morada** *n.* sitio donde se vive; hogar

**abominable** (ə-bŏm′ə-nə-bəl) *adj.* thoroughly detestable
  **abominable** *adj.* totalmente detestable

**abrasive** (ə-brā′sĭv) *adj.* harsh and rough
  **abrasivo** *adj.* áspero e irritante

**absolve** (əb-zŏlv′) *v.* to clear of guilt or blame
  **absolver** *v.* limpiar de culpa

**acquiescing** (ăk′wē-ĕs′ĭng) *adj.* consenting passively or without protest **acquiesce** *v.*
  **conforme** *adj.* que acepta pasivamente o sin protestar **conformarse** *v.*

**adamant** (ăd′ə-mənt) *adj.* stubborn; not giving in
  **obstinado** *adj.* terco; que no cede

**adversary** (ăd′vər-sĕr′ē) *n.* an opponent
  **adversario** *s.* opositor

**affiliate** (ə-fĭl′ē-ĭt) *n.* a person or organization associated with another
  **afiliado** *s.* persona u organización asociada a otra

**affinity** (ə-fĭn′ĭ-tē) *n.* a kinship or likeness
  **afinidad** *s.* parentesco o semejanza

**afflict** (ə-flĭkt′) *v.* to trouble or attack, causing physical or mental suffering
  **afligir** *v.* aquejar; afectar o atacar, causando daño físico o sufrimiento mental

**affronted** (ə-frŭn′tĭd) *adj.* intentionally insulted **affront** *v.*
  **afrontado** *adj.* insultado con intención **afrontar** *v.*

**aggressor** (ə-grĕs′ər) *n.* one that begins an attack or a quarrel
  **agresor** *s.* el que inicia un ataque o pleito

**aghast** (ə-găst′) *adj.* overcome with fear; terrified
  **horrorizado** *adj.* aterrorizado; lleno de miedo

**alleviation** (ə-lē′vē-ā′shən) *n.* a decrease in severity; relief
  **alivio** *s.* disminución de gravedad; mejoría

**allurement** (ə-lŏŏr′mənt) *n.* attraction; enticement
  **fascinación** *s.* atracción; encanto

**aloof** (ə-lŏŏf′) *adj.* distant
  **distante** *adj.* indiferente

**amiably** (ā′mē-ə-blē) *adv.* in a pleasant and friendly manner; good-naturedly
  **amigablemente** *adv.* de forma agradable y amable; cordialmente

**amicably** (ăm′ĭ-kə-blē) *adv.* in a friendly way
  **amigablemente** *adv.* de forma amistosa

**anarchy** (ăn′ər-kē) *n.* absence of any form of political authority
  **anarquía** *s.* ausencia total de autoridad política

**anguish** (ăng′gwĭsh) *n.* agonizing physical or mental pain
  **angustia** *s.* gran dolor físico o mental

**annihilate** (ə-nī′ə-lāt′) *v.* to destroy completely; wipe out
**aniquilar** *v.* destruir por completo; eliminar; arrasar

**anonymity** (ăn′ə-nĭm′ĭ-tē) *n.* a state of being unknown or unrecognized, without special or distinguishing qualities
**anonimato** *s.* estado en que no se es reconocido o identificado, sin cualidades distintivas o especiales

**antagonistic** (ăn-tăg′ə-nĭs′tĭk) *adj.* openly hostile and aggressive toward another
**antagónico** *adj.* abiertamente hostil y agresivo hacia otro

**aplomb** (ə-plŏm′) *n.* self-confidence
**aplomo** *s.* confianza en sí mismo

**appease** (ə-pēz′) *v.* to bring peace, quiet, or calm to; soothe
**apaciguar** *v.* aquietar, tranquilizar o calmar; confortar

**appraisal** (ə-prā′zəl) *n.* evaluation
**avalúo** *s.* evaluación

**apprehension** (ăp′rĭ-hĕn′shən) *n.* a suspicion of future evil; dread
**aprensión** *s.* sospecha de un mal futuro; recelo

**apprise** (ə-prīz′) *v.* to give notice to; inform
**informar** *v.* avisar; advertir

**arbitrary** (är′bĭ-trĕr′ē) *adj.* based on unpredictable decisions rather than on reason or law
**arbitrario** *adj.* basado en decisiones inesperadas o caprichosas, no en la razón o en la ley

**arbitrate** (är′bĭ-trāt) *v.* to judge or act as referee
**arbitrar** *v.* juzgar o actuar como árbitro

**arroyo** (ə-roi′ō) *n.* a deep gully cut by an intermittent stream; a dry gulch
**arroyo** *s.* barranco profundo cortado por un riachuelo intermitente; quebrada seca (este término se usa en inglés con el significado dado, que es distinto al significado en español: río pequeño)

**articulate** (är-tĭk′yə-lĭt) *adj.* clear and effective in speech
**elocuente** *adj.* que se expresa con claridad y convicción

**ascertain** (ăs′ər-tān′) *v.* to find out
**averiguar** *v.* investigar

**ascribe** (ə-skrīb′) *v.* to attribute to a specified cause or source
**atribuir** *v.* achacar a una causa u origen específico

**aspire** (ə-spīr′) *v.* to seek to achieve; strive
**aspirar** *v.* desear la realización de algo; empeñarse

**assurance** (ə-shŏŏr′əns) *n.* self-confidence
**seguridad** *s.* confianza en sí mismo

**atrocious** (ə-trō′shəs) *adj.* shockingly bad or lacking in taste; awful
**atroz** *adj.* muy malo o carente de gusto; horrible

**avalanche** (ăv′ə-lănch′) *n.* an overwhelming amount
**avalancha** *s.* cantidad abrumadora

**avarice** (ăv′ə-rĭs′) *n.* greed
**avaricia** *s.* codicia

**aversion** (ə-vûr′zhən) *n.* a strong dislike
**aversión** *s.* antipatía profunda

**avid** (ăv′ĭd) *adj.* having an intense desire or craving
**ávido** *adj.* con deseo o necesidad intensa

# B

**basely** (bās′lē) *adv.* dishonorably; meanly
**bajamente** *adv.* ruinmente; con maldad

**begrudge** (bĭ-grŭj′) *v.* to resent another person's possession of something
**envidiar** *v.* resentir que otra persona posea algo

**beguiling** (bĭ-gī′lĭng) *adj.* charming or delighting **beguile** *v.*
**encantador** *adj.* seductor; fascinante **encantar** *v.*

**beholden** (bǐ hōl' dən) *adj.* obliged to feel grateful; indebted
**agradecido** *adj.* obligado a sentir gratitud; endeudado

**beseech** (bǐ-sēch') *v.* to implore; beg
**suplicar** *v.* implorar; rogar

**bestowed** (bǐ-stōd') *adj.* applied; used **bestow** *v.*
**otorgado** *adj.* aplicado; usado **otorgar** *v.*

**blatantly** (blāt'nt-lē) *adv.* in an extremely obvious way; conspicuously
**evidentemente** *adv.* de forma sumamente obvia; conspicuamente

**blunder** (blŭn'dər) *n.* a mistake
**torpeza** *s.* metedura de pata

# C

**cajole** (kə-jōl') *v.* to persuade by pleasant words or flattery; coax
**engatusar** *v.* persuadir con bellas palabras; convencer con halagos o falsas promesas

**calamity** (kə-lăm'ĭ-tē) *n.* disaster
**calamidad** *s.* desastre

**callow** (kăl'ō) *adj.* lacking adult maturity or experience; immature
**inmaduro** *adj.* carente de madurez o experiencia; inexperto

**careen** (kə-rēn') *v.* to swerve, or cause to swerve, from side to side while in motion
**carenar** *v.* dar bandazos; ir de un lado a otro mientras se avanza

**cassock** (kăs'ək) *n.* an ankle-length garment, with close-fitting waist and sleeves, worn by clergymen
**sotana** *s.* prenda que llega al tobillo, de talle ajustado y mangas, usada por religiosos

**cauterize** (kô'tə-rīz') *v.* to burn or sear to destroy abnormal tissue
**cauterizar** *v.* quemar o chamuscar para destruir tejido anormal

**cavorting** (kə-vôr'tĭng) *adj.* prancing about; capering **cavort** *v.*
**retozador** *adj.* que da cabrioladas; que se divierte ruidosamente **retozar** *v.*

**censurer** (sĕn'shər-ər) *n.* one who expresses strong disapproval or harsh criticism
**censor** *s.* el que expresa fuerte desaprobación o crítica dura

**circumvent** (sûr'kəm-vĕnt') *v.* to avoid or get around by clever maneuvering
**evitar** *v.* salvar o rodear; evadir mediante maniobras ingeniosas

**cloister** (kloi'stər) *n.* a place devoted to religious seclusion; a monastery or convent
**claustro** *s.* lugar dedicado al encierro religioso; monasterio o convento

**cognizant** (kŏg'nĭ-zənt) *adj.* aware
**conocido** *adj.* sabido

**coherent** (kō-hîr'ənt) *adj.* understandable; logically consistent
**coherente** *adj.* comprensible; uniforme y lógico

**collusion** (kə-lōō'zhən) *n.* a secret agreement for a deceitful purpose
**colusión** *s.* acuerdo secreto con fines engañosos

**commission** (kə-mĭsh'ən) *v.* to assign a task or duty to
**comisionar** *v.* asignar una tarea u obligación

**commodity** (kə-mŏd'ĭ-tē) *n.* something useful; an article of commerce
**mercancía** *s.* producto útil; artículo comercial

**comply** (kəm-plī') *v.* to obey another's command, request, rule, or wish
**cumplir** *v.* obedecer la orden, solicitud, regla o deseo de otro

**composed** (kəm-pōzd') *adj.* calm; cool and collected
**sosegado** *adj.* calmado; tranquilo y sereno

**compound** (kŏm-pound') *v.* to form or make up; compose
**componer** *v.* formar o inventar; crear

**compulsory** (kəm-pŭl'sə-rē) *adj.* required without exception; mandatory
**obligatorio** *adj.* requerido sin excepciones; forzoso

**conceived** (kən-sēvd') *adj.* originated **conceive** *v.*
**concebido** *adj.* originado **concebir** *v.*

**conclude** (kən-klōōd') *v.* to arrive at a judgment or decision
**concluir** *v.* llegar a un juicio o decisión

**confederate** (kən-fĕd'ər-ĭt) *n.* one who assists in a plot; associate
**confederado** *s.* alguien que participa en una conjura; socio

**confront** (kən-frŭnt') *v.* to come up against; meet face to face
**confrontar** *v.* enfrentarse; encarar

**congenial** (kən-gēn'yəl) *adj.* suited to one's needs or nature; agreeable
**compatible** *adj.* adecuado a las necesidades o naturaleza de uno; agradable

**congruous** (kŏng'grōō əs) *adj.* fitting; suitable
**congruente** *adj.* conveniente; oportuno

**conjecture** (kən-jĕk'chər) *v.* to make a judgment on the basis of uncertain evidence; guess
**conjeturar** *v.* formarse un juicio con evidencia incierta; adivinar

**conscientious** (kŏn'shē-ĕn'shəs) *adj.* guided by conscience; honest
**concienzudo** *adj.* guiado por la conciencia; honesto

**consecrate** (kŏn'sĭ-krāt') *v.* to declare sacred
**consagrar** *v.* declarar sagrado

**consternation** (kŏn'stər-nā'shən) *n.* a state of paralyzing dismay; fear
**consternación** *s.* estado de profundo dolor emocional; miedo

**constitute** (kŏn'stĭ-tōōt') *v.* to amount to; equal
**constituir** *v.* representar; formar

**contagion** (kən-tā'jən) *n.* the spreading of disease
**contagio** *s.* difusión de una enfermedad

**contempt** (kən-tĕmpt') *n.* scorn; disdain
**desdén** *s.* burla; desprecio

**contemptuously** (kən-tĕmp'chōō-əs-lē) *adv.* in a way that shows disdain or disgust; scornfully
**desdeñosamente** *adv.* con desprecio

**contend** (kən-tĕnd') *v.* to compete; vie
**contender** *v.* competir; luchar

**contentious** (kən-tĕn'shəs) *adj.* quarrelsome
**contencioso** *adj.* discutidor; conflictivo

**contrite** (kən-trīt') *adj.* sorrowful for one's wrongdoing; repentant
**contrito** *adj.* afligido por errores propios; arrepentido

**copious** (kō'pē-əs) *adj.* in large amounts; abundant
**copioso** *adj.* en grandes cantidades; abundante

**coquettish** (kō-kĕt'ĭsh) *adj.* flirtatious
**coqueto** *adj.* seductor

**corroding** (kə-rō'dĭng) *adj.* gradually destructive **corrode** *v.*
**corrosivo** *adj.* que causa destrucción gradual **corroer** *v.*

**countenance** (koun'tə-nəns) *n.* the face, especially as an indicator of emotion
**semblante** *s.* cara, especialmente como indicador de emoción

**countenance** (koun'tə-nəns) *v.* to give or express approval; support
**aprobar** *s.* apoyar

**courtier** (kôr'tē-ər) *n.* a member of a royal court
**cortesano** *s.* miembro de una corte real

**credulity** (krĭ-dōō'lĭ-tē) *n.* an inclination to believe too readily
**credulidad** *s.* inclinación a creer fácilmente

# D

**dank** (dăngk) *adj.* unpleasantly damp; moist and chilly
**húmedo** *adj.* mojado y malsano; frío y mojado

**daunted** (dôn'tĭd) *adj.* intimidated or frightened **daunt** *v.*
**atemorizado** *adj.* intimidado o asustado **atemorizar** *v*

**dauntless** (dônt'lĭs) *adj.* fearless
**temerario** *adj.* sin miedo

**debilitated** (dĭ-bĭl'ĭ-tā'tĭd) *adj.* weakened; enfeebled
**debilitado** *adj.* frágil; endeble

**decorum** (dĭ-kôr'əm) *n.* proper and dignified behavior
**decoro** *s.* conducta adecuada y digna

**decrepit** (dĭ-krĕp'ĭt) *adj.* weakened, worn out, or broken down by old age or hard use
**decrépito** *adj.* débil, desgastado o roto por el tiempo o por mucho uso

**deferential** (dĕf'ə-rĕn'shəl) *adj.* extremely respectful
**deferente** *adj.* muy respetuoso

**deficiency** (dĭ-fĭsh'ən-sē) *n.* a lack
**deficiencia** *s.* carencia

**delectable** (dĭ-lĕk'tə-bəl) *adj.* highly pleasing; delightful
**deleitable** *adj.* muy agradable; delicioso

**deliberately** (dĭ-lĭb'ər-ĭt-lē) *adv.* in an unhurried and thoughtful manner
**deliberadamente** *adv.* de manera pensada y sin precipitación

**deliverance** (dĭ-lĭv'ər-əns) *n.* rescue from danger
**salvación** *s.* rescate de un peligro

**delve** (dĕlv) *v.* to conduct an investigation; search
**indagar** *v.* realizar una investigación; buscar

**denunciation** (dĭ-nŭn'sē-ā'shən) *n.* an act of condemning or accusing another; accusation
**denuncia** *s.* acto de condena o acusación

**deplore** (dĭ-plôr') *v.* to feel strong disapproval of or deeply regret
**deplorar** *v.* desaprobar fuertemente; lamentar profundamente

**deposition** (dĕp'ə-zĭsh'ən) *n.* a written statement by a witness
**declaración** *s.* testimonio escrito de un testigo

**derision** (dĭ-rĭzh'ən) *n.* harsh ridicule or mockery; scorn
**humillación** *s.* desprecio o desdén profundo; escarnio; burla aguda

**derisive** (dĭ-rī'sĭv) *adj.* mocking or ridiculing; scornful
**humillante** *adj.* desdeñable; despreciable

**derive** (dĭ-rīv') *v.* to obtain; get; receive
**derivar** *v.* obtener; recibir

**desolate** (dĕs'ə-lĭt) *adj.* without inhabitants; barren
**desolado** *adj.* inhabitado; vacío; yermo

**despotic** (dĭ-spŏt'ĭk) *adj.* like a dictator
**despótico** *adj.* como un dictador

**detract** (dĭ-trăkt') *v.* to take away; diminish
**detractar** *v.* quitar; disminuir

**devastation** (dĕv'ə-stā'shən) *n.* complete destruction
**devastación** *s.* destrucción total

**devious** (dē'vē-əs) *adj.* shifty; not straightforward
**taimado** *adj.* engañoso; deshonesto

**devotion** (dĭ-vō'shən) *n.* earnest dedication
**devoción** *s.* dedicación honesta

**diagnosis** (dī'əg-nō'sĭs) *n.* the identification of a physical disorder through an examination of its symptoms
**diagnóstico** *s.* identificación de un mal o enfermedad física mediante el examen de sus síntomas

**diaphanous** (dī-ăf'ə-nəs) *adj.* light or fragile in an unearthly way
**diáfano** *adj.* claro y limpio

**diffident** (dĭf'ĭ-dənt) *adj.* shy and timid; lacking self-confidence
**tímido** *adj.* turbado; inseguro

**digress** (dī-grĕs') *v.* to wander away from the main subject in a conversation or in writing; ramble
**desviarse** *v.* alejarse del tema central de una conversación; irse por las ramas

**dilapidated** (dĭ-lăp'ĭ-dā'tĭd) *adj.* in a state of disrepair; rundown
**dilapidado** *adj.* ruinoso; desgastado

**diligently** (dĭl'ə-jənt-lē) *adv.* in a persevering, painstaking manner
**diligentemente** *adv.* de manera perseverante, cuidadosa

**dirge** (dûrj) *n.* a slow, mournful piece of music; a funeral hymn
**canto fúnebre** *s.* pieza musical lenta y dolida; himno fúnebre

**discourse** (dĭ-skôrs') *v.* to speak
  **disertar** *v.* hablar en público

**disobedient** (dĭs'ə-bē'dē-ənt) *adj.* not
  obeying instructions or orders
  **desobediente** *adj.* que no obedece
  indicaciones u órdenes

**dispensation** (dĭs'pən-sā'shən) *n.*
  distribution; giving out
  **dispensación** *s.* distribución; reparto

**disproportionate** (dĭs'prə-pôr'shə-nĭt) *adj.* out
  of proportion; of an unequal size or amount
  **desproporcionado** *adj.* que no tiene la
  proporción debida

**dispute** (dĭ-spyōōt') *v.* to question or doubt
  **disputar** *v.* discutir; cuestionar o dudar

**disreputable** (dĭs-rĕp'yə-tə-bəl) *adj.* lacking
  respectability of character or behavior
  **desprestigiado** *adj.* carente de carácter o
  conducta respetable

**dissemble** (dĭ-sĕm'bəl) *v.* to disguise or
  conceal behind a false appearance
  **disimular** *v.* disfrazar u ocultar detrás de una
  apariencia falsa

**dissipation** (dĭs'ə-pā'shən) *n.* a reckless
  waste of resources; wastefulness
  **disipación** *s.* gasto descuidado de recursos;
  desperdicio

**dissolution** (dĭs'ə-lōō'shən) *n.* a breaking up;
  disintegration
  **disolución** *s.* ruptura; desintegración

**divining** (dĭ-vī'nĭng) *adj.* finding out through
  intuition; guessing from incomplete evidence
  **divine** *v.*
  **adivinado** *adv.* descubierto a través de la
  intuición; intuido sin tener todos los
  elementos **adivinar** *v.*

**divulge** (dĭ-vŭlj') *v.* to make known something
  private
  **divulgar** *v.* dar a conocer algo privado

**document** (dŏk'yə-mənt) *v.* to provide a
  detailed account of
  **documentar** *v.* dar información detallada

**dolefully** (dōl'fə-lē) *adv.* mournfully
  **lúgubremente** *adv.* tristemente

**dredge** (drĕj) *v.* to dig into; unearth
  **escarbar** *v.* sacar a la luz; desenterrar

**dubious** (dōō'bē-əs) *adj.* doubtful; suspicious
  **dudoso** *adj.* sospechoso; oscuro

## E

**edible** (ĕd'ə-bəl) *adj.* fit to eat
  **comestible** *adj.* que se puede comer

**edict** (ē'dĭkt') *n.* an order put out by a person
  in authority
  **edicto** *s.* orden de una persona de autoridad

**efface** (ĭ-fās') *v.* to rub or wipe out; erase
  **tachar** *v.* tallar o limpiar; borrar

**effrontery** (ĭ-frŭn'tə-rē) *n.* disrespectful and
  insulting boldness
  **desvergüenza** *s.* descaro irrespetuoso e
  insultante

**elemental** (ĕl'ə-mən'tl) *adj.* basic; like a
  natural force
  **elemental** *adj.* básico; como una fuerza natural

**eloquence** (ĕl'ə-kwəns) *n.* expressiveness
  **elocuencia** *s.* expresividad

**emaciated** (ĭ-mā'shē-ā'tĭd) *adj.* excessively
  thin; wasted away **emaciate** *v.*
  **emaciado** *adj.* en los huesos; muy delgado por
  pasar hambre **emaciarse** *v.*

**emancipate** (ĭ-măn'sə-pāt') *v.* to free; liberate
  **emancipar** *v.* liberar; dejar libre

**embody** (ĕm-bŏd'ē) *v.* to represent in bodily
  form
  **encarnar** *v.* representar en forma corporal

**embroidered** (ĕm-broi'dərd) *adj.* decorated
  with stitched designs **embroider** *v.*
  **bordado** *adj.* decorado con puntadas **bordar** *v.*

**emergence** (ĭ-mûr'jəns) *n.* the process of
  coming forth or coming into existence
  **emergencia** *s.* proceso de surgir o de nacer

**empower** (ĕm-pou'ər) *v.* to invest with authority
  **autorizar** *v.* investir de autoridad

**encroach** (ĕn-krōch') *v.* to advance beyond
  original limits; intrude
  **traspasar** *v.* ir más allá de los límites; cometer
  una intrusión

**endeavor** (ĕn-dĕv′ər) *v.* to make an earnest effort; strive
**esforzarse** *v.* hacer un esfuerzo honesto; empeñarse

**engender** (ĕn-jĕn′dər) *v.* to produce; bring about
**engendrar** *v.* producir; crear

**enterprising** (ĕn′tər-prī′zĭng) *adj.* possessing imagination and initiative
**emprendedor** *adj.* que posee imaginación e iniciativa

**environs** (ĕn-vī′rənz) *n.* a surrounding region
**alrededores** *s.* región cercana

**estrangement** (ĭ-strānj′mənt) *n.* separation; alienation
**alejamiento** *s.* distanciamiento; separación

**ethical** (ĕth′ĭ-kəl) *adj.* dealing with principles of right and wrong; moral
**ético** *adj.* relacionado con principios del bien y el mal; moral

**evade** (ĭ-vād′) *v.* to escape or avoid
**evadir** *v.* escapar o evitar

**evolve** (ĭ-vŏlv′) *v.* to develop gradually
**evolucionar** *v.* desarrollar gradualmente

**excommunication** (ĕks′kə-myōō′nĭ-kā′shən) *n.* banishment from a church
**excomunión** *s.* expulsión de una iglesia

**excruciatingly** (ĭk-skrōō′shē-ā′tĭng-lē) *adv.* in a way that causes great pain or distress
**atrozmente** *adv.* de forma que causa gran dolor o malestar

**exhilaration** (ĭg-zĭl′ə-rā′shən) *n.* a lively delight
**regocijo** *s.* dicha vivaz

**exploitation** (ĕk′sploi-tā′shən) *n.* use of another person or group for selfish purposes
**explotación** *s.* uso de otra persona o grupo con fines egoístas

**extenuating** (ĭk-stĕn′yōō-ā′tĭng) *adj.* lessening a fault by serving as a partial excuse
**atenuante** *adj.* que reduce una falta al servir como excusa parcial  **atenuar** *v.*

**exultingly** (ĭg-zŭl′tĭng-lē) *adv.* in a joyful and triumphant way
**exultantemente** *adv.* de manera gozosa y triunfal

## F

**faculty** (făk′əl-tē) *n.* a natural power or ability
**facultad** *s.* capacidad o habilidad natural

**fanatic** (fə-năt′ĭk) *n.* a person possessed by an excessive and irrational zeal, especially for a religious or political cause
**fanático** *s.* persona poseída por un fervor excesivo e irracional, especialmente por una causa religiosa o política

**feigned** (fānd) *adj.* not real; pretended
**fingido** *adj.* irreal; aparentado

**felicity** (fĭ-lĭs′ĭ-tē) *n.* happiness; bliss
**felicidad** *s.* alegría; dicha

**fitfully** (fĭt′fə-lē) *adv.* in an irregular way; unsteadily
**espasmódicamente** *adv.* de manera irregular; a intervalos

**flourish** (flûr′ĭsh) *v.* to thrive
**florecer** *v.* prosperar

**forlorn** (fər-lôrn′) *adj.* appearing sad or lonely
**abandonado** *adj.* con aspecto triste o desolado por la soledad

**formidable** (fôr′mĭ-də-bəl) *adj.* difficult to defeat
**formidable** *adj.* difícil de derrotar

**forte** (fôrt) *n.* something in which a person excels
**fuerte** *s.* tema o habilidad en que una persona destaca

**furtive** (fûr′tĭv) *adj.* secret; sneaky
**furtivo** *adj.* secreto; disimulado

**futile** (fyōōt′l) *adj.* useless
**fútil** *adj.* inútil

**futility** (fyōō-tĭl′ĭ-tē) *n.* uselessness
**futilidad** *s.* inutilidad

# G

**garrulously** (găr'ə-ləs-lē) *adv.* talking too much about trifles; talkative
**gárrulamente** *adv.* con mucha labia; locuazmente

**gaunt** (gônt) *adj.* thin and bony
**demacrado** *adj.* flaco y huesudo

**genetic** (jə-nĕt'ĭk) *adj.* relating to genes, the units that determine and transmit hereditary characteristics
**genético** *adj.* relacionado con los genes, las unidades que determinan y transmiten características hereditarias

**genial** (jēn'yəl) *adj.* having a friendly disposition
**cordial** *adj.* de disposición amable

**glib** (glĭb) *adj.* showing little thought, preparation, or concern
**superficial** *adj.* que muestra poca reflexión, preparación o interés

**grimace** (grĭm'ĭs) *n.* a twisting or distortion of the face
**mueca** *s.* torcimiento o distorsión de la cara

**grotesque** (grō-tĕsk') *adj.* having a bizarre, fantastic appearance
**grotesco** *adj.* de apariencia extraña, fantástica

**gullible** (gŭl'ə-bəl) *adj.* easily deceived or tricked
**crédulo** *adj.* fácil de engañar

# H

**harbor** (här'bər) *v.* to shelter; protect
**refugiar** *v.* amparar; proteger

**hue** (hyōō) *n.* appearance; color
**tinte** *s.* apariencia; color

# I

**immaculate** (ĭ-măk'yə-lĭt) *adj.* without stain; pure
**inmaculado** *adj.* sin mancha; puro

**impeccable** (ĭm-pĕk'ə-bəl) *adj.* flawless; perfect
**impecable** *adj.* sin fallas; perfecto

**impel** (ĭm-pĕl') *v.* to drive forward; force
**impeler** *v.* obligar; forzar

**impertinence** (ĭm-pûr'tn-əns) *n.* improper boldness; rudeness
**impertinencia** *s.* franqueza inadecuada; rudeza

**impertinent** (ĭm-pûr'tn ənt) *adj.* rude, ill-mannered
**impertinente** *adj.* rudo, grosero

**impervious** (ĭm-pûr'vē-əs) *adj.* incapable of being affected
**insensible** *adj.* que nada le afecta

**impetuosity** (ĭm-pĕch'ōō-ŏs'ĭ-tē) *n.* unthinking action
**impetuosidad** *s.* acción no pensada

**implacable** (ĭm-plăk'ə-bəl) *adj.* impossible to satisfy
**implacable** *adj.* imposible de satisfacer

**implicate** (ĭm'plĭ-kāt') *v.* to connect to an activity, especially one of an unsavory or criminal nature
**implicar** *v.* conectar con una actividad, especialmente si es dudosa o criminal

**implore** (ĭm-plôr') *v.* to beg; earnestly ask for
**implorar** *v.* rogar; pedir urgentemente

**inaccessible** (ĭn'ăk-sĕs'ə-bəl) *adj.* not obtained easily, if at all; unreachable
**inaccesible** *adj.* difícil de obtener; inalcanzable

**inanimate** (ĭn-ăn'ə-mĭt) *adj.* not alive; lifeless
**inanimado** *adj.* sin vida; muerto

**inaudibly** (ĭn-ô'də-blē) *adv.* unable to be heard clearly
**inaudiblemente** *adv.* que no se oye claramente

**incense** (ĭn-sĕns') *v.* to cause to be extremely angry
**encolerizar** *v.* causar enojo extremo

**incessant** (ĭn-sĕs'ənt) *adj.* ceaseless; continual
**incesante** *adj.* que no para; continuo

**inclination** (ĭn'klə-nā'shən) *n.* a favorable disposition; desire
**inclinación** *s.* disposición favorable; deseo

**inconceivable** (ĭn′kən-sē′və-bəl) *adj.* not able to be understood or imagined
**inconcebible** *adj.* que no se puede entender o imaginar

**incongruously** (ĭn-kŏng′grōō-əs-lē) *adv.* in a manner that is not fitting, suitable, or in agreement; incompatibly
**incongruentemente** *adv.* de forma inadecuada o inapropiada; incompatiblemente

**incorrigible** (ĭn-kôr′ĭ-jə-bəl) *adj.* impossible to correct or reform; uncontrollable
**incorregible** *adj.* imposible de corregir o reformar; incontrolable

**incredulously** (ĭn-krĕj′ə-ləs-lē) *adv.* in a manner showing a lack of belief
**incrédulamente** *adv.* sin fe o confianza

**indestructible** (ĭn′dĭ-strŭk′tə-bəl) *adj.* impossible to destroy
**indestructible** *adj.* imposible de destruir

**indictment** (ĭn-dīt′mənt) *n.* accusation
**denuncia** *s.* acusación

**indignant** (ĭn-dĭg′nənt) *adj.* filled with anger caused by something unjust or mean
**indignado** *adj.* lleno de ira causada por algo injusto o malo

**indiscretion** (ĭn′dĭ-skrĕsh′ən) *n.* a lack of good judgment in speech or behavior
**indiscreción** *s.* falta de juicio al hablar o actuar

**indiscriminately** (ĭn′dĭ-skrĭm′ə-nĭt-lē) *adv.* randomly
**indiscriminadamente** *adv.* al azar

**indoctrination** (ĭn-dŏk′trə-nā′shən) *n.* the process of being taught fundamentals, especially of military customs and discipline
**adoctrinamiento** *s.* proceso de enseñar los aspectos fundamentales, especialmente de las costumbres y la disciplina militar

**indomitable** (ĭn-dŏm′ĭ-tə-bəl) *adj.* not easily discouraged or defeated
**indomable** *adj.* que no se deja desalentar o vencer

**ineffable** (ĭn-ĕf′ə-bəl) *adj.* unable to be expressed in words
**inefable** *adj.* que no se puede expresar en palabras

**inexpedient** (ĭn′ĭk-spē′dē-ənt) *adj.* not useful for achieving a goal
**inoportuno** *adj.* inservible para alcanzar una meta

**inexplicable** (ĭn-ĕk′splĭ-kə-bəl) *adj.* difficult or impossible to explain
**inexplicable** *adj.* difícil o imposible de explicar

**infamous** (ĭn′fə-məs) *adj.* notorious
**infame** *adj.* de mala reputación; tristemente célebre

**infatuation** (ĭn-făch′ōō-ā′shən) *n.* the state of being completely carried away by foolish or shallow love or affection
**encaprichamiento** *s.* amor o afecto necio o superficial que domina el pensamiento

**infirmity** (ĭn-fûr′mĭ-tē) *n.* a sickness or weakness
**enfermedad** *s.* dolencia o debilidad

**inflict** (ĭn-flĭkt′) *v.* to cause to have or suffer; impose
**infligir** *v.* producir un daño; imponer

**ingenuous** (ĭn-jĕn′yōō-əs) *adj.* innocent; naive
**ingenuo** *adj.* inocente; candoroso

**ingratiate** (ĭn-grā′shē-āt′) *v.* to gain another's favor by deliberate effort
**congraciar** *v.* ganarse la aprobación de otro con un esfuerzo deliberado

**inherently** (ĭn-hîr′ənt-lē) *adv.* essentially
**inherentemente** *adv.* esencialmente

**iniquity** (ĭ-nĭk′wĭ-tē) *n.* wickedness; immorality
**iniquidad** *s.* maldad; inmoralidad

**insidious** (ĭn-sĭd′ē-əs) *adj.* treacherous
**insidioso** *adj.* traicionero

**insipid** (ĭn-sĭp′ĭd) *adj.* lacking in flavor; bland
**insípido** *adj.* sin sabor; aburrido

**insoluble** (ĭn-sŏl′yə-bəl) *adj.* having no solution; unsolvable
**insoluble** *adj.* que no tiene solución; irresoluble

**insurrection** (ĭn′sə-rĕk′shən) *n.* rebellion
**insurrección** *s.* rebelión

**intently** (ĭn-tĕnt′lē) *adv.* with concentrated attention
**atentamente** *adv.* con atención concentrada

**intercede** (ĭn′tər-sēd′) *v.* to plead on behalf of another or mediate in a dispute
**interceder** *v.* pedir a nombre de otro o mediar en una disputa

**interment** (ĭn-tûr′mənt) *n.* burial
**entierro** *s.* sepelio

**interminable** (ĭn-tûr′mə-nə-bəl) *adj.* endless
**interminable** *adj.* sin fin

**interpose** (ĭn′tər-pōz′) *v.* to interfere in order to help; intervene
**interponerse** *v.* interferir para ayudar; intervenir

**intimate** (ĭn′tə-māt) *v.* to make known indirectly; hint
**intimar** *v.* dar a conocer de manera indirecta; sugerir

**intuitively** (ĭn-tōō′ĭ-tĭv-lē) *adv.* without thinking; instinctively
**intuitivamente** *adv.* sin pensar; instintivamente

**inundate** (ĭn′ŭn-dāt′) *v.* to cover with water; overwhelm
**inundar** *v.* cubrir de agua; rebasar

**invest** (ĭn-vĕst′) *v.* to provide with a certain quality
**investir** *v.* dar cierta cualidad

**invincible** (ĭn-vĭn′sə-bəl) *adj.* unbeatable
**invencible** *adj.* que no se deja derrotar

**irresolution** (ĭ-rĕz′ə-lōō′shən) *n.* uncertainty; indecision
**irresolución** *s.* incertidumbre; indecisión

**irrevocable** (ĭ-rĕv′ə-kə-bəl) *adj.* impossible to take back or undo
**irrevocable** *adj.* imposible de retirar o deshacer

# J

**jubilant** (jōō′bə-lənt) *adj.* joyful and triumphant
**jubiloso** *adj.* gozoso y triunfal

# K

**kindred** (kĭn′drĭd) *n.* relatives or family
**parentela** *s.* parientes o familiares

# L

**laceration** (lăs′ə-rā′shən) *n.* a physical, mental, or emotional wound
**laceración** *s.* herida física, mental o emocional

**lament** (lə-mĕnt′) *v.* to grieve; wail
**lamentarse** *v.* dolerse; quejarse

**languish** (lăng′gwĭsh) *v.* to become weak
**languidecer** *v.* debilitar

**largesse** (lär-zhĕs′) *n.* generosity
**largueza** *s.* generosidad

**latent** (lāt′nt) *adj.* existing in a hidden form
**latente** *adj.* que existe en forma oculta

**lattice** (lăt′ĭs) *n.* an open framework made of spaced, crisscrossed strips
**rejilla** *s.* marco abierto hecho con tiras cruzadas

**legacy** (lĕg′ə-sē) *n.* something handed down from an ancestor or a predecessor or from the past
**legado** *s.* lo que se deja o transmite a los sucesores

**lethargy** (lĕth′ər-jē) *n.* a state of sluggishness and inactivity
**letargo** *s.* estado de sopor e inactividad

**license** (lī′səns) *n.* a lack of restrictions on behavior; freedom
**licencia** *s.* facultad o permiso para hacer una cosa; libertad

**linear** (lĭn′ē-ər) *adj.* resembling or arranged in a line
**lineal** *adj.* organizado en líneas

**list** (lĭst) *v.* to lean or tilt to one side
**inclinarse** *v.* hacerse hacia un lado

**loathsome** (lōth′səm) *adj.* arousing great dislike
**odioso** *adj.* que provoca mucho disgusto o rechazo; despreciado

**looming** (lōō′mĭng) *adj.* appearing to the mind in a large and threatening form **loom** *v.*
**imponente** *adj.* que parece grande y amenazante **imponer** *v.*

**ludicrous** (lōō′dĭ-krəs) *adj.* laughably absurd; ridiculous
**risible** *adj.* tan absurdo que causa risa; ridículo

**lurid** (lŏŏr′ĭd) *adj.* startling and sensational
**chillón** *adj.* llamativo y sensacional

**luxuriant** (lŭg-zhŏŏr′ē-ənt) *adj.* characterized by abundant growth
**exuberante** *adj.* que crececon lozanía

# M

**magnanimity** (măg′nə-nĭm′ĭ-tē) *n.* generosity
**magnanimidad** *s.* generosidad

**malicious** (mə-lĭsh′əs) *adj.* wicked; spiteful
**malicioso** *adj.* maligno; malo

**malinger** (mə-lĭng′gər) *v.* to pretend illness in order to avoid duty or work
**hacerse el enfermo** *v.* fingir enfermedad para evitar obligaciones o trabajo

**martial** (mär′shəl) *adj.* warlike
**marcial** *adj.* bélico; de guerra

**materialism** (mə-tîr′ē-ə-lĭz′əm) *n.* a preoccupation with worldly rather than spiritual concerns
**materialismo** *s.* preocupación por lo mundano en vez de lo espiritual

**mean** (mēn) *adj.* inferior in quality, value, or importance
**inferior** *adj.* de menor calidad, valor, o importancia

**mediocrity** (mē′dē-ŏk′rĭ-tē) *n.* a state of being only average in quality; moderate inferiority
**mediocridad** *s.* de calidad apenas promedio; inferioridad moderada

**meditation** (mĕd′ĭ-tā′shən) *n.* a thought or reflection
**meditación** *s.* pensamiento o reflexión profunda

**melancholy** (mĕl′ən-kŏl′ē) *adj.* gloomy; sad
**melancólico** *adj.* triste

**mercenary** (mûr′sə-nĕr′ē) *n.* a professional soldier hired to fight in a foreign army
**mercenario** *s.* soldado profesional contratado para pelear en un ejército extranjero

**mesa** (mā′ sə) *n.* a broad, flat-topped hill with clifflike sides
**meseta** *s.* planicie en lo alto de una montaña

**meticulous** (mĭ-tĭk′yə-ləs) *adj.* extremely careful and precise about details
**meticuloso** *adj.* sumamente cuidadoso, preciso y detallado

**mincing** (mĭn′sĭng) *adj.* acting refined or dainty
**remilgado** *adj.* refinado o afectado

**minutiae** (mĭ-nōō′shē-ē′) *n.* tiny elements, details, or parts
**minucias** *s.* elementos, detalles o piezas pequeñas

**misgiving** (mĭs-gĭv′ĭng) *n.* a feeling of doubt, mistrust, or uncertainty
**recelo** *s.* sentimiento de duda, desconfianza o incertidumbre

**mitigation** (mĭt′ĭ-gā′shən) *n.* lessening of something that causes suffering
**mitigación** *s.* lo que modera o suaviza algo que causa sufrimiento

**mollified** (mŏl′ə-fīd′) *adj.* pacified; made calm **mollify** *v.*
**apaciguado** *adj.* pacificado; calmado **apaciguar** *v.*

**monumental** (mŏn′yə-mĕn′tl) *adj.* great and lasting
**monumental** *adj.* grande y duradero

**morass** (mə-răs′) *n.* a difficult, confused, or entangled state of affairs; puzzling mess
**marisma** *s.* algo difícil, confuso o enredado; enredo incomprensible

**morose** (mə-rōs′) *adj.* gloomy and ill-tempered
**moroso** *adj.* triste y malhumorado

**multitude** (mŭl′tĭ-tōōd′) *n.* a great number of people
**multitud** *s.* gran cantidad de personas

# N

**narrative** (năr'ə-tĭv) *n.* a story
 **narrativa** *s.* narración

**nomadic** (nō-măd'ĭk) *adj.* without a fixed
 home; wandering
 **nómada** *adj.* sin hogar fijo; que va de un lugar
 a otro

**nominal** (nŏm'ə-nəl) *adj.* in name but not in
 reality
 **nominal** *adj.* de nombre pero no en la
 realidad

**nonconformist** (nŏn'kən-fôr'mĭst) *n.* one
 who does not follow generally accepted
 beliefs, customs, or practices
 **inconformista** *s.* el que no acepta los
 principios, costumbres y creencias de la
 sociedad en que vive

# O

**obliterate** (ə-blĭt'ə-rāt') *v.* to wipe out, leaving
 no trace
 **borrar** *v.* eliminar sin dejar huella

**obscure** (ŏb-skyŏŏr') *adj.* indistinct; not clearly
 understood
 **oscuro** *adj.* indistinto; que no se entiende
 claramente

**obscure** (ŏb-skyŏŏr') *v.* to cover over; hide
 **oscurecer** *v.* ocultar; confundir

**obstinate** (ŏb'stə-nĭt) *adj.* stubborn
 **obstinado** *adj.* terco

**obtuse** (ŏb-tōōs') *adj.* slow to understand; dull
 **obtuso** *adj.* lento para comprender; tonto

**odious** (ō'dē-əs) *adj.* arousing, or worthy of,
 strong dislike
 **odioso** *adj.* digno de odio; fastidioso

**ominous** (ŏm'ə-nəs) *adj.* threatening;
 menacing
 **ominoso** *adj.* amenazante; de mal agüero

**opaque** (ō-pāk') *adj.* not allowing light to pass
 through
 **opaco** *adj.* que no permite el paso de la luz

**oppressed** (ə-prĕst') *adj.* kept down by severe
 and unjust use of force or authority **oppress** *v.*
 **oprimido** *adj.* sometido por una fuerza o
 autoridad injusta **oprimir** *v.*

**opulent** (ŏp'yə-lənt) *adj.* characterized by
 abundance, extravagance, or wealth
 **opulento** *adj.* de gran abundancia,
 extravagancia o riqueza

**ostentation** (ŏs'tĕn-tā'shən) *n.* display meant
 to impress others; boastful showiness
 **ostentación** *s.* despliegue que tiene el fin de
 impresionar; alarde presuntuoso

**overwrought** (ō'vər-rôt') *adj.* excessively
 nervous or excited
 **sobreexcitado** *adj.* nerviosísimo; agotado por
 la emoción

# P

**pallid** (păl'ĭd) *adj.* abnormally pale
 **pálido** *adj.* descolorido

**palpable** (păl'pə-bəl) *adj.* that can be touched
 or felt
 **palpable** *adj.* que puede ser tocado o sentido

**panache** (pə-năsh') *n.* a sense of style; flair
 **brío** *s.* garbo; elegancia

**paradox** (păr'ə-dŏks') *n.* a seemingly
 contradictory statement that may
 nevertheless be true
 **paradoja** *s.* declaración que parece
 contradictoria pero que es verdadera

**parsimony** (pär'sə-mō'nē) *n.* extreme
 economy; stinginess
 **parsimonia** *s.* extrema economía; tacañería

**patent** (păt'nt) *adj.* obvious; apparent
 **patente** *adj.* obvio; aparente

**pathetic** (pə-thĕt'ĭk) *adj.* arousing pity or
 compassion
 **patético** *adj.* que despierta piedad o
 compasión

**peculiar** (pĭ-kyōōl'yər) *adj.* belonging
 particularly or primarily to one person, group,
 or kind
 **peculiar** *adj.* propio de una persona, grupo o
 clase

**perceptibly** (pər-sĕp'tə-blē) *adv.* in a way that can be perceived by the senses or the mind; noticeably
**perceptiblemente** *adv.* de forma que puede ser percibido por los sentidos o la mente; evidentemente

**perennial** (pə-rĕn'ē-əl) *adj.* lasting through the year or through many years; enduring
**perenne** *adj.* que dura todo el año o muchos años; duradero

**permeable** (pûr'mē-ə-bəl) *adj.* able to be passed through
**permeable** *adj.* que deja pasar

**perseverance** (pûr'sə-vîr'əns) *n.* persistence in the face of difficulty; determination
**perseverancia** *s.* persistencia frente a las dificultades; determinación

**perspective** (pər-spĕk'tĭv) *n.* a mental view or outlook; point of view
**perspectiva** *s.* visión mental o panorámica; punto de vista

**perturbation** (pûr'tər-bā'shən) *n.* a disturbance of the emotions; agitation; uneasiness
**perturbación** *s.* alteración de las emociones; agitación; incomodidad

**pervade** (pər-vād') *v.* to spread throughout
**penetrar** *v.* saturar por completo

**perverse** (pər-vûrs') *adj.* stubbornly opposed to what is right or reasonable; wrong-headed
**perverso** *adj.* opuesto tercamente a lo que es correcto o razonable; obstinado

**pestilence** (pĕs'tə-ləns) *n.* any epidemic disease that is usually fatal
**peste** *s.* enfermedad epidémica que suele ser mortal

**pestilential** (pĕs'tə-lĕn'shəl) *adj.* deadly; poisonous
**pestilente** *adj.* mortal; venenoso

**petulance** (pĕch'ə-ləns) *n.* ill temper; annoyance
**petulancia** *s.* mal humor; arrogancia

**piety** (pī'ĭ-tē) *n.* religious devotion; reverence for God
**piedad** *s.* devoción religiosa; reverencia a Dios

**pious** (pī'əs) *adj.* having or showing reverence for God
**piadoso** *adj.* que tiene o muestra reverencia a Dios

**placate** (plā'kāt') *v.* to soothe another's feelings; appease
**aplacar** *v.* calmar los sentimientos de otro; apaciguar

**placid** (plăs'ĭd) *adj.* undisturbed; calm or quiet
**plácido** *adj.* tranquilo; calmado o callado

**plague** (plāg) *v.* to annoy; harass
**plagar** *v.* molestar; fastidiar

**plaintiff** (plān'tĭf) *n.* the party that institutes a suit in court
**demandante** *s.* parte que inicia una demanda judicial

**poignant** (poin'yənt) *adj.* emotionally touching or moving
**conmovedor** *adj.* emotivo; enternecedor

**precarious** (prĭ-kâr'ē-əs) *adj.* risky; uncertain
**precario** *adj.* peligroso; incierto

**precept** (prē'sĕpt') *n.* a rule or principle prescribing a particular course of action
**precepto** *s.* regla o principio que dicta un curso de acción

**precipitately** (prĭ-sĭp'ĭ-tĭt-lē) *adv.* steeply
**precipitadamente** *adv.* empinadamente

**precipitous** (prĭ-sĭp'ĭ-təs) *adj.* steep; almost vertical
**escarpado** *adj.* empinado; casi vertical

**predilection** (prĕd'l-ĕk'shən) *n.* a personal preference
**predilección** *s.* preferencia personal

**predominate** (prĭ-dŏm'ə-nāt') *v.* to have controlling power or influence
**predominar** *v.* tener poder o influencia para controlar

**preeminently** (prē-ĕm'ə-nənt-lē) *adv.* above all; most importantly
**preeminentemente** *adv.* por encima de todo; con suma importancia

**preening** (prē'nĭng) *n.* dressing and grooming oneself with excessive care; primping **preen** *v.*
**acicalamiento** *s.* vestirse y arreglarse con cuidado excesivo **acicalar** *v.*

**preoccupied** (prē-ŏk'yə-pīd') *adj.* lost in thought; intensely concerned
**preocupado** *adj.* distraído; absorto

**prestige** (prĕ-stēzh') *n.* honor; admiration
**prestigio** *s.* honor; admiración

**presume** (prĭ-zōōm') *v.* to act overconfidently; go beyond the proper limits; dare
**presumir** *v.* actuar con demasiada seguridad; ir más allá de lo adecuado

**pretense** (prē'tĕns') *n.* the act of pretending; a false appearance or action intended to deceive
**fingimiento** *s.* acto de fingir; falsa apariencia o acción con el propósito de engañar

**preternaturally** (prē'tər-năch'ər-əl-ē) *adv.* more than naturally; extraordinarily
**sobrenaturalmente** *adv.* de modo sobrenatural; extraordinariamente

**probity** (prō'bĭ-tē) *n.* honesty; integrity
**probidad** *s.* honestidad; integridad

**procure** (prō-kyōōr') *v.* to get by special effort; obtain
**adquirir** *v.* conseguir por medio de esfuerzos especiales; obtener

**profoundly** (prə-found'lē) *adv.* deeply; intensely
**profundamente** *adv.* hondamente; intensamente

**profusion** (prə-fyōō'zhən) *n.* abundance; lavishness
**profusión** *s.* abundancia

**propitious** (prə-pĭsh'əs) *adj.* helpful or advantageous; favorable
**propicio** *adj.* que ayuda o es ventajoso; favorable

**providence** (prŏv'ĭ-dəns) *n.* an instance of divine care or guidance
**providencia** *s.* ejemplo de cuidado o guía divina

**provisional** (prə-vĭzh'ə-nəl) *adj.* temporary
**provisional** *adj.* temporal

**provocation** (prŏv'ə-kā'shən) *n.* something that arouses anger
**provocación** *s.* algo que despierta ira

**prowess** (prou'ĭs) *n.* superior strength, courage, or daring, especially in battle
**valentía** *s.* gran fuerza, valentía y arrojo, especialmente en la batalla

**punitive** (pyōō'nĭ-tĭv) *adj.* punishing or having to do with punishment
**punitivo** *adj.* que castiga o que se relaciona con el castigo

**purging** (pûr'jĭng) *n.* getting rid of something unwanted; cleansing **purge** *v.*
**purga** *s.* eliminación de algo no deseado; limpieza **purgar** *v.*

## Q

**qualm** (kwäm) *n.* a disturbing uneasiness or doubt
**remordimiento** *s.* duda que perturba

**quandary** (kwŏn'də-rē) *n.* a state of uncertainty
**dilema** *s.* estado de incertidumbre

**querulous** (kwĕr'ə-ləs) *adj.* given to complaining
**quejumbroso** *adj.* dado a quejarse

## R

**rakish** (rā'kĭsh) *adj.* dashingly or sportingly stylish; jaunty
**gallardo** *adj.* brioso o elegante; garboso

**rapt** (răpt) *adj.* deeply moved, delighted, or absorbed
**extasiado** *adj.* profundamente conmovido, encantado o absorto

**ravaged** (răv'ĭjd) *adj.* devastated; ruined **ravage** *v.*
**destruido** *adj.* devastado; arruinado **destruir** *v.*

**rebuff** (rĭ-bŭf') *v.* to reject bluntly; snub
**desairar** *v.* rechazar abiertamente; desdeñar

**recalcitrant** (rĭ-kăl'sĭ-trənt) *adj.* stubborn; hard to deal with
**recalcitrante** *adj.* terco; obstinado

**recommence** (rē'kə-měns') *v.* to begin again
**reiniciar** *v.* comenzar de nuevo

**regimentation** (rěj'ə-mən-tā'shən) *n.* the process of using discipline and control to organize into a rigid system
**reglamentación** *s.* proceso de organizar un sistema estricto con disciplina y control

**rend** (rěnd) *v.* to tear or split apart violently
**desgarrar** *v.* romper o dividir violentamente

**repercussion** (rē'pər-kŭsh'ən) *n.* a far-reaching effect
**repercusión** *s.* efecto de largo alcance

**repose** (rǐ-pōz') *v.* to rest or relax
**reposar** *v.* descansar o relajarse

**reproach** (rǐ-prōch') *n.* an expression of blame or disapproval
**reproche** *s.* expresión de culpa o desaprobación

**repudiate** (rǐ-pyōō'dē-āt') *v.* to reject the validity or authority of
**repudiar** *v.* rechazar la validez o autoridad

**resignation** (rěz'ǐg-nā'shən) *n.* an acceptance of something as unavoidable
**resignación** *s.* aceptación; conformidad

**resolute** (rěz'ə-lōōt') *adj.* firm or determined; unwavering
**resuelto** *adj.* firme o decidido; sin dudas

**resolve** (rǐ-zŏlv') *v.* to make a firm decision
**resolver** *v.* tomar una decisión firme

**respite** (rěs'pǐt) *n.* a brief period of rest or relief from pain or labor
**respiro** *s.* breve período de descanso o alivio de dolor o trabajo

**retaliating** (rǐ-tăl'ē-ā'tǐng) *n.* taking revenge **retaliate** *v.*
**represalia** *s.* venganza **vengarse** *v.*

**retraction** (rǐ-trăk'shən) *n.* a taking back of something said
**retractación** *s.* anulación de lo dicho

**reverberate** (rǐ-vûr'bə-rāt') *v.* to echo
**reverberar** *v.* hacer eco

**ritual** (rǐch'ōō-əl) *n.* a ceremonial act or a series of such acts
**ritual** *s.* acto ceremonial o serie de dichos actos

**robust** (rō-bŭst') *adj.* full of health and strength; vigorous
**robusto** *adj.* lleno de salud y fuerza; vigoroso

**rudiment** (rōō'də-mənt) *n.* an imperfect or undeveloped form
**rudimento** *s.* forma imperfecta o subdesarrollada

**rue** (rōō) *v.* to regret
**lamentar** *v.* arrepentirse

**ruminating** (rōō'mə-nā-tǐng) *adj.* turning a matter over and over in the mind **ruminate** *v.*
**rumión** *adj.* que da muchas vueltas a un asunto en la mente **rumiar** *v.*

**rummage** (rŭm'ǐj) *v.* to search through a confusion of objects
**hurgar** *v.* buscar revolviéndolo todo

## S

**sagacious** (sə-gā'shəs) *adj.* wise
**sagaz** *adj.* sabio

**scoff** (skŏf) *v.* to mock
**mofarse** *v.* burlarse

**scrupulously** (skrōō'pyə-ləs-lē) *adv.* in an extremely careful and thorough manner; conscientiously
**escrupulosamente** *adv.* de manera extremadamente cuidadosa y a fondo; concienzudamente

**scrutinize** (skrōōt'n-īz') *v.* to look over carefully; study
**escudriñar** *v.* revisar cuidadosamente; inspeccionar

**segregated** (sěg'rǐ-gā'tǐd) *adj.* separated according to race **segregate** *v.*
**segregado** *adj.* separado por razas **segregar** *v.*

**sentinel** (sěn'tə-nəl) *n.* a guard
**centinela** *s.* guardia

**serenity** (sə-rěn'ǐ-tē) *n.* a mental and spiritual calm; tranquillity
**serenidad** *s.* calma mental y espiritual; tranquilidad

**servile** (sur'vəl) *adj.* humbly submissive; slavish
**servil** *adj.* humildemente sumiso; abyecto

**servitude** (sûr′vĭ-tōōd′) *n.* the condition of one who is subject to a master; lack of freedom
**servidumbre** *s.* condición de quien está sujeto a un amo; falta de libertad

**shamble** (shăm′bəl) *v.* to walk or move awkwardly or clumsily
**arrastrar los pies** *v.* caminar o moverse con dificultad o torpeza

**sibilant** (sĭb′ə-lənt) *adj.* hissing
**sibilante** *adj.* que silba o suena a manera de silbido

**simper** (sĭm′pər) *v.* to smile in a shy or self-conscious way
**sonreír tontamente** *v.* sonreír con vergüenza o timidez

**singular** (sĭng′gyə-lər) *adj.* unusual or remarkable; unique
**singular** *adj.* inusual o notable; único

**solace** (sŏl′ĭs) *n.* comfort in sorrow or distress
**solaz** *s.* consuelo en la pena o la desgracia

**solicitous** (sə-lĭs′ĭ-təs) *adj.* full of desire; eager
**solícito** *adj.* lleno de deseo; atento

**sordid** (sôr′dĭd) *adj.* wretched; dirty; morally degraded
**sórdido** *adj.* miserable; sucio; degradado moralmente

**specimen** (spĕs′ə-mən) *n.* an example of a group
**espécimen** *s.* ejemplar de un grupo

**specter** (spĕk′tər) *n.* a ghostly vision; phantom
**espectro** *s.* visión fantasmagórica; fantasma

**spurn** (spûrn) *v.* to reject scornfully
**desdeñar** *v.* rechazar con desdén

**statute** (stăch′ōot) *n.* a law
**estatuto** *s.* ley

**stench** (stĕnch) *n.* a strong, foul odor
**hedor** *s.* olor desagradable y penetrante

**stigma** (stĭg′mə) *n.* a mark of disgrace
**estigma** *s.* marca de desgracia

**stiltedly** (stĭl′tĭd-lē) *adv.* in a stiffly dignified manner
**circunspectamente** *adv.* con dignidad tiesa

**stupendous** (stōo-pĕn′dəs) *adj.* of amazing size; enormous
**estupendo** *adj.* de sorprendente tamaño; enorme

**subdued** (səb-dōōd′) *adj.* made submissive; reduced in intensity; toned down **subdue** *v.*
**disminuido** *adj.* hecho sumiso; de menor intensidad o tono **disminuir** *v.*

**subjugation** (sŭb′jə-gā′shən) *n.* control by conquering
**subyugación** *s.* control por medio de la conquista

**sublime** (sə-blīm′) *adj.* of high spiritual, moral, or intellectual worth; noble
**sublime** *adj.* de elevado valor espiritual, moral o intelectual; noble

**subordinate** (sə-bôr′dn-ĭt) *n.* one who is lower in rank
**subordinado** *s.* el que es de rango inferior

**subservient** (səb-sûr′vē-ənt) *adj.* acting like a servant
**servil** *adj.* que se comporta como sirviente

**subsistence** (səb-sĭs′təns) *n.* livelihood
**subsistencia** *s.* forma de ganarse la vida

**subtle** (sŭt′l) *adj.* so slight as to be difficult to detect
**sutil** *adj.* delicado; tenue; difícil de detectar

**succulent** (sŭk′yə-lənt) *adj.* tasty; delicious
**suculento** *adj.* sabroso; delicioso

**succumb** (sə-kŭm′) *v.* to give up or give in; yield
**sucumbir** *v.* ceder o aceptar; rendirse

**suffuse** (sə-fyōōz′) *v.* to spread through
**difundir** *v.* bañar; cubrir

**sullenly** (sŭl′ən-lē) *adv.* resentfully; sulkily
**enfurruñadamente** *adv.* con mal humor y resentimiento

**sully** (sŭl′ē) *v.* to spoil; tarnish
**manchar** *v.* arruinar; ensuciar

**summarily** (sə-mĕr′ə-lē) *adv.* in a way that is quick and bypasses usual procedures
**sumariamente** *adv.* con rapidez y sin seguir los trámites normales

**sundry** (sŭn'drē) *adj.* various; miscellaneous
**diversos** *adj.* varios; misceláneos

**superficially** (soo'pər-fĭsh'ə-lē) *adv.* in a shallow way; concerned with only what is obvious
**superficialmente** *adv.* de manera ligera; con interés sólo en lo obvio

**surfeit** (sûr'fĭt) *n.* a fullness beyond the point of satisfaction
**hartura** *s.* saciedad más allá del punto de satisfacción

**surmise** (sər-mīz') *v.* to guess
**suponer** *v.* adivinar

**surreptitious** (sûr'əp-tĭsh'əs) *adj.* secret; stealthy
**subrepticio** *adj.* secreto; oculto

**synthesis** (sĭn'thĭ-sĭs) *n.* the combining of separate elements or substances to form a coherent whole
**síntesis** *s.* combinación de elementos o sustancias separadas para formar un todo coherente

# T

**tacitly** (tăs'ĭt-lē) *adv.* silently
**tácitamente** *adv.* silenciosamente

**tactful** (tăkt'fəl) *adj.* careful of others' feelings; considerate
**prudente** *adj.* cuidadoso de los sentimientos de otros; considerado

**tangible** (tăn'jə-bəl) *adj.* able to be touched or felt
**tangible** *adj.* que puede ser tocado o sentido

**taut** (tôt) *adj.* pulled tight; straight
**tirante** *adj.* estirado

**tedious** (tē'dē-əs) *adj.* boring because of dullness
**tedioso** *adj.* aburridor

**temerity** (tə-mĕr'ĭ-tē) *n.* foolish boldness
**temeridad** *s.* valentía tonta

**tempest** (tĕm'pĭst) *n.* a violent storm
**tempestad** *s.* tormenta violenta

**temporize** (tĕm'pə-rīz') *v.* to avoid immediate action or making a decision in order to gain time
**contemporizar** *v.* evitar acción inmediata; tomar una decisión a fin de ganar tiempo

**terminal** (tûr'mə-nəl) *adj.* final; fatal
**terminal** *adj.* final; fatal

**terrestrial** (tə-rĕs'trē-əl) *adj.* on the ground; earthly
**terrestre** *adj.* relativo al suelo o a la Tierra

**tersely** (tûrs'lē) *adv.* briefly
**concisamente** *adv.* brevemente

**theology** (thē-ŏl'ə-jē) *n.* a system of religious beliefs
**teología** *s.* sistema de creencias religiosas

**thwart** (thwôrt) *v.* to block or hinder; prevent the fulfillment of
**frustrar** *v.* bloquear u obstaculizar; impedir

**tousled** (tou'zəld) *adj.* messy; rumpled **tousle** *v.*
**desarreglado** *adj.* en desorden; revuelto **desarreglar** *v.*

**tranquil** (trăng'kwəl) *adj.* undisturbed; peaceful
**tranquilo** *adj.* imperturbable; pacífico

**transcribe** (trăn-skrīb') *v.* to make a handwritten or typed copy of
**transcribir** *v.* hacer una copia manuscrita o mecanografiada

**transient** (trăn'shənt) *adj.* lasting or existing for only a short time
**transitorio** *adj.* que dura o existe sólo por breve tiempo

**tremulous** (trĕm'yə-ləs) *adj.* marked by trembling, quivering, or shaking
**trémulo** *adj.* que tiembla o se sacude

**trepidation** (trĕp'ĭ-dā'shən) *n.* fearful uncertainty or worry
**trepidación** *s.* incertidumbre o preocupación que causa miedo

**truculent** (trŭk'yə-lənt) *adj.* eager for a fight; fierce
**agresivo** *adj.* deseoso de pelear; fiero

**tumultuous** (tōō-mŭl'chōō-əs) *adj.* wild and disorderly
**tumultuoso** *adj.* alborotado y desordenado

**tyrannical** (tĭ-răn′ĭ-kəl) *adj.* harsh; oppressive
**tiránico** *adj.* cruel; opresivo

# U

**unassailable** (ŭn′ə-sā′lə-bəl) *adj.* impossible to dispute or disprove; undeniable
**indiscutible** *adj.* imposible de disputar o desaprobar; innegable

**undulating** (ŭn′jə-lā′tĭng) *adj.* moving with a wavelike motion **undulate** *v.*
**ondulante** *adj.* con movimiento similar al de las olas **ondular** *v.*

**unintelligible** (ŭn′ĭn-tĕl′ĭ-jə-bəl) *adj.* incomprehensible; unable to be understood
**ininteligible** *adj.* incomprensible; imposible de ser entendido

**unobtrusive** (ŭn′əb-trōō′sĭv) *adj.* not noticeable; not calling attention to oneself
**discreto** *adj.* que no se nota; que no llama la atención hacia sí

**unrelenting** (ŭn′rĭ-lĕn′tĭng) *adj.* not stopping or weakening
**inexorable** *adj.* que no para ni se debilita

**unscrupulous** (ŭn-skrōō′pyə-ləs) *adj.* without principles; dishonorable
**inescrupuloso** *adj.* sin principios; deshonesto

**untenanted** (ŭn-tĕn′ən-tĭd) *adj.* not occupied
**desocupado** *adj.* vacío

**untoward** (ŭn-tôrd′) *n.* inappropriate
**adverso** *s.* inapropiado

**usurping** (yōō-sur′pĭng) *n.* taking another's place wrongfully **usurp** *v.*
**usurpador** *s.* el que toma el lugar de otro sin derecho **usurpar** *v.*

# V

**vacillating** (văs′ə-lā′tĭng) *adj.* swinging from one course of action or opinion to another; indecisive **vacillate** *v.*
**vacilante** *adj.* que cambia de opinión o de curso; indeciso **vacilar** *v.*

**vagabond** (văg′ə-bŏnd′) *n.* a wanderer; drifter
**vagabundo** *s.* persona que anda errante de un lugar a otro

**vanquish** (văng′kwĭsh) *v.* to defeat in battle
**vencer** *v.* derrotar en la batalla

**variant** (vâr′ē-ənt) *n.* something that differs slightly from others of its kind
**variante** *s.* algo que difiere un poco de otros de su tipo

**veneer** (və-nîr′) *n.* a thin surface layer that conceals what is below
**chapa** *s.* capa delgada en la superficie que oculta lo que está debajo; barniz

**venerable** (vĕn′ər-ə-bəl) *adj.* worthy of respect because of age, dignity, or character
**venerable** *adj.* digno de respeto por la edad, dignidad o carácter

**venture** (vĕn′chər) *v.* to dare to go
**aventurar** *v.* atreverse a ir

**vigilant** (vĭj′ə-lənt) *adj.* alert; watchful
**vigilante** *adj.* alerta; atento

**vindication** (vĭn′dĭ-kā′shən) *n.* the defense or justification of something, such as one's rights
**vindicación** *s.* defensa o justificación de algo, como los derechos propios

**vindictive** (vĭn-dĭk′tĭv) *adj.* wanting revenge; bearing a grudge
**vengador** *adj.* que desea venganza; que guarda resentimiento

**virulent** (vîr′yə-lənt) *adj.* extremely poisonous or harmful
**virulento** *adj.* extremadamente venenoso o dañino

**vivacious** (vĭ-vā′shəs) *adj.* full of energy; lively
**vivaz** *adj.* lleno de energía; vital

**void** (void) *n.* an empty space
**vacío** *s.* espacio sin nada

**vulgar** (vŭl′gər) *adj.* coarse; common
**vulgar** *adj.* rudo; común

# W

**wane** (wān) *v.* to decrease in size, intensity, or degree
**decaer** *v.* disminuir de tamaño, intensidad o grado

**whence** (hwĕns) *adv.* from where
**dónde** *adv.* de dónde

**wrath** (răth) *n.* fierce anger, or punishment resulting from such anger
**ira** *s.* cólera fuerte o castigo resultante de esa ira

**wretched** (rĕch′ĭd) *adj.* miserable
**desgraciado** *adj.* miserable

## Pronunciation Key

| Symbol | Examples | Symbol | Examples | Symbol | Examples |
|---|---|---|---|---|---|
| ă | at, gas | m | man, seem | v | van, save |
| ā | ape, day | n | night, mitten | w | web, twice |
| ä | father, barn | ng | sing, anger | y | yard, lawyer |
| âr | fair, dare | ŏ | odd, not | z | zoo, reason |
| b | bell, table | ō | open, road, grow | zh | treasure, garage |
| ch | chin, lunch | ô | awful, bought, horse | ə | awake, even, pencil, |
| d | dig, bored | oi | coin, boy | | pilot, focus |
| ĕ | egg, ten | ŏŏ | look, full | ər | perform, letter |
| ē | evil, see, meal | ōō | root, glue, through | | |
| f | fall, laugh, phrase | ou | out, cow | | **Sounds in Foreign Words** |
| g | gold, big | p | pig, cap | KH | *German* ich, auch; |
| h | hit, inhale | r | rose, star | | *Scottish* loch |
| hw | white, everywhere | s | sit, face | N | *French* entre, bon, fin |
| ĭ | inch, fit | sh | she, mash | œ | *French* feu, cœur; |
| ī | idle, my, tried | t | tap, hopped | | *German* schön |
| îr | dear, here | th | thing, with | ü | *French* utile, rue; |
| j | jar, gem, badge | *th* | then, other | | *German* grün |
| k | keep, cat, luck | ŭ | up, nut | | |
| l | load, rattle | ûr | fur, earn, bird, worm | | |

**Stress Marks**

′ This mark indicates that the preceding syllable receives the primary stress. For example, in the word *language,* the first syllable is stressed: lăng′gwĭj.

′ This mark is used only in words in which more than one syllable is stressed. It indicates that the preceding syllable is stressed, but somewhat more weakly than the syllable receiving the primary stress. In the word *literature,* for example, the first syllable receives the primary stress, and the last syllable receives a weaker stress: lĭt′ər-ə-chŏŏr′.

Adapted from *The American Heritage Dictionary of the English Language, Third Edition;* Copyright © 1992 by Houghton Mifflin Company. Used with the permission of Houghton Mifflin Company.

# Index of Fine Art

# Index of Skills

## Literary Concepts

Act, 161, 1342. *See also* Drama.
Allegory, 454, 462, 500, 1342
Alliteration. *See* Poetic elements.
Allusion, 262, 267, 307, 1005, 1025, 1136, 1146, 1232, 1342
Analogy, 254, 676, 863, 964, 1342
Anapest, 142, 1342. *See also* Poetic elements, meter.
Anaphora. *See* Figurative language.
Anecdote, 323, 806, 1227, 1342
Antagonist, 161, 329, 1168, 1178, 1343
Antihero, 1149, 1237, 1343
Aphorism, 340, 363, 367, 381, 1147, 1343
Archaic language, 138
Argumentation, 260–261, 1136
Aside, 162
Assonance. *See* Poetic elements.
Audience, 72, 78, 98, 152, 158, 323, 620, 959, 1178, 1343
Author's attitude. *See* Tone. *See also* Tone, recognizing *under* Reading and Critical Thinking Skills.
Author's perspective, 932, 937
Author's purpose (motivation), 100, 107, 116, 360, 562, 645, 950, 1343. *See also* Author's purpose (motivation) *under* Reading and Critical Thinking Skills.
Autobiographical essay. *See* Essay.
Autobiography, 70, 71, 99, 109, 116, 319, 381, 438, 562, 571, 1343
Ballad, 394, 618, 620, 731, 1344
Bias, 88, 144, 150
Biography, 70, 1344
Blank verse. *See* Poetic elements.
Caesura, 1344
Cast of characters, 161, 165, 1344
Catalog, 396, 404, 1344
Character(s), 48, 161, 190, 206, 228, 243, 251, 329, 360, 434, 516, 528, 544, 602, 637, 765, 788, 800, 804, 830, 833, 840, 860, 892, 1105, 1157, 1168, 1178, 1200, 1212, 1344
Characterization, 360, 516, 525, 539, 830, 833, 1345
Cliché, 442, 1345
Climax, 161, 243, 329, 1178, 1345. *See also* Plot.
Comedy, 161, 1345
Coming-of-age story, 788, 800, 1345
Conceit, 1345
Conflict, 48, 53, 88, 129, 161, 243, 544, 783, 788, 800, 894, 911, 1109, 1157, 1166, 1178, 1345
external and internal, 53, 88, 243, 329, 1105, 1109, 1166, 1345, 1348, 1254
Connotation, 150, 152, 908, 1346
Consonance. *See* Poetic elements.
Contrast, 289, 1346
*Corrido,* 702, 1346
Couplet. *See* Poetic elements.
Creation myth, 21, 24, 31, 1346
*Cuento,* 638, 643, 702, 1346

Cultural hero, 46, 702, 718, 1346
Dactyl, 142, 1346. *See also* Poetic elements, meter.
Deduction, 1136
Denotation, 908, 1346
Dénouement, 1346. *See also* Plot.
Description, 669, 676, 1223, 1346
Details, 70, 78, 93, 98, 100, 123, 251, 299, 300, 369, 438, 544, 669, 676, 824, 894, 973, 1168, 1215, 1221, 1223
Dialect, 593, 637, 679, 685, 1014, 1055, 1347
Dialogue, 162, 206, 329, 438, 544, 548, 562, 571, 620, 1006, 1014, 1018, 1023, 1095, 1150, 1155, 1347
Diary, 70, 81, 88, 1033, 1347
Diction, 78, 150, 421, 497, 571, 824, 863, 873, 967, 1025, 1198, 1232, 1347. *See also* Word choice.
Drama, 161–162, 329, 1347
Dramatic monologue, 162
Dynamic character, 840, 860, 892. *See also* Character.
Elegy, 394, 513, 1347
End rhyme, 344, 347, 466, 471, 620, 1360. *See also* Rhyme scheme.
Epic poem. *See* Poetry.
Epigram, 678
Epithet, 98, 829, 1348
Essay, 289, 369, 378, 950, 1221, 1348
autobiographical, 950, 957, 1343
critical, 973
nature writing, 381, 392, 1356
personal, 1215, 1221, 1357
Exaggeration, 685, 1348
Experimental poetry. *See* Poetry.
Exposition, 161, 1348. *See also* Plot.
Extended metaphor. *See* Figurative language.
External conflict. *See* Conflict.
Eyewitness report, 81, 120, 123, 609, 616, 1349
Fable, 21, 441, 1349
Falling action, 161, 1349. *See also* Plot.
Farce, 1349
Fiction, 62, 702, 1349
Figurative language, 282, 287, 293, 392, 438, 497, 562, 602, 750, 760, 860, 911, 943, 945, 1095, 1349
anaphora, 395, 971, 1342
extended metaphor, 760, 945, 948, 1348
hyperbole, 1351
metaphor, 287, 293, 347, 392, 497, 750, 757, 760, 815, 860, 911, 948, 1014, 1354
personification, 392, 602, 750, 760, 828, 860, 911, 1357
simile, 287, 392, 497, 602, 750, 760, 860, 911, 1361
Figures of speech, 602, 828
Flashback, 516, 548, 1350
Foil, 161, 228, 329, 1350
Folk tale, 39, 46, 638, 643, 644, 1350
Foot, 138, 142, 1013, 1350. *See also* Poetic elements, meter.
Foreshadowing, 500, 514, 525, 1350
Form, 394, 416, 553, 1006, 1350
Free verse. *See* Poetic elements.

Poetic elements. *See also* Figurative language; Imagery; Rhythm; Speaker.
- alliteration, 971, 1342
- assonance, 1343
- blank verse, 394, 1006, 1013, 1014, 1344
- consonance, 1346
- conventional form, 394
- couplet, 948, 1346
- free verse, 395, 396, 404, 1111, 1350
- iambic pentameter, 142, 943, 1006, 1013, 1351
- meter, 138, 142, 344, 347, 394, 395, 553, 620, 833, 1354
- octave, 943, 1356
- onomatopoeia, 1356
- organic form, 394
- parallelism, 396, 404, 1357
- quatrain, 620, 750, 761, 1359
- repetition, 33, 37, 396, 404, 620, 971, 1000, 1005, 1014, 1360
- rhyme, 347, 466, 471, 833, 971, 1360
- rhyme scheme, 142, 344, 347, 466, 471, 553, 750, 1360
- sestet, 943, 1361
- slant rhyme, 750, 761, 1361
- sound devices, 466, 471, 971, 1362
- stanza, 37, 344, 347, 553, 620, 1006, 1111, 1362
- structure, 416, 421, 1111, 1116, 1363
Poetry, 394–395, 1006
- epic, 309, 316, 394, 1348
- experimental, 410, 414, 1348
- lyric, 143, 838, 1353
- narrative, 316, 618, 830, 833, 1355
- protest, 578, 621, 731, 1359
Point of view, 88, 497, 580, 591, 833, 834, 1045, 1055, 1085, 1260
- first-person, 438, 580, 591, 731, 816, 1006, 1350
- limited, 580, 1045, 1055, 1191
- omniscient, 580, 591, 1085, 1191
- second-person, 1006
- third-person, 580, 591, 731, 815, 1006, 1045, 1055, 1085, 1191
Primary source. *See* Source.
Prop, 162, 163, 190, 1260
Prose, 423, 1260
Protest poem. *See* Poetry.
Protagonist, 161, 329, 1168, 1178, 1237, 1359
Quatrain. *See* Poetic elements.
Rationalism, 256–258, 270–276, 340, 446, 1359
Realism, 448, 636–637, 1359
Refrain, 414, 1359
Regional literature, 636
Repetition, 267, 497, 605, 607, 1018, 1360. *See also* Poetic elements.
Resolution, 129, 161, 329, 1360. *See also* Plot.
Rhetorical questions, 261–262, 1360
Rhyme. *See* Poetic elements.
Rhyme scheme. *See* Poetic elements.
Rhythm, 37, 138, 344, 394, 395, 396, 551, 750, 924, 928, 1000, 1005, 1013, 1014, 1095, 1118, 1120, 1360
Rising action, 161, 1360. *See also* Plot.

Romanticism, 340–342, 446, 1025, 1360
Sarcasm, 162
Satire, 1361
Scansion, 142, 943, 1013, 1361. *See also* Poetic elements, meter.
Scene, 161, 1361
Science fiction, 1361
Secondary source. *See* Source.
Sequence. *See* Chronological order *under* Reading and Critical Thinking Skills.
Sermon, 152, 1361
Sestet. *See* Poetic elements.
Setting, 55, 62, 78, 161, 162, 163, 251, 329, 544, 636–637, 669, 688, 697, 731, 830, 833, 1095, 1361
Short story, 117, 544–549, 1361
Simile. *See* Figurative language.
Slant rhyme. *See* Poetic elements, slant rhyme.
Slave narrative. *See* Narrative.
Social criticism, 1148–1149
Soliloquy, 162, 815, 1362
Song, 33
Sonnet, 940, 943, 948, 1362
- Italian (Petrarchan), 943, 1362
- Shakespearean (English or Elizabethan), 948, 1362
Sound devices. *See* Poetic elements.
Source
- primary, 81, 88, 91, 98, 616, 1260
- secondary, 91, 98, 1361
Speaker, 416, 421, 471, 804, 898, 967, 968, 1001, 1003, 1005, 1057, 1061, 1089, 1098, 1101, 1111, 1116, 1194, 1362
Stage directions, 162, 163, 190, 329, 1150
Stanza. *See* Poetic elements.
Static character, 840, 860, 892. *See also* Character.
Stereotype, 1362
Stream of consciousness, 1017, 1025, 1034, 1043, 1067, 1362
Structure, 55, 580, 591, 877, 892, 1227, 1232, 1363. *See also* Poetic elements.
Style, 62, 109, 497, 562, 571, 605, 607, 686, 750, 761, 938, 967, 971, 1014, 1018, 1023, 1067, 1118, 1120, 1363
Supernatural element, 24
Surprise ending, 786, 1363
Surrealism, 1363
Suspense, 496, 514, 1363
Symbol, 62, 404, 574, 578, 835, 838, 860, 1191, 1363
Synesthesia, 1363
Tall tale, 679, 685, 702, 1363
Theme, 2, 5, 62, 251, 289, 293, 298, 330, 347, 360, 638, 643, 763–764, 786, 830, 831, 894, 898, 967, 1057, 1058, 1061, 1076, 1085, 1191, 1237, 1364
Time frame. *See* Setting.
Title, 243, 330, 602, 894, 898, 1057, 1058, 1061, 1076, 1085, 1109, 1111, 1196, 1198, 1225, 1237, 1364
Tone, 295, 298, 307, 421, 497, 562, 571, 607, 824, 828, 838, 863, 932, 937, 957, 967, 971, 1018, 1023, 1088, 1093, 1148–1149, 1150, 1155, 1178, 1194, 1198, 1232, 1237, 1364. *See also* Tone *under* Reading and Critical Thinking Skills.
Tragedy, 161, 1364

Tragic hero, 1212, 1364
Transcendentalism, 340–342, 363, 1364
Transcript, 144, 148, 1365
Trickster tale, 21, 39, 46, 1365
Trochee, 142, 1365. *See also* Poetic elements, meter.
True rhyme. *See* Poetic elements, slant rhyme.
Understatement, 1365
Voice, 863, 873, 1227, 1232, 1365
Word choice, 150, 562, 571, 607, 971, 1000, 1005, 1018, 1118, 1120, 1365. *See also* Diction.

## Reading and Critical Thinking Skills

Analogies. *See also* Analogies *under* Vocabulary Skills.
    formulating, 254
    reading and understanding, 190, 964
Analyzing, 93, 129, 151, 158, 289, 293, 307, 360, 367, 378, 578, 580, 591, 760, 786, 932, 964, 971, 972, 1000, 1030, 1061, 1103, 1155, 1198, 1212, 1223, 1225, 1232
Arguments, evaluating, 300, 700, 1104, 1146
Author's attitude. *See* Tone, recognizing.
Author's purpose (motivation)
    analyzing, 571, 1241
    identifying, 100, 107, 562, 645, 652, 1241
Author's style. *See* Style, analyzing.
Bias, identifying, 144, 150
Brainstorming, 593, 932, 1095, 1150
Cause and effect, analyzing, 24, 31, 1093, 1254, 1258
Characterization, analyzing, 516, 525, 830, 833
Chronological order, 609, 1034, 1043, 1254, 1256
Classifying and categorizing
    chart, 24, 31, 37, 46, 48, 53, 55, 64, 88, 93, 109, 152, 163, 190, 228, 251, 268, 287, 289, 309, 318, 349, 369, 410, 421, 462, 471, 496, 500, 516, 562, 578, 593, 616, 658, 667, 669, 676, 688, 783, 802, 804, 806, 824, 830, 835, 863, 877, 892, 894, 928, 932, 940, 945, 973, 1000, 1006, 1018, 1025, 1076, 1095, 1157, 1200, 1221, 1225, 1232
    cluster diagram, 62, 81, 100, 940, 950, 967, 1057, 1120
    graph, 79, 602, 840, 875
    other diagram, 243, 279, 282, 498, 609, 638, 702, 705, 824, 1034, 1045, 1215
    Venn diagram, 148, 243, 294, 1005
    word web, 39, 289, 562, 605, 765, 875, 1223
Comparison and contrast
    characters, 55, 410, 528, 1056, 1200, 1215
    conflicts, 1061
    elements of literature, 31, 37, 46, 48, 78, 98, 100, 158, 228, 279, 293, 298, 309, 316, 342, 347, 367, 378, 392, 404, 414, 416, 421, 424, 434, 462, 496, 514, 516, 525, 539, 571, 578, 591, 602, 618, 620, 643, 652, 676, 685, 779, 782, 786, 804, 815, 828, 833, 838, 873, 876, 928, 937, 943, 948, 957, 959, 967, 973, 1005, 1043, 1055, 1085, 1093, 1101, 1105, 1111, 1118, 1155, 1194, 1198, 1215, 1223, 1225, 1227
    organizational pattern, 1254, 1257
Conclusions, drawing, 55, 62, 78, 158, 293, 295, 347, 360, 367, 434, 462, 471, 496, 514, 528, 667, 676, 685, 688, 697, 760, 815, 828, 833, 838, 894, 898, 932, 937, 957, 1013, 1055, 1061, 1076, 1085, 1101, 1116, 1120, 1146, 1155, 1157, 1166, 1178, 1191, 1212, 1215, 1225, 1232
Connections
    to current events, 150, 243, 287, 307, 574, 616, 620, 765, 783, 1136
    to historical events, 81, 243, 562, 605, 1095, 1105
    to personal experiences, 24, 33, 39, 53, 72, 93, 138, 144, 152, 262, 270, 282, 289, 295, 344, 363, 381, 396, 414, 454, 466, 473, 500, 580, 593, 645, 652, 658, 679, 688, 750, 830, 835, 840, 863, 924, 945, 950, 1000, 1006, 1025, 1034, 1045, 1168, 1180, 1194, 1240
Credibility of information sources, 1296
Critical analysis, 378, 404, 414, 471, 496, 525, 607, 760, 957, 1061, 1166, 1178, 1212, 1225
Cultural understanding
    connections, 77, 1083
    discussing themes and connections across cultures, 48, 377, 495, 702, 718, 1033
    shared characteristics, 718
Current events. *See* Connections, to current events.
Design features, 1241
Details
    analyzing, 93, 99, 107, 676, 697, 824, 838, 1178, 1225
    interpreting, 496, 828, 1101
Details, supporting, 93, 107, 496, 697, 786, 824, 973, 1061, 1215, 1221, 1254, 1255
Diagramming. *See* Classifying and categorizing.
Dialect, analyzing, 679
Fact and opinion, distinguishing, 150
Functional reading, 1241, 1260–1267
    instruction manual, 1260
    medicine label, 1265
    passport application, 1266–1267
    pay stub, 1264
    product advertisement, 1262
    product manual, 1263
    technical manual, 1261
Graphic organizers, interpreting, 875. *See also* Classifying and categorizing.
Images, interpreting, 779
Inferences, making, 48, 62, 63, 190, 206, 287, 298, 378, 410, 765, 779, 786, 877, 892, 971, 1018, 1023, 1118, 1120. *See also* Conclusions, drawing; Strategies for reading, predicting.
Interpretation, 31, 37, 46, 53, 62, 78, 88, 98, 107, 116, 142, 148, 158, 190, 206, 228, 243, 267, 279, 287, 293, 298, 316, 347, 360, 367, 378, 390, 404, 414, 434, 462, 471, 496, 514, 525, 539, 571, 578, 591, 602, 607, 620, 643, 652, 667, 676, 685, 697, 718, 760, 779, 786, 800, 804, 815, 828, 833, 838, 860, 873, 892, 898, 928, 937, 943, 948, 957, 964, 971, 1005, 1013, 1023, 1030, 1043, 1055, 1061, 1085, 1093, 1101, 1109, 1116, 1120, 1146, 1155, 1166, 1178, 1191, 1198, 1212, 1221, 1225, 1232. *See also* Judgments, making; Opinions, forming.
Judgments, making, 46, 78, 88, 107, 116, 148, 190, 206, 228, 243, 267, 293, 347, 434, 514, 602, 616, 643, 667, 676, 697, 702, 718, 760, 806, 815, 828, 830, 840, 937, 948, 964, 971, 1013, 1030, 1045, 1055, 1061, 1085, 1101, 1109, 1116, 1178, 1200, 1212, 1221

Vocabulary. *See* Vocabulary Skills.
Writer's motivation, stance, position. *See* Author's purpose (motivation).

## Vocabulary Skills

## Grammar, Usage, and Mechanics

## Writing Skills, Modes, and Formats

concluding paragraph, 515
interpretation, 393
literary review, 405, 435, 1213
missing scene, 244
new stanza, 579
new story ending, 32, 787
responding as a character, 299, 572, 617, 644, 687, 816, 834
review, 805
rewriting and extending, 1179
Writing from experience
analysis, 603
nature log, 405

## Inquiry and Research

Authority of sources
appropriateness, 1295, 1296
credibility, 984, 1296
Bibliography. *See* Works cited list.
Databases. *See* Electronic resources.
Dictionaries, 644
Documentary, 621
Electronic resources. *See also* LaserLinks *under* Viewing and Representing.
CD-ROMs, 379, 608, 687, 1288
online resources, 79, 149, 268, 379, 422, 452, 463, 572, 603, 657, 668, 677, 687, 748, 762, 816, 923, 929, 939, 945, 966, 977, 999, 1015, 1045, 1074, 1110, 1111, 1146
Encyclopedias, 268, 379, 608, 668, 939
Graphic organizers. *See also* Classifying and categorizing *under* Reading and Critical Thinking Skills.
chart, 24, 31, 37, 46, 48, 53, 55, 64, 88, 93, 109, 152, 163, 190, 228, 251, 268, 287, 289, 309, 318, 349, 369, 410, 462, 471, 496, 500, 516, 562, 578, 593, 616, 658, 667, 669, 676, 688, 783, 802, 804, 806, 824, 830, 835, 863, 877, 892, 894, 928, 932, 940, 945, 973, 1000, 1006, 1018, 1025, 1057, 1076, 1095, 1120, 1157, 1200, 1221, 1225, 1232
diagram, 62, 81, 100, 243, 279, 282, 498, 609, 702, 705, 824, 950, 967, 1034, 1045, 1057, 1120, 1215
graph, 79, 840, 875
Information organization and recording
chart, 24, 31, 37, 46, 48, 53, 55, 64, 88, 93, 109, 152, 163, 190, 228, 251, 268, 287, 289, 309, 318, 349, 369, 410, 462, 471, 496, 500, 516, 562, 578, 593, 616, 658, 667, 669, 676, 688, 783, 802, 804, 806, 824, 830, 835, 863, 877, 892, 894, 928, 932, 940, 945, 973, 1000, 1006, 1018, 1025, 1057, 1076, 1095, 1120, 1157, 1200, 1221, 1225, 1232
cluster diagram, 62, 81, 100, 940, 950, 967, 1057, 1120
graph, 79, 602, 840, 875
map, 677, 1117
notes, 985
other diagram, 243, 279, 282, 498, 609, 638, 702, 705, 824, 1034, 1045, 1215
Venn diagram, 148, 242, 294, 1005
word web, 39, 289, 562, 605, 765, 875, 1223

Internet, 79, 149, 268, 379, 422, 452, 463, 572, 603, 657, 668, 677, 748, 762, 816, 923, 929, 939, 945, 966, 977, 999, 1015, 1045, 1074, 1110, 1111, 1118, 1146, 1288, 1295
Interviewing, 816, 1062
Logical thinking, 1300
deductive arguments, 1300
inductive arguments, 1300
MLA guidelines, 1291
Note-taking, 985, 1288
Outlining, 986
Paraphrasing, 985, 1296
Plagiarism, avoiding, 987, 1297
Reports and research projects, topics for
anti-Semitism, 1086
antisocial personalities, 540
artistic visions, 159
Battle of Gettysburg, 608
Birmingham bombing, 621
the blues, 929
Brady, Mathew, 603
civil rights today, 1147
clothing styles, 861
con artists, 540
*corridos,* 719
creation myth, 32
Depression, 780
environmental effects of war, 1117
farm life, 1015
guerrilla tactics, 1101
Harlem Renaissance, 939
Harlem Renaissance artists, 944
hunting, 38
hypnosis, 668
impact of antiwar protests, 1121
inspirational speakers, 159
Japanese-American internment, 1102
Latin American cookbook, 1226
legal alien, 1198
*Mayflower,* 89
McCarthyism, 224
Michelangelo, 1031
Mississippi River, 667
mourning rituals, 1167
Native American music, 38
New Mexico, 38
"New South," 526
19th-century New England, 762
nonviolent resistance, 379
origin of the novel, 977
plague, 463
psychology, 472
Puerto Rico, 422
Puritan homes, 143
Puritan women, 143
Salem memorials, 149
Salem witch trials, 149, 244
shell shock, 1094
sibling rivalry, 816

## Speaking and Listening

## Viewing and Representing

# Index of Titles and Authors

# Acknowledgments *(continued)*

**Wylie Agency:** "The Man to Send Rain Clouds" by Leslie Marmon Silko. Copyright © 1981 by Leslie Marmon Silko. Reprinted with the permission of The Wylie Agency, Inc.

**N. Scott Momaday:** Excerpt from *The Way to Rainy Mountain* by N. Scott Momaday. Copyright © by N. Scott Momaday. Reprinted by permission of the author.

**Simon & Schuster:** Excerpts from *Cabeza de Vaca's Adventures in the Unknown Interior,* translated and annotated by Cyclone Covey. Copyright © 1961 by Macmillan Publishing Company. Reprinted with the permission of Simon & Schuster.

**Alfred A. Knopf:** Excerpts from *Of Plymouth Plantation* by William Bradford, edited by Samuel Eliot Morison. Copyright © 1952 by Samuel Eliot Morison, renewed 1980 by Emily M. Beck. Reprinted by permission of Alfred A. Knopf, Inc.

**Cowles Enthusiast Media:** "Women and Children First" by Alicia Crane Williams, *American History Illustrated,* November/December 1993. Copyright © American History Illustrated magazine. Reprinted with the permission of Cowles Enthusiast Media, Inc. (History Group), a PRIMEDIA publication.

**Little, Brown and Company:** Excerpt from *Blue Highways* by William Least Heat-Moon. Copyright © 1982 by William Least Heat-Moon. Reprinted by permission of Little, Brown and Company.

**Random House:** "My Sojourn in the Land of My Ancestors," from *All God's Children Need Traveling Shoes* by Maya Angelou. Copyright © 1986 by Maya Angelou. Reprinted by permission of Random House, Inc.

**The 21st Century:** "Vacation to Hell" by Joseph Saroufim, *The 21st Century,* November 1996. Copyright © The 21st Century newspaper. Reprinted through the courtesy of The 21st Century, Box 30, Newton, MA 02161.

## Unit Two

**USA Today:** "History Clashes with Commercialism" by Craig Wilson, *USA Today,* 24 October 1997. Copyright © 1997 USA Today. Reprinted with permission.

**Viking Penguin:** *The Crucible* by Arthur Miller. Copyright © 1952, 1953, 1954, renewed © 1980, 1981, 1982 by Arthur Miller. Used by permission of Viking Penguin, a division of Penguin Putnam Inc.

**Scott Renshaw:** "*The Crucible:* A Film Review by Scott Renshaw." Copyright © 1996 by Scott Renshaw. Reprinted by permission of the author.

**University of Illinois Press:** "The Declaration of the Rights of Woman" by Olympe de Gouges, from *Women in Revolutionary Paris, 1789–1795,* edited by Darline Levy, Harriet Applewhite, and Mary Johnson. Copyright © 1979 by the Board of Trustees of the University of Illinois. Reprinted by permission of the University of Illinois Press.

**University of Oklahoma Press:** "Lecture to a Missionary" by Red Jacket, from *American Indian Literature: An Anthology,* revised edition, edited by Alan R. Velie. Copyright © 1979, 1991 by the University of Oklahoma Press. Reprinted by permission of the University of Oklahoma Press.

**Writers House:** Excerpt from *Stride Toward Freedom* by Martin Luther King, Jr. Copyright © 1958 by Martin Luther King, Jr., renewed 1986 by Coretta Scott King. Reprinted by arrangement with the Heirs to the Estate of Martin Luther King, Jr., c/o Writers House Inc. as agent for the proprietor.

**Pathfinder Press:** Excerpt from "Necessary to Protect Ourselves" by Malcolm X, from *Malcolm X: The Last Speeches.* Copyright © 1989 by Betty Shabazz, Bruce Perry, and Pathfinder Press. Reprinted by permission of Pathfinder Press.

**Rodolfo Gonzales:** Excerpts from *I Am Joaquín/Yo Soy Joaquín* by Rodolfo Gonzales. Reprinted by permission of the author.

New York Times: "A Boy's School Project Aims to Revise History" by Lizette Alvarez, *New York Times*, 1 May 1998. Copyright © 1998 by The New York Times. Reprinted by permission.

**Unit Three**

**Navajivan Trust:** Excerpt from "Readiness for Satyagraha" by Mohandas K. Gandhi, from *The Essential Writings of Mahatma Gandhi,* edited by Raghavan Iyer. Used with the permission of the trustees of the Navajivan Trust.

**University of Alabama Press:** "Ode to Walt Whitman" by Pablo Neruda, from *Homage to Walt Whitman: A Collection of Poems from the Spanish,* translated by Didier Tisdel Jaén. Copyright © 1969 by the University of Alabama Press. Reprinted by permission of the University of Alabama Press.

**New Directions Publishing Corporation:** "Danse Russe" from *Collected Poems, 1909–1939,* vol. 1, by William Carlos Williams. Copyright © 1938 by New Directions Publishing Corp. Reprinted by permission of New Directions Publishing Corp.

"Spleen" by Charles Baudelaire (poem LXXXI from *The Flowers of Evil*), translated by Sir John Squires. Copyright © 1965 by New Directions Publishing Corp. Reprinted by permission of New Directions Publishing Corp.

**Liveright Publishing Corporation:** "anyone lived in a pretty how town," from *Complete Poems, 1904–1962* by E. E. Cummings, edited by George J. Firmage. Copyright 1940, © 1968, 1991 by the Trustees for the E. E. Cummings Trust. Reprinted by permission of Liveright Publishing Corporation.

**Firebrand Books:** "Ending Poem," from *Getting Home Alive* by Aurora Levins Morales and Rosario Morales. Copyright © 1986 by Aurora Levins Morales and Rosario Morales. Reprinted by permission of Firebrand Books, Ithaca, New York.

**Curbstone Press:** "Tía Chucha," from *The Concrete River* by Luis J. Rodriguez. Copyright © 1993 by Luis J. Rodriguez. Reprinted with permission of Curbstone Press. Distributed by Consortium.

**Ellen Levine Literary Agency:** "Gary Keillor," from *The Book of Guys* by Garrison Keillor. Copyright © 1993 by Garrison Keillor. Reprinted by permission of Ellen Levine Literary Agency on behalf of the author.

**Merlyn's Pen:** "Eternally Slow" by Stephanie Lauer. First appeared in *Merlyn's Pen* magazine. Copyright © by Merlyn's Pen, Inc. All rights reserved. Reprinted by permission of Merlyn's Pen, Inc.

**Stephen King:** Excerpt from *Danse Macabre* by Stephen King. Copyright © Stephen King. All rights reserved. Reprinted with permission.

**Random House:** "A Rose for Emily" by William Faulkner, from *The Collected Stories of William Faulkner.* Copyright © 1930 and renewed 1958 by William Faulkner. Reprinted by permission of Random House, Inc.

**Harcourt Brace & Company:** "The Life You Save May Be Your Own," from *A Good Man Is Hard to Find and Other Stories* by Flannery O'Connor. Copyright 1953 by Flannery O'Connor and renewed © 1981 by Regina O'Connor. Reprinted by permission of Harcourt Brace & Company.

**Sarah Mossberger:** "Reunited" by Sarah Mossberger, *Voices of Youth,* vol. 4. Used with permission of Sarah Mossberger.

**Unit Four**

**Doubleday:** Excerpt from *Coming of Age in Mississippi* by Anne Moody. Copyright © 1968 by Anne Moody. Used by permission of Doubleday, a division of Bantam Doubleday Dell Publishing Group, Inc.

**Liveright Publishing Corporation:** "Frederick Douglass," from *Angle of Ascent: New and Selected Poems* by Robert Hayden. Copyright © 1975, 1972, 1970, 1966 by Robert Hayden. Reprinted by permission of Liveright Publishing Corporation.

**Dudley Randall:** "Ballad of Birmingham" by Dudley Randall. Reprinted by permission of the author.

**Molly Ball:** *The Red Badge of Courage* by Molly Ball, *Statement*, Spring 1997. Reprinted with the permission of Molly Ball.

**Museum of New Mexico Press:** "The Indian and the Hundred Cows"/"El indito de las cien vacas" from *Cuentos: Tales from the Hispanic Southwest,* retold by José Griego y Maestas and translated by Rudolfo A. Anaya. Copyright © 1980 by the Museum of New Mexico Press. Reprinted with permission of the Museum of New Mexico Press.

**University of Nebraska Press:** "High Horse's Courting," from *Black Elk Speaks* by Black Elk and John G. Neihardt. Copyright © 1932, 1959, 1972 by John G. Neihardt, copyright © 1961 by the John G. Neihardt Trust. Reprinted by permission of the University of Nebraska Press.

**HarperCollins Publishers:** Chapter 11 from *The Autobiography of Mark Twain,* edited by Charles Neider. Copyright © 1917, 1940, 1958, 1959 by The Mark Twain Company, copyright 1924, 1945, 1952 by Clara Clemens Samossoud, copyright © 1959 by Charles Neider. Reprinted by permission of HarperCollins Publishers, Inc.

**University of Texas Press:** "The Legend of Gregorio Cortez," from *With His Pistol in His Hand: A Border Ballad and Its Hero* by Américo Paredes. Copyright © 1958, renewed 1986 by the University of Texas Press. Reprinted by permission of the author and the University of Texas Press.

**Unit Five**

**Little, Brown and Company; Harvard University Press; and the Trustees of Amherst College:** "After great pain, a formal feeling comes—" by Emily Dickinson, from *The Complete Poems of Emily Dickinson,* edited by Thomas Johnson. Copyright © 1929 by Martha Dickinson Bianchi, copyright © renewed 1957, 1963 by Mary L. Hampson. Used by permission of Little, Brown and Company. Reprinted by permission of the publishers and the Trustees of Amherst College from *The Poems of Emily Dickinson,* edited by Thomas H. Johnson (Cambridge: The Belknap Press of Harvard University Press). Copyright © 1951, 1955, 1979, 1983 by the President and Fellows of Harvard College.

**Feminist Press:** Excerpt from *Complaints and Disorders: The Sexual Politics of Sickness* by Barbara Ehrenreich and Deirdre English (New York: The Feminist Press at The City University of New York, 1973). Copyright © 1973 by Barbara Ehrenreich and Deirdre English. Reprinted by permission of The Feminist Press at The City University of New York.

**Rutgers University Press:** "Seventeen Syllables," from *Seventeen Syllables and Other Stories* by Hisaye Yamamoto. Copyright © by Hisaye Yamamoto. Reprinted by permission of Rutgers University Press.

**Rita Dove:** "Adolescence—III," from *The Yellow House on the Corner* by Rita Dove, published by Carnegie-Mellon University Press. Copyright © 1980 by Rita Dove. Reprinted by permission of the author.

**Delacorte Press/Seymour Lawrence:** "I Stand Here Ironing," from *Tell Me a Riddle* by Tillie Olsen, introduction by John Leonard. Copyright © 1956, 1957, 1960, 1961 by Tillie Olsen. Used by permission of Delacorte Press/Seymour Lawrence, a division of Bantam Doubleday Dell Publishing Group, Inc.

**Susan Bergholz Literary Services:** "Ironing Their Clothes," from *Homecoming* by

Julia Alvarez. Copyright © 1984, 1986 by Julia Alvarez. Published by Plume, an imprint of Dutton Signet, a division of Penguin Putnam Inc.; originally published by Grove Press. Reprinted by permission of Susan Bergholz Literary Services, New York. All rights reserved.

**Persea Books:** "Antigua: Almost Paradise" by Jillian Braithwaite, from *Starting With "I": Personal Essays by Teenagers.* Copyright © 1997 by Youth Communications/New York Center, Inc. Reprinted by permission of Persea Books, Inc.

"America and I" by Anzia Yezierska, from *How I Found America: Collected Stories of Anzia Yezierska.* Copyright © 1991 by Louise Levitas Henriksen. Reprinted by permission of Persea Books, Inc.

**Harcourt Brace & Company:** "Chicago," from *Chicago Poems* by Carl Sandburg. Copyright 1916 by Holt, Rinehart and Winston and renewed 1944 by Carl Sandburg. Reprinted by permission of Harcourt Brace & Company.

**Hilary Masters:** "Lucinda Matlock," from *Spoon River Anthology* by Edgar Lee Masters, originally published by The Macmillan Company. Reprinted by permission of Hilary Masters.

**Maxine Groffsky Literary Agency:** "In the American Society" by Gish Jen. First published in *The Southern Review,* Summer 1986. Copyright © 1986 by Gish Jen. Reprinted by permission of the author, c/o Maxine Groffsky Literary Agency.

**Far Corner Books:** "My Father and the Figtree" from *Words Under the Words: Selected Poems* by Naomi Shibab Nye, published by Far Corner Books, Portland, Oregon. Copyright © 1995 by Naomi Shibab Nye. Reprinted by permission of the publisher.

**Yvonne V. Sapia:** "Defining the Grateful Gesture," from *Valentino's Hair* by Yvonne Sapia. Reprinted with the permission of Yvonne V. Sapia.

**Arte Público Press:** "Refugee Ship" by Lorna Dee Cervantes, from *A Decade of Hispanic Literature: An Anniversary Anthology* (Houston: Arte Público Press—University of Houston, 1982). Reprinted by permission of the publisher.

**Unit Six**

**Alfred A. Knopf:** "I, Too," from *Collected Poems* by Langston Hughes. Copyright © 1994 by the Estate of Langston Hughes. Reprinted by permission of Alfred A. Knopf, Inc.

"Dream Deferred" ("Harlem"), from *Collected Poems* by Langston Hughes. Copyright © 1994 by the Estate of Langston Hughes. Reprinted by permission of Alfred A. Knopf, Inc.

"The Weary Blues," from *Collected Poems* by Langston Hughes. Copyright © 1994 by the Estate of Langston Hughes. Reprinted by permission of Alfred A. Knopf, Inc.

**Harold Ober Associates:** "Flute Players" by Jean-Joseph Rabéarivelo, translated by Langston Hughes, from *Poems from Black Africa.* Copyright © 1963 by Langston Hughes. Reprinted by permission of Harold Ober Associates Incorporated.

"A Black Man Talks of Reaping," from *Personals* by Arna Bontemps. Copyright © 1963 by Arna Bontemps. Reprinted by permission of Harold Ober Associates Incorporated.

**Chicago Tribune:** Excerpts from "Love, Langston" by Dahleen Glanton. Copyright © 1998 Chicago Tribune Company. All rights reserved. Used with permission.

**Hill and Wang:** Excerpt from "When the Negro Was in Vogue," from *The Big Sea* by Langston Hughes. Copyright © 1940 by Langston Hughes. Copyright renewed © 1968 by Arna Bontemps and George Houston Bass. Reprinted by permission of Hill and Wang, a division of Farrar, Straus & Giroux, Inc.

**Viking Penguin:** "My City," from *Saint Peter Relates an Incident* by James Weldon Johnson. Copyright 1935 by James Weldon Johnson, © renewed 1963 by Grace Nail Johnson. Used by permission of Viking Penguin, a division of Penguin Putnam Inc.

**GRM Associates:** "Any Human to Another," from *The Medea and Some Poems* by Countee Cullen. Copyright © 1935 by Harper & Brothers, copyright renewed 1963 by Ida M. Cullen. Reprinted by permission of GRM Associates, Inc., agents for the Estate of Ida M. Cullen.

**Archives of Claude McKay:** "If We Must Die" by Claude McKay, from *Selected Poems of Claude McKay.* Copyright © 1957 by Harcourt Brace. Used by permission of The Archives of Claude McKay, Carl Cowl, Administrator.

**Estate of Zora Neale Hurston:** "How It Feels to Be Colored Me" by Zora Neale Hurston, from *I Love Myself When I Am Laughing: A Zora Neale Hurston Reader,* edited by Alice Walker. Reprinted by permission of the Estate of Zora Neale Hurston.

**University of Illinois Press:** Excerpts from "Zora Neale Hurston: A Cautionary Tale and a Partisan View" by Alice Walker, foreword to *Zora Neale Hurston: A Literary Biography* by Robert E. Hemenway. Copyright © 1977 by the Board of Trustees of the University of Illinois. Used with the permission of the University of Illinois Press.

**James Baldwin Estate:** "My Dungeon Shook" by James Baldwin, originally published in *The Progressive.* Copyright © 1962 by James Baldwin, copyright renewed. Collected in *The Fire Next Time,* published by Vintage Books. Reprinted with the permission of the James Baldwin Estate.

**Gwendolyn Brooks:** "Life for My Child Is Simple," from *Blacks* by Gwendolyn Brooks (Chicago: Third World Press, 1991). Copyright © 1991 by Gwendolyn Brooks. Reprinted by permission of the author.

"Primer for Blacks," from *Primer for Blacks* by Gwendolyn Brooks (Chicago: Third World Press, 1991). Copyright © 1991 by Gwendolyn Brooks. Reprinted by permission of the author.

**Doubleday:** "Thoughts on the African-American Novel" by Toni Morrison, from *Black Women Writers (1950–1980)* by Mari Evans. Copyright © 1983 by Toni Morrison. Used by permission of Doubleday, a division of Bantam Doubleday Dell Publishing Group, Inc.

**Henry Holt & Company:** "Acquainted with the Night," "Mending Wall," and "'Out, Out—,'" from *The Poetry of Robert Frost,* edited by Edward Connery Lathem. Copyright 1944, 1956, 1958 by Robert Frost, copyright 1967 by Lesley Frost Ballantine, copyright 1916, 1928, 1930, 1939, © 1969 by Henry Holt and Company, Inc. Reprinted with the permission of Henry Holt and Company, Inc.

"The Death of the Hired Man" by Robert Frost, from *The Poetry of Robert Frost,* edited by Edward Connery Lathem. Copyright © 1958 by Robert Frost, copyright © 1967 by Lesley Frost Ballantine. Copyright 1930, 1939, © 1969 by Henry Holt & Company. Reprinted by permission of Henry Holt & Company, Inc.

Excerpts from "Some Science Fiction," "The Gift Outright," "After Apple-Picking," "Nothing Gold Can Stay," and "Fire and Ice," from *The Poetry of Robert Frost,* edited by Edward Connery Lathem. Copyright 1942, 1951, 1955, 1958, 1962 by Robert Frost, copyright © 1967, 1970 by Lesley Frost Ballantine, copyright 1923, 1930, 1939, © 1969 by Henry Holt & Company. Reprinted by permission of Henry Holt & Company, Inc.

**Scribner:** "The End of Something," from *In Our Time* by Ernest Hemingway. Copyright 1925 Charles Scribner's Sons, copyright renewed 1953 by Ernest Hemingway. Reprinted with the permission of Scribner, a division of Simon & Schuster.

**Faber and Faber:** "The Love Song of J. Alfred Prufrock," from *Collected Poems, 1909–1962* by T. S. Eliot. Reprinted by permission of Faber and Faber Ltd.

**Harcourt Brace & Company:** "The Jilting of Granny Weatherall," from *Flowering Judas and Other Stories* by Katherine Anne Porter. Copyright 1930 and renewed 1958 by Katherine Anne Porter. Reprinted by permission of Harcourt Brace & Company.

**HarperCollins Publishers:** "The Man Who Was Almost a Man," from *Eight Men* by Richard Wright. Copyright © 1961 by Richard Wright. Reprinted by permission of HarperCollins Publishers, Inc.

**HarperCollins Publishers and Faber and Faber:** "Mirror," from *Crossing the Water* by Sylvia Plath. Copyright © 1963 by Ted Hughes. Originally appeared in *The New Yorker.* Reprinted by permission of HarperCollins Publishers, Inc., and Faber and Faber Ltd.

**Houghton Mifflin Company:** "Self in 1958," from *Live or Die* by Anne Sexton. Copyright © 1966 by Anne Sexton. Reprinted by permission of Houghton Mifflin Company. All rights reserved.

**Unit Seven**

**Pantheon Books:** Excerpts from *The Good War* by Studs Terkel. Copyright © 1984 by Studs Terkel. Reprinted by permission of Pantheon Books, a division of Random House, Inc.

**Russell & Volkening:** "Armistice," from *The People and Uncollected Stories* by Bernard Malamud. Copyright © 1989 by Ann Malamud. Reprinted by permission of Russell & Volkening as agents for the author.

"Teenage Wasteland" by Anne Tyler, from *Seventeen* magazine, November 1983. Copyright © 1983 by Anne Tyler. Reprinted by permission of Russell & Volkening as agents for the author.

**Viking Penguin:** Excerpt from *If This Is a Man (Survival in Auschwitz)* by Primo Levi, translated by Stuart Woolf. Translation copyright © 1959 by Orion Press, Inc., © 1958 by Giulio Einaudi Editore SpA. Used by permission of Viking Penguin, a division of Penguin Putnam Inc.

"Symptoms" ("Why Soldiers Won't Talk"), from *Once There Was a War* by John Steinbeck. Copyright 1943, 1958 by John Steinbeck, renewed © 1971 by Elaine Steinbeck, John Steinbeck IV, and Thomas Steinbeck. Used by permission of Viking Penguin, a division of Penguin Putnam Inc.

**Farrar, Straus & Giroux:** "The Death of the Ball Turret Gunner," from *The Complete Poems* by Randall Jarrell. Copyright © 1969 by Mrs. Randall Jarrell. Reprinted by permission of Farrar, Straus & Giroux, Inc.

Excerpt from "Letter from Paradise, 21° 19' N., 157° 52' W.," from *Slouching Towards Bethlehem* by Joan Didion. Copyright © 1966, 1968 by Joan Didion. Reprinted by permission of Farrar, Straus & Giroux, Inc.

**Dwight Okita:** "In Response to Executive Order 9066," from *Crossing with the Light* by Dwight Okita (Chicago: Tía Chucha Press). Copyright © 1992 by Dwight Okita. Used by permission of the author.

**Houghton Mifflin Company/Seymour Lawrence:** "Ambush," from *The Things They Carried* by Tim O'Brien. Copyright © 1990 by Tim O'Brien. Reprinted by permission of Houghton Mifflin Co./Seymour Lawrence. All rights reserved.

**University Press of New England:** "Camouflaging the Chimera," from *Dien Cai Dau* by Yusef Komunyakaa, published by Wesleyan University Press. Copyright © 1988 by Yusef Komunyakaa. Reprinted by permission of the University Press of New England.

**Leona P. Schecter Literary Agency:** "Deciding," from *Shallow Graves* by Wendy Wilder Larsen and Tran Thi Nga. Reprinted by permission of the Leona P. Schecter Literary Agency.

**New Directions Publishing Corporation:** "At the Justice Department, November 15, 1969," from *Poems, 1968–1972* by Denise Levertov. Copyright © 1969 by Denise Levertov. Reprinted by permission of New Directions Publishing Corp.

**Wing Tek Lum:** "Chinese Hot Pot" by Wing Tek Lum, from *Chinese American Poetry,* edited by L. Ling-chi Wang and Henry Yiheng Zhao. Reprinted by permission of Wing Tek Lum.

**Writers House:** Excerpts from "Letter from Birmingham Jail" by Martin Luther King, Jr. Copyright © 1963 by Martin Luther King, Jr., renewed 1991 by Coretta Scott King. Reprinted by arrangement with the Heirs to the Estate of Martin Luther King, Jr., c/o Writers House Inc. as agent for the proprietor.

**William Morrow & Company:** "Revolutionary Dreams," from *The Women and the Men* by Nikki Giovanni. Copyright © 1970, 1974, 1975 by Nikki Giovanni. Reprinted by permission of William Morrow & Company, Inc.

**International Creative Management:** *Wandering* by Lanford Wilson. Copyright © 1967 by Lanford Wilson, renewed 1993. Reprinted by permission of International Creative Management, Inc.

**Random House:** "The Writer in the Family," from *Lives of the Poets* by E. L. Doctorow. Copyright © 1984 by E. L. Doctorow. Reprinted by permission of Random House, Inc.

**Alfred A. Knopf:** "Separating," from *Problems and Other Stories* by John Updike. Copyright © 1975 by John Updike. Reprinted by permission of Alfred A. Knopf, Inc.

"The Legend," from *The River of Heaven* by Garrett Hongo. Copyright © 1988 by Garrett Hongo. Reprinted by permission of Alfred A. Knopf, Inc.

**Chronicle Books:** "Mexicans Begin Jogging" by Gary Soto, from *Gary Soto: New & Selected Poems,* published by Chronicle Books, San Francisco. Copyright © 1995 by Gary Soto. Reprinted by permission of Chronicle Books.

**Arte Público Press:** "Legal Alien," from *Chants* by Pat Mora (Houston: Arte Público Press—University of Houston, 1985). Copyright © 1985 by Pat Mora. Reprinted by permission of the publisher.

"The Latin Deli" by Judith Ortiz Cofer, *The Americas Review* 19.1 (Houston: Arte Público Press—University of Houston, 1991). Reprinted by permission of the publisher.

**John Hawkins & Associates:** "Hostage," from *Heat and Other Stories* by Joyce Carol Oates, published by Plume. Copyright © 1992 The Ontario Review, Inc. Reprinted by permission of John Hawkins & Associates, Inc.

**Sandra Dijkstra Literary Agency:** "Mother Tongue" by Amy Tan. First appeared in *The Threepenny Review,* Fall 1990. Copyright © 1990 by Amy Tan. Reprinted by permission of Amy Tan and the Sandra Dijkstra Literary Agency.

**Susan Bergholz Literary Services:** "Straw into Gold: The Metamorphosis of the Everyday" by Sandra Cisneros. First published in *The Texas Observer,* 25 September 1987. Copyright © 1987 by Sandra Cisneros. Reprinted by permission of Susan Bergholz Literary Services, New York. All rights reserved.

The editors have made every effort to trace the ownership of all copyrighted material found in this book and to make full acknowledgment for its use. Omissions brought to our attention will be corrected in a subsequent edition.

## Art Credits

**Cover, Frontispiece**
Illustration copyright © 1998 Michael Steirnagle.

**Front Matter**
**viii** *left* Courtesy, University of Texas at Austin. Photo by Donald Codry, from *Mexican Masks* by Donald Codry, copyright © 1980. By permission of the University of Texas Press; *right* The Granger Collection, New York; **x** *top, A Morning View of Blue Hill Village* (1824), Jonathan Fisher. William A. Farnsworth Library and Art Museum, Rockland, Maine, museum purchase, 1965 (1965.134); *bottom* Teapot (about 1799) by Paul Revere. Silver, 7¼". Courtesy of the Museum of Fine Arts, Boston, gift of James Longley; **x–xi** Photofest; **xii** *left, The Wanderer* (1818), Caspar David Friedrich. Kunsthalle, Hamburg, Germany/Bridgeman/Art Resource, New York; *right* Smithsonian Institution, Washington, D.C.; **xiii** *Cliff Dwellers* (1913), George Bellows. Oil on canvas, 40³⁄₁₆" × 42¹⁄₁₆". Los Angeles County Museum of Art, Los Angeles County Fund. Copyright © 1995 Museum Associates, Los Angeles County Museum of Art, all rights reserved; **xiv** Corbis; **xv** Pictorial quilt (1895–1898), Harriet Powers. Pieced and appliquéd cotton embroidered with plain and metallic yarns, 69" × 105". Courtesy of Museum of Fine Arts, Boston, bequest of Maxim Karolik; **xvi** The Granger Collection, New York; **xviii** *left* Amherst College Library, Archives and Special Collections; *top right, Mr. and Mrs. Isaac Newton Phelps Stokes* (1897), John Singer Sargent. Oil on canvas, 85¼" × 39¾". The Metropolitan Museum of Art, bequest of Edith Minturn Phelps (Mrs. I. N.) Stokes, 1938 (38.104). Copyright © 1989 The Metropolitan Museum of Art, New York; **xx** Langston Hughes, Winold Reiss. National Portrait Gallery, Washington, D.C./Art Resource, New York; **xxi** The Granger Collection, New York; **xxii** *Ominous Omen* (1987), Rupert Garcia. Chalk, linseed oil, and oil paint on canvas, 47" × 130". Courtesy of the artist, Rena Bransten Gallery, San Francisco, and Galerie Claude Samuel, Paris. Copyright © Rupert Garcia; **2** *left* National Archives; *top right* From the collections of the Library of Congress; *bottom right* Photo by John Olson for *Life* magazine. Copyright © Time Inc.; **3** *top left, right* The Granger Collection, New York; *bottom left* Photo by Howard Sochurek for *Life* magazine. Copyright © Time Inc.; **6–7** *Child and Her Mother, Wapato, Yakima Valley, Washington* (1939), Dorothea Lange. From the collections of the Library of Congress.

**Unit One**
**18** *corn* The Granger Collection, New York; *cliff dwellings* Copyright © 1993 North Wind Pictures; **19** *compass* Copyright © Robert Frerck/Odyssey/Chicago; *foot warmer* Copyright © Winterthur Museum; **20** *top left* Colter Bay Indian Arts Museum at Grand Teton National Park, Wyoming; **21** Illustration by Rebecca McClellan; **22** *left* Copyright © 1993 Allen Russell/Profiles West; *right* AP/Wide World Photos; **28, 29** Details of *Creation Legend,* Tom (Two Arrows) Dorsey. Philbrook Museum of Art, Tulsa, Oklahoma (46.24); **32** *right* Illustration by David Cunningham; **39** Courtesy, University of Texas at Austin. Photo by Donald Codry, from *Mexican Masks* by Donald Codry, copyright © 1980. By permission of the University of Texas Press; **45** From *Mexican Masks* by Donald Codry, copyright © 1980. By permission of the University of Texas Press; **47** Historical Photograph Collections, Washington State University Libraries, Pullman, Washington; **54** Photo by Lee H. Marmon; **56** *initial M,* **58** *map* Illustrations by Gary Antonetti/Ortelius Design, Inc.; **58** *left* Dean Conger/Corbis; *right* Copyright © Gene Moore/Phototake, New York/PNI; **63** AP/Wide World Photos; **65** *left* From *Fool's Crow* by James Welch. Copyright © 1986 by James Welch. Used by permission of Viking Penguin, a division of Penguin Putnam Inc.; *right* Reprinted by

permission of Random House, Inc.; **66–67** Photo by Sharon Hoogstraten; **68** Newberry Library, Chicago; **79** *bottom* Detail of Indians forced to carry baggage and supplies of the Spanish invaders (1590), Theodor de Bry. Rare Books and Manuscripts Division, The New York Public Library, Astor, Lenox and Tilden Foundations; **80** The Granger Collection, New York; **82** *background* Copyright © D. Bowen/Westlight; *inset* Wood River Gallery, Mill Valley, California; **89** Detail of *View of Plymouth* (1627), Carl Sachs. American Heritage Picture Collection, New York; **90** Copyright © Culver Pictures; **93** Courtesy of Les Mansfield, Cincinnati, Ohio; **99** The Granger Collection, New York; **103, 105** From *Blue Highways* by William Least Heat-Moon. Copyright © 1982 by William Least Heat-Moon. By permission of Little, Brown and Company; **108** AP/Wide World Photos; **110, 110–111, 111, 112, 115** *fabrics* Photos by Sharon Hoogstraten; **117** UPI/Bettmann; **119** *left* From *The Great Explorers: The European Discovery of America* by Samuel Eliot Morison. Copyright © 1986 by Samuel Eliot Morison. Used by permission of Oxford University Press, Inc.; *right* Cover of *Blue Highways* by William Least Heat-Moon. Cover photograph copyright © Chuck Kuhn/The Image Bank. Cover reprinted by permission of Houghton Mifflin Company. All rights reserved; **120–124** Photos by Sharon Hoogstraten; **128** The Granger Collection, New York.

**Unit Two**

**132** *war* Copyright © 1993 North Wind Pictures; *Sir Isaac Newton* (18th century), unknown artist. Trinity College, Cambridge, U.K./Erich Lessing/Art Resource, New York; **133** *teapot* (about 1799) by Paul Revere. Silver, 7¼". Courtesy of the Museum of Fine Arts, Boston, gift of James Longley; *wig* Corbis-Bettmann; *watch* Copyright © Christie's Images; *statue* Copyright © Philip Jon Bailey; **137** Detail of chair seat cover (about 1725), embroidered by a member of the Bradstreet family. Cotton threads, linen warp, wool embroidery, 43 cm × 47 cm. Courtesy, Museum of Fine Arts, Boston, gift of Samuel Bradstreet; **138, 140–141** Copyright © David Fitzgerald/Tony Stone Images; **145, 149** Copyright © Culver Pictures; **151** Lee Snider/Corbis; **153, 157** Copyright © David Fitzgerald/Tony Stone Images; **159** The Granger Collection, New York; **160** Stock Montage; **161** The Granger Collection, New York; **164–165** Photofest; **166** Photo by Kim Britt; **169, 171, 176** Photofest; **179** Lee Snider/Corbis; **182** Photofest; **191** Copyright © Martin Rogers/National Geographic Image Collection; **193** Photofest; **207** Lee Snider/Corbis; **209, 220, 222–223** Photofest; **222** *bottom* Robbie Jack/Corbis; **225, 227** Photofest; **229** Copyright © ZEE/PNI; **238, 241** Photofest; **242** *bottom left* The Granger Collection, New York; *top right* Copyright © Twentieth Century Fox/Shooting Star. All rights reserved; **245** AP/Wide World Photos; **248–252** Photos by Sharon Hoogstraten; **256** *left, Portrait of Thomas Jefferson* (1805), Gilbert Stuart. Gift of the Regents of the Smithsonian Institution, the Thomas Jefferson Memorial Foundation, and the Enid and Crosby Kemper Foundation. National Portrait Gallery, Smithsonian Institution, Washington, D.C./Art Resource, New York; **257** *top, Abigail Adams* (1829), Jarvis F. Hanks. Courtesy, Charles Ames, Esq.; *bottom* The Granger Collection, New York; **260** *top* The Granger Collection, New York; *bottom* Howard Sochurek/*Life* magazine. Copyright © Time Inc.; **262** Detail of *Patrick Henry Before the Virginia House of Burgesses* (1851), Peter F. Rothermel. Red Hill, The Patrick Henry National Memorial, Brookneal, Virginia; **269** Stock Montage; **271** *left* Photo courtesy School Division, Houghton Mifflin Company; *right* Copyright © 1995 Smithsonian Institution; **274** Photo courtesy School Division, Houghton Mifflin Company; **275** Independence National Historical Park Collection; **281** *Thomas Jefferson*, Charles Févret de Saint-Mémin. Black chalk on paper, 23¹³⁄₁₆" × 17". Worcester Art Museum, Worcester, Massachusetts (1954.82); **284, 286** *signatures* The

Granger Collection, New York; **288** *top* From the collections of the Library of Congress; *bottom* National Gallery of Art, Washington, D.C.; **289** Detail of the Van Bergen Overmantel (1732–1733), attributed to John Heaten. Oil on wood (fireboard), 15¼″ × 73½″. Copyright © New York State Historical Association, Cooperstown, New York; **294** Stock Montage; **295** The Granger Collection, New York; **299** Courtesy of the Bureau of American Ethnology, Smithsonian Institution, Washington, D.C.; **308** *left* Stock Montage; *right* The Granger Collection, New York; **309, 313** *bottom* From the collections of the Library of Congress (LC-USF34-24829-D); **319** *left* Reprinted by permission of Dover Publications, Inc., Philip Smith, editor. Copyright © 1996 by Dover Publications, Inc.; *right* Reprinted by permission of HarperCollins Publishers, New York, from *The American Revolutionaries: A History in Their Own Words, 1750–1800* by Milton Meltzer. Copyright © 1987 by Milton Melzer; **320–324, 330** Photos by Sharon Hoogstraten.

**Unit Three**
**338** Smithsonian Institution, Washington, D.C.; **339** *cotton gin, telegraph* Smithsonian Institution, Washington, D.C.; *Levi's jeans* Courtesy of the Bancroft Library; *clock* Private collection/Art Resource, New York; *The Trail of Tears* (1942), Robert Lindneux. Oil on canvas. The Granger Collection, New York; **344** Detail of *En Mer* [At sea] (1898), Max Bohm. Courtesy of Alfred J. Walker Fine Art, Boston; **345, 346** *background* Copyright © D. Bowen/Westlight; **348** Stock Montage; **349, 350–351, 352, 353, 356, 359** Illustrations by Marlene Kay Goodman; **362** FPG International; **363** Detail of *Kindred Spirits* (1849), Asher B. Durand. Oil on canvas. Collection of The New York Public Library, Astor, Lenox and Tilden Foundations; **368** The New-York Historical Society; **370** Copyright © David Turnley/Corbis; **371** *top* AP/Wide World Photos; *bottom* Copyright © 1990 Joseph Cempa/Black Star/PNI; **374, 375** *left* UPI/Corbis-Bettmann; **375** *right* Copyright © Hulton Getty Picture Collection/Tony Stone Images; **380** National Portrait Gallery, Smithsonian Institution, Washington, D.C./Art Resource, New York; **381** Corbis-Bettmann; **382** *leaf* Copyright © John Shaw; **386** Copyright © Art Wolfe/Tony Stone Images; **387** Copyright © Jake Wyman/Photonica; **391** Copyright © John Shaw; **395** Copyright © 1993 Magnetic Poetry, Inc. All rights reserved. Photo by Sharon Hoogstraten; **397** Detail of *Cliff Dwellers* (1913), George Bellows. Oil on canvas. 40³⁄₁₆″ × 42¹⁄₁₆″. Los Angeles County Museum of Art, Los Angeles County Fund. Copyright © 1995 Museum Associates, Los Angeles County Museum of Art. All rights reserved; **405** Museum of The City of New York; **415** *left* National Archives; *right* By permission of the Houghton Library, Harvard University; **416** Detail of *Woman with Turban* (1985), Gilberto Ruiz. Mixed media on fabric, 36″ × 52″. Courtesy of Barbara Gillman Gallery, Miami Beach, Florida; **423** Copyright © 1986 Linda Haas; **435** FPG International; **437** *left* From *My First Summer in the Sierra* by John Muir, introduction by Gretel Ehrlich. Copyright © 1987 by Gretel Ehrlich. Used by permission of Viking Penguin, a division of Penguin Putnam Inc.; *right* Reprinted by permission of Harper & Row, Publishers, Inc., New York, from *Pilgrim at Tinker Creek* by Annie Dillard. Copyright © 1974 by Annie Dillard; **438–442, 450–454** *border* Photos by Sharon Hoogstraten; **450** *top* Corbis; *bottom* Corbis-Bettmann; **451** Hulton Deutsch Collection/Corbis; **452** *top* Weidenfeld and Nicolson Archive; *bottom* Edgar Allan Poe Museum, Richmond, Virginia; **453** *left* Copyright © Archive Photos; *right* AP/Wide World Photos; **454** *top* Copyright © 1986 Alberto Baudo/The Stock Market; **462–463** *border* Photo by Sharon Hoogstraten; **464–465** Copyright © 1986 Alberto Baudo/The Stock Market; **471–473** *border* Photo by Sharon Hoogstraten; **473, 474** *bottom left* Copyright © PhotoDisc; **474–475** Copyright © Anthony Howarth/Woodfin Camp/PNI; **476** Copyright © Gary L. Benson/AllStock/PNI; **479**

*background* Copyright © 1984 William Johnson/Stock Boston/PNI; **483** Copyright © PhotoDisc; **487** Copyright © Angelo Hornak/Corbis; **488** Copyright © Manuel Bellver/Corbis; **491** Copyright © Ann Rhoney/nonstock Inc./PNI. All rights reserved; **494** Copyright © William Johnson/Stock Boston/PNI; **496–499** *border* Photo by Sharon Hoogstraten; **497, 499** Courtesy of the collections of the Library of Congress; **500** Photo by Sharon Hoogstraten; **501** Detail of *La danse à la campagne* [The country dance] (1883), Pierre Auguste Renoir. Private collection; **502, 505** *bottom,* **506, 508, 511** *bottom left,* **512** Photos by Sharon Hoogstraten; **515** National Archives; **517** *background* Photo by Sharon Hoogstraten; **527** The Granger Collection, New York; **541** AP/Wide World Photos; **543** *left* From *Billy Budd* by Herman Melville. Copyright © 1948, 1956 by The President and Fellows of Harvard College. Used by permission of Viking Penguin, a division of Penguin Putnam Inc.; *right* Reprinted by permission of Random House, Inc; **544–548** Photos by Sharon Hoogstraten.

Unit Four

**556** *book* The Granger Collection, New York; **557** *money, poster* The Granger Collection, New York; *locomotive* Copyright © Chuck Place Photography; *clock* Bridgeman/Art Resource, New York; **558** *bottom, Battle of Franklin, Tennessee, 30 November 1864* (1891), Kurz and Allison. Lithograph. The Granger Collection, New York; **559** *bottom,* **560** *left* Courtesy of the U.S. Postal Service; **560** *right* Courtesy of Chicago Historical Society; **561** The Granger Collection, New York; **563** Corbis-Bettmann; **570** National Archives of Canada (C-28186); **573, 574** *top left* From the collections of the Library of Congress; **575** *background* Photograph by Sharon Hoogstraten; *left, right* The Granger Collection, New York; **576–577** Collection of The New-York Historical Society; **579** *left,* **580** From the collections of the Library of Congress; **587** Copyright © H. Abernathy/H. Armstrong Roberts; **590** *man* Chicago Historical Society; *woman* Merserve Collection, Library of Congress; **592** Culver Pictures; **593, 600** South Carolina Confederate Relic Room & Museum; **603** Corbis-Bettmann; **604** The Granger Collection, New York; **606** Gettysburg Historic Park/NARA Special Media Archives, Services Division (Still Pictures); **608** From the collections of the Library of Congress; **609** AP/Wide World Photos; **610–611** Illustration by Robert Tanenbaum; **612, 614** Photos by Sharon Hoogstraten; **621** Copyright © Layle Silbert; **624–628** Photos by Sharon Hoogstraten; **632** *center right* Collection of the New York Historical Society; **632–633** South Dakota State Historical Society; **633** *top* From the collections of the Library of Congress; **634–635** Photo by Sharon Hoogstraten; **636** *top* Library of Congress/Corbis; *bottom* The Granger Collection, New York; **642** Copyright © John Runne. Evergreen Art Company, Evergreen, Colorado; **653** *left* Smithsonian Institution, Washington, D.C.; *right* Photo by Ron Nicodemus; **654–658** *border* Photo by Sharon Hoogstraten; **654** *signature* Christie's Images; *top right* The Granger Collection, New York; *bottom center* Corbis-Bettmann; **655** *top* Copyright © Kelly Mooney Photography/Corbis; *bottom* The Granger Collection, New York; **656** *left, center* The Granger Collection, New York; *right* Charles E. Rotkin/Corbis; **657** *top* The Granger Collection, New York; *bottom* Corbis-Bettmann; **667–669, 670–671** David Muench/Corbis; **672, 675, 677** *left* The Granger Collection, New York; **677** *right* Copyright © Buddy Mays/Travel Stock; **684** The Granger Collection, New York; **685–687** *border* Photo by Sharon Hoogstraten; **687** The Granger Collection, New York; **689, 690, 694** Illustrations by Judith DuFour Love; **698** The Granger Collection, New York; **699** National Archives; **703, 717** Photo by Sharon Hoogstraten; **719** Arte Público Press; **722–726, 732** Photos by Sharon Hoogstraten.

## Unit Five

740 *Susan B. Anthony, statue* The Granger Collection, New York; 741 *poster, washing machine, automobile* The Granger Collection, New York; *watch* From *Pocket Watches* by Leonardo Leonardi and Gabriele Ribolini. Copyright © 1994, published by Chronicle Books; 742 *top* Copyright © Hulton Deutsch Collection; *bottom* The Granger Collection, New York; 743 *top* Culver Pictures; 744 *left* Courtesy of Chicago Historical Society; *right* The Granger Collection, New York; 746–750 *border* Photo by Sharon Hoogstraten; 746 *signature* The Granger Collection, New York; *top right* Amherst College Library, Archives and Special Collections; *bottom center* By permission of the Houghton Library, Harvard University; *bottom right* Corbis-Bettmann; 747 Jones Library, Special Collections, Amherst, Massachussetts; 748 *left* Corbis-Bettmann; *right* Amherst College Library, Archives and Special Collections; 749 Photofest; 757 *background* Corbis; 760–762 *border* Photo by Sharon Hoogstraten; 761, 762 Culver Pictures; 763 *top* Cover of *The Scarlet Letter* by Nathaniel Hawthorne. Used by permission of Dover Publications, Inc., New York; *bottom* Courtesy, Picture Research Consultants & Archive; 765 Detail of *A Woman Sewing in an Interior* (about 1900), Vilhelm Hammershøi. Christie's, London/Bridgeman/Art Resource, New York; 781 Stock Montage; 782 Culver Pictures; 787 Missouri Historical Society, St. Louis; 788 Photo by Russell Lee. Underwood Photo Archives, San Francisco; 801 Karen Huie; 805 Fred Viebahn; 816 Illustration copyright © 1990 by Mike Dooling, reprinted by permission of Scholastic Inc.; 817 AP/Wide World Photos; 819 *right* Reprinted by permission of Avon Books/Morrow, Inc.; 820 *bottom center,* 820–821 The Granger Collection, New York; 821 *top* Corbis-Bettmann; 822 The Granger Collection, New York; 824 *top left* Copyright © 1996 T. H. Benton & R. P. Benton Testamentary Trusts/Licensed by VAGA, New York; 829 *left* Stock Montage; *right* Illinois State Historical Library, Springfield; 834 Bettmann; 839 Moorland-Spingarn Research Center; 840 Illustration by Chuck Wilkinson; 862 National Archives; 864 Photo by Lewis W. Hine. Courtesy of George Eastman House, Rochester, New York; 867, 868 The Granger Collection, New York; 871 Photo by Lewis W. Hine. Courtesy of George Eastman House, Rochester, New York; 877, 885 Illustration by Roseann Litzinger; 893 Photo by Jerry Bauer; 901 *right* Book cover from *The Great Gatsby* (Authorized Text Edition) by F. Scott Fitzgerald (New York: Simon & Schuster, 1995). Reprinted with permission of Scribner, a division of Simon & Schuster; 902–906 Photos by Sharon Hoogstraten.

## Unit Six

914 *Nude Descending a Staircase, No. 2* (1912), Marcel Duchamp. Oil on canvas, 58″ × 35″. Philadelphia Museum of Art, Louise and Walter Arensberg Collection (50-134-59); *Louis Armstrong* The Bettmann Archive; 915 *woman* Corbis-Bettmann; *wristwatch* Private collection. Photo by Sharon Hoogstraten; *Charles Lindbergh* The Bettmann Archive; 916 *center left* Copyright © 1969 James Vander Zee. All rights reserved; *bottom* UPI/Bettmann; 917 UPI/Bettmann; 918 *top, bottom* AP/Wide World Photos; 920–924 *border* Photo by Sharon Hoogstraten; 920 *top, Langston Hughes,* Winold Reiss. National Portrait Gallery, Washington, D.C./Art Resource, New York; *bottom center* UPI/Corbis-Bettmann; *bottom right* The Granger Collection, New York; 921 *left* Corbis-Bettmann; *right* The Granger Collection, New York; 922 UPI/Corbis-Bettmann; 928–929 *border* Photo by Sharon Hoogstraten; 929 Copyright © 1995 Archive Photos/PNI; 931 Copyright © Chicago Tribune. Photo by Milbert Orlando Brown; 932 Copyright © Frank Driggs/Archive Photos/PNI; 934–935 *background* UPI/Corbis-Bettmann; 934 *left* Copyright © Culver Pictures; *center, right* Copyright © Frank Driggs/Archive Photos/PNI; 935 *left* Copyright © Archive Photos; *right*

UPI/Corbis-Bettmann; **937–939** *border* Photo by Sharon Hoogstraten; **938** The Granger Collection, New York; **939** National Portrait Gallery, Smithsonian Institution, Washington, D.C./Art Resource, New York; **944** *left* Fisk University; *right* National Portrait Gallery, Smithsonian Institution, Washington, D.C./Art Resource, New York; **945** Photo by Arthur Rothstein. From the collections of the Library of Congress; **949** *left* Yale Collection of American Literature, Beinecke Rare Book and Manuscript Library, Estate of Carl van Vechten, Joseph Solomon, Executor; *right* Fisk University; **950** Detail of *Bal Jeunesse* (about 1927), Palmer Hayden. Watercolor on paper, 14″ × 17″. Collection of Meredith and Gail Wright Sirmans; **955** *Mules and Men* by Zora Neale Hurston. Copyright © 1935 Zora Neale Hurston. Cover design by Suzanne Noli. Cover illustration copyright © David Diaz. Reproduced by permission of HarperCollins. All rights reserved; **958** Yale Collection of American Literature, Beinecke Rare Book and Manuscript Library, Estate of Carl van Vechten, Joseph Solomon, Executor; **960–963** *background* Photo by Sharon Hoogstraten; **965** Smith College Museum of Art, Northampton, Massachusetts, purchased 1943; **966** The Granger Collection, New York; **968** Copyright © 1992 Ron Rovtar/FPG International; **972** Howard Simmons; **975** *top left* Cover of *The Bluest Eye* by Toni Morrison. Copyright © 1989 Plume. Used with permission of Dutton Signet, a division of Penguin Books U.S.A. Cover illustration by Thomas Blackshear; *bottom left* Cover of *Beloved* by Toni Morrison. Copyright © 1988 New American Library. Used with permission of Dutton Signet, a division of Penguin Books U.S.A.; *right* Cover of *Song of Solomon* by Toni Morrison. Copyright © 1978 New American Library. Used with permission of Dutton Signet, a division of Penguin Books U.S.A.; **977** Copyright © Layle Silbert; **980–988** Photos by Sharon Hoogstraten; **992** *bottom* Copyright © Imperial War Museum; **993** The Bettmann Archive; **994** *left* National Archives; **996–1000** *border* Photo by Sharon Hoogstraten; **996** *signature* The Granger Collection, New York; *top* Copyright © Burt Glinn/Magnum Photos; *bottom right* Corbis-Bettmann; **997** *left* Hulton Deutsch Collection/Corbis; *right* From *New Hampshire* by Robert Frost (Henry Holt, Inc.); **998** *top* Copyright © Archive Photos; *bottom* Copyright © William Johnson/Stock Boston; **999** *top* UPI/Corbis-Bettmann; *bottom* John F. Kennedy Library/Corbis; **1002** Copyright © 1993 Thayer Syme/FPG International; **1005–1006** *border* Photo by Sharon Hoogstraten; **1012** *background* Photo by Emily Kling; **1013–1015** *border* Photo by Sharon Hoogstraten; **1014** The Granger Collection, New York; **1015** Copyright © Burt Glinn/Magnum Photos; **1016** The Granger Collection, New York; **1022** Copyright © D. J. McKay; **1024** National Archives; **1031, 1032, 1033, 1044** The Granger Collection, New York; **1045** AP/Wide World Photos; **1046–1047** Courtesy of *Life* magazine. Copyright © Margaret Bourke-White Estate; **1048** Courtesy of Sears, Roebuck and Co.; **1056** National Archives; **1057** Copyright © 1991 Photoworld/FPG International; **1059** *kitchen* Copyright © 1995 FPG International; **1059** *doll,* **1060** Photo by Sharon Hoogstraten; **1062** Copyright © Archive Photos; **1063** *left, right* AP/Wide World Photos; **1065** *left* Book cover of *The Nick Adams Stories* by Ernest Hemingway (New York: Charles Scribner's Sons, 1972). Reprinted with permission of Scribner, a division of Simon & Schuster; *right* Reprinted by permission of Random House, Inc.

**Unit Seven**
**1070** *mushroom cloud* AP/Wide World Photos; *John F. Kennedy* Copyright © 1960 Bob Henriques/Magnum Photos; **1071** *television* AP/Wide World Photos; *Twiggy, Richard Nixon* Copyright © Archive Photos; *watch* Private collection. Photo by Sharon Hoogstraten; **1072** *bottom* National Archives; **1073** Copyright © 1944 Robert Capa/Magnum Photos; **1074** Copyright © Donald J. Weber; **1076** Photo by Victor

Laredo; **1086** *top* Photo by George Skrigin; *bottom* UPI/Bettmann; **1087** AP/Wide World Photos; **1088, 1090, 1091, 1092** Copyright © 1968 Donald McCullin/Magnum Photos; **1094** *left* Copyright © 1995 Elliott Erwitt/Magnum Photos; *right* AP/Wide World Photos; **1095, 1099** *left, Evacuation Day, May 8, 1942,* Dorothea Lange. War Relocation Authority; **1099** *top right* AP/Wide World Photos; *bottom right* UPI/ Bettmann Newsphotos; **1100** *top left* UPI/Bettmann; *top right, Pledge of Allegiance at Rafael Weill Elementary* (1942), Dorothea Lange; *center right* Charles Mace/War Relocation Authority; *bottom, Manzanar Relocation Center* (1942), Dorothea Lange. War Relocation Authority; **1102** *left* AP/Wide World Photos; **1104** Corbis; **1108** *background* Copyright © Art Wolfe/Tony Stone Images; *woman* Copyright © 1969 Marc Riboud/Magnum Photos; *man* Copyright © Howard Grey/Tony Stone Images; **1110** Photo by Jerry Bauer; **1111** Photo by John Olson for *Life* magazine. Copyright © Time Inc.; **1117** *bottom left* Carolyn Wright; **1118** Photo by John Olson for *Life* magazine. Copyright © Time Inc.; **1124** Photo by Sharon Hoogstraten; **1125** *top* Copyright © Cantigny First Division Foundation; *bottom left, bottom right* Copyright © 1993 The Peace Museum; **1126-1128** Photos by Sharon Hoogstraten; **1132, 1133** AP/Wide World Photos; **1134** Illustration by J. W. Stewart; **1137, 1139, 1140, 1144** UPI/Corbis-Bettmann; **1148** Photo by John Olson for *Life* magazine. Copyright © Time Inc.; **1156** Photofest; **1158, 1159, 1160, 1165** Copyright © 1998 Curt Teich Postcard Archives, Lake County Museum, Illinois; **1167** Wyatt Counts/AP/Wide World Photos; **1168** *Portrait of Richard Freeman* (1974), Fairfield Porter. Oil on panel. Bowdoin College Museum of Art, Brunswick, Maine, anonymous gift (1986.74.1); **1179** AP/Wide World Photos; **1180** *The Table* (1970), Fairfield Porter. Collection of Elizabeth Feld; **1193, 1194** AP/Wide World Photos; **1199** *right* Arte Público Press; **1210–1211** Photos by Amy Ahlstrom; **1214, 1216–1217** AP/Wide World Photos; **1217** *bottom right* From *The Joy Luck Club* by Amy Tan. Copyright © 1989 by Amy Tan. Used by permission of Viking Penguin, a division of Penguin Putnam, Inc. Photo by Sharon Hoogstraten; **1222** Tom Herde/*The Boston Globe;* **1223, 1224** Copyright © William Schemmel/Stock South/PNI; **1226** Arte Público Press; **1231** Corbis; **1233** Photo by Rubén Guzmán.

**Reading Handbook**
**1240** right, **1252** Copyright © Corbis. **1343** © Volker Möhrke/Corbis; **1345** *top right Battle of Gettysburg* (1884). Color illustration. © Hulton Archives/Getty Images; *center right* Beverly R. Robinson Collection, United States Naval Academy Museum, Annapolis, Maryland; **1347, 1349** Mapquest.com; **1350, 1353** © Bettmann/Corbis; **1355** © PhotoDisc; **1357** *left* © Corbis; *right* © Bettmann/Corbis; **1359** © Corbis; **1361** *top right* © Bettmann/Corbis; *center right* From *The Jewish American.* © 1982 by Milton Meltze. Thomas Y. Crowell Junior Books/HarperCollins Children's Books; **1365** © Paul Conklin/PhotoEdit; **1370** Library of Congress.

Olga Y. Sanmaniego, English Department Chairperson, Burges High School, El Paso, Texas

Liz Sawyer-Cunningham, Los Angeles Senior High School, Los Angeles, California

Michelle Dixon Thompson, Seabreeze High School, Daytona Beach, Florida

## Teacher Review Panels (continued)

CALIFORNIA (continued)
Karen Buxton, English Department Chairperson, Winston Churchill Middle School, San Juan School District

Bonnie Garrett, Davis Middle School, Compton School District

Sally Jackson, Madrona Middle School, Torrance Unified School District

Sharon Kerson, Los Angeles Center for Enriched Studies, Los Angeles Unified School District

Gail Kidd, Center Middle School, Azusa School District

Corey Lay, ESL Department Chairperson, Chester Nimitz Middle School, Los Angeles Unified School District

Myra LeBendig, Forshay Learning Center, Los Angeles Unified School District

Dan Manske, Elmhurst Middle School, Oakland Unified School District

Joe Olague, Language Arts Department Chairperson, Alder Middle School, Fontana School District

Pat Salo, 6th Grade Village Leader, Hidden Valley Middle School, Escondido Elementary School District

FLORIDA
Judith H. Briant, English Department Chairperson, Armwood High School, Hillsborough County School District

Beth Johnson, Polk County English Supervisor, Polk County School District

Sharon Johnston, Learning Resource Specialist, Evans High School, Orange County School District

Eileen Jones, English Department Chairperson, Spanish River High School, Palm Beach County School District

Jan McClure, Winter Park High School, Orange County School District

Wanza Murray, English Department Chairperson (retired), Vero Beach Senior High School, Indian River City School District

Shirley Nichols, Language Arts Curriculum Specialist Supervisor, Marion County School District

Debbie Nostro, Ocoee Middle School, Orange County School District

Barbara Quinaz, Assistant Principal, Horace Mann Middle School, Dade County School District

*OHIO*

*Glyndon Butler,* English Department Chairperson, Glenville High School, Cleveland City School District

*Ellen Geisler,* English/Language Arts Department Chairperson, Mentor Senior High School, Mentor School District

*Dr. Paulette Goll,* English Department Chairperson, Lincoln West High School, Cleveland City School District

*Lorraine Hammack,* Executive Teacher of the English Department, Beachwood High School, Beachwood City School District

*Marguerite Joyce,* English Department Chairperson, Woodridge High School, Woodridge Local School District

*Sue Nelson,* Shaw High School, East Cleveland School District

*Dee Phillips,* Hudson High School, Hudson Local School District

*Carol Steiner,* English Department Chairperson, Buchtel High School, Akron City School District

*Nancy Strauch,* English Department Chairperson, Nordonia High School, Nordonia Hills City School District

*Ruth Vukovich,* Hubbard High School, Hubbard Exempted Village School District

TEXAS

*Dana Davis,* English Department Chairperson, Irving High School, Irving Independent School District

*Susan Fratcher,* Cypress Creek High School, Cypress Fairbanks School District

*Yolanda Garcia,* Abilene High School, Abilene Independent School District

*Patricia Helm,* Lee Freshman High School, Midland Independent School District

*Joanna Huckabee,* Moody High School, Corpus Christi Independent School District

*Josie Kinard,* English Department Chairperson, Del Valle High School, Ysleta Independent School District

*Mary McFarland,* Amarillo High School, Amarillo Independent School District

*Gwen Rutledge,* English Department Chairperson, Scarborough High School, Houston Independent School District

*Bunny Schmaltz,* Assistant Principal, Ozen High School, Beaumont Independent School District

*Michael Urick,* A. N. McCallum High School, Austin Independent School District

## Manuscript Reviewers *(continued)*

*Kathleen M. Anderson-Knight,* United Township High School, East Moline, Illinois

*Susan Arabie,* Marshall High School, Marshall, Texas

*Anita Arnold,* Thomas Jefferson High School, San Antonio, Texas

*Cassandra L. Asberry,* Dean of Instruction, Carter High School, Dallas, Texas

Jolene Auderer, Pine Tree High School, Longview, Texas

Don Baker, English Department Chairperson, Peoria High School, Peoria, Illinois

Beverly Ann Barge, Wasilla High School, Wasilla, Alaska

Louann Bohman, Wilbur Cross High School, New Haven, Connecticut

Rose Mary Bolden, Justin F. Kimball High School, Dallas, Texas

Lydia C. Bowden, Boca Ciega High School, St. Petersburg, Florida

Angela Boyd, Andrews High School, Andrews, Texas

Hugh Delle Broadway, McCullough High School, The Woodlands, Texas

Glyndon B. Butler, English Department Chairperson, Glenville High School, Cleveland, Ohio

Stephan P. Clarke, Spencerport High School, Spencerport, New York

Kathleen D. Crapo, South Fremont High School, St. Anthony, Idaho

Dr. Shawn Eric DeNight, Miami Edison Senior High School, Miami, Florida

JoAnna R. Exacoustas, La Serna High School, Whittier, California

Linda Ferguson, English Department Head, Tyee High School, Seattle, Washington

Ellen Geisler, English Department Chairperson, Mentor Senior High School, Mentor, Ohio

Ricardo Godoy, English Department Chairman, Moody High School, Corpus Christi, Texas

Meredith Gunn, Secondary Language Arts Instructional Specialist, Katy, Texas

Judy Hammack, English Department Chairperson, Milton High School, Alpharetta, Georgia

Robert Henderson, West Muskingum High School, Zanesville, Ohio

Martha Watt Hosenfeld, English Department Chairperson, Churchville-Chili High School, Churchville, New York

Janice M. Johnson, Assistant Principal, Union High School, Grand Rapids, Michigan

Eileen S. Jones, English Department Chair, Spanish River Community High School, Boca Raton, Florida

Paula S. L'Homme, West Orange High School, Winter Garden, Florida

Bonnie J. Mansell, Downey Adult School, Downey, California

Linda Maxwell, MacArthur High School, Houston, Texas

Ruth McClain, Paint Valley High School, Bainbridge, Ohio

Rebecca Miller, Taft High School, San Antonio, Texas

Deborah Lynn Moeller, Western High School, Fort Lauderdale High School

Bobbi Darrell Montgomery, Batavia High School, Batavia, Ohio

Bettie Moody, Leesburg High School, Leesburg, Florida

Margaret L. Mortenson, English Department Chairperson, Timpanogos High School, Orem, Utah

*Marjorie M. Nolan,* Language Arts Department Head, William M. Raines Sr. High School, Jacksonville, Florida

*Julia Pferdehirt,* Free-lance writer, former Special Education teacher, Middleton, Wisconsin

*Cindy Rodgers,* MacArthur High School, Houston, Texas

*Pauline Sahakian,* English Department Chairperson, San Marcos High School, San Marcos, Texas

*Jacqueline Y. Schmidt,* Department Chairperson and Coordinator of English, San Marcos High School, San Marcos, Texas

*David Schultz,* East Aurora High School, East Aurora, New York

*Milinda Schwab,* Judson High School, Converse, Texas

*John Sferro,* Butler High School, Vandalia, Ohio

*Brad R. Smedley,* English Department Chairperson, Hudtloff Middle School, Lakewood, Washington

*Faye S. Spangler,* Versailles High School, Versailles, Ohio

*Rita Stecich,* Evergreen Park Community High School, Evergreen Park, Illinois

*GayleAnn Turnage,* Abiline High School, Abiline, Texas

*Ruth Vukovich,* Hubbard High School, Hubbard, Ohio

*Kevin Walsh,* Dondero High School, Royal Oak, Michigan

*Charlotte Washington,* Westwood Middle School, Grand Rapids, Michigan

*Tom Watson,* Westbridge Academy, Grand Rapids, Michigan

*Linda Weatherby,* Deerfield High School, Deerfield, Illinois